The Only Portable Edition of the Internationally Renowned Dictionary

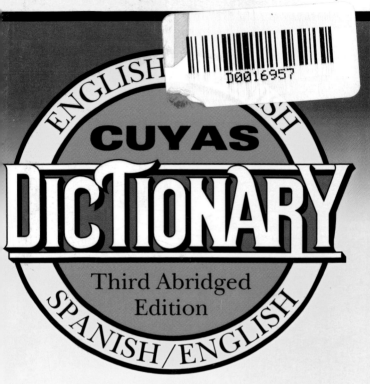

ENGLISH

CUYAS

DICTIONARY

Third Abridged Edition

SPANISH/ENGLISH

- Helpful guides to grammar and pronunciation

- Practical and contemporary

- Thousands of new entries

- Easy to read and use

Completely Revised and Updated

DICCIONARIO
Cuyás

INGLES-ESPAÑOL
ESPAÑOL-INGLES

TERCERA EDICION

Cuyás
DICTIONARY

ENGLISH-SPANISH
SPANISH-ENGLISH

THIRD EDITION

Edited by Roger J. Steiner, Professor Emeritus

MACMILLAN • USA

Third Edition

Macmillan General Reference
A Simon & Schuster Macmillan Company
1633 Broadway
New York, NY 10019-6785

MACMILLAN is a registered trademark of Macmillan, Inc.
Library of Congress Catalog No.: 98-68181
ISBN: 0-02-862627-3

Manufactured in the United States of America

1 2 3 4 5 6 7   99 00 01 02 03 04 05

CONTENTS

PARTE I
INGLES-ESPAÑOL

PART II
SPANISH-ENGLISH

Parte I
INGLES-ESPAÑOL

PREFACIO

Este diccionario está compuesto de acuerdo con el sistema empleado en los diccionarios Cuyás. Arturo Cuyás presentó su primer diccionario al Rey de España a principios de este siglo. Su hábil método inspiró a las ediciones de diccionarios bilingües español e inglés que le siguieron. La presente edición de bolsillo sigue esta tradición. Resulta fácil encontrar las referencias que se buscan en esta edición debido a que los datos están claramente organizados. El presente diccionario contiene más neologismos y expresiones de uso diario que cualquier otro diccionario bilingüe español e inglés del mismo tamaño. Por ejemplo, hay cuarenta usos para la palabra "papel." Además, en este diccionario se encuentran miles de vocablos que representan la traducción de expresiones provenientes de áreas tales como: la telecomunicación, el comercio, la medicina, los cohetes espaciales, el espacio, el turismo, los videos (o vídeos) y la informática. Las abreviaturas como **SIDA** y **ADN (DNA)** aparecen en castellano con sus correspondientes abreviaturas en inglés. El lenguaje popular usado en el mundo actual aparece en los siguientes ejemplos dados a continuación:

astronave	minusválido
autoedición	ordenador de mesa
banco de sangre	OVNI
camas gemelas	programación
computadora personal	reactor nuclear
conducta antideportiva	refugio fiscal
escáner	salida impresa
estereofónica	silla giratoria
estresado	teléfono celular
faxear	transbordador espacial
hard disk	videocámara
lluvia ácida	videojuego

Este diccionario advierte que se deben evitar las traducciones equívocas. A continuación damos cinco ejemplos:

El primer piso en español no es el primer piso en el inglés de Norteamérica, sino el segundo piso; el segundo piso en español es el tercer piso en el inglés de Norteamérica.

El "billón" castellano no es el "billion" del inglés de Norteamérica. El "billion" del lenguage norteamericano debe de traducirse con la expresión castellana "mil millones."

La palabra castellana "marrón" no representa la palabra inglesa "maroon." La palabra inglesa "maroon" representa el color que se podría designar como "burdeos" (color de las heces de vino).

La expresión española "¡oiga, señor!" no equivale a decir en inglés: "watch out, mister!" En inglés resulta grosero decirlo así. Este diccionario advierte que en un correcto inglés la palabra "mister" sólo se usa en combinación con el apellido, como por ejemplo: **Mr. Cruz** Sr. Cruz.

Este diccionario advierte que el vocablo castellano que quiere decir "hombre de raza negra" (**negro**) no debe de traducirse al inglés por el vocablo inglés "Negro," sino por la palabra de uso actual "Black," "African American" o "Afro-American."

Quedo agradecido a los muchos colaboradores y editores que hicieron posible la revisión de este diccionario para su tercera edición. En particular quisiera darle las gracias a Marie Butler-Knight, la editora de *Webster's New World Dictionary,* la cual organizó este proyecto y lo supervisó hasta su conclusión. También quisiera agradecer la colaboración de Sísi DiLaura Morris y de Alfred R. Wedel.

1 de septiembre 1998

Roger J. Steiner
Profesor Emérito
Universidad de Delaware

ADVERTENCIAS AL CONSULTANTE

1. *Distribución y orden.*   Para ahorrar espacio y poder incluir un mayor número de palabras hemos agrupado en familias todas aquellas que tienen una estrecha relación, ya de origen y significado, ya de ortografía, respetando, sin embargo, siempre, el orden alfabético. Todos los artículos principales van en negritas. Los modismos y giros van en itálica, alfabetizados por la primera palabra de la expresión. En las definiciones, la separación por medio de punto y coma indica áreas diferentes de significado; la coma, términos sinónimos dentro de cada área específica. Para ahorrar más espacio se ha omitido la parte común de las palabras que constituyen una misma familia. Las partes omitidas de las palabras que forman un grupo están referidas siempre al término que lo encabeza.

2. Todos los verbos irregulares van indicados por abreviaturas (*vti., vii., vai.*). Los números que van a continuación de las abreviaturas hacen referencia a la *Tablas de Verbos Irregulares,* en la página xxv.

3. *Adverbios.*   Todos los adverbios ingleses terminados en *-ly* se han omitido, excepto aquellos cuyo significado no tiene exacta correspondencia con el de sus equivalentes etimológicos en español.

4. *Abreviaturas.*   Todas las abreviaturas empleadas en el texto para indicar limitaciones de uso, geográficas o de otra índole (ex. *Méx.,* México; *aer.,* aeronática; *med.,* medicina) se hallarán explicadas en la lista de *Abreviaturas usadas en la parte 1ª* en la página xxx.

5. *Pronunciación.*   La pronunciación y acentuación de todas las palabras inglesas va indicada entre corchetes por medio de una adaptación simplificada del Alfabeto Fonético Internacional. En las páginas ix–x se incluye una Clave de las equivalencias españolas aproximadas de los sonidos ingleses representados por los símbolos fonéticos.

PRONUNCIACION INGLESA
CLAVE DE LOS SIMBOLOS FONETICOS

I. VOCALES

Símbolo	Grafías y Ejemplos	Equivalencia aproximada de sonido
[a]	a (father); e (sergeant); ea (heart); o (hot); ow (knowledge)	Como la a de pecado.
[ā]	a (legitimacy); ai (certain)	Entre e y a.
[ạ]	a (attire); ea (pageant)	Entre a y e.
[ắ]	a (forward, sofa)	Muy cercano a la a, pero más cerrado.
[æ]	a (man, that); ai (plaid); au (laugh)	Entre la a de caso y la e de guerra.
[ai]	ai (aisle); ay (aye); ei (height); ey (eye); i (life); ie (pie); uy (buy); y (by); ye (goodbye)	Como ai en vais.
[au]	ou (house); ow (cow)	Como au en causa.
[ɛ]	a (any); ae (aeronautics); ai (chair); ay (prayer); e (let); ea (head); ei (heifer); eo (leopard); ie (friend); u (bury)	Como la e de cerro.
[ē]	e (adequate, courtesy)	Muy cercana a la e.
[ẹ]	e (ardent); ea (sergeant)	Como la anterior.
[ei]	a (case); ai (train); au (gauge); ay (pay); e (fete)	Como ei en seis.
[i]	ae (alumnae); ay (quay); e (be); ea (clean); ee (sleep); ei (seize); eo (people); ey (key); i (machine); ie (fiend)	Como la i de vida.
[ị]	a (average); ay (Sunday); e (subsequent); ea (fear); ee (cheer); ei (sovereign); ey (money); i (bit); ie (sieve); o (women); oi (chamois); u (business); ui (guilt); y (very)	Como la i de sin, pero más breve y abierta.
[iu]	eau (beautiful); eu (feud); ew (few); iew (view); u (mute); ue (cue); ui (suit)	Como iu en ciudad o yu en yugo.
[o]	o (obese, notation)	Como la o de sola.
[ọ]	eo (dungeon); io (nation); o (atom)	Entre o y e.
[œ]	e (her); ea (earth); i (bird); o (word); ou (courage); u (burn); y (martyr)	Sonido parecido al de eu en francés (peur) o al de ö en aleman (schön).
[ou]	eau (beau); eo (yeoman); ew (sew); o (alone); oa (road); oe (foe); oo (brooch); ou (dough); ow (crow)	Como la o de loca seguida de una u leve.
[u]	eu (maneuver); ew (blew); o (do); oe (shoe); oo (food); ou (coupon); u (rude); ue (true); ui (juice)	Muy cercana a la u de suyo.
[ụ]	o (woman); oo (good); ou (could); u (bull)	Como la u de suyo, pero más cerrada.
[ǖ]	u (commensurate, corduroy)	Como iu en ciudad, pero más atenuado.
[ǚ]	u (censure, natural)	Lo mismo que el anterior, pero más relajado.
[wai]	oi (choir); uay (Paraguayan)	Como ua en guapa seguido de una i muy relajada.

[weɪ]	ua (pers*ua*de)	Como *ue* en s*ue*co seguido de una *i* muy relajada.
[yu]	eu (*eu*phemism); ew (*ew*e); ou (y*ou*); u (*u*nite)	Como *iu* en c*iu*dad o *yu* en *yu*go.
[yū]	u (reg*u*lar, sec*u*lar)	Como *iu* en c*iu*dad pero bastante más atenuado.
[ɔ]	a (*a*ll); au (l*au*nch); aw (l*aw*); o (s*o*ng); oa (br*oa*d)	Como la *o* de s*o*l pero más prolongada.
[ɔi]	oi (*oi*l); oy (t*oy*); uoy (b*uoy*)	Como *oy* en v*oy*.
[ʌ]	o (c*o*me); oe (d*oe*s); oo (fl*oo*d); ou (y*ou*ng); u (j*u*st)	Sonido entre *o* y *e*. Parecido al de la *o* francesa en h*o*mme.

II. CONSONANTES

Símbolo	Grafías y Ejemplos	Equivalencia aproximada de sonido
[b]	*b*aby; rob*b*er	Como la *b* de lum*b*re.
[ch]	*ch*urch; furni*t*ure; righ*t*eous; *ch*ristian; cat*ch*	Como la *ch* española.
[d]	*d*id; la*d*der	Como la *d* de on*d*a.
[dẑ]	ar*d*uous; gran*d*eur; bu*dg*e; a*dj*acent; *g*em; ju*dg*e	Sonido semejante al de la *y* de con*y*ugal o al de la *g* italiana en corti*g*iani.
[f]	*f*ar; rou*gh*; *ph*ilosophy	Como la *f* española.
[g]	*g*a*g*; wri*gg*le	Como la *g* de *g*ana.
[gz]	e*x*act; e*x*ample	Como la *g* de *g*ana seguida de la *s* francesa de mai*s*on.
[h]	*h*ere; be*h*ave; *wh*o; *wh*ole	Como la *j* española pero más aspirada y más suave.
[hw]	*wh*at; *wh*en	Como la *j* de *j*uez, pero más suave.
[ks]	e*x*cuse; ta*x*	Como la *x* de fle*x*ión.
[kw]	*qu*een; ac*qu*aint	Como *cu* en *cu*al o *qu* en *qu*e.
[l]	*l*ard; *l*ull; smal*l*	Como la *l* de *l*ado.
[m]	*m*an; ma*mm*al	Como la *m* española.
[n]	*n*un; ba*nn*er	Como la *n* española.
[ŋ]	a*n*chor; si*n*k; si*ng*; a*ng*le	Semejante al de la *n* de ba*n*co, pero más nasal.
[p]	*t*op; *p*e*pp*er	Como la *p* española.
[r]	*r*at; me*rr*y	Parecida a la *r* suave española.
[s]	*c*ent; *s*ister; mi*ss*; quart*z*; faça*d*e	Como la *s* de *s*ala, pero algo más tensa y larga.
[š]	o*c*ean; *ch*agrin; *s*ure; con*sc*ience; fi*sh*; mi*ss*ion; par*t*ial; an*x*ious	Como la *ch* francesa en *ch*aise.
[t]	fixe*d*; *t*aun*t*; ra*tt*le; *th*yme	Próxima a la *t* española de par*t*e.
[v]	o*f*; *v*i*v*id; o*v*er	Parecida a la *v* española, pero labiodental.
[w]	*w*e; a*w*ake	Como la *u* española.
[y]	on*i*on; *y*ear	Semejante a la *y* de a*y*er, pero más relajada.
[z]	riche*s*; di*s*cern; de*ss*ert; de*s*ert; an*x*iety; *z*eal; da*zz*le	Parecida a la *s* española de i*s*la.
[ẑ]	mira*g*e; plea*s*ure; vi*s*ion; a*z*ure	Como la *g* francesa de *g*enre.
[ð]	*th*is; wi*th*; mo*th*er	Muy semejante a la *d* de na*d*a.
[θ]	*th*in; *th*eater; tru*th*	Como la *z* de Castilla en *z*orro.

X

SINOPSIS DE LA GRAMÁTICA INGLESA

I. CONSIDERACIONES GENERALES

El idioma inglés no es tan exacto como el español. No hay reglas fijas para la pronunciación ni para la colocación del acento ni acentos ortográficos para ayudar en la pronunciación de una palabra. Consecuentemente, hay que aprender de memoria la pronunciación de un gran número de vocablos. (Véase la sección PRONUNCIACIÓN INGLESA, págs. ix–x.)

Se usan las mayúsculas en inglés como en español, y en los casos siguientes:
a) el pronombre sujeto I (*yo*) se escribe con mayúscula;
b) los nombres de los meses y días se escriben con mayúsculas;

Saturday, July 17   *el sábado, 17 de julio*

c) los gentilicios y todos los adjetivos formados de nombres propios se escriben con mayúsculas;

the Spaniards   *los españoles*

d) los títulos y tratamientos de cortesía se escriben con mayúsculas;

Mr.	*señor*
Mrs.	*señora*
Miss	*señorita*

e) todas las palabras en un título de libro, película, etc. se escriben con mayúsculas, exceptuando las palabras cortas si no van al principio.

From Here to Eternity

II. LAS PARTES DE LA ORACIÓN

A. Del artículo

1. El artículo indefinido en inglés carece de género; tiene las formas **a** y **an** (*un, una*). Cuando se antepone a una palabra comenzada en consonante se usa la forma **a**, y cuando se antepone a una palabra comenzada en vocal se usa la forma **an**. El plural de ambas formas es **some** (*unos, unas*).

a book	*un libro*
some books	*unos libros*
an airplane	*un avión*
some airplanes	*unos aviones*
a pen	*una pluma*

Generalmente, se usa el artículo indefinido en inglés como en español, aunque no tan frecuentemente. Algunas diferencias se citan a continuación:
a) no es necesario repetir el artículo indefinido antes de cada nombre;

I have a car, house and television *Tengo un coche, una casa y una televisión*

b) se usa el artículo indefinido antes de substantivos de cantidad como **a half** (*medio*), **a, one hundred** (*cien*), **a, one thousand** (*mil*);

There are a hundred soldiers here *Hay cien soldados aquí*

c) se usa el artículo indefinido cuando el nombre predicado no está modificado;

John is a doctor   *Juan es médico*

d) se usa el artículo indefinido cuando se sobrentiende que la cantidad aludida es uno;

He is wearing a coat	*Lleva abrigo*

e) se usa el artículo indefinido cuando se habla de precios.

He sells eggs at twenty cents a dozen	*Vende los huevos a veinte centavos la docena*

2. El artículo definido en inglés carece de género; tiene una única forma **the**, que corresponde indistintamente a los artículos definidos españoles *el, los, la, las y lo*.

the book	*el libro*
the books	*los libros*
the pen	*la pluma*
the pens	*las plumas*

No es tan corriente su uso en inglés como en español.

Mr. Martin is ill	*El señor Martínez está enfermo*
Love is not enough	*El amor no es suficiente*
Spanish	*El español*
It is one o'clock	*Es la una*
He goes to church on Sundays	*Va a la iglesia los domingos*
This coming year	*El año que viene*
Last Sunday	*El domingo pasado*

Se usa el artículo definido antes del número en un título.

Charles the Fifth	*Carlos V*

B. Del nombre

1. El nombre carece de género en el idioma inglés y generalmente sólo cambia para indicar el número. Por eso el artículo definido es siempre el mismo.

the house	*la casa*
the houses	*las casas*
the pencil	*el lápiz*
the pencils	*los lápices*

2. El plural de los nombres ingleses generalmente se forma añadiendo -s al final de la palabra.

SINGULAR		PLURAL	
chair	*silla*	**chairs**	*sillas*
book	*libro*	**books**	*libros*

Se forman algunos plurales añadiendo -es después de las terminaciones -s, -sh, -x, -j, -z y -ch.

SINGULAR		PLURAL	
dress	*vestido*	**dresses**	*vestidos*
bush	*arbusto*	**bushes**	*arbustos*
box	*caja*	**boxes**	*cajas*
birch	*abedul*	**birches**	*abedules*

Se forma el plural de los nombres terminados en -y (después de una consonante o de -qu) cambiando la -y por -i y añadiendo -es.

SINGULAR		PLURAL	
enemy	*enemigo*	**enemies**	*enemigos*
lady	*señora*	**ladies**	*señoras*
soliloquy	*soliloquio*	**soliloquies**	*soliloquios*

Se forma el plural de los nombres que terminan en -y precedida de vocal añadiendo una -s al final de la palabra.

SINGULAR		PLURAL	
donkey	*burro*	**donkeys**	*burros*

Se forma el plural de los nombres que terminan en -f, -fe, y -ff como sigue.

a) añadiendo -s al final de la palabra;

SINGULAR		PLURAL	
roof	techo	roofs	techos
chief	jefe	chiefs	jefes
cuff	puño de camisa	cuffs	puños de camisa

b) cambiando -f a -v y añadiendo -es.

SINGULAR		PLURAL	
knife	cuchillo	knives	cuchillos
leaf	hoja	leaves	hojas

N. B. Staff, scarf y wharf tienen dos formas para el plural. staffs y staves; scarfs y scarves; wharfs y wharves.

Se forma el plural de los nombres que terminan en -o precedida de vocal añadiendo -s al final de la palabra.

SINGULAR		PLURAL	
radio	radio	radios	radios

Se forma el plural de los nombres que terminan en -o precedida de consonante añadiendo -es al final de la palabra.

SINGULAR		PLURAL	
hero	héroe	heroes	héroes
potato	patata	potatoes	patatas

Se forma el plural de los números y letras añadiendo un apóstrofo y una -s.

There are ten 5's in this column	Hay diez cincos en esta columna
There are two s's in the word possible	Hay dos eses en la palabra possible

Algunos nombres, como los nombres de tribus, pueblos, razas y animales, tienen la misma forma para el singular que para el plural.

SINGULAR		PLURAL	
Chinese	chino	Chinese	chinos
Portuguese	portugués	Portuguese	portugueses
Norse	escandinavo	Norse	escandinavos
sheep	oveja	sheep	ovejas
deer	ciervo	deer	ciervos

Algunos nombres forman el plural de manera irregular.

SINGULAR		PLURAL	
child	niño	children	niños
tooth	diente	teeth	dientes
mouse	ratón	mice	ratones

En el caso de las palabras compuestas, generalmente se forma el plural de éstas pluralizando a la palabra principal.

SINGULAR		PLURAL	
mother-in-law	suegra	mothers-in-law	suegras
man-of-war	buque de guerra	men-of-war	buques de guerra

C. Del adjetivo

1. El adjetivo inglés no tiene ni género ni número; generalmente, se antepone al substantivo que modifica.

the red house	la casa roja
the red houses	las casas rojas
the white pencil	el lápiz blanco
the white pencils	los lápices blancos
the beautiful girl	la muchacha hermosa
the beautiful girls	las muchachas hermosas

2. *La comparación de los adjetivos*. Hay tres grados de comparación en inglés, que son: el positivo, comparativo y superlativo. El positivo de una o dos sílabas forma el comparativo añadiendo el sufijo **-er**. Los positivos con más de dos sílabas forman el comparativo anteponiendo el adverbio **more** (*más*). Los positivos de una o dos sílabas forman el superlativo añadiendo el sufijo **-est**, y los de dos o más sílabas forman el superlativo anteponiendo el adverbio **most** (*el más*). Se usa el comparativo **less** para indicar la cualidad de menos, y **least** para indicar el menos; ambas formas se anteponen al positivo.

POSITIVO		COMPARATIVO		SUPERLATIVO	
hard	*duro*	**harder**	*más duro*	**hardest**	*el más duro*
long	*largo*	**longer**	*más largo*	**longest**	*el más largo*
bright	*claro*	**brighter**	*más claro*	**brightest**	*el más claro*
capable	*capaz*	**more capable**	*más capaz*	**most capable**	*el más capaz*
clever	*listo*	**less clever**	*menos listo*	**least clever**	*el menos listo*

Se forma el comparativo y el superlativo de los adjetivos que terminan en **-y** después de una consonante cambiando la **-y** por **-i** y añadiendo los sufijos **-er** y **-est** respectivamente.

POSITIVO		COMPARATIVO		SUPERLATIVO	
pretty	*bonito*	**prettier**	*más bonito*	**prettiest**	*el más bonito*
happy	*feliz*	**happier**	*más feliz*	**happiest**	*el más feliz*

En algunos casos es necesario modificar la ortografía del positivo para acomodar a los grados del comparativo y superlativo. Generalmente, cuando el adjetivo de una o dos sílabas termina en consonante precedida de vocal, la consonante se dobla.

POSITIVO		COMPARATIVO		SUPERLATIVO	
drab	*pardo*	**drabber**	*más pardo*	**drabbest**	*el más pardo*
fat	*gordo*	**fatter**	*más gordo*	**fattest**	*el más gordo*

A continuación se dan algunos adjetivos de comparación irregular:

POSITIVO		COMPARATIVO		SUPERLATIVO	
bad	*mal*	**worse**	*peor*	**worst**	*el peor*
ill	*mal*	**worse**	*peor*	**worst**	*el peor*
evil	*mal*	**worse**	*peor*	**worst**	*el peor*
good	*bueno*	**better**	*mejor*	**best**	*el mejor*
many	*muchos*	**more**	*más*	**most**	*los más*
much	*mucho*	**more**	*más*	**most**	*el más*

D. Del adverbio

1. Se usa el adverbio en inglés, como en español, para modificar un verbo, un adjetivo u otro adverbio.

He ran quickly	*Corrió rápidamente*
The very good man	*El hombre muy bueno*
He ran very quickly	*Corrió rapidísimamente*

2. Generalmente, se forma el adverbio añadiendo el sufijo **-ly** a un adjetivo. La terminación **-ly** corresponde a la terminación *-mente* en español. Pero no todas las palabras terminadas en **-ly** son adverbios; algunas son adjetivos, como: **friendly** (*amigable*), **lovely** (*hermoso*), **kindly** (*bondadoso*), etc.

ADJETIVO		ADVERBIO	
strong	*fuerte*	**strongly**	*fuertemente*
regular	*regular*	**regularly**	*regularmente*

3. Algunas veces los adverbios toman la misma forma que los adjetivos.

ADJETIVO		ADVERBIO	
a slow watch	*un reloj atrasado*	**go slow**	*ve lentamente*
a late train	*un tren tardío*	**he arrived late**	*él llegó tarde*

4. El adverbio, como el adjetivo, tiene tres grados de comparación, que son: el positivo, comparativo y superlativo. Generalmente, se forma el comparativo y

superlativo añadiendo **more** (*más*) o **less** (*menos*) para el comparativo, y **most** (*el más*) o **least** (*el menos*) para el superlativo, antes del adverbio. No obstante, se forma el comparativo y superlativo de algunos adverbios añadiendo **-er** y **-est** respectivamente al final de la forma positiva.

POSITIVO		COMPARATIVO		SUPERLATIVO	
rapidly	*rápida-mente*	**more rapidly**	*más rápidamente*	**most rapidly**	*más rápida-mente*
easily	*fácilmente*	**more easily**	*más fácil-mente*	**most easily**	*más fácil-mente*
soon	*pronto*	**sooner**	*más pronto*	**soonest**	*más pronto*
easily	*fácilmente*	**less easily**	*menos fácil-mente*	**least easily**	*menos fácil-mente*

Los siguientes adverbios tienen comparaciones irregulares.

POSITIVO		COMPARATIVO		SUPERLATIVO	
far	*lejos*	**farther; further**	*más lejos*	**farthest; furthest**	*el más lejos*
ill, bad	*mal*	**worse**	*peor*	**worst**	*el peor*
little	*poco*	**less**	*menos*	**least**	*el menos*
much	*mucho*	**more**	*más*	**most**	*el más*
well	*bien*	**better**	*mejor*	**best**	*el mejor*

E. Del pronombre

1. *Los pronombres personales.* Los pronombres personales se dividen según el caso y son: el sujeto, objeto y posesivo. En inglés, es necesario usar el pronombre sujeto, porque los verbos no indican a la persona gramatical; se usa el mismo pronombre para el objeto directo que para el objeto indirecto. No hay equivalente inglés para las formas españolas *usted, Vd.* y *ustedes, Vds.* Se usa la forma del pronombre sujeto de segunda persona **you** (*tu, vosotros*) siempre, ya sea cuando se hable a una o a varias personas.

He is going tomorrow	*Irá mañana*
I see him now	*Le veo ahora*
I gave it to him	*Se lo di*
Do you speak Spanish?	*¿Habla Vd. español?*

A continuación se citan los pronombres personales que se usan ya como sujeto, ya como objeto directo o indirecto.

SINGULAR

	SUJETO		OBJETO DIRECTO E INDIRECTO	
primera persona	**I**	*yo*	**me**	*me*
segunda persona	**you**	*tú*	**you**	*te*
tercera persona	**he**	*él*	**him**	*lo, le; se*
	she	*ella*	**her**	*la, le; se*
	it	*ello*	**it**	*lo*

PLURAL

	SUJETO		OBJETO DIRECTO E INDIRECTO	
primera persona	**we**	*nosotros*	**us**	*nos*
segunda persona	**you**	*vosotros*	**you**	*vos, os*
tercera persona	**they**	*ellos*	**them**	*los, las; les*

Los pronombres posesivos en inglés carecen de género. Se refieren y concuerdan en número con el poseedor y no con la cosa poseída.

This book is mine	*Este libro es el mío*
Those books are mine	*Esos libros son los míos*
That dog is his	*Aquel perro es el suyo*
Are these pencils yours, Peter?	*¿Son estos lápices los tuyos, Pedro?*

PRONOMBRES POSESIVOS

mine	*el mío, la mía, los míos, las mías*
yours	*el tuyo, la tuya, los tuyos, las tuas; el vuestro, la vuestra, los vuestros, las vuestras*

his	*el suyo, los suyos*
hers	*la suya, las suyas*
ours	*el nuestro, la nuestra, los nuestros, las nuestras*
theirs	*el suyo, la suya, los suyos, las suyas*

Los adjetivos posesivos en inglés carecen de género. Concuerdan en número con el poseedor y no con la cosa poseída y preceden al substantivo que califican.

| **My books are in the drawer** | *Mis libros están en la gaveta* |
| **Our house is white** | *Nuestra casa es blanca* |

ADJETIVOS POSESIVOS

my	*mi, mis*
your	*tu, tus; vuestro, vuestros*
his	*su, sus*
her	*su, sus*
its	*su, sus*
our	*nuestro, nuestros*
their	*su, sus*

2. *Los pronombres relativos.* Los pronombres relativos sirven para referir a un nombre o pronombre que generalmente les precede en una oración. Los pronombres relativos se dividen en simples y compuestos.

a) Los pronombres relativos simples son:

who	*quien, que, cual, el que*
whom	*que, quien, el cual*
whose	*de quien, cuyo, del cual*
that	*que, cual, el que*
which	*que, quien, cual, el que*
what	*que, el que*

The man who came to dinner	*El hombre que vino a comer*
The man whom we saw is my brother	*El hombre que vinos es mi hermano*
The girl with whom he went to the movies is here	*La muchacha con quien fue al cine está aquí*
Give me what books you can	*Déme Vd. los libros que pueda*

b) Los pronombres relativos compuestos se forman añadiendo las terminaciones -ever y -soever a who, which y what (whoever, whichever, whatever) y se usan con carácter enfático.

c) Los pronombres relativos en inglés carecen de género y de número.

| **John and Charles, who are students, are on vacation** | *Juan y Carlos, quienes son estudiantes, están de vacaciones* |
| **Mary is the girl who sings** | *María es la muchacha que canta* |

d) Generalmente, **who** se refiere a una o algunas personas, **which** a una o algunas cosas, y **that** a ambas. **Whom** se puede usar tanto como objeto directo que indirecto. **Whose** se usa como posesivo.

Mary is the girl who sings	*María es la muchacha que canta*
Here is the book of which I spoke to you	*Aquí está el libro del cual te hablé*
Albert is the one that is playing the piano	*Alberto es el que toca el piano*
She is the girl to whom we gave the prize	*Ella es la muchacha a quien dimos el premio*
John, whose uncle is ill, is leaving tonight	*Juan, cuyo tío está enfermo, partirá esta noche*

3. *Los pronombres demostrativos.* Los pronombres demostrativos se usan para mostrar uno o varios objetos, a la vez que indican su proximidad o lejanía respecto a la persona que habla o de aquella a quien se habla. Los pronombres demostrativos en inglés carecen de género. Concuerdan en número con la cosa a la que se refieren.

	SINGULAR		PLURAL
this	éste, ésta, esto; cerca de la persona que habla	these	éstos, éstas
that	ése, ésa, eso; aquél, aquélla, aquello; lejos de la persona que habla	those	ésos, ésas; aquéllos, aquéllas

This is the pen	*Ésta es la pluma*
These are the books	*Éstos son los libros*
That is his	*Eso es suyo*
Those are hers	*Aquéllos son de ella*

4. *Los pronombres indefinidos.* Se usan los pronombres indefinidos en inglés como en español. A continuación se dan los pronombres indefinidos más usados en inglés:

all	*todo*	everybody	*todos*	nothing	*nada*
another	*otro*	everyone	*todos*	one	*uno*
any	*cualquier*	everything	*todo*	other	*otro*
anybody	*alquien, cualquiera*	few	*pocos*	some	*algunos*
anyone	*alguien, cualquiera*	many	*muchos*	somebody	*alguien*
anything	*algo, cualquier cosa*	neither	*ni uno ni otro*	someone	*alguien*
both	*ambos*	nobody	*ninguno, nadie*	something	*algo*
each	*cada uno, cada cual*	none	*ninguno, nadie*	such	*tal*
either	*uno u otro*	no one	*ninguno, nadie*		

One (*uno*) y other (*otro*) son los únicos que tienen plural.

These are the ones I like	*Estos son los que me gustan*
The others have already left	*Los otros ya se fueron*

5. *Los pronombres reflexivos o intensivos.* Los pronombres reflexivos, también llamados intensivos por su carácter enfático, carecen de género. Concuerdan en número con la persona a la que se refieren. Se forman de la unión del pronombre personal o del adjetivo posesivo con la terminación **-self** para el singular y **-selves** para el plural.

myself	*yo mismo; mí, mí mismo; me*
yourself	*tú mismo; Vd. mismo; ti, ti mismo; te, se*
himself	*él mismo; sí, sí mismo; se*
herself	*ella misma; sí, sí misma; se*
itself	*mismo; sí, sí mismo; se*
ourselves	*nosotros mismos; nos*
yourselves	*vosotros mismos; Vds. mismos; vos, os*
themselves	*ellos mismos; sí, sí mismos; se*
I did it myself	*Yo mismo lo hice*
It moves by itself	*Eso se mueve por sí mismo*
Did you do it yourself?	*¿Lo hizo Vd. mismo?*

F. Las palabras interrogativas

Las palabras interrogativas en inglés carecen de género y de número. A continuación se dan las de uso más frecuente.

how?	*¿cómo?*	where?	*¿dónde?*
how many?	*¿cuántos?*	which?	*¿cuál?*
how much?	*¿cuánto?*	who?	*¿quién?*
what?	*¿qué?*	why?	*¿por qué?*
when?	*¿cuándo?*		

How do you sell them?	¿A cómo los vende Vd.?
How many eggs are in that box?	¿Cuántos huevos hay en esa caja?
How much are they?	¿Cuánto cuestan?
What time is it?	¿Qué hora es?
When did you arrive?	¿Cuándo llegó Vd.?
Where are you going?	¿Dónde va Vd.?
Which sister did he marry?	¿Con cuál de las hermanas se casó?
Who goes there?	¿Quién va?
Why do you weep?	¿Por qué llora Vd.?

G. Del verbo

1. Los verbos en inglés pueden ser regulares o irregulares, según la conjugación. Cada verbo consta de tres partes principales: el presente, el pretérito y el participio pasado.

2. El infinitivo se forma con **to** y el presente del verbo.

| to change | cambiar | to play | jugar |
| to look | mirar | to use | usar |

El infinitivo se puede usar como substantivo; también puede hacer oficio de adjetivo o adverbio.

To play in the park is fun	El jugar en el parque es divertido
I have plenty of books to read	Tengo muchos libros que leer
The student came to learn English	El alumno vino a aprender inglés

3. El participio presente o gerundio del verbo generalmente se forma añadiendo **-ing** al presente.

PRESENTE	PARTICIPIO PRESENTE
look	looking
play	playing

Los verbos que tienen el presente terminado en **-e** muda generalmente pierden la **-e** y añaden **-ing** para formar el participio presente.

PRESENTE	PARTICIPIO PRESENTE
change	changing
use	using

Los verbos que doblan la consonante final para formar el pretérito y el participio pasado también doblan la consonante final para formar el participio presente.

PRESENTE		PARTICIPIO PRESENTE
stop	parar	stopping
tip	ladear	tipping

El participio presente se puede usar con el verbo auxiliar **to be** para formar un tiempo progresivo.

| I am playing cards | Estoy jugando a las cartas |
| I was playing football last week | Jugaba al fútbol la semana pasada |

4. El pretérito y el participio pasado generalmente se forman añadiendo **-d** o **-ed** al presente.

PRESENTE	PRETÉRITO	PARTICIPIO PASADO
change	changed	changed
look	looked	looked
play	played	played
use	used	used

Sin embargo, muchos verbos en inglés tienen formas irregulares para el pretérito y para el participio pasado. A continuación se da una descripción de algunos verbos que forman el pretérito y el participio pasado de manera irregular. No se incluyen los que forman el pretérito y el participio pasado de manera regular, aunque éstos tengan a la vez una forma alterna, a menos que ésta sea la preferida.

a) Algunos verbos duplican la consonante final del presente para formar el pretérito y el participio pasado.

PRESENTE	PRETÉRITO	PARTICIPIO PASADO
abet	**abetted**	**abetted**
abhor	**abhorred**	**abhorred**
acquit	**acquitted**	**acquitted**

Los verbos de esta clase incluidos en este diccionario, a excepción de sus compuestos, se dan a continuación.

admit	crib	grab	nip	sag	stem
allot	crop	grin	nod	sap	step
aver	dam	grip	occur	scan	stir
bag	defer	grit	omit	scar	stop
ban	deter	grub	outwit	scram	strap
bar	dim	gum	pad	scrap	strip
bed	din	gun	pan	scrub	strop
beg	dip	gut	pat	sham	strut
blab	dispel	handicap	patrol	shin	stub
blot	distil	hem	peg	ship	stud
blur	dog	hop	pen	shop	stun
bob	don	hug	pep	shrug	submit
bog	dot	impel	permit	shun	sum
bootleg	drag	incur	pet	sin	sun
brag	drip	infer	pin	skim	sup
brim	drop	inter	plan	skin	tag
bud	drug	jab	plod	slam	tan
bum	drum	jam	plot	slap	tap
can	emit	jar	plug	slip	tar
cap	equip	jet	pop	slop	thin
chap	excel	jig	prefer	slot	throb
char	expel	jot	prod	slug	tin
chat	extol	jut	prop	slum	tip
chip	fan	kid	propel	slur	top
chop	fat	knot	pun	smut	transfer
chum	fib	lag	quip	snag	transmit
clap	fit	lap	quiz	snap	trap
clip	flag	log	rag	snip	trim
clog	flap	lop	ram	snub	trot
clot	flat	lug	rap	sob	tug
club	flit	man	recur	sod	up
commit	flog	map	refer	sop	wad
compel	flop	mar	remit	span	wag
concur	fog	mob	rib	spar	war
confer	fret	mop	rig	spat	wed
control	fur	mud	rip	spot	whet
cop	gad	nab	rob	spur	whip
corral	gag	nag	rot	squat	whir
crab	gap	nap	rub	stab	whiz
cram	gem	net	rut	star	wrap

b) Algunos verbos cambian la **-y** final del presente en **-ied** para formar el pretérito y el participio pasado.

PRESENTE	PRETÉRITO	PARTICIPIO PASADO
accompany	**accompanied**	**accompanied**
acetify	**acetified**	**acetified**
acidify	**acidified**	**acidified**

Los verbos de esta clase incluidos en este diccionario, a excepción de sus compuestos, se dan a continuación:

ally	belly	carry	crucify	diversify
amnesty	bloody	certify	cry	dizzy
amplify	body	classify	defy	dry
apply	bully	codify	deny	eddy
baby	busy	comply	dignify	edify
beautify	candy	copy	dirty	electrify

empty	imply	mutiny	quarry	stratify
envy	indemnify	mystify	query	study
espy	intensify	notify	rally	supply
falsify	inventory	nullify	rectify	tally
fancy	jelly	occupy	rely	tarry
ferry	jolly	pacify	remedy	terrify
fortify	justify	parry	reply	testify
fry	levy	personify	sally	tidy
glorify	liquefy	pillory	sanctify	try
gratify	lobby	pity	satisfy	typify
gully	magnify	ply	shy	unify
harry	marry	prophesy	signify	vary
horrify	modify	pry	solidify	weary
humidify	mortify	purify	specify	worry
hurry	muddy	putty	spy	
identify	multiply	qualify	steady	

c) Algunos verbos no cambian en la formación del pretérito y del participio pasado. Los verbos de esta clase incluidos en este diccionario, a excepción de sus compuestos, se dan a continuación.

PRESENTE	PRETÉRITO	PARTICIPIO PASADO	PRESENTE	PRETÉRITO	PARTICIPIO PASADO
bid (ofrecer)	bid	bid	let	let	let
burst	burst	burst	put	put	put
cast	cast	cast	read	read	read
cost	cost	cost	set	set	set
cut	cut	cut	shed	shed	shed
hit	hit	hit	spread	spread	spread
hurt	hurt	hurt	thrust	thrust	thrust

d) Algunos verbos añaden -ked al presente para formar el pretérito y el participio pasado. Los verbos de esta clase incluidos en este diccionario se dan a continuación.

PRESENTE	PRETÉRITO	PARTICIPIO PASADO	PRESENTE	PRETÉRITO	PARTICIPIO PASADO
frolic	frolicked	frolicked	picnic	picnicked	picnicked
mimic	mimicked	mimicked	shellac	shellacked	shellacked
panic	panicked	panicked	traffic	trafficked	trafficked

e) Algunos verbos irregulares no siguen regla fija en la formación del pretérito y del participio pasado. Los verbos de este grupo incluidos en este diccionario, a excepción de sus compuestos, se dan a continuación.

PRESENTE	PRETÉRITO	PARTICIPIO PASADO	PRESENTE	PRETÉRITO	PARTICIPIO PASADO
abide	abode	abode	bite	bit	bitten
alight	alighted, alit	alighted, alit	bleed	bled	bled
			blow	blew	blown
arise	arose	arisen	break	broke	broken
awake	awoke, awaked	awoke, awaked	breed	bred	bred
			bring	brought	brought
be	was, were	been	build	built	built
bear	bore	born, borne	buy	bought	bought
			can	could	
beat	beat	beaten	catch	caught	caught
become	became	become	chide	chide, chided	chid, chidden, chided
begin	began	begun			
behold	beheld	beheld			
bend	bent	bent	choose	chose	chosen
beseech	besought, beseeched	besought, beseeched	cleave	cleft, cleaved, clove	cleft, cleaved, cloven
bid (ordenar)	bade	bidden	cling	clung	clung
bind	bound	bound	come	came	come

PRESENTE	PRETÉRITO	PARTICIPIO PASADO	PRESENTE	PRETÉRITO	PARTICIPIO PASADO
creep	crept	crept	pay	paid	paid
deal	dealt	dealt	pen	penned	pent
dig	dug, digged	dug, digged	(encerrar)		
			quit	quit	quitted
dive	dove, dived	dove, dived	rend	rent	rent
			rid	rid, ridded	rid, ridded
do	did	done	ride	rode	ridden
draw	drew	drawn	ring	rang	rung
drink	drank	drunk	rise	rose	risen
drive	drove	driven	run	ran	run
eat	ate	eaten	say	said	said
fall	fell	fallen	see	saw	seen
feed	fed	fed	seek	sought	sought
feel	felt	felt	sell	sold	sold
fight	fought	fought	send	sent	sent
find	found	found	shake	shook	shaken
flee	fled	fled	shine	shone, shined	shone, shined
fling	flung	flung			
fly	flew	flown	shoe	shod	shod
forbear	forbore	forborne	shoot	shot	shot
forbid	forbade	forbidden	show	showed	shown
forego	forewent	foregone	shrink	shrank, shrunk	shrunk, shrunken
foresee	foresaw	foreseen			
foretell	foretold	foretold	sing	sang	sung
foreget	forgot	forgotten	sink	sank, sunk	sunk, sunken
forgive	forgave	forgiven			
forsake	forsook	forsaken	sit	sat	sat
forswear	forswore	forsworn	slay	slew	slain
freeze	froze	frozen	sleep	slept	slept
get	got	got, gotten	slide	slid	slid, slidden
give	gave	given	sling	slung	slung
go	went	gone	slink	slunk	slunk
grind	ground	ground	sow	sowed	sown, sowed
grow	grew	grown			
hang	hung, hanged	hung, hanged	speak	spoke	spoken
			speed	sped, speeded	sped, speeded
have	had	had			
hear	heard	heard	spend	spent	spent
hide	hid	hid, hidden	spin	spun	spun
			spit	spat, spit	spat, spit
hold	held	held	spring	sprang, sprung	sprung
keep	kept	kept			
know	knew	known	stand	stood	stood
lay	laid	laid	steal	stole	stolen
lead	led	led	stick	stuck	stuck
(dirigir)			sting	stung	stung
leave	left	left	stink	stank, stunk	stunk
lend	lent	lent			
lie	lay	lain	strike	struck	struck, stricken
(echarse)					
light	lighted, lit	lighted, lit	string	strung	strung
lose	lost	lost	strive	strove, strived	striven, strived
make	made	made			
may	might		swear	swore	sworn
mean	meant	meant	sweep	swept	swept
meet	met	met	swell	swelled	swelled, swollen
mistake	mistook	mistaken			
pass	passed	passed, past	swim	swam	swum
			swing	swung	swung

xxi

PRESENTE	PRETÉRITO	PARTICIPIO PASADO	PRESENTE	PRETÉRITO	PARTICIPIO PASADO
take	took	taken	wear	wore	worn
teach	taught	taught	weave	wove	woven, wove
tear	tore	torn			
tell	told	told	weep	wept	wept
think	thought	thought	wet	wet, wetted	wet, wetted
thrive	throve, thrived	thrived, thriven	win	won	won
			wind	winded, wound	winded, wound
throw	threw	thrown			
tread	trod	trodden, trod	wit	wist, wiste	wist
understand	understood	understood	wring	wrung	wrung
wake	woke, waked	woken, waked	write	wrote	written

5. Los tiempos del modo indicativo. Hay seis tiempos principales, que son: el presente, el pretérito, el futuro, el presente perfecto, el pretérito perfecto y el futuro perfecto. Los tiempos se forman de las partes principales del verbo. Obsérvese que el verbo inglés no cambia su terminación para indicar a la persona gramatical, por eso es necesario usar siempre los pronombres personales.

a) *El presente.* El presente se usa para expresar una acción o estado actual, una acción habitual o una verdad.

John works in the garden   *Juan trabaja en el jardín*

SINGULAR		PLURAL	
primera persona	I play	we play	
segunda persona	you play	you play	
tercera persona	he, she plays	they play	

b) *El pretérito.* El pretérito expresa una acción terminada en el pasado.

Columbus discovered America   *Colón descubrió América*

SINGULAR		PLURAL	
primera persona	I played	we played	
segunda persona	you played	you played	
tercera persona	he, she played	they played	

No hay ningún tiempo en inglés que corresponda al imperfecto en español. La idea del imperfecto se expresa por medio del pretérito del verbo auxiliar **to be** y el participio presente del verbo conjugado.

SINGULAR		PLURAL	
primera persona	I was playing	we were playing	
segunda persona	you were playing	you were playing	
tercera persona	he, she was playing	they were playing	

c) *El futuro.* El futuro expresa una acción realizada después del momento actual. En inglés es necesario usar el verbo auxiliar **will** para formar el tiempo futuro.

He will work tomorrow   *El trabajará mañana*

SINGULAR		PLURAL	
primera persona	I will play	we will play	
segunda persona	you will play	you will play	
tercera persona	he, she will play	they will play	

En inglés no se usa el futuro para expresar probabilidad.

d) *El presente perfecto.* El presente perfecto expresa una acción pasada que se prolonga hasta el presente. Se forma con el presente del verbo auxiliar **to have** y el participio pasado del verbo conjugado.

I have played football many times   *He jugado al fútbol muchas veces*

SINGULAR		PLURAL	
primera persona	I have played	we have played	
segunda persona	you have played	you have played	
tercera persona	he, she has played	they have played	

xxii

e) *El pretérito perfecto.* El pretérito perfecto expresa una acción completada antes de algún momento indicado en el pasado. Se forma con el pretérito del verbo auxiliar **to have** y el participio pasado del verbo conjugado.

He had played the year before   *El había jugado el año anterior*

	SINGULAR	PLURAL
primera persona	**I had played**	**we had played**
segunda persona	**you had played**	**you had played**
tercera persona	**he, she had played**	**they had played**

f) *El futuro perfecto.* El futuro perfecto expresa una acción que habrá de completarse en algún momento indicado en el futuro. Este tiempo es de escaso uso en inglés.

	SINGULAR	PLURAL
primera persona	**I will have played**	**we will have played**
segunda persona	**you will have played**	**you will have played**
tercera persona	**he, she will have played**	**they will have played**

6. Los verbos auxiliares **to be** y **to have.** La conjugación del verbo **to be** es irregular en el presente y en el pretérito.

a) *El presente* de **to be** y **to have**

SINGULAR	PLURAL	SINGULAR	PLURAL
I am	**we are**	**I have**	**we have**
you are	**you are**	**you have**	**you have**
he, she, it is	**they are**	**he, she, it has**	**they have**

b) *El pretérito* de **to be**

I was	**we were**
you were	**you were**
he, she, it was	**they were**

7. *El modo subjuntivo y sus tiempos.* El modo subjuntivo expresa una duda, deseo, reproche, concesión, suposición o una condición contraria a la realidad. El subjuntivo es de escaso uso en inglés. En su lugar se emplean otras construcciones que sirven para expresar la misma idea. Se puede usar el indicativo para expresar la idea del subjuntivo.

He commands that I leave   *Él manda que yo salga*

También se puede expresar la idea del subjuntivo por medio de las palabras **should, would, could, might,** etc.

John should have come   *Juan debiera de haber venido*
He could have taken the train   *Él pudo haber tomado el tren*

Nótese que el modo potencial no existe en inglés. En su lugar se usa **would,** que equivale al presente, futuro o pretérito del subjuntivo, según las circunstancias.

If he had the money he would go   *Si él tuviera el dinero, iría*
Would you like to dance?   *¿Querría Vd. bailar?*

No se usa el subjuntivo en inglés para expresar probabilidad en el pasado.

It was probably three o'clock   *Serían las tres*

8. *El modo imperativo.* El modo imperativo expresa un mandato; sólo tiene el tiempo presente. Se forma con la segunda persona singular del verbo, sin el pronombre sujeto **you.**

go!   *¡ve! ¡id!*
come!   *¡ven! ¡venid!*

9. *La voz pasiva.* La voz pasiva se forma con el verbo auxiliar **to be** y el participio pasado del verbo conjugado.

The earth was seen clearly by the astronauts   *La tierra fue vista claramente por los astronautas*
This play has been performed many times   *Esta pieza teatral ha sido representada muchas veces*

H. De la conjunción

Las conjunciones son una parte invariable de la oración; se usan para enlazar dos o más palabras u oraciones. Las conjunciones se dividen en inglés, como en español, en *copulativas* y *disyuntivas*. Las conjunciones copulativas principales son: **and** (*y, e*), **but** (*pero, mas, sin embargo,* etc.) y **or** (*o, u*).

It was a black and white cat	*Era un gato negro y blanco*
John can play piano or guitar	*Juan toca piano o guitarra*

Las conjunciones disyuntivas principales son: **if** (*si, aunque,* etc.), **while** (*mientras que,* etc.), **although** (*bien que, aunque,* etc.), **though** (*bien que, aunque,* etc.), **when** (*cuando,* etc.), **until** (*hasta que*), **as** (*como; a medida que,* etc.), **since** (*desde que; puesto que,* etc.), **that** (*que; para que,* etc.) y **because** (*porque,* etc.).

I will play if you ask me	*Tocaré si Vd. me lo pide*
He didn't go out while it was raining	*Él no salió mientras que llovía*

I. De la preposición

La preposición sirve para denotar la relación entre dos palabras en una oración. Muchas preposiciones indican dirección o posición (**over**, *sobre, encima;* **behind**, *tras, detras de;* **from**, *de, desde;* **to**, **a**, *hasta, para;* **above**, *sobre, encima;* **below**, *bajo, debajo de;* **out**, *fuera de;* **in**, *en, mientras;* **around**, *cerca de, alrededor de;* **through**, *por, a través de;* **beyond**, *más allá de, tras;* **across**, *a través de;* **beside**, *al lado de, junto a,* etc.), y otras representan varios tipos de relación (**of**, *de;* **except**, *excepto, con excepción de;* **for**, *por, para;* **besides**, *además de, a más de,* etc.).

TABLAS DE VERBOS IRREGULARES INGLESES

El número que aparece en corchetes a la derecha de un verbo irregular indica la clase a que pertenece en las tablas siguientes.

CLASE 1

Los verbos de esta clase duplican la consonante final del infinitivo para formar el pretérito y el participio pasado. Ejemplos:

Presente	Pretérito	Participio	Presente	Pretérito	Participio
annul	annulled	annulled	quiz	quizzed	quizzed
bag	bagged	bagged	etc.	etc.	etc.
cap	capped	capped			

CLASE 2

Los verbos pertenecientes a esta clase pueden, al formar el pretérito y el participio pasado, duplicar la consonante final del infinitivo o dejarla simple. Ambas formas son aceptadas en el uso. Ejemplos:

Presente	Pretérito	Participio
anvil	anviled, anvilled	anviled, anvilled
bias	biased, biassed	biased, biassed
focus	focused, focussed	focused, focussed
kidnap	kidnaped, kidnapped	kidnaped, kidnapped
patrol	patroled, patrolled	patroled, patrolled
travel	traveled, travelled	traveled, travelled
etc.	etc.	etc.

CLASE 3

Presente	Pretérito	Participio	Presente	Pretérito	Participio
bet	bet, betted	bet, betted	quit	quit, quitted	quit, quitted
dig	dug, digged	dug, digged			
dip	dipped, dipt	dipped, dipt	rid	rid, ridded	rid, ridded
drip	dripped, dript	dripped, dript	shred	shredded, shred	shredded, shred
drop	dropped, dropt	dropped, dropt	wed	wedded	wedded, wed
knit	knitted, knit	knitted, knit	wet	wet, wetted	wet, wetted
pen (encerrar)	penned, pent	penned, pent	whip	whipped, whipt	whipped, whipt
wrap	wrapped, wrapt	wrapped, wrapt			

CLASE 4

Presente	Pretérito	Participio
alight	alighted, alit	alighted, alit
awake	awoke, awaked	awoke, awaked
bend	bent, bended	bent, bended
blend	blended, blent	blended, blent
broadcast	broadcast, broadcasted	broadcast, broadcasted
burn	burned, burnt	burned, burnt
chide	chided, chid	chided, chid, chidden
cleave	cleft, cleaved, clove	cleft, cleaved, cloven
clothe	clothed, clad	clothed, clad
dream	dreamed, dreamt	dreamed, dreamt
dress	dressed, drest	dressed, drest
dwell	dwelt, dwelled	dwelt, dwelled
forecast	forecast, forecasted	forecast, forecasted
gild	gilded, gilt	gilded, gilt
gird	girded, girt	girded, girt
grind	ground, grinded	ground, grinded
heave	heaved, hove	heaved, hove
kneel	knelt, kneeled	knelt, kneeled
lean	leaned, leant	leaned, leant
leap	leaped, leapt	leaped, leapt
learn	learned, learnt	learned, learnt
light	lighted, lit	lighted, lit
misspell	misspelled, misspelt	misspelled, misspelt
mix	mixed, mixt	mixed, mixt
outwork	outworked, outwrought	outworked, outwrought
overwork	overworked, overwrought	overworked, overwrought
plead	pleaded, pled, plead	pleaded, pled, plead
smell	smelled, smelt	smelled, smelt
speed	sped, speeded	sped, speeded
spell	spelled, spelt	spelled, spelt
spill	spilled, spilt	spilled, spilt
spoil	spoiled, spoilt	spoiled, spoilt
stave	staved, stove	staved, stove
stay	stayed, staid	stayed, staid
sunburn	sunburned, sunburnt	sunburned, sunburnt
sweat	sweat, sweated	sweat, sweated
thrive	throve, thrived	thrived, thriven
unclothe	unclothed, unclad	unclothed, unclad
work	worked, wrought	worked, wrought

CLASE 5

Presente	Pretérito	Participio	Presente	Pretérito	Participio
bide	bode, bided	bided	dive	dived, dove	dived
crow	crowed, crew	crowed	wake	waked, woke	waked
dare	dared, durst	dared			

CLASE 6

Presente	Pretérito	Participio	Presente	Pretérito	Participio
hew	hewed	hewed, hewn	shave	shaved	shaved, shaven
melt	melted	melted, molten	shear	sheared	sheared, shorn
mow	mowed	mowed, mown	show	showed	showed, shown
pass	passed	passed, past	sow	sowed	sowed, sown
prove	proved	proved, proven	strew	strewed	strewed, strewn
saw	sawed	sawed, sawn	swell	swelled	swelled, swollen
sew	sewed	sewed, sewn	weave	wove	wove, woven

CLASE 7

Los verbos pertenecientes a esta clase cambian la *y* final del infinitivo en *ied* para formar el pretérito y el participio pasado. Si la *y* se pronuncia [ai], *ied* se pronuncia [aid]. Cuando se pronuncia [i] el preterito y el participio se pronuncian [id]. Ejemplos:

bury	buried	buried	fancy	fancied	fancied
certify	certified	certified	worry	worried	worried
dirty	dirtied	dirtied	etc.	etc.	etc.

CLASE 8

Todos los verbos pertenecientes a esta clase añaden *ked* al infinitivo para formar el pretérito y el participio pasado. Ejemplos:

frolic	frolicked	frolicked	panic	panicked	panicked
mimic	mimicked	mimicked	etc.	etc.	etc.

CLASE 9

Los verbos pertenecientes a esta clase no varian en la formación del pretérito y el participio pasado. Ejemplos:

cut	cut	cut	put	put	put
hit	hit	hit	etc.	etc.	etc.
let	let	let			

CLASE 10

Presente	Pretérito	Participio	Presente	Pretérito	Participio
abide	abode	abode	drink	drank	drunk
arise	arose	arisen	drive	drove	driven
backbite	backbit	backbitten, backbit	eat	ate	eaten
			fall	fell	fallen
			feed	fed	fed
bear	bore	borne, born	feel	felt	felt
			fight	fought	fought
beat	beat	beaten, beat	find	found	found
			flee	fled	fled
become	became	become	fling	flung	flung
befall	befell	befallen	fly	flew	flown
begin	began	begun	forbear	forbore	forborne
behold	beheld	beheld	forbid	forbade, forbad	forbidden, forbid
beseech	besought	besought			
bid	bade, bid	bidden, bid	forego	forewent	foregone
bind	bound	bound	foresee	foresaw	foreseen
bite	bit	bitten, bit	foretell	foretold	foretold
bleed	bled	bled	forget	forgot	forgotten, forgot
blow	blew	blown			
break	broke	broken (roto), broke (arruinado)	forgive	forgave	forgiven
			forsake	forsook	forsaken
			forswear	forswore	forsworn
			freeze	froze	frozen
			get	got	gotten, got
breed	bred	bred	give	gave	given
bring	brought	brought	go	went	gone
build	built	built	grow	grew	grown
buy	bought	bought	hang	hung	hung
catch	caught	caught		(colgar)	
choose	chose	chosen	hear	heard	heard
cling	clung	clung	hide	hid	hidden, hid
come	came	come			
creep	crept	crept	hold	held	held
deal	dealt	dealt	inlay	inlaid	inlaid
draw	drew	drawn	keep	kept	kept

Presente	Pretérito	Participio	Presente	Pretérito	Participio
know	knew	known	seek	sought	sought
lay	laid	laid	sell	sold	sold
lead	led	led	send	sent	sent
leave	left	left	shake	shook	shaken
lend	lent	lent	shine	shone,	shone,
lie	lay	lain		shined	shined
(echarse)			shoe	shod	shod
lose	lost	lost	shoot	shot	shot
make	made	made	shrink	shrank,	shrunk,
make-up	made-up	made-up		shrunk	shrunken
mean	meant	meant	sing	sang, sung	sung
meet	met	met	sink	sank, sunk	sunk,
mislay	mislaid	mislaid			sunken
mislead	misled	misled	sit	sat	sat
mistake	mistook	mistaken	slay	slew	slain
misunder-	misunder-	misunder-	sleep	slept	slept
stand	stood	stood	slide	slid	sid, slidden
outbid	outbid	outbid-	sling	slung	slung
		den,	slink	slunk	slunk
		outbid	smite	smote	smitten,
outdo	outdid	outdone			smit
outgo	outwent	outgone	speak	spoke	spoken
outgrow	outgrew	outgrown	spellbind	spellbound	spellbound
outlay	outlaid	outlaid	spend	spent	spent
outrun	outran	outrun	spin	spun	spun
outshine	outshone	outshone	spit	spat, spit	spat, spit
overbear	overbore	overborne	spring	sprang,	sprung
overbid	overbid	overbid-		sprung	
		den,	stand	stood	stood
		overbid	steal	stole	stolen
overcome	overcame	overcome	stick	stuck	stuck
overdo	overdid	overdone	sting	stung	stung
overdraw	overdrew	overdrawn	stink	stank	stunk
overeat	overate	overeaten	stride	strode	stridden
overfeed	overfed	overfed	strike	struck	struck,
overgrow	overgrew	overgrown			stricken
overhang	overhung	overhung	string	strung	strung
overhear	overheard	overheard	strive	strove	striven
overlay	overlaid	overlaid	swear	swore	sworn
overrun	overran	overrun	sweep	swept	swept
oversee	oversaw	overseen	swing	swung	swung
overshoot	overshot	overshot	take	took	taken
oversleep	overslept	overslept	teach	taught	taught
overtake	overtook	overtaken	tear	tore	torn
overthrow	overthrew	over-	tell	told	told
		thrown	think	thought	thought
partake	partook	partaken	throw	threw	thrown
pay	paid	paid	tread	trod	trodden,
prepay	prepaid	prepaid			trod
rebuild	rebuilt	rebuilt	typewrite	typewrote	type-
remake	remade	remade			written
rend	rent	rent	undergo	underwent	undergone
repay	repaid	repaid	underpay	underpaid	underpaid
resell	resold	resold	undersell	undersold	undersold
retake	retook	retaken	understand	under-	under-
ride	rode	ridden		stood	stood
ring	rang	rung	undertake	undertook	under-
rise	rose	risen			taken
run	ran	run	undo	undid	undone
say	said	said	uphold	upheld	upheld
see	saw	seen	waylay	waylaid	waylaid

Presente	Pretérito	Participio	Presente	Pretérito	Participio
wear	wore	worn	withhold	withheld	withheld
weep	wept	wept	withstand	withstood	withstood
win	won	won	wring	wrung	wrung
wind	wound	wound	write	wrote	written
withdraw	withdrew	withdrawn			

CLASE 11 (Verbos auxiliares, anómalos y defectivos)

	Present	Preterit	Past Participle
to be	I am, you are, he is; (pl.) are	I was, you were, he was; (pl.) were	been
can	can	could	—
to do	I, you do, he does; (pl.) do	did	done
to have	I, you have, he has; (pl.) have	had	had
may	may	might	—
must	must	—	—
ought	ought	ought	—
shall	shall	should	—
will	will	would	—

ABREVIATURAS USADAS EN LA PARTE I

a.	adjetivo.
abrev.	abreviatura.
adv.	adverbio.
(aer.)	aeronáutica.
(aerosp.)	aeroespacial.
(agr.)	agricultura.
(alb.)	albañilería.
(álg.)	álgebra.
(Am.)	América.
(anat.)	anatomía.
(ant.)	anticuado.
(apl.)	aplícase.
(Arg.)	Argentina.
(arit.)	aritmética.
(arm.)	armería.
(arq.)	arquitectura.
art.	artículo.
(arti.)	artillería.
(astr.)	astronomía, astrología.
(aut.)	automovilismo.
aux.	auxiliar.
(b.a.)	bellas artes.
(biol.)	biología.
(bot.)	botánica.
(carp.)	carpintería.
(carr.)	carruajería.
(cine)	cine.
(cir.)	cirugía.
(coc.)	cocina.
(com.)	comercio.
comp.	comparativo.
(comput.)	computadora.
conj.	conjunción.
contr.	contracción.
(cost.)	costura.
defect.	defectivo.
(dep.)	deporte.
(despec.)	despectivo.
(elec.), (eléc.)	electricidad.
(electron.)	electrónica.
(esp.)	especialmente.
(E.U.)	Estados Unidos.
f.	femenino.
(fam.)	familiar.
(farm.)	farmacia.
(f.c.)	ferrocarriles.
(fig.)	figurado.
(filos.)	filosofía.
(fis.)	física.
(fisiol.)	fisiología.
(fon.)	fonética.
(for.)	voz forense.
(fort.)	fortificación.
(fot.)	fotografía.
(G.B.)	Gran Bretaña.
(gen.)	generalmente.
(geog.)	geografía.
(geol.)	geología.
(geom.)	geometría.
ger.	gerundio.
(gram.)	gramática.
(heráld.)	heráldica.
(hidr.)	hidráulica.
(hist.)	historia.
(hort.)	horticultura.
(humor.)	humorística.
(ict.)	ictiología.

(igl.)	iglesia.
imp.	imperfecto.
impers.	impersonal.
(impr.)	imprenta.
indic.	indicativo.
inf.	infinitivo.
(ing.)	ingeniería.
interj.	interjección.
interrog.	interrogativo.
(jer.)	jerga, argot.
(joy.)	joyería.
(lóg.)	lógica.
m.	masculino.
(mar.)	marina.
(mat.)	matemáticas.
(mec.)	mecánica.
(med.)	medicina.
mf.	masculino y femenino.
(mil.)	milicia.
(miner.)	minería, minerología.
(mús.), (mus.)	música, musical.
(ópt.)	óptica.
(orn.)	ornitología.
(p.ej.)	por ejemplo.
pers.	personal.
(pert.)	perteneciente (a).
pl.	plural.
(poét.)	poética.
(pol.)	política.
pos.	posesivo.
pp.	participio pasado.
pp. i.	participio pasado irregular.
prep.	preposición.
pret.	pretérito.
pron.	pronombre.
(quím.)	
(quim.)	química.
(rad.)	radiocomunicación.
refl.	reflejo o reflexivo.
rel.	relativo (gram.)
(rel.)	relativo a.
s.	substantivo.
sing.	singular.
(sociol.)	sociología.
subj.	subjuntivo.
super.	superlativo.
(teat.)	teatro.
(técn.)	técnica.
(tej.)	tejidos.
(tel.)	televisión.
(tlf.)	telefonía.
(tlg.)	telegrafía.
(TM)	marca de fábrica.
(Ú., ú.)	Úsase, úsase.
(V., *v.*)	Véa(n)se, véa(n)se.
va.	verbo auxiliar.
vai.	verbo auxiliar irregular.
(vg., v.g., v.gr.)	por ejemplo.
vi.	verbo intransitivo.
vii.	verbo intransitivo irregular.
vr.	verbo reflexivo o recíproco.
vri.	verbo reflexivo o recíproco irregular.
vt.	verbo transitivo.
vti.	verbo transitivo irregular.
(vulg.)	vulgar, obsceno.
(zool.)	zoología.

A

a [a(variante acentuado: ei)] (delante de sonido vocálico: **an**) *art.* un, una.—*from A to Z*, de pe a pa.—*such a man*, semejante hombre.—*twice a week* dos veces por semana.

aback [abǽk], *adv.* detrás, atrás.—*to take a.*, desconcertar, coger de improviso.

abandon [abǽndon], *vt.* abandonar, dejar.—*to a. oneself to*, entregarse a.—*s.*—*with wild a.*, desenfrenadamente.

abase [abéis], *vt.* abatir, humillar.—*to a. oneself*, humillarse.

abashed [abǽšt], *a.* avergonzado.—*to be a. at*, avergonzarse de.

abate [abéit], *vt.* reducir, rebajar; mitigar.—*vr.* disminuirse, calmarse.

abbey [ǽbi], *s.* abadía. —**abbot** [ǽbot], *s.* abad.

abbreviate [abrívieit], *vt.* abreviar, reducir, compendiar. —**abbreviation** [abriviéišon], *s.* (short form) abreviatura; (shortening) abreviación.

ABC [éibísi], **ABC's** [eibisíz], *s.* abecé.—*do you know your ABC's?*, ¿ya te sabes el abecé?

abdicate [ǽbdikeit], *vt.* y *vi.* abdicar.

abdomen [ǽbdomen], *s.* abdomen, vientre. —**abdominal** [æbdáminal], *a.* abdominal.

abduct [æbdákt], *vt.* secuestrar, raptar (a alguien).- —**ion** [æbdákšon], *s.* robo, secuestro; (anat.) abducción.

aberration [æbæréišon], *s.* error; desliz; aberración.

abet [abét], *vti.* [1] favorecer, apoyar; instigar.

abeyance [abéians], *s.* expectativa.—*in a.*, suspenso; latente.

abhor [æbhór], *vti.* [1] aborrecer, detestar, abominar.

abide [abáid], *vti.* [10] esperar, tolerar, sufrir.—*vii.* habitar, permanecer.—*to a. by*, atenerse a.

ability [abíliti], *s.* capacidad, talento.

abject [ǽbdžekt], *a.* abatido, servil.- —**ion** [æbdžékšon], *s.* abyección; servilismo.

abjure [æbdžúr], *vt.* abjurar, retractarse de; renunciar solemnemente a.—*vi.* retractarse; hacer renuncia solemne (del reino, etc.).

ablaze [abléiz], *adv.* en llamas.

able [éibl], *a.* capaz, apto, capacitado.—*a.-bodied*, robusto.—*to be a.*, poder, saber.

abnormal [æbnórmal], *a.* anormal, deforme, anómalo.

aboard [abórd], *adv.* a bordo.—*all a.!* ¡viajeros al tren!—*to go a.*, embarcarse.

abode [abóud], *s.* morada, residencia.—*pret.* y *pp.* de TO ABIDE.

abolish [abáliš], *vt.* abolir, revocar, anular. —**abolition** [æbolíšon], *s.* abolición, revocación, anulación.

A-bomb, *s.* bomba atómica.

abominable [abáminabl], *a.* abominable; aborrecible. —**abomination** [abaminéišon], *s.* abominación, odio.

abortion [abóršon], *s.* aborto; fracaso.

abound [abáund], *vi.* abundar.—*abounding in o with*, nutrido de.

about [abáut], *adv.* casi; poco más o menos; alrededor; por ahí (en el lugar, edificio, etc.).—*a.-face*, media vuelta (voz de mando).—*all a.*, por todas partes.—*prep.* de, acerca de; sobre, con respecto a; alrededor de; a eso de; por, en.—*to be a.*, estar para, al punto de.—*to think a.*, pensar en.—*to walk a. town*, pasear por el pueblo.

above [abáv], *a.* susodicho, precitado; precedente.—*s.* lo anterior, lo precedente.—*adv.* y *prep.* sobre, arriba (de), superior (a), fuera de, anteriormente.—*a. all*, sobre todo.—*from a.*, de lo alto, del cielo; desde arriba.

abrasion [abréižon], *s.* raspadura, desgaste. —**abrasive** [abréisiv], *a.* raspante.—*s.* abrasivo.

abreast [abrést], *adv.* de frente, en fila.—*four a.*, de cuatro en fondo.—*to keep a. of something*, estar al tanto de algo.

abridge [abrídž], *vt.* abreviar, condensar.- —**ment** [-ment], *s.* compendio, resumen.

abroad [abród], *adv.* en el extranjero, fuera de casa o del país; en público.—*to go a.*, salir del país, ir al extranjero.

abrupt [abrápt], *a.* brusco, repentino; escarpado; grosero.

1

abscess [ǽbsɛs], s. absceso.
absence [ǽbsɛns], s. ausencia, falta.—*in the a. of,* a falta de.—*leave of a.,* licencia, permiso.—**absent** [ǽbsɛnt], a. ausente.—*a.-minded,* distraído, abstraído, absorto; en Babia.—*to a. oneself,* retirarse (de), ausentarse.- —**absentee** [æbsɛntí], s. ausente.—*a. ballot,* voto por correo.—*a. landlord,* absentista, dueño ausentista.
absolute [ǽbsolut], a. absoluto, categórico, positivo.
absolution [æbsolúʃon], s. absolución.
absolve [æbsálv], vt. absolver.
absorb [æbsórb], vt. absorber; empapar; ocupar (el ánimo) intensamente.- —**ed** [-d], a. absorto, cautivado.- —**ent** [-ɛnt], s. y a. absorbente. —**absorption** [æbsórpʃon], s. absorción.
abstain [æbstéin], vi. abstenerse.
abstemious [æbstímiʌs], a. sobrio, abstemio.
abstinence [ǽbstinɛns], s. abstinencia.
abstract [ǽbstrækt], s. abstracción; sumario, extracto.—a. abstracto, distraído.—vt. [æbstrækt], abstraer; resumir, extractar; compendiar; separar.- —**ion** [æbstrǽkʃon], s. abstracción.
absurd [æbsʌ́rd], a. absurdo, ridículo, disparatado.- —**ity** [-iti], s. absurdo, disparate.
abundance [ʌbʌ́ndʌns], s. abundancia, exuberancia. —**abundant** [ʌbʌ́ndʌnt], a. abundante, copioso.
abuse [ʌbjúz], vt. abusar de; insultar; ultrajar, maltratar.—s. [ʌbjús], abuso; improperios, injurias, insultos.—*physical a.,* malos tratos.—*sexual a.,* abusos deshonestos. —**abusive** [ʌbjúsiv], a. abusivo, insultante, injurioso.
abyss [ʌbís], s. abismo; sima.
academic(al) [ækʌdémik(ʌl)], a. académico.—s. profesor de universidad. —**academy** [ʌkǽdɛmi], s. academia.
accede [æksíd], vi. acceder; subir o ascender (al trono).
accelerate [æksélɛreit], vt. acelerar, apresurar.—vi. darse prisa. —**acceleration** [ækselɛréiʃon], s. aceleración. —**accelerator** [æksélɛreito(r)], s. acelerador.
accent [æksɛnt], s. acento, dejo.—vt. [æksɛnt], acentuar. —**accentuate** [æksénchueit], vt. acentuar; dar énfasis a, recalcar.
accent mark, acento ortográfico, tilde.
accept [æksépt], vt. aceptar, admitir; reconocer.- —**able** [-ʌbl], a. aceptable, grato, admisible.- —**ance** [-ʌns], s. aceptación; buena acogida, aprobación.
access [ǽksɛs], s. acceso, entrada; aumento; acceso o ataque (de tos, etc.); (comput.) acceso. (comput.) obtener acceso a, entrar a.- —**ible** [æksésibl], a. accesible, asequible.- —**ion** [ækséʃon], s. aumento; subida (al trono); accesión; consentimiento.- —**ory** [æksésori], a. accesorio; secundario; adicional.—s. dependencia; cómplice.—pl. accesorios, repuestos, enseres; útiles (de cocina, etc.).
accident [æksidɛnt], s. accidente.—*by a.,* por casualidad.- —**al** [æksidéntal], a. accidental, casual.—s. (mus.) accidente.
acclaim [ækléim], vt. y vi. aclamar, aplaudir, proclamar.—s. aclamación. —**acclamation** [æklaméiʃon], s. aclamación, aplauso, proclamación.
acclimate [ækláimit], o **acclimatize** [ækláimʌtaiz], vt. y vi. aclimatar(se).
accommodate [ʌkámodeit], vt. acomodar, ajustar; componer; hacer un favor; (to provide lodgings) alojar, hospedar.—*to a. oneself,* conformarse, adaptarse. —**accommodation** [ʌkamodéiʃon], s. acomodamiento; favor; adaptación; ajuste; acuerdo.—pl. alojamiento, hospedaje.
accompaniment [ʌkámpaniment], s. acompañamiento. —**accompanist** [ʌkámpanist], s. acompañante. —**accompany** [ʌkámpani], vti. [7] acompañar.
accomplice [ʌkámplis], s. cómplice.
accomplish [ʌkámpliʃ], vt. efectuar, cumplir; completar; lograr, llevar a cabo.- —**ment** [-mɛnt], s. cumplimiento, enajenación, ejecución; proeza.—pl. conocimientos, habilidades; méritos.
accomplished [ʌkámpliʃt], a. consumado.
accord [ʌkórd], s. acuerdo, convenio; concierto; armonía; (mus.) acorde. —*in a.,* de mutuo acuerdo.—*of*

one's own a., espontáneamente.—
vt. acordar, conceder, otorgar.—
vi. concordar; convenir, avenirse,
concertar, estar de acuerdo.-
—ance [-ạns], **—ancy** [-ạnsị], *s.*
conformidad, armonía, acuerdo.—
in accordance with, de acuerdo con.
—ant [-ạnt], *a.* acorde, conforme,
propio.- **—ing** [íŋ], *a.* conforme,
acorde.—*a. as,* a medida que.—*a.
to,* según.- **—ingly** [-ịnlị], *adv.* en
conformidad, en efecto; de consiguiente; por ende.

accordion [ạkórdịọn], *s.* acordeón.

accost [ạkóst], *vt.* dirigirse a, abordar
(a alguien en la calle); acosar.

account [ạkáụnt], *vt.* tener por, considerar, estimar.—*vi.* dar cuenta y
razón.—*to a. for,* dar razón o responder de.—*s.* relato, relación; importancia, valor; explicación,
cuenta, razón; cálculo; consideración;
aprecio; (com.) cuenta.—*a.-
book,* libro de cuentas.—*by all accounts,* según el decir o la opinión
general.—*charge a.,* cuenta abierta
o corriente.—*of a.,* de nota, de importancia.—*on a. of,* a causa de.—
on my own a., por mi cuenta, por
mi cuenta y riesgo.—*on no a.,* de
ninguna manera.- **—able** [-ạbl],
a. responsable; explicable.- **—ant**
[-ạnt], *s.* contador; tenedor de libros.- **—ing** [-iŋ], *s.* contabilidad,
contaduría; estado de cuentas.—*to
ask an a.,* pedir rendición de
cuentas.

accredit [ækrédịt], *vt.* acreditar; dar
credenciales; dar crédito; atribuir a.

accrue [ækrú], *vi.* crecer, tomar incremento; acumularse.

accumulate [ạkjúmjụleịt], *vt.* y *vi.*
acumular(se), amontonar(se), atesorar; crecer. **—accumulation** [ạkju-
mjụléịṣọn], *s.* acumulación; (e.g. of
snow) montón.

accuracy [ǽkyụrǎsị], *s.* exactitud, precisión, esmero. **—accurate** [ǽkyụ-
rịt], *a.* exacto, preciso; certero (en
el tiro); exacto (en los cálculos).

accursed [ạkérst], *a.* maldito; execra-
ble; perverso, infame.

accusation [ækjuzéịṣọn], *s.* acusación. **—accuse** [ạkjúz], *vt.* acusar,
denunciar, (in)culpar.

accustom [ạkástọm], *vt.* y *vi.* acos-
tumbrar(se), habituar(se), ha-
cer(se)

ace [eịs], *s.* as (de naipes o dados); as
(el más sobresaliente en su activi-

dad); (tennis) ace.—*within an a. of,*
por poco, en un tris.—*a.* sobresaliente.

ache [eịk], *s.* dolor.—*vi.* doler.

achieve [ạchív], *vt.* realizar, lograr,
conseguir.- **—ment** [-mẹnt], *s.* realización, logro.

acid [ǽsịd], *s.* y *a.* ácido.—*s.* (jer.)
droga LSD.—*deoxyribonucleic a.,*
(DNA), ácido desoxirribonucleico
(ADN).- **—ity** [ǽsídịtị], *s.* acidez;
(med.) acedía.

acid rain, lluvia ácida.

acknowledge [æknálịdž], *vt.* reconocer; confesar, admitir; testificar.
—*to a. receipt,* acusar recibo. **—acknowledgment** [-mẹnt], *s.* reconocimiento; confesión; admisión;
acuse de recibo; testificación.

acolyte [ǽkolaịt], *s.* acólito; (fig.) seguidor.

acorn [éịkọrn], *s.* bellota.

acoustic [ạkústịk], *a.* acústico.—*s. pl.*
acústica; condiciones acústicas.

acquaint [ạkwéịnt], *vt.* avisar, informar.—*to a. oneself with,* ponerse al
corriente de, ponerse al tanto de.—
to be acquainted with somebody, conocer a alguien.—*to be acquainted
with something,* estar al corriente
de.- **—ance** [-ạns], *s.* conocimiento; familiaridad.

acquiesce [ækwịés], *vi.* asentir; consentir, conformarse.- **—nce**
[ækwịésẹns], *s.* acquiescencia,
asentimiento.

acquire [ạkwáịr], *vt.* adquirir, obtener,
contraer (hábitos, etc.). **—acquisition** [ækwịzíṣọn], *s.* adquisición.

**acquired immune-deficiency syndrome
(AIDS)** [ạkwáịrd], *s.* síndrome de
inmunodeficiencia adquirida
(SIDA).

acquit [ạkwít], *vti.* [1] absolver, dispensar; exonerar, relevar; pagar.—
to a. oneself, quedar bien; exone-
rarse.- **—tal** [-ạl], *s.* absolución.

acre [éịkọer], *s.* acre (medida de superficie). Ver Tabla.

acrimonious [ækrịmóụnịʌs], *a.* áspero, cáustico; enconado, amargo.

acrobat [ǽkrobæt], *s.* acróbata.

across [ạkrós], *adv.* a o de través; de
una parte a otra; al otro lado; en
crus.—*prep.* a través de; al otro lado
de; por.—*a. the way,* enfrente.

act [ækt], *s.* acción, acto, hecho;
(teat.) acto.—*s. (for.)* ley, decreto, acta.—*a. of God,* fuerza mayor.—*vi.* obrar, actuar, funcionar;

representar (en el teatro); simular; portarse.—*to a. as*, servir de, estar de.—*to a. up*, jaranear.—*vt.* hacer o desempeñar el papel de.- **—ing** [ǽktɪŋ], *s.* acción; (teat.) representación.—*a.* interino.- **—ion** [ǽkʃon], *s.* acción, acto; operación, funcionamiento; (teat.) argumento; (mil.) batalla; (mec.) mecanismo; (for.) demanda.—*to bring an a.*, entablar un pleito.—*to take a.*, proceder (contra).

activate [ǽktɪveɪt], *vt.* activar. **—active** [ǽktɪv], *a.* activo, diligente, ágil, eficaz. **—activity** [ǽktɪvɪtɪ], *s.* actividad, vigor.—*pl.* ocupaciones.

actor [ǽkto(r)], *s.* actor. **—actress** [ǽktrɪs] *s.* actriz.

actual [ǽkchuạl], *a.* real, verdadero; efectivo; existente.

actuary [ǽkchuẹrɪ], *s.* actuario (de seguros).

acumen [akɪúmɪn], *s.* perspicacia, sagacidad.

acupressure [ǽkyūéʃụr], *s.* digitopuntura.

acupuncture [ǽkyūpʌ́ŋkchụr], *s.* acupuntura.

acupuncturist [ǽkyūpʌ́nchụrist], *s.* acupuntor, acupunturista.

acute [akɪút], *a.* agudo.

A.D. (Anno Domini) [eɪdí], *abrev.* dC, d. de J.C. (después de Jesucristo).

ad [æd], *s.* (fam.) anuncio, aviso.

adamant [ǽdạmænt], *a.* firme, inflexible.

Adam's apple [ǽdamz], *s.* nuez de Adán, nuez de la garganta.

adapt [ạdǽpt], *vt.* adaptar, ajustar, amoldar; refundir.- **—ation** [ædạptíʃọn], *s.* adaptación, ajuste.

add [æd], *vt.* sumar, adicionar, totalizar; agregar, añadir.—*vi.* sumar.

added [ǽdɪd], *a.* adicional, extra, añadido.

addict [ǽdɪkt], *s.* adicto; (of sports, music, etc.) aficionado, fanático.—*drug a.*, narcómano.- **—ed** [ạdíktɪd], *a.* adicto, entregado o afecto a; partidario de.

adding machine [ǽdɪŋ], *s.* sumadora.

addition [ạdíʃọn], *s.* adición, añadidura; aditamento, adjunto, suma. —*in a.*, por añadidura.—*in a. to*, además de.— **—al** [-ạl], *a.* adicional.

address [ạdrés], *vt.* dirigir la palabra, arengar; dirigir o poner el sobre a una carta.—*s.* [ạdrés, ǽdres], dirección, señas; sobrescrito; membrete;

discurso; solicitud; memorial.— *business a.*, dirección profesional.— *home a.*, dirección particular, domicilio.— **—er** [-œ(r)], *s.* remitente (de una carta, etc.).

adept [ạdépt], *a.* adepto, perito.

adequacy [ǽdɛkwạsɪ], *s.* adecuación, suficiencia. **—adequate** [ǽdɛkwɪt], *a.* adecuado, proporcionado, suficiente.

adhere [ædhír], *vi.* adherirse, unirse; pegarse.- **—nce** [ædhírẹns], *s.* adhesión, apego, adherencia. **—adhesion** [ædhíʒọn], *s.* adhesión, adherencia. **—adhesive** [ædhísịv], *s.* adhesivo, sustancia adhesiva.—*a.* adhesivo, pegadizo, engomado (sello).—*a. plaster*, (GB) esparadrapo.—*a. tape*, cinta adhesiva.

adjacent [ædʒéɪsẹnt], *a.* adyacente.

adjective [ǽdʒɛktịv], *s.* adjetivo.

adjoin [ạdʒóɪn], *vt.* juntar, unir.—*vi.* (co)lindar con, estar contiguo.- **—ing** [-ɪŋ], *a.* contiguo.

adjourn [ạdʒœ́rn], *vt.* diferir, aplazar, clausurar, suspender o levantar la sesión.—*vi.* levantarse o suspenderse (una sesión).- **—ment** [-mẹnt], *s.* aplazamiento, traslación, suspensión.

adjunct [ǽdʒʌŋkt], *s.* aditamento, adjunto; ayudante; subalterno.—*a.* adjunto, auxiliar, subordinado.

adjust [ạdʒʌ́st], *vt.* ajustar, adaptar; acomodar, concertar, dirimir (disputas, etc.); regular.- **—ment** [-mẹnt], *s.* arreglo, adaptación, ajuste.

ad lib [ædlíb], *s.* improvisación.—*a.* improvisado.—*adv.* improvisando. —*vt.* y *vi.* improvisar.

administer [ædmínistœ(r)], *vt.* administrar; desempeñar (un cargo); suministrar; dar; aplicar (remedios, un castigo, etc.).—*to a. an oath*, tomar juramento. **—administration** [ædmɪnistréɪʃọn], *s.* administración; ministerio; gobierno; gerencia; manejo. **—administrative** [ædmínistreɪtịv], *a.* administrativo. **—administrator** [ædmínistreɪto(r)], *s.* administrador.

admirable [ǽdmirạbl], *a.* admirable.

admiral [ǽdmirạl], *s.* almirante.- **—Admiralty** [-tɪ], *s.* Almirantazgo, ministerio de marina del Reino Unido.

admiration [ædmiréɪʃọn], *s.* admiración. **—admire** [ædmáɪr], *vt.* admirar.—*vi.* admirarse de; sentir admiración por. —**admirer** [ædmáɪœ(r)], *s.* admirador; enamorado, pretendiente.

admission [ædmíʃən], *s.* admisión, entrada; acceso; precio de entrada; confesión, reconocimiento.—*a. fee,* cuota de entrada (en un club, etc.). —**admit** [ædmít], *vti.* [1] admitir, recibir; dar entrada; reconocer, admitir.- —**admittance** [ædmítəns], *s.* acceso, entrada.—*no. a.,* prohibida la entrada.

admonish [ædmániʃ], *vt.* amonestar, reprender. —**admonition** [ædmoníʃən], *s.* amonestación.

adolescence [ædolésəns], *s.* adolescencia. —**adolescent** [ædolésənt], *s. y a.* adolescente.

adopt [ədápt], *vt.* adoptar, prohijar.- —**ion** [ədápʃən], *s.* adopción, prohijamiento.

adorable [ədɔ́rəbl], *a.* adorable —**adoration** [ædɔréiʃən], *s.* adoración. —**adore** [ədɔ́r], *vt.* adorar.

adorn [ədɔ́rn], *vt.* adornar, ornamentar, embellecer, acicalar, aderezar.- —**ment** [-mənt], *s.* adorno, embellecimiento.

adrenaline [ædrénəlin], *s.* adrenalina.

adrift [ədríft], *adv.* al garete; abandonado; a la deriva.

adroit [ədrɔ́it], *a.* diestro, hábil, listo.

adulation [ædʒuléiʃən], *s.* adulación.

adult [ədʌ́lt], *a. y s.* adulto.—*adults only,* solo para adultos.

adulterate [ədʌ́ltœreit], *vt.* adulterar.—*a.* adulterado. —**adultery** [ədʌ́ltœri], *s.* adulterio.

advance [ædvǽns], *vt. y vi.* avanzar.—*vi.* avanzar, adelantarse; progresar; subir de valor o de precio.—*s.* avance; anticipo, adelanto.—*to pay in a.,* pagar por anticipado, pagar por adelantado.—*pl.* requerimientos amorosos, insinuaciones.—*a.* previo, anticipado.—*a. guard,* (mil.) avanzada.—*in a.,* anticipadamente; al frente; de antemano; (com.) por adelantado; anticipado.- —**d** [-t], *a.* avanzado, adelantado, desarrollado.—*a. in years,* entrado en años.- —**ment** [-mənt], *s.* progreso, adelantamiento; fomento; (in rank) ascenso.

advantage [ædvǽntjdʒ], *s.* ventaja, beneficio, delantera.—*to one's a.,* con provecho para uno.—*to take a. of,* aprovecharse de, sacar partido de.—*vt.* favorecer.—*vi.* medrar, sacar ventaja.- —**ous** [ædvəntéidʒʌs], *a.* provechoso, ventajoso, conveniente.

advent [ǽdvɛnt], *s.* advenimiento. —**Advent** (igl.) Adviento.

adventure [ædvénchŭr], *s.* aventura.- —**r** [-œ(r)], *s.* aventurero. —**adventurous** [-ʌs], *a.* aventurero; aventurado, arriesgado; atrevido.

adverb [ǽdvœrb], *s.* adverbio.

adversary [ǽdvœrseri], *s.* adversario. —**adverse** [ædvœrs], *a.* adverso. —**adversity** [ædvœrsiti], *s.* adversidad.

advertise [ǽdvœrtaiz], *vt.* anunciar, hacer propaganda o publicidad.- —**ment** [ædvœrtizmənt], *s.* anuncio.- —**r** [ǽdvœrtaizœ(r)], *s.* anunciante. —**advertising** [ǽdvœrtaizɪŋ], *s.* publicidad.

advice [ædváis], *s.* consejos.—*a piece of a.,* un consejo.

advisable [ædváizəbl], *a.* aconsejable, prudente; conveniente. —**advise** [ædváiz], *vt.* aconsejar; avisar, informar.—*vi.* aconsejar; (professionally) asesorar.—*to a. against,* desaconsejar. —**adviser** [ædvaizœ(r)], **advisor** [ædváizǫ(r)], *s.* consejero, consultor.—*legal a.,* asesor.

advocate [ǽdvokeit], *vt.* defender, recomendar.—*s.* defensor, partidario.

aeration [ɛréiʃən], *s.* aereado.

aerial [eííal], *a.* aéreo.—*a. photography,* aerofoto.—*s.* (rad./tel.) antena.

aerodynamics [erodainǽmiks], *s.* aerodinámica. —**aerobic** [erábik], *s.* aeróbico.—*a. exercises,* aerobismo, aerobics. —**aeronaut** [éronɔt], *s.* aeronauta. —**aeronautics** [eronɔ́tiks], *s.* aeronáutica. —**aeroplane** [éroplein], *s.* aeroplano. —**aerosol** [érosal], *s.* aerosol. —**aerospace** [érospeis], *a.* aerospacial.

aesthetic [esθétik], *a.* = ESTHETIC.- —**s** [-s], *s.* = ESTHETICS.

afar [əfár], *adv.* lejos, distante.—*a. off,* remoto.—*from a.,* desde lejos.

affable [ǽfabl], *a.* afable, atento.

affair [əfér], *s.* caso; (business) asunto, negocio; (love) affaire, aventura amorosa.—*a. of honor,* duelo.—*love a.,* amorío.

affect [əfékt], *vt.* afectar a; (an interest, mannerism, etc.) afectar.- —**ation** [æfɛktéiʃən], *s.* afectación.-

—**ed** [-ịd], *a.* afectado; amenerado.
– —**ion** [afékŝǫn], *s.* afecto, cariño. devoción, ternura; emoción; inclinación; impresión; (med.) afección, dolencia.- —**ionate** [afékŝǫnịt], *a.* afectuoso, cariñoso, amoroso.- —**ive** [aféktịv], *a.* afectivo.

affidavit [æfịdéịvịt], *s.* declaración jurada; testimonio.

affiliate [afílịeịt], *vt.* afiliar.—*vi.* y *vr.* afiliarse.—*s.* filial, afiliado.

affinity [afínịtị], *s.* afinidad.

affirm [afóerm], *vt.* afirmar, aseverar.— *vi.* afirmarse en alguna cosa; declarar formalmente ante un juez. – —**ation** [æfœrméịŝǫn], *s.* afirmación, aserto.— —**ative** [afóermạtịv], *a.* afirmativo.—*a. action,* discriminación positiva.

affix [afíks], *vt.* fijar; poner (firma o sello).—*s.* [æfịks], añadidura; (gram.) afijo.

afflict [aflíkt], *vt.* afligir. —**ion** [aflíkŝǫn], *s.* aflicción; desgracia.

affluence [æfluẹns], *s.* abundancia, opulencia. —**affluent** [æfluẹnt], *a.* opulento, afluente, abundante, copioso.—*s.* afluente, tributario.

afford [afórd], *vt.* dar, proporcionar, proveer; tener medios o recursos para una cosa, permitirse el lujo de.

affray [afréị], *s.* riña, pendencia.

affront [afrÁnt], *vt.* afrentar, insultar.—*s.* afrenta, insulto, agravio.

afield [afíld], *adv.* lejos de casa; descarriado.—*far a.,* muy lejos.

afire [afáịr], *adv.* en llamas.

aflame [afléịm], *adv.* en llamas.

afloat [aflóụt], *a.* y *adv.* a flote, flotante, a nado; inundado.

afoot [afút], *a.* y *adv.* a pie; en movimiento.

afraid [afréịd], *a.* acobardado, medroso, tímido.—*to be a.,* tener miedo, temer.—*I'm a. that Robert is not here,* lo siento, pero Roberto no está.

afresh [afréŝ], *adv.* de nuevo, otra vez.

African [æfrịkan], *s.* y *a.* africano.— *A.-American,* afroamericano.

Afro-American [æfroạmérịkan] *s.* y *a.* afroamericano.

aft [æft], *adv.* a popa o en popa.

after [æftœ(r)], *prep.* después de; detrás de, tras (de); al cabo de; en pos de; por, en busca de; según.—*a. all,* después de todo, de todas maneras.—*the day a. tomorrow,* pasado mañana.—*to be a. something,*

buscar algo.—*adv.* después, enseguida, seguidamente.—*soon a.,* poco después.—*conj.* después (de) que, así que.—*a.* posterior, siguiente; subsiguiente, resultante. —*a.-dinner,* de sobremesa.—*a.-effect,* resultado, consecuencia.— *a.-shave lotion,* loción para después del afeitado.- —**burner** [-boérnoer], *s.* dispositivo de postcombustión.—**math** [-mæθ], *s.* desenlace, consecuencia.- —**noon** [-nun], *s.* tarde.- —**taste** [-teịst], *s.* resabio (sabor).- —**ward(s)** [-wărd(z)], *adv.* después.

again [agén], *adv.* otra vez, aún, nuevamente, además; asimismo.—*a. and a.,* muchas veces.—*come a.,* vuelva Ud.

against [agénst], *prep.* contra; enfrente de; junto a (una pared, etc.); en contraste con; listo para.—*a. the grain,* a contrapelo; de mal grado.—*a. time,* dentro de tiempo limitado.

age [eịdž], *s.* edad; época, período, era, siglo; vejez, ancianidad; envejecimiento.—*A. of Aquarius,* siglo de Acuario.—*a. old,* secular, milenario.—*full a.,* mayoría de edad.— *of a.,* mayor (de edad).—*under a.,* minoría, menor (de edad).—*vi.* envejecerse; deteriorarse.—*vt.* madurar.- —**d** [eịdž(ị)d], *a.* anciano, añejo.

agency [eịdžẹnsị], *s.* agencia; gestión, influencia, medio.—*free a.,* libre albedrío. —**agenda** [adžénda], *s.* orden del día, agenda. —**agent** [eịdžẹnt], *s.* agente; representante, intermediario, apoderado; (for.) mandatario.

aggregate [ægrịgeịt], *a.* total, global.—*s.* agregado, total.—*in the a.,* en conjunto.—*vt.* y *vi.* agregar, sumar, juntar.

aggression [agréŝǫn], *s.* agresión. —**aggressive** [agrésịv], *a.* agresivo; dinámico, enérgico. —**aggressor** [agrésǫ(r)], *s.* agresor.

agile [ædžịl], *a.* ágil. —**agility** [adžílịtị], *s.* agilidad.

agitate [ædžịteịt], *vt.* agitar; inquietar.—*vi.* excitar la opinión pública. —**agitation** [ædžịtéịŝǫn], *s.* agitación; inquietud. —**agitator** [ædžịteịtǫ(r)], *s.* agitador; perturbador, alborotador; demagogo.

aglow [aglóụ], *y a.* resplandeciente.

ago [agóụ], *a.* y *adv.* pasado, en el pasado.—*a long time a.*, hace mucho tiempo.—*how long a.?* ¿cuánto tiempo hace?—*two years a.*, hace dos años.

agog [ǝgág], *s.*—*to be a.*, sentir gran curiosidad, estar ansioso.

agonize [ǽgǝnaiz], *vt.* atormentar.—*vi.* agonizar; penar, sufrir intensamente, retorcerse de dolor. —**agony** [ǽgǝni], *s.* agonía; angustia, tormento, zozobra.

agrarian [ǝgrérian], *s. y s.* agrario.—*s.* agrarista.

agree [ǝgrí], *vi.* concordar, coincidir, acordar; entenderse, avenirse; consentir; quedar o convenir en (precio, etc.); sentar (un precedente, etc.); sentarle a uno bien (ropa, clima, etc.); (gram.) concordar.—**able** [-ǝbl], *a.* agradable; satisfactorio; simpático; complaciente. —*a. to*, de acuerdo con.- —**ment** [-mǝnt], *s.* acuerdo, convenio, ajuste, concierto, avenencia; consentimiento; armonía; conformidad; (gram.) concordancia.—*in a.* (*with*), acorde con.

agricultural [ægrikálchŭrǝl], *a.* agrícola, agrario. —**agriculture** [ǽgrikálchŭ(r)], *s.* agricultura. —**agriculturist** [ægrikálchŭrist], *s.* agricultor.

ahead [ǝhéd], *adv.* delante, al frente, a la cabeza; adelante; hacia delante.

aid [eid], *vt. y vi.* ayudar, socorrer, auxiliar, apoyar.—*s.* ayuda, auxilio, concurso, socorro; subsidio; (mil.) ayudante.—*first a.*, primeros auxilios (médicos).

AIDS [eidz], *s.* (med.) SIDA (síndrome de inmunodeficiencia adquirida).

ail [eil], *vt.* (ant.) afligir, molestar (algún dolor).—*What ails you?*, ¿Que tienes?.—*vi.* estar enfermo o indispuesto.- —**ment** [éilmǝnt], *s.* dolencia, enfermedad.

aim [eim], *vt.* apuntar (con un arma); dirigir, asestar, encarar.—*vi.* apuntar, hacer puntería.—*to aim at o for*, apuntar a.—*to aim high/low*, apuntar alto/bajo; aspirar a mucho/a poco.—*s.* puntería; punta de mira; objetivo.—*accurate a.*, tino.—*to miss one's a.*, errar el tiro.- —**less** [éimlis], *a.* sin objeto, sin rumbo, a la ventura.

air [ɛr], *vt.* airear, ventilar, orear, aventar; secar (al aire o por calor); sacar a relucir, pregonar.—*s.* aire; atmósfera; brisa; semblante, ade-mán; (mús.) tonada.—*in the a.*, en vilo.—*in the open a.*, al aire libre; a la intemperie.—*to be on the a.*, estar trasmitiendo por radio.—*to put on airs*, darse tono o ínfulas.—*up in the a.*, indeciso; perplejo.—*a.* de aire, neumático; para aire; aéreo; aeronáutico, de aviación.—*a. bag*, (aut.) bolsa de aire.—*a. brakes*, frenos neumáticos.—*a. carrier*, portaaviones.—*a. conditioning*, acondicionamiento del aire, aire acondicionado.—*a. cooling*, enfriamiento por aire.—*a. drill*, taladro neumático.—*a. duct*, canal de aire. —*a. force*, aviación militar, fuerzas aéreas.—*a. hostess*, aeromoza, azafata.—*a. lane*, vía aérea.—*a. line*, línea o empresa aérea.—*a. liner*, avión de una empresa o línea aérea.—*a. mail*, correo aéreo.—*a.-mail service*, servicio aeropostal.— *a. plant*, talleres de aviación.—*a. pocket*, bache o cajón de aire.—*a. pressure*, presión atmosférica.—*a. proof*, hermético.—*a. raid*, ataque aéreo.—*a.-raid warning*, alarma aérea.—*a.-raid shelter*, refugio antiaéreo.—*a.-tight*, hermético.—*a.-to-a. missile*, misil de aire a aire.—*a. valve*, válvula (de admisión o salida) de aire.—*by a.-mail*, por vía aérea, por avión.- —**craft** [érkræft], *s.* máquina de volar (aeroplanos, dirigibles, etc.).—*a. carrier*, (mil. mar.) portaaviones.- —**field** [-fild], *s.* campo de aviación.- —**plane** [-plein], *s.* aeroplano, avión. —**port** [-port], *s.* aeropuerto; aeródromo.- —**sickness** [-siknis], *s.* mareo en viaje aéreo.- —**way** [-wei], *s.* ruta de aviación, vía aérea.—*pl.* red aérea.- —**y** [-i], *a.* aéreo, airoso; bien ventilado; etéreo; tenue; ligero; vanidoso, estirado.

aisle [áil], *s.* pasillo (de un teatro); nave (de una iglesia).—*a. seat*, asiento al lado de pasillo.—*to walk down the a.*, llegar al altar.

ajar [ǝdžár], *adv. y a.* entreabierto, entornado.—*to set a.*, entornar, entreabrir.

a.k.a., (also known as) alias.

akimbo [ǝkímbou], *a. y adv.* en jarras.

akin [ǝkín], *a.* consanguíneo, emparentado, afín; análogo, semejante.

alabaster [ælǝbǽstœ(r)], *s.* alabastro.

alarm [ǝlárm], *s.* alarma; rebato.—*a. clock*, (reloj) despertador.—*to sound* the a., dar la alarma, tocar a rebato.—vt. alarmar; asustar; inquietar.—vi. dar la alarma; asustarse.

Alaskan [alǽskan], s. natural de Alaska.—a. de o referente a Alaska.

alb [ælb], s. (igl.) alba.

Albanian [ælbéjnian], s. y a. albanés.—f. albanesa.

albatross [ǽlbɛtrɔs], s. albatros.

album [ǽlbʌm], s. alba.

alcohol [ǽlkohɔl], s. alcohol.— **—ic** [ælkohɔ́lik], a. alcohólico.— **—ism** [-izm], s. alcoholismo.

alcove [ǽlkouv], s. alcoba, nicho.

alderman [ɔ́ldœrman], s. regidor, concejal.

ale [eil], s. cerveza.

alert [alœ́rt], a. alerta, vigilante; cuidadoso.—on the a., sobre aviso.—s. alarma.—vt. poner sobre aviso.

algebra [ǽldžebrã], s. álgebra.

Algerian [ældžíriãn], a. y s. argelino.

alibi [ǽlibai], s. excusa; coartada.

alien [éjlyen], a. extraño, ajeno; extranjero, forastero.—s. extranjero, residente extranjero.— **—ate** [-ejt], vt. enajenar, traspasar; quitar, indisponer; alejar (a una persona de otra).

alight [aláit], vii. [4] descender, bajar, apearse; (con **on**) posarse (sobre); (aer.) aterrizar, acuatizar (un hidroavión).—a. y adv. encendido; iluminado.

align [aláin], vt. alinear(se).— **—ment** [-ment], s. alineación.

alike [aláik], adv. igualmente, del mismo modo; a la par.—a. semejante; igual.

alimony [ǽlimoni], s. (for.) alimentos, pensión a la mujer en el divorcio o separación.

alive [aláiv], a. vivo, viviente; encendido; animado; sensible.

alkali [ǽlkalai], s. (quím.) álcali.

all [ɔl], a. todo, todos; todo (el), todos (los).—s. y pron. todo, totalidad, conjunto; todos, todo el mundo; todo lo.—adv. completamente, enteramente.—above a., sobre todo, ante todo.—after a., después de todo, al fin y al cabo.—a. along, siempre, constantemente, sin cesar, por todo (el camino, tiempo, etc.).—a. around, en todo respecto.—a. at once, repentinamente; de un golpe; a un tiempo.—a. but, todo(s) menos, o sino; casi, por poco.—a. clear, cese

de alarma; (fig.) luz verde.—a. in, agotado, rendido de cansancio.—a. out, completamente; apagado (el fuego, un incendio).—a. out! ¡salgan todos!—a. out of, sin; desprovisto de.—a. over, terminado, acabado.—a.-purpose [-pœrpos], multiuso.—a. right, ciertamente, está bien, bueno.—a.-round, por todas partes; completo; acabado, consumado; de idoneidad general.—a. set, listo dispuesto.—a.-star [-star], estelar, de primeras figuras.—a. that, todo el (o lo) que, todos los que, cuanto(s).—a. the better (worse), tanto mejor (peor).—a. the same, a pesar de eso; lo mismo.—a.-time [-tajm], sin precedentes, de todos los tiempos.—a. told, en (con)junto, por todo.—not at a., de ningún modo, nada de eso; no por cierto; no hay de que.—once and for a., una vez por todas; definitivamente; para siempre.

Allah [álạ], m. Alá.

allay [aléj], vt. aliviar; calmar.

allegation [ælẹgéjšọn], s. alegación, argumento; (for.) alegato. **—allege** [alédž], vt. alegar; declarar; sostener; pretender; (for.) deducir.

allegiance [alídžạns], s. lealtad, homenaje, fidelidad.

allergic [alœ́rdžik], a. alérgico. **—allergy** [ǽlœrdžị], s. alergia.

alleviate [alívjejt], vt. aliviar, mitigar; aligerar.

alley [ǽlị], **alley-way** [ǽljwei], s. callejuela, callejón; (in a bowling alley) pista; (in a park) paseo.—a. cat, gato callejero.—blind alley, callejón sin salida.—bowling alley, bolera.

alliance [aláiạns], s. alianza. **—allied** [aláid], a. aliado, unido; relacionado.

alligator [ǽligeito(r)], s. caimán; yacaré.—a. pear, aguacate.—a. clip, pinza de contacto.

allocation [ælokéjšọn], s. colocación; asignación, distribución.

aloe [ǽlou], s. (bot.) áloe.— **—s** [-z], (sing. y pl.) áloe o acíbar.

allot [alát], vti. [1] distribuir, repartir, asignar.— **—ment** [-ment], s. asignación; distribución; ración; parcela.

allow [aláu], vt. permitir, consentir, dejar, conceder; dar, admitir; (com.) rebajar, deducir.—vi. (con **for**) tener en cuenta.— **—ance**

[-ạns], *s.* concesión; asignación; ración; pensión, mesada; permiso; indulgencia; descuento, bonificación, refacción; (tecn.) tolerancia.—*annual a.,* anualidad.—*monthly a.,* mensualidad.—*retirement a.,* jubilación, retiro.—*to make a. for,* tener en cuenta.

alloy [ælɔ́i], *s.* mezcla; (fund.) aleación; liga.—*vt.* alear, ligar (los metales).

All Saints' Day, *s.* día de Todos los Santos.

All Souls' Day, *s.* día de Difuntos, día de los Muertos.

allspice [ɔ́lspạis]. *s.* (bot.) pimienta de Jamaica; (coc.) pimienta inglesa.

allude [ạljúd], *vi.* aludir, referirse a.

allure [ạljúr], *vt.* halagar, atraer, seducir.—*s.* seducción, atractivo. **—alluring** [ạljúriŋ], *a.* seductivo, tentador.

allusion [ạljúʒọn], *s.* alusión.

ally [ạlái], *vti.* [7] unir.—*vii.* aliarse, coligarse.—*s.* aliado; pariente.

alma mater [ǽlmǽǽtœr], *s.* almamáter, antigua universidad.—*my a.,* mi (antigua) universidad.

almanac [ɔ́lmạnæk], *s.* almanaque.

almighty [ɔlmáiti], *a.* todopoderoso, omnipotente.—*s.* (con **the**) Dios.

almond [ámọnd], *s.* almendra.—*a.* **tres,** almendro.

almost [ɔ́lmoust], *adv.* casi, por poco.

alms [ams], *s.* limosna.

aloft [ạlɔ́ft], *adv.* arriba, en alto.

alone [ạlóun], *a.* y *adv.* solo, solitario; sólo, solamente.—*all a.,* a solas.—*to let a.,* dejar en paz, no molestar.

along [ạlɔ́ŋ], *prep.* por; a lo largo de; al lado de.—*adv.* a lo largo de; adelante.—*all a.,* todo el tiempo; de un extremo al otro.—*a. these lines,* en este sentido.—*a. with,* con, junto con.—*come a.,* venga conmigo.—*move a.!* ¡largo de aquí!—*to get a. with,* adelantar; ir tirando; llevarse (bien) con.- **—shore** [-ʃɔr], *adv.* a la orilla, a lo largo de la costa. - **—side** [-sạid], *adv.* y *prep.* a lo largo de, al lado, lado a lado.

aloof [ạlúf], *adv.* lejos, apartado, a distancia.—*a.* huraño, reservado.—*to stand o keep a.,* mantenerse apartado; aislarse.- **—ness** [-nịs], *s.* alejamiento, aislamiento.

aloud [ạláud], *adv.* alto, en vos alta.

alphabet [ǽlfạbet], *s.* alfabeto, abecedario, abecé.- **—ical** [ælfạbétịkạl], *a.* alfabético.

already [ɔlrédị], *adv.* ya, antes de ahora.

also [ɔ́lsou], *adv.* también, igualmente, además, asimismo.

altar [ɔ́ltạ(r)], *s.* altar, ara.—*a. boy,* monaguillo, acólito.—*a. bread,* pan de la eucaristía, hostia.—*a. rail,* comulgatorio.

alter [ɔ́ltœ(r)], *vt.* alterar, cambiar, modificar, mudar, variar.—*vi.* alterarse, cambiarse, variar.- **—ation** [-éiʃọn], *s.* alteración, cambio, mudanza; arreglo.

alternate [ǽltœrnẹit], *vt.* y *vi.* alternar; turnar; variar.—*a.* [ǽltœrnịt], alterno; alternativo.—*s.* suplente, sustituto. **—alternating** [ǽltœrnẹitiŋ], *a.* alternante, alternativo, alterno.—*a. current,* corriente alterna.—**alternative** [æltœrnǽtịv], *s.* alternativa.—*a.* alternativo.

although [ɔlðóu], *conj.* aunque, si (bien), bien que, no obstante, aun cuando.

altitude [ǽltịtiud], *s.* altura, altitud.

alto [ǽltou], *a.* alto.—*s.* contralto.

altogether [ɔltugéðœ(r)], *adv.* en conjunto; enteramente, del todo.

alumnus [ạlʌ́mnʌs], *s.* (*pl.* **alumni** [ạlʌ́mnai]), *f.* **alumna** [ạlʌ́mnạ], (*pl.* **alumnae** [ạlʌ́mni], ex-alumno; antiguo estudiante de una universidad o escuela.

aluminum [æljúmịnʌm], *s.* aluminio.

always [ɔ́lwejz], *adv.* siempre.

A.M. (ante meridiem) [eiém], *abrev.* de la mañana, p.ej., *9 A.M.,* las nueves de la mañana.

am [æm], (1ª pers. pres. ind. de TO BE), soy, estoy.

amalgamate [ạmǽlgạmẹit], *vt.* y *vi.* amalgamar, unir, incorporar.

amaranth [ǽmạrænθ], *s.* (bot.) amaranto, borlones; (color) púrpura oscura.

amass [ạmǽs], *vt.* acumular, amasar (riquezas, etc.); apilar.

amateur [ǽmạtịur], *s.* y *a.* aficionado, no profesional.

amaze [ạméjz], *vt.* asombrar, pasmar, dejar atónito o maravillado.- **—ment** [-ment], *s.* asombro, pasmo, aturdimiento. **—amazing** [ạméjzịŋ], *a.* asombroso, pasmoso.

ambassador [æmbǽsạdọ(r)], *s.* embajador.

amber [ǽmbœ(r)], *s.* ámbar; color de ámbar.—*a.* ambarino.

ambiguity [æmbi̯giúi̯ti], *s.* ambigüedad. **—ambiguous** [æmbígiu̯ʌs], *a.* ambiguo, equívoco; evasivo.

ambition [æmbíʂǫn], *s.* aspiraciones; ambición, codicia. **—ambitious** [æmbíʂʌs], *a.* lleno de aspiraciones; ambicioso, codicioso.

amble [æmbl], *vi.* andar; vagar.—*s.* (paso de) andadura.

ambulance [æmbi̯ulạns], *s.* ambulancia.

ambush [æmbu̯ŝ], *vt.* acechar, poner celada, emboscar.—*s.* emboscada, celada.

amen [ei̯mén, amén], *interj.* y *s.* amén.

amend [ạménd], *vt.* enmendar, rectificar, modificar, corregir, reformar.—*vi.* enmendarse, reformarse, restablecerse.— **—ment** [-mẹnt], *s.* enmienda, reforma.

American [ạmérikạn], *s.* y *a.* (South American) americano; (North American) norteamericano; (E.U.) estadounidense.—*A. Indian,* amerindio.

amethyst [æmẹ̄θi̯st], *s.* amatista; color de amatista.

amiable [éi̯mi̯ạbl], *a.* amable, afable.

amicable [æmi̯kạbl], *a.* amigable, amistoso.

amid [ạmíd], **amidst** [ạmídst], *prep.* entre, en medio de.

amiss [ạmís], *adv.* mal, fuera de lugar o de razón; impropiamente; de más.—*to take a.,* tomar a mal.—*a.* inoportuno, impropio, errado.

amity [æmi̯ti], *s.* amistad, concordia, armonía.

ammonia [ạmóu̯ni̯ạ], *s.* amoníaco.

ammunition [æmyuníʂǫn], *s.* munición, municiones.

amnesia [æmníʂi̯ạ], *s.* amnesia.

amnesty [æmnesti̯], *s.* amnistía.—*vt.* amnistiar.

amoebic [amíbi̯k], *a.* amebico.—*a. dysentery,* (med.) amebiasis, amebas.

among [ạmʌ́ŋ], **amongst** [ạmʌ́ŋst], *prep.* entre, mezclado con, en medio de.

amorous [æmorʌs], *a.* enamorado, amoroso, enamoradizo.

amortize [ạmórtai̯z], *vt.* amortizar.

amount [ạmáu̯nt], *s.* cantidad; importe, suma.—*vi.*—*to a. to,* ascender a, equivaler a, llegar a; venir a ser.

amperage [æmpíri̯dẑ], *s.* amperaje. **—ampere** [æmpír], *s.* amperio.—*a.-hour,* amperio-hora.

ampersand [æmpersænd], *s. el signo & (significando "y").*

amphibian [æmfíbi̯ạn], *s.* y *a.* anfibio.

amphitheater [æmfi̯θi̯ạtœ(r)], *s.* anfiteatro.

ample [æmpl], *a.* amplio; lato; abundante.

amplifier [æmpli̯fai̯œ(r)], *s.* amplificador, megáfono. **—amplify** [æmpli̯fai̯], *vti.* [7] amplificar; ampliar.

amputate [æmpi̯utei̯t], *vt.* amputar, desmembrar.

amputee [æmpi̯utí], *s.* persona con un miembro amputado.

amuse [ạmiúz], *vt.* entretener, distraer, divertir.—*to a. oneself,* divertirse.— **—ment** [-mẹnt], *s.* diversión, pasatiempo, entretenimiento. **—amusing** [ạmiúzi̯ŋ], *a.* divertido, recreativo; risible, gracioso.

an [æn], *art. (delante de sonido vocálico)* un, uno, una.

anachronism [ænækroni̯zm], *s.* anacronismo.

analog o **analogue** (aénạlɔg), *a.* (electron.) analógico.—*s.* (comput.) computadora analógica, ordenador analógico.

analogous [ạnælogʌs], *a.* análogo. **—analogy** [ạnælodẑi̯], *s.* analogía.

analysis [ạnǽli̯si̯s], *s.* análisis. **—analyze** [ǽnạlai̯z].—*vt.* analizar.

analyst [aénạli̯st], *s.* analista.

anarchist [ǽnạrki̯st], *s.* **anarchistic** [ænạrkísti̯k], *a.* anarquista. **—anarchy** [ǽnạrki̯], *s.* anarquís.

anathema [ạnǽθẹmạ], *s.* anatema; (fig.) abominación.

anatomy [ạnǽtomi̯], *s.* anatomía.

ancestor [ǽnsestǫ(r)], *s.* antepasado; (forerunner) antecesor. **—ancestral** [ænséstrạl], *a.* ancestral, hereditario. **—ancestry** [ǽnsestri̯], *s.* ascendencia, linaje.

anchor [æŋkǫ(r)], *vi.* anclar; asegurar.—*s.* ancla, áncora; artificio de sujeción o amarre; escape de reloj.—*to drop a.,* echar el ancla.—*to ride at a.,* estar fondeado o anclado.—*to weigh a.,* zarpar.— **—age** [-i̯dẑ], *s.* ancladero, fondeadero.— **—man** [-maen], *s.* (rad./tel.) presentador.— **—woman** [-wúmạn], *s.* presentadora.

anchovy [ǽnchou̯vi̯], *s.* anchos, anchova.

ancient [éi̯nŝent], *a.* antiguo, vetusto.—*the Ancients,* la Antigüedad.

and [ænd], *conj.* y, e.—*a. so forth*, o *a. so on*, etcétera, y así sucesivamente.—*ifs, ands or buts*, dimes y diretes.

Andalusian [ændəl̞iúẑən], *a.* y *s.* andaluz.

Andean [ændían], *a.* y *s.* andino.

andirons [ændaɪ̯ɔ͡ernz], *s. pl.* morillos.

anecdote [ænɪkdoʊt], *s.* anécdota.

anemia [ænímɪ̯ə], *s.* anemia, **—anemic** [æním̩k], *a.* anémico.

anesthesia [ænɛsθíẑɪ̯ə], *s.* anestesia. **—anesthetic** [ænɛsθétɪk], *a.* y *s.* anestésico.

anew [ænɪú], *adv.* nuevamente.

angel [éɪ̯nd̮ẑəl], *s.* ángel, serafín.— **—ic** [ænd̮ẑélɪk], *a.* angelical, angélico.

anger [ǽŋgœ(r)], *s.* enfado, enojo, ira, cólera.—*to provoke to a.*, encolerizar, enfadar.—*vt.* enfadar, enojar, encolerizar.

angina [ænd̮ẑáɪ̯nə, ænd̮ẑɪ̯nə], *s.* angina.—*a. pectoris*, angina de pecho.

angle [ǽŋgl], *vt.* sesgar.—*vi.* pescar con caña.—*s.* ángulo; punto de vista.—**r** [ǽŋglœ(r)], *s.* pescador (de caña).

angling [ǽŋglɪŋ], *s.* pesca con caña.

Anglo-Saxon [aeŋglɔ̄sæksʌn], *s.* y *a.* anglosajón.

angry [ǽŋgri], *a.* enojado, enfadado, encolerizado, bravo.—*to get a.*, enfadarse, enojarse, encolerizarse.

anguish [ǽŋgwɪ̑s], *s.* ansia, angustia.

angular [ǽŋgɪ̯ulə(r)], *a.* angular, anguloso.

aniline [ǽnɪs], *s.* anilina.

animal [ǽnɪ̯məl], *s.* y *a.* animal.

animate [ǽnɪ̯meɪt], *vt.* animar.— *a.* [ǽnɪ̯mɪt], animado, viviente. — **animation** [ǽnɪ̯méɪ̯s̮ən], *s.* animación. **—animism** [ǽnɪ̯mɪzm], *s.* animismo. **—animosity** [ænɪ̯másɪ̯tɪ], *s.* animosidad, rencor. **—animus** [ǽnɪ̯mʌs], *s.* ánimo, intención; animosidad.

anise [ǽnɪs], *s.* anís. **—anisette** [ænɪ̯zét], *s.* anís.

ankle [ǽŋkl], *s.* tobillo.—*a. sock*, calcetín corto, soquete.—*a. strap*, tirita tobillera.

annex [ænéks], *vt.* anexar, anexionar; (to add) adjuntar, añadir.—*s.* [ǽnɛks], anexo; añadidura; dependencia, pabellón separado.- **—ation** [ænɛkséɪ̯s̮ən], *s.* anexión, adición, unión.

annihilate [ənáɪ̯ɪleɪt], *vt.* aniquilar. **—annihilation** [ənaɪ̯ɪléɪ̯s̮ən], *s.* aniquilación.

anniversary [ænɪvœ́rsəri], *s.* aniversario.—*a.* anual.

annotate [ǽnoteɪt], *vt.* anotar; comentar, glosar. **—annotation** [ænotéɪ̯s̮ən], *s.* anotación, nota.

announce [ənáʊ̯ns], *vt.* anunciar.— **—ment** [-mᵊnt], *s.* anuncio.- **—r** [-œ(r)], *s.* (rad./tel.) comentarista.

annoy [ənɔ́ɪ̯], *vt.* molestar, incomodar, fastidiar.- **—ance** [-ᵊns], *s.* molestia, incomodidad, disgusto, fastidio.- **—ing** [-ɪŋ], *a.* fastidioso, molesto, incómodo, importuno, engorroso.

annual [ǽnyuᵊl], *a.* anual. **—annuity** [ənɪúɪ̯tɪ], *s.* anualidad;—*life a.*, renta vitalicia.

annul [ənʌ́l], *vti.* [1] anular.- **—ment** [-mᵊnt], *s.* anulación.

anodyne [ǽnodaɪ̯n], *a.* y *s.* (med.) anodino, calmante.

anoint [ənɔ́ɪ̯nt], *vt.* untar; (igl.) ungir.

anonymous [ənánɪmʌs], *a.* anónimo.

anorexia [ænorɛksɪ̯ə], *s.* anorexia.

another [ənʌ́ðœ(r)], *a.* otro; distinto, diferente.—*pron.* otro, uno más.— *a. such*, otro que tal.—*one a.*, uno(s) a otro(s).

answer [ǽnsœ(r)], *vt.* y *vi.* responder, contestar.—*to a. back*, replicar; refunfuñar.—*to a. for*, responder de, ser responsable de; (a person) responder por.—*to a. to the name of*, tener por nombre, llamarse.—*s.* respuesta, contestación; (mat.) solución, resultado.

ant [ænt], *s.* hormiga.—*a. hill*, hormiguero en forma de montículo.

antagonism [æntǽgonɪzm], *s.* antagonismo. **—antagonist** [æntǽgonɪst], *s.* antagonista, adversario. **—antagonize** [æntǽgonaɪ̯z], *vt.* y *vi.* contender, oponerse; contrariar; ser antagónico.

antarctic [æntárktɪk], *a.* antártico.

anteater [ǽntítœ(r)], *s.* oso hormiguero.

antecedent [æntɪsídᵊnt], *a.* y *s.* antecedente, precedente.

antechamber [ǽntɪ̯cheɪmbœ(r)], *s.* antecámara, antesala.

antedate [æntɪdéɪ̯t], *vt.* ser anterior a, preceder.

antelope [ǽntᵊloup], *s.* antílope.

antenna [ænténə], *s.* (rad./tel.) antena.- **—e** [ænténi], *pl.* (zool.) antenas.

anthem [ǽnθᵊm], *s.* himno.

anthology [ænθálod̮ẑɪ̯], *s.* antología, florilegio.

anthropology [ænθropáladʒi], s. antropología.

antiaircraft [æntjérkræft], a. antiaéreo.

antiballistic missile [æntjbalístik], s. mísil antibalístico, antimisil.

antibiotic [æntjbaiátik], a. y s. antibiótico.

antibody [æntjbadi], s. anticuerpo.

antic [æntik], s. zapateta, cabriola.— pl. travesuras; actos ridículos.

anticipate [æntísipeit], vt. esperar, prever; anticiparse a.—vi. anticiparse. —**anticipation** [æntjsipéiṣon], s. anticipación, previsión; expectación.

anticommunist [æntjkámyunist], s. y a. anticomunista.

antidote [æntidout], s. antídoto.

antifreeze [æntifriz], s. y a. anticongelante.

antihistamine [æntjhístamin], s. antihistamínico.

antiknock [æntinak], s. y a. antidetonante.

antimony [æntimouni], s. antimonio.

antinomy [æntínomi], s. antinomia; paradoja.

antipathy [æntípaθi], s. antipatía.

antipode [æntipoud], s. antípoda.

antiquarian [æntjkwérian], s. y a. anticuario. —**antiquated** [æntikweitid], a. anticuado. —**antique** [æntík], a. antiguo.—s. antigüedad, antigualla.—a. shop, tienda de antigüedades. —**antiquity** [æntíkwiti], s. antigüedad; ancianidad; la Antigüedad.

anti-Semite [æntjsémait], s. antisemita.

anti-Semitic [æntjsemítik], a. antisemítico.

anti-Semitism [æntjsémitism], s. antisemitismo.

antiseptic [æntjséptik], a. antiséptico.

antiskid [æntjskid], a. antideslizante.

antler [æntlœ(r)], s. asta (del ciervo, venado, etc.).

anus [éinʌs], s. ano.

anvil [ænvil], s. yunque.

anxiety [æŋgzáieti], s. ansiedad; anhelo, afán, ansias.

anxious [æŋkŝas], a. inquieto, impaciente, ansioso.

any [éni], a. y pron. cualquier(a), cualesquier(a); algún, alguno; todo.— a. longer, más tiempo, todavía; más.—a. more, más, aún; todavía.—a. way, de cualquier

modo.—at a. rate, o in a. case, de cualquier modo, de todos modos.—not a. longer, not a. more, ya no, no más.— —**body** [-badi], —**one** [-wʌn], pron. alguno, alguien, cualquiera; todo el mundo, toda persona.— —**how** [-hau], —**way** [-wei], adv. de cualquier modo; en cualquier caso; de todos modos; sea lo que sea; sin embargo.— —**thing** [-θiŋ], pron. algo alguna cosa, cualquier cosa; todo todo lo que.—a. else, cualquier otra cosa, algo más.—to be a. but, ser todo menos, no ser ni con mucho.— —**where** [-hwer], adv. donde quiera, en todas partes.—a. near, siquiera aproximadamente.—not a., en ninguna parte.

apart [apárt], adv. aparte; separadamente; de por sí; además; prescindiendo de; en pedazos, en partes.—to take a., desarmar, desmontar.

apartment [apártment], s. apartamento, piso.—a. building, edificio de apartamentos, casa de pisos.

apathy [æpaθi], s. apatía, indiferencia.

ape [eip], s. simio, mono; bruto; (fig.) imitador.— —**man** [-mæn], s. hombre mono.—vt. imitar, remedar.

aperitif [æperitíf], s. aperitivo.

aperture [æpœrchŭr], s. abertura, paso, rendija.

apex [éipeks], s. (pl. **apices** [æpisiz]) ápice, cúspide, punta, cima.

apiece [apís], adv. por persona, por cabeza; cada uno; sendos.

aplomb [aplóm], s. aplomo, seguridad; verticalidad.

apogee [æpodʒi], s. apogeo; auge.

apologetic(al) [apaladʒétik(al)], a. contrito; lleno de disculpas. —**apologize** [apáladʒaiz], vt. y vi. excusar(se), disculpar(se). —**apology** [apáladʒi], s. apología, excusa, disculpa, satisfacción.

apostasy [apástasi], s. apostasía.

apostle [apásl], s. apóstol. —**apostolic(al)** [æpostálik(al)], a. apostólico.—Apostolic See, (igl.) sede apostólica, la Santa Sede.

apostrophe [apástrofi], s. apóstrofe; apóstrofo.

apothecary [apáθēkeri], s. boticario.

appall [apól], vt. espantar, aterrar; consternar.— —**ing** [-iŋ], a. espantoso, aterrador.

apparatus [æpareitʌs], s. aparato.

apparel [apǽrᴇl], *s.* ropa.—*vti.* [2] vestir.

apparent [apérᴇnt], *a.* aparente, visible, manifiesto.—*a. horizon,* horizonte sensible.—*a. time,* tiempo solar.—*heir a.,* heredero forzoso.- **—ly** [-lị], *adv.* por lo visto, según parece, al parecer.

apparition [æparíʃon], *s.* aparición, aparecimiento; aparecido, fantasma, espectro.

appeal [apíl], *vi.* pedir o suplicar; despertar atención o simpatía.—*vt.* apelar de, apelar contra.—*s.* llamamiento; simpatía, atracción.

appear [apír], *vi.* aparecer(se), mostrarse, personarse; brotar, surgir; semejar; comparecer.—*to a. to be,* aparentar, representar.- **—ance** [-ạns], *s.* apariencia, aspecto, facha; aparición, comparecencia.

appease [apíz], *vt.* apaciguar, pacificar; calmar.- **—ment** [-mᴇnt], *s.* conciliación, apaciguamiento.- **—r** [-œ(r)], *s.* apaciguador.

append [apénd], *vt.* añadir, anexar; atar, colgar.- **—age** [-ịdž], *s.* pertenencia, dependencia, accesorio; colgajo, apéndice.- **—ectomy** [æpᴇndéktomị], *s.* apend(ic)ectomía.- **—ix** [apéndịks], *s.* (*pl.* appendices [apéndịsiz]) apéndice.

appetite [ǽpᴇtait], *s.* apetito. **—appetizer** [ǽpᴇtaizœ(r)], *s.* aperitivo. **—appetizing** [ǽpᴇtaizịŋ], *a.* apetitoso.

applaud [aplód], *vt.* aplaudir, aclamar. **—applause** [aplóz], *s.* aplauso, aclamación.

apple [ǽpl], *s.* manzana, poma.—*Adam's a.,* nuez, bocado de Adán.—*a. of discord,* manzana de la discordia.—*a. of one's eye,* niña del ojo.—*a. orchard,* manzanal, pomal.—*a. pie* o *tart,* pastel(illo) de manzana.—*a.-pie order,* orden perfecto.—*a. tree,* manzano.- **—jack** [-džæk], *s.* aguardiente de manzana.- **—sauce** [-sɔs], *s.* compota de manzana.

appliance [aplájans], *s.* aparato. **—applicable** [ǽplịkabl], *a.* aplicable. **—applicant** [ǽplịkant], *s.* solicitante, aspirante, candidato. **—application** [æplịkéjʃon], *s.* aplicación; uso, empleo; instancia, solicitud.—*a. blank, a. form,* formulario, planilla. **—applied** [apláịd], *a.* aplicado; adaptado, utilizado.—*a. for,* pedido, encargado.-

—apply [aplái], *vti.* y *vii.* [7] aplicar, poner, fijar; ser aplicable o pertinente.

appoint [apóịnt], *vt.* nombrar, **—ment** [-mᴇnt], *s.* nombramiento; puesto, empleo; cita.—*pl.* mobiliario.

appraise [apréjz], *vt.* (a)valuar, valorar, tasar. **—appraisal** [apreizal], *s.* tasación, valoración, evaluación. **—r** [-œ(r)], *s.* tasador.

appreciable [apríʃịabl], *a.* apreciable. **—appreciate** [apríʃịejt], *vt.* apreciar, valuar, tasar. **—appreciation** [apriʃịéjʃon], *s.* valuación, tasa; (rise in value) aumento en valor.

apprehend [æprịhénd], *vt.* y *vi.* comprender, entender; temer, recelar; aprehender, capturar. **—apprehension** [æprịhénʃon], *s.* aprensión, recelo, desconfianza; aprehensión, captura. **—apprehensive** [æprịhénsịv], *a.* aprensivo, receloso; penetrante, perspicaz.

apprentice [apréntịs], *s.* aprendiz.— *vt.* contratar como aprendiz.- **—ship** [-šịp], *s.* aprendizaje.

approach [apróųch], *vt.* acercarse a; (a subject or person) abordar.—*vi.* acercarse.—*s.* acercamiento; (to a problem) enfoque.

approbation [æprobéjʃon], *s.* aprobación.

appropriate [apróųprịejt], *vt.* apropiarse; (assign) asignar, destinar.— [apróųprịịt], *a.* apropiado, apto, pertinente. **—appropriation** [aproųprịéjʃon], *s.* apropiación, suma consignada.

approval [aprúval], *s.* aprobación; visto bueno; consentimiento.—*on a.,* a prueba. **—approve** [aprúv], *vt.* aprobar, sancionar.—*vi.*—*to a. of,* aprobar, sancionar.

approximate [apráksịmịt], *a.* aproximado, aproximativo.—*vt.* y *vi.* [apráksịmejt], aproximar(se), acercar(se).

apricot [éịprịkat], *s.* albaricoque, (Am.) chabacano.

April [éịprịl], *s.* abril.—*A. fool!,* ¡inocente!, ¡que la inocencia te valga!—*A. Fools' Day* (en E.U. y GB el primero de abril), el día de los Santos Inocentes.

apron [éịpron], *s.* delantal, mandil, plancha de protección; cubierta; (theat.) proscenio.—*tied to the a. strings,* dominado por la mujer o la madre.

apropos [æpropóų], *a.* pertinente,

oportuno.—*adv.*—*apropos of*, a propósito de.

apt [æpt], *a.* apto, apropiado; (clever) listo, capaz.—*to be a. to*, ser propenso a.- **—itude** [æptitjud], **—ness** [æptnɪs], *s.* aptitud.

aquamarine [ækwəmərín], *s.* (min.) aguamarina. **—aquarium** [əkwériʌm], *s.* acuario, pecera. **—aquatic** [əkwǽtɪk], *a.* acuático. **—aqueduct** [ǽkwɪdʌkt], *s.* acueducto.

aquaplane [ǽkwəplejn], *s.* esquí acuático.—*vi.* hacer esquí acuático.

Aquarius [əkwérɪʊs], *s.* (astr.) Acuario.

aquatic [əkwǽtɪk], *a.* acuático.

Arab [ǽrəb], *s.* árabe.- **—ian** [əréjbiʌn], *a.* árabe, arábigo.- **—ic** [ǽrəbɪk], *s.* árabe, lengua arábiga.—*a.* arábigo.—*A. numeral*, número arábigo.

Aragonese [ærəgoníz], *a.* y *s.* aragonés.

arbiter [árbɪtœ(r)], *s.* árbitro. **—arbitrary** [árbɪtreri], *a.* arbitrario, despótico. **—arbitrate** [árbɪtrejt], *vt.* y *vi.* arbitrar, terciar. **—arbitration** [arbɪtréjšon], *s.* arbitraje. **—arbitrator** [árbɪtrejto(r)], *s.* árbitro.

arbor [árbo(r)], *s.* (mec.) árbol, eje; (bot.) emparrado, glorieta.

arc [ark], *s.* arco.- **—ade** [arkéjd], *s.* arcada; arquería.

arch [arch], *vt.* y *vi.* arquear(se), enarcar(se), encorvar(se); abovedarse. —*s.* arco, bóveda.—*a.* travieso; astuto.

archaic [arkéiɪk], *a.* arcaico.

archangel [árkéjndžel], *s.* arcángel.

archbishop [árchbíšop], *s.* arzobispo.- **—ric** [-rɪk], *s.* arzobispado.

archer [árchœ(r)], *s.* arquero, flechero.- **—y** [-i], *s.* tiro de arco.

archetype [árkɪtajp], *s.* arquetipo.

arching [árchɪŋ], *a.* arqueado.—*s.* arqueo, curvatura.

archipelago [arkipélagou], *s.* archipiélago.

architect [árkɪtekt], *s.* arquitecto; (fig.) artífice.- **—ure** [árkɪtekchū(r)], *s.* arquitectura.

archive [árkajv], *s.* archivo, documento archivado. **—archivist** [árkɪvɪst], *s.* archivista, archivero.

archway [árchwej], *s.* arcada; pasadizo bajo un arco.

arctic [árktɪk], *a.* ártico, septentrional; frígido.—*s.* región ártica, círculo ártico.

ardent [árdent], *a.* ardiente; apasio-

nado. **—ardor** [árdo(r)], *s.* ardor, calor; pasión, ansia.

arduous [árdžuʌs], *a.* arduo, difícil; alto, escabroso, enhiesto.

are [ar], 2da. pers. sing., 1ra., 2da. y 3ra. pl., pres. ind. de TO BE.

area [érɪə], *s.* región, zona, área; (field) terreno; (mat.) área.—*a. code*, (tlf.) código de la zona, código territorial.

arena [ərínə], *s.* arena, liza, ruedo.

Argentine(an) [ardžéntin, ardžentíniən], *s.* y *a.* argentino.

argue [árgju], *vt.* y *vi.* debatir, disputar, discutir, argüir, argumentar; sostener; demostrar, indicar. **—argument** [árgjument], *s.* disputa, discusión.

arid [ǽrɪd], *a.* árido, seco.- **—ity** [ərídɪtɪ], *s.* aridez, sequedad.

Aries [ériz], *s.* (astr.) Aries.

arise [əráiz], *vii.* [10] levantarse, subir; surgir; proceder, provenir (de); suscitarse; originarse, sobrevenir; resucitar. **—arisen** [ərízen], *pp.* de TO ARISE.

aristocracy [ærɪstákrəsɪ], *s.* aristocracia. **—aristocrat** [ærístokræt], *s.* aristócrata. **—aristocratic(al)** [ærɪstokrǽtɪk(əl)], *a.* aristocrático.

arithmetic [ærɪstákrəsɪ], *s.* aritmética.- **—al** [ærɪθmétɪkəl], *a.* aritmético.- **—ian** [ærɪθmetíšən], *s.* aritmético.

ark [ark], *s.* arca.—*A. of the Covenant*, Arca de la Alianza.—*Noah's a.*, Arca de Noé.

arm [arm], *s.* brazo; rama, canal; (mil.) arma.—*pl.* (mil.) armas, armamentos; (heráld.) blasón. —*a. band*, brazalete.—*a. bone*, canilla o caña del brazo.—*a. in a.*, de bracete; cogido del brazo.—*a.'s reach*, alcance del brazo.—*vt.* armar.—*vi.* armarse.

Armada [armádə], *s.* armada, flota.— *the Spanish A.*, (hist.) la Armada Invencible.

armament [árməment], *s.* armamento; equipo.

armchair [ármcher], *s.* sillón, butaca.

armed [armd], *a.* armado.—*a. forces*, fuerzas armadas.—*a. robbery*, robo a mano armada.

Armenian [armínjen], *a.* y *s.* armenio.

armful [ármful], *s.* brazada, brazado.

armistice [ármɪstɪs], *s.* armisticio.

armor [ármo(r)], *s.* armadura; (plating) coraza, blindaje; (mil.) fuerzas blindadas.—*a.-clad*, blindado, acorazado.—*knights in a.*, caballeros con armaduras.—*vt.* acorazar, blindar.– **—ed** [-d], *a.* blindado, acorazado.– **—y** [-i], *s.* arsenal; (heráld.) armería; (E.U.) sala de prácticas.

armpit [ármpit], *s.* sobaco.

army [ármi], *s.* ejército; (fig.) multitud, muchedumbre.

aroma [aróumǝ], *s.* aroma, fragancia. – **—tic(al)** [ærǝmǽtik(al)], *a.* aromático.

arose [aróuz], *pret.* de TO ARISE.

around [aráund], *adv.* alrededor o en derredor, a la redonda; a la vuelta; allá, por todos lados; de un lado para otro.—*the other way a.*, al contrario, viceversa, al revés.—*prep.* al volver de, alrededor de, cerca de, en torno de.—*a. here*, por aquí.—*a. the corner*, a la vuelta de la esquina.

arouse [aráuz], *vt.* despertar; mover, excitar, alborotar.

arraign [arréin], *vt.* (jur.) presentar al tribunal– **—ment** [-ment], *s.* (jur.) presentación al tribunal.

arrange [arréindƷ], *vt.* arreglar, disponer; (mus.) arreglar, adaptar.—*vi.* prevenir, hacer arreglos; concertarse, convenir.– **—ment** [-ment], *s.* disposición; (agreement) convenio; (mus.) arreglo.—*pl.* planes, medidas, preparativos.—*flower a.*, arreglo.

array [arréi], *s.* orden de batalla, formación; pompa, adorno; conjunto, colección.—*vt.* poner en orden de batalla; ataviar, adornar.

arrears [arírz], *s. pl.* atrasos, cantidades vencidas y no pagadas.—*in a.*, atrasado en el pago.

arrest [arrést], *s.* prisión, arresto, reclusión; detención;—*under a.*, detenido, arrestado.—*vt.* impedir, detener, atajar, reprimir; arrestar, prender, recluir; atraer; fijar la atención.– **—ing** [-iŋ], *a.* impresionante, llamativo.

arrival [aráival], *s.* llegada; persona que llega.—*new a.*, recién llegado.—*on a.*, al llegar.—**arrive** [aráiv], *vi.* llegar; (succeed) tener éxito.

arrogance [ǽrogans], *s.* arrogancia. **—arrogant** [ǽrogant], *a.* arrogante.

arrow [ǽrou], *s.* flecha, saeta.—*a. wound*, flechazo.

arse [ars], (GB) (vulg.) culo; imbécil.—*you silly a.*, ¡burro!

arsenal [ársinal], *s.* arsenal.

arsenic [ársinik], *s.* y *a.* arsénico.

arson [árson], *s.* incendio premeditado.– **—ist** [-ist], *s.* incendiario.

art [art], *s.* arte.—*a. gallery*, museo de arte, museo de pintura.—*a. history*, historia del arte.– **—s** [arts],—*a. and crafts*, artes y oficios.—*a. and crafts fair*, una feria de artesanía.—*fine a.*, bellas artes.

artery [árteri], *s.* arteria.

artesian [artíƷan], *a.* artesiano.—*a. well*, pozo artesiano.

artful [ártful], *a.* artero, ladino; diestro.

arthritic [arθrítik], *a.* artrítico.

arthritis [arθráitis], *s.* artritis.

artichoke [ártichouk], *s.* alcachofa.

article [ártikl], *s.* artículo.—*a. of clothing*, prenda de vestir.

articulate [artíkjuleit], *vt.* articular; expresar claramente.—*vi.* articular.—*a.* [artíkjulit], articulado; claro, de expresión inteligible. **—articulation** [artikjuléiƷon], *s.* articulación.

artifice [ártifis], *s.* artificio. **—artificial** [artifíƷal], *a.* artificial; (smile, manner) afectado.—*a. insemination*, inseminación artificial.—*a. intelligence*, inteligencia artificial.—*a. leg*, pierna ortopédica.—*a. respiration*, respiración artificial.

artillery [artíleri], *s.* artillería.

artisan [ártizan], *s.* artesano. **—artist** [ártist], *s.* artista; artífice; actor. **—artistic** [artístik], *a.* artístico.

arum [érʌm], *s.* aro, (Am.) malanga.

Aryan [érian], *s.* y *a.* ario (pueblo e idioma).

as [æz], *adv., conj.* y *pron. rel.* como; a medida que, mientras (que), según, conforme; cuando; en el momento en que, al; hasta donde va, en lo que contiene.—*a. for*, en cuanto a, por lo que respecta a.—*a. from*, a partir de.—*a. if*, como si.—*a. it were*, por decirlo así.—*a. late a.*, tan recientemente como, apenas, no más.—*a. many a.*, tantos como, cuantos; hasta.—*a. much a. to say*, como quien dice.—*a. of*, con fecha de.—*a. per*, según, de acuerdo con.—*a. soon a. possible*, cuanto antes.—*a. such*, como tal.—*a. well*, también, además.—*a. well a.*, también como, lo mismo que; así como.—*a. yet*, todavía, aún, hasta ahora.

asbestic [æsbéstịk], *a.* incombustible.—**asbestos** [æsbéstọs], *s.* asbesto, amianto.

ascend [ạsénd], *vt.* subir.—*vi.* ascender, subir.— **—ancy** [-ạnsị], **—ency** [-ẹnsị], *s.* predominio, ascendiente. **—ascension** [ạsénsọn], *s.* ascensión. **—ascent** [ạsént], *s.* subida, ascensión; ascenso.

ascertain [æsœrtéịn], *vt.* averiguar, indagar.—*vi.* cerciorarse (de).

ascribe [ạskráịb], *vt.* atribuir, imputar.

ascetic [ạsétịk], *s.* asceta.—*a.* ascético.— **—ism** [ạsétịsịzm], *s.* ascetismo.

aseptic [ạséptịk], *a.* aséptico.

ash [æš], *s.* ceniza, cenizas.—*A. Wednesday,* Miércoles de Ceniza.— **—es** [ǽšịz], *s.* restos mortales.

ashamed [ạšéịmd], *a.* avergonzado, corrido.—*to be a.,* darle a uno vergüenza.

ash-blond [aéšblánd], *a.* rubio ceniza.

ashcan [aéškaen], *s.* cubo de la basura.

ashen [áešẹn], *a.* lívido, centiciento.

ashore [ạšór], *adv.* en tierra, a tierra.— *to go a.,* desembarcar.

ashtray [aéštreị], *s.* cenicero.

Asian [éịžạn], **Asiatic** [eịžịǽtịk], *a.* y *s.* asiático.

aside [ạsáịd], *adv.* a un lado; aparte.— *s.* aparte (en obras teatrales).

asinine [áesịnaịn], *a.* estúpido, necio.

ask [æsk], *vt.* y *vi.* preguntar, pedir, rogar; invitar, convidar.—*to a. one down, in, up,* rogar a uno que baje, entre, suba.

askance [ạskǽns], *adv.* de soslayo, recelosamente.—*to look a.,* no aprobar; mirar recelosamente.—**askew** [ạskjú], *adv.* de lado, de través.

asleep [ạslíp], *adv.* y *a.* dormido, durmiendo; entumecido.—*to fall a.,* dormirse.

asparagus [æspǽrạgʌs], *s.* espárrago.

aspect [ǽspekt], *s.* aspecto; apariencia.

as per, *prep.* de acuerdo con, segun.

asperity [æspérịtị], *s.* aspereza; rudeza, acrimonia.

asphalt [ǽsfɔlt], *s.* asfalto.

aspirant [ạspáịrạnt], *s.* y *a.* aspirante. **—aspiration** [æspịréịšọn], *s.* aspiración; anhelo.—**aspire** [ạspáịr], *vi.* aspirar, ambicionar, pretender.

aspirin [ǽspịrịn], *s.* aspirina.

ass [æs], *s.* asno; (fam.) imbécil.—*to make an a. of oneself,* quedar como un imbécil.—*you silly ass!,* ¡burro!; (vulg.) culo.

assail [ạséịl], *vt.* asaltar, atacar.- **—ant** [-ạnt], **—er** [-œ(r)], *s.* y *a.* asaltante, atracador.

assassin [ạsǽsịn], *s.* asesino.- **—ate** [-eịt], *vt.* asesinar.- **—ation** [-éịšọn], *s.* asesinato.

assault [ạsɔlt], *s.* asalto, ataque; agresión sexual, violación.—*a. and battery,* agresión con lesiones, maltrato de palabra y obra.—*vt.* (mil.) asaltar, atacar; (jur.) agredir, atacar; agredir sexualmente.

assay [ạséị], *vt.* ensayar.—*s.* ensaye.

assemble [ạsémbl], *vt.* juntar; convocar, congregar; montar maquinaria.—*vi.* reunirse, juntarse. **—assembly** [ạsémblị], *s.* reunión, asamblea.—*a. line production,* producción en serie.—*a. line,* línea de montaje.

assent [ạsént], *vi.* asentir, convenir.— *s.* asentimiento.

assert [ạsœrt], *vt.* afirmar, asegurar; hacer valer.—*to a. oneself,* hacerse valer.- **—ion** [ạsœršọn], *s.* aserto, afirmación.

assess [ạsés], *vt.* tasar, valorar, asignar impuestos.- **—ment** [-mẹnt], *s.* tasación, avaluación; impuesto.

asset [ǽset], *s.* cualidad, ventaja.— *pl.,* activo, haber, capital.

assiduous [ạsídžuạs], *a.* asiduo.

assign [ạsáịn], *vt.* asignar, señalar; adscribir; consignar, traspasar.- **—ment** [-mẹnt], *s.* asignación, señalamiento, cesión.

assimilate [ạsímịleịt], *vt.* y *vi.* asimilar(se); comparar(se).

assist [ạsịst], *vt.* asistir, ayudar.—*vi.* ayudar.- **—ance** [-ạns], *s.* auxilio, asistencia, ayuda.- **—ant** [-ạnt], *s.* y *a.* ayudante, auxiliar.

associate [ạsóuṣịeịt], *vt.* y *vi.* asociar(se), unir(se).—*a.* [ạsóuṣịịt], asociado.—*s.* compañero; (con)socio, colega; cómplice.—**association** [ạsouṣịéịšọn], *s.* asociación; unión; sociedad; conexión, relación.

assort [ạsórt], *vt.* surtir con variedad; clasificar.- **—ed** [-ịd], *a.* variado, surtido, mezclado.- **—ment** [-mẹnt], *s.* surtido variado, colección.

assume [ạsúm], *vt.* tomar, asumir; suponer, dar por sentado.—*vi.* arrogarse, atribuirse.- **—d** [-d], *a.* supuesto, presunto; falso, fingido. **—assumption** [ąsʌ́mpṣǫn], s. suposición, supuesto; asunción. **—Assumption,** (igl.) Asunción.

assurance [ąṣúrąns], s. seguridad, certeza; confianza; (GB) seguro. **—assure** [ąṣúr], vt. asegurar, garantizar; (GB) asegurar (contra riesgos). **—assured** [ąṣúrd], a. seguro, asegurado, confiado; (GB) asegurado (contra riesgos).—s. (GB) asegurado.

asterisk [ǽstęrisk], s. asterisco.

astern [ąstǫ́rn], adv. por la popa, a popa.

asteroid [aéstęrǫid], s. asteroide.

asthma [ǽzmą], s. asma.

astigmatism [ąstígmątizm], s. astigmatismo.

astonish [ąstániṣ], vt. asombrar.- **—ed** [-t], a. atónito.- **—ing** [-iŋ], a. sorprendente, asombroso.- **—ment** [-męnt], s. pasmo, asombro, sorpresa.

astound [ąstáund], vt. y vi. pasmar; aturdir, confundir.

astraddle [ąstrǽdl], adv. y a. a horcajadas.

astray [ąstréi], adv. y a. desviada o descarriadamente.—to go a., desviarse, perderse.—to lead a., llevar por el mal camino.

astride [ąstráid], adv. a horcajadas.

astrologer [æstrálodžœ(r)], s. astrólogo. **—astrology** [ąstrálodži], s. astrología.

astronomer [ąstránomœ(r)], s. astrónomo. **—astronomic(al)** [æstronámik(ąl)], a. astronómico. **—astronomy** [ąstránomi], s. astronomía.

Asturian [æstúriąn], s. y a. asturiano, astur.

asylum [ąsáilʌm], s. asilo.—insane a., (ant.) manicomio.

at [æt], prep. a; en; con; de; por.—angry a. me, enfadado conmigo.—a. his command, por orden suya.—a. last, por fin.—a. once, inmediatamente.—a. one stroke, de un golpe.—a. Rome, en Roma.—a. the door, a o en la puerta.—a. work, trabajando.

ate [eit], pret. de TO EAT.

atheism [éiθiizm], s. ateísmo. **—atheist** [éiθiist], s. ateo. **—atheistic(al)** [eiθiístik(ąl)], a. ateo, ateístico.

athlete [ǽθlit], s. atleta.—athlete's foot, (med.) pie de atleta, tiña po-

dal. **—athletic** [æθlétik], a. atlético.—a. supporter, (jockstrap) suspensorio. **—athletics** [æθlétiks], s. deportes, atletismo; gimnasia.

Atlantic [ætlǽntik], a. atlántico.—s. el mar Atlántico.

atlas [ǽtlas], s. atlas.

atmosphere [ǽtmosfir], s. atmósfera. **—atmospheric(al)** [ætmosférik(ąl)], a. atmosférico. **—atmospherics** [ætmosfériks], s. estática (rad.).

atoll [aétɔl], s. atolón.

atom [ǽtom], s. átomo.—a. bomb, bomba atómica.—a. splitting, fisión nuclear.- **—ic(al)** [atámik(ąl)], a. atómico.—atomic fisson, fisión atómica. **—ization** [ætomaizéiṣon], s. pulverización.- **—ize** [ǽtomaiz], vt. atomizar, pulverizar, rociar.- **—izer** [ǽtomaizœ(r)], s. pulverizador.

atone [ątóun], vt. y vi. expiar, purgar; reparar.- **—ment** [-męnt], s. expiación, etc.

atop [ątáp], adv. y prep. encima (de).

atrocious [ątróuṣʌs], a. atroz. **—atrocity** [ątrásiti], s. atrocidad.

attach [ątǽch], vt. (to fasten) sujetar; (to tie) atar, liar, ligar; (to join) unir; (importance) atribuir; (jur.) embargar bienes.- **—e** [ątaṣéi], s. agregado (diplomático).- **—ed** [ątǽcht], a. fijo; anejo, adjunto; (to someone) adicto, devoto.- **—ment** [ątǽchmęnt], s. atadura, unión; (device) accesorio; (fondness) cariño; (jur.) embargo de bienes.

attack [ątǽk], vt. y vi. atacar.—s. ataque.

attain [ątéin], vi. lograr, alcanzar, llegar a.- **—able** [-ąbl], a. asequible, accesible.- **—ment** [-męnt], s. logro, consecución.—pl. dotes, prendas.

attempt [ątémpt], vt. y vi. intentar, procurar, probar.—s. prueba, intento, tentativa, conato.

attend [ąténd], vt. asistir a.—vi. asistir.—to a. to, atender.—well-attended, muy concurrido (espectáculo, etc.).- **—ance** [-ąns], s. presencia, asistencia; público, concurrencia.- **—ant** [-ąnt], s. acompañante; sirviente; guarda, encargado.—a. comcomitante, acompañante.

attention [ąténṣon], s. atención.—to pay a., prestar atención, hacer caso.—interj. ¡atención!, ¡firmes!

—**attentive** [ətɛ́ntiv], *a.* atento.

—**attentiveness** [ətɛ́ntivnis], *s.* cortesia, atención.

attest [ətɛ́st], *vt.* atestiguar, atestar, autenticar.—*vi.* dar testimonio.

attic [ǽtik], *s.* desván, buhardilla; ático.—A., *a.* y *s.* ático.

attire [ətái(r)], *vt.* vestir, ataviar, adornar.—*s.* atavío, traje, ropa.

attitude [ǽtitjud], *s.* actitud, ademán, postura.

attorney [ətɕ́rni], *s.* abogado; apoderado.—*a. general,* fiscal nacional.— *district a.,* fiscal del distrito.— *A. General,* (USA) Ministro de Justicia.

attract [ətrǽkt], *vt.* y *vi.* atraer; cautivar.- —**ion** [ətrǽkʃon], *s.* atracción; atractivo, aliciente.- —**ive** [ətrǽktiv], *a.* atractivo; cautivador; simpático.- —**iveness** [ətrǽktivnis], *s.* atracción, atractivo.

attribute [ətríbjut], *vt.* atribuir, imputar, achacar.—*s.* [ǽtribjut], atributo, característica, distintivo.

attrition [ætríʃon], *s.* roce, rozadura, frotación; atrición.

attune [ətjún], *vt.* armonizar, afinar.

auburn [ɔ́bœrn], *a.* castaño rojizo.

auction [ɔ́kʃon], *s.* subasta, almoneda, remate.—*a. bridge,* bridge-remate.—*a. room,* sala de subastas.—*to put up for a.,* subastar.—*vt.* subastar, rematar.—*to a. off,* subastar, rematar. —**eer** [-ír], *s.* subastador; pregonero, rematador.—*vt.* vender en pública subasta.

audacious [ɔdéiʃʌs], *a.* audaz, osado; descarado. —**audacity** [ɔdǽsiti], *s.* audacia, osadía.

audible [ɔ́dibl], *a.* audible. —**audience** [ɔ́diɛns], *s.* auditorio, público; audiencia o entrevista. —**audit** [ɔ́dit], *s.* intervención y ajuste de cuentas.—*vt.* intervenir, revisar una cuenta. —**auditor** [ɔ́ditɔ(r)], *s.* oyente; interventor. —**auditorium** [ɔ̀ditɔ́riʌm], *s.* auditorio.

audio [ɔ́djou], *a.* y *s.* audio.—*a. system,* sistema audio, audiosistema.

audiofrequency [ɔ́djoufríkwensi], *s.* audiofrecuencia.

audiovisual [ɔ̀djouvíʒuəl], *a.* audiovisual.

auger [ɔ́gœ(r)], *s.* barrena; taladro.— *a. bit,* broca o mecha de taladro.

aught [ɔt], *s.* algo; cero; nada.—*adv.* absolutamente.

augment [ɔgmɛ́nt], *vt.* y *vi.* aumentar,

crecer.- —**ative** [-ātiv], *a.* aumentativo.

august [ɔgʌ́st], *a.* augusto, majestuoso. —**A.** [ɔ́gʌst], *s.* agosto (mes).

aunt [ænt, ant], *s.* tía.

aureola [ɔríolā], *s.* aureola, corona.

aureomycin [ɔrioumáiʃin], *s.* aureomicina.

auricular [ɔríkyūlā(r)], *a.* auricular; oíble; confidencial, secreto, dicho al oído.

auspices [ɔ́spisiz], *s. pl.* auspicios; dirección. —**auspicious** [ɔspíʃʌs], *a.* favorable, propicio.

austere [ɔstír], *a.* austero.- —**ness** [-nis], **austerity** [ɔstɛ́riti], *s.* austeridad.

Australian [ɔstréilyan], *a.* y *s.* australiano.

Austrian [ɔ́strian], *a.* y *s.* austríaco.

authentic(al) [ɔθɛ́ntik(al)], *a.* auténtico.- —**ity** [ɔθɛntísiti], *s.* autenticidad.

author [ɔ́θɔ(r)], *s.* autor.- —**ess** [-is], *s.* autora.

authoritative [ɔθɔ́riteitiv], *a.* autorizado. —**authority** [ɔθɔ́riti], *s.* autoridad. —**authorization** [ɔ̀θɔrizéiʃon], *s.* autorización. —**authorize** [ɔ́θɔraiz], *vt.* autorizar, facultar.

authorship [ɔ́θɔrʃip], *s.* autoría, paternidad literaria.

auto [ɔ́tou], *s.* coche, auto, automóvil, carro.

autocracy [ɔtákrasi], *s.* autocracia. —**autocrat** [ɔ́tokræt], *s.* autócrata.

autograph [ɔ́togræf], *a.* y *s.* autógrafo.—*vt.* autografiar.

automat [ɔ́tomæt], *s.* mecanismo automático; restaurante de servicio automático.- —**ed.** [ɔ́tomeitid], *s,* automatizado.—*a. teller machine (ATM),* cajero automático. —**ic(al)** [ɔtomǽtik(al)], *a.* automático.- —**ism** [ɔtǽmatizm], *s.* automatismo.- —**on** [ɔtámatan], *s.* autómata.

automobile [ɔ́tomoubil], *s.* automóvil.—*a. club,* automóvil club.—*a. industry,* industria automotriz, industria del automóvil.—*a. show,* salón del automóvil.

autonomous [ɔtánomʌs], *a.* autónomo. —**autonomy** [ɔtánomi], *s.* autonomía.

autopsy [ɔ́tapsi], *s.* autopsia.

autumn [ɔ́tʌm], *s.* otoño.

auxiliary [ɔgzílyāri], *a.* auxiliar.

avail [əvéil], *vt.* aprovechar, beneficiar,

valer.—*vi.* valer, servir, ser útil.—*to a. oneself of,* aprovecharse de.—*s.* provecho, utilidad.— **—able** [-abl], *a.* aprovechable, disponible.

avalanche [ǽvəlænch], *s.* alud, avalancha.

avarice [ǽvərɪs], *s.* avaricia, codicia. **—avaricious** [ævərɪ́ʃʌs], *a.* avaro, avariento.

avenge [əvéndʒ], *vt.* y *vi.* vengar(se).

avenue [ǽvənju], *s.* avenida, calzada; alameda.

aver [əvə́r], *vt.* asegurar, afirmar.

average [ǽvərɪdʒ], *s.* promedio; término medio.—*on an a.,* como promedio.—*a.* medio, común, corriente, típico.—*vt.* calcular el promedio o término medio; prorratear.

averse [əvə́rs], *a.* adverso, contrario; renuente. **—aversion** [əvə́rʒən], *s.* aversión.

avert [əvə́rt], *vt.* desviar, apartar; prevenir, conjurar.

aviary [éjvjerj], *s.* pajarera.

aviation [ejvjéjʃən], *s.* aviación. **—aviator** [éjvjejto(r)], *s.* aviador.

avid [ǽvjd], *a.* ávido, codicioso; ansioso.— **—ity** [əvídjtj], *s.* avidez, codicia; ansia.

avocado [ævokádou], *s.* aguacate.

avocation [ævokéjʃən], *s.* vocación; distracción, diversión.

avoid [əvɔ́jd], *vt.* evitar.— **—able** [-abl], *a.* evitable, eludible.— **—ance** [-ans], *s.* evitación.

await [əwéjt], *vt.* y *vi.* aguardar, esperar.

awake [əwéjk], *vti.* y *vii.* [4], **awaken** [əwéjkən], *vt.* y *vi.* despertar(se).—*a.* despierto, desvelado.— **—awakening** [əwéjkənjŋ], *s.* despertar, despertamiento.

award [əwɔ́rd], *vt.* y *vi.* otorgar, conferir, conceder, adjudicar.—*s.* premio; (awarding) concesión, adjudicación; (mil.) condecoración.

aware [əwér], *a.* consciente; enterado, sabedor; sobre aviso.

awash [əwáʃ], *a.* y *adv.* a flor de agua.

away [əwéj], *adv.* y *a.* lejos; a lo lejos; ausente, fuera.—*far a.,* muy lejos.—*right a.,* ahorita.—*to go a.,* alejarse.—*to take a.,* quitar.—*interj.* ¡fuera de aquí! ¡lárguese usted!

awe [ɔ], *s.* temor reverencial; pavor.—*a.-inspiring,* imponente.—*a.-struck,* despavorido, aterrado, espantado.—*to stand in a. of,* temer; reverenciar.—*vt.* infundir temor reverencial a.

awesome [ɔ́sʌm], *a.* imponente, formidable.

awful [ɔ́ful], *a.* tremendo; terrible, horrible, atroz.

awhile [əhwájl], *adv.* un rato, algún tiempo.

awkward [ɔ́kwərd], *a.* torpe, desmañado, desgarbado; embarazoso, delicado; difícil, incómodo.— **—ness** [-njs], *s.* torpeza, desmaña.

awl [ɔl], *s.* lezna; punzón; lengüeta.

awning [ɔ́njŋ], *s.* toldo.

awoke [əwóuk], *pret.* y *pp.* de TO AWAKE.

ax(e) [æks], *s.* hacha.

axiom [ǽksjəm], *s.* axioma, postulado sentencia.

axis [ǽksjs], *s.* (*pl.* axes [ǽksjz]) eje.

axle [ǽksl], *s.* eje, árbol.

aye, ay [aj], *adv.* sí.—*s.* voto afirmativo.

Aztec [ǽztɛk], *a.* y *s.* azteca.

azure [ǽʒ̱ɹ], *a.* y *s.* azur, azul celeste.

B

babble [bǽbl], *vt.* y *vi.* balbucear; charlar; murmurar (un arroyo).—*s.* charla, balbuceo, charlatanería; susurro, murmullo.— **—r** [bǽblœ(r)], *s.* charlatán, hablador; trapalero **—babbling** [bǽbljŋ], *a.* murmurante, balbuciente.—*s.* cháchara, garrulería, balbucencia.

babe [bejb], *s.* criaturita, nene, bebé.

baboon [bæbún], *s.* mandril.

baby [béjbj], *s.* criatura, crío, nene, nena, pequeñuelo, bebé, (Am.) guagua.—*a.* de niño; de, para o como nene; pequeño; de tierna edad; infantil.—*b. blue,* azul claro.—*b. boom,* boom de la natalidad.—*b. boomer,* persona nacida durante los veinte años 1945–1965 en los

E.U.—*b. carriage,* cochecillo de nene.—*b. face,* cara de niño.—*b.-sit,* hacer de canguro, cuidar niños.—*b. sitter,* canguro, baby-sitter.—*b. sitting,* canguros.—*b. grand piano,* piano de media cola.—*b. talk,* modo infantil de hablar, media lengua.—*b. tooth,* diente de leche.—*vti.* [7] tratar como niño; mimar.

baccalaureate [bækəlɔ́rɪ̯it], *s.* bachillerato.

bachelor [bǽchelo(r)], *s.* soltero, célibe; bachiller.

bacilli [bæsílaɪ], *s. pl.* bacilos, bacterias. **—bacillus** [bæsílʌs], *s.* bacilo, bacteria. **—bacillary** [bǽsɪleɪ], *a.* bacilar.

back [bæk], *s.* espalda; lomo, espinazo (de un animal); respaldo; dorso, revés (de la mano); reverso; parte posterior o de atrás, trasera; lomo (de un cuchillo, de un libro); (teat.) foro; (dep.) zaguero, defensa.—*behind one's b.,* por detrás, a espaldas de uno.—*in the b. of one's mind,* en lo recóndito del pensamiento.—*on one's b.,* a cuestas, boca arriba, de espaldas.—*to turn one's b.* (*on*), volver la espalda; negar ayuda (a).—*with one's b. to the wall,* entre la espada y la pared.—*a.* trasero, posterior, inferior; dorsal; atrasado; pasado (apl. al tiempo); lejano.—*b. alley,* callejón.—*b. door,* puerta trasera.—*b. pay,* sueldo atrasado.—*adv.* atrás, detrás; de nuevo; de vuelta.—*b. and forth,* de un lado a otro.—*to come b.,* volver, regresar.—*to give b.,* devolver.—*interj.* ¡atrás!—*vt.* hacer retroceder; apoyar, respaldar; endosar.—*vi.* (a veces con up) recular, retroceder, ciar.—*to b. down, to b. out,* volverse atrás; abandonar una empresa. **—ache** [bǽkeɪk], *s.* dolor de espalda. **—bite** [-baɪt], *vti. y vii.* [10] difamar, murmurar; morder.— **—biter** [-baɪtœ(r)], *s.* murmurador, difamador, detractor.— **—biting** [-baɪtɪŋ], *s.* murmuración, difamación, calumnia.— **—board** [-bɔrd], *s.* respaldo, espaldar.— **—bone** [-boʊn], *s.* espinazo; nervio; fundamento.— **—breaking** [-breɪkɪŋ], *a.* agobiante, abrumador.— **—date** [-deɪt], *vt.* pagar con retroactividad.— **—drop** [-drap], *s.* telón de fondo. **—ground** [-graʊnd], *s.* trasfondo; antecedentes; base,

fondo; lejanía.- **—seat** [-sít], *s.* asiento trasero. **—b. driver,** pasajero que moleste al conductor con sus indicaciones. **—side** [-saɪd], *s.* envés, vuelta, espalda; nalgas.- **—stage** [-steɪdʒ], *adv.* entre bastidores. **—track** [-traek], *vi.* retroceder; dar marcha atrás.—**stitch** [-stɪch], *s.* pespunte, punto atrás.—*vt. y vi.* pespuntar.- **—ward** [-wǎrd], *a.* vuelto o dirigido hacia atrás; retrógrado, atrasado; retraído; tardo, tardío.—*to go b. and forward,* ir y venir.- **—wardness** [-wǎrdnɪs], *s.* atraso; torpeza; retraimiento.- **—wards** [-wǎrdz], *adv.* atrás, de espaldas.—*to go b.,* retroceder, ir para atrás.

backer [bǽkẹr], *s.* partidario; patrocinador.

backfire [bǽkfaɪr], *vi.* producir detonaciones en el escape; (fig.) fracasar, salir mal.—*s.* petardeo, detonaciones.

backlash [bǽklæʃ], *s.* reacción violenta.

backlog [bǽklɔg], *s.* atraso.

bacon [béɪkɔn], *s.* tocino.—*to bring home the b.,* (fam.) ganar los garbanzos.

bacteria [bæktírɪ̯ä], *s. pl.* bacterias. **—bacterial** [bæktírɪ̯al], *a.* bacteriano, bactérico. **—bacteriological** [bæktɪrɪ̯oládʒɪ̯käl], *a.* bacteriológico.—*b. warfare,* guerra bacteriológica.

bad [bæd], *a.* mal(o), perverso, depravado; dañoso; enfermo, indispuesto; dañado, podrido.—*b. blood,* animosidad, encono.—*b. coin,* moneda falsa.—*bad off* (fam.) or *badly off,* malparado; muy enfermo; mal de dinero—*b. time,* mal rato.—*very b.,* pésimo. **—badly** [bǽdlɪ̯], *adv.* mal, gravemente.

bade [bæd], *pret.* de TO BID.

badge [bædʒ], *s.* condecoración, insignia, placa, distintivo.

badger [bǽdʒœ(r)], *vt.* molestar, cansar, fastidiar.—*s.* tejón.

baffle [bǽfl], *vt.* desconcertar; contrariar; frustrar, impedir. **—baffling** [bǽflɪŋ], *a.* desconcertante, desconcertador.

bag [bæg], *s.* saco, costal, talega; bolsa, zurrón; presa; saquito de mano.—*to be in the b.,* (fam.) ser cosa segura.—*to hold the b.,* (fam.) pagar los vidrios rotos.—*vti.* [1] ensacar, entalegar; cazar, cobrar (la caza).—*vii.* hacer bolsa o pliegue (la ropa).– **—gage** [bǽgidž], *s.* equipaje, maletas.—*b. check,* contraseña de equipaje.

bagel [beígel], *s.* bollo hecho de pan ácimo con forma de rosquilla.

bail [beíl], *s.* caución, fianza; fiador; cubo o vertedor para achicar (agua).—*on b.,* bajo fianza.—*to go b. for,* salir fiador de.—*vt.* dar fianza, caucionar; poner en libertad bajo fianza; achicar.—*vi.*—*to b. out,* (aer.) arrojarse de un avión.

bailiff [beílif], *s.* alguacil.

bait [beít], *vt.* cebar; atraer, tentar; molestar, acosar.—*s.* cebo, carnada; anzuelo, señuelo; pienso.—*to take the b.,* tragar el anzuelo, caer en un lazo.

baize [beíz], *s.* bayeta.—*green b.,* tapete verde.

bake [beík], *vt.* cocer o asar al horno, calcinar.—*vi.* hornear (como oficio); cocerse el horno.– **—d** [-t], *a.* horneado; cocido al horno. **—b.** *beans,* frijoles, judías.– **—r** [beíkœ(r)], *s.* panadero, hornero; pastelero.—*baker's dozen,* docena de fraile (trece).– **—ry** [-œri], *s.* horno, tahona, panadería, pastelería. **—baking** [-iŋ], *s.* hornada; cocción.—*b. powder,* polvo de hornear, levadura en polvo.

balance [bǽlans], *s.* balanza; equilibrio; balance, contrapeso; (com.) balance, saldo.—*b. wheel,* balancín, volante.—*vt.* equilibrar; balancear; contrapesar; (com.) saldar; pesar, considerar.—*vi.* equilibrarse; contrarrestarse; (com.) saldarse; balancearse, mecerse. **—balancing** [bǽlansiŋ], *s.* equilibrio; balanceo.—*a.* compensador.—*b. flap,* (aer.) alerón.

balcony [bǽlkoni], *s.* balcón; (teat.) galería, anfiteatro.

bald [bold], *a.* calvo; escueto; pelado, desnudo; desabrido.—*b. eagle,* águila norteamericana de cabeza blanca y alas oscuras.– **—headed** [boldhédid], *a.* calva.– **—ly** [lj], *adv.* sin rodeos, escuetamente.– **—ness** [-nis], *s.* calvicie.

bale [beíl], *s.* fardo; tercio (de tabaco); bala, paca (de algodón, de papel).—*vt.* embalar, empaquetar.

Balearic [bæliǽrik], *a.* balear.

baling [beíliŋ], *s.* embalaje; enfardeladura.

balk [bok], *vt.* frustrar, desbaratar.—*vi.* plantarse, encabritarse (un caballo); resistirse.—*s.* obstáculo, impedimento, fracaso; (carp.) viga.

ball [bol], *s.* bola, pelota, globo; yema (del dedo); baile; bala (de cañón). *b.-and-socket joint,* articulación de rótula.—*b. bearing,* cojinete de bola, cojinete a bolas, rodamiento (a bolas).—*b. game,* juego de pelota, de beisbol.—*b. of yarn,* ovillo.—*to b. up,* embrollar, confundir. **—park** [-park], estadio de béisbol.—*a b. figure,* cifra aproximada. **—player** [-pleíɘr], *s.* jugador de béisbol. **—point (pen)** [-point], bolígrafo, esferográfico, esfero, birome. **—room** [-rum], salón de baile.— *b. dance, b. dancing,* baile de salón.

ballad [bǽlad], *s.* balada, romance; copla, canción.

ballast [bǽlast], *s.* lastre; (f.c.) balasto.—*b. bed,* firme (de carretera).—*washed b.,* guijarro.—*vt.* lastrar; (f.c.) balastar.– **—ing** [-iŋ], *s.* lastre; balasto.

balloon [balún], *s.* globo (aerostático). – **—ist** [-ist], *s.* aeronauta.

ballot [bǽlot], *s.* cédula o boleta para votar; voto; votación.—*b. box,* urna electoral.—*vt.* y *vi.* votar.– **—ing** [-iŋ], *s.* votación.

balm [bam], *s.* bálsamo, ungüento fragante.– **—y** [bámi], *a.* balsámico, fragante; calmante; alocado, tonto.

ban [bæn], *s.* bando, edicto, proclama, pregón; excomunión.—*vti.* [1] prohibir, proscribir; excomulgar.

banal [beínal], *a.* trivial, vulgar.

banana [banǽnä], *s.* plátano, banano, guineo.—*b. plantation,* platanal, platanar.—*b. tree,* banano, plátano bananero.

band [bænd], *s.* banda, faja, tira; correa, cinta, franja, lista; abrazadera, zuncho; banda, pandilla, cuadrilla; (mús.) banda, charanga.—*vt.* y *vi.* juntar, congregar; fajar, atar.—*to b. together,* asociarse; formar pandilla.

bandage [bǽndidž], *s.* vendaje, venda, faja.—*vt.* vendar.

bandit [bǽndit], *s.* bandido, bandolero.– **—ry** [-ri], *s.* bandolerismo, bandidaje.

bane [bejn], s. ruina, azote, daño.-
—**ful** [béjnful], a. pernicioso, dañino, ponzoñoso, funesto.

bang [bæŋ], vt. golpear con ruido, hacer estrépito.—vi. dar estampido;
saltar.—s. golpe; estampido; portazo; ruido de un golpe; flequi-
llo.—with a b., con un golpe violento; con estrépito; de repente.—
interj. ¡pum!

banish [bǽnjš], vt. desterrar, deportar;
confinar.- —**ment** [-ment], s. destierro, deportación; confinamiento.

banister [bǽnjstœ(r)], s. baranda, pasamano.

bank [bæŋk], s. orilla, ribera, margen;
loma, cuesta; banco, bajío; (com.)
banco, casa de banca.—b. account,
cuenta bancaria.—b. book, libreta
de banco.—bank card, bank credit
card, tarjeta de crédito (expedida
por un banco).—b. note, billete
de banco.—vt. represar, estancar;
amontonar, apilar; depositar en un
banco.—vi. ocuparse en negocios
de banca; ser banquero.—vt. y vi.
(aer.) ladear(se).—to b. on, contar
con, confiar en.- —**er** [bǽŋkœ(r)],
s. banquero; cambista.- —**ing**
[-iŋ], s. banca, operaciones de
banco.—a. bancario.- —**rupt**
[-rʌpt], s. y a. quebrado, en quiebra, insolvente.—vt. quebrar, arruinar.- —**ruptcy** [-rʌptsj], s. bancarrota, quiebra.—to go into b., declararse en quiebra.

banner [bǽner], s. bandera, estandarte.

banns [bænz], s. pl. amonestaciones.

banquet [bǽŋkwit], s. banquete, festín.—vt. y vi. banquetear.

bantam [bǽntam], gallinilla de Bantam.- —**weight** [-wejt], peso gallo;
de los pesos gallo.

banter [bǽntœ(r)], vt. y vi. zum-
bar(se), dar matraca, chotear,
embromar.—s. zumba, burla,
chunga.- —**er** [-œ(r)], s. zumbón,
burlón.

baptism [bǽptjzm], s. bautismo, bautizo.- —**al** [bæptízmal], a. bautismal.—b. name, nombre de pila.
—**baptize** [bǽptajz], vt. bautizar.

bar [bar], s. barra; varilla; barra o pastilla (de chocolate, etc.); palanca;
impedimento; barrera; cantina,
bar, mostrador de taberna; reja, barrote; tribunal; abogacía, foro,

cuerpo de abogados; (for.) foro, es-
trados; recinto de los acusados;
(mus.) barra, raya de compás; (metal.) barra, lingote.—b. association,
colegio de abogados.—b. bell, palanqueta de gimnasio.—b. code, código de barras.—to be admitted to
the b., recibirse de abogado.—
vti. [1] trancar; estorbar, obstruir;
prohibir; excluir.—prep. excepto,
salvo.—b. none, sin excepción.

barb [barb], s. púa; lengüeta (de
saeta, anzuelo).

barbarian [barbérjan], a. y s. bárbaro,
barbárico. —**barbarism** [bárba-
rjzm], s. barbarie; barbarismo.
—**barbarity** [barbǽrjti], s. barbaridad, ferocidad. —**barbarous** [bár-
barʌs], a. bárbaro, inculto; cruel.

barbecue [bárbjkju], vt. hacer barbacoa, asar a la parrilla.—s. barbacoa.

barbed [barbd], a. barbado, armado
con lengüetas o púas.—b. wire,
alambre de púas, alambre de
espino.

barber [bárbœ(r)], s. barbero, peluquero.—b. shop, barbería, peluquería.

bard [bard], s. bardo, poeta.

bare [ber], a. desnudo; raso; pelado;
liso; sencillo; desarmado; descarnado; descubierto; público; desamueblado, vacío; mero, solo.—b.
of money, sin un cuarto, sin un
real.—vt. desnudar, descubrir,
despojar.- —**back** [bérbæk], a. y
adv. (montado) al pelo, sin silla.-
—**bonod** [-bound], a. muy flaco,
descarnado.- —**faced** [-fejst], a.
descarado, insolente, atrevido.-
—**facedness** [-fejstnjs], s. descaro,
desfachatez. —**back** [-bæk], adv. a
pelo, sin montura.- —**foot** [-fut],
a. descalzo.- —**handed** [-hǽndjd],
adv. sin guantes; sin herramienta.-
—**headed** [-hedjd], a. sin sombrero,
descubierto.- —**legged** [-legjd], a.
con las piernas descubiertas.- —**ly**
[-li], adv. apenas.- —**necked**
[-nekt], a. descotado, con escote.-
—**ness** [-njs], s. desnudez; flaqueza; miseria.

bargain [bárgjn], s. convenio, concierto; ganga; negocio, trato de
compra o venta; artículo muy reducido de precio.—at a b., baratísimo; en una ganga.—b. basement,
sección de rebajas, sección de ofer-
tas.—b. hunter, cazador de gan-

gas.—*to strike a b.*, cerrar un trato; hallar una ganga.—*vt.* y *vi.* concertar, negociar; regatear.—*to b. away*, permutar; vender regalado.- —**ing** [-iŋ], *s.* regateo; trato.

barge [bardž], *s.* lanchón, barcaza.— *vi.*—*to b. in*, entrometerse.

baritone [bǽritoun], *s.* barítono.

bark [bark], *s.* ladrido; (bot.) corteza; (naut.) velero.—*vt.* descortezar.— *to b. out* (an order) gritar.—*vi.* ladrar.—*his b. is worse than his bite*, perro que ladra no muerde.—*to b. up the wrong tree*, tomar el rábano por las hojas.

barkeeper [bárkipœ(r)], *s.* tabernero; barman, camarero.

barley [bárli], *s.* cebada.

barmaid [bármeid], *s.* camarera, moza de taberna; (Am.) mesera.

barn [barn], *s.* granero, pajar, troje; henil; establo (para ganado).—*b. owl*, lechuza.

barnacle [bárnakl], *s.* lapa, percebe.

barnyard [bárnyard], *s.* corral.

barometer [barámetœ(r)], *s.* barómetro.—**barometrical** [bæramétrikal], *a.* barométrico.

barrack [bǽrak], *s.* barraca, cabaña.— *pl.* cuartel.—*vt.* y *vi.* acuartelar(se).

barrage [baráž], *s.* descarga; cortina de fuego.—*a b. of questions*, un aluvión de preguntas.

barrel [bǽrel], *s.* barril, cuba, tonel; tambor de reloj; cañón (de arma de fuego).—*vti.* [2] ir como un bólido.

barren [bǽren], *a.* estéril, árido, infecundo.- —**ness** [-nis], *s.* esterilidad, infecundidad, aridez.

barricade [bǽrikéid], *s.* barricada, barrera, empalizada.—*vt.* cerrar con barricadas; obstruir el paso.

barrier [bǽriœ(r)], *s.* barrera; valla; obstáculo, estacada, atasco; límite.

bartender [bártɛndœ(r)], *s.* barman, camarero.

barter [bártœ(r)], *vt.* permutar, trocar, cambiar.—*s.* permuta, cambio, trueque.- —**er** [-œ(r)], *s.* traficante, cambalachero.

base [beis], *a.* bajo, ruín, villano; básico; (mus.) bajo, grave.—*b. court*, tribunal inferior.—*s.* basa, base, cimiento, fundamento; pedestal; zócalo; (mus.) bajo, grave; (beisbol) base.—*vt.* basar, apoyar, fundamentar.- —**ball** [béisbol], *s.* beisbol o basebol; pelota de beisbol.- —**board** [-bord], *s.* zócalo, plancha

que sirve de base; rodapié.- —**born** [-born], *a.* plebeyo; bastardo.- —**less** [-lis], *a.* desfondado; sin fundamento.- —**ment** [-mɛnt], *s.* sótano; basamento.- —**ness** [-nis], *s.* bajeza, vileza; ruindad.

bashful [bǽšful], *a.* vergonzoso, tímido.- —**ness** [-nis], *s.* vergüenza, timidez.

basic [béisik], *a.* básico, fundamental.

basilica [basílika], *s.* basílica.

basin [béisin], *s.* (al)jofaina, bacía, palangana; cubeta; pila (de agua bendita); taza, pilón; estanque, represa, dársena; charca; cuenca de un río.

basis [béisis], *s.* base; fundamento.

bask [bæsk], *vt.* y *vi.* asolearse, calentarse al sol, tomar el sol.

basket [bǽskit], *s.* cesto, canasta; cesta; (aer.) barquilla.- —**ball** [-bol], *s.* baloncesto, básquetbol.

Basque [bæsk], *a.* y *s.* vasco, vascongado; (lengua) vascuence.

bass [beis], *a.* (mus.) bajo, grave.—*b. clef*, clave de fa.—*b. drum*, bombo.—*b. horn*, tuba.—*b. string*, bordón.—*b. viol*, violón, contrabajo.—*s.* [bæs] (ict.) perca; [beis] bajo (apl. a la voz).

bassoon [basún], *s.* fagot.

bastard [bǽstard], *s.* bastardo, hijo natural.—*a.* bastardo; falso, espurio.- —**y** [-i], *s.* bastardía.

baste [beist], *vt.* hilvanar; echar grasa sobre el asado; (fam.) azotar.- —**basting** [béistiŋ], *s.* hilván; (fam.) paliza.

bastion [bǽschon], *s.* bastión, baluarte.

bat [bæt], *s.* bate de beisbol; garrote; murciélago; guata.—*vti.* y *vii.* [1] golpear; batear; pestañear.

batch [bæch], *s.* hornada; tanda; grupo.—*b. processing*, (comput.) procesamiento por lotes.

bath [bæθ], *s.* baño, cuarto de baño; bañadera.- —**e** [beið], *vt.* bañar, lavar.—*vi.* bañarse.- —**er** [béiðœ(r)], *s.* bañista. —**house** [bǽθhaus], *s.* casa de baño.- —**ing** [béiðiŋ], *s.* baño.- —**mat** [-mæt], *s.* estera de baño, alfombrilla.—*a.* de baño.— *b. resort*, balneario.—*b. suit*, traje de baño, (Am.) trusa.—*b. trunks*, calzón de baño.- —**robe** [bǽθroub], *s.* bata de baño, albornoz.- —**room** [-rum], *s.* cuarto de baño.—

b. fixtures, aparatos sanitarios.—
—tub [-tʌb], *s.* bañadera, bañera.

baton [bætán], *s.* bastón de mando;
(mus.) batuta.

battalion [bætǽlyǫn], *s.* batallón.

batter [bǽtœ(r)], *vt.* y *vi.* golpear, batir, majar.—*b. down*, demoler.—*s.* batido, masa culinaria; golpeadura.

battery [bǽtœri], *s.* (arti. y mec.) batería; (elec.) pila; batería, acumulador; asalto, agresión.

battle [bǽtl], *s.* batalla, combate; lucha.—*b. cruiser*, crucero de combate.—*vi.* y *vt.* batallar, combatir; luchar.— **—field** [-fild], **—ground** [-graund], *s.* campo de batalla.—**—ment** [-mǫnt], *s.* muralla almenada.— **—ship** [-ṣip], *s.* acorazado.

bawdy [bɔ́dị], *a.* subido de tono, verde.

bawl [bɔl], *vi.* (to weep) berrear. **—to b. out**, *vt.* regañar.—**bawling out** [-ịŋ], *s.* (fam.) rapapolvo, bronca.

bay [beị], *a.* bayo.—*v.t.* y *vi.* ladrar, aullar.—*s.* (geog.) bahía; (arch.) saliente, crujía; (bot.) laurel; (zool.) caballo bayo; (barking) ladrido, aullido.—*at b.*, acorralado; a raya.—*b. rum*, ron de malagueta.—*b. window*, mirador, ventana saliente.

bayonet [béịǫnịt], *s.* bayoneta.—*vt.* cargar o herir con bayoneta.

bazaar [bạzár], *s.* bazar, feria.

bazooka [bạzúka], *s.* bazuka.

B.C. (Before Christ) [bísí], *abrev.* aC, a. de J.C. (antes de Jesucristo).

be [bi], *vii.* [11] ser, existir; estar, encontrarse, hallarse, verse, quedar(se); haber; hacer; tener.—*he is no more*, ya no existe.—*it is cold, hot, etc.*, hace frío, calor, etc.—*there is no one there*, no hay nadie allí.—*to be American, Spanish, etc.*, ser americano, español, etc.—*to be astonished, surprised, etc.*, quedar(se) atónito, sorprendido, etc.—*to be cold, hungry, right, two years old, etc.*, tener frío, hambre, razón, dos años, etc.—*to be healthy, sick, etc.*, estar sano, enfermo, etc.—*to be in a serious situation, without money, etc.*, encontrarse, hallarse, verse en una situación seria, sin un centavo.

beach [bich], *s.* playa, costa, orilla.—*vt.* y *vi.* arrastrar a la playa; varar; encallar en la playa.

beacon [bíkǫn], *s.* faro; baliza, boya; fanal; señal luminosa.—*vt.* abalizar; iluminar, guiar.

bead [bid], *s.* cuenta (de rosario, collar), abalorio; burbuja; espuma; gota (de sudor); saliente.—*pl.* rosario.—*vt.* adornar con abalorios; redondear los bordes (de un tubo ensanchado).—*vi.* formar espuma; burbujear.— **—ing** [bídịŋ], *s.* abalorio; listón; moldura convexa; pestaña, reborde.

beadle [bídl], *s.* pertiguero o macero, muñidor, bedel, alguacil, ministril.

beak [bik], *s.* pico; hocico; (fam.) rostro; cabo; espolón (de buque).— **—ed** [-t], *a.* picudo.— **—er** [bíkœ(r)], *s.* vaso, copa.

beam [bim], *s.* rayo, destello; viga, tablón; (mar.) bao; manga de un buque; brazo de romana.—*on the b.*, ir bien encaminado.—*radio b.*, radio faro.—*vi.* destellar, fulgurar; rebosar de alegría.—*vt.* enviar; emitir, irradiar, radiar.— **—ing** [bímịŋ], *a.* radiante; brillante; alegre.— **—y** [-ị], *a.* radiante; alegre, vivo; macizo; (mar.) ancho de manga.

bean [bin], *s.* frijol, haba, habichuela, alubia, judía; grano, semilla; (fam.) cabeza, chola, cayuca.—*string b.*, habichuela verde, ejote, poroto.

bear [bɛr], *vti.* [10], sostener, sustentar; llevar; aguantar, soportar, sobrellevar; sufragar; producir; parir, dar a luz.—*to b. company*, acompañar.—*to b. in mind*, tener en cuenta.—*to b. out*, confirmar, corroborar.—*to b. with*, tener paciencia con.—*to b. witness*, dar testimonio.—*s.* oso; (com.) bajista (en la Bolsa).—*b. market*, mercado bajista, mercado en baja.— **—able** [bérạbl], *a.* sufrible, soportable.— **—er** [-œ(r)], *s.* portador; mensajero; soporte.— **—ing** [-ịŋ], *s.* cojinete, caja de bolas; paciencia, sufrimiento; porte, presencia; relación, conexión; cosecha; gestación.—*pl.* orientación, rumbo; línea de flotación.—*to find one's b.*, orientarse.—*a.* de apoyo, de contacto; productivo.—*fruit b.*, fructífero.

beard [bird], *s.* barba o barbas; (bot.) arista.

beast [bist], *s.* bestia; animal; cuadrúpedo; hombre brutal.—*b. of burden*, acémila.

beat [bit], *vti.* [10] batir; revolver; sacudir; pegar; golpear; ganar, vencer; aventajar; marcar (el compás).—

(caz.) dar una batida; sonar (el tambor).—*to b. a retreat*, batirse en retirada.—*vii.* latir, pulsar; batir (el sol, las olas); golpear repetidamente; sonar.—*to b. around the bush*, andar(se) con rodeos.—*to b. it*, (fam.) poner pies en polvorosa.—*s.* golpe; palpitación, latido; toque de tambor; ronda.—*a.* (fam.) fatigado, rendido de cansancio.—*pret.* y *pp.* de TO BEAT. **—beaten** [bíten], *pp.* de TO BEAT.—*a.* trillado; batido, vencido.- **—er** [-œ(r)], *s.* martillo, maza; molinillo; batidor, agitador, sacudidor.- **—ing** [-ɪŋ], *s.* paliza, zurra, tunda; latido, palpitación, pulsación; golpeo.

beatitude [bjǽtɪtjud], *s.* beatitud; bienaventuranza.—*the Beatitudes*, las bienaventuranzas.

beau [bou], *s.* pretendiente, acompañante, novio.

beautician [bjutíʃən], *s.* peluquero, peluquera. **—beautiful** [bjútɪful], *a.* bello, hermoso, precioso. **—beautify** [bjútɪfai], *vti.* [7] hermosear, embellecer, acicalar.—*vii.* hermosearse, pulirse, maquillarse. **—beauty** [bjútɪ], *s.* belleza, beldad, hermosura, preciosidad.—*b. parlor*, salón de belleza.

beaver [bívœ(r)], *s.* castor; piel de castor.—*eager b.*, trabajador entusiasta.—*to work like a b.*, trabajar como una hormiguita.- **—board** [-bɔrd], *s.* cartón de fibras para tabiques.

becalm [bɪkám], *vt.* calmar, sosegar; encalmarse (tiempo o viento).

became [bɪkéjm], *pret.* de TO BECOME.

because [bɪkɔ́z], *conj.* y *adv.* porque, pues, que.—*b. of*, a causa de.

beckon [békɔn], *vt.* llamar o mandar con (o por) señas.—*vii.* hacer señas o ademanes.—*s.* seña, ademán, llamada.

become [bɪkám], *vii.* [10] devenir; hacerse; llegar a ser; ponerse; volverse; convertirse en; quedarse (cojo, sordo, etc.).—*vti.* sentar bien, caer bien (trajes, vestidos, colores).—*pp.* de TO BECOME. **—becoming** [bɪkámɪŋ], *a.* propio, conveniente; favorecedor (vestido, color).

bed [bed], *s.* cama, lecho; (geol.) capa, estrato, yacimiento; cauce (de río); (mec.) asiento, lecho, fondo; armadura, base, cimiento; (ing.)

firme.—*double b.*, cama de matrimonio, cama camera.—*to go to b.*, acostarse.—*vti.* [1] acostar.- **—bug** [bédbʌg], *s.* chinche.- **—clothes** [-klouðz], *s. pl.* ropa de cama; (Am.). cobijas.

bedding [bédɪŋ], *s.* ropa de cama; cobijas (Am.).

bedlam [bédlam], *s.* casa de orates, manicomio; bullicio, confusión, belén.

Bedouin [bédwin], *s.* beduino.

bedpan [bédpaen], *s.* chata, cuña, silleta.

bedplate [bédplejt], *s.* (mec.) bancaza, platina.

bedraggled [bɪdrǽgld], *a.* enlodado.

bedridden [bédrɪden], *a.* postrado en cama. **—bedroom** [bédrum], *s.* alcoba, dormitorio, habitación, cuarto, pieza; (Mex.) recámara. **—bedside** [bédsaid], *s.* lado de cama; cabecera. **—bedsore** [bédsɔr], *s.* úlcera de decúbito. **—bedspread** [bédspred], *s.* colcha, cobertor. **—bedspring** [bédsprɪŋ], *s.* colchón de muelle. **—bedtime** [bédtajm], *s.* hora de acostarse.

bee [bi], *s.* abeja; (fam.) reunión, tertulia.—*b. line*, línea recta.

beech [bich], *s.* (bot.) haya.- **—nut** [bíchnʌt], *s.* nuez de haya, hayuco.

beef [bif], *s.* carne de res; res; queja.—*vi.* (fam.) jactarse; quejarse.

beefsteak [bífstejk], *s.* biftec, bistec, filete, churrasco.

beehive [bíhajv], *s.* colmena. **—beekeeper** [bíkipœ(r)], *s.* apicultor, colmenero. **—beekeeping** [bíkipɪŋ], *s.* apicultura.

been [bɪn], *pp.* de TO BE.

beer [bir], *s.* cerveza.—*b. garden*, patio abierto de un bar.

beet [bit], *s.* remolacha, (Mex.) betabel.

beetle [bítl], *s.* escarabajo. **—beetling** [bítlɪŋ], *s.* saliente, colgante; estampación.

beeswax [bízwæks], *s.* cera de abejas.

before [bɪfɔ́r], *adv.* delante, al frente; antes, con prioridad; (mar.) de proa.—*b.-mentioned*, antemencionado, susodicho.—*prep.* delante de, enfrente de; ante, en presencia de; antes de.—*b. the wind*, viento en popa.—*conj.* antes (de) que, primero.- **—hand** [-hænd], *adv.* de antemano; previamente, con antelación.—*a.* acomodado, con recursos.

befriend [bifrénd], *vt.* favorecer, patrocinar; brindar amistad.

beg [beg], *vii.* [1] mendigar, pordiosear, vivir de limosna.—*vti.* rogar, suplicar, pedir.—*to b. (leave) to,* permitirse.

began [bigǽn], *pret.* de TO BEGIN.

beggar [bégär], *s.* pordiosero, mendigo.— **—ly** [-li], *a.* pobre, miserable.—*adv.* pobremente. **—begging** [bégin], *s.* mendicidad, mendicación, pordioseo.

begin [bigín], *vti.* y *vii.* [10] comenzar, principiar, empezar, iniciar; (for.) incoar (un pleito).— **—ner** [-œ(r)], *s.* principiante; novicio, novato; (com.) meritorio.— **—ning** [-iŋ], *s.* comienzo, iniciación, principio, origen; génesis.—*from b. to end,* de cabo a rabo, de pe a pa.

begulle [bigáil], *vt.* engañar, seducir; defraudar; pasar el tiempo.

begun [bigán], *pp.* de TO BEGIN.

behalf [bihǽf], *s.—in* o *on behalf of,* por; a favor, en nombre de; en pro de; de parte de.

behave [bihéiv], *vt.* y *vi.* proceder, obrar, conducirse; (com)portarse (bien o mal).—*b. yourself!* ¡pórtate bien! **—behavior** [bihéivyor], *s.* conducta, comportamiento; funcionamiento.

behead [bihéd], *vt.* decapitar, degollar. **— —ing** [-iŋ], *s.* decapitación, degüello.

beheld [bihéld], *pret.* y *pp.* de TO BEHOLD.

behind [bihájnd], *adv.* atrás, detrás; en o a la zaga.—*to fall b.,* atrasarse, retrasarse.—*prep.* tras; detrás de; después de.—*b. one's back,* a espaldas de uno.—*b. the scenes,* entre bastidores.—*b. the time,* atrasado de noticias.—*s.* (coll.) nalgas, trasero.

behold [bihóuld], *vti.* [10] mirar, ver, contemplar.—*interj.* ¡he aquí! ¡mire Ud.!— **—er** [-œ(r)], *s.* espectador.

being [bíŋ], *ger.* de TO BE.—*for the time b.,* por el momento; por ahora.—*s.* ser, ente, criatura; existencia, vida.

belch [belch], *vi.* eructar; vomitar.—*vt.* arrojar; vomitar.—*s.* eructo.

belfry [bélfri], *s.* campanario.

Belgian [béldʒən], *s.* y *a.* belga.

belief [bilíf], *s.* fe, creencia, crédito; confianza; credo; opinión. **—believable** [bilívəbl], *a.* creíble. **—believe**

[bilív], *vt.* y *vi.* creer; pensar; opinar.—*to b. in,* creer en; tener fe en. **—believer** [bilívœ(r)], *s.* creyente, fiel.

bell [bel], *s.* campana; campanilla; timbre; cencerro; cascabel.—*b. boy,* botones.—*b. clapper,* badajo.—*b. ringer,* campanero.—*b. tower,* campanario.

belligerent [bilídʒerent], *s.* beligerante.—*a.* belicoso, guerrero.

bellow [bélou], *vi.* bramar, berrear; mugir, rugir; vociferar.—*s.* bufido, bramido, rugido.— **—s** [-z], *s. pl.* fuelle(s).

belly [béli], *s.* vientre; barriga, tripa, panza; estómago.—*vii.* [7] pandear.— **—ache** [-eik], *s.* dolor de vientre.— **—ful** [-ful], *s.* panzada, hartazgo.

belong [bilón], *vi,* pertenecer; tocar; corresponder.— **—ing** [-iŋ], *a.* perteneciente.—*s.* pertenencia, propiedad.—*pl.* bienes; efectos; bártulos.

beloved [bilǽv(i)d], *a.* querido, amado.—*s.* persona amada.

below [bilóu], *adv.* abajo, bajo, debajo, más abajo.—*prep.* bajo, debajo de; después de.—*b.-stated,* más adelante, o más abajo mencionado.

belt [belt], *s.* cinto o cinturón, faja, cincho; correa; tira; (mec.) correa de trasmisión; área, perímetro.—*b. shaft,* árbol de transmisión.—*vt.* fajar; ceñir; poner correa a (una máquina).

bench [bench], *s.* banco, banca; escaño; (for.) tribunal.—*b. warrant,* auto de prisión.

bend [bend], *vti.* y *vii.* [4] encorvar(se), curvar(se), doblar(se), plegar(se), torcer(se), inclinar(se); doblegar(se); someter(se).—*s.* combadura), encorvadura, curvatura; curva; recodo; codillo.—*to b. one's efforts,* redoblar uno sus esfuerzos.— **—er** [béndoer], *s.* (fam.) juerga.

beneath [biníθ], *adv.* abajo, debajo.—*prep.* bajo, debajo de; por bajo.

benediction [benidíkʃon], *s.* bendición.

benefactor [bénifæktœ(r)], *s.* benefactor, bienhechor.

benefice [bénifis], *s.* beneficio, prebenda.— **—nce** [binéfisens], *s.* beneficencia; caridad.— **—nt** [binéfisent], *a.* benéfico, caritativo. **—beneficial** [benifíʃəl], *a.* beneficioso, provechoso, ventajoso. **—benefit** [bénifit], *s.* beneficio.—*pl.* beneficios, (entitlements) prestaciones.—*for the b. of,* a beneficio de.—*vt.* beneficiar.—*vi.* sacar provecho.

benevolence [binévolens], *s.* benevolencia. **—benevolent** [binévolent], *a.* benévolo.

benign [bináin], *a.* benigno; afable.— **—ity** [binígniti], *s.* benignidad, bondad.

bent [bent], *pret. y pp.* de TO BEND.— *a.* curvo, encorvado, torcido; inclinado.—*s.* encorvadura, curvatura; inclinación, propensión, tendencia.

bequeath [bikwíð], *vt.* legar, donar (en testamento).— **—er** [-œ(r)], *s.* el que lega o dona (en testamento).— **bequest** [bikwést], *s.* manda, donación o legado.

berate [biréit], *vt.* reprender, reñir, regañar.

beret [beréi], *s.* boina.

berry [béri], *s.* baya (fresa, mora, etc.); grano (de café, etc.).

berth [bœrθ], *s.* litera, camarote; atracadero, dársena.—*vt. y vi.* atracar, llevar al puerto; dar camarote, pasaje o empleo a.

beseech [bisích], *vti.* [10] suplicar, rogar, implorar.

beset [bisét], *vti.* [9] acosar, perseguir; bloquear; rodear.—*pret. y pp.* de TO BESET.—*a.* acosado; engastado.

beside [bisáid], *adv.* cerca, al lado, a la mano.—*prep.* al lado de; junto a; en comparación de.—*b. himself,* fuera de sí.—*b. the point,* que no viene al caso.— **—s** [-z], *adv.* también, además.—*prep.* además de; sobre, por encima de; excepto.

besiege [bisídʒ], *vt.* sitiar; asediar, acosar.— **—r** [-œ(r)], *s.* sitiador; asediador.

besought [bisɔt], *pret. y pp.* de TO BESEECH.

best [best], *a. y adv. super.* de GOOD y WELL: mejor, del mejor modo, óptimo, óptimamente, superior (mente).—*b. man,* padrino de boda.—*b. seller,* éxito de venta, superventas; (book) éxito de librería, bestseller.—*the b. part of,* casi todo, la mayor parte de.—*you know b.,* Ud. sabe mejor que nadie.—*s.* [el, lo] mejor, [los] mejores, etc.—*at (the) b.,* a lo más, cuando más, aun en el mejor caso.—*to do one's b.,* hacer lo posible.—*to make the b. of,* sacar el mejor partido de.—*to the b. of*

my knowledge, según mi leal saber y entender.—*vt.* aventajar, vencer, ganar a.

bestial [béschal], *a.* bestial, brutal.— **—ity** [beschiǽliti], *s.* bestialidad, brutalidad.— **—ize** [béschalaiz], *vt.* embrutecer.

bestow [bistóu], *vt.* conceder, conferir; otorgar; agraciar; donar.—*to b. in abundance,* colmar (de).— **—al** [-al], *s.* otorgamiento; dádiva, presente.

bet [bet], *s.* apuesta.—*it's a good b.,* es cosa segura.—*vti. y vii.* [3] apostar.—*you b.,* (fam.) claro, ya lo creo.—*pret. y pp.* de TO BET.

Bethlehem [béθlehem], *s.* Belén.

betray [bitréi], *vt.* traicionar, vender; revelar, descubrir; engañar; dejar ver.— **—al** [-al], *s.* traición, perfidia; engaño; seducción.— **—er** [-œ(r)], *s.* traidor; seductor.

betroth [bitróθ], *vt. y vi.* desposar(se), contraer matrimonio o esponsales, comprometerse, dar palabra de casamiento.— **—al** [-al], *s.* esponsales, desposorio, compromiso, noviazgo.— **—ed** [-t], *s.* prometido, novio, futuro.

better [bétœ(r)], *a. y adv. comp.* de GOOD y WELL: mejor, de mejor modo; más bueno o bien; superior(mente).—*b. half,* cara mitad, costilla, media naranja (esposo o esposa).—*the b. part of,* casi todo.—*to be b.,* estar mejor.—*to know b.,* saber que no se deben hacer ciertas cosas.—*s.* superioridad, ventaja; persona superior (a uno).—*all o so much the b.,* tanto mejor.—*our betters,* nuestros superiores.—*vt.* mejorar; aventajar.—*vi.* mejorarse, progresar.— **—ment** [-ment], *s.* mejora; adelantamiento, superación.

betting [bétin], *s.* apuestas, el apostar, juego.

bettor [bétor], *s.* apostador.

between [bitwín], *adv.* en medio, de por medio, entre los dos.—*prep.* entre.—*b. now and then,* de acá para allá.

beverage [béviradʒ], *s.* bebida.

beware [biwér], *vi.* (Ú. sólo en *inf.*) guardarse, cuidarse de, estar alerta contra.—*interj.* ¡cuidado! ¡mucho ojo!

bewilder [biwíldœ(r)], *vt.* aturdir, azorar; desorientar.— **—ment** [-ment], *s.* aturdimiento, azoramiento, perplejidad.

bewitch [biwích], vt. embrujar, aojar; encantar, hechizar, embelesar.— **—er** [-œ(r)], s. brujo, encantador.— **—ing** [-iŋ], a. hechicero, encantador.

beyond [biyánd], adv. más allá, más lejos; allende.—s. lo que está más allá; la otra vida.—prep. más allá de, tras; después de; sobre; superior a; susceptible de.—b. (a) doubt, fuera de duda.—b. the seas, ultramarino.

bias [bájas], s. parcialidad, prejuicio; inclinación, preferencia; (in sewing) sesgo, diagonal.—vti. [2] influir en, torcer, afectar. **—biased o biassed** [bájast], a. parcial.

bib [bib], s. babero.

Bible [bájbl], s. Biblia.—the Holy B., la Santa Biblia, la Sagrada Biblia **—Biblical** [bíblikal], a. bíblico.

bibliography [biblijágræfi], s. bibliografía.

bicarbonate [bajkárbonit], s. bicarbonato.

bicker [bíkœ(r)], vi. altercar, reñir, pelear.— **—ing** [-iŋ], s. altercados, riñas, peleas.

bicycle [bájsikl], s. bicicleta.—vi. ir en bicicleta.—b. clip, pinza para ir en bicicleta.—b. rack, soporte para bicicleta.

bid [bid], s. postura, licitación; oferta; envite.—vti. [10] ofrecer, pujar licitar; envidar; mandar; rogar; invitar.—to b. farewell, good-bye, despedirse, decir adiós.—vii. hacer una oferta.—pret. y pp. de TO BID.— **—der** [-œ(r)], s. postor, licitador; the highest b., el mejor postor.— **—ding** [-iŋ], s. orden, mandato; invitación; licitación, postura.

bide [bajd], vii. [5] residir, quedarse; esperar.—to b. one's time, reservarse para mejor ocasión.

bidet [bidéj], s. (bathroom fixture) bidé; (zool.) jaca.

bier [bir], s. féretro.

bifocals [bájfoukalz], spl. anteojos bifocales, bifocales.

big [big], a. grande, gordo, grueso; importante, considerable; abultado, fatuo.—b. bang, (astr.) gran explosión.—b. brother, hermano mayor.—b. business, el gran capital.—b. cheese, b. shot, b. wheel, (fam.) pez gordo.—B. Dipper, (astr.) Osa Mayor.—b. game, caza mayor.—b.-headed, engreído.—b.-hearted, generoso.—b. league, liga

mayor.—b. top, carpa de circo.—b. wheel, (Ferris wheel) gran rueda, noria.

bigamist [bígamist], s. bígamo; bígama. **—bigamous** [bígamʌs], a. bígamo. **—bigamy** [bígami], s. bigamia.

bigot [bígot], s. fanático, persona intolerante.— **—ry** [-ri], s. fanatismo, intolerancia.

bigwig [bígwig], s. (fam.) pez gordo.

bile [bail], s. bilis, hiel; cólera, mal genio.

bilge [bildž], vi. (mar.) abrirse una vía de agua, hacer agua; combar.—vt. (mar.) quebrar el pantoque (de un buque); hacer combar.—s. (mar.) pantoque, sentina; barriga de barril.

bilingual [bailíŋgwal], a. bilingüe.

bilious [bílyʌs], a. bilioso.

bilk [bilk], vt. defraudar.

bill [bil], s. billete de banco; cuenta, factura; letra; giro; proyecto de ley; ley; certificado, documento; declaración; lista; cartel; pico (de ave); (teat.) programa.—b. of exchange, letra de cambio.—b. of fare, menú.—b. of indictment, acusación oficial escrita.—b. of lading, conocimiento de embarque.—b. of rights, declaración de derechos, ley fundamental.—b. of sale, escritura de venta.—vt. cargar en cuenta; anunciar por carteles; facturar, adeudar.—vi. juntar el pico (las aves).—to b. and coo, estar como dos tortolitos.- **—board** [bílbord], s. cartelera.- **—fold** [-fould], s. billetera, cartera.

billards [bílyârdz], spl. billar.—billiard table, mesa de billar.

billion [bílyon], s. (E.U.) mil millones, millar de millones (1,000,000,000); (G.B.) billón (millón de millones 1,000,000,000,000).

billow [bílou], s. oleada, ola grande; golpe de mar; onda.—vi. ondular o hincharse como una ola.- **—y** [-i], a. ondeante, ondulante.

billy goat [bíli gout], s. macho cabrío.

bin [bin], s. receptáculo; depósito.— coal b., carbonera.

binary [bájnari], a. binario.

bind [bajnd], vti. [10] atar; juntar; ligar; ceñir; obligar; vendar; ribetear; encuadernar, empastar; compeler.—to b. over, obligar a comparecer ante el juez.- **—er** [bájndœ(r)], s. encuadernador; portafolio, archivador; atadero.– **—ing** [-iŋ], s. atadura; venda, tira, cinta; encuadernación; ribete.—*half b.*, media pasta.—*paper b.*, encuadernación en rústica.—*a.* obligatorio; válido.

binoculars [bɪnákyūlắrz], s. pl. gemelos, binóculos.

biochemical [baɪoukémɪkạl], a., **biochemist** [baɪoukémɪst], s., **biochemistry** [baɪoukémɪstrɪ], s. bioquímica.

biographer [baɪágrạfœ(r)], s. biógrafo. **—biographical** [baɪogrǽfɪkạl], a. biográfico. **—biography** [baɪágrạfɪ], s. biografía.

biologic(al) [baɪoládʒɪk(ạl)], a. biológico. **—biologist** [baɪálodʒɪst], s. biólogo. **—biology** [baɪálodʒɪ], s. biología.

birch [bœrch], s. abedul; disciplina.— vt. azotar, fustigar.

bird [bœrd], s. ave, pájaro; (fam.) persona, tipo raro o singular.—*b. dog*, perro de caza.—*b. feeder*, comedero para pájaros.—*b. of prey*, ave de rapiña.—*b.'s eye view*, vista de pájaro. – **—bath** [-bæθ], s. pila para pájaros.– **—cage** [-keɪdʒ], s. jaula para pájaros; pajarera.– **—call** [-cɔl], s. reclamo.– **—lime** [-laɪm], s. liga (de caza).– **—seed** [-sid], s. alpiste.

biretta [bɪrét̬ạ], s. (igl.) birreta, birrete.

birth [bœrθ], s. nacimiento; origen; parto, alumbramiento; linaje. —*b. certificate*, partida de nacimiento.—*by b.*, de nacimiento.— *to give b. to*, dar a luz, parir.– **—day** [bœrθdej], s. cumpleaños, natalicio.– **—mark** [-mark], s. marca de nacimiento.– **—place** [-plejs], s. suelo natal.– **—rate** [-rejt], s. natalidad.– **—right** [-rajt], s. derechos de nacimiento.

Biscayan [bɪskéɪạn], s. y a. vizcaíno, vasco.

biscuit [bískɪt], s. (E.U.) bollo, panecillo; (G.B.) galleta, galletita.

bishop [bíʃọp], s. obispo; alfil (en el ajedrez).– **—ric** [-rɪk], s. obispado.

bit [bɪt], s. trozo; pizca; pedacito; poquito; momento; taladro, broca; bocado del freno.—*not a b.*, ni pizca.—*to smash to bits*, hacer añicos.—*pret.* y *pp.* de TO BITE.

bite [baɪt], vti. y vii. [10] morder, mordiscar; picar (un insecto, un pez, la pimienta).—s. mordedura, dentellada; mordisco; tentempié; picadura.– **—r** [bájtœ(r)], s. mordedor.

—biting [bájtɪŋ], a. penetrante; mordaz; picante; cáustico; mordedor. **—bitten** [bít̬ẹn], pp. de TO BITE.

bitter [bítœ(r)], a. agrio, amargo(so); áspero; agudo, mordaz; encarnizado; cortante.—s. pl. amargo.– **—ness** [-nɪs], s. amargor; acíbar, hiel; rencor; encono.

bitumen [bɪtjúmẹn], s. betún. **—bituminous** [bɪtjúmɪnʌs], a. bituminoso, abetunado.

blab [blæb], vii. [1] revelar.—vti. chismear. **—b. o blabber** [blǽbœ(r)], s. hablador; chismorreo.

black [blæk], s. negro.—*B.,* (person) negro.—*a.* negro; oscuro—*b. and blue,* amoratado.—*b. and white,* blanco y negro. —*b. market,* mercado negro.—*b. tie,* traje de etiqueta.—*in b. and white,* por escrito. – **—berry** [blǽkberɪ], s. (zarza) mora.– **—bird** [-bœrd], s. mirlo.– **—board** [-bɔrd], s. pizarrón, pizarra.– **—en** [-ẹn], vt. ennegrecer; teñir de negro; embetunar; difamar.—vi.—*to b. out,* perder el conocimiento.– **—head** [-hed], s. espinilla.– **—ish** [-ɪsh], a. negruzco, bruno.– **—mail** [-mejl], s. chantaje. – **—mailer** [-mejlœ(r)], s. chantajista.– **—ness** [-nɪs], s. negrura, oscuridad.– **—out** [-aut], s. apagón.– **—smith** [-smɪθ], s. herrero.– **—top** [-tap], s. asfalto.—vt. asfaltar.

bladder [blaédoer], s. vejiga.

blade [blejd], s. hoja (de navaja, espada, etc.); hoja (de hierba); pala (de remo, etc.); paleta (de hélice, turbina o ventilador).

blah [bla], s. (fam.) pamplinas.—*blah, blah, blah,* bla, bla, bla, bla.

blame [blejm], vt. (in)culpar; censurar.—s. (in) culpación; reproche, censura; culpa.– **—less** [bléjmlɪs], a. inocente; inculpado.

blanch [blænch], vt. blanquear; hacer palidecer.—vi. palidecer.– **—ing** [blǽnchɪŋ], s. blanqueo.

bland [blænd], a. blando, suave.

blank [blæŋk], a. en blanco; vacío; pálido; inexpresivo.—s. espacio en blanco; laguna, hueco; forma o papel en blanco, planilla; esqueleto. —*b. check,* cheque en blanco. —*b. verse,* verso libre o suelto.

blanket [blǽŋkɪt], s. manta, frazada, cobija.—vt. cubrir con manta.

blare [blaer], s. estridencia.—vt.—*to b. out,* vociferar; tocar muy fuerte.— vi. atronar.

blaspheme [blæsfím], *vt.* y *vi.* blasfemar. **—blasphemy** [blǽsfɪmi], *s.* blasfemia.

blast [blæst], *s.* ráfaga, bocanada; explosión, detonación; onda explosiva.—*b. furnace*, alto horno.—*vt.* volar, hacer saltar; maldecir.—*vi.*—*to b. off*, (aeroesp) despegar.

blaze [blejz], *s.* llama, llamarada; hoguera; fogata; ardor; arranque (ira, etc.).—*vt.* templar (acero); encender, inflamar; proclamar.—*vi.* arder con llama; resplandecer.

bleach [blich], *vt.* blanquear al sol; descolorar; aclarar (el pelo).—*vi.* ponerse blanco; desteñirse; palidecer.—*s.* blanqueamiento.- **—er** [blíchœ(r)], *s.* blanqueador.—*pl.* gradería, gradas o tendido de sol (deportes).

bleak [blik], *a.* desierto, desolado, inhóspito.

blear(ed) [blír(d)], **bleary** [blírɪ], *a.* nublado; bañado en lágrimas; legañoso, lacrimoso.—*b.-eyed*, con cara de sueño.

bleat [blit], *s.* balido.—*vi.* balar.

bled [bled], *pret.* y *pp.* de TO BLEED. **—bleed** [blid], *vii.* [10] sangrar, desangrarse.—*vti.* sangrar a (persona, planta); arrancarle a uno el dinero, chuparle la sangre.—*to b. white*, desangrar a.

blemish [blémɪ̂ʃ], *vt.* manchar.—*s.* mancha, imperfección.

blend [blend], *vti.* [4] mezclar, combinar, armonizar.—*vii.* combinarse, armonizarse.—*s.* mezcla, combinación.- **—er** [bléndœ(r)], *s.* licuadora.

bless [blɛs], *vt.* bendecir.- **—ed** [blésɪd], *a.* bendecido, bendito; bienaventurado.- **—ing** [-ɪŋ], *s.* bendición; gracia, favor. **—blest** [blɛst], *a.* = BLESSED.

blew [blu], *pret.* de TO BLOW.

blight [blajt], *s.* tizón, pulgón (parásito); contratiempo, malogro; ruina.—*vt.* y *vi.* destruir(se), agostar(se), frustrar(se).

blind [blajnd], *vt.* cegar; deslumbrar; ofuscar; encubrir; tapar; engañar.—*a.* ciego.—*b. alley*, callejón sin salida.—*b. date*, cita a ciegas, cita con un desconocido u una desconocida.—*b. flying*, vuelo a ciegas.—*b. man*, ciego (*b. woman*, ciega).—*b. man's buff*, la gallina ciega.—*b. spot*, punto ciego.—*s.* (for windows) persiana; (hideout) escondite.

blindage [blájndɪdʒ], *s.* blindaje.

blindfold [blájndfoʊld], *s.* venda para los ojos.—*a.* con los ojos vendados.—*vt.* vendar los ojos; ofuscar. **—blinding** [blájndɪŋ], *a.* deslumbrador, cegador. **—blindness** [blájndnɪs], *s.* ceguera, ceguedad.

blink [blɪŋk], *vi.* pestañear, parpadear; destellar.—*vt.* guiñar; mirar con los ojos entreabiertos.—*s.* pestañeo, guiño o guiñada; destello.- **—er** [blíŋkœ(r)], *s.* (aut.) intermitente, direccional.

blip [blip], *s.* bip, pitidito; (on radar screen) señal luminosa.

bliss [blɪs], *s.* gloria; bienaventuranza, felicidad; arrobamiento, deleite.- **—ful** [blísfʊl], *a.* dichoso.

blister [blístœ(r)], *s.* ampolla, vejiga, burbuja.—*vt.* y *vi.* levantar ampollas; ampollar(se).

blitz [blɪtz], *s.* (mil.) bombardeo aéreo.

blizzard [blízǝrd], *s.* ventisca, tormenta de nieve.

bloated [blóʊtɪd], *a.* hinchado, abotagado.

block [blak], *s.* bloque, trozo; obstáculo, obstrucción; lote; tableta o bloc de papel; plancha o estampa de impresión; horma; fajo; cuadra, manzana.—*vt.* bloquear; tapar; estorbar; planchar sobre horma; parar (una pelota, una jugada).—*to b. out*, esbozar, bosquejar.—*to b. the way*, impedir el paso.- **—ade** [-éjd], *s.* bloqueo, asedio.- **—buster** [-bʌstoer], *s.* éxito de taquilla; bestseller, superventas; bomba de demolición.- **—head** [blákhed], *s.* tonto, estúpido, mentecato.

blond(e) [bland], *a.* y *s.* rubio, (Am.) huero, catire.

blood [blʌd], *s.* sangre; linaje o parentesco; savia.—*b. bath*, massacre, baño de sangre.—*b. brother*, hermano de sangre.—*b. clot*, coágulo.—*b. count*, análisis cuantitativo de sangre.—*b.-curdling*, horripilante.—*b. pressure*, presión sanguínea, tensión arterial.—*b. pudding* o *sausage*, morcilla.—*b. relative*, pariente, consanguíneo.—*b. test*, análisis de sangre.—*b. vessel*, vaso sanguíneo.—*to get one's b. up*, encendérsele a uno la sangre.- **—hound** [-haʊnd], *s.* sabueso.- **—less** [blʌ́dlɪs], *a.* exangüe, desangrado.- **—shed** [ʃed], *s.* efusión o derramamiento de sangre.- **—shot**

[-šat], *a.* inyectado de sangre.-
—**stain** [-steɪn], *s.* mancha de sangre.- —**sucker** [-sʌkœ(r)], *s.* sanguijuela, usurero.- —**thirsty** [-θœrstɪ],
a. sanguinario.- —**y** [-ɪ], *a.* en-
sangrentado, sangriento, sanguinario.–*vti.* [7] ensangrentar.

bloom [blum], *s.* flor; floración; florecimiento; lozanía.–*vi.* florecer.-
—**ing** [blúmɪn], *a.* en flor; floreciente; fresco, lozano.

blossom [blásǫm], *s.* flor; floración.—
vi. florecer.— —**y** [-ɪ], *a.* lleno de flores, floreciente.

blot [blat], *s.* borrón; mancha, mancilla; tacha.—*vti.* [1] emborronar;
manchar; mancillar; empañar; secar con papel secante.—*to b. out,* tachar, borrar.—*vii.* correrse la tinta;
pasarse (el papel).– —**ch** [-ch], *s.*
mancha; borrón; pústula.–*vt.* marcar o cubrir con manchas o
ronchas.

blouse [blaus], *s.* blusa.

blow [bloʊ], *s.* golpe; contratiempo;
vendaval; (re)soplido; trompada;
trompetazo; fanfarrón–*at a b.,* de
un solo golpe.—*to come to blows,* venir a las manos.—*without striking a
b.,* sin dar un golpe, sin esfuerzo.—
vti. [10] (re)soplar; hacer sonar (un
instrumento de viento); ventear; divulgar; gastar con profusión; fanfarronear, alardear.—*to b. up,* estallar,
reventar.—*vt.* inflar; volar con dinamita.—*to b. one's nose,* sonarse
las narices.— —**er** [blóʊœ(r)], *s.* soplador; soplete.— —**ing** [-ɪn], *s.* soplo, soplido.–*a.* soplador. —**blown**
[bloʊn], *pp.* de TO BLOW.–*a.* jadeante, rendido; soplado, inflado.–
—**out** [-aut], *s.* reventón, escape
violento de aire, gas, etc.; (fam.)
(party) comilona, fiestón.— —**pipe**
[-paɪp], *s.* soplete.— —**torch** [-torch],
s. lámpara de soldar, soplete.– —**up**
[-ʌp], *s.* explosión; acceso de ira.–
—**y** [-ɪ], *a.* ventoso.

blubber [blábœr], *s.* esperma de ballena; (fam.) grasa.–*vi.* (fam.) lloriquear.

bludgeon [bládʒǫn], *s.* porra, garrote,
estaca.

blue [blu], *s.* azul.–*pl.* melancolía.—
a. azul; triste, melancólico.—*b.
chip,* de primer orden.—*b.-collar
worker,* obrero.—*b. jay,* urraca de
América.—*b. jeans,* vaqueros, tejanos, jeans.—*b. ribbon,* primer premio.–*vt.* azular; teñir de azul; añi-

lar.—*vi.* ponerse azul.- —**bell** [blú-
bel], *s.* campanilla (flor).- —**bird**
[-boerd], *s.* azulejo.- —**print**
[-prɪnt], *s.* ferroprusiato (impresión
de planos, etc.).

bluff [blaf], *a.* francote, brusco; escarpado.—*s.* escarpadura; fanfarro-
nada; fanfarrón; farsa; farsante; embaucador.—*vi.* conseguir algo a
fuerza de descaro; alardear, bala-
dronar; pretender, similar lo que
no se tiene.- —**er** [bláfœ(r)], *s.*
baladrón, fanfarrón, embaucador.

bluing [blúɪn], *s.* azul o añil para la
ropa. —**bluish** [blúɪš], *a.* azulado,
azulino.

blunder [blándœ(r)], *vt.* desatinar, disparatar, meter la pata.—*s.* disparate; patochada.

blunt [blant], *a.* embotado; romo;
brusco, descortés; lerdo.–*vt.* embotar; calmar o mitigar.- —**ness**
[blántnɪs], *s.* embotadura; franqueza.

blur [bloer], *s.* trazo borroso o confuso; borrón, mancha.—*vti.* [1] hacer borroso; embotar, entorpecer;
empañar; manchar.—*vii.* ponerse
borroso; nublarse; empañarse.

blurb [bloerb], *s.* anuncio efusivo, propaganda.

blurt [bloert], *vt.*—*to b. out,* descol-
garse con, revelar.

blush [blaš], *vi.* ruborizarse, sonrojarse; abochornarse.—*s.* rubor; bochorno; sonrojo.

bluster [blástœ(r)], *s.* bravatas, jactancia, fanfarronadas.—*vi.* fanfarronear, echar bravatas.- —**er**
[-œ(r)], *s.* fanfarrón.

boar [bor], *s.* verraco.—*wild b.,* jabalí.

board [bord], *s.* tabla; tablero; mesa;
comida(s); hospedaje; tribunal,
consejo, junta; cartón; bordo; bor-
da(da).—*pl.* escenario, tablas.—*b.
and lodging,* o *room and b.,* cuarto
y comida, pensión completa.—*vt.*
abordar; subir (a un tren, etc.); entablar, entarimar; dar manutención por dinero.—*vi.* estar a pupilaje.- —**er** [bórdœ(r)], *s.* huésped,
pupilo.- —**ing** [-ɪn], *s.* tablazón; tabique de tablas; pupilaje; abordaje.—*b. house,* casa de huéspedes,
pensión.—*b. pass,* tarjeta de embarque.

boast [boust], *vi.* alardear, jactarse.—
s. fanfarronada, alarde.- —**er** [bóʊ-
stœ(r)], *s.* fanfarrón.- —**ful** [-ful], *a.*

jactancioso.— **—fulness** [-fųlnįs], s. jactancia.

boat [boųt], s. barco, embarcación; buque, navío; bote.—vt. poner o llevar a bordo.—vi. navegar, remar, ir en bote.— **—house** [bóųthaųs], s. cobertizo para botes.— **—ing** [-įŋ], s. ir o pasear en bote; manejo de un bote; transporte en bote.— **—man** [-mąn], s. barquero, botero, etc.

bob [bab], vii. [1] moverse con sacudidas o de arriba abajo; cabecear.—to b. up, (fam.) aparecer.—s. corcho (en la pesca); meneo; borla; plomo de plomada; disco de un péndulo; melena.

bobbin [bábįn], s. bobina, canilla, broca.

bobsleigh [bábsleį], s. trineo.

bock beer [bak], s. cerveza de marzo.

bode [boųd], vt. presagiar, pronosticar, presentir.—vi. predecir; prometer.—to b. ill (o well), ser de mal (o buen) agüero.—pret. de TO BIDE.

bodily [bádįlį], a. corpóreo, corporal, físico.—adv. corporalmente; en persona; en conjunto; en peso.—

body [bádį], s. cuerpo; conjunto; gremio; cadáver; fuselaje; carrocería; parte principal o central; persona.—vti. [7] dar cuerpo o forma a; representar.— **—guard** [-gard], s. guardaespaldas.

bog [bag], s. pantano, fangal, atolladero; ciénaga.—vti. y vii. [1] hundir(se), atollar(se), atascar(se).

bogey [bóųgį], s. espantajo; fantasma; duende, coco.

bogus [bóųgʌs], a. falso, fingido.

Bohemian [bouhímįąn], a. y s. bohemio.

boil [boįl], vt. y vi. hervir, cocer, salcochar; agitarse, hervirle a uno la sangre.—s. hervor, ebullición; divieso, tumorcillo.— **—er** [bóįlœ(r)], s. olla; marmita; caldera; caldera de vapor.— **—ing** [-įŋ], a. hirviente.

boisterous [bóįstœrʌs], a. turbulento, ruidoso, revuelto.

bold [boųld], a. arrojado, valiente; descarado; escarpado; bien delineado.— **—face** [bóųldfeįs], s. descaro; persona desfachatada; letra negra, negrita o negrilla.— **—ness** [-nįs], s. arrojo, etc.; descaro.

Bolivian [bolívįąn], s. y a. boliviano.

bolster [bóųlstœ(r)], s. travesaño, cabezal.—vt. reforzar.

bolt [boųlt], s. cerrojo, pestillo, falleba; perno; clavija; proyectil; dardo; rayo; suceso repentino; pieza o rollo de paño.—vt. echar el cerrojo; escudriñar; engullir; arrojar, echar.—vi. saltar de repente; lanzarse; desbocarse; resistirse.

bomb [bam], s. bomba.—b. shelter, refugio contra bombardeos.—vt. bombardear.— **—ard** [bambárd], vt. bombear, bombardear.— **—ardier** [-bambȧ̦rdír], s. bombardero.— **—ardment** [bambárdmęnt], s. bombardeo, cañoneo.

bombast [bámbæst], s. ampulosidad.— **—ic** [bambæstįk], a. ampuloso, altisonante, campanudo.

bomber [bámœ(r)], s. avión de bombardeo; bombardero (avión o aviador).— **—ing** [-įŋ], s. bombardeo.— **—proof** [-pruf], a. a prueba de bombas.— **—sight** [-saįt], s. mira o visor de bombardeo.

bonanza [bonȧ̦nzą], s. mina de oro, filón, ganga; (miner.) bonanza.

bond [band], s. lazo, vínculo; unión; ligazón; bono, obligación; fiador; fianza.—pl. cadenas, cautiverio.— vt. unir; dar fianza; hipotecar; poner mercancías en depósito afianzado.— **—age** [bándįdʒ], s. cautiverio, esclavitud; obligación.— **—holder** [-hoųldœ(r)], s. accionista; rentista.— **—sman** [-zmąn], s. fiador, garante.

bone [boųn], s. hueso; espina de pez.—pl. osamenta.—vt. deshuesar.— **—ache** [bóųneįk], s. dolor de huesos.— **—d** [-d], a. deshuesado.— **—head** [-hed], s., **—headed** [-hędįd], a. mentecato, impécil.- **—less** [-lįs], a. sin huesos.

boner [bóųnœ(r)], s. (fam.) patochada, disparate.

bonfire [bánfaįr], s. hoguera, fogata.

bonnet [bánįt], s. gorra, gorro; sombrero de mujer; toca; solideo, bonete.

bonus [bóųnʌs], s. bonificación, prima.

bony [bóųnį], a. huesudo; óseo.

boo [bu], s. abucheo, grita, rechifla.— vt. y vi. dar grita, abuchear.—interj. ¡fuera!, ¡bu!

boob [bub], s., **booby** [búbį], s. y a. bobo, gaznápiro, papanatas.

book [bųk], s. libro.—b. stand o stall, puesto de libros.—b. worm, (fig.) ratón de biblioteca.—vt. asentar, inscribir; sacar, comprar o reservar (pasaje, localidades, etc.); contratar o apalabrar (a un artista, conferenciante, etc.)– **—binder** [búkbaindœ(r)], s. encuadernador.– **—binding** [-baindiŋ], s. encuadernación. – **—case** [-kejs], s. librero, estante para libros.– **—ing** [-iŋ], s. registro, asiento; compra o venta de billetes. – **—keeper** [-kipœ(r)], s. tenedor de libros.– **—keeping** [-kipiŋ], s. teneduría de libros.– **—let** [-lit], s. folleto.– **—maker** [-mejkœ(r)], **—ie** [-i], s. corredor de apuestas.– **—seller** [-sɛlœ(r)], s. librero, vendedor de libros.– **—store** [-stɔr], s. librería.– **—worm** [-wœrm], s. (fam.) ratón de biblioteca.

boom [bum], s. estampido; alza en el mercado; auge o prosperidad repentina.–vi. dar estampido; resonar; estar en auge; medrar.–vt. favorecer, fomentar.

boomerang [búmʤræŋ], s. bumerang.–vi. tener el efecto contrario al buscado.

boon [bun], s. dádiva, don; gracia; dicha, bendición.–a. jovial, festivo.

boor [bur], s. patán, rústico.– **—ish** [búrjʃ], a. rústico, agreste; tosco; guajiro, jíbaro.– **—ishness** [-jʃnjs], s. rusticidad; grosería.

boost [bust], vt. empujar; levantar; alzar desde abajo; fomentar, promover.–s. alza; ayuda, asistencia.– **—er** [bústœ(r)], s. impulsador; elevador de potencial o de tensión.–b. cable, cable de arranque.–b. rocket, cohete propulsor.–b. shot, (med.) vacuna de recuerdo.

boot [but], vt. y vi. aprovechar, valer, servir; calzarse uno las botas; dar patadas a. **—to b. up,** (comput.) cargar, hacer el cebado de.–s. bota; ganancia; (comput.) cebador.–to b., además, por añadidura.– **—black** [-blæk], s. limpiabotas.

booth [buθ], s. garita, casilla; puesto o mesilla de venta; cabina; reservado (restaurantes, etc.).

bootleg [bútleg], vti. y vii. [1] contrabandear (esp. en licorea).–a. de contrabando.

booty [búti], s. botín, despojo, presa.

border [bórdœ(r)], s. frontera; orilla; borde; margen; límite, confín; orla, ribete, cenefa.–vi. lindar; rayar, acercarse.–vt. orlar, ribetear, guarnecer; confinar.

bore [bɔr], vt. taladrar; barrenar, horadar; sondear; aburrir; dar la lata.–s. taladro, barreno; agujero hecho con taladro o barreno; calibre; diámetro interior de un cilindro.–pret. de TO BEAR.– **—d** [-d], a. taladrado; aburrido.– **—dom** [bórdom], s. fastidio; aburrimiento, tedio.– **—r** [-œ(r)], s. horadador; barrena; taladro; perforadora; cualquier animal que horada; pelmazo, latoso. **—boring** [bóriŋ], a. pesado, aburrido, latoso.–s. perforación; sondeo.–pl. partículas que se desprenden al taladrar o barrenar.

born [bɔrn], a. nacido; de nacimiento; por naturaleza.–pp. de TO BEAR.– to be b., nacer. **—borne** [bɔrn], pp. de TO BEAR.

borough [bárou], s. barrio; villa; municipio incorporado; distrito administrativo de una ciudad.

borrow [bárou], vt. pedir o tomar prestado; tomar fiado; apropiarse, copiar.– **—er** [-œ(r)], s. prestatario, el que pide o toma prestado.

bosom [búʒom], s. seno, pecho, corazón; buche, pechera; amor, inclinación.–a. íntimo, querido; secreto.

boss [bɔs], s. amo, capataz, patrón; jefe, cabecilla; cacique.–vt. mandar; dominar; regentear; dirigir.– **—ism** [bósjzm], s. caciquismo, caudillismo.– **—y** [-i], a. mandón, autoritario.

botany [bátanj], s. botánica.

botch [bach], vt.–to b. up, (fam.) hacer una chapuza de, chapucear.

both [boυθ], a. y pron. ambos, entrambos.–b. my father and his, tanto mi padre como el suyo.

bother [báðœ(r)], vt. y vi. incomodar(se), molestar(se); marear.–s. molestia, incomodidad; lata, pejiguera.

bottle [bátl], s. botella; frasco.–vt. embotellar.–to b. up, reprimir, contener.– **—bottling** [bátliŋ], embotellado.–b. plant, embotelladora.

bottom [bátom], s. fondo; suelo; lecho de un río, lago, etc.; parte inferior, lo más bajo; fundamento; trasero, nalgatorio; hez; asiento de una silla; pie (de página).–vt. poner fondo o asiento; cimentar, basar.–vi. apoyarse.– **—less** [-ljs], a. sin asiento; insondable.

bough [bau], s. rama, ramo.

bought [bɔt], *pret.* y *pp.* de TO BUY.

bouillon [búlyan], s. caldo.

boulder [bóuldœ(r)], s. peña, roca, pedrusco.

bounce [bauns], *vi.* rebotar; brincar, saltar; lanzarse; echar bravatas; fanfarronear.—*vt.* hacer (re)botar; echar a cajas destempladas, despedir.—*s.* (re)bote; salto, brinco; acto de arrojar a alguien violentamente. – —**r** [báunsœ(r)], s. (coll.) gorila, sacabullas (Mex.), guardián fornido a cargo de echar del lugar (cabaret, etc.) a los perturbadores.

bound [baund], s. límite, término; lindero; bote, brinco, corcovo.—*vt.* deslindar; parcelar; hacer saltar; confinar.—*vi.* saltar, (re)botar; corvetear.—*pret.* y *pp.* de TO BIND.—*a.* atado, sujeto; confinado; moral o legalmente obligado; encuadernado; destinado; resuelto (a).— —**ary** [báundari], s. límite, lindero, frontera; término.—*a.* limítrofe, divisorio.- —**less** [-lis], *a.* ilimitado, infinito.

bounteous [báuntiʌs], **bountiful** [báuntiful], *a.* liberal, generoso; copioso. —**bounteousness** [báuntiʌsnis], **bountifulness** [báuntifulnis], s. munificencia, liberalidad, generosidad; copiosidad. —**bounty** [báunti], s. generosidad, liberalidad; merced, gracia; subvención; prima.—*b. money* (mil.), enganche.

bouquet [bukéj], s. ramo, ramillete; aroma.

bourgeois [bŭrẑwá], *a.* y s. burgués.

bout [baut], s. encuentro, combate; asalto de esgrima o boxeo; ataque de enfermedad; vez, turno.

bow [bau], s. saludo, reverencia; zalema; proa.—*vi.* inclinarse; hacer una reverencia; agobiarse, ceder, someterse.—*s.* [bou], arco (flecha, violín, etc.); curva; lazada; lazo (de corbata, cinta, etc.).

bowels [báuelz], s. intestinos, tripas; entrañas; mondongo.—*to move one's b.*, mover el intestino, hacer *or* mover de vientre.

bower [báuœ(r)], s. glorieta, emparrado, cenador, enramada.

bowl [boul], s. escudilla, cuenco; concavidad; tazón de fuente; palangana, jofaina; bola, bocha; ponchera; (sport) estadio.—*pl.* juego de bolos.—*vi.* bolear, jugar a los bolos, al boliche, etc.—*vt.* (in bowling) lanzar.—*Anthony can b. 260*, Antonio puede hacer 260.—*to b. over*, derribar, tirar al suelo.- —**ing** [-iŋ], s. bolos, bowling.—*b. alley*, bolera, bowling.

bowman [bóumạn], s. arquero.

box [baks], s. caja, cajón; estuche; cofre, arca; apartado (de correos); casilla; compartimiento; taquilla; establo; manotazo, revés.—*b. seat*, asiento de palco.—*vt.* encajonar, embalar; abofetear.—*vi.* boxear.— —**er** [báksœ(r)], s. boxeador; embalador.—*b. shorts*, calzoncillos, calzones (Mex.), interiores (S.A.).- —**ing** [-iŋ], s. encajonamiento, empaque; madera para encajonar; boxeo, pugilismo; marco de puerta o de ventana. —**box tree, boxwood** [bákswụd], s. boj.

boy [bɔj], s. muchacho, niño, chico; hijo varón; mozo; criado; grumete.—*b. scout*, explorador, niño explorador. —**friend** [-frend], s. campañero, amigo; (of a woman) novio, pololo, amiguito.

boycott [bójkat], s. boicot, boicoteo.—*vt.* boicotear.

boyhood [bójhụd], s. niñez; pubertad, adolescencia.

brace [breis], *vt.* ligar, asegurar; reforzar; fortalecer; (teeth) poner aparatos a; encerrar en una llave o corchete.—*vi.* animarse.—*s.* abrazadera; berbiquí; tirante; corchete; llave; braguero; ligadura.- —**let** [bréislit], s. brazalete.

bracket [brækit], s. soporte, brazo o sostén (de lámpara, candelabro, etc.) asegurado en la pared; consola, repisa; ménsula; grupo, clase, nivel, categoría.—*pl.* corchetes; paréntesis angulares.—*vt.* poner entre paréntesis; unir; poner en una misma clase.

brackish [brækiš], *a.* salobre, salado.

brag [bræg], s. jactancia, fanfarronada; fanfarrón.—*vii.* [1] jactarse (de); fanfarronear; alardear; farolear.- —**gart** [brǽgart], s. mata siete.

braid [breid], *vt.* trenzar, entrelazar; galonear.—*s.* galón, trencilla, trenza.

braille, Braille [breil], s. braille, Braille.

brain [brein], s. cerebro, seso.—*b. dead*, clínicamente muerto.—*b.* sesos; inteligencia, juicio.—*to rack one's b.*, devanarse los sesos.

—storm [-stɔrm], s. (fam.) frenesí; (fig.) idea genial, idea luminosa.– **—storming** [-stɔrmin], s. brainstorming.– **—wash** [-wɔš], vt. lavarle el cerebro a, hacerle un lavado de cerebro.– **—washing** [-wɔsin], s. lavado de cerebro.– **—y** [bréjni], a. sesudo, inteligente.

brake [brejk], s. freno, retranca; grada, rastra; palanca.—b. lining, guarnición.—b. shoe, zapata de freno.—vt. frenar; gradar.- **—man** [bréjkman], s. guardafrenos, retranquero.

bramble [bræmbl], s. zarza.

bran [bræn], s. salvado, afrecho.

branch [brænch], s. rama; ramo; dependencia; división o sección; ramal, brazo; afluente; sucursal; bifurcación, ramal; arma (de las fuerzas armadas).—a. dependiente, tributario.—vi. ramificarse; echar astas o ramas.—to b. off, bifurcarse.

brand [brænd], s. sello o marca de fábrica; calidad; hierro de marcar reses; estigma, baldón.—b. name, marca conocida.—b.-new, nuevecito, flamante.—vt. herrar, marcar ganado, calimbar; tildar; infamar.— **—ing** [brændin], s. herradero, hierra.—b. iron, hierro de marcar ganado.

brandish [brændiš], vt. blandir; cimbrar, florear.—s. floreo, molinete.

brandy [brændi], s. coñac; aguardiente.

brass [bræs], s. latón; cualquier objeto de latón; descaro; calderilla (dinero); cobres (instrumentos de música).—b. band, banda, charanga.—b. knuckles, nudilleras de metal.—he's got a lot of b.!, (fam.) ¡que cara dura tiene!, ¡que jeta tiene!.—to get down to b. tacks, ir al grano.—vt. revestir de latón.

brassière [bræzír], s. sostén, corpiño, ajustador.

brat [bræt], s. rapaz, mocoso; niño travieso y díscolo.

bravado [brəvádou], s. bravata, baladronada.

brave [brejv], a. bravo, valiente; bizarro.—vt. desafiar, arrostrar.- **—ry** [bréjveri], s. valor; bizarría, heroísmo.

brawl [brɔl], s. alboroto, pendencia.—vi. alborotar, armar camorra.

bray [brej], vi. rebuznar.—s. rebuzno.- **—ing** [bréjin], s. rebuzno.

braze [brejz], vt. broncear; soldar; endurecer.- **—n** [bréjzen], a. descarado.

brazier [bréjzœ(r)], s. brasero.

Brazilian [brəzílian], a. y s. brasileño, brasilero.

breach [brich], s. brecha, abertura; infracción, violación; rompimiento. —b. of promise, violación de palabra de matrimonio.—vt. hacer brecha.

bread [bred], s. pan.—b. crumb, miga de pan.—vt. empanar; empanizar.—breaded cutlet, chuleta empanizada.—b. knife, cuchillo del pan.

breadth [bredθ], s. anchura, ancho; envergadura; latitud; amplitud.- **—wise** [brédθwajz], adv. a lo ancho.

break [brejk], vti. [10] romper, quebrantar, partir; infringir, violar (la ley, etc.); abrir brecha en; domar; arruinar; interrumpir; cambiar (un billete, etc.); moderar, amortiguar; exeder; descomponer.—to b. away, escaparse, fugarse.—to b. down, abatirse; (mec.) averiarse.—to b. in, forzar, romper o abrir empujando hacia adentro; domar (animales); entremeterse.—to b. into a house, escalar, allanar una casa.—to b. out, estallar.—to b. up, dividir en partes.—vii. romperse, quebrarse, frustrarse; descomponerse; rayar el día; brotar, florecer; dispersarse.— s. rotura, ruptura; abertura, grieta; comienzo, principio; intervalo, pausa; interrupción; baja en el mercado; casualidad, chiripa.—b. point, (tennis) punto de ruptura; (comput.) punto de-interrupción.- **—able** [bréjkabl], a. quebradizo, frágil.- **—age** [-jdẑ], s. fractura, rotura; indemnización por daños (tránsito, etc.).- **—down** [-daun], s. derrumbamiento; trastorno; interrupción o paralización de un servicio; avería; agotamiento.- **—er** [-œ(r)], s. rompiente (ola); infractor.- **—through** [-θru], s. gran avance; (mil) penetración.- **—water** [-wɔtœr], s. rompeolas.

breakfast [brékfast], s. desayuno.—vi. desayunarse.

breast [brest], s. pecho, seno; teta; mama; pechuga.—vt. amamantar; arrostrar resueltamente.—b. feed, amamantar, darle el pecho a.—b.-feeding, cría a los pechos.—**bone** [bréstboun], s. esternón.- **—stroke**

[-strouk], s. braza de pecho, estilo pecho.

breath [breθ], s. aliento, respiración, resuello; soplo; pausa, respiro; instante.—*b.-taking,* conmovedor, sorprendente.—*b. test,* prueba del alcohol. —**Breathalyzer** [bréθalaj-zœr]™, s. alcoholímetro.- —**e** [brið], vi. y vt. respirar, alentar; vivir; tomar aliento; soplar; aspirar; exhalar.- —**r** [brịðœ(r)], s. respirador; viviente; inspirador; tregua.- —**ing** [bríðịŋ], s. respiración; respiro, resuello.—*b. space,* respiro.- —**less** [bréθlịs], a. sin resuello; jadeante; muerto.- —**lessness** [-lịsnịs], s. jadeo, desaliento; muerte.

bred [bred], pret. y pp. de TO BREED.

breech [brich], s. (arti.) recámara, culata, cierre.

breeches [bríchịz], s. pl. calzones, bragas.

breed [brid], vti. [10] engendrar; criar; empollar; parir; producir; educar.—vii. multiplicarse.—s. casta, raza, progenie; prole.— —**er** [brídœ(r)], s. criador, ganadero; padre, reproductor o semental.- —**ing** [-ịŋ], s. cría, crianza; educación; maneras.

breeze [briz], s. brisa, airecillo. —**breezy** [brízị], a. airoso, ventilado; animado, vivo.

breviary [brívịerị], s. breviario.

brevity [brévịtị], s. brevedad; concisión.

brew [bru], vt. hacer, fabricar; preparar (té); fraguar, urdir, tramar.— vi. amenazar; formarse, prepararse.—s. cerveza; mezcla.- —**er** [brúœ(r)], s. cervecero.- —**ery** [-œrị], s. fábrica de cerveza, cervecería.- —**ing** [-ịŋ], s. elaboración de cerveza; señales de borrasca.

briar [brájặ(r)], s. rosal silvestre; zarza; brezo (para pipas).

bribe [brajb], s. cohecho, soborno.— vt. sobornar, cohechar.- —**ry** [brájbẹrị], s. cohecho, soborno.

brick [brịk], s. ladrillo(s).—vt. enladrillar.- —**bat** [bríkbæt], s. tejoleta, pedazo de ladrillo; insulto.- —**layer** [-lẹjœ(r)], s. albañil.

bridal [brájdặl], a. nupcial.—s. boda, fiesta nupcial.—**bride** [brajd], s. novia.—*the b. and groom,* los novios.—**bridegroom** [brájdgrum], s. novio. —**bridesmaid** [brájdzmẹjd], s. dama de honor.

bridge [brịdẑ], s. puente; caballete de la nariz; bridge.—*auction b.,* bridge subastado.—*b. toll,* peaje.—*contract b.,* bridge contrato.—*draw b.,* puente levadizo.- —**head** [-hẹd], s. cabeza de puente.—vt. tender un puente; atravesar.—*to b. a gap,* llenar un vacío.

bridle [brájdl], s. brida, freno; frenillo.—*b. path,* camino de herradura.—vt. enfrenar; reprimir; embridar.—vi. erguirse.

brief [brif], a. breve, conciso; fugaz.— s. epítome, resumen, memorial, informe; alegato.—*to hold no b. for,* no estar defendiendo o no ser defensor de.—vt. instruir, darle instrucciones a, informar.- —**case** [brífkẹjs], s. cartera.- —**ing** [-ịŋ], s. órdenes, instrucciones.

brigade [brịgéjd], s. brigada. —**brigadier** [brịgadír], s. brigadier, general de brigada.

bright [brajt], a. brillante, claro, lustroso; subido (colores); eximio; vivo, inteligente; halagüeño.- —**en** [brájtẹn], vt. pulir; alegrar, consolar; ennoblecer; mejorar.—vi. aclarar, despejarse (el cielo); animarse.- —**ness** [-nịs], s. lustre, lucidez; resplandor, claridad; agudeza.

brilliance [brílyặns], **brilliancy** [brílyặnsị], s. brillantez, brillo; resplandor; esplendor. —**brilliant** [brílyặnt], a. brillante; talentoso; excelente.—s. brillante; diamante.

brim [brịm], s. borde, margen; labio de un vaso; ala de sombrero.—vti. [1] llenar hasta el borde.—*to b. over,* rebosar; desbordar, derramar.

brimstone [brímstoun], s. azufre.

brine [brajn], s. salmuera; agua cargada de sal.—vt. salar.

bring [brịŋ], vti. [10] traer; llevar; conducir; persuadir; aportar; causar, producir.—*to b. about,* efectuar, poner por obra; lograr; dar lugar a; causar.—*to b. forth,* producir; parir; dar a luz.—*to b. forward,* empujar; llevar una suma a otra cuenta.—*to b. out,* presentar; publicar; poner en escena; descubrir.—*to b. over,* persuadir; convertir; traer.—*to b. up,* criar, educar.

brink [brịŋk], s. borde.—*on the b. of,* a punto de.- —**manship** [-maenşịp], s. política arriesgada.

brisk [brịsk], a. vivo, activo, enérgico; rápido; estimulante.- —**ness**

[brískni̯s], s. vivacidad, despejo; gallardía.

bristle [brísl], s. cerda.—vt. erizar, poner tieso.—vi. erizarse.

Briticism [brítisism], s. modismo o vocablo del inglés de Inglaterra.

British [brítis̆], a. británico.—spl.— the B., los británicos.

brittle [brítl], a. quebradizo; frágil; vidrioso.— **—ness** [-ni̯s], s. fragilidad.

broach [brouc̆], s. broca, mecha; punzón.—vt. mencionar por primera vez; introducir; hacer público; espetar; traer a colación.

broad [brɔd], a. ancho; amplio; claro; general; tolerante; indelicado; pronunciado, marcado; pleno.

broadcast [brɔ́dkæst], vti. y vii. [4] transmitir, emitir; (agr.) sembrar a voleo.—s. programa, emisión.— adv. por todas partes.- **—er** [-œ(r)], s. presentador, locutor, etc. (de radio o televisión).- **—ing** [-i̯ŋ], s. (radio) radiodifusión; (TV) televisión.

broadcloth [brɔ́dklɔθ], s. paño fino de lana o algodón.

broaden [brɔ́den], vt. y vi. ensanchar(se).

brocade [brokéi̯d], s. brocado.—vt. decorar con brocado.

broccoli [brákoli̯], s. bróculi, brécol.

brochure [brošúr], s. folleto.

broil [brɔi̯l],—vt. asar sobre las ascuas o en parrillas.—vi. asarse; asarse de calor.- **—er** [brɔ́i̯lœ(r)], s. parrilla(s); pollo propio para asar.- **—ing** [-i̯ŋ], a. extremadamente cálido, abrasador.

broke [brouk], pret. de TO BREAK.—a. tronado, sin blanca, sin un real. **—broken** [bróu̯ken], pp. de TO BREAK.—b.-down, averiado; destartalado—b.-hearted, destrozado, deshecho.—a. quebrado, roto; imperfecto; interrumpido; domado; mal pronunciado; debilitado; arruinado.- **—r** [bróu̯kœ(r)], s. corredor, cambista; agente de bolsa.- **—rage** [bróu̯kœri̯dž], s. corretaje, correduría.

bronchial [bránki̯al], a. bronquial.

bronze [branz], s. bronce.—vt. broncear.

brooch [brouc̆], s. broche, pasador.

brood [brud], a. clueca.—b. mare, yegua madre o paridera.—s. cría; pollada, nidada; camada; melancolía.—vt. empollar, incubar.—vi. preocuparse, ensimismarse.—to b. over, cavilar.

brook [bruk], s. arroyo, riachuelo; cañada, quebrada.—vt. sufrir, aguantar.- **—let** [brúkli̯t], s. arroyuelo.

broom [brum], s. escoba; retama.- **—stick** [brúmsti̯k], s. palo de escoba.

broth [brɔθ], s. caldo.

brothel [brɑ́ðel], s. burdel, lupanar.

brother [brɑ́ðœ(r)], s. hermano.— b.-in-law, cuñado.—interj. Dios mío!.- **—hood** [-hu̯d], s. fraternidad; (group) hermandad, cofradía. - **—ly** [-li̯], a. fraternal.

brought [brɔt], pret. y pp. de TO BRING.

brow [brau̯], s. ceja; frente; sien; arco superciliar.

brown [brau̯n], a. marrón, café (Am.); (hair) castaño; (skin) moreno; (suntanned) bronceado.—s. marrón, café.—vt. (coc.) dorar.—vi. (coc.) dorarse.—b. bear, oso pardo.—b. bread, pan negro.—b. rice, arroz integral.—b. sugar, azúcar negro, azúcar moreno.- **—ish** [bráu̯nis̆], a. pardusco.

brownie [bráu̯ni̯], s. bizcocho de chocolate y nueces.

browse [brau̯z], vt. y vi. curiosear; hojear (un libro).

bruise [bruz], vt. magullar; golpear; machacar; machucar; abollar; majar.—s. magulladura, etc.

brunette [brunét], a. moreno.—s. morena.

brush [brʌs̆], s. cepillo; escobilla; brocha; pincel; matorral; escaramuza; haz de leña menuda.—vt. (a)cepillar; frotar, restregar; pintar con brocha.—b. off, (jer.) desaire.—to give the b. to, (jer.) despedir noramala.—vi. moverse apresuradamente.—to b. aside, echar a un lado.—to b. away, restregar duro.— to b. up (on), repasar, refrescar; retocar.- **—wood** [brʌ́s̆wu̯d], s. broza, maleza.

brusque [braʌsk], a. brusco, abrupto.- **—ly** [-li̯], adv. con brusquedad.

brutal [brútal], a. brutal.- **—ity** [brutǽli̯ti̯], s. brutalidad.- **—ize** [brútalai̯z], vt. embrutecer; tratar cruelmente.—vi. embrutecerse.—brute [brut], s. bruto, bestia.—a. bruto, brutal. **—brutish** [brútis̆], a. bruto, brutal; embrutecido.

bubble [bɑ́bl], s. burbuja, pompa; ampolla; bagatela; engañifa.—vi. burbujear; hacer espuma; bullir; murmurar el río; ampollarse.—to b. over, rebosar; estar en efervescencia.—*to b. up*, ampollarse. —**bubbly** [bábli̱], *a.* burbujeante, espumoso.

bubonic [bjubáni̱k], *a.* bubónico.—*b. plague*, peste bubónica.

buck [bʌk], *s.* gamo; macho cabrío; macho de ciervo, alce, reno, etc.; corveta o respingo; topada.—*to pass the b.*, (coll.) echar al uno el muerto, pasar la pelota.—*vi.* encabritarse, respingar, corcovear.- —**shot** [-ṣat], *s.* perdigón.

bucket [bʌ́ki̱t], *s.* cubo, pozal, balde; contenido de un balde.—*b. seat*, asiento envolvente.—*to kick the b.*, (coll.) estirar la pata.

buckle [bʌ́kl], *s.* hebilla.—*vt.* abrochar con hebilla.—*vi.* doblarse, combarse.—*to b. up*, abrocharse el cinturón de seguridad.

bud [bʌd], *s.* yema, botón, capullo; brote, retoño.—*vii.* [1] brotar, retoñar; echar capullos.

buddy [bʌ́di̱], *s.* camarada, compañero.

budge [bʌdʒ], *vt.* mover.—*vi.* moverse, menearse; hacer lugar.

budget [bʌ́dʒi̱t], *s.* presupuesto.—*vt.* hacer presupuesto.

buff [bʌf], *s.* piel de ante, búfalo, etc.; color crema; pulidor.—*a.* de ante; de color crema.—*vt.* pulir, bruñir.

buffer [bʌ́fœ(r)], *s.* pulidor; amortiguador de choques.—*b. state*, estado tapón.—*b. zone*, zona parachoques.

buffet [buféj], *s.* bufet, bufé; (sideboard) aparador; [bʌ́fi̱t], bofetada; (fam.) sopapo; embote.—*vt.* abofetear; luchar contra.

buffoon [bʌfún], *s.* bufón.- —**ery** [-ęri̱], *s.* bufonada.

bug [bʌg], *s.* chinche, bicho; (med.) microbio; (comput.) fallo, error; (listening device) (coll.) micrófono oculto.

bugaboo [bágəbu], **bugbear** [bágbɛr], *s.* coco, espantajo, bu.

buggy [bági̱], *s.* coche ligero, calesa; vagón de cola.—*a.* lleno de chinches u otros insectos.

bugle [bjúgl], *s.* corneta de órdenes; trompeta; clarín.- —**r** [bjúglœr], *s.* trompetero, corneta.

build [bi̱ld], *vti.* y *vii.* [10] edificar, construir, fabricar.—*s.* estructura; forma; figura (de una persona).- —**er** [bíldœ(r)], *s.* constructor; maestro de obras.- —**ing** [-i̱ŋ], *s.* edificio, casa, obra, local.—*a.* constructor, para construcciones; relativo a casas o edificios. —**built** [bi̱lt], *pret.* y *pp.* de TO BUILD.

bulb [bʌlb], *s.* bulbo; ampolleta; bomb(ill)a, foco; pera de goma; ensanche.

Bulgarian [bʌlgéri̱ən], *s.* y *a.* búlgaro.

bulge [bʌldʒ], *s.* pandeo, comba.—*vt.* y *vi.* pandear(se); abultar(se). —**bulgy** [bʌ́ldʒi̱], *a.* combo, pandeado; saliente.

bulk [bʌlk], *s.* bulto, volumen; masa; parte principal; la mayor parte; el grueso.—*vi.* hincharse; aumentar (bulto, peso, importancia).- —**y** [bʌ́lki̱], *a.* abultado, voluminoso.

bull [buḻ], *s.* toro; (igl.) bula; (jer.) disparates, astupideces; (com.) alcista (en la Bolsa).—*b. market*, mercado alcista.—*b.'s eye*, diana, centro del blanco; tiro perfecto.—*to take the b. by the horns*, agarrar el toro por los cuernos.- —**dog** [buḻdɔg], *s.* perro dogo.- —**dozer** [-douzœ(r)], *s.* máquina razadora, bulldozer.

bullet [buḻi̱t], *s.* bala.

bulletin [buḻi̱ti̱n], *s.* boletín.—*b. board*, tablón de anuncios, tablero de anuncios.

bullfight [buḻfajt], *s.* corrida de toros.- —**er** [-œ(r)], *s.* torero.- —**ing** [-i̱ŋ], *s.* toreo, tauromaquia.

bullfrog [buḻfrag], *s.* rana toro.

bullock [buḻɔk], *s.* buey.

bullpen [buḻpen], *s.* toril. —**bullring** [buḻri̱ŋ], *s.* plaza de toros.

bully [buḻi̱], *s.* matón, bravucón, valentón.—*a.* magnífico, excelente.—*vti.* [7] intimidar. —**ing** [-i̱ŋ], *s.* intimidación, abuso.

bulwark [buḻwärk], *s.* baluarte, bastión; defensa.

bum [bʌm], *vti.* [1] (fam.) sablear, obtener (algo) graciosamente.—*vii.* (fam.) holgazanear; vivir parasitariamente.—*s.* (fam.) vago; golfo; atorrante.—*a.* (fam.) de calidad ínfima.

bumblebee [bʌ́mblbi̱], *s.* abejorro, moscardón.

bump [bʌmp], *s.* tope(tazo); chichón, protuberancia.—*vt.* chocar contra.—*to b. off*, (coll.) matar, despachar.- —**er** [bʌ́mpœ(r)], *s.* parachoques, defensa; lo que da golpes. —*a.* lleno; excelente; abundante.

bumpy [bʌ́mpi̱], *a.* desigual, con baches, áspero; (air) agitado.

bun [bʌn], *s.* buñuelo; friturita, bollo.

bunch [bʌnch], s. haz, manojo, atado; mazo, montón; racimo; ramillete; grupo; bulto.—vt. agrupar, juntar.—vi. arracimarse, amacollarse.

bundle [bándl], s. atado, lío; haz, mazo; fardo, bulto.—vt. liar, atar; empaquetar, envolver.—to b. up, abrigarse, taparse bien.

bungle [bángl], vt. chapucear, echar a perder.—vi. hacer chapucerías. —s. chapucería.— —r [bánglœ(r)], s. chapucero, chambón. —bungling [bángliŋ], a. chapucero.

bunion [bányon], s. juanete.

bunk [bʌŋk], s. tarima, litera; embuste; (fam.) baladronada, palabrería.—b. bed, litera, cucheta.

buoy [bój, búj], s. boya.—vt. aboyar.—vi. aboyarse, flotar, boyar.- —ancy [-ąnsi], s. flotabilidad; flotación; alegría, animación; fuerza ascensional.- —ant [-ąnt], a. boyante.

burden [bǿrden], s. carga, peso, gravamen; capacidad, tonelaje.—vt. cargar, agobiar, gravar.- —some [-sʌm], a. gravoso, oneroso, molesto.

bureau [bjúrou], s. buró, escritorio; oficina, despacho; agencia, negociado; ramo, división, departamento.- —cracy [bjurákrąsi], s. burocracia.- —crat [bjúrokræt], s. burócrata.- —cratic [bjuokrǽtik], a. burocrático.

burger [boérgœr], s. (coll.) hamburguesa.

burglar [boérglǫr], s. ladrón (de viviendas).- —y [-i], s. robo con escalo; hurto.

burial [bérjąl], s. entierro, inhumación, sepelio.

burlap [boérlæp], s. arpillera.

burlesque [bœrlésk], s. parodia; (E.U. teat.) espectáculo de variedades de carácter burlesco.—a. burlesco, paródico.—vt. chufar, parodiar.

burly [bǿrli], a. corpulento, fornido; nudoso.

Burmese [bǿrmiz], a. y s. birmano.

burn [bœrn], vti. y vii. [4] quemar(se), abrasar(se), incendiar(se); calcinar(se).—vi. arder.—s. quemadura; marca de hierro candente.- —er [bǿrnœ(r)], s. quemador, mechero, hornilla.

burnish [bǿrniš], vt. bruñir, pulir.— vi. tomar lustre.—s. bruñido.- —er [-œ(r)], s. bruñidor.

burrow [bǿrou], s. madriguera, cueva.—vt. hacer cueva(s) en.—vi. encuevarse; minar, horadar.

burst [bœrst], vti. y vii. [9] reventar(se), romper(se); abrir(se) violentamente.—to b. into flames, inflamarse.—to b. into tears, romper a llorar.—pret. y pp. de TO BURST.—s. reventón, estallido; ataque, arrebato.

bury [béri], vti. [7] enterrar, inhumar; sepultar; ocultar.

bus [bʌs], s. autobús, bus, camión.— vt. llevar en autobús.— —boy [-bɔj], s. ayudante decamarero.- —ing [-iŋ], s. transporte de escolares en autobús fuera de su zona para favorecer la integración racial.

bush [buš], s. arbusto; matorral; terreno cubierto de malezas, manigua.—to beat around the b., andar(se) con rodeos.

bushel [búšel], s. medida de áridos. Ver Tabla.

business [bíznis], s. negocio(s); cuestion de negocios; oficio, trabajo, profesión; comercio.—b. man, negociante, hombre de negocios o de empresas.

bust [bʌst], s. busto; pecho (de mujer); parranda, borrachera.

bustle [básl], vi. bullir, trajinar, ajetrearse.—s. bullicio, trajín; polisón.

busy [bízi], a. ocupado; activo; atareado.—b. signal, (tlf.) tono de ocupado, señal de ocupado, señal de comunicando.—b. street, calle concurrida, de mucho tráfico.—vti. [7] ocupar, emplear.- —body [-badi], s. entremetido; chismoso.

but [bʌt], conj., prep. y adv. pero, mas; sin embargo; excepto, menos; sólo, solamente, no más que; sino; que no; sin que; sin.—b. for, a no ser por.—none b., solamente.—s. objeción, pero.

butcher [búchœ(r)], s. carnicero.— b.'s shop, carnicería.—vt. matar reses; dar muerte cruel, hacer una carnicería.- —y [-i], s. carnicería, matanza; oficio de carnicero; matadero.

butler [bátlœ(r)], s. mayordomo.

butt [bʌt], s. culata (de rifle, etc.); colilla; cabo; mango; cabo; fin, límite; blanco (de las miradas, etc.); topetazo.—b. of ridicule, hazmerreir.—vt. topar; mochar.—vi. embestir.

butter [bátœ(r)], s. mantequilla, manteca (de nata de leche.)—vt. untar con mantequilla o manteca; adular.

butterfly [bátœ(r)flaj], s. mariposa.

buttermilk [bátœ(r)mjlk], s. suero de mantequilla. **—buttery** [bátœrj], s. bodega; despensa.—a. mantecoso; adulador.

buttock [bátok], s. nalga, trasero.— pl. posaderas.

button [báton], s. botón; tirador de puerta.—vt. abotonar.—vi. abotonarse.- **—hole** [-houl], s. ojal, presilla.—vt. abrir ojales; importunar.

buy [baj], vti. [10] comprar.—to b. off, sobornar.—s. compra.- **—er** [bájœ(r)], s. comprador, marchante.

buzz [bʌz], s. zumbido; susurro.—b. saw, sierra circular.—vi. zumbar; susurrar.- **—word** [-wœrd], s. palabra de moda.

buzzard [bázǎrd], s. buitre, aura, zopilote, carancho.

buzzing [bázjn], s. zumbido.

by [baj], prep. por; a, en; para, por, junto a, cerca de, al lado de; según, de acuerdo con.—adv. cerca, al lado; aparte, a un lado.—b. and b., pronto, luego.—b. day, de día.—b. God! ¡por Dios!—b. itself, por sí mismo.—b. means of, mediante.— b. much, con mucho.—b. the dozen, por docenas.—b. the way, apropósito, de paso, ya que viene al caso, etc.—b. then, para entonces.—b. this time, ahora, ya.—b. way of, por vía de.—days gone b., días pasados. - **—gone** [bájɡon], a. pasado.—let bygones be bygones, olvidemos lo pasado; pelillos a la mar.- **—law** [-lɔ], s. estatuto o reglamento.- **—path** [-pæθ], s. senda.- **—product** [-pradʌkt], s. producto accesorio, derivado, residual.- **—stander** [-stændœ(r)], s. espectador, circunstante, presente.

C

cab [kæb], s. taxi; coche de caballos; (for driver) cabina.—c. driver, taxista.—c. stand, parada de taxis.

cabal [kǎbǽl], s. cábala.

cabaret [kæbǎréj], s. cabaret.

cabbage [kæbjdž], s. berza, col, repollo.

cabby [kǽbj], s. (fam.), **cabdriver** [kǽbdrajvœ(r)], s. cochero; chofer de taxi.

cabin [kǽbjn], s. cabaña, barraca, choza; (mar.) cabina, camarote; (aut.) cabina.—c. boy, grumete.

cabinet [kǽbjnjt], s. escaparate, vitrina; armario; (pol.) gabinete; caja o mueble (de radio, T.V.).—c. council, consejo de ministros o del gabinete.—a. ministerial; secreto, reservado.- **—maker** [-mejkœ(r)], s. ebanista.- **—making** [-mejkjn], s. ebanistería.

cable [kéjbl], s. cable; cablegrama.— c. railway, funicular.—c. television, televisión por cable, cablevisión.— vt. y vi. cablegrafiar.- **—gram** [-græm], s. cablegrama, cable.

caboose [kǎbús], s. (f.c.) furgón de cola.

cackle [kǽkl], vi. cacarear; chacharear.—s. cacareo; cháchara.

cadaver [kǎdǽvœ(r)], s. cadáver.- **—ous** [-ʌs], a. cadavérico.

cadence [kéjdens], **cadency** [kéjdensj], s. cadencia, ritmo.

cadet [kǎdét], s. cadete.

caddie [kaédj], s. caddie.—vi. hacer de caddie.—to c. for, ser el caddie de.

cafeteria [kæfętírjǎ], s. cafetería, cantina; restaurante autoservicio, self-service.

cage [kejdž], s. jaula.—vt. enjaular.

cajole [kǎdžóul], vt. lisonjear, engatusar.

cake [kejk], s. torta, bizcocho, pastel, bollo, hojaldre; pastilla o pan de jabón, de cera, etc.; terrón.—c. mix, polvos para hacer pasteles.—vi. apelmazarse, formar costra.

calabash [kǽlǎbæš], s. calabaza.

calamitous [kǎlǽmjtʌs], a. calamitoso. **—calamity** [kǎlǽmjtj], s. calamidad.

calcium [kǽlsiʌm], *s.* calcio.
calculate [kǽlkiuleit], *vt.* calcular.—
  calculation [kælkiuléiṣon], *s.* cálculo, cómputo. —**calculator** [kǽlkiuleito(r)], *s.* calculista; calculador, (máquina) calculadora. —**calculus** [kǽlkiulʌs], *s.* cálculo.
caldron [kóldron], *s.* caldero, paila.
calendar [kǽlinda(r)], *s.* calendario; almanaque.—*c. year,* año natural, año civil.
calf [kæf], *s.* becerro, ternero; piel de becerro; pantorrilla.— *c. bound,* encuadernado en piel.- —**skin** [kǽfskin], *s.* piel de becerro curtida.
caliber [kǽliboe(r)], *s.* calibre; diámetro; (fig.) mérito. —**calibrate** [kǽlibreit], *vt.* calibrar. —**calibration** [kælibréiṣon], *s.* calibración.
calipers [kǽlipœrs], *s.* calibrador.
calk [kok], *vt.* calafatear.- —**ing** [kókin], *s.* calafateo, calafateadura.
call [kol], *vt.* llamar; visitar; denominar; apellidar; *—vi.* gritar.—*to c. again,* volver.—*to c. at,* (mar.) hacer escala, tocar (en un puerto).—*to c. back,* mandar volver; retirar.—*to c. for,* pedir; ir por; ir a buscar.—*to c. forth,* producir.—*to c. in,* hacer entrar.—*to c. names,* insultar.—*to c. off,* suspender; desistir de.—*to c. out,* gritar; hacer salir.—*to c. together,* convocar.—*to c. up,* recordar; llamar por teléfono.—*s.* llamada; llamamiento; citación; reclamo; vocación; señal, aviso; visita; (mil.) toque; (com.) demanda.—*on c.,* disponible; (com.) a solicitud, al pedir.—*to make* o *pay a c.,* hacer una visita.- —**er** [kólœ(r)], *s.* visitante.—*C. ID,* (tlf.) Identificación de Llamadas.- —**ing** [-iŋ], *s.* vocación; llamamiento; visita.
callous [kǽlʌs], *a.* calloso, córneo, encallecido; (fig.) duro, insensible. —**callus** [kǽlʌs], *s.* callo, dureza.
calm [kam], *s.* calma, serenidad, tranquilidad.—*a.* calmado, tranquilo, sereno.—*vt.* tranquilizar; calmar.—*to c. down,* calmarse, serenarse.- —**ness** [kámnis], *s.* = CALM.- —**y** [-i], *a.* tranquilo, apacible.
calorie [kǽlori], *s.* caloría.
calumny [kǽlʌmni], *s.* calumnia.
calves [kævz], *s. pl.* de CALF.
calyx [kéiliks], *s.* (bot.) cáliz.
cam [kæm], *s.* (mec.) leva.
camcorder [kǽmkorder], *s.* videocámara, camcórder.

came [keim], *pret.* de TO COME.
camel [kǽmel], *s.* camello.
camellia [kamílią], *s.* (bot.) camelia.
cameo [kǽmiou], *s.* camafeo; (cin.) actuación especial.
camera [kǽmerą], *s.* cámara fotográfica, máquina, fotográfica, máquina de fotos; (cin.) cámara.—*in c.,* (jur.) en la sala particular del juez; en secreto.—*on c.,* en imagen. - —**man** [-mæn], *s.* camarógrafo, cámara.
camomile [kǽmomail], *s.* manzanilla.
camouflage [kǽmuflaʒ], *s.* camuflaje; disfraz de protección.—*vt.* camuflar, disfrazar, encubrir.
camp [kæmp], *s.* campo, campamento.—*vt.* acampar.
campaign [kæmpéin], *s.* campaña (mil., pol., etc.).—*vi.* hacer campaña o propaganda.
camphor [kǽmfo(r)], *s.* alcanfor.—*c. ball,* = MOTH BALL.—*vt.* alcanforar.
campus [kǽmpʌs], *s.* (E.U.) campus.—*on c.,* en el campus.
can [kæn], *s.* (envase de) lata.—*c. opener,* abrelatas.—*vti.* [1] enlatar, envasar o conservar en latas; (fam.) despedir (de un empleo).—*v. def. i.* [11] poder, saber.
Canadian [kanéidian], *s.* y *a.* canadiense.
canal [kanǽl], *s.* canal; conducto.—*vti.* [2] canalizar; acanalar.
canary [kanéri], *s.* canario; (jer.) soplón.
cancel [kǽnsel], *vti.* [2] cancelar, revocar, rescindir; tachar; anular; suprimir.- —**lation** [kǽnseléiṣon], *s.* cancelación, rescisión; supresión.
cancer [kǽnsœ(r)], *s.* cáncer.—*C.,* (astr.) Cáncer.- —**ous** [-ʌS], *a.* canceroso.
candid [kǽndid], *a.,* sincero, franco, abierto.—*c. camera,* cámera indiscreta.
candidacy [kǽndidąsi], *s.* candidatura. —**candidate** [kǽndideit], *s.* candidato.
candied [kǽndid], *a.* azucarado, confitado.
candle [kǽndl], *s.* vela; (igl.) cirio.- —**light** [-lait], *s.—by c.,* a la luz de una vela.- —**stick** [-stik], *s.* palmatoria, candelero.
candor [kǽndo(r)], *s.* candor, candidez, franqueza; sinceridad.
candy [kǽndi], *s.* caramelo, bombón,

dulce, golosina.—*vti.* [7] almibarar, confitar, garapiñar.

cane [kéin], *s.* caña; bastón.—*c. field* o *plantation*, cañaveral.—*c. juice*, guarapo.—*sugar c.*, caña de azúcar.—*vt.* bastonear, apalear.

canine [kéinain], *a.* canino.—*s.* perro; (tooth) canino.

canned [kænd], *a.* enlatado.

cannibal [kǽnibal], *s.* caníbal, antropófago.- **—ism** [-izm], *s.* canibalismo.

cannon [kǽnon], *s.* cañón; (billar) carambola.—*c. bone*, canilla, caña.—*c. shot*, cañonazo.—*vt. y vi.* cañonear.- **—ade** [kǽnonéid], *s.* cañoneo.—*vt.* cañonear.

cannot [kǽnat], *fusión* de CAN (poder) y NOT.

canny [kǽni], *a.* astuto.

canoe [kanú], *s.* canoa, piragua; (Mex.) chalupa.—*vt. y vi.* llevar o pasear en canoa.

canon [kǽnon], *s.* canon; (clergyman) canónigo.—*c. law*, derecho canónico.- **—ize** [-aiz], *vt.* canonizar.

canopy [kǽnopi], *s.* dosel; palio; toldo; pabellón.

can't [kænt], *contr.* de CANNOT.

cant [kænt], *s.* jerga; hipocresías, gazmoñería; superficie inclinada.

cantaloupe [kǽntaloup], *s.* cantalupo.

canteen [kæntín], *s.* cantina, taberna; (water bottle) cantimplora

canter [kǽntœ(r)], *s.* medio galope.

canticle [kǽntikl], *s.* cántico, canto.

canton [kǽnton], *s.* cantón, distrito.

canvas [kǽnvas], *s.* lona; lienzo, cuadro; (mar.) vela, velamen.

canvass [kǽnvas], *s.* sondeo; solicitación; escrutinio.—*vt.*, sondear; solicitar; escudriñar.

canyon [kǽnyon], *s.* cañón.

cap [kæp], *s.* gorro, gorra; birrete; tapa; cima, cumbre; cápsula fulminante; casquillo, coronilla.—*vti.* [1] cubrir con gorra; poner tapa; poner cima o remate.

capability [keipabíliti], *s.* capacidad, idoneidad, aptitud. **—capable** [kéipabl], *a.* capaz; apto, competente.

capacious [kapéisʌs], *a.* capaz, espacioso. **—capacitate** [kapǽsiteit], *vt.* capacitar. **—capacity** [kapǽsiti], *s.* capacidad, cabida, espacio; inteligencia, disposición, suficiencia.

cape [keip], *s.* (geog.) cabo; capa.

caper [kéipœ(r)], *s.* cabriola; voltereta;

alcaparra.—*to cut a c.*, hacer una cabriola.—*vi.* dar brincos, retozar.

capillary [kǽpileri], *a.* capilar.

capital [kǽpital], *s.* capital; principal; excelente, magnífico.—*c. gains tax*, impuesto sobre la plusvalía.—*c. letter*, mayúscula.—*c. punishment*, pena de muerte.—*s.* capital (ciudad), cabecera (de un territorio o distrito); capitel; (com.) capital; fondos; caudal.—*to make c. (out) of*, sacar partido de.- **—ism** [-izm], *s.* capitalismo.- **—ist** [-ist], *s.* capitalista.- **—istic** [-ístik], *a.* capitalista (sistema, teoría, etc.).- **—ization** [-izéiʃon], *s.* capitalización; empleo de mayúsculas.- **—ize** [-aiz], *vt.* capitalizar.

capitol [kǽpitol], *s.* capitolio.

caprice [kaprís], *s.* capricho, antojo; fantasía.—**capricious** [kapríʃʌs], *a.* caprichoso.

Capricorn [kaéprikɔrn], *s.* (astr.) Capricornio.

capsize [kæpsáiz], *vi.* zozobrar, dar la vuelta.—*vt.* hacer zozobrar, volcar.

capsule [kǽpsiul], *s.* cápsula.

captain [kǽptin], *s.* capitán.—*vt.* capitanear.- **—cy** [-si], *s.* capitanía.

captious [kǽpʃʌs], *a.* criticón.

captivate [kǽptiveit], *vt.* cautivar, captar, fascinar. **—captivating** [kǽptiveitiŋ], *a.* cautivador, encantador, atractivo, seductivo. **—captivation** [kæptivéiʃon], *s.* encanto, fascinación. **—captive** [kǽptiv], *s. y a.* cautivo. **—captivity** [kæptíviti], *s.* cautiverio, cautividad, prisión. **—captor** [kǽpto(r)], *s.* captor, aprehensor. **—capture** [kǽpchū(r)], *s.* captura, apresamiento, prisión; presa.—*vt.* capturar, apresar, prender; (mil.) tomar.

car [kar], *s.* coche, auto, automóvil, carro; (of an elevator) cabina, carro, caja; (f.c.) vagón.

carafe [karǽf], *s.* garrafa, cantimplora.

caramel [kǽramel], *s.* caramelo.

carat [kǽrat], *s.* quilate.

caravan [kaéravæn], *s.* caravana; carricoche.

carbine [kárbain], *s.* carabina.

carbon [kárbon], *s.* copia al carbón; carbono; carbón (de lámpara de arco).—*c. copy*, copia al carbón.—*c. dioxide*, ahídrido carbónico.—*c. monoxide*, monóxido de carbono.—*c. paper*, papel carbón.- **—ic** [karbánjk], *a.* carbónico.– **—ization** [karbon̯izéjšon̯], *s.* carbonización.– **—ize** [kárbon̯ajz], *vt.* carbonizar.

carbuncle [kárbʌŋkl], *s.* (joy.) carbúnculo o carbunclo; (med.) carbunc(l)o.

carburetor [kárbjureito̯(r)], *s.* carburador.

carcass, carcase [kárkas], *s.* res muerta; esqueleto; despojo; caparazón (de ave); (mar.) casco o armazón.

card [kard], *s.* tarjeta, papeleta; naipe; carta; postal; ficha.—*c. catalogue,* catálogo de fichas.—*c. game,* juego de naipes.—*c. table,* mesa de baraja.—*to have a c. up one's sleeve,* tener algo (plan, etc.) en reserva. —*to play cards,* jugar a las cartas.- **—board** [kárdbɔrd], *s.* cartulina, cartón.—*vt.* verificar los papeles de; (técn.) cardar.

cardiac [kárdjæk], *a.* cardíaco.

cardinal [kárdjnal], *a.* cardinal, fundamental; rojo vivo.—*s.* cardenal.

care [ker], *s.* cuidado; atención, cautela; esmero; ansiedad; cargo, custodia.—*vi.* tener cuidado, ansiedad o interés por; querer; importarle a uno; estimar, apreciar; hacer caso.

career [karír], *s.* carrera.—*a.* de carrera.—*vi.* ir a toda velocidad.

carefree [kérfrí], *a.* despreocupado, alegre. **—careful** [kérful], *a.* cuidadoso, esmerado.—*to be c.,* tener cuidado. **—carefulness** [kérfulnjs], *s.* cuidado, cautela, atención. **—careless** [kérljs], *a.* descuidado, indiferente.—*to be c.,* descuidar. **—carelessness** [kérljsnjs], *s.* descuido, indiferencia.

caress [karés], *vt.* acariciar.—*s.* caricia.

caretaker [kértejkœ(r)], *s.* curador, guardián, custodio.

carfare [kárfer], *s.* dinero para el pasaje.

cargo [kárgou], *s.* carga, cargamento.

Carib [kǽrjb], *s.* caribe.– **—bean** [kǽrjbían], *a.* caribe, del mar Caribe.

caricature [kǽrjkachur], *s.* caricatura.—*vt.* caricaturizar. **—caricaturist** [-jst], *s.* caricaturista.

carload [kárloud], *s.* carga de un furgón o vagón (f.c.).

Carmelite [kármelajt], *s.* carmelita.

carnal [kárnal], *a.* carnal; sensual.

carnation [karnéjšon̯], *s.* clavel; color encarnado.

carnival [kárnjval], *s.* carnaval.

carnivore [kárnjvɔr], *s.* carnívoro. **—carnivorous** [karnívɔrʌs], *a.* carnívoro, carnicero.

carob [kǽrob], *s.* algarrobo.

carol [kǽrol], *s.* villancico; canto alegre.—*vti.* [2] cantar villancicos; cantar con alegría.

carouse [karáuz], *vi.* jaranear, andar de parranda; (fam.) correrla; embriagarse.—*s.* parranda; juerga; franchela.

carousel [karasél], *s.* caballitos; (in an airport) cinta transportadora, carrusel; carrete de diapositivas, carrusel.

carp [karp], *s.* (ict.) carpa.—*vi.* criticar.—*to c. at,* quejarse de.

carpenter [kárpentœ(r)], *s.* carpintero.—*vi.* carpintear. **—carpentry** [kárpentrj], *s.* carpintería.

carpet [kárpjt], *s.* alfombra.—*vt.* alfombrar, entapizar.– **—ing** [-jŋ], *s.* tela o tejido para alfombras; alfombrado.

carriage [kǽrjdž], *s.* carruaje, coche; conducción, acarreo, transporte; porte, aire de una persona; tren de aterrizaje; (of typewriter) carro. **—carrier** [kǽrjœ(r)], *s.* (trans)portador; arriero; carretero, cargador; empresa de transporte; mensajero; portaaviones; portador, agente transmisor de gérmenes; (rad.) onda de transmisión.—*c. pigeon,* paloma mensajera o correo.

carrion [kǽrjon̯], *s.* carroña.

carrot [kǽrot], *s.* zanahoria.

carry [kǽrj], *vti.* [7] llevar, conducir, transportar, acarrear; cargar; traer; llevar encima; contener; comprender; entrañar; dirigir; aprobar (una moción); ganar (las elecciones); tomar; aguantar, sostener; portarse. —*to c. away,* llevarse, entusiasmar, arrebatar.—*to c. off,* llevarse, retirar; ganar.—*to c. out,* llevar a cabo; sacar.—*to c. through,* llevar a cabo, completar.—*vii.* portear (como oficio); tener alcance (voz, tiro, etc.).

cart [kart], *s.* carro, carromato, carreta.—*c. load,* carretada.—*vt.* acarrear.– **—er** [-œr)], *s.* carretero.

cartilage [kártjljdž], *s.* cartílago.

carton [kárton̯], *s.* (caja de) cartón fino.

cartoon [kartún], *s.* (pint.) cartón, boceto; caricatura; chiste gráfico; (comics) tira cómica.—*vt.* y *vi.* caricaturizar.– **—ist** [-ịst], *s.* caricaturista; humorista.

cartridge [kártrịdž], *s.* (armas) cápsula, casquillo; cartucho.—*c. belt,* canana, cartuchera.

cartwright [kártrạit], *s.* carretero.

carve [karv], *vt.* y *vi.* esculpir; tallar; labrar; trinchar carne.– **—n** [kárvẹn], *a.* esculpido, entallado, grabado.– **—r** [kárvœr(r)], *s.* escultor; grabador, tallista; trinchante. **—carving** [kárvịŋ], *s.* escultura, talla; arte de trinchar.—*c. knife,* trinchante.

cascade [kæskéịd], *s.* cascada, catarata.

case [keis], *s.* caso; ejemplo; suceso; situación; causa, pleito, proceso; caja; vaina, funda, cubierta; bastidor.—*c. shot,* metralla.—*in c.,* caso (de) que, por si (acaso).—*in any c.,* de todos modos.—*in the c. of,* en cuanto *a,* respecto a.—*such being the c.,* siendo así.—*vt.* embalar, encajonar; enfundar.

cash [kæš], *s.* efectivo, dinero contante y sonante; (cont.) caja.—*c. balance,* saldo (en) efectivo.—*c. on delivery,* (C.O.D.), pago contra entrega.—*c. payment,* pago al contado.—*c. register,* caja registradora; contadora.—*in c.,* en efectivo.—*adv.* al contado.—*vt.* cambiar, cobrar, hacer efectivo (un cheque, etc.).– **—book** [kǽšbụk], *s.* libro de caja.– **—ier** [kæšír], *s.* cajero.—*c.'s check,* cheque de caja.

cashmere [kǽšmir], *s.* (tej.) casimir, cachemir(a).

casing [kéịsịŋ], *s.* envoltura, cubierta, funda; forro; marco de ventana o puerta.—*pl.* tripas para embutidos.

cask [kæsk], *s.* barril, tonel, casco.

casket [kǽskịt], *s.* cofrecito, estuche, joyero; ataúd, féretro.

casserole [kǽserọụl], *s.* cacerola; (utensil or food) cazuela; (food) guiso, guisado.

cassette [kạsét], *s.* cassette, cassete.—*on c.,* en cassette, grabado.—*c. deck,* platina, pletina.—*c. player,* pasacintas, cassette, pasacassettes, tocacassettes.—*c. recorder,* grabadora, grabador (de cassettes), casette.

cassock [kǽsọk], *s.* sotana.

cast [kæst], *vti.* [9] tirar, botar, emitir, lanzar; echar; tumbar, derribar; dirigir (la mirada o el pensamiento); vaciar, moldear (metales); calcular; (teat.) repartir (papeles); depositar (una boleta electoral).—*to c. anchor,* anclar, fondear.—*to c. aside,* desechar.—*to c. down,* abatir, descorazonar.—*to c. forth,* exhalar, despedir.—*to c. in one's teeth,* echar en cara.—*to c. in the rôle of,* adjudicar el papel de.—*to c. lots,* echar suerte.—*to c. off,* desamarrar, largar.—*to c. out,* echar fuera, arrojar.—*pret.* y *pp.* de TO CAST.—*a.* vaciado, fundido.—*c. iron,* hierro fundido.—*c. net,* atarraya.—*s.* lanzamiento, tirada; fundición; molde; mascarilla; aspecto, estampa; tinte; (teat.) reparto de papeles; actores (en un drama).

castanets [kæstạnéts], *s. pl.* castañuelas.

castaway [kǽstạweị], *s.* náufrago.

caste [kæst], *s.* casta.—*to lose c.,* desprestigiarse.

Castilian [kæstílịạn], *s.* y *a.* castellano.

castle [kǽsl], *s.* castillo; torre o roque de ajedrez.—*c. builder,* soñador.

castor [kǽstọ(r)], *s.* castor; paño o sombrero de castor.—*c. oil,* aceite de ricino.

casual [kǽžụal], *a.* casual, fortuito, ocasional; de paso.– **—ness** [-nịs], *s.* descuido, inadvertencia; indiferencia.– **—ity** [-tị], *s.* accidente, desastre; víctima (de un accidente); muerte violenta; (mil.) baja; pérdida; (for.) caso fortuito.

cat [kæt], *s.* gato.—*to bell the c.,* poner el cascabel al gato.—*to let the c. out of the bag,* revelar un secreto.—*to rain cats and dogs,* llover a cántaros.– **—ty** [-tị], *a.* malicioso.– **—walk** [-wɔk], *s.* pasarela; puente de trabajo.

catacombs [kǽtạkoụmz], *s. pl.* catacumbas.

Catalan [kǽtạlạn], *s.* y *a.* catalán.

catalog, catalogue [kǽtạlag], *s.* catálogo.—*c. showroom,* sala de muestras por los productos anunciados en un catálogo de venta por correspondencia.—*mail-order c.,* catálogo de venta por correspondencia.—*vt.* catalogar.

Catalonian [kætạlóụnịạn], *a.* y *s.* catalán.

cataract [kǽtạrækt], *s.* catarata.

catarrh [kạtár], *s.* catarro.

catastrophe [kạtǽstrọfị], *s.* catástrofe.

catcall [kǽtkɔl], *s.* silbido, rechifla.

catch [kæch], *vti.* [10] coger, agarrar; contraer, atrapar; pescar; sorprender.—*to c. in the act,* pescar in fraganti.—*to c. on*, comprender; popularizarse.—*to c. one's eye*, llamarle a uno la atención.—*vii.* engancharse; engranar; prenderse (fuego).—*to c. hold of*, agarrarse a, asirse de.—*to c. up* (*with*) alcanzar a, emparejarse (con); ponerse al día.—*s.* presa, captura; botín; redada; gancho, enganche; pestillo; cogida (de la pelota); trampa.—*c. phrase*, eslogan.— **—er** [káchœ(r)], *s.* cogedor; agarrador; receptor (de beisbol).— **—ing** [-iŋ], *s.* engranaje.—*a.* contagioso, pegadizo; seductor.

catechism [kátekizm], *s.* catecismo. **—catechize**[kátekaiz], *vt.* catequizar.

category [kátēgɔri], *s.* categoría, clase.

cater [kéitœ(r)], *vi. y vt.* abastecer, proveer, surtir (de viveres); complacer o halagar a uno en sus gustos.— **—er** [-œ(r)], *s.* proveedor, abastecedor, surtidor, despensero.

caterpillar [kátœrpilä(r)], *s.* oruga.

catgut [kátgʌt], *s.* cuerda de tripa.

cathartic [kaθártik], *a.* purgante.—*s.* purga, purgante.

cathedral [kaθídral], *s.* catedral.

Catholic [káθɔlik], *a. y s.* católico.—*a.* (c.) católico, universal.— **—ism** [kaθálisizm], *s.* catolicismo.

CAT (scanner) [skánœr], *s.* escáner TAC.

catsup [kátsʌp], *s.* salsa de tomate.

cattle [kátl], *s.* ganado, ganado vacuno, res.—*c. barn*, establo.—*c. bell*, cencerro, esquilón.—*c. raising*, ganadería.—*c. ranch*, hacienda de ganado, ganadería; (Am.) estancia.—*c. thief*, abigeo, cuatrero.—*c. tick*, garrapata.— **—man** [-mæn], *s.* ganadero.

Caucasian [kɔkéjžan], *s. y a.* caucásico.

caught [kɔt], *pret. y pp.* de TO CATCH.

cauliflower [kóliflauœ(r)], *s.* coliflor.

cause [kɔz], *s.* causa; (for.) proceso.—*vt.* causar; motivar; originar.

cauterize [kótœraiz], *vt.* cauterizar.

caution [kɔ́šɔn], *s.* cautela; cuidado; advertencia.—*vt.* advertir, precaver, prevenir.— **—cautious** [kɔ́šʌs], *a.* cauto, precavido, prudente.

cavalier [kævalír], *s.* caballero; galán.—*a.* altivo, desdeñoso.— **—cavalry** [kævalri], *s.* caballería.— **cavalryman** [kævalriman], *s.* soldado de caballería.

cave [kejv], *s.* cueva, caverna.—*c. man*, cavernícola; hombre grosero.—*c. painting*, pintura rupestre.—*c.-in*, hundimiento.—*vi.—to c. in*, hundirse. **—cavern** [kævœrn], *s.* caverna.

cavity [káviti], *s.* cavidad, hueco; caries.

caw [kɔ], *s.* graznido.—*vi.* graznar.

cay [kei, ki], *s.* cayo; isleta.

cayman [kéjman], *s.* caimán.

CD (compact disc) [sidí], *abbrev.* disco compacto.

cease [sis], *vi.* cesar (de), desistir o dejar de, parar (de).—*vt.* cesar, parar, suspenderse.— **—less** [síslis], *a.* incesante.

cedar [sídä(r)], *s.* cedro.

cede [sid], *vt.* ceder, traspasar, transferir.

ceiling [síliŋ], *s.* techo interior, cielo raso; límite, punto más alto.

celebrant [sélêbrant], *s.* celebrante. **—celebrate** [sélêbreit], *vt.* celebrar; festejar; alabar.—*vi.* celebrar; echar una cana al aire. **—celebrated** [sélêbreitid], *a.* célebre, famoso. **—celebration** [selêbréjšon], *s.* celebración. **—celebrity** [sēlébriti], *s.* celebridad, renombre.

celerity [sēlériti], *s.* celeridad.

celery [séleri], *s.* apio.

celestial [sēléschal], *a.* celeste; celestial.

celibacy [sélibasi], *s.* celibato, soltería.

cell [sel], *s.* celda, calabozo; célula; pila eléctrica.

cellar [sélä(r)], *s.* sótano, bodega.

cello [chélou], *s.* violoncelo.

cellophane [sélofein], *s.* celofán.

cellphone [sélfoun], *s.* teléfono celular.

cellular [séljulạr], *a.* celular.—*c. telephone*, teléfono celular.

celluloid [séljuloid], *s.* celuloide.

cellulose [séljulous], *s.* celulosa.

Celt [selt], *s.* Celta.— **—ic** [séltik], *a.* céltico.

cement [sēmént], *s.* cemento.—*vt.* cementar; recubrir con cemento; unir; pegar.—*vi.* pegarse; unirse.

cemetery [sémêteri], *s.* cementerio.

censor [sénsɔ(r)], *s.* censor; crítico.—*vt.* censurar, someter a la censura (cartas periódicos, etc.).— **—ship** [-šip], *s.* censura. **—censure** [sénšü(r)], *s.* censura, reprimendā, crítica.—*vt.* censurar, reprender, criticar.

census [sénsʌs], *s.* censo, empadronamiento, registro; catastro.—*vt.* empadronar, hacer el censo.

cent [sɛnt], s. centavo.—*per c.*, por ciento.

centennial [sɛnténjäl], a. y s. centenario.

center [séntœ(r)], s. centro.—*a.* central; céntrico.—*c. city*, centro de la ciudad.—*vt.* centrar, centralizar.—*vi.* concentrarse; estar o colocarse en el centro.— **—piece** [-pis], s. centro de mesa.

centigrade [séntigreid], s. centígrado.

centipede [séntipid], s. ciempiés.

central [séntṛạl], a. central, céntrico.— **—ize** [-aiz], vt. centralizar.—vi. centralizarse.

centrifugal [sɛntrífiugạl], a. centrífugo.

centripetal [sɛntrípetạl], a. centrípeto.

century [sénchūrị], s. siglo; centuria.

cereal [sírial], s. cereal, grano.—a. cereal.

ceremonial [sɛrēmóunjạl], a. y s. ceremonial; rito. **—ceremonious** [sɛrēmóunias], a. ceremonioso; ceremonioso. **—ceremony** [sérēmouni], s. ceremonia, ceremonial; cumplido, etiqueta.

certain [sœ́rtạn], a. cierto, alguno; seguro; positivo.—*for c.*, de fijo, con seguridad.— **—ity** [-ti], s. certeza, certidumbre; seguridad.

certificate [sœrtifikịt], **certification** [sœrtifikéisọn], s. certificado, testimonio; (for.) atestado, certificación, partida. —*certificate of residence*, carta de vecindad.—*certificate of stock*, bono, obligación. **—certify** [sœ́rtifai], vti. [7] certificar, atestiguar, responder de o por.— **—fied** [-faid], a. certificado.—*c. check*, cheque certificado.—*c. public accountant*, censor jurado de cuentas.

cervix [sœ́rviks], s. (anat.) cerviz, nuca.

cessation [sɛséisọn], s. cese, cesación.

cession [sésọn], s. cesión, traspaso.

cesspool [séspul], s. pozo negro, cloaca.

chafe [cheif], vt. excoriar, rozar; irritar.—vi. irritarse.—s. excoriación, rozadura; irritación.

chaff [chæf], s. hollejo, cáscara.—vt. y vi. embromar.

chagrin [şạgrín], s. mortificación, disgusto.—vt. mortificar, enfadar.

chain [chein], s. cadena.—pl. (fig.) prisiones; esclavitud.—*c. gang*, cuerda de presos, cadena de presos.—*c. letter*, carta de una cadena.—*c.-link*

fence, cercado eslabonado.—*c. mail*, cota de malla.—*c. reaction*, reacción en cadena.—*c. of mountains*, cordillera.—vt. encadenar; esclavizar.— **—saw** [-sɔ], s. motosierra, sierra de cadena.— **—smoker** [-smoukoer], s. cigarrista, fumador de un petillo tras otro.

chair [chɛr], s. silla; asiento; cátedra; sillón de la presidencia; (por extensión) presidencia, presidente (de una junta, etc.).—*folding c.*, silla de tijeras, silla plegable.—*rocking c.*, mecedora.—*to take the c.*, presidir (una junta).— **—man** [chérman], s. presidente.—*Madame C.*, Señora Presidenta.- **—manship** [-mạn-şip], s. presidencia.- **—person** [-pœrsọn], s. presidente.- **—woman** [-wuman], s. presidenta.

chalice [chǽlis], s. cáliz.

chalk [chɔk], s. tiza, yeso.—*c. for cheese*, gato por liebre.—vt. enyesar; dibujar o marcar con tiza; poner tiza (al taco).- **—y** [choki], a. yesoso; blanco.

challenge [chǽlindẑ], vt. desafiar, retar; disputar, contradecir; (for.) tachar, recusar; (mil.) dar el quién vive.—s. desafío, reto; (for.) recusación, tacha; (mil.) quién vive.- **—r** [-œ(r)], s. retador, desafiador; (for.) demandante.

chamber [chéjmbœ(r)], s. cámara; gabinete, alcoba, dormitorio; tribunal o sala de justicia; (mec.) depósito, cilindro.— **—lan** [-lin], s. camarero; chambelán.— **—maid** [-mejd], s. camarera, doncella de cuarto.

chameleon [kạmílịon], s. (zool.) camaleón.

chamois [şǽmi], s. gamuza.

champ [chæmp], s. (fam.) campeón.

champagne [şæmpéjn], s. champaña.

champion [chǽmpịon], s. campeón, adalid; defensor.—vt. defender.— **—ship** [-şip], s. campeonato.

chance [chæns], s. azar, casualidad; fortuna; ocasión, oportunidad; riesgo; probabilidad.—*by c.*, por casualidad; de chiripa.—*there is no c.*, no hay esperanza.—*to take chances*, correr un albur, aventurarse.—a. casual, fortuito.—vi. acontecer.—*to c. to have*, tener por casualidad.—*to c. upon*, topar (con).—vt. arriesgar.

chancellery [chǽnsɛlẹrị], s. cancillería. **—chancellor** [chǽnsɛlọ(r)], s.

canciller; ministro; magistrado; rector de universidad.

chandelier [šændęlír], *s.* araña de luces.

change [chęindž], *vt.* cambiar, alterar, modificar; substituir, reemplazar.— *to c. one's mind,* mudar de parecer.— *vi.* mudar, cambiar, alterarse.—*s.* cambio, alteración, mudanza; substitución, trueque; muda (de ropa, voz, etc.); vuelto; menudo; moneda suelta; novedad.—*c. of life,* menopausia.—*for a c.,* para variar, por cambiar.- **—able** [chęindžabl], *a.* variable; inconstante; alterable; (tej.) tornasolado.- **—less** [-lįs], *a.* inmutable.

channel [chænęl], *s.* canal; cauce; ranura; estría.—*vti.* [2] acanalar, estriar; conducir.

chant [chænt], *vt.* y *vi.* cantar (salmos, etc.).—*s.* canto llano; salmodia.

chaos [kéias], *s.* caos; gran confusión o desorden. **—chaotic** [kejátįk], *a.* caótico.

chap [chæp], *vti.* [1] rajar, agrietar.— *vii.* rajarse, cuartearse.—*s.* grieta, raja, hendidura; (fam.) chico; tipo.

chapel [chæpęl], *s.* capilla.

chaperon [šæperoun], *s.* acompañante, señora de compañía o respeto.—*vt.* acompañar a una o más señoritas en lugares públicos.

chaplain [chæplįn], *s.* capellán.

chaps [chæps], *s. pl.* (Am.) chaparreras, zamarros.

chapter [chæptœ(r)], *s.* capítulo; cabildo; filial (de una asociación).—*c. and verse,* con sus pelos y señales.

char [char], *vti.* y *vii.* [1] carbonizar(se), chamuscar(se).

character [kérįktœ(r)], *s.* carácter, genio; reputación; sujeto; (lit.) personaje; (teat.) papel; (fam.) tipo raro u original.- **—istic** [-ístįk], *a.* característico, propio.—*s.* característica, rasgo típico.- **—ize** [-aįz], *vt.* caracterizar.

charade [šaréid], *s.* payasada, farsa; (game) charada.

charcoal [chárkoul], *s.* carbón de leña.—*c. pencil,* carboncillo de dibujo.

charge [chardž], *vt.* cargar (armas, acumuladores, etc.); instruir; encargar; gravar; cobrar (precio); cargar en cuenta; acusar; atacar; embestir.—*vi.* pedir (precio); cargarse; cargar (a la bayoneta).—*s.* carga, embestida; carga (de un acumulador, etc.); cargo, custodia; encargo, encomienda; persona o cosa de que uno está encargado; impuesto; acusación, cargo.—*pl.* honorarios, gastos.—*c. account,* cuenta abierta.—*c. card,* tarjeta de pago.—*to take c. of,* encargarse de.

charlot [chérįot], *s.* carro antiguo de guerra o de carreras; cuádriga.

charisma [karízma], *s.* carisma.

charitable [chérįtabl], *a.* caritativo, benéfico. **—charity** [chérįti], *s.* caridad; limosna.

charlatan [šárlatan], *s.* charlatán, curandero.

charm [charm], *s.* encanto, hechizo; embeleso; talismán.—*vt.* hechizar; encantar, embelesar, prendar.- **—ing** [chármįn], *a.* encantador; fascinante, atractivo; seductor.

chart [chart], *vt.* poner en una carta náutica; cartografiar; trazar en un diagrama.—*s.* carta náutica; mapa plano; gráfica.

charter [chártœ(r)], *s.* cédula, título, carta de fuero o privilegio; estatuto, constitución.—*vt.* estatuir; fletar un barco; alquilar un tren, etc.—*c., member,* socio fundador.

charwoman [chárwuman], *s.* fregatriz, mujer de la limpieza.

chase [chęis], *vt.* cazar; perseguir.—*to c. away,* ahuyentar, espantar.—*s.* caza; persecución; ranura, muesca.- **—r** [chéįsœ(r)], *s.* cazador; perseguidor; (aer.) avión de caza.

chasm [kǽzm], *s.* abismo, precipicio.

chassis [šǽsį], *s.* armazón, bastidor, marco; chasis.

chaste [chęist], *a.* casto; honesto; puro.

chastise [chæstáįz], *vt.* castigar, corregir.- **—ment** [-ment], *s.* castigo, corrección.

chastity [chæstįti], *s.* castidad, pureza, honestidad.

chat [chæt], *vii.* [1] charlar, platicar.— *s.* charla, plática, palique.

chattels [chǽtęlz], *s. pl.* enseres, bienes muebles.

chatter [chǽtœ(r)], *vi.* castañetear o rechinar (los dientes); parlotear, charlar, (fam.) hablar por los codos; (mec.) vibrar.—*s.* charla, cháchara; vibración.- **—box** [baks], *s.* parlanchín, charlatán.

chauffeur [šoufér], *s.* chófer o chofer, conductor de automóvil.

chauvinism [šoúvįnįzm], *s.* chovinismo, patriotería.—*male c.,* machismo.

chauvinist [šoúvịnịst], *a.* y *s.* chovinista, patriotero; machista.—*male c. pig,* (fam.) machista asqueroso.

cheap [chip], *a.* barato; de pacotilla.—*c. shot,* (fam.) golpe bajo.—*to feel c.,* avergonzarse, sentirse inferior.—**en** [chípẹn], *vt.* y *vi.* abaratar(se), despreciar(se).—**ness** [-nịs], *s.* baratura, modicidad; vulgaridad.

cheat [chit], *vt.* engañar, embaucar; defraudar; timar.—*s.* trampa, fraude, engaño; timador.—**er** [chítœ(r)], *s.* estafador, embustero; tramposo, fullero.—**ing** [-ịŋ], *s.* engaño, fraude.

check [chɛk], *vt.* refrenar, reprimir; comprobar, confrontar, cotejar, verificar y marcar; registrar, facturar o depositar (equipajes, etc.); dar a guardar (el sombrero, etc.), recibiendo una contraseña; dar jaque (ajedrez).—*to c. in,* facturar el equipaje; (at hotel) registrarse.—*to c. out,* desocupar el cuarto de un hotel, etc.).—*vi.* detenerse; corresponder; rajarse; dar jaque.—*s.* cheque; póliza; comprobación, prueba; contraseña, talón de reclamo (de equipajes, etc.); cuenta (de restaurante); detención; rechazo; obstáculo; contratiempo; jaque (en el ajedrez); ficha (en el juego); grieta (en el hormigón); muesca.—*c.-in,* facturación de equipajes.—*c.-in desk, c.-in counter,* mostrador de facturación; (at hotel) recepción.—*c. mark,* marca, contraseña.—*c. up,* examen, comprobación.—**book** [chékbụk], *s.* talonario, chequera.—**er** [-œ(r)], *s.* cuadro, casilla; verificador; cada pieza del juego de damas.—*pl.* juego de damas.—**erboard** [-œ(r)bɔrd], *s.* tablero de damas.—**ing** [-ịŋ], *s.* comprobación.—*c. account,* cuenta corriente (en un banco).—**list** [-lịst], *s.* lista de control.—**mate** [-mejt], *vt.* dar (jaque) mate; desconcertar, derrotar.—*s.* (jaque) mate.—**out** [-aụt], *s.* revisión y pago.—*c. counter,* mostrador de revisión.—*c. person,* cajero, cajera.—*c. time,* hora de salida.—**point** [-pɔịnt], *s.* control.—**room** [-rum], *s.* guardarropa.

cheek [chik], *s.* carrillo, mejilla; (fam.) tupé, descaro; jamba (de puerta o ventana).—**bone** [chíkboụn], *s.* pómulo.

cheer [chir], *s.* alegría; jovialidad; consuelo.—*pl.* vivas, aplausos.—*vt.* alentar, alegrar; vitorear, aplaudir.—*vi.* alegrarse.—*c. up!* ¡ánimo! ¡valor!-—**ful** [chírfụl], *a.* alegre, animado, jovial.-—**fulness** [-fụlnịs], *s.* alegría, jovialidad.-—**leader** [-lidœr], *s.* animador.

cheese [chiz], *s.* queso.—**burger** [-bœrgœr], *s.* hamburguesa con queso.-—**cake** [chízkejk], *s.* quesadilla.-—**cloth** [-klɔθ], *s.* estopilla de algodón.

chemical [kémịkạl], *a.* químico.—*s.* producto químico.—*c. engineering,* ingeniería química.

chemise [šẹmíz], *s.* camisa de mujer.

chemist [kémịst], *s.* químico; farmacéutico.—**ry** [-rị], *s.* química.

cherish [chérịš], *vt.* apreciar, fomentar; abrigar, acariciar.

cherry [chérị], *s.* cereza (fruta y color); cerezo (árbol y madera).

cherub [chérʌb], *s.* querubín.

chess [ches], *s.* ajedrez.-—**board** [chésbɔrd], *s.* tablero de ajedrez.

chest [chest], *s.* pecho, torax; arca, cofre.—*c. of drawers,* cómoda, buró.

chestnut [chésnʌt], *s.* (bot.) castaña; castaño (árbol, madera; color).

chevron [ševrọn], *s.* (mil.) galón, insignia.

chew [chu], *vt.* y *vi.* mas(ti)car; rumiar; (fig.) meditar.—*to c. out,* (fam.) regañar, reñir.—*to c. the rag,* (fam.) charlar, estar dale que dale.—*s.* mascada; mordisco, bocado.—**ing** [chúịŋ], *s.* masticación; rumia.—*c. gum,* chicle, goma de mascar.

chic [šik], *a.* chic, elegante.

chick [chịk], *s.* polluelo, pollito; pajarito; (fam.) chica, pollita.-—**en** [chíkẹn], *s.* pollo, gallina (como alimento).—*c.-hearted,* cobarde, gallina.—*c. pox,* varicela, viruela loca.—*to c. out,* acobardarse, achicarse.—**pea** [-pi], *s.* garbanzo.

chief [chif], *s.* jefe; cabecilla; caudillo; cacique; (com.) principal.—*c. justice,* presidente del tribunal.—*c. of staff,* jefe del estado mayor.—*a.* principal; primero, en jefe.—**tain** [chíftịn], *s.* jefe, comandante; caudillo, capitán; cabeza.

chiffon [šịfán], *s.* gasa.

chignon [šínyan], *s.* moño, castaña.

chilblain [chílblejn], *s.* (med.) sabañón.

child [chajld], *s.* niño o niña; hijo o hija; criatura; chiquillo.—*c. abuse,* abuso (sexual) infantil.—*with* *c.*, embarazada, encinta.– **—birth** [chájldbœrθ], *s.* parto, alumbramiento.– **—hood** [chájldhụd], *s.* infancia, niñez.– **—ish** [-iŝ], *a.* pueril, frívolo.—*c. action*, chiquillada, niñería.– **—less** [-lis], *a.* sin hijos.– **—ren** [chíldren], *s. pl.* de CHILD.

Chilean [chílian], *s.* y *a.* chileno.

chili, chilli [chíli], *s.* (bot.) (Am.) chile, ají picante, mole.

chill [chil], *a.* frío, desapacible.—*s.* frío, (es)calofrío; enfriamiento; estremecimiento.—*chills and fever*, fiebre intermitente.—*vt.* enfriar, resfriar, helar; desanimar.—*vi.* dar escalofríos, calofriarse.– **—(i)ness** [chíl(i)nis], *s.* frialdad, calidad de frío.– **—y** [-i], *a.* frío, fresco; friolento.

chime [chajm], *s.* juego de campanas; campaneo, repique; armonía, conformidad.—*vt.* tocar, tañer las campanas.—*vi.* repicar (las campanas); sonar con armonía.

chimney [chímnį], *s.* chimenea.—*c. corner*, hogar, chimenea.—*c. flue*, cañón, tiro de la chimenea.—*c. sweep*, deshollinador.

chimpanzee [chįmpænzí], *s.* chimpancé.

chin [chin], *s.* barba, barbilla, mentón.—*c. cloth*, babero, babador.—*c. strap*, barboquejo.—*c. up!* ¡ánimo!

china [chájnạ], *s.* porcelana, loza fina, vajilla fina.—*c. cabinet*, chinero, vitrina.– **—ware** [-wer], *s.* = CHINA.—*C.*, China.– **—man** [-mạn], *s.* (despec) chino.– **—town** [-taụn], *s.* barrio chino.

chine [chajn], *s.* espinazo; lomo.

Chinese [chajníz], *s.* çhino (lengua y persona).—*a.* chino.—*C. lantern*, farolillo.

chink [chiŋk], *s.* grieta, resquicio.—*vt.* y *vi.* (hacer) sonar, (hacer) tintinar (copas, monedas, etc.).

chintzy [chíntzį], *a.* barato, ordinario.

chip [chip], *vti.* [1] desmenuzar, picar, astillar.—*vii.* quebrarse, desconcharse.—*s.* fragmento, astilla; desconchadura; viruta; ficha; tanto (en el juego).—*a c. off the old block*, de tal palo tal astilla.—*c. on one's shoulder*, propensión a pendencias.—*potato chips*, papas a la inglesa, rueditas de papas.

chipmunk [chípmʌnd], *s.* especie de ardilla.

chiropodist [kajrápodįst], *s.* pedicuro, callista, quiropedista.

chirp [chœrp], *vi.* chirriar, gorjear, piar.—*s.* chirrido; gorjeo; canto.

chisel [chízẹl], *s.* cincel; escoplo; buril.—*vti.* y *vii.* [2] cincelar; burilar; (fam.) estafar, timar.– **—(l)er** [-œ(r)], *s.* (fam.) estafador, timador.

chivalrous [ŝívạlrʌs], *a.* caballeroso, cortés, caballeresco.– **—chivalry** [ŝívạlrį], *s.* caballerosidad, cortesía, galantería.

chlorine [klórin], *s.* cloro. **—chloroform** [klórọfọrm], *s.* cloroformo. **—chlorophyll** [klórọfil], *s.* clorofila.

chock [chak], *s.* calzo, cuña; choque.—*vt.* afianzar, soportar, calzar.—*c.-full*, colmado, atestado, de bote en bote.

chocolate [cháklit], *s.* chocolate; bombón.—*c. pot*, chocolatera.

choice [chọįs], *s.* elección; selección; preferencia, opción; cosa elegida; lo selecto, lo más escogido; variedad.—*a.* escogido, selecto, exquisito.

choir [kwajr], *s.* coro, masa coral.—*c. practice*, ensayo de coro.– **—master** [-maestoer], *s.* director de coro, maestro de coro.

choke [chouk], *vt.* y *vi.* estrangular(se); ahogar(se); sofocar(se); atragantar(se), atorar(se); obturar(se) (el carburador).—*s.* estrangulación; ahogo; sofoco; estrangulador o ahogador (del automóvil).

cholera [kálerạ], *s.* cólera; cólera morbo. **—choleric** [kálẹrįk], *a.* colérico, irascible.

choose [chuz], *vti.* [10] escoger, preferir, seleccionar, optar por; desear.

chop [chap], *vt.* [1] tajar, cortar; picar carne; desbastar; hender.—*to c. off*, tronchar.—*vii.* dar cuchilladas.—*s.* prosión, parte; tajada; chuleta o costilla.—*pl.* quijadas (de animal).– **—per** [-pœr], *s.* (fam.) helicóptero.– **—pers** [-pœrz], *spl.* (fam.) dientes.– **—sticks** [stįks], *spl.* palillos.

choral [kórạl], *s.* y *a.* (mus.) coral.—*c. society*, orfeón, masa coral.

chord [kọrd], *s.* cordón, cuerda; (mus.) acorde.

chore [chọr], *s.* quehacer, faena, tarea.

chorus [kórʌs], *vt.* y *vi.* corear; componer o cantar música coreada; cantar o hablar a coro; hacer coro a.—*s.* (teat.) coro; estribillo.—*c. girl*, corista.—*in c.*, al unísono.

chose [chouz], *pret.* de TO CHOOSE. **—chosen** [chóuzẹn], *pp.* de TO CHOOSE.

chrism [krízm], *s.* (igl.) crisma.
Christ [krajst], *s.* Cristo.—*the C. child*, el niño Jesús. —**christen** [krísɛn], *vt.* bautizar. —**Christendom** [krísɛndom], *s.* cristiandad, cristianismo. —**christening** [krísɛnin], *s.* bautismo, cristianismo; bautizo.—*a.* bautismal. —**Christian** [kríschɑn], *a.* y *s.* cristiano.—*C. name*, nombre de pila o de bautismo. **Christianity** [krjschjǽnjtj], *s.* cristianismo, cristianidad. —**Christmas** [krísmɑs], *s.* Navidad.—*C. carol*, villancico, cántico de Navidad.—*C. Eve*, nochebuena.

chronic [kránjk], *a.* crónico, inveterado.
chronicle [kránjkl], *s.* crónica.—*vt.* escribir, registrar o narrar en forma de crónica.- —**r** [kránjklœ(r)], *s.* cronista, historiador.
chronologic(al) [kranoládʒjk(ɑl)], *a.* cronológico.
chronometer [kronámɛtœ(r)], *s.* cronómetro.
chrysalis [krísɑljs], *s.* (ent.) crisálida.
chrysanthemum [krjsǽnɛmʌm], *s.* crisantemo.
chubby [chábj], *a.* regordete, gordinflón, rechoncho.
chuck [chʌk], *vt.* desechar, tirar lo inútil; acariciar la barbilla.—*s.* mamola; echada, tirada; golpecito, caricia.—*c. hole*, bache.—*c. steak*, bisté de falda.- —**le** [chákl], *vi.* reir entre dientes.—*s.* risa ahogada, risita.
chum [chʌm], *vii.* [1] (fam.) ser camarada.—*s.* (fam.) camarada, compinche.
chunk [chʌŋk], *s.* pedazo corto y grueso, trozo; (fam.) persona fornida.- —**y** [chʌnjk], *a.* trabado, fornido, rechoncho.
church [chœrch], *s.* iglesia; templo; culto público, el clero.—*c. calendar*, santoral.- —**goer** [-gouɛr], *s.* practicante.- —**man** [chœrchmɑn], *s.* sacerdote, clérigo.- —**yard** [chœrchyard], *s.* cementerio (de parroquia).
churn [chœrn], *s.* mantequera.—*vt.* agitar, menear, revolver; batir manteca.—*vi.* agitarse, revolverse.- —**ing** [chœrnjn], *s.* batido; cantidad de manteca batida de una vez.
chute [šut], *s.* conducto; canal; tubo; sumidero; vertedero; paracaídas.
chyle [kajl], *s.* (fis.) quilo.

CIA [síajeí], *abrev.* (Central Intelligence Agency) CIA.
cider [sájdœ(r)], *s.* sidra.
cigar [sigár], *s.* cigarro, tabaco, puro, habano.—*c. case*, petaca.—*c. holder*, boquilla.—*c. lighter*, mechero, encendedor.—*c. store*, tabaquería, estanco.- —**ette** [sigarét], *s.* cigarrillo, pitillo, cigarro.—*c. case*, pitillera, cigarrera.
cinch [sjnch], *vt.* cinchar; apretar.—*s.* cincha; (fam.) ganga, cosa segura.
cinder [síndœ(r)], *s.* ceniza; carbón; brasa; rescoldo.—*pl.* pavesas, cenizas; carbón a medio quemar.—*vt.* reducir a cenizas. —**Cinderella** [sjndĕréla], *s.* la Cenicienta.
cinema [sínĕmǎ], *s.* cine, cinematógrafo.
cinnamon [sínamon], *s.* canela; árbol de la canela.
cipher [sájfœ(r)], *s.* cifra; (arit.) cero; nulidad.—*vt.* calcular; cifrar con clave.—*vi.* numerar.
circle [sœrkl], *s.* círculo; circunferencia, redondel, esfera; círculo (social); rueda, corro.—*vt.* circundar, cercar, rodear.—*vi.* dar vueltas, remolinear.
circuit [sœrkjt], *s.* circuito; vuelta, rodeo; radio; distrito; partido, jurisdicción.—*c. breaker*, interruptor automático.
circular [sœrkjulǎ(r)], *a.* circular; redondo.—*c. plate*, disco.—*s.* circular; carta, aviso o folleto circular.— **circulate** [sœrkjulejt], *vt.* propalar, propagar; poner en circulación.— *vi.* circular; propagarse. —**circulation** [sœrkjuléjšon], *s.* circulación; propaganda. —**circulatory** [sœrkjulǎtori], *a.* circulatorio, circular.
circumcise [sœrkʌmsajz], *vt.* circuncidar. —**circumcision** [sœrkʌmsíʒon], *s.* circuncisión.
circumference [sœrkʌmfɛrens], *s.* circunferencia, periferia; perímetro.
circumscribe [sœrkʌmskrájb], *vt.* circunscribir, fijar, limitar.
circumspect [sœkʌmspɛkt], *a.* circunspecto, discreto.
circumstance [sœrkʌmstæns], *s.* circunstancia, incidente, acontecimiento.—*under no circumstances*, jamás; de ningún modo.—*under the circumstances*, en las circunstancias presentes, siendo así las cosas. —**circumstantial** [sœrkʌmstǽnšal], *a.* circunstancial, accidental, inciden-

tal.—*c. evidence,* prueba de indicios.

circus [sœrkʌs], *s.* circo.

cistern [sístœrn], *s.* cisterna, aljibe.

citadel [sítạdẹl], *s.* ciudadela.

citation [sajtéjṣọn], *s.* cita, mención; (for.) citación, emplazamiento. —**cite** [sajt], *vt.* citar, referirse a (for.) citar a juicio.

citizen [sítịzẹn], *s.* ciudadano, vecino. – —**ship** [ṣịp], *s.* ciudadanía; nacionalidad.—*c. papers,* carta de ciudadanía o nacionalidad.

city [síti], *s.* ciudad, población, urbe; municipio.—*a.* municipal; citadino, urbano.—*c. council,* ayuntamiento, urbano.—*c. district,* barrio.—*c. hall,* ayuntamiento, casa consistorial.—*c. room,* (newsroom) redacción.

civic [sívịk], *a.* cívico.– —**ism** [sívịsịzm], *s.* civismo.– —**s** [sívịks], *s.* cívica, ciencia del gobierno civil. —**civil** [sívịl], *a.* civil, ciudadano; cortés, urbano.—*c. disobedience,* desobediencia civil.—*c. engineering,* ingeniería civil.—*c. liberties, c. rights,* derechos civiles.—*c. servant,* funcionario, empleado de servicio civil oficial.—*c. service,* administración pública, servicio civil oficial.—*c. war,* guerra civil.—*the C. War,* (E.U.) la guerra civil, la guerra de Secesión. —**civilian** [sịvílịyạn], *s.* paisano (no militar), civil.—*pl.* la población civil.—*a.* civil. —**civility** [sịvílịtị], *s.* civilidad, cortesía, urbanidad. —**civilization** [sịvịlịzéjṣọn], *s.* civilización. —**civilize** [sívịlajz], *vt.* civilizar. —**civvies** [sívez], *spl.* (fam.) traje de paisano, ropas civiles.—*in c.,* (fam.) de paisano, vestido de civil.

clad [klæd], *a.* vestido, aderezado.

claim [klejm], *vt.* demandar, pedir en juicio; reclamar; denunciar (una mina); sostener, pretender, alegar.—*to c. to be,* echárselas de.—*s.* demanda, reclamación, petición; pretensión, título, derecho; denuncia minera. – —**ant** [kléjmạnt], —**er** [-œ(r)], *s.* reclamante.

clairvoyance [klɛrvójạns], *s.* videncia, clarividencia. —**clairvoyant** [klɛrvójạnt], *a.* clarividente.

clam [klæm], *s.* almeja.

clamor [klǽmọ(r)], *s.* clamor(eo), gritería, vocería, algarabía; estruendo.—*vi.* clam(ore)ar, gritar, vociferar.— —**ous** [-ʌs], *s.* clamoroso, ruidoso, estruendoso.

clamp [klæmp], *s.* tornillo de banco; grampa; abrazadera; pinzas, tenazas; montón (de mineral, ladrillos, etc.); pisadas recias.—*vt.* empalmar; afianzar; sujetar.—*vi.* pisar recio.

clan [klæn], *s.* clan.

clang [klæŋ], *s.* retintín; campanada; campanillazo.—*vt. y vi.* (hacer) sonar, resonar o retumbar.

clap [klæp], *vti.* [1] batir; cerrar de golpe; aplaudir.—*to c. the hands,* batir palmas.—*vii.* aplaudir, dar palmadas, palm(ot)ear.—*s.* ruido o golpe seco; palmada, aplauso; (fam.) gonorrea.

claret [klǽrịt], *s.* clarete; burdeos, granate.

clarinet [klǽrịnet], *s.* clarinete.

clarity [klǽrịtị], *s.* claridad.

clash [klæṣ], *vi.* chocar, entrechocarse, encontrarse; discordar, oponerse.— *vt.* batir, golpear.—*s.* choque; encontrón, colisión; antagonismo, discordia.

clasp [klæsp], *s.* broche, presilla, traba, hebilla, abrazadera; cierre; (mec.) grapa; apretón, abrazo.—*vt.* abrochar, enganchar; asir, agarrar; asegurar; abrazar; ceñir; apretar (la mano).

class [klæs], *s.* clase; condición, rango; (mil.) promoción; las escuelas; (fam.) elegancia.—*c. action,* (jur.) acción popular, demanda colectiva.– —**mate** [-mejt], *s.* compañero de clase.– —**room** [-rum], *s.* sala de clase, aula.—*vt.* clasificar, calificar, ordenar.

classic [klǽsịk], *s. y a.* clásico.—*pl.* clásicas.– —**al** [-ạl], *a.* clásico.

classification [klǽsịfịkéjṣọn], *s.* clasificación. —**classified** [klǽsịfajd], *a.* clasificado; secreto, confidencial. —*c. ads,* anuncios clasificados (en secciones), avisos clasificados, anuncios por palabras. —**classify** [klǽsịfaj], *vti.* [7] clasificar, ordenar; clasificar como secreto.

classmate [klǽsmejt], *s.* condiscípulo. —**classroom** [klǽsrum], *s.* aula, clase.

clatter [klǽtœ(r)], *vi.* resonar ruidosamente, matraquear, guachapear; charlar.—*s.* ruido, estruendo; gritería; alboroto, bulla.

clause [klɔz], *s.* cláusula.

clavicle [klǽvɨkl], s. clavícula.
claw [klɔ], s. garra, zarpa, uña; pinza o tenaza (del cangrejo); gancho, garfio.—*c. hammer,* martillo de orejas.—*vt.* desgarrar; arañar; rasgar, despedazar.—*vi.* arañar.
clay [klej], s. arcilla, greda, barro.—*c. pigeon,* plato de barro.
clean [klin], *a.* limpio; puro; despejado; aseado; nítido; simétrico.—*c.-bred,* de pura raza.—*c.-handed,* con las manos limpias, sin culpa.—*to show a c. pair of heels,* tomar las de Villadiego.—*vt.* limpiar, asear, desengrasar, desenlodar.—*vi.* (gen. con up) limpiar(se), asear(se).— **er** [klínœ(r)], s. limpiador; mondador; tintorero; quitamanchas; depurador (de aire, etc.).— **ing** [-iŋ], s. aseo, limpieza; desengrase.— **liness** [klénlinɨs], s. limpieza, aseo, aliño; compostura; tersura.— **ly** [klénli], *a.* limpio, aseado; puro, delicado.— **ness** [-nɨs], s. limpieza, aseo; pureza. **cleanse** [kenz], *vt.* limpiar, purificar; purgar, depurar. **cleanser** [klénzœ(r)], s. limpiador, purificador.
clear [klɨr], *a.* claro, lúcido, transparente; despejado; (d)escampado; inocente; (com.) neto; sin deudas; puro; evidente.—*c.-headed,* inteligente, listo.—*c. profit,* beneficio neto.—*c.-sighted,* clarividente, perspicaz.—*c. track,* vía libre.—*s.* claro, espacio entre objetos.—*vt.* despejar, quitar estorbos; aclarar; justificar; salvar (un obstáculo); absolver; desenredar; desmontar; tumbar; obtener una ganancia líquida.—*to c. the table,* levantar la mesa.—*vi.* aclarar(se), serenar(se); liquidar cuentas.—*to c. off o up,* despejarse o escampar (el cielo).—*to c. out,* irse, escabullirse.— **ance** [klɨráns], s. despejo; despacho de aduana; beneficio líquido; (com.) venta de liquidación; (mec., ing.) juego, espacio libre.—*c. papers,* certificación del pago de derechos de aduana.— **ing** [-iŋ], s. aclaramiento, despejo; desmonte; claro, raso; justificación.— *c. house,* banco de liquidación.— **ness** [-nɨs], s. claridad; luz; despejo.
cleave [kliv], *vti.* [4] partir, rajar, tajar; penetrar.—*vii.* resquebrar, henderse; pegarse, adherirse.— **r**

[klívœ(r)], s. partidor; cuchilla o cortante de carnicero.
clef [klef], s. (mus.) clave, llave.
cleft [kleft], *pret. y pp.* de TO CLEAVE.— *a.* agrietado, partido.—*s.* grieta, fisura, rajadura, rendija.
clemency [klémɨnsi], s. clemencia, misericordia. **clement** [klémɨnt], *a.* clemente, misericordioso.
clench [klench], *vt.* agarrar; apretar o cerrar el puño; remachar.—V. CLINCH.—*s.* agarradera.— **er** [klénchœ(r)], s. agarrador; remachador; (fig.) argumento sin réplica.
clergy [klœrdʒi], s. clero.— **man** [-man], s. clérigo; cura, sacerdote.— **cleric** [klérik], s. clérigo.—*a.* clerical. **clerical** [klérikal], *a.* clerical; eclesiástico; burocrático, oficinesco.—*s.* clérigo.—*pl.* ropa clerical. **clerk** [klœrk], s. (sales clerk) dependiente de tienda, vendedor; (in an office) oficinista, escribiente; archivero; (jur.) escribano; (hist.) clérigo.—*C. of the Court,* actuario.— *vi.* trabajar como dependiente, oficinista, etc.
clever [klévœ(r)], *a.* diestro, hábil; avisado, listo; inteligente.— **ness** [-nɨs] s. talento; destreza, maña, habilidad.
cliché [klišéj], s. cliché, tópico, frase hecha, idea gastada, lugar común; (impr.) clisé.
click [klɨk], s. golpe seco; seguro, gatillo; gatillazo; chasquido de lengua.—*vt. y vi.* (hacer) sonar con uno o más golpes secos; hacer tictac; piñonear (un arma de fuego); (fam.) tener buen éxito.
client [klájɨnt], s. cliente; parroquiano.— **cle** [-él], s. clientela.
cliff [klɨf], s. farallón, risco, acantilado, precipicio.— **hanger** [-hænœr], s. situación tensa.
climate [klájmɨt], s. clima.
climax [klájmæks], s. clímax.
climb [klajm], *vt.* trepar, subir, escalar.—*vi.* trepar, subir, encaramarse, elevarse.—*s.* subida, ascenso.— **er** [klájmœ(r)], s. trepador, escalador; enredadera; oportunista.— **ing** [-iŋ], s. trepa, subida.—*a.* trepante, trepador.
clime [klajm], s. clima.
clinch [klɨnch], *vt.* remachar; agarrar; afianzar.—*vi.* agarrarse; (fam.) abrazarse estrechamente.—*s.* remache;

forcejeo, lucha cuerpo a cuerpo (esp. en el boxeo); (fam.) abrazo estrecho.– **—er** [klínchœ(r)], s. remachador; clavo remachado; argumento decisivo.

cling [kliŋ], vii. [10] asirse, adherirse, pegarse.– **—ing** [klíŋiŋ], a. colgante, pendiente; adhesivo.

clinic [klínik], s. clínica.– **—al** [-ạl], a. clínico.

clinker [klínkœ(r)], s. escoria.—vi. formar escorias.

clip [klip], vti. [1] trasquilar; tijeretear; cercenar; podar; pellizcar; agarrar.—s. tijeretazo; recorte; trasquila; cantonera; grapa, pinza, sujetapapeles; pasador o broche (de presión).—at a good c., a paso rápido.— c. joint, (jer.) cueva de ladrones, bar muy caro.– **—board** [-bɔrd], s. tabilla con sujetapapeles.– **—per** [klípœ(r)], s. trasquilador; cercenador, recortador.—pl. (for shearing) tijeras de trasquilar; (for hair) maquinilla (para cortar el pelo); (for nails) cortaúñas; (pruning shears) podaderas, tijeras de podar.– **—ping** [-iŋ], s. (shearing) esquileo; (act of cutting) tijereteo; (to read) recorte de prensa.—pl. recortes.

clique [klik], s. camarilla, compadraje.

cloak [klouk], s. capa, manto.—vt. encapotar; embozar; ocultar.– **—room** [klóukrum], s. guardarropa.

clock [klak], s. reloj (de mesa o pared).—c. dial o face, esfera.—c. radio, radiodespertador.—vt. medir o contar el tiempo de un acto.– **—maker** [klákmejkœ(r)], **—smith** [-smiθ], s. relojero.– **—wise** [-wajz], a. y adv. en el sentido de las agujas del reloj.– **—work** [-wœrk], s. maquinaria del reloj.

clod [klad], s. terrón; necio, gaznápiro.

clog [klag], vti. [1] embarazar; obstruir, entorpecer; amontonar.—vii. apiñarse, atestarse; amontonarse; atorarse; obstruirse; atascarse.—s. traba, obstáculo; carga; chanclo, zueco.—c. dance, zapateado.

cloister [klójstœ(r)], s. claustro; monasterio.—vt. enclaustrar.– **—ed** [-d], a. enclaustrado.

clone [kloun], s. clon.—vt. clonar.

close [klouz], vt. cerrar; tapar; terminar; levantar (una sesión); finiquitar (una cuenta).—vi. cerrar(se); unirse; terminar; fenecer.—to c.

with, cerrar (con el adversario).—s. fin, terminación; caída (de la tarde); clausura; cierre; coto; parcela.—a. [klous], cerrado; apretado; justo; íntimo (amistad); sofocante; mal ventilado; cercano, próximo; tupido, compacto; inmediato; sucinto; oculto; reservado; restringido; tacaño; casi empatado; parejo; reñido (combate, etc.).—at c. range, a quema ropa, a boca de jarro.—adv. cerca, de cerca; estrechamente.—c. by, muy cerca.—c. to, junto a; arrimado o pegado a; a raíz de.– **—d** [klouzd], a. cerrado; concluso.—c. chapter, asunto concluído.– **—ness** [klóusnjs], s. contigüidad; estrechez; falta de ventilación; firmeza; soledad; fidelidad (de copia o traducción).—close-out [klóuzaut], s. (com.) liquidación. **—closet** [klázjt], s. armario, alacena; excusado, retrete.—a. secreto, confidencial. —vt. encerrar a uno para conferenciar a puerta cerrada. **—close-up** [klóusʌp], s. fotografía de primer plano. **—closing** [klóuzjŋ], s. cierre; final, conclusión; clausura; remate (de cuentas).—a. de cierre; último; de clausura. **—closure** [klóuzɰ(r)], s. clausura; cierre; fin, conclusión.

clot [klat], s. coágulo, grumo.—vii. [1] coagularse, engrumecerse.

cloth [klɔθ], s. tela, paño, género, tejido.—c. binding, encuadernación en tela. **—clothe** [klouð], vti. [4] vestir; cubrir; arropar; revestir.—to c. with authority, investir de autoridad. **—clothed** [klouðd], pret. y pp. de TO CLOTHE.—es [klouðz], s. pl. vestido, vestuario, indumentaria; ropaje, ropa de toda especie.—c. chest, ropero.—c. hanger, perchero.—c. moth, polilla.—c. rack, perchero. **—esline** [klóuðzlajn], s. tendedera.– **—espin** [klóuðzpjn], s. pinzas para colgar ropa; (Cuba) palitos de tendedera. **—clothier** [klóuðjœ(r)], s. comerciante o fabricante de ropa; pañero, ropero. **—clothing** [klóuðjŋ], s. vestidos, ropa; vestuario, indumentaria.

cloud [klaud], s. nube; nublado, nubarrón; muchedumbre, multitud.— under a c., desacreditado, sospechoso.—in the clouds, abstraído; en las nubes.—vt. anublar, nublar; enturbiar; abigarrar; empañar.

—*vi.* nublarse, obscurecerse.— **-iness** [kláu̯dn̩is], *s.* nebulosidad, obscuridad.– **-less** [-li̯s], *a.* sin nubes, despejado, claro.– **-y** [-i̯], *a.* nublado, encapotado; nebuloso; turbio; obscuro; lóbrego; (fot.) velado.

clout [klau̯t], *s.* tortazo; peso, influencia.—*vt.* (fam.) dar un tortazo a.

clove [klou̯v], *s.* clavo de especia.—*c. of garlic,* diente de ajo.—*pret.* de TO CLEAVE. **—cloven** [klóu̯ven], *pp.* de TO CLEAVE.

clover [klóu̯vœ(r)], *s.* trébol.—*to be o live in c.,* vivir en la abundancia.

clown [klau̯n], *s.* payaso, bufón; gracioso.– **-ish** [kláu̯ni̯š], *a.* rudo, zafio.

cloy [klɔi̯], *vt.* empalagar; hastiar.

club [klʌb], *s.* porra, garrote, tranca; tolete; club, círculo; centro de reunión; palo o maza de golf.—*pl.* bastos (de baraja).—*c. sandwich,* sandwich club, sandwich de dos pisos.– **-foot** [-fu̯t], *s.* pie calcáneo, pie talo. **-house** [-hau̯s], *s.* casa club.— **-room** [-rum], *s.* sala de reuniones.— **-woman** [-wu̯man], *s.* clubista.—*vii.* [1] contribuir a gastos comunes; unirse o juntarse para un mismo fin.—*vti.* aporrear, golpear con garrote, apalear.

cluck [klʌk], *vt.* y *vi.* cloquear.—*s.* cloqueo.

clue [klu], *s.* indicio, pista; norte, guía.

clump [klʌmp], *s.* tarugo; terrón; aglutinación, masa, grupo; pisada recia.—*vt.* y *vi.* aglutinar(se); andar torpemente con fuertes pisadas.

clumsy [klámzi̯], *a.* desmañado, chapucero; incómodo; difícil de manejar.

clung [klʌŋ], *pret.* y *pp.* de TO CLING.

clunk [klʌŋk], *s.* golpetazo metálico.— *vi.* golpetear.

cluster [klástœ(r)], *s.* racimo; ramillete; grupo; caterva; enjambre.— *vi.* agruparse, arracimarse.—*vt.* apiñar, amontonar.

clutch [klʌch], *vt.* agarrar; apretar; embragar.—*to c. at,* tratar de empuñar.—*s.* agarro, presa; uña, garra; nidada; embrague.

clutter [klátœ(r)], *s.* baraúnda, batahola; desorden, confusión.—V. CLATTER.—*vi.* alborotar, hacer ruido o estrépito.—*vt.* poner en desorden, trastornar.

coach [kou̯ch], *s.* coche, carruaje; carroza; automóvil; (f.c.) vagón; maestro particular; (dep.) entrenador.—*vt.* adiestrar; aleccionar; entrenar.—*vi.* (dep.) entrenarse; servir de entrenador.– **-er** [kóu̯ch-œ(r)], *s.* preceptor; entrenador.— **-man** [-man], *s.* cochero.

coagulate [kou̯ǽgi̯u̯lei̯t], *vt.* y *vi.* coagular(se), cuajar(se).

coal [kou̯l], *s.* carbón, hulla, antracita.—*c. bin,* carbonera.—*c. brick,* briqueta, carbón prensado.—*c. dust,* cisco.—*c. tar,* alquitrán de hulla.—*vt.* y *vi.* echar carbón; hacer carbón; proveer(se) de carbón.

coalition [kou̯ali̯šon], *s.* coalición, liga.

coarse [kɔrs], *a.* basto, ordinario; toscovulgar; burdo.—*c. file,* lima de desbastar. **—ness** [kɔ́rsni̯s], *s.* tosquedad; vulgaridad, grosería, rudeza.

coast [kou̯st], *s.* costa, litoral.—*c. guard,* guarda de costas, servicio costanero; guardacostas.—*the c. is clear,* no hay moros en la costa.—*vt.* (mar.) costear.—*vi.* navegar a lo largo de la costa; deslizarse cuesta abajo.– **-al** [-al], *a.* costero.– **-er** [kóu̯stœ(r)], *s.* piloto práctico; barco de cabotaje; deslizador; (drink mat) posavasos.– **-line** [-lai̯n], *s.* costa, litoral.

coat [kou̯t], *s.* americana, chaqueta, saco; abrigo, sobretodo; (zool.) pelo, lana; capa o mano (de pintura, etc.).—*c. hanger,* perchero.— *c. of arms,* escudo de armas.—*to turn one's c.,* cambiar de casaca.— *vt.* vestir, revestir; dar una mano o capa de; azogar.– **-ing** [kóu̯ti̯ŋ], *s.* revestimiento, capa, mano de pintura.

coax [kou̯ks], *vt.* y *vi.* persuadir con halagos, engatusar.

coaxial [kou̯ǽksi̯al], *a.* coaxial.—*c. cable,* cable coaxial.

cob [kab], *s.* tusa o carozo de maíz; jaca.

cobble [kábl], *s.* guijarro.– **-stone** [-stou̯n], *s.* adoquín.

cobbler [káblœ(r)], *s.* zapatero de viejo, remendón; chapucero.

cobweb [kábweb], *s.* telaraña.

cocaine [kou̯kéi̯n], *s.* cocaína.

coccyx [káksi̯ks], *s.* (anat.) coxis, rabadilla.

cock [kak], *s.* gallo; macho de ave; espita (de agua, etc.); percusor o martillo de armas de fuego.—*c.-eyed*, bizco; (fam.) extravagante, loco.— *c. robin*, petirrojo.—*vt.* montar o amartillar (un arma de fuego); ladear (el sombrero).—*vi.* engreírse, gallear.

cockatoo [kakatú], *s.* cacatúa.

cockfight(ing) [kákfajt(iŋ)], *s.* riña(s) o pelea(s) de gallos. —**cockfighter** [kákfajtœ(r)], *s.* gallero.

cockpit [kákpit], *s.* (aer.) carlinga del avión; parte baja de popa de la cubierta (de un yate); cámara.

cockroach [kákrouch], *s.* cucaracha.

cockscomb [kákskoum], *s.* cresta (de gallo); gorro de bufón; (Am.) moco de pavo. —**cockspur** [kákspœ(r)], *s.* espuela (de gallo), espolón.

cocktail [káktejl], *s.* coctel; aperitivo.—*c. shaker*, coctelera.

cocky [káki], *a.* arrogante, hinchado.

cocoa [kóukou], *s.* cacao molido o en polvo; bebida de cacao.

coconut [kóukonʌt], *s.* coco; cocotero.—*c. plantation*, cocal.

cocoon [kökún], *s.* capullo (del gusano de seda, etc.).

COD [sioudí], *abbr.* (*collect on delivery*) entrega contra reembolso.

cod [kad], *s.* bacalao, abadejo.

coddle [kádl], *vt.* mimar, consentir.

code [koud], *s.* código; clave.

codeine [kóudin], *s.* codeína.

codfish [kádfiʃ], *s.* = COD.

codify [kádjfaj], *vt.* codificar.

coefficient [kouifíʃent], *s.* coeficiente.

coerce [kouérs], *vt.* forzar, obligar. —**coercion** [kouérʃon], *s.* coerción, coacción.

coexist [kouigzíst], *vi.* coexistir.— —**ence** [-ens], *s.* coexistencia.

coffee [kófi], *s.* café.—*c. plantation*, cafetal.—*c. pot*, cafetera.—*c. table*, mesa de centro, mesa de té, mesita baja.—*c. tree*, cafeto, cafe.- —**house** [-haus], *s.* café (establecimiento).- —**pot** [-pat], *s.* cafetera.

coffer [kófœ(r)], *s.* arca, cofre.

coffin [kófin], *s.* ataúd, féretro.

cog [kag], *s.* (mec.) diente o punto de rueda.- —**wheel** [kághwil], *s.* rueda dentada.

cohabitation [kouhæbitéjʃon], *s.* contubernio, cohabitación.

coherence [kohírens], **coherency** [kohírensi], *s.* coherencia. —**coherent** [kohírent], *a.* coherente.

cohesion [kouhíʒon], *s.* cohesión, adhesión, unión. —**cohesive** [kouhí-

siv], *a.* cohesivo, coherente, adherente.

coif [kójf], *s.* cofia, toca.

coiffure [kwafyúr], *s.* tocado, peinado.

coil [kojl], *s.* bobina, carrete; rosca; rollo; espiral de alambre.—*vt.* enrollar.—*vi.* enrollarse; enroscarse.

coin [kojn], *s.* moneda acuñada.—*vt.* acuñar; forjar (palabras o frases).- —**age** [kójnjdʒ], *s.* acuñación; moneda; sistema monetario; invención.

coincide [kouinsájd], *vi.* coincidir; estar de acuerdo. —**coincidence** [kouínsidens], *s.* coincidencia.

coke [kouk], *s.* cok (carbón).

colander [kálandœ(r)], *s.* colador; escurridor.

cold [kould], *a.* frío; helado; indiferente.—*c. cream*, crema cosmética.—*c. cuts*, fiambres variados. —*c.-blooded*, insensible, cruel, despiadado.—*c. feet*, (fam.) miedo, desánimo.—*c.-hearted*, insensible, impasible.—*c. shoulder*, (fam.) frialdad.—*c. snap*, corto rato de frío agudo.—*c. sore*, (med.) herpes labial, fuegos en la boca o los labios.— *c. storage*, almacenamiento en cámaras frigoríficas.—*c. sweat*, sudor frío.—*c. war*, guerra fría.—*c. wave*, ola de frío.—*s.* frío, frialdad; enfriamiento; resfriado, catarro, constipado.—*to catch c.*, resfriarse, acatarrarse.- —**ly** [-li], *adv.* con frialdad, fríamente.- —**ness** [kóuldnjs], *s.* frialdad; tibieza, indiferencia, despego.

colic [kálik], *s.* cólico.

coliseum [kalisíʌm], *s.* coliseo.

collaborate [kolæborejt], *vt.* colaborar. —**collaboration** [kolæboréjʃon], *s.* colaboración. —**collaborator** [kolæborejtọ(r)], *s.* colaborador.

collapse [kolǽps], *s.* derrumbamiento; desplome; fracaso; colapso.—*vi.* derrumbarse, desplomarse; fracasar; sufrir un colapso; hundirse.

collar [kálạ(r)], *s.* cuello (de camisa, etc.); collar de perro; collera; aro.- —**bone** [-boun], *s.* clavícula.—*vt.* poner cuello, aro; agarrar del cuello, acogotar.

collateral [kolǽteṛal], *a.* colateral.—*s.* garantía, resguardo.

collation [koléjʃon], *s.* cotejo; (igl.) colación; merienda; colación.

colleague [kálig], *s.* colega.

collect [kɔlékt], *vt.* colectar, recuadar; coleccionar; (re)copilar.—*c. on delivery* (C.O.D.), entrega contra reembolso, cóbrese al entregar.—*to c. one's self,* volver en sí, reponerse.—*s.* [kálekt], colecta.- **—ion** [kɔlékṣon], *s.* colección; colecta; montón; recaudación; cobranza; reunión.-*c. agency,* agencia de cobro.- **—ive** [kɔléktiv], *s.* (gram.) nombre colectivo.—*a.* colectivo.- **—or** [kɔléktɔ(r)], *s.* coleccionista; colector; recuadador; cobrador.

college [kálidẑ], *s.* colegio; colegio universitario.

collegiate [kálídẑat], *a.* universitario; (igl.) colegial, colgiado.

collet [kálit], *s.* (mec.) collar, mandril; (joy.) engaste.

collide [kɔláid], *vi.* chocar, topar; contradecir, estar en conflicto.

collision [kɔlíẑon], *s.* colisión, choque; antagonismo.

cologne [koloún], *s.* colonia.

colloquial [kɔlóukwial], *a.* familiar. coloquial.- **—ism** [-izm], *s.* expresión familiar, palabra familiar.

Colombian [kolámbian], *s.* y *a.* colombiano.

colon [kóulon], *s.* (gram.) dos puntos; (anat.) colon.

colonel [kǽrnel], *s.* coronel.

colonial [kɔlóunial], *a.* colonial. **—colonist** [kálonist], *s.* colono.—**colonize** [kálonaiz], *vt.* colonizar, poblar.—*vi.* establecerse en colonia.—**colony** [káloni], *s.* colonia.

color [kálo(r)], *s.* color; colorido; (naipes) palo.—*c. guard,* (mil.) portaestandarte.—*c. television,* televisión en colores, televisión a color.—*pl.* colores nacionales.—*c.-blind,* daltoniano.—*vt.* color(e)ar; teñir; iluminar; embellecer.—*vi.* ruborizarse.- **—ed** [-d], *a.* de color; (ant.) persona negra; engañoso, disfrazado; adornado.- **—ful** [-ful], *a.* lleno de colorido; pintoresco.- **—ing** [-iŋ], *s.* colorante, color; coloración; estilo o aire particular; colorido.- **—less** [-lis], *a.* descolorido; incoloro.

colossal [kolásal], *a.* colosal, descomunal.

colt [koult], *s.* potro.

Columbian [kolámbian], *a.* colombino, relativo a Colón.

Columbus Day [kolámbus], *s.* día de la Hispanidad, día de la raza.

column [kálʌm], *s.* columna.- **—ist** [kálʌm(n)ist], *s.* columnista.

comb [koum], *s.* peine; peineta; rastrillo; cresta de ave; panal de miel.— *vt.* peinar; cardar; rastrillar; escudriñar.

combat [kámbæt], *s.* combate.—*c. fatigue,* fatiga de combate.—*vt.* y *vi.* combatir.- **—ant** [kámbatant], *s.* y *a.* combatiente, luchador.- **—ive** [kámbætiv], *a.* combativo.

combination [kambinéiṣon], *s.* combinación. **—combine** [kombáin], *vt.* y *vi.* combinar(se); mezclar(se).

come [kʌm], *vii.* [10] venir, llegar; ir, acudir; provenir; aparecer, salir; acontecer.—*come in!* ¡entre(n)! ¡adelante!—*to c. about,* suceder.—*to c. across,* topar con.—*to c. back,* volver; retroceder.—*to c. by,* obtener; pasar junto a.—*to c. down,* bajar; descender.—*to c. down with,* enfermar de.—*to c. in,* entrar.—*to c. off,* desaparecer.—*to c. on,* seguir, progresar.—*to c. out,* salir, mostrarse.—*to c. over,* venir, cruzar.—*to c. through,* salir bien.—*to c. upon,* acometer, topar con.—*pp.* de TO COME.- **—back** [kámbæk], *s.* rehabilitación; regreso al puesto u oficio; repuesta aguda; motivo de queja.- **—down** [-daun], *s.* revés de fortuna; humillación, chasco.

comedian [komídian], *s.* comediante, actor cómico. **—comedy** [kámedi], *s.* comedia.

comet [kámit], *s.* cometa.

comfort [kámfort], *s.* comodidad; consuelo; bienestar.—*vt.* confortar; consolar.- **—able** [-abl], *a.* cómodo; consolador; adecuado.- **—er** [-œ(r)], *s.* edredón.- **—ing** [-iŋ], *a.* confortante.

comic [kámik], *a.* cómico.—*c. book,* revista de historietas, tebeo.—*c. opera,* ópera bufa, ópera cómica.—*c. strip,* tira cómica, historieta gráfica. - **—al** [-al], *a.* cómico.—*a.* y *s.* bufo.—*s. pl.* tiras cómicas, historietas.

coming [kámiŋ], *s.* venida, llegada.— *a.* próximo, venidero.

comma [kámä], *s.* (gram.) coma.

command [komǽnd], *vt.* mandar, ordenar, disponer; acaudillar, capitanear.—*vi.* imperar; imponerse.— *s.* mando; mandato, orden; comandancia; commando.- **—er** [-œ(r)], *s.* comandante, jefe supremo.- **—ment** [-ment], *s.* mandato, precepto.—*the Ten Commandments,* los diez Mandamientos.

ommemorate [kọmémoreịt], *vt.* conmemorar.—**commemoration** [kọmemoréịṣọn], *s.* conmemoración.

ommence [kọméns], *vt.* y *vi.* comenzar, iniciar.- —**ment** [-mẹnt], *s.* comienzo; inauguración; acto de distribución de diplomas.

ommend [kọménd], *vt.* encomendar, recomendar; alabar.- —**able** [-ạbl], *a.* loable.- —**ation** [kamẹndéịṣọn], *s.* elogio, alabanza.

omment [kámẹnt], *vt.* y *vi.* comentar; glosar, anotar.—*s.* comentario.- —**ary** [kámẹnteri], *s.* comentario.- —**ator** [kámẹnteịtọ(r)], —**er** [kámẹntœ(r)], *s.* comentarista.

ommerce [kámœrs], *s.* comercio.— **commercial** [kọmœ́rṣạl], *a.* comercial.

ommiseration [kọmịzẹréịṣọn], *s.* piedad, conmiseración.

ommissary [kámịseri], *s.* comisario, delegado.—**commission** [kọmíṣọn], *s.* comisión; misión; encargo; nombramiento.—*commissioned officer,* oficial del ejército. —**commissioner** [kọmíṣọnœ(r)], *s.* comisario; comisionado.

ommit [kọmít], *vti.* [1] cometer, perpetrar; encargar, encomendar.—*to c. one's self,* comprometerse.—*to c. to memory,* aprender de memoria.— *to c. to prison,* encarcelar, encerrar. —*to c. to writing,* poner por escrito.- —**ment** [-mẹnt], *s.* compromiso, obligación.

ommittee [kọmítị], *s.* comité, comisión, delegación.

ommodity [kọmádịtị], *s.* comodidad; mercancía.

ommon [kámọn], *a.* común, corriente; vulgar, trivial; público, general, comunal; inferior.—*c. law,* derecho consuetudinario.—*c. sense,* sentido común.—*c. soldier,* soldado raso.—*c. stock,* (com.) acción ordinaria, acciones ordinarias.—*s. pl.* ejido; refectorio, campo común.—*the C.,* (G.B.) la Cámara de los Comunes.- —**ness** [-nịs], *s.* comunidad; frecuencia; vulgaridad.- —**place** [-pleịs], *a.* común, vulgar.—*s.* lugar común.- —**weal** [-wil], *s.* el bien público.— —**wealth** [-welθ], *s.* estado; nación; comunidad de naciones; cosa pública.

ommotion [kọmóụṣọn], *s.* conmoción.

ommune [kọmiún], *vi.* comulgar; conversar, ponerse en contacto.

—**communicate** [kọmiúnịkeịt], *vt.* comunicar, dar parte de; contagiar; dar la comunión.—*vi.* comunicarse; tomar la comunión. —**communication** [kọmiunịkéịṣọn], *s.* comunicación.—**communion** [kọmiúnyọn], *s.* comunión.

communism [kámyunịzm], *s.* comunismo. —**communist** [kámyunịst], *a.* y *s.* comunista.

community [kọmiúnịtị], *s.* comunidad; vecindad; sociedad.

commuter [kọmiútœ(r)], *s.* abonado al ferrocarril; (elec.) conmutador.

compact [kámpækt], *s.* pacto, convenio; polvera de bolsillo; compresa.—*a.* [kọmpǽkt], compacto, conciso.—*c. disc* o *disk* (CD), disco compacto, compact-disc.

companion [kọmpǽnyọn], *s.* compañero; acompañante.- —**ship** [-ṣịp], *s.* compañerismo; compañía. —**company** [kámpạnị], *s.* compañía; sociedad; visita.—*ship's c.,* tripulación.—*present c. excepted,* mejorando lo presente.

comparable [kámpạrạbl], *a.* comparable. —**comparative** [kọmpǽrạtịv], *a.* comparativo, relativo; comparado. —**compare** [kọmpér], *vt.* comparar; comprobar, cotejar; equiparar.—*vi.* poderse comparar; ser comparable; ser igual.—*beyond c.,* sin igual o rival, sin par. —**comparison** [kọmpǽrịṣọn], *s.* comparación, cotejo; equiparación; símil; metáfora.

compartment [kọmpártmẹnt], *s.* compartimiento; departamento.

compass [kámpạs], *s.* compás de dibujo; brújula; circunferencia; alcance, ámbito.

compassion [kọmpǽṣọn], *s.* compasión.- —**ate** [-ịt], *a.* compasivo, misericordioso.

compatible [kọmpǽtịbl], *a.* compatible.

compatriot [kọmpéịtrịọt], *s.* y *a.* compatriota.

compel [kọmpél], *vti.* [1] compeler, obligar; dominar, someter.

compendium [kọmpéndiʌm], *s.* compendio, resumen.

compensate [kámpẹnseịt], *vt.* compensar; indemnizar.—*vi.* compensar; (con **for**) igualar, equivaler. —**compensation** [kampẹnséịṣọn], *s.* compensación; remuneración.

compete [kọmpít], *vi.* competir, rivalizar; (con **for**) disputarse.- —**nce** [kámpẹtẹns], —**ncy** [kámpẹtẹnsị], *s.*

competencia, suficiencia; subsistencia.- **—nt** [kámpẹtẹnt], *a.* competente, adecuado, calificado. **—competition** [kampẹtíšǫn], *s.* competición; rivalidad; certamen, concurso, oposición. **—competitive** [kǫmpétịtịv], *a.* competidor, que compite. **—competitor** [kǫmpétịtǫ(r)], *s.* competidor, rival, opositor.

compilation [kampịléjšǫn], *s.* compilación, recopilación. **—compile** [kǫmpáïl], *vt.* compilar, recopilar.

complacence [kǫmpléịsẹns], **complacency** [kǫmpléịsẹnsị], *s.* complacencia; presunción. **—complacent** [kǫmpléịsẹnt], *a.* complaciente; satisfecho de sí mismo.

complain [kǫmpléịn], *vi.* quejarse, lamentarse; querellarse.- **—t** [-t], *s.* queja; lamento; querella; enfermedad.

complement [kámplẹmẹnt], *s.* complemento; accesorio.—*vt.* complementar, completar.

complete [kǫmplít], *a.* completo.—*vt.* completar, rematar; perfeccionar. - **—ness** [-nịs], *s.* perfección, minuciosidad. **—completion** [kǫmplíšǫn], *s.* terminación, cumplimiento; completamiento.

complex [kámpleks], *a.* complejo, complicado.—*s.* complejo; obsesión.

complexion [kǫmplékšǫn], *s.* tez; cutis.

complexity [kǫmpléksịtị], **complexness** [kǫmpléksnịs], *s.* complejidad.

compliance [kǫmpláịans], *s.* sumisión; complacencia; acatamiento; anuencia.—*in c. with,* de acuerdo con, accediendo a. **—compliant** [kǫmpláịant], *a.* complaciente.

complicate [kámplịkẹjt], *vt.* complicar, enredar.—*a.* complicado.- **—d** [kámplịkẹjtịd], *a.* complicado, enredado. **—complication** [kamplịkéjšǫn], *s.* complicación.

compliment [kámplịmẹnt], *s.* halago, alabanza; cumplimiento.—*pl.* saludos, recados.—*c. of the author,* homenaje del autor, obsequio del autor.—*vt.* cumplimentar.- **—ary** [-ạrị], *a.* lisonjero; de cortesía, gratuito.—*c. copy,* ejemplar de cortesía.—*c. ticket,* pase de cortesía.

comply [kǫmpláị], *vii.* [7] obedecer a; cumplir con.

component [kǫmpóụnẹnt], *a.* y *s.* componente.

compose [kǫmpóụz], *vt.* componer; conciliar, sosegar.- **—d** [-d], *a.* sose-

gado, sereno; compuesto (de).- **—**[-œ(r)], *s.* autor, compositor. **—composite** [kǫmpázịt], *a.* compuest mixto.—*s.* compuesto, cosa con puesta; mixtura. **—compositic** [kampozíšǫn], *s.* composició tema; componenda.

composure [kǫmpóụzŭ(r)], *s.* compo tura, calma, sangre fría.

compost [kámpoụst], *s.* (agr.) abon compuesto, abono vegetal.

compote [kámpoụt], *s.* compot dulce.

compound [kámpaụnd], *s.* compuest mezcla; palabra compuesta; cuerp compuesto.—*a.* compuesto; me clado.—*vt.* [kampáụnd], compo ner, combinar, mezclar.—*vi.* av nirse, transigir.

comprehend [kamprịhénd], *vt.* con prender; abarcar, incluir. **—cor prehensible** [kamprịhénsịbl], comprensible, inteligible. **—cor prehension** [kamprịhénšǫn], *s.* con prensión. **—comprehensive** [kan prịhénsịv], *a.* compre(he)nsiv inclusivo; amplio; perspicaz.

compress [kǫmprés], *vt.* comprimi apretar, condensar.—*s.* [kámpres compresa.- **—ion** [kǫmpréšǫn], compresión.

comprise [kǫmpráịz], *vt.* incluir, co tener, comprender; constar de.

compromise [kámpromaịz], *s.* con promiso, arreglo.—*vt.* compromete ter.—*vi.* transigir.

comptroller [kǫntróụlœ(r)], *s.* inte ventor, contralor.

compulsion [kǫmpálšǫn], *s.* compu sión, apremio. **—compulsive** [kǫn pálsịv], *a.* compulsivo. **—compu sory** [kǫmpálsǫrị], *a.* obligatorio.

compunction [kǫmpáŋkšǫn], *s.* con punción, remordimiento, escr pulo.

computation [kampịutéjšǫn], *s.* con putación, cálculo. **—compute** [kǫn pịút], *vt.* computar, calcular. **—con puter** [kǫmpịútœ(r)], *s.* ordenado computadora.—*c. chip,* micropl quita.—*c. dating service,* agenc matrimonial por ordenador.—*con puter game,* video juego.—*c. grapl ics,* grafismo por computadora.— *language,* lenguaje de ordenado lenguaje de programación, le guaje de máquina.—*c. literac* capacidad de operar con un o denador.—*c. program,* programa d ordenador.—*c. programmer,* progra mador de ordenador.—*c. programming*, programación de ordenadores.—*c. science*, informática.—*c. virus*, virus de ordenadores.– **—ize** [-aiz], *vt.* computarizar, computerizar.

omputing [kompiútiŋ], *s.* informática, computación.—*c. skills*, competencia en el uso de computadoras.—*c. time*, tiempo máquina.

omrade [kámræd], *s.* camarada, compañero.– **—ship** [-šip], *s.* camaradería.

on [kan], *s.* (fam.) estafa, timo; (jer.) presidiario, preso; contra.—*c. game*, (fam.) estafa, timo.—*the pros and cons*, los pros y los contras.—*vt.* (fam.) estafar, timar.

oncave [kánkeiv], *a.* cóncavo. **—concavity** [kankǽviti], *s.* concavidad.

onceal [konsíl], *vt.* ocultar, esconder, encubrir.– **—ment** [-ment], *s.* ocultación; encubrimiento.

oncede [konsíd], *vt.* conceder, admitir.—*vi.* asentir; convenir.

onceit [konsít], *s.* presunción, engreimiento, ínfulas; vanagloria; concepto.– **—ed** [-id], *a.* vanidoso, engreído.

onceivable [konsívabl], *a.* concebible.—**conceive** [konsív], *vt.* y *vi.* concebir.

oncentrate [kánsentreit], *vt.* (re)concentrar.—*vi.* reunirse.—*s.* substancia concentrada.– **—d** [kánsentreitid], *a.* concentrado. **—concentration** [kansentréišon], *s.* (re)concentración; recogimiento.

oncept [kánsept], *s.* concepto.– **—ion** [konsépšon], *s.* concepción.

oncern [konsǿrn], *vt.* concernir; afectar; interesar; inquietar.—*s.* interés; inquietud; asunto; incumbencia; compañía, firma; importancia, consecuencia.—*of what c. is it to you?* ¿qué le importa? ¿qué más le da a Ud.?– **—ed** [-d], *a.* inquieto, preocupado; interesado; comprometido.—*as far as I am c.*, en cuanto a mí.– **—ing** [-iŋ], *prep.* por lo concerniente a, respecto a.

oncert [kánsœrt], *s.* concierto.— *in c.*, de concierto.– **—master** [-mǽstœr], *s.* (mus.) concertino.— *vt.* [konsǿrt], concertar.

oncession [konséšon], *s.* concesión, privilegio.– **—ary** [-ɛri], *s.* concesionario.– *a.* otorgado por concesión.

onch [kaŋk, kanch], *s.* caracola; (arq.) concha.

conciliate [konsíliejt], *vt.* conciliar; apaciguar. **—conciliation** [konsiliéišon], *s.* conciliación. **—conciliatory** [konsíliatɔri], *a.* conciliatorio.

concise [konsáis], *a.* conciso, sucinto. – **—ness** [-nis], *s.* concisión, laconismo.

conclude [konklúd], *vt.* y *vi.* concluir(se). **—conclusion** [konklúžon], *s.* conclusión; decisión; deducción. **—conclusive** [konklúsiv], *a.* concluyente; decisivo.

concord [kánkɔrd], *s.* concordia; armonía; concordancia.– **—ance** [kankɔ́rdans], *s.* concordancia, conformidad.

concrete [kánkrit], *a.* fraguado; cuajado; de hormigón.—*s.* concreto; hormigón; cemento.—*c. steel* o *reinforced c.*, hormigón armado.

concur [konkǿr], *vii.* [1] concurrir; convenir con, estar de acuerdo; unirse, juntarse.

concussion [konkášon], *s.* sacudida, golpe, conmoción.

condemn [kondém], *vt.* condenar; expropiar.– **—ation** [kandemnéišon], *s.* condenación; confiscación. – **—atory** [kondémnatɔri], *a.* condenatorio.

condensation [kandenséišon], *s.* condensación. **—condense** [kondéns], *vt.* y *vi.* condensar(se). **—condenser** [kondénsœ(r)], *s.* condensador.

condescend [kandisénd], *vi.* condescender. **—condescencion** [kandisénšon], *s.* condescendencia.

condiment [kándiment], *s.* condimento.

condition [kondíšon], *s.* condición; estado; requisito; nota o calificación provisional.—*vt.* estipular; acondicionar; reprobar (en un examen).– **—al** [-al], *a.* condicional.

condole [kondóul], *vi.* condolerse, dar el pésame.– **—nce** [kondóulens], *s.* condolencia, pésame.

condom [kándom], *s.* preservativo, condón.

condominium [kandomíni∧m], *s.* propiedad horizontal; apartamento, piso en régimen de propiedad horizontal.

condor [kándo(r)], *s.* cóndor.

conduce [kondjús], *vi.* conducir a, favorecer, tender a. **—conducive** [kondjúsiv], *a.* conducente, conveniente, apropiado.

conduct [kondákt], *vt.* conducir, guiar; (mus.) dirigir.—*vr.* conducirse, comportarse.—*vi.* ser conductor; llevar la batuta.—*s.* [kándʌktʃ], conducta, comportamiento; manejo, conducción.- **—ion** [kondákʃon], conducción.- **—or** [kondáktoҩ(r)], *s.* conductor; director de orquesta; revisor o inspector de boletines. **—conduit** [kándit], *s.* conducto.

cone [koun], *s.* cono; cucurucho; barquillo.—*pine c.,* piña (del pino).

confection [konfékʃon], *s.* confección, hechura; confite, confitura.- **—er** [-œ(r)], *s.* confitero.- **—ery** [-ɛri], *s.* dulces, confites; confitería.

confederacy [konfédœrᶏsi], *s.* confederación. **—confederate** [konfédœrei̯t], *vt.* y *vi.* confederar(se).—*a.* y *s.* [konfédœri̯t], confederado. **—confederation** [konfedœréi̯ʃon], *s.* confederación.

confer [konfœ́r], *vii.* [1] conferenciar,—*vti.* conferir.- **—ence** [kánfᶏrᶏns], *s.* conferencia.

confess [konfés], *vt.* y *vi.* confesar(se).- **—ion** [konféʃon], *s.* confesión.- **—ional** [konféʃonal], **—ionary** [konféʃonᶏri], *s.* confes(i)onario.- **—or** [konféʃo(r)], *s.* confesor.

confetti [kᶏnféti], *s.* confeti.

confidant [kanfidǽnt], *s.* confidente. **—confide** [konfái̯d], *vt.* y *vi.* confiar(se), fiar(se). **—confidence** [kánfidᶏns], *s.* confianza; confidencia.— *c. game,* (fam.) estafa, timo. **—confident** [kánfidᶏnt], *a.* cierto, seguro; confiado.—*s.* confidente. **—confidential** [kanfidénʃal], *a.* confidencial.

confine [konfái̯n], *vt.* y *vi.* confinar.— *to be confined in bed,* guardar cama.—*s. pl.* [kánfai̯nz], confín, límite.- **—ment** [konfái̯nment], *s.* confinamiento, encierro; restricción; ahogo.

confirm [konfœ́rm], *vt.* confirmar.- **—ation** [kanfœrméi̯ʃon], *s.* confirmación; ratificación.

confiscate [kánfiskei̯t], *vt.* confiscar.

conflagration [kanflᶏgréi̯ʃon], *s.* conflagración.

conflict [kánflikt], *s.* conflicto, choque, oposición.—*vi.* [konflíkt], luchar, estar en pugna.- **—ing** [konflíktiŋ], *a.* antagónico; contradictorio.

confluence [kánfluᶏns], *s.* confluencia.

conform [konfórm], *vt.* y *vi.* conformar(se), ajustar(se).- **—ity** [-iti], *s.*

conformidad, concordancia; resignación.

confound [konfáu̯nd], *vt.* confundir; aturrullar; trabucar.- **—ed** [-i̯d], *a.* maldito, condenado.

confront [konfrʌ́nt], *vt.* afrontar; confrontar; carear.

confuse [konfjúz], *vt.* confundir.- **—d** [-d], *a.* confuso; confundido, turbado. **—confusing** [konfjúziŋ], *a.* confuso, desconcertante. **—confusion** [konfjúʒon], *s.* confusión, desorden.

congeal [kondžíl], *vt.* y *vi.* congelar(se), helar(se); cuajar(se).

congenial [kondžíni̯al], *a.* congenial, agradable, simpático.- **—ity** [kondžini̯ǽliti], **—ness** [-nis], *s.* simpatía, congenialidad.

congest [kondžést], *vt.* y *vi.* congestionar(se), apiñar(se).- **—ed** [-i̯d], *a.* congestionado, apiñado.- **—ion** [kondžéschon], *s.* congestión; apiñamiento.

congratulate [kongrǽchulei̯t], *vt.* felicitar, congratular.—*to c. on,* felicitar por. **—congratulation** [kongræchuléi̯ʃon], *s.* felicitación, congratulación.

congregate [káŋgrigei̯t], *vt.* y *vi.* congregar(se). **—congregation** [kaŋgrigéi̯ʃon], *s.* congregación; asamblea, reunión; grey.

congress [káŋgris], *s.* convención, congreso, asamblea; (C.) Congreso, Parlamento.- **—ional** [koŋgréʃonal], *a.* perteneciente o relativo a congreso.- **—man** [káŋgrisman], **—woman** [káŋgriswumᶏn], *s.* congresista, diputado; miembro de un congreso.

congruent [káŋgruᶏnt], *a.* congruente.

conjecture [kondžékchūr], *s.* conjetura.—*vt.* conjeturar.

conjugate [kándzugei̯t], *vt.* conjugar.- **—conjugation** [kandzugéi̯ʃon], *s.* conjugación. **—conjunction** [kondžʌ́ŋkʃon], *s.* conjunción; unión, liga.

conjuration [kandžuréi̯ʃon], *s.* conjuro; sortilegio, encantamiento. **—conjure** [kondžúr], *vt.* rogar o pedir con instancia, conjurar; [kándzu(r)], exorcizar.—*vi.* [kándzu(r)], conjurar; escamotear, hacer juegos de mano.

connect [konékt], *vt.* y *vi.* conectar(se), unir(se), acoplar(se); relacionar(se), comunicar(se); entroncar(se); em palmar(se).– **—ion** [kǫnékṣǫn], s. conexión; enlace; relación, parentesco.

connivance [kǫnáivǫns], s. connivencia. **—connive** [kǫnáiv], vi. hacer la vista gorda, tolerar.**—conniver** [kǫnáivœ(r)], s. consentidor, cómplice.

connoisseur [kanǐsœr], s. conocedor.

conquer [kánkœ(r)], vt. conquistar; vencer.—vi. triunfar.— **—ing** [-iŋ], a. conquistador, victorioso.– **—or** [-ǫ(r)], s. conquistador, vencedor. **—conquest** [kánkwest], s. conquista.

conscience [kánṣens], s. conciencia (moral). **—conscientious** [kanṣįénṣʌs], a. concienzudo. **—conscious** [kánṣʌs], a. consciente. **—consciousness** [kánṣʌsnįs], s. conocimiento, conciencia.

conscript [kǫnskrípt], vt. reclutar, alistar.—a. y s. [kánskrįt], conscripto, recluta.– **—ion** [kǫnskrípṣǫn], s. conscripción, reclutamiento.

consecrate [kánṣēkreįt], vt. consagrar; ungir; canonizar. **—consecration** [kanṣēkréįṣǫn], s. consagración; dedicación; canonización.

consecutive [kǫnṣékyutįv], a. consecutivo, sucesivo.

consent [kǫnṣént], s. consentimiento.—by common c., de común acuerdo.—vi. consentir.

consequence [kánṣēkwens], s. consecuencia; importancia. **—consequent** [kánṣēkwent], a. y s. consecuente, consiguiente.

conservation [kanṣœrvéįṣǫn], s. conservación, preservación. **—conservative** [kǫnṣœrvǫtįv], s. y a. conservador. **—conservatory** [kǫnṣœrvǫtǫrį], s. conservatorio, academia; invernadero. **—conserve** [kǫnṣœrv], vt. conservar, preservar; hacer conserva.—s. [kánṣœrv], conserva, dulce.

consider [kǫnṣídœ(r)], vt. considerar; tratar con respeto.—vi. pensar, reflexionar.– **—able** [-ǫbl], a. considerable; notable.– **—ate** [-it], a. considerado, (muy) mirado.– **—ation** [-éįṣǫn], s. consideración, miramiento; deliberación.– **—ing** [-iŋ], prep. en consideración a, en vista de.—c. that, en vista de que.

consign [kǫnṣáįn], vt. consignar; confiar, traspasar; relegar.– **—ment** [-ment], s. (com.) consignación, partida, envío.

consist [kǫnṣíst], vi. consistir (en), constar (de).– **—ence** [-ens], **—ency** [-ensį], s. consistencia; consecuencia; firmeza, estabilidad.– **—ent** [-ent], a. consecuente, conveniente; armonizable; coherente, consistente, denso.

consistory [kǫnṣístǫrį], s. consistorio; asamblea, congreso.

consolation [kanṣoléįṣǫn], s. consuelo. **—console** [kǫnṣóųl], vt. consolar.—s. [kánṣoųl], consola.

consolidate [kǫnṣálįdeįt], vt. y vi. consolidar(se); unir(se); fundir(se). **—consolidation** [kǫnṣalįdéįṣǫn], s. consolidación; unión; fusión.

consoling [kǫnṣóųliŋ], a. consolador.

consonant [kánṣonǫnt], s. y a. consonante.

consort [kánṣɔrt], s. consorte, cónyuge.—vi. [kǫnṣórt], asociarse; armonizar.—vt. asociar, casar.

conspicuous [kǫnṣpíkyuʌs], a. conspicuo, eminente, notorio, manifiesto.

conspiracy [kǫnṣpírǫsį], s. conspiración, complot. **—conspirator** [kǫnṣpírǫtǫ(r)], s. conspirador. **—conspire** [kǫnṣpáįr], vi. conspirar.—vt. maquinar, tramar.

constable [kánṣtǫbl], s. alguacil, agente de policía; condestable.

constancy [kánṣtǫnsį], s. constancia; lealtad. **—constant** [kánṣtǫnt], a. constante.—s. (mat.) constante.

constellation [kanṣtɛléįṣǫn], s. constelación.

consternation [kanṣtœrnéįṣǫn], s. consternación.

constipate [kánṣtįpeįt], vt. estreñir. **—constipation** [kanṣtįpéįṣǫn], s. estreñimiento.

constituent [kǫnṣtíchuent], s. elemento, ingrediente o componente.—a. constitutivo; constituyente (asamblea, etc.). **—constitute** [kánṣtįtjut], vt. constituir, establecer. **—constitution** [kanṣtįtjúṣǫn], s. constitución; complexión, naturaleza (de una persona); estatutos. **—constitutional** [kanṣtįtjúṣǫnǫl], a. constitucional; constituyente.—s. (fam.) paseo higiénico.

constrain [kǫnṣtréįn], vt. constreñir, compeler, forzar.– **—t** [-t], s. fuerza, constreñimiento.

constrict [kǫnṣtríkt], vt. apretar, estrechar, encoger.

construct [kǫnṣtrákt], vt. construir; fabricar.– **—ion** [kǫnṣtrákṣǫn], s.

construcción.- **—ive** [kɔnstráktįv], a. constructivo.

construe [kɔnstrú], vt. interpretar, explicar; inferir; construir, componer.

consul [kánsʌl], s. cónsul.- **—ar** [kánsįulǎ(r)], a. consular.- **—ate** [kánsįulįt], s. consulado.

consult [kɔnsált], vt. consultar.—vi. asesorarse, consultarse, aconsejarse (con); conferenciar.- **—ant** [-ʌnt], **—er** [-œ(r)], s. consultante, consultor.- **—ation** [kansʌltéjʂɔn], s. consulta(ción), junta; deliberación.

consume [kɔnsįúm], vt. y vi. consumir(se).- **—r** [kɔnsįúmœ(r)], s. consumidor.

consummate [kánsʌmejt], vt. consumar, acabar, completar.—a. [kansʌmįt], consumado. **—consummation** [kansʌméjʂɔn], s. consumación.

consumption [kɔnsʌmpʂɔn], s. consunción; consumo, gasto; tisis. **—consumptive** [kɔnsʌmptįv], a. consuntivo, destructivo.—s. y a. tísico.

contact [kántækt], s. contacto.—pl. relaciones.—vt. y vi. tocar(se), poner(se) en contacto.

contagion [kɔntéjdʐɔn], s. contagio; infección, peste. **—contagious** [kɔntéjdʐʌs], a. contagioso.

contain [kɔntéjn], vt. contener, caber, tener cabida para; abarcar; reprimir; ser exactamente divisible.- **—er** [-œ(r)], s. recipiente, vasija, envase.

contaminate [kɔntǽmįnejt], vt. contaminar; viciar. **—contamination** [kɔntǽmįnéjʂɔn], s. contaminación.

contemplate [kántemplejt], vt. contemplar; proyectar, tener la intención de. **—contemplation** [kantempléjʂɔn], s. contemplación, especulación; intención, proyecto.

contemporary [kɔntémporerį], a. y s. contemporáneo, coetáneo.

contempt [kɔntémpt], s. desprecio, menosprecio, desdén.—c. of court, (for.) contumacia; rebeldía.- **—ible** [-įbl], a. despreciable, desdeñable.- **—uous** [kɔntémpchuʌs], a. desdeñoso, despreciativo.

contend [kɔnténd], vt. sostener o afirmar.—vi. contender.- **—er** [-œ(r)], s. contendiente, competidor.

content [kɔntént], a. contento, satisfecho.—vt. (com)placer, conten-

tar.—s. contento, satisfacción; [kántent], cantidad, proporción, volumen.—pl. contenido.—table of contents, índice general.- **—ed** [kɔnténtįd], a. contento, placentero.

contention [kɔnténʂɔn], s. contención, argumento.

contentment [kɔnténtment], s. contentamiento, satisfacción.

contest [kántest], s. contienda, debate; certamen, competencia; litigio.—vt. [kɔntést], disputar; discutir; litigar.—vi. contender; competir; rivalizar con. **—contestant** [kɔntéstʌnt], s. contendiente, opositor; litigante.

context [kántekst], s. contexto.

contiguous [kɔntígįuʌs], a. contiguo.

continent [kántįnent], s. continente.—a. casto, continente.- **—al** [kantįnéntʌl], a. continental.

contingency [kɔntíndʐensį], s. contingencia. **—contingent** [kɔntíndʐent], a. y s. contingente.

continual [kɔntínyuʌl], a. continuo, incesante. **—continuance** [kɔntínyuʌns], s. (for.) aplazamiento; continuación. **—continuation** [kɔntįnyuéjʂɔn], s. continuación, prolongación. **—continue** [kɔntínyu], vt. continuar; mantener, prolongar; (for.) aplazar.—vi. continuar; durar; proseguir. **—continuity** [kantįnįúįtį], s. continuidad; coherencia **—continuous** [kɔntínyuʌs], a. continuo, ininterrumpido.

contour [kántur], s. contorno; curva de nivel.—vt. contorn(e)ar, perfilar.

contraband [kántrʌbænd], s. contrabando.—a. prohibido, ilegal.- **—ist** [-įst], s. contrabandista.

contract [kántrækt], s. contrato, convenio, pacto, ajuste; contrata.—vt. [kɔntrǽkt], contratar, pactar; contraer (enfermedad, deuda, etc.).—vi. contraerse, encogerse; comprometerse por contrato.- **—ion** [kɔntrǽkʂɔn], s. contracción, encogimiento, estrechamiento.- **—or** [kɔntrǽkto(r)], s. contratista.

contradict [kántrʌdíkt], vt. contradecir, desmentir, llevar la contraria a.- **—ion** [kantrʌdíkʂɔn], s. contradicción.- **—ory** [kantradíktorį], a. contradictorio; contrario.

contrary [kántrerį], a. contrario; testarudo, porfiado.—c.-minded, de di versa opinión.—*s.* contrario.—*on the c.,* al contrario.

contrast [kántræst], *s.* contraste, contraposición.—*vt.* y *vi.* [kọntræst], contrastar.

contribute [kọntríbiut], *vt.* y *vi.* contribuir. —**contribution** [kantribiúșọn], *s.* contribución; colaboración literaria, donativo. —**contributor** [kọntríbiutọ(r)], *s.* colaborador, contribuidor.

contrite [kántrait], *a.* contrito. —**contrition** [kọntríșọn], *s.* contrición.

contrivance [kọntráivạns], *s.* idea, plan, invención; artefacto, dispositivo; traza, artificio; estratagema. —**contrive** [kọntráiv], *vt.* idear, inventar; tramar, urdir.—*vi.* darse maña o trazas (de); maquinar.

control [kọntróul], *s.* mando, dirección, dominio; regulación, inspección; restricción.—*pl.* mandos, controles.—*a.* regulador; de gobierno; de comprobación.—*vti.* [1] controlar, gobernar, dirigir, regular; reprimir, restringir.– —**ler** [-œ(r)], *s.* interventor, registrador, contralor; aparato de manejo y control.

controversy [kántrovœrsi], *s.* controversia, debate.

contumacy [kántiumași], *s.* contumacia, terquedad.

contusion [kọntúžọn], *s.* contusión.

convalesce [kanvalés], *vi.* convalecer. – —**nce** [kanvalésẹns], *s.* convalecencia.– —**nt** [kanvalésẹnt], *a.* y *s.* convaleciente.

convene [kọnvín], *vt.* convocar, citar; emplazar.—*vi.* reunirse. —**convenience** [kọnvínyẹns], **conveniency** [kọnvínyẹnsi], *s.* comodidad, conveniencia.—*at one's earliest convenience,* en la primera oportunidad que uno tenga, tan pronto como sea posible.—**convenient** [kọnvínyẹnt], *a.* conveniente.

convent [kánvẹnt], *s.* convento.

convention [kọnvénșọn], *s.* convención, congreso; convenio; costumbre.– —**al** [-ạl], *a.* convencional.

conversant [kánvœrsạnt], *a.* versado, experto, entendido. —**conversation** [kanvœrséišọn], *s.* conversación, plática. —**converse** [kọnvœrs], *vi.* conversar.—*a.* [kánvœrs], inverso, contrario.—*s.* (fam.) conversa; (lóg.) inversa, recíproca.

conversion [kọnvœržọn], *s.* conver-

sión. —**convert** [kọnvœrt], *vt.* convertir; transmutar; reducir a; cambiar (valores).—*vi.* convertirse, transformarse.—*s.* [kánvœrt], neófito, converso. —**convertible** [kọnvœrtibl], *a.* convertible, conversible.

convex [kánvẹks], *a.* convexo.

convey [kọnvéi], *vt.* conducir, acarrear, transportar; transmitir, comunicar; dar a entender.– —**ance** [-ạns], *s.* vehículo, conducción; transmisión; traspaso; escritura de traspaso.

convict [kánvikt], *s.* reo convicto; presidiario.—*vt.* [kọnvíkt], condenar; probar la culpabilidad.– —**ion** [kọnvíkșọn], *s.* convicción; fallo condenatorio.

convince [kọnvíns], *vt.* convencer. —**convincing** [kọnvínsiŋ], *a.* convincente.

convocation [kanvokéišọn], *s.* convocación, llamamiento. —**convoke** [kọnvóuk], *vt.* convocar, citar.

convoy [kọnvói], *vt.* escoltar, convoyar.—*s.* [kánvoi], convoy, escolta.

convulsion [kọnválšọn], *s.* convulsión. —**convulsive** [kọnválsiv], *a.* convulsivo.

coo [ku], *s.* arrullo.—*vi.* arrullar, decir ternezas.

cook [kuk], *vt.* y *vi.* cocinar, cocer, guisar.—*to c. up,* tramar, urdir.—*what's cooking?* (fam.) ¿qué se trama? ¿qué pasa?—*s.* cocinero, cocinera.– —**ery** [kúkœri], *s.* arte de la cocina.– —**ie** [-i], —**y** [i], *s.* gallet(it)a, bizcochito.– —**ing** [-iŋ], *s.* arte culinario; cocción.—*a.* de la cocina.—*c. pan,* cacerola, cazuela.

cool [kul], *a.* fresco; frío, indiferente; sereno.—*c.-headed,* sereno.—*s.* frescura.—*vt.* enfriar, refrescar.—*to c. one's heels,* hacer antesala, esperar mucho tiempo.—*vi.* enfriarse, calmarse.– —**er** [kúlœ(r)], *s.* enfriadera; enfriadero; refrigerante; nevera.– —**ing** [-iŋ], *a.* refrescante, refrigerante.—*s.* enfriamiento, refrigeración.– —**ness** [-nịs], *s.* frialdad; sangre fría; tibieza, despego.

coon [kun], *s.* mapache o coatí.—*old c.,* viejo marrullero.

coop [kup], *s.* jaula.—*chicken c.,* gallinero.—*vt.* (**in** o **up**) enjaular, encerrar.

coöperate [koápẹreit], *vi.* cooperar.

—**coöperation** [koapⱸréiŝǫn], s. cooperación. —**coöperative** [koápⱸrātįv], a. cooperativo, cooperante.—s. cooperativa. —**coöperator** [koápⱸrⱸito(r)], s. cooperador.

coördinate [koórdįneįt], vt. coordinar.—s. [koórdįnįt], igual, semejante; coordenada.—a. coordenado; relativo a las coordenadas. —**coördination** [koordįnéiŝǫn], s. coordinación.

cop [kap], s. (fam.) polizonte.—vti. [1] (fam.) coger, prender; (jer.) hurtar, robar.—to c. a plea, (law) (fam.) declararse culpable para obtener una sentencia más leve.—vii.—to cop out, (jer.) resbalarse, escabullirse, rajarse.

copartner [koupártnⱸ(r)], s. (con)socio; copartícipe.

cope [koup], vi. hacer frente a, habérselas con.—I cannot c. with this, no puedo con esto.

copilot [koupáįlǫt], s. copiloto, segundo piloto.

copious [kóųpįʌs], a. copioso, abundante.

copper [kápœ(r)], s. cobre; (fam.) policía.—a. de cobre, cobrizo.- —**smith** [kápœrsmį̊θ], s. calderero.

copulation [kapyūléiŝǫn], s. cópula o coito; unión.

copy [kápį], s. copia; ejemplar (de una obra); imitación; número de un periódico.—c. book, copiador (para cartas, cuentas, etc.); libreta, cuaderno.—vti. y vii. [7] copiar; imitar.- —**right** [-rajt], s. derechos de propiedad literaria, artística o intelectual; derechos del autor; derecho de reproducción; copyright.—vt. registrar como propiedad literaria o artística, inscribir en el registro de la propiedad literaria, obtener el copyright de.—a. (o **copyrighted** [kápįrajtįd]) protegido por los derechos del autor, derechos registrados.—c. reserved, es propiedad, reservados todos los derechos, copyright.

cord [kɔrd], s. cordel, cuerda; tendón.- —**less** [lɛs], a. inalámbrico.—c. telephone, teléfono inalámbrico, teléfono sin hilos.

cordial [kórdžal], s. cordial, tónico.— a. cordial, sincero.- —**ity** [kordžǽlįtį], s. cordialidad.

cordovan [kórdovan], s. cordobán.— (C.), a. y s. cordobés.

corduroy [kórdūrɔj], s. pana.

core [kɔr], s. centro, corazón, parte central; fondo, núcleo.—vt. quitar el corazón o centro; despepitar (fruta).

cork [kɔrk], s. corcho; tapón de corcho.—vt. tapar con corcho.- —**screw** [kórkskru], s. tirabuzón, sacacorchos.

corn [kɔrn], s. maíz; grano, cereal; callo (de los pies o manos); (fam.) sensiblería, cursilería. —**cob** [-kab], s. mazorca de maíz.- —**field** [-fild], s. maizal.- —**starch** [-starch], s. almidón de maíz.—vt. salar, curar; granular.- —**ed** [-d], a. acecinado, curado.—c. beef, cecina.

corner [kórnœ(r)], s. esquina; rincón; recodo; aprieto o apuro; monopolio.—c. bracket, rinconera.—to cut corners, echar por el atajo, atajar; economizar.—to drive into a c., poner entre la espada y la pared.— vt. arrinconar; copar; monopolizar. - —**ed** [-d], a. anguloso, esquinado; acorralado, en aprietos; copado.- —**stone** [-stoun], s. piedra angular; primera piedra.- —**wise** [-wajz], adv. diagonalmente.

cornet [kɔrnét], s. corneta; cornetín.

cornice [kórnįs], s. cornisa.

cornucopia [kɔrnúpiǎ], s. cornucopia, cuerno de la abundancia.

corny [kórnį], a. de maíz; de trigo; calloso; (coll.) afectado, exageradamente sentimental; inferior, de mala calidad o gusto; manido.

corolla [korálǎ], s. (bot.) corola.- —**ry** [károlⱸrį], s. corolario.

coronation [karonéiŝǫn], s. coronación.

coroner [káronœ(r)], s. médico forense.

corporal [kórporal], a. corporal, corpóreo.—s. (mil.) cabo.

corporate [kórporįt], a. corporativo; colectivo; de la empresa, de la compañía; empresarial.—the c. image, la imagen corporativa.

corporation [kɔrporéiŝǫn], s. corporación; (com.) sociedad anónima.

corps [kour], s. cuerpo o grupo organizado.—army c., cuerpo de ejército.

corpse [kɔrps], s. cadáver.

corpuscle [kórpʌsl], s. corpúsculo.

corral [korǽl], vt. acorralar.—s. corral.

correct [korékt], vt. corregir; reprender, castigar; reparar, remediar.—a. exacto; correcto.- —**ion** [korékŝǫn],

s. enmienda, corrección.— **—ional** [kǫrékṣǫṇạl], *a.* correccional, penal.—**ness** [kǫréktnịs], *s.* corrección.— **—or** [-ǫ(r)], *s.* revisor, corrector.

correlate [kárḛleịt], *vt.* correlacionar.—*vi.* tener correlación.—**correlative** [kǫrélạṭịv], *a.* y *s.* correlativo.—**correlation** [karḛléịṣǫṇ], *s.* correlación.

correspond [karḛspánd], *vi.* corresponder; mantener correspondencia.— **—ence** [-ḛns], **—ency** [-ḛnsị], *s.* correspondencia; reciprocidad.— **—ent** [-ḛnt], *a.* correspondiente.— *s.* corresponsal, correspondiente.

corridor [kárịdǫ(r)], *s.* corredor, galería, pasillo.

corroborate [kǫrábǫreịt], *vt.* corroborar, confirmar.—**corroboration** [kǫrabǫréịṣǫṇ], *s.* corroboración.

corrode [kǫróụd], *vt.* y *vi.* corroer(se). **—corrosive** [kǫróụṣịv], *a.* corrosivo; mordaz.

corrugated [kórụgeịtịd], *a.* ondulado.

corrugation [karugéịṣǫṇ], *s.* corrugamiento; contracción.

corrupt [kǫrápt], *a.* corrompido; depravado.—*vt.* corromper.—*vi.* corromperse, prodrirse.— **—ion** [kǫrápṣǫṇ], *s.* corrupción.

cortege [kǫrtéž], *s.* comitiva, séquito.

cortisone [kórtịsoụn], *s.* cortisona.

corvette [kǫrvét], *s.* (mar.) corbeta.

cosmetic [kazmétịk], *a.* y *s.* cosmético.

cosmic(al) [kázmịk(ạl)], *a.* cósmico.

cosmopolitan [kazmǫpálịṭạn], **cosmopolite** [kazmápolaịt], *a.* y *s.* cosmopolita.

cost [kǫst], *s.* costo, coste, costa; precio, importe.—*at all costs,* a toda costa.—*c. of living,* costo de la vida.—*vii.* [9] costar.—*pret.* y *pp.* de TO COST.— **—liness** [kóstlịnịs], *s.* suntuosidad, carestía.— **—ly** [-lị], *a.* costoso, caro.

co-star [koụ́star], *s.* coprotagonista.— *vi.* coprotagonizar.

costume [kástịum], *s.* vestuario; disfraz.—*c. jewelry,* bisutería, alhajas de fantasía.

cot [kat], *s.* cabaña, choza; catre, camilla.

coterie [kóụṭeṛị], *s.* camarilla, claque.

cottage [kátịdž], *s.* casita, cabaña, choza; casa de campo.—*c. cheese,* requesón.

cotton [kátǫṇ], *s.* algodón (planta y fibra); ropa o género de algodón.—

c. belt, (E.U.), región algodonera.— *c. candy,* algodón de azúcar.—*c. wool,* algodón en rama.—*c. yarn,* hilaza.

couch [kaụch], *s.* diván; sofá, canapé.—*studio c.,* sofá-cama.

cougar [kúgạr], *m.* puma.

cough [kǫf], *s.* tos.—*c. drop,* pastilla para la tos.—*whooping c.,* tosferina.—*vi.* toser.—*to c. up,* expectorar; (fam.) pagar.— **—ing** [kófịŋ], *s.* acceso de tos.

could [kụd], *pret.* de CAN.

council [kaụ́nsịl], *s.* concilio; consejo; concejo.—*city c.,* consejo municipal.—*c. of war,* consejo de guerra.— **—man** [-mạn], *s.* concejal.— **—(l)or** [-ǫ(r)], *s.* concejal; consejero.

counsel [kaụ́nsẹl], *s.* consejo; deliberación; dictamen; abogado consultor.—*vti.* [2] aconsejar, recomendar; asesorar.— **—(l)or** [-ǫ(r)], *s.* consultor; asesor.—*c. at law,* abogado.

count [kaụnt], *vt.* contar, numerar, calcular.—*vi.* valer.—*to count on* o *upon,* contar con, confiar en.—*s.* cuenta, cómputo; cargo.

countenance [kaụ́nṭenạns], *s.* semblante, cara; talante, aspecto.—*out of c.,* desconcertado.—*to give c.* apoyar, favorecer.—*vt.* aprobar; apoyar.

counter [kaụ́ntœ(r)], *s.* mostrador, tablero; ficha; contador.—*adv.* contra, al contrario, en contra.—*to run c. to,* oponerse, violar.—*a.* contrario.—*vt.* contradecir; rechazar; prevenir.—*vi.* oponerse.

counteract [kaụntœrǽkt], *vt.* contrariar; neutralizar, contrarrestar.

counterattack [kaụntœratǽk], *vt.* y *vi.* contraatacar, hacer un contraataque.—*s.* contraataque.

counterbalance [kaụntœrbǽlạns], *vt.* contrapesar, compensar.—*s.* [kaụ́ntœrbǽlạns], contrapeso, equilibrio, compensación.

counterfeit [kaụ́ntœrfịt], *vt.* falsificar.—*s.* falsificación; moneda falsa.—*a.* falsificado. **—counterfeiter** [kaụ́ntœrfịtœ(r)], *s.* falsificador, monedero falso.

countermand [kaụntœrmǽnd], *s.* contraorden.—*vt.* revocar.

countermarch [kaụ́ntœrmarch], *s.* contramarcha.

counterpart [kaụ́ntœrpart], *s.* contraparte.

counterpoint [kaụ́ntœrpǫịnt], *s.* contrapunto.

counterrevolution [kaʊntœrrɛvoliúṣ̣ọn], s. contrarrevolución.

counterstroke [káʊntœrstroʊk], s. contragolpe.

countess [káʊntis], s. condesa.

countless [káʊntlis], a. innumerable, sin cuento.

country [kántri], s. país, nación; región, tierra, patria; campo.—c. club, club de campo.—a. campestre.— **—man** [-man], s. compatriota, coterráneo; campesino, aldeano.— **—side** [-said], s. campo; distrito rural.

county [káʊti], s. condado, jurisdicción.—c. seat, cabecera de distrito o jurisdicción.

couple [kápl], s. pareja, par.—vt. acoplar, (a)parear.—vi. acoplarse, formar pareja. **—coupling** [káplịŋ], s. acoplamiento; cópula; unión, junta.

courage [kœ́ridʒ], s. coraje, valor.— **—ous** [kʌréidʒʌs], a. corajudo, valiente, valeroso.— **—ousness** [kʌréidʒʌsnịs], s. valor, brío.

courier [kúriœ(r)], s. mensajero, propio.

course [kɔrs], s. curso; marcha; rumbo, dirección; progreso.—in due c., a su tiempo.—matter of c., cosa de cajón, de rutina.—of c., por supuesto, desde luego, etc.

court [kɔrt], s. tribunal de justicia, juzgado, corte, audiencia; pista, cancha, campo de juego (tenis, etc.); séquito; patio, plazoleta; cortejo, galanteo.—c.-martial, consejo de guerra.—to pay c. to, hacer la corte a.—to put out of c., demostrar la falsedad de.— **—house** [-haʊs], s. juzgado, palacio de justicia, casa de tribunales.— **—ly** [-li], a. distinguido, fino.—c. love, amor cortés.— **—room** [-rum], s. sala de tribunal, sala de justicia.—vt. cortejar, galantear; atraerse, captar.

courteous [kœ́rtịʌs], a. cortés. **—courtesy** [kœ́rtẹsi], s. cortesía; reverencia.

courtier [kórtịœ(r)], s. cortesano; palaciego.

courtship [kórtʃịp], s. cortejo, galanteo.

courtyard [kórtyard], s. patio, atrio.

cousin [kázịn], s. primo o prima.—first c., primo hermano o carnal.

couturier [kutụryé], s. modisto.

cove [koʊv], s. cala, ensenada.

covenant [kávẹnạnt], s. contrato, convenio, pacto; escritura de contrato.

cover [kávœ(r)], vt. cubrir; tapar, ocultar; cobijar, proteger; forrar; abarcar; recorrer (distancias, etc.); empollar; ponerse el sombrero; (con **up**) encubrir.—s. cubierta, tapa; forro; envoltura; capa, pretexto; albergue; cubierto; funda; cobertor, tapete.—c. charge, (precio de) cubierto (en restaurantes, etc.).—to take c., buscar abrigo.— **—ing** [-ịŋ], s. funda, cubierta; envoltura; ropa, abrigo.— **—t** [kávœrt], a. encubierto, disimulado.

covet [kávịt], vt. codiciar.— **—ous** [-ʌs], a. codicioso.

cow [kaʊ], s. vaca; hembra de otros cuadrúpedos grandes (elefantes, etc.).—vt. acobardar, intimidar.

coward [káʊard], a. y s. cobarde.— **—ice** [-ịs], **—liness** [-lịnịs], s. cobardía.

cowbell [káʊbel], s. cencerro. **—cowboy** [káʊbɔj], s. vaquero, montero.

cower [káʊœ(r)], vi. agacharse; aplastarse de miedo.

cowhide [káʊhạjd], s. cuero, vaqueta.

cowpox [káʊpaks], s. vacuna. **—cowshed** [káʊʃed], s. establo de vacas.

coxcomb [kákskoʊm], s. petimetre.

coy [kɔj], **coyish** [kɔ́jịʃ], a. recatado, modesto; tímido.

cozy, cozey [kóʊzị], a. cómodo, agradable.

crab [kræb], s. cangrejo; (fig.) cascarrabias.—c. apple, manzana silvestre.—a. agrio, áspero.—vii. [1] regañar. pescar crustáceos.

crack [kræk], s. grieta, rajadura; crujido, chasquido; trueno, estampido; chanza.—at the c. of dawn, al romper el día.—a. de calidad superior.—c. shot, tirador certero.—vt. romper; rajar; chasquear, restallar; crujir; trastornar.—to c. jokes, gastar bromas.—vi. agrietarse; rajarse, partirse; traquetear.— **—ed** [-t], a. agrietado, cuarteado; chiflado; (voz) cascada, desapacible.— **—er** [krækœ(r)], s. galleta.— **—le** [krǽkl], vt. hacer crujir.—vi. crujir, crepitar, restallar.—s. crujido, crepitación.

cradle [kréjdl], s. cuna.—vt. acunar.—vi. mecerse en la cuna.

craft [kræft], s. artificio; maña, habilidad; arte u oficio; gremio; embarcación, embaracaciones.— **—sman**

[krǽftsmạn], *s.* artífice, artesano.– **—y** [-i], *a.* astuto, taimado.

crag [kræg], *s.* despeñadero, risco.– **—gy** [krǽgi], *a.* escarpado.

cram [kræm], *vti.* y *vii.* [1] rellenar(se), hartar(se), atracar(se); cebar(se); (fig.) preparar(se) rápidamente para un examen.

cramp [kræmp], *s.* calambre; grapa.— *a.* contraído, apretado.—*vt.* comprimir, apretar; estrechar; sujetar con grapa.

cranberry [krǽnberi], *s.* arándano agrio de los pantanos.

crane [krejn], *s.* grulla; grúa.—*vt.* levantar con la grúa; estirar, extender (el cuello).—*vi.* estirarse, alargarse.

cranium [kréjnịʌm], *s.* cráneo.

crank [kræŋk], *s.* manija; manubrio; biela; cigüeña, manivela; maniático, caprichoso; capricho, chifladura.—*c. axle,* cigüeñal.– **—case** [krǽŋkkejs], *s.* cárter del cigüeñal.– **—shaft** [-šæft], *s.* cigüeñal.– **—y** [-i], *a.* chiflado.

cranny [krǽni], *s.* grieta, resquicio.

crape [krejp], *s.* = CREPE.

crash [kræš], *vi.* romperse, caerse estrepitosamente, estrellarse; estallar; quebrar; aterrizar violentamente.— *vt.* romper o despedazar estrepitosamente, estrellar; echar a pique.—*to c. the gate,* colarse.—*s.* estallido, estampido, estrépito; quiebra; aterrizaje violento; choque, estrellamiento.—*c. landing,* aterrizaje forzoso, aterrizaje de emergencia.

crass [kraes], *a.* craso; burdo, grosero.

crate [krejt], *s.* canasto, jaula de embalaje; huacal.—*vt.* embalar (en huacales, etc.).

crater [kréjtœ(r)], *s.* cráter.

cravat [krʌvǽt], *s.* corbata; chalina.

crave [krejv], *vt.* anhelar, desear; apetecer vehementemente.—*vi.* pedir o desear con vehemencia, suspirar por.

craven [kréjvịn], *a.* cobarde.

crawl [krɔl], *vi.* arrastrarse, andar a gatas; serpear; humillarse; ir a paso de tortuga.—*s.* arrastramiento; natación marinera.

crayfish [kréjfîš], *s.* cangrejo de río, ástaco; cangrejo de mar, cámbaro, pequeña langosta.

crayon [kréjọn], *s.* lápiz de color, creyón; tiza; dibujo al pastel.

craze [krejz], *vt.* y *vi.* enloquecer(se).— *s.* locura, manía; moda.– **—d** [-d], *a.*

enloquecido, loco. **—crazy** [kréjzị], *a.* loco.

creak [krik], *vi.* crujir, rechinar, chirriar.—*s.* crujido, rechinamiento.

cream [krim], *s.* crema, nata.—*c. cheese,* queso crema.—*c. of tartar,* crémor tártaro.—*cold c.,* crema cosmética.—*c. puff,* bollo de crema.— *vi.* criar nata.—*vt.* desnatar.– **—ery** [krímœri], *s.* lechería.– **—y** [-i], *a.* cremoso.

crease [kris], *s.* pliegue; arruga; raya (del pantalón, etc.).—*vt.* y *vi.* plegar(se); arrugar(se).

create [krjéjt], *vt.* crear o criar. **—creation** [krjéjšọn], *s.* creación. **—creative** [krjéjtịv], *a.* creador. **—creativeness** [krjéjtịvnịs], *s.* facultad creadora. **—creator** [krjéjtọ(r)], *s.* creador.—*the C.,* el Creador, Dios. **—creature** [kríchū(r)], *s.* criatura.

creche [kreš], *s.* (igl.) belén.

credence [krídẹns], *s.* creencia; crédito. **—credentials** [krẹdénšạlz], *s. pl.* cartas credenciales.

credibility [kredịbílịti], *s.* credibilidad.—*c. gap,* margen de credibilidad.

credit [krédịt], *s.* crédito, fe; (com.) activo, haber.—*c. card,* tarjeta de crédito.—*on c.,* al fiado, a plazos.—*vt.* creer; atribuir; reconocer; acreditar; abonar en cuenta; dar al fiado.– **—able** [-ạbl], *a.* estimable, loable.– **—ed** [-id], *a.* acreditado.– **—or** [-ọ(r)], *s.* acreedor.

credulous [krédjuḷʌs], *a.* crédulo.

creed [krid], *s.* credo, creencia.

creek [krik], *s.* cala; riachuelo, arroyo.

creep [krip], *vii.* [10] arrastrarse; gatear; trepar; moverse cautelosamente; someterse abyectamente. —*s.* arrastramiento.—*pl.* hormigueo; pavor.– **—er** [krípœ(r)], *s.* reptil; enredadera; trepadora, trepador.

cremate [krímejt], *vt.* incinerar. **—cremation** [krịméjšọn], *s.* incineración.

creole [kríoụl], *s.* y *a.* criollo.

crepe [krejp], *s.* crespón; (for mourning) brazalete negro; (coc.) crep, crêpe, panqueque.

crept [krept], *pret.* y *pp.* DE TO CREEP.

crepuscular [krepʌ́skjuḷạ(r)], *a.* crepuscular. **—crepuscule** [krepʌ́skjul], *s.* crepúsculo.

crescent [krésẹnt], *a.* creciente.—*s.* (cuarto) creciente; media luna.

cress [kres], *s.* mastuerzo, berro.

crest [krest], *s.* cresta; penacho; cima;

blasón.- **—fallen** [kréstfɔlen], *a.* cabizbajo, abatido.

cretonne [krítan], *s.* (tej.) cretona.

crevice [krévɪs], *s.* hendedura, grieta.

crew [kru], *s.* tripulación o dotación; marinería; cuadrilla de obreros.— *pret.* de TO CROW.

crib [krɪb], *s.* pesebre; camita de niño; granero; arcón; casucha; plagio.—*c. death,* muerte de cuna.—*vti.* [1] hurtar; plagiar; enjaular; estribar.

cricket [kríkɪt], *s.* grillo; cri(c)quet.

crime [kraɪm], *s.* crimen, delito. — **criminal** [krímɪnəl], *a.* y *s.* criminal.

crimp [krɪmp], *vt.* rizar, encrespar, engrifar.—*a.* rizado.—*s.* rizo.

crimson [krímzɔn], *a.* y *s.* carmesí.

cripple [krípl], *s.* cojo o manco; tullido.—*vt.* lisiar, derrengar, baldar.

crisis [kráɪsɪs], (*pl.* **crises** [kráɪsiz]) *s.* crisis.

crisp [krɪsp], *a.* quebradizo; tostado; crespo; vivo, animado.—*vt.* encrespar; hacer frágil. **—y** [krɪspɪ], *a.* crespo, frágil; fresco.

criterion [kraɪtírɪɔn], *s.* criterio.

critic [krítɪk], *s.* crítico; censor; crítica.- **—al** [-əl], *a.* crítico, criticón; difícil; decisivo.- **—ism** [krítɪsɪzm], *s.* crítica; juicio crítico; censura.- **—ize, -ise** [krítɪsaɪz], *vt.* y *vi.* criticar.

croak [krouk], *vi.* graznar; croar; gruñir.—*s.* graznido, canto de ranas.

crochet [kroʃeɪ], *s.* crochet.—*c. hook,* aguja de crochet.—*vt.* tejer a crochet.

crock [krak], *s.* vasija de barro.- **—ery** [krákœrɪ], *s.* loza, cacharros.

crocodile [krákodaɪl], *s.* cocodrilo; caimán.

crony [króunɪ], *s.* (fam.) compinche, amigote.

crook [kruk], *s.* falsario, estafador; fullero; maleante; gancho, curva (tura).—*vt.* y *vi.* encorvar(se); torcer(se).- **—ed** [krúkɪd], *a.* encorvado; torcido; pícaro.

croon [krun], *vt.* cantar suavemente.— *vi.* cantar con voz suave.

crop [krap], *s.* cosecha; látigo; buche de ave.—*c. dusting,* aerofumigación, fumigación aérea.—*vti.* [1] segar, cosechar.—*vii.* dar frutos.

croquette [kroukét], *s.* (coc.) croqueta.

crosier [króuʒœ(r)], *s.* báculo pastoral.

cross [krɔs], *s.* cruz (sentidos recto y figurado); cruce; querella, encuentro; cruzamiento (de razas).—*a.* relativo o perteneciente a la cruz; atravesado, transversal; cruzado; malhumorado.—*c.-country,* a campo traviesa.—*c.-eyed,* bizco.—*c.-fertilization,* fecundación cruzada.—*c.-fertilize,* fecundar mediante fecundación cruzada.—*crossword puzzle,* crucigrama.—*vt.* cruzar, atravesar; marcar con una cruz; cruzar (razas); eliminar tachando; poner el trazo transversal a una letra; santiguarse; hacerse cruces.—*vi.* cruzarse.- **—bar** [krɔsbar], *s.* travesaño.- **—beam** [-bim], *s.* viga transversal.- **—fire** [-faɪr], *s.* fuego cruzado.—*to be caught in the c.,* estar entre dos fuegos.

crossing [krɔsɪŋ], *s.* cruce, intersección; paso, vado; travesía, acción de cruzar; cruzamiento (razas); santiguamiento. **—crossroad** [krɔsroud], *s.* cruce de dos caminos.

crouch [krautʃ], *vi.* agacharse, agazaparse; rebajarse.

crow [krou], *s.* cuervo; canto del gallo.—*c.'s foot,* pata de gallo (arrugas).—*vii.* [5] cantar el gallo.—*vi.* cantar victoria, alardear.- **—bar** [króubar], *s.* barra o palanca de hierro.

crowd [kraud], *s.* gentío, multitud; apiñamiento.—*vt.* amontonar, apiñar.—*vi.* apiñarse.- **—ed** [kráudɪd], *a.* apiñado; lleno de bote en bote.

crown [kraun], *s.* corona; diadema; guirnalda; monarca; soberanía; coronilla; copa de sombrero; cima.— *c. prince,* príncipe heredero.—*vt.* coronar.

crucible [krúsɪbl], *s.* crisol.

crucifix [krúsɪfɪks], *s.* crucifijo. **—crucify** [krúsɪfaɪ], *vti.* [7] crucificar.

crude [krud], *a.* crudo; imperfecto; tosco.- **—ness** [krúdnɪs], *s.* crudeza, tosquedad.

cruel [krúel], *a.* cruel.- **—ty** [-tɪ], *s.* crueldad.

cruet [krúɪt], *s.* ampoll(et)a; vinajera; vinagrera.—*c. stand,* convoy de mesa.

cruise [kruz], *vi.* cruzar, viajar de crucero; andar de un lado a otro.—*s.* crucero, viaje.—*c. missile,* misil de crucero.—*c. ship,* transatlántico.— *cruising speed,* velocidad de crucero—*world c.,* crucero alrededor del mundo.- **—r** [krúzœ(r)], *s.* (mar.) crucero.

crumb [krʌm], *s.* migaja, migajón;

pizca.—vt. desmig(aj)ar; desmenuzar.— **-le** [krámbl], vt. desmigar, desmenuzar.—vi. desmoronarse.

crumple [krámpl], vt. arrugar.—vi. contraerse, apabullarse.

crunch [kranch], vi. crujir; mascullar.—vt. tascar; cascar.—s. crujido.

crusade [kruséjd], s. cruzada.— **-r** [kruséjdœ(r)], s. cruzado.

crush [kraʃ], vt. romper por compresión; aplastar, machacar; estrujar; majar; abrumar.—vi. aplastarse; romperse o deformarse por compresión.—s. estrujamiento o deformación por compresión o choque.

crust [krast], s. costra; postilla; corteza (pan, queso, etc.); mendrugo; carapacho, concha.—vt. encostrar, incrustrar.—vi. encostrarse.

crustacean [krastéjʃjan], a. y s. crustáceo.

crusty [krásti], a. costroso; sarroso; brusco, malhumorado.

crutch [krach], s. muleta; arrimo; muletilla; horquilla; horcajadura, entrepierna.

cry [kraj], vti. y vii. [7] gritar; llorar; exclamar; lamentarse; vocear; pregonar.—s. grito; lloro, llanto; pregón.—a far c. from, muy lejos de.— **-ing** [krájiŋ], a. llorón, gritón; enorme; urgente.

crypt [kript], s. gruta, cripta.— **-ic** [kríptik], a. enigmático, oculto.

crystal [krístal], s. cristal; cristal de roca; cristal de reloj.—a. de cristal.—c. ball, bola de cristal.— **-line** [-in], a. cristalino.— **-lization** [-iʒéjʃon], s. cristalización.— **-lize** [-ajz], vt. y vi. cristalizar(se).

cub [kab], s. cachorro (de fiera).

Cuban [kjúban], a. y s. cubano.

cube [kjub], s. cubo.—c. root, raíz cúbica.— **-cubic** [kjúbik], a. cúbico.

cuckold [kákold], s. marido cornudo; cabrón, cuclillo.—vt. encornudar.

cuckoo [kúku], s. cuco; cucú (canto).—a. (fam.) chiflado.

cucumber [kjúkambœ(r)], s. pepino.—cool as a c., fresco como una lechuga.

cud [kad], s. rumia.—c.-chewing, rumiante.—to chew the c., rumiar; charlar.

cuddle [kádl], vt. abrazar con ternura; acariciar, mimar.—vi. abrazarse; estar abrazados.—s. abrazo.

cudgel [kádʒel], s. garrote, estaca, porra, cachiporra.

cue [kju], s. señal, indicación; (teat.) pie, apunte; indirecta, sugestión.—billiard c., taco de billar.

cuff [kaf], s. trompada; puño de camisa; bocamanga; vuelta del pantalón.—c. buttons o links, gemelos.—pl. manillas, esposas.—vt. abofetear; maniatar.—vi. darse puñetazos.

culinary [kjúlineri], a. culinario.

culminate [kálminejt], vi. culminar.—**culmination** [kalminéjʃon], s. culminación.

culprit [kálprit], s. reo, delincuente, culpable.

cult [kalt], s. culto, devoción; secta.

cultivate [káltivejt], vt. cultivar. —**cultivation** [kaltivéjʃon], s. cultivo.—**cultivator** [káltivejtœ(r)], s. labrador, cultivador; máquina cultivadora.

culture [kálchū(r)], s. cultura; cultivo (de bacterias, etc.).— **-d** [-d], a. culto, cultivado.

cumbersome [kámbœ(r)sam], a. pesado, engorroso.

cumulus [kjúmyūlas], s. montón; (meteor.) cúmulo.

cunning [kániŋ], a. astuto; socarrón; sutil; sagaz; gracioso, mono (aplícase a los niños).—s. astucia; sagacidad.

cup [kap], s. taza, jícara, pocillo; cubeta; cáliz; trago; (deportos) copa.—**board** [kábord], s. aparador.

cupola [kjúpolá], s. (arq.) cúpula, domo.

cur [kœr], s. perro callejero; canalla, bellaco.

curate [kjúrit], s. cura. —**curator** [kjúrejtœ(r)], s. conservador (de museo).

curb [kœrb], s. borde o encintado (de la acera); freno, restricción; barbada; brocal de pozo.—vt. refrenar, contener; poner freno o coto a.

curd [kœrd], s. cuajada; requesón.—vt. y vi. cuajar(se), coagular(se).—**le** [kœrdl], vt. y vi. cuajar(se), coagular(se); helar(se).

cure [kjur], s. cura, curación; remedio.—vt. curar; vulcanizar.—vi. vulcanizarse; curarse; sanarse.

curfew [kœrfju], s. toque de queda.

curio [kjúrjou], s. objeto curioso y raro.— **-sity** [kjurjásiti], s. curiosidad; rareza.— **-us** [kjúrjas], a. curioso; entremetido; cuidadoso; raro.

curl [kœrl], s. bucle, rizo; ondulación.—*vt.* rizar; fruncir.—*vi.* enroscarse; rizarse.

curlew [kɔ́erlju], *s.* chorlito.

curly [kɔ́erli], *a.* rizado, crespo.

currant [kɔ́erənt], *s.* grosella.

currency [kɔ́erensi], *s.* moneda corriente; dinero en circulación; uso corriente; valor corriente. **—current** [kɔ́erent], *a.* corriente, común; actual, en curso.—*c. account,* cuenta corriente.—*c. events,* sucesos de actualidad.—*s.* corriente (de aire, agua, etc.).—*direct c.,* corriente continua.

curriculum [kʌríkyūlʌm], *s.* plan de estudios.

curse [kœrs], *vt.* maldecir.—*vi.* renegar; blasfemar.—*s.* maldición; terno.—**d** [kœrsi̯d], *a.* maldito.

curt [kœrt], *a.* brusco; conciso.— **—ail** [kœrtéi̯l], *vt.* cortar; abreviar; restringir.

curtain [kɔ́ertin], *s.* cortina; (teat.) telón.—*c. call,* (teat.) salida a escena.—*pl.* cortinaje.

curvature [kɔ́ervachu̱(r)], *s.* curvatura, encorvamiento. **—curve** [kœrv], *vt.* curvar, combar, encorvar.—*vi.* encorvarse; torcerse.—*s.* curva; curvadura, comba. **—curved** [kœrvd], *a.* curvo; encorvado; combado.

cushion [kúši̱on], *s.* cojín; almohadilla; almohadón; amortiguador.—*vt.* acojinar, suavizar, amortiguar.

cusp [kʌsp], *s.* cúspide.

custard [kʌ́stərd], *s.* flan, natillas.—*c. apple,* guanábana, anona.

custody [kʌ́stodi̱], *s.* custodia, guardia.

custom [kʌ́stom], *s.* costumbre; usanza; clientela o parroquia. —*c.-made,* hecho a la medida; (furniture) hecho de encargo.—*pl.* derechos de aduana o arancelarios.- **—ary** [-eri̱], *a.* habitual, acostumbrado.- **—er** [-œ(r)], *s.* parroquiano, cliente.- **—shouse** [-shaus], *s.* aduana.

cut [kʌt], *vti.* [9] cortar; dividir, partir; rebanar; grabar; labrar, tallar; segar; desbastar; recortar; negar el saludo a; cortar los naipes; rebajar, reducir (sueldos, gastos, etc.); cortar (trajes).—*to c. across,* cruzar, atravesar, cortar al través.—*to c. a figure,* descollar; hacer buen papel.—*to c. asunder,* separar cortando, despedazar.—*to c. away,* recortar.—*to c. capers,* hacer cabriolas.—*to c. down,* tumbar; talar; mermar, rebajar, cercenar.—*to c. off,* cercenar; aislar; interceptar (la comunicación); interrumpir; suspender los abastecimientos; desheredar.—*to c. up,* trinchar; despedazar.—*vii.* hacer un corte o incisión; ser cortante.— *pret.* y *pp.* de TO CUT.—*s.* corte; cortadura, incisión; tajo; ofensa; cosa o palabra hiriente; ausencia (de una clase, etc.); pedazo, cosa cortada; atajo; rebaja (sueldos, gastos, etc.); clisé, grabado; talla.—*a.* cortado.—*c. and dried,* preparado, convenido de antemano.—*c. glass,* cristal tallado.

cute [kjut], *a.* lindo, mono, gracioso; listo.

cuticle [kjútikl], *s.* cutícula; película.

cutlass [kátlas], *s.* alfanje.

cutler [kátlœ(r)], *s.* cuchillero.- **—y** [-i], *s.* cuchillería, cuchillos; tienda del cuchillero.

cutlet [kátli̱t], *s.* chuleta.

cutoff [kátɔf], *s.* atajo.—*c. date,* fecha límite.—*c. point,* límite.

cutter [kátœ(r)], *s.* cortador; herramienta o máquina para cortar. **—cutting** [kátiɲ], *a.* cortante; de cortar; incisivo, mordaz.—*s.* cortadura; corte; incisión.

cuttlefish [kátlfi̱š], *s.* (ict.) pulpo.

cyanide [saíanai̱d], *s.* cianuro.

cycle [sái̱kl], *s.* ciclo; bicicleta.—*vi.* andar en bicicleta. **—cycling** [sái̱kliɲ], *s.* ciclismo.

cyclone [sái̱kloun], *s.* ciclón.

cyclotron [sái̱klotran], *s.* ciclotrón.

cylinder [síli̱ndœ(r)], *s.* cilindro; rodillo; tambor.

cymbal [símbal], *s.* címbalo, platillo.

cynic [síni̱k], *s.* cínico.- **—al** [-al], *a.* cínico.- **—ism** [síni̱si̱zm], *s.* cinismo.

cypress [sái̱pres], *s.* ciprés.

Czech [chɛk], *s.* y *a.* checo.— **—oslovak(ian)** [-oslovák(i̱an)], *s.* y *a.* checo(e)slovaco.

D

dab [dæb], s. toque ligero.—vt. tocar ligeramente.- **—ble** [-běl], vt. salpicar, rociar, mojar.—to d. in, meterse en.- **—r** [dǽblœ(r)], s. aficionado, diletante.

dad [dæd], **daddie, daddy** [dǽdi], s. papá, papaíto; (Am.) papacito, tata.

dado [déjdou], s. (arq.) rodapié.

daffodil [dǽfodil], s. narciso.

daft [dæft], a. tonto, bobo; loco.

dagger [dǽgœ(r)], s. daga, puñal.

daily [déjli], a. diario, cotidiano, diurno.—s. periódico diario.—adv. diariamente.

daintiness [déjntinis], s. delicadeza, elegancia. **—dainty** [déjnti], a. delicado, elegante, refinado; sabroso; melindroso.—s. golosina.

dairy [déri], s. lechería; quesería; vaquería.

daisy [déjzi], s. margarita; (fam.) primor.—d. wheel, (impr.) margarita.

dale [dejl], s. valle; cañada.

dam [dæm], s. (re)presa, embalse, dique; central hidroeléctrica.—vti. [1] represar, embalsar.

damage [dǽmidž], s. daño, perjuicio, deterioro; pérdida; avería.—pl. daños y perjuicios.—vt. dañar, averiar, deteriorar; perjudicar; damnificar.—vi. dañarse, averiarse.

dame [déjm], s. dama, señora; (col.) tía, fulana.

damn [dæm], vt. maldecir; reprobar.—d. it! ¡maldito sea!—vi. renegar, maldecir.—s. maldición.

damp [dæmp], a. húmedo, mojado.—s. humedad; desaliento. **—d.** o **—dampen** [dǽmpen], vt. humedecer, mojar; desanimar, desalentar; amortiguar.—vi. humedecerse.- **—er** [-œ(r)], a. registro, regulador de tiro de chimenea; sordina; desalentador; amortiguador.- **—ness** [-nis], s. humedad, relente.

damsel [dǽmzěl], s. damisela, doncella.

dance [dæns], vi. bailar, danzar.—s. danza, baile. **—r** [dǽnsœ(r)], s. bailarín(a); bailador(a).

dandelion [dǽndilajon], s. (bot.) diente de león.

dandruff [dǽndrʌf], s. caspa.

dandy [dǽndi], s. dandi, petimetre, lechuguino.—a. (fam.) excelente, magnífico.

Dane [dejn], s. danés, dinamarqués.—great D., perro danés.

danger [déjndžœ(r)], s. peligro, riesgo.- **—ous** [-ʌs], a. peligroso, arriesgado; grave, de cuidado.

dangle [dǽngl], vt. colgar, suspender.—vi. pender, bambolearse; andar al retortero.

Danish [déjniš], a. danés, dinamarqués.—D. pastry, bollo cubierto de azúcar glaseado.—s. danés; lengua danesa.

dapple(d) [dǽpl(d)], a. rodado, tordo, con manchas, salpicado.

dare [der], vii. [5] osar, atreverse, arriesgarse.—vti. retar, desafiar; provocar.—s. reto, desafío.- **—devil** [dérdevil], a. y s. temerario, osado. **—daring** [dérin], a. osado, temerario; denodado.—s. osadía, bravura.

dark [dark], a. oscuro; trigueño, moreno; sombrío, tenebroso; siniestro.—dark horse, ganador sorpresa.—the D. Ages, la Alta Edad Media, la Edad de las tinieblas.—to be left in the d., dejar en ayunas, en la ignorancia.—to grow d., anochecer, oscurecer.—to keep it d., ocultar algo.—s. oscuridad; tinieblas; noche; anochecer; ignorancia, secreto.- **—en** [dárkn], vt. oscurecer, ensombrecer; cegar; nublar; denigrar, manchar.—vi. oscurecerse, nublarse.- **—ness** [-nis], s. oscuridad, sombra, tinieblas; ofuscación; ceguera; ignorancia.- **—room** [-rum], s. (fot.) cuarto oscuro.

darling [dárlin], a. querido, amado.—s. querido, el predilecto.—my d., vida mía, amor mío.—you are a d., eres un encanto.

darn [darn], vt. zurcir, remendar; (fam.) maldecir.—s. zurcido.—I don't give a d., me importa un bledo.

darnel [dárněl], s. (bot.) cizaña.

darning [dárnin], s. zurcido, remiendo.

dart [dart], s. dardo, saeta; banderilla; movimiento rápido; (cost.) sisa.—

d. thrower, banderillero.—*vt.* lanzar, flechar.—*vi.* lanzarse, precipitarse.— **—board** [-bɔrd], *s.* diana.

dash [dæš], *vt.* arrojar, tirar, lanzar; estrellar, romper; magullar; frustrar (esperanzas); rociar, salpicar; sazonar.—*to d. out,* tachar.—*to d. to pieces,* hacer añicos.—*vi.* chocar, estrellarse; lanzarse; saltar.—*s.* arremetida; ataque; choque, embate; guión, raya; energía; condimento; poquito, pizca; carrera corta.— **—board** [dǽšbɔrd], *s.* (aut.) tablero de instrumentos, cuadro de mandos.

data [déjtə, dǽtə], *s.* (*pl.* de DATUM [déjtʌm]) datos, información; (comput.) datos.—*d. bank,* banco de datos.—*d. capture,* formulación de datos, toma de datos.—*d. dictionary, d. directory,* guía de datos.—*d. file,* archivo de datos.—*d. link,* medio de transmisión de datos.—*d. preparation,* preparación de datos.—*d. processing,* proceso de datos.—*d. procesor,* procesador de datos.—*d. protection,* protección de datos.—*d. transmission,* transmisión de datos, telemática.— **—base** [-bejs], *s.* base de datos.

date [dejt], *s.* fecha; cita, compromiso; época; (bot.) dátil.—*d. palm,* palma datilera.—*down to d.,* hasta la fecha, hasta ahora.—*out of d.,* anticuado, pasado de moda.—*up to d.,* hasta ahora; al día.—*vt.* datar, fechar; computar; dar cita a uno.—*vi.* (con **from**) datar (de), remontarse a.

datum [déjtʌm], *s.* dato.

daub [dɔb], *vt.* embadurnar; untar; pintarrajear.

daughter [dɔ́tœ(r)], *s.* hija.—*d.-in-law,* nuera.

dawn [dɔn], *vi.* amanecer, alborear, clarear; asomar, mostrarse.—*to d. (up)on,* ocurrírsele a uno, caer en la cuenta.—*s.* alba, aurora, madrugada; albores.— **—ing** [dɔ́nin], *s.* alborada.

day [dej], *s.* día.—*d. after tomorrow,* pasado mañana.—*d. bed,* sofá cama.—*d. before yesterday,* anteayer.—*d. in, d. out,* día tras día, sin cesar.—*d. laborer,* jornalero.—*days of obligation,* fiestas de guardar.—*d.-star,* lucero del alba.—*d. wages,* jornal.—*every other d.,* cada dos días.— **—book** [déjbuk], *s.* libro de cuentas diarias.— **—break** [-brejk],

s. amanecer.– **—dream** [-drim], *s.* ensueño, ilusión.—*vi.* soñar despierto.— **—light** [-lajt], *s.* luz del día, luz natural.—*d. saving time,* hora de verano (E.U.).

daze [dejz], *vt.* ofuscar, aturdir, trastornar.—*s.* deslumbramiento, ofuscamiento.

dazzle [dǽzl], *vt.* deslumbrar, ofuscar, encandilar; camuflar.—*s.* deslumbramiento.

deacon [díkɔn], *s.* diácono.

dead [ded], *a.* muerto; inerte; marchito.—*d. center,* punto muerto.—*d. end,* callejón sin salida.—*d. eye,* tirador certero.—*d. pan (face),* (cara) inalterable.—*d. stop,* parada en seco.—*d. weight,* carga onerosa; tara.—*d. wood,* leña seca; material inútil; gente inútil.—*s. pl.* los muertos.—*the d. of night,* lo más profundo de la noche.—*adv.* entera o absolutamente; del todo; repentinamente.—*d. drunk,* borracho perdido.—*d. tired,* agotado.– **—en** [dédn], *vt.* amortiguar; quitar brillo, sonido, etc.— **—beat** [-bit], *s.* (fam.) gorrón; (fam.) holgazán.– **—line** [-lajn], *s.* línea vedada; término, plazo final.– **—lock** [-lak], *s.* detención, paro, estancamiento.– **—ly** [-li], *a.* mortal; fatal; fulminante; implacable.– **—ness** [-njs], *s.* inercia; amortiguamiento.

deaf [def], *a.* sordo.—*d.-mute,* sordomudo.– **—en** [défn], *vt.* ensordecer.— **—ening** [-ɛnin], *a.* ensordecedor.— **—ness** [-njs], *s.* sordera; ensordecimiento.

deal [dil], *s.* trato, negocio; pacto o convenio; mano (en el juego de naipes); porción; parte.—*a great d.,* mucho, una gran cantidad.—*vti.* [10] distribuir, repartir; dar (los naipes); asestar (un golpe).—*to d. out,* dispensar.—*vii.* negociar, traficar, gestionar; mediar; dar (en el juego de baraja).— **—er** [dílœ(r)], *s.* comerciante, negociante, agente de comercio; el mano (en el juego de baraja).— **—ing** [-iŋ], *s.* conducta; trato; negocio.—*pl.* negocios; transacciones. **—dealt** [delt], *pret.* y *pp.* de TO DEAL.

dean [din], *s.* deán; decano.

dear [dir], *a.* querido, amado; costoso, caro.—*s.* persona querida, bien amado.—*d. me!* ¡válgame Dios!—*d. sir(s),* muy señor(es) mío(s), o nuestro(s).

dearth [dœrθ], *s.* carestía, escasez.

death [dɛθ], *s.* muerte; defunción, fallecimiento; mortandad.—*d. certificate*, partida de defunción.—*d. dealing*, mortífero.—*d. knell*, toque de difuntos.—*d. mask*, mascarilla.—*d. rate*, mortalidad.—*d. rattle*, estertor.—*d. row*, pabellón de los condenados a muerte.—*d. struggle*, agonía.—*d. wound*, herida mortal.—*to be in the d. house*, estar en capilla.- **—bed** [-bɛd], *s.* lecho de muerte.- **—less** [dɛθlɪs], *a.* inmortal.- **—watch** [-wach], *s.* velorio.

debarkation [dɪbarkéɪʃŏn], *s.* = DISEMBARKATION.

debase [dɪbéɪs], *vt.* rebajar, deshonrar.

debatable [dɪbéɪtǎbl], *a.* discutible, disputable. **—debate** [dɪbéɪt], *s.* discusión, debate, disputa.—*vt.* disputar, controvertir; considerar.—*vi.* deliberar, discutir.

debauchery [dɛbɔ́chěrɪ], *s.* libertinaje, corrupción.

debenture [dɪbénchŭ(r)], *s.* bono; obligación; pagaré del gobierno.

debit [débɪt], *s.* débito, cargo; egreso; debe (de una cuenta).—*d. balance*, saldo deudor.—*vt.* adeudar, cargar en cuenta.

debonair [dɛbonér], *a.* cortés, afable; elegante, gallardo.

debrief [dɛbríf], *vt.* interrogar para conseguir datos informativos.- **—ing** [-ɪŋ], *s.* interrogación para conseguir datos informativos.

debris [dǎbrí], *s.* escombros, restos, ruinas; despojos.

debt [dɛt], *s.* deuda, débito; obligación.—*to run into d.*, endeudarse, entramparse.- **—or** [déto(r)], *s.* deudor.

debug [dɛbág], *vt.* localizar y retirar los micrófonos ocultos de; (comput.) depurar.

debunk [dɛbáŋk], *vt.* (jer.) desacreditar; desenmascarar.

debut [dǎbiú], *s.* estreno; presentación de una señorita en sociedad.

decade [dékeɪd], *s.* decenio, década.

decadence [dɪkéɪdens], *s.* decadencia. **—decadent** [dɪkéɪdɛnt], *a.* decadente, decaído.

decaffeinated [dɛkáefĕneɪtɪd], *a.* descafeinado, sin cafeína.

decant [dɪkǽnt], *vt.* decantar.- **—er** [-ɛr], *s.* garrafa, licorera.

decapitate [dɪkǽpɪteɪt], *vt.* decapitar,

degollar. **—decapitation** [dɪkæpɪtéɪʃŏn], *s.* decapitación.

decathlon [dɛkáeθlon], *s.* decatlón.

decay [dɪkéɪ], *vi.* decaer, declinar; deteriorarse; carcomerse; cariarse; pudrirse, dañarse; picarse.—*s.* decaimiento, decadencia; ruina; caries; podredumbre.

decease [dɪsís], *s.* fallecimiento, defunción.—*vi.* morir, fallecer.- **—d** [-t], *s. y a.* difunto, finado.

deceit [dɪsít], *s.* engaño, fraude, falacia, trampa.- **—ful** [-fŭl], *a.* engañoso, falso; mentiroso. **—deceive** [dɪsív], *vt.* engañar, embaucar, defraudar.

December [dɪsémbœ(r)], *s.* diciembre.

decency [dísensɪ], *s.* decencia; pudor.

decennial [dɪsénjąl], *a.* decenal.

decent [dísent], *a.* decente; razonable, módico.

deception [dɪsépʃŏn], *s.* engaño, fingimiento, impostura.

decide [dɪsáɪd], *vt. y vi.* decidir, determinar, resolver.- **—d** [-ɪd], *a.* decidido, resuelto.

decimal [désɪmąl], *s. y a.* decimal.—*d. point*, punto decimal; (usually a comma is used for the decimal point in Spanish) coma decimal, coma de decimales. **—decimate** [désɪmeɪt], *vt.* diezmar.

decipher [dɪsáɪfœ(r)], *vt.* descifrar, interpretar; aclarar.

decision [dɪsíʒŏn], *s.* decisión, resolución; entereza; (for.) fallo, auto, providencia. **—decisive** [dɪsáɪsɪv], *a.* decisivo; terminante, perentorio.

deck [dɛk], *vt.* ataviar, engalanar.—*s.* cubierta (de un buque); baraja.—*d. chair*, (mar.) silla de cubierta, perezosa.—*d. hand*, marinero de cubierta.

declaim [dɪkléɪm], *vi.* declamar, perorar.

declaration [deklạréɪʃŏn], *s.* declaración; exposición; manifiesto. **—declare** [dɪklér], *vt. y vi.* declarar, manifestar; deponer.

declassify [dɪklǽsɪfaɪ], *vt.* levantar el secreto oficial de.

declension [dɪklénʃŏn], *s.* (gram.) declinación.

decline [dɪkláɪn], *vt.* rehusar; (gram.) declinar.—*vi.* rehusar, negarse (a); declinar, decaer.—*s.* declinio; declive. **—declivity** [dɪklívɪtɪ], *s.* declive.

dècolletage [deikaltáʒ], *s.* escote; traje escotado.

decompose [dikọmpóuz], *vt.* descomponer; pudrir.—*vi.* pudrirse, corromperse. **—decomposition** [dikampozíʃọn], *s.* descomposición; corrupción, putrefacción.

decongestant [díkọndžéstạnt], *a.* y *s.* descongestionante.

decorate [dékoreit], *vt.* decorar, adornar; condecorar. **—decoration** [dɛkoréiʃọn], *s.* decoración; adorno, ornamento, condecoración, insignia. **—decorative** [dékorạtiv], *a.* decorativo, ornamental. **—decorator** [dékoreitọ(r)], *s.* decorador.

decorous [dékọrʌs], *a.* decoroso.

decorum [dikórʌm], *s.* decoro, honor; corrección.

decoy [dikói], *vt.* atraer con señuelo o añagaza.—*s.* señuelo, añagaza, reclamo.

decrease [dikrís], *vi.* decrecer.—*vi.* y *vt.* disminuir, reducir, mermar.—*s.* disminución; merma; menguante; decadencia.

decree [dikrí], *vt.* y *vi.* decretar, mandar.—*s.* decreto, edicto, mandato, ley.

decrepit [dikrépit], *a.* decrépito, caduco.

dedicate [dédikeit], *vt.* dedicar; aplicar. **—dedication** [dedikéiʃọn], *s.* dedicación, dedicatoria.

deduce [didiús], *vt.* deducir, inferir; derivar.

deduct [didákt], *vt.* deducir, restar, su(b)straer, rebajar, descontar.– **—ion** [didákʃọn], *s.* deducción; su(b)stracción; descuento, rebaja; conclusión.

deed [did], *s.* acto, hecho, hazaña; (for.) escritura.

deep [dip], *a.* profundo, hondo; abstruso, recóndito; intenso (color); (mus.) grave; sagaz.—*d. blue,* turquí.—*d.-freeze,* congelar, ultracongelar.—*d. freezer,* congelador, freezer.—*d. freezing,* congelación, ultracongelación.—*d.-fry,* freír en aceite abundante.—*d. fryer,* freidora.—*d. sea,* alta mar.—*d.-sea fishing,* pesca mayor, pesca de profundidad.—*d. space,* (astr.) espacio interplanetario.—*d. structure,* (ling.) estructura profunda.— *adv.* profundamente.—*d.-rooted, d.-seated,* profundamente arraigado. —*d. in thought,* abstraído.—*s.* profundidad(es); piélago, mar.– **—en**

[dipn], *vt.* profundizar, ahondar; oscurecer; entristecer.—*vi.* hacerse más hondo, más profundo o más intenso.– **—ly** [-li], *adv.* profundamente.- **—ness** [-nịs], *s.* profundidad, hondura; intensidad.

deer [dir], *s.* venado, ciervo.

deface [diféis], *vt.* afear, desfigurar, mutilar.

default [difólt], *s.* omisión; incumplimiento de una obligación; insolvencia; falta; (for.) rebeldía.—*vt.* y *vi.* faltar; no pagar; (for.) no comparecer.— **—er** [-œ(r)], *s.* desfalcador; rebelde.

defeat [difít], *s.* derrota; frustración; (for.) anulación.—*vt.* derrotar, vencer; frustrar; anular.- **—ist** [-ist], *s.* y *a.* derrotista.

defect [difékt], *s.* defecto, falta, tacha.– **—ion** [difékʃọn], *s.* deserción; defección; abandono.- **—ive** [diféktiv], *a.* defectuoso; falto de inteligencia; (gram.) defectivo.- **—or** [-ọr], *s.* desertor.

defend [difénd], *vt.* defender, proteger.- **—ant** [-ạnt], *a.* acusado; que defiende.—*s.* demandado, acusado, procesado.- **—er** [-œ(r)], *s.* defensor, protector. **—defense** [diféns], *s.* defensa, protección.—*d. attorney,* abogado defensor. **—defenseless** [difénslịs], *a.* indefenso; inerme. **—defensive** [difénsiv], *a.* defensivo.—*s.* defensiva.

defer [difœr], *vti.* [1] diferir, aplazar, retrasar; remitir.—*vii.* demorarse; (con **to**) ceder, acatar, consentir.- **—ence** [défẹrẹns], *s.* deferencia, acatamiento, respeto.

defiance [difáiạns], *s.* desafío, reto; oposición. **—defiant** [difáiạnt], *a.* retador, provocador.

deficiency [difíṣẹnṣị], *s.* deficiencia, defecto. **—deficient** [difíṣẹnt], *a.* deficiente; defectuoso.

defile [difáil], *vi.* (mil.) desfilar.—*vt.* manchar, profanar, viciar, corromper.—*s.* desfiladero.

define [difáin], *vt.* definir; limitar; fijar; determinar. **—definite** [définit], *a.* definido, exacto, categórico, preciso. **—definition** [definíʃọn], *s.* definición. **—definitive** [difínitiv], *a.* definitivo, decisivo, terminante.

deflate [difléit], *vt.* desinflar; reducir (valores, etc.). **—deflation** [difléiʃọn], *s.* deflación; desinflación.

deflect [diflékt], *vt.* y *vi.* desviar(se), apartar(se), ladear(se).

deflower [dɪfláuœ(r)], vt. desflorar; violar.

deform [dɪfórm], vt. deformar, desfigurar, afear.– **—ation** [dɪforméjṣọn], s. deformación, desfiguración.– **—ed** [dɪfórmd], a. deformado, desfigurado; deforme, contrahecho.– **—ity** [dɪfórmɪtɪ], s. deformidad; deformación; fealdad.

defraud [dɪfród], vt. defraudar, estafar.– **—er** [-œ(r)], s. defraudador, estafador.

defray [dɪfréj], vt. costear, sufragar.

defrost [dɪfróst], vt. descongelar, deshelar.

deft [deft], a. diestro, hábil.– **—ness** [déftnɪs], s. destreza, habilidad.

defunct [dɪfʌ́ŋkt], a. y s. difunto.

defy [dɪfái], vti. [7] desafiar, retar.

degenerate [dɪdʒénereɪt], vi. degenerar.—s. y a. [dɪdʒénerɪt], degenerado.

degradation [degrȧdéjṣọn], s. degradación; degeneración; corrupción. **—degrade** [dɪgréjd], vt. degradar; rebajar.—vi. degenerar; envilecerse.

degree [dɪgrí], s. grado; título; cuantía.—*by degrees*, gradualmente, poco a poco.—*to take a d.*, graduarse.

dehumidifier [diyumídɪfajœr], s. deshumedecedor.

deign [dejn], vt. y vi. dignarse, condescender.

deity [díjtɪ], s. deidad, divinidad.

dejected [dɪdʒéktɪd], a. acongojado, abatido.— **—dejection** [dɪdʒékṣọn], s. melancolía, abatimiento, desaliento; deposición.

delay [dɪléj], vt. dilatar, demorar, retardar; entretener.—vi. tardar, demorarse.—s. dilación, tardanza, demora.

delectable [dɪléktȧbl], a. delicioso, deleitable. **—delectation** [dɪlektéjṣọn], s. deleite, deleitación.

delegate [délēgeɪt], vt. delegar, comisionar.—a. y s. delegado, comisorio. **—delegation** [delēgéjṣọn], s. delegación, comisión.

delete [dɪlít], vt. tachar, borrar, suprimir.

deliberate [dɪlíbereɪt], vt. y vi. deliberar, reflexionar.—a. [dɪlíberɪt], deliberado, premeditado; cauto. **—deliberation** [dɪlɪberéjṣọn], s. deliberación, reflexión, premeditación.

delicacy [délɪkȧsɪ], s. delicadeza; sua-

vidad; ternura; fragilidad; manjar, golosina. **—delicate** [délɪkɪt], a. delicado, frágil; suave; fino; tierno; exquisito. **—delicatessen** [delɪkȧtésẹn], s. delicatessen, charcutería, fiambrería y rotisería, salsamentaria, salchichonería.

delicious [dɪlíʌs], a. delicioso, sabroso, rico.

delight [dɪlájt], s. deleite, delicia, encanto.—vt. deleitar, encantar, recrear.—vi. deleitarse, recrearse, complacerse (en).— **—ed** [-ɪd], a. encantado, contentísimo.—*to be d. to,* tener mucho gusto en; alegrarse muchísimo de.— **—ful** [-fʊl], a. delicioso, encantador.

delineate [dɪlínjeɪt], vt. delinear, trazar, diseñar. **—delineator** [dɪlínjeto(r)], s. delineante.

delinquency [dɪlíŋkwẹnsɪ], s. delincuencia. **—delinquent** [dɪlíŋkwẹnt], s. y a. delincuente.

delirious [dɪlíriʌs], a. delirante, desvariado.—*to be d.,* delirar, desvariar. **—delirium** [dɪlíriʌm], s. delirio, desvarío; devaneo.

deliver [dɪlívœ(r)], vt. entregar; libertar; pronunciar (conferencia, discurso, etc.); descargar, asestar (un golpe); despachar (un pedido); transmitir (energía, etc.).—*to d. a baby,* dar a luz.– **—ance**[-ạns], s. rescate, liberación.– **—er** [-œ(r)], s. libertador; repartidor, mensajero.– **—y** [-ɪ], s. entrega; distribución o reparto; remesa; liberación, rescate; dicción, forma de expresión; cesión; parto; (mec.) descarga, proyección.—*d. man,* recadero, mensajero.

dell [dɛl], s. cañada.

delude [dɪliúd], vt. engañar, alucinar.

deluge [déljudʒ], s. diluvio, inundación; calamidad.—vt. inundar.

delusion [dɪliúʒọn], s. error; ilusión; decepción, engaño.

demagogue [démȧgag], s. demagogo. **—demagogy** [démagadʒɪ], s. demagogia.

demand [dɪmænd], vt. demandar; exigir, reclamar.—s. demanda; exigencia.—*on d.,* a la presentación; a solicitud.—*to be in d.,* tener demanda, ser solicitado.– **—ing** [-ɪŋ], a. exigente.

demeanor [dɪmínọ(r)], s. conducta, comportamiento, proceder; porte, semblante.

demented [dɪméntɪd], a. demente.

demerit [dímẹrịt], *s.* demérito, desmerecimiento.

demijohn [démịdẑan], *s.* botellón.

demise [dimáịz], *s.* defunción, fallecimiento.

demobilize [dimóųbịlaịz], *vt.* desmovilizar.

democracy [dimákrạsị], *s.* democracia. **—democrat** [démokræt], *s.* demócrata. **—democratic** [dɛmokrǽtịk], *a.* democrático.

demolish [dimálịš], *vt.* demoler, derribar.– **—er** [-œ(r)], *s.* demoledor. **—demolition** [dɛmolíšọn], *s.* demolición, derribo, arrasamiento.

demon [dímọn], *s.* demonio, diablo.

demonstrate [démọnstreịt], *vt.* demostrar, probar. **—demonstration** [dɛmọnstréišọn], *s.* demostración, muestra; prueba; manifestación pública. **—demonstrative** [dịmánstrạtịv], *a.* demostrativo; efusivo. **—demonstrator** [démọnstreịto(r)], *s.* manifestante.

demoralization [dịmarạlịzéišọn], *s.* desmoralización. **—demoralize** [dịmáralaịz], *vt.* desmoralizar.

demur [dịmœr], *vi.* objetar.

demure [dịmyúr], *a.* recatado, modesto; sobrio, grave.

den [dɛn], *s.* cueva, guarida, cuchitril, pocilga; gabinete (de estudio).

dengue [déŋgeị], *s.* (med.) dengue.

denial [dịnáịal], *s.* negación, negativa, desmentida; denegación.

denominate [dịnámịneịt], *vt.* denominar, nombrar.–*a.* denominado. **—denomination** [dịnamịnéišọn], *s.* denominación, título, designación; confesión. **—denominator** [dịnámịneịto(r)], *s.* (arit.) denominador.

denote [dịnóųt], *vt.* denotar, señalar.

denouement [deịnúman], *s.* desenlace.

denounce [dịnáųns], *vt.* denunciar, delatar.

dense [dɛns], *a.* denso, espeso, tupido; estúpido. **—density** [dénsịtị], *s.* densidad, espesura; estupidez.

dent [dɛnt], *s.* abolladura; mella; hendidura.—*vt.* y *vi.* abollar(se), mellar(se).

dental [déntạl], *a.* dental.—*d. floss,* hilo dental.—*d. plate,* dentadura postiza.—*d. surgeon,* cirujano dentista. **—dentist** [déntịst], *s.* dentista, odontólogo. **—dentistry** [déntịstrị], *s.* odontología. **—denture** [dénchų(r)], *s.* dentadura postiza.

denunciation [dịnʌnsịéišọn], *s.* denuncia, acusación.

deny [dịnáị], *vti.* [7] negar; denegar; desmentir; negarse a.—*vii.* negar.

deodorant [dióụdọrạnt], *s.* desodorante.

depart [dịpárt], *vi.* irse, partir, salir; apartarse, desviarse; morir.—*the departed,* los difuntos.

department [dịpártmẹnt], *s.* departamento; compartimiento; sección (en una tienda, etc.); oficina, negociado; ministerio; distrito.—*d. store,* grandes almacenes, bazar.

departure [dịpárhü(r)], *s.* partida, salida, ida, marcha; desviación.

depend [dịpénd], *vi.* depender.—*to d. on* o *upon,* depender de; contar con; confiar en; necesitar (de); ser mantenido por.– **—able** [-ạbl], *a.* formal, seguro, digno de confianza.– **—ence** [-ẹns], *s.* dependencia; confianza; sostén, apoyo.– **—ency** [-ẹnsị], *s.* dependencia.– **—ent** [-ẹnt], *a.* y *s.* dependiente, subalterno.—*s.* familiar mantenido.

depict [dịpíkt], *vt.* pintar; representar; describir.

deplorable [dịplórạbl], *a.* deplorable; lastimoso. **—deplore** [dịplór], *vt.* deplorar.

deploy [dịplóị], *vt.* y *vi.* (mil.) desplegar(se).—*s.* despliegue.

depopulate [dịpápyuleịt], *vt.* y *vi.* despoblar(se).

deport [dịpórt], *vt.* deportar.—*v.* (com)portarse, conducirse.– **—ation** [-éịšọn], *s.* deportación.– **—ment** [-mẹnt], *s.* conducta, comportamiento.

depose [dịpóųz], *vt.* deponer; destronar; (for.) declarar, atestiguar.—*vi.* deponer, testificar.

deposit [dịpázịt], *vt.* depositar.—*vi.* depositarse.—*s.* depósito; sedimiento; (geol., min.) yacimiento, filón. **—deposition** [depozíšọn], *s.* deposición, testimonio; destitución. **—depositor** [dịpázịtọ(r)], *s.* depositante.

depot [dípoụ], *s.* depósito, almacén; paradero de tren.

deprave [dịpréịv], *vt.* depravar, pervertir.– **—d** [-d], *a.* depravado. **—depravity** [dịprǽvịtị], *s.* depravación.

depreciate [dịpríšịeịt], *vt.* depreciar, abaratar; menospreciar.—*vi.* abaratarse; depreciarse.

depress [dịprés], *vt.* deprimir, abatir;

abaratar, rebajar el precio de; hundir.– **—ion** [dɪpréṣǝn], s. depresión, abatimiento; concavidad; hondonada.

deprivation [dɛprɪvéiṣǝn], s. privación; pérdida. **—deprive** [dɪpráɪv], vt. privar, despojar.

depth [dɛpθ], s. profundidad; hondura; fondo; espesor, grueso (de una cosa); viveza (color); gravedad (sonido); penetración.—*d. bomb*, carga de profundidad.

deputy [dépɪutɪ], s. diputado; delegado, agente.

derail [dɪréɪl], vt. y vi. descarrilar(se).– **—ment** [-mǝnt], s. descarrilamiento.

derange [dɪréndz], vt. desarreglar; volver loco, desquiciar.– **—d** [dɪréndzd], a. trastornado, desquiciado.– **—ment** [-mǝnt], s. desarreglo; trastorno mental.

derby [dʌrbɪ], s. sombrero hongo; carrera.

derelict [dérɛlɪkt], a. negligente.—s. persona sin amparo; golfo, indigente.

deride [dɪráɪd], vt. ridiculizar, escarnecer, burlarse o mofarse de.– **—r** [dɪráɪdœ(r)], s. burlón. **—derision** [dɪríẓǝn], s. mofa, escarnio. **—derisive** [dɪráɪsɪve], a. burlesco.

derive [dɪráɪv], vt. deducir (una conclusión); derivar.—vi. derivar, provenir, emanar.

derrick [dérɪk], s. grúa, cabria; armazón de un pozo de petróleo.

descend [dɪséndl], vt. y vi. descender, bajar; (con **to**) rebajarse a; (con **up o upon**) invadir, caer en o sobre.– **—ant** [-ǝnt], s. descendiente.– **—ent** [-ǝnt], a. descend(i)ente; originario (de). **—descent** [dɪsént], s. descenso, bajada; descendimiento; declive; alcurnia, descendencia, sucesión.

describe [dɪskráɪb], vt. describir, pintar. **—description** [dɪskrípṣǝn], s. descripción; trazado; clase. **—descriptive** [dɪskrípṭɪv], a. descriptivo.

desecrate [désɛkreɪt], vt. profanar.– **—desecration** [desɛkréṣǝn], s. profanación.

desegregate [dɪségrɛgeɪt], vt. eliminar la segregación racial de.—vi. dejar de practicar la segregación racial.

desegregation [dɪsɛgrɛgéiṣǝn], s. abolición de la segregación racial.

desensitize [dɪsénsɪtaɪz], vt. insensibilizar.

desert [dézœrt], s. desierto, yermo; páramo.—a. desierto, yermo, desolado.—*d. island*, isla desierta.—vt. [dɪzœrt], desamparar, abandonar. —vt. y vi. desertar.– **—er** [dɪzœrtœ(r)], s. desertor. **—ion** [dɪzœrṣǝn], s. deserción, abandono.– **—s** [dɪzœrt(s)], s. mérito, merecimiento.—*to get one's d.*, llevar su merecido. **—deserve** [dɪzœrv], vt. merecer.—vi. tener merecimientos. **—deserving** [dɪzœrvɪŋ], a. meritorio; merecedor o digno.—s. mérito, merecimiento.

design [dɪzáɪn], vt. diseñar, delinear; concebir; proyectar.—vi. hacer proyectos, diseños, planos.—s. diseño; proyecto; disposición, arreglo, construcción; plan; propósito, designio; plano.—*by o through d.*, adrede, intencionalmente.– **—er** [-œ(r)], s. dibujante; diseñador; proyectista.—*custom d.* figurinista.—*stage d.*, escenógrafo.— **—ing** [-ɪŋ], a. insidioso, astuto, intrigante.

designate [dézɪgneɪt], vt. designar, destinar; señalar. **—designation** [dezɪgnéiṣǝn], s. designación, señalamiento, nombramiento.

desirable [dɪzáɪrǝbl], a. deseable, apetecible, conveniente. **—desire** [dɪzáɪr], s. deseo, anhelo, ansia, antojo.—vt. desear, anhelar, ansiar. —vi. sentir deseo. **—desirous** [dɪzáɪrʌs], a. deseoso, anheloso.

desist [dɪsíst], vi. desistir.

desk [desk], s. escritorio, pupitre, buró.—*d. clerk*, recepcionista.—*d. pad*, bloc de notas.– **—top** [-tap], a. de escritorio, de sobremesa.—*d. publishing*, autoedición, edición electrónica.

desolate [désoleɪt], vt. desolar, arrasar; despoblar; desconsolar.—a. [désōlɪt], desolado; solitario; triste.— **desolation** [desoléiṣǝn], s. desolación; desconsuelo; soledad; aflicción.

despair [dɪspér], s. desesperanza, desesperación.—vi. desesperar, perder toda esperanza.– **—ing** [-ɪŋ], a. desesperante; sin esperanza.

despatch, s., vt. = DISPATCH.

desperado [dɛspɛréidou], s. foragido; prófugo; malhechor. **—desperate** [déspɛrɪt], a. desesperado; arrojado, arriesgado o temerario. **—desperation** [despɛréiṣǝn], s. desesperación; furor.

despicable [déspɪkǝbl], a. despreciable, vil. —**despise** [dispáiz], *vt.* despreciar, menospreciar.

despite [dispáit], *s.* despecho, inquina.—*prep.* a pesar de, a despecho de.

despoil [dispóil], *vt.* despojar, expoliar.

despondence, despondency [dispándens(i)], *s.* desaliento, abatimiento. —**despondent** [dispándent], *a.* desalentado, abatido, desesperanzado.

despot [déspat], *s.* déspota.— **ic** [despátik], *a.* despótico.— **ism** [déspotizm], *s.* despotismo; absolutismo.

dessert [dizœrt], *s.* postre.

destination [destinéison], *s.* destino; paradero. —**destine** [déstin], *vt.* destinar; dedicar. —**destiny** [déstini], *s.* destino, hado, sino.

destitute [déstitjut], *a.* destituido, necesitado; (con **of**) falto, desprovisto de. —**destitution** [destitjúson], *s.* indigencia, privación.

destroy [distrói], *vt.* destruir, destrozar, desbaratar, acabar con.— —**er** [-œ(r)], *s.* destructor; (mar.) destructor, cazatorpedero. —**destruction** [distrákson], *s.* destrucción, ruina, destrozo. —**destructive** [distráktiv], *a.* destructor; destructivo; dañino.

detach [ditéch], *vt.* separar, despegar o desprender; (mil.) destacar.— —**ed** [-t], *a.* suelto, separado; imparcial; desinteresado.— —**able** [-abl], *a.* separable, desmontable, de quita y pon.— —**ment** [-ment], *s.* separación; indiferencia; desinterés, despego; (mil.) destacamento.

detail [ditéil], *vt.* detallar, particularizar, promenorizar.—*s.* detalle, pormenor; (mil.) destacamento.

detain [ditéin], *vt.* detener; retardar, atrasar; retener.

detect [ditékt], *vt.* descubrir; averiguar; (rad.) rectificar.— —**ion** [ditékson], *s.* averiguación, descubrimiento; rectificación.— —**ive** [-iv], *s.* detective, agente de policía secreta o particular.—*d. story,* novela policíaca, novela policial.— —**or** [-o(r)], *s.* descubridor; indicador de nivel; rectificador; (elec.) detector.

detente [deitánt], *s.* (pol.) distensión.

deter [ditœr], *vti.* [1] disuadir; desanimar, acobardar.

detergent [ditœrdzent], *a.* y *s.* detergente.

deteriorate [ditíriioreit], *vt.* y *vi.* deteriorar(se), desmejorar(se). —**dete-**

rioration [ditirioréison], *s.* deterioro, desperfecto, desmejora.

determination [ditœrminéison], *s.* determinación, decisión. —**determinative** [ditœrminativ], *a.* determinativo, determinante. —**determine** [ditœrmin], *vt.* determinar, decidir; (for.) definir.—*vi.* resolverse, decidirse. —**determined** [ditœrmind], *a.* determinado, decidido, resuelto.

deterrent [ditérent], *s.* freno, impedimento.

detest [ditést], *vt.* detestar, aborrecer.— —**able** [-abl], *a.* detestable, aborrecible.

detonate [détoneit], *vi.* detonar, estallar.—*vt.* hacer estallar. —**detonating** [détoneitin], *a.* detonante. —**detonation** [detonéison], *s.* detonación. —**detonator** [détoneito(r)], *s.* detonador.

detour [ditúr], *s.* desviación, desvío, rodeo.—*vt.* y *vi.* (hacer) desviar o rodear.

detract [ditrǽkt], *vt.* disminuir o quitar.—*vi.* detractar.— —**or** [-o(r)], *s.* detractor.— —**ion** [ditrǽkson], *s.* detracción.

detriment [détriment], *s.* detrimento; per juicio.

deuce [djus], *s.* dos (en naipes o dados); pata (en otros juegos); (fam.) diantre, demontre.

devaluate [divǽlyueit], *vt.* depreciar, desvalorizar. —**devaluation** [divælyuéison], *s.* depreciación, desvalorización. —**devalue** [divǽlyu], *vt.* depreciar.

devastate [dévasteit], *vt.* devastar, asolar. —**devastating** [dévasteitin], *a.,* **devastator** [dévasteito(r)], *s.* devastador, asolador. —**devastation** [devastéison], *s.* devastación, desolación, ruina.

develop [divélop], *vt.* desenvolver, desarrollar; mejorar; fomentar; explotar (minas, etc.); revelar (fotos). —*vi.* progresar; avanzar; desarrollarse.— —**er** [-œ(r)], *s.* (fot.) revelador.— —**ing** [-in], *a.*—*d. nations,* naciones en vías de desarrollo.— —**ment** [-ment], *s.* desarrollo, evolución, progreso; fomento; explotación; revelado.

deviant [dívient], *a.* desviado.

deviate [dívieit], *vt.* y *vi.* desviar(se), apartar(se). —**deviation** [divjéison], *s.* desviación; deriva; desvío, extravío.

device [diváis], *s.* artefacto, artificio; invento; proyecto; expediente, recurso; ardid; dibujo; patrón; lema, divisa.—*pl.* deseo, inclinación.

devil [dévil], *s.* diablo; demonio; manjar muy picante.—*between the d. and the deep sea,* entre la espada y la pared.—*d's advocate,* abogado del diablo.—*the D.,* Satanás.—*the d. take the hindmost,* el que venga atrás, que arree.- **—ish** [-iŝ], *a.* diabólico; perverso; travieso.- **—try** [-tri], **—ment** [-ment], *s.* diablura; travesura; maldad.

devious [dívɅs], *a.* desviado, descarriado; tortuoso.

devise [diváiz], *vt.* idear, trazar; proyectar; (for.) legar.—*vi.* urdir, maquinar.

devoid [divóid], *a.* libre, exento; desprovisto (de).

devote [divóut], *vt.* dedicar; consagrar.—*vr.* dedicarse, consagrarse (a). - **–d** [-id], *a.* devoto, ferviente; leal, afecto.—**devotion** [divóuŝon], *s.* devoción, piedad; dedicación; lealtad, afecto.

devour [diváur], *vt.* devorar, engullir.

devout [diváut], *a.* piadoso, devoto.

dew [dju], *s.* rocío; relente, sereno.—*vt.* rociar; refrescar.- **—drop** [djúdrap], *s.* gota de rocío.

dewlap [djúlæp], *s.* papada.

dewy [djúi], *a.* lleno de rocío.

dexterity [dekstériti], *s.* destreza, habilidad, maña, tino. **—dexterous** [dékstɛrɅs], *a.* diestro, hábil.

diabetes [daiabítiz], *s.* diabetes.

diabetic [daiabétik], *a.* y *s.* diabético.

diabolic(al) [daiabálik(al)], *a.* diabólico.

diagnose [daiægnóus], *vt.* diagnosticar. **—diagnosis** [daiægnóusis], *s.* diagnosis.

diagonal [daiægonal], *a.* y *s.* diagonal.

diagram [dáiagræm], *s.* diagrama; gráfico.

dial [dáial], *s.* esfera de reloj; cuadrante; disco del teléfono; indicador.—*d. tone,* tono de marcar, tono dediscado.—*vt.* sintonizar; marcar (en el disco de llamada), (Am.) discar.—*sun d.,* reloj de sol.

dialect [dáialekt], *s.* dialecto.

dialogue [dáialag], *s.* diálogo.

dialysis [daiǽlesis], *s.* diálisis.—*d. machine,* dializador.

diameter [daiǽmɛtœ(r)], *s.* diámetro.

diamond [dáimond], *s.* diamante; bri-

llante; oros (de baraja); (geom.) rombo.

diaper [dáiapœ(r)], *s.* pañal, braguita.

diaphragm [dáiafræm], *s.* diafragma.

diarrhea [daiaríǽ], *s.* diarrea.

diary [dáiari], *s.* diario.

dice [dais], *s.* (*pl.* de DIE) dados.—*d. box,* cubilete.—*vt.* cortar en forma de cubos menudos.

dictate [díkteit], *vt.* y *vi.* dictar; mandar, imponer(se).—*s.* dictamen. **—dictation** [diktéiŝon], *s.* dictado; mando arbitrario. **—dictator** [díkteito(r)], *s.* dictador. **—dictatorial** [diktatórial], *a.* dictatorial. **—dictatorship** [diktéitorŝip], *s.* dictadura.

diction [díkŝon], *s.* dicción; locución.- **—ary** [-eri], *s.* diccionario.

did [did], *pret.* de TO DO.

die [dai], *vi.* morir(se), expirar, fallecer; marchitarse.

die [dai], *s.* (*pl.* **dice** [dais]) dado (para jugar); (*pl.* **dies** [daiz]) cuño, troquel; molde.—*the d. is cast,* la suerte está echada.

diet [dáiet], *s.* dieta, régimen alimenticio; (pol.) dieta.—*vt.* poner a dieta.—*vi.* estar a dieta- **—ary** [-ari], *a.* alimenticio; dietético.

differ [dífœ(r)], *vi.* diferir; diferenciarse, distinguirse.—*to d. from,* o *with,* no estar de acuerdo con.- **—ence** [-ens], *s.* diferencia; distinción (de personas, etc.); discrepancia; desacuerdo; (arit.) residuo.—*it makes no d.,* no importa.- **—ent** [-ent], *a.* diferente, distinto.- **—ential** [-énŝal], *s.* diferencial.- **—entiate** [-énŝieit], *vt.* y *vi.* diferenciar(se), distinguir(se).

difficult [dífikɅlt], *a.* difícil; penoso.- **—y** [-i], *s.* dificultad; tropiezo; reparo.—*pl.* aprieto, apuro.

diffuse [difjúz], *vt.* difundir; desparramar.—*vi.* difundirse; disiparse.—*a.* [difjús] difundido, esparcido; difuso. **—diffusion** [difjúžon], *s.* difusión; dispersión; prolijidad.

dig [dig], *vti.* [3] cavar, excavar; ahondar; escarbar.—*to d. out,* desentrañar.—*to d. up,* desenterrar.—*vii.* cavar; (fam.) matarse a trabajar.—*s.* empuje; (fam.) observación sarcástica.

digest [dáidžest], *s.* compendio, resumen; recopilación.—*vt.* [daidžést], recopilar, abreviar y clasificar; digerir.—*vi.* digerirse; asimilarse.- **—ible** [daidžéstibl], *a.* digerible, digestible.- **—ion** [daidžéschon], s. digestión; asimilación.- **—ive** [daidžéstiv], a. y s. digestivo.

digit [dídžit], s. (math.) dígito; (anat.) dedo.- **—al** [-al], a. digital.—*d. clock,* reloj digital.—*d. computer,* ordenador digital.—*d. scanner,* lector digital.

digitalis [didžitǽlis], s. (farm.) digital.

dignified [dígnifaid], a. serio, grave; digno. **—dignify** [dígnifai], vti. [7] dignificar, honrar, exaltar. **—dignitary** [dígniteri], s. dignatario. **—dignity** [dígniti], s. dignidad; nobleza, majestuosidad; rango o cargo elevado.

digress [daigrés], vi. divagar.- **—ion** [daigréšon], s. divagación o digresión.

dike [daik], s. dique, represa; zanja; malecón.—vt. represar; canalizar.

dilapidate [dilæpideit], vt. dilapidar.- **—d** [-id], a. destartalado, arruinado.

dilate [dailéit], vt. dilatar, ensanchar.—vi. dilatarse, extenderse.

dilemma [dilémá], s. dilema.

diligence [dílidžens], s. diligencia; coche diligencia. **—diligent** [dílidžent], a. diligente, aplicado; activo.

dill [dil], s. (bot.) eneldo.—*d. pickle,* pepino encurtido sazonado con eneldo.

dilute [diliút], vt. desleír, diluir; aguar.—vi. desleírse, diluirse.—a. diluido.

dim [dim], a. oscuro; borroso; empañado; deslustrado; (fot.) velado.—vti. [1] oscurecer; empañar, deslustrar; amortiguar o reducir la intensidad de una luz.—vii. oscurecerse, etc.

dime [daim], s. (E.U. y Canadá) moneda de diez centavos.

dimension [diménšon], s. dimensión, extensión, tamaño.

diminish [dimíniš], vt. disminuir, (a)minorar; rebajar, degradar.—vi. disminuir(se), menguar, (a)minorarse, decrecer. **—diminution** [diminjúšon], s. di(s)minución, rebaja, reducción. **—diminutive** [dimínyutiv], a. diminuto; diminutivo.—s. (gram.) diminutivo.

dimness [dímnis], s. ofuscamiento; penumbra.

dimple [dímpl], s. hoyuelo.—vt. y vi. formar o formarse hoyuelos.

din [din], s. estrépito, alboroto.—vti. [1] ensordecer; aturdir.—vii. alborotar; (re)sonar con estrépito.

dine [dain], vi. comer (la comida principal), cenar.- **—r** [dáinœ(r)], s. comedor; comensal. **—dining-car** [dáininkar], s. coche comedor. **—dining room** [dáinin rúm], s. comedor.

dinghy [díngi], s. lancha o bote pequeño.

dingy [díndži], a. empañado, deslustrado; manchado, sucio; oscuro.

dinky [dínki], a. pequeño, diminuto.

dinner [dínœ(r)], s. comida (principal), cena; cubierto.—*d. bell,* campana de la cena.—*d. dance,* cena con baile.—*d. jacket,* smoking, esmoquin.—*d. pail,* fiambrera, portaviandas.—*d. plate,* plato grande.—*d. roll,* panecillo.—*d. table,* mesa de comedor.—*d. theater,* sala de espectáculos con servicio de restaurante.—*d. time,* hora de cenar, hora de comer.

dinosaur [dáinosor], s. dinosaurio.

diocese [dáiosis], s. diócesis.

dip [dip], vti. [3] sumergir; bañar, humedecer, mojar, zambullir; saludar con la bandera; (mar.) achicar.—vii. sumergirse, zambullirse; hundirse; hojear (en un libro, etc.); inclinarse hacia abajo.—s. inmersión, zambullida; baño corto; inclinación.- **—stick** [-stik], s. varilla de nivel. caída, pendiente.

diphtheria [difθíriá], s. difteria.

diphthong [dífθon], s. diptongo.

diploma [diplóumá], s. diploma; título.

diplomacy [diplóumási], s. diplomacia; tacto. **—diplomat** [díplomæt], s. diplomático. **—diplomatic** [diplomǽtik], a. diplomático.

dipper [dípœ(r)], s. cazo, cucharón.

dire [dair], a. extremo, angustioso; horrendo; de mal agüero.

direct [dirékt], a. directo; derecho; en línea recta (descendencia, sucesión, etc.).—*d. current,* corriente continua.—*d. mail,* publicidad por correo.—*d. object,* (ling.) complemento directo.—vt. dirigir; encaminar; gobernar.—vi. dirigir; servir de guía.- **—ion** [dirékšon], s. dirección; rumbo; gobierno, administración; instrucción.—*d. finder,* (rad.) radiogoniómetro.- **—ive** [-iv], a. directivo.—s. instrucción, mandato. - **—or** [-o(r)], s. director; gerente; administrador; vocal de una junta directiva; director de orquesta.—*board of directors,* consejo de administración.—a. (mat.) director, directriz.- **—ory** [-ọri], *s.* directorio; guía comercial.

dirt [dœrt], *s.* basura; mugre; tierra; lodo; polvo; bajeza.—*d. cheap*, (fam.) baratísimo, regalado. **—dirty** [dœrti], *a.* sucio; manchado; enlodado; indecente; puerco; vil.—*d. trick*, (fam.) perrada.—*d. word*, palabrota, mala palabra.—*vti.* [7] emporcar, ensuciar.

disability [dịsạbịlịtị], *s.* incapacidad; inhabilidad, impotencia. **—disable** [dịséịbl], *vt.* imposibilitar; inhabilitar; (for.) incapacitar legalmente.

disadvantage [dịsạdvǽntịdẑ], *s.* desventaja, detrimento.—*at a d.*, en situación desventajosa.- **—d** [-d], *a.* desfavorecido, carenciado.

disagree [dịsạgrí], *vi.* disentir, discrepar, diferir, desavenirse; estar en pugna.—*to d. with*, no estar de acuerdo con; no sentar bien a.- **—able** [-ạbl], *a.* desagradable; descortés, desapacible. **—ment** [-mẹnt], *s.* desacuerdo, desavenencia; discordia; disensión; discrepancia.

disappear [dịsạpír], *vi.* desaparecer (se).- **—ance** [-ạns], *s.* desaparición.

disappoint [dịsạpóịnt], *vt.* chasquear; decepcionar, desilusionar; defraudar una esperanza.—*to be disappointed*, verse contrariado; estar desilusionado o decepcionado.- **—ment** [-mẹnt], *s.* desengaño, desilusión, decepción, contratiempo; chasco.

disapproval [dịsạprúvạl], *s.* desaprobación, censura. **—disapprove** [dịsạprúv], *vt.* y *vi.* desaprobar.

disarm [dịsárm], *vt.* desarmar; (fig.) apaciguar, sosegar.—*vi.* deponer las armas; licenciar tropas.- **—ament** [-ạmẹnt], *s.* desarme.

disarrange [dịsạréịndẑ], *vt.* desarreglar, descomponer, desordenar.- **—ment** [-mẹnt], *s.* desarreglo, desorden.

disassemble [dịsạsémbl], *vt.* desarmar, desmontar (un reloj, una máquina).

disaster [dịzǽstœr(r)], *s.* desastre; siniestro. **—disastrous** [dịzǽstrʌs], *a.* desastroso, funesto.

disband [dịsbǽnd], *vt.* licenciar las tropas.—*vi.* dispersarse, desbandarse.

disburse [dịsbœrs], *vt.* desembolsar, pagar, gastar.- **—ment** [-mẹnt], *s.* desembolso; gasto;—*pl.* (com.) egresos.

disc [dịsk], *s.* (anat.) disco; = DISK.—*d. jockey*, disc-jockey, pinchadiscos.— **—co** [-koụ], discoteca, disco.

discard [dịskárd], *vt.* descartar; despedir.—*vi.* descartarse (en el juego).— *s.* [dịskárd] descarte (en el juego).

discern [dịzœrn], *vt.* y *vi.* discernir, percibir, distinguir.- **—ment** [-mẹnt], *s.* discernimiento; criterio.

discharge [dịschárdẑ], *vt.* descargar; disparar; cumplir, desempeñar, ejecutar; despedir; exonerar, eximir; dispensar; arrojar, vomitar; (mil.) licenciar.—*vi.* descargarse; vaciarse; desaguar.—*s.* descarga; disparo; (com.) descargo; carta de pago; desempeño; remoción, despido; (mil.) licencia absoluta; absolución, exoneración; derrame, desagüe.

disciple [dịsáịpl], *s.* discípulo.

discipline [dísiplin], *s.* disciplina; enseñanza; castigo; materia de estudio.—*vt.* disciplinar, instruir; castigar.

disclose [dịsklóụz], *vt.* descubrir, destapar; revelar, publicar. **—disclosure** [dịsklóụẑụ(r)], *s.* descubrimiento, revelación.

discolor [dịskálọ(r)], *vt.* y *vi.* descolorar(se), desteñir(se).- **—ation** [-éị̣ṣọn], *s.* descoloramiento.

discomfort [dịskámfọrt], *s.* incomodidad; malestar, molestia.—*vt.* incomodar; molestar.

disconcert [dịskọnsœrt], *vt.* desconcertar, confundir.

disconnect [dịskọnékt], *vt.* desconectar; desunir o separar.- **—ed** [-ịd], *a.* desconectado; inconexo, incoherente.

disconsolate [dịskánsolịt], *a.* desconsolado, inconsolable, desolado.

discontent [dịskọntént], *s.* descontento, desagrado.—*a.* descontento; quejoso, disgustado.—*vt.* descontentar, desagradar.- **—ed** [-ịd], *a.* descontent(adiz)o; disgustado.- **—ment** [-mẹnt], *s.* descontento, mal humor.

discontinue [dịskọntínyu], *vt.* y *vi.* interrumpir, descontinuar; suspender; desabonarse.

discord [dískɔrd], *s.* discordia; desacuerdo, (mus.) disonancia.—*to sow d.*, cizañar.—*vi.* [dịskɔ́rd], discordar.- **—ance** [dịskɔ́rdạns], **—ancy** [dịskɔ́rdạnsị], *s.* discordia; discordancia; disensión.- **—ant** [dịskɔ́rdạnt], *a.* discorde, desconforme; discordante, disonante.

discotheque [dískŏték], s. discoteca, disco.

discount [dískaunt], vt. descontar; rebajar, deducir; dar poca importancia a.—s. descuento, rebaja.—d. rate, tipo de descuento.

discourage [diskŏérid̂], vt. desalentar; desaprobar, oponerse a.——d [-d], a. desanimado, desalentado.——ment [-mȩnt], s. desaliento, desánimo, obstáculo.

discourse [dískŏrs], s. discurso; plática, conversación; disertación.—vi. [diskŏrs], discurrir, discursar; disertar; conversar, razonar.—vt. hablar de proferir, expresar.

discourteous [diskŏértjʌs], a. descortés, grosero. **—discourtesy** [diskŏértȩsi], s. descortesía.

discover [diskávœ(r)], vt. descubrir.——er [-œ(r)], s. descubridor.——y [-i], s. descubrimiento, hallazgo.

discredit [diskrédit], s. descrédito, desconfianza; deshonra; oprobio.—vt. desacreditar; desautorizar, desvirtuar.

discreet [diskrít], a. discreto, prudente, juicioso.——ness [-nȩs], s. = DISCRETION.

discrepancy [diskrépȩnsi], s. discrepancia, diferencia; variación.

discretion [diskréȿǫn], s. discreción, juicio, prudencia.

discriminate [diskrímineit], vt. discriminar, prejuzgar; discernir, distinguir.—a. [diskríminit], definido, distinguible; discernidor. **—discrimination** [diskriminéiȿǫn], s. discriminación, prejuicio; discernimiento; distinción, diferencia.

discuss [diskás], vt. discutir, debatir; tratar.——ion [diskáȿǫn], s. discusión, debate; exposición, ventilación.

disdain [disdéin], vt. desdeñar, despreciar.—vi. desdeñarse, esquivarse.—s. desdén, desprecio, esquivez.——ful [-ful], a. desdeñoso; altivo, altanero.

disease [dizíz], s. enfermedad, afección, dolencia.—vt. enfermar, hacer daño.——d [-d], a. enfermo; morboso.

disembark [disembárk], vt. y vi. desembarcar(se).——ation [-éiȿǫn], s. desembarco o desembarque.

disembowel [disembáuȩl], vti. [2] destripar, desentrañar, sacar las entrañas.

disengage [disengéid̂], vt. desunir;

desasir; (mec.) desembragar; desenganchar.—vi. soltarse, desligarse, zafarse.

disentangle [disentǽŋgl], vt. desenredar, desenmarañar, desembrollar.

disfigure [disfígyŭ(r)], vt. desfigurar, afear.

disgorge [disgŏrd̂], vt. desembuchar; vomitar.

disgrace [disgréis], s. ignominia, vergüenza; deshonra, estigma.—vt. deshonrar; desacreditar.——ful [-ful], a. vergonzoso, oprobioso.

disguise [disgáiz], vt. disfrazar, enmascarar; desfigurar; encubrir.—s. disfraz, máscara; embozo.

disgust [disgást], s. repugnancia; asco, náusea; disgusto.—vt. repugnar; fastidiar, hastiar.——ed [-id], a. disgustado, fastidiado.——ing [-iŋ], a. repugnante, asqueroso; odioso.

dish [diȿ], s. plato, fuente; manjar.—pl. vajilla, loza.—d. antenna, antena parabólica.—d. drainer o rack, escurreplatos.—d. towel, secador, paño de cocina.——cloth [-klɔθ], s. estropajo.——pan [-pæn], s. pileta, paila de lavar platos.——rag [-ræg], s. estropajo.——washer [-wŏœr], s. lavaplatos; (mec.) lavaplatos, lavavajillas.

dishearten [dishártȩn], vt. desanimar, descorazonar.

dishevel [diȿévȩl], vti. [2] desgreñar, desmelenar.

dishonest [disánist], a. falto de honradez, pícaro; fraudulento, falso.——y [-i], s. improbidad, picardía; fraude.

dishonor [disánǫ(r)], s. deshonor, deshonra; afrenta.—vt. deshonrar; afrentar.——able [-ȩbl], a. deshonroso, ignominioso; deshonrado, infamado.

dishwasher [diȿwǎȿœ(r)], s. lavaplatos; (mec.) lavaplatos, lavavajillas.

disillusion [disiljúȥǫn], vt. desilusionar, desengañar.——ment [-mȩnt], s. desilusión, desengaño, decepción.

disinfect [disinfékt], vt. desinfectar.——ant [-ȩnt], a. y s. desinfectante.——ion [disinfékȿǫn], s. desinfección.

disinherit [disinhérit], vt. desheredar.

disinterment [disintérmȩnt], s. exhumación, desenterramiento.

disjoin [disdʒŏin], vt. desunir, apartar, disgregar.——t [-t], vt. descoyuntar, dislocar.——ted [-tid], a. dislocado, descoyuntado; sin ilación.

disk [dísk], *s.* disco; rodaja.—*d. drive,* (comput.) unidad de disco, disquetera.

diskette [dískét], *s.* (comput.) disquete.

dislike [disláik], *s.* aversión, antipatía.—*vt.* tener aversión, no gustar de.

dislocate [díslokeit], *vt.* dislocar, descoyuntar.—**dislocation** [dislokéiṣon], *s.* dislocación, luxación.

dislodge [disládʒ], *vt.* desalojar, echar fuera.—*vi.* mudarse.

disloyal [dislóial], *a.* desleal.-—**ty** [-ti], *s.* deslealtad.

dismal [dízmal], *a.* lúgubre, triste.—*s.* pantano.

dismantle [dismǽntl], *vt.* desguarnecer; desmantelar; desmontar.

dismay [disméi], *s.* desaliento, desmayo; consternación.—*vt.* desanimar, espantar, aterrar.

dismiss [dismís], *vt.* despedir, destituir; descartar; despachar; dar de baja.-—**al** [-al], *s.* despido, remoción, destitución.

dismount [dismáunt], *vt.* desmontar; desarmar.—*vi.* apearse, descabalgar.

disobedience [disobídiens], *s.* desobediencia.—**disobedient** [disobídient], *a.* desobediente.—**disobey** [disobéi], *vt.* y *vi.* desobedecer.

disorder [disórdœ(r)], *s.* desorden; irregularidad; alboroto; enfermedad.—*vt.* desordenar; inquietar, perturbar.-—**ly** [-li], *a.* desordenado, desarreglado; escandaloso, perturbador.—*d. house,* burdel.—*adv.* desordenadamente, etc.

disown [disóun], *vt.* repudiar, negar, desconocer; renunciar, renegar de.

disparity [dispǽriti], *s.* disparidad.

dispatch [dispǽch], *vt.* despachar, expedir; remitir.—*s.* despacho; mensaje, comunicación.

dispel [dispél], *vti.* [1] dispersar; disipar, desvanecer.

dispensary [dispénsari], *s.* dispensario.—**dispensation** [dispenséiṣon], *s.* dispensa, exención; designio divino.—**dispense** [dispéns], *vt.* distribuir, repartir; administrar (justicia); dispensar, eximir.—*to d. with,* prescindir de.-—**r** [dispénsœr], *s.* dispensador; (mec.) distribuidor automático.

dispersal [dispœrsal], *s.* dispersión.—**disperse** [dispœrs], *vt.* dispersar; esparcir.—*vi.* dispersarse; disiparse.—*a.* disperso. —**dispersion** [dispœrṣon], *s.* dispersión; esparcimiento; difusión.

displace [displéis], *vt.* desplazar; (a bone) dislocar.-—**d** [-t], *a.*—*d. person,* desplazado. *a.*-—**ment** [-ment], *s.* desplazamiento; dislocación.

display [displéi], *vt.* desplegar, extender; exhibir, lucir.—*s.* despliegue; ostentación, exhibición.—*d. window,* escaparate, vidriera.—*on d.,* en exhibición.

displease [displíz], *vt.* y *vi.* desagradar, disgustar.—**displeasure** [displéʒu(r)], *s.* desagrado, disfavor.

disposal [dispóuzal], *s.* disposición; colocación, arreglo; venta (de bienes); donación. —**dispose** [dispóuz], *vt.* arreglar, disponer; inclinar el ánimo; ordenar, mandar.—*vi.* disponer.—*to d. of,* acabar con; deshacerse de; dar, vender, traspasar; disponer de. —**disposition** [dispozíṣon], *s.* disposición; arreglo, ordenación; índole.

dispossess [dispozés], *vt.* desposeer, desalojar; (for.) desahuciar, lanzar.

disprove [disprúv], *vt.* refutar.

dispute [dispiút], *vt.* refutar, impugnar.—*vi.* disputar, discutir.—*s.* disputa, discusión; litigio, pleito.

disqualify [diskwálifai], *vti.* [7] descalificar, inhabilitar.

disregard [disrigárd], *vt.* desatender, hacer caso omiso de; desairar, despreciar.—*s.* desatención, descuido, omisión; desprecio, desaire.

disrepair [disrepér], *s.* mal estado.

disreputable [disrépyütabĕl], *a.* de mala fama; vergonzoso.

disrepute [disrĕpyút], *s.* mala fama, descrédito.—*to bring into d.,* desacreditar.—*to fall into d.,* caer en descrédito.

disrespect [disrispékt], *s.* desatención, falta de respeto.—*vt.* desacatar, desairar; faltar el respeto a.-—**ful** [-ful], *a.* irrespetuoso, irreverente.

disrupt [disrápt], *vt.* romper; rajar, reventar; hacer pedazos; desorganizar, desbaratar.-—**ion** [disrápṣon], *s.* desgarro, rotura; desorganización o rompimiento.—**ive** [disráptiv], *a.* destructor, disolvente.

dissatisfaction [disætisfǽkṣon], *s.* descontento, disgusto.—**dissatisfy** [disǽtisfai], *vti.* [7] desagradar, descontentar.

dissect [disékt], *vt.* disecar, anatomizar; analizar.-—**ion** [disékṣon], *s.*

disección, disecación, anatomía; análisis.

dissension [dɪsénʃǝn], s. disensión, discordia. **—dissent** [dɪsént], vi. disentir, disidir.—s. disensión, desavenencia.

dissertation [dɪsœrtéiʃǝn], s. disertación; (for a degree) tesis.

dissimulation [dɪsɪmyʊléiʃǝn], s. disimulo, disfraz; tolerancia afectada.

dissipate [dɪsipeit], vt. y vi. disipar(se), dispersar(se), desintegrar(se), desvanecer(se).—vt. desperdiciar, derrochar.— **—d** [dɪsipeitid], a. disipado, disoluto. **—dissipation** [dɪsipéiʃǝn], s. disipación; libertinaje.

dissociate [dɪsóuʃieit], vt. disociar, dividir, separar.

dissolute [dɪsoljut], a. disoluto, libertino, licencioso. **—dissolution** [dɪsoljúʃǝn], s. disolución. **—dissolve** [dɪzálv], vt. disolver; disipar; dispersar; desleír; derogar, revocar, anular.—vi. disolverse; descomponerse; desvanecerse; languidecer.

dissonance [dɪsǝnǝns], s. disonancia; desconcierto, discordia. **—dissonant** [dɪsǝnǝnt], a. disonante, discordante; contrario, discorde.

distaff [dɪstǽf], s. rueca.—d. o d. side, sexo débil.

distance [dɪstǝns], s. distancia; alejamiento; lejanía, lontananza; trecho; intervalo.—at a d., de lejos.—in the d., en lontananza, a lo lejos.—to keep one's d., guardar las distancias.—vt. alejar, apartar; espaciar; tomar la delantera. **—distant** [dɪstǝnt], a. distante, alejado; esquivo, frío.

distaste [dɪstéist], s. fastidio, aversión, disgusto.— **—ful** [-fʊl], a. enfadoso.

distend [dɪsténd], vt. y vi. tender(se), ensanchar(se), dilatar(se), hinchar(se); distender(se).

distill [dɪstíl], vt. y vi. destilar.— **—ation** [dɪstɪléiʃǝn], s. destilación.— **—ery** [-œri], s. destilería.

distinct [dɪstíŋkt], a. distinto, claro, preciso;—d. from, distinto a.— **—ion** [dɪstíŋkʃǝn], s. distinción; discernimiento; diferencia; honor.— **—ive** [dɪstíŋktiv], a. distintivo, característico. **—distinguish** [dɪstíŋgwiʃ], vt. distinguir, discernir; honrar. **—distinguished** [dɪstíŋgwiʃt], a. distinguido; prestigioso; especial, señalado.

distort [dɪstórt], vt. (re)torcer; defor-

mar; falsear, tergiversar.— **—ion** [dɪstórʃǝn], s. distorsión; esguince; deformación, tergiversación.

distract [dɪstrǽkt], vt. distraer; perturbar, interrumpir.— **—ion** [dɪstrǽkʃǝn], s. distracción; perturbación; diversión, pasatiempo.

distress [dɪstrés], s. pena, dolor; angustia; desgracia, miseria; embargo, secuestro.—vt. angustiar, afligir; poner en aprieto; embargar, secuestrar.

distribute [dɪstríbjut], vt. distribuir.—vi. hacer distribución.— **—r** [dɪstríbjutœr(r)], **distributor** [dɪstríbjutǝr(r)], s. distribuidor, repartidor. **—distribution** [dɪstrɪbjúʃǝn], s. distribución, reparto.

district [dɪstríkt], s. distrito, comarca, territorio; barriada, barrio; región, jurisdicción.

distrust [dɪstrást], vt. desconfiar, recelar.—s. desconfianza, recelo; descrédito.— **—ful** [-fʊl], a. desconfiado, receloso; suspicaz.

disturb [dɪstœrb], vt. alborotar, (per)turbar; distraer, interrumpir; desordenar, revolver.— **—ance** [-ǝns], s. disturbio, conmoción, desorden.— **—er** [œr(r)], s. perturbador.

disuse [dɪsyús], s. desuso.—to fall into d., caer en desuso, perder vigencia.—vt. [dɪsyúz], desusar; cesar de usar.

ditch [dɪch], s. zanja; cuneta; trinchera; foso; acequia.—vt. zanjar; abandonar, desembarazarse de; (fam.) dar calabazas a.

ditto [dítou], s. ídem; lo mismo; marca (") o abreviatura (id.); duplicado, copia fiel.—vt. duplicar, copiar.—adv. como ya se dijo; asimismo.

divan [dáivæn, dɪvǽn], s. diván.

dive [daiv], vii. [5] za(m)bullirse, echarse o tirarse de cabeza; bucear; enfrascarse, profundizar; (aer.) picar.—s. za(m)bullidura, buceo; (aer.) picada; (jer.) antro.—d. bomb, bombardear en picado.—d. bomber, bombardero en picado.—d. bombing, bombardeo en picado.— **—r** [dáivœr(r)], s. saltador, zambullidor; (in a diving suit) buceador, buzo. **—diving** [dáiviŋ], s. saltos de trampolín, clavados, zambullida; buceo, submarinismo.—d. bell, campana de buzo.—d. board, trampolín.—d. suit, escafandra, traje de buzo.

diverge [dɪvœrdʒ], vi. divergir, diferir, desviarse.— **—nce** [dɪvœrdʒǝns],

—ncy [djvǽrdẑensi], s. divergencia.- **—nt** [djvǽrdẑent], a. divergente.

divers [dájvœrz], a. varios, diversos.

diverse [djvǽrs], a. diverso, variado, distinto. **—diversify** [djvǽrsifaj], vti. [7] diversificar, variar. **—diversion** [djvǽrʒon], s. desviación; diversión, entretenimiento.—**diversity** [djvǽrsiti], s. diversidad, variedad; diferencia. **—divert** [djvǽrt], vt. desviar; divertir. **—diverting** [djvǽrtiŋ], a. divertido, entretenido, recreativo.

divide [djvájd], vt. dividir; desunir, separar; repartir, compartir.—vi. dividirse.- **—nd** [dívjdend], s. dividendo.

divine [djvájn], a. divino; teólogo.— vt. adivinar; vaticinar. **—divinity** [djvíniti], s. divinidad; deidad; atributo divino; teología.

division [djvíʒon], s. división; distribución, repart(imient)o; ramo, negociado, departamento; sección; desunión, desacuerdo.

divorce [djvɔrs], s. divorcio.—vt. y vi. divorciar(se).- **—e** [djvɔrsí], s. persona divorciada.

divulge [djváldʒ], vt. divulgar, propalar.

dizziness [dízinjs], s. vértigo, vahído; desvanecimiento. **—dizzy** [dízi], a. vertiginoso, desvanecido.—vti. [7] causar vértigos; aturdir.

DNA abrev. (**deoxyribonucleic acid**) ADN, DNA.

do [du], vti. [11] hacer; ejecutar; obrar; finalizar; producir; despachar; cumplir; arreglar; cocer, guisar.—vii. hacer; comportarse; proceder; hallarse.—how d. you d.? ¿cómo está Ud?—that will d., eso basta, bastará.

docile [dásjl], a. dócil, sumiso.

dock [dak], s. dique, dársena; muelle, desembarcadero; banquillo de los acusados.—vt. cortar, cercenar; reducir, rebajar; (mar.) poner en dique.—vt. y vi. atracar, entrar en muelle.- **—er** [dákœ(r)], s. estibador, trabajador de muelle.

docket [dákit], s. minuta, sumario; rótulo, marbete.

dockyard [dákyard], s. astillero, arsenal.

doctor [dáktọ(r)], s. médico; doctor.— vt. medicinar, tratar; falsificar, adulterar; componer.- **—ate** [-it], s. doctorado.

doctrine [dáktrin], s. doctrina, dogma; teoría.

document [dákyụment], s. documento.—vt. [dákyụment], documentar; probar con documentos.— **—al** [dakyụméntạl], a., **—ary** [dakyụméntạri], a. documental.—s. (película) documental.- **—ation** [dakyụmentéjṣon], s. documentación.

dodge [dadẑ], vt. esquivar, soslayar, evadir.—vi. escabullirse; dar un quiebro o esquinazo; hurtar el cuerpo.

doe [dou], s. hembra del gamo, de la liebre, del conejo, del canguro y del antílope.—**skin** [dóuskin], s. ante; tejido fino de lana.

dog [dɔg], s. perro; macho de los cánidos (zorro, lobo, chacal, etc.); calavera, tunante.—d.-cheap, baratísimo.—d. collar, collar de perro; (fam. y humor.) alzacuello, clergyman.—d. days, canícula.—d.-eared, (fam.) sobado y con las esquinas dobladas.—d. in the manger, (fam.) el perro del hortelano.—d. racing, carrera de galgos.—d. show, exposición canina.—d. tired, cansadísimo.—to put on the d., darse ínfulas.—vti. [1] seguir los pasos; espiar, perseguir.- **—catcher** [-kaechoer], s. perrero.- **—fight** [dɔ́gfajt], s. riña de perros; combate entre aviones de caza. **—dogged** [dɔ́gid], a. terco, tenaz.—**doggy** [dɔ́gi], a. perruno.—d. bag, bolsita de sobras (proporcionado en un restaurante).- **—house** [-haus], s. caseta de perro.—in the d., en desgracia.

dogma [dɔ́gmạ], s. dogma.- **—tic** [dɔgmǽtik], a. dogmático.

dolly [dɔ́li], s. mantelillo individual.

doings [dúins], s. pl. acciones, obras; acontecimientos, cosas que ocurren.

dole [doul], s. distribución, reparto; porción; sopa boba; limosna; ración.—vt. repartir, distribuir, dar (limosna).- **—ful** [dóulfụl], a. dolorido; lúgubre, triste.

doll [dal], s. muñeca, muñeco.—d's house, dollhouse, casa de muñecas.—to d. up, acicalarse, emperifollarse.- **—y** [dáli], s. muñequita; plataforma rodante.

dollar [dálạr], s. dólar.—d. bill, billete de un dólar.—d. sign, signo del dólar.

dolphin [dálfin], s. delfín.

domain [doméin], s. dominio; heredad.

dome [doum], s. cúpula.

domestic [doméstik], a. doméstico, familiar; del país, nacional; interno, interior.—s. doméstico, sirviente.——**ate** [-eit], vt. domesticar; hacer adquirir costumbres caseras.

domicile [dámisil], s. domicilio.

dominant [dáminant], a. dominante. ——**dominate** [dámineit], vt. y vi. dominar. ——**domination** [daminéişon], s. dominación, dominio, imperio. ——**domineer** [daminír], vt. y vi. dominar, tiranizar. ——**domineering** [daminírin], a. dominante, tiránico, mandón. ——**dominion** [domínyon], s. dominio; territorio; distrito; posesión, propiedad.

don [dan], vti. [1] vestirse, ponerse, calarse.—s. caballero; don (título).

donate [dóuneit], vt. donar, contribuir. ——**donation** [dounéişon], s. donación, donativo, dádiva.

done [dʌn], pp. de TO DO.—a. hecho, ejecutado; acabado; bien cocido o asado.—d. for, agotado, rendido; perdido.—d. up, envuelto; fatigado.

donkey [dánki], s. asno, burro.

donor [dóuno(r)], s. donante, donador.

doom [dum], vt. sentenciar a muerte; predestinar a la perdición.—s. sentencia, condena; sino, destino; perdición, ruina.- ——**sday** [dúmzdei], s. día del juicio final.

door [dor], s. puerta; portezuela; entrada.—d. mat, felpudo.—d.-to-d., de puerta a puerta, a domicilio.- ——**bell** [dórbel], s. timbre o campanilla de llamada.- ——**keeper** [-kipœ(r)], ——**man** [-man], s. portero. - ——**knob** [-nab], s. tirador o perilla de puerta.- ——**plate** [-pleit], s. placa de puerta.- ——**sill** [-sil], s. umbral.- ——**step** [-step], s. escalón de la puerta.- ——**way** [-wei], s. entrada; portal.

dope [doup], s. estupefaciente, narcótico; menjurje; (fam.) datos, informes; tonto, estúpido.—d. addict, o fiend, narcómano.—d. racket, tráfico ilícito de drogas.—vt. narcotizar; pronosticar; conjeturar. ——**dopy** [dóupi], a. (fam.) narcotizado, aletargado.

dormitory [dórmitori], s. (bedroom)

dormitorio; (student's residence) residencia de estudiantes, colegio mayor.

dormouse [dórmaus], s. (zool.) lirón.

dorsal [dórsal], a. dorsal, espinal.

dosage [dóusidž], s. dosificación. ——**dose** [dous], s. dosis; (fig.) mal trago.—vt. administrar una dosis.— vi. medicarse con frecuencia.

dot [dat], s. punto.—on the d., en punto, a la hora exacta.—to a d., perfectamente, absolutamente.— vti. [1] puntear; poner punto (a una letra).

dotage [dóutidž], s. chochera; cariño excesivo. ——**dote** [dout], vi. chochear.

double [dábl], a. doble, duplicado; falso, engañoso.—d. agent, doble agente.—d. bed, cama de matrimonio.—d. boiler, baño Maria.— d.-breasted, (sast.) cruzado, de dos filas.—d. check, volver a revisar; verificar dos veces.—d.-cross, tración hecha a un cómplice.—d. chin, papada.—d. dealer, falso, traidor.—d. entry, partida doble.—d. meaning, doble sentido; equívoco; segunda intención.—d.-park, aparcar en doble fila.—d. talk, (fam.) galimatías; (fam.) habla ambigua para engañar.—adv. doblemente.—s. doble, duplo; (teat., cine) doble.—vt. doblar, duplicar.—vi. doblarse, duplicarse; volver atrás.

doubt [daut], vt. y vi. dudar; desconfiar.—s. duda.—if o when in d., en caso de duda.—ful [dáutful], a. dudoso. ——**less** [-lis], a. indudable, cierto; confiado.—adv. sin duda, indudablemente, probablemente.

douche [duš], s. jeringa o lavado vaginal; ducha, (Am.) regadera.—vt. y vi. duchar(se).

dough [dou], s. pasta, masa; (fam.) plata, dinero.- ——**nut** [dóunʌt], s. buñuelo, rosquilla, donut.- ——**y** [-i], a. pastoso.

dove [dʌv], s. paloma, tórtola.— [douv], pret. de TO DIVE.

dowel [dáuel], s. clavija, espiga.

down [daun], adv. abajo; hacia abajo; al sur.—d. below, allá abajo.—d. from, desde.—d. to, hasta.—d. to date, hasta la fecha.—to boil d., reducir la ebullición.—to cut d., recortar, rebajar.—to go o come d., bajar.—to lie d., acostarse.—interj. ¡abajo!—d.

with the King! ¡muera el Rey!—prep. en sentido descendente; por, al largo de, hacia abajo.—d. the street, calle abajo.—a. pendiente, descendente; abatido, alicaído; de abajo; atrasado, atrás.—d. and out, fuera de combate; vencido; arruinado.—d. payment, primer plazo, paga al contado.—to be d. on, tener inquina a.—s. plumón; bozo; lana fina o pelo suave, pelusa; revés de fortuna, baja, caída; colina, duna.—d. bed, colchón de plumas.—vt. derribar; vencer; tragar; creer sin previo examen.— **—cast** [dáunkæst], a. alicaído, cabizbajo.— **—fall** [-fɔl], s. caída; ruina.— **—grade** [-grejd], a. y adv. cuesta abajo.—s. bajada, descenso.— **—hearted** [-hartįd], a. abatido, descorazonado.— **—hill** [-hįl], a. pendiente, en declive. —s. declive, bajada.—adv. cuesta abajo.— **—pour** [-pɔr], s. aguacero, chaparrón.— **—right** [-rajt], a. vertical; claro, categórico; absoluto, completo.—adv. claramente, completamente.- **—sizing** [-sajzįŋ], s. reducción de personal.— **—stairs** [-stérz], adv. abajo, en el piso de abajo.—s. piso inferior, primer piso. - **—town** [-taun], a. y adv. de o en la parte baja de la ciudad; del centro.

dowry [dáurį], s. dote; arras.

doze [douz], vi. dormitar, descabezar el sueño.—s. sueño ligero; sopor.

dozen [dázęn], s. docena.

drab [dræb], a. pardusco; monótono; ordinario, sin atractivos.—s. color entre gris pardo y amarillento.

draft [dræft], s. corriente de aire; tiro (de chimenea, etc.); succión; trago; (mar.) calado, tracción; carretada; trazado, dibujo; plan, plano; borrador, minuta; proyecto, propuesta (de ley, reglamento, etc.); letra de cambio, libranza; (mil.) reclutamiento, leva; destacamento.—d. ale o beer, cerveza de tonel o de barril.— d. dodger, emboscado; prófugo del servicio militar.—vt. proyectar, bosquejar; hacer un borrador o diseño, esquema, plan; reclutar; redactar.— **—sman** [dræftsmęn], s. dibujante, delineante, diseñador.

drag [dræg], vti. [1] arrastrar, tirar; rastrear, rastrillar.—to d. in, traer por los cabellos.—to d. on u out, prolongar.—vii. arrastrarse por el suelo; ir

tirando; atrasarse, ir en zaga; pasar con penosa lentitud, ser interminable.—s. rastra; draga; rémora, cosa que retarda o dificulta.

drain [drejn], vt. drenar, desaguar; desecar; escurrir; colar; achicar; agotar; consumir, disipar.—to d. off, vaciar.—vi. desaguarse, vaciarse, escurrirse.—s. desagüe, escurridor; sumidero, alcantarilla; consumo; agotamiento.—d. plug, tapón de desagüe.—a. de desagüe.- **—age** [dréjnįdž], s. drenaje, desagüe.- **—er** [-œ(r)] s. colador, coladero.- **—pipe** [-paip], s. tubo de desagüe.

drake [drejk], s. pato o ánade macho.

drama [drámǎ], s. drama.— **—tic** [dramǽtįk], a. dramático.- **—tics** [dramǽtįks], s. dramática.— **—tist** [drǽmǎtįst], s. dramaturgo.— **—tize** [drǽmǎtajz], vt. dramatizar.

drank [dræŋk], pret. de TO DRINK.

drape [drejp], vt. revestir, entapizar; colgar (cortinas, etc.); formar pliegues artísticos.— **—ry** [dréjpœrį], s. cortinaje, ropaje, colgaduras, tapicería, etc.

draught [dræft], s., vt. = DRAFT.

draw [drɔ], vti. [10] tirar; atraer; estirar; sacar; inferir, deducir; desenvainar; hacer salir; chupar o mamar; aspirar, respirar; cobrar (un sueldo); sacarse (un premio); echar (suertes); procurarse, proporcionarse; correr o descorrer (cortinas, etc.); dibujar; trazar; redactar, extender (un cheque, etc.); devengar (intereses, etc.); retirar (fondos); girar, librar; tender (un arco); destripar (aves).—to d. along, arrastrar.—to d. aside, llevar aparte.—to d. back, hacer retroceder.—to d. in, atraer, seducir, embaucar.—to d. up, redactar.—vii. tirar; atraer gente; (dep.) empatar; dibujar.—to d. away, alejarse.—to d. back, retroceder.—to d. near, acercarse.—to d. up, pararse, detenerse.—s. tracción; atracción; empate; sorteo.- **—back** [drɔbæk], s. desventaja, inconveniente.- **—bridge** [-brįdž], s. puente levadizo o giratorio.- **—er** [-œ(r)], s. gaveta, cajón.—pl. calzoncillos.- **—ing** [-įŋ], s. dibujo; sorteo; giro; cobranza; extracción.—d. account, cuenta corriente.—d. board, tablero de dibujo.—d. room, sala, salón. **—drawn** [drɔn], pp. de TO DRAW.

drawl [drɔl], s. habla lenta y pesada.— vt. pronunciar lenta y pesadamente.—vi. hablar lenta y pesadamente.

dread [dred], s. miedo, pavor.—a. terrible, espantoso.—vt. y vi. temer, tener miedo a.- **—ful** [drédfʊl], a. terrible, espantoso.- **—locks** [-laks], spl. rizos al estilo de los rastafaris.

dream [drim], s. sueño, ensueño.—vti. y vii. [4] soñar; ver en sueños; fantasear, forjar(se).—to d. of, soñar con. - **—er** [drímœ(r)], s. soñador.— **y** [-i], a. contemplativo, soñador; propio de un sueño.

dreary [dríri], a. triste, melancólico; monótono, pesado.

dredge [dredʒ], vt. dragar; rastrear; polvorear.—s. draga; rastra.

dregs [dregz], s. pl. heces; sedimento; desperdicios; hez, gentuza.

drench [drench], vt. empapar; mojar; remojar.—s. empapada; mojadura.

dress [dres], vti. [4] vestir; ataviar; adornar; curar (heridas); preparar, arreglar; aliñar, aderezar; curtir; amortajar; arreglar (el pelo).—to d. down, poner como nuevo (a alguien).—vii. vestirse; ataviarse; adornarse; alinearse.—to d. up, vestirse de etiqueta, prenderse de veinticinco alfileres.—s. vestido; traje; indumentaria.—d. ball, baile de etiqueta o de trajes.—d. rehearsal, (teat.) ensayo general.—d. suit, traje de etiqueta.- **—er** [-oer], s. cómoda con espejo; tocador.—to be a good d., vestir con elegancia, vestirse con mucho estilo.- **—ing** [-iŋ], s. aderezamiento, adorno; (for salad) aliño; (stuffing) relleno; (med.) apósito; (med.) vendaje; (agr.) abono; (of leather) curtido.—d.-down, regaño.- **—maker** [-mejkoer], s. costurera, modista.- **—making** [-mejkiŋ], s. costura, modistería.- **—y** [drési], a. (fam.) elegante, vistoso.

drew [dru], pret. de TO DRAW.

dried [drajd], a. seco; secado; desecado. **—drier** [drájœ(r)], s. secador, secadora; secadero; secante; desecante.

drift [drift], s. rumbo, tendencia; impulso; deriva; montón (de nieve, arena).—to get the d. of, comprender lo esencial de algo; enterarse sólo a medias.—vi. (ser., mar.) derivar, ir a la deriva; vagar; apilarse,

amontonarse o esparcirse con el viento.- **—wood** [dríftwʊd], s. madera flotante; madera de playa.

drill [dril], vt. taladrar, barrenar, horadar; fresar; sembrar, plantar en hileras o surcos; ejercitar, dar instrucción (ejército, etc.), entrenar.—vi. (mil.) hacer la instrucción, practicar, ejercitarse.—s. taladro, fresa, barrena; práctica, ejercicio; disciplina; adiestramiento; (tela de) dril.

drink [driŋk], vti. y vii. [10] beber.—s. bebida; trago, copa.— **—able** [dríŋkabl], a. potable.- **—er** [-œ(r)], s. bebedor; borrachín.- **—ing** [iŋ], s. beber, el beber.—d. fountain, fuente de agua corriente para beber.—d. song, canción de taberna.—d. trough, abrevadero.—d. water, agua potable.—no drinking allowed, se prohibe el consumo de bebidas alcohólicas.

drip [drip], vti. y vii. [3] gotear.—s. gota; goteo; gotera.—d. coffee, café de maquinilla.—d.-dry, de lava y pon, de lavar y poner, lavilisto, no retorcer, cuélguelo mojado y déjelo escurrir.- **—ping** [dríp̣iŋ], s. goteo.—pl. líquidos que gotean; grasa.—a. (fam.) empapado, chorreantes.

drive [drajv], vti. [10] guiar, conducir, manejar (automóviles, etc.); impulsar, empujar; echar, arrojar; inducir; forzar (a); arrear; meter, clavar, hincar.—vii. andar o ir de paseo (automóvil, etc.); saber guiar, manejar o conducir vehículos.—to d. at, aspirar a, tender a; querer decir.—to d. away, ahuyentar, echar; alejarse (en un vehículo).—s. paseo en automóvil; capacidad de mando, energía; calzada para vehículos; presión, exigencia; tendencia, anhelo; campaña pública; conducción de vehículos.—d.-in, autocine; cafetería que sirve directamente en el automóvil.—d.-in bank, autobanco.

drivel [drível], vii. [2] babear; bobear.— s. baba; ñoñería; cháchara.

driven [dríven], pp. de TO DRIVE. **—driver** [drájvœ(r)], s. conductor, chófer; (of carriage) cochero; (of cart) carretero; (of racer) piloto; (of taxi) taxista.—driver's license, permiso de conducir, licencia de conducción.—*driver's seat,* asiento del chofer.—*pile d.,* martinete. **—driveway** [dráįvweį], *s.* vía de acceso a un garage; calzada.

drizzle [drízl], *vi.* lloviznar.—*s.* llovizna.

drone [drouȵ], *s.* zángano; haragán; zumbido.—*vi.* haraganear; zumbar; hablar en tono monótono.

droop [drup], *vi.* inclinarse, caer; colgar, pender; decaer, desanimarse; languidecer, marchitarse.

drop [drap], *s.* gota; zarcillo; caída, declive, pendiente; pastilla; (com.) baja, caída.—*a d. in the bucket,* una gota en el mar.—*d. curtain,* telón de boca.—*d. hammer,* martinete.—*vti.* [3] verter a gotas; soltar, dejar caer; desprenderse de; renunciar a, desistir de; despedir, echar.—*to d. a letter,* echar una carta en el buzón.—*to d. a line,* escribir unas líneas.—*to d. in,* hacer una visita inesperadamente.—*to d. out,* desaparecer; separarse.—*vii.* gotear; descender; detenerse.- **—let** [dráplįt], *s.* gotita.- **—out** [-aųt], *s.* marginado; alumno que no completa los estudios.

drought [draųt], **drouth** [draųθ], *s.* sequía; aridez, sequedad.

drove [drouv], *s.* manada, recua, hato, piara; gentío.—*pret.* de TO DRIVE.- **—r** [dróųvœ(r)], *s.* ganadero.

drown [draųȵ], *vt.* y *vi.* ahogar(se); anegar(se); sumergir(se).

drowse [draųz], *vt.* y *vi.* adormecer(se), amodorrar(se). **—drowsiness** [dráųsįnįs], *s.* modorra, somnolencia, pesadez. **—drowsy** [dráųzí], *a.* soñoliento, amodorrado; soporífero.

drudge [drʌdʒ], *vi.* afanarse, fatigarse.—*s.* ganapán, esclavo del trabajo.

drug [drʌg], *s.* droga, medicamento; narcótico; artículo de poca venta.—*d. addict,* drogadicto, toxicómano.—*d. store,* farmacia, botica, droguería.—*vti.* [1] mezclar con drogas; narcotizar.—*vii.* tomar drogas. **—druggist** [drʌgįst], *s.* droguero, farmacéutico.

drum [drʌm], *s.* tambor; redoblante; cuñete; cuerpo de columna; tímpano (del oído).—*d. major,* jefe de la banda; (mil.) tambor mayor—*vti.* y *vii.* [1] tocar el tambor; tam-

borilear; repetir, machacar; teclear.—**drummer** [-œ(r)], *s.* batería, baterista; (mil.) tambor, tamborilero; viajante de comercio.—**stick** [-stįk], *s.* baqueta, palillo (coc.) muslo, pata.

drunk [drʌȵk], *pp.* de TO DRINK.—*s.* borrachín; parranda, borrachera.—*a.* ebrio, borracho.- **—ard** [drʌȵkård], *s.* borracho, borrachín.- **—en** [-ęn], *a.* ebrio, borracho.—*d. driving,* conducir en estado de embriaguez, conducir borracho, manejar borracho.- **—enness** [-ęnnįs], *s.* embriaguez; ebriedad.

dry [draį], *a.* árido, seco.—*d. cell,* pila o elemento seco.—*d. cleaner,* tintorería.—*d. cleaning,* limpieza en seco.—*d. goods,* lencería; víveres.—*d. ice,* hielo seco.—*d. run,* simulacro.—*d. wall,* muro de mampostería sin mortero.—*vti.* [7] secar, desecar; enjugar; desaguar; acecinar.—*vii.* secarse, enjugarse.—*to d. up,* secarse completa y rápidamente. **—er** [dráįœ(r)], *s.* (hand-held) secador; (mec.) secadora.—*s.* = DRIER.- **—ness** [-nįs], *s.* sequedad, aridez.

dubious [djúbįʌs], *a.* dudoso; incierto; ambiguo.

duchess [dáchįs], *s.* duquesa.

duck [dʌk], *s.* pato, ánade; acción de agacharse.—*vt.* chapuzar; evitar (un golpe, deber, etc.).—*vi.* agacharse, chapuzar(se).- **—ling** [dáklįȵ], *s.* patito.

ductile [dáktįl], *a.* dúctil.

dud [dʌd], *s.* (fam.) persona o cosa floja o inútil; fiasco; bomba o granada que no estalla.—*pl.* (fam.) ropa.

dude [djud], *s.* petimetre, lechuguino.

due [dju], *a.* cumplido, vencido; pagadero; apto, propio, conveniente, oportuno; legítimo; esperado, que debe llegar.—*d. bill,* pagaré.—*adv.* exactamente.—*s.* deuda u obligación; derechos, tributo.—*to get one's d.,* llevar su merecido castigo.

duel [djúęl], *s.* duelo, desafío; certamen.—*vi.* batirse en duelo.

duet [djuét], *s.* dúo, dueto.

duffel [dáfęl], *s,—d. bag,* talego, tula, bolso marinero.

dug [dʌg], *pret.* y *pp.* de TO DIG.—*s.* teta, ubre.- **—out** [-aųt], *s.* chabola; (mar.) piragua.

duke [djuk], *s.* duque.

dull [dʌl], *a.* embotado, obtuso, sin

punta, sin filo; apagado, sordo; lerdo; insípido, soso, insulso; flojo, perezoso; lánguido; (colores) desvaído, mate; insensible; triste; deslustrado, empañado; opaco, nebuloso; soñoliento; (com.) inactivo, muerto.—*vt.* y *vi.* embotar(se); entorpecer(se); ofuscar(se); empañar(se).– **—ard** [dálạrd], *a.* estúpido.– **—ness** [-nịs], *s.* embotamiento; estupidez; aburrimiento; somnolencia, pesadez.

dumb [dʌm], *a.* mudo; callado; estúpido.—*deaf and d,* sordomudo.—*d. show,* pantomima.– **—bell** [-bel], *s.* halterio; (jer.) estúpido.– **—found** [-faund], *vt.* dejar sin habla, confundir.– **—ness** [dámnịs], *s.* mudez; silencio; estupidez.– **—waiter** [-weịtoer], *s.* montaplatos.

dummy [dámị], *a.* imitado, fingido, contrahecho.—*s.* maniquí; testaferro; (in printing) maqueta; (in cards) muerto; imitación; (jer.) estúpido, bobo.—*ventriloquist's d.,* muñeco de ventrílocuo.

dump [dʌmp], *vt.* vaciar de golpe; descargar; vender a precios inferiores a los corrientes.—*s.* montón de basuras; (landfill) basurero; (mil.) depósito de municiones.—*d. truck,* volquete, dumper.—*pl.* melancolía, morriña.– **—ing** [dámpịn], *s.* vaciamiento; inundación del mercado con artículos de precios rebajados; competir comercialmente con precios ínfimos.—*d. ground,* vertedero, basurero.

dumpling [dámplịn], *s.* bola de pasta hervida.

dumpy [dámpị], *a,* regordete.

dun [dʌn], *a.* (color) pardo.—*vt.* requerir para el pago.

dunce [dʌns], *s.* zopenco, tonto.

dune [djun], *s.* duna.—*d. buggy,* buggy (para transitar por la arena).

dung [dʌŋ], *s.* estiércol, boñiga.—*d. heap o yard,* estercolero, muladar.

dungarees [dʌŋgạríz], *spl.* overol, mono; pantalón de peto.

dungeon [dándzọn], *s.* calabozo, mazmorra.

dunghill [dáŋhịl], *s.* estercolero, muladar.

dunk [dʌŋk], *vt.* (coll.) mojar, ensopar; tirar al agua.

dupe [djup], *s.* incauto, primo.—*vt.* engañar, embaucar.

duplicate [djúplịkeịt], *vt.* duplicar.— *s.* [djúplịkịt], duplicado, copia.—*in d.,* por duplicado.—*a.* duplicado, doble, en pares. **—duplicity** [djuplísịtị], *s.* duplicidad, engaño, segunda intención.

durability [djurạbílịtị], *s.* durabilidad duración; permanencia. **—duration** [djuréịsọn], *s.* duración. **—during** [djúrịn], *prep.* durante, mientras.

dusk [dʌsk], *a.* oscuro (poet.).—*s.* crepúsculo vespertino; oscuridad.— *d.-to-dawn,* del anochecer, a la madrugada.– **—y** [dáskị], *a.* oscuro; moreno; pardo.

dust [dʌst], *s.* polvo; cenizas, restos mortales.—*d. brush,* plumero.—*d. cloud,* polvareda.—*vt.* sacudir o quitar el polvo; (es)polvorear.—*to d. one's jacket,* zurrar a uno.– **—bin** [-bịn], *s.* receptáculo para polvo o cenizas.– **—er** [dástœ(r)], *s.* paño del polvo; plumero; guardapolvos. – **—y** [-ị], *a.* empolvado, polvoriento.

Dutch [dʌch], *s.* y *a.* holandés.—*D. tile,* azulejo.—*D. treat,* convite a escote.—*to go D.,* ir a medias.- **—man** [dáchmạn], *s.* holandés.

duty [djútị], *s.* deber, obligación; incumbencia; impuesto, derechos de aduana; trabajo, servicio (mec.).— *d. free,* libre de impuestos.—*in d. bound,* moralmente obligado.—*off d.,* libre, franco de servicio.—*on d.,* de guardia o de servicio.

dwell [dwel], *vii.* [4] habitar, morar.

dwarf [dwɔrf], *s.* enano, pigmeo.—*a.* diminuto, enano.

dwindle [dwíndl], *vi.* menguar, disminuirse; degenerar; decaer; consumirse.—*vt.* mermar.

dye [daị], *vt.* teñir.—*s.* tinte.- **—r** [dáịœ(r)], *s.* tintorero.

dying [dáịịn], *a.* moribundo; mortecino; mortal.—*s.* muerte.

dynamic [daịnǽmịk], *a.* dinámico; enérgico.

dynamite [dáịnạmaịt], *s.* dinamita.— *vt.* volar con dinamita, dinamitar.

dynamo [dáịnạmou], *s.* dínamo, generador.

dynasty [dáịnạstị], *s.* dinastía.

dysentery [dísẹnterị], *s.* disentería.

E

each [ich], *a.* cada, todo.—*pron.* cada uno, cada cual, todos.—*e.* **for him-self,** cada cual por su cuenta, o por su lado.—*e.* **other,** mutuamente; unos a otros.—*adv.* por persona, por cabeza, cada cual.

eager [ígœ(r)], *a.* ansioso, anhelante, deseoso.— **—ness** [-n̩s], *s.* ansia, anhelo, afán, ahinco; vehemencia.

eagle [ígl̩], *s.* águila.- **—t** [íglit], *s.* aguilucho.

ear [ir], *s.* oreja; oído; espiga.—*by the* **ears,** en pugna abierta.—*e.* **muff,** orejera.—*to be all ears,* (fam.) aguzar los oídos o las orejas.- **—ache** [-ek], *s.* dolor de oído.- **—drops** [-drapz], *spl.* gotas para los oídos.- **—drum** [ir̩drʌm], *s.* tímpano.

earl [œrl], *s.* conde.

early [œ́rli], *a.* primitivo, primero; tempran(er)o; próximo.—*e.* **bird,** (fig.) madrugador.—*e.* **warning,** de alerta avanzada, de alerta precoz. —*e.-warning system,* sistema de alarma anticipada, sistema de alerta avanzada.—*the e. part of,* el principio de.—*adv.* temprano, pronto, antes de la hora; al principio.—*as e. as possible,* lo más pronto posible.

earn [œrn], *vt.* ganar; merecer.

earnest [œ́rn̩st], *a.* serio, formal.—*s.* seriedad, buena fe; prenda, señal.- **—ness** [-n̩s], *s.* seriedad; sinceridad; celo.

earnings [œ́rniŋz], *s. pl.* salario, sueldo, paga, jornal; ganancias.

earphone [írfoun], *s.* auricular; audífono.

earring [íriŋ], *s.* pendiente, arete.

earth [œrθ], *s.* tierra (materia; planeta); mundo; suelo.- **—enware** [œ́rθ̩nwɛr], *s.* loza de barro, cacharros.- **—ly** [-li], *a.* terreno; terrenal, mundano.- **—quake** [-kwejk], *s.* temblor de tierra, terremoto.- **—ward** [-wǎrd]. *a. y adv.* hacia la tierra.- **—worm** [-wœrm], *s.* lombriz de tierra.- **—y** [-i], *a.* terroso; mundano, primario.

ease [iz], *s.* tranquilidad; comodidad, alivio, descanso; facilidad, desenvoltura, naturalidad.—*at e.,* descansadamente, a sus anchas.—*with e.,* con facilidad.—*vt.* aliviar, mitigar, aligerar, desembarazar, facilitar.—*vi.* disminuir, apaciguarse, suavizarse.

easel [ízel̩], *s.* caballete de pintor; atril.

east [ist], *s.* este, levante, oriente.—*a.* oriental; del este.—*E. Indian,* indio, hindú.—*E. Indies,* spl. Indias Orientales.—*adv.* hacia el este.

Easter [ístœ(r)], *s.* Pascua florida o de Resurrección.—*E. egg,* huevo de Pascua.—*E. Saturday,* Sábado Santo.—*E. Sunday,* Domingo de Resurrección.

eastern [ístœrn], *a.* oriental. **—East-erner** [ístœrnœ(r)], *s.* oriental; habitante del este (de los E.U.).

easy [ízi], *a.* fácil; cómodo; suelto, libre; tranquilo; aliviado.—*e. chair,* butaca, poltrona.—*e. going,* lento; calmado, sereno.—*adv.* e *interj.* despacio, qued(it)o.

eat [it], *vti.* [10] comer, tomar.—*to e. away, into* o *through,* corroer.—*to e. breakfast, lunch, dinner, supper,* desayunarse, almorzar, comer, cenar.—*to e. one's heart out,* sufrir en silencio.—*to e. one's words,* retractarse.—*to e. up,* devorar, tragar.—*vii.* comer, alimentarse, sustentarse. **—eaten** [íten̩], *pp.* de TO EAT.

eaves [ivz], *s. pl.* alero.— **—drop** [ívzdrap], *vii.* [1] escuchar solapadamente, fisgonear.

ebb [eb], *vi.* menguar la marea; decaer.—*s.* menguante, marea baja, reflujo; decadencia.—*e. of life,* vejez.—*e. tide,* marea menguante.

ebony [éboni], *s.* ébano.

eccentric [ikséntrik], *s.* persona excéntrica o rara; (mec.) excéntrica.—*a.* also **—al** [-al̩], *a.* (geom. y mec.) excéntrico; extravagante, estrafalario.

ecclesiastic [iklizíǽstik], *s.* eclesiástico. **—e.,** **—al** [-al̩], *a.* eclesiástico.

echo [ékou], *s.* eco.—*vi.* repercutir, resonar.—*vt.* repetir con aprobación; hacer eco.

eclipse [iklíps], *s.* eclipse.—*vt.* eclipsar.

ecocide [ékosajd], *s.* ecocidio.

ecological [ikǒládʒikǎl], *a.* ecológico.

ecology [ikǎdʒi], s. ecología.

economic(al) [ikonámik(al)], a. económico; moderado, módico. **—economics** [ikonámiks], s. economía política. **—economist** [ikánomist], s. economista. **—economize** [ikánomajz], vt. y vi. economizar, ahorrar. **—economy** [ikánomi], s. economía, ahorro.

ecstasy [ékstasi], s. éxtasis.

ecstatic [ɛkstaétik], a. extático, extasiado.

Ecuadorian [ɛkwadórian], a. y s. ecuatoriano.

eddy [édi], s. remanso; remolino.—vi. arremolinarse; remansarse.

edge [edʒ], s. filo; canto; borde, orilla, margen.—on e., de canto; impaciente, ansioso.—to set the teeth on e., dar dentera.—vt. incitar; (cost.) orlar.—vi. avanzar de lado, escurrirse.— **—wise** [édʒwajz], adv. de filo o de canto. **—edging** [édʒin], s. orla(dura), pestaña.

edible [édibl], a. y s. comestible.

edict [idikt], s. edicto, mandato; bando.

edifice [édifis], s. edificio. **—edify** [édifaj], vti. [7] edificar; instruir moralmente.

edit [édit], vt. redactar; editar; dirigir (un periódico); corregir (manuscritos).— **—ion** [idíʃon], s. edición; tirada.— **—or** [-o̩(r)], s. redactor; director de un periódico o revista; editor.— **—orial** [-ɔ́rial], a. editorial.—e. rooms o staff, redacción.— s. editorial, artículo de fondo.

educate [édjukejt], vt. educar; instruir. **—education** [edjukéjʃon], s. educación; enseñanza, instrucción. **—educational** [edjukéjʃonal], a. docente; educativo.—e. institution, plantel, centro docente. **—educator** [édjukejto̩(r)], s. educador.

eel [il], s. anguila.

eerie [iri], a. misterioso, espectral.

effect [ɛfékt], s. efecto; impresión; eficiencia.—pl. efectos. bienes.—in e., vigente; en realidad.—into e., en vigor, en práctica.—of no e., sin resultado; vano.—to the e. that, de que, en el sentido de que.—vt. efectuar, realizar, llevar a cabo.— **—ive** [-iv], a. efectivo, eficaz; vigente.

effeminate [ɛféminit], a. afeminado.

efficacy [éfikasi], s. eficacia.

efficiency [ɛfíʃensi], s. eficiencia; eficacia; (mec.) rendimiento. **—efficient** [ɛfíʃent], a. eficiente; eficaz, competente; (mec.) de gran rendimiento.

effigy [éfidʒi], s. efigie.

effort [éfort], s. esfuerzo, empeño.

effrontery [efrántœri], s. desfachatez, descaro.

effusion [ɛfiúʒon], s. efusión, derrame; expansión. **—effusive** [ɛfiúsiv], a. expansivo, efusivo.

egg [eg], s. huevo.—e. dealer, huevero.—e.-laying, postura.—e. white, clara de huevo.—e. yolk, yema de huevo.—hard boiled e., huevo duro.—poached e., huevo escalfado.—soft-boiled e., huevo pasado por agua.- **—head** [-hed], s. (jer.) cerebro.- **—nog** [égnag], s. ponche de huevo.- **—plant** [-plænt], s. berenjena.- **—shell** [-ʃel], s. cáscara de huevo.

egotism [ígoṳtizm], s. egolatría, egotismo. **—egotist** [ígoṳtist], s. ególatra, egotista.

Egyptian [idʒípʃan], a. y s. egipcio.

eight [et], a. y s. ocho. **—eighth** [etθ], a. y s. octavo. **—eight hundred,** ochocientos.—e. one, ochocientos uno.

eighteen [etín], a. y s. dieciocho, diez y ocho. **—eighteenth** [etínθ], a. y s. décimoctavo. **—eighty** [éti], a. y s. ochenta. —e.-one, ochenta y uno. **—eightieth** [étiiθ], a. y s. octogésimo; ochentavo.

either [íðœ(r), ájðœ(r)], a. y pron. uno u otro, cualquiera de los dos.— conj. o, ora, ya.—adv. (después de not, nor) tampoco.

ejaculate [idʒǽkyūlejt], vt. exclamar, proferir; (med.) eyacular. **—ejaculation** [idʒækyūléjʃon], s. exclamación; eyaculación.

eject [idʒékt], vt. arrojar, lanzar, expulsar.- **—ion** [idʒékʃon], s. expulsión, evacuación.

elaborate [ilǽbɔrejt], vt. elaborar; explicar detalladamente.—a. [ilǽbɔrit], elaborado, trabajado, detallado, esmerado; recargado. **—elaboration** [ilæbɔréjʃon], s. elaboración; obra acabada.

elapse [ilǽps], vi. pasar, transcurrir.

elastic [ilǽstik], a. elástico.—s. cinta de goma, elástico.- **—ity** [ilǽstisiti], s. elasticidad.

elate [iléjt], *vt.* exaltar; alborozar; elevar.- **—d** [-jd], *a.* exaltado, alborozado.

elbow [élbou], *s.* codo; recodo, ángulo; brazo de sillón.—*at one's e.,* a la mano, muy cerca.—*e. room,* espacio suficiente, holgura.—*vt.* dar codazos.—*to e. one's way,* abrirse paso a codazos.—*vi.* codear; formar recodos o ángulos.

elder [éldœ(r)], *a.* mayor, de más edad; antiguo, anterior.—*s.* anciano; soñor mayor; dignatario.—*pl.* ancianos, mayores, antepasados.- **—ly** [-lj], *a.* mayor, de edad madura o avanzada. **—eldest** [éldjst], *a.* mayor de todos, [el] de más edad.—*e. son,* hijo primogénito.

elect [jlékt], *vt.* elegir, escoger.—*a.* y *s.* electo o elegido.- **—ive** [-iv], *a.* electivo.—*s.* (elective course) optativa.- **—ion** [jlékšon], *s.* elección.- **—or** [-o̱(r)], *s.* elector.- **—oral** [-o̱ral], *a.* electoral.- **—orate** [-o̱rjt], *s.* electorado.

electric [jléktrik], *a.* eléctrico.—*e. blanket,* cobija eléctrica.—*e. chair,* silla eléctrica.—*e. clock,* reloj eléctrico.—*e. eel,* anguila eléctrica.—*e. eye,* célula fotoeléctrica.—*e. fence,* cercado electrificado.—*e. guitar,* guitarra eléctrica.—*e. ray,* torpedo.—*e. razor (o e. shaver),* máquina de afeitar eléctrica.—*e. shock,* descarga eléctrica.—*e. shock treatment,* tratamiento por electrochoque.—*e. tape,* cinta aislante.- **—al** [-al], *a.* eléctrico.—*e. engineer,* electricista, ingeniero electrotécnico, ingeniero electroísta.—*e. engineering,* electrotecnia, ingeniería eléctrica, ingeniería electricista.—*e. storm,* tormenta eléctrica. **—electrician** [jlektríšan], *s.* electricista. **—electricity** [jlektrísiti], *s.* electricidad. **—electrification** [jlektrjfjkéjšon], *s.* electrización; electrificación. **—electrify** [jléktrjfaj], *vti.* [7] electrizar; electrificar. **—electrocardiogram** [jlektrokárdjograem], *s.* electrocardiograma. **—electrocute** [jléktrokjut], *vt.* electrocutar. **—electrocution** [jlektrokjúšon], *s.* electrocución. **—electrode** [jléktroud], *s.* electrodo. **—electrolysis** [jlektrálẹsjs], *s.* electrólisis.- **—electromagnetic** [jlektromaegnétjk], *a.* electromagnético.

electron [jléktran], *s.* electrón.—*e. beam,* haz de electrones.—*e. gun,* cañón de electrones.—*e. microscope,* microscopio electrónico.- **—ic** [-jk], *a.* electrónico.—*e. mail,* correo electrónico. **—electronics** [jlektránjks], *s.* electrónica.

electroshock [jléktrošak], *s.* electrochoque.—*e. therapy,* terapía de electrochoque.

elegance [éligans], *s.* elegancia. **—elegant** [éligant], *a.* elegante.

element [éljment], *s.* elemento; componente.—*pl.* nociones, rudimentos.- **—al** [eljméntal], **—ary** [eljménterj], *a.* elemental, primordial, rudimentario.—*e. school,* escuela de enseñanza primaria.

elephant [éljfant], *s.* elefante.

elevate [éljvejt], *vt.* elevar; alzar, exaltar. **—elevated** [éljvejtjd], *a.* elevado.—*e. railroad,* ferrocarril elevado. **—elevation** [eljvéjšon], *s.* elevación; exaltación; altura; eminencia. **—elevator** [éljvejto(r)], *s.* ascensor; elevador.—*e. shaft,* caja o pozo del ascensor.—*grain e.,* silo.

eligible [éljdžjbl], *a.* elegible.

eliminate [jlímjnejt], *vt.* eliminar, suprimir. **—elimination** [jljmjnéjšon], *s.* eliminación, supresión. **—eliminatory** [jlímjnatorj], *a.* eliminatorio.

eleven [jlévẹn], *a.* y *s.* once.- **—eleventh** [jlévẹnθ], *a.* y *s.* undécimo.

elf [ɛlf], *s.* geniecillo, elfo. **—elves** [ɛlvz], *spl.* geniecillos.

elite [ilít], *a.* y *s.* elite, élite.

elk [ɛlk], *s.* alce o ante.

elm [ɛlm], *s.* olmo.

elocution [ɛlokjúšon], *s.* elocución; declamación.

elope [jlóup], *vi.* fugarse, huir con un amante.- **—ment** [-mẹnt], *s.* fuga amorosa.

eloquence [élokwẹns], *s.* elocuencia, oratoria, (fam.) labia. **—eloquent** [élokwẹnt], *a.* elocuente.

else [ɛls], *a.* otro, diferente; más.—*anything e.,* algo más; cualquiera otra cosa.—*nobody e.,* no one e.,* ningún otro.—*adv.* y *conj.* más, además; en vez de.—*how e.?,* ¿de qué otro modo?.—*or e.,* o bien, o en su lugar, de otro modo, en otro caso; si no.- **—where** [élswer], *adv.* en, a o de otra parte.

elude [jljúd], *vt.* eludir, evadir, evitar,

sortear. —**elusive** [iljúsiv], **elusory** [iljúsori], *a.* evasivo, fugaz.

emaciate(d) [iméişieit(id)], *a.* demacrado, macilento, flaco; extenuado.

e-mail or **E-mail** [ímeil], *s.* correo electrónico.

emancipate [imǽnsipeit], *vt.* emancipar.—**emancipation** [imænsipéişǫn], *s.* emancipación. —**emancipator** [imǽnsipeitǫ(r)], *s.* emancipador, libertador.

embalm [embám], *vt.* embalsamar.- —**ment** [-mǫnt], *s.* embalsamamiento.

embankment [embǽŋkmǫnt], *s.* dique; terraplén.

embarcation [embarkéişǫn], *s.* = EMBARKATION.

embargo [embárgou], *s.* embargo, detención, prohibición.—*vt.* embargar, detener.

embark [embárk], *vt.* y *vi.* embarcar(se).- —**ation**, [-éişǫn], *s.* embarque.

embarrass [embǽrǫs], *vt.* turbar, desconcertar; embarazar.- —**ment** [-mǫnt], *s.* turbación; embarazo, estorbo; (com.) apuros.

embassy [émbǫşi], *s.* embajada.

embed [embéd], *vti.* [1] eneajar, empotrar.

embellish [embéliş], *vt.* embellecer.- —**ment** [-mǫnt], *s.* embellecimiento.

ember [émbœ(r)], *s.* ascua, pavesa.— *pl.* rescoldo.

embezzle [embézl], *vt.* desfalcar.- —**ment** [-mǫnt], *s.* desfalco.- —**r** [embézlœ(r)], *s.* desfalcador.

embitter [embitœ(r)], *vt.* emargar.

emblem [émblǫm], *s.* emblema, símbolo.

embody [embadi], *vti.* [7] dar cuerpo, encarnar; incorporar; incluir, englobar.—*vii.* unirse, incorporarse.

embolus [émbǫlʌs], *s.* (med.) émbolo.

emboss [embós], *vt.* repujar, realzar, estampar en relieve.- —**ment** [-mǫnt], *s.* realce, relieve.

embrace [embréis], *vt.* abrazar; abarcar, rodear.—*vi.* abrazarse.—*s.* abrazo.

embrasure [embréiş̂ų(r)], *s.* (fort.) tronera, aspillera; (arq.) alféizar.

embroider [embróidœ(r)], *vt.* bordar, recamar.—*vi.* hacer labor de bordado.- —**er** [-œ(r)], —**ess** [-is], *s.* bordador; bordadora.- —**y** [-i], *s.* bordado, bordadura, labor.

embroil [embróil], *vt.* embrollar, enredar.- —**ment** [-mǫnt], *s.* embrollo intriga.

embryo [émbriou], *s.* embrión.- —**nic** [embriánik], *a.* embrionario.

emendation [imendéişǫn], *s.* enmienda, corrección.

emerald [émerǫld], *s.* esmeralda.

emerge [imœ́rdž], *vi.* emerger, brotar, surgir.

emergency [imœ́rdžensi], *s.* emergencia, aprieto o necesidad urgente.—*e. hospital,* hospital de urgencia casa de socorros.—*e. landing,* aterrizaje forzoso. —**emergen** [imœ́rdžǫnt], *a.* emergente; urgente.

emeritus [imérițŭs], *a.* emérito.—*professor,* profesor emérito.

emery [émęri], *s.* esmeril.

emigrant [émigrǫnt], *a.* emigrante.- *s.* emigrante, emigrado. —**emigrat** [émigreit], *vi.* emigrar, expatriarse —**emigration** [emigréişǫn], *s.* emigración.

eminence [émiņens], *s.* altura, cima eminencia. —**eminent** [émiņent] *a.* eminente.

emissary [émiseri], *s.* emisario —**emission** [imíşǫn], *s.* emisión salida. —**emit** [imít], *vti.* [1] emitir.

emotion [imóuşǫn], *s.* emoción. —**al** [-ǫl], *a.* emocional, emotivo sensible; sentimental.

emperor [émpœrǫ(r)], *s.* emperador.

emphasis [émfasis], *s.* énfasis. —**emphasize** [émfasaiz], *vt.* enfatiza poner énfasis; recalcar, acentua. —**emphatic** [emfǽtik], *a.* enfático energético; categórico.

empire [émpair], *s.* imperio.

employ [emplói], *vt.* emplear; usa dedicar.—*s.* empleo; ocupación oficio.— —**ce** [-í], *s.* empleado.- —**er** [-œ(r)], *s.* patrón, patrono. —**ment** [-mǫnt], *s.* empleo, colocación; uso, aplicación.

empower [empáuœ(r)], *vt.* autoriza facultar, dar poder.

empress [émpris], *s.* emperatriz.

empty [émpti], *a.* vacío, desocupado vacante; vano; vacuo, frívolo.—*e headed,* tonto.—*vti.* [7] vaciar, de socupar, evacuar.—*vii.* vaciarse; de saguar, desembocar.

emulsion [imálşǫn], *s.* emulsión.

enable [enéibl], *vt.* habilitar, capac tar, permitir.

enact [enǽkt], *vt.* promulgar, da

(una ley); decretar; (teat.) hacer el papel de.

enamel [ɛnǽmel], *vti.* [2] esmaltar.— *s.* esmalte.

encamp [ɛnkǽmp], *vt.* y *vi.* (mil.) acampar.— **—ment** [-ment], *s.* campamento.

enchant [ɛnchǽnt], *vt.* encantar, hechizar; fascinar, embelesar.— **—er** [-œ(r)], *s.* encantador, hechicero.— **—ment** [-ment], *s.* encantamiento, hechicería, hechizo; encanto.— **—ress** [-ris], *s.* maga; encantadora, seductora, hechicera.

encircle [ɛnsǿrkl], *vt.* cercar, rodear.

enclose [ɛnklóuz], *vt.* cercar; rodear, circundar; encerrar; incluir, adjuntar o enviar adjunta una cosa. **—enclosure** [ɛnklóuẑū(r)], *s.* vallado, tapia; cercado; recinto; lo adjunto (en carta, etc.), contenido.

encompass [ɛnkámpas], *vt.* circundar, rodear, encerrar; abarcar.

encore [ánkor], *s.* (teat) bis, repetición.—*interj.* ¡bis!; ¡que se repita!—*vt.* (teat.) pedir la repetición de, pedir la repetición a.

encounter [ɛnkáutœ(r)], *s.* encuentro, choque; combate.—*vt.* y *vi.* encontrar; salir al encuentro de; topar o tropezar con.

encourage [ɛnkǿridẑ], *vt.* animar, alentar; fomentar.— **—ment** [-ment], *s.* aliento, ánimo; fomento.

encumber [ɛnkámboer], *vt.* cargar, estorbar.

encumbrance [ɛnkámbraens], *s.* estorbo; impedimento.

encyclopedia [ɛnsaiklopídia], *s.* enciclopedia.

end [end], *s.* fin; extremidad; punta; remate; desenlace, final; fondo; propósito, objeto.—*at loose ends,* en desorden, desarreglado.—*at the e. of,* al cabo de.—*e. line,* línea de límite.—*no e. of,* un sinfín de, muchísimo(s), la mar de.—*to make both ends meet,* pasar con lo que se tiene.—*to no e.,* sin efecto, en vano.—*vt.* y *vi.* acabar, concluir, terminar, finalizar.

endear [ɛndír], *vt.* hacer(se) querer.

endeavor [ɛndévǿ(r)], *s.* esfuerzo, conato, empeño, tentativa.—*vt.* intentar, pretender, tratar de.—*vi.* esforzarse, hacer un esfuerzo (por).

ending [ɛndiŋ], *s.* fin, conclusión; terminación; desenlace.

endive [ɛndaiv], *s.* (bot.) escarola.

endless [ɛndlis], *a.* sin fin; interminable, perpetuo.

endorse [ɛndórs], *vt.* = INDORSE. **—endorsement** [ɛndórsment], *s.* = INDORSEMENT.

endow [ɛndáu], *vt.* dotar; fundar.— **—ment** [-ment], *s.* dotación; fundación; dote, prenda, atributo, gracia.

endurance [ɛndiúrans], *s.* paciencia; resistencia; duración.—*to be beyond* o *past e.,* ser insoportable o inaguantable. **—endure** [ɛndiúr], *vt.* soportar, sufrir, resistir, tolerar.—*vi.* durar, perdurar; tener paciencia.

enema [ɛnemä], *s.* (med.) enema, lavativa.

enemy [ɛnemi], *s.* enemigo, adversario.

energetic(al) [ɛnœrdẑétik(al)], *a.* enérgico, vigoroso. **—energy** [ɛnœrdẑi], *s.* energía, vigor, carácter.—*e. crisis,* crisis de energía, crisis energética.

enervate [ɛnœrveit], *vt.* enervar, debilitar; desvirtuar, embotar.

enfold [ɛnfóuld], *vt.* = INFOLD.

enforce [ɛnfórs], *vt.* dar fuerza o vigor; poner en vigor; cumplimentar, observar o ejecutar (una ley); hacer hincapié en.— **—ment** [-ment], *s.* ejecución de una ley; observancia forzosa.

engage [ɛngéidẑ], *vt.* ajustar, apalabrar, comprometer; contratar; emplear; entretener; atraer; (mil.) librar o trabar batalla o combate, entrar en lucha con; (mec.) engranar con.—*vi.* obligarse, dar palabra, comprometerse; ocuparse, entregarse a; pelear.— **—d** [-d], *a.* ocupado; comprometido; comprometido para casarse; engranado.— **—ment** [-ment], *s.* contrato; compromiso, noviazgo; cita; engranaje; batalla, acción.

engender [ɛndẑéndœ(r)], *vt.* engendrar, procrear.—*vi.* engendrarse, producirse.

engine [ɛndẑin], *s.* máquina; locomotora; motor; instrumento.— **—er** [-ír], *s.* ingeniero; maquinista.—*vt.* manejar, dirigir.—*vi.* hacer de ingeniero o maquinista.— **—ering** [-íriŋ], *s.* ingeniería; manejo.

English [íngliš], *s.* y *a.* inglés.—*E. Channel,* Canal de la Mancha.—*s.* idioma inglés.—*E. speaking,* de habla inglesa.– **—man** [-mạn], s. inglés.– **—woman** [-wụmạn], s. inglesa.

engrave [ɛngréịv], vt. grabar; cincelar, esculpir.– **—r** [-œ(r)], s. grabador. **—engraving** [ɛngréịvịn̩], s. grabado; lámina, estampa.

enhance [ɛnhǽns], vt. realzar, aumentar; mejorar; (comput.) procesar.– **—d** [ɛnhaénst], a. mejorado; (comput.) procesado.– **—ment** [-mẹnt], s. realce, aumento, ampliación; mejora.

enigma [ịnígmạ], s. enigma, intríngulis.

enjoin [ɛnd̂ɔ́ịn], vt. mandar, ordenar; imponer.—to e. from, (for.) prohibir.

enjoy [ɛndʒɔ́ị], vt. gozar de; gustar de; gustarle a uno; disfrutar de; saborear.—to e. oneself, gozar, divertirse. – **—able** [-ạbl], a. deleitable, agradable.– **—ment** [-mẹnt], s. goce, disfrute, placer; usufructo.

enlarge [ɛnlárdʒ], vt. agrandar, ensanchar; ampliar o amplificar.—vi. ensancharse o agrandarse; explayarse (en).– **—ment** [-mẹnt], s. agrandamiento, ensanchamiento; ampliación.– **—r** [-œ(r)], s. (fot.) ampliador(a).

enlighten [ɛnláịtẹn], vt. iluminar, instruir, ilustrar, alumbrar, esclarecer.

enlist [ɛnlíst], vt. alistar; enrolar; reclutar.—vi. enrolarse; sentar plaza.– **—ment** [-mẹnt], s. alistamiento, enganche, enrolamiento, reclutamiento.

enliven [ɛnláịvẹn], vt. animar, alentar, avivar.

enmity [ɛ́nmịtị], s. enemistad.

ennoble [ɛnóųbl], vt. ennoblecer.

enormity [ịnɔ́rmịtị], s. enormidad; atrocidad. **—enormous** [ịnɔ́rmʌs], a. enorme; atroz.

enough [ịnʌ́f], a. bastante, suficiente.—to be e., bastar.—s. lo suficiente.—interj. ¡basta! ¡no más!.— adv. bastante, harto.

enquire [ɛnkwáịr], vt. = INQUIRE. **—enquirer** [ɛnkwáịrœ(r)], s. = INQUIRER.

enrage [ɛnréịdʒ], vt. enfurecer, encolerizar.

enrapture [ɛnrǽpchū(r)], vt. arrobar, embelesar, extasiar.

enrich [ɛnrích], vt. enriquecer.– **—ment** [-mẹnt], s. enriquecimiento.

enroll [ɛnróụl], vt. y vi. alistar(se), enrolar(se); matricular(se); envol-

ver(se); enrollar(se).—vi. alistarse enrolarse; inscribirse, matricularse.– **—ment** [-mẹnt], s. alistamiento, enrolamiento; matrícula registro.

ensign [ɛ́nsaịn], s. bandera, enseña pabellón; [ɛ́nsịn], alférez; subteniente.—e. bearer, abanderado.

enslave [ɛnsléịv], vt. esclavizar.

ensue [ɛnsjú], vi. suceder, sobrevenir.

entail [ɛntéịl], s. vinculación.—vt vincular, perpetuar; acarrear, imponer.

entangle [ɛntǽn̩gl], vt. enredar, embrollar, enmarañar.– **—men** [-mẹnt], s. enredo, embrollo, complicación.

enter [ɛ́ntœ(r)], vt. entrar a, por o en penetrar; asentar, registrar; hacerse miembro de, ingresar en.—vi. entrar, introducirse; (teat.) salir al escenario, entrar en escena.

enterprise [ɛ́ntœrpraịz], s. empresa **—enterprising** [ɛ́ntœrpraịzịn̩], a emprendedor.

entertain [ɛntœrtéịn], vt. entretener divertir; festejar, agasajar (en casa).—to e. hopes, ideas, abrigar o acariciar esperanzas o ideas.– **—e** [-œ(r)], s. artista de variedades; an fitrión.– **—ment** [-mẹnt], s. entretenimiento.

enthrone [ɛnθróụn], vt. entron(iz)ar.

enthusiasm [ɛnθjúzịæzm], s. entusiasmo. **—enthusiast** [ɛnθjúzịæst] s. entusiasta. **—enthusiastic(al)** [ɛn θịuzịǽstịk(al)], a. entusiástico, en tusiasta; entusiasmado.

entice [ɛntáịs], vt. atraer, seducir, ha lagar; engatusar.

entire [ɛntáịr], a. entero, cabal, com pleto, íntegro, todo.– **—ty** [-tị] s. entereza, integridad, totalidad todo.

entitle [ɛntáịtl], vt. titular; dar de recho a, autorizar.—to be entitled titularse.—to be entitled to, tene derecho a.– **—ment** [mẹnt], s. de recho, autorización.

entity [ɛ́ntịtị], s. entidad; ente, ser.

entrails [ɛ́ntreịlz], s. entrañas, vísce ras; tripas.

entrance [ɛ́ntrạns], s. entrada; in greso; portal, puerta.—e. hall, za guán, vestíbulo.—no e., se prohib la entrada.

entrance [ɛntrǽns], vt. extasiar, he chizar.

entrap [ɛntraép], vt. entrampar; (to deceive) hacer caer en la trampa (jur.) incitar a la comisión de un delito.- **—ment** [-mẹnt], s. (jur.) incitación por agentes de la ley a la comisión de un delito.

entreat [entrít], vt. rogar, suplicar, implorar, instar.- **—y** [-ị], s. ruego, súplica, instancia.

entree [ántreị], s. entrada; privilegio de entrar; (coc.) principio o entrada.

entrench [entrénch], vt. y vi. atrincherar(se).—e. on o upon, invadir, infringir.- **—ment** [-mẹnt], s. atrincheramiento, trinchera.

entrust [entrÁst], vt. (con **to** o **with**) entregar, encargar (de), (con)fiar, depositar.

entry [éntrị], s. entrada; acceso; ingreso; asiento, anotación; registro; partida; bervete (catálogo, diccionario, etc.).

entwine [entwáịn], vt. entrelazar, entretejer.

enumerate [injúmereịt], vt. enumerar. **—enumeration** [injumẹréịšọn], s. enumeración; catálogo.

envelop [envélọp], vt. envolver.- **—e** [énvẹloup], s. envoltura; cubierta; sobre(carta).

enviable [énviạbl], a. envidiable. **—envious** [énvịʌs], a. envidioso.

environment [enváịrọnmẹnt], s. cercanía; ambiente o medio ambiente. **—environs** [enváịrọns], s. pl. alrededores, suburbios, afueras.

envoy [énvoị], s. enviado.

envy [énvị], vti. [7] envidiar; codiciar.—s. envidia.

epaulet [épɔlɛt], s. (mil.) charretera.

epic [épịk], a. épico.—s. epopeya.

epidemic [epịdémịk], a. epidémico.— s. epidemia, peste, plaga.

epigram [épịgræm], s. epigrama.

epileptic [epịléptịk], a. y s. epiléptico.

epilogue [épịlag], s. epílogo.

epiphany [ipífạnị], s. (igl.) Epifanía.

episcopal [ipískọpạl], a. episcopal.

episode [épịsoud], s. episodio.

epistle [ipísl], s. epístola. **—epistolary** [ipístoleɹị], a. epistolar.

epitaph [épịtæf], s. epitafio.

epithet [épịθɛt], s. epíteto.

epitome [ipítọmị], s. epítome. **—epitomize** [ipítọmaịz], vt. abreviar, epitomar.

epoch [épọk], s. época, era.—e.-making, trascendental, que forma época.

equal [íkwạl], a. igual; parejo; adecuado.—e. sign, igual, signo de igual.—s. igual; cantidad igual.— vt. igualar; emparejar; igualarse a, ponerse al nivel de; ser igual a.- **—ity** [ikwálịtị], s. igualdad; uniformidad; paridad.- **—ization** [ikwạlịzéịšọn], s. igualación, compensación.- **—ize** [íkwạlaịz], vt. igualar; compensar.

equanimity [ikwạnímịtị], s. ecuanimidad.

equate [íkweịt], vt. (mat.) igualar; (to compare) equiparar, identificar.

equation [ikwéịšọn], s. ecuación; igualdad.

equator [ikwéịtọ(r)], s. ecuador.- **—ial** [ikwạtóɹịạl], a. ecuatorial.

equilibrium [ikwịlíbrịʌm], s. equilibrio.

equip [ikwíp], vti. [1] equipar.- **—ment** [-mẹnt], s. equipo, habilitación; conjunto de aparatos, accesorios, etc.

equitable [ékwịtạbl], a. equitativo. **—equity** [ékwịtị], s. equidad, justicia.

equivalence [ikwívạlẹns], s. equivalencia. **—equivalent** [ikwívạlẹnt], a. y s. equivalente.

equivocal [ikwívọkạl], a. equívoco, ambiguo. **—equivocate** [ikwívọkeịt], vi. usar palabras o frases equívocas.

era [írạ], s. era, época.

eradicate [irǽdịkeịt], vt. desarraigar; destruir, extirpar. **—eradication** [irǽdịkéịšọn], s. desarraigo, extirpación.

erase [iréịs], vt. borrar, raspar.- **—r** [-œ(r)], s. borrador, goma de borrar; raspador. **—erasure** [iréịšų(r)], s. borradura, raspadura.

erect [irékt], vt. erigir, edificar; montar, instalar; erguir, alzar.—a. erecto, erguido; vertical.

ermine [œrmịn], s. armiño.

erosion [iróụžọn], s. erosión; desgaste; corrosión.

erotic [erátịk], a. erótico.

err [œr], vi. errar; equivocarse; descarriarse, pecar.- **—and** [érạnd], s. recado, mandado, diligencia.—e. boy, mandadero, recadero.- **—ant** [érạnt], a. errante.—knight e., caballero andante.- **—atic** [irǽtịk], a. irregular; excéntrico; errático.- **—oneous** [eróụnịʌs], a. errado, erróneo.- **—or** [érọ(r)], s. error, yerro, equivocación; pecado.

erupt [irÁpt], vi. salir con fuerza; hacer erupción.- **—ion** [irÁpšọn], s. erupción; irrupción.

escalator [éskạlẹitọ(r)], *s.* escalera móvil.

escapade [ɛskạpéid], *s.* travesura; correría, aventura; fuga. **—escape** [eskéip], *vi.* escaparse o librarse de; fugarse, huir.—*vt.* evadir, evitar, esquivar.—*to e. notice,* pasar inadvertido.—*s.* escapada; fuga o escape.

escarpment [ɛskárpmẹnt], *s.* escarpa, acantilado.

escort [éskɔrt], *s.* escolta; acompañante.—*vt.* [ɛskɔ́rt] escoltar; acompañar.

Eskimo [éskịmou], *s.* y *a.* esquimal.

espionage [éspịọnịdẑ], *s.* espionaje.

esplanade [ɛsplạnéid], *s.* explanada, paseo.

espy [ɛspái], *vi.* [7] divisar, columbrar.—*vii.* mirar alrededor, observar.

esquire [ɛskwáir], *s.* escudero.—Esq., (abrev.) Sr. Don, e.g., *Anthony Sweet, Esq.,* Sr. Don Antonio Sweet. (E.U.: empleado *esp.* por los nombres de abogados.)

essay [ɛséj], *vt.* ensayar.—*s.* [éseị] ensayo literario; tentativa.- **—ist** [éseịịst], *s.* ensayista.

essence [ésẹns], *s.* esencia.—*in e.,* esencialmente. **—essential** [ɛsénṣạl], *a.* esencial; indispensable.—*s.* esencial, substancia.—*to stick to essentials,* ir al grano.

establish [ɛstǽblịŝ], *vt.* establecer.—*vr.* establecerse, radicarse.- **—ment** [-mẹnt], *s.* establecimiento; fundación; institución; pensión o renta vitalicia.

estate [ɛstéit], *s.* bienes, propiedades; patrimonio, herencia; finca, hacienda; estado, clase o condición. —*country e.,* finca rústica.—*real e.,* bienes raíces.

esteem [ɛstím], *vt.* estimar, apreciar; tener en o por, creer.—*s.* estimación, aprecio; mérito; juicio, opinión. **—estimable** [éstịmạbl], *a.* estimable; calculable. **—estimate** [éstịmẹjt], *vt.* estimar, apreciar, valorar; calcular aproximadamente.—*s.* [éstịmịt], estimación, cálculo; opinión; presupuesto aproximado. **—estimation** [ɛstịméjṣọn], *s.* estima, aprecio; opinión; suposición; valuación; presupuesto.

esthetic [ɛsθétịk], *a.* estético.- **—s** [-s], *s.* estética.

estrange [ɛstréjndẑ], *vt.* extrañar, alejar; enajenar.

estuary [éschị̣ụẹri], *s.* estuario, ría.

etch [ɛch], *vt.* y *vi.* grabar al agua fuerte.- **—er** [échœ(r)], *s.* grabador aguafortista.- **—ing** [-ịŋ], *s.* grabado al agua fuerte.

eternal [ịtœ́rnạl], *a.* eterno. **—eternity** [ịtœ́rnịti], *s.* eternidad.

ether [íθœ(r)], *s.* éter.- **—eal** [ịθíṛịạl] *a.* etéreo.

ethical [éθịkạl], *a.* ético, moral. **—ethics** [éθịks], *s.* ética, moral.

Ethiopian [iθịóụpịạn], *s.* y *a.* etíope.

ethnic [éθnịk], *a.* étnico.

etiquette [étịket], *s.* etiqueta.

etymology [etịmálodẑị], *s.* etimología.

eucalyptus [yucạlíptạs], *s.* eucalipto.

eulogy [yúlọdẑị], *s.* elogio, panegírico.

Eurasian [yuréjẑịạn], *s.* y *a.* eruasio eurasiático.

European [yuropíạn], *s.* y *a.* europeo.

euthanasia [yuθạnéịzịạ], *s.* eutanasia.

evacuate [ịvǽkyụejt], *vt.* evacuar.—*vi* vaciarse; retirarse. **—evacuation** [ịvǽkyụéjṣọn], *s.* evacuación.

evade [ịvéjd], *vt.* evadir, eludir, esquivar.

evaluate [ịvǽlyụejt], *vt.* evaluar, tasar **—evaluation** [ịvǽlyụéjṣọn], *s.* evaluación.

evangelic(al) [ịvǽndẑélik(ạl)], *a.* evangélico.

evangelist [ịvaéndẑịẹlịst], *s.* evangelizador (predicador); (bib.) evangelista.

evaporate [ịvǽpọrẹjt], *vt.* y *vi.* evaporar(se); desvanecer(se). **—evaporation** [ịvǽporéjṣọn], *s.* evaporación.

evasion [ịvéjẑọn], *s.* evasión; evasiva **—evasive** [ịvéjṣịv], *a.* evasivo.

eve [iv], *s.* noche; vigilia; víspera.—*Christmas E.,* Nochebuena.—*on the e. of,* en vísperas de.

even [ívẹn], *a.* llano, plano, nivelado; liso; igual, uniforme, imparcial; apacible; cabal, justo; constante; (número) par; parejo (con.).—*of e. date,* de la misma fecha.—*to be even with,* estar en paz, mano a mano con.—*to get e. with,* desquitarse.- *adv.* aun, hasta, incluso.—*e. as,* así como.—*e. if,* aun cuando, aunque.—*e. now,* ahora mismo.—*e. so,* así; aun así.—*e. though,* aunque.- *not e.,* ni siquiera.—*vt.* igualar, emparejar, allanar, nivelar; liquidar.

evening [ívnịŋ], *s.* tarde; (primeras horas de la) noche.—*last e.,* anoche.- *a.* de la tarde; vespertino.

event [ịvént], *s.* acontecimiento, suceso; caso; consecuencia, resul tado.—*at all events, in any e.,* sea lo que fuere, en todo caso, de cualquier modo.– **—ful** [-fụl], *a.* memorable, lleno de acontecimientos.– **—ual** [ivénchuạl], *a.* último, final. **—uality** [ivenchuǽliti], *s.* eventualidad.

ever [évœ(r)], *adv.* siempre; alguna vez, en cualquier tiempo; nunca.— *as e.,* como siempre.—*e. since,* desde que; desde entonces.—*for e. and e.,* por siempre jamás, por los siglos de los siglos.—*hardly e.,* casi nunca.— *nor e.,* ni nunca.– **—green** [-grin], *a.* siempre verde.—*s.* planta de hoja perenne.– **—lasting** [-lǽstiŋ], *a.* perpetuo, perdurable, duradero.— *s.* eternidad.– **—more** [-mɔr], *adv.* eternamente; por siempre jamás.

every [évri], *a.* cada; todo, todos los.— *e. once in a while,* de vez en cuando.—*e. one of them,* todos, todos sin excepción.—*e. other,* cada dos, uno sí y otro no.– **—body** [-badi], *pron.* todos, todo el mundo; cada uno, cada cual.– **—day** [-dei], *a.* diario, cuotidiano.– **—one** [-wʌn], *pron.* todo el mundo; todos. – **—thing** [-θiŋ], *pron.* todo.– **—where** [-hwer], *adv.* en o por todas partes, dondequiera.

evict [ivíkt], *vt.* desalojar, desahuciar; expulsar.– **—ion** [ivíkʃọn], *s.* desalojamiento; desahucio; expulsión.

evidence [évidẹns], *s.* evidencia; prueba.– **evident** [évidẹnt], *a.* evidente, claro.

evil [ívịl], *a.* malo; maligno, perverso; nocivo; aciago.—*e. deed,* mal hecho.—*e. eye,* mal de ojo.—*s.* mal; infortunio; maldad.—*the E. One,* el diablo.—*adv.* mal; malignamente.– **—doer** [-duœ(r)], *s.* malhechor.

evoke [ivóụk], *vt.* evocar.

evolution [evoljúʃọn], *s.* evolución, desarrollo.– **—ism** [-ịzm], *s.* evolucionismo. **—evolve** [iválv], *vt.* desenvolver, desarrollar; producir por evolución.—*vi.* desarrollarse; evolucionar.

ewe [yu], *s.* oveja.

exacerbation [egzæsœrbéjʃọn], *s.* exacerbación; agravación; exasperación.

exact [egzǽkt], *a.* exacto; justo; puntual.—*vt.* exigir, imponer.– **—ing** [-iŋ], *a.* exigente.

exaggerate [egzǽdʐẹreịt], *vt. y vii.* exagerar, ponderar. **—exaggeration** [egzǽdʐẹréjʃọn], *s.* exageración.

exalt [egzólt], *vt.* exaltar, enaltecer; regocijar; reforzar.– **—ation** [-éjʃọn], *s.* exaltación; enaltecimiento.

exam [egzǽm], *s.* examen.– **—ination** [-inéjʃọn], *s.* examen; investigación; reconocimiento; ensayo, prueba; (for.) interrogatorio.– **—ine** [-in], *vt.* examinar; indagar; reconocer; preguntar, inquirir; analizar.– **—iner** [-inœ(r)], *s.* examinador, inspector.

example [egzǽmpl], *s.* ejemplo, ejemplar; lección, escarmiento.

exasperate [egzǽspẹreịt], *vt.* exasperar; irritar; agravar. **—exasperation** [egzǽspẹréjʃọn], *s.* exasperación; agravación.

excavate [ékskạveịt], *vt.* excavar, (so)cavar; vaciar, ahondar. **—excavation** [ékskạvéjʃọn], *s.* excavación; desmonte; zanja.

exceed [eksíd], *vt.* exceder; aventajar, sobrepujar; (sobre)pasar; rebasar.— *vi.* excederse, propasarse; preponderar.– **—ing** [-iŋ], *a.* excesivo; extraordinario.

excel [eksél], *vti. y vii.* [1] aventajar, superar; ser superior a; sobresalir.– **—lence** [éksẹlẹns], *s.* excelencia.– **—lent** [éksẹlẹnt], *a.* excelente.

except [eksépt], *vt.* exceptuar, excluir, omitir.—*prep.* excepto, con excepción de, fuera de.– **—ing** [-iŋ], *prep.* a excepción de, salvo, exceptuando.– **—ion** [eksépʃọn], *s.* excepción, salvedad; objeción.—*to take e.,* objetar, oponerse, desaprobar.– **—ional** [eksépʃọnạl], *a.* excepcional.

excess [eksés], *s.* exceso; excedente; inmoderación o destemplanza; desorden; demasía; sobrante.–*a.* excesivo, sobrante; suplemental, de recargo.—*e. profits tax,* impuesto sobre las ganancias excesivas.– **—ive** [-iv], *a.* excesivo.

exchange [ekschéịndʐ], *vt.* cambiar; canjear, permutar; trocar, intercambiar.—*s.* cambio, trueque, permuta; canje; (com.) lonja, bolsa; cambio (de la moneda).—*bill of e.,* letra de cambio.—*e. rate,* tipo de cambio.— *stock e.,* bolsa de cambios.

excite [eksáịt], *vt.* excitar; provocar, suscitar, estimular.– **—d** [-ịd], *a.* excitado, acalorado.– **—ment** [-mẹnt], *s.* excitación; estimulación; agitación; acaloramiento.– **—exciting** [-iŋ], *a.* excitante, estimulante, incitante; emocionante.

exclaim [ekskléịm], *vt. y vi.* exclamar,

clamar. —**exclamation** [ɛksklaméíṣon], s. exclamación.—*e. point*, signo de admiración.

exclude [ɛksklúd], vt. excluir. —**exclusion** [ɛksklúȥon], s. exclusión. —**exclusive** [ɛksklúsiv], a. exclusivo; privativo; selecto.—*e. of,* exclusive, sin contar. —**exclusiveness** [ɛksklúsivnis], s. exclusividad; exclusiva.

excommunicate [ɛkskomjúnikeit], vt. excomulgar.—a. y s. excomulgado. —**excommunication** [ɛkskomjunikéíṣon], s. excomunión.

excrement [ɛ́kskriment], s. excremento, heces.

excursion [ɛkskœ́rȥon], s. excursión, romería; expedición.

excusable [ɛkskjúȥabl], a. excusable, disculpable. —**excuse** [ɛkskjúz], vt. excusar, disculpar; sincerar, justificar; eximir; paliar; despedir.—s. [ɛkskjús], excusa; pretexto.

execration [ɛksikréíṣon], s. abominación.

execute [ɛ́ksikjut], vt. ejecutar, llevar a cabo; legalizar, formalizar; ajusticiar. —**execution** [ɛksikiúṣon], s. ejecución, cumplimiento; mandamiento judicial; legalización; ajusticiamiento.—**executioner** [ɛksikiúṣonœ(r)], s. verdugo. —**executive** [ɛgzékyutiv], a. ejecutivo.—s. poder ejecutivo; funcionario ejecutivo. —**executor** [ɛgzékyuto(r)], s. ejecutor; albacea.

exempt [ɛgzémpt], vt. eximir, franquear.—a. exento; libre, franco, inmune.- —**ion** [ɛgzémpṣon], s. exención, franquicia, inmunidad.

exercise [ɛ́ksœrsaiz], s. ejercicio.—vt. ejercer; ejercitar; adiestrar; preocupar, causar ansiedad.—vi. adiestrarse, ejercitarse; hacer ejercicio.

exert [ɛgzœ́rt], vt. esforzar; ejercer.— vr. empeñarse, esforzarse.- —**ion** [ɛgzœ́rṣon], s. esfuerzo, empeño, ejercicio.

exhale [ɛkshéjl], vt. exhalar, espirar.— vi. vah(e)ar; disiparse, desvanecerse.

exhaust [ɛgzɔ́st], vt. agotar, vaciar; gastar, consumir; debilitar, cansar.—s. vapor de escape; tubo de escape; (fís. y mec.) vacío.- —**ion** [ɛgzɔ́schon], s. agotamiento; debilitación, postración; (mec.) vaciamiento.- —**ive** [-iv], a. exhaustivo; agotador; completo, cabal.

exhibit [ɛgzíbit], vt. exhibir; presentar, manifestar; exponer, mostrar.—vi. dar una exhibición.—s. exhibición; manifestación; (for.) pruebas en un juicio.- —**ion** [ɛksibíṣon], s. exhibición, exposición; manifestación; estentación.

exhilarate [ɛgzílareit], vt. alegrar, regocijar o alborozar; animar, estimular.

exile [égzail], s. destierro, expatriación; desterrado, expatriado.—vt. desterrar, expatriar

exist [ɛgzíst], vi. existir, subsistir, vivir. - —**ence** [-ɛns], s. existencia, vida, subsistencia; ente, ser.- —**ent** [-ɛnt], —**ing** [-iŋ], a. existente, actual, presente.

exit [éksit], s. salida; (teat.) mutis, vase.—vi. salir.

exodus [éksodʌs], s. éxodo.

exonerate [ɛgzánereit], vt. exonerar; relevar.

exorbitance [ɛgzórbitans], s. exorbitancia, exceso. —**exorbitant** [ɛgzórbitant], a. exorbitante excesivo.

exotic [ɛgzátik], a. exótico.

expand [ɛkspǽnd], vt. y vi. extender(se), expandir(se). —**expanse** [ɛkspǽns], s. extensión, espacio. —**expansion** [ɛkspǽnṣon], s. expansión, dilatación; desarrollo. —**expansive** [ɛkspǽnsiv], a. expansivo, efusivo.

expatriate [ɛkspéjtrieit], vt. y vr. expatriar(se), desnaturalizar(se), desterrar(se).—s. y a. [ɛkspéjtriit] expatriado, desterrado.

expect [ɛkspékt], vt. esperar; contar con.- —**ance** [-ans], —**ancy** [-ansi], s. expectativa.- —**ant** [-ant], a. expectante; embarazada, encinta.- —**ation** [-éíṣon], s. expectación, expectativa, esperanza.

expectorate [ɛkspéktoreit], vt. y vi. expectorar, escupir.

expedience [ɛkspídiens], **expediency** [ɛkspídiensi], s. conveniencia. —**expedient** [ɛkspídient], a. oportuno, conveniente; prudente, propio.—s. expediente, medio, recurso.

expedition [ɛkspidíṣon], s. expedición.- —**ary** [-ɛri], a. y s. expedicionario.

expel [ɛkspél], vti. [1] expeler, expulsar; despedir.

expend [ɛkspénd], vt. gastar, consumir; desembolsar.- —**iture** [-ichu(r)], s. gasto, desembolso. —**expense** [ɛkspéns], s. gasto, coste, costa, costo; desembolso.—*at any e.*, a toda costa. —**expensive** [ɛkspénsɪv], *a.* costoso; caro, dispendioso.

experiment [ɛkspérɪment], *s.* experimento.—*vi.* experimentar.— —**al** [ɛksperɪméntal], *a.* experimental. —**experience** [ɛkspírɪens], *s.* experiencia; conocimiento; pericia; lance, incidente personal.—*vt.* experimentar; sentir. —**experienced** [ɛkspírɪenst], *a.* experimentado, perito; hábil; avezado; amaestrado o aleccionado. —**expert** [ɛkspœrt], *a.* experto; pericial.—*s.* [ɛkspœrt], experto, perito.

expiate [ɛkspɪejt], *vt.* expiar.

expiration [ɛkspɪréiʃon], *s.* expiración; vencimiento; espiración; muerte. —**expire** [ɛkspáɪr], *vt.* espirar, expeler.—*vi.* expirar, terminar; fallecer, morir.

explain [ɛkspléɪn], *vt.* explicar. —**explanation** [ɛksplanéiʃon], *s.* explicación. —**explanatory** [ɛksplǽnatɔri], *a.* explicativo.

explode [ɛksplóʊd], *vt.* volar, hacer estallar o explotar; refutar, confundir.—*vi.* estallar, hacer explosión; reventar.

exploit [ɛksplɔit], *s.* hazaña, proeza.— *vt.* [ɛksplɔit], explotar, sacar partido de; abusar.— —**ation** [ɛksplɔitéiʃon], *s.* explotación, aprovechamiento.— —**er** [ɛksplɔitœ(r)], *s.* explotador.

exploration [ɛksplɔréiʃon], *s.* exploración. —**explorator** [ɛksplɔrejtɔ(r)], **explorer** [ɛksplɔrœ(r)], *s.* explorador. —**explore** [ɛksplór], *vt.* explorar; averiguar; sondear.—*vi.* dedicarse a exploraciones.

explosion [ɛksplóʊʒon], *s.* explosión, voladura; detonación; reventón. —**explosive** [ɛksplóʊsɪv], *a.* y *s.* explosivo.

exponent [ɛkspóʊnent], *s.* exponente.

export [ɛkspórt], *vt.* exportar.—*s.* [ɛkspɔrt] exportación.

expose [ɛkspóʊz], *vt.* exponer, exhibir; poner en peligro; revelar, sacar a luz; desenmascarar. —**exposé** [ɛkspozéj], *s.* revelación comprometedora o escandalosa. —**exposition** [ɛkspozíʃon], *s.* exposición, exhibición. —**exposure** [ɛkspóʊʒụ(r)], *s.* exposición; acción de exponer(se); estar expuesto a (la intemperie); orientación, situación; revelación. —*e. meter*, exposímetro.

expound [ɛkspáʊnd], *vt.* exponer, explicar.

express [ɛksprés], *vt.* expresar, manifestar; enviar por expreso.—*vi.* expresarse.—*a.* expreso; claro, explícito; especial; hecho de encargo; llevado por expreso; pronto, rápido. —*adv.* por expreso; expresa o especialmente.—*s.* tren, autobús, ascensor, etc. expreso o exprés; expreso, servicio de transporte de mercancías.— —**ion** [ɛkspréʃon], *s.* expresión; semblante, talante; dicción, locución, giro.— —**ive** [ɛksprésɪv], *a.* expresivo.

expropriate [ɛkspróʊprɪejt], *vt.* enajenar, expropiar.

exquisite [ɛkskwɪzɪt], *a.* exquisito.

extend [ɛksténd], *vt.* extender; amplificar; prolongar; ampliar.—*vi.* extenderse, prolongarse; dar de sí.— —**ed** [-ɪd], *a.* extenso, prolongado; diferido. —**extension** [ɛksténʃon], *s.* extensión; dilatación; expansión; prolongación; prórroga.—*e. cord*, (elec.) cordón de extensión, extensión, alargador. —**extensive** [ɛksténsɪv], *a.* extens(iv)o. —**extent** [ɛkstént], *s.* extensión; alcance; grado, punto, límite.—*to a certain e.*, hasta cierto punto.—*to a great e.*, en sumo grado, grandemente.—*to the full e.*, en toda su extensión, completamente.

exterior [ɛkstírɪo(r)], *a.* exterior, externo; manifiesto.—*s.* exterior; exterioridad, aspecto.

exterminate [ɛkstœrmɪnejt], *vt.* exterminar. —**extermination** [ɛkstœrmɪnéiʃon], *s.* exterminio. —**exterminator** [ɛkstœrmɪnejtɔ(r)], *s.* exterminador.

external [ɛkstœrnal], *a.* externo, exterior; extranjero.—*s.* exterior; exterioridad.

extinct [ɛkstíŋkt], *a.* extinto; extinguido, apagado.— —**ion** [ɛkstíŋkʃon], *s.* extinción. —**extinguish** [ɛkstíŋgwɪʃ], *vt.* extinguir; apagar; sofocar; suprimir, destruir; oscurecer. —**extinguisher** [ɛkstíŋgwɪʃœ(r)], *s.* extintor de incendios; apagador; matacandelas.

extol [ɛkstóʊl], *vti.* [1] ensalzar, enaltecer, elogiar.

extort [ɛkstórt], *vt.* extorsionar; sacar u obtener por fuerza; arrebatar; exigir dinero sin derecho.— —**ion** [ɛkstórʃon], *s.* extorsión; exacción.

extra [ékstră], *a.* extraordinario; suplementario; de repuesto o de reserva.—*e. charge,* recargo.—*s.* exceso; recargo, sobreprecio; gasto extraordinario.—*adv.* excepcionalmente, en exceso.

extract [ekstrǽkt], *vt.* extraer; extractar.—*s.* [ékstrækt], extracto; resumen.

extradite [ékstrădait], *vt.* entregar o reclamar por extradición —**extradition** [ekstrădíșon], *s.* extradición.

extraordinary [ekstrórdineri], *a.* extraordinario.

extraterrestrial [ekstrătĕréstriăl], *a.* extraterrestre, del espacio.

extravagance [ekstrǽvagans], **extravagancy** [ekstrǽvagansi], *s.* lujo desmedido, derroche; extravagancia; disparate. —**extravagant** [ekstrǽvagănt], *a.* extravagante.

extreme [ekstrím], *a.* extremo, extremado; riguroso, estricto. —**extremity** [ekstrémiti], *s.* extremidad; rigor; necesidad, apuro.—*pl.* medidas extremas; extremidades.

exult [egzált], *vi.* saltar de alegría, regocijarse.- —**ant** [-ant], *a.* regocijado, alborozado; triunfante.- —**ation**

[-éișon], *s.* regocijo, transporte; triunfo.

eye [ai], *s.* ojo.—*an e. for an e.,* ojo por ojo.—*before one's eyes,* en presencia de uno, a la vista.—*by e.,* a ojo.—*e. shade,* visera, guardavista.—*e. socket,* órbita o cuenca del ojo.—*half an e.,* ojeada, vistazo.—*to keep an e. on,* vigilar.—*to make eyes at,* mirar amorosamente o con codicia; comerse con los ojos.—*to see e. to e.,* ser del mismo parecer.—*to shut one's eyes to,* hacer la vista gorda.—*with an e. to,* con la intención de, pensando en, con vistas a.—*vt.* mirar de hito en hito; clavar la mirada a; hacer ojos o agujeros a.- —**ball** [áibɔl], *s.* globo del ojo.- —**brow** [-brau], *s.* ceja.- —**glass** [-glæs], *s.* ocular; anteojo.—*pl.* lentes, espejuelos, gafas, anteojos.- —**lash** [-læ̂s], *s.* pestaña. - —**lid** [-lid], *s.* párpado.- —**sight** [-sait], *s.* vista; alcance de la vista.- —**sore** [-sɔr], *s.* cosa que ofende la vista.- —**strain** [-strein], *s.* vista fatigada.- —**tooth** [-tuθ], *s.* colmillo.- —**wash** [-wâ̂], *s.* colirio, loción para los ojos; (fam.) patraña.- —**witness** [-wítnis], *s.* testigo presencial.

F

fable [féibl], *s.* fábula, ficción.- —**d** [féibĕld], *a.* legendario, fabuloso.

fabric [fǽbrik], *s.* tejido, género; fábrica, edificio; textura.- —**ate** [-eit], *vt.* fabricar; construir; inventar, mentir.- —**ation** [-éișon], *s.* fabricación; edificio; invención, mentira.

fabulous [fǽbyulʌs], *a.* fabuloso, ficticio.

façade [fasád], *s.* (arq.) fachada.

face [feis], *s.* cara, rostro; faz; lado; superficie; fachada, frente; aspecto; apariencias; prestigio; esfera (de reloj); descaro; mueca.—*f. card,* figura (en la baraja).—*f. down(ward),* boca abajo.—*f. powder,* polvos de arroz o de tocador.—*f. value,* (com.) valor nominal; significado literal.—*in the f. of,* ante; luchando contra, a pesar de.—*to lose f.,* desprestigiarse.—*vt.* volverse o mirar hacia; arrostrar, afrontar, enfrentarse o encararse con; (for.) responder (a un cargo);

cubrir, forrar.—*to f. out,* persistir en o sostener descaradamente.—*to f. the music,* (fam.) hacer frente a las consecuencias.—*vi.* volver la cara; dar o mirar (a, hacia).—*to f. about,* voltear la cara; cambiar de frente.- —**t** [fǽsit], *s.* faceta.

facetious [fasî̂ʌs], *a.* jocoso, chistoso, humorístico.

facial [féișal], *a.* facial.—*s.* limpieza de cutis.

facilitate [fasíliteit], *vt.* facilitar, allanar, expedir. —**facility** [fasíliti], *s.* facilidad; (building) complejo, centro.

facsimile [fæksímili], *s.* facsímile.

fact [fækt], *s.* hecho; realidad.—*in f.,* en efecto, en realidad; de hecho.—*in the very f.,* en el mero hecho.—*matter of f.,* hecho positivo.—*the f. remains that,* ello es que, es un hecho, a pesar de todo.

faction [fǽkșon], *s.* facción, bando; alboroto. —**factious** [fǽkʃʌs], *a.* faccioso, sedicioso, revoltoso.

factor [fǽktǝ(r)], *s.* elemento, factor; agente comisionado.

factory [fǽktǝri], *s.* fábrica; factoría.

factual [fǽkchuǝl], *s.* exacto; real.

faculty [fǽkʌlti], *s.* facultad; (teaching corps) cuerpo docente, profesorado.

fad [fæd], *s.* novedad, moda; manía.

fade [fejd], *vt.* marchitar; desteñir.— *vi.* desteñirse, descolorarse; marchitarse; (rad.) apagarse la intensidad.—*f.-out,* desaparición u oscurecimiento gradual.—*to f. away,* desvanecerse, desaparecer. —**fading** [féidiŋ], *s.* pérdida gradual de intensidad, sonido, etc.; (rad.) fluctuación en la intensidad de las señales.

fag [fæg], *s.* (despec.) maricón. — **fagged** [fǽgd], *pp.*—*to be all f. out,* estar reventado, estar hecho polvo.

faggot, fagot [fǽgot], *s.* (sticks) haz de leña; (despec.) maricón.

fail [fejl], *vt.* abandonar, dejar; frustrar; (fam.) reprobar, suspender (en los estudios).—*vi.* faltar; fallar; fracasar; frustrarse; consumirse, decaer; (com.) quebrar; salir mal, ser reprobado (en examen, etc.).—*s.* falta; defecto; fracaso.—*f.-safe,* de seguridad; infalible, a toda prueba.— *without f.,* sin falta.- —**ure** [féjlyǝ(r)], *s.* fracaso, malogro; suspenso (en un examen); falta, omisión, descuido; (com.) quiebra, bancarrota; (mec.) avería, defecto (de motor, etc.).

faint [fejnt], *vi.* desmayarse; desfallecer.—*a.* lánguido, abatido; indistinto, tenue; desfallecido.—*f.-hearted,* medroso, pusilánime.—*s.* desmayo, desfallecimiento.—*fainting fit to spell,* síncope, desmayo.—*in a f.,* desmayado.- —**ness** [féjntnjs], *s.* falta de claridad; languidez, desaliento.

fair [fɛr], *a.* claro, despejado; rubio; limpio; favorable, próspero; bello; justo, imparcial; razonable; regular, pasable.—*f. and square,* honrado a carta cabal.—*f. complexion,* tez blanca.—*f. name,* nombre honrado, sin tacha.—*f. play,* proceder leal, juego limpio.—*f. sex,* bello sexo.— *f. trade,* comercio recíproco.—*f. weather,* buen tiempo, bonanza.—*f. wind,* viento favorable.—*to give f. warning,* prevenir,

avisar de antemano.—*to make a f. copy,* poner en limpio.—*adv.* justamente, honradamente; claramente; bien.—*f.-minded,* imparcial, justo.—*s.* feria; exposición.- —**grounds** [-graundz], *spl.* recinto ferial, real de la feria.- —**ness** [fɛrnjs], *s.* hermosura, belleza; honradez; justicia, imparcialidad.- —**y** [-i], *s.* hada, duende; (fam.) afeminado.—*a.* de hadas, de duendes.— *f. tale,* cuento de hadas.- —**yland** [-jlænd], *s.* país de las hadas.

faith [fejθ], *s.* fe; confianza; creencia, religión; fidelidad.—*f. healer,* curandero, santero.—*to break f. with,* faltar a la palabra dada a.—*upon my f.,* a fe mía.- —**ful** [féjθful], *a.* fiel; leal; exacto; justo, recto.- —**fully** [-fuli], *adv.* fielmente, firmemente; puntualmente.- —**fulness** [-fulnjs], *s.* fidelidad, honradez; exactitud.- —**less** [-ljs], *a.* infiel, desleal, pérfido.

fake [fejk], *s.* (fam.) falsificación, fraude, impostura; imitación, copia; patraña, farsa. *V.* FAKER.—*vt.* y *vi.* (fam.) falsificar; fingir, contrahacer.—*a.* falso, fraudulento.- —**r** [féjkœr], *s.* (fam.) farsante; falsario, imitador; embustero.

falcon [fólkǝn], *s.* halcón.

fall [fol], *vii.* [10] caer(se); bajar, decrecer, disminuir; decaer.—*to f. asleep,* dormirse.—*to f. back,* retroceder, retirarse.—*to f. back on,* o *upon,* recurrir a, echar mano de.—*to f. behind,* rezagarse.—*to f. down,* postrarse; caerse.—*to f. due,* (com.) vencer(se). —*to f. for,* (fam.) prendarse de; ser engañado por.—*to f. in,* (mil.) alinearse; expirar, caducar.—*to f. in line,* formar cola; seguir la corriente.—*to f. in love,* enamorarse.—*to f. in price,* abaratarse.—*to f. in with,* convenir, estar de acuerdo con.—*to f. out,* desavenirse, reñir.—*to f. short,* faltar; errar el tiro.—*to f. sick,* enfermar.— *to f. through,* fracasar, malograrse.— *s.* caída, bajada, descenso; salto de agua; otoño; ruina; desnivel; desembocadura de un río; (com.) baja de precios; (mús.) cadencia; disminución del sonido.- —**off** [-ɔf], *s.* dismunición, reducción.- —**out** [-aut], *s.* lluvia radiactiva, precipitación radiactiva; (side effect) secuela.—*f. shelter,* refugio antinuclear.—*a.* otoñal. —**fallen** [fólęn], *pp.* de TO FALL.—**falling** [fɔliŋ], *a.* cayente.—*f.-out*, pelea.

fallow [fǽlou], *a.* descuidado, abandonado.—*s.* barbecho.—*vt.* barbechar.

false [fɔls], *a.* falso, fingido, engañoso; postizo; (mus.) desafinado, discordante.—*f. alarm*, falsa alarma.—*f. bottom*, fondo doble.—*f. claim*, pretensión infundada.—*f.-faced*, hipócrita, falso.—*f. friend*, (ling.) falso amigo.—*f.-hearted*, pérfido.—*f. hem*, dobladillo falso.—*f. pregnancy*, embarazo psicológico.—*f. rib*, costilla falsa.—*f. start*, intento fallido; (sports) salida en falso.—*f. step*, desliz; imprudencia.—*f. teeth*, dentadura postiza.—**hood** [fɔ́lshud], *s.* falsedad, embuste.— **ness** [-nis], *s.* falsedad, perfidia.— **tto** [-étou], *s.* (mús.) falsete. —**falsification** [fɔlsifikéíṣǫn], *s.* falsificación. —**falsify** [fɔ́lsifai], *vti.* [7] falsificar; falsear.—*vii.* mentir.

falter [fɔ́ltœ(r)], *vt.* balbucear.—*vi.* vacilar; tartamudear.—*s.* vacilación, temblor.

fame [feim], *s.* fama.—*vt.* afamar; celebrar.— **d** [-d], *a.* afamado, famoso, renombrado; célebre.

familiar [fəmílyă(r)], *a.* familiar, íntimo; confianzudo.—*f. with*, acostumbrado o versado o ducho en, conocedor de, al tanto de.—*s.* familiar.— **ity** [fəmiljǽriti], *s.* familiaridad, intimidad; confianza, llaneza; (con *with*) conocimiento (de). —**family** [fǽmili], *s.* familia.— *a.* familiar, casero, de la familia.—*f. man*, padre de familia.—*f. name*, apellido.—*f. tree*, árbol genealógico.—*in the f. way*, (fam.) encinta, embarazada.

famine [fǽmin], *s.* hambre, carestía. —**famished** [fǽmiʃt], *a.* famélico, hambriento.

famous [féimʌs], *a.* famoso, afamado, célebre; (fam.) excelente.

fan [fæn], *s.* abanico; ventilador; aventador; aficionado, entusiasta, admirador.—*f. club*, club de fans, club de admiradores.—*vti.* [1] abanicar; ventilar; aventar.

fanatic [fənǽtik], *s.* y *a.* fanático.— **(al)** [-(ạl)], *a.* fanático.—**ism** [fənǽtisizm], *s.* fanatismo.

fanciful [fǽnsiful], *a.* imaginativo, caprichoso; fantástico. —**fancy** [fǽnci], *s.* fantasía, imaginación,

antojo, capricho; afición, afecto.—*to take a f. to*, aficionarse a; coger cariño a.—*a.* fantástico; de fantasía; elegante; de lujo, costoso.—*f. ball*, baile de trajes.—*f. dress*, disfraz.—*vti.* [7] imaginar; gustar de, aficionarse a; antojarse, fantasear.—*vii.* tener un antojo o capricho; creer o imaginar algo sin prueba.

fang [fæŋ], *s.* colmillo (de animal, fiera); diente (de serpiente, del tenedor).— **ed** [-d], *a.* colmilludo.

fanny [fǽni], *s.* (fam.) trasero.

fantastic [fæntǽstik], *a.* fantástico; caprichoso; ilusorio, imaginario. — **fantasy** [fǽntəsi], *s.* fantasía.

far [far], *adv.* lejos; a lo lejos; en alto grado.—*as f. as, so f. as*, hasta; en la medida que, en cuanto a, según.—*by f.*, con mucho.—*f. and wide*, por todas partes.—*f. away*, muy lejos.—*the F. East*, el Lejano Oriente, el Extremo Oriente.—*f. flung*, vasto, extenso.—*f. from*, ni con mucho.—*f. off*, a lo lejos; muy lejos; distante, remoto.—*so f., thus f.*, hasta ahora; hasta aquí; hasta ahí.—*a.* lejano, distante, remoto.—*a f. cry (from)*, muy lejos de.

faraway [fárạwei], *a.* lejano, alejado; abstraído, distraído.

farce [fars], *s.* (teat.) farsa; comedia, engaño.

fare [fer], *vi.* pasarlo, irla a uno (bien o mal); acontecer.—*s.* pasaje o tarifa (precio); pasajero; comida, plato.— *bill of f.*, menú.— **well** [férwel], *interj.* ¡adiós! ¡vaya con Dios!—*a.* de despedida.—*f. performance*, función de despedida.—*s.* despedida, adiós.

farm [farm], *s.* finca de labor, granja; (Am.) chácara.—*f. hand*, peón o mozo de labranza, bracero.—*vt.* cultivar, labrar.—*vi.* cultivar la tierra y criar animales.—*to f. out*, ceder por contrato, encargar.— **er** [fármœ(r)], *s.* labrador, granjero, agricultor.—*tenant f.*, colono.— **house** [-haus], *s.* granja, alquería. – **ing** [-iŋ], *s.* cultivo, labranza, agricultura.—*a.* agrícola; de labranza.– **stead** [-sted], *s.* granja, alquería.

farther [fárðœ(r)], *adv.* más lejos, a mayor distancia; además de, demás de.—*f. on*, más adelante.—*a.* más lejano; ulterior.— **most** [-moust], *a.* más lejano o remoto. **—farthest** [fárðist], *a.* más lejano o remoto; más largo o extendido.—*adv.* lo más lejos, a la mayor distancia.

fascinate [fásineit], *vt.* fascinar, hechizar. **—fascinating** [fásineitiŋ], *a.* fascinador, hechicero. **—fascination** [fasinéišon], *s.* fascinación, hechizo.

fascism [fášizẽm], *s.* fascismo.

fascist [fášist], *a.* y *s.* fascista.

fashion [fášon], *s.* moda, estilo; elegancia; manera.—*f. model,* modelo, maniquí.—*f. plate,* figurín.—*f. shop,* tienda de modas.—*f. show,* desfile de modas, desfile de modelos.—*in f.,* de moda.—*out of f.,* pasado de moda.—*to be the f.,* ser (de) moda.—*vt.* adaptar; formar; idear.- **—able** [-ḁbl], *a.* de moda; elegante, de buen tono.

fast [fæst], *vi.* ayunar, hacer abstinencia.—*s.* ayuno, abstinencia, vigilia.—*a.* firme, seguro, fuerte; fijo, indeleble; apretado; constante, fiel; profundo (sueño); veloz, ligero, rápido; adelantado (reloj); derrochador; disoluto.—*f. food,* comida rápida.—*f.-forward button,* botón de avance rápido.—*f. lane,* carril para automoviles rápidos.—*f.-talk,* (fam.) engatusar, embaucar.—*to live in the f. lane,* (fam.) vivir a toda máquina.—*adv.* fuertemente, firmemente; estrechamente; para siempre; aprisa, rápidamente.—*f. by,* cerca de, junto a.- **—en** [fǽsn], *vt.* afirmar, asegurar, sujetar; pegar; atar, amarrar; trabar, unir; abrochar.—*vi.* fijarse; agarrarse, pegarse.

fastidious [fæstídiʌs], *a.* escrupuloso, melindroso; descontentadizo; quisquilloso.

fasting [fǽstiŋ], *s.* ayuno, abstinencia.

fat [fæt], *a.* gordo; obeso; graso, mantecoso; opulento, rico; lucrativo.— *s.* gordura; grasa, manteca, sebo.— *vti.* y *vii.* [1] engordar.

fatal [féitʌl], *a.* fatal; mortal; inevitable.- **—ism** [-izm], *s.* fatalismo.- **—ist** [-ist], *s.* fatalista.- **—ity** [feitǽliti], *s.* fatalidad; desgracia; muerte.

fate [feit], *s.* hado, destino, sino; suerte, fortuna; parca.- **—d** [féitid], *a.* predestinado; fatal, aciago.

father [fáðœr], *s.* padre.—*f.-in-law,* suegro.—*Father's Day,* el día del Padre.—*vt.* engendrar; pronijar; tratar como hijo.—*to f. on* o *upon,* achacar, atribuir a.- **—hood** [-hud], *s.* paternidad.- **—land** [-lænd], *s.* (madre)patria, suelo natal.- **—less** [-lis], *a.* huérfano de padre; bastardo.- **—ly** [-li], *a.* paternal, paterno.—*adv.* paternalmente.

fathom [fáðom], *s.* braza.—*vt.* sondar, sondear; profundizar.- **—less** [-lis], *a.* insondable, impenetrable.

fatigue [fatíg], *s.* fatiga, cansancio; (mil.) faena.—*pl.* (mil.) traje de faena.—*vt.* y *vi.* fatigar(se), cansar(se).

fatness [fátnis], *s.* gordura. **—fatten** [fátn], *vt.* engordar, cebar.—*vi.* engordar, echar carnes. **—fattening** [fátniŋ], *s.* ceba, engorde (del ganado).—*a.* engordador.

faucet [fósit], *s.* grifo, llave, espita.

fault [folt], *s.* falta, culpa; defecto, tacha; (geol.) falla; (elec.) fuga de corriente.—*at f.* o *in f.,* culpable, responsable.—*to a f.,* excesivamente, con exceso.—*to find f. with,* culpar; hallar defecto en.- **—finder** [fólt-faindœr], *s.* censurador, criticón.- **—less** [-lis], *a.* sin tacha, impecable.- **—y** [-i], *a.* defectuoso, imperfecto.

favor [féivo(r)], *vt.* hacer un favor; agraciar, favorecer; patrocinar, sufragar.—*s.* favor; fineza, cortesía; auspicio, apoyo; (com.) carta, grata, atenta.—*in f. of,* a favor de; (com.) pagadero a.—*to be in f. with,* disfrutar del favor de.—*to lose f.,* caer en desgracia.- **—able** [-ḁbl], *a.* favorable, propicio.- **—ed** [-d], *a.* favorecido; valido.—*well (ill)-f.,* bien (mal) parecido.- **—ite** [-it], *a.* favorito, preferido.—*s.* favorito, protegido.—*f. son,* hijo predilecto.- **—itism** [-itizm], *s.* favoritismo.

fawn [fon], *s.* cervato, cervatillo; color de cervato.—*vi.* halagar, adular.

fax [fæks], *s.* fax, telefax, telefacsímil.—*f. machine,* telereproductor de imágenes.—*to send someone a f.,* mandarle un fax a alguien.—*vt.* faxear, enviar por fax, mandar por fax.

FBI [éfbíaí], *abrev.* (Federal Bureau of Investigation) FBI.

fear [fír], *s.* temor, miedo, pavor, recelo.—*vt.* y *vi.* temer, recelar.- **—ful** [fírful], *a.* miedoso; tímido, temeroso; horrendo, espantoso, terrible.- **—less** [-lịs], *a.* intrépido; sin temor, arrojado.- **—lessness** [-lịsnịs], *s.* intrepidez, arrojo.

feasible [fízịbl], *a.* factible, hacedero, practicable, viable.—*adv.* de modo factible.

feast [fist], *s.* fiesta; festejo, función; (fam.) comilona.—*vt.* festejar, agasajar.—*vi.* comer opíparamente.

feat [fit], *s.* acción; hazaña, proeza; juego de manos.—*pl.* suertes.

feather [féðœ(r)], *s.* pluma; plumaje; (carp.) lengüeta, barbilla.—*a f. in one's cap,* un triunfo, un timbre de orgullo para uno.—*f. duster,* plumero.—*to show the white f.,* volver las espaldas, huir.—*vt.* emplumar.—*to f. one's nest,* hacer su agosto; sacar tajada.- **—brain** [-brein], *s.* imbécil, tonto.- **—less** [-lịs], *a.* desplumado; implume.- **—weight** [-weịt], *a.* y *s.* ligero de peso; (dep.) peso pluma.- **—y** [-i], *a.* plumado; ligero.

feature [fíchū(r)], *s.* rasgo, carácter distintivo; (teat.) pieza o película principal.—*pl.* facciones, fisonomía.—*vt.* destacar, poner en primer plano; exhibir, mostrar (como lo más importante).

February [fébrueri], *s.* febrero.

fecund [fíkʌnd], *a.* fecundo, fértil.- **—ity** [fịkʌ́ndịtị], *s.* fecundidad; fertilidad, abundancia.

fed [fed], *pret.* y *pp.* de TO FEED.

federal [fédœrạl], *a.* federal. **—federate** [fédœreịt], *vt.* y *vi.* (con)federar(se). **—federation** [fedœréíṣọn], *s.* (con)federación, liga.

fee [fi], *s.* honorarios; derechos; cuota.

feeble [fíbl], *a.* débil; enfermizo; flojo, endeble; delicado.

feed [fid], *vti.* [10] alimentar, mantener, dar de comer a; dar pienso.—*vii.* comer, alimentarse; pacer, pastar.—*s.* forraje, pienso, comida.—*f. bag,* morral.—*f. cock* o *tap,* grifo de alimentación.—*f. pump,* bomba de alimentación.—*f. rack,* pesebre, comedero.- **—er** [fídœ(r)], *s.* alimentador; cebador (de ganado).- **—ing** [-iŋ], *s.* alimentación; forraje, pasto.—*a.* nutritivo, de alimentación.—*f. bottle,* biberón.

feel [fil], *vti.* [10] sentir; experimentar; tocar, palpar; percibir.—*to f. one's way,* ir a tientas.—*to f. the effects of,* resentirse de.—*vii.* sentirse, encontrarse.—*to f. angry, happy,* etc., estar enfadado, contento, etc.—*to f. ashamed, joyous,* etc., avergonzarse, alegrarse, etc.—*to f. bad,* sentirse mal; estar triste, entristecerse.—*to f. cold, warm, hungry, thirsty,* tener frío, calor, hambre, sed.—*to f. for,* condolerse de.—*to f. like* (*having* o *doing*), sentir deseos de, tener gana(s) de, querer.—*s.* tacto; sensación, percepción.- **—er** [fílœ(r)], *s.* el que toca o palpa; tentativa; tentáculo, antena.- **—ing** [-iŋ], *s.* tacto; sensación; sentimiento, sentido, emoción, sensibilidad; ternura, compasión; presentimiento, sospecha.—*to hurt one's feelings,* herir el amor propio, tocar en lo vivo.—*a.* sensible, tierno, conmovedor.

feet [fit], *s. pl.* de FOOT.

felicitate [fịlísịteịt], *vt.* felicitar, cumplimentar. **—felicitation** [fịlịsịtéíṣọn], *s.* felicitación, enhorabuena. **—felicity** [fịlísịtị], *s.* felicidad, bienaventuranza, dicha; ocurrencia oportuna.

fell [fɛl], *pret.* de TO FALL.—*vt.* derribar, tumbar, cortar (un árbol); (cost.) sobrecoser.

fellow [félou], *a.* asociado; compañero de o en.—*f. boarder,* compañero de pupilaje.—*f. citizen,* conciudadano.—*f. countryman,* compatriota.—*f. man, being* o *creature,* prójimo, semejante.—*f. member,* compañero, colega.—*f. partner,* consocio.—*f. scholar,* o *student,* condiscípulo.—*f. traveler,* compañero de viaje; (pol.) simpatizante (del partido communista).—*s.* compañero, camarada; socio o individuo de un colegio, sociedad, etc.; (fam.) hombre, sujeto, tipo.—*a good f.,* (fam.) buen chico.—*a young f.,* un joven, un muchacho.- **—ship** [-ṣip], *s.* confraternidad, compañerismo; asociación; sociedad; beca de investigación.—*f. holder,* becario, becado.

felony [félọni], *s.* crimen, delito, felonía.

felt [fɛlt], *s.* fieltro.—*f. pen, f.-tip pen,* rotulador, marcador.—*pp.* y *pret.* de TO FEEL.—*a.* de fieltro.

female [fímeịl], *s.* hembra (mujer, animal, o planta).—*a.* hembra; femenino.—*f. dog, donkey,* etc., perra, burra, etc.

feminine [féminịn], *a.* femenino, femenil; afeminado.—*s.* (gram.) (género) femenino. **—femininity** [fe-mjnínjtj], s. feminidad. **—feminism** [fémjnjzem], s. feminismo. **—feminist** [fémjnjst], a. y s. feminista.

femur [fímœ(r)], s. fémur.

fence [fens], s. cerea, cere(ad)o, valla, vallado; estacada; seto; (fam.) comprador de efectos robados; (mec.) resguardo.—f. season, tiempo de veda.—to be on the f., estar indeciso.—vt. (gen. con in) cercar, vallar.—vi. esgrimir.—**r** [fénsœ(r)], s. esgrimista. **—fencing** [fénsjŋ], s. esgrima; materiales para cercar; valladar.—f. foil, florete.

fender [féndœ(r)], s. guardafango, guardabarros; guardafuegos de chimenea; (mar.) defensas.

fennel [fénel], s. (bot.) hinojo.

ferment [fœrmént], vt. (hacer) fermentar.—vi. fermentar.—s. [fœrment] fermento; levadura; fermentación.—**ation** [-éjšon], s. fermentación.

fern [fœrn], s. helecho.

ferocious [fjróúšʌs], a. feroz, brutal, fiero. **—ferocity** [fjrásjtj], s. ferocidad, ensañamiento, fiereza salvaje.

ferret [férjt], s. (zool.) hurón; (cost.) listón, ribete.—vt. (con out) indagar, averiguar; escudriñar.

Ferris [férjs] **wheel,** s. noria, rueda de feria.

ferry [férj], vti. [7] balsear (un río); pasar (viajeros, mercancías o trenes de ferrocarril) a través del río; llevar, transportar; (aer.) transportar (tropas, etc.) por avión.—vi. cruzar el río en barca.—s. embarcadero, balsadero; transbordador; balsa o barco de pasar el río; balso o barco portatrén. **—ferryboat** [férjbout], s. barca o balsa de pasar el río; barco o balsa portatrén; transbordador, barco de transbordo.

fertile [fœrtjl], a. fértil, fecundo. **—fertility** [fœrtíljtj], s. fertilidad. **—fertilization** [fœrtjljzéjšon], s. fertilización, abono; (biol.) fecundación. **—fertilize** [fœrtjlajz], vt. fertilizar, fecundar; abonar. **—fertilizer** [fœrtjlajzœ(r)], s. abono, fertilizador.

fervent [fœrvent], a. ferviente, fervoroso; ardiente. **—fervor** [fœrvo(r)], s. fervor, devoción; ardor, calor.

fester [féstœ(r)], vi. enconarse, ulcerarse, supurar.—s. llaga, úlcera.

festival [féstjval], s. fiesta, festival, festividad. **—festive** [féstjv], a. festivo,

regocijado. **—festivity** [festívjtj], s. regocijo, júbilo; fiesta, festividad.

fetch [fech], vt. ir a buscar; traer; coger; aportar.—vi. moverse, menearse.—s. tirada, alcance; estratagema; aparecido.

fete [fejt], vt. festejar.—s. fiesta.

fetish [fétjš], s. fetiche; (fig.) manía.

fetter [fétœ(r)], vt. engrillar, encadenar; impedir.—s. traba, grillete.—pl. grillos, prisiones.

fetus [fítʌs], s. feto.

feud [fjud], s. contienda, enemistad entre familias, tribus, etc.; feudo.

fever [fívœ(r)], s. fiebre; calentura.—**ish** [-jš], a. febril, calenturiento.

few [fju], a., pron. o s. pocos; no muchos, contados.—a f., (alg)unos, unos cuantos, unos pocos.

fiancé [fjanséj], s. prometido, novio.—**e** [fjanséj], s. prometida, novia.

fiat [fíæt], s. orden, decreto.

fib [fjb], s. embuste, filfa, bola.—vii. [1] contar embustes.

fiber [fájbœ(r)], s. fibra, filamento.—f.-optics, transmisión por fibra óptica.—**board** [-bord], s. cartón madera.—**glass** [-glaes], s. fibra de vidrio.—**fibrous** [fájbrʌs], a. fibroso.

fickle [fíkl], a. voluble, inconstante, veleidoso.

fiction [fíkšon], s. ficción; literatura novelesca; novela. **—fictitious** [fjktíšʌs], a. ficticio.

fiddle [fjdl], s. (fam.) violín.—fit as a f., en buena condición física.—vi. (fam.) tocar el violín.—to f. away, malgastar el tiempo.—**r** [-œ(r)], s. (fam.) violinista.

fidelity [fjdéljtj], s. fidelidad; veracidad.

fidget [fídžjt], vt. inquietar.—vi. ajetrearse, afanarse; moverse nerviosamente.—s. (gen. pl.) afán, agitación, inquietud, impaciencia.—**y** [-j], a. inquieto, agitado.

fief [fif], s. feudo.—**dom** [-dom], s. feudo.

field [fild], s. campo (en todas sus acepciones).—f. artillery, artillería de campaña.—f. day, día de ejercicios atléticos; (mil.) día de maniobras; (fig.)—to have a f., obtener un gran éxito; divertirse muchísimo; hacer su agosto.—f. glasses, gemelos, anteojos.—f. goal, (basketball) canasta; (football) gol de campo.—f. hockey, hockey sobre hierba.—f. hospital, hospital de campaña, hospital de sangre.—f. kitchen, (mil.)

cocina de campaña.—*f. trip*, viaje de estudio.—*f. work*, trabajo científico de campo o en el terreno.- **—er** [-œr], *s.* (baseball) jardinero.- **—worker** [-wœrkœr], *s.* trabajador de campo, investigador de campo.

fiend [find], *s.* demonio, diablo; monstruo.—*dope f.*, narcómano.- **—ish** [fíndiŝ], *a.* diabólico, malvado.

fierce [firs], *a.* fiero, feroz; bárbaro; furioso; vehemente.- **—ness** [fírsnjs], *s.* fiereza, ferocidad; vehemencia.

fiery [fáiri], *a.* ardiente; vehemente; feroz, furibundo.

fifteen [fiftín], *a.* y *s.* quince. **—fifteenth** [fiftínθ], *a.* decimoquinto.— *s.* quinceavo.

fifth [fifθ], *a.* y *s.* quinto.—*f. column*, (pol.) quinta columna.

fiftieth [fíftjeθ], *a.* quincuagésimo.—*s.* cincuentavo.

fifty [fífti], *a.* y *s.* cincuenta.—*f.-f.*, mitad y mitad, a medias.—*f.-one*, cincuenta y uno.

fig [fig], *s.* higo.—*f. tree*, higuera.

fight [fait], *vti.* [10] pelear, combatir o luchar con (contra); librar (una batalla); lidiar (toros).—*to f. off*, rechazar.—*to f. out*, llevar la lucha hasta lo último.—*vii.* batallar, luchar; pelear; torear, lidiar.—*to f. against odds*, luchar con desventaja.—*s.* batalla, lucha, combate, lidia; pelea, riña.- **—er** [fájtœr], *s.* guerrero; peleador; lidiador, luchador, combatiente.—*f. plane*, avión de combate o de caza.- **—ing** [-iŋ], *a.* combatiente; agresivo; luchador.— *f. cock*, gallo de pelea, gallo de riña.—*s.* combate, riña, pelea.

figurative [fígyuṛaṭiv], *a.* figurativo; (language, meaning) figurado.

figure [fígyu(r)], *s.* figura; forma; talle; representación; personaje; (arit.) cifra, número; (com.) precio, valor.— *f. of speech*, tropo; metáfora.—*f. skating*, patinaje artístico.—*to cut a f.*, descollar.—*vt.* figurar, delinear; representar; calcular.—*to f. out*, hallar por cálculo, resolver.—*to f. up*, computar, calcular.—*vi.* figurar; (fam.) figurarse, imaginarse; calcular; (mús.) florear.

filament [fílament], *s.* filamento; hilacha.

file [fail], *s.* lima; escofina; archivo; carpeta o cubierta (para archivar papeles); legajo; actas; protocolo (de

notario, etc.); fila, hilera.—*f. case*, archivador; fichero.—*f. card*, ficha o tarjeta (de fichero).—*vt.* limar; archivar; acumular; presentar, registrar, anotar; protocolar.—*vi.* marchar en filas.—*to f. past*, desfilar.

filial [fíljal], *a.* filial. **—filiation** [filjéiŝon], *s.* filiación.

filibuster [fílíbʌstœr], *vi.* (E.U.) hacer obstrucción en un cuerpo legislativo prolongando el debate.—*s.* obstruccionista u obstrucción parlamentaria; filibustero, pirata.

filigree [fíligri], *s.* filigrana.

filing [fáiliŋ], *s.* limado, acción de limar; acción de archivar; (gen. *pl.*) limaduras, limalla.—*f. card*, ficha, tarjeta para archivo.

Filipino [filipínou], *s.* y *a.* filipino.

fill [fil], *vt.* llenar; rellenar; desempeñar, ocupar (un puesto); preparar (una receta); despachar (un pedido); hinchar, inflar; empastar (un diente).—*to f. in*, terraplenar; rellenar; insertar.—*to f. out*, completar; llevar a cabo.—*to f. up*, colmar; llenar un impreso; tapar.—*to f. up the time*, emplear el tiempo.—*vi.* (a menudo con up) llenarse, henchirse; saciarse.—*s.* terraplén; hartura; abundancia.

fillet [fílet], *s.* (cook.) filete.

filling [fíliŋ], *s. a.* (food) sólido, que llena.—*s.* (stuffing) relleno; (mec.) empaquetadura; (in tooth) empaste.—*f. station*, estación de servicio.

film [film], *s.* película; telilla, velo; membrana; nube en el ojo.—*f. star*, estrella de cine.- **—strip** [-strip], *s.* tira de película, tira proyectable.— *vt.* cubrir con película; rodar una película; fotografiar.

filter [fíltœr], *vt.* filtrar, colar.—*vi.* (in)filtrarse.—*s.* filtro.

filth [filθ], *s.* suciedad, inmundicia, porquería, mugre.- **—y** [fílθi], *a.* sucio, puerco, asqueroso; inmundo.

fin [fin], *s.* aleta (de pez); barba de ballena.

final [fáinal], *a.* final, terminante, definitivo, decisivo.—*s.* final.- **—ist** [-jst], *s.* finalista en un torneo deportivo.- **—ity** [fainæljti], *s.* finalidad; decisión, determinación.- **—ly** [fáinali], *adv.* finalmente, en fin, en conclusión, por último.

finance [fináens], *s.* finanza.—*pl.* finanzas; fondos.—*vt.* financiar.

—**financial** [fínǽnŝəl], *a.* financiero, monetario. —**financier** [fínænsír], *s.* financiero, financista, hacendista. —**financing** [fínǽnsiŋ], *s.* financiamiento, (Am.) refacción.

find [faind], *vti.* [10] encontrar, hallar.—*to f. fault with,* censurar o criticar a.—*to f. out,* descubrir; averiguar, enterarse (de).—*vii.* (for.) juzgar, fallar.—*s.* hallazgo, descubrimiento; encuentro.- —**er** [fáindœ(r)], *s.* el que encuentra; (fot.) visor, enfocador.- —**ing** [-iŋ], *s.* descubrimiento; (for.) fallo.

fine [fain], *a.* fino; refinado; excelente, admirable; primoroso; guapo, gallardo; claro; agradable.—*f. arts,* bellas artes.—*f. print,* letra pequeña, letra menuda.—*f.-tooth comb,* peine de dientes muy finos.—*with a f.-tooth comb,* (fig.) a fondo. —*f.-tune,* poner a punto, ajustar; afinar.—*f. weather,* tiempo despejado.—*s.* multa.—*vt.* afinar, refinar; multar.—*to be fined,* incurrir en multa.—*adv.* finamente; (fam.) de primera; muy bien (apl. a la salud).—*f.-tongued,* zalamero.—*interj.* ¡bien! ¡magnífico!.- —**ness** [fáinnis], *s.* fineza, delicadeza; primor, excelencia; perfección; finura (de arena, cemento, etc.).- —**ry** [fáinœri], *s.* gala, adorno, atavío.- —**sse** [finés], *s.* diplomacia, astucia; refinamiento; discernimiento; (in cards) impase.—*vt.* hacer el impase a; (fig.) lograr por medio de trucos.

finger [fíngœ(r)], *s.* dedo (de las manos).—*f. bowl,* lavafrutas.—*f. food,* tapas.—*little f.,* (dedo) meñique.—*middle f.,* dedo (del) corazón.—*to have a f. in the pie,* meter la cuchara; tener participación en un asunto.—*to have at one's finger tips,* tener o saber al dedillo.—*vt.* tocar, manosear; hurtar; (mus.) pulsar, teclear.- —**nail** [-nejl], *s.* uña del dedo.- —**print** [-prínt], *s.* huella dactilar; impresión digital.—*vt.* tomar las impresiones digitales de.- —**printing** [-príntiŋ], *s.* dactiloscopia.

finicky [fíniki], *a.* (fam.) delicado, melindroso.

finish [fíniŝ], *vt.* acabar, terminar, rematar; pulir, retocar, perfeccionar.—*to f. off,* rematar.—*to f. up,* darle la última mano a; retocar; terminar.—*vi.* acabar, finalizar; fenecer.—*s.* fin, término, remate; pulimento, última mano, acabado.—*f. line,* (dep.) meta.- —**ed** [-t], *a.* acabado, perfeccionado, pulido.- —**ing** [-iŋ], *s.* consumación; perfección; última mano, repaso.—*a.* último, de remate; de acabar.—*f. blow,* golpe de gracia.—*f. coat,* (pint.) última mano.—*f. nail,* puntilla francesa.

Finn [fin], *s.* finlandés, finlandesa.- —**ish** [fíniŝ], *a.* y *s.* finlandés.

fir [fœr], *s.* abeto; pino.

fire [fair], *s.* fuego; lumbre; incendio, quema; chispa; ardor, pasión.—*f. alarm,* alarma de incendios.—*f. department,* servicio de bomberos.—*f. drill,* ejercicio para caso de incendio.—*f. engine,* bomba de incendios.—*f. escape,* escalera de incendios.—*f. extinguisher,* matafuego.—*f. house,* cuartel de bomberos, estación de incendios.—*f. hydrant,* boca de incendio.—*f. plug,* boca de agua.—*f. power,* (mil.) potencia de fuego.—*f. sale,* venta de mercancías averiadas en un incendio.—*f. screen,* pantalla de chimenea.—*f. wall,* cortafuego.—*to catch f.,* encenderse, inflamarse.—*to set f., to set on f.,* pegar fuego a, incendiar.—*to take f.,* encenderse; acalorarse.—*under f.,* (mil., fig.) expuesto al fuego; atacado; censurado.—*vt.* incendiar; encender; disparar; enardecer; (fam.) despedir, echar (empleados).—*to f. up,* encender.—*vi.* encenderse; inflamarse; disparar, hacer fuego; enardecerse.—*to f. up,* enfurecerse.- —**arm** [fájrarm], *s.* arma de fuego.- —**brand** [-brænd], *s.* tea, tizón; incendiario.- —**bug** [-bʌg], *s.* (fam.) incendiario.- —**cracker** [-krækœ(r)], *s.* triquitraque, buscapiés, cohete.- —**fly** [-flaj], *s.* luciérnaga.- —**house** [-haus], *s.* estación o cuartel de bomberos.- —**man** [-man], *s.* bombero; fogonero. —**place** [-plejs], *s.* hogar, chimenea.- —**proof** [-pruf], *a.* incombustible, a prueba de fuego, refractario.—*vt.* hacer refractario o incombustible.- —**side** [-sajd], *s.* hogar, fogón; vida doméstica.—*a.* casero, íntimo.- —**trap** [-træp], *s.* edificio sin medios adecuados de escape en caso de incendio.- —**warden** [-wɔrdən], *s.* vigía de incendios.- —**water** [-wɔtœr], *s.* aguardiente.-

—**wood** [-wụd], s. leña.- —**works** [-wærks], s. fuegos artificiales. —**firing** [fáịrịŋ], s. descarga, tiroteo.—*f. squad*, (mil.) pelotón o piquete de fusilamiento.

firm [fœrm], a. firme; fijo, estable; sólido; persistente; tenaz, inflexible.—s. (com.) casa o empresa de comercio; firma, razón social.

firmament [fœrmạmẹnt], s. firmamento.

firmness [fœrmnịs], s. firmeza; estabilidad, fijeza, solidez; entereza, tesón.

first [fœrst], a. primero; primario; primitivo.—*f.-aid kit*, botiquín de urgencia o de primeros auxilios.— *f.-born*, primogénito.—*f. cousin*, primo hermano.—*f. floor*, planta baja.—*f.-hand*, de primera mano.— *f. lady*, primera dama.—*f. name*, nombre de pila.—*written in the f. person*, escrito en primera persona.—*adv.* primero; en primer lugar; al principio; antes; por, o la, primera vez.—*at f.*, al principio, al pronto.—*f. of all*, en primer lugar, ante todo.—*f. or last*, tarde o temprano.—*f.-rate*, de primera clase.

fiscal [fískạl], a. fiscal.—*f. year*, año fiscal.

fish [fịʃ], s. pez; pescado.—*f. bait*, cebo o carnada.—*f. hatchery*, vivero, criadero.—*f. market*, pescadería.— *f. pole*, caña de pescar.—*f. story*, cuento increíble.—*f. tank*, pecera.—*neither f. nor fowl*, ni carne ni pescado.—*shell-f.*, marisco.—*vt.* y *vi.* pescar. —**bone** [fíʃboụn], s. espina de pescado.- —**erman** [-œrmạn], s. pescador.- —**ery** [-œrị], s. industria pesquera; pesquero.- —**hook** [-hụk], s. anzuelo; garfio; bichero.- —**ing** [-ịŋ], s. pesca, pesquería.—*a.* de pescar; pesquero (barco, industria).—*f. line*, sedal o tanza de pescar.—*f. reel*, carrete.—*f. rod*, caña o vara de pescar.- —**monger** [-mʌŋgœ(r)], s. pescadero.- —**worm** [-wœrm], s. lombriz para pescar.- —**y** [-ị], a. que huele o sabe a pescado; abundante en peces; (fam.) sospechoso.

fission [fíʃọn], s. fisión.

fissure [fíʃū̱(r)], s. fisura, grieta, rajadura.—*vi.* agrietararse.

fist [fịst], s. puño; (impr.) llamada, manecilla,—*f. fight*, lucha a puñetazos.

- —**ful** [-fụl], s. puñado.- —**icuffs** [fístịkafs], s. puñetazos; riña a puñetazos.

fit [fịt], s. ataque, convulsión; arranque, arrebato; corte, talle; ajuste, encaje; conveniencia, adaptación.—*by fits (and starts)*, a tontas y a locas.—*a.* apto, idóneo, a propósito, adecuado, conveniente; capaz; apropiado; en buena salud, bien.—*f. for a king*, digno de reyes.—*f. to be tied*, (fam.) loco de atar.—*vti.* [1] ajustar, encajar, acomodar; adaptar; surtir, equipar; preparar; (cost.) entallar un vestido, probar.—*to f. out*, equipar; armar.—*to f. up*, ajustar, componer; ataviar; amueblar.—*vii.* convenir; ajustarse, entallarse, venir, sentar o caer bien o mal.—*to f. into*, encajar en.—*to f. in with*, concordar con.— —**ness** [fítnịs], s. aptitud, idoneidad, disposición; conveniencia; adaptabilidad.- —**ting** [-ịŋ], a. propio, adecuado, conveniente.—*s.* ajuste; unión o conexión de tubería; (cost.) corte, prueba.—*f. room*, probador.—*pl.* guarniciones; accesorios; avíos o herrajes.

five [faịv], a. y s. cinco. —**five hundred**, quinientos.—*f. one*, quientos uno. —**fiver** [faívœr], s. (jer.) cinco dólares.

fix [fịks], vt. fijar; asegurar; señalar (una fecha); arreglar; reparar, componer; (fam.) ajustar las cuentas.— *to f. up*, componer, arreglar; equipar.—*s.* apuro, aprieto.- —**ed** [-t], a. fijo, estable, permanente.- —**ings** [-ịŋz], spl. (fam.) (cook.) guarnición, acompañamiento.- —**ture** [fịkschū̱(r)], s. cosa fija o enclavada en un sitio; adorno. —*pl.* muebles y enseres; instalaciones.

flabby [flǽbị], a. fiojo, fofo, blando.

flaccid [flaésịd], a. fláccido, débil, flojo.

flag [flǽg], s. bandera; pabellón; banderola.—*F. Day*, Día de la Bandera.—*vti.* [1] izar bandera; hacer señales con banderola; enlosar; (comput.) señalar con un indicador o una bandera.—*to f. down*, parar.—*vii.* flaquear; decaer.

flagpole [flǽgpoụl], s. asta de bandera.

flagrant [fléịgrạnt], a. notorio, escandaloso; fiagrante.

flagship [flǽgŝɪp], s. nave capitana.
—**flagstaff** [flǽgstæf], s. asta de
bandera. —**flagstone** [flǽgstoun],
s. losa grande de embaldosar; laja.

flair [fler], s. sagacidad; aptitud, propensión.

flake [fleɪk], s. escama; copo de nieve;
hojuela, laminilla.—*f. of ice,* carámbano.—*vt.* y *vi.* formar hojuelas o escamas. —**flaky** [fléɪkɪ], a. escamoso.

flame [fleɪm], s. llama(rada), flama;
ardor, pasión.—*f. retardant,* ignífugo.—*f. thrower,* lanzallamas.—*vt.*
quemar, chamuscar.—*vi.* arder,
flamear, llamear; brillar, fulgurar;
inflamarse.– —**less** [fléɪmlɪs], a.
sin llama. —**flaming** [fléɪmɪn], a.
flamante, llameante; encendido,
inflamado; apasionado.– —**proof**
[-pruf], a. ininflamable; resistente
al fuego.

flamingo [flæmíngou], s. (orn.) flamenco.

flange [flændǯ], s. borde, reborde,
pestaña, oreja.—*f. joint,* junta de
pestañas.—*f. nut,* tuerca de reborde.—*vt.* rebordear, poner pestaña o reborde.—*vi.* sobresalir, hacer reborde.

flank [flæŋk], s. ijar, ijada; flanco, costado.—*a.* de lado, de costado o por
el flanco.—*vt.* estar a cada lado de;
(mil.) flanquear.—*vi.* (con on) lindar con.

flannel [flǽnəl], s. franela, bayeta.

flap [flæp], s. (sast.) cartera; faldeta,
faldón; aleta; ala de sombrero; hoja
plegadiza de mesa; oreja de zapato;
revés, cachete; (cir.) colgajo.—*f.
door,* trampa.—*f.-eared,* orejudo.—
f.-mouthed, hocicudo, morrudo.—
vti. [1] batir (las alas), sacudir,
pegar; agitar.—*to f. the wings,* aletear.—*vii.* batir; colgar.

flare [fler], *vt.* chamuscar; acampanar.—*vi.* brillar; fulgurar; resplandecer.—*to f. up,* encenderse; encolerizarse.—*s.* llama, llamarada,
fulgor; luz de Bengala; cohete de
señales; brillantez.—*f. up,* llamarada; arrebato de cólera; jarana.

flash [flæŝ], s. llamarada, destello, resplandor; fogonazo; (period.) breve
despacho telegráfico; (cine) incidencia.—*f. bulb,* bombilla de
flash.—*f. of lightning,* relámpago.—
f. of the eye, ojeada, vistazo.—*f. of
wit,* agudeza, ingenio.—*vt.* encender; enviar o despedir con celeridad; hacer brillar.—*vi.* relampaguear; brillar, fulgurar, destellar;
pasar o cruzar como un relámpago.
– —**ing** [flǽŝɪn], a. centelleante; relampagueante.—*s.* centelleo; relampagueo.– —**light** [-laɪt], s. linterna.– —**y** [-ɪ], a. charro, llamativo.

flask [flæsk], s. frasco grande; matraz; caneca.

flat [flæt], s. apartamento, piso;
(mús.) bemol.—*f. of the hand,*
palma de la mano.—*a.* llano, plano,
llano, liso; chato, aplastado; extendido; categórico; insulso, insípido;
(mús.) bemol; desafinado; monótono; menor o disminuído.—*f.-
bottomed,* de fondo plano.—
f.-footed, de pies planos; (fam.)
resuelto, determinado.—*f.-nosed,*
chato, ñato.—*f. rate,* tipo o tarifa
fijos; precio alzado.—*f. tax,* impuesto único.—*f. tire,* pinchazo;
neumático desinflado.— —**foot**
[-fut], s. (jer. y despec.) agente de
policía.—*adv.* terminantemente;
resueltamente; (com.) sin interés.—*vti.* [1] (mús.) bemol(iz)ar;
achatar.—*vii.* (mús.) desafinar por
lo bajo; aplastarse.— —**boat** [flǽtbout], s. bote o barco de fondo
plano.– —**car** [-kar], s. (f.c.) (vagón
de) plataforma.– —**iron** [-aɪœrn], s.
plancha (de planchar).– —**ly** [-lɪ],
adv. categóricamente, rotundamente.– —**ness** [-nɪs], s. llanura,
lisura, insipidez, insulsez.– —**ten**
[-n], *vt.* aplastar, achatar, aplanar;
deprimir; enderezar (un avión).—
vi. aplanarse; (aer.) enderezarse.

flatter [flǽtœ(r)], *vt.* y *vi.* adular, lisonjear.– —**er** [-œ(r)], s. adulador;
lisonjero, zalamero.– —**y** [-ɪ], s.
adulación, lisonja, halago.

flattop [flǽttap], s. (fam.) portaaviones.

flaunt [flɔnt], *vt.* y *vi.* ostentar, lucir;
desplegar, ondear.—*s.* ostentación.

flavor [fléɪvo(r)], s. sabor; sazón.—*vt.*
saborear; sazonar.

flaw [flɔ], s. defecto, falta, mancha;
grieta, pelo, paño, paja; ráfaga, racha.—*vt.* afear; estropear; agrietar.—*vi.* agrietarse; estropearse.–
—**less** [flɔlɪs], a. entero; intachable,
irreprochable; perfecto.

flax [flæks], s. lino.

flay [fleɪ], *vt.* desollar, despellejar.

flea [fliː], s. pulga.– **—bag** [-bæg], s. (jer. y despec.) piojoso, piojento; hotel de mala muerte.

fled [fled], pret. y pp. de TO FLEE.. **—flee** [fliː], vti. [10] huir de, evitar.—vii. huir; fugarse; desaparecer.

fleece [fliːs], s. vellón, lana.—Golden F., Toisón de Oro.—vt. esquilar; despojar, esquilmar. **—fleecy** [flíːsi], a. lanudo.

fleet [fliːt], s. armada, escuadra, flota, flotilla.—a. veloz, rápido.– **—ing** [flíːtiŋ], a. fugaz, efímero.

Flemish [flémiʃ], a. y s. flamenco.—s. idioma flamenco.

flesh [fleʃ], s. carne; pulpa (de las frutas).—f. and blood, carne y hueso; sangre, parentela, progenie.—f. wound, herida superficial.—in the f., vivo; en persona.—to put on f., echar carnes.—**pots** [-pɔts], spl. (humor.) antros de perdición.– **—y** [fléʃi], a. gordo, carnoso; pulposo.

flew [fluː], pret. de TO FLY.

flexibility [flèksibíliti], s. flexibilidad. **—flexible** [fléksibl], a. flexible. **—flexion** [flékʃɔn], s. flexión.

flick [flik], vt. golpear o sacudir levemente.—vi. revolotear.—s. golpecito.– **—er** [flíkœ(r)], vi. flamear; fluctuar, vacilar; aletear; revolotear.—s. llama vacilante; pestañeo, parpadeo.; (fam.) película.—pl. (fam.)—the f., el cine.

flier [flái̯œ(r)], s. volador; aviador; fugitivo; (mec.) volante; hoja o papel volante; cosa veloz.

flight [flait], s. vuelo; escuadrilla aérea; bandada de pájaros; ímpetu; arranque; huída, evasión.—f. attendant, auxiliar de vuelo.—f. of stairs, tramo de escalera.

flimsy [flímzi], a. débil, endeble; baladí, frívolo.

flinch [flinch], vi. vacilar; acobardarse; retroceder.—s. titubeo.

fling [fliŋ], vti. [10] arrojar, tirar, lanzar, echar.—to f. about, desparramar, esparcir.—to f. away, desechar.—to f. open, abrir de repente.—to f. out, arrojar con fuerza; hablar violentamente, echar chispas.—to f. up, abandonar, dejar.—vii. lanzarse.—s. tiro; lanzamiento; indirecta; tentativa.—to go on a f., echar una cana al aire.

flint [flint], s. pedernal.

flirt [flœrt], vi. coquetear, (neol.) flirtear; dejarse tentar (por una idea, etc.).– **—ation** [-éiʃɔn], s. coqueteo, galanteo.

flit [flit], vii. [1] revolotear; volar; deslizarse velozmente.

float [flout], vt. poner, mantener o llevar a flote; (com.) emitir, poner en circulación.—vi. flotar, sobrenadar.—s. flotador; boya; balsa salvavidas; corcho de una caña de pescar; carroza.—a. de flotador.

flock [flak], s. hato, manada, rebaño; grey; bandada; congregación; multitud; pelusilla.—vi. congregarse.

flog [flag], vti. [1] azotar.– **—ging** [flágiŋ], s. azotaina, paliza.

flood [flʌd], s. diluvio; avenida, creciente, inundación; torrente; pletora.—f. light, reflector.—f. tide, pleamar.—vt. inundar; anegar; abarrotar.—vi. desbordar.– **—gate** [flʌ́dgeit], s. compuerta.

floor [flɔr], s. suelo; piso; pavimento.—boarded f., entarimado.—first f., ground f., planta baja, piso bajo.—f. board, (aut.) tabla de piso.—f. lamp, lámpara de pie.—f. plan, planta.—f. show, espectáculo de cabaret.—second f., primer piso, piso principal.—to have the f., tener la palabra. **—walker** [-wɔ́koer], s. jefe de vendedores.—vt. derribar, tirar al suelo; entarimar; echar al suelo; derrotar; dejar turulato.

flop [flap], vti. [1] batir, sacudir.—vii. aletear; caer flojamente; colgar; caerse, venir abajo.—to f. down, tumbarse, dejarse caer.—to f. up, voltear(se).—s. fracaso, fiasco; golpe seco.– **—house** [-hau̯s], s. (jer.) albergue para vagabundos.– **—py** [flápi], a. (fam.) flojo, blando, flexible.—f. disk, (comput.) disquete, disco flexible, disco floppy.

florist [flórist], s. florista.

floss [flɔs], s. seda floja; penacho del maíz.—dental f., hilo dental.

flounce [flauns], s. volante, fleco, cairel.

flounder [fláundœ(r)], s. (ict.) lenguado.—vi. forcejar torpemente; tropezar y caer; revolcarse.

flour [flau̯r], s. harina.—vt. enharinar.—vi. pulverizarse.

flourish [flœ́riʃ], vt. florear, blandir; embellecer.—vi. florecer; medrar, prosperar; (mus.) florear.—*s.* rasgo; rúbrica; floreo, adorno; (esgr.) molinete.

floury [fláu̯ri], *a.* harinoso.

flout [flau̯t], *vt.* burlarse de, mofarse de.

flow [flou̯], *vi.* fluir, manar; correr; seguirse; ondear, flotar; abundar; crecer (la marea).—*to f. away,* deslizarse, pasar.—*to f. from* o *out,* brotar, salir, nacer, manar de.—*to f. into,* desembocar.—*to f. with,* rebosar de.—*vt.* inundar; derramar; hacer fluir.—*s.* corriente; torrente; flujo; desagüe; abundancia.

flower [fláu̯œ(r)], *s.* flor; planta en flor; flor y nata.—*f. pot,* tiesto.—*f. vase,* florero, búcaro.—*vi.* florecer.—**-y** [-i], *a.* florido, ornado.

flowing [flóu̯iŋ], *a.* corriente, fluente, fluido; suelto; colgante.—*s.* derrame; salida; corriente; flujo; fluidez.

flown [flou̯n], *pp.* de TO FLY.—*a.* vidriado.

flu [flu], *s.* (fam.) influenza, gripe.

fluctuate [flákchue̯it], *vi.* fluctuar; oscilar, ondear. —**fluctuation** [flʌkchué̯iṣọn], *s.* fluctuación.

flue [flu], *s.* cañón de chimenea; tubo de caldera; pelusa, borra; conducto; cañón de órgano.

fluency [flúe̯nṣi], *s.* fluidez; afluencia; labia. —**fluent** [flúe̯nt], *a.* facundo; suelto, corriente; copioso; fluido.

fluff [flʌf], *s.* pelusa, lanilla, vello, plumón.—*vt.* mullir, esponjar.—**-y** [flʌfi], *a.* cubierto de plumón o vello; mullido, esponjoso.

fluid [flúi̯d], *s.* flúido; líquido; gas.—*a.* flúido; líquido; gaseoso.—**-ity** [fluídi̯ti], —**ness** [flúi̯dnịs], · *s.* fluidez.

flung [flʌŋ], *pret.* y *pp.* de TO FLING.

flunk [flʌŋk], *s.* fracaso.—*vt.* reprobar, suspender; fracasar en un examen. -—**(e)y** [flʌ́ŋki], *s.* lacayo; adulón.

fluorescence [fluo̯résẹns], *s.* fluorescencia. —**fluorescent** [fluo̯résẹnt], *a.* fluorescente.

flurry [flœ́ri], *s.* chaparrón, ráfaga, nevisca; agitación, frenesí; lluvia.—*vt.* agitar, aturdir.

flush [flʌš], *vi.* sonrojarse, abochonarse; inundarse; nivelar(se).—*vt.* limpiar con un chorro de agua.—*to f. the toilet,* tirar de la cadena.—*a.* nivelado, parejo; copioso.—*s.*

rubor; animación; flujo rápido; abundancia; flux (de naipes).

fluster [flʌ́stœr], *s.* confusión, aturdimiento.—*vt.* confundir, aturdir.

flute [flut], *s.* flauta; estria de una columna; rizado, pliegue.—*vt.* estriar, acanalar; rizar, plegar.

flutter [flʌ́tœ(r)], *vt.* agitar, menear, sacudir; aturdir.—*vi.* agitarse, menearse; aletear, revolotear; flamear, ondular.—*s.* agitación; vibración; palpitación; aleteo; ondulación.

flux [flʌks], *s.* flujo; diarrea.

fly [flai̯], *vti.* [10] hacer volar; elevar (una cometa, etc.); enarbolar; evitar, huir de; dirigir (un avión); cruzar o atravesar en avión.—*vii.* volar; lanzarse, precipitarse; pasar rápidamente; escaparse; desaparecer, desvanecerse.—*to f. around,* ir de un lado a otro.—*to f. at,* arrojarse o lanzarse sobre.—*to f. away,* irse volando, escaparse.—*to f. from,* huir de.—*to f. into a passion* o *rage,* montar en cólera; irse del seguro.— *to f. off,* desprenderse súbitamente; separarse, sublevarse.—*to f. open,* abrirse repentinamente.—*to f. out,* dispararse, salir a espetaperros.—*s.* mosca; vuelo; bragueta.—*f.-speck,* cagadita de mosca.- —*away* [flái̯a̯we̯i], *a.* tremolante; inconstante.— —**er** [-œ(r)], *s.* = FLIER.- —**ing** [-iŋ], *a.* volante, volador, volátil; flameante, ondeante; rápido, veloz; breve.—*f. fish,* pez volador.—*s.* aviación; vuelo.- —**leaf** [-lif], *s.* guarda de un libro.

foam [fou̯m], *s.* espuma.—*f. rubber,* goma espuma.—*vt.* hacer espuma.—*vi.* espumar, echar espuma(rajos).- —**-y** [fóu̯mi], *a.* espumoso.

focus [fóu̯kʌs], *s.* foco; distancia focal.—*out of f.,* desenfocado.—*vti.* y *vii.* [2] enfocar(se); concentrar(se).

fodder [fádœ(r)], *s.* forraje, pienso.—*vt.* dar forraje a.

foe [fou̯], *s.* enemigo.

fog [fag], *s.* niebla, neblina, bruma; velo; confusión, perplejidad.—*vti.* [1] oscurecer; velar.—*vii.* ponerse brumoso; velarse.- —**gy** [fági], *a.* brumoso, neblinoso; velado.

foil [fɔi̯l], *vt.* frustrar, contrarrestar.—*s.* hoja delgada de metal; oropel; chapa; hoja de oro o plata; florete; rastro; contraste.

fold [fould], s. doblez, pliegue; redil; hato, rebaño.—vt. doblar, plegar; encerrar, envolver; meter en redil.—to f. the arms, cruzar los brazos.—vi. doblarse, plegarse.— **—er** [fóuldœ(r)], s. plegador, plegadera; carpeta; cuadernillo; circular.— **—ing** [-iŋ], a. plegadizo.—f. bed, catre de tijera.—f. chair, silla plegadiza.—f. screen, biombo.—s. plegado, doblamiento; repliegue.

foliage [fóuḷiḏ], s. follaje, frondosidad, fronda.

folk [fouk], s. gente; nación, raza, pueblo.—pl. parientes, parentela.—a. popular, tradicional, del pueblo.— f. music, música folklórica.—f. tale, conseja.

follow [fálou], vt. seguir; venir después de; perseguir; ejecutar, poner por obra; resultar de; ejercer.—to f. out, llevar hasta el fin.—to f. suit, jugar el mismo palo (en los naipes); seguir el ejemplo; seguir la corriente.—to f. up, llevar hasta el fin; continuar.— vi. ir detrás; seguirse.—to f. on, perseverar.— **—er** [-œ(r)], s. seguidor; acompañante; secuaz.—pl. comitiva, séquito.— **—ing** [-iŋ], a. siguiente; próximo.—s. adhesión; séquito; oficio, profesión.

folly [fáli], s. tontería, locura, desatino.

foment [fomént], vt. fomentar.

fond [fand], a. aficionado, enamorado; tierno, cariñoso; querido, acariciado.—to be f. of, ser amigo de o aficionado a; ser afecto a, estar encariñado con.— **—le** [fándl], vt. mimar, acariciar, hacer fiestas a.— **—ness** [fándnis], s. afición, cariño.

font [fant], s. pila de bautismo o de agua bendita; (impr.) fundición, torta.

food [fud], s. alimento, comida, sustento.—f. poisoning, intoxicación por alimentos—f. stamps, cupones alimenticios (vales gubernamentales canjeables por alimentos).— **—stuff** [fúdstʌf], s. producto o sustancia alimenticia.—pl. víveres, comestibles.

fool [ful], s. tonto, necio; inocente, bobo; badulaque; (teat.) gracioso; bufón.—f's gold, pirita de hierra.— vt. chasquear; embromar; engañar.—to f. away, malbaratar; perder el tiempo.—vi. tontear, divertirse,

chancear.— **—ery** [fúlœri], s. tontería.— **—hardy** [-hardi], a. arriesgado, temerario.— **—ish** [-iš], a. tonto; disparatado; badulaque; bobo.— **—ishness** [-iŝniŝ], s. simpleza, tontería, disparate.— **—proof** [-pruf], a. a prueba de impericia; (fam.) infalible.

foot [fut], s. (pl. **feet** [fit]) pie; pata; base.—by f., a pie.—f. by f., paso a paso.—f.-loose, sin trabas u obligaciones, andariego.—f. race, carrera a pie.—f. soldier, soldado de infantería.—on f., de pie; a pie; progresando.—to put one's f. in it, meter la pata.— **—ball** [fútbɔl], s. football, balompié, balón.—f. player, futbolista.— **—ing** [-iŋ], s. base, fundamento; cimiento; posición firme.—on the same f., en pie de igualdad.— **—lights** [-laits], s. candilejas; el teatro, las tablas.— **—man** [-man], s. lacayo.— **—note** [-nout], s. nota al pie de una página.— **—pace** [-peis], s. descanso de escaleras; paso lento.— **—path** [-paθ], s. senda para peatones.— **—print** [-print], s. pisada, rastro.— **—rest** [rɛst], s. apoyapiés, descansapié.—**—step** [-step], s. huella, pisada, paso.— **—stool** [-stul], s. escabel, taburete.— **—walk** [-wɔk], **—way** [-wei], s. senda de peatones; acera.— **—wear** [-wɛr], s. calzado.— **—work** [-wœrk], s. juego o manejo de los pies (boxeo, baile, etc.)

fop [fap], s. petimetre, currutaco.

for [fɔr], prep. por; para; durante; por espacio de; de; con, a pesar de, no obstante; —as f., en cuanto a.—as f. me, por mi parte.—but f., a no ser, sin.—f. all that, no obstante, con todo, a pesar de eso.—f. good, para siempre.—what f.? ¿para qué?— conj. porque, puesto que, pues; en efecto.

forage [fáriḏ], vt. y vi. forrajear, proveer(se) de forraje; apacentar(se); saquear.—s. forraje.

forbad o forbade [fɔrbǽd], pret. de TO FORBID.

forbear [fɔrbér], s. antepasado, antecesor.—vti. y vii. [10] abstenerse de, tener paciencia; reprimirse.

forbid [fɔrbíd], vti. [10] prohibir; impedir, estorbar; excluir de. **—forbidden** [fɔrbídǝn], pp. de TO FORBID.—a. prohibido, vedado, ilícito.

– **—ding** [-iŋ], *a.* prohibitivo; repulsivo, aborrecible, repugnante.

forbore [fɔrbór], *pret.* de TO FORBEAR. **—forborne** [fɔrbórn], *pp.* de TO FORBEAR.

force [fɔrs], *s.* fuerza; necesidad; personal; cuerpo (de tropas, de policía, etc.).—*pl* fuerzas (militares o navales).—*by f. of*, a fuerza de.—*in f.*, vigente, en vigor.—*vt.* forzar, obligar; violar; impulsar; embutir.—*to f. along*, hacer avanzar o adelantar.—*to f. away*, obligar a alejarse.—*to f. back*, rechazar, hacer retroceder.—*to f. the issue*, hacer que el asunto se discuta o decida pronto, que se vaya al grano sin demora.– **—ed** [-t], *a.* forzado, forzoso; fingido.– **—ful** [fórsfu̱l], *a.* enérgico, potente, violento. **—forcible** [fórsi̱bl], *a.* fuerte, enérgico; violento; de peso.

ford [fɔrd], *s.* vado.—*vt.* vadear.

fore [fɔr], *a.* anterior, delantero; proel.—*adv.* delante, hacia delante; de proa.—*s.* delantero, frente.—*interj.* ¡fore!— **—arm** [fórarm], *s.* antebrazo.—*vt.* [fɔrárm], armar de antemano.– **—bode** [-bóu̱d], *vt.* y *vi.* pronosticar, presagiar; presentir.– **—boding** [-bóu̱diŋ], *s.* presentimiento, corazonada.—*a.* agorero.– **—cast** [fórkæst], *vti.* y *vii.* [4] pronosticar, prever, predecir; proyectar, trazar.— *pret.* y *pp.* de TO FORECAST.—*s.* pronóstico, predicción; proyecto, plan.– **—doom** [-dum], *s.* predestinación, sino.– **—father** [-faðœ(r)], *s.* ascendiente, antepasado.– **—finger** [-fiŋgœ(r)], *s.* dedo índice. – **—foot** [-fut], *s.* mano o pata delantera.– **—front** [-frʌnt], *s.* vanguardia, primera fila.– **—go** [-góu̱], *vii.* [10] privarse de, renunciar a; ceder, abandonar.– **—gone** [-gón], *a.* predeterminado; inevitable, seguro.–*pp.* de TO FOREGO.– **—ground** [-grau̱nd], *s.* primer plano.– **—head** [-i̱d], *s.* frente; parte delantera.

foreign [fári̱n], *a.* extranjero; exterior; extraño; advenedizo; remoto.—*f. commerce*, comercio exterior.—*f. exchange*, cambio extranjero. —*f. to the case*, ajeno al caso.– **—er** [-œ(r)], *s.* extranjero, extraño, forastero.

forelock [fórlak], *s.* guedeja.

foreman [fórma̱n], *s.* capataz; encargado; mayoral; presidente del jurado.

foremost [fórmou̱st], *a.* delantero, primero; principal, más notable.

forenoon [fórnun], *s.* [la] mañana.

forerunner [fɔrránœ(r)], *s.* precursor; presagio, pronóstico.

foresaid [fórsed], *a.* antedicho, susodicho.

foresaw [fɔrsó], *pret.* y *pp.* de TO FORESEE. **—foresee** [fɔrsí], *vti.* [10] prever.—*vii.* tener previsión. **—foreseen** [fɔrsín], *pp.* de TO FORESEE. **—foresight** [fórsajt], *s.* previsión, perspicacia.

forest [fári̱st], *s.* selva, bosque, floresta.—*f. ranger*, guardabosques.— *vt.* arbolar.

forester [fári̱stœ(r)], *s.* silvicultor; guardamonte; habitante del bosque. **—forestry** [fári̱stri̱], *s.* silvicultura; ingeniería forestal.

foretell [fɔrtél], *vti.* y *vii.* [10] predecir, adivinar.– **—er** [-œ(r)], *s.* profeta. **—foretold** [fɔrtóu̱ld], *pret.* y *pp.* de TO FORETELL.

forever [fɔrévœ(r)], *adv.* siempre; para o por siempre; perpetuidad.—*f. and a day*, o *f. and ever*, eternamente, por siempre jamás.

forewarn [fɔrwórn], *vt.* prevenir, advertir, avisar.

forewent [fɔrwént], *pret.* de TO FOREGO.

foreword [fórwœrd], *s.* prefacio.

forfeit [fórfi̱t], *s.* prenda perdida; multa; decomiso; pérdida legal de cosa o derecho por incumplimiento de obligaciones.—*pl.* juego de prendas.—*a.* confiscado, perdido por incumplimiento.—*vt.* perder algo por incumplimiento de obligaciones.

forgave [fɔrgéjv], *pret.* de TO FORGIVE.

forge [fɔrdʒ], *s.* fragua; forja; herrería.—*vt.* forjar, fraguar; falsificar, falsear; inventar; tramar.—*to f. ahead*, abrirse paso, avanzar.– **—ry** [fórdʒœri̱], *s.* falsificación.

forget [fɔrgét], *vti.* y *vii.* [10] olvidar (se de).—*f. it*, no piense más en eso; no se preocupe, descuide Ud.—*to f. oneself*, excederse, propasarse; ser distraído; ser abnegado.– **—ful** [-fu̱l], *a.* olvidadizo.– **—fulness** [-fu̱lni̱s], *s.* olvido, descuido;

calidad de olvidadizo. **—f.-me-not** [-mįnat], s. (bot.) nomeolvides.

forgive [fɔrgív], vti. [10] perdonar, dispensar, condonar. **—forgiven** [fɔrgíven], pp. de TO FORGIVE.- **—ness** [-nįs], s. perdón; clemencia, misericordia. **—forgiving** [fɔrgívįŋ], a. magnánimo, clemente, de buen corazón, perdonador.

forgot [fɔrgát], pret. de TO FORGET. **—forgotten** [fɔrgáten], pp. de TO FORGET.

fork [fɔrk], s. tenedor; horquilla; bifurcación; confluencia de un río.— vt. cargar heno con la horquilla. —to f. out, (fam.) desembolsar, aflojar.—vi. bifurcarse.

forlorn [fɔrlɔ́rn], a. abandonado; infeliz, desdichado.—f. hope, empresa desesperada.

form [fɔrm], s. forma; figura; hechura; hoja, modelo que ha de llenarse; condición; estado; práctica, ritual, formalidad; estilo; horma, matriz, patrón; porte, modales.—vt. formar, construir, labrar, modelar, idear, concebir; constituir, integrar.—vi. formarse.- **—al** [fɔ́rmal], a. formal.- **—ality** [-ǽlįtį], s. formalidad, etiqueta, cumplimiento.- **—alize** [-ạlaịz], vt. formalizar.- **—at** [-æt], s. formato.- **—ation** [-éịṣ̌ǫn], s. formación; desarrollo; arreglo.

former [fɔ́rmœ(r)], a. primero; precedente, anterior; antiguo; ex-, que fue.—the f., aquél, aquélla, aquéllos, etc.- **—ly** [-lį], adv. antiguamente, antes, en tiempos pasados.

formula [fɔ́rmyulặ], s. fórmula, receta. - **—te** [fɔ́rmyuleịt], vt. formular.

forsake [fɔrséịk], vti. [10] abandonar, desamparar; separarse de; renegar de; desechar; dar de mano a. **—forsaken** [fɔrséịken], pp. de TO FORSAKE.—a. abandonado. **—forsook** [fɔrsų̃k], pret. de TO FORSAKE.

forswear [fɔrswér], vti. [10] abjurar, renunciar o negar solemnemente.—vii. perjurar(se). **—forswore** [fɔrswór], pret. de TO FORSWEAR. **—forsworn** [fɔrswórn], pp. de TO FORSWEAR.

fort [fɔrt], s. fuerte, fortaleza, fortín.

forth [fɔrθ], adv. delante; adelante; fuera, afuera; a la vista, públicamente; hasta lo último.—and so f., y así sucesivamente; etcétera.- **—coming** [-kámįŋ], a. venidero, futuro, próximo.—s. aparición, acercamiento, proximidad.- **—with** [-wįð], adv. inmediatamente.

fortieth [fɔ́rtįẹθ], a. cuadragésimo.— s. cuarentavo.

fortification [fɔrtįfįkéịṣ̌ǫn], s. fortificación; fortalecimiento; fortaleza. **—fortify** [fɔ́rtįfaị], vti. [7] fortificar; fortalecer; reforzar; corroborar.— vii. construir defensas.

fortitude [fɔ́rtįtįud], s. fortaleza, fuerza, ánimo.

fortnight [fɔ́rtnaịt], s. quincena, dos semanas.—ly [-lį], a. quincenal, bisemanal.—adv. quincenalmente. —s. revista bisemanal.

fortress [fɔ́rtrįs], s. fortaleza, plaza fuerte.

fortunate [fɔ́rchụnįt], a. afortunado, dichoso. **—fortune** [fɔ́rchụn], s. fortuna; dicha; sino; caudal, bienes.— f. cookie, galletita china.—f. hunter, (despec.) cazafortunas.- **—teller** [-telœr], s. adivino.—vt. dotar con una fortuna.

forty [fɔ́rtį], a. y s. cuarenta.—f.-one, cuarenta y uno.

forum [fɔ́rʌm], s. plaza; foro; tribunal; reunión para debatir un asunto.

forward [fɔ́rwạrd], adv. adelante, en adelante, hacia adelante, más allá.—a. delantero; adelantado; precoz; anterior; activo; desenvuelto; emprendedor; radical.—s. delantero.—vt. (a career) promover, fomentar; (mail) enviar, reexpedir.—please forward, hágase seguir.

foster [fástœ(r)], vt. fomentar, promover; criar.—a. adoptivo.—f. child, niño criado como si fuera hijo.—f. daughter, hija de leche, hija adoptiva.—f. home, hogar de adopción.—f. son, hijo de leche, hijo adoptivo.—to place in a f. home, colocar con una familia de acogida.

fought [fɔt], pret. y pp. de TO FIGHT.

foul [faụl], a. sucio, impuro; fétido; viciado (aire); detestable, vil; injusto, sin derecho; contrario, desagradable; obsceno; lleno de errores y correcciones.—f.-dealing, dolo, mala fe.—f. language, lenguaje soez.—f.-mouthed, mal hablado.— f. play, juego sucio o desleal.—f. weather, mal tiempo.—s. acción de ensuciar; violación de las reglas establecidas.—vt. ensuciar; trabar;

violar las reglas.—*vi.* ensuciarse; trabarse; chocar.—*s.* (sports) falta.

found [faṷnd], *pret.* y *pp.* de TO FIND.— *vt.* cimentar, fundamentar; fundar, instituir; apoyar en; fundir, derretir.—*the Founding Fathers,* (E.U.) los fundadores de la nación americana.- **—ation** [-éiṣọn], *s.* fundación, establecimiento; fundamento, base; dotación; cimiento. —*f. stone,* piedra fundamental.- **—er** [fáṷndœ(r)], *s.* fundador; fundidor.—*vt.* (mar.) hacer zozobrar.— *vi.* irse a pique, zozobrar; fracasar.- **—ry** [-ri], *s.* fundición (fábrica).

fountain [fáṷntịn], *s.* fuente; manantial; fontanar; pila.—*f. pen,* pluma estilográfica, pluma fuente, estilográfica.- **—head** [-hed], *s.* fuente, origen.

four [fọr], *a.* y *s.* cuatro. —**four hundred,** cuatrocientos.—*f. one,* cuatrocientos uno. **—fourth** [fọrθ], *a.* y *s.* cuarto.

foursquare [fọrskwér], *a.* cuadrado; (fig.) franco, sincero; (fig.) firme, constante.

fourteen [fọrtín], *a.* y *s.* catorce. — **fourteenth** [fọrtínθ], *a.* decimocuarto.—*s.* catorzavo.

fowl [faṷl], *s.* gallo, gallina; aves; carne de ave.

fox [faks], *s.* zorra, raposa; zorro, taimado.- **—hole** [fákshoṵl], *s.* trinchera individual.- **—y** [-i], *a.* taimado, astuto.

foyer [fóiœ(r)], *s.* salón de entrada; (teat.) salón de descanso.

fraction [frǽkṣọn], *s.* fracción, quebrado; fragmento.—*vt.* fraccionar.- **—al** [-ạl], *a.* fraccionario; fraccionado.

fracture [frǽkchụ(r)], *s.* fractura, rotura, ruptura, quiebra.—*vt.* y *vi.* fracturar(se), quebrar(se).

fragile [frǽdžịl], *a.* frágil.- **—ness** [-nịs], **fragility** [frạdžílịti], *s.* fragilidad; debilidad.

fragment [frǽgmẹnt], *s.* fragmento; trozo.- **—ary** [-ẹri], *a.* fragmentario.

fragrance [fréigrạns], *s.* fragancia.- **—fragrant** [fréigrạnt], *a.* fragante.

frail [freịl], *a.* frágil; endeble.—*s.* canasta, espuerta.- **—ty** [fréịlti], *s.* fragilidad; debilidad.

frame [freịm], *vt.* enmarcar, encuadrar; formar, construir; armar; forjar, idear; arreglar clandestinamente (el resultado de un juego,

etc.); incriminar por medio de una estratagema.—*s.* marco; armazón; estructura; figura; armadura, esqueleto; bastidor.—*f. of mind,* estado de ánimo.—**up** [fréịmʌp], *s.* conspiración, fraude.

franc [frǽŋk], *s.* franco (moneda).

franchise [frǽnchaịz], *s.* derecho político; franquicia, privilegio; concesión; exención.

frank [frǽŋk], *a.* franco, sincero; francote, campechano.—*s.* franquicia postal; (cook.) salchicha de Frankfurt.—*vt.* franquear (una carta).

frankfurter [frǽŋkfœrtœ(r)], *s.* salchicha de Frankfurt, salchicha alemana.

frankness [frǽŋknịs], *s.* franqueza.

frantic [frǽntịk], *a.* frenético, furioso.

fraternal [frạtœrnạl], *a.* fraternal, fraterno. **—fraternity** [frạtœrnịti], *s.* (con)fraternidad; hermandad; (group of young men) asociación estudiantil. **—fraternize** [frǽtœrnaịz], *vi.* y *vt.* (con)fraternizar, hermanar(se).

fraud [frọd], *s.* fraude; farsante, trampista.- **—ulent** [frɔ́džụlẹnt], *a.* fraudulento.

fray [freị], *s.* riña, refriega; raedura, desgaste.—*vt.* ludir, raer.—*vi.* deshilacharse.

freak [frik], *s.* capricho, antojo; rareza; monstruo, fenómeno; (fam.) bicho raro; (fam.) fanático, e.g., *tennis f.,* fanático del tenis.—*f. of nature,* aborto de la naturaleza.—*a.* raro; anormal.- **—ish** [fríkịṣ], *a.* caprichoso, antojadizo; raro.

freckle [fréckl], *s.* peca.—*f.-faced,* pecoso.—*vt.* motear.—*vi.* ponerse pecoso.- **—d** [-d], *a.* pecoso; moteado.

free [fri], *a.* libre; franco; vacante; exento; gratuito; desocupado; liberal, generoso.—*f. enterprise,* libre empresa.—*f. of charge,* gratis.—*f. on board,* franco a bordo, libre a bordo.—*vt.* librar, libertar; eximir; desembarazar.—*adv.* libremente, gratis.— **—dom** [frídọm], *s.* libertad; exención, inmunidad; libre uso.

freelance [frílæns], *a.* por cuenta propia.—*vi.* trabajar por cuenta propia.

Freemason [frímáịsọn], *s.* masón.

freeze [friz], *vti.* [10] congelar, helar.—*vii.* helarse; helar, escarchar.—*s.* helada. **—dried** [-draịd], *pp.* liofilizado.- **—dry** [-draj], *vt.* liofilizar.- **—r** [frízœ(r)], *s.* congelador, freezer. **—freezing** [frízıŋ], *a.* congelante, frigorífico; glacial.—*s.* helamiento, congelación.

freight [frejt], *vt.* fletar; cargar.—*s.* carga, cargazón; flete.—*by f.*, como carga.—*f. car* o *train*, carro, tren de mercancías.—*f. elevator*, montacargas.- **—er** [fréjtœ(r)], *s.* buque de carga.

French [french], *a.* y *s.* francés.—*F. fries*, patatas fritas.—*s.* idioma francés.- **—man** [fréncḥmṇn], *s.* francés.- **—woman** [-wụmṇn], *s.* francesa.

frenzy [frénzj], *s.* frenesí.

frequency [fríkwẹnsj], *s.* frecuencia.—*f. modulation*, frecuencia modulada, modulación de frecuencia. **—frequent** [fríkwẹnt], *a.* frecuente.—*vt.* [frịkwént], frecuentar; concurrir a.

fresh [freš], *a.* fresco; reciente; nuevo; refrescante; desahogado, entremetido.—*f. air*, aire puro; aire libre.—*f. from*, acabado de llegar, sacar, etc.—*f. hand*, novicio.—*f. water*, agua dulce.- **—en** [fréšẹn], *vt.* refrescar, refrigerar.—*vi.* refrescarse, avivarse.- **—ly** [-lj], *adv.* frescamente, con frescura; nuevamente, recientemente.- **—man** [-mṇn], *s.* estudiante de primer año; novato, novicio.- **—ness** [-nịs], *s.* frescura, frescor; lozanía, verdor; descaro.

fret [fret], *vti.* [1] rozar, raer; desgastar; enojar, irritar; adornar con calados.—*vii.* apurarse, inquietarse; incomodarse, impacientarse; agitarse.—*s.* roce; raedura; desgaste; irritación, enojo; hervor; relieve, realce; traste de guitarra.—*f. saw*, segueta, sierra caladora.- **—ful** [frétfụl], *a.* displicente, irritable, enojadizo.

friar [fráịạ(r)], *s.* fraile.

fricassee [frịḳạsí], *s.* fricasé.—*vt.* hacer fricasé.

friction [fríkšọn], *s.* fricción; frotación; roce; desavenencia.—*f. tape*, (elec.) cinta aisladora.

Friday [frájdj], *s.* viernes.—*girl F.*, chica para todo.—*man Friday*, servidor fiel et muy adicto.

friend [frend], *s.* amigo, amiga.- **—less** [fréndlịs], *a.* desamparado, desvalido, sin amigos.- **—liness** [-lịnịs], *s.* amistad.- **—ly** [-lj], *a.* amistoso,

amigable, cordial.—*f. fire*, (mil.) fuego amigo.—*adv.* amistosamente.- **—ship** [-šịp], *s.* amistad.

fright [frajt], *s.* susto, espanto, pavor; espantajo.- **—en** [frájtẹn], *vt.* espantar, asustar, amilanar.—*to f. away*, ahuyentar.- **—ful** [-fụl], *a.* espantoso, terrible.- **—fulness** [-fụlnịs], *s.* espanto, terror.

frigid [fríḏžịd], *a.* frío, frígido; indiferente.- **—ity** [frịḏžíḏịtị], *s.* frialdad, frigidez; indiferencia.

fringe [frinḏž], *s.* fleco, pestaña; orla, borde.—*vt.* guarnecer con flecos; orlar.

frisk [frịsk], *vi.* saltar, brincar, retozar.—*vt.* registrar los bolsillos, cachear.—*s.* retozo; brinco, salto.- **—y** [frískj], *a.* retozón, vivaracho.

fritter [frítœ(r)], *s.* fritura, fruta de sartén.—*to f. away*, desperdiciar o malgastar a poquitos.

frivolity [frịválịtị], *s.* frivolidad. **—frivolous** [frívọlʌs], *a.* frívolo.

fro [frou], *adv.* atrás, hacia atrás.—*to and f.*, de una parte a otra, de acá y allá.

frock [frak], *s.* vestido (de mujer).—*f. coat*, levita.

frog [frag], *s.* rana; alamar.—*f. in the throat*, carraspera, ronquera, gallo en la garganta.- **—man** [-mæn], *s.* hombre rana, submarinista.

frolic [frálịk], *s.* juego, retozo, travesura.—*a.* alegre, juguetón, travieso.—*vii.* [8] juguetear, retozar, triscar. **—frolicked** [frálịkt], *pret.* y *pp.* de TO FROLIC.- **—some** [-sʌm], *a.* retozón, travieso.

from [fram], *prep.* de; desde; de parte de; a fuerza de; a partir de; a causa de.—*f. memory*, de memoria.—*f. now on*, de ahora en adelante, en lo sucesivo.—*f. nature*, del natural.

frond [frand], *s.* fronda.- **—age** [-idž], *s.* frondosidad, follaje, frondas.

front [frʌnt], *s.* frente (*m.*); frontispicio, fachada, portada.—*in f.*, delante, enfrente.—*in f. of*, delante de, ante.—*shirt f.*, pechera.—*a.* anterior, delantero; frontero; frontal.—*f. door*, puerta principal, puerta de entrada.—*f.-wheel drive*, (aut.) tracción delantera.—*f. matter*, preliminares.—*f. page*, primera plana.—*f. porch*, soportal.—*f. row*, delantera, primera fila.—*f.-runner*, favorito; (sports) puntero.—*f. seat*, asiento delantero.—*f. steps*, quicio, pretorio.—*f.* view, vista de frente.— *vt.* hacer frente a.—*to f.* towards, mirar hacia; dar o caer a.—*vi.* estar al frente de.

frontier [frʌntír], *s.* frontera.- **—sman** [frʌntírzmæn], *s.* habitante de la frontera, colonizador, explorador.—*a.* fronterizo.

frost [frɔst], *s.* escarcha; helada.- **—bite** [-bajt], *s.* congelación.— **—bitten** [-bjten], congelado, helado.—*vt.* cubrir de escarcha.—*vi.* escarchar, helar, congelarse.- **—y** [frɔ́stj], *a.* escarchado; helado.

froth [frɔθ], *s.* espuma; bambolla.—*vi.* espumar, hacer espuma; echar espuma.- **—y** [frɔ́θj], *a.* espumoso; frívolo, vano.

frown [fraʊn], *s.* ceño, entrecejo.—*vi.* fruncir el entrecejo.—*to f. at, on,* o *upon,* desaprobar, mirar con ceño.- **—ing** [fráʊnjŋ], *a.* ceñudo.

froze [froʊz], *pret.* DE TO FREEZE. **—frozen** [fróʊzen], *pp.* DE TO FREEZE.

fructification [frʌktjfjkéjṣon], *s.* fructificación; fruto.

frugal [frúgal], *a.* frugal.- **—ity** [frugǽljtj], *s.* frugalidad.

fruit [frut], *s.* fruta; fruto; provecho; resultado.—*as nutty as a f. cake,* (fam.) más loco que una cabra.—*f. cake,* torta de frutas.—*f. fly,* mosca de la fruta.—*f. juice,* jugo de frutas.—*f. tree,* árbol frutal.- **—ful** [frútful], *a.* fructífero, feraz; productivo; prolífico, fecundo; fructuoso, provechoso.- **—ion** [fruíṣon], *s.* fruición, buen término.- **—less** [-ljs], *a.* infructuoso, estéril, vano.

frustrate [frʌ́strejt], *vt.* frustrar. **—frustration** [frʌstréjṣon], *s.* frustración.

fry [fraj], *s.* fritada; brete, sofocón; cría, pececillos recién nacidos; enjambre, muchedumbre.—*small f.,* chiquillería, gente menuda.- **—fries** [frajz], *spl.* papas fritas, patatas fritas, papas a la francesa.—*vti.* y *vii.* [7] freir(se), archicharrar(se).—*frying pan,* sartén.—*out of the f. into the fire,* de Guatamala para meterse en Guatepeor.

fudge [fʌdž], *s.* jarabe o dulce de chocolate; embuste, cuento.

fuel [fiúel], *s.* combustible; pábulo, aliciente.—*f. oil,* aceite combustible.—*f. tank,* depósito de combustible.—*vt.* y *vi.* abastecer(se) de combustible.

fugitive [fjúdžjtjv], *a.* y *s.* fugitivo.

fulfill [fulfíl], *vt.* colmar, llenar; realizar.- **—ment** [-ment], *s.* cumplimiento, desempeño, ejecución; realización; colmo.

full [ful], *a.* lleno; completo, cabal, repleto; pleno; cumplido; amplio; rotundo; harto, ahito; maduro, perfecto.—*f. age,* mayoría de edad.— *f.-blooded,* de sangre pura, pura raza.—*f.-length,* de cuerpo entero.—*f. moon,* luna llena, plenilunio.—*f. name,* nombre y apellido.—*f. scope,* carta blanca, rienda suelta.—*f. speed,* a toda velocidad.—*f. stop,* punto final; detención total de un vehículo.—*f. time,* tiempo o período completo, horas normales de trabajo.—*adv.* enteramente, del todo; de lleno; totalmente, en pleno; derechamente.—*f.-blown,* abierta del todo (una flor).—*f.-grown,* maduro, crecido; completamente desarrollado.- **—ness** [fúlnjs], *s.* plenitud, abundancia; hartura, saciedad; complemento.

fulsome [fúlsʌm], *a.* empalagoso; de mal gusto.

fume [fjum], *s.* tufo, gas, emanación; vapores, gases, emanaciones deletéreas.—*vt.* fumigar, sahumar, exhalar.—*vi.* exhalar vapores; encolerizarse.

fumigate [fjúmjgejt], *vt.* fumigar, sahumar. **—fumigation** [fjumjgéjṣon], *s.* fumigación; sahumerio.

fun [fʌn], *s.* broma, chanza, burla; diversión.—*f.-loving,* amante de las diversiones, gozador.—*in f.,* por gusto, por divertirse.—*to have fun,* divertirse.—*to poke fun at,* burlarse de.

function [fʌ́ŋkṣon], *s.* función, ejercicio, ocupación; ceremonia, acto; potencia, facultad.—*vi.* funcionar.- **—al** [-al], *a.* funcional.- **—ary** [-erj], *s.* funcionario.

fund [fʌnd], *s.* fondo (dinero).—*pl.* fondos.—*vt.* consolidar (una deuda).

fundament [fʌ́ndament], *s.* fundamento.- **—al** [fʌndaméntal], *a.* fundamental.—*s.* fundamento.

funeral [fiúneral], *a.* funeral, funerario, fúnebre.—*f. director,* director de funeraria, director de pompas fúnebres.—*f. home* o *parlor,* funeraria.—*f. procession,* cortejo fúnebre.—*s.* funeral(es), exequias; entierro; duelo. **—funereal** [fɹunírɹal], *a.* fúnebre.

fungicide [fʌ́ndʒisaid], *s.* fungicida.

fungus [fʌ́ŋgʌs], *s.* (*pl.* **fungi** [fʌ́ndʒai]) hongo.

funnel [fʌ́nel], *s.* embudo; cañón de chimenea.—*vti.* y *vii.* [2] encauzar(se); concentrar(se).

funny [fʌ́ni], *a.* cómico, divertido, gracioso, ocurrente, chusco; (fam.) extraño, curioso.—*f. business,* treta; picardía, fraude.

fur [fœr], *s.* piel, pelo (de los animales); sarro.—*vti.* [1] cubrir, forrar o adornar con pieles.—*vii.* formarse incrustaciones.

furious [fjúrɹʌs], *a.* furioso, enfurecido.

furl [fœrl], *vt.* plegar, recoger.

furlough [fœrlou], *s.* (mil.) licencia.—*vt.* licenciar.

furnace [fœ́rnis], *s.* horno (industrial).—*blast f.,* alto horno.

furnish [fœ́rniʃ], *vt.* surtir, suministrar; aparejar, equipar; amueblar.

furniture [fœ́rnichur], *s.* muebles, mueblaje, arreos, avíos.—*a piece of f.,* un mueble.—*f. polish,* pulimento para muebles.

furrow [fœ́rou], *s.* surco; zanja; arruga; muesca; mediacaña.—*vt.* surcar; estriar; arar.

further [fœ́rðœ(r)], *a.* ulterior, más distante; más amplio; nuevo, adicional.—*adv.* más; más lejos, más allá; además; además de eso.—*vt.* fomentar, adelantar, promover.- **—ance** [-ans], *s.* adelantamiento, promoción.- **—more** [-mór], *adv.* además; otrosí. **—furthest** [fœ́rðist], *a.* y *adv.* (el) más lejano; (el) más remoto; (lo) más lejos.

furtive [fœ́rtiv], *a.* furtivo, secreto.

fury [fjúri], *s.* furia; frenesí.

fuse [fjuz], *vt.* y *vi.* fundir(se).—*s.* espoleta; mecha; fusible.—*f. box,* caja de fusibles.

fuselage [fjúzelidʒ], *s.* fuselaje.

fusion [fjúʒion], *s.* fusión, fundición; unión; (nuclear) fusión.

fuss [fʌs], *s.* bulla, bullicio; melindre; agitación o actividad inútil.—*f. budget,* persona exigente o fastidiosa.—*vi.* inquietarse por pequeñeces; hacer melindres.- **—y** [fʌ́si], *a.* inquieto; remilgado, exigente.

futile [fjútil], *a.* fútil. **—futility** [fjutíliti], *s.* futilidad.

future [fjúchu(r)], *a.* futuro.—*s.* futuro, porvenir.—*in f.,* en lo sucesivo; de aquí en adelante.—*in the near f.,* en fecha próxima.

fuzz [faz], *vi.* soltar pelusa o borra.—*s.* pelusa, borra, vello; (jer. y despec.) polizonte.- **—y** [fázi], *a.* velloso, cubierto de pelusa; crespo.

G

gabardine [gæbərdín], *s.* gabardina (tejido y sobretodo).

gabble [gǽbl], *vt.* y *vi.* charlar; graznar (los gansos).—*s.* algarabía; charla; graznido.

gable [géibl], *s.* (arq.) arguilón, remate triangular de edificio o pared; pared lateral.—*g. end,* alero.—*g. roof,* tejado de dos aguas.

gad [gæd], *vii.* [1] callejear.- **—about** [gǽdəbaut], *a.* callejero.—*vi.* corretear, callejear.—*s.* placero, persona callejera. **—fly** [-flai], *s.* tábano.

gadget [gǽdʒit], *s.* (fam.) dispositivo, artefacto, artificio.

gaff [gæf], *s.* arpón o garfio; (mar.) botavara.

gag [gæg], *vti.* [1] amordazar; hacer callar; (teat.) meter morcilla.—*vii.* arquear, dar náuseas.—*s.* mordaza; asco; (teat.) morcilla; (fam.) chuscada; payasada; chiste.

gage, *s.* y *vt.* = GAUGE. **—gager,** *s.* = GAUGER.

gaiety [géieti], *s.* jovialidad, alegría, alborozo; viveza. **—gaily** [géili], *adv.* alegremente, jovialmente.

gain [gein], *s.* ganancia, beneficio, provecho.—*vt.* ganar, adquirir; lograr, conseguir.—*vi.* ganar.—*to g. weight,* echar carnes, engordar.- **—ful** [géinful], *a.* lucrativo, ventajoso.- **—ings** [-iŋz], *s. pl.* ganancias.

gait [geit], *s.* marcha, paso, andadura.—*at a good g.,* a buen paso.

ale [geil], *s.* ventarrón, viento fuerte; (of laughter) estallido.

alician [galíʃan], *s.* y *a.* gallego.

all [gɔl], *s.* hiel, bilis; odio; (fam.) descaro.—*g. bladder,* vesícula biliar.—*vt.* y *vi.* irritar, hostigar.

allant [gǽlant], *a.* galante, cortés; galanteador; gallardo, bizarro; valeroso, valiente.—*s.* galán.— **-ry** [-ri], *s.* valentía, gallardía, valor; galantería.

allery [gǽleri], *s.* galería; tribuna; pasadizo; (teat.) paraíso, cazuela, gallinero; público que ocupa el paraíso.

alley [gǽli], *s.* (mar.) galera; (mar.) cocina; (imp.) galera.—*g. slave,* galeote.

allon [gǽlon], *s.* galón. Ver Tabla.

allop [gǽlop], *s.* galope.—*vi.* galopar.—*vt.* hacer galopar.

allows [gǽlouz], *s.* horca; patíbulo.

alore [galór], *adv.* en abundancia.

aloshes [galáʃès], *s.* chanclos altos de goma o de tela engomada.

alvanize [gǽlvanaiz], *vt.* galvanizar.

amble [gǽmbl], *vt.* aventurar (una cosa) en el juego, jugarse.—*vi.* jugar por dinero.—*s.* (fam.) jugada.— **-r** [gǽmblœ(r)], *s.* jugador.—*a compulsive g.,* un jugador empedernido.— **-gambling** [gǽmbliŋ], *s.* juego (por dinero).—*g. debts,* deudas de juego.—*g. den,* garito.—*g. house,* garito, casa de juego.

ambol [gǽmbol], *vi.* brincar, saltar; cabriolar; juguetear.—*s.* cabriola, brinco, travesura.

ame [geim], *s.* juego; pasatiempo; partido o partida de juego; caza (piezas, vivas o muertas).—*g. bird,* ave de caza.—*g. of chance,* juego de azar, juego de suerte.—*g. plan,* estrategia.—*g. preserve,* vedado, vedado de caza.—*g. show,* programa concurso.—*g. warden,* guardabosque.—*to make g. of,* burlarse de, mofarse de.—*vt.* y *vi.* jugar; jugar fuerte.—*a.* relativo a la caza o al juego; dispuesto a pelear; valeroso.—*to die g.,* morir peleando.— **-cock** [géimkak], *s.* gallo de pelea, gallo de riña. — **-keeper** [-kipœ(r)], *s.* guardamonte, guardabosque.

ander [gǽndœ(r)], *s.* ánsar, ganso.

ang [gæŋ], *s.* cuadrilla, pandilla; juego (de herramientas, etc.); grupo.—*vt.* y *vi.* formar cuadrilla.

angplank [gǽŋplæŋk], *s.* pasarela, pasamano, plancha.

gangrene [gǽŋgrin], *vt.* y *vi.* gangrenar(se).—*s.* gangrena.

gangster [gǽŋstœ(r)], *s.* pandillero, pistolero.

gangway [gǽŋwei], *s.* (mar.) pasamano, portalón, tilla.—*interj.* ¡afuera!, ¡abran paso!, ¡paso libre!

gap [gæp], *s.* portillo, abertura, brecha; vacío, laguna; barranca, hondonada.—*vti.* [1] hacer una brecha en.

gape [geip], *vi.* quedarse boquiabierto; embobarse; bostezar.—*s.* bostezo; boqueada; brecha, abertura.

garage [garáž], *s.* garaje; taller mecánico o de reparaciones.—*g. sale,* venta de garage *(venta de objetos usados).*—*vt.* dejar en garage.

garb [garb], *s.* vestido, vestidura; apariencia exterior, aspecto.—*vt.* vestir, ataviar.

garbage [gárbidž], *s.* basura, desperdicios, bazoña.—*g. can,* cubo, bote de basura.—*g. dump,* vertedero, basurero.—*g. truck,* camión basurero.— **-man** [-mæn], *s.* basurero.

garden [gárdn], *s.* jardín; huerta, huerto.—*g. of Eden,* paraíso terrenal.—*g. path,* sendero.—*to lead up the g. path,* embaucar, engañar.—*g. stuff,* hortalizas, legumbres, verduras.—*vt.* y *vi.* cultivar jardines o huertos.— **-er** [-œ(r)], *s.* jardinero; hortelano.— **-ing** [-iŋ], *s.* jardinería; horticultura.

gardenia [gardíniǎ], *s.* gardenia.

gargle [gárgl], *vt.* y *vi.* gargarizar, hacer gárgaras.—*s.* gárgara, gargarismo.

garland [gárland], *s.* guirnalda.

garlic [gárlik], *s.* ajo.

garment [gármęnt], *s.* prenda de vestir; vestido.—*pl.* ropa, vestimenta.

garnish [gárnišˌ], *vt.* (coc.) aderezar, adornar; (jur.) notificar; (jur.) embargar.—*s.* adorno; (coc.) aderezo, condimento de adorno.

garnet [gárnit], *s.* granate.

garret [gǽrit], *s.* buhardilla, desván.

garrison [gǽrison], *s.* (mil.) guarnición.—*vt.* (mil.) guarnecer; guarnicionar.

garrote [garóut], *s.* garrote.—*vt.* agarrotar; estrangular para robar.

garter [gártœ(r)], *s.* liga (para las medias).

gas [gæs], *s.* gas; gasolina.—*g. burner,* mechero de gas.—*g. chamber,* cámara de gases.—*g. engine,* motor de gas.—*g. guzzler,* (jer.) esponja (con-

sumo de mucha gasolina).—*g. heat,*
calefacción por gas.—*g. mask,* máscara antigás.—*g. meter,* contador
de gas.—*g. pedal,* acelerador.—*g.
pump,* surtidor, poste distribuidor.—*g. range,* o *g. stove,* fogón o cocina de gas.—*g. station,* estación de
servicio, estación gasolinera.—*g.
tank,* depósito de gasolina, tanque
de gasolina.—*tear g.,* gas lacrimógeno.—*vti.* [1] (mil.) asfixiar, envenenar o atacar con gas.- **—eous**
[gǽsjʌs], *a.* gaseoso; aeriforme.

gash [gæš], *vt.* hacer un tajo en, acuchillar, herir con arma blanca.—*s.*
cuchillada, tajo, corte profundo.

gasket [gǽskit], *s.* (mec.) junta, empaquetadura.

gaslight [gǽslait], *s.* luz de gas; mechero de gas. **—gasoline** [gǽsolin],
s. gasolina.

gasp [gæsp], *vt.* jadear, boquear; emitir sonidos entrecortados.—*s.* boqueada, jadeo.

gate [geit], *s.* puerta; portón; (aer.)
puerta de embarque; (f.c.) barrera;
(hidr.) compuerta; entrada de taquilla (*número de asistentes*).—*to
crash the g.,* (jer.) colarse de gorra.-
—crasher [-kræšoer], *s.* (jer.) intruso, colado, paracaidista.-
—keeper [géitkipœr)], *s.* portero;
(f.c.) guardabarrera.- **—way** [-wei],
s. entrada, paso (con portillo).

gather [gǽðœr)], *vt.* reunir, recoger,
coger; acumular; recolectar; juntar,
congregar; (cost.) fruncir; colegir,
deducir.—*to g. breath,* tomar
aliento.—*vi.* unirse, reunirse, juntarse, congregarse; amontonarse,
acumularse; concentrarse.—*s.*
(cost.) pliegue, frunce.—**-ing** [-iŋ],
s. asamblea; reunión; agrupación;
(re)colección, acopio; fruncimiento; (cost.) fruncido.

Gaucho [gáuçhou], *s.* gaucho.

gaudy [gódj], *a.* vistoso; llamativo,
chillón.

gauge [geidž], *s.* medida; calibre; calibrador; indicador; (mar.) calado;
(m.v.) manómetro; (f.c.) ancho de
vía; aforo, arqueo.—*g. pressure,* presión manométrica.—*vt.* calibrar;
medir; estimar, apreciar.

gaunt [gɔnt], *a.* flaco, delgado, demacrado.

gauntlet [góntlit], *s.* guantelete;
guante con puño.—*to run the g.,* correr baquetas.

gauze [gɔz], *s.* gasa, cendal.

gave [geiv], *pret.* de TO GIVE.

gavel [gǽvel], *s.* mazo, martillo.

gawk [gɔk], *vi.* (fam.) bobear, comete
torpezas.- —*s.* bobo, torpe.- —
[góki], *s.* papanatas.—*a.* bobo
tonto, torpe, desgarbado.

gay [gei], *a.* y *s.* gay, homosexual.—
(ant.) alegre, festivo. **—gayety,** *s.*
GAIETY.

gaze [geiz], *vi.* mirar con fijeza, clava
la mirada.—*s.* contemplación, m
rada fija o penetrante.

gazebo [gazíbo], *s.* mirador; cenado
glorieta.

gazette [gazét], *s.* gaceta.

gazelle [gazél], *s.* gacela.

gear [gir], *s.* engranaje; mecanism
de tra(n)smisión; rueda dentad
(mar.) aparejo; equipo, pertrecho
aperos; atavíos.—*g. box* o *g. caj
de engranajes; (aut.) caja de veloc
dades.—*g. shifting,* cambio de velo
cidad o de marcha.—*g. wheel,* rued
dentada.—*in g.,* engranado.—*lan
ing g.,* tren de aterrizaje.—*out of g
desengranado.—*to put in g.,* relaci
nar; engranar, embragar.—*to thro
out of g.,* desengranar, desembraga
- **—shift** [-šift], *s.* palanca de can
bio, palanca de velocidades.—*v
aparejar; equipar; montar, a
mar; engranar, embragar.—*vi.* e
granar.

geese [gis], *s. pl.* de GOOSE.

gel [džel], *s.* gel.—*vi.* cuajarse en form
de gel, gelificarse.

gelatin(e) [džélatin], *s.* gelatina.

gem [džem], *s.* gema; alhaja.—*vti.* [
adornar con piedras preciosas.

Gemini [džéminai], *s.* (astr.) Géminis.

gendarme [žándarm], *s.* gendarm
polizonte armado.

gender [džéndœr)], *s.* (gram.) géner

gene [džin], *s.* gen, gene.

genealogy [džinjálodži], *s.* genealogí

general [džéneral], *a.* general, fr
cuente.—*g. delivery,* lista de c
rreos.—*g. practitioner,* médico d
medicina general.—*g. purpose,* pa
toda clase de objetivos.—*g. stor
tienda de variedades.—*s.* (mil.) g
neral.—*in g.,* en general, por reg
general.- **—ity** [džéneraliti], *s.* g
neralidad.- **—ize** [džéneralaiz], *v
generalizar.

generate [džénereit], *vt.* engendra
producir, causar. **—generati**
[džénerišon], *s.* generación.—

gap, brecha generacional.—*G. X,* personas nacidas despues de 1965. **—generator** [džéneˌreiˌto(r)], *s.* generador, dinamo.

eneric [dženérik], *a.* genérico; (farm.) no de marca.—*s.* producto no de marca.

enerosity [dženerásiti], *s.* generosidad, largueza. **—generous** [dženérʌs], *a.* generoso; noble, magnánimo; amplio.

enesis [dženěsịs], *s.* génesis.

enetic [dženétịk], *a.* genético.—*g. engineering,* ingeniería genética.—*genetics s. sing.* genética.

enial [džíniʌl], *a.* genial, afable.— **—ity** [džiniæliti], *s.* afabilidad.

enital [dženịtʌl], *a.* genital.—*pl.* genitales, partes pudendas.

enius [džínyʌs], *s.* genio; prototipo.

enteel [džentíl], *a.* cortés, gentil; gallardo, airoso, elegante; cursi.

entile [džéntail], *s.* y *a.* gentil, pagano.

entle [džéntl], *a.* suave, dulce, benévolo; dócil, manso; bien nacido.- **—man** [-mạn], *s.* caballero; señor.- **—manliness** [-mạnlịnịs], *s.* caballerosidad,   hidalguía.- **—manly** [-mạnlị], *a.* caballeroso.- **—men** [-mẹn], *s. pl.* de GENTLEMAN; señores; (en cartas) muy señores míos (nuestros).—*g.'s agreement,* pacto de caballeros.- **—ness** [-nịs], *s.* dulzura, suavidad; docilidad, mansedumbre; urbanidad. **—gently** [džéntlị], *adv.* dulcemente, suavemente; poco a poco, despacio.

enuflect [dženŭflekt], *vi.* hacer una genuflexión.

enuine [dženyuịn], *a.* genuino, auténtico; sincero.

enus [džínŭs], *s.* género.

eographer [džiágrafoe(r)], *s.* geógrafo. **—geographic(al)** [džiográefịk(ạl)], *a.* geográfico. **—geography** [džiágrafị], *s.* geografía. **—geologist** [džiálodžịst], *s.* geólogo. **—geology** [džiálodžị], *s.* geología. **—geometric(al)** [džiométrịk(ạl)], *a.* geométrico. **—geometry** [džiámetrị], *s.* geometría.

eranium [džeréinịʌm], *s.* geranio.

erman [džóermạn], *s.* y *a.* alemán.—*s.* lengua alemana.—*G. measles,* roseola.

erm [džóerm], *s.* germen; microbio. **—g. warfare,** guerra bacteriológica.- **—icide** [džóermịsaid], *s.* germicida.

germinate [džóermịneit], *vi.* germinar. **—germination** [džóermịnéišọn], *s.* germinación.

gerund [džérʌnd], *s.* (gram.) gerundio.

gestation [džestéišọn], *s.* gestación.

gesture [džéschū(r)], *s.* gesto, ademán, signo.—*vi.* accionar; gesticular o hacer gestos.

get [get], *vti.* [10] conseguir, obtener, adquirir; agarrar, atrapar; ganar; llevar (premio, ventaja, etc.); recibir; procrear; hacer que; incitar; procurar, lograr; ir por, traer; entender.— *to g. back,* recobrar.—*to g. down,* descolgar, bajar; tragar.—*to g. on,* ponerse (ropa).—*to g. out,* publicar, editar, sacar.—*to g. the worse* o *the worst,* llevar la peor parte, quedar mal parado.—*to g. wind of,* recibir aviso de, tener noticia de.—*vii.* ganar dinero; llegar; ponerse o volverse; hacerse, ser; hallarse, estar; introducirse, meterse.—*g. out!* ¡fuera! ¡largo de aquí!—*g. up!* ¡arre!—*to g. along,* ir pasando.—*to g. along well (badly) with,* llevarse bien (mal) con.—*to g. married,* casarse.— *to g. off,* salir de un asunto; escapar; salir; bajar(se), apearse.—*to g. on,* adelantar; ponerse encima de; subir; montar; entrar en un coche.— *to g. out,* salir, salirse.—*to g. out of order,* desajustarse, descomponerse. —*to g. out of the way,* apartarse o hacerse a un lado.—*to g. ready,* disponerse, aprestarse.—*to g. rid of,* zafarse o librarse de, acabar con, quitar de encima.—*to g. through,* pasar, penetrar; terminar.—*to g. together,* juntarse, reunirse.—*to g. up,* levantarse.—*to g. well,* curar, sanar, ponerse bueno.- **—away** [gétawei], *s.* ida, partida; escape; arranque (de un auto).- **—up** [-ʌp], *s.* arreglo, disposición; atavío; traje.

ghastly [gǽstlị], *a.* lívido, cadavérico; horrible, espantoso.—*adv.* horriblemente; mortalmente.

ghost [goŭst], *s.* fantasma, espectro, sombra; espíritu.—*the Holy G.,* el Espíritu Santo.—*not a g. of a doubt,* ni sombra de duda.—*to give up the g.,* entregar el espíritu, morir(se).- **—ly** [góŭstlị], *a.* espectral, fantástico, de duendes o aparecidos.

giant [džáiạnt], *a.* gigantesco, gigante.—*s.* gigante.

giblets [džíblịts], *s. pl.* menudillos.

giddiness [gídịnịs], *s.* vértigo, vahido;

desvarío. —**giddy** [gídi], *a.* vertiginoso; voluble, inconstante.

gift [gift], *s.* regalo, dádiva; donación; don, dote, talento.—*g. certificate*, vale, cheque-regalo.—*gift of gab*, (fam.) facundia, labia.—*g. shop*, tienda de objetos de regalo.—*g. tax*, impuesto sobre donaciones.—*g.-wrap*, envolver en paquete regalo.- —**ed** [gíftid], *a.* talentoso, genial; agraciado.

gigantic [dʒaigǽntik], *a.* gigantesco.

giggle [gígl], *vi.* reírse sin motivo, reírse por nada.—*s.* risa nerviosa, risita.

gild [gild], *vti.* [4] dorar.

gill [gil], *s.* agalla, branquia.

gilt [gilt], *pret.* y *pp.* de TO GILD.—*a.* dorado, áureo.—*s.* dorado; oropel; falso brillo.

gin [dʒin], *s.* ginebra (licor de enebro).

ginger [dʒíndʒœ(r)], *s.* jengibre.—*g. ale*, cerveza de jengibre.- —**bread** [-bred], *s.* pan de jengibre.—*a.* recargado, de mal gusto.

gipsy [dʒípsi], *s.* = GYPSY.

giraffe [dʒi̯rǽf], *s.* jirafa.

gird [gœrd], *vti.* [4] ceñir; rodear.- —**le** [gœrdl], *s.* faja; ceñidor; cinto.—*vt.* ceñir, cercar, fajar, circundar.

girl [gœrl], *s.* muchacha, niña; (fam.) sirvienta, criada.—*g. scout*, niña exploradora.- —**friend** [-frend], *s.* (of a man) novia, amiguita; (of a woman) amiga.—*live-in g.*, compañera.- —**hood** [gœrlhud], *s.* doncellez; vida o edad de muchacha; la juventud femenina.- —**ish** [-iš], *a.* juvenil; de niña.

girt [gœrt], *pret.* y *pp.* de TO GIRD.—*a.* (mar.) amarrado.

girth [gœrθ], *s.* cincha; faja; cinto; gordura; circunferencia, periferia.—*vt.* cinchar, ceñir.

gist [dʒist], *s.* substancia, esencia, enjundia.

give [giv], *vti.* [10] dar.—*to g. advice*, dar consejo; asesorar.—*to g. a lift to one*, ayudar a uno a levantarse o a levantar algo; llevarle (en coche, etc.).—*to g. a piece of one's mind to*, decir las verdades del barquero, decir cuántas son cinco.—*to g. away*, regalar; deshacerse de; vender regalado; divulgar un secreto.—*to g. back*, restituir, devolver.—*to g. birth*, dar a luz, parir; producir.—*to g. chase*, perseguir.—*to g. ear to*, prestar oídos a.—*to g. forth*, publicar, divulgar.—*to g. oneself away*, (fam.)

enseñar la oreja.—*to g. oneself up*, rendirse; abandonarse, desesperarse.—*to g. out*, publicar, divulgar, proclamar.—*to g. over*, abandonar, desistir de; desahuciar.—*to g. pause*, dar en qué pensar; hacer pensar.—*to g. place*, dejar el puesto (a).—*to g. rise to*, dar lugar a, ocasionar.—*to g. the slip*, dar esquinazo; echar.—*to g. up*, renunciar a; entregar; resignar.—*to g. up the ghost*, morir; darse por vencido.—*to g. voice to*, decir, expresar.—*s.* acción de dar de sí, ceder físicamente (como una cuerda); elasticidad. **g.-and-take** [gívanteik], *s.* concesiones mutuas, componenda. —**given** [gíven], *pp.* de TO GIVE.—*a.* dado; citado, especificado; (mat.) conocido.—*g. name*, nombre de pila.—*g. that*, suponiendo que, sabiendo que.—*g. to*, adicto o aficionado a. —**give** [gívœ(r)], *s.* donante, donador.

gizzard [gízǝrd], *s.* molleja (de ave).

glacial [gléišǝl], *a.* glacial; (geol.) glaciario. —**glacier** [gléišœ(r)], *s.* glaciar, ventisquero.

glad [glæd], *a.* alegre, contento, gozoso.—*to be g.*, alegrarse, tener gusto.- —**den** [glædn], *vt.* alegrar, regocijar, recrear.

glade [gleid], *s.* claro, raso o pradera (en un bosque).

gladiolus [glædióulʌs], *s.* (bot.) gladiolo, espadaña.

gladness [glǽdnis], *s.* alegría, placer, gozo.

glamor [glǽmǫ(r)], *s.* encanto, hechizo, embrujo; embeleso.—*vt.* encantar, hechizar.- —**ous** [-ʌs], *a.* encantador, hechicero.

glance [glæns], *s.* mirada, ojeada, vistazo; vislumbre; fulgor.—*at first g.*, a primera vista.—*vt.* mirar de o al soslayo, o de refilón.—*vi.* dar un vistazo o una ojeada; centellear; tocar o herir oblicuamente.

gland [glænd], *s.* glándula.

glare [glɛr], *vi.* relumbrar, brillar; tener colores chillones; (con **at**) mirar echando fuego por los ojos.—*s.* resplandor; resol; mirada feroz y penetrante.—*a.* liso, lustroso y resbaladizo. —**glaring** [glériŋ], *a.* deslumbrador; evidente, notorio; penetrante, furioso.

lass [glæs], *s.* vidrio; cristal; vaso; copa; espejo; lente, catalejo.—*pl.* anteojos, gafas, espejuelos, lentes.—*dark g.,* espejuelos de sol.—*g. blower,* soplador de vidrio.—*g. ceiling,* techo de cristal; (fig) tope, barreras.—*g. cutter,* diamante de vidriero.—*a.* de vidrio.—*g. window,* vidriera, escaparate.- —**ful** [glǽsful], *s.* vaso (su contenido).- —**ware** [-wɛr], *s.* vajilla de cristal, cristalería.- —**wort** [-wœrt], *s.* (bot.) sosa, matojo.—**y** [-i], *a.* vítreo, vidrioso. —**glaze** [glejz], *vt.* poner vidrios a una ventana; vidriar; glasear; (cerá.) esmaltar.—*s.* superficie lisa y lustrosa; lustre; capa de hielo. —**glazier** [gléiẑœ(r)], *s.* vidriero.

leam [glim], *s.* destello, fulgor, viso, centelleo.—*vi.* centellear, fulgurar, destellar.

ean [glin], *vt.* espigar; recoger; juntar.

lee [gli], *s.* alegría, gozo, júbilo; (mús.) canción para voces solas.— *g. club,* cantoría, coro; orfeón.

lib [glib], *a.* suelto de lengua, locuaz.

lide [glaid], *vi.* deslizarse; (aer.) planear.—*s.* deslizamiento; (aer.) planeo.- —**r** [gláidœ(r)], *s.* (aer.) planeador, deslizador.

limmer [glímœ(r)], *vi.* rielar, centellear.—*s.* luz trémula; vislumbre.

limpse [glimps], *s.* ojeada, vistazo; vislumbre.—*vt.* vislumbrar.—*vi.* ojear.

lint [glint], *vi.* brillar, destellar.—*s.* destello, relumbre.

listen [glisn], *vi.* brillar, resplandecer.

litter [glítœ(r)], *vi.* resplandecer, centellear, rutilar, brillar.—*s.* brillo, resplandor, centelleo.

litz [glits], *s.* (fam.) oropel.- —**y** [glítsi], *a.* deslumbrante, glamoroso.

lobal [glóubəl], *a.* global; esférico.— *the g. village,* la aldea mundial.—*g. warming,* calentamiento global, calentamiento del planeta. —**globe** [gloub], *s.* esfera, globo. —**globetrotter** [glóubtratœ(r)], *s.* trotamundos. —**globular** [glábyulə(r)], *s.* globular, esférico. —**globule** [glábyul], *s.* glóbulo.

gloom [glum], **gloominess** [glúminis], *s.* oscuridad, lobreguez, tenebrosidad, tinieblas; melancolía, tristeza. —**gloomy** [glúmi], *a.* tenebroso, sombrío, lóbrego; nublado, triste, melancólico.

glorify [glórifai], *vti.* [7] glorificar, exaltar, alabar. —**glorious** [glóriʌs], *a.* glorioso; (fam.) excelente, magnífico. —**glory** [glóri], *s.* gloria.—*vii.* [7] gloriarse, vanagloriarse, jactarse.

gloss [glɔs], *s.* lustre, brillo; pulimento; apariencia; glosa; comentario.—*vt.* pulir, pulimentar, satinar.—*vt. y vi.* glosar, comentar.—*to g. over,* minimizar, disimular.- —**ary** [glásari], *s.* glosario.- —**y** [glósi], *a.* lustroso, satinado; (fot.) brillante.

glove [glʌv], *s.* guante.—*g. compartment,* (aut.) guantera.—*to be hand and g.,* ser uña y carne.—*to handle with kid gloves,* tratar con mucho miramiento.—*to handle without gloves,* tratar sin contemplaciones.—*vt.* enguantar.

glow [glou], *vi.* brillar o lucir suavemente; fosforecer; ponerse incandescente; enardecerse.—*s.* brillo sin llama; incandescencia; calor intenso; vehemencia.- —**ing** [glóuiŋ], *a.* incandescente, encendido; ardiente.- —**worm** [-wœrm], *s.* luciérnaga, (Am.) cocuyo.

glower [glauœr], *s.* ceño fruncido, mirada hosca.—*vi.* tener la mirada hosca.—*to g. at,* mirar hoscamente.

glue [glu], *s.* cola, engrudo o goma de pegar.—*vt.* encolar; engomar.- —**y** [glúi], *a.* pegajoso, viscoso.

glut [glʌs], *s.* superabundancia.—*vt.* saturar, inundar.

glutton [glátən], *s.* glotón, tragón, comelón.- —**ous** [-ʌs], *a.* glotón; goloso.- —**y** [-i], *s.* glotonería, gula.

G-man [dzímæn], *s.* agente del FBI.

gnarled [narld], *a.* nudoso, retorcido.

gnash [næ͡ʃ], *vt.* rechinar o crujir los dientes.

gnat [næt], *s.* (Am.) jején; mosquito.

gnaw [nɔ], *vt.* roer.—*vi.* morder.—*to g. at,* roer.- —**er** [nɔœ(r)], *s.* roedor.

gnome [noum], *s.* gnomo.

GNP [dzíénpí], *abrev.* (**gross national product**) PNB.

go [gou], *vii.* [10] ir, irse; andar; marcharse, partir; (mec.) funcionar; acudir.—*to g. abroad,* ir al extranjero.—*to g. across,* cruzar.—*to g. af-*

ter, seguir a.—*to g. ahead,* adelantar, proseguir.—*to g. along,* seguir, proseguir; irse, marcharse.—*to g. around,* alcanzar para todos.—*to g. astray,* extraviarse.—*to g. away,* desaparecer; irse, marcharse.—*to g. back,* regresar; volverse atrás.—*to g. in for,* dedicarse a.—*to g. into,* entrar en.—*to g. near,* acercarse.—*to g. off,* irse, largarse; dispararse.—*to g. on,* avanzar, continuar, proseguir.— *to g. out,* salir; apagarse.—*to g. to pot,* arruinarse.—*to g. under,* quedar arruinado; hundirse; ser vencido; pasar por debajo de.—*to g. up,* subir, ascender.—*to g. without saying,* sobreentenderse.—*s.* usanza, energía, empuje; buen éxito.—*is it a g.?* ¿está resuelto? ¿estamos convenidos?— *it is no g.,* es inútil, esto no marcha.—*on the g.,* en actividad.

goad [goud], *s.* aguijón, puya.—*g. spur,* acicate.—*g. stick,* garrocha, rejo.—*vt.* aguijonear; estimular.

goal [goul], *s.* meta, fin, objeto, objetivo, propósito; (dep.) gol, tanto.

goat [gout], *s.* cabra; chiva.—*billy g.,* macho cabrío.—*to be the g.,* cargar con la culpa ajena.- **—ee** [goutí], *s.* pera, perilla.

gobble [gábl], *vt.* engullir, tragar.—*vi.* hacer ruido con la garganta como los pavos.—*s.* voz del pavo.- **—r** [gáblœ(r)], *s.* glotón, tragón; pavo.

go-between [góubitwin], *s.* mediador; alcahuete.

goblet [gáblit], *s.* copa de mesa, vaso de pie.

goblin [gáblin], *s.* trasgo, duende.

gocart [góukart], *s.* carretilla.

god, God [gad], *s.* dios, Dios.—*G. be with you,* vaya usted con Dios.—*G. forbid,* no lo quiera Dios.—*G. willing,* Dios mediante, si Dios quiere.- **—child** [gádchajld], *s.* ahijado, ahijada.- **—dess** [-is], *s.* diosa.- **—father** [-faðœ(r)], *s.* padrino.- **—less** [-lis], *a.* ateo, impío.- **—lessness** [-lisnis], *s.* impiedad, ateísmo. - **—like** [-lajk], *a.* divino.- **—liness** [-linis], *s.* piedad, santidad.- **—ly** [-li], *a.* divino; devoto, piadoso.- **—mother** [-mʌðœ(r)], *s.* madrina.- **—parents** [-peɾents], *s.* padrinos.- **—ship** [-šip], *s.* divinidad.- **—son** [-sʌn], *s.* ahijado.

go-getter [góugétœ(r)], *s.* buscavidas.

going [góuin], *a.* y *ger.* de TO GO; activo, que funciona.—*a g. concern,* una

empresa que funciona o marcha.— *s.* paso, andar; marcha, ida; partida; estado del camino.—*g. out,* salida.

goiter [gójtœ(r)], *s.* bocio, papera; (Am.) buche.

gold [gould], *s.* oro; color de oro.—*g. dust,* oro en polvo.—*g. leaf,* pan d• oro finísimo.—*g. mine,* mina d• oro.—*g. rush,* fiebre de oro.- **—digger** [-digoe(r)], *s.* buscador de oro• (fam. y despec.) cazafortunas.—*g. standard,* patrón de oro.—*g. work* orfebrería.- **—en** [góulden], *a.* áu• reo, de oro, dorado; rubio, ama• rillento.—*g. mean,* punto medio• justo medio.—*g. rule,* regla de la ca• ridad cristiana.—*g. wedding anniver• sary,* bodas de oro.- **—finch** [-fjnch] *s.* cardelina; jilguero amarillo.- **—fish** [-fiš], *s.* pececillo(s) d• colores; carpa dorada.- **—smith** [-smjθ], *s.* orfebre.

golf [galf], *s.* golf.—*g. ball,* pelota de golf.—*g. club,* palo de golf.—*g. course, g. links,* campo de golf.- **—e•** [gálfoer], *s.* golfista.

gondola [gándolá], *s.* góndola; (aer.• barquilla o cabina; (f.c.) vagón d• mercancías. **—gondolier** [gandolír]• *s.* gondolero.

gone [gɔn], *pp.* de TO GO.—*a.* ido; per• dido, arruinado; pasado; apagado.

gong [gan], *s.* batintín, gong.

gonorrhea [ganoriá], *s.* gonorrea.

good [gud], *a.* bueno; apto, conve• niente; genuino, válido, valedero• digno.—*a g. deal,* mucho, bas• tante.—*a g. turn,* un favor, una gra• cia.—*as g. as,* casi.—*g. afternoon* buenas tardes.—*g. enough,* sufi• cientemente bueno, pasadero, su• ficiente.—*g. evening,* buenas tardes buenas noches.—*G. Friday,* Viernes Santo.—*g. for nothing,* inútil, sin va• lor; haragán.—*g.-looking,* guapo• bien parecido.—*g.-luck charm*• amuleto de la buena suerte.—*g• morning,* buenos días.—*g. nature*• bondad, buen corazón.—*g.-na• tured,* afable, bonachón.—*g. night*• buenas noches.—*g. sense,* sensa• tez.—*s.* bien; provecho, ventaja.— *pl.* géneros, mercancías, efectos.— *for g.,* para siempre.—*for g. and all*• terminantemente, una vez por to• das.—*it's no g.,* no vale, es inútil.— *interj.* ¡bueno! ¡muy bien!- **—by,** **bye** [gudbái], *s.* e *interj.* adiós; hasta la vista; vaya usted con Dios.- **—l•**

ness [gúdljnįs], s. belleza, gracia, elegancia.- **—ness** [-njs], s. bondad, benevolencia; fineza.—*interj.* ¡Ave María! ¡Dios mío!- **—y** [-į], a. y s. bonachón, Juan Lanas.—*g.-g.,* santurrón, beato.—*pl.* dulces, golosinas.—*interj.* (fam.) ¡viva!, ¡yupi!, ¡que alegría!.

goose [gus], s. ganso, oca; necio.—*g. flesh,* carne de gallina (aplicado a la piel humana).—*g. pimples,* carne de gallina.—*g. step,* paso de ganso.— *g.-step,* marchar con paso de ganso. - **—berry** [gúzberį], s. grosella.

gore [gɔr], s. cuajarón de sangre; (cost.) cuchillo, nesga; pedazo triangular de terreno.—*vt.* herir con los cuernos; poner nesga o cuchillo.

gorge [gɔrdʒ], s. garganta, desfiladero.—*vt.* atiborrar; hartar, saciar.—*vi.* hartarse, saciarse.

gorgeous [gɔrdʒʌs], a. vistoso, magnífico, suntuoso.

gorilla [gorílį], s. gorila.

gory [górį], a. sangriento, sanguinolento.

gospel [gáspɘl], s. evangelio; cosa cierta e indudable.—*g. truth,* verdad palmaria.- **—(l)er** [-œ(r)], s. evangelista.

gossip [gásįp], s. chismografía, murmuración; chismoso; chisme.—*vi.* chismear, murmurar.– **—ing** [-įŋ], **—y** [-į], a. chismoso, murmurador.

got [gat], *pret.* y *pp.* de TO GET.

goth [gaθ], s. godo. **—Gothic** [gáθįk], a. gótico.—s. lengua goda.

gotten [gátn], *pp.* de TO GET.

gouge [gaudʒ], s. gubia; ranura, canal, estría.—*vt.* escoplar; arrancar, sacar, vaciar; engañar.

gourd [gɔrd], s. calabaza; (Am.) güiro.

gourmet [gurmeí], s. gastrónomo, buen paladar.

gout [gaut], s. gota, artritis.- **—y** [gaúti], a. gotoso.

govern [gávœrn], vt. y vi. gobernar, regir.– **—ess** [-įs], s. institutriz.– **—ment** [-mɘnt], s. gobierno, gobernación; administración, dirección; régimen.—*g. in exile,* gobierno exiliado.- **—or** [-ǫ(r)], s. gobernador; regulador.

gown [gaun], s. traje de mujer; túnica, toga, vestidura talar.—*dressing g.,* bata.—*evening g.,* traje de fiesta.— *wedding g.,* traje de novia.—*vt.* y vi. togar(se).

grab [græb], vti. [1] asir, agarrar; arrebatar; posesionarse.—s. agarrón, toma, asimiento; presa; arrebatiña; copo; gancho, garfio; (fam.) robo.— *g. bag,* bolsa de sorpresas.

grace [greįs], s. gracia, garbo; favor, concesión, privilegio; talante.— *good graces,* favor, amistad, bienquerencia.—*g. note,* s. (mus.) apoyatura, nota de adorno.—*to say g.,* bendecir la mesa.—*with a bad (good) g.,* de mala (buena) gana.- **—ful** [gréįsfų], a. gracioso, agraciado; garboso; fácil, natural; decoroso.- **—fulness** [-fųlnįs], s. donosura, garbo, elegancia.

gracious [gréįʃʌs], a. bondadoso, benigno; afable; gracioso, grato.—*g. me!* o *good(ness) g.!* ¡válgame Dios! ¡caramba!

gradation [greįdéįʃǫn], s. graduación; grado; serie; escalonamiento; (mús. y pint.) gradación. **—grade** [greįd], s. grado; clase; nota o calificación; declive.—*at g.,* a nivel.—*down g.,* cuesta abajo.—*g. crossing,* paso a nivel.—*g. school,* escuela primaria.— *highest g.,* de primera clase o calidad.—*up g.,* cuesta arriba.—*vt.* clasificar u ordenar; graduar; (ing.) nivelar. **—gradual** [grǽdʒų̜ɘl], a. gradual; graduado. **—graduate** [grǽdʒų̜eįt], vt. graduar.—*vi.* graduarse.—*a.* [grǽdʒų̜it], graduado.—s. graduado. **—graduation** [grǽdʒų̜éįʃǫn], s. graduación.

graft [græft], s. injerto; tejido injertado; parte donde se hace el injerto; malversación; (Am.) peculado; latrocinio; soborno político.—*vt.* y vi. injertar; malversar; traficar con puestos públicos; cometer peculado.

graham cracker [greíặm], s. galleta integral.

grail [greįl], s. grial.—*the holy G.,* el santo Grial.

grain [greįn], s. grano; fibra o veta de la madera, el mármol, etc.—*pl.* cereales, granos en general.—*across the g.,* transversalmente a la fibra.- **—y** [greínį], a. graneado; granular; veteado.

gram [græm], s. gramo.

grammar [grǽmặ(r)], s. gramática; elementos de una ciencia.—*g. school,* escuela pública de enseñanza elemental.- **—ian** [grǽmériạn], s. gramático. **—grammatical** [grạmǽtįkạl], a. gramatical.

granary [grǽnari], s. granero.

grand [grænd], a. grande, grandioso; magnífico; ilustre, augusto; (mus.) piano de cola; (jer.) mil dólares.— *baby g.*, piano de media cola.—*g. finale*, final espectacular.—*g. jury*, jurado de acusación.—*g. lodge*, gran oriente.—*g. opera*, gran ópera.—*g. piano*, piano de cola.- **—aunt** [grǽndænt], s. tía abuela.- **—child** [-chaild], s. nieto, nieta.- **—daughter** [-dɔtœ(r)], s. nieta.- **—ee** [grændí], s. noble, grande.- **—father** [-faðœ(r)], s. abuelo.—*g. clock*, reloj de pie.- **—ma** [-ma], s. (fam.) abuelita.- **—mother** [-mʌðœ(r)], s. abuela.- **—nephew** [-nɛfju], s. sobrino nieto.- **—ness** [-nis], s. grandiosidad.- **—niece** [-nis], s. sobrina nieta.- **—pa** [-pa], s. (fam.) abuelito.- **—parent** [-pɛrent], s. abuelo, abuela.- **—sire** [-sair], s. antepasado.- **—son** [-sʌn], s. nieto.- **—stand** [-stænd], s. tribuna, tendido, gradería de asientos para espectadores.- **—uncle** [-ʌŋkl], s. tío abuelo.

grange [greindʒ], s. granja, cortijo, alquería; asociación de agricultores.- **—r** [greindʒœ(r)], s. granjero.

granite [grǽnit], s. granito.

granny [grǽni], s. (fam.) abuelita; comadre; viejecita.—*g. knot*, nudo corredizo.

grant [grænt], vt. conceder; permitir; ceder, transferir; asentir, convenir en.—*to take for granted*, dar por supuesto.—s. concesión, donación; otorgamiento, subvención, franquicia, asentimiento; documento que confiere un privilegio o concesión.—*g.-in-aid*, pensión, subvención, subsidio.—*granting that*, dado que, supuesto que.

granulate [grǽnyuleit], vt. granular, granear.—vi. granularse; (med.) encarnar. **—granule** [grǽnyul], s. granito, gránulo.

grape [greip], s. uva; vid.- **—fruit** [grǽipfrut], s. toronja.- **—shot** [-šat], s. (art.) metralla.- **—vine** [-vain], s. vid, parra; noticia que circula por vías secretas.

graph [græf], s. gráfica; diagrama.—vt. construir la gráfica de, representar gráficamente.- **—ic(al)** [grǽfik(al)], a. gráfico.- **—ics** [grǽfiks], spl. diseño gráfico; (comput.) gráficos.— *high-resolution g.*, gráficos de alta resolución.- **—ite** [-ait], s. grafito.

grapple [grǽpl], vt. agarrar, asir; ama rrar.—vi. agarrarse; (mar.) atracarse abordarse.—s. lucha, riña.

grasp [græsp], vt. empuñar, asir; apre sar, apoderarse de, usurpar; ve entender.—vi. agarrarse fuerte mente.—s. asimiento; presa; usur pación; puñado; garras; com presión.

grass [græs], s. hierba; pasto, cés ped.—*g. grown*, cubierto d hierba.—*g. snake*, culebra.—*the g roots*, el pueblo, la gente común, le bases.—vt. cubrir de hierba; apa centar.—vi. pacer; cubrirse d hierba.- **—hopper** [grǽshapœ(r)] s. saltamontes, langosta.- **—lan** [-lænd], s. campo de pastoreo, pra dera.- **—y** [-i], a. herboroso; her báceo.

grate [greit], s. reja, verja, enrejad parrilla.—vt. enrejar, poner enre jado; (coc.) rallar; raspar; emparrill lar.—vi. rozar; raer; rechinar, ch rriar.—*to g. on*, molestar, irritar.

grateful [gréitful], a. agradecid grato, gustoso.- **—ness** [-nis], gratitud, agrado.

grater [gréitœ(r)], s. rallador, rallo.

gratify [grǽtifai], vti. [7] satisface complacer, dar gusto; gratificar.

grating [gréitiŋ], a. rechinante, ch rriante, discordante; irritante, ás pero.—s. reja, rejilla, verja, enre jado; emparrillado; escurrider chirrido, rechinamiento; retícul (de microscopio, etc.); ralladura.

gratis [gréitis], adv. gratis.—a. gra tuito.

gratitude [grǽtitiud], s. gratitud, rec nocimiento.

gratuitous [gratiúitʌs], a. gratuito; ir justificado. **—gratuity** [gratiúiti], gratificación; propina.

grave [greiv], s. sepultura, sepulcr tumba; acento grave.—a. grave, s rio; solemne; (mus.) bajo, pr fundo.- **—clothes** [gréivklouðž], pl. mortaja.- **—digger** [-digœ(r)], sepulturero, enterrador.

gravel [grǽvel], s. cascajo, grav (med.) cálculos.

graveyard [gréivyard], s. cementerio.

gravitate [grǽviteit], vi. gravita **—gravitation** [grǽvitéišon], s. grav tación. **—gravity** [grǽviti], s. grav dad; seriedad; importancia.

gravy [gréivi], s. salsa o caldillo de u guiso de carne.

gray [grei], vt. y vi. ponerse gris o can

encanecer.—*a.* gris, pardo; tordo, rucio; cano, encanecido.—*g.-haired,* o *-headed,* canoso; envejecido.—*s.* color gris; animal gris.- —**hound** [-haund], *s.* galgo.—*g. racing,* carreras de galgos.- —**ish** [gréjiŝ], *a.* pardusco, grisáceo; entrecano; tordillo.

'raze [greiz], *vt.* apacentar, pastorear; rozar.—*vi.* pacer, pastar; rozarse.

rease [gris], *s.* grasa; lubricante.— *vt.* engrasar; lubrificar.- —**greasy** [grísi], *a.* grasiento, pringoso.- —**paint** [-peint], *s.* maquillaje teatral.

reat [greit], *a.* gran, grande; magno; admirable; excelente; espléndido.—*a g. deal,* mucho, gran cantidad.—*a g. many,* muchos.—*a g. way off,* muy lejos.—*a g. while,* un largo rato.—*G. Bear,* Osa Mayor.—*G. Britain,* Gran Bretaña. —**g.-grandchild** [-grǽndchaild], *s.* biznieto. —**g.-grandfather** [-grǽndfaðœ(r)], *s.* bisabuelo. —**g.-grandmother** [-grǽndmʌðœ(r)], *s.* bisabuela.— —**ness** [gréitnis], *s.* grandeza; grandiosidad; magnitud, extensión; fausto.

recian [gríŝan], *s.* y *a.* griego.

reed [grid], *s.* voracidad, gula; codicia, avidez.- —**ily** [grídili], *adv.* vorazmente; codiciosamente; vehementemente, con ansia.- —**y** [-i], *a.* voraz; anhelante, ávido, codicioso.

reek [grik], *s.* griego; (fam.) lenguaje o cosa ininteligible.—*a.* griego.

reen [grin], *a.* verde (de color y de sazón); fresco; inexperto, bisoño.—*g. card,* carta verde; (E.U.) permiso de residencia y trabajo.—*g. corn,* maíz tierno; trigo nuevo.—*g.-eyed,* ojiverde, celoso.—*g. goods,* verduras.—*g. hand,* novicio.—*g. thumb,* pulgares verdes (*don de criar plantas*).—*s.* color verde; verdor, verdura; prado o pradera; césped.—*pl.* verduras, hortalizas.—*vt.* pintar o teñir de verde.—*vi.* verdear.- —**back** [-bæk], *s.* (fam.) dólar, verde. - —**ery** [-ěrj], *s.* verdura.- —**horn** [-horn], *s.* (fam.) novato, pardillo.- —**house** [grínhaus], *s.* invernadero. - —**ish** [-iŝ], *a.* verdoso, verdusco.- —**ly** [-li], *adv.* nuevamente, recientemente; sin madurez.- —**ness** [-nis], *s.* verdor; vigor, frescura; falta de experiencia; novedad.

reet [grit], *vt.* saludar, dar la bienvenida.—*vi.* encontrarse y saludarse.- —**ing** [grítiŋ], *s.* salutación, sa-

ludo.—*g. card,* tarjeta de buen deseo.—*pl.* ¡salud! ¡saludos!

grenade [grenéid], *s.* (mil.) granada.

grew [gru], *pret.* de TO GROW.

grey [grei], *a.* gris; pardo; canoso.—v. GRAY.- —**hound** [gréihaund], *s.* galgo.—*g. racing,* carreras de galgos. - —**ish** [-iŝ], *a.* v. GRAYISH.

grid [grid], *s.* red; parrilla; reja, rejilla. - —**dle** [grídl], *s.* tapadera de fogón; tortera.- —**iron** [grídaiœrn], *s.* parrillas; andamiaje; (dep.) campo, cancha.- —**lock** [-lak], *s.* paralización total del tráfico; (fig.) punto muerto.

grief [grif], *s.* pesar, aflicción, dolor, sentimiento.—*g.-stricken,* desconsolado, apesadumbrado.—*to come to g.,* pasarlo mal; malograrse.

grievance [grívans], *s.* injusticia, perjuicio; agravio. —**grieve** [griv], *vt.* afligir, lastimar; apesadumbrar.— *vi.* apesadumbrarse, dolerse, penar. —**grievous** [grívʌs], *a.* penoso, doloroso; oneroso; fiero, atroz, cruel.

griffin [grífin], **griffon** [grífon], *s.* (mit. griega) grifo.

grill [gril], *vt.* asar en parrillas; atormentar con fuego o calor; interrogar severamente y sin tregua.—*s.* parrilla; manjar asado en parrilla; restaurante.- —**ing** [-iŋ], *s.* interrogatorio.- —**room** [grílrum], *s.* restaurante especializado en asados a la parrilla.

grim [grim], *a.* ceñudo, austero, severo; horrendo; sombrío; deprimente.

grimace [griméis], *s.* mueca.—*vi.* hacer muecas.

grime [graim], *s.* tizne, mugre, porquería.—*vt.* ensuciar, tiznar. —**grimy** [grájmi], *a.* tiznado, sucio, manchado.

grimness [grímnis], *s.* horror; lo funesto; austeridad, severidad; crueldad, fiereza.

grin [grin], *vii.* [1] hacer muecas mostrando los dientes; sonreír satisfecha, aprobativa o sarcásticamente.— *s.* mueca (de ira, dolor, etc.); sonrisa expresiva.

grind [graind], *vti.* [4] moler, quebrantar, triturar; pulverizar; picar carne; hacer crujir (los dientes); afilar, amolar; vaciar; rallar, estregar; pulir, esmerilar; mascar; acosar, oprimir; (fam.) dar lata o matraca.— *vii.* hacer molienda; rozar; pulirse con el roce.—*s.* molienda; (fam.) trabajo pesado.— **—er** [gráindœ(r)], s. molinero; moledor; esmerilador; piedra de molino o de amolar; molino; amolador; muela.— **—ing** [-iŋ], s. molienda; afilamiento; esmerilado; pulimiento; rechinamiento.— a. opresivo.

grip [grip], s. apretón de mano; agarrón, asimiento; presa; saco de mano; mango, puño, agarradera; capacidad de agarrar, comprender o retener.—*to come to grips with*, luchar a brazo partido con.—*vti.* [1] agarrar, empuñar.—*vii.* agarrarse con fuerza.

gripe [graip], *vt.* agarrar, empuñar; pellizear; (mec.) morder; dar cólico; afligir.—*vi.* agarrar fuertemente; padecer cólico; quejarse, refunfuñar de vicio.—s. grapa, abrazadera; puño, mango, manija, agarradera; aprieto.—*pl.* retortijón, cólico.

grippe [grip], s. gripe, influenza.

grisly [grízli], a. espantoso, terrible.

grist [grist], s. (ant.) molienda.—*to be g. to one's mill*, (fam.) serle a uno de mucho provecho.

gristle [grísl], s. cartílago, ternilla.

grit [grit], s. arena, cascajo; firmeza; entereza; valor.—*pl.* sémola.—*vti.* y *vii.* [1] (hacer) rechinar o crujir (los dientes, etc.).

grizzle [grízl], s. color gris; mezclilla. **—grizzly** [grízli], a. grisáceo, pardusco.—*g. bear*, oso gris.

groan [groun], *vi.* gemir; lanzar quejidos.—s. gemido, quejido.

grocer [gróusœ(r)], s. tendero (de ultramarinos o comestibles).— **—y** [-i], s. tienda de ultramarinos, tienda de comestibles.—*pl.* comestibles, víveres, provisiones.

groom [grum], s. novio (en el acto de la boda); mozo de mulas; lacayo.— *vt.* cuidar, almohazar los caballos; peinar y vestir, acicalar.— **—sman** [grúmzman], s. padrino de boda.

groove [gruv], s. muesca, ranura, estría; surco; rutina.—*g. and tongue*, (carp.) ranura y lengüeta.—*in the g.*, (fam.) envena, en plena forma.

grope [group], *vt.* y *vi.* tentar, andar a tientas; buscar tentando.

gross [grous], a. total; flagrante, burdo; craso; ordinario, grosero; obeso, gordísimo; denso, espeso; (com.) bruto.—*g. national product*, producto national bruto.—*g. profit*, ganancia bruta.—*g. weight*, peso bruto.—s. gruesa (doce docenas);

totalidad, conjunto.—*vt.* tener una entrada bruta de.

grotto [grátou], s. gruta; antro, covacha.

grouch [grauch], s. gruñón, descontento.—*to have a g.*, estar de mal humor.

ground [graund], *pret.* y *pp.* de TO GRIND.—*g. glass*, vidrio esmerilado.—*g. meat*, carne picada (molida).—s. tierra, terreno, suelo, base, fundamento; razón, motivo (pint.) fondo o campo; baño, capa (elec. y radio) toma de tierra; (mil.) campo de batalla.—*pl.* poso, sedimento, heces; jardín, parque, terrenos; cancha.—*g. floor*, planta baja.—*to break g.*, desmontar, roturar; empezar un trabajo.—*to come o fall to the g.*, caer al suelo; fracasar.— *to gain g.*, ganar terreno.—*to give o to lose g.*, perder terreno, retroceder atrasar.—*to take the g.*, (mar.) encallar.—*vt.* fundar, apoyar, establecer poner en tierra; (elec. y rad.) conectar con tierra.—*vi.* encallar, varar.— **—less** [gráundlis], a. infundado.

group [grup], s. grupo, agrupación conjunto.—*vt.* y *vi.* agrupar(se) reunir(se).

grouse [graus], s. (orn.) chocha; (Am. guaco.—*vi.* (fam.) quejarse.

grove [grouv], s. arboleda, bosquecillo.

grovel [grável], *vi.* arrastrarse, prosternarse.

grow [grou], *vti.* [10] cultivar; criar.— *vii.* crecer; aumentar; desarrollarse nacer, darse (frutas, plantas, etc.) —*to g. crazy*, volverse loco.—*to g dark*, anochecer.—*to g. late*, hacerse tarde.—*to g. less*, disminuir.—*to g old*, envejecer.—*to g. on o upon*, apoderándose de; ganar o aventajar a.—*to g. up*, crecer, hacerse hombre.—*to g. young again*, remozarse

growl [graul], *vi.* gruñir, rezongar.—*v* decir gruñendo.—s. gruñido, rezongo.

grown [groun], *pp.* de TO GROW.—*g* crecido, espigado; cubierto o llen de hierbas, malezas, etc.—*g.-up* crecido, adulto. **—growth** [grouθ], s crecimiento, desarrollo; aumento producto, producción; tumor, ex crecencia.—*g. area*, sector en ex pansion.—*g. industry*, industria e crecimiento.

grub [grʌb], s. (ent.) gorgojo; larv (fam.) manducatoria.— **—by** [-bi], sucio, mugriento.—*vti.* y *vii.* [1] rozar; cavar; emplearse en oficios bajos; (fam.) manducar.

grudge [grʌdž], *vt.* envidiar, codiciar; escatimar, dar de mala gana.—*s.* rencor, inquina; renuencia, mal grado.

gruesome [grúsʌm], *a.* macabro; horripilante.

gruff [grʌf], *a.* ceñudo, áspero; grosero; (b)ronco (voz).— **—ness** [gráfnis], *s.* aspereza, mal humor.

grumble [grámbl], *vi.* refunfuñar, rezongar.—*s.* regaño, refunfuñadura.— **—r** [grámblœ(r)], *s.* refunfuñador, rezongador, malcontento.

grunt [grʌnt], *vi.* gruñir; refunfuñar.—*s.* gruñido.

guano [gwánou], *s.* guano.

Guarani [gwaraní], *s.* guaraní.

guarantee [gærʌntí], *vt.* garantizar; afianzar; responder de o por; dar fianza.—*s.* garantía, fianza; persona de quien otra sale fiadora.

guard [gard], *vt.* y *vi.* guardar, custodiar; vigilar; estar prevenido; guardarse.—*to g. against,* guardarse de.—*s.* guarda, guardia; guardián, custodio; protección, defensa; vigilancia; centinela; cautela; estado de defensa; guarnición de un vestido o de una espada; conductor de tren.—*g. dog,* perro guardián.—*on g.,* alerta; en guardia.—*a.* de guardia, de protección.— **—ian** [gárdjʌn], *s.* guardián, custodio; tutor.—*a.* que guarda, tutelar.—*g. angel,* ángel de la guarda.— **—ianship** [-jʌnšịp], *s.* tutela; protección, custodia.— **—rail** [-reil], *s.* barandilla; barrera de seguridad.— **—sman** [gárdzmaen], *s.* soldado de la Guardia Nacional.

Guatemalan [gwatɛmálʌn], *a.* and *s.* guatemalteco.

guava [gwávạ], *s.* guayaba; guayabo.

guerrilla [gɛrílạ], *s.* guerrilla; guerrillero.

guess [gɛs], *vt.* y *vi.* conjeturar, suponer; adivinar; acertar.—*s.* conjetura, suposición; adivinación.

guest [gɛst], *s.* huésped, invitado; forastero, visita; pensionista.

guffaw [gufŏ], *s.* carcajada, risotada.—*vi.* reír a carcajadas.

guidance [gájdạns], *s.* guía, dirección, conducta.— **—guide** [gajd], *vt.* guiar, dirigir, encaminar; adiestrar; arreglar, gobernar.—*guided missile,* proyectil dirigido.—*guided tour,* visita guiada.—*s.* guía, mentor; ba-

quiano; (mec.) corredera; (impr.) mordante.—*g. dog,* perro guía, perro lazarillo. **—guidebook** [gájdbụk], *s.* guía del viajero. **—guideline** [gaídlajn], *s.* pauta, directriz.

guild [gild], *s.* gremio; cofradí, hermandad; corporación; colegio profesional (de médicos, abogados, etc.); sociedad benéfica.

guile [gajl], *s.* astucia, maña.- **—less** [-les], *a.* cándido, sincero.

guilt [gilt], *s.* delito; culpa, culpabilidad.- **—less** [gíltlịs], *a.* inocente, libre de culpa.- **—y** [-i], *a.* culpable.

guinea pig [gínị píg], *s.* conejillo de Indias.

guitar [gitár], *s.* guitarra.- **—ist** [-ịst], *s.* guitarrista.

gulch [gʌlch], *s.* quebrada, cañada.

gulf [gʌlf], *s.* golfo; seno; sima.—*G. Stream,* corriente del golfo.

gull [gʌl], *vt.* engañar, timar, estafar.—*s.* gaviota; bobo, primo.

gullet [gálịt], *s.* fauces; gaznate; zanja, trinchera profunda.

gullible [gálịbl], *a.* crédulo, simple.

gully [gálị], *vti.* [7] formar canal.—*s.* zanja honda; barranco, barranca.

gulp [gʌlp], *vt.* engullir, tragar; sofocar (un sollozo).—*vi.* entrecortar el resuello.—*s.* trago, sorbo.

gum [gʌm], *s.* goma; encía.—*chewing g.,* chicle, goma de mascar.—*vti.* [1] engomar; pegar con goma.

gumbo [gámbou], *s.* (Am.) quimbombó.

gummy [gámị], *a.* gomoso, engomado.

gun [gʌn], *s.* arma de fuego (cañón; fusil; escopeta; pistola o revólver).—*vti.* [1] hacer fuego.—*vii.* cazar con escopeta o rifle. **—boat** [gánbout], *s.* cañonero.— **—fight** [-fait], *s.* pelea a tiros; (duel) duelo.— **—fire** [-fair], *s.* fuego, disparos; cañoneo.- **—man** [-mạn], *s.* pistolero.- **—ner** [-œr(r)], *s.* artillero; ametrallador.- **—powder** [-paụdœ(r)], *s.* pólvora.- **—smith** [-smịθ], *s.* armero.

gurgle [gœrgl], *vi.* borbotar, gorgotear.—*s.* gorgoteo; borbotón; gluglú.

gush [gʌš], *vt.* derramar, verter.—*vi.* brotar, fluir, chorrear; (fam.) ser extremoso.—*s.* chorro, borbotón; (fam.) efusión, extremo.

gust [gʌst], *s.* ráfaga, bocanada; acceso, arrebato.

gusto [gástou], *s.* entusiasmo, satisfacción, celo, deleite, gusto.

gut [gʌt], *s.* intestino, tripa; cuerda de

tripa; (mar.) estrecho.—*pl.* (fam.) entrañas; valor ánimo.—*vti.* [1] destripar; desentrañar.- **—less** [-lɛs], *a.* cobarde, sin agallas.

gutter [gátœ(r)], *s.* canal, canalón; gotera; cuneta; arroyo de la calle; albañal; acequia; estría, canal de ebanistería; (fig.) bajos fondos.—*vt.* acanalar, estriar; construir albañales, etc.—*vi.* acanalarse; manar, gotear.

guy [gai], *s.* cable de retén, tirante; viento; (fam.) tipo, sujeto, tío; adefesio, mamarracho.—*vt.* sujetar con vientos; hacer burla o mofa.

gym [dʒim], *s.* gimnasio.

gymnasium [dʒimnéiziʌm], *s.* gimnasio. **—gymnast** [dʒimnæst], *s.* gimnasta. **—gymnastic(al)** [dʒimnǽstik(al)], *a.* gimnástico. **—gymnastics** [dʒimnǽstiks], *s.* gimnasia, gimnástica.

gynecology [gainekálodʒi], *s.* ginecología.

H

haberdasher [hǽbœrdæšœ(r)], *s.* camisero, mercero, tendero.- **—y** [-i], *s.* camisería, mercería.

habit [hǽbit], *s.* hábito, costumbre; vicio; vestido.—*by* o *from* (*force of*) *h.*, de vicio.—*to be in the h. of,* soler, acostumbrar.

habitable [hǽbitabl], *a.* habitable. **—habitation** [hǽbitéišɔn], *s.* habitación, domicilio, morada. **—habitat** [hǽbitæt], *s.* (biol.) hábitat.

habitual [habíchual], *a.* habitual, acostumbrado. **—habituate** [habíchueit], *vt.* y *vi.* habituar(se).

hack [hæk], *s.* caballo de alquiler, rocín; tos seca; plumífero, autor mercenario; taxi.—*h. stand,* punto o parada de taxis.—*h. saw,* sierra para cortar metal.—*vt.* tajar, picar.—*vi.* cortar; toser con tos seca; alquilarse.- **—saw** [-sɔ], *s.* sierra de armero, sierra de arco.

hacker [hǽkœ(r)], *s.* (comput. y fam.) pirata informático.

hacking [hǽkiŋ], *s.* (comput. y fam.) piratería informática.

hackle [hǽkl], *s.* rastrillo; plumas de cuello de ciertas aves; mosca para pescar.—*vt.* rastrillar; tajar; mutilar.

hackneyed [hǽknid], *a.* trillado, gastado, manido.

had [hæd], *pret.* de TO HAVE.

haggard [hǽgärd], *a.* trasnochado, macilento, ojeroso, flaco.

haggle [hǽgl], *vt.* tajar.—*vi.* regatear.

hail [heil], *s.* granizo; saludo; grito, llamada.—*H. Mary,* Ave María.—*within hailing distance,* al habla, al alcance de la voz.—*interj.* ¡salve! ¡salud!—*vt.* saludar; aclamar; llamar.—*vi.* granizar; vocear.—*to h. from,* ser oriundo de.- **—storm** [héilstɔrm], *s.* granizada.

hair [her], *s.* pelo; vello; cabello, cabellera; cerda; hebra, filamento; pelusa.—*against the h.,* a contrapelo.—*h. dryer,* secador.—*h. net,* redecilla.—*h.-raising,* espeluznante, horripilante.—*h. remover,* depilatorio.—*h. spray,* laca, fijador.—*h. stroke,* rasgo muy fino.—*to a h.,* exactamente, perfectamente.- **—brush** [hérbrʌš], *s.* cepillo de cabeza. **—cloth** [-klɔθ], *s.* tela de crin.- **—cut** [-kʌt], *s.* pelado, corte de pelo.- **—do** [-du], *s.* peinado.- **—dresser** [-dresœ(r)], *s.* peluquero, peluquera, peinador o peinadora.- **—dressing** [-dresiŋ], *s.* peinado.- **—less** [-lis], *a.* pelón; sin pelo, lampiño.- **—line** [-lain], *s.* nacimiento del pelo; (fine line) línea delgada.- **—pin** [-pin], *s.* horquilla, (Am.) gancho del pelo.- **—y** [-i], *a.* peludo, velludo.

Haitian [héitian], *a.* y *s.* haitiano.

hake [heik], *s.* (ict.) merluza.

hale [heil], *a.* sano, robusto.—*vt.* llevar por la fuerza.

half [hæf], *s.* mitad; medio.—*h. and h.,* mitad y mitad; de medio a medio, en partes iguales.—*a.* y *adv.* medio, semi.—*h.-baked,* a medio cocer o asar, etc.—*h. binding,* (enc.) media pasta.—*h. brother,* medio hermano.—*h.-closed,* entornado.—*h. dozen,* media docena.—*h. fare,* medio billete.—*h.-full,* mediado.—*h. hearted,* poco entusiasta, sin ánimo.—*h. hour,* media hora; de media hora.—*h.-mast,* media asta (la bandera); poner a media asta.— *h.-open(ed),* entreabierto.—*h.-past one, two, etc.,* la una, las dos, etc. y media.—*h. price,* mitad de precio.— *h. shell,* concha; *on the h.,* en su concha.—*h. sister,* media hermana.— *h.-staff,* media asta.—*h. tone,* semitono.—*h.-truth,* verdad a medias.—*h.-way,* a medio camino; medio; *halfway house,* centro de reinserción social.—*h.-witted,* tonto, imbécil.—*to h.-open,* entreabrir.– **—way** [hǽfwei], *a.* y *adv.* equidistante, a medio camino; parcial(mente).

halibut [hǽlibʌt], *s.* (ict.) mero.

hall [hɔl], *s.* pasillo, corredor; vestíbulo, zaguán; salón (para reuniones, funciones, etc.). edificio (de un colegio u universidad).—*city h.,* o *town h.,* ayuntamiento, alcaldía.— *h. of fame,* galería de personajes famosos.– **—mark** [-mark], *s.* marca de contraste; (fig.) sello.

hallelujah [hæelilúya], *interj.* ¡aleluya!

hallo [halóu], *interj.* ¡hola! ¡oiga!

hallow [hǽlou], *vt.* consagrar.

Hallowe'en [hæloún], *s.* víspera de Todos los Santos.

hallucination [hæljusinéiṣon], *s.* alucinación. **—hallucinate** [hæljúsineit], *vi.* alucinar.

halo [héilou], *s.* halo, nimbo, aureola.

halt [hɔlt], *vi.* hacer alto.—*vt.* parar, detener.—*s.* parada, alto.—*interj.* ¡alto!

halter [hɔ́ltœ(r)], *s.* cabestro, ronzal, jáquima; dogal.

halve [hæv], *vt.* dividir o partir en dos partes iguales; (carp.) machihembrar.– **—s** [-z], *s. pl.* de HALF.

ham [hæm], *s.* jamón, pernil; (anat.) corva; (teat.) comediante pamplinero.—*pl.* nalgas.—*vi.* sobreactuar.—*to h. up,* interpretar sobreactuando.

hamburger [hǽmbœrgœ(r)], *s.* hamburguesa; carne de vaca picada y frita.

hamlet [hǽmlit], *s.* aldea, caserío.

hammer [hǽmœ(r)], *s.* martillo; martinete.—*vt.* martillar; machacar; clavar; forjar.—*to h. one's brains,* devanarse los sesos.—*vi.* martillar, dar golpes; repiquetear.– **—head** [-hed], *s.* pez martillo, cornuda.

hammock [hǽmok], *s.* hamaca.

hamper [hǽmpœ(r)], *s.* canasta, cesto,

cuévano.—*vt.* embarazar, estorbar; encestar, encanastar.

hand [hænd], *s.* mano; palmo; ajecución; mano de obra; manecilla o aguja del reloj; operario, obrero, bracero; carácter de letra; firma; mano (en los naipes).—*at h.,* o *near at h.,* a la mano, cerca.—*by h.,* a mano; con biberón.—*h. and glove,* uña y carne.—*h. baggage,* equipaje de mano.—*h. in h.,* parejas; junto; de acuerdo.—*h. over head,* inconsideradamente.—*hands off,* no tocar; no meterse.—*hands off policy,* política de no intervención.—*h. to h.,* cuerpo a cuerpo, a brazo partido.— *h.-wrestle,* pulsear.—*in h.,* de contado.—*on the one h.,* por una parte.—*on the other h.,* por otra parte; en cambio; al contrario.—*to h.,* a la mano; listo.—*to set the h. to,* emprender; firmar.—*vt.* dar, entregar, poner en manos (de alguien).— *to h. down,* transmitir; entregar; dictar (un fallo).—*to h. over,* entregar, alargar.—*a.* de mano; hecho a mano; manual.—*h. glass,* lente de aumento, lupa.– **—ball** [hǽndbɔl], *s.* pelota, juego de pelota.– **—bag** [-bæg], *s.* maletín; bolsa de mano.– **—bill** [-bil], *s.* volante.– **—book** [-buk], *s.* manual; prontuario; guía. – **—cuff** [-kʌf], *s.* manilla.—*pl.* esposas.—*vt.* maniatar, esposar.— **—ful** [-ful], *s.* puñado, manojo.— **—set** [-set], *s.* microteléfono.

handicap [hǽndikæp], *vti.* [1] (dep.) emparejar ventajas entre competidores; poner obstáculos.—*s.* (dep.) ventaja en carreras o torneos; desventaja, impedimento, obstáculo. **—handicapped** [hǽndikæpt], *a.* impedido; que sufre de algún impedimento físico o mental.

handiwork [hǽndiwœrk], *s.* artefacto; trabajo manual.

handkerchief [hǽŋkœrchif], *s.* pañuelo.

handle [hǽndl], *vt.* tocar, manosear; manipular, manejar; tratar; dirigir; comerciar en; poner mango a.— *vi.* manejarse.—*s.* mango, puño, asa, manigueta, manubrio, tirador; (Am.) cacha (de arma). **—handling** [hǽndliŋ], *s.* manejo; manoseo; maniobra; manipulación.

handmade [hǽndméid], *a.* hecho a mano. **—handmaid** [hǽndmeid], *s.* criada de mano, asistenta. **—hand-**

rail [hǽndreil], s. pasamano, baranda, barandilla. —**handsaw** [hǽndsɔ], s. serrucho, sierra de mano. —**handshake** [hǽndʃeik], s. apretón de manos.

handsome [hǽndsʌm], a. hermoso; guapo; bien parecido; generoso.

handwriting [hǽndraitiŋ], s. carácter de letra; escritura cursiva, caligrafía.

handy [hǽndi], a. manuable, fácil de manejar; próximo, a la mano; diestro, hábil. —**h.-man**, factótum. —**to come in h.**, venir al pelo.

hang [hæŋ], vt. ahorcar. —vi. ser ahorcado. —vti. [10] colgar, suspender; fijar (en la pared); empapelar; poner colgaduras. —**to h. out**, enarbolar; colgar. —**to h. up**, levantar; colgar. —vii. colgar, pender, caer. —**to h. around**, rondar, haraganear. —**to h. up**, colgar el auricular. —s. caída (de un vestido, cortina, etc.); (fam.) maña, destreza; quid. —**h. gliding**, vuelo con ala delta.

hangar [hǽŋǎ(r)], s. hangar.

hanger [hǽŋœ(r)], s. perchero, colgadero. —**hanging** [hǽŋiŋ], s. muerte en la horca. —pl. colgaduras, tapices, cortinaje. —a. colgante. —**hangman** [hǽŋman], s. verdugo. —**hangover** [hǽŋouvœ(r)], s. (Am.) resaca, cruda, ratón.

hank [hæŋk], s. madeja.

happen [hǽpn], vi. acontecer, suceder; hallarse por casualidad en. —**to h. on**, encontrarse o tropezar con. —**whatever happens**, suceda lo que suceda. —**-ing** [-iŋ], s. suceso, acontecimiento.

happily [hǽpili], adv. feliz o dichosamente; afortunadamente. —**happiness** [hǽpinis], s. felicidad, dicha, alegría. —**happy** [hǽpi], a. feliz, dichoso, alegre, contento; afortunado. —**h. birthday!**, ¡feliz cumpleaños! —**h.-go-lucky**, imperturbable, despreocupado.

harangue [haráeŋ], s. arenga, perorata. —vt. arengar a.

harass [haráes], vt. acosar, hostigar; (with worries) atormentar, perseguir; (mil.) hostilizar, picar. —**-ed** [haráest], a. (with worries) nervioso, tenso; (look) preocupado. —**-ment** [mɛnt], s. acoso; tormento continuo; (mil.) hostigamiento. —**sexual h.**, acoso sexual.

harbinger [hárbindʒœ(r)], s. heraldo.

harbor [hárbɔ(r)], s. puerto; asilo, abrigo. —**h. master**, capitán del puerto. —**h. pilot**, práctico. —vt. abrigar; albergar.

hard [hard], a. duro, endurecido; difícil, arduo; penoso; fuerte, recio; riguroso, severo; inflexible. —**h. cash**, metálico, dinero contante y sonante. —**h.-core**, empedernido; incondicional, a ultranza; explícito, duro. —**h. drink**, bebida fuertemente alcohólica; licor. —**h. hat**, casco protector; (fam.) trabajador de construcción. —**h. labor**, trabajo forzado. —**h. luck**, mala suerte. —**h.-luck story**, historia lacrimógena. —**h. of hearing**, duro de oído. —**h. rubber**, ebonita, vulcanita. —**h. sausage**, salchichón. —**h. to deal with**, intratable. —**h. water**, agua cruda. —**h. words**, palabras injuriosas. —adv. mucho; con ahínco, con impaciencia; difícilmente; con fuerza, fuertemente; duramente. —**h.-bitten**, (fam.) endurecido, aguerrido. —**h.-boiled**, duro, insensible. —**h.-boiled egg**, huevo duro. —**h. by**, inmediato, muy cerca. —**h.-headed**, astuto. —**h.-hearted**, duro de corazón. —**h. pressed**, acosado, apurado. —**h.-won**, ganado a pulso. —**h.-working**, trabajador. —**h.-up**, (fam.) alcanzado, apurado. —**h.-won**, ganado a pulso. —**h.-working**, trabajador. —**to rain h.**, llover a cántaros. —**-back** [-bæk], a. encuadernado. —s. libro encuadernado. —**-en** [hárdn], vt. y vi. endurecerse. —**-ening** [-niŋ], s. endurecimiento. —**-ly** [-li], adv. difícilmente, apenas, a duras penas, escasamente; duramente. —**-ness** [-nis], s. dureza, endurecimiento; crudeza (del agua). —**-ship** [-ʃip], s. penalidad, trabajo; privaciones. —**-ware** [-wer], s. ferretería, quincallería; (comput.) hardware, soporte físico, equipo. —**h. store**, ferretería, quincallería. —**-wareman** [-werman], s. ferretero, quincallero. —**-y** [-i], a. fuerte, robusto; bravo, intrépido.

hare [her], s. liebre. —**-brained** [hérbreind], a. cabeza de chorlito, ligero de cascos. —**-lip** [-lip], s. labio leporino.

harem [hérem], s. harén.

harlot [hárlot], s. ramera, prostituta.

harm [harm], s. daño, perjuicio, mal. —vt. dañar, perjudicar; ofender, herir. —**-ful** [hármful], a. da-

ñoso, dañino, nocivo, perjudicial.—
—**less** [-lįs], *a.* inocuo; inofensivo;
ileso; sano y salvo.

harmonic [harmánįk], *s.* (mús.) armónico, tono secundario.—*pl.* armonía.—*a.* armónico.—**a** [-ą̈], *s.* (mús.) armónica. —**harmonious** [harmóuņįʌs], *a.* armónico; armonioso; proporcionado. —**harmonize** [hármonąįz], *vt.* armonizar, concertar.—*vi.* armonizarse, congeniar; armonizar, convenir, corresponder. —**harmony** [hármonį], *s.* armonía, acuerdo.

harness [hárnįs], *s.* arreos, guarniciones (de caballerías); arnés; (mec.) aparejo; (fig.) servicio activo.—*h. maker,* guarnicionero.—*h. race,* carrera con sulky.—*vt.* enjaezar; poner los arreos.

harp [harp], *s.* arpa.—*vi.* tocar el arpa.—*to h. on* o *upon,* repetir, machacar.

harpoon [harpún], *s.* arpón.

harpy [hárpį], *s.* arpía.

harrow [hǽrou], *s.* grada, rastrillo; rodillo para desterronar.—*vt.* gradar, rastrillar; perturbar, atormentar.

harry [hǽrį], *vti.* [7] asolar, saquear; acosar, molestar.

harsh [harš], *a.* áspero; tosco.— —**ness** [háršnįs], *s.* aspereza; severidad.

harvest [hárvįst], *s.* cosecha; siega, agosto; fruto, recolección.—*h. festival,* fiesta de la cosecha.—*h. moon,* luna llena.—*h. time,* mies.—*vt.* recoger la cosecha, segar; cosechar.— —**er** [-œ(r)], *s.* cosechero, segador; segadora, máquina de segar.

has-been [hǽzben], *s.* (fam. y despec.) nombre del pasado.

hash [hǽš], *s.* picadillo, jigote.—*vt.* picar, hacer picadillo.

haste [hejst], *s.* prisa.—*in h.,* de prisa.— —**n** [héjsn], *vt.* apresurar.—*vi.* darse prisa, apresurarse. —**hasty** [héjstį], *a.* apresurado; precipitado.

hat [hæt], *s.* sombrero.—*bowler h.,* sombrero hongo.—*h. box,* sombrerera.—*h. rack,* perchero.—*Panama h.,* jipijapa.—*silk h.* o *top h.,* sombrero de copa.—*soft h.,* sombrero flexible.

hatch [hæch], *vt.* criar, empollar, incubar; fraguar, tramar, maquinar.—*s.* cría; nidada; pollada; compuerta; portezuela; trampa; escotilla.— —**ery** [héchœrį], *s.* incubadora; vivero.

hatchet [hǽchįt], *s.* hacha pequeña, hachuela.—*to bury the h.,* hacer las paces.

hatchway [hǽchwej], *s.* escotilla.

hate [hejt], *vt.* odiar, aborrecer.—*s.* odio, aborrecimiento.— —**ful** [héjtful], *a.* aborrecible, odioso. —**hatred** [héjtrįd], *s.* odio, aborrecimiento.

hatter [hǽtœ(r)], *s.* sombrerero.

haughtiness [hótįnįs], *s.* arrogancia, altanería, altivez; ínfulas, humos. —**haughty** [hótį], *a.* arrogante; altivo, altanero.

haul [hɔl], *vt.* tirar de, arrastrar; transportar; (mar.) halar.—*to h. down the colors,* arriar la bandera.—*to h. the wind,* (mar.) ceñir el viento.—*s.* tirón o estirón, arrastre, transporte; redada; (fam.) buena pesca.

haunch [hɔnch], *s.* anca; pernil, pierna, pata.

haunt [hɔnt], *vt.* frecuentar; rondar, vagar por; perseguir.—*s.* guarida, nidal.— —**ed** [hóntįd], *a.* embrujado, encantado.—*h. house,* casa de fantasmas.

have [hæv], *vai.* [11] haber.—*vti.* tener; contener; tomar (comer, beber); recibir (carta, noticia, etc.). —*to h. in hand,* tener entre manos.— *to h. on,* tener puesto (traje, etc.).—*to h. one's way,* salirse uno con la suya.—*to h. something done,* mandar hacer algo.—*to h. to,* tener que.

haven [héjvn], *s.* puerto, fondeadero, abra; abrigo, asilo.

haversack [hǽvœrsæk], *s.* mochila.

havoc [hǽvok], *s.* estrago, ruina.—*to play h. with,* hacer estragos.

Hawaiian [hawájyan], *a.* y *s.* hawaiano.

hawk [hɔk], *s.* halcón; gavilán.—*h.-nosed,* de nariz aguileña.—*vt.* y *vi.* pregonar mercancías; cazar con halcón.— —**sbill** [hóksbįl], *s.* carey.

hawthorn [hóθɔrn], *s.* espino, oxiacanta.

hay [hej], *s.* heno; paja de heno u otras hierbas para forraje.—*h. fever,* fiebre del heno.— —**field** [-fild], *s.* henar, campo de heno.— —**fork** [héjfɔrk], *s.* horca, tridente.— —**loft** [-lɔft], *s.* henil, pajar.— —**stack** [-stæk], *s.* almiar; montón de heno.

hazard [hǽzәrd], *s.* azar, albur; peligro, riesgo; obstáculo (en el golf, etc.).— *vt.* arriesgar, aventurar. —**ous** [-ʌs], *a.* arriesgado, peligroso.

haze [hejz], *s.* niebla, bruma.—*vi.*

abrumarse la atmósfera.—*vt.* dar novatadas (en los colegios).

hazel [héizl], *s.* avellano.—*a.* castaño claro, avellanado; de avellano.- **—nut** [-nʌt], *s.* avellana.

hazing [héjziŋ], *s.* novatada (en los colegios). **—hazy** [héizi], *a.* nublado, brumoso; confuso, vago.

he [hi], *pron. pers.* él.—*h.*-*bear*, oso (macho).—*h.*-*goat*, macho cabrío. —*h.*-*man*, (fam.) hombre cabal, todo un hombre.—*h. who, h. that*, el que, aquel que, quien.

head [hed], *s.* cabeza; cima; parte superior o principal; cabecera (de cama, mesa, río); jefe, caudillo; director; punta (de flecha, etc.); puño (de bastón).—*a h.*, por barba, por persona.—*at the h.* (*of*), al frente (de).—*h. over heels*, precipitadamente.—*heads or tails?*, ¿cara o cruz?, ¿águila o sol? (Mex.).—*to bring to a h.*, ultimar.—*to come to a h.*, llegar a un estado definitivo o a una crisis; (med.) madurar.—*a.* principal; de o para la cabeza; de frente; (mar.) de proa.—*h. cold*, romadizo, coriza, resfriado.—*vt.* encabezar; dirigir, presidir; descabezar; poner título; podar.—*to h. off*, detener, prevenir.—*vi.* (con **for**) dirigirse a.- **—ache** [hédejk], *s.* jaqueca, dolor de cabeza.- **—board** [-bɔrd], *s.* cabecera de cama.- **—dress** [-dres], *s.* cofia, tocado, redecilla.- **—first** [-fœrst], *adv.* de cabeza.- **—iness** [-inis], *s.* terquedad, obstinación; encabezamiento del vino.- **—ing** [-iŋ], *s.* título, encabezamiento; membrete.- **—less** [-lis], *a.* descabezado, degollado; acéfalo. - **—light** [-lajt], *s.* (aut.) faro o farol delantero; (f.c.) farol, fanal.- **—line** [-lajn], *s.* titular, cintillo; título, encabezamiento.- **—long** [-lɔŋ], *a.* temerario, arrojado, precipitado.— *adv.* de cabeza, precipitadamente, irreflexivamente.- **—master** [-mǽstœ(r)], *s.* director de escuela.- **—mistress** [-místris], *s.* directora.- **—quarters** [-kwɔrtœrz], *s.* (mil.) cuartel general; jefatura (de policía, etc.); oficina principal de operaciones.— **—stone** [-stoun], *s.* lápida mortuoria.— **—strong** [-strɔŋ], *a.* terco, testarudo, obstinado.- **—way** [-wej], *s.* (mar.) salida, marcha de un buque; avance; progreso; adelanto,

ventaja.—*to make h.*, adelantar, progresar.- **—y** [-i], *a.* temerario, arrojado; violento, impetuoso.

heal [hil], *vt.* curar; componer.—*vi.* sanar; recobrar la salud.—*to h. up*, cicatrizarse.- **—ing** [híliŋ], *a.* sanativo, curativo.—*s.* cura, curación.

health [helθ], *s.* salud; sanidad.—*h. insurance*, seguro de enfermedad.- **—ful** [hélθful], *a.* sano, saludable, salubre.- **—iness** [-inis], *s.* salubridad, sanidad.- **—y** [-i], *a.* sano; saludable.

heap [hip], *s.* montón, pila, acumulación; multitud.—*in heaps*, a montones.—*vt.* amontonar, apilar, acumular.—*h. up*, colmar.

hear [hir], *vti.* [10] oír; oír decir; escuchar; tener noticia de.—*vii.* oír.—*to h. from someone*, saber de, tener noticias de alguien. **—heard** [hœrd], *pret.* y *pp.* de TO HEAR.- **—er** [híroe(r)], *s.* oyente.- **—ing** [-iŋ], *s.* sentido del oído; audiencia; (for.) vista (de un pleito o causa); examen de testigos; audición.- **—say** [-sej], *s.* rumor, fama.—*by h.*, de oídas.

hearse [hœrs], *s.* coche fúnebre.

heart [hart], *s.* corazón; ánimo; (fig.) entraña(s).—*at h.*, en el fondo, esencialmente; en verdad.—*by h.*, de memoria.—*from one's h.*, de todo corazón, con sinceridad.—*h. and soul*, en cuerpo y alma.—*h.-lung machine*, bomba corazon-pulmón.—*h.-rending*, doloroso, desgarrador.—*h.-to-h. talk*, charla íntima y franca.—*h.-warming*, alentador, reconfortante.—*to take h.*, cobrar ánimo.—*to take to h.*, tomar a pechos.- **—ache** [hártejk], *s.* dolor de corazón; angustia, congoja, pesar.- **—beat** [-bit], *s.* latido del corazón, palpitación; profunda emoción.- **—broken** [-broukn], *a.* acongojado, transido de dolor, (fig.) muerto de pesar; desengañado.- **—burn** [-bœrn], *s.* (med.) acedía, acidez.- **—en** [-n], *vt.* animar, confortar.- **—felt** [-felt], *a.* cordial, sincero; sentido.- **—sick** [-sik], *a.* abatido, muy afectado.- **—throb** [-θrɔb], *s.* (fam.) ídolo.

hearth [harθ], *s.* hogar, fogón, chimenea.

heartily [hártili], *adv.* cordialmente, de corazón.— **—heartless** [hártlis], *a.* sin

corazón; cruel; pusilánime.
—**hearty** [hárti], *a.* cordial, sentido, sincero; sano, vigoroso; gustoso, grato.

heat [hit], *s.* calor; ardor, vehemencia; celo (de los animales); hornada; colada; (dep.) carrera o corrida eliminatoria.—*vt.* y *vi.* calentar(se), caldear(se); acalorar(se).— —**er** [hítœ(r)], *s.* calentador, calefactor.

heathen [híðęn], *s.* y *a.* pagano.

heating [hítiŋ], *s.* calefacción.—*a.* caluroso; de calefacción.—*h. pad,* almohadilla o bolsa eléctrica.

heave [hiv], *vti.* alzar, levantar (con esfuerzo); (mar.) izar; lanzar, arrojar; exhalar, prorrumpir.—*vii.* suspirar hondo; palpitar; jadear; tener náuseas; (mar.) virar.—*to h. in sight,* (mar.) aparecer, asomar.—*s.* alzadura, levantamiento; náusea.

heaven [hévn], *s.* cielo, paraíso.—*pl.* firmamento, las alturas.—*for h.'s sake!* ¡por Dios!— —**ly** [-li], *a.* celeste; celestial.—*adv.* celestialmente.— —**ward** [-wärd], *adv.* hacia el cielo, hacia las alturas.

heaviness [hévinis], *s.* pesantez, pesadez, peso; abatimiento; opresión, carga.—**heavily** [hévili], *adv.* pesadamente; lentamente; tristemente; excesivamente.— —**heavy** [hévi], *a.* pesado; grueso; opresivo; molesto; denso, espeso; pesaroso; indigesto.—*h. duty,* servicio o trabajo fuerte (de una máquina).—*h. rain,* lluvia, chaparrón, aguacero. —**heavyweight** [hévi̭weit̯], *a.* (dep.) de peso pesado o máximo.—*s.* (boxeo) peso completo.

Hebrew [híbru], *a.* y *s.* hebreo; israelita; judío.—*s.* lengua hebrea.

hedge [hedž], *s.* seto, vallado.—*vt.* cercar con seto, vallar; circundar.- —**hog** [hédžhag], *s.* (zool.) erizo.

heed [hid], *vt.* atender.—*vi.* prestar atención.—*s.* cuidado, atención.

heel [hil], *s.* talón o calcañar; tacón; talón de una media.—*heels over head,* patas arriba.—*vt.* poner talón a.—*to be well heeled,* (fam.) estar bien provisto de dinero.—*vi.* escorarse.—*to h. over,* zozobrar.

heifer [héfœ(r)], *s.* vaquilla, novilla.

height [hait], *s.* altura, elevación; estatura, talla.—*the h. of folly,* el colmo de la locura.- —**en** [háit̯n], *vt.* realzar, elevar; exaltar; avivar.

heinous [héinʌs], *a.* atroz, nefando.

heir [ɛr], *s.* heredero.—*h. apparent,* heredero forzoso.- —**ess** [éris], *s.* heredera.- —**loom** [-lum], *s.* reliquia de familia.

held [held], *pret.* y *pp.* de TO HOLD.

helicopter [hélikaptœ(r)], *s.* helicóptero.

helium [hílʌm], *s.* (quim.) helio.

hell [hɛl], *s.* infierno.- —**ish** [hélįš], *a.* infernal.

hello [hɛlóu], *interj.* ¡hola!; ¡buenos días!; (tlf.) ¡dígame!; (tlf.) ¡bueno!

helm [hɛlm], *s.* (mar.) timón; yelmo.

helmet [hélmi̭t], *s.* casco, yelmo.

help [help], *vt.* ayudar, auxiliar, socorrer; aliviar; remediar.—*I can't h. it,* no puedo evitarlo.—*to h. one to,* servir a uno; proporcionar.—*vi.* ayudar, contribuir; servir (en la mesa).—*I can't h. saying,* no puedo (por) menos de decir.—*s.* ayuda, auxilio, socorro; remedio; fuerza de trabajo (criados, obreros, empleados, dependientes).—*there is no h. for it,* eso no tiene remedio.- —**er** [hélpœ(r)], *s.* asistente, ayudante.- —**ful** [-ful], *a.* útil, servicial; provechoso; saludable.- —**ing** [-iŋ], *s.* ayuda; porción (de comida) que uno se sirve o le sirven.- —**less** [-lis], *a.* desvalido; imposibilitado; inútil; irremediable.- —**lessness** [-lisnis], *s.* desamparo; impotencia.

hem [hem], *s.* (cost.) dobladillo, jaretón, borde.—*vti.* [1] dobladillar, bastillar; (gen. con **in**) rodear, encerrar.—*vii.* fingir tos.—*interj.* ¡ejem!- —**line** [-lain], *s.* bastilla, ruedo.

hemisphere [hémisfįr], *s.* hemisferio. —**hemispheric(al)** [hemisférik(al)], *a.* hemisférico.

hemlock [hémlak], *s.* (bot.) abeto; cicuta.

hemorrhage [hémoridž], *s.* hemorragia. —**hemorrhagic** [hemorǽdžik], *a.* hemorrágico.

hemorrhoids [hémorɔidz], *s. pl.* hemorroides, almorranas.

hemp [hemp], *s.* (bot.) cáñamo.—*h. cord,* bramante.—*h. sandal,* alpargata.

hen [hen], *s.* gallina; hembra de ave.—*h. party,* fiesta de mujeres.—*h.-pecked,* dominado por su mujer.

hence [hens], *adv.* de aquí; desde aquí; de ahí que, por tanto, en consecuencia.- **—forth** [hénsfɔrθ], *adv.* (de aquí) en adelante.

henchman [hénchmən], *s.* secuaz, paniaguado.

hepatitis [hepätáitịs], *s.* hepatitis.

her [hœr], *pron.* la, le, a ella, (después de *prep.*) ella.—*a.* su, de ella.

herald [hérald], *s.* heraldo.—*vt.* anunciar, pregonar, proclamar.- **—ry** [-rị], *s.* heráldica, blasón.

herb [(h)œrb], *s.* hierba, yerba.

herd [hœrd], *s.* manada, rebaño; multitud.—*vi.* ir en manadas.—*vt.* reunir el ganado en rebaños.- **—sman** [hœrdzmạn], *s.* pastor.

here [hịr], *adv.* aquí; acá; por aquí; ahora, en este momento, en este punto; ¡presente!—*h. it is*, he aquí; aquí tiene Ud.—*h.'s to you!*, ¡a la salud de Ud.!—*that is neither h. nor there*, eso no viene al caso. **—abouts** [-ạbáuts], *adv.* por aquí, por aquí cerca.- **—after** [-áeftœ(r)], *adv.* (de aquí) en adelante, en lo sucesivo.— *s.* el más allá.- **—by** [-bái], *adv.* por éstas, por la presente.

hereditary [hịrédịterị], *a.* hereditario. **—heredity** [hịrédịti], *s.* (biol.) herencia.

heresy [héresị], *s.* herejía. **—heretic** [héretịk], *s.* hereje.—*a.* herético.

heritage [hérịtịdž], *s.* herencia.

hermit [hœrmịt], *s.* ermitaño.- **—age** [-ịdž], *s.* ermita.

hernia [hœrnịä], *s.* hernia.

hero [hịrou], *s.* héroe; protagonista.- **—ic(al)** [hịróuịk(ạl)], *a.* heróico, épico.- **—ics** [hịrouịks], *spl.* actos heroicos.- **—ine** [hérojn], *s.* heroína, protagonista.- **—ism** [hérojzm], *s.* heroísmo, heroicidad; proeza.

heron [héron], *s.* garza.

herpes [hárpiz], herpes, herpe.

herring [hérịŋ], *s.* arenque.

hers [hœrz], *pron. pos.* suyo, suya, (de ella); el suyo, la suya, los suyos, las suyas (de ella).- **—elf** [hœrsélf], *pron.* ella misma, ella, sí misma.

hesitant [hézịtạnt], *a.* vacilante, indeciso. **—hesitate** [héjtejt], *vi.* vacilar, titubear. **—hesitation** [hezịtéjšọn], *s.* titubeo, vacilación.

heterogeneous [heterọdžínʌs], *a.* heterogéneo.

hew [hju], *vti.* [6] tajar, cortar, picar piedra; desbastar; labrar.—*to h. in*

pieces, destrozar, destroncar.—*vii.* golpear.—*to h. right and left*, acuchillar a diestra y siniestra.

hex [hɛks], *s.* maleficio.—*vt.* hacerle un maleficio a.- **—agon** [héksạgạn], *s.* hexágono.

hey [hej], *interj.* ¡eh! ¡oiga! ¡digo!

hi [haj], *interj.* ¡hola!

hiatus [hajeítṷs], *s.* paréntesis, pausa; abertura, laguna; hiato.

hibernate [hájbœrnejt], *vi.* invernar. **—hibernation** [hajbœrnéjšọn], *s.* invernada.

hiccough, hiccup [híkʌp], *s.* hipo.—*vi.* hipar, tener hipo.

hickory [híkọrị], *s.* nogal americano.

hid [hịd], *pret.* y *pp.* de TO HIDE.

hidden [hídn], *pp.* de TO HIDE.—*a.* oculto, escondido, secreto. **—hide** [hajd], *vti.* [10] esconder, ocultar. —*vii.* esconderse, ocultarse; (con out) estarse escondido.—*s.* escondite; cuero, piel, pellejo.- **—bound** [-baund], *a.* rígido, cerrado, dogmático. **—hideaway** [hájdạwej], *s.* escondite, escondrijo.

hideous [hídịʌs], *a.* horrible, espantoso, feo.

hierarchy [hájẹrarkị], *s.* jerarquía.

hieroglyphic [hajẹrọglífịk], *s.* y *a.* jeroglífico.

high [haj], *a.* alto; de alto; elevado; encumbrado o eminente, superior; solemne; supremo, sumo; vivo, intenso; arrogante; poderoso.—*h. altar*, altar mayor.—*h. and dry*, en seco.—*h. blood pressure*, hipertensión arterial.—*h.-brow*, intelectual.—*h-class*, de lujo; de primera calidad; de categoría.— *h. command*, alto mando.—*h. diving*, saltos desde grandes alturas.—*h. fidelity*, alta fidelidad.—*h. hat*, sombrero de copa.—*h. heels*, zapatos de tacón.—*h. jump*, salto de altura, salto alto.—*H. Mass*, misa cantada o mayor.—*h. priest*, sumo sacerdote.—*h. rank*, categoría, alto rango.—*h. rise*, alto, de muchas plantas.—*h. rise*, torre de apartamentos.—*h.-risk*, de alto riesgo.—*h. school*, escuela secundaria.—*h. sea*, mar gruesa.—*h. seas*, alta mar.—*h.-tech*, de alta tecnología.—*h. tide*, pleamar.—*h. treason*, alta traición.—*h. water mark*, línea de pleamar; (highest point) cénit, apogeo.—*h. wire act*, número en la cuerda floja.—*h.-wire artist*, equilibrista, funámbulo.—*h. words,* palabras ofensivas o asperas.—*in h. gear,* (aut.) en directa.—*in h. terms,* en términos lisonjeros.—*it is h. time to,* ya es hora de.—*adv.* alto; en lo alto; altamente; muy, sumamente; a grande altura; arrogantemente; a precio elevado; lujosamente.—*h. and low,* de arriba abajo; por doquiera.—*h.-handed,* despótico, arbitrario.—*h.-minded,* magnánimo, noble, idealista.—*h.-priced,* caro.— *h.-seasoned,* picante.—*h.-sounding,* altisonante.—*s.* alza, subida; punto o lugar alto; valor o precio máximo. — **ball** [hájbɔl], *s.* whiskey, ron, etc., mezclado con soda y hielo.— **boy** [-bɔi], *s.* cómoda alta con patas altas.— **chair** [-chɛr], *s.* silla alta (*para niño*).— **er** [haíçœ(r)], *comp.* h. education, enseñanza superior.— **land** [-lænd], *s.* región montañosa.—*pl.* tierras altas, montañas.— **lander** [-lændœ(r)], *s.* montañés de Escocia.— **landish** [-lændiʃ], *a.* montañés.— **light** [-lajt], *vt.* realzar, hacer destacar, subrayar.—*s.* punto de destaque, o de resalto.— **lighter** [-lajtœ(r)], *s.* rotulador, marcador.— **ly** [-li], *adv.* altamente; levantadamente, elevadamente; sumamente; arrogantemente; ambiciosamente; encarecidamente. — **ness** [-nis], *s.* altura, elevación; celsitud; Alteza (título).— **way** [-wej], *s.* carretera, calzada; camino real; vía pública.

hike [hajk], *s.* (fam.) caminata; marcha; excursión.—*vi.* dar una caminata o paseo largo; ir de excursión.—*vt.* levantar, arrastrar; aumentar de pronto.— **r** [hájkœ(r)], *s.* excursionista.

hilarious [hilériŭs], *a.* divertidísimo, comiquísimo; regocijado, jubiloso.

hijack [hájdʒæk], *vt.* secuestrar.— **er** [hájdʒækœ(r)], *s.* secuestrador; (aer) pirata aéreo.— **ing** [hájdʒækiŋ], *s.* secuestros; (aer) piratería aéreo.

hill [hil], *s.* collado, colina, cerro, cuesta, otero, altozano.—*vt.* aporcar.—*vi.* amontonarse.— **billy** [-bili], *s.* (fam.) rústico, paleto.— **man** [hílman], *s.* serrano, arribeño.— **ock** [-ɔk], *s.* altillo, loma, montecillo, otero.— **side** [-sajd], *s.* ladera, flanco de una colina.— **top** [-tap], *s.* cima, cumbre de una co-

lina.— **y** [-i], *a.* montañoso, montuoso.

hilt [hilt], *s.* puño, empuñadura.—*up to the h.,* a fondo; por completo.

him [him], *pron.* le, (a, para, con, etc.) él.— **self** [himsélf], *pron.* él, él mismo, se, sí, sí mismo.—*by h.,* solo, por sí, por su cuenta.—*for h.,* por su cuenta, por cuenta propia.— *he h.,* él mismo; en persona.—*he said to h.,* se dijo a sí mismo.

hind [hajnd], *a.* trasero, zaguero, posterior.—*h. foremost,* lo de atrás delante.—*s.* cierva.— **brain** [hájndbrejn], *s.* cerebelo; parte posterior del encéfalo.— **er** [híndœ(r)], *vt.* impedir, estorbar, obstaculizar; oponerse.—*a.* [hájndœ(r)], posterior, trasero.— **ermost** [-œrmoṷst], **most** [-moṷst], *a.* postrero, último.— **sight** [-sajt], *s.* percepción a posteriori, percepción tardía, retrospección.

hindrance [híndrans], *s.* impedimento, obstáculo, estorbo.

Hindu [híndu], *s.* y *a.* hindú, indostánico.

hinge [hindʒ], *s.* gozne, gonce, bisagra; punto principal o capital.—*vt.* engoznar, poner goznes.—*vi.* girar sobre goznes.—*to h. on,* depender de.

hint [hint], *vt.* insinuar, indicar.—*vi.* echar una indirecta.—*to h. at,* aludir a.—*s.* indirecta, insinuación.

hip [hip], *s.* cadera.— **bone** [-boṷn], *s.* hueso de la cadera.

hire [hajr], *vt.* alquilar; arrendar; emplear; contratar.—*to h. out,* alquilar(se).—*s.* alquiler, arriendo; salario; paga; jornal.

his [hiz], *a.* y *pron.* su, sus (de él); suyo, etc.; el suyo, la suya, los suyos, las suyas (de él).

Hispanic [hispǽnik], *a.* hispánico, hispano.

hiss [his], *vt.* y *vi.* silbar, (re)chiflar; sisear.—*s.* silbido, silba; siseo.

historian [histórian], *s.* historiador. — **historic(al)** [histárjk(al)], *a.* histórico. — **history** [hístori], *s.* historia.

hit [hit], *vti.* [9] dar, pegar, golpear; atinar, acertar; encontrar, dar con o en; denunciar.—*to h. it off,* avenirse, simpatizar, hacer buenas migas.— *vi.* rozar, chocar; acaecer o acontecer felizmente; salir bien; encontrar por casualidad; acertar.—*h. or miss,* al azar; atolondradamente.—*to h. against*, dar contra alguna cosa, chocar.—*to h. on* o *upon*, dar con, hallar; ocurrírsele a uno; acordarse de.—*pret.* y *pp.* de TO HIT.—*s.* golpe, choque, coscorrón; rasgo de ingenio.

hitch [hich], *vt.* atar, ligar; enganchar; mover a tirones.—*vi.* moverse a saltos; enredarse; congeniar, llevarse bien con otro.—*s.* alto, parada; tropiezo, dificultad; tirón.- **—hike** [híchhajk], *vi.* hacer autostop.- **—hiker** [híchhajkœ(r)], *s.* autoestopista.- **—hiking** [híchhajkiŋ], *s.* autostop.

hither [híðœ(r)], *adv.* acá, hacia acá.—*a.* citerior.- **—most** [-moust], más cercano o próximo.- **—to** [-tu], *adv.* hasta ahora, hasta aquí.

HIV [eíchájví], *abrev.* (Human Immunodeficiency Virus) VIH.

hive [hajv], *s.* colmena; enjambre; emporio.—*pl.* urticaria.—*vt.* enjambrar; atesorar, acumular.—*vi.* vivir juntos como en colmena.

hoard [hɔrd], *vt.* y *vi.* acaparar; atesorar, acumular y guardar.—*s.* provisión; montón; acumulación; tesoro escondido.- **—er** [hɔ́rdœ(r)], *s.* acaparador; atesorador.

hoarse [hɔrs], *a.* ronco.- **—ness** [hɔ́rsnis], *s.* ronquera, carraspera.

hoary [hɔ́rj], *a.* blanco, blanquecino; cano, canoso; escarchado; venerable.

hobble [hábl], *vt.* poner trabas.—*vi.* cojear.—*s.* cojera, traba; dificultad.

hobby [hábj], *s.* hobby, afición, pasatiempo.- **—horse** [-hɔrs], *s.* caballito; (favorite topic) caballo de batalla, monotema.

hobgoblin [hábgablin], *s.* duende, trasgo.

hock [hak], *s.* vino del Rin; corvejón, jarrete (del caballo, etc.); (anat.) corva.—*in h.*, (E.U., fam.) empeñado.—*vt.* (E.U., fam.) empeñar, dar en prenda.

hockey [hakj], *s.* hockey.—*h. stick*, palo de hockey.—*ice h.*, hockey sobre hielo.

hodgepodge [hádʒpadʒ], *s.* mezcolanza, baturrillo.

hoe [hou], *s.* azada, azadón, escardillo.—*vt.* azadonar.

hog [hag], *s.* cochino, cerdo; (fam.) persona sucia, tragona o egoísta;

(aer.) vuelta hacia abajo.- **—gish** [hágíʃ], *a.* porcino; egoísta; comilón.- **—gishness** [-iʃniʃ], *s.* porquería, cochinada; glotonería; egoísmo.- **—shead** [hágzhed], *s.* pipa, tonel.

hoist [hɔjst], *vt.* alzar, elevar; izar, enarbolar.—*s.* cabria, pescante, grúa, montacargas; levantamiento; ascención.—*h. bridge*, puente levadizo.

hold [hould], *vti.* [10] tener, asir, coger, agarrar; retener, reservar; detener, contener; sostener, apoyar; tener de reserva; restringir; encerrar; mantener; tener cabida o capacidad para; opinar, juzgar, reputar, entender; poseer, ocupar, disfrutar; celebrar (sesión, reunión); continuar, seguir; conservar; guardar, observar; obligar; hacer (responsable, etc.).—*to h. a bet* o *wager*, apostar.—*to h. a candle to*, (fam.) poder compararse con.—*to h. at bay*, tener a raya.—*to h. back*, retener; contener.—*to h. down*, oprimir, tener sujeto; conservar, no perder.—*to h. forth*, expresar, publicar; mostrar.—*to h. in*, sujetar, refrenar, contener.—*to h. off*, apartar, alejar.—*to h. out*, ofrecer, proponer; extender.—*to h. over*, tener suspendido o en suspenso; diferir, aplazar; prolongar una nota musical.—*to h. sway*, gobernar, mandar.—*to h. up*, levantar, alzar; apoyar, sostener; asaltar para robar, atracar.—*vii.* valer, ser válido, estar en vigor; mantenerse firme, sostenerse, aguantar; seguir, proseguir; estar en posesión; refrenarse, abstenerse; aplicarse, ser aplicable.—*s.* presa, asimiento; asa, mango; influencia, dominio; freno; refugio; posesión; custodio; celda; (mus.) calderón.- **—er** [hóuldœ(r)], *s.* tenedor, posesor; mantenedor; asidero, mango, asa; porta-(*lamp h.*, portalámpara, etc.); sostén; propietario; arrendatario; inquilino.—*h. of a bill*, tenedor de una letra.—*h. of a share*, accionista.- **—ing** [-iŋ], *s.* arrendamiento.—*h. company*, compañía tenedora, sociedad de control.- **—ings** [iŋz], *spl.* valores habidos.- **—up** [-ʌp], *s.* detención; (jer.) atraco, asalto.

hole [houl], *s.* agujero, orificio; cavidad, hueco, hoyo; bache; perforación; pozo, charco (de un río, arroyo, etc.); cueva, madriguera, guarida (de animales); (fam.) atolladero, aprieto, brete.—*vt.* agujerear, taladrar, perforar; meter una bola de billar en la tronera.—*vi.* encuevarse; hacer un agujero u hoyo.

holiday [hálįdeį], *s.* día festivo, festividad.—*pl.* vacaciones, asueto.—*a.* alegre, festivo.

holiness [hóulįnįs], *s.* santidad, beatitud.—*His H.,* Su Santidad.

hollow [hálou], *a.* hueco, vacío; cóncavo; hundido; sordo (ruido); falso, insincero.—*h.-chested,* de pecho hundido.—*h.-hearted,* solapado.—*h. punch,* sacabocados.—*h. ware,* ollas, pucheros, marmitas.—*s.* cavidad, canal, ranura; hueco; valle; cañada.—*vt.* excavar; ahondar; ahuecar.— **—ness** [-nįs], *s.* cavidad, oquedad, vaciedad; doblez, falsía.

holly [hálį], *s.* acebo; agrifolio.— **—hock** [-hak], *s.* malva loca u hortense.

holster [hóustœ(r)], *s.* pistolera, funda (de pistola).

holy [hóulį], *a.* santo, pío; puro, inmaculado; sacro, sagrado; consagrado; santificado; bendito.—*h. cross,* santa cruz.—*h. cup,* cáliz.—*h. orders,* órdenes sacerdotales.—*H. Ghost,* Espíritu Santo.—*h. rood,* crucifijo; santa cruz.—*h. water,* agua bendita.—*H. Week,* Semana Santa.—*H. Writ,* la Sagrada Escritura.

homage [hámįdž], *s.* homenaje, reverencia, culto.—*to do* o *pay h.,* acatar, rendir homenaje.

home [houm], *s.* hogar, casa; morada; domicilio, residencia, habitación; asilo, albergue, refugio; (dep.) meta, límite o término.—*at h.,* en casa; en el país de uno; con toda comodidad; en su elemento.—*h. computer,* computadora doméstica, ordenador doméstico.—*h.-made,* hecho en casa.—*h. movie,* película casera.— *h. owner,* propietario.—*h. plate,* (dep.) base del bateador, home.—*h. run,* (dep.) cuadrangular, home run.—*h. town,* ciudad natal, pueblo natal.—*to hit* o *strike h.,* llegar al alma, herir en lo vivo.—*a.* doméstico, de casa, casero; nativo, natal, regional, del país; certero, que llega a la meta.—*adv.* a casa; en casa; al

país o en la tierra de uno; en su lugar.— **—land** [hóumlænd], *s.* patria, tierra natal.— **—less** [-lįs], *a.* sin casa ni hogar; mostrenco.— **—like** [-laįk], *a.* como en casa; sosegado y cómodo.— **—liness** [-lįnįs], *s.* simpleza, sencillez; fealdad, mal aspecto.— **—ly** [-lį], *a.* casero, doméstico; sencillo, llano; feo; rústico, inculto, vulgar.— **—made** [-méįd], *a.* casero, hecho en casa; fabricado en el país.— **—maker** [-meįkoe(r)], *s.* ama de casa.— **—sick** [-sįk], *a.* nostálgico.— **—sickness** [-sįknįs], *s.* nostalgia, añoranza.— **—stead** [-sted], *s.* casa de habitación y sus terrenos; heredad; hogar.— **—ward** [-wärd], *adv.* hacia casa, hacia su país; de vuelta.—*h.-bound,* de regreso.— **—work** [-wœrk], *s.* trabajo, tarea, estudio, etc. para hacer en la casa.

homicidal [hámįsaįdǝl], *a.* homicida. **—homicide** [hámįsaįd], *s.* homicidio; homicida.

homogeneity [houmodžęnéíįtį], *s.* homogeneidad. **—homogeneous** [houmodžíníʌs], *a.* homogéneo. **—homogenize** [homádžęnaįz], *vt.* homogenizar.

homosexual [homǫsékšyǝl], *a.* y *s.* homosexual.

Honduran [handúrǝn], *a.* y *s.* hondureño.

hone [houn], *s.* piedra de afilar.—*vt.* afilar, asentar, pulir, esmerilar.

honest [ánįst], *a.* honrado, probo, recto; honesta (mujer).— **—ly** [-lį], *adv.* honradamente; de veras; francamente; honestamente.— **—y** [-į], *s.* honradez, probidad; franqueza; honestidad; bonhomía.

honey [hánį], *s.* miel de abejas; dulzura; querido, querida.— **—comb** [-koųm], *s.* panal de miel.— **—ed** [-d], *a.* dulce, meloso, melifluo.— **—moon** [-mun], *s.* luna de miel.— **—suckle** [-sʌkl], *s.* madreselva.

honk [haŋk], *s.* pitazo, bocinazo (automóvil); graznido.—*vt.* y *vi.* pitar o sonar la bocina; graznar.

honor [ánǫ(r)], *s.* honor, honra; honradez, rectitud; lauro.—*pl.* distinción (en estudios, etc.).—*h. bright,* (fam.) de veras, a fe de caballero.—*on* o *upon my h.,* por mi fe, por mi palabra.—*your H.,* usía, vuestra señoría.—*vt.* honrar; laurear, condecorar; respetar.– **—able** [-ạbl], a. honorable; pundonoroso; honrado; honorífico, honroso, (H.) honorable (tratamiento).– **—ary** [-εrị], a. honorario, honorífico; honroso.

hood [hụd], s. capucha, capucho, caperuza; muceta; fuelle de carruaje; (aut.) cubierta del motor; cubierta, tapa; campana del hogar.—vt. cubrir con caperuza, capucha, etc.; tapar, ocultar.– **—wink** [-wịŋk], vt. engañar.

hoodoo [húdu], s. mal de ojo.—vt. hacer mal de ojo; traer mala suerte.

hoof [hụf], s. casco, uña (del caballo, etc.); pezuña; animal ungulado.— on the h., en pie (ganado), vivo.

hook [hụk], s. gancho, garabato, garfio; anzuelo; grapón; garra; corchete; atractivo, aliciente; (mús.) rabo de una corchea.—vt. enganchar; atraer, engatusar; dar una cornada, coger; pescar; encorvar.—to h. up, conectar; enganchar.— **—ed** [-t], a. enganchado; encorvado, ganchudo, ganchoso; adicto a las drogas; our friends are h. on video games, nuestros amigos están enviciado con los videojuegos.– **—up** [húkʌp], s. (rad.) trasmisión en cadena; cadena de emisoras.— **—y** [-ị], a. ganchudo.—to play h., hacer novillos o rabona, no ir a la escuela o a la clase.

hooligan [húligạn], s. rufián, truhán.—a. de rufianes, truhanesco.– **—ism** [-ịzm], s. truhanería, rufianismo.

hoop [hup], s. aro; fleje, (mec.) collar(ín); anilla, argolla; sortija; miriñaque; grito.—vt. poner aro a; enzunchar; ceñir.—vi. gritar; ojear.

hoot [hut], vi. gritar, ulular, huchear; dar grita; sonar la bocina o el pito.— vt. ridiculizar, abuchear.—s. grita, ruido, clamor, chillido.— **—ing** [hútịŋ], s. grita, rechifla, abucheo.

hop [hap], vti. [1] saltar, brincar; (fam.) alzar el vuelo en (un avión), poner en marcha.—vii. saltar en un pie, andar a saltitos; cojear.—s. salto, brinco; (fam.) baile; lúpulo; (aer.) trayecto de vuelo; (fam.) vuelo.— pl. (com.) lúpulo.

hope [houp], s. esperanza; expectativa.—h. chest, arcón del ajuar.—in hopes, en o con la esperanza.—vt. y vi. esperar, tener esperanza.—to h. against h., esperar lo imposible.–

—ful [hóupfụl], a. esperanzado, confiado.—s. (fam.) joven que promete.– **—fully** [-fụlị], adv. con esperanza.– **—less** [-lịs], a. desahuciado; desesperante, desespera(nza)do; incurable; irremediable.– **—lessness** [-lịsnịs], s. desesperanza; falta de esperanza o remedio.

horde [hɔrd], s. horda; enjambre; hato o manada; muchedumbre.

horizon [horáịzọn], s. horizonte.– **—tal** [harịzántạl], a. y s. horizontal. – **—tality** [harịzantǽlịtị], s. horizontalidad.

hormone [hɔ́rmoụn], s. hormona.

horn [hɔrn], s. cuerno, asta; tentáculo; palpo o antena; (mus.) trompa; corneta de monte. bocina.—pl. cornamenta.—vt. poner cuernos; dar una cornada; dar una cencerrada.

hornet [hɔ́rnịt], s. avispón, moscardón.

horrible [hárịbl], a. horrible, horroroso.– **—horrid** [hárịd], a. horrible, hórrido; ofensivo; dañoso.– **—horrify** [hárịfaị], vti. [7] horrorizar. **—horrifying** [hárịfaịịŋ], a. horripilante. **—horror** [hárọ(r)], s. horror.—h.-stricken, horrorizado.

horse [hɔrs], s. caballo; (mil.) caballería; potro (de carpintero, gimnasia, etc.); caballete, burro, banco.—h. breaker, domador de caballos.—h. dealer, chalán.—h. race, carrera de caballos.—h. racing, carreras de caballos.—h. sense, (fam.) gramática parda, sentido común.— h. show, concurso hípico.—h. thief, cuatrero. **—back** [hɔ́rsbæk], s. lomo de caballo.—to ride h., montar a caballo.– **—fly** [-flaị], s. tábano.– **—hide** [-haịd], s. piel de caballo.– **—laugh(ter)** [-læf(tœ(r))], s. risotada, carcajada.– **—man** [-mạn], s. jinete.– **—manship** [-mạnšịp], s. equitación.– **—power** [-paụœ(r)], s. caballo de fuerza.– **—radish** [-rædịš], s. rábano picante o rústico.– **—shoe** [-šu], s. herradura.– **—tail** [-teịl], s. cola de caballo.– **—whip** [-hwịp], s. látigo, fuete, fusta.—vti. [1] dar fuetazos, azotar con el látigo, etc.– **—woman** [-wụmạn], s. amazona.– **—horsiness** [hɔ́rsịnịs], s. afición a los caballos.– **—horsy** [hɔ́rsị], a. caballar, caballuno; hípico, aficionado a caballos.

hose [hoụz], s. calceta; medias o calzas; manguera, manga de bomba o de riego; tubo flexible de goma.—*h. reel,* carretel de manguera. **—hosiery** [hóu̯ʒœri], *s.* calcetería.

hospice [háspis], *s.* hospicio.

hospitable [háspitabl], *a.* hospitalario. - **—ness** [-nis], *s.* hospitalidad. **—hospital** [háspital], *s.* hospital. **—hospitality** [haspitǽliti], *s.* hospitalidad.

host [houst], *s.* hospedero, huésped; anfitrión; multitud; (H.) (igl.) hostia.

hostage [hástidʒ], *s.* rehén.

hostess [hóustis], *s.* posadera, mesonera; anfitriona; (aer.) azafata.

hostile [hástil], *a.* hostil, enemigo, adverso. **—hostility** [hastíliti], *s.* hostilidad.—*pl.* (actos de) guerra.

hot [hat], *a.* caliente, cálido; caluroso; ardiente, fogoso; picante, acre; violento, furioso; (fam.) intolerable; en caliente; (fam.) cercano (de algo que se busca).—*h.-blooded,* apasionado.—*h. dog,* (fam.) = FRANK-FURTER.—*h.-headed,* fogoso, exaltado.

hotel [hotél], *s.* hotel.—*h. keeper* o *manager,* hotelero, fondista.

hothouse [háthous], *s.* invernadero.

hound [haund], *s.* sabueso, podenco; hombre vil.—*vt.* cazar con perros; soltar los perros; seguir la pista; perseguir; azuzar.

hour [au̯r], *s.* hora.—*pl.* horas (rezos).—*h. hand,* horario (del reloj).- **—ly** [áu̯rli], *adv.* a cada hora; por horas.—*a.* frecuente, por horas.

house [haus], *s.* casa, domicilio, vivienda; familia; linaje; casilla (tablero de damas y ajedrez); casa comercial, razón social; cámara de un cuerpo legislativo; (teat.) sala, público; (mec.) caja, cubierta.—*h. arrest,* arresto domiciliario.—*h. call,* visita a domicilio.—*H. of Commons,* (Lords, Peers, Representatives), Cámara de los Comunes, (Lores, Pares, Cámara de Represen-tantes).—*vt.* albergar, alojar; poner a cubierto; almacenar.- **—breaker** [háu̯sbreı̯kœ(r)], *s.* escalador.- **—breaking** [háu̯sbreı̯kiŋ], *s.* escalo, allanamiento de morada.- **—hold** [-hould], *s.* casa, familia.- **—keeper** [-kipœ(r)], *s.* ama de gobierno o de llaves; mujer de casa.- **—keeping** [-kipiŋ], *s.* manejo doméstico; (comput.) tareas de reorganización de los ficheros.—*a.* doméstico, ca-

sero, provisto de facilidades para cocinar.- **—top** [-tap], *s.* tejado, techo, azotea.- **—wife** [-wai̯f], *s.* ama de casa; madre de familia.- **—work** [-wœrk], *s.* tareas domésticas. **—housing** [háu̯ziŋ], *s.* alojamiento, vivienda; almacenaje.

hove [houv], *pret.* y *pp.* de TO HEAVE.

hovel [hável], *s.* cobertizo, choza, cabaña, casucha, tugurio.

hover [hávœ(r)], *vt.* cubrir con las alas.—*vi.* revolotear; cernerse (las aves, y fig.) rondar; estar suspenso; dudar.- **—ing** [-iŋ], *s.* revoloteo.

how [hau̯], *adv.* cómo; cuán, cuánto; a cómo.—*h. about it?* ¿qué le parece? ¿y si lo hiciéramos?—*h. do you do?* ¿cómo le va? ¿cómo está usted?—*h. early?* ¿cuándo, a más tardar?—*h. far?* ¿a qué distancia? ¿hasta dónde?—*h. late? ¿a qué hora? ¿hasta qué hora? ¿cuándo?—h. long?* ¿cuánto tiempo? ¿cuánto demo-rará?—*h. many?* ¿cuántos?—*h. much?* ¿cuánto?—*h. now?* ¿y bien? ¿pues qué? ¿qué significa eso?—*h. often?* ¿con qué frecuencia? ¿cuántas veces?—*h. pretty!* ¡qué bonito! —*h. so?* ¿cómo así?—*h. soon?* ¿cuándo? ¿con qué rapidez?—*h. well!* ¡qué bien!—*s.* cómo, modo, manera.- **—belt** [hau̯bít], *adv.* sea como fuere; no obstante.- **—ever** [hau̯évœ(r)], *adv.* como quiera que, de cualquier modo; por muy.— *conj.* no obstante, sin embargo.

howitzer [háu̯isœ(r)], *s.* (arti.) obús.

howl [hau̯l], *vi.* aullar, dar alaridos; ulular; rugir; bramar.—*vt.* gritar; condenar o echar a gritos.—*s.* aullido; alarido; gemido; rugido; bramido.

hub [hʌb], *s.* cubo de la rueda; por extensión, centro, eje; calzo.- **—bub** [hábʌb], *s.* grita, alboroto, bulla.

huckster [hákstœ(r)], *s.* vendedor ambulante; sujeto ruin.

huddle [hádl], *vt.* amontonar desordenadamente atrabancar.—*vi.* acurrucarse; apiñarse.—*s.* tropel, confusión; (fam.) junta o reunión secreta.

hue [hju], *s.* matiz, tinte; grita, clamor.—*h. and cry,* alarma, vocerío.— *many-hued,* matizado.

hug [hʌg], *vti.* [1] abrazar; abrazarse a; navegar muy cerca de la costa. —*to h. one's self,* congratularse.—*s.* abrazo apretado.

huge [hjudʒ], a. inmenso, enorme, vasto, colosal.– **—ness** [hjúdʒnis], s. enormidad, inmensidad.

hulk [hʌlk], s. casco de barco; barco viejo; armatoste.– **—ing** [hálkiŋ], a. tosco, grueso.

hull [hʌl], s. cáscara, corteza; vaina de legumbre; casco (de un buque); flotador (de aeroplano); armazón.— vt. descascarar; desvainar; deshollejar.

hum [hʌm], vti. [1] canturrear, tararear.—vii. zumbar; susurrar.—s. zumbido; susurro; voz inarticulada (¡hum!); (fam.) engaño, filfa, chasco.

human [hjúman], a. humano.—h. being, ser humano.—h. race, género humano.—s. mortal, ser humano. – **—e** [hjuméjn], a. humano, benévolo, compasivo; humanitario.– **—itarian** [hjúmænitérian], a. humanitario.—s. filántropo.– **—itarianism** [hjúmænitérianizm], s. humanitarismo.– **—ity** [hjumǽniti], s. humanidad.—pl. humanidades.– **—ize** [hjúmanajz], vt. y vi. humanizar(se).– **—kind** [hjúmankajnd], s. humanidad, género humano.

Human Immunodeficiency Virus (HIV), virus de inmunodeficiencia humana (VIH).

humble [hámbl], a. humilde.—vt. humillar, someter.—vi. bajar la cerviz. – **—ness** [-nis], s. humildad.

humbug [hámbʌg], s. farsa, patraña, fraude; farsante.

humdrum [hámdrʌm], a. monótono, pesado, cansado.—s. fastidio, lata, aburrimiento; posma.

humid [hjúmid], a. húmedo. **—humidify** [hjumídifaj], vti. [7] humedecer.— **—ity** [hjumíditi], s. humedad.

humiliate [hjumíljeit], vt. humillar. **—humiliation** [hjumiljéjṣọn], s. humillación. **—humility** [hjumíliti], s. humildad, sumisión.

humming [hámiŋ], s. zumbido; susurro; canturreo.—a. zumbador; (fam.) muy activo, intenso. **—hummingbird** [hámiŋbœrd], s. colibrí, pájaro mosca, tominejo.

humor [hjúmọ(r)], s. humor, carácter; humorada, fantasía, capricho; humorismo; agudeza, chiste; (med.) humor.—to be in a bad h. o out of h., estar de mal humor.—vt. contemporizar, seguir el humor, consentir,

mimar.– **—ous** [-ʌs], a. humorístico.

hump [hʌmp], s. giba, joroba.—vi. encorvarse.– **—back** [hámpbæk], s. giba, joroba; jorobado.– **—backed** [-bækt], a. jorobado, giboso, corcovado.– **—y** [-j], a. giboso.

hunch [hʌnch], vt. empujar, dar empellones; doblar la espalda.—vi. moverse o avanzar a tirones o a sacudidas; abalanzarse.—s. giba, corcova; pedazo o trozo grueso; (fam.) corazonada, presentimiento.– **—back** [hánchbæk], s. joroba; jorobado.– **—backed** [-bækt], a. jorobado.

hundred [hándred], a. cien(to).—s. ciento; (arit.) centena, centenar.— by hundreds, a (o por) centenares.— by the h., por ciento(s); por centenares.—h. and one, ciento uno.—one h., ciento.– **—fold** [-foṵld], s. céntuplo.– **—th** [-θ], a. y s. centésimo, céntimo; ciento (ordinal).– **—weight** [-wejt], s. quintal. Ver Tabla.

hung [hʌŋ], pret. y pp. de TO HANG (colgar).

Hungarian [hʌŋgérian], a. y s. húngaro.—s. lengua húngara.

hunger [háŋgœ(r)], s. hambre.—h. strike, huelga de hambre.—vt. hambrear.—vi. hambrear, tener hambre.—to h. for, anhelar, tener hambre de. **—hungry** [háŋgri], a. hambriento; deseoso; estéril, pobre.—to be o feel h., tener hambre, estar hambriento.

hunk [hʌŋk], s. (fam.) buen pedazo; rebanada gruesa.

hunt [hʌnt], vt. cazar; perseguir, seguir; recorrer buscando.—to h. up, buscar.—to h. up and down, buscar por todas partes.—vi. cazar; buscar.—to h. after, buscar, anhelar.—to h. counter, ir contra la pista.—s. caza, cacería; acosamiento.– **—er** [hántœ(r)], s. cazador, montero; podenco; caballo de caza.– **—ing** [-iŋ], s. montería, caza, cacería.—h.-box, pabellón de caza.– **—ress** [-ris], s. cazadora.– **—sman** [-sman], s. montero, cazador.

hurdle [hœrdl], s. valla (portátil); (fig.) obstáculo.—pl. (dep.) carrera de obstáculos.

hurdy-gurdy [hœrdi gœrdi], s. organillo; zanfona.

hurl [hœrl], vt. tirar, lanzar, arrojar,

echar; proferir.—*vr.* lanzarse, abalanzarse.—*s.* tiro, lanzamiento.

hurrah [hurá], *interj.* ¡viva! ¡hurra!—*vt.* y *vi.* aclamar, vitorear.

hurricane [hǽrikein], *s.* huracán, ciclón.—*h. lamp,* farol.

hurried [hǽrid], *a.* precipitado, apresurado, hecho de prisa. **—hurry** [hǽri], *vti.* y *vii.* [7] apresurar(se); dar(se) prisa; obrar a la carrera o con precipitación.—*to h. after,* correr detrás o en pos de.—*to h. away,* salir precipitadamente.—*to h. back,* volver de prisa; apresurarse a volver.— *to h. off,* huir, salir o hacer marchar de prisa.—*to h. on,* apresurar, precipitar; impulsar; apresurarse.—*to h. over,* (hacer) pasar rápidamente; despachar, expedir.—*to h. up,* apresurarse, darse prisa.—*s.* prisa, premura, precipitación, apuro.—*there is no h. about it,* no corre prisa.—*to be in a h.,* tener prisa.

hurt [hœrt], *vti.* [9] dañar, hacer mal o daño, lastimar, herir; injuriar, ofender; perjudicar.—*to h. one's feelings,* herirle a uno el amor propio, ofenderlo.—*vii.* doler.—*pret.* y *pp.* de TO HURT.—*s.* lesión, herida, contusión; daño, perjuicio.—*a.* lastimado, herido, perjudicado.

husband [hǽzband], *s.* marido, esposo. **– —ry** [-ri], *s.* labranza, agricultura.

hush [hʌʃ], *vt.* apaciguar, aquietar; hacer callar.—*to h. up,* tapar, ocultar; mantener secreto.—*vi.* estar quieto, callar.—*s.* silencio, quietud.—*h. money,* dinero para soborno o cohecho.—*very h.-h.,* muy secreto.

husk [hʌsk], *s.* cáscara, vaina, pellejo, hollejo; bagazo; desperdicio.—*vt.* descascarar, desvainar, pelar.– **—y** [háski], *a.* cascarudo; ronco.—*a.* y *s.* (fam.) fuerte, fornido.—*s.* perro esquimal; un dialecto esquimal.

hussy [hʌsi], *s.* sota, mujerzuela.

hustle [hʌsl], *vt.* mezclar, confundir; empujar, atropellar, sacudir.—*vi.* andar a empellones; (fam.) patear.—*h. and bustle,* vaivén.

hut [hʌt], *s.* choza, cabaña, barraca; cobertizo; (Am.) bohío.

hyacinth [háiasinθ], *s.* jacinto.

hybrid [háibrid], *a.* y *s.* híbrido.

hyena [haíná], *s.* hiena.

hydrant [háidrant], *s.* boca de riego. **—hydraulic(al)** [haidrólik(al)], *a.* hidráulico. **—hydrocarbon** [haidrocárbon], *s.* hidrocarburo. **—hydrogen** [háidrodžin], *s.* hidrógeno. **—hydroplane** [-plein], *s.* hidroplano.

hygiene [háidžin], **hygienics** [haidziéniks], *s.* higiene.

hymen [háimen], *s.* himeneo; himen.

hymn [him], *s.* himno.

hyphen [háifen], *s.* raya, guión.

hypocrisy [hipákrisi], *s.* hipocresía. **—hypocrite** [hípokrit], *s.* hipócrita. **—hypocritical** [hipokrítikal], *a.* hipócrita.

hypothesis [haipáθesis], *s.* hipótesis, supuesto.

hysteria [histíria], *s.* histeria. **—hysteric(al)** [histérik(al)], *a.* histérico. **—hysterics** [histériks], *s.* = HYSTERIA.

I [ai], *pron. pers.* yo.

Iberian [aibírian], *a.* ibérico.—*a.* y *s.* ibero.

ice [ais], *s.* hielo; (coc.) sorbete.—*i. age,* época glacial.—*i. bag,* bolsa para hielo.—*i. cream,* helado.—*i.-cream cone,* cucurucho de helado, barquillo de helado.—*i.-cream sundae,* copa de helado.—*i. cube,* cubito de hielo.—*i. hockey,* hockey sobre patines.—*i. skate,* patín de cuchilla.—*vi.* patinar sobre hielo.—*i.*

skater, patinador.—*i. skating,* patinaje sobre hielo.—*i. tray,* bandejito de hielo.—*i. water,* agua helada.—*to skate on thin i.,* (fam.) buscar el peligro.—*vt.* helar, enfriar con hielo; (coc.) garapiñar.– **—berg** [aisbœrg], *s.* banquisa, iceberg.– **—boat** [-bout], *s.* rompehielos.– **—box** [-baks], *s.* nevera.– **—breaker** [-breikœr], *s.* rompehielos.– **—d** [-t], *a.* congelado; enfriado con hielo.

Icelander [áislạndœ(r)], s. islandés.
—**Icelandic** [aislǽndik], a. y s. islandés.—s. lengua islandesa.

iceman [áismæn], s. vendedor de hielo. —**icicle** [áisikl], s. carámbano. —**iciness** [áisinis], s. frigidez. —**icing** [áisiŋ], s. (coc.) garapiña. —**icy** [áisi], a. helado, frío; cubierto de hielo.

idea [aidíạ], s. idea.—**l** [aidíạl], s. y a. ideal.—**lism** [aidíạlizm], s. idealismo.—**list** [aidíạlist], s. idealista.—**lize** [aidíạlaiz], vt. idealizar.

identical [aidéntikạl], a. idéntico. —**identification** [aidentifikéisọn], s. identificación. —**identify** [aidéntifai], vti. [7] identificar. —**identity** [aidéntiti], s. identidad.

ideological [aidioládžikạl], a. ideológico. —**ideology** [aidiálodži], s. ideología.

idiocy [ídiọsi], s. idiotez; imbecilidad.

idiom [ídiọm], s. modismo, idiotismo; habla, lenguaje.

idiot [ídiọt], s. idiota.—**ic** [idiátik], a. idiota.

idle [áidl], a. ocioso; inútil, vano, frívolo.—i. money, capital improductivo.—vi. holgazanear o haraganear; holgar, estar ocioso; (aut.) marchar en ralentí, marchar en vacío.—vt. (generalmente con away) gastar ociosamente.- —**ness** [-nis], s. ociosidad, ocio; pereza, holgazanería, haraganería; inutilidad.- —**r** [áidlœ(r)], s. holgazán, perezoso. —**idly** [áidli], adv. ociosamente; desidiosamente; inútilmente.

idol [áidọl], s. ídolo.- —**ater** [aidálạtœ(r)], s. idólatra.- —**atry** [aidálạtri], s. idolatría.- —**ize** [áidọlaiz], vt. idolatrar.

if [if], conj. si; supuesto que; con tal que; aunque; aun cuando.—as i., como si.—even i., aunque.—i. so, si es así.—s. hipótesis, suposición; condición.

ignite [ignáit], vt. encender.—vi. encenderse. —**ignition** [igníşọn], s. ignición; encendido (del motor).—i. switch, interruptor de encendido.

ignoble [ignóubl], a. innoble.

ignorance [ígnorạns], s. ignorancia. —**ignorant** [ígnorạnt], a. ignorante. —**ignore** [ignór], vt. pasar por alto, no hacer caso de.

illegal [ilígạl], a. ilegal, ilícito.- —**ity** [iligǽliti], s. ilegalidad.

illegible [ilédžibl], a. ilegible.

illegitimacy [ilidžítimạsi], s. ilegitimidad. —**illegitimate** [ilidžítimit], a. ilegítimo.

ill [il], a. enfermo; malo.—i. fame, mala fama.—i. health, mala salud.—i. will, mala voluntad.—s. mal.—adv. mal.—i.-advised, desaconsejado.—i. at ease, incómodo.—i.-bred, malcriado.—i.-considered, desconsiderado.—i.-disposed, malintencionado.—i.-fated, aciago, funesto.—i.-gotten, mal ganado. —i. humored, malhumorado.—i.-mannered, de malos modales.—i. spent, malgastado.—i.-starred, malhadado.—i.-tempered, de mal genio.—i.-timed, inoportuno.—to i.-treat, maltratar.—to take i., tomar a mal; caer enfermo.

illicit [ilísit], a. lícito; ilegal.

illiteracy [ilíterạsi], s. analfabetismo; ignorancia. —**illiterate** [ilíterit], a. y s. analfabeto; ignorante.

illness [ílnis], s. enfermedad, mal.

illogical [iládžikạl], a. ilógico.

illuminate [iljúmineit], vt. iluminar, alumbrar; (a manuscript) iluminar, minear. —**illumination** [iljuminéişọn], s. iluminación.

illusion [iljúżọn], s. ilusión.—to cause i., ilusionar. —**illusive** [iljúsiv], a. ilusivo. —**illusory** [iljúsori], a. ilusorio.

illustrate [ílʌstreit], vt. ilustrar, explicar, esclarecer con ejemplos. —**illustration** [ilʌstréişọn], s. ejemplo, aclaración; (b.a.) grabado, ilustración, lámina. —**illustrator** [ílʌstreitọ(r)], s. ilustrador. —**illustrious** [ilástriʌs], a. ilustre, preclaro.

image [ímidž], s. imagen.—the very i. of, la propia estampa de.- —**ry** [-ri], s. fantasía; conjunto de imágenes. —**imaginable** [imǽdžinạbl], a. imaginable. —**imaginary** [imǽdžineri], a. imaginario. —**imagination** [imædžinéişọn], s. imaginación; inventiva. —**imaginative** [imǽdžineitiv], a. imaginativo; imaginario. —**imagine** [imǽdžin], vt. imaginarse, figurarse.—vt. imaginar.

imbecile [ímbisil], a. y s. imbécil. —**becility** [imbisíliti], s. imbecilidad.

imbibe [imbáib], vt. embeber, absorber; empapar(se); saturarse de.

imitate [ímiteit], vt. imitar, remedar. —**imitation** [imitéişọn], s. imitación.—a. de imitación. —**imitator** [ímiteitọ(r)], s. imitador.

immaculate [imǽkyulit], a. inmaculado, sin mancha; impecable.

immaterial [imatírial], a. inmaterial; poco importante.—to be i., no importar, ser indiferente.

immature [imachúr], a. inmaturo, verde; prematuro.

immediate [imídiit], a. inmediato, cercano; próximo.— —ly [-li], adv. inmediatamente, en seguida.

immense [iméns], a. inmenso, vasto. —immensity [ménsiti], s. inmensidad.

immerse [imórs], vt. sumergir. —immersion [imórshon], s. inmersión; bautismo por inmersión.

immigrant [ímigrant], a. y s. inmigrante. —immigrate [ímigreit], vi. inmigrar. —immigration [imigréishon], s. inmigración.

imminent [íminent], a. inminente.

immobile [imóubil], a. inmóvil, inmovible, inmoble. —immobility [imoubíliti], s. inmovilidad. —immobilize [imóubilaiz], vt. inmovilizar.

immodest [imádist], a. inmodesto.

immoral [imáral], a. inmoral.— —ity [imorǽliti], s. inmoralidad.

immortal [imórtal], a. y s. inmortal.— —ity [imortǽliti], s. inmortalidad.— —ize [imórtalaiz], vt. inmortalizar.

immovable [imúvabl], a. inamovible; inquebrantable.

immune [imjún], a. y s. inmune. —immunity [imjúniti], s. inmunidad. —immunization [imjunizéishon], s. inmunización. —immunize [ímjunaiz], vt. inmunizar.

imp [imp], s. diablillo, trasgo.

impact [ímpækt], s. impacto, choque.

impair [impér], vt. empeorar, deteriorar.— —ment [-ment], s. empeoramiento, deterioro.

impart [impárt], vt. impartir, comunicar, hacer saber.

impartial [impárshal], a. imparcial.— —ity [imparshiǽliti], s. imparcialidad.

impassable [impǽsabl], a. intransitable.

impassioned [impǽshond], a. apasionado, vehemente.

impassive [impǽsiv], a. impasible.

impatience [impéishens], s. impaciencia. —impatient [impéishent], a. impaciente.

impeach [impích], vt. residenciar.— —ment [-ment], s. residencia.

impeccable [impékabl], a. impecable.

impede [impíd], vt. estorbar, dificultar.

—impediment [impédiment], s. impedimento.—speech i., defecto del habla.

impel [impél], vti. [1] impeler, impulsar.

impending [impéndin], a. inminente.

impenetrable [impénitrabl], a. impenetrable.

impenitent [impénitent], a. impenitente.

imperative [impérativ], a. imperativo, imperioso.—s. imperativo.

imperceptible [impœrséptibl], a. imperceptible.

imperfect [impœrfikt], a. y s. imperfecto.— —ion [impœrfékshon], s. imperfección.

imperial [impírial], a. imperial.- —ism [-izm], s. imperialismo.- —ist [-ist], s. imperialista.

imperious [impíriʌs], a. imperioso.

impersonal [impœrsonal], a. impersonal.

impersonate [impœrsoneit], vt. personificar; (teat.) representar; imitar. —impersonation [impœrsonéishon], s. imitación.

impertinence [impœrtinens], impertinency [impœrtinensi], s. impertinencia. —impertinent [impœrtinent], a. impertinente.

imperturbable [impœrtœrbabl], a. imperturbable.

impervious [impœrviʌs], a. impermeable.—i. to, insensible a.

impetuosity [impechuásiti], s. impetuosidad. —impetuous [impéchuʌs], a. impetuoso. —impetus [ímpitʌs], s. ímpetu.

impiety [impáieti], s. impiedad. —impious [ímpiʌs], a. impío.

implacable [impléikabl], a. implacable.

implement [ímpliment], s. herramienta, utensilio; instrumento.—vt. poner por obra, llevar a cabo.

implicate [ímplikeit], vt. implicar, envolver. —implication [implikéishon], s. consecuencia; implicación.

implicit [implísit], a. implícito, tácito; incondicional, absoluto, ciego.

implore [implór], vt. implorar, suplicar.

imply [impláí], vti. [7] querer decir, dar a entender, insinuar; implicar.

impolite [impoláit], a. descortés.

import [impórt], vt. (com.) importar; significar.—vi. importar.—s. [ímport], significación, importancia; artículo importado.- —ance [im-

pórtans], s. importancia.——ant [im-
pórtant], a. importante.- —ation
[importéişon], s. (com.) importación.- —er [impórtœ(r)], s. importador.
importune [importjún], vt. y vi. importunar.
impose [impóuz], vt. imponer.—to i.
on o upon, abusar de. —imposing
[impóuzin], a. imponente. —imposition [impozíşon], s. imposición;
abuso, molestia.
impossibility [impasibíliti], s. imposibilidad. —impossible [impásibl], a.
imposible.
impostor [impásto(r)], s. impostor.
—imposture [impáschu(r)], s. impostura.
impotence [ímpotens], s. impotencia.
—impotent [ímpotent], a. impotente.
impoverish [impávœriş], vt. empobrecer.
impracticable [impræktikabl], a. impracticable; intratable.
impregnate [imprégneit], vt. impregnar; fecundizar, empreñar.
impress [imprés], vt. imprimir; grabar;
impresionar.- —ion [impréşon],
s. impresión.- —ionable [impréşonabl], a. impresionable. —ive
[imprésiv], a. impresionante.
imprint [imprínt], vt. imprimir, estampar.—s. [ímprint], impresión; pie
de imprenta.
imprison [imprízon], vt. encarcelar.-
—ment [-ment], s. encarcelamiento.
improbable [imprábabl], a. improbable.
impromptu [imprámptyu], a. improvisado.—adv. de improviso.—s. improvisación; (mus.) impromptu.
improper [imprápœ(r)], a. impropio;
indecoroso.
improve [imprúv], vt. mejorar; perfeccionar.—vi. mejorarse; mejorar.-
—ment [-ment], s. mejoramiento;
mejoría.
improvisation [impravizéişon], s. improvisación. —improvise [improváiz], vt. improvisar.
imprudence [imprúdens], s. imprudencia, indiscreción. —imprudent
[imprúdent], a. imprudente.
impudence [ímpjudens], s. insolencia,
descaro.—impudent [ímpjudent], a.
descarado, insolente.
impulse [ímpals], s. impulso; estímulo. —impulsive [impálsiv], a. impulsivo.

impure [impiúr], a. impuro. —impurity
[impiúriti], s. impureza.
in [in], prep. en, de, por, con, mientras,
dentro de.—i. haste, de prisa.—i. so
far as, o insofar as, en cuanto (a),
hasta donde.—adv. dentro, adentro; en casa.—i. here, there, etc., aquí
dentro, allí dentro, etc.—to be all i.,
estar rendido, agotado.—to be i., haber llegado; estar (en casa, en la oficina, etc.).—to be i. with someone,
gozar del favor de alguien.
inability [inabíliti], s. inhabilidad, incapacidad, ineptitud.
inaccessible [inæksésibl], a. inaccesible.
inaccurate [inækyurit], a. inexacto,
erróneo, incorrecto.
inactive [inæktiv], a. inactivo. —inactivity [inæktíviti], s. inactividad.
inadequate [inædikwit], a. inadecuado.
inadmissible [inædmísibl], a. inadmisible.
inadvertence [inædvœrtens], s. inadvertencia. —inadvertent [inædvœrtent], a. inadvertido, accidental.
inalienable [inéilyenabl], a. inalienable.
inanimate [inénimit], a. inanimado.
inasmuch as [inazmách az], adv. en
cuanto; tanto como; como quiera
que, puesto que, visto que, por
cuanto.
inaugural [inógiural], a. inaugural.
—inaugurate [inógiureit], vt. inaugurar. —inauguration [inogiuréişon], s. inauguración; toma de posesión.
inborn [ínborn], a. innato, ingénito.
Inc., abrev. (**Incorporated** constituido
en sociedad anónima) S. A. (Sociedad Anónima).
Inca [inkã], s. inca.—a. inca, incaico.
incalculable [inkǽlkiuabl], a. incalculable.
incandescent [inkændésent], a. incandescente, candente.
incapable [inkéipabl], a. incapaz. —incapacitate [inkapǽsiteit], vt. incapacitar, inhabilitar. —incapacity
[inkapǽsiti], s. incapacidad.
incarcerate [inkársereit], vt. encarcelar.
incarnate [inkárneit], vt. encarnar.—
a. [inkárnit], encarnado; personificado. —incarnation [inkarnéişon],
s. encarnación.
incendiary [inséndjeri], a. y s. incendiario.

incense [ínsens], s. incienso.—vt. [in-séns], exasperar, irritar.

incentive [inséntiv], a. y s. incentivo.

incessant [insésant], a. incesante.

incest [ínsest], s. incesto.

inch [inch], s. pulgada.—by inches, paso a paso, con gran lentitud.—every i., cabal, en todo respecto.—i. by i., palmo a palmo, pulgada por pulgada.—within an i. of, a dos dedos de.—a. de una pulgada.—vi. (con along) avanzar poquito a poquito.

incident [ínsident], s. incidente.— **al** [insidéntal], a. incidental; concomitante.—s. pl. gastos imprevistos; circunstancias imprevistas.

incinerator [insínereito(r)], s. incinerador.

incision [insíẑon], s. incisión. —**incisor** [insáiẑo(r)], a. y s. incisivo.

incite [insáit], vt. incitar, instigar.

inclination [inklinéiẑon], s. inclinación; pendiente, declive. —**incline** [inkláin], vt. inclinar.—vi. inclinarse, ladearse.—s. [ínklain], declive, pendiente.

inclose [inklóuz], vt. = ENCLOSE. —**inclosure** [inklóuẑu(r)], s. = ENCLOSURE.

include [inklúd], vt. incluir, comprender. —**inclusion** [inklúẑon], s. inclusión. —**inclusive** [inklúsiv], a. inclusivo.

incoherent [inkohírent], a. incoherente, inconexo.

income [ínkʌm], s. ingresos, entrada, renta, rédito, utilidades.—gross i., entrada bruta.—i. tax, impuesto sobre los ingresos, impuesto sobre rentas.—i. tax return, declaración de impuesto sobre rentas.—taxable i., renta gravable.

incomparable [inkámparabl], a. incomparable, sin igual.

incompetence [inkámpitens], s. incompetencia. —**incompetent** [inkámpitent], a. incompetente.

incomplete [inkomplít], a. incompleto.

incomprehensible [inkamprihénsibl], a. incomprensible.

incongruous [inkángruʌs], a. incongruente; inapropiado, extraño, raro.

inconsiderate [inkonsídœrit], a. desconsiderado; desatento.

inconsistency [inkonsístensi], s. inconsistencia; inconsecuencia. —**inconsistent** [inkonsístent], a. inconsistente; inconsecuente.

inconstancy [inkánstansi], s. inconstancia. —**inconstant** [inkánstant], a. inconstante, vario.

inconvenience [inkonvíniens], s. inconveniencia, inconveniente; incomodidad, molestia.—vt. incomodar, estorbar, molestar. —**inconvenient** [inkonvíniǝnt], a. inconveniente, inoportuno, molesto, incómodo.

incorporate [inkórporeit], vt. incorporar; constituir en sociedad anónima.—vi. incorporarse; constituirse en sociedad anónima. —**incorporation** [inkɔrporeíẑon], s. incorporación; constitución en sociedad anónima.

incorrect [inkorékt], a. incorrecto.

increase [inkrís], vt. y vi. aumentar(se); multiplicarse.—s. [ínkris], aumento, incremento. —**increasingly** [inkrísinli], adv. cada vez más.

incredible [inkrédibl], a. increíble. —**incredulity** [inkridiúliti], s. incredulidad. —**incredulous** [inkrédẓulʌs], a. incrédulo.

increment [ínkriment], s. incremento.

incriminate [inkrímineit], vt. incriminar.

incubation [inkiubéiẑon], s. incubación. —**incubator** [ínkiubeito(r)], s. incubadora.

incumbency [inkámbensi], s. incumbencia. —**incumbent** [inkámbent], s. titular.—a.—to be i. on, incumbir a.

incur [inkœr], vti. [1] incurrir (en); atraerse.—to i. a debt, contraer una deuda.

incurable [inkiúrabl], a. y s. incurable.

incursion [inkœrẑon], s. incursión, correría.

indebted [indétid], a. adeudado; obligado.

indecency [indísensi], s. indecencia. —**indecent** [indísent], a. indecente; indecoroso.—i. exposure, (jur.) exhibicionismo.

indecision [indisíẑon], s. indecisión.

indeed [indíd], adv. verdaderamente, claro.—interrog. ¿de veras? ¿es posible?—interj. ¡de veras!

indefatigable [indifǽtigabl], a. incansable, infatigable.

indefensible [indifénsibl], a. indefendible, insostenible.

indefinite [indéfinit], a. indefinido.

indelible [indélibl], a. indeleble.

indelicate [indélikit], a. indelicado.

indemnify [indémnifai], vti. [7] indemnizar. —**indemnity** [indémnɪti], s. indemnización.

Indent [indént], vt. dentar, endentar; (impr.) sangrar.

Independence [indipéndəns], s. independencia. —**independent** [indipéndənt], a. independiente.

indescribable [indiskráibəbl], a. indescriptible.

indeterminate [indɪtœrmɪnɪt], a. indeterminado.

index [índeks], s. índice.—*i. card,* ficha, tarjeta índice.—*i. finger,* dedo índice.—*i. tab,* pestaña.—vt. poner índice a; poner en un índice; clasificar; (com.) indexar, indiciar.

India [índiə], s. la India.—*I. ink,* tinta china.

Indian [índiən], a. y s. indio.—*I. file,* fila india; en fila india.—*I. Ocean,* Océano Indico.—*I. summer,* veranillo de San Martín.

indicate [índikeit], vt. indicar. —**indication** [indikéiʃən], s. indicación. —**indicative** [indíkətiv], a. y s. indicativo.

indict [indáit], vt. (for.), procesamiento; (for.) auto de acusación formulado por el gran jurado; crítica. procesar. —**ment** [-mənt], s. (for.) acusación.

indifference [indífərəns], s. indiferencia. —**indifferent** [indífərənt], a. indiferente; pasadero, mediano.

indigenous [indídʒənʌs], a. indígena.

indigestion [indidʒéschən], s. indigestión.

indignant [indígnənt], a. indignado.—**ly** [-li], adv. con indignación. —**indignation** [indignéiʃən], s. indignación. —**indignity** [indígniti], s. indignidad.

indigo [índigou], a. azul de añil.—s. índigo.

indirect [indirékt], a. indirecto.

indiscreet [indiskrít], a. indiscreto. —**indiscretion** [indiskréʃən], s. indiscreción.

indispensable [indispénsəbl], a. indispensable, inprescindible; de rigor.

indispose [indispóuz], vt. indisponer. —**d** [-d], a. indispuesto; maldispuesto. —**indisposition** [indispozíʃən], s. indisposición; malestar.

indistinct [indistíŋkt], a. indistinto.

individual [individʒuəl], a. individual.—s. individuo.— **ity** [individʒuǽliti], s. individualidad, personalidad.

indivisible [indivízibl], a. indivisible.

Indo-Chinese [índou chainíz], a. y s. indochino.

indoctrinate [indáktrineit], vt. adoctrinar.

indolence [índoləns], s. indolencia. —**indolent** [índolənt], a. indolente.

indomitable [indámitəbl], a. indomable.

indoor [índɔr], a. interior; casero.- —**s** [índɔrz], adv. (a)dentro; en casa; bajo techado, bajo cubiero.

indorse [indɔrs], vt. (com.) endosar; apoyar, aprobar.- —**e** [-í], s. endosatario.- —**ment** [-mənt], s. endoso; apoyo, aprobación. —**r** [indɔrsœ(r)], s. endosante.

induce [indjús], vt. inducir, persuadir.- —**ment** [-mənt], s. aliciente, estímulo, incentivo.

induct [indʌkt], vt. instalar; iniciar.- —**ion** [indákʃən], s. (elec. y lóg.) inducción.—*i. valve,* válvula de admisión.

indulge [indáldʒ], vt. mimar; gratificar;—vi. (con **in**) entregarse a; gustar de.- —**nce** [indáldʒəns], s. indulgencia; exceso, complacencia, favor.- —**nt** [indáldʒənt], a. indulgente.

industrial [indástriəl], a. industrial.- —**ist** [-ist], s. industrial.- —**ization** [-izéiʃən], s. industrialización.- —**ize** [-aiz], vt. industrializar. —**industrious** [indástriʌs], a. industrioso, aplicado. —**industry** [índʌstri], s. industria.

ineffective [inɛféktiv], a. ineficaz, inefectivo. —**ineffectual** [inɛfékchuəl], a. ineficaz, fútil. —**inefficacy** [inéfikəsi], **inefficiency** [inɛfíʃənsi], s. ineficacia; futilidad. —**inefficient** [inɛfíʃənt], a. ineficaz, de mal rendimiento.

ineligible [inélidʒibl], a. inelegible.

inept [inépt], a. inepto.- —**itude** [-itjud], s. ineptitud, inhabilidad.

inequality [inikwáliti], s. desigualdad.

inert [inœrt], a. inerte.- —**ia** [inœrʃiə], s. inercia.

inestimable [inéstiməbl], a. inestimable, inapreciable.

inevitable [inévitəbl], a. inevitable.

inexpensive [inɛkspénsiv], a. barato.

inexperience [inɛkspíriəns], s. inexperiencia.- —**d** [-t], **inexpert** [inɛkspœrt], a. inexperto, bisoño. —**inexpertness** [inɛkspœrtnis], s. impericia.

inexplicable [inéksplikabl], a. inexplicable.

inexpressible [ineksprésibl], a. inexpresable, indecible, inefable.

infallibility [infælibíliti], s. infalibilidad. —**infallible** [infælibl], a. infalible.

infamous [ínfamʌs], a. infame. —**infamy** [ínfami], s. infamia.

infancy [ínfansi], s. infancia. —**infant** [ínfant], s. infante.—a. infantil; naciente. —**infantile** [ínfantil], a. infantil.

infantry [ínfantri], s. infantería.— —**man** [-man], s. soldado de infantería.

infect [infékt], vt. infectar, inficionar. —**ion** [infékšon], s. infección.— —**ious** [infékšʌs], a. infeccioso.

infer [infœr], vti. [1] inferir, colegir, deducir.— —**ence** [ínferens], s. inferencia.— —**entially** [inferénšali], adv. por inferencia.

inferior [infírio(r)], s. and a. inferior.— —**ity** [infiriáriti], s. inferioridad.

infernal [infœrnal], a. infernal. —**inferno** [infœrnou], s. infierno.

infest [infést], vt. infestar, plagar.

infidel [ínfidel], a. y s. infiel. —**ity** [infidéliti], s. infidelidad.

infield [ínfild], s. (dep.) cuadro interior.

infighting [ínfaitin], s. luchas internas; (dep.) combate cerrado.

infiltrate [ínfiltreit], vt. y vi. infiltrar(se) (en). —**infiltration** [infiltréišon], s. infiltración.

infinite [ínfinit], a. y s. infinito. —**infinitive** [infínitiv], s. y a. infinitivo. —**infinity** [infíniti], s. infinidad. (mat.) infinito.

infirm [infœrm], a. achacoso, inferme. —**ary** [-ari], s. enfermería.— —**ity** [-iti], s. enfermedad, dolencia, achaque.

inflame [infléim], vt. inflamar. —**inflammable** [inflæmabl], a. inflamable. —**inflammation** [inflaméišon], s. inflamación.

inflate [infléit], vt. inflar.—vi. inflarse. — —**d** [infléitid], a. inflado, exagerado; (with air or gas) inflado, hinchado. —**inflation** [infléišon], s. inflación.

inflect [inflékt], vt. torcer, doblar; modular; (gram.) declinar, conjugar.— —**ion** [inflékšon], s. inflexión, dobladura; acento, modulación; flexión, conjugación, declinación.

inflexibility [infleksibíliti], s. inflexibilidad. —**inflexible** [infléksibl], a. inflexible.

inflict [inflíkt], vt. infligir, imponer.— —**ion** [inflíkšon], s. imposición.

influence [ínfluens], s. influencia.— vt. influir; sobre, influenciar. —**influential** [influénšal], a. influyente.

influenza [influénzǎ], s. influenza.

influx [ínflʌks], s. (in)flujo; afluencia.

inform [infórm], vt. informar, comunicar; avisar.—vi. soplar, delatar.—to i. against, denunciar a, delatar a.— —**al** [-al], a. sin ceremonia.— —**ality** [infórmæliti], s. informalidad.— —**ation** [infórméišon], s. informes, información.— —**er** [infórmœ(r)], s. delator; denunciante; (fam.) soplón, chivato.

infraction [infrækšon], s. infracción.

infrequent [infríkwent], a. raro, poco frecuente.

infringe [infríndž], vt. infringir, violar.—to i. upon, invadir, usurpar.— —**ment** [-ment], s. infracción, violación.

infuriate [infúrieit], vt. enfurecer.

ingenious [indžínjas], a. ingenioso; hábil. —**ingenuity** [indžinjúiti], s. ingeniosidad.

ingenuous [indžényuʌs], a. ingenuo.— —**ness** [-nis], s. ingenuidad.

ingoing [íngouin], a. entrante.

ingot [íngot], s. lingote.

ingrained [ingréind], a. arraigado; (dirt) incrustado.

ingratiate [ingréišeit], vr.—to i. oneself with, congraciarse con. —**ingratiating** [ingréišeitin], a. insinuante, obsequioso.

ingratitude [ingrætitjud], s. ingratitud.

ingredient [ingrídient], s. ingrediente.

inhabit [inhæbit], vt. habitar, poblar.—vi. residir.— —**able** [-abl], a. habitable.— —**ant** [-ant], s. habitante.

inhalation [inhǎléišon], s. inspiración; (med.) inhalación. —**inhale** [inhéil], vt. inspirar, inhalar, aspirar.

inhere [inhír], vi. ser inherente.— —**nt** [inhírent], a. inherente, inmanente.

inherit [inhérit], vt. y vi. heredar.— —**ance** [-ans], s. herencia.—i. tax, impuesto sucesorio.— —**or** [-o(r)], s. heredero.

inhibit [inhíbit], vt. inhibir, prohibir.— —**ion** [inhibíšon], s. inhibición.

inhospitable [inháspitabl], a. inhospitalario; inhóspito.

inhuman [inhjúman], a. inhumano.–
—e [inhjuméin], a. inhumano.
—ity [inhjumǽniti], s. inhumanidad.
inimical [inímikal], a. hostil, enemigo.
inimitable [inímitabl], a. inimitable.
initial [iníʃal], a. y s. inicial.—vti. [2] firmar con sus iniciales.**—ly** [-i], adv. al principio. **—initiate** [iníʃieit], vt. iniciar, entablar.—[iníʃiet], s. iniciado. **—initiation** [iniʃiéiʃon], s. iniciación. **—initiative**[iníʃiativ], s. iniciativa.
inject [indʒékt], vt. inyectar; introducir.– **—ion** [indʒékʃon], s. inyección.
injunction [indʒáŋkʃon], s. mandato; (jur.) mandamiento judicial, entredicho.
injure [índʒur], vt. dañar; lastimar, lesionar, herir; (to offend) agraviar. **—injurious** [indʒúriʌs], a. perjudicial, dañoso; (offensive) agravioso. **—injury** [índʒuri], s. daño; herida, lesión; (offense) agravio.
injustice [indʒʌ́stis], s. injusticia.
ink [iŋk], s. tinta.—vt. entintar.– **—ling** [íŋkliŋ], s. insinuación; sospecha; vislumbre, indicio, noción vaga.– **—stand** [-stænd], s. escribanía; tintero.– **—well** [-wɛl], s. tintero.
inland [ínland], a. y s. interior.—adv. tierra adentro.
in-law [ínlɔ], s. (fam.) pariente político.
inlay [inléi], vti. [10] embutir; incrustar; hacer ataujía o mosaico.—s. [ínlei], taracea, embutido.
inlet [ínlet], s. caleta, ensenada.
inmate [ínmeit], s. asilado, recluso; presidiario, preso.
inmost [ínmoust], a. más íntimo.
inn [in], s. mesón, posada.
innate [inéit], a. innato, ingénito.
inner [ínœ(r)], a. secreto; interior.—i. spring mattress, colchón de muelles interiores.—i. tube, cámara (de neumático).
inning [íniŋ], s. entrada, turno, mano.
innkeeper [ínkipœ(r)], s. posadero, mesonero, fondista.
innocence [ínosens], s. inocencia. **—innocent** [ínosent], s. y a. inocente.
innovate [ínoveit], vt. innovar. **—innovation** [inovéiʃon], s. innovación.
innuendo [inyuéndou], s. indirecta, insinuación.

innumerable [injúmerabl], a. innumerable, incontable.
inoculate [inákjuleit], vt. y vi. inocular. **—inoculation** [inakjuléiʃon], s. inoculación.
inoffensive [inoffénsiv], a. inofensivo.
inopportune [inaportjún], a. inoportuno, intempestivo.
inorganic [inɔrgǽnik], a. inorgánico.
input [ínput], s. aportación, aporte; (comput., elec.) entrada.
inquire [inkwáir], vt. y vi. inquirir, preguntar, averiguar.—to i. about, after o for, preguntar por.—to i. into, investigar, examinar, informarse.—to i. of, dirigirse a. **—inquiry** [inkwáiri], s. pregunta; averiguación, encuesta.
inquisition [inkwiziʃon], s. inquisición. **—inquisitive** [inkwízitiv], a. curioso, preguntón. **—inquisitiveness** [inkwízitivnis], s. curiosidad, manía de preguntar.
insane [inséin], a. loco, insano. **—insanity** [insǽniti], s. locura, insania.
inscribe [inskráib], vt. inscribir; dedicar. **—inscription** [inskrípʃon], s. inscripción; dedicatoria.
inscrutable [inskrútabl], a. inescrutable, insondable.
insect [ínsekt], s. insecto.—i. repellent, repelente de insectos.—i. spray, insecticida en aerosol.– **—icide** [inséktisaid], a. y s. insecticida.
insecure [insikiúr], a. inseguro. **—insecurity** [insikiúriti], s. inseguridad, incertidumbre; riesgo.
insensitive [insénsitiv], a. insensible. **—insensitivity** [insensitíviti], s. falta de sensibilidad.
inseparable [inséparabl], a. inseparable.
insert [ínsœrt], s. inserción.—vt. [insœrt], insertar.– **—ion** [insœ́rʃon], s. inserción; (cost.) entredós.
inshore [inʃɔ́r], a. cercano a la orilla.— adv. hacia o cerca de la orilla.
inside [insáid], a. interior, interno; secreto.—i. information, informes confidenciales.—s. interior.—insides, (fam.) entrañas.—on the i., (fam.) en el secreto de las cosas.— adv. adentro, dentro, en el interior.—i. out, al revés.—prep. dentro de.– **—r** [insáidœ(r)], s. persona enterada.
insidious [insídiʌs], a. insidioso.
insight [ínsait], s. penetración.
insignia [insígniä], s. pl. insignias.
insignificance [insignífikans], s. insig-

nificancia. —**insignificant** [insig-nífikant], a. insignificante.

insinuate [insínyueit], vt. insinuar.— *to i. oneself into,* introducirse en. —**insinuation** [insinyuéiṣon], s. insinuación.

insipid [insípid], a. insípido.

insist [insíst], vi. insistir.— —**ence** [-ens], s. insistencia.— —**ent** [-ent], a. insistente.

insolence [ínsolens], s. insolencia. —**insolent** [ínsolent], a. insolente.

insomnia [insámniä], s. insomnio.

inspect [inspékt], vt. inspeccionar. —**ion** [inspékṣon], s. inspección.— —**or** [inspéktǫ(r)], s. inspector.

inspiration [inspiréiṣon], s. inspiración. —**inspire** [inspáir], vt. y vi. inspirar.

instability [instabíliti], s. inestabilidad.

install [instól], vt. instalar.— —**ation** [-éiṣon], s. instalación; (pol.) investidura. —**instal(l)ment** [instólment], s. instalación; entrega.—*in installments,* por entregas; a plazos.—*i. plan,* pago a plazos, compra a plazos.—*on the i. plan,* con facilidades de pago.

instance [ínstans], s. ejemplo, caso;— *for i.,* por ejemplo.

instant [ínstant], a. inmediato,—*i. coffee,* café instantáneo.—*i. replay,* (dep.) repetición de la jugada.— s. instante, momento.— —**aneous** [-éiniʌs], a. instantáneo.

instead [instéd], adv. preferiblemente; en su lugar.—*i. of,* en lugar de, en vez de.

instep [ínstep], s. empeine.

instigate [ínstigeit], vt. instigar. —**instigation** [instigéiṣon], s. instigación.

instinct [ínstiŋkt], s. instinto.— —**ive** [instíŋktiv], a. instintivo.

institute [ínstitiut], vt. instituir.—s. instituto. —**institution** [institiúṣon], s. institución.

instruct [instrΛkt], vt. instruir.— —**ion** [instrΛkṣon], s. instrucción.—*pl.* instrucciones; órdenes; consigna.— —**ive** [-iv], a. instructivo.— —**or** [-ǫ(r)], s. instructor.

instrument [ínstrument], s. instrumento.—*i. panel,* tablero de mandos.— —**al** [instruméntal], a. (mus.) instrumental.—*to be i. in,* jugar un papel deciso en, ser instrumento eficaz para, contribuir materialmente a.

instrumentalist [instrŭméntalist], s. instrumentista.

insubordinate [insΛbórdinit], a. insubordinado. —**insubordination** [insΛbordinéiṣon], s. insubordinación.

insufficiency [insΛfíṣensi], s. insuficiencia. —**insufficient** [insΛfíṣent], a. insuficiente.

insulate [ínsiuleit], vt. aislar. —**insulation** [insiuléiṣon], s. aislamiento. —**insulator** [ínsiuleitǫ(r)], s. aislador.

insult [ínsΛlt], s. insulto.—vt. [insΛlt], insultar.

insuperable [insiúperabl], a. insuperable.

insurance [inṣúrans], s. seguro.—*i. against,* provisión contra.—*i. agent,* agente de seguros.—*i. company,* compañía de seguros.—*i. policy,* póliza de seguro. —**insure** [inṣúr], vt. asegurar.— —**r** [inṣúrer], s. asegurador.

insurgent [insórdżent], a. y s. insurgente.

insurrection [insoerékṣon], s. insurrección.

intact [intǽkt], a. intacto, íntegro.

intake [ínteik], s. entrada; toma, admisión.—*i. valve,* válvula de admisión.

integral [íntigral], a. íntegro; (mat.) entero (número, función, etc.). —**integrity** [intégriti], s. integridad.

intellect [íntelekt], s. intelecto; (person) intelectual.— —**ual** [intelékchual], s. y a. intelectual. —**intelligence** [intélidżens], s. inteligencia; información; policía secreta. —**intelligentsia** [intelidżénsiä], s. intelectualidad. —**intelligent** [intélidżent], a. inteligente.

intemperance [intémperans], s. intemperancia. —**intemperate** [intémpœrit], s. intemperante; riguroso.

intend [inténd], vt. intentar, proponerse; destinar; querer decir.

intendancy [inténdansi], s. intendencia. —**intendant** [inténdant], s. intendente.

intense [inténs], a. intenso. —**intensification** [intensifikéiṣon], s. intensificación. —**intensify** [inténsifai], vti. y vii. [7] intensificar(se). —**intensity** [inténsiti], s. intensidad. —**intensive** [inténsiv], a. intensivo.

intent [intént], a. atento; intenso.—*i. on,* resuelto a.—s. intento; acepción, sentido.—*to all intents and purposes*, en realidad, de verdad. **—ion** [inténʂǫn], *s.* intención. **—ional** [inténʂǫnal], *a.* intencional.

inter [intǫer], *vti.* [1] enterrar.

intercede [intǫersíd], *vi.* interceder.

intercept [intǫersépt], *vt.* interceptar.- **—ion** [intǫersépʂǫn], *s.* interceptación.

intercession [intǫerséʂǫn], *s.* intercesión.

interchange [intǫerchéjndʐ], *vt.* intercambiar.—*vi.* intercambiarse.—*s.* [íntǫerchejndʐ], intercambio; (on a highway) correspondencia.

intercourse [íntǫerkɔrs], *s.* communicación, trato; intercambio. (copulation) cópula, comercio.

interdict [íntǫerdjkt], **interdiction** [intǫerdjkʂǫn], *s.* entredicho.— [íntǫerdjkt], *vt.* interdecir.

interest [íntǫerjst], *vt.* interesar.—*s.* interés.—*the interests*, las grandes empresas.- **—ed** [-jd], *a.* interesado. — **—ing** [-jŋ], *a.* interesante.

interface [íntoerfejs], *s.* punto de contacto; interrelación; (comput.) interfaz.

interfere [intǫerfír], *vi.* inmiscuirse; (fis.) interferir; (vet.) tropezar un pie con otro (los caballos).- **—nce** [intǫerfírens], *s.* injerencia, intromisión; (fis., rad.) interferencia.

interim [íntǫerjm], *a.* interino.—*s.* intermedio, ínterin.

interior [intírjǫ(r)], *a.* y *s.* interior.

interjection [intǫerdʐékʂǫn], *s.* interjección; interposición.

interlace [intǫerléjs], *vt.* entrelazar.

interlock [íntǫerlák], *vt.* trabar.—*vi.* trabarse.

interlude [íntǫerljud], *s.* intervalo; (teat.) intermedio; (mus.) interludio.

intermediary [intǫermídjerj], *a.* y *s.* intermediario. **—intermediate** [intǫermídjjt], *a.* intermedio.

interminable [intǫermjnabl], *a.* interminable.

intermingle [intǫermjŋgl], *vt.* entremezclar.—*vi.* entremezclarse.

intermission [intǫermjʂǫn], *s.* intermisión, intervalo; (teat.) descanso.

intermittent [intǫermjtent], *a.* intermitente.

intermix [intǫermjks], *vt.* entremezclar.—*vi.* entremezclarse.

intern [intǫern], *vt.* internar, recluir.—

s. [íntǫern], interno de hospital. **—al** [intǫernal], *a.* interno.

international [intǫernǽʂǫnal], *a.* internacional.- **—ize** [-ajz], *vt.* internacionalizar.

interne [íntǫern], *s.* = INTERN.

interpose [intǫerpóuz], *vt.* interponer

interpret [intǫerprjt], *vt.* interpretar. **—ation** [-éjʂǫn], *s.* interpretación. **—er** [-œ(r)], *s.* intérprete.

interrogate [intérǫgejt], *vt.* y *vi.* interrogar. **—interrogation** [interǫgéjʂǫn], *s.* interrogatorio.—*i. point* signo de interrogación. **—interrogative** [interágǫtjv], *a.* interrogativo.—*s.* palabra interrogativa.

interrupt [intǫrápt], *vt.* interrumpir.- **—ion** [intǫrápʂǫn], *s.* interrupción.— **—or** [-ǫ(r)], *s.* interruptor disyuntor.

intersect [intǫrsékt], *vt.* cortar.—*vi* (geom.) cortarse.— **—ion** [intǫrsékʂǫn], *s.* intersección; cruce.

intertwine [intǫertwájn], **intertwist** [intǫertwíst], *vt.* entrelazar.—*vi.* entrelazarse.

interval [íntǫervǫl], *s.* intervalo.—*a intervals*, de vez en cuando; de trecho en trecho.

intervene [intǫervín], *vi.* intervenir. **—intervention** [intǫervénʂǫn], *s.* intervención.

interview [íntǫervju], *s.* entrevista, interviú.—*vt.* entrevistarse con.- **—er** [-œ(r)], *s.* entrevistador; reportero, periodista.

intestine [intéstjn], *s.* (anat.) intestino, tripa.

intimacy [íntjmǫsj], *s.* intimidad. **—intimate** [íntjmjt], *a.* íntimo.—*s.* amigo íntimo.—*vt.* [íntjmejt], insinuar, intimar. **—intimation** [intjm-éjʂǫn], *s.* insinuación.

into [íntu], *prep.* en, dentro, adentro hacia el interior de.—*i. the bargain*, por añadidura.

intolerable [intálerǫbl], *a.* intolerable, insufrible. **—intolerance** [intálerans], *s.* intolerancia. **—intolerant** [intálerant], *a.* intolerante.

intonation [intonéjʂǫn], *s.* entonación.

intoxicate [intáksjkejt], *vt.* embriagar. **—intoxication** [intaksjkéjʂǫn], *s.* embriaguez; (med.) intoxicación, envenenamiento.

intransitive [intrǽnsjtjv], *a.* (gram.) intransitivo.

intrepid [intrépjd], *a.* intrépido.

intricate [íntrjkjt], *a.* intrincado.

ntrigue [intríg], *s.* intriga; galanteo, lío amoroso.—*vt.* (to arouse the curiosity of) intrigar.—*vi.* intrigar; tener intrigas amorosas.— **—r** [intrígœ(r)], *s.* intrigante.

ntroduce [introdiús], *vt.* introducir; presentar (una persona a otro).—**introduction** [introdákson], *s.* introducción; presentación.

ntrude [intrúd], *vi.* entremeterse.— **—r** [intrúdœ(r)], *s.* intruso, entremetido.—**intrusion** [intrúʒon], *s.* intrusión, entremetimiento. **—intrusive** [intrúsiv], *a.* intruso.

ntrust [intrást], *vt.* = ENTRUST.

ntuition [intjuíson], *s.* intuición.—**intuitive** [intjúitiv], *a.* intuitivo.

nundate [ínʌndeit], *vt.* inundar, anegar.

nvade [invéid], *vt.* invadir.— **—r** [invéidœ(r)], *s.* invasor.

nvalid [invǽlid], *a.* inválido, nulo.— *a.* y *s.* [ínvalid], inválido.— **—ate** [invǽlideit], *vt.* invalidar, anular.

nvaluable [invǽlyuabl], *a.* inestimable, inapreciable.

nvariable [invériabl], *a.* invariable.

nvasion [invéiʒon], *s.* invasión.

nvective [invéktiv], *s.* invectiva.

nvent [invént], *vt.* inventar.— **—ion** [invénson], *s.* invención, invento.— **—ive** [-iv], *a.* inventivo.— **—or** [-ɔ(r)], *s.* inventor.

nventory [ínventɔri], *s.* inventario.— *vti.* [7] inventariar.

nverse [invœrs], *a.* inverso. **—invert** [invœrt], *vt.* invertir.—*s.* [ínvœrt], invertido.—*inverted commas,* comillas.

nvest [invést], *vt.* (com.) invertir; investir, conferir; (mil.) sitiar, cercar.

nvestigate [invéstigeit], *vt.* investigar. **—investigation** [investigéison], *s.* investigación. **—investigator** [invéstigeitɔ(r)], *s.* investigador.

nvestment [invéstment], *s.* (com.) inversión; (mil.) sitio, cerco; investidura. **—investor** [invéstɔ(r)], *s.* (com.) inversionista.

nveterate [invéterit], *a.* inveterado, empedernido.

nvigorate [invígoreit], *vt.* vigorizar.

nvincible [invínsibl], *a.* invencible.

nvisibility [invizibíliti], *s.* invisibilidad. **—invisible** [invízibl], *a.* invisible.—*i. ink,* tinta simpática.

nvitation [invitéison], *s.* invitación, convite. **—invite** [inváit], *vt.* convidar, invitar. **—inviting** [inváitiŋ], *a.*

atractivo; incitante; (coc.) apetitoso.

invocation [invokéison], *s.* invocación.

invoice [ínvɔis], *s.* (com.) factura.—*vt.* facturar.

invoke [invóuk], *vt.* invocar; evocar, conjurar.

involuntary [inválʌnteri], *a.* involuntario.

involve [inválv], *vt.* envolver, comprometer.

inward(s) [ínwærd(z)], *adv.* hacia adentro, hacia lo interior; adentro. **—inward**, *a.* interior, interno.—*s.* el interior.—*pl.* entrañas.

iodin(e) [áiodain], *s.* yodo o iodo.

iota [aióutä], *s.* jota, punto, tilde.

IOU [aióuyú], *abrev.* (I owe you) pagaré.

I.Q. [aíkyú], *abrev.* (intelligence quotient) cociente intelectual.

irascible [airǽsibl], *a.* irascible.

irate [áireit], *a.* airado, iracundo. **—ire** [air], *s.* ira, furia.

iridescent [iridésent], *a.* iridiscente.

iris [áiris], *s.* (anat.) iris; (rainbow) arco iris; (bot.) lirio.

Irish [áiriš], *a.* y *s.* irlandés.—*s.* lengua irlandesa.

irk [œrk], *vt.* fastidiar, molestar.— **—some** [œrksʌm], *a.* fastidioso, enfadoso.

iron [áiœrn], *s.* hierro; plancha (de planchar).—*strike while the i. is hot,* a hierro caliente batir de repente.—*a.* ferreo, de hierro; relativo al hierro.—*i. curtain,* (pol.) telón de acero.—*vt.* planchar.—*to i. out,* allanar. **—irons** [áiœrnz], *spl.* hierros, grilletes.

ironic(al) [airánik(al)], *a.* irónico.

ironing [áiœrniŋ], *s.* planchado, ropa.

irony [áironi], *s.* ironia.

irradiate [iréidieit], *vt.* y *vi.* irradiar. **—irradiation** [ireidiéison], *s.* irradiación.

irrational [irǽšonal], *a.* irracional.

irregular [irégyulä(r)], *a.* irregular.— **—ity** [iregyulǽriti], *s.* irregularidad.

irrelevancy [irélevansi], *s.* inaplicabilidad. **—irrelevant** [irélevant], *a.* inaplicable, impertinente.

irreligious [irilídžʌs], *a.* irreligioso.

irreplaceable [iripleísibl], *a.* insubstituible, irreemplazable.

irresponsible [irispánsibl], *a.* irresponsable.

irreverence [iréverens], *s.* irreverencia. **—irreverent** [iréverent], *a.* irreverente.

irrevocable [irévọkạbl], *a.* irrevocable.

irrigate [írigeit], *vt.* regar. **—irrigation** [irigéişǫn], *s.* irrigación.

irritable [íritabl], *a.* irritable.— **—ness** [-nịs], *s.* irritabilidad. **—irritate** [íriteit], *vt.* irritar. **—irritation** [iritéişǫn], *s.* irritación.

Islam [ízlam], el Islam. **—Islamic** [izlámịk], *a.* islámico.

island [áiland], *s.* isla.— **—er** [-œ(r)], *s.* isleño. **—isle** [ail], *s.* ínsula. **—islet** [áilịt], *s.* isleta, cayo.

isolate [áisoleịt], *vt.* aislar. **—isolation** [aisoléişǫn], *s.* aislamiento. **—isolationism** [aisoléişǫnịzm], *s.* aislacionismo.

Israeli [izréilị], *a.* y *s.* israelí.— **—te** [ízriẹlait], *s.* israelita.

issue [íşu], *s.* (impr.) edición, tirada, impresión; número (de una revista, etc.); prole; (com.) emisión de valores; (for.) beneficios, rentas; salida, egreso; (med.) flujo; fuente, nacimiento; evento, consecuencia; decisión; tema de discusión.—*vt.* echar, arrojar; dar; dictar, expedir; (com.) librar, emitir; dar a luz, publicar.—*vi.* salir, fluir, provenir; nacer; resultar; resolverse.

isthmus [ísmʌs], *s.* istmo.

it [it], *pron. neutro* él, ella, eso, ello, lo, la, le.—*i. is four o'clock*, son las cuatro.—*i. is late*, es tarde.—*i. rain*, llueve.—*what time is i.?* ¿qué hora es?

Italian [itályạn], *a.* y *s.* italiano.— lengua italiana. **—italic** [itálịk], (impr.) bastardilla, itálica (letra); (I) itálico, italiano. **—italicize** [itálisaịz], *vt.* poner en letra itálica o bastardilla; subrayar, dar énfasis. **—italics** [itálịks], *s. pl.* (impr.) letra itálica, bastardilla o cursiva.

itch [ich], *s.* comezón, picazón; prurito.—*vi.* picar, sentir picazón o comezón; antojarse; desear vehementemente.— **—y** [íchị], *a.* sarnoso; picante.

item [áitem], *s.* partida; artículo; párrafo; detalle; renglón.— **—ize** [-aịz], *vt.* especificar, particularizar, pormenorizar.

itinerary [aịtínẹreri], *a.* y *s.* itinerario.

its [its], *a. posesivo neutro* su, sus (de él, de ella, de ello).— **—elf** [itsélf], *pron* (él) mismo, (ella) misma; sí mismo, sí misma; sí; se.—*it moves of i.*, eso se mueve por sí mismo.

ivory [áivorị], *s.* marfil.—*pl.* cosas hechas de marfil.—*a.* marfileño.

ivy [áivị], *s.* hiedra.

J

jab [dẓæb], *vti.* [1] pinchar, punzar.— *s.* punzada, pinchazo.

jack [dẓæk], *s.* macho del burro y otros animales; (mec.) gato, cric; sota de la baraja; (mar.) bandera de proa (rad,/tel.) jack.—*every man j.*, cada hijo de vecino.—*j.-of-all-trades*, aprendiz de todo y oficial de nada.—*j.-o'-lantern*, fuego fatuo; linterna hecha de una calabaza, con cara grotesca.—*j. plane*, (carp.) garlopa.—*j.-pot*, premio gordo, premio mayor.—*j. rabbit*, liebre americana.—*to hit the j.-pot*, (jer.) ponerse las botas.—*vt.* alzar un objeto con el gato.

jackal [dẓákạl], *s.* chacal.

jackass [dẓékæs], *s.* asno, borrico, burro; (fig.) estúpido, necio.

jackdaw [dẓékdɔ], *s.* grajo.

jacket [dẓékịt], *s.* chaqueta, chamarra; envoltura; forro; sobrecubierta.

jackknife [dẓæknaịf], *s.* navaja de bolsillo; (dep.) salto de carpa.

jade [dẓeid], *s.* (min.) jade; rocín, jamelgo; mujerzuela, sota.—*vt.* cansar.— **—d** [dẓéịdịd], *a.* ahito, saciado.

jagged [dẓǽgịd], *a.* mellado, dentado, serrado.

jail [dẓeil], *s.* cárcel.—*vt.* encarcelar. **—bird** [-bœrd], *s.* (fam.) preso; (fam.) infractor habitual.— **—** [dẓéịlœ(r)], *s.* carcelero.

jam [dẓæm], *s.* compota, conserva; agolpamiento; atascamiento; atascadero; situación peliaguda.—*vt.* [1] apiñar; apretar, apachurrar, estrujar; atorar; (rad.) causar interferencia en.—*vii.* atorarse, trabarse, agolparse.—*to j. on the brakes*, frenar de golpe.

Jamaican [dẓạméịkạn], *a.* y *s.* jamaiquino.

jamb [dẓæm], *s.* jamba.

ammed [dʒæmd], *a.* atorado, trabado; de bote en bote, repleto.

anitor [dʒænitǫ(r)], *s.* portero; conserje.

anuary [dʒænyʉeri], *s.* enero.

ar [dʒar], *vti.* [1] sacudir, agitar, hacer vibrar o trepidar.—*vii.* chirriar, hacer ruido desagradable; vibrar, trepidar.—*s.* jarro o jarra; pote, tarro; vibración; sacudida; chirrido.

argon [dʒárgon], *s.* jerga, jerigonza.

asmin(e) [dʒǽsmin], *s.* jazmín.

asper [dʒǽspœ(r)], *s.* (min.) jaspe.

aundice [dʒɔ́ndis], *s.* icterícia; predisposición.—*vt.* causar icterícia; predisponer.- —**d** [-t], *a.* ictericiado; (fig.) avinagrado.

aunt [dʒɔnt], *s.* excursión, caminata.- —**y** [-i], *a.* airoso, garboso.

avanese [dʒavanís], *a.* y *s.* javanés.

avelin [dʒǽvlin], *s.* jabalina, venablo.

aw [dʒɔ], *s.* quijada, mandíbula; (mec.) mordaza.—*vt.* y *vi.* (jer.) regañar.- —**breaker** [-breikœr], *s.* (fam.) (candy) hinchabocas; (fam.) (word) trabalenguas.- —**bone** [dʒɔ́boun], *s.* maxilar, quijada, mandíbula. —**jaws** [dʒɔz], *spl.* boca, garganta.

ay [dʒei], *s.* (fam.) rústico; simplón; (orn.) grajo.- —**walk** [-wɔk], *vi.* cruzar la calle descuidamente.- —**walker** [dʒéiwɔkœ(r)], *s.* (fam.) peatón descuidado o imprudente.

azz [dʒæz], *s.* (mus.) jazz; (fam.) animación, vivez.—*to j. up*, (fam.) animar, dar viveza a.- —**y** [dʒǽzi], *a.* chillón; de última moda.

ealous [dʒélʌs], *a.* celoso, envidioso.—*to be j.*, tener celos.—*to become j.*, encelarse, ponerse celoso.- —**y** [-i], *s.* celos; envidia.

ean [dʒin], *s.* (tej.) dril.—*pl.* pantalones de dril, jeans, vaqueros, tejanos.—*a pair of j.*, unos jeans, unos vaqueros, unos tejanos.

eep [dʒip], *s.* Jeep, jip (pequeño automóvil, todo terreno, que se maniobra con gran facilidad y en poco espacio).

eer [dʒir], *vt.* y *vi.* mofar, befar, escarnecer, burlarse.—*s.* befa, mofa, burla, escarnio, choteo.

elly [dʒéli], *s.* jalea.—*vti.* y *vii.* [7] convertir(se) en jalea. —**jellyfish** [dʒélifiš], *s.* medusa, aguamala.

eopardize [dʒépardaiz], *vt.* arriesgar, exponer. —**jeopardy** [dʒépardi], *s.* riesgo, peligro.

erk [dʒœrk], *s.* tirón, arranque, estirón; tic, espasmo muscular; (fam.)

estúpido, idiota.—*by jerks*, a sacudidas.—*vt.* dar un tirón; sacudir; traquetear; hacer tasajo.—*vi.* moverse a tirones.—*jerked beef*, tasajo.- —**y** [dʒœrki], *a.* espasmódico; (fam.) estúpido, atontado.

jersey [dʒœrzi], *s.* tejido de punto.

jest [dʒest], *vi.* bromear, chancearse.—*s.* chanza, broma, guasa.- —**er** [dʒéstœ(r)], *s.* bufón; burlón; guasón.

Jesuit [dʒéʒuit], *s.* jesuita.

jet [dʒet], *s.* chorro; surtidor; (min.) azabache.—*j.-black*, azabachado.—*j. engine*, motor a chorro, motor de reacción.—*j. lag*, jet lag, desfase horario, cansancio del desfase (debido a un largo viaje en avion).—*j. plane*, avión de chorro, avión a reacción.—*j. propulsion*, propulsión a chorro.—*j. ski*, moto acuática.—*vii.* [1] salir en chorro; volar en avión de chorro.

jetty [dʒéti], *s.* malecón, rompeolas; muelle, espolón.

Jew [dʒu], *s.* judío.

jewel [dʒúel], *s.* joya, alhaja; gema, piedra preciosa.—*j. box*, joyero.—*vti.* [2] enjoyar, adornar con piedras preciosas.

Jewish [dʒúiš], *a.* judío.

jiffy [dʒífi], *s.* (fam.) instante, periquete.—*in a j.*, en un santiamén.

jig [dʒig], *s.* giga (música y danza).—*j. saw*, sierra de vaivén.—*the j. is up*, (jer.) ya se acabo todo, estamos perdidos.- —**saw** [-sɔ], *s.*—*j. puzzle*, rompecabezas.—*vti.* [1] cantar o tocar una jiga; sacudir de abajo hacia arriba.—*vii.* bailar una jiga.

jilt [dʒilt], *vt.* dar calabazas a (un novio).

jingle [dʒíngl], *vt.* y *vi.* sonar o resonar.—*s.* retintín, sonido metálico; (rad., T.V., etc.) anuncio rimado y cantado.—*j. bell*, cascabel.—*vt.* hacer sonar.—*vi.* cascabelear.

jinx [dʒinks], *s.* gafe.—*vt.* (fam.) traer mala suerte a.

job [dʒab], *s.* tarea, faena; empleo, ocupación, trabajo; empresa.—*by the j.*, a destajo.- —**ber** [dʒábœ(r)], *s.* corredor o comisionista al por mayor.

jockey [dʒáki], *s.* jinete, jockey.—*vt.* montar (un caballo) en la pista; maniobrar hábilmente para sacar alguna ventaja, engañar.

jockstrap [dʒákstræp], *s.* suspensorio.

jocose [dʒokóս̩s], a. jocoso.

join [dʒoịn], vt. juntar, unir, ensamblar, acoplar; asociar; afiliarse o unirse a.—to j. battle, librar batalla.—to j. company, incorporarse.—to j. the colors, (fam.) alistarse, enrolarse.—vi. asociarse, unirse.— **t** [-t], s. juntura, junta, unión, empalme, ensambladura, acopladura; conexión, enganche; coyuntura, articulación; nudillo; gozne, bisagra; charnela; cuarto de un animal; encuentro de un ave.—out of j., dislocado, descoyuntado.—a. unido, agrupado, colectivo; copartícipe; asociado; mixto; conjunto.—j. account, cuenta en común.—j. property, propiedad mancomunada.—j. stock company, sociedad anónima.

joke [dʒoս̩k], s. broma, burla, chanza, chiste, chuscada.—in j., en chanza, de broma.—j. book, libro de chistes.—vi. bromear, chancear(se), gastar bromas.— **r** [dʒóս̩kœ(r)], s. burlón, bromista, guasón; (naipes) comodín; equívoco o falla de ley o contrato a cuyo amparo pueden ser burlados legalmente. —**jokingly** [dʒóս̩kịŋlị], adv. por burla, en chanza.

jolly [dʒáli], a. alegre, festivo, jovial; jaranero; divertido; (fam.) excelente, magnífico.—adv. (fam.) muy, sumamente.—vti. y vii. [7] (fam.) engatusar, lisonjear; seguir el humor (a).

jolt [dʒoս̩lt], vt. y vi. traquetear, sacudir, dar sacudidas.—s. sacudida, traqueteo.

jonquil [dʒánkwil], s. (bot.) junquillo.

jostle [dʒásl], vt. y vi. empujar, empellar, codear.—s. empellón, empujón.

jot [dʒat], s. pizca, jota (cosa mínima).—I don't care a j. (about), me importa un bledo.—vti. [1]—to j. down, apuntar, anotar.

journal [dʒœ́rnạl], s. diario, periódico diario; revista (publicación); acta; diario (apuntes personales); (com.) diario (libro).— **ism** [-ịzm], s. periodismo, diarismo, la prensa.— **ist** [-ịst], s. periodista.— **istic** [-ístịk], a. periodístico.— **ize** [-aịz], vt. (com.) pasar al diario.—vi. apuntar en un diario.

journey [dʒœ́rnị], s. viaje.—vi. viajar.

joust [dʒʌst, dʒaս̩st], s. justa, torneo.—vi. justar.

jovial [dʒóս̩vịạl], a. jovial.

jowl [dʒaս̩l], s. carrillo; quijada papada.

joy [dʒɔị], s. alegría, júbilo, regocijc felicidad.—j. ride, (fam.) paseo d recreo en coche; (fam.) paseo alo cado en coche.— **ful** [dʒɔịfս̩l], a alegre, gozoso; placentero.— **ou** [-ʌs], a. alegre, gozoso.

Jr. abrev. (Junior) hijo, p.ej., —**Dary Wayne Brown, Jr.** Daryl Wayn Brown, hijo.

jubilant [dʒúbịlạnt], a. jubiloso. —**ju bilee** [dʒúbịli], s. jubileo.

Judaic(al) [dʒụdéjịk(ạl)], a. judaicc —**Judaism** [dʒúdịjsm], s. judaísmo.

judge [dʒʌdʒ], s. juez.—vt. juzgar; sen tenciar, fallar.—vi. juzgar.— **judg ment** [dʒʌdʒmẹnt], s. juicio. (for.) fa llo, sentencia.

judicial [dʒụdíʃạl], a. judicial.—**judici ary** [dʒụdíʃịeri], a. judiciario; jud cial.—s. judicatura; poder judicia —**judicious** [dʒụdíʃʌs], a. juicioso.

jug [dʒʌg], s. botijo; jarro, cacharrc cántaro, porrón; (fam.) chiron (cárcel).

juggle [dʒʌgl], vi. hacer juegos de ma nos, escamotear; engañar, hace trampas. —**juggling** [dʒʌglịŋ], s. jue gos malabares.— **r** [dʒʌglœ(r)], malabarista; impostor.

jugular [dʒʌgyụla(r)], a. and s. yugula

juice [dʒus], s. zumo, jugo; (jer.) elec tricidad. —**juicy** [dʒúsị], a. jugoso zumoso; (spicy) picante.

jukebox [dʒúkbaks], s. tocadiscos aute mático de moneda.

July [dʒụláj], s. julio.

jumble [dʒʌmbl], vt. emburujar, revo ver.—s. revoltijo, masa confusa.

jumbo [dʒʌmboս̩], s. (fam.) (fam.) ot jeto enorme.—a. colosal, giga tesco, enorme.

jump [dʒʌmp], vt. saltar por encima d o al otro lado de; hacer saltar; sa tarse, omitir; comer un peón (en juego de damas).—to j. the trac descarrilar.—vi. saltar, brincar; c briolar; subir rápidamente (precio etc.); (con **with**) convenir, conco dar.—to j. at, apresurarse a aprov char.—to j. on, arremeter; (fam.) p ner como nuevo.—to j. over, salt por encima de.—to j. to a conclusio sacar precipitadamente una concl sión.—s. salto, cabriola, brinc (dep.) pista de saltos (esquí); (fam ventaja.—on the j., de un salto, vuelo.—to get o have the j. on,

la delantera a, adelantársele a uno.—
—er [dʒʌ́mpœ(r)], s. saltador; blusa de obrero o de mujer; zamarra de pieles; narria, rastra.— **—y** [-i], a. nervioso o excitable en exceso.

nction [dʒʌ́ŋkʃon], s. conexión, juntura, unión; acopladura; bifurcación; entronque, empalme, confluencia de vías. **—Juncture** [dʒʌ́ŋkchū(r)], s. junta, juntura; coyuntura, articulación; ocasión, oportunidad.

ne [dʒun], s. junio.

ngle [dʒʌ́ŋgl], s. jungla, selva. (Am.) manigua; maraña, matorral.

nior [dʒúnyo(r)], s. menor; socio menor; joven; estudiante de tercer año (en escuela superior, colegio o universidad).—a. más joven; hijo — **Daryl Wayne Brown, Junior** Daryl Wayne Brown, hijo.—j. college, colegio para los dos primeros años universitarios.—j. high school, escuela secundaria inferior (intermedia entre la elemental y la secundaria).—j. partner, socio menor.

nk [dʒʌŋk], s. (mar.) junco; hierro viejo, chatarra; (useless stuff) trastos viejos, baratijas viejas.—j. dealer, chatarrero, chapucero.—j. yard, chatarrería.—vt. (fam.) descartar por inservible.

ridic(al) [dʒuríḍik(al)], a. jurídico, judicial. **—jurisdiction** [dʒuriṣdíkṣon], s. jurisdicción; potestad; fuero; competencia. **—jurisprudence** [dʒuriṣprúḍens], s. jurisprudencia. **—jurist** [dʒúriṣt], s. jurista,

jurisconsulto. **—juristic** [dʒuríṣtik], a. jurídico. **—juror** [dʒúro(r)], s. (for.) jurado (individuo). **—jury** [dʒúri], s. (for.) jurado (cuerpo e institución).

just [dʒʌst], a. justo, honrado, recto, justiciero; justificado; legal; legítimo; exacto, cabal.—adv. justamente, exactamente; casi; sólo, no más que; apenas; simplemente; hace un momento.—j. about, poco más o menos; o poco menos.—j. as, al momento que; cuando; no bien; lo mismo que, semejante a.—j. beyond, un poco más allá.—j. by, al lado, al canto, aquí cerca.—j. now, ahora mismo, hace poco.—j. so, ni más ni menos.—to have j. time enough, tener el tiempo preciso.—to have j. arrived, acabar de llegar.— **—ice** [dʒʌ́stis], s. justicia; razón, derecho; (for.) juez; magistrado.—j. of the peace, juez de paz.— **—ifiable** [-ifajabl], a. justificable.— **—ification** [-iḟikéiʃon], s. justificación; descargo, defensa; razón de ser. **—justify** [-ifaj], vti. [7] justificar.

jut [dʒʌt], vii. [1] sobresalir, resaltar; combarse; proyectar.—s. salidizo, proyección.

jute [dʒut], s. yute, cáñamo de Indias.

juvenile [dʒúvenjl], a. juvenil, joven.—j. delinquency, delincuencia de menores.—s. mocito, joven; (teat.) galancete.

juxtapose [dʒʌkstạpóus], vt. yuxtaponer. **—juxtaposition** [dʒʌkstạpouzjṣon], s. yuxtaposición.

K

leidoscope [kạláiḍoskoup], s. calidoscopio.

ngaroo [kæŋgạrú], s. canguro.

el [kil], s. quilla.—vi.—to k. over, (naut.) dar de quilla, zozobrar; (fig.) volcarse; (fam.) desmayarse.

en [kin], a. afilado; aguzado; agudo; sutil; perspicaz; ansioso; mordaz.— **—ness** [kínnjs], s. agudeza; sutileza, perspicacia; anhelo.

ep [kip], vti. [10] conservar; quedarse con; guardar; tener (criados, secretario, un perro); llevar (cuentas, libros); cumplir (la palabra, una

promesa); detener, mantener.—to k. an eye on, vigilar.—to k. back, detener; ocultar; impedir.—to k. down, sujetar.—to k. from, mantener lejos de; impedir (cambiando el giro).—to k. in, mantener dentro; no dejar salir.—to k. in mind, recordar; tener en cuenta.—to k. informed (of), tener al corriente o al tanto (de).—to k. on, mantener; continuar.—to k. one's distance, mantenerse dentro de propios límites, no tomarse libertades.—to k. one's hands off, no tocar, no meterse en.—to k. one's temper, contenerse; obrar con calma.—*to k. one's word,* cumplir su palabra, tener palabra.—*to k. out,* no dejar entrar; excluir.—*to k. up,* mantener, conservar.—*vii.* mantenerse, sostenerse; continuar; permanecer.—*to k. along,* continuar, proseguir.—*to k. at home,* quedarse en casa.—*to k. away,* mantenerse apartado, no acercarse.—*to k. from,* abstenerse de; no meterse en.—*to k. in,* permanecer dentro; estarse en casa.—*to k. off,* no entrar a; no tocar; mantenerse fuera o lejos de.—*to k. on,* seguir, proseguir.—*to k. out of,* no meterse en, o evitar.—*to k. out of the way,* estarse o hacerse a un lado.—*to k. up,* mantenerse firme; persistir; no cejar.—*s.* manutención, subsistencia.—*for keeps,* para siempre; para guardar, para quedarse con ello.— **—er** [kípœ(r)], *s.* guarda, guardián, custodio; carcelero.— **—ing** [-iŋ], *s.* custodia, mantenimiento; cuidado, preservación.—*in k. with,* en armonía con, al mismo tenor que.— **—sake** [-sejk], *s.* regalo, recuerdo.

keg [keg], *s.* cuñete, barrilito.—*k. beer,* cerveza de barril.

kennel [kénel], *s.* perrera.

kept [kept], *pret.* y *pp.* de TO KEEP.

kerchief [kœrchịf], *s.* pañuelo.

kernel [kœrnel], *s.* grano de cereal; médula, núcleo.

kerosene [kérosin], *s.* keroseno.

kettle [kétl], *s.* caldera, marmita, olla; (teakettle) tetera.— **—drum** [-drʌm], *s.* (mús.) timbal, tímpano.

key [ki], *s.* llave; clave; fundamento; tono (de la voz); (mec.) llave; (elec.) conmutador; tecla (del piano, de máquina de escribir, etc.); (mar.) cayo, isleta.—*in k.,* templado, de acuerdo, en armonía.—*k. ring,* llavero.—*K. West,* Cayo Hueso.—*k. word,* palabra clave.—*pass k.,* llave maestra.—*a.* principal; fundamental; estratégico.—*vt.* poner llaves; afinar.— **—board** [kíbɔrd], *s.* teclado. — **—hole** [-houl], *s.* ojo de la cerradura.— **—note** [-nout], *s.* (mus.) nota tónica; idea fundamental.—*k. speech,* discurso de apertura.— **—stone** [-stoun], *s.* clave, espinazo; (fig) piedra angular.

khaki [kǽkị], *s.* kaki, caqui.

kibitzer [kíbịtsœ(r)], *s.* (fam.) mirón, molesto; entremetido.

kick [kịk], *vt.* acocear, dar patadas a.—

to k. the bucket, (fam.) estirar ﬂ pata.—*vi.* cocear, patear, dar o tira〈 coces; oponerse; quejarse.—*s.* p〈 tada, coz; puntapié; oposición ﬁ queja; estímulo, aliento.

kid [kịd], *s.* cabrito, chivato; cabritill〈 (piel); (fam.) niño; muchachit〈 chico, chica.—*vti.* y *vii.* [1] (fam〈 embromar, tomar el pelo; bromea〈

kidnap [kídnæp], *vti.* [2] secuestrar — **(p)er** [-œ(r)], *s.* secuestrador — **(p)ing** [-iŋ], *s.* secuestro.

kidney [kídnị], *s.* riñón.—*k. bea〈* judía.

kill [kịl], *vt.* matar; destruir; amort〈 guar; suprimir; producir una impr〈 sión irrestible en.—*s.* matanz〈 ataque final; (caza) pieza muerta.- *k.-joy,* aguafiestas.— **—er** [kílœ(r)]〈 matador.— **—ing** [-iŋ], *a.* matad〈 destructivo; (fam.) muy dive〈 tido.—*s.* matanza; (fam.) gran g〈 nancia.

kiln [kịl], *a.* horno.

kilogram [kílougræm], *s.* kilo(gramc 〈 Ver Tabla. **—kilometer** [kílom〈 tœ(r)], *s.* kilómetro. **—kilowa〈** [kílowat], *s.* kilovatio.

kimono [kịmóunou], *s.* quimon〈 bata.

kin [kịn], *s.* parentesco; parentela, ﬁ milia.—*the next of k.,* los parient〈 (más) próximos.—*a.* parient〈 allegado.

kind [kaịnd], *a.* bondadoso, benévol〈 amable; afectuoso.—*k. regards,* cc 〈 dial saludo; sentimientos de con〈 deración.—*s.* género, clase, cas〈 índole, calidad.—*nothing of the ﬁ* nada de eso; no hay tal.

kindergarten [kíndœrgartịn], *s.* e〈 cuela de párvulos, jardín de la i〈 fancia.

kindle [kíndl], *vt.* encender.—*vi.* e〈 cenderse. **—kindling** [kíndliŋ]〈 encendajas.—*k. wood,* le〈 menuda.

kindly [káịndlị], *adv.* amable o bonc 〈 dosamente; cordialmente.—*tell ﬁ k.,* tenga la amabilidad de c〈 cirme.—*a.* bondadoso, benév〈 favorable. **—kindness** [káịndnịs]〈 bondad.

kindred [kíndrịd], *s.* parentesco, cc 〈 sanguinidad; parentela.—*a.* e〈 parentado, deudo, consanguín〈 afin.

king [kịŋ], *s.* rey; rey (en el ajedre〈 dama (en el juego de damas〈

—**dom** [kíndǫm], s. reino.— **-ly** [-li], a. real, regio; majestuoso.—adv. regiamente, majestuosamente.— **—pin** [-pin], s. pivote central; (bowling) bolo delantero; (fam.) persona principal.— **—ship** [-šip], s. majestad; monarquía; reinado.

inky [kínki], a. ensortijado, crespo.

insfolk [kínzfouk], s. parentela. **—kinship** [kínšip], s. parentesco. **—kinsman** [kínzmǎn], s. pariente, deudo. **—kinswoman** [kínzwǔmǎn], s. parienta.

iosk [kiásk], s. kiosco o quiosco.

iss [kis], vt. besar.—to k. away, borrar con besos.—vi. besarse.—s. beso; (candy) dulce.

it [kit], s. cartera de herramientas; estuche; equipaje; (for first aid) botiquín; (mil.) equipo.

itchen [kíchęn], s. cocina.—k. boy, pinche.—k. garden, huerta.—k. range o stove, cocina económica.— k. sink, fregadero.— **—ette** [-ét], s. cocina reducida o pequeña.— **—ware** [-wer], s. utensilios de cocina, batería de cocina.

ite [kait], s. cometa, papalote; milano.

itten [kítn], s. gatito. **—ish** [-iš], a. retozón. **—kitty** [kíti], s. gatito, minino; (en el juego) puesta.

nack [næk], s. tino, don, destreza.

napsack [næpsæk], s. mochila.

nave [neiv], s. bribón, bellaco; sota (de los naipes).— **—ry** [néivǫeri], s. picardía, bribonada, bellaquería.

nead [nid], vt. amasar, sobar.—k. trough, artesa, amasadura.

nee [ni], s. rodilla; codillo (de cuadrúpedo); (mec.) codo, angular, escuadra; (mar.) curva.—k. deep, hasta la rodilla.—k. high, hasta la rodilla.—k. jerk, reflejo rotuliano. **—kneel** [nil], vii. [4] arrodillarse, hincar la rodilla.

nell [nel], s. doble, toque de difuntos; clamoreo; mal agüero.—vt. yvi. doblar, tocar a muerto.

new [niu], pret. de TO KNOW.

nicknack [níknæk], s. chuchería, baratija, juguete.

nife [naif], s. cuchillo.—k. sharpener, afilador, afilón.—vt. acuchillar; (fam.) frustrar o arruinar por intrigas.

night [nait], s. caballero; caballo (del ajedrez).—k. commander, comendador.—k. errant, caballero an-

dante.—k. errantry, caballería andante.—vt. armar caballero; conferir el título de Sir.— **—hood** [náithud], s. caballería.— **-ly** [-li], a. caballeresco.—adv. caballerosamente.

knit [nit], vti. y vii. [3] hacer malla, media o calceta; atar, enlazar, entretejer; contraer; unirse, trabarse; soldarse (un hueso); tejer a punto de aguja.—to k. one's brow, fruncir las cejas, arrugar el entrecejo.— **—knitting** [nítiŋ], s. trabajo de punto.—k. machine, máquina de hacer tejidos de punto. **—knitwear** [nítwer], s. artículo(s) de punto.

knives [naivz], s. pl. de KNIFE.

knob [nab], s. prominencia, bulto, protuberancia; nudo en la madera; borlita o borlilla; perilla, tirador.

knock [nak], vt. y vi. golpear; tocar, llamar a una puerta; (fam.) criticar, hablar mal de.—to k. down, derribar, tumbar; atropellar (con un auto, etc.); (mec.) desarmar, desmontar.—to k. out, hacer salir a golpes; acogotar; destruir; dejar o poner fuera de combate.—s. golpe; aldabonazo, llamada; (fam.) crítica.— **—er** [nákoe(r)], s. golpeador; llamador, aldaba.— **—out** [-aut], s. golpe decisivo, puñetazo decisivo; (dep.) nocaut, K.O.; (fam.) real moza.

knoll [noul], s. loma, otero.

knot [nat], s. nudo; lazo, vínculo.— vti. y vii. [1] anudar(se).— **—hole** [-houl], s. agujero en la madera.— **—ty** [-i], a. nudoso; intrincado, difícil.

know [nou], vti. [10] conocer; saber; discernir.—to k. how to (swim, sing, etc.), saber (nadar, cantar, etc.).—to k. the ropes, conocer los detalles, estar al tanto, (fig.) saber el juego.— vii. saber.—as far as I k., que yo sepa.—to be in the k., estar informado o en el secreto.—to k. best, ser el mejor juez, saber lo que más conviene.—to k. better, saber que no es así; saber lo que debe hacerse o como debe uno portarse.—to k. of, saber de, tener noticia o conocimiento de; conocer de oídas.— **—how** [-hau], s. conocimiento, destreza, habilidad.- **—ingly** [nóuiŋli], adv. hábilmente, sabiamente; a sabiendas, con conocimiento de causa.- **—ledge** [náljdž], s. conocimiento, saver, sapiencia; ciencia,

erudición.—*to the best of my k.*, según mi leal saber y entender.
—**known** [noun], *pp.* de TO KNOW.
knuckle [nʌ́kl], *s.* nudillo, artejo, articulación de los dedos; jarrete de ternero o cerdo; (mec.) charnela.—*vi.* someterse; abandonar la partida.— *to k. down*, o *to*, consagrarse o emprender con vehemencia.—*to k.*

(*under*) *to*, doblegarse ante; cede a.
K.O. [keíoú], *abrev.* (knockout) K.C (nocaut).
Korean [koríạn], *a.* y *s.* coreano.
kosher [koúŝer], *a.* autorizado por l ley judía; (fam.) genuino.
kudos [kjúḍạs], *s.* (fam.) gloria, re nombre, fama.

L

label [léịbẹl], *s.* marbete, rótulo, etiqueta; marca.—*vti.* [1] rotular o marcar; apodar; designar, clasificar; poner etiqueta a.
labial [léịbịạl], *a.* labial.
labor [léịbọ(r)], *s.* trabajo; [el] obrerismo; mano de obra; labor; obra.—*l. union*, sindicato o gremio obrero.—*vi.* trabajar; estar de parto.—*vt.* elaborar; hacer trabajar, activar.
laboratory [lǽb(o)rạtɔrị], *s.* laboratorio.
labored [léịbọrd], *a.* hecho con dificultad; forzado. **—laborer** [léịbọrœ(r)], *s.* peón, jornalero, bracero; obrero, operario, trabajador. **—laborious** [lạbórịạs], *a.* laborioso, trabajoso, ímprobo; diligente, industrioso.
labyrinth [lǽbịrịnθ], *s.* laberinto.
lace [leịs], *s.* encaje; cordón, cinta; cordón del corsé o del zapato.—*vt.* atar, abrochar (corsé, zapatos, vestidos, etc.) con lazos o cordones; enlazar; galonear; entrelazar.
lack [lǽk], *vt.* y *vi.* carecer, necesitar, faltar.—*s.* falta, carencia, escasez; necesidad.- **—ing** [lǽkịn], *a.* falto, carente, defectuoso.—*to be l. in*, hacerle falta a uno; carecer de.
lackey [lǽkị], *s.* lacayo.—*vt.* y *vi.* servir como lacayo; ser criado.
laconic [lạkánịk], *a.* lacónico.
lacquer [lǽkœ(r)], *vt.* dar laca; barnizar.—*s.* laca, barniz.
lacy [léịsị], *a.* de o parecido al encaje.
lad [lǽd], *s.* mozo, mozalbete, chico.
ladder [lǽdœ(r)], *s.* escalera o escala (de mano).—*l. truck,* carro de escaleras de incendio.
laden [léịdn], *a.* cargado, abrumado, oprimido.

ladle [léịdl], *s.* cucharón, cazo; (fund caldero.—*vt.* sacar o servir con cu charón.
lady [léịdị], *s.* señora, dama.—*l. i waiting,* camarera de la reina.—*F killer,* tenorio, conquistador. **—like** [-lạịk], *a.* delicado, tierno, el gante; afeminado.- **—love** [-lʌv], amada, mujer querida.
lag [lǽg], *s.* retraso; retardación d movimiento.—*vii.* [1] retrasarse, r zagarse, quedarse atrás.- **—ga** [lǽgạrd], *a.* tardo, perezoso, holg zán.—*s.* rezagoado, holgazán.
lager beer [lágœr], *s.* cerveza reposad
lagoon [lạgún], *s.* laguna, charca.
laity [leịịtị], *s.* legos, laicos.
laid [leịd], *pret.* y *pp.* de TO LAY.—*l. u* almacenado; (fam.) encamado p estar enfermo.
lain [leịn], *pp.* de TO LIE (echarse).
lair [lɛr], *s.* cubil, guarida.
lake [leịk], *s.* lago.
lamb [lǽm], *s.* cordero, borrego **—kin** [lǽmkịn], *s.* corderito.
lame [leịm], *a.* cojo, renco; lisiado, e tropeado.—*vt.* lisiar, estropear **—ness** [léịmnịs], *s.* cojera; defect imperfección.
lament [lạmént], *vt.* y *vi.* lamen tar(se).—*s.* lamento.- **—ab** [lǽmẹntạbl], *a.* lamentable, depl rable, desconsolador.- **—atị** [lǽmẹntéịŝọn], *s.* lamento, lame tación.
laminate [lǽmịneịt], *vt.* y *vi.* (metạl laminar.
lamp [lǽmp], *s.* lámpara; farol; li terna.—*l. burner,* mechero.—*l. po* farola de la calle.—*l. shade,* pantạ de lámpara.- **—black** [lǽmpblæk s.* negro de humo.- **—wick** [-wịk], mecha de lámpara.

mpoon [læmpún], *s.* pasquín, sátira.—*vt.* pasquinar, satirizar.

nce [læns], *s.* lanza; pica.—*vt.* lancear, dar una lanzada; abrir con bisturí.— **—r** [lǽnsœ(r)], *s.* lancero.— **—t** [lǽnsįt], *s.* (cir.) lanceta.

nd [lænd], *s.* tierra; terreno; suelo; país, nación; región, territorio.—*l. breeze,* terral.—*l. surveying,* agrimensura.—*l. surveyor,* agrimensor.—*vt.* desembarcar; echar en tierra.—*vi.* desembarcar; tomar tierra; (aer.) aterrizar; amarar (un avión).— **—holder** [lǽndhoųldœ(r)], *s.* hacendado, terrateniente.— **—ing** [-įŋ], *s.* descanso, rellano de escalera; desembarco, desembarque; desembarcadero; aterrizaje; amaraje.—*a.* de desembarque, de aterrizaje.—*l. beacon,* radiofaro de aterrizaje.—*l. craft,* barcaza militar de desembarque.—*l. forces,* tropas de desembarco.—*l. gear,* tren de aterrizaje.—*l. strip,* faja de aterrizaje.— **—fall** [-fɔl], *s.* aterrada; tierra vista desde el mar; aterraje.— **—lady** [-leįdį], *s.* casera, ama, patrona; arrendadora, propietaria.— **—lord** [-lɔrd], *s.* propietario o dueño de tierras o casas; arrendador; casero, patrón.— **—mark** [-mark], *s.* mojón, señal; (mar.) marca; punto o acontecimiento culminante.— **—owner** [-oųnœ(r)], *s.* hacendado, terrateniente, propietario.— **—scape** [-skeįp], *s.* paisaje.— **—slide** [-slaįd], *s.* derrumbamiento, derrumbe; (pol.) victoria arrolladora.

ne [leįn], *s.* senda, vereda; calle, callejuela; ruta; (aut.) carril; (mar.) ruta; (aer.) corredor aéreo, pasillo.

nguage [lǽŋgwįdʒ], *s.* lengua, idioma; lenguaje.

nguette [lǽŋgwet], *s.* (mus.) lengüeta.

nguid [lǽŋgwįd], *a.* lánguido. **—languish** [lǽŋgwįʃ], *vi.* languidecer, consumirse. **—languishing** [lǽŋgwįʃįŋ], *s.* languidez.—*a.* lánguido, decaído. **—languor** [lǽŋgǫ(r)], *s.* desfallecimiento, languidez, debilidad.

nk [læŋk], *a.* flaco, seco; alto y delgado.—*l. hair,* cabellos largos y lacios.— **—y** [lǽŋkį], *a.* larguirucho, langaruto, delgaducho.

ntern [lǽntœrn], *s.* linterna, farol; (mar.) faro, fanal.—*l. jack,* fuego fatuo.

lap [læp], *s.* falda; regazo; (dep.) vuelta completa de la pista; lamedura.—*l. dog,* perrillo faldero.—*vti.* [1] lamer; envolver; sobreponer, solapar.

lapel [ląpél], *s.* (sast.) solapa.

Laplander [lǽplændœ(r)], *s.* lapón.

lapse [læps], *s.* lapso; intervalo de tiempo, transcurso; desliz, equivocación, falta; (for.) prescripción, caducidad de la instancia.—*in the l. of time,* con el transcurso del tiempo, andando el tiempo.—*vi.* pasar, transcurrir; decaer, deslizarse; caer en desliz o error; (for.) prescribir, caducar.

laptop [lǽptap], *a. y s.* (comput.) portátil.

larceny [lársenį], *s.* ratería, hurto.

lard [lard], *s.* manteca (de cerdo), (tocino) gordo.—*vt.* mechar.— **—er** [lárdœ(r)], *s.* despensa.

large [lardʒ], *a.* grande.—*l. intestine,* intestino grueso.— **—ly** [lárdʒlį], *adv.* en gran parte, en buena parte.— **—ness** [-nįs], *s.* grandeza.

lariat [lǽrįąt], *s.* lazo, reata, mangana.

lark [lark], *s.* alondra, calandria; (fam.) francachela, parranda, holgorio.

larva [lárvą], *s.* (*pl.* **larvae** [lárvį]) larva.

laryngitis [lærįndʒáįtįs], *s.* laringitis, afonía, ronquera. **—larynx** [lǽrįŋks], *s.* laringe.

lascivious [ląsívįąs], *a.* lascivo.

lash [læʃ], *s.* látigo, flagelo; azote, latigazo; chasquido; pestaña (del ojo).—*vt.* dar latigazos; azotar, flagelar; atar; (mar.) amarrar, trincar.—*vi.* chasquear el látigo.

lass [læs], *s.* doncella, moza, muchacha, chica.

lassitude [lǽsįtįud], *s.* lasitud.

lasso [lǽsou], *vt.* (en)lazar.—*s.* lazo, mangana, (Am.) guaso.

last [læst], *a.* último; final, supremo; pasado.—*l. evening,* ayer por la noche, anoche.—*l. name,* apellido.—*l. night,* anoche.—*l. straw,* acábose, colmo.—*the L. Supper,* la Cena.—*l. will and testament,* última disposición.—*l. word,* última palabra.—*next to the l.,* penúltimo.—*adv.* por la última vez, por último, al fin.—*at l.,* por fin, al cabo.—*s.* fin, término; (lo, el) último; (zap.) horma.—*to the l.,* hasta el fin, hasta lo último.—*vi.* durar, perdurar, permanecer, subsistir.—*vt.* (zap.) ahormar, poner en la horma.— **—ing** [lǽstįŋ], *a.* duradero, perdurable.— **—ly** [-lį], *adv.* en conclusión, por fin, finalmente, por último.

latch [læch], *s.* aldaba, pestillo, cerrojo, picaporte.—*l. key,* llavín.—*vt.* cerrar con aldaba o pestillo.

late [leịt], *a.* tardío; tardo; último, postrero; reciente; difunto.—*l. arrival, l.-comer,* recién llegado.—*adv.* tarde; poco ha, últimamente.—*l. in the year,* al fin del año.—*to be l.,* llegar tarde, retrasarse, estar atrasado; ser tarde.—*too l.,* (demasiado) tarde.— **—ly** [léịtli], *adv.* poco ha, no ha mucho; recientemente, últimamente.

latent [léịtent], *a.* latente.

later [léịtœ(r)], *adv.* y *a.* (*comp.* de LATE) más tarde; luego, después, posterior.—*l. on,* más trade, después.

lateral [léteṛal], *a.* lateral.

latest [léịtịst], *a.* y *adv.* (*superl.* de LATE) último; novísimo.—*at the l.,* a más tardar.

lath [læθ], *s.* lata, listón, enlistonado.

lathe [leịð], *s.* torno.—*l. bed,* banco del torno.

lather [læðœ(r)], *vt.* enjabonar (para afeitar).—*vi.* hacer espuma.—*s.* jabonadura, espuma de jabón.

Latin [lætịn], *a.* y *s.* latino.—*s.* latín.— *L. America,* Latinoamérica, la América Latina.—*L. American,* latinoamericano.

latitude [lætịtịud], *s.* latitud; amplitud; libertad.

latrine [latrín], *s.* letrina.

latter [lætœ(r)], *a.* posterior; segundo.—*the l.,* éste, ésta, esto.

lattice [lætịs], *s.* enrejado, celosía.

laud [lɔd], *s.* (canto de) alabanza; loa.—*vt.* alabar, loar, elogiar.— **—able** [lɔ́dabl], *a.* laudable, loable.

laugh [læf], *vi.* reír(se).—*to l. loudly,* reírse a carcajadas.—*vt.* ahogar en o con risa.—*s.* risa; risotada.— **—able** [læfabl], *a.* risible, irrisorio; divertido.— **—ing** [-ịn], *s.* risa, reír.—*l. gas,* gas hilarante.— **—stock** [-stak], *s.* hazmerreír.— **—ter** [-tœ(r)], *s.* risa.

launch [lɔnch], *vt.* botar o echar al agua (un barco); dar principio a, acometer; lanzar.—*vi.* lanzarse.—*s.* lancha, chalupa.— **—ing** [lɔ́nchịn], *s.* lanzamiento; (mar.) botadura.—*l. pad,* plataforma de lanzamiento.

launder [lɔ́ndœ(r)], *vt.* lavar y planchar; (money) blanquear, lavar. **—laundress** [lɔ́ndrịs], *s.* lavandera. **—laundry** [lɔ́ndrị], *s.* lavadero, lavandería; ropa lavada o para la

var.—*l. basket,* cesto de la ropa su cia. **—laundryman** [lɔ́ndrịmạn], *s* lavandero.

laureate [lɔ́rịịt], *a.* laureado. **—laure** [lɔ́rel], *s.* laurel.—*to rest on one's lau rels,* dormirse sobre sus laurele tinción.

lava [lávạ], *s.* lava.

lavatory [lǽvạtoṛị], *s.* lavatorio, la vabo; (washroom) lavamanos; (to let) excusado.

lavender [lǽvẹndœ(r)], *s.* espliego, la vanda, alhucema.

lavish [lǽvịš], *a.* pródigo.—*vt.* prod gar.— **—ness** [-nịs], *s.* prodigalidad profusión.

law [lɔ], *s.* ley; derecho; leyes (en gene ral); justicia, jurisprudencia.—*l abiding,* observante de la ley.—*l. nations,* derecho internacional; de recho de gentes.—*l. school,* Facultar de Derecho.— **—breaker** [lɔ́breịk œ(r)], *s.* transgresor, infractor. **—ful** [-fųl], *a.* legal, lícito; pe mitido, válido.— **—less** [-lịs], *a.* ilegal; desenfrenado, licencioso. **—maker** [-meịkœ(r)], *s.* legislador. **—making** [-meịkịn], *s.* legisla ción.—*a.* legislativo.

lawn [lɔn], *s.* césped, prado.—*l. mowe* cortacésped, tundidora de césped.

lawsuit [lɔ́sịut], *s.* pleito, litigio, juicic **—lawyer** [lɔ́yœ(r)], *s.* abogado.—*l. bill,* minuta.—*l.'s office,* bufete, de pacho de abogado.

lax [læks], *a.* suelto, flojo; laxo, r lajado.— **—ative** [lǽksạtịv], *a.* y *s.* l xante.— **—ity** [-ịtị], **—ness** [-nịs], *s* aflojamiento; relajamiento; rel jación.

lay [leị], *pret.* de TO LIE (echarse).

lay [leị], *vti.* [10] poner, colocar; tende (tuberías, rieles, etc.), instalar; derr bar; poner (un huevo, la mesa, etc. enterrar; calmar; imponer (carga tributos).—*to l. against,* acusar d achacar a.—*to l. apart,* reservar, pe ner aparte.—*to l. aside,* desecha arrinconar; ahorrar.—*to l. off,* tr zar, delinear; despedir.—*to l. or gastar, emplear; exhibir; trazar; pr yectar.—*vii.* poner (las gallina etc.); apostar; (mar.) situarse, col carse.—*to l. off,* parar (en el tr bajo).—*to l. over,* demorarse, di tenerse; sobrepasar.—*a.* laico, seglar; profano, incompetente.— *brother,* donado, lego.—*l. sister,* nada.—*s.* situación, orientació

—**er** [léįœ(r)], s. capa, estrato, mano; gallina ponedora. — —**ing** [-įŋ], s. colocación; postura (del huevo).– —**man** [-mạn], s. lego, seglar. – —**off** [-ɔf], s. despedida o despido (de obreros).– —**out** [-aųt], s. plan, disposición, arreglo, trazado.– —**over** [-oųvœ(r)], s. parada en un viaje.

azily [léįzįlį], adv. perezosamente. —**laziness** [léįzįnįs], s. pereza, holgazanería. —**lazy** [léįzį], a. perezoso, holgazán; pesado.—l. bones, perezoso.

ead [lid], s. primacía, primer lugar; dirección, mando; delantera; (teat.) papel principal, protagonista; [led], plomo; mina o grafito del lápiz; (mar.) sonda, escandallo; plomada.—l. pencil, lápiz.—l. poisoning, (med.) cólico saturnino.—vti. [10] [lid], llevar de la mano; guiar, dirigir; mandar, acaudillar; ir a la cabeza de; enseñar; amaestrar; llevar (buena, mala vida); inducir.—to l. a new life, enmendarse.—to l. astray, descarriar, seducir.—to l. off o out, desviar; principiar.—vii. guiar, enseñar el camino; sobresalir; ir adelante; conducir; dominar; ser mano en el juego de naipes.—to l. (up) to, conducir a, dar a.– —**en** [lédn], a. plomizo; aplomado; pesado.

eader [lídœ(r)], s. jefe, (neol.) líder; guía, conductor; guión; caballo delantero; (imp.) puntos suspensivos. – —**ship** [-šįp], s. jefatura, (neol.) liderato; dirección, primacía. —**leading** [lídįŋ], a. director; principal; dominante, sobresaliente.—l. edge, (aer.) borde de ataque.—l. lady, (teat.) primera actriz.—l. man, jefe, cabecilla; (teat.) galán, protagonista.—l. question, pregunta tendenciosa.

eaf [lif], s. hoja.—l. tobacco, tabaco en rama.—to turn over a new l., hacer libro nuevo.—vi. echar hojas; hacerse frondoso.—vt. hojear (un libro).– —**less** [líflįs], a. deshojado.– —**let** [-lįt], s. (impr.) folleto, volante, circular; (bot.) hojuela.– —**y** [-į], a. frondoso; de forma de hoja.

ague [lig], s. liga; legua (unas 3 millas).—vi. asociarse, ligarse.

eak [lik], s. gotera en un techo; fuga o escape de gas, vapor, etc.; (mar.) vía de agua.—vi. gotear; (mar.) hacer agua; salirse; dejar escapar (el agua,

vapor, etc.), escurrirse.—to l. out, (fig.) divulgarse, saberse, traslucirse. – —**age** [líkįdẑ], s. goteo, escape, fuga, salida; (com.) avería, merma, derrame.

lean [lin], vii. [4] apoyarse, recostarse, inclinarse; ladearse, encorvarse.— vti. apoyar, reclinar; inclinar; encorvar.—a. flaco; magro; enjuto, delgado.– —**ing** [-įŋ], a. inclinado.—s. inclinación.– —**to** [-tóų], s. colgadizo.

leap [lip], vii. [4] saltar, brincar, dar un salto o brinco.—vti. (hacer) saltar, cubrir el macho a la hembra.—s. salto, brinco; cabriola, zapateta.— by leaps and bounds, a saltos; a pasos agigantados.—l. year, año bisiesto.

learn [lœrn], vti. y vii. [4] aprender; enterarse de, saber; instruirse.— —**ed** [lœrnįd], a. docto, erudito, sabio.— l. journal, revista científica.—l. word, cultismo, voz culta. —**ing** [-įŋ], s. saber, ciencia conocimientos, erudición; aprendizaje.

lease [lis], s. arriendo, contrato de arrendamiento.—l. holder, arrendatario.—vt. arrendar.—vi. arrendarse.

leash [liš], s. traílla, correa.

least [list], a. (super. de LITTLE) mínimo; ínfimo; (el) más pequeño.—not in the l., de ninguna manera, bajo ningún concepto.— adv. menos.—s. (lo) menos.—at l., al menos, por lo menos.

leather [léðœ(r)], s. cuero.—a. de cuero.—l. belt, correa, cinturón.—l. strap, correa.– —**n** [-n], a. de cuero.

leave [liv], s. licencia, permiso, venia.—l. of absence, licencia.—l.-taking, despedida.—on l., (mil.) con licencia.—vti. [10] dejar; abandonar; salir o partir de ; separarse de.— to l. alone, dejar quieto o en paz; no meterse con.—to l. off, cesar, suspender; dejar (un vicio, una costumbre).—to l. out, omitir, excluir.—to l. word, dejar dicho.—vii. irse, marcharse, salir, partir.

leaven [lévn], s. levadura.—vt. leudar. – —**ing** [-įŋ], s. levadura.

leaves [livz], s. pl. de LEAF.

leaving [lívįŋ], s. partida, marcha.—pl. sobras, desechos, desperdicios.

lecherous [léchœrʌs], a. lujurioso, lascivo. —**lechery** [léchœrį], s. lujuria, lascivia.

lecture [lékchų(r)], s. conferencia;

sermoneo.—*l. hall* o *room,* aula, cátedra, salón de conferencias.— *vt.* sermonear.—*vi.* dar una conferencia.— **—r** [lékchŭrœ(r)], *s.* conferenciante; lector (de universidad o iglesia).

led [led], *pp.* y *pret.* de TO LEAD.

ledge [ledž], *s.* retallo; cama de roca; arrecife.

ledger [lédžœ(r)], *s.* (com.) libro mayor.

lee [li], *s.* sotavento, socaire.

leech [lich], *s.* sanguijuela.

leer [lir], *s.* mirada de soslayo.—*vi.*— *to l. at,* mirar de soslayo, mirar injuriosamente. **—ingly** [lírinli], *adv.* de soslayo.- **—y** [-i], *a.* (fam.) receloso, suspicaz.

leeward [líwǎrd, (mar.) lúǎrd], *a.* sotavento.

leeway [líweị], *s.* (aer. y mar.) deriva; tiempo de sobra; (fam.) libertad de acción.

left [left], *pret.* y *pp.* de TO LEAVE.—*l. behind,* rezagado.—*l. off,* desechado.—*to be l.,* quedar(se).—*a.* izquierdo.—*l. field,* (dep.) jardín izquierdo.—*l. hand,* izquierdo (lado, etc.); con la mano izquierda.—*l.- handed,* zurdo; torpe, desmañado; insincero, malicioso.—*l. wing,* (pol.) bando izquierdista o radical, las izquierdas.—*s.* mano izquierda, lado izquierdo; (pol.) izquierda(s).—*at, on,* o *to the l.,* a la izquierda.— **—ist** [léftịst], *a.* y *s.* izquierdista.- **—over** [-oụvœ(r)], *s.* sobrante, sobra, rezago.—*a.* sobrante, sobrado.

leg [leg], *s.* pierna; pata o pie (animales y objetos); trayecto, jornada.—*not to have a l. to stand on,* no tener justificación alguna.—*on* o *upon its legs,* en pie, firmemente establecido.— *on one's last legs,* acabándose; agonizando; sin recursos.—*to pull someone's leg,* tomarle el pelo a uno.

legacy [légasị], *s.* legado.

legal [lígǎl], *a.* legal.—*l. tender,* curso legal.- **—ity** [ligǽlịtị], *s.* legalidad.- **—ization** [-ịzéịšǫn], *s.* legalización.- **—ize** [-aịz], *vt.* legalizar.

legate [légịt], *s.* legado.— **legation** [ligéịšǫn], *s.* legación.

legend [lédžęnd], *s.* leyenda; letrero, inscripción.- **—ary** [-ɛrị], *a.* legendario.

legerdemain [ledžœrdịméịn], *s.* juego de manos, prestidigitación.

legging [légịn], *s.* polaina.

legible [lédžịbl], *a.* legible.

legion [lídžǫn], *s.* legión.- **—ary** [-ɛrị] *a.* y *s.* legionario.

legislate [lédžịsleịt], *vi.* legislar. **—le gislation** [ledžịsléịšǫn], *s.* legislación. **—legislative** [lédžịsleịtịv], *a.* legislativo. **—legislator** [lédžịsleị tǫ(r)], *s.* legislador. **—legislatur** [lédžịslejchū(r)], *s.* asamblea legisla tiva, cuerpo legislativo.

legitimate [lịdžítịmịt], *a.* legítimo.- *vt.* [lịdžítịmeịt], legitimar.

leisure [lížū(r)], *s.* ocio, desocupa ción.—*at one's l.,* a la comodidad d uno.—*l. class,* gente acomodada.- *l. hours,* horas libres o desocupadas ratos perdidos.—*to be at l.,* esta desocupado.- **—ly** [-lị], *a.* pau sado, deliberado.—*adv.* despacio cómoda o desocupadamente; a su anchas.

lemon [lémǫn], *s.* limón.—*l. tree,* limo nero, limón.- **—ade** [-éịd], *s.* l¹ monada.

lend [lend], *vti.* [10] prestar, dar pres tado.—*to l. a hand,* dar una mano ayudar.— **—er** [léndœ(r)], *s.* presta dor, prestamista.

length [lenθ], *s.* longitud, largo(r); ex tensión, distancia; duración d tiempo; alcance (de un tiro, etc. (mar.) eslora.—*at full l.,* a lo larg de todo el largo.—*at l.,* al fin, f nalmente; extensamente.- **—e** [lénθn], *vt.* y *vi.* alargar(se), prolon gar(se).- **—ways** [-weịz], **—wis** [-waịz], *adv.* longitudinalmente; a l largo; de largo a largo.- **—y** [-i], larg o; larguísimo.

leniency [líniẹnsị], *s.* indulgencia, le nidad.— **lenient** [líniẹnt], *a.* indu gente, clemente.

lens [lenz], *s.* lente; cristalino (del ojo

lent [lent], *pret.* y *pp.* de TO LEND.—(L. *s.* cuaresma.

lentil [léntịl], *s.* (bot.) lenteja.

Leo [líou], *s.* (astr.) Leo.

leopard [lépǎrd], *s.* leopardo.

leotard [líotard], *s.* leotardo.

leper [lépœ(r)], *s.* leproso. **—lepros** [léprǫsị], *s.* lepra. **—leprous** [léprʌs *a.* leproso, lazarino.

lesion [lížǫn], *s.* lesión.

less [les], *a.* (*comp.* de LITTLE) meno menos, inferior.—*adv.* menos; e grado más bajo.—*l. and l.,* cada ve menos.—*s.* (el o lo) menos.—*pre* menos; sin.

essee [lesí], *s.* arrendatario, inquilino.

essen [lésn], *vt.* aminorar, disminuir, mermar; rebajar.—*vi.* mermar, disminuirse; rebajarse, degradarse. **—lesser** [lésœ(r)], *a. (comp.* de LITTLE*)* menor, más pequeño.

esson [léson], *s.* lección.

essor [léso(r)], *s.* arrendador.

est [lest], *conj.* para que no, por miedo de que, por temor a que, no sea que.

et [let], *vti.* [9] dejar, permitir; arrendar, alquilar.—*l. alone,* cuanto más, ni mucho menos.—*l. us go!* ¡vamos! ¡vámonos!—*to l. alone,* dejar en paz.—*to l. be,* no molestar; no meterse con.—*to l. down,* dejar caer; bajar; abandonar.—*to l. go,* soltar.—*to l. in,* dejar entrar, admitir.—*to l. know,* hacer saber, avisar.—*to l. off,* disparar, descargar; dispensar, indultar.—*to l. out,* dejar salir, soltar; arrendar; divulgar (un secreto). —*to l. the cat out of the bag,* revelar un secreto.—*vii.* alquilarse o arrendarse.—*pret.* y *pp.* de TO LET.

letdown [létdoun], *s.* disminución, aminoramiento, decepción, desilusión; descenso.

lethal [líθəl], *a.* mortal, mortífero.

lethargic [liθárdʒik], *a.* letárgico. **—lethargy** [léθərdʒi], *s.* letargo, apatía.

letter [létœ(r)], *s.* letra; carta.—*l. bomb,* carta explosiva.—*l. box,* buzón; apartado.—*l. carrier,* cartero.—*l. of license,* moratoria, espera.—*l. opener,* abrecartas.—*to the l.,* al pie de la letra, a la letra.—*vt.* rotular; poner letras, título o letreros a.**—head** [-hed], *s.* membrete.**—ing** [-iŋ], *s.* letrero, inscripción, rótulo.

lettuce [létis], *s.* lechuga.

letup [létʌp], *s.* (fam.) pausa.—*without l.,* sin cesar.

leukemia [ljukímjə], *s.* leucemia.

Levant [livænt], *s.* Levante, Oriente.**—ine** [-in], *a.* y *s.* levantino.

levee [lévi], *s.* ribero, dique.

level [lévəl], *a.* plano, llano, igual, parejo; a nivel.—*l. crossing,* (f.c.) paso a nivel.—*l.-headed,* juicioso, discreto.—*s.* nivel (instrumento, altura); puntería.—*on the l.,* abiertamente, sin dolo.—*adv.* a nivel, a ras.—*vti.* [2] igualar, allanar; nivelar; apuntar.—*vii.* apuntar (un arma); nivelar, hacer nivelaciones.

lever [lévœ(r)], *s.* palanca; escape de reloj.—*control l.,* palanca de mando.—*vt.* apalancar.- **—age** [-idz], *s.* apalancamiento; (fig.) ventaja.

Levite [lívait], *s.* levita.

levity [léviti], *s.* frivolidad, ligereza.

levy [lévi], *s.* leva, reclutamiento; impuesto, recaudación; (for.) embargo.—*vti.* [7] imponer, recaudar; reclutar; (for.) embargar.

lewd [ljud], *a.* lujurioso, lascivo.**—ness** [ljúdnis], *s.* lujuria, lascivia.

lexical [léksikəl], *a.* léxico.

lexicographer [leksikágrəfœr], *s.* lexicógrafo. **—lexicographic(al)** [leksikográfik(əl)], *a.* lexicográfico.

lexicography [leksikágrəfi], *s.* lexicografía. **—lexicology** [leksikálodzi], *s.* lexicología. **—lexicon** [léksikon], *s.* léxico, vocabulario, diccionario.

liability [laiəbíliti], *s.* riesgo; obligación, responsabilidad.—*l. insurance,* seguro de responsabilidad civil.—*pl.* (com.) pasivo, deudas. **—liable** [láiəbl], *a.* sujeto, expuesto; obligado, responsable; propenso.—*to be l. to + inf.,* (fam.) amenazar + *inf.*

liaison [líazan], *s.* enlace; relaciones amorosas.

liar [láiər], *s.* embustero, mentiroso.

libel [láibel], *s.* libelo; difamación.—*vti.* [2] difamar.- **—(l)ous** [-ʌs], *a.* difamatorio.

liberal [líberəl], *a.* liberal; tolerante; (pol.) liberal.—*s.* liberal.- **—ism** [-izm], *s.* liberalismo.- **—ity** [libəréliti], *s.* liberalidad.

liberate [líbereit], *vt.* libertar, librar. **—liberation** [libəréiʃon], *s.* liberación. **—liberator** [líbəreito(r)], *s.* libertador.

libertine [líbœrtin], *a.* y *s.* libertino.

liberty [líbœrti], *s.* libertad.—*to take the l. to,* tomarse la libertad de.

Libra [láibra] o [líbra], *s.* (astr.) Libra.

librarian [laibrérian], *s.* bibliotecario. **—library** [láibreri], *s.* biblioteca.

libretto [librétou], *s.* libreto.

Libyan [líbian], *s.* y *a.* libio; líbico.

lice [lais], *s. pl.* de LOUSE.

license, licence [láisens], *s.* licencia, permiso; licencia, libertinaje.—*driver's l.,* carnet de chófer, permiso de conducir.—*l. plate,* chapa de circulación, placa de matrícula.—*vt.* licenciar. **—licentious** [laisénʃʌs], *a.* licencioso, desenfrenado, disoluto.

licit [lísit], *a.* lícito.

lick [lik], *vt.* lamer; (fam.) cascar, dar una tunda o zurra; vencer.—*to l. the dust,* morder el polvo.—*vi.* flamear.—*s.* lamedura, lengüetada; lamedero; (fam.) bofetón.- **—ing** [líkiŋ], *s.* tunda, paliza; derrota.

licorice [líkoris], *s.* regaliz, orozuz.

lid [lid], *s.* tapa, tapadera; párpado.

lie [lai], *s.* mentira, embuste.—*l. detector,* detector de mentiras.—*to give the l. to,* dar un mentís a.—*white l.,* mentira inocente, mentirilla.—*vi.* mentir.—*vii.* [10] echarse, estar tendido; yacer; descansar, hallarse.—*to l. down,* echarse, acostarse.

lien [lin], *s.* (for.) embargo; derecho de retención.

lieutenant [liuténant], *s.* teniente; lugarteniente.—*l. commander,* capitán de fragata.

life [laif], *s.* vida; modo de vivir; vivacidad, animación.—*for l.,* de por vida; vitalicio; (fam.) del natural.—*still l.,* naturaleza muerta, bodegón.—*a.* de la vida; vitalicio.—*l. annuity,* renta vitalicia.—*l. belt,* cinturón salvavidas.—*l. imprisonment,* cadena perpetua.—*l. insurance,* seguro sobre la vida.—*l. preserver,* salvavidas.—*l. sentence,* cadena perpetua.—*l.-size,* de tamaño natural. **—boat** [láifbout], *s.* bote o lancha salvavidas, o de salvamento.- **—guard** [-gard], *s.* salvavidas (persona).- **—less** [-lis], *a.* sin vida, muerto, inanimado; deshabitado.- **—lessness** [-lisnis], *s.* falta de vida; falta de animación o vigor.- **—like** [-laik], *a.* que parece vivo, natural.- **—long** [-lɔŋ], *a.* de toda la vida, perpetuo.- **—saver** [-seivœ(r)], *s.* bañero, salvavidas (persona).— **style** [-stail], *s.* estilo de vida.- **—time** [-taim], *s.* curso de la vida; toda la vida.—*a.* vitalicio, vital; perpetuo.

lift [lift], *vt.* alzar, levantar, elevar; (fam.) hurtar; plagiar.—*l.-off,* despegue vertical.—*to l. up,* alzar; soliviar.—*to l. (up) the hand,* prestar juramento levantando la mano; orar; hacer un esfuerzo.—*vi.* disiparse (la niebla).—*s.* elevación; alza; aparejo o gancho de alzar; ascensión.—*to give one a l.,* ayudar a uno; alentar o animar a uno; llevar a uno gratis en un vehículo.

ligament [lígament], (anat.) liga mento.

ligature [lígachur], *s.* ligaduro; ligado

light [lait], *s.* luz; claridad, resplandor lumbre; alumbrado; día, alba.—*i this l.,* desde este punto de vista.—*bulb,* bombilla.—*l.-year,* año luz.—*a.* ligero, leve; sutil; llevadero, fáci fútil, frívolo, superficial; ágil, li viano; inconstante, mudable; ale gre, vivo; incontinente; claro (co lores; piel).—*l.-haired,* pelirrubio.- *l.-headed,* ligero de cascos; atolon drado.—*l.-headedness,* atolondra miento, aturdimiento.—*l.-hearted* alegre, festivo.—*l.-witted,* chalade cascabelero.—*vti.* [4] encende alumbrar, iluminar.—*vii.* encen derse; iluminarse; descender, po sarse; apearse.- **—en** [láitn], *vt.* ilu minar, alumbrar; aclarar; aligera aliviar; regocijar.—*vi.* ponerse li gero; relampaguear, centellear.- **—er** [-œ(r)], *a.* (comp. de LIGHT).— encendedor.- **—house** [-haus], faro.- **—ing** [-iŋ], *s.* alumbrado, luz iluminación.- **—ness** [-nis], *s.* leve dad, ligereza; agilidad; frivolidad, l viandad.- **—ning** [-niŋ], *s.* relám pago; relampagueo.- **—weigh** [-weit], *a.* ligero; de entretiempo.

likable [láikabl], *a.* amable, simpático agradable.- **—like** [laik], *a.* seme jante; análogo, igual; lo mismo que equivalente.—*it looks l. rain,* parec que va a llover.—*to feel l. going,* tene ganas de ir.—*s.* semejanza; seme jante, igual.—*pl.* gustos, simpatía aficiones.—*adv.* y *prep.* como, seme jante a; a (la) manera de, a guisa de en son de; al igual que, del mism modo que, a semejanza de; (fam probablemente.—*l. as,* como, a como.—*l. mad,* como loco, furic samente.—*l. this,* así, de es modo.—*that is (just) l. him,* eso e muy propio de él.—*what are they l.* ¿cómo son ellos?—*vt.* gustarle uno; gustar de; tener gusto en o af ción a; aprobar; querer, simpatiza con.—*to l. best, better,* gustarle uno) más.—*vi.* gustar, agradar.—*you l.,* como usted quiera, como usted guste.—*if you l.,* si le parec (bien).—*she had l. to die* o *have die* (fam.) por poco se muere. **—likeli hood** [láiklihud], *s.* probabilidad verosimilitud; apariencia. **—likel**

[lájkli], *a.* probable, verosímil, fácil; prometedor; apto, idóneo, a propósito.—*adv.* probablemente.—*l. enough,* no sería extraño. —**liken** [lájkn], *vt.* asemejar, comparar. —**likeness** [lájknis], *s.* semejanza, parecido; igualdad; apariencia, aire; retrato. —**likewise** [lájkwajz], *adv.* también, asímismo, además, igualmente; otrosí. —**liking** [lájkin], *s.* afición, gusto, agrado, inclinación; simpatía; preferencia.

lilac [lájlak], *s.* (bot.) lila.—*a.* de color de lila.

Lilliputian [lilipiúsan], *a.* y *s.* liliputiense.

lily [líli], *s.* (bot.) lirio, azucena; flor de lis.—*l.-livered,* cobarde, ruin.—*l. pad,* hoja de nenúfar.

Lima bean [laíma], *s.* judía de la peladilla, frijol de media luna.

limb [lim], *s.* miembro (del cuerpo); rama (de árbol); miembro, individuo; limbo; borde, orilla.—*vt.* desmembrar.— **—er** [límbœ(r)], *a.* flexible, blando.—*vi.* (up) ponerse flexible.— **—erness** [límbœrnis], *s.* flexibilidad.

lime [lajm], *s.* (bot) limero; (fruit) lima; (calcium oxide) cal; (linden tree) tila o tilo.— **—light** [lájmlajt], *s.*—*to be in the l.,* estar a la vista del público.

limerick [límĕrik], *s.* quintilla jocosa.

limit [límit], *s.* límite.—*vt.* limitar.—*limited-access highway,* carretera de vía libre.— **—ation** [-éjšon], *s.* limitación.— **—less** [-lis], *a.* ilimitado.

limp [limp], *s.* cojera.—*a.* débil, flojo; fláccido.—*vi.* cojear.

limpid [límpid], *a.* diáfano, cristalino, límpido.— **—ity** [límpíditi], **—ness** [límpidnis], *s.* limpidez, diafanidad.

line [lajn], *s.* línea; tubería, cañería; raya; veta; renglón; sedal (de pescar); frontera, límite; (com.) renglón, ramo, clase; surtido, artículos; (f.c., etc.) recorrido, trayecto; método, plan; línea de conducta; hilera, fila; verso; especialidad.— *along these lines,* en este sentido.— *in a l.,* en línea.—*in l.,* alineado; de acuerdo; dispuesto.—*in one's line,* dentro de la especialidad o conocimientos de uno.—*on the lines of,* conforme a, a tenor de.—*out of one's line,* ajeno a la especialidad o tarea

de uno; asunto de que uno no entiende.—*vt.* trazar líneas, rayar; alinear; ir a lo largo o en los bordes u orillas de.—*to l. out,* marcar con rayas.—*to l. up,* alinear.—*vi.* alinearse; estar alineado; (up) formar fila, estar en fila o haciendo cola; formar, ponerse en formación.- **—age** [líniidž], *s.* linaje, alcurnia.- **—ar** [líniá(r)], *a.* lineal; longitudinal; (zool. y bot.) linear.- **—d** [lajnd], *a.* rayado; forrado.- **—up** [-ʌp], *s.* agrupación, formación; (of prisoners) rueda.

linen [línen], *s.* lienzo, lino; hilo de lino; ropa blanca; ropa de cama.—*l. closet,* armario para la ropa blanca.

liner [lájnœ(r)], *s.* transatlántico, vapor de travesía.

linger [língœ(r)], *vi.* demorarse, ir despacio; subsistir, persistir.—*vt.* (out o away) prolongar, demorar.

lingerie [lændzęrí], *s.* ropa interior de mujer.

linguist [língwist], *s.* linguista; políglota.— **—ic** [lingwístik], *a.* lingüístico.- **—ics** [lingwístiks], *s.* lingüística.

lining [lájnin], *s.* forro; revestimiento; (aut.) guarnición.

link [link], *s.* eslabón.—*pl.* campo de golf.—*vt.* y *vi.* eslabonar(se), enlazar(se).- **—age** [línkidž], *s.* eslabonamiento.

linnet [línit], *s.* pardillo.

linoleum [linóuliʌm], *s.* linóleo.

linotype [lájnotajp], *s.* linotipo; (mec.) linotipia.— **linotypist** [-ist], *s.* linotipista.

linseed [línsid], *s.* linaza.—*l. oil,* aceite de linaza.

lint [lint], *s.* hilas; pelusilla de la ropa.

lion [lájon], *s.* león.— **—ess** [-is], *s.* leona.— **—ize** [-ajz], *vt.* poner por las nubes.

lip [lip], *s.* labio.—*l.-read,* vt. y vi. leer en los labios.—*l. reading,* labiolectura.—*to give l.-service,* defender de dientes para fuera, de boquilla.- **—stick** [lípstik], *s.* lápiz de labios, lápiz labial.

liquefy [líkwifaj], *vti.* y *vii.* [7] liquidar, liquidarse; derretir, fundirse.

liqueur [likœ́(r)], *s.* licor; bebida cordial.

liquid [líkwid], *s.* líquido.—*a.* líquido; (com.) realizable. **—liquidate** [líkwideit], vt. liquidar. —**liquidation** [likwidéiŝon], s. liquidación.

liquor [líkor(r)], s. licor.—hard l., licor espiritoso.

lisp [lisp], vt. y vi. cecear; balbucir o balbucear.—s. ceceo; balbuceo, balbucencia.

list [list], s. lista; (tej.) orilla, borde; lista, tira; (mar.) escora, inclinación.—l. price, precio de catálogo, precio de tarifa.—pl. liza, palestra.—vt. registrar. poner en lista; catalogar; (mil.) alistar.—vi. (mar.) irse a la banda.

listen [lísn], vi. escuchar, oir; obedecer.—to l. in, escuchar a escondidas; escuchar por radio.— —**er** [-œ(r)], s. oyente.—radio l., radioyente.

listless [lístlis], a. desatento; indiferente, descuidado.— —**ness** [-nis], s. descuido, indiferencia.

litany [lítani], s. (igl.) letanía.

liter [lítœ(r)], s. litro. Ver Tabla.

literacy [líterasi], s. capacidad de leer y escribir. —**literal** [líteral], a. literal. —**literalism** [líteralizm], s. exactitud literal; realismo extremo. —**literally** [líterali], adv. literalmente. —**literary** [líterœri], a. literario. —**literate** [líterit], a. que sabe leer y escribir. —**literature** [líterachur], s. literatura.

lithe [laiθ], a. flexible, cimbreño.

lithography [liθágrafi], s. litografía.

litigate [lítigeit], vt. y vi. litigar. —**litigation** [litigéiŝon], s. litigio.

litre [lítœ(r)], s. = LITER.

litter [lítœ(r)], s. desorden; basura, papelería; (stretcher) camilla, parihuela; (vehicle) litera; (bedding) cama, paja; (zool.) camada, ventregada.—vt. esparcir (colillas, desechos, etc.); desordenar, desaliñar.—vi. parir.

little [lítl], a. pequeño; poco.—a. l. (bit), un poco, un poquito.—a l. sugar, un poquito de azúcar.—a l. while, un rato, un ratico.—l. finger, dedo auricular, dedo meñique.—adv. poco.—l. by l., poco a poco.—s. poco; porción o parte pequeña.

liturgy [lítŭrdzi], s. liturgia.

live [liv], vt. vivir, llevar (tal o cual vida).—vi. vivir, existir; habitar, morar, residir; mantenerse, subsistir.—a. [laiv], vivo, viviente; de la vida, vital; encendido, en ascua; activo, listo; de interés actual.—l. wire, alambre cargado; (jer.) trafa-

gón.—adv. (rad./tel.) en directo, en vivo.- —**lihood** [láivlihud], s. vida, subsistencia.— —**liness** [láivlinis], s. vida, vivacidad, viveza, animación; agilidad, actividad.- —**ly** [láivli], a. vivo, vivaz, vivaracho; gallardo, airoso; rápido; animado.—adv. enérgicamente; vivamente; aprisa. - —**n** [láiven], vt. animar, regocijar. —vi. animarse, regocijarse.- —**r** [lívœ(r)], s. (anat., zool.) hígado; vividor.

livery [lívœri], s. librea.

lives [laivz], s. pl. de LIFE.

livestock [láivstak], s. ganadería.

livid [lívid], a. lívido.

living [lívin], s. vida.—the l., los vivos, los seres vivientes.—a. vivo, viviente.—l. room, sala.—l. wage, salario decoroso.

lizard [lízărd], s. lagarto.

llama [lámä], s. (zool.) llama.

load [loud], s. carga; peso; (o)presión.—loads of, (fam.) montones de, gran cantidad o número.—vt. y vi. cargar; recargar.- —**d** [lóudęd], a. cargado; (jer.) muy borracho; (jer.) muy rico.—l. dice, dados cargados.

loaf [louf], s. pan.—l. of sugar, pilón de azúcar.—vi. haraganear, holgazanear.- —**er** [lóufœ(r)], s. holgazán; zapato deportivo (sin cordones).

loam [loum], s. suelo franco.

loan [loun], s. préstamo; (com.) préstito.—l. shark, (fam.) usurero, garrotero.—vt. prestar.

loath [louθ], a. poco dispuesto, renuente.- —**e** [louð], vt. detestar, abominar.- —**some** [lóuðsʌm], a. abominable, asqueroso.

loaves [louvz], s. pl. de LOAF.

lobby [lábi], s. vestíbulo; salón de entrada; paso, pasillo; pórtico; (pol.) cabilderos.—vti. y vii. [7] politiquear.- —**ing** [-iɳ], s. cabildeo.- —**ist** [-ist], s. cabildero.

lobster [lábstœ(r)], s. langosta; bogavante.

local [lóukạl], a. local; vecinal; regional.—l. horizon, horizonte sensible o visible.—l. train, tren ordinario o de escalas.- —**ity** [lokélịti], s. situación; localidad; lugar.- —**ization** [-izéiŝon], s. localización.— —**ize** [-aiz], vt. localizar.- —**locate** [lóukeit], vt. y vi. ubicar(se). —**location** [lokéiŝon], s. localidad; localización; colocación.—on l., (cin.) en exteriores.

lock [lak], *s.* cerradura; llave o pestillo (de las armas de fuego); chaveta; esclusa, compuerta; abrazo estrecho y apretado; buele, guedeja.—*l. nut,* (mec.) contratuerca.—*l. step,* marcha en fila apretada.—*l. stitch,* punto de cadeneta.—*l. washer,* (mec.) arandela de seguridad.—*under l. and key,* bajo llave.—*vt.* cerrar con llave; poner cerradura; juntar, entrelazar, atar, trabar; abrazar; fijar, trincar; cerrar.—*to l. in,* encerrar, poner bajo llave.—*to l.* (one) *out,* cerrar la puerta a uno; dejar en la calle o sin trabajo.—*to l. up,* encerrar, encarcelar.—*vi.* cerrarse con llave; unirse; trabarse; sujetarse.— **—er** [lákœr], *s.* armario cerrado con llave.— **—et** [lákit], *s.* medallón, guardapelo.— **—jaw** [-dʒɔ̄], *s.* trismo. - **—out** [-aut], *s.* huelga patronal.— **—smith** [-smiθ], *s.* cerrajero.- **—up** [-ʌp], *s.* calabozo; cárcel; encarcelamiento.

locomotive [loukomóutjv], *s.* locomotora.—*l. engineer,* maquinista.

locust [lóukʌst], *s.* langosta, langostón, saltamontes; cigarra.

locution [lokiúsǫn], *s.* locución.

lode [loud], *s.* filón, venero, veta.- **—star** [-star], *s.* estrella polar, estrella de guía.

lodge [ladʒ], *vt.* alojar, albergar; colocar; plantar, introducir, fijar; dar a guardar.—*to l. a complaint,* dar una queja.—*vi.* hospedarse; tenderse, echarse.—*s.* casa de guarda; pabellón; portería; logia.— **—r** [ládʒœr], *s.* inquilino, huésped. **—lodging** [ládʒiŋ], *s.* posada, hospedería; hospedaje, alojamiento; morada, residencia.

loft [lɔft], *s.* ático, sobrado, desván; almacén.- **—iness** [lɔ́ftjnis], *s.* altura; nobleza; altanería.- **—y** [-i], *a.* alto, encumbrado; altivo, soberbio.

log [lɔg], *s.* leño, palo; tronco, madero; (mar.) corredera; (aer.) diario de vuelo.—*l. cabin, l. hut,* cabaña rústica.—*l. driving,* flotaje.—*to sleep like a l.,* dormir como un leño.—*vti.* [l] registrar; recorrer.— **—book** [-buk], *s.* (mar.) cuaderno de bitácora; (aer.) libro de vuelo.- **—ger** [lɔ́gœr], *s.* leñador, maderero; grúa de troncos; tractor.— **—gerheads** [lɔ́gœrhedz], *spl.*—*at l.,* reñidos.- **—ging** [lɔ́giŋ], *s.* tala de árboles, explotación forestal; comercia en maderas.- **—jam** [-dzæm], *s.* atasco de rollizos; (fig.) estancación.

logic [ládʒik], *s.* lógica.- **—al** [-ạl], *a.* lógico.- **—ian** [lodʒịṣan], *s.* lógico.

loin [lɔjn], *s.* lomo.—*l. cloth,* taparrabo.

loiter [lɔ́jtœ(r)], *vi.* remolonear, holgazanear.—*vt.* (away) malgastar (tiempo).- **—er** [-œ(r)], *s.* vagabundo, holgazán.

loll [lal], *vi.* apoyarse, recostarse, tenderse; pender, colgar (la lengua de un animal).—*vt.* dejar colgar (la lengua).

lollipop [lálipap], *s.* paleta, pirulí.

lone [loun], *a.* solitario, solo; soltero.—*l. wolf,* (fig.) lobo solitario.— **—liness** [lóunlinis], *s.* soledad; tristeza del aislamiento.- **—ly** [-li], *a.* solitario; triste, desamparado.- **—some** [-sʌm], *a.* solitario, desierto; triste.

long [lɔŋ], *a.* largo; de largo; extenso, prolongado; tardío, dilatorio; excesivo, de más; distante; (com.) recargado, esperando alza de precios.—*how l.?* ¿de qué largo (medida)?—*in the l. run,* a la larga.—*it is a l. way,* dista mucho, está muy lejos.—*l.-distance call,* (tlf.) llamada a larga distancia.—*l. dozen,* docena de fraile, trece.—*l. face,* (fam.) cara triste.—*l. hundred,* ciento viente.— *l.-suffering,* paciencia, resignación, aguante.—*l. suit,* fuerte, especialidad de una persona.—*l. time,* mucho tiempo, largo rato.—*l.-winded,* difuso, palabrero.—*adv.* a gran distancia; mucho; (durante) mucho tiempo.—*all* o *the whole day, year, etc.* l., todo el santo día, todo el año, etc.—*as l. as,* mientras.—*before* o *ere l.,* en breve, antes de mucho.—*how l.?* ¿cuánto tiempo?—*how l. is it since?* ¿cuánto (tiempo) hace que?—*l. after,* mucho (tiempo) después.—*l. ago,* hace mucho (tiempo).—*l.-drawn,* lento, pesado, prolongado.—*l. live!* ¡viva!—*l.-lived,* longevo.—*l.-range,* de largo alcance.—*l.-sighted,* sagaz, previsor. *—l.-standing,* de larga duración.— *l.-term,* (com.) a largo plazo.—*not l. ago* o *since,* no hace mucho.—*not l. before,* poco tiempo antes.—*so l. as,* mientras que, en tanto que.—*s.* longitud, largo.—*pl.* (com.) los que guardan acciones en espera de alza.—*vi.* (for, o to) anhelar, suspirar (por), codiciar, apetecer, ansiar; añorar.– **—er** [lɔ́ŋɡœ(r)], a. más largo.—adv. más tiempo, más rato.—how much l.? ¿cuánto tiempo más?—no l., ya no, no más.– **—evity** [lɔndžévɨ̯ɨ], s. longevidad.– **—hand** [-hǽnd], s. escritura a mano.– **—ing** [lɔ́ŋɨŋ], s. deseo vehemente, anhelo, ansia, ansiedad.—a. anhelante, ansioso, vehemente.– **—itude** [lándžɨ̯tɨ̯ud], s. longitud.

longshoreman [lɔ́ŋšɔrmạn], s. estibador, cargador del muelle.

look [lŭk], vt. mirar, pasar la vista a; causar o expresar con la mirada o el ademán.—to l. daggers, echar chispas; (at) mirar echando chispas.—to l. in the face, mirar cara a cara, sin vergüenza.—to l. one's age, representar uno los años que tiene.—to l. over, mirar ligeramente o por encima.—to l. up, buscar, averiguar; (fam.) visitar a uno.—vi. mirar, ver; parecer, aparentar; poner cuidado o tener cuidado; lucir (bien, mal); tener cara de.—as it looks to me, a mi ver.—to l. about, observar, mirar alrededor.—to l. about one, estar alerta, vigilar.—to l. after, cuidar, atender a, mirar por; prestar atención; inquirir, investigar.—to l. alike, parecerse a.—to l. alive, darse prisa.—to l. at, mirar; tender la vista a; considerar.—to l. back, reflexionar; mirar atrás.—to l. bad, tomar mal cariz; parecer feo; tener mala cara.—to l. down upon, despreciar.—to l. for, buscar; esperar.—to l. into, estudiar, examinar, averiguar.—to l. like, parecerse a; tener cara o traza de; dar o haber señales de.—to l. on, considerar; estimar; juzgar; mirar, ver; ser espectador.—to l. out of, asomarse a.—to l. sharp, tener ojo avizor.—to l. through, examinar, inspeccionar, hacer un registro de.—to l. to, cuidar de, velar por; atender a; hacer responsable; esperar de; acudir a.—to l. up to, respetar, estimar.—s. mirada, ojeada, vistazo.—pl. aspecto, apariencia, semblante, traza.—to have a l. at, mirar, echar una ojeada a.– **—ing** [lŭ́kɨŋ], s. miramiento; busca; examen.—a. de o para mirar.—good (bad)-l., bien (mal) parecido.—l. glass, espejo.– **—out** [-aŭt], s. vigía, vigilancia; observación; mirador; centinela.— that's his l., (fam.) eso le concierne (a

él); allá él, con su pan se lo coma.— to be on the l., estar a la mira.

loom [lum], s. telar.—vi. vislumbrarse; parecer inevitable, amenazar.– **—ing** [lúmɨŋ], s. espejismo.

loon [lun], s. bobo, tonto.— **—y** [lúnɨ], s. y a. (fam.) bobo, loco rematado.

loop [lup], s. gaza, lazo, bucle; ojal, presilla, alamar; onda; punto; curva, vuelta; (mec.) abrazadera, anilla; (aer.) rizo.—vt. asegurar con presilla; hacer gazas en; formar festones o curvas en.—to l. in, (elec.) intercalar (en un circuito).—to l. the l., (aer.) rizar el rizo, dar una vuelta vertical.—vi. andar haciendo curvas; formar gaza.— **—hole** [lúphoụl], s. abertura, mirador; aspillera, tronera; escapatoria, excusa.

loose [lus], vt. desatar, desprender; aflojar; aliviar; soltar, libertar, librar; desenredar; desocupar.—to l. one's hold, soltar.—a. suelto; desatado; flojo, holgado; vago, indefinido; libre, disoluto; negligente.—l. end, cabo suelto; at loose ends, desarreglado, indeciso.—l.-leaf notebook, cuaderno de hojas cambiables.— l.-tongued, largo de lengua, ligero de lengua.—s. libertad, soltura.— on the l., (fam.) libre; sin trabas; de parranda.– **—n** [lúsn], vt. aflojar, soltar, desunir; laxar, relajar; librar.—vi. desunirse, aflojarse, desatarse.– **—ness** [-nɨs], s. aflojamiento, flojedad, holgura; relajamiento; soltura; flujo de vientre; vaguedad.

loot [lut], vt. y vi. saquear.—s. botín; saqueo, pillaje.

lop [lap], vti. [1]—to l. off, cortar, podar.—vii. colgar.—l.-eared, de orejas gachas.– **—sided** [lápsaɪ̯dẹd], a. ladeado, sesgado; desproporcionado, asimétrico.

loquacious [lokwéɪ̯šʌs], a. locuaz. **—loquacity** [lokwǽsɨ̯ɨ], s. locuacidad.

lord [lɔrd], s. señor; lord (pl. lores).— L.'s Prayer, Padrenuestro.—L.'s Supper, Cena del Señor, sagrada communión.—vt. y vi.—to l. it over, dominar imponerse a.– **—ly** [lɔ́rdlɨ], a. señoril; imperioso.—adv. señorilmente; altiva o imperiosamente.– **—ship** [-šɨp], s. señoría, excelencia.—your l., usía, vuecencia.

lore [lɔr], s. erudición, saber, ciencia.

lorgnette [lɔrnyét], s. impertinentes; gemelos de teatro con mango.

lose [luz], vti. [10] perder.—*to l. face,* desprestigiarse.—*to l. heart,* descorazonarse.—*to l. oneself,* perderse, extraviarse.—*to l. one's temper,* encolerizarse.—*to l. sight of,* perder de vista.—*vii.* perder, tener una pérdida; atrasar (un reloj).—*to l. out,* (fam.) llevarse chasco, ser derrotado.- **—r** [lúzœ(r)], s. perdedor. **—losing** [lúzịŋ], a. perdedor, perdidoso; vencido. **—loss** [lɔs], s. pérdida; perjuicio, daño; privación. —*at a l.,* perdiendo, con pérdida; perplejo, indeciso, en duda.—*at a l. to,* sin acertar a.—*l. of face,* pérdida de prestigio. **—lost** [lɔst], pret. y pp. de TO LOSE.—a. perdido, extraviado, descarriado; desorientado; perplejo; malogrado; desperdiciado.—*l. and found department,* oficina de objetos perdidos.

lot [lat], s. solar, terreno, lote, porción, parte; grupo (de personas); suerte, hado, sino.—*a l.,* (fam.) mucho.—*a l. of,* (fam.) gran número de, gran cantidad de.—*by lots,* enchando suertes, a la suerte.—*lots of,* (fam.) mucho, muchos.—*to draw* o *to cast lots,* echar suertes.—*to fall to one's l.,* tocarle a uno en suerte.

lotion [lóųʃọn], s. loción.

lottery [látœrị], s. lotería, rifa. **—lotto** [látoų], s. lotería.

loud [laųd], a. ruidoso; recio, fuerte; chillón; (fam.) urgente; llamativo; subido de color.—*l. laugh,* risotada, carcajada.—*adv.* ruidosamente; en alta voz; a gritos.- **—mouthed** [laųdmaúθd], a. vocinglero.- **—ness** [láųdnịs], s. ruido, sonoridad; (fam.) vulgaridad, mal gusto. **—loudspeaker** [láųdspíkœ(r)], s. altavoz, altoparlante; megáfono.

lounge [laųndʒ], vi. holgazanear; repatingarse; ponerse uno a sus anchas.—s. salón de fumar o descansar; sofá, canapé.

louse [laųs], s. piojo. **—lousy** [láųzị], a. piojoso; (fam.) vil, ruin; (fam.) chapucero.

louver [lúvœr], s. lumbrera; tablilla de persiana.

lovable [lávạbl], a. amable. **—love** [lʌv], vt. amar, querer; (fam.) gustar de, tener afición a.—vi. amar.—s. amor.—*for l. or money,* por buenas o por malas; a cualquier precio.—*in l. with,* enamorado de.—*l. affair,* intriga amorosa, amorío.—*l. bird,* pe-

riquito.—*l. seat,* confidente.—*l. song,* canción de amor.—*not l. or money,* por nada del mundo.—*to make l. to,* enamorar, galantear, cortejar. **—loveliness** [lávlịnịs], s. amabilidad, agrado, encanto; belleza. **—lovely** [lávlị], a. amable, cariñoso; hermoso, bello; (fam.) agradable, atractivo; ameno. **—lover** [lávœ(r)], s. amante; galán; aficionado. **—lovesick** [lávsịk], a. enfermo de amor, herido de amor. **—loving** [lávịŋ], a. amante, amoroso, cariñoso, afectuoso; aficionado; apacible.

low [loų], a. bajo; abatido; gravemente enfermo; malo (dieta, opinión, etc.); módico (precio); muerto, grosero; vil, rastrero; pobre, humilde; débil, debilitado.—*in l. gear,* (aut.) en primera.—*l. comedy,* farsa, sainete.—*l.-down,* (fam.) bajo, vil.—*l. spirits,* abatimiento.—*l. tide,* bajamar.—*l. trick,* mala pasada.—*l. water,* marea baja.—*adv.* bajo; en la parte inferior; a precio bajo; vilmente; sumisamente; en voz baja; en tono profundo.—*l.-minded,* ruin.—*vi.* mugir, berrear.—s. mugido, berrido; punto o lugar bajo; valor o precio mínimo; (aut.) primera velocidad.—*l.-down,* (fam.) información confidencial o de primera mano; los hechos verdaderos. - **—born** [lóųbɔrn], a. de humilde cuna.- **—bred** [-bred], a. malcriado; vulgar.- **—brow** [-braų], a. poco intelectual.- **—er** [-œ(r)], vt. humillar, abatir, deprimir; bajar, poner más bajo; rebajar, disminuir; [láųœ(r)], mirar amenazadoramente.—*to l. the flag,* abatir la bandera.—vi. menguar, disminuirse.—a. más bajo; inferior.- **—erclassman** [lóųœrklǽsmạn], s. estudiante de primero o segundo año.- **—ering** [lóųœrịŋ], a. encapotado, nebuloso; amenazador.- **—land** [lóųlạnd], s. tierra baja. - **—liness** [-lịnịs], s. humildad; bajeza, vileza.- **—ly** [-lị], a. humilde; vil, bajo.—adv. humildemente; vilmente.

loyal [lóịạl], a. leal, fiel, constante.- **—ty** [-tị], s. lealtad, fidelidad.

lozenge [lázẹndʒ], s. pastilla; rombo.

lubricant [ljúbrịkạnt], s. y a. lubri(fi)-cante. **—lubricate** [ljúbrịkẹịt], vt. lubri(fi)car, engrasar.

lucid [ljúsịd], a. luciente; diáfano; brillante; lúcido; claro, inteligible.-

—ity [ljusíditi], **—ness** [ljúsjdnjs], s. lucidez; claridad mental; transparencia; brillantez.

luck [lʌk], s. suerte; buen suerte.—*to be in l.*, estar de buena suerte.—*to be out of l.*, estar de mala suerte.- **—lly** [lʌkjlj], adv. afortunadamente.- **—y** [-j], a. afortunado; de buen agüero.—*l. break,* (fam.) chiripa, coyuntura favorable.

lucrative [ljúkrątjv], a. lucrativo.

ludicrous [ljúdjkrʌs], a. ridículo, risible.

lug [lʌg], s. (fam.) tirón, estirón; cosa tirada; cosa lenta y pesada; (mec.) oreja, argolla; saliente; agarradera.—vt. tirar de, halar.

luggage [lʌgjdž], s. equipaje.

lukewarm [ljúkwɔrm], a. tibio, templado; indiferente, frío.

lull [lʌl], vt. arrullar; aquietar.—vi. calmarse, sosegarse.—s. momento de calma o de silencio.- **—aby** [lʌlạbaj], s. arrullo; canción de cuna, nana.

lumber [lámbœ(r)], s. madera aserrada; maderaje; armatoste; trastos o muebles viejos.—vt. amontonar trastos viejos.—vi. andar pesadamente; avanzar con ruido sordo.- **—ing** [-jŋ], a. pesado.- **—jack** [-džæk], s. leñador, hachero.

luminary [ljúmjnerj], s. astro; lumbrera.

lump [lʌmp], s. masa, bulto, burujón; protuberancia, chichón; hinchazón; pitón; terrón.—*a l. in the throat,* un nudo en la garganta.—*by the l.,* a bulto, en globo, a ojo, por junto.—*in a o in the l.,* todos juntos, sin distinción.—*l. of sugar,* terrón de azúcar.—*l. sum,* suma redonda.— vt. amontonar; comprar a bulto, en globo.—*to l. it,* (fam.) soportarlo, tragar saliva.—vi. trabajar como estibador; apelotonarse, aterronarse. - **—y** [lámpj], a. aterronado.

lunacy [ljúnạsj], s. locura. **—lunar** [ljúnạ̈(r)], a. lunar; lunario; lunado; lunático. **—lunatic** [ljúnạtjk], s. y a. loco, lunático.

lunch [lʌnch], s. almuerzo; colación,

merienda.—*l. basket,* fiambrera.- **—room** [-rum], s. cantina, merendero.—vi. almorzar; merendar, tomar una colación.

luncheon [lánchɔn], s. almuerzo; almuerzo de ceremonia.

lung [lʌŋ], s. pulmón.

lunge [lʌndž], s. estocada; arremetida.—vi. dar una estocada, tirarse a fondo; arremeter, abalanzarse.

lurch [lœrch], s. sacudida, vaivén; bandazo, guiñada.—*to leave in the l.,* plantar, dejar en las astas del toro o en la estacada.—vi. andar tambaleando; dar bandazos.

lure [ljur], s. añagaza, señuelo; cebo.— vt. atraer, inducir, tentar.

lurid [ljúrjd], a. cárdeno; espeluznante, siniestro.

lurk [lœrk], vi. acechar; moverse furtivamente; emboscarse.

luscious [lʌ́šʌs], a. sabroso, delicioso; meloso; empalagoso.

lush [lʌš], a. suculento, jugoso; fresco y lozano; exuberante.

lust [lʌst], s. lujuria, concupiscencia; codicia; anhelo vehemente.—vi. (for o after) codiciar.

luster [lʌ́stœ(r)], s. lustre, brillo.—pl. realce, lucimiento; araña de cristal; lustro.—vt. lustrar. **—lustrous** [lʌ́strʌs], a. lustroso, brillante.

lusty [lʌ́stj], a. lozano, vigoroso.

lute [ljut], s. laúd.

Lutheran [ljúθœrạn], s. y a. luterano.

luxuriant [lʌkŝúrjạnt], a. exuberante; superfluo; frondoso; lujuriante. **—luxurious** [lʌkŝúrjʌs], a. lujoso. **—luxury** [lʌ́kŝụrj], s. lujo.

lye [laj], s. lejía.

lying [lájjŋ], a. mentiroso.—*l. down,* acostado.—*l.-in hospital,* casa de maternidad.—s. el mentir.

lynch [ljnch], vt. linchar.—*l. law,* justicia de la soga.

lynx [ljŋks], s. lince.

lyre [lajr], s. (mus.) lira. **—lyric(al)** [lírjk(ạl)], a. lírico. **—lyric** [lírjk], s. poema lírico. **—lyricism** [lírjsjzm], s. lirismo. **—lyricist** [lírjcjst], s. letrista; poeta lírico.

M

ma [ma], s. (fam.) mamá.

ma'am [mæm], s. contr. de MADAM, señora.

macabre [mǝkábr], a. macabro.

macadam [mǝkǽdǝm], s. macadán.

macaroni [mækǝróuni], s. pl. macarrones.

macaroon [mækǝrún], s. almendrado.

macaw [mǝkɔ́], s. guacamayo.

mace [meis], s. maza; (bot.) macis.— M., gas para defensa personal.— **—bearer** [-berẹr], s. macero.

macerate [mǽsẹreit], vt. macerar. **—maceration** [mæsẹréiṣǫn], s. maceración.

machinate [mǽkineit], vt. y vi. maquinar. **—machination** [mækinéiṣǫn], s. maquinación, intriga. **—machine** [mǝṣín], s. máquina, aparato; vehículo, automóvil, avión, etc.—m. gun, ametralladora.—to m.-gun, ametrallar.—m.-made, hecho a máquina.—m. shop, taller mecánico.—m. translation, traducción automática. **—machinery** [mǝṣínœri], s. maquinaria; mecanismo, aparato; organización, sistema. **—machinist** [mǝṣínist], s. maquinista, mecánico; tramoyista.

mackerel [mǽkẹrel], s. caballa, (Am.) macarela, pintada.

mad [mæd], a. loco, demente; furioso, rabioso; insensato; enojado, encolerizado.—to go m., enloquecerse, volverse loco; (zool.) rabiar.

madam [mǽdǝm], s. celestina; dueña de un burdel; señora.

madame [mǽdǝm, mædǽm], s. señora.

madcap [mǽdkæp], a. y s. fogoso; temerario; calavera, tarambana. **—madden** [mǽdn], vt. y vi. enloquecer(se), enfurecer(se).

made [meid], pret. y pp. de TO MAKE.— a. hecho, fabricado.—m.-over, rehecho; reformado.—m.-to-order, hecho de encargo; hecho a la medida. **—made-up** [méidʌp], a. artificial; ficticio; maquillado, pintado; (con of) compuesto (de).

madhouse [mǽdhaus], s. manicomio. **—madman** [mǽdmǝn], s. loco, orate. **—madness** [mǽdnis], s. locura, demencia; furia, rabia.

Madrilenian [mædrilíniǝn], a. y s. madrileño.

magazine [mægǝzín], s. revista; (arti.) cámara para los cartuchos; almacén militar.—m. rifle, rifle de repetición.—powder m., polvorín; santabárbara.

magic [mǽdžik], s. magia; prestidigitación.—a. mágico, encantador.— m. wand, varita mágica, varita de virtud.- **—ian** [mǝdžíṣǝn], s. mágico; ilusionista, prestidigitador.

magistrate [mǽdžistreit], s. magistrado; juez.

magnanimous [mægnǽnimʌs], a. magnánimo.

magnet [mǽgnit], s. imán, magneto.- **—ic** [mægnétik], a. magnético; atractivo.- **—ism** [mǽgnitizm], s. magnetismo.- **—ize** [mǽgnitaiz], vt. magnetizar, imantar.—vi. imantarse.

magnificence [mægnífisẹns], s. magnificencia. **—magnificent** [mægnífisẹnt], a. magnífico.

magnify [mǽgnifai], vti. [7] aumentar, ampliar; (the voice) amplificar; (igl.) magnificar.—magnifying glass, vidrio de aumento, lupa.

magnitude [mǽgnitiud], s. magnitud.

magpie [mǽgpai], s. urraca; (fig.) hablador, cotorra.

mahogany [mǝhágǝni], s. caoba, caobo.

maid [meid], s. doncella; criada, sirvienta, doméstica.—m. of honor, primera madrina de boda; doncella de honor; dama de honor.- **—en** [méidn], s. doncella.—a. soltera.— m. aunt, tía soltera.—m. lady, soltera.—m. name, apellido de soltera.

mail [meil], s. correo; correspondencia; cota de malla.—by return m., a vuelta de correo.—m. bag, valija.— m. carrier, cartero.—m. order, pedido postal.—vt. echar al correo; enviar por correo.- **—box** [méilbaks], s. buzón.- **—ing** [-iŋ], s.—m. list, lista de envío, banco de direcciones.- **—man** [-mæn], s. cartero.

maim [meim], vt. estropear, lisiar, tullir.

main [mein], a. principal; esencial; de mayor importancia.—m. course, plato principal, plato fuerte,—*m. deck,* cubierta principal.—*m. floor,* planta baja.—*m. office,* (com.) casa matriz.—*m. street,* calle principal, calle mayor.—*m. wall,* pared maestra.—*the m. thing,* lo principal, lo esencial.—*s.* cañería maestra, conducto; océano, alta mar.—*in the m.,* mayormente.- **—land** [méjnlənd], *s.* continente, tierra firme.- **—stay** [-stej], *s.* sostén, apoyo.

maintain [mejntéjn], *vt.* mantener, guardar; sostener, afirmar. **—maintenance** [méjntənəns], *s.* mantenimiento; manutención; sostén, sustento, sostenimiento; conservación (de vía, máquina, camino, etc.).

maize [mejz], *s.* maíz.

majestic [mədžéstik], *a.* majestuoso. **—majesty** [mædžisti], *s.* majestad.

major [méjdžo(r)], *a.* mayor, más grande; principal.—*s.* comandante, mayor; mayor de edad; curso de especialización (en universidad o colegio).—*m.-domo,* mayordomo.— *m. general,* general de división.—*vi.* (con in) especializarse en un estudio o asignatura.- **—ity** [mədžáriti], *s.* mayoría, el mayor número (de); (for.) mayoría, mayor edad.

make [mejk], *vti.* [10] hacer; confeccionar; formar; poner (triste, alegre); decir, pronunciar (un discurso, etc.); dar, prestar (escusas, juramento); cometer (error, equivocación).—*to m. a clean breast of,* confesar, admitir francamente un error.—*to m. a fool of,* engañar; poner en ridículo.—*to m. a hit,* (fam.) causar buena impresión.—*to m. fun of,* burlarse de.—*to m. good,* abonar, subsanar.—*to m. haste,* darse prisa.—*to m. known,* hacer saber; dar a conocer.—*to m. love to,* enamorar, cortejar, hacer el amor a.—*to m. money,* ganar dinero.—*to m. no difference,* no importar, ser indiferente.—*to m. off with,* llevarse, arrebatar.—*to m. one's way,* avanzar; progresar; abrirse paso; salir bien.— *to m. out,* distinguir; entender, comprender.—*to m. out a check to,* hacer el cheque pagadero a favor de.—*to m. room for,* dar paso a; dejar campo, lugar o puesto para; dar lugar o puesto a.—*to m. sense,* tener sentido (una frase); parecer acertado; (con **of**) comprender.—*to m. sure,* cerciorar, asegurar.—*to m. the most of,*

aprovecharse de.—*to m. up,* inventar (cuentos); conciliar, apaciguar; saldar, ajustar.—*to m. up for,* compensar, indemnizar.—*to m. up one's mind,* resolverse, determinar.—*to m. way,* abrir paso; abrir paso.—*vii.* (con **at, for,** o **toward**) dirigirse o encaminarse a, abalanzarse a; (con **for** o **to**) contribuir a, servir para.—*to m. merry,* divertirse; regodearse.—*to m. out,* (jer.) besuquearse; qué tal, p.ej., *how did you make out?* ¿qué tal te fue? (en el examen, con los niños, etc.).—*to m. sure,* asegurarse, cerciorarse.—*s.* hechura, forma, figura; fabricación; manufactura; marca, nombre de fábrica.- **—believe** [-bjlív], *a.* fingido, falso, de mentirijillas.—*s.* artificio, fingimiento.—*vt.* fingir.- **—r** [méjkœ(r)], *s.* hacedor; artífice; fabricante; autor; librador (de cheque, pagaré, etc.); otorgante (de escritura).- **—shift** [-šjft], *a.* provisional, de fortuna.—*s.* expediente.- **—up** [-ʌp], *s.* conjunto; carácter, modo de ser; (teat.) caracterización; afeite, maquillaje.—*vti.* y *vii.* [10] maquillar(se).

making [méjkiŋ], *s.* fabricación.—*pl.* elementos, materiales.

malady [mélədi], *s.* mal, enfermedad.

maladjustment [mælədžástmənt], *s.* inadaptación, desadaptación.

malaria [mələria], *s.* malaria, paludismo.

Malay(an) [məléj(ən)], *a.* y *s.* malayo, de Malaca.

male [mejl], *a.* masculino; macho.— *m. child,* hijo varón.—*m. nurse,* enfermero.—*s.* macho; varón.

malediction [mælidíkšon], *s.* maldición.

malefactor [mélifæktœ(r)], *s.* malhechor.

malevolent [məlévolent], *a.* malévolo.

malice [mélis], *s.* malicia.—*m. aforethought,* (for.) premeditación. **—malicious** [məlíšʌs], *a.* malicioso, maligno. **—malign** [məláin], *a.* maligno.—*vt.* calumniar. **—malignant** [məlignənt], *a.* maligno.

malinger [məlíŋgœ(r)], *vi.* fingirse enfermo, hacer la zanguanga.

mall [mɔl], *s.* alameda, paseo de árboles; (com.) centro comercial, galería.

malleable [mæliəbl], *a.* maleable.

mallet [mælit], *s.* mazo; (dep.) mallete.

malt [mɔlt], *s.* malta.—*malted milk,* leche malteada.

man(m)a [mámạ, mạmá], *s.* mamá.

mammal [mǽmạl], *s.* mamífero.

mammoth [mǽmǫθ], *a.* enorme, gigantesco.—*s.* mamut.

mammy [mǽmị], *s.* mamita, mamá; (E.U.) niñera o criada negra.

man [mæn], *s.* hombre; (in chess) pieza; (in checkers) pieza, peón.—*m. about town*, bulevardero.—*m. and wife*, marido y mujer.—*m. Friday*, criado fiel.—*m. hunt*, caza al hombre.—*m. in the moon*, cara or cuerpo de hombre imaginarios en la luna llena.—*m. of God*, hombre de iglesia, cura.—*m. of straw*, testaferro.—*m. of war*, buque de guerra.—*man overboard!*, ¡hombre al agua!—*to a m.*, hasta el último hombre.—*vti.* [1] tripular, dotar; armar; poner guarnición a.

manacle [mǽnạkl], *s.* manilla.—*pl.* esposas.—*vt.* poner esposas a.

manage [mǽnịdž], *vt.* manejar.—*vi.* arreglarse.- **—able** [-ạbl], *a.* manejable.- **—ment** [-mẹnt], *s.* manejo, dirección, gerencia; la empresa, la parte patronal, los patronos.- **—r** [mǽnịdžœ(r)], *s.* administrador, director; empresario; superintendente; (com.) gerente; (dep.) manager.- **—rial** [-rịạl], *a.* empresarial.

mandate [mǽndeịt], *s.* mandato.—*vt.* asignar por mandato. **—mandatory** [mǽndạtọrị], *a.* (for.) preceptivo, obligatorio.

mane [meịn], *s.* crines; melena.

maneuver [mạnúvœ(r)], *s.* maniobra.—*vt.* y *vi.* maniobrar.

manful [mǽnfụl], *a.* varonil; resuelto.

manganese [mǽngạnís], *s.* manganeso.

mange [meịndž], *s.* sarna, roña.

manger [méịndžœ(r)], *s.* pesebre.

mangle [mǽngl], *vt.* lacerar, aplastar.—*s.* planchadora mecánica.

mango [mǽngoụ], *s.* (bot.) mango.

mangrove [mǽngroụv], *s.* mangle.

mangy [méịndžị], *a.* sarnoso, roñoso.

manhole [mǽnhoụl], *s.* caja de registro, pozo de inspección.

manhood [mǽnhụd], *s.* virilidad; los hombres.

mania [méịnịạ], *s.* manía.- **—c** [méịnịæk], *a.* y *s.* maníaco.

manicure [mǽnịkiụr], *s.* manicura.—*vi.* hacer la manicura. **—manicurist** [mǽnịkiụrịst], *s.* manicuro, manicura.

manifest [mǽnịfest], *a.* manifesto, claro.—*s.* (com.) manifiesto.—*vt.*

manifestar.- **—o** [mænịféstoụ], *s.* manifesto, proclama.

manifold [mǽnịfoụld], *a.* múltiple, vario.—*s.* copia, ejemplar; (aut.) colector, múltiple.

manikin [mǽnịkịn], *s.* maniquí; enano.

manipulate [mạnípyụleịt], *vt.* manipular. **—manipulation** [mạnịpyụléịṣọn], *s.* manipulación.

mankind [mænkáịnd], *s.* (la) humanidad, (el) género humano; [mǽnkaịnd], los hombres, el sexo masculino. **—manliness** [mǽnlịnịs], *s.* virilidad, masculinidad. **—manly** [mǽnlị], *a.* varonil, masculino.

manned spaceship [mǽnd], *s.* astronave tripulada.

mannequin [mǽnĕkịn], *s.* maniquí.

manner [mǽnœ(r)], *s.* manera.—*pl.* modales, crianza.—*after the m. of*, como, a la manera de, a la, a lo.—*by no m. of means*, de ningún modo.—*in a m.*, en cierto modo, hasta cierto punto.—*in a m. of speaking*, como quien dice, por decirlo así.- **—ism** [-ịzm], *s.* amaneramiento, manerismo.

mannish [mǽnịṣ], *a.* hombruno.

manor [mǽnọ(r)], *s.* señorío; (hist.) feudo.—*m. house*, casa solariega.

mansion [mǽnṣọn], *s.* mansión; casa grande; hotel, palacio; (manor house) casa solariega.

manslaughter [mǽnslǫtœ(r)], *s.* homicidio sin premeditación.

mantel(piece) [mǽntl(pis)], *s.* repisa o tablero de chimenea.

mantilla [mæntílạ], *s.* mantilla.

mantle [mǽntl], *s.* manto, capa.

manual [mǽnyụạl], *a.* manual.—*m. training*, enseñanza de los artes y oficios.—*s.* manual; (mus.) teclado manual.

manufacture [mænyụfǽkchụ(r)], *s.* fabricación; manufactura.—*vt.* manufacturar, fabricar.- **—r** [-œ(r)], *s.* fabricante. **—manufacturing** [-ịŋ], *a.* manufacturero, industrial.—*s.* fabricación, manufactura.

manure [mạnịúr], *vt.* estercolar.—*s.* estiércol.

manuscript [mǽnyụskrịpt], *a.* y *s.* manuscrito.

many [ménị], *a.*, *pron.* y *s.* muchos, muchas.—*a great m.*, muchos, muchísimos.—*as m.*, igual número, otros tantos.—*as m. as*, tantos como; cuantos; más que; hasta.—*how m.?* ¿cuántos?—*one, two, etc., too m.*,

uno, dos, etc., de más o de sobra.—
so m., tantos.—*the m.*, la mayoría, la
mayor parte de la gente; las masas,
la muchedumbre.—*too m.*, demasiados.—*twice as m.*, dos veces más.

map [mæp], *s.* mapa; plano (de una
ciudad).—*m. maker*, cartógrafo.—
vti. [1] trazar el mapa de; indicar en
el mapa.—*to m. out*, trazar el plan
de.

maple [méjpl], *s.* arce.

mar [mar], *vti.* [1] estropear, desfigurar.

marauder [marɔ́dœ(r)], *s.* merodeador.
—**marauding** [marɔ́djn], *s.* merodeo, pillaje.

marble [márbl], *s.* mármol; canica o
bolita de vidrio o mármol.—*pl.*
juego de canicas o bolitas.—*a.* marmóreo, de mármol.

march [march], *vt.* poner en marcha,
hacer marchar.—*vi.* marchar, caminar.—*to m. in*, entrar.—*to m. off*,
irse, marcharse.—*to m. out*, salir o
hacer salir.—*s.* marcha; progreso,
adelanto; (mil. mús.) marcha, paso-
doble; (M.) marzo.

marchioness [márʂɔnjs], *s.* marquesa.

mare [mɛr], *s.* yegua.

margarine [márdʐarin], *s.* margarina.

margin [márdʐjn], *s.* margen; (com.)
doble.—*m. release*, tecla de escape.–
—**al** [-al], *a.* marginal.

marigold [mærjgould], *s.* (bot.) caléndula, maravilla.

marihuana o marijuana [marjhwána], *s.*
mariguana, marijuana.

marine [marín], *a.* marino, marítimo,
naval.—*s.*marina (mercante) soldado de infantería de marina.—*M.
Corps*, Infantería de Marina.

marital [mærjtal], *a.* matrimonial.—
m. status, estado civil.

maritime [mærjtajm], *a.* marítimo.

marjoram [márdʐɔram], *s.* mejorana.

mark [mark], *s.* marca; signo; seña o señal; huella, impresión; nota; calificación; marco (moneda); blanco o
diana.—*birth m.*, antojo, lunar.—
question m., punto de interrogación
(?).—*up to the m.*, (fam.) enteramente satisfactorio, perfectamente
bueno o bien.—*vt.* marcar, señalar;
acotar; advertir, notar.—*to m. down*,
poner por escrito, anotar; marcar a
un precio más bajo.—*to m. out*, elegir o escoger; cancelar, borrar.—
—**down** [-daun], *s.* reducción de precio.– —**er** [márkœ(r)], *s.* marcador;
marca; jalón.– —**up** [-ʌp], *s.* aumento de precio.

market [márkjt], *s.* mercado.—*m.
price*, precio corriente.—*m. woman*,
verdulera.—*on the m.*, de o en
venta.—*vt.* llevar al, o vender en el
mercado; hallar mercado para.—*vi.*
comprar o vender en un mercado;
hacer compras en un mercado o
tienda de víveres.- —**ing** [-jn], *s.* comercio; mercadeo, comercializa-
ción; mercología, mercadotecnia.

marketable [márkɛtabĕl], *a.* comercia-
ble, vendible.

marksman [márksman], *s.* buen tirador.- —**ship** [-ʂjp], *s.* buena puntería.

marmalade [mármaleid], *s.* mermelada.

marmot [mármɔt], *s.* (zool.) marmota.

maroon [marún], *s.* y *a.* granate, burdeos, rojo oscuro.—*vt.* abandonar a
uno en una costa desierta.

marquee [markí], *s.* marquesina.

marquetry [márkɛtrj], *s.* marquetería.

marquis [márkwjs], *s.* marqués.- —**e**
[markíz], *s.* marquesa.

marriage [mærjdʐ], *s.* matrimonio;
casamiento.—*m. articles*, capitula-
ciones matrimoniales. —**married**
[mærjd], *a.* casado; matrimonial,
conyugal.—*m. couple*, cónyuges,
marido y mujer.—*to get m.*, casarse.

marrow [mærou], *s.* tuétano, médula,
meollo; substancia, esencia.

marry [mærj], *vti.* [7] casar, unir en matrimonio; casarse con.—*vii.* casarse,
contraer matrimonio.

marsh [marʂ], *s.* pantano, ciénaga.

marshal [márʂal], *s.* mariscal; oficial de
justicia; cursor de procesiones, maestro de ceremonias.—*vti.* [2] ordenar, poner en orden; conducir con
ceremonia.

marshmallow [márʂmælou], *s.* bombón de merengue y gelatina; bombón de malvavisco.

marshy [márʂj], *a.* pantanoso, cenagoso.

mart [mart], *s.* mercado; emporio.

martial [márʂal], *a.* marcial.—*m. law*,
ley marcial.

martyr [mártœ(r)], *s.* mártir.—*vt.* martirizar; atormentar.- —**dom** [-dɔm],
s. martirio.

marvel [márvɛl], *s.* maravilla.—*vii.* [2]
maravillarse.- —**(l)ous** [-ʌs], *a.* maravilloso; (fam.) excelente.

mascot [mæskat], *s.* mascota.

masculine [mæskjuljn], *a.* masculino;
varonil. —**masculinity** [mæskjulí-
njtj], *s.* masculinidad.

mash [mæʂ], *s.* masa; (for brewing)

malta remojada; (for animals) afrecho remojado.—*vt.* machacar, majar.—*mashed potatoes,* puré de papas o patatas.

mask [mæsk], *s.* máscara, careta, antifaz; disfraz.—*m.,* mascarilla.—*masked ball,* baile de máscaras.—*vt.* enmascarar, disfrazar; encubrir.—*vi.* andar disfrazado.

mason [méjson], *s.* albañil; (M.) masón.—**ry** [-rj], *s.* albañilería; mampostería; (M.) masonería.

masquerade [mæskęréjd], *s.* mascarada, comparsa de máscaras; máscara, disfraz.—*m. ball,* baile de máscaras.—*vi.* enmascararse, disfrazarse.

mass [mæs], *s.* masa, montón, mole; bulto, volumen; (M.) misa.—*M. book,* libro de misa; misal.—*m. meeting,* reunión en masa, mitin popular.—*m. noun,* nombre no numerable.—*m. production,* producción o fabricación en serie.—*the masses,* el pueblo, las masas.—*vt.* juntar, reunir en masa, amasar.

massacre [mæsȧkœ(r)], *s.* matanza, carnicería.—*vt.* matar, degollar.

massage [mȧsáž], *s.* masaje.—*vt.* masar, masajear.—**masseur** [mæsœ́r], **masseuse** [mæsœ́z], *s.* masajista.

massif [mæsif], *s.* macizo. —**massive** [mǽsjv], *a.* macizo, abultado, sólido.

mast [mæst], *s.* mástil, palo.

master [mǽstœ(r)], *s.* amo, dueño, señor; maestro; director; señorito; perito, experto.—*m. bedroom,* alcoba de respeto.—*m. builder,* maestro de obras.—*m. key,* llave maestra.—*M. of Arts,* licenciado, maestro en artes.—*m. of ceremonies,* maestro de ceremonias; animador.—*a.* maestro, superior.—*vt.* dominar; conocer a fondo.—**ful** [-ful], *a.* dominante; experto; excelente.—**mind** [-maind], *s.* mente directora.—*vt,* planear y organizar.—**ly** [-lj], *a.* magistral; maestro.—*adv.* con maestría; magistralmente.—**piece** [-pis], *s.* obra maestra.—**y** [-j], *s.* dominio, poder; maestría, destreza; conocimiento.

mastiff [mǽstif], *s.* mastín.

mat [mæt], *s.* estera, esterilla, felpudo; rejilla; colchón gimnástico.—*vt.* enmarañar.—*vi.* enmarañarse.

match [mæch], *s.* fósforo, cerilla; pareja; igual, semejante; (dep.) partido, juego, contienda; concurso, certamen.—*drawn m.,* empate.—*m. point,* (dep.) tanto o punto decisivo.—*to meet one's m.,* encontrar la horma de su zapato.—*vt.* hermanar, aparear; igualar a, equiparar; competir con.—*vi.* armonizar, hacer juego, casar.—**book** [-buk], *s.* librito de fósforos; librito de cerillas.—**box** [-baks], *s.* fosforera; (of wax matches) cerillera.—**less** [mǽchljs], *a.* incomparable, sin igual, sin par.—**maker** [-mejkœ(r)], *s.* casamentero; organizador de encuentros deportivos.

mate [mejt], *s.* consorte, cónyuge; compañero, compañera; macho o hembra entre los animales; mate (ajedrez); (mar.) piloto.—*vt.* casar; aparear.—*vi.* aparearse; casarse.

material [mȧtíriȧl], *a.* material; sustancial, esencial.—*s.* material; materia; tela, tejido.—**ize** [-ajz], *vi.* materializarse, realizarse.

maternal [mȧtœ́rnȧl], *a.* maternal, materno. —**maternity** [mȧtœ́rnjti], *s.* maternidad.

mathematic(al) [mæθjmǽtik(ȧl)], *a.* matemático. —**mathematician** [mæθjmȧtíšȧn], *s.* matemático. —**mathematics** [mæθjmǽtjks], *s.* matemática(s).

matinée [mætjnéj], *s.* matiné, función de tarde.

mating [méjtjŋ], *s.* apareamiento; casamiento.—*m. season,* época de celo.

matriarch [méjtrjȧrk], *s.* matriarca.

matriculate [mȧtríkyulejt], *vt. y vi.* tricular(se). —**matriculation** [mȧtrjkyuléjšȯn], *s.* matrícula, inscripción.

matrimony [mǽtrjmonj], *s.* matrimonio.

matrix [méjtrjks], *s.* (*pl.* **matrices** [méjtrisiz]) matriz; molde.

matron [méjtrȯn], *s.* matrona.

matt [mæt], *a.* mate.

matter [mǽtœ(r)], *s.* materia; substancia; asunto, cuestión; material; cosa, negocio; importancia; pus.—*as a m. of fact,* a decir verdad; de hecho; en realidad.—*m. of course,* cosa natural, de rutina.—*m. of fact,* realidad, hecho cierto.—*m.-of-fact,* positivista, práctico, prosaico; sensato.—*(it is) no m.,* no importa.—*no m. how (much, good, etc.),* por (bueno, mucho, muy bueno, etc.) que.—*small m.,* cosa sin importancia; menudencia.—*to make matters* *worse,* para colmo de desdichas.—*what is the matter?* ¿qué pasa? ¿qué ocurre?—*vi.* importar; convenir, hacer al caso.—*what does it m.?* ¿qué importa?

matting [mǽtiŋ], *s.* estera; orla o marco de cartón (para cuadros, grabados).

mattress [mǽtris], *s.* colchón; jergón.

mature [matiúr], *a.* maduro; (com.) vencido, pagadero.—*vt.* madurar, sazonar.—*vi.* madurar(se), sazonarse; (com.) vencer, cumplirse un plazo. —**maturity** [-iti], *s.* madurez; (com.) vencimiento.

maudlin [módlin], *a.* lacrimoso, sensiblero; chispo y lloroso.

maul [mɔl], *vt.* aporrear, maltratar.

mausoleum [mɔsolíum], *s.* mausoleo.

maw [mɔ], *s.* buche; vejiga de aire.

maxim [mǽksim], *s.* máxima.

maximum [mǽksimʌm], *s.* y *a.* máximo.

may [mei], *vai.* [11] poder, tener facultad o permiso, ser posible o permitido.—*m. I come in?* ¿se puede entrar?—*m. you have a good trip,* que tenga Ud. buen viaje.—*s.* (M.) mayo.—*M. day,* el primero de mayo.

Mayan [máyan], *a.* y *s.* maya, de los mayas.

maybe [méibi], *adv.* acaso, quizá, tal vez.

mayonnaise [meionéiz], *s.* mayonesa.

mayor [méio(r)], *s.* alcalde.- —**ess** [-is], *s.* alcaldesa.

maze [meiz], *s.* laberinto.

me [mi], *pron. pers.* me, mí.—*do me the favor,* hágame Ud. el favor.—*for me,* para mí.—*with me,* conmigo.

meadow [médou], *s.* vega, prado.- —**land** [-lænd], *s.* pradera.

meager [mígœ(r)], *a.* escaso, pobre, insuficiente; magro, flaco.- —**ness** [-nis], *s.* escasez; delgadez; pobreza.

meal [mil], *s.* comida; harina.—*m. time,* hora de comer.- —**y** [míli], *a.* harinoso.

mean [min], *a.* humilde; mediano; inferior; bajo, vil; malo, desconsiderado; de mal humor; despreciable; tacaño, mezquino; insignificante; medio; intermedio.—*m.-spirited,* ruin, bajo.—*s.* medio; mediocridad, medianía; término medio.—*pl.* modos; fondos, medios, recursos.—*by all means,* sin duda, por supuesto; por todos los medios posibles.—*by means of,* por medio de; mediante.—*by no means,* de ningún modo.—*to live on one's means,* vivir de sus rentas.—*vti.* [10] significar, querer decir; pensar, proponerse, pretender; destinar a; envolver, encerrar; decir de veras.—*I didn't m. to do it,* lo hice sin pensar, o sin querer.—*I m. it,* hablo en serio o formalmente.—*what do you m.?* ¿qué quiere Ud. decir? ¿qué se propone Ud.?—*you don't m. it!* ¡calla!- —**ing** [míniŋ], *s.* intención; sentido, significado, significación.- —**ingless** [míninlis], *a.* sin sentido, vacío.- —**ness** [mínnis], *s.* bajeza; vileza; miseria, mezquindad; mal genio. —**meant** [ment], *pret.* y *pp.* de TO MEAN.—*to be m. for,* o *to,* servir para; haber nacido para; tener por objeto.—*who is m.?* ¿de quién se trata?- —**time** [míntaim], —**while** [mínhwail], *adv.* mientras tanto, entretanto, por de (o lo) pronto.—*s.* ínterin.—*in the m.,* mientras tanto, en el ínterin, hasta entonces.

meander [miǽndœr], *vi* serpentear; vagar.

measles [mízlz], *s. pl.* sarampión.

measurable [mézŭrabl], *a.* mensurable; apreciable. —**measurably** [mézŭrabli], *adv.* perceptiblemente. —**measure** [mézŭ(r)], *s.* medida; compás, cadencia; proyecto de ley; (mús.) compás.—*pl.* medios.—*beyond m.,* con exceso, sobremanera.—*in a great m.,* en gran manera; en gran parte.—*in some m.,* hasta cierto punto, en cierto modo.—*vt.* medir; calibrar, graduar; (mar.) arquear, cubicar (un barco).—*vi.* medir, tener tal o cual dimensión. —**measured** [mézŭrd], *a.* acompasado, medido; moderado; rítmico. —**measurement** [mézŭrment], *s.* medición; dimensión; medida; (mar.) arqueo, cubicación.

meat [mit], *s.* carne; sustento (en general); substancia, jugo.—*cold meats,* fiambres.—*m. ball,* albóndiga.—*m. market,* carnicería.- —**y** [míti], *a.* carnoso; jugoso, substancioso.

Mecca [méka], *s.* La Meca.

mechanic [mikǽnik], *a.* y *s.* mecánico. - —**al** [-al], *a.* mecánico, maquinal.—*m. pencil,* lapicero.- —**s** [-s],

s. mecánica. **—mechanism** [mékạnịzm], s. mecanismo; maquinaria. **—mechanization** [mekạnịzéíṣọn], s. mecanización; maquinismo; (mil.) motorización. **—mechanize** [mékạnaịz], vt. mecanizar; (mil.) motorizar.

medal [médạl], s. medalla; condecoración.- **—lion** [mịdǽlyọn], s. medallón.

meddle [médl], vi. (gen. con **with** o **in**) meterse, entremeterse.- **—r** [médlœ(r)], s. entremetido.- **—some** [médlsʌm], a. entremetido, oficioso.

median [mídịạn], a. intermedio, medio.—s. punto medio, número medio.—m. strip, faja central, faja divisoria.

mediate [mídịeịt], vt. y vi. mediar, intervenir, intermediar.—a. [mídịịt], mediato, medio; interpuesto. **—mediation** [mịdịéíṣọn], s. mediación, intercesión; intervención; tercería. **—mediator** [mídịeịtọ(r)], s. mediador, intercesor, medianero.

medical [médịkạl], a. médico, medicinal.—m. corps, cuerpo de sanidad.—m. kit, botiquín. **—medicate** [médịkeịt], vt. medicinar. **—medication** [mẹdịkéíṣọn], s. medicación; medicamento. **—medicine** [médịsịn], s. medicina; medicamento.—m. cabinet, armario botiquín.—m. man, curandero, hechicero. **—medicinal** [mịdísịnạl], s. medicinal.

medieval [mịdịívạl], a. medieval.

mediocre [mídịokœ(r)], a. mediocre. **—mediocrity** [mịdịákrịtị], s. mediocridad.

meditate [médịteịt], vt. y vi. meditar, reflexionar. **—meditation** [mẹdịtéíṣọn], s. meditación.

Mediterranean [mẹdịtẹréínịạn], a. mediterráneo.

medium [mídịʌm], s. medio, instrumento; médium o medio (en el espiritismo) medio; medium, medio.—a. intermedio; (coc.) a medio asar, a punto, término medio.—m. rare, (coc.) medio hecho, sonrosado, más bien poco hecho.

medley [médlị], s. mezcolanza; (mus.) popurrí.

meek [mik], a. manso, humilde, dócil. - **—ness** [míknịs], s. mansedumbre, humildad, docilidad.

meet [mit], vti. [10] encontrarse con; encontrar, topar o chocar con; satis-

facer, llenar (requisitos); pagar, saldar (un pagaré, etc.); sufragar (los gastos, etc.); ir a esperar (un tren, vapor, persona, etc.); combatir o pelear con; conocer o ser presentado.—to m. a charge, refutar, responder a una acusación.—to m. the eye, saltar a la vista.—vii. encontrarse, verse; reunirse, chocarse, tocarse; confluir.—till we m. again, hasta la vista, hasta más ver(nos).— to m. halfway, partir la diferencia.— **—ing** [mítịŋ], s. reunión; junta, asamblea; encuentro; duelo o desafío.—m. place, lugar de reunión.—to call a m., convocar a junta.

megaphone [mégạfoụn], s. megáfono.

melancholy [mélạnkạlị], s. melancolía.

mellow [méloụ], a. maduro; sazonado; meloso, blando, suave.—vt. y vi. suavizar(se).

melodious [mẹlóụdịʌs], a. melodioso. **—melody** [mélọdị], s. melodía.

melon [mélọn], s. melón.

melt [melt], vti. y vi. [6] derretir(se), fundir(se); deshelar(se); disolver-(se).—to m. into tears, deshacerse en lágrimas.

member [mémbœ(r)], s. miembro.- **—ship** [-ṣịp], s. asociación; número de miembros; personal.—m. dues, cuota.

membrane [mémbreịn], s. membrana.

memento [mịméntoụ], s. recordatorio, recuerdo. **—memo** [mémoụ], s. apunte, membrete. **—memoir** [mémwar], s. memoria; biografía.— pl. memorias. **—memorable** [mémorạbl], a. memorable. **—memorandum** [memorǽndʌm], s. apunte, membrete. **—memorial** [mịmɔ́rịạl], a. conmemorativo.—s. monumento conmemorativo; memorial, instancia, petición.—m. arch, arco triunfal. **—memorize** [mémoraịz], vt. aprender de memoria. **—memory** [mémorị], s. memoria.—from m., de memoria.

men [mɛn], s. pl. de MAN.—m.'s room, lavabo para caballeros.

menace [ménịs], vt. y vi. amenazar.— s. amenaza.

mend [mɛnd], vt. remendar; repasar; zurcir; arreglar, componer; reformar, mejorar.—vi. reformarse, mejorar.—s. remiendo.—on the m., mejorando(se).- **—ing** [-iŋ], s. remiendo, zurcido.

menial [mín̯i̯al̯], *a.* servil, bajo.—*s.* criado, doméstico.

menstruate [ménstru̯e̯it̯], *vi.* menstruar. **—menstruation** [mɛnstru̯é̯išǫn], *s.* menstruación.

mental [mént̯al̯], *a.* mental.—*m. illness,* enfermedad mental.—*m. test,* prueba de inteligencia. **mentality** [mɛnt̯ǽ̯lit̯i̯], *s.* mentalidad.

mention [méns̯ǫn], *s.* mención.—*vt.* mencionar.—*don't m. it!* ¡no hay de qué! ¡de nada!—*not to m.,* sin contar.

menu [ményu], *s.* menú.

meow [miáu̯], *s.* maullido.—*vi.* maullar.

mercantile [mœ́rk̯ant̯il̯], *a.* mercantil.

mercenary [mœ́rsenɛr̯i̯], *a.* mercenario.—*s.* mercenario.

merchandise [mœ́rchandaiz], *s.* mercancía(s), mercadería. **—merchant** [mœ́rchant], *s.* mercader, mercante.—*a.* mercante.—*m. marine,* marina mercante.- **—man** [-mæn], *s.* buque mercante.

merciful [mœ́rsi̯ful̯], *a.* misericordioso. **—merciless** [mœ́rsi̯lis̯], *a.* despiadado, cruel, implacable.

mercurial [mœrki̯ú̯ri̯al̯], *a.* mercurial; (fig.) vivo, volátil. **—mercury** [mœ́rki̯ur̯i̯], *s.* mercurio, azogue.

mercy [mœ́rs̯i̯], *s.* misericordia; merced, gracia.—*m. killing,* eutanasia.

merge [mœrdž], *vt.* y *vi.* unir(se), fusionar(se).- **—r** [mœ́rdžœ(r)], *s.* fusión de empresas.

meridian [mi̯ríd̯i̯an̯], *s.* meridiano; mediodía; (fig.) cenit, auge.—*a.* meridiano.

meringue [mœ́ræ̯ŋ], *s.* merengue.

merit [mérit̯], *s.* mérito.—*on its (his, etc.) own merits,* por sí mismo.—*vt.* merecer.- **—orious** [-ór̯i̯ʌs̯], *a.* meritorio.

mermaid [mœ́rme̯id̯], *s.* sirena. **—merman** [mœ́rmæn], *s.* tritón.

merrily [mér̯i̯li̯], *adv.* alegremente. **—merriment** [mér̯i̯ment̯], *s.* alegría, regocijo; diversión. **—merry** [mér̯i̯], *a.* alegre, regocijado.—*M. Christmas!,* ¡Felices Pascuas!, ¡Felices Navedades!.—*m.-go-round,* tiovivo, caballito.—*to make m.,* divertirse, ir de parranda. **—merrymaker** [mér̯i̯me̯ik̯œ(r)], *s.* fiestero, parrandero. **—merrymaking** [mér̯i̯me̯ik̯i̯ŋ], *s.* fiesta, parranda, holgorio.—*a.* regocijado, parrandero.

mesh [mɛš], *s.* malla; punto u obra de malla; redecilla; (mec.) engranaje.—*pl.* red, trampas, lazos.—*vt.* enredar, coger con red; (mec.) endentar.—*vi.* enredarse; (mec.) endentar, engranar.

mess [mɛs], *s.* cochinería; fregado, lío, embrollo; (coc.) rancho.—*m. hall,* sala de rancho; comedor de militares.—*m. kit,* utensilios de rancho. —*to make a m. of,* ensuciar; echar a perder.—*vt.* ensuciar.—*to m. up,* desarreglar, desordenar, echar a perder.—*vi.* comer.—*to m. around,* ocuparse en fruslerías.

message [mési̯dž], *s.* mensaje; recado. **—messenger** [mésendžœ(r)], *s.* mensajero; mandadero.

messy [mési̯], *a.* sucio, puerco; desordenado, revuelto.

met [met], *pret.* y *pp.* de TO MEET.

metal [mét̯al̯], *s.* metal.—*a.* metálico, de metal.—*m. polish,* limpiametales.- **—lic** [mét̯ǽlik̯], *a.* metálico.- **—lurgic(al)** [metalœ́rdžik̯(al̯)], *a.* metalúrgico.- **—lurgy** [mét̯alœr̯džị̯], *s.* metalurgia.- **—work** [-wœrk], *s.* metalistería.

metamorphose [metamórfouz], *vt.* metamorfosear. **—metamorphosis** [mɛtamórfosis], *s.* metamorfosis.

metaphor [métafo(r)], *s.* metáfora.

meteor [mít̯i̯o̯(r)], *s.* meteoro; estrella fugaz.- **—ological** [-oládžik̯al̯], *a.* meteorológico.- **—ologist** [-álodžist̯], *s.* meteorólogo.- **—ology** [-álodžị̯], *s.* meteorología.

meter [mítœr], *s.* metro; contador; (mus.) compás, tiempo.—*m. reader,* lector del contador.—*vt.* medir (con contador).- **—ing** [-iŋ], *s.* medición.

methane [méθe̯in̯], *s.* metano.

method [méθǫd], *s.* método.- **—ic(al)** [mɛθádik̯(al̯)], *a.* metódico, sistemático.

meticulous [mit̯íkyu̯lʌs̯], *a.* meticuloso.

metre [mítœ(r)], *s.* = METER.

metric(al) [métrik̯(al̯)], *a.* métrico.

metronome [métronou̯m], *s.* metrónomo.

metropolis [mɛtrápol̯is̯], *s.* metrópoli; urbe. **—metropolitan** [metropálit̯an̯], *a.* metropolitano.—*s.* (igl.) metropolitano.

mettle [métl̯], *s.* brío, ánimo.- **—some** [-sʌm], *a.* brioso, animoso.

mew [mi̯u], *s.* maullido.—*vi.* maullar, mayar.

Mexican [méksik̯an̯], *a.* y *s.* mejicano.

mezzanine [méząnin], *s.* entresuelo.

mice [majs], *s. pl.* de MOUSE.

microbe [májkroub], *s.* microblo.

microcard [majkrocard], *s.* microficha.

microchip [majkrochip], *s.* chip, microchip, pastilla de silicio.

microcomputer [majkrokǫmpyútœr], *s.* microordenador, microcomputadora.

microcosm [majkrokazěm], *s.* microcosmo.

microfiche [maíkrofiš], *s.* microficha.

microfilm [maíkrofilm], *s.* microfilm, micropelícula.

microgroove [majkrogruv], *s.* microsurco.

microphone [májkrofoun], *s.* micrófono.

microscope [májkroskoup], *s.* microscopio. — **microscopic(al)** [majkroskápik(ąl)], *a.* microscópico.

microsurgery [majkroscœrdžěrį], *s.* microcirugía.

microwave [majkrowejv], *s.* microonda. — *m. oven*, horno de microondas.

mid [mjd], *a.* medio. — *(in) m. air*, (en) el aire. — *m.-course*, media carrera o medio camino. — *m.-sea*, alta mar. — **—day** [míddej], *s.* mediodía. — *a.* del mediodía. — **—dle** [mídl], *a.* medio, intermedio, mediano; de en medio. — *m.-aged*, de edad madura. — *M. Ages*, Edad Media. — *m.-class*, de la clase media. — *m. class*, clase media, burguesía. — *M. East*, Oriente Medio. — *m. finger*, dedo del corazón. — *m. ground*, posición intermedia. — *m.-sized*, de mediana estatura o tamaño. — *s.* centro, medio, mitad. — *about o towards the m. of*, a mediados de. — *m. of*, mediados de. — *m. of the road*, posición intermedia. — *m.-of-the-road*, moderado, enemigo de extremos. — **—dleman** [mídlmæn], *s.* intermediario; (com.) corredor; revendedor; agente de negocios. — **—dlemost** [mídlmoust], *a.* del medio; en el medio o más cercano a él. — **—dleweight** [mídlwejt], *s.* (dep.) de peso medio (hasta 160 lbs.). — *s.* peso medio. — **—dling** [mídlįŋ], *a.* mediano, regular, pasadero. — **—man** [-mæn], *s.* intermediario.

middy [mídį], *s.* (fam.) guardiamarina; blusa marinera.

midget [mídžįt], *s.* enanillo, liliputiense.

midland [mídlænd], *a.* de tierra adentro. — *s.* región central.

midnight [mídnajt], *s.* medianoche. — *a.* nocturno; negro.

midriff [mídrįf], *s.* (anat.) diafragma; talle.

midshipman [mídšįpmąn], *s.* guardia marina; aspirante de marina.

midst [mjdst], *s.* medio, centro; (fig.) seno; presión, rigor. — *in our, their, your m.*, en medio de nosotros, ellos, ustedes. — *in the m. of*, en medio de, en lo más recio de. — *adv.* en medio. — *prep.* (poét.) entre.

midstream [mjdstrím], *s.* — *in m.*, en pleno río.

midsummer [mídsámœ(r)], *s.* pleno verano.

midway [mídwej], *s.* mitad del camino; (of a fair) avenida central. — *a.* situado a mitad del camino. — *adv.* a mitad del camino.

midweek [míwik], *s.* mediados de la semana.

midwife [mídwajf], *s.* partera, comadrona.

midwinter [mįwíntœr], *s.* pleno invierno.

midyear [mídyir], *a.* de mediados del año. — *s.* mediados del año.

mien [min], *s.* semblante, aire.

miff [mjf], *vt.* ofender.

might [majt], *pret.* y *pres. opcional* de MAY. — *s.* poder, poderío, fuerza. — *with m. and main*, con todas sus fuerzas, a más no poder. — **—ily** [májtįlį], *adv.* poderosamente. — **—y** [-į], *a.* potente, poderoso; enorme. — *adv.* (fam.) muy.

migraine [májgrejn], *s.* jaqueca, migraña.

migrant [májgrąnt], *s.* emigrante; ave migratoria o de paso. — *a.* nómada; (e)migratorio. — **migrate** [májgrejt], *vi.* emigrar; trasplantarse. — **migration** [majgréjšǫn], *s.* (e)migración; trasplante. — **migratory** [májgratɔrį], *a.* (e)migratorio; nómada.

mike [majk], *s.* (fam.) micrófono = MICROPHONE.

milch [mjlch], *a.* lechera. — *m. cow*, vaca lechera.

mild [majld], *a.* suave, blando; leve, ligero, dócil, manso; (climate) templado.

mildew [míldju], *s.* moho; mildeu.

mildness [majldnįs], *s.* suavidad, lenidad; apacibilidad; mansedumbre.

mile [majl], *s.* milla inglesa. Ver Tabla. – **—age** [májlidž], *s.* recorrido en millas. – **—stone** [-stoun], *s.* piedra miliaria.—*to be a m.,* hacer época.

militant [mílitant], *a.* y *s.* militante. **—military** [mílitęrj], *a.* militar.—*m. coup* o *uprising,* pronunciamiento, cuartelazo.—*s.* los militares. **—militia** [mílíšą], *s.* milicia. **—militiaman** [mílíšąman], *s.* miliciano.

milk [mjlk], *s.* leche.—*m. can,* lechera.—*m. diet,* régimen lácteo.—*m. pail,* ordeñadero.—*m. shake,* batido de leche.—*vt.* ordeñar; (fam.) extraer de; chupar; abusar de, explotar. – **—er** [mílkœ(r)], *s.* ordeñador. – **—ing** [-iŋ], *s.* ordeño. – **—maid** [-mejd], *s.* lechera. – **—man** [-mæn], *s.* lechero. – **—y** [-j], *a.* lácteo, lechoso.—*M. Way,* Vía Láctea.

mill [mjl], *s.* (grain) molino; (steel) fábrica; (fabics) hilandería; (wood) aserradero; (sugar) ingenio; (to grind coffee) molinillo; (part of a dollar) milésima.—*to go through the m.,* someter a un entrenamiento riguroso. – **—stone** [-stoun], *s.* muela de molino; (fig.) carga pesada.—*vt.* moler; acordonar, cerrillar; laminar; triturar; fresar; batir.—*vi.—to m. around,* arremolinarse.

miller [mílœ(r)], *s.* molinero; mariposa con manchas blancas.

milliner [mílinœ(r)], *s.* modista de sombreros. – **—y** [mílinęrj], *s.* artículos para sombreros femeninos; sombrerería femenina; ocupación en este sector; tienda de sombreros femeninos.

milling [míliŋ], *s.* molienda; acordonamiento, acuñación (moneda); cordoncillo de la moneda; fresado.—*m. around,* remolino.—*a.* de moler, fresar, etc.—*m. cutter* o *tool,* fresa.—*m. machine,* fresadora.—*m. saw,* sierra.

million [mílyon], *s.* millón. – **—aire** [-ér], *s.* y *a.* millonario. **—millionth** [mílyonθ], *a.* y *s.* millonésimo.

millpond [mílpand], *s.* represa de molino. **—millrace** [mílrejs], *s.* caz.

mime [majm], *s.* mimo.—*vt.* remedar.

mimic [mímjk], *vti.* [8] remedar, imitar.—*s.* imitador, remedador.—*a.* mímico, imitativo, burlesco. **—mimicked** [mímjkt], *pret.* y *pp.* de TO MIMIC. – **—ry** [-rj], *s.* mímica, remedo.

mince [mjns], *vt.* desmenuzar; picar (carne), hacer picadillo; medir (las palabras); atenuar.—*m. pie,* pastel relleno de carne picada con frutas.—*not to m. words,* hablar sin rodeos.—*vi.* andar remilgadamente; hablar remilgadamente. – **—meat** [mínsmit], *s.* cuajado, picadillo.—*to make m. of,* destruir, aniquilar. **—mincingly** [mínsjŋlj], *adv.* a pedacitos; a pasitos; con afectación.

mind [majnd], *s.* mente, espíritu.—*m. reader,* adivinador del pensamiento ajeno, lector mental.—*of one m.,* unánimes.—*of sound m.,* en su cabal juicio.—*out of m.,* olvidado.—*out of one's m.,* loco; fuera de juicio.—*to bear in m.,* tener en cuenta, tener presente.—*to call to m.,* recordar, traer a la memoria.—*to change one's m.,* mudar de parecer.—*to give someone a piece of one's m.,* decirle a alguien cuántas son cinco, ponerle como nuevo.—*to have a m. to,* tener gana de, querer; proponerse.—*to have in m.,* recordar; tener en consideración; pensar en.—*to keep in m.,* tener presente o en cuenta.—*to make up one's m.,* decidirse.—*to my m.,* a mi juicio, a mi ver.—*with one m.* unánimemente.—*vt.* notar, observar; atender a; cuidar; cuidarse de; tener inconveniente en; hacer caso a, o de.—*to m. one's business,* meterse uno en lo que le importa.—*vi.* atender obedecer, hacer caso; tener cuidado.—*I don't m.,* no me importa.—*never m.,* no importa; no se moleste, no se preocupe. – **—ful** [májndful], *a.* atento, cuidadoso.

mine [majn], *pron. pos.* mío, mía, míos; mías; el mío, etc.; lo mío.—*of m.,* mío, mía.

mine [majn], *s.* mina.—*m. field,* campo de minas.—*m. sweeper,* dragaminas.—*vt.* minar; extraer. – **—r** [májnœ(r)], *s.* minero; zapador. – **—ral** [mínęral], *s.* y *a.* mineral. – **—alogy** [mjnęrálodžj], *s.* mineralogía.

mingle [míŋgl], *vt.* mezclar, confundir.—*vi.* mezclarse, asociarse.

miniature [mínjachųr], *s.* miniatura.—*a.* en miniatura; diminuto.

miniaturization [mjnjątchǔrjzejšon], *s.* miniaturización.

minimal [mínjmal], *a.* mínimo.

minimize [mínjmajz], *vt.* atenuar, quitar importancia; reducir al mínimo; achicar; menospreciar. **—minimum** [mínimʌm], s. y a. mínimo.—*m. wage*, jornal mínimo.

mining [máiniŋ], s. minería; acto de sembrar minas explosivas.—a. minero, de mina.

minister [mínistœ(r)], s. ministro; clérigo, pastor.—vt. y vi. ministrar.—vi. atender, auxiliar; socorrer. **—ministry** [mínistri], s. ministerio.

mink [miŋk], s. visón; piel de visón.

minnow [mínou], s. pececillo.

minor [máinɔ(r)], a. menor; secundario, inferior; leve.—*m. key*, tono menor.—s. menor de edad.- **—ity** [majnáriti], s. minoridad, menoría (de edad); minoría.

minstrel [mínstrel], s. juglar, trovador, ministril.

mint [mint], s. casa de moneda; (bot.) menta, hierbabuena; pastilla de menta.—*a m. of money*, un dineral.—vt. acuñar.

minus [máinʌs], prep. menos; falto de; sin.—a. (mat. y elec.) negativo; deficiente.—*m. sign*, signo de restar.—*to be, come out, etc. m.* (something), salir perdiendo (algo).—s. cantidad negativa; deficiencia; signo menos.

minute [mainjút], a. menudo, minúsculo; nimio, minucioso.—s. [mínit], minuto, momento, instante; (geom. etc.) minuto; minuta, nota, apunte.—pl. actas, minutas; memoria auténtica.—*m. book*, minutario, libro de actas.—*m. hand*, minutero.—*this* (very) *m.*, ahora mismito.

miracle [mírakl], s. milagro.—*m. play*, auto. **—miraculous** [mirǽkyulʌs], a. milagroso.

mirage [miráz̆], s. espejismo.

mire [mair], s. lodo, fango.—vt. enlodar.—vi. atascarse.

mirror [mírɔ(r)], s. espejo; ejemplar, modelo.—vt. reflejar.

mirth [mœrθ], s. alegría, regocijo.- **—ful** [mœrθful], a. alegre, gozoso.- **—less** [-lis], a. triste, abatido.

miry [máiri], a. lodoso, fangoso.

misadventure [misʌdvénchū(r)], s. desventura, desgracia.

misbehave [misbiheív], vi. conducirse mal, portarse mal.

miscarriage [miskǽridz̆], s. aborto, malparto; fracaso, malogro. **—miscarry** [miskǽri], vii. [7] frustrarse, malograrse; abortar, malparir.

miscellaneous [miseléinjʌs], a. misceláneo.

mischief [mískʃif], s. mal, daño; malicia; travesura. **—mischievous** [mískʃivʌs], a. dañino; malicioso; travieso.

misdeal [mísdil], s. repartición errónea.—[misdíl], vt. y vi. repartir mal.

misdeed [mísdíd], s. fechoría, delito.

misdemeanor [mísdimínɔ(r)], s. mala conducta; (for.) falta, delito de menor cuantía.

miser [máizœ(r)], s. avaro, verrugo. **—able** [mízœrabl], a. miserable; (fam.) achacoso, indispuesto.- **—ly** [máizœrli], a. avariento, mezquino. - **—y** [mízœri], s. miseria.

misfortune [misfórchun], s. desgracia.

misgiving [misgíviŋ], s. mal presentimiento, rescoldo.

mishap [mishǽp], s. accidente, percance.

misinterpret [misintœrprit], vt. y vi. interpretar mal, tergiversar.- **—ation** [-éişon], s. tergiversación.

misjudge [misdz̆ádz̆], vt. y vi. juzgar mal.

mislead [mislíd], vti. [10] extraviar, descaminar; alucinar, engañar; seducir, inducir al mal; engañar. **—ing** [-iŋ], a. engañoso. **—misled** [misléd], pret. y pp. de TO MISLEAD.—a. engañado.

mismanagement [mismǽnidz̆ment], s. mala administración, desgobierno.

misnomer [misnoúmœr], s. nombre impropia, mal nombre.

misplace [mispléis], vt. colocar fuera de sitio; (fam.) extraviar, perder.

misprint [misprínt], vt. imprimir con erratas.—s. error de imprenta.

mispronounce [mispronáuns], vt. y vi. pronunciar mal. **—mispronunciation** [mispronʌnsiéişon], s. pronunciación incorrecta.

misrepresent [misreprizént], vt. tergiversar, falsificar.- **—ation** [-éişon], s. falsedad, tergiversación.

Miss [mis], s. Srta., Sta. **—miss**, señorita.

miss [mis], vt. errar (el tiro, el golpe, etc.); no acertar con, no comprender; equivocar; perder (el tren, la función, etc.); echar de menos; pasar sin, abstenerse, carecer de; pasar por alto, dejar de hacer.—*to m. the mark*, errar el blanco o el tiro.—vi. frustrarse, salir mal; marrar, errar, faltar; fallar.—*to m. out*, (fam.) llevarse chasco; llegar tarde.—*s.* malogro, fracaso; tiro fallido.

missal [mísạl], *s.* misal.

misshapen [miṣšéịpn], *a.* deforme, contrahecho.

missile [mísil], *a.* arrojadizo.—*s.* proyectil; arma arrojadiza; projectil dirigido.

missing [mísiŋ], *a.* extraviado, perdido; desaparecido; ausente.—*m. link*, hombre mono.—*m. persons*, desaparecidos.—*to be m.*, hacer falta, haber desaparecido.

mission [míšọn], *s.* misión.— **—ary** [-ɛṛị], *s.* misionario, misionero.—*a.* misional.—*m. station*, (igl.) misión.

missive [mísịv], *s.* misiva.

misspell [miṣspél], *vti.* [4] deletrear mal, escribir mal.

mist [mist], *s.* neblina; (fine spray) vapor.—*vt.* empañar.—*vi.* lloviznar.

mistake [mistéịk], *vti.* [10] equivocar, comprender mal; trabucar, tomar una cosa por otra.—*s.* equivocación, error. **—mistaken** [mistéịkn], *pp.* de TO MISTAKE.—*a.* erróneo, incorrecto, desacertado.

mister [místœ(r)], *s.* (fam.)—*got a light, m.?* ¿tiene fuego, caballero?.—*hey, m.!* ¡oiga!.—*watch out, m.!* ¡cuidado, socio!* [no es de buena educación decir 'mister' sin el apellido.]

mistletoe [mísltou], *s.* muérdago; cabellera.

mistook [mistúk], *pret.* de TO MISTAKE.

mistress [místrịs], *s.* dueña, ama; querida, moza, manceba; (GB) maestra de escuela.

mistrust [mistrÁst], *s.* desconfianza.—*vt.* desconfiar de, dudar de.- **—ful** [-fụl], *a.* desconfiado, receloso.

misty [místị], *a.* brumoso, neblinoso.

misunderstand [misʌndœrstǽnd], *vti.* [10] etender mal, no comprender. **—misunderstood** [misʌndœrstúd], *pret.* y *pp.* de TO MISUNDERSTAND.—*a.* mal entendido o comprendido.- **—ing** [-iŋ], *s.* malentendido; desavenencia.

misuse [misyús], *s.* mal uso; abuso; maltrato. (com.) malversación.— *vt.* [misyúz], abusar de; maltratar; (com.) malversar.

mite [mait], *s.* pizca; óbolo; (insect) ácaro.

mitigate [mítịgeit], *vt.* mitigar, calmar.—*vi.* calmarse, mitigarse.

mitt [mit], *s.* mitón; guante de beisbol.

mitten [mítn], *s.* mitón, confortante.—*pl.* (fam.) guantes de boxeo (fam.) las manos.

mix [miks], *vti.* y *vii.* [4] mezclar(se) unir(se).—*to m. up*, confundir, equivocar.—*s.* mezcla; proporciones de los ingredientes de una mezcla —*m.-up*, (fam.) lío, confusión agarrada.- **—ed** [mikst], *a.* mixto mezclado; (candy) variados.—*m company*, reunión de personas de ambos sexos.—*m. drink*, bebida mezclada.- **—ture** [míkschū(r), *s* mezcla; mixtura; mezcolanza.

moan [moun], *s.* gemido.—*vi.* gemir.

moat [mout], *s.* foso.

mob [mab], *s.* chusma, populacho gentuza; (fam.) turbamulta; multitud.—*vti.* [1] atropellar.—*vii.* formar tropel, tumulto, alboroto.

mobile [móụbịl], *a.* móvil.—*m. home* caravana fija, casa rodante. **—mobility** [mobíḷịtị], *s.* movilidad. **—mobilization**[mobịlịzéịšọn], *s.* movilización. **—mobilize** [móụbịlaịz], *vt* movilizar.—*vi.* movilizar, movilizarse.

moccasin [mákạsịn], *s.* mocasín.

mock [mak], *vt.* burlarse de, mofarse de; despreciar; engañar.—*to m. at* mofarse de.—*a.* simulado, fingido.—*m. orange*, jeringuilla, celinda.—*m.-up*, maqueta.- **—ery** [mákœṛị], *s.* mofa, burla, escarnio **—ing** [-iŋ], *a.* burlón. **—ingbird** [-iŋbœrd], *s.* (Am.) sinsonte.

mode [moud], *s.* modo, manera, procedimiento; moda; uso, costumbre (gram. fil. mús.) modo; (mús.) modalidad.- **—l** [mádẹl], *s.* modelo ejemplar o patrón; prototipo muestra; horma; patrón, figurín modelo vivo.—*a.* modelo, ejemplar.—*m. airplane*, aeromodelo.— *vti.* [2] modelar; moldear.—*vii.* servir de modelo, modelar.- **—l(i)ing** [mádẹliŋ], *s.* modelado.—*a.* modelador.

modem [moúdɛm], *s.* módem.

moderate [mádẹṛịt], *a.* moderado, regular, ordinario; razonable, sobrio; módico (en precio).—*s.* moderado.—*vt.* y *vi.* [mádẹṛeịt], moderar(se), calmar(se): presidir **—moderation** [mádẹṛéịšọn], *s.* moderación; sobriedad; presidencia, acto de presidir. **—moderator** [mádẹṛeịtœr], *s.* presidente; árbitro (fis.) moderador.

modern [mádœrn], *a.* moderno.—
—**ize** [-aįz], *vt.* modernizar.

modest [mádįst], *a.* modesto.— —**y**
[-į], *s.* modestia.

modification [madįfįkéįṣǫn], *s.* modificación. —**modifier** [mádįfaįœ(r)],
s. modificante. —**modify** [mádįfaį],
vti. [7] modificar, cambiar.

modulate [mádžųleįt], *vt.* y *vi.* modular.

mohair [móuhɛr], *s.* mohair (pelo de la
cabra de Angora): tela de este material.

Mohammedan [mouhǽmedǫn], *s.* y *a.*
(despec. y ant.) *var.* de Muhammad.

moist [mɔįst], *a.* húmedo; lloroso; lluvioso.— —**en** [mɔ́įsn], *vt.* humedecer, mojar ligeramente.— —**ure**
[mɔ́įschụ(r)], *s.* humedad.

molar [móulǎ(r)], *a.* molar.—*s.* muela.

molasses [molǽsįz], *s.* melaza, miel de
purga.—*m. candy,* (Am.) melcocha.

mold [mould], *s.* molde, matriz;
moho; tierra vegetal.—*vt.* moldear,
vaciar, amoldar.—*vi.* enmohecerse.
— —**er** [móuldœ(r)], *vi.* convertirse
en polvo, desmoronarse, consumirse.—*vt.* convertir en polvo, consumir, desgastar.— —**ing** [-įŋ], *s.*
moldura; amoldamiento; moldea-
miento, vaciado.— —**y** [-į], *a.* mohoso, enmohecido.

mole [moul], *s.* lunar o mancha en la
piel; muelle, malecón, espolón;
topo.—*m.-eyed,* cegato.—*m. hill,*
topinera.

molecule [málįkjul], *s.* molécula.

molest [molést], *vt.* molestar, vejar;
faltar al respeto (a una mujer); meterse con, dañar.

mollify [málįfaį], *vt.* apaciguar, aplacar.

mollusk [málʌsk], *s.* molusco.

molt [moult], *vi.* mudar la pluma.—
—**ing** [móųltįŋ], *s.* muda.

molten [móųltęn], *pp.* de TO MELT.—*a.*
fundido, derretido (metales).

moment [móųmęnt], *s.* momento, instante; importancia, peso.—*at any
m.,* de un momento a otro.— —**ary**
[-erį], *a.* momentáneo.— —**ly** [-lį],
adv. por momentos.— —**ous** [mo-
méntʌs], *a.* importante, grave, trascendental.— —**um** [moméntʌm], *s.*
impulso, ímpetu; (mech.) cantidad
de movimiento.

monarch [mánǎrk], *s.* monarca.— —**y**
[-į], *s.* monarquía.

monastery [mánǎsterį], *s.* monasterio.

—**monastic** [monǽstįk], *a.* monástico.

Monday [mándį], *s.* lunes.

monetary [mánįterį], *a.* monetario, pe-
cuniario. —**money** [mánį], *s.* dinero; moneda.—*m. changer, dealer,
o jobber,* cambista.—*m. lender,* prestamista, usurero.—*m.-maker,* cosa
con que se gana dinero; persona
que gana y acumula dinero, acauda-
lada; persona metalizada.—*m. order,* giro postal.—*to make m.,* ganar
dinero; dar dinero (una empresa).

mongrel [máŋgręl], *a.* y *s.* mixto, mestizo.—*s.* (perro) de raza indefinida.

monitor [mánįtœr], *s.* monitor.—*vt.*
controlar; escuchar; superentender.

monk [mʌŋk], *s.* monje, fraile.

monkey [máŋkį], *s.* mono, macaco,
mico.—*m. wrench,* llave inglesa.—
to play the m., hacer monadas.—*vt.*
y *vi.* (fam.) remedar; hacer payasa-
das o monerías.—*to m. with,* meterse con; bregar con.— —**shine**
[-šaįn], *s.* (fam.) monería.

monocle [mánokęl], *s.* monóculo.

monogamy [monágamį], *s.* monogamia.

monogram [mánogrǽm], *s.* monograma.

monologue [mánolag], *s.* monólogo,
soliloquio.

monopolize [monápolaįz], *vt.* monopolizar, acaparar. —**monopoly** [mo-
nápolį], *s.* monopolio, estanco.

monorail [mánoreįl], *s.* monorriel.

monosyllable [manosílabl], *s.* monosílabo.

monotonous [monátǫnʌs], *a.* monótono. —**monotony** [monátǫnį], *s.*
monotonía.

monster [mánstœ(r)], *s.* monstruo.
—*a.* monstruoso. —**monstrosity**
[manstrásįtį], *s.* monstruosidad.
—**monstrous** [mánstrʌs], *a.* monstruoso.

month [manθ], *s.* mes.— —**ly** [mánθlį],
a. mensual.—*adv.* mensual-
mente.—*s.* publicación mensual.—
pl. las reglas, menstruo.

monument [mányụment], *s.* monumento.— —**al** [manyụméntǎl], *a.*
monumental.

moo [mu], *vi.* mugir.—*s.* mu, mugido.

mood [mud], *s.* genio, humor; (gram.)
modo.— —**y** [múdį], *a.* caprichoso;
caviloso; triste, hosco, melancólico, taciturno.

moon [mun], *s.* luna.—*m.-blind,* cegato, corto de vista.—*m.-mad, m.-struck,* lunático, loco.—*m. shot,* lanzamiento a la Luna.- **—beam** [-bim], *s.* rayo lunar.- **—light** [múnlajt], *s.* luz de la luna.- **—lighting** [múnlajtiŋ], *s.* multiempleo, pluriempleo.- **—lit** [-lit], *a.* iluminado por la luna.- **—rise** [-rajz], *s.* salida de la luna.- **—scape** [-skejp], *s.* paisaje lunar.- **—set** [-set], *s.* puesta de la luna.- **—shine** [-šajn], *s.* claridad de la luna; desatino; (fam.) cháchara, música celestial; (fam.) licor destilado ilegalmente.- **—walk** [-wɔk], *s.* caminata exploratoria sobre la superficie lunar.- **—y** [-i], *a.* claro como la luna; lunático; simplón; soñador.

moor [mur], *s.* páramo; brezal; (M.) moro.—*vt.* (mar.) amarrar, aferrar, afirmar con anclas.—*vi.* (mar.) anclar, atracar.

moose [mus], *s.* alce, ante.

mop [map], *s.* aljofifa, fregasuelos, estropajo; (of hair) espesura.—*vti.* [1] aljofifar; enjugarse.—*to m. up,* limpiar de enemigos.—*mopping-up,* (mil.) operación de limpieza.

mope [moup], *vi.* andar abatido, entregarse a la melancolía.

moral [máraḷ], *a.* moral, ético; virtuoso; honrado, recto.—*s.* moral, moraleja.—*pl.* moral.- **—e** [morǽel], *s.* moral, estado de ánimo, espíritu.- **—ity** [morǽliti], *s.* moralidad.- **—ize** [máraḷajz], *vt.* y *vi.* moralizar.

morbid [mórbid], *a.* morboso, malsano, horripilante.

more [mɔr], *a.* más, adicional.—*adv.* más, en mayor grado; además.—*s.* mayor cantidad o número.—*m. and m.,* cada vez más.—*m. or less,* poco más o menos.—*no m.,* no más; ya no; se acabó.—*so much the m.,* tanto más, cuanto más.—*the m.,* tanto más.- **—over** [-óʊvœ(r)], *adv.* además, por otra parte.

morgue [mɔrg], *s.* depósito de cadáveres.

Mormon [mórmon], *a.* y *s.* mormón.

morning [mórniŋ], *s.* mañana; madrugada.—*good m.!* ¡buenos días!—*m. glory,* dondiego de día.—*m. sickness,* vómitos del embarazo.—*a.* matinal.

Moroccan [morákan], *a.* y *s.* marroquí.

moron [móron], *s.* morón; (fam.) imbécil.

morphine [mórfin], *s.* morfina.

morrow [mároʊ], *s.* mañana.—*on th m.,* en el día de mañana; el día si guiente.

Morse code [mɔrs], *s.* código morse.

morsel [mórseḷ], *s.* bocadito; pedacit

mortal [mórtaḷ], *a.* y *s.* mortal.- **—it** [mortǽliti], *s.* mortalidad; mortar dad.—*m. rate,* mortalidad.

mortar [mórtḁ(r)], *s.* mortero, almirez (arti.) mortero, obús.—*m. piec* (alb.) mortero, mezcla.

mortgage [mórgidž], *s.* hipoteca.—*n loan,* préstamo hipotecario.—*vt.* h potecar.

mortician [mortíšan], *s.* empresario d pompas fúnebres.

mortify [mórtifaj], *vti.* [7] mortifica: humillar, abochornar.

mortuary [mórchueri], *s.* depósito d cadáveres.—*a.* mortuorio.

mosaic [mozéijk], *a.* y *s.* mosaico.

Moslem [mázlem], (ant.) *var.* d Muslim.

mosque [mask], *s.* mezquita.

mosquito [moskítoʊ], *s.* mosquito.- *m. net,* mosquitero.

moss [mɔs], *s.* musgo.- **—y** [mósi], *c* musgoso.

most [moʊst], *a.* más; lo más, los má: el mayor número (de); casi todo(s la mayor parte (de).—*for the m. par* principalmente, generalmente.- *adv.* más, lo más, sumamente, muy (fam.) casi.—*s.* lo principal, l: mayor parte, el mayor número, **l** más, el mayor valor.—*at* (the) *m.,* lo más, a lo sumo, cuando más.- **—ly** [móʊstli], *adv.* en su mayo parte, casi todo(s), principalmente

moth [mɔθ], *s.* polilla.—*m. ball,* bol de alcanfor, bola de naftalina.—*m eaten,* apolillado.—*m. hole,* apol lladura.

mother [mʌ́ðœ(r)], *s.* madre.—*m country,* madre patria, metrópoli.- *M. Goose,* supuesta autora de un colección de cuentos infantile como *Cuentos de Calleja.*—*m.-i* *law,* suegra.—*M. Nature,* la Natur leza, la Madre Naturaleza.—*m of-pearl,* nácar, madreperla.— materno, maternal; nativo, nata vernáculo, nacional; metropol tano.—*M.'s Day,* el día de la M. dre.—*M. Superior,* madre superior (monjas).—*m. tongue,* lengua m terna.—*vt.* servir de madre a.— criar madre (vino, etc.).- **—hoc**

[-húd], s. maternidad.– **—less** [-lĭs], a. huérfano de madre.– **—ly** [-lĭ], a. maternal, materno.—adv. maternalmente.

motif [motíf], s. motivo, asunto, tema.

motility [motílĭtĭ], s. movilidad. **—motion** [móuʃọn], s. movimiento; signo, señal, seña; moción, proposición; (for.) pedimento.—m. picture, película cinematográfica.—on the m. of, a propuesta de.—to set in m., poner en marcha.—vi. hacer señas. **—motionless** [móuʃọnlĭs], a. inmóvil; yerto.

motivate [móutĭvejt], vt. motivar. **—motive** [móutĭv], a. motor, motriz.—m. power, fuerza motriz.—s. motivo, móvil, porqué; pie, tema, idea.

motley [mátlĭ], a. abigarrado; mezclado, variado, diverso; vestido de colorines.—s. traje de payaso; mezcla de colores; mezcolanza.

motor [móutọr], s. motor.—a. motriz, motor; de motor.—m. boat o launch, gasolinera, lancha automóvil.—m. scooter, motoneta.—vi. ir en automóvil. **—cade** [-kejd], s. caravana de automóviles.– **—car** [-kar], s. automóvil, auto.– **—coach** [-kouʧ], s. autobús, ómnibus.– **—cycle** [-sajkl], s. motocicleta.– **—ist** [-ĭst], s. automovilista, motorista.– **—ization** [moutọrĭzéjʃọn], s. motorización.– **—ize** [-ajz], vt. motorizar.– **—man** [-mạn], s. motorista, conductor (de tranvía o tren eléctrico).

mottle [mátl], vt. motear, vetear, manchar.—s. mota, veta, mancha.

motto [mátou], s. mote, lema, divisa.

mould [mould], s., vt. y vi. = MOLD. **—moulder** [móuldœr], vi. y vt. = MOLDER. **—moulding** [móuldĭŋ], s. = MOLDING. **—mouldy** [móuldĭ], a. = MOLDY.

moult [moult], vi. = MOLT. **—moulting** [móultĭŋ], s. = MOLTING.

mound [maund], s. montón de tierra; montículo; baluarte; túmulo.—vt. amontonar; atrincherar, fortalecer.

mount [maunt], s. monte, montaña; baluarte, terraplén; montadura; caballería; montura; apeadero; (mil.) monta; toque de clarín.—vt. cabalgar; armar, montar; subir, alzar, elevar; enaltecer; engastar, montar (joyas); (teat.) poner en escena; preparar una cosa para usarla o exhi-

birla.—vi. ascender, elevarse; montar a caballo; subir, montar, ascender (una cuenta, etc.).– **—ain** [máuntĭn], s. monte, montaña.—a. montés, montañés; de montaña.—m. bike, bicicleta de montaña.—m. chain, m. range, sierra, cordillera, cadena de montañas.—m. climber, alpinista.—m. climbing, alpinismo.– **—aineer** [-ĭnír], s. montañés, serrano.– **—ainous** [-ĭnʌs], a. montañoso.– **—ing** [-ĭŋ], s. montura; papel de soporte; (mec.) montaje.

mourn [mourn, mɔrn], vt. lamentar, llorar, sentir.—vi. lamentarse, dolerse; vestir o llevar luto.—to m. for, llevar luto por; lamentar, llorar.– **—ful** [mórnfụl], a. triste, plañidero; apesadumbrado; fúnebre, lúgubre. – **—ing** [-ĭŋ], s. luto; duelo; dolor, aflicción.—in m., de luto, de duelo; fúnebre.—m. band, brazal de luto.

mouse [maus], s. ratón; (comput.) ratón.– **—trap** [máustræp], s. ratonera.

moustache [mʌstǽʃ], s. = MUSTACHE.

mouth [mauθ], s. boca; abertura; bocadura o desembocadura de un río.—m. organ, armónica de boca.– **—ful** [máuθfụl], s. bocado; buchada; migaja, pizca.– **—piece** [-pis], s. boquilla, embocadura; vocero, portavoz.– **—wash** [-wɔ̂ʃ], s. enjuague, enjuagadientes.

movability [muvǎbĭlĭtĭ], s. movilidad. **—movable** [múvabl], a. movible; móvil; movedizo.—s. pl. muebles, menaje, mobiliario, efectos. **—move** [muv], s. movimiento; paso; jugada, lance, turno de jugar.—on the m., en marcha, en movimiento; de viaje.—to get a m. on, (fam.) darse prisa, empezarse a mover.—to make a m., dar un paso; hacer una jugada.—vt. mover; remover; trasladar, mudar; hacer una moción; conmover; persuadir.—to m. to, causar (cólera, etc.), poner (colérico, etc.).—vi. moverse; mudarse; ir, andar, caminar, ponerse en marcha; obrar, entrar en acción; avanzar, progresar; mover el vientre; hacer una jugada.—to m. away, alejarse; irse; trasladarse; mudar de casa.—to m. in, entrar; entrar a habitar una casa. **—movement** [múvmẹnt], s. movimiento; aparato de relojería; (of the bowels) evacuación; (of a symphony) tiempo.

—**movie** [múvi], s. película.—*pl.* cine.—*m. camera*, cámara; filmadora.—*m. star*, estrella de cine.—*m. theater*, cine. —**goer** [-gouœr], s. aficionado al cine. —**moving** [múviņ], a. conmovedor, emocionante, patético.—*m. parts*, piezas movibles.—*m. picture*, película cinematográfica.—s. movimiento, moción; traslado, mudanza.

mow [mou], *vti.* [6] segar, guadañar, cortar la hierba.- —**er** [móuœe(r)], s. segador; segadora mecánica.

Mr. [místœr], *abrev.* (**Mister**) Sr. (Señor), p.ej., **Mr. Cruz** Sr. Cruz. [no es de buena educación decir 'Mr.' sin el apellido]

Mrs. [mísiz], s. Sra., p.ej., **Mrs. Somavilla** Sra. Somavilla. [no es de buena educación decir 'Mrs.' sin el apellido]

Ms. [miz], nueva abreviatura que se aplica igualmente a **Miss** y **Mrs.**

much [mʌch], a. mucho, abundante, copioso.—*adv.* mucho; muy; con mucho, en gran manera.—*as m. as*, tanto como.—*as m. more*, otro tanto más.—*how m.?* ¿cuánto?—*m. as*, por más que, a pesar de.—*m. the same*, casi lo mismo—*m. too*, demasiado.—*not so m. as*, no tanto como; ni siquiera.—*so m.*, tanto—*this m. more*, esto más, tanto así más.—s. mucho.

muck [mʌk], s. abono, estiércol; cieno; porquería, basura.

mucous [mjúkʌs], a. mucoso. —**mucus** [mjúkʌs], s. mocoso.

mud [mʌd], s. fango, lodo, barro.—*m. wall*, tapia.- —**dle** [mádl], *vt.* embrollar, confundir; revolver; atontar.—*to m. through*, hacer algo malamente, salir del paso a duras penas.—s. embrollo, confusión.- —**dy** [mádi], a. lodoso, sucio; turbio, confuso.—*vti.* [7] enturbiar, ensuciar, embarrar.

muff [mʌf], s. manguito (para las manos); chabacanería, torpeza; (baseball) fallar la bola.—*vt.* desperdiciar (una ocasión); dejar escapar (la pelota); (fam.) hacer algo torpemente.

muffin [máfin], s. panecillo, mollete.

muffle [máfl], *vt.* embozar; encubrir; apagar o atenuar un sonido.—*to m. up*, embozarse.- —**d** [-d], a. apagado, sordo.- —**r** [máflœe(r)], s. bu-

fanda; (aut.) silenciador; (mús. sordina.

mug [mʌg], s. pichel, jarra, tarr (Mex.); (jer.) jeta, hocico; (jer rufián.—*m. shot*, foto (de archiv policial).—*vt.* (jer.) atracar, asalta (jer.) fotografiar.—*vi.* (jer.) hace muecas.

Muhammad [mŭhǽmad], s. Ma homa.

Muhammadan [mŭhǽmadan], s. (ant musulmán, islámico.

Muhammadanism [mŭhǽmadanizm s. (ant.) el Islam, islamismo.

mulatto [mulǽtou], a. y s. mulato.

mulberry [málberi], s. mora.—*m. tre* moral.

mule [mjul], s. mulo, mula.- —**te** [mjuletír], s. arriero, mulatero.

mull [mʌl], s.—*vt.* calentar con esp cias.—*vi.—to m. over*, reflexiona sobre.

multilingual [mʌltilíŋgwal], a. mult lingüe, plurilingüe; políglota.

multiple [máltipl], s. múltiplo.— múltiple; (mat.) múltiplo.—*n choice*, de opción múltiple.—*n sclerosis*, esclerosis múltiple. —**m tiplication** [mʌltiplikéiʃon], multiplicación.—*m. table*, tabla (multiplicar. —**multiplicity** [mʌl plísiti], s. multiplicidad, sinnún ero. —**multiply,** *vti.* y *vii.* [7] multipl car(se).

multitude [máltitjud], s. multitud.

mum [mʌm], *interj.* ¡chitón! ¡sile cio!—a. callado, silencioso.—*m the word*, punto en boca.—*to ke m.*, callarse.

mumble [mámbl], *vt.* y *vi.* masculla mascujar.

mummy [mámi], s. momia.

mumps [mʌmps], s. (med.) paperas.

munch [mʌnch], *vt.* ronzar.

municipal [mjunísipal], a. municipal —**ity** [mjunisipǽliti], s. municip municipalidad.

munificence [mjunífisens], s. muni cencia. —**munificent** [mjunífisen a. munífico.

munition [mjuníʃon], s. munición. *vt.* municionar.

mural [mjúral], a. mural.—s. pintu mural; decoración mural.

murder [mérdœe(r)], s. asesinat homicidio.—*vt.* asesinar; (fam.) (tropear.—*vi.* cometer homicidi —**er** [-œe(r)], s. asesino, homicida

—**ess** [-įs], s. asesina.— —**ous** [-ʌs], a. asesino, sanguinario.

murky [mœ́rki], a. oscuro, lóbrego.

murmur [mœ́rmœr], s. murmullo.— vt. y vi. murmurar.

muscat [mʌ́skąt], s. moscatel (uva y pasa). —**muscatel** [mʌskątél], s. moscatel (vino y uva).

muscle [mʌ́sl], s. músculo; (fig.) fuerza muscular.—m.-bound, demasiado musculoso. —**muscular** [mʌ́skju-lą̈(r)], a. muscular; musculoso.—m. dystrophy, distrofia muscular.

muse [mjuz], s. musa.—the Muses, las Musas.—vi. meditar, reflexionar.— to m. on, contemplar.

museum [mjuzíʌm], s. museo.

mush [mʌʃ], s. gachas de harina de maíz; (fam.) sentimentalismo exagerado.

mushroom [mʌ́ʃrum], s. seta, hongo.—m. cloud, nube-hongo.— vi. aparecer de la noche a la mañana.—to m. into, convertirse rapide-rápidamente en.

mushy [mʌ́ʃi], a. pastoso; exageradamente sentimental.

music [mjúzįk], s. música.—m. hall, salón de conciertos; café cantante.—m. stand; tablado para una orquesta. —**al** [-ąl], a. musical.—m. comedy, zarzuela, comedia musical.- —**ian** [mjuzíʃąn], s. músico.

musk [mʌsk], s. almizcle.—a. almizclero.

muskmelon [mʌ́skmelon], s. melón. —**muskrat** [mʌ́skræt], s. almizclera.

Muslim [mázlįm], a. y s. musulmán, muslime, islámico.—M. calendar, calendario islámico.

muslin [mázlįn], s. muselina.

muss [mʌs], s. (fam.) desorden, confusión; arrebatiña.—vt. (fam.) desordenar, manosear, arrugar.

mussel [mʌ́sęl], s. mejillón.

must [mʌst], vai. [11] deber, tener que; haber que; deber (de).—he m. have gone, debió ir, debe (de) haber ido.— it m. be very late, será muy tarde.— she m. have missed the train, habrá perdido el tren.—s. mosto; moho.

mustache [mʌstǽʃ], s. bigote, mostacho.

mustard [mʌ́stąrd], s. mostaza.

muster [mʌ́stœ(r)], vt. reunir; (mil.) juntar para pasar lista, revista,

etc.—to m. in o into service, (mil.) alistar.—to m. up, tomar (valor, fuerza, etc.).—vi. (mil.) juntarse; pasar lista.—s. asamblea; matrícula de revista.—m. roll, lista de revista.—to pass m., llenar los requisitos.

musty [mʌ́sti], a. mohoso; añejo; rancio; pasado; mustio, triste.

mutability [mjutąbíliti], s. inconstancia, veleidad. —**mutable** [mjútąbl], a. inconstante, veleidoso. —**mutation** [mjutéĭʃon], s. mutación.

mute [mjut], a. y s. mudo.—vt. poner sordina a.

mutilate [mjútįlejt], vt. mutilar. —**mutilation** [mjutįléĭʃon], s. mutilación.

mutineer [mjutįnír], s. amotinado.

mutinous [mjútįnʌs], a. amotinado. —**mutiny** [mjútįni], vii. [7] amotinarse.—s. motín, amotinamiento.

mutter [mʌ́tœ(r)], vt. y vi. murmurar.

mutton [mʌ́ton], s. carne de carnero.—m. broth, caldo de carnero.—m. chop, chuleta de carnero.

mutual [mjúchµąl], a. mutuo, recíproco, mutuo.—m. aid, apoyo mutuo.—m. benefit association, mutualidad.—m. friend, amigo común.—m. fund, (com.) fondo de inversión mobiliaria.—m. savings bank, caja de ahorros mutuos.

muzzle [mázl], s. morro, hocico; bozal; boca (de arma de fuego).—vt. abozalar, poner bozal; amordazar.

my [maj], a. pos. mi, mis.

myopia [majóupįą], s. miopía. —**myopic** [majápįk], a. miope, corto de vista.

myriad [mírįąd], s. miríada; diez mil; millares, un gran número.—a. innumerable, numeroso.

myrrh [mœr], s. mirra, goma resinosa.

myrtle [mœ́rtl], s. mirto, arrayán.

myself [majsélf], pron. yo mismo; me, mí, mí mismo.—I myself did it, yo mismo lo hice.—I said to myself, me dije a mí mismo o para mí.

mysterious [mįstírįʌs], a. misterioso. —**mystery** [místeri], s. misterio.

mystic [místįk], a. y s. místico. —**mystify** [místįfaj], vti. [7] confundir, desconcertar; intrigar; mixtificar.

myth [mįθ], s. mito; fábula; ficción.- —**ical** [míθįkąl], a. mítico; fabuloso; imaginario.- —**ological** [mįθọládžį-kąl], a. mitológico. —**ology** [mįθá-lodžį], s. mitología.

N

nab [næb], *vti.* [1] (fam.) prender, atrapar, agarrar, echar mano a.

nag [næg], *s.* jaco, rocín, caballejo; (fam.) penco, jamelgo.—*vti.* y *vii.* [1] regañar.

nail [nejl], *s.* clavo; (of finger) uña.—*n. brush,* cepillo de uñas.—*n. file,* lima para las uñas.—*n. polish,* esmalte para las uñas.—*to hit the n. on the head,* dar en el clavo.—*vt.* clavar.

naive [naív], *a.* ingenuo, cándido.

naked [néjkjd], *a.* desnudo; descubierto; descamisado; patente.—*stark n.,* en cueros, (fam.) en pelota.—*the n. truth,* la verdad pura y simple.—(with the) *n. eye,* (a) simple vista.- **—ness** [-njs], *s.* desnudez.

name [nejm], *s.* nombre; (first name) nombre de pila; (last name) apellido; fama, renombre.—*by* u *of the n. of,* llamado, nombrado.—*Christian n.,* nombre de pila.—*in God's name,* por el amor de Dios.—*in n.,* de nombre.—*n. day,* día del santo, onomástico.—*n.-tag,* etiqueta; chapa.—*to call names,* maltratar de palabra.—*what is your n.?* ¿cómo se llama usted?—*vt.* nombrar; fijar.- **—less** [néjmljs], *a.* sin nombre, anónimo.- **—ly** [-lj], *adv.* especialmente; a saber, o sea, es decir.- **—sake** [-sejk], *s.* tocayo; homónimo.

nap [næp], *s.* (tej.) lanilla; sueñecillo.—*to take a n.,* descabezar un sueñecillo.—*vii.* [1] echar un sueñecillo.

nape [nejp], *s.* nuca, cogote; testuz.

naphtha [næfθǎ], *s.* nafta.- **—lene** [-lin], *s.* naftalina.

napkin [næpkjn], *s.* servilleta.

narcissus [narsísas], *s.* narciso.

narcotic [narkátjk], *s.* y *a.* narcótico.

narrate [næréjt], *vt.* y *vii.* narrar, relatar. **—narration** [næréjšon], *s.* narración, relato. **—narrative** [nǽrạtjv], *a.* narrativo.—*s.* narración, narrativa, relato. **—narrator** [næréjto(r)], *s.* narrador.

narrow [nǽrou], *a.* angosto, estrecho; tacaño, mezquino; intolerante.—*n. gauge,* (f.c.) de vía estrecha.—*n.-minded,* estrecho de miras.—*n. pass,* desfiladero.—*to have a n. escape,* salvarse en una tabla.—*s. pl.* pasaje angosto; desfiladero; estrecho.—*vt.* estrechar, contraer, encoger; limitar.—*vi.* estrecharse, encogerse, reducirse.- **—ly** [-lj], *adv.* estrechamente; por poco, escasamente.- **—ness** [-njs], *s.* angostura; estrechez, pobreza.

nasal [néjzạl], *a.* y *s.* nasal.- **—ize** [-ajz], *vt.* nasalizar.—*vi.* ganguear.

nasty [nǽstj], *a.* malévolo; sucio, asqueroso; ofensivo, obsceno, indecente; (tiempo) inclemente.

natal [néjtạl], *a.* nativo; natal.

nation [néjšon], *s.* nación.- **—al** [nǽšonạl], *a.* nacional.—*n. anthem,* himno nacional.—*n. debt,* deuda pública.—*s.* ciudadano; súbdito.- **—alism** [nǽšonạljzm], *s.* nacionalismo.- **—ality** [nǽšonǽljtj], *s.* nacionalidad; origen, tradición.- **—alization** [nǽšonạljzéjšon], *s.* nacionalización; naturalización.- **—alize** [nǽšonạlajz], *vt.* nacionalizar.

native [néjtjv], *a.* nativo, natal, natural, oriundo; indígena; del país, patrio.—*N. American,* amerindio.—*n. country* o *land,* patria, país natal, terruño.—*s.* natural, nativo, indígena. **—nativity** [nejtívjtj], *s.* nacimiento, natividad; (N.) Navidad.

natural [nǽchurạl], *a.* natural; nativo; sencillo, sin afectación; normal, ordinario; ilegitimo, bastardo.—*s.* (mús.) becuadro; tecla blanca.- **—ism** [-jzm], *s.* naturalismo.- **—ist** [-jst], *s.* naturalista.- **—ization** [-jzéjšon], *s.* naturalización; nacionalización.—*n. papers,* carta de naturaleza.- **—ize** [-ajz], *vt.* naturalizar; nacionalizar.- **—ly** [-lj], *adv.* naturalmente; desde luego.- **—ness** [-njs], *s.* naturalidad; sencillez. **—nature** [néjchŭ(r)], *s.* naturaleza; natural, índole, genio; especie, género, clase.

naught [nɔt], *s.* nada; cero.—*to set at n.,* hacer tabla rasa de.

naughtiness [nɔ́tjnjs], *s.* maldad, perversidad; picardía, travesura. **—naughty** [nɔ́tj], *a.* desobediente, díscolo; pícaro, travieso; libre, picaresco; (story) verde.

nausea [nɔ́ŝi̯ă], s. náusea.— **—te** [nɔ̂ŝi̯eit̯], vt. dar náuseas a.—vi. nausear.— **—ting** [nɔ̂ŝi̯eit̯in̯], a. nauseabundo, asqueroso.

nautical [nɔ́t̯ikl̯], a. náutico, marino.

naval [néival̯], a. naval; de marina.— N. Academy, Escuela Naval Militar.—n. officer, oficial de marina.— n. station, apostadero.

nave [neiv], s. (arq.) nave.

navel [néivel̯], s. ombligo.—n. orange, naranja de ombligo.

navigable [nǽvigabl̯], a. navegable.— **—navigate** [nǽvigeit̯], vt. y vi. navegar. **—navigation** [nǽvigéiŝon̯], s. navegación; náutica. **—navigator** [nǽvigeit̯o(r)], s. navegante; piloto; tratado de náutica. **—navy** [néivi], s. marina de guerra; marina; azul oscuro o marina.—n. blue, azul marino.—n. yard, arsenal de puerto.

nay [nei], adv. no; de ningún mode; más aún, y aún.—s. voto negativo.

nazi [nátsi] a. y s. nazi, nacista.

N-bomb [énbam], s. bomba de neutrones.

near [nir], prep. cerca de, junto a, próximo a, por, hacia.—adv. cerca; proximamente; (fam.) casi.—n. at hand, a (la) mano, cerca.—N. East, Cercano Oriente, Próximo Oriente.—n. miss, casi una colisión.—a. cercano, próximo, inmediato; allegado; íntimo, estrecho; a punto de, por poco.—vt. y vi. acercar(se).— **—by** o **n.-by** [nírbai], prep. cerca de.—adv. cerca, a (la) mano.—a. cercano, contiguo, próximo.— **—ly** [-li], adv. cerca, cerca de; estrechamente; casi; de cerca; próximamente, aproximadamente.— **—ness** [-ni̯s], s. proximidad, cercanía.— **—sighted** [-sáit̯id], a. miope, corto de vista.— **—sightedness** [-sáit̯idni̯s], s. miopía.

neat [nit], a. limpio, aseado, pulero; pulido; mondo, lirondo; nítido, claro; esmerado; puro, sin mezcla.— **—ness** [nítni̯s], s. aseo, pulcritud, nitidez, limpieza.

nebula [nébyu̯lă], s. (astr.) nebulosa; nube en el ojo. **—nebulous** [nébyu̯lʌs], a. nebuloso.

necessarily [néseseri̯li], adv. necesariamente. **—necessary** [néseseri], a. necesario, preciso, forzoso.—to be n., ser menester, hacer falta. **—necessitate** [ni̯sési̯teit̯], vt. necesitar, exigir. **—necessity** [ni̯sési̯ti], s. necesi-

dad.—pl. artículos de primera necesidad, requisitos indispensables.

neck [nɛk], s. cuello, garganta; pescuezo; gollete (de botella); (cost.) escote; istmo, cabo, península; (of violin or guitar) mástil; desfiladero.—n. and n. (dep.) parejos.—n. of land, lengua de tierra.—in u on the n. of, a raíz de.—to break one's n., (fam.) matarse trabajando.—to stick one's n. out, (fam.) descubrir el cuerpo.—vi. (jer.) acariciarse (dos enamorados). **—lace** [nɛklis], s. collar, gargantilla.— **—tie** [-tai], s. corbata.—n. pin, alfiler de corbata.

nectarine [nɛktarín], s. griñon.

need [nid], s. necesidad; carencia, falta; pobreza, miseria.—if n. be, si hubiere necesidad, si fuere necesario.—in n., necesitado.—vt. necesitar; hacer falta.—vi. ser necesario; estar en la necesidad, carecer de lo necesario.— **—ful** [nídful̯], a. necesario; necesitado.

needle [nídl̯], s. aguja.—n. bath, ducha en alfileres.—n. case, alfiletero.—n. point, bordado al pasado; encaje de mano.

needless [nídli̯s], a. inútil, innecesario.—n. to say, excusado es decir.

needlework [nídlwœrk], s. costura; labor, bordado de aguja.

needy [nídi], a. necesitado, menesteroso.

ne'er [ner], adv. contr. de NEVER. **—n.-do-well** [nérduwel̯], s. haragán, holgazán, perdido, perdulario.

nefarious [ni̯férias], a. nefando, malvado.

negation [ni̯géiŝon̯], s. negación, negativa. **—negative** [négat̯iv], a. negativo.—s. negativa; electricidad negativa, borne negativo; (gram.) negación; (mat.) término negativo; (foto.) prueba negativa.

neglect [ni̯glékt], s. descuido, negligencia; abandono, dejadez.—vt. descuidar, desatender; abandonar.— **—ful** [-ful̯], a. negligente, descuidado. **—negligence** [négli̯ḑęns], s. negligencia. **—negligent** [négli̯ḑęnt], a. negligente.

negotiable [ni̯góuŝi̯abl̯], a. negociable. **—negotiate** [ni̯góuŝi̯eit̯], vt. negociar; gestionar, agenciar; (fam.) vencer, superar.—vi. negociar. **—negotiation** [ni̯gouŝi̯éiŝon̯], s. negociación; negocio, gestión.

Negro [nígrou], s. y a. negro.

neigh [nei], *vi.* relinchar.—*s.* relincho.

neighbor [néibo(r)], *s.* vecino; prójimo.- **—hood** [-hud], *s.* vecindad; vecindario; barrio; cercanías, alrededores.—*in the n. of,* en las inmediaciones de; (fam.) casi, como, aproximadamente.- **—ing** [-iŋ], *a.* vecino, vecinal, colindante, próximo o cercano.- **—ly** [-li], *a.* buen vecino, amable, sociable.

neither [níðœ(r), náiðœ(r)], *a.* ningún, ninguno de los dos.—*conj.* ni; tampoco, ni siquiera.—*n. he nor she,* ni él ni ella.—*pron.* ninguno, ni uno ni otro, ni el uno ni el otro.

Neo-Latin [niolǽtin], *s.* y *a.* neolatino.

neologism [niálodžizm], *s.* neologismo.

neon [nían], *s.* neo, neón.

nephew [néfju], *s.* sobrino.

nerve [nœrv], *a.* nervioso.—*s.* nervio; vigor, fibra; valor, ánimo; (fam.) desfachatez, descaro.—*pl.* excitabilidad nerviosa.—*n.-racking,* horripilante. **—nervous** [nœrvʌs], *a.* nervioso.—*n. breakdown,* colapso nervioso. **—nervousness** [nœrvʌsnis], *s.* nerviosidad; estado nervioso o irritable.

nest [nest], *s.* nido; nidada.—*n. egg,* nidal; (fig.) ahorros, hucha.—*n. of tables,* juego de mesas.—*to feather one's n.,* hacer todo para enriquecerse.—*vi.* anidar; anidarse.

nestle [nésl], *vt.* abrigar, poner en un nido.—*vi.* anidar(se).

net [net], *s.* red; redecilla; malla; (com.) ganancia líquida; (fig.) trampa; (tej.) tul.—*vti.* [1] enredar o coger con red; cubrir con redes o mallas; coger; obtener; producir (una ganancia líquida).—*a.* (com.) neto, líquido; de punto de malla.— *n. amount,* importe neto.—*n. balance,* saldo líquido o neto.—*n. profit,* ganancia o utilidad líquida, beneficio líquido.- **—ting** [-iŋ], *s.* red; tejido de malla.

nettle [nétl], *s.* (bot.) ortiga.—*vt.* picar; irritar, provocar.

network [nétwœrk], *s.* red, malla; (rad., T.V., f.c., etc.) cadena, red, sistema.

neurasthenia [njurasθíniä], *s.* neurastenia.

neurosis [njuróusis], *s.* neurosis. **—neurotic** [njurátik], *a.* neurótico.

neuter [njútœ(r)], *a.* neutro; neutral. **—neutral** [njútral], *a.* neutral; neutro; indiferente.—*s.* neutral.—*in n.* (aut.) en punto muerto. **—neutrality** [njutrǽliti], *s.* neutralidad. **—neutralize** [njútralaiz], *vt.* neutralizar.

neutron [níutron], *s.* neutrón.—*n. bomb,* bomba de neutrones, bomba neutrónica.

never [névœ(r)], *adv.* nunca, jamás; no, de ningún modo.—*n. again,* nunca más, otra vez no.—*n. ending,* interminable, sin fin.—*n. fear,* no hay cuidado, no hay miedo.—*n. mind,* no importa.— **—more** [nevœr mór], *adv.* jamás, nunca más. **—theless** [nevœrðélés], *adv.* y *conj.* no obstante, con todo, sin embargo; a pesar de eso.

new [nju], *a.* nuevo; moderno; fresco; reciente, recién; distinto.—*n. moon,* luna nueva, novilunio.—*what's n.?* ¿qué hay de nuevo? **—born** [njú bórn], *a.* recién nacido.- **—comer** [njúkʌmœ(r)], *s.* recién llegado.— **—fangled** [njúfǽŋgld], *a.* recién inventado.- **—ly** [njúli], *adv.* nuevamente, recientemente, recién.—*n. arrived,* recién llegado; advenedizo.- **—lywed** [-liwed], *s.* recién casado; recién casada.- **—ness** [-nis], *s.* novedad; innovación.- **—s** [-z], *s.* noticia, noticias; noticia fresca (newspaper, radio, television) noticias.—*n. agency,* agencia de noticias.—*n. bulletin,* boletín informativo.—*n. coverage,* reportaje.—*the six o'clock news,* (rad./tel.) las noticias, el informativo, el noticiario o el noticiario de las seis.—*the sport n.,* la información deportiva.—*no news is good n.,* la falta de noticias es buena noticia.—*what's the n.?* ¿qué hay de nuevo? ¿qué noticias hay? **—sboy** [-zbɔi], *s.* chiquillo vendedor de periódicos.- **—scast** [njúzkæst], *s.* noticiario radiofónico.—*vt.* radiodifundir (noticias).- **—spaper** [-zpeipœ(r)], *s.* periódico, diario.— *n. man,* periodista; reportero, reportero.—*n. serial,* folletín.- **—print** [-print], *s.* papel-prensa. **—sreel** [-zril], *s.* noticiario cinematográfico.- **—sstand** [-zstænd], *s.* quiosco o puesto de periódicos, revistas, etc. - **—sworthy** [njúzwœrθi], *a.* de gran actualidad, de interés periodístico. **—sy** [-zi], *a.* informativo, lleno de novedades.

New Year's Day, *s.* el Día de Año Nuevo.

New Year's Eve, s. la noche vieja, la víspera de año nuevo.

New York [yɔrk], a. neoyorkino.—s. Nueva York.—*N. Yorker,* neoyorkino.

New Zealander [níu zíländœ(r)], s. neozelandés.

next [nekst], a. siguiente; entrante; próximo, contiguo, inmediato; subsiguiente, futuro, venidero.—n. door, la puerta o (casa) al lado.—n. month, (week, year), el mes (la semana, el año) entrante, próximo o que viene.—n. time, otra vez, la próxima vez.—the n. life, la otra vida.—to be n., seguir en turno, tocarle a uno.—adv. luego, después, inmediatamente después, en seguida, a renglón seguido.—n. best, lo mejor a falta de eso.—n. to, junto a, al lado de; después de; casi.—n. to impossible, punto menos que imposible.—what n.? ¿y ahora (o luego) qué?

Niagara Falls [najǽgarǝ], s. las Cataratas del Niagara.

nibble [níbl], vt. mordiscar, mordisquear; pacer.—vi. picar, morder.—to n. at, picar de o en.—s. mordisco.

Nicaraguan [nikarágwǝn], a. y s. nicaragüense.

nice [najs], a. fino, sutil; delicado; diligente, solícito; esmerado, pulcro, refinado; agradable, lindo; simpático, gentil, amable.—n.-looking, hermoso, guapo, bien parecido.—ly [nájslį], adv. muy bien, con delicadeza, finamente.—to get along n. with, llevarse bien con.- —ness [-nįs], s. finura, delicadeza, amabilidad; esmero; refinamiento; sutileza. - —ty [nájsetį], s. primor, cuidado; finura, delicadeza; remilgo.

niche [nich], s. nicho, hornacina; colocación conveniente.

nick [nik], s. muesca, mella, corte, picadura.—in the n. of time, en el momento justo o crítico.—vt. mellar, hacer muescas en; cortar.

nickel [níkel], s. níquel; (fam.) moneda de cinco centavos (E.U.).—n. steel, acero níquel.—to n.-plate, niquelar.

nickname [níknejm], s. mote, apodo.—vt. motejar, apodar.

nicotine [níkotin], s. nicotina.

niece [nis], s. sobrina.

nifty [níftį], a. (jer.) elegante; (jer.) excelente.

niggard [nígärd], a. y s. tacaño.

night [najt], s. noche.—last n., anoche.—n. before last, anteanoche.—tomorrow n., mañana por la noche.—a. nocturno; de noche.—n. blindness, ceguera nocturna.—n. clothes, ropa de dormir.—n. club, café cantante, cabaret.—n. owl, buho, lechuza, mochuelo; (fam.) trasnochador.—n. shift, turno de noche.—n. watch, sereno, guardia nocturno; guardia nocturna; acción de trasnochar.—n. watchman, sereno, vigilante nocturno.- —cap [nájtkæp], s. gorro de dormir; trago antes de acostarse, sosiega.- —fall [-fɔl], s. anochecida, anochecer, caída de la tarde.- —gown [-gaun], s. camisa de dormir.- —hawk [-hɔk], s. chotacabras; (fam.) trasnochador.- —ingale [-iŋgejl], s. ruiseñor.- —ly [-lį], adv. por las noches, todas las noches.- a. nocturno, de noche.- —mare [-mer], s. pesadilla. - —shirt [-šœrt], s. camisa de dormir.- —time [-tajm], s. noche.—in the n., de noche.

nil [nil], s. nada.

nimble [nímbl], a. vivo, listo, ágil, veloz, expedito.—n.-witted, despierto, inteligente. —**nimbly** [nímblį], adv. ligeramente, ágilmente.

nincompoop [nínkompup], s. badulaque, papirote.

nine [najn], a. y s. nueve. —**nine hundred,** a. y s. novecientos.—n. one, novecientos uno. —**ninth** [najnθ], a. y s. noveno.

ninepins [nájnpįnz], s. bolos.

nineteen [najntín], a. y s. diecinueve. —**nineteenth** [najntínθ], a. y s. decimonoveno, decimonono; (fraction) diecinueveavo, diecinueveava parte.

ninety [nájntį], a. y s. noventa.—n.-one, noventa y uno. —**ninetieth** [najntįeθ], a. y s. nonagésimo, noventavo.

ninny [nínį], s. simplón, tonto.

nip [nip], vt. [1] pellizcar; asir, sujetar; recortar, desmochar; helar, escarchar; marchitar.—to n. in the bud, cortar en flor.—to n. off, desmochar.—s. pellizco; pedacito; trago, traguito; dentellada; helada, escarcha; cogida; daño repentino (plantas y sembrados).—n. and tuck, (dep.) empate.

nipple [nípl], s. pezón; tetilla; mamadera; (mec.) tubo roscadó de unión.

Nipponese [nɪpaníz], s. y a. nipón, japonés.

nit [nɪt], s. liendre.

nitrate [nájtreịt], s. nitrato. **—nitric** [nájtrɪk], a. nítrico, azoico. **—nitrogen** [nájtrɒdʒɪn], s. nitrógeno, ázoe.

no [noụ], adv. no.—*no longer,* ya no.—*n. more,* nada más.—*n. sooner,* no bien.—*a.* ninguno, ningún.—*n.-account,* (fam.) sin valor, deleznable.—*n. dogs allowed,* no se admiten perros.—*n.-fault,* libre de culpa (divorcio, seguro, accidente de tráfico).—*n. fooling,* sin broma, fuera de broma.—*n. matter,* no importa.—*n. matter how much,* por mucho que.—*no man's land,* terreno sin reclamar; (mil.) la terra de nadie.—*n. one,* nadie, ninguno.—*n. payment,* no delivery, sin pago no hay (o habrá) entrega.—*n. show,* s. pasajero no presentado.—*n. smoking,* se prohibe fumar, prohibido fumar.—*n.-trump,* sin triunfo.—*to n. purpose,* sin objeto.—*with n. money,* sin dinero.—*s.* no, voto negativo.

nobility [nobɪ́lɪtɪ], s. nobleza; hidalguía. **—noble** [noúbl], a. y s. noble; hidalgo. **—nobleman** [noúblmạn], s. noble, hidalgo. **—nobleness** [noúblnɪs], s. nobleza, caballerosidad. **—noblesse** [noblés], s. nobleza. **—nobly** [noúblɪ], adv. noblemente.

nobody [noúbadɪ], pron. nadie, ninguno.—*n. else,* nadie más, ningún otro.—*s.* persona insignificante, (fam.) quídam.

nocturnal [naktǽrnạl], a. nocturno.— *n. emission,* polución nocturna. **—nocturne** [náktœrn], s. nocturno.

nod [nad], vti. [1] hacer una seña afirmativa o llamativa con la cabeza; inclinar (una rama, etc.).—*vii.* cabecear, inclinar la cabeza; descabezar un sueño, dormitar.—*s.* cabeceo; cabezada; señal afirmativa con la cabeza; inclinación de cabeza.— *to get the n.,* recibir el visto bueno.

node [noụd], s. bulto, protuberancia, chichón; nudo; tumor, dureza, nódulo; nodo.

noise [nɔɪz], s. ruido.—*it's being noised about that,* corre el rumor de que, se rumora que.—**less** [nɔ́ɪzlɪs], a. silencioso, sin ruido. **—noisily** [nɔ́ɪzɪlɪ], adv. ruidosamente. **—noisy**

[nɔ́ɪzɪ], a. ruidoso, turbulento, estrepitoso.

nomad [noúmæd], a. y s. nómada.

nominal [námɪnạl], a. nominal. **—nominate** [námɪneịt], vt. nombrar, designar; postular como candidato. **—nomination** [namɪnéịʃọn], s. nombramiento, nominación; propuesta. **—nominative** [námɪnạtɪv], a. y s. (gram.) nominativo. **—nominee** [namɪní], s. candidato; persona nombrada.

nonchalance [nánʃạlạns], s. indiferencia, desenvoltura. **—nonchalant** [nánʃạlạnt], a. indiferente, desenvuelto.

noncom [nánkam], s. (fam.) clase, suboficial.

noncombatant [nankámbạtạnt], a. y s. no combatiente.

noncommissioned officer [nankạmíʃọnd], s. clase, suboficial.

noncommittal [nankọmítạl], a. reservado, evasivo, reticente.

nondescript [nándɪskrɪpt], a. indefinido, inclasificable.

none [nʌn], pron. nadie, ninguno; nada; nada de.—*adv.* no, de ninguna manera, absolutamente no.— *n. the less,* no obstante, sin embargo, no menos.—*to be n. the better (worse),* no hallarse mejor (peor), no salir o quedar mejor (peor) librado, no ganar (perder).

nonexistent [nanɪgzístẹnt], a. inexistente.

nonpayment [nanpeímẹnt], s. falta de pago.

nonplus [nanplás], vt. dejar estupefacto, dejar pegado a la pared.

nonprofit [nanpráfɪt], a. sin fin lucrativo.

nonrefillable [nanrẹfílạbẹl], a. irrellenable.

nonrusting [nanrástɪŋ], a. inoxidable.

nonsectarian [nansektérɪạn], a. no sectario.

nonsense [nánsɛns], s. disparate, desatino; tontería, absurdo; (fam.) música celestial.—*interj.* ¡qué disparate! ¡bah! **—nonsensical** [nansénsɪkạl], a. disparatado, desatinado.

nonskid [nanskíd], a. antideslizante.

nonstop [nanstáp], a. y s. sin parar, sin escala.

nonsupport [nansʌpórt], s. falta de manutención.

nonunion [nanyunyọn], a. no agremiado u opuesto a los sindicato obreros; de fuera de los sindicatos obreros.

oodle [núdl], s. tallarín, fideo, pasta alimenticia; tonto, mentecato; (fam.) cabeza.—*n. soup,* sopa de pastas, sopa de fideos.

ook [nuk], s. rincón; escondrijo.

oon [nun], s. mediodía; las doce del día; (poét.) medianoche; (fig.) culminación, apogeo.—*at high n.,* en pleno mediodía.—*a.* meridional.- **—day** [núndej], s. mediodía (mitad del día).—*a.* meridional, de mediodía.- **—time** [-tajm], s. mediodía.

oose [nus], s. lazo corredizo; dogal.— *n. snare,* trampa.—*vt.* lazar; coger con lazo corredizo o trampa; ahorcar.

or [nɔr], *conj.* ni.—*n. I,* yo tampoco.

ordic [nórdjk], *a.* y s. nórdico.

orm [nɔrm], s. norma, modelo, tipo.- **—al** [nórmal], *a.* normal, regular, corriente; típico, ejemplar; perpendicular.—s. norma, estado normal. **—alize** [-alajz], *vt.* normalizar.

orth [nɔrθ], s. norte, septentrión.—*a.* septentrional.—*N. American,* norteamericano.—*adv.* al norte, hacia el norte.- **—east** [nɔrθíst], s. y a. nordeste.- **—erly** [nórðœerlj], **—ern** [nórðœern], *a.* septentrional, norteño, nórtico; nordista; del norte o hacia el norte.—*northern lights,* aurora boreal.- **—erner** [nórðœernœ(r)], s. habitante del norte.- **—land** [nórθlænd], s. tierra o región del norte.- **—west** [nɔrθwést], s. y a. noroeste o norueste.- **—western** [nɔrθwéstœern], *a.* del noroeste.

orwegian [nɔrwídžjan], s. y a. noruego.

ose [nouz], s. nariz; (animal) hocico; olfato; sagacidad.—*n. bag,* cebadera, morral.—*n. cone,* cono de proa.—*n. dive,* (aer.) picada.—*n. ring,* nariguera.—*vt.* y *vi.* oler, olfatear; entremeterse.—*to n. about,* husmear, curiosear.—*to n.-dive,* (aer.) picar.—*to n. out,* descubrir; vencer por poco.- **—bleed** [-blid], s. hemorragia nasal.- **—y** [nóuzj], *a.* (fam.) curioso, husmeador.

ostalgia [nastáldžả], s. nostalgia. **—nostalgic** [nastáldžjk], *a.* nostálgico.

ostril [nástrjl], s. ventana de la nariz; nariz.

ot [nat], *adv.* no; ni, ni siquiera.—*is it n.?* ¿no es así? ¿no es eso? ¿ver-

dad?—*n. a little,* no poco, bastante.—*n. any,* ninguno.—*n. at all,* nada; de ningún modo; de nada (contestación a *thank you*).—*n. even,* ni siquiera.—*n. one,* ni uno (sólo).—*n. so much as,* ni siquiera.— *n. to,* sin, por no.

notability [nóutảbíliti], s. notabilidad. **—notable** [nóutảbl], *a.* y s. notable.

notarize [nóutảrajz], *vt.* abonar con fe notarial.

notary (public) [nóutari (páblik)], s. notario (público). **—notation** [notéjšǫn], s. notación; anotación.

notch [nach], s. muesca, corte; ranura; mella.—*vt.* hacer muescas en, mellar.

note [nout], s. nota; marca, señal; anotación, apunte; comunicación, nota diplomática; esquela; aviso, conocimiento; distinción, importancia; (mus.) nota; (com.) billete; letra; vale, pagaré.—*n. paper,* papel de cartas.—*vt.* marcar, distinguir; observar, advertir; apuntar, anotar, asentar, registrar.- **—book** [nóutbuk], s. libreta, cuaderno.- **—d** [nóutjd], *a.* notable, afamado, insigne.- **—worthy** [-wœerðj], *a.* notable, digno de atención.

nothing [náθjŋ], s. nada; cero; nadería, friolera.—*for n.,* gratis; inútilmente, sin provecho.—*good for n.,* inservible; despreciable.—*n. but,* sólo, no más que.—*n. else,* ninguna otra cosa; nada más.—*n. less than,* lo mismo que, no menos que.—*n. much,* no mucho, poca cosa.—*(there is) n. to* o *in it,* eso no vale nada, no asciende a nada.—*sweet nothings,* ternezas.—*that is n. to me,* eso nada me importa.—*there is n. else to do* o *n. for it but,* no hay más remedio (que).—*adv.* de ningún modo, en nada.

notice [nóutjs], s. nota, observación; atención; aviso, anuncio, noticia, informe, notificación; mención; artículo, suelto; llamada; consideración, cortesía.—*at the shortest n.,* al momento, tan pronto como sea posible.—*on short n.,* con poco plazo o tiempo, con poco tiempo de aviso.—*to take n.,* prestar atención; hacer caso; notar, observar.—*until further n.,* hasta más aviso.—*vt.* notar, reparar en, caer en la cuenta de; atender a, cuidar de; hacer mención de.- **—able** [-abl], *a.* digno de atención, notable; perceptible. **—notifi-**

cation [nouṭifikéjṣọn], s. notificación; cita. **—notify** [nóuṭifaj], vti. [7] notificar, avisar; prevenir; requerir; citar.

notion [nóuṣọn], s. noción; idea; parecer, opinión; preocupación; intención, inclinación.—pl. mercería, novedades, baratijas.—*notions counter,* sección de mercería.

notoriety [noutọráịeti], s. notoriedad, mala reputación. **—notorious** [notórịʌs], a. de mala fama, mal reputado; bien conocido.

notwithstanding [natwiǒstǽndiŋ], adv. no obstante, sin embargo.—prep. a pesar de, a despecho de.—conj. aun cuando, aunque, bien que; por más que.—n. that, aunque.

nought [nɔt], s. nada; cero; la cifra O.

noun [naụn], s. (gram.) nombre, sustantivo.

nourish [nóẹrịṣ], vt. nutrir, alimentar; alentar, fomentar.- **—ment** [-mẹnt], s. alimento, nutrimento.

novel [nável], a. novel, nuevo; insólito, extraño, original.—s. novela.- **—ist** [-ịst], s. novelista.- **—ty** [-ti], s. novedad; innovación.—pl. novedades, artículos de fantasía.

November [novémbœ(r)], s. noviembre.

novice [návịs], s. novicio, novato, aprendiz. **—novitiate** [novíṣịejt], s. (igl.) noviciado.

now [naụ], adv. ahora; ya; hoy día, actualmente; al instante; después de esto; ahora bien, esto supuesto.—from n. on, de aquí en adelante.—just n., ahora mismo, poco ha.—n. and again o then, de vez en cuando.—n. rich, n. poor, ya rico, ya pobre; tan pronto rico como pobre; ora rico, ora pobre.—n. then, y bien, ahora bien, bien, pues bien.—conj. (con that) ya que, ahora que, puesto que.—s. actualidad, momento presente.- **—adays** [náụadejz], adv. hoy (en) día.

nowhere [nóụhwer], adv. en ninguna parte.—n. else, en ninguna otra parte.—n. near, ni con mucho.—**nowise** [nóụwajz], adv. de ningún modo, de ninguna manera, de modo alguno.

noxious [nákṣʌs], a. nocivo.

nozzle [názl], s. (on hose) boquillo, lanza; (on rocket, jet engine) tobera; (jer.) nariz.

nth [ɛnθ], a. n^{mo} (enésimo).—to the nth degree, elevado a la potencia n; a má... no poder.

nuance [nyúạns], s. matiz.

nub [nʌb], s. protuberancia; pedazo.

nuclear [njúklẹar], a. nuclear.—n. fal... out, lluvia nuclear.—n. physics física nuclear.—n.-powered, nuclea... —n. reactor, reactor nuclear.—n. tes... ban, proscripción de las pruebas nu cleares.—n. umbrella, sombrilla nu clear.

nucleus [njúklịʌs], s. núcleo.

nude [njud], a. desnudo.—s. (b.a.) des nudo, figura humana desnuda.—i... the n., desnudo.

nudge [nʌdž], vt. dar un codazo suav... a, empujar suavemente.—s. codaz suave.

nudism [njúdịzm], s. nudismo, desn... dismo (culto o práctica). **—nudis** [njúdịst], s. y a. desnudista. **—nudit** [njúdịti], s. desnudez.

nugget [nágit], s. (min.) pepita.

nuisance [njúsʌns], s. molestia, e... torbo; persona o cosa fastidiosas.

null [nʌl], a. nulo, sin fuerza legal.— and void, nulo, irrito, nulo y sin va... lor.- **—ification** [-ịfịkéjṣọn], s. an... lación, invalidación. **—nullify** [nál... faj], vti. [7] anular, invalidar.

numb [nʌm], a. entumecido.—vt. e... tumecer.

number [námbœ(r)], vt. numerar; a cendera.—s. número.- **—less** [-lịs a. innumerable.

numbness [námnịs], s. entumec... miento, adormecimiento.

numeral [njúmẹral], a. numeral.— número. **—numeric(al)** [njúmér k(al)], a. numérico. **—numero** [njúmẹrʌs], a. numeroso.

numskull [námskʌl], s. (fam.) bod... que, mentecato.

nun [nʌn], s. monja.

nunnery [náncẹri], s. convento.

nuptial [nápṣal], a. nupcial.—n. sor... epitalamio.—pl. nupcias, bodas.

nurse [nœrs], s. enfermera, enfe... mero.—wet n., ama de cría, n... driza.—vt. criar, amamantar; cuid... o asistir enfermos; cultivar (u... planta).- **—maid** [nœrsmejd], s. ... ñera, (Am.) manejadora.- **—r** [nœrsœri], s. cuarto de los niñ... institución o lugar para párvulos lactantes; semillero; vivero (plantas).—n. school, escuela de p... vulos (previa al kindergarten).— tales, cuentos para niño... **—rymaid** [nœrscẹrịmejd], s. = N...

SEMAID. **—nursing** [nŕrsiŋ], s. crianza, lactancia; asistencia, profesión de enfermera.—n. bottle, biberón.—n. home, clínica de reposo.

urture [nŕrchŭ(r)], s. alimentación, nutrimento; educación, crianza.— vt. nutrir, alimentar; criar, educar.

ut [nʌt], s. nuez; tuerca; cejilla de violín o guitarra; (jer.) estrafalario.—a hard n. to crack, (fam.) hueso duro de roer. **—meg** [nʌ́tmeg], s. nuez moscada.

utrient [njútrient], a. nutritivo. **—nu-**

triment [njútriment], s. alimento. **—nutrition** [njutríʃon], s. nutrición. **—nutritious** [njutríʃʌs], **nutritive** [njútritiv], a. nutricio, nutritivo.

nutshell [nʌ́tʃel], s. cáscara de nuez.— in a n., en pocas palabras.

nutty [nʌ́ti], a. abundante en nueces; con sabor a nueces; (jer.) loco, chiflado.—n. about, (jer.) loco por.

nuzzle [nʌ́zĕl], vt. y vi. hocicar.

nylon [náilon], s. nilón.—pl. medias de nilón.

nymph [nimf], s. ninfa.

O

ak [ouk], s. roble, encina.—o. grove, encinar, robledo.

ar [ɔr], s. remo.—vt. y vi. remar, bogar.— **—sman** [órzman], s. remero.

asis [oéisis], s. oasis.

at(s) [out(s)], s. avena.

ath [ouθ], s. juramento; blasfemia, terno.—on o upon o., bajo juramento.—to take o make an o., jurar, prestar juramento.

atmeal [óutmil], s. harina de avena; gachas de avena.

bedience [obídiens], s. obediencia. **—obedient** [obídient], a. obediente.

beisance [obéisans], s. cortesía, reverencia; homenaje; deferencia.

belisk [ábelisk], s. obelisco; (impr.) cruz.

bese [obís], a. obeso, gordo. **—obesity** [obísiti], s. obesidad, gordura.

bey [obéi], vt. obedecer.—vi. ser obediente.

bituary [obíchueri], a. y s. obituario, necrología.

bject [ábdžekt], s. objeto; (gram.) complemento.—o. ball, mingo (en el billar).—vt. [obdžékt], objetar.— vi. poner objeciones. **—ion** [obdžékšon], s. objeción, reparo.— **—ive** [obdžéktiv], a. objetivo.—o. case, (gram.) caso complementario.—s. (ópt., mil.) objetivo; objeto, propósito.

bligate [ábligeit], vt. obligar. **—obligation** [abligéišon], s. obligación. **—obligatory** [oblígatori], a. obligatorio. **—oblige** [obláidž], vt. obligar; complacer.—much obliged, muchas gracias. **—obliging** [obláidžiŋ], a.

servicial, complaciente, condescendiente, cortés.

oblique [oblík], a. oblicuo.

obliterate [oblíterejt], vt. borrar, tachar; destruir, arrasar.

oblivion [oblívion], s. olvido. **—oblivious** [oblívias], a. olvidadizo.

obnoxious [obnákšʌs], a. ofensivo, detestable.

obscene [obsín], a. obsceno. **—obscenity** [obséniti], s. obscenidad.

obscure [obskiúr], a. oscuro.—vt. oscurecer; ocultar. **—obscurity** [obskiúriti], s. oscuridad.

obsequies [ábsikwiz], s. pl. exequias.

obsequious [obsíkwias], a. obsequioso, zalamero, servil, rastrero.

observance [obzœ́rvans], s. observancia, cumplimiento; rito o ceremonia. **—observant** [obzœ́rvant], a. observador; observante. **—observation** [abzœrvéišon], s. observación. **—observatory** [obzœ́rvatori], s. observatorio. **—observe** [obzœ́rv], vt. observar; guardar (una fiesta). **—observer** [obzœ́rvœ(r)], s. observador.

obsess [absés], vt. obsesionar.— **—ion** [abséson], s. obsesión.

obsolete [ábsolit], a. desusado, caído en desuso.

obstacle [ábstakl], s. obstáculo.

obstetrician [abstetríšon], s. tocólogo, obstetra. **—obstetrics** [obstétriks], s. obstetricia, tocología.

obstinacy [ábstinäsi], s. obstinación. **—obstinate** [ábstinit], a. obstinado.

obstruct [obstrʌ́kt], vt. obstruir. **—obstruction** [obstrʌ́kšon], s. obstrucción.

obtain [ǫbtéin], vt. obtener.—vi. prevalecer, existir.

obtuse [ǫbtiús], a. obtuso.

obviate [ábviẹit], vt. obviar. **—obvious** [ábviʌs], a. obvio.

occasion [ǫkéiʒǫn], s. ocasión.—as o. requires, en caso necesario, cuando llegue la ocasión.—on o., en su oportunidad o a su debido tiempo.—on the o. of, con motivo de.—to give o., dar pie.—vt. ocasionar, causar, acarrear.- **—al** [-ạl], a. ocasional, casual; alguno que otro; poco frecuente.- **—ally** [-ạli], adv. a veces, de vez en cuando, ocasionalmente.

occident [áksịdẹnt], s. occidente.- **—al** [aksịdéntạl], a. occidental.

occlusion [ǫklúʒǫn], s. obstrucción; (med.) oclusión.

occult [ǫkált], a. oculto.

occupancy [ákyūpansị], s. ocupación. **—occupant** [ákyūpạnt], s. ocupante; inquilino. **—occupation** [akyūpéiʃǫn], s. ocupación. **—occupy** [ákyūpai], vti. [7] ocupar; habitar.

occur [ǫkǿr], vii. [1] ocurrir; suceder, acontecer, acaecer; ocurrir.—to o. to someone, ocurrírse.- **—rence** [-ẹns], s. ocurrencia; suceso, caso, acontecimiento.

ocean [óuʃạn], s. océano.—o. liner, transatlántico, buque transoceánico. **—oceanic** [ouʃịǽnịk], a. oceánico.

o'clock [ǫklák], contr. de OF THE CLOCK. por el reloj.—it is one o., es la una.—it is eight o., son las ocho.

octave [áktịv], s. (mús.) octava.

October [aktóuḅoǝ(r)], s. octubre.

octopus [áktǫpʌs], s. (zool.) pulpo.

ocular [ákyūlạ̄(r)], a. y s. ocular. **—oculist** [ákyūlịst], s. oculista, oftalmólogo.

odd [ad], a. suelto; (odd number) impar, non; (that doesn't match) dispar; casual, accidental; extraordinario, singular, raro; extraño.—o. jobs, pequeñas tareas.—o. lot, lote inferior al centenar.—twenty o., veinte y tantos, veinte y pico.- **—ity** [ádịtị], s. singularidad, rareza.- **—s** [adz], s. pl. desigualdad, diferencia, disparidad; partido o apuesta desigual; ventaja, exceso; disputa.—by all o., con mucho; sin duda.—o. and ends, retazos.—the o. are that, las probabilidades son, es lo más probable

que.—to be at o., estar de punta, estar encontrados.

ode [oud], s. oda.

odious [óudiʌs], a. odioso, abominable.

odor [óudǫ(r)], s. olor.—bad o., mal olor.- **—ous** [-ʌs], a. oloroso.

odyssey [ádisị], s. odisea.

o'er [ouɾ], contr. de OVER.

of [av], prep. de; a; en.—it tastes o. wine, sabe a vino.—o. course, por supuesto, desde luego.—o. late, últimamente.—o. mine, mío, mía.—to dream o., soñar con.—to think o. pensar en.

off [ɔf], adv. lejos, a distancia, fuera; de menos.—day o., día libre.—far o. lejos (de).—hands o., no tocar.—o and on, de vez en cuando, algunas veces; a intervalos.—six miles o., seis millas de distancia.—to be badl (o well) o., andar mal (bien) de dinero.—to be o., irse, marcharse, salir.—to be o. key, desafinar, estar desafinando.—to put o., diferir aplazar.—to see someone o., despedir a alguien.—to turn o. the water (th light, the gas), cortar el agua (la luz, e gas).—two dollars o., un descuent de dos dólares.- **—beat** [-bit], (jer.) insólito, chocante, original. **—chance** [-chæns], s. posibilidac poco probable.- **—color** [-kalǫr], descolorido; indispuesto; (inde cent) colorado, subido de color.- prep. lejos de; fuera de; de; desde frente a, cerca de.—o. the track (fam.) despistado, por los cerros d Úbeda.

offend [ofénd], vt. y vi. ofender. **—** [-ǿ(r)], s. delincuente, ofensor, ir fractor. **—offense** [oféns], ofensa.—no o., sin ofender a uste no lo dijo por tanto.—to take o. a ofenderse de. **—offensive** [ofénsiv a. ofensivo.—s. ofensiva.

offer [ófǿ(r)], vt. ofrecer; (resistance oponer; (igl.) rezar.—vi. ofrecers presentarse.—s. oferta, ofrec miento; declaración de amor; pr puesta.- **—ing** [-iŋ], s. ofrec miento, oferta; ofrenda.

offhand [ófhǽnd], a. y adv. improv sado, de repente; sin pensarlo, c improviso.

office [ófis], s. oficio; ministerio cargo; oficina, despacho; neg ciado, departamento.—pl. servici favor; buenos oficios.—doctor's consultorio médico.—*lawyer's o.*, bufete.—*o. boy*, mandadero, mensajero (de oficina).—*o. hours*, horas de oficina; (med.) horas de consultorio.—*o. seeker*, aspirante, pretendiente.—*o. supplies*, suministros para oficinas.- **—holder** [-houldœ(r)], *s.* empleado público, funcionario, burócrata.- **—r** [ɔ́fisœ(r)], *s.* oficial; funcionario; guardia, agente de policía.—*vt.* mandar (como oficial o jefe); proveer de oficiales y jefes. **—official** [ɔfíʃəl], *a.* oficial.—*s.* oficial público; funcionario autorizado o ejecutivo. **—officiate** [ɔfíʃieit], *vi.* oficiar, celebrar (la misa); ejercer o desempeñar un cargo. **—officious** [ɔfíʃʌs], *a.* oficioso, entremetido, intruso.

ff-peak load, *s.* (elec.) carga de las horas de valle.

ffprint [ɔ́fprint], *s.* sobretiro, separata.

ff season, *s.* temporada baja.—*o. rates,* tarifas de temporada baja, tarifas de fuera de temporada.

ffset [ɔ́fset], *s.* balance, compensación, equivalencia.—*a.* fuera de su lugar; desalineado; (impr.) offset. láminas de caucho.—*vti.* [9] [ɔfsét], compensar; imprimir por offset.

ffshoot [ɔ́fʃut], *s.* descendiente; (branch) ramal; consecuencia; (bot.) retoño, renuevo.

ffshore [ɔ́fʃɔr], *a.* costero; (fishing) de bajura; (wind) terral.—*adv.* a lo largo.

ffspring [ɔ́fspriŋ], *s.* hijo(s), vástago(s), prole, progenie o descendencia.

ffstage [ɔ́fsteidʒ], *a.* de entre bastidores.

ff-street parking, *s.* estacionamiento fuera de la vía pública.

ff-the-record, *a.* extraoficial, confidencial.

ff-the-wall, *a.* (fam.) estrambótico.

ff-white, *a.* y *s.* color hueso.

ften [ɔ́fn], *adv.* frecuentemente, a menudo, muchas veces.—*as o. as,* siempre que, tantas veces (o tan a menudo) como.—*how o.?* ¿cuántas veces? ¿con qué frecuencia?—*not o.,* rara vez.—*so o.,* tantas veces.—*too o.,* con demasiada frecuencia.

gle [oúgĕl], *vt.* y *vi.,* ojear; mirar amorosamente.

gre [oúgœr], *s.* ogro.

hm [oum], *s.* ohmio.

il [ɔil], *s.* aceite; petróleo; óleo.—*o.*

can, bidón o lata de aceite.—*o. cup,* (mec.) lubri(fi)cadora, copilla.—*o. painting,* pintura o cuadro al óleo; arte de pintar al óleo.—*o. tanker,* barco petrolero.—*vt.* aceitar, engrasar, lubri(fi)car; (fam.) untar (la mano), sobornar.- **—cloth** [ɔ́ilkloθ], *s.* encerado, hule.- **—y** [-i], *a.* aceitoso, oleoso, oleaginoso; grasiento.

ointment [ɔ́intmənt], *s.* ungüento.

O.K., OK, okay [oúkéi], *a.* (fam.) correcto; conforme; bueno, que sirve.—*adv.* bien.—*it is O.K.,* está bien.—*s.* (Vᵒ.Bᵒ.) visto bueno.—*vt.* aprobar; dar o poner el visto bueno a. *pret.* y *pp.* **O.K.'d;** *ger.* **O.K.'ing.**

okra [oúkrä], *s.* (bot.) (Am.) quimbombó.

old [ould], *a.* viejo, anciano; antiguo; añejo.—*how o. is he?* ¿cuántos años tiene?—*of o.,* de antiguo, de atrás.—*o. age,* vejez, ancianidad.—*o. boy,* (fam.) chico, (Am.) viejo (expresión de amistad).—*o.-fashioned,* chapado a la antigua; anticuado.—*o. fogey,* persona un poco ridícula por sus ideas o costumbres atrasadas.— *O. Glory,* la bandera de los Estados Unidos.—*o. hand,* práctico, veterano.—*o. lady,* anciana; (despec.) madre, esposa.—*o. maid,* solterona.—*o. man,* anciano, viejo; (fam.) padre, marido.—*o.-timer,* antiguo residente, veterano; (fam.) persona chapada a la antigua.—*o. wives' tale,* cuento de viejas.—*o.-world,* del Viejo Mundo.

olive [áliv], *s.* (bot.) olivo, aceituno; aceituna, oliva.—*o. branch,* ramo de olivo; (peace) oliva.—*o.-colored,* aceitunado.—*o. grove,* olivar.—*o. oil,* aceite de oliva.—*a.* aceitunado; verde olivo.

Olympic [olímpik], *a.* olímpico.—*O. games,* Olimpíadas, juegos Olímpicos.- **—s** [olímpiks], *spl.* Olimpíadas.

omelet [ámlit], *s.* tortilla (de huevos).

omen [oúmin], *s.* agüero, augurio. **—ominous** [áminəs], *a.* ominoso.

omission [omíʃən], *s.* omisión.—**omit** [omít], *vti.* [1] omitir.

omnibus [ámnibʌs], *s.* ómnibus; (Mex.) camión, (Arg.) colectivo, (Cuba) guagua.

omnipotent [amnípotənt], *a.* omnipotente.

on [an], *prep.* sobre, encima de; en; a, al; bajo; por; contra.—*o. account* (*of*), a cuenta (de).—*o. an average*, por término medio.—*o. hand*, entre manos.—*o. leaving*, al salir.—*o. my part*, por mi parte.—*o. my responsibility*, bajo mi responsabilidad.—*o. purpose*, a propósito, adrede.—*o. record*, registrado; que consta.—*o. the contrary*, por el contrario.—*o. the road*, de viaje, viajando.—*o. the table*, sobre la mesa.—*to draw o. my bank*, girar contra mi banco.—*a.* y *adv.* puesto; encendido; funcionando; en contacto.—*and so o.*, y así sucesivamente; etcétera.—*o. and off*, a intervalos, de vez en cuando.—*o. and o.*, continuamente, sin cesar.—*to have one's hat o.*, tener el sombrero puesto.—*to turn o. the light (the radio, etc.)*, encender la luz (el radio, etc.).

once [wʌns], *adv.* y *s.* una vez; en otro tiempo.—*at o.*, en seguida, al instante, inmediatamente; a un mismo tiempo, simultáneamente.—*o. and again*, varias veces.—*o. for all*, por última vez, de una vez para siempre.—*o. in a while*, de cuando en cuando.—*o.-over*, (fam.) examen rápido.—*o. upon a time*, había una vez, érase que se era.—*this o.*, (siquiera) esta vez. —*a.* de otro tiempo, pasado, que fue.—*conj.* una vez que, tan pronto como.

one [wʌn], *a.* un, uno, una; solo, único; cierto; igual.—*it is all o. to me*, lo mismo me da; me es lo mismo.—*o. day*, cierto día, un día; algún día, un día de éstos.—*o.-eyed*, tuerto.—*o.-handed*, manco; con una sola mano.—*o.-sided*, parcial, injusto, (for.) leonino; unilateral; de un solo lado; desigual.—*o.-track mind*, una sola idea en la cabeza.—*o. way*, de una sola dirección; (f.c., avión, etc.) billete o boleto de ida o sencillo.—*s.* y *pron.* uno.—*a better o.*, uno mejor.—*all o.*, lo mismo.— *o. and all*, todos, todos sin excepción.—*o. and the same*, idéntico.— *o. another*, uno(s) a otros.—*o. by o.*, uno a uno, uno por uno.—*o. (for) each*, sendos, uno para cada uno.— *o. or two*, unos pocos.—*o.'s*, de uno, su.—*that o.*, ése; aquél.—*the white o.*, el blanco.—*this o.*, éste.

onerous [ánɛrʌs], *a.* oneroso.

oneself [wʌnsélf], *pron.* se, sí, sí mismo, (a) uno mismo.—*by o.*, solo, por sí solo.—*with o.*, consigo.

ongoing [áŋgouiŋ], *a.* en curso, actual progresivo, en marcha.

onion [ányon], *s.* cebolla.— —skin [-skịn], *s.* papel cebolla.

onlooker [ánlụkœ(r)], *s.* espectador, observador; (fam.) mirón.

only [óµnli], *a.* único, sólo.—*adv.* (tan) sólo, solamente, únicamente; no más que (o de).—*if o.*, ojalá, si.—*no o . . . but also*, no sólo . . . sino también.—*conj.* sólo que, pero.

onset [ánset], *s.* embestida, arremetida, carga; principio.

onto [ántu], *prep.* a; encima de, sobre en.

onward [ánwặrd], *a.* avanzado; progresivo.— —(s) [-(z)], *adv.* adelante, hacia adelante; en adelante.

ooze [uz], *vt.* y *vi.* escurrir(se); exudar(se), rezumar(se); manar, fluir.— *s.* cieno, limo.

opal [óµpal], *s.* ópalo.

opaque [opéịk], *a.* opaco; obscuro.

open [óµpn], *vt.* abrir; destapar; desplegar; empezar, iniciar; entablar.— *vi.* (a veces con **out**) abrirse, entreabrirse; desplegarse; empezar.—*to o. on* o *upon*, caer, dar o mirar a.—*to o. with*, empezar con.—*a.* abierto; sincero, franco; descubierto; expuesto a un ataque; público, descampado.—*in the o. air*, al aire libre, a la intemperie.—*in the o. field*, campo raso.—*o.-eyed*, alerta, vigilante; con ojos asombrados.—*o.- handed*, maniabierto, liberal.—*o.- hearted*, franco, sincero.—*o. house* coliche.—*o.-minded*, razonable, liberal.—*o.-mouthed*, boquiabierto —*o. port*, puerto franco.—*o. question*, cuestión discutible; asunto en duda.—*o. sea*, alta mar.—*o. season*, temporada de caza, pesca.—*o. secret*, secreto a voces.—*o. shop*, taller franco.—*o. winter*, invierno templado.—*wide o.*, de par en par.—? claro, raso, lugar abierto.—*can opener*, abrelatas.—*in the o.*, a campo raso; al aire libre, a la intemperie; a descubierto, abiertamente.— —ing [-iŋ], *s.* abertura, brecha; boca, orificio; salida; claro, campo abierto inauguración, apertura; empleo vacante.—*a.* preliminar, inicial; inaugural.—*o. night*, noche de estreno —*o. number*, primer número.—*o. performance*, (teat.) estreno.—*o. price*, primer curso, precio de apertura.

opera [ápɛrặ], *s.* ópera.—*o. glasses*, ge

melos de teatro.—*o. hat,* clac, sombrero de muelles.—*o. house,* teatro de la ópera.

operable [áperabl], *a.* operable. **—operate** [ápereit], *vt.* operar, hacer funcionar, mover; (min.) explotar; manejar.—*vi.* (con **in, on** o **upon**) obrar, operar; producir efecto; funcionar; (cir.) operar; (com.) operar, especular; (mil.) operar, maniobrar.—*operated by,* (mec.) accionado por. **—operating** [ápereitin], *a.* operante, actuante; operatorio.—*o. room,* quirófano.—*o. table,* mesa operatoria. **—operation** [apéréison], *s.* operación; funcionamiento; manejo, manipulación. **—operator** [ápereitor(r)], *s.* operario; maquinista; telegrafista; telefonista; ascensorista; cirujano; empresario de minas; (fam.) manipulador.

operatic [aperátik], *a.* operístico.

operetta [aperétá s], *s.* opereta, zarzuela.

opiate [óupiit], *s.* narcótico, opiato. **—opium** [óupiam], *s.* opio.—*o. den,* fumadero de opio.

opinion [opínyon], *s.* opinión.—*in my o.,* a mi parecer. **—ated** [-eitid], *a.* terco, porfiado, obstinado.

opossum [opásam], *s.* zarigüeya, oposúm.

opponent [opóunent], *s.* contrario.

opportune [aportiún], *a.* oportuno, a propósito, conveniente. **—opportunity** [aportiúniti], *s.* oportunidad; ocasión.

oppose [opóuz], *vt.* oponerse a. **—opposite** [ápozit], *a.* opuesto, contrario; de enfrente, al otro lado.—*prep.* enfrente de.—*s.* contrario.—*the o.,* lo opuesto, lo contrario. **—opposition** [apozíson], *s.* oposición.

oppress [oprés], *vt.* oprimir. **—ion** [oprésòn], *s.* opresión. **—ive** [oprésiv], *a.* opresivo; sofocante. **—or** [opréso(r)], *s.* opresor, tirano.

opt [opt], *vi.* optar.—*to o. for or to,* optar por.

optic(al) [áptik(al)], *a.* óptico. **—optician** [aptísan], *s.* óptico. **—optics** [áptiks], *s.* óptica.

optimism [áptimizm], *s.* optimismo. **—optimist** [áptimist], *s.,* **—optimistic** [aptimístik], *a.* optimista.

option [ápsòn], *s.* opción. **—al** [-al], *a.* facultativo, potestativo.

opulence [ápyulens], *s.* opulencia. **—opulent** [ápyulent], *a.* opulento.

or [or], *conj.* o, u; si no, de lo contrario.—*o. else,* o bien.

oracle [árakl], *s.* oráculo.

oral [óral], *a.* oral; verbal, hablado; bucal.—*s.* examen oral.

orange [áràndž], *s.* naranja; color naranja, anaranjado.—*o. blossom,* azahar.—*o. grove,* naranjal.—*o. juice,* zumo de naranja.—*o. pekoe,* té negro de Ceilán.—*o. tree,* naranjo.—*a.* perteneciente a las naranjas; anaranjado. **—ade** [-éjd], *s.* naranjada.

orang-utan [oráŋutæn], *s.* orangután.

oration [oréison], *s.* oración, discurso. **—orator** [árator(r)], *s.* orador. **—oratory** [áratori], *s.* oratoria, elocuencia; oratorio, capilla.

orb [orb], *s.* orbe.

orbit [órbit], *s.* órbita.

orchard [órchard], *s.* huerto, vergel.

orchestra [órkistra], *s.* orquesta; (teat.) patio de butacas, (Am.) platea.—*o. seat,* luneta, butaca de platea.

orchid [órkid], *s.* orquídea.

ordain [ordéin], *vt.* decretar; (igl.) ordenar.

ordeal [ordíl], *s.* prueba muy difícil.

order [órdoe(r)], *s.* orden; (com.) orden, pedido.—*pl.* órdenes sagradas o sacerdotales; sacramento.—*in (good) o.,* en regla, en orden, en buen estado.—*in o. to* o *that,* para, a fin de que, para que, porque, con (el) objeto de.—*in working o.,* en buen estado.—*money o.,* giro postal.—*on the o. of,* de la clase de.—*o. blank,* hoja de pedidos.—*o. of knighthood,* orden de caballería.—*out of o.,* descompuesto; que no funciona; desordenado, desarreglado.—*to give* o *place an o.,* hacer un pedido.—*to o.,* a propósito, especialmente;(com.) a la orden, por encargo especial, según se pida, a la medida.—*vi.* dar órdenes.—*vt.* ordenar, mandar; poner en orden; mandar hacer; encargar, pedir (mercancías, un coche, el almuerzo, etc.).—*to o. away,* despedir a uno, decirle que se vaya.—*to o. in,* mandar entrar; mandar traer.—*to o. out,* mandar salir; mandar llevar; echar. **—ly** [-li], *a.* ordenado, metódico; bien arreglado; obediente, disciplinado; tranquilo.—*s.* ordenanza, asistente.—*adv.* ordenadamente, metódicamente, en orden. **—ordinal** [órdinal], *a.* ordinal.—*s.* numeral ordinal; (igl.) libro ritual. **—ordinance** [órdinans], *s.* ordenanza, ley, reglamento; rito, ceremonial; ordenación, disposición.

ordinary [ɔ́rdjneɹj], *a.* ordinario.

ordnance [ɔ́rdnəns], *s.* (mil.) artillería, cañones; trechos de guerra.

ore [ouɹ], *s.* mena, mineral metalífero.

organ [ɔ́rgən], *s.* órgano.—*barrel o.*, organillo.—*o.-grinder*, organillero.— **—ic(al)** [ɔrgǽnjk(əl)], *a.* orgánico; organizado; sistematizado; constitutivo o fundamental.- **—ism** [-jzm], *s.* organismo.- **—ist** [-jst], *s.* (mus.) organista.- **—ization** [-jzéjʃən], *s.* organización; estructura orgánica; constitución; organismo; cuerpo, entidad, compañía, corporación.- **—ize** [-ajz], *vt.* organizar.— *vi.* organizarse, constituirse.- **—izer** [-ajzœ(r)], *s.,* **—izing** [-ajzjŋ], *a.* organizador.

organdy [ɔ́rgəndj], *s.* organdí.

orgasm [ɔ́rgæzm], *s.* orgasmo.

orgy [ɔ́rdʒj], *s.* orgía.

orient [óuɹjent], *s.* oriente, este, levante.—*the O.,* el Oriente.— *vt.* orientar.- **—al** [orjéntal], *a.* y *s.* oriental.- **—ate** [óuɹjentejt], *vt.* orientar.- **—ation** [orjentéjʃən], *s.* orientación.

orifice [áɹjfjs], *s.* orificio, abertura.

origin [ɔ́rjdʒjn], *s.* origen.- **—al** [orjdʒi-nal], *a.* original; primitivo, primero, originario.—*s.* original; prototipo.— **—ality** [orjdʒjnǽljtj], *s.* originalidad.- **—ally** [orjdʒjnəlj], *adv.* originariamente, en el principio; originalmente.- **—ate** [orjdʒjnejt], *vt.* originar.—*vi.* originarse, dimanar.- **—ator** [orjdʒjnejtœ(r)], *s.* originador, iniciador.

oriole [óuɹjoul], *s.* oropéndola.

ornament [ɔ́rnəment], *s.* ornamento, adorno.—*vt.* [ɔ́rnəment], ornamentar, adornar.- **—al** [ɔrnəm'ntal], *a.* ornamental, decorativo.—*s.* cosa, planta, etc. de adorno.— **ornate** [ɔrnéjt], *a.* muy ornado; florido.

ornithology [ɔrnjθálodʒj], *s.* ornitología.

orphan [ɔ́rfən], *a.* y *s.* huérfano.—*vt.* dejar huérfano a.- **—age** [-jdʒ], *s.* orfandad; orfanato.

orthodox [ɔ́rθodaks], *a.* ortodoxo; convencional.- **—y** [-j], *s.* ortodoxia.

orthographic(al) [ɔrθográfjk(əl)], *a.* ortográfico.- **—orthography** [ɔrθágrafj], *s.* ortografía.

oscillate [ásjlejt], *vt.* oscilar.—**oscillation** [asjléjʃən], *s.* oscilación.

osmosis [asmóusjs], *s.* ósmosis.

ostensible [asténsjbl], *a.* aparente; pretendido.—**ostentation** [astentéjʃən], *s.* ostentación, jactancia, alarde.—**ostentatious** [astentéjʃʌs], *a.* ostentoso, fastuoso; jactancioso.

ostracism [ástrasjzm], *s.* ostracismo.—**ostracize** [ástrasajz], *vt.* aislar; desterrar, condenar al ostracismo.

ostrich [ástrjtʃ], *s.* avestruz; (Am.) ñandú, suri.

other [ʌ́ðœ(r)], *a.* y *pron.* otro, otra (otros, otras).—*each o.,* uno a otro, el uno al otro, unos a otros.—*every o. day,* en días alternos, un día sí y otro no.—*o. than,* otra cosa que; más que.—*some o. day,* cualquier otro día.- **—wise** [-wajz], *adv.* de otra manera, de otro modo; de lo contrario, si no; o bien.—*a.* otro, diferente.

otter [átœ(r)], *s.* nutria; piel de nutria.

ouch [ach], *interj.* ¡ax!

ought [ɔt], *vai.* [11] deber; convenir.— *it o. to be so,* así debería (o debiera) ser.—*you o. not to go,* usted no debe (debiera, debería) ir.—*you o. to know,* usted debería saberlo.—*pret.* de OUGHT.

ought [ɔt], *s.* y *adv.* algo, alguna cosa; nada; cero.—*for o. I know,* por lo que yo puedo comprender, en cuanto yo sé.

ounce [auns], *s.* onza. Ver Tabla.

our(s) [auɹ(z)], *a.* y *pron. pos.* (el, los) nuestro(s), (la, las) nuestra(s).—*a friend of ours,* un amigo nuestro.— **ourselves** [auɹsélvz], *pron.* nosotros mismos, nosotras mismas; a nosotros mismos; nos (reflexivo).

oust [aust], *vt.* desposeer, desanuciar, desalojar; echar fuera, despedir.

out [aut], *adv.* fuera, afuera; hacia fuera.—*prep.* fuera de; más allá de.—*a.* exterior; ausente; fuera de moda; errado (cálculos, etc.); cesante; (declarado) en huelga.—*a way o.,* escapatoria.—*four o. of five,* de cada cinco, cuatro.—*o. and away,* con mucho.—*o. and o.,* cabal, completo; declarado; redomado.—*o. at interest,* puesto a interés.—*o. at the elbows,* andrajoso, roto por los codos.—*o. loud,* en voz alta.—*o. of fear,* por miedo.—*o. of money,* sin dinero.—*o. of print,* agotado (libros).—*time is o.,* el tiempo (la hora) ha pasado; el plazo ha expirado.—

to be o., estar fuera o ausente; no estar en boga; quedar cesante; quedarse cortado; salir perdiendo; estar apagado o extinguido; haberse agotado o acabado; haberse publicado, haber salido (libro, periódico, etc.); estar reñidos.—*to be o. of,* no tener más, habérsele acabado a uno.—*to run o. of,* acabársele a uno, quedarse sin.—*interj.* ¡fuera!—*o. with it!* ¡fuera con ello! hable sin rodeos.—*s.* exterior, parte de afuera; esquina, lugar exterior; exterioridad; cesante; dimisionario (fam.) pero, defecto; (impr.) olvido, omisión.—*pl.* (pol.) la oposición.

outbalance [au̯tbǽlans], *vt.* sobrepujar, exceder.

outbid [au̯tbíd], *vti.* [10] mejorar, pujar, ofrecer más dinero (en subasta, etc.).—*pret.* y *pp.* de TO OUTBID. —**outbidden** [au̯tbídn], *pp.* de TO OUTBID.

outboard motor [au̯tbɔrd], *s.* motor fuera de borda.

outbreak [áu̯tbrei̯k], *s.* erupción, brote; ataque violento; pasión; tumulto, disturbio; principio (de una guerra, epidemia, etc.).

outburst [áu̯tbœrst], *s.* explosión, erupción, estallido; acceso; arranque.

outcast [áu̯tkæst], *a.* desechado, inútil; proscripto; perdido.—*s.* paria.

outcome [áu̯tkʌm], *s.* resultado.

outcry [áu̯tkrai̯], *s.* clamor(eo); grita; alboroto, gritería; protesta.

outdated [au̯tdéi̯těd], *a.* fuera de moda, anticuado.

outdid [au̯tdíd], *pret.* de TO OUTDO.

outdistance [au̯tdístans], *vt.* dejar atrás, adelantarse a.

outdo [au̯tdú], *vti.* [10] exceder, sobrepujar, descollar, eclipsar, vencer.— *to o. oneself,* superarse, encontrarse a sí mismo.—**outdone** [au̯tdʌ́n], *pp.* de TO OUTDO.

outdoor [áu̯tdɔr], *a.* externo, fuera de la casa, al aire libre.– —**s** [-z], *s.* campo raso, aire libre.—*adv.* fuera de casa, a la intemperie.

outer [áu̯tœ(r)], *a.* exterior, externo.— *o. space,* espacio exterior.—**most** [-mou̯st], *a.* extremo; [lo] más exterior.

outfit [áu̯tfit], *s.* equipo, apresto, tren; ropa, vestido, traje; habilitación; pertrechos; avíos.—*vti.* [1] equipar, habilitar, pertrechar.

outgoing [áu̯tgou̯iŋ], *s.* ida, salida, partida.—*a.* saliente, que cesa; que sale, de salida; extrovertido.

outgrew [au̯tgrú], *pret.* de TO OUTGROW.—**outgrow** [au̯tgróu̯], *vti.* [10] crecer más que; pasar la edad de, ser ya viejo para, ser demasiado grande para; curarse de con la edad o con el tiempo.—**outgrown** [au̯tgróu̯n], *pp.* de TO OUTGROW.—*he has o. his crib,* la cuna ya le queda pequeña.—**outgrowth** [áu̯tgrou̯θ], *s.* excrecencia; resultado, consecuencia.

outhouse [áu̯thau̯s], *s.* accesoria; retrete situado fuera de la casa.

outing [áu̯tiŋ], *s.* salida; paseo, caminata, excursión, jira.

outlaid [au̯tléi̯d], *pret.* y *pp.* de TO OUTLAY.

outlandish [au̯tlǽndiš], *a.* estrafalario, extraño, ridículo; de aspecto extranjero o exótico; remoto.

outlast [au̯tlǽst], *vt.* durar más que; sobrevivir a.

outlaw [áu̯tlɔ], *s.* forajido, facineroso; proscrito; fuera de la ley; rebelde.— *vt.* proscribir; declarar fuera de la ley.

outlay [áu̯tlei̯], *s.* desembolso.—*vti.* [10] [áu̯tléi̯], desembolsar.

outlet [áu̯tlet], *s.* salida; orificio de salida; escape; desagüe; sangrador; toma (de agua, corriente eléctrica); (com.) punto de venta; punto de venta a precios reducidos.

outline [áu̯tlai̯n], *s.* contorno, perfil; croquis, esbozo, bosquejo, plan general, reseña.—*vt.* bosquejar, delinear, esbozar, reseñar, trazar.

outlive [au̯tlív], *vt.* sobrevivir a, durar más que.

outlook [áu̯tluk], *s.* vista, perspectiva, aspecto; punto de vista; probabilidades.

outlying [áu̯tlai̯iŋ], *a.* distante, remoto; lejos del centro; extrínseco; exterior.

outmoded [au̯tmóu̯děd], *a.* fuera de moda.

outnumber [au̯tnʌ́mbœ(r)], *vt.* exceder en número, ser más que.

out-of-date, *a.* fuera de moda, anticuado.

out-of-door, *a.* al aire libre.

out-of-doors, *s.* aire libre, campo raso.

out-of-print, *a.* agotado.

out-of-the-way, *a.* apartado, remoto; poco usual.

out of tune, *a.* desafinado.—*adv.* desafinadamente.

out of work, *a.* desempleado, sin trabajo

outpatient [áu̯tpei̯ʃe̜nt], *s.* paciente de consulta externa.

outpost [áu̯tpost], *s.* (mil.) avanzada.

outpouring [áu̯tpɔriŋ], *s.* chorro, chorreo, efusión; desahogo.

output [áu̯tput], *s.* producción; rendimiento; (comput., elec.) salida; (mec.) potencia neta o útil.

outrage [áu̯trei̯dʒ], *vt.* ultrajar; maltratar; violar, desflorar.—*s.* ultraje; desafuero; atrocidad; violación, rapto.- **—ous** [au̯tréi̯dʒʌs], *a.* ultrajante, injurioso; atroz; desaforado.

outran [au̯træn], *pret.* de TO OUTRUN.

outrank [au̯trǽŋk], *vt.* exceder en rango o grado.

outrider [áu̯trai̯dœr], *s.* carrerista.

outright [áu̯trai̯t], *a.* completo; directo; sincero, franco.—*adv.* [áu̯tráj̇t], completamente; abiertamente; sin reserva; sin tardanza, al momento.

outrun [au̯trán], *vti.* [10] correr más que; pasar, ganar, exceder.—*pp.* de TO OUTRUN.

outset [áu̯tset], *s.* principio; salida.

outshine [au̯tʃái̯n], *vti.* [10] dejar deslucido, eclipsar.—**outshone** [au̯tʃóu̯n], *pret. y pp.* de TO OUTSHINE.

outside [áu̯tsái̯d], *a.* exterior, externo; superficial; extremo; ajeno, neutral.—*s.* exterior, parte de afuera; superficie; apariencia; extremo.—*at the o.,* (fam.) a lo sumo, a más tirar.—*adv.* afuera, fuera.—*o. of,* (fam.) con excepción de.—*prep.* fuera de; (fam.) excepto.- **—r** [áu̯tsái̯dœr], *s.* forastero, extraño; intruso.

outsize [áu̯tsai̯z], *s.* prenda de vestir de tamaño fuera de lo común.—*a.* de tamaño extraordinario; (fam.) inmenso.

outskirt [áu̯tskœrt], *s.* borde, linde.—*pl.* afueras, suburbios, arrabales, inmediaciones.

outspoken [áu̯tspóu̯kn], *a.* abierto, franco(te).—*to be o.,* (fam.) no tener pelos en la lengua.

outstanding [au̯tstǽndiŋ], *a.* sobresaliente, prominente; (com.) sin pagar, sin cobrar.

outstretch [au̯tstréch], *vt.* extender, alargar, estirar.

outstrip [au̯tstríp], *vti.* [1] pasar, rezagar; aventajar, ganar.

outward [áu̯twǝrd], *a.* exterior, visible; aparente, superficial; extraño; extrínseco; corpóreo.—*adv.* fuera, afuera, exteriormente; superficialmente; (mar.) de ida; para el extranjero.

outweigh [au̯twéi̯], *vt.* pesar más que; contrapesar, compensar.

outwit [au̯twít], *vti.* [1] ser más listo que; burlar; despistar.

outworn [au̯twɔ́rn], *a.* ajado, gastado, usado; anticuado.

oval [óu̯vǝl], *s.* óvalo.—*a.* oval, ovalado.—*the O. Office,* (E.U.) el despacho oval, el despacho del presidente.

ovary [óu̯vǝri], *s.* ovario.

ovation [ovéi̯ʃǝn], *s.* ovación.

oven [ávn], *s.* horno.

overall [óu̯vœrɔl], *a.* global, total, de conjunto.—*s. pl.* traje de mecánico, mono(s); pantalones de trabajo.

over [óu̯vœ(r)], *prep.* sobre, encima, por encima de; allende, al otro lado de; a causa o por motivo de; a pesar de; más de; mientras, durante; por, en.—*o. all,* total, de extremo a extremo.—*o. night,* durante la noche, hasta el otro día.—*adv.* al otro lado; al lado, parte o partido contrario; enfrente; encima; al revés; más, de más, de sobra; otra vez, de nuevo; demasiado, excesivamente; acabado, terminado; a la vuelta, al dorso.—*to be* (all) *o.,* haber pasado; haberse acabado, terminar(se).—*to be left o.,* quedar, sobrar.—*to be o. and above,* sobrar.—*a.* acabado, terminado; demasiado; sobrante, en exceso de superior; exterior.—*it is all o.,* ya pasó; se acabó.

overate [ou̯vœréi̯t], *pret.* de TO OVEREAT.

overbearing [ou̯vœrbériŋ], *a.* imperioso, dominante, arrogante.

overbid [ou̯vœrbíd], *vti.* [10] ofrecer más que, pujar.—*vii.* ofrecer demasiado.—*pret. y pp.* de TO OVERBID.—*s.* [óu̯vœrbid], puja.—**overbidden** [ou̯vœrbídn], *pp.* de TO OVERBID.

overboard [óu̯vœrbɔrd], *adv.* (mar.) al mar, al agua.—*man o.!* ¡hombre al agua!

overburden [ou̯vœrbœ́rden], *vt.* sobrecargar; oprimir.

overcame [ou̯vœrkéi̯m], *pret.* de TO OVERCOME.

overcast [ou̯vœrkǽst], *vti.* [9] anublar, oscurecer; entristecer; cicatrizar; sobrehilar.—*vii.* anublarse.—*pret. y* *pp.* de TO OVERCAST.—*a.* [óuvœr-kæst], nublado, encapotado; sombrío.

overcharge [ouvœrchárdž], *vt.* cobrar demasiado; recargar el precio; sobrecargar.—*s.* [óuvœrchardž], cargo excesivo; cargo adicional; recargo; carga eléctrica excesiva.

overcoat [óuvœrkout], *s.* sobretodo, gabán, abrigo.

overcome [ouvœrkám], *vti.* [10] vencer, rendir; sojuzgar, subyugar; superar, vencer, salvar (obstáculos).—*vii.* sobreponerse; ganar, vencer; hacerse superior.—*pp.* de TO OVERCOME.—*s.* agobiado, confundido.

overconfidence [ouvœrkánfidẹns], *s.* presunción, excesiva confianza.— **overconfident** [ouvœrkánfidẹnt], *a.* demasiado confiado.

overcrowd [ouvœrkráud], *vt.* apiñar, atestar.

overdid [ouvœrdíd], *pret.* de TO OVERDO.—**overdo** [ouvœrdú], *vii.* [10] hacer más de lo necesario; extralimitarse.—*vti.* agobiar, abrumar de trabajo; exagerar; (coc.) recocer, requemar.—**overdone** [ouvœrdán], *a.* demasiado trabajado; (coc.) recocido, requemado, demasiado asado.—*pp.* de TO OVERDO.

overdose [óuvœrdous], *s.* dosis excesiva.

overdraft [óuvœrdræft], *s.* sobregiro, giro en descubierto.—**overdraw** [ouvœrdró], *vti.* [10] sobregirar. exagerar (en el dibujo, la descripción, etc.).—**overdrawn** [ouvœrdrón], *pp.* de TO OVERDRAW.

overdress [ouvœrdrés], *vt.* adornar con exceso.—*vi.* vestirse con exceso.—*s.* [óuvœrdres], sobreprenda.

overdrew [ouvœrdrú], *pret.* de TO OVERDRAW.

overdue [óuvœrdjú], *a.* vencido y no pagado, atrasado.

overeat [ouvœrít], *vii.* [10] comer con exceso.—**overeaten** [ouvœrítn], *pp.* de TO OVEREAT.

overestimate [ouvœréstimeit], *vt.* estimar en valor excesivo.—*s.* [ouvœréstimit], estimación exagerada.

overexcite [ouvœriksáit], *vt.* sobreexcitar.- —**ment** [-mẹnt], *s.* sobreexcitación.

overexposure [ouvœrikspóužu(r)], *s.* (fot.) sobreexposición.

overfed [ouvœrféd], *pret.* y *pp.* de TO OVERFEED.—**overfeed** [ouvœrfíd], *vti.* [10] sobrealimentar.

overflow [ouvœrflóu], *vi.* rebosar, desbordarse.—*vt.* inundar.—*s.* [óuvœrflou], rebosamiento, derrame; caño de reboso.

overfly [ouvěrflái], *vt.* sobrevolar.

overgrown [ouvěgróun], *a.* demasiado grande para su edad; denso, frondoso.

overhang [ouvœrhǽn], *vti.* [10] sobresalir horizontalmente por encima de; colgar, suspender; mirar a, dar a, caer a; ser inminente, amenazar.— *vii.* colgar o estar pendiente.—*s.* [óuvœrhæn], (arq.) alero; vuelo.

overhaul [ouvœrhól], *vt.* repasar, registrar, recorrer; componer, remendar; desarmar y componer; alcanzar.—*s.* [óuvœrhol], recorrido, revisión, reparación; alcance.

overhead [ouvœrhéd], *adv.* arriba, en lo alto; más, o hasta más, arriba de la cabeza.—*a.* [óuvœrhed], de arriba; de término medio; de techo.—*s.* gastos generales.

overhear [ouvœrhír], *vti.* [10] oír por casualidad o espiando.—**overheard** [ouvœrhóerd], *pret.* y *pp.* de TO OVERHEAR.

overheat [ouvœrhít], *vt.* recalentar.— *vi.* recalentarse.

overhung [óuvœrhʌn], *pret.* y *pp.* de TO OVERHANG.—*a.* colgado o suspendido por arriba.

overjoy [ouvœrdžói], *vt.* alborozar, regocijar.- —**ed** [-d], *a.* lleno de alegría.—*to be o.,* no caber de contento.

overlaid [ouvœrléid], *pret.* y *pp.* de TO OVERLAY.

overland [óuvœrlænd], *a.* y *adv.* por tierra, por vía terrestre.

overlap [ouvœrlǽp], *vti.* [1] sobreponer, sobremontar, superponer.—*vii.* superponerse.—*s.* [óuvœrlæp], superposición.

overlay [ouvœrléi], *vti.* [10] cubrir, extender sobre; dar una capa o mano (pintura, etc.); echar un puente sobre.—*s.* [óuvœrlei], capa o mano.

overload [ouvœrlóud], *vt.* sobrecargar.—*s.* [óuvœrloud], sobrecarga.

overlook [ouvœrlúk], *vt.* mirar desde lo alto; tener vista a, dar, dominar (con la vista); examinar; cuidar de; pasar por alto, disimular, tolerar; hacer la vista gorda; no hacer caso de; no notar.

overly [oúvẽrlị], *adv.* (fam.) excesivamente, demasiado.

overnight [ouvœrnájt], *adv.* toda la noche; de la noche a la mañana.—*a.* [óuvœrnajt], de una noche; de la noche anterior.—*o. bag*, saco de noche.

overpass [oúvẽrpæs], *s.* viaducto.

overpower [ouvœrpáuœ(r)], *vt.* sobreponerse a, vencer, superar; sujetar; embargar (los sentidos).— **-ing** [-iŋ], *a.* abrumador, arrollador, irresistible.

overproduction [ouvœrprodákšọn], *s.* superproducción, sobreproducción.

overqualified [ouvĕrkwálịfajd], *a.* con más titulación de la requerida.

overran [ouvœrrǽn], *pret.* de TO OVERRUN.

overrate [ouvœrréjt], *vt.* encarecer; exagerar el valor de.

overreach [ouvœrrích], *vt.* ser más listo que; engañar; alargar demasiado; tirar alto.—*to o. oneself*, excederse, ir más allá de lo necesario.

overreact [ouvĕrrẹ sǽkt], *vi.* reaccionar de forma exagerada.— **-ion** [ouvĕrrẹǽkšọn], *s.* reacción exagerada.

overrule [ouvœrrúl], *vt.* (for.) denegar, no admitir; predominar, dominar; gobernar.

overrun [ouvœrrán], *vti.* [10] invadir, infestar; saquear; excederse; desbordarse.—*vii.* rebosar, estar muy abundante.—*pp.* de TO OVERRUN.

oversaw [ouvœrsɔ́], *pret.* de TO OVERSEE.

oversea(s) [óuvœrsí(z)], *adv.* allende los mares.—*a.* de ultramar, ultramarino; extranjero.

oversee [ouvœrsí], *vti.* [10] inspeccionar, vigilar; descuidar, pasar por alto.—**overseen** [ouvœrsín], *pp.* de TO OVERSEE.— **-r** [óuvœrsiœ(r)], *s.* superintendente, director.

overshadow [ouvĕršǽdou], *vt.* sombrear; (fig.) eclipsar.

overshoe [óuvœršu], *s.* chanclo; zapato de goma.

oversight [óuvœrsajt], *s.* inadvertencia, descuido; vigilancia, cuidado.

oversleep [ouvœrslíp], *vii.* [10] dormir demasiado; no despertarse a tiempo.

overslept [ouvœrslépt], *pret.* y *pp.* de TO OVERSLEEP.

overstate [ouvœrstéjt], *vt.* exagerar.

overstep [ouvœrstép], *vti.* [1] traspasar, excederse.

overstock [ouvœrsták], *vt.* abarrotar.

overt [óuvœrt], *a.* abierto, público; premeditado.—*o. act*, (for.) acción premeditada; acto hostil.

overtake [ouvœrtéjk], *vti.* [10] dar alcance, alcanzar; atajar; (fam.) atrapar.—**overtaken** [ouvœrtéjkn], *pp.* de TO OVERTAKE.

over-the-counter, *a.* vendido directamente al comprador; comprado sin receta.

overthrew [ouvœrθrú], *pret.* de TO OVERTHROW.—**overthrow** [ouvœrθróụ], *vti.* [10] echar abajo, abatir, demoler, derribar; derrocar, destronar; vencer.—*s.* [óuvœrθrou], derribo, derrocamiento; caída; derrota, ruina; subversión; destronamiento; (dep.) lanzamiento o boleo demasiado alto.—**overthrown** [ouvœrθróụn], *pp.* de TO OVERTHROW.

overtime [óuvœrtajm], *s.* horas extraordinarias de trabajo; tiempo suplementario; pago por trabajo hecho fuera de las horas regulares.—*adv.* fuera del tiempo estipulado.—*a.* en exceso de las horas regulares de trabajo.

overtook [ouvœrtúk], *pret.* de TO OVERTAKE.

overture [óuvœrchụr], *s.* insinuación, proposición o propuesta formal; (mús.) obertura.

overturn [ouvœrtœrn], *vt.* volcar; echar abajo; trastornar.—*vi.* volcarsè; (mar.) zozobrar.—*s.* [óuvœrtœrn], vuelco, volteo; trastorno.

overweight [óuvœrwejt], *s.* exceso de peso; sobrepeso.—*a.* [ouvœrwéjt], que pesa demasiado.

overwhelm [ouvœrhwélm], *vt.* abrumar, agobiar, anonadar; sumergir, hundir.— **-ing** [-iŋ], *a.* abrumador, (fam.) aplastante.—*s.* abrumamiento, anonadación.

overwork [ouvœrwœrk], *vti.* [4] hacer trabajar excesivamente, esclavizar.—*vii.* trabajar demasiado.—*s.* [óuvœrwœrk], trabajo excesivo o hecho fuera de las horas reglamentarias.—**overworked** [ouvœrwœrkt], *a.* recargado, muy elaborado; agobiado de trabajo.

ow [au], *interj.* ¡ax!

owe [ou], *vt.* deber, adeudar; (to) ser

deudor de; estar obligado a.—*owing to,* debido a, con motivo de, por causa de.—*to be owing to,* ser debido, imputable o atribuible a.—*vi.* estar endeudado, deber.

owl [aul], *s.* lechuza, buho, mochuelo.

own [oun], *a.* propio, particular, de mi, su, etc. propiedad.—*a house of his o.,* una casa de su propiedad.—*to be on one's o.,* no depender de otro, trabajar por su (propic) cuenta.—*to hold one's o.,* mantenerse firme.—*vt.* poseer, ser dueño de, tener; reconocer, confesar.—*owned by,* propiedad de.—*to o. up,* confesar de plano.—**er** [óunœ(r)], *s.* propietario, amo, dueño.- **ership** [-œrȿip], *s.* propiedad, pertenencia.

ox [aks], *s.* (*pl.* **oxen** [áksn]) buey.—*o. driver,* boyero.

oxidation [aksidéiȿɔn], *s.* oxidación. —**oxygen** [áksidȥɛn], *s.* oxígeno.— *o. tent,* cámara o tienda de oxígeno.

oyster [óistœ(r)], *s.* ostra, (Am.) ostión.—*o. bed,* ostrero.—*o. cocktail,* ostras en su concha.—*o. fork,* desbullador.—*o. knife,* abreostras.—*o. shell,* desbulla.—*o. stew,* sopa de ostras.

ozone [óuȥoun], *s.* ozono; (fam.) aire fresco.—*the o. layer,* la capa de ozono.—*o.-hole,* agujero en la capa de ozono.

P

pa [pa], *s.* (fam.) papá.

pace [peis], *s.* paso; modo de andar.— *vt.* recorrer o medir a pasos; marcar el paso.—*vi.* pasear, andar, marchar. - **maker** [péismeikœ(r)], *s.* (med.) marcapaso.

pacific [pasífik], *a.* pacífico.—**pacifier** [pǽsifaiœ(r)], *s.* pacificador, apaciguador; chupete (para niños).— **pacifist** [pǽsifist], *a.* y *s.* pacifista. - **pacify** [pǽsifai], *vti.* [7] pacificar, apaciguar, calmar.

pack [pæk], *s.* lío, fardo; paquete; cajetilla o paquete de cigarrillos; jauría; manada; cuadrilla (de pícaros).—*p. animal,* acémila, animal de carga.— *p. cloth,* arpillera.—*p. train,* recua, reata.—*vt.* empacar, empaquetar; embalar, envasar; apretar; cargar (una acémila).—*to p. off,* o *to send packing,* enviar, despedir, despachar; poner de patitas en la calle.— *vi.* empaquetar; hacer el baúl, arreglar el equipaje.—*to p. away* u *off,* largarse.- **age** [pǽkidȥ], *s.* fardo, bulto, lío; paquete.—*vt.* empacar, empaquetar.- **er** [-œ(r)], *s.* embalador, empaquetador, empacador, envasador.—*meat p.,* frigorífico.- **et** [-it], *s.* paquete, cajetilla; fardo pequeño.- **ing** [-iŋ], *s.* embalaje; envase; (mec.) empaquetadura, relleno.—*p. box* o *case,* caja de embalaje.—*p. house* o *plant,* frigorífico.— *p. slip,* hoja de embalaje.

packsaddle [pǽksædl], *s.* albarda.

pact [pækt], *s.* pacto, convenio, tratado.

pad [pæd], *s.* cojinete o cojincillo, almohadilla; (sast.) hombrera, relleno; bloc (de papel); pata (de ciertos animales).—*vti.* [1] forrar, rellenar.—*vii.* caminar (penosa o cansadamente). **ding** [-iŋ], *s.* (cost.) relleno, almohadilla; algodón guata; ripio (en un escrito).

paddle [pǽdl], *vt.* y *vi.* bogar o remar con canalete; chapotear.—*s.* canalete, remo corto.—*p. wheel,* rueda de paletas.

padlock [pǽdlak], *s.* candado.—*vt.* echar el candado, cerrar con candado.

pagan [péigan], *s.* pagano.- **ism** [-izm], *s.* paganismo.

page [peidȥ], *s.* página; paje; botones.—*vt.* paginar; vocear, buscar llamando.

pageant [pǽdȥant], *s.* espectáculo, público.

paginate [pǽdȥineit], *vt.* paginar, foliar.

paid [peid], *pret.* y *pp.* de TO PAY.

pail [peil], *s.* cubo, balde.

pain [pein], *vt.* doler; causar dolor; apenar, afligir.—*vi.* doler.—*s.* dolor.—

on p. of, so pena de.—*to be in p.,* tener dolor, estar con dolor.— **—ful** [péjnful], *a.* penoso; doloroso; arduo, laborioso.—*to be p.,* doler.— **—killer** [-kjlœr], *s.* (fam.) remedio contra el dolor.— **—less** [-ljs], *a.* sin pena, sin dolor.— **—s** [-z], *s. pl.* trabajo; esmero; cuidado; ansiedad; dolores de(l) parto.— **—staking** [-ztejkjŋ], *a.* cuidadoso, industrioso; esmerado.—*s.* esmero.

paint [pejnt], *vt.* pintar; pintarse el rostro.—*p. remover,* sacapintura, quitapintura.—*to p. the town red,* (fam.) ir de parranda, correrla.—*vi.* pintar, ser pintor; pintarse, maquillarse, darse colorete.—*s.* pintura; color; colorete, arrebol.— **—brush** [péjntbrʌs], *s.* brocha, pincel.— **—er** [-œ(r)], *s.* pintor.— **—ing** [-jŋ], *s.* pintura.

pair [per], *s.* par; pareja.—*p. of scissors,* tijeras.—*p. of trousers,* pantalones.—*vt.* y *vi.* (a)parear(se), hermanar(se).

pajamas [pɑdʒáməz], *s. pl.* pijama.

pal [pæl], *s.* (fam.) compañero, compinche.

palace [pæljs], *s.* palacio.

palatable [pælātabl], *a.* sabroso, apetitoso; agradable.—**palatal** [pælátal], *a.* y *s.* palatal.—**palate** [pæljt], *s.* paladar, cielo de la boca.

palaver [pɑlævœ(r)], *s.* palabrería, labia; embustes.

pale [pejl], *a.* pálido; descolorido.—*to grow p.,* ponerse pálido.—*vi.* palidecer; perder el color.— **—face** [-fæs], *s.* (despec.) carapálida, rostropálida.— **—ness** [péjlnjs], *s.* palidez, descoloramiento.

palette [pæljt], *s.* (pint.) paleta.—*p. knife,* espátula.

palisade [pæljséjd], *s.* (em)palizada, estacada.—*pl.* risco.

pall [pol], *s.* paño mortuorio; (igl.) palio.—*vt.* quitar el sabor; hartar, empalagar.—*vi.* hacerse insípido, perder el sabor.— **—bearer** [pólbœrœ(r)], *s.* portaféretro.

pallet [pæljt], *s.* jergón, cama pobre.

pallid [pæljd], *a.* pálido, descolorido.

pallium [pæljʌm], *s.* (igl.) palio.

pallor [pælo(r)], *s.* palidez.

palm [pam], *s.* palma, palmera; palma de la mano.—*p. grove,* palmar.—*p. leaf,* palma, hoja de la palmera.—*P. Sunday,* domingo de Ramos.—*vt.* escamotear; (con *off, on* o *upon*)

engañar, defraudar con.— **—ist** [pámjst], *s.* quiromántico.— **—istry** [-jstrj], *s.* quiromancia.— **—y** [-j], *a.* floreciente, próspero.

palpable [pælpabl], *a.* palpable, evidente.

palpate [pælpejt], *vt.* palpar.

palpitate [pælpjtejt], *vi.* palpitar, latir.—**palpitation** [pælpjtéjʃon], *s.* palpitación, latido.

pamper [pæmpœ(r)], *vt.* mimar, consentir.

pamphlet [pæmfljt], *s.* folleto, panfleto.

pan [pæn], *s.* cacerola, cazuela; perol; caldero.—*frying p.,* sartén.—*vii.* [1] (con *out*) (fam.) dar buen resultado o provecho.—*vti.* (fam.) criticar o poner como nuevo.

Panama [pænjma], *s.* Panamá.—*P. Canal,* Canal de Panamá.—*P. hat,* panamá.

Panamanian [pænaméjnjan], *s.* y *a.* panameño.

Pan-American [pænamérjkan], *a.* panamericano.

pancake [pænkejk], *s.* hojuela, torta delgada, (Am.) panqué o panqueque.—*p. landing,* aterrizaje aplastado, aterrizaje en desplome.—*vt.* (aer.) desplomarse.

pane [pejn], *s.* hoja de vidrio o cristal de ventana o vidriera; entrepaño de puerta, etc.

panel [pænel], *s.* panel; entrepaño, tablero; (cost.) paño en un vestido; (for.) jurado.—*vti.* [2] artesonar, formar tableros.

pang [pæŋ], *s.* angustia, congoja, dolor, tormento.—*pl.* ansias.

panic [pænjk], *a.* y *s.* pánico.—*p.-stricken,* sobrecogido de terror, preso de pánico.—*vti.* [8] consternar, sobrecoger de terror.—**panicked** [pænjkt], *pret.* y *pp.* de TO PANIC.— **—ky** [pænjkj], *a.* aterrorizado.

pansy [pænzj], *s.* (bot.) pensamiento; (fam. y despec.) marica, mariquita.

pant [pænt], *vi.* jadear, resollar; palpitar.—*to p. for* o *after,* suspirar por, desear con ansia.

panther [pænθœ(r)], *s.* pantera, leopardo; (Am.) puma.

panties [pæntiz], *s. pl.* pantaloncillos de mujer, bragas, bombachas.

panting [pæntjŋ], *a.* jadeante.—*s.* jadeo.

pantomime [pæntomajm], *s.* pantomima; mímica.

pantry [pǽntri], s. despensa.

pants [pænts], s. pl. pantalones.

pap [pæp], s. (coc.) papilla; (fig.) tonterías.

papa [pápä, papá], s. (fam.) papá.

papacy [péipəsi], s. papado, pontificado.—**papal** [péipəl], a. papal, pontifical.

papaya [papáyä], s. (Am.) lechosa, papaya.

paper [péipœ(r)], s. papel; memoria; disertación, ensayo; diario, periódico; (com.) valor negociable.—pl. papeles, documentos, credenciales.—on p., escrito; por escrito; en teoría.—p. bag, bolsa de papel.—p. clip, grapa, sujetapapeles.—p. currency o money, papel moneda.—p. cutter, cortapapeles, guillotina.—p. doll, muñeca de papel.—p. hanger, empapelador, papelista.—p. knife, cortapapeles.—p. work, papeleo.—p.-thin, delgadísimo.—p. tiger, tigre de papel.—a. de papel; para papel; escrito.—vt. empapelar.—**back** [-bæk], s. libro en rústica.—**boy** [-bɔi], s. vendedor de periódicos.—**weight** [-weit], s. pisapapeles.

paprika [pǽprikä], s. pimentón.

par [par], s. equivalencia, paridad; (com.) par.—p. value, valor a la par, valor nominal.—to be on a p. with, ser igual a, correr parejas con.

parable [pǽrəbl], s. parábola.

parachute [pǽrəšut], s. paracaídas.—p. jump, salto en paracaídas.—**parachutist** [pǽrəšutist], s. paracaidista.

parade [paréid], s. (mil.) parada; desfile, procesión; paseo público.—p. ground, plaza de armas.—vt. y vi. formar en parada; pasar revista; desfilar; pasear; ostentar.

paradise [pǽrədais], s. paraíso.

paradox [pǽrədaks], s. paradoja.

paraffin [pǽrəfin], s. parafina.

paragraph [pǽrəgræf], s. párrafo.—vt. dividir en párrafos.

Paraguayan [pærəgwéiən, pærəgwáiən], a. y s. paraguayo.

parakeet [pǽrəkit], s. periquito, perico.

parallel [pǽrəlɛl], a. paralelo.—p. bars, paralelas (gimnasia).—s. línea paralela; (geog.) paralelo.—vti. [2] ser paralelo o igual a; cotejar.

paralysis [parǽlisis], s. parálisis.—**paralytic** [pærəlítik], s. y a. paralítico.—**paralyzation** [pærəlizéišon], s. pará-

lisis; paralización.—**paralyze** [pǽrə-laiz], vt. paralizar.—**paralyzed** [pǽrəlaizd], a. paralítico.

paramount [pǽrəmaunt], a. primordial, supremo, principalísimo.

paranoiac [pærənɔiæk], a. y s. paranoico.

parapet [pǽrəpet], s. parapeto.

paraphernalia [pærəfœrnéiliä], s. pl. avíos, trastos.

parasite [pǽrəsait], s. parásito.—**parasitic(al)** [pærəsítik(əl)], a. parásito.

parasol [pǽrəsɔl], s. parasol, quitasol.

paratrooper [pǽrətrupœ(r)], s. paracaidista.—**paratroops** [pǽrətrups], s. pl. tropas paracaidistas.

parcel [pársɛl], s. paquete; bulto; partida.—p. of ground o land, parcela o lote de terreno, solar.—p. post, paquetes postales.—vti. [2] (con **out** o **into**) partir, dividir; empaquetar; parcelar, dividir en parcelas.

parch [parch], vt. y vi. (re)secar(se); tostar(se), quemar(se).—to be parched with thirst, morirse de sed.

parchment [párchmɛnt], s. pergamino.

pardon [párdon], vt. perdonar; indultar; disculpar, dispensar.—p. board, junta de perdones.—p. me! ¡perdone Ud.! ¡Ud. dispense!—s. perdón, absolución, indulto.—I beg your p.! ¡Ud. dispense! ¡perdone Ud.!; ¿cómo decía Ud.?—**able** [párdonəbl], a. perdonable.

pare [per], vt. cortar, recortar; mondar; pelar; adelgazar; reducir (gastos).

parent [pérɛnt], s. padre o madre; autor, fuente.—pl. padres.—a. madre, matriz, principal.—**age** [-idž], s. ascendencia, alcurnia, origen.—**al** [paréntəl], a. paternal o maternal.

parenthesis [parénθesis], s. paréntesis.—**parenthetical** [pærenθétikəl], a. entre paréntesis.

paring [périŋ], s. peladura, mondadura; recorte.—p. knife, cuchillo para mondar.

parish [pǽriš], s. parroquia.—p. priest, (cura) párroco.—**ioner** [pærí-šonœ(r)], s. feligrés, parroquiano.

Parisian [parísiən], a. y s. parisiense.

parity [pǽriti], s. paridad.

park [park], s. parque.—vt. y vi. estacionar(se) (un coche), (Am.) parquear.—**ing** [párkiŋ], s. estacionamiento (de un vehículo).—no p., prohibido estacionarse.—p. brake, freno de mano.—*p. garage*, parking, estacionamiento.—*p. lights*, (aut.) faros de situación.—*p. lot*, parking, estacionamiento.—*p. meter*, reloj de estacionamiento, parquímetro.— *p. ticket*, aviso de multa.- **—land** [-lænd], *s.* zona verde, parques; jardines.- **—way** [-wej], *s.* avenida ajardinada, paseo; (expressway) carretera de vía libre.

parley [párli], *vi.* parlamentar.—*s.* parlamento.

parliament [párliment], *s.* parlamento. - **—ary** [parliméntari], *a.* parlamentario.

parlor [párlo(r)], *s.* (ant.) sala, salón.

parochial [paróukial], *a.* parroquial; de criterio estrecho, limitado.

parody [párodi], *s.* parodia.—*vt.* parodiar.

parole [paróul], *s.* libertad bajo palabra.—*vt.* poner en libertad bajo palabra.

parrot [párot], *s.* papagayo, loro.—*p. fever*, psitacosis.—*vt.* y *vi.* repetir o hablar como loro.

parry [péri], *vti.* y *vii.* [7] (esgr.) parar, rechazar, quitar.—*s.* parada, quite.

parsley [pársli], *s.* perejil.

parsnip [pársnip], *s.* chirivía.

parson [párson], *s.* clérigo; cura, párroco; pastor protestante.

part [part], *s.* parte; pedazo, trozo; región, lugar; (teat.) papel; raya del cabello.—*pl.* prendas, cualidades.—*p. and parcel*, parte integrante; uña y carne, carne y hueso.—*p. owner*, condueño.—*p.-time*, por horas, parcial (trabajo).—*to do one's p.*, cumplir uno con su obligación; hacer cuanto pueda.—*to take p.* (*in*), participar o tomar parte (en).—*vt.* separar, dividir.—*to p. company*, separarse.—*to p. one's hair*, hacerse la raya.—*to p. with*, deshacerse de.— *vi.* separarse; despedirse.—*to p. with*, desprenderse o deshacerse de.

partial [páršal], *a.* parcial; amigo; aficionado.- **—ity** [parš(i)æliti], *s.* parcialiadad; afición.- **—ly** [páršali], *adv.* parcialmente, en parte; parcialmente, con parcialidad.

participant [partísipant], *a.* y *s.* participante, (co)partícipe.—**participate** [partísipejt], *vt.* y *vi.* participar. —**participation** [partisipéišon], *s.* participación.

participle [pártisipl], *s.* participio.

particle [pártikl], *s.* partícula; pizca.

particular [partíkyulä(r)], *a.* particular,

peculiar; preciso, exacto; delicado escrupuloso; detallado; exigente quisquilloso.—*s.* particular, particularidad, detalle, pormenor.—*in p.*, particularmente, en particular específicamente.—*to go into particulars*, entrar en detalles.

parting [pártin], *s.* separación; partida; despedida.

partisan [pártizan], *a.* y *s.* partidario, adepto.—*s.* (mil.) guerrillero.

partition [partíšon], *s.* partición, repartimiento; división, separación; demarcación; (alb.) tabique; (carp.) mampara.—*p. wall*, tabique; pared medianera.—*vt.* partir, dividir; repartir, distribuir.

partly [pártli], *adv.* en parte.

partner [pártnœ(r)], *s.* socio; compañero; pareja (de baile, tenis, etc.); (wife or husband) cónyuge.—**ship** [-šip], *s.* (com.) compañía; sociedad; consorcio.—*to enter into a p. with*, asociarse con.

partridge [pártridž], *s.* perdiz.

part-time [párttaim], *a.* por horas, parcial.

party [párti], *s.* partido político; reunión o fiesta privada; partida (de campo, teatro, etc.); (for.) parte, parte interesada; partida, facción; cómplice.

pass [pæs], *vti.* [6] pasar; pasar de; pasar por; aprobar (un proyecto, a un alumno); promulgar (una ley); traspasar (un negocio); ser aprobado (en un examen, una materia); admitir, dar entrada.—*to p. by*, pasar por; pasar de largo.—*to p. each other*, o *one another*, cruzarse.—*to p. over*, atravosar, cruzar, salvar; traspasar; omitir, pasar por alto; excusar.—*to p. sentence*, dictar o pronunciar sentencia.—*to p. the buck*, (fam.) echarle la carga o el muerto a otro.—*to p. the time away*, gastar o pasar el tiempo.—*vii.* pasar; correr, transcurrir (el tiempo, etc.); ser aprobado (un proyecto, un alumno); ser admitido; (esgr.) dar una estocada, hacer un pase.—*to p. away*, fallecer.—*to p. through*, pasar por; atravesar; colarse.—*s.* paso; desfiladero; pase (billete, permiso; de manos, de esgrima, en el juego); (mil.) licencia, salvoconducto; aprobación (en un examen).- **—able** [pæsabl], *a.* pasable, transitable; pasadero, regular.- **—age** [-idž], *s.* pasaje; paso, tránsito; travesía; pasillo, pasadizo; callejón pasaje (de un libro, etc.); trámite y aprobación de un proyecto de ley.**—ageway** [-ídzwei], s. pasadizo, pasaje.

passbook [pǽsbuk], s. libro de cuenta y razón; libreta de banco.

passenger [pǽsendżœ(r)], s. pasajero.**—pl.** pasajeros, el pasaje.**—passer(-by)** [pǽsœ(r) bái], s. transeúnte, viandante.

passer-by [pǽsěrbái], s. transeúnte.

passion [pǽşon], s. pasión; cólera.**—p. flower,** pasionaria.**—P. Week,** semana de Pasión, semana santa.**—ate** [-it], a. apasionado.

passive [pǽsiv], a. pasivo; inerte.**—s.** (gram.) voz pasiva.**—ness** [-njs], **passivity** [pæsíviti], s. pasividad; inercia.

passkey [pǽski], s. llave maestra.

Passover [pǽsouvœ(r)], s. pascua (de los hebreos).

passport [pǽsport], s. pasaporte.**—password** [pǽswœrd], s. santo y seña; (comput.) contraseña.

past [pæst], pp. de TO PASS.**—a.** pasado, último; ex, que fue (presidente, director, etc.).**—p. master of,** experto o sobresaliente en.**—p. participle,** participio pasivo.**—p. tense,** pretérito.**—s.** (lo) pasado; antecedentes, historia; (gram.) pretérito; pasado.**—in the p.,** antes, en tiempos pasados.**—prep.** más de, después de (tiempo); más allá de, fuera de (lugar).**—half** (quarter, etc.) p. two, las dos y media (cuarto, etc.).**—p. remedy,** irremediable.

paste [peist], s. pasta; engrudo.**—vt.** empastar, pegar con engrudo.**—board** [péistbord], s. cartón.

pastel [pæstél], s. (b.a.) pastel; pintura al pastel.

pasteurization [pæstœrizéişon], s. pasteu(ri)zación.**—pasteurize** [pǽstœraiz], vt. paste(u)rizar.

pastille [pæstíl], s. pastilla, tableta.

pastime [pǽstaim], s. pasatiempo.

pastor [pǽsto(r)], s. pastor, cura, clérigo.**—al** [-al], a. y s. pastoral.

pastry [péistri], s. pastelería.**—p. cook,** pastelero.**—p. shop,** pastelería, repostería.

pasture [pǽschŭ(r)], s. pasto, pastura.**—p. ground** o lands, pradera, dehesa, prado, pastizal.**—vt.** pastar, apacentar, pastorear.**—vi.** pastar, pacer.

pasty [péisti], a. pastoso; pálido.

pat [pæt], a. oportuno, propio, (fam.)

pintiparado, al pelo; fijo, firme; fácil.**—adv.** justamente, convenientemente, a propósito.**—to stand p.,** mantenerse en sus trece; (in poker) no querer cambiar ninguna carta.**—s.** golpecito, palmadita; caricia; porción pequeña de mantequilla.**—p. on the back,** (fam.) felicitación, enhorabuena.**—vti.** [1] dar palmaditas a, acariciar, pasar la mano sobre.

patch [pæch], vt. remendar.**—vi.** echar remiendos.**—s.** parche; remiendo; material para remiendos; sembrado (de trigo, etc.).**—p. of land** o ground, pedazo de terreno.

pate [peit], s. coronilla.

patent [pǽtent], a. patente, palmario, manifiesto; de patente, patentado.**—p. leather,** charol.**—s.** patente.**—p. medicine,** especialidad medicinal.**—p. pending,** patente solicitada.**—p. rights,** derechos de patente.**—vt.** patentar.

paternal [pǽtœrnal], a. paternal, paterno.**—paternity** [pǽtœrniti], s. paternidad.

path [pæθ], s. senda, sendero; camino; trayectoria.

pathetic [pǽθétik], a. patético.

pathological [pæθoládžikal], a. patológico.**—pathology** [pǽálodži], s. patología.**—pathos** [péiθas], s. patetismo.

pathway [pǽθwei], s. senda, vereda.

patience [péişens], s. paciencia.**—patient** [péişent], a. paciente.**—s.** paciente, enfermo.

patriot [péitriot], s. patriota.**—ic** [peitriátik], a. patriótico.**—ism** [péitriotizm], s. patriotismo.

patrol [patróul], s. patrulla; ronda.**—vti.** y vii. [2] patrullar; hacer la ronda.**—man** [-mæn], s. guardia municipal, vigilante de policía.

patron [péitron], s. patrón, patrocinador, protector; padrino; cliente, parroquiano.**—p. saint,** patrón, santo titular.**—age** [-idž], s. (igl.) patronato; patrocinio; clientela habitual; (pol.) control de nombramientos por el partido de gobierno.**—ess** [-is], s. patrona, protectora; patrocinadora, madrina.**—ize** [-aiz], vt. patrocinar, apadrinar; tratar con condescendencia; ser parroquiano habitual de.

patsy [pǽtsi], s. (jer.) cabeza de turco, chivo expiatorio, pánfilo; presa fácil.

patter [pǽtœr], s. golpeteo; charla, palabrería.—*vi.* golpetear; charlar, parlotear.

pattern [pǽtœrn], *s.* modelo, norma; patrón, molde, plantilla, diseño.—*vt.* copiar, imitar.—*to p.* oneself after, tomar como modelo a.

paunch [pɔnch], *s.* panza, barriga.—**y** [pɔ́nchi], *a.* barrigón, panzudo.

pauper [pɔ́pœr], *s.* indigente, pobre.

pause [pɔz], *s.* pausa.—*vi.* hacer pausa, detenerse brevemente; vacilar.

pave [peiv], *vt.* pavimentar, adoquinar, enlosar, embaldosar.—*paved road*, carretera pavimentada, camino asfaltado.—*to p. the way*, facilitar, preparar el terreno, abrir el camino.—**ment** [péivment], *s.* pavimento.

pavilion [pavílyon], *s.* pabellón.

paw [pɔ], *s.* garra, zarpa, pata; (fam.) mano.—*vt.* y *vi.* patear, piafar; (fam.) manosear.

pawn [pɔn], *vt.* empeñar, pignorar, dar en prenda.—*s.* prenda, empeño; (in chess) peón.—*p. ticket*, papeleta de empeño.—**broker** [pɔ́nbroukœr], *s.* prestamista, prendero.—**shop** [-šap], *s.* casa de empeños.

pay [pei], *vti.* [10] pagar, remunerar; costear; abonar, saldar; producir ganancia o provecho a.—*to p. a call o a visit*, hacer una visita.—*to p. a compliment*, hacer un cumplido; (fam.) piropear.—*to p. attention*, prestar atención; fijarse o reparar (en), hacer caso (de).—*to p. back*, devolver, reembolsar; pagar en la misma moneda.—*to p. court*, hacer la corte, enamorar.—*to p. for*, pagar, costear.—*to p. off*, pagar; pagar por completo; vengarse de, ajustarle a uno las cuentas.—*to p. one's respects*, presentar u ofrecer sus respetos.—*to p. up*, pagar por completo.—*to p. the piper*, pagar el pato, pagar los vidrios rotos.—*vii.* pagar (a veces con **off**) compensar, tener cuenta, ser provechoso; valer la pena.—*to p. dearly*, costarle a uno caro.—*s.* paga; sueldo, salario, jornal; recompensa.—*bad (good) p.*, mal (buen) pagador, (fam.) mala (buena) paga.—*p. roll*, nómina, lista de jornales.—**able** [péiabl], *a.* pagadero; reembolsable.—**check** [-chek], *s.* cheque en pago de sueldo.—**day** [-dei], *s.* día de pago.—**ee** [peií], *s.* (com.) tenedor, portador (de un giro).—**er** [peíœr], *s.* pagador.—

master [-mǽstœr], *s.* pagador.—*p.'s office*, pagaduría.—**ment** [-ment], *s.* pago, paga.—*p. in advance*, anticipo, pago adelantado.—*p. in full*, pago total.

PC = personal computer.

PD = Police Department.

pea [pí], *s.* guisante, chícharo.—*p. gun* o *shooter*, cerbatana.—*p. soup*, sopa de guisantes; (fam.) neblina espesa y amarillenta.—*sweet p.*, guisante de olor.

peace [pis], *s.* paz.—*P. Corps*, Cuerpo de Paz.—*p. of mind*, serenidad del espíritu.—*p. pipe*, pipa ceremonial.—*public p.*, orden público.—**able** [písabl], *a.* pacífico, tranquilo.—**ful** [-ful], *a.* tranquilo, pacífico, apacible.—**keeping** [-kipiŋ], *s.* mantenimiento de la paz.—**maker** [-meikœr], *s.* conciliador.—**time** [-taim], *s.* época de paz, tiempos de paz.

peach [pich], *s.* melocotón, durazno; (fam.) persona o cosa admirable.—*p. tree*, melocotonero; duraznero.

peacock [píkak], *s.* pavo real.

peak [pik], *s.* cima, cumbre, pico, picacho; cúspide.—*s.* y *a.* máximo.—*p. hour*, hora punta.—*p. load*, (elec.) carga de punta.

peal [pil], *s.* repique de campanas; estruendo, estrépito.—*p. of laughter*, carcajada, estrepitosa.—*p. of thunder*, trueno.—*p.-ringing*, repiqueteo.—*vt.* y *vi.* repicar, repiquetear.

peanut [pínʌt], *s.* cacahuete, (Am.) maní.—*p. butter*, mantequilla de maní, mantequilla de cacahuete.—*p. vendor*, manisero.

pearl [pœrl], *s.* perla.—*p. button*, botón de nácar.—*p.-colored*, perlino.—**ly** [pœrli], *a.* perlino; nacarado.

peasant [pézant], *s.* y *a.* campesino, rústico.

peat [pit], *s.* turba.

pebble [pébl], *s.* guijarro, china.

pecan [pikán], *s.* (bot.) pacana.

peck [pek], *s.* medida de áridos, celemín; picotazo, picotada.—*vt.* picotear, picar.—*vi.* picotear.

peculiar [pikiúlyä(r)], *a.* peculiar, singular, raro.—**ity** [pikiuláeriti], *s.* peculiaridad, particularidad.

pedagogue [pédagag], *s.* pedagogo.—**pedagogy** [pédagoudži], *s.* pedagogía.

pedal [pédal], *s.* pedal.—*vii.* [2] pedalear.

peddle [pédl], *vt.* vender de puerta en

puerta.—*vi*. ser vendedor ambulante.- **—r** [pédlœ(r)], *s*. baratiller vendedor ambulante.

pedestal [pédestạl], *s*. pedestal.

pedestrian [pịdéstrịạn], *s*. peatón.—*a*. pedestre.

pedigree [pédịgri], *s*. pedigrí; linaje; árbol genealógico; fuente; origen; expediente, historial.

peck [pik], *vi*. mirar a hurtadillas.—*s*. mirada rápida y furtiva.

peel [pil], *vt*. (a veces con **off**) descortezar, pelar, mondar.—*vi*. desconcharse, descascararse, pelarse.—*s*. corteza, cáscara; piel.- **—ing** [pílịŋ], *s*. peladura, mondadura; desconchado.

peep [pip], *vi*. atisbar, mirar a hurtadillas; asomar; piar.—*not to p.*, (fam.) no chistar.—*s*. atisbo; mirada, ojeada; pío, piada.—*p. show*, mundonuevo.- **—hole** [píphoụl], *s*. mirilla; atisbadero.

peer [pịr], *vi*. atisbar mirar detenidamente.—*to p. at*, mirar con ojos de miope.—*s*. par, igual; Par del Reino.- **—less** [pírlịs], *a*. sin par, incomparable.

peeve [piv], *s*. (fam.) cojijo.—*pet p.*, manía.—*vt*. (fam.) enojar, irritar.

peg [peg], *s*. espiga, taco; tarugo; (mar.) cabilla; (mus.) clavija; (coll.) (beisbol) tiro.—*p. leg*, pierna o pata de palo.—*to take someone down a p.*, humillar, bajarle a uno los humos.—*vti*. [1] estaquillar, clavar; estacar, jalonear; tirar o lanzar (la pelota).—*vii*. (gen. con **away**) afanarse; trabajar con ahinco.

pelican [péljkạn], *s*. pelícano, alcatraz.

pellet [péljt], *s*. píldora, pelotilla; bola, bolita; perdigón.

pell-mell [pélmél], *a*. tumultuoso.—*adv*. atropelladamente.

pelt [pelt], *s*. piel, cuero; golpe violento.—*vt*. apedrear.—*vi*. arrojar alguna cosa; caer con fuerza.—*p. box o case*, estuche.

pen [pen], *s*. pluma; (for animals) corral, redil.—*ball-point p.*, bolígrafo, birome, pluma atómica.—*fountain p.*, pluma estilográfica, pluma fuente.—*p. name*, seudónimo.—*p. pal*, (fam.) amigo por correspondencia.—*p. point*, punta de la pluma.—*p. stroke*, plumazo. —*vti*. [1] escribir (con pluma); redactar.—*to p. in o up*, acorralar, encerrar.

penal [pínạl], *a*. penal.- **—ize** [-ajz],

vt. penalizar, castigar; perjudicar; (dep.) sancionar.- **—ty** [pénạlti], *s*. pena, castigo; (for late payment) recargo; (dep.) sanción.

penance [pénạns], *s*. penitencia.

penchant [pénšạnt], *s*. afición, inclinación.

pencil [pénsịl], *s*. lápiz.—*mechanical p.*, lapicero.—*p. sharpener*, sacapuntas, afilalápices.—*vti*. [2] dibujar, marcar o escribir con lápiz.

pendant [péndạnt], *s*. medallón, colgante; pendiente; araña (de luces).—*a.* = PENDENT.

pending [péndịŋ], *a*. pendiente.—*prep*. durante; hasta.

pendulum [péndžụlʌm], *s*. péndulo.

penetrate [pénẹtrejt], *vt*. y *vi*. penetrar.—**penetrating** [pénẹtrejtịŋ], *a*. penetrante.—**penetration** [penẹtréjšọn], *s*. penetración.

penguin [péngwịn], *s*. pingüino.

penholder [pénhoụldœr], *s*. portalápices; (to hold nib) portaplumas.

penicillin [penịsílịn], *s*. penicilina.

peninsula [pịnínšụlậ], *s*. península.- **—r** [-(r)], *a*. peninsular.

penis [pínịs], *s*. pene, miembro viril.

penitence [pénịtẹns], *s*. penitencia; contrición.—**penitent** [pénịtẹnt], *a*. y *s*. penitente.—**penitentiary** [penịténšạri], *a*. penitenciario; de castigo, penal.—*s*. penitenciaría, presidio.

penknife [pénnajf], *s*. cortaplumas.

penmanship [pénmạnšịp], *s*. escritura, caligrafía.

pennant [pénạnt], *s*. gallardete, banderola; (fig.) campeonato.

penniless [pénịlịs], *s*. sin un real; en la miseria; sin dinero.—**penny** [pénị], *s*. (E.U.) centavo.

pension [pénšọn], *s*. pensión; jubilación; retiro.—*vt*. (a veces con **off**) pensionar, jubilar.

pensive [pénsịv], *a*. pensativo, meditabundo.

Pentecost [péntịkɔst], *s*. el Pentecostés.

penthouse [pénthaụs], *s*. penthouse, ático, casa de azotea; alpende, colgadizo.

peony [píọnị], *s*. peonía.

people [pípl], *s*. pueblo; gente; personas; los habitantes (de un país).—*p. say*, dicen, se dice, dice la gente.—*the common p.*, el pueblo, el vulgo, la plebe.—*the p.*, el público, la gente.—*vt*. poblar.

pep [pɛp], *s.* (fam.) ánimo, brío; energía, vigor.—*vti.* [1] (con **up**) (fam.) animar, estimular.

pepper [pépœ(r)], *s.* (bot.) pimienta; pimiento.—*green p.,* ají, pimiento.—*p.-and-salt cloth,* tejido de mezclilla.—*red p.,* chile, pimentón.—*vt.* sazonar con pimienta; acribillar. **—mint** [-mint], *s.* menta.—**y** [-i], *a.* picante; mordaz; irascible.

per [pœr], *prep.* por.—*p. annum,* al año.—*p. capita,* per cápita.—*p. cent,* por ciento.—*p. diem,* por día.—*what p. cent of . . . ?* ¿qué porcentaje de . . . ?

perambulator [pœræmbjuleito(r)], *s.* cochecito de niño.

percale [pœrkéjl], *s.* percal.

perceive [pœrsjv], *vt.* percibir; percatar(se) (de); comprender, entender.

percentage [pœrséntjdž], *s.* (com.) tanto por ciento, porcentaje.

perceptible [pœrséptjbl], *a.* perceptible, sensible.**—perception** [pœrsépšon], *s.* percepción.

perch [pœrch], *s.* (ict.) perca; percha (para las aves).—*vi.* posarse.

perchance [pœrchǽns], *adv.* acaso, tal vez, quizá, por ventura.

percolate [pœrkoleit], *vt.* y *vi.* (tras)colar, (in)filtrar, pasar, rezumarse. **—percolator** [pœrkoleito(r)], *s.* percolador, cafetera filtradora, cafetera eléctrica.

percussion [pœrkášon], *s.* percusión.

peremptory [pœrémptorj], *a.* perentorio; terminante, definitivo.

perennial [pœrénjal], *a.* perenne; (bot.) vivaz.—*s.* planta vivaz.

perfect [pœrfjkt], *a.* perfecto; completo.—*s.* (gram.) tiempo perfecto.—*vt.* [pœrfékt], perfeccionar, mejorar.—**ion** [pœrfékšon], *s.* perfección.

perforate [pœrforeit], *vt.* perforar.— **perforation** [pœrforéišon], *s.* perforación.

perform [pœrfórm], *vt.* ejecutar; (teat.) representar.—**ance** [-ans], *s.* ejecución; funcionamiento; (teat.) función, representación.—*first p.,* (teat.) estreno.—**er** [-œ(r)], *s.* ejecutor, ejecutante; actor, actriz.

perfume [pœrfjum], *s.* perfume.— [pœrfjúm], *vt.* perfumar.

perhaps [pœrhǽps], *adv.* tal vez, quizá(s), acaso, por ventura.

peril [péril], *s.* peligro.—*vti.* [2] poner

en peligro.- **—ous** [-ʌs], *a.* peligroso.

perimeter [pœrímɛtœ(r)], *s.* perímetro.

period [píriod], *s.* período; época, tiempo; (impr.) punto; menstruación.- **—ic(al)** [pirjádjk(al)], *a.* periódico.- **—ical** [pirjádjkal], *s.* periódico, revista periódica.

periscope [périskoup], *s.* periscopio.

perish [périš], *vi.* perecer.- **—able** [-abl], *a.* perecedero.—*pl.* mercancías corruptibles.

perjure [pœrdžur], *vt.* perjurar.**—perjury** [pœrdžurj], *s.* perjurio.—*vi.—to p. oneself,* perjurarse.

perk [pœrk], *vt.* erguir, levantar (la cabeza, la oreja).—*vi.* (fam.) (coffee) hacerse, filtrarse; (con **up**) animarse, avivarse, levantar la cabeza. **—s** [pœrks], *spl.* beneficios extras, ventajas.- **—y** [pœrki], *a.* animado, despabilado.

permanence [pœrmanens], *s.* permanencia.**—permanent** [pœrmanent], *a.* permane(cie)nte, duradero; indeleble.—*s.* ondulado permanente.

permeate [pœrmieit], *vt.* y *vi.* penetrar.

permissible [pœrmjsibl], *a.* permisible, lícito.**—permission** [pœrmíšon], *s.* permiso.**—permit** [pœrmít], *vti.* [1] permitir, autorizar.—*s.* [pœrmjt], permiso, licencia, pase.

pernicious [pœrníšʌs], *a.* pernicioso.

perpendicular [pœrpendíkyulà(r)], *a.* y *s.* perpendicular.

perpetrate [pœrpɛtreit], *vt.* perpetrar.**—perpetrator** [pœrpɛtreito(r)], *s.* perpetrador.

perpetual [pœrpéchual], *a.* perpetuo.**—perpetuate** [pœrpéchueit], *vt.* perpetuar.—**perpetuity** [pœrpɛtújti], *s.* perpetuidad.

perplex [pœrpléks], *vt.* dejar perpleo.- **—ed** [-t], *a.* perplejo.- **—ity** [-iti], *s.* perplejidad, confusión, duda.

persecute [pœrsɛkjut], *vt.* perseguir.— **persecution** [pœrsɛkjúšon], *s.* persecución.**—persecutor** [pœrsɛkjuto(r)], *s.* perseguidor.

perseverance [pœrsɛvírans], *s.* perseverancia.**—persevere** [pœrsɛvír], *vi.* perseverar.

Persian [pœržan], *s.* y *a.* persa.

persist [pœrsjst], *vi.* persistir.- **—ence** [-ens], *s.* persistencia.- **—ent** [-ent], **—ing** [-iŋ], *a.* persistente.

person [pœrson], *s.* persona.—*p.-to-p.,*

(tlf.) particular a particular.— **—age**
[-idž], s. personaje.— **—al** [-ạl], a.
personal; de uso personal.—p. *com-*
puter, computadora personal, ordenador personal.—*p. property,* bienes
muebles.— **—ality** [pœrsọnǽliti], s.
personalidad.—**personify** [pœrsán-
ifaị], vti. [7] personificar.— **—nel**
[pœrsọnél], s. personal.

personnel [pœrsọnél], s. personal.—*P.*
(department), sección de personal.—
p. manager, jefe de personal.

perspective [pœrspéktịv], s. perspectiva.

perspicacious [pœrspịkéjšʌs], a. perspicaz.—**perspicacity** [pœrspịkǽ-
sịtị], s. perspicacia.

perspiration [pœrspịréjšọn], s. sudor,
transpiración.—**perspire** [pœrs-
pájr], vt. y vi. sudar, transpirar.—
perspiring [pœrspájrịŋ], a. sudoroso.

persuade [pœrswéjd], vt. persuadir.
—**persuasion** [pœrswéjžọn], s. persuasión; creencia, opinión.—**per-**
suasive [pœrswéjsịv], a. persuasivo.

pert [pœrt], a. atrevido, descarado, insolente; listo, despierto.

pertain [pœrtéjn], vi. pertenecer.—
pertaining to, perteneciente a.

pertinent [pœrtịnẹnt], a. pertinente.

perturb [pœrtœ́rb], vt. perturbar.

perusal [pẹrúzạl], s. lectura cuida-
dosa.—**peruse** [pẹrúz], vt. leer con
cuidado.

Peruvian [pẹrúvịạn], s. y a. peruano.

pervade [pœrvéjd], vt. penetrar, llenar.—**pervasive** [pœrvéjsịv], a. penetrante.

perverse [pœrvœ́rs], a. perverso.—
pervert [pœrvœ́rt], vt. pervertir.—s.
[pœ́rvœrt], pervertido.

pessimism [pésịmịzm], s. pesi-
mismo.—**pessimist** [pésịmịst], s.,
pessimistic [pesịmístịk], a. pesimista.

pest [pest], s. peste; insecto nocivo;
(bore) machaca.— **—er** [péstœ(r)],
vt. molestar, importunar.— **—ilence**
[-ịlẹns], s. pestilencia.— **—ilent**
[-ịlẹnt], a. pestilente.

pet [pet], s. animal mimado, animal
casero; niño mimado; favorito.—p.
shop, pajerería.—a. mimado; favorito.—*p. name,* nombre de cariño.—
vti. [1] mimar, acariciar.—vii. (jer.)
besuquearse.

petal [pétạl], s. pétalo.

petition [pẹtíšọn], s. petición, demanda, súplica; instancia, solicitud.—vt. suplicar, rogar; pedir.

petroleum [pịtróuliạm], s. petróleo.

petticoat [pétịkout], s. refajo;
enagua(s).

pettiness [pétịnịs], s. pequeñez, mezquindad.—**petty** [pétị], a. insignificante, mezquino, despreciable; subordinado, inferior.—*p. cash,*
(com.) caja chica.—*p. larceny,*
hurto, ratería.—*p. officer,* suboficial,
oficial subalterno de marina.

petulance [péchụlạns], s. mal genio,
impaciencia; petulancia.—**petulant**
[péchụlạnt], a. enojadizo, malhumorado.

petunia [pịtúnịạ], s. petunia.

pew [pju], s. banco de iglesia.

phalanx [féjlæŋks], s. falange.

phantom [fǽntọm], s. fantasma.

Pharaoh [férou], s. Faraón.

pharmacist [fármạsịst], s. farmacéutico,—**pharmaceutical** [farmạsyútị-
kạl], a. farmacéutico.—**pharmacy**
[fármạsị], s. farmacia.

pharynx [fǽrịŋks], s. faringe.

phase [fejz], s. fase.—vt. poner en
fase.—*to f. out,* deshacer paulatina-
mente.

pheasant [fézạnt], s. faisán.

phenomena [fịnámẹnạ], s. pl. de PHE-
NOMENON.— **—l** [fịnámẹnạl], a. fenomenal.—**phenomenon** [fịnámẹ-
nạn], s. fenómeno.

philanthropist [fịlǽnθrọpịst], s. filántropo.—**philanthropy** [fịlǽnθrọpị],
s. filantropía.

philharmonic [fịlharmánịk], a. filarmónico.

philology [fịlálọdžị], s. filología.

philosopher [fịlásọfœ(r)], s. filósofo.
—**philosophic(al)** [fịlọsáfịk(ạl)], a.
filosófico.—**philosophy** [fịlásọfị], s.
filosofía.

phlegm [flem], s. flema, gargajo.—*to*
cough up p., gargajear.

phone [foun], s. teléfono.—*p. call,* llamada telefónica.—vt. y vi. telefonear.

phonetics [fonétịks], s. fonética.

phonograph [fóunọgræf], s. fonógrafo.

phony [fóunị], a. (fam.) falso, contrahecho.—s. (jer.) farsa; (fam.) farsante.

phosphate [fásfejt], s. fosfato.—**phos-**
phorus [fásfọrʌs], s. (quím.) fósforo.

photo [fóutou], s. retrato, foto, fotografía.— **—finish** [-fịnịš], s. (dep.) llegada a la meta, determinada me-

diante el fotofija; (fig.) competencia muy reñida.—*p. camera,* fotofija.-
—**graph** [fóutogræf], *vt.* fotografiar, retratar.—*s.* fotografía, retrato.-
—**grapher** [fotágrafœ(r)], *s.* fotograío.- —**graphic** [fotográfik], *s.* fotográfico.- —**graphy** [fotágrafj], *s.* fotografía (arte).- —**meter** [fotámẹtœ(r)], *s.* fotómetro.- —**stat** [fóutọstæt], *s.* fotocopia.

phrase [freiz], *s.* frase.—*vt.* frasear.

physic [fízik], *s.* purgante; medicina.-
—**al** [-ạl], *a.* físico.- —**ian** [fizíșạn], *s.* médico, facultativo.- —**ist** [fízjsjst], *s.* físico.- —**s** [fízjks], *s.* física.

physiologic(al) [fizioládʒjk(ạl)], *a.* fisiológico.—**physiology** [fiziálodʒj], *s.* fisiología.

physique [fizík], *s.* físico, figura, talle, exterior.

pianist [píænjst], *s.* pianista.—**piano** [piǽnou], *s.* piano.—*p. stool,* banqueta de piano.—*p. tuner,* afinador.

piccolo [píkolou], *s.* flautín.

pick [pik], *vt.* picar, picotear; abrir (una cerradura) con ganzúa; escoger, elegir; coger, recoger; mondar o limpiar; descañonar (un ave).—*to p. out,* escoger, entresacar.—*to p. pockets,* robar carteras.—*to p. up,* alzar, recoger; coger; recobrar (el ánimo, las carnes).—*to p. up speed,* acelerar la marcha, aumentar la velocidad.—*vi.* picar, comer bocaditos.—*to p. up,* restablecerse, recobrar la salud; cobrar carnes; desarrollar velocidad.—*s.* (zapa)pico (herramienta); ganzúa; lo más escogido, la flor y nata; cosecha.- —**ax(e)** [píkæks], *s.* zapapico, piqueta.- —**et** [-it], *s.* piquete; estaca.—*p. fence,* cerca de estacas puntiagudas.—*p. line,* línea de piquetes.—*vt.* y *vi.* cercar con estacas; (mil.) colocar de guardia; estacionar o poner piquetes de vigilancia y propaganda.

pickle [píkl], *s.* escabeche; salmuera; encurtido; (fam.) lio, enredo, brete, apuro.—*vt.* escabechar; encurtir.—*pickled fish,* pescado en escabeche.

pickpocket [píkpakjt], *s.* carterista, ratero.—**pickup** [píkʌp], *s.* (aut.) aceleración; (electron.) pick-up, fonocaptor.—*p. truck,* camioneta de reparto.

picnic [píknjk], *s.* jira campestre, partida de campo, romería.—*vii.* [8] hacer una jira al campo, merendar en el campo. —**picnicked** [píknjkt] *pret.* y *pp.* de TO PICNIC.

picture [píkchǔ(r)], *s.* pintura, cuadro; retrato, fotografía; (fig.) estampa, imagen; lámina, grabado; película, film.—*pl.* (fam.) cine.—*p. frame,* marco, cuadro.—*p. gallery,* galería de pinturas.—*p. post card,* postal ilustrada.—*p. signal,* videoseñal.—*p. tube,* tubo de imagen, tubo de televisión.—*p. window,* ventana panorámica.—*to be out of the p.,* no figurar ya en el asunto.—*vt.* pintar, dibujar; describir; imaginar.-
—**sque** [pjkchŭrésk], *a.* pintoresco.

pie [pai], *s.* pastel; (impr.) pastel.—*p. in the sky,* castillos en el aire.—*to be easy as p.,* ser pan comido.—*to have a finger in the p.,* estar metido en el asunto.

piece [pis], *s.* pieza, pedazo, trozo sección, parte; cualquier moneda (teat.) pieza; ficha (del dominó o de las damas).—*of a p.,* de la misma clase, del mismo tenor.—*p. of advice,* consejo.—*p. of furniture,* mueble.—*p. of ground o land,* parcela, solar.—*p. work,* destajo.—*to go to pieces,* desarmarse, desbaratarse. —*vt.* remendar.—*to p. on,* pegar o poner a.

pier [pir], *s.* muelle, embarcadero; espigón; (arq.) pila, machón; entrepaño de pared.

pierce [pirs], *vt.* agujerear, taladrar; acribillar; atravesar, traspasar.—*pierced with holes,* acribillado.—*vi.* penetrar, internarse, entrar a la fuerza.—**piercing** [pírsjŋ], *a.* penetrante, cortante.

piety [páiẹtj], *s.* piedad, devoción.

pig [pig], *s.* cochino, cerdo, puerco, marrano.—*a.p. in a poke,* trato a ciegas.—*p.-headed,* terco, cabezudo.—*p. iron,* arrabio, hierro en lingotes.

pigeon [pídʒọn], *s.* paloma, palomo; pichón.- —**hole** [-houl], *s.* casilla, casillero.—*vt.* encasillar, poner en una casilla; (fig.) archivar; dar carpetazo (a un proyecto de ley, etc.).

piggy [pígj], *s.* lechón, cochinito, cochinillo.—*p. bank,* alcancía.-
—**back** [-bæk], *adv.* a cuestas, en hombros.

pigment [pígmẹnt], *s.* pigmento.

pigmy [pígmj], *s.* = PYGMY.

pigpen [pígpen], *s.* zahurda, pocilga, chiquero, (coll.) cochiquero.—**pigskin** [pígskjn], *s.* piel de cochino o de cerdo; pelota de fútbol.—**pigsty** [pígstaı], *s.* = PIGPEN.—**pigtail** [pígteıl], *s.* cola de cerdo; trenza, coleta.

pike [paık], *s.* pica, garrocha; (ict.) especie de lucio o sollo; (fam.) carretera; camino de barrera.

pile [paıl], *s.* pila, montón; pilote; pelillo, pelusa.—*pl.* hemorroides, almorranas.—*p. driver, p. engine,* martinete para clavar pilotes.—*vt.* hincar pilotes en; amontonar, apilar; acumular.—*vi.* amontonarse, acumularse.

pilfer [pílfœ(r)], *vt.* y *vi.* ratear, hurtar.

pilgrim [pílgrım], *s.* peregrino.- —**age** [-ıdž], *s.* peregrinación, romería.

pill [pıl], *s.* píldora; sinsabor, mal trago; (fam.) persona fastidiosa.

pillage [pílıdž], *s.* pillaje, saqueo.—*vt.* pillar, saquear.—*vi.* rapiñar.

pillar [pílä(r)], *s.* columna, pilar.—*from p. to post,* de la Ceca a la Meca.

pillbox [pílbaks], *s.* caja para píldoras; (mil.) fortín de ametralladoras.

pillory [pílorı], *s.* cepo, picota.—*vti.* [7] empicotar; exponer a la vergüenza pública.

pillow [pílou], *s.* almohada; almohadón; cojín.—*vt.* poner sobre una almohada.- —**case** [-keıs], *s.* funda de almohada.

pilot [páılot], *vt.* pilotear, timonear; dirigir, guiar.—*s.* piloto; práctico (de puerto); guía.

pimp [pımp], *s.* chulo, alcahuete.—*vi.* alcahuetear.

pimple [pímpl], *s.* grano, barro.

PIN [pın], *abrev.* (**Personal Identification Number**) número de identificación personal.

pin [pın], *s.* alfiler; prendedor, broche; (mec.) perno, pasador, espiga; bolo; (mar.) cabilla; (mus.) clavija.—*I don't care a p.,* no se me da un bledo, no me importa un pito.—*p. money,* (dinero para) alfileres.—*vti.* [1] prender con alfileres; fijar, clavar; enclavijar.—*to p. one's faith to* u *on,* confiar absolutamente en.—*to p. up,* asegurar o prender con alfileres o tachuelas.- —**ball** [-bol], *s.* billar romano, bagatela.

pincers [pínsœrz], *s. pl.* pinzas, tenacillas; alicates, tenazas.

pinch [pınch], *vt.* pellizcar; apretar con pinzas o tenazas; estrechar; escatimar; (fam.) prender, arrestar.—*vi.* pellizcar; apretar.—*my shoes p. me,* me aprietan los zapatos.—*s.* pe-

llizco; pizca; aprieto, apuro; dolor, punzada.—**pinch-hit** [pínch hít], *vii.* [9] batear por otro, batear de emergente; (fig.) servir en lugar de otro en caso de necesidad.—*pret.* y *pp.* DE TO PINCH-HIT.—**pinch-hitter** [pínch hítœ(r)], *s.* bateador emergente.

pincushion [pínkųšǫn], *s.* acerico.

pine [paın], *s.* pino y su madera.—*p. cone,* piña.—*p. grove,* pinar.—*p. kernel* o *nut,* piñón.—*p. needle,* pinocha.—*vi.* (con **away**), consumirse; (con **for**) anhelar.—**apple** [pájnæpl], *s.* piña, ananá(s).

ping [pıŋ], *s.* silbido de bala.—*p.-pong,* ping-pong, pin-pón.

pinhead [pínhɛd], *s.* cabecilla de alfiler; (fam.) bobalicón, cabeza de chorlito.

pining [pájnıŋ], *s.* languidez, nostalgia.

pinion [pínyon], *s.* (mec.) piñón; ala de ave.—*p. drive,* transmisión por engranajes.—*vt.* atar las alas; atar los brazos.

pink [pıŋk], *s.* estado perfecto; (pol.) comunistoide; (bot.) clavel, clavellina.—*a.* rosado, sonrosado; (pol.) de extrema izquierda, rojo.

pinking [pínkıŋ], *s.* (cost.) picadura.

pinnacle [pínakl], *s.* (arq.) pináculo, remate; cima, cumbre.

pinpoint [pínpoınt], *s.* punta de alfiler.—*vt.* y *vi.* señalar con precisión.—*a.* exacto, preciso.

pinprick [pínprık], *s.* alfilerazo.

pint [paınt], *s.* cuartillo, pinta (medida de líquidos). Ver Tabla.

pinto [píntou], *a.* pintado, pinto.—*s.* caballo o frijol pinto.

pinwheel [pínhwil], *s.* (fireworks) rueda de fuegos artificiales, girándula; (child's toy) molinete, molinillo.

pioneer [paıonír], *s.* pionero, colonizador; precursor.—*vt.* y *vi.* colonizar; promover.

pious [pájʌs], *a.* pío, piadoso, devoto.

pip [pıp], *s.* pepita; (on card or dice) punto; (radar signal) señal (silbido corto); (veterinary medicine) pepita; (fam.) joya, perla.

pipe [paıp], *s.* tubo, caño; tubería; cañería; pipa de fumar, cachimba; (mús.) cañón (de órgano); (mús.) caramillo, flauta.—*pl.* gaita; tubería.—*p. cleaner,* limpiapipas.—*p. dream,* esperanza imposible.—*p. line,* tubería, cañería; oleoducto;

fuente de informes confidenciales.—*p. organ,* órgano.—*p. wrench,* llave para tubos;—*vt.* conducir por medio de cañerías o tubos; instalar cañerías en.—*vi.* pitar; gritar.—*to p. down,* (fam.) callarse.- **—r** [pájpœ(r)], *s.* flautista; gaitero.—**piping** [pájpiŋ], *a.* agudo.—*p. hot,* en (o muy) caliente, hirviendo.—*s.* (fam.) llanto, gemido; cañería, tubería; (cost.) vivo, cordoncillo.

pippin [pípin], *s.* camuesa.

pipsqueak [pípskwik], *s.* (fam.) mequetrefe.

pique [pik], *s.* pique, resentimiento, rencilla.—*vt.* picar, irritar; excitar (interés, curiosidad, etc.).—*vi.* (aer.) picar, descender en picada.—*vr.* (gen. con **on** o **upon**) preciarse, jactarse; picarse, ofenderse.

piracy [pájṛ̣ạsi], *s.* piratería.—**pirate** [pájṛit], *s.* pirata.—*vt.* y *vi.* piratear.

Pisces [pájsiz], *s.* (astr.) Piscis.

pistil [pístil], *s.* pistilo.

pistol [pístọl], *s.* pistola; revólver.—*p. holster,* funda, cartuchera.

piston [pístọn], *s.* pistón, émbolo.—*p. ring,* aro de émbolo.—*p. rod,* vástago del émbolo.—*p. stroke,* carrera del émbolo.

pit [pit], *s.* hoyo; hoya; foso; abismo; hueso de ciertas frutas; (teat.) platea.

pitch [pich], *s.* grado de inclinación, pendiente, declive; paso (de tornillo, hélice, etc.); (mús.) tono; diapasón; (beisbol) lanzamiento, tiro; pez, betún, brea, alquitrán; resina.—*p. dark,* oscuro como boca de lobo.—*p. pine,* pino tea.—*p. pipe,* (mus.) diapasón.—*vt.* tirar, arrojar; (beisbol) lanzar la pelota al bateador; armar (tienda, etc.); embrear, embetunar; graduar el tono, dar el diapasón.—*to p. tents,* (mil.) acampar.—*vi.* caerse de cabeza; establecerse; cabecear (el buque).—*to p. in,* (fam.) poner manos a la obra.—*to p. into,* (fam.) arremeter a, embestir; sermonear.—*to p. (up)on,* escoger.- **—er** [píchœ(r)], *s.* jarro, cántaro; (beisbol) lanzador.— **fork** [-fɔrk], *s.* (agr.) horca, horquilla; tridente.

piteous [pítiʌs], *a.* lastimero, lastimoso.

pitfall [pítfɔl], *s.* trampa, hoyo cubierto; peligro latente.

pith [piθ], *s.* meollo, médula; tuétano; (fig.) fuerza, vigor; substancia, la parte esencial, el quid.

pitiful [pítiful], *a.* lastimoso, enterne-

cedor; pobre, despreciable. —**pitiless** [pítilis], *a.* despiadado, cruel.

pittance [pítans], *s.* pitanza, ración, porción.

pity [píti], *s.* piedad, lástima, compasión.—*for p.'s sake,* por piedad.—*it is a p.,* es lástima, es de sentirse.—*vti.* [7] compadecer.—*vii.* apiadarse, tener piedad o compadecerse de.

pivot [pívọt], *s.* espiga, pivote, muñón.—*p. chair,* silla giratoria.—*vt.* colocar sobre un eje, o por medio de un pivote.—*vi.* girar sobre un pivote.

pixie [píksi], *s.* duendecillo.

placard [plǽkard], *s.* cartel, letrero, rótulo.—*vt.* publicar por medio de carteles; fijar (cartel o aviso).

place [plejs], *s.* lugar, sitio; puesto; posición, empleo, colocación; grado; espacio, asiento; cubierto (en la mesa).—*in p. of,* en lugar de, en vez de.—*in that p.,* allí, allá.—*in the first p.,* en primer lugar.—*in the next p.,* luego, después.—*out of p.,* fuera de lugar; impropio, indebido.—*p. card,* tarjetita con el nombre.—*p. name,* nombre de lugar, topónimo.—*p. setting,* cubierto.—*to take p.,* tener lugar.- **—bo** [plasíbou], *s.* placebo.- **—ment** [-ment], *s.* colocación.—*vt.* colocar, poner, situar; dar colocación o empleo a; dar salida a.—*to p. across,* atravesar.—*to p. before,* anteponer.

placid [plǽsịd], *a.* plácido, apacible, sereno.

plagiarism [pléjdż(i)ạrizm], *s.* plagio. —**plagiarist** [pléjdż(i)ạrist], *a.* y *s.* plagiario. —**plagiarize** [pléjdż(i)ạrajz], *vt.* y *vi.* plagiar.

plague [plejg], *s.* plaga, peste; miseria, calamidad.—*vt.* importunar, fastidiar; infestar, plagar.

plaid [plæd], *s.* manta escocesa; género escocés.—*a.* a cuadros escoceses.

plain [plejn], *a.* llano, simple, sencillo; franco; corriente, ordinario; puro, sin mezcla; claro.—*in p. English,* sin rodeos, en plata.—*in p. sight,* en plena vista.—*p.-clothes man,* detective, policía secreta.—*p. speaking,* franqueza.—*p.-spoken,* claro, franco(te).—*p. truth,* pura verdad.— *adv.* llanamente; sencillamente; claramente.—*s.* llano, llanura, planicie; vega; (Am.) pampa, sabana.- **—sman** [pléjnzmæn], *s.* llanero.

plaintiff [pléjntjf], *s.* (for.) demandante.

plait [plejt], *s.* pliegue, doblez, alforza; trenza.—*vt.* plegar; tejer, trenzar.

plaintive [pléjntjv], *a.* dolorido, quejumbroso.

plan [plæn], *s.* plan, proyecto, programa; plano, dibujo.—*vti.* [1] idear, proyectar, planear, proponerse; pensar, resolver.—*vii.* hacer planes.

plane [plejn], *s.* superficie plana, plano; (carp.) cepillo, garlopa; aeroplano.—*a.* plano, llano.—*p. tree,* plátano falso.—*vt.* cepillar; desbastar; alisar.—*vi.* alisar, cepillar; (aer.) planear.

planet [plǽnjt], *s.* planeta.

plank [plæŋk], *s.* tablón, tabla gruesa; tablazón; (pol.) postulados en el programa de un partido.—*vt.* entablar, enmaderar; (min.) encofrar.- **—ing** [plǽŋkjŋ], *s.* tablaje, tablazón, forro; encofrado.

plant [plænt], *s.* planta, mata; fábrica.—*vt.* plantar, sembrar; instalar; fundar, establecer.- **—ation** [-éjşǫn], *s.* plantación; (Am.) ingenio; siembra, plantío; criadero de árboles.- **—er** [plǽntœ(r)], *s.* plantador, sembrador, cultivador.

plaque [plæk], *s.* placa.

plasma [plǽzmǎ], *s.* plasma; protoplasma.

plaster [plǽstœ(r)], *s.* yeso; argamasa, mezcla; parche, emplasto.—*mustard p.,* sinapismo.—*p. cast,* (med.) vendaje enyesado; (b.a.) yeso.—*p. of Paris,* estuco de París.—*vt.* enyesar, enlucir; (fig.) embarrar, emba- durnar; cubrir (paredes, etc.) con carteles o anuncios; poner emplastos, emplastar.- **—board** [-bɔrd], *s.* cartón de yeso y fieltro.- **—ing** [-iŋ], *s.* enyesado, enlucido; (med.) emplastadura.

plastic [plǽstjk], *s.* y *a.* plástico.—*p. surgery,* cirugía estética.

plate [plejt], *s.* plato; plancha, chapa, lámina; placa; (dent.) dentadura postiza.—*p. armor,* blindaje.—*p. glass,* vidrio o cristal cilindrado.—*vt.* platear, dorar, niquelar, platinar; unir con planchas de metal; blindar.

plateau [plætóu], *s.* meseta, mesa, altiplanicie, altiplano.

plateful [pléjtfʊl], *s.* un plato lleno; ración.

platform [plǽtfɔrm], *s.* plataforma, ta- blado; tarima; terraplén; andén; (pol.) plataforma electoral.

platinum [plǽtjnʌm], *s.* platino.—*p. blond,* rubia platino.

platitude [plǽtjtjud], *s.* perogrullada, trivialidad, lugar común.

Platonic [plǎtánjk], *a.* platónico; (p. o P.) platónico.

platoon [plǎtún], *s.* (mil.) pelotón.

platter [plǽtœ(r)], *s.* fuente, platón.

plausible [plɔ́zjbl], *a.* plausible, razonable; verosímil.

play [plej], *vt.* jugar (algún juego); practicar (un deporte); (teat.) representar; desempeñar (un papel); (mus.) ejecutar, tocar; manipular.— *p. off,* (dep.) partido de desempate.—*to p. a joke on,* hacer una burla a, dar una broma a.—*to p. one a (bad, dirty, mean) trick,* jugarle una mala pasada.—*to p. the fool,* hacerse el tonto, hacer el papel de bobo.—*to p. tricks,* hacer suertes; hacer travesuras.—*vi.* jugar, juguetear; entretenerse; burlarse, bromear; (mus.) tocar; (teat.) representar.—*s.* juego; jugada; (teat.) pieza.—*at p.,* jugando.—*in p.,* chanza, de burlas.—*p. actor,* actor cómico.—*p. upon words,* equívoco, juego de palabras.- **—back** [-bæk], *s.* lectura; aparato de lectura.- **—bill** [pléjbjl], *s.* cartel, programa.- **—boy** [-bɔj], *s.* joven rico y ocioso; calavera.- **—er** [-œ(r)], *s.* jugador; actor, actriz, cómico, comediante; (mus.) ejecutante, músico.—*piano p.,* pianista.—*p. piano,* autopiano.- **—ful** [-fʊl], *a.* jugetón, retozón, travieso.- **—goer** [-goʊœr], *s.* aficionado al teatro.- **—ground** [-graʊnd], *s.* campo o patio de recreo; campo de deportes.- **—house** [-haʊs], *s.* teatro; casita de muñecas.- **—ing** [iŋ],—*p. card,* naipe.—*p. field,* campo de deportes.- **—mate** [-mejt], *s.* compañero de juego.- **—pen** [-pɛn], *s.* corral, parque.- **—thing** [-θiŋ], *s.* juguete, niñería.- **—time** [-tajm], *s.* hora de recreo o juego.- **—wright** [-rajt], *s.* dramaturgo, autor dramático, comediógrafo.

plea [pli], *s.* ruego, súplica; disculpa, pretexto; (for.) alegato, defensa.— *p. bargaining,* (for.) un acuerdo con el fiscal para reducir los cargos.— **plead** [plid], *vti.* [4] defender (un pleito, una causa); alegar; aducir como razón, motivo o excusa.—*vii.*

suplicar, implorar; abogar (por).—
to p. guilty, confesarse culpable.—*to
p. not guilty,* declararse inocente.

pleasant [pléžạnt], *a.* grato, agradable,
ameno; simpático, afable.—*p. journey* o *trip!* ¡feliz viaje!—*p. weather,*
buen tiempo.- **—ry** [-rị], *s.* broma,
humorada, chanza. **—please** [pliz],
vt. agradar; complacer, dar gusto, satisfacer, complacer.—*to be pleased
to,* tener gusto en, o el gusto de; alegrarse de, complacerse en.—*to be
pleased with,* estar satisfecho o contento de o con.—*vi.* querer, servirse,
ser gustoso en, placerle a uno.—*if
you please,* por favor, si usted tiene la
bondad, si usted me hace el favor.—
to speak as one pleases, hablar como
a uno le da la gana. **—pleasing**
[plízịŋ], *a.* complaciente; agradable, ameno.—*to be p.,* gustar, dar
gusto; caer bien. **—pleasure** [plé-
žụ(r)], *s.* placer, gusto, deleite; complacencia.—*at one's (own) p.,* como
uno quiera, como le plazca.—*p.
seeker,* amigo de los placeres.—*with
p.,* con mucho gusto.

pleat [plit], *vt.* (cost.) plegar, hacer
pliegues, plisar.—*s.* pliegue.- **—ing**
[plítịŋ], *s.* (cost.) plegado, plisado.

plebeian [plịbíạn], *a.* y *s.* plebeyo.

plebiscite [plébịsạịt], *s.* plebiscito.

pledge [pledž], *s.* prenda, señal; empeño, fianza; rehén; promesa.—*vt.*
pignorar, empeñar, dar en prenda;
dar fianza; comprometerse a, dar
(la palabra).

plentiful [pléntịfụl], *a.* copioso, abundante; fértil, feraz. **—plenty** [plénti],
s. abundancia, profusión, afluencia.—*the Horn of P.,* el Cuerno de la
Abundancia.—*a.* (fam.) copioso,
abundante.

pleurisy [plúrịsị], *s.* pleuresía.

pliable [plájạbl], *a.* flexible; plegable;
dócil. **—pliancy** [plájạnsị], *s.* flexibilidad, docilidad, blandura.
—pliant [plájạnt], *a.* flexible, cimbreño; dócil, blando, tratable,
manual.

pliers [plájơrz], *s. pl.* alicates.

plight [plajt], *s.* apuro, aprieto; promesa (de matrimonio).—*vt.* empe-
ñar o dar (palabra).

plod [plad], *vii.* [1] avanzar con lentitud; afanarse, ajetrearse, trabajar
con ahinco.

plot [plat], *s.* solar, parcela; plano de
un terreno; conspiración, complot;
trama o argumento (de drama o

novela).—*vti.* [1] tramar, urdir,
fraguar; hacer el plano, la gráfica
o el diagrama.—*vii.* conspirar, maquinar.

plow [plaụ], *s.* arado.—*vt.* arar, labrar,
surcar; (mar. y fig.) surcar. **—man**
[pláụmạn], *s.* labrador; yuguero;
patán.- **—share** [-šẹr], *s.* reja de
arado.

pluck [plʌk], *vt.* arrancar; pelar; desplumar; (mus.) puntear, pulsar;
(fam.) robar, estafar, dejar sin un
cuarto, (fam.) arrancar.—*to p. up
courage,* cobrar ánimo; hacer de tripas corazón, sacar fuerzas de flaqueza.—*vi.* (at) tirar de, dar un tirón.—*s.* valor, ánimo, resolución;
arranque, tirón.- **—y** [plʌkị], *a.* animoso, resuelto.

plug [plʌg], *s.* tapón, tarugo, taco;
cuña, espita; (dent.) empaste o em-
pastadura; porción de tabaco comprimido; cala (frutas); cierre (de válvula); (elec.) enchufe, adaptador,
tomacorriente; conectador; tapón o
fusible; (aut.) bujía; (fam.) rocín,
penco.—*vti.* [1] ataruga, obturar;
(dent.) empastar, orificar; (elec.)
(in) enchufar, conectar; calar (me-
lones, etc.).

plum [plʌm], *s.* ciruela; golosina, gollería; lo mejor; la nata; puesto muy
ventajoso; dividendo jugoso.—*p.
pudding,* pudín inglés con pasas.—
p. tree, ciruelo.

plumage [plúmịdž], *s.* plumaje.

plumb [plʌm], *a.* vertical, a plomo.—*p.
bob,* plomada.—*p. level,* nivel de albañil.—*p. line,* cuerda de plomada.—*s.* plomada; sonda.—*off p.,
out of p.,* desviado de la vertical.—
adv. a plomo, verticalmente; (fam.)
completa o rematadamente.—*vt.*
sondear; aplomar; emplomar, sellar
con plomo; instalar cañerías. **—er**
[plʌmœ(r)], *s.* plomero.- **—ing**
[-ịŋ], *s.* plomería; instalación sani-
taria; conjunto de cañerías.—*p. fixtures,* artefactos sanitarios.

plume [plum], *s.* pluma; plumaje, penacho.—*vt.* adornar con plumas;
desplumar.

plummet [plʌmịt], *s.* plomo, plomada;
sonda.

plump [plʌmp], *a.* rollizo, regordete;
gordinflón.—*adv.* de golpe; a
plomo; directamente.—*vt.* soltar,
dejar caer; engordar, hinchar.—*vi.*
caer a plomo; hincharse, engordar,
llenarse.

plunder [plándœ(r)], *vt.* despojar, saquear, entrar a saco; expoliar.—*s.* pillaje, saqueo, rapiña; botín.

plunge [plʌndž], *vt.* zambullir, sumergir, chapuzar; hundir; precipitar; sumir.—*vi.* sumergirse, zambullirse; precipitarse, arrojarse, lanzarse.—*s.* sumersión, zambullida; salto, arrojo, embestida; tanque para bañarse.- **—r** [plándœ(r)], *s.* buzo; (mec.) émbolo; jugador o bolsista desenfrenado.

plunk [plʌŋk], *adv.* (fam.) con un golpe seco.—*vt.* (fam.) empujar o dejar caer pesadamente.—*vi.* sonar con un ruido de golpe seco.

plural [plúral], *a.* y *s.* plural.- **—ity** [plʊrǽliti], *s.* pluralidad; mayoría relativa (de votos); multitud.- **—ize** [plúralaiz], *vt.* pluralizar.

plus [plʌs], *prep.* más; además de, con, con la añadidura de.—*a.* (mat. y elec.) positivo; (fam.) y más, con algo de sobra; más otras cosas.—*to be, come out,* etc. *p.* (*something*), (fam.) salir ganando (algo). —*s.* signo más (+); cantidad positiva.

plush [plʌš], *s.* felpa; pana.—*a.* afelpado; (fam.) lujoso, suntuoso.—*a.* afelpado.

ply [plai], *vti.* [7] trabajar en con ahinco; ejercer, practicar; emplear, ocupar; manejar (la aguja, el remo); importunar, acosar (con preguntas, etc.); convidar a beber varias veces; atacar tenazmente; plegar.—*vi.* ir y venir regularmente; estar constantemente ocupado o funcionando; solicitar o aguardar compradores; (mar.) hacer la travesía.—*s.* pliegue, doblez; propensión; capa (de tejido, goma, etc.).- **—wood** [-wud], *s.* chapeado, madera laminada.

P.M. o **p.M.** *abrev.* (**post meridiem**) de la tarde, p.ej., *4 P.M.*, las cuatro de la tarde; de la noche, p.ej., *10 P.M.*, las diez de la noche.

pneumatic [njumǽtik], *a.* neumático.—*p. drill*, martillo neumático. **—pneumonia** [njumóuniə], *s.* pulmonía, neumonía.

poach [pouč], *vt.* escalfar; cazar o pescar en vedado; invadir.—*vi.* encenagarse; atollarse o meterse en un fangal.- **—er** [póučœ(r)], *s.* cazador furtivo.

pock [pak], *s.* pústula, postilla, viruela.—*p.-marked*, picado de viruelas.

pocket [pákit], *s.* bolsillo, faltriquera; cavidad, bolsón; bolsa; nasa; hoyo; hondonada, depresión; callejón sin salida; tronera.—*in p.*, con ganancia.—*out of p.*, con pérdida.—*p. calculator*, bolsicalculadora, calculadora de bolsillo.—*p. clip*, sujetador (de lápiz, etc.).—*p. money*, dinero para gastos personales.—*p. picking*, ratería de carterista.—*p. veto*, veto presidencial tácito.—*vt.* embolsar, meter en el bolsillo; tomar, apropiarse; tragarse (una injuria).- **—book** [-buk], *s.* portamonedas, bolsa; cartera, billetera; (fig.) dinero, recursos; libro que cabe en el bolsillo.- **—knife** [-naif], *s.* cortaplumas.

pod [pad], *s.* vaina (de frijol, etc.); capullo (de gusano de seda).—*vi.* llenarse, hincharse; criar vainas.

poem [póuim], *s.* poema, composición poética.—*pl.* versos, rimas. **—poet** [póuit], *s.* poeta. **—poetess** [póuitis], *s.* poetisa. **—poeti(cal)** [pouétik(al)], *a.* poético. **—poetics** [pouétiks], *s.* (arte) poética. **—poetry** [póuitri], *s.* poética; poesía.

pogrom [póugrom], *s.* (hist.) pogromo.

poignant [pɔ́in(y)ənt], *a.* acerbo, punzante; conmovedor, patético.

point [pɔint], *s.* punto; punta; fin, objeto; peculiaridad; grado (de una escala); momento crítico; instante.— *to be beside the p.*, no venir al caso.— *to get the p.*, caer en la cuenta, verle la gracia.—*to get to the p.*, venir o ir al grano.—*what's the p.?* ¿a qué viene eso? ¿de o para qué sirve?—*vt.* aguzar, afilar (lápiz, arma, etc.); (con **at**, **to** o **toward**) apuntar, señalar, indicar; encarar, dirigir, asestar.—*to p. out*, apuntar, señalar, mostrar.—*vi.* apuntar; propender, inclinarse a; dar, mirar hacia; (med.) madurarse (un absceso).- **—blank** [pɔ́intblǽŋk], *a.* horizontal; directo, claro, categórico.—*adv.* a quema ropa, a boca de jarro; sin ambages.- **—ed** [pɔ́intid], *a.* puntiagudo; en punta; picante, satírico; directo, acentuado, enfático.- **—er** [-œ(r)], *s.* indicador, índice; manecilla, aguja; fiel (de balanza); apuntador, puntero; buril; perro de caza; (fam.) indicación o consejo útil.- **—less** [-lis], *a.* inútil, vano; sin objeto.

poise [pɔiz], *s.* equilibrio; estabilidad; aplomo, serenidad; porte, talante.

—vt. equilibrar, estabilizar.—vi. quedar en equilibrio.

poison [pójzǝn], s. veneno, ponzoña.—p. ivy, tosiguero.—p.-pen letter, (fam.) carta anónima ofensiva.—vt. envenenar; (fig.) corromper, inficionar.- —er [-œ(r)], s. envenenador.- —ing [-iŋ], s. envenenamiento.- —ous [-ʌs], a. venenoso, ponzoñoso.

poke [pouk], s. empuje, empujón; persona indolente; saquito; vejiga de aire.—vt. picar, aguijonear; atizar, hurgonear; asomar, sacar (la cabeza, etc.).—to p. fun at, mofarse de.—to p. one's nose into, meter las narices en; entremeterse, curiosear.—vi. rezagarse; andar a tientas.- —r [póukœ(r)], s. atizador; entremetido; juego de naipes.

pok(e)y [póuki], a. (fam.) flojo, pesado, lento; apretado, ahogado (cuarto); desaliñado (vestido).—s. (fam.) chirona.

polar [póulǝ(r)], a. polar.—p. bear, oso blanco.—p. lights, aurora boreal o austral.

polarity [polǽriti], s. polaridad.

pole [poul], s. (geog. y elec.) polo; pértiga, palo largo, asta, estaca; poste; jalón; (P.) polaco.—p. vault, salto con garrocha.

police [polís], s. (cuerpo de) policía.— p. officer, agente de policía, vigilante.—p. state, estado-policía.—p. station, cuartel de policía, comisaría, jefatura de policía.—a. policíaco, policial.—vt. vigilar, mantener el orden (con la policía).- —man [-man], s. (agente de) policía, vigilante.

policy [pálisi], s. sagacidad; curso o plan de acción; política; regla, sistema, costumbre; póliza de seguro.—p. holder, asegurado, tenedor de póliza.

polio [póuliou], s. (med.) polio.

polish [páliš], vt. pulir, pulimentar; lustrar; educar; civilizar.—vi. recibir lustre o pulimento.—s. pulimento, tersura, lustre; urbanidad; cultura; betún o bola para zapatos; embolada, acción de lustrar (zapatos). —Polish [póuliš], a. polaco, polonés.—s. polaco (idioma).

polite [poláit], a. cortés, bien educado, atento.- —ness [-nis], s. cortesía, urbanidad, buena crianza, buena educación.—for p.'sake, por cortesía.

politic [pálitik], a. político; sagaz, astuto, hábil; apropiado, atinado.- —al [polítikal], a. político; (desp.) politiquero.- —ian [palitíšan], s. político, estadista; (desp.) politicastro, politiquero.- —s [pálitiks], s. política; asuntos, métodos o intereses políticos; (desp.) politiquería; maniobras de partido o facción.

poll [poul], s. lista electoral; votación; escrutinio; encuesta.—pl. lugar donde se vota; urnas electorales; elecciones.—p. tax, capitación, impuesto sobre el voto.—vt. dar o recibir votos; contar los votos, escrutar; someter a votación.—vi. votar en las elecciones.

pollen [pálen], s. polen.

pollute [polút], vt. contaminar; mancillar; profanar. —pollution [polúšon] s. contaminación, corrupción, mancilla, mancha; polución.

polo [póulou], s. (dep.) polo.—p. player, polista, jugador de polo.—water p., polo acuático.

Polynesian [palinížan], s. y a. polinesi(an)o.

pomade [poméjd], s. pomada.

pomegranate [pámgrænit], s. (bot.) granada.

pommel [pámel], s. pomo (de espada), perilla (de arzón).

pomp [pamp], s. pompa, fausto.- —osity [-ásiti], —ousness [pámpʌsnis], s. pomposidad, fausto, ostentación; afectación, altisonancia (de estilo).- —ous [-ʌs], a. pomposo, ostentoso.

poncho [pánchou], s. (Am.) poncho, manta.

pond [pand], s. charca, laguito, estanque; vivero (de peces).

ponder [pándœ(r)], vt. examinar, estudiar, pesar, (fig.) rumiar.—vi. (con on u over) considerar, deliberar, reflexionar (acerca de).- —ous [-ʌs] a. pesado; voluminoso; tedioso.

poniard [pányärd], s. puñal.

pontiff [pántif], s. pontífice. —pontifical [pantífikal], a. pontifical; papal.

pontoon [pantún], s. pontón; barcaza; (aer.) flotador.

pony [póuni], s. jaca; caballito; copa o vaso pequeño, o el licor que se sirve en ellos.

poodle [púdl], s. perro de lanas o de aguas.

pool [pul], vt. formar una puesta (en ciertos juegos); pagar a escote; mancomunar intereses.—vi. formar un charco; resbalarse.—*s.* charco; alberca; estanque; piscina; puesta; fusión de intereses o de empresas, piña; combinación para especular; (game) trucos.—*p. table,* mesa de trucos.— **—room** [-rum], *s.* sala de trucos.

oop [pup], *s.* (mar.) popa.—*to be pooped,* (fam.) estar hecho polvo.

oor [puɾ], *a.* pobre, necesitado, indigente; deficiente, falto, escaso; en mal estado; de poco mérito; malo, de mala calidad; estéril (tierra); enfermizo.—*s.* (con **the**) los pobres.— **—house** [púrhaụs], *s.* hospicio, asilo, casa de beneficencia.— **—ly** [-lị], *a.* (fam.) indispuesto, enfermizo.—*adv.* pobremente; malamente.—*p. off,* escaso de dinero.

op [pap], *s.* chasquido, ruido seco, detonación; pistoletazo; taponazo; bebida gaseosa; (fam.) papá; (fam.) concierto popular.—*vti.* [1] soltar, espetar, disparar; chasquear; hacer saltar un tapón.—*vii.* entrar o salir de sopetón; saltar un tapón; dar chasquidos o estallidos; detonar; reventar.—*to p. off,* (fam.) morir; dormirse.—*to p. up,* (fam.) aparecer de repente.—**corn** [pápkɔrn], *s.* maíz reventón; rosetas, flores o palomitas de maíz.

ope [poup], *s.* papa, sumo pontífice.

opiar [páplạ(r)], *s.* álamo.—*black p.,* chopo.—*p. grove,* alameda.

oplin [páplịn], *s.* popelina.

oppy [pápị], *s.* amapola.

opulace [pápyụlịs], *s.* pueblo, plebe; populacho, chusma.—**popular** [pápyụlạ(r)], *a.* popular, democrático; populachero; en boga, de moda. **—popularity** [papyụlǽrịtị], *s.* popularidad, prestigio, buena acogida general. **—popularization** [papyụlärịzéịṣọn], *s.* popularización, vulgarización. **—popularize** [pápyụláraịz], *vt.* popularizar, divulgar, hacer popular. **—populate** [pápyụleịt], *vt.* poblar. **—population** [papyụléịṣọn], *s.* población, vecindario. **—populous** [pápyụlʌs], *a.* populoso.

orcelain [pórselịn], *s.* porcelana.

orch [pɔrch], *s.* pórtico, porche.

orcupine [pórkyụpaịn], *s.* puerco espín.

ore [pɔr], *s.* poro.—*vi.* (con **on, upon, over**) escudriñar, estudiar escrupulosamente.

ork [pɔrk], *s.* carne de puerco.—*p. chop,* chuleta de cerdo.

porous [pórʌs], *a.* poroso.

porpoise [pórpʌs], *s.* delfín, marsopa.

porridge [párịdʒ], *s.* gachas de avena.

port [pɔrt], *s.* puerto; babor, lado izquierdo de una embarcación; porte, talante; oporto.—*p. of call,* escala.— *p. wine,* vino de Oporto.

portable [pórtạbl], *a.* portátil.

portal [pórtạl], *s.* portal.

portent [pórtent], *s.* presagio, augurio.— **—ous** [pɔrténtʌs], *a.* portentoso, prodigioso; de mal agüero, amenazante.

porter [pórtœ(r)], *s.* mozo de cuerda, maletero; camarero, mozo de servicio (trenes, hoteles, etc.); portero.

portfolio [pɔrtfóuḷịọu], *s.* cartera.

porthole [pórthoụl], *s.* portilla, porta.

portion [pórṣọn], *s.* porción, parte; cuota; dote.

portly [pórtlị], *a.* corpulento; majestuoso, grave.

portrait [pórtrịt], *s.* retrato.—*p. painter,* retratista.—*to sit for a p.,* posar para un retrato. **—portray** [pɔrtréị], *vt.* retratar, pintar. **—portrayal** [pɔrtréịạl], *s.* representación gráfica, dibujo, pintura; descripción.

Portuguese [pórchụgez], *a.* y *s.* portugués.—*s.* lengua portuguesa.

pose [poụz], *vt.* (b.a.) posar; proponer, afirmar; plantear (un problema); confundir con preguntas difíciles.—*vi.* colocarse en cierta postura; tomar posturas afectadas.—*to p. as,* hacerse pasar por; echárselas de.—*s.* postura, posición, actitud.

position [pọzíṣọn], *s.* posición; puesto, empleo; opinión.

positive [pázịtịv], *a.* positivo.

posse [pásị], *s.* fuerza civil armada.

possess [pozés], *vt.* poseer.— **—ion** [pozéṣọn], *s.* posesión.—*pl.* patrimonio, propiedades, bienes.— **—ive** [-ịv], *s.* y *a.* posesivo.—*a.* posesorio; posesional.— **—or** [-ọ(r)], *s.* poseedor, posesor.

possibility [pasịbílịtị], *s.* posibilidad. **—possible** [pásịbl], *a.* posible.—*as far as o as much as p.,* en lo posible.— *as soon as p.,* cuanto antes.

post [poụst], *s.* poste, pilar; (mil.) puesto, plaza, guarnición, avanzada; empleo, cargo; correo, estafeta, propio.—*p. card,* tarjeta postal.—*p.-free,* franco de porte.—*p. office,* correo, casa de correos, administración de correos, estafeta.—*p.-office box,* apartado de correos.—*vt.* pegar o fijar carteles; anunciar; poner en lista; apostar, situar; echar al correo; prohibir la entrada a (un terreno, etc.); estigmatizar; (com.) pasar los asientos al libro mayor; (fam.) informar, tener al corriente; poner al tanto de.—*p. no bills,* se prohibe fijar carteles.— **—age** [póus-tĭdž], *s.* franqueo, porte de correos.—*p. meter,* franqueadora.—*p. stamp,* sello de correo, estampilla, timbre.— **—al** [-ạl], *a.* postal.—*p. card,* tarjeta postal.—*p. permit,* franqueo concertado.— **—box** [-baks], *s.* buzón; apartado.— **—date** [-dẹịt], *s.* posfecha.—*vt.* posfechar.

poster [póustœ(r)], *s.* cartel, cartelón, letrero, rótulo.

posterior [pastírịọ(r)], *a.* posterior.— *pl.* nalgas. **—posterity** [pastérịtị], *s.* posterioridad.

posthumous [páschŭmŭs], *a.* póstumo.

postman [póustmạn], *s.* cartero. **—postmark** [póustmark], *s.* matasellos. **—postmaster** [póust-mæstœ(r)], *s.* administrador de correos.— **—mortem** [-mɔrtem], *s.* autopsia.

postpaid [póustpẹịd], *a.* con porte pagado, franco de porte.

postpone [poustpóun], *vt.* aplazar.— **—ment** [-mẹnt], *s.* aplazamiento.

postscript [póustskrịpt], *s.* posdata.

postulate [páschŭlẹjt], *vt.* postular.— *s.* [páschŭlịt], postulado.

posture [páschŭ(r)], *s.* postura.—*vi.* adoptar poses, asumir una pose.

postwar [póustwɔ́r], *a.* de la posguerra.

posy [póuzị], *s.* ramillete, flor.

pot [pat], *s.* marmita, olla; pote; cacharro; tiesto (para flores); orinal; cantidad contenida en una olla; crisol; (en el juego) puesta.—*p.-bellied,* panzudo, barrigón.—*to go to p.,* (fam.) arruinarse, desbaratarse, (fig.) irse a pique.

potash [pátæš], *s.* potasa. **—potassium** [potǽsịʌm], *s.* potasio.

potato [potéịtou], *s.* patata, papa.— *sweet p.,* batata, boniato.

potbellied [pátbelíd], *a.* barrigón, panzudo.

potency [póutẹnsị], *s.* potencia. **—potent** [póutẹnt], *a.* potente. **—potentate** [póutẹntẹjt], *s.* potentado. **—potential** [poténšạl], *a.* **—potentiality** [potenšịǽlịtị], *s.* potencialidad.

pothole [páthoʊl], *s.* bache.

potion [póușọn], *s.* poción.

potpourri [poupurí, patpúri], *s.* ba... turrillo, miscelánea, popurrí.

potter [pátœ(r)], *s.* alfarero.—*p.'s fiel...* cementerio de los pobres.—*p. wheel,* torno de alfarero.– **—y** [-i], alfarería; cacharros de alfarería.

pouch [pauch], *s.* bolsa, saquillo (anat. y zool.) bolsa, saco.

poultice [póultịs], *s.* cataplasma.

poultry [póultrị], *s.* aves de corral.— *yard,* corral, gallinero.

pounce [pauns], *s.* zarpada; salto zarpa, garra.—*vi.—to p. on,* salta... sobre.

pound [paund], *s.* libra. Ver Tabla; go... pazo.—*p. sterling,* libra esterlina.- *vt.* golpear; machacar, majar, ap... rrear; poner a buen recaudo.—... golpear; batir con violencia (el cor... zón); andar pesadamente; avanza... continua o enérgicamente.

pour [pɔr], *vt.* derramar; verter, vacia... trasegar; escanciar; gastar pródig... mente.—*vi.* fluir, caer copiosa o r... pidamente; llover a cántaros; salir borbotones.

pout [paut], *s.* pucherito; berrinche.- *vi.* hacer pucheros; enfurruñars... poner mal gesto.

poverty [pávœrtị], *s.* pobreza.

powder [páudœ(r)], *s.* pólvora; polv... polvos.—*p. keg,* barril de pólvor... (fig.) polvorín.—*p. magazine,* po... vorín, santabárbara.—*p. puff,* bor... para empolvarse.—*p. room,* cuart... tocador, cuarto aseo.—*vt.* pulve... zar; empolvar; polvorear; espolv... rear.—*vi.* pulverizarse; ponerse po... vos.— **—y** [-i], *a.* polvoriento; e... polvado; deleznable, quebradizo.

power [páụœ(r)], *s.* fuerza, poder, p... derío; potencia (nación); (mat... mec.) potencia.—*vt.* accionar, im... pulsar.—*p. brake,* servofreno.—... *dive,* picado con motor.—*p.-dive,* ... car con motor a toda marcha.—... *drill,* taladro eléctrico; perforado... mecánica.—*p. lawnmower,* motos... gadora.—*p. line,* (elec.) sector ... distribución.—*p. mower,* motoseg... dora.—*p. of attorney,* (for.) poder.— *p. pack,* (elec.) transformador port... til.—*p. plant,* (elec.) central elé... trica, estación generadora; (ae... grupo motopropulsor; (aut.) grup... motor.—*p. shovel,* pala mecánic... excavadora.—*p. station = pow... plant.—*p. steering,* (aut.) servodire...

ción.—*p. tool,* herramienta motriz.—*the powers that be,* las autoridades, los que mandan.—*p. plant,* planta de fuerza motriz.- **—ful** [-fuł], *a.* poderoso, potente, fuerte; influyente.- **—house** [-haus], *s.* central eléctrica; (fig.) motor, motriz, fuente, puntal; (fig.) persona de mucha energía.- **—less** [-lis], *a.* impotente; ineficaz.

owwow [paúwau], *s.* (fig.) conferencia, consejo.

ox [paks], *s.* cualquier enfermedad que causa erupciones pustulosas.—*chicken p.,* varicela.—*small p.,* viruela.

racticable [præktikabl], *a.* practicable, factible, viable; accesible, transitable. **—practical** [præktikał], *a.* práctico; de hecho, real; positivo, prosaico.—*p. joke,* broma pesada.—*p. politics,* política de realidades; politiquería. **—practice** [præktis], *s.* práctica, uso, costumbre; ejercicio; experiencia; sistema, regla, método; clientela.—*in p.,* en la práctica.—*vt.* y *vi.* practicar, ensayar(se), adiestrar(se), ejercitar(se); ejercer (una profesión).

ractitioner [præktíʃøncer], *s.* (med.) práctico.

airie [préri], *s.* llanura, pradera, pampa, sabana.—*p. dog,* ardilla ladradora.—*p. wolf,* coyote.

aise [preiz], *s.* alabanza, loa, elogio; fama, renombre.—*vt.* alabar, encomiar, ensalzar.- **—worthy** [préizwcerði], *a.* laudable, plausible.

ance [præns], *vi.* cabriolar, corvetear.—*s.* cabriola, corveta.

ank [prænk], *s.* travesura; jugarreta.—*to play pranks,* hacer diabluras.- **—ish** [prænkiʃ], *a.* travieso.

ate [preit], *vi.* charlar, parlotear.—*s.* charla. **—prattle** [prætl], *vi.* parlotear, (fam.) chacharear; balbucear; murmurar (un arroyo).—*s.* parloteo, (fam.) cháchara.

awn [prɔn], *s.* camarón.

ay [prei], *vt.* rogar, suplicar; implorar.—*vi.* rezar, orar; (for) hacer votos por.—*p. tell me,* sírvase decirme.- **—er** [prer], *s.* oración, rezo, plegaria; súplica, ruego.—*the Lord's P.,* el Padrenuestro.—*p. beads,* rosario.—*p. book,* devocionario.—*p. desk,* reclinatorio.

each [prich], *vt.* y *vi.* predicar; sermonear.- **—er** [príchœ(r)], *s.* predi-

cador.- **—ing** [-iŋ], *s.* predicación; sermón.

preamble [príæmbl], *s.* preámbulo.

prearrange [priaréindʒ], *vt.* arreglar de antemano, predisponer, prevenir.

precarious [prikériʌs], *a.* precario.

precaution [prikóʃøn], *s.* precaución.

precede [prisíd], *vt.* y *vi.* preceder.- **—nce** [prisídens, présedens], *s.* precedencia.- **—nt** [présedent], *s.* precedente.—*a.* precedente.

precept [prísept], *s.* precepto.

precinct [prísiŋkt], *s.* distrito electoral, barriada.—*police p.,* comisaría.

precious [préʃʌs], *a.* precioso; preciado; de gran valor; caro, querido.—*adv.* (fam.) muy.

precipice [présipis], *s.* precipicio, despeñadero. **—precipitate** [prisípiteit], *vt.* precipitar.—*vi.* precipitarse.—[prisípitat], *a.* precipitado. **—precipitation** [prisipitéiʃøn], *s.* precipitación. **—precipitous** [prisípitʌs], *a.* escarpado; (hurried) precipitoso.

precise [prisáis], *a.* preciso; meticuloso. **—precision** [prisíʒøn], *s.* precisión.

predatory [prédatɔri], *a.* predatorio.

predecessor [prédisesɔ(r)], *s.* predecesor, antecesor; antepasado.

predetermine [priditcérmin], *vt.* predeterminar, prefijar.

predicament [pridíkament], *s.* apuro, situación difícil. **—predicate** [prédikeit], *vt.* proclamar; predicar; basar o fundar en algo; afirmar un predicado.—*vi.* afirmarse.—*s.* [prédikit], (gram. y log.) predicado, atributo.

predict [pridíkt], *vt.* predecir.- **—ion** [pridíkʃøn], *s.* predicción, pronóstico, profecía.

predilection [predilékʃøn], *s.* predilección.

predispose [pridispóuz], *vt.* predisponer, prevenir. **—predisposition** [pridispozíʃøn], *s.* predisposición.

predominance [pridáminʌns], *s.* predominio; ascendiente, influencia. **—predominant** [pridáminant], *a.* predominante. **—predominate** [pridámineit], *vi.* predominar, prevalecer.

prefabricate [prifæbrikeit], *vt.* prefabricar.- **—d** [-id], *a.* prefabricado.

preface [préfis], *s.* prefacio, advertencia.—*vt.* introducir, empezar.

prefer [prifcér], *vti.* [1] preferir; exaltar;

presentar, ofrecer; dar preferencia.—*to p. a charge,* presentar una denuncia.—*to p. a claim,* presentar una demanda.- **—able** [préfrabl], *a.* preferible, preferente.- **—ence** [préfrens], *s.* preferencia, predilección.

prefix [prífiks], *vt.* prefijar, anteponer.—*s.* [prífiks], prefijo.

pregnancy [prégnansi], *s.* preñez, embarazo. **—pregnant** [prégnant], *a.* preñada, embarazada; (fig.) elocuente, cargado.—*p. with,* repleto, lleno de.

prejudge [pridźÁdź], *vt.* prejuzgar.

prejudice [prédźudis], *s.* prejuicio; perjuicio (detrimento).—*without p.,* (jur.) sin detrimento de sus propios derechos.—*vt.* predisponer, prevenir; perjudicar.

prelate [prélit], *s.* prelado.

preliminary [prilímineri], *a.* preliminar; preparatorio.—*s.* preliminar.—*pl.* exámenes preliminares; pruebas eliminatorias.

prelude [préljud], *s.* preludio.—*vt.* preludiar.

premature [primachúr], *a.* prematuro.—*p. baby,* niño sietemesino.

premeditate [priméditeit], *vt.* y *vi.* premeditar. **—premeditation** [primeditéiśon], *s.* premeditación.

premier [prímice(r)], *s.* primer ministro, jefe de gobierno.—*a.* primero, principal.

premiere [primír], *s.* estreno.

premise [prémis], *s.* premisa.—*on the premises,* en el local mismo.

premium [prímiʌm], *s.* premio; (com.) prima.—*at a p.,* muy escaso, de gran valor.

premonition [primoníśon], *s.* advertencia; presentimiento, corazonada.

preoccupation [priakyūpéiśon], *s.* preocupación.

prepaid [pripéjd], *a.* con porte pagado; pagado por adelantado.—*pret.* y *pp.* de TO PREPAY.

preparation [prepəréiśon], *s.* preparación; preparativo; (farm.) preparado. **—preparatory** [pripǽratɔri], *a.* preparatorio; previo, preliminar. **—prepare** [pripér], *vt.* preparar, apercibir; disponer, prevenir; aderezar, adobar, confeccionar.—*vi.* prepararse, disponerse, hacer preparativos. **—preparedness** [pripéridnis], *s.* preparación, prevención, apercibimiento.

prepay [pripéj], *vti.* [10] pagar por adelantado; franquear (una carta).

preponderance [pripándərans], *s.* preponderancia. **—preponderate** [pripándereit], *vi.* preponderar.

preposition [prepozíśon], *s.* preposición.

prepossessing [pripozésiŋ], *a.* simpático, atractivo.

preposterous [pripástərʌs], *a.* absurdo, ridículo, descabellado.

prep school [prep], *s.* escuela preparatorio.

prerequisite [prirékwizit], *a.* previamente necesario.—*s.* requisito previo.

prerogative [prirágətiv], *s.* prerrogativa.

presage [présidź], *s.* presagio.—*vt.* presagiar.

prescribe [priskrájb], *vt.* y *vi.* prescribir. **—prescription** [priskrípśon], *s.* prescripción; (farm.) receta.

presence [prézens], *s.* presencia.—*p. of mind,* presencia de ánimo, aplomo, serenidad. **—present** [prézent], *a.* presente; actual, corriente (mes, semana, etc.).—*at the p. time,* hoy (por hoy), en la actualidad.—*p. company excepted,* mejorando lo presente.—*p.-day,* actual, (del día) de hoy.—*p. participle,* participio activo o de presente, gerundio.—*to be p.* (at), asistir (a); presenciar; concurrir.—*s.* presente; (gram.) tiempo presente; regalo, obsequio, presente.—*at p.,* al presente, actualmente, (por) ahora.—*for the p.,* por ahora, por el (o lo) presente.—*vt.* [prizént], presentar, introducir, dar a conocer; dar, regalar, obsequiar. **—presentation** [prezentéiśon], *s.* presentación.

presentiment [prizéntiment], *s.* presentimiento.

presently [prézentli], *adv.* luego, ya, dentro de poco.

preservation [prezœrvéiśon], *s.* preservación, conservación. **—preservative** [prizœrvativ], *a.* preservativo.—*s.* preservativo, salvaguardia. **—preserve** [prizœrv], *vt.* preservar; proteger; reservar; conservar, mantener; salar, curar; confitar, almibarar.—*vi.* hacer conservas de fruta.—*s.* (gen. *pl.*) conserva, dulce, compota, confitura; vedado, coto. **—preserved** [prizœrvd], *a.* conservado, en conserva.

preside [prizáid], *vi.* and *vt.* presidir.—*to p. at* o *over a meeting*, presidir una reunión o asamblea. **—presidency** [prézidênsi], *s.* presidencia. **—president** [prézidênt], *s.* presidente. **—presidential** [prezidénŝal], *a.* presidencial.

press [pres], *vt.* prensar; comprimir; exprimir; pisar (el acelerador, la uva, el pedal, etc.); oprimir (el botón); planchar (ropa); abrumar, oprimir, presionar, obligar, apremiar; acosar; hostigar; abrazar, dar un apretón.—*pressed for money*, apurado de dinero.—*vi.* pesar, ejercer presión; urgir, apremiar; apiñarse; ser importuno; influir en el ánimo.—*to p. forward* or *on*, avanzar, adelantarse; arremeter, embestir.—*s.* muchedumbre; apiñamiento; empuje, apretón; prisa, presión, urgencia; cúmulo de negocios; (mec.) prensa; imprenta; prensa (periódica); escaparate, armario; (mil.) leva, enganche.—*p. agent*, agente de publicidad.—*p. box*, tribuna de la prensa.—*p. clipping*, recorte de periódico.—*p. conference*, conferencia de prensa.—*p. release*, comunicado de prensa.—**—ing** [présin], *a.* urgente, apremiante.—*s.* planchado.—**ure** [préŝu(r)], *s.* presión; urgencia; apretón; opresión; fuerza electromotriz.

prestige [prestíž], *s.* prestigio, fama.

prestidigitator [prestidídžiteito(r)], *s.* prestidigitador.

presumable [prizjúmabl], *a.* presumible. **—presume** [prizjúm], *vt.* presumir, suponer; (con **to**) atreverse a.—*vi.* jactarse, presumir; obrar presuntuosamente; (con **on** o **upon**) abusar de. **—presumption** [prizámpŝon], *s.* presunción; pretensión. **—presumptuous** [prizámpchuas], *a.* impertinente, confianzudo, desenvuelto.

presuppose [prisapóuz], *vt.* presuponer. **—presupposition** [prisapozíŝon], *s.* conjetura, presunción.

pretend [priténd], *vt.* aparentar, fingir, simular; alegar o afirmar falsamente.—*vi.* fingir; presumir, alardear.—*to p. to*, pretender, reclamar, aspirar a.—*to p. to be*, echárselas de, darse por, hacerse el.—**er** [-œ(r)], *s.* pretendiente (a la corona o trono); el que finge. **—pretense** [priténs, prítens], *s.* fingimiento; pretexto, excusa; máscara, capa, velo; pretensión; ostentación; afectación, simulación.—*under false pretenses*, con falsas apariencias, con dolo.—*under p. of*, so pretexto de, a título de. **—pretentious** [priténŝas], *a.* presuntuoso, presumido, de o con pretensiones.

preterit(e) [préterit], *a.* y *s.* pretérito.

pretext [prítekst], *s.* pretexto, excusa.

prettily [prítili], *adv.* lindamente, bonitamente. **—prettiness** [prítinis], *s.* lindeza, galanura. **—pretty** [príti], *a.* lindo, bonito, (fam.) mono; bello, bueno, grande.—*a p. mess you made*, buena la hizo usted.—*a p. penny*, (fam.) una buena suma.—*adv.* algo; un poco, bastante.—*p. good*, bastante bueno.—*p. much*, bastante casi.—*p. well*, medianamente, así así.

prevail [privéil], *vi.* prevalecer, preponderar; ser muy frecuente; estar en boga; (con **over** o **against**) vencer a, triunfar de; sobresalir, predominar.—*to p. on, upon* o *with*, persuadir, inducir, convencer. **—prevalence** [prévalens], *s.* predominio, preponderancia; frecuencia. **—prevalent** [prévalent], *a.* corriente, común.

prevent [privént], *vt.* impedir.—*vi.* obstar.—**ion** [privénŝon], *s.* prevención; medidas de precaución.—**ive** [privéntiv], *a.* y *s.* preservativo.

previous [prívias], *a.* previo, anterior.

prey [prei], *s.* presa; víctima.—*vi.* (con **on** o **upon**) devorar (la presa); rapiñar, robar.

price [prais], *s.* precio.—*p. control*, intervención de precios.—*p. cutting*, reducción de precios.—*p. fixing*, fijación de precios.—*p. war*, guerra de precios.—*vt.* apreciar, estimar; fijar el precio de, poner precio a.—**less** [práislis], *a.* inapreciable; sin precio; (fam.) absurdo, divertido.

prick [prik], *vt.* punzar, picar, pinchar; marcar, indicar o calcar con agujerillos; causar una punzada (dolor punzante); puntear (marcar con puntos).—*to p. up one's ears*, aguzar, erguir o enderezar las orejas.—*vi.* sentir una punzada (dolor punzante); erguirse o estar erguido; picarse (el vino).—*s.* aguijón; espiche; púa; pinchazo; agujerillo.—**le** [príkl], *s.* pincho, púa, espina.—*vt.*

y *vi.* producir o sentir picazón.– **—ly** [príklị], *a.* lleno de púas o puntas, espinoso.—*p. heat,* salpullido.—*p. pear,* higo chumbo; (Am.) tuna.

pride [praịd], *s.* orgullo; arrogancia.—*the p. of,* la flor y nata de.—*to take p. in,* ufanarse o preciarse de.—*vr.*—*to p. oneself on* o *upon,* enorgullecerse de.– **—ful** [práịdfụl], *a.* orgulloso, arrogante, vanidoso.

priest [prist], *s.* sacerdote.– **—hood** [prísthụd], *s.* sacerdocio.

prig [prịg], *s.* pedante, gazmoño.– **—gish** [prígịŝ], *a.* pedantesco; gazmoño.

prim [prịm], *a.* relamido, estirado.

primacy [práịmạsị], *s.* primacía; supremacía; precedencia. **—primal** [práịmạl], *a.* primordial; principal.

primarily [práịmɛrịlị], *adv.* primariamente, en primer lugar. **—primary** [práịmɛrị], *a.* primario, elección preliminar; (elec.) primario.

prime [praịm], *s.* flor; albor, principio; alba, aurora, amanecer; la flor y nata, lo mejor; (igl.) (Hora) prima; número primo; (esgr.) primera; (impr.) virgulilla, signo (′).—*p. of life,* edad viril, flor de edad.—*a.* primero, principal; primoroso, de primera clase; selecto; original, prístino; (mat.) primo; (impr.) marcado con el signo (′).—*p. minister,* primer ministro.—*vt.* informar, instruir previamente; cebar (un carburador, arma, etc.); dar la primera capa de pintura; poner el signo (′).

primer [prịmœ(r)], *s.* cartilla.—[praịmœr], *s.* aprestador; (mec.) cebador.

primitive [prịmịtịv], *a.* primitivo. (biol.) rudimentario.—*s.* y *a.* (b.a.) primitivo (artista u obra).

primp [prịmp], *vt.* y *vi.* vestir(se) con afectación; acicalar(se); portarse afectadamente.

primrose [prịmrouz], *s.* (bot.) primavera; color amarillo claro.—*a.* florido, gayo.—*p. path,* vida sensual.

prince [prịns], *s.* príncipe.—*p. of the royal blood,* infante.—*P. of Wales,* príncipe de Gales.– **—ly** [prịnslị], *a.* principesco, regio.—*adv.* principescamente.– **—ss** [prịnsịs], *s.* princesa.

principal [prịnsịpạl], *a.* principal.—*s.* principal, jefe; director o rector (de escuela o colegio primarios o secundarios); (for.) causante, constituyente; (com.) capital o principa (puesto a interés); (arq.) jamba d fuerza. **—principle** [prịnsịpl], *s.* prin cipio, origen; fundamento, motivo razón; principio (regla, ley); (quim principio activo.

print [prịnt], *vt.* estampar, imprimir; t rar, hacer una tirada; publicar; escr bir imitando letra de molde.—*s.* im presión, estampa; tipo o letra d molde; impreso, folleto, volant periódico, etc.; grabado; estam pado; molde; (fot.) tiraje.—*pl.* es tampados.—*in p.,* impreso, publ cado; en letra de molde.—*out p.,* (edición) agotada.—*printed ma ter,* impresos.– **—er** [prịntœ(r)], impresor, tipógrafo; (comput.) im presora.—*p.'s devil,* aprendiz de im prenta.– —*p.'s ink,* tinta de im prenta. **—ing** [-ịŋ], *s.* imprenta, t pografía impresión; tirada; im preso; estampado.—*p. pres* prensa, imprenta.—*a.* de imprent de imprimir.– **—out** [-aụt], *s.* (com put.) salida impresa, listado.

prior [práịọ(r)], *a.* anterior, prec dente.—*p. to,* antes de.—*s.* prior **—ity** [praịárịtị], *s.* prioridad.

prism [prízm], *s.* prisma.

prison [prízọn], *s.* prisión, cárcel.—*p. van,* coche celular.– **—er** [-œ(r)], prisionero, preso.

pristine [prístin], *a.* prístino.

privacy [práịvạsị], *s.* retiro, aisl miento, retraimiento; independen cia de la vida privada; el derecho esa independencia; reserva, secret **—private** [práịvịt], *a.* privado; part cular; personal, confidencial.— soldado raso.—*pl.* partes pudenda **—privation** [praịvéịŝọn], *s.* priv ción; carencia.

privilege [prívịlịdẑ], *s.* privilegio.—*v* privilegiar; (from) eximir.– **—d** [-d *a.* privilegiado, exento.

privy [prívị], *a.* (con **to**) informado, e terado (en); particular, propio, pe sonal; (ant.) privado, secreto, exc sado.—*s.* (ant.) retrete, letrina.

prize [praịz], *s.* premio, galardó presa, botín.—*p. fight,* partido boxeo profesional.—*p. fighter,* b xeador profesional.—*vt.* aprecia estimar; valuar, tasar.

pro [proụ], *adv.* en favor; por.—*s.* vo afirmativo; (dep. fam.) profesi nal.—*p. and con,* en pro y en contr

probability [prabạbílịtị], *s.* probabi

dad. **—probable** [prábəbl], *a.* probable.

probation [probéjʃən], *s.* libertad vigilada; período de prueba.**—on p.**, a prueba.

probe [proub], *s.* (cir.) sonda, cánula; prueba, ensayo; indagación.**—vt.** (cir.) sondear, explorar; indagar.

probity [próubiti], *s.* probidad.

problem [práblem], *s.* problema.**—atic(al)** [prablemǽtik(əl)], *a.* problemático.

procedure [prosídžu(r)], *s.* procedimiento. **—proceed** [prosíd], *vi.* proceder. **—proceeding** [prosídiŋ], *s.* procedimiento.—*pl.* actas; diligencias. **—proceeds** [próusidz], *s.* producto, ganancia.

process [práses], *s.* procedimiento; proceso, progreso.**—p. server**, entregador de la citation. elaborar.

procession [proséʃən], *s.* procesión; desfile; cortejo.

prochoice [prouchɔ́is], *a.* permitiendo el aborto con el derecho de decidir.

proclaim [prokléjm], *vt.* proclamar. **—proclamation** [praklaméjʃən], *s.* proclamación, proclama.

proclivity [proklíviti], *s.* propensión, inclinación, proclividad.

procrastinate [prokrǽstineit], *vt. y vi.* diferir de un día para otro.—*vi.* dejar las cosas para más tarde.

procreate [próukrieit], *vt. y vi.* procrear.

procure [prokjúr], *vt.* procurar, obtener, conseguir.—*vt. y vi.* alcahuetear.**—r** [-œ(r)], *s.* alcahuete.**—ss** [-is], *s.* alcahueta.

prod [prad], *vti.* [1] punzar, picar, aguijonear.—*s.* aguijada; empuje.

prodigal [prádigəl], *a. y s.* pródigo.**—ity** [pradigǽliti], *s.* prodigalidad.

prodigious [prodídžʌs], *a.* prodigioso; enorme, inmenso. **—prodigy** [prádidžj], *s.* prodigio.

produce [prodjús], *vt.* producir; presentar; (com.) rendir, rentar; (teat.) montar o poner en escena una obra; (geom.) prolongar.—*vi.* producir; fructificar.—*s.* [prádjus], producto, fruto; productos agrícolas, provisiones.**—r** [prodjúsœ(r)], *s.* productor; (teat.) empresario; generador, gasógeno. **—product** [prádʌkt], *s.* producto. **—production** [prodákʃən], *s.* producción; (teat.) representación. **—productive** [prodáktiv], *a.* productivo.

profane [proféjn], *a.* profano; blasfemo, irreverente.—*vt.* profanar. **—profanity** [profǽniti], *s.* blasfemia.

profess [profés], *vt. y vi.* profesar.**—ion** [proféʃən], *s.* profesión. **—ional** [proféʃənal], *a.* profesional; perito, experto; de profesión.—*s.* profesional; deportista de profesión.**—or** [-ɔ(r)], *s.* catedrático; profesor universitario; (fam.) maestro.**—orship** [-ɔrʃip], *s.* profesorado, cátedra.

proffer [práfœ(r)], *vt.* proponer, ofrecer.—*s.* oferta, propuesta.

proficiency [profíʃensi], *s.* competencia. **—proficient** [profíʃent], *a.* experto, perito, diestro, hábil.

profile [próufail], *s.* perfil.**—in p.**, de perfil.—*vt.* perfilar.

profit [práfit], *s.* provecho, beneficio, ganancia, utilidad.**—at a p.**, con ganancia.—*to make a p.* o *to show a p.*, ganar dinero.—*vt.* ser de utilidad a, servir.—*vi.* sacar utilidad o provecho, ganar.—*to p. by*, sacar partido de, beneficiarse de.**—able** [-əbl], *a.* provechoso.**—eer** [prafitír], *vi.* explotar, lograr.—*s.* explotador, logrero.

pro forma [proufórma], *a.* meramente formal.

profound [profáund], *a.* profundo.**—ness** [-nis], **profundity** [profánditi], *s.* profundidad.

profuse [profjús], *a.* profuso; pródigo. **—ness** [-nis], **profusion** [profjúžən], *s.* profusión, abundancia; prodigalidad.

progeny [prádženi], *s.* progenie, prole.

program [próugræm], *s.* programa.—*vt.* programar.

programer o **programmer** [próugræmœr], *s.* (comput. y electron.) programador. **—programing** o **programming** [prougræmiŋ], (comput. y rad./tel.) programación.

progress [prágres], *s.* progreso; progresos. **—ive** [progrésiv], *a.* progresivo; progresista.—*s.* progresista.

prohibit [prouhíbit], *vt.* prohibir.**—ion** [prou(h)jbíʃən], *s.* prohibición. **—ive** [prouhíbjtiv], *a.* prohibitivo.

project [prodžékt], *vt.* proyectar.—*s.* [prádžekt], proyecto.—*vi.* proyectarse. **—ile** [prodžéktil], *s.* proyectil. **—ion** [prodžékʃən], *s.* proyección. **—or** [prodžéktɔ(r)], *s.* proyector.

proletarian [prouletérian], *a. y s.* proletario. **—proletariat** [prouletériat], s. proletariado.

prolific [prolífik], a. prolífico.

prologue [próulag], s. prólogo.—vt. prologar.

prolong [prolón], vt. prolongar.- **—ation** [prolɔŋgéiʃon], s. prolongación.

promenade [pramenád], vi. pasear (se).—s. paseo; baile de gala.—p. deck, (mar.) cubierta de paseo.

prominence [prámɪnens], s. prominencia; importancia. **—prominent** [prámɪnent], a. prominente.

promiscuous [promískyuʌs], a. promiscuo.

promise [prámɪs], s. promesa.—vt. y vi. prometer. **—promising** [prámɪsɪŋ], a. que promete, prometedor, halagüeño. **—promissory** [prámɪsɔri], a. promisorio.—p. note, pagaré, vale.

promontory [prámontɔri], s. (geog.) promontorio.

promote [promóut], vt. promover; fomentar.- **—r** [-œ(r)], s. promotor; empresario. **—promotion** [promóuʃon], s. promoción; fomento.

prompt [prampt], a. pronto, listo, expedito; puntual.—vt. impulsar, mover, incitar; (teat.) apuntar.- **—er** [prámptœ(r)], s. (teat.) apuntador.—p.'s box, (teat.) concha.- **—ness** [-nɪs], s. prontitud; puntualidad.

prone [proun], a. postrado boca abajo; dispuesto, propenso.

prong [praŋ], s. punta (de tenedor, horquilla, etc.).

pronoun [próunaun], s. pronombre.

pronounce [pronáuns], vt. pronunciar. **- —d** [-t], a. pronunciado, marcado, fuerte, subido.- **—ment** [-ment], s. declaración; decisión, opinión. **—pronunciation** [pronʌnsiéiʃon], s. pronunciación.

proof [pruf], s. prueba.—to be p. against, ser o estar a prueba de.—to put to the p., poner a prueba.—a. de prueba.—p. against, a prueba de.— p. sheet, prueba de imprenta.- **—read** [prúfrid], vti. y vii. [9] leer y corregir pruebas.—[prúfred], pret. y pp. de TO PROOFREAD. **—reader** [-ridœ(r)], s. corrector de pruebas.- **—reading** [-ridiŋ], s. corrección de pruebas.

prop [prap], vti. [1] apuntalar, apoyar.—s. apoyo, puntal.—pl. (teat.) accesorios.

propaganda [prapagǽndä], s. propaganda. **—propagandist** [prapagǽndɪst], s. y a. propagandista. **—propagate** [prápageit], vt. propagar.—vi propagarse. **—propagation** [prapagéiʃon], s. propagación.

propel [propél], vti. [1] propulsar, impeler, empujar.- **—ler** [-lœr], s. hélice.

proper [prápœ(r)], a. propio, conveniente; decoroso; justo, exacto;- **—ty** [-ti], s. propiedad.—personal p., bienes muebles.—pl. (teat.) accesorios.

prophecy [práfesi], s. profecía. **—prophesy** [práfesai], vti. y vii. [7] profetizar. **—prophet** [práfit], s. profeta **—prophetic(al)** [profétik(al)], a. profético.

prophylactic [proufilǽktik], a. y s. profiláctico.

propitiate [propíʃieit], vt. propiciar **—propitious** [propíʃʌs], a. propicio.

proportion [propórʃon], s. proporción.—pl. tamaño, dimensiones.— in p. as, a medida que.—out of p. desproporcionado.—vt. proporcionar.- **—al** [-al], a. proporcional.

proposal [propóuzal], s. propuesta oferta de matrimonio. **—propose** [propóuz], vt. proponer.—vi. proponer matrimonio. **—proposition** [prapozíʃon], s. proposición, propuesta.

propound [propáund], vt. proponer.

proprietor [propráietɔ(r)], s. propietario. **—propriety** [propráieti], s. propiedad, corrección; decoro, decencia.—pl. normas o cánones (de arte, sociales, etc.).

propulsion [propʌ́lʃon], s. propulsión.

prorate [prouréit], vt. prorratear.

prosaic [prozéiik], a. prosaico.

proscribe [proskráib], vt. proscribir.

prose [prouz], s. prosa.—a. prosaico.

prosecute [prásikiut], vt. llevar a cabo (for.) procesar. **—prosecution** [prasikiúʃon], s. prosecución. **—prosecutor** [prásikiutɔ(r)], s. (for.) acusador demandante; fiscal.—prosecuting attorney, acusador público, fiscal.

prosody [prásodi], s. prosodia; métrica.

prospect [práspekt], vt. y vi. (min. prospectar.—to p. for, buscar.—s perspectiva, panorama; probabilidad de éxito; expectativa; situación orientación; (min.) indicación o señal de veta; (com.) cliente, compra dor probable.– **—ive** [prospéktiv], *a*. anticipado, venidero, en perspectiva; presunto.– **—or** [práspekto(r)], *s*. explorador o buscador de minas, petróleo, etc.– **—us** [prospéktʌs], *s*. prospecto, programa.

prosper [práspœ(r)], *vi*. prosperar.– **—ity** [praspériti], *s*. prosperidad.– **—ous** [-ʌs], *a*. próspero.

prostitute [prástitiut], *vt*. y *vi*. prostituir(se).—*s*. prostituta. **—prostitution** [prastitiúshon], *s*. prostitución.

prostrate [prástreit], *a*. postrado, prosternado.—*vt*. postrar (med.) postrar, debilitar.—*to p. oneself*, postrarse.—*s*. (anat.) próstata. **—prostration** [prastréjshon], *s*. postración.

protagonist [protǽgonist], *s*. protagonista.

protect [protékt], *vt*. proteger.– **—ion** [protékshon], *s*. protección.– **—ive** [-iv], *a*. protector; (e.p.) proteccionista.– **—or** [-o(r)], *s*. protector.– **—orate** [-orit], *s*. protectorado.

protégé [próutǽžei], *s*. protegido.

protein [próuti(i)n], *s*. proteína.

pro-tempore [proutémporē], *a*. interino.

protest [protést], *vt*. y *vi*. protestar.—*s*. [próutest], protesta.– **—ant** [prátistant], *a*. y *s*. (P.) (igl.) protestante.– **—antism** [prátistantizm], *s*. (P.) protestantismo.– **—ation** [pratestéjshon], *s*. protesta(ción); declaración.

protocol [próutokal], *s*. protocolo, registro.

protoplasm [próutoplæzm], *s*. protoplasma.

prototype [próutotaip], *s*. prototipo.

protract [protrǽkt], *vt*. prolongar.

protrude [protrúd],—*vi*. resaltar.

protuberance [protiúberans], *s*. protuberancia.

proud [praud], *a*. orgulloso; soberbio; glorioso.—*p. flesh*, carnosidad, bezo.—*to be p. of*, enorgullecerse de, ufanarse de.

prove [pruv], *vti*. [6] probar.—*vii*. resultar.—*to p. to be*, venir a ser, resultar.

proverb [právœrb], *s*. proverbio.

provide [prováid], *vt*. proporcionar, suministrar.—*vi*.—*to p. for*, proveer a; asegurarse (el porvenir).—*provided (that)*, con tal que, a condición de que, siempre que.

providence [právidens], *s*. providen-

cia. **—providential** [pravidénshal], *a*. providencial.

provider [prováidœ(r)], *s*. proveedor, abastecedor. **—providing** [prováidiŋ], *conj*. con tal que.

providing = provided

province [právins], *s*. provincia, región; competencia. **—provincial** [provínshal], *a*. provincial.—*s*. provinciano.

provision [provížon], *s*. provisión, condición, estipulación.—*pl*. provisiones, comestibles.– **—al** [-al], *a*. provisional, interino.

proviso [prováiso], *s*. condición, estipulación, salvedad.

provocation [pravokéjshon], *s*. provocación; excitación, estímulo. **—provocative** [provákativ], *a*. provocativo.– **—provoke** [provóuk], *vt*. provocar. **—provoking** [provóukiŋ], *a*. provocador, irritante.

prow [prau], *s*. proa.

prowess [práuis], *s*. proeza; destreza.

prowl [praul], *vt*. y *vi*. rondar (para robar o vigilar); merodear; andar acechando; vagar.—*s*. ronda, merodeo.—*on the p.*, buscando algo.—*p. car*, coche patrulla.– **—er** [práulœ(r)], *s*. merodeador, rondador.

proximity [praksímiti], *s*. proximidad, inmediación.

proxy [práksi], *s*. poder, poderhabiente.

prude [prud], *s*. mojigato, gazmoño.

prudence [prúdens], *s*. prudencia. **—prudent** [prúdent], *a*. prudente.

prudery [prúdœri], *s*. mojigatería, gazmoñería. **—prudish** [prúdiš], *a*. gazmoño, mojigato.

prune [prun], *vt*. y *vi*. podar, escamondar.—*s*. ciruela pasa.

Prussian [práshan], *a*. y *s*. prusiano.

pry [prai],—*vti*. [7]—*to p. into*, fisgar, fiscalizar, curiosear, entremeterse. —*to p. off*, despegar.—*to p. open*, forzar con la alzaprima o palanca.—*to p. out of*, arrancar (un secreto) a (una persona).—*vi*. entremeterse.– **—ing** [práiiŋ], *a*. fisgón, entremetido.—*s*. fisgoneo, curioseo.

psalm [sam], *s*. salmo, himno.

Psalter [sóltœr], Salterio.

pseudo [súdou], *a*. falso, supuesto, fingido.– **—nym** [súdonim], *s*. seudónimo.

psych [saik], *vt*. (fam.)—*to p. out*, poner nervioso.—*to p. oneself*, mentalizarse.

psyche [sájki], s. psique; mente. —**psychiatric(al)** [saikiǽtrik(al)], a. psiquiátrico. —**psychiatrist** [saikájatrist], s. psiquiatra. —**psychiatry** [saikájatri], s. psiquiatría. —**psychoanalysis** [saikoanǽlisis], s. psicoanálisis. —**psychoanalyst** [saikoǽnalist], s. psicoanalista. —**psychoanalyze** [saikoǽnalaiz], vt. psicoanalizar. —**psychologic(al)** [saikoládʒik(al)], a. psicológico. —**psychologist** [saikálodʒist], s. psicólogo. —**psychology** [saikálodʒi], s. psicología. —**psychopath** [sáikopæθ], s. psicópata. —**psychosis** [saikóusis], s. psicosis. —**psychotherapy** [saikoθérapi], s. psicoterapia. —**psychotic** [saikátik], s. y a. psicótico, psicopático.

puberty [piúbœrti], s. pubertad.
public [páblik], a. y s., público.—p. library, biblioteca municipal.—p. school, (E.U.) escuela pública; (G.B.) internado privado con dote.—p. speaking, elocución, oratorio.—p. toilet, quiosco de necesidad.—p. utility, empresa de servicio público.— —**ation** [-éjʃon], s. publicación.— —**ist** [páblisist], s. publicista.— —**ity** [pablísiti], s. publicidad. —**publicize** [páblisaiz], vt. publicar. —**publish** [pábliʃ], vt. publicar. —**publisher** [pábliʃœ(r)], s. editor. —**publishing** [pábliʃiŋ], a. editorial, de publicaciones.—p. house, casa editorial.— p. house, casa editora, editorial.

puck [pak], s. duende travieso; disco de goma (en el hockey sobre hielo).
pucker [pákœ(r)], vt. (cost.) fruncir, plegar, recoger, arrugar.—vi. arrugarse.—s. (cost.) fruncido, pliegue, fuelle, arruga; (fam.) agitación.
pudding [púdiŋ], s. budín, pudín.—p. dish o pan, flanera, tortera.
puddle [pádl], s. charco, poza.
pudgy [pádʒi], a. (fam.) regordete, gordinflón.
puerile [piúéril], a. pueril.
Puerto Rican [pwérto ríkan], a. y s. puertorriqueño.
puff [paf], s. resoplido; soplo, bufido; bocanada, fumada; elogio exagerado; (cost.) bullón; especie de buñuelo.—powder p., polvera, borla de polvos.—p. adder, víbora venenosa.—p. box, polvera, caja de polvos.—p. of wind, ráfaga, soplo, racha; ventolera.—vt. inflar; engreír; dar bombo; (cost.) abollonar; dar chupadas (pipa, tabaco, etc.).—vi.

inflarse; engreírse; bufar; resoplar; jadear, hipar; echar bocanadas; fumar.—to p. up, hincharse, henchirse.— —**y** [páfi], a. hinchado, inflado.

pug [pag], s. moño (del pelo); (alb.) torta.—p. nose, nariz respingada.
pugilist [piúdʒilist], s. pugilista.
pugnacious [pagnéiʃʌs], a. belicoso, peleador, discutidor. —**pugnacity** [pagnǽsiti], s. pugnacidad.
puke [piuk], vt. y vi. vomitar.
pull [pul], vt. tirar de, halar; estirar; sacar, arrancar (un diente, etc.); pelar, desplumar; bogar, remar; (fam.) sorprender, copar (un garito, etc.); prender (a uno); sacar (un arma).— to p. a face, hacer una mueca.—to p. asunder o away, arrancar o quitar con violencia.—to p. back, tirar hacia atrás; hacer recular o cejar.—to p. down, derribar, demoler; degradar; humillar, abatir.—to p. in, tirar hacia dentro; contener, refrenar.—to p. in o to pieces, hacer trizas, despedazar.—to p. one's leg, (fam.) tomarle el pelo a uno.—to p. oneself together, recobrar la calma; arreglarse, componerse.—to p. out, sacar, arrancar.—to p. the trigger, apretar el gatillo.—to p. through, sacar de dificultades o de un aprieto.—to p. together, llevarse bien; obrar de acuerdo.—to p. up, extirpar, desarraigar; contener, refrenar (un caballo); arrimar (una silla); subir (las persianas).—vi. tirar con esfuerzo; tironear, dar un tirón; ejercer tracción.—to p. apart, romperse por tracción.—to p. for, abogar por (una persona).—to p. in, llegar (un tren); contenerse, refrenarse.—to p. through, salir de un apuro.—s. tirón, estirón; tirador (de puerta, etc.); tracción; (fam.) influjo, influencia; (impr.) impresión con la prensa de mano; (dep.) ejercicio de remos, boga.— —**er** [púlœ(r)], s. el o lo que tira, saca o arranca; extractor.
pullet [púlit], s. polla.
pulley [púli], s. polea.
pullover [púlouvœ(r)], s. jersey, suéter.
pulmonary [pálmonɛri], a. pulmonar.
pulp [palp], s. pulpa; (to make paper) pasta; (of tooth) bulbo.
pulpit [púlpit], s. púlpito.
pulsate [pálseit], vi. pulsar; vibrar. —**pulsation** [palséiʃʌn], s. pulsación, latido.—**pulse** [pals], s. pulso; pulsación; (bot.) legumbres colecti-

vamente.—to feel o take the pulse of, tomar el pulso a.

pulverize [pálveʒraįz], vt. pulverizar.

pumice stone [pámįs], s. piedra pómez.

pummel [pámĕl], vt. apuñear, aporrear.

pump [pʌmp], s. bomba (de agua, aire, etc.); zapatilla, escarpín.—p. water, agua de pozo.—vt. y vi. dar a la bomba, (Am.) bombear.—to p. in, inyectar (aire, etc.).—to p. out, achicar, sacar a bomba.—to p. up, inflar (un neumático, etc.).

pumpkin [pámpkįn, páŋkįn], s. calabaza común.

pun [pʌn], s. equívoco, retruécano, juego de vocablos.—vii. [1] decir retruécanos o equívocos, jugar del vocablo.

punch [pʌnch], vt. punzar, taladrar, horadar con punzón; dar un puñetazo a.—s. punzón, sacabocado(s), máquina o aparato de taladrar; ponche (bebida); puñetazo; (fam.) energía, actividad.—p. bowl, ponchera.—p. card, tarjeta perforada. —p. clock, reloj registrador de tarjetas.—p.-drunk, atonado; completamente aturdido.—p. line, broche de oro, colofón del artículo; remate (de un chiste).- —ing [-įŋ], s.—p. bag, punching, boxibalón.

punctual [páŋkchu̧al], a. puntual, exacto. —**punctuality** [pʌŋkchu̧-æliti], s. puntualidad.

punctuate [páŋkchu̧ejt], vt. y vi. puntuar. —**punctuation** [pʌŋkchu̧éjšǫn], s. (gram.) puntuación.

puncture [páŋkchu̧(r)], s. pinchazo, perforación; puntura, punzadura, picad(ur)a.—vt. pinchar, perforar, picar.

pungency [pándžęnsį], s. picante; mordacidad. —**pungent** [pándžęnt], a. picante; estimulante.

punish [pánįš], vt. castigar.- —**ment** [-męnt], s. castigo; (fam.) maltrato.

punk [pʌnk], a. (jer.) malo, de mala calidad.—s. yesca, pebete; (jer.) pillo, gamberro.

puny [pjúnį], a. encanijado; diminuto; mezquino.

pup [pʌp], s. cachorro, perrillo.—p. tent, (fam.) tienda de campaña.

pupil [pjúpįl], s. (anat.) pupila; alumno.

puppet [pápįt], s. títere; muñeco; maniquí.—p. show, función de títeres.

puppy [pápį], s. cachorro, perrillo.—p. love, primeros amores.

purchase [pǿrchįs], vt. comprar; adquirir.—s. compra; agarre firme. —r [-œ(r)], s. comprador, marchante.

pure [pįur], a. puro.

purgative [pǿrgatįv], a. y s. purgante. —**purgatory** [pǿrgatɔrį], s. purgatorio. —**purge** [pœrdž], vt. purgar.—s. (med.) purgante; purgación; depuración.

purification [pįurįfįkéjšǫn], s. purificación. —**purify** [pįúrįfaį], vti. [7] purificar. —**Puritan** [pįúrįtan], s. y a. puritano. —**puritanical** [pįurįtǽnį-kạl], a. puritano, riguroso, rígido, severo. —**purity** [pįúrįtį], s. pureza.

purple [pǿrpl], a. purpurado, rojo morado.—m. púrpura, rojo morado.

purport [pǿrpɔrt], s. significado; tenor, sustancia.—vt. y vi. [pœrpórt], significar, querer decir.

purpose [pǿrpǫs], s. propósito, fin, objeto, intención.—on p., de propósito, aposta.—to no p., inútilmente.—vt. y vi. proponer(se), intentar.- —**ful** [-ful], a. determinado, tenaz. —**ly** [-lį], adv. adrede, de propósito.

purr [pœr], s. ronroneo.—vi. ronronear.

purse [pœrs], s. bolsa, bolso de bolsillo; portamonedas; talega, bolsa de dinero; colecta; (prize money) premio.—p. snatcher, carterista.—p. strings, cordones de la bolso.—to hold the p. strings, tener las llaves de la caja.- —r [pǿrsœ(r)], s. contador de navío, comisario de a bordo.

pursue [pœrsįú], vt. y vi. perseguir, dar caza, acosar; (pro)seguir, continuar; seguir (una carrera), dedicarse a, ejercer; (for.) demandar, poner pleito, procesar.- —r [-œ(r)], s. perseguidor. —**pursuit** [pœrsįút], s. perseguimiento, persecución, caza; práctica, ejercicio; prosecución; busca; ocupación; pretensión; empeño.—pl. ocupaciones, estudios, investigaciones, actividades.

purvey [pœrvéj], vt. proveer, suministrar.- —**or** [-ǫ(r)], s. proveedor, abastecedor.

pus [pʌs], s. pus.

push [pųš], vt. empujar; propugnar, promover, activar; oprimir, pulsar; apremiar, obligar; importunar, molestar.—to p. ahead o through, pujar.—to p. in, encajar, hacer entrar.—to p. off, apartar con la mano; desalojar.—to p. on, incitar, aguijonear; apresurar.—to p. out, empujar hacia afuera; echar, expulsar.—*vi.* empujar, dar un empujón, dar empellones; apresurarse; acometer.— *to p. forward,* adelantarse dando empujones; adelantar, avanzar.—*to p. further,* seguir adelante.—*to p. in,* entremeterse.—*to p. off,* (mar.) desatracar.—*s.* impulso; empuje, empujón; arremetida; apuro, aprieto; (fam.) energía, iniciativa; (mil.) ofensiva.—*p. button,* botón de llamada, botón interruptor.- **—cart** [púškart], *s.* carretilla de mano.- **—er** [-æ(r)], *s.* persona emprendedora o agresiva.- **—ing** [-iŋ], *a.* activo, emprendedor; agresivo, entremetido.- **—over** [-oúvœr], *s.* bollo, incauto.—*to be a pushover,* ser pan comido.

pussy(cat) [púsị(kæt)], *s.* gatito, minino.—*p. willow,* sauce norteamericano de amentos muy sedosos.

put [pụt], *vti.* poner; disponer, colocar; proponer, presentar; expresar, declarar; (dep.) lanzar (el peso).—*to p. across,* (fam.) realizar, llevar a cabo.—*to p. after,* poner detrás de (sitio); posponer a (tiempo).—*to p. a question,* hacer una pregunta.—*to p. back,* atrasar, retardar; devolver, reponer.—*to p. by,* guardar; arrinconar; desviar, apartar.—*to p. down,* poner (en el suelo, etc.); sofocar, reprimir; deprimir, abatir; depositar; anotar, apuntar; rebajar, disminuir; hacer callar.—*to p. forward,* adelantar; proponer como candidato.—*to p. in,* poner en, echar en o a, meter; poner, insertar, introducir, intercalar; presentar, hacer (reclamo, etc.); colocar (en un empleo, etc.); interponer (palabra, observación); (top., dib.) trazar (una curva, etc.); pasar o gastar (tiempo, haciendo algo).—*to p. in a word for,* interceder por, hablar en favor de.—*to p. in gear,* (aut.) hacer engranar.—*to p. in print,* imprimir.—*to p. off,* diferir, dilatar, aplazar; desechar, apartar; evadir, entretener (con promesas); quitarse, desprenderse de (ropa,

etc.).—*to p. on,* poner sobre; ponerse (ropa, etc.); calzar (zapatos, etc.); echar, poner, dar, aplicar (vapor, el freno, etc.); instigar a; fingir, disimular; encender (las luces, el radio, etc.); (teat.) producir, representar, poner en escena.—*to p. out,* brotar, echar retoños; despedir, despachar, echar; apagar (la luz, el fuego); publicar; cegar; borrar, tachar; cortar, desconcertar; sacar de quicio; poner (dinero a interés), dar (a logro); extender, sacar, mostrar; enojar, irritar.—*to p. out of order,* descomponer, desordenar.—*to p. to flight,* poner en fuga, ahuyentar.— *to p. together,* juntar, acumular; (mec.) armar, montar; coordinar.— *to p. to it,* causar dificultad.a, poner al parir.—*to p. to shame,* avergonzar.—*to p. up,* poner en su lugar, conservar; preparar, confeccionar; construir, erigir; (mec.) montar; presentar (como candidato); ofrecer, elevar; levantar (la mano); alojar, hospedar; envainar; ofrecer resistencia; (fam.) poner dinero en una apuesta; tramar, urdir.—*to p. up to,* incitar, instigar a; presentar o someter a; (fam.) dar instrucciones.— *to p. up with,* aguantar, soportar.— *vi.* (mar.) dirigirse, seguir rumbo. —*pret.* y *pp.* de TO PUT.—*s.* accion del verbo TO PUT en cualquiera de sus acepciones.

putter [pátœr], *s.* (dep.) putter.—*vi.* trabajar sin orden ni sistema.—*to p. around,* ocuparse en fruslerías.

putty [pátị], *s.* masilla.—*p. knife,* espátula.—*vti.* [7] enmasillar.

puzzle [pázl], *s.* acertijo, rompecabezas; enigma, misterio, (fam.) problema arduo.—*vt.* confundir, poner perplejo; enmarañar, embrollar.— *to p. out,* descifrar.—*vi.* estar perplejo.—*to p. over,* tratar de descifrar.

pygmy [pígmị], *s.* pigmeo.

pyramid [píramịd], *s.* pirámide.—*vt.* y *vi.* aumentar(se), acumular(se).

python [paíθon], *s.* pitón.

Q

quack [kwæk], *vi.* graznar.—*s.* graznido del pato.—*s. y a.* charlatán.—*s.* curandero; medicucho, medicastro.— **—ery** [kwǽkœri], *s.* charlatanismo; fraude.

quadrant [kwádrant], *s.* cuadrante.

quadroon [kwadrún], *s.* cuarterón.

quadruped [kwádruped], *s. y a.* cuadrúpedo.

quadruple [kwádrupl], *a.* cuádruple, cuádruplo.—*vt. y vi.* cuadruplicar(se).— **—ts** [kwádruplits], *s. pl.* gemelos cuádruples.

quagmire [kwǽgmair], *s.* tremedal, cenagal; atolladero.

quail [kweil], *s.* codorniz.—*vi.* acobardarse.

quaint [kweint], *a.* singular, curioso; pintoresco; original, raro.— **—ness** [kwéintnis], *s.* rareza, singularidad, pintorequismo.

quake [kweik], *s.* temblor, terremoto.—*vi.* temblar.

Quaker [kwéikœr], *a. y s.* cuáquero.

qualification [kwalifikéişon], *s.* calificación, requisito; c(u)alidad, capacidad, idoneidad; título, habilitación; atenuación, mitigación; limitación; salvedad.—*without q.,* sin reservas o reparos. **—qualify** [kwalifai], *vti.* [7] capacitar, habilitar; calificar; modificar, limitar, restringir.—*vii.* habilitarse, llenar los requisititularse; (dep.) clasificarse.— **—ing** [-iŋ], *a.* (dep.) eliminatorio. **—qualitative** [kwálițeițiv], *a.* cualitativo. **—quality** [kwaliți], *s.* c(u)alidad; clase, casta, jaez; propiedad, poder o virtud; categoría, distinción, alta posición social.

quantitative [kwántițeițiv], *a.* cuantitativo. **—quantity** [kwántiți], *s.* cantidad.

quantum [kwántŭm], *a.* cuántico.—*s.* cuanto, quántum.

quarantine [kwárantin], *s.* cuarentena; estación de cuarentena.—*vt.* poder en cuarentena.

quarrel [kwárel], *s.* riña, disputa.—*vii.* [2] pelear, reñir, disputar.— **—some** [-sʌm], *a.* pendenciero.

quarry [kwari], *s.* cantera, pedrera; caza, presa.—*vti.* [7] sacar de una cantera; extraer, sacar.

quart [kwɔrt], *s.* cuarto de galón (Ver Tabla); (mus.) cuarta.- **—er** [kwɔ́rtœ(r)], *s.* cuarto, cuarta parte; arroba (Ver Tabla); trimestre; cuarto de hora; moneda de 25 centavos; cuarto de luna, etc.; origen, procedencia; región, comarca, distrito; barrio, barriada, vecindad; (carp.) entrepaño; cuartel, merced, clemencia.—*pl.* domicilio, vivienda, morada; (mil.) cuartel; alojamiento.—*a.* cuarto.—*vt.* descuartizar, hacer cuartos; dividir en cuatro partes iguales o en cuarteles; (mil.) acuartelar, acantonar; alojar, hospedar.- **—erly** [-œrli], *a.* trimestral. —*q. payment,* trimestre.—*s.* publicación trimestral.—*adv.* trimestralmente; en cuartos, por cuartos.- **—ermaster** [-œrmæstœ(r)], *s.* (mil.) comisario; furriel.—*q. general,* intendente del ejército.- **—et(te)** [kwɔrtét], *s.* cuatro personas o cosas de una misma clase; (mus., poét.) cuarteto.

quartet [kwɔrtét], *s.* cuarteto.

quartz [kwɔrts], *s.* cuarzo, sílice.

quasar [kwéişar], *s.* (astr.) objeto del espacio, fuente cuasiestelar de radio.

quash [kwaş], *vi.* solocar, reprimir; anular, invalidar.

quatrain [kwátrein], *s.* cuarteta, redondilla.

quaver [kwéivœ(r)], *vi.* estremecerse, temblar.—*s.* temblor, estremecimiento; trémolo, vibración.

quay [ki], *s.* muelle; (des)embarcadero.

Quechuan [kéchwan], *s. y a.* quechua.

queen [kwin], *s.* reina.

queer [kwir], *a.* extraño, raro; indispuesto, desfalleciente; (fam.) chiflado, excéntrico, estrafalario; (fam.) sospechoso, misterioso; (fam.) falso; (despec.) afeminado.—*s.* (fam.) moneda falsa.—*vt.* (jer.) comprometer; (jer.) echar a perder.

quell [kwel], *vt.* reprimir, sofocar; mitigar.

quench [kwench], *vt.* apagar; sofocar, reprimir; (electron.) amortiguar.

query [kwíri], *s.* pregunta; duda; (imp.) signo interrogante (?).—*vti.* [7] marcar con signo de interrogación;

preguntar, indagar, pesquisar.—*vii.* expresar una duda; preguntar.

quest [kwest], *s.* búsqueda, demanda.—*in q. of,* en busca de.

question [kwéschọn], *s.* pregunta; cuestión; asunto, proposición.— *beside the q.,* ajeno al asunto.—*beyond* o *without q.,* fuera de duda, indiscutible.—*out of q.,* sin duda, de veras.—*q.-begging,* de carácter o círculo vicioso.—*q. mark,* signo de interrogación.—*to ask a q.,* hacer una pregunta.—*to be out of the q.,* ser indiscutible; no haber que pensar en.—*to put the q.,* interrogar; torturar; someter a votación.—*vt.* interrogar; cuestionar.—*vi.* inquirir, preguntar, escudriñar.- **—able** [-ạbl], *a.* cuestionable. **—naire** [kwɛschọnér], *s.* cuestionario.

queue [kyụ], *s.* cola.—*vi.* hacer cola.

quibble [kwíbĕl], *vi.* sutilizar.

quick [kwịk], *a.* rápido, veloz, ágil; vivo; despierto, listo.—*s.* carne viva;—*the q. and the dead,* los vivos y los muertos.—*to cut* (*hurt, offend, etc.*) *to the q.,* herir en lo vivo, en el alma o profundamente.—*adv.* con presteza, prontamente, velozmente.—*q.-sighted,* de vista aguda, penetrante.—*q.-tempered,* de genio vivo, irascible.—*q.-witted,* vivo de ingenio, listo, agudo, perspicaz.- **—en** [kwíkn], *vt.* acelerar, avivar; animar.—*vi.* acelerarse, animarse. **—lime** [-lạim], *s.* cal viva.— **—ly** [-lị], *adv.* rápidamente, pronto.- **—ness** [-nịs], *s.* presteza, vivacidad, prontitud, celeridad; sagacidad, viveza, penetración. **—sand** [-sænd], *s.* arena movediza.- **—silver** [-sịlvœ(r)], *s.* azogue, mercurio.

quiet [kwáịẹt], *a.* quieto; silencioso; (com.) encalmado.—*to be q.,* callarse; guardar silencio.—*s.* quietud; silencio.—*on the q.,* a las calladas.— *vt.* acallar; aquietar.—*vi.* aquietarse; callarse.—*to q. down,* calmarse.-

—ness [-nịs], *s.* sosiego, tranquilidad.

quill [kwịl], *s.* pluma de ave; cañón de pluma; (zool.) púa.

quilt [kwịlt], *s.* colcha, edredón.—*vt.* acolchar.

quince [kwịns], *s.* membrillo.

quinine [kwáịnạin], *s.* quinina.

quintessence [kwịntésẹns], *s.* quintaesencia.

quintuple [kwíntịupl], *a.* y *s.* quíntuplo.—*vt.* y *vi.* quintuplicarse.- **—ts** [kwịntịúplẹts], *spl.* gemelos quíntuplos, quintillizos.

quip [kwịp], *s.* pulla, chufleta.—*vt.* decir en son de burla.—*vii.* [1] echar pullas.

quirk [kwʌrk], *s.* excentricidad, rareza; sutileza; vuelta repentina.

quit [kwịt], *vti.* [3] dejar.—*vii.* irse; (fam.) dejar de trabajar.—*pret.* y *pp.* de TO QUIT.—*a.* libre, descargado.— *to be quits,* estar en paz; quedar vengado; no deberse nada.—*to call it quits,* dar (algo) por terminado.

quite [kwạit], *adv.* enteramente; verdaderamente; (fam.) bastante, muy.—*q. a bit,* considerable, bastante.

quitter [kwịtœ(r)], *s.* remolón; desertor (de una causa, etc.).

quiver [kwívœ(r)], *s.* carcaj, aljaba; temblor.—*vi.* temblar.

quixotic [kwịksátịk], *a.* quijotesco.

quiz [kwịz], *s.* examen; interrogatorio.—*q. game,* torneo de preguntas y respuestas.—*q. program,* programa de preguntas y respuestas.- **—ical** [-ịkạl], *a.* curioso; socarrón, burlón.—*vti.* [1] examinar; interrogar.

quota [kwóụtạ̈], *s.* cuota.

quotation [kwoụtéịʃọn], *s.* cita; (com.) cotización.—*q. marks,* comillas. **—quote** [kwoụt], *vt.* y *vi.* citar; (com.) cotizar.—*s.* (fam.) cita.—*pl.* (fam.) comillas.

quotient [kwóụʃẹnt], *s.* (mat.) cociente.

R

rabbi [rǽbaj], s. rabí, rabino.— **—nical** [ræbínjkal], a. rabínico.

rabbit [rǽbjt], s. conejo.—r. ears, (rad.) antena de conejo.—r. hole, conejera.

rabble [rǽbl], s. canalla, chusma, populacho.—r. rouser, populachero, alborotapueblos.

rabid [rǽbjd], a. (med.) rabioso; fanático, violento, feroz. **—rabies** [réjbiz], s. rabia, hidrofobia.

raccoon [rækún], s. mapache, oso lavador.

race [rejs], s. raza; estirpe; carrera, corrida, regata.—r. course o track, pista de carreras; hipódromo.—r. horse, caballo de carreras.—r. riot, disturbio racista.—r. track, pista de carreras.—vt. hacer competir en una carrera; hacer correr deprisa.—vi. correr deprisa; competir en una carrera.— **—r** [réjsœ(r)], s. corredor; caballo de carrera; coche de carreras.

racial [réjšal], a. racial, étnico.

rack [ræk], s. percha, colgador; bastidor; potro del tormento; dolor, pena, angustia; (mec.) cremallera.—r. bar, cremallera.—to be on the r., estar en angustias.—vt. atormentar; agobiar.—to r. one's brains, devanarse los sesos.

racket [rǽkjt], s. raqueta; confusión, baraúnda; (fam.) parranda, franca-chela; (fam.) negocio turbio, trapisonda.—vi. meter bulla.– **—eer** [rǽkjtịr], s. bandido urbano que explota la extorsión, (Am., neol.) raquetero.—vi. extorsionar, extraer por la intimidación y la violencia.

racy [réjsị], a. picante.

radar [réjda(r)], s. radar.

radial [réjdjal], a. radial.

radiance [réjdịans], s. brillo, resplandor, esplendor. **—radiant** [réjdjant], a. radiante; resplandeciente, brillante. **—radiate** [réjdjejt], vt. emitir, irradiar.—vi. radiar, brillar. **—radiation** [rejdjéjšọn], s. radiación, irradiación.—r. sickness, enfermedad de radiación, mal de rayos. **—radiator** [réjdjejtọ(r)], s. aparato de calefacción; (aut., etc.) radiador.—r. cap, tapón de radiador.

radical [rǽdjkạl], a. y s. radical.

radio [réjdjou], s. radio; radiocomunicación.—by r., por radio, radiado. —r. amateur, fan o ham, radioaficionado.—r. announcer, locutor, anunciador.—r. beacon, radiofaro.—r. frequency, radiofrecuencia.—r. listener, radioyente, radioescucha.—r. station, (estación) emisora o difusora.—vt. y vi. radiar, radiodifundir.– **—active** [-ǽktịv], a. radioactivo.– **—activity** [-æktívịtị], s. radioactividad.– **—logist** [-álodžịst], s. radiólogo.

radish [rǽdjš], s. rábano.

radium [réjdjʌm], s. (quím.) radio.

radius [réjdjʌs], s. (geom. y anat.) radio; alcance.

raffle [rǽfl], vt. y vi. rifar.—s. rifa, sorteo.

raft [ræft], s. balsa, almadía.—vt. transportar en balsa; pasar en balsa.

rafter [rǽftœ(r)], s. viga (de techo).

rag [ræg], s. trapo, andrajo, harapo; persona andrajosa; (mús.) tiempo sincopado.—r. doll, muñeca de trapo.—vti. [1] rasgar; poner en música sincopada o musiquilla.—vii. tocar musiquilla o música sincopada.– **—weed** [-wid], s. ambrosía.

ragamuffin [rǽgamʌfịn], s. galopín, golfo; pelafustán, pelagatos.

rage [rejdž], s. rabia, furor, cólera; (fam.) boga, moda.—vi. rabiar, bramar, encolerizarse, enfurecerse.

ragged [rǽgịd], a. andrajoso; cortado en dientes.

raging [réjdžịŋ], a. rabioso, furioso.

raid [rejd], vt. invadir; (fam.) entrar o apoderarse por fuerza legal; allanar.—vi. hacer una irrupción. —s. correría, irrupción, incursión; (fam.) invasión repentina.—air r., ataque aéreo.

rail [rejl], s. pasamano, barandilla; antepecho; (f.c.) riel, rail, carril; ferrocarril.—by r., por ferrocarril.—r. fence, cerca hecha de palos horizontales.—vt. (a veces con in u of) poner barandilla, barrera o verja.—vi. (con at o against) injuriar; protestar contra.– **—ing** [réjlịŋ], s. barandilla, pasamano.

raillery [réjlœrị], s. zumba, chocarrería.

railroad [réilroud], *s.* ferrocarril, vía férrea.—*a.* ferroviario, de ferrocarril, para ferrocarriles.—*r. crossing*, paso a nivel.—*r. junction*, entronque.—*vt.* (fam.) apresurar; hacer aprobar (una ley, etc.) con precipitación; hacer encarcelar falsamente.

railway [réilwei], *a.* ferroviario.—*s.* ferrocarril.

rain [rein], *vi.* llover.—*r. or shine*, que llueva o no; con buen o mal tiempo.—*to r. cats and dogs*, llover a cántaros.—*s.* lluvia.—*r. forest*, selva tropical; bosque pluvial.—*r. water*, agua lluvia.- **—bow** [réinbou], *s.* arco iris.- **—coat** [-kout], *s.* impermeable, (Am.) capa de agua.- **—drop** [-drap], *s.* gota de agua.- **—fall** [-fɔl], *s.* aguacero; lluvias; cantidad de lluvia caída.- **—y** [-i], *a.* lluvioso.—*for a r. day*, por lo que pueda tronar.

raise [reiz], *vt.* levantar, alzar, poner en pie; elevar; construir, erigir; aumentar, subir; promover, ascender; criar, cultivar; hacer brotar; reclutar, alistar; reunir, recoger o juntar (dinero); levantar (en la caza); fermentar (pan).—*to r. a point*, presentar una cuestión, hacer una observación.—*to r. Cain*, o *a racket*, o *a rumpus*, (fam.) armar un escándalo, un alboroto; armar un lío.—*s.* aumento.

raisin [réizin], *s.* pasa, uva seca.

rake [reik], *s.* rastro, rastrillo; calavera, libertino, perdido.—*vt.* rastrillar; barrer; atizar (el fuego); (mil.) enfilar, barrer.—*to r. over the coals*, (fam.) despellejar, poner como un trapo.—*vi.* pasar el rastrillo; llevar una vida disoluta.—*r.-off* (jer.) dinero obtenido ilícitamente.

rally [réli], *vti.* [7] (mil.) reunir y reanimar; recobrar.—*vii.* (mil.) reunirse, rehacerse; recobrar las fuerzas, revivir. recobrarse (los precios en la Bolsa).—*s.* unión o reunión (de tropas dispersas o de gente); recuperación.; reunión política.

ram [ræm], *s.* carnero padre, morueco; (mec.) martinete, pisón; ariete hidráulico; (mar.) espolón.—*vti.* [1] apisonar; meter por la fuerza; atestar.

RAM [ræm], *abrev.* (comput.) (**random-access memory**) memoria de acceso aleatorio o directo.

ramble [ræmbl], *vi.* vagar, callejear; divagar, ir por las ramas; discurrir.—*s.* paseo.- **—r** [ræmbloe(r)], *s.* vagabundo, callejero; paseador.

ramp [ræmp], *s.* rampa.

rampart [ræmpart], *s.* (fort.) terraplén; muralla; amparo, defensa.

ramrod [ræmrad], *s.* baqueta.

ramshackle [ræmšækl], *a.* desvencijado, destartalado, ruinoso.

ran [ræn], *pret.* DE TO RUN.

ranch [ranch], *s.* (Am.) rancho, estancia; hacienda, granje.—*vi.* tener hacienda de ganado.- **—er** [ránchœ(r)], *s.* (Am.) ranchero; ganadero.

rancid [ránsid], *a.* rancio.

rancor [ránkɔ(r)], *s.* rencor, encono, inquina.- **—ous** [-ʌs], *a.* rencoroso.

random [rándom], *a.* fortuito, casual, impensado; sin orden ni concierto.—*at r.*, a la ventura, al azar.—*r. access*, acceso aleatorio o directo.—*r.-access memory*, (comput.) memoria de acceso aleatorio o directo.- **—ized** [-aizd], *a.* aleatorio.

randy [rándi], *a.* (fam.) calentón, cachondo, arrecho.

rang [ræŋ], *pret.* DE TO RING (tocar).

range [reindž], *vt.* recorrer; poner en posición; poner en fila; (a veces con **in**) alinear; arreglar, clasificar.—*vi.* vagar; estar en línea; estar a la misma altura; variar, fluctuar; (arti.) tener alcance (un proyectil).—*s.* distancia; extensión, recorrido; alcance (de un arma o proyectil); pastizal; radio de acción; fila, hilera; clase, orden; cocina económica.— *at close r.*, a quema ropa.—*r. finder*, (arti.) telémetro.—*r. of mountains*, cadena de montañas, cordillera.— *to be within the r. of*, estar a tiro, al alcance de.- **—r** [réindžœ(r)], *s.* guardabosque; vigilante.

rank [ræŋk], *s.* rango, posición (social, etc.); (mil.) grado, graduación, categoría; línea, hilera; (mil.) fila.—*the ranks, the r. and file*, la tropa, los soldados de fila; gente común, pueblo.—*vt.* clasificar, ordenar; colocar por grados; poner en fila.—*vi.* tener tal o cual grado o clasificación; ocupar (primero, segundo, etc.) lugar; (con **with**) estar al nivel de; (con **high, low**) ocupar (alta, baja) posición.—*a.* rancio; lozano; espeso, grosero; completo; fétido.

rankle [ræŋkl], *vt.* enconar, irritar.—*vi.* enconarse.

ransom [rǽnsọm], s. rescate.—vt. rescatar.

rant [rænt], vi. desvariar, despotricar.

rap [ræp], vti. y vii. [1] golpear, dar un golpe seco; (fam.) criticar, zaherir.—to r. at the door, tocar o llamar a la puerta.—s. golpe corto y seco; (fam.) crítica mordaz.—I don't care a r., no me importa un bledo.—r. music, rap.—to take the r., (fam.) pagar los vidrios rotos.

rapacious [rạpéịʃʌs], a. rapaz.

rape [reip], s. violación, estupro.—vt. violar, estuprar.

rapid [rǽpịd], a. rápido.—s. pl. rápidos (de un río), rabión.- —**ity** [rạpíḍịtị], s. rapidez, velocidad.

rapt [ræpt], a. arrebatado o extasiado.—r. in thought, absorto.- —**ure** [rǽpchụ(r)], s. rapto, arrobamiento, embeleso, éxtasis.

rare [rɛr], a. raro; precioso; extraordinario; (coc.) poco asado, a medio pasar.—r. bird, mirlo blanco.- —**ly** [rérlị], adv. raramente, rara vez.- —**rarity** [rérịtị], s. rareza; curiosidad.

rascal [rǽskạl], s. pícaro, bribón, bellaco, pillo.- —**ity** [ræskǽlịtị], s. bribonería, bellaquería.

rash [ræʃ], a. temerario, imprudente, precipitado.—s. salpullido, erupción.- —**ness** [rǽʃnịs], s. temeridad, imprudencia, precipitación.

rasp [ræsp], s. chirrido, sonido estridente; ronquera; escofina, raspador.—vt. escofinar; decir con voz ronca.

raspberry [rǽzberị], s. (bot.) frambuesa; (fam.) trompetilla, sonido de mofa.—r. bush, frambueso.

rat [ræt], s. rata; (fam.) postizo para el pelo.—r. poison, matarratas.—r. trap, ratonera.—to smell a r., recelar, haber gato encerrado.

rate [reit], s. tarifa, precio o valor fijo; tipo (de interés, etc.); preporción, tanto (por ciento, por unidad, etc.); modo, manera; clase.—at any r., de todos modos, sea como sea, en todo caso.—at that r., en esa proporción; de ese modo; a ese paso.—at the r. of, a razón de.—r. of exchange, cambio, tipo del cambio.—vt. tasar, valuar; clasificar; considerar, justipreciar; fijar precio, tarifa, etc.—vi. ser considerado (como); estar clasificado (como).

rather [rǽðœ(r)], adv. bastante, un poco, algo; más bien, mejor dicho; antes bien.—(I) had r. o would r., preferiría, más bien quisiera.—r. than, más bien que, en vez de, mejor que.—interj. ¡ya lo creo!

ratification [rætịfịkéịʃọn], s. ratificación.—**ratify** [rǽtịfai], vti. [7] ratificar, confirmar.

rating [réịtịn], s. justiprecio; clasificación (de un buque, marinero, etc.); (mec.) capacidad o potencia normal; clase, rango.

ratio [réịʃọu], s. razón; cociente.

ration [rǽʃọn, réịʃọn], s. (mil.) ración.—r. book o card, cartilla o tarjeta de racionamiento.—vt. racionar.

rational [rǽʃọnạl], a. racional.- —**ization** [ræʃọnạlịzéịʃọn], s. explicación racional de acciones, creencias, etc.—**ize** [rǽʃọnạlaịz], vt. interpretar racionalmente; buscar explicación racional o justificativa de.

rationing [rǽʃọnịn, réịʃọnịn], s. racionamiento.

rattan [rætǽn], s. bejuco.

rattle [rǽtl], vt. hacer sonar como una matraca; batir o sacudir con ruido; (fam.) atolondrar, aturrullar; (con off) decir a la carrera.—vi. matraquear; parlotear.—s. cascabel (de crótalo); sonajero, (Am.) maruga (juguete); matraca; estertor.—r.-brained, casquivano; r.-headed, ligero de cascos, casquivano.- —**snake** [-sneịk], s. culebra o serpiente de cascabel.

raucous [rɔ́kʌs], a. ronco.

ravage [rǽvịdʒ], vt. saquear, pillar, asolar, destruir.—s. ruina, estrago, destrucción; saqueo, pillaje.

rave [reiv], vi. delirar, desvariar; disparatar; bramar, salirse de sus casillas.—to r. over o about, entusiasmarse locamente por, deshacerse en elogios de.

raven [réịvn], s. cuervo.—a. negro brillante.

ravenous [rǽvẹnʌs], a. voraz, famélico; rapaz.

ravine [rạvín], s. cañón, hondonada.

ravioli [rævịóúlị], n. ravioles.

ravish [rǽvịʃ], vt. arrebatar, atraer, encantar; violar, estuprar.- —**ing** [-ịn], a. embriagador, arrebatador.

raw [rɔ], a. crudo; pelado, despellejado; descarnado; desapacible; fresco, nuevo; novato, bisoño (recluta, etc.); vulgar.—r.-boned, huesudo.—r. cotton (silk), algodón (seda) en rama.—*r. deal,* (jer.) mala pasada.—*r. flesh,* en carne viva.—*r. material,* materia prima.—**hide** [róhajd], *a.* de cuero sin curtir.—*s.* cuero crudo; látigo de cuero crudo.

ray [rej], *s.* rayo (de luz, calor, etc.); (ict.) raya.

rayon [réjan], *s.* rayón.

raze [rejz], *vt.* arrasar, demoler, destruir.

razor [réjzo(r)], *s.* navaja de afeitar.—*r. blade,* hoja o cuchilla de afeitar.

razz [ræz], *vt.* mofarse de.- **ing** [-iŋ], *s.* (jer.) irrisión.

reach [rich], *vt.* llegar a o hasta; alcanzar, lograr, conseguir; penetrar.—*to r. out one's hand,* tender la mano.— *vi.* extenderse, alcanzar.—*to r. into,* penetrar en.—*s.* alcance; extensión; poder.—*beyond one's r.,* fuera del alcance de uno.—*within one's r.,* al alcance de uno; dentro del poder de uno.

react [rjækt], *vi.* reaccionar.- **ion** [rjækšon], *s.* reacción.- **ionary** [rjækšoneri], *a.* y *s.* reaccionario.

reactor [rjækto(r)], *s.* (quím.) reactivo.—*nuclear r.,* reactor nuclear.

read [rid], *vti.* [9] leer; marcar, indicar.—*r.-only memory (ROM),* (comput.) memoria ROM, memoria de acceso aleatorio.—*the thermometer reads 20°,* el termómetro marca 20°.—*to r. law,* estudiar derecho.— *to r. proofs,* corregir pruebas.—*vii.* leer.—[red], *pret.* y *pp.* de TO READ.- **able** [rídabl], *a.* legible; ameno, entretenido.- **er** [-œ(r)], *s.* lector; libro de lectura (de texto).—*optical character r.,* (comput.) lector.

readily [rédji], *adv.* fácilmente; luego; con placer, de buena gana. **readiness** [rédjnis], *s.* disposición, buena voluntad; prontitud; facilidad.—*in r.,* listo; preparado.

reading [ridiŋ], *s.* lectura; conferencia, disertación; lectura de un proyecto de ley; apertura de un testamento.—*r. matter,* material de lectura; sección de lectura (de un periódico).—*r. room,* salón de lectura.

readjust [riadžást], *vt.* ajustar de nuevo; readaptar.- **ment** [-ment], *s.* readaptación; reajuste.

readout [rídaut], *s.* (comput.) lectura.

ready [rédj], *a.* listo, pronto, preparado, dispuesto; inclinado, propenso; al alcance; útil, disponible.—*r. cash,* dinero a la mano, dinero contante y sonante.—*r.-made,* ya hecho, confeccionado.— *r.-made clothing,* ropa hecha.—*r.-made suit,* traje hecho.—*r.-mix,* (coc.) de sobre, de paquete.

reagent [riéjdžent], *s.* (quím.) reactivo.

real [ríal], *a.* real, verdadero, auténtico, genuino, legítimo.—*r. estate,* bienes raíces o inmuebles.—*r. estate agent,* agente inmobiliario.—*r. time,* (comput.) tiempo real.—*adv.* (fam.) muy, bastante.- **ism** [-jzm], *s.* realismo.- **ist** [-jst], *s.* realista.- **ity** [rjæljti], *s.* realidad, verdad.—*in r.,* en realidad, de veras, efectivamente.- **ization** [-jzéjšon], *s.* realización; comprensión.- **ize** [-ajz], *vt.* realizar, efectuar; darse cuenta, hacerse cargo de; comprender; (com.) realizar.

realm [relm], *s.* reino.

realtor [ríalto(r)], *s.* corredor de bienes raíces.

ream [rim], *s.* resma.—*pl.* (fam.) montones.—*vt.* escariar. agrandar un agujero.

reanimate [riénjmejt], *vt.* reanimar, resucitar.

reap [rip], *vt.* segar; cosechar.- **er** [rípœ(r)], *s.* segador; segadora mecánica.- **ing** [-iŋ], *s.* siega, cosecha.

reappear [riapír], *vi.* reaparecer.- **ance** [-ans], *s.* reaparición.

reapportionment [riapóršonment], *s* nuevo prorrateo.

rear [rir], *a.* de atrás, trasero, posterior; último, de más atrás.—*r. admiral,* contra(a)lmirante.—*r. guard,* retaguardia.—*s.* fondo; espalda, parte de atrás o posterior; trasero; cola.— *r. view mirror,* (aut.) espejo retrovisor.—*r. window,* (aut.) luneta posterior.—*vt.* levantar; alzar; criar, educar.—*vi.* encabritarse (el caballo).

rearm [riárm], *vt.* rearmar.- **ament** [-ament], *s.* rearme.

rearrange [riaréjndž], *vt.* volver a arreglar; cambiar el arreglo o el orden de; refundir.

reason [rízon], *s.* razón; causa, motivo, porqué; argumento.—*by r. of,* con motivo de, a causa de, en virtud de.—*in (all) r.,* con justicia, con razón.—*it stands to r.,* está puesto en razón.—*r. why,* el porqué.—*to bring to r.,* meter en razón.—*within r.,* con moderación; dentro de los términos de la razón;—*vi.* razonar; discurrir.— **able** [-abl], *a.* razonable.- **ably**

[-əbli], *adv.* razonablemente; bastante.- **—ing** [-iŋ], *s.* razonamiento, raciocinio.

reassure [riəṣúr], *vt.* tranquilizar; volver a asegurar.

rebate [ríbeit], *vt.* y *vi.* rebajar, descontar.—*s.* rebaja, descuento.

rebel [rébəl], *a.* y *s.* rebelde.—*vii.* [1] [ribél], rebelarse.- **—lion** [ribélyən], *s.* rebelión, sublevación.- **—lious** [ribélyʌs], *a.* rebelde.

rebirth [ribŕθ], *s.* renacimiento.

rebound [ribáund], *vi.* (re)botar; repercutir.—*s.* [ríbaund], (re)bote; repercusión.

rebuff [ribáf], *s.* desaire, repulsa.—*vt.* desairar, rechazar.

rebuild [ribíld], *vti.* [10] reedificar, reconstruir.- **—rebuilt** [ribílt], *pret.* y *pp.* de TO REBUILD.

rebuke [ribiúk], *vt.* reprender.—*s.* represión.

recall [rikól], *vt.* revocar, anular; recordar, acordarse de.—*to r. an ambassador,* retirar a un embajador.—*s.* recordación; revocación; (mil.) toque o aviso de llamada.

recant [rikǽnt], *vt.* y *vi.* retractar(se).

recap [ríkæp], *s.* neumático recauchutado; (fam.) resumen.—[rikǽp], *vt.* recauchutar; (fam.) resumir.—*vi.* (fam.) resumir.

recast [rikǽst], *vti.* [9] volver a fundir; refundir, volver a escribir; volver a hacer; (teat.) volver a repartir (papeles.).—*pret.* y *pp.* de TO RECAST.

recede [risíd], *vi.* retroceder; retirarse, alejarse; desistir, volverse atrás; bajar (los precios).

receipt [risít], *s.* recibo; carta de pago; receta, fórmula.—*pl.* ingresos, entradas.—*on r. of,* al recibo de.—*to acknowledge r.,* acusar recibo.—*vt.* y *vi.* firmar o extender recibo; poner el recibí. **—receive** [risív], *vt.* recibir.—*received payment,* recibí. **—receiver** [risívœ(r)], *s.* recibidor; (tlf.) auricular, receptor; radiorreceptor; (for.) depositario, síndico.

recent [rísənt], *a.* reciente.- **—ly** [-li], *adv.* recientemente.—*r. married,* recién casados.

receptacle [riséptəkl], *s.* receptáculo. **—reception** [risépṣon], *s.* recepción; recibimiento.—*r. desk,* recepción. **—receptionist** [risépṣoniṣt], *s.* recepcionista.

recess [risés] o [ríses], *s.* hueco, nicho; hora de recreo; lugar escondido; interrupción, intermisión; receso.—

[risés], *vt.* poner en un nicho.—*vi.* suspender la sesión; suspenderse.- **—ion** [risésôn], *s.* retroceso, retirada; (com.) recesión, contracción económica.

recharge [richárdž], *vt.* recargar.

recipe [résipi], *s.* receta (de cocina).

recipient [risípient], *a.* y *s.* destinatario, recipiente, recibidor.

reciprocal [risíprokəl], *a.* recíproco. **—reciprocate** [risíprokeit], *vt.* reciprocar. **—reciprocity** [resiprásiti], *s.* reciprocidad.

recital [risáital], *s.* recitación; (mus.) recital; relación, narración. **—recitation** [resitéiṣôn], *s.* recitación, declamación. **—recite** [risáit], *vt.* y *vi.* narrar, relatar; recitar; declamar; dar o decir la lección.

reckless [réklis], *a.* imprudente, temerario; atolondrado.- **—ness** [-nis], *s.* temeridad; imprudencia.

reckon [rékon], *vt.* y *vi.* contar, enumerar; calcular; estimar; suponer, creer; (con **on** o **upon**) contar con, fiar en.—*to r. with,* tener en cuenta; habérselas con.- **—ing** [-iŋ], *s.* cuenta; cómputo, cálculo; ajuste de cuentas.—*day of r.,* día del juicio (final).

reclaim [rikléim], *vt.* (for.) reclamar (derechos, etc.); (rei)vindicar; mejorar y utilizar (tierras); utilizar (material usado). **—reclamation** [rekləméiṣon], *s.* reclamación; mejoramiento.

recline [rikláin], *vt.* y *vi.* reclinar(se), recostar(se).- **—r** [rikláinœr], *s.* asiento abatible o reclinable.

recognition [rekogníṣon], *s.* reconocimiento. **—recognize** [rékognaiz], *vt.* reconocer.

recoil [ríkoil], *s.* rechazo, reculada; (arti.) retroceso, culatazo.—*vi.* [rikóil], recular; retirarse; retroceder; culatear, patear (un arma de fuego).

recollect [rekolékt], *vt.* y *vi.* recordar; [rikolékt], recoger.- **—ion** [rekoléksôn], *s.* recuerdo.

recommend [rekoménd], *vt.* recomendar.- **—ation** [-éiṣon], *s.* recomendación.

recompense [rékompens], *vt.* recompensar.—*s.* recompensa.

reconcile [rékonsail], *vt.* reconciliar. **—reconciliation** [rekonsiliéiṣon], *s.* reconciliación.

recondition [rikondíṣon], *vt.* (mec.) reacondicionar; restaurar, reparar.

reconnaissance [rikánəṣans], *s.* reconocimiento. —**reconnoiter** [rikǫn-óitœ(r)], vt. reconocer.

record [rikórd], vt. registrar, inscribir; protocolizar (documentos); archivar; grabar (un disco, etc.).—*recorded music*, música en discos.—s. [rékǫrd], registro; partida, inscripción, anotación; acta; documento; crónica, historia; hoja de servicios, antecedentes de una persona; disco (fonográfico); (for.) memorial, informe; testimonio; memoria; (dep.) marca.—*pl.* archivo, protocolo; actas, autos; memorias, datos.—*of r.*, que consta (en el expediente, en la escritura, etc.).—*off the r.*, confidencialmente, extraoficialmente.—*on r.*, registrado; de que hay o queda constancia.—*r. breaker*, plusmarquista.—*r. changer*, cambiadiscos.—*r. holder*, recordman.—*r. library*, discoteca.—*r. player*, tocadiscos.— **ed** [-ĕd], a. grabado; escrito, documentado.— **er** [rikórdœ(r)], s. registrador, archivero; dulzaina, caramillo.—*r. of deeds*, registrador de la propiedad.—*tape r.*, grabadora de cinta magnetofónica.— **ing** [-iŋ], a. registrador; magnetofónico.—*r. secretary*, secretario escribiente, secretario de actas.—s. registro; grabación o grabado.

recount [rikáunt], vt. contar, referir, relatar; [rikáunt], recontar, hacer un recuento.—s. [ríkaunt], recuento.

recoup [rikúp], vt. resarcir, recobrar; indemnizar; desquitarse de.

recourse [rikɔrs], s. recurso, remedio, auxilio, refugio; (for.) recurso.—*to have r. to*, recurrir a, apelar a, valerse de.—*without r.*, (com.) sin responsabilidad (de parte del endosante).

recover [rikʌ́vœ(r)], vt. recobrar, recuperar.—vi. recobrar la salud; reponerse, restablecerse.— **y** [-i], s. recobro, recuperación.

recreate [rékrieit], vt. y vi. recrear(se), divertir(se). —**recreation** [rekriéišǫn], s. recreación, recreo; diversión; esparcimiento.

recruit [rikrút], vt. y vi. (mil.) alistar, reclutar.—s. (mil.) recluta; novicio, novato.- **ing** [-iŋ], s. reclutamiento.

rectangle [réktæŋgl], s. rectángulo. —**rectangular** [rektǽŋgyülǎ(r)], a. rectangular.

rectification [rektifikéišǫn], s. rectificación. —**rectify** [réktifai], vti. [7] rectificar.

rector [réktǫ(r)], s. rector (de universidad, orden religiosa); cura párroco. — **y** [-i], s. casa del párroco.

rectum [réktʌm], s. (anat.) recto.

recuperate [rikiúpereit], vt. recuperar, recobrar.—vi. recuperar la salud, reponerse. —**recuperation** [rikiuperéišǫn], s. recuperación.

recur [rikœ́r], vii. [1] repetirse, volver a ocurrir; (med.) recaer.

recurrent [rikœ́rent], a. repetido; periódico; (med.) recurrente.

red [red], a. rojo, encarnado, colorado; rojo (comunista).—*r. ball*, mingo (en el billar).—*r.-blooded*, fuerte, valiente, vigoroso.—*r.* (blood) *cell*, hematíe, glóbulo rojo.—*R. Cross*, Cruz Roja.—*r.-haired*, pelirrojo.—*r.-handed*, con las manos en la masa; en flagrante.—*r.-hot*, candente, enrojecido al fuego; acérrimo; muy entusiasta o enardecido; reciente (informe, noticia, etc.).—*r.-letter day*, día memorable.—*r.-light district*, zona de tolerancia, barrio de los lupanarez.—*r. pepper*, pimentón.—*R. Ridinghood*, Caperucita Roja.—*r. tape*, expedienteo, burocratismo, formulismo dilatorio.—*r. wine*, vino tinto.—s. color rojo; (pol.) rojo, comunista.—*to see r.*, (fam.) enfurecerse.- **cap** [-kæp], s. mozo de estación.- **coat** [-kout], s. (hist.) soldado inglés.- **den** [rédn], vt. teñir de rojo.—vi. ponerse colorado; ruborizarse.- **dish** [-iš], a. rojizo.- **head** [-hed], s. pelirrojo.

redeem [ridím], vt. redimir; desempeñar (un objeto); reseatar; cumplir (lo prometido).- **er** [-œ(r)], s. redentor.—*the R.*, el Redentor, el Salvador. —**redemption** [ridémpšǫn], s. redención.

redeploy [ridiplɔ́i], vt. dar nuevo destino a, reorientar.

redness [rédnis], s. rojez.

redo [ridú], vt. rehacer.

redolent [rédolent], a. fragante; sugestivo, evocador.

redouble [ridábl], vt. redoblar; repetir.—vi. redoblarse.

redoubt [ridáut], s. (fort.) reducto.

redound [ridáund], vi. redundar (en), resultar (en), contribuir (a).

redraft [rídræft], s. nuevo dibujo, copia o borrador; (com.) resaca.—vt. [ridrǽft], redactar, dibujar de nuevo.

redress [ridrés], vt. enderezar; reparar,

resarcir; remediar, compensar, desa-graviar; hacer justicia.—*s.* [rídres], reparación, satisfacción, desagravio; remedio; compensación.

reduce [ridjús], *vt.* someter.—*vt. y vi.* reducir(se); disminuir, aminorar, rebajar; mermar.—*vi.* adelgazar. **—reduction** [ridákṣon], *s.* reducción; rebaja, disminución.

redundance [ridándans], *s.* redundancia. **—redundant** [ridándant], *s.* redundante.

redwood [rédwud], *s.* secoya, pino gigantesco de California (árbol y madera).

reed [rid], *s.* caña, junquillo, (Am.) bejuco; (mús.) lengüeta; caramillo; instrumento de lengüeta.

reef [rif], *s.* arrecife, escollo.

reek [rik], *vi.* (gen. con **of** o **with**) humear, exhalar, oler a; oler mal.—*s.* tufo; vaho; hedor.

reel [ril], *s.* carrete; carretel; broca; canilla; devanadera; cinta (cinematográfica).—*vt.* aspar, enrollar, devanar.—*vi.* hacer eses, tambalear, bambolear.

reelect [riĕlékt], *vt.* reelegir. **—ion** [riĕlékṣon], *s.* reelección.

reentry [riéntri], *s.* reingreso, nueva entrada; (of a space vehicle) reentrada.

reestablish [riestǽbliṣ], *vt.* restablecer, instaurar.

refer [rifœ́r], *vti.* [1] referir, remitir; trasladar.—*vii.* referirse, remitirse, aludir; acudir; dar referencias.—*referred to,* mencionado; a que se hace referencia, a que uno se refiere.—**ee** [referí], *s.* árbitro; juez de campo.—*vt. y vi.* arbitrar; servir de árbitro.—**ence** [réferens], *s.* referencia; recomendación; alusión, mención; persona que sirve como referencia o fiador.—*in* o *with r. to,* respecto de, en cuanto a.—*a.* de referencia; de consulta (libro, etc.).—**endum** [referéndʌm], *s.* plebiscito, referendum.

refill [rifíl], *vt.* llenar de nuevo, rellenar, reenvasar; recambiar.—*s.* [rífil], recambio, repuesto.

refine [rifáin], *vt. y vi.* refinar(se).— **—d** [-d], *a.* refino, refinado; fino, cortés. **—ment** [-ment], *s.* refinamiento, cortesía; purificación, refinación.—**ry** [rifáinœri], *s.* refinería. **—refining** [rifáininŋ], *s.* refinación, depuración.

reflect [riflékt], *vt.* reflejar; reflexio-nar.—*vi.* reflexionar, meditar; reflejar.—*to r. on* o *upon,* desprestigiar; desdecir de.— **—ion** [riflékṣon], *s.* reflexión; reflejo; reproche, tacha.—*on* o *upon r.,* después de pensarlo; bien pensado.— **—or** [rifléktƟ(r)], *s.* reflector. **—reflex** [rífleks], *a.* reflejo.—*s.* acción refleja; reflejo, reverberación. **—reflexive** [rifléksiv], *a.* (gram.) reflexivo, reflejo.

reform [rifórm], *vt. y vi.* reformar(se), corregir(se), enmendar(se).—*s.* reforma, enmienda.—*r. school,* reformatorio, casa de corrección.—**ation** [refɔrméjṣon], *s.* reforma; (R. hist.) Reforma.—**er** [rifɔ́rmœ(r)], *s.* reformador, reformista.

refrain [rifréjn], *vi.* refrenarse, abstenerse de, contenerse.—*s.* (poét.) estribillo; (fam.) cantinela.

refresh [rifréṣ], *vt.* refrescar, renovar; aliviar.—*vr.* refrescarse.— **—ing** [-iŋ], *a.* refrescante; alentador, placentero.— **—ment** [-ment], *s.* refrigerio, tentempié; refresco.

refried beans [rífrajd], *spl.* frijoles refritos.

refrigerate [rifrídẓereit], *vt.* refrigerar, enfriar. **—refrigeration** [rifrídẓeréjṣon], *s.* refrigeración, enfriamiento. **—refrigerator** [rifrídẓereitƟ(r)], *s.* refrigerador, nevera; frigorífico; refrigerante.

refuel [rifiúel], *vt. y vi.* reabastecer(se) de combustible.

refuge [réfiudẓ], *s.* refugio, amparo, asilo.— **—e** [refiudẓí], *s.* refugiado; asilado.

refund [rífʌnd], *s.* reembolso, restitución.—*vt.* [rifʌ́nd], restituir, reintegrar, reembolsar; amortizar; consolidar una deuda.— **—able** [rifʌ́ndabl], *a.* reembolsable.

refusal [rifiúzal], *s.* negativa, denegación; desaire; opción, exclusiva.—**refuse** [rifiúz], *vt. y vi.* rehusar; rechazar; desechar; denegar; negarse a.—*s.* [réfius], desecho, basura, desperdicio; sobra.—*r. dump,* escombrera.—*a.* desechado, de desecho.

refute [rifiút], *vt.* refutar, rebatir.

regain [rigéjn], *vt.* recobrar, recuperar.

regal [rígal], *a.* real, regio.

regale [rigéil], *vt.* regalar, agasajar, festejar; recrear, deleitar.—*vi.* regalarse.

regalia [rigéiliǎ], *s. pl.* regalía; insignias, distintivos; galas.—*in full r.,* (fig.) de punta en blanco; de gran gala.

regard [rigárd], *vt*. observar, mirar; considerar, reputar, juzgar; tocar a, referirse a, concernir, relacionarse con.—*as regards*, tocante a, en cuanto a, por (o en) lo que respecta a.—*s*. miramiento, consideración; estimación; respeto; relación; mirada.—*pl*. memorias, afectos, recuerdos.—*in o with r. to*, (con) respecto a o de, tocante a.—*in this r.*, a este respecto.—*with* (*best, kind*) *regards*, con los mejores afectos; con saludos cariñosos.—*without* (*any*) *r. to*, sin miramientos por, sin hacer caso de.— **—ing** [-iŋ], *prep*. en cuanto a, respecto de.— **—less** [-lis], *a*. descuidado, desatento.—*r. of*, sin hacer caso de, haciendo caso omiso de; a pesar de.

regatta [rigátǎ], *s*. regata.

regency [rídžensi], *s*. regencia.

regent [rídžent], *a*. y *s*. regente.

regime [rejzím], *s*. régimen.

regimen [rédžimen], *s*. régimen.

regiment [rédžiment], *s*. regimiento. —*vt*. regimentar.— **—al** [-al], *a*. regimental.—*spl*. uniforme militar.

region [rídžon], *s*. región.—*in the r. of*, en las cercanías de.— **—al** [-al], *a*. regional.

register [rédžistœ(r)], *s*. registro, inscripción, matrícula; lista, archivo; protocolo; padrón, nómina; registrador; indicador, contador; (mús.) registro (de la voz y del órgano).— *vt*. registrar, inscribir, matricular; protocolar; marcar (según escala o graduación); certificar (una carta). —*registered letter*, carta certificada.— *registered nurse*, enfermera diplomada.—*vi*. inscribirse; matricularse.—**registrar** [rédžistrar], *s*. registrador, archivero. **—registration** [redžistréjšon], *s*. asiento, registro; inscripción; matrícula.—*r. fee*, derechos de matrícula.

regret [rigrét], *s*. pena, pesar, sentimiento; remordimiento.—*pl*. excusa (que se envía para rehusar una invitación).—*vti*. [1] sentir, deplorar, lamentar.— **—table** [-abl], *a*. lamentable, sensible.

regular [régyŭlă(r)], *a*. regular, ordinario, normal, corriente; ordenado, metódico.—*s*. (mil.) soldado de línea; obrero permanente.—*pl*. tropas regulares.— **—ity** [regyŭlǽriti],

s. regularidad. **—regulate** [régyŭlejt], *vt*. regular(izar), reglamentar. **—regulation** [regyŭléjšon], *s*. regulación; orden, regla.—*pl*. reglamento.—*a*. reglamentario, de reglamento. **—regulator** [régyŭlejtǫ(r)], *s*. regulador (de una máquina, turbina, etc.); registro (de reloj).

rehearsal [rihœ́rsal], *s*. (teat.) ensayo. **—rehearse** [rihœ́rs], *vt*. (teat.) ensayar; repasar; repetir.—*vi*. ensayarse.

reheat [rihít], *vt*. recalentar; calentar de nuevo.

reign [rejn], *vi*. reinar; prevalecer, imperar, predominar.—*s*. reinado.- **—ing** [réjniŋ], *a*. reinante, imperante.

reimburse [riimbœ́rs], *vt*. reembolsar, reintegrar.— **—ment** [-ment], *s*. reembolso, reintegro.

rein [rejn], *s*. rienda; brida; (fig.) dirección; sujeción, freno.—*to give r. to*, dar rienda suelta a.—*vt*. gobernar, refrenar (un caballo); llevar las riendas de.

reindeer [réjndir], *s*. reno.

reinforce [riinfórs], *vt*. reforzar, fortalecer.—*reinforced concrete*, hormigón armado.- **—ment** [-ment], *s*. refuerzo.

reinsurance [riinšúrans], *s*. reaseguro. **—reinsure** [riinšúr], *vt*. reasegurar.

reissue [ríšu], *s*. reimpresión; nueva edición o emisión.—*vt*. volver a publicar o emitir.

reiterate [rítereit], *vt*. reiterar.— **—reiteration** [ritteréjšon], *s*. reiteración, repetición.

reject [ridžékt], *vt*. rechazar.- **—ion** [ridžékšon], *s*. rechazamiento, rechazo.

rejoice [ridžóis], *vt*. y *vi*. regocijar(se), alegrar(se).— **—rejoicing** [ridžóisiŋ], *s*. regocijo, júbilo.

rejoin [ridžóin], *vt*. reunir con, volver a la compañía de.—*vi*. [ridžóin], replicar.- **—der** [ridžóindœ(r)], *s*. respuesta, réplica.

relapse [rilǽps], *vi*. recaer; reincidir (en un error, etc.).—*s*. recaída; reincidencia.

relate [riléjt], *vt*. relatar, contar, narrar; relacionar; emparentar.- **—d** [riléjtid], *a*. relacionado; afín; emparentado, allegado. **—relation** [riléjšon], *s*. relación; relato, narración; parentesco; pariente.—*pl*. parentela, parientes; tratos, comunicaciones.— *in r. to*, con relación a, con respecto

a. **—relationship** [rĭléĭṣǫnṣ̌ĭp], s. relación; parentesco. **—relative** [rélǫtĭv], a. relativo.—s. pariente, deudo, allegado; (gram.) relativo, pronombre relativo. **—relativity** [rĕlǫtívĭtĭ], s. relatividad.

relax [rĭlǽks], vt. y vi. relajar.— **—ation** [-éĭṣǫn], s. distracción; relajación.

relay [rĭléĭ], s. relevo; (elec.) relevador.—r. race, (dep.) carrera de relevos o de equipos.—vt. retransmitir (un mensaje, etc.).

release [rĭlís], vt. soltar; poner en libertad; relevar; renunciar a o abandonar; aliviar; poner en circulación.— s. liberación; exoneración; alivio; (m.v.) escape.

relegate [rélĕgĕĭt], vt. relegar. **—relegation** [rĕlĕgéĭṣǫn], s. relegación.

relent [rĭlént], vi. aplacarse; ceder, ablandarse, enternecerse.- **—less** [-lĭs], a. implacable, inexorable.— **—lessness** [-lĭsnĭs], s. inexorabilidad.

relevance [rélĕvǫns], **relevancy** [rélĕvǫnṣĭ], s. pertinencia. **—relevant** [rélĕvǫnt], a. pertinente, a propósito, apropiado; que hace o viene al caso.

reliability [rĭlĭáĭǝbílĭtĭ], **reliableness** [rĭláĭǝblnĭs], s. confiabilidad; calidad de seguro o digno de confianza; formalidad; precisión; veracidad. **—reliable** [rĭláĭǝbl], a. seguro, digno de confianza, confiable, fidedigno, formal. **—reliance** [rĭláĭǝns], s. confianza, seguridad. **—reliant** [rĭláĭǝnt], a. confiado (en sí mismo).

relic [rélĭk], s. reliquia, vestigio.

relief [rĭlíf], s. ayuda, auxilio; subsidio de paro forzoso; auxilio social; consuelo; socorro, limosna; descanso; (mil.) relevo; (b.a.) relieve, realce.— r. agencies, agencias de auxilio o de socorro.—r. valve, válvula de seguridad.—to be on r., recibir auxilio social. **—relieve** [rĭlív], vt. relevar, socorrer, aliviar; mitigar; realzar, hacer resaltar; (mil.) relevar.

religion [rĭlĭdžǫn], s. religión. **—religious** [rĭlĭdžʌs], a. y s. religioso. **—religiousness** [rĭlĭdžʌsnĭs], s. religiosidad.

relinquish [rĭlíŋkwĭṣ̌], vt. abandonar, dejar, ceder.- **—ment** [-mĕnt], s. abandono, dejación, renuncia.

relish [rélĭṣ̌], s. buen gusto, sabor grato, dejo; sazón, condimento; entremés; goce, saboreo.—vt. saborear, paladear; gustar de; sazonar, condimentar.—vi. saber bien, ser sabroso; gustar.

reload [rilóud], vt. recargar.

reluctance [rĭlʌ́ktǫns], s. repugnancia, aversión.—with r., de mala gana. **—reluctant** [rĭlʌ́ktǫnt], a. renuente, maldispuesto. **—reluctantly** [rĭlʌ́ktǫntlĭ], adv. de mala gana, a regañadientes.

rely [rĭláĭ], vii. [7] (con on o upon) confiar o fiar en, fiarse de, contar con.

remade [riméĭd], pret. y pp. de TO REMAKE.

remain [riméĭn], vi. quedar(se), restar o faltar; sobrar; estarse, permanecer; continuar.- **—der** [-dœ(r)], s. resto, restante, residuo, sobra(nte).- **—s** [-z], s. pl. restos, sobras, despojos; reliquias; ruinas.

remake [riméĭk], vti. [10] rehacer.

remark [rĭmárk], s. observación.—vt. y vi. observar.—to r. on, aludir a, comentar.- **—able** [-ǝbl], a. notable, extraordinario, admirable, señalado.

remedy [rémĕdĭ], s. remedio, medicamento; cura.—vti. [7] curar, remediar.

remember [rĭmémbœ(r)], vt. recordar, acordarse de.—vi. acordarse, hacer memoria. **—remembrance** [rĭmémbrǫns], s. memoria; recordación; recuerdo.

remind [rĭmáĭnd], vt. recordar.- **—er** [-œ(r)], s. recordatorio; advertencia.

reminiscence [rĕmĭnĭsĕns], s. reminiscencia.—pl. memorias. **—reminiscent** [rĕmĭnĭsĕnt], a. evocador, rememorativo.

remiss [rĭmĭs], a. remiso, descuidado. - **—ion** [rĭmĭṣ̌ǫn], s. remisión, perdón; (com.) remesa.—to go into r., (med.) entrar en remisión. **—remit** [rĭmĭt], vti. [1] (com.) remesar; remitir; perdonar, condonar; eximir; relajar.—vii. (com.) hacer remesas; girar. **—remittance** [rĭmĭtǫns], s. remesa, envío, giro.

remnant [rémnǫnt], s. remanente, resto, residuo; vestigio; retazo.

remodel [rimádĕl], vt. [2] modelar de nuevo; rehacer, reconstruir; renovar.

remorse [rĭmórs], s. remordimiento, cargo de conciencia.- **—ful** [-fǔl], a. arrepentido, con remordimientos.- **—less** [-lĭs], a. sin remordimientos.

remote [rĭmóut], a. remoto.—r. control, mando a distancia, control remoto telemando.—*r.-controlled*, teledirigido, con mando a distancia, con control remoto.- **—ness** [-nis], s. lejanía; improbabilidad.

removable [rimúvabl], a. separable; amovible; de quita y pon. **—removal** [rimúval], s. acción de quitar o levantar; remoción; deposición; eliminación; alejamiento; traslado, mudanza, cambio de domicilio. **—remove** [rimúv], vt. remover; quitar; eliminar; alejar, mudar, cambiar, trasladar; destituir, deponer; apartar; sacar, extirpar.—vi. mudarse, trasladarse, alejarse; cambiar de sitio o domicilio. **—removed** [rimúvd], a. apartado, alejado, distante; destituído. **—remover** [rimúvœ(r)], s. removedor.

remunerate [rimjúnereit], vt. remunerar. **—remuneration** [rimjuneréjʃon], s. remuneración.

renaissance [renāsáns], **renascence** [rinǽsens], s. renacimiento; (R.) Renacimiento.

rend [rend], vti. y vii. [10] rasgar(se), desgarrar(se); rajar(se).

render [réndœ(r)], vt. hacer; dar, prestar, rendir; (mus.; teat.) interpretar, ejecutar; traducir; derretir; (com.) enviar, girar (una cuenta).—*to r. assistance*, prestar auxilio, auxiliar.- **—ing** [-iŋ], s. traducción; interpretación. **—rendition** [rendíʃon], s. versión o traducción; (mus.; teat.) interpretación, ejecución; rendición, entrega.

rendezvous [rándēvu], s. cita; (in space) encuentro, reunión.—vi. reunirse en una cita, encontrarse.

renegade [rénigeid], s. renegado.

renew [rinjú], vt. renovar; restaurar; reanudar; (com.) extender, prorrogar.- **—al** [-al], s. renovación; reanudación; (com.) prórroga.

renounce [rináuns], vt. renunciar.- **—ment** [-ment], s. renuncia, renunciamiento.

renovate [rénoveit], vt. renovar.

renown [rináun], s. renombre.

rent [rent], vt. alquilar, arrendar, dar o tomar en arrendamiento.—s. renta, alquiler; arrendamiento; rasgadura; raja, grieta.—*for r.*, se alquila o arrienda.—*pret.* y *pp.* de TO REND.- **—al** [réntal], s. renta; arrendamiento, alquiler.

reopen [rióupn], vt. y vi. reabrir(se); volver a abrir(se); reanudar (una discusión, etc.).- **—ing** [-iŋ], s. reapertura.

reorganization [riɔrganizéjʃon], s. reorganización. **—reorganize** [riɔrganajz], vt. reorganizar.

repaid [ripéid], *pret.* y *pp.* de TO REPAY.

repair [ripér], vt. reparar, restaurar, componer, remendar.—s. reparo, reparación, restauración; compostura, remiendo.—*out of r.*, descompuesto, en mal estado. **—reparation** [reparéjʃon], s. reparación; satisfacción, desagravio.

reparation [rĕparéjʃon], s. reparación.

repartee [repartí], s. conversación, plática; respuesta viva; agudeza y gracia en responder.

repatriate [ripéitrieit], vt. repatriar.

repay [ripéi], vti. [10] pagar, reembolsar; reintegrar; pagar en la misma moneda.- **—ment** [-ment], s. pago, devolución, retorno.

repeal [ripíl], vt. derogar, revocar, abrogar, abolir.—s. revocación, derogación, abrogación.

repeat [ripít], vt. repetir.—s. repetición.- **—edly** [-idli], adv. repetidamente, repetidas veces, a menudo.

repel [ripél], vti. [1] repeler, rechazar.—vii. ser repelente o repulsivo.- **—lent** [-ent], a. repelente.

repent [ripént], vt. y vi. arrepentirse (de).- **—ance** [-ans], s. arrepentimiento.- **—ant** [-ant], a. arrepentido, contrito.

repertory [répœrtɔri], s. repertorio.

repetition [repitíʃon], s. repetición.

replace [ripléis], vt. reemplazar; suplir; reponer.- **—able** [-abl], a. reemplazable; renovable.- **—ment** [-ment], s. reemplazo, sustitución; reemplazante; pieza de repuesto; restitución, reposición.

replenish [ripléniʃ], vt. rellenar; llenar o surtir nuevamente. **—replete** [riplít], a. repleto; ahito.

replica [réplikā], s. (b.a.) réplica.

reply [riplái], s. respuesta; réplica.—*r. coupon*, vale respuesta.—vti. y vii. [7] contestar, responder; replicar.

report [ripórt], vt. informar acerca de, dar parte de; denunciar; comunicar; relatar; redactar un informe o dictamen; reseñar.—*it is reported*, corre la voz, se dice.—vi. presentar informe o dictamen; servir como reportero; comparecer, personarse.—s. relato, parte, noticia; comunicado; reseña; informe, dictamen; voz, rumor; reportaje; detonación.—*by r.*, según se dice.—*r. card*, certificado escolar.- **—er** [-œ(r)], *s.* repórter, reportero; noticiero; relator.

epose [ripóuz], *vt.* descansar; poner (confianza o esperanza).—*vi.* descansar.—*s.* descanso.

epository [ripázitɔri], *s.* depósito, almacén, repositorio.

eprehend [reprehénd], *vt.* reprender.

epresent [reprizént], *vt.* representar; significar, exponer; [ripriʒént], presentar de nuevo.— **—ation** [reprizentéjʃon], *s.* representación.- **—ative** [repriʒéntativ], *a.* representativo, típico; representante.—*s.* representante; símbolo, tipo, ejemplar; **(R.)** diputado, representante.

epress [riprés], *vt.* reprimir.— **—ion** [ripréʃon], *s.* represión.

eprieve [riprív], *vt.* aplazar la ejecución de; suspender; aliviar (un dolor).—*s.* aplazamiento de ejecución de sentencia; tregua; suspensión; alivio.

eprimand [réprimænd], *vt.* reprender, reconvenir, (fam.) sermonear.—*s.* reprimenda, regaño, censura.

eprint [ripríni], *vt.* reimprimir.—*s.* [ripríni], reimpresión; tirada aparte (de un artículo).

eprisal [ripráizal], *s.* represalia.

eproach [ripróuch], *vt.* reprochar; oprobiar.—*s.* reproche; oprobio.— *above r.*, intachable, irreprochable.

eprobate [réprobejt], *s.* réprobo, malvado, disoluto, depravado.

eproduce [riprodjús], *vt.* reproducir; duplicar, copiar.—*vi.* reproducirse. **—reproduction** [riprodákʃon], *s.* reproducción; (b.a.) copia.

eproof [riprúf], *s.* reprobación.—**reprove** [riprúv], *vt.* reprobar.

eptile [réptil], *s. y a.* reptil.

epublic [ripábljk], *s.* república.- **—an** [-an], *a. y s.* republicano.

epudiate [ripiúdjeit], *vt.* repudiar; (for.) negarse a reconocer.

epugnance [ripágnans], *s.* repugnancia; aversión.—**repugnant** [ripágnant], *a.* repugnante.

epulse [ripáls], *s.* repulsa, repulsión; denegación.—*vt.* desechar, rechazar, repeler.—**repulsive** [ripálsiv], *a.* repulsivo, repugnante, repelente.

eputable [répjūtabl], *a.* honroso, honrado, intachable; lícito.—**reputation** [repjūtéjʃon], *s.* reputación; crédito, estimación, prestigio.—**re**

pute [ripiút], *vt.* reputar, juzgar, tener por.—*s.* reputación, fama, crédito.

request [rikwést], *s.* súplica, ruego; petición, instancia, solicitud; (com.) demanda.—*at the r. of,* o *by r.*, a petición, a solicitud o instancia de.—*on r.*, en boga, muy solicitado, pedido o buscado.—*vt.* rogar, suplicar, solicitar.

require [rikwáir], *vt.* requerir, demandar, exigir, necesitar.- **—ment** [-ment], *s.* demanda, requerimiento, exigencia; requisito, necesidad; formalidad; estipulación. **—requisite** [rékwizit], *a.* necesario, forzoso, indispensable.—*s.* requisito.—**requisition** [rekwiziʃon], *s.* pedimento, petición, demanda; (mil.) requisa; necesidad, requisito, menester; (com.) demanda, solicitud; (for.) requisitoria.—*vt.* (mil.) requisar.—**requite** [rikwáit], *vt.* corresponder a; vengarse de.

resale [ríseil], *s.* reventa.

rescind [risínd], *vt.* rescindir.

rescue [réskiu], *vt.* rescatar, redimir; salvar, librar.—*s.* rescate, redención, salvación, libramiento, recobro; socorro.—*r. party,* pelotón de salvamento.- **—r** [-œ(r)], *s.* salvador, libertador.

research [risœrch], *s.* investigación.— *vt.* investigar.

resell [risél], *vti. y vii.* [10] revender.

resemblance [rizémblans], *s.* parecido, semejanza.—**resemble** [rizémbl], *vt.* (a)semejarse a, parecerse a; salir (uno) a (su padre, etc.).

resent [rizént], *vt.* resentirse de o por.- **—ful** [-ful], *a.* resentido.- **—ment** [-ment], *s.* resentimiento.

reservation [rezœrvéjʃon], *s.* reservación; reserva; excepción, restricción (mental); pasaje (sitio, alojamiento, etc.) reservados de antemano. **—reserve** [rizœrv], *vt.* reservar, guardar, retener, conservar; exceptuar, excluir.—*s.* reserva.—**reservoir** [rézœrvwar], *s.* depósito; receptáculo; cubeta; (com.) surtido de reserva; alberca; cisterna, aljibe; depósito (de gas, petróleo, etc.).

reset [risét], *vti.* [9] montar de nuevo.—*pret. y pp.* de TO RESET.

reside [rizáid], *vi.* residir, vivir, habitar.- **—nce** [rézidens], *s.* residencia, domicilio; casa; estancia, mansión; quedada, permanencia.- **—nt** [rézident], *a.* residente.—*s.* habitante, vecino; (dipl.) ministro residente.

residual [rizídžual], *a.* restante, remanente.—**residue** [rézidiu], *s.* residuo, resto, sobrante, remanente.

resign [rizáin], *vt.* dimitir, renunciar.—*vi.* presentar la dimisión.—*vr.* resignarse, rendirse, someterse, conformarse.- —**ation** [rezignéišon], *s.* dimisión, renuncia, dejación; resignación, conformidad.

resilience [rizíliens], *s.* elasticidad, resorte, rebote; capacidad de recobrar la figura y el tamaño original después de deformación.—**resilient** [rizílient], *a.* elástico; (fig.) alegre, animado.

resin [rézin], *s.* resina.

resist [rizíst], *vt.* resistir; resistir a.—*vi.* resistirse.- —**ance** [-ans], *s.* resistencia.- —**ant** [-ant], *a.* resistente.

resold [risóuld], *pret.* y *pp.* de TO RESELL.

resole [risóul], *vt.* sobresolar.

resolute [rézoliut], *a.* resuelto, determinado, firme, denodado.—**resolution** [rezoliúšon], *s.* resolución.—*good resolutions*, buenos propósitos.—**resolve** [rizálv], *vt.* y *vi.* resolver(se).

resonance [rézonans], *s.* resonancia.—**resonant** [rézonant], *a.* resonante.

resort [rizórt], *vi.* (con **to**) acudir, recurrir, frecuentar; pasar a, recorrer a, hacer uso de, echar mano de.—*s.* recurso, medio, expediente; lugar de temporada o muy frecuentado, estación.

resound [rizáund],—*vi.* resonar.

resource [risórs], *s.* recurso, medio, expediente.—*pl.* fondos, recursos; riquezas, recursos naturales.- —**ful** [-ful], *a.* listo, ingenioso, dotado de inventiva.- —**fulness** [-fulnis], *s.* inventiva, iniciativa.

respect [rispékt], *vt.* respetar, venerar, estimar; acatar, observar, guardar; corresponder, tocar, concernir, atenerse a.—*s.* respeto, estimación; reverencia, veneración, culto; acatamiento, miramiento; honra, homenaje; respecto, asunto.—*pl.* memorias, recuerdos, respetos.—*in other respects,* por lo demás.—*in r. that,* puesto que.—*in some r.,* de algún modo, hasta cierto punto.—*out of r. for* o *to,* en obsequio de, por consideración a.- —**ability** [rispektabíliti], *s.* respectabilidad.- —**able**

[rispéktabl], *a.* respetable, forma estimable, honroso; acreditado autorizado; bastante bueno; cons derable.- —**ful** [-ful], *a.* resp tuoso.—**respectfully** [rispéktfuli], respectuosamente.—*r. yours,* de V atento y seguro servidor.- —**in** [-in], *prep.* con respecto a, en cuant a, por lo que toca a, (en lo) tocante - —**ive** [-iv], *a.* respectivo; partic lar, individual; sendos.

respiration [respiréišon], *s.* respir ción, respiro.—**respire** [rispáir], *vt. vi.* resollar, respirar; espirar, exhala

respite [réspit], *s.* tregua, esper pausa; plazo, prórroga, respiro.

respond [rispánd], *vi.* responder.—**re ponse** [rispáns], *s.* respuesta.—**re ponsibility** [rispansibíliti], *s.* respo sabilidad; obligación, deber; so vencia.—**responsible** [rispánsibl *a.* responsable; de responsabil dad.—*r. for,* responsable de.

rest [rest], *s.* descanso, reposo; tregu pausa; paz, quietud; apoyo, bas resto, residuo, sobra; (poét.) cesur (con **the**) los demás, los otros; resto.—*at r.,* en paz (apl. a los muer tos).—*r. cure,* cura de reposo.— *home,* sanatorio; asilo de ancia nos.—*r. room,* sala de descanso; ex cusado, retrete; (of a theater) salon cillo.—*r. stop,* parada de descanso área de servicio o descanso.—*v* descansar, reposar; yacer, reposar e el seno de la muerte; cesar, parar; e tar en paz, vivir tranquilo; posarse asentarse; apoyarse (en), cargar (s bre); confiar (en), contar (con); de pender (de); permanecer.—*to assured,* perder cuidado.—*vt.* y *v* descansar, proporcionar descans apoyar o asentar; (for.) terminar l presentación de pruebas.

restaurant [réstorant], *s.* restaurante.

restful [réstful], *a.* reposado, quieto tranquilo, descansado.

restitution [restitiúšon], *s.* restitución

restless [réstlis], *a.* inquieto, impa ciente; bullicioso, levantisco insomne.- —**ness** [-nis], *s.* inquie tud, impaciencia, desasosiego; in somnio.

restoration [restoréišon], *s.* restaura ción; reintegración.—**restore** [r stór], *vt.* restaurar.

restrain [ristréin], *vt.* refrenar, repri mir, cohibir; represar; moderar, li mitar, coartar; (for.) prohibir vedar a.— **-t** [-t], *s.* moderación; sujeción, restricción; coerción, prohibición.—**restrict** [ristríkt], *vt.* restringir.—**restriction** [ristríkʃən], *s.* restricción.

sult [rizʌ́lt], *vi.* resultar.—*to r. in*, dar por resultado, parar en.—*s.* resultado.—*as a r. of*, de resultas de.

sume [rizjúm], *vt.* reasumir; reanudar; recuperar; resumir, compendiar.—*vi.* tomar el hilo; empezar de nuevo.—**résumé** [rezuméj], *s.* resumen.—**resumption** [rizʌ́mpʃən], *s.* reanudación; recobro.

surface [risʌ́rfas], *vt.* dar nueva superficie a.—*vi.* volver a emerger.

surrect [rezʌrékt], *vt. y vi.* resucitar.—**resurrection** [rezʌrékʃən], *s.* resurrección.

suscitate [risʌ́siteit], *vt. y vi.* resucitar.

tail [rítejl], *vt.* detallar, vender al por menor.—*vi.* vender(se) al por menor.—*s.* venta al por menor.—*a. y adv.* al por menor.— **-er** [-œ(r)], *s.* comerciante al por menor, detallista.

tain [ritéjn], *vt.* retener; contratar (a un abogado).— **-er** [-œ(r)], *s.* partidario; criado, dependiente; (for.) anticipo.

take [ritéjk], *vti.* [10] volver a tomar; reasumir, recoger; (fot. y cine) volver a fotografiar o filmar.—**retaken** [ritéjkn], *pp.* de TO RETAKE.

taliate [ritǽljeit], *vi.* desquitarse, vengarse; tomar represalias.—**retaliation** [ritæljéjʃən], *s.* desquite, venganza.

tard [ritárd], *vt.* retardar.—*s.* retardo.—[rítard], *s.* (fam.) tarado.— **-ed** [id], *a.* retrasado, débil.—*the r.*, los retrasados.

ticence [rétisens], *s.* reticencia, reserva.—**reticent** [rétisent], *a.* reticente, reservado, circunspecto.

tina [rétinǎ s], *s.* retina.

tinue [rétinju], *s.* comitiva, séquito.

tiral [ritájral], *s.* retiro, retirada; (com.) recogida.—**retire** [ritájr], *vi.* retirarse, irse a acostar; retirarse de la vida activa, de un empleo, etc.; jubilarse; retraerse, retroceder, recogerse, apartarse, separarse.—*vt.* (com.) recoger, retirar de la circulación; jubilar.—**retirement** [ritájrment], *s.* retiro; retraimiento; recogida, recogimiento; lugar retirado; jubilación.

retook [ritúk], *pret.* de TO RETAKE.

retort [ritórt], *vt.* replicar.—*s.* respuesta pronta y aguda, réplica; (quim.) retorta.

retouch [ritách], *vt.* retocar.—*s.* retoque.

retrace [ritréjs], *vt.* desandar, volver atrás; buscar el origen de; repasar; volver a trazar.—*to r. one's steps*, volver sobre sus pasos.

retract [ritrǽkt], *vt.* desdecirse de, retractarse de.—*vi.* retractarse, desdecirse.

retreat [ritrít], *s.* retiro; soledad, retraimiento; refugio, asilo; (mil.) retirada; retreta.—*vi.* retirarse.

retribution [retribjúʃən], *s.* retribución, pago; justo retorno, pena incurrida.

retrievable [ritrívabl], *a.* recuperable; reparable.—**retrieve** [ritrív], *vt.* recuperar, recobrar; restaurar, remediar; cobrar (la caza).—*vi.* cobrar la caza.—**retriever** [ritrívœ(r)], *s.* perro cobrador, perro traedor.

retroactive [retroǽktjv], *a.* retroactivo.

retrofiring [retrofájriŋ], *s.* retrodisparo.

retrogress [retrogrés], *vi.* retroceder; empeorar.

retrorocket [retrorákět], *s.* retrocohete.

retrospect [rétrospekt], *s.* mirada retrospectiva.—*in r.*, en retrospectiva.— **-ive** [retrospéktjv], *a.* retrospectivo.

return [ritœrn], *vt.* (de)volver; corresponder a, pagar, dar en cambio, recompensar; dar (gracias, fallo, respuesta, etc.); (pol.) elegir, enviar (al congreso, etc.).—*to r. a call*, pagar una visita.—*to r. a kindness*, corresponder a un favor.—*to r. a verdict*, dictar un fallo, dar un veredicto.—*vi.* volver, regresar; reaparecer; responder, replicar.—*vt. y vi.* volver otra vez; dar otra vuelta o doblez.—*s.* vuelta, regreso; correspondencia (a un favor, etc.), pago, recompensa; respuesta; devolución; reaparición; utilidad, rédito; cambio, trueque; informe o parte oficial; curva, vuelta; desviadero; (arq.) ala, vuelta de moldura, marco, etc.; (pol.) elección.—*pl.* resultado, cifras (de elecciones).—*by r. mail*, a vuelta de correo.—*happy returns*, felicidades en su cumpleaños.—*income tax r.*, declaración de impuesto sobre rentas.—*in r.,* en cambio, en pago, en recompensa.—*many happy returns of the day!,* ¡que cumpla muchos más!—*r. address,* señas del remitente.—*r. bout o engagement,* combate revancha.—*r. game,* desquite.—*r. ticket,* billete de vuelta; billete de ida y vuelta.—*r. trip,* viaje de vuelta.

reunion [rįyúnyọn], *s.* reunión.—**reunite** [rįyụnáįt], *vt.* reunir.—*vi.* reunirse.

Rev., *abrev.* (Reverend) Rvdo., Rdo.

revamp [rĕvǽmp], *vt.* componer, renovar, remendar.

reveal [rįvíl], *vt.* revelar; dar a conocer.— **-ing** [-iŋ], *a.* revelador; impúdico, sugestivo (vestido).

reveille [rĕvĕli], *s.* (mil.) toque de diana.

revel [rĕvẹl], *vii.* [2] jaranear, ir de parranda; gozarse (en).—*s.* algazara, jarana, parranda.

revelation [rẹvẹléįšọn], *s.* revelación; visión; (**R.**) Apocalipsis.

revelry [rĕvẹlri], *s.* jarana, gresca, francachela, orgia, borrachera.

revenge [rįvéndž], *vt.* y *vi.* vengar(se); desquitarse, satisfacerse o vengarse de.—*s.* venganza, desquite.- **—ful** [-fụl], *a.* vengativo.

revenue [rĕvẹnju], *s.* rentas públicas; (com.) renta; rédito; entrada, ingreso; beneficio, recompensa.—*r. officer,* aduanero; agente fiscal o del fisco.—*r. stamp,* sello fiscal, sello de impuesto.

reverberate [rĕvĕrbĕreit], *vi.* reverberar.

revere [rįvír], *vt.* reverenciar, venerar.- **—nce** [rĕvrẹns], *s.* reverencia, veneración; reverencia (saludo); (**R.**, igl.) Reverencia (tratamiento).—*to pay r.,* rendir homenaje.—*vt.* reverenciar, venerar.- **—nd** [rĕvrẹnd], *a.* reverendo, venerable; (**R.**, igl.) Reverendo (tratamiento).—*s.* (fam.) clérigo.- **—nt** [rĕvrẹnt], *a.* reverente.

reverie [rĕvẹri], *s.* ensueño; embelesamiento, arrobamiento; (mus.) fantasía.

reversal [rįvérsạl], *s.* reversión; inversión; (for.) revocación; cambio (de opinión, etc.).—**reverse** [rįvérs], *vt.* trastocar, invertir; trastornar; (for.) revocar.—*vi.* volver a un estado anterior, invertirse.—*a.* reverso, invertido; opuesto, contrario; (mec.) de inversión o contramarcha.—*s.* lo

contrario, lo opuesto, respaldo dorso, reverso; reversión, inversión contratiempo, revés.—**revert** [rį vĕrt], *vi.* retroceder, volver, resurtir (biol.) saltar atrás; (for.) revertir.— **revertible** [rįvĕrtįbl], *a.* reversible.

review [rįvjú], *vt.* rever, remirar; repa sar (estudios, etc.); revisar; censurar reseñar, criticar o analizar (un libro etc.); (mil.) revistar, pasar revista a.—*vi.* reseñar, escribir para una re vista.—*s.* repaso; examen, análisis reseña; censura, juicio crítico; re vista; (for.) revisión.— **-er** [-œ(r)], *s* crítico, revistero (literario, teatral etc.).

revile [rĕvaíl], *vt.* ultrajar, vilipendiar.

revise [rįvájz], *vt.* revisar, releer, repa sar; corregir, enmendar.—**revisio** [rįvížọn], *s.* revisión, repaso; en mienda; edición revisada.

revival [rįvájvạl], *s.* renacimiento, re novación, reavivamiento; (teat.) re posición o reestreno; desperta miento religioso.—**revive** [rįvájv] *vt.* hacer revivir, (re)avivar, resuci tar; restablecer, restaurar; desperta hacer recordar.—*vi.* revivir; res tablecerse, reanimarse; volver en s renacer.

revocable [rĕvọkạbl], *a.* revocable **—revoke** [rįvóųk], *vt.* revoca derogar.—*vi.* (en los naipes) renur ciar.

revolt [rįvóụlt], *vi.* rebelarse, suble varse; sentir repugnancia o repul sión.—*vt.* rebelar, sublevar; causa asco o repulsión; indignar.—*s.* su blevación, alzamiento, rebelión. **—ing** [-iŋ], *a.* odioso, repugnant asqueroso.

revolution [revọljúšọn], *s.* revolucióx revuelta; (mec.) giro.- **—ary** [-ẹri], y *s.* revolucionario.- **—ist** [-įst], revolucionario.

revolve [rįvǽlv], *vi.* girar, dar vuelta rodar; moverse en ciclos, sucede periódicamente.—*vt.* voltear, hac girar o rodar; revolver (en la cabeza considerar bajo todos los aspectos. **—r** [-œ(r)], *s.* revólver (arma).— **volving** [-iŋ], *a.* giratorio.—*r. boo case,* giratoria.—*r. door,* puer giratoria.—*r. fund,* fondo rotativo.

reward [rįwórd], *vt.* premiar, recon pensar.—*s.* recompensa, premi rescate; hallazgo.- **—ing** [-iŋ], remunerador, provechoso, agr decido.

rewind [ríwaįnd], *s.* (mec. y cine) retr

ceso.—[riwáind], *vt.* (film) rebobinar.

hapsody [rǽpsodi], *s.* rapsodia.

heostat [ríostæt], *s.* reóstato.

hesus [rísʌs], *s.* macaco de la India.

hetoric [rétorik], *s.* retórica.—**al** [ri-
tárikal], *a.* retórico.

heumatic [rumǽtik], *a.* y *s.* reumático.

heumatism [rúmatizm], *s.* reumatismo.

hinestone [ráinstoun], *s.* diamante de
imitación hecho de vidrio.

hinoceros [rainásǝros], *s.* rinoceronte.

hombus [rámbas], *s.* rombo.

hubarb [rjúbarb], *s.* ruibarbo.

hyme [raim], *s.* rima; verso; poesía.—
without r. or reason, sin ton ni son.—
vt. y *vi.* rimar.

hythm [ríðm], *s.* ritmo; (med.) perio-
dicidad.- —**ic(al)** [ríðmik(al)], *a.*
rítmico.

ib [rib], *s.* costilla; (arq.) faja, listón,
nervio, nervadura; viga de tejado;
arco; saliente; varilla (de abanico o
paraguas); tirante; (mec.) pestaña,
reborde; (cost.) vivo; (bot.) nervadura de las hojas; (cost.) costilla, esposa.—*vti.* [1] marcar con rayas,
listones o filetes; afianzar con
rebordes o pestañas; (cost.) poner
vivos; (fam.) embromar, burlarse
de.

ibald [ríbald], *a.* grosero y obsceno.

ibbon [ríbon], *s.* cinta.

ice [rais], *s.* arroz.

ich [rich], *a.* rico; costoso; precioso;
suntuoso, cuantioso; exquisito;
vivo (color, etc.); muy sazonado,
dulce, fuerte, etc.; fértil; (fam.) muy
divertido; risible.—*to get r.,* enriquecerse.—*s. pl.* riqueza(s); bienes; opulencia; sazón, dulzura, suculencia.

ckets [ríkits], *s.* raquitis.

ckety [ríkiti], *a.* desveneijado, destartalado; (med.) raquítico.

d [rid], *vti.* [3] desembarazar, quitar
de encima, zafar.—*to be r. of,* estar libre o exento de.—*pret.* y *pp.* de TO
RID.- —**dance** [rídans], *s.* supresión,
liberación de una pejiguera o peligro.

dden [rídn], *pp.* de TO RIDE.

ddle [rídl], *s.* acertijo, enigma, adivinanza, rompecabezas; (fam.) busi-
lis, quisicosa; misterio; criba.—*vt.*
resolver, adivinar; acribillar.—*vi.*
hablar enigmáticamente.

de [raid], *vti.* [10] cabalgar, montar; ir
montado en o sobre; pasear o reco-

rrer (a caballo, en automóvil,
etc.).—*to r. down* u *over,* pasar por
encima de, derribar y hollar; pisotear, atropellar; mandar con arrogancia.—*to r. out,* hacer frente a,
resistir bien (el viento).—*vii.* cabalgar; pasear (a caballo o en un
vehículo); ir en automóvil, coche,
etc.; flotar; (mec.) rodar, tener
juego, funcionar.—*s.* paseo (a caballo, en auto, etc.).- —**r** [ráidœ(r)], *s.*
jinete; pasajero; cláusula adicional;
condición.

ridge [ridʒ], *vt.* (agr.) formar camello-
nes; acanalar, arrugar.—*vi.* tener ca-
mellones.—*s.* cerro, colina, cordillera, serranía; escollo, arrecife;
arruga, costurón; camellón; caballete del tejado.—*r. roof,* tejado a dos
vertientes o aguas.—*r. tile,* teja aca-
nalada.— —**pole** [-poul], *s.* parhilera.

ridicule [rídikjul], *s.* ridículo, mofa, rechifla.—*vt.* ridiculizar, mofarse de,
rechiflar.—**ridiculous** [ridíkyūlʌs],
a. ridículo, risible, grotesco.

riding [ráidiŋ], *s.* equitación.—*r.
academy,* escuela de equitación.—*r.
boots,* botas de montar.—*r. habit,*
amazona, traje de montar.

rife [raif], *a.* común, corriente.—*r.
with,* abundante en, lleno de.

riffraff [rífræf], *s.* canalla, gentuza.

rifle [ráifl], *s.* rifle, fusil; espiral de rifle;
piedra de afilar.—*vt.* robar, arreba-
tar.- —**man** [-man], *s.* fusilero.

rift [rift], *s.* abertura; desacuerdo.

rig [rig], *vti.* [1] equipar, aparejar; en-
jarciar (un velero); arreglar de una
manera fraudulenta.—*to r. oneself
up,* ataviarse, emperifollarse.—*s.*
equipo, aparejo; traje, atavío; aparato.- —**ging** [rígiŋ], *s.* (mar.) aparejo, cordaje, jarcia; (mec.) aparejo
(de poleas); equipo de arrastre (de
trozas).

right [rait], *a.* recto, justo, equitativo;
propio, conveniente; correcto,
exacto; cierto, real, genuino, legal,
legítimo; derecho, directo; ordenado, ajustado; derecho (lado,
mano); verdadero; derecho (contrario de revés).—*all r.,* bueno, conforme.—*it is r.,* está bien; es justo.
—*r. and left,* a diestra y siniestra.
—*r. angle,* ángulo recto.—*r. field,* jardín derecho.—*r. hand,* diestra; de
la mano derecha.—*r.-hand man,*
(fam.) hombre de confianza, brazo
derecho.—*r. mind,* entero juicio.—
r. of way, derecho de tránsito o de

paso; servidumbre de paso o vía.—
to yield the r., ceder el paso.—**r.** *or wrong,* con razón o sin ella; bueno o malo.—*r. side,* lado derecho; lado de afuera, cara; haz (telas, etc.).—*r.-wing,* derechista.—**r.-winger,** (fam.) derechista.—*to be r.,* tener razón.—*interj.* ¡bien! ¡bueno!—*adv.* rectamente, justamente; exactamente, perfectamente, precisamente; bien; correctamente; debidamente; derechamente; a la derecha.—*r. about face,* media vuelta.—*r. now,* ahora mismo.—*r. there,* allí mismo.—*to go r. home,* ir derechito para la casa.—*s.* derecho; justicia; rectitud; propiedad, dominio, título; poder, autoridad; privilegio, prerrogativa; opción; (la) diestra, (la) derecha; (pol.) derecha(s).—*vt.* hacer justicia; enderezar.—*to r. a wrong,* enderezar un entuerto, corregir un abuso.— **—eous** [ráich∧s], *a.* justo, recto, equitativo; virtuoso, honrado, probo.— **—eousness** [ráich∧snis], *s.* rectitud, virtud, honradez, probidad.— **—ful** [ráitful], *a.* legítimo.— **—ist** [-ist], *s. y a.* (pol.) derechista.

rigid [rídžid], *a.* rígido, inflexible, yerto; austero, estricto, riguroso.— **—ity** [ridžíditi], *s.* rigidez.

rigmarole [rígmaroul], *s.* galimatías.

rigor [rígo(r)], *s.* rigor; inclemencia; severidad, austeridad; tesón, terquedad; exactitud; (med.) escalofrío.— **—ous** [-∧s], *a.* rigoroso o riguroso; recio (tiempo); estricto, severo.

rill [ril], *s.* riachuelo, arroyuelo.

rim [rim], *s.* canto, borde, margen, orilla; llanta, aro; cerco, reborde, pestaña; ceja.

rime [raim], *s.* escarcha; = RHYME.

rind [raind], *s.* corteza, cáscara.

ring [riŋ], *s.* anillo, argolla, anilla; (joy.) anillo, sortija; circo, arena, liza; cerco; corro o corrillo; ojera; campaneo, repique; juego de campanas; campanilleo; toque de timbre; sonido metálico.—*r. finger,* dedo anular.—*vt.* rodear, circundar; poner una anilla a; anillar, ensortijar.—*vi.* moverse en círculo o en espiral; formar círculo.—*vti.* [10] tocar, sonar, tañer, repicar (campanas, timbre, campanilla); repetir, reiterar.—*to r. up,* llamar (a uno) por teléfono; (teat.) levantar el telón.—*vii.* sonar, tañer, campanillear; retumbar, resonar; zumbar (los oídos).—

to r. off, terminar (una conversación telefónica); (fam.) cesar de hablar.—*to r. true,* sonar bien (una moneda, etc.); sonar a verdad.— **—ing** [-iŋ], *a.* resonante.—*s.* (of bells) tañido; (of buzzer) toque; (of phone) timbre; (in the ears) retintín, zumbido.- **—leader** [-lídœr], *s.* cabecilla.- **—let** [ríŋlit], *s.* anillejo, círculo; sortija, bucle, rizo; (Am.) crespo.- **—master** [-mæstœr], *s.* (in a circus) maestro de ceremonias.- **—side** [-said], *s.* cercanías de cuadrilátero.- **—seat,** asiento junto al cuadrilátero.- **—worm** [-wœrm], s. tiña.

rink [riŋk], *s.* pista de patinar.

rinse [rins], *vt.* enjuagar; lavar; aclarar (la ropa).—*s.* enjuague, aclaración

riot [ráiot], *s.* tumulto; alboroto; (of colors) exhibición brillante.—*to run r.,* desenfrenarse; crecer lozanamente.—*vi.* armar motines; alborotarse.— **—er** [-œ(r)], *s.* amotinado, alborotador.- **—ous** [-∧s], *a.* bullicioso; desenfrenado; alborotado.

rip [rip], *vti. y vii.* [1] rasgar(se), rajar(se), romper(se); descoser(se); soltar(se); arrancar(se).—*to r. off,* rasgar, arrancar; cortar.—*to r. out a seam,* descoser, desbaratar una costura.—*s.* laceración, rasgadura, rasgón; (fam.) persona, caballo o cosa que no vale nada.

ripe [raip], *a.* maduro; en sazón; hecho, acabado; preparado, a propósito; rosado, colorado; (agr.) espigado.- **—n** [ráipn], *vt. y vi.* madurar, sazonar(se).- **—ness** [-nis], *s.* madurez, sazón.

ripple [rípl], *vt.* rizar, ondear.—*vi.* agitarse, rizarse la superficie del agua; murmurar.—*s.* escarceo, onda, rizo (del agua); murmullo.

rise [raiz], *vii.* [10] ascender, subir, elevarse, remontarse; levantarse, ponerse en pie; levantarse (de la cama); alzarse, sublevarse; suspender una sesión; salir (el sol); nacer, brotar (las plantas o los manantiales); surgir, aparecer, presentarse; sobrevenir, suscitarse (una disputa); ascender, mejorar de posición; aumentar de volumen; subir de precio.—*to r. early,* madrugar.—*to r. to one's feet,* ponerse en pie, levantarse.—*s.* ascensión, elevación; levantamiento, insurrección; crecimiento o desarrollo; cuesta, subida;

nacimiento (de un manantial); altura, eminencia; salida (de un astro); encarecimiento, alza de precios; crecimiento (de un río, etc.); origen, causa; ascenso; elevación de la voz.—*h. rise,* torre (de apartamentos).—*to give r. to,* dar origen a, ocasionar.—**risen** [rízn], *pp.* de TO RISE.—**riser** [rаіzœr], *s.*—*early r.,* madrugador.—*late r.,* dormilón.

isk [rіsk], *s.* riesgo, peligro.—*to run a take the r.,* correr riesgo, correr peligro.—*vt.* arriesgar, aventurar, exponer; arriesgarse en.- **—y** [rískj], *a.* peligroso, arriesgado, aventurado, imprudente, temerario.

isqué [rіskeí], *a.* escabroso, subido de tono.

ite [rаіt], *s.* rito, ceremonia.—*last rites,* honras fúnebres.—**ritual** [ríchu̯al], *a.* y *s.* ritual, ceremonial.

itzy [rítzi], *a.* (fam.) lujoso.

ival [rа́іva̯l], *s.* rival.—*a.* competidor, opuesto.—*vti.* [2] rivalizar con.—*vii.* rivalizar.- **—ry** [-ri], *s.* rivalidad.

iver [rívœ(r)], *s.* río.—*down the r.,* río abajo.—*up the r.,* río arriba.—**side** [-sa̯id], *s.* ladera, ribera u orilla de un río.

ivet [rívit], *s.* remache.—*vt.* remachar; (fig.) asegurar, afianzar.

ivulet [rívyu̯l̯it], *s.* riachuelo, arroyuelo.

R.N. [áren], *abrev.* (registered nurse) enfermera diplomada.

oach [rou̯ch], *s.* cucaracha.

oad [rou̯d], *s.* camino, vía; carretera.—*r. hog,* loco del volante.—*r. map,* mapa itinerario.—*r. sign,* señal de carretera, poste indicador.- **—bed** [-bed], *s.* firme; (f.c.) infræstructura.- **—block** [-blak], *s.* barricada; obstáculo.- **—side** [ro̯u̯dsa̯id], *s.* orilla o borde del camino.- **—way** [-we̯і], *s.* carretera, calzada.

oam [rou̯m], *vt.* y *vi.* vagar, andar errante.

oar [rɔr], *vi.* rugir, bramar.—*s.* rugido, bramido; estruendo, estrépito.

oast [rou̯st], *vt.* asar; tostar; calcinar; (fam.) hablar mal de; ridiculizar.—*a.* asado; tostado.—*s.* asado.—*r. beef,* rosbif.- **—er** [róu̯stœ(r)], *s.* asador; tostador.

ob [rab], *vti.* y *vii.* [1] robar.—*to r. one of,* robar, hurtar o quitarle a uno (el dinero, etc.).- **—ber** [rábœ(r)], *s.* ladrón; salteador, bandido.—*r. baron,*

capitalista inescrupuloso.- **—bery** [-œri], *s.* robo.

robe [rou̯b], *s.* manto; túnico o túnica; ropón, toga, traje talar; bata; corte de vestido; manta de coche.—*vt.* vestir de gala o de ceremonia; vestir, ataviar.—*vi.* vestirse; cubrirse.

robin [rábin], *s.* petirrojo; (E.U.) primavera.

robot [rou̯bat], *s.* robot.

robust [robást], *a.* robusto, vigoroso, fuerte.

rock [rak], *s.* roca, peña, peñasco; arrecife, escollo; (fig.) amparo, protección; (jer.) diamante, piedra preciosa; (mus.) rock.—*r.-bottom,* el mínimo, el más bajo.—*r. candy,* azúcar cande.—*r. crystal,* cristal de roca.—*r. garden,* jardín entre rocas.—*R. of Gibraltar,* peñón de Gibraltar.—*r. salt,* sal de compás, sal gema.—*r.wool,* lana mineral.—*on the rocks,* (bebidas) con hielo; arruinado, tronado.—*vt.* mecer, balancear; arrullar; sosegar.—*vi.* mecerse, bambolear, oscilar.- **—er** [rákœ(r)], *s.* arco; mecedora (silla); balancín.

rocket [rákit], *s.* cohete, volador.—*r. bomb,* (mil.) bomba cohete.—*r. launcher,* lanzacohetes.—*r. plane,* avión cohete.—*r.-propelled,* propulsado por un cohete.—*r. ship,* aeronave cohete.—*vi.* volar o ascender verticalmente en el aire.

rocking [rákіŋ], *a.* mecedor; oscilante.—*r. chair,* mecedora, sillón de hamaca.—*r. horse,* caballo mecedor.—*s.* mecedura, balance, balanceo.

rocky [rákі], *a.* peñascoso, rocoso, pedregoso, duro, endurecido.

rod [rad], *s.* vara, varilla; cetro; bastón de mando; varilla de virtudes; caña de pescar; barra de cortina; vara de medir; (mec.) vástago, barra; azote; (fig.) disciplina, castigo; linaje.

rode [rou̯d], *pret.* de TO RIDE.

rodent [róu̯dent], *a.* y *s.* roedor.

roe [rou̯], *s.* hueva, ovas de pescado.—*r. deer,* corzo.

rogue [rou̯g], *s.* bribón, pícaro, pillo, golfo, villano; (fam.) pilluelo, perillán.—*r.'s gallery,* archivo fotográfico de delincuentes.—**roguish** [róu̯gіš], *a.* picaresco, (fam.) tuno, travieso.

role o **rôle** [rou̯l], *s.* (teat.) papel.—*to play a r.,* desempeñar un papel.

roll [rou̯l], *vt.* hacer rodar; girar, voltear; enrollar, abarquillar; (fund.) laminar; alisar, emparejar con rodillo; apisonar (el césped); liar; envolver, fajar; redoblar (el tambor); hacer vibrar (lengua o voz); poner (los ojos) en lanco.—*to r. over*, (com.) refinanciar.—*to r. up*, enrrollar; (fam.) cumular; revolver.—*vi.* rodar; agitarse (las olas); ondular, fluctuar; retumbar, retemblar; bambolearse, balancearse; arrollarse, abarquillarse; dar un redoble de tambores.—*to r. about*, rodar, divagar, andar de acá para allá.—*to r. down*, bajar rodando.—*to r. in money*, nadar en la abundancia.—*to r. to a stop*, seguir rodando hasta pararse.—*s.* rollo; rol, lista, nómina, matrícula, registro; bollo, panecillo; echada; (mec.) rodillo, cilindro de emparejar allanar o laminar; laminador; maza de trapiche; redoble (de tambores); retumbo del trueno; balanceo, bamboleo; oleaje (cir.) mecha.—*pl.* archivos.—*r. call*, lista, el pasar lista.—*r.-top desk*, escritorio de cortina corrediza.— **—er** [róulœ(r)], s. rodillo, tambor, cilindro; aplanadera; alisador; ola larga; (cir.) venda, faja.—*r. bearing*, cojinete de rodillos.—*r. coaster*, montaña rusa.—*r. skate*, patín de ruedas.—*r. towel*, toalla sin fin.

rolling [róuliŋ], *a.* rodante; ondulante.—*r. mill*, taller de laminación.—*r. pin*, rodillo, hataca.—*r. stock*, (f.c.) material móvil.—*r. stone*, piedra movediza.

ROM [roum], *abrev.* (read-only memory) (comput.) memoria de acceso ROM, memoria de acceso aleatorio.

Roman [róumạn], *a.* romano; católico romano.—*r. candle*, vela romana.—*R. Empire*, Imperio romano.—*R. nose*, nariz aquilina.—*s.* romano.

romance [roméns], *s.* romance; novela, ficción, cuento, fábula; (mús.) romanza; aventura, drama, episodio extraño y conmovedor; (fam.) amorío, idilio.—*vi.* mentir; fingir fábulas; hablar o pensar románticamente.—*a.* (**R.**) romance; neolatino.—*R. language*, lengua neolatina o románica.

Romanesque [roumạnésk], *a.* (arq.) románico.

romantic [romántik], *a.* romántico, novelesco; sentimental; fantástico.

— **—ism** [romántjsjzm], s. romanticismo.— **—ist** [romántjsjst], s. (escritor, músico, etc.) romántico.

romp [ramp], *vi.* juguetear, retozar.—*s.* retozo.

roof [ruf], *s.* tejado, techo, azotea; bóveda, cielo; cubierta; casa, hogar, habitación.—*r. garden*, pérgola; azotea de baile y diversión.—*r. of the mouth*, bóveda palatina, paladar.—*r. tile*, teja.—*vt.* techar; abrigar, alojar.— **—ing** [rúfiŋ], s. techado, techumbre.

rook [ruk], *s.* (bird) grajo; (in chess) roque.—*vt.* trampear.— **—ie** [-i], *s.* (jer.) recluta; novato.—*r. cop*, policía novato.

room [rum], *vi.* vivir, hospedarse, alojarse.—*s.* habitación, cuarto, aposento, sala, cámara, pieza; lugar, espacio, puesto; paraje, sitio; causa, motivo, razón; tiempo, ocasión, oportunidad.—*r. and board*, pensión completa.—*r. clerk*, recepcionista.— **—er** [rúmœ(r)], s. huésped, inquilino.— **—iness** [-injs], s. espaciosidad, holgura, amplitud.— **—mate** [-mejt], s. compañero de cuarto.— **—y** [-i], *a.* espacioso, capaz, amplio, bolgado.

rooming house [rúmiŋ], s. pensión.

roost [rust], *s.* percha de gallinero; lugar de descanso; sueño, descanso (de la aves domésticas).—*vi.* dormir o descansar (las aves) en una percha.— **—er** [rústœ(r)], s. gallo.

root [rut], *s.* raíz.—*r. and branch*, por completo.—*vi.* y *vt.* echar o criar raíces, arraigar(se); hozar.—*to r. for*, (fam.) aplaudir, alabar, vitorear.—*to r. up* o *out*, arrancar de raíz, desarraigar; extirpar.—*to take r.*, radicar, arraigar(se).

rope [roup], *s.* soga; cuerda, cordel, cabo; driza; reata; sarta, ristra, trenza; hilera, fila.—*r. ladder*, escala de cuerdas.—*r. sandal*, alpargata.—*to know the ropes*, (fam.) saber todas las tretas.—*vt.* atar con una cuerda, rodear con soga; coger con lazo.—*to r. in*, (fam.) atraer, embaucar, engañar.—*to r. off*, cercar con cuerdas.—*vi.* hacer hebras o madeja.— **—walker** [-wɔkœr], s. funámbulo, volatinero.

rosary [róuzạri], *s.* rosario.— **rose** [rouz], s. rosa; color de rosa.—*r. garden*, rosaleda, rosalera.—*r. tree*, rosal.—**rosebay** [róuzbej], s. adelfa

—**rosebud** [róʊzbʌd], s. pimpollo, botón o capullo de rosa; niña adolescente.—**rosebush** [róʊzbʊ̌š], s. rosal.

osemary [róʊzmeri], s. (bot.) romero.

osette [roʊzét], s. rosa, roseta; escarapela, moña; (arq.) rosetón, florón.

osin [rázin], s. resina.

oster [rástœr], s. lista, registro; horario escolar.

ostrum [rástrʌm], s. tribuna.

osy [róʊzi], a. rosado, sonrosado; alegre.

ot [rat], vti. y vii. [1] pudrir(se), corromper(se).—s. podredumbre; (jer.) tontería.

otary [róʊtari], a. giratorio, rotativo, rotatorio.—**rotate** [róʊtejt], vi. girar; alternar(se).—vt. hacer girar, dar vuelta(s) a; alternar; (agr.) sembrar o cultivar en rotación.—**rotation** [roʊtéjšon], s. rotación, giro; turno; alternativa.—by r., in r., por turnos, alternadamente; (agr.) en rotación.

ote [roʊt], s. lo que se aprende de memoria.—by r., de memoria o de coro; mecánicamente.

otten [rátn], a. podrido; (fam.) malísimo; dañado; en mal estado.

otund [rotánd], a. redondo; regordete; rotundo, sonoro.

ouge [ruž], s. colorete.—a. colorado, encarnado.—vt. y vr. arrebolar(se), pintar(se), dar(se) colorete.

ough [rʌf], a. áspero; tosco; fragoso, escabroso; erizado; encrespado; desapacible; rudo, inculto, grosero, brusco; tempestuoso, borrascoso, agitado; chapucero; aproximativo, general; preliminar, preparativo.—as o at a r. guess, a ojo de buen cubero.—r. diamond, diamante en bruto; persona ruda pero de buen fondo.—r. draft, boceto, bosquejo; borrador.—s. matón, rufián.—in the r., en bruto, sin pulimento.—vt. poner áspero, tosco, escabroso; labrar toscamente; (fam.) molestar, irritar.—to r. it, pasar trabajos, vivir sin comodidades.— —**cast** [-kæst], s. mezcla gruesa; modelo tosco.— —**en** [rʌfn], vt. y vi. poner(se) áspero o tosco; picar, rascar.— —**ly** [-li], adv. aproximadamente; brutalmente; asperamente.— —**ness** [-nis], s. aspereza, rudeza; brusquedad. severidad, dureza.

oulette [rulét], s. ruleta.

round [raʊnd], a. redondo, circular, cilíndrico, esférico, orbicular; rollizo; rotundo; sonoro; cabal, grande, cuantioso; franco, llano, ingenuo; vivo, veloz; justo, honrado.—r. numbers, cifras globales.—R. Table, Tabla Redonda.—r. trip, viaje de ida y vuelta.—r. trip ticket, billete de ida y vuelta.—to go r. and r., dar vuelta tras vuelta.—s. círculo, esfera; círculo de personas o cosas; redondez; vuelta, giro, rotación; peldaño (de escala); liston o travesaño (de silla); rodaja de carne; (arq.) mediacaña; (mil.) ronda; andanada, salva, disparo, descarga; cartucho con bala; ruta, camino, circuito; rutina, serie; (dep.) tanda, suerte, turno; (boxeo, etc.) asalto; (naipes) mano; (mus.) rondó; danza.—adv. alrededor, en derredor, por todos lados; a la redonda.—all-r., cumplido, que sirve para todo; cabal.—r. about, por el lado opuesto; por todos lados, a la redonda.—r.-shouldered, cargado de espaldas.—prep. alrededor de; a la vuelta de.—vt. redondear, dar vuelta; doblar (un cabo, una esquina); acabar, perfeccionar.—to r. up, recoger, juntar, reunir; coger; recoger el ganado.—vi. redondearse; desarrollarse, perfeccionarse; dar vueltas; rondar.—to r. out, llenarse, redondearse.— —**about** [ráʊndạbaʊt], a. indirecto, vago; desviado.—s. chaqueta; tiovivo; rodeo.— —**house** [-haʊs], s. cocherón, casa de máquinas, depósito de locomotoras.— —**ness** [-nis], s. redondez.— —**up** [-ʌp], s. rodeo de ganado; recogida, junta; apresuramiento, aprehensión.

rouse [raʊz], vt. despertar, animar, excitar, suscitar; levantar (la caza); (mar.) halar.—vi. despertar(se), despabilarse, animarse, moverse.

rousing [raʊ́ziŋ], a. vehemente; caluroso, entusiasta.

roustabout [raʊ́stạbaʊt], s. obrero inexperto, trabajador sin experiencia; bracero, peón.

route [rut, raʊt], s. ruta, vía; rumbo, derrotero; marcha, curso.—vt. encaminar, señalar ruta, pista, vía (a trenes, aviones, etc.).

routine [rutín], a. rutinario.—s. rutina; costumbre, hábito.

rove [roʊv], vi. corretear, vagar, vagabundear.—s. correría, paseo.- **—r** [róʊvœ(r)], s. vagabundo; persona inconstante.

row [roʊ], s. hilera, fila; paseo en lancha o bote; remadura; [raʊ], camorra, trifulca.—vt. [roʊ], conducir remando.—vi. [roʊ], remar, bogar; [raʊ], armar camorra.- **—boat** [róʊboʊt], s. bote de remos.- **—dy** [ráʊdi], a. y s. gamberro.- **—dyism** [ráʊdiizm], s. rufianismo.- **—er** [róʊœ(r)], s. remero.

royal [rɔ́ial], a. real, regio, magnífico.—to have a r. time, divertirse en grande, o a cuerpo de rey.- **—ist** [-ist], s. (pol.) realista.- **—ty** [-ti], s. realeza.—pl. derechos de autor o de inventor.

rub [rʌb], vti. [1] estregar, frotar, friccionar; raspar, raer; incomodar, fastidiar.—to r. away, quitar frotando.—to r. down, dar un masaje; alisar frotando.—to r. in, hacer penetrar frotando; (fam.) machacar.—to r. off, quitar; limpiar frotando.—to r. out, borrar.—to r. the wrong way, frotar a contrapelo; irritar; incomodar.—to r. up, aguijonear, excitar; retocar, pulir.—vii. pasar raspando, rozar; ser desagradable o molesto; ir a contrapelo.—s. frotación, roce, tropiezo, dificultad; sarcasmo, denuesto.- **—ber** [rʌ́bœ(r)], a. de caucho.—r. band, faja de goma, elástico, liga.—r. eraser, goma de borrar.—r. plant, árbol del caucho.—r. plantation, cauchal.—r. stamp, estampilla, sello o cuño de goma; (fig.) el que aprueba ciegamente.—to r.-stamp, estampar con un sello de goma; (fam.) aprobar ciegamente.—s. caucho, goma elástica; masajista; goma de borrar; estropajo; escofina; jugada decisiva.—pl. chanclos, zapatos de goma.- **—neck** [-nek], vi. (despec.) curiosear, fisgonear.

rubbish [rʌ́biʃ], s. basura, desperdicio(s), desecho, escombro, cascajo ripio; (fam.) tontería.

rubble [rʌ́bl], s. piedra en bruto o sin labrar; escombros; cascote, casca.

rubdown [rʌ́bdaʊn], s. masaje, fricción.

rube [rub], s. (jer.) rústico, isidro.

ruby [rúbi], s. rubí; carmín, color rojo vivo.—a. rojo.

rudder [rʌ́dœ(r)], s. timón (de barco).

ruddiness [rʌ́dinis], s. rojez, rubicundez.—**ruddy** [rʌ́di], a. rojo, rojizo rubicundo.

rude [rud], a. rudo, brusco, descortés, tosco, chabacano; inculto; fuerte vigoroso.- **—ness** [rúdnis], s. grosería; descortesía; rudeza, aspereza rusticidad, crudeza.

rudiment [rúdiment], s. rudimento, (biol.) embrión, germen.- **—ary** [rudiméntari], a. rudimentario.

rue [ru], vt. lamentar, arrepentirse de.

ruffian [rʌ́fian], a. y s. rufián.

ruffle [rʌ́fl], vt. (cost.) fruncir un volante, rizar; ajar, arrugar, desordenar; encrespar; desazonar, enfadar vejar; redoblar (el tambor).—vi. rizarse, arrugarse; desarreglarse; tremolar; enojarse, incomodarse.—s (cost.) volante fruncido; desazón enojo; escarceo del agua; redoble de tambor.

rug [rʌg], s. alfombra.

rugged [rʌ́gid], a. áspero, escarpado abrupto; tosco, basto; inculto; desa pacible; descomedido; arrugado ceñudo, regañón; desgreñado; ro busto, vigoroso; tempestuoso, bo rrascoso.- **—ness** [-nis], s. escabro sidad; rudeza; robustez.

ruin [rúin], s. ruina, bancarrota; es trago, destrucción; degradación perdición.—pl. ruinas, escombros —vt. arruinar; echar a perder; estro pear.—vi. arruinarse; decaer.- **—ous** [-ʌs], a. ruinoso.

rule [rul], s. regla; gobierno, mando dominio; soberanía; régimen, rei nado; estatuto, precepto; regulari dad, buen orden; (fig.) norma, guía modelo; (for.) auto, fallo; (impr. pleca, filete; raya, línea trazada.—a a r., por regla general.—r. book, re glamento.—r. of thumb, regla o mé todo empírico.—to be the r., ser la regla; ser de reglamento.—vt. go bernar, mandar, regir; reprimi (for.) decidir, determinar, disponer dirigir, guiar; arreglar, ordenar; ra yar (papel).—to r. out, excluir; des cartar.—vi. gobernar, mandar; esta blecer una regla, formular una deci sión; prevalecer, estar en boga (com.) mantenerse a un tipo.—to over, mandar, gobernar, dominar. **—r** [rúlœ(r)], s. soberano, príncipe gobernador, gobernante; pauta, re gla (para trazar líneas).—**rulin**

[rúliŋ], s. (for.) decisión, fallo, disposición; rayadura; rayado.—a. gobernante, imperante.

rum [rʌm], s. ron.

Rumanian [ruméjnjan], a. y s. rumano (persona e idioma).

rumble [rʌmbl], vi. retumbar, rugir; avanzar con estruendo.—vt. hacer retumbar, etc.—s. retumbo; rugido; estruendo; (jer.) riña entre pandillas.

ruminant [rúminant], a. y s. rumiante.—**ruminate** [rúminejt], vt. y vi. rumiar; considerar, reflexionar.

rumor [rúmǫ(r)], s. rumor, runrún.—vt. divulgar, propalar.—it is rumored, se dice, corre la voz.

rump [rʌmp], s. anca, nalga; (cut of beef) cuarto trasero.

rumple [rʌmpl], vt. arrugar, ajar.—s. arruga, doblez, estrujadura.

rumpus [rʌmpʌs], s. (fam.) batahola, jaleo, escándalo, alboroto.—r. room, cuarto de juegos.

run [rʌn], vti. [10] correr, hacer correr; mover, poner en movimiento; dejar correr o salir; meter, clavar, introducir; empujar, echar; cazar, perseguir; tirar, trazar (una línea, en el papel o el terreno); pasar (la vista); atravesar, cruzar; derramar, manar; correr (un peligro); fundir, moldear; (cost.) bastear; tener o proponer como candidato; mandar, dominar; manejar, dirigir (una máquina, institución, empresa).—to r. a blockade, violar o burlar un bloqueo.—to r. a temperature, tener fiebre.—to r. down, dar caza; (mar.) echar a pique; difamar, hablar mal de; quebrantar, postrar; gastar (la salud, etc.).—to r. for office, aspirar a un cargo electivo.—to r. in, recorrer; encerrar; (fam.) prender.—to r. into the ground, meter en la tierra; extender hasta más abajo del suelo; (fam.) llevar al exceso.—to r. off, desviar; desecar, vaciar; repetir, decir de coro; imprimir.—to r. out, agotar; desperdiciar; (fam.) echar.—to r. over, atropellar, pasar encima de; hojear, repasar, revisar de prisa.—to r. through, ver, examinar, presentar, etc. a la ligera; atravesar, pasar de parte a parte; traspasar; hojear, leer por encima; gastar, derrochar, malbaratar.—to r. up, (cost.) remendar, repasar; incu-

rrir, hacer subir (una cuenta); sumar, hacer una suma; montar o edificar de prisa; (mar.) izar.—vii. correr; pasar, deslizarse; marchar, andar, funcionar, moverse (un buque, reloj, máquina, etc.); derretirse, fluir, gotear o chorrear; derramarse; correrse (un color); competir, lidiar; ser candidato, presentarse como tal; (med.) supurar; (teat.) representarse consecutivamente; extenderse, ir, llegar (hasta), correr, transcurrir; tener predilección; continuar, durar; rezar, decir; tener curso, circular; salirse, dejar fugar el agua, etc.; ir, andar (en manadas, etc.).—to r. about, andar de lugar en lugar; corretear.—to r. across, atravesar corriendo; hallar; dar o tropezar con.—to r. against, chocar, topar, dar contra; oponerse; ser contrario a.—to r. ahead, correr delante; llevar ventaja.—to r. away, huir, escapar, zafarse; desbocarse.—to r. away with, arrebatar; fugarse con; (fam.) llevarse la palma en, ser el protagonista en.—a. extraído; vaciado; derretido; (fam.) de contrabando.—s. corrida, carrera; curso, marcha; batida de caza; (mil.) marcha forzada; vuelta, viajecito, jornada; recorrido, trayecto; distancia; (mec.) marcha, movimiento, funcionamiento; serie, continuación; duración, vida; hilo (del discurso); (teat.) serie de representaciones consecutivas de una pieza; lo que sale o se saca cada vez (hornada, vaciado, etc.); mando, dirección; (béisbol) carrera; arribazón (de peces); clase, tipo; aspecto, carácter.—in the long r., a la larga.—the (common) r., el común de las gentes; lo común, lo corriente.—pp. de TO RUN.—**away** [rʌnąwej], a. y s. fugitivo, desertor.—s. fuga; rapto, secuestro; desbocamiento; caballo desbocado.

rundown [rʌndaun], s. resumen.—a. desmedrado; agotado; desmantelado; sin cuerda, distendido; descargado.

rung [rʌŋ], pp. de TO RING (tocar).—s. travesaño; radio, rayo; (fig.) peldaño.

runner [rʌnœ(r)], s. corredor; andarín; pieza o parte giratoria o corrediza; mensajero; (fam.) correve(i)dile; fugitivo; contrabandista; agente, factor; alguacil; corredera.

running [ránin], s. carrera, corrida; contrabando; funcionamiento.—a. que corre; que fluye o mana; que funciona.—r. board, estribo.—r. expenses, gastos corrientes.—r. start, (dep.) salida lanzada.—r. water, agua corriente.

runoff [ránɔf], s. residuo líquido; (dep.) eliminatoria.—r. election, segunda votación.

runproof [ránpruf], a. indesmallable.

runt [rʌnt], s. enano; paloma; (little child) redrojo.

runway [ránwej], s. lecho, madre, cauce; senda; rampa; (aer.) pista de aterrizaje.

rupture [rápchū(r)], s. ruptura; quebradura.—vt. romper, fracturar; reventar.—vi. romperse, rajarse, reventar.

rural [rúr̯al], a. rural.—r. free delivery, distribución gratuita del correo en el campo.

rush [rʌ̂s], s. ímpetu, embestida, acometida; prisa, precipitación; torrente, tropel, agolpamiento, asedio; lucha, rebatiña; tierra rica en oro; (bot.) junco; friolera, bagatela.—r. hour, hora de aglomeración, horas de punta.—r. order, pedido urgente.—with a r., de golpe; de repente.—vi. lanzarse, abalanzarse, precipitarse; embestir, acometer; agolparse.—to r. forward, lanzarse.—to r. in, entrar de rondón.—to r. in upon, sorprender.—to r. out, salir con precipitación.—to r. through, lanzarse por entre o a través de.—vt. empujar o arrojar con violencia; activar.—to r. through, ejecutar deprisa.

Russian [rʌ̂ʃan], a. y s. ruso (persona e idioma).

rust [rʌst], s. herrumbre, orín, moho.—vt. y vi. enmohecer(se); entorpecer(se), embotar(se).

rustic [rástik], a. rústico, rural; agrario, agreste; campesino; sencillo; inculto.—s. rústico, campesino.

rustle [rásl], vt. y vi. susurrar, crujir (la seda), murmurar (las hojas); (fam.) hurtar ganado.—s. susurro, crujido, murmullo.

rusty [rásti], a. mohoso, herrumbroso; rojizo o amarillento; entorpecido, torpe por falta de práctica.

rut [rʌt], vti. [1] hacer rodadas o surcos.—vii. bramar (los venados, etc.), estar en celo.—s. rodada, surco, bache; rutina, costumbre; brama, celo (de los animales).

ruthless [rúθlis], a. cruel, despiadado.—**-ness** [-nis], s. crueldad, empedernimiento.

rye [raj], s. centeno; whisky de centeno.

S

Sabbath [sǽbæθ], s. sábado; domingo.—**sabbatical** [sabǽtikal], s. año sabático (de los profesores).

saber [séjbœ(r)], s. sable.

sable [séjbl], s. (zool.) marta cibelina.

sabot [sǽbou], s. zueco.

sabotage [sǽbotaʒ], s. sabotaje.—vt. cometer sabotaje (contra, en).

saboteur [sæbotœ́r], s. saboteador.

saccharin [sǽkarin], s. sacarina.—**-e** [sǽkarin], a. dulzón; empalagoso.

sack [sæk], s. saco, costal, talega; (mil.) saqueo, saco.—vt. saquear.—**-cloth** [sǽkklɔθ], s. arpillera.

sacrament [sǽkrament], s. sacramento; eucaristía.—**sacred** [séjkrid], a. (con)sagrado, sacro(santo).

sacrifice [sǽkrifais], vt. y vi. sacrificar, inmolar.—s. sacrificio, inmolación.—at a s., haciendo un sacrificio; perdiendo, con pérdida.

sacrilege [sǽkrilidʒ], s. sacrilegio.—**sacrilegious** [sækrilídʒʌs], a. sacrílego.

sacristan [sǽkristan], s. sacristán.—**sacristy** [sǽkristi], s. sacristía.

sacrum [séjkrʌm], s. (anat.) sacro.

sad [sæd], a. triste, pesaroso; cariacontecido; aciago, nefasto.—s sack, (fam.) inútil.—**-den** [sædn] vt. y vi. entristecer(se).

saddle [sædl], s. silla de montar, montura; silla o sillín (de bicicleta o motocicleta).—s. horse, caballo de silla o cabalgadura.—vt. ensillar; enalbardar.—to s. with, hacer cargar con.

—bag [-bæg], s. alforja, jaque.—
—cloth [-klɔθ], s. mantilla (de silla).— **—r** [sǽdlœ(r)], s. talabartero.

sadism [sǽdjzm], s. sadismo. **—sadistic** [sædístjk], a. sádico, sadista.

sadness [sǽdnjs], s. tristeza.

safe [seif], s. caja de caudales, caja fuerte.—a. seguro; salvo, ileso; sin peligro; intacto; digno de confianza.—s. and sound, sano y salvo.—s.-conduct, salvoconducto, salvaguardia.—s. deposit box, caja de seguridad (en el banco).—
—guard [séjfgard], s. salvaguardia; resguardo; defensor, escolta; defensa, abrigo.—vt. salvaguardar, proteger; escoltar.— **—ty** [-tj], s. seguridad, protección; seguro (de arma de fuego).—a. de seguridad.—s. pin, imperdible.—s. match, fósforo de seguridad.—s. razor, maquinilla de seguridad (de afeitarse).

saffron [sǽfron], s. (bot.) azafrán.

sag [sæg], vti. [1] combar, pandear.—vii. combarse, pandearse; aflojarse, doblegarse; hundirse.—s. comba, pandeo.

sage [seidʒ], s. sabio; (bot.) salvia.—a. sabio; sagaz; cuerdo, prudente.

Sagittarius [sædʒjtériŭs], s. (astr.) Sagitario.

said [sed], pret. y pp. de TO SAY.—a. (el) mencionado o citado; (for.) dicho, antedicho.—s. and done, dicho y hecho.

sail [seil], s. (mar.) vela; excursión o paseo en barco.—pl. velamen.—under full s., a toda vela, a todo trapo.—vi. hacerse o darse a la vela; zarpar; salir (un buque); navegar.—to s. before the wind, navegar viento en popa.—to s. close with the wind, ceñir el viento, bolinear.—vt. navegar por, surcar.— **—boat** [séjlbout], s. barco de vela, balandro, velero.—**—fish** [-fjʃ], s. aguja de mar, (Am.) pez vela, aguja de abanico.— **—ing** [-jŋ], s. navegación (a vela); salida o partida de un barco.—clear o plain s., coser y cantar.— **—or** [-ǫ(r)], s. marinero; marino.

saint [seint], s. santo.—s.'s day, día del santo, onomástico.—a. san, santo.—vt. canonizar.—**—hood** [séjnthud], s. santidad.— **—liness** [-ljnjs], s. santidad.— **—ly** [-lj], a. santo.

sake [seik], s. causa, motivo, fin, objeto, razón; amor, respeto, consideración.—for God's s., por Dios, por el amor de Dios.—for mercy's s., por piedad, por misericordia.—for the s. of, en consideración a.

salad [sǽlad], s. ensalada.—s. bowl, ensaladera.—s. dressing, aliño, aderezo para ensalada.

salamander [sǽlamændœ(r)], s. salamandra.

salami [salámj], s. salchichón.

salary [sǽlarj], s. sueldo, salario, pago.

sale [seil], s. venta; liquidación, saldo; (com.) realización.—sales slip, recibo, comprobante.—sales talk, palabrería de vendedor.—sales tax, impuesto sobre las ventas.—for s. u on s., de venta, en venta.— **—sclerk** [seílsklœrk], s. vendedor, dependiente.— **—zlady** [seílzlejdj], s. vendedora, dependienta.— **—sman** [séjlzman], s. vendedor; dependiente de tienda.— **—smanship** [seílzmænʃip], s. arte de vender.— **person** [seílzpœrson], s. vendedor, vendedora, dependiente, dependienta; representante, corredor, corredora.— **—sroom** [seílzrum], s. salón de ventas; salón de exhibición.

saliva [saláivä], s. saliva.

sallow [sǽlou], a. cetrino.

sally [sǽlj], vii. [7] (a veces con **forth**) salir, hacer una salida.—s. salida.

salmon [sǽmon], s. salmón.

saloon [salún], s. salón; cámara de un vapor; (E.U.) taberna, cantina, tugurio.

salt [sɔlt], s. sal; agudeza, ingenio chispeante.—old s., lobo de mar.—pl. sales medicinales; sal de higuera, sulfato de magnesia.—a. salado; salobre; curado o conservado con sal.—salted peanuts, saladillos.—s. pork, tocino salado.—s. shaker, salero (de mesa).—vt. salar; (fig.) sazonar.—to s. away, ahorrar.— **—ed** [sɔltjd], a. salado.— **—peter** [-pítœ(r)], s. nitro, salitre.— **—y** [-j], a. salado; salobre.

saltine [sɔltín], s. galletita salada.

salutation [sælyutéjʃon], s. salutación.—**salute** [salĭút], vt. y vi. saludar; cuadrarse.—s. saludo.

Salvadoran [sælvadóran], **Salvadorian** [sælvadórian], s. y a. salvadoreño.

salvage [sǽlvjdʒ], s. salvamento.—vt. salvar; recobrar. **—salvation** [sælvéjʃon], s. salvación.

salve [sæv, sav], s. ungüento.—vt. curar (una herida) con ungüentos; preservar; aliviar.

salvo [sǽlvou], s. salva.

Samaritan [səmǽritən], a. y s. samaritano.

same [seim], a. y pron. mismo; igual, idéntico.—*all the s.*, a pesar de eso, a pesar de todo.—*it is all the s. to me*, me es igual, lo mismo me da.—*just the s.*, del mismo modo; a pesar de eso.—*much the s. as*, casi como.—*the s.*, lo mismo; el mismo, los mismos; otro tanto.

sample [sǽmpl], s. muestra.—*s. book*, muestrario.—*s. copy*, ejemplar muestra.—*vt.* probar, catar.

sanctify [sǽŋktifai], vti. [7] santificar. —**sanctimonious** [sæŋktimóuniʌs], a. mojigato, santurrón. —**sanctimoniousness** [sæŋktimóuniʌsnis], s. mojigatería.

sanction [sǽŋkšən], s. sanción.—*vt.* sancionar.

sanctity [sǽŋktiti], s. santidad. —**sanctuary** [sǽŋkchueri], s. santuario.

sand [sænd], s. arena.—*s. bank*, banco de arena.—*s. blast*, chorro de arena; limpiar con chorro de arena.—*s. bar*, barra, banco de arena.—*s. blasting*, limpiadura por chorro de arena.—*s. box*, (f.c.) arenero.—*s. dune*, duna, médano.—*s. glass*, reloj de arena, ampolleta.—*s. pit*, arenal.—*vt.* (en) arenar; (gen. con **down**) alisar con papel de lija.- —**al** [sǽndal], s. sandalia.- —**bag** [-bæg], s. saco de arena.—*vt.* proteger con sacos de arena; (jer.) engañar.

sandpaper [sǽndpeipœ(r)], s. papel de lija.—*vt.* lijar. —**sandstone** [sǽndstoun], s. piedra arenisca. —**sandstorm** [sǽndstɔrm], s. tempestad de arena.

sandwich [sǽndwich], vt. intercalar, insertar.—s. emparedado, sandwich.

sandy [sǽndi], a. arenoso, arenisco.

sane [sein], a. cuerdo; sano.

sang [sæŋ], pret. de TO SING.

sanguinary [sǽŋgwineri], a. sanguinario. —**sanguine** [sǽŋgwin], a. confiado, lleno de esperanza; sanguíneo.

sanitarium [sænitériʌm], s. enfermería, sanatorio. —**sanitary** [sǽniteri], a. sanitario; higiénico. —s. napkin, compresa higiénica. —**sanitation** [sæniteišən], s. saneamiento; sanidad. —**sanity** [sǽniti], s. cordura; sensatez; sanidad.

sank [sæŋk], pret. de TO SINK.

sap [sæp], vti. [1] zapar, minar; agotar, debilitar.—s. savia; (fort.) zapa. (fam.) tonto.

sapling [sǽpliŋ], s. árbol muy joven.

sapphire [sǽfair], s. zafiro.

Saracen [sǽrasen], s. sarraceno.

sarcasm [sárkæzm], s. sarcasmo. —**sarcastic** [sarkǽstik], a. sarcástico.

sardine [sardín], s. sardina.

sash [sæš], s. (mil.) faja, banda; cinturón, ceñidor; (carp.) bastidor o marco de ventana.—s. window, ventana de guillotina.

sat [sæt], pret. y pp. de TO SIT.

satanic [seitǽnik], a. satánico.

satchel [sǽchel], s. maletín; bolsa.

sate [seit], vt. hartar, saciar; hastiar.

sateen [sætín], s. (tej.) satén, rasete.

satellite [sǽtelait], s. satélite.—s. country, país satélite.—s. dish, antena parabólica.—s. spy s., satélite espía.—weather s., satélite meteorológico.

satiate [seišieit], vt. saciar.- —d [seišieitid], a. ahito, harto.

satin [sǽtin], s. (tej.) raso.

satire [sǽtair], s. sátira. —**satiric(al)** [satírik(al)], a. satírico. —**satirize** [sǽtiraiz], vt. satirizar.

satisfaction [sætisfǽkšən], s. satisfacción. —**satisfactory** [sætisfǽktori], a. satisfactorio; suficiente.—a. satisfecho, contento. —**satisfy** [sǽtisfai], vti. y vii. [7] satisfacer.—to oneself that, convencerse de que.

saturate [sǽchūreit], vt. saturar; empapar, impregnar. —**saturation** [sæchūréišən], s. saturación.

Saturday [sǽtœrdi], s. sábado.

satyr [séitœ(r), sǽtœ(r)], s. sátiro.

sauce [sɔs], s. salsa.—vt. condimentar, sazonar.- —dish [sósdiš], s. salsera. —pan [-pæn], s. cacerola.- —[sósœ(r)], s. platillo. —saucines [sósinis], s. insolencia. —sauc[sósi], a. descarado, insolente.

sauerkraut [sáuŗkraut], s. chucruta.

sausage [sósidž], s. salchicha; embutido; chorizo; longaniza; morcilla.

savage [sǽvidž], a. y s. salvaje.- —[-ri], s. salvajismo.

savanna(h) [səvǽnə], s. (Am.) sabana.

save [seiv], vt. salvar; guardar, conservar; evitar; ahorrar, economizar.—prep. salvo, excepto.—conj. sino, menos que, a no ser que. —**savin**

[-iŋ], *a.* ahorrativo, frugal, económico; *salvador.—s.* economía, ahorro; salvedad.—*pl.* ahorros.—*s. account,* cuenta de ahorros.—*s. and loan company,* sociedad de ahorros y préstamos.—*savings bank,* caja de ahorros.—*prep.* con excepción de, fuera de, excepto, salvo. **—savior** [séivᵩo(r)], *s.* salvador.—*the Saviour,* el Salvador (Jesucristo).

avor [séivᵩr], *s.* sabor.—*vt.* saborear.—*vi.*—*to s. of,* oler a, saber a.— **—ory** [séivᵩri], *a.* sabroso; picante; fragante.—*s.* (bot.) ajedrea.

aw [sɔ], *s.* (carp.) sierra.—*vti.* [6] serrar, aserrar.—*pret.* de TO SEE.— **—buck** [sɔ́bʌk], *s.* caballete de aserrar, tijera; (fam.) billete de diez pesos.— **—dust** [-dʌst], *s.* (a)serrín.— **—horse** [-hɔrs], *s.* = SAWBUCK.— **mill** [-mil], *s.* aserradero, aserrío.— **sawn** [sɔn], *pp.* de TO SAW.—*a.* aserrado.— **—pit** [-pit], *s.* aserradero.

axon [sǽkson], *a. y s.* sajón.

axophone [sǽksofoun], *s.* saxofón.

ay [sei], *vt.* y *vii.* [10] decir.—*I s.!* ¡digo!—*it is said, they s.,* se dice, dicen.—*s.!* ¡oiga!—*so to s.,* por decirlo así.—*to s. good-bye,* despedirse, decir adiós.—*to s. in one's sleeve,* decir para su capote.—*to s. nothing of,* sin mencionar.—*to s. on,* continuar hablando.—*that is to s.,* es decir, esto es.—*you don't s. (so)!* ¡calle Ud.! ¡no es posible!—*s.* uso de la palabra; expresión de opinión; afirmación.— *s.-so,* (fam.) opinión o juicio personal; declaración autorizada.— **—ing** [séiiŋ], *s.* dicho; aserto; decir, refrán.—*as the s. goes,* como dice el refrán.

cab [skæb], *s.* (cir.) costra, postilla; (despec.) esquirol, rompehuelgas, carnero.

cabbard [skǽbᵩrd], *s.* vaina, funda.

cabby [skǽbi], *a.* costroso, postilloso.

cables [skéibiz], *s.* sarna.

cabrous [skǽbrᵩs], *a.* escabroso, áspero, rugoso; (not for polite society) escabroso.

cads [skædz], *spl.* (fam.) montones, pilas.

caffold [skǽfould], *s.* andamio, tablado; cadalso, patíbulo.— **—ing** [-iŋ], *s.* andamiada, andamiaje; paral.

cald [skɔld], *vt.* escaldar; (coc.) escalfar; esterilizar.— **—ing** [-iŋ], *a.* hirviendo.—*s.* quemadura, escaldadura.

scale [skeil], *s.* escala; gama; platillo de balanza; (gen. en *pl.*) balanza, báscula; escama (de peces, reptiles); (med.) costra, laminita, plancha, hojuela.—*to s.,* (dib.) según escala.—*vt.* escamar o des(es)camar; cubrir con escamas; incrustar o desincrustar; escalar; (con **down**) reducir según escala; pesar.—*vi.* (a veces con **off**) descostrarse; desconcharse, pelarse.

scallop [skǽlop], *s.* (molusco) vieira; concha de peregrino; venera; (thin slice of meat) escalope; (cost.) festón, onda.—*vt.* festonear, ondear; (coc.) asar ostras empanadas.— **—ed** [skǽlopt], *a.* festoneado.—*s. potatoes,* papas o patatas gratinadas o al gratén.

scalp [skælp], *s.* cuero cabelludo.—*vt.* arrancar el cuero cabelludo; comprar y revender (acciones, billetes de f.c., teatro, etc.) a precios extraoficiales.

scaly [skéili], *a.* escamoso; herrumbroso.

scamp [skæmp], *s.* bribón, golfo.

scamper [skǽmpᵩr], *vi.* escaparse precipitadamente.—*to s. away,* escaparse precipitadamente.

scan [skæn], *vti.* [1] escudriñar; hojear, repasar; medir (versos); (med.) hacer un escáner de, hacer un scanner de, hacer una ecografía de; (astr., comput., mil.) explorar.—*s.* escudriñamiento; (med.) escáner, scanner, escanograma; ecografía; (astr., comput., mil.) exploración.—*s. form,* ficha de scanner.- **—ner** [skǽnᵩr], *s.* (electron, tel. radar) explorador, unidad exploradora; (ing.) analizdor; (med.) escáner, scanner, escanógrafo; ecógrafo; (comput.) analizador de léxico, explorador.

scandal [skǽndᵩl], *s.* escándalo.- **—ize** [-aiz], *vt.* escandalizar.- **—ous** [-ʌs], *a.* escandaloso.

Scandinavian [skændinéiviᵩn], *a. y s.* escandinavo.

scapula [skǽpüᵩlᵩ], *s.* escápula, omóplato.

scar [skar], *s.* cicatriz; costurón.—*vti.* [1] marcar o una cicatriz.

scarce [skers], *a.* raro, escaso, contado. **—scarcely** [skérsli], *adv.* apenas; probablemente no; ciertamente no.—*s. ever,* raramente. **—scarcity** [skérsiti], *s.* carestía, escasez; rareza.

scare [sker], *vt.* asustar, espantar; amedrentar, intimidar.—*to s. away,* espantar, ahuyentar.—*s.* susto, sobresalto, espanto.- **—crow** [skérkrou], *s.* espantajo; (fam.) esperpento.

scarf [skarf], *s.* bufanda; chalina; tapete (de mesa).—*vt.* (carp.) acoplar.

scarlet [skárlit], *s.* escarlata, grana.— *a.* de color escarlata.—*s. fever,* escarlatina.

scary [skéri], *a.* (fam.) medroso, asustadizo; (causing fright) (fam.) espantoso.

scathing [skeíθiŋ], *a.* acerbo, duro.

scatter [skǽtœ(r)], *vt.* y *vi.* esparcir(se), diseminar(se), desparramar(se), desperdigar(se); dispersar(se).—*s.-brained,* atolondrado, ligero de cascos.

scattered showers [skǽtœrd], lluvias aisladas.

scene [sin], *s.* escena, vista; escenario; decoración.—*behind the scenes,* entre bastidores.—*to make a s.,* dar un escándalo.- **—ry** [sínœri], *s.* vista, paisaje; (teat.) decoraciones, decorado.—**scenic** [sínik], *a.* escénico; teatral; pintoresco.

scent [sent], *s.* olfato; olor, perfume; fragancia; rastro, pista.—*to throw off the s.,* despistar.—*vt.* y *vi.* oler, olfatear, husmear, ventear; rastrear.

scepter [séptœ(r)], *s.* cetro.

sceptic [sképtik], *s.* y *a.* escéptico.- **—al** [sképtikal], *a.* escéptico.

schedule [skédʒul], *vt.* inventariar, catalogar; fijar el tiempo para; establecer un itinerario.—*s.* cédula; horario (de f.c., etc.), itinerario; suplemento; plan, programa; lista; tarifa.

scheme [skim], *s.* plan, proyecto, programa; planta, esquema; diseño; bosquejo; ardid, treta, artificio.—*vt.* y *vi.* proyectar, trazar; urdir, tramar.- **—r** [skímœr], *s.* proyectista; intrigante.

schism [sízm], *s.* cisma, escisión.- **—atic** [sizmǽtik], *a.* y *s.* cismático.

scholar [skálǎ(r)], *s.* escolar, estudiante, colegial; becario; hombre erudito, docto.- **—ly** [-li], *a.* erudito, ilustrado, docto.—*adv.* cruditamente, doctamente.- **—ship** [ʃip], *s.* saber, erudición; beca.— **scholastic** [skolǽstik], *a.* escolástico; escolar. **—school** [skul], *s.* escuela; colegio; facultad de universidad.—*boarding s.,* colegio de internos.—*s. age,* edad escolar.—*s.*

board, junta de instrucción pú blica.—*s. bus,* ómnibus escolar.—*s. day,* día lectivo.—*s. of fishes,* banco de peces.—*s. year,* año escolar.—*a* escolar; de escuela; para escuela.—*s board,* junta de educación.—*s. desk,* pupitre.—*secondary s.,* instituto de segunda enseñanza.—*vt.* instruir enseñar, aleccionar, adiestrar **—schoolboy** [skúlbɔi], *s.* muchacho de escuela, colegial. **—schoolgirl** [skúlgœrl], *s.* niña de escuela, colegiala. **—schoolhouse** [skúlhaus], *s.* escuela (edificio). **—schooling** [skúliŋ], *s.* instrucción elemental, educación, enseñanza. **—school mate** [skúlmejt], *s.* condiscípulo. **—schoolroom** [skúlrum], *s.* aula, sala de clase. **—schoolteacher** [skúl tichœ(r)], *s.* maestro de escuela.

schooner [skúnœ(r)], *s.* goleta.

scintillate [síntileit], *vi.* chispear, centellear.

scion [saion], *s.* vástago.

science [sáiens], *s.* ciencia. **—scien tific** [saientífik], *a.* científico **—scientist** [sáientist], *s.* científico hombre de ciencia.

scissors [sízo(r)z], *s. pl.* tijeras.

scoff [skaf], *vi.* (con at) mofarse o bur larse de; befar.— *s.* mofa, escarnio burla, befa.- **—law** [skáflɔ], *s.* per sona que hace caso omiso de las leyes.

scold [skould], *vt.* y *vi.* regañar, reñir reprender.—*s.* regañón; regañona.- **—ing** [skóuldiŋ], *s.* regaño, repren sión.—*a.* regañón.

scoop [skup], *s.* pala de mano; cuchara o cucharón de draga; paletada. (fam.) hallazgo, ganancia; primicia noticia sensacional exclusiva (en un periódico).—*vt.* sacar con pala o cuchara; achicar; ahuecar, cavar, ex cavar.

scoot [skut], *vi.* (fam.) salir pitando irse a toda prisa.- **—er** [skútœ(r)], *s.* patinete, escuter, monopatín.

scope [skoup], *s.* alcance, extensión campo, espacio o esfera de acción (fig.) envergadura.

scorch [skɔrch], *vt.* chamuscar; abra sar.—*vi.* chamuscarse, abrasarse.- *s.* quemadura superficial, chamus quina.- **—ing** [-iŋ], *a.* abrasador acerbo, duro, mordaz.

score [skɔr], *s.* línea, raya; cuenta, tan tos (en el juego); (dep.) anotación punteo, tanteo; resultado final (mús.) partitura; veintena.—*on that s.*, a ese respecto, en cuanto a eso.—*on the s. of*, con motivo de.—*s. keeper*, (dep.) anotador, tanteador.—*to settle a s.*, ajustar cuentas; saldar una cuenta.—*vt.* rayar; tantear, ganar tantos en un juego; (mús.) instrumentar.—*to s. a point*, (dep.) ganar un tanto; obtener un triunfo.—*vi.* marcar; llevar una cuenta; marcar los tantos en un juego; (fig.) recibir buena acogida, merecer aplausos.- **—board** [-bɔrd], *s.* marcador, cuadro indicador.- **—r** [skɔ́rœ(r)], *s.* marcador.

scorn [skɔrn], *vt.* y *vi.* despreciar, menospreciar, desdeñar.—*s.* desdén, menosprecio, desprecio.- **—ful** [skɔ́rnfuḷ], *a.* desdeñoso, despreciativo.

Scorpio [skɔ́rpiou], *s.* (astr.) Escorpio, Escorpión.

scorpion [skɔ́rpiọn], *s.* escorpión, alacrán.

Scot [skat], *s.* escocés.—*scot-free*, impune.—*to get away scot-free*, salir ileso; quedar impune. **—Scottish** [skátiš], *a.* escocés.- **—Scotland** [skátḷand], *s.* Escocia. **—Scots** [skats], *s.* (language) escocés. **—Scotsman** [skátsmæn], *s.* escocés. **—Scotswoman** [skátswụmạn], *s.* escocesa.—**the Scottish**, los escoceses.

scotch [skach], *vt.* acallar, poner fin a.—*s.* whisky escocés.—*Scotch o Scotch whisky*, whisky escocés.—*Scotch tape* (trademark), cinta Scotch. **—Scotch** [skatch], *a.* escocés.—*s.* (language) escocés. **—Scotchman** [skáchmæn], *s.* escocés.

scoundrel [skáụndreḷ], *s.* pícaro, bribón.

scour [skaụr], *vt.* y *vi.* fregar, estregar; explorar detenidamente.- **—er** [skáụrœ(r)], *s.* limpiador, desengrasador.

scourge [skœrdž], *s.* azote.—*vt.* azotar.

scout [skaụt], *s.* (mil.) explorador, batidor, escucha; niño explorador.— *S.* explorador, boy scout.—*vt.* y *vi.* (mil.) explorar; reconocer.- **—master** [-mæstœr], *s.* jefe de tropa de niños exploradores.

scowl [skaụl], *vi.* fruncir el ceño o el entrecejo; enfurruñarse; tener mal cariz.—*s.* ceño, entrecejo; mal cariz.

cram [skræm], *vii.* [1] (fam.) irse de prisa.—*interj.* ¡largo! ¡fuera!

scramble [skræmbl], *vt.* recoger de prisa o confusamente; embrollar; (coc.) hacer un revoltillo.—*scrambled eggs*, revoltillo, huevos revueltos.—*vi.* (bot.) trepar; andar a la rebatiña, bregar.—*s.* contienda, rebatiña.

scrap [skræp], *s.* migaja, mendrugo; pedacillo, fragmento; sobras; material viejo o de deshecho; (fam.) riña, camorra.—*s. iron*, hierro viejo, chatarra.—*s. paper*, papel para apuntes; papel de desecho.—*vti.* [1] echar a la basura; descartar; desbaratar, desmantelar (un buque).—*vii.* (fam.) reñir, armar camorra.- **—book** [skræpbụk], *s.* álbum de recortes.

scrape [skrejp], *vt.* y *vi.* raspar, rozar; rasguñar, arañar; (a veces con up o together) recoger, amontonar poco a poco; tocar mal (un instrumento de cuerda); restregar los pies.—*to s. acquaintance*, trabar amistad.—*to s. along*, (fam.) ir tirando, ir escapando.—*s.* raspadura, rasguño, arañazo; enredo, lío, aprieto, apuro.- **—r** [skréjpœ(r)], *s.* raspador, rascador; (fam.) rascatripas; (mar.) rasqueta.

scratch [skræch], *vt.* y *vi.* rascar, raspar; arañar; rasguñar; rayar (el vidrio); escribir mal, garrapatear; escarbar; borrar.—*s.* rasguño, arañazo; marca o raya; (dep.) línea de arrancada en una carrera.—*s. paper* o *pad*, papel o cuadernillo de apuntes.—*to start from s.*, empezar sin nada, o de (la) nada; comenzar desde el principio.—*up to s.*, en buenas o excelentes condiciones.

scrawl [skrɔl], *vt.* garrapatear, garabatear.—*s.* garabato, garrapato.

scrawny [skrɔ́ni], *a.* huesudo, flaco.

scream [skrim], *vt.* y *vi.* chillar; gritar.—*s.* grito, alarido, chillido; (fam.) cosa o persona jocosa.

screech [skrich], *vi.* chillar, ulular.—*s.* chillido, alarido.- **—y** [skríchi], *a.* chillón, agudo.

screen [skrin], *s.* biombo, mampara; pantalla; resguardo; criba, cedazo, tamiz.—*s. star*, (cine) estrella o astro de la pantalla.—*the s.*, el cine, el celuloide, la pantalla.—*vt.* cribar, cerner, tamizar; escudar, proteger; filmar; proyectar en la pantalla.

screw [skru], *s.* tornillo.—*a.* de tornillo.—*s. bolt*, perno roscado.—*s. nut*, rosca, hembra de tornillo.—*s. plate*, terraja o tarraja.—*s. propeller*, hélice.—*s. thread*, rosca (de tornillo).—*vt.* atornillar, (Am.) tornillar; torcer, retorcer.—*to s. off*, des(a)tornillar.- **—ball** [-bɔl], *s.* (jer.) estrafalario, excéntrico.- **—driver** [skrúdraįvœ(r)], *s.* destornillador.- **—y** [-į], *a.* (jer.) descabellado, chiflado.

scribble [scríbl], *vt.* y *vi.* escribir de prisa; garrapatear, garabatear, emborronar.—*s.* garabato, garabateo.

scribe [skaįb], *s.* escriba; escribiente; (humor.) escribidor.

scrimp [skrįmp], *vt.* y *vi.* escatimar.

script [skrįpt], *s.* guión de película; (teat.) manuscrito; (rad.) libreto; letra cursiva; (for.) escritura; material escrito a máquina. **—Scripture** [skrípchūr], *s.* (Sagrada) Escritura.- **—writer** [-raįtœr], *s.* guionista, cinematurgo.

scrofula [skráfyūlǎ], *s.* escrófula, (Am.) lamparón.

scroll [skrouļ], *s.* rollo de papel o pergamino; rasgo, rúbrica; (arq.) cinta, voluta.—*a.* en espiral; de caracol.

scrooge [skrudẑ], *s.* (fam.) miserable.

scrub [skrʌb], *vti.* [1] fregar, estregar; restregar.—*a.* achaparrado, desmirriado; inferior.—*s. oak*, chaparro.—*s. woman*, fregona.—*s. team*, (dep.) equipo de jugadores novicios o suplentes.—*s.* estropajo, escoba vieja; animal de raza mixta e inferior; persona mezquina o inferior.

scruff [skrʌf], *s.* nuca, pescuezo.

scruple [skrúpl], *s.* escrúpulo.—*vi.* tener escrúpulos. **—scrupulous** [skrúpyūlʌs], *a.* escrupuloso; puntilloso.

scrutinize [skrútįnaįz], *vt.* escudriñar, escrutar. **—scrutiny** [skrútįnį], *s.* escrutinio.

scuff [skʌf], *vt.* rascar.—*s. mark*, rozadura, rascadura.- **—le** [skʌfęl], *s.* lucha, sarracina.—*vi.* forcejear, luchar.

sculptor [skálptǫ(r)], *s.* escultor. **—sculpture** [skálpchū(r)], *s.* escultura.—*vt.* esculpir, cincelar.

scum [skʌm], *s.* espuma, nata; hez, escoria.—*the s. of the people*, la canalla.—*vt.* y *vi.* espumar.

scurvy [skœ́rvį], *s.* escorbuto.

scuttle [skátl], *s.* escotillón; trampa; barreno, agujero; carrera corta; cubo, balde (para carbón).—*vt.* barrenar, dar barreno a.—*vi.* echar a correr.

scythe [saįð], *s.* guadaña.

sea [si], *s.* mar.—*a.* de mar, marino, marítimo.—*beyond the s.* o *seas*, allende el mar; fuera de aguas jurisdiccionales.—*s. biscuit*, galleta de barco.—*s. breeze*, brisa de mar, virazón.—*s. chart*, carta náutica o de marear.—*s. dog*, (zool.) foca; (fam.) marinero viejo, lobo de mar.—*s. food*, pescado y mariscos comestibles.—*s. green*, verdemar, glauco.— *s. gull*, gaviota.—*s. legs*, pie marino.—*s. level*, nivel del mar.—*s. lion*, foca, león marino.—*s. mile*, milla náutica.- **—board** [síbɔrd], *a.* costanero, litoral.—*s. costa*; litoral.- **—coast** [-kouşt], *s.* costa, litoral.- **—farer** [-ferœr], *s.* marinero; viajero por mar.- **—going** [-gouįŋ], *a.* de alta mar.

seal [siļ], *s.* sello; timbre; precinto; firma; (zool.) foca.—*under the hand and s. of*, firmado y sellado por.—*vt.* sellar, precintar; estampar; cerrar una carta o paquete (con goma o lacre).- **—ing wax** [síļįŋ wæks], *s.* lacre.

seam [sim], *s.* costura, cosedura; sutura; cicatriz, marca; (min.) filón, veta; yacimiento; (mec.) junta, costura (de un tubo, una caldera, etc.).

seaman [símąn], *s.* marinero, marino.

seamless [símlįs], *a.* sin costura. **—seamstress** [símstrįs], *s.* costurera; modistilla. **—seamy** [símį], *a.* con costuras.—*the s. side*, el lado malo.

séance [seįans], *s.* sesión de espiritistas.

seaplane [sípleįn], *s.* hidroavión. **—seaport** [sípɔrt], *s.* puerto de mar.

sear [sįr], *a.* seco, marchito.—*vt.* secar, marchitar; tostar, chamuscar; cauterizar.

search [sœrch], *vt.* y *vi.* buscar, explorar, escudriñar; registrar (una casa), investigar, indagar.—*to s. after*, preguntar por; indagar, inquirir.—*to s. for*, buscar; solicitar, procurar.—*to s. out*, buscar hasta descubrir.—*s.* te registro, reconocimiento; pesquisa, indagación o investigación; búsqueda, busca.—*in s. of*, en busca de.—*s. for arms*, cacheo.—*s. warrant*, auto de registro domiciliario; orden de allanamiento.- **—ing** [sœrchįŋ], *a.* penetrante, escrutador.- **—light** [-laįt], *s.* reflector lumínico (orientable); luz proyectada por éste.

seashore [síʃɔr], s. playa, litoral, ribera, costa, orilla del mar. **—seasick** [sísɪk], a. mareado.—*to get s.,* marearse. **—seasickness** [sísɪknɪs], s. mareo. **—seaside** [sísaɪd], s. = SEASHORE.

season [sízɔn], s. estación (del año); sazón; temporada.—*in s.,* en sazón; a su tiempo.—*s. ticket,* billete de abono.—*vt.* (coc.) sazonar, condimentar, aliñar; aclimatar, habituar. *vi.* sazonarse, madurarse, habituarse.— **—al** [-al], a. estacional.- **—ing** [-ɪŋ], s. (coc.) condimento, aliño, aderezo, sazón; sal, chiste. cura (de la madera).

seat [sit], s. asiento; silla; escaño; (teat.) localidad; (sast.) fondillo de los calzones; nalga; sede (de diócesis); sitio; paraje; mansión, quinta.—*s. belt,* cinturón de asiento.—*s. cover,* funda de asiento, cubreasiento.—*s. of war,* teatro de la guerra.—*vt.* sentar, asentar; colocar en asientos; tener asientos o cabida para; ajustar (una válvula) en su asiento; poner asiento a (una silla, etc.); echar fondillos (a un pantalón).—*vi.* asentar, ajustar en su asiento (una válvula etc.).

seaway [síwej], s. ruta marítima; estela; mar gruesa.

seaweed [síwid], s. alga marina.

seaworthy [síwœrθi], a. marinero, en condiciones de navegar.

secede [sisíd], vi. separarse, retirarse. **—secession** [siséʃɔn], s. secesión.

seclude [sikljúd], vt. apartar, recluir.— *vi.* alejarse de otros.- **—d** [sikljúdjd], a. alejado o apartado; retirado, solitario, recogido. **—seclusion** [sikljúʒɔn], s. reclusión, aislamiento, soledad; retiro.

second [sékɔnd], a. segundo, secundario; inferior.—*every s. day,* cada dos días; un día sí y otro no.—*on s. thought,* segundo de repensarlo; después de pensarlo bien.—*s. childhood,* chochera, senilidad.—*s.-best,* (el) mejor después del primero.—*s.-class,* de segunda clase.—*S. Coming,* (igl.) segundo Advenimiento.—*s. cousin,* primo segundo.—*s. fiddle,* (fig.) (el) mejor después del primero.—*s. floor,* (E.U.) primer piso—(G.B.) segundo piso.—*s.-guess,* cuestionar a posteriori.—*s. hand,* segundero.—*s. lieutenant,* alférez, subteniente.—*s. mortgage,* segunda hipoteca.—*s. nature,* naturaleza arraigada, instinto.—*s.-rate,* de segundo orden; de calidad inferior.— *s. sight,* clarividencia.—*s.-string,* de reserva, suplente.—*s. teeth,* segunda dentición.—*s. wind,* nuevo aliento.—*s. segundo;* momento, instante; brazo derecho; ayudante; padrino (en un duelo); segundo (de tiempo).—*vt.* apoyar, apadrinar; secundar o apoyar (una proposición).—*adv.* en segundo lugar.- **—ary** [-eri], a. secundario.—*s. school,* escuela secundaria o de segunda enseñanza.- **—hand** [-hænd], a. de segunda mano, usado; indirecto, por conducto ajeno o de oídas.- **—ly** [-li], adv. en segundo lugar.

secrecy [síkresi], s. secreto, reserva; sigilo. **—secret** [síkrit], a. secreto; escondido, oculto, recóndito.—*s. agent,* agente secreto.—*s. police,* policía secreta.—*s. service,* servicio secreto, servicios de inteligencia. —*s.* secreto. **—secretary** [sékreteri], s. secretario, secretaria. **—secrete** [sikrít], vt. esconder, ocultar, encubrir; (fisiol.) secretar. **—secretion** [sikríʃɔn], s. (fisiol.) secreción. **—secretive** [sikrítiv], a. callado, reservado; secretorio.

sect [sɛkt], s. secta.- **—arian** [sɛktériɑn], a. o sectario.

section [sékʃɔn], s. sección, división; porción; tajada muy delgada; departamento, negociado; (dib.) corte, sección.—*vt.* seccionar, dividir en secciones.

secular [sékjulɑ(r)], a. y s. secular.

secure [sikjúr], a. seguro; confiado; firme, fuerte.—*vt.* asegurar, resguardar; afianzar, fijar; garantizar; procurarse, obtener. **—security** [sikjúriti], s. seguridad, seguro (social); protección o defensa; fianza, garantía, prenda; fiador.—*pl.* (com.) valores, obligaciones.—*public securities,* efectos públicos.—*securities in hand,* valores en cartera.

sedan [sidǽn], s. (aut.) sedán.—*s. chair,* silla de manos.

sedate [sidéjt], a. sentado, sosegado, serio. **—sedative** [sédativ], a. y s. (med.) sedativo, sedante, calmante.

sedge [sɛdʒ], s. (bot.) junco.

sediment [sédiment], s. sedimento, borra.

sedition [sidíʃɔn], s. sedición. **—seditious** [sidíʃʌs], a. sedicioso.

seduce [sįdjús], vt. seducir, deshonrar. – **—r** [-œ(r)], s. seductor, burlador. **—seduction** [sįdÁkšǫn], s. seducción. **—seductive** [sįdÁktįv], a. seductivo.

see [si], vti. y vii. [10] ver.—s.? (fam.) ¿comprende? ¿sabe?—to s. about, pensar en; averiguar.—to s. (a person) home, acompañar (a una persona) a su casa.—to s. (a person) off, ir a despedir (a una persona).—to s. red, echar chispas, montar en cólera.—to s. through (a proposition), comprender (una proposición).—to s. through (a person), (fig.) leer, adivinar el pensamiento (a una persona).—to s. (a person) through, ayudar (a una persona) a salir del paso, o hasta lo último.—to s. (a thing) through, llevar (una cosa) hasta el cabo; estar (en una cosa) hasta lo último.—to s. to, atender a, tener cuidado de; cuidarse de.—to s. to it that, atender a que, ver que, hacer que.— I see, ¡ya! ya veo, comprendo.—let me s., vamos a ver; déjeme pensar.— s. (igl.) silla, sede.

seed [sid], s. semilla, simiente; grano; pepita.—s. plot, semillero.—to go o run to s., granar; agotarse, envejecerse.—vt. sembrar; despepitar.— vi. hacer la siembra.- **—bed** [-bed], s. semillero.- **—ling** [sídlįŋ], s. planta de semilla; planta de semillero; retoño, brote.- **—y** [-į], a. lleno de granos; (fam.) andrajoso, raído.

seeing [síįŋ], s. vista, visión.—conj.— s. that, visto que, siendo así que, puesto que, ya que.—a. vidente, que ve.—S. Eye Dog, perro-lazarillo.

seek [sik], vti. y vii. [10] buscar; pedir; procurar, solicitar, aspirar a.—to s. after, buscar, tratar de obtener.—to s. for, buscar.

seem [sim], vi. parecer; parecerle a uno.—it seems to me, me parece.- **—ingly** [símįnlį], adv. aparentemente, al parecer.

seen [sin], pp. de TO SEE.

seep [sip], vi. rezumarse, escurrirse.

seer [sįr], s. profeta, vidente.

seesaw [sísɔ], s. vaivén, columpio, balancín.—a. de vaivén, de balance.—vi. columpiarse; alternar; vacilar.

seethe [sið], vi. hervir, bullir; burbujear.

segment [ségmęnt], s. segmento.

segregate [ségrēgeit], vt. y vi. segregar(se).—a. segregado. **—segregation** [segrēgéišǫn], s. segregación.

seismic [sájzmįk], a. sísmico. **—seismograph** [sájzmǫgræf], s. sismógrafo.

seize [siz], vt. asir, agarrar, coger; capturar, prender; apoderarse de; aprovecharse de; (for.) secuestrar, embargar, decomisar, incautarse de (bienes, etc.).—to be seized of, (for.) obtener posesión de.—to be seized with, sobrecogerse de.—vi. (gen con **on** o **upon**) agarrar, coger; apoderarse de. **—seizure** [síž̦(r)], s. aprehensión, prisión; captura, presa; (mil.) toma; (for.) embargo, secuestro, (de)comiso; (med.) ataque, acceso súbito de una enfermedad.

seldom [séldǫm], adv. raramente, rara vez, por rareza.

select [sęlékt], vt. seleccionar, escoger, entresacar.—a. selecto, escogido.- **—ion** [sęlékšǫnț], s. selección, elección.

self [self], a. uno mismo; se; sí mismo.—s. uno mismo, sí mismo.—s.-addressed envelope, sobre con el nombre y dirección del remitente.—s.-centered, egocéntrico. —s.-conscious, consciente de sí mismo; afectado, falto de naturalidad.—s.-consistent, consecuente consigo mismo.—s.-control, continencia; imperio sobre sí mismo. —s.-defense, defensa propia, autodefensa.—s.-denial, abnegación. —s.-determination, autodeterminación. —s.-discipline, autodisciplina.—s.-employed, que trabaja por su propia cuenta.—s.-evident, patente, manifiesto.—s.-explanatory, que se explica por sí mismo.—s.-important, altivo, arrogante.—s.-interest, egoísmo, interés personal.—s.-made man, hijo de sus propias obras.—s.-possession, sangre fría, serenidad, aplomo.—s.-respect, pundonor, dignidad, decoro, respeto de sí mismo.—s.-righteous, santurrón.—s.-satisfied, pagado de sí mismo.—s.-winding, de cuerda automática (apl. a relojes).- **—ish** [sélfįš], a. egoísta, interesado.- **—ishness** [-įšnįs], s. egoísmo.- **same** [-séjm], a. idéntico, mismísimo.

sell [sel], vti. y vii. [10] vender(se).—to

s. on trust, fiar, vender al fiado o al crédito.—*to s. out,* realizar, hacer venta de realización; venderlo todo. – **—er** [sélœ(r)], *s.* vendedor.– **—ing** [-iŋ], *s.* venta.– **—out** [aut], *s.* (fam.) saldo; (jer.) traición; (teat.) éxito de taquilla.

selves [selvz], *s. pl.* de SELF.

semantic [semǽntik], *a.* semántico.– **—s** [semǽntiks], *s.* semántica.

semen [símen], *s.* semen, esperma; (bot.) simiente, semilla.

semester [seméstœ(r)], *s.* semestre.

semicircle [sémisœrkl], *s.* semicírculo.

semicolon [sémikoulon], *s.* punto y coma (;).

seminar [séminar], *s.* seminario.

seminary [sémineri], *s.* seminario.

Semite [sémait], *s.* semita. **—Semitic** [semítik], *a.* semítico.

semitrailer [sémitreilœr], *s.* semi-remolque.

senate [sénit], *s.* senado.**—senator** [sénato(r)], *s.* senador.

send [send], *vti.* [10] enviar, despachar, expedir; lanzar, arrojar.—*to s. away,* despedir, poner en la calle.—*to s. back,* devolver; enviar de vuelta.— *to s. forth,* echar (retoños, etc.); emitir, despedir (luz, vapores); enviar, despachar.—*to s. in,* hacer entrar; introducir.—*to s. off,* despachar, expedir.—*to s. one about one's business,* enviar a paseo.—*to s. up,* mandar subir; (fam.) enviar a la cárcel.—*to s. word,* mandar recado; avisar; enviar a decir.—**er** [séndœ(r)], *s.* remitente; (elec.) transmisor.

send-off [sendɔf], *s.* (fam.) despedida ceremonial; (fam.) despedida afectuosa.

senile [sínail], *a.* senil, caduco, chocho. **—senility** [seníliti], *s.* senilidad, senectud.

senior [sínyo(r)], *a.* mayor, de mayor edad; más antiguo.—*s. citizens,* gente de edad.—*s.* señor mayor, anciano; socio más antiguo o principal; (E.U.) escolar del último año; (abreviado Sr.) padre, p.ej., **John Cruz, Senior** Juan Cruz, padre.— **ity** [sinyóriti], *s.* precedencia, prioridad; antigüedad.

sensation [senséişon], *s.* sensación.— *to be a s.,* ser un exitazo.– **—al** [-al], *a.* sensacional; escandaloso; emocionante. **—sense** [sens], *s.* sentido; razón, juicio; sensación; sentimiento; significado, interpre-

tación.—*in a s.,* hasta cierto punto.—*to be out of one's senses,* haber perdido el juicio, no estar en sus cabales.—*vt.* percibir por los sentidos; (fam.) sentir. **—senseless** [sénslis], *a.* insensible, privado, sin conocimiento; sin sentido, absurdo; insensato, necio. **—sensibility** [sensibíliti], *s.* sensibilidad. **—sensible** [sénsibl], *a.* cuerdo, razonable; sensato; sensible; sensitivo. **—sensibly** [sénsibli], *adv.* perceptiblemente, sensiblemente; con sensatez o sentido común. **—sensitive** [sénsitiv], *a.* sensitivo; sensible, impresionable; susceptible; tierno; delicado; (fot.) sensibilizado. **—sensitiveness** [sénsitivnis], *s.* sensibilidad; susceptibilidad; finura, delicadeza.

sensual [sénşual], *a.* sensual, lascivo, lujurioso; carnal.– **—ity** [sensuǽliti], *s.* sensualidad, lascivia; lujuria.

sent [sent], *pret.* y *pp.* de SEND.

sentence [séntens], *s.* (gram.) oración, cláusula; (for.) sentencia, fallo; condena (de presidio).—*vt.* sentenciar, condenar.

sentiment [séntiment], *s.* sentimiento; afecto, simpatía; opinión, sentir; sentido, sentimental.– **—al** [sentiméntal], *a.* sentimental.– **—ality** [sentimentǽliti], *s.* sentimentalismo.

sentinel [séntinel], **sentry** [séntri], *s.* (mil.) centinela.—*s. box,* garita (de centinela).

separate [sépareit], *vt.* y *vi.* separar(se); apartar(se).—*a.* [séparit], separado, aparte, suelto; distinto, diferente. **—separation** [separéişon], *s.* separación.

September [septémbœ(r)], *s.* septiembre.

septic [séptik], *a.* séptico.—*s. tank,* pozo séptico o negro o ciego, fosa séptica.

septuplet [septáplit], *s.* septillizo.

sepulcher [sépʌlkœ(r)], *s.* sepulcro, sepultura.

sequel [síkwel], *s.* secuela, consecuencia, efecto; continuación. **—sequence** [síkwens], *s.* secuencia; serie, orden de sucesión; arreglo; encadenamiento, ilación; efecto; (en los naipes) runfla de un palo.

sequin [síkwin], *s.* lentejuela.

sequoia [sikwóiä], *s.* abeto gigantesco de California, secoya.

serape [serápei], *s.* sarape.

Serb [sœrb], **Serbian** [sœrbian], s. y a. servio.

serenade [serenéid], s. (mús.) serenata.—vt. dar serenata a.

serene [sērín], a. sereno, despejado; sosegado, tranquilo. **—serenity** [serénịtị], s. serenidad; tranquilidad, calma, quietud.

serf [sʌrf], s. siervo de la glega.

serge [sœrdž], s. estameña.

sergeant [sárdžęnt], s. (mil.) sargento.

serial [sírịạl], a. de o en serie; de orden (número, marca, etc.); consecutivo; formando serie; que se publica por entregas.—s. number, número de serie.—s. obra que se publica por entregas; película por episodios. **—series** [sírịz], s. serie; sucesión, cadena; ciclo.—in s., (elec.) en serie.

serious [sírịʌs], a. serio; formal; grave, de peso.- **—ness** [-nịs], s. seriedad; formalidad; gravedad.

sermon [sœrmon], s. sermón.

serpent [sœrpęnt], s. serpiente o sierpe.

serum [sírʌm], s. suero.

servant [sœrvant], s. criado, sirviente; servidor.—pl. servidumbre.—s. girl, s. maid, criada, sirvienta, doncella. (Am.) mucama. **—serve** [sœrv], vt. servir; manejar, hacer funcionar (un cañón, etc.); abastecer, surtir; cumplir (una condena).—it serves you right, (en tono de represión) te está bien empleado; bien se lo merece Ud.—to s. an office, desempeñar un cargo.—to s. a warrant, ejecutar un auto de prisión.—to s. one a trick, jugar a uno una mala partida.—to s. notice (on), avisar o dar aviso, hacer saber, advertir, notificar.—to s. time, cumplir una condena en presidio.—vi. servir; bastar, ser suficiente o apto; (dep.) efectuar el saque, sacar.—to s. for, servir de; hacer oficio de.—s. (dep.) saque. **—server** [sœrvœ(r)], s. servidor. **—service** [sœrvịs], s. servicio; (dep.) saque; vajilla, servicio de mesa; juego (de café, etc.); entrega legal de una citación.—at your s., a su disposición, a sus órdenes, servidor de Ud.—it is of no s., no vale nada, de nada sirve.—out of s., (mec.) que no funciona, descompuesto.—s. record, hoja de servicios.—s. station, (aut.) estación de servicio, taller de reparaciones.—vt. atender a, suministrar lo necesario a o para. **—ser-**

viceable [sœrvịsạbl], a. servicial, servible, útil; duradero. **—man** [-mæn], s. reparador, mecánico; militar. **—servile** [sœrvịl], a. servil, bajo, abyecto. **—servitude** [sœrvịtjud], s. servidumbre; esclavitud; vasallaje; (for.) servidumbre.

sesame [sésami], s. sésamo.—open s.!, ¡sésamo ábrete!

session [sésọn], s. sesión; período escolar.—to be in s., sesionar.

set [set], vti. [9] poner; colocar, asentar; instalar, establecer; fijar, inmovilizar; señalar; engastar, montar (piedras preciosas); arreglar; regular, ajustar; establecer; componer (tipos de imprenta); poner en música; (med.) reducir (fracturas).—to s. afire, poner fuego a, incendiar.—to s. ajar, entornar, entreabrir.—to s. an example, dar ejemplo.—to s. a price on, fijar precio a; poner precio, ofrecer premio por.—to s. aside, poner aparte.—to s. a trap, armar una trampa.—to s. back, hacer retroceder; atrasar, retrasar.—to s. eyes on, ver; mirar; clavar los ojos en.—to s. fire to, poner o prender fuego a, incendiar; inflamar (las pasiones).—to s. forth, manifestar; exponer; publicar.—to s. in, (joy.) montar, engastar.—to s. off, poner aparte, separar; poner en relieve; disparar.—to s. up the drinks, (fam.) convidar (a beber).—vii. ponerse (un astro); cuajarse, solidificarse; endurecerse; fraguar (el hormigón, etc.); correr, moverse o fluir (una corriente); empollar (las aves); (fam.) ajustar, caer bien (una prenda de vestir).—to s. forth, avanzar, ponerse en marcha.—to s. in, comenzar, aparecer, sobrevenir; cerrar (la noche).—to set off (fig.), salir, partir.—to s. on o upon, salir, partir; emprender un viaje o un negocio.—to s. to work, poner manos a la obra; emprender el trabajo.—to s. up, establecerse; principiar.—pret. y pp. de TO SET.—a. resuelto; fijo, invariable; establecido arreglado, ajustado; puesto, colocado; rígido, (mec.) armado; (joy.) montado, engastado.—to be (all) s. to, estar listo o preparado.—s juego, surtido, colección, serie grupo, clase; equipo; aparato (de radio); (astr.) puesta; curso, dirección (teat.) decoración; (dep.) partida (danz.) tanda; fraguado (del ce

mento, etc.).—s. of books, colección de libros.—s. of diamonds, terno.-
—back [sétbæk], s. retroceso, revés, contrariedad; contracorriente.

setback [sétbæk], s. revés, contrariedad.

settee [seti], s. canapé, diván.

setter [sétœ(r)], s. perro perdiguero.

setting [sétiŋ], s. puesta de un astro, ocaso; (teat.) puesta en escena, decoraciones; (joy.) engaste, montadura; (fam.) nidada.—s. sun, sol poniente.—s. up, establecimiento; (mec.) montaje.—s.-up exercises, ejercicios sin aparatos, gimnasia sueca.

settle [sétl], vt. asentar; fijar, asegurar; arreglar; establecer, estatuir; casar; colonizar, poblar; sosegar, calmar; resolver (dudas); solucionar (un problema); señalar, fijar; saldar, finiquitar, ajustar (cuentas); componer.—to s. on o upon, señalar, asignar, dar en dote.—vi. asentarse; establecerse, radicarse; instalarse, poner casa; calmar; determinarse; saldar una cuenta.—to s. differences, avenirse, hacer las paces.—to s. down, asentarse; posarse (un hidroavión o ave).- —ment [-mǝnt], s. establecimiento; colonización; colonia; caserío, poblado; (for.) asiento, domicilio; dote; empleo, destino; ajuste, arreglo; (com.) saldo, liquidación, finiquito, pago.—s. house, casa de beneficencia.- —r [sétlœ(r)], s. poblador, colono; fundador.

seven [sévǝn], a. y s. siete.—seven hundred, a. y s. setecientos.—s. one, setecientos uno.—seventh [sévǝnθ], a. y s. séptimo.

seventeen [sevǝntín], a. y s. diecisiete, diez y siete.—seventeenth [sevǝntínθ], a. y s. decimoséptimo, diecisieteavo.

seventy [sévǝnti], a. y s. setenta.—s.-one, setenta y uno.—seventieth [sévǝntjjǝθ], a. y s. septuagésimo, setentavo.

sever [sévœ(r)], vt. separar, desunir, dividir; cortar, romper.—vi. separarse, desunirse; partirse.

several [sévœrǝl], a. varios, diversos; distinto(s), respectivo(s).—s. varios, cada uno en particular.

severe [sévír], a. severo, riguroso; duro; rígido, estricto, austero; grave, serio; recio, fuerte. —severity [sēvériti], s. severidad, rigor; rigidez, austeridad; seriedad, gravedad.

sew [sou], vti. y vii. [6] coser.

sewage [sujdʒ], s. aguas negras, aguas residuales.—s. disposal, tratamiento de aguas residuales.

sewer [sjúœ(r)], s. albañal, cloaca, alcantarilla. —age [-jdʒ], s. alcantarillado.

sewing [sóuiŋ], s. costura.—a. de coser; para coser.—s. basket, cesta de costura.—s. machine, máquina de coser. —sewn [soun], pp. de TO SEW.

sex [seks], s. sexo.—s. appeal, atracción sexual.—the fair s., el bello sexo.

sexagenarian [seksǝdʒenérjǝn], a. y s. sexagenario.

sexton [sékstǝn], s. sacristán.

sexual [séks[u]ǝl], a. sexual.—s. harassment, acosamiento sexual.—s. intercourse, comercio sexual. —sexy [séksi], a. (jer.) sicalíptico, erótico.

shabby [ʃæbi], a. usado, gastado, raído; andrajoso; ruin, vil.

shack [ʃæk], s. choza, casucha.

shackle [ʃækl], vt. encadenar; poner esposas o grilletes a; trabar; poner obstáculos, estorbar.—s. grillete, grillo, esposa; traba; impedimento.—pl. hierros, prisiones.

shad [ʃæd], s. sábalo, alosa.

shade [ʃeid], s. sombra; matiz, tinte; visillo, cortina; pantalla de lámpara; visera.—vt. sombrear, dar sombra; resguardar de la luz; matizar. —shading [ʃéidiŋ], s. (b.a.) sombreado. —shadow [ʃædou], s. sombra (proyectada por un objeto); oscuridad; imagen reflejada (en agua o espejo).—vt. oscurecer, sombrear; espiar, seguir a uno como su sombra; (b.a.) sombrear, matizar.—vi. oscurecerse; cambiar gradualmente de color. —shady [ʃéidi], a. sombreado, sombrío; (fam.) sospechoso.—to keep s., (fam.) guardar oculto.

shaft [ʃæft], s. pieza larga y estrecha o parte larga y estrecha de la misma (mango, cabo, etc. de un arma o herramienta); flecha o saeta; lanza, vara (de coche, carretón, etc.); fuste (de una columna o carruaje); (mec.) eje árbol; pozo, tiro (de mina, ascensor, etc.); cañón de chimenea.

shaggy [ʃægi], a. peludo, velludo, hirsuto; lanudo; áspero.

shake [ʃeik], vti. [10] sacudir o menear,

cimbrear; hacer temblar; hacer vacilar o flaquear; agitar.—*to s. hands,* estrecharse la mano.—*to s. one's head,* cabecear, mover la cabeza.— *to s. up,* sacudir; agitar; (fam.) regañar, sermonear.—*vii.* temblar; estremecerse; cimbrearse; vacilar, titubear; (fam.) dar(se) la mano.—*to s. in one's shoes o boots,* temblar de miedo.—*to s. with cold,* tiritar.—*to s. with laughter,* desternillarse o reventar de risa.—*s.* sacudida; sacudimiento; temblor; apretón de manos; instante; batido (de leche, fruta, chocolate, etc.).—*s. up,* (fam.) gran reorganización; (fam.) cambio de personal, reorganización completa.- **—down** [-daun], *s.* prueba; (jer.) exacción, concusión, timo, estafa.- **—shaken** [šéikn], *pp.* de TO SHAKE. **—shaky** [šéiki], *a.* trémulo; vacilante, movedizo; indigno de confianza.

shall [šæl], *vai.* [11] (se usa para formar el futuro o para expresar obligación).—*they s. not pass,* no pasarán.—*you s. do it,* tiene Ud. que hacerlo.—(V. SHOULD.)

shallow [šælou], *a.* bajo, poco profundo; superficial.—*s.-brained,* ligero de cascos.—*s.* (mar.) bajío, bajo.- **—ness** [-nis], *s.* poca profundidad; superficialidad; frivolidad.

sham [šæm], *vti.* y *vii.* [1] simular, fingir.—*s.* fingimiento, ficción; (fam.) bambolla, farsa.—*a.* fingido, disimulado; falso, postizo.—*s. battle,* (mil.) simulacro de combate.

shame [šeim], *s.* vergüenza; ignominia, deshonra; bochorno.—*for s.! s. on you!* ¡qué vergüenza¡—*it is a s.,* es una vergüenza; es una lástima.— *what a s.!* ¡qué lástima!—*vt.* avergonzar, abochornar; deshonrar.— **ful** [šéimful], *a.* vergonzoso, escandaloso.- **—less** [-lis], *a.* desvergonzado, sin vergüenza, descarado.

shampoo [šæmpú], *s.* champú.—*vt.* lavar la cabeza a, lavar.

shamrock [šæmrak], *s.* trébol.

shank [šæŋk], *s.* caña o canilla de la pierna; zanca; (mec.) asta o astil, mango, vástago, caña.

shanty [šænti], *s.* casucha, choza, chabola.

shape [šeip], *vt.* formar; dar forma a.— *vi.* (a veces con **up**) empezar a tomar, formar o mostrar progreso.—*s.* forma, figura, hechura (de una persona); estado, manera, modo.- —

less [šéiplis], *a.* informe; disforme.- **—ly** [-li], *a.* bien formado, esbelto.

share [šer], *vt.* repartir; compartir; (con in) participar de, tener o tomar parte en.—*vi.* participar o tener parte.—*s.* parte, porción; (com.) acción; participación.—*to go shares,* ir a medias.- **—holder** [šérhouldœ(r)], *s.* (com.) accionista.

shark [šark], *s.* tiburón; estafador; (fam.) experto, perito.—*loan s.,* usurero, agiotista.

sharp [šarp], *a.* agudo; puntiagudo; cortante, afilado; sagaz; vivo, astuto; incisivo, penetrante; acre, agrio; mordaz, sarcástico; distinto, claro, bien delineado o definido; (mús.) sostenido; punzante (dolor); abrupto, pronunciado (pendiente, curva, etc.).—*s. features,* facciones enjutas.—*s.* (mús.) sostenido; estafador, fullero.—*adv.* V. SHARPLY.—*at four o'clock s.,* (fam.) a las cuatro en punto.—*s.-edged,* afilado.—*s.-pointed,* puntiagudo.—*s.-witted,* penetrante, perspicaz.- **—en** [šárpn], *vt.* afilar; aguzar, sacar punta a, amolar.—*vi.* aguzarse; afilarse.- **—ener** [-ęnœ(r)], *s.* afilador, aguzador.—*pencil s.,* sacapuntas.— **—er** [-œ(r)], *s.* tahúr, fullero; estafador.- **—ly** [-li], *adv.* con filo; prontamente; brusca y mordazmente; agudamente, vivamente; sutil o ingeniosamente.- **—ness** [-nis], *s.* agudeza, sutileza, perspicacia; mordacidad; acidez; rigor; inclemencia.- **— shooter** [-šutœ(r)], *s.* tirador certero.

shatter [šætœ(r)], *vt.* destrozar, hacer pedazos o añicos; estrellar, romper; quebrantar (la salud).—*vi.* hacerse pedazos, quebrarse, romperse. —*s.* fragmento, pedazo.- **—proof** [-pruf], *a.* inastillable.

shave [šeiv], *vti.* [6] rasurar o afeitar; rapar; (carp.) (a)cepillar; desbastar.—*vii.* rasurarse, afeitarse.—*s.* afeitado, (Am.) afeitada.—*to have a close s.,* salvarse en una tabla, escapar por casualidad. **—shaving** [šéiviŋ], *s.* afeitado, rasura(ción), (Am.) afeitada.—*pl.* virutas, acepilladuras.

shawl [šɔl], *s.* chal, mantón.—*Spanish s.,* mantón de Manila.

she [ši], *pron. pers.* ella; (delante de who o that) la que, aquella que.—*s. cat (-goat, -ass, etc.)* gata (cabra, burra, etc.).

sheaf [šif], *s.* gavilla; atado.

shear [šịr], *vti*. [6] rapar, esquilar, trasquilar; tonsurar; cortar (gen. con tijeras o cizallas).– **—er** [šị́rœ(r)], *s*. esquilador.– **—s** [-z], *s. pl*. tijeras grandes; (mec.) cizallas.

sheath [šiθ], *s*. vaina; funda, estuche, cubierta.– **—e** [šið], *vt*. envainar, enfundar.

sheaves [šivz], *pl*. de SHEAF.

shed [šed], *vti*. [9] desprenderse de, largar; mudar; verter, derramar; esparcir.—*vii*. mudar (los cuernos, la piel, las plumas).—*s*. cobertizo; tejadillo.—*pret*. y *pp*. de TO SHED.

sheen [šịn], *s*. lustre, viso.

sheep [šịp], *s*. oveja, carnero; ovejas; ganado lanar; (fig.) rebaño, grey.— *s. dog*, perro de pastor.—*s. tick*, garrapata.– **—fold** [šịpfouḷd], *s*. redil, aprisco, majada.– **—ish** [-iš], *a*. avergonzado; tímido, pusilánime.– **—skin** [-skịn], *s*. piel de borrego; (fam.) diploma.

sheet [šịt], *s*. lámina (de metal); sábana; pliego u hoja (de papel); extensión de agua.—*s. lightning*, fucilazo(s); relampagueo.—*s. metal*, metal laminado.—*s. music*, música en hojas sueltas.

shelf [šelf], *s*. anaquel, estante, repisa, tabla, entrepaño; saliente (de roca).

shell [šel], *s*. concha, carapacho; casco (de embarcación); cáscara (de nuez, huevo, etc.); vaina (de legumbres); cubierta, corteza; armazón (de edificio); (arti.) bomba, granada, proyectil; cápsula para cartuchos; bote o canoa para regatas.—*s. shock*, neurosis de guerra.—*vt*. descascarar, desvainar, mondar, pelar; (arti.) bombardear.—*vi*. descascararse.— *to s. out*, (fam.) aflojar la mosca.

shellac [šelǽk], *s*. (goma) laca.—*vti*. [8] barnizar con laca. **—shellacked** [šelǽkt], *pret*. y *pp*. de TO SHELLAC.

shellfish [šélfiš], *s*. marisco(s).

shelter [šéltœ(r)], *s*. resguardo; refugio, abrigo, asilo;—*air-raid s*., refugio antiaéreo.—*to take s*., abrigarse, refugiarse.—*vt*. guarecer, abrigar, amparar, proteger.

shelve [šelv], *vt*. poner sobre un estante o anaquel; (fig.) poner a un lado, dar carpetazo, archivar, arrinconar.– **—s** [-z], *pl*. de SHELF.

shepherd [šépœrd], *s*. pastor; zagal; (fig.) párroco, cura.—*s. dog*, perro de pastor.—*s.'s hut*, turgurio.– **—ess** [-is], *s*. pastora; zagala.

sherbet [šœ́rbịt], *s*. sorbete.

sheriff [šérịf], *s*. alguacil mayor.

sherry [šérị], *s*. vino de Jerez.

shield [šịld], *s*. escudo; broquel, rodela; resguardo, defensa; protector.—*vt*. escudar, resguardar, proteger.

shift [šịft], *vt*. cambiar; desviar; trasladar; mudar la ropa; (teat.) cambiar de decoración.—*to s. about*, revolverse, girar.—*to s. for oneself*, ingeniarse, darse maña, componérselas.—*to s. gears*, (aut.) cambiar de marcha.—*to s. into high*, (aut.) meter la directa.—*vi*. moverse; cambiar de puesto, mudarse; mudar, cambiar, variar.—*to s. for oneself*, ingeniarse, arreglárselas.—*s*. cambio; desviación; maña, subterfugio; turno o tanda de obreros; (aut.) palanca de cambio.—*s. key*, tecla de mayúsculas.—*s. work*, trabajo por turnos.– **—less** [-les], *a*. desidioso, perezoso.– **—y** [šịftị], *a*. evasivo, furtivo; astuto; ingenioso.

shilling [šílịŋ], *s*. chelín.

shin [šịn], *s*. espinilla (de la pierna).— *s. bone*, tibia, canilla, caña.—*vti*. y *vii*. [1] trepar.

shine [šạịn], *vii*. [10] (re)lucir, brillar, fulgurar, resplandecer; hacer sol o buen tiempo.—*vt*. pulir, bruñir; dar lustre (a los zapatos); limpiar (el calzado), (Méx.) embolar.—*s*. resplandor, lustre, brillo.

shingle [šíŋgl], *s*. ripia, teja de madera; tejamaní; pelo a la garçonne; (fam.) letrero de oficina.—*pl*. (med.) zona.—*to hang out one's s*., (fam.) abrir una oficina.—*vt*. cubrir con ripias; cortar (el pelo) a la garçonne.

shining [šáịnịŋ], *a*. brillante, luciente.

shiny [šáịnị], *a*. lustroso, brillante.

ship [šịp], *s*. barco, buque, nave, navío; vapor; aeronave.—*vti*. [1] embarcar; (com.) enviar, despachar, remesar.—*vii*. embarcarse.– **—board** [šípbord], *s*. (mar.) bordo.—*on s*., a bordo.– **—builder** [-bịldœ(r)], *s*. ingeniero naval, constructor de buques.– **—mate** [-mejt], *s*. compañero de a bordo.– **—ment** [-mẹnt], *s*. (com.) embarque; cargamento, partida; envío, despacho, consignación, remesa.– **—owner** [-ounœ(r)], *s*. naviero, armador.– **—per** [-œ(r)], *s*. embarcador, fletador; expedidor, remitente.– **—ping** [-ịŋ], *s*. (com.) embarque; envío, despacho.—*a*. naval, marítimo, de marina mercante.—*s. agent*, consignatario de buques.- **—shape** [-šeip], *a.* y *adv.* en buen orden. **—wreck** [-rēk], *s.* naufragio.—*vt.* hacer naufragar o zozobrar; echar a pique.—*shipwrecked person*, náufrago.- **—yard** [-yard], *s.* astillero, varadero.

shirk [šœrk], *vt.* y *vi.* evadir(se de), eludir, evitar.

shirt [šœrt], *s.* camisa; blusa.—*in s. sleeves*, en mangas de camisa.

shiver [šívœ(r)], *s.* temblor, (es)calofrío, estremecimiento.—*vi.* tiritar, temblar.

shoal [šoul], *s.* bajío, banco de arena.

shock [šak], *s.* choque; sacudida, sacudimiento; golpe; susto, sobresalto, emoción; ofensa; (med.) choque, postración nerviosa.—*s. absorber*, (mec. y aut.) amortiguador.—*s. dog*, perro de lanas.—*s. treatment*, (med.) terapia de electrochoque.—*s. troops*, tropas (escogidas) de asalto.—*vt.* y *vi.* sacudir, dar una sacudida; chocar, ofender, disgustar; conmover; escandalizar, horrorizar; (agr.) hacinar.- **—ing** [šákiŋ], *a.* espantoso, horrible; chocante, ofensivo.

shod [šad], *pret.* y *pp.* de TO SHOE.- **—dy** [-di], *a.* falso, de imitación.

shoe [šu], *s.* zapato; herradura.—*s. blacking*, betún para zapatos, bola.—*s. lace*, cordón, lazo (de zapatos).—*s. polish*, lustre, betún, bola.—*s. store*, zapaterí.—*s. tree*, horma.—*to be in his (their, etc.) shoes*, estar en su pellejo.—*vti.* [10] herrar (un caballo); calzar (a una persona, el ancla).- **—horn** [šúhɔrn], calzador.- **—maker** [-meikœ(r)], *s.* zapatero.- **—shine** [-šain], *s.* brillo, lustre.—*s. boy*, limpiabotas, lustrabotas.- **—string** [-striŋ], *s.* cordón, lazo (de zapato).

shone [šoun], *pret.* y *pp.* de TO SHINE.

shoo [šu], *vt.* y *vi.* oxear.—*interj.* ¡zape!, ¡úscale!—*s.-in*, asegurado.

shook [šuk], *pret.* de TO SHAKE.

shoot [šut], *vti.* [10] tirar, disparar; descargar; herir o matar con arma de fuego; fusilar, pasar por las armas; arrojar, lanzar; emitir (un rayo); rodar, filmar (una escena o película).—*to s. down*, tumbar a balazos.—*to s. off*, tirar, descargar (arma de fuego); llevarse.—*vii.* tirar, disparar armas de fuego; pasar o correr rápidamente; nacer, brotar, germinar; punzar (un dolor).—*to s. forth*, lanzarse o abalanzarse.—*to s. out*, bro-

tar, germinar.—*to s. up*, nacer, crecer; madurar.—*s.* vástago, retoño.- **—er** [šutœ(r)], *s.* tirador.- **—ing** [-iŋ], *s.* tiroteo, tiro(s), descarga; (cine) filmación de una escena.—*s. gallery*, galería de tiro al blanco.—*s. match*, certamen de tiro al blanco.—*s.-out*, tiroteo, balacera.—*s. star*, estrella fugaz.—*the whole s. match*, (jer.) absolutamente todo.

shop [šap], *s.* tienda; taller.—*s. window*, escaparate.—*a.* de tienda; de taller.—*vii.* [1] ir de tiendas o de compras, hacer compras.- **—keeper** [šápkipœ(r)], *s.* tendero.- **—lifter** [-liftœr], *s.* mechero, ratero de tiendas. **—ping** [-iŋ], *s.* compras.—*to go s.*, ir de tiendas o de compras.—*s. center*, centro comercial.—*s. district*, barrio comercial.- **—worn** [-wɔrn], *a.* sobado, deslucido por el manoseo y trajín de la tienda.

shore [šɔr], *s.* costa, ribera, playa, orilla, litoral; (constr.) puntal.—*s. dinner*, comida de pescado y mariscos.—*vt.* apuntalar, acodalar.

shorn [šɔrn], *pp.* de TO SHEAR.—*a.* mocho, chamorro.

short [šɔrt], *a.* corto; bajo de estatura; diminuto, pequeño; falto, escaso; breve, conciso; próximo, cercano.—*in a o within a s. time o while*, en un rato; en poco tiempo; dentro de poco.—*in s. order*, prontamente.—*on s. notice*, prontamente, con poco tiempo de aviso.—*on s. term*, (com.) a corto plazo.—*s. circuit*, cortocircuito.—*s. cut*, atajo; método abreviado o corto.—*s.-lived*, de breve vida.—*s. of this*, fuera de esto.—*s.-range*, de poco alcance.—*s. sale*, (com.) venta al descubierto.—*s. story*, cuenta.—*s. tempered*, de mal genio.—*s.-term*, a corto plazo.—*to be s.*, para abreviar.—*to be s. of*, estar lejos de; no responder a; estar escaso de.—*to cut s.*, interrumpir, abreviar.—*to fall s. of*, ser inferior a, no corresponder a o no alcanzar.—*to grow s.*, acortarse, disminuir.—*s.* resumen, (com.) déficit.—*for s.*, para abreviar, para mayor brevedad.—*in s.*, en resumidas cuentas.—*pl.* pantalones cortos, calzoncillos; (cine) películas cortas.—*adv.* brevemente.—*s.-handed*, escaso de personal.—*s.-tempered*, irascible.—*s.-winded*, asmático, corto de respiración.- **—age** [šɔrtiḍẑ], *s.* déficit; carestía, escasez, falta, merma.– **—cake** [-keįk], *s.* (coc.) torta de frutas.– **—change** [-cheįndẑ], *vt.* no devolver la vuelta debida a; (fam.) no ser justo con.– **—coming** [-kʌmįŋ], *s.* defecto; negligencia, descuido; falta.– **—en** [-n], *vt.* y *vi.* acortar(se), abreviar(se), disminuir(se), encoger(se).– **ening** [-enįŋ], *s.* acortamiento; abreviación; (coc.) manteca o grasa con que se hacen hojaldres, etc.– **—hand** [-hænd], *s.* taquigrafía, estenografía.—*a.* taquigráfico.– **—ly** [-lį], *adv.* luego, al instante, dentro de poco; brevemente; en breve.—*s. after*, a poco de.—*s. afterward*, al poco rato.—*s. before*, poco antes.– **—ness** [-nįs], *s.* cortedad; pequeñez; brevedad; deficiencia.– **—sighted** [-saįtįd], *a.* miope, cegato; falto de perspicacia.

shot [šat], *pret.* y *pp.* de TO SHOOT.—*vti.* [1] cargar con perdigones.—*s.* perdigón; munición, perdigones; bala, proyectil; tiro, disparo; escopetazo; balazo; alcance (de pistola, etc.); tirada, jugada (en el billar); inyección; (fam.) trago (de licor).—*a good s.*, un tirador certero.—*like a s.*, como un rayo; disparado.—*not by a long s.*, (fam.) ni por asomo, ni por pienso.—*s.-put*, (dep.) tiro de la pesa.—*to take s. at*, hacer un tiro a; echar una púa, burla o indirecta a.– **—gun** [šátgʌn], *s.* escopeta.—*to ride s.*, (jer.) viajar como guardia armado.

should [šųd], *vai.* [11] (se usa para formar el condicional o para expresar obligación).—*I said that I s. go*, dije que iría.—*you s. tell him*, Ud. debe (o debería) decírselo.—V. SHALL.

shoulder [šóųldœ(r)], *s.* hombro; encuentro (de un ave); pernil, cuarto delantero (de un cuadrúpedo); saliente o contenes (de carretera, camino, etc.).—*pl.* espalda(s), hombros.—*on one's shoulders*, a cuestas.—*s. blade*, omóplato u omoplato, paletilla.—*s. pad*, hombrera.—*s. to s.*, hombro con hombro; unidamente.—*to put one's s. to the wheel*, arrimar el hombro, echar una mano.—*vt.* echarse a la espalda, cargar al hombro, llevar a hombros; (fig.) cargar con, asumir.—*s. arms*, (mil.) armas al hombro.

shout [šaųt], *vt.* y *vi.* vocear, gritar, vociferar; vitorear.—*s.* grito, alarido; aclamación.

shove [šʌv], *vt.* y *vi.*, empujar, dar empujones o empellones.—*to s. away*, rechazar, alejar.—*to s. off*, echar afuera (una embarcación); alejarse de, dejar.—*to s. out*, empujar hacia afuera, hacer salir.—*s.* empellón, empujón, empuje.

shovel [šável], *s.* pala.—*vti.* [2] traspalar, (Am.) palear.– **—ful** [-fųl], *s.* palada.

show [šoų], *vti.* [6] mostrar, enseñar; señalar; exhibir; indicar, probar, demostrar; poner en escena, representar (un drama); poner, proyectar (una película).—*to s. forth*, exponer, mostrar; publicar.—*to s. in*, introducir, hacer entrar (a una persona).— *to s. off*, hacer gala de.—*to s. one's cards o hand*, mostrar el juego; (fig.) dejarse ver (las intenciones).—*to s. up*, hacer subir (a una persona); denunciar, descubrir, arrancar la careta a.—*vii.* aparecer, mostrarse, asomarse.—*to s. off*, alardear; pavonearse.—*to s. through*, transparentarse; entrelucir.—*to s. up*, aparecer, presentarse.—*s.* exhibición, exposición; espectáculo público; (teat.) función; ostentación; apariencia; (fam. E.U.) oportunidad.—*s. bill*, cartel, cartelón, rótulo.—*s.-off*, (fam.) pinturero.—*s. window*, escaparate de tienda, vidriera.– **—case** [šóųkeįs], *s.* aparador, vitrina.– **—down** [-daųn], *s.* acción perentoria o definitiva; hora de la verdad.– **—room** [-rum], *s.* sala de muestras, sala de exhibición.– **—y** [šóųį], *a.* aparatoso, cursi, ostentoso.

shower [šáųœ(r)], *s.* chubasco, chaparrón; (baño de) ducha.—*heavy s.*, aguacero.—*s. bath*, ducha, baño de ducha.—*vt.* llover, regar, derramar con abundancia.—*vi.* llover, caer un chubasco.

shown [šoųn], *pp.* de TO SHOW. **—showy** [šóųį], *a.* ostentoso, vistoso, suntuoso, rimbombante; chillón, charro.

shrank [š ræŋk], *pret.* de TO SHRINK.

shrapnel [šræpnel], *s.* (arti.) metralla; granada de metralla.

shred [šred], *vti.* [3] picar, desmenuzar, hacer trizas o tiras.—*s.* triza, jirón, tira, retazo; fragmento, pizca.

shrew [ŝru], *s.* arpía, virago, mujer de mal genio; (zool.) musaraña.

shrewd [ŝrud], *a.* perspicaz, sagaz; astuto; agudo, cortante.– **—ness** [ŝrúdnįs], *s.* sagacidad, astucia, sutileza.

shriek [ŝrik], *vi.* chillar, gritar.—*s.* chillido, grito agudo.

shrill [ŝrįl], *a.* chillón, estridente, agudo, penetrante.—*vt.* y *vi.* chillar.

shrimp [ŝrįmp], *s.* (zool.) camarón; (fam.) renacuajo.

shrine [ŝrajn], *s.* relicario; sepulcro de santo; lugar sagrado.

shrink [ŝrįŋk], *vii.* [10] encogerse, contraerse; disminuir, mermar; (con **from**) evadir, apartarse o huir de; retroceder.—*to s. back*, retirarse, retroceder.—*vti.* encoger, contraer.– **—age** [ŝr[ŋkįdž], *s.* encogimiento o contracción; (com.) merma, pérdida.

shrivel [ŝrível], *vti.* [2] arrugar, fruncir, doblar, encoger; estrechar; marchitar.—*vii.* arrugarse, fruncirse, encogerse, deshincharse; marchitarse.

shroud [ŝraud], *s.* mortaja, sudario.— *vt.* amortajar; (fig.) cubrir, ocultar.

shrub [ŝrʌb], *s.* arbusto.– **—bery** [ŝrábœrį], *s.* arbustos; grupo de arbustos; maleza.

shrug [ŝrʌg], *vii.* [1] encogerse de hombros.—*s.* encogimiento de hombros.

shrunk [ŝrʌŋk], *pret.* y *pp.* DE TO SHRINK. **—shrunken** [ŝráŋkęn], *pp.* DE TO SHRINK.

shudder [ŝʌ́dœ(r)], *vi.* estremecerse, temblar.—*s.* temblor, estremecimiento.

shuffle [ŝʌfl], *vt.* y *vi.* barajar (naipes); mezclar, revolver.—*to s. along*, arrastrar los pies, chancletear; ir tirando o pasando.—*s.* evasiva, salida; mezcla, confusión; restregamiento de los pies en el suelo, chancleteo.

shuffleboard [ŝáflbɔrd], *s.* juego de tejo.

shun [ŝʌn], *vti.* y *vii.* [1] huir, rehuir, esquivar, evitar.

shut [ŝʌt], *vti.* y *vii.* [9] cerrar(se).—*to s. down*, cesar en el trabajo, parar.—*to s. from*, excluir.—*to s. in*, encerrar, confinar.—*to s. off*, impedir la entrada, interceptar; cortar (el agua, etc.); interrumpir (a uno) en el teléfono, cortarle el circuito.—*to s. out*, cerrar la puerta (a uno); excluir.—*to s. up*, hacer callar; cerrar; acabar; tapar; encerrar; callarse.—*pret.* y *pp.* de TO SHUT.—*a.* cerrado.– **—down** [ŝátdaun], *s.* paro, cesación o suspensión de trabajo (en una fábrica, etc.).– **—ter** [-œ(r)], *s.* cerrador; persiana; contraventana; postigo; (foto.) obturador.

shuttle [ŝátl], *s.* (tej.) lanzadera; vehículo que hace trayectos cortos entre dos puntos.—*s. flight*, puente aéreo.—*s. service*, servicio de enlace.—*s. space s.*, transbordador espacial, lanzadera espacial.—*vt.* transportar, llevar (en viaje corto).—*vi.*—*to s. back and forth*, ir y venir.– **—cock** [-kak], *s.* (dep.) volante.

shy [ŝaj], *a.* tímido; asustadizo; cauteloso; esquivo, arisco; vergonzoso; (fam.) ñoño.—*vti.* [7] (con **off**) hacer desviar, apartar; lanzar o arrojar.—*vii.* respingar (un caballo); asustarse.— **—ness** [ŝájnįs], *s.* timidez; recato; esquivez; vergüenza, (fam.) noñez.

shyster [ŝájstœ(r)], *s.* (fam. E.U.) picapleitos, trapisondista, leguleyo; sinvergüenza, granuja.

Siamese [sajamíz], *s.* y *a.* siamés.—*S. twins*, hermanos siameses.

Sicilian [sįsílyan], *a.* y *s.* siciliano.

sick [sįk], *a.* enfermo; malo; nauseado; (con of) cansado, disgustado, fastidiado.—*s. leave*, licencia por enfermedad.—*s. room*, enfermería. —*to be s. to one's stomach*, tener náuseas.—*vt.* azuzar, excitar o incitar (a un perro).— **—bed** [-bed], *s.* lecho de enfermo.– **—en** [síkn], *vt.* enfermar; dar asco; debilitar, extenuar.—*vi.* enfermarse; nausear, tener asco.– **—ening** [-ęnįŋ], *a.* nauseabundo, repugnante.

sickle [síkl], *s.* hoz.

sickly [síklį], *a.* enfermizo, achacoso; enclenque; nauseabundo. **—sickness** [síknįs], *s.* enfermedad, dolencia; náusea.

sickness [síknɛs], *s.* enfermedad; náuseas.

side [sajd], *s.* lado, costado; flanco; ladera, falda; facción, partido, bando; banda (de un barco).—*by the s.*, al lado de; cerca de.—*on all sides* u *on every s.*, por todos lados, por todas partes.—*on that s.*, a, de, en o por ese lado.—*on the other s.*, del o al otro lado; más allá; a la otra parte.—*on the s. lines*, sin tomar parte.—*on this s.*, a, de en o por este lado; más acá.—*s. by s.*, lado a lado; hombro a hombro, juntos.—*a.* lateral; de lado; oblicuo; secundario, incidental.—*s. arms*, armas blancas.—*s. dish*, plato de entrada.—*s. door*, puerta lateral; puerta excusada.—*s. effect*, efecto secundario perjudicial.—*s. glance*, mirada de soslayo.—*s. issue*, cuestión secundaria.—*s. light*, luz lateral; información o detalle incidental.—*s. line*, negocio o actividad incidentales; (dep.) línea o límite del torreno de juego.—*s. show*, función secundaria, espectáculo de atracciones.—*s. view*, perfil, vista de lado.—*vt.* y *vi.* (con **with**) tomar parte por, declararse por, ser de la opinión de.— **board** [sájdbɔrd], *s.* aparador.— **burns** [-bœrnz], *s. pl.* patillas.

sidesaddle [sájdsædl], *a.* sillón, silla de amazona.— **sidesplitting** [sajdspljtiŋ], *a.* desternillante.— **sideswipe** [sájdswajp], *vt.* (fam.) chocar o rozar oblicuamente.—*s.* choque o rozamiento oblicuo.— **sidetrack** [sájdtræk], *vt.* desviar; echar a un lado, arrinconar; (f.c.) meter en un desviadero.— **sidewalk** [sájdwɔk], *s.* acera, (Am.) banqueta; (Am.) vereda.—*s. café*, terraza, café en la acera.— **sideways** [sájdwejz], *a.* y *adv.* de lado, lateral(mente), de soslayo, al través.— **siding** [sájdiŋ], *s.* (f.c.) apartadero, desviadero, vía muerta.— **sidle** [sájdl], *vi.* ir de lado.

siege [sidʒ], *s.* sitio, asedio, cerco.—*to lay s.*, poner sitio o cerco.

sierra [sjérầ], *s.* sierra, cordillera.

siesta [sjéstầ], *s.* siesta, siestecilla.

sieve [sjv], *s.* cedazo, tamiz, criba.—*vt.* = SIFT.— **sift** [sjft], *vt.* cerner, cribar, tamizar.—*to s. out*, investigar.—*vi.* pasar al través de un tamiz.

sigh [saj], *vi.* suspirar.—*s.* suspiro.

sight [sajt], *s.* vista; visión, perspectiva; escena; espectáculo; modo de ver; mira (de armas de fuego); agujero o abertura para mirar.—*at s.*, a la vista (letra, giro, etc.); a primera vista; al ver, cuando se vea.—*s.-read*, leer un libro abierto; (mus.) ejecutar a la primera lectura.—*thirty days after s.*, (com.) a treinta días vista.—*to be a s.*, (fam.) parecer o estar como un adefesio; ser extraordinario o extraño.—*a.* visual; (com.) a la vista.—*vt.* alcanzar con la vista,

avistar, divisar.—*to s. land*, (mar.) recalar.—*vi.* apuntar; dirigir una visual.- **—seeing** [sájtsjiŋ], *s.* visita turística a lugares de interés.- **seer** [-sícœr], *s.* turista, excursionista.

sign [sajn], *s.* signo; señal, seña; rastro, indicio; muestra, letrero, rótulo.—*s. language*, lenguaje gestual o de gestos, lenguaje por señas.—*s. of the cross*, señal de la cruz.—*to talk in s. language*, hablar por señas.—*vt.* firmar; rubricar; suscribir (un tratado, etc.); (con **off** o **away**) firmar la cesión o traspaso de.—*vi.* firmar. **—al** [sígnặl], *a.* señalado, notable, memorable.—*s.* seña, señal.—*s. tower*, (f.c.) garita de señales.—*vti.* y *vii.* [2] hacer señas, señalar, indicar. **—signatory** [sígnặtɔrj], *a.* y *s.* firmante, signatario.— **signature** [sígnặchụr], *s.* firma; rúbrica.- **signer** [sájnœ(r)], *s.* firmante, signatario.- **signing** [sájnjŋ], *s.* firma, rúbrica; lenguaje de gestos. **—post** [-poụst], hito, poste de guía.

signet [sígnjt], *s.* sello; timbre.

significance [sjgnífjkặns], *s.* significación; significado. **—significant** [sjgnífjkặnt], *a.* significante, significativo. **—signify** [sígnjfaj], *vti.* y *vii.* [7] significar.

silence [sájlẹns], *s.* silencio.—*s. gives consent*, quien calla otorga.—*vt.* imponer silencio, mandar o hacer callar; sosegar, aquietar. **—silent** [sájlẹnt], *a.* silencioso; taciturno; tácito.—*s. movie*, cine mudo.—*s. partner*, socio comanditario.

silhouette [sjluét], *vt.* hacer aparecer en silueta; perfilar.—*s.* silueta.

silicon [sílikọn], *s.* silicio.—*s. chip*, pastilla de silicio.

silk [sjlk], *s.* seda.—*pl.* sedería, géneros de seda.—*a.* de seda.—*s.-stocking*, aristocrático.- **—en** [sílkn], *a.* de seda; sedoso.- **worm** [-wœrm], *s.* gusano de seda.- **—y** [-i], *a.* sedoso, sedeño; de seda.

sill [sjl], *s.* umbral de puerta; solera, mesilla.—*window s.*, antepecho de ventana.

silliness [sílịnjs], *s.* necedad, tontería, simpleza.— **silly** [sílị], *a.* necio, tonto.

silo [sáílo], *s.* silo.

silver [sílvœ(r)], *s.* plata; vajilla de plata o plateada.—*a.* de plata; plateado.—*s. lining*, aspecto agradable de una condición desgraciada o triste.—*vt.* platear; azogar (un espejo, etc.).— **—smith** [-smiθ], *s.* platero, orfebre. **—ware** [-wɛr], *s.* vajilla de plata; artículos de plata.— **—y** [-i], *a.* plateado; argentino, argentado.

simian [símiạn], *s.* simio, mono.

similar [símilạ(r)], *a.* similar, semejante, análogo, parecido.— **—ity** [similéṛiti], *s.* semejanza, analogía, parecido.— **—ly** [símilạrli], *adv.* semejantemente, asimismo, de igual manera.— **—simile** [símili], *s.* símil. **—similitude** [símílitiud], *s.* similitud, semejanza.

simmer [símœ(r)], *vi.* hervir a fuego lento.

simper [símpœr], *s.* sonrisa boba.—*vi.* sonreir bobamente.

simple [símpl], *a.* simple; sencillo; llano; ingenuo, cándido; mentecato, necio; insignificante, ordinario.—*s.*-minded, cándido, confiado, candoroso.—*s.*-mindedness, candor, sencillez.—*s.* simplón, gaznápiro, bobo; simple.— **—ton** [-tọn], *s.* bobalicón, simplón, papanatas, gaznápiro.—**simplicity** [simplísiti], *s.* sencillez, llaneza; simplicidad; simpleza, bobería.—**simplify** [símplifai], *vti.* [7] simplificar.

simulate [símjuleit], *vt.* simular, fingir.

simultaneity [saimʌltaníiti], *s.* simultaneidad. —**simultaneous** [saimʌltéịnịʌs], *a.* simultáneo.

sin [sin], *s.* pecado, culpa.—*vii.* [1] pecar.

since [sins], *adv.* hace; desde entonces.—*four days s.*, hace cuatro días.—*not long s.*, no hace mucho, hace poco.—*s. when? how long s.?* ¿de cuándo acá? ¿desde cuándo?— *prep.* desde, después de, a contar de.—*conj.* desde que, después que; puesto que, como, como quiera que, ya que, en vista de que.

sincere [sinsír], *a.* sincero; serio. —**sincerity** [sinsériti], *s.* sinceridad.

sine [sain], *s.* (mat.) seno.

sinew [sínyu], *s.* tendón; fibra, nervio.

sinful [sínful], *a.* pecaminoso; pecador.

sing [siŋ], *vii. y vt.* [10] cantar.

singe [sind̂ẑ], *vt.* chamuscar; quemar (las puntas del pelo).—*s.* chamusquina.

singer [síŋœ(r)], *s.* cantante, cantor(a). **—singing** [síŋiŋ], *a.* cantante, de canto; cantor.—*s. bird*, ave canora.

single [síŋgl], *a.* único, solo; particular, individual; sencillo (no doble, etc.); soltero.—*s. file*, hilera; en hilera, uno tras otro.—*s.-handed*, solo, sin ayuda.—*vt.* (gen. con *out*) singularizar; particularizar; escoger.—*s.* billete de un dólar.—*pl.* partido de individuales (no parejas) (en el tenis, etc.). **—singly** [síŋgli], *adv.* individualmente, uno a uno, separadamente.

singsong [síŋsɔŋ], *s.* sonsonete.

singular [síŋgiulạ(r)], *a.* singular; extraño, extraordinario, raro; único.—*s.* (gram.) (número) singular.

sinister [sínistœ(r)], *a.* siniestro.

sink [siŋk], *vti.* [10] hundir, sumergir; (mar.) echar a pique a o fondo; sumir; cavar, abrir (un pozo); clavar, enterrar.—*vii.* hundirse, sumirse; (mar.) naufragar, zozobrar, irse a pique.—*to s. on one's knees*, caer de rodillas.—*s.* sumidero, vertedero; fregadero.— **—er** [síŋkœ(r)], *s.* plomada de pescar; el que o lo que se hunde.— **—ing** [-iŋ], *s.* hundimiento; abertura (de un pozo, etc.); acción de hundirse, echar a pique.—*a.* que (se) hunde.

sinless [sínles], *a.* impecable.

sinner [sínœ(r)], *s.* pecador(a).

sinus [sáinʌs], *s.* cavidad, abertura; (anat.) seno, cavidad ósea.

sip [sip], *vti.* [1] sorber, libar, chupar.— *s.* sorbo.

siphon [sáifọn], *s.* sifón.—*vt. y vi.* sacar líquidos con sifón.

sir [sœr], *s.* señor, caballero.—*Dear Sir*, (en cartas) Muy Señor mío (nuestro).

siren [sáiṛen], *s.* sirena.

sirloin [sœ́rlɔịn], *s.* solomillo, lomo.

sissy [sísi], *s. y a.* (fam.) marica, afeminado.

sister [sístœ(r)], *s.* hermana; sor; monja.—*s.-in-law*, cuñada.

sit [sit], *vti.* [10] sentar; dar asiento a; tener capacidad o espacio para.— *vii.* sentarse; estar sentado; posarse; empollar (las aves); reunirse, celebrar junta o sesión; formar parte de un congreso, tribunal, etc.; sentar, caer bien o mal (un vestido, etc.); descansar, apoyarse.—*s.-down strike*, huelga de sentados, huelga de brazos caídos.—*to s. by*, sentarse o estar sentado cerca de, junto o al lado de.—*to s. down*, sentarse.—*to s. for*, servir de modelo, posar.—*to s. still*, estarse quieto, no moverse; no levantarse Ud.—*to s. tight*, (fam.) esperar sin decir nada, tenerse firme.—*to s. up*, incorporarse.- **—e** [sajt], *s.* sitio, situación, local; asiento.- **—ting** [sítiŋ], *s.* acción o modo de sentarse; sesión, junta; (a)sentada; nidada.—*s. duck*, pato sentado en el agua; (fam.) blanco de fácil alcance.—*s. room*, sala de estar.

situate [síchụẹjt], *vt.* situar; fijar sitio o lugar para.- **—d** [síchụẹjtid], *a.* situado, sito, ubicado. **—situation** [sịchụéjṣọn], *s.* situación; ubicación, posición; colocación, plaza, empleo.

six [sịks], *a.* y *s.* seis.—*s.-pack*, caja de seis botellas o latas.—*s.-shooter*, revólver de seis tiros. **—six hundred**, *a.* y *s.* seiscientos. **—s. one**, seiscientos uno. **—sixth** [sịksθ], *a.* y *s.* sexto.

sixteen [sịkstín], *a.* y *s.* dieciséis, diez y seis. **—sixteenth** [sịkstínθ], *a.* y *s.* decimosexto, dieciseisavo.

sixty [síkstị], *a.* y *s.* sesenta.—*s.-one*, sesenta y uno. **—sixtieth** [síkstịẹθ], *a.* y *s.* sexagésimo, sesentavo

sizable [sájẓạbl], *a.* de tamaño razonable, adecuado; considerable. **—size** [sajẓ], *s.* tamaño, medida, dimensiones; diámetro (de un tubo, alambre, etc.); apresto, cola, talla, estatura.—*vt.* clasificar o separar según el tamaño o estatura; valuar, justipreciar; aprestar, encolar.

sizzle [sịzl], *vi.* chirriar (al freírse); (fam.) estar muy caliente.—*s.* chirrido (al freírse).

skate [skejt], *vi.* patinar.—*s.* patín.- **—r** [skéjtoe(r)], *s.* patinador. **—skating** [skéjtiŋ], *s.* patinaje.—*a.* de o para patinar.—*s. rink*, pista o sala de patinar.

skein [skejn], *s.* madeja.

skeleton [skéleton], *s.* esqueleto; armazón.—*s. key*, ganzúa, llave maestra.

skeptic [sképtik], *s.* y *a.* escéptico.- **—al** [-ạl], *a.* escéptico.

sketch [skẹch], *s.* diseño, bosquejo, boceto, croquis; (teat.) pieza corta o ligera; drama o cuadro dramático de radio.—*vt.* diseñar, esbozar, delinear, bosquejar, hacer un croquis

de.- **—book** [-bụk], libro de bocetos; libro de esbozos literarios.

skewer [skjúœ(r)], *s.* pincho.—*vt.* espetar.

ski [ski], *s.* esquí.—*vi.* esquiar.

skid [skịd], *vii.* [1] deslizar; patinar (una rueda); (aut.) patinar o resbalar lateralmente.—*s.* patinazo.

skier [skíœ(r)], *s.* esquiador.

skiff [skịf], *s.* esquife.

skiing [skíjŋ], *s.* esquiismo.

ski jacket, *s.* plumífero.

ski jump, *s.* salto de esquí; cancha de esquiar; trampolín.

ski lift, *s.* telesquí.

skill [skịl], *s.* habilidad, destreza, pericia, maña.- **—ed** [skịld], *a.* práctico, instruido, experimentado, experto.

skillet [skílịt], *s.* sartén; cacerola pequeña.

skillful [skílfụl], *a.* diestro, hábil, experto, ducho.

skim [skịm], *vti.* [1] desnatar; espumar; examinar superficialmente, hojear (un libro).—*vii.* deslizarse o pasar rasando.—*to s. over*, resbalar, rozar.

ski mask, *s.* pasamontaña.

skim milk, *s.* leche desnatada.

skimp [skịmp], *vt.* escatimar; chapucear.—*vi.* economizar, apretarse; chapucear. **—y** [ị], *a.* escaso; tacaño, mezquino.- **—y**

skin [skịn], *s.* piel (cutis, epidermis, tez); odre, pellejo; cuero; cáscara.—*s. deep*, superficial.—*s. diver*, submarinista.—*vti.* [1] desollar, despellejar; pelar, mondar; (fam.) sacar dinero a, pelar.—*vii.* mudar la piel; (fam.) ser embaucador o engañador; (fam.) (gen. con **out**) escabullirse.- **—flint** [skínflịnt], *s.* avaro.- **—ny** [-ị], *a.* flaco, descarnado; pellejudo.

skip [skịp], *vti.* [1] saltar, omitir; saltar por encima de, pasar por alto.—*vii.* saltar, brincar.—*s.* cabriola, salto, brinco; omisión.—*s. bombing*, bombardeo de rebote. **—per** [skípœ(r)], *s.* (mar.) patrón.

skirmish [skœrmịṣ], *s.* (mil.) escaramuza, refriega.—*vi.* (sos)tener una escaramuza.

skirt [skœrt], *s.* falda, faldellín, saya; orilla, margen, borde.—*pl.* (fam.) mujer, faldas.—*vt.* seguir la orilla de; costear; (cost.) orillar.—*vi.* (con **along, near**, etc.) ladear, (mar.) costear.

skit [skịt], *s.* boceto burlesco, paso cómico.

skittish [skịtịš], *a.* espantadizo; tímido; retozón; caprichudo, voluble.

skull [skʌl], *s.* cráneo; calavera.— **—cap** [skʌ́lkæp], *s.* bonete, solideo.

skunk [skʌŋk], *s.* mofeta, zorrillo; (fam.) canalla, persona ruin.

sky [skaj], *s.* cielo, firmamento.—*s.-blue, s.-colored,* azul celeste, cerúleo.—*to praise to the skies,* poner en, o sobre, las nubes.— **—lark** [skájlark], *s.* alondra, calandria.— **—light** [-lajt], *s.* claraboya, tragaluz.— **—line** [-lajn], *s.* línea de los edificios contra el cielo.— **—rocket** [-rakịt], *s.* cohete, volador.— **—scraper** [-skrejpœ(r)], *s.* rascacielos.— **—Skylab** [skájlæb], *s.* laboratorio espacial.— **—writing** [-rajtịŋ], *s.* escritura aérea.

slab [slæb], *s.* losa, baldosa; lonja, tajada gruesa; plancha, tablón; laja, lancha.

slack [slæk], *a.* flojo; poco firme, aflojado; remiso, tardo.—*s.* (mar.) seno de un cabo; flojedad; (com.) período de poca actividad; estación o tiempo muerto.—*pl.* pantalones flojos.—*s.,* **slacken** [slǽkn], *vt.* aflojar, relajar, desapretar; disminuir.— *vi.* aflojarse, relajarse; disminuir; retardarse; flojear.

slag [slæg], *s.* escoria.

slain [slejn], *pp.* de TO SLAY.

slake [slejk], *vt.* apagar (la cal, la sed); refrescar; desleír (la cal); moderar.— *slaked lime,* cal muerta o apagada.— *vi.* apagarse (la cal).

slam [slæm], *vti.* [1] cerrar de golpe.— *vii.* cerrarse de golpe y con estrépito.—*s.* portazo; (fam.) crítica severa.—*s.-bang,* (fam.) de golpe y porrazo.

slander [slǽndœ(r)], *vt.* calumniar, difamar.—*s.* calumnia, difamación.— **—ous** [-ʌs], *a.* calumnioso, difamatorio.

slang [slæŋ], *s.* vulgarismo; jerga, jerigonza, germanía.

slant [slænt], *vt.* y *vi.* sesgar(se), inclinar(se).—*s.* oblicuidad; inclinación; sesgo; declive; punto de vista.

slap [slæp], *vti.* [1] abofetear, acachetear.—*s.* bofetada, bofetón, manotada, manotazo.—*a s. in the face,* bofetada; insulto.—*adv.* de golpe y porrazo, de sopetón.— **—dash** [slǽpdæš], *a.* y *adv.* descuidado, chapucero; de prisa, descuidadamente.

slash [slæš], *vt.* acuchillar, dar cuchilladas; cortar, hacer un corte largo en; rebajar, reducir radicalmente (sueldos, gastos, precios, etc.).—*vi.* tirar tajos y reveses.—*s.* cuchillada; corte, cortadura.

slat [slæt], *s.* tablilla, lámina.

slate [slejt], *s.* pizarra; pizarra para escribir; (E.U. pol.) lista de candidatos; candidatura.—*s. roof,* empizarrado.

slaughter [slótœ(r)], *s.* carnicería, matanza, (fam.) degollina.—*vt.* matar, sacrificar (las reses); hacer una carnicería o matanza; destrozar.— **—house** [-haụs], *s.* matadero.

Slav [slav], *a.* y *s.* eslavo.

slave [slejv], *s.* esclavo.—*s. driver,* negrero.—*s. trade,* trato de esclavos.— *s. trader,* negrero.—*vi.* trabajar como esclavo.— **—holder** [-houldœr], *s.* dueño de esclavos.

slaver [slǽvœ(r)], *s.* baba.—*vi.* babear.

slavery [sléjvœrị], *s.* esclavitud.

Slavic [slávịk], *s.* lengua eslava.—*a.* eslavo.

slavish [sléjvịš], *a.* servil, abyecto; esclavizado.

slay [slej], *vti.* [10] matar.— **—er** [sléjœ(r)], *s.* matador; asesino.

sled [sled], *vti.* y *vii.* [1] ir o llevar en trineo.—*s.* trineo, rastra.—*s. hammer,* acotillo, mazo.

sleek [slik], *a.* liso, bruñido, alisado; suave, zalamero.—*vt.* alisar, pulir, suavizar.

sleep [slip], *vti.* y *vii.* [10] dormir.—*to s. off,* curar durmiendo (un dolor de cabeza, etc.); dormirla (la borrachera, etc.).—*to s. on* o *upon,* descuidarse o no hacer caso de; consultar con la almohada.—*to s. out,* dormir fuera de casa; saciarse de dormir.— *to s. over,* consultar con la almohada.—*to s. soundly,* dormir profundamente o a pierna suelta.—*s.* sueño.— **—er** [slípœ(r)], *s.* persona dormida; (f.c.) coche dormitorio, coche cama; (f.c.) traviesa, (Am.) durmiente.— **—ily** [-ịlị], *adv.* con somnolencia o soñolencia.— **—iness** [-inịs], *s.* soñolencia o somnolencia, sueño, modorra.— **—ing** [-ịŋ], *a.* durmiente; dormido.—*s. bag,* saco de dormir.—*s. car,* coche-cama.—*s. pill,* píldora para dormir.—*s. partner,* socio comanditario.—*s. sickness,* encefalitis letárgica.- **—less** [-lịs], *a.* desvelado, insomne.- **—walker** [-wɔkœ(r)], *s.* so(m)námbulo.- **—y** [-i], *a.* soñoliento, amodorrado.—*to be s.,* tener sueño.- **—head** [-hɛd], *s.* dormilón.

sleet [slit], *s.* aguanieve.—*vi.* caer aguanieve.

sleeve [sliv], *s.* (sast.) manga.- **—less** [slívlịs], *a.* sin mangas.

sleigh [slej], *s.* trineo.—*s. bell,* cascabel.—*s. ride,* paseo en trineo.—*vi.* pasearse en trineo.

sleight [slajt], *s.* habilidad; ardid, estratagema.—*s. of hand,* juego de manos, prestidigitación.

slender [sléndœ(r)], *a.* delgado; esbelto; sutil; escaso; insuficiente.

slept [slept], *pret.* y *pp.* de TO SLEEP.

sleuth [sliuθ], *s.* detective; agente de policía secreta o investigador privado.

slew [sliu], *pret.* de TO SLAY.

slice [slajs], *vt.* rebanar, cortar en tajadas; tajar, cortar.—*s.* rebanada, tajada, lonja.

slick [slịk], *vt.* alisar, pulir.—*vi.* (gen. con *up*) (fam.) componerse, acicalarse.—*a.* liso, terso, lustroso; resbaladizo, aceitoso; meloso; (fam.) diestro, mañoso; (fam.) de primera. - **—er** [slíkœ(r)], *s.* impermeable flojo; (fam.) embaucador, farsante.

slid [slịd], *pret.* y *pp.* de TO SLIDE. **—slidden** [slídn], *pp.* de TO SLIDE. **—slide** [slajd], *vii.* [10] resbalar(se), deslizarse, caer(se); patinar.—*vti.* hacer resbalar; (con *let*) dejar correr, no hacer caso de.—*s.* tapa corrediza; (foto.) diapositiva, transparencia; platina de microscopio; resbalón, resbaladura; resbaladero; (geol.) falla; desmoronamiento, alud; (mús.) ligado.—*a.* corredizo; de corredera.—*s. rule,* regla de cálculo. **—sliding** [slájdịŋ], *s.* deslizamiento, resbalo.—*a.* corredizo, deslizante. —*s. door,* puerta corrediza.

slight [slajt], *a.* ligero, leve; pequeño, fútil, débil, delgado.—*s.* desaire, desatención, feo, desprecio.—*vt.* menospreciar, despreciar, desairar; desatender, descuidar.

slim [slịm], *a.* delgado; baladí; delicado; escaso.

slime [slajm], *s.* limo, lama, cieno,

fango, babaza.—*vt.* y *vi.* enfangar, enlodar. **—slimy** [slájmị], *a.* viscoso, fangoso, limoso; mucoso.

sling [slịŋ], *s.* honda; (cir.) cabestrillo; (mar.) eslinga.—*vti.* [10] tirar con honda; tirar, arrojar; eslingar, izar.- **—shot** [slíŋšat], *s.* tirador, tiragomas, tiraflechas.

slink [slịŋk], *vii.* [10] escabullirse, escaparse, escurrirse.

slip [slịp], *vti.* [1] deslizar; soltarse, zafarse, soltar, desatar; irse de (la memoria, etc.).—*to s. a cog,* equivocarse.—*to s. in,* introducir o meter (esp. secretamente).—*to s. off,* quitarse de encima, soltar.—*to s. on,* ponerse (vestido, etc.) de prisa.—*to s. one's arm around* o *through,* pasar el brazo por (la cintura, etc.).—*vii.* resbalar, deslizarse; salirse de su sitio; cometer un desliz; errar o equivocarse; olvidársele a uno.—*to s. into,* introducirse, entrometerse.—*to s. out,* salir sin ser observado; dislocarse un hueso.—*s.* resbalón; deslizamiento; tropiezo, traspié; desliz; resbaladero; declive; falta, error, descuido; lapso; (agr.) plantón; tira o pedazo (de papel); funda de almohada; combinación (de vestir); boleta, papeleta.—*s.* cover, funda (de muebles, etc.).—*s. of the tongue,* error de lengua.- **—knot** [slípnat], *s.* lazo o nudo corredizo.- **—per** [slípœ(r)], *s.* pantufla, chancleta, babucha; zapatilla.- **—pery** [slípœri], *a.* resbaladizo, resbaloso; evasivo, zorro; voluble.- **—shod** [-šad], *a.* descuidado, desaliñado; tosco, mal hecho.

slit [slịt], *vti.* [9] rajar, hender; cortar en tiras; rasgar (un vestido).—*s.* cortadura larga; hendedura, tajo; ranura, abertura.—*pret.* y *pp.* de TO SLIT.

slob [slab], *s.* (jer.) sujeto desaseado, puerco.- **—ber** [-bœr], *vi.* babear, babosear.

slogan [slóugan], *s.* consigna; lema.

sloop [slup], *s.* balandro, chalupa.

slop [slap], *vti.* [1] derramar; ensuciar, enlodar.—*vii.* derramarse; chapalear (por el fango, agua nieve, etc.).—*s.* líquido derramado en el suelo; mojadura.—*pl.* agua sucia; aguachirle, lavazas; té o café flojo.

slope [sloup], *s.* (geol. y min.) inclinación; (f.c.) talud; declive, bajada; cuesta, falda, ladera; agua, vertiente (de tejado); (fort.) rampa.—*vt.* y *vi.* inclinar(se).

sloppy [slápi], *s.* mojado y sucio; desgalichado; chapucero.

slot [slat], *s.* (mec.) muesca, ranura, abertura, hendedura.—*s. machine*, tragamonedas.—*vti.* [1] acanalar, hacer una ranura en.

sloth [slɔθ], *s.* pereza, haraganería; (zool.) perezoso.

slouch [slauch], *s.* postura relajada.— *vi.* andar caído de hombres; repanchigarse.

slough [slau], *s.* lodazal, cenagal, cieno; estado de degradación; [slju] (E.U.) charca cenagosa; [slʌf], piel o camisa que muda la serpiente; (med.) tejido muerto.—*vi.* y *vt.* echar de sí tejido muerto o la piel.

Slovak [slóuvæk], *a.* y *s.* eslovaco.

slovenliness [slávenlinis], *s.* desaliño, suciedad. **—slovenly** [slávenli], *a.* desaliñado, descuidado.

slow [slou], *vt.* y *vi.* (con *up* o *down*) retardar, aflojar el paso, ir más despacio.—*a.* lento, despacioso; tardo; atrasado (el reloj); calmoso, cachazudo; lerdo, estúpido.—*s. motion*, velocidad reducida; (cine) cámara lenta.—*adv.* despacio, lentamente. **- —down** [daun], *s.* retraso, retardación.—*s. strike*, huelga de brazos caídos.- **—ly** [slóuli], *adv.* despacio, lentamente, pausadamente.- **—ness** [-nis], *s.* lentitud, retraso; cachaza; torpeza.- **—poke** [-pouk], *s.* tardón.

slug [slʌg], *s.* cualquier cosa, animal o persona de movimiento(s) lento(s); (zool.) babosa; (arti.) posta; bala; (impr.) lingote.—*vti.* [1] (arti.) cargar con posta; (fam.) aporrear.- **—gard** [slʌɡ̆ərd], *s.* haragán, holgazán, pelmazo.- **—gish** [-giš], *a.* inactivo, indolente; pachorrudo.

sluice [sljus], *s.* esclusa; compuerta; canal; (fig.) salida.—*s. gate*, compuerta.

slum [slʌm], *s.* vivienda miserable.— *pl.* arrabales, barrios bajos.—*vii.* [1] visitar los barrios bajos.—*to go slumming*, recorrer tugurios o lugares de mala vida.

slumber [slámbœ(r)], *vi.* dormitar; dormir; dormirse o descuidarse.—*s.* sueño ligero y tranquilo.

slump [slʌmp], *vi.* hundirse el pie en una materia blanda; aplastarse, rebajarse; caer, bajar.—*vt.* arrojar violentamente; hacer bajar (precios) súbitamente.—*s.* hundimiento; aplastamiento; disminución de actividad o vigor; (com.) baja repentina en los valores, bajón, desplome.

slung [slʌŋ], *pret.* y *pp.* de TO SLING.

slunk [slʌŋk], *pret.* y *pp.* de TO SLINK.

slur [slœr], *vti.* [1] menospreciar, rebajar; pasar por encima, suprimir; comerse sílabas o letras.—*s.* reparo, pulla; estigma; mancilla o mancha ligera en la reputación.

slush [slʌš], *s.* lodo blando; fango; aguanieve fangosa; desperdicios de cocina; (fam.) tonterías sentimentales.

slut [slʌt], *s.* mujerzuela, ramera; mujer sucia; perra.

sly [slai], *a.* astuto, taimado, socarrón.—*on the s.*, a hurtadillas, a la chiticallando.- **—ness** [sláinis], *s.* socarronería, astucia, disimulo.

smack [smæk], *vt.* y *vi.* manotear, golpear; besar ruidosamente; hacer sonar o chasquear (un beso, golpe, latigazo, etc.); rechupetear, saborear; saborearse.—*vi.* (con *of*) saber (a), tener gusto, dejo (de); oler (a).—*s.* sabor, gusto, gustillo; beso sonado; rechupete; manotada; chasquido de látigo.

small [smɔl], *a.* pequeño, diminuto, chico; menor; bajo de estatura; corto; insignificante; despreciable, mezquino.—*s. change*, suelto, dinero menudo.—*s. fry*, gente menudo.—*s. intestine*, intestino delgado.—*s. print*, tipo menudo.— *s.-town*, lugareño, apegado a cosas lugareñas.- **—ness** [smólnis], *s.* pequeñez; bajeza, ruindad.- **—pox** [-paks], *s.* viruela(s).

smart [smart], *a.* vivo, listo, hábil; despabilado, astuto, ladino; inteligente, talentoso; agudo, sutil; punzante, mordaz; elegante, de buen tono.—*s. aleck*, (fam.) fatuo, sabihondo.—*s. set*, gente chic.—*s.* escozor; dolor, aflicción.—*vi.* escocer, picar; requemar.- **—ness** [smártnis], *s.* agudeza, viveza; ingenio, talento; astucia; elegancia, buen tono.

smash [smæš], *vt.* y *vi.* romper, quebrar, aplastar, destrozar.—*s.* rotura, destrozo; fracaso; ruina, quiebra.— *s. hit*, (fam.) éxito rotundo.—*to go to s.*, arruinarse; hacerse añicos. **- —up** [-ʌp], *s.* colisión violenta.

smattering [smǽterin], s. tintura.

smear [smĭr], vt. untar, embarrar, tiznar, manchar.—s. *campaign*, campaña de calumnias.—s. embarradura, mancha.

smell [smel], vti. y vii. [4] oler.—*to s. a rat*, haber gato encerrado.—*to s. of*, oler a.—s. olfato; olor (bueno o malo).—*smelling salts*, sales aromáticas. —**smelt** [smelt], vt. fundir o derretir (metales). —**smelter** [sméltœ(r)], s. fundidor; alto horno. – —**y** [sméli], a. hediondo, maloliente.

smile [smáil], vi. sonreír(se).—s. sonrisa. —**smiling** [smáilin], a. risueño, sonriente. —**smilingly** [smáilinli], adv. con cara risueña.

smirch [smœrch], vt. ensuciar, tiznar; mancillar, deslucir.—s. mancilla, tizne.

smith [smiθ], s. forjador, herrero. – —**y** [smiθi], s. fragua, forja; herrería.

smitten [smítn], pp. de TO SMITE.—a. afligido; (fam.) muy enamorado.

smock [smak], s. bata corta, blusa.

smoke [smouk], s. humo.—s. *detector*, detector de humo.—*to have a s.*, dar una fumada; fumar.—vt. fumar; curar al humo; sahumar; (con **out**) ahumar, ahogar con humo; hacer salir con humo.—vi. fumar; humear, echar humo.– —**less** [smóuklis], a. sin humo.—s. *powder*, pólvora sin humo.– —**r** [smóukœ(r)], s. fumador; (f.c.) coche o salón de fumar; (fam.) tertulia en que se fuma. – —**stack** [-stæk], s. chimenea. —**smoking** [smóukin], s. acción de fumar.—a. humeante.—s. *car*, (f.c.) coche fumador.—s. *jacket*, batín.—s. *room*, cuarto o salón de fumar. —**smoky** [smóuki], a. humeante; humoso, ahumado.

smolder [smóuldœ(r)], vi. arder en rescoldo; estar latente.

smooth [smuð], a. liso, pulido; parejo, plano, igual; uniforme; suave; tranquilo (agua, etc.); cortés, afable.—s.-*shaven*, bien afeitado.—s.-*sliding*, que se desliza con suavidad e igualdad.—vt. allanar, alisar, suavizar; (gen. con **over**) zanjar, atenuar.– —**ness** [smúðnis], s. lisura, tersura, igualdad; suavidad, blandura; dulzura.

smote [smout], pret. de TO SMITE.

smother [smáðœ(r)], vt. y vi. ahogar(se), asfixiar(se); sofocar(se).

smoulder [smóuldœ(r)], vi. = SMOLDER.

smudge [smʌdʒ], vt. tiznar, ensuciar o manchar con tizne, tinta u hollín; fumigar, ahumar.—s. tiznajo, tiznadura, tiznón; fumigación o ahumadura.

smug [smʌg], a. pagado de sí mismo; petulante.

smuggle [smʌgl], vt. pasar o meter de contrabando.—vi. hacer contrabando, contrabandear.– —**r** [smʌglœ(r)], s. contrabandista.

smuggling [smʌglin], s. contrabando.

smut [smʌt], s. tiznón, tiznadura, mancha; obscenidad, indecencia; (bot., agr.) tizón.—vti. [1] tiznar, manchar; (fig.) mancillar.– —**ty** [-i], a. tiznado; indecente, verde.

snack [snæk], s. bocad(ill)o, refrigerio, (fam.) tente(e)mpié, piscolabis.

snag [snæg], s. nudo que sobresale en la madera; tocón o tronco sumergido; obstáculo oculto ignorado.—vti. [1] rasgar o dañar, chocando contra algo sumergido; impedir, obstruir; arrancar troncos o tocones (de un río).

snail [sneil], s. caracol.

snake [sneik], s. serpiente, culebra.—vi. serpentear, culebrear. —**snaky** [snéiki], a. tortuoso; solapado, astuto.

snap [snæp], vti. [1] chasquear, hacer estallar; dar, apretar o cerrar con golpe o estallido; romper con ruido y violencia; atrapar, arrebatar, echar la zarpa a; interrumpir; fotografiar instantáneamente.—*to s. one's fingers*, castañetear con los dedos.—*to s. up*, comprar, aceptar, etc. con avidez; cortar, interrumpir (a uno) con una réplica mordaz.—vii. chasquear, dar un chasquido; estallar, romperse con estallido; romperse una cosa tirante; chispear (los ojos); hablar fuerte; fallar un tiro.—*to s. at*, tirar mordiscos a, pegar una dentellada a; hablar mordazmente o con aspereza (a uno); aceptar una oferta con entusiasmo y de prisa.—*to s. in two*, romperse en dos pedazos.—*to s. off*, soltarse, saltar, abrirse de golpe.—s. chasquido; castañeteo (con los dedos); estallido; cierre de resorte; dentellada, mordiscón; (fam.) vigor, energía; período corto (de frío); (fam.) ganga, cosa fácil.—a. hecho de repente, de golpe o instantáneamente.—s. *fastener*, cierre automático.– —**shot** [snǽpšat], s. foto in-

stantánea.—**py** [-ị], *a.* (fam.) vivo,
enérgico; elegante, garboso; mordedor; enojadizo; acre, picante; chispeante.

snare [snɛr], *s.* trampa, lazo; bordón,
tirante.—*s. drum*, caja clara.—*vt.*
enredar, tender trampas o lazos.

snarl [snarl], *vi.* gruñir, regañar; refunfuñar; hacer fu (el gato).—*vt.* enredar, enmarañar; embutir, estampar
(artículos huecos de metal).—*vi.*
enredarse, enmarañarse.—*s.* gruñido, regaño; (fam.) riña; maraña,
hilo enredado; complicación, enredo; nudo en la madera.

snatch [snæch], *vt.* arrebatar; (fam.)
raptar.—*to s. off*, arrebatar.—*vi.*
(con **at**) tratar de agarrar o arrebatar.—*s.* arrebatamiento; arrebatiña;
(fam.) rapto; pedacito; ratito.—*by
snatches*, a ratos.

sneak [snik], *vi.* (con **in**) entrarse
a hurtadillas; (con **out** o **away**) salirse a hurtadillas, escurrir el bulto;
obrar solapada o bajamente; arrastrarse.—*vt.* ratear, cometer ratería, hurtar.—*s.* (fam.) persona solapada.—*s. thief*, ratero.

sneaker [sníkœr], *s.* sujeta solapado.
—**sneakers** [sníkœrz], *spl.* zapatillas
(de deporte).

sneaky [sníkị], *a.* solapado, furtivo.

sneer [snịr], *vi.* hacer un gesto de desprecio; echar una mirada despec-
tiva; mofarse de.—*vt.* expresar con
un gesto de desprecio.—*s.* gesto,
mirada o expresión de desprecio;
mofa.

sneeze [sniz], *vi.* estornudar.—*not
to be sneezed at*, no ser de despreciar, no ser un cualquiera.—*to s. at*,
despreciar, menospreciar.—*s.* estornudo.

snicker [sníkœr], *s.* risa tonta.—*vi.*
reírse tontamente.

sniff [snịf], *vt.* husmear, olfatear,
oliscar; inspirar o aspirar audi-
blemente.—*vi.* resollar, oler; sor-
berse los mocos; (con **at**) desdeñar, mostrar desprecio con re-
soplidos.—*s.* olfateo; cosa olfa-
teada.—**le** [snífl], *vi.* sorber por las
narices; moquear; lloriquear.—*s.*
moquita; lloriqueo.

snip [snịp], *vti.* [1] tijeretear; cortar con
tijeras.—*to s. off*, cortar o recortar de
un golpe.—*s.* tijeretada; recorte, retazo; pedacito; parte; (fam.) persona pequeña o insignificante.

snipe [snaip], *vt.* y *vi.* disparar o hacer

fuego desde un escondite o apostadero.—**r** [snáipœ(r)], *s.* francotirador, paco.

snippet [snípịt], *s.* recorte.

snippy [snípị], *a.* (fam.) arrogante, desdeñoso; (fam.) acre, brusco.

snitch [snịch], *vt.* y *vi.* (jer.) escamotear, ratear.

snivel [snívẹl], *vii.* [2] lloriquear, llorar
como una criatura.—*s.* moco.

snob [snab], *s.* esnob, persona con pretensiones.—**bery** [snábœrị], *s.* esnobismo, pretensiones.—**bish**
[-bịš], *a.* esnob, esnobista.

snoop [snup], *s.* (fam.) entremetido;
fisgón, curioso.—*vi.* entremeterse;
husmear, fisgonear.—**y** [-ị], *a.*
(fam.) curioso, entremetido.

snooze [snuz], *vi.* (fam.) echar un
sueñecito.—*s.* (fam.) sueñecito.

snore [snɔr], *vi.* roncar.—*s.* ronquido.

snot [snat], *s.* moco.—**ty** [tị], *a.*
(fam.) mocoso; (fam.) asqueroso,
sucio; (jer.) engreído.

snout [snaut], *s.* hocico, morro, jeta;
trompa de elefante; cañón de un
fuelle; lanza de manguera; embocadura de un cañón.

snort [snɔrt], *vt.* y *vi.* resoplar, bufar.—
s. bufido, resoplido.

snow [snou], *s.* nieve; nevada.—*vi.*
nevar.—*vt.* (con **in, over, under** o **up**)
cubrir, obstruir, detener o aprisionar con nieve.—*to s. under*, derrotar por completo.—**ball** [snóubɔl],
vt. lanzar bolas de nieve a.—*s.* pelota de nieve.—**drift** [-drịft], *s.*
ventisca, ventisquero.—**fall** [-fɔl],
s. nevada.—**flake** [-fleịk], *s.* copo
de nieve.—**plow** [-plau], *s.* (máquina) quitanieves.—**shoe** [-šu],
s. raqueta de nieve.—**storm**
[-stɔrm], *s.* nevada, tormenta de
nieve.—**y** [-ị], *a.* níveo; puro, sin
mancha; nevoso; cargado de nieve.

snub [snʌb], *vti.* [1] desairar, tratar con
desprecio estudiado o afectada arrogancia; reprender; (con **up**) parar de
repente.—*s.* desaire, repulsa; (fam.)
nariz chata.—*a.* romo, chato.

snuff [snʌf], *s.* moco, pabilo o pavesa
de candela o vela; tufo, olor; rapé.—
up to s., (fam.) despabilado.—*vt.* olfatear, oler, ventear; sorber por la
nariz; despabilar (una vela).—*vi.*
aspirar; tomar rapé.—*to s. it* o *out*,
(fam.) morirse.—**le** [snʌfl], *vi.*
ganguear.—*s.* gangueo.—*pl.*
catarro nasal, romadizo.

snug [snʌg], *a.* cómodo, abrigado;

bien dispuesto; acomodado; apretado, ajustado.— **—gle** [snágl], *vi.* apretarse.—*to s. up to,* arrimarse a.

so [soμ], *adv.* y *pron.* así; de esta manera; pues bien, conque; tan; (fam.) muy, tan.—*how s.?* ¿cómo así? ¿cómo es eso?—*if s.,* si así es, si lo fuere, en tal caso.—*I hope s.,* I think s., así lo espero, lo creo.—*is that s.?* ¿así? ¿de veras?—*just s.,* ni más ni menos; exactamente.—*not s.,* no es así, eso no es verdad.—*S.-and-S.,* Fulano de tal.—*s. as to,* para, a fin de.—*s. be it,* amén, así sea.—*s. big,* de este tamaño, así de grande.—*s.-called,* así llamado, llamado, según se llama.—*s. far,* hasta aquí, hasta ahí; hasta ahora; tan lejos.—*s. far as,* tan lejos como; hasta, hasta donde.—*s. forth,* etcétera; y así sucesivamente.—*s. long,* hasta luego, hasta más ver; hasta aquí (ahí).—*s. long as,* mientras que.—*s. many,* tantos.—*s. much,* tanto.—*s. much a,* tanto por.—*s. much as,* por mucho que; tanto como; siquiera.—*s. much for,* eso en cuanto a, eso basta en cuanto a.—*s. much s. o that,* tanto que.—*s. much the better,* tanto mejor.—*s. much the less,* tanto menos.—*s. much the worse,* tanto peor.—*s. or s.,* de un modo u otro.—*s.-s.,* así así, tal cual, regular, medianamente.—*s. that,* de suerte que, de modo que; para que, a fin de que.—*s. then,* así pues, conque, por tanto.—*s. to say* o *speak,* por decirlo así.—*conj.* con tal que; (fam.) para que; (fam.) por lo tanto; de modo que.

soak [soμk], *vt.* empapar; remojar; (con **in** o **up**) embeber, absorber; (con **through**) calar, poner hecho una sopa; (fam.) cobrar precios exorbitantes (a uno); (fam.) beber con exceso.—*vi.* estar en remojo; (con in, to o through) remojarse, esponjarse, calarse; (fam.) empinar el codo.—*to be soaked to the skin,* estar calado hasta los huesos.—*s.* remojo, calada; (fam.) bebedor, borracho; orgía.

so-and-so [soμandsoμ], *s.* fulano, fulano de tal; tal cosa.

soap [soμp], *s.* jabón; (fam.) adulación; (fam.) dinero.—*s. bubble,* burbuja de jabón.—*s. dish,* jabonero.—*s. flakes,* copos de jabón.—*s. opera,* (fam.) telenovela, radionovela, serial lacrimógeno.—*vt.* enjabonar,

lavar con jabón; (fam.) adular.—**—suds** [-sμdz], *spl.* jabonaduras.—**—y** [soμpi], *a.* jabonoso.

soar [sɔr], *vi.* remontarse, cernerse; encumbrarse, aspirar; (aer.) planear horizontalmente sin motor.—*s.* vuelo o remonte.

sob [sab], *s.* sollozo.—*s. sister,* (fam.) escritora de sentimentalismo cursi.—*vii.* [1] sollozar.—*vti.* decir sollozando.

sober [sóμbœr], *a.* cuerdo; sobrio; sereno; templado, moderado; de sangre fría; sombrío; de color apagado.—*in s. earnest,* de veras, con seriedad, formalmente.—*s.-minded,* desapasionado.—*vt.* y *vi.* desemborrachar(se); poner(se) grave, serio o pensativo; volverse sobrio, cuerdo, moderado.—*to s. down,* serenar(se); hacer volver o volverse cuerdo; sosegar(se).— **—ness** [-nịs], **sobriety** [sobrájẹti], *s.* sobriedad, templanza, moderación; cordura; seriedad; calma.

sobriquet [sóμbrịkẹi], *s.* sobrenombre, apodo.

soccer [sákœr], *s.* fútbol.

sociable [sóμʃabl], *a.* sociable, afable, comunicativo. **—social** [sóμʃal], *a.* social; sociable; (zool.) que vive en comunidad; (bot.) que ocupa grandes áreas; de agregación densa.—*s. register,* guía social.—*s. security,* seguridad social.—*s. worker,* asistente social.—*s. tertulia,* reunión informal. **—socialism** [sóμʃalizm], *s.* socialismo. **—socialist** [sóμʃalịst], *a.* y *s.* socialista. **—society** [sosájẹty], *s.* sociedad; comunidad; asociación, gremio; consorcio; círculos del buen tono; compañía, conversación o trato amenos. **—sociology** [soʃjálodʒị], *s.* sociología.

sock [sak], *s.* calcetín; escarpín; (fam.) porrazo, golpe; zapato ligero.—*vt.* (fam.) pegar, golpear con fuerza.

socket [sákịt], *s.* cuenca (del ojo); casquillo; portalámpara; enchufe.—*s. wrench,* llave de caja, llave de cubo.

sod [sad], *vti.* [1] cubrir de césped.—*s.* césped; témpano de tierra vegetal.

soda [sóμdạ], *s.* soda, sosa; gaseosa.—*s. fountain,* fuente de sodas.

sodium [sóμdịʌm], *s.* sodio.—*s. bicarbonate,* bicarbonato de sodio.

sodomy [sádọmị], *s.* sodomía.

sofa [sóμfạ], *s.* sofá.

soft [sɔft], *a.* blando; muelle; dúctil;

suave; liso; dulce, grato al oído; fofo; tierno, delicado; mimoso; afeminado; apocado; de matices delicados o apagados.—*s.-boiled eggs,* huevos pasados por agua.—*s. coal,* hulla grasa.—*s. drink,* bebida no alcohólica.—*s.-pedal,* (mus.) usar el pedal suave; (fig.) minimizar, moderar.—*s. soap,* jabón blando; (fam.) adulación.—*s.-soap,* (fam.) darle jabón a.—*s. water,* agua blanda.— **—ware** [-wɛr], *s.* (comput.) software, logical.— **—en** [sɔ́fn], *vt.* ablandar; reblandecer; mitigar, suavizar; enternecer; afeminar; amortiguar o apagar (colores).— *vi.* ablandarse; reblandecerse; templarse; amansarse; enternecerse.— **—ly** [sɔ́ftli], *adv.* blandamente; callando; suavemente, sin ruido; lentamente.— **—ness** [-nis], *s.* blandura; suavidad; pastosidad; maleabilidad; dulzura; ternura; morbidez.

soggy [sági], *a.* empapado, mojado; esponjoso.

soil [sɔil], *vt.* y *vi.* manchar(se), ensuciar(se), empañar(se).—*s.* terreno, tierra vegetal, suelo; país, región; suciedad; mancha; abono; pantano en que se refugia la caza.

solace [sɔ́lis], *s.* solaz.—*vt.* solazar.

solar [sóulǎr], *a.* solar.—*s. battery,* fotopila.—*s. home,* casa solar.

sold [sould], *pret.* y *pp.* de TO SELL.—*s. out,* (com.) agotado.—*to be s. on,* (fam.) estar convencido de, o convertido a.

solder [sádœr], *vt.* soldar.—*s. soldadura.—* **—ing** [-iŋ], *s.* soldadura.—*s. iron,* soldador, cautín.

soldier [sóuldžœr], *s.* soldado, militar.—*s. of fortune,* aventurero militar.—*pl.* tropa, fuerza.— **—ly** [-li], *a.* militar, marcial.— **—y** [-i], *s.* soldadesca.

sole [soul], *vt.* echar suelas.—*s.* planta del pie; suela; suelo; lenguado.—*a.* único, solo; (for.) soltero; absoluto; exclusivo.—*s. agency* o *right,* (com.) exclusiva, exclusividad.—*s. agent,* agente exclusivo.— **—ly** [-li], *adv.* solamente, únicamente.

solemn [sálem], *a.* solemne.— **—ity** [solémniti], *s.* solemnidad; formalidad; pompa; rito, ceremonia.

solicit [solísit], *vt.* solicitar.—*vi.* pretender, hacer una solicitud.— **—or** [-ǫr], *s.* agente, solicitador; pre-

tendiente.— **—ous** [-ʌs], *a.* solícito, cuidadoso.— **—ude** [-jud], *s.* solicitud, cuidado, afán.

solid [sálid], *s.* sólido.—*a.* sólido; puro (oro, plata, etc.); macizo; cúbico; unánime; (fam.) completo, verdadero.—*s. for,* unánimemente en favor de.—*s. geometry,* geometría del espacio.— **—arity** [salidǽriti], *s.* solidaridad. **—solidify** [solídifai], *vti.* vii. [7] solidificar(se).— **—ity** [solíditi], *s.* solidez.

soliloquy [solílokwi], *s.* soliloquio, monólogo. **—solitaire** [sáliter], *s.* (joy., naipes) solitario. **—solitary** [sáliteri], *a.* solitario; retirado; solo; aislado; incomunicado.—*s.* solitario, ermitaño. **—solitude** [sálitjud], *s.* soledad; vida solitaria. **—solo** [sóulou], *s.* (mús.) solo. **—soloist** [sóulouist], *s.* (mús.) solista.

soluble [sályübl], *a.* soluble. **—solution** [soljúšon], *s.* solución.

solve [salv], *vt.* resolver; solucionar; desentrañar, desenredar, aclarar.

solvency [sálvensi], *s.* solvencia. **—solvent** [sálvent], *a.* solvente.—*s.* (quím.) disolvente.

somber [sámbœr], *a.* sombrío, lóbrego, lúgubre, oscuro, tétrico.

some [sʌm], *a.* algo de, un poco; algún, alguno; unos pocos, varios; ciertos; algunos, unos.—*he is some man,* (fam.) es todo un hombre.—*s. difficulty,* cierta dificultad.—*s. fine day,* el mejor día, cuando menos se piensa.—*s. house,* (fam.) gran casa.—*pron.* algunos; parte, una parte, una porción, un poco, algo (de).—*adv.* (fam.) cerca de, como; poco más o menos.— **—body** [sámbadi], *s.* alguien, alguno; un personaje.—*s. else,* algún otro.— **—how** [-hau], *adv.* de algún modo, de alguna manera.—*s. or other,* de un modo u otro.— **—one** [-wʌn], *pron.* alguien, alguno.

somersault [sámœrsolt], *s.* salto mortal, tumbo, voltereta.—*vt.* dar un salto mortal.

something [sámθiŋ], *s.* alguna cosa, algo.—*s. else,* otra cosa; alguna otra cosa; algo más.—*adv.* algo, algún tanto. **—sometime** [sámtaim], *adv.* algún día, oportunamente, alguna vez.—*s. last week,* durante la semana pasada.—*s. soon,* un día de éstos, en breve, sin tardar mucho.— **—sometimes** [sámtaimz], *adv.* algu-

nas veces, a veces, de vez en cuando.
—**somewhat** [sʌ́mhwat], s. alguna
cosa, algo; un poco.—*adv.* algo, algún tanto, un poco. —**somewhere**
[sʌ́mhwɛr], *adv.* en alguna parte.—
s. else, en alguna otra parte.

somnolence [sámnolɛns], s. somnolencia. —**somnolent** [sámnolɛnt], *a.*
soñoliento; soporífero.

son [sʌn], s. hijo.—*s.-in-law,* yerno,
hijo político.

song [sɔŋ], s. canción, canto, cantar,
copla; balada, poema lírico; poesía,
verso; bagatela, nimiedad, bicoca.–
—**bird** [-bœrd], s. ave canora. —**ster**
[sɔ́ŋstœ(r)], s. cantor, cantante, cancionista; pájaro cantor.

sonic [sánik], *a.* sónico.—*s. boom,*
(aer.) estampido sónico.

sonnet [sánit], s. soneto.

sonny [sʌ́ni], s. hijito.

sonorous [sonórʌs], *a.* sonoro.

soon [sun], *adv.* pronto, prontamente;
de buena gana.—*as s. as,* tan pronto
como; así que, no bien.—*how s.?*
¿cuándo? ¿cuándo, a más tardar?—
s. after, poco después (de).

soot [sut], s. hollín, tizne.

soothe [suð], vt. calmar, sedar; consolar; desenfadar. —**soothing** [súðiŋ],
a. calmante, sedante.

soothsayer [súθseiœ(r)], s. adivino.

sooty [súti], *a.* tiznado, hollíniento.

sop [sap], s. sopa (cosa empapada); soborno, regalo para sobornar o apaciguar a alguien.—*vti.* [1] ensopar,
empapar.—*to be sopping wet,* estar
hecho una sopa, estar calado hasta
los huesos.—*to s. up,* absorber.

sophism [sáfizm], s. sofisma. —**sophisticate** [sofístikeit], *vt.* falsificar,
adulterar. —**sophisticated** [sofísti-
keitid], *a.* con experiencia, avezado
al mundo; afectado, artificial. —**sophistication** [sofistikéiʃon], s. mundanidad, experiencia; afectación.
—**sophistry** [sáfistri], s. sofistería.—
pl. retóricas.

sophomore [sáfomɔr], s. estudiante de
segundo año.

soporific [souporífik], *a.* soporífero;
soñoliento.

sopping [sápiŋ], *a.* empapado.—*s. wet,*
hecho una sopa.

soprano [soʊprɑ́noʊ], s. tiple, soprano.—*a.* de soprano.

sorcerer [sɔ́rsœrœ(r)], s. hechicero,
brujo. —**sorceress** [sɔ́rsœris], s.
bruja, hechicera. —**sorcery** [sɔ́r-

sœri], s. sortilegio; brujería, hechicería.

sordid [sɔ́rdid], *a.* sórdido; vil, bajo; interesado, mezquino.

sore [sɔr], s. llaga, úlcera; lastimadura;
mal, dolor; matadura (del ganado);
encono; pena, espina, memoria do-
lorosa; disgusto.—*a.* enconado,
dolorido, sensible; apenado, ape-
sarado; (fam.) enojado, sentido, picado; doloroso, penoso; molesto;
vehemente.—*s. throat,* mal de garganta; carraspera.—*to be s. at,* estar
enojado con.—*to be sorely in need of,*
necesitar urgentemente.– —**ness**
[sɔ́rnis], s. dolor, mal; calidad de dolorido, enconado o sensible; amargura de una pena.

sorrel [sárel], *a.* alazán, roano.—*s.*
color alazán o roano; animal alazán.

sorrily [sárili], *adv.* mal, malamente,
lastimosamente. —**sorrow** [sároʊ],
s. pesar, dolor, pena; duelo, luto;
desgracia, infortunio. —*s.-stricken,*
afligido, agobiado de dolor.—*to my
s.,* con gran sentimiento mío.—*vi.*
afligirse, sentir pena. —**sorrowful**
[sároʊful], *a.* afligido, angustiado;
triste, doloroso. —**sorry** [sári], *a.*
apesadumbrado; arrepentido; lamentable; malo, miserable, ruin, de
inferior calidad; despreciable, ridículo.—*I am s.,* lo siento, estoy
apenado.

sort [sɔrt], s. clase, especie, suerte;
manera, modo, forma.—*after a s.* o
in a s., de cierto modo, hasta cierto
punto.—*all sorts of,* toda clase de.—
in like s., de modo análogo.—*of
sorts,* de varias clases; de mala
muerte.—*out of sorts,* indispuesto;
malhumorado; triste.—*they are a
bad s.,* son mala gente.—*vt.* (con
over) separar, dividir, distribuir en
grupos, clasificar; (con **out**) escoger,
seleccionar; colocar; arreglar.—*vi.*
corresponder, ajustar; estar de
acuerdo; rozarse) adaptarse.

so-so [soúsou], *a.* mediano, regular,
talcualillo.—*adv.* así así, tal cual.

sot [sat], s. borrachín.

sought [sɔt], *pret.* y *pp.* de TO SEEK.

soul [souŋ], s. alma; psiquis; (fig.) corazón; esencia, virtud principal; inspiración; personificación; individuo,
persona; vecino, habitante.—*All
Souls' Day,* Día de Difuntos.—*not a
s.,* nadie, ni un alma.—*on* o *upon my
s.,* por vida mía.– —**ful** [sóulful], *a.*

sentimental, espiritual.– **—less** [-lis], *a.* desalmado, vil.

sound [sau̯nd], *a.* sano, bueno; sólido, firme; ileso, incólume; puro, ortodoxo; cierto, justo; firme; cabal; (com.) solvente.—*of s. mind,* en su cabal juicio.—*safe and s.,* sano y salvo.—*s. business,* negocio seguro.—*s. film,* película sonora.—*s. sleep,* sueño profundo.—*adv.* sanamente, vigorosamente.—*s.* (geog.) estrecho; (mar. y cir.) sonda; son, sonido, tañido; ruido; vejiga natatoria (peces).—*vt.* sonar, tocar, tañer; dar el toque de; entonar; proclamar; celebrar; probar por el sonido; sondear; auscultar.—*to s. a note,* dar señal, avisar; formular, enunciar.—*vi.* sonar; resonar, divulgarse; dar toque de aviso o llamada. – **—ing** [sáu̯ndiŋ], *a.* sonante, resonante.—*high-s.,* retumbante.—*s.* sondeo, sondaje.— **—ly** [-li], *adv.* sanamente.—*to sleep s.,* dormir profundamente.– **—ness** [-nis], *s.* sanidad, salud; vigor; firmeza, solidez, estabilidad; verdad, rectitud, pureza; fuerza, validez; rectitud, justicia; pureza de la fe, ortodoxia; (com.) solvencia.

soup [sup], *s.* sopa.—*in the s.,* (fam.) en apuros.—*s. kitchen,* comedor de beneficencia.—*s. spoon,* cuchara de sopa.

sour [sau̯r], *a.* agrio; ácido, fermentado, rancio; desabrido, acre, huraño, malhumorado.—*s. grapes!,* ¡están verdes les uvas!.—*vt.* agriar, cortar (la leche, etc.); irritar, indisponer (los ánimos); desagradar; hacer fermentar.—*vi.* agriarse, cortarse; fermentar; irritarse, enojarse; corromperse.

source [sɔrs], *s.* fuente, nacimiento, origen, causa, procedencia, germen.

sourness [sáu̯rnis], *s.* agrura, acedía, acidez; acritud, acrimonia.

south [sau̯θ], *s.* sur o sud; comarca o región situada al sur.—*a.* meridional, austral.—*S. American,* sudamericano.—*adv.* hacia el sur; del sur (viento).– **—east** [-íst], *s.* y *a.* sudeste.– **—eastern** [-ístœrn], *a.* y *adv.* del sudeste.– **—ern** [sáðœrn], *a.* meridional, del sur.– **—erner** [sáðœrnœ(r)], *s.* habitante del sur.– **—ermost** [sáðœrnmou̯st], *a.* de más al sur, más meridional.– **—paw** [-pɔ], *a.* y *s.* (dep.) zurdo.– **—ward** [-wård], *a.* situado hacia el sur.—

adv. hacia el mediodía.– **—west** [-wést], *s.* y *a.* sudoeste.– **—western** [-wéstœrn], *a.* en, hacia o del sudoeste.

souvenir [súvɛnịr], *s.* memoria, prenda de recuerdo.

sovereign [sávrịn], *s.* soberano, monarca.—*a.* soberano, independiente; preeminente; eficacísimo.– **—ty** [-tị], *s.* soberanía; estado soberano.

soviet [sóu̯vịɛt], *s.* sóviet.—*a.* soviético.

sow [sau̯], *s.* (zool.) puerca, cerda, marrana.—*vti.* y *vii.* [6] [sou̯], (agr.) sembrar; desparramar, esparcir, diseminar.

soy [sɔi̯], *s.* soja, soya; salsa de soja.– **—bean** [sójbin], *s.* soja, soya.

space [spei̯s], *a.* espacial, del espacio.—*s.* espacio.—*in the s. of,* por espacio de.—*vt.* espaciar.—*outer s.,* espacio exterior.—*s. age,* era de exploración espacial.—*s. bar,* espaciador, tecla de espacios.—*s. capsule,* cápsula espacial.—*s. center,* centro espacial.—*s. heater,* calentador unitario, calentador de espacio.—*s. platform,* plataforma espacial.—*s. probe,* sonda espacial.—*s. program,* programa de exploración espacial.—*s. shuttle,* transbordador espacial, lanzadera espacial.—*s. station,* estación espacial.—*s. suit,* vestido o traje espacial, escafandra espacial.—*s. telescope,* telescopio espacial.—*s.-time,* espacio-tiempo.— *s. travel,* viajes por el espacio, navegación espacial.—*s. vehicle,* vehículo interplanetario.—*s. walk,* paseo espacial.—*s.-walk,* pasear por el espacio.– **—craft** [-kræft], *s.* nave espacial, astronave.– **—man** [-mæn], *s.* astronauta; visitante a la Tierra del espacio exterior.– **—port** [-pɔrt], *s.* estación de lanzamiento.– **—ship** [-šịp], *s.* astronave, nave espacial.

spacious [spéi̯ʃʌs], *a.* espacioso, amplio, extenso. **—spaciousness** [spéi̯ʃʌsnịs], *s.* espaciosidad, extensión.

spade [spei̯d], *s.* pala, laya; (playing card) espada.—*to call a s. a s.,* llamar al pan, pan y al vino, vino.—*vt.* layar, revolver con pala.– **—work** [-wɔrk], *s.* trabajo preliminar.

spaghetti [spʌgéti], *s.* espaguetis, spaghetti.

span [spæn], *s.* palmo; lapso, espacio,

trecho; (arq.) luz; (aer.) envergadura, dimensión máxima transversal; ojo, apertura de puente, arco o bóveda; pareja (de caballos).—*vti.* [1] medir a palmos; atravesar; abarcar, llegar de un lado a otro de; extenderse sobre; ligar, atar.

pangle [spǽngl], *s.* lentejuela.

paniard [spǽnyård], *s.* español (persona española).

paniel [spǽnyel], *s.* perro de aguas.

panish [spǽnįš], *s.* español (idioma).—*a.* español (de España), hispánico, hispano.—*S.* moss, barba española.—*S.-speaking,* de habla española, hispanohablante.—*S. shawl,* mantón de Manila.

pank [spæŋk], *vt.* azotar, zurrar.

par [spar], *s.* (mar.) mástil, palo; (min.) espato; pugilato; riña, pelea.—*vi.* boxear, pelear.

pare [sper], *vt.* ahorrar, economizar; escatimar; prescindir de, pasarse sin; conceder, dedicar (tiempo); perdonar; no abusar de, compadecer; evitar, ahorrar trabajo o molestia a; usar con moderación; eximir de.—*there's no time to s.,* no hay tiempo que perder.—*to have time to s.,* tener tiempo de sobra o libre.—*to s. oneself,* cuidarse de sí mismo, ahorrarse trabajo, molestia, etc.—*a.* disponible, sobrante; de reserva, de repuesto; enjuto; económico, mezquino; escaso; sobrio.—*s. parts,* piezas de repuesto o de cambio.—*s. room,* cuarto de reserva.

park [spark], *s.* chispa; pizca; petimetre o pisaverde.—*pl.* (fam.) radiotelegrafista.—*s. plug,* bujía.—*vt.* (fam.) galantear, enamorar.—*vi.* echar chispas, centellear.— **—le** [spárkl], *s.* centelleo, destello, chispa.—*vi.* centellear, brillar, relampaguear; ser espumoso (vinos, etc.).— **—ling** [-lįŋ], *a.* centelleante; brillante; agudo, ingenioso; espumoso.

parrow [spǽrou], *s.* gorrión, pardal.—*s. hawk,* esparaván, gavilán, cernícalo.—*s. shot,* mostacilla.

parse [spars], *a.* esparcido, desparramado; claro, ralo.

partan [spártan], *a.* y *s.* espartano.

pasm [spæzm], *s.* espasmo.

pastic [spǽstįk], *a.* espástico.

pat [spæt], *pret.* y *pp.* de TO SPIT (escupir).—*vti.* y *vii.* [1] (fam.) reñir, disputar ligeramente.—*s.* huevas de los mariscos; palmadita; mano-

tada, sopapo, bofetada; riña, disputa.—*pl.* botines; polainas cortas.

spatial [spéišąl], *a.* espacial, del espacio.

spatula [spǽchulą], *s.* espátula.

spawn [spɔn], *s.* huevas; pececillos.—*vt.* y *vi.* desovar.

speak [spik], *vti.* y *vii.* [10] hablar; decir; conversar; comunicar(se); recitar.—*so to s.,* por decirlo así.—*s.-easy,* (jer.) taberna clandestina.—*to s. about* u *of,* hablar o tratar de.—*to s. brokenly,* chapurr(e)ar.—*to s. daggers,* decir improperios, echar chispas.—*to s. for,* hablar en favor de; hablar en nombre de; ser recomendación para; solicitar.—*to s. out,* hablar claro.—*to s. to the point,* ir al grano.—*to s. up,* hablar en alta voz; interponer; decir claridades.- **—er** [spíkœ(r)], *s.* hablante, orador; presidente (de un cuerpo legislativo); (rad.) altavoz.

spear [spir], *s.* lanza; venablo; arpón de pesca; brizna, brote, retoño.—*vt.* alancear, herir con lanza.—*vi.* (bot.) brotar.- **—head** [-hed], *s.* punta de lanza.—*vt.* dirigir, conducir; dar impulso a.- **—mint** [spírmint], *s.* (bot.) hierbabuena, menta verde.

special [spéšąl], *a.* especial; extraordinario, peculiar; diferencial; hecho especialmente.—*s. delivery,* correo exprés, correo expreso.—*s. students,* (education) alumnos que requieren una atención deferenciada.—*s. warrant,* orden de arresto.—*s.* persona o cosa especial; (fam., com.) ganga, saldo.- **—ist** [-įst], *s.* y *a.* especialista, especializado.- **—ize** [-aįz], *vt.* y *vi.* especializar(se); tener por especialidad.- **—ness** [-nįs], *s.* especialidad.- **—ity** [spešįǽlįtį], *s.* especialidad, peculiaridad, rasgo característico.

specie [spíšį], *s.* efectivo, numerario.

species [spíšįz], *s.* (biol., lóg.) especie; clase, género, suerte, variedad; forma, naturaleza. **—specific** [spįsífįk], *a.* específico, preciso; especificativo, determinado; peculiar.—*s.* (med.) específico. **—specify** [spésífaį], *vti.* [7] especificar; estipular, prescribir. **—specimen** [spésįmęn], *s.* espécimen, muestra; ejemplar.

speck(le) [spék(l)], *s.* manchita, mácula; motita; nube (en un ojo); lunar, señal; pizca, punto.—*vt.* manchar, motear.

spectacle [spéktąkl], *s.* espectáculo.—

pl. espejuelos. **—spectacular** [spɛk-tǽkyūlǎ(r)], *a.* espectacular; aparatoso. **—spectator** [spɛ́ktejtọ(r)], *s.* espectador, mirón.

specter [spɛ́ktœ(r)], *s.* espectro, visión. **—spectrum** [spɛ́ktrʌm], *s.* (opt.) espectro.

speculate [spɛ́kyūlejt], *vt.* y *vi.* especular. **—speculation** [spɛkyūléjṣọn], *s.* especulación. **—speculative** [spɛ́kyūlejtjv], *a.* especulativo; (com.) especulador. **—speculator** [spɛ́kyūlejtọ(r)], *s.* téorico; (com.) especulador; (teat.) revendedor de billetes.

sped [spɛd], *pret.* y *pp.* de TO SPEED.

speech [spich], *s.* palabra, lenguaje, idioma; voz; discurso, arenga, perorata; disertación; (teat.) parlamento.—*s. correction,* rehabilitación del habla.- **—less** [spíchljs], *a.* mudo; callado.

speed [spid], *vti.* [4] ayudar, favorecer; acompañar, despedir; despachar, expedir; acelerar, apresurar, dar prisa, avivar.—*vii.* correr, apresurarse, darse prisa; andar o moverse con presteza; (aut.) exceder la velocidad permitida; adelantar, progresar.—*s.* velocidad; rapidez; presteza; progreso, buen éxito.—*s. gear,* (aut.) cambio de velocidades.—*s. limit,* velocidad máxima permitida; límite de velocidad.—*s. trap,* (aut.) control inesperado de velocidad por radar.- **—ily** [-jlj], *adv.* rápidamente, de prisa; pronto.- **—ometer** [spidámetọ(r)], *s.* velocímetro, cuentaquilómetros, indicador de velocidad.- **—y** [-j], *a.* veloz, rápido, vivo.

spell [spɛl], *vti.* [4] deletrear; descifrar, leer con dificultad; indicar, significar; hechizar, encantar; (fam.) relevar, reemplazar.—*to s. the watch,* relevar a la guardia.—*vii.* deletrear; (fam.) descansar por un rato.—*s.* hechizo, encanto, ensalmo; fascinación; turno, tanda; (fam.) poco tiempo, rato, trecho.—*by spells,* por turnos; a ratos.—*under a s.,* fascinado.- **—bind** [spélbajnd], *vti.* [10] fascinar, embelesar, hechizar.- **—binder** [-bájndœr], *s.* (fam.) orador fascinante, orador persuasivo.- **—bound** [spélbaund], *pret.* y *pp.* de TO SPELLBIND.—*a.* fascinado, embelesado, hechizado.- **—er** [spélœ(r)], *s.* silabario; libro de deletrear.- **—ing** [-jŋ], *s.* deletreo, ortografía, grafía.

spelunker [spjlʌ́ŋkœr], *s.* espeleólogo de afición.

spend [spɛnd], *vti.* [10] gastar; consumir, agotar; pasar, emplea (tiempo, etc.)—*spending money* dinero para gastos menudos.—*vii.* gastar dinero, hacer gastos; gastarse, consumirse; desovar.- **—e** [spéndœr], *s.* gastador.- **—thr** [spéndθrjft], *s.* pródigo, derrochador, manirroto. **—spent** [spɛnt] *pret.* y *pp.* de TO SPEND.—*a.* agotado rendido.

sperm [spœrm], *s.* esperma, semen aceite de ballena.—*s. whale,* ca chalote.

spew [spyu], *vt.* y *vi.* vomitar.

sphere [sfjr], *s.* esfera; orbe; astro; es fera o círculo de acción. **—spherica** [sférjkal], *a.* esférico.

sphinx [sfjŋks], *s.* esfinge.

spice [spajs], *s.* especia; (poét.) aroma fragancia.—*s. box,* especiero.—*vt* condimentar con especias. **—spic** [spájsj], *a.* aromático, especiado (fig.) sabroso, picante.

spick-and-span [spíkandspǽn], *a* flamante; limpio, pulcro.

spider [spájdœ(r)], *s.* araña, arácnido sartén; cubo y rayos (de un rueda).—*s. web, s.'s web,* telaraña.

spiffy [spífj], *a.* (jer.) guapo, elegante.

spigot [spígot], *s.* grifo.

spike [spajk], *s.* (bot.) espiga; alcayata escarpia, espigón, clavo largo perno; pico.—*vt.* clavetear; emper nar, enclavijar; anular, poner fin a.

spikenard [spájknard], *s.* (bot.) nardo

spiky [spájkj], *a.* erizado, puntiagudo armado de púas.

spill [spjl], *s.* astilla; clavija; mecha (fam.) vuelco, caída (del caballo ● de un vehículo); derramamiento.—*vti.* [4] derramar, verter; desparra mar, esparcir; (fam.) divulga volcar.—*vii.* derramarse, rebosar. **—way** [-wej], *s.* bocacaz, canal d desagüe.

spin [spjn], *vti.* [10] hilar; (mec.) to near.—*to s. a yarn,* hilar; contar u cuento increíble.—*to s. out,* alar gar, prolongar; retorcer; hacer baila (un trompo).—*vii.* hilar; girar, dar rápidamente; (aut.) girar si avanzar (las ruedas); bailar (u trompo); (aer.) entrar en barrena.– *s.* giro, vuelta; (fam.) paseo en coch o bicicleta; (aer.) barrena.

spinach [spínjch], *s.* espinaca.

spinal [spájnǎl], *a.* (anat.) espinal.—●

column, columna vertebral o espina dorsal.—s. cord, médula espinal.

pindle [spíndl], s. huso; eje.

pine [spain], s. espinazo, espina dorsal; (bot.) espina; (zool.) púa.— **less** [spáinlis], a. sin espinazo; pusilánime; servil.

pinner [spínœ(r)], s. hilandero; hiladera, máquina de hilar; cebo artificial para pescar. **—spinning** [spínin], s. hilandería, arte de hilar; (aut.) rotación estacionaria de las ruedas.

pinster [spínstœ(r)], s. soltera, solterona; hilandera.- **—hood** [-hud], s. soltería.

piral [spáiral], s. espiral; (aer.) vuelo en espiral.—a. espiral; en espiral; de caracol.—s. staircase, escalera de caracol.—vii. [2] (aer.) volar en espiral; tomar forma o curso espiral.

pire [spair], s. (arq.) aguja; brizna de hierba; cúspide, cima, ápice; espiga, espiral, caracol.—vi. rematar en punta; (bot.) germinar.

pirit [spírit], s. espíritu; aparecido, espectro; inclinación, vocación; temple; intención; ánimo, brío, valor.—s. level, nivel de burbuja.— pl. espíritus, vapores; bebidas espirituosas; estado de ánimo.—high spirits, alegría, animación.—vt. (con away) arrebatar, hacer desaparecer (como por ensalmo).- **—ed** [-id], a. vivo, brioso; animoso.- **—ual** [spírichual], a. espiritual; mental, intelectual; místico; piadoso, religioso; espiritualista.- **—ualism** [spírichualizm], s. espiritismo; espiritualismo.- **—uous** [spírichuas], a. espirituoso, alcohólico; embriagador.

pit [spit], vti. [10] escupir, esputar.— vii. escupir; chisporrotear.—vt. y pp. de TO SPIT.—vti. [1] espetar, ensartar.—s. saliva, salivazo, escupitajo; lengua de tierra; asador, espiche.—the s. and image o the spitting image, (fam.) el vivo retrato, la imagen viva.

pite [spait], s. rencor, despecho, ojeriza.—(in) s. of, a pesar de, a despecho de, no obstante.—vt. mostrar resentimiento, mortificar.- **—ful** [spáitful], a. rencoroso; malicioso; malévolo.

pitfire [spítfair], s. fierabrás; mujer colérica.

pittle [spítl], s. saliva, escupitajo. **—spittoon** [spitún], s. escupidera.

splash [splæš], vt. salpicar, rociar, enlodar; chapotear, humedecer.—vi. chapotear.—s. salpicadura, rociada; chapoteo.- **—board** [splǽšbɔrd], s. guardabarros, (Am.) guardafangos.- **—down** [-daun], s. acuatizaje.

spleen [splin], s. bazo; mal humor; tristeza, esplín.

splendid [spléndid], a. espléndido; esplendente, brillante; ilustre, glorioso; excelente. **—splendor** [spléndo(r)], s. esplendor.

splice [splais], vt. empalmar; empotrar; (fam.) casar.—s. junta o empalme.

splint [splint], vt. (cir.) entablillar.—s. tira plana y delgada; astilla; (cir.) tablilla.- **—er** [splíntœ(r)], vt. astillar; (cir.) entablillar.—vi. hacerse pedazos, romperse en astillas.—s. astilla; esquirla (de hueso); brizna; astilla clavada en la carne.—s. group, grupo disidente.

split [split], vti. [9] hender, partir; rajar, cuartear, separar; dividir, repartir; (quim.) escindir, desdoblar; descomponer.—to s. off o up, desunir, desamistar.—vii. henderse, escindirse, rajarse, romperse a lo largo, cuartearse, resquebrajarse; estallar, reventar; dividirse; (fam.) disentir; (fam.) ser traidor, revelar secretos.— pret. y pp. de TO SPLIT.—s. hendidura, grieta, rendija, cuarteadura; división, cisma, rompimiento.—a. hendido, partido, rajado, cuarteado; curado (pescado).—s. fee, (med.) dicotomía.—s. personality, personalidad desdoblada.

splitting [splítin], a. partidor; agudo; penetrante; (headache) enloquecedor.

splotch [splach], s. mancha grande.— vt. manchar.

splurge [splʌrdž], s. (fam.) fachenda, ostentación.—vi. (fam.) fachendear.

spoil [spɔil], vti. [4] echar a perder; estropear, desgraciar; inutilizar; viciar, corromper; malcriar, consentir; despojar, saquear.—vii. inutilizarse, estropearse; podrirse.—s. saqueo; botín.—pl. beneficios de un cargo público.—spoils system, premio de servicios políticos con empleos públicos.- **—age** [spɔ́ilidž], s. desperdicio, daño, inutilización.

spoke [spouk], s. rayo, radio (de rueda).—pret. de TO SPEAK. **—spoken** [spóukn], pp. de TO SPEAK.- **—sman**

[-smən], s. interlocutor; vocero, portavoz; el que lleva la palabra.

spoliation [spouljéįşǫn], s. despojo, rapiña; (for.) expoliación.

sponge [spʌndž], s. esponja; (fam.) gorrón, parásito.—s. *cake*, bizcocho.—vt. lavar o mojar con esponja esponjar.—*to s. up*, absorber, chupar; (fam.) comer de gorra, sablear; sacar (dinero, etc.).—vi. embeberse; (fam.) vivir o comer a expensas de otro, darle un sablazo a uno.— —**r** [spándžœ(r)], s. (fam.) gorrista, sablista, pegote. —**spongy** [spándžį], a. esponjoso, esponjado.

sponsor [spánsǫ(r)], s. fiador; patrocinador, patrón, patrono; (rad. y T.V.) entidad que patrocina un programa; padrino o madrina; defensor, apadrinador, fomentador.—vt. salir fiador de, ser responsable de; apadrinar, ser padrino de; promover, fomentar, patrocinar; (rad. y T.V.) costear o presentar un programa comercial.— —**ship** [-ŝįp], s. patrocinio.

spontaneous [spanteįnęǔs], a. espontáneo.

spool [spul], s. carretel, bobina.—vt. devanar, ovillar.

spoon [spun], s. cuchara.—vt. sacar con cuchara.—vi. pescar con cuchara; (fam.) acariciarse, besarse.— —**ful** [spúnfųl], s. cucharada, cucharadita.

sporadic o **sporadical** [sporǽdįkǫl], a. esporádico.

spore [spǫr], s. espora.

sport [spǫrt], s. deporte.—pl. deportismo.—*for* o *in s.*, de burlas, en broma.—s. *clothes*, trajes de sport.—s. *fan*, (fam.) aficionado al deporte, deportista.—*to be a good s.*, ser buen compañero; saber perder (en el juego).—*to make s. of*, burlarse de.—vt. (fam.) hacer alarde de, lucir, ostentar.—vi. divertirse, jugar; bromear, chancearse.—a. deportivo.- —**ing** [įn], s.—s. *chance*, (fam.) riesgo de buen perededor.— s. *goods*, artículos de deporte.— —**s** [-s], a. deportivo; de o para deportes.—s. *news*, noticiario deportivo.—s. *writer*, cronista deportivo.— —**caster** [-kǽstœr], s. locutor deportivo.- —**wear** [-wer], s. trajes deportivos.- —**sman** [spórtsmǝn], s. deportista.

spot [spat], s. sitio, lugar, paraje,

puesto, punto; mancha, borrón, tacha; grano; lunar.—*in spots*, (fam.) en algunos respectos; aquí y allí.—*on* o *upon the s.*, ahí mismo, allí mismo, en el acto, al punto, inmediatamente.—s. *cash*, dinero contante.—*to be on the s.*, (fam.) hallarse en un aprieto; estar en peligro de muerte; estar en el lugar de los hechos.—a. (com.) en existencia, listo para entregarse.—s. *cash*, dinero contante; pago al contado.— vti. [1] motear; manchar, macular; (fam.) observar, notar, distinguir.— vii. salir manchas; mancharse.— —**less** [spátlįs], a. inmaculado.— —**light** [-lajt], s. (teat., fot., aut., etc.) reflector (móvil). —**spotted** [spátįd], a. manchado.

spouse [spaųs], s. cónyuge, consorte.

spout [spaųt], s. chorro, surtidor, caño, conducto, espita; (arq.) gárgola; cuello de vasija, pico de cafetera o tetera.—*to go up the s.*, (fam.) fracasar.—vt. y vi. arrojar o echar (un líquido); surgir, brotar, correr a chorro; (fam.) recitar, declamar.

sprain [spreįn], vt. torcer, producir un esguince.—s. (med.) torcedura, esguince.

sprang [sprǽŋ], pret. de TO SPRING.

sprawl [sprɔl], vt. y vi. tender(se); despatarrar(se); (agr.) desparramarse.

spray [spreį], vt. y vi. rociar, pulverizar un líquido.—s. rociada, rocío; espuma del mar; salpicadura; rociador, pulverizador; líquido de rociar; ramaje.—s. *gun*, pistola pulverizadora.

sprayer [spreíœr], s. pulverizador, vaporizador, rociador.

spread [spred], vti. y vii. [9] tender(se), extender(se), desplegar(se), deservolver(se); desparramar(se), esparcir(se); diseminar, propalar(se).— *to s. apart*, abrir(se), separar(se).— *to s. something (butter, etc.) on*, untar con; dar una capa de.—*to s. out the tablecloth*, extender el mantel.—*to s. with*, untar con; cubrir de.—pret. pp. de TO SPREAD.—a. extendido, desparramado; (joy.) de poco brillo.—s. extensión, amplitud; propagación; diseminación; cobertor de cama; tapete de mesa, mantel; (fam.) festín, comilona; (com.) diferencia; anuncio con encabezamiento a través de dos páginas.— —**sheet** [-ŝit], s. (comp.) hoja de cálculo.

spree [spri], s. borrachera; juerga, parranda.—*to go on a s.,* ir (o andar) de juerga, parranda o farra.

sprig [sprig], s. ramita.

sprightly [spráitli], a. alegre, vivo, garboso.

spring [spriŋ], vti. [10] soltar (un resorte o muelle); sacar o presentar de golpe; hacer volar (una mina); combar; rendir un palo o verga; (arq.) vaciar (un arco); insertar o meter doblando o forzando; saltar por encima de; pasar saltando; ojear (la caza); asegurar o montar con resortes o muelles.—*to s. a leak,* tener un escape; (mar.) empezar a hacer agua.—*to s. a surprise on someone,* coger de sorpresa a alguien, coger a alguien de improviso.—vii. saltar, brincar; salir, brotar, manar (un líquido); dimanar, provenir; presentarse súbitamente; combarse, rendirse; nacer, crecer; levantarse, elevarse.—*to s. at,* abalanzarse sobre; saltar a.—*to s. away,* saltar a un lado; lanzarse de un salto.—*to s. forward,* abalanzarse, dispararse.—*to s. up,* nacer, brotar, desarrollarse; salir a luz; subir, engrandecerse.—*to s. upon,* abalanzarse sobre; saltar a.—s. muelle, resorte; elasticidad; salto, corcovo, bote; vuelta a su posición anterior; motivo, móvil; primavera; fuente, manantial; origen, nacimiento; surtidor; combadura.—*s. fever,* (humor.) ataque primaveral.—a. primaveral; de manantial.—**board** [bɔrd], s. trampolín.—**time** [-taim], s. primavera.

sprinkle [spríŋkl], vt. rociar; regar; salpicar, polvorear.—vi. lloviznar.—s. rocío, rociada; llovizna; una pizca, un poquito.—**r** [spríŋklœ(r)], s. rociador, regadera; (igl.) hisopo, aspersorio; carro de riego. — **sprinkling** [spríŋkliŋ], s. rociada, aspersión; pizca.—*s. can,* regadera, rociadera.

sprout [spraut], vt. hacer germinar o brotar; (agr.) desbotonar.—vi. retoñar, echar botones o renuevos; crecer; ramificarse.—s. renuevo, retoño, botón.—*Brussels sprouts,* coles de Bruselas.

spruce [sprus], a. garboso, apuesto, majo.—s. abeto.—*to s. up,* vestir(se) con esmero, emperifollar(se), poner(se) majo.

sprung [sprʌŋ], *pret.* y *pp.* de TO SPRING.

spun [spʌn], *pret.* y *pp.* de TO SPIN.

spunk [spʌŋk], s. (fam.) ánimo, coraje, corazón.

spur [spœr], s. espuela, acicate; incentivo, estímulo; excitación; espolón (del gallo); uña puntiaguda; pincho; (geog.) estribación; (arq.) puntal.—*on the s. of the moment,* sin pensarlo, impulsivamente.—vti. y vii. [1] espolear, acicatear, aguijonear; incitar, estimular; calzarse las espuelas; apretar el paso.—*to s. on,* espolear, estimular.

spurious [spœriǔs], a. espurio.

spurn [spœrn], vt. y vi. despreciar; menospreciar; rechazar a puntapiés; coccar.

spurt [spœrt], vt. y vi. arrojar o salir un chorro o chorros; brotar, surgir; hacer un esfuerzo supremo.—s. chorro; arrebato, esfuerzo supremo; rato, momento.

sputter [spátœ(r)], vt. y vi. espurrear, rociar con la boca; chisporrotear; farfullar, barbotear.—s. chisporroteo; chispeo de saliva; farfulla.

sputum [spiútʌm], s. saliva; (med.) esputo.

spy [spai], s. espía.—vti. [7] atisbar, divisar; espiar, observar; (con out) explorar, reconocer un país.—vii. espiar; ser espía.— **glass** [spáiglæs], s. anteojo de larga vista.

squab [skwab], s. (orn.) pichón; persona gordiflona; cojín, otomana.

squabble [skwábl], vt. (imp.) empastelar.—vi. reñir, disputar.—s. pendencia, riña, disputa.

squad [skwad], s. (mil.) escuadra, patrulla, pelotón; partida; equipo.—**ron** [skwádrɔn], s. (mar.) escuadra, armada, flota; (mil.) escuadrón; cuadro; soldados en formación; (aer.) escuadrilla.

squalid [skwálid], a. escuálido; miserable, sucio, asqueroso.

squall [skwɔl], vt. y vi. chillar, berrear.—vi. haber borrasca.—s. chillido, berrido; borrasca; (mar.) racha, turbonada, chubasco.

squalor [skwálɔ(r)], s. miseria; porquería, mugre.

squander [skwándœ(r)], vt. y vi. malgastar, despilfarrar, desparramar, disipar.— **er** [-œ(r)], s. derrochador, manirroto.

square [skwɛr], a. cuadrado; en cuadro; rectangular; a escuadra; perfecto, exacto, justo, cabal; íntegro, honrado, equitativo; (fam.) completo, abundante; (com.) saldado, en paz; (mar.) en cruz; (mat.) elevado al cuadrado.—*s. dance,* baile de figuras.—*s. deal(ing),* buena fe, equidad, justicia, honradez, juego limpio.—*s. meal,* (fam.) comida abundante.—*s.-shooter,* (fam.) persona honrada.—*to get s. with,* (fam.) desquitarse de, hacérselas pagar a.—*s.* cuadrado; cuadro; plaza, plazoleta; casilla (de tablero de damas, etc.); manzana de casas; escuadra, cartabón; proporción debida, orden, exactitud; honradez, equidad; (mil.) cuadro.—*on the s.,* (fam.) honradamente, de buena fe; a escuadra.—*out of s.,* fuera de escuadra.—*vt.* cuadrar, formar un cuadro; escuadrar; (mat.) cuadrar, elevar al cuadrado; (b.a.) cuadricular; (com.) saldar, ajustar, arreglar (cuentas); pasar balance; justificar; poner de acuerdo; medir superficies en pies, metros, etc., cuadrados.—*to s. one's self,* sincerarse, justificarse, dar satisfacción.—*vi.* estar en ángulo recto; cuadrar, encajar, convenir, estar de acuerdo.

squash [skwaš], *s.* (bot.) calabaza.—*vt.* aplastar, (fam.) despachurrar.

squat [skwat], *vii.* [1] agacharse, agazaparse, sentarse en cuclillas; establecerse sin derecho en un local.—*a.* agachado, puesto en cuclillas; rechoncho.—*s.* posición del que está en cuclillas. —**ter** [-tœr], *s.* advenedizo, intruso, colono usurpador.

squawk [skwɔk], *vi.* graznar; (fam.) quejarse ruidosamente.—*s.* graznido; (fam.) queja o protesta ruidosa.

squeak [skwik], *vi.* chirriar, rechinar; (fam.) delatar.—*s.* chillido, chirrido.—*to have a narrow s.,* escapar en una tabla. —**squeal** [skwil], *vi.* chillar; (fam.) delatar.—*s.* chillido.

squeamish [skwímiš], *a.* remilgado, delicado, escrupuloso.- —**ness** [-nis], *s.* remilgo, escrúpulo; náusea.

squeeze [skwiz], *vt.* apretar, comprimir; estrechar; estrujar, exprimir, prensar; acosar, agobiar; rebajar (jornales).—*to s. in,* hacer entrar apretando.—*to s. through,* forzar al través de.—*vi.* pasar, entrar o salir apretando.—*s.* apretadura, apretón; abrazo fuerte.- —**r** [skwízœr], *s.* exprimidera.

squelch [skwɛlch], *vt.* aplastar; sofo-

car; (fam.) hacer callar, paraliza (fig.) desconcertar.—*vi.* ser vencid desconcertado; chapotear.

squid [skwjd], *s.* calamar.

squint [skwjnt], *s.* estrabismo; mirad bizca; mirada furtiva o de soslayo.-*vt.* y *vi.* mirar bizco, bizquear; mira achicando los ojos; mirar de través de soslayo.—*squint-eyed,* bizco, bi sojo, estrábico; avieso; ambiguo.

squirm [skwœrm], *vi.* retorcerse, se pentear; trepar.—*to s. out of a di ficulty,* esforzarse para vencer un dificultad o salir de un aprieto.—*s* retorcimiento.

squirrel [skwœręl], *s.* ardilla.

squirt [skwœrt], *vt.* y *vi.* (hacer) salir chorros; chorrear; jeringar.—*s* chisguete, chorretada; (fam.) jerin gazo.—*s. gun,* jeringa.

Sr., *abrev.* (**Senior**) padre, p.ej., **Joh Cruz, Sr.** Juan Cruz, padre.

stab [stæb], *vti.* y *vi.* [1] herir con arm blanca, dar de puñaladas.—*s.* puña lada; estocada.—*s. in the back,* pu ñalada trapera.

stability [stabíliti], *s.* estabilidad; fi meza, consistencia, solidez; asien to. —**stabilize** [stéjbilajz], *vt.* es tabilizar. —**stabilizer** [stéjbilaja œ(r)], *s.* estabilizador. —**stab** [stéjbl], *a.* estable.—*s.* establo, cua dra.—*vt.* y *vi.* poner o estar en es tablo.

stack [stæk], *s.* montón, pila, rimer hacina (de heno); cañón de chime nea; (fam.) abundancia; (mil.) pabe llón de fusiles.—*vt.* hacinar, apila amontonar; poner las armas en pa bellón.

stadium [stéjdjʌm], *s.* estadio, camp deportivo; grado de progreso o ade lanto.

staff [stæf], *s.* báculo, bordón, cayad apoyo, sostén; vara, bastón d mando; pértiga; vara de medir; ast (de bandera o lanza); baliza, jaló de mira; estado mayor, plana ma yor; personal; facultad; junt cuerpo.—*vt.* proveer de persona funcionarios u oficiales.

stag [stæg], *s.* venado, ciervo; (fam hombre, varón, macho.—*s. part* (fam.) tertulia de hombres solos.

stage [stejdž], *s.* (teat.) escenario, e cena, tablas; (fig.) teatro (arte y pr fesión); escena de acción; tablad entarimado, plataforma, estrad andamio; etapa, jornada; grado, e tado; período (de una enfermedad); platina (de microscopio); diligencia, ómnibus; (arq.) escalón, paso de escalera; (rad.) elemento, unidad; (mec.) grado.—*by short stages,* a pequeñas etapas, a cortas jornadas.—*s. door,* entrada de los artistas.—*s. fright,* trac, miedo al público.—*s. manager,* director de escena.—*s. scenery* o *setting,* decoración, decorado.—*s.-struck,* fascinado por el teatro; que se muere por ser actor o actriz.—*s. whisper,* susurro en voz alta.—*vt.* preparar; ejecutar, efectuar; (teat.) poner en escena, montar, escenificar; (re)presentar.

stagecoach [stéidʒkouch], *s.* diligencia, ómnibus.

stagehand [stéidʒhænd], *s.* tramoyista, metemuertos, metesillas.

stagger [stǽgœ(r)], *vi.* hacer eses, tambalear, bambolear; vacilar, titubear.—*vt.* causar vértigos o vahídos; asustar; hacer vacilar; hacer tambalear; disponer o arreglar (plantas, etc.) al tresbolillo; alternar; espaciar (horas de trabajo, etc.).—*s.* tambaleo, vacilación.- **—ing** [-iŋ], *a.* tambaleante; sorprendente.

stagnant [stǽgnạnt], *a.* estancado. **—stagnate** [stǽgneit], *vi.* estancarse, estacionarse. **—stagnation** [stægnéidʒǫn], *s.* estancamiento, paralización.

staid [steid], *pret.* y *pp.* de TO STAY.—*a.* grave, serio, sosegado, formal.

stain [stein], *vt.* y *vi.* manchar, macular; teñir; tiznar; mancillar, desdorar.—*stained glass,* vidrio de color.—*s.* mancha, mácula; tinte; solución colorante; borrón, estigma.- **—less** [stéinlịs], *a.* limpio; inmaculado; que no se mancha.—*s. steel,* acero inoxidable.

stair [ster], *s.* escalón, peldaño.—*pl.* escalera.- **—case** [stérkeis], **—way** [-wei], *s.* escalera; escalinata (exterior).

stake [steik], *s.* estaca; (fig.) hoguera, pira; apuesta, posta o puesta; azar, riesgo; premio del vencedor; (com.) interés, ganancia o pérdida contingente.—*at s.,* en juego, envuelto, comprometido, en peligro.—*vt.* jugarse, apostar; aventurar, arriesgar; (fam.) establecer a uno en los negocios, etc.; darle o prestarle dinero.

stale [steil], *a.* añejo; rancio, pasado;

viciado (el aire); gastado, anticuado, trillado; improductivo.—*s. bread,* pan duro.—*s. wine,* vino picado.- **—mate** [-meit], *s.* mate ahogado.—*vt.* dar mate ahogado a.

stalk [stɔk], *vt.* cazar al acecho.—*vi.* taconear, andar con paso majestuoso.—*s.* tallo, pedúnculo, peciolo; troncho de hortalizas; pie de copa; paso majestuoso, taconeo.

stall [stɔl], *s.* pesebre, casilla de establo; casilla, puesto (en el mercado, etc.); tabla (de carnicero); (teat.) luneta o butaca, (igl.) sitial de coro; (min.) galería; (aer.) disminución de velocidad.—*vt.* meter en cuadra o establo; poner puestos o casillas; atascar, atollar; poner obstáculos.—*to s. off,* evitar, eludir, tener a raya.—*vi.* estar atascado; (aut.) pararse, ahogarse (el motor); (aer.) bajar de la velocidad mínima de vuelo.—*to s. for time,* (fam.) dar largas; demorar para ganar tiempo o no hacer una cosa.

stallion [stǽlyǫn], *s.* caballo semental.

stalwart [stɔ́lwärt], *a.* fornido, membrudo; (pol.) leal, firme, fiel.

stamina [stǽminạ], *s.* nervio, fibra, vigor.

stammer [stǽmœ(r)], *vt.* y *vi.* tartamudear; balbucear.—*s.* tartamudeo; balbuceo.- **—er** [-œ(r)], *s.* tartamudo, gago.

stamp [stæmp], *vt.* estampar; marcar, señalar; imprimir; sellar, estampillar; timbrar (papel, cartas); poner el sello (de correo); acuñar; patear (el suelo, etc.); estigmatizar.—*stamping grounds,* (jer.) territorio, guarida.—*to s. out,* extirpar, suprimir.—*vi.* patalear; piafar.—*s.* sello, estampilla; timbre; impresión, marca, estampa; estampador; cuño, troquel; mano de mortero; (fig.) temple, suerte, clase; laya, calaña.—*s. duties,* derechos del timbre.—*s. duty,* impuesto del timbre.—*s. pad,* tampón.—*s.-vending machine,* máquina expendedora de sellos.

stampede [stæmpíd], *vt.* y *vi.* espantar(se); dispersar(se) en desorden.—*s.* estampida; huida en tropel; determinación repentina y unánime.

stance [stæns], *s.* postura.

stanch [stænch], *vt.* restañar; estancar.—*a.* [stanch], firme, fiel, adicto.

stand [stænd], *vti.* [10] poner derecho,

colocar o poner de pie; resistir, hacer frente a; aguantar, tolerar; sostener, defender; (fam.) sufragar.—*to s. one's ground,* resistir, defender su puesto o posición, mantenerse en su puesto.—*to s. treat,* (fam.) pagar la convidada.—*to s. up,* (fam.) dejar plantado a uno.—*vii.* estar, estar situado; ponerse o estar de pie; tenerse derecho; mantenerse, durar, perdurar; sostenerse; quedarse; pararse, detenerse; quedar suspenso; ponerse o estar en cierta posición; erguirse, enderezarse.—*to s. about,* rodear, cercar.—*to s. against,* hacer frente a.—*to s. aloof (from),* retraerse (de).—*to s. aside,* apartarse.—*to s. back,* retroceder; quedarse atrás.—*to s. by,* ser o permanecer fiel a; estar listo; sostener, favorecer; atenerse a; sostenerse en; someterse a; estar de mirón; estar cerca, quedarse allí; mantenerse listo.—*to s. fast,* no cejar o ceder.—*to s. for,* estar en lugar de; significar, querer decir; tolerar; aprobar, favorecer; solicitar, pretender; presentarse como candidato u opositor; sostener, defender; apadrinar; llevar rumbo hacia.—*to s. forth,* adelantarse, avanzar; presentarse.—*to s. in good stead,* servir, ser útil.—*to s. in line,* hacer cola.—*to s. in the way,* cerrar el paso; estorbar.—*to s. in with,* juntarse o estar aliado con; estar en gracia de.—*to s. off,* mantenerse a distancia, apartarse; negar, denegar.—*to s. on o upon,* estar colocado sobre, estar en; adherirse a; interesar, concernir, pertenecer; estimar, valuar; fijarse en; picarse de, tener su orgullo en; insistir en.—*to s. on end,* erizarse; ponerse de punta; mantenerse derecho.—*to s. on one's own feet,* valerse a sí mismo.—*to s. on tiptoe,* ponerse o estar de puntillas.—*to s. out,* mantenerse firme; apartarse; denegar; resaltar, destacarse, estar en relieve.—*to s. over,* aplazar; plantarse al lado de para vigilar o apurar.—*to s. pat,* mantenerse en sus trece.—*to s. up,* levantarse, alzarse.—*s.* puesto, sitio, lugar, posición, estación; tarima, estrado, plataforma; tribuna, grada, galería (de espectadores); mostrador, puesto en un mercado; velador, mesita, pie, estante, pedestal, sostén, soporte; actitud, opinión; parada, pausa, alto; término;

inactividad, estancamiento; oposición, resistencia.—*s.-in,* (teat. y cine) doble; (fam.) buenas aldabas.—*to make a s.,* pararse y resistir.

standard [stǽndạrd], *s.* norma, tipo, pauta, patrón, modelo; (mec.) soporte, madrina, pie, montante, árbol; bandera, estandarte, pendón.—*s. of living,* nivel o norma de vida.—*a.* normal, de ley; patrón (vara, libra, etc.); clásico.—*s.-bearer,* abanderado; cacique, jefe político.—*s. book o work,* obra de autoridad reconocida; obra clásica.—*s. equipment,* equipo regular o de uso corriente.—*s. gauge,* marca o medida que sirve de norma.—*s. pitch,* (mús.) diapasón normal.—*s. time,* hora legal, hora oficial.—**ization** [stǽndạrdịzéjṣọn], *s.* uniformación, normalización, reducción a un patrón común.— —**ize** [-ạjz], *vt* (Am.) estandarizar; normalizar.

standee [stændí], *s.* espectador o pasajero de pie.

standing [stǽndịŋ], *a.* derecho o en pie; levantado, de pie; erecto; con pedestal o pie; permanente, fijo, establecido; duradero, estable; parado; estancado, encharcado; (for.) vigente.—*s.* posición, reputación; categoría; puesto, sitio, paraje; duración, antigüedad; alto, parada.—*of long s.,* (que existe, dura, etc.) desde hace mucho tiempo.—*s. army,* ejército permanente.—*s. room,* sitio para estar de pie.—**standpoint** [stǽndpɔjnt], *s.* punto de vista. —**standstill** [stǽndstịl], *s.* parada, detención, alto; punto muerto, impasse.—*to come to a s.,* cesar, pararse.

stank [stæŋk], *pret.* de TO STINK.

stanza [stǽnzạ], *s.* estrofa.

staple [stéjpl], *s.* artículo o producto principal, renglón de comercio; elemento o asunto principal; materia prima o bruta; hembra de cerrojo; grapa, aro, argolla; grapa de alambre (para sujetar papeles).—*pl.* artículos de primera necesidad.—*a.* (com. corriente, de consumo o uso general; principal, prominente; establecido, reconocido; vendible.—*vt* asegurar (papeles, etc.) con grapas; coser con alambre; clasificar hebras textiles por su longitud.— —**r** [stéjplẹr], *s.* engrapador, cosepapeles grapador.

star [star], s. estrella; cosa o persona principal; asterisco; mancha en la frente de un animal.—*shooting s.*, estrella fugaz.—*s.-spangled*, tachonado de estrellas.—*S.-Spangled Banner*, bandera estrellada (nombre dado a la bandera y el himno de E.U.A.).—*vti.* [1] adornar con estrellas; marcar con asterisco; (teat., cine) introducir como estrella.—*vii.* ser estrella (teat. cine, etc.).—*a.* sobresaliente, excelente.

starboard [stárbɔrd], s. (mar.) estribor.

starch [starch], s. almidón, fécula; (fig.) entereza, vigor; rigidez.—*vt.* almidonar.— **—y** [stárchi], a. feculento; estirado, entonado.

stare [ster], *vt.* clavar o fijar la vista en o a; encararse con; mirar de hito en hito o descaradamente.—*vi.* abrir grandes ojos; mirar con fijeza, asombro o insolencia; saltar a la vista; ser muy vivo o chillón (un color); erizarse (el pelo).—*s.* mirada fija o de hito en hito; encaro.

starfish [stárfiʃ], s. estrella de mar.

stark [stark], a. tieso, rígido; (fig.) inflexible, severo; completo, cabal; puro.—*s.-naked*, en pelota, en cueros.

starlight [stárlajt], s. luz de las estrellas.

starling [stárliŋ], s. estornino.

starry [stári], a. estrellado; como estrellas, centelleante, rutilante.

Star Spangled Banner, s. bandera estrellada (de los E.U.).

start [start], *vt.* empezar, iniciar; poner en marcha; dar la señal de salida; levantar (la caza).—*to s. a row*, armar una gresca.—*vi.* comenzar; partir, salir; arrancar (un motor, etc.); sobresaltarse, asustarse; provenir, proceder de; aflojarse; descoyuntarse; combarse.—*to s. after*, salir tras o en busca de; seguir a.—*to s. back*, dar un respingo; emprender el viaje de regreso.—*to s. for*, ponerse en camino hacia.—*to s. off*, partir, ponerse en marcha.—*to s. out*, salir, partir; principiar a.—*to s. up*, levantarse precipitadamente; salir de repente; ponerse en movimiento, arrancar.—*s.* principio, comienzo; salida, partida; arranque; sobresalto, susto; respingo; ímpetu, arranque, pronto; ventaja, delantera; grieta, raja.—*at the s.*, al primer paso, al principio.—*by fits and starts*, a saltos y corcovos; a ratos.— **—er** [stártœ(r)], s. iniciador; el que da la señal de partida; (dep.) juez de salida; comienzo; cosa con que se principia; (aut.) arranque, mecanismo de arranque.— **—ing** [-iŋ], a. de salida; de arranque.—*s. point*, punto de partida, arrancadero.—*s.* puesta en marcha.

startle [stártl], *vt.* y *vi.* espantar(se), dar(se) un susto; sobrecoger(se); alarmar(se).

startling [stártliŋ], a. alarmante, asombroso.

starvation [starvéjʃon],—*s.* hambre, inanición.—*s. diet*, régimen, de hambre; cura de hambre. **—starve** [starv], *vi.* morir de hambre; hallarse en la inopia.—*vt.* matar de hambre.

starving [stárviŋ], a. hambriento, famélico.

state [stejt], s. estado; situación, condición; pompa, ceremonia.—*in a s. of nature*, desnudo; en pecado; indomado; incivilizado.—*in (great)* con (gran) pompa, de (gran) ceremonia.—*in s. of to*, en estado de.—*s. of mind*, estado de ánimo.—*to lie in s.*, estar de cuerpo presente.—*a.* de estado; del estado; estatal; político, público; de lujo o gala; perteneciente a los estados o a cada estado.—*vt.* y *vi.* decir, expresar; consignar; rezar (un texto); formular (un principio, ley, etc.); enunciar, plantear.— **—liness** [stéjtliniʃ], s. majestad, dignidad.— **—ly** [-li], a. augusto, majestuoso.— **—ment** [-ment], s. declaración, exposición; afirmación, aserto; manifestación; cuenta, estado de cuenta; relato, información, memoria; planteo, enunciado; proposición; (com.) balance.— **—room** [-rum], s. (mar.) camarote; (f.c.) salón; salón de recepción de un palacio.— **—sman** [-sman], s. estadista.

static [stǽtik], s. (rad.) estática.—*a.* estático.— **—s** [-s], s. (mec.) estática.

station [stéjʃon], s. estación (de f.c., radio, policía, vía crucis, etc.); sitio, puesto; rango o posición social; (mar.) apostadero; (mil.) puesto.—*s. break*, (rad./tel.) descanso, intermedio.—*s. house*, cuartelillo de policía.—*s. identification*, (rad./tel.) indicativo de la emisora.—*s. master*, jefe de estación.—*s. wagon*, rubia, coche rural, vagoneta, ranchera, familiar, camioneta.—vt. estacionar, colocar, situar, apostar.- **—ary** [-ɛrɪ], a. estacionario, fijo.—to re-main s., estacionarse, quedarse inmóvil.- **—er** [-œ(r)], s. papelero.- **—ery** [ɛrɪ], s. papelería, objetos de escritorio; papel de cartas.—s. store, papelería.

statistic(al) [stətístɪk(əl)], a. estadístico.—**statistics** [stətístɪks], s. estadística; datos estadísticos.

statuary [stǽchuɛrɪ], s. estatuaria; estatuario, escultor. **—statue** [stǽchu], s. estatua.

stature [stǽchu(r)], s. estatura, altura, tamaño; alzada; importancia.

status [stéɪtʉs], condición, estado; categoría; situación social, legal o profesional.

statute [stǽchʉt], s. estatuto, ley, reglamento.—s. law, derecho escrito.

statutory [stǽchʉtori], a. estatutario, legal.

staunch [stɔnch], vt. y a. restañar; estancar.—a. firme, fiel, adicto.

stave [steɪv], vti. [4] desfondar, abrir boquete; poner duelas (a un barril).—to s. off, rechazar, parar; retardar, diferir.—vii. desfondarse, hacerse pedazos.—s. duela de barril; escalón, peldaño (de escala); (mus.) pentagrama; (poét.) estrofa.

stay [steɪ], vti. [4] parar, impedir; sostener, apoyar, reforzar; aplazar; (for.) sobreseer.—vii. quedarse, permanecer; parar(se); tardar(se); alojarse.— to s. away, mantenerse alejado; no volver.—to s. in, quedarse en casa, no salir.—to s. out, quedarse fuera, no entrar.—to s. put, (fam.) estarse quieto o en un mismo sitio.—to s. up, velar, no acostarse.—s. estancia, residencia, permanencia; suspensión, espera, parada; (for.) sobreseimiento; impedimento, obstáculo; refuerzo, sostén, soporte; ballena de corsé; estabilidad, fijeza.

stead [sted], s. (con in) lugar, sitio; utilidad; ayuda.—in his (her) s., en su lugar.—in s. of, en lugar de, en vez de, haciendo las veces de.—to stand in (good) s., ser útil o de provecho.- **—fast** [stédfæst], a. constante, inmutable; resuelto, determinado.- **—ily** [-ɪlɪ], adv. constantemente; de firme; regular o progresivamente.- **—iness** [-ɪnɪs], s. estabilidad, firmeza; entereza; constancia.- **—y** [-ɪ], a. firme, fijo, seguro; juicioso, formal; constante, uniforme, con-

tinuo.—s.-going, metódico, constante.—vti. [7] reforzar; impedir el movimiento de; calmar; fortalecer.

steak [steɪk], s. biftec, bisté.

steal [stil], vti. y vii. [10] hurtar, robar; pasar furtivamente.—s. (fam.) hurto, robo.—th [stɛlθ], s. cautela, reserva.—by s., a hurtadillas.— **thy** [stélθɪ], a. furtivo, escondido, clandestino.

steam [stim], s. vapor; vaho.—a. de vapor; para vapor; por vapor.—s. engine, máquina de vapor.—s. heating), calefacción por vapor.—s. shovel, pala mecánica de vapor.—s. table, (coc.) plancha caliente.—vt. proveer de vapor; cocinar al vapor; limpiar con vapor.—vi. generar o emitir vapor; funcionar por vapor.- **—boat** [stímbout], s. buque de vapor.- **—ship** [stímʃip], s. buque de vapor.- **—er** [-œ(r)], s. buque o máquina de vapor; baño (de María).—s. trunk, baúl de camarote.

steed [stid], s. corcel.

steel [stil], s. acero.—a. de acero.—s. wool, virutillas de acero, estopa de acero.—vt. acerar, revestir de acero; acorazar; fortalecer; hacer insensible.- **—y** [stílɪ], a. acerado, duro, inflexible.- **—yard** [-yard], s. romana.

steep [stip], a. empinado, pendiente, escarpado; (fam.) exorbitante.—vt. impregnar, remojar, macerar; poner en infusión.- **—le** [stípl], s. aguja, torre, campanario.—steeplechase, carrera de campanario, carrera de obstáculos.—steeplejack, escalatorres.- **—ness** [stípnɪs], s. calidad de empinado o pendiente; inclinación.

steer [stɪr], s. novillo.—vt. guiar, dirigir, conducir; timonear; (mar.) patronear (un barco).—vi. navegar, timonear; gobernarse, conducirse; obedecer al timón.- **—ing** [stírɪŋ], s. dirección (automóvil), gobierno (buque).—power s., (aut.) dirección hidráulica o movida por motor.—s. wheel, (aut.) volante; (mar.) rueda del timón.—a. de dirección o gobierno.

steerage passenger [stírɪdẑ], s. (mar.) pasajero de entrepuente.

stem [stém], s. (bot.) tallo, vástago; caña, varita; estirpe, linaje; (mec. y carp.) espiga, caña; pie (de copa); (gram.) raíz (mac.) tajamar.—vti. [1] ir contra, hacer frente a; embestir con la proa; represar, contener; desgranar (uvas, etc.).—*vii.* detenerse, contenerse.

stench [stench], *s.* hedor, hediondez.

stencil [sténsjl], *s.* estarcido.—*vti.* [2] estarcir.

stenographer [stenágrœfœ(r)], *s.* estenógrafo, taquígrafo. —**stenography** [stenágráfj], *s.* estenografía.

step [step], *vti.* [1] plantar (el pie).—*to s. down*, reducir, disminuir; escalonar; hacer escaleras en.—*to s. off,* medir a pasos.—*to s. up,* acelerar (el paso); (elec.) elevar (la tensión de una corriente).—*vii.* dar un paso; pisar; andar, caminar.—*to s. after,* seguir o ir detrás.—*to s. aside,* apartarse, hacerse a un lado.—*to s. back,* retroceder.—*to s. down,* bajar, descender.—*to s. forth,* avanzar.—*to s. in,* entrar; intervenir; entrometerse.—*to s. on,* poner el pie sobre; pisar; andar sobre.—*to s. on the gas,* (aut.) pisar el acelerador; (fam.) menearse, darse prisa.—*to s. out,* salir; apearse (de un vehículo); apretar el paso; (fam.) andar de parranda.—*to s. over,* atravesar.—*to s. up,* subir.—*s.* paso; escalón; grada, peldaño; estribo; umbral (de la puerta de entrada); pisada, huella; comportamiento; (mús.) intervalo; diente de una llave; (rad.) elemento, unidad.—*pl.* medios, pasos, gestiones; gradería; escalinata.—*s. by s.,* paso a paso; punto por punto.- —**brother** [stépbrʌdœ(r)], *s.* medio hermano, hermanastro.- —**child** [-chajld], *s.* hijastro, hijastra.- —**daughter** [-dɔtœ(r)], *s.* hijastra.- —**father** [-fadœ(r)], *s.* padrastro.- —**ladder** [-lædœ(r)], *s.* escala, escalera de mano.- —**mother** [-mʌdœ(r)], *s.* madrastra.

stepping stone, *s.* estriberón; (fig.) escalón, escabel.

stepsister [stépsjstœ(r)], *s.* media hermana, hermanastra. —**stepson** [stépsʌn], *s.* hijastro.

stereo [stérjo], *s.* equipo estereofónico, estéreo; sonido estereofónico, estéreo.—*in s.,* en estéreo.—*a.* estéreo, estereofónico; estereoscópico. —*s.* esterioscopio.

stereophonic [sterjofánjk], *a.* estereofónico.

stereoscope [stérjoskoup], *s.* estereoscopio. —**stereoscopic** [sterjoskápjk], *a.* estereoscópico.

stereotype [stérjotajp], *vt.* estereotipar.

sterile [stérjl], *a.* estéril. —**sterility** [sterjljtj], *s.* esterilidad. —**sterilization** [sterjljzéjšon], *s.* esterilización. —**sterilize** [stérjlajz], *vt.* y *vi.* esterilizar.

sterling [stœrljn], *a.* esterlina; genuino, de ley.

stern [stœrn], *a.* austero, severo; firme.—*s.* (mar.) popa; (fam.) rabo. - —**ness** [stœrnnjs], *s.* severidad, rigor.

stethoscope [stéθoskoup], *s.* estetoscopio.

stevedore [stívẹdɔr], *s.* estibador.

stew [stju], *vt.* y *vi.* estofar; (fam.) inquietarse; achicharrarse.—*s.* estofado, guisado, puchero; (fam.) ansiedad; agitación mental.

steward [stjúwård], *s.* administrador; mayordomo; despensero; camarero (en aviones, vapores, etc.).—*s.'s room,* despensa.- —**ess** [-js], *s.* camarera (de buque o avión); aeromoza, azafata.

stick [stjk], *s.* palo, estaca; garrote, porra; vara, bastón (de mando); varilla; palillo (de tambor); barra (de lacre, tinta china, etc.); batuta; estique de escultor; (mus.) arco de contrabajo; (mar.) verga; pinchazo; adhesión; parada, demora; escrúpulo; (teat.) mal actor.—*pl.* leña menuda.—*the sticks,* (fam.) las afueras, despoblado.—*vti.* [10] pegar, adherir; clavar, hincar; prender (con alfiler); fijar (con tachuelas, etc.); meter, introducir; matar o herir de una puñalada; picar, punzar; llenar de puntas; (fam.) aturrullar.—*s.-up,* (jer.) asalto, atraco.—*to s. out,* sacar, asomar, mostrar; perseverar hasta el fin.—*to s. up,* (fam.) atracar, parar para robar.—*to s. up one's hands,* poner las manos arriba en señal de entrega.—*to s. up one's nose at,* hacer ascos, despreciar, hacer un gesto despreciativo.—*vii.* estar clavado o prendido o pegado; pegarse, adherirse; permanecer fijo; ser constante; vacilar; atollarse.—*to s. at,* detenerse, sentir escrúpulos de.—*to s. at it,* (fam.) persistir.—*to s. by,* sostener, apoyar; pegarse (a alguno).—*to s. close,* mantenerse juntos.—*to s. fast,* adherirse fuertemente.—*to s. out,* salir, sobresalir, proyectarse.— *to s. to one's guns,* seguir uno en sus trece; mantenerse firme.—*to s. up for,* (fam.) volver por; salir a la defensa de.- —**er** [stjkœr], *s.* etiqueta engomada, marbete engomado; punta, espina; (fam.) problema arduo.- **—y** [-i], *a.* pegajoso, viscoso.

stiff [stɪf], *a.* tieso; duro, firme; embotado; yerto, aterido; rígido, inflexible; tenso; chabacano, ceremonioso, afectado; almidonado; espeso; terco; (fam.) peliagudo; bravo (viento, etc.); fuerte, cargado (bebidas, etc.); (com.) firme (mercado, precios); (fam.) caro.—*s.* (fam.) cadáver.- **—en** [stɪfn], *vt.* atiesar; endurecer; espesar; aterir; dificultar.—*vi.* atiesarse; endurecerse; enderezarse; espesarse; obstinarse; aterirse.- **—ness** [-nɪs], *s.* tiesura; rigidez; aterimiento; (med.) rigor; obstinación; dureza de estilo; espesura.

stifle [stáɪfl], *vt.* sofocar, ahogar; asfixiar; apagar; suprimir, callar, ocultar.—*vi.* ahogarse, sofocarse, asfixiarse.

stigma [stɪgmä], *s.* estigma.- **—tize** [stígmätaɪz], *vt.* estigmatizar.

stiletto [stɪlétou], *s.* estilete.

still [stɪl], *vt.* acallar, hacer callar; amortiguar; aquietar; detener; destilar.—*vi.* acallarse; aquietarse.— *adv.* todavía, aún; aun; no obstante, sin embargo, a pesar de eso.—*a.* inmóvil; tranquilo, silencioso; fijo; apacible; suave, sordo (ruido); no espumoso (vino); muerto, inanimado.—*s. life,* (pint.) naturaleza muerta.—*s.* silencio, quietud; alambique.- **—birth** [-bœrθ], *s.* parto muerto.- **—born** [-bɔrn], *a.* nacido muerto.- **—ness** [stɪlnɪs], *s.* silencio, quietud, calma.

stilt [stɪlt], *s.* zanco; soporte; ave zancuda.- **—ed** [stɪltɪd], *a.* altisonante, pomposo.

stimulant [stɪ́myūlänt], *a.* y *s.* estimulante. **—stimulate** [stɪ́myūleɪt], *vt.* estimular. **—stimulation** [stɪmyūléɪṣön], *s.* estímulo, excitación.(med.) estimulación. **—stimulus** [stɪ́myūläs], *s.* estímulo; incentivo; (med.) estimulante; (bot.) aguijón.

sting [stɪŋ], *vti.* y *vii.* [10] picar; punzar, pinchar; estimular, aguijonear; herir, atormentar; remorder la conciencia.—*to s. the quick,* herir en lo vivo.—*s.* aguijón; picada, picadura; picazón; (bot.) púa; remordimiento de conciencia; estímulo.

stinginess [stɪ́ndẓɪnɪs], *s.* tacañería, mezquindad, avaricia. **—stingy**

[stɪ́ndẓɪ], *a.* mezquino, tacaño, avaro; escaso, nimio.

stink [stɪŋk], *vii.* [10] heder, apestar.— *s.* hedor, hediondez.- **—er** [stɪ́nkœ(r)], *s.* cosa o persona hedionda; (fam.) sujeto vil o despreciable.

stint [stɪnt], *vt.* restringir, escatimar; asignar una tarea.—*vi.* ser económico o parco; estrecharse.—*s.* cuota, tarea; límite, restricción.

stipend [stáɪpɛnd], *s.* estipendio, sueldo.

stipple [stɪpl], *vt.* puntear, granear.—*s.* picado, punteado.

stipulate [stɪ́pyūleɪt], *vt.* estipular, especificar. **—stipulation** [stɪpyūléɪṣön], *s.* estipulación, condición; convenio.

stir [stœr], *vti.* [1] agitar, menear, batir; hurgar, revolver; perturbar, excitar, incitar; conmover; ventilar, discutir.—*to s. up,* conmover, excitar; aguijonear; poner en movimiento; revolver; suscitar (interés, etc.).— *vii.* moverse, menearse.—*s.* movimiento, conmoción, excitación, alboroto, revuelo.

stirrup [stɪ́rʌp], *s.* estribo.—*s. bone,* (anat.) estribo, huesecillo del oído.

stitch [stɪch], *vt.* coser, hilvanar.—*to s. up,* remendar, (cir.) dar puntos.—*vi.* dar puntadas, coser.—*s.* puntada, punto; (med.) dolor punzante; (agr.) caballón, surco.

stock [stak], *s.* (bot. y hort.) tronco, cepa; patrón; injerto; linaje, estirpe; (com.) acciones, valores; capital comercial; surtido (de mercancías); mercancías almacenadas, existencias; (teat.) repertorio; enseres, muebles.—*in s.,* (com.) en existencia.—*out of s.,* (com.) agotado.—*s. car,* (aut.) coche de serie; (f.c.) vagón para el ganado.—*s. company,* (com.) sociedad anónima; (teat.) compañía de repertorio.—*s. dividend,* acción liberada.—*s. exchange,* bolsa; asociación de corredores de bolsa.—*s. in hand,* mercancías en almacén, existencias.—*s. market,* bolsa, mercado de valores.—*s. split,* reparto de acciones gratis.—*to lay in a s. (of),* almacenar, proveerse (de).—*a.* perteneciente o relativo a la bolsa, la ganadería o el teatro de repertorio; normal, usual; muy usado; estereotipado; (com.) de surtido.—*vt.* poner o llevar en surtido;

surtir; acumular, juntar, acopiar.–
—**ade** [stakéid], vt. empalizar.
—s. empalizada; vallado.— **broker**
[stákbrouḳœ(r)], s. corredor de
bolsa, bolsista.– —**holder** [-hoụld-
œ(r)], s. accionista, tenedor de títulos o acciones.—s. of record, accionista que como tal figura en el libro-
registro de la compañía.

stocking [stákiŋ], s. media, calceta.

stockpile [stákpaịl], reserva de materias primas.—vt. acumular—vi.
acumular materias primas.

stockroom [stákrum], s. almacén; sala
de exposición.

stocky [stáki], a. rechoncho, fornido.

stockyard [stákyard], s. corral de concentración de ganado.

stoic [stóụik], s. y a. estoico. —**stoicism** [stóụịsịzm], s. estoicismo; es-
toicidad.

stoke [stouḳ], vt. y vi. atizar (el fuego);
alimentar, cargar (un horno).– —**r**
[stóụḳœ(r)], s. fogonero.

stole [stoụl], pret. de TO STEAL.—s. es-
tola. —**stolen** [stóụlẹn], pp. de TO
STEAL.

stomach [stámạk], s. estómago.—vt.
sufrir, aguantar, tolerar.

stone [stoụn], s. piedra; hueso (de las
frutas).—s.-blind,   enteramente
ciego.—s.-broke, (fam.) tronado, arrancado.—s.-dead, muerto como
una piedra.—s.-deaf, sordo como
una tapia, enteramente sordo.—s.-
dumb, enteramente mudo.—s. mason, albañil, cantero.—s. quarry,
cantera, pedrera.—s.'s cast, s.'s
throw, tiro de piedra, corta distancia.—vt. apedrear; deshuesar
(frutas); (alb.) revestir de piedras.—
to s. to death, matar a pedradas, lapi-
dar. —**stony** [stóụni], a. pedregoso;
pétreo, de piedra; duro, insensible.
—**y** [stóụni], a. pedregoso; duro,
empedernido.

stood [stụd], pret. y pp. de TO STAND.

stool [stul], s. banquillo, taburete, escabel; banqueta; inodoro, bacín;
(caza) señuelo.—pl. evacuación de
vientre, deposiciones.—s. pigeon,
(fam.) soplón, espía.—vt. atraer con
añagazas o señuelos.—vi. echar tal-
los, retoños, etc.; evacuar (el vientre); atraer con señuelos; (fam.) actuar como soplón.

stoop [stup], vi. agacharse, doblar o inclinar el cuerpo; ir encorvado, ser
cargado de espaldas; encorvarse;

humillarse, rebajarse; condescender; arrojarse sobre la presa.—vt. rebajar, degradar.—s. inclinación de
hombros, cargazón de espaldas;
descenso, caída; abatimiento; gradería, escalinata de entrada.—s.-
shouldered, cargado de espaldas.

stop [stap], vti. [1] parar; detener, atajar; suspender, paralizar; contener,
reprimir; obstruir, tapar, estancar,
represar.—to s. short, detener brusca
o repentinamente.—to s. up, tapar, cerrar, tupir, obturar.—vii. pa-
rar(se); detenerse, hacer alto; demorarse; cesar; acabarse; (fam.)
quedarse algún tiempo, alojarse.—
to s. (working, etc.), cesar o dejar de
(trabajar, etc.).—s. parada, detención; cesación; pausa, alto; interrupción; suspensión; paro (de trabajo); obstáculo, impedimento; represión; (gram.) punto; (mec.)
retén; tope, lengüeta; seguro; (mús.)
tecla; llave; traste (de guitarra); registro (de órgano).—s. light, luz de
parada.—s. sign, señal de alto, señal
de parada.—s. watch, reloj de segundos muertos, cronómetro.– —**cock**
[-kak], s, llave de cierre, llave de
paso.– —**gap** [-gæp], s. substituto
provisional.– —**over** [stápouvœ(r)],
s. parada temporal en un lugar.– —
page [-idž], s. cesación, interrupción; paro (del trabajo); detención,
interceptación; obstrucción, impedimento; represa; retención (sobre
un pago); (med.) estrangulación.—
—**per** [-œ(r)], vt. entaponar.—s. tapón; taco, tarugo.

storage [stórịdž], s. (derechos de) almacenaje.—s. battery, (elec.) acumulador.—to keep in s., almacenar.

store [stɔr], s. tienda; almacén, depósito; acopio.—pl. pertrechos, equipos;   víveres,   provisiones.—vt.
proveer o abastecer; pertrechar;
acumular; tener en reserva; almacenar.– —**house** [stórhaụs], s. almacén.– —**keeper** [-kipœ(r)], s. guar-
daalmacén; jefe de depósito; tendero, comerciante; (mar.) pañolero.
– —**room** [-rum], s. despensa; bodega; almacén; (mar.) pañol de
víveres.

stork [stɔrk], s. (orn.) cigüeña.

storm [stɔrm], s. tempestad, temporal, tormenta o borrasca; vendaval; arrebato, frenesí; tumulto;
(mil.) ataque, asalto.—s. cloud, nu-

barrón.—s. door, contrapuerta, guardapuerta.—s. sash, contravidriera.—s. troops, tropas de asalto.—s. window, guardaventana, sobrevidriera.—vt. (mil.) asaltar, tomar por asalto.—vi. haber tormenta; estallar de cólera.- **—y** [stórmj], a. tempestuoso, borrascoso; violento, turbulento.

story [stórj], s. cuento, historia, historieta; fábula, conseja, (fam.) cuento de viejas; hablilla, rumor; enredo, trama o argumento; (fam.) mentira, embuste; (fam.) artículo (escrito); (arq.) alto, piso, planta.- **—teller** [-telœr], s. narrador; (fam.) mentiroso.

stout [staʊt], a. fornido, forzudo; gordo, corpulento; fuerte, sólido, firme; resuelto, intrépido.—s. cerveza fuerte.

stove [stoʊv], s. estufa, hornillo, cocina o fogón de hierro.—pret. y pp. de TO STAVE.- **—pipe** [-paɪp], s. tubo de estufa, tubo de hornillo.

stow [stoʊ], vt. colocar, meter, alojar; esconder, ocultar; (mar.) estibar, acomodar la carga en el barco; rellenar.—to s. away on a ship, esconderse en un barco, embarcarse clandestinamente.- **—away** [stóuawej], s. (mar.) polizón.

straddle [strǽdl], vt. montar a horcajadas; (fam.) tratar de favorecer ambas partes en (un pleito, una disputa, etc.).

strafe [streif], vt. bombardear violentamente.

straggle [strǽgl], vi. extraviarse; rezagarse.- **—r** [-œ(r)], s. rezagado.

straight [streit], a. derecho, recto; directo, en línea recta; lacio (pelo); erguido; equitativo; íntegro, honrado; exacto; sin estorbos; ininterrumpido.—s. face, cara seria.—s. line, línea recta.—s.-line, en línea recta; de movimiento en línea recta.—s. off, luego, en seguida.—s.-out, sincero; intransigente.—s. razor, navaja barbera.—adv. directamente, en línea recta; inmediatamente, al punto.—s. ahead, todo derecho; enfrente.—s. away, en seguida, inmediatamente.—s. off, sin vacilar, sin demora.—s. runfla de cinco naipes del mismo palo.- **—en** [stréitn], vt. enderezar; poner en orden, arreglar.- **—forward** [-fórwärd], a. recto, derecho; íntegro, honrado, sincero.—adv. de frente.-

—ness [-njs], s. derechura, calidad de recto o derecho; rectitud, probidad, honradez.- **—way** [-wej], adv. inmediatamente, en seguida.

strain [streɪn], vt. hacer fuerza a ; poner tirante; poner, consagrar (la atención, etc.); forzar (la vista, etc.); estirar; forzar; extremar; perjudicar por esfuerzo excesivo; colar; tamizar, cribar; apretar; agarrar; (mec.) deformar.—to s. a point, excederse; hacer una concesión; hacer violencia (a la lógica, la conciencia, etc.).—vi. esforzarse; estar sometido a esfuerzo; pasar o meterse por, infiltrarse.—to s. at, esforzarse por.—s. tensión, tirantez; esfuerzo violento; (med.) lesión por esfuerzo violento o excesivo; (mec.) esfuerzo; deformación; indicio; (mus.) aire, tonada; rasgo racial; parte distintiva de un poema; tono; modo de hablar; genio o disposición heredada. - **—ed** [streɪnd], a. forzado; tirante. - **—er** [stréɪnœ(r)], s. colador, filtro, tamiz.

strait(s) [streɪt(s)], s. (geog.) estrecho; apuro, aprieto; estrechez.—strait jacket, camisa de fuerza.—straitlaced, estrecho, mojigato.

strand [strænd], vt. y vi. (mar.) encallar; dejar o quedarse desamparado; trenzar (un cordel).—s. costa, playa, ribera; cabo, hebra, hilo; sarta; ramal (de cable, etc.). **—stranded** [strǽndjd], a. desprovisto, desamparado; (mar.) encallado.

strange [streɪndʒ], a. extraño, singular; forastero; ajeno; desconocido; reservado, esquivo.—s. to say, lo cual es extraño; (es) cosa extraña.- **—ness** [stréɪndʒnjs], s. extranjería; extrañeza, rareza; reserva, esquivez; maravilla.- **—r** [stréɪndʒœ(r)], s. extranjero, extraño, forastero; desconocido.

strangle [strǽŋgl], vt. estrangular; dar garrote; ahogar, sofocar.—vi. morir estrangulado, estrangularse.

strap [stræp], s. correa, tira, faja, banda; abrazadera; precinta; (mec.) cabeza de biela.—vti. [1] atar con correas; precintar; asentar (navajas de afeitar).

stratagem [strǽtɑdʒem], s. estratagema, artimaña. **—strategic(al)** [stratídʒjk(al)], a. estratégico. **—strategy** [strǽtjdʒj], s. estrategia.

stratify [strǽtjfaj], vti. [7] estratificar.

stratosphere [strǽtosfɪr], s. estratosfera.

straw [strɔ], s. paja.—*not to care a s.*, no importarle a uno un comino.—*s. hat*, sombrero de paja.—*s. man*, hombre de paja, testaferro.—*s. vote*, sondeo informal de opinión.—*the last s.*, el golpe de gracia, el acabóse.—*a.* de paja; pajizo.

strawberry [strɔ́beri], s. fresa.

stray [strej], vi. descarriarse, extraviarse; desmandarse (el ganado). —*a.* extraviado, descarriado.—*s.* persona o animal descarriado o perdido.

streak [strik], s. raya, lista, línea, faja, veta; rayo de luz; vena, rasgo de ingenio; traza, pizca; antojo, capricho.—*like a s.*, veloz como un relámpago.—*s. of luck*, racha.—*vt.* rayar, listar; abigarrar.—*vi.* pasar o viajar con suma rapidez.- —**y** [stríkí], a. listado, rayado; entreverado.

stream [strim], s. corriente; arroyo, corriente de agua; flujo, chorro (de líquido, gas, luz, etc.); curso.—*down s.*, agua abajo.—*up s.*, agua arriba.—*vt.* y *vi.* correr, manar, fluir, brotar; salir a torrentes; derramar con abundancia; lavar en agua corriente; ondear, flotar, flamear, tremolar (una bandera); pasar dejando un rastro de luz.- —**er** [strímœ(r)], s. banderola, gallardete; aurora boreal; cinta (que flota en el aire); serpentina.

streamlined [strímlajnd], a. aerodinámico, perfilado.

street [strit], s. calle.—*s. cleaner*, basurero; (mec.) barredera.—*s. clothes*, traje de calle.—*s. floor*, piso bajo, planta baja.—*s. lamp*, farol (de la calle).—*s. sprinkler*, carricuba, carro de riego.- —**car** [strítkar], s. tranvía.- —**walker** [-wɔkœr], s. cantonera, carrerista.

strength [streŋθ], s. fuerza, vigor; reciedumbre; pujanza; fuerza legal; (ing.) resistencia; aguante; solidez; intensidad; vehemencia; (quim.) concentración, grado de concentración; seguridad, confianza; (mil.) efectivos.—*on* o *upon the s. of*, fundándose en, confiando en.- —**en** [stréŋθn], vt. fortalecer, fortificar; consolidar; corroborar, reforzar; confortar, alentar.—*vi.* fortalecerse; reforzarse; arreciar(se). —**strenuous**

[strényuʌs], a. fuerte; activo, enérgico; acérrimo, tenaz.

stress [stres], s. fuerza, peso, importancia; (ing., mec.) esfuerzo; tensión; énfasis.—*vt.* someter a esfuerzo; recalcar, subrayar, poner de relieve.

stretch [strech], vt. extender, alargar, tender; estirar, atesar; ensanchar, dilatar; violentar, forzar; (fam.) exagerar, llevar al extremo.—*to s. a point*, excederse; ceder un poco.—*to s. forth*, alargar, extender.—*to s. oneself*, desperezarse.—*to s. out*, extender, estirar, alargar.—*vi.* alargarse, dar de sí, dilatarse; (fig.) esforzarse, exagerar.—*to s. out*, extenderse, llegar (hasta); echarse (en la cama, etc.).—*s.* alargamiento; dilatación; elasticidad; tirantez; violencia o interpretación forzada; alcance, trecho, distancia; lapso, tirada; (confinement in jail) (jer.) condena.—*at a s.*, de una vez, de un tirón.- —**er** [stréchœ(r)], s. estirador, dilatador, atesador; camilla, andas; ladrillo o losa (planos); (carp.) viga, madero largo, tirante; (pint.) bastidor.—*s.-bearer*, camillero.

strew [stru], vt. [6] regar, esparcir, derramar; rociar, salpicar.

striate [strájejt], vt. estriar.

stricken [stríkn], pp. de TO STRIKE.—*a.* herido (por un proyectil); atacado (por dolencias); agobiado; afligido.

strict [strikt], a. estricto; exacto, riguroso, escrupuloso; estirado, tirante; (zool.) ceñido, limitado.

stridden [strídn], pp. de TO STRIDE. —**stride** [strajd], vti. [10] cruzar a grandes trancos; montar a horcajadas.—*vii.* andar a trancos.—*s.* paso largo, tranco, zancada.

strident [strájdẹnt], a. estridente.

strife [strajf], s. contienda; rivalidad, porfía.

strike [strajk], vti. [10] golpear; percutir; batir, tocar, sonar; dar contra, chocar con; encender (un fósforo); acuñar (monedas).—*to s. off*, cortar, quitar, cercenar; cerrar (un trato).—*to s. oil*, encontrar petróleo; (fam.) hacerse rico de pronto.—*to s. through*, traspasar, atravesar; calar.—*to s. up*, (mús.) tocar, tañer.—*to s. work*, hallar trabajo.—*vii.* golpear; dar golpes; sonar (una campana); encontrarse; ir delante, avanzar; brotar, estallar, manifestarse (una epidemia, etc.); declararse en huelga; rehusar, resistirse, plantarse; rendirse, arriar el pabellón; arraigar.—*to s. at,* acometer.—*to s. back,* dar golpe por golpe.—*to s. for,* (fam.) dirigirse hacia; acometer.—*to s. in,* meterse; juntarse, unirse; interrumpir; conformarse con.—*to s. into,* comenzar de repente; penetrar.—*to s. on,* dar contra; descubrir.—*to s. out,* tomar una resolución; arrojarse; lanzarse.—*s.* golpe; ataque rápido o inesperado; huelga, paro; (min.) descubrimiento.—*s. breaker,* obrero que reemplaza a los huelguistas.- **—r** [stráikœ(r)], *s.* huelguista; golpeador, percusor. **—striking** [stráikįŋ], *a.* sorprendente, notable; llamativo; vívido; que está en huelga; conspicuo.

string [striŋ], *s.* cuerda; cordel, bramante; ristra, sarta; hilera, fila; recua, fibra, nervio, tendón.—*pl.* (mus.) instrumentos de cuerda; (fam.) condiciones, estipulaciones. —*s. bean,* habichuela verde, judía verde, (Am.) poroto; alubia.—*to have on a s.,* (fam.) tener (a uno) en un puño.—*vti.* [10] encordar; templar (un instrumento); ensartar, enhebrar; encordelar; atar con cordel; tender (alambre, etc.); estirar, atesar; quitar las fibras.—*to s. (along),* (fam.) tomarle el pelo a uno; hacer esperar a uno.—*to s. out,* extender.—*to s. up,* (fam.) ahorcar.—*vii.* extenderse en línea.

stringed instrument, *s.* instrumento de cuerda.

stringent [stríndžent], *a.* riguroso, severo, estricto.

strip [strip], *vti.* [1] desnudar; despojar, quitar; desguarnecer; robar; descortezar; ordeñar hasta agotar; desgarrar o cortar en tiras; desvenar, despalillar (tabaco); (mec.) desmontar.—*to s. off,* desnudar; deshojar.—*vii.* desnudarse, despojarse (de).—*s.* tira, faja, listón, lista; lonja (de carne).—*s. mining,* mineraje a tajo abierto.

stripe [straip], *vt.* rayar.—*s.* raya, lista, banda, franja, tira; (mil.) galón, barra; cardenal (en el cuerpo); calaña, clase.- **—d** [-t], *a.* rayado, listado, a rayas.

strive [straiv], *vii.* [10] esforzarse, hacer lo posible; disputar; oponerse;

contrarrestar. **—striven** [strívn], *pp* de TO STRIVE.

strode [stroud], *pret.* de TO STRIDE.

stroke [strouk], *s.* golpe; toque; boga, remada; rasgo, trazo; (med.) ataque fulminante.—*at one s.,* de un golpe, de un tirón.—*at the s. of twelve,* al dar las doce.—*s. of a bell,* campanada.—*s. of a pen o brush,* plumazo, pincelada.—*s. of the hand,* caricia.—*s. of wit,* rasgo de ingenio, chiste, gracia.—*vt.* pasar la mano por, acariciar; frotar suavemente; (cost.) alisar un plegado.

stroll [stroul], *vi.* vagar, callejear; pasearse.—*s.* paseo, vuelta.- **—er** [stroulœ(r)], *s.* vagabundo; paseante, cochecito de bebé; cómico de la legua.- **—ing** [stróuliŋ], *a.* ambulante.

strong [strɔŋ], *a.* fuerte; firme; recio, fornido; enérgico; vivo, subido (colores); (com.) con tendencia a la alza.—*s. drink,* bebida alcohólica.- *s.-minded,* independiente.- **—box** [-baks], *s.* cofre fuerte, caja de caudales.- **—hold** [-hould], *s.* plaza fuerte.

strop [strap], *vti.* [1] asentar (navajas).—*s.* asentador; (mar.) estrobo.

strove [strouv], *pret.* de TO STRIVE.

struck [strʌk], *pret.* y *pp.* de TO STRIKE.

structural [strákchŭral], *a.* estructural, de estructura; relativo a la estructura; (ing.) de construcción, de construcciones. **—structure** [strákchŭ(r)], *s.* construcción (edificio, puente, etc.); estructura; (fig.) textura, hechura.

struggle [strágl], *vi.* luchar, pugnar, bregar; esforzarse; contender; agitarse.—*s.* esfuerzo; disputa, contienda; pugna, forcejeo; lucha, conflicto.

strum [strum], *vt.* arañar sin arte.- **—pet** [-pet], *s.* ramera.

strung [strʌŋ], *pret.* y *pp.* de TO STRING.

strut [strʌt], *vii.* [1] contonearse, pavonearse; ensoberbecerse, inflarse.—*vti.* (ing., etc.) apuntalar.- *s.* contoneo; poste, puntal; columna.

stub [stʌb], *s.* (agr.) tocón, cepa; zoquete; fragmento, resto; colilla (de cigarro, etc.); talón.—*vti.* [1]—*to s. one's toe,* dar un tropezón.

stubble [stábl], *s.* (agr.) rastrojo; (of beard) cañón.

stubborn [stáborn], *a.* obstinado,

terco, tesonero, contumaz; reñido; inquebrantable.— **—ness** [-nis], s. obstinación, testarudez, contumacia.

stucco [stákou], vt. (alb.) estucar.—s. estuco.

stuck [stʌk], pret. y pp. de TO STICK.—s.-up, (fam.) estirado, orgulloso.

stud [stʌd], s. (carp.) paral, montante, pie derecho; perno, pasador; tachón, clavo de adorno; botón de camisa o cuello, gemelo de puño; caballeriza; (zool.) yeguada, caballada; (elec.) tornillo de contacto.—vti. [1] tachonar.

student [stiúdẹnt], s. estudiante; alumno, escolar.—s. body, alumnado, estudiantado.—a s. of Shakespeare, un estudioso de Shakespeare. **—studio** [stiúdjou], s. estudio, taller; gabinete. **—studious** [stiúdjʌs], a. estudioso; aplicado; estudiado. **—study** [stádi], s. estudio; materia que se estudia; meditación profunda; despacho, gabinete.—vti. [7] estudiar; cursar (una asignatura, etc.).—to s. up, considerar, meditar; proyectar.—vii. estudiar; meditar.

stuff [stʌf], s. material; materia, sustancia, elemento fundamental; cosa, objeto; cachivaches, baratijas; desechos, desperdicios; cosas, ideas o sentimientos sin valor; mejunje, pócima.—vt. henchir, llenar; rellenar (un pavo, etc.); hartar; atestar; disecar (un animal).—stuffed shirt, (jer.) tragavirotes.—vi. y vr. atracarse, hartarse, engullir, tupirse.- **—ing** [stáfiŋ], s. relleno; (mec.) empaquetado.- **—y** [-i], a. sofocante, mal ventilado; (fam.) estirado, afectado.

stumble [stámbl], vi. tropezar, dar un traspié.—to s. on o upon, encontrar o tropezar con.—s. traspié, tropezón; desliz; desatino.—stumbling block, escollo.

stump [stʌmp], s. tocón, cepa; muñón (de brazo o pierna); raigón (de una muela); poste; (b.a.) difumino; tope de cerradura; tribuna pública; arenga electoral; (fam.) desafío, reto.—s. speaker, orador callejero.—s. speech, arenga electoral.—vt. confundir, dejar patidifuso; cercenar, mutilar.—to s. the country, recorrer el país diciendo discursos políticos.—vi. renquear; (fam.) pronun-

ciar discursos políticos.- **—y** [stámpi], a. lleno de tocones; rechoncho, cachigordete; (Am.) chaparro.

stun [stʌn], vti. [1] aturdir, atontar; pasmar, privar; atronar, ensordecer.—s. choque, golpe o sacudimiento (emotivos); aturdimiento.

stung [stʌŋ], pret. y pp. de TO STING.—a. (fam.) chasqueado, burlado, engañado.

stunk [stʌŋk], pret. y pp. de TO STINK.

stunning [stániŋ], a. (fam.) sorprendente; magnífico, excelente; elegante, hermoso.

stunt [stʌnt], vt. impedir el crecimiento o desarrollo de; no dejar medrar.—vi. (fam.) hacer ejercicicios malabares o gimnásticos; hacer suertes o maniobras sensacionales.—s. falta de crecimiento o desarrollo; animal o planta raquíticos; (fam.) suerte, ejercicio o acción de habilidad; maniobra sensacional (de aviación, etc.).—s. flying, vuelos acrobáticos.—s. man, (cine) doble que hace suertes peligrosas.

stupefaction [stiupẹfǽkṣọn], s. estupefacción. **—stupefy** [stiúpẹfai], vti. [7] atontar, atolondrar.

stupid [stiúpid], a. estúpido; necio.- **—ity** [stiupídịti], s. estupidez; necedad; inepcia.

stupor [stiúpọ(r)], s. estupor; atontamiento.

sturdy [stœrdi], a. fuerte, robusto; tenaz, porfiado.

stutter [státœ(r)], vi. tartamudear.—s. tartamudeo.- **—er** [-œ(r)], s. tartamudo.- **—ing** [-iŋ], s. tartamudeo.—a. tartamudo, balbuciente.

sty [stai], s. pocilga, cuchitril; lupanar; (también stye [stai]), (med.) orzuelo.

style [stail], s. estilo; uso, moda; género, escuela; (cir.) estilete.—to be in s., estilarse, estar de moda.—vt. (in)titular, nombrar, llamar. **—stylish** [stáiliṣ], a. elegante; a la moda.

styptic pencil [stíptik], s. lápiz estíptico.

suave [swav], a. suave; afable, fino.

subconscious [sʌbkánṣʌs], a. subconsciente.—s. subconsciencia.

subdivide [sʌbdiváid], vt. subdividir.

subdue [sʌbdiú], vt. subyugar, sojuzgar, dominar; domar o amansar; mejorar (tierras); suavizar.

subject [sʌbdžékt], vt. sujetar; sojuzgar, avasallar; exponer, presentar; supeditar, subordinar.—*a.* [sʌ́bdʒɛct], sujeto; propenso; supeditado.—*s. to,* sujeto a, afecto *a.*—*s.* súbdito; vasallo; materia, tópico; asignatura (de estudios); (gram.) sujeto.—*s. matter,* asunto, materia de que se trata.— **—ion** [sʌbdʒɛ́kʃɔn], *s.* sujeción, supeditación, dependencia; sometimiento; ligadura.- **—ive** [sʌbdʒɛ́ktiv], *a.* subjetivo.

subjugate [sʌ́bdʒugeit], *vt.* subyugar, sojuzgar, someter.

subjunctive [sʌbdʒʌ́ŋktiv], *a.* y *s.* subjuntivo.

sublease [sʌblis], *s.* subarriendo.—*vt.* [sʌblís], subarrendar. **—sublet** [sʌblét], *vti.* [9] subarrendar.—*pret.* y *pp.* de TO SUBLET.

sublimate [sʌ́blimeit], *vt.* (quím.) sublimar; (fig.) refinar, purificar. — **sublime** [sʌbláim], *a.* sublime.—*s.* sublimidad, lo sublime.—*vt.* y *vi.* sublimar, exaltar; (quím.) sublimar(se).

submarine [sʌ́bmarin], *s.* y *a.* submarino.—*s. chaser,* cazasubmarinos.

submerge [sʌbmœrdʒ], *vt.* y *vi.* sumergir(se), hundir(se). **—submersible** [sʌbmœ́rsjbl], *a.* sumergible. **—submersion** [sʌbmœ́rʃɔn], *s.* sumersión.

submission [sʌbmíʃɔn], *s.* sumisión. **—submissive** [sʌbmísjv], *a.* sumiso, obediente, dócil. **—submit** [sʌbmít], *vti.* [1] someter; presentar, exponer, proponer.—*vri.* y *vii.* someterse, conformarse.

subordinate [sʌbórdjnit], *a.* y *s.* subalterno, subordinado.—*vt.* [sʌbórdjneit], subordinar.

suborn [sʌbórn], *vt.* (for.) sobornar, cohechar.- **—ation** [sʌbɔrnéjʃɔn], *s.* soborno, cohecho.—*s. of perjury,* (for.) soborno de testigo.

subpoena [sʌ̆pína], *s.* comparendo.—*vt.* mandar comparecer.

subscribe [sʌbskráib], *vt.* y *vi.* suscribir(se); firmar; aprobar; abonar(se).—*to s. for,* suscribirse a.—*to s. ten dollars,* prometer una contribución de diez dólares (para una colecta, etc.).- **—r** [sʌbskráibœ(r)], *s.* suscritor, abonado; firmante, el que suscribe. **—subscription** [sʌbskrípʃɔn], *s.* suscripción, abono; cantidad suscrita; firma.

subsequent [sʌ́bsjkwent], *a.* subsecuente, subsiguiente.—*s. to,* con posterioridad a, después de.

subside [sʌbsáid], *vi.* calmarse, atenuarse; bajar (el nivel); disminuir; irse al fondo, asentarse, (quím.) precipitarse.

subsidize [sʌ́bsjdaiz], *vt.* subvencionar. **—subsidy** [sʌ́bsjdi], *s.* subvención, subsidio.

subsist [sʌbsíst], *vi.* subsistir; perdurar; sustentarse, mantenerse.—*vt.* alimentar o mantener.

substance [sʌ́bstans], *s.* sustancia. **—substantial** [sʌbstǽnʃal], *a.* sólido, fuerte, resistente; importante, valioso; considerable; seguro; responsable; existente, real; duradero; esencial; corpóreo, material; sustancial, sustancioso.—*s.* realidad; parte esencial. **—substantiate** [sʌbstǽnʃieit], *vt.* comprobar, establecer, verificar.**—substantive** [sʌ́bstantiv], *a.* y *s.* sustantivo.

subterranean [sʌbtɛréjnian], *a.* subterráneo.

subtle [sʌ́tl], *a.* sutil; perspicaz; apto; ingenioso.- **—ty** [-tj], *s.* sutileza; astucia.

subtract [sʌbtrǽkt], *vt.* y *vi.* sustraer, quitar, (mat.) restar, sustraer.- **—ion** [sʌbtrǽkʃɔn], *s.* sustracción; resta.

suburb [sʌ́bœrb], *s.* suburbio; barrio residencial.- **—an** [sʌbœ́rban], *a.* y *s.* suburbano.

subversion [sʌbvœ́rʒɔn], *s.* subversión. **—subversive** [sʌbvœ́rsjv], *a.* subversivo.—*s.* persona subversiva. **—subvert** [sʌbvœ́rt], *vt.* subvertir.

subway [sʌ́bwei], *s.* subterráneo; ferrocarril subterráneo, metropolitano, (fam.) el metro, (Am.) el subte.

succeed [sʌksíd], *vt.* suceder o seguir a.—*vi.* salir bien, tener buen éxito.—*to s. in,* lograr, conseguir. **—success** [sʌksés], *s.* buen éxito, logro; prosperidad; triunfo; persona o asunto que tiene buen éxito. **—successful** [sʌksésful], *a.* próspero, afortunado; productivo, satisfactorio. **—succession** [sʌksésɔn], *s.* sucesión, serie; continuación; descendencia; herencia. **—successive** [sʌksésjv], *a.* sucesivo. **—successor** [sʌkséso(r)], *s.* sucesor; heredero.

succumb [sʌkám], *vi.* sucumbir.

such [sʌch], *a.* tal; semejante; dicho, mencionado.—*no s. (a) thing,* no hay tal.—*s. a,* (fam.) tan.—*such a*

bad man, un hombre tan malo.—*s. a man,* tal hombre, semejante hombre.—*s. and s.,* o *s. or s.,* tal(es) y tal(es), tal o cual.—*s. as,* (tal) como.—*there is s. a thing as,* hay algo que se llama; hay casos en que.—*pron.* tal.—*s. as,* los que, quienes.—*s. is life,* tal (o así) es la vida.

suck [sʌk], *vt.* y *vi.* chupar; librar; mamar; (mec.) aspirar.—*to s. in,* embeber, absorber, chupar.—*to s. out o up,* chupar, extraer por succión. — **er** [sákœ(r)], *s.* lechón o cochinillo que todavía mama; chupador; mamador; mamón, chupón; dulce que se chupa; (fam.) primo, bobo.- **le** [sákl], *vt.* amamantar, criar.—*vi.* lactar, mamar.— **ling** [-liŋ], *a.* y *s.* mamón, recental.—*a.* de teta, de cría.—*s. pig,* cerdo de leche.—**suction** [sákšɘn], *s.* succión.

sudden [sádn], *a.* repentino, súbito; apresurado; (med.) fulminante.— *all of a s.,* de repente.

suds [sʌdz], *s. pl.* jabonaduras; (fam.) cerveza.

sue [sju], *vt.* y *vi.* (for.) demandar.—*to s. to, to s. for,* rogar, pedir, tratar de persuadir.

suede [sweid], *s.* gamuza, ante.

suet [sjúit], *s.* sebo en rama; grasa, gordo.

suffer [sáfœ(r)], *vt.* y *vi.* sufrir, padecer; soportar, tolerar.—*to s. from,* adolecer de.- **er** [-œ(r)], *s.* paciente, sufridor; víctima; perjudicado; el que tolera tácitamente.- **ing** [-iŋ], *s.* sufrimiento, padecimiento, pena, suplicio.—*a.* paciente, sufriente.

suffice [sʌfáis], *vt.* y *vi.* bastar, ser suficiente.—*s. it to say,* baste decir. —**sufficiency** [sʌfíʃɘnsi], *s.* suficiencia; lo suficiente; eficacia; presunción. —**sufficient** [sʌfíʃɘnt], *a.* suficiente, bastante.

suffix [sʌfíks], *vt.* añadir como sufijo.—*s.* [sáfiks], (gram.) sufijo, afijo.

suffocate [sáfokeit], *vt.* sofocar, asfixiar, ahogar; apagar (un fuego). —*vi.* sofocarse, asfixiarse, ahogarse. —**suffocation** [sʌfokéiʃɘn], *s.* sofocación, asfixia, ahogo.

suffrage [sáfridʒ], *s.* sufragio, voto; aprobación; (igl.) sufragio.- **tte** [sáfradʒét], *s.* mujer sufragista.

sugar [šúgä(r)], *s.* azúcar.—*lump of s.,* terrón de azúcar.—*s. bowl,* azucarero, azucarera.—*s. cane,* caña de azúcar.—*s. making* (*season*), zafra.— *vt.* azucarar, endulzar.—*to s.-coat,* confitar, garapiñar; (fig.) dorar la píldora.—*vi.* cristalizarse (el almíbar), (Am.) azucararse.- **plum** [-plʌm], *s.* merengue, confite, dulce.

suggest [sʌgdʒést], *vt.* sugerir, insinuar; evocar.- **ion** [sʌgdʒéschɘn], *s.* sugestión; sugerencia, insinuación.- **ive** [sʌgdʒéstiv], *a.* sugestivo; sugerente.

suicidal [sjuisáidɘl], *a.* suicida. —**suicide** [sjúisaid], *s.* suicidio; suicida.— *to commit s.,* suicidarse.

suit [sjut], *s.* petición, súplica; galanteo; (for.) pleito, juicio; colección, serie, juego, surtido; (sast.) traje completo, (Am.) flus; (naipes) palo.—*s. of clothes,* traje completo.—*vt.* y *vi.* convenir, acomodar, adaptar(se).—*to s. oneself,* hacer uno lo que guste.- **able** [sjútɘbl], *a.* adecuado, satisfactorio, a propósito.- **case** [-keis], *s.* maleta, valija.- **e** [swit], *s.* serie, juego; séquito, comitiva.—*s. of rooms,* serie de departamentos o habitaciones; habitación o pieza (gen. muy lujosa).- **or** [sjúto(r)], *s.* (for.) demandante, parte actora; pretendiente, novio; aspirante.

sulfa [sálfa], *s.* (farm.) sulfa.—*s. drugs,* medicamentos sulfas.

sulfate [sálfeit], *s.* sulfato. —**sulfur** [sálfœ(r)], *s.* azufre.

sullen [sálɘn], *a.* hosco, arisco; lento (río); sombrío, tétrico.- **ness** [-nis], *s.* hosquedad.

sulphate [sálfeit], *s.* = SULFATE.—**sulphur** [sálfœ(r)], *s.* = SULFUR.

sultry [sáltri], *a.* bochornoso, sofocante (verano, calor, etc.).

sum [sʌm], *s.* suma; cantidad; sustancia, esencia.—*in s.,* en esencia, suma o resumen.—*s. total,* suma total, monta o monto.—*vti.* y *vii.* [1] sumar.—*to s. up,* recapitular, resumir, compendiar; (for.) presentar su alegato.- **marize** [sámaraiz], *vt.* resumir.- **mary** [-ari], *s.* sumario, resumen, recopilación, reseña (de un libro).

summer [sámœ(r)], *a.* estival, veraniego.—*s.* verano, estío; (arq.) viga maestra; dintel.—*s. boarder,* veraneante.—*s. resort,* lugar de veraneo.—*s. school,* escuela de verano.—*vi.* veranear.

summit [sámit], *s.* cima, cumbre, cúspide, ápice.—*s. conference,* conferencia en al cumbre.

summon [sámọn], *vt.* (for.) citar, apercibir; llamar, convocar; mandar, requerir; (mil.) intimar.—*to s. up,* evocar; despertar, excitar (valor, fuerza, etc.).— **—s** [-z], *s.* (for.) citación, apercibimiento; (mil.) intimación (de rendición).

sumptuous [sámpchŭʌs], *a.* suntuoso.

sun [sʌn], *s.* sol.—*vti.* [1] (a)solear.—*to s. oneself,* tomar el sol.— **—bath,** baño de sol.- **—beam** [-bim], *s.* rayo de sol.- **—bonnet** [-banet], *s.* papalina.- **—burn** [sánbœrn], *vti.* y *vit.* [4] quemar(se) o tostar(se) con el sol.—*s.* quemadura de sol.- **—burned** [sánbœrnd], **—burnt** [sánbœrnt], *a.* quemado, tostado o bronceado por el sol.—*pret.* y *pp.* de TO SUNBURN. **—Sunday** [sándị], *s.* domingo.—*S. best,* ropa dominguera.—*S. school,* escuela dominical.- **—dae** [sándị], *s.* helado con frutas, jarabes o nueces.— **—dial** [-daịạl], *s.* reloj de sol, cuadrante solar.- **—down** [-daụn], *s.* puesta de sol.

sundries [sándrịz], *s. pl.* (com.) géneros varios. **—sundry** [sándrị], *a.* varios, diversos.—*all and s.,* todos y cada uno.

sunflower [sánflaụœ(r)], *s.* (bot.) girasol.

sunglasses [sánglæsẹz], *spl.* gafas de sol. **—sun lamp** [sánlæmp], *s.* lámpara de rayos ultravioletas.

sung [sʌŋ], *pret.* y *pp.* de TO SING.

sunk [sʌŋk], *pret.* y *pp.* de TO SINK. **—sunken** [sáŋkn], *a.* sumido, hundido.—*pp. de* TO SINK.

sunless [sánlịs], *a.* sombrío; sin luz; sin sol, nublado. **—sunlight** [sánlaịt], *s.* luz del sol. **—sun porch** [sánpɔrch], *s.* solana. **—sunny** [sánị], *a.* de sol (día); asoleado; resplandeciente; alegre, risueño; halagüeño.—*s. side,* lado del sol; lado bueno, aspecto favorable.—*s. side up,* (huevos) fritos. **—sunrise** [sánraịz], *s.* salida del sol, amanecer; (poét.) Oriente. **—sunset** [sánset], *s.* puesta del sol, ocaso. **—sunshine** [sánṣaịn], *s.* luz del sol, claridad del sol; día. **—sunstroke** [sánstroụk], *s.* (med.) insolación, (fam.) tabardillo.

sup [sʌp], *vti.* [1] sorber.—*vit.* cenar.

super [sịúpœ(r)], *s.* (com.) cosa excelente; alta calidad; (abrev. fam.) de SUPERINTENDENT.—*a.* (fam.) excelente.

superb [sịupœ́rb], *a.* soberbio, grandioso; (fam.) de primera.

supercargo [sịupœrkárgoụ], *s.* (mar.) sobrecargo.

supercilious [sịupœrsílịŭs], *a.* arrogante, altanero.

superficial [sịupœrfíṣạl], *a.* superficial, somero.

superfluous [sụpœ́rflụʌs], *a.* superfluo.

superheat [sịupœrhít], *vt.* recalentar.

superhuman [sịupœrhjúmạn], *a.* sobrehumano.

superimpose [sịupœrịmpóụz], *vt.* superponer, sobreponer.

superintend [sịupœrịnténd], *vt.* estar encargado de, dirigir. **—ent** [-ẹnt], *s.* superintendente; inspector; capataz; encargado de un edificio de apartamentos.

superior [sụpírịọ(r)], *a.* y *s.* superior. **—ity** [sụpịrịárịtị], *s.* superioridad.

superlative [sịupœ́rlạtịv], *a.* y *s.* superlativo.

superman [sịúpœrmæn], *s.* superhombre.

supernatural [sịupœrnǽchụrạl], *a.* sobrenatural.—*s.* lo sobrenatural.

superposition [sịupœrpọzíṣọn], *s.* superposición.

supersede [sịupœrsíd], *vt.* reemplazar; desalojar; invalidar; (for.) sobreseer.

superstition [sịupœrstíṣọn], *s.* superstición. **—superstitious** [sịupœrstíṣʌs], *a.* supersticioso.

supervise [sịupœrváịz], *vt.* supervisar. **—supervision** [sịupœrvíṣọn], *s.* supervisión. **—supervisor** [sịupœrváịzọ(r)], *s.* supervisor.

supper [sápœ(r)], *s.* cena.

supplant [sʌplǽnt], *vt.* suplantar.

supple [sápl], *a.* flexible; dócil, obediente; servil.

supplement [sáplẹmẹnt], *s.* suplemento; apéndice.—*vt.* [sáplemẹnt], suplementar.

suppli(c)ant [sáplị(k)ạnt], *s.* y *a.* suplicante. **—supplication** [sáplịkáịṣọn], *s.* súplica, ruego; (igl.) preces, rogativa.

supplier [sʌplájœ(r)], *s.* proveedor, abastecedor. **—supplies** [sʌplajz], *s. pl.* (mil.) pertrechos; materiales, efectos; provisiones, víveres, enseres. **—supply** [sʌpláị], *vti.* [7] abastecer, proveer (de); suministrar, habilitar; suplir, reemplazar.—*s.* suministro, provisión, abastecimiento; substituto, suplente; (com.) abasto; oferta; repuesto; surtido.

support [sʌpórt], *vt.* sostener, aguantar, apoyar; mantener (a una persona, etc.), proveer para; resistir, tolerar; abogar por, defender; probar, confirmar; justificar.—*s.* sostén, soporte; sustento, manutención.— **er** [-œ(r)], *s.* mantenedor; defensor; partidario; sostén, soporte.

suppose [sʌpóuz], *vt.* suponer; dar por sentado o existente; poner por caso; creer, imaginar. **—supposition** [sʌpozíʃon], *s.* suposición, supuesto, hipótesis.

suppository [sʌpázitəri], *s.* supositorio.

suppress [sʌprés], *vt.* suprimir, acabar con; reprimir, contener; eliminar.— **ion** [sʌpréʃon], *s.* supresión; (med.) suspensión.

suppurate [sʌpyʉreit], *vi.* supurar. **—suppuration** [sʌpyʉréiʃon], *s.* supuración; pus.

supremacy [sjuprémasi], *s.* supremacía. **—supreme** [sjuprím], *a.* supremo, sumo.—*S. Being,* Ser Supremo.

sure [ʃʉr], *a.* seguro, cierto, infalible; firme; certero.—*be s. to come,* o *be s. and come,* no deje(n) de venir, venga(n) sin falta.—*for s.,* de fijo, con seguridad.—*adv.* (fam.) ciertamente, indudablemente.—*s. enough,* a buen seguro, con certeza; en efecto, en realidad de verdad.— **ty** [ʃʉrti], *s.* (for. y com.) fiador; fianza, garantía; seguridad, certeza.—*of a s.,* de seguro, como cosa cierta.—*to be o go s. for,* ser fiador, salir garante de.

surf [sœrf], *s.* oleaje, resaca, marejada; espuma del mar.—*s.-riding,* patinaje sobre las olas.— **board** [-bɔrd], *s.* patín de mar.

surface [sœrfis], *s.* superficie.—*vt.* allanar, alisar; poner superficie a.— *vt.* y *vi.* (hacer) emerger, surgir o salir a la superficie.

surge [sœrdʒ], *s.* (mar.) oleaje u oleada; (elec.) sobretensión.—*vi.* agitarse o embravecerse (el mar); romper (las olas).—*vt.* hacer ondular; (mar.) largar.

surgeon [sœrdʒon], *s.* cirujano. **—surgery** [sœrdʒœri], *s.* cirugía. **—surgical** [sœrdʒikəl], *a.* quirúrgico.

surly [sœrli], *a.* áspero, rudo, hosco.

surmise [sœrmáiz], *vt.* conjeturar, su-

poner, vislumbrar.—*s.* conjetura, suposición, vislumbre.

surmount [sœrmáunt], *vt.* vencer, superar, salvar; coronar, poner (algo) sobre.

surname [sœrneim], *s.* apellido; sobrenombre.—*vt.* apellidar, llamar.

surpass [sœrpǽs], *vt.* sobrepasar, superar, aventajar.

surplus [sœrplʌs], *s.* sobrante, excedente; (com.) superávit.—*a.* excedente, de sobra, sobrante.

surprise [sœrpráiz], *s.* sorpresa; novedad; extrañeza; asombro.—*by s.,* de sorpresa.—*s. party,* fiesta sorpresa.—*vt.* sorprender.

surrender [sʌréndœ(r)], *vt.* rendir, entregar; ceder.—*vi.* rendirse, entregarse; (mil.) capitular.—*s.* rendición, entrega; (mil.) capitulación; (for.) cesión.—*s. value,* valor de rescate (de un seguro, etc.).

surreptitious [sʌreptíʃʉs], *a.* subrepticio.

surrogate [sóerogeit], *a.* sucedáneo.— *s. mother,* madre de alquiler.

surround [sʌráund], *vt.* circundar, cercar, rodear, ceñir.— **ing** [-iŋ], *a.* circunstante, circunvecino.—*s. pl.* alrededores, contornos, inmediaciones; medio, circunstancias que rodean (a una persona, hecho o lugar).

surtax [sœrtæks], *s.* recargo; impuesto adicional.

surveillance [sœrvéilans], *s.* vigilancia.—*vt.* vigilar.

survey [sœrvéi], *vt.* inspeccionar, examinar, reconocer; medir o deslindar terrenos.—*vi.* ejecutar operaciones topográficas.—*s.* [sœrvei], examen, estudio; encuesta (de la opinión pública); medición o deslinde (de terrenos).— **or** [sœrvéio(r)], *s.* topógrafo; agrimensor.

survival [sœrvájval], *s.* supervivencia; sobreviviente; reliquia.—*s. of the fittest,* supervivencia del más apto. **—survive** [sœrvájv], *vt.* y *vi.* sobrevivir; salir o quedar vivo. **—survivor** [sœrvájvo(r)], *s.* sobreviviente, superviviente.

suspect [sʌspékt], *vt.* y *vi.* sospechar (de), desconfiar (de); maliciar.—*s.* [sʌspekt], persona sospechosa.—*a.* sospechoso.

suspend [sʌspénd], *vt.* suspender.— **ers** [-œrz], *s. pl.* tirantes del pantalón. **—suspense** [sʌspéns], *s.* suspensión; impaciencia; ansiedad; (for.) entredicho. **—suspension** [sʌspénʃǫn], s. suspensión.

suspicion [sʌspíʃǫn], s. sospecha, recelo. **—suspicious** [sʌspíʃʌs], a. sospechoso; suspicaz.

sustain [sʌstéin], vt. sostener, aguantar; tener, mantener; sufrir (una desgracia, pérdida, etc.); (mus.) prolongar, sostener; apoyar; confortar; alimentar; defender; establecer, probar. **—sustenance** [sʌ́stęnans], s. sustento, mantenimiento, subsistencia; alimentos.

suture [sjúchū(r)], vt. (cir.) suturar.— s. sutura.

swab [swab], s. escobón; (cir.) tapón de algodón.—vt. limpiar; (cir.) limpiar con algodón.

swagger [swǽgœ(r)], vi. fanfarronear; pavonearse.—s. jactancia, baladronada; pavoneo.

swallow [swálou], vt. y vi. tragar(se); engullir.—to s. up, tragar(se); absorber.—s. bocado, trago; deglución; (orn.) golondrina.

swam [swæm], pret. de TO SWIM.

swamp [swamp], s. pantano, ciénaga, fangal.—vt. empantanar, encharcar; abrumar, recargar; inundar.— vi. empantanarse; zozobrar.– **—y** [swámpi], a. pantanoso, cenagoso.

swan [swan], s. cisne.—s. dive, salto de ángel.—s. song, canto del cisne; obra última.

swap [swap], vti. [1] cambiar, cambalachear, permutar.—vii. hacer trueques o cambalaches.—s. trueque, (fam.) cambalache.

swarm [swɔrm], s. enjambre; (fig.) hormiguero, multitud.—vt. y vi. enjambrar; pulular, bullir, hormiguear; (fam.) trepar.

swarthy [swɔ́rθi], a. moreno, trigueño.

swat [swat], s. (fam.) golpe violento.—vt. (fam.) golpear con fuerza; (a fly) aplastar (una mosca).

swath [swaθ], s. ringla o ringlera de mies segada; guadañada.—to cut a wide s., hacer alarde u ostentación.

sway [swej], vt. inclinar, ladear; influir en el ánimo de (alguno), inducir; blandir, cimbrar; gobernar, regir; (mar.) izar, guindar.—vi. ladearse, inclinarse; torcerse; oscilar, mecerse; ondular; flaquear, tambalear.—s. poder, predominio, influjo; vaivén, oscilación, ondula-

ción, balanceo.—to give full s. to, dar ancho campo a.– **—backed** [swéjbækt], a. derrengado.

swear [swer], vti. y vii. [10] jurar.

sweat [swet], vti. y vii. [4] sudar; hacer sudar; trabajar duro.—s. sudor.— **—er** [-œ(r)], s. suéter.

Swede [swid], s. sueco. **—Swedish** [swídiš], a. sueco.—s. idioma sueco.

sweep [swip], vti. [10] barrer; deshollinar (chimeneas); recorrer, pasar la vista por.—to s. away, robar sin dejar nada; arrastrar con todo.—to s. the bottom, dragar.—vi. barrer; pasar o deslizarse rápidamente; pasar arrasando; pasar con paso o ademán majestuosos.—to s. down, descender precipitadamente. —s. barrido; alcance, extensión.— **—er** [swípœr], s. barrendero; (mec.) barredera.– **—ing** [-iŋ], a. arrebatador; comprensivo, extenso.—pl. barreduras.

sweet [swit], a. dulce; fragante; melodioso; bonito, lindo; agradable; amable, bondadoso; fresco; (mec.) suave y sin ruido; fértil (tierra).—s. corn, maíz tierno.—s. herbs, hierbas olorosas.—s. pea, guisante de olor.—s. potato, batata, boniato, (Am.) camote.—s.-scented, perfumado.—s.-smelling, fragante.—s.-spoken, melifluo.—to have a s. tooth, ser goloso.—s. dulzura; deleite; persona querida; golosina, dulce. —pl. dulces, golosinas.– **—bread** [swítbred], s. lechecilla o molleja de ternera.– **—en** [-n], vt. endulzar, dulcificar; (farm.) edulcorar; mitigar; hacer salubre.—vi. endulzarse. – **—heart** [-hart], s. novia, prometida; novio, prometido; persona querida, amante.—a. querido; cielo, vida.— **—meat** [-mit], s. dulce, confitura, golosina.— **—ness** [-nis], s. dulzura, melosidad, suavidad, delicadeza, bondad.

swell [swel], vti. y vii. [6] hinchar(se), inflar(se), henchir(se); engreír(se). —to s. out, arrojar (el árbol) sus hojas; ampollarse; bufar.—a. elegante, de buen tono; magnífico.—s. hinchazón; oleada, marejada; prominencia; ondulación del terreno.– **—ing** [swéliŋ], s. hinchazón; tumefacción, turgencia, abotagamiento; bulto, chichón, protuberancia.

swept [swept], pret. y pp. de TO SWEEP.

swerve [swœrv], vt. y vi. desviar(se),

apartar(se), extraviar(se), virar(se), torcer(se).—s. desviación, viraje.

swift [swɪft], a. rápido, ligero, raudo; veloz, volador; vivo, diligente; sumarísimo; (mar.) velero.- **—ness** [swɪ́ftnɪs], s. velocidad, rapidez, prontitud.

swig [swɪg], s. (fam.) trago, tragantada.—vt. y vi. (fam.) beber a grandes tragos.

swim [swɪm], vii. [10] nadar; flotar; dejarse ir o llevar; deslizarse suavemente; tener la cabeza ida; tener mareo o vértigo; padecer vahídos.—vti. pasar a nado; hacer nadar o flotar.—s. natación; nadada; nadadera de pez; movimiento de deslizarse; vida social.—to be in the s., estar en la corriente o marcha de las cosas.—to take a s., ir a nadar.- **—mer** [swɪ́mœ(r)], s. nadador.- **—ming** [-ɪŋ], a. que nada, natatorio; para nadar.—s. pool, piscina, (Am.) alberca, pileta.—s. suit, traje de baño.

swindle [swɪ́ndl], vt. estafar, timar.—s. estafa, timo.- **—r** [swɪ́ndlœ(r)], s. estafador, timador.

swine [swaɪn], s. marrano(s), puerco(s), cerdo(s); persona soez.- **—herd** [swáɪnhœrd], s. porquero, porquerizo.

swing [swɪŋ], vti. y vii. [10] columpiar(se), mecer(se); balancear(se), bambolear(se); girar, hacer girar.—vti. blandir.—to s. about, dar una vuelta.—to s. clear, evitar un choque.—s. oscilación, vaivén, balanceo; columpio, mecedor; libertad de acción, libre curso; autoridad, control; (mec.) juego, recorrido, alcance.—in full s., en plena operación, en su apogeo.

swipe [swaɪp], s. (fam.) golpe fuerte.—to take a s. at, (fam.) dar un golpe fuerte a.—vt. (com.) pasar (una tarjeta electrónica) por la ranura de una máquina en el mostrador de revisión y pago; (fam.) hurtar, robar.

swish [swɪš], s. chasquido.—vt. y vi. chasquear.

Swiss [swɪs], a. y s. suizo, helvético.— S. cheese, Gruyère, queso suizo.

switch [swɪč], s. latiguillo, fusta; trenza postiza; fustazo; (f.c.) cambiavía, agujas; (elec.) interruptor, conmutador; acción de desviar, cambiar, conmutar (un tren, una corriente).—s. engine, locomotora de patio o de maniobras.—vt. fustigar, dar latigazos; (f.c.) desviar; (elec.) cambiar.—to s. off, desconectar, cortar (la corriente); apagar (las luces).—to s. on, conectar; encender (las luces).—vi. (off) desviarse, cambiarse.- **—board** [swɪ́chbɔrd], s. (elec.) pizarra o cuadro de distribución; (tlf.) cuadro conmutador.

swivel [swɪ́vĕl], s. eslabón giratorio.— vi. girar sobre un eje.—s. chair, silla giratoria.

swollen [swóŭln], pp. de TO SWELL.

swoon [swun], vi. desmayarse, desfallecer.—s. desmayo, síncope.

sword [sɔrd], s. espada.—s. belt, cinturón.—s. swallower, tragasable.—s. thrust, estocada.- **—fish** [-fɪš], s. pez espada.

swore [swɔr], pret. de TO SWEAR. **—sworn** [swɔrn], pp. de TO SWEAR.

swum [swʌm], pp. de TO SWIM.

swung [swʌŋ], pret. y pp. de TO SWING.

syllable [sɪ́labl], s. sílaba.

symbol [sɪ́mbol], s. símbolo; emblema; (teol.) credo.- **—ic(al)** [sɪmbáli-k(al)], a. simbólico.- **—ism** [sɪ́mbolɪzm], s. simbolismo.

symmetrical [sɪmétrɪkal], a. simétrico. **—symmetry** [sɪ́mɪtrɪ], s. simetría.

sympathetic(al) [sɪmpaθétɪk(al)], a. simpático; compasivo. **—sympathize** [sɪ́mpaθaɪz], vi.; compadecerse. **—sympathy** [sɪ́mpaθɪ], s. compasión, conmiseración.

symphony [sɪ́mfonɪ], s. sinfonía.

symptom [sɪ́mptom], s. síntoma.

synagogue [sɪ́nagag], s. sinagoga.

synchronization [sɪŋkronɪzéɪšon], s. sincronización.- **—synchronize** [sɪ́ŋkronaɪz], vt. y vi. sincronizar.

syndicate [sɪ́ndɪkeɪt], vt. y vi. (com.) sindicar(se).—s. [sɪ́ndɪkɪt], (com.) sindicato.

synonym [sɪ́nonɪm], s. sinónimo. **—synonymous** [sɪnánɪmʌs], a. sinónimo.

synopsis [sɪnápsɪs], s. sinopsis.

syntax [sɪ́ntæks], s. sintaxis.

synthesis [sɪ́nθesɪs], s. síntesis. **—synthetic** [sɪnθétɪk], a. sintético.

syphilis [sɪ́fɪlɪs], s. sífilis.

syringe [sɪ́rɪndž], s. (med.) jeringa.

syrup [sɪ́rʌp], s. jarabe; almíbar; sirope.- **—y** [-ɪ], a. almibarado; meloso.

system [sɪ́stĕm], s. sistema.- **—atic(al)** [sɪstɛmǽtɪk(al)], a. sistemático.- **—atize** [sɪ́stɛmataɪz], vt. sistematizar.

T

tab [tæb], *s.* apéndice, proyección; marbete; (fam.) cuenta.

tabby [tǽbi], *s.* gato atigrado; gata.

tabernacle [tǽbœrnækl], *s.* tabernáculo.

table [téjbl], *s.* mesa; tabla (matemática, de materias, etc.).—*t. d'hôte*, comida a precio fijo.—*t. linen*, mantelería.—*t. manners*, modales que uno tiene en la mesa.—*t. of contents*, índice de materias, tabla de materias.—*t. setting*, vajil.—*t. talk*, conversación de sobremesa.—*t. tennis*, tenis de mesa.—*vt.* aplazar la discusión de.– **—cloth** [-klɔθ], *s.* mantel.– **—land** [-lænd], *s.* meseta.– **—spoon** [-spun], *s.* cuchara.– **—spoonful** [-spunful], *s.* cucharada.– **—t** [tǽblit], *s.* tableta, pastilla, comprimido; (pad) bloc; (slab) plancha, lápida.– **—ware** [-wɛr], *s.* servicio de mesa, artículos para la mesa.

tabloid [tǽblɔid], *s.* periódico sensacional.

taboo [tabú], *a.* proscrito, prohibido.—*s.* tabú.—*vt.* declarar tabú; (fig.) prohibir, excluir.

tabulate [tǽbyuleit], *vt.* tabular. **—tabulator** [tǽbyuleitɔ(r)], *s.* tabulador.

tacit [tǽsit], *a.* tácito.– **—urn** [-œrn], *a.* taciturno.

tack [tæk], *vt.* clavar con tachuelas; (mar.) cambiar de rumbo; (cost.) puntear, pegar, coser, hilvanar.—*to t. on*, añadir.—*s.* tachuela, puntilla; hilván; nuevo plan de acción; (mar.) cambio de rumbo.

tackle [tǽkl], *vt.* agarrar, asir; atacar, abordar (un problema, etc.), luchar con; atajar a un adversario.—*s.* aparejo; (football) atajo, agarrada; atajador.—*fishing t.*, avíos de pescar.

tact [tækt], *s.* tacto; tino, tiento, ten con ten.– **—ful** [tǽktful], *a.* discreto, cauto, político.– **—ical** [-ikal], *a.* táctico.

tactics [tǽktiks], *s. pl.* táctica.

tactless [tǽktlis], *a.* falto de tacto o de tino, impolítico.

tadpole [tǽdpoul], *s.* (zool.) renacuajo.

taffeta [tǽfitä], *s.* tafetán.

tag [tæg], *s.* marbete, etiqueta; herrete; pingajo.—*to play t.*, jugar al tócame tú.—*vti.* [1] marcar con marbete; tocar a (un jugador).—*vii.* [1]—seguir de cerca.

tail [teil], *s.* cola, rabo.—*pl.* frac.; (of a coin) cruz.—*at the t. end*, al final.— *t. end*, cola, extremo; conclusión.— *t. light*, faro trasero.—*t. spin*, (aer.) barrena picada.—*vt.* seguir de cerca.—*vi.*—*to t. after*, pisar los talones a.– **—gate** [-geit], *vt.* ir pisándole los talones a.—*vi.* manejar pegado al vehículo de delante.—*s.* (aut.) puerta trasera. **—tailgating** o **tailgate party** [téilgeitiŋ], *s.* (fam.) merienda al lado del coche.

tailor [téilɔ(r)], *s.* sastre.—*vt.* entallar (un traje); adaptar.—*t.-made*, hecho a la medida.—*t.-made suit*, traje sastre, traje hecho a medida. **—tailored** [téilɔrd], *a.* entallado.

taint [teint], *vt.* y *vi.* manchar(se), inficionar(se), corromper(se).— *tainted food*, alimentos pasados, echados a perder.—*s.* mácula, mancha, corrupción.

take [teik], *vti.* [10] tomar; coger, asir, agarrar; recibir, aceptar; apropiarse, apoderarse de; percibir o cobrar; llevar, conducir, acompañar; restar, deducir; usar, emplear, adoptar; considerar, tener por; admitir; adaptarse o hacerse a; coger, contraer (una enfermedad); sacar (un retrato, una copia); dar (un salto, un paso, un paseo).—*to t. aback*, desconcertar.—*to t. advantage of*, aprovecharse de.—*to t. down*, bajar; descolgar; desmontar.—*to t. for granted*, dar por sentado; no apreciar.—*to t. heart*, animarse, cobrar valor.—*to t. hold of*, asir, agarrar; tomar posesión de; encargarse de.—*to t. in*, entrar; aceptar, recibir; comprender; engañar; abarcar.—*to t. into account*, tomar en consideración.—*to t. into consideration*, tener en cuenta.—*to t. offense*, ofenderse.—*to t. on*, emprender; contratar.—*to t. out*, sacar; llevar a paseo; extraer.—*to t. over*, tomar posesión de.—*to t. pains*, esmerarse.—*to t. pity on*, apiadarse, compadecerse de.—*to t. place*, celebrarse, verificarse.—*to t. the floor*, tomar la palabra.—*to t. the trouble to,* tomarse la molestia.—*to t. to heart,* tomar a pecho.—*to t. to task,* reprender.—*to t. up,* subir; dedicarse a; recoger.—*vii.* ser poseedor, adquirir propiedad; pegar bien, tener buen éxito, (fam.) cuajar; prender (la vacuna, el fuego, etc.); hacer su efecto, ser eficaz; (fam.) picar (el pez); sacar buen o mal retrato; pegar, adherirse; arraigar (las plantas).—*to t. after,* parecerse a, salir a; imitar, a seguir el ejemplo de; ser como.—*to t. ill,* caer enfermo.—*to t. off,* partir, salir; (aer.) despegar, hacerse al aire.—*to t. to,* aficionarse a; tomar cariño o recurrir a; dedicarse a.—*s.* toma; cogida, redada; entrada, producto, ingresos (de una función, etc.).—*t.-in,* (fam.) fraude, engaño; estafador; entrada, ingresos.—*t.-off,* (fam.) imitación burlesca; (aer.) despegue; (dep., gimn.) trampolín; raya de donde se salta. **—taken** [téjkn], *pp.* de TO TAKE.—*to be t. ill,* caer enfermo.—*to be t. off o away,* morir(se).—*to be t. with,* prendarse o estar prendado de. **—taking** [téjkiŋ], *a.* atractivo, seductor; (fam.) contagioso.—*s.* toma; (for.) embargo.—*t. for,* afición, inclinación, afecto; (fam.) arrebato, agitación.—*pl.* ingresos.

talcum [tǽlkʌm], *s.* talco.—*t. powder,* polvos de talco.

tale [tejl], *s.* cuento, relato; embuste, mentira.- **—bearer** [téjlbercœ(r)], *s.* chismoso, cuentista.

talent [tǽlent], *s.* talento, ingenio; aptitud.—*t. scout,* cazatalentos.- **—ed** [-jd], *a.* talentoso, de talento; hábil.

talisman [tǽlismən], *s.* talismán.

talk [tɔk], *vt.* y *vi.* hablar; charlar, conversar.—*to t. away,* malgastar el tiempo hablando; disipar con la palabra.—*to t. into,* convencer de, inducir a.—*to t. out of,* disuadir; sonsacar.—*to t. over,* discutir, conferenciar acerca de.—*to t. to,* hablar a; reprender.—*to t. to the purpose,* hablar al alma.—*to t. up,* alabar. —*s.* conversación, plática; habla; charla; tema de una conversación; discurso; comidilla (objeto de chismes, etc.).- **—ative** [tɔ́kətjv], *a.* locuaz, charlatán.- **—ativeness** [-ətjvnjs], *s.* locuacidad.- **—er** [-œ(r)], *s.* conversador; decidor; orador; charlatán.

tall [tɔl], *a.* alto; (fam.) grande.—*six feet t.,* seis pies de alto o de altura.

tallow [tǽlou], *vt.* ensebar.—*s.* sebo.

tally [tǽlj], *s.* cuenta.—*t. sheet,* hoja de cuentas o apuntes.—*vti.* [7] llevar la cuenta.—*vii.* cuadrar, concordar, estar conforme.—*to t. up,* sumar, contar.

talon [tǽlọn], *s.* garra.

tamale [tạmálị], *s.* (Am.) tamal.

tambourine [tæmbọrín], *s.* pandero, pandereta.

tame [tejm], *a.* manso, domesticado; dócil, tratable; insustancial, insípido; (fam.) moderado.—*vt.* domar, amansar, domesticar; avasallar; suavizar; represar (un río).- **—ness** [téjmnjs], *s.* mansedumbre, docilidad.- **—r** [-œ(r)], *s.* domador.

tamp [tæmp], *vt.* apisonar.

tamper [tǽmpœ(r)], *vi.* (con **with**) meterse en o con; falsificar, adulterar; tocar lo que no se debe; sobornar.

tampon [tǽmpan], *s.* (cir.) tapón; (farm.) tampón.—*vt.* (cir.) taponar.

tan [tæn], *vti.* [1] curtir; zurrar; tostar, requemar.—*a.* tostado, de color de canela.—*s.* color de canela; tostadura del sol.

tang [tæŋ], *s.* dejo, gustillo, sabor.

tangent [tǽndʒent], *a.* y *s.* tangente.— *to fly o go off on a t.,* salirse por la tangente.

tangerine [tændʒerín], *s.* mandarina.

tangible [tǽndʒjbl], *a.* tangible, palpable.

tangle [tǽŋgl], *vt.* y *vi.* enredar(se), enmarañar(se); confundir(se).—*to t. with,* venir a las manos (con).—*s.* enredo, embrollo; confusión; alga marina.

tank [tæŋk], *s.* tanque, depósito; (mil.) tanque, carro de combate.—*t. car,* carro cuba, vagón cisterna.

tanner [tǽnœ(r)], *s.* curtidor. **—tannery** [tǽnœrị], *s.* tenería, curtiduría.

tantalize [tǽntạlajz], *vt.* torturar lentamente con lo inasequible. **—tantalizing** [tǽntạlajzjŋ], *a.* tentador e inasequible.

tantrum [tǽntrʌm], *s.* (fam.) berrinche, pataleta.

tap [tæp], *vti.* [1] perforar (un barril, etc. para sacar líquido) o sangrar (un árbol); unir o conectar con (para tomar agua, corriente, etc. o para interceptar o transmitir mensajes telefónicos, etc.); sacar de, tomar de; (cir.) sajar o punzar (un absceso, etc.); golpear ligeramente, dar una palmadita.—*vii.* tocar o golpear ligeramente.—*s.* espita; tapón o tarugo; (mec.) macho de terraja; toma (de agua, elec., etc.), derivación; golpecito, palmadita.—*beer on t.,* cerveza del barril o de sifón.—*t. dance,* zapateado, zapateo.—*t. dancer,* bailarín de zapateado o de claqué.—*t. room,* bar.—*t. water,* agua de grifo.

tape [téip], *s.* cinta, cintilla; cinta de papel o de metal.—*adhesive t.,* tela o cinta adhesiva, esparadrapo.— *blank t.,* cinta virgen.—*red t.,* burocratismo, formulismo dilatorio.—*t. deck,* platina, pletina.—*t. measure,* cinta para medir, cinta métrica.—*t.-record,* grabar en cinta.—*t. recorder,* grabadora (de cinta), magnetófono.—*t. recording,* grabación en cinta.—*vt.* sujetar con cinta adhesiva; (med.) vendar; medir con la cinta métrica; grabar en cinta magnetofónica.

taper [téipœ(r)], *s.* velita, candela; cirio; ahusamiento de un objeto.—*vt.* afilar, adelgazar, ahusar.—*vi.* rematar en punta, tener forma ahusada; cesar poco a poco.

tapestry [tǽpistri], *s.* tapiz, tapicería, colgadura.

tapeworm [téipwœrm], *s.* (lombriz) solitaria, tenia.

tapioca [tǽpióukǎ], *s.* tapioca.

tar [tar], *s.* alquitrán, brea o pez líquida; (fam.) marinero.— *t. paper,* papel alquitranado.— *vti.* [1] alquitranar, embrear, embetunar.

tardiness [tárdinis], *s.* tardanza, lentitud. **—tardy** [tárdi], *a.* tardío, moroso, lento.

target [tárgit], *s.* blanco a que se tira; (fig.) objetivo.—*t. practice,* tiro al blanco.—*vt.* dirigir.

tariff [tǽrif], *s.* tarifa; arancel; impuesto.—*a.* arancelario, aduanero.—*vt.* tarifar; afectar por razón de impuestos.

tarnish [tárniš], *vt.* deslustrar.—*vi.* deslustrarse.—*s.* deslustre.

tarpaulin [tarpólin], *s.* lona embreada.

tarry [tǽri], *vii.* [7] demorarse, tardar, entretenerse.

tart [tart], *a.* acre, ácido; agridulce; mordaz.—*s.* tarta; pastelillo de fruta; (jer.) puta.

task [tæsk], *s.* tarea, faena, labor.—*to take to t.,* amonestar, regañar.

tassel [tǽsel], *s.* borla.—*vti.* [2] adornar con borlas.

taste [téist], *vt.* gustar; saborear, probar, catar.—*vi.* saber a, tener sabor o gusto.—*s.* gusto; sabor; (fig.) paladar; saboreo, paladeo; prueba, sorbo, trago, pedacito; muestra; gusto, discernimiento; afición.—*in bad t.,* de mal gusto.—*to have a t. for,* gustar de.- **—ful** [téistful], *a.* elegante, de buen gusto.- **—less** [-lis], *a.* insípido; desabrido, sin gracia; de mal gusto. **—tasty** [téisti], *a.* sabroso, gustoso.

tatter [tǽtœ(r)], *s.* andrajo, harapo, guiñapo, jirón.- **—ed** [-d], *a.* andrajoso, harapiento.

tattle [tǽtl], *vi.* chismear, comadrear; descubrir o revelar secretos indiscretamente.—*s.* charla, cháchara; chismografía.- **—r** [-œ(r)], *s.* chismoso.

tattoo [tætú], *s.* tatuaje; (mil.) retreta.—*vt.* tatuar.

taught [tɔt], *pret. y pp.* de TO TEACH.

taunt [tɔnt], *vt.* vilipendiar, vituperar; mofarse de; reprender.—*s.* vituperio; dicterio; sarcasmo.

Taurus [tórǔs], *s.* (astr.) Tauro.

taut [tɔt], *a.* tirante, tenso; listo, preparado, en regla.

tavern [tǽvœrn], *s.* taberna; mesón, posada, figón.

tawdry [tódri], *a.* cursi, charro.

tax [tæks], *s.* impuesto, tributo, contribución, gabela; carga, exacción.—*t. base,* base imponible, base impositiva.—*t. collector,* recaudador de impuestos.—*t. cut,* reducción de impuestos.—*t.-deductible,* desgravable.—*t. deduction,* gasto deducible.—*t. evader,* burlador de impuestos.—*t. evasion,* evasión fiscal, evasión de impuestos.—*t.-exempt,* exento de impuestos.—*t. exemption,* desgravación fiscal, deducción impositiva.—*t.-free,* libre de impuestos.—*t. haven,* paraíso fiscal.—*t. rate,* tipo impositivo.—*t. return,* declaración de la renta, declaración de impuestos.—*t. shelter,* refugio fiscal, inversión que reduce el impuesto a pagar.—*vt.* imponer contribuciones a; (for.) tasar; abusar de; reprender; reprobar; (fam.) pedir como precio.—*to t. with,* acusar, tachar, imputar.- **—able** [tǽksabẹl], *a.* imponible.- **—ation** [-éišọn], *s.* tributación; imposición de contribuciones.

taxi(cab) [tǽksǐ(kæb)], s. auto de alquiler, taxímetro.—*t. driver,* taxista.—*t. stand,* parada de taxis.

taxpayer [tǽkspejœ(r)], s. contribuyente, tributario.

tea [ti], s. te; reunión en que se sirve te; infusión, cocimiento.—*t. bag,* bolsita de té.- **—cart** [-kart], s. mesita de té.

teach [tich], vti. [10] enseñar, instruir; aleccionar.—vii. ser maestro, enseñar.- **—er** [tíchœ(r)], s. maestro.— *teacher's pet,* alumno mimado.- **—ing** [-iŋ], a. docente, enseñado; aleccionador.—s. enseñanza, instrucción, magisterio; doctrina.

teacup [tíkʌp], s. taza para te. **—teakettle** [tíketl], s. marmita, olla de calentar agua.

team [tim], s. (dep.) equipo (de jugadores); conjunto de personas que trabaja coordinadamente; tronco, par, yunta (de animales de tiro).— vt. uncir, enganchar, enyugar.—vi. guiar un tronco o yunta.—*to t. up,* asociarse (con) para formar un equipo.- **—mate** [-mejt], s. compañero de equipo.- **—ster** [tímstœ(r)], s. tronquista; carretero; camionero.- **—work** [-wœrk], s. cooperación, esfuerzo coordinado de un equipo.

teapot [típat], s. tetera.

tear [tir], s. lágrima.—*in tears,* llorando.—*t. bomb* (gas), bomba lacrimógena (gas lacrimógeno).—vi. llorar, derramar lágrimas.—vti. [10] [ter], desgarrar, rasgar.—*to t. asunder,* separar con violencia.—*to t. away,* arrancar, desmembrar.—*to t. down,* derribar, demoler.—*to t. one's hair,* mesarse los cabellos.—*to t. out,* arrancar, separar con violencia.—*to t. up,* arrancar, desarraigar; deshacer, desbaratar.—vii. rasgarse; andar precipitadamente.—s. rasgadura, desgarradura; precipitación; (fam.) borrachera.- **—ful** [tírfu̧l], a. lloroso, lacrimoso.

tease [tiz], vt. embromar, tomar el pelo a; provocar, tentar.- **—r** [tízœr], s. bromista; (puzzle) rompecabezas.- **—teasing** [tízi̧ŋ], s. tomaduras de pelo; burlas.

teaspoon [tíspun], s. cucharita, cucharilla.- **—ful** [-fu̧l], s. cucharadita.

teat [tit], s. teta; tetilla; pezón; ubre.

technical [téknį̇kal], a. técnico, tecnológico.— **—ity** [teknį̇kǽlįti], s. detalle ténico. **—technician** [tekníʃan],

s. técnico, experto. **—technique** [tekník], s. técnica, ejecución.

tedious [tídjʌs], a. tedioso, fastidioso.

teem [tim], vi. bullir, hormiguear.

teens [tíns], s. números de trece a diecinueve; edad de trece a diecinueve años.—*teen-age,* adolescencia, de trece a diecinueve años de edad.— *teenager,* adolescente, persona de trece a diecinueve años de edad.

teeth [tiθ], pl. de TOOTH.- **—teethe** [tið], vi. endentecer.- **—ing** [tíði̧ŋ], s. dentición.—*t. ring,* chupete.

teetotaler [titóu̧t̪alœ(r)], s. abstemio.

telegram [télǝgræm], s. telegrama. **—telegraph** [télǝgræf], vt. y vi. telegrafiar; enviar por telégrafo.—s. telégrafo. **—telegraphic** [telǝgrǽfik], a. telegráfico. **—telegraphy** [telég-ræfi̧], s. telegrafía.

telepathy [telépa̧θi̧], s. telepatía.

telephone [télǝfou̧n], vt. y vi. telefonear.—s. teléfono.—*t. booth,* cabina telefónica, locutorio.—*t. call,* llamada telefónica.—*t. directory,* anuario telefónico, guía telefónica.—*t. exchange,* central telefónica.—*t. operator,* telefonista, operadora.— *t. receiver,* receptor telefónico.— *t. table,* mesita portateléfono.

teleprinter [télǝpri̧ntœr], s. teleimpresor.

telescope [télǝskou̧p], s. telescopio.— vt. y vi. encajar(se), enchufar(se) un objeto en otro. **—telescopic** [telǝs-kápi̧k], a. telescópico; de enchufe.

teletype [télǝtaip], s. teletipo.—vt. y vi. transmitir por teletipo.

televise [télǝvaiz], vt. televisar. **—television** [telǝvíẑ̧on], s. televisión.—*t. screen,* pantalla televisora.—*t. set,* televisor, telerreceptor.

tell [tel], vti. y vii. [10] decir; contar; expresar; explicar; revelar, descubrir; adivinar, decidir, determinar.—*to t. off,* contar, recontar; (mil.) designar.—*to t. on,* descubrir, delatar a; dejarse ver en, afectar a.—*to t. one (where to get) off,* decir a uno cuántas son cinco, cantárselas claras, soltarle cuatro frescas.—*to t. tales out of school,* revelar secretos.—*to t. volumes,* ser muy significativo.- **—er** [télœ(r)], s. relator, narrador; escrutador de votos; pagador o cobrador de un banco.—*t.'s window,* taquilla.- **—ing** [-i̧ŋ], a. eficaz, notable.—*a t. argument,* un argumento convincente.- **—tale** [-tejl], s. soplón, chismoso.—a. revelador.

temerity [tēmériti], s. temeridad.

temper [témpœ(r)], vt. moderar, mitigar, calmar; (pint.) mezclar; modificar, ajustar; (a)temperar, ablandar; (metal) templar.—s. mal genio; índole, humor, disposición; genio; condición; calma, ecuanimidad; temple; punto (grado de densidad).—to lose one's t., perder la paciencia, enojarse.— **—ament** [témp(œ)rament], s. temperamento; complexión, naturaleza; composición; disposición; temple.— **—ance** [témp(œ)rans], s. templanza, temperancia, sobriedad.— **—ate** [témp(œ)rit], a. sobrio, abstemio; templado, benigno; moderado.

temperature [témp(œ)rachū(r)], s. temperatura.—to have o run a t., tener fiebre o calentura.

tempest [témpist], s. tempestad.—vt. agitar, conmover violentamente.— **—uous** [tempéschuʌs], a. tempestuoso, borrascoso; impetuoso.

temple [témpl], s. templo; (anat.) sien.

temporal [témporal], a. temporal.—s. hueso temporal.

temporary [témporeri], a. temporáneo, temporario, provisional, interino.

tempt [tempt], vt. tentar.— **—ation** [-éjšon], s. tentación.

ten [ten], a. y s. diez. **—tenth** [tenθ], décimo.

tenacious [tinéišʌs], a. tenaz. **—tenacity** [tinǽsiti], s. tenacidad.

tenant [ténant], s. arrendatario, inquilino; morador, residente.

tend [tend], vt. guardar, vigilar, cuidar; atender.—vi. tender, propender; dirigirse; atender.—to tend on, o upon, asistir, servir a.- **—ency** [téndensi], s. tendencia, propensión; dirección.

tender [téndœ(r)], a. tierno; delicado; muelle; benigno, compasivo; sensible.—t.-hearted, de corazón tierno.—t. of u over, cuidadoso de, solicito de los sentimientos ajenos.—s. oferta, ofrecimiento, propuesta.—vt. ofrecer, presentar, proponer; enternecer, ablandar.— vi. hacer una oferta; enternecerse.- **—loin** [-lɔjn], s. filete.- **—ness** [-nis], s. terneza, ternura; sensibilidad; delicadeza; benevolencia.

tendon [téndon], s. tendón.

tendril [téndril], s. (bot.) zarcillo.

tenement [ténɛment], s. casa de vecindad; vivienda (barata).

tenet [ténit], s. dogma, principio, credo.

tennis [ténis], s. tenis.—t. court, campo de tenis.—t. player, tenista.

tenor [téno(r)], s. (mus.) tenor; tendencia; texto, contenido.—a. (mus.) de enor.

tense [tens], a. tenso, tirante.—s. (gram.) tiempo. **—tension** [ténšon], s. tensión, tirantez.

tent [tent], s. toldo; tienda de campaña, (Am.) carpa.

tentacle [téntakl], s. tentáculo.

tentative [téntativ], a. tentativo, de ensayo.—s. tentativa, ensayo, tanteo.

tenuous [tényuʌs], a. tenue, sutil; raro.

tenure [tényū(r)], s. ejercicio; (for.) tenencia; (pol.) inamovilidad.

tepid [tépid], a. tibio, templado.

term [tœrm], s. término; (imprisonment) condena; semestre, período escolar; (ling.) término; (pol.) mandato, período.—pl. condiciones; (com.) facilidades de pago.—to be on good (bad) terms with, llevarse bien (mal) con; estar en buenas (malas) relaciones con.—to bring to terms, imponer condiciones a, hacer arreglos con.—to come to terms, arreglarse, convenirse.—vt. nombrar, llamar, calificar de.- **—inal** [tœrminal], a. terminal.—s. término, final; (f.c. y elec.) terminal.- **—inate** [-ineit], vt. y vi. terminar.- **—ination** [-inéjšon], s. terminación o fin; (gram.) desinencia.- **—inus** [-inŭs], s. término.

termite [tœrmajt], s. termita, comején.

tern [tœrn], s. golondrina de mar; terno.

terrace [téris], vt. terraplenar.—s. terraplén; terraza; azotea.

terrain [teréjn], s. terreno, campo.

terramycin [teramáisin], s. terramicina.

terrible [téribl], a. terrible; (fam.) muy desagradable.

terrier [térjœ(r)], s. perro de busca; zorrero.

terrific [terífik], a. terrífico, espantoso; (fam.) excelente, tremendo, formidable. **—terrify** [térifaj], vti. [7] aterrar, aterrorizar, espantar.

territory [téritɔri], s. territorio.

terror [téro(r)], s. espanto, terror.- **—ism** [-izm], s. terrorismo.- **—ist** [-ist], s. terrorista.- **—ize** [-ajz], vt. aterrorizar, atemorizar.

erry cloth s.albornoz.

erse [tœrs], a. breve, sucinto.

est [tɛst], s. prueba, ensayo, experimento; examen; comprobación; (quím.) análisis; resultado de un análisis; reacción, reactivo.—t. flight, (aer.) vuelo experimental o de prueba.—t. pilot, (aer.) piloto de pruebas.—t. tube, probeta, tubo de ensayo.—the acid t., la prueba suprema o decisiva.—vt. ensayar, comprobar, hacer la prueba de; someter a prueba; examinar (a un estudiante, etc.); (for.) atestiguar.

estament [téstamęnt], s. testamento.

esticle [téstikl], s. testículo.

estify [téstifaj], vti. y vii. [7] testificar, atestiguar, atestar. **—testimonial** [testimóunjal], s. atestación; certificado; encomio; recomendación. **—testimony** [testimóunj], s. testimonio, declaración.—in t. whereof, en fe de lo cual.

etanus [tétanʌs], s. tétano, tétanos.

ext [tɛkst], s. texto.- **—book** [tékstbuk], s. libro de texto.

extile [tékstjl], a. textil, tejido; de tejer, de tejidos.—s. tejido; material textil. **—texture** [tékschur], s. textura.

hal [tái, taj], s.

han [ðæn], conj. que; de; del que, de la que, que.—fewer than ten, menos de diez.—I am taller than he, soy más alto que él.—less time than they expected, menos tiempo del que esperaban.—more than once, más de una vez.

hank [ðæŋk], vt. agradecer, dar gracias a.—t. you, gracias.- **—ful** [-fuļ], a. agradecido. **—fulness** [ðæŋkfulnįs], s. agradecimiento, gratitud.- **—less** [-ljs], a. desagradecido; ingrato.- **—s** [-s], s. gracias.—t. to, gracias a, merced a, debido a.- **—sgiving** [ðæŋksgívįŋ], s. acción de gracias.—Thanksgiving Day, día de acción de gracias.

hat [ðæt], a. ese, esa, aquel, aquella.—t. way, por aquel camino; por allí; de ese modo.—pron. ése, ésa, eso; aquél, aquélla, aquello; que, quien, el que, la que, lo que; el cual, la cual, lo cual.—t. is (to say), es decir.—t. is how, así es como se hace.—t. is t., eso es lo que hay, no hay más que hablar, etc.—t. of John, el de Juan.—t. of yesterday, el o lo de ayer.—t. which, el que, la que, etc.—conj. que; para que, a fin de que, con el objeto de.—in t., en que, a causa de que, por cuanto.—not but t., no es decir que.—save t., salvo que.—so t., para que, con tal que; de modo que, de suerte que.—adv. tan.—not t. far, no tan lejos.—t. large, así de grande, de este tamaño.—t. many, tantos.—t. much, tanto.

thatch [θǽch], paja, paja (para techos).—vt. techar con paja.—thatched roof, techumbre de paja.

thaw [θɔ], vt. y vi. deshelar(se), derretir(se).—to t. out, hacer(se) más tratable, menos reservado o ceremonioso, abrirse.—s. deshielo, derretimiento.

the [ði, ðę], art. el, la, lo, los, las.—adv. cuanto, tanto, mientras más, etc.—t. less you say, t. better, cuanto menos diga, tanto mejor.—t. more he spoke, t. more we admired him, mientras más hablaba, más lo admirábamos.—t. more the merrier, cuanto más mejor.—t. more . . . t. more, cuanto más . . . tanto más.

theater, theatre [θíątœ(r)], s. teatro; arte dramático.- **—goer** [-gouœr], s. teatrero. **—theatrical** [θiǽtrikąl], a. teatral.—s. pl. funciones teatrales.

thee [ði], pron. (ant.) te, a ti.—for t., para ti; por ti.—with t., contigo.

theft [θɛft], s. hurto, robo, latrocinio.

their [ðer], a. su, sus, suyo(s), suya(s) (de ellos, de ellas).- **—s** [-z], pron. el suyo (de ellos), la suya (de ellas), los suyos (de ellos), las suyas (de ellas).

them [ðɛm], pron. los, las, les; ellos, ellas (precedidos de preposición).

theme [θim], s. tema.—t. song, tema central.

themselves [ðɛmsélvz], pron. ellos mismos, ellas mismas; sí (mismos, mismas) (después de prep.); se (refl.). —with t., consigo.—V. HIMSELF, HERSELF.

then [ðɛn], adv. entonces, en aquel tiempo, a la sazón; después, luego, en seguida; en otro tiempo; además; en tal caso; pues, conque; por consiguiente, por esta razón.—but t., por otra parte, sin embargo, si bien es cierto que.—by t., para entonces.—now and t., de cuando en cuando; de vez en cuando.—now t., ahora bien; tenemos pues.—t. and there, allí mismo, al punto.—conj. pues, en tal caso.

thence [ðɛns], adv. desde allí; desde entonces; por eso.- **—forth** [-fórθ], *adv.* de allí en adelante; desde entonces.

theological [θioládʒiḳạl], *a.* teológico, teologal. —**theology** [θiálodʒi], *s.* teología.

theorem [θíorɛm], *s.* teorema. —**theoretical** [θiorétiḳạl], *a.* teórico, especulativo. —**theory** [θíori], *s.* teoría.

therapeutic [θɛrạpiútiḳ], *a.* terapéutico.– —**s** [-s], *s.* terapéutica. —**therapy** [θɛ́rạpi], *s.* terapia.

there [ðɛr], *adv.* ahí, allí, allá; en eso, en cuanto a eso.—*down t.,* ahí (allí) abajo.—*over t.,* ahí.—*t. is, t. are,* hay.—*t. you are,* (fam.) eso es todo; ahí nos (me, etc.) tiene; ahí está el busilis.—*up t.,* ahí (allí) arriba.– —**abouts** [ðɛrạbáuts], *adv.* por ahí, por allí, cerca; acerca de eso; aproximadamente.- —**after** [ðɛræftœ(r)], *adv.* después, después de eso; conforme.- —**by** [ðɛrbái], *adv.* con eso, con lo cual; de tal modo, así; allí, por allí cerca; acerca de eso.- —**for** [ðɛrfór], *adv.* por es(t)o; para es(t)o.- —**fore** [ðérfɔr], *adv.* por es(to), por (lo) tanto, por ende, por consiguiente, en consecuencia, luego.- —**from** [ðɛrfrám], *adv.* de allí, de ahí; de eso. - —**in** [ðɛrín], *adv.* allí dentro; en esto, en eso.- —**of** [ðɛráv], *adv.* de esto, de eso.- —**on** [ðɛrán], *adv.* sobre o encima de él, ella, etc.; por encima; por lo tanto; luego, al punto.- —**upon** [ðɛrʌpán], *adv.* sobre o encima de él, ella, etc.; por lo tanto, por consiguiente; sobre lo cual, luego, al punto.- —**with** [ðɛrwíθ], *adv.* con eso, con esto; en eso, entonces, luego, inmediatamente.

thermodynamic [θœrodainǽmiḳ], termodinámico.

thermometer [θœrmámɛtœ(r)], *s.* termómetro. —**thermos** [θǿrmos], *s.* termo(s).—*t. bottle,* botella termos. —**thermostat** [θǿrmostæt], *s.* termóstato.

thermonuclear [θœrmonyúklĕạr], *a.* termonuclear.

thesaurus [θɛ́sɔ̃rŭs], *s.* tesauro, tesoro.

these [ðiz], *a. pl.* de THIS: estos, estas.— *pron.* éstos, éstas.

thesis [θísis], *s.* tesis.

they [ðei], *pron. pl.* de HE, SHE, IT: ellos, ellas.—*t. say,* se dice, dicen.

thick [θiḳ], *a.* grueso; espeso; tupido, denso; atestado, lleno; estúpido; apagado (voz, etc.); impenetrable;

profundo (sombra, etc.); (fam.) íntimo.—*t.-and-thin,* cabal, a toda prueba.—*s.* grueso, espesor; lo más denso, nutrido, tupido o recio.— *adv.* frecuentemente, continuadamente; densa o tupidamente.—*t.-headed,* espeso, torpe.—*t.-lipped,* bezudo, (Am.) bembón.—*t.-set,* rechoncho.—*t.-skinned,* insensible sinvergüenza.—*to lay it on t.,* exagerar.- —**en** [θíkn], *vt.* y *vi.* espesar(se), condensar(se), engrosar(se); reforzar(se); enturbiar(se); complicar(se).- —**et** [-it], *s.* maleza, espesura, matorral, broza.- —**ness** [-nis], *s.* espesor; densidad; grosor; cuerpo, consistencia; capa (superpuesta); (fam.) estupidez.

thief [θif], *s.* ladrón. —**thieve** [θiv], *vt.* y *vi.* hurtar, robar. —**thievery** [θívĕri], *s.* latrocinio, hurto, robo. —**thieves** [θivz], *s. pl.* de THIEF.

thigh [θai], *s.* muslo.—*t. bone,* fémur.

thimble [θímbl], *s.* dedal.

thin [θin], *a.* delgado, fino, tenue; flaco, descarnado; ligero, transparente; aguado; (mus.) débil, poco resonante; apagado (color); escaso, pequeño.—*vti.* y *vii.* [1] enrarecer(se); adelgazar(se); fluidificarse.—*to t. out,* aclarar, entresacar (el monte, etc.).

thine [ðain], *pron.* y *a.* (ant.) tuyo, el tuyo; tu, tus.

thing [θiŋ], *s.* cosa, objeto; asunto, acontecimiento, hecho.

think [θiŋḳ], *vti.* y *vii.* [10] pensar; proponerse; creer, juzgar, conjeturar.— *as you t. fit,* como a usted le parezca mejor, como Ud. quiera.—*to t. better of,* cambiar de opinión acerca de, formar mejor opinión de.—*to t. over,* pensarlo, meditarlo.—*to t. nothing of,* mirar con desprecio, tener en poco; creer fácil, no dar importancia a.—*to t. on* o *upon,* acordarse de, recordar; pensar en; reflexionar acerca de; meditar, considerar.—**able** [θíŋḳabl], *a.* concebible. —**er** [-œ(r)], *s.* pensador.– —**ing** [-iŋ], *s.* pensamiento, reflexión; concepto, juicio.—*to my t.,* en mi opinión.

thinness [θínnis], *s.* tenuidad, delgadez; poca consistencia; debilidad.

third [θœrd], *a.* y *s.* tercero. —**thirdly** [θœ́rdli], *adv.* en tercer lugar.—*t. degree,* (fam.) interrogatorio bajo tortura.—*t. party,* (for.) tercera persona

sona; (pol.) tercer partido.—*T. World*, Tercer Mundo.

thirst [θɚrst], *s.* sed; ansia, anhelo.— *vi.* tener o padecer sed; ansiar anhelar.—*to t. for*, tener sed de; anhelar.- **—y** [θɚrstị], *a.* sediento.—*to be t.*, tener sed.

thirteen [θɚrtịn], *a.* y *s.* trece. **—thirteenth** [θɚrtínθ], *a.* y *s.* decimotercero, trezavo.

thirty [θɚrti], *a.* y *s.* treinta.—*t.-one*, treinta y uno. **—thirtieth** [θɚrtịịθ], *a.* y *s.* trigésimo, treintavo.

this [ðịs], *a.* este, esta.—*pron.* éste, ésta, esto.—*t. way*, por aquí.

thistle [θịsl], *s.* cardo, abrojo.—*t. bird*, *t. finch*, jilguero.

tho' [ðou], *conj.* = THOUGH.

thong [θaŋ], *s.* correa, tira de cuero, látigo.

thorax [θóræks], *s.* tórax, pecho.

thorn [θɔrn], *s.* (bot.) espina, púa; espino, abrojo; (fig.) pesadumbre, zozobra.— **—y** [θórnị], *a.* espinoso; arduo.

thorough [θɚrou], *a.* cabal, completo, acabado, perfecto; cuidadoso, concienzudo.- **—bred** [-bred], *a.* de pura raza, casta o sangre; bien nacido.—*s.* (un) pura sangre (caballo, etc.).- **—fare** [-fɛr], *s.* vía pública, paso, tránsito.—*no t.*, no hay paso; calle cerrada.

those [ðouz], *a. pl.* de THAT: aquellos, aquellas; esos, esas.—*pron.* ésos, ésas, aquéllos, aquéllas.—*t. that*, *t. which*, *t. who*, los que, aquellos que, quienes.

thou [ðau], *pron.* (ant.) tú.

though [ðou], *conj.* aunque, bien que, si bien, aun cuando.—*as t.*, como si.—*adv.* (fam.) sin embargo; a pesar de eso.

thought [θɔt], *pret.* y *pp.* de TO THINK.— *s.* pensamiento; meditación, reflexión; idea; intención, propósito; recuerdo; cuidado, solicitud; poquito, pizca.—*to take t. for*, pensar en, proveer para.- **—ful** [θɔtful], *a.* pensativo; considerado; precavido.- **—fulness** [-fulnịs], *s.* calidad de meditativo, precavido o considerado; consideración; cuidado, atención; previsión.- **—less** [-lịs], *a.* atolondrado, descuidado; irreflexivo; inconsiderado.- **—lessness** [-lịsnịs], *s.* descuido o inadvertencia; falta de consideración; atolondramiento; indiscreción, ligereza.

thrash [θræʃ], *vt.* zurrar, apalear; (fam.) vencer decisivamente.—*vi.* arrojarse, agitarse.—*to t. out a matter*, ventilar un asunto.- **—ing** [θréʃịŋ], *s.* trilla; paliza.

thread [θred], *s.* hilo; fibra, hebra, filamento.—*screw t.*, rosca (de un tornillo).—*t. lace*, encaje de hilo.—*vt.* enhebrar, enhilar, ensartar; colarse a través de, pasar por; (mec.) roscar, aterrajar.—*vi.* colarse en, llegar hasta.- **—bare** [θrédbɛr], *a.* raído, gastado.

threat [θret], *s.* amenaza.- **—en** [θrétn], *vt.* y *vi.* amenazar, amagar.- **—ening** [θrétnịŋ], *a.* amenazador.

three [θri], *a.* y *s.* tres.—*t. R's*, lectura, escritura y aritmética. **—three hundred**, *a.* y *s.* trescientos.—*t. one*, trescientos uno.

threefold [θrífould], *a.* trino, triple; tres veces más.—*adv.* tres veces. **—threescore** [θrískór], *s.* tres veintenas, sesenta.

thresh [θreʃ], *vt.* (agr.) trillar, desgranar.—*vi.* trillar el grano.- **—ing** [θréʃịŋ], *s.* trilla.—*t. floor*, era.—*t. machine*, máquina trilladora.- **—er** [-œ(r)], *s.* trillador; máquina trilladora.

threshold [θréʃould], *s.* umbral; entrada; (fig.) comienzo.

threw [θru], *pret.* de TO THROW.

thrice [θrajs], *adv.* tres veces.

thrift [θrift], *s.* economía, ahorro.- **—y** [θríftị], *a.* económico, ahorrativo.

thrill [θrịl], *vt.* emocionar vivamente, hacer estremecer.—*vi.* emocionarse, conmoverse.—*s.* emoción, estremecimiento.- **—er** [θrílœ(r)], *s.* novela o película melodramática.- **—ing** [-ịŋ], *a.* emocionante, conmovedor.

thrive [θrajv], *vii.* [4] medrar, prosperar, tener buen éxito.

throat [θrout], *s.* garganta.—*to clear one's t.*, aclarar la voz.

throb [θrab], *vii.* [1] latir, palpitar.—*s.* latido, pulsación, palpitación.

throes [θrouz], *spl.* agonía, angustia.— *in the t. of*, en medio de.

thrombosis [θrambóusịs], *s.* trombosis.

throne [θroun], *s.* trono.

throng [θraŋ], *s.* tropel de gente, muchedumbre.

throttle [θrátl], *s.* regulador, obturador, válvula reguladora.—*t. valve*, válvula de estrangulación, válvula

reguladora; (aut.) acelerador.—vt.
ahogar, estrangular.—vi. ahogarse,
asfixiarse.

through [θru], a. continuo, que va
hasta el fin.—t. ticket, (f.c., etc.) billete, boleto o boletín directo.—adv.
de o al través, de parte a parte, de un
lado a otro; desde el principio hasta
el fin; enteramente, completamente.—t. and t., enteramente; en
todo; hasta los tuétanos.—to be t.,
haber terminado; (fam.) no poder
más.—prep. por; a través de; de un
extremo (o lado) a otro de; por conducto o por medio de, mediante,
por entre; por causa de, gracias a,
por mediación de.— **—out** [-áut],
prep. por todo, en todo; a lo largo de;
durante todo.—adv. en todas partes; desde el principio hasta el fin;
de parte a parte; en todo respecto.

throw [θrou], vti. y vii. [10] arrojar,
tirar, disparar, lanzar; echar.—to
t. about, esparcir.—to t. aside,
desechar.—to t. away, arrojar; desperdiciar, malgastar; desechar, arrinconar.—to t. back, rechazar; devolver.—to t. out, proferir, insinuar;
expeler, excluir; esparcir, exhalar,
emitir.—to t. out of gear, (mec.) desengranar, desconectar; (fig.) trastornar.—to t. up, echar al aire; elevar, levantar; renunciar a, abandonar; (fam.) vomitar.—s. tirada,
echada, lance; cobertor ligero. —
thrown [θroun], pp. de to THROW.

thrush [θraʃ], s. tordo.

thrust [θrʌst], vii. [9] acometer, embestir (con espada, etc.); tirar una estocada (con); meterse, pasar abrién-
dose campo.—vti. meter; empujar;
forzar; atravesar; clavar, hincar.—to
t. aside, rechazar; empujar a un
lado.—to t. forward, empujar, echar
adelante.—to t. in, meter, introducir.—to t. on, incitar, empujar.—to t.
out, echar fuera; sacar (la lengua,
etc.).—to t. through, apuñalar, atravesar de parte a parte.—to t. upon,
imponer.—pret. y pp. de TO
THRUST.—s. empuje, empujón; estocada, cuchillada, lanzada, etc.; arremetida; derrumbe.

thud [θʌd], s. sonido apagado; golpe
sordo.—vt. y vi. golpear con ruido
sordo.

thug [θʌg], s. asesino; ladrón, salteador.

thumb [θʌm], s. pulgar.—t. index, es-

calerilla, índici con pestañas.—under the t. of, dominado por, bajo el
talón de.—vt. hojear (un libro) con
el pulgar; manosear con poca destreza; emporcar con los dedos.- —
tack [ʋámtæk], s. chinche (de
dibujo).

thump [θʌmp], s. golpazo, porrazo;
golpe sordo.—vt. y vi. aporrear,
acachetear; latir con violencia (el
corazón).

thunder [θándœ(r)], s. trueno, tronido;
estruendo, estampido.—vi. tronar;
retumbar.—vt. (fig.) tronar; fulmi-
nar.- **—bolt** [-bouļt], s. rayo, centella.- **—ous** [-ŭs], a. atronador, tro-
nitoso.- **—ing** [-iŋ], **—ous** [-ʌs], a.
atronador; fulminante.- **—storm**
[-storm], s. tronada.

Thursday [θœrzdi], s. jueves.

thus [ðʌs], adv. así, de este modo; por
eso, por lo tanto; en estos términos;
hasta ese punto, tanto, a ese grado;
siendo así, en este caso.—t. and so,
tal y tal cosa; de tal y tal modo.—t.
far, hasta ahora; hasta aquí.

thwart [θwort], vt. impedir, desbaratar, frustrar.

thy [ðai], a. (ant.) tu, tus.

thyme [taim], s. (bot.) tomillo.

thyroid gland [θaíroid], s. glándula tiroides.

thyself [ðaisélf], pron. (ant.) tú mismo,
ti mismo.

tibia [tíbiậ], (anat.) tibia; (ent.) cuarta
articulación.

tick [tik], s. tictac; (insect) garrapata;
funda de colchón; (fam.) crédito,
fiado.—t.-tock, tictac.—vt. hacer sonar produciendo tictac.—vi. hacer
sonido de tictac; batir, latir; (fam.)
vender o comprar al fiado.—to t. off,
marcar.- **—ing** [-iŋ], s. cutí, terliz.

ticket [tíkịt], s. billete, (Am.) boleto
(de tren, teatro, etc.); rótulo, marbete; marca; candidatura de un partido político; papeleta o (Am.)
balota (para votar).—t. agent, taquillero.—t. collector, revisor.—t. office,
taquilla, despacho de billetes.—t.
scalper, revendedor de billetes de
teatro.—t. window, taquilla, ventanilla.

tickle [tíkl], vt. hacer cosquillas a; halagar, lisonjear; divertir; agradar.—
vi. hacer, tener o sentir cosquillas.—
s. cosquillas. **—ticklish** [tíkliʃ], a.
cosquilloso; inseguro; delicado,
difícil.

tidal wave [taídạl], s. ola de marea; (fig.) ola.

tide [taid], s. marea; corriente; curso, marcha; flujo; tiempo, estación, sazón.—*tidal wave,* marejada, aguaje.—*vt.* llevar, conducir (la marea).—*vi.* navegar o flotar con la marea.

tidiness [táidịnịs], s. limpieza, aseo; orden.

tidings [táidịŋs], *s. pl.* nuevas, noticias.

tidy [táidi], *a.* limpio, pulcro, ordenado; (fam.) considerable.—*s.* cubierta de respaldar.—*vti.* y *vii.* [7] asear, poner en orden.

tie [tai], *vt.* atar, amarrar, liar; unir, enlazar, encadenar, vincular; restringir, limitar; (pol., dep.) empatar.— *to t. the knot,* (fam.) casarse.—*to t. tight,* apretar.—*to t. up,* amarrar, asegurar; recoger; impedir, obstruir, paralizar (el tránsito, la industria, etc.); envolver; vincular (con).—*vi.* liarse; relacionarse; empatarse.—*s.* lazo, nudo, ligadura; vínculo, conexión; apego, adhesión; (dep., etc.) empate; corbata; (mus.) ligadura.—*pl.* zapatos bajos. - **—pin** [-pịn], s. alfiler de corbata.

tier [tir], s. fila, hilera, ringlera; (teat.) fila de palcos.

tiger [táigœ(r)], s. tigre.—*t. lily,* azucena atigrada.

tight [tait], *a.* bien cerrado, hermético; tirante, tieso; apretado, estrecho; compacto; (com.) escaso, difícil de obtener; (fam.) apurado, difícil, grave; tacaño; borracho.—*t.-fitting,* muy ajustado.—*t. squeeze,* (fam.) aprieto.- **—en** [táitn], *vt.* y *vi.* estrechar(se), apretar(se); estirar(se), atesar(se).- **—ness** [-nịs], s. tensión, tirantez; estrechez; apretadura; impermeabilidad; (fam.) tacañería. - **—rope** [-roup], s. cuerda tirante. **—s** [-s], s. traje de malla, calzas.

tilde [tíldẹ], s. (gram.) tilde.

tile [tail], s. azulejo, baldosa; teja; mosaico; bloque hueco; tubo de barro cocido.—*t. roof,* tejado, techo de tejas.—*vt.* tejar; embaldosar.

till [til], s. gaveta o cajón para guardar dinero.—*prep.* hasta.—*conj.* hasta que.—*vt.* cultivar, labrar.- **—age** [tíljdʒ], s. labranza, labor; cultivo.

tilt [tilt], s. inclinación, declive; justa, torneo; lanzada; toldo, tendal.—*vt.* y *vi.* ladear(se), inclinar(se).—*vt.* y *vi.* (over) volcar(se).

timber [tímbœ(r)], s. madera o materiales de construcción; palo, fuste; maderamen, maderaje; monte, bosque, árboles de monte; viga, madero; armazón; mango de madera; (fig.) cualidades.—*t. line,* límite del bosque maderable.—*t. yard,* maderería, taller de maderas.—*vt.* enmaderar.- **—land** [-lænd], s. bosque maderable.

time [taim], s. tiempo; época; período, estación; hora; vez, turno; oportunidad, ocasión; (com.) prórroga; plazo; (mús.) compás.—*at a t., at the same t.,* a la vez, al mismo tiempo.— *at no t.,* nunca.—*at times,* a veces.— *behind the times,* atrasado de noticias; anticuado.—*behind t.,* atrasado, retardado.—*between times,* en los intervalos.—*for the t. being,* por ahora.—*from t. to t.,* de cuando en cuando.—*in good t.,* temprano.—*on t.,* a la hora debida; (com.) a plazos.—*t. bomb,* bomba-reloj.—*t. clock,* reloj registrador.—*t. exposure,* exposición de tiempo.—*t. fuse,* espoleta de tiempos.—*t. signal,* señal horaria.—*t. zone,* huso horario.—*to beat t.,* llevar el compás.—*to be on time,* ser puntual.—*to have a good t.,* pasar un buen rato; divertirse.— *what t. is it?* ¿qué hora es?—*vt.* adaptar al tiempo, hacer con oportunidad; regular, poner a la hora; contar o medir el tiempo de; (mús.) llevar el compás.- **—card** [-kard], s. hoja de presencia, tarjeta registradora.- **—keeper** [táimkipœ(r)], s. cronometrista.- **—less** [-lịs], *a.* eterno.- **—liness** [-lịnịs], s. oportunidad.- **—ly** [-li], *adv.* oportunamente; a tiempo.—*a.* oportuno, conveniente.- **—piece** [-pis], s. cronómetro, reloj.- **—table** [-tejbl], s. horario, itinerario. **—worn** [-wɔrn], *a.* gastado por el tiempo.

timid [tímịd], *a.* tímido.- **—ity** [tịmídịtị], s. timidez. **—timorous** [tímorʌs], *a.* miedoso, tímido.

tin [tịn], s. estaño; (hoja de) lata, hojalata; objeto de hojalatería; (fam.) dinero, moneda.—*t. can,* (recipiente de) lata.—*t. foil,*—*t. can,* lata, envase de hojalata.—*t. cup,* taza de hojalata.—*t. foil,* hojuela de estaño, papel de estaño.—*t. roof,* tejado de hojalata.—*t. soldier,* soldadito de plomo.—*vti.* [1] estañar, cubrir con estaño; enlatar.- **—smith** [-smịθ], s.

hojalatero.- **—type** [-taip], s. ferrotipo. **—ware** [-wɛr], s. objetos de hojalata.

tincture [tíŋkchū(r)], s. tintura; tinte.—*t. of iodine,* tintura de iodo.—*vt.* teñir; impregnar, imbuir.

tinder [tíndœ(r)], s. yesca; mecha.— **—box** [-baks], s. caja de la yesca; (fig.) polvorín, barril de pólvora.

tinge [tindž], *vi.* y *vt.* colorar, teñir, matizar.—*s.* tinte, matiz; gustillo, dejo.

tingle [tíŋgl], *vi.* y *vt.* sentir o producir hormigueo o picazón; zumbar los oídos.—*s.* picazón, hormigueo, comezón; retintín.

tinker [tíŋkœr], s. calderero.—*vi.* ocuparse vanamente.

tinkle [tíŋkl], *vt.* hacer retiñir.—*vi.* retiñir.—*s.* retintín.

tinsel [tínsɛl], s. oropel, relumbrón; talco; lentejuelas.—*a.* de oropel; de relumbrón.

tint [tint], *vt.* teñir, colorar, matizar.— *s.* tinte, color, matiz; (b.a.) media tinta.

tiny [táini], *a.* diminuto, minúsculo.

tip [tip], s. punta, extremidad, cabo; casquillo, regatón; yema del dedo; puntera (zapato); propina, gratificación; aviso confidencial; palmadita, golpecito.—*vti.* [1] ladear, inclinar, voltear; dar un golpecito a; dar propina a; informar confidencialmente; guarnecer.—*to t. off,* (fam.) advertir en confianza o en secreto.—*to t. over,* volcar(se).—*vii.* ladearse, inclinarse; dar propina.

tipsy [típsi], *a.* achispado; vacilante; ladeado.

tiptoe [típtou], s. punta del pie.—*on t.,* de o en puntillas; ansioso.—*vi.* andar de puntillas.

tiptop [típtap], *a.* (fam.) de primera, excelente.—*s.* cima, cumbre.

tirade [taireíd], s. diatriba, invectiva.

tire [táir], s. llanta, neumático, goma.—*t. chain,* cadena de llanta.—*t. gauge,* indicador de presión de inflado.—*t. pressure,* presión de inflado.—*t. pump,* bomba para inflar neumáticos.—*vt.* cansar, fatigar; aburrir, fastidiar.—*to t. out,* rendir de cansancio.—*vi.* cansarse; aburrirse, fastidiarse.- **—d** [-d], *a.* cansado, fatigado; aburrido; provisto de llantas.- **—less** [táirlis], *a.* infatigable, incansable; sin llanta.- **—some** [-sʌm], *a.* tedioso, cansado, aburrido.

tissue [tíšu], s. (biol.) tejido; gasa, tisú; (fig.) serie conexa, encadenamiento.—*t. paper,* papel de seda. —*vt.* entretejer.

tithe [táið], s. diezmo; minucia, pizca.—*vi.* pagar el diezmo.

title [táitl], s. título; (dep.) campeonato.—*t. deed,* título de propiedad.—*t. page,* portada, frontispicio.—*t. rôle,* (teat.) papel principal.- **—holder** [-houldœr], s. titulado; (dep.) campeón.

to [tu], *adv.* hacia adelante.—*to and fro,* de un lado para otro; yendo y viniendo.—*to come to,* volver en sí.— *prep.* a, para; por; hasta; en; con; según; menos.—*five minutes to four,* las cuatro menos cinco.—*from house to house,* de casa en casa.—*he wishes to go,* desea ir.—*kind to her,* amable o bondadoso con ella.—*to a certain extent,* hasta cierto punto.— *to be or not to be,* ser o no ser.—*to my way of thinking,* según mi modo de pensar.

toad [tóud], s. sapo.- **—stool** [-stul], s. hongo no comestible.

toast [toust], *vt.* tostar; brindar por.— *vi.* tostarse; calentarse; brindar, beber a la salud de.—*s.* tostadas; (drink) brindis.—*a piece of t.,* una tostada.- **—er** [tóustœ(r)], s. el que brinda; tostador; tostadera, parrilla **- —master** [-mæstœ(r)], s. el que preside un banquete; maestro de ceremonias.

tobacco [tobǽkou], s. (bot.) tabaco.— *t. pouch,* petaca.

toboggan [tobágan], s. tobogán.—*vi.* deslizarse en tobogán.

today [tudéi], s. y *adv.* hoy; hoy en día.

toddle [tádl], *vi.* (del niño o viejo) titubear.- **—r** [-œ(r)], s. niño, niña.

toe [tou], s. dedo del pie; puntera, punta (del pie, de media, de zapato); pie, base (de un terraplén, etc.); (mec.) saliente, brazo.—*t.-in,* dedo gordo del pie.—*t.-in,* convergencia.—*toes up,* muerto.—*vt.* tocar con la punta del pie; dar un puntapié; poner punteras.—*vi.* (con **in**) andar con la punta de los pies hacia adentro; (mec.) converger (una rueda).- **—nail** [tóuneil], s. uña (de los dedos de los pies).

together [tugéðœr], *adv.* juntamente; a un tiempo; sin interrupción.—*t. with,* a una con, juntos, junto con.—*a.* juntos.

toil [tɔil], *vi.* afanarse, trabajar asidua-
mente; moverse con dificultad.—
vt. conseguir a duras penas.—*s.*
faena, trabajo; pena, afán; obra la-
boriosa.– **—er** [tɔilœ(r)], *s.* trabajador, el que se afana.

toilet [tɔilit], *s.* vestido, tocado, atavío;
acto de vestirse; tocador; excusado,
retrete.—*t. case,* neceser.—*t. paper* o
tissue, papel higiénico.—*t. set,*
juego de tocador.—*t. soap,* jabón de
olor, jabón de tocador.—*t. water,*
agua de colonia.

token [tóukn], *s.* señal, muestra,
prueba; prenda, recuerdo; ficha,
disco metálico (usado en tranvías,
teléfonos, etc.).—*as a t. of,* en
prenda de.—*t. payment,* pago parcial (en señal de buena fe y de
adeudo).– **—ism** [-izm], *s.* formulismo.

told [tould], *pret.* y *pp.* de TO TELL.

tolerable [tálœrabl], *a.* tolerable, sufrible; mediano, pasadero. **—tolerance** [tálœrans], *s.* tolerancia.
—tolerant [tálœrant], *a.* tolerante. **—
tolerate** [tálœreit], *vt.* tolerar. **—toleration** [talœréišon], *s.* tolerancia, indulgencia.

toiletries [tóilĕtriz], *spl.* artículos de tocador, artículos de perfumería.

toll [toul], *s.* peaje, portazgo, pontazgo; (fig.) pérdida, número de
víctimas (en un siniestro, etc.); tañido o doble de campanas.—*t.
bridge,* puente de peaje.—*t. call,*
(tlf.) llamada a larga distancia.—*to
take a heavy t.,* (fig.) costar caro (en
víctimas, etc.).—*vt.* y *vi.* cobrar o pagar peaje o portazgo; tañer o doblar
(las campanas).—*to t. the hour,* dar la
hora.– **—gate** [-geit], *s.* barrera de
peaje.

tomato [toméitou], *s.* tomate.

tomb [tum], *s.* tumba, sepulcro.

tomboy [támbɔi], *s.* muchacha traviesa.

tombstone [túmstoun], *s.* losa, lápida
sepulcral.

tomcat [támkæt], *s.* gato macho.

tome [tóum], *s.* tomo, volumen.

tomorrow [tumárou], *s.* y *adv.* mañana.—*day after t.,* pasado mañana.—*t. afternoon (morning, noon,
night),* mañana por la tarde (por la
mañana, al mediodía, por la
noche).

ton [tʌn], *s.* tonelada.

tone [toun], *s.* tono; sonido, metal o

timbre de la voz.—*vt.* dar o modificar el tono, entonar; templar, afinar.—*to t. down,* (pint.) suavizar
el tono; (mus.) amortiguar el
sonido; modificar la expresión.—*to
t. up,* subir de tono; vigorizar, robustecer; (med.) entonar, tonificar.
—*vi.* corresponder en tono o
matiz.

tongs [tanz], *s. pl.* tenazas, tenacillas;
pinzas, alicates; mordazas.

tongue [tʌn], *s.* lengua; lengüeta; badajo de campana.—*t. twister,* trabalenguas.

tonic [tánik], *a.* y *s.* tónico.

tonight [tunáit], *adv.* y *s.* esta noche;
durante esta noche.

tonnage [tánidž], *s.* tonelaje; (com.)
derechos de tonelaje.

tonsil [tánsil], *s.* amígdala, tonsila.– **—
itis** [-áitis], *s.* (med.) tonsilitis, amigdalitis.

too [tu], *adv.* también, además, asímismo; demasiado.—*(it is) too bad,*
es lástima, es de sentirse.—*t. many,*
demasiados.—*t. much,* demasiado.

took [tuk], *pret.* de TO TAKE.

tool [tul], *s.* herramienta; utensilio o
instrumento.—*pl.* útiles, bártulos,
aperos.

toot [tut], *s.* toque, bocinazo; (f.c.) pitazo.—*I don't give a toot!* (jer.) ¡me da
igual!.—*vt.* y *vi.* sonar.

tooth [tuθ], *s.* diente, muela.—*to have
a sweet t.,* ser muy goloso, gustar de
los dulces.—*t. and nail,* con todo tesón, con empeño.—*t. decay,* caries
dental.– **—ache** [túθeik], *s.* dolor de
muelas o de diente.– **—brush**
[-brʌš], *s.* cepillo de dientes.– **—ed**
[-t], *a.* dentado, serrado, dentellado.
– **—less** [-lis], *a.* desdentado.– **—
paste** [-peist], *s.* pasta de dientes.–
—pick [-pik], *s.* mondadientes, palillo.

top [tap], *s.* cima, cumbre, pico, cúspide, vértice, cabeza, cresta (de una
montaña); ápice, punta, remate,
parte superior; superficie; cabeza
(de una página); tabla (de mesa); coronilla (de la cabeza); copa (de árbol); cielo (de un automóvil, etc.);
auge, apogeo; primer puesto, último grado; tupé; trompo, peonza;
(aut.) capota, fuelle; cofa; tope.—*at*
o *from the t.,* por arriba.—*on t.,* con
buen éxito.—*on t. of,* encima de;
además de.—*t.-flight, t.-notch,* de
primera fila, sobresaliente.—*t. hat,*

(fam.) sombrero de copa, chistera.—*t.-heavy,* más pesado arriba que abajo.—*vti.* [1] desmochar (un árbol, etc.); cubrir, coronar, rematar; llegar a la cima de, coronar; aventajar, exceder.—*to t. off,* rematar, terminar.—*vii.* erguirse, ser eminente; predominar.—*to t. off with,* terminar con.— **—knot** [-nat], *s.* moño.— **—mast** [-mæst], *s.* (mar.) mastelero.— **—most** [-moṇst], *a.* (el) más alto.— **—sail** [-seḷl], *s.* (mar.) gavia.— **—soil** [-sɔil], *s.* capa superficial del suelo.

topaz [tóupæz], *s.* topacio.

topcoat [tápkout], *s.* saco; sobretodo, gabán.

toper [tóupœ(r)], *s.* borrachín.

topic [tápik], *s.* asunto, materia, tema.

topsy-turvy [tápsị tœ́rvị], *adv.* y *a.* trastornado, desbarajustado, patas arriba.

torch [tɔrch], *s.* antorcha.— **—bearer** [-bɛrœr], *s.* hachero.— **—light** [-lait], *s.* luz de antorcha.

tore [tɔr], *pret.* de TO TEAR.

torment [tɔrmént], *vt.* atormentar, torturar; afligir.—*s.* [tɔ́rment], tormento, suplicio, tortura; pena, angustia.

torn [tɔrn], *pp.* de TO TEAR.

tornado [tɔrnéjdou], *s.* tornado, huracán.

torpedo [tɔrpídou], *s.* torpedo.—*vt.* torpedear.

torpid [tórpịd], *a.* torpe; entorpecido; adormecido, aletargado. **—torpor** [tórpɔ(r)], *s.* torpeza; entorpecimiento; adormecimiento; letargo, apatía.

torrent [tárent], *s.* torrente; raudal, agolpamiento.

torrid [tárịd], *a.* tórrido; abrasador, ardiente.

tortoise [tórtịs], *s.* tortuga, galápago; tortuga de tierra, (Am.) jicotea.

tortuous [tórchuʌs], *a.* tortuoso, sinuoso.

torture [tórchụ(r)], *s.* tortura, tormento, suplicio.—*vt.* torturar, dar tormento; tergiversar.— **—r** [-œ(r)], *s.* atormentador, verdugo.

toss [tɔs], *vt.* tirar, lanzar al aire; menear, agitar, sacudir.—*to t. aside,* echar a un lado.—*to t. in a blanket,* mantear.—*to t. in o up the sponge,* darse por vencido; desistir.—*to t. off,* tragar de golpe; echar a un lado,

no hacer caso de; hacer sin esfuerzo ni esmero.—*to t. out,* derrocar (un gobierno, etc.).—*vi.* corcovear; mecerse.—*to t. for, to t. up,* echar o jugar a cara o cruz.—*s.* echada, alcance de una echada.—*t.-up,* cara o cruz; probabilidad igual.

tot [tat], *s.* chiquitín, nene, nena.

total [tóụtal], *a.* y *s.* total.— **—itarian** [toụtæḷịtérịan], *s.* y *a.* totalitario.— **—itarianism** [toụtæḷịtérịanịzm], *s.* totalitarismo.— **—ity** [toụtǽḷịtị], *s.* totalidad.

totter [tátœ(r)], *vi.* tambalear, temblar, vacilar.

touch [tʌch], *vt.* tocar; tentar, palpar, manosear; alcanzar, herir; conmover, enternecer; igualar, aproximarse a; (b.a.) delinear, esbozar; tratar (un asunto); concernir, importar; aludir a, tratar por encima; afectar.—*to t. for,* (fam.) dar un blazo; pedir prestado a; robar a.—*to t. off,* descargar (arma); hacer o acabar de prisa; bosquejar.—*to t. up,* retocar; corregir.—*vi.* tocar(se); estar en contacto.—*to t. and go,* tratar de un asunto ligeramente.—*to t. on* o *upon,* tocar en; tratar ligeramente de; concernir; acercarse a.—*s.* tacto (sentido); toque; dolorcito, punzada; indirecta; prueba, examen; corazonada; pincelada; dejo; (fam.) sablazo.—*t.-and-go,* montado al pelo; precario; ligero de cascos.— **—iness** [táchịnịs], *s.* susceptibilidad, delicadeza.— **—ing** [-iŋ], *prep.* tocante a, en cuanto a, acerca de.—*a.* patético, conmovedor.—*s.* toque; tacto; contacto.— **—wood** [-wụd], *s.* yesca.— **—y** [-i], *a.* quisquilloso, susceptible.

tough [tʌf], *a.* correoso, duro; vigoroso, (fam.) de pelo en pecho; resistente; testarudo, tenaz; flexible y fuerte; (metal) trabajable; (fam.) difícil, penoso; rudo, vulgar.—*t. break, t. luck,* (fam.) mala pata o suerte.—*s.* villano, rufián.— **—en** [táfn], *vt.* y *vi.* hacer(se) correoso; endurecer(se).— **—ness** [-nịs], *s.* tenacidad; endurecimiento; rigidez; flexibilidad; resistencia; rudeza.

toupee [tupé], *s.* tupé, peluca.

tour [tụr], *s.* viaje de turismo, excursión; jira de inspección; vuelta, circuito; turno.—*vt.* viajar por, recorrer.—*vi.* viajar por distracción.-

—ist [túrĭst], *a.* turístico, de turismo.—*s.* turista.– **—ism** [-ĭzm], *s.* turismo.

ournament [túrnạmẹnt], *s.* (dep.) torneo; justa.

ourniquet [túrnĭket], *s.* (cir.) torniquete.

ousle [táu̯zĕl], *vt.* despeinar, enmarañar.

ow [tou̯], *s.* estopa; remolque; lo que va remolcado.—*t. plane,* avión de remolque.—*t. truck,* camión-grúa.—*vt.* remolcar.– **—age** [-ĭdž], *s.* derechos de remolque.– **—boat** [-bout], *s.* remolcador.– **—line** [-lạin], *s.* cable de remolque.– **—rope** [-roup], *s.* cuerda de remolque.

oward(s) [tɔrd(z), tuwɔrd(z)], *prep.* hacia; con, para con; cosa de, alrededor de; tocante a.

owel [tau̯l], *s.* toalla.—*t. rack,* toallero.

ower [táu̯œr], *s.* torre; (mil.) torreón.—*bell t.,* campanario.—*vi.* descollar, sobresalir, destacarse; remontarse.– **—ing** [-ĭŋ], *a.* encumbrado; sobresaliente.—*t. rage,* furia violenta.

owing service [tóu̯ĭŋ], *s.* servicio de grúa.

own [tau̯n], *s.* ciudad; villa, pueblo, aldea; municipio; la ciudad, el pueblo.—*t. council,* concejo municipal.—*t. hall,* casa de ayuntamiento.—*t. planning,* urbanismo.– **—ship** [-šĭp], *s.* distrito municipal.– **—people** [-pipĕl], *spl.* vecinos del pueblo.

oxic [táksĭk], *a.* tóxico.

oy [tɔi̯], *s.* juguete.—*t. soldier,* soldado de juguete.—*a.* de juego; diminuto.—*vi.* jugar, juguetear, retozar.

race [trei̯s], *s.* rastro, huella, pisada, pista; vestigio, señal, indicio; una pizca, un ápice.—*vt.* trazar, delinear; calcar; rastrear, seguir la pista; plantear, indicar; reconstruir, determinar el origen de.

rachea [tréi̯kĭạ], *s.* tráquea.

rack [træk], *s.* vestigio, rastro, pista, huella, pisada; carril; rumbo, ruta; curso (de cometa, etc.); senda, vereda; (f.c.) vía, rieles o carriles; estera o banda (de tractor oruga); atletismo; pista (de atletismo, carreras, etc.).—*off the t.,* descarrilado; desviado, extraviado.—*on the t.,* sobre la pista, en el rastro.—*t. meet,* concurso de carreras y saltos.—*vt.* rastrear.—*to t. down,* descubrir (el origen, escondite, etc. de).

tracking [trǽkĭŋ], *s.* seguimiento.—*t. station,* estación de seguimiento (de vehículos espaciales).

tract [trækt], *s.* trecho; región, comarca, terreno; (anat.) área, canal, sistema; folleto.

traction [trǽkšǫn], *s.* tracción. **—tractor** [trǽktǫ(r)], *s.* tractor.

trade [trei̯d], *s.* comercio; ramo o giro; trueque, trato, negocio; movimiento mercantil; oficio; gremio.—*t. agreement,* tratado comercial (entre naciones); pacto entre patronos y gremios obreros.—*t. name,* razón social; nombre comercial o de fábrica.—*t. school,* escuela industrial o de artes y oficios.—*t. union,* gremio, sindicato.—*t. winds,* vientos alisios.—*vt.* y *vi.* negociar, comerciar, traficar; cambiar.—*to t. in,* negociar en; entregar un objeto (auto, radio, etc.) en pago total o parcial de otro.—*to t. off,* cambalachear.—*to t. on,* aprovecharse de.– **—mark** [-mark], *s.* marca de fábrica, marca registrada.– **—r** [tréi̯dœr], *s.* negociante, comerciante, traficante, mercader; buque mercante.– **—sman** [tréi̯dzmạn], *s.* tendero, mercader; artesano, menestral.

trading [tréi̯dĭŋ], *s.* movimiento comercial; (on the stock exchange) contratación, operaciones.—*t. post,* factoría.

tradition [trạdíšǫn], *s.* tradición.– **—al** [-ạl], *a.* tradicional.

traffic [trǽfĭk], *s.* tráfico.—*t. circle,* glorieta de tráfico.—*t. court,* juzgado de tráfico.—*t. jam,* embotellamiento, tapón de tráfico.—*t. light,* luz de tráfico, semáforo.—*t. sign* o *signal,* señal de tráfico.—*t. ticket,* aviso de multa.—*vti.* y *vii.* [8] traficar. **—trafficked** [trǽfĭkt], *pret.* y *pp.* de TO TRAFFIC.

tragedy [trǽdžĭdĭ], *s.* tragedia. **—tragic(al)** [trǽdžĭk(ạl)], *a.* trágico.

trail [trei̯l], *vt.* arrastrar; remolcar; traer, llevar (barro, etc.) en los pies, zapatos, etc.; asentar (la yerba) con el andar hasta formar vereda; rastrear, seguir la pista; (f.c.) agregar (vagones) a un tren.—*vi.* ir arrastrando; dejar rastro; rezagarse; seguir el rastro; arrastrarse, trepar (una planta).—s. rastro, huella; cola (de vestido, cometa, etc.); sendero, vereda; carretera; indicio.- **—blazer** [-bleịzœr], s. pionero.- **—er** [tréịlœ(r)], s. rastreador; carro o coche remolcado; remolque.—t. truck, camión con remolque.

train [treịn], vt. adiestrar, entrenar; apuntar (un arma); enfocar (un anteojo).—vi. adiestrarse, entrenarse. —s. tren; séquito, comitiva; cabalgata; recua; reguero de pólvora; serie, sucesión, curso (de las ideas, acontecimientos, etc.); cola (de ave, vestido, cometa); (mec.) juego, movimiento.- **—ee** [treịní], s. persona a quien se entrena o adiestra; (mil.) soldado recluta.- **—er** [tréịnœ(r)], s. entrenador; domador.- **—ing** [-ịŋ], s. adiestramiento, entrenamiento, preparación.—a. de entrenamiento, de instrucción.

trait [treịt], s. rasgo, característica, cualidad; golpe, toque.

traitor [tréịtǫ(r)], s. traidor.

trajectory [trạdʒéktǫrị], s. trayectoria.

tram [træm], s. (min.) vagoneta.

tramp [træmp], vt. y vi. pisar con fuerza; caminar; vagabundear.— s. marcha pesada; ruido de pisadas; caminata; vagabundo.- **—le** [træmpl], vt. hollar, pisar, pisotear, conculcar.—vi. pisar fuerte.—to t. on, atropellar, hollar, pisotear.—s. pisoteo; atropello.

trance [træns], s. rapto, arrobamiento; (med.) síncope, catalepsia; estado hipnótico.

tranquil [trǽŋkwịl], a. tranquilo, sereno.- **—lity** [træŋkwílịtị], s. tranquilidad, calma, serenidad, sosiego. - **—ize** [trǽŋkwịlaịz], vt. y vi. tranquilizar(se).- **—izer** [trǽŋkwịlizœr], s. tranquilizante.

transact [trænzǽkt], vt. transar, negociar.- **—ion** [trænzǽkṣǫn], s. transacción, negociación.

transatlantic [trænzætlǽntịk], a. transatlántico.—t. liner, (vapor o buque) transatlántico.

transcontinental [trænzkantịnéntạl], a. transcontinental.

transcribe [trænskráịb], vt. transcribir. **—transcript** [trænskrípt], s. copia, traslado.—**transcription** [trænskrípṣǫn], s. transcripción.

transfer [trǽnsfœr], vti. [1] transferir, pasar, trasladar; transbordar; (for.)

traspasar, ceder.—s. [trǽnsfœ(r)] transferencia; traslado; transbordo (for.) traspaso, cesión.—t. paper, pa pel de calcar.

transform [trænsfórm], vt. y vi. trans formar(se).- **—able** [-ạbl], a. trans formable.- **—ation** [-éịṣǫn], s transformación.- **—er** [-œr], s transformador.

transfusion [trænzfjúʒǫn], s. transfu sión.—blood t., transfusión de sangre.

transient [trǽnṣẹnt], a. pasajero, trán sitorio; que está de paso o de trán sito; transeúnte.—s. transeúnte **—transistor** [trænzístœr], s. transis tor. **—transit** [trǽnsịt], s. tránsito.— in t., en tránsito.—**transition** [trænzíṣǫn], s. tránsito, paso; transi ción. **—transitive** [trǽnsịtịv], a (gram.) transitivo. **—transitory** [trǽnsịtǫrị], a. transitorio; provi sional.

translate [trænsléịt], vt. traducir; tras ladar.—to t. from Spanish to English traducir del español al inglés **—translation** [trænsléịṣǫn], s. tra ducción; traslación. **—translator** [trænsléịtǫ(r)], s. traductor.

transmission [trænsmíṣǫn], s. trans misión. **—transmit** [trænsmít], vt [1] transmitir. **—transmitter** [træns mítœ(r)], s. remitente; transmisor.

transom [trǽnsǫm], s. montante, cla raboya.

transparency [trænspǽrẹnsị], s. trans parencia; (foto.) diapositiva **—transparent** [trænspǽrẹnt], a transparente; (fig.) claro.

transpire [trænspaịr], vi. transpira (fam.) tener lugar.

transplant [trænsplǽnt], v trasplantar.

transport [trænspórt], vt. transpo tar.—s. [trǽnspǫrt], s. transport rapto, paroxismo.- **—ation** [træns portéịṣǫn], s. transporte; boleto, b llete, pasaje.

transpose [trænspoúz], vt. transpo ner; (mus.) transportar.

transverse [trænsvǿers], a. transve sal, transverso.

trap [træp], s. trampa, garlito, re lazo.—mouse t., ratonera.—t. shoo ing, tiro de pichón; tiro al vuelo a u blanco movible.—vti. [1] coger co trampa; atrapar; hacer caer en e garlito.—vii. armar lazos, trampas asechanzas.– **—door** [trǽpdɔr], s. escotillón, trampa; (min.) puerta de ventilación.

rapeze [trapíz], s. trapecio (de gimnasia o circo). **—trapezoid** [trǽpēzɔid], s. trapezoide.

rapper [trǽpœr], s. cazador de alforja.

rappings [trǽpiŋz], s. pl. arreos, aderezos, galas.

rapshooting [trǽpšutiŋ], s. tiro al vuelo.

rash [trǽš], s. basura, desecho; (junk) cachivaches; (nonsense) disparates; (worthless people) gentuza.—t. can, basurero.– **—y** [trǽši], a. despreciable, baladí.

rauma [tráuma], s. trauma.– **—tic** [traumǽtik], a. traumático.

ravel [trǽvɛl], vti. y vii. [2] viajar; recorrer.—s. viaje; excursión; jornada; (mec.) recorrido.—pl. correrías; relación de un viaje.—t. bureau, oficina de turismo.—t.-worn, fatigado por el viaje.—**er** [-œ(r)], s. viajero; viajante.—traveler's check, cheque de viajeros.—traveling salesman, viajante de comercio, agente viajero.

raverse [trævœrs], a. transversal.—t. board, rosa náutica o de los vientos.—adv. de través, en sentido transversal.—s. travesaño.—vt. atravesar.

ray [trei], s. bandeja; (Am.) batea; (foto.) cubeta.

reacherous [tréchœrʌs], a. traidor, traicionero. **—treachery** [tréchœri], s. traición, perfidia, deslealtad.

read [tred], vti. y vii. [10] pisar, hollar; andar, caminar.—s. paso; pisada, huella; escalón; superficie de rodadura (de rueda, neumático, etc.); banda o cadena (de tractor oruga).– **—le** [trédl], s. (mec.) pedal.

reason [trízɔn], s. traición.—high t., lesa patria; lesa majestad.– **—able** [-ʌbl], a. pérfido, desleal, traidor.

reasure [tréžū(r)], s. tesoro.—t.-trove, tesoro hallado.—vt. atesorar; acumular riquezas; guardar como un tesoro.– **—r** [trézûrœ(r)], s. tesorero. **—treasury** [tréžūri], s. tesorería; erario; (com.) caja; (T.) Ministerio de Hacienda o del Tesoro.

reat [trit], vt. y vi. tratar (bien o mal); curar; convidar, invitar.—s. placer; obsequio; convite.– **—ise** [trítis], s. tratado (libro).– **—ment** [-ment], s.

tratamiento, trato; (med.) cura, cuidado.– **—y** [-i], s. tratado, pacto.

treble [trébl], a. triple; (mus.) atiplado.—t. clef, clave de sol.—s. (mus.) tiple.—vt. triplicar.—vi. triplicarse.

tree [tri], s. árbol.—shoe t., horma de zapato.—up a tree, puesto entre la espada y la pared.– **—less** [trílis], a. pelado, sin árboles.- **—top** [-tap], s. copa.

trellis [trélis], s. enrejado; emparrado.

tremble [trémbl], vi. temblar; estremecerse; tiritar; trinar.—s. temblor.

tremendous [triméndʌs], a. tremendo.

tremolo [trémolou], s. (mús.) trémolo.

tremor [trémɔ(r)], s. tremor, temblor, estremecimiento; vibración, trepidación. **—tremulous** [trémyūlʌs], a. trémulo, tembloroso.

trench [trench], vt. y vi. surcar; hacer zanjas o fosos; (mil.) atrincherar.— s. foso, zanja; tajo; presa (de riego); trinchera.—t. coat, trinchera.- **—ant** [trénchant], a. mordaz, punzante; enérgico, bien definido.

trend [trend], vi. dirigirse, tender, inclinarse.—s. dirección, rumbo, curso, tendencia.

trespass [tréspas], vi. (con on o upon) violar, infringir; invadir, rebasar o traspasar los límites; (con against) pecar, faltar.—no trespassing!, ¡prohibida la entrada!—s. transgresión, translimitación; infracción, violación; culpa, pecado.

tress [tres], s. trenza; rizo, bucle.—pl. cabellera.

trestle [trésēl], s. caballete.

trial [trájal], s. prueba, ensayo, tanteo, tentativa; desgracia, aflicción; (for.) proceso, juicio, vista.—a. de prueba; experimental.—by t., al tanteo.—on t., (com.) a prueba; (for.) enjuiciado.—t. and error, método de tanteos.—t. balloon, globo sonda.

triangle [trájæŋgl], s. triángulo. **—triangular** [trajæŋgyūlä(r)], s. triangular.

tribal [trájbal], a. tribal, de tribu. **—tribe** [trajb], s. tribu.

tribulation [tribyūléjšon], s. tribulación.

tribunal [tribjúnal], s. (for.) sala, juzgado; tribunal; foro.

tributary [tríbyūteri], a. y s. tributario; subordinado, subalterno. **—tribute**

[tríbįut], s. tributo; contribución, impuesto; homenaje.

trice [traįs], s. momento, instante.— *in a t.*, en un periquete.

trichina [trįkáįnǎ], s. triquina.

trick [trįk], s. treta; ardid, truco; trampa; juego de manos, chasco; burla; travesura, jugarreta; destreza, maña; marrullería; (naipes) baza; (mar.) guardia del timonel.—*to do the t.*, resolver el problema, dar en el busilis.—*vt.* engañar, embaucar.—*to t. out*, ataviar, componer, asear.—*vi.* trampear, vivir de trampas.— **—ery** [trįkœrį], s. ardid, engaño, astucia.

trickle [trįkl], s. goteo, chorro delgado.—*vi.* gotear, escurrir; pasar gradualmente e irregularmente.— *to t. in*, llegar en pequeñas cantidades; llegar en pequeños grupos.

tricky [trįkį], a. falso, tramposo, marrullero; intrincado.

tricycle [tráįsįkl], s. triciclo.

tried [traįd], a. probado, seguro, fiel.

trifle [tráįfl], s. bagatela, fruslería, friolera, baratija.—*vt.* (con **away**) malgastar (el tiempo, etc.).—*vi.* holgar(se).—*to t. with*, jugar con, burlarse de. **—trifling** [tráįflįŋ], a. frívolo, trivial.

trigger [trígœ(r)], s. gatillo, disparador.—*vt.* poner en movimiento, provocar.

trigonometry [trįgonámetrį], s. trigonometría.

trill [trįl], s. trino, gorjeo, (fam.) gorgorito; (fon.) vibración.—*vt.* vibrar (la r).—*vi.* trinar, gorjear; gotear.

trillion [trílyon], s. (E.U.) billón; (G.B.) trillón.

trilogy [trílodžį], s. trilogía.

trim [trįm], a. ajustado, bien acondicionado; ataviado, acicalado.—*vti.* [1] componer, arreglar, pulir, ajustar, adaptar; (carp.) desbastar, acepillar; (agr.) podar; recortar (cabellos, barba); (cost.) adornar, guarnecer, ribetear; (fam.) reprender, zurrar; (fam.) derrotar; sacar ventaja a.—*to t. off*, recortar; atusar.—*to t. up*, adornar, hermosear, componer.—*vii.* vacilar, titubear; nadar entre dos aguas.—*s.* atavío, adorno; traje, vestido; estilo; condición, estado; (cost.) franja, ribete, guarnición; (arq.) molduras.– **—ming** [trímįŋ], s. (cost.) guarnición, cenefa; ajuste,

arreglo; (agr.) poda; recorte (de pelo, barba); (fam.) derrota.

trinity [trínįtį], s.—*the (Holy) Trinity*, l (Santísima) Trinidad.

trinket [trįŋkįt], s. baratija, chuchería.

trio [tríou], s. terno; (mus.) trío.

trip [trip], vti. [1] hacer caer a uno (cor una zancadilla, hacer tropezar; ar mar un lazo o zancadilla; coger uno en falta; (mec.) disparar, soltar desatar; (mar.) zarpar, levar an clas.—*vii.* tropezar; equivocarse, co meter un desliz o descuido; (mar. zarpar; correr, ir aprisa.—*s.* viaj corto, excursión; tropiezo, traspiés paso falso, desliz; zancadilla; paso movimiento ágil.

tripe [traįp], s. (coc.) callos, mon dongo; (fam.) cosa sin valor, nece dades.

triple [trípl], a. triple.—*vt.* triplicar **—tripod** [tráįpad], s. trípode.

trite [traįt], a. trillado, gastado; trivial vulgar.– **—ness** [tráįtnįs], s. vulgari dad, trivialidad.

triumph [tráįʌmf], s. triunfo, victo ria.—*vi.* triunfar; vencer, salir victo rioso.– **—al** [traįʌmfál], a. triunfal.- **—ant** [traįʌmfant], a. triunfante.

trivia [trívįa], spl. bagatelas, triviali dades.

trivial [trívįal], a. trivial, frívolo, fútil.

trod [trad], *pret.* y *pp.* de TO TREAD **—trodden** [trádn], *pp.* de TO TREAD.

troll [troul], vt. y vi. pescar a la cacea.

trolley [trálį], s. (elec.) polea de trole coche o tranvía de trole.—*t. car*, (co che de) tranvía.

trombone [trámboun], s. (mus. trombón.

troop [trup], s. tropa; cuadrilla, grupo compañía (de actores); (mil.) escua drón de caballería.—*vi.* apiñarse, i en tropel.– **—er** [trúpœr], s. soldade de caballería; agente (de policía).

trophy [tróufį], s. trofeo; recuerdo.

tropic [trápįk], s. trópico.—*pl.* zon tropical.– **—al** [-al], a. tropical.

trot [trat], vti. [1] hacer trotar.—*t. ou* (fam.) sacar a exhibir.—*vii.* trotar, i al trote.—*s.* trote.—*at a t.*, al trote.

troubadour [trúbador], s. trovador.

trouble [trʌbl], vt. (per)turbar, distur bar; enturbiar; enfadar, hostigar atribular, preocupar; molestar, im portunar.—*to t. oneself*, tomarse la molestia; inquietarse.—*vi.* incomo darse, darse molestia, apurarse.—*s* perturbación; disturbio, inquietud; enfermedad, mal; (mec.) avería; cuita, pena, congoja; disgusto, desavenencia; dificultad, molestia; impertinencia, engorro.—*t. spot,* lugar de conflicto.—*to be in t.,* hallarse en dificultades.- **—maker** [-mejkœ(r)], *s.* perturbador, agitador.- **—shooter** [-šútœr], *s.* localizador de averías; componedor.- **—some** [-sʌm], *a.* penoso, pesado; importuno; dificultoso, fastidioso, molesto; pendenciero.

ough [trɔf], *s.* artesa; comedero (para animales); abrevadero, bebedero; seno de dos olas; canal (artificial); canalón (del tejado); (meteor.) mínimo de presión.

oupe [trup], *s.* compañía de actores o de circo.

ousers [tráuzœrz], *s. pl.* pantalones.

ousseau [trúsou], *s.* ajuar de novia.

out [traut], *s.* trucha.

owel [tráuel], *s.* (alb.) llana, paleta.

uancy [trúansi], *s.* ausencia sin permiso de la escuela o del deber.- **—truant** [trúant], *s.* novillero, que se ausenta de la escuela.—*to play t.,* hacer novillos, capear la escuela.

uce [trus], *s.* (mil.) tregua.

uck [trʌk], *vt. y vi.* acarrear.—*s.* camión; carretón; carretilla de mano; carreta; efectos para vender o trocar; hortalizas para el mercado; (fam.) cosas sin valor.—*t. driver,* camionista.—*t. garden,* huerto de hortalizas.

uculent [trákjülent], *a.* truculento.

udge [trʌdž], *vi.* caminar, ir a pie.—*to t. along,* marchar con pena y trabajo.

ue [tru], *a.* verdadero, cierto, real, efectivo; ingenuo, sincero; exacto; justo, a plomo, a nivel, alineado, bien arreglado; legítimo, genuino; fiel, leal.—*t. copy,* copia fiel.—*t.-hearted,* fiel, leal, sincero.—*t. to life,* verosímil; al natural.- **—love** [-lʌv], *s.* fiel amante; (bot.) hierba de París.—*t. knot,* lazo de amor.

uffle [tráfl], *s.* trufa.

uism [trújzm], *s.* perogrullada.- **—truly** [trúli], *adv.* verdaderamente, en verdad; realmente, exactamente; sinceramente, de buena fe.—*yours t.,* de Vd. atto. y S.S., su seguro servidor; (fam.) este cura (yo).

ump [trʌmp], *s.* triunfo (naipes); (fam.) real mozo, excelente persona; (poét.) trompeta; trompetazo.—*vt.* (naipes) matar con triunfo; engañar.—*to t. up,* forjar; inventar.—*vi.* (naipes) jugar un triunfo, matar.

trumpet [trámpit], *s.* (mus.) trompa, trompeta, clarín (instrumento y músico); bocina, megáfono.—*vi.* trompetear.—*vt.* (fig.) divulgar.

truncate [tráŋkejt], *vt.* truncar.

truncheon [tránchon], *s.* porra, tranca.

trunk [trʌŋk], *s.* tronco; baúl; trompa de elefante.—*pl.* calzones cortos para deportes.—*t. line,* línea principal (f.c., elec., telf., etc.).—*a.* troncal.

trust [trʌst], *s.* confianza, fe; creencia; (com.) crédito; (for.) fideicomiso, cargo, depósito; (com.) combinación monopolista.—*in t.,* en confianza; en depósito.—*t. company,* banco fideicomisario, banco de depósitos.—*vt. y vi.* confiar (en), contar con; tener confianza en o hacer confianza de; encargar y fiar; fiarse (de); creer, dar crédito a; vender al fiado.- **—ee** [trʌstí], *s.* síndico, fideicomisario, fiduciario, depositario; miembro de un patronato.- **—eeship** [trʌstíšip], *s.* cargo de administrador, fideicomisario.- **—ful** [trástful], *a.* confiado.- **—worthy** [-wœrði], *a.* fiable, confiable; fidedigno.- **—y** [-i], *a.* fiel; íntegro, confiable; firme, seguro.—*s.* presidiario fidedigno.

truth [truθ], *s.* verdad, realidad; veracidad; exactitud.- **—ful** [trúθful], *a.* verídico; verdadero, exacto.- **—fulness** [-fulnis], *s.* veracidad; exactitud; realismo.

try [traj], *vti.* [7] probar, ensayar; procurar, tratar de, intentar; exasperar, cansar; comprobar, (for.) procesar; ver (una causa); (metal.) purificar, refinar.—*to t. on,* probarse (ropa).—*to t. one's hand,* hacer uno la prueba.—*to t. out,* probar, someter a prueba.—*vii.* probar, ensayar; procurar, hacer lo posible; (mar.) capear.—*s.* prueba, ensayo.- **—ing** [trájiŋ], *a.* de prueba; molesto, exasperador, irritante; angustioso, penoso.

tryst [trajst], *s.* cita; lugar de cita.

tub [tʌb], *s.* cuba; batea; tina; cubeta; bañera; (fam.) acto de bañarse.

tube [tjub], *s.* tubo; cámara de llanta o

neumático; (rad.) válvula, bombillo, tubo.

tuber [tjúbœ(r)], s. (bot.) tubérculo; (anat.) tubérculo, hinchazón, prominencia.– **—cle** [-kl], s. tubérculo.– **—cular** [tjubœrkyūlǎ(r)], a. tuberculoso, tísico.– **—culosis** [tjubœrkyūlóųsįs], s. tuberculosis.

tubing [tjúbįŋ], s. tubería. **—tubular** [tjúbyūlǎ(r)], a. tubular.

tuck [tʌk], s. (cost.) alforza.—vt. alforzar; arropar; doblar, aprestar.—to t. up, arremangar.– **—er** [tʌ́kœ(r)], s. (cost.) escote.—vt. (E.U., fam.) (a menudo con **out**) cansar, fatigar.

Tuesday [tjúzdį], s. martes.

tuft [tʌft], s. penacho, cresta; borla; manojo, ramillete; tupé, moño; macizo (de plantas).

tug [tʌg], vti. [1] tirar de, arrastrar; remolcar.—vii. esforzarse, tirar con fuerza.—s. tirón, estirón; (mar.) remolcador.—t. of war, lucha de la cuerda.– **—boat** [-boųt], s. remolcador.

tuition [tjuíšǫn], s. enseñanza; precio de la enseñanza.

tulip [tjúlįp], s. tulipán.

tulle [tul], s. tul.

tumble [tʌ́mbl], vi. caer, dar en tierra.—to t. down, desplomarse; voltear, rodar; dar saltos, brincar; revolcarse; (fam.) comprender, caer en ello.—to t. out, (fam.) levantarse.— t.-down, destartalado, desvenciado.—vt. revolver; tirar, arrojar.— to t. over o about, tumbar, derribar; volcar; desarreglar, trastornar; ajar o arrugar (la ropa); cazar al vuelo; pulir por fricción.—s. caída, tumbo; vuelco, voltereta; desorden, confusión.– **—r** [tʌ́mblœ(r)], s. vaso (de mesa); cubilete; acróbata, saltimbanqui, titiritero.

tumor [tjúmǫ(r)], s. tumor.

tumult [tjúmʌlt], s. tumulto, escándalo; agitación.– **—uous** [tjumálchųʌs], a. tumultuoso, alborotado.

tun [tʌn], s. tonel, cuba.

tuna [túnǎ], s. (ict.) atún; (bot.) tuna; nopal.—t. fish, atún.

tune [tjun], s. (mús.) aire, tonada, son, melodía; afinación, concordancia, armonía.—in t., templado, afinado.—out of t., destemplado, desafinado, desentonado.—to the t. of, al son de, tocando o entonando.—

vt. templar, afinar, entonar; ajusta adaptar; (rad.) sintonizar.—to t. u (mec.) poner a punto el motor.—v armonizar, modular.—to t. in, (rad. sintonizar.– **—r** [tjúnœ(r)], s. af nador, templador; (rad.) sintoni zador.

tungsten [tʌ́ŋstęn], s. (quím.) tungs teno.

tunic [tjúnįk], s. túnica; (mil.) casaca guerrera.

tuning [tjúnįŋ], s. (mús.) acto de tem plar, afinación; (rad.) sintoniza ción.—t. fork, (mús.) diapasón.

tunnel [tʌ́nęl], s. túnel; (min.) soca vón.—vti. y vii. [2] horadar; cons truir o abrir un túnel.

tunny [tʌ́nį], s. atún.—striped t bonito.

turban [tœ́rbąn], s. turbante.

turbid [tœ́rbįd], a. turbio, espeso; tur bulento.

turbine [tœ́rbįn], s. turbina.

tureen [turín], s. sopera, salsera.

turf [tœrf], s. césped; terrón (con cés ped); carreras de caballos, hipé dromo.

Turk [tœrk], s. turco.

turkey [tœ́rkį], s. pavo.

Turkish [tœ́rkįš], a. turco.—T. towe toalla rusa, toalla de felpa gruesa.– s. idioma turco.

turmoil [tœ́rmɔįl], s. disturbio, tu multo, alboroto.

turn [tœrn], vt. voltear, hacer gira transformar; (mec.) tornear; inve tir (posición); revolver (en l mente); doblar (una esquina etc.).—to t. against, predisponer e contra de; causar aversión a o con tra.—to t. around, voltear, dar vuelt a.—to t. aside, desviar, hacer a u lado.—to t. away, despedir, echa desviar.—to t. back, devolver, rest tuir; volver atrás.—to t. down, ple gar, doblar; poner boca abajo; baja disminuir (intensidad de una llama etc.); (fam.) abandonar; rechaza rehusar.—to t. from, desviar o aleja de.—to t. in, replegar; doblar haci adentro; entregar.—to t. into, cor vertir en, cambiar en.—to t. off, cor tar (el agua, el vapor, etc.); cerrar (l llave del agua, etc.); desconectar apagar (la luz, el radio, etc.); (mec tornear.—to t. on, abrir (la llave de agua, etc.); dar (vapor, etc.); conec tar o encender (la luz, el radio, etc. establecer el servicio (de electric dad, etc.).—*to t. out*, echar, expeler, arrojar; sacar hacia afuera; apagar (la luz, etc.); producir; volver al revés; doblar, torcer; echar al campo (los animales).—*to t. over*, transferir, pasar, trasladar; invertir, volcar; revolver.—*to t. up*, voltear; levantar; cavar (el suelo); arremangar; subir (el cuello).—*vi.* girar, rodar, voltear; torcer, seguir otra dirección; voltearse; convertirse en; ponerse (pálido, colorado, etc.); mudar (de posición, opinión, etc.).—*my head turns (round)*, se me va la cabeza.—*to t. about* o *around*, volverse; voltearse.—*to t. against*, volverse contra.—*to t. aside*, desviarse.—*to t. back*, retroceder; volverse.—*to t. down a street*, torcer por una calle.— *to t. in*, guarecerse; entrar; llegar a casa; (fam.) irse a la cama.—*to t. into*, entrar en; transformarse en.— *to t. off*, torcer, desviarse.—*to t. on*, depender de; volverse contra; acometer a.—*to t. out*, resultar; asistir; acudir; estar vuelto hacia afuera; (fam.) salir de casa; levantarse.—*to t. over*, revolverse, dar vueltas; volcarse (un auto, etc.).—*to t. short*, dar media vuelta.—*to t. to*, recurrir o acudir a; dirigirse hacia o a; convertirse en; redundar en.—*to t. up*, acontecer; aparecer; tirar hacia arriba (la nariz).—*to t. upon*, estribar, depender de; recaer sobre.—*s.* vuelta, giro; rodeo; recodo; turno; tanda; lance; ocasión; cambio, mudanza; torcedura; curso, dirección; fase, aspecto, cariz; proceder, procedimiento; partida o pasada (buena o mala) hecha a alguno; inclinación, propensión; giro de frase; vuelta, paseo corto; (teat.) pieza corta; (dep.) contienda, partido; (com.) transacción.—*a friendly t.*, un favor.—*at every t.*, a cada instante.—*to take another t.*, cambiar de aspecto, tomar otro sesgo o cariz.—*to take turns*, turnarse, alternar.—*t. signal*, (aut.) intermitente.

turnbuckle [tǽrnbʌkl], *s.* (mec.) torniquete. —**turncoat** [tǽrnkout], *s.* desertor, renegado, tránsfuga. —**turner** [tǽrnœ(r)], *s.* (mec.) tornero.

turnip [tǽrnip], *s.* nabo.

turnover [tǽrnouvœ(r)], *a.* doblado o vuelto hacia abajo.—*s.* vuelco, voltereta; (com.) movimiento de mercancías; ciclo de compra y venta;

cambio (de personal); reorganización; empleo parcial turnado.

turnpike [tǽrnpaik], *s.* autopista de peaje.

turnstile [tǽrnstail], *s.* torniquete (en una entrada, etc.). —**turntable** [tǽrnteibl], *s.* placa giratoria; platillo del gramófono.

turpentine [tǽrpentain], *s.* trementina; aguarrás.—*oil of t.*, aguarrás.

turpitude [tǽrpityud], *s.* torpeza, infamia, vileza.

turquoise [tǽrkwɔiz], *s.* (min.) turquesa.

turret [tǽrit], *s.* torre(cilla); (fort.) roqueta; (mar. y aer.) torre blindada.

turtle [tǽrtl], *s.* tortuga de mar, carey. — **dove** [-dʌv], *s.* tórtola.

tusk [tʌsk], *s.* colmillo (de elefante, jabalí, etc.).

tussle [tásl], *s.* lucha, agarrada.—*vi.* forcejear, tener una agarrada.

tutor [tiútǝ(r)], *s.* tutor, ayo, preceptor; (for.) curador.—*vt.* enseñar, instruir.— **ing** [-iŋ], *s.* instrucción.

tuxedo [tʌksídou], *s.* esmoquin, smoking.

TV [tiví], *abrev.* (television) tele, TV.

twang [twæŋ], *s.* tañido; timbre nasal.

tweed [twid], *s.* paño de lana de dos colores.—*a.* hecho de este paño.

tweet [twit], *s.* pío.—*vi.* piar.— **er** [twítœr], *s.* altavoz para audiofrequencias elevadas.

tweezers [twízœrz], *s. pl.* tenacillas, pinzas.

twelve [twelv], *a.* y *s.* doce. —**twelfth** [twelfθ], *a.* y *s.* duodécimo, doceavo.

twenty [twénti], *a.* y *s.* veinte.—*t.-one*, (number and game) veintiuno. —**twentieth** [twéntiiθ], *a.* y *s.* vegésimo.

twice [twais], *adv.* dos veces; al doble.

twiddle [twidel], *vt.* revolver ociosamente, juguetear con.

twig [twig], *s.* (bot.) ramita, vástago; varilla.

twilight [twáilait], *s.* crepúsculo.—*by t.*, entre dos luces.—*a.* oscuro, sombrío.

twin [twin], *s.* y *a.* gemelo.

twine [twain], *vt.* retorcer; enroscar.— *vi.* enroscarse; ensortijarse; caracolear.—*to t. about*, abrazar.—*s.* cuerda, cordel.

twinge [twindž], *vt.* y *vi.* causar o sentir un dolor agudo; atormentar; sufrir.—s. dolor agudo, punzada; re-mordimiento.

twinkle [twíŋkl], vt. y vi. destellar, (hacer) centellear, rutilar, titilar; (hacer) parpadear, pestañear.—s. destello, centelleo; pestañeo; guiño, guiñada; momento, instante.

twirl [twœrl], vt. y vi. (hacer) girar.—s. rotación, vuelta; rasgueo.

twist [twist], vt. (re)torcer, enroscar, entretejer, enrollar; doblar, doblegar; trenzar; ceñir.—vi. enroscarse, torcerse, envolverse; virar; ensortijarse; serpentear, caracolear.—s. torsión, torcedura; tirón, sacudida; cordoncillo; peculiaridad; contorsión, quiebro; rosca de pan, pan retorcido; efecto dado a la pelota (en baseball).— **—er** [-œr], s. (fam.) tornado.

twit [twit], vt.—to t. someone about, tomarle el pelo a alguien por.

twitch [twich], vt. tirar o sacudir bruscamente.—vi. crisparse.—s. tirón, sacudida; contracción espasmódica.— **—ing** [twíchiŋ], s. tic nervioso.

twitter [twítœ(r)], vi. gorjear (pájaros); temblar de agitación.—s. gorjeo; inquietud.

two [tu], a. y pron. dos.—s. dos.—to put t. and t. together, atar cabos, sacar la conclusión evidente.—t.-bit, (fam.) de tres al cuarto, de chicha y nabo, de poca monta.—t. bits, veinticinco centavos; cantidad insignificante. —t.-car garage, garaje de dos plazas.—t.-cylinder, de dos cilindros.— t.-edged, de dos filos.—t. faced, (fam.) falso, doble.—t. hundred, doscientos.—t. hundred one,

doscientos uno.—t. hundredth, du centésimo.—t.-time, (jer.) engaña en amor, ser infiel a.— **—fol** [-fould], a. doble; duplicado; de do: clases o aspectos.—adv. dos veces duplicadamente, al doble.— **—some** [-sʌm], s. pareja; pareja de jugado res; juego de dos.

tycoon [taikún], s. (E.U., fam.) mag nate industrial.

type [taip], s. tipo.—vt. y vi. mecano grafiar.— **—face** [-feis], s. tipo de le tra.— **—script** [-skript], s. materia escrito a máquina.— **—sette** [-setœr], s. cajista; máquina de com poner.— **—write** [-rait], vti. y vii. [10 mecanografiar.— **—writer** [táip raitœ(r)], s. máquina de escribir.—t ribbon, cinta para máquinas de es cribir.— **—writing** [-raitiŋ], s. meca nografía; trabajo de mecanógrafo.- **—written** [táipritn], pp. de TO TYPE WRITE.—a. mecanografiado.- **wrote** [táiprout], pret. de TO TYPE WRITE.

typhoid [táifɔid], a. (med.) tifoideo.- t. fever, fiebre tifoidea.

typhoon [taifún], s. tifón.

typhus [táifʌs], s. (med.) tifus, (Am. tifo.

typical [típikal], a. típico.— **—typify** [típifai], vti. [7] representar, ejem plificar, simbolizar.

typist [táipist], s. mecanógrafo.

typographical [taipográfikal], a. tipo gráfico.—t. error, error de imprenta

tyrannical [tiránikal], a. tiránico, ti rano.— **—tyranny** [tírani], s. tiranía **—tyrant** [táirant], s. tirano.

tyro [taíro], s. tirón, novicio.

U

ubiquitous [yubíkwitŭs], a. ubicuo.
udder [ʌ́dœ(r)], s. ubre.
UFO [yúefóu], abrev. (**Unidentified Flying Object**) OVNI (objeto volador no identificado).
ugliness [ʌ́gliŋis], s. fealdad; (fam.) malhumor. **—ugly** [ʌ́gli], a. feo; (fam.) malhumorado.
ulcer [ʌ́lsœ(r)], s. úlcera, llaga.- **—ate** [-eit], vt. y vi. ulcerar(se).

ulterior [ʌltírio(r)], a. ulterior. **—ulti mate** [ʌ́ltimit], a. último.
ultrasonic [ʌltrasánik], a. ultrasónico **—ultraviolet** [ʌltravájolit], a. ultra violeta.
umbilical [ʌmbílikal], a.—u. cord, cor dón umbilical.
umbrella [ʌmbrélặ], s. paraguas; (mil. sombrilla protectora.
umpire [ámpair], s. árbitro; arbitra dor.—vt. y vi. arbitrar.

umpteen [ʌ́mptin], *a.* (fam.) tropecientos.

UN [yúén], *abrev.* (**United Nations**) ONÚ.

unable [ʌnéjbl], *a.* inhábil, incapaz, impotente; imposibilitado.—*to be u.*, no poder, serle a uno imposible.

unabridged [ʌnạbrídẓd], *a.* íntegro, sin abreviar.

unaccustomed [ʌnạkástọmd], *a.* desacostumbrado; inhabituado.

unadulterated [ʌnạdʌ́ltœreịtịd], *a.* genuino, puro, sin mezcla.

unaffected [ʌnạféktịd], *a.* inafectado; franco, natural; impasible.

unanimity [yunạnímịtị], *s.* unanimidad. —**unanimous** [yụnǽnịmʌs], *a.* unanime.

unanswerable [ʌnǽnsœrạbl], *a.* incontestable, incontrovertible.

unarmed [ʌnármd], *a.* desarmado, indefenso, inerme.

unassuming [ʌnạsjúmịŋ], *a.* modesto.

unattainable [ʌnạtéjnạbl], *a.* inasequible, irrealizable.

unattractive [ʌnạtrǽktịv], *a.* desagradable, poco atractivo.

unauthorized [ʌnɔ́θ̣θọraịzd], *a.* sin autorización.

unavailable [ʌnạvéịlạbl], *a.* inasequible. —**unavailing** [ʌnạvéịlịŋ], *a.* inútil, vano, infructuoso.

unavoidable [ʌnạvóịdạbl], *a.* inevitable, ineludible.

unaware [ʌnạwér], *a.* ignorante o inconsciente de, ajeno a.

unbalanced [ʌnbǽlạnst], *a.* desequilibrado; (fam.) chiflado; (com.) no balanceado.

unbearable [ʌnbérạbl], *a.* intolerable, insufrible.

unbecoming [ʌnbịkámịŋ], *a.* indecoroso; impropio, indigno; que sienta mal (vestido, etc.).

unbelievable [ʌnbẹlívạbĕl], *a.* increíble.

unbending [ʌnbéndịŋ], *a.* inflexible.

unbias(s)ed [ʌnbájạst], *a.* imparcial.

unbound [ʌnbáụnd], *a.* no encuadernado, en rústica; suelto, desatado.

unbreakable [ʌnbréịkạbl], *a.* irrompible; impenetrable. —**unbroken** [ʌnbróụkṇn], *a.* intacto, entero; inviolado; continuo; invicto; indómito.

unbutton [ʌnbátṇn], *vt.* desabotonar, desabrochar.

uncalled-for [ʌnkɔ́ldfɔr], *a.* innecesario, no justificado; insolente.

uncanny [ʌnkǽnị], *a.* misterioso, pavoroso; espectral; maravilloso.

unceasing [ʌnsísịŋ], *a.* incesante.— **—ly** [-lị], *adv.* sin cesar.

uncertain [ʌnsÉrtạn], *a.* incierto; perplejo, indeciso.— **—ty** [-tị], *s.* incertidumbre; (lo) incierto; irresolución; inseguridad.

unchangeable [ʌnchéịndẓạbl], *a.* inalterable, inmutable; igual. —**unchanged** [ʌnchéịndẓd], *a.* inalterado.

uncharitable [ʌnchǽrịtạbl], *a.* no caritativo, duro.

unchecked [ʌnchékt], *a.* desenfrenado, sin control.

uncivil [ʌnsívịl], *a.* incivil, descortés, grosero.— **—ized** [-aịzd], *a.* bárbaro, salvaje.

unclaimed [ʌnkleịmd], *a.* sin reclamar; (mail) rechazado, sobrante.

unclassifiable [ʌnklǽsịfaịạbl], *a.* inclasificable.

uncle [ʌ́ŋkl], *s.* tío.

unclean [ʌnklín], *a.* sucio, desaseado, impuro; obsceno.

uncoil [ʌnkóịl], *vt.* desenrollar.

uncollectable [ʌnkọléktạbl], *a.* incobrable.

uncomfortable [ʌnkámfọrtạbl], *a.* incómodo, molesto; intranquilo; indispuesto, con malestar.

uncommon [ʌnkámọn], *a.* poco común, raro, infrecuente.

unconcern [ʌnkọnsœ́rn], *s.* indiferencia, frialdad.

unconcerned [ʌnkọnsœ́rnd], *s.* despreocupado, indiferente.

unconditional [ʌnkọndíṣọnạl], *a.* absoluto, incondicional; a discreción.

uncongenial [ʌnkọndžínịạl], *a.* antipático, incompatible.

unconnected [ʌnkọnéktịd], *a.* inconexo.

unconquerable [ʌnkáŋkœrạbl], *a.* invencible, insuperable, inconquistable.

unconscionable [ʌnkanṣọnạbĕl], *a.* inescrupuloso; desrazonable, excesivo.

unconscious [ʌnkánṣʌs], *a.* inconsciente; privado, sin conocimiento; que ignora; desconocido, involuntario.—*the u.*, (psic.) lo inconsciente.— **—ness** [-nịs], *s.* insensibilidad; inconsciencia.

unconstitutional [ʌnkanstịtịúṣọnạl], *a.*

inconstitucional.– **—ity** [ʌnkans-tițiușọnǽliți], s. inconstitucionalidad.

unconventional [ʌnkọnvénšọnạl], a. despreocupado, informal, libre.

uncork [ʌnkɔ́rk], vt. descorchar, destapar.

uncouth [ʌnkúθ], a. tosco, zafio, grosero, desgarbado, torpe, descorchar.

uncover [ʌnkávœ(r)], vt. destapar, descubrir; desabrigar; poner al descubierto.—vi. descubrirse, desabrigarse.

unction [ʌ́ŋkšọn], s. unción. **—unctuous** [ʌ́ŋkchuʌs], a. untuoso, craso; zalamero.

uncultivated [ʌnkʌ́ltịveițịd], a. yermo, inculto; rústico, grosero.

uncultured [ʌnkʌ́lchụrd], a. inculto, ignorante.

uncut [ʌnkʌ́t], a. sin cortar; sin tallar, en bruto (gemas).

undamaged [ʌndǽmịdẑd], a. ileso, indemne.

undaunted [ʌndɔ́ntịd], a. denodado, impávido, intrépido.

undecided [ʌndịsáịdịd], a. indeciso; irresoluto.

undeniable [ʌndịnáịạbl], a. innegable.

under [ʌ́ndœ(r)], a. inferior, de abajo.—u.-secretary, subsecretario. —adv. debajo; más abajo; menos.— prep. debajo de, bajo; so; menos de o que; a; en; en tiempo de, en la época de; conforme a, según.—to be u. an obligation, deber favores, estar obligado.—u. a cloud, en aprietos.—u. arms, bajo las armas.—u. color of, so color de.—u. consideration, en consideración.—u. contract, bajo contrato; conforme al contrato.—u. cover, al abrigo, a cubierto.—u. fire, en combate; bajo el fuego del enemigo; (fig.) atacado, criticado, en aprietos.—u. steam, al vapor.—u. way, en camino, en marcha; andando; principiando.– **—age** [-eịdẑ], a. menor de edad.– **—brush** [-brʌš], s. maleza, broza.– **—clothes** [-klouðz], **—clothing** [-klouðịŋ], s. ropa interior. – **—cover** [-kʌvœr], a. secreto.– **—developed** [-devélopt], a. subdesarrollado.– **—dog** [-dɔg], s. el que pierde; el más débil.—the underdogs, los de abajo.– **—done** [-dʌn], a. (coc.) a medio asar, soasado.– **—estimate** [-éstịmeịt], vt. menospreciar, subestimar.– **—fed** [-féd], a. malnutrido.– **—go** [-góu], vti. [10] sufrir, padecer; aguantar, sobrellevar; pa-

sar por, ser sometido a; arrostrar.– **—gone** [-gɔn], pp. de TO UNDERGO.– **—graduate** [-grǽdẑuịt], s. alumno no graduado de universidad.—a. no graduado; (course) para el bachillerato.– **—ground** [-graund], a. subterráneo; secreto.—u. movement, organización clandestina de resistencia política o patriótica.—adv. bajo tierra; ocultamente.– **—growth** [-grouθ], s. maleza.– **—handed** [-hǽndịd], a. disimulado, clandestino.– **—line** [-láịn], vt. subrayar.– **—lying** [-láịịŋ], a. subyacente; fundamental.– **—mine** [-máịn], vt. socavar, minar, zapar; debilitar, arruinar subrepticiamente. – **—neath** [-níθ], adv. debajo.—prep. debajo de, bajo.– **—nourished** [-nœrịšt], a. desnutrido.– **—paid** [-péịd], pret. y pp. de TO UNDERPAY.– **—pass** [-pǽs], s. paso inferior. **—underpay** [ʌndœrpéị], vti. [10] pagar insuficientemente.– **—privileged** [-prívịledẑd], a. desheredado, desamparado.– **—rate** [-réịt], vt. menospreciar, desestimar, rebajar. **—undersell** [-sél], vti. [10] malbaratar; vender a menor precio que.– **—shirt** [-šœrt], s. camiseta.– **—sign** [-sáịn], vt. su(b)scribir.—the undersigned, el que firma, el infrascrito, el suscrito, el abajo firmado.– **—sized** [-sáịzd], a. de tamaño o estatura menor que lo normal.– **—skirt** [-skœrt], s. enagua(s); refajo, sayuela.– **—sold** [-sóụld], pret. y pp. de TO UNDERSELL.

understand [ʌndœrstǽnd], vti. y vii. [10] entender, comprender; saber, ser sabedor, hacerse cargo, tener conocimiento de, tener entendido (que); sobrentender.– **—able** [-ạbl], a. comprensible.– **—ing** [-ịŋ], s. entendimiento, inteligencia; modo de ver o entender; comprensión; acuerdo, arreglo; armonía, mutua comprensión.—a. entendedor, inteligente, comprensivo. **—understood** [ʌndœrstúd], pret. y pp. de TO UNDERSTAND.

understudy [ʌndœrstʌ́dị], s. (teat.) actor suplente.

undertake [ʌndœrtéịk], vti. y vii. [10] emprender, acometer, intentar; comprometerse a, responder de, encargarse de. **—undertaken** [ʌndœrtéịkn], pp. de TO UNDERTAKE.– **—r** [ʌndœrtéịkœ(r)], s. empresario de pompas fúnebres; contratista. **—un-**

dertaking [ʌndœrtéikiŋ], *s.* empresa; contratación; empresa funeraria; (for.) compromiso, promesa; empeño o garantía. **—undertook** [ʌndœrtúk], *pret.* de TO UNDERTAKE.

undertow [ándœrtou], *s.* resaca.

undervalue [ʌndœrvǽlyu], *vt.* desestimar, menospreciar, despreciar; tasar en menos del valor real.

underwear [ándœrwer], *s.* ropa interior.

underwent [ʌndœrwént], *pret.* de TO UNDERGO.

underworld [ándœrwœrld], *s.* hampa, vida del vicio, bajos fondos de la sociedad; el mundo terrenal; antípodas; averno, infierno.

underwriter [ándœrwraitœr], *s.* asegurador; compañía aseguradora.

undeserved [ʌndizœrvd], *a.* inmerecido. **—undeserving** [ʌndizœrviŋ], *a.* indigno.

undesirable [ʌndizáirabl], *a.* indeseable; inconveniente, desventajoso; pernicioso.

undetermined [ʌnditœrmind], *a.* indeterminado.

undeveloped [ʌndivélopt], *a.* no desarrollado, rudimentario; inexplotado.

undid [ʌndíd], *pret.* de TO UNDO.

undignified [ʌndígnifaid], *a.* indecoroso, falto de dignidad.

undisciplined [ʌndísiplind], *a.* indisciplinado; falto de corrección; sin instrucción.

undisturbed [ʌndistœrbd], *a.* imperturbable, impasible; intacto, sin cambio.

undo [ʌndú], *vti.* [10] anular, desvirtuar, contrarrestar; reparar (un daño); arruinar, perder; causar pesadumbre a; deshacer; desatar; (mec.) desmontar. **—undone** [ʌndán], *pp.* de TO UNDO.—*a.* sin hacer; sin terminar; deshecho.—*to be u.,* estar perdido o arruinado.—*to come u.,* deshacerse, desatarse.—*to leave nothing u.,* no dejar nada por hacer.

undoubtedly [ʌndáutidli], *adv.* indudablemente.

undress [ʌndrés], *vt.* desnudar, desvestir; (cir.) desvendar.—*vi.* desnudarse.—*s.* paños menores; ropa de casa.

undue [ʌndjú], *a.* indebido, desmedido; ilícito, injusto; (com.) por vencer.

undulate [ándjuleit], *vi.* ondular, on-

dear, fluctuar.—*vt.* hacer ondear.—*a.* [ándjulit], ondeado, ondulado.

unduly [ʌndjúli], *adv.* indebidamente; irregularmente, ilícitamente.

undying [ʌndáiiŋ], *a.* imperecedero.

unearth [ʌnœ́rθ], *vt.* desenterrar.- **—ly** [-li], *a.* sobrenatural; fantástico; extraordinario.

uneasily [ʌnízili], *adv.* inquietamente; incómodamente, penosamente. **—uneasiness** [ʌnízinis], *s.* inquietud, desasosiego, ansiedad; incomodidad, disgusto, malestar. **—uneasy** [unízi], *a.* inquieto, ansioso; molesto, incómodo; desgarbado; difícil, pesado.—*to be u.,* no tenerlas todas consigo.

uneducated [ʌnédžukeitid], *a.* falto de educación, indocto, ignorante.

unemployed [ʌnimplóid], *a.* sin empleo, desocupado, cesante; ocioso. **—unemployment** [ʌnimplóiment], *s.* desempleo, desocupación.

unending [ʌnéndiŋ], *a.* interminable.

unequal [ʌníkwal], *a.* desigual, dispar; ineficaz, insuficiente, inferior; desproporcionado; injusto, parcial; falto de uniformidad.—*to be u. to,* no tener fuerzas para, ser incapaz de.

unerring [ʌnœ́riŋ], *a.* infalible.

uneven [ʌníven], *a.* desigual; escabroso; irregular, poco uniforme; non, impar (número).- **—ness** [-nis], *s.* desigualdad; escabrosidad, aspereza; abolladura; desnivel; irregularidad.

unexpected [ʌnikspéktid], *a.* inesperado, impensado; repentino.

unexpurgated [ʌnékspœrgeitid], *a.* sin expurgar, íntegro.

unfailing [ʌnféiliŋ], *a.* inagotable; indefectible; seguro, infalible.

unfair [ʌnfér], *a.* doble, falso, desleal; injusto; (for.) leonino.

unfaithful [ʌnféiθful], *a.* infiel; desleal; inexacto.- **—ness** [-nis], *s.* infidelidad, deslealtad; inexactitud.

unfamiliar [ʌnfamílyä(r)], *a.* poco familiar, poco común; no conocido; poco conocedor.

unfashionable [ʌnfǽšonabl], *a.* pasado de moda.

unfasten [ʌnfǽsn], *vt.* desatar, desabrochar, desenganchar, desprender, soltar, aflojar, zafar.

unfathomable [ʌnfǽðomabl], *a.* insondable; sin fondo; impenetrable.

unfavorable [ʌnféivorabl], *a.* desfavorable, contrario, adverso.

unfeeling [ʌnfílɪŋ], *a.* insensible.

unfit [ʌnfít], *a.* inepto, incapaz, incompetente; impropio, inoportuno; inadaptable, inadecuado, inservible.

unfold [ʌnfóuld], *vt.* desplegar, desdoblar, desenvolver, desarrollar, abrir; extender; descifrar, poner en claro; manifestar, explicar.—*vi.* abrirse, desenvolverse, desarrollarse.

unforeseen [ʌnfɔrsín], *a.* imprevisto, impensado, inesperado.

unforgettable [ʌnfɔrgétabl], *a.* inolvidable.

unforgivable [ʌnfɔrgívabl], *a.* imperdonable.

unfortunate [ʌnfɔ́rchʊ̯nɪt], *a.* desafortunado, infeliz, desventurado; infausto, aciago.—*s.* desventurado, desgraciado.- —**ly** [-lɪ], *adv.* por desgracia.

unfounded [ʌnfáu̯ndɪd], *a.* infundado; (for.) improcedente.

unfreeze [ʌnfríz], *vt.* deshelar; (com.) desbloquear.

unfriendly [ʌnfréndlɪ], *a.* poco amistoso; hostil, enemigo; desfavorable, perjudicial.—*an u. act,* un acto hostil.

unfurl [ʌnfœ́rl], *vt.* desplegar, desarrollar, desdoblar, extender.

unfurnished [ʌnfœ́rnɪ̯ʃt], *a.* desamueblado; desprovisto.

ungodly [ʌngádlɪ], *a.* impío, irreligioso; (fam.) atroz.

ungrateful [ʌngréjtfʊl], *a.* desagradecido, ingrato; desagradable.

unguent [ʌ́ŋgwɛnt], *s.* ungüento.

unhandy [ʌnhǽndɪ], *a.* inmane jable; desmañado.

unhappiness [ʌnhǽpɪnɪs], *s.* infelicidad, desgracia, desdicha. —**unhappy** [ʌnhǽpɪ], *a.* infeliz, desgraciado, desdichado; infausto, aciago.

unharmed [ʌnhármd], *a.* ileso, incólume, sano y salvo; a salvo, sin daño.

unharness [ʌnhárnɪs], *vt.* desguarnecer, desenganchar.

unhealthy [ʌnhélθɪ], *a.* enfermizo, achacoso; insalubre, malsano.

unheard [ʌnhœ́rd], *a.* que no se ha oído.—*u. of,* inaudito, desconocido.

unhinge [ʌnhíndẑ], *vt.* desquiciar, sacar de quicio; desequilibrar, trastornar (el juicio).

unhitch [ʌnhích], *vt.* descolgar, desatar; desenganchar, desaparejar.

unhook [ʌnhúk], *vt.* desenganchar, desabrochar; descolgar.

unhoped-for [ʌnhoúptfɔr], *a.* inesperado, no esperado.

unhurt [ʌnhœrt], *a.* ileso, indemne.

uniform [yúnɪfɔrm], *a.* y *s.* uniforme.—*in full u.,* de gran uniforme.—*vt.* uniformar.- —**ity** [yunɪfɔ́rmɪtɪ], *s.* uniformidad. —**unify** [yúnɪfaɪ], *vti.* [7] unificar.

unilateral [yunɪlǽteṛal], *a.* unilateral.

unimaginable [ʌnɪmǽdẑɪ̯nabl], *a.* inimaginable.

unimportant [ʌnɪmpɔ́rtant], *a.* de poca o ninguna importancia, insignificante.

uninhabitable [ʌnɪnhǽbɪtabl], *a.* inhabitable. —**uninhabited** [ʌnɪnhǽbɪtɪd], *a.* deshabitado.

uninjured [ʌníndẑʊrd], *a.* ileso, incólume; sin daño.

unintelligible [ʌnɪntélɪdẑɪbl], *a.* ininteligible.

unintentional [ʌnɪnténṣoṇal], *a.* involuntario; no intencional.

uninteresting [ʌníntrɪstɪ̯ŋ], *a.* poco interesante.

union [yúnyön], *s.* unión; conformidad, concordia; mancomunidad, fusión; (E.U.) las estrellas de la bandera nacional; sindicato, gremio.

unique [yʊ̯ník], *a.* único en su género, original.

unison [yúnɪ̯ṣön], *s.* unisonancia; (fig.) concordancia, armonía.—*in u.,* todos juntos, a una.

unit [yúnɪt], *s.* unidad.—*a.* unitario.

unite [yʊ̯nájt], *vt.* unir.—*vi.* unirse. —**unity** [yúnɪtɪ], *s.* unidad.

United Kingdom, Reino Unido.

United Nations, Naciones Unidas.

United States, *a.* estadounidense.—*s.—the U. is,* los Estados Unidos son (o están).

universal [yunɪvœ́rṣal], *a.* universal. —**universe** [yúnɪvœrs], *s.* universo. —**university** [yunɪvœ́rsɪtɪ], *s.* universidad.—*a.* universitario.

unjust [ʌndẑʌ́st], *a.* injusto.- —**ifiable** [ʌndẑʌstɪfájabl], *a.* injustificable.

unkempt [ʌnkémpt], *a.* desgreñado; desaseado; tosco.

unkind [ʌnkájnd], *a.* duro, brutal, intratable.- —**ness** [-nɪs], *s.* dureza, brutalidad, falta de amabilidad.

unknown [ʌnnóu̯n], *a.* desconocido, ignoto.—*u. quantity,* (mat.) incógnita.—*u. soldier,* soldado desconocido.—*u. to one,* sin saberlo uno.—

s. cosa o persona desconocida; (mat.) incógnita.

unleaded [ʌnlédɪd], *a.* sin plomo.

unless [ʌnlés], *conj.* a menos que, a no ser que, como no sea, no siendo.

unlike [ʌnláɪk], *a.* diferente, dispar.— *prep.* a diferencia de.— **-ly** [-lɪ], *adv.* improbablemente.—*a.* improbable.

unlimited [ʌnlímɪtɪd], *a.* ilimitado; sin restricción.

unload [ʌnlóʊd], *vt.* y *vi.* descargar.

unlock [ʌnlák], *vt.* abrir.

unlucky [ʌnlákɪ], *a.* de mala suerte; desgraciado; infausto, de mal agüero.

unmanageable [ʌnmǽnɪdʒ̣ǝbl], *a.* inmanejable.

unmarried [ʌnmǽrɪd], *a.* soltero.

unmerciful [ʌnmɚsɪful], *a.* inclemente, despiadado; cruel.

unmerited [ʌnmérɪtɪd], *a.* inmerecido.

unmistakable [ʌnmɪstéɪkǝbl], *a.* inequívoco, inconfundible, evidente.

unmoved [ʌnmúvd], *a.* inmovible, fijo; inmutable; inflexible, inexorable.

unnatural [ʌnnǽchʊrǝl], *a.* forzado, artificial o afectado; contranatural, monstruoso; desnaturalizado.

unnecessary [ʌnnésɛsɛrɪ], *a.* innecesario, inútil, superfluo.

unnoticed [ʌnnóʊtɪst], *a.* inadvertido.

unoccupied [ʌnákɪupaɪd], *a.* desocupado o vacante.

unofficial [ʌnofíʃǝl], *a.* oficioso, extraoficial.

unorthodox [ʌnórθǝdaks], *a.* heterodoxo.

unpack [ʌnpǽk], *vt.* desempaquetar, desembalar.

unpaid [ʌnpéɪd], *a.* no pagado o por pagar.

unparalleled [ʌnpǽrǝleld], *a.* único, sin igual, sin paralelo.

unpardonable [ʌnpárdǝnǝbl], *a.* imperdonable.

unpatriotic [ʌnpeɪtrɪátɪk], *a.* antipatriótico.

unpaved [ʌnpéɪvd], *a.* sin pavimentar, desempedrado.

unpleasant [ʌnplézǝnt], *a.* desagradable.— **-ness** [-nɪs], *s.* calidad de desagradable; desagrado o desazón; (fam.) riña, desavenencia.

unpopular [ʌnpápyʊlǝ(r)], *a.* impopular.— **-ity** [ʌnpapyʊǽrɪtɪ], *s.* impopularidad.

unprecedented [ʌnprésɛdentɪd], *a.* sin precedente, inaudito, nunca visto.

unprepared [ʌnprɪpérd], *a.* desprevenido, desapercibido.

unprincipled [ʌnprínsɪpld], *a.* sin principios, sin conciencia.

unprofitable [ʌnpráfɪtǝbl], *a.* no lucrativo; inútil, vano.

unprotected [ʌnprotéktɪd], *a.* sin protección, sin defensa.

unpublished [ʌnpáblɪʃt], *a.* inédito, no publicado.

unqualified [ʌnkwálɪfaɪd], *a.* inepto; incompetente; sin títulos; sin reservas, incondicional; entero, completo.

unquestionable [ʌnkwéschǝnǝbl], *a.* incuestionable, indiscutible.

unravel [ʌnrǽvl], *vti.* [2] desenredar, desenmarañar; aclarar; descifrar.— *vii.* desenredarse; desenlazarse.

unreal [ʌnríǝl], *a.* irreal, quimérico, ilusorio; inmaterial, incorpóreo; insincero.— **-ity** [ʌnriǽlɪtɪ], *s.* irrealidad.

unreasonable [ʌnrízǝnǝbl], *a.* fuera de razón, irrazonable; irracional; exorbitante. **—unreasoning** [ʌnrízǝnɪŋ], *a.* irracional.

unrecognizable [ʌnrékɔgnaɪzǝbl], *a.* irreconocible; desconocido.

unrefined [ʌnrɪfáɪnd], *a.* no refinado, impuro, en bruto; inculto, grosero, ordinario.

unreliable [ʌnrɪláɪǝbl], *a.* indigno de confianza, informal.

unrepentant [ʌnrɪpéntǝnt], *a.* impenitente.

unrest [ʌnrést], *s.* inquietud, desasosiego.

unripe [ʌnráɪp], *a.* verde, agraz; prematuro.

unrivaled [ʌnráɪvǝld], *a.* sin rival, sin par.

unroll [ʌnróʊl], *vt.* desarrollar, desenrollar, desenvolver, desplegar.—*vi.* abrirse, desarrollarse.

unruffled [ʌnráféld], *a.* tranquilo, sereno.

unruly [ʌnrúlɪ], *a.* indócil, inmanejable, ingobernable, indómito; revoltoso, levantisco; intratable; desarreglado.

unsafe [ʌnséɪf], *a.* peligroso, inseguro.

unsalable [ʌnséɪlǝbl], *a.* invendible.

unsanitary [ʌnsǽnɪtɛrɪ], *a.* antihigiénico; insalubre.

unsatisfactory [ʌnsætɪsfǽktorɪ], *a.* insatisfactorio; malo, inaceptable.

unsatisfied [ʌnsǽtɪsfaɪd], *a.* insatisfecho.

unscrew [ʌnskrú], vt. des(a)tornillar, desenroscar.

unscrupulous [ʌnskrúpjulʌs], a. sin escrúpulos, desaprensivo.

unseasonable [ʌnsízonabl], a. intempestivo; prematuro; indebido, inconveniente.—at u. hours, a deshora. —**unseasoned** [ʌnsízond], a. sin sazonar, insípido; verde (madera).

unseat [ʌnsít], vt. desarzonar; echar abajo (de un puesto).

unseemly [ʌnsímli], a. impropio, indecoroso, indigno.

unseen [ʌnsín], a. invisible, oculto.

unselfish [ʌnsélfiʃ], a. desinteresado, generoso, abnegado.– —**ness** [-nis], s. desinterés, generosidad, abnegación.

unserviceable [ʌnsœrvisabl], a. inútil, inservible.

unsettle [ʌnsétl], vt. perturbar, trastornar.– —**d** [-d], a. inestable, variable, inconstante; desarreglado, descompuesto; no establecido, no instalado, sin residencia fija; indeciso; incierto; (com.) por pagar, no liquidado, pendiente; turbio, revuelto; inhabitado; despoblado; lunático.

unshaken [ʌnʃéikn], a. firme, inmovible.

unshaven [ʌnʃéivn], a. sin afeitar.

unsheltered [ʌnʃéltœrd], a. desamparado, desvalido. —**unsheltering** [ʌnʃéltœriŋ], a. inhospitalario.

unsightly [ʌnsáitli], a. feo, repugnante.

unskilled [ʌnskíld], a. inexperto.—u. laborer, bracero, peón. —**unskillful** [ʌnskílful], a. desmañado.

unsociable [ʌnsóuʃabl], a. insociable, huraño.

unsold [ʌnsóuld], a. invendido.

unsophisticated [ʌnsofístikeitid], a. sencillo, ingenuo.

unsound [ʌnsáund], a. defectuoso, erróneo, falso; poco firme, falto de fuerza.

unspeakable [ʌnspíkabl], a. indecible, inefable; (atrocious) incalificable.

unsportsmanlike conduct, [ʌnspórtsmanlaik], s. (dep.) conducta antideportiva.

unstable [ʌnstéjbl], a. inestable.

unsteady [ʌnstédi], a. inestable, inseguro, no firme; vacilante, tambaleante; inconstante, veleidoso.

unsuccessful [ʌnsʌksésful], a. infructuoso, sin éxito; desafortunado.

unsuitable [ʌnsjútabl], a. inapropiado, inadaptable; incompetente.

unsuspected [ʌnsʌspéktid], a. insospechado. —**unsuspecting** [ʌnsʌspéktiŋ], a. cándido, confiado.

untamed [ʌntéjmd], a. indómito, bravío, cerrero.

untaught [ʌntót], a. indocto; no enseñado, sin instrucción, ignorante.

unthinkable [ʌnθíŋkabl], a. inimaginable. —**unthinking** [ʌnθíŋkiŋ], a. descuidado, irreflexivo.

untidy [ʌntáidi], a. desaliñado, desarreglado, falto de pulcritud.

untie [ʌntái], vt. desatar, desligar; deshacer (un nudo); aflojar, soltar, zafar.

until [ʌntíl], prep. hasta.—conj. hasta que.—not u., no antes que.

untimely [ʌntáimli], a. intempestivo.

untiring [ʌntáiriŋ], a. infatigable.

untold [ʌntóuld], a. nunca dicho; indecible, incalculable.

untouchable [ʌntáchabl], a. intocable, intangible. —**untouched** [ʌntácht], a. intacto, ileso; insensible, impasible.

untoward [ʌntórd], a. adverso, desfavorable.

untrained [ʌntréjnd], a. indisciplinado; inexperto, imperito.

untranslatable [ʌntrænsléjtabl], a. intraducible.

untried [ʌntráid], a. no probado o ensayado; no experimentado; novel.

untroubled [ʌntrábld], a. no molestado o perturbado; tranquilo; claro, transparente.

untrue [ʌntrú], a. falso; mendaz; engañoso.

untruth [ʌntrúθ], s. falsedad, mentira; infidelidad.– —**ful** [-ful], a. falso, mentiroso.

unused [ʌnyúzd], a. inusitado, insólito; no usado, nuevo; desacostumbrado. —**unusual** [ʌnyúʒual], a. raro, extraordinario, extraño; excepcional; insólito, inusitado; desacostumbrado.

unveil [ʌnvéjl], vt. quitar el velo a, revelar, descubrir; inaugurar (un monumento).—vi. quitarse el velo, descubrirse.

unwarranted [ʌnwórantid], a. injustificado; no autorizado; sin garantía.

unwary [ʌnwéri], a. incauto, imprudente, irreflexivo.

unwelcome [ʌnwélkʌm], *a.* mal recibido o acogido; desagradable, incómodo, importuno.

unwholesome [ʌnhóulsʌm], *a.* dañino, nocivo, malsano, insalubre.

unwieldy [ʌnwíldj], *a.* pesado, difícil de manejar.

unwilling [ʌnwílin], *a.* renuente.— **—ly** [-lj], *adv.* de mala gana.— **—ness** [-njs], *s.* mala gana, repugnancia, renuencia.

unwise [ʌnwáiz], *a.* imprudente; ignorante.

unwittingly [ʌnwítinlj], *adv.* sin saber, inconscientemente.

unworthiness [ʌnwɛ́rðinjs], *s.* indignidad, falta de mérito. **—unworthy** [ʌnwɛ́rðj], *a.* indigno, desmerecedor.

unwrap [ʌnræp], *vti.* [1] desenvolver.

unwritten [ʌnrítn], *a.* no escrito; en blanco; tradicional.—*u. law,* derecho consuetudinario; derecho natural.

unyielding [ʌnyíldin], *a.* inflexible, inexorable, inconmovible, firme; reacio, terco.

unzip [ʌnzíp], *vt.* bajar la cremallera.

up [ʌp], *a.* que va hacia arriba; levantado (de la cama); empinado; erecto; ascendente (tren, etc.).—*adv.* arriba, hacia arriba, para arriba; en pie, derecho; de pie, levantado; (fam.) bien enterado, competente, a la altura de; llegado, acabado, concluido; enteramente, totalmente, completamente.—*it is all u.,* todo se acabó.—*on the u.-and-u.,* mejorándose; abiertamente, sin dolo.—*time is u.,* se ha cumplido el tiempo; ha expirado el plazo; ha llegado la hora.—*to be u. in on, to be up on,* estar al corriente de, al día de o versado en.—*to be u. to,* ser suficiente o competente para; estar a la altura de; estar haciendo o urdiendo, andar (en travesuras, intrigas, etc.).—*to be u. to one,* (fam.) depender de, ser asunto de, o tocarle a uno.—*u. above,* arriba, más arriba.—*u.-and-coming,* prometedor.—*u.-and-doing,* emprendedor.—*u.-and-down,* vertical, de vaivén; (fam.) franco, claro.—*u. to,* hasta; capaz de; tramando; al corriente de, sabedor de.—*u. to date,* hasta la fecha.—*u.-to-date,* moderno, al día.—*what's u.?* ¿qué hay? ¿de qué se trata?—*prep.* hacia arriba de; a lo largo de; en

lo alto de.—*u. one's sleeve,* en secreto, para sí.—*vti.* [1] subir, elevar; aumentar (precios, etc.).—*s.* prosperidad.—*ups and downs,* vaivenes, altibajos, vicisitudes.—*interj.* ¡arriba! ¡aúpa!

upbringing [ʌ́pbrinin], *s.* crianza, educación.

update [ʌpdéit], *vt.* poner al día, actualizar.

upheaval [ʌphívəl], *s.* solevantamiento; trastorno, cataclismo.

upheld [ʌphéld], *pret.* y *pp.* de TO UPHOLD.

uphill [ʌphíl], *adv.* cuesta arriba.—*a.* ascendente; penoso, dificultoso.

uphold [ʌphóuld], *vti.* [10] sostener, apoyar, defender.

upholster [ʌphóulstœ(r)], *vt.* rellenar y cubrir muebles; tapizar; poner colgaduras, cortinas, etc.— **—y** [-j], *s.* tapicería.

upkeep [ʌ́pkip], *s.* conservación, mantenimiento.

uplift [ʌplíft], *vt.* elevar, levantar, alzar.—*s.* [ʌ́plift], levantamiento, elevación.

upon [ʌpán], *prep.* en, sobre, encima de.

upper [ʌ́pœ(r)], *a.* superior, de encima o de arriba; (más) alto.—*to have the u. hand,* tener vara alta.—*u. classes,* altas clases.—*u. middle class,* alta burguesía.— **—most** [-moust], *a.* (el) más alto; (el) principal.—*adv.* en lo más alto; primero, en primer lugar.

uppish [ʌ́pjʃ], *a.* (fam.) copetudo, arrogante.

upright [ʌ́prajt], *a.* derecho, vertical, recto; probo, honrado.—*s.* montante, pieza vertical; soporte, apoyo.— **—ness** [-njs], *s.* calidad de vertical; rectitud, probidad.

uprising [ʌpráizin], *s.* levantamiento (acto de levantar algo); levantamiento, insurrección; cuesta, pendiente.

uproar [ʌ́prɔr], *s.* grita, bulla, bullicio, conmoción; (fig.) rugido.— **—ious** [ʌprɔ́rjʌs], *a.* ruidoso, tumultuoso; bullanguero.

uproot [ʌprút], *vt.* desarraigar.

upset [ʌpsét], *vti.* [9] trastornar, desbaratar; volcar, derribar; desconcertar, turbar; (mar.) zozobrar.—*vi.* volcarse; (mar.) zozobrar.—*pret.* y *pp.* de to UPSET.—*a.* trastornado; volcado; turbado; erigido; fijo, determinado.—*u. price,* precio mínimo fijado en una subasta.—s. [ápset], vuelco; trastorno.

upsetting [ʌpsétiŋ], a. desconcertante.

upside [ápsajd], s. parte superior, lo de arriba.—u. down, lo de arriba abajo; al revés, invertido; (fam.) patas arriba; en confusión, trastornado.

upstairs [ápstérz], adv. arriba, en el piso de arriba.—a. alto (piso, etc.); de arriba (de las escaleras).

upstanding [ʌpstǽndiŋ], a. derecho; gallardo; probo, recto.

upstart [ápstart], a. y s. advenedizo.

up-to-date [áptɔdejt], a. corriente, moderno, de última hora.

up-to-the-minute [áptɔðĕmínit], a. al día, de actualidad.

upturn [áptœrn], s. vuelta hacia arriba; alza.—vt. [áptœrn], volver hacia arriba; trastornar; volcar. **—ed** [áptœrnd], a. respingada (nariz).

upward [ápwǎrd], a. vuelto hacia arriba; ascendente.- **—(s)** [-(z)], adv. hacia arriba; más.—from ten cents u., de diez centavos en adelante.

uranium [yʊréjniʌm], s. uranio.

urban [œrban], a. urbano.- **—e** [œrbéjn], a. fino, cortés.- **—ity** [œrbǽniti], s. urbanidad.

urchin [œrchin], s. rapaz, granuja, pilluelo, golfillo; (zool.) erizo.

urge [œrdʒ], vt. urgir, apresurar, apremiar; incitar; acosar; solicitar; recomendar con ahinco.—vi. apresurarse; estimular; presentar argumentos o pretensiones.—s. impulso, estímulo; ganas.- **—ncy** [œrdʒensi], s. urgencia.- **—nt** [œrdʒent], a. urgente, apremiante.

urinal [yʊrinal], s. urinario.- **—urinate** [yúrinejt], vt. y vi. orinar. **—urine** [yúrin], s. orina, orines.

urn [œrn], s. urna; jarrón.

Uruguayan [yʊrʊgwéjan, yʊrʊgwájan], a. y s. uruguayo.

us [ʌs], pron. nos; nosotros.

U.S.A. o **USA** [yúésej], abrev. (**United States of America**) E.U.A., EEUU, EE.UU.

usage [yúsidʒ], s. trato, tratamiento; uso, usanza. **—use** [yus], s. uso; aprovechamiento; aplicación; servicio, utilidad, provecho; necesidad; ocasión de usar; costumbre, uso.—no u. (of) talking, es inútil dis-

cutirlo.—to have no u. for, no necesitar o no servirse de; (fam.) no tener muy buena opinión de, tener en poco.—vt. [yuz], usar, utilizar; hacer uso, servirse de; acostumbrar, soler.—to u. up, gastar, consumir, agotar.—vi. soler, acostumbrar. —he used to come every day, el venía todos los días o acostumbraba venir todos los días.—the city used to be smaller, antes la ciudad era más pequeña. **—used** [yuzd], a. usado. —u. to, acostumbrado a. **—useful** [yúsful], a. útil, provechoso. **—usefulness** [yúsfulnis], s. utilidad. **—useless** [yúslis], a. inútil; ocioso; inservible; inepto. **—uselessness** [yúslisnis], s. inutilidad. **—user** [yúzœ(r)], s. el que usa o utiliza; consumidor; comprador.

usher [ʌ̂œ(r)], s. (teat., etc.) acomodador.—vt. acomodar.—to u. in, anunciar, introducir.

usual [yúʒual], a. usual, acostumbrado, común.—as u., como de costumbre, como siempre.

usurp [yuzœrp], vt. usurpar; arrogarse. **—er** [-œ(r)], s. usurpador.

usury [yúʒuri], s. usura.

utensil [yuténsil], s. utensilio.—pl. útiles.

uterus [yúterʌs], s. útero.

utilitarian [yutjilitérian], a. utilitario. **—utility** [yutjíliti], s. utilidad; servicio. **—utilize** [yútjilajz], vt. utilizar, hacer uso de, aprovechar.

utmost [átmoust], a. extremo, sumo; mayor, más grande; más posible; más distante.—s. lo sumo, lo mayor.—to the u., hasta no más.

utopia [yutoúpia], s. utopía.- **—n** [yutoúpian], a. utópico, utopista.

utter [átœ(r)], a. total, entero, cabal, completo; absoluto; terminante.— vt. proferir, pronunciar; decir, expresar; dar (un grito, etc.); descubrir, publicar, revelar; engañar, defraudar con (moneda falsa); hacer pasar fraudulentamente; emitir, poner en circulación.- **—ance** [-ans], s. pronunciación; expresión; lenguaje; aserción, declaración.- **—ly** [-li], adv. completamente, de remate.

uvula [yúvyülä], s. (anat.) campanilla, úvula, galillo.

V

vacancy [véik̯ansi], s. vacío; vacante; empleo vacante; local o cuarto desocupado. —**vacant** [véik̯ant], a. vacío, vacante; desocupado; libre. —**vacate** [véik̯eit], vt. evacuar, dejar vacío; desocupar; abandonar; dejar vacante; (for.) anular, rescindir, revocar.—vi. salir, irse, marcharse; desalojar; vacar; desocupar. —**vacation** [veik̯éiṣon], s. vacación, asueto; (for.) anulación, revocación.

vaccinate [væksịneit], vt. vacunar. —**vaccination** [væksịnéiṣon], s. vacunación, inoculación. —**vaccine** [væksin], s. vacuna.

vacillate [væsịleit], vi. vacilar. —**vacillation** [væsịléiṣon], s. vacilación.

vacuum [vǽkyụʌm], s. vacío.—a. de vacío; (mec.) aspirante.—in a v., en el vacío.—v. cleaner, aspirador (de polvo), limpiador al vacío.

vagabond [vǽgaband], a. vagabundo, errante; fluctuante.—s. vago, (fam.) pelafustán. —**vagrancy** [véigransi], s. vagancia. —**vagrant** [véigrant], s. y a. vago, vagabundo.

vague [veig], a. vago, indefinido, impreciso; incierto, dudoso.- —**ness** [véignịs], s. vaguedad.

vain [vein], a. vano, vanidoso; inútil; fútil, insustancial.—in v., en vano.

valentine [vǽlentain], s. tarjeta amorosa o jocosa del día de San Valentín.—Valentine Day, día de los corazones (14 de febrero).

valiant [vǽlyant], a. valiente, valeroso, bravo; (fam.) de puños.

valid [vǽlịd], a. válido; valedero.- —**ate** [-eit], vt. validar.- —**ity** [valídịti], s. validez; fuerza legal.

valise [valís], s. maleta.

valley [vǽli], s. valle.

valor [vǽlọ(r)], s. valor, ánimo.- —**ous** [-ʌs], a. valeroso.

valuable [vǽlyụabl], a. valioso; precioso, apreciable, preciado.—s. pl. joyas u otros objetos de valor. —**valuation** [vælyụéiṣon], s. justiprecio, tasación, valoración. —**value** [vǽlyụ], s. mérito, valor; precio, valuación; aprecio, estimación; (mus.) valor de una nota.—v. added tax, impuesto al valor agregado.—

vt. tasar, valorar; hacer caso de, tener en mucho; considerar.

valve [vælv], s. válvula; ventalla; valva.

vamp [væmp], s. (fam.) sirena, mujer peligrosa.- —**ire** [vǽmpair], s. vampiro; estafador.

van [væn], s. carro de cargo, camión de mudanzas.

vane [vein], s. veleta; aspa (de molino); paleta (de hélice).

vanguard [vǽngard], s. vanguardia.

vanilla [vanílạ], s. vainilla.

vanish [vǽnịṣ], vi. desvanecerse.

vanity [vǽnịti], s. vanidad; tocador.—v. case, estuche de afeites, neceser de belleza.

vanquish [vǽŋkwịṣ], vt. y vi. vencer.

vapor [véipọ(r)], s. vapor.- —**ize** [-aiz], vt. y vi. vaporizarse.- —**izer** [-aizœ(r)], s. vaporizador.

variable [vériabl], s. y a. variable. —**variance** [vérians], s. variación, cambio; desavenencia, discrepancia.—to be at v., estar en desacuerdo (con). —**variation** [veriéiṣon], s. variación; variedad; (gram.) flexión.

varicose [vérikous], a. varicoso.—v. vein, varice, várice.

varied [vérịd], a. variado, vario; alterado; (zool., orn.) abigarrado, multicolor. —**variegated** [vérigeitịd], a. abigarrado, jaspeado, veteado; diverso, diversificado.—**variety** [varáieti], s. variedad, diversidad; surtido; tipo, clase, especie.—v. show (teat.) función de variedades. —**various** [vériʌs], a. varios, algunos, unos cuantos; desemejante, diferente; inconstante; veteado.

varnish [várnịṣ], s. barniz.—vt. barnizar.

varsity [vársịti], a. (dep.) universitario.—s. (dep.) equipo principal de la universidad.

vary [véri], vti. y vii. [7] variar, cambiar; diversificar(se); desviar(se).

vase [veis], s. jarrón, vaso; florero, búcaro.

Vaseline [vǽselin], s. (TM) vaselina.

vast [væst], a. vasto; inmenso.

vat [væt], s. tina, tanque, cuba.

vaudeville [vóudvil], s. función de variedades.

vault [vɔlt], s. (arq.) bóveda, cúpula; cueva, bodega, subterráneo; tumba; (igl.) cripta; (fig.) cielo, firmamento; (dep.) voltereta, salto con garrocha.—vt. (arq.) abovedar, voltear.—vt. y vi. (dep.) voltear, saltar (con garrocha o apoyando las manos).

veal [vil], s. (carne de) ternera.—v. *cutlet,* chuleta de ternera.

veer [vir], vi. desviarse; cambiar (el viento, etc.).—vt. y vi. (mar.) virar.

vegetable [védẓtabl], s. vegetal, planta.—pl. verduras, hortalizas, legumbres.—a. vegetal; de hortalizas. —**vegetarian** [vedẓētérian], a. y s. vegetariano. —**vegetate** [védẓēteit], vi. vegetar. —**vegetation** [vedẓētéiṣon], s. vegetación.

vehemence [víhịmens], s. vehemencia. —**vehement** [víhịment], a. vehemente, impetuoso, extremoso.

vehicle [víhịkl], s. vehículo; medio; (farm.) excipiente.

veil [veil], vt. velar, cubrir con velo; encubrir, disimular, tapar.—s. velo.

vein [vein], s. vena; veta; (fig.) humor, genio.- —**ed** [-d], a. venoso; veteado, jaspeado.

vellum [vélʌm], s. vitela, pergamino.

velocity [vilásịti], s. velocidad.

velum [vílʌm], s. cubierta membranosa; velo del paladar.

velvet [vélvịt], s. terciopelo.—a. de terciopelo. —**y** [-i], a. aterciopelado.

vender [véndœ(r)], s. vendedor ambulante. —**vending machine,** distribuidor automático. —**vendor** [véndǫ(r)], s. (for.) vendedor, cedente.

veneer [venír], vt. enchapar.—s. chapa; apariencia.

venerable [vénęrabl], a. venerable; sagrado; antiguo. —**venerate** [vénęreit], vt. venerar, reverenciar. —**veneration** [venęréiṣon], s. veneración.

venereal [venírial], a. venéreo.

Venetian [venísán], a. y s. veneciano.—*Venetian blind,* persiana.

Venezuelan [venezwéilan], a. y s. venezolano.

vengeance [véndẓans], s. venganza.—*with a v.,* con violencia, con toda su alma; con creces, extremadamente. —**vengeful** [véndẓful], a. vengativo.

venial [vínial], a. venial; perdonable.

venom [vénǫm], s. veneno; rencor, malignidad.- —**ous** [-ʌs], a. venenoso; dañoso; maligno.

vent [vent], s. respiradero, abertura,

lumbrera; salida, paso; fogón de arma de fuego; (zool.) ano; emisión; desahogo.—vt. expresar, desahogar, (fam.) desembuchar.—*to v. one's spleen,* descargar su bilis.- —**ilate** [véntịleịt], vt. ventilar.- —**ilation** [-ịléiṣon], s. ventilación.- —**ilator** [-ịleịtǫ(r)], s. ventilador.

ventriloquist [ventrílokwịst], s. ventrílocuo.

venture [vénchū(r)], s. riesgo, ventura, albur; (com.) pacotilla; operación o empresa arriesgada; especulación.—vt. arriesgar, aventurar.—vi. osar, atreverse; aventurarse, arriesgarse.

venue [vényụ], s. (for.) lugar donde se reúne el jurado.—*change of v.,* (for.) traslado de jurisdicción.

veranda [vịrǽndǎ], s. pórtico, soportal, porche, mirador.

verb [vœrb], s. verbo.- —**al** [vœrbal], a. verbal; oral; literal.

verbatim [verbéịtịm], a. textual.—adv. palabra por palabra, al pie de la letra.

verbena [vœrbínǎ], s. (bot.) verbena.

verdant [vœrdạnt], a. verde, verdoso; inocente, sencillo.

verdict [vœrdịkt], s. veredicto, fallo.

verdigris [vœrdịgris], s. verdín. —**verdure** [vœrdẓụr], s. verdor.

verge [vœrdẓ], s. borde, margen; confín; (arq.) fuste; vara, báculo.—*on o upon the v. of,* al borde de; a punto de.—vi.—*to v. on o upon,* llegar casi hasta.

verify [vérịfaj], vti. [7] verificar, constatar. (for.) afirmar bajo juramento.

veritable [vérịtabl], a. verdadero. —**verity** [vérịtị], s. verdad, realidad.

vermin [vœrmịn], s. miseria, musaraña; bichos, piojos, chinches, etc.

vernacular [vœrnǽkyụlǎ(r)], a. vernáculo, nativo; (med.) local.—s. idioma vernáculo.

versatile [vœrsạtịl], a. versátil, de variados talentos o aptitudes; adaptable; voluble. —**versatility** [vœrsạtílịtị], s. versatilidad, adaptabilidad, variedad de talentos; veleidad.

verse [vœrs], s. verso; (igl.) versículo.- —**d** [-t], a. versado, perito. —**versicle** [vœrsịkl], s. versículo. —**versification** [vœrsịfikéiṣon], s. versificación. —**version** [vœrẓǫn], s. versión; interpretación; (cir.) versión.

versus [vœrsʌs], prep. contra.

vertebra [vœrtẽbrǎ], s. (pl. **vertebrae**

[vɔ́ertjbri]) vértebra.– **—te** [vɔ́ertj-breit], s. y a. vertebrado.

vertex [vɔ́erteks], s. (pl. **vertices** [vɔ́ertjsiz]) vértice; cima, cumbre, cúspide, ápice.

vertical [vɔ́ertjkal], a. vertical.– **—ity** [vɔ́ertjkǽlitj], s. verticalidad.

vertigo [vɔ́ertjgou], s. (med.) vértigo.

vervain [vɔ́ervein], s. (bot.) verbena.

very [vérj], a. mismo, propio, idéntico; verdadero, real; mismísimo.—for that v. reason, por lo mismo.—the v. idea of doing it, sólo la idea, o la mera idea de hacerlo.—this v. day, hoy mismo.—adv. muy, mucho, muchísimo.—v. many, muchísimos.—v. much, mucho, muchísimo.—sumamente, muy.—v. much so, muy mucho, muchísimo, en sumo grado.

vesicle [vésjkl], s. vesícula.

vespers [véspœrz], s. vísperas.

vessel [vésel], s. embarcación, barco, buque; vasija, vaso.

vest [vest], s. chaleco; (G.B.) camiseta.—v.-pocket, de bolsillo, en miniatura.—vt. vestir.—to v. in, conceder (poder) a.—to v. with, investir de.—vested interests, intereses creados.—vi. vestirse.—to v. in, pasar a.

vestibule [véstjbjul], s. vestíbulo; zaguán.

vestige [véstjdž], s. vestigio.

vestments [véstmènts], spl. (igl.) vestiduras.

vestry [véstrj], s. vestuario, sacristía; junta parroquial.

veteran [véterạn], s. y a. veterano.

veterinarian [veterjnérjạn], a. y s. veterinario.

veto [vítou], vt. vetar.—s. veto.

vex [veks], vt. irritar, vejar.– **—ation** [ve kséjšon], s. irritación, vejación.

via [váijạ], prep. vía.– **—duct** [váijạdʌkt], s. viaducto.

vial [váijạl], s. redoma, frasco pequeño.

vibrate [váibreit], vt. y vi. vibrar. **—vibration** [vaibréjšon], s. vibración.

vice [vais], s. vicio, inmoralidad; defecto, falta; resabio (caballo, etc.).—prefijo vice-.—v.-admiral, vicealmirante.—v.-president, vicepresidente.—v. versa, viceversa.– **—roy** [váisrɔj], s. virrey.

vicinity [visínjtj], s. vecindad.

vicious [víšʌs], a. vicioso.—v. dog, perro bravo.

vicissitude [visísjtjud], s. vicisitud.

victim [víktjm], s. víctima.

victor [víktɔ(r)], s. vencedor.– **—ious**

[viktórjʌs], a. victorioso.– **—y** [víktorj], s. victoria.

video [vídèou], a. de video.—s. video, vídeo.—vt. grabar.—v. camera, videocámara.—v. film, película de video, videofilm.—v. game, videojuego.—v. library, videoteca.—v. piracy, videopiratería.—v. recorder, aparto de video.—v. recording, (tape) video; (process) grabación en video. – **—cassette** [kạsét], s. videocasete.—v. recorder, magnetoscopia, video.– **—phone** [-foun], s. vídeófono.– **—projector** [-prodžéctœr], s. videoproyector.– **—tape** [-teip], s. cinta de video, videocinta.—vt. grabar en video.—v. recorder, video, videograbadora.—v. recording, video, videograma; (act) videograbación.– **—taping** [-teipin], s. videograbación.

vie [vai], vi. competir, rivalizar, disputar(se), emular.

view [vju], vt. mirar, ver; contemplar; examinar, inspeccionar, reconocer; considerar, especular.—s. vista, mirada; inspección; contemplación; visión; escena, panorama, paisaje; perspectiva; alcance de la vista; modo de ver, criterio; opinión, parecer; fase, aspecto; mira, intento, propósito.—v. finder, (foto.) visor.– **—point** [vjúpɔint], s. punto de vista.

vigil [vídžjl], s. vigilia.– **—ance** [-ạns], s. vigilancia.– **—ant** [-ạnt], a. vigilante.

vignette [vinyét], s. viñeta.

vigor [vígo(r)], s. vigor.– **—ous** [-ʌs], a. vigoroso.

vile [vail], a. vil; asqueroso, repugnante; (weather) muy malo.

villa [vílạ], s. villa, quinta.– **—ge** [vílidž], s. aldea.– **—ger** [vílidžœr(r)], s. aldeano.

villain [vílạn], s. malvado; (teat.) malo, traidor. **—ous** [-ʌs], a. malvado.– **—y** [-i], s. maldad, perfidia.

vim [vim], s. fuerza, vigor, brío.

vindicate [víndjkeit], vt. vindicar. **—vindictive** [vjndíktjv], a. vengativo.

vine [vain], s. (bot.) enredadera; vid, parra.– **—gar** [vínjgǎ(r)], s. vinagre. – **—yard** [vínyǎrd], s. viña, viñedo. **—vintage** [víntjdž], s. vendimia.– v. wine, vino añejo. **—vintner** [víntnœr(r)], s. vinatero.

vinyl [vaínjl], s. vinilo.

violate [váijoleit], vt. violar. **—violation**

[vajoléjṣon], s. violación. **—violence** [vájolẹns], s. violencia. **—violent** [vájolẹnt], a. violento.

violet [vájolịt], s. (bot.) violeta; color violado.—a. violado, violáceo.

violin [vajolín], s. violín; violinista.— **—ist** [-ịst], s. violinista. **—violoncello** [violanchélou], s. violoncelo.

VIP [víaipí], abrev. (**very important person**) VIP.

viper [vájpœ(r)], s. víbora.

virgin [vœrdẓịn], a. y s. virgen.—v. birth, parto virginal de María Santísima; (zool.) partenogénesis.— **—al** [-ạl], a. virginal.- **—ity** [vœrdẓínịtị], s. virginidad.

Virgo [vœrgou], s. (astr.) Virgo.

virile [víril], a. viril. **—virility** [vịrílịtị], s. virilidad.

virtual [vœrchuạl], a. virtual.

virtue [vœrchụ], s. virtud. **—virtuoso** [vœrchụóụsoụ], s. (mús.) virtuoso. **—virtuous** [vœrchụʌs], a. virtuoso.

virulence [vírụlẹns], s. virulencia; malignidad, acrimonia. **—virulent** [vírụlẹnt], a. virulento, ponzoñoso; maligno, cáustico. **—virus** [vájrʌs], s. virus.

visa [vízạ], s. visa, visado.—transit v., visado de tránsito.

viscera [vísẹrạ], s. pl. vísceras.- **—l** [vísẹrạl], a. visceral.

viscosity [vịskásịtị], s. viscosidad.

viscount [vájkaụnt], s. vizconde.- **—ess** [-ịs], s. vizcondesa.

viscous [vískʌs], a. viscoso, pegajoso.

visibility [vịzịbílịtị], s. visibilidad. **—visible** [vízịbl], a. visible. **—vision** [vízọn], s. visión, vista; clarividencia, perspicacia, previsión; fantasma; fantasía; revelación profética; (cine) representación de los pensamientos o sueños de un actor. **—visionary** [vízọnẹrị], a. y s. visionario.

visit [vízịt], vt. visitar; (to afflict) afligir.—vi. visitarse; hacer visitas, ir de visita.—s. visita.—s. visita.- **—ation** [-éjṣọn], s. visitación; gracia o castigo del cielo.- **—ing** [-ịŋ], s. visitas.—v. card, tarjeta de visita.—v. hours, horario de visitas.—v. nurse, enfermera ambulante.- **—or** [-ọ(r)], s. visitante, visitador.—v. center, centro de informaciones.

visor [vájzọ(r)], s. visera.

vista [vístạ], s. vista, panorama.

visual [víẓuạl], a. visual.- **—ize** [-aịz], vt. visualizar, imaginar, representarse en la mente.

vital [vájtạl], a. vital, fundamental; decisivo.—pl. órganos vitales; (fam.) las tripas; (humor.) las partes, los bajos.- **—ity** [vajtǽlịtị], s. vitalidad, energía vital.- **—ize** [vájtạlaịz], vt. vitalizar.

vitamin [vájtạmịn], s. vitamina.

vitiate [víṣịejt], vt. viciar; inficionar, infectar, corromper; (for.) viciar, invalidar.

vitreous [vítrịʌs], a. vítreo, vidrioso.

vitriol [vítrịọl], s. vitriolo.- **—ic** [vịtrịálịk], a. ferozmente mordaz.

viva [vívạ], interj. ¡viva!

vivacious [vịvéjṣʌs], a. vivo, vivaracho, vivaz. **—vivacity** [vịvǽsịtị], s. vivacidad, viveza. **—vivid** [vívịd], a. vivo.

V-neck [vínɛk], a. de escote en pico, de escote en V.

vocabulary [vokǽbyụlẹrị], s. vocabulario.

vocal [vóụkạl], a. vocal; expresivo.- **—ist** [-ịst], s. vocalista.- **—ize** [-aịz], vt. y vi. vocalizar.

vocation [vokéjṣọn], s. oficio, profesión; vocación.

vogue [voụg], s. moda, boga.—in v., de moda, en boga.

voice [vɔịs], s. voz.—with one v., a una voz.—vt. expresar; (fon.) sonorizar. - **—less** [-lịs], a. sin voz; mudo; silencioso; (fon.) sordo.

void [vɔịd], a. vacío; vano; (for.) nulo, inválido.—v. of, desprovisto de.—s. vacío; (gap) hueco, laguna.—vt. (for.) anular, invalidar; vaciar, evacuar.—vi. excretar.

volatile [válạtịl], a. volátil. **—volatilize** [válạtịlaịz], vt. y vi. volatilizar(se).

volcanic [valkǽnịk], a. volcánico. **—volcano** [valkéjnoụ], s. volcán.

volition [volíṣọn], s. voluntad.

volley [válị], s. (mil.) descarga; (dep.) voleo.- **—ball** [-bɔl], s. volibol.—vt. y vi. (dep.) volear.

volt [voụlt], s. (elec.) volt, voltio; (equit.) vuelta.- **—age** [vóụltịdẓ], s. voltaje, tensión.

volume [vályụm], s. volumen; tomo; volumen sonoro.—to speak volumes, ser muy significativo. **—voluminous** [volịúmịnʌs], a. voluminoso.

voluntary [válʌntẹrị], a. voluntario.- **—volunteer** [valʌntír], s. voluntario.—vt. contribuir u ofrecer voluntariamente.—vi. ofrecerse o hacer algo; servir como voluntario.

volute [volịút], s. (arq.) voluta.

vomit [vámịt], *vt.* y *vi.* vomitar.—*s.* vómito; vomitivo, emético.

voracious [voréiȿʌs], *a.* voraz.

vortex [vórteks], *s.* (*pl.* **vortices** [vórtịsiz]) vórtice.

vote [voṳt], *s.* voto; votación.—*vt.* votar por; (fam.) dominar el voto de.— *to v. down,* rechazar por votación.— *vi.* votar, dar voto.- **—r** [vóṳtœ(r)], *s.* votante. **—voting** [vóṳtịŋ], *s.* votación.

vouch [vaṳch], *vt.* garantizar.—*vi.*—*to v. for,* responder por; responder de.- **—er** [váṳchœ(r)], *s.* comprobante; garante.

vow [vaṳ], *s.* voto.—*to take vows,* tomar el hábito religioso.—*vt.* (vengeance) jurar; (igl.) votar.—*vi.* votar.—*to v. to,* hacer votos de.

vowel [váṳel], *s.* vocal.

voyage [vóiịdž], *s.* viaje; viaje travesía.—*vi.* viajar.- **—r** [vóiịdžœ(r)], *s.* viajero.

vulcanization [vʌlkạnịzéiȿọn], *s.* vulcanización. **—vulcanize** [válkạnaiz], *vt.* vulcanizar.

vulgar [válgä(r)], *a.* grosero; público, generalmente sabido; vernáculo.- **—ity** [vʌlgǽrịtị], *s.* grosería.

vulnerable [válnerabl], *a.* vulnerable.

vulture [válchṳ(r)], *s.* buitre.

W

wad [wad], *s.* taco; bolita; pelotilla; rollo (de papeles, billetes de banco, etc.); material para rellenar muebles (guata, etc.); (fam.) dinero, dineral, ahorros.—*vti.* [1] (cost.) acolchar, enguatar; rellenar (muebles, colchones, etc.); (arti.) atacar.

waddle [wádl], *vi.* anadear.—*s.* anadeo.

wade [weịd], *vt.* y *vi.* vadear; meterse en agua baja y andar en ella.—*to w. in* o *through,* andar con dificultad (en el lodo, etc.); terminar con dificultad o con tedio.—*to w. into,* (fam.) atacar resueltamente.

wafer [wéifœ(r)], *s.* oblea; (igl.) hostia; (coc.) barquillo; (farm.) sello.

waffle [wáfěl], *s.* barquillo.—*w. iron,* barquillero.

wag [wæg], *vti.* [1] sacudir, mover o menear ligeramente.—*to w. the tail,* mover la cola o rabo.—*vii.* oscilar, balancearse; ir pasando, deslizarse; (fam.) irse.—*s.* meneo; coleo; movimiento de cabeza; bromista, burlador.

wage [weịdž], *vt.* emprender, sostener; hacer (guerra), dar (batalla).—*s.* (gen. **wages**) salario, paga, jornal.— *w. earner,* asalariado.

wager [wéịdžœ(r)], *vt.* y *vi.* apostar.— *s.* apuesta.—*to lay a w.,* hacer una apuesta.

wagon [wǽgọn], *s.* vagón, carro, carretón, carreta, carromato; furgón.

walf [weịf], *s.* niño, animalito u objeto extraviado o abandonado.

wail [weịl], *vt.* y *vi.* deplorar, llorar, lamentar(se).—*s.* lamentación, gemido.

waist [weịst], *s.* (anat.) cintura; talle; (cost.) cinto, corpiño.—*w.-deep,* hasta la cintura.- **—coat** [wéịstkoṳt, wéskọt], *s.* chaleco.- **—line** [-lain], *s.* cintura.

wait [weịt], *vt.* esperar, aguardar.—*vi.* estar aguardando; atender; estar listo; servir; ser criado, sirviente o mozo (de fonda).—*to w. at table,* servir a la mesa.—*to w. for,* esperar.—*to w. on* o *upon,* ir a ver o presentar sus respetos a; servir a; atender a, despachar (en una tienda); (fam.) acompañar.- **—ing** [-iŋ], *s.* espera.—*w. list,* lista de espera.—*w. room,* sala de espera; (med.) antesala.—*s.* espera; (fam.) plantón; demora.—*in w.,* al o en acecho.- **—er** [wéịtœ(r)], *s.* mozo de café o restaurante, camarero.- **—ress** [-rịs], *s.* moza de café, camarera.

waive [weịv], *vt.* renunciar a; desistir de; diferir, posponer; repudiar.- **—r** [wéịvœ(r)], *s.* renuncia.

wake [weịk], *vti.* y *vii.* [5] despertar(se).—*to w. up,* despertar(se), animar(se).—*s.* vel(at)orio; (mar.) estela.—*in the w. of,* tras; inmediatamente después de; a raíz de.- **—ful** [wéịkful], *a.* vigilante, en vela; desvelado.- **—n** [-n], *vt.* y *vi.* despertar(se).

wale [weịl], *s.* cardenal, verdugo, verdugón; (tej.) relieve.

Wales [weilz], s. Gales.—*W.*, el país de Gales.—*the Prince of Wales,* el Príncipe de Gales.

walk [wɔk], vi. andar, caminar, ir a pie; pasear(se); (equit.) ir al paso; conducirse, portarse.—*to w. away,* irse, marcharse.—*to w. back,* regresar.—*to w. out,* salir, irse; declararse en huelga.—*to w. over,* ir al paso (caballo); (fam.) ganar fácilmente; abusar de.—*to w. up,* subir (a pie); acercarse.—*to w. up and down,* pasearse, ir y venir.—vt. hacer andar, (sacar a) pasear; recorrer, andar o pasar de una parte a otra de; andar por; hollar; llevar (un caballo) al paso.—s. paseo, caminata; modo de andar; paso del caballo; paseo, alameda; acera; carrera, oficio, empleo, estado, condición; método de vida, conducta, porte.—*w.-on,* figurante; extra; (dep.) jugador que se alista voluntario (no reclutado).— **—er** [wɔkœr], s. peatón; (mec.) andador.— **—ie-talkie** [wɔkitɔki], s. transmisor-receptor portátil, walkie-talkie.— **—ing** [-iŋ], a. a pie; para andar.—s. andar; caminata, paseo.—*w. papers,* nota de despido.—*w. stick,* bastón.— **—out** [-aut], s. huelga; retirada en señal de protesta.

wall [wɔl], s. pared; tabique; muro o tapia; muralla.—*low mud w.,* tapia.—*to drive, push o thrust to the w.,* poner entre la espada y la pared; acosar.—*to go to the w.,* hallarse acosado; verse obligado a ceder; (com.) quebrar.—vt. emparedar, tapiar, murar.— **—board** [-bɔrd], s. cartón tabla, madera prensada, panel.

wallet [wálit], s. cartera; bolsa de cuero; mochila; alforja.

wallflower [wólflauœr], s. (bot.) al(h)elí.—*to be a w.,* comer pavo, planchar el asiento.

wallop [wálop], vt. (fam.) golpear fuertemente; (fam.) vencer decisivamente.—s. (fam.) golpe rudo, bofetón; tunda; fuerza.

wallow [wálou], vi. revolcarse; chapotear (en el lodo); estar encenagado o sumido en el vicio.—s. revolcadura; revolcadero.

wallpaper [wólpeipœr], s. papel de empapelar, papel pintado.—vt. empapelar.

walnut [wólnʌt], s. (bot.) nuez; nogal.

walrus [wólrʌs], s. morsa.

waltz [wɔlts], vi. valsar.—s. vals.

wan [wan], a. pálido, macilento; débil.

wand [wand], s. vara; varilla de virtudes; batuta.

wander [wándœr], vi. errar, vagar; perderse, extraviarse.—vt. recorrer, andar por.- **—er** [-œr], s. vagabundo; peregrino.

wane [wein], vi. menguar (la luna); declinar, decaer.—s. disminución; decadencia; menguante (de la luna); (carp.) bisel.

want [want], vt. necesitar; querer, desear; pedir con urgencia, exigir.—vi. estar necesitado, pasar necesidades; faltar.—s. necesidad, carencia; privación, indigencia; exigencia; solicitud, demanda.—*for w. of,* a o por falta de.—*to be in w.,* estar necesitado.—*w.ad.,* anuncio clasificado.- **—ing** [wántiŋ], a. falto, defectuoso; deficiente; menguado; necesitado, escaso.—*to be w.,* faltar.

wanton [wántọn], a. inconsiderado, desconsiderado; disoluto, lascivo.

war [wɔr], s. guerra; arte militar.—*w. cloud,* amenaza de guerra.—*w. lord,* jefe militar.—*w. mother,* madrina de guerra.—*W. of the Roses,* guerra de las dos Rosas.—*w.-torn,* devastado por la guerra.—a. de o relativo a la guerra; bélico, marcial.—vii. [1] guerrear, estar en guerra.—*to w. on,* hacer la guerra a.

warble [wórbl], vi. trinar, gorjear; murmurar (un arroyo).—s. gorjeo, trino.- **—r** [-œr], s. ave cantora.

ward [wɔrd], vt. (off) resguardarse de; evitar, parar o desviar (un golpe).—s. pupilo o menor en tutela; barriada, barrio o distrito de ciudad; sala, división de hospital, etc.; tutela; protección; defensa, posición defensiva.- **—en** [wórden], s. custodio, celador, capataz; alcaide, carcelero; conserje; bedel.

wardrobe [wórdroub], s. guardarropa, ropero, armario; vestuario, ropa.

warehouse [wérhaus], s. almacén, depósito.—vt. almacenar.

warfare [wórfer], s. guerra; arte militar; operaciones militares; lucha, combate. **—warlike** [wórlaik], a. bélico(so), marcial.

warm [wɔrm], a. caluroso, caliente, cálido; templado, tibio; acalorado; fogoso, violento; conmovido, apasionado; expresivo; afectuoso; (pint.) que tira a rojo o amarillo; reciente, fresco; (fam.) cercano al objeto buscado; molesto; peligroso.—*to be w.,* tener calor; estar o ser caliente (una cosa); (con it por sujeto) hacer calor.—*w.-blooded,* apasionado; (zool.) de sangre caliente.—*w.-hearted,* afectuoso.—*w.-up,* calentón.—*vt.* calentar; caldear, abrigar; entusiasmar; (fam.) zurrar.—*to w. over* o *up,* calentar (comida fría).—*vi.* (con **up**) entusiasmarse; acalorarse; tomar bríos.—*to w. to(ward),* simpatizar con; cobrar cariño o afición a.- **—th** [-θ], *s.* calor (moderado); celo, entusiasmo; cordialidad; enojo.

warmonger [wɔ́rmʌŋɡœr], *s.* belicista.

warn [wɔrn], *vt.* avisar, prevenir, advertir, poner sobre aviso; aconsejar, amonestar; (for.) apercibir.—*vi.* servir de escarmiento.- **—ing** [wɔ́rniŋ], *s.* aviso, advertencia; escarmiento.—*a.* de alarma.

warp [wɔrp], *s.* torcedura, comba; (tej.) urdimbre; (mar.) remolque, calabrote.—*w. and woof,* (tej.) trama y urdimbre.—*vt.* (re)torcer; encorvar, combar, alabear; prevenir el ánimo; (tej.) urdir; (mar.) remolcar.—*vi.* torcerse; combarse; desviarse, alejarse; (tej.) urdir; (mar.) ir a remolque.

warpath [wɔ́rpæθ], *s.—to be on the w.,* (Native Americans) estar en pie de guerra; (humor.) estar buscando camorra.

warplane [wɔ́rpleįn], *s.* avión de guerra.

warrant [wárant], *vt.* garantizar, responder por; aseverar, certificar; justificar; autorizar.—*s.* (for.) auto, mandamiento, orden, cédula; autorización, poder; documento justificativo; testimonio; sanción; motivo, razón.- **—y** [-i̦], *s.* garantía; seguridad; autorización.

warrior [wɔ́rio̦(r)], *s.* guerrero. **—warship** [wɔ́rŝip], *s.* navío o buque de guerra.

wart [wɔrt], *s.* verruga.

wartime [wɔ́rtaim], *s.* período o tiempo de guerra.—*a.* relativo a dicho período; de guerra. **—warworn** [wɔ́rwɔrn], *a.* agotado por el servicio militar.

wary [wéri̦], *a.* cauto, cauteloso; prudente, precavido, prevenido.—*to be w. of,* desconfiar de.

was [waz, wʌz], (*1a.* y *3a. pers. sing.*) *pret.* de TO BE.

wash [waŝ], *vt.* lavar; fregar.—*to w. away, off* o *out,* lavar, borrar, hacer

desaparecer; quitar lavando; llevarse (el agua o un golpe de mar).—*washed-out,* desteñido; (fam.) debilitado, rendido.—*washed-up,* (fam.) agotado, deslomado.—*vi.* lavarse; lavar ropa; no perder el color o no estropearse cuando se lava.—*s.* lavado, lavadura; ropa lavada o para lavar; lavatorio, lavazas, agua sucia.—*w. and wear,* de lava y pon.— *w. basin,* palangana.—*w. stand,* lavabo.—*w. tub,* tina.—*w. water,* lavazas.—*a.* de o para lavar; lavable. - **—able** [wáŝ♭l], *a.* lavable.- **—er** [-œ(r)], *s.* (machine) lavadora; lavador; (mec.) arandela, zapatilla.—*w. woman,* lavandera.- **—ing** [-iŋ], *s.* lavado, lavamiento; ropa lavada; ropa sucia.—*w. machine,* lavadora, máquina de lavar.- **—cloth** [-klɔθ], *s.* paño para lavarse.- **—day** [-dej], *s.* día de la colada.- **—out** [-aut], *s.* derrubio; (fig.) fracaso.- **—rag** [-ræg], *s.* paño para lavarse; paño de cocina.- **—room** [-rum], *s.* gabinete de aseo, lavabo.

wasp [wasp], *s.* avispa.—*wasp's nest,* avispero.

waste [wejst], *vt.* malgastar, derrochar, desperdiciar; gastar, consumir; desolar, talar.—*vi.* gastarse, consumirse; desgastarse, dañarse.—*to w. away,* demacrarse, consumirse; ir a menos, menguar.—*a.* desechado, inútil; yermo; desolado; arruinado; sobrante.—*to lay w.,* devastar, asolar.—*s.* despilfarro; decadencia; merma, pérdida; despojos, desperdicios; erial; extensión, inmensidad; devastación; escombros.—*w. paper,* papeles usados, papel de desecho.- **—basket** [-bæskĕt], *s.* papelera.- **—ful** [wéjstful], *a.* manirroto, pródigo; ruinoso, antieconómico; destructivo.- **—fulness** [-fulni̦s], *s.* prodigalidad, derroche.

watch [wach], *s.* reloj (de bolsillo); vela, desvelo o vigilia; velorio; vigilancia, cuidado, observación; centinela, vigilante; cuarto, guardia, turno de servicio.—*to be on the w.,* estar alerta.—*to keep w. over,* vigilar a.—*w. charm,* dije.—*w. crystal,* cristal de reloj.—*w. wrist w.,* reloj de pulsera.—*vt.* vigilar, observar; ver, oír (T.V., radio, etc.); atisbar, espiar; cuidar, guardar.—*to w. one's step,* tener cuidado, andarse con tiento.—*vi.* estar alerta; hacer guardia; velar; *to w. for,* esperar; buscar.—*to w. out* for, tener cuidado con.—*to w. over,* guardar, vigilar; velar por, cuidar de; inspeccionar; estar a cargo de.—*w. out!* ¡cuidado!- **—case** [-keis], *s.* caja de reloj.- **—dog** [-dɔg], *s.* perro de guarda; (fig.) guardián fiel.— **—ful** [wáchfᵤl], *a.* despierto, vigilante, observador, que está alerta; desvelado.- **—maker** [-meíkœr], *s.* relojero.- **—man** [-mᵤn], *s.* sereno, guardián.- **—tower** [-tauœ(r)], *s.* atalaya; mirador.- **—word** [-wœrd], *s.* santo y seña; lema.

water [wɔ́tœ(r)], *s.* agua; extensión de agua (lago, río, etc.); marea; líquido semejante al agua (lágrimas, etc.).— *like w.,* en abundancia.—*w. closet,* inodoro, excusado, retrete.—*w. color,* acuarela; color para acuarela.— *w.-cooled,* enfriado por agua.—*w. front,* barrio de los muelles.—*w. ice,* sorbete.—*watering can,* regadera.— *w. lily,* ninfea, nenúfar.—*w. line,* línea de flotación; nivel de agua.— *w. main,* cañería de agua.—*w. polo,* polo de agua.—*w. power,* fuerza de agua, hulla blanca.—*w.-repellent, w.-resistant,* impermeabilizado, hidrófugo; (finish) impermeable.—*w. ski,* esquí acuático.—*w.-ski,* hacer esquí acuático.—*w. tower,* arco de agua.—*w. wheel,* rueda de agua; turbina de agua; (mar.) rueda de paletas.—*vt.* regar; humedecer, mojar, aguar, diluir; echar agua a; abrevar; dar agua a (un barco, locomotora, etc.).—*vi.* chorrear agua o humedad; tomar agua (un barco, etc.); beber agua (los animales).—*my eyes w.,* me lloran los ojos.—*my mouth waters,* se me hace la boca agua.— **—cress** [-krɛs], *s.* berros.- **—fall** [-fɔl], *s.* cascada, catarata, salto de agua.- **—mark** [-mark], *s.* filigrana, marca de agua; marca de nivel de agua.- **—melon** [-mɛlɔn], *s.* sandía, melón de agua.- **—proof** [-pruf], *a.* a prueba de agua, impermeable.—*vt.* impermeabilizar.- **—spout** [-spaᵤt], *s.* tromba; remolino.- **—tight** [-tajt], *a.* hermético, estanco.- **—way** [-wej], *s.* vía acuática o fluvial; canal o río navegable.- **—y** [-i], *a.* acuoso, aguado; insípido, soso; lloroso.

watt [wat], *s.* vatio.

wave [wejv], *s.* ola; onda, ondulación; movimiento de la mano, ademán; (tej. y joy.) aguas, visos.—*vt.* y *vi.* (hacer) ondear o flamear, blandir(se); ondular (el pelo, etc.); hacer señas o señales.—*to w. good-bye,* agitar la mano, el pañuelo, etc. en señal de despedida.- **—r** [wéjvœ(r)], *vi.* ondear, oscilar; tambalear, balancearse; vacilar, titubear, fluctuar. **—wavy** [wéjvi], *a.* ondeado, rizado; ondulante.

wax [wæks], *s.* cera; cerumen; parafina.—*a.* de cera, ceroso; encerado.—*w. paper,* papel encerado, papel parafinado.—*vt.* encerar; encerotar (hilo).—*vi.* crecer (la luna); hacerse, ponerse.- **—works** [-wœrks], *s.* museo de cera.

way [wej], *s.* vía; camino, senda; conducto, paso; espacio recorrido; rumbo, dirección; marcha, andar, velocidad (de un buque, etc.); modo, medio, manera; uso, costumbre.—*all the w.,* en todo el camino; del todo; hasta el fin.—*a long w. off,* muy lejos.—*by the w.,* a propósito, ya que viene al caso; de paso.—*by w. of,* por la vía de, pasando por; por vía de, a modo de; a título de.—*every w.,* por todas partes, de todos lados; de todos modos.—*no w.,* de ningún modo, de ninguna manera.—*on the w.,* de camino, de paso.—*on the w. to,* rumbo a, camino de.—*that w.,* por ahí, por allí; de ese modo, así.—*the other w. around,* al contrario, al revés.—*this w.,* por aquí; así, de este modo.—*to be in the w. of,* impedir, estorbar.—*to give w.,* ceder.—*to have one's (own) w.,* hacer uno lo que quiera; salirse con la suya.—*to make w.,* abrir paso.—*under w.,* en camino, en marcha; empezado, haciéndose.— *w. in,* entrada.—*w. out,* salida.—*w. through,* pasaje. **—wayfarer** [wéjferœr], *s.* caminante. **—waylaid** [wejléjd], *pret.* y *pp.* de TO WAYLAY. **—waylay** [wejléj], *vti.* [10] estar en acecho para asaltar o robar; asaltar; detener a alguien en su camino. - **—side** [wéjsajd], *s.* orilla o borde del camino.—*a.* que está junto al camino.- **—ward** [wéjwärd], *a.* descarriado; díscolo, voluntarioso; vacilante.

we [wi], *pron.* nosotros, nosotras.

weak [wik], *a.* débil, flaco.- **—en** [wíkn], *vt.* debilitar, enflaquecer.— *vi.* debilitarse, enflaquecerse.- **—ly** [-li], *adv.* débilmente.- **—ness**

[-nịs], *s.* debilidad, flaqueza; afición, gusto.

wealth [wélθ], *s.* riqueza.— **—y** [wélθị], *a.* rico.

wean [win], *vt.* destetar.—*to w. away from,* apartar poco a poco de.

weapon [wépọn], *s.* arma.

wear [wer], *vti.* [10] llevar o traer puesto (un traje, etc.), usar, gastar (bigote, sombrero, etc. habitualmente); desgastar, deteriorar.—*to w. away,* gastar o consumir.—*to w. down,* (des)gastar (por rozamiento).—*vii.* gastarse, consumirse; durar, perdurar; pasar, correr (el tiempo).—*to w. away,* decaer; gastarse, consumirse.—*to w. off,* usarse, gastarse; borrarse; desaparecer.—*to w. well,* durar largo tiempo, ser duradero.—*s.* uso, gasto, deterioro; moda, boga; prendas de vestir; durabilidad.—*w. and tear,* uso y desgaste.— **—iness** [wírịnịs], *s.* cansancio; aburrimiento.— **—ing** [wérịŋ], *s.* uso; desgaste, deterioro;—*w. apparel,* ropa, prendas de vestir.— **—isome** [wírịsọm], *a.* fatigoso; tedioso, pesado.— **—weary** [wírị], *a.* cansado.—*vt.* cansar.—*vi.* cansarse.

weasel [wízẹl], *s.* comadreja.—*w. words,* palabras ambiguas.

weather [wéðœ(r)], *s.* tiempo (estado atmosférico).—*pl.* vicisitudes de la suerte.—*it is good (bad) weather,* hace buen (mal) tiempo.—*a.* del tiempo, relativo al tiempo.—*w.-beaten,* curtido por la intemperie.—*w.-bound,* detenido por el mal tiempo.—*w. bureau,* observatorio, oficina metereológica.—*w. forecast(ing),* predicción o pronóstico del tiempo.—*w. report,* parte meteorológico.—*w. stripping,* burlete, cierre hermético.—*w. vane,* veleta.—*vt.* aguantar (el temporal).— **—man** [-mæn], *s.* meteorologista, pronosticador del tiempo.

weave [wiv], *vti.* y *vii.* [6] tejer.—*s.* tejido.—*vii.* tejer, trabajar en telar.—*s.* tejido.— **—r** [wívœ(r)], *s.* tejedor.

web [web], *s.* tela, tejido; (orn.) membrana.—*spider's w.,* tela de araña.—*w.-footed,* palmípedo, de pie palmeado.— **—bed** [-d], *a.* unido por una telilla o membrana; (orn.) palmípedo.

wed [wed], *vti.* [3] casarse con; casar.—*vii.* casarse.—*pp.* de TO WED. **—wedded** [wédịd], *a.* casado; conyugal.—*w. to,* (fig.) empeñado en, declarado por, aferrado en.- **—ding** [wédịŋ], *s.* bodas, nupcias, matrimonio.—*w. cake,* pastel de boda.—*w. day,* día de bodas.—*w. march,* marcha nupcial.—*w. night,* noche de bodas.—*w. ring,* anillo nupcial.—*a.* nupcial.- **—lock,** matrimonio.

wedge [wedʒ], *s.* cuña, calzo; prisma triangular.—*entering w.,* cuña, entrada, medio de entrar; para abrir brecha.—*vt.* acuñar, meter cuñas, calzar.

wedlock [wédlak], *s.* matrimonio.

Wednesday [wénzdị], *s.* miércoles.

wee [wi], *a.* pequeñito, diminuto.

weed [wid], *s.* mala hierba.—*vt.* desherbar, escardar.

week [wik], *s.* semana.—*w. in w. out,* semana tras semana.— **—day** [-dej], *s.* día laborable.- **—end** [-end], *s.* fin de semana.—*vi.* pasar el fin de semana.— **—ly** [wíklị], *a.* semanal.—*adv.* semanalmente, por semana.—*s.* revista semanal, semanario.

weep [wip], *vti.* y *vii.* [10] llorar.— **—er** [wípœ(r)], *s.* llorón.— **—ing** [-ịŋ], *s.* llanto, lloro.—*a.* plañidero, llorón.—*w. willow,* sauce llorón.

weevil [wívịl], *s.* gorgojo.

weft [weft], *s.* (tej.) trama.

weigh [wej], *vt.* pesar; considerar, reflexionar acerca de.—*to w. anchor,* levar anclas.—*to w. down,* exceder en peso; sobrepujar; sobrecargar, agobiar, oprimir.—*to w. out,* pesar, clasificar por peso.—*vi.* pesar, ser pesado; ser importante.—*to w. down,* hundirse por su propio peso.—*to w. on,* gravar, ser gravoso; levar anclas, hacerse a la vela.- **—t** [-t], *vt.* cargar, gravar; aumentar el peso de; poner un peso a.—*s.* peso; pesa; carga, gravamen; lastre; importancia, autoridad.- **—lifter** [-lịftœr], *s.* levantador de pesas, halterófilo.- **—lifting** [-lịftịŋ], *s.* levantamiento de pesas, halterofilia.- **—tless** [wejtlẹs], *a.* ingrávido.- **—tlessness** [wejtlẹsnẹs], *s.* ingravidez.- **—ty** [wéjtị], *a.* de peso, pesado; grave, serio, importante.

weird [wịrd], *a.* misterioso, horripilante, sobrenatural, raro, fantástico.

welcome [wélkʌm], *a.* bienvenido; grato, agradable.—*you are w.,* (respuesta a "muchas gracias", etc.) de nada, no hay de que; sea usted bienvenido.—*you are w. to it,* está a su disposición; se lo doy o presto con gusto; (irónico) buen provecho le haga.—*s.* bienvenida, buena acogida.—*vt.* dar la bienvenida a, recibir con agrado.—*interj.* ¡bienvenido!

weld [wɛld], *vt.* soldar con autógena; (fig.) unir.—*vi.* soldarse.— **—er** [wɛ́ldœ(r)], *s.* soldador.— **—ing** [-iŋ], *s.* soldadura.

welfare [wɛ́lfœr], *s.* bienestar; (pol.) asistencia, beneficencia.—*to be on w.,* vivir de la asistencia pública.—*w. state,* gobierno socializante, estado de beneficencia.

well [wɛl], *vi.* manar, brotar, fluir.—*s.* pozo; manantial, ojo de agua; aljibe, cisterna; origen; tintero.—*a.* bueno, en buena salud; salvo, sano; satisfactorio, conveniente; agradable; provechoso, ventajoso.—*it is just as w.,* menos mal.—*w. and good,* bien está, santo y muy bueno.—*w.-being,* bienandanza, felicidad, bienestar.—*w.-doer,* bienhechor.—*w.-doing,* benéfico; beneficencia.—*adv.* bien; muy; favorablemente; suficientemente; convenientemente; con propiedad, razonablemente; en sumo grado.—*as w.,* también.—*as w. as,* tanto como; además de.—*she is w. over forty,* anda por encima de los cuarenta años.—*w.-appointed,* bien provisto o bien equipado.—*w.-attended,* muy concurrido.—*w.-behaved,* de buena conducta.— *w.-being,* bienestar.—*w.-bred,* bien criado, cortés.—*w.-done,* bien hecho; (coc.) bien asado.—*w.-informed,* versado, bien enterado. —*w.-intentioned,* bien intencionado.—*w.-kept,* bien cuidado; (secret) bien guardado.—*w.-known,* bien conocido; familiar.—*w.-meaning,* bien intencionado.—*w.-nigh,* casi.—*w.-read,* leído, muy leído.—*w.-spent,* bien empleado.— *w.-thought of,* bien mirado.— *w.-timed,* oportuno.—*w.-to-do,* acomodado.—*w.-wisher,* amigo, favorecedor.—*w.-worn,* usado, trillado, gastado.—*interj.* ¡vaya, vaya! ¡qué cosa!

Welsh [wɛlʃ], *a.* galés.—*to w. on,* (jer.) dejar de cumplir con.—*s.* idioma galés.— **—man** [wɛ́lʃmən], *s.* galés.

welt [wɛlt], *s.* roncha, verdugón; (cost.) ribete, vivo; (carp.) refuerzo; (fam.) costurón; azotaina, tunda.— *vt.* ribetear; (fam.) azotar levantando ronchas.— **—er** [wɛ́ltœr], *s.* confusión, conmoción.—*w.-weight,* (dep.) peso mediano ligero.

wen [wɛn], *s.* lobanillo.

wend [wɛnd], *vt.*—*to w. one's way,* dirigir sus pasos, seguir su camino.

went [wɛnt], *pret.* de TO GO.

wept [wɛpt], *pret. y pp.* de TO WEEP.

were [wœr], *pret. sing.* de *2a* pers. y *pl.* de *indic.* y *sing.* y *pl.* de *subj.* de TO BE.—*as it w.,* por decirlo así; como si fuese.—*if I w. you,* yo en su caso, si yo fuera usted.—*there w.,* había, hubo.

west [wɛst], *s.* oeste, poniente, occidente, ocaso.—*a.* occidental, del oeste.—*W. Indian,* natural de las Antillas inglesas.—*adv.* a o hacia el poniente; hacia el occidente.— **—ern** [wɛ́stœrn], *a.* occidental.—*s.* novela o película del oeste o de vaqueros.— **—erner** [-œrnœ(r)], *s.* natural o habitante del oeste.— **—ward** [-wärd], *a.* que tiende o está al oeste.—*adv.* hacia el oeste.

wet [wɛt], *a.* mojado; húmedo; lluvioso.—*w. blanket,* aguafiestas.—*w. nurse,* ama de cría o de leche.—*w. through,* empapado, hecho una sopa.—*s.* humedad; lluvia; antiprohibicionista (enemigo de la Ley Seca en E.U.).—*vti.* [3] mojar, humedecer.—*pret. y pp.* de TO WET.— **—back** [-bæk], *s.* (despec.) mojado, espalda mojada. **—ness** [wɛ́tniʃ], *s.* humedad.

whack [hwæk], *vt.* (fam.) pegar, golpear.—*vi.* dar una tunda; ajustar cuentas; participar de.—*s.* (fam.) golpe; participación; porción; tentativa.

whale [hweil], *s.* ballena; cachalote; algo enorme, descomunal o de magnífica calidad.— **—bone** [-boun], *s.* ballena.

wharf [hwɔrf], *s.* muelle, (des)embarcadero, descargadero.

what [hwat], *pron., a. y adv.* qué; qué que; cuál; cómo; cualquiera.—*he knows w.'s w.,* sabe lo que se trae, sabe cuántas son cinco.—*w. a boy,* ¡qué muchacho!—*w. else?* ¿qué más?—*w. for?* ¿para qué? ¿por qué?—*w. of it?* ¿y qué? ¿y eso qué importa?—*w. people may say,* el qué dirán.— **—(so)ever** [hwat(so)-

évœ(r)], *pron.* cuanto, cualquier cosa que, todo lo que; sea lo que fuere, que sea.—*a.* cualquier(a).—*w. you say,* diga Ud. lo que diga.

wheat [hwit], *s.* trigo.—*w. field,* trigal.

wheedle [hwídl], *vt.* y *vi.* engatusar, hacer zalamerías, halagar.

wheel [hwil], *s.* rueda; rodaja; torno; polea.—*steering w.,* volante (de automóvil); rueda del timón.—*w. base,* batalla, paso, distancia entre ejes.—*w. chair,* silla de ruedas, cochecillo para inválidos.—*vt.* (hacer) rodar; transportar sobre ruedas; (hacer) girar; poner ruedas.—*vi.* rodar, girar; (fam.) ir en bicicleta.—*to w. about* o *around,* cambiar de rumbo o de opinión.- **—barrow** [hwílbærou], *s.* carretilla.—**wheeler-dealer** [hwíleٍrdíleٍr], *s.* (jer.) negociante de gran influencia e independencia.

wheeze [wiz], *s.* resuello ronco.—*vi.* resollar produciendo un silbido.

whelp [hwelp], *s.* (zool.) cachorro; osezno (de oso).—*vi.* parir (la hembra de animal carnívoro).

when [hwɛn], *adv.* y *conj.* cuando, al tiempo que, mientras que; que, en que; en cuanto, así que, tan pronto como; y entonces.—*since w.?* ¿desde cuándo? ¿de cuándo acá?- **—ce** [-s], *adv.* de donde o desde donde, de que o quien; de qué causa; de ahí que, por eso es por lo que; por consiguiente.- **—(so)ever** [-(so)évœ(r)], *adv.* cuando quiera que, siempre que, en cualquier tiempo que sea, todas las veces que.

where [hwɛr], *adv.* donde, dónde; en donde, por donde; en dónde, por dónde; adonde, adónde.- **—abouts** [hwɛٍrabauts], *s.* paradero.—*adv.* donde, dónde, en qué lugar.- **—abouts** [-abauts], *s.* paradero.- **—as** [hwɛræz], *conj.* considerando, por cuanto, visto que, en vista de que, puesto que, siendo así que; mientras que, al paso que.- **—by** [hwɛrbái], *adv.* por lo cual, con lo cual, por donde, de que; por medio del cual; ¿por qué? ¿cómo?- **—fore** [hwérfɔr], *adv.* por lo cual; por eso.—*s.* porqué, causa, motivo.- **—in** [hwɛrín], *adv.* donde, en donde, en lo cual; en qué, (en) dónde.- **—of** [hwɛráv], *adv.* de lo cual, de (lo) que; cuyo; de qué, de quién.- **—on** [hwɛrán], *adv.* en que, sobre lo cual,

sobre que; en qué.- **—upon** [hwɛrʌpán], *adv.* sobre lo cual, después de lo cual, con lo cual; entonces; en qué, sobre qué.- **—ver** [hwɛrévœ(r)], *adv.* dondequiera que o por dondequiera que, adondequiera que.- **—withal** [hwɛrwiðɔ́l], *adv.* con que, con lo cual, ¿con qué?—*s.* [hwɛrwiðɔl], dinero necesario.

whet [hwɛt], *vti.* [1] afilar amolar; estimular, incitar; aguzar o abrir el apetito.

whether [hwéðœ(r)], *conj.* si; sea, sea que, ora, ya.—*w. you will or not,* que quieras que no quieras, tanto si quieres como si no quieres.

whetstone [hwétstoun], *s.* piedra de afilar, piedra de amolar.

whey [hwej], *s.* suero.

which [hwich], *pron.* y *a.* qué, cuál; el cual, la cual, lo cual, los cuales, las cuales; que; el que, la que, lo que, los que, las que.—*all of w., all w.,* todo lo cual.—*w. of them?* ¿cuál de ellos? —*w. way?* ¿por dónde? ¿por qué camino?- **—ever** [hwichévœ(r)], *pron.* y *a.* cualquiera (que); el que.

while [hwajl], *s.* rato; lapso o espacio de tiempo.—*a (little) w. ago,* hace poco rato, no hace mucho.—*all this w.,* en todo este tiempo.—*for a w.,* por algún tiempo.—*to be worth w.,* valer la pena.—*conj.* mientras (que), en tanto que, al mismo tiempo que; aun cuando, si bien.— *to w. away,* pasar, entretener el tiempo.

whim [hwiٍm], *s.* antojo, capricho; fantasía.

whimper [hwímpœ(r)], *vi.* sollozar; lloriquear, gimotear.—*vt.* decir lloriqueando.—*s.* quejido, lloriqueo, gimoteo.

whimsical [hwímzikaٍl], *a.* caprichoso, fantástico.

whine [hwajn], *vi.* gemir, quejarse, lamentarse; lloriquear, gimotear.—*s.* quejido, lamento, lloriqueo, gimoteo.

whip [hwip], *vti.* [3] azotar, fustigar, flagelar; zurrar; (fam.) vencer, ganar a; batir (leche, huevos, etc.); sobrecoser; envolver (una soga, etc.) con cuerdecilla.—*to w. away,* arrebatar, llevarse.—*to w. in,* meter con violencia; reunir; hacer juntar; mantener juntos.—*to w. off,* ahuyentar a latigazos; quitar de re-

pente; despachar prontamente.—
to w. on, ponerse rápidamente.—*to
w. out,* arrebatar; sacar prontamente.—*to w. up,* coger de repente;
preparar en el momento; batir.—
whipped cream, nata, crema batida.—*whipper-snapper,* (ant.) arra-
piezo, mequetrefe.—*whipping boy,*
cabeza de turco, víctima inocente.—*whipping post,* poste de flagelación.—*s.* azote; látigo; latigazo;
movimiento circular de vaivén.— —
lash [-læš], *s.* tralla.— —**poorwill** [hw-
íporwil], *s.* chotacabras norteamericano.

whir [hwœr], *vti. y vii.* [1] zumbar.—*s.*
zumbido; aleteo.— —**l** [-l], *vt. y vi.* girar, rodar, voltejear, remolin(e)ar.—
s. giro, vuelta, volteo, remolino.
—**whirlpool** [hwœrlpul], *s.* vórtice,
vorágine, remolino. —**whirlwind**
[-wind], *s.* torbellino, remolino de
viento.

whisk [hwisk], *s.* escobilla, cepillo;
movimiento rápido.—*w. broom,* escobilla.—*vt.* cepillar, barrer.—*vi.*
menear la cola; marcharse deprisa.

whisker [hwískœ(r)], *s.* pelo de la
barba.—*pl.* barbas; (on the side of
face) patillas; (zool.) bigotes.

whiskey [hwíski], *s.* whisky.

whisper [hwíspœ(r)], *vt. y vi.* cuchichear, secretear; murmurar, susurrar; apuntar, soplar, sugerir.—*s.*
cuchicheo, susurro, murmullo.-
—**ing** [-iŋ], *a. y s.* susurrón.

whistle [hwísl], *vt. y vi.* silbar; chiflar.—*to w. for,* llamar silbando;
(fam.) buscar en vano.—*s.* silbo,
silbido; silbato, pito; (fam.) gaznate.—*w. stop,* apeadero, pueblecito.

whit [hwit], *s.* ápice, pizca, jota, etc.

white [hwait], *a.* blanco; puro, inmaculado.—*w.-collar,* oficinesco.—*w.
feather,* (fig.) cobardía o señal de cobardía.—*w. lead,* albayalde.—*w. lie,*
mentirilla, mentira blanca o venial.—*w. lily,* azucena.—*w.-livered,*
pálido, débil; cobarde.—*w. meat,*
pechuga, carne de la pechuga del
ave.—*w. plague,* tuberculosis.—*w.
slavery,* trata de blancas.—*s.* blanco
(color); persona blanca; clara del
huevo; esclerótica; (impr.) espacio
en blanco. —**caps** [-kæps], *spl.* cabrillas, palomas.- —**n** [hwáitn], *vt.
y vi.* blanquear(se), emblanque-
cer(se).- —**ness** [-nis], *s.* blancura,

albura, albor; palidez; pureza, candor.- —**wash** [-waš], *s.* lechada,
blanqueo.—*vt.* (alb.) blanquear, enlucir, encalar, dar lechada a; encubrir (las faltas de alguno).

whither [hwíθœr], *adv.* adónde.—*conj.*
adonde.

whitish [hwáitiš], *a.* blanquecino.

whittle [hwítl], *vt.* mondar; sacar pedazos (a un trozo de madera); aguzar,
sacar punta.—*to w. away* o *down,*
cortar o reducir poco a poco.

whiz [hwiz], *vii.* [1] zumbar (por la gran
velocidad); (fig.) pasar o ir muy de
prisa.—*s.* zumbido (debido a la velocidad); (fam.) fenómeno, persona
muy destacada, cosa muy buena.

who [hu], *pron.* quién, quiénes; quien,
quienes; que; el, la, los, las que; el, la,
cual, los, las cuales.—*w. goes there,*
¿quién vive?.— —**ever** [huévœ(r)]
pron. quienquiera que, cualquiera
que; quien, el que, la que, etc.

whole [houl], *a.* todo, entero, completo, total; íntegro, intacto; enterizo, continuo; sano; ileso.—
w.-hearted, sincero, enérgico, activo.—*w.-heartedly,* de todo corazón; con tesón.—*s.* totalidad, todo,
conjunto.—*as a w.,* en conjunto.—
on o upon the w., en conjunto, en general.- —**sale** [hóulseil], *a. y adv.*
(com.) (al) por mayor; en grande.—
s. venta o comercio (al) por mayor.—*vt. y vi.* vender (al) por mayor
- —**saler** [-seilœr], *s.* comerciante al
por mayor.- —**some** [-sʌm], *a.*
sano, saludable, salutífero; edificante. —**wholly** [hóuli], *adv.* totalmente, del todo, por completo.

whom [hum], *pron.* (a) quién, (a) quiénes; (a) quien, (a) quienes; que; al (a
la, a los, a las) que; al (a la) cual, a lo
(a las) cuales.- —**ever** [-évœr], *pron.*
rel. a quienquiera que.

whoop [hup], *s.* grito; alarido; esterto-
de la tosferina; chillido del buho.—
vt. y vi. gritar, vocear.—*vi.* respira
ruidosamente (después de un paro
xismo de tos).—*to w. it up,* arma
una gritería.—*whooping cough,* tos
ferina, coqueluche.

whore [hɔr], *s.* puta.

whose [huz], *pron.* cuyo, cuya, cuyos
cuyas; de quien, de quienes; de
quién, de quiénes.

why [hwai], *adv.* ¿por qué? ¿para qué?
¿a qué? por qué, por el cual, etc.—
the reason w., la razón por la cual.-

we don't know w., no sabemos por qué.—*s.* porqué, causa, razón, motivo.—*interj.* ¡cómo . . . ! ¡pero . . . ! ¡si . . . !—*w., I just saw her!* pero si la acabo de ver!

Ick [wik], *s.* mecha, pabilo, toreida.

Icked [wíkid], *a.* malo, malvado, inicuo; travieso, picaresco.– **—ness** [-nis], *s.* maldad, iniquidad.

Icker [wíkœ(r)], *a.* de mimbre, tejido de mimbres.—*s.* mimbre.

Icket [wíkit], *s.* portillo, postigo, portezuela.

Ide [waid], *a.* ancho, anchuroso; holgado; vasto.—*five inches w.,* cinco pulgadas de ancho.—*adv.* lejos, a gran distancia; anchamente; extensamente; descaminadamente; fuera de lugar o del caso.—*far and w.,* por todas partes.—*w.-angle,* granangular.—*w.-awake,* despabilado.—*w.-open,* abierto de par en par.– **—ly** [wáidli], *adv.* lejos, a gran distancia; extensivamente; muy, mucho; ancha u holgadamente.– **—n** [-n], *vt.* ensanchar, extender, ampliar, dilatar.—*vi.* ensancharse, dilatarse.– **spread** [-spred], *a.* esparcido, diseminado; general, extenso.

Idow [wídou], *s.* viuda.– **—ed** [-d], *a.* viudo; enviudado.– **—er** [-œ(r)], *s.* viudo.

Idth [widθ], *s.* anchura, ancho.

Ield [wild], *vt.* esgrimir; manejar; (fig.) empuñar (el cetro); mandar, gobernar.

Ife [waif], *s.* esposa, mujer.

Ig [wig], *s.* peluca.

Iggle [wígl], *vt.* y *vi.* menear(se) rápidamente; culebrear.—*s.* meneo rápido.

Ild [waild], *a.* salvaje, silvestre, selvático, montés; fiero, feroz, bravo; inculto, desierto, despoblado; turbulento, borrascoso; alocado; descabellado; desenfrenado; insensato; impetuoso, violento.—*w. boar,* jabalí.—*w. card,* comodín; (comput.) comodín; (fig.) imponderable.—*w. flower,* flor del campo.—*w.-goose chase,* empresa quimérica.—*w. oats,* excesos de la juventud.– **—cat** [wáildkæt], *s.* gato montés; negocio arriesgado; pozo (de petróleo) de exploración; (fam.) locomotora sin vehículos.—*a.* atolondrado, sin fundamento; ilícito, no autorizado.—*w. strike,* huelga repentina, no autorizada

por el sindicato.– **—erness** [wíldœrnis], *s.* desierto, vermo; despoblado, soledad.– **—fire** [-fair], *s.* fuego fatuo; fucilazo; incendio descontrolado.—*to spread like w.,* correr como pólvora en reguero.– **—life** [-laif], *s.* animales salvajes.– **—ness** [wáildnis], *s.* escabrosidad, fragosidad; tosquedad; rudeza, ferocidad; travesura; desvarío, locura.

wile [wail], *vt.* engañar, sonsacar; (fam.) engatusar.—*to w. away,* pasar (el rato).—*s.* ardid, red, superchería, treta, fraude, engaño; astucia.

will [wil], *s.* voluntad; albedrío; decisión; intención; gana, inclinación; precepto, mandato; (for.) testamento.—*w. power,* fuerza de voluntad.—*vt.* querer; legar.—*vai.* y *v. defect.* [11] (como auxiliar forma el futuro): *he w. speak,* él hablará; (como defectivo se traduce en el presente por 'querer'): *w. you sit down?* ¿quiere Ud. sentarse?

willful [wílful], *a.* voluntarioso, testarudo; premeditado, voluntario.– **—ness** [-nis], *s.* testarudez; premeditación.– **—willing** [wíliŋ], *a.* gustoso; complaciente; espontáneo.– **—willingly** [wíliŋli], *adv.* de buena voluntad.– **—willingness** [wíliŋnis], *s.* buena voluntad, gusto, complacencia.

will-o'-the-wisp [wil o ðe wísp], *s.* fuego fatuo.

willow [wílou], *s.* sauce.– **—y** [-i], *a.* esbelto, cimbreante.

willy-nilly [wíliníli], *adv.* de grado o por fuerza.

wilt [wilt], *vt.* marchitar.—*vi.* marchitarse.

wily [wáili], *a.* astuto, marrullero.

wimple [wímpl], *s.* toca.

win [win], *vti.* y *vii.* [10] ganar, vencer; lograr, conquistar; persuadir, atraer; prevalecer.—*to w. out,* triunfar, salir bien, lograr buen éxito.—*s.* (fam.) victoria.

wince [wins], *vi.* retroceder, recular; respingar.—*s.* respingo.

winch [winch], *s.* montacargas, malacate, cabria, cabrestante; manubrio, cigüeña.

wind [wind], *s.* viento, aire; aliento; flatulencia; palabrería.—*pl.* (mús.) instrumentos de viento; los músicos que los tocan.—*between w. and water,* a flor de agua.—*to catch* o *get one's w.,* recobrar el aliento.—*to get* *w. of,* husmear, descubrir.—*w. aft,* viento en popa.—*vti.* [10] [waind], quitar el resuello; olfatear; devanar, ovillar; enrollar; tejer; (re)torcer; dar cuerda a; manejar, dirigir, gobernar; perseguir, seguir las vueltas o los rodeos de.—*to w. off,* desenrollar.—*to w. out,* desenmarañar, desenredar, salir de un enredo.—*to w. up,* concluir; devanar, ovillar; dar cuerda (a un reloj).—*vii.* enrollar, arrollarse; (con up) enroscarse; culebrear; ir con rodeos; insinuarse; (re)torcerse, ensortijarse.—*to w. about,* enrollarse.—*to w. along,* serpentear, culebrear.— **—bag** [windbæg], *s.* (fam.) charlatán; palabreo vano.— **—break** [-breik], *s.* guardavientos.— **—ed** [wíndĕd], *a.* falto de respiración, sin resuello. **—fall** [wíndfɔl], *s.* fruta caída del árbol; ganga, ganancia inesperada, (fam.) chiripa.— **—ing** [wáindin], *s.* vuelta, revuelta, giro, rodeo; recodo, recoveco, tortuosidad; combadura; (elec., etc.) arrollamiento; (min.) extracción del mineral.—*w. up,* acto de dar cuerda (a un reloj); liquidación; conclusión, desenlace.—*a.* sinuoso; enrollado; en espiral.— **—lass** [wíndlas], *s.* torno.- **—mill** [wíndmil], *s.* molino de viento; (aer.) turbina de aire.—**—storm** [-storm], *s.* ventarrón.—**—ward** [-ward], *s.* barlovento.

window [wíndou], *s.* ventana; ventanilla; vidriera, escaparate (de tienda).—*w. blind,* persiana, celosía (en el interior); postigo, contraventana, puertaventana (en el exterior).—*w. dressing,* escaparatismo.—*w. frame,* marco de ventana.—*w. screen,* alambrera, sobrevidriera.—*w. shade,* visillo, transparente de resorte.—*w.-shop,* mirar los escaparates sin comprar.—*w. shutter,* contraventana.—*w. sill,* repisa de ventana. **—pane** [-pein], *s.* cristal o vidrio de ventana.- **—windpipe** [wíndpaip], *s.* tráquea; gaznate. **—windshield** [wíndšild], *s.* (aut.) parabrisa(s).—*w. wiper,* limpiavidrios del parabrisas. **—windy** [wíndi], *a.* ventoso; ventiscoso; borrascoso; expuesto al viento; pomposo; flatulento.—*it is w.,* hace viento.

wine [wain], *s.* vino; color de vino, rojo oscuro.—*w. cellar,* bodega.—*w. skin,* bota o pellejo de vino.- —

glass [-glæs], *s.* copa para vino.- —

growing [-grouin], *s.* vinicultura.· **—y** [wáinĕri], *s.* lagar.- **—ski** [-skin], *s.* odre.- **—taster** [-teistœr] *s.* catavinos.

wing [win], *s.* ala; flanco; lado; aspa (d molino); (teat.) bastidor; bamba lina.—*w. chair,* sillón de orejas.—*w nut,* tuerca de aletas.- **—sprea** [-spred], *s.* envergadura.

wink [wink], *vi.* pestañear, parpadear guiñar; centellear, dar luz tré mula.—*to w. at,* hacer la vist gorda.—*s.* pestañeo, parpadeo; u abrir y cerrar de ojos; guiño, gui ñada; siestecita.

winner [wínœ(r)], *s.* ganador, vence dor. **—winning** [wínin], *s.* triunfo.- *pl.* ganancias.—*a.* victorioso, triun fante; ganancioso; atractivo; per suasivo.—*w. back,* desquite.—*w manners,* don de gente.

winnow [wínou], *vt.* aventar; entre sacar.

winsome [wínsʌm], *a.* atractivo, sim pático.

winter [wíntœ(r)], *s.* invierno.—*a* hibernal, invernal.—*vi.* inverna **—wintry** [wíntri], *a.* invernal; com de invierno.- **—green** [-grin], *s* gaultería; escencia de gaultería.

wipe [waip], *vt.* limpiar frotando; en jugar; frotar, restregar.—*to w. awa* secar (frotando).—*to w. off,* borra cancelar; limpiar, lavar.—*to w. ou* borrar, cancelar, suprimir; destrui extirpar, aniquilar, exterminar; ago tar.- **—r** [waipœr], *s.* paño, trapo.

wire [wair], *s.* alambre; (fam.) tele grama.—*barbed w.,* alambre d púas.—*to pull wires,* (fam.) toca resortes.—*w. cutter,* cortaalambre —*w. gauze, w. screening,* tela mett lica.—*w.-haired,* de pelo áspero.- *w. pulling,* (fam.) empleo de reso tes.—*w. recorder,* grabadora de alan bre.—*w. tapping,* escuchas tel fónicas.—*vt.* poner alambres; ata con alambre; instalar conductore eléctricos.—*vt.* y *vi.* telegrafiar.- **less** [wájrlis], *s.* radiocomunica ción; telégrafo o teléfono sin h los.—*a.* inalámbrico, sin hilos alambres; de o por radiocomunica ción.- **—tap** [-tæp], *vt.* (tlf.) inte venir. **—wiring** [wáirin], *s.* (elec alambraje.- **—wiry** [-i], *a.* de alambr como un alambre; tieso, tenso; flac pero fuerte.

wisdom [wízdom], *s.* sabiduría, si

piencia; discernimiento, juicio, cordura; prudencia, sentido común; máxima, apotegma.—**w. tooth,** muela del juicio. —**wise** [wajz], *a.* sabio, docto, erudito; cuerdo, sensato, discreto; atinado; (fam.) vivo, listo.—*the three W. Men,* los tres Reyes Magos.—*w. guy,* (jer.) sabelotodo.—*s.* modo, manera.—*in any w.,* de cualquier modo.—*in no w.,* de ningún modo, absolutamente.- —**acre** [-ejkœr], *s.* sabihondo.- **crack** [wájzkræk], *s.* (fam.) agudeza, chiste, dicho u observación agudos.—*vi.* (fam.) decir agudezas.

wish [wiš], *vt.* y *vi.* desear, querer; hacer votos por; pedir.—*to w. for,* apetecer, ansiar, anhelar, querer, hacer votos por.—*s.* deseo, anhelo; cosa deseada; voto; súplica.—*to make a w.,* pensar en algo que se desea.- —**bone** [wíšbọụn], *s.* espoleta de la pechuga de las aves, (fam.) hueso de la suerte.- —**ful** [-fụl], *a.* deseoso; ávido, ansioso.—*w. thinking,* optimismo a ultranza.

wistful [wístfụl], *a.* anhelante, ansioso, ávido; pensativo, triste.

wit [wit], *s.* rasgo de ingenio, agudeza; ingenio; hombre de ingenio.—*pl.* juicio, sentido, razón; industria.—*to be at one's wits' end,* no saber uno qué hacer o decir; (fam.) perder la chaveta.—*to live by one's wits,* vivir de gorra, ser caballero de industria.

witch [wich], *s.* bruja; (fam.) mujer encantadora o fascinante; niña traviesa.—*w. hazel,* (bot.) nogal de la brujería; hamamelina, hazelina.- —**craft** [wíchkræft], *s.* brujería; sortilegio; fascinación.

with [wiδ], *prep.* con; para con; en compañía de.—*a man w. good sense,* un hombre de juicio.—*that country abounds w. oil,* ese país abunda en petróleo.—*the lady w. the camellias,* la dama de las camelias.—*to part w.,* separarse de.—*to struggle w.,* luchar contra.—*w. all speed,* a toda prisa, a toda velocidad.

withdraw [wiδdró], *vti.* [10] retirar; apartar, quitar, sacar, privar de; desdecirse de, retractar o retractarse de.—*vii.* retirarse, separarse; irse, salir.- —**al** [-ạl], *s.* retiro, retirada; recogida.—*w. symptom,* síntoma de abstinencia. —**withdrawn** [wiδdrón], *pp.* de TO WITHDRAW. —**withdrew** [wiδdrú], *pret.* de TO WITHDRAW.

wither [wíδœ(r)], *vt.* marchitar; ajar, deslucir; debilitar; avergonzar, sonrojar.—*vi.* marchitarse, secarse.

withheld [wiδhéld], *pret.* y *pp.* de TO WITHHOLD. —**withhold** [wiδhóụld], *vti.* [10] retener; negar, rehusar; apartar; detener; impedir.—*vii.* reprimirse, contenerse.—*to w. one's consent,* negar la aprobación, no dar el consentimiento.—*withholding tax,* impuesto deducido del sueldo, impuesto de retención.

within [wiδín], *prep.* dentro de, en lo interior de, en el espacio de; a la distancia de; al alcance de; a poco de; casi a, cerca de.—*w. an inch,* pulgada más o menos; (fig.) a dos dedos (de).—*w. bounds,* a raya.—*w. hearing,* al alcance de la voz.—*adv.* dentro, adentro; dentro de uno; en casa, en la habitación.

without [wiδáut], *prep.* sin; falto de; fuera de, más allá de.—*to do w.,* pasarse sin, prescindir de.—*adv.* fuera, afuera, por fuera, hacia afuera, de la parte de afuera; exteriormente.— *conj.* (fam.) si no, a menos que.

withstand [wiθstǽnd], *vt.* aguantar, resistir.

witness [wítnịs], *s.* testigo; espectador; testimonio.—*in w. whereof,* en fe de lo cual.—*w. stand,* banquillo o estrado de los testigos.—*vt.* presenciar; dar fe.

witty [wíti], *a.* satírico, sarcástico; ingenioso, agudo; gracioso, ocurrente.

wives [wajvz], *s. pl.* de WIFE.

wizard [wízạrd], *a.* hechicero, mágico.—*s.* hechicero, mago, brujo.- —**ry** [-ri], *s.* hechicería, magia.

wobble [wábl], *vi.* balancearse, tambalearse; (fam.) vacilar.—*vt.* hacer tambalear(se) o vacilar.—*s.* bamboleo, tambaleo.

woe [wọu], *s.* infortunio, miseria, pesar, calamidad.—*w. is me!* ¡desgraciado de mí!- —**begone** [wóụbịgọn], *a.* cariacontecido, triste.

woke [wọuk], *pret.* de TO WAKE.

wolf [wulf], *s.* lobo; (fam.) mujeriego, libertino.—*to cry w.,* dar falsa alarma.—*w. cub,* lobezno, lobato.— *vt.* (fam.) engullir, devorar. — **wolves** [wulvz], *s. pl.* de WOLF.

woman [wúmạn], *s.* mujer.—*w. hater,* misógino.—*w. voter,* electora.—*w. writer,* escritora.- —**hood** [-hụd], *s.* estado o condición de mujer adulta; sexo femenino, las mujeres.- —

kind [-kaɪnd], *s.* las mujeres; el sexo femenino.— **-ly** [-lɪ], *a.* mujeril, de mujer, femenino.—*adv.* mujerilmente; femenilmente.

womb [wum], *s.* útero, matriz; (fig.) madre; caverna; seno, entrañas.

women [wímɪn], *s. pl.* de WOMAN.

won [wʌn], *pret.* y *pp.* de TO WIN.

wonder [wʌndœ(r)], *vt.* desear saber; sorprenderse, maravillarse de; preguntarse.—*I* w. *what he means,* ¿qué querrá decir?—*vi.* admirarse.—*to w. at,* extrañar, maravillarse de.—*s.* admiración; maravilla, portento, milagro; enigma, cosa extraña o inexplicable.—*no w.,* no es extraño, no es mucho.—*w. drugs,* drogas milagrosas.— **-ful** [-fʊl], *a.* maravilloso, asombroso; admirable, excelente.— **-land** [-lænd], *s.* tierra de las maravillas.— **-ment** [-mɛnt], *s.* asombro, sorpresa.

wont [wʌnt], *a.* acostumbrado.—*to be w.,* soler, tener la costumbre.—*s.* uso, costumbre, hábito.

won't [woʊnt], *contr.* de WILL NOT.

woo [wu], *vt.* y *vi.* cortejar, galantear, enamorar; pretender a una mujer; solicitar, importunar; esforzarse por obtener (fama, etc.).

wood [wʊd], *s.* madera; leña; madero.—*pl.* bosque, selva, monte.—*a.* de o para madera o para almacenarla, transportarla o labrarla; de monte, que vive o crece en la selva.—*to be out of the woods,* haber puesto una pica en Flandes; estar a salvo.—*w. carving,* talla en madera.—*w. engraving,* grabado en madera.—*w. screw,* tornillo tirafondo.— **-chuck** [-chʌk], *s.* marmota de América.— **-cut** [wúdkʌt], *s.* grabado en madera.— **-cutter** [-kʌtœ(r)], *s.* leñador; grabador en madera.— **-ed** [-ɪd], *a.* provisto de madera; arbolado; boscoso.— **-en** [-n], *a.* de palo o madera; grosero, rudo; estúpido, inexpresivo.— **-en** [wúdĕn], *a.* de madera; torpe, sin ánimo.—*w. leg,* pata de palo.—*w. shoe,* zueco.— **-land** [-lænd], *s.* arbolado, monte, bosque, selva.—*a.* [-lǎnd], de bosque, selvático.— **-(s)man** [-(z)mǎn], *s.* leñador, hachero.— **-pecker** [-pɛkœ(r)], *s.* pájaro carpintero, picaposte, picamaderos.— **-pile** [-paɪl], *s.* montón de leña.— **-shed** [-ʃĕd], *s.* leñero.— **wind** [-wɪnd], *s.* (mus.) instrumento

de viento de madera.— **-work** [-wœrk], *s.* enmaderamiento, maderaje, maderamen; obra de carpintería; ebanistería.

woof [wuf], *s.* (tej.) trama, textura. **-woofer** [wúfœr], *s.* alatvoz para audiofrecuencias bajas.

wool [wʊl], *s.* lana.—*all-w.,* de pura lana.—*a.* lanar; de lana.—*w. bearing,* lanar.— **-(l)en** [wúlɪn], *a.* de lana; lanudo; lanero.—*w. yarn,* estambre.—*s.* paño o tejido de lana.—*pl.* ropa o prendas de lana.— **-ly** [-ɪ], *a.* lanudo; lanar; de lana; crespo, pasudo (cabello); (b.a.) falto de detalles; aborregado (cielo).

word [wœrd], *s.* palabra; vocablo, voz; aviso, recado, mensaje; noticia(s); santo y seña; voz de mando, orden, mandato.—*pl.* contienda verbal; (mús.) letra (de una canción, etc.).—*by w. of mouth,* de palabra.—*in so many words,* textualmente; claramente, sin ambages.—*in the words of,* según las palabras de como dice.—*on my w.,* bajo mi palabra, a fe mía.—*to have a w. with,* hablar con.—*to have words,* (fam.) tener unas palabras, disputar.—*to leave w.,* dejar dicho.—*w. count,* recuento de vocabulario.—*w. order,* orden de colocación.—*w. processor,* procesador de textos o de palabras.—*vt.* expresar; redactar.— **-iness** [wœrdɪnɪs], *s.* verbosidad.— **-ing** [-ɪŋ], *s.* redacción, fraseología, expresión, términos.— **-y** [wœrdɪ], *a.* verboso.

wore [wɔr], *pret.* de TO WEAR.

work [wœrk], *vti.* [4] trabajar; laborar; explotar (una mina, etc.); fabricar, elaborar; obrar sobre, influir en; hacer trabajar o funcionar; manipular; surtir efecto; resolver (un problema).—*to w. one's way through,* abrirse camino por o en; pagar uno con su trabajo los gastos de.—*to w. through,* penetrar; atravesar a fuerza de trabajo.—*vii.* trabajar; funcionar; tener buen éxito, ser eficaz; ir (bien o mal); obrar u operar (un remedio).—*to w. at,* trabajar en; ocuparse en o de.—*to w. down,* bajarse.—*to w. free,* aflojarse o soltarse con el movimiento o el uso.—*to w. loose,* aflojarse, soltarse con el uso.—*to w. out,* tener buen éxito; surtir efecto; resultar.—*s.* trabajo; tarea, empresa, labor; obra; (cost.

labor.—*out of w.,* sin trabajo, cesante.—*(to be) at w.,* (estar) ocupado, trabajando o funcionando.—*to be hard at w.,* estar muy atareado.—*w. force,* mano de obra; personal obrero.—*w. of art,* obra de arte.- **—able** [-aběl], *a.* practicable; laborable.- **—bench** [-bench], *s.* banco de trabajo o taller.- **—day** [-dei], *s.* día de trabajo; (number of hours) jornada.- **—er** [wœrkœ(r)], *s.* trabajador, obrero, operario; abeja u hormiga obrera.- **—ing** [-iŋ], *s.* obra, trabajo; funcionamiento; laboreo, explotación; maniobra.—*a.* que trabaja, trabajador; de trabajo; fundamental.—*w. class,* clase obrera.—*w. day,* día de trabajo o laborable; jornada.- **—ingman** [-iŋman], *s.* obrero, jornalero, operario.- **—man** [-man], *s.* trabajador, obrero, operario.- **—manship** [-manŝip], *s.* hechura, mano de obra; artificio; primor o destreza del artífice.- **—out** [-aut], *s.* ensayo, prueba; (physical exercise) ejercicio.- **—room** [-rum], *s.* taller, obrador; gabinete de trabajo.- **—shop** [-ŝap], *s.* taller, obrador.

orld [wœrld], *s.* mundo.—*w. affairs,* asuntos internacionales.—*world's fair,* exposición mundial.—*W. War,* guerra mundial.—*w.-wide,* mundial, global, de alcance mundial.— *W.-Wide Web,* (comput.) teleraña mundial.—*w. without end,* para siempre jamás; por los siglos de los siglos.- **—ly** [wœrldli], *a.* mundano, mundanal, carnal, terreno, terrenal, terrestre; seglar, profano.—*w.-wise,* que tiene mucho mundo.—*adv.* mundanalmente, profanamente.

orm [wœrm], *s.* gusano; lombriz; oruga; polilla, carcoma; gorgojo.— *w.-eaten,* carcomido, picado de gusanos.—*vt.* y *vi.* insinuarse, introducirse o arrastrarse (como un gusano).—*to w. a secret out of a person,* arrancar mañosamente un secreto a una persona.—*vi.* trabajar u obrar lentamente y por bajo mano.

orn [wɔrn], *pp.* de TO WEAR.—*w.-out,* gastado, raído; estropeado; cansado; agotado.

orrisome [wœrisʌm], *a.* inquietante; aprensivo, inquieto.

orry [wœri], *vti.* y *vii.* [7] preocu-

par(se), inquietar(se); apurar(se), afligir(se).—*s.* preocupación, inquietud, cuidado, apuro.

worse [wœrs], *a.* peor, más malo; inferior; en peor situación.—*to be w. off,* estar en peores circunstancias, o quedar peor.—*to get w.,* empeorar(se).—*to make o render w.,* empeorar.—*w. and w.,* de mal en peor; peor que nunca; cada vez peor.—*adv.* peor; menos.—*s.* menoscabo, detrimento; (lo) peor.—*to change for the w.,* empeorar(se).

worship [wœrŝip], *s.* culto, adoración; reverencia, respeto.—*your w.,* usía; vuestra merced.—*vti.* [2] adorar; reverenciar, honrar.—*vii.* adorar; profesar culto o religión.- **—(p)per** [-œ(r)], *s.* adorador, devoto.

worst [wœrst], *a.* pésimo, malísimo.— *the w.,* el, o la, o lo peor.—*adv.* del peor modo posible; pésimamente. —*vt.* vencer, rendir o derrotar a; triunfar de.

worsted [wústid], *s.* estambre.

worth [wœrθ], *s.* mérito; consideración, importancia; valor, valía; monta, precio; nobleza, excelencia, dignidad.—*a.* que vale o posee; equivalente a; de precio o valor de; digno de, que vale la pena de.—*to be w.,* valer, costar; merecer; tener.- **—less** [wœrθlis], *a.* inútil, inservible; sin valor; indigno, despreciable.- **—while** [-hwail], *a.* de mérito, digno de atención.—*to be w.,* valer la pena. - **—y** [wœrði], *a.* digno; apreciable, benemérito; merecedor.

would [wud], *vai.,* *pret.* de WILL (forma el modo condicional): *she said she w. come,* dijo que vendría.—*v. defect., pret.* de WILL.—*w.-be,* llamado; supuesto; presumido.—*w. you sit down?* ¿querría Ud. sentarse?

wound [waund], *pret.* y *pp.* de TO WIND (devanar).—*s.* [wund], herida; llaga, lesión; ofensa, golpe, daño.— *vt.* y *vi.* herir, lesionar, llagar, lastimar; ofender, agraviar.

wove [wouv], *pret.* y *pp.* de TO WEAVE. **—woven** [wóuvn], *pp.* de TO WEAVE.

wrangle [ræŋgl], *vi.* reñir; disputar.—*s.* pendencia, riña; disputa, altercado.

wrap [ræp], *vti.* [3] arrollar o enrollar; envolver.—*to w. up,* arrollar; envolver; arropar; embozar; cubrir, ocultar.—*vii.* arrollarse; envolverse.—*to w. up (in),* envolverse (en).—*s.* bata; abrigo.—*pl.* abrigos y mantas (de viaje, etc.).– **—per** [ráepœ(r)], *s.* envoltura, cubierta; faja de periódico; bata, peinador; pañal de niño.– **—ping** [ráepiŋ], *a.* de envolver, de estraza (papel).—*s.* envoltura, cubierta.

wrath [ræθ], *s.* ira, cólera.– **—ful** [ráeθful], *a.* airado, colérico.

wreath [riθ], *s.* corona, guirnalda; festón; trenza; espiral.– **—e** [rið], *vt.* enroscar, entrelazar, tejer (coronas o guirnaldas); ceñir, rodear.—*vi.* enroscarse, ensortijarse.

wreck [rek], *s.* naufragio; destrozo, destrucción; buque naufragado, barco perdido; restos de un naufragio.—*vt.* hacer naufragar; arruinar, echar a pique; demoler, desbaratar.—*vi.* naufragar, zozobrar, irse a pique; fracasar.– **—ing** [-iŋ], *a.*—*w. ball,* bola rompedora.—*w. crane,* grúa de auxilio.

wrench [rench], *vt.* arrancar, arrebatar; (re)torcer; dislocar, sacar de quicio.—*to w. one's foot,* torcerse el pie.—*s.* arranque, tirón; torcedura; (mec.) llave de tuercas.—*monkey w.,* llave inglesa.

wrest [rest], *vt.* arrebatar, arrancar violentamente.

wrestle [résl], *vt.* luchar con; forcejear contra.—*vi.* luchar a brazo partido; esforzarse; disputar.– **—r** [réslœ(r)], *s.* luchador. **—wrestling** [résliŋ], *s.* (dep.) lucha grecorromana; lucha a brazo partido.—*w. match,* partido de lucha.

wretch [rech], *s.* infeliz, desventurado, miserable; ente vil, despreciable.– **—ed** [réchjd], *a.* infeliz, miserable; calamitoso; vil, despreciable; perverso; mezquino; malísimo, detestable. **—wretchedness** [réchjdnjs], *s.* miseria; desgracia; vileza.

wriggle [rígl], *vt.* menear, retorcer, hacer colear.—*vi.* colear, culebrear, undular; retorcerse.

wring [riŋ], *vti.* [10] torcer, retorcer; arrancar; estrujar, exprimir, escurrir; forzar; atormentar, aquejar.—*to w. out,* exprimir. **—er** [riŋœr], *s.* exprimidor.

wrinkle [ríŋkl], *s.* arruga; surco, buche; (fam.) capricho, maña; artificio; idea, ocurrencia; indicio, insinuación.—*vt.* arrugar, fruncir.—*to w. up,* arrugar, plegar.—*vi.* arrugarse; encarrujarse.

wrist [rjst], *s.* (anat.) muñeca; (mec.)

muñón.—*w. watch,* reloj de pulsera

writ [rjt], *s.* (for.) escrito, orden, auto mandamiento, decreto judicial.– *Holy W.,* Sagrada Escritura.

write [rajt], *vti.* [10] escribir; descri bir.—*to w. after,* copiar de.—*to w. good hand,* hacer o tener buena le tra.—*to w. off,* (com.) cancelar, sal dar.—*to w. out,* redactar; copia transcribir; escribir completo (si abreviar).—*to w. up,* narrar, relata describir; (fam.) ensalzar por es crito; (com.) poner al día (el libr mayor); valorar en demasía una par tida del activo.—*vii.* escribir, tene correspondencia; ser escritor o au tor.—*to w. back,* contestar a un carta.—*to w. on,* continuar escri biendo; escribir acerca de.– **—** [rájtœ(r)], *s.* escritor; literato, hom bre de letras, autor.—*writer's cramp* grafospasmo.—*w.-up,* crítica, re seña; artículo, reportaje.

writhe [rajð], *vt.* (re)torcer.—*vi.* re torcerse; contorcerse (por algún do lor). **—writhing** [rájðiŋ], *s.* retorci miento, contorsión.

writing [rájtiŋ], *s.* escritura; letra; es crito; (el arte de) escribir.—*a.* de para escribir.—*at the present w. o a this w.,* al tiempo que esto se escribe ahora mismo.—*(to put) in w.,* (po ner) por escrito.—*w. desk,* escrito rio.—*w. pad,* block de papel.—*v paper,* papel de escribir, papel d cartas. **—written** [rítn], *pp.* de T WRITE.

wrong [rɔŋ], *s.* injusticia, sinrazór agravio; mal, daño, perjuicio culpa; error; falsedad.—*to be in th w.,* no tener razón.—*to do w.,* obrar hacer mal; hacer daño, perjud car.—*a.* erróneo, desacertado; in justo; censurable; falso; irregula equivocado; inconveniente; ma hecho, mal escrito, etc.—*he took th w. book,* cogió el libro que no era, se equivocó de libro.—*w. numbe* número equivocado.—*w. side,* cor trahaz, revés; (of the street) lac contrario.—*adv.* mal, sin razón causa; injustamente; al revés.—*v* causar perjuicio a; hacer mal ofender; agraviar; ser injusto con. **—doing** [-duiŋ], *s.* malheche maldad.

wrote [rout], *pret.* de TO WRITE.

wrought [rɔt], *pret.* y *pp.* de TO WORK.— *a.* forjado, labrado, trabajado.—

iron, hierro forjado.—*w.-up*, (sobre)excitado, perturbado.

wrung [rʌŋ], *pret. y pp.* de TO WRING.

wry [raj], *a.* torcido, doblado, sesg(ad)o; pervertido, tergiversado.—*w. face*, gesto, visaje, mueca, mohín.

X

xenophobia [zɛnofoúbia], *s.* xenofobia.

Xerox (TM) [zíraks], *s.* Xerox.—*to make a X. (copy)* of, xerocopiar, xerografiar.—*X. copy*, Xerox, fotocopia.—*X. machine*, fotocopiadora.

Xmas [krísmas], *s.* = CHRISTMAS.

X-rated [éksrejtjd], *a.* sólo para adultos.

X ray [éksrej], *s.* rayo X; radiografía.

X-ray [éksrej], *a.* radiográfico, de rayos X.—*vt.* radiografiar, fotografiar con los rayos X.—*X. photograph,* radiografía.

xylophone [zájlofoun], *s.* xilófono; (Am.) especie de marimba.

Y

yacht [yat], *s.* yate.—*y. club,* club náutico.

yam [yæm], *s.* ñame; boniato, camote.

yank [yæŋk], *s.* tirón.—*vt.* sacar de un tirón.

Yankee [yǽŋki], *a. y s.* (fam.) yanqui (natural del Norte de los EE.UU.).

yard [yard], *s.* corral; patio; cercado; yarda (medida). Ver Tabla.—**—stick** [yárdstjk], *s.* yarda graduada de medir; patrón, modelo; criterio.

yarn [yarn], *s.* hilaza; hilo, hilado; estambre; (fam.) cuento increíble.

yaw [yo], *vi. y vi.* (mar.) guiñar.—*s.* guiñada.—*pl.* (med.) frambesia, pián.

yawn [yon], *vi.* bostezar; abrirse, desmesuradamente.—*s.* bostezo.

yea [yej], *adv. y s.* sí.

year [yjr], *s.* año.—*y. in, y. out,* año tras año.—*pl.* años, edad; vejez.—*to be . . . years old,* cumplir . . . años.— **—book** [yírbuk], *s.* anuario.— **—ly** [-lj], *a.* anual.—*adv.* anualmente.

yearn [yœrn], *vi.* suspirar, anhelar.—*to y. for,* suspirar por, anhelar por.— **—ing** [yœ́rnjŋ], *s.* anhelo, deseo ardiente.

yeast [yist], *s.* levadura.

yell [yel], *vt. y vi.* decir a gritos.—*s.* grito.

yellow [yélou], *a.* amarillo; sensacional, escandaloso (periódico, etc.); (fam.) cobarde, blanco.—*y. fever,* fiebre amarilla.—*s.* amarillo (color).—*vi.* amarillecer.– **—ish** [-iŝ], *a.* amarillento.

yelp [yɛlp], *vi.* gañir.—*s.* gañido.

yeoman [yóumạn], *s.* (*pl.* **yeomen** [yóumẹn]), (mar.) pañolero; (E.U.) (mar.) oficinista de a bordo.—*y. service,* servicio leal o notable.

yes [yes], *adv.* sí.—*y. indeed,* sí por cierto, ya lo creo.—*s.* respuesta afirmativa o favorable.—*y. man,* hombre servil, que obedece ciegamente.—*vt.* decir sí a.—*vi.* decir sí.

yesterday [yéstœrdj], *s. y adv.* ayer. **—yesteryear** [yéstœryjr], *adv.* antaño.

yet [yet], *conj.* con todo, sin embargo, no obstante; mas, pero, empero; aun así.—*adv.* aún, todavía, hasta ahora; a lo menos; más, además, más que.—*as y.,* hasta ahora, hasta aquí, todavía.—*not y.,* todavía no, aún no.

yield [yild], *vt.* producir; redituar, rendir.—*vi.* entregarse, rendirse, someterse; acceder, ceder, consentir; producir.—*s.* producción, rendimiento; (crop) cosecha; (income) rédito; (traffic sign) ceda el paso.

yoke [youk], *s.* yugo; (fig.) yugo; (zool.) yunta; (of a shirt) hombrillo.—*vt.* uncir.

yolk [youk], *s.* yema.

yonder [yándœ(r)], *adv.* allí, allá, acu-llá.—*a.* aquel, aquella, aquellos, aquellas.

yore [yɔr], *s.*—*in days of y.*, de otro tiempo; de antaño.

you [yu], *pron.* tú, usted, vosotros, ustedes; te, a ti, le, la, a usted, os, a vosotros, les, a ustedes; se, uno.

young [yʌŋ], *a.* joven.—*y. fellow*, joven, mozo.—*y. lady*, muchacha, señorita, jovencita (joven).—*y. man*, muchacho, joven.—*s.*—*the y.*, los jóvenes, la gente joven.—*y. people*, jóvenes, gente joven.— **—ster** [yʌ́ŋstœ(r)], *s.* jovencito, mozalbete; niño, chiquillo.

your [yųr], *a.* tu(s), vuestro(s), vuestra(s); su(s), de usted(es).— **—s** [-z], *pron.* el tuyo, la tuya, los tuyos, las tuyas; el vuestro, etc.; el, la, lo, los o las de usted(es); el suyo, etc.—*y. affectionately*, su afectísimo.—*y. truly*, de Vd. atto. y S.S., su seguro servidor; (fam.) este cura (yo).— **—self** [-sélf], *pron.* tú mismo, tú misma; usted mismo, usted misma.— **—selves** [-sélvz], *s. pl.* vosotros, vosotras o ustedes mismos (mismas).

youth [yuθ], *s.* juventud, jóvenes.— **—ful** [yúθfųl], *a.* juvenil, mocil.

Yuletide [yúltajd], *s.* la Pascua de Navidad.

Z

zany [zéjnį], *a.* y *s.* cómico, bufo.

zap [zæp], *vt.* (fam.) liquidar; (comput.) eliminar, borrar.—*interj.* (fam.) ¡zas!

zeal [zil], *s.* celo, entusiasmo.— **—ot** [zélọt], *s.* entusiasta, fanático.— **—ous** [zélʌs], *a.* entusiasta, fervoroso.

zebra [zíbrą], *s.* cebra.

zebu [zíbĳu], *s.* cebú.

zenith [zínįθ], *s.* cenit; (fig.) apogeo.

zephyr [zefœ(r)], *s.* céfiro.

zeppelin [zɛpělįn], *s.* zepelín.

zero [zírou], *s.* cero.—*z. gravity*, gravedad nula.

zest [zest], *s.* entusiasmo; gusto, sabor; (peeling) cáscara, peladura.—*to give z. to*, dar gusto o sabor a.

zigzag [zígzæg], *a.* y *adv.* en zigzag.—*vi.* zigzaguear.

zinc [zįŋk], *s.* cinc o zinc.

zip [zįp], *s.* (fam.) silbido, zumbido; (fam.) energía, brío.—*z. code*, código postal.—*vt.* cerrar o abrir con cierre relámpago.—*vi.* silbar, zumbar; (fam.) moverse con energía.—*to z. by*, (fam.) pasar rápidamente.—*to z. up*, cerrarse con una cremallera.

zipper [zípœ(r)], *s.* cierre cremallera automático o relámpago.

zodiac [zóųdjæk], *s.* zodíaco.

zone [zouŋ], *s.* zona; distrito postal.—*vt.* dividir en zonas.

zoo [zu], *s.* jardín o parque zoológico.— **—logic(al)** [zoųoládžik(ąl)], *a.* zoológico.— **—logist** [zoųálodžįst], *s.* zoólogo.— **—logy** [zoųálodžį], *s.* zoología.

zoom [zum], *s.* zumbido.—*vi.* zumbar (aer.) empinarse.

NOMBRES GEOGRAFICOS QUE DIFIEREN
EN ESPAÑOL Y EN INGLES

A

Abyssinia [æbịsíniậ], Abisinia.
Adriatic [ejdriǽtik], Adriático.
Ægean [idžíận], Egeo.
Afghanistan [æfgǽnịstæn], Afganistán.
Africa [ǽfrịkậ], Africa.
Alexandria [ælegzǽendriậ], Alejandría.
Algeria [ældžíriậ], Argelia.
Algiers [ældžírz], Argel.
Alps [ælps], Alpes.
Alsace-Lorraine [ælséịs o ælsǽs / loréịn], Alsacia Y Lorena.
Amazon [ǽmạzan], (Río de las) Amazonas.
America [ạmérịkậ], América.
Andalusia [ændạlúžậ], Andaluća.
Antilles [æntíliz], Antillas.
Antwerp [ǽntwŒrp], Amberes.
Apennines [ǽpenạjnz], Apeninos.
Appalachians [æpạlǽchịạnz], (Montañas) Apalaches.
Asia Minor [éịžậ / májnọ(r)], Asia Menor.
Assyria [ạsíriậ], Asiria.
Athens [ǽθịnz], Atenas.
Atlantic [ætlǽntịk], Atlántico.

B

Babylon [bǽbịlan], Babilonia.
Balearic Islands [bæliǽrịk], Islas Baleares.
Balkans [bólkạnz], Balcanes.
Baltic [bóltịk], Báltico.
Barbary [bárbạrị], Berbería.
Basel [bázẹl], Basilea.
Bavaria [bạvérịậ], Baviera.
Belgium [béldž(j)ʌm], Bélgica.
Belgrade [belgréịd], Belgrado.
Belize [belíz], Belice, Beliza.
Berlin [bŒrlín], Berln.
Bern [bŒrn], Berna.
Bethlehem [béθlị(h)em], Belén.
Biscay [bískej], Vizcaya.
Black Sea, Mar Negro.
Bologna [boụlónyậ], Bolonia.
Bonn [ban], Bona.
Bordeaux [bordó], Burdeos.
Bosporus [básporʌs], Bósforo.
Brazil [brạzíl], Brasil.
Bretagne [bretány], **Brittany** [brítạni], Bretaña.
British Columbia [brítịš kolámbịậ], Columbia Británica.
British Honduras [handúrạs], Honduras Británicas.
British Isles, Islas Británicas.
Brussels [brásẹlz], Bruselas.
Bucharest [bjukarést], Bucarest.
Burgundy [bǽrgʌndị], Borgoña.

Burma [bŒrmä], Birmania.
Byzantium [bịzǽnšiʌm], Bizancio.

C

Calcutta [kælkátậ], Calcuta.
Cameroons [kæmẹrúnz], Camerún, Kamerún.
Canada [kǽnạdậ], Canadá.
Canary Islands, Canarias.
Cape Horn, Cabo de Hornos.
Cape of Good Hope, Cabo de Buena Esperanza.
Caribbean [kærịbíạn, kạríbịạn], Caribe.
Carthage [kárθịdž], Cartago.
Caspian [kǽspịạn], Caspio.
Castile [kæstíl], Castilla.
Catalonia [kætạlónịậ], Cataluña.
Caucasus [kókạsạs], Cáucaso.
Cayenne [kajén, kején], Cayena.
Ceylon [sịlán], Ceilán.
Chaldea [kældíậ], Caldea.
Champagne [šæmpéịn], Champaña.
Cologne [kọlón], Colonia.
Constantinople [kanstæntịnópl], Constantinopla.
Copenhagen [kọpẹnhéịgẹn], Copen(h)ague.
Corinth [kórịnθ], Corinto.
Corsica [kórsịkậ], Córcega.
Crete [krit], Creta.
Croatia [kro{é}íšậ], Croacia.
Curaçao [ky.rạsó], Curazao.
Cyprus [sáịprʌs], Chipre.
Czechoslovakia [chekoslovǽkịậ], Checoslovaquia.

D

Dalmatia [dælméịšậ], Dalmacia.
Damascus [dạmǽskạs], Damasco.
Danube [dǽnjub], Danubio.
Dardanelles [dardạnélz], Dardanelos.
Dead Sea, Mar Muerto.
Delphi [délfaị], Delfos.
Denmark [dénmark], Dinamarca.
Douro River [dóry], Duero (Río).
Dover [dóvŒ (r)], Duvres.
Dresden [drézdẹn], Dresde.
Dunkirk [dánkŒrk], Dunquerque.

E

East Indies [índịz], Indias Orientales.
Edinburgh [édịnbŒrọ], Edimburgo.
Egypt [ídžịpt], Egipto.
Elbe [élbậ], Elba.
England [íŋglænd], Inglaterra.
English Channel, Canal de la Mancha, Paso de Calais.

361

Escurial [eskýriəl], Escorial.
Ethiopia [iθiópiə], Etiopa, Abisinia.
Euphrates [yufréitiz], Eufrates.
Europe [yúrop], Europa.

F

Finland [fínlənd], Finlandia.
Flanders [flǽndœrz], Flandes.
Florence [flɔ́rens], Florencia.
France [fræns], Francia.
Frankfort-on-the-Main [frǽŋkfort], Francfort del Mein.

G

Galilee [gǽlili], Galilea.
Gascony [gǽskoni], Gascuña.
Gaul [gɔl], Galia.
Geneva [dʒenívə], Ginebra.
Genoa [dʒénowə], Génova.
Germany [dʒœ́rməni], Alemania.
Ghent [gent], Gante.
Gold Coast [gold kost], Costa de Oro.
Great Britain [greit brítn], Gran Bretaña.
Greece [gris], Grecia.
Greenland [grínlənd], Groenlandia.
Guadeloupe [gwadəlúp], Guadalupe.
Guam [gwam], Guaján, Guam.
Guiana [giǽnə, giánə], Guayana.

H

Hague [heig], (La) Haya.
Haiti [héiti], Haití, Isla Española.
Hamburg [hǽmbœrg], Hamburgo.
Havana [havǽnə], La Habana.
Hawaii [hawáii], Hawá, Hauá.
Hebrides [hébridiz], Hébridas.
Hindustan [hindstǽn], Indostán.
Hispaniola [hispanyólə], La Española.
Holland [hálənd], Holanda.
Holy Land, Tierra Santa.
Hungary [hǽŋgəri], Hungría.

I

Iceland [áislənd], Islandia.
India [índiə], India, Indostán.
Indian Ocean, (Mar de las) Indias, (Océano) Índico.
Ionia [aióniə], Jonia.
Ireland [áirlənd], Irlanda.
Istanbul [istænbúl], Estambul.
Italy [ítəli], Italia.
Ivory Coast, Costa del Marfil.
Izmir [ízmir], Esmirna.

J

Japan [dʒəpǽn], Japón.
Jericho [dʒériko], Jericó.
Jerusalem [dʒirúsələm], Jerusalén.
Jugoslavia [yugoslǽviə], = YUGOSLAVIA.
Jutland [dʒátlənd], Jutlandia.

K

Kashmir [kæ̂šmír], Cachemira.
Khartoum [kartúm], Kartum.
Key West, Cayo Hueso.
Korea [koríə], Corea.
Kurdistan [kœ́rdistæn], Kurdistán.

L

Labrador [lǽbrədɔr], Tierra del Labrador.
Lapland [lǽplənd], Laponia.

Lausanne [lozǽn], Lausana.
Lebanon [lébənon], Líbano.
Leghorn [léghɔrn], Liorno.
Leningrad [léningræd], Leningrado.
Lesser Antilles [lésœ(r) æntíliz], Las Pequeñas Antillas.
Lhasa [lásə], Lasa.
Libya [líbiə], Libia.
Liége [liéž, liéž], Lieja.
Lisbon [lízbon], Lisboa.
Lithuania [liθéiniə], Lituania.
Lombardy [lámbərdi], Lombardia.
London [lándon], Londres.
Lorraine [loréin], Lorena.
Louisiana [luiziǽnə], Luisiana.
Low Countries, Países Bajos, Holanda.
Lower California [lóœ(r) kæljfɔ́rnyə], Baja California.
Lucerne [lusœ́rn], Lucerna.
Luxemburg [láksembœrg], Luxemburgo.

M

Madeira [mədírə], Madera.
Majorca [mədʒɔ́rkə], Mallorca.
Malay [méilei, máléi], Malaca.
Marseilles [marséi(lz], Marsella.
Martinique [martiník], Martinica.
Mecca [mékə], Meca.
Mediterranean [mediteréiniən], Mediterráneo.
Memphis [mémfis], Menfis.
Mexico [méksiko], México, Méjico.
Minorca [minɔ́rkə], Menorca.
Mississippi [misisípi], Misisipí.
Missouri [mizúri], Misurí.
Mobile [mobl], Mobila.
Montpellier [monpelyé], Mompellier.
Morocco [moɾǽko], Marruecos.
Moscow [máskə], Moscú.
Moselle [mozél], Mosela.
Musqat [mʌskǽt], Omán.

N

Naples [néiplz], Nápoles.
Navarre [nəvár], Navarra.
Nazareth [nǽzəreθ, nǽzriθ], Nazaret.
Netherlands [néðœrləndz], Páses Bajos, Holanda.
New Castile, Castilla la Nueva.
New England, Nueva Inglaterra.
Newfoundland [niúfándlænd], Terranova.
New Mexico, Nuevo México (o Méjico).
New Orleans [ɔ́rliənz, orlínz], Nueva Orleáns.
New South Wales, Nueva Gales del Sur.
New York [yórk], Nueva York.
New Zealand [zílənd], Nueva Zelandia.
Nice [nis], Niza.
Nile [nail], Nilo.
Normandy [nɔ́rməndi], Normandía.
North America, América del Norte.
North Carolina [kærəláinə], Carolina del Norte.
North Dakota [dəkótə], Dakota del Norte.
Norway [nɔ́rwei], Noruega.
Nova Scotia [nóvə skóšə], Nueva Escocia.
Nyasaland [nyásəlænd], Niaslandia.

O

Oceania [ošiǽniə], Oceanica [ošiǽnikə], Oceaña.

Old Castile, Castilla la Vieja.
Olympus [olímpʌs], Olimpo.
Ostend [asténd], Ostende.

P

Pacific [pʌsífɪk], Pacífico.
Palestine [pǽlestaɪn], Palestina.
Panama [pǽnʌmǽ], Panamá.
Paris [pǽrɪs], París.
Parnassus [parnǽsʌs], Parnaso.
Peking [pikɪŋ], Pekín.
Peloponnesus [pelopanísʌs], Peloponeso.
Pennsylvania [pensɪlvéɪnjǽ], Pensilvania.
Persian Gulf [pŒ̃rʒan], Golfo Pérsico.
Peru [perú], Perú.
Philadelphia [fɪlǽdélfjǽ], Filadelfia.
Philippines [fílipinz], Filipinas.
Phoenicia [finíʃǽ], Fenicia.
Poland [pólǽnd], Polonia.
Polynesia [palɪníʃǽ], Polinesia.
Pompeii [pampéji], Pompeya.
Port-au-Prince [pɔrt o prɪns], Puerto Príncipe.
Porto Rico [pórtɑ ríkɑ], Puerto Rico.
Prague [prag], Praga.
Provence [prɑváns], Provenza.
Providence [právɪdens], Providencia.
Prussia [prʌ́ʃǽ], Prusia.
Pyrenees [píréniz], Pireneos.

R

Red Sea, Mar Rojo.
Rhine [raɪn], Rin o Rhin.
Rhineland [ráɪnlænd], Renania.
Rhodes [rɑdz], Rodas.
Rhodesia [rɑdíʒǽ], Rodesia.
Rhone [rɑn], Ródano.
Rocky Mountains, Montañas Rocosas o Rocallosas.
Rome [rɑm], Roma.
Rouen [ruán], Ruán.
Russia [rʌ́ʃǽ], Rusia.

S

Saragossa [sǽrǽgásǽ], Zaragoza.
Sardinia [sardínjǽ], Cerdeña.
Saudi Arabia [saúdi ǽréjbjǽ], Arabia Saudita.
Saxony [sǽksɔnɪ], Sajonia.
Scandinavia [skǽndɪnéjvjǽ], Escandinavia.
Scotland [skátlǽnd], Escocia.
Seine [seɪn, sen], Sena.
Seoul [sɑl], Seúl.
Serbia [sŒ̃rbjǽ], Servia.
Seville [sevɪl], Sevilla.
Sicily [sísɪlɪ], Sicilia.
Sierra Leone [sjérǽ ljón(ɪ)], Sierra Leona.
Slavonia [slǽvɔ́njǽ], Eslavonia.
Slovakia [slovákjǽ], Eslovaquia.
Slovenia [slovínjǽ], Eslovenia.
South Africa, Sud-África.
South America, América del Sur, Sud-América, Sur-América.
South Carolina [kǽrolájnǽ], Carolina del Sur.
South Dakota [dǽkɔ́tǽ], Dakota del Sur.
Soviet Union [sɔ́vjet], Unión Soviética.
Spain [speɪn], España.

Spanish America, Hispano-América, América Española.
Sparta [spártǽ], Esparta.
Spoleto [spoléjtɑ], Espoleto.
Stockholm [stákhɑ(l)m], Estocolmo.
Strait of Magellan [mǽdʒélǽn], Estrecho de Magallanes.
Sudan [sudǽn], Sudán.
Sweden [swíden], Suecia.
Switzerland [swɪtsŒrlǽnd], Suiza.
Syracuse [sírǽkjus], Siracusa.
Syria [sírjǽ], Siria.

T

Tagus [téjgʌs], Tajo.
Tahiti [tahíti], Tahití.
Tanganyika [tæŋgǽnyíkǽ], Tanganica.
Tangier [tændʒír], Tánger.
Texas [téksǽs], Tejas.
Thailand [tájlǽnd], Thailandia.
Thames [temz], Támesis.
Thebes [θibz], Tebas.
Thrace [θreɪs], Tracia.
Tobago [tɑbéjgɑ], Tabago.
Tokyo [tɔ́kjɑ], Tokio.
Toulouse [tulúz], Tolosa.
Trent [trent], Trento.
Troy [trɔj], Troya.
Tunis(ia) [t(j)únɪs; t(j)uníʃǽ], Túnez (ciudad, país).
Turkey [tŒ̃rkɪ], Turquía.
Tuscany [tʌ́skǽnɪ], Toscana.
Tyrol [tírǽl, tirɔ́l], Tirol.

U

Ukraine [yúkreɪn, yukréɪn], Ucrania.
Union of South Africa, Unión Sudafricana.
United Kingdom, Reino Unido.
United States of America, Estados Unidos de América.
Upper Volta [vɔ́ltǽ], Alto Volta.
USSR [yu es ɛs ar], URSS.

V

Venice [vénɪs], Venecia.
Versailles [vŒrséjlz, versáy], Versalles.
Vesuvius [vɛsúvjʌs], Vesubio.
Vienna [vjénǽ], Viena.
Virgin Islands, Islas Vírgenes.

W

Wales [weɪlz], Gales.
Warsaw [wɔ́rsɔ], Varsovia.
Watling Island [wátlɪŋ], Isla de San Salvador.
West Indies [índɪz], Antillas.
West Virginia [vŒrdʒínyǽ], Virginia Occidental.

Y

Yugoslavia [yugɔslávjǽ], Yugoeslavia.

Z

Zanzibar [zǽnzɪbar], Zanzíbar.
Zealand [zílǽnd], Zelandia.
Zion [zájɔn], Sion.
Zululand [zúlulænd], Zululandia.

NOMBRES PROPIOS DE PERSONAS
Y DE PERSONAJES HISTORICOS,
LITERARIOS Y MITOLOGICOS

(Sólo se incluyen los que difieren en ambas lenguas. Se excluyen los diminutivos y afectivos que se forman añadiendo "ito," "illo," etc., v.gr. Agustinito, Juanillo, Juanico, etc.)

A

Abelard [ǽbelard], Abelardo.
Abraham [éjbrahæm], Abrahán.
Achilles [akíliz], Aquiles.
Adam [ǽdam], Adán.
Æneas [inías], Eneas.
Æschylus [éskilas], Esquilo.
Æsop [ísop, ísap], Esopo.
Agatha [ǽgaθa], Agueda, Ágata.
Agnes [ǽgnis], Inés.
Alan [ǽlan], Alano.
Albert [ǽlbɛrt], Alberto.
Alexander [æligzǽndœ(r)], Alejandro.
Alfred [ǽlfrid], Alfredo.
Alice [ǽlis], Alicia.
Allan [ǽlan], **Allen** [ǽlen], Alano.
Alphonso [ælfánso], Alfonso, Alonso, Ildefonso.
Andrew [ǽndru], Andrés.
Angel [éjndƷel], Angel.
Anne [æn], **Anna** [ǽnä], Ana.
Anthony [ǽnθoni], Antonio.
Archimedes [arkimídiz], Arquímedes.
Aristophanes [æristáfaniz], Aristófanes.
Aristotle [ǽristatl], Aristóteles.
Arnold [árnold], Arnaldo, Arnoldo.
Arthur [árθœ(r)], Arturo.
Attila [ǽtilä], Atila.
Augustine [ɔ́gastin, ɔgástin], Augustín.
Augustus [ɔgástas], Augusto.

B

Bacchus [bǽkas], Baco.
Bartholomew [barθálomju], Bartolomé.
Basil [bǽzil], Basilio.
Beatrice [bíatris], Beatriz.
Benedict [bénedikt], Benito.
Benedicta [benedíktä], Benita.
Benjamin [béndƷamin], Benjamín.
Bernard [bɛrnard, bernárd], Bernardo.
Bertha [bɛrθä], Berta.
Bonaventura [bánavenchúrä], Buenaventura, Ventura.
Brutus [brútas], Bruto.
Buddha [búdä], Buda.

C

Caesar [síza(r)], César.
Calvin [kǽlvin], Calvino.
Camille [kamíl], Camila.

Camillus [kamílas], Camilo.
Caroline [kǽrolajn], Carolina.
Cassandra [kasǽndrä], Casandra.
Catharine [kǽθarin], **Catherine** [kǽθerin], Catalina.
Cato [kéjto], Catón.
Catullus [katálas], Catulo.
Cecile [sisíl], Cecilia.
Charlemagne [šárlemejn], Carlomagno.
Charles [charlz], Carlos.
Charlotte [šárlot], Carlota.
Christ [krajst], Cristo.
Christine [kristín], Cristina.
Christopher [krístofœ(r)], Cristóbal.
Cicero [sísero], Cicerón.
Claire, Clare [kler], Clara.
Claude [klɔd], Claudio.
Clement [klément], Clemente.
Clovis [klɔ́vis], Clodoveo.
Columbus [kolámbas], Colón.
Confucius [konfjúšas], Confucio.
Constance [kánstans], Constanza, Constancia.
Constantine [kánstantajn], Constantino.
Cyrus [sájras], Ciro.

D

Daisy [déjzi], Margarita.
Delilah [dilájlä], Dalila.
Demosthenes [dimásθeniz], Demóstenes.
Dennis [dénis], Dionisio.
Diogenes [dajádƷeniz], Diógenes.
Dionysius [dajonšías], Dionisio.
Dominic [dáminik], Domingo.
Dorothy [dɔ́roθi], dároθi], Dorotea.

E

Edith [ídiθ], Edita.
Edmund [édmand], Edmundo.
Edward [édwärd], Eduardo.
Eleanor, Elinor [élino(r)], Leonor.
Eliza [ilájzä], Elisa.
Elizabeth [ilízabeθ], Isabel.
Ellen [élen], Elena.
Eloise [éloiz], Elósa.
Em(m)anuel [imǽnyɛl], Manuel.
Emil [éjmil], Emilio.
Emily [émili], Emilia.
Emma [émä], Ema, Manuela.
Epicurus [epikýras], Epicuro.

Erasmus [iræzmʌs], Erasmo.
Ernest [ŒrnjsT], Ernesto.
Ernestine [Œrnestin], Ernestina.
Esther [éstŒ(r)], Ester.
Euclid [yúkljd], Euclides.
Eugene [yudžín], Eugenio.
Eugénie [Œ̆žéní], Eugenia.
Eve [iv], Eva.

F

Felicia [fjlíšjạ̈], Felisa, Felicia.
Ferdinand [fŒrdjnænd], Fernando.
Florence [flɔ́rens], Florencia.
Frances [frænsjs], Francisca.
Francis [frænsjs], Frank [fræŋk], Francisco.
Frederica [fredẹríkạ̈], Federica.
Frederick [fréḍẹrjk], Federico.

G

Galen [géjlẹn], Galeno.
George [džɔrdž], Jorge.
Geraldine [džéraldin], Gerarda.
Gerard [džjrárd], Gerardo.
Gertrude [gŒrtrud], Gertrudis.
Gilbert [gjlbŒrt], Gilberto.
Godfrey [gádfrj], Godofredo.
Gracchus [grǽkas], Graco.
Grace [grejs], Engracia.
Gregory [grégorj], Gregorio.
Gustave [gástav], Gustavus [gʌstéjvʌs], Gustavo.

H

Hadrian [héjdrjạn], Adriano.
Hannah [hǽnạ̈], Ana.
Hannibal [hǽnjbạl], Aníbal.
Harold [hǽrọld], Haroldo.
Helen [héljn], Elena.
Henrietta [henrjétạ̈], Enriqueta.
Henry [hénrj], Enrique.
Herbert [hŒrbŒrt], Heriberto.
Herman [hŒrmạn], Arminio.
Herod [hérọd], Herodes.
Herodotus [hjrádọtas], Herodoto.
Hezekiah [hezẹkájạ̈], Ezequías.
Hippocrates [hjpákrạtiz], Hipócrates.
Homer [hómŒ(r)], Homero.
Horace [hɔ́rjs], Horacio.
Hortense [hɔrténs], Hortensia.
Hubert [hjúbŒrt], Huberto.
Humbert [hámbŒrt], Humberto.
Humphrey [hámfrj], Hunfredo.

I

Ignatius [jgnéjšʌs], Ignacio.
Inez [ájnez, ínez], Inés.
Innocent [ínosẹnt], Inocencio.
Isabella [jzabélạ̈], Isabel.
Isidore [jzjdọr], Isidro, Isidoro.

J

James [džejmz], Jaime, Jacobo, Santiago.
Jane [džejn], Juana.
Jasper [džǽspŒ(r)], Gaspar.
Jeffrey [džéfrj], Geofredo.
Jehovah [džjhóvạ̈], Jehová.
Jeremiah [džerẹmájạ̈], Jeremías.
Jerome [džjróm, džérọm], Jerónimo, Gerónimo.
Jesus Christ [džízʌs], Jesucristo.

Joachim [yóạkjm], Joaqún.
Joan [džọn], Juana.
Joan of Arc [ark], Juana de Arco.
John [džan], Juan.
Jonathan [džánạθạn], Jonatán, Jonatás.
Joseph [džózẹf], José.
Josephine [džózẹfin], Josefina.
Joshua [džášjạ̈], Josué.
Judith [džúdjθ], Judit.
Julian [džúlyạn], Julián; Juliano (emperador).
Juliet [džúlyet, džuljét], Julia, Julieta.
Julius [džúlyạs], Julio.
Justinian [džʌstínjạn], Justiniano.

K

Katharine [kǽθạrjn], Katherine [kǽθẹrjn], Catalina.

L

Laurence, Lawrence [lɔ́rens], Lorenzo.
Lazarus [lǽzạras], Lázaro.
Lenore [ljnɔ́r], Lenora.
Leo [líọ], León.
Leonard [lénạrd], Leonardo.
Leonora [lionórạ̈], Lenora.
Leopold [líọpọld], Leopoldo.
Lewis [lújs], Luis.
Livy [ljvj], Livio.
Louis [lújs, lúj], Luis.
Louise [luíz], Luisa.
Lucan [lúkạn], Lucano.
Lucian [lúšạn], Luciano.
Lucretia [lukríšạ̈], Lucrecia.
Lucretius [lukríšʌs], Lucrecio.
Lucy [lúsj], Lucía.
Luke [luk], Lucas.
Luther [lúθŒ(r)], Lutero.

M

Magdalen [mǽgdạlẹn], Magdalena.
Magellan [mạdžélạn], Magallanes.
Margaret [márgạrjt], Margarita.
Marian [mérjạn], Marion [mérjọn], Mariana.
Marjorie [márdžọrj], Margarita.
Mark [mark], Marco, Marcos.
Martha [márθạ̈], Marta.
Mary [mérj], María.
Matthew [mǽθju], Mateo.
Maurice [mɔ́rjs], Mauricio.
Messiah [mesájạ̈], Mesías.
Michael [májkẹl], Miguel.
Michelangelo [majkelǽndželọ], Miguel Angel.
Miriam [mírjạm], María.
Mohammed [mọhǽmid], Mahoma.
Moses [mózjz], Moisés.

N

Nathan [néjθạn], Natán.
Nathaniel [nạθǽnyẹl], Nataniel.
Nebuchadnezzar [neby,kạdnézạ̈(r)], Nabucodonosor.
Nero [nírọ], Nerón.
Nicholas [níkọlạs], Nicolás.
Noah [nóạ̈], Noé.

O

Octavius [aktéjvjʌs], Octavio.
Oliver [áljvŒ(r)], Oliverio.

365

Otto [átọ], Otón.
Ovid [ávịd], Ovidio.

P

Patrick [pǽtrịk], Patricio.
Paul [pɔl], Pablo.
Pauline [pɔln], Paula, Paulina.
Perseus [pŒrsus], Perseo.
Peter [pítŒ(r)], Pedro.
Philip [fílịp], Felipe, Felipo (de Macedonia).
Philippa [fílípặ], Felipa.
Pilate [pájlặt], Pilatos.
Pindar [píndặ(r)], Píndaro.
Pius [pájʌs], Pío.
Plato [pléjtọ], Platón.
Plautus [plɔ́tʌs], Plauto.
Pliny [plínị], Plinio.
Plutarch [plútark], Plutarco.
Prometheus [promíθus], Prometeo.
Ptolemy [tálẹmị], Tolomeo, Ptolomeo.
Pythagoras [pịθǽgọrạs], Pitágoras.

Q

Quentin [kwéntịn], Quintín.

R

Rachel [réjchẹl], Raquel.
Ralph [rælf], Rodolfo.
Randolph [rǽndalf], Randolfo.
Raphael [réjfjẹl], Rafael.
Raymond [réjmọnd], Raimundo, Ramón.
Rebecca [rịbékặ], Rebeca.
Reginald [rédžịnạld], Reinaldo.
Reuben [rúbịn], Rubén.
Richard [rịchặrd], Ricardo.
Robert [rábŒrt], Roberto.
Roderick [rádẹrịk], Rodrigo.
Roger [rádžŒ(r)], Rogelio, Rogerio.
Roland [rólạnd], Rolando, Orlando.
Romulus [rámyūlʌs], Rómulo.
Ronald [ránạld], Renaldo.
Rosalie [rózạlị], Rosalía.
Rosary [rózạrị], Rosario.
Rose [rọz], Rosa.
Rubin [rúbịn], Rubén.
Rudolph [rúdalf], Rodolfo.

S

Saladin [sǽlạdịn], Saladino.
Salome [sạlómị], Salomé.
Samson [sǽmsọn], Sansón.
Sarah [sérặ], Sara.

Satan [séjtạn], Satanás.
Scipio [sípịọ], Escipión.
Solomon [sálomọn], Salomón.
Sophia [sọ́fịặ], Sofía.
Sophocles [sáfokliz], Sófocles.
Stephen, Steven [stívẹn], Esteban.
Strabo [stréjbọ], Estrabón.
Stradivarius [strædịvérịʌs], Estradivario.
Suleiman [sulẹịmán], Solimán.
Susan [súzạn], Susana.
Sylvester [sịlvéstŒ(r)], Silvestre.

T

Tacitus [tǽsịtʌs], Tácito.
Tamerlane [tǽmŒrlejn], Tamerlán.
Terence [térẹns], Terencio.
Theodore [θíodɔr], Teodoro.
Theresa [tịrísặ], Teresa.
Thomas [támạs], Tomás.
Thucydides [θusídịdiz], Tucídides.
Tiberius [tajbírịʌs], Tiberio.
Timothy [tịmoθị], Timoteo.
Titian [tíšạn], el Ticiano.
Tristram [trístrạm], Tristán.

U

Ulysses [yulísiz], Ulises.
Urban [Œrbạn], Urbano.

V

Valentine [vǽlẹntajn], Valentín.
Vergil [vŒrdžịl], Virgilio.
Vespucci [vespútchị], Vespucio.
Vincent [vínsẹnt], Vicente.
Virgil [vŒrdžịl], Virgilio.
Vivian [vívịạn], Bibiana.

W

Walter [wɔ́ltŒ(r)], Gualterio.
Wilhelmina [wịlhelmínặ], Guillermina.
William [wílyạm], Guillermo.

X

Xavier [zéjvịŒ(r), zǽvịŒ(r)], Javier.
Xenophon [zénofan], Jenofonte.
Xerxes [zŒrksiz], Jerjes.

Z

Zachary [zǽkạrị], Zacarías.
Zeno [zínọ], Zenón, Cenón.
Zoroaster [zóroæstŒ(r)], Zoroastro.

ABREVIATURAS MAS USUALES EN INGLES

A

a., acre(s).
A.B., Bachelor of Arts.
abbr., abbreviation.
abr., abridgment, abridged.
A.C., alternating current; Air Corps.
acct., account.

Adm., admiral(ty).
Afr., Africa(n).
aft., afternoon.
agcy., agency.
agr(ic)., agriculture; agricultural.
agt., agent.

Ala., Alabama.
Alas., Alaska.
a.m., ante meridiem (before noon).
A.M., Master of Arts; before noon; amplitude modulation.

amp., ampere; amperage.
amt., amount.
anat., anatomy.
anon., anonymous.
ans., answer.
A.P., Associated Press.
app., appendix; appointed.
Apr., April.
apt., apartment.
Ar., Arabic; Aramaic.
arith., arithmetic(al).
Ariz., Arizona.
Ark., Arkansas.
assn., association.
assoc., association; associate.
asst., assistant.
att., attorney.
Att.Gen., Attorney General.
atty., attorney.
Aug., August.
ave., avenue.

B

b., base; book; born; brother.
B., British.
B.A., Bachelor of Arts.
bal., balance.
B.B.A., Bachelor of Business Administration.
B.C., before Christ.
bd., board; bond; bound.
b.e., B/E, bill of exchange.
bet., between.
Bibl., Biblical; bibliographical.
biog., biographical; biography.
biol., biological; biology.
bk., book.
b.l., B/L, bill of lading.
bldg., building.
blvd., boulevard.
b.p., bills payable; boiling point.
Br., British; Britain.
Bro(s)., brother(s).
b.s., balance sheet; bill of sale.
B.S(c)., Bachelor of Science.
bus., business.
bx., box.

C

c., cent; chapter; cubic; current; center.
C., Cape; Catholic; centigrade.
C.A., Central America; Chartered Accountant.
cal., calorie; caliber.
Cal(if)., California.
Can., Canada; Canadian.
cap., capital; capitalize(d); Chapter.
Capt., Captain.
Cath., Catholic.
cent., centigrade; central; century.
cert., certificate; certify.
cf., confer; compare.

C.F.I., cost, freight, and insurance.
C.G., Coast Guard.
Ch., Church.
chap., chapter.
chem., chemical, chemistry.
C.I.F., cost, insurance, and freight (c.i.f., o c.s.f. costo, seguro y flete).
c.o., c/o., care of; carried over.
C.O., Commanding Officer.
Co., company; county.
C.O.D., collect (o cash) on delivery (cóbrese a la entrega).
Col., Colonel; Colorado.
Colo., Colorado.
com., commerce.
Com., Commander; Commission(er); Committee; Commodore.
comp., comparative; compare; compound.
con., conclusion; contra (against, opposing).
Cong., Congress(ional).
Conn., Connecticut.
cont., containing; contents; continent; continue(d).
cor., corrected; correction; corresponding; corner.
Corp., Corporal; corporation.
cp., compare.
C.P.A., Certified Public Accountant.
Cpl., Corporal.
cr., credit(or).
C.S.A., Confederate States of America.
C.S.T., Central Standard Time.
ct., cent.
Ct., Connecticut.
cts., cents; certificates.
c.w.o., cash with order.

D

d., died; dime; dollar.
D.A., District Attorney.
Dan., Danish.
D.C., District of Columbia; direct current.
D.D., Doctor of Divinity.
D.D.S., Doctor of Dental Surgery.
Dec., December.
deg., degree(s).
Del., Delaware.
Dem., Democrat(ic).
dep., department; deputy.
dept., department.
der(iv)., derivation; derivative.
D.H.C., Doctor Honoris Causa.
dial., dialect(al).
diam., diameter.
diff., difference; different.

disc., discount; discovered.
dist., distance; district.
div., divided; dividend; division.
D.Lit., Doctor of Literature.
D.Litt., Doctor of Letters.
doz., dozen(s).
Dr., Doctor.
dup., duplicate.
D.V., Deo volente (God willing).
dz., dozen(s).

E

E., east(ern); English.
ea., each.
econ., economic(s); economy.
ed., edition; editor.
educ., education(al).
e.g., exempli gratia (for example), v.g.
elec(t)., electric(al); electricity.
Eng., England; English.
esp(ec)., especially.
est., established.
E.S.T., Eastern Standard Time.
etc., et cetera (and so forth).
Eur., Europe(an).
ex., example; exception; executive.
exc., except(ed); exception.
exch., exchange.
exp., export(ed); express; expenses.

F

F., Fahrenheit; Father; French; Friday.
Fahr., Fahrenheit.
FBI, Federal Bureau of Investigation.
Feb., February.
Fed., Federal.
ff., following.
fin., financial.
Fla., Florida.
F.M., frequency modulation.
f.o.b., free on board (libre a bordo).
fol(l)., following.
fr., francs; from.
Fr., France; French.
Fri., Friday.
ft., foot, feet.
Ft., fort.

G

G., German.
Ga., Georgia.
gal(l)., (pl., gals.), gallon(s).
G.B., Great Britain.
Gen., General.
geog., geographic(al); geography.
Ger., German(y).
Gov., government; Governor.

Govt., government.
G.P.O., General Post Office.
Gt.Br(it)., Great Britain.

H

hdqrs., headquarters.
H.E., His Eminence; His
Excellency.
H.H., His (o Her) Highness;
His Holiness.
H.I., Hawaiian Islands.
H.M., His (o Her) Majesty.
H.M.S., His (o Her) Majesty's
service, ship o steamer.
Hon., Honorable.
h.p., horse power; high
pressure.
H.Q., headquarters.
H.R., House of
Representatives.
hr(s)., hour(s).
ht., height; heat.

I

I., Island.
Ia., Iowa.
Ice(l)., Iceland(ic).
Id(a)., Idaho.
Ill., Illinois.
inc., incorporated;
including; increase.
Ind., Indiana; India; Indian;
Indies.
ins., insurance.
inst., instant; institute.
int., interest; international.
inv., invented; inventor;
invoice.
I.O.U., I owe you.
I.Q., intelligence quotient.
Is(l)., Island(s); Isle(s).
It(al)., Italian; Italy.
ital., italic.

J

Jam., Jamaica.
Jan., January.
Jap., Japan(ese).
J.C., Jesus Christ; Julius
Caesar.
J.P., Justice of the Peace.
Jr., Junior.
Jul., July.
Jun., June; Junior.

K

K., King; Knight(s).
Kan(s)., Kansas.
Ken., Kentucky.
Knt., Knight.
k.o., knockout.
kt., carat.
Kt., Knight.
Ky., Kentucky.

L

l., latitude; length; line.
L., lake; Latin.
La., Louisiana.

lat., latitude.
Lat., Latin.
Leg(is)., legislature;
legislative.
Lieut., Lieutenant.
liq., liquid; liquor.
lon(g)., longitude.
Lt., Lieutenant.
Ltd., Limited.

M

M., Monday; member.
M.A., Master of Arts.
mag., magazine; magnetism.
Maj., Major.
Mar., March.
Mass., Massachusetts.
M.C., Master of Ceremonies;
Member of Congress.
M.D., Medical Doctor.
Md., Maryland.
mdse., merchandise.
Me., Maine.
Mex., Mexican; Mexico.
mfg., manufacturing.
Mgr., manager.
Mich., Michigan.
Minn., Minnesota.
misc., miscellaneous;
miscellany.
Miss., Mississippi.
Mo., Missouri; Monday.
mo(s)., month(s).
Mon., Monday.
Mont., Montana.
M.P., Member of Parliament;
Military Police.
m.p.h., miles per hour.
Mr., Mister, Master.
Mrs., Mistress.
M.S(c)., Master of Science.
Mt(s)., Mount, Mountain(s).

N

N., North(ern).
N.A(m)., North America(n).
nat(l)., national.
NATO, North Atlantic Treaty
Organization.
N.B., New Brunswick; nota
bene (note well).
N.C., North Carolina.
N.Dak., North Dakota.
Neb(r)., Nebraska.
N.Eng., New England.
Neth., Netherlands.
Nev., Nevada.
n.g., (fam.) no good.
N.G., National Guard.
N.H., New Hampshire.
N.J., New Jersey.
N.M(ex)., New Mexico.
No. (pl., nos.), number.
noncom.,
noncommissioned officer.
Norw., Norwegian; Norway.
Nov., November.
nt.wt., net weight.
N.Y., New York.

N.Y.C., New York City.
N.Z(eal)., New Zealand.

O

O., Ohio; Ontario; Ocean.
O.A.S., Organization of
American States.
obs., observation;
observatory; obsolete.
Oct., October.
O.K., all right; correct.
Okla., Oklahoma.
Ont., Ontario.
ord., order; ordinance.
Ore(g)., Oregon.

P

p., page; part; pint.
Pa., Pennsylvania.
Pac., Pacific.
payt., payment.
p.c., per cent; post card.
pd., paid.
Penn., Pennsylvania.
Ph.D., Doctor of Philosophy
photog., photographic;
photography.
phys., physician; physics.
P.I., Philippine Islands.
pkg(s)., package(s).
pl., place; plate; plural.
P.M., Postmaster; paymaster
post meridiem (after
noon).
P.O.D., Post Office
Department; pay on
delivery.
pop., population.
pos., positive.
pp., pages.
P.R., Porto Rico o Puerto
Rico.
pr., pair; price.
pres., present; presidency.
Pres., President.
prin., principal.
Prof., Professor.
Prot., Protestant.
pro tem., pro tempore
(temporarily).
prov., province; provincial
P.S., postscript.
pt., part; payment; point;
pint; port.
pub., public; published;
publisher.
P.X., (military) post
exchange.

Q

Q., Quebec; Queen.
qt., quantity; quart.
qu., quart(er); queen; query
question.
Que., Quebec.
ques., question.
quot., quotation.
q.v., quod vide (which see)
qy., query.

368

R

R., Republican; river; Royal.
R.A., Rear Admiral; Royal
 Academy.
R.C., Roman Catholic; Red
 Cross.
Rd., Road.
rec., receipt.
rec'd., recd., received.
ref., reference; referred;
 reformed.
reg., registry; regular.
Reg(t)., regiment.
Rep., Representative;
 Republic(an).
Rev., Reverend.
R.I., Rhode Island.
R.I.P., rest in peace.
R.N., registered nurse.
r.p.m., revolutions per
 minute.
R.R., railroad.
R.S.V.P., Répondez, s'il vous
 plaît (please answer).
Ry., railway, railroad.

S

S., Saturday; Sunday;
 South(ern).
S.A., South America(n);
 South Africa; South
 Australia; Salvation Army.
Sab., Sabbath.
S.Am., South America.
Sat., Saturday.
S.C., South Carolina;
 Supreme Court.
Scot., Scotch, Scottish;
 Scotland.
S.Dak., South Dakota.
SEATO, Southeast Asia
 Treaty Organization.
sec., second(ary); secretary;
 section.
Sen., Senate; Senator.
Sep(t)., September;
 Septuagint.
seq., sequel; the following.
Serg(t)., Sergeant.
serv(t)., servant.
Sgt., Sergeant.
S.I., Staten Island.
Soc., Society.
Sp., Spain; Spanish.

spt., seaport.
Sr., senior; sir.
S.S., steamship; Sunday
 School.
St., Saint; Street.
str., steamer.
sub., substitute; suburban.
Sun(d)., Sunday.
sup., superior.
Supp., Supplement.
Supt., superintendent.

T

tbs., tablespoon(s).
tel., telegram; telegraph;
 telephone.
teleg., telegram; telegraph.
Tenn., Tennessee.
Ter(r)., Territory.
Tex., Texas.
Th., Thur(s)., Thursday.
tp., township.
trans., translation;
 translated; transaction.
treas., treasurer; treasury.
tsp., teaspoon(s).
Tu(es)., Tuesday.

U

U., University.
U.K., United Kingdom.
ult., ultimate.
ult(o)., ultimo (the past
 month) (el mes pasado).
Univ., University.
U.P.I., United Press
 International.
U.S., United States.
U.S.A., United States of
 America; United States
 Army; Union of South
 Africa.
U.S.A.F., United States Air
 Force.
U.S.C.G., United States
 Coast Guard.
U.S.M., United States Mail.
U.S.M.C., United States
 Marine Corps.
U.S.N., United States Navy.
U.S.S., United States Ship;
 United States Senate.
U.S.S.R., USSR, Union of
 Soviet Socialist Republics.

usu., usual(ly).
Ut., Utah.

V

v., verse; versus; volume.
Va., Virginia.
V.A., Veterans'
 Administration.
var., variant; variation;
 variety; various.
vet., veteran; veterinary.
Vice Pres., Vice President.
vid., vide (see).
viz., videlicet (namely).
vocab., vocabulary.
vol., volume; volunteer.
V.P., Vice President.
vs., versus.
Vt., Vermont.

W

w., week; weight; with.
W., Wednesday; Welsh;
 west(ern).
Wash., Washington (estado).
Wed., Wednesday.
W.I., West Indian; West
 Indies.
Wis(c)., Wisconsin.
wk., week; work.
wt., weight.
W.Va., West Virginia.
Wy(o)., Wyoming.
wk., week; work.
wt., weight.
W.Va., West Virginia.
Wy(o)., Wyoming.

X

Xn., Xtian., Christian.

Y

Y., Young Men's Christian o
 Hebrew Association.
y., yard; year.
Y.M.C.A., Young Men's
 Christian Association.
Y.M.H.A., Young Men's
 Hebrew Association.
yr., year; your.

Z

Z., Zone.

TABLAS DE PESOS Y MEDIDAS (TABLES OF WEIGHTS AND MEASURES)

Avoirdupois Weights
(Unidades comunes de peso)

1 ounce (oz.) = 28,35 gramos (g.)
1 pound (lb.) = 16 ounces = 435,59 gramos
1 hundredweight (cwt.) = 112 pounds = 50,8 kilogramos

Troy and Apothecaries' Weights
(Unidades de peso usadas en joyería y farmacia)

1 ounce = 31,10 gramos
1 pound = 12 ounces = 373,24 gramos

Liquid and Dry Measures
(Medidas de capacidad para líquidos y áridos)

Liquid (Líquidos)

1 pint (pt.) = 0,47 litros (l.)
1 quart (qt.) = 2 pints = 0,94 litros
1 gallon (gal.) = 4 quarts = 3,78 litros
1 barrel (b.) = 31.5 gallons = 119,07 litros

Dry (Áridos)

1 pint (pt.) = 0,55 litros
1 quart (qt.) = 2 pints = 1,1 litros
1 gallon (gal.) = 4 quarts = 4,40 litros
1 peck (pk.) = 2 gallons = 8.80
1 bushel = 4 pecks = 35 litros

Linear Measures
(Medidas de longitud)

1 inch (in.) o 1″ = 2,54 centímetros (cm.)
1 foot (ft.) o 1′ = 12 inches = 30,48 centímetros
1 yard (yd.) = 3 feet = 91,44 centímetros
1 mile (m.) = 1,760 yards = 1,609 kilómetros (km.)

Square Measures
(Medidas de superficie)

1 square inch (sq.in.) = 6,45 centímetros cuadrados (cm.²)
1 square foot (sq.ft.) = 144 square inches = 0,93 metros cuadrados
1 square yard (sq.yd.) = 9 square feet = 0,836 metros cuadrados (m.²)
1 acre = 4,830 square yards = 40,468 hectáreas
1 square mile (sq.m.) = 640 acres = 2,59 kilómetros cuadrados (km.²)

TERMOMETRO

32° Fahrenheit (punto de congelación) = 0° centígrados
212° Fahrenheit (punto de ebullición) = 100° centígrados
Para reducir grados Fahrenheit a grados centígrados multiplíquese por 5/9 e réstense 32°.

Part II
SPANISH-ENGLISH

PREFACE

This dictionary has been compiled in the tradition of the well-known Cuyás dictionaries. Arturo Cuyás presented his first dictionary to the King of Spain at the turn of the century and its sound workmanship inspired later editions, of which this portable version is an offspring. The user has here a convenient reference because it is easy to find one's way among carefully selected entries. Nevertheless, this dictionary offers a concentration of neologisms and words and expressions in everyday use that is perhaps more extensive than in any other Spanish and English dictionary of comparable size. There are forty entries for the Spanish word for 'paper'. Thousands of entries provide translations of new words that have come into use in fields of endeavor such as audio, commerce, computers, medicine, rocketry, space travel, television, and video. Abbreviations such as AIDS and DNA appear with their equivalent Spanish abbreviations. The real language of the real world of today is exemplified in the following two dozen entry words chosen at random from this dictionary:

automated teller (ATM)	oxygen tent
bagel	personal computer
camcorder	random-access memory (ROM)
cellular telephone	scanner
child abuse	septuplets
downsizing	signing
fax	space shuttle
garage sale	stereo
hacker	tax shelter
jeans	unsportsmanlike conduct
microchip	video game
nuclear reactor	to zap

This dictionary is careful to warn the user about misleading translations. Here are five examples:

The first floor in Spanish is not the first floor in American English—it is the second floor, and the second floor in Spanish is the third floor in American English, and so on.

The Spanish billón looks like the English "billion" but in North America it is a "trillion." And the American English billion must be translated by Spanish words for a thousand million ("mil millones").

One of the commonly used words for the color "brown" in Spanish is marrón, sometimes interpreted wrongly as "maroon" in English. But maroon in English is translated into Spanish as "granate."

Without the help of the information provided by this dictionary, a Spanish speaker learning English might think that it is polite to say: "Watch out, mister!" But Spanish señor is equivalent to "mister" only when it is used with the last name and abbreviated: Sr. Cruz = Mr. Cruz. The expression "¡oiga!" might be used as a translation for "Watch out, mister!"

Many dictionaries but not this dictionary give the impression that "Negro" is an up-to-date translation of Spanish negro whereas the correct translation is "black," "African-American," or "Afro-American."

Thanks are herewith given to the many informants, helping hands, and editors who have enabled this new revision to be published as the third edition. Marie Butler-Knight, Publisher of *Webster's New World Dictionary*, organized this project and used her expertise in seeing it through to the final stages. Professor Alfred R. Wedel provided important information. Special mention should also be made of Professor Sísi DiLaura Morris for her significant help.

September 1, 1998

Roger J. Steiner
Professor Emeritus,
University of Delaware

ADVICE TO THE USER

1. *Arrangement.* In order to save space and make our dictionary richer in entries, we have grouped together families of words closely related in origin and meaning or in spelling, whenever this arrangement did not interfere with alphabetical order. For further saving of space, the common parts of words of the same family have been omitted. The omitted part is always referred to the head entry of the group. All main entries are in boldface type. Idioms and expressions within entries are italicized and alphabetized by the first word. In definitions, semicolons are used to separate different areas of meaning; commas for synonyms within areas.

2. *Gender of Nouns.* In the Spanish-English section the gender of Spanish nouns is indicated as follows: *m.* for nouns that are exclusively masculine (ex., **hombre, banco, buey, sofá, amor**), *f.* for nouns that are only feminine (ex., **mujer, casa, fe, libertad, costumbre**), *mf.* for those which have a masculine and a feminine meaning without change in form (ex., **artista, amante, testigo**), and *n.* for those which have a masculine form ending in *o* and a corresponding feminine form ending in *a* (ex., **obrero, abogado**), in which case only the masculine form is entered. Nouns having a gender inflexion different from the above are listed separately for the masculine and feminine (ex., **actor, actriz**).

3. *Diminutives.* Diminutives are entered only when they have special meanings or when they have become nouns in their own right (ex., **ahorita, eucharilla, ventanilla, portezuela**).

4. *Verbs.* All irregular verbs are identified by the abbreviations *vti., vii., vri.,* and *vai.* The numbers and letters in brackets next to the abbreviations refer to the *Table of Irregular Verbs* on page xxi.

5. *Adverbs.* All Spanish adverbs of manner are formed by adding *-mente* to the feminine singular form of the corresponding adjective (ex., **rápido: rápida, rápidamente**). Only those Spanish adverbs not conforming to the above or whose meaning does not correspond to their English cognates are entered.

6. *Abbreviations.* All abbreviations used to indicate limitations of range, geographic or otherwise (ex., *Mex.,* Mexico; *aer.,* aeronautics; *med.,* medicine), are fully identified in the list of *Abbreviations used in Part II* on page xxx.

7. *Pronunciation.* Spanish being a quasi-phonetic language, the transcription of each individual word has been considered unnecessary. A clear, simple explanation of approximate English equivalents of Spanish phonemes is given on page v.

8. *Accentuation.* Words ending in a vowel, *n,* or *s* are stressed in the next to the last syllable (ex., **casa, comen, puertas.**) Words ending in a consonant other than *n* or *s* are stressed in the last syllable (ex., **comprar, atroz, pastel**). Stresses that do not follow these two rules are indicated by a written acute accent (ex., **árbol, acción, rápido.**)

SPANISH PRONUNCIATION

I. VOWELS

Approximate English Equivalents

a About midway between the *a* in f*a*ther and the *a* in c*a*t.

e About midway between the *a* in h*a*te and the *e* in b*e*t.

i Very like the *i* in mach*i*ne or the *ee* in t*ee*th.

o Somewhat similar to the *o* in n*o*te or the *o* in *o*r.

Approximate English Equivalents

u Very close to the *oo* in m*oo*n or the *u* in r*u*le. It is always silent after *q* and also after *g*, unless marked with dieresis (ex., ver-güenza).

y It is a vowel when standing alone or at the end of a word, and as such it is pronounced as *i* above.

II. CONSONANTS

b As in English but slightly softer at the beginning of a word or when preceded by *m* or *n*. Between vowels or preceded by a vowel and followed by *l* or *r* it is pronounced without the lips coming into complete contact.

c Before *e* or *i* it has the sound of the *th* of *th*ink in the Castilian speech of Spain. In the popular speech of many parts of Spain and in all Spanish America it is pronounced like the English *s* in *s*ay. Before *a*, *o* and *u* and at the end of a syllable or a word it is always like the English *k* in *k*ey.

ch It is considered a single letter and always pronounced like the *ch* in *ch*urch.

d Similar to English *d* in *d*ance. Between vowels or at the end of a word it has the sound of the English *th* in mo*th*er.

f As English *f*.

g Before *a*, *o* and *u* or preceding a consonant it is like the *g* in *g*o. Before *e* and *i* it sounds like the *ch* in the Scottish word lo*ch*.

h Always silent.

j Like *g* above before *e* or *i*.

l As English *l*.

ll Treated like a single letter. Sounds very close to the *lli* in mi*lli*on or in bri*lli*ant in the Castilian speech of Spain. In many parts of Spain and in most of Spanish America it is pronounced like the *y* in *y*et.

m As English *m*.

n As English *n* but before *b* or *v* it is sounded like an *m*.

ñ It sounds very similar to the *ny* in ca*ny*on or the *ni* in o*ni*on.

p As in English but somewhat softer.

q Occurs only in the combinations *que*, *qui* in which the *u* is silent. It has the sound of the English *k* in *k*ey.

r At the beginning of a word or preceded by *l*, *n*, or *s* it is strongly rolled. Otherwise it is pronounced with a single touch of the tongue.

rr It is treated as a single letter, and it is strongly trilled.

s Like the English *s* in *s*ee.

t Similar to the English *t* but less explosive.

v Same as *b* above.

x Sounds like *ks* or *gs* when placed between vowels. When followed by a consonant it is pronounced as the English *s* in *s*ame.

y (See Vowels above.) Preceding a vowel it is similar to the English *y* in *y*ear.

z In Castile it is pronounced like the *th* of *th*ick. In many parts of Spain and in all Spanish America it sounds like the English *s* in *s*ase.

PRONUNCIATION OF THE
SPANISH ALPHABET

The IPA symbols show you how the letters of the alphabet should be read.

a	[α]	j	['xota]	r	['ere]
b	[be] or [be 'larga]	k	[kα]	s	['ese]
c	[se] or [Өe]	l	['ele]	t	[te]
d	[de]	m	['eme]	u	[u]
e	[e]	n	['ene]	v	[be] or [be 'korta]
f	['efe]	ñ	['eŋe]	w	['doβle βe]
g	[xe]	o	[o]	x	['ekis]
h	['atʃe]	p	[pe]	y	[i grʲega]
i	[i]	q	[ku]	z	[seta] or [Өeta]

SYNOPSIS OF SPANISH GRAMMAR

I. GENERAL REMARKS

The Spanish alphabet consists of 26 separate symbols. The **w** of the English alphabet is not a part of the Spanish alphabet, and **rr**, though considered a separate symbol, does not occupy a separate place in the Spanish alphabet. The double consonants in Spanish are **cc** and **nn**. Each letter or symbol has a fixed pronunciation that is, under clearly defined rules, invariable. There is no gliding or blending of sounds, as in English, nor do changes occur in the pronunciations of the same letters when they appear in different words, as is so often the case in English. (See pp. v–vi SPANISH PRONUNCIATION, for a description of the pronunciation of individual Spanish letters and combinations of letters.) The differences between the Spanish of Spain and that of other Spanish-speaking countries consist in minor variations of pronunciation and in additions to the vocabulary that arise from geographical location and ethnic background.

A written accent over a vowel indicates that the syllable containing the vowel is accented, as: **lápiz** (*pencil*), **biología** (*biology*), **automóvil** (*automobile*), **termómetro** (*thermometer*), **condición** (*condition*). When a syllable is added to a word that has no written accent, as in forming certain plurals, a written accent may be added to show retention of the original stress, as: **germen, gérmenes; virgen, vírgenes.** Words without a written accent and ending in a vowel, **-n** or **-s**, have the accent on the next to the last syllable. Accordingly, certain words that add a syllable in the plural or in forming the feminine, drop the written accent, as: **condición, condiciones; japonés, japonesa.** All other words are accented on the last syllable.

There are three genders in Spanish: masculine, feminine and neuter.

Capital letters are used in Spanish as in English, with the following exceptions:

a) the subject pronouns **yo, usted** and **ustedes** are not capitalized except at the beginning of a sentence, or when **usted** and **ustedes** are abbreviated, as they usually are. **Vd.** and **Vds.** are commonly used abbreviations for **usted** and **ustedes** respectively.

b) names of months and days of the week are masculine and are not capitalized;

   El sábado, 17 de julio   *Saturday, July 17*

   Only **sábado** (*Saturday*) and **domingo** (*Sunday*) of the days of the week have plural forms;

c) adjectives formed from proper nouns are not capitalized, even when used as nouns, as: **los españoles** (*the Spaniards*);

d) titles spelled out (**señor, señora, señorita, don, doña**) are not capitalized except when they begin a sentence. When these titles are abbreviated, they are capitalized (**Sr., Sra., Srta., D., Da.**);

e) book and film titles are not capitalized except for the first word and proper names;

   La verdad sospechosa
   El capitán veneno

Punctuation in Spanish is much the same as in English, except that the Spanish add an inverted question mark and an inverted exclamation point before a question and an exclamation respectively.

| ¿Qué cosa quiere? | What does he want? |
| ¡Fuego! | Fire! |

II. PARTS OF SPEECH

A. Articles

1. The indefinite articles in Spanish are **un**, **una**, **unos** and **unas**. They agree in gender and number with the nouns and are generally repeated before each noun.

un libro (masculine)	a book
un ojo (masculine)	an eye
una pluma (feminine)	a pen
una manzana (feminine)	an apple
unos muchachos (masculine)	some boys
unas pinturas (feminine)	some paintings
Tengo un coche, una casa y una televisión	I have a car, house and television

It is not necessary to use the indefinite article in the following cases:
a) when denoting a quantity, as: **otro** (*another*), **medio** (*half*), **cien**, **ciento** (*a, one hundred*), and **mil** (*a, one thousand*);

| Hay cien soldados aquí | There are a hundred soldiers here |
| Necesito otro lápiz | I need another pencil |

b) when a predicate noun is unmodified;

| Juan es médico | John is a doctor |

c) when the meaning of *one* is obvious;

| Lleva abrigo | He is wearing a coat |

2. The definite articles in Spanish are **el**, **los**, **la**, **las** and the neuter form **lo**. Every Spanish noun has its corresponding article. The article appears in conjunction with the noun in most cases and agrees with it in gender and number.

el libro (masculine)	the book
la pluma (feminine)	the pen
los muchachos (masculine)	the boys
las pinturas (feminine)	the paintings
lo útil (neuter)	the useful
Los libros, los lápices y la pluma están en la mesa	The books, pencils and pen are on the desk
El señor Martínez está enfermo	Mr. Martin is ill
Vende los huevos a veinte centavos la docena	He sells eggs at twenty cents a dozen
Va a la iglesia los domingos	He goes to church on Sundays
El año que viene	Next year
Es la una	It is one o'clock

The definite article is not generally used with **mediodía** (*noon*) and **medianoche** (*midnight*).

| Es medianoche | It is midnight |

The definite article **el** replaces **la** before feminine nouns beginning with stressed **a** or **ha**.

| El agua está fría | The water is cold |

El following the preposition **a** contracts to **al**.

| Juan va al taller | John is going to the shop |

El following the preposition **de** contracts to **del**.

Él lleva el abrigo del padre   *He is wearing his father's coat*

The neuter form **lo** is used with an adjective to form a noun.

Lo importante es estudiar mucho   *The important thing is to study a great deal*

The definite article is not used:

a) with **don** and **doña**;

Doña María está aquí   *Madam Mary is here*

b) when speaking directly to a person;

¿Cómo está Vd., señor Martínez?   *How are you, Mr. Martin?*

c) when the noun is preceded by a possessive or demonstrative pronoun or adjective;

Este libro es negro   *This book is black*

d) before a numeral in a title.

Carlos Quinto   *Charles the Fifth*

B. Nouns

1. Spanish nouns are masculine or feminine or have one form for both genders; there are no neuter nouns. Nouns ending in **-o** are usually masculine. Nouns ending in **-dad**, **-ción** and **-sión** are feminine. Nouns ending in **-a**, **-ie**, **-ud** and **-umbre** are usually feminine. The gender is indicated in the vocabulary of this dictionary.

2. The plural of Spanish nouns is generally formed by adding **-s** to the singular of those that end in an unaccented vowel, and **-es** to those that end in an accented vowel or a consonant. Those ending in **-z** change the **-z** to **-c** and add **-es**. Some nouns (generally those ending in **-s** in the singular) have the same form for both the singular and the plural.

SINGULAR		PLURAL	
la casa	*house*	las casas	*houses*
la decisión	*decision*	las decisiones	*decisions*
la dificultad	*difficulty*	las dificultades	*difficulties*
el libro	*book*	los libros	*books*
la raíz	*root*	las raíces	*roots*
el lápiz	*pencil*	los lápices	*pencils*
el paraguas	*umbrella*	los paraguas	*umbrellas*

The masculine plural is used to indicate both masculine and feminine when both genders are included collectively.

Mis primos   *My cousins*
Mis hermanos   *My brothers and sisters*

C. Adjectives

1. Adjectives agree in gender and number with the nouns they modify and generally, but not necessarily, follow the noun. Those that end in **-o** are generally masculine; those that end in **-a** are generally feminine. An adjective ending in **-o** changes **-o** to **-a** to form the feminine and adds an **-s** to form the plural.

la casa roja	*the red house*
el libro rojo	*the red book*
las casas rojas	*the red houses*
los libros rojos	*the red books*

Some adjectives have only one ending and are both masculine and feminine.

una situación artificial	*an artificial situation*
un satélite artificial	*an artificial satellite*
un pintor modernista	*a modernistic painter*
las tendencias modernistas	*modernistic tendencies*

ix

Some adjectives lose their masculine singular ending when preceding the noun they modify.

el buen hombre	*the good man*
el primer piso	*the first floor*
un mal paso	*a false step*

2. *Comparison of adjectives.* The comparative and superlative degrees of adjectives in Spanish are formed by placing **más** (*more*) or **menos** (*less*), for the comparative degree, and **el más** (*most*) or **el menos** (*least*), for the superlative degree, before the positive form of the adjective.

POSITIVE		COMPARATIVE		SUPERLATIVE	
bonito	*pretty*	más bonito	*prettier*	el más bonito	*prettiest*
feliz	*happy*	más feliz	*happier*	el más feliz	*happiest*
listo	*clever*	menos listo	*less clever*	el menos listo	*least clever*

Comparisons employing **que** (*than*) as a conjunction are expressed by **más** (or **menos**) . . . **que**.

Hablo más despacio que él	*I speak slower than he*
Este libro es menos interesante que ése	*This book is less interesting than that one*

Comparisons employing **tan** (*as*) are expressed by **tan . . . como**.

Mi casa es tan grande como la tuya	*My house is as big as yours*

In Spanish there is an absolute superlative which is formed by placing **muy** (*very*) before the adjective, or by adding the endings **-ísimo** or **-érrimo** to the positive degree of the adjective. These endings are not equivalent to the *-est* of English superlatives. They have an intensive force and are translated by *very* or *extremely* followed by the adjective.

POSITIVE		COMPARATIVE	
hermoso	*beautiful*	más hermoso	*more beautiful*
difícil	*difficult*	más difícil	*more difficult*
célebre	*famous*	más célebre	*more famous*

SUPERLATIVE		ABSOLUTE SUPERLATIVE	
el más hermoso	*most beautiful*	muy hermoso	*very beautiful*
		hermosísimo	*extremely beautiful*
el más difícil	*most difficult*	muy difícil	*very difficult*
		dificilísimo	*extremely difficult*
el más célebre	*most famous*	celebérrimo	*extremely famous*

The comparison of some adjectives is irregular.

POSITIVE		COMPARATIVE		SUPERLATIVE	
bueno	*good*	mejor	*better*	el mejor	*best*
grande	*big, great*	más grande	*bigger, greater*	el más grande	*biggest, greatest*
		mayor	*greater, older*	el mayor	*greatest, oldest*
malo	*bad*	peor	*worse*	el peor	*worst*
pequeño	*small*	más pequeño	*smaller*	el más pequeño	*smallest*
		menor	*smaller, younger*	el menor	*smallest, youngest*

3. *Possessive adjectives.* Like all adjectives in Spanish, the possessive adjectives agree in number and gender with the nouns they modify. The Spanish possessive adjectives are:

SINGULAR		PLURAL
mi	*my*	mis
tu	*your*	tus
su	*his, her, your, its*	sus
nuestro	*our*	nuestros
vuestro	*your*	vuestros
su	*their, your*	sus

D. Adverbs

As in English, Spanish adverbs modify a verb, an adjective or another adverb. Many adverbs are formed by adding -mente to the feminine singular form of the adjective.

ADJECTIVE		ADVERB	
clara	*clear*	**claramente**	*clearly*
rápida	*rapid*	**rápidamente**	*rapidly*

The comparative and superlative degrees of adverbs are formed in the same manner as the comparative and superlative degrees of adjectives, but the superlative degree of adverbs is seldom used.

POSITIVE		COMPARATIVE		SUPERLATIVE	
claramente	*clearly*	**más claramente**	*more clearly*	**el más claramente**	*most clearly*
rápidamente	*rapidly*	**más rápidamente**	*more rapidly*	**el más rápidamente**	*most rapidly*

The comparison of some adverbs is irregular.

POSITIVE		COMPARATIVE		SUPERLATIVE	
bien	*well*	**mejor**	*better*	**mejor**	*best*
mal	*bad*	**peor**	*worse*	**peor**	*worst*
mucho	*much*	**más**	*more*	**más**	*most*
poco	*little*	**menos**	*less*	**menos**	*least*

E. Pronouns

1. *Personal pronouns.* Personal pronouns serve as subjects, direct objects of a verb, indirect objects of a verb, and possessives. In Spanish, the verb ending indicates the subject. It is therefore unnecessary to use a subject pronoun with the verb, unless clarity or emphasis is desired. *It*, when used as a subject, is never translated. The third person, **usted, Vd.** and **ustedes, Vds.** (*you*), is generally used when addressing persons. The second person singular or plural (the *you* of English) is the familiar form in Spanish and is limited in use. The following table lists personal pronouns used as the subject and as the direct object of a verb.

SINGULAR

	SUBJECT		DIRECT OBJECT	
1st person	**yo**	*I*	**me**	*me*
2nd person	**tú**	*you*	**te**	*you*
3rd person	**él**	*he*	**lo**	*him*
	ella	*she*	**la**	*her*
	usted, Vd.	*you*	**lo, la**	*him, her*
	ello	*it* (seldom used)	**lo**	*it*

PLURAL

1st person	**nosotros**	*we*	**nos**	*us*
2nd person	**vosotros**	*you*	**os**	*you*
3rd person	**ellos**	*they*	**los**	*them*
	ellas	*they*	**las**	*them*
	ustedes, Vds.	*you*	**los, las**	*them*

Direct object pronouns follow, and are attached to, an infinitive, a present participle, or a verb in the affirmative command.

Él quiere traerlo después	*He wants to bring it later*
Estoy buscándola	*I am looking for her*
Hágalo ahora	*Do it now*

In other cases, they are placed before the verb.

Nos llamaron ayer	*They called us yesterday*

Indirect object pronouns are placed in the same order in a sentence as direct object pronouns. The indirect object pronouns are:

	SINGULAR		PLURAL	
1st person	**me**	*to me*	**nos**	*to us*
2nd person	**te**	*to you*	**os, vos**	*to you*
3rd person	**le, se**	*to him, her, you*	**les**	*to them, you*

Se as a 3rd person indirect object pronoun should not be confused with the reflexive **se**. Since **le** and **se** mean *to him, to her* or *to you*, it may be necessary in a sentence to add a clarifying phrase, **a él, a ella,** or **a Vd.** Possessive pronouns agree in gender and number with the object possessed. They are as follows:

SINGULAR		PLURAL	
el mío	*mine*	**los míos**	
la mía	*mine*	**las mías**	
el tuyo	*yours*	**los tuyos**	
la tuya	*yours*	**las tuyas**	
el suyo	*his*	**los suyos**	
la suya	*hers*	**las suyas**	
el nuestro	*ours*	**los nuestros**	
la nuestra	*ours*	**las nuestras**	
el vuestro	*yours*	**los vuestros**	
la vuestra	*yours*	**las vuestras**	
el suyo	*theirs*	**los suyos**	
la suya	*theirs*	**las suyas**	

Éste es mi libro y ése es el suyo (de Vd.)	*This is my book and that one is yours*

2. *Relative pronouns.* Relative pronouns refer to nouns or pronouns that are antecedents in a sentence, and may be the subject or the object of a verb. The most common relative pronouns are:

que	*which, that, who, whom, when*
cual	*which, as, such as*
quien	*who, whom, whoever, whomever, which, whichever*
cuyo	*whose, of which, of whom, whereof*

Que and **cual** are used without distinction as to gender. **Que** refers to persons or things and may be the subject or the object of a verb; it has no plural.

El hombre que vino a comer	*The man who came to dinner*
El hombre que vimos es mi hermano	*The man whom we saw is my brother*

The prepositions **a, de** and **en** are used with **que** when referring to things.

El cine delante del que . . .	*The movie in front of which . . .*

Lo que and **lo cual** are used when referring to a clause or an idea.

No comió esta mañana, lo que me sorprendió	*He didn't eat this morning, which surprised me*

The following are interchangeable forms; the article indicates gender.

el que	*who, whom, which*	**el cual**
la que		**la cual**
los que		**los cuales**
las que		**las cuales**

Quien is both masculine and feminine. In both its singular (**quien**) and plural (**quienes**) forms, it may serve as the object of a preposition.

La muchacha con quien fue al cine está aquí	*The girl with whom he went to the movies is here*

Quien is sometimes used in the singular with a plural antecedent. **Cuyo** has masculine (**cuyo**), feminine (**cuya**) and plural (**cuyos, cuyas**) forms, and agrees in gender and number with its antecedent.

3. *Demonstrative pronouns.* Demonstrative pronouns specify particular persons or objects and indicate their relative distance from the speaker or from the person addressed. Demonstrative pronouns become demonstrative adjectives when preceding a noun and are written without an accent.

DEMONSTRATIVE PRONOUNS			DEMONSTRATIVE ADJECTIVES	
SINGULAR	PLURAL		SINGULAR	PLURAL
éste (*m.*)	éstos	*this, these,* near speaker	este	estos
ésta (*f.*) esto (*neut.*)	éstas		esta	estas
ése (*m.*)	ésos	*that, those,* near person addressed	ese	esos
ésa (*f.*) eso (*neut.*)	ésas		esa	esas
aquél (*m.*)	aquéllos	*that, those,* away from speaker and addressee	aquel	aquellos
aquélla (*f.*) aquello (*neut.*)	aquéllas		aquella	aquellas

The neuter forms, **esto, eso** and **aquello** carry no accent and are used to refer to some general idea or to an object not yet identified.

tal	tales	*such, such a one, such things*
tanto	tantos	*that*

Tal and **tanto** are adjectives as well as pronouns and carry no accent as either.

4. *Indefinite Pronouns.* Indefinite pronouns have the same function in Spanish as in English. They are:

alguien	*somebody, someone*
nadie	*nobody, no one, none*
cualquiera	*any one*
quienquiera	*whoever*
algo	*some*
nada	*nothing*

Alguien, nadie, algo and **nada** have the same form for the masculine and feminine. They have no plural forms. Other parts of speech may also act as indefinite pronouns, among these are the interrogatives **cuál** (*which*) and **quién** (*who*), the demonstrative pronoun **tal** (*such a*), and the adjectives **alguno** (*some*), **ninguno** (*none*), **todo** (*all*), **mucho** (*many*), **demasiado** (*too much, too many*), **bastante** (*sufficient, enough*), **harto** (*sufficient*), and **poco** (*few*).

F. Interrogatives

Interrogatives in Spanish always carry an accent. Some common interrogatives are:

¿qué?	*what? which?*	¿cuándo?	*when?*
¿quién?	*who? whom?*	¿cómo?	*how?*
¿de quién?	*whose?*	¿dónde?	*where?*
¿cuál	*which one?*	¿adónde?	*to where?*
¿cuánto?	*how much?*	¿por qué?	*why?*

Quién, cuál and **cuánto** have the plural forms **quiénes, cuáles** and **cuántos,** and are used as pronouns. The other interrogatives have no plural form. **Qué** may be used as an adjective or a pronoun and may refer to either persons or things.

G. Verbs

Verbs in Spanish are regular, radical-changing, orthographic-changing, and irregular in their conjugations. The following remarks describe some of the more important characteristics of verbs and their conjugations. A table of model conju-

xiii

gations of regular, radical-changing, orthographic-changing and irregular verbs at the end of this section.

1. Many verbs require a preposition before an infinitive. Some of the most common are:

a) those that require the preposition **a**;

acertar	to manage, succeed	enviar	to send
acostumbrarse	to accustom oneself, get used to	invitar	to invite
acudir	to come to, resort to	ir	to go
aprender	to learn	llegar	to arrive
apresurarse	to hasten	negarse	to refuse
atreverse	to dare	obligar	to compel
ayudar	to help	pasar	to pass, go by
bajar	to come down	persuadir	to persuade
comenzar	to begin	ponerse	to start
correr	to run	proceder	to proceed
disponerse	to prepare	subir	to go up
echar(se	to start	tornar	to return, turn
empezar	to begin	venir	to come
enseñar	to teach	volar	to fly
entrar	to enter	volver	to return, do again

b) those that require the preposition **de**;

acabar	to finish, conclude	dejar	to discontinue, leave
acordarse	to remember	encargarse	to undertake, take on oneself
alegrarse	to be glad	extrañarse	to be surprised
avergonzarse	to be ashamed	gozar	to enjoy
cesar	to cease	olvidarse	to forget
concluir	to conclude, finish	tratar	to try

Acabar de is also used to mean *to have just*.

Acabo de llegar a Nueva York   *I have just come to New York*

c) those that require the preposition **en**;

acordar	to agree	pensar	to think
complacerse	to take pleasure	persistir	to persist
consentir	to consent	quedar	to agree, decide
empeñarse	to persist, insist	tardar	to be slow, delay
insistir	to insist	vacilar	to hesitate

d) those that require the preposition **con**.

contar	to count on, rely
soñar	to dream

2. The infinitive of the verb is sometimes used as a noun, and often takes **el** in this case.

El estudiar es difícil   *Studying is difficult*

The infinitive follows most common verbs (**poder, saber, desear, esperar,** etc.) without a preposition, but some verbs require a preposition before the infinitive, see above.

3. The present participle (gerund) is formed by adding **-ando** to the stem of verbs whose infinitives end in **-ar**, and **-iendo** to the stem of verbs whose infinitives end in **-er** and **-ir**.

INFINITIVE		PRESENT PARTICIPLE
hablar	to speak	hablando
comer	to eat	comiendo
vivir	to live	viviendo

Some verbs having an irregular form of the present participle are:

INFINITIVE	PRESENT PARTICIPLE	INFINITIVE	PRESENT PARTICIPLE
caer	cayendo	oír	oyendo
corregir	corrigiendo	pedir	pidiendo
creer	creyendo	poder	pudiendo
decir	diciendo	seguir	siguiendo
divertirse	divirtiéndose	sentir	sintiendo
dormir	durmiendo	servir	sirviendo
ir	yendo	traer	trayendo
leer	leyendo	venir	viniendo

The present participle is used with some tense of **estar** to form a progressive tense.

Estoy hablando   *I am speaking*

4. The past participle is formed by adding **-ado** to the stem of verbs whose infinitives end in **-ar**, and **-ido** to the stem of verbs whose infinitives end in **-er** and **-ir**.

INFINITIVE		PAST PARTICIPLE
hablar		hablado
comer		comido
vivir		vivido

Some verbs having an irregular form of the past participle are:

INFINITIVE	PAST PARTICIPLE	INFINITIVE	PAST PARTICIPLE
abrir	abierto	poner	puesto
cubrir	cubierto	proveer	provisto
decir	dicho	pudrir	podrido
escribir	escrito	romper	roto
freír	frito	soltar	suelto
hacer	hecho	ver	visto
imprimir	impreso	volver	vuelto
morir	muerto		

The past participles of compounds of the above verbs, as **entreabrir, descubrir, describir,** etc., are also irregular.

5. There are three regular conjugations in Spanish.

a) The first conjugation includes the verbs ending in **-ar** in the infinitive.

INFINITIVE		PRESENT PARTICIPLE	PAST PARTICIPLE
hablar	*to speak*	hablando	hablado
estudiar	*to study*	estudiando	estudiado
caminar	*to walk*	caminando	caminado

b) The second conjugation includes the verbs ending in **-er** in the infinitive.

INFINITIVE		PRESENT PARTICIPLE	PAST PARTICIPLE
comer	*to eat*	comiendo	comido
entender	*to understand*	entendiendo	entendido
beber	*to drink*	bebiendo	bebido

c) The third conjugation includes the verbs ending in **-ir** in the infinitive.

INFINITIVE		PRESENT PARTICIPLE	PAST PARTICIPLE
vivir	*to live*	viviendo	vivido
partir	*to depart*	partiendo	partido
subir	*to go up*	subiendo	subido

6. *Tenses of the indicative mood.*

Present Tense. The present tense is used to express action in the present, habitual or customary action, or a general truth.

Juan trabaja en el jardín   *John works in the garden*

It is formed by dropping the infinitive endings and adding personal endings. Verbs of the first regular conjugation add **-o, -as, -a, -amos, -áis, -an;** verbs of the second regular conjugation add **-o, -es, -e, -emos, -éis, -en;** verbs of the third regular conjugation add **-o, -es, -e, -imos, -ís, -en.**

b) *Imperfect Tense.* The imperfect tense is used to describe the past, a continuing action in the past, or what was habitual or customary in the past.

La ventana estaba abierta	*The window was open*
Caminaba por la calle	*I was walking down the street*
Jugábamos cuando estábamos de vacaciones	*We played when we were on vacation*

It is formed by dropping the infinitive endings and adding personal endings. Verbs of the first regular conjugation add -aba, -abas, -aba, -ábamos -abais, -aban; verbs of the second and third regular conjugations add -ía -ías, -ía, -íamos, -íais, -ían. Ir, ser and ver (and its compounds) are irregularly conjugated in the imperfect tense, see the Verb Table.

c) *Preterit (Past) Tense.* The preterit tense is used to express an action completed in the past and to form the passive voice in the past.

Concha cerró la puerta	*Concha closed the door*
América fue descubierta por Colón	*America was discovered by Columbus*

It is formed by dropping the infinitive endings and adding personal endings. Verbs of the first regular conjugation add -é, -aste, -ó, -amos, -asteis -aron; verbs of the second and third regular conjugations add -í, -iste, -ió -imos, -isteis, -ieron.

d) *Future Tense.* The future tense is used as in English. In addition, it expresses probability or conjecture in the present; its use corresponds exactly to that of the conditional in the past.

Él trabajará mañana	*He will work tomorrow*
¿Qué hora será?	*I wonder what time it is*
Serán las tres	*It is probably three o'clock*

It is formed by adding the personal endings -é, -ás, -á, -emos, -éis, -án to the infinitive. The future endings are the same for all verbs, whether regular or irregular.

7. *Conditional Mood.* The conditional mood is used as in English. It also expresses probability in the past. Its use corresponds exactly to that of the future tense.

Si fuera Vd. lo compraría	*If I were you, I would buy it*
Serían las siete	*It was probably seven o'clock*

It is formed by adding the personal endings of the imperfect tense of the second and third conjugations to the infinitive, -ía, -ías, -ía, -íamos, -íais -ían.

8. *Subjunctive mood and tenses.* The subjunctive mood expresses wish, obligation, or a condition improbable or contrary to fact.

a) The tense of the subjunctive in a subordinate clause is determined by the tense of the verb in the main clause. When the verb in the main clause is in the present or in the future tense, the verb in the subordinate clause will be in the present subjunctive. When the verb in the main clause is in the preterit imperfect or conditional, the verb in the subordinate clause will be in the imperfect subjunctive.

b) When futurity is implied, the subjunctive is required following such adverbs or adverbial locutions, of time as:

cuando	*when*
después que	*after*
hasta que	*until*
luego que	*as soon as*
mientras que	*while*
antes (de) que	*before* (always followed by the subjunctive)
Lo veré cuando él venga	*I shall see him when he comes*

c) The subjunctive is required following such conjunctive locutions as:

a menos que	*unless*
antes (de) que	*before*
para que	*in order that*
como si	*as if, as though*

xvi

con tal que	provided that, as long as
sin que	without
Me habló como si fuera mi padre	He spoke to me as though he were my father
Lo haré con tal que me ayude	I shall do it provided you help me

4) The subjunctive is used in noun clauses introduced by **que** (*that*) when the following conditions exist at the same time:
1. the sentence contains two clauses;
2. the subject in the subordinate clause differs from the subject of the main clause;
3. when a verb of emotion or feeling, command, request, permission, prohibition, approval, advice, necessity, cause, denial, doubt, or an impersonal locution in the main clause, affects the subject and/or the verb of the subordinate clause.

Me alegro de que ellos se vayan	I am glad that they are going
Ellos temían que no llegásemos a tiempo	They feared that we would not arrive on time
Dígale a Pedro que me ayude	Tell Peter to help me
No creo que él diga la verdad	I don't believe he is telling the truth
Es posible que le escribamos	It is possible that we will write to him

) *Present Subjunctive*. In addition to its uses in subordinate clauses, the present subjunctive expresses a command.

| No sea Vd. tonto | Don't you be silly |
| Escriban Vds. la lección | Write the lesson |

It is formed by dropping the infinitive endings and adding personal endings. Verbs of the first regular conjugation add **-e, -es, -e, -emos, -éis, -en**; verbs of the second and third regular conjugations add **-a, -as, -a, -amos, -áis, -an.**

) *Imperfect Subjunctive*. The imperfect subjunctive is formed by dropping the ending **-ron** of the third person plural of the preterit and adding personal endings. There are two sets of endings that are usually interchangeable, but the form in **-ra** is the more commonly used in modern Spanish. The two sets of endings are the same for all three conjugations. They are: **-ra, -ras, -ra, -ramos, -rais, -ran** and **-se, -ses, -se, -semos, -seis, -sen.** The imperfect subjunctive is rarely used by itself, but it may appear in such simple sentences as:

Quisiera verlo	I should like to see him
Debiera Vd. ir	You should go
¿Pudiera Vd. decírmelo?	Would you be able to tell it to me?

) *Future Subjunctive*. The future subjunctive is formed by dropping the infinitive endings and adding personal endings. Verbs of the first regular conjugation add **-are, -ares, -are, -áremos, -areis, -aren**; verbs of the second and third conjugations add **-iere, -ieres, -iere, -iéremos, -iereis, -ieren.**

9. *Imperative Mood*. The imperative mood expresses a command. There is one ·nse only, the present. The forms of the imperative mood are the second person ·ngular and plural (familiar form) and they are formed by dropping the infinitive ·nding and adding **-a** and **-ad** respectively in the first conjugation, **-e** and **-ed** in ·he second conjugation, and **-e** and **-id** in the third conjugation.

10. *Compound Tenses*. The compound tenses express a completed action. ·here is a corresponding compound tense for each of the simple tenses. They are ·rmed with the auxiliary verb **haber** (regularly conjugated) and the uninflected ·ast participle of the verb.

	PERFECT INDICATIVE	
	SINGULAR	PLURAL
1st person	**he amado**	**hemos amado**
2nd person	**has amado**	**habéis amado**
3rd person	**he amado**	**han amado**

	PLUPERFECT INDICATIVE	
1st person		**había amado**
2nd person		**habías amado** etc.

xvii

1st person	**hube amado**
2nd person	**hubiste amado** etc.

FUTURE PERFECT INDICATIVE

1st person	**habré amado**
2nd person	**habrás amado** etc.

CONDITIONAL PERFECT

1st person	**habría amado**
2nd person	**habrías amado** etc.

PERFECT SUBJUNCTIVE

1st person	**haya amado**
2nd person	**hayas amado** etc.

PLUPERFECT SUBJUNCTIVE

1st person	**hubiera amado**
2nd person	**hubieras amado**etc.

FUTURE PERFECT SUBJUNCTIVE

1st person	**hubiere amado**
2nd person	**hubieres amado** etc.

11. *The Passive Voice.* The passive voice is formed with the auxiliary verb **se** (*to be*) and an inflected past participle; it is seldom used in Spanish. It should b noted that not all constructions employing **ser** and a past participle are passiv for some past participles have an active meaning in certain constructions. Th same can be said of the verb **ser** when used with the past participle of an intrans tive verb.

Los libros fueron escritos por Cervantes	*The books were written by Cervantes*
La niña está acompañada por su madre	*The girl is accompanied by her mother*

12. *Radical-changing Verbs.* In these verbs a change occurs in the radica when the tonic accent (voice stress) falls on the radical vowel **-e** or **-o**. Radica changing verbs are divided into three classes.
a) To the first class belong those verbs ending in **-ar** and **-er** whose radical vow els **-e** or **-o** change to **-ie** and **-ue** respectively when the radical receives th stress. The changes occur in all of the singular and in the third person plura of the present indicative, in the present subjunctive, and in the imperativ singular. See **acertar** and **volver** in the Verb Table.
b) To the second class belong those verbs ending in **-ir** whose radical vowels or **-o** change to **-ie** and **-ue** respectively when the radical receives the stres The changes occur as in the verbs of the first class. They also change **-e** to and **-o** to **-u** in the first and second persons plural of the present subjunctiv in the third person singular and plural of the preterit, in all of the imperfe subjunctive, and in the present participle. See **sentir** and **dormir** in the Ver Table.
c) To the third class also belong those verbs ending in **-ir** whose radical vow **-e** changes to **-i** when the radical receives the stress. The change occurs in a of the singular and in the third person plural of the present indicative, in a of the present subjunctive, in the third person singular and plural of the pre erit, in all of the imperfect subjunctive, in the imperative singular, and in th present participle. See **pedir** in the Verb Table. Other verbs of this class a those ending in **-eír**. See **reír** in the Verb Table.
Note. Most common verbs that have **-e** or **-o** in the radical are radica changing verbs.

13. *Orthographic-changing Verbs.* Orthographic-changing verbs are thos which undergo a change in spelling in order to maintain the sound of the fin consonant before the infinitive ending.
a) Verbs ending in **-car** change the **-c** to **-qu** before an **-e**. See **embarcar** in th Verb Table.
b) Verbs ending in **-gar** change the **g** to **-gu** before an **-e**. See **amargar** in th Verb Table.

c) Verbs ending in **-zar** change the **-z** to **-c** before an **-e**. See **alcanzar** in the Verb Table.

d) Verbs ending in **-guar** change the **-gu** to **-gü** before an **-e**. See **averiguar** in the Verb Table.

e) Verbs ending in **-cer** or **-cir** preceded by a consonant change the **-c** to **-z** before **-a** and **-o**. See **mecer** and **zurcir** in the Verb Table.

f) Verbs ending in **-cer** or **-cir** preceded by a vowel change the **-c** to **-zc** before **-a** and **-o**. See **agradecer** and **conducir** in the Verb Table. Some notable exceptions to this rule are: **cocer** and its compounds, and **mecer**, in which the **-c** changes to **-z**, and **hacer** and **decir**, which are highly irregular. See the Verb Table.

g) Verbs ending in **-ger** or **-gir** change the **-g** to **-j** before **-a** and **-o**. See **recoger** in the Verb Table.

h) Verbs ending in **-guir** change the **-gu** to **-g** before **-a** and **-o**. See **distinguir** in the Verb Table.

i) Verbs ending in **-quir** change the **-qu** to **-c** before **-a** and **-o**. See **delinquir** in the Verb Table.

j) Verbs ending in **-eer** change the **-i** of the ending to **-y**. See **leer** in the Verb Table.

k) Verbs ending in **-uir** (except those ending in **-guir** and **-quir**) insert **-y** before **-a**, **-e** and **-o**, and replace an unstressed **-i** between vowels with **-y**. See **construir** in the Verb Table.

14. *Reflexive Verbs.* Reflexive verbs are used more frequently in Spanish than in English. Verbs that are intransitive in English are often reflexive in Spanish. Some Spanish verbs are always reflexive. Others may be reflexive or not, depending on the use. Reflexive verbs always occur in conjunction with a reflexive pronoun.

PRESENT INDICATIVE

	SINGULAR	PLURAL
1st person	yo me lavo	nosotros nos lavamos
2nd person	tú te lavas	vosotros os (vos) laváis
3rd person	él se lava	ellos se lavan

Lavar is an example of a verb that may be reflexive or not. In the sample conjugation above, it is reflexive, in the sense of *to wash oneself*. It can also be used transitively and without the reflexive pronoun.

When the subject of a reflexive verb is two or more persons or things, and the action of the verb falls upon the plural subject, the verb is used with a reciprocal meaning.

Las muchachas se visitan	*The girls visit each other*
José, Pedro y Juan se escriben	*Joseph, Peter and John write each other*

15. *Impersonal Verbs.* These verbs are used only in the infinitive and in the third person singular. They are generally used in a causative sense, their subject being implied but not stated. The verbs **haber** and **hacer**, when used impersonally, mean *there is* or *there are*. Some impersonal verbs are used transitively but only in a metaphorical sense. The pronoun **se** and the active form of the verb is also used to form some impersonal constructions.

Llueve hoy	*It is raining today*
Nieva	*It is snowing*
Hay polvo	*It is dusty*
Se prohibe fumar	*It is forbidden to smoke*

Some typical impersonal verbs are:

alborear	to dawn	helar	to freeze
amanecer	to dawn	llover	to rain
anochecer	to grow dark	lloviznar	to drizzle
diluviar	to rain heavily	nevar	to snow
escarchar	to frost	relampaguear	to lighten
granizar	to hail	tronar	to thunder

16. *Defective Verbs.* These are verbs that lack some tenses and persons. They must not be confused with some verbs that, while not being truly defective, are

xix

seldom used in some of their persons. Defective verbs are sometimes used in metaphorical sense. Some typical defective verbs are:

abolir	*to abolish*
agredir	*to assault*
aguerrir	*to accustom to war*
arrecirse	*to become stiff with cold*
atañer	*to concern*
aterirse	*to become stiff with cold*
balbucir	*to stammer*
concernir	*to concern*
despavorir	*to be aghast*
embaír	*to deceive*
empedernir	*to harden*
garantir	*to guarantee*
manir	*to keep meat until it becomes gamey*
soler	*to be in the habit of*
transgredir	*to transgress*
usucapir	*to usucapt*

17. *Ser and Estar.* Each of these verbs means *to be,* but they are not interchangeable. **Ser** denotes a permanent state or condition.

La casa es blanca	*The house is white*

Estar denotes a temporary state or condition.

La puerta está abierta	*The door is open*

18. *Negation.* In Spanish, the negative **no** always precedes the verb.

No quiero ir	*I don't want to go*
No la veo	*I don't see her*

H. Prepositions

Some common prepositions are:

a	*at, to, for*	hacia	*towards*
antes, ante	*before*	hasta	*until*
con	*with*	para	*for, to*
contra	*against*	por	*by, for, through*
de	*of, from*	según	*according*
desde	*from*	sin	*without*
en	*in, on, at*	sobre	*on, upon*
entre	*between, among*	tras, detrás	*behind*

I. Conjunctions

Some common conjunctions are:

que	*that*	porque, que	*because*
también	*also*	pues, pues que	*since*
además	*moreover*	por	*by, for*
y, e	*and*	por tanto	*therefore*
ni	*neither, nor*	por cuanto	*whereas*
o, u, ya	*or, either, whether*	para que	*that*
sea que	*whether*	a fin de	*in order that*
tampoco	*neither*	si	*if*
mas, pero	*but*	sino	*but*
aun, cuando, aun cuando	*even*	con tal que	*provided*
aunque	*although, though*		
a menos de, a menos que	*unless*	como, así como	*as*
pues, puesto que	*since*	así	*so*

E is used instead of **y** when the following word begins with **i** or **hi.** **U** is employed instead of **o** when the word immediately following begins with **o** or **ho.**

XX

IRREGULAR VERBS

KEY FOR THE IDENTIFICATION OF TENSES AND PARTS OF SPANISH VERBS

A	Present Indicative.	F	Conditional.
B	Present Subjunctive.	G	Imperfect Subjunctive.
C	Imperfect Indicative.	H	Imperative.*
D	Preterite Indicative.	I	Past Participle.
E	Future Indicative.	J	Gerund.

* For all positive and negative imperative forms with *usted*, *ustedes*, and *nosotros* and for the negative forms with *tú* and *vosotros* the present subjunctive is used.

Reflexive and reciprocal verbs attach the object pronouns (**me, te, se, nos, os, se**) at the end of the infinitive (*peinarse; amarse*), the positive imperative (*péinate, péinese; amaos*), and the gerund (*peinándose; amándose*). In all the tenses of the indicative and the subjunctive these pronouns are detached and placed before the verb (me *peino*, te *peinas*, se *peina*, **nos** *peinamos*, **os** peináis, se *peinan*; nos *amamos*, os *amáis*, se *aman*, etc.).

SPANISH IRREGULAR AND ORTHOGRAPHIC CHANGING VERBS

) A number placed next to the entry indicates that the irregular verb follows the pattern of conjugation of the model given under that number in Part I below. (Example: **pensar** [1], behaves like the model **acertar**—changes **e** to **ie**—in the same tenses A, B, H.)

) A letter placed next to the entry indicates that the orthographic changing verb follows the spelling irregularities of the model verb given under that letter in Part II below. (Example: **aplazar** [a], behaves like the model **alcanzar**.)

) A number and a letter placed next to the entry indicate that the verb belongs to both of the above categories. (Example: **almorzar** [12-a], behaves like both **contar** *and* **alcanzar**.)
Only the irregular forms are given.

I. IRREGULAR VERBS

No.	Verb	Irregular Tenses (See Key)	
1	acertar	A	acierto, aciertas, acierta; aciertan.
		B	acierte, aciertes, acierte; acierten.
		H	acierta, acierta; acierten.
2	adquirir	A	adquiero, adquieres, adquiere; adquieren.
		B	adquiera, adquieras, adquiera; adquieran.
		H	adquiere, adquiera; adquieran.
3	agradecer	A	agradezco.
		B	agradezca, agradezcas, agradezca; agradezcamos, agradezcáis, agradezcan.
		H	agradezca; agradezcamos, agredezcan.
4	andar	D	anduve, anduviste, anduvo; anduvimos, anduvisteis, anduvieron.
		G	anduviera or anduviese, anduvieras or anduvieses, anduviera or anduviese; anduviéramos or anduviésemos, anduvierais or anduvieseis, anduvieran or anduviesen.

No.	Verb	Irregular Tenses (See Key)	
5	asir	A	asgo.
		B	asga, asgas, asga; asgamos, asgáis, asgan.
6	bendecir	A	bendigo, bendices, bendice; bendicen.
		B	bendiga, bendigas, bendiga; bendigamos, bendigáis, be digan.
		D	bendije, bendijiste, bendijo; bendijimos, bendijisteis, be dijeron.
		G	bendijera or bendijese, bendijeras or bendijeses, bendije or bendijese; bendijéramos or bendijésemos, bendijera or bendijeseis, bendijeran or bendijesen.
		H	bendice, bendiga; bendigamos, bendigan.
		I	bendito (also the regular: benedecido).
		J	bendiciendo.
7	caber	A	quepo.
		B	quepa, quepas, quepa; quepamos, quepáis, quepan.
		D	cupe, cupiste, cupo; cupimos, cupisteis, cupieron.
		E	cabré, cabrás, cabrá; cabremos, cabréis, cabrán.
		F	cabría, cabrías, cabría; cabríamos, cabríais, cabrían.
		G	cupiera or cupiese, cupieras or cupieses, cupiera or cupie cupiéramos or cupiésemos, cupierais or cupieseis, cup ran or cupiesen.
		H	quepa, quepamos, quepan.
8	caer	A	caigo.
		B	caiga, caigas, caiga; caigamos, caigáis, caigan.
		H	caiga; caigamos, caigan.
9	ceñir	A	ciño, ciñes, ciñe; ciñen.
		B	ciña, ciñas, ciña; ciñamos, ciñáis, ciñan.
		D	ciñó; ciñeron.
		G	ciñera or ciñese, ciñeras or ciñeses, ciñera or ciñese; ciñ ramos or ciñésemos, ciñerais or ciñeseis, ciñeran or ñesen.
		H	ciñe, ciñe; ciñamos, ciñan.
		J	ciñendo.
10	cerner, cernir	A	cierno, ciernes, cierne; cernimos, cernís, ciernen.
		B	cierna, ciernas, cierna; ciernan.
		E	cerneré, cernirás, cernirá; cerniremos, cerniréis, cernirán.
		F	cerniría, cernirías, cerniría; cerniríamos, cerniríais, cern rían.
		H	cierne, cierna; ciernan.
11	conducir	A	conduzco.
		B	conduzca, conduzcas, conduzca; conduzcamos, cond cáis, conduzcan.
		D	conduje, condujiste, condujo; condujimos, condujiste condujeron.
		G	condujera or condujese, condujeras or condujeses, co dujera or condujese; condujéramos or condujésem condujerais or condujeseis, condujeran or condujesen
		H	conduzca; conduzcamos, conduzcan.
12	contar	A	cuento, cuentas, cuenta; cuentan.
		B	cuente, cuentes, cuente; cuenten.
		H	cuenta, cuente; cuenten.

No.	Verb	Irregular Tenses (See Key)	
13	dar	A	doy.
		D	di, diste, dio; dimos, disteis, dieron.
		G	diera or diese, dieras or dieses, diera or diese; diéramos or diésemos, dierais or dieseis, dieran or diesen.
14	decir	A	digo, dices, dice; dicen.
		B	diga, digas, diga; digamos, digáis, digan.
		D	dije, dijiste, dijo; dijimos, dijisteis, dijeron.
		E	diré, dirás, dirá; diremos, diréis, dirán.
		F	diría, dirías, diría; diríamos, diríais, dirían.
		G	dijera or dijese, dijeras or dijeses, dijera or dijese; dijéramos or dijésemos, dijerais or dijeseis, dijeran or dijesen.
		H	di, diga; digamos, digan.
		I	dicho.
		J	diciendo.
15	desosar	A	deshueso, deshuesas, deshuesa; deshuesan.
		B	deshuese, deshueses, deshuese; deshuesen.
		H	deshuesa, deshuese; deshuesen.
16	discernir	A	discierno, disciernes, discierne; disciernen.
		B	discierna, disciernas, discierna; disciernan.
		H	discierne, discierna; disciernan.
17	dormir	A	duermo, duermes, duermo; duermen.
		B	duerma, duermas, duerma; durmamos, durmáis, duerman.
		D	durmió; durmieron.
		G	durmiera or durmiese, durmieras or durmieses, durmiera or durmiese; durmiéramos or durmiésemos, durmierais or durmieseis, durmieran or durmiesen.
		H	duerme, duerma; durmamos, duerman.
		J	durmiendo.
18	entender	A	entiendo, entiendes, entiende; entienden.
		B	entienda, entiendas, entienda; entiendan.
		H	entiende, entienda; entiendan.
19	erguir	A	yergo, yergues, yergue; yerguen.
		B	yerga, yergas, yerga; irgamos, irgáis, yergan.
		D	irguió; irguieron.
		G	irguiera or irguiese, irguieras or irguieses, irguiera or irguiese; irguiéramos or irguiésemos, irguierais or irguieseis, irguieran or irguiesen.
		H	yergue, yerga; irgamos, yergan.
		J	irguiendo.
20	estar	A	estoy, estás, está; están.
		B	esté, estés, esté; estén.
		D	estuve, estuviste, estuvo; estuvimos, estuvisteis, estuvieron.
		G	estuviera or estuviese, estuvieras or estuvieses, estuviera or estuviese; estuviéramos or estuviésemos, estuvierais or estuvieseis, estuvieran or estuviesen.
		H	está, esté; estén.
21	haber	A	he, has, ha or hay (impersonal form); hemos or habemos, han.
		B	haya, hayas, haya; hayamos, hayáis, hayan.
		D	hube, hubiste, hubo; hubimos, hubisteis, hubieron.
		E	habré, habrás, habrá; habremos, habréis, habrán.

No.	Verb	Irregular Tenses (See Key)	
		F	habría, habrías, habría; habríamos, habríais, habrían.
		G	hubiera or hubiese, hubieras or hubieses, hubiera or hubiese; hubiéramos or hubiésemos, hubierais or hubieseis hubieran or hubiesen.
		H	he, haya; hayamos, hayan.
22	hacer	A	hago.
		B	haga, hagas, haga; hagamos, hagáis, hagan.
		D	hice, hiciste, hizo; hicimos, hicisteis, hicieron.
		E	haré, harás, hará; haremos, haréis, harán.
		F	haría, harías, haría; haríamos, haríais, harían.
		G	hiciera or hiciese, hicieras or hicieses, hiciera or hiciese; hiciéramos or hiciésemos, hicierais or hicieseis, hicierar or hiciesen.
		H	haz, haga; hagamos, hagan.
		I	hecho.
23	huir	A	huyo, huyes, huye; huyen.
		B	huya, huyas, huya; huyamos, huyáis, huyan.
		H	huye, huya; huyamos, huyan.
24	ir	A	voy, vas, va; vamos, vais, van.
		B	vayas, vaya; vayamos, vayáis, vayan.
		C	iba, ibas, iba; íbamos, ibais, iban.
		D	fui, fuiste, fue; fuimos, fuisteis, fueron.
		G	fuera or fuese, fueras or fueses, fuera or fuese; fuéramos o fuésemos, fuerais or fueseis, fueran or fuesen.
		J	yendo.
25	jugar	A	juego, juegas, juega; juegan.
		B	juegue, juegues, juegue; jueguen.
		H	juega, juegue; jueguen.
26	mover	A	muevo, mueves, mueve; mueven.
		B	mueva, muevas, mueva; muevan.
		H	mueve, mueva; muevan.
27	mullir	D	mulló; mulleron.
		G	mullera or mullese, mulleras or mulleses, mullera or mullese; mulléramos or mullésemos, mullerais or mulleseis mulleran or mullesen.
		J	mullendo.
28	oir	A	oigo, oyes, oye; oyen.
		B	oiga, oigas, oiga; oigamos, oigáis, oigan.
		H	oye, oiga; oigamos, oigan.
28′	oler	A-B-H	It is conjugated in the same way that No. 26 (mover) but with an "h" before diphthong "ue": huelo, hueles, etc.
29	pedir	A	pido, pides, pide; piden.
		B	pida, pidas, pida; pidamos, pidáis, pidan.
		D	pidió; pidieron.
		G	pidiera or pidiese, pidieras or pidieses, pidiera or pidiese pidiéramos or pidiésemos, pidierais or pidieseis, pidiera or pidiesen.
		H	pide, pida; pidamos, pidan.
		J	pidiendo.

No.	Verb	Irregular Tenses (See Key)	
30	placer	A	plazco.
		B	plazca, plazcas, plazca (or plegue or plega); placamos, placáis, plazcan.
		D	plugo (or plació); pluguieron (or placieron).
		G	pluguiera or pluguiese (or placiera or placiese).
		H	plazca; plazcamos, plazcan.
31	poder	A	puedo, puedes, puede; pueden.
		B	pueda, puedas, pueda; puedan.
		D	pude, pudiste, pudo; pudimos, pudisteis, pudieron.
		E	podré, podrás, podrá; podremos, podréis, podrán.
		F	podría, podrías, podría; podríamos, podríais, podrían.
		G	pudiera or pudiese, pudieras or pudiese, pudiera or pudiese; pudiéramos or pudiésemos, pudierais or pudieseis, pudieran or pudiesen.
		H	puede, pueda; puedan.
		J	pudiendo.
32	poner	A	pongo.
		B	ponga, pongas, ponga; pongamos, pongáis, pongan.
		D	puse, pusiste, puso; pusimos, pusisteis, pusieron.
		E	pondré, pondrás, pondrá; pondremos, pondréis, pondrán.
		F	pondría, pondrías, pondría; pondríamos, pondriais, pondrían.
		G	pusiera or pusiese, pusieras or pusieses, pusiera or pusiese; pusiéramos or pusiésemos, pusieseis, pusieran or pusiesen.
		H	pon, ponga; pongamos, pongan.
		I	puesto.
33	pudrir or podrir	I	podrido. (When the infinitive used is "podrir," the verb is conjugated as "pudrir," which only is irregular in its p.p.)
34	querer	A	quiero, quieres, quiere; quieren.
		B	quiera, quieras, quiera; quieran.
		D	quise, quisiste, quiso; quisimos, quisisteis, quisieron.
		E	querré, querrás, querrá; querremos, querréis, querrán.
		F	querría, querrías, querría; querríamos, querríais, querrían.
		G	quisiera or quisiese, quisieras or quisieses, quisiera or quisiese; quisiéramos or quisiésemos, quisierais or quisieseis, quisieran or quisiessen.
		H	quiere, quiera; quieran.
35	reir	A	río, ríes, ríe; ríen.
		B	ría, rías, ría; riamos, riáis, rían.
		D	rio; rieron.
		G	riera or riese, rieras or rieses, riera or riese; riéramos or riésemos, rierais or rieseis, rieran or riesen.
		H	ríe, ría; riamos, rían.
		J	riendo.
36	roer	A	It is a regular form, but it can be conjugated "roigo" and "royo" in the first person singular.
		B	It is a regular form too but it can be conjugated "roiga" and "roya," etc.
37	saber	A	sé.
		B	sepa, sepas, sepa; sepamos, sepáis, sepan.

No.	Verb	Irregular Tenses (See Key)	
		D	supe, supiste, supo; supimos, supisteis, supieron.
		E	sabré, sabrás, sabrá; sabremos, sabréis, sabrán.
		F	sabría, sabrías, sabría; sabríamos, sabríais, sabrían.
		G	supiera or supiese, supieras or supieses, supiera or supiese; supiéramos or supiésemos, supierais or supieseis, supieran or supiesen.
		H	sepa; sepamos, sepan.
38	salir	A	salgo.
		B	salga, salgas, salga; salgamos, salgáis, salgan.
		E	saldré, saldrás, saldrá; saldremos, saldréis, saldrán.
		F	saldría, saldrías, saldría; saldríamos, saldríais, saldrían.
		G	sal, salga; salgamos, salgan.
39	sentir	A	siento, sientes, siente; sienten.
		B	sienta, sientas, sienta; sintamos, sintáis, sientan.
		D	sintió; sintieron.
		G	sintiera or sintiese, sintieras or sintieses, sintiera or sintiese; sintiéramos or sintiésemos, sintierais or sintieseis, sintieran or sintiesen.
		H	siente, sienta; sintamos, sientan.
		J	sintiendo.
40	ser	A	soy, eres, es; somos, sois, son.
		B	sea, seas, sea; seamos, seáis, sean.
		C	era, eras, era; éramos, erais, eran.
		D	fui, fuiste, fue; fuimos, fuisteis, fueron.
		G	fuera or fuese, fueras or fueses, fuera or fuese; fuéramos or fuésemos, fuerais or fueseis, fueran or fuesen.
		H	sea; seamos, sean.
41	tañer	D	tañó; tañeron.
		G	tañera or tañese, tañeras or tañeses, tañera or tañese; tañéramos or tañésemos, tañerais or tañeseis, tañeran or tañesen.
		J	tañendo.
42	tener	A	tengo, tienes, tiene; tienen.
		B	tenga, tengas, tenga; tengamos, tengáis, tengan.
		D	tuve, tuviste, tuvo; tuvimos, tuvisteis, tuvieron.
		E	tendré, tendrás, tendrá; tendremos, tendréis, tendrán.
		F	tendría, tendrías, tendría; tendríamos, tendríais, tendrían.
		G	tuviera or tuviese, tuvieras or tuvieses, tuviera or tuviese; tuviéramos or tuviésemos, tuvierais or tuvieseis, tuvieran or tuviesen.
		H	ten, tenga; tengamos, tengan.
43	traer	A	traigo.
		B	traiga, traigas, traiga; traigamos, traigáis, traigan.
		D	traje, trajiste, trajo; trajimos, trajisteis, trajeron.
		G	trajera or trajese, trajeras or trajeses, trajera or trajese; trajéramos or trajésemos, trajerais or trajeseis, trajeran or trajesen.
		H	traiga; traigamos, traigan.
44	valer	A	valgo.
		B	valga, valgas, valga; valgamos, valgáis, valgan.

No.	Verb	Irregular Tenses (See Key)	
		E	valdré, valdrás, valdrá; valdremos, valdréis, valdrán.
		F	valdría, valdrías, valdría; valdríamos, valdríais, valdrían.
		H	val(e), valga; valgamos, valgan.
5	venir	A	vengo, vienes, viene; vienen.
		B	venga, vengas, venga; vengamos, vengáis, vengan.
		D	vine, viniste, vino; vinimos, vinisteis, vinieron.
		E	vendré, vendrás, vendrá; vendremos, vendréis, vendrán.
		F	vendría, vendrías, vendría; vendríamos, vendríais, vendrían.
		G	viniera or viniese, vinieras or vinieses, viniera or viniese; viniéramos or viniésemos, vinierais or vinieseis, vinieran or viniesen.
		H	ven, venga; vengamos, vengan.
		J	viniendo.
6	ver	A	veo.
		B	vea, veas, vea; veamos, veáis, vean.
		C	veía, veías, veía; veíamos, veíais, veían.
		H	vea; veamos, vean.
		I	visto.
7	volver	A	vuelvo, vuelves, vuelve; vuelven.
		B	vuelva, vuelvas, vuelva; vuelvan.
		H	vuelve, vuelva; vuelvan.
		I	vuelto.
8	yacer	A	yazco (or yazgo or yago).
		B	yazca (yazga, yaga), yazcas (yazgas, yagas), yazca (yazga, yaga); yazcamos (yazgamos, yagamos), yazcáis (yazgáis, yagáis), yazcan (yazgan, yagan).
		H	yace (or yaz), yazca (yazga, yaga); yazcamos (yazgamos, yagamos), yazcan (yazgan, yagan).

No. 49   Verbs with Irregular Participles

Verbs	Regular Participle	Irregular Participle
abrir	—	abierto
absolver	—	absuelto
absorber	absorbido	absorto
abstraer	abstraído	abstracto
adscribir	—	adscrito
afligir	afligido	aflicto
circunscribir	—	circunscrito
cubrir	—	cubierto
descubrir	—	descubierto
despertar	despertado	despierto
devolver	—	devuelto
disponer	—	dispuesto
elegir	elegido	electo
encubrir	—	encubierto
enjugar	enjugado	enjuto
entreabrir	—	entreabierto
entrever	—	entrevisto
escribir	—	escrito
excluir	excluido	excluso
eximir	eximido	exento
expresar	expresado	expreso

xxvii

Verbs with Irregular Participles

Verbs	Regular Participle	Irregular Participle
extender	extendido	extenso
extinguir	extinguido	extinto
freír	freído	frito
fijar	fijado	fijo
hartar	hartado	harto
imponer	—	impuesto
imprimir	imprimido	impreso
incluir	incluído	incluso
inscribir	—	inscrito
insertar	insertado	inserto
interponer	—	interpuesto
invertir	invertido	inverso
maldecir	maldecido	maldito
matar	matado	muerto
morir	—	muerto
nacer	nacido	nato
poner	—	puesto
posponer	—	pospuesto
predecir	—	predicho
predisponer	—	predispuesto
prender	prendido	preso
prescribir	—	prescrito
presumir	presumido	presunto
presuponer	—	presupuesto
pretender	pretendido	pretenso
prever	—	previsto
propender	propendido	propenso
proponer	—	propuesto
proscribir	—	proscrito
prostituir	prostituído	prostituto
proveer	proveído	provisto
reabrir	—	reabierto
reelegir	reelegido	reelecto
rehacer	—	rehecho
reimprimir	—	reimpreso
reponer	—	repuesto
resolver	—	resuelto
romper	—	roto
sobreponer	—	sobrepuesto
sofreír	sofreído	sofrito
sujetar	sujetado	sujeto
superponer	—	superpuesto
suponer	—	supuesto
surgir	surgido	surto
suscribir	—	suscrito
suspender	suspendido	suspenso
sustituir	sustituído	sustituto
transcribir	—	transcripto
tra(n)sponer	—	tra(n)spuesto
truncar	truncado	trunco
yuxtaponer	—	yuxtapuesto

No. 50   Defective Verbs or Verbs Which Have Some Especial Characteristics

Verbs	
abolir	Only tenses having endings with "i" are used; abolió, abolía, aboliré, etc.
acaecer	Used only in the infinitive and in the third person of all tenses.
acontecer	See *Acaecer.*
agredir	See *Abolir.*
atañer	Used only in the third person of all tenses, especially "atañe," "atañen."
aterirse	See *Abolir.*
balbucir	Persons of this verb which do not have the ending "i" are conjugated in the same way as the regular verb "balbucear."
concernir	Only the gerund (concerniendo) and the third person of all tenses are used, especially: concierne, conciernes; concernía, concernían; concierna, conciernan.

ranizar	See *Acaecer*.	
reterir	See *Abolir*.	
oler	Used only in the present and imperfect indicative. The participle "solido" is used only in the present perfect tense.	
ransgredir	See *Abolir*.	

II. ORTHOGRAPHIC CHANGING VERBS

Verbs marked with letter		
a	"z" changes to "c" before "e" and "i," and "c" changes to "z" before "a," "o," "u."	alcanzar; alcance, alcancemos, etc. mecer: mezo, mezas, etc. zurcir: zurza, zurzo, etc.
b	1) Verbs ending -**gar**: "g" changes to "gu" before "e," "i." 2) Verbs ending -**guar**: "gu" changes to "gü" before "e," "i." 3) The group "gu" changes to "g" before "a," "o."	1) amargar: amargue, amarguen, etc. 2) averiguar: averigüe, averigüemos, etc. 3) distinguir: distingo, distingamos, etc.
c	"g" changes to "j" before "a," "o."	recoger: recojo; recojas, etc.
d	"qu" changes to "c" before "a," "o." "c" changes to "qu" before "e," "i."	delinquir: delinco; delinca, etc. embarcar: embarque, embarquemos, etc.
e	verbs ending -**aer**, -**eer**, -**uir**: tonic "i" of verb ending changes to "y" in the gerund and in the third person of tenses "D" and "G."	caer: cayó; cayera or cayese; cayendo. construir: construyó; construyera or construyese; construyendo. leer: leyó; leyera or leyese; leyendo.

ABBREVIATIONS USED IN PART II

a.	adjective.	(math.)	mathematics.
abbr.	abbreviation.	(mech.)	mechanics.
adv.	adverb.	(med.)	medicine.
(aer.)	aeronautics.	(metal.)	metallurgy.
(aerosp.)	aerospace.	(Mex.)	Mexico.
(agr.)	agriculture.	*mf.*	noun (not inflected to show gender).
(alg.)	algebra.		
(Am.)	Spanish America(n).	(mil.)	military.
(anat.)	anatomy.	(min.)	mining, mineralogy.
(app.)	applied.	(mus.)	music.
(arch.)	architecture.	*n.*	noun (inflected, usually *-o* to *-a*, to show gender).
(Arg.)	Argentina.		
(arith.)	arithmetic.	(naut.)	nautical.
art.	article.	(neol.)	neologism.
(artil.)	artillery.	*neut.*	neuter.
(astr.)	astronomy; astrology.	*nom.*	nominative case.
aug.	augmentative.	(obs.)	obsolete.
(aut.)	automotive.	(of.)	offensive.
(bib.)	Biblical.	(opt.)	optics.
(biol.).	biology.	(ornith.).	ornithology.
(bot.)	botany.	(pej.)	pejorative.
(carp.)	carpentry.	(p.ej.).	for example.
(chem.)	chemistry.	*pers.*	person; personal.
(cine.)	cinema, movies.	(pert.).	pertaining (to).
(coll.)	colloquial.	(pharm.)	pharmaceutical.
(collect.)	collectively.	(philos.).	philosophy.
(com.)	commerce.	(phon.)	phonetics.
comp.	comparative.	(phot.)	photography.
(comput.)	computer.	(phys.)	physics.
conj.	conjunction.	(physiol.)	physiology.
(contempt.)	contemptuous.	*pl.*	plural.
contr.	contraction.	(poet.)	poetry.
(cook.)	cooking.	(pol.)	politics.
defect.	defective.	*poss.*	possessive.
dim.	diminutive.	*pp.*	past participle.
(eccl.).	ecclesiastic.	*prep.*	preposition.
(econ.).	economics.	*pret.*	preterit.
(elec.).	electricity.	(print.)	printing.
(electron.)	electronics.	*pron.*	pronoun.
(eng.)	engineering.	(rad.)	radio.
(esp.)	especially.	(ref.)	referring (to).
f.	feminine; feminine noun.	*refl.*	reflexive.
(fam.).	familiar.	*rel.*	relative (pronoun).
(fig.)	figurative(ly).	(rhet.)	rhetoric.
(fort.).	fortifications.	(R.R.)	railroad.
fut.	future.	(S.A.)	South America(n).
(G.B.)	Great Britain.	(sew.)	sewing.
(gen.)	generally.	*sing.*	singular.
(geog.)	geography.	(sl.).	slang.
(geol.)	geology.	(Sp.)	Spain, Spanish.
(geom.)	geometry.	(sports)	sports.
ger.	gerund.	*subj.*	subject; subjunctive.
(gram.)	grammar.	*super.*	superlative.
(herald.).	heraldry.	(surg.)	surgery.
(hist.)	history.	(tech.)	technology.
(hort.)	horticulture.	(tel.)	telegraph(y); telephone.
(humor.)	humorous.	(theat.)	theater.
(hydraul.)	hydraulics.	(TM)	trademark.
(ichth.)	ichthyology.	(TV)	television.
imp.	imperfect.	(USA)	United States of America.
imper.	imperative.	*V.*	see.
impers.	impersonal.	*va.*	auxiliary verb.
ind.	indicative.	*vai.*	irregular auxiliary verb.
inf.	infinitive.	*vi.*	intransitive verb.
interj.	interjection.	*vii.*	irregular intransitive verb.
interrog.	interrogative.	*vr.*	reflexive verb.
(jewel.)	jewelry.	*vri.*	irregular reflexive verb.
(law)	legal system.	*vt.*	transitive verb.
(lit.)	literally.	*vti.*	irregular transitive verb.
m.	masculine; masculine noun.	(vulg.)	vulgar, obscene.
(mason.)	masonry.	(zool.)	zoology.

A

a, *prep.* to; in; at; according to; by; for; of; on; toward.—*a beneficio de,* for the benefit of.—*a caballo,* on horseback.—*a la derecha,* at the right.—*a máquina,* by machine.—*a mi gusto,* according to my taste.—*a oscuras,* in the dark.—*a tiempo,* on time.—*al anochecer,* toward the evening.—*di el libro a Pedro,* I gave the book to Peter.

bacería, *f.* grocery.—**abacero,** *n.* grocer.

abad, *m.* abbot.—**abadía,** *f.* abbey.

abajo, *adv.* under, underneath, below, down.—*a. de,* beneath.—*boca a.,* face down.—*de arriba a a.,* from top to bottom.—*venirse a.,* to fall.—*el a. firmante, los a. firmantes,* the undersigned.

balanzar, *vti.* [a] to balance; to hurl, impel.—*vri.* to rush on or upon; to venture on.

balorio, *m.* glass bead; bead work.

abandonado, *a.* negligent; slovenly.—**abandonar,** *vt.* to abandon, desert; to give up.—*vi.* to despair; to give oneself up to; to be neglectful.—**abandono,** *m.* abandon; neglect; despondency.

abanicar, *vti.* [d] to fan.—**abanico,** *m.* fan.

abanico, *m.* fan; fanlight; (mar.) derrick; (fig.) range.—*a. de chimenea,* fire screen.—*en a.,* fanned out.

baratar, *vt.* to cheapen; to abate.—*vr.* to fall in price.

abarcar, [d] *vti.* to clasp, embrace, contain; to comprise.

barrotar, *vt.* to stow; to overstock; (fig.) to cram, stuff.—**abarrotero,** *n.* (Am.) storekeeper.—**abarrotes,** *m. pl.* (Am.) groceries; (Am.) grocery store.

bastecedor, *n.* supplier.—**abastecer,** *vti.* [3] to supply.—**abastecimiento,** *m.* supply; supplying.—**abasto,** *m.* supply of provisions; (fig.) abundance.—*dar a.,* to be sufficient (for); to provide, furnish.

batido, *a.* depressed.—**abatimiento,** *m.* depression.—**abatir,** *vt.* to throw down; to knock (bring, shoot) down; to humble, abase; to discourage; to lower, strike (a flag).—*vr.* to become disheartened; to swoop down.

abdicación, *f.* abdication.—**abdicar,** *vti.* [d] to abdicate.

abdomen, *m.* abdomen.—**abdominal,** *a.* abdominal.

abducción, *f.* (logic & anat.) abduction.

abecé, *m.* alphabet, ABC.—*¿ya te sabes el a.?,* do you know your ABCs?

abedul, *m.* birch.

abeja, *f.* bee.—*a. obrera,* worker bee.—*a. reina,* queen bee.—**abejar,** *m.* apiary.—**abejón,** *m.* drone.—**abejorro,** *m.* bumblebee.

aberración, *f.* aberration; error.

abertura, *f.* opening; slit; gap.

abeto, *m.* spruce; fir; hemlock.

abierto, *pp.* of ABRIR.—*a.* open.

abigarrado, *a.* variegated, motley.

abismado, *a.* dejected; amazed; lost in thought.—**abismal,** *a.* abysmal. **abismar,** *vt.* to depress; to amaze.—*vr.* to be immersed (in thought, grief, etc.).—**abismo,** *m.* abyss; chasm; (igl.) Hell.

ablandamiento, *m.* softening.—**ablandar,** *vt. & vi.* to soften.—*vr.* to soften, relent.

abnegación, *f.* self-denial, abnegation.

abobado, *a.* silly; bewildered.

abochornar, *vt.* to overheat; to shame; to embarrass.—*vr.* to blush; to become embarrassed.

abofetear, *vt.* to slap.

abogacía, *f.* law.—**abogado,** *n.* lawyer.—*a. criminalista, a. penalista,* criminal lawyer.—*a. defensor,* defense lawyer.—*a. del diablo,* devil's advocate.—*a. de oficio,* public defender.—**abogar,** *vii.* [b] to advocate, plead (as a lawyer).

abolengo, *m.* ancestry.

abolición, *f.* abolition.—**abolir,** *vti.* [50] to abolish.

abolladura, *f.* dent; bump; bruise; embossing.—**abollar,** *vt.* to emboss; to dent.

abominable, *a.* abominable.—**abominación,** *f.* abomination.—**abominar,** *vt.* to abominate, abhor.

abonado, *n.* subscriber; commuter.—*a.* reliable, apt, inclined; (agr.) rich (soil).—**abonar**, *vt.* (com.) to credit with; to pay; to guarantee, indorse, answer for; (agr.) to manure.—*a. con fe notarial*, to notarize.—*vr.* to subscribe; to buy a season or commutation ticket.—**abono**, *m.* surety; assurance; payment; subscription; indorsement; fertilizer; installment.—*a. compuesto* or *vegetal*, compost.

abordaje, *m.* the act of boarding a ship.—**abordar**, *vt.* (naut.) to ram, collide with, board (a ship); to broach (a subject), enter upon (a matter); to accost, approach (a person).

aborrecer, *vti.* [3] to hate, abhor. —**aborrecible**, *a.* hateful; abhorrent. —**aborrecimiento**, *m.* abhorrence, hatred.

abortar, *vi.* to miscarry, abort; (med.) to have a miscarriage; to have an abortion.—**abortista**, *a.* pro-choice.—*mf.* pro-choicer; doctor who carries out abortions.—*f.* woman who has had an abortion. —**abortivo**, *a.* abortive, producing abortion.—**aborto**, *m.* miscarriage, abortion; monster, freak.—*a. espontáneo*, miscarriage.

abotagarse, **abotargarse**, *vri.* [b] to swell; to bloat.

abotonar, *vt.* to button.—*vi.* to bud.— *vr.* to button up.

abrasador, *a.* burning, extremely hot.—**abrasar**, *vt.* to burn; to parch, scorch; to dry up.—*vr.* to burn (with); to boil (with) (any violent passion); to burn up, down.

abrasivo, *m.* & *a.* abrasive.

abrazadera, *f.* clasp, clamp, cleat. —**abrazar**, *vti.* [a] to embrace, hug. —**abrazo**, *m.* hug, embrace.

abrecartas, *m.* letter opener.—**abreostras**, *m.* oyster knife.

abrelatas, *m. sing.* can opener.

abreviación, *f.* abbreviation; abridgment; shortening.—**abreviar**, *vt.* to abridge, abbreviate.—**abreviatura**, *f.* abbreviation.

abridor, *m.* bottle opener.—*a. de latas*, can opener.

abrigar, *vti.* [b] to shelter, shield; to keep warm; to cherish.—*vri.* to take shelter; to cover up.—**abrigo**, *m.* overcoat; shelter, protection.—*al a. de*, sheltered from, shielded by.

abril, *m.* April.

abrillantar, *vt.* to polish, shine; t(brighten; to add splendor.

abrir, *vti.* [49] to open, unlock, unfas ten, uncover; to cut open; to dig.— *a. paso*, to make way, to clear the way.—*vii.* to open; to clear (o(weather).—*vri.* to open, expand; t(crack.

abrochar, *vt.* to clasp, button, fasten.

abrojo, *m.* (bot.) thistle, thorn prickle.—*pl.* hidden reefs.

abrumador, *a.* overwhelming, crush ing; wearisome.—**abrumar**, *vt.* t(crush, overwhelm, oppress; t(annoy.—*vr.* to become foggy.

abrupto, *a.* abrupt; steep; rugged.

absenta, *f.* absinthe.—**absentismo**, *m* **escolar**, truancy.—**absentista**, *m* absentee; absentee landlord.

absceso, *m.* abscess.

absolución, *f.* absolution.

absolutismo, *m.* absolutism.—**absc luto**, *a.* absolute.—*en a.*, unquali fiedly; absolutely; (in negativ(sentences) (not) at all.—*lo a.*, th(absolute.

absolver, *vti.* [47–49] to absolve; t(acquit.

absorber, *vti.* [49] to absorb.—**absc ción**, *f.* absorption.—**absorto**, *pp.* of ABSORBER.—*a.* absorbed; er grossed.

abstemio, *a.* abstemious.—*n.* teete taler.

abstenerse, *vri.* [42] to abstain.—**a stinencia**, *f.* abstinence.

abstracción, *f.* abstraction; concentra tion.—**abstracto**, *pp. i.* de A STRAER.—*a.* & *m.* abstract.—**a straer**, *vti.* [43–49] to abstrac —**abstraído**, *a.* withdrawn, preoccu pied; absent-minded.

absuelto, *pp.* of ABSOLVER.—*a.* acqui ted, absolved.

absurdo, *a.* absurd.—*m.* absurdity.

abuchear, *vt.* to boo, hoot.—**abuchec** *m.* booing, hooting.

abuela, *f.* grandmother; (fig.) ol woman.—**abuelo**, *m.* grandfathe (fig.) old man;—**abuelos**, ancestor:

abultar, *vt.* to enlarge.—*vi.* to be bulk

abundamiento, *m.* abundance.— *mayor a.*, furthermore; with all th more reason.—**abundancia**, *f.* abur dance, plenty.—**abundante**, *a* abundant, plentiful, teemin —**abundar**, *vi.* to abound.

aburrido, *a.* bored; boring.—**aburr**

miento, *m.* boredom.—**aburrir,** *vt.* to bore.—*vr.* to get bored.

abusar, *vi.* to exceed, go too far; to take undue advantage.—*a. de,* to abuse, use wrongly; to betray (a confidence); to take undue advantage of; to impose upon.—**abusivo,** *a.* abusive; outrageous.—**abuso,** *m.* abuse.—*a. de confianza,* breach of trust.—*a. (sexual) infantil,* child abuse.—*abusos deshonestos,* sexual abuse.

abyección, *f.* abjection, abjectness; degradation.—**abyecto,** *a.* abject, servile, slavish.

acá, *adv.* here; hither.—*¿de cuándo a.?* since when?—*por a.,* here, hereabouts; this way.

acabado, *a.* perfect, faultless; wasted; dilapidated.—*m.* (art) finish.—**acabamiento,** *m.* completion, end; physical decline.—**acabar,** *vt. & vi.* to finish; to complete; to end.—*a. con,* to finish, destroy.—*a. de* (foll. by *inf.*), to have just (foll. by *pp.*).—*a. por,* to end by, to . . . finally.—*vr.* to be finished; to end, be over; to grow feeble or wasted; *acabársele a uno* (*el dinero, la paciencia, etc.*) to run out of (money, patience, etc.).

academia, *f.* academy; school.—*a. de corte y confección,* dressmaking school.—*a. de idiomas,* language school.—*a. militar,* military academy.—**académico,** *a. & n.* academic; academician.

acaecer, *vii.* [3–50] to happen, come to pass.—**acaecimiento,** *m.* event.

acallar, *vt.* to silence, to quiet.

acalorado, *a.* heated; excited, hot under the collar.—*n.* (fig.) hothead.—**acaloramiento,** *m.* ardor, heat, excitement.—**acalorar,** *vt.* to heat, inflame, excite.—*vr.* to grow warm; to get overheated; to get excited.

acampar, *vt., vi. & vt.* to encamp.

acanalado, *a.* striated, fluted, corrugated, grooved.—**acanalar,** *vt.* to make a channel in; to flute, corrugate, groove.

acantilado, *m.* cliff; escarpment.—*a.* steep, sheer.

acantonar, *vt.* to quarter (troops).

acaparador, *a.* greedy, selfish.—*n.* monopolizer; hoarder.—**acaparar,** *vt.* to monopolize; to corner, control (the market); to hoard, stockpile.

—**acaparamiento,** *m.* hoarding; monopolizing.

acariciar, *vt.* to fondle, caress; to cherish.

acarrear, *vt.* to carry, cart, transport; to give rise to.—*vr.* to bring upon oneself.—**acarreo,** *m.* carrying, transportation; cartage.

acaso, *m.* chance, accident.—*adv.* perhaps; by chance, by accident.—*por si a.,* just in case.

acatamiento, *m.* obeisance, respect, homage.—**acatar,** *vt.* to obey; to accept; to respect.

acatarrarse, *vr.* to catch cold.

acaudalado, *a.* rich, opulent.

acaudillar, *vt.* to command, lead.

acceder, *vi.* to accede, agree, consent.—*a. a,* to succeed to (the throne); to gain access to; (comput.) to access.—**accesible,** *a.* accessible, approachable; attainable.—**acceso,** *m.* access; entrance; admittance; (med.) access, fit, attack.—*a. aleatorio,* (comput.) random access.—*a. secuencial,* (comput.) sequential access.—*obtener a. a,* (comput.) to access.—*prohibido el a.,* no admittance.—**accesorio,** *a.* accessory; secondary.—*pl.* spare parts; accessories; (theat.) props.

accidentado, *a.* seized with a fit; rugged, uneven (ground); troubled, eventful; injured.—*n.* injured person.—**accidentarse,** *vr.* to have a fit or stroke.—**accidente,** *m.* accident; chance; sudden fit; (gram.) inflection.—*a. aéreo,* plane crash.—*a. de circulación, a. de tráfico,* traffic accident.—*a. ferroviario,* train crash.—*a. geográfico,* geographical feature.—*por a.,* accidentally, by chance.

acción, *f.* action; feat; lawsuit; battle; (lit.) plot; (com.) stock, share.—*a. de gracias,* thanksgiving.—*a. ordinaria, a. primitiva,* common stock.—*a. liberada,* stock dividend.—*a. preferente,* preferred stock.—**accionar,** *vi.* to gesticulate.—*vt.* (mech.) to operate, move.—**accionista,** *mf.* stockholder, shareholder.

acechanza, *f.* waylaying; snare, trap.—**acechar,** *vt.* to lie in ambush for; to spy on.—**acecho,** *m.* waylaying, lying in ambush.—*al a.* or *en a.,* in wait, in ambush.

acedía, *f.* acidity.

aceitar, *vt.* to oil; to rub with oil. **—aceite,** *m.* oil; essential oil.—*a. combustible,* fuel oil.—*a. de oliva,* olive oil.—*a. de parafina,* mineral oil.—*a. de ricino,* castor oil.—*a. solar,* suntan lotion.**—aceitera,** *f.* oil cruet; oil can.**—aceitoso,** *a.* oily.**—aceituna,** *f.* olive.**—aceitunado,** *a.* olive-colored.

aceleración, *f.* acceleration; haste. **—acelerador,** *a.* accelerating.—*m.* accelerator; (aut.) gas pedal. **—acelerar,** *vt.* to accelerate; to hasten, hurry, rush.—*vr.* to move fast; to make haste.

acémila, *f.* pack animal.

acendrado, *a.* purified, refined; unspotted, stainless.**—acendrar,** *vt.* to purify or refine; to free from stain or blemish.

acento, *m.* accent, stress; way of speaking; written accent.—*a. agudo,* acute accent.—*a. circunflejo,* circumflex accent.—*a. ortográfico,* accent mark.**—acentuación,** *f.* accentuation.**—acentuar,** *vt.* to accentuate; to emphasize; to write accents.

acepción, *f.* sense, meaning.

aceptable, *a.* acceptable, admissible.**—aceptación,** *f.* acceptation; acceptance, approval, applause.— **aceptar,** *vt.* to accept, admit; (com.) to honor.

acera, *f.* sidewalk; row of houses on either side of a street.

acerado, *a.* steely; strong; hard; sharp.

acerbo, *a.* tart; harsh, cruel; poignant; scathing.

acerca de, *prep.* about, with regard to.**—acercamiento,** *m.* approximation, approach, rapprochement. **—acercar,** *vti.* [d] to bring or place near or nearer.—*vri.* to draw near, come, approach.

acerico, *m.* pincushion.

acero, *m.* steel; sword; courage.

acérrimo, *a. super.* very strong (taste, odor); very harsh; very vigorous; very stanch or stalwart.

acertado, *a.* fit; proper; wise.**—acertar,** *vti.* [1] to hit the mark; to do the right thing; to guess, be right.—*vii.* to guess right.—*a. con,* to find, come upon.**—acertante,** winner.— **acertijo,** *m.* riddle.

achacar, *vti.* [d] to attribute.—*a. la culpa a uno,* to lay the blame on someone.**—achacoso,** *a.* sickly, ailing.**—achaque,** *m.* indisposition; minor chronic ailment; excuse, pretext; motive; subject, matter.

achatar, *vt.* to flatten, squash.

achicar, *vti.* [d] to diminish, lessen; to shorten; to humble, belittle; to bail, drain.—*vri.* to humble oneself; to be cowed.

achicharrar, *vt. & vr.* to burn to a crisp.

aciago, *a.* unfortunate, sad; fateful.

acíbar, *m.* aloes; bitterness; displeasure.

acicalar, *vt.* to embellish.—*vr.* to dress in style; (coll.) to doll up.

acicate, *m.* inducement; goad.

acidez, *f.* acidity, tartness.**—ácido,** *m.* acid.—*a.* acid; sour; harsh.

ácido, *m.* acid.—*a. cítrico,* citric acid.—*a. clorhídrico,* hydrochloric acid.—*a. desoxirribonucleico,* deoxyribonucleic acid, DNA.—*a. sulfúrico,* sulfuric acid.

acierto, *m.* good judgment; accuracy; rightness; skill; good aim; good guess.

aclamación, *f.* acclamation.**—aclamar,** *vt.* to shout, applaud, acclaim.

aclaración, *f.* explanation.**—aclarar,** *vt.* to make clear; to explain; to thin; to rinse.—*vi.* to clear up; to recover brightness.

aclimatar, *vt.* to acclimatize.—*vr.* to get acclimatized.

acobardar, *vt.* to intimidate, frighten.—*vr.* to become frightened, intimidated.

acogedor, *a.* welcoming, kindly. **—acoger,** *vti.* [c] to receive; (fig.) to harbor, shelter.—*vri.* to take refuge.**—acogida,** *f.,* **acogimiento,** *m.* reception; admittance, acceptance; refuge, shelter.—*tener buena (mala) a.,* to be well (unfavorably) received.

acogotar, *vt.* to break the neck of; to choke, to strangle.

acojinar, *vt.* (mech.) to cushion.

acolchado, *a.* quilted.**—acolchar, acolchonar,** *vt.* to quilt.

acólito, *m.* altar boy, acolyte.

acometedor, *a.* aggressive; enterprising.**—acometer,** *vt.* to attack, rush on, (coll.) go for; to undertake. **—acometida,** *f.,* **acometimiento,** *m.* attack, assault; branch or outlet (in a sewer).

acomodado, *a.* convenient, fit; wealthy; reasonable.**—acomodador,**

n. usher.—**acomodar,** *vt.* to arrange; to accommodate; to set to rights; to place; to reconcile; to furnish, supply; to take in, lodge.—*vi.* to fit; to suit.—*vr.* to condescend; to adapt oneself; to put up with; to settle. —**acomodaticio,** *a.* compliant, accommodating.—**acomodo,** *m.* arrangement; string pulling; soft job.

acompañamiento, *m.* accompaniment; retinue; attendance.—**acompañante,** *mf.* chaperon; companion; (mus.) accompanist.—*a.* accompanying.—**acompañar,** *vt.* to accompany; to attend, escort; to enclose (in letters).

acompasado, *a.* measured; rhythmical; slow.

acondicionado, *a.*—*bien a.,* nice, friendly; in good condition.—*mal a.,* bad-tempered; in bad condition.—*aire a.,* air-conditioned.— **acondicionador,** *m.*—*a. de aire,* air conditioner.—*a. de pelo,* hair conditioner.—**acondicionar,** *vt.* to condition; to prepare, equip, fit out; to air condition.

acongojar, *vt.* to afflict, grieve.—*vr.* to become anguished; to grieve.

aconsejable, *a.* advisable.—**aconsejar,** *vt.* to advise, counsel.—*vr.* (con) to consult (with).

acontecer, *vii.* [3–50] to happen, come about.—**acontecimiento,** *m.* event, happening.

acopio, *m.* gathering; storing; assortment; collection; supply; stock.

acoplamiento, *m.* coupling; joint; scarfing.—**acoplar,** *vt.* to couple, join, connect; to hitch, yoke; to scarf (timber); to reconcile; to pair; to mate (animals).—*vr.* to settle a difference, come to an agreement; to mate (of animals).

acoquinar, *vt.* to cow, intimidate.—*vr.* to be cowed.

acorazado, *m.* battleship.—*a.* ironclad.—**acorazar,** *vti.* [a] to armor.

acordar, *vti.* [12] to resolve; to agree upon; to remind; to tune, harmonize.—*vii.* to agree.—*vri.* (de) to remember, *e.g., ¿te acuerdas de mí?* do you remember me?—*si mal no me acuerdo,* if I remember rightly. —**acorde,** *a.* agreed; in tune; in accord.—*m.* chord; harmony of sounds and colors.—**acordeón,** *m.* accordion.

acordonar, *vt.* to lace; to mill (a coin); to cord; to cordon or rope off.

acorralar, *vt.* to corral; to surround; to corner.

acortar, *vt.* to shorten, lessen, reduce; to obstruct.—*a. la marcha,* to slow down.—*vr.* to shrivel, contract; to be bashful; to fall back.

acosamiento, acoso, *m.* relentless pursuit; harassing, hounding.—*a. sexual,* sexual harassment.—*operación de a. y derribo,* (mil.) search and destroy operation.—**acosar,** *vt.* to pursue relentlessly; to harass, hound.—*a. sexualmente,* to harass sexually.

acostado, *a.* reclining, lying down; in bed.—**acostar,** *vti.* [12] to lay down; to put to bed.—*vri.* to lie down; to go to bed.

acostumbrado, *a.* habitual, customary; accustomed.—*a. a,* used to, accustomed to.—**acostumbrar,** *vt.* to accustom, train.—*vi.* to be accustomed, to be in the habit of.—*vr.* to get used to, become accustomed to.

acotación, *f.* stage direction (in a play); marginal note; elevation marked on a map.—**acotamiento,** *m.* enclosure, reservation; boundary mark.—**acotar,** *vt.* to set boundary marks on; to mark out; to annotate; to select.

acre, *a.* sour; acrimonious; tart; mordant.—*m.* (medida inglesa = .4 hectárea) acre.

acrecentamiento, *m.* increase.—**acrecentar,** *vti.* [1] to increase; to improve.

acreditado, *a.* reputable.—**acreditar,** *vt.* to assure, affirm; to verify, prove; (com.) to recommend, answer for, guarantee; to accredit, authorize.— *vr.* to establish one's reputation.

acreedor, *a.* meritorious, deserving.— *n.* creditor.—*a. hipotecario,* mortgagee.

acribillar, *vt.* to perforate; to riddle; to cover with wounds.

acrílico, *a.* & *m.* acrylic.

acrisolado, *a.* honest, virtuous, upright.

acrobacia, *f.* acrobatics.—**acróbata,** *mf.* acrobat.—**acrobático,** *a.* acrobatic.

acta, *f.* document; minutes; certificate.—*a. de matrimonio,* (Mex.) marriage certificate.—*a. de naci-*

miento, (Mex.) birth certificate.—*a. notarial,* affidavit.—*levantar a.,* to draw up the minutes; to note, set down.

actltud, *f.* attitude; position, posture.

activar, *vt.* to make active; to expedite, hasten.—**actividad,** *f.* activity, energy.—*en a.,* in operation.—**activo,** *a.* active.—*m.* (com.) assets.

acto, *m.* act, action, deed; public function.—*a. inaugural,* opening ceremony.—*a. reflejo,* reflex action.—*a. seguido,* immediately after.—*en el a.,* at once.—**actor,** *m.* player, actor.—*hacer a. de presencia,* to attend, be present.—*parte actora,* plaintiff.—**actriz,** *f.* actress.—**actuación,** *f.* actuation; action; part played.—*pl.* (law) proceedings.

actuación, *f.* action; performance.—*pl.* (leg.) proceedings.—**actualizar,** *vt.* to update.

actual, *a.* present, of the present time.—**actualidad,** *f.* present time.—*de a.,* up-to-the-minute.—*en la a.,* nowadays.—*pl.* current affairs; newsreel.—**actualmente,** *adv.* nowadays, at the present time.

actuar, *vi.* to act; to perform judicial acts.—*vt.* to put in action, actuate.

actuario, *n.* actuary; clerk of the court.

acuanauta, *mf.* aquanaut.

acuaplano, *m.* surfboarding.

acuarela, *f.* water color (painting).

acuario, *m.* aquarium.—**A.,** (astr.) Aquarius.

acuartelamiento, *m.* quartering or billeting (of troops); quarters.—**acuartelar,** *vt.* to quarter, billet.

acuático, *a.* aquatic.—**acuatije,** *m.* splashdown.—**acuatizar,** *vii.* [a] (aer.) to land on the water.

acuchillar, *vt.* to cut, hack; to slash, cut open; to knife.

acudir, *vi.* to go; to come; to attend; to respond (to a call); to go or come to the rescue; to resort; to have recourse.

acueducto, *m.* aqueduct.

acuerdo, *m.* agreement.—*de a.,* in agreement.—*¡de acuerdo!* agreed!

acumulación, *f.* accumulation; gathering.—**acumulador,** *n.* accumulator.—*m.* battery.—**acumular,** *vt.* to accumulate, gather, pile up.—**acumulativo,** *a.* cumulative; joint.

acuñación, *f.* coining, minting; wedging.—**acuñar,** *vt.* to coin, mint; to wedge.

acuoso, *a.* watery.

acupunturista or **acupuntor,** *mf.* acupuncturist.—**acupuntura,** *f.* acupuncture.

acurrucarse, *vri.* [d] to huddle up.

acusación, *f.* accusation.—**acusado,** *n.* & *a.* defendant, accused.—**acusador,** *n.* acuser;—*a. público,* prosecuting attorney.—**acusar,** *vt.* to accuse; to prosecute; to indict; to acknowledge (receipt).—*vr.* (de) to confess (to).—**acuse,** *m.* acknowledgment (of receipt).

acústico, *a.* acoustic.—*m.* hearing aid.—*f.* acoustics.

adagio, *m.* adagio; proverb, maxim; (mus.) adagio.

adán, *m.* (fig.) slovenly man.—**A.,** Adam.

adaptabilidad, *f.* versatility.—**adaptable,** *a.* adaptable; versatile.—**adaptación,** *f.* adaptation.—**adaptar,** *vt.* to adapt, fit.—*vr.* to adapt oneself.

a. de C., *abbr.* (**antes de Cristo**) B.C. (Before Christ).

adecuación, *f.* fitness; adequateness.—**adecuado,** *a.* adequate, suitable, proper.—**adecuar,** *vt.* to fit; to adapt.

adefesio, *m.* (coll.) nonsense, absurdity; blunder; queer person; ridiculous attire.

adelantado, *a.* anticipated; advanced; far ahead; proficient; precocious; bold, forward; (of a clock) fast; early (fruits, plants).—*por a.,* in advance.—**adelantamiento,** *m.* advance; progress; improvement; increase; anticipation; promotion.—**adelantar,** *vt.* & *vi.* to progress, advance; to grow; to keep on; to anticipate; to pay beforehand; to improve; to go fast; (of a clock) to gain.—*vr.* to take the lead; to come forward.—*a. a,* to surpass, outdo.—**adelante,** *adv.* ahead; farther on; forward.—*de a.,* ahead, in the front; forward, head (as a.).—*de aquí en a., de hoy en a.,* or *en a.,* henceforth, from now on, in the future.—*llevar a.,* to go ahead with, carry on.—*más a.,* farther on.—*salir a.,* to come through, come out well or ahead.—*interj.* forward! go on!—**adelanto,** *m.* advance, progress; improvement; (com.) advance payment.

adelfa, *f.* rosebay.

adelgazamiento, *m.* slimming; thinness.—**adelgazar,** *vti.* [a] to make slender; to thin out; to lessen.—*vri.* to become thin or slim.

ademán, *m.* gesture; attitude.—*pl.* manners.

además, *adv.* moreover, furthermore, besides.—*a. de,* besides.

adenoides, *fpl.* adenoids.

adentro, *adv.* within, inside.—*mar a.,* out to sea.—*tierra a.,* inland.—*interj.* come in! let's go in!—*m. pl.* innermost thoughts.

adepto, *n.* follower, supporter.

aderezar, *vti.* [a] to dress, embellish, adorn; to prepare; to cook, season; to dress (salad).—**aderezo,***m.* dressing; adorning; preparation; set of jewelry; seasoning.

adeudado, *a.* indebted; in debt.—**adeudar,** *vt.* to owe; (com.) to be subject to duty; to charge, debit.—*vr.* to run into debt.—**adeudo,** *m.* debit.

adherencia, *f.* adhesion; adherence.—**adherir,** *vti.* [39] & *vri.* to adhere; to stick.—**adhesión,** *f.* adhesion; attachment; following.—**adhesivo,** *a.* & *m.* adhesive.

adición, *f.* addition; (Am.) bill, check.—**adicional,** *a.* additional.—**adicionar,** *vt.* to add.

adicto, *a.* addicted, devoted.—*n.* addict; supporter, follower.

adiestramiento, *m.* training; practice; drill.—**adiestrar,** *vt.* to instruct, train.—*vr.* to practice, train.

adinerado, *a.* rich, wealthy.

¡adiós!, *interj.* good-bye!; (fam.) hello!—*m.* good-bye, farewell.

aditamento, *m.* addition, adjunct.

adivinación, *f.* divination, foretelling.—**adivinador,** *n.*—*a. del pensamiento ajeno,* mind reader.—**adivinanza,** *f.* riddle.—**adivinar,** *vt.* to guess; to divine; to solve (a riddle).—**adivino,** *n.* diviner; fortuneteller; soothsayer.

adjetivo, *n.* & *a.* adjective.

adjuntar, *vt.* to enclose, send enclosed or with something else.—**adjunto,** *a.* adjoined; enclosed, attached; adjunct.—*n.* assistant.

administración, *f.* administration, management; board (of directors); central office.—*a. de correos,* postoffice station.—*a. pública,* civil service.—**administrador,** *n.* administrator; manager; director; trustee.—*a. de aduanas,* collector of customs.—

a. de correos, postmaster.—**administrar,** *vt.* to administer, govern.—**administrativo,** *a.* administrative.

admirable, *a.* admirable, excellent.—**admiración,** *f.* admiration; wonder.—*punto de a.,* exclamation point (!).—**admirador,** *n.* admirer.—**admirar,** *vt.* to admire.—*vr.* (de) to be surprised, amazed at.

admisible, *a.* admissible.—**admisión,** *f.* admission, acceptance.—**admitir,** *vt.* to receive; to admit; to let in; to accept.

admonición, *m.* warning, reprimand.—**admonitorio,** *a.* warning (signal, voice, etc.).

ADN, *abbr.* (**ácido desoxirribonucleico**) DNA.

adobar, *vt.* to dress, prepare or cook (food); to pickle (meat, fish); to marinade; to tan (hides).

adobo, *m.* dressing for seasoning or pickling (meat, fish); mending, repairing.

adocenado, *a.* common, ordinary.

adoctrinar, *vt.* to instruct, indoctrinate.

adolecer, *vii.* [3] (de) (fig.) to suffer from.

adolescencia, *f.* adolescence.—**adolescente,** *mf.* & *a.* adolescent.

adonde, *adv.* (interr. **¿adónde?**) where; (where to?).—**adondequiera,** *adv.* wherever.

adopción, *f.* adoption.—**adoptado,** *n.* adopted child.—**adoptar,** *vt.* to adopt; to embrace (an opinion).—**adoptivo,** *a.* adoptive, adopted.

adoquín, *m.* cobblestone; (coll.) blockhead.—**adoquinado,** *m.* & *a.* pavement; paved.—**adoquinar,** *vt.* to pave.

adorable, *a.* adorable.—**adoración,** *f.* adoration, worship.—**adorar,** *vt.* to adore, worship.

adormecedor, *a.* soporific.—**adormecer,** *vti.* [3] to make sleepy; to numb.—*vri.* to fall asleep; to grow numb.—**adormecimiento,** *m.* drowsiness; sleepiness; numbness.—**adormilado,** *a.* drowsy.

adornar, *vt.* to adorn, ornament, trim. to garnish.—**adorno,** *m.* adornment, ornament; trimming.

adquirir, *vti.* [2] to acquire, obtain, get.—**adquisición,** *f.* acquisition; purchase.—**adquisitivo,** *a.*—*poder a.,* purchasing power.

adrede, *adv.* purposely, intentionally.

adrenalina, *f.* adrenaline.
adscribir, *vti.* [49] to inscribe; to add as an employee.—**adscrito,** *pp.* of AD-SCRIBIR.—*a.* written after.
aduana, *f.* customs; customs house.—*libre de a.,* customs-free.—**aduanero,** *n.* customs officer.—*a.* customs.
adueñarse, *vr.* to take possession.
adulación, *f.* flattery, adulation.—**adulador,** *n.* flatterer, adulator.—**adular,** *vt.* & *vi.* to flatter.—**adulón,** *a.* fawning, cringing.—*n.* toady, creep.
adulteración, *f.* adulteration.—**adulterar,** *vt.* to adulterate; to corrupt; to sophisticate; to tamper with.—**adulterio,** *m.* adultery.—**adúltero,** *n.* adulterer, adulteress.
adulto, *n.* & *a.* adult.
adusto, *a.* austere, stern; sullen.
advenedizo, *n.* newcomer; upstart.—*a.* newly arrived.—**advenimiento,** *m.* advent, coming.
adventicio, *a.* adventitious.
adverbial, *a.* adverbial.—**adverbio,** *m.* adverb.
adversario, *m.* opponent, adversary.—**adversidad,** *f.* adversity.—**adverso,** *a.* adverse.
advertencia, *f.* advice; warning; notice; foreword.—**advertido,** *a.* forewarned; sharp, wise.—**advertir,** *vti.* [39] to take notice of; to advise; to give notice or warning; to point out.
Adviento, *m.* (eccl.) Advent.
adyacente, *a.* adjacent.
aeración, *f.* aeration.
aéreo, *a.* serial; airy; aeronautical; air.—*por correo a.,* by air mail.—*fuerza a.,* air force.—**aerodinámica,** *f.* aerodynamics.—*a.* streamline(d).—**aerobic,** *m.* aerobics.—**aeróbico,** *a.* aerobic.—**aerobio,** *a.* aerobic.—**aerobismo,** *m.* aerobics.—**aerobús,** *m.* airbus.—**aeroclub,** *m.* flying club.—**aerodeslizador, aerodeslizante,** *m.* hovercraft.—**aeródromo,** *m.* airfield.—**aeroespacial,** *a.* aerospace.—**aerofumigación,** *f.* crop dusting.—**aerograma,** *m.* airmail letter.—**aerolínea,** *f.* airline.—**aeromodelo,** model airplane.—**aeromozo,** *n.* flight attendant.—**aeronauta,** *mf.* aeronaut.—**aeronáutica,** *f.* aeronautics.—**aeronave,** *f.* airship, dirigible.—*a. cohete,* rocket ship.—**aeroplano,** *m.* airplane, aircraft.—**aeropuerto,** *m.* airport.—**aerosol,** *m.* aerosol.—**aerostación,** *f.* ballooning.—**aeróstata,** *mf.* bal-

loonist.—**aerotaxi,** *m.* air taxi.—**aerotansportado,** *a.* airborne.
afabilidad, *f.* affability, friendliness.—**afable,** *a.* affable, kind, friendly.
afamado, *a.* celebrated, noted, famous.
afán, *m.* anxiety, eagerness.—**afanarse,** *vr.* to act or work eagerly or anxiously; to toil.—**afanoso,** *a.* laborious, painstaking.
afear, *vt.* to make ugly or faulty; to decry, censure.
afectación, *f.* affectation.—**afectado,** *a.* affected.—**afectar,** *vt.* to affect, concern; to move; to affect, feign, put on.—**afectividad,** *f.* affection.—**afectivo,** *a.* emotional, easily moved.—**afecto,** *m.* affection, love, fondness.—*a.* affectionate; (a) fond (of), inclined (to).—**afectuoso,** *a.* affectionate.
afeitado, *m.* shave, shaving.—**afeitar,** *vt.* to shave.—*vr.* to shave (oneself).—**afeite,** *m.* cosmetic, make-up.
afelpado, *a.* velvety, plush.
afeminado, *a.* effeminate.—*m.* effeminate person.—**afeminamiento,** *m.,* **afeminación,** *f.* effeminacy.
aferrado, *a.* headstrong, obstinate.—**aferramiento,** *m.* grasping, seizing; attachment; obstinacy.—**aferrar,** *vt.* to moor, anchor.—*vr.* to cling.
afianzamiento, *m.* fastening, securing.—**afianzar,** *vti.* [a] to fasten, secure.—*vri.* to steady oneself.
afición, *f.* fondness; taste, inclination; affection.—*tomar a. a,* to become fond of.—**aficionado,** *n.* & *a.* amateur; (sports) fan.—*a. a,* fond of.—**aficionar,** *vt.* to inspire affection, fondness or liking.—*vr.* (a) to fancy; to become fond of.
afijo, *m.* affix.
afilado, *a.* sharp.—*m.* sharpening.—**afilador,** *m.* sharpener.—*a. de lápices,* pencil sharpener.—**afilar,** *vt.* to sharpen, whet, grind.
afilalápices, *m.* pencil sharpener.
afiliar, *vt.* (a) to affiliate (with).—*vr.* (a) to join, affiliate oneself (with).
afín, *a.* skin, kindred; related.
afinación, *f.* finishing touch, refining; tuning.—**afinador,** *n.* piano tuner; tuning key.—**afinamiento,** *m.* refinement.—**afinar,** *vt.* to perfect; to refine; to tune.—*vr.* to become polished.

afinidad, *f.* affinity; resemblance.

afirmación, *f.* affirmation.—**afirmar,** *vt.* to affirm, assert; to make fast, secure, fasten.—*vr.* to hold fast; to steady oneself or make oneself firm; to maintain firmly.—**afirmativo,** *a.* affirmative.

aflicción, *f.* affliction, sorrow, grief. —**aflictivo,** *a.* distressing.—**afligir,** *vti.* [49-c] to afflict, upset.—*vri.* to grieve, become despondent.

aflojamiento, *m.* relaxation; loosening, slackening.—**aflojar,** *vt.* to loosen, slacken, relax, let loose.— *vi.* to let up, ease off.—*vr.* to abate, weaken, flag.

afluencia, *f.* flowing; influx.— **afluente,** *m.* affluent, tributary. —**afluir,** *vii.* [23-e] (a) to flock (in); to flow (into).

afonía, *f.* hoarseness, loss of voice.

afortunado, *a.* lucky, fortunate.

afrenta, *f.* affront, outrage; disgrace. —**afrentar,** *vt.* to affront; to insult.— *vr.* to be ashamed; to blush.—**afrentoso,** *a.* insulting, outrageous.

africano, *n.* & *a.* African.

afro, *a. invar.* Afro.—**afroamericano,** *a.* Afro-American, African-American.

afrontar, *vt.* to confront; to face.

afta, *f.* (med.) sore.

afuera, *adv.* out; outside; in public.— *interj.* out! clear the way! one side!— *f. pl.* suburbs, outskirts.

agachar, *vt.* to lower, bend.—*vr.* to bend down; to yield, give in.

agalla, *f.* gill; tonsil.—*pl.* (coll.) guts.—*tener a.* (coll.) to have guts; (Am.) to be greedy; to be shrewd.

agarrada, *f.* run-in, fight.—**agarradero,** *n.* holder, handle.—**agarrado,** *a.* (coll.) stingy, close-fisted.—**agarrar,** *vt.* to grasp, seize; (coll.) to obtain; to catch; to come upon.—*vr.* to hold on; (coll.) to have a fight.— *¡agárrate bien!* hold tight!

agarrotar, *vt.* to tie firmly; to strangle; to stiffen.—*vr.* to stiffen up.

agasajar, *vt.* to treat well, to give a royal welcome to.—**agasajo,** *m.* friendly treatment; royal welcome.

agazaparse, *vr.* to crouch down.

agencia, *f.* agency; bureau, office; branch.—*a. de cobro,* collection agency.—*a. de colocaciones,* employment agency.—*a. de información, a. de noticias, a. de prensa,* news agency.—*a. de publicidad, a. publicitaria,* advertising agency.—*a. de* turismo, a. de viajes, travel agency.— a. funeraria, funeral parlor, funeral home.—**agenciar,** *vt.* to solicit, promote, negotiate.—**agenda,** *f.* diary, notebook; agenda.—*a. cultural,* entertainment guide.—*a. de trabajo,* engagement book.—**agente,** *m.* agent; policeman.—*a. de bolsa, a. de cambio,* stockbroker.—*a. de publicidad, a. publicitario,* advertising agent.—*a. de viajes,* travel agent.—*a. inmobiliario,* real estate agent.—*a. literario,* literary agent.— *a. secreto,* secret agent.

ágil, *a.* nimble, fast, light.—**agilidad,** *f.* agility, nimbleness.

agiotista, *mf.* loan shark.

agitación, *f.* agitation; excitement. —**agitador,** *n.* agitator, rouser.—*a.* agitating, stirring.—**agitar,** *vt.* to agitate; to stir, shake up; to ruffle.—*vr.* to flutter; to become excited.

agobiar, *vt.* to weigh down; to overwhelm; to oppress.—*vr.* to bow; to crouch.—**agobio,** *m.* bending down; oppression, burden, nervous strain.

agonía, *f.* agony; death struggle; violent pain; anxious desire.—**agonizante,** *a.* & *mf.* dying person.—**agonizar,** *vii.* [a] to be dying, in the throes of death.

agostar, *vt.* to scorch, wither.—*vr.* to become parched; to dry up, wilt. —**agosto,** *m.* August.—*hacer su a.,* to feather one's nest.

agotamiento, *m.* draining; exhaustion.—**agotado,** *a.* exhausted; sold out; out of print.—**agotar,** *vt.* to drain; to exhaust, use up.—*vr.* to become exhausted; to give out; to wear oneself out; to be out of print.

agraciado, *a.* graceful, gracious; charming; lucky.—*n.* grantee.— **agraciar,** *vt.* to adorn, grace; to grant, reward.

agradable, *a.* agreeable; pleasing, pleasant.—**agradar,** *vi.* to be pleasing; to please.

agradecer, *vti.* [3] to thank for; to be grateful for.—**agradecido,** *a.* thankful.—**agradecimiento,** *m.* gratitude.

agrado, *m.* affability, agreeableness; pleasure; liking.—*ser del a. de uno,* to like someone.

agrandamiento, *m.* enlargement.— **agrandar,** *vt.* to enlarge; to increase; to let out (dress).

agrario, *a.* agrarian.

agravar, *vt.* to aggravate; to make worse, more serious.—*vr.* to get worse, more serious.

agraviar, *vt.* to wrong, offend, insult. *vr.* to take offense.—**agravio,** *m.* offense, insult, affront.

agraz, *a.* unripe.—*m.* unripe grape; (coll.) displeasure.

agredir, *vti.* [50] to attack, assault.

agregado, *m.* aggregate; assistant; attaché.—**agregar,** *vti.* [b] to add, join; to collect, gather; to aggregate.

agresión, *f.* aggression.—*a. con lesiones,* assault and battery.—*a. sexual,* sexual assault.—**agresivo,** *a.* aggressive, offensive.—**agresor,** *n.* aggressor, assaulter.

agreste, *a.* rustic, wild; rude, uncouth.

agriar, *vt.* to make sour or tart; to irritate, exasperate.—*vr.* to sour, turn acid.

agrícola, *a.* agricultural.—**agricultor,** *n.* farmer, agriculturist.—**agricultura,** *f.* agriculture, farming.

agridulce, *a.* bittersweet.

agrietarse, *vr.* to crack; to chap (skin).

agrimensor, *m.* land surveyor.—**agrimensura,** *f.* land surveying.

agrio, *a.* sour, tart; sour, sharp, disagreeable.

agrupación, *f.* group; association; gathering.—**agrupar,** *vt.* to group; to gather, assemble.—*vr.* to crowd together; to form groups.

agua, *f.* water; liquid; rain; slope of a roof.—*pl.* luster of diamonds; clouds (in silk, etc.); gloss (in feathers, stones).—*a. abajo,* downstream.—*a. arriba,* upstream.—*a. bendita,* holy water.—*a. blanda,* soft water.—*a. corriente,* running water.—*a. de colonia,* eau de cologne, toilet water.—*a. destilada,* distilled water.—*a. de grifo,* tap water.—*a. dulce,* fresh water.—*a. dura,* hard water.—*a. helada,* ice water.—*a. mineral,* mineral water.—*a. nieve,* sleet.—*a. oxigenada,* hydrogen peroxide.—*a. pesada,* heavy water.—*agua potable, a. para beber,* drinking water.—*a. salada,* salt water.—*aguas negras, aguas residuales, aguas servidas,* sewage.—*aguas pluviales,* rainwater.—*aguas hasta el cuello,* to be in a fix, in difficulties.—*estar entre dos aguas,* to be undecided, be on the fence.—*hacer*

aguas, to urinate.—*¡hombre al a.!* man overboard!—**aguacate,** *m.* avocado, alligator pear.—**aguacero,** *m.* heavy rain.—**aguachirle,** *m.* inferior wine.—**aguada,** *f.* watering station; drinking water source.—**aguado,** *a.* watery, watered.—**aguafuerte,** *m.* etching.—**aguafiestas,** *mf.* spoilsport.—**aguamarina,** *f.* aquamarine.

aguantar, *vt.* to bear, endure; to resist; to maintain; to hold.—*vr.* to forbear.—**aguante,** *m.* strength, resistance; patience, endurance.

aguar, *vt.* [b] to water down; to spoil, mar.—*vr.* to be spoiled.

aguardar, *vt.* to wait for.—*vi.* to await.

aguardentoso, *a.* smelling of alcohol; drunken (voice).—**aguardiente,** *m.* brandy, eau-de-vie.—*a. de caña,* rum.—*a. de manzana,* applejack.

aguarrás, *m.* turpentine.

aguazal, *m.* marsh, fen.

agudeza, *f.* sharpness; fineness; wit, witticism; repartee; high pitch; shrillness.—**agudo,** *a.* sharp, acute; keen-edged; shrill, screechy; witty, clever, sparkling.

agüero, *m.* omen.—*de buen a.,* lucky.

aguerrido, *a.* battle-tested, veteran.

aguijón, *m.* sting (of insect); prick; spur, goad.—**aguijonazo,** *m.* sting.—**aguijonear,** *vt.* to prick, goad; to push, urge.

águila, *f.* eagle.—*á. caudal, á. real,* golden eagle;—*¿á. o sol?,* (Mex.) heads or tails?—*á. ratonera,* buzzard.—**aguileño,** *a.* aquiline.—**aguilucho,** *m.* eaglet.

aguinaldo, *m.* Christmas or New Year's present; tip; pocket money; (Am.) Christmas bonus; (Am.) Christmas carol.

aguja, *f.* needle; hatpin; spire, steeple; bodkin; obelisk; hornfish; needle shell; hand (of a clock); magnetic compass; (R.R.) switches; spindle.—*a. de calceta, media, punto* or *tejer,* knitting needle.—*a. de capotera* or *zurcir,* darning needle.—*a. de crochet, ganchillo* or *gancho,* crochet hook.—*a. de mechar,* trussing needle.—*a. de marear, a. de bitácora, a. magnética,* compass needle, ship's compass.—*a. hipodérmica,* hypodermic needle.—**agujerear,** *vt.* to pierce, perforate.—**agujero,** *m.* hole; dugout.—*a. en la capa de* *ozono,* ozone-hole.—**agujeta,** *f.* little needle.—*pl.* charley horse, pain from over-exercise.

agusanarse, *vr.* to become worm-eaten, putrid.

aguzador, *n.* sharpener.—*a.* sharpening.—**aguzar,** *vti.* [a] to whet, sharpen; to urge, excite.—*a. las orejas,* to prick up one's ears.

aherrojar, *vt.* to chain, put in irons.

ahí, *adv.* there; yonder.—*de a.,* hence.—*por a.,* somewhere around here; that way; over there; more or less.

ahijado, *n.* godchild; protegé.—*m.* godson.—**ahijada,** *f.* goddaughter.

ahinco, *m.* earnestness, eagerness.

ahito, *a.* gorged, sated.—*m.* indigestion; satiety.

ahogado, *a.* drowned; close, unventilated; suffocated.—*estar* or *verse a.,* to be overwhelmed or swamped.—*n.* suffocated or drowned person.—**ahogar,** *vti.* [b] to drown; to choke, throttle, smother; to oppress; to quench, extinguish.—*vri.* to drown; to be suffocated.—**ahogo,** *m.* drowning; shortness of breath; financial difficulty.

ahondar, *vt.* to deepen; to dig; to go deep into.—*vi.* to go deep, penetrate; to progress in knowledge.

ahora, *adv.* now.—*a. bien,* now, now then.—*a. mismo,* right now, just now; at once.—*hasta a.,* so far; hitherto, until now.—*por a.,* for the present.

ahorcado, *n. & a.* hanged (person). —**ahorcar,** *vti.* [d] to hang (execute by hanging).—*vri.* to hang, be hanged; to hang oneself.

ahorita, *adv.* (Am.) just now.—*a. mismo,* this very minute, just now; at once.

ahormar, *vt.* to fit, shape, adjust; to last, break in (shoes); to bring to reason.

ahorrar, *vt.* to save, economize; to spare; to avoid.—*vi.* to save money.—**ahorrativo,** *a.* thrifty, frugal.—**ahorro,** *m.* economy.—*pl.* savings.—*caja de ahorros,* savings bank.

ahuecar, *vti.* [d] to make hollow, scoop out; to loosen.—*a. la voz,* to speak in a deep, solemn tone.—*vri.* to become hollow; to put on airs.

ahumado, *a.* smoky; smoked.—**ahumar,** *vt.* to smoke; to cure in smoke.—*vi.* to fume; to emit smoke.—*vr.* to be blackened by smoke.

ahuyentar, *vt.* to put to flight; to drive away.

aindiado, *a.* resembling Native Americans.

airado, *a.* angry, wrathful.

aire, *m.* air; atmosphere; wind; air, appearance; carriage, gait; tune.—*a. acondicionado,* air conditioning.—*a. comprimido,* compressed air.—*a. fresco,* fresh air.—*a. puro,* clean air.—*a. viciado,* stale air.—*a. de familia,* family resemblance.—*al a. libre,* outdoors.—*de buen,* or *mal a.,* in a good, or a bad humor.—*en el a.,* in suspense, in the air.—*tomar el a.,* to take a walk.—**aireado,** *m.* aeration.—**airear,** *vt.* to air; to ventilate; to aerate.—*vr.* to take the air; to cool oneself.—**airoso,** *a.* airy, windy; graceful, gracious; successful.

aislado, *a.* isolated; insulated.—**aislador,** *m.* isolator; insulator.—*a.* isolating; insulating.—**aislamiento,** *m.* isolation; insulation; insulating material.—**aislar,** *vt.* to isolate; to insulate.—*vr.* to become isolated; to seclude oneself.

ajar, *vt. & vr.* to crumple; to wilt, wither.

ajedrecista, *n.* chess player.—**ajedrez,** *m.* chess; chess set.

ajeno, *a.* another's; alien, foreign; unaware, ignorant; oblivious.

ajetrearse, *vr.* to tire oneself out; to rush around.—**ajetreo,** *m.* hustle and bustle.

ají, *m.* (Am.) green pepper.

ajo, *m.* garlic; swear word.—*echar ajos (y cebollas),* to swear, curse.

ajuar, *m.* trousseau; household furniture.

ajustado, *a.* agreed upon; tight; fitted.—**ajustar,** *vt.* to adjust; to adapt, fit; to regulate; to agree about, concert; to tighten; to engage, hire.—*vr.* to settle; to conform; to be engaged or hired.—**ajuste,** *m.* adjustment; fitting; agreement; engagement; settlement.—*pl.* couplings.

ajusticiar, *vt.* to execute, put to death.

al, (*contr.* of **a** & **el**) to the; on, at; about.—*le dí la carta al criado,* I gave the letter to the servant.—*al llegar,* on arrival.—*al amanecer,* at daybreak.—*estoy al partir,* I am about to leave.

ala, *f.* wing; row; wing (of a building); brim (of a hat); leaf (of a door, table).—*a. abierta,* (sports) wide receiver.—*a. cerrada,* (sports) tight end.—*a. delta,* hang gliding; (apparatus) hang glider.—**Alá,** Allah.—*cortar las alas a uno,* to clip one's wings.—*dar alas,* to embolden, encourage.

alabanza, *f.* praise.—**alabar,** *vt.* to praise, commend.—*vr.* to boast.

alabastro, *m.* alabaster.

alabear, *vt.* & *vr.* to warp.

alacena, *f.* cupboard; closet; cabinet.

alacrán, *m.* scorpion.

alado, *a.* winged.

alambicado, *a.* distilled; (fig.) refined, precious; affected.—**alambicamiento,** *m.* distillation; (fig.) subtlety; affectation.—**alambicar,** *vti.* [d] to distill; to overrefine, exaggerate.—**alambique,** *m.* still.

alambrada, *f.* wire fence; wire defenses.—**alambrado,** *m.* wire cover; electric wiring.—**alambraje,** *m.* (elec.) wiring.—**alambrar,** *vt.* to fence with wire.—**alambre,** *m.* wire.—*a. cargado,* live wire.—*a. de espino* or *púas, a. espinoso,* barbed wire.—*a. forrado,* insulated wire.—*a. de tierra,* ground (wire).—**alambrera,** *f.* wire netting; wire screen, window screen.

alameda, *f.* alameda, mall, public walk shaded with trees; poplar grove.—**álamo,** *m.* poplar.

alarde, *m.* ostentation, boasting, bluff.—*hacer a.,* to boast; to show off.—**alardear,** *m.* to boast.

alargador, *m.* extension cord.

alargar, *vti.* [b] to lengthen; to extend; to stretch out; to protract, prolong.—*vri.* to be prolonged; to drag; to become longer; to enlarge.

alarido, *m.* howl, shriek, yell.

alarma, *f.* alarm.—*a. aérea,* air-raid warning.—*a. antirrobo, a. de ladrones,* burglar alarm.—*a. contra incendios, a. de incendios,* fire alarm.—*a. roja,* red alert.—*falsa a.,* false alarm.—**alarmante,** *a.* alarming, startling.—**alarmar,** *vt.* to alarm.—*vr.* to become alarmed.—**alarmista,** *n.* alarmist.

alazán, *a.* & *m.* sorrel.

alba, *f.* dawn; alb.—*al a.,* or *al rayar el a.,* at daybreak.

albacea, *mf.* (law) executor, executrix.

albanés, *n.* & *a.* Albanian.

albañil, *m.* mason, bricklayer.—**albañilería,** *f.* masonry (occupation or work).

albarda, *f.* packsaddle.

albaricoque, *m.* apricot.

albatros, *m.* albatross.

albayalde, *m.* white lead.

albedrío, *m.* will; free will; impulsiveness.—*libre a.,* free will.

alberca, *f.* pond, reservoir; (Am.) swimming pool.

albergar, *vti.* [b] to lodge, shelter, harbor; to take in (lodgers).—*vr.* to lodge; to find shelter or lodging.—**albergue,** *m.* lodging; shelter; (animal) den.

albóndiga, *f.* meat ball.

albor, *m.* dawn; whiteness; beginning.—**alborear,** *vi.* to dawn.

albornoz, *m.* hooded cloak; bathrobe; terry cloth.

alborotador, *n.* agitator, rioter.—*a.* rowdy.—**alborotar,** *vt.* to disturb, agitate.—*vi.* to create an uproar.—*vr.* to become excited; to fuss; to riot.—**alboroto,** *m.* excitement; riot, brawl, commotion.

alborozar, *vti.* [a] to gladden, exhilarate.—*vri.* to rejoice.—**alborozo,** *m.* merriment, gaiety, joy.

album, *m.* album.—*a. de recortes,* scrapbook.—*a. de sellos, a. de estampillas,* stamp album.

albur, *m.* risk, chance.—*correr un a.,* to venture, chance, risk.

alcachofa, *f.* artichoke.

alcahueta, *f.* procuress; go-between; gossip.—**alcahuete,** *m.* procurer, pimp; go-between, front man; fence, receiver of stolen goods.—**alcahuetear,** *vt.* & *vi.* to aid, abet; to pander.

alcaide, *m.* warden; jailer.

alcalde, *m.* mayor.—**alcaldesa,** *f.* mayoress; wife of the mayor.—**alcaldía,** *f.* mayor's office; city hall.

álcali, *m.* alkali.—**alcalino,** *a.* alkaline.

alcance, *m.* reach; overtaking; pursuit; arm's length; range (of fire arms, etc.); deficit; scope, sweep.—*pl.* mental powers; ability.—*al a. de,* within reach of.—*a largo a.,* long term.—*dar a.,* to catch up with.

alcancía, *f.* piggy bank; money box.

alcanfor, *m.* camphor; (Am.) procurer, pimp.

alcantarilla, *f.* sewer; drain.—**alcantarillado,** *m.* sewer system, drains, sewerage.—**alcantarillar**, *vt.* to lay sewers in, to provide drains for.

alcanzado, *a.* needy; in debt; hard-up.—**alcanzar**, *vti.* [a] to reach; to overtake, come up to; to obtain, attain.—*a. a uno algo*, to hand, pass something to someone.

alcaparra, *f.* caper.

alcatraz, *m.* gannet.

alcayata, *f.* hook, spike.

alcázar, *m.* fortress; royal palace.

alce, *m.* elk; moose.

alcista, *a.* upward.—*mf.* bull (on the stock market).

alcoba, *f.* alcove; bedroom.—*a. de respeto*, master bedroom.

alcohol, *m.* alcohol.—**alcohólico**, *a.* alcoholic.—*pl. A. Anonimos*, Alcoholics Anonymous.—**alcoholímetro**, *m.* Breathalyzer (TM).

alcornoque, *m.* cork tree; (coll.) blockhead.

alcurnia, *f.* lineage.

aldaba, *f.* knocker (of a door); latch; handle (door, furniture).—*tener buena a.*, or *buenas aldabas*, to have powerful friends.—**aldabonazo**, *m.* knocking.

aldea, *f.* village, hamlet.—*a. mundial*, global village.—**aldeano**, *n.* villager, peasant.—*a.* rustic, unpolished.

aleación, *f.* alloy; alloying.

alebrestarse, *vr.* (Am.) to cut capers; to become frightened or excited.

aleccionador, *a.* instructive.—**aleccionamiento**, *m.* instruction, coaching.—**aleccionar**, *vt.* to teach, instruct, coach.

aledaño, *a.* bounding, bordering.—*m.* boundary, border.

alegación, *f.* (law.) declaration.—*a. de culpabilidad*, (Mex.) plea of guilty.—*a. de inocencia*, (Mex.) plea of not guilty.—**alegar**, *vti.* [b] to allege, affirm; to quote; to adduce; to argue.—**alegato**, *m.* claim; plea, argument; (law) indictment.

alegoría, *f.* allegory.—**alegórico**, *a.* allegorical.

alegrar, *vt.* to make merry, exhilarate; to enliven; to brighten.—*vr.* (de) to rejoice (at); to be glad (of or to); to be happy; to get tipsy.—**alegre**, *a.* merry, joyful; lively; cheerful; bright (of colors); tipsy.—**alegría**, *f.* mirth, merriment; happiness, joy.—**alegrón**, *m.* (coll.) sudden, unexpected joy.

alejamiento, *m.* removal to a distance;

receding; retiring; withdrawal.—**alejar**, *vt.* to remove to a distance; to move away; to separate; to estrange.—*vr.* to recede; to withdraw or move away.

alelarse, *vr.* to become stupefied.—**alelado**, *a.* spellbound, bewildered.

alelí, *m.* = ALHELÍ.

aleluya, *m.* halleluja.

alemán, *n. & a.* German.

alentador, *a.* encouraging, cheering.—**alentar**, *vii.* [1] to breathe.—*vti.* to encourage, cheer; to inspire.

alergia, *f.* allergy.—*a. a la primavera*, hayfever.—**alérgico**, *a.* allergic.

alero, *m.* eaves, overhang; splashboard of a carriage.

alerón, *m.* (aer.) aileron; (anat.) armpit.

alerta, *m.* alarm, alert.—*a.* watchful, vigilant, alert.—*interj.* look out! watch out!—**alertar**, *vt.* to render vigilant; to put on guard.

aleta, *f.* fin; (mech.) leaf of a hinge; blade (of a propeller); fender (of a car).

aletargar, *vti.* [b] to cause drowsiness.—*vri.* to become drowsy, sluggish.

aletazo, *m.* blow with the wing; flapping.—**aletear**, *vi.* to flutter (wings or fins).—**aleteo**, *m.* fluttering (of wings or fins).

alevosía, *f.* perfidy, treachery.—**alevoso**, *a.* treacherous.

alfabético, *a.* alphabetical.—**alfabeto**, *m.* alphabet.—*a. Morse*, Morse code.—*a. de los sordomudos*, sign language.—**alphabetizar**, *vt.* to teach to read and write; to put in alphabetical order.

alfanje, *m.* scimitar, cutlass.

alfarería, *f.* pottery; potter's art.—**alfarero**, *n.* potter.

alféizar, *m.* window sill or embrasure.

alfeñique, *m.* sugar paste; wimp.

alférez, *m.* second lieutenant.—*a. de fragata*, ensign.

alfil, *m.* bishop (in chess).

alfiler, *m.* pin; scarfpin; brooch.—*a. de corbata*, necktie pin.—*a. de seguridad, gancho*, or *nodriza*, safety pin.—*pegar* or *prender con alfileres*, to do in a slipshod way.—**alfilerazo**, *m.* pinprick.—**alfiletero**, *m.* pincase, needle case; pincushion.

alfombra, *f.* carpet.—*a. de baño*, bathmat.—*a. mágica*, magic carpet.—**alfombrar**, *vt.* to carpet.

alforja, f. saddlebag.

alforza, f. pleat, tuck; (coll.) scar.

alga, f. seaweed.

algarabía, f. jargon; din, hubbub.

algarroba, f. carob.—**algarrobo,** m. locust tree; carob tree.

algazara, f. din, clamor; jubilation, joy.

álgebra, f. algebra.—**algebraico,** a. algebraic.

algo, pron. something.—adv. somewhat, a little.—a. es a., every little bit counts.

algodón, m. cotton; cotton plant.—a. de azúcar, cotton candy.—a. en rama, raw cotton.—**algodonal,** m. cotton plantation.—**algodonero,** a. pertaining to cotton.—m. cotton plant; cotton dealer, planter, or farmer.

alguacil, m. constable; bailiff; governor.

alguien, pron. somebody, someone.

algún, alguno, a. some, any.—alguna que otra vez, sometimes, once in a while.—**alguno,** pron. somebody, someone.—a. que otro, a few, some.—pl. some, some people.

alhaja, f. jewel, gem; valuable object.

alharaca, f. clamor, fuss, ado.

alhelí, m. (bot.) wallflower.

alhucema, f. lavender.

aliado, n. & a. ally, allied.—**alianza,** f. alliance; agreement; wedding ring.—**aliarse,** vr. to become allied; to form an alliance.

alias, m. alias.—adv. alias, e.g., Roberto alias 'el Grande', Robert alias 'the Great One'.

alicaído, a. drooping, weak; dejected, crestfallen.

alicates, m. pl. pliers.

aliciente, m. attraction, inducement.

alienado, a. alienated; mentally ill.—n. mentally ill person.—**alienista,** mf. psychiatrist.

aliento, m. breath, wind; breathing; encouragement; bravery.—dar a., to encourage.—nuevo a., second wind.—sin a., breathless.

aligeramiento, m. alleviation, lightening.—**aligerar,** vt. to lighten; to alleviate; to hasten; to shorten.

alimaña, f. destructive animal, pest.—pl. vermin.

alimentación, f. feeding; food, nourishment.—**alimentar,** vt. to feed, nourish; to nurture; to encourage; to foster.—**alimenticio,** a. nourishing; nutritious; dietary.—**alimento,** m. food, nourishment.—a. chatarra, (Mex.) junk food.—pl. alimony.

alineación, f. alignment.—**alinear,** vt. to align; to line up; to put into line.—vr. to fall in line; to form a line.

aliñar, vt. to dress or season (food); to adorn.—**aliño,** m. dressing or seasoning; ornament, decoration; cleanliness.

alisar, vt. to plane, smooth; to polish, burnish.

alisios, m. pl. trade winds.

alistamiento, m. enrollment; (mil.) enlistment, recruitment; (mil.) draft.—**alistar,** vt. & vr. to enlist, enroll; to get or make ready.

aliviar, vt. to alleviate, relieve, soothe; to lighten; to reprieve.—**alivio,** m. alleviation, easement, mitigation; relief; reprieve.

aljibe, m. cistern, tank; well; (Am.) dungeon.

aljofifa, f. mop.—**aljofifar,** vt. to mop.

allá, adv. there; thither, over there.—a. en mi niñez, in the old times of my childhood.—a. por el año de 1900, about 1900.—a. veremos, we shall see.—a. voy, I am coming.—el más a., the beyond.—más a., farther.—muy a., much beyond, far beyond.

allanamiento, m. leveling; smoothing; (law) breaking and entering; (law) raid.—**allanar,** vt. to level, smooth; to flatten; to remove or overcome (difficulties); to pacify, subdue; (law) to break into (a house); (law) to raid, search.—vr. to abide (by), acquiesce.

allegado, a. near, related.—n. relative; ally.—**allegar,** vti. [b] to reap; to collect; gather together.—vri. to agree with; to adhere to.

allende, adv. beyond, over, on the other side.—a. los mares, overseas.

allí, adv. there, in that place; thereto.—por a., that way; through there, thereabouts.

alma, f. soul; human being; inhabitant; essence, core; bore of a gun.—a. de cántaro, fool.—a. de Dios, kind-hearted person; harmless creature.—a. en pena, ghost.—a. mía, mi a., my dearest; my love.

almacén, m. store, shop; warehouse, repository; storage house, depot, grocery store; stockroom; dockyard.—*pl.* department store.—**almacenaje,** *m.* storage.—**almacenar,** *vt.* to store; to lay up, hoard; to put in storage.—**almacenista,** *m.* wholesaler; department store or warehouse owner.

alma-máter, *f.* driving force; university; (antigua universidad) alma mater.

almanaque, *m.* almanac, calendar.

almeja, *f.* clam.

almena, *f.* battlement.

almendra, *f.* almond.—**almendrado,** *a.* almond-shaped.—*m.* macaroon. —**almendro,** *m.* almond tree.

almíbar, *m.* syrup.—**almibarado,** *a.* syrupy, sugary; flattering.

almidón, *m.* starch.—**almidonado,** *a.* starched; stiff; straightlaced, stuffy.—**almidonar,** *vt.* to starch.

almirantazgo, *m.* admiralty.—**almirante,** *m.* admiral.

almirez, *m.* mortar.

almizcle, *m.* musk.—**almizclero,** *a.* musk.

almohada, *f.* pillow.—*consultar con la a.,* to sleep on the matter.—**almohadilla,** *f.* pincushion; pad; ink pad; small pillow.—**almohadón,** *m.* cushion.

almorranas, *f. pl.* hemorrhoids, piles.

almorzar, *vii.* [12-a] to lunch, to have lunch.—*vti.* to have for lunch.—**almuerzo,** *m.* lunch.—*a. de ceremonia,* luncheon.

alocado, *a.* crazy, wild, reckless, nuts.

alojamiento, *m.* accomodations; (mil.) billeting.—**alojar,** *vt.* to get rooms for, to book; to put up (at one's home); to accommodate (a certain number of persons); to quarter (troops).—*vr.* to stay, to room.

alondra, *f.* lark.

alpargata, *f.* hemp sandal.

alpinismo, *m.* mountain climbing. —**alpinista,** *mf.* mountain climber.

alpiste, *m.* birdseed.

alquilar, *vt.* to rent; to hire;—*vr.* to be a wage earner.—**alquiler,** *m.* wages; rent, rental; renting, hiring.—*de a.,* for hire.

alquitrán, *m.* tar.—**alquitranado,** *a.* tarry.

alrededor, *adv.* around.—*a. de,* about, around, (coll.) approximately.—**alrededores,** *m. pl.* environs, outskirts.

alta, *f.* (med.) discharge (from hospital); (mil.) certificate of enlistment.—*darse de a.,* to be admitted (in a profession, social club), to become a member.

altanería, *f.* haughtiness, arrogance. —**altanero,** *a.* haughty, arrogant.

altar, *m.* altar.—*a. mayor,* high altar.

altavoz, *m.* loudspeaker.—*a. para audiofrecuencias bajas/elevadas,* woofer/tweeter.

altea, *f.* marshmallow.

alterable, *a.* alterable, changeable. —**alteración,** *f.* alteration; strong emotion; commotion.—*a. del orden público,* public disturbance.—**alterado,** *a.* disturbed, agitated.—**alterar,** *vt.* to alter, change, transform; to disturb, stir up.—*vr.* to change, go bad; to get upset.

altercado, *m.* altercation, quarrel.—**altercar,** *vii.* to argue, dispute, quarrel.

alternador, *m.* (elec.) alternator.—**alternar,** *vt., vi.* & *vr.* to alternate.—**alternativa,** *f.* alternative, choice; service by turn.—**alternativo, alterno,** *a.* alternate, alternating.—*corriente alterna,* alternating current.

alteza, *f.* height; nobility.—*si, A.,* yes, your Highness.

altibajos, *m. pl.* unevenness of ground; ups and downs.

altiplanicie, *f.* **altiplano,** *m.* high plateau.

altisonante, *a.* high-sounding.

altitud, *f.* height; altitude.

altivez, *f.* haughtiness, pride.—**altivo,** *a.* haughty, proud, arrogant.

alto, *a.* high; elevated; tall; eminent; lofty; loud.—*alta cocina,* haute cuisine.—*alta costura,* haute couture.—*a. fidelidad,* high fidelity.—*a. frecuencia,* high frequency.—*a. mar,* high seas.—*altas esferas,* upper echelons.—*altas horas,* the small hours.—*alto mando,* high-ranking officer.—*altos hornos,* blast furnaces.—*de lo a.,* from above.—*las altas finanzas,* high finance.—*m.* height, elevation; hill; top; story, floor; summit; mountain top, crest; top floor; heap, pile; (mil.) halt; place or time of rest.—*dar el a. a alguien,* (mil.) to order someone to halt.—*hacer a.,* to halt.—*pasar por a.,* to overlook, forget.—*adv.* high, high up; loud, loudly; (voice) high.—*interj.* (mil. command) halt!—**altoparlante,** *m.* v. ALTAVOZ.—**altozano,** *m.* hillock, knoll; height.—**altura,** *f.* height, altitude;

tallness, stature; summit, top; (naut.) the latitude; altitude; level, standard.—*estar a la a. de*, to be equal to.—*pl.* the heavens, Heaven.—*a estas alturas*, at this moment.

alucinación, *f.* hallucination.—**alucinar**, *vt.* & *vr.* to dazzle, fascinate, delude.—*vi.* to hallucinate.

alud, *m.* avalanche.

aludido, *a.* referred, aforementioned.—**aludir**, *vi.* to allude, refer.

alumbrado, *m.* illumination, lighting.—*a. público*, street lighting.—*a.* lit, lighted; tipsy.—**alumbramiento**, *m.* childbirth; lighting.—**alumbrar**, *vt.* to light; to illuminate, light up; to enlighten.—*vi.* to give, or shed light; to give birth.—*vr.* to get tipsy.

aluminio, *m.* aluminum.

alumno, *n.* pupil, student.—*a. mimado*, teacher's pet.

alusión, *f.* allusion, reference, hint.—**alusivo**, *a.* allusive, hinting.

aluvión, *m.* flood, barrage.

alza, *f.* rise (in price).—**alzada**, *f.* height (of horse); (law) appeal.—**alzado**, *a.* & *n.* (of) a lump sum; revolted, insurgent.—**alzamiento**, *m.* lifting, raising; insurrection.—**alzar**, *vti.* [a] to raise; to lift; to pick up; (eccl.) to elevate the host.—*a. cabeza*, to recover from a calamity or a disease.—*a. velas*, to sail away; to move.—*vri.* to revolt; to rise; (law) to appeal.—*alzarse con*, to run off with something, steal something.

ama, *f.* mistress of the house; landlady; (woman) owner.—*a. de casa*, housewife, homemaker.—*a. de cría o de leche*, wet nurse.—*a. de llaves*, housekeeper.

amabilidad, *f.* amiability, affability; kindness.—**amable**, *a.* amiable, affable; kind.

amado, *a.* beloved, dear.—*n.* sweetheart, lover.

amaestrar, *vt.* to train, break in (animals); to train, coach.

amagar, *vti.* [b] to threaten; to hint.—*vii.* to threaten; to be impending; to feign.—**amago**, *m.* threat; hint; indication, sign.

amalgama, *f.* amalgam.—**amalgamar**, *vt.* to amalgamate.

amamantar, *vt.* to nurse, suckle, breast-feed.

amanecer, *vii.* [3] to dawn.—*m.* dawn,

daybreak.—*al a.*, at dawn, at daybreak.

amanerado, *a.* full of mannerisms.—**amanerarse**, *vr.* to adopt mannerisms; to become affected.

amansamiento, *m.* taming; breaking (horses).—**amansar**, *vt.* to tame, domesticate; to break (a horse); to pacify, soothe.—*vr.* to calm down; to become subdued.

amante, *mf.* & *a.* lover; mistress, loving.

amanuense, *m.* scribe, amanuensis.

amañar, *vt.* to do cleverly.—*vr.* to be handy; to manage things cleverly.

amapola, *f.* poppy.

amar, *vt.* to love.

amaranto, *m.* amaranth.

amarar, *vi.* to set down on water.

amargar, *vti.* [b] to make bitter.—*vri.* to become bitter.—**amargo**, *a.* bitter.—*m.* bitterness; bitters; (Am.) mate tea.—**amargor**, *m.*, **amargura**, *f.* bitterness.

amarillear, *vi.* to show a yellow tinge.—**amarillento**, *a.* yellowish.—**amarillez**, *f.* yellowness.—**amarillo** *a.* & *n.* yellow.

amarra, *f.* cable; rope.—**amarradero** *m.* hitching post; tying or fastening place; mooring berth.—**amarrar**, *vt.* to tie, fasten; to lash, moor.—**amarre**, *m.* tying; mooring; mooring line or cable.

amartillar, *vt.* to hammer; to cock (gun).

amasar, *vt.* to knead; to mash; to amass, accumulate.—**amasijo**, *m.* batch of dough; (act of) kneading; mash, mixture; medley; hodgepodge, jumble.

amatista, *f.* amethyst.

amatorio, *a.* amatory.

amazona, *f.* Amazon; horsewoman; riding habit.—**amazónico**, *a.* Amazonian.

ambages, *m. pl.* circumlocution; maze; beating around the bush.—*sin a.*, in plain language.

ámbar, *m.* amber.—**ambarino**, *a.* amberlike.

ambición, *f.* ambition; aspiration —**ambicionar**, *vt.* to seek eagerly; aspire to; to covet.—**ambicioso**, *a* ambitious, aspiring; covetous greedy.

ambidextro, ambidiestro, *a.* ambidextrous.

ambiente, *m.* atmosphere; air; env

ronment.—*a. artificial,* air conditioning.

ambigüedad, *f.* ambiguity.—**ambiguo,** *a.* ambiguous, uncertain, doubtful.

ámbito, *m.* bounds, area; scope.

ameba, *f.* amoeba.

amebico, *a.* amoebic.—**amebiasis** or **amebas,** amoebic dysentery.

ambos, *a.* & *pron. pl.* both.

ambrosía, *f.* ambrosia; ragweed.

ambulancia, *f.* ambulance; field hospital.—**ambulante,** *a.* walking; shifting; roving, wandering; moving.

amedrentar, *vt.* to scare, frighten, intimidate.

amén, *m.* amen, so be it.—*a. de,* besides; aside from.

amenaza, *f.* threat, menace.—**amenazador,** *a.* threatening, menacing.—**amenazar,** *vti.* [a] to threaten, menace; to be impending.

amenguar, *vti.* [b] to diminish, to lessen; to dishonor, to belittle.

amenidad, *f.* amenity.—**amenizar,** *vti.* [a] to render pleasant or agreeable.—**ameno,** *a.* pleasant, agreeable; readable.

América, *f.* America.—*A. Central,* Central America.—*A. del Norte,* North America.—*A. del Sur,* South America.—*A. Latina,* Latin America.

americano, *a.* & *n.* American; South American.—*a la a.,* crew cut (haircut).—*pagar a la a.,* to go Dutch.

amerindio, *n.* American Indian, Native American.

ametralladora, *f.* machine gun, tommy gun.—**ametrallar,** *vt.* to shell; to machine-gun.

amianto, *m.* asbestos.

amiga, *f.* female friend; mistress.—**amigable,** *a.* friendly; fit, affable.

amígdala, *f.* tonsil.—**amigdalitis,** *f.* tonsilitis.

amigo, *m.* friend.—*ser a. de,* to be a friend of; to have a taste for.—*a. del alma, de confianza,* or *íntimo,* close friend.—*a. por correspondencia,* pen pal.—*a. en la prosperidad,* fairweather friend.—*interj.* well!, well!.—**amigote,** *m.* pal, chum.

amilanamiento, *m.* abject fear; terror.—**amilanar,** *vt.* to frighten; to cow.—*vr.* to become terrified; to cower, quail; to flag.

aminorar, *vt.* to lessen; to enfeeble.

amistad, *f.* friendship, friendliness.—*pl.* friends.—*hacer a.,* or *amistades,* to become acquainted; to make

friends.—*hacer las amistades,* to make up, become reconciled.—**amistoso,** *a.* friendly, amicable.

amnesia, *f.* amnesia.

amnistía, *f.* amnesty.—**amnistiar,** *vt.* to pardon, grant amnesty.

amo, *m.* master; boss.

amodorrado, *a.* drowsy, sleepy.—**amodorrarse,** *vr.* to become drowsy.

amohinarse, *vr.* to sulk.

amolador, *n.* & *a.* grinder, sharpener, whetter; grinding, sharpening, whetting.—**amoladura,** *f.* whetting, grinding.—**amolar,** *vti.* [12] to grind, sharpen, hone.

amoldar, *vt.* to mold, shape; to adjust; to adapt.—*vr.* to conform, adapt oneself.

amonestación, *f.* admonition, warning.—*pl.* banns.—*correr las amonestaciones,* to publish the banns.—**amonestar,** *vt.* to admonish, warn, advise; to publish the banns.

amoníaco, *m.* ammonia.

amontonamiento, *m.* heaping; piling; crowding.—**amontonar,** *vt.* & *vr.* to heap up, pile up; to crowd.

amor, *m.* love; lover, love; lovemaking.—*pl.* love affair.—*a. cortes,* courtly love.—*primeros a.,* puppy love.—*a. propio,* self-respect, self-esteem.—*con* or *de mil amores,* with all one's heart.

amoratado, *a.* livid, bluish.—*ojo a.,* black eye.—**amoratarse,** *vr.* to turn black and blue.

amordazar, *vti.* [a] to gag, muzzle.

amorío, *m.* love affair, romance.—**amoroso,** *a.* affectionate, loving, tender; cute, sweet.

amortajar, *vt.* to shroud (a corpse).

amortiguación, *f.,* **amortiguamiento,** *m.* softening, muffling, cushioning, deadening.—**amortiguador,** *m.* shock absorber; muffler.—**amortiguar,** *vti.* [b] to muffle; to soften; to tone down; to deaden; to cushion.

amortización, *f.* amortization.—**amortizar,** *vti.* [a] to amortize; to pay on account; to redeem (debt, etc.).

amoscarse, *vri.* [d] to get peeved, annoyed.

amotinado, *a.* mutinous, rebellious.—*n.* mutineer.—**amotinamiento,** *m.* mutiny.—**amotinar,** *vt.* to incite to mutiny or rebellion.—*vr.* to mutiny, rebel.

amovible, *a.* removable, detachable.

amparar, *vt.* to shelter; to protect,

help.—*vr.* to enjoy protection; to defend oneself; to seek shelter. **—amparo,** *m.* aid; protection; shelter.

amperaje, *m.* amperage.—**amperímetro,** *m.* amperimeter.—**amperio,** *m.* ampere.

ampliación, *f.* enlargement.—**ampliador,** *n.* amplifier.—*a.* amplifying.—**ampliar,** *vt.* to amplify; to enlarge; to magnify.—**amplificador,** *a.* amplifying.—*n.* amplifier, loudspeaker.—**amplificar,** *vti.* [d] = AMPLIAR.—**amplio,** *a.* ample, roomy, extensive, large.—**amplitud,** *f.* largeness, fullness; amplitude; extent.

ampolla, *f.* blister; decanter; water bubble; bulb.—**ampollar,** *vt.* to blister; to make hollow.—*vr.* to bubble up.—**ampolleta,** *f.* small vial; sandglass.

ampulosidad, *f.* verbosity.—**ampuloso,** *a.* pompous, bombastic.

amputación, *f.* amputation.—**amputar,** *vt.* to amputate.

amueblar, *vt.* to furnish (a room, a house, etc.).

amuleto, *m.* amulet, charm.—*a. de la buena suerte,* good-luck charm.

anacrónico, *a.* anachronistic.—**anacronismo,** *m.* anachronism.

ánade, *n.* duck; goose.

anal, anal.

analfabetismo, *m.* illiteracy.—**analfabeto,** *a.* & *n.* illiterate (person).

analgésico, *a.* analgesic.

análisis, *mf.* analysis.—*a. de sangre,* blood test.—**analista,** *mf.* analyst.—**analítico,** *a.* analytical.—**analizador,** *m.* analyzer.—**analizar,** *vti.* [a] to analyze.

analogía, *f.* analogy; resemblance.—**analógico,** *a.* (comput.) analogue.—**análogo,** *a.* analogous, similar.

anaquel, *m.* shelf.—**anaquelería,** *f.* shelving, case of shelves.

anaranjado, *a.* orange-colored.—*n.* orange (color).

anarquía, *f.* anarchy.—**anárquico,** *a.* anarchical.—**anarquismo,** *m.* anarchism.—**anarquista,** *n.* & *a.* anarchist(ic).

anatema, *m.* anathema, excommunication.—**anatematizar,** *vti.* [a] to anathematize.

anatomía, *f.* anatomy; dissection.—**anatómico,** *a.* anatomical.

anca, *f.* haunch, croup (animals); rump; hip.

ancestral, *a.* ancestral.

ancho, *a.* broad, wide—*m.* width, breadth.—*a sus anchas,* with absolute freedom.

anchoa, anchova, *f.* anchovy.

anchura, *f.* width, breadth.—**anchuroso,** *a.* vast, spacious, extensive.

ancianidad, *f.* old age.—**anciano,** *n.* & *a.* aged; old (man, woman).

ancla, áncora, *f.* anchor.—*echar anclas,* to anchor.—*levar anclas,* to weigh anchor.—**anclar,** *vi.* to anchor.

andada, *f.* walk, track, trail.—*pl.* footprints.—*volver a las andadas,* to go back to one's old tricks.—**andadura,** *f.* gait; amble (of horses).

andaluz, *n.* & *a.* Andalusian.

andamiada, *f.,* **andamiaje,** *m.* scaffolding.—**andamio,** *m.* scaffold.

andanada, *f.* broadside; grandstand for spectators; reproof; tirade.

andante, *a.* walking; (mus.) andante.—**andanza,** *f.* occurrence, event.—*pl.* rambles, wanderings.—**andar,** *vii.* [4] to walk, go; (watch, machine, etc.) to run, work, move, go; to act, behave; to elapse, pass; to be; to get along, be going.—*¡anda! ¡anda!* move on! get up! go ahead!—*a. en,* to be attending to, or engaged in; to be going on, be near; to ride in (a carriage, automobile, etc.).—*andarse con rodeos,* or *por las ramas,* to beat around the bush.—*a todo a.,* at full speed.—**andariego,** *a.* restless, roving; fast walker, runner.—**andarín,** *m.* professional walker, runner.

andas, *f. pl.* stretcher; litter; bier.

andén, *m.* sidewalk by a road, wharf or bridge; platform (of a RR. station).

andino, *a.* & *n.* Andean, of the Andes.

andrajo, *m.* rag, tatter; despicable person.—**andrajoso,** *a.* ragged, in tatters.

andurriales, *m. pl.* byroads, lonely places.

anécdota, *f.* anecdote.—**anecdótico,** *a.* anecdotal.

anegado, *a.* overflowed; wet soaked.—**anegar,** *vt.* to inundate; flood; to submerge; to flush; to drown, sink.—*vr.* to become wet or soaked; to be flooded.

anejo, *a.* = ANEXO.

anemia, *f.* anemia.—**anémico,** *a.* anemic.

anestesia, *f.* anesthesia.—**anestesia**

vt. to anesthetize.—**anestésico,** m. & a. anesthetic.

•exar, vt. to annex.—**anexión,** f. annexation.—**anexo,** a. annexed, joined.

•fibio, n. amphibian.—a. amphibious.

•fiteatro, m. amphitheater, lecture hall, auditorium.

•fitrión, m. host.—**anfitriona,** f. hostess.

•garillas, f. pl. handbarrow; panniers; cruet stands.

•gel, m. angel.—a. custodio, guardián, or de la guarda, guardian angel. —**angélico,** a. angelic(al).

•gina, f. angina.—pl. sore throat.—a. de pecho, angina pectoris.

•glófono, angloparlante, a. English-speaking.

•glosajón, a. & m. Anglo-Saxon.

•gostar, vt. & vr. to narrow; to become narrow, contract.—**angosto,** a. narrow.—**angostura,** f. narrowness; narrows (in a river, etc.).

•guila, f. eel.—a. eléctrica, electric eel.

•gular, a. angular.—a. muerto, blind spot.—a. recto, right angle.—piedra a., cornerstone.—**ángulo,** m. angle.—**anguloso,** a. angular, sharp; full of bends.

•gustia, f. anguish, grief, sorrow. —**angustiar,** vt. to cause anguish, distress.—**angustioso,** a. full of, or causing, anguish.

•helante, a. eager, yearning, longing.—**anhelar,** vi. to desire anxiously, long for, covet.—**anhelo,** m. strong desire; longing; panting.— **anheloso,** a. anxious, panting.

•idar, vi. to nest; to nestle; to dwell; to shelter.—vr. to nest; to settle (in a place).

•ilina, f. aniline.

•illa, f. ring; curtain ring; hoop. —**anillado,** a. in the form of a ring, annulated.—**anillo,** m. ring.—a. de boda, a. nupcial, wedding ring.—a. de compromiso, a. de pedida, engagement ring.

•ima, f. soul; (mil.) bore (of a gun). —**animación,** f. activity, liveliness; (cin.) animation.—**animado,** a. lively, animated.—**animador,** m. master of ceremonies, presenter; events organizer; cheerleader.—a. encouraging.—**animadversion,** f. animosity, antagonism.

•imal, m. animal; dunce, blockhead.—a. mimado or casero, pet.— a. animal; stupid, brutish.

animar, vt. to animate, give life; to encourage.—vr. liven up; to cheer up.—**ánimo,** m. spirit, soul; courage.—**animosidad,** f. animosity; courage.—**animoso,** a. brave, spirited.

aniñado, a. childish.—**aniñarse,** vr. to become childish.

aniquilamiento, m. destruction, annihilation.—**aniquilar,** vt. to annihilate, wipe out.

anís, m. anise, anisette; licorice.

aniversario, m. anniversary.—a. annual, yearly.

ano, m. anus.

anoche, adv. last night.—**anochecer,** vii. [3] to grow dark (at the approach of night).—m. nightfall, dusk.— **anochecida,** f. nightfall.

anodino, n. & a. anodyne; insignificant.

anonadamiento, m. annihilation; crushing.—**anonadar,** vt. to annihilate; to crush, overwhelm.

anónimo, a. anonymous.—m. anonymous letter.

anormal, a. abnormal.—**anormalidad,** f. abnormality.

anotación, f. note; (Am.) goal, touchdown, point.—**anotar,** vt. to make a note of.—vi. (Am.) to score.—vr. to sign up.

ansia, f. anxiety; eagerness; anguish; longing.—pl. nausea.—**ansiar,** vt. to long for.—**ansiedad,** f. anxiety; worry.—**ansioso,** a. anxious; eager.

antagónico, a. antagonistic.—**antagonismo,** m. antagonism.—**antagonista,** mf. antagonist; opponent.

antaño, adv. yesteryear; yore.

antártico, a. antarctic.

ante, prep. before; in the presence of.—a. todo, above all.—m. elk; buffalo; buffalo skin; suede.

anteanoche, adv. night before last.

anteayer, adv. day before yesterday.

antebrazo, m. forearm.

antecámara, f. antechamber; lobby.

antecedente, a. & m. antecedent. —**antecesor,** n. predecessor, forefather.

antedatar, vt. to antedate.

antedicho, a. aforesaid.

antelación, f. precedence in order of time.

antemano, a. beforehand.—de a., beforehand.

antena, *f.* antenna, aerial.—*a. de conejo,* (rad./TV) rabbit ears.—*a. parabólica,* dish antenna, satellite dish.

antenoche, *adv.* = ANTEANOCHE.

anteojo, *m.* telescope.—**anteojos,** *m. pl.* eyeglasses, spectacles.—*a. bifocales,* bifocals.—*a. de larga vista,* binoculars.—*a. de sol,* sunglasses —*a. de teatro,* opera glasses.—*a. opticos,* prescription glasses.—*a. oscuros,* dark glasses.

antepasado, *a.* (of time) passed.—*año a.,* year before last.—*n.* ancestor.

antepecho, *m.* railing; window sill.

anteponer, *vti.* [32] to prefer; to place before.

anterior, *a.* previous; earlier; former; above, preceding.—**anterioridad,** *f.* priority.—*con a.* beforehand.

antes, *adv.* before; formerly; first; rather.—*a. bien,* on the contrary; rather.—*a. de Cristo,* Before Christ (B.C.).

antesala, *f.* anteroom, waiting room.—*hacer a.,* to be kept waiting.

antiácido, *a.* & *m.* antacid.

antiadherente, *a.* nonstick.

antiaéreo, *a.* antiaircraft.

antibalas, *a.* bulletproof.

antibalístico, *a.* antiballistic.

antibelicista, *a.* antiwar.—*mf.* pacifist.

antibiótico, *m.* & *a.* antibiotic.

anticipación, *f.* anticipation.—*con a.,* in advance.—**anticipado,** *a.* early, ahead of time.—*por a.,* in advance.—**anticipar,** *vt.* to anticipate (in the sense of "to do, cause to happen," etc., before the regular time); to advance (money, payment); to lend; to move up (a date).—*vr.* to anticipate, act first; to happen earlier than the expected time.—**anticipo,** *m.* advance; advance payment; (law) retainer.

anticomunista, *mf.* & *a.* anticommunist.

anticongelante, *m.* & *a.* antifreeze.

anticuado, *a.* antiquated, old-fashioned; obsolete.—**anticuario,** *n.* & *a.* antiquarian.

anticuerpo, *m.* antibody.

antideslizante, *m.* & *a.* antiskid, nonskid.

antidetonante, *m.* & *a.* antiknock.

antídoto, *m.* antidote.

antier, *adv.* (Am.) V. ANTEAYER.

antiestético, *a.* unattractive.

antifaz, *m.* veil that covers the face; mask.

antigualla, *f.* piece of junk, relic.—**antigüedad,** *f.* antiquity; ancien times; antique; seniority.—**antiguo** *a.* antique; ancient, old.—*a la a.* after the manner of the ancients, i an old-fashioned manner.—*A. Tes tamento, m.* (igl.) Old Testament.—*de a.,* since old times.—*los antiguos* the ancients.

antihigiénico, *a.* unsanitary.

antihistamínico, *a.* antihistamine.

antillano, *n.* & *a.* West Indian.

Antillas, *fpl.* West Indies.

antílope, *m.* antelope.

antimanchas, *a.* stain-resistant.

antimateria, *f.* antimatter.

antimisil, *a.* antiballistic.—*m.* antiba listic missile.

antimonio, *m.* antimony.

antinomía, *f.* antinomy; contradic tion; paradox.

antipatía, *f.* antipathy; dislike, aver sion.—**antipático,** *a.* unfriendly disagreeable.

antipatriótico, *a.* unpatriotic.

antípoda, *a.* antipodal.—*m. pl.* an típodes.

antisemita, *a.* anti-Semitic.—*mf.* ant Semite.

antisemítico, *a.* anti-Semitism.

antisemitismo, *m.* anti-Semitism.

antiséptico, *n.* & *a.* antiseptic.

antojadizo, antojado, *a.* capriciou whimsical, fanciful.—**antojarse,** *v* to arouse a fancy; to cause a capr cious desire.—*se me antojó,* I took fancy to.—**antojo,** *m.* whim, fanc birth mark.—*a su a.,* as one please arbitrarily.

antología, *f.* anthology.

antorcha, *f.* torch.

antracita, *f.* anthracite.

antro, *m.* bar, dive.—*a. de corrupcio* den of iniquity.

antropología, *f.* anthropology.

antropófago, *a.* cannibalistic.—*m* cannibal.

anual, *a.* annual, yearly.—**anualidad,** *f.* annuity.—**anuario,** *m.* yearboo trade or professional directory.—*telefónico,* telephone directory.

anudar, *vt.* to knot; to tie, unite.

anuencia, *f.* compliance, consent.

anulación, *f.* annulment; cancellatio overturning.—**anular,** *vt.* to annu make void; to cancel, quash.—ring-shaped.—*dedo a.,* ring finger.

anunciador, *n.* & *a.* announcer, a nouncing; advertiser, advert ing.—**anunciante,** *n.* announce advertiser.—**anunciar,** *vt.* to announce; to advertise; to foretell.—**anuncio,** *m.* announcement; notice; advertisement.—*anuncios breves, clasificados,* or *por palabras,* classified advertisements, want ads.

zuelo, *m.* fishhook; lure.

adidura, *f.* addition, increase; extra, over.—*por a.,* in addition, to make matters worse.—**añadir,** *vt.* to add, join.

ejo, *a.* old; of old vintage; stale.

cos, *m. pl.* shreds, fragments.—*hacer a.,* to shatter.

l, *m.* indigo; indigo blue.—**añilar,** *vt.* to blue (clothes).

o, *m.* year.—*al a.,* by the year; after a year.—*a. bisiesto,* leap year.*a. económico,* or *fiscal,* fiscal year.—*a. escolar,* school year.—*a. luz,* light year.—*A. Nuevo,* New Year.—*¡Feliz A. Nuevo!,* Happy New Year!—*a. sabático,* (de los profesores) sabbatical.—*tener 10 años,* to be 10 years old.—**añoso,** *a.* old, aged.

oranza, *f.* yearning.—**añorar,** *vt.* to yearn for.—*vi.* to pine, grieve.

abullar, *vt.* to flatten, crush.

acentar, *vti.* [1] to graze, pasture; (fig.) to nourish.

achurrar, *vt.* to squash.

acible, *a.* gentle, placid, calm.

aciguamiento, *m.* pacification, appeasement.—**apaciguar,** *vti.* [b] to appease, pacify.

adrinar, *vt.* to sponsor; to favor; to protect; to be godfather at a christening; to be best man at a wedding; to act as a second in a duel.

agado, *a.* switched off; extinct; muffled; lifeless, spiritless.

agar, *vti.* [b] to put out, extinguish; to turn off; to soften; to deaden.—*vri.* to become extinguished, die out; to go out.—**apagón,** *m.* blackout.

aisado, *a.* squat, flattened.

alabrar, *vt.* to make an arrangement; to come to an agreement; to speak about, discuss; to engage.

alancar, *vti.* [d] to jack up, to jack open.

alear, *vt.* to beat up; to thrash.

añar, *vt.* to grasp, seize; to fix, rig; to cover up.

arador, *m.* sideboard, buffet; store window.

arato, *m.* apparatus; appliance; pomp, show; system.—*a. eléctrico,* thunder and lightning.—*aparatos sanitarios,* bathroom fixtures.—**aparatoso,** *a.* pompous, showy.

aparcamiento, *m.* parking; parking lot.—**aparcar,** *vt.* & *vi.* to park.—*a. en doble fila;* to double-park.—*prohibido a.* no parking.

aparear, *vt.* to match, mate; to pair.

aparecer, *vii.* & *vri.* [3] to appear, show up, turn up.—**aparecido,** *n.* ghost, specter.

aparejado, *a.* fit; ready; equipped.—**aparejar,** *vt.* qto prepare; to saddle or harness; to rig; to equip.—*vr.* to get ready; to equip oneself.—**aparejo,** *m.* preparation; harness; gear; packsaddle; tackle; rigging.—*pl.* equipment, trappings.

aparentar, *vt.* to feign, pretend.—**aparente,** *a.* apparent.

aparición, *f.* apparition; appearance (coming in sight); ghost.

apariencia, *f.* appearance, aspect; probability; semblance.

apartadero, *m.* (RR.) siding.

apartado, *a.* distant, remote, isolated.—*m.* section, paragraph.—*a. de coreos, a. postal,* post office box.—*a. de localidades,* (teat.) ticket agency.—**apartamento,** *m.* apartment.—**apartamiento,** *m.* separation; retirement; aloofness; secluded place; (Am.) apartment.—**apartar,** *vt.* to set apart; to separate, divide; to dissuade; to remove; to sort.—*vr.* to withdraw; to hold off; to desist; to retire; to separate.—**aparte,** *m.* paragraph; (theat.) aside.—*adv.* separately; aside.

apartheid, *m.* apartheid.

apasionado, *a.* passionate; impassioned, warm-blooded; partial.—*n.* admirer.—**apasionamiento,** *m.* passion; partiality.—**apasionar,** *vt.* to rouse, excite, thrill; to fill with passion.—*vr.* to become impassioned, passionately fond; to fall passionately in love.

apatía, *f.* apathy.—**apático,** *a.* apathetic.

apeadero, *m.* whistle stop, halt.—**apear,** *vr.* to get off; to climb down.

apechugar, *vti.* [b] to face up to.—*a. con,* to put up with something courageously; to accept.

apedrear, *vt.* to stone.

apegarse, *vri.* [b] to become attached to; to become fond of.—**apego,** *m.* attachment, fondness.

apelable, *a.* appealable.—**apelación,** *f.* appeal; remedy, help.—**apelar,** *vt.* &

vi. to appeal; to have recourse to.
—apelativo, *m.* name.

apellidado, *a.* named (last name), by the name of.**—apellidar,** *vt.* to call by name (last name).**—vr.** to be called (have the last name of). **—apellido,** *m.* family name, last name.

apelotonar, *vt.* & *vr.* to form into balls; to pile up.

apenar, *vt.* & *vr.* to cause pain, sorrow; to grieve; (Am.) to cause embarrassment, shame.

apenas, *adv.* scarcely, hardly; no sooner than; as soon as.

apéndice, *m.* appendix.**—apendicitis,** *f.* appendicitis.

apercibimiento, *m.* readiness; warning; summons.**—apercibir,** *vt.* to provide; to prepare; to warn, advise; to summon.**—vr.** (a) to get ready (to).**—a. de,** to notice.

apergaminado, *a.* like parchment; dried up.

aperitivo, *m.* apertif; appetizer.

apero, *m.* farm implement; tool.**—pl.** equipment (for an activity).

apertura, *f.* (act of) opening or beginning; (fot.) aperture.

apesadumbrar, *vt.* & *vi.* to grieve; to make (become) sad, grief-stricken.

apestado, *a.* & *n.* pestered, annoyed; satiated.**—apestar,** *vt.* to infect with the plague; to corrupt, turn putrid; to annoy, bother; to sicken, nauseate.**—vi.** to stink.**—apestoso,** *a.* stinking, sickening; offensive; boring.

apetecer, *vti.* [3] to hunger for; to like; to desire.**—vii.** to be desirable, appetizing.**—apetecible,** *a.* desirable; appetizing.**—apetencia,** *f.* appetite, hunger; desire.**—apetito,** *m.* appetite; appetence.**—apetitoso,** *a.* appetizing, inviting, palatable.

apiadarse, *vr.* (de) to pity, take pity (on).

ápice, *m.* apex, summit, top; pinnacle.

apilar, *vt.* to heap, pile up.

apiñado, *a.* crowded, close together. **—apiñamiento,** *m.* pressing together; crowding, congestion.**—apiñar,** *vt.* & *vr.* to press together; crowd.

apio, *m.* celery.

apisonadora, *f.* road roller, steamroller.

apisonar, *vt.* to roll flat, to tamp down.

aplacar, *vti.* [d] to appease, soothe.

aplanamiento, *m.* leveling, flattening.**—aplanar,** *vt.* to make

level.**—vr.** to tumble down; to g●
depressed.

aplastante, *a.* crushing, overpowe●
ing.**—aplastar,** *vt.* to smash, crush
squash; to confound.**—vr.** to fla●
ten; to collapse.

aplaudir, *vt.* to applaud, clap; to ap●
prove; to praise.**—aplause,** *m.* ap●
plause; clapping; approbation.

aplazamiento, *m.* postponement; a●
journment.**—aplazar,** *vti.* [a] t●
postpone; to adjourn.

aplicable, *a.* applicable, suitable, fi●
ting.**—aplicación,** *f.* application
studiousness; diligence.**—aplicad●
a. applied, studious; industriou●
—aplicar, *vti.* [d] to apply; to put on
—vri. to apply oneself.

aplomado, *a.* self-confident. plumbe●
vertical.**—aplomar,** *vt.* to mak●
straight or vertical, to plumb.**—v**
to plumb, be vertical.**—vr.** to settl●
down.**—aplomo,** *m.* self-assuranc●
aplomb; verticalness.

apocado, *a.* pusillanimous, timi●
—apocar, *vti.* [d] to lessen; to b●
little.**—vri.** to belittle oneself.

apodar, *vt.* to nickname.

apoderado, *n.* proxy; attorney.**—ap●
derar,** *vt.* to empower; to gra●
power of attorney to.**—apoderars**
de, to take possession of, seize.

apodo, *m.* nickname.

apogeo, *m.* apogee; height.

apolillado, *a.* motheaten.**—apolill●
dura,** *f.* moth hole.**—apolillarse, ●
to be motheaten.

apolítico, *a.* non-political.

apología, *f.* apologia, defense, praise.

apoltronarse, *vr.* to grow lazy.

aporreado, *a.* miserable.**—aporrear,**
to beat; to pester.**—vr.** to overwor●
to become overtired.**—aporreo, r●
beating.

aportación, *f.,* **aporte,** *m.* contrib●
tion.**—aportar,** *vi.* to contribute; ●
make port; to arrive.

apósito, *m.* (med.) dressing.

aposta, *adv.* on purpose.

apostadero, *m.* naval station.

apostador, *m.* bettor.**—apostar,** v●
[12] to bet; to post, station.**—a.**
que, to bet that.**—apostárselas a, ●
con, to compete with.

apostasia, *f.* apostasy.**—apóstata, m**
& *a.* apostate.

apóstol, *m.* apostle.**—apostolado, r●
apostleship.**—apostólico,** *a.* apo●
tolic.

apostrofar, *vt.* to apostrophize.**—apo●**

trofe, *f.* apostrophe.—**apóstrofo,** *m.* apostrophe (').

apostura, *f.* natural elegance, graceful bearing.

apoyapiés, *m.* footrest.

apoyar, *vt.* to rest, lean, support; to back, defend; to aid; to abet.—*vi.* (en or sobre) to rest (on).—*vr.* (en) to rest (on); to lean (on or against); to be supported (by); to be based (on).—**apoyo,** *m.* prop, stay; support; protection, aid; backing.

apoyatura, *f.* (mus.) grace note.

apreciable, *a.* appreciable, considerable; worthy of esteem; valuable. —**apreciación,** *f.* estimation, valuation; appreciation.—**apreciar,** *vt.* to appreciate, price, value; to esteem.—**aprecio,** *m.* esteem, high regard; appraisement, valuation.

aprehender, *vt.* to apprehend, arrest, seize.—**aprehensión,** *f.* seizure, capture; apprehension; fear.

apremiante, *a.* urgent, pressing.— **apremiar,** *vt.* to press, urge; to compel, oblige.—**apremio,** *m.* pressure, constraint; judicial compulsion.

aprender, *vt. & vi.* to learn.—**aprendiz,** *n.* apprentice.—**aprendizaje,** *m.* apprenticeship.

aprensión, *f.* apprehension; scruple; fear; distrust, suspicion.—**aprensivo,** *a.* apprehensive, overanxious.

apresar, *vt.* to seize, grasp; to capture; to imprison.

aprestar, *vt.* to prepare, make ready; to size.—*vr.* to get ready.

apresurado, *a.* hasty, quick.—**apresuramiento,** *m.* hastiness, quickness.—**apresurar,** *vt.* to hurry, hasten.—*vr.* to make haste, hurry up.

apretado, *a.* tight; dense; difficult. —**apretar,** *vti.* [1] to tighten; to press down, compress; to clench (teeth, fist); to grip (hand in greeting); to squeeze; to urge.—*vii.* to pinch (of shoes, etc.); to be tight (of clothes).—**apretón,** *m.* struggle, conflict; squeeze; short run, spurt.—*a. de manos,* handshake. —**apretujar,** *vt.* (coll.) to squeeze tightly.—**aprieto,** *m.* predicament.

aprisa, *adv.* quickly, hurriedly, promptly; fast.

aprisionar, *vt.* to imprison; to trap.

aprobación, *f.* approval, consent.— **aprobar,** *vti.* [12] to approve; to pass (in an examination).

aprontar, *vt.* to prepare quickly; to make ready; to expedite.

apropiación, *f.* appropriation.—**apropiado,** *a.* appropriate. —**apropiar,** *vt.* to adapt; to fit.—*apropiarse de,* to take illegal possession of.

aprovechable, *a.* available, usable.— **aprovechado,** *a.* saving, thrifty, studious.—*n.* go-getter.—**aprovechamiento,** *m.* utilization, exploitation.—**aprovechar,** *vt.* to utilize, make good use of.—*vi.* to be useful, profitable or beneficial; to progress, get ahead.—*aprovecharse de,* to take advantage of, make the most of.

aprovisionar, *vt.* to supply.

aproximación, *f.* approximation; approach.—**aproximado,** *a.* approximate.—**aproximar,** *vt.* to place or bring near; to approximate.—*vr.* to get approach.

aptitud, *f.* aptitude, natural ability.— *pl.* qualifications.—**apto,** *a.* suitable; capable.

apuesta, *f.* bet, wager.

apuesto, *a.* elegant, stylish; handsome.

apuntación, *f.* note; musical notation.—**apuntador,** *n.* (theat.) prompter.

apuntalar, *vt.* to prop; to shore up.

apuntar, *vt.* to aim, level; to point out, mark; to note, make a note of; to hint; to sketch; (theat.) to prompt.—*vi.* to begin to appear. —**apunte,** *m.* annotation, memorandum; rough sketch.

apuñalar, *vt.* to stab.—**apuñear,** *vt.* (fam.) to punch, pummel.

apurado, *a.* worried; needy; exhausted; difficult; in haste; hard up.—**apurar,** *vt.* to drain to the last drop; to exhaust (a subject); to press, hurry; to worry, annoy.—*vr.* to hurry up; to get worried.—**apuro,** *m.* need, want; worry; plight, predicament, quandary; rush, hurry.

aquejar, *vt.* to grieve, afflict, ail.

aquel (*fem.* **aquella**), *a.* that (over there).—*pl.* those (yonder).—**aquél** (*fem.* **aquélla**), *pron.* that one; the former; those.—**aquello,** *pron. neut.* that, that thing, that matter.

aquí, *adv.* here; hither.—*de a. en adelante,* from now on, hereafter.— *hasta a.,* up till now.—*por a.,* this way, through here.

aquiescencia, *f.* (law) acquiescence.

aquietar, *vt.* to quiet; to pacify.—*vr.* to become calm; to quiet down.

aquilatar, *vt.* to examine closely; to assay.

ara, *f.* altar.

árabe, *mf.* Arab.—*a.* Arabian; Arabic.—**arábigo,** *a.* Arabian, Arabic.—*número a.*, Arabic numeral.

arado, *m.* plow; (Am.) piece of cultivated land.

aragonés, *n.* & *a.* Aragonese.

arancel, *m.* tariff.—*a. de aduanas,* customs, duty.—**arancelario,** *a.* pertaining to tariff.

arandela, *f.* (mech.) washer; pan of a candlestick; sconce.

araña, *f.* spider; chandelier.

arañar, *vt.* to scratch.—**arañazo,** *m.* scratch.

arar, *vt.* to plow.

arbitraje, *m.* arbitration.—**arbitrar,** *vt.* to arbitrate; to umpire; to act unhampered; to contrive.—**arbitrariedad,** *f.* arbitrariness; arbitrary act.—**arbitrario,** *a.* arbitrary; arbitral.—**arbitrio,** *m.* free will; means; arbitration; bond; compromise; discretion, judgment.—**árbitro,** *m.* arbitrator, arbiter, umpire, referee.

árbol, *m.* tree; mast; upright post; axle or shaft; arbor; spindle; drill.—*á. del caucho,* rubber plant.—*a. de Navidad, a. de Pascua,* Christmas tree.—*a. genealógico,* family tree.—**arbolado,** *a.* wooded; masted.—*á. muy joven,* sapling.—*m.* woodland.—**arboleda,** *f.* grove.—**arbusto,** *m.* shrub.

arca, *f.* ark; chest, coffer.—*a. de agua,* water tower.—*A. de la Alianza,* Ark of the Covenant.—*A. de Noé,* Noah's Ark.

arcada, *f.* arcade; row of arches.—*pl.* retching.

arcaico, *a.* archaic.

arcángel, *m.* archangel.

arcano, *a.* arcane.—*m.* mystery.

arce, *m.* maple, maple tree.

archimillonario, *a.* & *n.* multimillionaire.

archipiélago, *m.* archipelago.

archivar, *vt.* to file; to deposit in archives.—**archivero,** *n.* archivist; filecase, file-drawers.—**archivo,** *m.* archives; file; public records.—*a. de datos,* data file.—*a. de delincuentes, a. fotográfico,* rogues' gallery.

arcilla, *f.* clay.

arco, *m.* arc; arch; bow.—*a. iris,* rainbow.—*a. triunfal, a. de triunfo,* triumphal arch, memorial arch.

arcón, *m.* large chest; bin, bunker.—*a. del ajuar,* hope chest.

arder, *vi.* to burn; to rage (of war, etc.); to be consumed.—*a. en rescoldo,* to smolder.

ardid, *m.* trick, scheme, stratagem.

ardiente, *a.* ardent, burning; passionate, fervent.

ardilla, *f.* squirrel.—*a. ladradora,* prairie dog.

ardor, *m.* ardor; hotness, heat; dash, valor.—**ardoroso,** *a.* ardent; fiery, vigorous.

arduo, *a.* arduous.

área, *f.* area; square decameter (See Table).—*a. de reposo,* rest area.—*a. de servicio,* service area.

arena, *f.* sand, grit; arena.—*a. movediza,* quicksand.—**arenal,** *m.* sandy ground; desert; sand pit.—**arenero,** *m.* sand dealer; (R.R.) sandbox.

arenga, *f.* harangue, speech.—**arengar,** *vii.* [b] to harangue, deliver a speech.

arenque, *m.* herring.

arete, *m.* earring.

argamasa, *f.* mortar.

argelino, *a.* & *n.* Algerian.

argentado, *a.* silvered, silver-plated.—**argentar,** *vt.* to plate or adorn with silver; to polish like silver.—**argentino,** *a.* & *n.* Argentinian.—*a.* silvery.

argolla, *f.* ring; staple; hoop.

argótico, *a.* slang.

aguardiente, *m.* eau-de-vie; firewater.

argucia, *f.* trick, subtlety.

argülr, *vii.* & *vti.* [23-e] to argue, indicate, imply.—**argumentación,** *f.* argumentation; reasoning.—**argumentar,** *vi.* to argue, dispute.—**argumento,** *m.* argument; summary; plot (of a play, etc.).

aridez, *f.* barrenness, aridity.—**árido,** *a.* arid, dry, barren.—*pl.* dry goods; grains.

Aries, *m.* (astr.) Aries.

ariete, *m.* battering ram.

ario, *n.* & *a.* Aryan.

arisco, *a.* unfriendly, unsociable.

arista, *f.* sharp edge or angle.

aristocracia, *f.* aristocracy.—**aristócrata,** *mf.* & *a.* aristocrat.

aritmética, *f.* arithmetic.—**aritmético,** *a.* arithmetical.—*m.* arithmetician.

arma, *f.* weapon, arm; means, power, reason.—*pl.* armed forces; military profession.—*a. de fuego,* firearm.—**armada,** *f.* navy; fleet; squadron.—*A. Invencible,* Spanish Armada.—**armador,** *n.* ship owner; adjuster, fitter, assembler.—**armadura,** *f.* armor; framework, shell of a building; (mus.) key signature.—**armamento**, *m.* armament.—**armar**, *vt.* to arm; to man; to bind; to assemble, mount; to adjust, set, frame; to reinforce (concrete); to form, prepare; to start, cause; (naut.) to equip, fit out, put in commission.—*vr.* to prepare oneself; to arm oneself.

armario, *m.* wardrobe; clothes closet; cabinet; bookcase.—*a. cerrado con llave*, locker.—*a. para la ropa blanca*, linen closet.

armatoste, *m.* hulk; unwieldy piece of furniture.

armazón, *f.* framework, skeleton, frame; hulk (of a ship).

armenio, *a.* & *n.* Armenian.

armería, *f.* museum of arms; gunsmith's shop.—**armero**, *m.* armorer, gunsmith; keeper of arms.

armiño, *m.* ermine.

armisticio, *m.* armistice.

armonía, *f.* harmony.—**armónica**, *f.*—*a. de boca*, mouth organ.—**armónico**, *a.* harmonious.—**armonio**, *m.* harmonium, reed organ.—**armonioso**, *a.* harmonious.—**armonización**, *f.* harmonization.—**armonizar**, *vti.* & *vii.* [a] to harmonize.

arnés, *m.* harness; coat of mail.

aro, *m.* hoop, rim; staple; earring; wedding band; arum.—*entrar por el a.*, to be forced to yield.

aroma, *m.* aroma; perfume, fragrance.—**aromático**, *a.* aromatic, fragrant.—**aromatizar**, *vti.* [a] to perfume.

arpa, *f.* harp.

arpía, *f.* shrew, harpy; fiend.

arpillera, *f.* sackcloth, burlap.

arpón, *m.* harpoon.—**arponear**, *vt.* to harpoon.—**arponero**, *n.* harpooner.

arquear, *vt.* to arch; to beat (wool); to gauge (ships).—*vr.* to arch, become arched.—**arqueo**, *m.* arching; balance (in accounting); (naut.) tonnage.

arquería, *f.* series of arches; arcade; archery.—**arquero**, *n.* cashier; archer; (sports) goalkeeper.

arquetipo, *m.* archetype.

arquitecto, *m.* architect.—**arquitectónico**, *a.* architectural.—**arquitectura**, *f.* architecture.

arrabal, *m.* outlying district.—*pl.* outskirts, slums.—**arrabalero**, *a.* ill-bred.

arracimarse, *vr.* to cluster.

arraigado, *a.* inveterate, fixed.—

arraigar, *vii.* [b] to take root.—*vri.* to settle, establish oneself; to take root.—**arraigo**, *m.* establishment, hold, influence; property, land.

arrancada, *f.* sudden start.—**arrancado**, *a.* (Am.) broke, penniless.—**arrancadero**, *m.* starting point.—**arrancar**, *vti.* [d] to root out, extirpate; to pull out, tear off.—*vii.* to start.—**arranque**, *m.* sudden start, sudden impulse; (aut.) starter.

arrasar, *vt.* to level, raze, demolish.—*vi.* to clear up (of sky).

arrastrado, *a.* miserable, wretched.—*n.* downcast one.—**arrastrar**, *vt.* to drag; to drag down, degrade.—*vi.* to drag along the ground; to play a trump (in cards).—*vr.* to crawl, creep, drag along; to grovel.—**arrastre**, *m.* dragging; haulage.

arrayán, *m.* myrtle.

¡arre! *interj.* gee, get up!—**arrear**, *vt.* to drive (horses, etc.).

arrebatado, *a.* rash, impetuous; sudden, violent.—**arrebatador**, *a.* ravishing.—**arrebatar**, *vt.* to snatch; to enrapture, captivate.—*vr.* to be carried away by passion.—**arrebato**, *m.* sudden attack, fit; rapture, ecstasy.

arrebol, *m.* redness; rouge; red sky or clouds.—**arrebolar**, *vr.* to redden.

arrebujar, *vt.* to jumble together; to wrap.—*vr.* to wrap oneself up.

arrechucho, *m.* fit of anger.

arreciar, *vt.* & *vi.* to increase in strength or intensity.

arrecife, *m.* reef.

arredrar, *vt.* to scare, intimidate.—*vr.* to be intimidated.

arreglar, *vt.* to arrange; to adjust, settle; to regulate.—*vr.* to tidy oneself up; to turn out right; to settle differences, come to an agreement; to compromise.—**arreglo**, *m.* disposition, arrangement; adjustment; repair; (com.) agreement; compromise, settlement.—*a. floral*, flower arrangement.—*con a. a*, according to; in accordance with.

arrellanarse, *vr.* to sit at ease, make oneself comfortable.

arremangar, *vti.* [b] to tuck up, turn up, roll up (the sleeves, etc.).—*vri.* to roll up one's sleeves.

arremeter, *vt.* to assail, attack.—**arremetida**, *f.* attack, assault.

arremolinarse, *vr.* to whirl; to crowd together; to mill around.

arrendador, *n.* hirer; tenant.—**arren-**

dar, *vti.* [1] to rent, let, lease, hire.—**arrendatario**, *n.* lessee, tenant.

arreo, *m.* ornament, decoration.—*pl.* harness, trappings, accessories.—*adv.* successively, uninterruptedly.

arrepentido, *a.* remorseful, repentant.—**arrepentimiento**, *m.* repentance.—**arrepentirse**, *vri.* [39] to repent, regret.

arrestado, *a.* bold, audacious. —**arrestrar**, *vt.* to arrest, imprison.—*vr.* (Am.) to dare.—**arresto**, *m.* imprisonment, arrest; spirit, enterprise.—*a. domiciliario*, house arrest.—*a. preventivo*, preventive detention.

arriar, *vt.* to lower, strike (a flag).

arriba, *adv.* up, above, high; upstairs; upwards; overhead.—*a. de*, above; higher up.—*cuesta a.*, uphill.—*de a. a abajo*, from top to bottom; up and down.—*para a.*, upwards.—*por a.*, at, or from, the top.—*por a. de*, above, over.—*interj.* up!—**arribada**, *f.* arrival (of a ship).—**arribar**, *vi.* to put into port; to reach; to recover; to prosper by dubious means.—**arribo**, *m.* = ARRIBADA.

arriendo, *m.* renting; lease; rent.

arriero, *m.* muleteer.

arriesgar, *vti.* [b] to risk, hazard, jeopardize.—*vri.* to venture; to dare; to run a risk.

arrimar, *vt.* to place near; to stow; to put away, lay aside.—*vr.* to go near (to); to seek the protection (of); to join.—**arrimo**, *m.* support, protection.

arrinconar, *vt.* to corner; to put away, lay aside.—*vr.* to retire.

arriscado, *a.* bold, rash; craggy.

arroba, *f.* weight of twenty-five pounds.

arrobador, *a.* enchanting, entrancing.—**arrobamiento, arrobo**, *m.* rapture, bliss; trance.—**arrobarse**, *vr.* to be enraptured.

arrocero, *m.* rice planter or dealer.—*a.* pertaining to rice.

arrodillar, *vr.* to kneel down.

arrogancia, *f.* arrogance; stately carriage.—**arrogante**, *a.* arrogant; imposing, spirited, dashing.

arrogar, *vri.* to assume (power or rights).

arrojado, *a.* rash, dashing, fearless. —**arrojar**, *vt.* to throw, fling; to cast out; to dismiss, drive out.—*vr.* to throw oneself.—*a. a, a en*, to rush or plunge into.—**arrojo**, *m.* fearlessness, dash, boldness.

arrollador, *a.* overwhelming, violent, sweeping.—**arrollar**, *vt.* to roll up; to carry off, sweep away; to trample, run over; to defeat, destroy.

arropar, *vt.* to cover, wrap.—*vr.* to wrap oneself, bundle up.

arrostrar, *vt.* to defy, face.

arroyo, *m.* small stream, brook; gutter.—**arroyuelo**, *m.* rivulet, rill.

arroz, *m.* rice.—*a. con leche*, rice pudding.—*a. integral*, brown rice.—*a. salvaje*, wild rice.—**arrozal**, *m.* rice field.

arruga, *f.* wrinkle, crease.—**arrugar**, *vti.* [b] to wrinkle; to crease, crumple.—*vri.* to become wrinkled, creased or crumpled; (Am.) to become intimidated.

arruinar, *vt.* to ruin; to bankrupt.—*vr.* to become ruined.

arrullador, *a.* lulling, soothing.—**arrullar**, *vt.* to lull; to coo.—**arrullo**, *m.* cooing; lullaby.

arrumaco, *m.* caress, fondling.

arrumbar, *vt.* to put away as useless; to silence; to remove from a trust; (naut.) to determine the direction.—*vi.* to take bearings.

arsenal, *m.* shipyard, navy yard; arsenal, armory.

arsénico, *a.* arsenic.

arte, *m.* art; skill, craft; trade, profession; artifice, device; intrigue.—*a. de vender*, salesmanship.—*pl.* arts.—*a. de pesca*, (mar.) nets.—*a. menores*, crafts.—*a. y oficios*, arts and crafts.—*bellas artes*, fine arts.—**artefacto**, *m.* artefact; device; appliance.—*artefactos de baño, artefactos sanitarios*, bathroom fixtures.

arteria, *f.* artery; trunk or main line; main highway.

artería, *f.* cunning, artfulness.—**artero**, *a.* cunning, artful.

artesa, *f.* trough.

artesanía, *f.* workmanship, artisanship.—*pl.* handicrafts, craftwork.—**artesano**, *n.* artisan, craftsman.

artesiano, *a.* artesian.

artesonado, *a.* paneled (ceiling).

ártico, *a.* arctic.

articulación, *m.* articulation, joint.—*a. de rótula*, ball-and-socket joint.—**articulado**, *a.* jointed; articulate.—**articular**, *vt.* to unite, join; to articulate.—*a.* articular.—**artículo**, *m.* article.—*a. de fondo*, editorial.—*a. determinado* or *definido*, definite article.—*a. indeterminado* or *indefinido*, indefinite article.—*artículos de deporte*, sporting goods.—*artículos de perfumeria* or *tocador*, toiletries.

artifice, *mf.* artisan, craftsman.—**artificial,** *a.* artificial; sophisticated.—**artificio,** *m.* workmanship; craft; artifice; cunning; trick, ruse; contrivance, device.—**artificioso,** *a.* skillful, ingenious; artful, cunning, contrived.

artillar, *vt.* to mount (cannon).—**artillería,** *f.* artillery.—*a. antiaérea*, antiaircraft artillery.—**artillero,** *m.* artilleryman, gunner.

artimaña, *f.* trap, snare, trick.

artista, *a.* & *mf.* artist; actor; actress.—**artístico,** *a.* artistic.

artrítico, *a.* arthritic.—*n.* arthritis sufferer.

artritis, *f.* arthritis.

arveja, *f.* (Am.) green pea.

arzobispado, *m.* archbishopric.—**arzobispo,** *m.* archbishop.

as, *m.* ace.

asa, *f.* handle.

asado, *m.* & *a.* roast.—*bien a.*, (cook.) well-done.—**asador,** *m.* spit (rod); roaster.—**asadura,** *f.* entrails.

asalariado, *a.* wage-earning, salaried.—*n.* salaried person, wage earner.—**asalariar,** *vt.* to put on the payroll.

asaltante, *mf.* assailant, assaulter; robber.—**asaltar,** *vt.* to assault, storm, assail; to rob.—**asalto,** *m.* assault; attack.

asamblea, *f.* assembly; meeting.—*a. de accionistas*, stockholders' meeting.—**asambleísta,** *mf.* assemblyman.

asar, *vt.* to roast.—*vr.* to be roasting; to be very hot.

asaz, *adv.* enough; greatly, very.

asbesto, *m.* asbestos.

ascendencia, *f.* lineage.—**ascendente,** *a.* ascendant, ascending.—**ascender,** *vii.* [18] to ascend, climb; to be promoted.—*vti.* to promote.—**ascendiente,** *mf.* ancestor.—*m.* influence.—**ascensión,** *f.* ascension.—**ascenso,** *m.* promotion; ascent.—**ascensor,** *m.* elevator.

asceta, *m.* ascetic, hermit.—**ascetismo,** **ascetismo,** *m.* asceticism.

asco, *m.* nausea, disgust, loathing; disgusting thing.—*darle a uno a.*, to make one sick.—*estar hecho un a.*, to be very dirty.—*hacer ascos*, to turn up one's nose.

ascua, *f.* red-hot coal, ember.—*estar en ascuas*, to be on tenterhooks.

aseado, *a.* clean, neat.—**asear,** *vt.* to clean; to adorn, embellish.—*vr.* to clean oneself up.—**aseo,** *m.* cleanliness, neatness, tidiness.

asechanza, asechar, asecho, = ACECHANZA, ACECHAR, ACECHO.

asediar, *vt.* to besiege, blockade.—**asedio,** *m.* siege, blockade.

asegurado, *n.* & *a.* insured (person).—**asegurador,** *n.* & *a.* insurer; insuring; underwriter.—**asegurar,** *vt.* to assure; to secure, fasten; to affirm; to insure.—*vr.* to make sure; to hold fast; to be insured, take out insurance.

asemejar, *vt.* to liken, compare.—*vr.* (a) to look like, resemble.

asentaderas, *f. pl.* buttocks.—**asentador,** *m.* razor strop.—**asentar,** *vti.* [1] to place, seat; to adjust; to arrange, settle; to enter (an account, etc.); to hone.—*vii.* to fit, settle.—*vri.* to establish oneself, settle.

asentimiento, *m.* assent.—**asentir,** *vii.* [39] to agree, to assent.

aseo, *m.* cleanliness, cleanness, tidiness.

asepsia, *f.* asepsis.—**aséptico,** *a.* aseptic.

asequible, *a.* obtainable, affordable; approachable.

aserción, *f.* assertion, affirmation.

aserradero, *m.* sawmill; sawpit; sawhorse.—**aserrar,** *vti.* [1] to saw.—**aserrín,** *m.* sawdust.

asesinar, *vt.* to murder; to assassinate.—**asesinato,** *m.* murder; assassination.—**asesino,** *a.* murderous, homicidal.—*n.* murderer; assassin.—*a. a sueldo*, hitman.—*a. en serie*, serial killer.

asesor, *n.* consultant, adviser. —**asesorar,** *vt.* to give legal advice.—*vr.* to take advice.—*a. de*, *a. con*, to consult.—**asesoría,** *f.* office, pay and fees of a consultant.

aserto, *m.* assertion, affirmation.

asestar, *vt.* to point, aim; to level.—*a. un golpe*, to deal a blow.

aseveración, *f.* asseveration, assertion.—**aseverar,** *vt.* to asseverate, affirm, assert.

asfaltar, *vt.* to asphalt, to blacktop.—

asfalto, *m.* asphalt; blacktop. asphalt.

asfixia, *f.* asphyxia.—**asfixiante,** *a.* asphyxiating.—**asfixiar,** *vt.* to asphyxiate, suffocate.—*vr.* to be asphyxiated.

así, *adv.* so, thus, in this manner, like this; therefore.—*a. a.,* so-so, middling.—*a. como,* as soon as, just as.—*a. como a.,* just like that, without rhyme or reason.—*a. no más,* so so, just so.—*a. que,* so that.—*a. y todo,* and yet; just the same.

asiático, *n.* & *a.* Asian, Asiatic.

asidero, *m.* hold; handle; pretext.

asiduidad, *f.* assiduity, perseverance.—**asiduo,** *a.* assiduous, persevering.

asiento, *m.* seat; site; solidity; settling; bottom; sediment; treaty, contract; entry; registry; stability, permanence; list, roll.—*a. abatible,* recliner.—*a. de atrás, a. trasero,* front seat.—*a. delantero,* back seat.—*a. de palco,* box seat.—*a. envolvente,* bucket seat.—*a. expulsor, proyectable,* or *de eyección,* ejection seat.—*a. junto al cuadrilátero,* ringside seat.—*a. reservado,* reserved seat.

asignación, *f.* assignment; allocation of money.—**asignar,** *vt.* to assign; to appoint; to ascribe.—**asignatura,** *f.* subject (in school curriculum).

asilar, *vt.* to shelter; to place in an asylum.—**asilo,** *m.* asylum; refuge; shelter; private hospital, nursing home.—*a. de ancianos, a. de la tercera edad,* old people's home, retirement home for senior citizens.—*a. político,* political asylum.

asimilable, *a.* assimilable.—**asimilación,** *f.* assimilation.—**asimilar,** *vt.* to assimilate.

asimismo, *adv.* likewise, in like manner.

asir, *vti.* [5] & *vii.* to grasp or seize; to hold; to take root.—*vri.* (de) to take hold (of); to avail oneself of.

asistencia, *f.* attendance, presence; assistance, aid.—**asistente,** *mf.* assistant, helper; military orderly.—*a. social,* social worker.—**asistir,** *vi.* to attend, be present (at).—*vt.* to tend; to attend; to take care of; to assist, help, serve; to accompany.

asma, *f.* asthma.—**asmático,** *a.* asthmatic.

asno, *m.* donkey, ass.

asociación, *f.* association; fellowship;

union.—*a. sindical,* labor union.—**asociado,** *n.* & *a.* associate(d).—**asociar,** *vt.* to associate.—*vr.* to associate; to form a partnership; to join.

asolar, *vti.* [12] to raze, devastate, lay waste.

asolear, *vt.* to sun.—*vr.* to be sunburned; to take a sunbath.

asomar, *vi.* to begin to appear.—*vt.* to show (one's face); to stick out (one's head).—*vr.* to loom; to show up; to lean; to take a look.

asombradizo, *a.* timid, shy.—**asombrar,** *vt.* to astonish, amaze; to frighten.—*vr.* (de) to wonder, be astonished (at).—**asombro,** *m.* amazement or astonishment; dread, fear.—**asombroso,** *a.* astonishing, marvelous.

asomo, *m.* indication, sign; conjecture, suspicion.—*ni por a.,* not even remotely.

asonada, *f.* attack of a mob, mobbing; violent protest.

aspa, *f.* vane of a windmill; reel; cross stud.—**aspaviento,** *m.* exaggerated wonder or fear; fuss.

aspecto, *m.* aspect, look, appearance.

aspereza, *f.* asperity; roughness; severity; harshness, rough place.—**áspero,** *a.* rough; harsh; uneven; gruff.—**asperón,** *m.* scourer.

aspillera, *f.* loophole; embrasure.

aspiración, *f.* aspiration, ambition; breathing in; (ling.) aspiration;—**aspirador,** *m.* vacuum cleaner.—**aspirante,** *mf.* candidate, applicant.—*a. de marina,* midshipman.—*bomba a.,* suction pump.—**aspirar,** *vt.* to inhale; to aspire; to covet; to aspirate; to suck.—*vi.* to aspire; to draw, breathe in, inhale.

aspirina, *f.* aspirin.

asquear, *vt.* to disgust, nauseate, sicken.—**asquerosidad,** *f.* filthiness, baseness.—**asqueroso,** *a.* filthy, loathsome, squalid; vile, revolting.

asta, *f.* horn; antler; mast, pole, flagstaff; lance.—*a media a,* at half-mast, at half-staff.

asterisco, *m.* asterisk.

asteroide, *m.* asteroid.

astigmatismo, *m.* astigmatism.

astilla, *f.* chip, splinter.—**astillar,** *vt.* to splinter.—*vr.* to break into splinters.—**astillero,** *m.* shipyard, dockyard.

astro, *m.* star; planet; heavenly

body.—**astrología,** *f.* astrology.— **astrólogo,** *n.* astrologer.—**astronauta,** *mf.* astronaut, spaceman. —**astronave,** *f.* spaceship, spacecraft.—*a. tripulada,* manned spaceship.—**astronomía,** *f.* astronomy. —**astronómico,** *a.* astronomic.— **astrónomo,** *n.* astronomer.

astucia, *f.* astuteness, cunning.

astur, asturiano, *n.* & *a.* Asturian.

astuto, *a.* astute, cunning, sly, crafty, sneaky.

asueto, *m.* time off; vacation.

asumir, *vt.* to assume, take upon oneself (command, responsibilities, etc.); to raise, elevate.

asunción, *f.* acceptance, adoption; assumption, taking on.—*ceremonia de a. del mando,* inauguration ceremony.—*la A.,* (eccl.) the Assumption.

asunto, *m.* topic, theme, subject, matter; affair, business.

asustadizo, *a.* scary, easily frightened.—**asustar,** *vt.* to frighten, scare.—*vr.* to be frightened.

atacar, *vti.* [d] to attack; to button; to fit; to ram (gun); to corner.

atadijo, *m.* loose bundle.—**atado,** *m.* bundle, parcel.—*a.* shy, irresolute; fastened, tied.—**atadura,** *f.* fastening, binding; knot.

atajar, *vt.* to intercept; to interrupt; to take a short cut.—**atajo,** *m.* short cut; interception; cutoff.

atalaya, *f.* watchtower; height.—*m.* guard; lookout.

atañer, *vii.* [50] to relate, affect; to belong, pertain, concern.

ataque, *m.* attack; fit, seizure;—*a. cardíaco, a. al corazón,* heart attack.

atar, *vt.* to tie, fasten, bind; to lace; to deprive of motion.

atarantado, *a.* astonished; dizzy.— **atarantar,** *vt.* to astound, dumbfound.—*vr.* to be or become dumbfounded.

atardecer, *m.* late afternoon.—*vii.* [3] to draw towards evening.

atareado, *a.* busy.—**atarear,** *vt.* to give a job to.—*vr.* to work hard.

atascadero, *m.* muddy place; obstruction.—**atascar,** *vti.* [d] to stop up; to jam, obstruct.—*vri.* to get stuck; to stick; to jam, become obstructed; to stall.—**atasco,** *m.* traffic jam; blockage; logjam.

ataúd, *m.* coffin, casket.

ataviar, *vt.* to adorn; to deck out, trim.—*vr.* to dress up.—**atavío,** *m.* dress; finery, gear.

ateísmo, *m.* atheism.

atemorizar, *vti.* [a] to scare, frighten.

atemperar, *vt.* to temper, soften; to accommodate.

atención, *f.* attention; civility; kindness.—*pl.* affairs, business.—*interj.* attention!.—**atender,** *vii.* [18] to attend, be attentive; to pay attention.—*vti.* to take care of; to show courtesy to; to wait on; to attend to, pay attention to.

atenerse (a), *vri.* [42] to follow, adhere to; to abide (by), stick (to).

atentado, *m.* offense, violation, transgression; crime.—**atentar,** *vt.* to attempt, try.

atento, *a.* attentive; polite, courteous.—*de Vd. a. y seguro servidor,* respectfully yours.

ateo, *n.* & *a.* atheist(ic).

aterciopelado, *a.* velvety.

aterido, *a.* stiff with cold.—**aterirse,** *vri.* [50] to become stiff with cold.

aterrador, *a.* frightful, terrifying, dreadful.—**aterrar,** *vt.* to terrify; to awe; to appall.—*vr.* to be filled with terror, to be awed or appalled.

aterrizaje, *m.* landing.—*a. aplastado* or *en desplome,* pancake landing.— *a. forzoso, a. de emergencia,* crash landing.—**aterrizar,** *vii.* [a] to land.

aterrorizar, *vti.* [a] to frighten, terrify, terrorize.—*vri.* to be terrified.

atesorar, *vt.* to treasure; to hoard.

atestación, *f.* testimonial.—**atestado,** *m.* attestation.—**atestar,** *vt.* to attest, witness; to cram, stuff.

atestiguar, *vti.* [b] to depose, witness, attest; (law) to testify.

atiborrar, *vt.* to stuff.—*vr.* to stuff oneself.

ático, *a.* Attic; elegant.

atildamiento, *m.* meticulousness in dress or style.—**atildarse,** *vr.* to dress up.

atinar, *vi.* to hit the mark; to guess right; to say or do the right thing.— *a. con,* to find, hit upon.

atisbar, *vt.* to watch, pry; to scrutinize.—**atisbo,** *m.* sign, indication; glimpse, peek.

atizador, *m.* poker.—**atizar,** *vti.* [a] to poke (the fire); to snuff or trim (a candle, etc.); to rouse, stir.—*a. un golpe,* to deliver a blow.

atizonarse, *vr.* (of plants) to become mildewed.

atlántico, *n.* & *a.* Atlantic.

atlas, *m.* atlas.

atleta, *mf.* athlete.—**atlético,** *a.* athletic.—**atletismo,** *m.* athletics.

atmósfera, *f.* atmosphere.—**atmosférico,** *a.* atmospheric.

atolladero, *m.* morass, quagmire, bog.—**atollarse,** *vr.* to get bogged down; to be in a quandary.

atolón, *m.* atoll.

atolondrado, *a.* hare-brained, bewildered.—**atolondramiento,** *m.* thoughtlessness, bewilderment.—**atolondrar,** *vt.* to confound, stun.—*vr.* to become confused, stunned.

atómico, *a.* atomic.—**átomo,** *m.* atom.

atomizador, *m.* atomizer.—**atomizar,** *vt.* to spray.

atónito, *a.* astonished, amazed, aghast.

atontado, *a.* foolish, stupid.—**atontamiento,** *m.* stupefaction, stunning.—**atontar,** *vt.* to stun, stupefy; to confound, confuse.—*vr.* to become stupid, dull, stunned.

atorar, *vt.* (Am.) to obstruct; to jam, choke, clog.—*vr.* to stick in the mire; to fit the bore closely; to choke; to stuff oneself.

atormentador, *n.* torturer, tormentor.—**atormentar,** *vt.* to torment, torture; to afflict.

atornillar, *vt.* to screw; to screw on.

atosigar, *vti.* [b] to harass, pester.

atrabancar, *vti.* [d] to rush.—*vri.* to be in a fix.

atrabiliario, *a.* ill-tempered.

atracar, *vti.* [d] to dock, moor; to come alongside; to cram; to hold up, rob.—*vri.* to overeat, stuff oneself with food.—**atraco,** *m.* holdup, robbery.—*a. a mano armada,* armed robbery.—**atracón,** *m.* overeating.—*darse un a.,* to gorge, stuff oneself.

atracción, *f.* attraction.—**atractivo,** *a.* attractive.—**atraer,** *vti.* [43] to attract; to allure.

atragantarse, *vr.* to choke.

atrancar, *vti.* [d] to bar, bolt (a door); to obstruct.—*vri.* to lock oneself in; to get stuck.

atrapar, *vt.* to catch, grab; to trap; to overtake; to deceive.

atrás, *adv.* back; aback; backward, behind; past; ago.—**atrasado,** *a.* late; behind time; backward.—**atrasar,** *vt.* to retard, delay; to set, put back (timepiece).—*vi.* (of timepiece) to lose or be slow.—*vr.* to remain, be left or fall behind; to lose time; to be late.—**atraso,** *m.* lateness; tardiness; delay; backlog; backwardness.—*pl.* arrears.

atravesar, *vti.* [1] to place across; to go through; to cross; to pierce.—*vr.* to lie across, be in the way; to break in, interrupt, intrude (in); to meddle.

atrayente, *a.* attractive.

atreverse, *vr.* to dare; to venture.—*a. con,* to be insolent to.—**atrevido,** *a.* bold, fearless; forward, insolent.—**atrevimiento,** *m.* nerve.

atribución, *f.* attribution; attribute; power, authority.—**atribuir,** *vti.* [23-e] to attribute, ascribe, impute.—*vri.* to take to or on oneself.

atribular, *vt.* to grieve, afflict, distress.—*vr.* to be or become grieved or distressed.

atributo, *m.* attribute, quality.

atrición, *f.* contrition; attrition.

atril, *m.* music stand; lectern.

atrincheramiento, *m.* entrenchment; trenches.—**atrincherar,** *vt.* & *vr.* to entrench; to mound.

atrio, *m.* hall, vestibule; atrium.

atrocidad, *f.* atrocity.

atronador, *a.* thundering, stunning.—**atronar,** *vti.* [12] to deafen, stun.

atropellamiento, *m.* confusion.—**atropellar,** *vt.* to trample under foot; to knock down; to run over, hit, injure; to push through; to outrage.—*vr.* to move or act hastily or recklessly; to rush.—**atropello,** *m.* trampling, running over; injuring, abuse, outrage.

atroz, *a.* atrocious; huge, enormous.

atuendo, *m.* dress, garb, attire.

atún, *m.* tuna, tuna fish.

aturdido, *a.* hare-brained, reckless.—**aturdimiento,** *m.* bewilderment; confusion.—**aturdir,** *vt.* to bewilder, daze; to stun.—*vr.* to become bewildered.

aturrullar, *vt.* to confound, bewilder.

atusar, *vt.* to trim; to comb and smooth (the hair).—*vr.* to overdress.

audacia, *f.* audacity, boldness.—**audaz,** *a.* bold, fearless, audacious.

audiencia, *f.* audience, hearing; court.—*a. nacional,* supreme court.—*a. pública,* public hearing.—*a. territorial,* police court.—**auditivo,** *a.* auditory.—**auditor,** *n.* judge.—**auditorio,** *m.* audience, assembly of listeners.

audio, *m.* audio; (rad./tel.) sound.

audiofrecuencia, *f.* audiofrequency.

audiosistema, *m.* audio system.

audiovisual, *a.* audiovisual.

auge, *m.* apogee; culmination; summit.—*ir en a.,* to be on the increase.

aula, *f.* classroom; lecture room.

aullar, *vi.* to howl; to yell, cry.—**aullido, aúllo,** *m.* howl.

aumentar, *vt.* & *vr.* to augment, increase,enlarge, magnify.—**aumentativo,** *a.* increasing; (gram.) augmentative.—**aumento,** *m.* increase, augmentation, etc.

aún (aun), *adv.* & *conj.* even.—*adv.* yet, still; as yet.—*a. cuando,* even though.

aunar, *vt.* to unite, join; to combine; to unify.—*vr.* to be united or confederated.

aunque, *conj.* (al)though, notwithstanding, even if.

aúpa, *interj.* up!

aura, *f.* gentle breeze; applause, acclamation; (Am.) buzzard.

aureola, *f.* aureola, halo.

aureomicina, *f.* aureomycin.

auricular, *a.* auricular.—*m.* telephone receiver.—*pl.* headphones; earphones.

auscultar, *vt.* to sound (with stethoscope).

ausencia, *f.* absence.—**ausentarse,** *vr.* to absent oneself.—**ausente,** *a.* absent; distracted.—*mf.* absentee; missing person.—**ausentismo,** *m.* absenteeism.—*a. escolar,* truancy.—**ausentista,** *a.* absentee.

auspiciar, *vt.* to sponsor; to promote.—*auspiciado por,* under the auspices of, sponsored by.—**auspicios,** *m. pl.* auspices, sponsorship; presage; omens.

austeridad, *f.* austerity.—**austero,** *a.* austere.

australiano, *n.* & *a.* Australian.

austríaco, *n.* & *a.* Austrian.

autenticar, *vti.* [d] to authenticate; to attest.—**autenticidad,** *f.* authenticity.—**auténtico,** *a.* authentic, genuine.

auto, *m.* automobile; judicial decree or sentence; edict; (hist.) miracle play.—*a. de registro domiciliario,* search warrant.—*pl.* (law) records of a case.

autobús, *m.* bus.—*a. de dos pisos,* double-decker bus.—**autocamión,** *m.* truck.

autocine, *m.* drive-in movie.

autocracia, *f.* autocracy.—**autócrata,** *mf.* autocrat.

autóctono, *a.* aboriginal, native.

autodefensa, *f.* self-defense.

autodromo, *m.* automobile race course.

autoedición, *f.* desktop publishing.

auto-escuela, *f.* driving school.

autoestima, *f.* self-esteem.

autógrafo, *m.* autograph.

autómata, *m.* robot, automaton.—**automático,** *a.* automatic.

automóvil, *m.* automobile.—**automovilismo,** *m.* motoring.—**automovilista,** *n.* devotee of motoring.—*a.* automotive.

autonomía, *f.* autonomy; home rule; self-determination.

autopiano, *m.* player piano.

autopista, *f.* expressway.—*a. de peaje,* turnpike.

autopsia, *f.* autopsy, postmortem.

autor, *m.* author.—**autora,** *f.* authoress.—**autoridad,** *f.* authority.—**autoritario,** *a.* authoritarian; authoritative; overbearing.—**autorización,** *f.* authorization.—**autorizar,** *vti.* [a] to authorize, empower; to legalize; to prove by quotation; to approve, exalt.

autoservicio, *m.* supermarket; self-service restaurant.

autostop or **auto-stop,** *m.* hitchhiking.—*hacer a.,* to hitchhike.

aval, *m.* guarantee; indorsement.

auxiliar, *vt.* to aid, help,assist; to attend.—*a.* auxiliary, assisting.—*mf.* helper, assistant.—*a. de vuelo,* flight attendant.—**auxilio,** *m.* aid, assistance, help.

avalar, *vt.* to vouch for.

avalorar, *vt.* to estimate, value, appraise.

avaluar, *vt.* to estimate, assess, appraise.—**avalúo,** *m.* valuation, appraisal.

avance, *m.* advance; improvement; attack.—**avanzada, avanzadilla,** *f.* (mil.) outpost; advance guard.—**avanzar,** *vii.* [a] to advance, progress; to improve.—*vti.* to advance, push forward.

avaricia, *f.* avarice.—**avaricioso, avariento,** *a.* avaricious, miserly.—**avaro,** *n.* miser.—*a.* avaricious, miserly.

avasallador, *a.* overwhelming, dominating.—**avasallar,** *vt.* to subject, dominate, enslave, subdue.

ave, *f.* fowl; bird.—*a. canora,* songbird.—*a. de corral,* poultry.—*a. negra,* (fam.) trickster.

avecindarse, *vr.* to settle, become a resident; to establish oneself.

avejentar, *vt.* & *vr.* to age.

avellana, *f.* hazelnut.—**avellanado,** *a.* nutbrown; wrinkled.—**avellano,** *m.* hazelnut tree.

avemaría, *f.* Hail Mary; rosary bead. —**¡Ave María!** *interj.* Good Heavens!

avena, *f.* oats.

avenencia, *f.* agreement.

avenida, *f.* avenue; way of access; flood.—*a. ajardinada,* parkway. —**avenido,** a.—*bien* or *mal avenidos,* on good or bad terms.—**avenirse,** *vri.* [45] to settle differences; to agree; to compromise.

aventajar, *vt.* to advance, improve; to surpass; to prefer.—*vr.* to excel, exceed; to advance, rise.

aventar, *vti.* [1] to fan, blow; to winnow.—*vii.* to breathe hard.—*vri.* to be inflated or puffed up; to escape, run away.

aventura, *f.* adventure; contingency, chance, event, risk.—**aventurar,** *vi.* to venture, hazard, risk.—*vr.* (a) to run the risk of.—**aventurero,** *n.* adventurer.—*a.* adventurous.

avergonzar, *vti.* [12-a-b] to shame.—*vr.* to be ashamed.

averiguación, *f.* investigation.—**averiguar,** *vti.* [b] to inquire, investigate, ascertain, find out.

avería, *f.* damage; mischief; misfortune.—**averiar,** *vt.* to damage.—*vr.* to be damaged; to spoil (foods).

aversión, *f.* aversion, dislike.

avestruz, *f.* ostrich.

avezado, *a.* accustomed; trained; practiced.

aviación, *f.* aviation.—**aviador,** *n.* aviator.—*f.* aviatrix.

aviar, *vt.* to equip; to lend, advance money to; to supply; to prepare; to go, get on the way.

avidez, *f.* covetousness, avidity.—**ávido,** *a.* (de) avid, eager, anxious.

aviejarse, *vr.* to age, grow old.

avieso, *a.* perverse; mischievous; crooked, irregular.

avinagrado, *a.* sour, acrimonious. —**avinagrar,** *vt.* to sour, acidulate.—*vr.* to become sour.

avío, *m.* preparation, provision; money advanced.—*pl.* gear, utensils; paraphernalia.

avión, *m.* airplane.—*a. de caza,* pursu[it] plane.—*a. de chorro, a. a chorro, a. [de] reacción,* jet plane, jet.—*a. de guerr[a]* warplane.—*a. de remolque,* to[w] plane.—*por a.,* airmail.

avisado, *a.* cautious, sagacious, clea[r]sighted.—**avisar,** *vt.* to inform announce, give notice of; to war[n] advise.—**aviso,** *m.* information, n[o]tice; advertisement; advice, warn[ing].—*a. de multa,* parking ticket.

avispa, *f.* wasp.—**avispado,** *a.* livel[y] brisk, clever.—**avisparse,** *vr.* to [be] on the alert; to fret.—**avispero,** *m.* nest of wasps; carbuncle.

avistar, *vt.* to sight at a distance.—[vr.] to have an interview, meet.

avituallar, *vt.* to provide food.

avivar, *vt.* to quicken, enliven; to e[n]courage; to revive.—*vr.* to revive; [to] cheer up.

avizor, *a.* alert, watchful.—**avizorar,** [vt.] to watch; to keep a sharp lookout.

ax, *interj.* ouch!, ow!

axila, *f.* armpit.

axioma, *m.* axiom; maxim.

ay, *m.* moan, lament.—*interj.* ouch alas!

aya, *f.* governess, instructress.—**ay[o]** *m.* tutor or guardian; teacher.

ayer, *adv.* yesterday.

ayuda, *f.* help, aid.—*a. decamarer[o]* busboy.—**ayudante,** *mf.* assistan[t] helper; adjutant.—**ayudar,** *vt.* to ai[d] help, assist.

ayunar, *vi.* to fast.—**ayuno,** *m.* fast, a[b]stinence.—*a.* (de) uninformed (o[f]) ignorant (of); unaware (of).—*est[ar] en ayunas,* to fast; to be uni[n]formed.—*quedarse en ayunas,* not [to] catch on; to miss the point.

ayuntamiento, *m.* municipal gover[n]ment; town hall; sexual inte[r]course.

azabachado, *a.* jet-black.—**azabach[e]** *m.* jet (stone).

azada, *f.* hoe.—**azadón,** *m.* hoe, spud

azafata, *f.* flight attendant.

azafrán, *m.* saffron.

azahar, *m.* orange or lemon blossom

azar, *m.* hazard, chance; disaster; acc[i]dent.—*al a.,* at random.—*correr (e[l]* or *el) a.,* to take (that) chance, ru[n] the risk.—**azaroso,** *a.* unlucky; ha[z]ardous.

ázoe, *m.* nitrogen.

azogar, *vti.* [b] to silver with me[r]cury.—**azogue,** *m.* mercury, quic[k]silver.

azoramiento, *m.* excitement, confusion.—**azorar,** *vt.* to disturb, startle; to confound, embarrass; to bewilder.—*vr.* to become embarrassed, uneasy, or startled.

azotaina, *f.* drugging, flogging, spanking.—**azotar,** *vt.* to whip, lash; to thrash.—**azotazo,** *m.* lash.—**azote,** *m.* whip; scourge; stroke, blow.

azotea, *f.* flat roof.

azteca, *mf.* & *a.* Aztec.

azúcar, *m.* sugar.—*a. en cubos, en pancitos, en terrones,* sugar lumps.—*a. glasé,* confectioners' sugar.—*a. morena, a. moreno,* brown sugar.—**azucarado,** *a.* sugary; affectedly sweet

or affable.—**azucarar,** *vt.* to sugar; to sweeten; to coat or ice with sugar. —**azucarera,** *f.* sugar bowl.—**azucarero,** *m.* sugar master; sugar bowl; sugar producer or dealer.—*a.* sugar.

azucena, *f.* white lily.—*a. atigrada,* tiger lily.

azufre, *m.* sulfur; brimstone.

azul, *a.* & *m.* blue.—*a. celeste,* sky blue.—*a. marino,* navy blue.—**azulado,** *a.* bluish.

azulejado, *a.* tiled.—**azulejo,** *m.* glazed tile; bluebird.

azur, *a.* azure.

azuzar, *vti.* [a] to urge, set (dogs) on; to incite, goad.

B

baba, *f.* drivel, spittle, saliva; slime. —**babear,** *vi.* to drivel; to slaver. —**babero,** *m.* bib, feeder.

Babia, *f.*—*estar en B.,* to be woolgathering.—**babieca,** *m.* ignorant, stupid fellow.

babor, *m.* (naut.) port, portside.—*de b. a estribor,* athwart ship.

babosa, *f.* (zool.) slug.—**babosear,** *vi.* = BABEAR.—**baboso,** *a.* driveling, slavering; silly; overaffectionate.

babucha, *f.* slipper.

bacalao, *m.* cod.

bache, *m.* deep hole, pothole, rut (in the road).

bachiller, *n.* bachelor (degree); babbler, prater.—**bachillerato,** *m.* baccalaureate, B.A. degree.

bacía, *f.* metal basin; shaving dish.

bacilo, *m.* bacillus.

bacín, *m.* (obs.) chamber pot.

bacteria, *f.* bacterium.—**bacteriano,** *a.* bacterial.—**bacteriología,** *f.* bacteriology.—**bacteriológico,** *a.* bacteriological.—**bacteriólogo,** *n.* bacteriologist.

báculo, *m.* walking stick, staff; support, aid.—*b. pastoral,* bishop's crosier.

badajo, *m.* clapper of a bell.

badana, *f.* dressed sheepskin.

badulaque, *a.* foolish; good-for-nothing.—*m.* fool.

bagaje, *m.* beast of burden; (mil.) baggage.

bagatela, *f.* trifle; pinball.—*pl.* trivia.

bahía, *f.* bay, harbor.

bailable, *a.* (of music) composed for dancing.—*m.* ballet.—**bailador,** *n.* dancer.—**bailar,** *vi.* to dance, spin.— *b. al son que le toquen,* to adapt oneself to circumstances.—*b. claqué,* to tap dance.—*b. como un trompo,* to dance well.—**bailarín,** *n.* dancer; ballet dancer.—*b. de claqué,* tap dancer.—**baile,** *m.* dance, ballet; ball.—*b. de etiqueta,* formal dance.—*b. de máscaras,* masquerade, masked ball.—*b. de salón,* ballroom dance, ballroom dancing.— *b. de trajes,* fancy-dress ball.—**bailotear,** *vi.* (coll.) to dance clumsily, frequently.—**bailoteo,** *m.* awkward dancing.

baja, *f.* fall in price; (mil.) casualty; vacancy.—*b. por maternidad,* maternity leave.—*dar de b.,* to drop (a person from a list, etc.).—*darse de b.,* to drop out, resign from.—**bajada,** *f.* descent; slope.—**bajamar,** *f.* low water, low tide.—**bajar,** *vi.* to descend; to fall; to come or go down; to drop, lessen, diminish.—*vt.* to lower, reduce; to bring or take down, let down.—*vr.* to bend over, stoop; to crouch, grovel; to alight; to get out (of a vehicle); to get down; to bow down.

bajeza, *f.* meanness; vile act or remark; low action.

bajío, *m.* sandbank.—*pl.* lowlands.

bajista, *a.* downward.—*mf.* bass player; bear (on the stock market).

bajo, *a.* low, shallow; short; abject; base; common; (of color) dull; (of sound) deep, low; coarse, vulgar; downcast; late (Middle Ages).—*b. forma,* bad shape, poor form.—*bajos fondos,* underworld.—*por lo b.,* on the sly; in an undertone.—*adv.* softly, in a low voice.—*prep.* under.—*m.* bass (voice, singer, instrument); ground floor; sand bank.— *pl.* underskirts; trousers' cuffs.

bala, *f.* bullet, shot, ball; bale.—*b. de fogueo* or *de salva,* blank.—*b. perdida,* stray bullet; (fig.) a good-for-nothing.

balada, *f.* ballad.

baladí, *a.* trivial, petty.

baladronada, *f.* boast, bravado.

balance, *m.* oscillation, rolling, rocking, swinging; balance; balance sheet; (Cuba) rocking chair; (aer.) rolling.—**balancear,** *vt.* to balance; to put into equilibrium.—*vi.* & *vr.* to roll, rock, swing; to waver.—**balanceo,** *m.* rocking, rolling; wobbling.—**balancín,** *m.* balancing pole; rocker arm; seesaw; rocking chair.

balandro, *n.* sloop.

balanza, *f.* scales; balance.—*b. comercial,* balance of trade.—*b. de baño,* bathroom scales.

balar, *vi.* to bleat., to baa.

balastar, *vt.* to ballast.—**balasto,** *m.* (RR.) ballast.

balazo, *m.* shot, bullet wound.

balbucear, *vi.,* **balbucir,** *vii.* [11] to hesitate in speech, stammer.—**balbuceo,** *m.* stammer, babble.—**balbuciente,** *a.* stammering, stuttering.

balcón, *m.* balcony; porch.

baldar, *vt.* to cripple.

balde, *m.* bucket, pail.—*de b.,* gratis; free.—*en b.,* in vain, with no result.—**baldear,** *vt.* to wash (floors, decks).—**baldeo,** *m.* washing (floors, decks).

baldío, *a.* untilled, uncultivated; barren.—*m.* wasteland.

baldón, *m.* affront, insult; disgrace.

baldosa, *f.* paving tile; floor tile; flagstone.

balear, *a.* & *mf.* Balearic; person of or from the Balearic Islands.—*vt.* (Am.) to shoot (wound or kill).

balido, *m.* bleating, bleat.

balístico, *a.* ballistic.

baliza, *f.* buoy.—**balizaje,** *m.* (aer.) runway lights.—**balizar,** *vti.* [a] to mark with buoys.

ballena, *f.* whale; whalebone.—**ballenato,** *m.* young whale.—**ballenera** *f.* whaleboat.—**ballenero,** *a.* whaling.—*n.* whaler.—*m.* whaleboat.

ballesta, *f.* crossbow.

ballet, *m.* ballet.

balneario, *a.* & *m.* spa, resort.

balompié, *m.* soccer.—**balón,** *m.* football; (auto) balloon tire.—*b. de gas* gas bag.—**baloncesto,** *m.* basketball. Also BASKETBOL.—**balonmano** *m.* handball.—**balonvolea,** volleyball.

balsa, *f.* raft; pool, pond.—**balsadero** *m.* ferry.—**balsear,** *vt.* to ferry, to cross (a river).

bálsamo, *m.* balsam, balm.

baluarte, *m.* bastion, bulwark.

balumba, *f.* bulk, heap; jumble.

bambalinas, *fpl.* (theat.) flies, borders.

bambolear, *vi.* & *vr.* to swing, sway —**bamboleo,** *m.* swinging, swaying

bambolla, *f.* show, sham, bragging.

banana, *f.,* banana.—**banano,** *m.* banana tree.

banca, *f.* bench; stand; (com.) banking.—*b. de hielo,* iceberg.—**bancario,** *a.* banking; financial.— **bancarrota,** *f.* bankruptcy; failure.

banco, *m.* bench; settee; pew; (mech.) bed, table; pedestal; school of fish shoal; (com.) bank.—*b. de ahorros* savings bank.—*b. de arena,* sand bank.—*b. de compensaciones,* clearing house.—*b. de coral,* coral reef.— *b. de datos,* data bank.—*b. de direcciones,* mailing list.—*b. de esperma* or *semen,* sperm bank.—*b. de sangre* blood bank.—*b. de trabajo,* work bench.—*b. fideicomisario,* trust company.—*B. Mundial,* World Bank.

banda, *f.* band; ribbon; sash; scarf band, gang; covey; edge; side of ship; cushion (of a billiard table).— *b. sonora,* sound track.—**bandada,** covey; flock of birds.—**bandazo,** *m.* (of ship) violent roll to side.—**bandear,** *vi.* to band.—*vr.* to conduct for oneself.

bandeja, *f.* tray; salver.

bandera, *f.* flag, banner; colors.—*b. a popa,* ensign.—*b. f.* band faction.—**banderilla,** *f.* baiting dart (bullfight).—*poner a uno una b.,* taunt or provoke one.—**banderín,** *m.* camp colors; flag; railway signal; recruiting post.—**banderola,** *f.* streamer; pennant; signal flag.

bandidaje, *m.* banditry; gang.—**bandido,** *m.* bandit, robber.

bando, *m.* proclamation; faction, side.

bandolera, *f.* woman bandit; bandoleer, shoulder belt.—**bandolerismo,** *m.* banditry.—**bandolero,** *m.* highwayman, brigand.

banquero, *n.* banker.

banqueta, *f.* backless bench; stool; footstool; (Mex.) sidewalk.

banquete, *m.* banquet.—**banquetear,** *vt.*, *vi.* & *vr.* to banquet, feast.

banquillo, *m.* little stool.—**b. de los acusados,** defendant's seat.—**b. de los testigos,** witness stand.—**banquito,** *m.* stool, footstool.

bañadera, *f.* (Am.) bathtub.—**bañar,** *vt.* to bathe, wash; to dip; to apply a coating to.—*vr.* to take a bath. —**bañera,** *f.* bathtub.—**bañista,** *mf.* bather.—**baño,** *m.* bath; bathing; bathtub; bathroom.—**b. de sangre,** blood bath.—**b. de sol,** sun bath.— **b. María,** double boiler.—*pl.* bathhouse; spa.

baqueano, *n.* & *a.* = BAQUIANO.

baqueta, *f.* ramrod.—*pl.* drumsticks.—**a la b.,** harshly, despotically.

baquiano, *n.* (Am.) guide.—*a.* expert.

bar, *m.* bar; liquor cabinet.

barahúnda, *f.* uproar, tumult.

baraja, *f.* pack or deck (of cards).—**barajar,** *vt.* to shuffle (the cards); to jumble together.

baranda, *f.* railing; banister.—**barandilla,** *f.* balustrade, railing.

barata, *f.* (fam.) barter, exchange; (Am.) bargain sale.—**baratear,** *vt.* to sell cheap; to haggle.—**baratijas,** *f. pl.* trifles, trinkets.—**baratillero,** *n.* peddler; seller of secondhand goods or articles.—**baratillo,** *m.* secondhand shop; remnant sale; bargain counter.—**barato,** *a.* cheap; low (priced), reasonable.—*adv.* cheaply.—*m.* bargain sale, bargain counter.—**cobrar el b.,** to sell protection by compulsion.—**baratura,** *f.* cheapness.

barba, *f.* chin; beard; whiskers; wattle.—*pl.* beard, whiskers; fibers; rough edges of paper.—**b. corrida** or **cerrada,** thick beard.—**b. de ballena,** whalebone.—**b. española,** Spanish moss.—**en sus barbas,** to his face.— **tener pocas barbas,** to be young or inexperienced.

barbacoa, *f.* (Am.) barbecue; barbecued meat.

barbaridad, *f.* barbarity; atrocity; cruelty; rudeness; (Am.) excess (in anything); nonsense; blunder.—**barbarie,** *f.* fierceness; cruelty; barbarity; lack of culture.—**barbarismo,** *m.* barbarism; barbarousness.—**barbarizar,** *vti.* [a] to barbarize.—*vii.* to make wild statements.—**bárbaro,** *a.* barbarous, barbaric.—*n.* barbarian.

barbechar, *vt.* to plow for seeding; to fallow.—**barbecho,** *m.* fallow.

barbería, *f.* barbershop.—**barbero,** *m.* barber.—**barbilla,** *f.* point of the chin.—**barboquejo,** *m.* chin strap; hat guard.

barbotar, *vt.* & *vi.* to mumble.

barbudo, *a.* heavy-bearded.

barca, *f.* boat, barge, bark.—**b. chata,** ferryboat.—**barcaza,** *f.* (naut.) barge.

barco, *m.* boat, vessel, ship.

bardo, *m.* bard, poet.

barítono, *m.* baritone.

barloventear, *vi.* to turn to windward; to wander around.—**barlovento,** *m.* windward.

barniz, *m.* varnish.—**barnizar,** *vti.* [a] to varnish.

barométrico, *a.* barometric.—**barómetro,** *m.* barometer.

barquero, *m.* boatman.—**barquichuelo,** *m.* small barge or boat.— **barquilla,** *f.* small boat; (naut.) log; (aer.) nacelle.

barquillo, *m.* thin rolled wafer; waffle.—**b. de helado,** ice-cream cone. —**barquillero,** *m.* waffle iron.

barra, *f.* bar; (mech., eng.) bar, beam, rod, crowbar; stripe; stick; (Arg.) gang (of boys); railing in a court room.—**b. de labios,** lipstick.—**b. espaciadora,** space bar.

barrabasada, *f.* serious mischief; reckless, harmful action.

barraca, *f.* barrack, cabin, hut.—**barracón,** *m.* stall, booth.

barranca, *f.,* **barrancal, barranco,** *m.* deep hollow; cliff; gorge, ravine; precipice; great difficulty, obstacle.

barredera, *f.* (mech.) street cleaner.

barredura, *f.* sweeping.—*pl.* sweepings, chaff.

barreminas, *m.* minesweeper (ship).

barrena, *f.* drill; auger; gimlet; (aer.)

spin; spinning dive.—*b. de gusano*, wimble; rock drill.—*b. grande*, borer, auger.—*b. picada*, tail spin.—*entrar en b.*, (aer) to spin.—**barrenado**, *a*. bored, drilled.—*m*. boring, drilling.—**barrenador**, *m*. auger or borer.—**barrenar**, *vt*. to drill, bore; to foil; to infringe (a law).—*b. una roca*, or *mina*, to blast a rock or a mine.

barrendero, *n*. sweeper, dustman (woman).

barrenillo, *m*. boring insect.—**barreno**, *m*. large borer, drill or auger; bored hole, blast hole.

barreña, *f.*, **barreño**, *m*. earthenware basin.

barrer, *vt*. to sweep; (naut.) to rake.—*al b.*, (com.) on an average.

barrera, *f*. barricade, barrier, parapet; turnpike, tollgate; clay pit.—*b. de peaje*, tollgate.—*b. de seguridad*, guardrail.

barriada, *f*. district, quarter, neighborhood.

barrica, *f*. cask, keg.

barricada, *f*. barricade.

barrido, *m*. sweeping.

barriga, *f*. belly; pregnancy.—**barrigón**, **barrigudo**, *a*. big-bellied, paunchy.

barril, *m*. barrel; keg.—*b. de pólvora*, powder keg.

barrio, *m*. district, ward, quarter; suburb.—*barrios bajos*, slums.—*b. comercial*, shopping district.—*b. de los lupanares*, red-light district.—*el otro b.*, the other world; eternity.

barro, *m*. mud; clay; earthenware.—*pl*. pimples on the face.

barrote, *m*. short and thick iron bar; round rung (of a ladder).

barruntar, *vt*. to conjecture, guess.—**barrunto**, *m*. conjecture; presentiment; guess; hint; indication, sign.

bártulos, *m. pl*. household goods.

barullo, *m*. confusion, disorder.

basamento, *m*. (arch.) base and pedestal.—**basar**, *vt*. to support, give a base to; to base; (surv.) to refer (operation, etc.) to a base line.—*vr*. (*en*) to base one's opinion (on).

basca, *f*. nausea; squeamishness.

base, *f*. base, basis; (mil., chem., alg., geom.) base.—*b. de datos*, database.—*b. del bateador*, (sports) home plate.—*b. imponible* or *impositiva*, tax base.—**básico**, *a*. basic.

basílica, *f*. basilica.

basilisco, *m*. basilisk.—*estar hecho un b.*, to be furious.

basketbol, **basquetbol**, *m*. basketball.—**basketbolista**, *mf*. basketball player.

¡basta!, stop! that will do!

bastante, *a*. sufficient, enough.—*adv*. enough; rather, fairly, pretty.

bastar, *vi*. to suffice; to be enough.

bastardilla, *f*. italics.—*a*. italic.—**bastardo**, *a*. & *n*. bastard.

bastidor, *m*. frame; easel; embroidery frame; stretcher for canvas; wing of stage scenery; window sash.—*entre bastidores*, behind the scenes; in the wings, offstage, backstage.

bastilla, *f*. hem; hemline.

bastión, *m*. bulwark, bastion.

basto, *m*. packsaddle; pack; (cards) club.—*pl*. a suit of cards named **bastos**.—*a*. coarse, rude; homespun.

bastón, *m*. cane, walking stick; baton.—**bastonazo**, *m*. blow with a cane.

basura, *f*. sweepings, litter, rubbish; garbage, refuse.—**basurero**, *m*. garbage dump, landfill; trash can; rubbish collector.

bata, *f*. house coat; smock; wrap; dressing gown; lounging robe.

batacazo, *m*. fall; thud; bump.

batahola, *f*. racket, hubbub, uproar.

batalla, *f*. battle, struggle.—*b. campal*, pitched battle.—**batallador**, *n*. & *a*. battler; battling; fighter; fighting.—**batallar**, *vi*. to battle, fight, struggle.—**batallón**, *m*. battalion.

batata, *f*. sweet potato.

bate, *m*. (Am.) baseball bat.

batea, *f*. tray; foot tub; flat-bottomed boat; (R.R.) flatcar.

bateador, *n*. (Am.) batter.—**batear**, *vt*. & *vi*. to bat.

batería, *f*. battery; (mus.) percussion instruments; (Am. baseball) battery; footlights.—*b. de cocina*, kitchen utensils.

batiburrillo, *m*. = BATURRILLO.

batida, *f*. hunting party.—**batido**, *a*. beaten, trodden (as roads).—*m*. batter of flour, eggs, etc.—*b. de leche*, milkshake.—**batidor**, *m*. beater; scout; ranger; leather beater; stirring rod.—**batiente**, *m*. jamb (of a door); leaf (of a door).

batintín, *m*. (Am.) gong.

batir, *vt*. to beat, pound; to defeat; to strike; to demolish; to flap; to stir;

to reconnoiter.—*b. el record,* to beat, or break the record.—*b. palmas,* to clap the hands.—*vr.* to fight; to duel.

baturrillo, *m.* hodgepodge; confusion.

batuta, *f.* baton.—*llevar la b.,* to lead; to preside.

baúl, *m.* trunk, chest.—*b. de camarote,* steamer trunk.

bautismal, *a.* baptismal.—**bautismo,** *m.* baptism, christening.—**bautista,** *mf.* Baptist.—**bautizar,** *vti.* [a] to baptize, christen; to nickname.—**bautizo,** *m.* baptism; christening party.

baya, *f.* berry, any small globular fruit.

bayeta, *f.* baize, thick flannel.

bayo, *a.* bay, cream-colored.—*m.* bay horse.

bayoneta, *f.* bayonet.—**bayonetazo,** *m.* bayonet thrust or wound.

baza, *f.* card trick.—*meter la b.,* to butt in.—*no dejar meter b.,* not to let one put in a single word.

bazar, *m.* bazaar, market place.

bazo, *m.* spleen; milt.

bazofia, *f.* scraps; garbage; waste meat; refuse.

beatería, *f.* sanctimoniousness, false piety.—**beatitud,** *f.* beatitude, blessedness, holiness.—**beato,** *a.* blessed; beatified; devout; bigoted; prudish.—*n.* beatified person; devout person; bigot; prude; (fam.) churchgoer.

bebé, *m.* baby; doll.

bebedero, *m.* watering place; watering trough.—**bebedor,** *n.* drinker; hard drinker.—**beber,** *vt. & vi.* to drink; to swallow; to pledge, toast.—*b. como una esponja,* to drink like a fish.—*m.* drink, drinking.—**bebida,** *f.* drink, beverage; potion.—**bebido,** *a.* drunk; intoxicated.

beca, *f.* scholarship; fellowship; academic sash.—*b. de investigación,* fellowship.—**becario,** *n.* scholar, fellow.

becerro, *m.* yearling calf; calfskin.

becuadro, *m.* (mus.) natural sign.

bedel, *m.* beadle, warden; usher (at school, etc.).

beduíno, *n. & a.* Bedouin; uncivil.

befa, *f.* jeer, scoffing.

befo, *a.* = BELFO.

beisbol, *m.* baseball (game).—**beisbolero,** *n.* **beisbolista,** *mf.* baseball player.

bejuco, *m.* rattan.

beldad, *f.* beauty.

belén, *m.* nativity scene, crèche; confusion, bedlam.—*B.,* Bethlehem.

belfo, *a.* having a thick lower lip.—*m.* lip of an animal.

belga, *mf. & a.* Belgian.

bélico, *a.* warlike.—**belicista,** *mf.* warmonger.—**belicoso,** *a.* warlike, bellicose; quarrelsome.

beligerancia, *f.* belligerency.—**beligerante,** *mf. & a.* belligerent.

bellaco, *a.* artful, sly, cunning, roguish.—*m.* rogue, villain, knave.—**bellaquear,** *vi.* to cheat, swindle.—**bellaquería,** *f.* cunning, slyness; wickedness.

belleza, *f.* beauty.—**bello,** *a.* beautiful, fair.

bello, *a.* beautiful.—*bellas artes,* fine arts, beaux-arts.—*el b. sexo,* the fair sex.

bellota, *f.* acorn.

bembo, *a.* (pej.) thick-lipped.—**bembón,** *a.* (pej.) thick-lipped.

bemol, *m.* (mus.) flat.—*tener bemoles,* (coll.) to be a touch job.

bencina, *f.* benzine.

bendecir, *vti.* [6] to bless.—**bendición,** *f.* blessing, benediction.—**bendito,** *pp. i.* of BENDECIR.—*a.* blessed; sainted; simple-minded.

benedícite, *m.* grace.—*rezar el b.,* to say grace.

benefactor, *n.* benefactor.

beneficencia, *f.* beneficence, charity; department of public welfare.—**beneficiar,** *vt.* to benefit; to cultivate, develop, exploit; to purchase.—*vr.* to profit.—**beneficiario,** *n.* beneficiary.—**beneficio,** *m.* benefit; profits; favor, benefaction.—*b. bruto,* gross profit.—*b. neto,* clear profit.—**beneficioso,** *a.* beneficial, profitable.—**benéfico,** *a.* beneficent, charitable.

benemérito, *a.* meritorious, worthy.

beneplácito, *m.* approval, consent.

benevolencia, *f.* benevolence, kindness.—**benévolo,** *a.* benevolent, kind.

benignidad, *f.* benignity, kindness; mildness.—**benigno,** *a.* benign, kind; mild.

beodo, *a.* drunk.—*n.* drunkard.

berbiquí, *m.* drill brace; wimble.

berenjena, *f.* eggplant.—**berenjenal,** *m.* bed of eggplants.—*meterse en un b.,* to get into a mess.

bergante, *m.* scoundrel, rascal.

bermejo, *a.* bright red.

bermellón, bermillón, *m.* vermilion.

berrear, *vi.* to cry like a goat, bellow.
—**berrido,** *m.* bleat; shriek.

berrinche, *m.* tantrum; rage, temper.

berro, *m.* watercress.

berza, *f.* cabbage.

besar, *vt.* & *vi.* to kiss.—**beso,** *m.* kiss.

bestia, *f.* beast.—*b. de carga,* beast of
burden.—*mf.* dunce.—**bestial,** *a.*
bestial, beastly; (fam.) terrific, fabulous; gigantic.—**bestialidad,** *f.* brutality; stupid notion.

besugo, *m.* sea bream; red gilthead.

besuquear, *vt.* & *vi.* (fam.) to neck, to
smooch.—**besuqueo,** *m.* necking,
smooching.

betabel, *f.* (Mex.) beet.

betún, *m.* bitumen, pitch; shoe-
blacking; coarse wax.—**betunar,** *vt.*
to pitch, tar.

biberón, *m.* nursing bottle.

Biblia, *f.* Bible.—**bíblico,** *a.* Biblical.
—**bibliografía,** *f.* bibliography.—**biblioteca,** *f.* library.—*b. municipal,*
public library.—**bibliotecario,** *n.* librarian.

bicarbonato, *m.* bicarbonate.

bichero, *m.* boat hook.

bicho, *m.* bug, insect; grub; simpleton; brat.

bicicleta, *f.* bicycle.

bidé, *m.* (mueble de tocador) bidet
(bathroom fixture).

biela, *f.* connecting rod; crank.

bien, *m.* good, supreme goodness;
benefit; righteousness; object of
love.—*en b. de,* for the sake, good, or
benefit of.—*pl.* property; possessions; estate.—*bienes de fortuna,*
worldly possessions.—*bienes ga-
nanciales,* matrimonial common
property.—*bienes inmuebles,* real estate.—*bienes muebles,* personal
property.—*hombre de b.,* honest
man.—*adv.* well; all right; right;
very; happily; perfectly.—*b. que,*
although.—*encontrar,* or *hallar b.,*
approve.—*más b.,* rather.—*o b.,*
or else; otherwise.—*si b.,* while,
though,—*y b.,* well, now then.

bienaventurado, *a.* blessed; fortunate.—**bienaventuranza,** *f.* beatitude; bliss; well-being.—*pl.* beatitudes.—**bienestar,** *m.* comfort;
well-being.—**bienhechor,** *n.* benefactor.—**bienvenida,** *f.* welcome;
safe arrival.—**bienvenido,** *a.*
welcome.

bifocales, *mpl.* bifocals.

biftec, *m.* beefsteak.

bifurcación, *f.* a forking or branching
out.—**bifurcarse,** *vri.* [d] to branch
off, fork; to divide into two
branches.

bigamia, *f.* bigamy.—**bígamo,** *a.* & *n.*
bigamous; bigamist.

bigornia, *f.* two-horn anvil.

bigote, *m.* mustache.—*pl.* whiskers (of
a cat).

bilingüe, *a.* bilingual.

bilioso, *a.* bilious.—**bilis,** *f.* bile.

billar, *m.* billiards.—*b. romano,* pinball.—**billarista,** *mf.* billiard player.

billete, *m.* bill, bank note; note, brief
letter; ticket.—*b. de abono,* season
ticket.—*b. de ida y vuelta,* round-trip
ticket.—*b. de vuelta,* return ticket.—
medio b., half fare.—**billetera,** *f.* wallet, billfold.

billón, *m.* (E.U.) trillion (a million million: 1,000,000,000,000); (G.B.)
billion.

bimensual, *a.* occurring twice a
month.—**bimestral, bimestre,** *a.* bi-
monthly.—**bimestre,** *m.* a period of
two months.

binario, *a.* binary.

binóculos, *m. pl.* opera glasses; binoculars.

biodegradable, *a.* biodegradable.

biografía, *f.* biography.—**biográfico,** *a.*
biographical.—**biógrafo,** *n.* biographer.

biología, *f.* biology.—**biólogo,** *n.* biologist.

biombo, *m.* folding screen.

bioquímica, *f.* biochemistry.—**bio-
químico,** *a.* biochemical.—*n.* biochemist.

bip, *m.* blip; beep.

bipartición, *f.* fission, splitting.

birlar, *vt.* to rob, pilfer; to kill or knock
down at one blow; (fam.) to outwit.

birlocha, *f.* kite.

birmano, *n.* & *a.* Burmese.

birome, *f.* ballpoint pen.

birreta, *f.* biretta.—**birrete,** *m.* motar-
board, academic cap.

bis, *a.*—*viven en el 17 b.,* they live at
number 17A.—*adv.* twice.—*m.* en-
core.—*interj.* encore!

bisabuela, *f.* great-grandmother.—**bisabuelo,** *m.* great-grandfather.

bisagra, *f.* hinge.

bisbisar, *vi.* to mutter.—**bisbiseo,** *m.*
muttering.

bisel, *m.* bevel, bevel edge.—**biselado,**
m. beveling.—**biselar,** *vt.* to bevel.

bisiesto, *a.*—*año b.,* leap year.

bisnieto, *n.* great-grandchild.—*m.* great-grandson.—*f.* great-grand-daughter.

bisojo, *a.* cross-eyed, squint-eyed.

bisoño, *n.* & *a.* novice; inexperienced.

bistec, *m.* beefsteak.

bisturí, *m.* scalpel.

bizarría, *f.* bravery; magnanimity.—**bizarro,** *a.* brave; gallant.

bizco, *a.* cross-eyed, squint-eyed.

bizcocho, *m.* biscuit; sponge cake.

blanco, *a.* white.—*n.* white person.—*m.* white (color); aim, goal.—*b. y negro,* black and white.—*dar en el b.,* to hit the mark.—*de punta en b.,* cap-a-pie; in full regalia.—*quedarse en b.,* to be frustrated, disappointed.—**blancura,** *f.* whiteness.—**blancuzco,** *a.* whitish.

blandengue, *a.* (fam.) bland, soft.

blandir, *vt.* & *vr.* to brandish.

blando, *a.* soft, pliant; smooth; bland; indulgent; flabby; sensual; (fam.) cowardly; (fam.) tender, gentle (eyes).—**blanducho, blandujo,** *a.* flabby.—**blandura,** *f.* softness; delicacy; gentleness; mild weather.

blanqueador, *m.* blancher, white-washer; bleacher.—**blanqueadura,** *f.,* **blanqueamiento, blanqueo,** *m.* whitening, bleaching, whitewashing.—**blanquear,** *vt.* to whiten; to whitewash; to bleach.—*vi.* to show white; to begin to turn white.—**blanquecino,** *a.* whitish.—**blanquillo,** *m.* (Mex.) egg.

blasfemar, *vi.* to blaspheme.—**blasfemia,** *f.* blasphemy.—**blasfemo,** *n.* & *a.* blasphemer; blasphemous.

blasón, *m.* coat of arms; honor, glory; heraldry.—**blasonar,** *vi.* to boast, brag.

bledo, *m.*—*no me importa un b.,* I don't give a darn.

blindado, *n.* & *a.* iron-clad.—**blindaje,** *m.* blindage; armor.—**blindar,** *vt.* to armor; to protect with blindage.

bloc, *m.* pad, tablet.—*b. de notas,* desk pad, note pad.

bloque, *m.* block; coalition.—**bloqueador,** *n.* & *a.* blockader; blocking.—**bloquear,** *vt.* to blockade; to block, freeze (funds).—**bloqueo,** *m.* blockade.

blusa, *f.* blouse.

boardilla, *f.* dormer window; garret.

boato, *m.* ostentation, pomp.

bobina, *f.* bobbin; coil.—**bobinar,** *vt.* to wind.

bobada, bobería, *f.* foolish speech or action.—**bobalicón,** *n.* blockhead, simpleton.—**bobear,** *vi.* to act or talk foolishly; fritter away (time).—**bobo,** *a.* foolish, simple.—*n.* fool, booby.

boca, *f.* mouth; entrance; opening.—*a b. de jarro,* at close range.—*andar de b. en b.,* to be the talk of the town.—*b. abajo,* prone, face downwards.—*b. arriba,* supine, on one's back.—*b. de agua,* fire plug.—*b. del estómago,* pit of the stomach.—*b. de incendio,* fire hydrant.—*b. de riego,* hydrant.—*no decir esta b. es mía,* to be mum.—**bocacalle,** *f.* opening of a street or street intersection.—**bocadillo,** *m.* mid-morning luncheon or small luncheon; sandwich, roll.—**bocado,** *m.* mouthful, morsel, bite; bit (of a bridle).—**bocamanga,** *f.* part of a sleeve near the wrist.—**bocanada,** *f.* mouthful (of liquor); puff (of smoke).

boceto, *m.* sketch.—*b. burlesco,* skit.

bocha, *f.* bowl, ball for playing at bowls or bowling.

bochinche, *m.* tumult, hubbub.

bochorno, *m.* embarrassment; sultry weather.—**bochornoso,** *a.* embarrassing; shameful; sultry; humiliating.

bocina, *f.* horn; trumpet; speaking tube; megaphone.

bocio, *m.* goiter.

bocón, *n.* braggart; wide-mouthed person.

boda, *f.* wedding, nuptials.—*bodas de oro,* golden wedding anniversary.

bodega, *f.* wine vault or cellar; winery; retail grocery; storeroom, warehouse; hold (of ship).—**bodegón,** *m.* tavern; still life.—**bodeguero,** *m.* keeper of a wine vault; liquor dealer; grocer.

bodoque, *m.* pellet; wad; lump; dunce, idiot.

bofe, *m.* lung; (Am. coll.) snap, easy job.—*echar los bofes,* to toil; to pant, be out of breath.

bofetada, *f.* **bofetón,** *m.* slap in the face, buffet.

boga, *f.* rowing.—*en b.,* in vogue.—*mf.* rower.—**bogar,** *vii.* [b] to row.

bogavante, *m.* lobster; oar stroke.

bohemio, *n.* & *a.* Bohemian.

bohío, *m.* Indian hut, hovel, cabin.

boicot, *m.* boycott.—**boicoteador,** *n.* & *a.* boycotter; boycotting.—**boicotear,** *vt.* & *vi.* to boycott.—**boicoteo,** *m.* boycott(ing).

boina, f. beret.

boj, m. box tree, boxwood.

bola, f. ball; marble; globe; falsehood, fib; (Mex.) shoe blacking; (Mex.) tumult, riot.—*b. de cristal,* crystal ball.—*b. de naftalina,* mothball.—*b. de nieve,* snowball.—*b. de partido,* match point.—*b. rompedora,* wrecking ball.—**bolazo,** m. blow with a ball; fib, lie.—**boleada,** f. (Mex.) shoeshine.—**boleador,** m. bowler; (Mex.) bootblack.—**bolear,** vi. to bowl; to boast; to lie, fib.—**boleo,** m. bowling.—**bolera,** f. bowling alley.—**bolero,** m. bolero; (Mex.) bootblack.

boleta, f. ballot; pass; pay order; certificate; lodging billet.—**boletería,** f. box, or ticket, office.—**boletín,** m. bulletin; ticket.—*b. informativo,* news bulletin.—**boleto,** m. ticket.

boliche, m. bowl, bowling alley; saloon; gambling joint; small stove.

bolígrafo, m. ballpoint pen.

boliviano, n. & a. Bolivian.

bollo, m. small loaf or roll, muffin, bun; biscuit; lump; tuft; dent; swelling; fritter.—*b. de crema,* cream puff.

bolo, m. (bowling) a ninepin; dunce.—pl. bowls, bowling.

bolsa, f. purse; pouch, bag, satchel; stock exchange; exchange center.—*b. de aire,* (aut.) air bag.—*b. para hielo,* ice bag.—*b. de papel,* paper bag.—**bolsicalculadora,** f. pocket calculator.—**bolsillo,** m. pocket; purse.—*rascarse el b.,* to spend much money.—**bolsista,** m. stockbroker; speculator.—**bolsita,** f. small bag.—*b. de sobras,* doggy bag.—*b. de té,* teabag.—**bolso,** m. moneybag; purse.

bomba, f. pump; bomb; fire engine; skyrocket; high hat.—*a prueba de b.,* bomb proof, indestructible.—*b. atómica,* atomic bomb.—*b. corazonpulmón,* heart-lung machine.—*b. de acción retardada,* time bomb.—*b. de aire,* pump.—*b. de neutrones,* N-bomb, neutron bomb.—*b. de tiempo,* time bomb.—*b. H. or de hidrógeno,* hydrogen bomb, H-bomb.—*b. neumática,* air pump.—*b. trampa,* booby-trap bomb.—*fruta b.,* papaya.—**bombardear,** vt. to bombard; to bomb.—*b. en picado,* to dive-bomb.—**bombardeo,** m. bombardment.—*b. de robote,* skip bombing.—*b. en picado,* dive bombing.—**bombardero,** m. bomber (airplane); bombardier.—**bombazo,** m explosion; bomb hit; bad news—**bombear,** vt. to pump.—**bombeo,** m. pumping; curving; bulging.—**bombero,** m. fireman.—**bombilla,** f. electric light bulb.—*b. de flash,* flash bulb.

bombo, m. large drum; bass drum; pomp, ostentation.—*dar b.* to flatter, praise excessively.—a. dazed, stunned; stupid; lukewarm.

bombón, m. chocolate, bonbon, sweet.—**bombonera,** f.

bonachón, a. good-natured, kind; innocent.

bonanza, f. fair weather; prosperity; bonanza.

bondad, f. goodness; kindness.—*tener la b. (de),* please.—**bondadoso,** a. kind, kind-hearted.

bonete, m. bonnet, cap; skullcap; candy dish.

bonhomía, f. honesty, kindliness.

boniato, m. sweet potato.

bonificación, f. discount; allowance; bonus.—**bonificar,** vti. [d] to discount (the price of something).

bonitamente, adv. brazenly; craftily; neatly.—**bonito,** a. pretty.—m. bonito, striped tunny.

boñiga, f. cow dung; castings.

boom [bum], m. boom.—*b. de natalidad,* baby boom.

boqueada, f. gasp, gasping.—**boquear,** vi. to gape, gasp; to breathe one's last; to end.—**boquera,** f. crack in the corner of the mouth.—**boquete,** m. gap, narrow entrance.—**boquiabierto,** a. astonished; openmouthed.—**boquilla,** f. cigar or cigarette holder; mouthpiece of a wind instrument; small mouth.

borbotar, vi. to gush out; to boil or bubble fiercely; to spurt.—**borbollón, borbotón,** m. bubbling, gushing up of water.—*a borbotones,* impetuously.

borceguí, m. high laced shoe.

bordado, m. embroidery; embroidering.—*b. al pasado,* needlepoint.—a. embroidered.—**bordador,** n. embroiderer.—**bordadura,** f. embroidery.—**bordar,** vt. to embroider.

borde, m. border, edge, rim; brim; flange.—*al b. de,* on the verge of.—**bordear,** vt. to skirt, go along the edge of; to approach, get near.

bordo, m. board, the side of a ship.—*a b.,* on board, aboard.

bordón, *m.* walking staff; bass-string of guitar.

borinqueño, *n.* & *a.* Puerto Rican.

borla, *f.* tassel, tuft; powder puff; doctorate.—*tomar la b.,* to graduate.

borra, *f.* sediment, waste; yearling ewe; coarse wool.

borrachera, *f.* drunkenness; madness, great folly.—**borrachín, borrachón,** *m.* drunkard; sot.—**borracho,** *n.* drunkard.—*a.* drunk.

borrador, *m.* eraser; rough draft.—**borradura,** *f.* erasure, striking out, deletion.—**borrar,** *vt.* to erase, rub out, cross out, blot out.

borrasca, *f.* storm; hazard.—**borrascoso,** *a.* stormy.

borrego, *n.* yearling sheep; simpleton.

borricada, *f.* drove of donkeys; stupid word or action.—**borrico,** *m.* donkey; blockhead.

borrón, *m.* blot; rough draft; stigma.—**borroso,** *a.* blurred, indistinct.

boscaje, *m.* cluster of trees; thicket.

bosque, *m.* woods, forest.—*b. maderable,* timberland.—*b. pluvial,* rain forest.

bosquejar, *vt.* to sketch, outline; to plan; to make a rough model of.—**bosquejo,** *m.* sketch; rough outline.

bostezar, *vii.* [a] to yawn, gape.—**bostezo,** *m.* yawn, yawning.

bota, *f.* boot; small leather wine bag.—*ponerse las botas,* to hit the jackpot.

botadero, *m.*—*b. de basuras,* garbage dump, landfill site.

botadura, *f.* launching (of a ship).

botánica, *f.* botany.—**botánico,** *a.* botanical.—*n.* botanist.

botar, *vt.* to cast, pitch, throw; to throw out (of a job), fire; to launch; to misspend; to throw away.—*vi.* & *vr.* (of unbroken horse) to jump and kick, caper; to bound; to rebound.—**botarate,** *m.* spendthrift; madcap.

botavara, *f.* (mar.) gaff; boat hook.

bote, *m.* leap, bound, bounce; rearing of a horse; can or jar; rowing boat.—*b. de basura,* garbage can.—*de b. en b.,* crowded, crammed.

botella, *f.* bottle.—*b. termos,* thermos bottle.—**botellón,** *m.* demijohn.

botica, *f.* drug store.—**boticario,** *n.* apothecary, druggist.

botija, *f.* earthen round, short-necked jug; fat person.

botillería, *f.* refreshment stand.—**botillero,** *n.* ice-cream vendor.

botín, *m.* booty, spoils of war; spats; bootee.—**botina,** *f.* woman's boot.—**botinería,** *f.* shoe store.

botiquín, *m.* medicine chest; first-aid kit; (Am.) wine shop.

botón, *m.* button; knob; sprout, bud, blossom.—*b. de avance rápido,* fast-forward button.—*b. de llamada,* push button.—*b. interruptor,* push button.—**botonadura,** *f.* set of buttons.—**botones,** *m. sing.* bellboy.

bóveda, *f.* arch; vault; vault for the dead.

boxeador, *n.* boxer, pugilist.—**boxear,** *vi.* to box.—**boxeo,** *m.* boxing.—**boxibalón,** *m.* punching bag.

boya, *f.* buoy.

boyada, *f.* herd of oxen.

boyante, *a.* buoyant, floating; prosperous.—**boyar,** *vi.* to buoy; to float.

boyero, *m.* ox driver.

bozal, *m.* muzzle (for dogs, etc.).—*a.* of pure breed, unmixed; newly immigrating; inexperienced; simple, half-witted; coarse; wild.

bozo, *m.* down (on face); mustache; area around the lips.

braceada, *f.* violent stretching out of the arms.—**bracear,** *vi.* to move or swing the arms.—**braceo,** *m.* repeated swinging of the arms.—**bracero,** *m.* day laborer; roustabout; unskilled laborer.—*de b.,* or *de bracete,* arm in arm.

bragas, *f. sing.* & *pl.* breeches; child's diaper; hoisting rope.—**braguero,** *m.* truss, bandage for a rupture.—**bragueta,** *f.* fly of trousers.

braille, Braille, *m.* braille, Braille.

bramante, *a.* roaring.—*m.* twine, packthread.—**bramar,** *vi.* to roar, groan, bellow.—**bramido,** *m.* roar, bellow.

brasa, *f.* ember; red-hot coal or wood.—*estar en brasas,* to be on tenterhooks.—**brasero,** *m.* brazier; fire pan.

brasileño, brasilero, *n.* & *a.* Brazilian.

bravata, *f.* bravado, boast; bluster, threat.—**braveza, bravura,** *f.* bravery; courage; anger.—**bravío,** *a.* ferocious, wild.—**bravo,** *a.* brave; angry; wild, fierce.—**bravucón,** *m.* & *a.* bully; boaster; boasting.

braza, *f.* fathom (measure).—**brazada,** *f.* stroke (swimming, rowing); uplifting of the arms; armful.—*b. de pecho,* breaststroke.—*b. mariposa,* butterfly (swimming stroke).—**brazado,** *m.* armful.—**brazal,** *m.* arm-

band; bracer; armlet.—**brazalete,**
m. bracelet.—**brazo,** *m.* arm (of the
body, a chair, etc.); branch, bough;
strength, power.—*pl.* workmen,
hands.—*a b. partido,* hand to hand,
with all one's strength.—*del b.,* by
the arm; arm in arm.

brea, *f.* pitch, tar.

brebaje, *m.* beverage, potion.

brecha, *f.* breach, opening, gap.

brécol, *m.* broccoli.—**brecolera,** *f.*
flowering broccoli.

brega, *f.* struggle; fight.—*andar a,* or
en, la b., to work hard.—**bregar,** *vii.*
[b] to contend, struggle; to
overwork.

breña, *f.,* **breñal, breñar,** *m.* craggy and
brambled ground.—**breñoso,** *a.*
craggy and brambled.

bresca, *f.* honeycomb.

brete, *m.* fetter, shackle; difficulty.—
en un b., in a difficult situation, hard
pressed to do it.

bretón, *n.* & *a.* Breton.

breva, *f.* early fruit of a fig tree; choice
cigar; advantage, profit.

breve, *a.* brief, short.—*en b.* shortly, in
a little while.—**brevedad,** *f.* brevity,
briefness.—**breviario,** *m.* breviary;
epitome.

brezal, *m.* moor, heath.—**brezo,** *m.*
(bot.) heath, heather.

bribón, *n.* loafer, crook.—**bribonada,** *f.*
loafing, crookedness.—**bribonear,**
vi. to loaf around, to be crooked.—
bribonería, *f.* rascality; vagrancy.

brida, *f.* bridle, rein.

brigada, *f.* brigade; group of people
doing a task together; sub-
lieutenant.—**brigadier,** *m.* brigadier
general.

bridge, *m.* bridge.—*b. contrato,* contract bridge.—*b. subastado,* auction
bridge.

brillante, *a.* brilliant, bright; shining,
sparkling.—*m.* brilliant, diamond.
—**brillantez,** *f.* dazzle, brilliance.—
brillo, *m.* shine, brightness, luster,
sparkle; shoeshine.—**brillar,** *vi.* to
shine, sparkle, glitter; excel.

brincar, *vii.* [d] to leap, jump, caper,
skip.—**brinco,** *m.* leap, jump, hop,
caper.

brindar, *vt.* to toast, drink the health;
to offer.—**brindis,** *m.* drinking the
health of another; toast.

brío, *m.* vigor, enterprise, courage.
—**brioso,** *a.* vigorous, courageous,
spirited.

brisa, *f.* breeze.

británico, *a.* & *n.* British; Britisher.

britano, *n.* & *a.* Briton; British.

brizna, *f.* fragment; splinter or chip;
string (of beans, etc.); shred.

broca, *f.* reel, bobbin; drill bit.

brocado, *m.* (gold or silver) brocade.

brocal, *m.* curbstone of a well.

brocha, *f.* brush; loaded dice.—*de b.
gorda,* crude, badly done.—**bro-
chada,** *f.,* **brochazo,** *m.* stroke of the
brush.

broche, *m.* clasp; hook and eye; fastener; brooch.—*b. de oro,* punch
line.

bróculi, *m.* broccoli.

broma, *f.* joke, jest; gaiety, fun;
prank.—**bromear,** *vi.* to joke, jest,
make fun.—**bromista,** *mf.* joker,
wag; teaser.—*a.* joking, waggish,
prankish.

bronca, *f.* quarrel, wrangle; dispute.

bronce, *m.* bronze.—**bronceado,** *a.*
bronzed; bronze-colored.—*m.*
bronzing.—**broncear,** *vt.* to bronze,
to adorn with brass.

bronco, *a.* rough, unpolished; morose;
rude; hard; abrupt; hoarse; wild (of
horse).

bronconeumonía, *f.* bronchopneumo-
nia.—**broncopulmonía,** *f.* bronchial
pneumonia.

bronquedad, *f.* harshness; brittleness.

bronquial, *a.* bronchial.—**bronquio,**
m. bronchus.—**bronquitis,** *f.* bron-
chitis.

broquel, *m.* shield, buckler; support,
protection.

brotar, *vt.* to bud, germinate, shoot
forth; to gush, rush out; to break
out; to issue, appear.—**brote,** *m.* germination of vines; bud of trees;
shoot; outbreak (of a disease).

broza, *f.* rotted branches, leaves, etc.
on the ground; rubbish, chaff; undergrowth, brushwood.

bruces, *n. pl.*—*caer de b.,* to fall flat on
one's face.—*de b.,* forward; face
downward; on one's stomach.

bruja, *f.* witch.—**brujería,** *f.* witchcraft,
sorcery.—**brujo,** *m.* sorcerer, con-
jurer, wizard; witch doctor.

brújula, *f.* magnetic needle; compass.

bruma, *f.* mist, fog.—**brumoso,** *a.*
foggy, misty.

bruno, *m.* & *a.* dark brown, blackish.

bruñir, *vti.* [27] to polish, burnish.

brusco, *a.* brusque, gruff; sudden,
sharp (curve).

rusquedad, f. brusqueness, gruffness; suddenness; sharpness (of a curve).

rutal, a. brutal, brutish.—m. animal (quadruped).—**brutalidad,** f. brutality; brutishness, unkindness; brutal or stupid action.—**bruto,** a. brutish; crude (of oil, etc.); gross (profits, etc.); unpolished.—en b., in a rough state, in the rough.—m. beast, brute; blockhead.

ruza, f. horse brush; stove brush; scrubbing brush; printer's brush.

u, m. bugaboo.—hacer el b., to scare, frighten.

ubón, m. bubo.—**bubónico,** a. bubonic.

úcaro, m. flower vase.

ucear, vi. to dive, plunge.—**buceo,** m. diving; searching under water.

uchada, f. mouthful.—**buche,** m. belly; (coll.) bosom; mouthful (of liquids); double chin; (Am.) goiter.

ucle, m. ringlet, curl, lock of hair.

udismo, m. Buddhism.—**budista,** mf. & a. Buddhist.

uen(o), a. good; kind; suited, fit; appropriate; well, in good health; in good condition.—buenos días, good morning, good day.—buenas noches, good evening.—buenas tardes, good afternoon.—de buenas a primeras, unexpectedly.—adv. all right; that is enough.—**buenamente,** adv. freely, spontaneously.—**buenaventura,** f. good luck; fortune (as told by a fortune teller).

uey, m. ox, bullock.

ufanda, f. scarf, muffler.

ufar, vi. to puff and blow with anger; to snort.

ufet, bufé, m. (cook.) buffet; cafeteria; sideboard.

ufete, m. desk or writing table; lawyer's office or clientele.

ufido, m. snort, bellow, roar.

ufo, a. & n. comic; farcical; clownish; crude.

ufón, m. buffoon; jester.—a. funny, comical.—**bufonada,** f. buffoonery; jest.

uho, m. owl.

uhonero, m. peddler, hawker.

ultre, m. vulture.

ujía, f. spark plug; candlestick; candle; candle power.

ula, f. papal bull.

ulbo, m. bulb.

úlgaro, n. & a. Bulgarian.

bulla, f. chatter, noise, shouting; noisy crowd.—**bullanga,** f. noise, tumult.—**bullanguero,** a. fond of noisy merriment.—**bullicio,** m. noise, bustle.—**bullicioso,** a. boisterous riotous; merry and noisy.

bullir, vii. [27] to boil, bubble up; to swarm, teem; to bustle; to stir, move about.

bulto, m. bulk, volume, size; bundle; package; lump, swelling; indistinct shape or form.—escurrir, huir, or sacar el b., to sneak out; to dodge.

bumerang, m. boomerang.

buñuelo, m. fritter, bun; anything poorly done or spoiled; failure.

buque, m. vessel, ship; steamer.—b. mercante, merchantman.—b. transoceánico, ocean liner.

burbuja, f. bubble.—b. de jabón, soap bubble.—**burbujear,** vi. to bubble. —**burbujeo,** m. bubbling.

burdel, m. brothel.

burdo, a. coarse, rough.

burgués, a. & n. bourgeois.—**burguesía,** f. bourgeoisie, middle class.—alta b., upper middle class.

buril, m. chisel; graver.—**burilar,** vt. to engrave.

burla, f. scoffing, mockery, taunt, gibe; jest, fun; trick, deception.—pl. teasing.—**burlador,** n. seducer; jester.— b. de impuestos, tax evader.—**burlar,** vt. to ridicule, mock, scoff; to abuse; to deceive; to evade.—vr. (de) to mock, laugh (at), make fun (of). —**burlesco,** a. burlesque, ludicrous. —**burlete,** m. weather stripping. —**burlón,** a. bantering, waggish, mocking.—n. scoffer; joker, teaser.

buró, m. bureau; writing desk.—**burocracia,** f. bureaucracy.—**burocrático,** a. bureaucratic.—**burocratismo,** m. red tape.

burrada, f. stupid action or saying. —burro, n. ass, donkey; windlass.— a. stupid.

bursátil, a. relating to the stock exchange.

busca, f. search; pursuit.—**buscapleitos,** mf. trouble maker.—**buscar,** vti. [d] to seek, search for.—vri. to bring upon oneself.—**buscavidas,** mf. busybody; hustler; thrifty person.

busilis, m. (coll.) difficulty, difficult point, snag.

búsqueda, f. search.

busto, m. bust, bosom.

butaca, *f.* armchair; easy-chair; (theater) orchestra seat.

butifarra, *f.* sausage.

buzo, *m.* diver.

buzón, *m.* letter drop; letter box; plug stopper.

C

cabal, *a.* just, complete; perfect, thorough; full; faultless.—*estar en sus cabales,* to be in one's right mind.

cábala, *f.* premonition; cabal, intrigue.

cabalgadura, *f.* riding horse or mule. —**cabalgar,** *vii.* [b] to ride on horseback.

caballa, *f.* horse mackerel.

caballeresco, *a.* knightly, chivalrous; gentlemanly.—**caballería,** *f.* riding animal; cavalry; horsemanship; mount; horse; knighthood; chivalry; (Am.) land measure (about 33 ½ acres).—**caballeriza,** *f.* stable. —**caballerizo,** *m.* head groom of a stable.—**caballero,** *m.* knight; cavalier; gentleman; (sl.) buddy, mister, mac.—*a.* riding, mounted; gentlemanly.—*c. de industria,* defrauder, swindler.—**caballerosidad,** *f.* chivalry, quality of a gentleman; nobleness.—**caballeroso,** *a.* noble, generous; gentlemanly.—**caballete,** *m.* ridge of a roof; sawhorse; trestle; easel; gallows of a printing press.—**caballista,** *m.* horseman; expert in horses.—**caballito,** *m.* rocking horse; hobbyhorse.—*pl.* carousel, merry-go-round.—*c. del diablo,* dragonfly.—*c. de mar,* sea horse.—**caballo,** *m.* horse; playing card depicting a mounted prince (equivalent to a queen in a French or English deck); (chess) knight.—*a mata c.,* at breakneck speed.—*c. de batalla,* favorite idea.—*c. de carreras,* race horse.—*c. mecedor,* rocking horse.

cabaña, *f.* cabin, hut; hovel.

cabaret, *m.* cabaret, nightclub.

cabecear, *vi.* to nod; to raise or lower the head (pert. to horses); to incline to one side; (naut., aer.) to pitch, tilt.—**cabeceo,** *m.* nodding, nod of the head; (naut., aer.) pitching.

cabecera, *f.* head-board of a bed; seat of honor; chief city of a district.

cabecilla, *f.* small head.—*m.* ringleader.

cabellera, *f.* head of hair; wig.—**cabello,** *m.* a hair; hair of the head.— *asirse de un c.,* to catch at trifles.— *traer por los cabellos,* to drag in irrele vantly.—**cabelludo,** *a.* hairy.—*cuer c.,* scalp.

caber, *vii.* [7] to fit into, go into; to be contained; to have enough room for.—*c. la posibilidad,* to be within possibility.—*no cabe duda,* there is no doubt.—*no c. en sí,* to be filled with conceit.

cabestrillo, *m.* sling (for injured arm).—**cabestro,** *m.* halter; bullock rope, cord.

cabeza, *f.* head; leader; upper part; intelligence.—*c. de alfiler,* pinhead.— *c. de chorlito,* harebrained.—*c. de puente,* bridgehead.—*c. de turco,* (sl.) patsy, fall guy.—*de c.,* headfirst headlong.—*de pies a c.,* all over.— *levantar c.,* to be restored in health or fortune.—*ni pies ni c.,* neither rhyme nor reason.—**cabezada,** *f* butt (with the head); nod; headshake; headgear (of a harness); headstall of a bridge; (naut.) pitching.—**cabezazo,** *m.* blow with the head.—**cabezón, cabezota, ca bezudo,** *a.* & *n.* largeheaded (one) headstrong (one).

cabida, *f.* content, capacity; space room.—*tener c.,* to be appropriate to fit.

cabildear, *vi.* to lobby.—**cabildeo,** *m* lobbying.—**cabildero,** *n.* lobby ist.—**cabilderos,** *mpl.* lobby.

cabildo, *m.* chapter of a cathedral o collegiate church; municipal coun cil; city hall.

cabilla, *f.* (naut.) dowel, pin; (mason. reinforcement pin; iron rod.

cabina, *f.* (mar.) cabin; (aut.) (fo driver) cab, cabin; car (of an eleva tor).—*c. telefónica* or *de teléfonos* telephone booth.

abizbajo, *a.* crestfallen; thoughtful; melancholy.

able, *m.* cable.—*c. coaxial,* coaxial cable.—*c. de arranque,* booster cable.—*c. de remolque,* towline.—**cablegrafiar,** *vt.* to cable.—**cablegrama,** *m.* cablegram.—**cablevisión,** *f.* cable television.

cabo, *m.* extreme; tip; bit; cape, headland; handle; piece of rope; corporal; end.—*al c.,* at last.—*al c. de,* at the end of.—*dar c. a,* to finish.—*de c. a rabo,* from head to tail, from the beginning to the end.—*llevar a c.,* to carry out; to accomplish.

cabotaje, *m.* coasting trade; pilotage.

cabra, *f.* goat.—**cabria,** *f.* crane, winch.—**cabrillas,** *fpl.* whitecaps. —**cabrío,** *m.* herd of goats.—*a.* goatish.—**cabriola,** *f.* caper, hop, somersault.—**cabritilla,** *f.* kid, dressed kidskin.—**cabritillo, cabrito,** *m.* kid. —**cabrón,** *m.* buck, he-goat; (fig.) acquiescing cuckold.

cabuya, *f.* (Am.) sisal or hemp cord.

cacahual, *m.* cacao plantation.

cacahuate, cacahué, cacahuete, *m.* peanut.

cacao, *m.* cacao; cacao tree; chocolate.

cacarear, *vi.* to cackle; (coll.) to brag, boast.—**cacareo,** *m.* cackling; boast, brag.

cacatúa, *f.* cockatoo.

cacería, *f.* hunt, hunting.

cacerola, *f.* casserole; saucepan.

cacha, *f.* each of the two leaves of a knife or gun (handle).

cachalote, *m.* sperm whale.

cacharrería, *f.* crockery store; collection or stock of earthen pots.—**cacharro,** *m.* coarse earthen pot; (Am.) cheap trinket; (Cuba) jalopy.

cachaza, *f.* first froth on cane juice when boiled; slowness, tardiness. —**cachazudo,** *a.* slow, calm, phlegmatic.

cachemir, *m.* cashmere.

cacheo, *m.* search for hidden arms.

cachetada, *f.* slap on the face.—**cachete,** *m.* cheek; punch in the face or head.—**cachetudo,** *a.* plump-cheeked, fleshy.

cachimba, *f.* smoking pipe.

cachiporra, *f.* cudgel.

cachivache, *m.* piece of junk; (Am.) trinket.—*pl.* trash.

cacho, *m.* slice, piece; (Chile) unsold goods.

cachorro, *n.* cub; puppy; small pistol.

cachucha, *f.* small rowboat; slap.

cacique, *m.* Indian chief; (coll.) political boss.—**caciquismo,** *m.* caciquism; political bossism.

caco, *m.* pickpocket; thief.

cacumen, *m.* acumen, keen insight.

cada, *a.* every, each.—*c. cual, c. uno,* each; every one.—*c. vez que,* every time; whenever.

cadalso, *m.* gallows; scaffold for capital punishment.

cadáver, *m.* corpse, cadaver.—**cadavérico,** *a.* cadaverous.

caddie, *mf.* caddie.—*hacer de caddie,* to caddy.—*ser el caddie de,* to caddy for.

cadena, *f.* chain; range (of mountains).—*c. llanta,* tire chain.—*c. de montaje,* assembly line.—*c. de presos,* chain gang.—*tirar de la c.,* to flush the toilet.—*c. perpetua,* imprisonment for life.—*c. radial,* broadcasting system.

cadencia, *f.* cadence; rhythm; flow of verses or periods; (mus.) cadenza. —**cadencioso,** *a.* rhythmical.

cadeneta, *f.* lace or needlework worked in form of chain.

cadera, *f.* hip.

cadete, *m.* cadet.

caducar, *vii.* [d] to dote; to be worn out by service; to fall into disuse; to become obsolete or extinct; to prescribe; (law) to lapse; to expire.—**caducidad,** *f.* (law) lapse, expiration. —**caduco,** *a.* senile; decrepit; perishable.

caer, *vii.* [8-e] to fall, drop; to fall off; to hang down, droop; to fall due; to befall.—*c. bien,* to create a good impression; to fit; to be becoming.—*c. de la noche,* nightfall.—*c. en cama,* or *enfermo,* to be taken ill.—*c. en gracia,* to please.—*c. en la cuenta,* to understand the situation; to realize.—*c. redondo,* to drop unconscious.—*dejar c.,* to drop; to let fall.—*vri.* to fall down or off; to tumble; to become downcast.—*c. de su peso,* to be self-evident, to be obvious; to fall by itself.—*caérsele a uno la cara de vergüenza,* to be deeply ashamed.

café, *m.* coffee (tree, berry, beverage); coffee house; café.—*c. en la acera,* sidewalk café.—*c. retinto,* black coffee.—*c. soluble,* instant coffee.—**cafeína,** *f.* caffein.—**cafetal,** *m.* coffee plantation.—**cafetera,** *f.* coffeepot.—**cafetería,** *f.* retail coffee shop;

cafeteria.—**cafetero,** *m.* coffee merchant.—**cafetín,** *m.* small café.—**cafeto,** *m.* coffee tree.

cagadita, *f.*—*c. de mosca,* fly-speck.

calda, *f.* fall; falling; tumble; drop; droop; descent.—*a la c. del sol,* at sunset.—*la c. de la tarde,* at the close of the afternoon.—**caído,** *a.* languid; downfallen.

caimán, *m.* cayman; alligator.

caimito, *m.* star apple.

caja, *f.* box; case; cash box or safe; (com.) cash, funds; cashier's office; printer's case; shell, block (of a pulley).—*c. clara,* snare drum.—*c. contadora, c. registradora,* cash register.—*c. de ahorros mutuos,* mutual savings bank.—*c. de alquiler* or *de seguridad,* safety deposit box.—*c. de caudales* or *c. fuerte,* safe, strongbox.—*c. de escalera,* stairwell.—*c. de fusibles,* fuse box.—*c. de la yesca,* tinderbox.—*c. de música,* music box.—*c. de pensiones,* pension fund.—*c. de registro,* manhole.—*c. de reloj,* watchcase.—*c. de sorpresas,* jack-in-the-box.—*c. negra,* (aer.) black box, flight recorder.—*con cajas destempladas,* roughly, without ceremony.—*en c.,* cash, cash kept in the safe.—**cajero,** *n.* cashier; box maker; checkout person.—**cajetilla,** *f.* package (of cigarettes).—**cajista,** *mf.* compositor (in printing); typesetter.—**cajón,** *m.* large box, case; drawer; locker; mold for casting.—*c. de sastre,* odds and ends.—**cajuela,** *f.* small box; (Am.) automobile trunk.

cal, *f.* lime.—*c. viva,* quicklime.

cala, *f.* cove, small bay; creek; fishing ground; sample slice (of a fruit).

calabacín, *m.* calabash.

calabaza, *f.* pumpkin; (fig.) nincompoop.—*dar calabazas,* to jilt (a suitor); to flunk (a student).

calabozo, *m.* dungeon; prison cell; calaboose.

calado, *m.* open work in metal, stone, wood, or linen; draught of a vessel; lace trimmings.

calafate, calafateador, *m.* calker.—**calafatear,** *vt.* to calk.—**calafateo,** *m.* calking.

calamar, *m.* squid.

calambre, *m.* cramp (of muscles), spasm.

calamidad, *f.* calamity.—**calamitoso,** *a.* calamitous; unfortunate.

calandria, *f.* lark, skylark.

calar, *vt.* to penetrate, soak through, drench; to go through; to make open work in (metal, wood, linen or paper); to fix (the bayonet); to see through (a person); to take or cut out a sample of.—*vi.* (of ships) to draw.—*vr.* to become drenched.

calavera, *f.* skull; madcap; rake, profligate; (Mex.) tail light.—**calaverada,** *f.* foolishness, rash action.

calaña, *f.* sort, kind, quality; (fig.) evil moral character.

calcar, *vti.* [d] to trace; to imitate.

calceta, *f.* hose, stocking.—*hacer c.,* to knit.—**calcetín,** *m.* sock.

calcio, *m.* calcium.

calco, *m.* tracing, transfer; copy, imitation; near image.

calculador, *n.* calculator, computer.—**calcular,** *vt.* to calculate, compute; to estimate.—**calculadora,** *f.* calculator.—*c. de bolsillo,* pocket calculator.—**calculista,** *mf.* calculator; designer, schemer.—**cálculo,** *m.* calculation; conjecture; calculus (differential, integral, etc.); (med.) calculus, (kidney, etc.) stone.

caldear, *vt.* to heat; to weld.—*vr.* to become warm; to become overheated; to become overexcited.

caldera, *f.* caldron; kettle; boiler.—**calderero,** *m.* coppersmith; boiler maker; tinker.—**calderilla,** *f.* any copper coin.—**caldero,** *m.* semispherical caldron or boiler; caldronful.

caldo, *m.* broth; gravy; bouillon.

calefacción, *f.* heating system; heating, warming.—*c. por gas,* gas heat.

calendario, *m.* calendar, almanac.

caléndula, *f.* marigold.

calentador, *m.* heater.—*c. unitario* or *de espacio,* space heater.—**calentamiento,** *m.* (sports) warm-up.—*c. global, c. del planeta,* global warming.—**calentar,** *vti.* [1] to heat, warm; (fig.) to give a beating.—*vr.* to become hot; to become excited or angry; to be in heat.—**calentón,** *a.* (vulg.) horny, randy.—*m.* (fam.) fit of anger; warm-up.—**calentura,** *f.* fever.—**calenturiento,** *a.* feverish.

caletre, *m.* (coll.) judgment, acumen.

calibrador, *m.* gauge (instrument); calipers.—**calibrar,** *vt.* to calibrate (a firearm); to gauge.—**calibre,** *m.* caliber; bore (of a cylinder); gauge; diameter (of a wire).

calicanto, *m.* stone masonry.

calidad, *f.* quality; grade; rank; importance.—*pl.* conditions; personal qualifications; parts.

cálido, *a.* warm; hot.

calidoscopio, *m.* kaleidoscope.

caliente, *a.* warm, hot; (Am.) angry.—*en c.* at once.

calificación, *f.* qualification; judgment; mark (in an examination).—**calificar,** *vti.* [d] to qualify; to rate, class; to judge.—**calificativo,** *a.* qualifying; descriptive.

caligrafía, *f.* calligraphy.

calina, *f.* haze, mist, fog.

cáliz, *m.* chalice; communion cup; (bot.) calyx.

callandito, *adv.* quietly, stealthily, softly.—**callar,** *vi.* & *vr.* to be silent, keep silent; to stop, cease (talking, singing, etc.); to shut up.—*vt.* & *vr.* to hush, conceal; to suppress, keep secret.—*vt.* to silence; to gag.—*dar la callada por respuesta,* to answer by silence.

calle, *f.* street; passage; lane.—*abrir c.,* to clear the way.—*c. abajo,* down the street.—*c. de dirección única* or *c. de sentido único,* one-way street.—*c. de travesía,* cross street.—*c. mayor,* main street.—*dejar en la c.,* to leave penniless.—*echar a la c.,* to put out of the house.—*llevarse de c.,* to sweep away.—**callejear,** *vi.* to saunter, loiter about the streets.—**callejero,** *n.* loiterer; loafer.—**callejón,** *m.* alley.—*c. sin salida,* blind alley; dead end.—**callejuela,** *f.* lane; passage; dingy street.

callista, *mf.* chiropodist.—**callo,** *m.* corn, callus (on foot); callus, hard skin.—*pl.* tripe (food).—**callosidad,** *f.* callousness.—**calloso,** *a.* callous; hard-skinned.

calma, *f.* calm; calmness, tranquility; lull, quiet.—*c. chicha,* dead calm.—*con c.,* calmly, quietly.—*en c.,* (of the sea) calm, smooth.—**calmado,** *a.* quiet, calm, still.—**calmante,** *a.* mitigating; quieting, soothing.—*m.* & *a.* sedative; narcotic.—**calmar,** *vt.* to calm, quiet, pacify; to mitigate, soothe.—*vi.* to abate; to be becalmed.—*vr.* to quiet down; to calm oneself, be pacified.—**calmoso,** *a.* calm; slow; phlegmatic.

calor, *m.* heat; warmth, ardor.—*c. de una batalla,* brunt of a battle.—*tener c.,* to be, feel warm.—**caloría,** *f.* calo-

rie.—**calórico,** *m.* caloric.—**calorífero,** *m.* heater, radiator.—**caluroso,** *a.* warm, hot; cordial, enthusiastic.

calumnia, *f.* calumny, slander.—**calumniador,** *n.* & *a.* slander(ing).—**calumniar,** *vt.* to slander.

calva, *f.* baldhead; clearing.

calvario, *m.* Calvary; tribulation.

calvicie, *f.* baldness.—**calvo,** *a.* bald; barren.—*m.* baldhead.

calza, *f.* wedge, shoehorn.—*pl.* tights.—**calzada,** *f.* paved road; highway.—**calzado,** *m.* footwear.—**calzador,** *m.* shoehorn.—**calzar,** *vti.* [a] to put on (shoes, etc.); to make steady by wedging.—**calzo,** *m.* wedge.

calzón, *m.,* **calzones,** *m. pl.* breeches; pants, trousers.—*calzón corto,* knee breeches; shorts.—*tener los calzones bién puestos,* to have the heart in the right place.—**calzoncillos,** *m. pl.* drawers, men's shorts, boxer shorts, boxers, underpants.

cama, *f.* bed; couch; cot.—*c. de agua,* water bed.—*c. de matrimonio* or *c. doble,* double bed.—*c. elástica,* trampoline.—*camas gemelas,* twin beds.—*guardar,* or *hacer c.,* to be confined to bed.—**camada,** *f.* brood, litter; gang.

camafeo, *m.* cameo.

camaleón, *m.* chameleon.

cámara, *f.* chamber; parlor; bedroom; camera; inner tube; association, council; (aer.) cockpit.—*c. agrícola,* farmers' union, grange.—*c. ardiente,* funeral parlor.—*c. cinemática,* film camera.—*c. de cine,* film camera.—*c. de combustión,* combustion chamber.—*c. de comercio,* chamber of commerce.—*c. de compensación,* clearing house.—*c. de descompresión,* decompression changer.—*c. de disco,* disk camera.—*c. de gas,* gas chamber.—*c. de las máquinas,* (mar.) engine room.—*C. de los Comunes,* House of Commons.—*C. de los Lores,* House of Lords.—*c. de oxígeno,* oxygen tent.—*C. de Representantes,* House of Representatives.—*C. de Senadores,* Senate.—*c. de televisión,* television camera.—*c. de video,* video camera.—*c. fotográfica,* camera.—*c. frigorífica,* cold-storage room, icebox.—*c. indiscreta,* candid camera.—*camaras,* loose bowels.—*s. séptica,* septic tank.—*mf.* cameraman, camerawoman, camera-person.

camarada, *n.* comrade; pal, chum. **—camaradería,** *f.* comradeship; companionship.

camarera, *f.* chambermaid; wait-ress.**—camarero,** *m.* waiter; valet.

camarilla, *f.* small room; coterie; clique.

camarón, *m.* shrimp, prawn.

camarote, *m.* cabin, berth, stateroom.

cambalache, *m.* (coll.) barter, swap. **—cambalachear,** *vt.* to barter, to swap.**—cambalachero,** *n.* barterer.

cambiante, *a.* bartering, exchanging; changing.—*m. pl.* iridescent sheen or colors.**—cambiar,** *vt.* to change; to barter; to exchange; to alter.—*vi.* to change, shift.—*c. de marcha,* to shift gear.—*c. de opinión,* to change one's mind.**—cambio,** *m.* change; barter; exchange; rate of exchange (of money); alteration.—*en c.,* in return; on the other hand.—*en c. de,* in lieu of, instead of.**—cambista,** *mf.* banker, money broker.

cambiadiscos, *m.* record changer.

camcórder, *m.* camcorder.

camelar, *vt.* to flirt; to court, woo; to seduce.

camelia, *f.* camellia.

camello, *m.* camel.**—camellón,** *m.* ridge turned up by plow.

camilla, *f.* stretcher, litter; couch; cot.**—camillero,** *m.* stretcher-bearer.

caminante, *m.* traveler, walker, way-farer.**—caminar,** *vi.* to journey, walk, travel, go, move along.—*c. con pies de plomo,* to act cautiously.**—cami-nata,** *f.* long walk; hike; jaunt.**—camino,** *m.* road; highway; course; passage; way; journey.—*c. de herra-dura,* bridle path.—*c. de hierro,* rail-road.—*de c., en c.,* on the way.—*po-nerse en c.,* to set out, start.

camión, *m.* truck; (Mex.) bus.—*c. ba-surero,* garbage truck.—*c. de mudan-zas,* van.—*camión-grúa,* tow truck. **—camionero,** *m.* truck driver.**—camioneta,** *f.* small or delivery truck; station wagon; (Am.) bus.**—camionista,** *mf.* truck driver.

camisa, *f.* shirt, chemise.—*c. de fuerza,* strait jacket.—*c. de vapor,* steam jacket.**—camisería,** *f.* haber-dashery.**—camisero,** *n.* shirt maker. **camiseta,** *f.* undershirt.**—camisón,** *m.* nightshirt; nightgown; chemise.

camorra, *f.* quarrel.**—camorrista,** *mf.* noisy, quarrelsome person.

camote, *m.* (Am.) sweet potato.

campamento, *m.* encampment; camp.

campana, *f.* bell.—*c. de buzo,* diving bell.—*c. de la cena,* dinner bell.—*c. de rebato,* alarm bell.**—campanada,** *f.* stroke of a bell, clang.**—campana-rio,** *m.* belfry.**—campanear,** *vi.* to ring the bells frequently.—*vt.* to di-vulge; to noise about.**—campanero,** *m.* bellman; bell founder.**—cam-panilla,** *f.* small bell; hand bell; uvula; (bot.) bellflower.**—campani-llazo,** *m.* violent ringing of a bell. **—campanilleo,** *m.* ringing, tinkling of small bells.

campante, *a.* cheerful; self-satisfied.

campanudo, *a.* high-flown, bombas-tic.

campar, *vi.* to excel; to encamp.—*c. por sus respetos,* to act as one pleases, be subject to no control.

campaña, *f.* campaign; countryside, fields, open country.—*c. de calum-nias,* smear campaign.

campear, *vi.* to be in the field; to frisk about; to be prominent.

campechano, *a.* frank; cheerful; hearty; open.

campeón, *m.* champion; defender. **—campeonato,** *m.* championship, title.

campesino, *a.* rural, rustic.—*n.* coun-tryman (-woman); peasant; farmer.**—campestre,** *a.* rural, bu-colic.**—campiña,** *f.* field; country. **—campo,** *m.* country; countryside; field; space, camp; flat land.—*a c. raso,* in the open air.—*a c. traviesa,* across country.—*c. de deportes,* play-ing field.—*c. de golf,* golf course.—*c. de minas,* mine field.—*c. de tenis,* tennis court.—*c. santo,* or *campo-santo,* cemetery.**—campus,** *m.* cam-pus.

camuesa, *f.* pippin (apple).

camuflaje, *m.* camouflage.**—camuflar,** *vt.* to camouflage.

cana, *f.* gray hair.—*echar una c. al aire,* to go on a lark.

canadiense, *mf. & a.* Canadian.

canal, *m.* channel; canal; strait; groove.—*abrir en c.,* to cut from top to bottom.—*f.* slot in metal work; drinking trough.

canalete, *m.* bladed paddle for canoe-ing.

canalizar, *vti.* [a] to construct channels or canals in or for; to channel.

canalla, f. rabble, riffraff; mob.—m. mean fellow, cur.—**canallada,** f. base, despicable act.—**canallesco,** a. base, churlish.

canana, f. cartridge belt.

canapé, m. couch; lounge; settee.

canario, m. canary.—n. & a. (native) of the Canary Islands.

canasta, f. basket; crate; (basket.) field goal.—**canasto,** m. large basket, crate.—c. de la ropa, hamper.—**¡canastos!** interj. gracious! confound it!

cáncamo, m. (Am.) ringbolt.

cancela, f. front door grating or screen.

cancelación, f. cancellation.—**cancelar,** vt. to cancel.

cáncer, m. cancer.—**C.,** (astr.) Cancer.—**canceroso,** a. cancerous.

cancha, f. (tennis, handball, etc.) court; (bowling) alley; game grounds; (Am.) roasted corn or beans.—c. de esquiar, ski jump.

canciller, m. chancellor.—**cancillería,** f. chancellery.

canción, f. song; love poem.—c. de amor, love song.—**cancionero,** m. song book; song writer.—**cancionista,** mf. composer or singer of songs, songster.

candado, m. padlock.

candela, f. candle; fire; light.—**candelabro,** m. candelabrum; bracket.—**candelero,** m. candlestick.

candente, a. incandescent, red-hot.

candidato, n. candidate.—**candidatura,** f. candidacy.

candidez, f. ingenuousness; naiveté; candor.—**cándido,** a. candid; simple, innocent; white; unsuspecting.

candil, m. oil lamp; hand lamp.—**candileja,** f. oil receptacle of a lamp.—pl. footlights of a theater.

candor, m. pure whiteness; candor; innocence.—**candoroso,** a. sincere; innocent; pure-minded.

canela, f. cinnamon.

cangrejo, m. crab.

canguro, m. kangaroo; baby sitter.—hacer de c. or hacer c., to baby-sit.—pl. baby sitting.

caníbal, m. cannibal, man-eater.

canica, f. marble; little ball.

canícula, f. dog days.

canilla, f. tibia; shinbone; (Am.) faucet; spool (for thread).—**canillera,** f. (baseball) shin guard.

canino, a. canine.—tener un hambre canina, to be ravenous.

canje, m. exchange; interchange.—

canjear, vt. to exchange, interchange.

cano, a. gray-haired.

canoa, f. canoe.

canon, m. canon; rule, precept; catalogue.—**canónigo,** m. (eccl.) canon.—**canonización,** f. canonization.—**canonizar,** vti. [a] to canonize; to consecrate.

canoso, a. gray-haired.

cansado, a. tired; tiring; tiresome; boring.—**cansancio,** m. weariness; fatigue.—c. del desfase, jet lag.—**cansar,** vt. to weary, tire, fatigue; to bore.—vr. to become tired or weary.—vi. to be tiring or tiresome.

cantalup or **cantalupe,** m. cantaloupe.

cantante, mf. singer, songster, vocalist.—**cantar,** m. song; epic poem.—ese es otro c., that is a horse of another color.—vt. to sing.—cantarlas claras, not to mince words.—vi. to sing; to speak out; (coll.) to squeal.—c. de plano, to make a full confession.

cántaro, m. pitcher; jug.—llover a cántaros, to rain cats and dogs.

cantera, f. (stone) quarry.—**cantero,** m. stone mason.

cántico, m. canticle.

cantidad, f. quantity; amount; large portion; sum of money.

cantimplora, f. canteen; carafe; wine flask.

cantina, f. canteen; bar room, saloon; lunch room; railroad station restaurant; lunch-box.—**cantinero,** n. bartender.

canto, m. singing; song; canto; chant or canticle; end, edge, border; back of a knife; front edge of a book; stone; pebble; quarry stone, block.—de c., on edge.

cantón, m. canton; corner.

cantonera, f. corner cupboard; streetwalker.

cantor, n. singer, songster; minstrel.—a. that sings.

caña, f. cane; reed; reed spear; stem, stalk; walking stick; sugar cane brandy.—c. brava, bamboo.

cañada, f. dell, ravine; cattle path.

cáñamo, m. hemp; cloth made of hemp.—**cañamón,** m. hemp seed; birdseed.

cañaveral, m. cane or reed field.

cañería, f. conduit; pipe line.—c. de agua, water main.—**caño,** m. tube, pipe; spout; (Am.) branch of a river, stream.

cañón, *m.* cannon, gun; barrel of a gun; canyon; flue of a chimney; quill; beard's stubble.—*c. antiaéreo,* anti-aircraft gun.—*c. de electrones,* electron gun.—*c. laser,* laser gun.—**cañonazo**, *m.* cannon shot.—**cañonear**, *vt.* to cannonade, bombard.—*vr.* to cannonade each other.—**cañoneo**, *m.* bombardment; cannonade.—**cañonero**, *m.* cañonera, *f.* gunboat.

caoba, *f.* mahogany.

caos, *m.* chaos.—**caótico**, *a.* chaotic.

capa, *f.* cloak, mantle, cape; layer; coat, coating; cover; coat of paint; disguise; pretense.—*andar de c. caída,* to go downhill.—*c. de ozono,* ozone layer.

capacidad, *f.* capacity; contents; ability.—**capacitación**, *f.* training.—**capacitar**, *vt.* & *vr.* to enable, qualify, prepare; to empower.

capar, *vt.* (coll.) to castrate.

caparazón, *m.* shell of crustaceans; caparison.

capataz, *m.* foreman; overseer.

capaz, *a.* capable, able, competent; roomy, large.

capcioso, *a.* captious; insidious; artful.

capellán, *m.* chaplain; clergyman; priest.

Caperucita Roja, Red Ridinghood.

caperuza, *f.* pointed hood.

capilar, *a.* capillary.

capilla, *f.* chapel; hood.

capirote, *m.* hood.—*tonto de c.,* dunce.

capital, *m.* capital, funds.—*f.* capital (city).—*a.* capital; main; leading; great.—*pena c.,* death sentence.—**capitalismo**, *m.* capitalism.—**capitalista**, *mf.* & *a.* capitalist(ic).—**capitalización**, *f.* capitalization.—**capitalizar**, *vti.* [a] to capitalize.

capitán, *m.* captain; commander.—*c. de corbeta,* lieutenant commander.—*c. de fragata,* navy commander.—*c. de navío,* navy captain.—*c. general del ejército,* field marshal.—**capitanear**, *vt.* to command; to lead.—**capitanía**, *f.* captainship; captaincy.

capitel, *m.* spire over the dome of a church; capital of a column or pilaster.

capitolio, *m.* capitol.

capítulo, *m.* (book or organization) chapter.

caporal, *m.* ringleader; (Mex.) foreman of a ranch.

capota, *f.* top of convertible vehicles.

capote, *m.* cloak with sleeves; bullfighter's cape.—*dar c.,* to deceive.—*decir para su c.,* to say to oneself.

capricho, *m.* caprice, whim, fancy; (mus.) capriccio.—**caprichoso**, **caprichudo**, *a.* capricious, whimsical; stubborn.

Capricornio, *m.* (astr.) Capricorn.

cápsula, *f.* cartridge shell; capsule.—*c. espacial,* space capsule.

captar, *vt.* to captivate, attract, win over; to tune in (radio station).—**captura**, *f.* capture, seizure.—**capturar**, *vt.* to arrest; to apprehend.

capucha, *f.* hood.

capullo, *m.* cocoon; flower bud; acorn cup.

caqui, *m.* & *a.* khaki.

cara, *f.* face; countenance; front; facing; surface.—*buena c.,* good appearance.—*c. de pocos amigos,* churlish look.—*c. o cruz,* heads or tails; (fig.) toss-up.—*de c.,* facing.—*echar en c.* to reproach, blame.—*sacar la c. por alguien,* to defend another person.

carabina, *f.* carbine.—*la c. de Ambrosio,* a worthless thing.—**carabinero**, *m.* customs armed guard.

caracol, *m.* snail.—*escalera de c.,* winding staircase.—**caracola**, *f.* shell of sea snails.—**caracolear**, *vi.* (of horses) to caracole, to prance.—**caracoleo**, *m.* caracoling, prancing about.—**¡caracoles!** *interj.* good gracious!

carácter, *m.* character; temper; energy.—*caracteres de imprenta,* printing types.—**característica**, *f.* characteristic; feature.—**característico**, *a.* characteristic, distinctive.—*n.* character actor or actress.—**caracterizar**, *vti.* [a] to characterize; (theat.) to act a part.—*vti.* & *vri.* (theat.) to make up, dress up for a part.

¡caramba!, *interj.* (coll.) gracious! great guns!

carámbano, *m.* icicle.

carambola, *f.* carom in billiards.—*por c.,* (coll.) indirectly; by chance.

caramelo, *m.* caramel.

caramillo, *m.* small flute; (mus.) recorder; confused heap of things.

carapacho, *m.* shell (of crabs, lobsters, etc.).

carapálida, *f.* (pej.) paleface.

carátula, *f.* title page of a book; mask; (Am.) dial of a watch.

caravana, *f.* caravan, convoy, motorcade; trailer.—*c. de automóviles,* motorcade.—*c. fija,* mobile home.

caray!, *interj.* good gracious!

carbón, *m.* coal; carbon.—*c. de leña,* charcoal.—**carbonera,** *f.* coal cellar, coal bin.—**carbonería,** *f.* coal yard.—**carbonero,** *a.* pert. to coal or charcoal.—*n.* coal or charcoal seller.—**carbonilla,** *f.* coal dust, cinder.—**carbonizar,** *vti.* [a] & *vri.* to carbonize; to char.—**carbono,** *m.* carbon.

carbunclo, carbunco, *m.* carbuncle; anthrax.

carburador, *m.* carburetor.—**carburante,** *m.* fuel oil.—**carburar,** *vt.* to carburize.—**carburo,** *m.* carbide.

carcaj, *m.* quiver (for arrows).

carcajada, *f.* outburst, or peal, of laughter; guffaw.

cárcel, *f.* jail; prison.—**carcelero,** *n.* jailer, warden.

carcoma, *f.* wood borer.—**carcomido,** *a.* worm-eaten; consumed; decayed.

cardador, *n.* carder, comber.—**cardar,** *vt.* to card or comb wool.

cardenal, *m.* cardinal; cardinal bird; welt, bruise.

cardenillo, *m.* verdigris.—**cárdeno,** *a.* livid; dark purple.

cardíaco, *a.* cardiac.

cardinal, *a.* cardinal (point); main, fundamental.

cardo, *m.* thistle.

carear, *vt.* to confront (criminals).—*vr.* to meet face to face.

carecer, *vii.* [3] (de) to lack, to be wanting in.—**carencia,** *f.* lack; scarcity; deficiency.—**carente,** *a.* lacking, wanting.

carero, *a.* overcharging; profiteering.—*m.* profiteer.—**carestía,** *f.* scarcity, dearth; famine; high price.

careta, *f.* mask.

carey, *m.* hawksbill; tortoise; hawksbill or tortoise shell.

carga, *f.* charge (all meanings); load; burden; freight; cargo; loading; impost, duty, tax; obligation.—*c. de punta,* (elec.) peak load.—*volver a la c.,* to insist; to harp on a subject. —**cargado,** *a.* full; loaded; fraught; strong, thick.—*c. de espaldas,* stoop-shouldered.—**cargador,** *m.* shipper; carrier; stevedore; porter; ramrod.—**cargamento,** *m.* cargo; shipment.—**cargar,** *vti.* [b] & *vii.* to load; to burden; to carry (a load); to charge (all meanings); to ship; to

bore; to be burdensome.—*vii.* to incline, lean towards; to be supported by; (con) to assume responsibility; to bear the blame.—*vri.* (of sky) to become overcast; to be full of; to load oneself (with).—**cargazón,** *f.* cargo; abundance.—*c. de cabeza,* heaviness of the head.—*c. del tiempo,* cloudy, thick weather.—

cargo, *m.* post, position; duty, responsibility; (com.) debit; charge, custody; accusation.—*c. de administrador* or *fideicomisario,* trusteeship.—*c. de conciencia,* remorse, sense of guilt.—*hacerse c. de,* to take charge of; to take into consideration; to realize.—**carguero,** *a.* freight-carrying.—*n.* beast of burden.

cariacontecido, *a.* sad, mournful, downcast, woebegone.

caribe, *mf.* Carib; savage.

caricatura, *f.* caricature; cartoon.—**caricaturista,** *mf.* caricaturist; cartoonist.—**caricaturizar,** *vti.* [a] to caricature, mock.

caricia, *f.* caress; petting.

caridad, *f.* charity, charitableness. —**caritativo,** *a.* charitable.

caries, *f.* bone decay, tooth decay.

cariño, *m.* love, fondness, affection. —**cariñoso,** *a.* affectionate, loving.

carisma, *s.* charisma.

cariz, *m.* aspect.

carlinga, *f.* (aer.) cockpit.

carmelita, *n.* & *a.* Carmelite.—*m.* & *a.* (Cuba, Chile) brown.

carmesí, carmín, *m.* & *a.* crimson, bright red.

carnada, *f.* bait.

carnal, *a.* carnal, sensual.—*primo c.,* first cousin.

carnaval, *m.* carnival; Mardi gras.—**carnavalesco,** *a.* pertaining to a carnival or Mardi gras.

carnaza, *f.* bait.

carne, *f.* flesh; meat; pulp (of fruit).—*c. de cañón,* cannon fodder.—*c. blanca,* white meat.—*c. de gallina,* (fig.) goose flesh.—*c. de res* (Am.) beef.—*c. fiambre,* cold meat.—*c. magra,* lean meat.—*c. viva,* quick or raw flesh in a wound.—*c. y hueso,* flesh and blood.—*ni c. ni pescado,* neither fish nor fowl; insipid.—*ser uña y c.,* to be hand and glove, to be one.—**carné,** *m.* identity card.—*c. de chófer, c. de conducir,* driver's license.—*c. de socio,* membership card; library card.—**carnero,** *m.*

sheep, mutton, ram.—**carnicería,** f. meat market, butcher's shop; slaughter.—**carnicero,** a. carnivorous; sanguinary, cruel.—n. butcher.—**carnívoro,** n. carnivore. —a. carnivorous.—**carnosidad,** f. fleshiness; proud flesh.—**carnoso,** a. fleshy; meaty; fat.

caro, a. dear, expensive, costly; dear, beloved.—*cara mitad,* better half.— *adv.* dearly, at a high price or cost.

carozo, m. core of an apple, pear, etc.; corn cob.

carpa, f. (ichth.) carp; canvas tent; circus tent.

carpeta, f. table cover; portfolio; desk pad; folder.—**carpetazo,** m.—*dar c.,* to lay aside; to pigeonhole.

carpintería, f. carpentry; carpenter's shop.—**carpintero,** m. carpenter.— *pájaro c.,* woodpecker.

carraspear, vi. to clear one's throat; to be hoarse.—**carraspera,** f. (coll.) hoarseness; sore throat.

carrera, f. run, running race; course; race track; profession, career.—*a la c., de c.,* hastily, hurriedly.—*c. a pie,* foot race.—*c. de campanario, c. de obstáculos,* steeplechase.—*c. de galgos,* dog racing.

carrerista, mf. outrider; racing cyclist; racegoer; streetwalker.

carreta, f. wagon, cart.—**carretada,** f. cartful.—*pl.* great quantities.—*a carretadas,* (coll.) copiously, in abundance.—**carrete,** m. spool, bobbin, reel; coil; carousel (for slides).—**carretel,** m. fishing reel.— **carretera,** f. highway; drive.—*c. de vía libre,* limited-access highway, parkway, thruway, expressway, turnpike.—**carretero,** m. cart driver; cartwright.—**carretilla,** f. wheelbarrow, handcart; (RR.) go-cart.—*de c.,* mechanically, by rote.—**carretón,** m. wagon, cart.

carricuba, f. street sprinkler.

carril, m. rut; furrow; lane; (R.R.) rail.—**carrilera,** f. rut (in road).

carrillo, m. cheek; small cart.

carro, m. cart, cart; (Am.) automobile; carriage (of typewriter); cartload.— *c. cuba,* (R.R.) tank car.—*c. de cargo,* van.—*c. de combate,* (mil.) tank.—*c. de riego,* street sprinkler.—*untar el c.,* (fig.) to grease the palm, to bribe. —**carrocería,** f. (auto) body.—**carromato,** m. low, strong cart, covered wagon.

carroña, f. carrion, putrid carcass.

carroza, f. carriage for state occasions.—*c. morturria,* hearse.—**carruaje,** m. vehicle; carriage; car.—**carrusel,** m. carousel, slide tray; carousel, merry-go-round; carousel (for baggage).

carta, f. letter; map, chart; playing card; charter.—*c. blanca,* carte blanche, full powers.—*c. bomba,* letter bomb.—*c. certificada,* registered letter.—*c. de marear, c. náutica,* sea chart.—*c. de pago,* acquittance, receipt.—*c. de una cadena,* chain letter.—*c. explosiva,* letter bomb.—*c. verde,* (permiso de residencia y trabajo) green card.—*tomar cartas,* to take part; to take sides.

cartabón, m. carpenter's square; drawing triangle.

cartapacio, m. memorandum book; student's notebook; dossier.

cartear, vr. to write to each other, correspond.

cartel, m. poster, handbill; placard, cartel.—**cartelera,** f. billboard.— **cartelón,** m. show bill.

cartera, f. brief case; pocketbook, handbag; wallet; portfolio; office and position of a cabinet minister.—**carterista,** m. pickpocket, purse snatcher.—**cartero,** m. letter carrier, postman.

cartílago, m. cartilage; parchment.

cartilla, f. primer; identity card; passbook.

cartografía, f. cartography.—**cartógrafo,** m. cartographer.

cartón, m. pasteboard; cardboard; cartoon.—*c. madera,* fiberboard.—*c. piedra,* paper-mâché.—*c. tabla,* wallboard.—**cartoné,** m.—*en c.* hard-back (book).—**cartulina,** f. bristol board, thin cardboard.

cartuchera, f. cartridge box or belt; gun holster.—**cartucho,** m. paper cone or bag; cartridge.

casa, f. house; home; household; firm, concern.—*c. club,* club house.—*c. consistorial,* city hall.—*c. de ayuntamiento,* town hall.—*c. de beneficencia,* children's home.—*c. de corrección,* reform school.—*c. de empeños,* pawnshop.—*c. de fantasmas,* haunted house.—*c. de huéspedes,* boarding house.—*c. de máquinas,* roundhouse.—*c. de moneda,* mint.—*c. de socorro,* emergency hospital.—*c. de vecindad,* tenement house.—*c. editorial,* publishing house.—*c. pública,* brothel.—

rodante, mobile home.—*c. solar*, solar home.

ᵢsaca, *f.* dresscoat.

ᵢsado, *a.* & *n.* married (person).—**casamentero**, *n.* matchmaker.—**casamiento**, *m.* marriage; wedding.—**casar**, *vi.* & *vr.* to marry, get married.—*vt.* to marry off; to couple.

ᵢscabel, *m.* jingle bell; sleigh bell; snake's rattle; rattlesnake.—*poner el c. al gato*, to bell the cat.—**cascabelero**, *a.* light-witted.

ᵢscada, *f.* cascade, waterfall.

ᵢscado, *a.* broken, burst; decayed.

ᵢscajo, *m.* gravel; fragments; rubbish.

ᵢscanueces, *m.* nutcracker.—**cascar**, *vti.* [d] to crack, break into pieces; to crunch; (coll.) to beat, strike.—*vi.* (coll.) to talk too much.—*vri.* to break open.

áscara, *f.* peel, shell, rind, hull, husk; bark (of trees).—*c. de huevo*, eggshell.—*pl. interj.* by Jove!—**cascarilla**, *f.* powdered eggshell for cosmetic.—**cascarón**, *m.* eggshell.

ascarrabias, *mf.* crab, irritable person.

ascarudo, *a.* having a thick shell, hull, etc.

asco, *m.* skull; broken fragment of glassware; hull (of a ship); helmet; hoof.—*calentarse los cascos*, to bother one's brain.—*c. protector*, hard hat.—*ligero de cascos*, featherbrained.

ᵢasera, *f.* housekeeper; landlady; caretaker.—**caserío**, *m.* village, settlement; group of houses.—**casero**, *m.* landlord; caretaker; tenant farmer.—*a.* domestic; home-bred; home-made; homely, homey, informal; household (of articles).—**caseta**, *f.* small house; cabin; booth.

ᵢasi, *adv.* almost, nearly.—*c. c.*, very nearly.

ᵢasilla, *f.* ticket office; post office box; hut; stall; booth; pigeonhole; square of chessboard.—*sacar a uno de sus casillas*, (coll.) to vex beyond one's patience.—**casillero**, *m.* desk or board with pigeonholes.

casimir, *m.* cashmere.

ᵢaso, *m.* case; occurrence; event; matter, question, point.—*c. que*, in case.—*dado el c. que*, supposing that.—*el c. es que*, the fact is that.—*en tal c.*, in such a case.—*en todo c.*, at all events, anyway.—*hacer c.*, to mind, obey, pay attention.—*no*

venir al c., to have nothing to do with the case.—*poner por c.*, to assume, suppose.—*vamos al c.*, let us come to the point.—*verse en el c. de*, to be obliged to, have to.

casorio, *m.* (coll.) wedding.

caspa, *f.* dandruff.

casquillo, *m.* empty cartridge; cap; socket.

cassette or **cassete**, cassette, audio cassette; cassette recorder or player.—*en c.*, taped, recorded, audiotaped.

casta, *f.* breed, lineage, caste; pedigree; quality.

castaña, *f.* chestnut; (fig.) chignon.

castañetear, *vt.* to rattle the castanets.—*vi.* to chatter (the teeth); to creak (the knees).—**castañeteo**, *m.* sound of castanets; chattering of the teeth.

castaño, *m.* chestnut tree and wood.—*a.* hazel, brown, auburn.

castañuela, *f.* castanet.

castellano, *m.* Spanish language.—*n.* native of Castile.—*a.* Castilian; Spanish (lang., gram., etc.).

castidad, *f.* chastity.

castigar, *vti.* [b] to chastise, punish, castigate.—**castigo**, *m.* chastisement, punishment; penalty.

castillo, *m.* castle.—*c. de cartas* or *naipes*, house of cards.

castizo, *a.* pure, correct (language); of good breed.

casto, *a.* chaste.

castor, *m.* beaver; castor.

castrar, *vt.* to castrate, geld.

castrense, *a.* military.

casual, *a.* accidental; occasional, chance.—**casualidad**, *f.* chance event; accident; coincidence.—*por c.*, by chance.

casucha, *f.* hut, shack, hovel.

cataclismo, *m.* upheaval; catastrophe.

catacumbas, *f.* catacombs.

catador, *m.* taster, sampler.—**catadura**, *f.* act of tasting; (coll.) aspect, looks.—**catar**, *vt.* to sample, try by tasting.

catalán, *n.* & *a.* Catalan, Catalonian.

catalejo, *m.* telescope.

catalogar, *vti.* [b] to catalogue, list.—**catálogo**, *m.* catalogue, list.—*c. de fichas*, card catalogue.—*c. de venta por correspondencia*, mail-order catalogue.

cataplasma, *f.* poultice; (fig.) nuisance, vexer.

catarata, *f.* cataract, cascade, waterfall; cataract of the eye.—*las Cataratas del Niagara,* Niagara Falls.

catarro, *m.* catarrh; cold, snuffles.

catastro, *m.* census of real property of a county or state.

catástrofe, *f.* catastrophe.

catavinos, *mf.* winetaster.

catecismo, *m.* catechism.

cátedra, *f.* subject taught by a professor; professorship; seat or chair of a professor.—**catedrático,** *n.* full professor.

catedral, *f.* cathedral.

categoría, *f.* category; class, condition; rank.—*de c.,* of high rank, prominent.—**categórico,** *a.* categorical; positive.

catequizar, *vti.* [a] to catechize; to proselytize by religious instruction; to persuade, induce.

caterva, *f.* multitude; crowd, throng; herd.

catire, *a.* & *n.* (Am.) blond, blonde.

católico, *a.* catholic; universal.—*n.* & *a.* (Roman) Catholic.—*no estar muy c.,* to feel under the weather.—**catolicismo,** *m.* Catholicism.

catorce, *a.* & *s.* fourteen.—**catorzavo,** *a.* fourteenth.

catre, *m.* small bedstead; cot.—*c. de tijera,* folding cot.

caucásico, *n.* & *a.* Caucasian.

cauce, *m.* bed of a river; river course.

cauchal, *m.* rubber plantation.

caución, *f.* caution, precaution; surety, guarantee; bail.

caucho, *m.* rubber (material and tree).

caudal, *m.* volume (of water); abundance; fortune, wealth.—**caudaloso,** *a.* carrying much water; copious, abundant; wealthy.

caudillaje, caudillismo, *m.* leadership; bossism; tyranny.—**caudillo,** *m.* leader, chief; political boss.

causa, *f.* cause; motive, reason; lawsuit, case; trial (at law).—*a* or *por c. de,* on account of, because of, due to.—**causante,** *mf.* originator; (law) the person from whom a right is derived; constituent, principal.—**causar,** *vt.* to cause.

cáustico, *a.* caustic, burning.—*m.* caustic.

cautela, *f.* caution, prudence; cunning.—**cauteloso,** *a.* cautious, prudent, wary.

cauterizar, *vti.* [a] to cauterize; to blame.

cautivador, cautivante, *a.* captivating,

charming.—**cautivar,** *vt.* to captivate, charm; to take prisoner.—**cautiverio,** *m.,* **cautividad,** *f.* captivity.—**cautivo,** *n.* captive.

cauto, *a.* cautious, prudent, wary.

cavar, *vt.* to dig, excavate.—*vi.* to dig, to get to the bottom (of a subject, etc.).

caverna, *f.* cave, cavern.—**cavernícola,** *mf.* caveman, cave dweller.—**cavernoso,** *a.* cavernous; hollow.—*voz cavernosa,* deep-throated voice.

cavidad, *f.* cavity.

cayo, *m.* key, cay, island reef.—*C. Hueso,* Key West.

cayuco, *m.* (Am.) dugout canoe.

caz, *m.* channel; millrace.

caza, *f.* hunt(ing); wild game.—*dar c.* to pursue.—**cazador,** *a.* hunting.—*n.* hunter.—*c. de alforja,* trapper.—**cazafortunas,** *mf.* (pej.) fortune hunter.—**cazar,** *vti.* [a] to chase, hunt; to catch; to pursue.—**caza submarinos,** submarine chaser.—**cazatalentos,** *mf.* talent scout.—**cazatorpedero,** *m.* destroyer.

cazo, *m.* dipper; pan; pot.

cazón, *m.* small shark.

cazuela, *f.* cooking pan; stewing pan; stew; crock; casserole; (theat.) top gallery.

cazuz, *m.* ivy.

cebada, *f.* barley.—**cebadera,** *f.* nose bag.—**cebado,** *m.*—*cargar* or *hacer el cebado de,* (comput.) to boot up.—**cebador,** *m.* (comput.) boot.—**cebar,** *vt.* & *vi.* to fatten (animals); to stuff; to feed (a fire, lamp); to prime (a firearm); to excite and cherish (a passion); to bait (a fish hook).—*vr.* to gloat over (a victim).—**cebo,** *m.* bait; incentive; fodder.

cebolla, *f.* onion; onion bulb.—**cebolleta,** *f.* spring onion; scallion.

cebra, *f.* zebra.

cebú, *m.* zebu.

cecear, *vi.* to lisp.—**ceceo,** *m.* lisping, lisp.

cecina, *f.* corned, dried beef.

cedazo, *m.* sieve.

ceder, *vt.* to transfer, cede, yield.—*vi.* to yield, submit; to fail; to slacken; to abate.

cedro, *m.* cedar.

cédula, *f.* scrip; bill; charter; order; decree; warrant; share.—*c. de identidad,* or *c. personal,* official identity document.

céfiro, *m.* zephyr, west wind; breeze.

cegar, *vii.* [1-b] to grow or go blind.—*vti.* to blind; to confuse; to close up, stop up, block up, fill up.—*vri.* to become or be blinded (by passion, etc.).—**cegato,** *a.* (coll.) short-sighted.—**ceguedad, ceguera,** *f.* blindness; ignorance.—*c. nocturna,* night blindness.

ceja, *f.* eyebrow.—*quemarse las cejas,* to burn the midnight oil.—*tener entre c. y c.,* to dislike; to think constantly about.

cejar, *vi.* to give up; to give in, yield; to cede; to relax, slacken.

cejijunto, *a.* frowning, scowling; with knitted eyebrows.

celada, *f.* ambush; artful trick; trap; helmet.—**celador,** *n.* watchman (-woman); caretaker.—**celar,** *vt.* to watch over zealously or jealously; to watch, keep under guard; to protect; to conceal.

celda, *f.* cell (in a convent, prison, etc.).—**celdilla,** *f.* cell in beehives; (bot.) cell.

celebración, *f.* celebration; praise; applause.—**celebrar,** *vt.* to celebrate; to praise, applaud; to revere; to rejoice at; to say (mass); to hold (formal meeting).—**célebre,** *a.* famous, renowned.—**celebridad,** *f.* celebrity; renown, fame.

celeridad, *f.* celerity, quickness.

celeste, *a.* celestial, heavenly.—*azul c.,* sky-blue.—**celestial,** *a.* celestial, heavenly.

celestina, *f.* procuress; go-between.

celibato, *m.* celibacy.—**célibe,** *a.* & *mf.* unmarried (person); bachelor.

celo, *m.* zeal; devotion; mating, heat (of animals).—*pl.* jealousy.—*dar celos,* to inspire jealousy.

celofán, *m.* cellophane.

celosía, *f.* lattice work; venetian blind.

celoso, *a.* jealous; zealous, eager; suspicious.

celta, *n.* & *a.* Celt(ic).—**céltico,** *a.* Celtic.

célula, *f.* (biol.) cell.—**celular,** *a.* cellular.—*c. fotoeléctrica,* electric eye.

celuloide, *m.* celluloid.

celulosa, *f.* cellulose.

cementar, *vt.* to cement.

cementerio, *m.* cemetery, graveyard.—*c. de los pobres,* potter's field.

cemento, *m.* cement, concrete.—*c. armado,* reinforced concrete.

cena, *f.* late dinner, supper.—*c. con baile,* dinner dance.—*C. del Señor,* Lord's Supper, Holy Communion.—*la C.,* (eccl.) the Last Supper.

cenagal, *m.* quagmire, slough; arduous, unpleasant affair.

cenagoso, *a.* muddy, miry, marshy.

cenar, *vi.* to sup.—*vt.* to take supper.

cencerrada, *f.,* **cencerreo,** *m.* serenade with cowbells, pots and pans, etc.—**cencerro,** *m.* cowbell.

cendal, *m.* gauze, crepe.

cenefa, *f.* border; fringe; valance.

cenicero, *m.* ashtray; ash pan.—**cenicienta,** *f.* thing or person ill-treated.—*la C.,* Cinderella.—**ceniciento,** *a.* ash-colored, ashen.

cenit, *m.* zenith.

ceniza, *f.* ash(es), cinder(s).—**cenizo,** *a.* ash-colored.

censo, *m.* census.

censor, *m.* censor, critic.—*c. jurado de cuentas,* certified public accountant.—**censura,** *f.* censorship; censure, blame, reproach.—**censurable,** *a.* reprehensible, blameworthy.—**censurar,** *vt.* to review, criticize; to censure, blame.

centavo, *m.* cent.

centella, *f.* lightning; thunderbolt.—**centell(e)ante,** *a.* sparkling, flashing.—**centellar, centellear,** *vi.* to twinkle, sparkle.—**centelleo,** *m.* sparkling; twinkling.

centena, *f.* a hundred.—**centenario,** *a.* & *m.* centennial.

centeno, *m.* rye.

centesimal, *a.* (of a number) between one and one hundred.—**centésimo,** *n.* & *a.* (a) hundredth.

centígrado, *a.* centigrade.—**centigramo,** *m.* centigram.—**centilitro,** *m.* centiliter.—**centímetro,** *m.* centimeter. (See Table of Measures.)

céntimo, *m.* penny; hundredth part.

centinela, *m.* sentry, sentinel.

central, *a.* central.—*f.* main office of a public service; (Am.) sugar mill.—*c. eléctrica,* powerhouse, power plant.—**centralización,** *f.* centralization.—**centralizar,** *vti.* [a] to centralize.—**centrar,** *vt.* to center.—**céntrico,** *a.* central.

centrífugo, *a.* centrifugal.

centrípeto, *a.* centripetal.

centro, *m.* center; middle; midst.—*c. comercial,* shopping center, mall.—*c. de informaciones,* visitor center.—*c. de mesa,* centerpiece (for table).—*c. espacial,* space center.—*estar en*

su c., to be in one's element.—
centroamericano, *n.* & *a.* Central American.

centuria, *f.* century (period of time); division of Roman army.

ceñir, *vti.* [9] to gird; to surround, girdle; to fit tight; to hem in.—*vri.* to confine or limit oneself.

ceño, *m.* frown; scowl.—*fruncir el c.,* to frown; to scowl.—**ceñudo,** *a.* frowning; scowling.

cepa, *f.* stump, stub; vinestock; stock of a family.—*de buena c.,* on good authority; of good stock.

cepillar, *vt.* to brush; to plane; to polish.—**cepillo,** *m.* brush; (carp.) plane; charity box.—*c. de uñas,* nail brush.

cepo, *m.* stocks, pillory; stock (of an anchor); trap, snare; clamp.

cera, *f.* wax; wax tapers.—*pl.* honeycombs.—*c. de abejas,* beeswax.

cerámica, *f.* ceramic art; ceramics.

cerbatana, *f.* pea shooter; blowgun; ear trumpet for the deaf.

cerca, *f.* fence; hedge; enclosure.—*adv.* near, close by, nigh.—*c. de,* closely, close at hand.—**cercado,** *m.* fence; stone wall; enclosure.—*c. eslabonado,* chain-link fence.—**cercanía,** *f.* nearness; surroundings, neighborhood.—*cercanías de cuadrilátero,* ringside.—**cercano,** *a.* near, close; neighboring.—**cercar,** *vti.* [d] to fence in; to circle, gird; to surround; to besiege.

cercenar, *vt.* to clip, trim, pare; to sever, mutilate; to reduce, curtail.

cerciorar, *vt.* to assure, affirm.—*vr.* (de) to ascertain, make sure of.

cerco, *m.* fence; ring; circle; rim, border; blockade, siege.—*levantar el c.,* to raise a blockade.—*poner c. a,* to lay siege to, to blockade.

cerda, *f.* bristle; horse's hair.

cerdo, *m.* hog, pig; pork.—*c. de leche,* suckling pig.

cerdoso, *a.* bristly; hairy.

cereal, *m.* cereal.

cerebro, *m.* brain.—*lavarle el c. a,* to brainwash.

ceremonia, *f.* ceremony; formality.—*guardar c.,* to comply with the formalities.—**ceremonial,** *a.* & *m.* ceremonial.—**ceremonioso,** *a.* ceremonious, formal.

cereza, *f.* cherry.—**cerezo,** *m.* cherry tree, cherry wood.

cerilla, *f.* wax match; wax taper; ear wax.—**cerillo,** *m.* (Am.) wax match.

cerner, cernir, *vti.* [10] to sift.—*vii.* to drizzle.—*vri.* to soar.

cero, *m.* zero, naught.

cerquillo, *m.* hair bangs.

cerquita, *adv.* very near; at a short distance.

cerrado, *a.* incomprehensible, obscure; close; closed; obstinate; inflexible; cloudy; overcast; stupid.—*a puerta cerrada,* closed (meeting, etc.).—**cerradura,** *f.* lock; closure.—**cerrajería,** *f.* locksmith's shop or forge.—**cerrajero,** *m.* locksmith.—**cerrar,** *vti.* [1] & *vi.* to close, shut, fasten, lock; to fold and seal (a letter).—*vri.* to close; to remain firm in one's opinion; to become cloudy and overcast; to get close to each other.—*cerrársele a uno todas las puertas,* to find all avenues closed.—**cerrazón,** *f.* dark and cloudy weather preceding a storm.

cerrero, *a.* untamed; wild; unbroken (horse).

cerro, *m.* hill.

cerrojo, *m.* bolt, latch.

certamen, *m.* contest; competition.—*c. de tiro al blanco,* shooting match.

certero, *a.* well-aimed; accurate; sure; skillful; unfailing.

certeza, *f.* certainty; assurance.—**certidumbre,** *f.* certainty, conviction.

certificación, *f.* certificate, affidavit.—**certificado,** *m.* certificate, attestation; testimonial; piece of registered mail.—*c. de defunción,* death certificate.—*c. escolar,* report card.—**certificar,** *vti.* [d] to certify, attest; to register (a letter); to prove by a public instrument.

cervato, *m.* fawn.

cervecería, *f.* brewery; alehouse; beer tavern.—**cervecero,** *a.* beer.—*n.* brewer; beer seller.—**cerveza,** *f.* beer, ale.—*c. de barril,* keg beer.—*c. de marzo,* bock beer.—*c. reposada,* lager beer.

cerviz, *f.* cervix, nape of the neck.—*doblar la c.,* to humble oneself.

cesación, *f.* cessation, discontinuance, stop, pause.—**cesante,** *a.* ceasing.—*mf.* dismissed civil servant.—**cesantía,** *f.* dismissal from a post.—**cesar,** *vi.* to cease, stop; to desist; to retire; to leave a post or employment.—**cese,** *m.* cease; cessation of payment (pension, salary).—*c. de alarma,* all clear.

cesión, *f.* cession, transfer, conveyance; concession.—**cesionario,** *n.* grantee, assignee, transferee.—**cesionista,** *mf.* transferrer, assigner, grantor.

césped, *m.* lawn; turf; grass; grass plot.

cesta, *f.* basket, pannier; basketful.—*c. de costura,* sewing basket.—**cesto,** *m.* large basket; hutch; hamper; laundry basket.

cetrino, *a.* sallow; jaundiced.

cetro, *m.* scepter; reign.

chabacanería, *f.* coarseness; bad taste; vulgar expression or action.—**chabacano,** *a.* coarse, crude, vulgar.—*m.* (Am.) apricot.

chabola, *f.* hut; dugout.

chacal, *m.* jackal.

cháchara, *f.* chitchat, idle talk.—**chacharear,** *vi.* to chatter.

chacota, *f.* mockery; ridicule.—*hacer ch. de,* to mock at.—**chacotear,** *vi.* to make merry; to joke boisterously.

chacra, *f.* (Am.) small piece of farm land.

chafar, *vt.* to flatten, crush; to cut short.

chaflán, *m.* bevel (in buildings).

chal, *m.* shawl.

chalado, *a.* lightwitted, crazy.

chalán, *m.* cattle trader; horsedealer; huckster.

chaleco, *m.* vest.

chalina, *f.* cravat; scarf.

chalupa, *f.* sloop; long boat; small canoe.

chamaco, *m.* (Am.) youngster.

chamarra, *f.* windbreaker; wool jacket; leather jacket.—**chamarreta,** *f.* a short, loose jacket.

chambón, *a.* clumsy, bungling, lucky.—*n.* bungler.

champaña, *m.* champagne.

champú, *m.* shampoo.

chamuscar, *vti.* [d] to singe or scorch.—**chamusquina,** *f.* scorching.

chancear, *vi.* & *vr.* to jest, joke, fool. —**chancero,** *a.* merry, jolly.

chancho, *n.* (Am.) pig; dirty person.—*a.* dirty, unclean.

chanchullero, *n.* trickster; smuggler. —**chanchullo,** *m.* unlawful conduct; vile trick; (coll.) racket.

chancla, *f.* old shoe with worn-down heel.—**chancleta,** *f.* slipper.—**chancleteo,** *m.* clatter of slippers.—**chanclo,** *m.* overshoe.

changador, *m.* (Am.) carrier, porter; handy man.

chantaje, *m.* blackmail.—**chantajista,** *mf.* blackmailer.

chanza, *f.* joke, jest, fun.

chapa, *f.* veneer; plate, sheet (of metal); rosy spot on the cheek; name tag; badge; nameplate; top, cap (of a bottle).—*c. de circulación,* license plate.—**chapado,** *a.* veneered; having red cheeks.—*ch. a la antigua,* old fashioned.

chapapote, *m.* mineral tar, asphalt.

chaparrear, *vi.* to shower; to pour.

chaparreras, *f. pl.* chaps.

chaparro, *a.* & *n.* short, stocky (person).—*m.* (bot.) scrub oak.

chaparrón, *m.* violent shower, downpour.

chapotear, *vi.* to paddle in the water, dabble.—**chapoteo,** *m.* splash, splatter.

chapucear, *vt.* to botch, bungle.—**chapucería,** *f.* bungle; clumsy fib.—**chapucero,** *a.* rough, unpolished, slapdash; clumsy; rude.

chapurrar, chapurrear, *vt.* to jabber (a language); to speak brokenly; to mix drinks.

chapuza, *f.* (fam.) botched job.—*hacer una c. de,* to botch up.—**chapuzar,** *vti.* [a] to duck.—*vii.* & *vri.* to dive, duck.

chaqueta, *f.* jacket; sack coat; (mech.) casing, jacket.—**chaquetear,** *vi.* to run away in fright.

charada, *s.* charade.

charanga, *f.* military brass band; fanfare.

charca, *f.* pool, basin, pond.—**charco,** *m.* pool, puddle.

charcutería, *f.* delicatessen.

charla, *f.* prattle, chat; informal address; patter.—**charlador,** *n.* prater, talker.—*a.* prating, talking.—**charlar,** *vi.* to chat, prattle, prate; to patter.—**charlatán,** *n.* prater, babbler, windbag; charlatan, humbug.—**charlatanería,** *f.* garrulity, verbosity; charlatanism, humbug.—**charlatanismo,** *m.* quackery; verbosity.

charnela, *f.* hinge.

charol, *m.* patent leather.—**charola,** *f.* (Am.) tray.—**charolar,** *vt.* to varnish.

charro, *n.* churl; coarse, ill-bred person; (Mex.) cowboy.—*a.* showy, flashy.

chascarrillo, *m.* joke, spicy anecdote.

chasco, *m.* failure, disappointment; trick, prank.

chasquear, *vt.* to crack or snap (a whip).—*vi.* to crack, snap.—*vt.* to fool; to play a trick on; to disappoint, fail; to cheat.—**chasquido,** *m.* crack of a whip or lash; crack.

chata, *f.* bedpan; barge; (RR.) flatcar.—**chatarrería,** *f.* junk yard.—**chatarrero,** *n.* junk dealer.—**chato,** *a.* flat; flat-nosed.

chayote, *m.* vegetable pear; silly fool, dunce.

checo, checo(e)slovaco, *n.* & *a.* Czechoslovak, Czechoslovakian.

chelín, *m.* shilling.

cheque, *m.* check.—*c. certificado* or *conformado,* certified check.—*c. de viaje* or *viajeros,* traveler's check.—*c. en blanco,* blank check.—*c.-regalo,* gift certificate.—*c. sin fondos,* bad check, bounced check.—**chequear,** *vt.* (Am.) to check, verify; to check (mark).

chicha, *f.* (Am.) a popular fermented beverage (made from maize, pineapple, etc.).

chícharo, *m.* pea.

chicharra, *f.* locust; horse fly; (fig.) talkative woman.

chicharrón, *m.* crackling, fried scrap; overroasted meat.

chichón, *m.* bump; bruise.

chico, *a.* little, small.—*n.* (*f.* chica) child; boy; youngster; fellow; chap.

chicotazo, *m.* blow with a whip; lash.—**chicote,** *m.* whip; cigar; cigar butt.

chiflado, *a.* flighty, crazy.—**chifladura,** *f.* eccentricity; mania, craziness.—**chiflar,** *vi.* to hiss, whistle.—*vr.* to become mentally unbalanced; to lose one's head.—*vt.* (a) to show noisy disapproval to someone (artist, etc.).—**chiflido,** *m.* shrill whistling sound.

chile, *f.* red pepper.

chileno, *n.* & *a.* Chilean.

chillar, *vi.* to screech, scream; to crackle, creak.—**chillido,** *m.* screech, scream; bawling of a woman or child.—**chillón,** *n.* screamer, bawler; whiner.—*a.* whining; screechy; showy; loud (of colors).

chimenea, *f.* chimney; fireplace.

chimpancé, *m.* chimpanzee.

china, *f.* pebble; Chinese woman; porcelain, chinaware; (Mex.) girl, sweetheart; (Am.) orange.

chinche, *f.* bedbug; thumbtack; tedious, pestering person.

chinchín, *m.* (Am.) drizzle.

chinchorro, *m.* small dragnet; small fishing boat.

chinela, *f.* slipper.

chino, *n.* & *a.* Chinese.—*m.* Chinese language.

chiquero, *m.* pigpen; hut for goats; bullpen.

chiquillada, *f.* childish speech or action.—**chiquillería,** *f.* swarm of children.—**chiquillo,** *n.* child.—**chiquitín,** *n.* baby boy; baby girl; very little child.—**chiquito,** *a.* small, little; very small.—*n.* little boy (girl), little one.

chiribitil, *m.* garret; small room.

chirigota, *f.* jest, joke, fun.

chiripa, *f.* stroke of good luck; chance or unexpected event.—*de ch.,* by chance.

chirivía, *f.* parsnip.

chirle, *a.* insipid, tasteless.—**chirlo,** *m.* wound or scar on the head.

chirona, *f.* (coll.) prison, jail.

chirriar, *vi.* to squeak, creak; to sizzle.—**chirrido,** *m.* squeak; screech.

chisguete, *m.* squirt.

chisme, *m.* gossip, piece of gossip; gadget.—**chismear, chismorrear,** *vi.* & *vt.* to gossip, to blab; to tattle.—**chismorreo,** *m.* gossiping, blabber.—**chismoso,** *n.* talebearer, telltale, gossip.—*a.* gossiping.

chispa, *f.* spark; very small diamond; little bit; cleverness, wit; state of drunkenness.—*coger una ch.,* to get drunk.—*echar chispas,* to show anger, to be furious.—**chispeante,** *a.* sparkling, sparkling.—**chispear,** *vi.* to spark; to sparkle.—**chisporrotear,** *vi.* to sputter sparks.—**chisporroteo,** *m.* sputtering of sparks.

chistar, *vi.* to mumble, mutter; to open one's lips.

chiste, *m.* joke, jest; witty saying.—**chistoso,** *a.* witty.

chistera, *f.* top hat; fish basket.

¡chitón!, *interj.* hush! not a word!

chiva, *f.* she-goat; (Am.) goatee.—**chivato,** *n.* informer, talebearer.—**chivo,** *m.* he-goat.

chocante, *a.* disagreeable; strange, surprising.—**chocar,** *vii.* [d] to strike; to collide; to meet, fight; to happen upon; to irritate; to surprise.

chocarrería, *f.* raillery; coarse jest. **—chocarrero,** *a.* vulgar, scurrilous.

chocha, *f.* (orn.) grouse.

chochear, *vi.* to drivel, act senile; to dote.**—chochera, chochez,** *f.* senility; dotage.**—chocho,** *a.* doting, senile.

chocolate, *m.* chocolate.

chofer, chófer, *mf.* chauffeur.

cholo, *n.* (Am.) mestizo, half-breed.— *a.* coarse; uncouth; dark-skinned.

chopo, *m.* black poplar.

choque, *m.* impact; collision; clash; dispute, clash.

chorizo, *m.* red pork sausage.

chorlito, *m.* curlew.**—*cabeza de c.,*** harebrained.

chorrear, *vi.* to spout; to drip; to be dripping wet.**—chorro,** *m.* spurt, jet, gush; stream, flow.**—*a chorros,*** abundantly.**—*c. delgado,*** trickle.

chotacabras, *f.* (ornith.) nighthawk; whippoorwill.

chotear, *vt.* to banter, gibe; to make fun of.**—choteo,** *m.* joking; jeering.

choucroute, or **chucruta,** *f.* sauerkraut.

chovinismo, *m.* (patriotería) chauvinism.

chovinista, *mf.* (patriotero) chauvinist.**—*a.* chauvinistic, chauvinist.

choza, *f.* hut, hovel.

chubasco, *m.* squall, shower.

chuchería, *f.* trifle, trinket.

chucho, *m.* dog; whip; railway switch; electric switch.

chueco, *a.* crooked, bent; (Am.) left-handed.

chuleta, *f.* chop; cutlet; slap.

chulo, *a.* (Am.) pretty, nice, attractive.**—*n.* lower-class native of Madrid.**—*m.* pimp; bully.

chunga, *f.* jest, joke.

chupar, *vt.* to suck; to absorb; to sip; to sponge on.**—chupete,** *m.* pacifier (for children); teething ring.**—chupón,** *a.* sucking.**—*n.* sponger.

churrasco, *m.* piece of broiled meat. **—churrasquear,** *vi.* to barbecue, roast over coals; to prepare (meat) for barbecuing; to eat barbecued meat.

churre, *mf.* filth.**—churriento,** *a.* dirty, greasy.

chuscada, *f.* pleasantry, joke.— **chusco,** *a.* merry, funny.

chusma, *f.* rabble, mob.

chuzo, *m.* (mil.) pike.

cianuro, *m.* cyanide.

cibelina, *f.* sable.

cicatería, *f.* niggardliness, stinginess.**—cicatero,** *a.* niggardly, stingy.

cicatriz, *f.* scar.**—cicatrización,** *f.* healing.**—cicatrizar,** *vii.* [a] to heal.

ciclismo, *m.* bicycling.**—ciclista,** *mf.* cyclist.

ciclo, *m.* cycle; period of time.

ciclón, *m.* cyclone; hurricane.

ciclotrón, *m.* cyclotron.

cicuta, *f.* hemlock.

ciego, *a.* blind; blinded.**—*n.* blind person; (anat.) blind gut.**—*a ciegas,*** blindly, in the dark.

cielo, *m.* sky; firmament; heaven(s); ceiling; glory; paradise; roof.**—*llovido del c.,*** godsend.**—*ver el c. abierto,*** to find an unforeseen opportunity.

ciempiés, *m.* centipede.

ciénaga, *f.* marsh, moor.

ciencia, *f.* science; knowledge; certainty.**—*a c. cierta,*** with certainty.

cieno, *m.* mud, mire, slime; slough.

científico, *a.* scientific.**—*n.* scientist.

ciento, *a.* & *s.* hundred, one hundred.**—*c. uno,*** one hundred and one, hundred and one.**—*por c.,*** per cent.

cierre, *m.* act and mode of closing; shutting, locking; fastener; clasp; plug of a valve.**—*c. hermético,*** weather stripping.

cierto, *a.* sure, positive; certain; true; a certain.**—*de c.,*** certainly, surely.— *lo c. es que,* the fact is that.**—*no por c.,*** certainly not.**—*por c. que,*** indeed; by the way.

cierva, *f.* hind, doe.**—ciervo,** *m.* deer, stag.

cierzo, *m.* cold northerly wind.

cifra, *f.* figure, number; cipher; symbol.**—cifrar,** *vt.* to write in cipher; to abridge.**—*c. las esperanzas,*** to place one's hopes.

cigarra, *f.* locust.

cigarrera, *f.* cigar cabinet; pocket cigar or cigarette case; woman cigarette maker or dealer.**—cigarrero,** *m.* cigarette maker or dealer.**—cigarrillo,** *m.* cigarette.**—cigarro,** *m.* cigar; cigarette.

cigüeña, *f.* stork; crane; bell-crank; crank.**—cigüeñal,** *m.* crankshaft.

cilíndrico, *a.* cylindrical.**—cilindro,** *m.* cylinder; roller; press roll; chamber.

cima, *f.* summit, peak; top, tiptop.—

dar c., to conclude successfully, crown.

címbalo, *m.* cymbal.

cimbrar, *vt.* = CIMBREAR.—**cimbreante,** *a.* willowy.—**cimbrear,** *vt.* to brandish; to shake; to sway; to arch.—*vr.* to bend; to vibrate; to shake.—**cimbreño,** *a.* pliant, flexible.—**cimbreo,** *m.* act of bending, brandishing, swaying, vibrating.

cimentación, *f.* foundation; laying of a foundation.—**cimentar,** *vti.* [1] to lay the foundations of; to found; to ground.—**cimiento,** *m.* foundation; groundwork, bed; base; root.

cinc, *m.* zinc.

cincel, *m.* chisel; engraver.—**cincelar,** *vt.* to chisel, engrave, carve.

cincha, *f.* girth, cinch.—**cinchar,** *vt.* to girth, cinch up.

cinco, *a.* & *m.* five.—**cincuenta,** *a.* & *m.* fifty.—*c. y uno,* fifty-one.—**cincuentavo,** *a.* & *m.* fiftieth.

cincuentón, *a.* fifty-year old.—*n.* fifty-year-old person.

cine, cinema, *m.* moving picture, "movie"; movie theater.—*c. mudo,* silent movie.—*c. sonoro* or *hablado,* sound movie, talkie.—**cinematografía,** *f.* cinematography.—**cinematógrafo,** *m.* cinematograph; moving-picture.—**cinematurgo,** *n.* scriptwriter.

cínico, *a.* cynical; impudent; barefaced.—*n.* cynic.—**cinismo,** *m.* cynicism.

cinta, *f.* ribbon; tape, band, strip, sash; (moving-picture) film, reel.—*c. adhesiva,* adhesive tape.—*c. aisladora,* friction tape.—*c. aislante,* electric tape.—*c. de teleimpresor,* ticker tape.—*c. de video,* video tape.—*c. transportadora,* conveyor belt; carousel (for baggage).—*c. virgen,* blank tape.—**cintarazo,** *m.* slap with a belt.—**cintillo,** *m.* hatband; coronet; headline.—**cinto,** *m.* belt, girdle.—**cintura,** *f.* waist, waistline.—*meter en c.,* to control, to discipline.—**cinturón,** *m.* belt; (fig.) girdle; sword belt.—*c. de asiento,* seat belt.

ciprés, *m.* cypress.—**cipresal,** *m.* cypress grove.

circo, *m.* circus.

circuito, *m.* circuit.—*c. cerrado de televisión,* closed-circuit television.—*c. impreso,* printed circuit.

circulación, *f.* circulation; currency; traffic.—**circulante,** *a.* circulatory, circulating.—*biblioteca c.,* lending library.—**circular,** *vi.* to circulate, move.—*vt.* to circulate, pass round.—*a.* circular; circulatory; circling.—*f.* circular letter, notice.—**circulatorio,** *a.* circulatory.—**círculo,** *m.* circle; circumference; ring; social circle, club, association.—*c. vicioso,* vicious circle.

circuncidar, *vt.* to circumcise.—**circuncisión,** *f.* circumcision.

circundar, *vt.* to surround, encircle.

circunferencia, *f.* circumference.

circunscribir, *vti.* [49] to circumscribe.

circunspección, *f.* circumspection, prudence.—**circunspecto,** *a.* circumspect, cautious.

circunstancia, *f.* circumstance.—**circunstancial,** *a.* circumstantial.

circunstante, *a.* surrounding; present, attending.—*m. pl.* bystanders; audience.

cirio, *m.* wax taper.

ciruela, *f.* plum.—*c. pasa,* prune.—**ciruelo,** *m.* plum tree.

cirugía, *f.* surgery.—**cirujano,** *n.* surgeon.—*c. dentista,* dental surgeon.

cisco, *m.* coal dust; (coll.) bedlam.

cisma, *m.* schism; discord.—**cismático,** *n.* & *a.* schismatic.

cisne, *m.* swan.

cisterna, *f.* cistern; reservoir; underground water tank.

cisura, *f.* incision.

cita, *f.* appointment, engagement, date; quotation; rendezvous.—*c. a ciegas,* blind date.—**citación,** *f.* citation, quotation; summons; judicial notice.—**citar,** *vt.* to make an appointment with; to convoke; to quote; to summon; to give judicial notice.

ciudad, *f.* city.—*c. balneario,* coastal resort.—*c. estado,* city-state.—*c. natal,* home town.—**ciudadanía,** citizenship.—**ciudadano,** *a.* pertaining to a city.—*n.* citizen.—**ciudadela,** *f.* citadel; tenement house.

cívico, *a.* civic.

civil, *a.* polite.—**civilización,** *f.* civilization.—**civilizador,** *a.* & *n.* civilizing; civilizer.—**civilizar,** *vti.* [a] to civilize.—**civismo,** *m.* good citizenship.

cizaña, *f.* darnel; weed; discord.—**cizañar,** *vi.* to sow discord.—**cizañero,** *n.* troublemaker.

clamar, *vi.* to whine; to clamor, vociferate.—*c. por,* to demand, cry out for.—**clamor,** *m.* clamor, outcry; whine; toll of bells, knell.—**clamorear,** *vi.* to clamor; to toll, knell.—**clamoreo,** *m.* repeated or prolonged clamor; knell.—**clamoroso,** *a.* clamorous, loud, noisy.

clan, *m.* clan; (fam.) clique.

claqué, *m.* tap dancing, tap.

clara, *f.* glair, white of an egg.—*a las claras,* clearly, openly.

claraboya, *f.* skylight; transom; bull's-eye.

clarear, *vt.* to give light to.—*vi.* to dawn; to clear up.—*vr.* to be transparent, translucent.

clarete, *m.* claret.

claridad, *f.* brightness, splendor, light; clearness.—*pl.* plain language, plain truths.—**clarificar,** *vti.* [d] to brighten; to clarify; to purify.

clarín, *m.* bugle, clarion; bugler.—**clarinada,** *f.* tart remark.—**clarinete,** *m.* clarinet; clarinet player.

clarividencia, *f.* clairvoyance; clear-sightedness; second sight.—**clarividente,** *a.* clairvoyant; clear-sighted.—**claro,** *a.* clear, distinct; bright, cloudless; light (color); transparent; thin; spaced out; frank; outspoken; obvious, evident; open.—*m.* clearing; light spot; clear spot in the sky.—*adv.* clearly.—*¡c. (está)!* of course, naturally.—*pasar la noche en c.,* not to sleep a wink.—*poner en c.,* to make plain.—*sacar en c.,* to conclude, to arrive at a conclusion.

clase, *f.* class, kind, sort; class in school; classroom.—*c. alta,* upper class.—*c. baja,* lower class.—*c. dirigente,* ruling class.—*c. media,* middle class.—*c. particular,* private lesson.—*de c.,* of distinction, of high standing.

clásico, *a.* classic(al).—*n.* classicist.

clasificación, *f.* classification.—**clasificar,** *vti.* [d] to classify; to class.

claudicar, *vii.* [d] to halt, limp; to bungle; to yield.

claustro, *m.* cloister; faculty of a university; monastic state.

cláusula, *f.* period; sentence; clause; article.—*c. adicional,* rider (in a contract).

clausura, *f.* cloister; inner recess of a convent; closing; clausure, confinement.—**clausurar,** *vt.* to close, conclude, adjourn.

clavar, *vt.* to nail; to fix, fasten; to stick; pin, prick; to pierce; (coll.) to cheat, deceive.—*c. la vista,* or *los ojos,* to stare.

clave, *f.* key of a code; (mus.) key; clef; keystone.—*c. de do en cuarta línea,* tenor clef.—*c. de fa,* bass clef.—*c. de sol,* trebel clef.

clavel, *m.,* **clavellina,** *f.* pink, carnation.

clavetear, *vt.* to nail; to decorate or stud with nails.

clavícula, *f.* clavicle, collar bone.

clavija, *f.* pin, peg; peg of a string instrument.—*apretar las clavijas,* to put on the thumb screws; to dress down.

clavo, *m.* nail; spike; clove.—*dar en el c.,* to hit the nail on the head.—*un c. saca otro c.,* one grief cures another.

clemencia, *f.* clemency, mercy.—**clemente,** *a.* merciful.

cleptómano, *n.* & *a.* kleptomaniac.

clerical, *a.* clerical, pert. to the clergy.—**clérigo,** *m.* clergyman.—**clero,** *m.* clergy.

cliente, *mf.* client; customer.—**clientela,** *f.* following, clientele; customers; practice (of lawyers, doctors).

clima, *m.* climate, clime.

clímax, *m.* climax.

clínica, *f.* clinic; private hospital; doctor's or dentist's office; nursing home.

clisé, *m.* cliché; stereotype plate; (phot.) negative.

cloaca, *f.* sewer; cesspool.

clon, *m.* clone.—**clonación,** *f.* cloning.—**clonaje,** *m.* cloning.—**clonar,** *vt.* to clone.

cloquear, *vi.* to cluck, cackle.

cloro, *m.* chlorine.—**clorofila,** *f.* chlorophyll.—**cloroformar,** *vt.,* **cloroformizar,** *vti.* [a] to chloroform.—**cloroformo,** *m.* chloroform.

club, *m.* private club.—*c. de campo,* country club.—*c. náutico,* yacht club.—**clubista,** *f.* clubwoman.

clueca, *f.* brooding hen.—**clueco,** *a.* broody; (coll.) decrepit.

coacción, *f.* force; coercion.—**coactivo,** *a.* forcible; coercive.

coagular, *vt.* to coagulate; to curdle.—*vr.* to coagulate, clot; to curdle.

coalición, *f.* coalition.

coartada, *f.* alibi.—**coartar,** *vt.* to limit, restrain.

coba, *f.* (coll.) fawning, adulation.—*dar c.,* to flatter.

cobarde, *mf.* coward; poltroon.—*a.* cowardly.—**cobardía,** *f.* cowardice.

cobertizo, *m.* shed, hut; penthouse.—**cobertor,** *m.* bedcover.—**cobertura,** *f.* cover, wrapper, covering, coverlet.

cobija, *f.* cover; (Am.) blanket.—*c. eléctrica,* electric blanket.—**cobijar,** *vt.* to cover; to shelter; to lodge.—*vr.* to take shelter.

cobrador, *m.* collector, receiving teller.—**cobranza,** *f.* receipt, collection (of money).—**cobrar,** *vt.* to collect (bills, debts); to receive (what is due); to retrieve (shot game); to gain; to charge (price, fee); to cash (check).—*c. ánimo,* to take courage.—*c. fuerzas,* to gather strength.

cobre, *m.* copper; brass kitchen utensils; brass instruments of an orchestra.—*batir el c.,* to hustle.—**cobrizo,** *a.* coppery; copper-colored.

cobro, *m.* receipt, collection (of money); cashing.—*poner en c.,* to put in a safe place.—*ponerse en c.,* to seek a safe place; to withdraw to safety.

coca, *f.* coca; coca leaves.—**cocaína,** *f.* cocaine.

cocal, *m.* coconut plantation.

cocción, *f.* cooking.

cocear, *vt.* & *vi.* to kick.

cocer, *vti.* [26-a] to boil; to bake; to cook; to calcine (brick, etc.).—*vii.* to boil, cook.—**cocido,** *a.* boiled, baked, cooked.—*bien c.,* (cook.) well-done.—*m.* a Spanish stew.

cochambre, *m.* (coll.) greasy, dirty thing.—**cochambroso,** *a.* filthy, smelly.

coche, *m.* carriage; coach; car.—*c. antiguo* or *de época,* classic (car).—*c. bomba,* car bomb.— *c. cama,* (R.R.) sleeping car.—*c. celular,* prison van.—*c. de carreras,* racer.—*c. de serie,* stock car.—*c. familiar* or *rural,* station wagon.—*c. fúnebre* or *mortuorio,* hearse.—**cochecillo,** *m.—c. para inválidos,* wheel chair.—**cochero,** *m.* coachman.

cochinada, *f.* (coll.) hoggishness; dirty action, dirty trick.—**cochinilla,** *f.* cochineal.—**cochinillo,** *n.* suckling pig.—*c. de Indias,* guinea pig.—**cochino,** *n.* hog (sow), pig.—*a.* & *n.* dirty, vile (person).—**cochiquera,** *f.* (coll.) hog sty, pigpen.

cociente, *m.* quotient.—*c. intelectual,* intelligence quotient (I.Q.).

cocimiento, *m.* boiling, concoction.—**cocina,** *f.* kitchen; cuisine, cookery.—*c. de campaña,* (mil.) field kitchen.—**cocinar,** *vt.* & *vi.* to cook.—**cocinero,** *n.* cook; chef.

coco, *m.* coconut (tree, shell, fruit); bogey.

cocodrilo, *m.* crocodile.

cocotero, *m.* coconut tree.

coctel, *m.* cocktail.—**coctelera,** *f.* cocktail shaker.

cocuyo, *m.* firefly.

codazo, *m.* blow with the elbow.—**codear,** *vi.* to elbow.—*vt.* to nudge.—*vr.* to rub shoulders, be on intimate terms.—**codeo,** *m.* elbowing; familiarity.

codeína, *f.* codeine.

codiciar, *vt.* & *vi.* to covet.—**codicioso,** *a.* covetous, greedy; ambitious.

codificar, *vti.* [d] to codify.—**código,** *m.* code.—*c. barrado* or *de barras,* bar code.—*c. civil,* civil law.—*c. de comercia,* commercial law.—*c. genético,* genetic code.—*c. militar,* military law.—*c. morse,* Morse code.—*c. penal,* penal code.—*c. postal,* ZIP code.—*c. territorial* or *de la zona,* (tel.) area code.

codo, *m.* elbow; bend.—*alzar* or *empinar el c.,* to drink too much.—*hablar por los codos,* to talk too much.

codorniz, *f.* quail.

coeducación, *f.* coeducation.

coeficiente, *m.* coefficient.

coerción, *f.* coercion.

coetáneo, *a.* contemporary.

coexistencia, *f.* coexistence.—**coexistir,** *vi.* to coexist.

cofia, *f.* coif; hair net.

cofrade, *mf.* member (of a confraternity, brotherhood, etc.).—**cofradía,** *f.* brotherhood, sisterhood; guild.

cofre, *m.* coffer; trunk; chest.—**cofrecito,** *m.* casket, jewel box.

coger, *vti.* [c] to catch; to seize, grasp; to gather up, collect; to take, receive, hold.—*cogerse una cosa,* to steal something.—**cogida,** *f.* toss or goring by bull; a catch of the ball by a baseball player.

cogollo, *m.* heart of garden plants; shoot of a plant; sugar cane top, used as forage.

cogote, *m.* back of the neck, nape.

cohechar, *vt.* to bribe.—**cohecho,** *m.* bribery.

coherencia, *f.* coherence; connection.—**coherente,** *a.* coherent.—**co-**

heslón, *f.* cohesion.—**cohesivo,** *a.* cohesive.

ohete, *m.* skyrocket; rocket.—*c. propulsor,* booster rocket.—*c. sonda,* space probe.

ohibición, *f.* reserve, shyness; restraint.—**cohibido,** *a.* inhibited; embarrassed, uneasy.—**cohibir,** *vt.* to restrain, inhibit.

oincidencia, *f.* coincidence.—**coincidente,** *a.* coincident.—**coincidir,** *vi.* to coincide.

oito, *m.* copulation.

ojear, *vi.* to limp.—*c. del mismo pie,* to have the same weakness.—**cojera,** *f.* limp, lameness.

ojín, *m.* cushion; pad.—**cojinete,** *m.* bearing; pillow block; small cushion.—*c. de bola* or *c. a bolas,* ball bearing.—*c. de rodillos,* roller bearing.

ojo, *a.* lame, crippled; one-legged; (of table, etc.) unsteady, tilting.—*n.* cripple.

ok, *m.* coke.

ol, *f.* cabbage.

ola, *f.* tail; queue, line of people; glue.—*estar a la c.,* to be in the last place.—*hacer c.,* to stand in line, to queue (up).—*tener* or *traer c.,* to have serious consequences.

olaboración, *f.* collaboration; contribution (to a periodical, etc.).—**colaborador,** *m.* collaborator; contributor (to a periodical, etc.).—**colaborar,** *vi.* to collaborate.

olación, *f.* collation; lunch, light meal.—*ceremonia de c. de grados,* graduation ceremony.—*traer a c,* to bring up for discussion.

oladera, *f.* strainer, sieve.—**colador,** *m.* colander.—**colar,** *vti.* & *vii.* [12] to strain, drain, pass through, percolate.—*vri.* to slip in or out, sneak in.

olapso, *m.* collapse.—*c. nervioso,* nervous breakdown.

olateral, *a.* collateral.

olcha, *f.* coverlet, quilt, bedspread; saddle and trappings.

olchón, *m.* mattress.

olear, *vi.* to wag (the tail).—*vt.* to pull down (cattle) by the tail.

olección, *f.* collection.—**coleccionador, coleccionista,** *n.* collector (of stamps, etc.).—**coleccionar,** *vt.* to form a collection of, collect.—**colecta,** *f.* collection of voluntary contributions, tax assessment.—**colectar,** *vt.* to collect.—**colectividad,** *f.* collectivity; mass of people; community.—**colectivo,** *a.* collective.—**colector,** *m.* collector, gatherer.

colega, *mf.* colleague; fellow worker.

colegial, *a.* collegiate.—*n.* first or secondary school student; (coll.) inexperienced person, greenhorn.—**colegiatura,** *f.* membership in a professional association (bar, medical, engineering, etc.).—**colegio,** *m.* body of professional men; school, academy; elementary or secondary school.—*c. mayor,* residence hall, dorm.

colegir, *vti.* [29-c] to deduce, infer, conclude.

cólera, *f.* anger, rage, fury.—*m.* cholera.—**colérico,** *a.* angry, irascible; choleric.

coleta, *f.* pigtail.—*cortarse la c.,* to retire, quit the profession (esp. bullfighters).—**coletilla,** *f.* postscript; small queue (hair).

coleto, *m.* leather jacket; inner self.—*decir para su c.,* to say to oneself.—*echarse al c.,* to drink down; to devour.

colgadizo, *m.* lean-to.

colgado, *a.* suspended, hanging; disappointed.—**colgadura,** *f.* tapestry; bunting.—**colgajo,** *m.* tatter or rag hanging from (clothes, etc.).—**colgante,** *m.* drop; pendant; hanger; king post.—*a.* hanging.—**colgar,** *vti.* [12-b] to hang up; to impute, charge with; to kill by hanging; to flunk a student.—*vii.* to be suspended; to dangle; to flag, droop.—*vri.* to hang oneself.

colibrí, *m.* hummingbird.

coliche, *m.* open house, at-home.

cólico, *m.* colic.

coliflor, *f.* cauliflower.

coligarse, *vri.* [b] to band together, become allies.

colilla, *f.* cigar stub; cigarette butt.

colina, *f.* hill.

colindante, *a.* contiguous, adjacent, abutting.—**colindar,** *vi.* (**con**) to be contiguous, or adjacent (to); to abut (on).

coliseo, *m.* theater, opera house; coliseum.

colisión, *f.* collision, clash.

collado, *m.* height, hill.

collar, *m.* necklace; collar, collet.—**collarín,** *m.* collar of a coat; (mech.) tube, sleeve; ruff.—**collera,** *f.* horse collar.

colmado, *a.* (**de**) abundant; full (of), filled (with).—*m.* specialty eating house (gen. for sea food); grocery store, supermarket.—**colmar,** *vt.* (**de**) to heap up, fill to the brim (with); to fulfill, make up; to bestow liberally.

colmena, *f.* beehive, (Am.) bee.—**colmenar,** *m.* apiary.

colmillo, *m.* eyetooth; fang; tusk.

colmo, *m.* fill; overflowing; overmeasure; limit; climax, extreme, acme.—*a. c.,* abundantly.—*llegar al c., ser el c.,* to be the limit.

colocación, *f.* situation, position; employment, job; placing, setting, arrangement; placement.—**colocar,** *vti.* [d] to arrange, put in due place or order; to place, provide with employment, take on (in a job).—*vri.* to take (a job); to place oneself.

colombiano, *n.* & *a.* Colombian.

colombino, *a.* pertaining to Columbus; pertaining to pigeons or doves.

colonia, *f.* settlement, colony; plantation; cologne water.—**colonial,** *a.* colonial.—**colonización,** *f.* settlement, colonization.—**colonizador,** *n.* & *a.* colonizer; colonizing.—**colonizar,** *vti.* [a] to colonize, settle.—**colono,** *m.* colonist, settler; tenant farmer.

coloquial, *a.* colloquial.—**coloquio,** *m.* conversation, dialogue.

color, *m.* color; paint; rouge; coloring tint; pretext.—*c. hueso,* off-white.—*sacarle los colores a uno,* to shame, make one blush.—**coloración,** *f.* coloration, coloring, painting.—**colorado,** *a.* red; ruddy; colored; (Mex.) risqué, off-color.—*ponerse c.,* to blush.—**colorante,** *m.* color, paint; coloring tint.—*a.* coloring.—**colorar, colorear,** *vt.* to color, paint, dye, stain; to make plausible; to palliate.—**coloreado,** *a.* colored.—**colorete,** *m.* rouge.—**colorido,** *m.* coloring or color; pretext, pretense.

colosal, *a.* colossal, huge.

columbrar, *vt.* to perceive faintly, discern at a distance; to conjecture.

columna, *f.* column, pillar.—*c. vertebral,* or *dorsal,* spine.

columpiar, *vt.* & *vr.* to swing.—**columpio,** *m.* swing; seesaw.

coma, *f.* comma (,).—*m.* coma, unconsciousness.—*c. decimal, c. de decimales,* comma used as a decimal point in Spanish.

comadre, *f.* mother and godmoth〈 with respect to each other; midwif〈 gossip; go-between.—**comadrea**〈 *vi.* to gossip, tattle.—**comadreja,** weasel.—**comadreo,** *m.* gossipin〈—**comadrón,** *m.* male midwife, a〈 coucheur.—**comadrona,** *f.* midwife

comandancia, *f.* command; office of commander; province or district 〈 a commander.—**comandante,** *n*〈 commander, commandant.—**c〈 mandar,** *vt.* to command.

comandita, *f.* (com.) silent partne〈 ship.—**comanditario,** *a.* (com.) pe〈 taining to a silent partnership.

comando, *m.* military command.

comarca, *f.* territory, region.

comba, *f.* curvature, warp, bend.〈—**combadura,** *f.* bending, bend.〈—**combar,** to bend, curve.—*vr.* 〈 warp, bulge; to sag.

combate, *m.* combat, fight, battl〈 struggle.—*c. revancha,* (boxing) r〈 turn bout, return engagement.〈—**combatiente,** *mf.* & *a.* combatan〈 fighter; fighting.—**combatir,** *vt.* 〈 *vi.* to combat, fight; to attack, o〈 pose; to struggle.

combinación, *f.* combination; conne〈 tion; compound; plan; slip (unde〈 wear).—**combinar,** *vt.* & *vr.* to con〈 bine, unite.

combustible, *m.* fuel.—*a.* combus〈 ible.—**combustión,** *f.* combustion.

comedero, *m.* feeding-trough; (col〈 eating place.—*c. para pájaros,* bi〈 feeder.—*a.* edible, eatable.

comedia, *f.* comedy; farce; play.—**c**〈 **mediante,** *mf.* actor, actress, com〈 dian; hypocrite.—*a.* (coll.) hyp〈 critical.

comedido, *a.* courteous, polite; pr〈 dent, moderate.—**comedimient**〈 *m.* moderation; politeness.—**com**〈 **dirse,** *vri.* [29] to govern oneself; 〈 be moderate, polite.

comedor, *m.* dining room.—*c. de ben*〈 *ficencia,* soup kitchen.—*c. de mi*〈 *tares,* (mil.) mess hall.—*n.* & 〈 eater; eating.

comején, *m.* termite.

comensal, *n.* table guest; companio〈 at meals.

comentar, *vt.* to comment; to ann〈 tate, expound.—**comentario,** *〈 commentary.—**comentarista,** *〈 commentator; (rad. & TV) a〈 nouncer.

comenzar, *vti.* [1-a] & *vii.* to co〈 mence, begin.

comer, vt. to eat; to take (in chess, checkers, etc.).—c. pavo, (fam.) to be a wallflower.—vi. to eat; to lunch, dine.—vr. to eat up; to omit, skip.—dar de c., to feed.—ganar para c., to make a living.

comercial, a. commercial.—**comerciante,** mf. trader, dealer; storekeeper.—c. al por mayor, wholesaler.—**comerciar,** vi. to trade, engage in commerce.—**comercio,** m. commerce, trade; marketing.—c. sexual, sexual intercourse.

comestible, a. eatable, edible.—m. pl. food, provisions, groceries.

cometa, m. comet.—f. kite.

cometer, vt. to commit, perpetrate.—**cometido,** m. commission; charge; task, duty.

comezón, f. itch(ing); longing, desire.

comicios, m. pl. elections, primaries; district assemblies.

cómico, m. player, actor, comedian.—a. comic; comical, funny.

comida, f. eating; food; luncheon, dinner, supper.—c. rápida, fast food.

comienzo, m. start, beginning.—dar c., to begin, start.

comillas, f. pl. quotation marks (" ").

comilón, m. great eater, glutton.

comino, m. cumin (plant, seed).—no valer un c., not to be worth a bean.

comisaría, f. police station; office of the commissary.—**comisario,** m. commissary; police inspector; purser.

comisión, f. commission; committee; assignment; perpetration.—c. permanente, standing committee.—**comisionado,** m. commissioner.—a. commissional or commissionary; commissioned.—**comisionar,** vt. to commission; to appoint.—**comisionista,** mf. commission merchant; commission agent; commissioner.

comité, m. committee; commission.

comitiva, f. retinue; group of attendants or followers.

como, adv. & conj. how; in what manner; to what degree; as; since; like; as if; about, approximately; if; such as; inasmuch as; as.—c. quiera que, although; since.—**cómo,** interrog. what? how? why?—¿a cómo? how much?—¿a cómo estamos? what is the date?—¿cómo? what is it? what did you say?—¿cómo así? how? how so?—¿cómo no? why not? of course.—interj. why! is it possible!

cómoda, f. chest of drawers, bureau.—c. alta con patas altas, highboy.—c. con espejo, dresser.

comodidad, f. comfort, convenience; commodity.—**comodín,** m. joker (in a card deck); wild card; gadget, jigger; excuse, alibi; (comput.) wild card.—**cómodo,** a. comfortable; cozy; convenient.

comodoro, m. commodore.

compacto, a. compact.

compadecer, vti. [3] to pity, be sorry for.—vri. (de) to pity; (con) to conform, agree, tally.

compadraje, compadrazgo, m. alliance for mutual protection and advancement (used in a bad sense); clique.—**compadre,** m. godfather and father of a child with respect to each other; friend, pal.

compaginar, vt. to arrange in proper order; to unite, join.

compañerismo, m. good fellowship, comradeship.—**compañero,** m. companion, pal; fellow member; partner; one of a pair, mate.—c. de armas, comrade-in-arms.—c. de cama, bedfellow.—c. de clase, classmate.—c. de cuarto, habitación, or piso, roommate.—c. de equipo, teammate.—c. de juego, playmate.—c. de trabajo, coworker.—c. de viaje, traveling companion; (pol. & pej.) fellow traveler.—**compañía,** f. company; partnership; co-partnership.—c. de actores o de circo, troupe.—c. tenedora, holding company.

comparación, f. comparison.—**comparar,** vt. to compare; to confront.—**comparativo,** a. comparative.

comparecencia, f. appearance.—**comparecer,** vii. [3] to appear (before a judge, etc.).—**comparendo,** m. summons, subpoena.

comparsa, f. (theat.) retinue of persons.—mf. (theat.) extra, supernumerary actor.

compartimiento, m. division of a whole into parts; compartment; department.—**compartir,** vt. to divide into equal parts; to share.

compás, m. compass; measure; beat, meter.—llevar el c., to beat time.

compasión, f. compassion, pity.—**compasivo,** a. compassionate, merciful.

compatibilidad, f. compatibility.—**compatible,** a. compatible, suitable.

compatriota, mf. compatriot, fellow-countryman.

compeler, vt. to compel, force.

compendiar, vt. to abridge, condense.—**compendio**, m. compendium, abridgment.

compenetración, f. intermixture.—**compenetrarse**, vr. to pervade, intermix; to be in full agreement.

compensación, f. compensation; recompense, reward.—**compensar**, vt. & vi. to compensate, recompense; to counterbalance; to balance, equilibrate; to indemnify.

competencia, f. competition, rivalry; competence, aptitude; jurisdiction; dispute.—**competente**, a. competent, apt; applicable (to); adequate.—**competición**, f. competition.—**competidor**, n. opponent, competitor.—a. competing.—**competir**, vii. [29] to compete, vie, rival.

compilación, f. compilation.—**compilador**, n. & a. compiler, compiling.—**compilar**, vt. to compile.

compinche, m. bosom friend, pal.

complacencia, f. pleasure, satisfaction; complacency.—**complacer**, vti. [3] to please, accommodate.—vri. (en) to be pleased (with or to); to delight (in); to take pleasure (in).—**complaciente**, a. pleasing, kind, agreeable.

complejidad, f. complexity.—**complejo**, a. complex; intricate, arduous.—m. complex.

complementario, a. complementary.—**complemento**, m. complement.—c. directo, (ling.) direct object.

completar, vt. to complete, perfect, finish.—**completo**, a. complete, unabridged; completed; unqualified.—por c., completely.

complexión, f. constitution; temperament, nature.

complicación, f. complication, complexity.—**complicar**, vti. [d] to complicate; to jumble together.—vri. to become difficult, confused.

cómplice, mf. accomplice.—**complicidad**, f. complicity.

complot, m. plot, conspiracy.

componenda, f. adjustment, compromise.—**componente**, mf. & a. component.—**componer**, vti. [32] to compose; to compound; to prepare; to repair; to heal, restore; to brace up; to trim, fit up; to reconcile.—vri. to prink, (coll.) doll up; to calm oneself.

comportamiento, m. behavior.—**comportar**, vr. to behave.

composición, f. composition; repair.—**compositor**, n. composer (of music).—**compostura**, f. composure; repair, repairing; cleanliness, neatness of dress.

compota, f. compote, stewed fruits; preserves.

compra, f. purchase; buying; shopping.—hacer compras, to shop.—ir or salir de compras, to go shopping.—**comprado**, a. purchased, bought.—c. sin receta, over-the-counter.—**comprador**, m. buyer; purchaser; user.—**comprar**, vt. to buy, purchase; to shop.

comprender, vt. to understand, comprehend; to comprise, include, cover.—**comprensible**, a. comprehensible, understandable.—**comprensión**, f. comprehension, understanding, comprehensiveness; act of comprising or containing.—**comprensivo**, a. comprehensive; capable of understanding; containing.

compresa, f. compress.—c. higiénica, sanitary napkin.

compresión, f. compression.—**comprimir**, vt. to compress.—vr. to become compact.

comprobación, f. verification, checking; proof, substantiation.—**comprobante**, m. proof, evidence; voucher; sales slip.—**comprobar**, vti. [12] to verify, confirm, check.

comprometer, vt. to compromise; to endanger; to arbitrate; to engage; to risk; to expose, jeopardize.—vr. to commit oneself; to undertake; to expose oneself; to become engaged; to become involved; to expose oneself to risk.—**compromiso**, m. compromise; obligation; embarrassment; engagement, appointment.

compuerta, f. hatch or half-door; lock, floodgate.

compuesto, pp. of COMPONER.—m. compound, preparation, mixture.—a. compound; composed; repaired; arranged; made up.

compungirse, vri. [c] to feel compunction or remorse.

computación, f. (comput.) computing.—curso de c., course in computing.—experto en c., computer expert.

computadora, f. **computador**, m. computer.—c. de a bordo, onboard computer.—c. de mesa, desktop computer.—c. doméstica, home computer.—*c. personal,* personal computer.—*c. portátil,* laptop computer.

computar, *vt.* to compute, calculate. —**computarizado** or **computerizado,** *a.* computerized.—**computarizar** or **computerizar,** *vt.* to computerize. —**cómputo,** *m.* computation, calculation.

comulgar, *vii.* [b] to take communion; to commune.—**comulgatorio,** *m.* altar rail.

común, *a.* common, public; usual, customary; current; vulgar.—*por lo c.,* usually.

comunicación, *f.* communication; communiqué, official statement.— *pl.* means of communication. —**comunicado,** *m.* letter to a paper; communiqué.—*c. de prensa,* press release.—**comunicar,** *vti.* [d] to communicate; to notify.—*vri.* to communicate; to connect; to be in touch.—**comunicativo,** *a.* communicative, talkative.

comunidad, *f.* the common people; community; corporation; religious group.—**comunión,** *f.* communion; political party.—*Sagrada C.,* (eccl.) Holy Communion.—**comunismo,** *m.* communism.—**comunista,** *mf.* & *a.* communist(ic).—**comunistoide,** *a.* & *mf.* (pol.) commie, pink, fellow traveler.

con, *prep.* with; (when followed by infinitive) by; although.—*c. que,* and so, then, so then.—*c. tal que,* provided that.—*c. todo,* nevertheless, notwithstanding.

conato, *m.* endeavor; effort, exertion; attempt, attempted crime.

concavidad, *f.* hollowness, concavity.—**cóncavo,** *a.* hollow, concave.—*m.* concavity.

concebible, *a.* conceivable.—**concebir,** *vti.* [29] & *vii.* to conceive, become pregnant; to imagine; to comprehend.

conceder, *vt.* to concede, admit; to give, grant.

concejal, *m.* councilman.—**concejo,** *m.* municipal council; civic body of a small town; board of aldermen.

concentración, *f.* concentration. —**concentrar,** *vt.* to concentrate.— *vr.* to concentrate (mentally); to come together.—**concéntrico,** *a.* concentric.

concepción, *f.* conception; idea.— **concepto,** *m.* concept, thought;

judgment, opinion.—**conceptuar,** *vt.* to judge, think, form an opinion of.—**conceptuoso,** *a.* witty; overelaborate.

concerniente, *a.* (a) concerning, relating (to).—*en lo c. a,* with regard to, as for.—**concernir,** *vii.* [50] to concern, relate to.

concertar, *vti.* [1] to concert, arrange by agreement, adjust, settle.— *vii.* to agree, accord.—*vri.* to come to an agreement; to go hand in hand.

concertino, *m.* (mus.) concertmaster, first violin.

concesión, *f.* concession, grant.—**concesionario,** *m.* concessionary.

concha, *f.* shell; shell-fish; tortoise-shell, conch; (theat.) prompter's box.—*c. marina,* sea shell.

conciencia, *f.* conscience; conscientiousness; consciousness.—**concienzudo,** *a.* conscientious.

concierto, *m.* concert; agreement; good order and arrangement.

conciliábulo, *m.* unlawful meeting, or agreement.—**conciliar,** *vt.* to conciliate; to reconcile.—*c. el sueño,* to get to sleep.—**concilio,** *m.* (eccl.) council.

concisión, *f.* conciseness, succinctness.—**conciso,** *a.* concise, succinct.

concitar, *vt.* to excite, stir up, agitate.

conciudadano, *n.* fellow citizen, countryman.

concluir, *vti.* [23-e] to conclude, bring to an end; to decide finally, determine; to infer, deduce.—*vii.* & *vri.* to come to an end, finish.—**conclusión,** *f.* conclusion (all senses).— **concluyente,** *a.* concluding, conclusive.

concomitancia, *f.* concomitance.

concordancia, *f.* concordance; harmony; concord, agreement.—**concordar,** *vti.* [12] to reconcile; to make agree; to harmonize.—*vii.* to be in accord; to agree.—**concordia,** *f.* concord, harmony; agreement; peace, good will.

concretar, *vt.* to summarize, sum up; to combine, unite.—*vr.* to limit or confine oneself (to a subject).—**concreto,** *a.* concrete (not abstract).— *en c.,* concretely; in brief, in a few words.—*m.* concrete (building material).

concubina, *f.* concubine, mistress. —**concubinato** *m.* concubinage.

conculcar, *vti.* [d] to trample underfoot; to violate, infringe.

concupiscencia, *f.* lust.—**concupiscente**, *a.* sensual.

concurrencia, *f.* attendance; concurrence; audience, gathering, assembly.—**concurrido**, *a.* frequented; (of a meeting, etc.) well-attended.—**concurrir**, *vi.* to concur, agree; to meet in one point, time or place; to attend.

concurso, *m.* competitive contest or examination; concourse; aid, assistance; call for bids (on a piece of work, a service, etc.); gathering.—*c. de carreras y saltos*, track meet.

condado, *m.* earldom; county; dignity of a count.—**conde**, *m.* count, earl.

condecoración, *f.* medal; badge; decoration.—**condecorar**, *vt.* to bestow a medal or insignia on; to decorate.

condena, *f.* penalty; sentence, term of imprisonment.—**condenable**, *a.* condemnable.—**condenación**, *f.* condemnation; punishment; damnation.—**condenado**, *n.* & *a.* damned (in hell); convict; condemned; convicted.—**condenar**, *vt.* to condemn; to damn; to declare guilty; to censure, disapprove; to nail or wall up (a door, etc.); to annoy.—*vr.* to be damned (to hell).

condensación, *f.* condensation.—**condensador**, *a.* condensing.—*m.* (steam, elec., etc.) condenser.—**condensar**, *vt.* to condense, thicken.—*vr.* to be condensed.

condesa, *f.* countess.

condescendencia, *f.* condescension; compliance.—**condescender**, *vii.* [18] to condescend; to yield, comply.

condición, *f.* condition, state; temper; constitution; rank; stipulation; status.—**condicionado**, *a.* conditioned; conditional.—**condicional**, *a.* conditional.—**condicionar**, *vi.* to impose conditions; to agree, accord.

condimentar, *vt.* to season or dress (foods).—**condimento**, *m.* seasoning, condiment.

condiscípulo, *n.* schoolmate, fellow student.

condolencia, *f.* condolence, expression of sympathy.—**condolerse**, *vri.* [26] (**de**) to condole (with), be sorry (for), sympathize (with).

condominio, *m.* joint ownership.

condón, *m.* condom.

cóndor, *m.* condor.

conducción, *f.* conveyance; carriage, transportation; leading, guiding; conducting; driving; conduit.—**conducente**, *a.* conducive, conducent.—**conducir**, *vti.* [11] & *vii.* to convey, carry; to take, accompany; to direct, lead; to manage, conduct; to drive.—*vii.* (**a**) to conduce, contribute (to); to be suitable (for); to lead, tend (to).—*c. en estado de embriaguez* or *c. borracho*, to drive while drunk, drunk driving.—*vri.* to behave, act, conduct oneself.—**conducta**, *f.* conduct, behavior.—*c. antideportiva*, unsportsmanlike conduct.—*de buena c.*, well-behaved.—**conducto**, *m.* duct, conduit, pipe.—**conductor**, *n.* (Am.) conductor (RR., bus, etc.); leader; driver.—*a.* conducting, conductive (of heat, electricity, etc.).

conectar, *vt.* to connect.

conejo, *m.* rabbit.—*conejillo de Indias*, guinea pig.

conexión, *f.* connection; joint; coherence.

confección, *f.* any handwork; workmanship; fancy work, ready-made article.—**confeccionar**, *vt.* to make, prepare; to compound.

confederación, *f.* confederacy, confederation.—**confederado**, *m.* & *a.* confederate.—**confederar**, *vt.* & *vr.* to confederate, join, form a confederacy.

conferencia, *f.* conference, meeting, interview; lecture.—*c. en la cumbre*, summit conference.—**conferenciante**, **conferencista**, *mf.* lecturer.—**conferenciar**, *vi.* to consult together, hold a conference; to lecture.

conferir, *vti.* [39] to confer; to give, bestow.

confesar, *vti.* [1] to confess, hear confession.—*vri.* to confess or make confessions.—**confesión**, *f.* confession.—**confesionario**, *m.* confessional.—**confesor**, *m.* father confessor.

confeti, *m.* confetti.

confiable, *a.* trusty, reliable.—**confiado**, *a.* unsuspecting, trusting; confident.—**confianza**, *f.* confidence; familiarity, informality.—**confianzudo**, *a.* (coll.) fresh, overfriendly.—**confiar**, *vii.* (**en**) to rely (on), to trust (in).—*vt.* to confide;

to commit to the care of another.—**confidencia,** *f.* trust, confidence; confidential information.—**confidencial,** *a.* confidential.—**confidente,** *mf.* confidant; police spy.—*m.* love seat.—*a.* faithful, trusty.

confín, *m.* limit, boundary, border.—*a.* bordering; limiting.—**confinamiento,** *m.* confinement.—**confinar,** *vt.* & *vr.* to confine; to banish to a definite place; to border on.

confirmación, *f.* confirmation; corroboration.—**confirmar,** *vt.* to confirm.

confiscación, *f.* confiscation.—**confiscar,** *vti.* [d] to confiscate.

confitar, *vt.* to candy; to preserve (fruit); to sweeten.—**confite,** *m.* candy, bonbon; sweets.—**confitería,** *f.* confectionery; confectioner's shop.—**confitura,** *f.* confection.

conflagración, *f.* conflagration.

conflicto, *m.* conflict.

confluencia, *f.* confluence.—**confluente,** *a.* confluent.—**confluir,** *vii.* [23-e] to join (rivers and sea currents); to assemble in one place.

conformación, *f.* conformation; shape.—**conformar,** *vt.* to conform, adjust, fit.—*vi.* to suit, fit, conform.—*vr.* to comply; to submit; to resign oneself.—**conforme,** *a.* alike, similar; correct, acceptable; compliant; resigned.—*adv.* in due proportion; agreeably, accordingly.—**conformidad,** *f.* likeness; conformity; agreement; resignation, submission.

confortar, *vt.* to comfort; to console; to strengthen.

confrontar, *vt.* to confront; to collate; to compare, check.

confundir, *vt.* to confound; to perplex, confuse; to mystify.—*vr.* to be bewildered, perplexed; to become ashamed and humbled.—**confusión,** *f.* confusion, disorder; perplexity; embarrassment.—**confuso,** *a.* confused, confounded; unintelligible; perplexed.

congelación, *f.* freezing; deep freezing; frostbite.—**congelador,** *m.* freezer, deep freezer.—**congelar,** *vt.* & *vr.* to freeze; to deep-freeze; to congeal.

congénere, *a.* kindred, of like kind.

congeniar, *vi.* to be congenial; to get along well (with).

congestión, *f.* congestion.—**congestionar,** *vt.* to congest.—*vr.* to get congested.

congoja, *f.* anguish, sorrow, grief.

congraciarse, *vr.* (**con**) to ingratiate oneself, to win favor.

congratulación, *f.* congratulation.—**congratular,** *vt.* to congratulate.—*vr.* to congratulate oneself, rejoice.

congregación, *f.* congregation; meeting, assembly; religious fraternity, brotherhood.—**congregar,** *vti.* [b] & *vri.* to assemble, congregate.—**congresista,** *mf.* congressman, congresswoman.—**congreso,** *m.* congress; convention, assembly.—*C. de los Diputados,* House of Representatives.

congruencia, *f.* congruence; convenience; fitness.—**congruente,** *a.* congruent, corresponding.

congruencia, *f.* congruence; convenience; fitness.—**congruente,** *a.* congruent, corresponding.

cónico, *a.* conical, conic.

conjetura, *f.* conjecture.—**conjeturar,** *vt.* to conjecture.

conjugación, *f.* conjugation.—**conjugar,** *vti.* [b] to conjugate.

conjunción, *f.* conjunction, union; act of coupling or joining together.

conjunto, *a.* united.—*m.* whole, aggregate.—*en c.,* altogether, as a whole.

conjura, conjuración, *f.* conspiracy, conjuration, plot.—**conjurado,** *m.* conspirator.—**conjurar,** *vi.* to conspire.—*vt.* to exorcise, conjure; to entreat, implore; to avert, ward off.—**conjuro,** *m.* conjuration; exorcism; entreaty.

conllevar, *vt.* to aid; to bear with patience.

conmemoración, *f.* remembrance; commemoration; anniversary.—**conmemorar,** *vt.* to commemorate.

conmensurable, *a.* commensurable.

conmigo, *pron.* with me, with myself.

conmiseración, *f.* commiseration, pity.

conmoción, *f.* commotion, excitement.—**conmovedor,** *a.* touching; sad, pathetic; exciting, thrilling.—**conmover,** *vti.* [26] to touch, move; to appeal to; to disturb, shock; to excite, stir.

conmutación, *f.* commutation, exchange.—**conmutador,** *m.* electric switch; telegraph key.—**conmutar,** *vt.* to exchange, barter.

connivencia, *f.* connivance; plotting.

cono, *m.* cone.

conocedor, *a.* (**de**) familiar (with), expert (in).—*n.* expert, connoisseur.—**conocer,** *vti.* [3] to know; to meet; to experience, comprehend.—*vii.* to know, be competent.—*vri.* to know oneself.—**conocido,** *a.* prominent, well-known.—*n.* acquaintance.—**conocimiento,** *m.* knowledge; skill, ability; acquaintance; bill of lading.—*poner en c. de,* to inform, notify.

conque, *conj.* so then; now then; and so; well then; therefore.

conquista, *f.* conquest, subjugation; conquered territory, thing or person.—**conquistador,** *m.* & *a.* conqueror, conquering; (fig.) Don Juan.—

conquistar, *vt.* to conquer; to win, acquire; to win over, persuade.

consabido, *a.* well-known; in question; before-mentioned, aforesaid.

consagración, *f.* consecration.—**consagrar,** *vt.* to consecrate; to deify; to devote, dedicate.—*vr.* to devote or give oneself to (study, work, etc.).

consanguíneo, *a.* related by blood.—**consanguinidad,** *f.* blood relationship.

consciencia, *f.* consciousness.—**consciente,** *a.* conscious.

consecución, *f.* attainment, obtaining, acquisition.—**consecuencia,** *f.* consequence; consistency; result.—*a c. de,* because of.—*en* or *por c.,* consequently, therefore.—**consecuente,** *m.* effect, issue, consequence.—*a.* consequent, following; logical, consistent.—**consecutivo,** *a.* consecutive, successive.

conseguir, *vti.* [29-b] to attain, get, obtain; to succeed in.

conseja, *f.* story, fairy tale, fable, old wives' tale.

consejero, *m.* counsellor, member of a council; adviser.—**consejo,** *m.* counsel, advice; council, consulting body.—*c. de guerra,* court martial; council of war.—*c. de ministros,* cabinet.—*c. escolar,* school board.—*presidente del c.,* prime minister.

consenso, *m.* general assent; consensus; verdict.

consentido, *a.* & *n.* spoiled (child); cuckold.—**consentidor,** *m.* complier, conniver; coddler.—**consentimiento,** *m.* consent; coddling; acquiescence.—**consentir,** *vti.* [40] to consent, permit; to acquiesce in; to accept, admit; to pamper, spoil.

conserje, *n.* doorman, janitor, porter.

conserva, *f.* canned food, preserve, jam; pickle.—**conservación,** *f.* conservation; preservation; maintenance, upkeep.—**conservador,** *m.* conservator, preserver; curator.—*m.* & *a.* conservative.—**conservar,** *vt.* to conserve, maintain, preserve; to guard; to preserve or pickle (fruit); to can.—*vr.* to keep young, be well preserved; to last, keep well.—**conservatorio,** *m.* (music) conservatory.

considerable, *a.* considerable, important.—**consideración,** *f.* consideration; importance; respect.—**considerado,** *a.* prudent; considerate; thoughtful; esteemed, distinguished.—**considerar,** *vt.* to consider; to treat with consideration.

consigna, *f.* watchword, password; slogan; (RR.) checkroom.—**consignación,** *f.* consignment, shipment.—**consignar,** *vt.* to consign, assign; to deliver; to check (baggage); to set apart.

consigo, *pron.* with oneself (himself, herself, itself, themselves, yourself, yourselves).

consiguiente, *m.* (log.) consequence, result, effect.—*a.* consequent.—*por c.,* therefore.

consistencia, *f.* consistence, consistency.—**consistente,** *a.* consistent, firm, solid.—**consistir,** *vi.* to consist; to be comprised, contained.—*c. en,* to consist in, to be a matter of.

consistorio, *m.* consistory; municipal council, board of aldermen.

consocio, *n.* partner.

consola, *f.* console; bracket shelf.

consolación, *f.* consolation.—**consolador,** *a.* consoling.—**consolar,** *vti.* [12] to console, comfort.

consolidación, *f.* consolidation.—**consolidar,** *vt.* to consolidate; to harden, strengthen; to fund (debts).—*vr.* to consolidate, grow firm; to unite.

consonante, *m.* rhyming word; (mus.) consonant or corresponding sound.—*f.* & *a.* (letter) consonant; harmonious.

consorcio, *m.* syndicate, partnership.

consorte, *n.* consort, mate.

conspicuo, *a.* conspicuous; prominent.

conspiración, *f.* conspiracy, plot.—**conspirador,** *n.* conspirator.—*a.* conspiring.—**conspirar,** *vi.* to conspire, plot.

constancia, *f.* written evidence; con

stancy, perseverance.—**constante,** *a.* constant; uninterrupted; firm.

constar, *vi.* to be clear, evident, certain; to be recorded, registered; (**de**) to be composed (of), consist (of).

constatar, *vt.* to verify, confirm.

constelación, *f.* constellation.

consternación, *f.* consternation.—**consternar,** *vt.* to dismay; to amaze; to distress, grieve.

constipado, *m.* head cold.—*a.* suffering from a cold.—**constipar,** *vr.* to catch cold.—*vt.* to cause a cold.

constitución, *f.* constitution.—*c. en sociedad anónima,* incorporation.—**constitucional,** *a.* constitutional.—**constitucionalidad,** *f.* constitutionality.—**constituir,** *vti.* [23-e] to constitute.—*c. en sociedad anónima,* to incorporate.—*vri.* (**en**)(en), to set oneself up as.—**constituyente,** *mf.* & *a.* constituent.

constreñir, *vti.* [9] to constrain, compel, force; to contract.

construcción, *f.* construction; act and art of constructing; structure; building.—**constructor,** *m.* builder; maker.—**construir,** *vti.* [23-e] to construct, build, form.

consuelo, *m.* consolation, relief, solace; joy.

consuetudinario, *a.* customary, generally practiced.

cónsul, *mf.* consul.—**consulado,** *m.* consulate.

consulta, *f.* consultation, conference; office hours of a doctor).—**consultante,** *mf.* consulter.—*a.* consulting.—**consultar,** *vt.* to consult.—**consultor,** *n.* consulter.—*a.* consulting.—**con-sultorio,** *m.* clinic, doctor's office.

consumación, *f.* consummation; extinction.—**consumar,** *vt.* to consummate, finish, perfect; to commit (a crime).

consumidor, *n.* & *a.* consumer, user; consuming.—**consumir,** *vt.* to consume; to waste away.—*vr.* to be consumed, exhausted; to run out; to languish.—**consumo,** *m.* consumption (of provision, fuel, merchandise).

consunción, *f.* consumption, wasting away.

consustancial, *a.* consubstantial.

contabilidad, *f.* bookkeeping, accounting.—**contable,** *a.* countable.—*mf.* bookkeeper, accountant.

contacto, *m.* contact.

contado, *a.* scarce, race.—*al c.,* cash.—*por o de c.,* of course, as a matter of course.—**contador,** *m.* accountant; auditor; paymaster; purser; counter; meter (for gas, water, etc.).—*caja contadora,* or **contadora,** cash register.—*c. de navío,* purser.—**contaduría,** *f.* office of a cashier, paymaster or treasurer; box office (in a theater, etc.); accountant's or auditor's office.

contagiar, *vt.* to infect, contaminate; to corrupt, pervert.—*vr.* (**de**) to become infected (with).—**contagio,** *m.* contagion; corruption of morals.—**contagioso,** *a.* contagious; perverting.

contaminación, *f.* contamination, pollution; defilement.—**contaminado,** *a.* corrupted, contaminated.—**contaminar,** *vt.* to contaminate; to pervert; to infect by contagion.

contante, *a.* (money) ready.—*m.* cash.—*dinero c.,* or *dinero c. y sonante,* cash.—**contar,** *vti.* [12] to count; to relate, tell.—*vii.* to compute, figure.—*c. con,* to depend on, rely on; to reckon with; to take into account; to possess, have at one's disposal.

contemplación, *f.* contemplation, meditation; complaisance.—**contemplar,** *vt.* to contemplate; to meditate; to be lenient or complaisant with; to humor.—**contemplativo,** *a.* contemplative; studious; lenient.—*n.* contemplator.

contemporáneo, *n.* & *a.* contemporary.—**contemporización,** *f.* temporizing, compliance.—**contemporizar,** *vii.* [a] to temporize; to comply; to adapt oneself.

contender, *vii.* [18] to fight, combat; to contend, debate.—**contendiente,** *mf.* fighter, disputant; opponent.—*a.* fighting.

contener, *vti.* [42] to contain; to include; to curb, stop.—*vri.* to control oneself, to refrain.—**contenido,** *a.* moderate, restrained.—*n.* content(s).

contentar, *vt.* to content, satisfy, make happy.—*vr.* to be contented, satisfied; to become reconciled, make up.—**contento,** *a.* content, contented; satisfied; happy.—*m.* contentment, satisfaction.

contera, *f.* metal tip (of umbrella, cane, etc.).

conterráneo, *n.* = COTERRANEO.

contestación, *f.* answer, reply.—**contestar,** *vt.* to answer, reply.

contexto, *m.* context.—**contextura,** *f.* texture.

contienda, *f.* struggle, fight; debate, dispute.

contigo, *pron.* with you [thee]; with yourself [thyself].

contigüidad, *f.* contiguity, closeness.—**contiguo,** *a.* contiguous, next, adjacent.

continencia, *f.* continence, self-control; abstinence; moderation; chastity.

continente, *m.* continent; container; countenance.—*a.* abstemious, continent; chaste; moderate.

contingencia, *f.* contingency, risk, possibility.—**contingente,** *m.* quota, contingent, share.—*a.* contingent, accidental.

continuación, *f.* continuation, continuance; stay.—*a c.,* immediately, right after; as follows.—**continuar,** *vt.* & *vi.* to continue; to go on; to pursue; to endure, last, remain; to prolong.—**continuidad,** *f.* continuity.—**continuo,** *a.* continuous, uninterrupted; connected; steady, constant.

contonearse, *vr.* to walk with a waddle; to strut.—**contoneo,** *m.* strut, waddle.

contornear, *vt.* to trace the contour or outline of.—**contorno,** *m.* outline, contour; neighborhood; environs of a place.

contorsión, *f.* contortion, twist; grotesque gesture.

contra, *prep.* against, in opposition to, contrary to, opposite to, versus.—*m.* opposite sense; opposite opinion.—*f.* difficulty, obstacle.—*c. viento y marea,* against all odds.—*el pro y el c.,* the pros and cons.—*en c. (de),* against, in opposition to.—*hacer* or *llevar la c.,* to oppose; to contradict.

contraalmirante, *m.* rear admiral.

contraataque, *m.* counterattack.

contrabajo, *m.* bass fiddle.

contrabandear, *vi.* to smuggle.—**contrabandista,** *mf.* smuggler, contrabandist.—**contrabando,** *m.* smuggling, running.

contracción, *f.* contraction, shrinking; corrugation; abbreviation.

contrachap(e)ado, *a.*—*madera c.,* plywood.

contradecir, *vti.* [14] to contradict.

—**contradicción,** *f.* contradiction.

—**contradicho,** *pp.* of CONTRADECIR.

—**contradictorio,** *a.* contradictory.

contraer, *vti.* [43] & *vii.* to contract; to catch; to reduce.—*vri.* to contract, diminish; to shrink.

contrafuerte, *m.* buttress; spur (of a mountain).

contragolpe, *m.* back or reverse stroke.

contrahacer, *vti.* [22] to counterfeit, forge; to copy, imitate.—**contrahaz,** *f.* wrong side.—**contrahecho,** *pp.* of CONTRAHACER.—*a.* deformed; counterfeit, forged.

contralor, *m.* (Am.) controller, comptroller.

contraluz, *f.* view (of thing) seen against the light.

contramaestre, *m.* overseer, foreman, boatswain.

contramarcha, *f.* countermarch.

contraorden, *f.* countermand.

contraparte, *f.* counterpart.

contrapartida, *f.* emendatory or corrective entry.

contrapelo, *m.*—*a c.,* against the grain.

contrapesar, *vt.* to counterbalance; to counteract, offset.—**contrapeso,** *m.* counterweight, counterbalance, balancing weight.

contraproducente, *a.* self-defeating, producing the opposite of the desired effect.

contrapuerta, *f.* storm door.

contrapuesto, *a.* compared, contrasted (with); opposed (to).

contrapunto, *m.* counterpoint, harmony.

contrariar, *vt.* to contradict, oppose; to disappoint.—**contrariedad,** *f.* disappointment; impediment; set back.—**contrario,** *a.* contrary; adverse.—*m.* opponent.—*al c.,* or *por lo c.,* on the contrary.—*de lo c.,* otherwise.

contrarrestar, *vt.* to oppose, resist; to check, arrest; to counteract.

contrarrevolución, *f.* counterrevolution.

contrasentido, *m.* contradiction in terms; conclusion contrary to premises.

contraseña, *f.* (comput.) password; (mil.) countersign, watchword, password; check for hat or baggage.—*c. de salida,* pass-out ticket.

contratación, *f.* hiring; transactions, trading (on the stock market).

contrastar, *vt.* to contrast; to test

(scales, etc.); to assay (metals).—**contraste**, *m.* contrast, opposition; inspector (of weights); assayer; assayer's office.

contrata, *f.* contract, agreement.—**contratación**, *f.* contractual transaction.—**contratar**, *vt.* to contract for; to engage, hire; to trade.

contratiempo, *m.* disappointment, setback.

contratista, *mf.* contractor.—**contrato**, *m.* contract.

contraveneno, *m.* antidote.

contravenir, *vti.* [45] to contravene.

contraventana, *f.* window shutter.

contraventor, *n.* transgressor.

contravidriera, *f.* storm sash.

contrayente, *mf.* contracting party (to a marriage).—*a.* engaged (to be married).

contribución, *f.* contribution; tax, scot.—**contribuir**, *vii.* [23-e] to contribute.—**contribuyente**, *a.* contributing; contributory.—*mf.* taxpayer.

contrición, *f.* contrition, compunction.

contrincante, *mf.* opponent, competitor, rival.

contrito, *a.* contrite, penitent.

control, *m.* control; checkpoint.—*con c. remoto*, remote-controlled.—*c. remoto*, remote control.—**controlar**, *vt.* to control; to monitor.

controversia, *f.* controversy, debate. —**controvertible**, *a.* controvertible, disputable.

contubernio, *m.* cohabitation; infamous alliance.

contumacia, *f.* obstinacy; contumacy; persistence in error; (law) contempt of court.—**contumaz**, *a.* obstinate; contumacious.

contundente, *a.* producing contusion; forceful; conclusive, decisive; trenchant.

conturbar, *vt.* to perturb, disturb.—*vr.* to become uneasy, agitated, anxious.

contusión, *f.* contusion, bruise.—**contuso**, *a.* bruised.

conuco, *m.* (Am.) patch of cultivated ground (maize field, etc.).

convalecencia, *f.* convalescence.—**convalecer**, *vii.* [3] to be convalescing.—**convaleciente**, *mf.* & *a.* convalescent.

convalidar, *vt.* to confirm, ratify.

convecino, *m.* neighbor.—*a.* neighboring, near.

convencer, *vti.* [a] to convince.—*vri.* to become convinced.—**convencimiento**, *m.* belief, conviction.

convención, *f.* convention; assembly; pact, agreement.—**convencional**, *a.* conventional.—**convencionalismo**, *m.* conventionalism, conventionality.

convenido, *a.* agreed.—**conveniencia**, *f.* convenience; utility; self-interest; agreement.—**conveniente**, *a.* useful; advantageous; suitable, befitting.—**convenio**, *m.* convention, agreement.—**convenir**, *vii.* [45] to befit; to agree; to convene, gather; to coincide; to be a good thing to.—*vri.* to agree, make a deal; to suit one's interests.

convento, *m.* convent.

conversación, *f.* conversation, talk.—*c. de sobremesa*, table talk.—**conversador**, *n.* talker.—*a.* conversational.—**conversar**, *vi.* to talk, converse; chat.

conversión, *f.* conversion; change. —**convertir**, *vti.* [39] to convert; to change.—*vri.* to become converted; to turn into, become.

convexidad, *f.* convexity.—**convexo**, *a.* convex.

convicción, *f.* conviction.—**convicto**, *a.* convicted, guilty.

convidada, *f.* invitation to drink, treat.—**convidado**, *n.* & *a.* invited (guest).—**convidar**, *vt.* to invite.

convincente, *a.* convincing.

convite, *m.* invitation; treat; banquet.

convocación, *f.* convocation, calling.—**convocar**, *vti.* [d] to convoke, convene, call together.—**convocatoria**, *f.* call, notice of a meeting.

convoy, *m.* convoy.—*c. de mesa*, cruet stand.—**convoyar**, *vt.*, to convoy, escort.

convulsión, *f.* convulsion.—**convulsivo**, *a.* convulsive.—**convulso**, *a.* convulsed; agitated.

conyugal, *a.* conjugal, wedded.—**cónyuge**, *mf.* spouse, consort.—*m. pl.* husband and wife.

coñac, *m.* brandy, cognac.

cooperación, *f.* cooperation.—**cooperador**, *n.* & *a.* cooperator, cooperating, cooperative.—**cooperar**, *vi.* to cooperate.—**cooperativa**, *f.* cooperative (society).—**cooperativo**, *a.* cooperating.

coordinación, *f.* coordination.—**coordinar**, *vt.* to coordinate.

copa, *f.* goblet, wineglass; drink (of liquor); treetop; crown of a hat;

(sports) cup.—*c. (de) helado*, ice-cream sundae.—*pl.* a suit of cards named **copas**.

copar, *vt.* to cut off and capture; to cover (the whole bet); to sweep (all posts in an election); to corner.

copartícipe, *mf.* participant, co-partner.

copete, *m.* tuft, bun (hair); forelock; crest; summit.—*de alto c.*, of high rank, aristocratic.—**copetudo**, *a.* tufted, crested; haughty.

copia, *f.* copy, imitation; abundance.—*c. al carbon*, carbon copy.—*c. fiel*, true copy.—**copiar**, *vt.* to copy.

copiloto, *m.* copilot.

copiosidad, *f.* copiousness, abundance.—**copioso**, *a.* copious, abundant.

copista, *mf.* copyist, transcriber.

copla, *f.* short popular folk song; certain kind of stanza (poetry).

copo, *m.* small bundle of cotton, flax, etc.; snowflake.—*copos de jabón*, soap flakes.

coprotagonista, *mf.* co-star.—**coprotagonizar**, *vi.* to co-star.

cópula, *f.* joining, coupling two things together; connection; copulation.—**copular**, *vi.* to mate (of animals).

coqueluche, *f.* whooping cough.

coqueta, *f.* flirtatious girl.—**coquetear**, *vi.* to flirt.—**coqueteo**, *m.* flirtation.—**coquetería**, *f.* flirtation; affectation.—**coquetón**, *a.* kittenish.—*m.* lady-killer.

coraje, *m.* courage, bravery; anger.

coral, *m.* coral; a white-and-red poisonous snake.—*a.* choral.

coraza, *f.* armor plating; carapace; armor (of a vessel, cable, etc.).

corazón, *m.* heart; core, center; (fig.) courage; love; charity.—*anunciar*, or *decir el c. algo*, to have a presentiment.—*arrancársele a uno el c.*, to be heartbroken.—*de c.*, heartily.—**corazonada**, *f.* premonition, hunch.

corbata, *f.* necktie, cravat.

corbeta, *f.* corvette.—*capitán de c.*, lieutenant commander.

corcel, *m.* war-horse, charger, steed.

corchete, *m.* clasp, hook, hook and eye; snaplock; bracket.

corcho, *m.* cork; cork stopper.

corcova, *f.* hump, hunch.—**corcovado**, *a.* & *n.* humpback(ed), hunchback(ed).

cordaje, *m.* cordage; rigging.

cordal, *m.* wisdom tooth.

cordel, *m.* cord; thin rope; land measure.—*a c.*, in a straight line.—*da c.*, to banter.

cordero, *m.* lamb; lambskin.

cordial, *a.* hearty, cordial.—*m.* cordial tonic.—**cordialidad**, *f.* cordiality.

cordillera, *f.* mountain range.

cordobán, *m.* cordovan, goatskin—**cordobés**, *n.* & *a.* Cordovan; o Córdoba.

cordón, *m.* cord, braid, string; cordon (of soldiers); chord.—*c. de extensión*, extension cord.—*c. umbilical*, um bilical cord.—**cordoncillo**, *m.* mill ing on edge of a coin; twisted o small cord; lacing; braid.

cordura, *f.* prudence, practical wis dom, sanity.

coreano, *a.* & *n.* Korean.

corear, *vt.* to chorus, accompany with a chorus; to answer in chorus.—*v* to chorus.—**coreografía**, *f.* choreog raphy.—**coreográfico**, *a.* choreo graphic.—**coreógrafo**, *n.* choreogra pher.—**corista**, *n.* chorister; mem ber of a chorus.—*f.* chorus girl.

coriza, *f.* head cold.

cornada, *f.* thrust with the horns, gor ing.—**cornamenta**, *f.* horns, ant lers.—**cornear**, *vt.* to butt; to gore.

córneo, *a.* hornlike, horny.

corneta, *f.* cornet, bugle.—*m.* bu gler.—**cornetín**, *m.* cornet; co netist.

cornisa, *f.* cornice.

cornucopia, *f.* cornucopia.

cornudo, *a.* horned.—*m.* (fig. cuckold.

coro, *m.* choir; chorus.

corola, *f.* corolla.—**corolario**, *m.* co ollary.

corona, *f.* crown; wreath; tonsure.—**coronación**, *f.* coronation; crown ing.—**coronar**, *vt.* to crown; to top to complete.

coronel, *m.* colonel.

coronilla, *f.* top of the head.—*esta hasta la c.*, to be fed up.

corpiño, *m.* bodice.

corporación, *f.* corporation; inst tution.

corporal, *a.* corporal.

corporativo, *a.* corporate.

corpóreo, *a.* corporeal, bodily.

corpúsculo, *m.* corpuscle.

corral, *m.* corral; yard; poultry yar pen; playpen.—*c. de concentració de ganado*, stockyard.

correa, *f.* leather strap; leash; belt.—

tener c., to be able to endure a lot.—**correaje,** *m.* a set of straps.—**correazo,** *m.* a blow with a strap.

corrección, *f.* correction; correctness.—**correccional,** *a.* corrective.—*m.* reformatory.—**correcto,** *a.* polite, well-bred; proper; correct. —**corrector,** *m.* corrector, amender; proofreader.

corredizo, *a.* running; sliding.—**corredor,** *m.* runner; gallery; corridor, lane; covert way; broker.—*c. de la muerte,* death row.—*a.* running.

corregir, *vt.* [29-c] to correct; to adjust (an instrument); to remedy; to rebuke, reprove; to punish.—*c. pruebas* (print.) to read proofs.—*vri.* to mend, reform.

correlación, *f.* correlation.—**correlativo,** *a.* correlative.

correntón, *m.* gadder; man about town.

correo, *m.* post, mail; correspondence; courier; letter carrier; post office.— *c. aéreo,* airmail.—*c. certificado,* registered mail.—*c. electrónico,* electronic mail, E-mail.—*echar al c.,* to mail, post.

correr, *vi.* to run; to race; to flow; to extend, expand; to pass, elapse; to go on, continue; to be said, be common talk.—*c. a cargo de,* to be the concern of.—*c. con,* to charge oneself with a matter, take care of.—*c. la voz,* to be said or rumored.—*c. por cuenta de uno,* to be one's affair.—*vt.* to run or move swiftly; to race (a horse, car, etc.); to slide; to pursue, chase; to throw out.—*vr.* to file right or left; to slide, go through easily; to become embarrassed; to run away, to flee.—**correría,** *f.* incursion, foray, raid; excursion.—*pl.* youthful escapades.

correspondencia, *f.* correspondence, relation; interchange; mail, correspondence.—**corresponder,** *vi.* (a) to reciprocate (a favor, etc.); to match, correspond; to respond (to); to fit, suit; to pertain (to); to concern; to agree.—*vr.* to correspond, keep in contact by mail.—**correspondiente,** *a.* corresponding, respective.—*mf.* correspondent.—**corresponsal,** *mf.* correspondent; newspaper correspondent.

corretaje, *m.* brokerage.—**corretear,** *vi.* to walk the streets, ramble; to romp.—**correvedile, correveidile,** *mf.* talebearer; gossip.

corrida, *f.* course, run, running, race; career.—*c. de toros,* bullfight.

corrido, *a.* experienced, wise; embarrassed, ashamed; continuous, flowing, unbroken.—*m.* Mexican folk ballad.

corriente, *a.* current; running, fluent, flowing; present, current (month or year); plain, easy; generally received, admitted; ordinary, common; regular, standard.—*f.* current (river, electricity, etc.); tendency; course; trend.—*c. alterna,* alternating current.—*c. direct* or *c. continua,* direct current.—**-mente,** *adv.* usually, normally; commonly, often.

corrillo, *m.* group of talkers; clique. —**corro,** *m.* group of gossipers or spectators; circular space.

corroboración, *f.* corroboration.—**corroborar,** *vt.* to corroborate.

corroer, *vt.* to corrode.—*vr.* to corrode, decay.

corromper, *vt.* to corrupt; to vitiate; to debauch.—*vr.* to rot, putrefy; to become corrupt(ed).

corrosivo, *a.* corrosive.

corrugado, *a.* corrugated.

corrupción, *f.* corruption; putrefaction; depravity, immorality.—**corruptela,** *f.* corrupt practice.—**corruptible,** *a.* corruptible; perishable.—**corrupto,** *a.* corrupt, rotten.

corsé, *m.* corset.

cortaalambres, *m.* wire cutter.

cortacésped, *m.* lawnmower.

cortada, *f.* (Am.) cut, slash, gash. —**cortador,** *m.* (tailoring, bootmaking, etc.) cutter.—**cortadura,** *f.* cut; cutting, incision.—**cortafuego,** *m.* fire wall.—**cortante,** *a.* cutting, sharp, trenchant.—**cortapapeles,** *m.* paper cutter; paper knife.—**cortapisa,** *f.* obstacle, restriction.—**cortaplumas,** *m.* pocketknife; penknife.—**cortar,** *vt.* to cut, cut down, cut off, cut out, cut open; to disjoin, separate; to interrupt, stop.—*vr.* to be ashamed, confused.—**cortaúñas,** *mpl.* nail clippers.—**corte,** *m.* cutting edge; cutting; cut; material necessary for a garment; style (clothing); sectional view.—*f.* royal court; (Am.) court of justice.—**cortedad,** *f.* smallness; pusillanimity; timidity.

cortejar, *vt.* to woo, court; to curry favor.—**cortejo,** *m.* courtship; cortege, retinue; procession.

cortés, *a.* polite, courteous; urbane.—

cortesano, *a.* courtly.—*m.* courtier.—*f.* prostitute.—**cortesía**, *f.* courtesy.—*de c.*, complimentary (copy, ticket, etc.).

corteza, *f.* bark of a tree; peel, rind, skin; crust of bread, pies, etc.; outward appearance.

cortina, *f.* curtain.—*c. de ducha*, shower curtain.—**cortinaje**, *m.* curtains, hangings.

cortisona, *f.* cortisone.

corto, *a.* short; brief; scanty; timid, bashful.—*c. de alcances*, stupid—*a la corta o a la larga*, sooner or later.—**cortocircuito**, *m.* short circuit.

corva, *f.* back of the knee.—**corvadura**, *f.* curvature.

corvejón, *m.* hock joint of a quadruped.

corveta, *f.* curvet, leap, buck or bound of a horse.

corvo, *a.* bent; arched.

corzo, *n.* roe deer, fallow deer.

cosa, *f.* thing, matter, affair.—*como si tal c.*, as if nothing had happened.—*c. de*, about, approximately.—*no es c.*, it is not worth anything.—*otra c.*, something else.—*poca c.*, matter of slight importance; weak or timid person.

coscorrón, *m.* blow on the head.

cosecha, *f.* harvest, crop, yield; results.—**cosechar**, *vt.* & *vi.* to reap, gather in; to harvest.—**cosechero**, *m.* owner or reaper of a crop, harvester; grower.

cosepapeles, *m.* stapler.

coser, *vt.* to sew (up, on); to stitch.

cosmético, *m.* & *a.* cosmetic.

cósmico, *a.* cosmic.

cosmopolita, *a.* & *mf.* cosmopolitan.

coso, *m.* arena, ring.

cosquillas, *f.* tickling.—*buscarle a uno las c.*, to tease.—*hacer c.*, to tickle.—**consquillear**, *vt.* to tickle.—**cosquilleo**, *m.* tickling sensation.—**cosquilloso**, *a.* ticklish; touchy.

costa, *f.* coast, shore; cost, price.—*a c. de*, at the expense of.

costado, *m.* side, flank.

costal, *m.* sack or large bag.—**costalada**, *f.* (a) falling flat on the ground.

costar, *vii.* [12] to cost.—*c. trabajo*, to be difficult.

costarricence, *mf.* & *a.* Costa Rican.

coste, *m.* cost, price, expense.

costear, *vt.* to pay the cost.—*vi.* to pay, be profitable; to sail along the coast.

costeño, costero, *a.* coastal, offshore.

costilla, *f.* rib; chop; cutlet; (fig.) wife.—*c. falsa*, false rib.—*medirle a uno las costillas*, to cudgel one.—**costillaje, costillar**, *m.* the ribs, or rib system; frame of a ship.

costo, *m.* cost, price; expense.—**costoso**, *a.* expensive.—*c. de la vida*, cost of living.

costra, *f.* crust; deposit; scab.—**costroso**, *a.* crusty, scabby.

costumbre, *f.* custom; habit.

costura, *f.* sewing; seam; stitching; needlework; suture.—**costurera**, *f.* seamstress, dressmaker.—**costurero**, *m.* sewing box, table or room.—**costurón**, *m.* large, coarse seam; big scar.

cota, *f.* = CUOTA; coat of mail; coat of arms; number indicating elevation above sea level, etc.—*c. de malla*, coat of mail.

cotarro, *m.*—*alborotar el c.*, to cause disturbance; to produce riot.

cotejar, *vt.* to compare, collate; to confront.—**cotejo**, *m.* comparison, collation.

coterráneo, *a.* fellow citizen.

cotidiano, *a.* daily; quotidian.

cotización, *f.* quotation of prices; current price.—**cotizar**, *vti.* [a] to quote prices; to call out current prices in the stock exchange; to pay (one's share).

coto, *m.* enclosed pasture; preserve; landmark, boundary.—*poner c. a*, to put a stop to.

cotorra, *f.* parrot; (fig.) chatterbox.—**cotorrear**, *vi.* to chatter; to gossip.—**cotorreo**, *m.* chattering; gossiping.

covacha, *f.* small cave or hollow underground; grotto; (fig.) den.

coxis, *m.* coccyx.

coyunda, *f.* strap for yoking oxen; dominion; matrimonial union.

coyuntura, *f.* joint; occasion; nick of time.

coz, *f.* kick; drawback; unprovoked bruskness.

cráneo, *m.* cranium, skull.

craso, *a.* crass, inexcusable.

cráter, *m.* crater.

creaclón, *f.* creation.—**creador**, *n.* & *a.* creator, creating, creative.—**crear**, *vt.* to create, establish, found.

crecer, *vii.* [3] to grow; to bud forth; to increase.—*vr.* to swell with pride, authority, etc.—**creces**, *f.*

pl. augmentation, excess.—*con c.*, amply.—**crecida,** *f.* swelling of rivers.—**crecido,** *a.* grown, increased.—**creciente,** *a.* growing, increasing; waxing (moon); crescent (moon).—*f.* flood of rivers; crescent (of the moon).—**crecimiento,** *m.* growth; growing; increase.

credencial, *f.* letter or document of appointment to a post.—*pl.* credentials.

crédito, *m.* credit; reputation; credence, belief.—*dar c.,* to believe.

credo, *m.* creed, articles of faith, tenet.—**credulidad,** *f.* credulity.—**crédulo,** *a.* credulous.—**creencia,** *f.* belief; creed; religion.—**creer,** *vti.* [e] to believe; to credit; to think; to assume.—*¡ya lo creo!,* of course.

crema, *f.* cream of milk; custard; select society; cold cream; dieresis.—*c. batida,* whipped cream.

cremación, *f.* cremation, incineration.

cremallera, *f.* ratchet, rack; toothed bar; zipper.—*bajar la c.,* to unzip.

crematorio, *m.* crematory; incinerator.

crémor, *m.*—*c. tártaro,* cream of tartar.

crencha, *f.* parting of the hair into two parts; each of these parts.

crepuscular, *a.* crepuscular.—**crepúsculo,** *m.* crepuscule, twilight; dawn; dusk.

crespo, *a.* curly; crispy.—*m.* curl.

crespón, *m.* crepe.

cresta, *f.* comb (of a bird); cockscomb; crest of a helmet; wave crest; top; crest or summit of a mountain.

cretona, *f.* cretonne.

creyente, *mf.* & *a.* believer, believing.

creyón, *m.* crayon; charcoal pencil.

cría, *f.* act of nursing; breeding; bringing up; rearing; brood; litter of animals; suckling; nursing; infant. —*c. a los pechos,* breast-feeding. —**criada,** *f.* female servant, maid. —**criadero,** *m.* breeding place; tree nursery; hatchery.—**criado,** *a.* bred.—*m.* male servant.—**crianza,** *f.* nursing, suckling; secretion of milk; breeding; manners, education, upbringing.—**criar,** *vt.* to breed; to bring up; to nurse; to foster.—**criatura,** *f.* creature; baby; infant; child; tool; puppet.

criba, *f.* sieve, screen.—**cribar,** *vt.* to sift, sieve.

cricquet, *m.* = CRIQUET.

crimen, *m.* crime; murder.—**criminal,** *mf.* & *a.* criminal; murderer.—**crimi-**

nalidad, *f.* criminality.—**criminalista,** *m.* criminologist, penologist.

crin, *f.* mane, horsehair.

crío, *m.* (coll.) nursing baby.

criollo, *m.* Spanish-American native; Creole.—*a.* national, traditional (in Spanish America).

cripta, *f.* crypt.

criquet, *m.* (sport) cricket.

crisálida, *f.* pupa, chrysalis.

crisantemo, *m.* chrysanthemum.

crisis, *f.* crisis.—*c. energética,* energy crisis.

crisma, *m.* chrism.—*f.* (coll.) head.—*romperse la c.,* to break one's neck.

crisol, *m.* crucible, melting pot; hearth of a furnace.

crispar, *vt.* to contract (muscles); to clench (fists).—*vi.* to twitch.

cristal, *m.* crystal; glass; lens; (window) pane.—*c. cilindrado,* plate glass.—*c. de reloj,* watch crystal.—*c. de roca,* rock crystal.—*c. tallado,* cut glass.—**cristalería,** *f.* glassware; glass store.—**cristalino,** *a.* crystalline, clear.—*m.* crystalline of the eye.—**cristalización,** *f.* crystalization.—**cristalizar,** *vii.* [a] & *vri.* to crystalize.

cristiandad, *f.* Christendom; Christianity.—**cristianismo,** *m.* Christianity; the body of Christians.—**cristiano,** *a.* & *n.* Christian (person).

criterio, *m.* criterion; judgment, discernment.

crítica, *f.* criticism; critique; censure.—**criticar,** *vti.* [d] to criticize; to judge.—**crítico,** *a.* critical; decisive.—*m.* critic, reviewer.—**criticón,** *m.* & *a.* faultfinder; faultfinding.

croar, *vi.* to croak.

crónica, *f.* chronicle.—**crónico,** *a.* chronic.—**cronista,** *mf.* chronicler, annalist, historian.—*c. deportivo,* sports writer.

cronología, *f.* chronology.—**cronológico,** *a.* chronological, chronologic.—**cronométrico,** *a.* chronometric.—**cronómetro,** *m.* chronometer, timepiece; stop watch.

croqueta, *f.* croquette, fritter.

croquis, *m.* sketch, rough draft.

cruce, *m.* crossing; crossroads; crossbreeding.—**crucero,** *m.* transept; crossroads; railroad crossing; crosspiece; cruiser; cruise, cruising.—**crucificar,** *vti.* [d] to crucify, torture; to sacrifice; to ruin.—**crucifijo,** *m.*

crucifix.—**crucigrama**, *m.* crossword puzzle.

cruda, *f.* (Am.) hangover.—**crudeza**, *f.* crudity, crudeness; rawness.—**crudo**, *a.* raw; crude; uncooked; harsh.

cruel, *a.* cruel, remorseless.—**crueldad**, *f.* cruelty.

crujido, *m.* crack, creak, crackling, creaking; rustle; crunch.—**crujir**, *vi.* to crackle, creak; to rustle.

cruz, *f.* cross; (fig.) affliction; tails (of coin).—*C. Roja*, Red Cross.—*echar a cara o c.*, to toss up.—**cruzada**, *f.* crusade; holy war; campaign.—**cruzamiento**, *m.* crossing.—**cruzar**, *vti.* [a] to cross; to go across, pass; to cruise; to interbreed.

cuadernillo, *m.* quire of paper.—**cuaderno**, *m.* writing book, memorandum book; note or exercises book; booklet.—*c. de bitácora*, (naut.) logbook.—*c. de hojas cambiables*, looseleaf notebook.

cuadra, *f.* stable; city block, block of houses; hospital or prison ward.

cuadrangular, *m.* (sports) home run.

cuadrado, *a.* square; perfect.—*m.* square; quadrate; foursquare; (print.) quad, quadrat.—**cuadrante**, *m.* quadrant; sundial.—**cuadragésimo**, *a.* & *m.* fortieth.—**cuadrar**, *vt.* & *vi.* to square; to form into or reduce to a square; to please, suit; to fit in; to correspond.—*vr.* to stand at attention.—**cuadricular**, *vt.* to divide or design into squares.—**cuadriga**, *f.* chariot.—**cuadrilla**, *f.* gang, party; crew; band of armed men; team of bullfighters.—**cuadruplicado**, *a.* quadrupled.—**cuadro**, *m.* square; picture, painting; frame; scene; impressive spectacle; vivid description; (Am.) blackboard.—*c. interior*, (sports) infield.—**cuadrúpedo**, *m.* & *a.* quadruped.—**cuádruple, cuádruplo**, *a.* quadruple, fourfold.

cuajada, *f.* curd.—**cuajar**, *vt.* to coagulate; to curd, curdle; to yell; to overdecorate.—*vi.* to succeed, materialize.—*vr.* to coagulate; to curdle; to fill, become full.—**cuajarón**, *m.* clot.—**cuajo**, *m.* rennet; curd; thickening (of a liquid).—*de c.*, radically; by the roots.

cual (*pl.* **cuales**), *rel. pron.* which, such as, as.—*cada c.*, each one.—*c. más c. menos*, some people more, others less.—*el c., la c., los cuales, las cuales,* which, who.—*lo c.* which.—*adv.* as, like.—*c. si*, as if.—*¿cuál?* *pron. interr.* which one? what?

cualidad, *f.* quality; trait.

cualquier(a), (*pl.* **cualesquier, cualesquiera**), *a.* any.—*pron.* any(one), anybody; someone, somebody; whichsoever, whoever.—*un cualquiera*, a nobody, a person of no account.

cuando (interr. *¿cuándo?*), *adv.* when; at, or during the time of; in case that, if; though, although, even; sometimes.—*c. más*, at most.—*c. menos*, at the least.—*de c. en c.*, from time to time.

cuantía, *f.* amount, quantity; rank, importance, degree.—**cuantioso**, *a.* numerous, abundant.—**cuanto**, *a.* as much as, all the, whatever.—*pl.* as many as, all the, whatever.—*pron.* all that, everything that.—*pl.* all those, who or which.—**cuánto, cuánta**, *a.* & *pron. interr.* how much.—*pl.* how many.—*adv.* as, the more.—*c. antes* as soon as possible.—*c. más que*, all the more so.—*en c.*, as soon as.—*en c. a*, as for, as regards.—*por c.*, therefore, inasmuch.

cuanto, *m.* quantum.

cuáquero, *a.* & *n.* Quaker.

cuarenta, *a.* & *s.* forty.—*c. y uno*, forty-one.—**cuarentavo**, *a.* fortieth —**cuarentena**, *f.* forty days; quarantine.—**cuarentón**, *n.* & *a.* (man or woman) in the forties.

cuaresma, *f.* Lent.

cuarta, *f.* fourth; fourth part; span of the hand; short whip.—**cuartazo** *m.* blow with a whip.—**cuartear**, *vt* to quarter, divide into four parts; to whip.—*vr.* to split, crack, rive.

cuartel, *m.* quarter, fourth part; barracks; mercy; district, ward.—*c. de bomberos*, fire house.—*c. de policía* police station.—*no dar c.*, to give no quarter.—**cuartelada**, *f.*, **cuartelazo** *m.* military coup d'état.

cuartelillo, *m.* (de policía) station house.

cuarteta, *f.* quatrain.—**cuarteto**, *m* (mus.) quartet.

cuartilla, *f.* sheet of paper; (print. sheet of copy; fourth part of an *arroba* (about 6 lbs.).—**cuartillo**, *m* pint. (See Table of Measures).

cuarto, *m.* & *a.* fourth; fourth part quarter.—*m.* room, chamber.—*pl* cash, money.—*c. de reserva*, spare room.—*c. trasero*, (cook.) rump.—*no tener un c.*, not to be worth a cent.

cuarzo, *m.* quartz.

cuate, *m.* (Mex.) twin.—*eso no tiene c.*, that has no match.

cuatrero, *m.* horse thief, cattle thief.

cuatro, *a.* & *s.* four.—**cuatrocientos**, *a.* & *m.* four hundred.—*c. uno*, four hundred one.

cuba, *f.* cask; big-bellied person; drunkard.

cubano, *n.* & *a.* Cuban.

cubeta, *f.* small barrel or cask.

cubicación, *f.* measurement; volume, capacity; cubing of a number.

cúbico, *a.* cubic.

cubierta, *f.* cover, covering; lid; deck of ship; book wrapper.—*c. de paseo*, (naut.) promenade deck.—*c. principal*, main deck.

cubierto, *pp.* of CUBRIR.—*m.* covert; place setting.

cubil, *m.* lair, den.

cubilete, *m.* dicebox.

cúbito, *m.* ulna, larger bone of forearm.—**cubito**, *m.*—*c. de hielo*, ice cube.

cubo, *m.* cue; pail, bucket; hub of a wheel; shaft case; millpond; bastion of a castle.—*c. de la basura*, ashcan; garbage can.

cubreasiento, *m.* seat cover.—**cubrecama**, *f.* coverlet, bedspread.—**cubremesa**, *f.* table cover.

cubrir, *vti.* [49] to cover; to coat; to hide; to roof; to meet (a bill or check).—*vri.* to cover oneself; to protect oneself; to hedge; to put on one's hat.

cucaña, *f.* greased pole to climb for a prize; the sport itself.

cucaracha, *f.* cockroach.

cuchara, *f.* spoon; ladle; scoop.—*c. de sopa*, soup spoon.—*meter la c.*, or *su c.*, to meddle, intrude.—**cucharada**, *f.* spoonful.—**cucharadita**, *f.* teaspoonful.—**cucharilla**, *f.* teaspoon, coffee spoon.—**cucharón**, *m.* ladle; large spoon; scoop.

cuchichear, *vi.* to whisper.—**cuchicheo**, *m.* whisper, whispering.

cuchilla, *f.* cleaver; blade of a knife; any cutting blade; razor blade; penknife.—*c. de pan*, bread knife.—*c. para mondar*, paring knife.—**cuchillada**, *f.* a cut with a knife; stab; slash; gash.—**cuchillería**, *f.* cutlery, cutler's shop.—**cuchillo**, *m.* knife; gusset.

cuchitril, *m.* narrow hole or corner; very small room; hut; den.

cuchufleta, *f.* joke, jest, fun.

cuclillas, —*en c.*, in a crouching or squatting position.

cuclillo, cuco, *a.* cunning; prim.—*m.* cuckoo; (Am.) peach, peach tree.

cucurucho, *m.* wrapping in the form of a cone; paper or cardboard cone.—*c. de helado*, ice-cream cone.

cuelga, *f.* cluster of grapes; string (of garlic, onion, etc.); (Am.) (coll.) birthday present.

cuello, *m.* neck; collar.

cuenca, *f.* wooden bowl; socket of the eye; river basin; deep valley.—**cuenco**, *m.* earthen or wooden bowl.

cuenta, *f.* computation, calculation; account; bill, (coll.) tab; note; bead (of a rosary, etc.).—*a fin de cuentas*, in the end.—*caer en la c.*, (coll.) to catch on, get the point.—*c. de ahorros*, savings account.—*c. en común*, joint account.—*correr de la c. de uno*, to be one's responsibility.—*darse c.*, to realize.—*en resumidas cuentas*, in short.—*no tenerle a uno c.*, to be of no profit to one.—*por c. propia*, freelance.—*rendir c.*, to inform, report.—*tener* or *tomar en c.*, to take into account.—*tomar una cosa por su c.*, to take upon oneself.

cuento, *m.* tale; story; short story; piece of gossip.—*dejarse de cuentos*, to come to the point.—*sin c.*, numberless.—*traer a c.*, to bring to bear upon the subject; to drag into the subject.—*venir a c.*, to be pertinent.

cuerda, *f.* cord, rope, string; chord; watch spring.—*bajo c.*, or *por debajo de c.*, underhandedly, deceitfully.—*c. de presos*, chain gang.—*c. de remolque*, towrope.—*c. tirante*, tightrope.—*dar c. a*, to wind up (a watch, etc.).

cuerdo, *a.* sane; prudent, wise.

cuerno, *m.* horn; antenna, feeler.—*mandar al c.*, to send to the devil.—*poner cuernos*, to be unfaithful (to a husband).

cuero, *m.* rawhide, skin; leather; wineskin.—*en cueros*, or *en cueros vivos*, or *en el puro c.*, stark-naked.

cuerpo, *m.* body; bulk; corps.—*a. c. descubierto*, without cover or shelter.—*c. a c.*, hand to hand; in single combat.—*C. de Paz*, Peace Corps.—*c. docente*, faculty (teaching corps).—*en c. y alma,* wholly, sincerely, with pleasure.—*estar de c. presente,* to lie in state.—*tomar c.,* to increase, to grow, to thicken.

cuervo, *m.* crow; raven; (Am.) buzzard.

cuesco, *m.* kernel; stone (of a fruit); the breaking of wind.

cuesta, *f.* hill, slope, grade.—*c. abajo,* downhill.—*c. arriba,* uphill.—*a cuestas,* on one's back.

cuestación, *f.* petition; solicitation or collection for a charitable purpose.

cuestión, *f.* question, dispute, controversy; matter, problem, affair. —**cuestionario,** *m.* questionnaire.

cueva, *f.* cave, grotto, cavern; cellar.— *c. de ladrones,* (sl.) clipjoint.

cuidado, *m.* care, attention; custody; carefulness, caution; worry, anxiety.—*no hay c. (de que)* there is no danger that.—*¡no pase c.!* or *¡pierda c.!* don't worry!—*tener c.,* to be careful; to be worried.—*interj.* look out! beware!—**cuidadoso,** *a.* careful.— **cuidar,** *vt.* to care for, tend, mind, keep; to execute with care.—*c. de,* to take care of.—*vr.* to take care of oneself.—*cuidarse de,* to look out for, to guard against; to avoid.

culta, *f.* care, grief, affliction, trouble.—**cuitado,** *a.* unfortunate, wretched.

cuje, *m.* withe; pole supported by two vertical ones for hanging tobacco.—*pl.* hop poles.

culata, *f.* butt, stock (of a firearm); (Am.) rear (of car, house).—**culatazo,** *m.* blow with the butt; recoil of a firearm.

culebra, *f.* snake; coil; grass snake.— **culebrear,** *vi.* to twist, wriggle (as a snake).

culero, *m.* baby's diaper.

culinario, *a.* culinary.

culminación, *f.* culmination.—**culminar,** *vi.* to culminate.

culo, *m.* buttocks; bottom; anus; bottom of anything.

culpa, *f.* fault; guilt; blame.—*echar la c. a,* to blame.—*tener la c. de,* to be to blame, or responsible for.—**culpabilidad,** *f.* culpability, guilt.—**culpable,** *a.* guilty.—**culpar,** *vt.* to blame, accuse; to condemn.

cultivar, *vt.* to cultivate; to farm, till, grow.—**cultivo,** *m.* cultivation; farming.—**culto,** *a.* cultivated; cultured.—*m.* cult, worship.—**cultura,** *f.* culture; cultivation.

cumbre, *f.* top, tiptop, summit, crest.

cumpleaños, *m.* birthday.—*¡feliz c.!* or *¡c. feliz!,* happy birthday!

cumplido, *a.* fulfilled, expired; polite; faultless; large, ample.—*m.* compliment; courtesy.—**cumplimentar,** *vt.* to compliment; to show courtesy; to congratulate.—**cumplimiento,** *m.* fulfillment, completion, performance; expiration; courtesy, compliment.—**cumplir,** *vt.* to fulfill, carry out; to reach (age).—*¡que cumpla(s) muchos más!,* many happy returns of the day!.—*¡que los complas muy feliz!,* have a very happy birthday!—*vi.* to fall due, expire; to do one's duty.—*c. años,* to have a birthday.—*vr.* to be realized, come to an end.

cúmulo, *m.* heap, pile; large quantity or number; cumulus (clouds).

cuna, *f.* cradle; place of birth; lineage, origin.

cundir, *vi.* to spread, propagate; to yield abundantly; to grow, expand.

cuneta, *f.* road drain; side ditch; gutter.

cuña, *f.* wedge; splinter; bedpan.

cuñada, *f.* sister-in-law.—**cuñado,** *m.* brother-in-law.

cuño, *m.* die (for coining money); impression made by die; (fig.) stamp.

cuota, *f.* quota, share; dues, fee.

cuotidiano, *a.* = COTIDIANO.

cupo, *m.* quota; tax rate; contents, capacity.

cupón, *m.* coupon.

cúpula, *f.* dome, cupola.

cura, *m.* curate, priest.—*c. de hambre,* starvation diet.—*f.,* or **curación,** *f.* healing; cure.—**curador,** *m.* caretaker.—**curandero,** *n.* faith-healer; witch doctor, medicine man; (pej.) quack, charlatan.—**curar,** *vt. & vi.* to treat, heal, cure; to season, dry (meats, woods, etc.).—*vr.* to recover from sickness; to heal.—**curativo,** *a.* curative, healing.

curiosear, *vi.* to pry, snoop, spy, peek, peer.—**curiosidad,** *f.* curiosity; curious thing; rare object or person. —**curioso,** *a.* curious, prying; careful, diligent, skillful; rare; neat, clean.

cursar, *vt.* to study; to attend a course of study; to transmit, expedite. —**curso,** *m.* course, direction, career; course of study; scholastic year.—*en c.,* ongoing, underway, in progress.—*primer c.,* opening price.

cursi, *a.* ridiculously pretentious in appearance, behavior or taste.

curtido, *m.* tanning; tanned leather. —**curtidor,** *m.* tanner.—**curtir,** *vt.* to tan; to bronze the skin; to harden; to inure.—*vr.* to become tanned, sunburned, weather-beaten; to become hardened or experienced.

curva, *f.* curve; curvature; bend.—**curvatura,** *f.* curvature; curving.—**curvo,** *a.* curved; bent; arched.

cúspide, *f.* cusp, apex, top, peak, summit.

custodia, *f.* custody, safe-keeping; guardian; (eccl.) monstrance.—**custodiar,** *vt.* to guard; to convoy; to take care of.—**custodio,** *m.* guard, custodian; watchman; caretaker.

cutí, *m.* ticking.

cutícula, *f.* cuticle.

cutis, *m.* skin, complexion.

cuyo, cuya (*pl.* **cuyos, cuyas**), *pron. poss.* of which, of whom, whose, whereof.

D

dable, *a.* possible, practicable; grantable.

dactilógrafo, *n.* typist.

dádiva, *f.* gift, gratification.—**dadivoso,** *a.* bountiful, liberal.

dado, *m.* die; block.—*pl.* dice.—*d. cargados,* loaded dice.

dador, *n.* giver, donor; bearer (of letter).

daga, *f.* dagger.

daltonismo, *m.* color blindness.

dama, *f.* lady; gentlewoman; mistress; (theat.) leading lady.—*d. de honor,* bridesmaid; lady-in-waiting.— *juego de damas,* checkers.—**damisela,** *f.* young woman, damsel.

damnificar, *vti.* [d] to hurt, damage, injure.

dandi, *m.* dandy, fop, coxcomb.

danés, *a.* Danish.—*n.* Dane.

danza, *f.* dance.—*d. del vientre,* belly dance.—**danzante,** *mf.* dancer; (coll.) busybody.—**danzar,** *vii.* [a] to dance; to whirl.—**danzarín,** *n.* dancer.

dañado, *a.* spoiled, tinted; dammed.

dañar, *vt.* to hurt, damage; to harm; to spoil; to weaken.—*vr.* to spoil; to be damaged; to hurt oneself.—**dañino,** *a.* destructive, harmful; vicious.—**daño,** *m.* damage, hurt, loss, spoilage; nuisance.—**dañoso,** *a.* injurious.

dar, *vti.* [13] to give; to hand; to grant; to emit; to hit, strike; to yield.—*d. a conocer,* to make known.—*d. a entender,* to insinuate; to suggest.—*d. a luz,* to give birth to.—*d. comienzo,* to begin.—*d. con,* to find, come

upon.—*d. cuerda a,* to wind up (clock, watch, etc.).—*d. de baja,* to dismiss.—*d. de comer,* to feed animals.—*d. de sí,* to give, stretch.—*d. fin a,* to complete, finish.—*d. (frente) a,* to face, look out on.— *d. golpes a,* to beat, thrash.—*d. gritos,* to shout.—*d. la razón a,* to say (a person) is right, agree with.—*d. largas a,* to postpone.—*d. las espaldas,* to turn one's back.—*darle a uno por,* to take to.—*d. lugar a,* to give rise to.—*d. parte (de),* to report (about), communicate.—*d. pasos,* to take steps.—*d. prestado,* to lend.—*d. que decir,* to give occasion for censure or criticism.—*d. que hacer,* to give trouble.—*d. que pensar,* to give food for thought.—*d. satisfacciones,* to apologize.—*no d. pie con bola,* not to do a thing right, to make a mess of it.—*vri.* to yield, surrender; to devote oneself.— *darse cuenta de,* to realize.—*darse por,* to consider oneself as.—*darse por vencido,* to give up.—*darse prisa,* to hurry.—*darse tono,* to put on airs.

dardo, *m.* dart, arrow.

dársena, *f.* dock; yacht basin, marina.

data, *f.* date; item in an account.—**datar,** *vt.* to date; (com.) to credit on account.—*vi.* to take origin, date from.

dátil, *m.* date.—**datilera,** *f.* date palm.

dato, *m.* datum.—*pl.* data.

de, *prep.* of; from; for; by; than; in.

deán, *m.* (ecl.) dean.

debajo, *adv.* beneath, underneath.— *d. de,* under, beneath.—*por d.,* from below; underneath.—*por d. de,* under; below.

debate, *m.* debate; altercation.—**debatir,** *vt.* to argue, discuss, debate.—*vr.* to struggle.

debe, *m.* debit.—**deber,** *vt.* to owe; to have to, be obliged to, must, ought, should.—*d. de,* must have, must be.—*m.* duty, obligation.—**debido,** *a.* fitting, right, just.—*d. a,* owing to, on account of; due to.

débil, *a.* weak, feeble, sickly.—**debilidad,** *f.* weakness, feebleness.—**debilitación,** *f.,* **debilitamiento,** *m.* weakening.—**debilitar,** *vt.* to weaken.—*vr.* to grow weaker.

débito, *m.* debt; debit.

debut, *m.* debut.—**debutar,** *vi.* to make one's debut.

década, *f.* decade; series of ten.

decadencia, *f.* decadence, decay, decline.—**decadente,** *a.* decaying, decadent, declining.—**decaer,** *vii.* [8-e] to decay, fail; to fall off.—**decaimiento,** *m.* decay; weakness.

decano, *n.* dean (of a University); senior member of a group or organization.

decantar, *vt.* to decant.

decapitación, *f.* beheading.—**decapitar,** *vt.* to behead, decapitate.

decatlón, *m.* decathlon.

decena, *f.* series of ten.—**decenio,** *m.* decade; decennial.

decencia, *f.* decency; modesty; honesty.—**decente,** *a.* decent; honest; modest.

decepción, *f.* disappointment; disillusionment.—**decepcionar,** *vt.* to disappoint.

dechado, *m.* model; sample, pattern.

decidir, *vt.* to decide, determine, resolve.—*vr.* to decide, make up one's mind; to be determined.

decima, *f.* tenth; (eccl.) tithe.—**decimal,** *a.* & *m.* decimal.—**decimo,** *a.* & *m.* tenth.—**decimoctavo,** *a.* & *m.* eighteenth.—**decimocuarto,** *a.* & *m.* fourteenth.—**decimonono** or **decimonoveno,** *a.* & *m.* nineteenth.—**decimoquinto,** *a.* & *m.* fifteenth.—**decimoséptimo,** *a.* & *m.* seventeenth.—**decimosexto,** *a.* & *m.* sixteenth.—**decimotercero,** *a.* & *m.* thirteenth.

decir, *vti.* [14] & *vii.* to say, tell; to speak; to name.—*como quien dice,* as if meaning.—*d. bien,* to be right.—*d. mal,* to be wrong.—*d. para sí o*

para su capote, to say oneself.—*d. por d.,* to talk for the sake of talking.—*d. sí a,* to yes.—*d. sí,* to yes.—*es d.,* that is to say, that is.—*querer d.,* to mean, signify.—*por decirlo así,* so to speak.—*m.* saying, proverb.—*al d. de,* according to.

decisión, *f.* decision, determination, resolution, issue.—**decisivo,** *a.* decisive, final.

declamación, *f.* declamation, speech; reading, recitation.—**declamador,** *n.* orator; reciter.—**declamar,** *vi.* to declaim; to recite.

declaración, *f.* declaration; statement; manifestation; (law) deposition.—*d. de derechos,* bill of rights.—*d. de impuesto sobre rentas, d. de la renta, d. de impuestos,* tax return.—**declarado,** *a.* declared.—**declarante,** *a.* declaring, expounding.—*mf.* declarer; witness.—**declarar,** *vt.* to declare, make known; (law) to testify.—*vr.* to declare one's opinion; (coll.) to make a declaration of love.—**declarativo,** *a.* declarative.

declinación, *f.* declination, fall, decline; (gram.) declension, inflection.—**declinar,** *vi.* to decline; to decay; to wane; to diminish.—*vt.* (gram.) to decline.

declive, *m.* declivity; slope, fall; (RR.) grade.—*en d.,* slanting, sloping.

decomisar, *vt.* to confiscate.—**decomiso,** *m.* confiscation.

decoración, *f.* decoration; ornament; (theat.) setting.—**decorado,** *m.* decoration, ornamentation.—**decorador,** *n.* & *a.* decorator; decorating.—**decorar,** *vt.* to decorate; to adorn, embellish.—**decorativo,** *a.* decorative.

decoro, *m.* decency, decorum; honor; propriety.—**decoroso,** *a.* decorous, decent.

decrecer, *vii.* [3] to decrease, diminish.—**decreciente,** *a.* diminishing, decreasing.

decrépito, *a.* decrepit.—**decrepitud,** *f.* decrepitude.

decretar, *vt.* to decree, resolve; to decide.—**decreto,** *m.* decree; decision.

d. de C., *abbr.* (**después de Cristo**) A.D. (Anno Domini).

dedal, *m.* thimble.

dedicación, *f.* dedication; consecration.—**dedicar,** *vti.* [d] to dedicate, devote; to autograph (a literary work).—*vri.* (**a**) to devote oneself (to); to make a specialty (of).—**dedicatoria,** *f.* dedication; dedicatory inscription.

dedillo, *m.*—*saber al d.,* to know perfectly.—**dedo,** *m.* finger; toe; finger's breadth; small bit.—*d. anular,* ring finger.—*d. gordo,* (fam.) big toe; thumb.—*d. índice,* forefinger, index finger.—*d. medio,* middle finger.—*d. auricular* or *d. meñique,* little finger.—*d. pulgar,* thumb.

deducción, *f.* deduction, inference, conclusion.—*d. impositiva,* tax exemption.—**deducir,** *vti.* [11] to deduce, infer; to draw; to offer as a plea; to deduct.

defecto, *m.* defect, imperfection.—*d. del habla,* speech impediment.—**defectuoso,** *a.* defective, imperfect, unsound.

defender, *vti.* [18] to defend.—**defensa,** *f.* defense; protection; shelter; bumper; (football) back.—*d. personal,* self-defense.—**defensiva,** *f.* defensive.—**defensivo,** *a.* defensive.—*m.* defense.—**defensor,** *n.* defender; supporter; (law) counsel for the defense, defender.

deferencia, *f.* deference.—**deferir,** *vii.* [2] to yield, submit.—*vti.* to communicate; to delegate.

deficiencia, *f.* deficiency.—**deficiente,** *a.* deficient, faulty.

definición, *f.* definition.—**definible,** *a.* definable.—**definido,** *a.* definite.—**definir,** *vt.* to define; to establish, determine.—**definitivo,** *a.* definitive.—*en definitiva,* in conclusion; in short.

deflación, *f.* deflation.

deformación, *f.* deformation, distortion; deformity.—**deformar,** *vt.* to deform, disfigure.—*vr.* to become deformed, change shape.—**deforme,** *a.* deformed, disfigured; hideous.—**deformidad,** *f.* deformity; ugliness.

defraudación, *f.* defrauding; fraud, deceit.—**defraudador,** *n.* defrauder, defaulter.—**defraudar,** *vt.* to defraud; to rob of.

defunción, *f.* death, demise.

degeneración, *f.* degeneration, degeneracy.—**degenerado,** *n.* & *a.* degenerate.—**degenerar,** *vi.* to degenerate.

deglución, *f.* swallowing.—**deglutir,** *vt.* to swallow.

degollación, *f.* beheading.—**degollar,** *vti.* [12] to behead, decapitate.—**degollina,** *f.* slaughter; butchery.

degradación, *f.* degradation, humiliation, debasement; depravity, degeneracy.—**degradante,** *a.* degrading.—**degradar,** *vt.* to degrade, debase; humiliate, revile.—*vr.* to degrade or lower oneself.

degüello, *m.* beheading, throatcutting.

dehesa, *f.* pasture ground.

deidad, *f.* deity; goddess.—**deificar,** *vti.* [d] to deify.

dejación, *f.* abandonment, relinquishment.—*d. de bienes,* (law) assignment.—**dejadez,** *f.* slovenliness, neglect.—**dejado,** *pp.* of DEJAR.—*a.* slovenly; indolent, negligent.—**dejar,** *vt.* to leave; to let; to let go, relinquish; to permit, allow; to abandon, quit; to forsake; to yield; to omit.—*d. atrás,* to outdistance.—*d. caer,* to drop.—*d. de,* to stop; to fail to.—*vr.* to be slovenly; to abandon oneself.—**dejo,** *m.* aftertaste; trace; slight accent.

del, *contraction of* DE *and* EL; of the.

delación, *f.* accusation, information.

delantal, *m.* apron.

delante, *adv.* before, ahead, in front.—*d. de prep.* before, in front of, in the presence of.—**delantera,** *f.* front, fore end; front seats in theaters, etc.; lead, advantage.—**delantero,** *a.* foremost, first; front.—*m.* front part; (sport) forward.

delatar, *vt.* to accuse, denounce.—**delator,** *n.* informer, accuser, denouncer.

delegación, *f.* delegation; proxy; office of a delegate.—**delegado,** *n.* delegate, proxy.—**delegar,** *vti.* [b] to delegate.

deleitable, *a.* delectable, delightful.—**deleitación,** *f.* delectation, pleasure, delight.—**deleitar,** *vt.* to delight, please.—*vr.* to delight or please.—**deleite,** *m.* pleasure, delight; lust.—**deleitoso,** *a.* delightful, pleasing.

deletrear, *vt.* to spell.—**deletreo,** *m.* spelling.

deleznable, *a.* ephemeral; worthless; negligible; contemptible.

delfín, *m.* porpoise; dolphin.

delgadez, *f.* thinness; slenderness; leanness.—**delgado,** *a.* thin; lean; slender, slim.—**delgaducho,** *a.* thinnish, lanky.

deliberación, *f.* deliberation.—**deliberar,** *vi.* to deliberate, ponder; to consult or take counsel together.

delicadeza, *f.* delicacy, refinement; softness; tenderness.—**delicado,** *a.* delicate; gentle; tender; sickly, frail; dainty; exquisite.

delicia, *f.* delight, pleasure.—**delicioso,** *a.* delicious; delightful.

delincuencia, *f.* delinquency.—*d. de menores,* juvenile delinquency.—**delincuente,** *mf.* delinquent, offender.—*d. juvenil,* juvenile delinquent.—*a.* delinquent, guilty.

delineación, *f.* delineation, draft, sketch.—**delineador,** *m.* (de ojos) eye liner.—**delineante,** *mf.* draftsman, designer.—**delinear,** *vt.* to delineate, sketch.

delirante, *a.* delirious.—**delirar,** *vi.* to be delirious; to talk nonsense; to rave.—**delirio,** *m.* delirium; frenzied rapture; nonsense.

delito, *m.* crime, offense.—*d. de sangre,* violent crime.

demacrado, *a.* emaciated.—**demacrarse,** *vr.* to waste away.

demagogia, *f.* demagogy.

demanda, *f.* (law) claim, complaint; petition; question, inquiry; (com.) demand.—*la oferta y la d.,* supply and demand.—**demandado,** *n.* defendant.—**demandante,** *mf.* plaintiff, complainant.—**demandar,** *vt.* to demand, ask, solicit; to desire; (law) to sue.

demás, *a.* other.—*estar d.,* to be useless; to be unwelcome, not wanted.—*lo d.,* the rest.—*los d., las d.,* the rest; the others.—*por lo d.,* aside from this; furthermore.—*todo lo d.,* everything else.—*y d.,* and other things, or persons; and so forth.—*adv.* besides, moreover.—**demasía,** *f.* excess, surplus; insolence, outrage.—*en d.,* excessively.—**demasiado,** *a.* excessive; too much.—*pl.* too many.—*adv.* too, excessively; too much.

demencia, *f.* madness, insanity.—**demente,** *a.* insane, mad.—*mf.* lunatic.

demérito, *m.* demerit.

democracia, *f.* democracy.—**demócrata,** *mf.* democrat.—**democrático,** *a.* democratic.

demoledor, *n.* & *a.* demolisher; demolishing.—**demoler,** *vti.* [26] to demolish, destroy, raze.—**demolición,** *f.* demolition.

demonio, *m.* demon; devil.

demora, *f.* delay.—**demorar,** *vt.* to delay.—*vi.* to delay, tarry.—*vr.* to linger, tarry; to be delayed.

demostración, *f.* demonstration; proof.—**demostrar,** *vti.* [12] to demonstrate, show; to prove.

demudado, *a.* wan, pale (from illness, fright, etc.).—**demudarse,** *vr.* to lose one's calm; to turn pale.

denegación, *f.* denial, refusal.—**denegar,** *vti.* [1-b] to deny, refuse.

dengoso, *a.* fastidious; coy.—**dengue,** *m.* fastidiousness; coyness; (med.) dengue.—*hacer dengues,* to act coy.

denodado, *a.* daring, intrepid.

denominación, *f.* denomination.—**denominador,** *m.* denominator.—**denominar,** *vt.* & *vr.* to call, give a name to.

denostar, *vti.* [12] to insult; to revile.

denotar, *vt.* to denote, express.

densidad, *f.* density.—**denso,** *a.* dense, thick; close, compact.

dentado, *a.* toothed, serrated.—**dentadura,** *f.* set of teeth.—*d. postiza,* false teeth, denture.—**dental,** *a.* dental.—**dentellada,** *f.* bite; tooth marks.—**dentera,** *f.* teeth on edge; (coll.) envy.—**dentición,** *f.* teething.—*segunda d.,* second teeth.—**dentífrico,** *m.* toothpaste or toothpowder.—**dentista,** *mf.* dentist.

dentro, *adv.* inside, within.—*de d.,* from inside.—*d. de,* within; inside.—*d. del año,* in the course of the year.—*d. de poco,* shortly, soon.—*hacia d.,* inwards.—*por d.,* inside; inwardly.

denuedo, *m.* boldness, bravery, courage.

denuesto, *m.* affront, insult.

denuncia, *f.* accusation, arraignment; denunciation; (min.) claim.—**denunciante,** *mf.* denouncer; accuser.—*a.* denouncing; accusing.—**denunciar,** *vt.* to denounce; to advise, give notice; to squeal; (min.) to claim.

deparar, *vt.* to offer, afford, furnish, present.

departamento, *m.* department; compartment, section; apartment.

departir, *vi.* to chat, converse.

dependencia, *f.* dependence, dependency; subordination; branch office; outbuildings.—**depender,** *vi.* (de) to depend, rely (on).—**de-**

pendiente, *a.* dependent, subordinate.—*mf.* clerk, salesman (-woman), salesclerk; retainer.

eplorable, *a.* deplorable.—**deplorar,** *vt.* to deplore, regret.

eponer, *vti.* [32] to depose; to declare; to attest; to lay down.

eportación, *f.* deportation.—**deportar,** *vt.* to deport.

eporte, *m.* sport.—**deportista,** *mf.* sportsman (-woman); sports fan. —**deportivo,** *a.* athletic, sportive.

eposición, *f.* assertion, affirmation; testimony; removal from office; bowel movement.

epositar, *vt.* to deposit; to entrust; to lay aside.—*vr.* (chem.) to settle. —**depositario,** *n.* depositary, trustee. —**depósito,** *m.* deposit, trust; depot, repository, warehouse; storage; sediment.—*d. de agua,* reservoir.—*d. de cadáveres,* morgue.—*d. de combustible,* fuel tank.—*d. de locomotoras,* roundhouse.

epravación, *f.* depravity, viciousness.—**depravar,** *vt.* to deprave, corrupt.

epreciación, *f.* depreciation.—**depreciar,** *vt.* & *vr.* to depreciate.

epresión, *f.* depression.—**depresivo, deprimente,** *a.* depressive, depressing.—**deprimir,** *vt.* to depress; to belittle.—*vr.* to become depressed or compressed.

epuesto, *pp.* of DEPONER.

epuración, *f.* purifying; purge.—**depurar,** *vt.* to purify; to purge.

erecha, *f.* right hand; right side; (pol.) right-winger; right-wing.—*a derechas,* right; rightly.—**derechista,** *mf.* rightist.—**derecho,** *a.* straight; right (opposite to left); right-handed; vertical; upright.— *adv.* straight ahead, straightaway.— *m.* right; (**D.**) the Law; entitlement.—*tener d. a,* to be entitled to.—*d. de matrícula,* registration fee.—*d. de reproducción,* copyright.—*d. de tránsito o de paso,* right of way.—*pl.* fees, dues, duties.—*d. arancelarios* or *de aduana,* customs duties.—*d. de autor* or *de inventor,* copyright; royalties.—*d. de nacimiento,* birthright.—*d. de patente,* patent rights.—*d. civiles,* civil liberties, civil rights.—*d. de remolque,* towage.—**derechura,** *f.* straightness.

eriva, *f.* ship's course; deviation, drift; (aer. & naut.) leeway.—**deriva-**

ción, *f.* derivation.—**derivar,** *vi.* & *vr.* to derive.—*vi.* to drift.—*vt.* to derive, trace to its origin.

derogación, *f.* derogation, repeal. —**derogar,** *vt.* [b] to derogate; to annul, revoke, repeal.

derramamiento, *m.* pouring out; spilling, shedding; overflow; scattering.—*d. de sangre,* bloodshed.—**derramar,** *vt.* to pour out; to spill; to shed; to scatter; to spread.—*vr.* to overflow, run over; to be scattered or spread.—**derrame,** *m.* overflow; scattering; shedding; leakage; (med.) discharge.

derredor, *m.* circuit.—*al d.,* or *en d.,* round about.—*al d. de,* or *en d. de,* about, around.

derrengado, *a.* crooked; lame, crippled; swaybacked.—**derrengar,** *vti.* [1-b] to injure the back; to cripple; to make crooked.

derretir, *vti.* [29] to melt, fuse.—*vr.* to melt, fuse; to be deeply in love.

derribar, *vt.* to demolish, knock down; to overthrow.—**derribo,** *m.* wrecking, demolition; debris.

derrocamiento, *m.* throwing down, overthrow.—**derrocar,** *vti.* [12-d] to pull down; to oust; to overthrow.

derrochador, *n.* spendthrift, squanderer.—*a.* extravagant, prodigal. —**derrochar,** *vt.* to waste, squander. —**derroche,** *m.* waste, squandering, wastefulness.

derrota, *f.* defeat; (naut.) ship's course.—**derrotar,** *vt.* to defeat; (naut.) to cause to drift.—**derrotero,** *m.* (naut.) collection of seacharts; ship's course; course of action, way.—**derrotista,** *mf.* defeatist.

derruir, *vti.* [23-e] to demolish, tear down.

derrumbamiento, *m.* landslide; collapse; downfall.—**derrumbar,** *vt.* to throw down headlong.—*vr.* to tumble down; to crumble away; to cave in.—**derrumbe,** *m.* tumbling down, collapse; landslide.

desabonarse, *vr.* to cancel a subscription.

desabotonar, *vt.* to unbutton.

desabrido, *a.* harsh, sour; ill-humored; tasteless.—**desabrimiento,** *m.* ill humor; tastelessness.

desabrigar, *vti.* [b] to uncover; to strip.—*vri.* to take off outer clothing, expose oneself to cold.

desabrochar, *vt.* to unclasp, unfasten.—*vr.* to unclasp, or unfasten oneself; to become unclasped or unfastened.

desacatar, vt. to treat disrespectfully.—**desacato,** m. disrespect; lack of reverence.

desacertado, a. unwise, mistaken. —**desacierto,** m. error, mistake, blunder.

desaconsejado, a. ill-advised.

desacostumbrado, a. unusual; unaccustomed.

desacreditar, vt. to discredit.

desacuerdo, m. discordance, disagreement.

desafiar, vt. to challenge; to defy; to compete with.

desafinación, f. discordance, being out of tune.—**desafinado,** a. out of tune.—**desafinadamente,** adv. out of tune.—**desafinar,** vi. to be discordant, out of tune.—vr. to get out of tune.

desafío, m. challenge; duel; struggle, contest, competition.

desaforado, a. disorderly; lawless; outrageous.

desafortunado, a. unfortunate, unlucky.

desafuero, m. excess, outrage.

desagradable, a. disagreeable, unpleasant, unattractive.—**desagradar,** vt. to displease, offend, miff.

desagradecido, a. ungrateful.

desagrado, m. discontent, displeasure.

desagraviar, vt. to apologize; to make amends for.—**desagravio,** m. apology, satisfaction; reparation.

desaguar, vti. [b] to drain.—vii. to empty (rivers); to urinate.—**desagüe,** m. drainage; drain, outlet; waste.

desaguisado, m. outrage, wrong.

desahuciado, a. despaired of, hopeless; given over; evicted.—**desahuciar,** vt. to give over; to evict.—**desahucio,** m. eviction.

desahogado, a. free, unencumbered; comfortable; well-off; impudent, brazen-faced.—**desahogar,** vt. [b] to ease, relieve.—vri. to unbosom oneself; to give a piece of one's mind; to relieve oneself.—**desahogo,** m. ease, relief; unburdening; relaxation; comfort.

desairar, vt. to disregard; to slight; to scorn; to rebuff.—**desaire,** m. slight, rebuff, disdain.

desajustar, vt. to disarrange, disor-

der.—vr. to get out of order o adjustment.—**desajuste,** m. disar rangement, lack of adjustment.

desalentador, a. dispiriting, discourag ing.—**desalentar,** vti. [1] to discou age; to dismay.—vri. to jade, be come exhausted.—**desaliento,** m dismay, depression of spirits, dis couragement; faintness.

desaliñado, a. slipshod.—**desaliñar,** vt & vr. to disarrange, disorder, ruffle to make slovenly.—**desaliño,** m slovenliness, negligence of dress disarray; neglect.

desalmado, a. soulless, merciless, in human; impious.

desalojamiento, desalojo, m. dislodg ing; displacement.—**desalojar,** vt. t dislodge, oust; to displace.

desalquilado, a. unrented, vacant.— vacant.—**desalquilarse,** vr. to be come vacant.

desamarrar, vt. to untie; (naut.) to un moor; to unbend (a rope).—vr. t untie oneself; to get loose.

desamparado, a. forsaken; defense less, vulnerable; underprivileged homeless.—**desamparar,** vt. to for sake, abandon.—**desamparo,** m abandonment; helplessness.

desamueblado, a. unfurnished.—**des amueblar,** vt. to strip of furniture.

desandar, vti. [4] to retrace one's steps

desangramiento, m. bleeding to ex cess.—**desangrar,** vt. to bleed; t drain.—vr. to bleed to death.

desanimación, f. lack of enthusiasm dullness.—**desanimado,** a. dull, flat discouraged.—**desanimar,** vt. to dis courage, dishearten.—vr. to get dis couraged; to jade.

desapacible, a. disagreeable unpleasant.

desaparecer, vii. [3] & vri. to disappea vanish; to get out of sight.—**desa parición,** f. disappearance, van ishing.

desapercibido, a. unaware; unpre pared, unguarded; unnoticed.

desaplicado, a. indolent, careless, ne glectful.

desaprensivo, a. unscrupulous.

desapretar, vti. [1] to slacken, loosen loose.

desaprobación, f. disapproval.—**desa probar,** vti. [12] to disapprove of; t condemn.

desarmado, a. unarmed.—**desarma** vt. to disarm; to dismount; to disas semble.—**desarme,** *m.* disarmament.

desarraigar, *vti.* [b] to eradicate, root out.

desarrapado, *a.* ragged.

desarreglado, *a.* slovenly, disorderly; disarranged; immoderate.—**desarreglar,** *vt.* to disarrange, disorder.—**desarreglo,** *m.* disarrangement, disorder.

desarrollar, *vt.* to develop, unfold; to expound.—*vr.* to develop; to evolve; to unfold.—**desarrollo,** *m.* development; unfolding; expounding.

desarzonar, *vt.* to unseat (from a saddle).

desaseado, *a.* untidy, slovenly.—**desaseo,** *m.* untidiness, slovenliness.

desasir, *vti.* [5] to loosen.—*vri.* (de) to get loose (from); to extricate oneself (from).

desasosiego, *m.* restlessness, uneasiness.

desastrado, *a.* shabby, ragged.—**desastre,** *m.* disaster.—**desastroso,** *a.* disastrous.

desatar, *vt.* to untie, unfasten, loosen.—*vr.* to loosen; to break loose, break out (as a storm).—*d. en,* to break out into, to pour out (insults, etc.).

desatascar, *vti.* [d] to pull or draw out of the mud.

desatención, *f.* inattention; discourtesy.—**desatender,** *vti.* [18] to pay no attention to; to disregard, slight, neglect.—**desatento,** *a.* inattentive, careless, discourteous.

desatinado, *a.* nonsensical; foolish.—**desatinar,** *vt.* to rattle, bewilder.—*vi.* to get rattled or bewildered; to talk nonsense.—**desatino,** *m.* foolish act or expression; nonsense.

desatracar, *vti.* [d] to sheer off; to bear away; to unmoor.

desautorizado, *a.* unauthorized.—**desautorizar,** *vti.* [a] to disauthorize.

desavenencia, *f.* discord, disagreement.—**desavenido,** *a.* discordant, disagreeing.

desayunarse, *vr.* to have breakfast.—**desayuno,** *m.* breakfast.

desazón, *f.* displeasure; uneasiness; insipidity.—**desazonar,** *vt.* to displease, annoy.—*vr.* to become indisposed; to become uneasy.

desbancar, *vti.* [d] to break the bank; to supplant, oust.

desbandada, *f.* disbanding.—*a la d.,* in disorder.—**desbandarse,** *vr.* to disband, disperse, scatter.

desbarajuste, *m.* disorder, confusion.

desbaratar, *vt.* to break to pieces, smash.—*vr.* to fall to pieces.

desbarrar, *vi.* to act foolishly; to talk nonsense.

desbastar, *vt.* to hew, pare, trim.

desbloquear, *vt.* to clear; to release, to free; (com.) to unfreeze.

desbocado, *a.* runaway (horse); foulmouthed, indecent.—**desbocar,** *vti.* [d] & *vri.* to run away.—*vr.* to use abusive language, unloosen one's tongue.

desbordamiento, *m.* overflowing, flooding.—**desbordar,** *vi.* & *vr.* to overflow; to lose one's self-control.

desbulla, *f.* oyster shell.—**desbullador,** *m.* oyster fork.

descabalgar, *vii.* [b] to dismount (from a horse).

descabezar, *vti.* [a] to behead; to cut the upper parts or points of.—*d. el sueño,* to take a nap, grab forty winks.

descabellado, *a.* illogical, absurd.

descafeinado, *a.* decaffeinated; watered-down, diluted.—*m.* decaffeinated coffee.

descalabradura, *f.* wound on the head.—**descalabrar,** *vt.* to wound on the head; to injure; to defeat.—*vr.* to injure one's skull.—**descalabro,** *m.* calamity; misfortune.

descalificar, *vti.* [d] to disqualify.

descalzar, *vti.* [a] to unshoe, to pull off the shoes.—*vr.* to take off one's shoes.—**descalzo,** *a.* barefoot, shoeless.

descaminado, *a.* misguided, illadvised, mistaken.

descamisado, *a.* shirtless, ragged.—*m.* (coll.) ragamuffin.

descampado, *a.* disengaged, open, clear.—*en d.,* in the open air.

descansar, *vi.* to rest, lean upon; to depend.—*vt.* to place or set down on a support or base.—**descanso,** *m.* rest; relief; landing of stairs; (mech.) support; (teat.) intermission; (rad./TV) station break.

descarado, *a.* impudent, barefaced.

descarga, *f.* unloading, unburdening; (mil.) volley, barrage; (elec.) discharge.—*d. eléctrica,* electric shock.—**descargar,** *vti.* [b] to unload, unburden; to ease, lighten; to empty; (mil.) to fire; to discharge or unload firearms; (elec.) to discharge; to acquit.—*vii.* to strike with violence (as a storm).—**descargo**, *m.* (com.) acquittance, receipt; (law) plea or answer to an impeachment.

descarnar, *vt.* to remove flesh from; to eat away.—*vr.* to lose flesh, become emaciated.

descaro, *m.* impudence, barefacedness; effrontery.

descarriar, *vt.* to lead astray, misguide, mislead; to separate (cattle).—*vr.* to be separated; to go astray.

descarrilamiento, *m.* derailment.—**descarrilar,** *vt.* to derail.—*vi. & vr.* to run off the track, be derailed.

descartar, *vt.* to discard; to lay aside.—*vr.* to discard (at cards).

descascar, descascarar, *vt.* to peel, shell.—*vr.* to peel off, shell off.

descendencia, *f.* descent, origin; descendants.—**descendente,** *a.* descending.—**descender,** *vii.* [18] to descend; to get, come or go down; to drop (of temperature); to derive, come from.—**descendiente,** *a.* descending.—*mf.* descendant, offspring.—**descendimiento,** *m.* descent, lowering.—**descenso,** *m.* descent; lowering; fall.

descifrar, *vt.* to decipher, make out.

descocado, *a.* bold, forward.—**descoco,** *m.* impudence, sauciness.

descolgar, *vti.* [12-b] to unhang; to take down; to lower.—*vri.* to climb down (a rope, etc.); to turn up unexpectedly.

descollar, *vii.* [12] & *vti.* to tower, excel, surpass.

descolorar, *vt. & vr.* to discolor; to lose color, fade.—**descolorido,** *a.* pale, faded.

descomedido, *a.* excessive, disproportionate; rude, impolite.—**descomedimiento,** *m.* rudeness, incivility.

descompasado, *a.* excessive, disproportionate; out of tune or time.

descomponer, *vti.* [32] to disarrange, upset; to put out of order; (chem.) to decompose.—*vri.* to decompose, rot; to get out of order; to lose one's temper.—**descomposición,** *f.* disarrangement; disorder; decomposition, decay.—**descompuesto,** *pp.* of DESCOMPONER.—*a.* insolent; out of temper; immodest; out of order.

descomulgar, *vti.* [b] to excommunicate.

descomunal, *a.* extraordinary; monstrous, enormous.

desconcertante, *a.* disconcerting, baffling.—**desconcertar,** *vti.* [1] to disarrange, disturb, confuse; to disconcert, baffle, mystify; to disjoint.—*vri.* to become perplexed, confused.—**desconcierto,** *m.* discord, disagreement; disorder, confusion.

desconectar, *vt.* to disconnect.

desconfiado, *a.* distrustful; mistrustful.—**desconfianza,** *f.* diffidence; distrust.—**desconfiar,** *vi.* (de) to mistrust; to have no confidence (in); to suspect, doubt.

desconforme, *a.* = DISCONFORME.—**desconformidad,** *f.* = DISCONFORMIDAD.

descongelar, *vt.* to defrost.

descongestionante, *a. & m.* decongestant.

desconocer, *vti.* [3] to fail to recognize; to disregard, ignore; to not know; to disown.—**desconocido,** *a.* unknown.—*n.* unknown person, stranger.—**desconocimiento,** *m.* ignorance; disregard.

desconsideración, *f.* inconsiderateness.—**desconsiderado,** *a.* inconsiderate; thoughtless.

desconsolado, *a.* disconsolate, grief-stricken, downhearted.—**desconsolador,** *a.* discouraging; lamentable.—**desconsolar,** *vti.* [12] to afflict.—*vri.* to despair, be disconsolate.—**desconsuelo,** *m.* affliction, disconsolateness.

descontar, *vti.* [12] to discount, deduct; to take for granted.—*vri.* to miscount.

descontentadizo, *a.* hard to please.—**descontentar,** *vt.* to displease.—**descontento,** *a.* discontent, displeased.—*m.* discontent, displeasure.

descontinuar, *vt.* to discontinue, leave off.

descorazonar, *vt.* to dishearten, discourage.

descorchar, *vt.* to uncork; to break open.

descortés, *a.* impolite, discourteous.—**descortesía,** *f.* discourtesy.

descortezar, *vti.* [a] to strip bark; to take off the crust of.

descoser, *vt.* to rip, unstitch, unseam.—*vr.* to rip.

descoyuntar, *vt.* to dislocate or disjoint.—*vr.* to become disjointed.—*d. de risa,* to split one's sides with laughter.

descrédito, *m.* discredit.

descreer, *vti.* [e] to disbelieve; to deny due credit to.—**descreído,** *n.* & *a.* unbeliever; infidel; unbelieving.

describir, *vti.* [49] to describe, depict.—**descripción,** *f.* description; sketch.—**descriptivo,** *a.* descriptive.—**descrito,** *pp.* of DESCRIBIR.—*a.* described.

descuartizamiento, *m.* quartering; breaking or cutting in pieces; carving.—**descuartizar,** *vti.* [a] to quarter; to carve; to cut into pieces.

descubierto, *pp.* of DESCUBRIR.—*a.* discovered; uncovered; unveiled; bareheaded; manifest; exposed.—*m.* deficit; overdraft.—*al d.,* openly; in the open.—*en d.,* overdrawn.—**descubridor,** *n.* discoverer.—**descubrimiento,** *m.* discovery; invention; find.—**descubrir,** *vti.* [49] to discover; to disclose; to uncover; to reveal.—*vri.* to take off one's hat.

descuento, *m.* discount; deduction, allowance.

descuidado, *a.* careless, negligent, slapdash; slovenly; unthinking.—**descuidar,** *vt.* to neglect.—*¡descuide!* don't worry.—*vi.* to lack attention or diligence; to be careless.—*vr.* to be careless, negligent.—**descuido,** *m.* carelessness; oversight, slip; lack of attention.—*al d.,* unobserved, on the sly; carelessly.

desde, *prep.* since, from.—*d. ahora,* from now on.—*d. entonces,* since then, ever since.—*d. luego,* of course.—*d. que,* since, ever since.

desdecir, *vii.* [14] to be unworthy (of); to detract (from).—*vri.* to retract, recant.

desdén, *m.* disdain, slight, scorn.

desdentado, *a.* toothless.

desdeñable, *a.* contemptible, despicable.—**desdeñar,** *vt.* to disdain, scorn.—**desdeñoso,** *a.* disdainful, contemptuous.

desdicha, *f.* misfortune, ill luck.—**desdichado,** *a.* unfortunate; unlucky; wretched.—*n.* wretch; poor devil.

desdoblar, *vt.* to unfold, spread open.

desdoro, *m.* dishonor, blemish, stigma.

deseable, *a.* desirable.—**desear,** *vt.* to desire, wish.

desecar, *vti.* [d] to drain; to dry.

desechar, *vt.* to reject; to exclude; to put or lay aside; to throw away; to cast off.—**desecho,** *m.* waste; surplus, remainder; junk.—*de d.,* cast off, discarded; scrap (iron, etc.).—*desechos militares,* army surplus.—*desechos nucleares,* nuclear waste.—*d. radioactivos,* radioactive waste.

desembalar, *vt.* to unpack, open.

desembarazar, *vti.* [a] to free, ease.—*vri.* to rid oneself of difficulties.

desembarcar, *vti.* [d] to unload; to put ashore.—*vii.* to land, disembark, go ashore.

desembocadura, *f.* outlet; mouth (of a river, canal, etc.).—**desembocar,** *vii.* [d] (en) to flow (into); to end (at), lead (to).

desembolsar, *vt.* to pay out, disburse.—**desembolso,** *m.* disbursement, expenditure.

desembragar, *vti.* [b] to disengage the clutch.

desembrollar, *vt.* to unravel, clear, disentangle.

desembuchar, *vt.* to disgorge; to turn out of the maw; (coll.) to tell all.

desempacar, *vti.* [d] to unpack.

desempatar, *vt.* to decide a tie vote; to run, play, or shoot off a tie.

desempedrado, *a.* unpaved.

desempeñar, *vt.* to redeem (from pawn).—*d. un cargo,* to fill a post.—*d. un papel,* to play a part.—*vr.* to extricate oneself from debt.—**desempeño,** *m.* redemption (of a pledge); discharge (of an obligation).

desempleado, *n.* & *a.* unemployed, out of work.—**desempleo,** *m.* unemployment.

desempolvar, *vt.* to dust, remove dust or powder from.

desencadenar, *vt.* to unchain; to free, liberate.—*vr.* to break loose, free oneself from chains; to break out with fury (as a storm); to come down in torrents (the rain).

desencajado, *a.* disjointed; ill-looking, emaciated.

desenfado, *m.* freedom, ease, naturalness.

desenfrenado, *a.* ungoverned, unchecked, wanton; riotous.—**desenfreno,** *m.* rashness, wantonness, licentiousness.

desenganchar, *vt.* to unhook, unfasten; to unhitch, unharness.

desengañar, *vt.* to undeceive, set right;

to disillusion.—*vr.* to become disillusioned.—**desengaño**, *m.* disillusionment, disappointment.

desengrasar, *vt.* to remove the grease from.

desenlace, *m.* conclusion, end, ending.—**desenlazar**, *vti.* [a] to unlace, untie, loose; to unravel.

desenmarañar, *vt.* to disentangle; to unravel, make clear.

desenmascarar, *vt.* to unmask.

desenredar, *vt.* to untangle, unravel.—*vr.* to extricate oneself.

desenroscar, *vti.* [d] to untwist; to unscrew.

desensillar, *vt.* to unsaddle.

desentenderse, *vri.* [18] (**de**) to have nothing to do with; to ignore; to pay no attention (to).—*hacerse el desentendido*, to pretend not to see, notice or understand.

desenterrar, *vti.* [1] to dig up, unearth.

desentonación, *f.* dissonance.—**desentonado**, *a.* out of tune; discordant.—**desentonar**, *vi.* to be off key, out of tune; to clash (in colors); to be out of keeping with.

desentrañar, *vt.* to penetrate or dive into; to bring out, reveal, dig out.

desenvoltura, *f.* sprightliness, ease; impudence.—**desenvolver**, *vti.* [47] to unfold, unwrap, unroll; to unravel; to develop.—*vri.* to behave with self-assurance; to unfold, unroll.—**desenvolvimiento**, *m.* unfolding, development.—**desenvuelto**, *pp.* of DESENVOLVER.—*a.* forward; free, easy.

deseo, *m.* desire, wish.—**deseoso**, *a.* desirous, eager.

desequilibrado, *a.* unbalanced; deranged.—**desequilibrar**, *vt.* to put out of balance.—*vr.* to become deranged.—**desequilibrio**, *m.* lack of balance; derangement.

deserción, *f.* desertion.—**desertar**, *vt.* to desert; *vt.* to abandon.—*vi.* (**de**) to desert (from).—**desertor**, *n.* deserter.

desesperación, *f.* despair, desperation; anger.—**desesperado**, *a.* desperate, despairing; hopeless.—**desesperante**, *a.* causing despair; maddening.

desesperanza, *f.* despair.—**desesperanzado**, *a.* discouraged; hopeless, in despair.

desesperar, *vi.* to lose hope, despair.—*vt.* to make one despair; to discourage hope; (coll.) to drive crazy.—*vr.* to despair, despond; to fret.—**desespero**, *m.* despair; vexation.

desestimar, *vt.* to undervalue; to reject, deny.

desfachatado, *a.* impudent, saucy.—**desfachatez**, *f.* effrontery, impudence.

desfalcar, *vti.* [d] to embezzle.—**desfalco**, *m.* embezzlement.

desfallecer, *vii.* [3] to pine; to weaken; to faint.—**desfalleciente**, *a.* pining, languishing.—**desfallecimiento**, *m.* languor; dejection; swoon.

desfase, *m.* (phys.) phase lag.—*d. horario*, jet lag.

desfavorable, *a.* unfavorable; untoward.—**desfavorecido**, *a.* disadvantaged.

desfigurar, *vt.* to disfigure, deform; to deface; to disguise (as the voice); to distort.

desfiladero, *m.* defile, gorge; road at the side of a precipice.—**desfilar**, *vi.* to file past; to march in review, parade.—**desfile**, *m.* parade, procession.

desflorar, *vt.* to tarnish; to deflower; to violate.

desfogar, *vri.* [b] to vent one's anger.—*vti.* to vent.

desfondar, *vt.* to break or take off the bottom of.

desgaire, *m.* carelessness, indifference.—*al d.*, in an affectedly careless manner; disdainfully.

desgajar, *vt.* to tear, break off (branches).—*vr.* to be torn off; to fall off.

desgañifarse, **desgañitarse**, *vr.* to shriek, scream at the top of one's voice.

desgarbado, *a.* ungraceful, uncouth, gawky.

desgarrador, *a.* tearing; heartbreaking, heart-rending.—**desgarradura**, *f.* laceration, tear, break.—**desgarrar**, *vt.* to rend, tear; to claw; to expectorate.—*vr.* to tear.—**desgarrón**, *m.* large rent or tear (in clothing, etc.).

desgastar, *vt.* to wear away, consume, waste by degrees.—*vr.* to lose strength and vigor; to wear down or away.—**desgaste**, *m.* slow waste; abrasion; wear and tear; erosion.

desgobierno, *m.* mismanagement; misrule.

desgracia, *f.* misfortune, wretchedness; affliction; disgrace.—**desgraciado,** *a.* & *n.* unfortunate (person), wretched (person).—**desgraciar,** *vt.* to ruin; to maim; to spoil.—*vr.* to disgrace; to lose favor; to become a cripple.

desgranar, *vt.* to remove the grain from; to thrash, thresh (corn, etc.); to shell (peas, etc.).—*vr.* to shed the grains; to scatter about (as beads).

desgravable, *a.* tax-deductible.—**desgravación,** *f.* tax relief.—*d. fiscal,* tax exemption.

desgreñar, *vt.* to dishevel.

desguarnecer, *vti.* [3] to disarm (an opponent); to unharness; to strip of trimmings and ornaments.

deshabitado, *a.* uninhabited, untenanted, deserted.

deshacer, *vti.* [22] to undo; to destroy; to untie.—*vri.* to be consumed, destroyed; to wear oneself out; to grieve, mourn; to outdo oneself.—*deshacerse de,* to get rid of.

desharrapado, *a.* shabby, ragged, tattered.

deshecho, *pp.* of DESHACER.—*a.* ruined, destroyed, in pieces; undone; worn-out.

deshelar, *vti.* [1] &*vri.* to thaw; to melt; to unfreeze.

desherbar, *vti.* [1] to weed.

desheredar, *vt.* to disinherit.

deshermanar, *vt.* to unmatch, spoil a pair.

deshielo, *m.* thaw, thawing.

deshilachar, *vt.* to ravel.—*vr.* to fuzz; to ravel.

deshilar, *vt.* to ravel; to scrape (lint).—*vr.* to fuzz; to grow thin.

deshilvanado, *a.* disconnected, incoherent (of speech).

deshinchar, *vt.* to reduce the swelling of; to deflate.—*vr.* to become deflated; to go down (of anything swollen).

deshojar, *vt.* to strip off the leaves.—*vr.* to shed leaves.

deshollejar, *vt.* to husk, hull; to peel.

deshollinador, *m.* chimney sweep.

deshonestidad, *f.* dishonesty; indecency.—**deshonesto,** *a.* dishonest, dishonorable; lewd.

deshonor, *m.* dishonor, disgrace; insult, affront.—**deshonra,** *f.* dishonor; seduction or violation (of a woman).—**deshonrar,** *vt.* to affront, insult, defame; to dishonor, disgrace; to seduce or ruin (a woman).—**deshonroso,** *a.* dishonorable.

deshora, *f.* inconvenient time.—*a d.,* or *a deshoras,* untimely, extemporarily.

deshuesar, *vt.* to bone (an animal); to take the pits out of (fruits).

deshumedecedor, *m.* dehumidifier.

desidia, *f.* laziness, indolence.—**desidioso,** *a.* lazy, indolent.

desierto, *m.* desert.—*a.* uninhabited, deserted, lonely.

designación, *f.* designation.—**designar,** *vt.* to appoint, designate.—**designio,** *m.* design, purpose, intention.

desigual, *a.* unequal, unlike; uneven, rough; changeable; (road) bumpy.—**desigualdad,** *f.* inequality, difference; roughness, unevenness.

desilusión, *f.* disappointment, disillusionment.—**desilusionar,** *vt.* to disillusion.—*vr.* to become disillusioned.

desinfección, *f.* disinfection; disinfecting.—**desinfectante,** *m.* & *a.* disinfectant; disinfecting.—**desinfectar,** *vt.* to disinfect; to sterilize.

desenrollar, *vt.* to unroll, uncoil.

desinflamar, *vt.* & *vr.* to remove the inflammation of.

desinflar, *vt.* & *vr.* to deflate.

desintegración, *f.* disintegration.—**desintegrar,** *vt., vi.* & *vr.* to disintegrate.

desinteresado, *a.* disinterested, impartial; unselfish, generous; uninterested.

desistir, *vi.* (de) to desist (from).

desleal, *a.* disloyal; perfidious.—**deslealtad,** *f.* disloyalty, treachery, unfaithfulness.

desleir, *vti.* [35-e] to dilute; to dissolve.—*vri.* to become diluted.

deslenguado, *a.* impudent; foulmouthed.

desligar, *vti.* [b] to loosen, untie.—*vri.* to get loose; to give way.

deslindar, *vt.* to mark the boundaries of; to clear up, define.—**deslinde,** *m.* demarcation, determination of boundaries.

desliz, *m.* slip, slide; false step.—**deslizamiento,** *m.* slip, slipping; glide; skidding, sliding.—**deslizante,** *a.* gliding, sliding.—**deslizar,** *vii.* [a] &

vri. to slip; to slide; to skid; to glide; to act or speak carelessly.—*vri.* to shirk, evade.

deslucido, *a.* dull, shabby, shopworn; unsuccessful.—**deslucir,** *vti.* [3] to tarnish, dull; to discredit.—*vri.* to fail, be a failure.

deslumbrador, *a.* dazzling, glaring.—**deslumbramiento,** *m.* glare, dazzling; confusion of sight or mind.—**deslumbrante,** *a.* dazzling.—**deslumbrar,** *vt.* to dazzle.

deslustrar, *vt.* to tarnish; to obscure, dim; to remove the glaze from; to stain (reputation, etc.).

desmadejamiento, *m.* languishment, weakness.—**desmadejar,** *vt.* to enervate.—*vr.* to languish.

desmán, *m.* misbehavior; excess.

desmandar, *vr.* to be impudent; to lose moderation or self-control.

desmantelamiento, *m.* dismantling; dilapidation.—**desmantelar,** *vt.* to dismantle; to abandon.

desmañado, *a.* clumsy, awkward.

desmayar, *vi.* to falter, lose heart.—*vr.* to faint.—**desmayo,** *m.* swoon, faint; discouragement.

desmejorar, *vt.* to debase; to make worse.—*vi.* & *vr.* to decline, become worse; to deteriorate.

desmelenado, *a.* disheveled.

desmemoriado, *a.* forgetful.

desmentir, *vti.* [39] to give the lie to; to contradict.—*vri.* to recant, retract.

desmenuzar, *vti.* [a] to crumble; to shred; to tear into bits; to examine minutely.—*vri.* to crumble, fall into small pieces.

desmerecer, *vti.* [3] to become unworthy of.—*vii.* to deteriorate; to compare unfavorably.—**desmerecimiento,** *m.* demerit, unworthiness.

desmesurado, *a.* disproportionate, excessive.

desmigajar, *vt.* & *vr.* to crumb; to crumble.

desmochar, *vt.* to lop or cut off the top of (a tree, etc.).—**desmoche,** *m.* cutting off.

desmontar, *vt.* to clear (a wood); to uncock (firearms); to take apart (machines).—*vi.* to dismount; to alight (from a horse, mule, etc.).

desmoralización, *f.* demoralization.—**desmoralizar,** *vti.* [a] to demoralize, corrupt.—*vri.* to become demoralized.

desmoronamiento, *m.* crumbling.—

desmoronar, *vt.* to demolish gradually; to destroy.—*vr.* to fall, crumble.

desmovilizar, *vti.* [a] to demobilize.

desnivel, *m.* unevenness, drop.—**desnivelado,** *a.* unlevel.—**desnivelar,** *vt.* to make uneven.—*vr.* to lose its level.

desnucar, *vti.* [d] to break the neck of.—*vri.* to break one's neck.

desnudar, *vt.* & *vr.* to strip, undress, unclothe.—**desnudez,** *f.* nudity, nakedness.—**desnudismo,** *m.* nudism.—**desnudista,** *mf.* nudist.—**desnudo,** *a.* nude, naked; bare, evident.

desnutrición, *f.* malnutrition.—**desnutrido,** *a.* undernourished.

desobedecer, *vti.* [3] & *vii.* to disobey.—**desobediencia,** *f.* disobedience.—**desobediente,** *a.* disobedient.

desocupación, *f.* leisure; unemployment.—**desocupado,** *a.* idle, without occupation; vacant, unoccupied.—*n.* unemployed person; idler.—**desocupar,** *vt.* to vacate; to evacuate; to empty.—*vr.* to retire (from a business or occupation).

desodorante, *m.* & *a.* deodorant.

desoír, *vti.* [28-e] to pretend not to hear; not to heed.

desolación, *f.* desolation; destruction; affliction.—**desolado,** *a.* desolate; disconsolate.—**desolar,** *vti.* [12] to lay waste.—*vri.* to grieve.

desollar, *vti.* [12] to flay, skin.

desorden, *m.* disorder, confusion; lawlessness; disturbance, riot.—**desordenar,** *vt.* to disorder, disturb, disarrange.

desorientación, *f.* disorientation, loss of bearings; perplexity.—**desorientar,** *vt.* to mislead, confuse.—*vr.* to lose one's bearings.

desosar, *vti.* [15] = DESHUESAR.

desovar, *vii.* [15] to spawn.

despabilado, *a.* vigilant; wakeful; lively, smart.—**despabilar,** *vt.* to trim or snuff (a candle); to rouse; to enliven.—*vr.* to wake up.

despachar, *vt.* to dispatch; to expedite; to attend to; to wait on (as in a shop); to dismiss, discharge.—*vr.* to make haste.—**despacho,** *m.* dispatch; study; office; salesroom; telegram; communiqué; shipment.—*d. de billetes,* ticket office.—*d. oval del presidente (E.U.),* the Oval Office.

despachurrar, *vt.* to squash, smash, crush.

despacio, *adv.* slowly; deliberately.—**despacioso**, *a.* slow.—**despacito**, *adv.* very slowly, gently, softly.

desparpajo, *m.* self-confidence, pertness, cockiness.

desparramar, *vt.* & *vr.* to scatter, disseminate, spread.

despatarrarse, *vr.* (coll.) to sprawl, go sprawling.

despavorido, *a.* terrified.

despechar, *vt.* to spite.—*vr.* to be spited.—**despecho**, *m.* spite.—*a despecho de*, in spite (of), despite.

despectivo, *a.* contemptuous.

despedazar, *vti.* [a] to tear to pieces, cut up.—*vri.* to break or fall to pieces.

despedida, *f.* leave-taking, farewell; send-off; dismissal.—**despedir**, *vti.* [29] to dismiss; to emit; to see a person off (at a station, airport, etc.).—*vri.* to take leave (of), say goodbye (to); to leave (a post).

despegado, *a.* unglued; unaffectionate, unfeeling.—**despegar**, *vti.* [b] to unglue, disjoin.—*vii.* to rise, take off (of a plane).—*vri.* to come off; to become indifferent.—**despego**, *m.* coolness, indifference; aversion.—**despegue**, *m.* take-off (of a plane).—*d. vertical,* lift-off.

despeinado, *a.* uncombed.—**despeinar**, *vt.* & *vr.* to disarrange the hair.

despejado, *a.* smart; clear, cloudless; unobstructed.—**despejar**, *vt.* to remove impediments from, clear; (math.) to find the value of.—*vr.* to become bright and smart; to clear up.

despellejar, *vt.* to flay, skin; to speak ill of.

despensa, *f.* pantry; storeroom (for food); food, provisions.—**despensero**, *n.* butler; (naut.) steward.

despeñadero, *m.* precipice, crag.—**despeñar**, *vt.* to precipitate, to hurl down.—*vr.* to throw oneself headlong.

desperdiciar, *vt.* to squander, waste, misspend.—**desperdicio**, *m.* waste, spoilage; profusion.—*pl.* garbage.

desperdigar, *vti.* [b] to separate, disjoin; to scatter.

desperezarse, *vri.* [a] to stretch one's limbs.

desperfecto, *m.* deterioration; slight injury or damage, imperfection.

despertador, *m.* alarm clock.—**despertar**, *vti.* [1–49] to wake up; to arouse, to stir up.—*vii.* & *vri.* to wake up.

despiadado, *a.* unmerciful, pitiless.

despido, *m.* dismissal, firing; lay-off; severance pay.

despierto, *a.* awake; watchful; diligent; smart.

despilfarrar, *vt.* to waste, squander.—**despilfarro**, *m.* extravagance, squandering; waste.

despintar, *vt.* to take the paint off.—*vr.* to lose color, fade.

despistar, *vt.* to throw off the scent.

desplazado, *a.* displaced.—*n.* displaced person.—**desplazamiento**, *m.* displacement.—**desplazar**, *vti.* [a] to displace.

desplegar, *vti.* [1–b] to unfold, unfurl; to display.—*vri.* to deploy (as troops).—**despliegue**, *m.* unfurling, unfolding; deployment.

desplomar, *vr.* to tumble down, collapse.—**desplome**, *m.* tumbling down, downfall, collapse.

desplumar, *vt.* & *vr.* to pluck (a bird); to fleece, skin; to strip of property.

despoblación, *f.* depopulation.—**despoblado**, *m.* uninhabited place, wilderness.—*a.* uninhabited, desolate.—**despoblar**, *vti.* [12] to depopulate; to despoil or desolate.—*vri.* to become depopulated.

despojar, *vt.* to despoil, strip of property; to deprive of; to cut off from.—*vr.* (de) to take off (as a coat).—**despojo**, *m.* spoliation; spoils.—*pl.* leavings, scraps from the table; giblets of fowl; remains.

desposado, *n.* betrothed; bride; bridegroom.—**desposar**, *vt.* to marry (to perform the marriage ceremony for).—*vr.* to be betrothed, or married.

desposeer, *vti.* [e] to dispossess, oust.

déspota, *m.* despot.—**despótico**, *a.* despotic.—**despotismo**, *m.* despotism, tyranny.

despreciable, *a.* contemptible, despicable, insignificant.—**despreciar**, *vt.* to despise, scorn.—**desprecio**, *m.* scorn, contempt.

desprender, *vt.* to unfasten; to separate.—*vr.* to give way; to issue (from), come out (of); to follow, be a consequence (of).—**desprendimiento**, *m.* detachment, landslide; disinterestedness.

despreocupación, *f.* freedom from bias; unconventionality.—**despreocupado,** *a.* unprejudiced; unconventional; carefree, unconcerned. —**despreocuparse,** *vr.* to become unbiased, lose prejudice; (de) to ignore; to pay no attention (to).

desprestigiar, *vt.* to discredit.—*vr.* to lose reputation or prestige.—**desprestigio,** *m.* loss of reputation or prestige.

desprevenido, *a.* unprovided; unprepared.

despropósito, *m.* absurdity, nonsense.

desprovisto, *a.* (de) unprovided (with),lacking (in); stranded.

después, *adv.* after, afterward; next, then, later.—*d. de,* after; next to.— *d. de Cristo,* A.D.—*d. de que,* or *d. que,* after.

despuntar, *vt.* to blunt; to crop.—*vi.* to sprout or bud; to be outstanding; to excel.

desquiciar, *vt.* to unhinge; to unsettle.—*vr.* to become unhinged; to fall down.

desquitarse, *vr.* (de) to win one's money back, recoup; to get even. —**desquite,** *m.* compensation; recovery of a loss; revenge; return game or bout.

destacamento, *m.* (mil.) detachment.—**destacar,** *vti.* [d] to bring out, make conspicuous; (mil.) to detach.—*vri.* to stand out, be conspicuous; to be outstanding.

destajo, *m.* piece work, task.—*a d.,* by the job, piece work.

destapar, *vt.* to uncover, uncork, take off (cover, lid, cap).—*vr.* to become uncovered.

destartalado, *a.* handled, jumbled; ramshackle, scantily and poorly furnished; tumbledown.

destellar, *vi.* to flash, twinkle, gleam.—**destello,** *m.* flash, sparkle, gleam.

destemplado, *a.* inharmonious; out of tune; out of tone; intemperate; without its temper (of metal). —**destemplanza,** *f.* indisposition.

desteñir, *vti.* [9] & *vri.* to discolor, fade.

desternillante, *a.* sidesplitting.—**desternillarse (de risa),** *vr.* to split one's sides with laughter.

desterrar, *vti.* [1] to banish, exile. —**desterrado,** *n.* exile, outcast.

destetar, *vt.* to wean.—**destete,** *m.* weaning.

destiempo, *adv.*—*a d.,* unseasonably, untimely, inopportunely.

destierro, *m.* exile.

destilar, *vt.* to distill; to filter.—*vi.* to distill, to drip, drop; to ooze.—**destilería,** *f.* distillery.

destinar, *vt.* to destine; to appoint; to assign.—**destinatario,** *n.* addressee; consignee.—**destino,** *m.* destiny; destination; employment.—*con d. a,* bound for, going to.

destitución, *f.* dismissal from employment, office or charge.—**destituir,** *vti.* [23-e] to dismiss from office.

destornillador, *m.* screwdriver.—**destornillar,** *vt.* to unscrew.

destrabar, *vt.* to loosen, to unfetter.

destreza, *f.* skill, dexterity, ability; nimbleness.

destripar, *vt.* to disembowel, gut; to smash, crush.

destrozar, *vti.* [a] to break into pieces, smash up.—**destrozo,** *m.* destruction; havoc.

destrucción, *f.* destruction.—**destructivo,** *a.* destructive.—**destructor,** *m.* destroyer.—*a.* destroying.— **destruir,** *vti.* [23-e] to destroy; to ruin; to demolish, raze.

desusado, *a.* unusual; obsolete, out of date.—**desuso,** *m.* disuse.—*caído en desuso,* obsolete.

desvalido, *a.* helpless, unprotected, unsheltered.

desvalijar, *vt.* to rob.

desván, *m.* attic; loft; garret.

desvanecer, *vti.* [3] to dispel; to fade; to cause to vanish.—*vri.* to vanish, disappear; to faint.

desvariar, *vi.* to rave, be delirious; to rant.—**desvarío,** *m.* delirium, raving; madness; absurdity.

desvelar, *vt.* to keep awake.—*vr.* to go without sleep; to pass a sleepless night; to be watchful or vigilant. —**desvelo,** *m.* insomnia, lack of sleep; watchfulness; anxiety, uneasiness.

desvencijado, *a.* ramshackle, rickety, loose-jointed.

desventaja, *f.* disadvantage.—**desventajoso,** *a.* disadvantageous.

desventura, *f.* misfortune, mishap.— **desventurado,** *a.* unfortunate, unlucky, faint-hearted.

desvergonzado, *a.* impudent; shameless.—**desvergüenza,** f. impudence; shamelessness.

desvestir, vti. [29] & vri. to undress.

desviación, f. deviation.—**desviadero,** m. (RR.) siding.—**desviado,** a. deviant.—**desviar,** vt. to deflect; to sway; to dissuade; (fencing) to ward off; (RR.) to switch.—vr. to turn aside; to deviate; to swerve; to drift (away from).—**desvío,** m. deviation, turning away; coldness, indifference; (RR.) siding, side track.

desvirtuar, vt. to impair; to lessen the merit of; to detract from the value of.

desvivirse, vr. (por) to have excessive fondness (for); to do one's utmost (in behalf of); to be dying (for, to).

detallar, vt. to detail, relate minutely; to specify; to retail.—**detalle,** m. detail, particular; (com.) retail.—**detallista,** mf. (com.) retailer; one addicted to details (painter, etc.).

detective, mf. detective.—**detector,** m. (elec., radio) detector.—d. de incendios, smoke detector.—d. de mentiras, lie detector.—d. de metales, metal detector.—d. de minas, mine detector.

detención, f. delay, stop, halt, holdup; arrest, detention.—d. domiciliaria, house arrest.—d. preventiva, police custody, preventive detention.—**detener,** vti. [42] to stop, detain; to arrest; to retain, reserve.—vri. to tarry, stay; to stop, halt; to pause.—**detenimiento,** m. care, thoroughness.

detergente, a. & m. detergent.

deteriorar, vt. & vr. to deteriorate, spoil, wear out.—**deterioro,** m. deterioration, damage, wear and tear.

determinación, f. determination; resolution; firmness.—**determinado,** a. determined, decided; resolute, purposeful; settled, definite.—**determinar,** vt. to determine, fix; to limit; to specify; to distinguish, discern; to assign (as time and place); to resolve, decide.—vr. to determine, resolve; to make up one's mind.

detestable, a. detestable, hateful.—**detestar,** vt. to detest.

detonación, f. detonation.—**detonante,** a. detonating.—**detonar,** vi. to detonate, explode.

detracción, f. detraction, defamation.—**detractor,** n. & a. detractor, slanderer.—a. detracting.

detrás, adv. behind; back, in the rear.—d. de, behind, in back of.—por d., from the rear, from behind; behind one's back.

detrimento, m. detriment, damage.

deuda, f. debt; indebtedness.—deudas incobrables, bad debts.—**deudo,** m. relative, kinsman.—**deudor,** n. & a. debtor; indebted.

devanar, vt. to reel, wind.—devanarse los sesos, to rack one's brain.

devaneo, m. delirium, giddiness; frenzy; dissipation; love affair.

devastación, f. devastation, destruction.—**devastador,** n. & a. devastator; devastating.—**devastar,** vt. to devastate, ruin, lay waste.

devengar, vti. [b] to earn, draw (as salary, interest, etc.)

devenir, vii. [45] to become; to happen; to befall.

devoción, f. devotion, piety; faithful attachment.—**devocionario,** m. prayer book.

devolución, f. return, restitution; devolution.—**devolver,** vti. [47–49] to return, give back; to restore; to pay back.

devorador, n. devourer.—a. devouring, ravenous.—**devorar,** vt. to devour, swallow up, gobble, wolf.

devoto, a. devout, pious; devoted.

devuelto, pp. of DEVOLVER.

día, m. day.—al d., up to date; by the day.—a los pocos días, a few days later.—al otro d., on the following day.—d. de bodas, wedding day.—d. de entresemana, weekday.—d. de trabajo, workday.—de d., by day.—d. festivo, public holiday.—d. hábil or laborable, workday.—d. lectivo, school day.—d. libre, day off.—d. sandwich, day taken as vacation between two public holidays.—el d. de Año Nuevo, New Year's Day.—el d. de Difuntos, el d. de los Muertos, All Souls' Day.—el d. de la Hispanidad, el d. de la raza, Columbus Day.—el d. de la Madre, Mother's Day.—el d. del Padre, Father's Day.—el d. de San Valentín, el d. de los enamorados, Valentine's Day.—el d. de Todos los Santos, All Saints' Day.—el d. menos pensado, when least expected.—el mejor d., some fine day.—en su d., at the proper time.—hoy (en) d., nowadays.—poner al d., to update.—por d., per diem.—un d. sí y otro no, every other day.

diabetes, f. diabetes.—**diabético,** a. diabetic.

diablo, m. devil.—**diablura,** f. deviltry, mischief, wild prank.—**diabólico,** a. diabolical, devilish.

diácono, m. deacon.

diafragma, m. diaphragm.

diagnosticar, vti. [d] to diagnose.—**diagnóstico,** m. diagnosis.—a. diagnostic.

diagonal, a. diagonal; oblique.—f. (geom.) diagonal.

diagrama, m. diagram.

dialecto, m. dialect.

diálisis, f. dialysis.—**dializador,** m. dialysis machine.

dialogar, vii. [b] to dialogize; to chat, converse.—**diálogo,** m. dialogue.

diamante, m. diamond.

diámetro, m. diameter.

diana, f. target, bull's eye; dartboard; reveille.

diapasón, m. tuning fork; pitch pipe.

diapositiva, f. lantern slide; (phot.) plate.

diario, a. daily.—m. journal, diary; daily newspaper; daily expense.—d. de a bordo or de navegación, (naut.) log, logbook.—d. de vuelo, (aer.) log.—a d., daily, every day.

diarrea, f. diarrhea.

dibujante, mf. designer, draftsman.—d. publicitario, commercial artist.—**dibujar,** vt. to draw, sketch; to depict.—**dibujo,** m. drawing; sketch; delineation.

dicción, f. diction.—**diccionario,** m. dictionary.—d. bilingüe, bilingual dictionary.—d. de ideas afines, d. de sinónimos, d. ideológico, thesaurus.

dicha, f. happiness; good luck.

dicharachero, a. witty; wisecracking.—**dicharacho,** m. smart remark; wisecrack.—**dicho,** pp. of DECIR.—a. (the) said, mentioned; this.—m. saying, proverb.

dichoso, a. lucky, fortunate; happy.

diciembre, m. December.

dicotomía, f. dichotomy; (med.) split fee.

dictado, m. dictation.—pl. dictates, promptings.—**dictador,** n. dictator.—**dictadura,** f. dictatorship.—**dictamen,** m. judgment, opinion.—**dictaminar,** vi. to express an opinion, pass judgment.—**dictar,** vt. to dictate.

dicterio, m. taunt; insult.

diecinueve, a. & m. nineteen.—**dieciocho,** a. & m. eighteen.—**dieciséis,** a. & m. sixteen.—**diecisiete,** a. & m. seventeen.

diente, m. tooth; tusk.—decir or hablar entre dientes, to mumble, to mutter.—de dientes afuera, without sincerity, as mere lip service.

diestra, f. right hand.—**diestro,** m. bullfighter.—a. skillful, able; right.

dieta, f. diet; traveling allowance.

diez, a. & m. ten.—m. (eccl.) decade (of a rosary).

diezmar, vt. to decimate.—**diezmo,** m. tithe; tenth part.

diez y nueve, a. & m. nineteen.—**diez y ocho,** a. & m. eighteen.—**diez y seis,** a. & m. sixteen.—**diez y siete,** a. & m. seventeen.

diferencia, f. difference; disagreement.—**diferenciación,** f. differentiation.—**diferenciar,** vt. to differentiate, distinguish between.—vi. to differ, disagree.—vr. to be different.—**diferente,** a. different.

diferido, —en d., prerecorded.

diferir, vti. [39] to defer, postpone; to procrastinate.—vii. to differ.

difícil, a. difficult, hard.—**dificultad,** f. difficulty.—**dificultar,** vt. to make difficult; to impede.—**dificultoso,** a. difficult, hard.

difteria, f. diphtheria.

difundir, vt. & vr. to diffuse, spread out; to spread (as news); to divulge, publish; to broadcast.

difunto, a. defunct, dead.—n. corpse.

difusión, f. diffusion; diffusiveness; dispersion; broadcasting.—**difuso,** a. diffuse; wordy; widespread.

digerir, vti. [39] to digest.—**digestión,** f. digestion.

digital, a. digital; finger.—f. digitalis.—**digitar,** (fam.) to rig, orchestrate.—**dígito,** m. digit.—**digitopuntura,** f. acupressure.

dignarse, vr. to condescend.—**dignatario,** n. dignitary.—**dignidad,** f. dignity; high rank; stateliness.—**digno,** a. meritorious, worthy; fitting, appropriate.

digresión, f. digression.

dije, m. trinket; locket; charm.

dilación, f. delay.

dilapidación, f. dilapidation; squandering.—**dilapidar,** vt. to dilapidate; to squander.

dilatación, f. dilatation, expansion; enlargement.—**dilatado,** a. vast, extensive; drawn out.—**dilatar,** vt. &

vr. to dilate; to prolong; to retard, delay.

dilema, *m.* dilemma.

diligencia, *f.* diligence; activity; stage-coach; errand; judicial proceeding.—*hacer d.,* or *la d.,* to try.—**diligente,** *a.* diligent; prompt, swift.

diluir, *vti.* & *vri.* [23-e] to dilute.

diluvio, *m.* flood; deluge.

dimanar, *vi.* (**de**) to spring or flow (from); to originate (in).

dimensión, *f.* dimension; extent, size.

diminución, *f.* diminution.—**diminutivo,** *a.* diminishing; diminutive.—*m.* (gram.) diminutive.—**diminuto,** *a.* tiny.

dimisión, *f.* resignation (from post). —**dimitir,** *vt.* to resign, give up (post).

dinamarqués, *n.* & *a.* Dane, Danish.

dinámico, *a.* dynamic, energetic.

dinamita, *f.* dynamite.

dínamo, dínamo, *f.* (gen. *m.* in Am.) dynamo.

dinastía, *f.* dynasty.

dineral, *m.* a lot of money.—**dinero,** *m.* money; currency; wealth.—*d. contante y sonante, d. a la mano,* ready money, cash.—*d. de bolsillo,* pocket money.—*d. en efectivo* or *en efectivo, cash.—d. negro* or *sucio,* undeclared income.—*d. suelto,* small change.

dinosaurio, *m.* dinosaur.

dintel, *m.* lintel, doorhead.

diócesis, *f.* diocese.

dios, *m.* god; (**D.**) God.—*D. mediante,* God willing.—*¡D. mío!* my God! —**diosa,** *f.* goddess.

diploma, *m.* diploma; bull, patent, license; title.—**diplomacia,** *f.* diplomacy.—**diplomado,** *a.* qualified.— *n.—d. universitario de enfermería,* registered nurse.—**diplomático,** *a.* diplomatic.—*n.* diplomat.

diptongo, *m.* diphthong.

diputado, *n.* deputy, representative, delegate; assignee.

dique, *m.* dike; dry dock; check, restraint.—*d. marítimo,* sea wall.

dirección, *f.* direction, course; management; postal address; office of a director.—*d. asistida,* (aut.) power steering.—*d. particular,* home address.—*d. profesional,* business address.—**directivo,** *a.* directive, managing.—*f.* governing board, board of directors, management.—*n.* member of a board of directors; officer of a society, club, etc.—**direc-**

cional, *a.* directional.—*f.* (aut.) turn signal, directional signal.—**directo,** *a.* direct; straight.—*en d.,* (rad./TV) live.—**director,** *n.* & *a.* director; directing.—*n.* director, manager; chief; editor (of a newspaper); principal (of a school); conductor (of an orchestra).—*d. de coro,* choir director.—*d. de escena,* (theat.) stage manager.—*d. de funeraria, d. de pompas fúnebres,* funeral director.—**directorio,** *a.* directive, directorial.— *m.* directory; directorate.—**dirigente,** *a.* directing, leading; ruling.—*mf.* leader.—**dirigir,** *vti.* [c] to direct; to address (a letter, etc.); to command; to govern, manage.— *vri.* (**a**) to address, speak (to); to apply, resort (to); to go (to or toward).

dirimir, *vt.* to solve (a difficulty); to settle (a controversy).

discar, *vti.* [d] (tel.) to dial.

discernimiento, *m.* discernment, judgment.—**discernir,** *vii.* [16] to discern, discriminate.

disciplina, *f.* discipline, training; obedience; rule of conduct; any art or science.—*pl.* whip, scourge.—**disciplinar,** *vt.* to discipline, educate; to drill.

discípulo, *n.* disciple, follower; pupil.

disco, *m.* record; (comput.) disk; (sports) discus; road sign.—*d. compacto* or *digital,* compact disk (CD).—*d. de arranque,* (comput.) boot disk.—*d. duro,* hard disk.—*d. fijo,* fixed disk.—*d. flexible* or *floppy,* floppy disk.—*d. óptico,* video disk.—*d. rígido,* hard disk.—*d. volador,* flying saucer.—*f.* disco, discothèque.—**disc-jockey,** *m.* disk jockey.—**discoteca,** *f.* disco, discothèque; record collection; record store; record library.

díscolo, *a.* ungovernable; undisciplined.

disconforme, *a.* discordant, disagreeing.—**disconformidad,** *f.* non-conformity; disparity; disagreement.

discontinuo, *a.* discontinuous.

discordancia, *f.* disagreement, discord; maladjustment.—**discordante,** *a.* discordant, dissonant. —**discordar,** *vii.* [12] to be in discord, disagree.—**discorde,** *a.* discordant; dissonant.—**discordia,** *f.* discord, disagreement.

discreción, *f.* discretion; prudence;

liberty of action and decision.—*a d.*, at will, unconditionally.

discrepancia, *f.* discrepancy.—**discrepante,** *a.* disagreeing, differing.—**discrepar,** *vi.* to differ, disagree.

discreto, *a.* discreet, prudent, unobtrusive; fairly good.

discriminación, *f.* discrimination.—*d. positiva,* (para eliminar la discriminación racial y sexual) affirmative action.—**discriminar,** *vt.* to discriminate against; to differentiate, distinguish.—*vi.* to discriminate.

disculpa, *f.* apology, excuse.—**disculpable,** *a.* excusable; pardonable.—**disculpar,** *vt.* & *vr.* to exculpate (oneself); to excuse (oneself); to apologize.

discurrir, *vi.* to roam, ramble about; to flow (as a river); to reflect, think; to discourse.—*vt.* to invent; to infer.

discurso, *m.* speech; dissertation; space of time; discourse.

discusión, *f.* discussion.—**discutible,** *a.* controvertible, disputable.—**discutidor,** *n.* & *a.* arguer; arguing.—**discutir,** *vt.* & *vi.* to discuss; to argue.

disecación, *f.* = DISECCION.—**disecar,** *vti.* [d] to dissect; to stuff (dead animals).—**disección,** *f.* dissection; anatomy.

diseminación, *f.* scattering, spreading.—**diseminar,** *vt.* to spread, scatter.

disensión, *f.* dissent; contest, strife.

disentería, *f.* dysentery.

disentir, *vii.* [39] to dissent, disagree, differ.

diseñador, *n.* designer, delineator.—**diseñar,** *vt.* to draw; to sketch, outline.—**diseño,** *m.* design, sketch, outline; description.

disertación, *f.* dissertation.—**disertar,** *vi.* (**sobre or acerca de**) to discourse (on), treat (of), discuss.

disforme, *a.* deformed; hideous; out of proportion.

disfraz, *m.* disguise, mask; costume; dissimulation.—**disfrazar,** *vti.* [a] to disguise; to misrepresent.—*vri.* to disguise oneself; to masquerade.

disfrutar, *vt.* to benefit by; to have the benefit of; to enjoy (good health, etc.).—*vi.* (**de**) to enjoy; to have.—**disfrute,** *m.* use, benefit.

disgregación, *f.* separation; dissociation.—**disgregar,** *vti.* [b] to separate, disperse.

disgustar, *vt.* to displease; to annoy; to offend.—*vr.* to be, or become displeased, hurt or annoyed; to fall out (with each other).—**disgusto,** *m.* disgust; affliction; displeasure; unpleasantness; quarrel; annoyance; grief.

disimular, *vt.* to dissimulate; to tolerate, overlook; to misrepresent.—**disimulo,** *m.* dissimulation; tolerance.

disipación, *f.* dissipation; waste.—**disipar,** *vt.* & *vr.* to dissipate; to vanish.—*vt.* to squander.

disjockey, *mf.* disc jockey, DJ.

diskette, *m.* (comput.) diskette, floppy disk.

dislocación, *f.* dislocation; sprain.—**dislocar,** *vti.* [d] & *vri.* to dislocate, disjoint; to sprain.

disminución, *f.* diminution; retrenchment.—**disminuir,** *vti.* [23-e] to diminish, lessen; to detract from.—*vii.* to diminish, decrease.

disociación, *f.* separation, dissociation.—**disociar,** *vt.* to dissociate, separate.

disolución, *f.* dissolution; solution.—**disoluto,** *a.* dissolute.—**disolvente,** *m.* solvent.—**disolver,** *vti.* [47] to dissolve; to break up (as a meeting); to separate.—*vri.* to dissolve; to break up.

disonancia, *f.* harsh sound; discord; dissonance.—**disonante,** *a.* dissonant; discordant.

dispar, *a.* unlike; unequal; unmatched.

disparador, *m.* shooter; trigger; ratchet wheel.—**disparar,** *vt.* & *vi.* to shoot, discharge, fire; to throw, hurl.—*vr.* to dart off; to run away (as a horse); to go off (as a gun).

disparatar, *vi.* to talk nonsense; to blunder.—**disparate,** *m.* blunder; absurdity, nonsense.—**disparatero,** *n.* bungler.

disparejo, *a.* uneven.

disparidad, *f.* disparity, inequality.

disparo, *m.* shooting, discharge; shot; sudden dash.

dispendio, *m.* extravagance, prodigality.—**dispendioso,** *a.* costly; extravagant.

dispensa, *f.* exemption, dispensation.—**dispensar,** *vt.* to dispense; to excuse, pardon.—**dispensario,** *m.* dispensary; clinic.

dispersar, *vt.* to disperse, scatter, put to flight.—*vr.* to disperse, disband.—**disperso,** *a.* dispersed; scattered.

displicencia, *f.* disagreeableness; indifference.—**displicente**, *a*. disagreeable, unpleasant; peevish.

disponer, *vti*. [32–49] & *vii*. to dispose; to arrange; to resolve, direct, order.—*d. de*, to have at one's disposal.—*vri*. (**para** or **a**) to prepare oneself; to get ready (to); to make one's will.—**disponible**, *a*. available, disposable.—**disposición**, *f*. disposition, arrangement; disposal; aptitude; temper; proportion, order; specification.—**dispositivo**, *m*. device; mechanism; appliance.—**dispuesto**, *pp*. de DISPONER.—*a*. ready, disposed; fit; smart, clever; skillful.

disputa, *f*. dispute, controversy; debate.—**disputar**, *vt*. & *vi*. to dispute, debate, argue; to quarrel.

disquete, disquette, *f*. (comput.) diskette, floppy disk.—**disquetera**, *f*. (comput.) disk drive.

distancia, *f*. distance; interval; range.—*a d.*, from afar.—**distante**, *a*. distant, far.—**distar**, *vi*. to be distant; to be different.

distender, *vti*. [18] & *vri*. to distend, to expand.—**distensión**, *f*. distention, expansion; detente.

distinción, *f*. distinction; honor, award.—**distinguido**, *a*. distinguished, outstanding; refined, courtly, elegant.—**distinguir**, *vti*. [b] to distinguish, tell apart; to see clearly at a distance, make out, spot; to esteem.—*vri*. to distinguish oneself, to excel; (**de**) to differ, be distinguished.—**distintivo**, *a*. distinctive.—*m*. distinctive mark; badge, insignia.—**distinto**, *a*. distinct; clear; different.

distracción, *f*. absent-mindedness; lack of attention; pastime; oversight.—**distraer**, *vti*. [43] to distract; to amuse; to entertain; to lead astray.—*vri*. to be absent-minded; to be inattentive; to amuse oneself.—**distraído**, *a*. inattentive; absent-minded.

distribución, *f*. distribution.—**distribuidor**, *n*. & *a*. distributor; distributing.—*d. automático*, vending machine.—**distribuir**, *vti*. [23-e] to distribute, deal out; to sort (as mail).

distrito, *m*. district.

distrofia, *f*. dystrophy.—*d. muscular*, muscular dystrophy.

disturbio, *m*. disturbance.—*d. racista*, race riot.—*pl*. riot, disturbances.

disuelto, *pp*. of DISOLVER.—*a*. dissolved, melted.

disyuntiva, *f*. dilemma; alternative.

diurno, *a*. daily.

divagación, *f*. wandering, digression.—**divagar**, *vii*. [b] to roam, ramble; to digress.

diván, *m*. couch, divan.

divergencia, *f*. divergence, divergency.—**divergente**, *a*. divergent; dissenting.—**divergir**, *vii*. [c] to diverge; to dissent.

diversidad, *f*. diversity, variety.—**diversificar**, *vti*. [d] to diversify, vary.

diversión, *f*. entertainment, amusement.—**divertido**, *a*. amusing.—**divertir**, *vti*. [39] to amuse, entertain.—*vri*. to amuse oneself; to have a good time.

diverso, *a*. diverse, different; various.

dividendo, *m*. dividend.—**dividir**, *vt*. & *vi*. to divide.—*vr*. to divide; to split; to be divided; to separate (from), part company (with).

divinidad, *f*. divinity.—**divinizar**, *vti*. [a] to deify.—**divino**, *a*. divine.

divisa, *f*. badge, emblem.—*pl*. foreign currency.

divisar, *vt*. to sight, make out, perceive.

división, *f*. division; distribution; section; disunity.—**diviso**, *a*. divided, disunited.—**divisor**, *n*. divider.—*a*. dividing.

divo, *n*. celebrity, star; prima donna.

divorciar, *vt*. to divorce; to separate.—*vr*. to get divorced.—**divorcio**, *m*. divorce; breach.

divulgación, *f*. disclosure, divulgation; publication.—**divulgar**, *vti*. [b] to divulge; to disclose; to publish; to popularize.—*vri*. to become widespread.

dizque, diz que, *a*. (fam.) so-called.—*adv*. (fam.) apparently; they say; so they said.

dobladillo, *m*. (sewing) hem, border; trousers cuff.—*d. falso*, false hem.—**doblar**, *vt*. to double; to fold; to crease; to bend; to subdue.—*d. la esquina*, to turn the corner.—*vi*. to toll the knell.—*vr*. to bend; to bow, stoop; to submit.—**doble**, *a*. double, twofold, duplicate; thick, heavy; thick-set, strong.—*d. barba*, (fam.) double chin.—*d. contabilidad*, double-entry bookkeeping.—*d. fondo*, false bottom.—*d. juego*, double-dealing.—*d. nacionalidad*, dual nationality.—*d. personalidad*, split personality.—*d. tracción*, four-wheel drive.—*mf*. double; (theat. & cine) stand-in.—*d. que hace suertes* *peligrosas,* stunt man.—**doblegar,** *vti.* [b] to sway, dominate, force to yield; to fold, bend.—*vr.* to yield, give in; to fold, bend.—**doblez,** *m.* crease, fold.—*f.* double-dealing; hypocrisy.

doce, *a.* & *m.* twelve.—**doceavo,** *a.* & *m.* twelfth.—**doceno,** *a.* twelfth.

docena, *f.* dozen.—*d. de fraile,* (trece) baker's dozen.

docente, *a.* educational; teaching.

dócil, *a.* docile; obedient; pliable, malleable.—**docilidad,** *f.* docility, tameness.

docto, *a.* learned, well-informed. —**doctor,** *n.* (academic) doctor. —**doctorado,** *m.* doctorate.—**doctorar,** *vt.* to confer (*vr.* to obtain) the degree of doctor.

doctrina, *f.* doctrine.

documentación, *f.* documentation; documents.—**documentado,** *a.* documented; well-informed; having the necessary documents or vouchers.—**documental,** *a.* documentary.—**documento,** *m.* document.

dogal, *m.* halter; hangman's noose.

dogma, *m.* dogma, tenet.—**dogmático,** *a.* dogmatical or dogmatic.

dólar, *m.* dollar.

dolencia, *f.* aching; disease, ailment. —**doler,** *vii.* [26] to pain, ache; to hurt, grieve.—*vri.* to repent; to regret; to be moved, take pity; to complain.—**doliente,** *a.* aching, suffering; sorrowful; sick.—*mf.* mourner; sick person.—**dolor,** *m.* pain, aching, ache; sorrow, affliction.—*d. de oído,* earache.—**dolorido,** *a.* doleful; afflicted; painful.—**doloroso,** *a.* painful; pitiful.

doma, *f.* breaking in (of a horse).—**domador,** *n.* horsebreaker, tamer.—**domar,** *vt.* to tame; to break in; to subdue.—**domeñar,** *vt.* to tame, subdue; to dominate.—**domesticar,** *vti.* [d] to domesticate.—*vri.* to become tame.—**doméstico,** *a.* domestic.— *n.* household servant.

domiciliar, *vt.* to lodge.—*vr.* to take up residence; to dwell, reside.—**domiciliario,** *a.* domiciliary.—**domicilio,** *m.* domicile; home; residence.—*reparto a domicilio,* home-delivery service, we deliver.

dominación, *f.* dominion, domination; rule; power.—**dominante,** *a.* domineering; prevailing; dominant.—**dominar,** *vt.* to dominate; to

stand out above (as a hill); to master (a subject, language, etc.); to subdue, repress.—*vr.* to control oneself.

dominio, *m.* domain; dominion; power, authority.

domingo, *m.* Sunday.—**dominguero,** *a.* done on Sunday; pertaining to Sunday.—**dominical,** *a.* pertaining or relative to Sunday.—**dominicano,** *n.* & *a.* Dominican.

don, *m.* gift, present; natural gift, knack; Don (title for a gentleman, equivalent to Mr. or Esq. in English, used only when the given name is mentioned).

donación, *f.* donation; contribution.

donado, *n.* lay brother, lay sister.

donaire, *m.* gracefulness, gentility. —**donairoso,** *a.* graceful, elegant; witty.

donante, *mf.* & *a.* giver; giving.—**donar,** *vt.* to donate, bestow.—**donativo,** *m.* donation, gift.

doncella, *f.* maidservant; maiden.—*d. de honor,* maid of honor (attendant on a princess).—*a.* virginal.—**doncellez,** *f.* maidenhood.

donde (*interr.* **dónde**), *adv.* where; wherein; in which; wherever.—*a d.,* where, whereto.—*¿de dónde?* where from, whence?—*¿en dónde?* where?.—*¿por dónde?* whereabout? by what way or road?—**dondequiera,** *adv.* anywhere; wherever.— *por d.,* everywhere, in every place.

dondiego, *m.* (bot.) four-o'clock, marvel-of-Peru.—*d. de día,* (bot.) morning glory.

Doña, *f.* title given to a lady, equivalent to the English Mrs. or Miss, used only when the given name is mentioned.

dorado, *a.* gilt, golden.—*m.* gilding.— **dorar,** *vt.* to gild; to palliate.

dormilón, *n.* (coll.) sleepy head, late riser.—**dormir,** [17] *vii.* to sleep.— *vri.* to go to sleep, fall asleep.—**dormitar,** *vi.* to doze, nap.—**dormitorio,** *m.* bedroom; dormitory (large bedroom).

dorsal, *a.* dorsal.—**dorso,** *m.* spine; back.

dos, *a.* & *m.* two.—**doscientos,** *a.* & *m.* two hundred.—*doscientos uno,* two hundred one.

dosel, *m.* canopy; portiere.—**doselera,** *f.* valance.

dosificación, *f.* proportioning; dosage.—**dosificar,** *vti.* [d] to measure

dot–ecl

out the doses of.—**dosis** f. dose; quantity.

dotación, f. endowment, foundation; equipment; crew of warship; personnel (of office, etc.).—**dotado,** a. endowed with, gifted with.—**dotar,** vt. to bestow; to endow; to give a dowry to.—**dote,** m. & f. dowry.—f. pl. gifts, natural talents.

draga, f. dredge.—**dragado,** m. dredging.—**dragaminas,** m. minesweeper.—**dragar,** vti. [b] to dredge.

drama, m. drama; play.—**dramático,** a. dramatic.—**dramatizar,** vti. [a] & vii. to dramatize.—**dramaturgo,** n. dramatist; playwright.

drenaje, m. drainage.—**drenar,** vt. to drain.

dril, m. drill, strong cloth.

droga, f. drug; medicine; trick.—*drogas milagrosas,* wonder drugs.—**drogadicto,** m. drug addict.—**droguería,** f. drug store; drug trade.—**droguero,** n. **droguista,** mf. druggist; impostor.

ducentésimo, a. & m. two hundredth.

ducha, f. douche; shower bath.—*d. en alfileres,* needle bath.

ducho, a. skillful, expert.

dúctil, a. ductile, malleable.

duda, f. doubt.—**dudar,** vi. & vt. to doubt; to hesitate.—**dudoso,** a. doubtful, dubious; hazardous.

duelo, m. duel; sorrow, affliction; mourning; mourners; condolence.

duende, m. elf, hobgoblin.—**duendecillo,** m. pixie, little elf.

dueño, n. owner.—*d. ausentista,* absentee landlord.—*d. de esclavos,* slaveholder.

dueto, m. duet.

dulce, a. sweet; fresh (of water); pleasing; ductile (of metals).—m. confection, sweetmeat, candy.—**dulcería,** f. confectionery shop.—**dulcero,** n. confectioner.—**dulcificar,** vti. [d] to sweeten.

dulzaina, f. (mus.) recorder.

dulzón, a. saccharine.—**dulzura,** f. sweetness; kindliness.

duna, f. dune.

duodécimo, a. & m. twelfth.

duplicación, f. duplication, doubling.—**duplicado,** m. copy, duplicate; counterpart.—*por d.,* in duplicate.—**duplicar,** vti. [d] to double, duplicate; to repeat.—**duplo,** m. double, twice as much.

duque, m. duke.—**duquesa,** f. duchess.

durabilidad, f. durability, permanence.—**durable,** a. durable, lasting.—**duración,** f. duration.—*ser de d.,* to wear well, last.—**duradero,** a. lasting, durable.—**durante,** prep. during.—**durar,** vi. to last; to endure; to wear well (of clothes).

durazno, m. peach; peach tree.

dureza, f. hardness, solidity; cruelty, unkindness.—**duro,** a. hard, steely; solid, firm; rigorous; rude.—*a duras penas,* with difficulty; scarcely.

durmiente, a. sleeping.—mf. sleeper.—f. (RR.) tie.

E

e, conj. and (used only before words that begin with i or hi not followed by e).

ebanista, mf. cabinetmaker.—**ebanistería,** f. cabinetwork.—**ébano,** m. ebony.

ebrio, a. intoxicated, drunk.

ebullición, f. boiling.

echada, f. throw, cast; toss; (Mex.) boast.—**echar,** vt. to throw, cast; to expel; to dismiss, fire; to pour (as wine); to put (in, into); to turn (as a key); to give off, emit, eject; to bear (shoots, fruit); to play one's turn (in games).—*e. a,* to start, begin to.—*e.*

abajo, to overthrow; to tear down, demolish.—*e. a perder,* to spoil, ruin.—*e. a pique,* to sink a ship.—*e. a uno el muerto,* (fam.) to pass the buck.—*e. de menos,* to miss.—*e. de ver,* to notice.—*e. el bofe,* to work very hard.—*e. la cuenta,* to balance the account.—*e. mano,* to seize, grab.—*e. mano de,* to resort to.—*e. suertes,* to draw lots.—vr. to lie down; to throw oneself down.—*e. a perder,* to spoil; to become ruined.—*echárselas de,* to fancy oneself as.

eclesiástico, a. ecclesiastical.—m. clergyman, priest.

eclipsar, *vt.* to eclipse; to outshine. —*vr.* to be eclipsed.—**eclipse,** *m.* eclipse.

eco, *m.* echo.—*hacer e.,* to become important or famous.

ecocidio, *m.* ecocide.—**ecología,** *f.* ecology.—**ecológico,** ecological.

economía, *f.* economy.—*e. doméstica,* home economics, domestic science.—*e. política,* economics.—*pl.* savings.—**económico,** *a.* economic(al); saving, thrifty.—**economista,** *mf.* economist.—**economizar,** *vti.* [a] to economize; to save.

ecuación, *f.* equation.

ecuador, *m.* equator.

ecuánime, *a.* equable, calm, serene. —**ecuanimidad,** *f.* equanimity.

ecuatoriano, *n.* & *a.* Ecuadorian.

edad, *f.* age.—*e. del espacio,* space age.—*e. de piedra,* Stone Age.—*e. escolar,* school age.—*e. madura,* middle age.—*la Alta E. Media, la E. de las tinieblas,* the Dark Ages.— *mayor de e.,* of (legal) age.—*menor de e.,* under age, minor.

edición, *f.* edition, issue; publication.—*e. de bolsillo,* pocket edition.—*e. eléctronica,* desktop publishing.—*e. numerada,* limited edition.—*e. príncipe,* first edition.

edicto, *m.* edict, proclamation.

edificación, *f.* edification; construction.—**edificante,** *a.* edifying; erecting.—**edificar,** *vti.* [d] & *vii.* to edify; to build, construct.—**edificio,** *m.* edifice, building, structure.

editar, *vt.* to publish.—**editor,** *n.* & *a.* publisher; publishing.—**editorial,** *mf.* & *a.* editorial.—*f.* publishing house.—*a.* publishing.

edredón, *m.* comforter, quilted blanket.

educación, *f.* education, upbringing; good breeding, politeness.—*e. a distancia,* correspondence courses, distance learning.—*e. especial,* special education (for children with special needs).—*e. física,* physical culture.—*e. preescolar,* preschool education.—*e. superior,* higher education.—**educador,** *n.* & *a.* educator; educating.—**educar,** *vti.* [d] to educate, instruct, raise, train.—**educativo,** *a.* educational.

EE. UU., *abbr.* (**Estados Unidas**) U.S.

efectivo, *a.* effective; real, actual.— *hacer e.,* to cash (a check, etc.).—*m.* cash, specie.—*en e.,* in cash, in coin.—**efecto,** *m.* effect; impression; end, purpose.—*e. invernadero,* greenhouse effect.—*e. óptico,* optical illusion.—*e. secundario perjudicial,* side effect.—*pl.* assets; goods; drafts.—*efectos especiales,* special effects.—*efectos públicos,* public securities.—*efectos sonoros,* sound effects.—*en e.,* as a matter of fact, actually.—*tener e.,* to become effective.—**efectuar,** *vt.* to effect, carry out, do, make.

eficacia, *f.* efficacy, efficiency.—**eficaz,** *a.* efficacious, effective, telling.—**eficiencia,** *f.* efficiency, effectiveness.—**eficiente,** *a.* efficient, effective.

efigie, *f.* effigy, image.

efusión, *f.* effusion, shedding; warmth of manner.—*e. de sangre,* bloodshed.—**efusivo,** *a.* effusive.

egipcio, *n.* & *a.* Egyptian.

egocéntrico, *a.* self-centered.

egoísmo, *m.* selfishness, self-interest.—**egoísta,** *a.* selfish.—*mf.* egoist.—**ególatra,** *mf.* = EGOTISTA. —**egolatría,** *f.* = EGOTISMO.—**egotismo,** *m.* egotism.—**egotista,** *mf.* & *a.* egotist; egotistic.

eje, *m.* axis; axle; (fig.) main point.—*e. de transmission,* drive shaft.

ejecución, *f.* execution; carrying out.—**ejecutar,** *vt.* to execute; to perform, carry out; (law) to levy, seize property.—*e. a la primera lectura,* (mus.) to sight-read.—**ejecutivo,** *a.* executive; executory.—*m.* executive (power or person).—**ejecutor,** *n.* executor; executer.— *e. de la justicia,* executioner.— **ejecutoria,** *f.* sentence, judgment; pedigree.

ejemplar, *a.* exemplary.—*m.* specimen, sample; copy.—**ejemplificar,** *vti.* [d] to be an example, typify. —**ejemplo,** *m.* example, instance.— *dar e.,* to set an example.—*e. de cortesía,* complimentary copy.—*e. muestra,* sample copy.

ejercer, *vti.* [a] to practice (a profession); to perform; to exert.—**ejercicio,** *m.* exercise; practice.—*e. de tiro,* rifle practice.—*e. fiscal,* fiscal year.—*hacer e.,* to exercise; (mil.) to drill.—**ejercitar,** *vt.* to exercise, to put into practice; to drill (troops); to train.—*vr.* to practice.—**ejército,** *m.* army.—*e. permanente,* standing army.

ejido, *m.* common, public land.

ejote, *m.* (Mex.) stringbean.

el, *art. m. sing.* (*pl.* **los**) the.—**él,** *pron. m. sing.* (*pl.* **ellos**) he.

elaboración, *f.* elaboration, manufacture.—**elaborar,** *vt.* to elaborate; to manufacture.

elasticidad, *f.* elasticity.—**elástico,** *a.* elastic, springy.—*pl.* suspenders.

elección, *f.* election; choice.—**electivo,** *a.* elective.—**electo,** *ppi.* of ELEGIR.—*a.* elect, chosen.—**elector,** *n.* & *a.* elector; electing.—*m.* elector, voter.—**electorado,** *m.* electorate.—**electoral,** *a.* electoral.

electricidad, *f.* electricity.—**electricista,** *mf.* electrician, electrical engineer.—**eléctrico,** *a.* electric(al). —**electrificación,** *f.* electrification. —**electrificar,** *vti.* [d] to electrify.— **electrización,** *f.* electrification.— **electrizar,** *vti.* [a] to electrify.—*vri.* to become electrified.—**electrocardiograma,** *m.* electrocardiogram.— **electrochoque,** *m.* electroconvulsive therapy.—**electrocutar,** *vt.* to electrocute.—**electrodo,** *m.* electrode.—**electrólisis,** *f.* electrolysis. —**electromagnético,** *a.* electromagnetic.—**electrón,** *m.* electron.— **electrónica,** *f.* electronics.—**electrotecnia,** *f.* electrical engineering.

elefante, *n.* elephant.

elegancia, *f.* elegance, gracefulness; neatness.—**elegante,** *a.* elegant, stylish, graceful, chic.

elegible, *a.* eligible.—**elegir,** *vti.* [29–49-c] to choose.

elemental, *a.* elemental, elementary; fundamental.—**elemento,** *m.* element.—*pl.* elements, rudiments.

elenco, *m.* (theat.) cast; catalogue.

elevación, *f.* elevation; altitude; rise; rapture.—**elevado,** *a.* elevated.— **elevador,** *m.* (Am.) elevator, hoist. —**elevar,** *vt.* to raise, heave; to exalt.—*vr.* to rise, soar.

elfo, *m.* elf.

eliminación, *f.* elimination.—**eliminar,** *vt.* to eliminate.—**eliminatorio,** *a.* qualifying, preliminary.—*f.* qualifying round, heat, runoff.

elite or **élite,** *f.* elite; top-class.—*tropas de e.,* crack troops.

elocución, *f.* elocution; effective diction, style.—**elocuencia,** *f.* eloquence.—**elocuente,** *a.* eloquent.

elogiar, *vt.* to praise, extol.—**elogio,** *m.* praise, eulogy.

elote, *m.* (Mex., C.A.) ear of green corn; corn on the cob.

eludir, *vt.* to elude, avoid.

ella, *pron. f. sing.* (*pl.* **ellas**) she.—**ello,** *pron. neut. sing.* it.—*e. dirá,* the event will tell.—*e. es que,* the fact is that.—**ellos,** *pron. m. pl.;* **ellas,** *pron. f. pl.* they.

emancipación, *f.* emancipation.— **emancipar,** *vt.* to emancipate.—*vr.* to free oneself; to become free or independent.

embadurnar, *vt.* to smear.

embajada, *f.* embassy; errand, mission.—**embajador,** *n.* ambassador.

embalador, *n.* packer.—**embalaje,** *m.* packing, baling.—**embalar,** *vt.* to bale, pack.

embaldosado, *m.* tile floor.—**embaldosar,** *vt.* to pave with tiles or flagstones.

embalsamamiento, *m.* embalming.— **embalsamar,** *vt.* to embalm; to perfume.

embalse, *m.* dam.

embarazada, *a.* pregnant.—**embarazar,** *vti.* [a] to embarrass, hinder; to make pregnant.—**embarazo,** *m.* impediment; embarrassment, confusion; perplexity; pregnancy.—*e. psicológico,* false pregnancy.—**embarazoso,** *a.* embarrassing; entangled, cumbersome.

embarcación, *f.* boat, ship; embarkation.—**embarcadero,** *m.* wharf, pier.—**embarcador,** *n.* shipper.— **embarcar,** *vti.* [d] to ship; to embark.—*vri.* to embark; to board (ship or train).

embargar, *vti.* [b] to restrain, suspend; (law) to embargo; to seize.—**embargo,** *m.* embargo, seizure.—*sin e.,* notwithstanding, however, nevertheless.

embarque, *m.* shipment (of goods).

embarrancar, *vii.* [d] & *vri.* to run aground.

embarrar, *vt.* to smear; to daub; to vilify.—*vr.* to be covered with mud; to lose one's self-respect.

embate, *m.* dashing of the waves; sudden impetuous attack.—*embates de la fortuna,* sudden reverses of fortune.

embaucador, *n.* impostor.—**embaucar,** *vti.* [d] to deceive, trick, fool.

embebecimiento, *m.* amazement; rapture; absorption.—**embeber,** *vt.* to imbibe, absorb; to soak.—*vi.* to shrink.—*vr.* to be enraptured; to be absorbed.

embelesamiento, *m.* rapture, ecstasy.—**embelesar,** *vt.* to charm, delight.—*vr.* to be charmed, or delighted.—**embeleso,** *m.* rapture, delight; charm.

embellecer, *vti.* [3] to beautify, embellish.—**embellecimiento,** *m.* embellishment, beautifying.

emberrenchinarse, emberrincharse, *vr.* (coll.) to throw a tantrum.

embestida, *f.* assault, violent attack, onset.—**embestir,** *vti.* [29] to assail, attack; to make a drive on.—*vii.* to attack, rush.

embetunar, *vt.* to blacken; to polish (shoes).

emblema, *m.* emblem, symbol.

embobar, *vt.* to enchant, fascinate.—*vr.* to be struck with astonishment.

embocadura, *f.* entrance by a narrow passage; mouthpiece of a wind instrument; mouth of a river.—**embocar,** *vti.* [d] to enter through a narrow passage.

emborrachar, *vt.* to intoxicate.—*vr.* to become intoxicated, get drunk.

émbolo, *m.* piston; (med.) embolus.

embolsar, *vt.* to put into a purse.—*vr.* to pocket, put into one's pocket.

emborronar, *vt.* to blot.—*vt. & vi.* to scribble.

emboscada, *f.* ambush, ambuscade.—**emboscar,** *vti.* [d] to place in ambush.—*vri.* to lie in ambush.

embotado, *a.* blunt, dull.—**embotamiento,** *m.* blunting; bluntness, dullness.—**embotar,** *vt.* to blunt, to dull (an edge or point); to enervate, debilitate; to dull.—*vr.* to become dull.

embotellado, *m.* bottling.—**embotelladora,** *f.* bottling plant.—**embotellamiento,** *m.* traffic jam.—**embotellar,** *vt.* to bottle; to bottle up, to block.

embozado, *a.* muffled, with face covered (with a cloak).—**embozar,** *vti.* [a] to muffle; to cloak; to muzzle.—*vr.* to muffle oneself up.

embragar, *vti.* [b] to throw in the clutch.—**embrague,** *m.* clutch; coupling.

embreado, *a.* tarry.—**embrear,** *vt.* to tar.

embriagador, *a.* spirituous, intoxicating; ravishing.—**embriagar,** *vti.* [b] to intoxicate; to enrapture.—*vri.* to get drunk.—**embriaguez,** *f.* intoxication, drunkenness; rapture.

embrión, *m.* embryo.

embrollar, *vt.* to entangle, mess up; to ensnare, embroil.—**embrollo,** *m.* tangle; trickery, deception; embroilment.

embromar, *vt.* to banter, tease; to vex, annoy; (Am.) to harm.—*vr.* to be annoyed, disgusted.

embrujar, *vt.* to bewitch.—**embrujo,** *m.* bewitchment.

embrutecer, *vti.* [3] to brutalize; to stupefy, stultify.—*vri.* to become brutalized; to grow stupid.

embudo, *m.* funnel.

embullar, *vt.* (Am.) to incite to revelry.—*vi.* (Am.) to make noise.—*vr.* (Am.) to revel, make merry.—**embullo,** *m.* (Am.) gaiety, revelry.

embuste, *m.* lie; trick, fraud.—**embustero,** *n.* liar; trickster, cheat.

embutido, *m.* sausage; inlaid work.—**embutir,** *vt.* to inlay, emboss; to insert; to stuff; (coll.) to cram; to eat much.

emergencia, *f.* emergence, emergency.—**emergente,** *a.* emergent, issuing.—**emerger,** *vii.* [c] to emerge, arise.

emérito, *a.* emeritus.—*profesor e.,* professor emeritus.

emigración, *f.* emigration.—**emigrado,** *n.* emigrant; emigré.—**emigrante,** *mf. & a.* emigrant.—**emigrar,** *vi.* to emigrate.

eminencia, *f.* eminence; height; outstanding person.—**eminente,** *a.* eminent; high, lofty.

emisario, *m.* emissary.—**emisión,** *f.* emission; issue (of paper money, bonds, etc.); radiation.—*emisiones radiofónicas,* broadcasting.—**emisor,** *a.* emitting; broadcasting.—*m.* radio transmitter.—*f.* broadcasting station.—**emitir,** *vt.* to emit, send forth; to issue (as bonds, etc.); to broadcast.

emoción, *f.* emotion.—**emocional,** *a.* emotional.—**emocionante,** *a.* moving, impressive, thrilling.—**emocionar,** *vt.* to touch, move, shock.—*vr.* to be moved, touched.—**emotivo,** *a.* moving, emotive.

empacador, *n.* packer.—**empacar,** *vti.* [d] to pack; to bale.—*vri.* (Am.) (coll.) to put on airs.

empachar, *vt.* to embarrass; to cram; to cause indigestion.—*vr.* to be embarrassed; to suffer indigestion.—**empacho,** *m.* bashfulness; embarrassment; indigestion.—*sin e.,* without ceremony; unconcernedly.

empadronar, *vt.* to register, take the census of.

empalagar, *vti.* [b] to pall, cloy; to bother.—**empalagoso**, *a.* cloying, too rich or sweet; wearisome, boresome.

empalizada, *f.* palisade, stockade.

empalmar, *vt.* to couple, join; to splice.—*vi.* (RR.) to branch; to join.—**empalme**, *m.* joint, connection; (RR.) junction.

empanada, *f.* meat pie.—**empanadilla**, *f.* small meat pie.—**empanar**, *vt.*, **empanizar**, *vti.* [a] to bread.

empañar, *vt.* to dim, blur, mist; to soil (reputation).

empapar, *vt.* to imbibe; to soak, drench.—*vr.* (**en**) to imbibe; to be soaked (in); to steep oneself (in).

empapelador, *n.* paperhanger.—**empapelar**, *vt.* to wallpaper, to paper; to wrap up in paper.

empaque, *m.* packing; appearance, air; (Am.) boldness, impudence.—**empaquetador**, *n.* packer.—**empaquetadura**, *f.* packing; gasket.—**empaquetar**, *vt.* to pack; to stuff.—*vr.* to dress up.

emparedado, *a.* & *n.* recluse.—*m.* sandwich.—**emparedar**, *vt.* to wall, shut up.

emparejar, *vt.* & *vi.* to level, smooth; to match.

emparentar, *vii.* [1] to become related by marriage.

emparrado, *m.* vine arbor.

empastar, *vt.* to fill a tooth; to paste; to bind books.—**empaste**, *m.* filling (of a tooth); binding.

empatar, *vt.* to equal; to tie (in voting or games); (Am.) to join, tie.—**empate**, *m.* tie (in voting or games); joint.

empecinado, *a.* stubborn.—**empecinarse**, *vr.* (**en**) to persist (in), be stubborn (about).

empedernido, *a.* hard-hearted; hardened, compulsive, inveterate, confirmed, hard-core.

empedrado, *m.* stone pavement.—**empedrar**, *vti.* [1] to pave with stones.

empeine, *m.* instep.

empellón, *m.* jostle, shove.—*a empellones*, pushing, by pushing rudely.

empeñado, *a.* determined, persistent.—**empeñar**, *vt.* to pawn; to pledge; to engage.—*vr.* (**en**) to persist (in); to insist; to begin (a battle); to go into debt.—**empeño**, *m.*

pledge, pawn; engagement; earnest desire; persistence; determination.—*casa de empeños*, pawnshop.—*con e.*, eagerly.

empeoramiento, *m.* deterioration.—**empeorar**, *vt.* to impair; to make worse.—*vi.* & *vr.* to grow worse.

empequeñecer, *vti.* [3] to make smaller, diminish; to belittle.

emperador, *m.* emperor.—**emperatriz**, *f.* empress.

emperchar, *vt.* to hang on a perch.—*vr.* (coll.) to dress up.

emperejilar, **emperifollar**, *vt.* & *vr.* to dress elaborately, to doll up.

emperramiento, *m.* obstinacy.—**emperrarse**, *vr.* (**en**) (coll.) to be obstinate or stubborn (about).

empezar, *vti.* [1-a] & *vii.* to begin.

empicotar, *vt.* to pillory; to picket.

empinado, *a.* steep; high, lofty.—**empinar**, *vt.* to raise; to tip, incline.—*e. el codo*, to drink heavily.—*vr.* to stand on tiptoe; to tower, rise high; (aer.) to zoom.

emplasto, *m.* plaster, poultice.

emplazamiento, *m.* (law) summons.—**emplazar**, *vti.* [a] to summon.

empleada, *f.* maid.—*e. con cama*, live-in maid.—**empleado**, *n.* employee.—*e. bancario*, bank clerk.—*e. de hogar*, domestic servant.—*e. del Estado* or *e. público*, civil servant.—**emplear**, *vt.* to employ; to engage, hire.—*vr.* to be employed.—**empleo**, *m.* employ, employment, job; use.

emplomar, *vt.* to lead; to put lead seals on.

emplumar, *vt.* to feather; to tar and feather.

empobrecer, *vti.* [3] to impoverish.—*vri.* to become poor.—**empobrecimiento**, *m.* impoverishment.

empolvar, *vt.* & *vr.* to cover with dust; to powder.

empollar, *vt.* to hatch, brood.

emponzoñamiento, *m.* poisoning.—**emponzoñar**, *vt.* to poison; to corrupt.

empotrar, *vt.* to embed; to fix in a wall; to splice.

emprendedor, *n.* & *a.* enterpriser; enterprising.—**emprender**, *vt.* to undertake, engage in.—*e. a*, or *con*, to address, accost.

empreñar, *vt.* to make pregnant.

empresa, *f.* enterprise, undertaking; company, firm; management.—*e. de servicios públicos*, public utility.—

libre e., free enterprise.—**empresa-rial,** *a.* managerial, business.—**em-presario,** *n.* promoter; contractor; theatrical manager; impresario.—*e. de pompas fúnebres,* mortician, funeral director.

empréstito, *m.* loan.—*e. público,* government loan.

empujar, *vt.* to push, impel, shove.—**empuje,** *m.* push, shove; energy; (eng.) thrust.—**empujón,** *m.* push, violent shove.—*a empujones,* pushing, jostling.

empuñadura, *f.* hilt (of a sword); handle, grip.—**empuñar,** *vt.* to clinch, grip.

emulsión, *f.* emulsion.—**emulsionar,** *vt.* to emulsify.

en, *prep.* in; at; on, upon; to; into.

enagua(s), *f.* petticoat, slip.

enajenación, *f.,* **enajenamiento,** *m.* alienation (of property); absence of mind; rapture.—*e. mental,* mental derangement.—**enajenar,** *vt.* to alienate; to transfer (property); to transport, enrapture.—*vr.* to be enraptured.

enaltecer, *vti.* [3] to extol, exalt.

enamoradizo, *a.* inclined to fall in love.—**enamorado,** *a.* in love, enamored.—*n.* lover; sweetheart.—**enamoramiento,** *m.* love, being in love; courting, love-making.—**enamorar,** *vt.* to inspire love in; to make love to, woo.—*vr.* to fall in love.—**enamoriscarse,** *vri.* [d] (coll.) to become infatuated.

enano, *a.* dwarfish, small.—*n.* dwarf, manikin.

enarbolar, *vt.* to hoist, raise high, hang out (a flag, etc.).

enardecer, *vti.* [3] to fire with passion, excite, inflame.—*vri.* to be kindled, get excited, inflamed (with passion).—**enardecimiento,** *m.* ardor; passion; inflaming; excitement.

encabezamiento, *m.* headline, heading, title; tax roll.—**encabezar,** *vti.* [a] to draw up (a tax roll); to put a heading or title to; to head, lead.

encabritarse, *vr.* to rear, rise up on the hind legs.

encadenamiento, *m.* chaining; linking.—**encadenar,** *vt.* to chain; to enslave; to link together (as thoughts).

encajar, *vt.* to fit in, insert, adjust; to join.—*vi.* to fit snugly; to fit, suit, be appropriate.—*vr.* to intrude; to squeeze oneself in.—**encaje,** *m.*

lace, inlaid work; adjusting, fitting or joining together; socket.—*e. de mano,* needlepoint.

encajonar, *vt.* to box; to case; to narrow.

encallado, *a.* (naut.) stranded.—**encallar,** *vi.* (naut.) to run aground.

encallecer, *vti.* [3] & *vii.* to get corns or calluses.—*vri.* to become hardened or callous.

encaminar, *vt.* to guide; to direct.—*vr.* (a) to take the road (to); to be on the way (to).

encandilar, *vt.* to dazzle; to daze, bewilder; (coll.) to stir (the fire).

encanecer, *vii.* [3] to grow gray-haired; to grow old.

encanijamiento, *m.* frailty, lack of development.—**encanijar,** *vt.* to weaken (a baby) by poor nursing.—*vr.* to pine; to become emaciated.

encantado, *a.* enchanted, delighted, charmed; haunted.—**encantador,** *n.* charmer; enchanter.—*a.* charming; delightful.—**encantamiento,** *m.* enchantment.—**encantar,** *vt.* to enchant, charm; to delight; to bewitch.—**encanto,** *m.* enchantment, charm; delight.

encañonar, *vt.* to level a gun at.

encapotamiento, *m.* cloudiness.—**encapotarse,** *vr.* to become cloudy.

encapricharse, *vr.* to indulge in whims; to be stubborn.

encaramar, *vt.* & *vr.* to raise; to elevate; to extol; to climb; to perch upon.

encarar, *vi.* to face.—*vt.* to aim.—*vr.* (con) to face, be face to face.

encarcelación, *f.,* **encarcelamiento,** *m.* imprisonment.—**encarcelar,** *vt.* to imprison, incarcerate, jail.

encarecer, *vti.,* [3] *vii.* & *vri.* to raise the price; to extol; to enhance.—**encarecidamente,** *adv.* eagerly, earnestly.—**encarecimiento,** *m.* enhancement.

encargado, *a.* in charge.—*n.* person in charge; agent; foreman; (E.U.) superintendent.—**encargar,** *vti.* [b] to entrust, put under the care (of a person); to order (goods, etc.).—*vri.* to take charge.—**encargo,** *m.* charge, commission; errand; assignment; (com.) order.

encariñamiento, *m.* fondness, attachment.—**encariñarse,** *vr.* (con) to become fond (of).

encarnación, *f.* incarnation; personification.—**encarnado,** *a.* incarnate;

flesh-colored; red.—**encarnar,** vi. to become incarnate.—vt. to incarnate; to embody; to bait (a fish-hook).

encarnizado, a. bloody; fierce, hard-fought.—**encarnizarse,** vri. [a] to become enraged; to fight with fury.— e. con or en, to be merciless to; to treat inhumanely.

encarrilar, vt. to put on the right track; to set right.

encasillar, vt. to pigeonhole; to include in a list of (candidates).

encasquetar, vt. & vr. to pull down (one's hat) tight.

encasquillar, vr. to stick, get stuck (a bullet in a gun).

encastillado, a. lofty, haughty.—**encastillarse,** vr. to shut oneself up in a castle; to be unyielding or headstrong.

encausar, vt. to prosecute, indict.

encauzar, vti. [a] to channel; to conduct through channels; to guide, direct.

encenagarse, vri. [b] to wallow in dirt, mire, or vice.

encendajas, f. pl. kindling.

encendedor, m. (cigarette, etc.) lighter.—**encender,** vti. [18] to light, kindle.—vri. to take fire; to light up.—**encendido,** a. inflamed; red.—m. (engine) ignition.

encerado, a. waxed; wax-colored.—m. oilcloth; tarpaulin; blackboard.—**encerar,** vt. to wax.

encerrar, vti. [1] to lock or shut up; to confine; to contain, involve.—vri. to live in seclusion; to be locked up.—**encerrona,** f. allurement.

enchapado, m. veneer; plates or sheets forming a cover or lining.—**enchapar,** vt. to veneer; to cover with metal plates or sheets.

encharcarse, vri. [d] to form puddles.

enchilada, f. (Mex.) pancake of maize with chili.

enchufar, vt. & vr. to plug in; to fit (a tube) into another; to telescope.—**enchufe,** m. socket joint; sliding of one thing into another; (elec.) plug; socket; outlet.

encía, f. gum (of the mouth).

enciclopedia, f. encyclopedia.

encierro, m. confinement; act of closing or locking up; retreat; prison; fold (of cattle).

encima, adv. above; at the top; overhead; over and above, besides; in addition, to boot.—e. de, on, upon.—por e., superficially, hastily.—por e. de, over, above; regardless of.

encina, f. evergreen oak, live oak.

encinta, a. pregnant.

encintado, m. sidewalk curb.

enclenque, a. weak, feeble, sickly.

encoger, vti. [c] to contract, shorten, shrink.—vri. to shrink; to shrivel.—encogerse de hombros, to shrug the shoulders.—**encogimiento,** m. contraction, shrinkage; bashfulness.

encolado, m., **encoladura,** f. gluing; priming, sizing.—**encolar,** vt. to glue; to stick.

encolerizar, vti. [a] to anger.—vri. to become angry.

encomendar, vti. [1] to entrust, commend.—vri. to entrust oneself; to pray.

encomiar, vt. to praise, eulogize.—**encomio,** m. praise, testimonial, eulogy.

encomienda, f. commission, charge.—e. postal, (Am.) parcel post.

enconar, vt. to inflame; to infect.—vr. to rankle; to fester, become infected.—**encono,** m. rancor, ill-will; soreness; sore spot.

encontrado, a. opposite; in front; opposed.—**encontrar,** vti. [12] to find; to meet.—vii. to meet; to collide.—vri. to meet; to collide; to be, find oneself; to feel (app. to health); to be opposed to each other; to conflict; to find; (con) to meet, come across or upon.—**encontronazo,** m. collision; bump.

encopetado, a. presumptuous; of high social standing.

encordar, vti. [12] to string (instruments); to lash or bind with ropes.

encorvar, vt. & vr. to bend, curve.

encrespamiento, m. curling; fury, roughness (of the sea, etc.).—**encrespar,** vt. to curl; to set (the hair) on end; to ruffle (the feathers).—vr. to become rough (the sea, the waves).

encrucijada, f. crossroads, ambush.

encuadernación, f. binding (books); bindery.—**encuadernado,** a. hardback (book).—**encuadernador,** n. bookbinder.—**encuadernar,** vt. to bind (books).

encubierto, ppi. of ENCUBRIR.—**encubridor,** n. & a. concealer; concealing; accomplice.—**encubrimiento,** m.

concealment.—**encubrir**, *vti.* [49] to conceal, hide, cloak.

encuentro, *m.* encounter, meeting; collision, clash; find, finding; (mil.) encounter, fight; rendezvous (in space); —**salir al e. de**, to go to meet; to encounter.

encumbrado, *a.* high, elevated; lofty. **encumbramiento**, *m.* elevation, exaltation; height, eminence.—**encumbrar**, *vt.* to raise, elevate.—*vi.* to ascend.—*vr.* to rise; to be proud, rate oneself high.

encurtido, *m.* pickle.—**encurtir**, *vt.* to pickle.

endeble, *a.* feeble, weak; flimsy.

endemoniado, *a.* devilish, fiendish, perverse.—**endemoniar**, *vt.* & *vr.* (coll.) to irritate.

endentado, *a.* serrated.—**endentar**, *vti.* [1] & *vii.* to gear, engage.—**endentecer**, *vi.* teethe.

enderezamiento, *m.* straightening; setting right.—**enderezar**, *vti.* [a] to straighten; to right, set right.—*vri.* to straighten up.

endeudarse, *vr.* to contract debts.

endiablado, *a.* devilish, diabolical; perverse, wicked.

endilgar, *vti.* [b] to spring something on (a person).

endiosar, *vt.* to deify.—*vr.* to be elated with pride.

endosar, *vt.* to indorse (a draft, etc.). —**endosatario**, *n.* indorsee.—**endose, endoso**, *m.* indorsement.

endulzar, *vti.* [a] to sweeten; to soften.

endurecer, *vti.* [3] & *vri.* to harden; to inure.—**endurecido**, *a.* hard, hardy; inured.—**endurecimiento**, *m.* hardness; hardening; hard-heartedness.

eneldo, *m.* (bot.) dill.

enema, *m.* enema.

enemigo, *a.* hostile; inimical.—*n.* enemy, foe.—*m.* (mil.) enemy.—*el e. malo*, the devil.—**enemistad**, *f.* enmity, hatred.—**enemistar**, *vt.* to make enemies of.—*vr.* (**con**) to become an enemy (of); to fall out (with).

energía, *f.* energy; power.—**enérgico**, *a.* energetic, lively.

energúmeno, *n.* violent, impulsive person; person possessed with a devil.

enero, *m.* January.

enervar, *vt.* to enervate, weaken.—*vr.* to become weak.

enfadar, *vt.* to vex, anger.—*vr.* to become angry.—**enfado**, *m.* vexation, anger; trouble, drudgery.—**enfadoso**, *a.* annoying, troublesome.

enfangar, *vti.* [b] & *vri.* to soil with mud; (coll.) to soil one's reputation.—*vr.* to vice, etc.).

enfardar, *vt.* to pack, bale.

énfasis, *m.* emphasis.—**enfático**, *a.* emphatic; bombastic.

enfermar, *vi.* (Am. *vr.*) to fall ill, be taken ill.—*vt.* to make ill.—**enfermedad**, *f.* illness, sickness.—*e. de legionario*, Legionnaires' disease.— *e. del sueño*, sleeping sickness.—*e. de radiación*, radiation sickness.—*e. mental*, mental illness.—*e. nerviosa* nervous disorder.—*e. profesional* occupational disease.—*e. venérea* venereal disease, VD.—**enfermera** *f.* nurse.—*e. ambulante*, visiting nurse.—*e. diplomada*, registered nurse.—**enfermería**, *f.* infirmary sanitarium.—**enfermero**, *m.* male nurse.—**enfermizo**, *a.* sickly; unhealthful.—**enfermo**, *a.* ill, sick.—*e. de amor*, lovesick.—*n.* patient.

enfiestarse, *vr.* (Am.) to have a good time; to go on a spree.

enfilar, *vt.* to place in a row or line.

enflaquecer, *vti.* [3] to make thin or lean.—*vii.* & *vri.* to become thin lose weight; to weaken.—**enflaquecimiento**, *m.* loss of flesh; thinness.

enfocar, *vti.* [d] to focus, focus on.— **enfoque**, *m.* focusing; approach (to a problem, etc.).

enfrascarse, *vri.* to be entangled or involved; to be absorbed, engrossed (in work, affairs, etc.).

enfrentar, *vt.* to confront, put face to face; to face.—*vr.* to confront, face meet face to face.—*e. con*, to face; to oppose.—**enfrente**, *adv.* opposite in front.—*de e.*, opposite, across (the street, etc.).

enfriamiento, *m.* refrigeration; cooling; cold, chill (illness).—**enfriar**, *vt* to cool.—*vr.* to cool; to cool off or down; to become chilled.

enfundar, *vt.* to case, put into a case (a a pillow); to fill up, stuff.

enfurecer, *vti.* [3] to enrage, make furious.—*vri.* to rage; to become furious or stormy.

enfurruñarse, *vr.* (coll.) to become angry; to grumble.

engalanar, *vt.* to adorn, deck; (naut.) to dress.—*vr.* to dress up, doll up.

engallado, *a.* erect, upright

haughty.—**engallarse,** *vr.* to draw oneself up arrogantly.

nganchar, *vt.* to hook, hitch; to ensnare; to press into military service.—*vr.* to engage; to enlist in the army.—**enganche,** *m.* hooking; enlistment in the army.

ngañador, *n.* & *a.* deceiver; deceiving.—**engañar,** *vt.* to deceive; to cheat; to fool, hoax; to while away (time).—*vr.* to deceive oneself; to make a mistake, be mistaken.—**engaño,** *m.* deceit, fraud; hoax; mistake, misunderstanding.—**engañoso,** *a.* deceitful, artful, misleading.

ngarce, *m.* linking; setting (of precious stone).

ngarzar, *vti.* [a] to link; to set (precious stone).

ngarrotarse, *vr.* to become numb with cold; (fig.) to be very cold, frozen.

ngastar, *vt.* to set (jewels).—**engaste,** *m.* setting (of stones).

ngatusar, *vt.* (coll.) to inveigle, wheedle, cajole.

ngendrar, *vt.* to father, sire, engender, generate, procreate; to bear.—**engendro,** *m.* shapeless embryo; badly-made thing.

nglobar, *vt.* to inclose, embody.

ngolfarse, *vr.* to become engrossed, absorbed into.

ngomar, *vt.* to gum, to size; to glue.

ngordar, *vt.* to fatten.—*vi.* & (Am.) *vr.* to become fat.

ngorro, *m.* embarrassment, nuisance.—**engorroso,** *a.* troublesome, annoying.

ngranaje, *m.* gear, gearing.—**engranar,** *vi.* to gear; to interlock.

ngrandecer, *vti.* [3] to aggrandize; to enlarge; to exalt, extol; to magnify.—**engrandecimiento,** *m.* increase, enlargement; exaltation.

ngrapador, *m.* stapler.

ngrasador, *m.* oiler, lubricator.—**engrasar,** *vt.* to grease, oil, lubricate.—**engrase,** *m.* lubrication, oiling, greasing.

ngreído, *a.* conceited.—**engreimiento,** *m.* conceit, presumption, vanity.—**engreír,** *vti.* [35] to encourage the conceit of, to make vain; to elate.—*vri.* to become vain or conceited.

ngrifar, *vt.* & *vr.* to curl, crisp.

ngrosar, *vti.* [12] to enlarge; to increase; to thicken, broaden.—*vii.* & (Am.) *vri.* to become fat; to increase, swell.

engrudo, *m.* paste, glue.

engullir, *vti.* [27] to gobble, gorge, wolf.

enhebrar, *vt.* to thread; to string.

enhiesto, *a.* erect, upright.

enhorabuena, *f.* congratulation, felicitation.

enigma, *m.* enigma, riddle.—**enigmático,** *a.* enigmatic.

enjabonadura, *f.* soaping.—**enjabonar,** *vt.* to soap; to wash with soap; (coll.) to soft-soap.

enjaezar, *vti.* [a] to harness.

enjambre, *m.* swarm of bees; crowd, agglomeration.

enjaular, *vt.* to cage; to confine.

enjuagar, *vti.* [b] & *vri.* to rinse, rinse the mouth.—**enjuagatorio,** *m.* rinsing; mouth wash; finger bowl.—**enjuague,** *m.* rinse, rinsing; mouthwash; plot, scheme.

enjugar, *vti.* [b-49] to dry; to wipe.—*vri.* to dry oneself.

enjuiciamiento, *m.* (law) indictment.—**enjuiciar,** *vt.* to indict; to carry on (a case); to pass judgment on.

enjundia, *f.* grease or fat of fowl; substance.

enjuto, *ppi.* of ENJUGAR.—*a.* dried; lean, skinny.

enladrillar, *vt.* to pave with bricks.

enlace, *m.* connection; tie; link; marriage; (mil.) scout.

enlatar, *vt.* to can.

enlazar, *vti.* [a] to lace, bind; to rope, lasso.—*vri.* to interlock, join; to marry.

enlodar, *vt.* to soil with mud.—*vr.* to get muddy.

enloquecer, *vti.* [3] to madden, drive insane.—*vii.* & *vri.* to become insane.—**enloquecimiento,** *m.* madness.

enlosado, *m.* flagstone pavement.—**enlosar,** *vt.* to pave with tiles or slabs.

enlutar, *vt.* to put in mourning; to darken, sadden.—*vr.* to go into mourning.

enmarañamiento, *m.* entanglement.—**enmarañar,** *vt.* to tangle (as hair, etc.); to entangle, involve in difficulties; to embroil.

enmascarar, *vt.* to mask.—*vr.* to masquerade, put on a mask.

enmasillar, *vt.* to putty, cement.

enmendar, *vti.* [1] to amend, correct; to repair; to reform.—*vri.* to mend, reform.—**enmienda,** *f.* emendation, correction, amendment.

enmohecer, *vti.* [3] & *vri.* to rust; to mold.—**enmohecimiento,** *m.* rusting; molding.

enmudecer, *vti.* [3] hush, silence.—*vii.* to become dumb; to be silent.

ennegrecer, *vti.* [3] to blacken; to darken, obscure.—**ennegrecimiento,** *m.* blackening.

ennoblecer, *vti.* [3] to ennoble; to impart dignity to.

enojadizo, *a.* fretful, peevish, ill-tempered.—**enojado,** *a.* angry, cross.—**enojar,** *vt.* to make angry, irritate; to annoy.—**enojo,** *m.* anger; annoyance.—**enojoso,** *a.* troublesome; annoying.

enorgullecer, *vti.* [3] to make proud. —*vri.* to be proud; to swell with pride.—**enorgullecimiento,** *m.* pride; haughtiness.

enorme, *a.* enormous.—**enormidad,** *f.* enormousness, great quantity or size; enormity, atrocity.

enraizar, *vii.* [a] & *vri.* to take root.

enramada, *f.* bower, arbor; grove.

enrarecer, *vti.* [3] to thin, rarefy.—*vri.* to become thin or rarefied.—**enrarecimiento,** *m.* rarefaction, rarity.

enredadera, *f.* (bot.) climber; vine.—**enredador,** *n.* entangler; tattler.—**enredar,** *vt.* to entangle, snarl; to puzzle; to mess up, involve in difficulties; to lay, set (snares, nets).—*vr.* to get entangled, snarled; to get involved.—**enredo,** *m.* tangle, entanglement; puzzle; mischievous lie; plot.

enrejado, *m.* railing, grating; lattice.—**enrejar,** *vt.* to fence with railings; to put a trellis or lattice on.

enrevesado, *a.* frisky; difficult.

enriquecer, *vti.* [3] to enrich.—*vri.* to become rich.

enrojecer, *vti.* [3] to redden; to make red-hot.—*vri.* to blush; to turn red.

enrolar, *vt.* to sign on (a crew); to enroll; to enlist.—*vr.* to become a crew member.

enrollar, *vt.* to roll, wind, wrap up.

enronquecer, *vti.* [3] to make hoarse.—*vii.* & *vri.* to get hoarse.—**enronquecimiento,** *m.* hoarseness.

enroscar, *vti.* [d] to twine, to twist.—*vri.* to curl up, roll up.

ensalada, *f.* salad; hodgepodge, medley.—**ensaladera,** *f.* salad dish o bowl.

ensalmo, *m.* enchantment, spell charm.—*como por e.,* or *por e.,* as i miraculously, suddenly and unex pectedly.

ensalzar, *vti.* [a] to extol, exalt, praise.

ensambladura, *f.,* **ensamble,** *m.* join ery; joint.—**ensamblar,** *vt.* to join couple, connect.

ensanchamiento, *m.* widening, en largement, expansion.—**ensan char,** *vt.* to widen, enlarge.—*e. el cor azón,* to cheer up.—*vr.* to expand enlarge.—**ensanche,** *m.* enlarge ment, widening, expansion.

ensangrentar, *vti.* [1] & *vri.* to stain with blood.—*vri.* to cover onesel with blood.

ensañamiento, *m.* ferocity, cruelty —**ensañarse,** *vr.* to vent one's fury to be merciless.

ensartar, *vt.* to string (as beads); t thread; to link.

ensayar, *vt.* to practice, try, rehearse to test; to assay.—*vr.* to train one self, practice.—**ensayista,** *mf.* essa writer.—**ensayo,** *m.* test; essay; tria experiment; rehearsal; preparator practice.—*e. de coro,* choir prac tice.—*e. general,* (theat.) dress re hearsal.

ensenada, *f.* creek; cove.

enseña, *f.* standard, colors, ensign.

enseñado, *a.* accustomed; trained —**enseñanza,** *f.* teaching; edu cation.—*e. a distancia,* correspon dence courses, distance learning.— *e. de los artes y oficios,* manual train ing.—*e. media* or *secundaria,* sec ondary education.—*e. primaria,* el ementary education.—*e. progra mada,* programmed learning.—*e superior,* higher education.—*p teachings.*—**enseñar,** *vt.* to teach; t train; to show, point out.

enseñorear, *vt.* to lord; to domineer.– *vr.* to take possession (of a thing).

enseres, *m. pl.* chattels; fixtures, acces sories; implements; househol goods.

enseriarse, *vr.* (Am.) to become seri ous; to become angry.

ensillar, *vt.* to saddle.

ensimismarse, *vr.* to become absorbe in thought.

ensoberbecer, *vti.* [3] to mak proud.—*vri.* to become proud an haughty.

ensopar, *vt.* to steep, soak; to drench.

ensordecedor, *a.* deafening.—**ensordecer,** *vti.* [3] to deafen.—*vii.* & *vri.* to become deaf.—**ensordecimiento,** *m.* deafness.

ensortijar, *vt.* & *vr.* to curl, form ringlets.

ensuciar, *vt.* to stain, soil, dirty.—*vr.* to soil one's bed, clothes, etc.; to get dirty; (coll.) to be dishonest.—*vi.* to fit.

ensueño, *m.* dream; illusion, fantasy.

entablar, *vt.* to cover with boards; to plank; to initiate, start (as a negotiation, etc.); to bring (a suit or action).—**entablillar,** *vt.* (surg.) to splint.

entallar, *vt.* to notch, to carve; to tailor.—*vi.* to fit.

entarimado, *m.* parquet floor.—**entarimar,** *vt.* to floor with boards, parquet.

ente, *m.* entity, being; (coll.) guy.

enteco, *a.* sickly; thin, skinny.

entenada, *f.* (Am.) stepdaughter.—**entenado,** *m.* (Am.) stepson.

entendederas, *f. pl.* understanding, brains.—**entender,** *vti.* [18] & *vii.* to understand.—*dar a e.,* to insinuate, hint.—*e. de,* to be an expert in, know.—*vri.* to understand one another; to be understood; to be meant.—*entenderse con,* to have to do with; to deal with.—*m.* understanding, opinion.—*a mi e., según mi e.,* in my opinion, according to my understanding.—**entendido,** *a.* expert; able; posted.—*tener e.,* to understand.—**entendimiento,** *m.* intellect, mind; understanding; comprehension.

enterado, *a.* posted, informed.—*bien e.,* well-informed.—*no darse por e.,* to ignore; to pretend not to understand.—**enterar,** *vt.* to inform, acquaint, advise.—*enterarse de,* to learn, become informed about or familiar with, find out about.

entereza, *f.* entirety; integrity; fortitude, firmness; presence of mind.

enterizo, *a.* of, or in, one piece; whole.

enternecedor, *a.* moving, touching.—**enternecer,** *vti.* [3] to soften; to touch, move to pity.—*vri.* to be moved to pity; to be affected.—**enternecimiento,** *m.* compassion, pity, softening.

entero, *a.* entire, whole; perfect; honest, upright; unqualified, complete; pure; strong, vigorous; uncastrated

(animal).—*por e.,* entirely, fully.—*m.* (arith.) integer.

enterrador, *m.* gravedigger.—**enterramiento,** *m.* burial, funeral.—**enterrar,** *vti.* [1] to bury, inter.

entibiar, *vt.* to make lukewarm; to temper.—*vr.* to cool down.

entidad, *f.* entity; value, importance.

entierro, *m.* burial; funeral.—*e. de residuos,* landfill.

entintar, *vt.* to ink, ink in (a drawing); to tint or dye.

entoldar, *vt.* to cover with an awning; to adorn with hangings.—*vr.* to swell with pride.

entonación, *f.* modulation; intonation.—**entonado,** *a.* haughty, snobbish; (fig.) starchy.—**entonar,** *vt.* to modulate, intone; to sing in tune; to harmonize colors.—*vr.* to put on grand airs.—**entono,** *m.* harmony; snobbishness.

entonces, *adv.* then, at that time; in that case.—*interrog.* then what? and then?—*desde e.,* from then on.—*hasta e.,* up to that time.—*por e.,* at the time.

entornar, *vt.* to half-close; to set ajar.

entorpecer, *vti.* [3] to make numb; to stupefy; to obstruct.—**entorpecimiento,** *m.* torpor, numbness, stupefaction; dullness, stupidity.

entrada, *f.* entrance; gate; admission; admittance; entry; arrival; beginning (of a season); entrée (course at dinner); (com.) entry (in a book); (comp.) input.—*e. bruta,* gross income.—*e. de los artistas,* stage door.—*e. de taquilla,* (número de asistentes) gate.—*pl.* receding hair at temples; (com.) income.

entrambos, *a.* & *pron.* both.

entrampar, *vt.* to ensnare, entrap; to trick, deceive; to entangle; to encumber with debts.—*vr.* (coll.) to get into debt; to get into difficulties.

entrante, *a.* entering; coming.—*mes e.,* next month.

entraña, *f.* entrail.—*pl.* entrails; humaneness; (fig.) heart; affection; the inmost recess of anything.—*hijo de mis entrañas,* child of my heart.—*sin entrañas,* heartless.—**entrañable,** *a.* most affectionate; deep (affection).

entrar, *vi.* (**a, en, por**) to go (in), come (in), enter; to go (into); to flow (into); to be admitted or have free entrance (to); to join; to begin; to fit (of shoes, garment).—*vt.* to introduce, put in.

entre, *prep.* between, among, amongst, amidst; within, in.—*e. manos,* in hand.—*e. tanto,* in the meantime, meanwhile.

entreabierto, *ppi.* of ENTREABRIR.—*a.* half-opened, ajar.—**entreabrir,** *vti.* [49] to half-open, to set ajar.

entreacto, *m.* intermission.

entrecano, *a.* grayish (hair or beard).

entrecejo, *m.* space between inclosures; scowl.

entrecortado, *a.* confused, hesitating; breathless.—**entrecortar,** *vt.* to cut without severing; to interrupt at intervals.

entrecruzar, *vti.* [a] to intercross; to interlace, interweave.

entredicho, *m.* interdiction.

entrega, *f.* delivery, conveyance; installment of a publication; surrender.—*e. contra reembolso,* collect on delivery (COD).—**entregador,** *a.* delivering.—*n.* deliverer.—*e. de la citación,* process server.—**entregar,** *vti.* [b] to deliver; to give up, surrender; to hand (over); (com.) to transfer; to pay.—*a e.,* (com.) to be supplied.—*vri.* to deliver oneself up, surrender, give in.—*entregarse a,* to abandon oneself to or devote oneself to.

entrelazar, *vti.* [a] to interlace, entwine.—**entremés,** *m.* (theat.) one-act farce; side dish.

entremeter, *vt.* to place between.—*vr.* to intrude; to meddle.—**entremetido,** *a.* meddlesome.—*n.* meddler; intruder; busybody.—**entremetimiento,** *m.* intrusion; meddlesomeness.

entremezclar, *vt.* to intermingle, intermix.

entrenador, *n.* trainer, coach.—**entrenamiento,** *m.* training, coaching.—**entrenar,** *vt., vi.* & *vr.* to train.

entrepaño, *m.* panel; shelf.—**entrepiernas,** *f.* crutch, fork of legs.—**entresacar,** *vti.* [d] to pick out or choose; to select; to sift; to thin out.—**entresuelo,** *m.* mezzanine.—**entretanto,** *adv.* & *m.* meanwhile.—**entretejer,** *vt.* to intertwine, interweave.—**entretela,** *f.* (sewing) interlining.

entretener, *vti.* [42] to amuse, entertain; to allay (pain); to delay.—*vri.* to amuse oneself; to tarry.—**entrete-**nido, *a.* entertaining, pleasant; amusing; readable.—**entretenimiento,** *m.* amusement, entertainment, pastime.

entretiempo, *m.* spring or fall (autumn).

entrever, *vti.* [46–49] to glimpse; to see vaguely.

entreverado, *a.* streaky; intermixed.—**entreverar,** *vt.* to intermix, intermingle.

entrevista, *f.* interview, meeting.—**entrevistador,** *n.* interviewer.—**entrevistar,** *vt.* to interview.—**entrevisto,** *ppi.* of ENTREVER.

entristecer, *vti.* [3] to sadden, afflict.—*vri.* to become sad.—**entristecimiento,** *m.* sadness; fretting.

entrometer, *vt.* & *vr.* = ENTREMETER.—**entrometido,** *a.* & *n.* = ENTREMETIDO.—**entrometimiento,** *m.* = ENTREMETIMIENTO.

entroncar, *vii.* [d] (RR.) to form a junction.—**entronque,** *m.* connection; (RR.) junction.

entronizar, *vti.* [a] to enthrone; to exalt.

entubar, *vt.* to provide with casing (oil well, etc.)

entumecer, *vti.* [3] to make numb.—*vri.* to become numb (the limbs), go to sleep.—**entumecimiento,** *m.* torpor; deadness; numbness; swelling.—**entumirse,** *vr.* to become numb.

enturbiar, *vt.* to muddle; to make muddy; to dim, confuse.—*vr.* to get muddy.

entusiasmado, *a.* enthusiastic.—**entusiasmar,** *vt.* to make enthusiastic; to enrapture.—*vr.* to become enthusiastic.—**entusiasmo,** *m.* enthusiasm.—**entusiasta,** *mf.* enthusiast.—*a.* enthusiastic.

enumeración, *f.* enumeration.—**enumerar,** *vt.* to enumerate.

enunciación, *f.,* **enunciado,** *m.* statement.—**enunciar,** *vt.* to state.

envainar, *vt.* to sheathe.

envalentonar, *vt.* to encourage; to make bold.—*vr.* to become bold; to brag.

envanecer, *vti.* [3] to make vain.—*vri.* to become vain.—**envanecimiento,** *m.* conceit.

envasador, *n.* filler, packer; funnel.—**envasar,** *vt.* to put into a container; to pack, to can; to sack (grain).—**envase,** *m.* container; filling, bottling;

packing.—*e. de hojalata,* tin can.—*e. no recuperable* or *retornable,* nonreturnable bottle.

nvejecer, *vti.* [3] to make old; to make look old.—*vii.* & *vri.* to grow old; to look older.—**envejecimiento,** *m.* oldness, age; aging.

nvenenador, *n.* & *a.* poisoner; poisoning.—**envenenamiento,** *m.* poisoning.—**envenenar,** *vt.* to poison.

nvergadura, *f.* breadth of the sails; wingspread of birds; (aer.) span; forcefulness.

nvés, *m.* back or wrong side; back; shoulders.

nviado, *n.* envoy; messenger.—**enviar,** *vt.* to send; to ship.

nviciar, *vt.* to corrupt; to vitiate.—*vr.* (en) to acquire bad habits; to take (to) (drinking, etc.).

nvidia, *f.* envy.—**envidiar,** *vt.* to envy.—**envidioso,** *a.* envious.

nvilecer, *vti.* [3] to vilify, debase.—*vri.* to degrade oneself.—**envilecimiento,** *m.* vilification, debasement.

nvío, *m.* remittance; consignment of goods, shipment.

nvite, *m.* stake at cards; invitation; push.—*al primer e.,* at once; at the start.

nviudado, *a.* widowed.—**enviudar,** *vi.* to become a widower or widow.

nvoltorio, *m.* bundle.—**envoltura,** *f.* cover, wrapper.—**envolver,** *vti.* [47] to wrap; to swaddle; to imply; to contain, carry with it; (mil.) to surround.—*vri.* to be implicated, involved.—**envuelto,** *pp.* of ENVOLVER.

nyesado, *m.* plasterwork; plaster, plastering.—**enyesadura,** *f.* plastering.—**enyesar,** *vt.* to plaster; to chalk; to whitewash.

pica, *f.* epic poetry.—**épico,** *a.* epic.

pidemia, *f.* epidemic.

pifanía, *f.* Epiphany; Twelfth Night.

pigrama, *m.* epigram; witticism.—**epigramático,** *a.* epigrammatic.

piléptico, *n.* & *a.* epileptic.

pílogo, *m.* epilogue; summing up.

piscopal, *a.* episcopal; Episcopal.

pisodio, *m.* episode; incident.

pístola, *f.* epistle, letter.

pitafio, *m.* epitaph.

pitalamio, *m.* nuptial song.

píteto, *m.* epithet.

pítome, *m.* epitome.

poca, *f.* epoch, era.—*é. de paz,* peacetime.—*é glacial,* ice age.—*hacer e.,* to be a turning point.

epopeya, *f.* epic poem.

equidad, *f.* equity; justice.

equilibrar, *vt.* to equilibrate; to counterpoise, counterbalance.—**equilibrio,** *m.* equilibrium, balance, counterbalance.—**equilibrista,** *mf.* juggler; acrobat.

equipaje, *m.* baggage; luggage.—*e. de mano,* hand baggage.—**equipar,** *vt.* to fit out, equip, furnish.—**equipo,** *m.* equipment; team: work crew.

equiparación, *f.* comparison, collation.—**equiparar,** *vt.* to compare, collate; to equate.

equipo, *m.* equipment, outfit; team, crew, squad, gang.—*e. de alta fidelidad,* hi-fi system.—*e. de novia,* trousseau.—*e. de urgencia,* first-aid kit.—*e. móvil,* outside broadcasting unit.

equitación, *f.* horsemanship; riding.

equitativo, *a.* equitable, fair, just.

equivalencia, *f.* equivalence.—**equivalente,** *a.* equivalent, tantamount.—**equivaler,** *vii.* [44] to be equivalent.

equivocación, *f.* mistake, error; equivocation.—**equivocar,** *vti.* [d] to mistake; to confuse; to equivocate.—*vri.* to be mistaken; to make a mistake.—**equívoco,** *m.* equivocation; quibble; pun.—*a.* equivocal, ambiguous.

era, *f.* era, age; threshing floor.—*e. de exploración espacial,* space age.

erario, *m.* public treasury.

erección, *f.* erection; erectness, elevation.

erguir, *vti.* [19] to erect; to set up straight.—*vri.* to straighten up; to stand or sit erect; to swell with pride.

erial, *m.* unimproved land.—*a.* uncultivated.

erigir, *vti.* [c] to erect, raise; to build; to found, establish.—*erigirse en,* to set oneself up as.

erizado, *a.* covered with bristles, spiky.—*e. de,* beset with; covered with; bristling with.—**erizar,** *vti.* [a] to set on end; to bristle.—*vri.* to bristle; to stand on end (of the hair).—**erizo,** *m.* hedgehog; prickly husk.

ermita, *f.* hermitage.—**ermitaño,** *n.* hermit.

erogación, *f.* expense.

erosión, *f.* erosion, wearing away.

erótico, *a.* erotic(al).—**erotismo,** *m.* eroticism.

errado, *a.* mistaken; erroneous.—**er-**

rante, *a.* wandering, nomadic; errant.—**errar**, *vti.* [1-e] to miss (the target, blow, etc.); to fail in (one's duty to).—*vii.* to wander.—*vii. & vri.* to be mistaken; to commit an error.—**errata**, *f.* mistake, error; misprint.—*e. de imprenta*, printer's error, misprint.—**erróneo**, *a.* erroneous, mistaken; unsound.—**error**, *m.* mistake; (comput.) bug.—*e. craso*, gross error.—*e. de hecho*, factual error.—*e. de imprinta*, printer's error.—*e. tipográfico*, typographical error.

eructar, *vi.* to belch.—**eructo**, *m.* belching.

erupción, *f.* eruption; bursting forth; rash.

esa, V. ESE.

esbelto, *a.* slender, svelte, willowy.

esbirro, *m.* bailiff; henchman.

esbozar, *vti.* [a] to sketch.—**esbozo**, *m.* sketch, outline; rough draft.

escabechar, *vt.* to pickle; to stab and kill.—**escabeche**, *m.* pickle; pickled fish.

escabel, *m.* footstool; (fig.) stepping stone.

escabrosidad, *f.* unevenness, ruggedness; harshness; wildness.—**escabroso**, *a.* uneven; craggy; rude; off-color.—scabrous.

escabullirse, *vii.* [27] to slip away; to scamper, sneak away; to cop out (sl.).

escafandra, *f.* diving suit.—*e. espacial*, space suit.

escala, *f.* ladder, stepladder; graduated rule or instrument; port of call; stopover; scale.—*hacer e. en*, to touch, or stop at (a place).

escalación, *f.* escalation.

escalador, *n.* climber; housebreaker.

escalafón, *m.* roster, roll, register.

escalar, *vt.* to scale; to break in.—*vi.* to climb.—*vr.* to escalate.—**escalatorres**, *n.* steeplejack, human fly.—**escaldar**, *vt.* to burn, scald; to make red-hot.—*vr.* to get scalded.

escalera, *f.* staircase; stairs; stairway; ladder.—*e. de caracol* or *e. espiral*, spiral staircase.—*e. de incendios*, fire escape.—*e. de mano*, stepladder, ladder.—*e. mecánica* or *móvil*, escalator.

escalerilla, *f.* thumb index; (aer.) steps; (naut.) gangway.

escalfar, *vt.* to poach (eggs).

escalinata, *f.* flight of stairs (outside of a building).

escalo, *m.* second-story housebreaking.—**escalofrío**, *m.* chill.

escalón, *m.* step of a stairway; rung; rank; social position; (mil.) echelon; (fig.) stepping stone.—**escalonar**, *vt.* (mil.) to form in echelon; to stagger, spread out; to terrace.—**escalope**, *m.* scallop, thin slice of meat.

escalpelo, *m.* scalpel, dissecting knife.

escama, *f.* fish or reptile scale; suspicion.—**escamar**, *vt.* to scale (fish); to cause suspicion.—**escamoso**, *a.* scaly.

escamoteador, *n.* juggler, prestidigitator; swindler.—**escamotear**, *vt.* (in juggling) to palm; to rob by artful means.

escampar, *vi.* to stop raining.

escandalizar, *vti.* [a] to scandalize shock.—*vri.* to be shocked, scandalized.—*vii.* to create commotion to behave noisily.—**escándalo** *m.* scandal; licentiousness; tumult, commotion.—**escandaloso** *a.* scandalous, shocking; turbulent.

escandinavo, *n. & a.* Scandinavian.

escáner, *m.* scanner.—*e. TAC*, CAT scanner.

escaño, *m.* bench (with back).

escapada, *f.* escape, flight, escapade.—*en una e.*, in a minute, in jiffy.—**escapar**, *vi. & vr.* to escape; to run away.—**escaparate**, *m.* shop window, store window.—**escaparatismo**, *m.* window dressing.—**escapatoria**, *f.* escape, fleeing; excuse subterfuge; way out (of difficulty etc.).—**escape**, *m.* escape, flight subterfuge; exhaust (of steam etc.).—*a e.*, or *a todo e.*, at full speed in great haste.

escápula, *f.* scapula.

escapulario, *m.* (eccl., med.) scapular.

escarabajo, *m.* black beetle.

escaramuza, *f.* skirmish; dispute.

escarapela, *f.* badge, rosette in lapel quarrel ending in blows.

escarbar, *vt.* to scrape or scratch (as fowl); to dig; to poke (the fire); to dig into, investigate.

escarcha, *f.* frost, rime; icing.—**escarchar**, *vi.* to freeze.—*vt.* to ice frost (cakes, etc.).

escardillo, *n.* gardener's hoe.

escariar, *vt.* to ream.

escarlata, *f. & a.* scarlet, red.—**escarlatina**, *f.* scarlet fever.

escarmentar, *vii.* [1] to learn by experience; to take warning.—*vti.* to in flict an exemplary punishment on.—**escarmiento**, *m.* warning, lesson, punishment.

escarnecer, *vti.* [3] to scoff, mock. —**escarnio**, *m.* scoffing, gibe, mockery.

escarola, *f.* endive; ruff, frill.

escarpa, *f.* slope, bluff; (mil.) scarp. —**escarpado**, *a.* steep, craggy, rugged.

escarpín, *m.* thin-soled shoe; dancing pump; woolen socks.

escasear, *vi.* to be scarce; to diminish.—**escasez**, *f.* scarcity, shortage; niggardliness; want; scantiness. —**escaso**, *a.* small, limited; little; scarce; niggardly.

escatimar, *vt.* to curtail, lessen.

escayola, *f.* stucco, plasterwork.

escena, *f.* stage; scenery; scene; sight, view.—**escenario**, *m.* (theat.) stage.

escepticismo, *m.* skepticism.—**escéptico**, *n.* & *a.* skeptic.

escindir, *vt.* & *vr.* to split (an atom, etc.).

escisión, *f.* division; schism; fission.

esclarecer, *vti.* [3] to lighten, illuminate; to enlighten, elucidate; to ennoble.—**esclarecido**, *a.* illustrious, prominent.—**esclarecimiento**, *m.* enlightening; elucidation; ennoblement.

esclavina, *f.* short cape.

esclavitud, *f.* slavery.—**esclavizar**, *vti.* [a] to enslave, overwork.—**esclavo**, *n.* slave.

esclerosis, *f.* sclerosis.—*e. múltiple,* multiple sclerosis.

esclusa, *f.* lock; sluice, floodgate.

escoba, *f.* broom.—**escobazo**, *m.* blow with a broom.—**escobilla**, *f.* whisk broom; (elec.) brush of a dynamo.—**escobón**, *m.* swab.

escocer, *vii.* [26-a] to sting, burn; to smart.

escocés, *n.* & *a.* Scot; Scottish.—*m.* Scottish, Scotch (language).—**Escocia**, *f.* Scotland.

escofina, *f.* rasp, file.—**escofinar**, *vt.* to rasp.

escoger, *vti.* [c] to choose, select; to elect.

escolar, *mf.* pupil, student.—*a.* scholastic, school.

escollo, *m.* reef; difficulty, danger.

escolta, *f.* escort, guard.—**escoltar**, *vt.* to escort, guard.

escombrar, *vt.* to clear of rubbish.—**escombro**, *m.* rubbish.

esconder, *vt.* to hide, conceal; to in-

clude, contain.—*vr.* to hide; to skulk.—**escondidas, escondidillas,** *f. pl.*—*a e.,* on the sly, secretly.—**escondite, escondrijo,** *m.* lurking place; hiding place.—*jugar al e.,* to play hide-and-seek.

escopeta, *f.* shotgun, fowling piece. —**escopetazo**, *m.* gunshot; gunshot wound.

escoplo, *m.* chisel.

escorar, *vt.* (naut.) to prop; to shore up.

escorbuto, *m.* scurvy.

escoria, *f.* dross, slag, scum.

Escorpio or **Escorpión**, *m.* (astr.) Scorpio.—**escorpión**, *m.* scorpion.

escotar, *vt.* to cut a dress low in the neck.—**escote**, *m.* low neck, décolletage; tucker; scot, share, quota.—*e. en pico, e. en V,* V-neck.— **escotilla**, *f.* (naut.) hatchway.— **escotillón**, *m.* scuttle, trapdoor; stage trap.

escozor, *m.* burning, smarting.

escriba, *m.* scribe.—**escribano**, *m.* actuary; court clerk.—**escribiente**, *mf.* clerk.—**escribir**, *vti.* [49] to write.— *e. a máquina,* to type.—*vri.* to carry on correspondence with each other.—**escrito**, *ppi.* of ESCRIBIR.— *m.* writing; manuscript; literary composition.—*por e.,* in writing.— **escritor**, *n.* writer, author.—**escritorio**, *m.* writing desk; countinghouse; office.—*e. de cortina corrediza,* rolltop desk.—**escritura**, *f.* writing, handwriting; deed, instrument; (**E.**) Scripture.—*e. aérea,* skywriting.—*e. a mano,* longhand.

escrófula, *f.* scrofula.

escrúpulo, *m.* scruple, hesitation; squeamishness.—**escrupulosidad**, *f.* scrupulousness; exactness, thoroughness.—**escrupuloso**, *a.* scrupulous, thorough, particular; squeamish.

escrutar, *vt.* to scrutinize; to count (the ballots.).—**escrutinio**, *m.* scrutiny; count.

escuadra, *f.* carpenter's square; drawing triangle; angle iron; knee, angle brace; (mil.) squad; (naut.) squadron, fleet.—**escuadrón**, *m.* (mil.) squadron.

escuálido, *a.* weak; squalid; emaciated.

escucha, *f.* listening.—*e. telefónica,* wire tap, phone tap.—*escuchas telefónicas,* wire tapping, phone tapping.—*mf.* scout.—**escuchar**, *vt.* to listen to; to mind, heed.—*vi.* to listen.

escudar, *vt.* to shield, protect.—**escudero**, *m.* shield-bearer, squire.—**escudo**, *m.* shield; escutcheon; protection; coin of different values.—*e. de armas,* coat of arms.

escudriñar, *vt.* to scrutinize, search, pry into, rummage through; to survey, scan, canvass.

escuela, *f.* school; schoolhouse; (art) school, style.—*e. de conductores,* driving school.—*e. de enseñanza primaria* or *primera enseñanza,* primary school.—*e. de equitación,* riding school or academy.—*e. de verano,* summer school.—*e. diferencial,* school for children with special needs.—*e. dominical,* Sunday school.—*e. militar,* military academy.—*e. naval,* naval academy.—*e. nocturna,* night school.—*e. normal,* teachers' college.—*e. técnica,* technical college.—*e. vocacional,* vocational school.

esculpir, *vt. & vi.* to sculpture; to engrave.—**escultor**, *n.* sculptor, (*f.*) sculptress.—**escultórico, escultural,** *a.* sculptural.—**escultura,** *f.* sculpture; carved work.

escupidera, *f.* spittoon.—**escupir,** *vt. & vi.* to spit.—**escupitajo,** *m.* spit, spittle, phlegm.

escurridizo, *a.* slippery.—**escurridor,** *m.* colander; dish-draining rack. —**escurriduras,** *f. pl.* rinsings, dregs. —**escurrir,** *vt.* to drain off; to strain off; to wring (as clothes).—*e. el bulto,* to sneak away.—*vr.* to drop, drip; to slip, slide; to escape, sneak away.

ese, *m.* **esa,** *f.* (*pl.* **esos, esas**), *a. dem.* that.—*pl.* those; **ése, ésa** (*pl.* **ésos, ésas**), *pron. dem.* that (one); (*pl.* those); the former.—**eso,** *pron. dem. neut.* that.—*e. es,* that's it.—*e. mismo,* that's right, precisely.—*ni por ésas,* in no way.—*por eso,* so, therefore.

esencia, *f.* essence.—**esencial,** *a.* essential.

eses, *s. pl.,* reeling of a drunken man.—*hacer e.,* to reel.

esfera, *f.* sphere; clock dial.—**esférico,** *a.* spherical.—**esfero,** *m.* ballpoint pen.—**esterográfico,** *m.* ballpoint pen.

esfinge, *f.* sphinx.

esforzar, *vti.* [12-a] to strengthen; to

encourage.—*vri.* to exert oneself, make efforts, try hard.—**esfuerzo,** *m.* courage, spirit; effort, strong endeavor.

esfumar, *vt.* (art) to shade.—*vr.* to vanish, disappear.

esgrima, *f.* fencing.—**esgrimir,** *vt.* to fence; to wield, brandish (a weapon).

eslabón, *m.* link of a chain; steel for striking fire with a flint.—*e. giratorio,* swivel.—**eslabonamiento,** *m.* linking, uniting; connection, sequence.—**eslabonar,** *vt.* to link; to join.

eslavo, *n. & a.* Slav.

eslogan, *m.* slogan, catch phrase.

eslovaco, *n. & a.* Slovak.

esmaltar, *vt.* to enamel; to embellish.—**esmalte,** *m.* enamel; enamel work.—*e. para las uñas,* nail polish.

esmerado, *a.* careful; carefully done; painstaking.

esmeralda, *f.* emerald.

esmerarse, *vr.* to do one's best, to take pains (with).

esmeril, *m.* emery.—**esmerilar,** *vt.* to polish with emery.

esmero, *m.* careful attention, nicety.

esmoquin, *m.* tuxedo, dinner jacket.

esnob, *mf.* snob.—**esnobista,** *a.* snobbish.—**esnobismo,** *m.* snobbery.

eso, V. ESE.

espaciador, *m.* space bar.—**espacial,** *a.* spatial; space.—**espaciar,** *vt.* to space; to space out; to lengthen intervals; (print.) to lead.—**espacio,** *m.* space, room; space, gap; area; (rad./TV) slot, program.—*e. aéreo,* airspace.—*e. exterior* or *sideral,* outer space.—*el e.,* space.—*e. interplanetario,* (astr.) deep space.— *e.-tiempo,* space-time.—*e. vital,* lebensraum, living space.—*por e. de,* in the space of.—**espaciosidad,** *f.* spaciousness.—**espacioso,** *a.* spacious, roomy; ample.

espada, *f.* sword; swordsman; swordfish; matador.—*pl.* a suit of cards named **espadas.**—**espadachín,** *m.* dexterous swordsman; bully.

espadaña, *f.* (bot.) gladiolus.

espalda, *f.* (anat.) back.—*pl.* back or back part.—*a espaldas,* treacherously.—*de espaldas,* backwards; from behind.—*e. mojada,* (pej. & off.) wetback.—**espaldar,** *m.* back of a seat.

espantada, *f.* stampede, running

away.—**espantadizo**, a. timid, skittish.—**espantajo**, m. scarecrow; fright.—**espantar**, vt. to scare; to chase or drive away.—vr. to be astonished.—**espanto**, m. fright; horror; threat.—**espantoso**, a. frightful; fearful.

España, f.—la E., Spain.

español, n. & a. Spanish.—n. Spaniard (f.) Spanish woman.

esparadrapo, m. adhesive tape, court plaster.

esparcimiento, m. scattering; amusement, relaxation.—**esparcir**, vti. [a] to scatter, spread; to divulge.

espárrago, m. asparagus.

espartano, a. & n. Spartan.

espasmo, m. spasm.—**espasmódico**, a. spasmodic, convulsive.

espástico, a. spastic.

espátula, f. spatula; (art) palette knife; putty knife.

specia, f. spice.—pl. medicinal drugs.

special, a. special.—en e., specially, in particular.—**especialidad**, f. specialty; course, subject (of study).—**especialista**, mf. specialist.—**especialización**, f. specialization; specializing.—**especializar**, vti. [a] to specialize.—vri. (en) to specialize (in).

specie, f. species; kind, sort; piece of news; statement.—en e., in kind.—**especiero**, m. spice box.—**especificar**, vti. [d] to specify.—**específico**, a. specific.—m. (med.) specific.—**espécimen**, m. specimen, sample.

spectacular, a. spectacular.—**espectáculo**, m. spectacle, show.—e. de atracciones, side show.—e. de cabaret, floorshow.—**espectador**, n. spectator.—e. de pie, standee.—pl. audience.

spectral, a. ghostly, eerie; uncanny.—**espectro**, m. specter; spectrum.

speculación, f. speculation.—**especulador**, n. & a. speculator; speculating.—**especular**, vt. & vi. to speculate.—**especulativo**, a. speculative.

spejismo, m. mirage; illusion.—**espejo**, m. mirror, looking glass.—**espejuelos**, m. pl. (Am.) eyeglasses.—e. de sol, sun glasses, dark glasses.

speleólogo, n. spelunker.

speluznante, a. hair-raising.

spera, f. waiting; stay, pause.—en e. de, waiting for.—sala de e., waiting room.—**esperanza**, f. hope; (often

pl.) prospects.—dar esperanza(s), to promise.—**esperanzar**, vti. [a] to give hope to.—**esperar**, vt. to wait for; to hope.—vi. to wait; to hope.—vr. to wait, stay.

esperma, f. sperm; tallow.—e. de ballena, blubber.

esperpento, m. hideous thing or person; absurdity, nonsense.

espesar, vt. to thicken, curdle.—vr. to thicken; to condense.—**espeso**, a. thick, dense; dull, heavy.—**espesor**, m. thickness.—**espesura**, f. thicket, close wood; thickness, density; mop (of hair).

espetar, vt. to skewer, spit; to spring (something) on (one).—**espetera**, f. kitchen rack.

espía, mf. spy.—**espiar**, vt. to spy on; (coll.) to tail.

espiga, f. tassel, ear (as of corn, wheat); pin; dowel; spigot.—**espigado**, a. tall, grown; (agr.) eared, ripe.—**espigar**, vii. [b] to glean; to tenon; to tassel (as corn).—vri. to grow tall; to go to seed.

espina, f. thorn; fishbone; spine; splinter; suspicion.—dar mala e., to cause suspicion or anxiety.—**espinaca**, f. spinach.—**espinazo**, m. spine, backbone.—**espinilla**, f. shinbone; blackhead.—**espino**, m. hawthorn.—**espinoso**, a. thorny; arduous; dangerous.

espionaje, m. espionage, spying.

espiral, a. spiral, winding.

espirar, vt. & vi. to breathe, exhale; to emit.

espíritu, m. spirit; soul; genius; essence; courage.—pl. spirits.—**espiritual**, a. spiritual; soulful; ghostly.—**espirituoso**, a. spirituous; ardent; spirited.

espita, f. faucet, spigot; tap; drunkard.

esplendidez, f. splendor; abundance; liberality.—**espléndido**, a. splendid, generous; resplendent.—**esplendor**, m. splendor; nobleness.—**esplendoroso**, a. splendid, radiant.

espliego, m. lavender.

espolazo, m. violent prick with a spur.—**espolear**, vt. to spur; to incite.—**espoleta**, f. fuse (of a bomb).—e. de tiempos, time fuse.—**espolón**, m. cock's spur; (naut.) ram; breakwater; buttress.

espolvorear, vt. to sprinkle with powder.

esponja, f. sponge; (sl.) gas guzzler.

—**esponjar,** *vt.* to sponge.—*vr.* to swell.—**esponjoso,** *a.* spongy, porous; springy.

esponsales, *m. pl.* betrothal, engagement.

espontáneo, *a.* spontaneous.

esporádico, *a.* sporadic, sporadical.

espora, *f.* spore.

esposa, *f.* spouse, wife.—*pl.* manacles, handcuffs.—**esposar,** *vt.* to shackle.—**esposo,** *m.* spouse, husband.

espuela, *f.* spur; incitement.

espuerta, *f.* two-handled fruit basket.—*a espuertas,* abundantly.

espulgar, *vti.* [b] to clean lice or fleas from; to examine closely.

espuma, *f.* foam; lather; suds; froth; scum.—**espumadera,** *f.* skimmer, colander.—**espumar,** *vt.* to skim, to scum.—*vi.* to froth, foam.—**espumarajo,** *m.* foam or froth from the mouth.—**espumoso,** *a.* foamy, frothy; sparkling (wine).

espurio, *a.* spurious.

esputar, *vt.* & *vi.* to expectorate, spit. —**esputo,** *m.* spittle, saliva; sputum.

esquela, *f.* billet, note.

esquelético, *a.* thin; skeletal.—**esqueleto,** *m.* skeleton; very thin person.

esquema, *m.* scheme, plan; outline.— **esquemático,** *a.* schematic.—**esquematizar,** *vti.* [a] to sketch, outline.

esquí, *m.* ski.—*e. acuático,* water ski, aquaplane.—**esquiador,** *n.* skier. —**esquiar,** *vi.* to ski.—**esquismo,** *m.* skiing.

esquife, *m.* skiff, small boat.

esquila, *f.* small bell; cattle bell; sheep shearing.—**esquilador,** *n.* shearer. —**esquilar,** *vt.* to shear, crop, clip. —**esquileo,** *m.* shearing, clipping.

esquilmar, *vt.* to impoverish; to exploit.

esquilón, *m.* cattle bell.

esquimal, *n.* & *a.* Eskimo.

esquina, *f.* corner, angle (outside).— **esquinazo,** *m.* corner.—*dar e.,* to evade.

esquirla, *f.* splinter of a bone.

esquirol, *mf.* (pej.) scab, strikebreaker.

esquivar, *vt.* to elude, avoid; to shun.—*vr.* to disdain, withdraw. —**esquivez,** *f.* disdain; aloofness; coldness.—**esquivo,** *a.* elusive, evasive; cold.

estabilidad, *f.* stability.—**estable,** *a.* stable, steady.

establecer, *vti.* [3] to establish, found; to decree.—*vri.* to establish or settle oneself.—**establecimiento,** *m.* establishment; institution.

establo, *m.* stable; cattle barn.

estaca, *f.* stake, pole; stick, cudgel —**estacada,** *f.* palisade; paling fence work.—*dejar (a uno) en la e.,* to leave (one) in the lurch.

estación, *f.* season (of the year); moment, time; (RR., radio, tel., police, etc.) station; resort.—*e. de esquí,* ski resort.—*e. de lanzamiento,* spaceport.—*e. de seguimiento,* tracking station.—*d. de servicio,* (aut.) service station.—*e. de trabajo,* work station.—*e. espacial,* space station.—*e. ferroviaria,* railroad station.—*e. generadora,* power plant, power station.—*e. meteorológica,* weather station.—*e. orbital,* orbital space station.—*e. terminal* or *término,* terminus.—**estacional,** *a.* seasonal.—**estacionamiento,** *m.* (auto) parking; stationing, settling.—**estacionar,** *vt.* to park (a car, etc.).—*vr* to park; to remain stationary; to stagnate.—**estacionario,** *a.* stationary, motionless.

estada, estadía, *f.* stay, sojourn, detention; demurrage; cost of such stay.—**estadio,** *m.* stadium.—*e. de béisbol,* ballpark.

estadista, *m.* statesman.

estadística, *f.* statistics.—**estadístico,** *a.* statistical.

estado, *m.* state, condition (of persons or things); estate, class, rank; status, state, commonwealth; state, government; statement, account, report.—*e. benefactor* or *bienestar,* welfare state.—*e. ciudad,* city-state.—*e. civil,* marital status.—*e. de ánimo,* state of mind.—*e. de beneficencia* welfare state.—*e. de coma,* coma.— *e. de cuenta,* bank statement.—*e. de derecho,* democracy.—*e. de emergencia* or *excepción,* state of emergency.—*e. mayor,* (mil.) staff.—*e. policía,* police state.—*estar en e.,* to be pregnant.—*e. tapón,* buffer state.—*hombre de e.,* statesman.— *mal e.,* disrepair.

Estados Unidos, *m. pl.* United States.

estadounidense, estadunidense, *mf.* & *a.* of the U.S., North American.

estafa, *f.* swindle, con, con game —**estafador,** *n.* swindler, sharper shark, con artist.—**estafar,** *vt.* to swindle, con.

estafermo, *m.* idle fellow.

estafeta, f. post office.

estallar, vi. to explode, burst; (of fire, etc.) to break out.—**estallido,** m. outburst.

estambre, m. worsted, woolen yarn; stamen.

estameña, f. serge.

estampa, f. print, stamp; image; picture; engraving.—**estampado,** m. cotton print, calico; stamping; cloth printing.—**estampar,** vt. to print, stamp.

estampida, f. stampede.—**estampido,** m. report of a gun; outburst.—e. sónico, sonic boom.

estampilla, f. rubber stamp; seal; (Am.) postage stamp.

estancación, f. standstill, halt, logjam, blockage, gridlock.—**estancamiento,** m. stagnation.—**estancar,** vti. [d] to stanch, check, stem.—vri. to stagnate; become stagnant.

estancia, f. stay; dwelling, habitation; ranch.—**estanciero,** n. (Am.) ranch owner, cattle raiser.

estanco, a. watertight.—m. monopoly; store for monopolized goods; cigar store.

estandarte, m. standard, banner, colors.

estanque, m. pool, reservoir, pond.—**estanquillo,** m. cigar store; small shop.

estante, m. shelf; bookcase.—**estantería,** f. shelving, shelves.

estaño, m. tin.

estar, vii. [20] to be.—¿a cómo estamos? ¿a cuánto estamos? what day is it? what is the date?—¿estamos? is it agreed? do you understand?—e. bien, to be well.—e. con, to live in company with; to have a (disease), to be ill with; to be in a state of (hurry, anger, etc.).—e. de más, to be out of place, in the way.—e. para, to be about to; to be in a mood or in condition to or for.—e. por, to be in favor of; to feel like.—e. por ver, to remain to be seen.—e. sobre sí, to be on one's guard.—vri. to be, to keep; to stay, to remain.

estarcido, m. stencil.—**estarcir,** vti. [a] to stencil.

estatal, a. pertaining to the state.

estática, f. statics.—**estático,** a. static, statical.

estatua, f. statue.

estatuir, vti. [23-e] to establish, ordain, enact.

estatuario, a. statutory.

estatura, f. stature, height of a person.

estatuto, m. statute, ordinance.

este, m. east, orient.

este, dem. a. (f. **esta;** pl. **estos, estas**) this (pl. these).—**éste,** dem. pron. (f. **ésta;** pl. **éstos, éstas;** neut. **esto**) this, this one; the latter (pl. these; the latter).—a todo esto, meanwhile.—en esto, at this juncture, point; herein (to).—esto es, that is; that is to say.—por esto, for this reason; on this account.

estela, f. wake of a ship.

estenografía, f. stenography.—**estenógrafo,** n. stenographer.

estera, f. mat, matting.—e. de baño, bathmat.

estercolero, m. dung heap.

estéreo, a. & m. stereo.—grabación en e, stereo recording.—**estereofónico,** a. stereophonic.—equipo e., sonido e., stereo.

estereoscópico, a. stereoscopic.—**estereoscopio,** m. stereoscope.

estereotipar, vt. to stereotype; to print from stereotypes.

estéril, a. sterile, barren; unfruitful.—**esterilidad,** f. sterility, barrenness, unfruitfulness.—**esterilizar,** vti. [a] to sterilize.

esterlina, a. sterling.

esternón, m. breastbone.

estero, m. inlet, estuary.

estertor, m. death rattle.

estética, f. esthetics.—**estético,** a. esthetic.

estetoscopio, m. stethoscope.

estiba, f. stowage.—**estibador,** n. stevedore, longshoreman.—**estibar,** vt. to stow.

estiércol, m. dung, manure.

estigma, m. birthmark; stigma, mark of infamy; (bot.) stigma.—**estigmatizar,** vti. [a] to stigmatize.

estilar, vi. & vr. to be customary.

estilete, m. stiletto (dagger); small chisel; (surg.) flexible probe.

estilista, mf. stylist.—**estilo,** m. style.—al e. de, in the style of.—e. de vida, lifestyle.—e. libre, (swimming) freestyle.—e. mariposa, (swimming) butterfly.—e. pecho, (swimming) breaststroke.—por el e., or por ese e., of that kind, like that.—**estilográfica,** f. fountain pen.

estima, f. esteem.—**estimable,** a. estimable, worthy.—**estimación,** f. esteem, regard; estimate.—**estimar,** vt. to estimate, value; to esteem; to judge, to think.

estimulante, *a.* stimulating.—*m.* stimulant.—**estimular,** *vt.* to stimulate; to goad, incite, encourage.—**estímulo,** *m.* stimulus; inducement; incitement; stimulation.

estío, *m.* summer.

estipendio, *m.* stipend, fee.

estíptico, *a.* styptic; constipated.

estipulación, *f.* stipulation.—**estipular,** *vt.* to stipulate, specify.

estirpe, *f.* lineage, pedigree.

estirado, *a.* affected, pompous, stuffy; haughty; (fig.) starchy.—**estiramiento,** *m.* stretching.—**estirar,** *vt.* to stretch, lengthen.—*e. la pata,* (fam.) to kick the bucket.—**estirón,** *m.* pull(ing); haul(ing); rapid growth.

estival, *a.* summer.

esto, V. ESTE.

estocada, *f.* stab, sword thrust.

estofa, *f.* quality, class, sort; stuff, cloth.—**estofado,** *m.* stew.—**estofar,** *vt.* to stew; to quilt.

estoicismo, *m.* stoicism.—**estoico,** *n.* & *a.* stoic(al).

estolidez, *f.* stupidity.—**estólido,** *a.* stupid, imbecile.

estómago, *m.* stomach.

estopa, *f.* tow; burlap; oakum.—*e. de acero,* steel wool.

estoque, *m.* rapier; matador's sword.

estorbar, *vt.* to hinder; to obstruct; to impede.—**estorbo,** *m.* hindrance, obstruction, nuisance.

estornino, *m.* starling.

estornudar, *vi.* to sneeze.—**estornudo,** *m.* sneeze.

estrado, *m.* dais; lecturing platform.—*e. de los testigos,* witness stand.

estrafalario, *a.* odd, eccentric.

estragar, *vti.* [b] to deprave, spoil.—**estrago,** *m.* ravage, ruin, havoc; wickedness.

estrambótico, *a.* odd, eccentric.

estrangulación, *f.* strangling; strangulation; throttling.—**estrangular,** *vt.* to strangle, choke, throttle.

estratagema, *f.* stratagem; trick.

estrategia, *f.* strategy.—**estratégico,** *a.* strategic.

estratificar, *vti.* [d] & *vri.* to stratify.—**estrato,** *m.* stratum; layer.

estratosfera, *f.* stratosphere.

estrechar, *vt.* to tighten; to narrow; to take in (a coat, etc.); to constrain.—*e. la mano,* to shake hands; to greet.—*vr.* to narrow; to bind oneself strictly.—**estrechez,** *f.* narrowness; tightness; poverty.—**estrecho,** *a.* narrow, tight.—*m.* strait, channel.

estregar, *vti.* [1-b] to rub; to scour.—**estregón,** *m.* rough rubbing.

estrella, *f.* star.—*e. de cine,* film star.—*e. fugaz,* shooting star.—*e. de mar,* starfish.—*e. polar* or *de guía,* Pole Star, North Star, lodestar.—**estrellar,** *vt.* to dash to pieces, smash up.—*vr.* to fail; to smash; (**contra**) to crash or dash (against), be shattered (by).

estremecer, *vti.* [3] & *vri.* to shake, tremble, shudder.—**estremecimiento,** *m.* trembling, shaking, shudder(ing).

estrenar, *vt.* to use or to do for the first time.—*vr.* to begin to act in some capacity; to make one's debut; (of a play) to open.—**estreno,** *m.* inauguration; first performance; debut.

estreñimiento, *m.* constipation.—**estreñir,** *vti.* [9] to constipate.

estrépito, *m.* noise, din; crash.—**estrepitoso,** *a.* noisy, deafening; boisterous.

estriar, *vt.* to flute; to gutter.—*vr.* to become grooved, striated.

estribación, *f.* spur of a mountain.—**estribar,** *vi.* (**en**) to rest (on); to be based (on); to lie (in).

estriberón, *m.* stepping stone.

estribillo, *m.* refrain of a song.

estribo, *m.* stirrup; runningboard, step or footboard of a coach; (anat.) stirrup bone; abutment; support.—*perder los estribos,* to talk nonsense; to lose one's head.

estribor, *m.* (naut.) starboard.

estricto, *a.* strict.

estridente, *a.* strident.

estrobo, *m.* loop; oarlock.

estrofa, *f.* (poet.) stanza.

estropajo, *m.* swap; esparto scrubbing pad; worthless thing; dishcloth, dishrag.

estropear, *vt.* to maim, cripple; to damage, spoil.—*vr.* to get out of order, damaged.—**estropicio,** *m.* breakage, crash.

estructura, *f.* structure.—**estructural,** *a.* structural.

estruendo, *m.* din, clatter; uproar.—**estruendoso,** *a.* obstreperous, noisy.

estrujamiento, *m.* crushing, squeezing.—**estrujar,** *vt.* to squeeze, crush.—**estrujón,** *m.* crush, squeeze.

estuario, *m.* estuary, inlet.

estuche, *m.* fancy box or case (as for jewelry, etc.).

estuco, *m.* stucco; plaster.—*e. de Paris,* plaster of Paris.

estudiante, *mf.* student.—**estudiantil,** *a.* student, pertaining to students.—**estudiar,** *vt.* to study.—**estudio,** *m.* study; reading room; studio.—**estudioso,** *a.* studious.—*n.* scholar, expert, student.

estufa, *f.* stove; heater; hothouse; drying chamber; small brazier.

estupefacción, *f.* stupefaction, numbness.—**estupefaciente,** *a. & m.* narcotic.—**estupefacto,** *a.* motionless; stupefied.

estupidez, *f.* stupidity.—**estúpido,** *a. & n.* stupid (person).

estupor, *m.* stupor; amazement.

estupro, *m.* ravishment, rape.

etapa, *f.* stage; station, stop.

éter, *m.* ether.—**etéreo,** *a.* ethereal.

eternidad, *f.* eternity.—**eternizar,** *vti.* [a] to prolong indefinitely.—*vri.* to be everlasting; to be exceedingly slow; to stay forever.—**eterno,** *a.* eternal, everlasting, timeless.

ética, *f.* ethics.—**ético,** *a.* ethical.

etimología, *f.* etymology.—**etimológico,** *a.* etymological.

etíope, *mf.* Ethiopian.—**etiópico,** *a.* Ethiopic, Ethiopian.

etiqueta, *f.* etiquette, formality; formal dress; label, tag; name tag.—*de e.,* ceremonious; formal.—*e. engomada,* sticker.—*poner e. a,* to label.

étnico, *a.* ethnic.—**etnología,** *f.* ethnology.

E.U., *abbr.* (**Estados Unidos**) U.S.—E.U.A., *abbr.* (**Estados Unidos de América**) U.S.A.

eucalipto, *m.* eucalyptus.

eurasiático, eurasio, *n. & a.* Eurasian.—**europeo,** *n. & a.* European.

eutanasia, *f.* mercy killing, euthanasia.

evacuación, *f.* evacuation; exhaustion.—**evacuar,** *vt.* to evacuate, empty; to quit, leave, vacate.

evadir, *vt.* to evade, elude, avoid.—*vr.* to escape; to sneak away.

evaluación, *m.* appraisal, valuation.—**evaluar,** *vt.* to rate, value, appraise; to price.

evangélico, *a.* evangelical.—**evangelio,** *m.* gospel.—**evangelista,** *m.* (bib.) Evangelist.—**evangelizador,** *m.* evangelist.—**evangelizar,** *vti.* [a] to evangelize.

evaporación, *f.* evaporation.—**evaporar,** *vt. & vr.* to evaporate, vaporize.

evasión, *f., evasiva,* *f.* evasion, dodge, escape.—*e. fiscal, e. de impuestos,* tax evasion.—**evasivo,** *a.* evasive, elusive.

evento, *m.* event, contingency.—**eventual,** *a.* contingent; fortuitous.—**eventualidad,** *f.* contingency.

evidencia, *f.* evidence, proof; obviousness.—**evidenciar,** *vt.* to prove, make evident.—**evidente,** *a.* evident.

evitable, *a.* avoidable.—**evitar,** *vt.* to avoid; to shun; to prevent.

evocación, *f.* evocation, evoking.—**evocar,** *vti.* [d] to evoke.

evolución, *f.* evolution; change.—**evolucionar,** *vi.* to evolve; to change; to develop; to perform evolutions or maneuverings.

exacerbación, *f.* exasperation; exacerbation.—**exacerbar,** *vt.* to irritate, exasperate; to aggravate (disease, etc.).

exactitud, *f.* exactness; punctuality; accuracy.—**exacto,** *a.* exact; accurate; precise; punctual.

exageración, *f.* exaggeration.—**exagerar,** *vt.* to exaggerate, overstate.

exaltación, *f.* exaltation.—**exaltado,** *a.* hot-headed; ultra-radical.—**exaltar,** *vt.* to exalt; to praise.—*vr.* to become excited, upset.

examen, *m.* examination; inquiry.—**examinar,** *vt.* to examine; investigate.—*vr.* to take an examination.

exánime, *a.* spiritless, lifeless.

exasperación, *f.* exasperation.—**exasperar,** *vt.* to exasperate.—*vr.* to become exasperated.

excavación, *f.* excavation.—**excavar,** *vt.* to excavate.

excedente, *a.* exceeding.—*m.* surplus.—**exceder,** *vt.* to exceed, surpass; to overstep.—*e. en rango or grado,* to outrank.—*vr.* to go too far; to overstep one's authority.

excelencia, *f.* excellence; excellency (title).—**excelente,** *a.* excellent, first-rate, tiptop.—*interj.* good! fine!

excelso, *a.* elevated, sublime, lofty.

excentricidad, *f.* eccentricity.—**excéntrico,** *a.* eccentric(al); odd.

excepción, *f.* exception.—**excepcional,** *a.* exceptional, unusual.—**excepto,** *adv.* excepting, except, with the exception of.—**exceptuar,** vt. to except.

excesivo, a. excessive.—**exceso,** m. excess; atrocity; surplus.

excitable, a. excitable.—**excitación,** f. excitation, exciting; excitement. —**excitante,** a. exciting, stimulating.—**excitar,** vt. to excite.—vr. to become excited.

exclamación, f. exclamation.—**exclamar,** vi. to exclaim.

excluir, vti. [23-e] to exclude; to bar. —**exclusión,** f. exclusion, shutting out, debarring.—**exclusiva,** f. refusal; rejection, exclusion; sole right or agency.—**exclusivo,** a. exclusive.

excomulgar, vti. [b] to excommunicate.—**excomunión,** f. excommunication.

excremento, m. excrement.

exculpar, vt. & vr. to exonerate.

excursión, f. excursion, trip, tour. —**excursionista,** mf. excursionist.

excusa, f. excuse.—**excusado,** a. unnecessary; reserved, private.—m. toilet, rest room.—**excusar,** vt. to excuse.—vr. to excuse oneself; to apologize.

exención, f. exemption.—**exento,** ppi. of EXIMIR.—a. exempt; free.—e. de impuestos, tax-exempt.

exequias, f. pl. obsequies.

exhalación, f. exhalation; bolt of lightning; shooting star; fume, vapor, emanation.—**exhalar,** vt. to exhale, breathe forth, emit.

exhausto, a. exhausted.

exhibición, f. exhibition, exposition.—**exhibir,** vt. to exhibit, expose; to show.

exigencia, f. demand; requirement; unreasonable request.—**exigente,** a. demanding; exacting.—**exigir,** vti. [c] to require; to exact, demand.

eximio, a. famous, most excellent.

eximir, vti. [49] to exempt, excuse, except.

existencia, f. existence.—pl. (com.) stock in hand.—en e., in stock. —**existente,** a. existent, existing; in stock.—**existir,** vi. to exist, to be.

éxito, m. success; issue, result.—é. de venta, é. de librería, best-seller.—é. rotundo, (fam.) smash hit.

éxodo, m. exodus, emigration; (E.), Exodus.

exoneración, f. exoneration.—**exonerar,** vt. to exonerate.

exorbitancia, f. exorbitance.—**exorbitante,** a. exorbitant, excessive.

exótico, a. exotic, foreign.

expansión, f. expansion, extension; recreation.—**expansivo,** a. expansive; communicative, sociable.

expatriación, f. expatriation.—**expatriar,** vt. to expatriate.—vr. to emigrate, leave one's country.

expectación, f. expectation, expectancy.—**expectante,** a. expectant. —**expectativa,** f. expectation, expectancy, hope.

expectoración, f. expectoration; sputum.—**expectorar,** vt. & vi. to expectorate.

expedición, f. expedition; dispatch; journey.—**expedicionario,** a. expeditionary.—**expediente,** m. file of papers bearing on a case; dispatch; (law) action, proceeding; means; pretext.—cubrir el e., to keep up appearances.—**expedienteo,** m. (coll.) red tape.—**expedir,** vti. [29] to expedite; to issue; to draw out; to ship, send.—**expeditivo,** a. expeditious, speedy.

expeler, vt. to expel, eject.

expender, vt. to spend; to sell.—**expensas,** f. pl. expenses, charges, costs.— a e. de uno, at one's expense.

experiencia, f. experience; experiment.—e. de la vida, sophistication.—**experimental,** a. experimental.—**experimentar,** vt. to experience; to experiment, test.—**experimento,** m. experiment, test.—**experto,** n. & a. expert.

expiación, f. expiation.—**expiar,** vt. to expiate, atone for.

expiración, f. expiration.—**expirar,** vi. to expire; to die.

explanada, f. lawn; esplanade.

explayar, vt. to extend.—vr. to expatriate; to have a good time; to confide (in a person).

explicable, a. explainable.—**explicación,** f. explanation.—**explicar,** vti. [d] to explain.—vri. to explain oneself; to understand (the reason, cause, etc.).—**explícito,** a. explicit, clear; hard-core, explicit.

exploración, f. exploration; (astr., comput., mil.) scan.—**explorador,** n. & a. explorer; exploring; scout; Scout, Boy Scout; (comput., electron., radar, TV) scanner.—**explorar,** vt. to explore; to scout.

explosión, f. explosion.—hacer e., to

explode.—**explosivo,** *m.* & *a.* explosive.—**explotación,** *f.* exploitation; development, working (of a mine, etc.); plant, works; operation, running (of a factory, RR., etc.).—**explotador,** *n.* & *a.* exploiter; exploiting.—**explotar,** *vt.* to exploit; to work (a mine, etc.); to operate, run (a business, RR., etc.); to exploit (to one's own advantage); (Am.) to explode, detonate.—*vi.* to explode.—*hacer e.,* to explode.

expoliación, *f.* spoliation.—**expoliar,** *vt.* to plunder, despoil.

exponente, *m.* & *a.* exponent.—**exponer,** *vti.* [32–49] to expose; to show; to jeopardize.—*vri.* to run a risk, lay oneself open to.

exportación, *f.* exportation, export.—**exportar,** *vt.* to export.

exposición, *f.* exposition, statement; risk, jeopardy; exposure; exhibition.—*e. canina,* dog show.—*e. comercial* or *industrial,* trade fair.—*e. de tiempo,* (phot.) time exposure.—*e. mundial* or *universal,* world's fair.

exposímetro, *m.* exposure meter.

expresar, *vti.* [49] to express.—*vri.* to express oneself; to speak.—**expresión,** *f.* expression; wording; statement; form; phrase, utterance.—**expreso,** *ppi.* of EXPRESAR.—*a.* expressed; express, clear; fast (train, etc.).—*m.* express (train, etc.).

exprimidor, *m.* or **exprimidora,** *f.* squeezer, lemon squeezer, juicer; wringer.

exprimir, *vt.* to squeeze, press out.

expropiar, *vt.* to expropriate.

expuesto, *ppi.* of EXPONER.—*a.* on display; exposed, liable; dangerous; in danger.

expulsar, *vt.* to expel, eject.—**expulsión,** *f.* expulsion, ejection.

expurgar, *vt.* to expurgate.—*sin e.,* unexpurgated.

exquisito, *a.* exquisite, delicious.

extasiar, *vt.* & *vr.* to enrapture, delight.—**éxtasis,** *m.* ecstasy.—**extático,** *a.* ecstatic.

extemporáneo, *a.* untimely, inopportune.

extender, *vti.* [18–49] to extend; to unfold; to spread out; to stretch out; to draw up or issue (a document).—*vri.* to extend, last; to spread, become popular.—**extensión,** *f.* extension; extent, length; expanse, spaciousness; stretch; duration.—

extensivo, *a.* extensive; ample.—**extenso,** *ppi.* of EXTENDER.—*a.* extended, extensive; spacious.

extenuación, *f.* attenuation; exhaustion.—**extenuar,** *vt.* to exhaust, weaken.—*vr.* to languish, waste away.

exterior, *a.* exterior; external, outer; foreign.—*m.* outside; personal appearance; foreign countries.—*en exteriores,* (cine) on location.—**exteriorizar,** *vti.* [a] to externalize, make manifest.—*vri.* to unbosom oneself.

exterminador, *n.* & *a.* exterminator; exterminating.—**exterminar,** *vt.* to exterminate; to raze.—**exterminio,** *m.* extermination, ruin.

externo, *a.* external, outward; exterior.—*n.* day pupil.

extinción, *f.* extinction; extinguishing.—**extinguir,** *vti.* [49-b] & *vri.* to quench, extinguish; to suppress, destroy.—**extinto,** *ppi.* of EXTINGUIR.—*a.* extinct.—**extintor,** *m.* fire-extinguisher.

extirpar, *vt.* to extirpate, root out, eradicate.

extorsión, *f.* extortion.

extracción, *f.* extraction.—**extractar,** *vt.* to epitomize, abstract.—**extracto,** *m.* summary, abstract; extract.

extradición, *f.* extradition.

extraer, *vti.* [43] to extract, draw out, remove.

extralimitarse, *vr.* to overstep one's authority; to take advantage of another's kindness.

extranjero, *a.* foreign, alien.—*n.* foreigner.—*en el e.,* abroad.

extrañar, *vt.* to banish; to estrange; to wonder at, find strange; to miss.—**extrañeza,** *f.* oddity; surprise; estrangement.—**extraño,** *a.* strange; foreign; extraneous; unaccountable.—*n.* stranger, foreigner, outsider.

extraoficial, *a.* unofficial.

extraordinario, *a.* extraordinary.—*m.* extra.—*horas extraordinarias,* overtime.

extraterrestre, *a.* extraterrestrial.

extravagancia, *f.* oddness; folly; eccentricity.—**extravagante,** *a.* eccentric; unusual, odd.

extraviar, *vt.* to mislead, misguide; to misplace, mislay; to embezzle.—*vr.* to go astray; to lose one's way; to miscarry (as a letter); to deviate; to err.—**extravío**, *m.* deviation; aberration; misconduct; misplacement.

extremar, *vt.* to carry to an extreme.—*vr.* to exert oneself to the utmost, take special pains.—**extremidad**, *f.* extremity; end; edge, border; extreme or remotest part.—**extremo**, *a.* extreme, last; furthest; greatest; utmost.—*m.* extreme, highest degree; apex; furthest end, extremity; greatest care.—*con* or *en e.*, extremely.—*hacer extremos*, to express one's feelings with vehemence, to gush.—**extremoso**, *a.* extreme, vehement.

exudar, *vi.* & *vt.* to exude; to ooze out.

eyaculación, *f.* ejection; ejaculation.—**eyacular**, *vt.* to eject; to ejaculate.

F

fábrica, *f.* fabrication; structure; factory; mill.—**fabricación**, *f.* manufacturing; manufacture.—**fabricante**, *mf.* & *a.* maker, manufacturer; making, manufacturing.—**fabricar**, *vti.* [d] to manufacture, make; to build, construct.—**fabril**, *a.* manufacturing.

fábula, *f.* fable, tale, fiction.—**fabuloso**, *a.* fabulous; marvelous; mythical.

facción, *f.* faction, turbulent political party.—*pl.* features, lineaments.—**faccioso**, *a.* factious.—*n.* rebel.

faceta, *f.* oblique side; facet.

facha, *f.* (coll.) appearance, look, aspect.—**fachada**, *f.* (arch.) façade; (coll.) outward appearance.

fachenda, *f.* vanity, boastfulness.—**fachendoso**, *a.* vain, boastful.

facial, *a.* facial.

fácil, *a.* easy; docile, handy; yielding; likely.—**facilidad**, *f.* ease; facility.—*dar facilidades*, to facilitate.—**facilitar**, *vt.* to facilitate, make easy; to provide.

facineroso, *a.* wicked, villainous.

facsímil, facsímile, *m.* facsimile; fax.

factible, *a.* feasible, practicable.

factor, *m.* factor, element, cause; (com.) agent, commissioner.—**factoría**, *f.* agency; trading post; factory.

factótum, *m.* handyman; busybody.

factura, *f.* invoice, bill; workmanship.—**facturación**, *f.* invoicing; turnover; registration; (aer.) check in.—*f. de equipajes*, baggage check in.—**facturar**, *vt.* (com.) to invoice; to bill; (RR.) to check (baggage).—*f. el equipaje*, to check in.

facultad, *f.* faculty; power; branch, school.—**facultar**, *vt.* to empower, authorize.—**facultativo**, *a.* facultative; optional; pertaining to a faculty.—*m.* physician.

facundia, *f.* eloquence.—**facundo**, *a.* eloquent, fluent.

faena, *f.* work, labor, task.

fago, *m.* bassoon.—*mf.* bassoonist.

faisán, *m.* pheasant.

faja, *f.* band; sash; girdle; (geog.) zone; belt.—*f. central* or *divisoria*, media strip (of a highway).—*f. de aterrizaje*, landing strip.—**fajar**, *vt.* to band, belt, girdle.—*vr.* (Am.) (coll.) to fight.—**fajo**, *m.* sheaf; bundle.

falacia, *f.* fallacy, fraud, deceit.—**falaz**, *a.* deceitful, false, fallacious.

falange, *f.* phalanx.

falda, *f.* skirt, flap; the lap; slope; loin (of beef).—*pl.* (fig.) women.—**faldeta**, *f.* small skirt; covering cloth or canvas, flap.—**faldón**, *m.* coattail, shirttail; flap.

falla, *f.* fault, defect; failure; (geol.) fault, slide.—**fallar**, *vt.* to pass sentence, render a verdict on.—*vi.* to fail, be deficient or wanting; to miss, fail to hit; to give way.

falleba, *f.* shutter bolt.

fallecer, *vii.* [3] to die.—**fallecimiento**, *m.* decease, death.

fallido, *a.* disappointed, frustrated.

fallo, *m.* verdict, judgment, decision; mistake, error; defect, fault; (in cards) void; (comput.) bug.—*f. cardiaco*, heart failure.

falsario, *n.* forger; liar.—**falsear**, *vt.* to forge; to misrepresent.—*vi.* to slacken.—**falsedad**, *f.* falsehood, lie; deceit.—**falsete**, *m.* (mus.) falsetto.—**falsificación**, *f.* falsification, counterfeit, forgery.—**falsificador**, *n.* counterfeiter, falsifier, forger.—**falsificar**, *vti.* [d] to counterfeit, falsify, forge; to sophisticate.—**falso,** *a.* false, untrue; incorrect; deceitful, untruthful; forged, counterfeit; sham, imitation (as jewels); unsound.—*f. alarma,* false alarm.—*f. amigo,* (ling.) false friend.

falta, *f.* lack, want, dearth; fault, mistake; defect; offense, misdemeanor; (law) default; (sport) fault.—*a f. de,* for lack of.—*f. de manutención,* nonsupport.—*f. de pago,* nonpayment.—*hacer f.,* to be necessary.—*sin f.,* without fail.—**faltar,** *vi.* to be wanting, lacking; to be needed; to fall short; to fail in; to commit a fault; to offend; to be absent or missing.—*falta un cuarto para las dos,* it is quarter to two.—*f. a la verdad,* to lie.—*f. al respeto,* to treat disrespectfully.—*¡no faltaba más!* (coll.) of course! that would be the limit!—**falto,** *a.* short; deficient.—*f. de respiración,* winded, out of breath.

faltriquera, *f.* pocket.

fama, *f.* fame; reputation.—*de mala f.,* disreputable, notorious.—*mala f.,* disrepute, ill fame.

famélico, *a.* hungry, ravenous.

familia, *f.* family.—*f. de acogida,* foster family.—*f. extensa,* extended family.—*f. monoparental,* single-parent family.—*f. nuclear,* nuclear family.—**familiar,** *a.* familiar; domestic; common, frequent; well-known; homelike; colloquial.—*mf.* relative.—*m.* (aut.) station wagon.—**familiaridad,** *f.* familiarity.—**familiarizar,** *vti.* [a] to acquaint, accustom, familiarize.—*vri.* to accustom, habituate oneself; to become familiar.

famoso, *a.* famous; (coll.) great, excellent.

fanal, *m.* lighthouse; lantern; headlight; bell glass.

fanático, *n.* & *a.* fanatic; (sports) fan. —**fanatismo,** *m.* fanaticism.

fanega, *f.* Spanish grain measure (roughly equivalent to a bushel); land measure.

fanfarrón, *n.* blusterer, swaggerer; boaster.—**fanfarronada,** *f.* boast, bluff, swagger.—**fanfarronear,** *vi.* to brag, swagger.—**fanfarronería,** *f.* bragging.

fangal, *m.* marsh, slough, quagmire. —**fango,** *m.* mire, mud.—**fangoso,** *a.* muddy, miry.

fantasear, *vi.* to fancy; to imagine.—

fantasía, *f.* fantasy, fancy, whim, imagination.

fantasma, *m.* phantom, ghost.—**fantasmagórico,** *a.* phantasmagoric. —**fantasmón,** *m.* an inflated, presumptuous person.

fantástico, *a.* fantastic; whimsical.

fantoche, *m.* vain and insignificant person; puppet.

farallón, *m.* headland; cliff.

farándula, *f.* strolling troop of players.—**farandulero,** *n.* comedian, player.

Faraón, *m.* Pharaoh.

fardo, *m.* bale, bundle; load.

farfullar, *vi.* (coll.) to gabble, jabber.

faringe, *f.* pharynx.

farmacéutico, *a.* pharmaceutical.—*n.* pharmacist, druggist.—**farmacia,** *f.* pharmacy; drugstore.

faro, *m.* lighthouse; beacon; (auto) light, headlight.—*faros de situación,* parking lights.—*f. trasero,* (aut.) tail light.—**farol,** *m.* lantern, light; street lamp; hurricane lamp; bluff.—*echar un f.,* to bluff.—**farola,** *f.* street lamp; lighthouse.—**farolear,** *vi.* (coll.) to boast, brag.

farra, *f.* spree.

farsa, *f.* farce; company of players; sham, humbug.—**farsante,** *mf.* & *a.* humbug; fake.

fascinación, *f.* fascination, enchantment.—**fascinador,** *n.* & *a.* fascinator, charmer; fascinating, charming.—**fascinante,** *a.* fascinating, charming.—**fascinar,** *vt.* to fascinate, bewitch, charm.

fascismo, *s.* fascism.—**fascista,** *a.* & *mf.* fascist.

fase, *f.* phase, aspect.

fastidiar, *vt.* to annoy, bore.—*vr.* to weary; to become vexed, bored or displeased.—**fastidio,** *m.* dislike; weariness; nuisance, annoyance.—**fastidioso,** *a.* annoying; tiresome; displeased, bothersome.

fastuoso, *a.* magnificent, lavish; pompous, ostentatious.

fatal, *a.* fatal; mortal; disastrous; fated.—**fatalidad,** *f.* fatality; fate, destiny; calamity.

fatiga, *f.* fatigue, weariness; hardship; anxiety; hard breathing.—**fatigar,** *vti.* [b] to fatigue, tire.—*vri.* to tire, get tired.—**fatigoso,** *a.* tiring; tiresome, boring; tired, fatigued.

fatuo, *a.* foolish, conceited.—*fuego f.,* will-o'-the-wisp.

fauces, *f. pl.* gullet.

favor, *m.* favor; help, aid; grace; compliment.—*a f. de,* in behalf of; in favor of.—*f. de, hágame el f.* or *por f.,* please.—**favorable,** *a.* favorable.—**favorecer,** *vti.* [3] to favor; to help, befriend; to abet; (of colors, clothes, etc.) to be becoming.—**favoritismo,** *m.* favoritism.—**favorito,** *n.* & *a.* favorite; front-runner.

fax, *m.* fax.—*enviar por f.,* mandar por *f.,* to fax.—*mandar un f. a alguien,* to send someone a fax.—**faxear,** *vt.* to fax.

faz, *f.* face; outside.

fe, *f.* faith, faithfulness; testimony.—*dar f.,* to attest, certify; to witness.—*f. de bautismo* or *de nacimiento,* baptism or birth certificate.

fealdad, *f.* ugliness, homeliness.

febrero, *m.* February.

febril, *a.* feverish.

fecha, *f.* date; standing.—*f. límite,* deadline, closing date, cutoff date.—**fechar,** *vt.* to date.

fechoría, *f.* misdeed, villainy.

fécula, *f.* starch.—**feculento,** starchy.

fecundación, *f.* fecundation, fertilization.—*f. cruzada,* cross-fertilization.—**fecundar,** *vt.* to fertilize, fecundate.—**fecundidad,** *f.* fecundity, fertility, fruitfulness.—**fecundo,** *a.* fecund, fertile; abundant, copious.

federación, *f.* federation, confederation.—**federal,** *a.* federal.

felicidad, *f.* happiness, felicity.—*¡felicidades!* congratulations!—**felicitación,** *f.* congratulation, felicitation.—**felicitar,** *vt.* to congratulate, felicitate.

feligrés, *n.* parishioner.

feliz, *a.* happy, fortunate.—*¡Felices Pascuas!, ¡Felices Navedades!,* Merry Christmas!

felonía, *f.* felony, treachery.

felpa, *f.* plush.—**felpilla,** *f.* chenille.—**felpudo,** *a.* plushy.—*m.* doormat.

femenino, *a.* feminine.—**feminidad,** *f.* femininity.

feminismo, *m.* feminism.—**feminista,** *mf.* feminist.

fenecer, *vii.* [3] to die; to end.

fenomenal, *a.* phenomenal, extraordinary.—**fenómeno,** *m.* phenomenon; (coll.) freak.

feo, *a.* ugly, homely; improper; offensive.—*m.* slight, affront.—*hacerle un f. a alguien,* to slight someone.

feraz, *a.* fertile, fruitful; abundant, plentiful.

féretro, *m.* bier, coffin.

feria, *f.* fair, market, bazaar.—**feriado,** *a.*—*día f.,* holiday.

fermentación, *f.* fermentation.—**fermentar,** *vi.* & *vt.* to ferment.—**fermento,** *m.* ferment, leavening; (chem.) enzyme.

ferocidad, *f.* ferocity.—**feroz,** *a.* ferocious, fierce.

férreo, *a.* of or containing iron; harsh, severe.—*vía férrea,* railroad.—**ferretería,** *f.* hardware; hardware shop.—**ferretero,** *n.* hardware dealer.

ferrocarril, *m.* railroad, railway.—*f. de cremallera,* rack railroad.—*f. elevado,* elevated railroad.—**ferrocarrilero, ferroviario,** *a.* pertaining to a railroad.—*n.* railroad employee.—**ferrotipo,** *m.* tintype.

fértil, *a.* fertile; plentiful.—**fertilidad,** *f.* fertility; abundance.—**fertilizante,** *m.* & *a.* fertilizer; fertilizing.—**fertilizar,** *vti.* [a] to fertilize, make fruitful.

ferviente, fervoroso, *a.* fervent; zealous; devout.—**fervor,** *m.* zeal, fervor.

festejar, *vt.* to entertain; to feast; to woo; to celebrate.—**festejo,** *m.* feast, entertainment; courtship.

festín, *m.* banquet, feast.

festival, *m.* festival.—**festividad,** *f.* festivity; gaiety; holiday.—**festivo,** *a.* festive, gay; humorous, witty; festival.—*día f.,* holiday.

festón, (sew.) scallop (trim).—**festonear,** *vt.* (sew.) to scallop.

fetiche, *m.* fetish.

fétido, *a.* fetid, stinking.

feto, *m.* fetus.

feudo, *m.* fief; fiefdom.

fiado, *m.*—*al f.,* on credit, on trust.—**fiador,** *n.* bondsman, guarantor, surety.—*salir f.,* to go surety.

fiambre, *m.* cold food, cold meats; (coll.) old or late news.—**fiambrera,** *f.* lunch basket; dinner pail.—**fiambrería y rotisería,** *f.* delicatessen.

fianza, *f.* surety, bail; caution; security.—*bajo f.,* on bail.—**fiar,** *vt.* to trust; to bail; to sell on trust, give credit for; to entrust, confide.—*vi.* to confide; to sell on trust, give credit.—*ser de f.,* to be trustworthy.—*vr.* (**de**) to have confidence (in), depend (on), trust.

fibra, *f.* fiber, filament; energy, stamina, vigor; (min.) vein of ore.—**fibroso,** *a.* fibrous.—*f. de vidrio,* fi-

berglass.—*f. óptica,* optical fiber.—
transmisión por f. óptica, fiber-optics.

ficción, *f.* fiction; tale, story.—**ficticio,**
a. fictitious.

ficha, *f.* chip, man, counter, checker,
domino (in games); (tel.) token; index card; personal record; rascal.—
f. médica, medical records.—*f. policial,* police record.—**fichar,** *vt.* to file
a card of personal record (police,
etc.); (coll.) to blacklist.—**fichero,**
m. card index, catalogue.

fidedigno, *a.* trustworthy; creditable.

fidelidad, *f.* fidelity, faithfulness; accuracy.—*alta f.,* high fidelity.

fideos, *m. pl.* vermicelli; spaghetti;
noodles.

fiebre, *f.* fever; intense excitement.—
f. del heno, hay fever.—*f. de oro,* gold
rush.—*f. palúdica,* malaria.

fiel, *a.* faithful, devoted; true, accurate; (pol.) stalwart.—*m.* pointer of
a balance or steelyard.—*al f.,* equal
weight, even balance.

fieltro, *m.* felt; felt hat.

fiera, *f.* wild beast; vicious animal or
person.—**fierabrás,** *m.* (coll.) spit-
fire, bully; wayward child.—**fiereza,**
f. fierceness, ferocity.—**fiero,** *a.*
fierce, cruel; ferocious; huge; wild,
savage.

fierro, *m.* V. HIERRO.

fiesta, *f.* feast, entertainment, party;
festivity, holiday.—*aguar la f.,* to
mar one's pleasure.—*f. de la cosecha,*
harvest festival.—*f. sorpese,* surprise
party.—*hacer fiestas,* to caress; to
wheedle, to fawn on.—**fiestero,** *a.*
gay, jolly.—*n.* jolly person.

figura, *f.* figure; shape; build; image;
face card.—**figurado,** *a.* figurative,
metaphorical.—**figurar,** *vt.* to shape,
fashion; to represent.—*vi.* to figure.—*vr.* to fancy, imagine to occur,
come to mind; to seem.—**figurativo,**
a. figurative.—**figurín,** *m.* fashion
plate; well-dressed man.

fijador, *n.* & *a.* fixer; fastener; fixing;
fastening;—*m.* hair tonic; hair
spray.—**fijar,** *vti.* [49] to fix, fasten;
to determine, establish; to post
(bills); to set (a date).—*vri.* (en) to
settle (in); to fix one's attention
(on); to stare at; to take notice (of),
pay close attention (to).—**fijeza,** *f.*
firmness, stability; steadfastness.—
fijo, *ppi.* of FIJAR.—*a.* fixed; settled;
permanent; (mech.) stationary.—*a
punto f.,* exactly; with certitude.—*de*

f., certainly.—*hora fija,* time agreed
on.

fila, *f.* row, tier, line; (mil.) rank; hatred.—*en f.,* in a row.—*primera f.,*
front row.

filamento, *m.* filament.

filantropía, *f.* philanthropy.—**filántropo,** *n.* philanthropist.

filarmónico, *a.* philharmonic.

filete, *m.* (arch.) fillet; (sewing) narrow
hem; edge, rim; (print.) ornamental
line; (cook.) tenderloin, fillet.

filfa, *f.* (coll.) fib, hoax, fake.

filiación, *f.* filiation; personal description.—**filial,** *a.* filial.

filibustero, *m.* filibuster; buccaneer.

filigrana, *f.* filigree; watermark in paper; fanciful thing.

filipino, *n.* & *a.* Filipino.

filmar, *vt.* (neol.) to film (a moving
picture).

filo, *m.* cutting edge.—*de dos filos,*
two-edged.

filología, *f.* philology.

filón, *m.* (geog.) vein, lode; bonanza.

filoso, *a.* (Am.) sharp.

filosofía, *f.* philosophy.—**filosófico,** *a.*
philosophic(al).—**filósofo,** *n.* philosopher.

filtración, *f.* filtration, leak(age).—**filtrar,** *vt.* & *vi.* to filter.—*vi.* to percolate, filter.—*vr.* to leak out; to disappear; to filter through.—**filtro,** *m.*
filter.

fin, *m.* end, conclusion; object, purpose.—*a f. de,* in order to, so as to.—
a f. de que, so that, to the end that.—
al f., at last.—*al f. y al cabo,* at last;
lastly; after all.—*en f.,* finally, lastly;
in short; well.—*F.,* The End.—*f. de
año,* New Year's Eve.—*f. de semana,*
weekend.—*poner f.,* to put an end
to, stop, get rid of.—*por f.,* at last,
finally.—*sin f.,* endless.—**final,** *a.*
final; conclusive.—*m.* end, conclusion.—*pl.* (sports) finals.—**finalidad,** *f.* finality; intention.—**finalista,** *mf.* (sports) finalist.—**finalizar,**
vti. [a] to finish, conclude; (law) to
execute (a contract, deed).—*vii.* to
end, to be finished or concluded.

financiamiento, *m.* financing.—**financiar,** *vt.* (Am.) to finance.—**financiero,** *a.* financial.—*n.* financier.—
financista, *mf.* (Am.) financier.—**finanzas,** *f. pl.* public finances.

finca, *f.* real estate, land; country estate, farm, ranch.

finés, *a.* Finnish.—*n.* Finn.

fineza, *f.* fineness; kindness, courtesy; gift, favor.

fingimiento, *m.* simulation, pretense, sham.—**fingir,** [c] *vti.* & *vri.* to feign, dissemble; to affect; to imagine.

finiquitar, *vt.* to settle and close (an account).

finlandés, *a.* Finnish.—*n.* Finn.

fino, *a.* fine; thin; subtle; delicate, nice; affectionate; sharp (as a point); polite, urbane.—**finura,** *f.* fineness; politeness; courtesy.

firma, *f.* signature; hand (as hand and seal); act of signing; (com.) firm, house; firm name.

firmamento, *m.* firmament, sky.

firmante, *mf.* signer, subscriber.—**firmar,** *vt.* to sign; to subscribe, set one's hand.

firme, *a.* firm, stable; hard; unyielding; resolute.—*m.* groundwork, bed; roadbed.—*en f.*, definitive, final, in final form.—*adv.* firmly, strongly. —**firmeza,** *f.* firmness; hardness.

fiscal, *a.* fiscal.—*m.* attorney general; district attorney, public prosecutor.—**fiscalización,** *f.* discharge of a FISCAL'S duties; control.—**fiscalizar,** *vti.* [a] to prosecute; to criticize, censure; to control.

fisgar, *vii.* [b] to snoop; to peep; to pry.—**fisgón,** *n.* snooper; busybody.—*a.* snooping.—**fisgonear,** *vi.* to pry; to snoop.

física, *f.* physics.—*f. nuclear,* nuclear physics.—**físico,** *a.* physical.—*n.* physicist.—*m.* (coll.) physical appearance, physique.

fisiología, *f.* physiology.—**fisiológico,** *a.* physiological.

fisión, *f.* fission.

fisonomía, *f.* features; face.

fisura, *f.* (geol.) fissure, cleft; (surg.) fissure of bone.

fláccido, *a.* flaccid.

flaco, *a.* thin, lean; feeble; frail.—*m.* weak point, weakness.—**flacura,** *f.* thinness.

flagrante, *a.* flagrant.—*en f.*, in the act.

flama, *f.* V. LLAMA.—**flamante,** *a.* flaming, bright; brand-new.—**flamear,** *vi.* to flame, blaze; to flutter (banners, sails, etc.).

flamenco, *a.* & *n.* Flemish.—*n.* flamingo.—*cante f.*, Andalusian gypsy singing.

flan, *m.* rich custard.

flanco, *m.* side; flank.

flanera, *f.* pudding pan.

flanquear, *vt.* to flank.

flaquear, *vi.* to flag, weaken; to slacken.—**flaqueza,** *f.* leanness, thinness; weakness; frailty.

flatulencia, *f.* belch, wind.

flauta, *f.* flute.—**flautín,** *m.* piccolo. —**flautista,** *mf.* flute player.

fleco, *m.* fringe, purl, flounce.

flecha, *f.* arrow.—**flechar,** *vt.* to shoot an arrow; (fig.) to inspire sudden love.—**flechazo,** *m.* arrow wound; love at first sight.

fleje, *m.* iron hoop or strap.

flema, *f.* phlegm.—**flemático,** *a.* phlegmatic.

flemón, *m.* gumboil.

fletar, *vt.* to charter (a ship); to freight; to hire.—*salir fletado,* to escape fast; to leave on the run.—**flete,** *m.* freight, freightage; hire price (for transporting freight, cargo).

flexibilidad, *f.* flexibility.—**flexible,** *a.* flexible; docile; lithe.—**flexión,** *f.* flection, flexure.

flirtear, *vi.* (neol.) to flirt.

flojear, *vi.* to slacken; to grow weak.— **flojedad, flojera,** *f.* weakness, feebleness; laxity, negligence.—**flojo,** *a.* loose, lax; weak; flaccid; lazy; cowardly.

floppy, *m.* (comput.) floppy disk.

flor, *f.* flower; blossom; prime; compliment.—*decir,* or *echar flores,* to pay compliments, to flatter.—*f. de edad,* prime of life.—*f. del campo,* wild flower.—*la f. y nata de,* the pride of.—**floreado,** *a.* flowered, figured (goods); made of the finest flour.— **florear,** *vt.* to flower; to bolt (flour); to flourish; to pay compliments to.—**florecer,** *vii.* [3] to flower, bloom; to prosper.—**floreciente,** *a.* flourishing, thriving.—**florecimiento,** *m.* flowering; flourishing.— **floreo,** *m.* idle talk; compliment; (fencing, mus.) flourish.—**florero,** *n.* (Am.) flower vendor.—*m.* flowerpot; flower vase; flower stand. —**floresta,** *f.* wooded field.—**florete,** *m.* fencing foil.—**florido,** *a.* flowery; full of flowers, in bloom; choice, select.—**florista,** *mf.* florist.

flota, *f.* fleet.—**flotación,** *f.* flotation, floating.—*linea de f.,* waterline.— **flotador,** *n.* & *a.* floater; floating. —*m.* float.—**flotante,** *a.* floating. —**flotar,** *vi.* to float; to waft.

fluctuación, *f.* fluctuation; wavering.—**fluctuar,** *vi.* to fluctuate; waver.

fluente, *a.* fluent, flowing.—**fluidez,** *f.* fluidity; fluency.—**fluido,** *a.* fluid; fluent.—*m.* fluid.—**fluir,** [23-e] *vii.* to flow.—**flujo,** *m.* flux, flow.

flúor, fluor, *m.* fluorine; floride.—**fluoración,** *f.* fluoridation.—**fluorescencia,** *f.* fluorescence.—**fluorescente,** *a.* fluorescent.

FM, *abbr.* (**frecuencia modulada**) *f.* FM.

foca, *f.* (zool.) seal; sea dog.

foco, *m.* focus; center, source; electric-light bulb.

fofo, *a.* spongy, soft.

fogarada, fogata, *f.* bonfire, blaze.—**fogón,** *m.* fireside; cooking place, cooking stove, kitchen range; touchhole of a gun; firebox (of a boiler, locomotive, etc.).—**fogonazo,** *m.* powder flash.—**fogonero,** *n.* fireman, stoker.—**fogosidad,** *f.* fieriness, heat, vehemence.—**fogoso,** *a.* fiery; ardent; impetuous; spirited.

follar, *vt.* to paginate, number the pages of a book, etc.—**folio,** *m.* folio.

follaje, *m.* foliage; leafage.

folletín, *m.* newspaper serial.—**folleto,** *m.* pamphlet, booklet, brochure.

fomentar, *vt.* to foment; to warm; to promote, encourage.—**fomento,** *m.* fomentation; promotion; development.

fonda, *f.* inn; eating house; second-rate hotel.

fondeadero, *m.* anchoring ground; haven.—**fondear,** *vt.* (naut.) to sound; to search (a ship).—*vi.* to cast anchor.—**fondeo,** *m.* (naut.) search; casting anchor.

fondillo, *m.* seat of trousers; (coll.) bottom, posterior.

fondista, *mf.* innkeeper.

fondo, *m.* bottom; depth; background; nature (of a person); principal or essential part of a thing; fund, capital.—*f. de comercio,* good will.—*f. de inversión mobiliaria,* mutual fund.—*f. de pensiones,* pension fund.—*f. de reptiles,* slush fund.—*F. Monetario Internacional,* International Monetary Fund, IMF.—*f. rotativo,* revolving fund.—*pl.* funds, resources.—*a f.,* thoroughly.—*andar mal de fondos,* to be short of money.—*en f.,* abreast.

fonética, *f.* phonetics.—**fonético,** *a.* phonetic.—**fónico,** *a.* phonic, acoustic.

fonocaptor, *m.* (electron.) pickup.

fonógrafo, *m.* phonograph.

fontana, *f.* fountain, spring, water jet.—**fontanar,** *m.* water spring.

football, *m.* football.

forajido, *n.* outlaw, fugitive; bandit.

forastero, *a.* foreign.—*n.* stranger; outsider.

forcejar, forcejear, *vi.* to struggle, strive; to contest, contend; to resist; to tussle.

forestal, *a.* pertaining to a forest.—*ingeniería, f.,* forestry.

forja, *f.* smelting furnace; smithy; forge; forging.—**forjador,** *n.* blacksmith, forger.—**forjar,** *vt.* to forge; to frame, form.

forma, *f.* form, shape; manner; method, order; pattern, mold; format; block (for hats, etc.).—*pl.* (of persons) figure.—*de f. que,* so as, so that.—*en f.,* in due form; in a thorough and proper manner.—*tomar f.,* to develop, to materialize.—**formación,** *f.* formation, forming.—**formal,** *a.* formal, regular, methodical; proper; serious; truthful, reliable; well-behaved.—**formalidad,** *f.* formality; exactness, punctuality; seriousness, solemnity; requisite; established practice.—**formalismo,** *m.* formalism.—**formalista,** *mf.* formalist.—**formalizar,** *vti.* [a] to put in final form; to legalize.—*vri.* to become serious or earnest.—**formar,** *vt.* to form; to shape.—*f. parte de,* to be a member of.—*vr.* to develop; to take form.—**formativo,** *a.* formative.—**formato,** *m.* format (of a book).

fórmula, *f.* formula; recipe, prescription.—**formulación,** *f.* formulation.—*f. de datos,* (comput.) data capture.—**formular,** *vt.* to formulate.—**formulismo,** *m.* formulism; red tape.

fornido, *a.* robust, husky, stout, stalwart.

foro, *m.* forum; court of justice; bar, the legal profession; back (in stage scenery).

forraje, *m.* forage, fodder; foraging.

forrar, *vt.* to line (as clothes); to cover (as a book, umbrella, etc.); (anat.) to sheathe.—**forro,** *m.* lining, doubling; cover.

fortalecedor, *n.* & *a.* fortifier; fortifying.—**fortalecer,** *vti.* [3] to fortify, strengthen, corroborate.—**fortalecimiento,** *m.* fortifying; fortification, defenses.—**fortaleza,** *f.* fortitude; strength, vigor; fortress, fort.—**fortificación,** fortification; fort; military architecture.—**fortificar,** *vti.* [d] to strengthen; (mil.) to fortify.—**fortín,** *m.* small fort.

fortuna, *f.* fortune; good luck; wealth.—*por f.,* fortunately.

forúnculo, *m.* = FURUNCULO.

forzar, *vti.* [12-a] to force, break in (as a door); to compel; to subdue by force; to ravish.—**forzoso,** *a.* obligatory, compulsory; unavoidable.—**forzudo,** *a.* strong, vigorous.

fosa, *f.* grave.—*f. común,* common grave; pauper's grave.—*f. nasal,* nostril.—*f. séptica,* septic tank.

fosco, *a.* frowning; cross.

fosfato, *m.* phosphate.

fosforescencia, *f.* phosphorescence.—**fosforecer,** *vii.* [3] to phosphoresce.—**fosforera,** *f.* matchbox.—**fósforo,** *m.* phosphorous; friction match.—*f. de seguridad,* safety match.

foso, *m.* pit; stage pit; moat.

foto, *f.* photo (photograph).—**fotocopia,** *f.* photocopy.—**fotocopiadora,** *f.* photocopier.—**fotocopiar,** *vt.* to photocopy.—**fotoeléctrico,** *a.* photoelectric.—**fotofija,** *f.* photo-finish camera.—**fotogénico,** *a.* photogenic.—**fotograbado,** *m.* photoengraving, photogravure.—**fotografía,** *f.* photography; photograph.—*f. con los rayos X,* X-ray.—**fotografiar,** *vt.* to photograph.—**fotógrafo,** *n.* photographer.—**fotopila,** *f.* solar battery.

frac, *m.* tail coat.

fracasar, *vi.* to fail.—**fracaso,** *m.* downfall; failure.

fracción, *f.* fragment; fraction.—**fraccionamiento,** *m.* division into fractions.—**fraccionario,** *a.* fractional.

fractura, *f.* fracture; breaking, crack.—**fracturar,** *vt.* & *vi.* to fracture, break.

fragancia, *f.* fragrance, scent.—**fragante,** *a.* fragrant.

frágil, *a.* brittle, breakable, fragile.—**fragilidad,** *f.* fragility; frailty.

fragmentario, *a.* fragmentary.—**fragmento,** *m.* fragment.

fragor, *m.* clamorous noise; blare.

fragosidad, *f.* roughness; impenetrability, thickness, wildness (of a forest); craggedness.—**fragoso,** *a.* craggy, rough; full of brambles and briers, roaring.

fragua, *f.* forge; smithy.—**fraguar,** *vt.* to forge; to hammer out; to plan, plot.—*vi.* (of concrete, etc.) to set.

fraile, *m.* friar, monk.

frambuesa, *f.* (bot.) raspberry.

francachela, *f.* (coll.) lark, spree; gala meal.

francés, *a.* French.—*m.* French language.—*n.* Frenchman (-woman).

franco, *a.* frank, open; franc; free, clear, disengaged; exempt.—*f. a bordo,* free on board.—*m.* franc.

francotirador, sniper.

franela, *f.* flannel.

franja, *f.* fringe, trimming, band; stripe; strip (of land).

franqueadora, *f.* postage meter.—**franquear,** *vt.* to exempt; to grant immunity to; to enfranchise; to prepay (postage); to open, clear.—*vr.* to unbosom oneself.—**franqueo,** *m.* postage.—*f. concertado,* postal permit.—**franqueza,** *f.* frankness.—*con f.,* frankly.—**franquicia,** *f.* exemption from taxes; franchise, grant.

frasco, *m.* flask, vial.

frase, *f.* phrase.—*f. hecha,* cliché; set phrase.—**fraseología,** *f.* phraseology; verbosity; wording.

fraternal, *a.* brotherly, fraternal.—**fraternidad,** *f.* fraternity, brotherhood.—**fraternizar,** *vii.* [a] to fraternize.

fraude, *m.,* **fraudulencia,** *f.* fraud.—**fraudulento,** *a.* fraudulent.

frazada, *f.* blanket.

frecuencia, *f.* frequency.—*con f.,* frequently.—**frecuentar,** *vt.* to frequent.—**frecuente,** *a.* frequent.

fregadero, *m.* kitchen sink.—**fregar,** *vti.* [1-b] to rub; to wash; to scrub, scour; (Am.) to annoy, bother.—**fregasuelos,** *m.* mop.—**fregona,** *f.* kitchenmaid; dishwasher; scrubwoman.

freidora, *f.* deep fryer.—**freir,** *vti.* & *vri.* [35–19] to fry.—*f. en aceite,* to deep-fry.

frenar, *vt.* to brake, apply the brake to; to restrain; to bridle.

frenesí, *m.* frenzy, fury, madness; folly; (fam.) brainstorm.—**frenético,** *a.* mad, frantic, frenzied.

freno, *m.* brake; bridle or bit of the bridle; curb, restraint, control, deterrent.—*f. de mano,* parking brake.—*frenos asistidos,* power brakes.

frente, *f.* forehead; countenance.—*m.* front, fore part, façade.—*al f.,* opposite; carried forward.—*al f. de,* in front of; in charge of.—*de f.,* from the front; front; facing; abreast.—*f. a,* opposite, facing.—*f. a f.,* face to face.—*f. por f.,* directly opposite.—*hacer f.,* to face (a problem, etc.); to meet (a demand, etc.).

fresa, *f.* strawberry; (mech.) drill, bit, milling tool.

fresca, *f.* cool air, fresh air; fresh remark.—**fresco,** *a.* fresh; (of weather, etc.) cool; just made, finished, or gathered.—*m.* cool or fresh air; (art) fresco.—*hacer f.,* to be cool.—*tomar el f.,* to get or go out for some fresh air.—**frescor,** *m.* cool; freshness.—**frescura,** *f.* freshness; impudence; unconcern.

fresno, *m.* ash tree; ash wood.

frialdad, *f.* coldness; unconcern, coolness.

fricasé, *m.* fricassee.

fricción, *f.* friction, rubbing.—**friccionar,** *vt.* to rub.

friega, *f.* friction, rubbing.

frigidez, *f.* frigidity.—**frígido,** *a.* frigid.—**frigorífico,** *a.* refrigerating.—*m.* refrigerator, storage house or room.

frijol, *m.* bean.—*f. colorado,* kidney bean.—*f. de media luna,* Lima bean.—*pl.* beans; food.—*f. refritos,* refried beans.

frío, *a.* cold; frigid; indifferent, unemotional; dull.—*m.* cold, coldness.—*hacer f.,* to be cold.—*tener f.,* to feel cold.—**friolento,** *a.* chilly; very sensitive to cold.

friolera, *f.* trifle, bauble.

frisar, *vi.* (en) to approach; to be near (to).

frita, *f.* (Am.) hamburger.—**fritada,** *f.* fry; dish of anything fried.—**frito,** *ppi.* of FREÍR.—*estar f.,* to be lost; to be annoyed.—*m.* fry.—**fritura,** *f.* fry, fritter.

frivolidad, *f.* frivolity.—**frívolo,** *a.* frivolous, trifling.

fronda, *f.* leaf; frond.—*pl.* foliage, verdure.—**frondosidad,** *f.* frondage, leafy foliage.—**frondoso,** *a.* leafy, luxuriant.

frontal, *a.* frontal, pertaining to the forehead.—*m.* (eccl.) frontal; (anat.) frontal bone.

frontera, *f.* frontier, border.—**fronterizo,** *a.* frontier; facing, opposite.—**frontero,** *a.* opposite, facing.

frontis, *m.* frontispiece, façade.—**frontispicio,** *m.* frontispiece.

frontón, *m.* main wall of a handball court; Jai-Alai court.

frotación, *f.* rubbing.—**frotamiento,** *m.* rubbing.—**frotar,** *vt.* to rub.

fructífero, *a.* fruit-bearing; fruitful.—**fructificación,** *f.* fructification.—**fructificar,** *vii.* [d] to bear fruit; to yield profit.

frugal, *a.* frugal.—**frugalidad,** *f.* frugality, thrift.

fruición, *f.* fruition, enjoyment.

fruncimiento, *m.* wrinkling; shirring.—**fruncir,** *vti.* [a] to wrinkle; to gather in pleats; to shrivel.—*f. el ceño,* or *f. las cejas,* to frown.—*f. los labios,* to curl or pucker the lips.

fruslería, *f.* trifle, bauble, tidbit.

frustración, *f.* frustration.—**frustrar,** *vt.* to frustrate.—*vr.* to fail.

fruta, *f.* fruit.—**frutal,** *a.* fruit-bearing; fruit.—*m.* fruit tree.—**frutería,** *f.* fruit store.—**frutero,** *n.* fruit seller; fruit basket, fruit dish.—**fruto,** *m.* fruit; fruits, result; benefice, profit.

fucilazo, *m.* wildfire, sheet lightning.

fuego, *m.* fire; (Am.) skin eruption; firing of firearms; passion.—*estar entre dos fuegos,* to be caught in the crossfire.—*f. amigo,* (mil.) friendly fire.—*f. cruzado,* crossfire.—*f. fatuo,* will-o'-the-wisp.—*fuegos artificiales,* fireworks.—*hacer f.,* to fire, shoot.—*romper f.,* to start shooting.

fuelle, *m.* bellows; blower; puckers in clothes.

fuente, *f.* water spring; fountain; source; serving dish, platter.—*beber en buenas fuentes,* to be well-informed.—*f. de sodas,* soda fountain.

fuera, *adv.* out, outside.—*de f.,* from the outside.—*f. de,* besides, in addition.—*f. de sí,* beside oneself; aghast.—*hacia f.,* outward.—*por f.,* on the outside.—*interj.* out! away! put him out! get out!

fuero, *m.* statute, law; jurisdiction; privilege or exemption; compilation of laws.

fuerte, *a.* strong; powerful; intense; firm, compact; hard, not malleable.—*m.* fort, fortress; strong point;

(mus.) forte.—*adv.* strongly, hard, copiously.—**fuerza**, *f.* force; power; strength; stress; violence; firmness; (mil.) force(s).—*a f. de*, by dint of, by force of.—*a la f., a viva f.*, by main force, forcibly.—*f. aceleratriz*, acceleration.—*f. de agua*, water power.—*f. de inercia*, inertia.—*f. de voluntad*, will power.—*f. mayor*, superior force.—*f. retadatriz*, deceleration.—*f. viva*, kinetic energy.—*fuerzos del orden* or *de orden público*, police.

fuetazo, *m.* (Am.) blow with a whip. —**fuete**, *m.* horsewhip, riding whip.

fuga, *f.* flight; escape; runaway; elopement; leak, leakage; fugue.—**fugacidad**, *f.* brevity.—**fugarse**, *vri.* [b] to flee, run away; to escape, leak out.—**fugaz**, *a.* brief.—**fugitivo**, *n.* & *a.* fugitive, runaway.—*a.* brief, perishable, unstable.

fulano, *n.* (Mr.) so-and-so.—*f. de tal*, so-and-so.

fulgor, *m.* brilliancy.—**fulgurar**, *vi.* to flash, shine with brilliancy.

fullero, *a.* (coll.) shady, dishonest.—*n.* cheat, sharper; card sharp.

fumada, *f.* puff, whiff, (of smoke).—**fumadero**, *m.* smoking room.—**fumador**, *n.* smoker.—*a.* addicted to smoking.—**fumar**, *vt.* & *vi.* to smoke (cigars, etc.).

fumigación, *f.* fumigation.—*f. aérea*, crop dusting.—**fumigar**, *vti.* [b] to fumigate.

funámbulo, *m.* tightrope walker.

función, *f.* function; duty; functioning; religious ceremony; (theat.) performance, play.—*f. secundario*, side show.—**funcional**, *a.* functional.—**funcionamiento**, *m.* functioning, working, operation, performance.—**funcionar**, *vi.* to function; to work, run.—**funcionario**, *n.* functionary, public official.

funda, *f.* case, sheath, cover, envelope, slip.—*f. de almohada*, pillowcase.—*f. de asiento*, seat cover.

fundación, *f.* foundation; founding; beginning, origin.—**fundador**, *n.* founder.—**fundamental**, *a.* fundamental, basal.—**fundamentar**, *vt.* to establish on a basis; to base; to set firm.—**fundamento**, *m.* basis; reason, fundamental principle; root; good behavior, orderliness.—**fundar**, *vt.* to found; to raise; to establish, institute; to base, ground. —*vr.* (**en**) to base one's opinion (on).

fundición, *f.* smelting; foundry.—**fundir**, *vt.* to fuse or melt; to merge, blend; to be ruined.

fúnebre, *a.* funereal, mournful; funeral; dark, lugubrious.—**funeral(es)**, *m.* funeral.—**funeraria**, *f.* funeral parlor.—**funerario, funeral**, *a.* funeral.—**funesto**, *a.* ill-fated; fatal; mournful; regrettable.

fungicida, *a.* & *m.* fungicide.

fungir, *vii.* [c] to act in some capacity.

fungosidad, *f.* fungus, fungous growth; spongy morbid growth.

funicular, *m.* funicular railway; cable car, cable railway.

furgón, *m.* wagon; boxcar.—*f. de cola*, (RR.) caboose.

furia, *f.* fury, rage; ill-tempered person.—**furibundo, furioso**, *a.* furious; frantic.—**furor**, *m.* furor, fury, anger; enthusiasm; exaltation of fancy.—*hacer f.*, to be the rage.

furtivo, *a.* furtive, clandestine.

furúnculo, *m.* (med.) boil.

fuselaje, *m.* fuselage.

fusible, *a.* fusible.—*m.* (elec.) fuse.

fusil, *m.* rifle, gun.—**fusilamiento**, *m.* execution by shooting.—**fusilar**, *vt.* to shoot, execute by shooting.—**fusilazo**, *m.* rifle shot.—**fusilería**, *f.* (mil.) guns, rifles.—**fusilero**, *m.* rifleman.

fusión, *f.* fusion, melting; union; merger; (phys.) fusion.—*f. de empresas*, merger.—*f. fría*, cold fusion.—*f. nuclear*, nuclear fusion.—**fusionar**, *vt.* to unite, merge.—*vr.* to merge, form a merger.

fusta, *f.* whiplash.—**fustigar**, *vti.* [b] to lash.

fútbol, *m.* soccer.—*f. americano*, (American) football.—**futbolista**, *mf.* soccer player; football player. —**futbolístico**, *a.* soccer; football.

futesa, *f.* trifle, bagatelle.—**fútil**, *a.* trifling, trivial.

futuro, *a.* future.—*n.* betrothed, future husband (wife); future.—*en lo f.*, in the future, hereafter.

G

gabacho, *a.* (coll.) Frenchlike.—*m.* (coll.) Frenchman.

gabán, *m.* overcoat.

garbardina, *f.* gabardine.

gabinete, *m.* cabinet (of a government); sitting room; private parlor; studio, study; dentist's or doctor's office.—*g. de aseo,* washroom, powder room.—*g. de trabajo,* workroom.

gacela, *f.* gazelle.

gaceta, *f.* official gazette.—**gacetilla,** *f.* personal-news column; gossip; newspaper squib.—**gacetillero,** *n.* **gacetista,** *mf.* newsmonger, gossip.

gachas, *f. pl.* porridge, mush.

gacho, *a.* bent; drooping; turned down.—*a gachas,* (coll.) on all fours.—*con las orejas gachas,* (coll.) crestfallen.

gafas, *f. pl.* spectacles.—*g. de sol,* sunglasses.

gago, *n.* stammerer, stutterer.—**gaguear,** *vi.* to stutter.—**gaguera,** *f.* stuttering.

gaita, *f.* hurdy-gurdy.—*asomar la g.,* to stick out one's neck.—*g. gallega,* bagpipe.—**gaitero,** *n.* piper, bagpipe player.

gaje, *m.*—*pl.* fees.—*gajes del oficio,* fisherman's luck.

gajo, *m.* torn off branch (of a tree); bunch of fruit; segment of fruit.

gala, *f.* full dress; array; gala.—*pl.* trappings.—*galas de novia,* bridal trousseau.—*hacer g. de,* to be proud of, glory in, boast of.

galán, *m.* gallant; lover, wooer; (theat.) leading man.—**galante,** *a.* gallant, polished, attentive to ladies.—**galantear,** *vt.* to court, woo.—**galanteo,** *m.* gallantry, courtship, wooing.—**galantería,** *f.* gallantry, courtesy, politeness; compliment to a lady.

galápago, *m.* fresh-water tortoise.

galardón, *m.* reward, prize.

galaxia, *f.* galaxy.

galeno, *m.* (coll.) physician.

galeote, *m.* galley slave.

galera, *f.* (naut., print.) galley; wagon, van; prison.—**galerada,** *f.* (print.) galley; galley proof.

galería, *f.* gallery, lobby, corridor; (theat.) gallery; art museum; collection of paintings; (com.) shopping center, mall.—*g. de alimentación,* indoor food market.—*g. de tiro al blanco,* shooting gallery.

galerna, *f.* (naut.) stormy northwest wind.

galés, *n.* & *a.* Welshman; Welsh.

Gales, *m.*—*el país de G.,* Wales.—*el Príncipe de Gales,* the Prince of Wales.

galgo, *n.* greyhound, grayhound.—*carreras de g.,* greyhound racing, dog racing, dog races.

gallardete, *m.* pennant, streamer.

gallardía, *f.* gracefulness; bravery; nobleness.—**gallardo,** *a.* graceful, elegant; lively; brave.

gallear, *vi.* to raise the voice in anger; to crow; to bully.

gallegada, *f.* a Galician dance and its tune.—**gallego,** *n.* & *a.* Galician; (fam.) Spaniard.—*m.* Galician (language).

galleta, *f.* cracker, biscuit, hardtack; cookie; slap.—**galletica,** *f.* small or fine cracker or biscuit.—**galletita,** *f.*—*g. china,* fortune cookie.—*g. salada,* saltine.

gallina, *f.* hen.—*g. de Guinea* or *guineo,* guinea hen.—*mf.* coward.—*la g. ciega,* blindman's buff.—**gallinero,** *m.* poultry yard, hen coop or house; (coll., theat.) top gallery.—**gallito,** *m.* small cock; cock of the walk, bully.—**gallo,** *m.* cock, rooster; false note in singing; bully.—*g. de pelea,* or *inglés,* gamecock.—*patas de g.,* wrinkles in the corner of the eye.

galillo, *m.* uvula, soft palate.

galocha, *f.* galosh, clog.

galón, *m.* gallon; braid, tape, binding lace; stripe, chevron (on uniforms).—**galonear,** *vt.* (sewing) to bind; to trim with braid.

galopar, *vi.* to gallop.—**galope,** *m.* gallop; haste, speed.—*a g.,* hurriedly, speedily.—**galopín,** *m.* ragamuffin; rascal; shrewd fellow.

galpón, *m.* (Am.) shed.

galvanizar, *vti.* [a] to galvanize; to electroplate.

gamo, m. buck of the fallow deer.

gamuza, f. chamois; chamois skin; suede.

gana, f. appetite, hunger; desire; mind.—*dar g.,* or *ganas de,* to arouse desire to.—*de buena g.,* willingly.—*de mala g.,* unwillingly.—*no me da la g.,* I don't want to, I won't.—*tener g.,* or *ganas de,* to desire; to wish to.

ganadería, f. cattle raising; cattle ranch; cattle brand.—**ganadero,** n. cattleman; cattle dealer; stock farmer.—a. pertaining to cattle.—**ganado,** m. cattle; herd.—*g. bovino* or *vacuno,* cattle.—*g. caballar* or *equino,* horses.—*g. cabrío* or *caprino,* goats.—*g. lanar* or *ovino,* sheep.—*g. porcino,* or *cerda,* pigs, hogs, swine.—*pp.*—*g. a pulso,* hard-won.

ganador, n. & a. winner; winning.—**ganancia,** f. gain, profit.—*g. líquida,* (com.) net.—**ganancioso,** a. lucrative, profitable; gaining.—**ganapán,** m. drudge; common laborer; coarse man.—**ganar,** vt. to win; to gain; to earn.—*g. el pan, la vida,* or *el sustento,* to make a living.

gancho, m. hook; crook; crotch.—*echar el g.,* (fig.) to catch; to hook.—*g. del pelo,* hairpin.—*tener g.,* (coll.) to be attractive.

gandul, n. (coll.) idler, loafer, tramp.—**gandulería,** f. idleness, laziness.

ganga, f. bargain; windfall.

gangoso, a. twangy.

gangrena, f. gangrene.—**gangrenarse,** vr. to become gangrenous.

ganguear, vi. to snuffle; to speak nasally.—**gangueo,** m. snuffle; nasal speech.

gansada, f. (coll.) stupidity.—**ganso,** n. goose, gander; silly person; ninny.

ganzúa, f. picklock, skeleton key; burglar.

gañán, m. farm hand; rustic; (fig.) uncouth, brutal person.

gañote, m. (coll.) throat.

garabateo, m. scribbling, scrawling.—**garabato,** m. scrawl, scribble; hook.

garaje, m. garage.—*g. de dos plazas,* two-car garage.

garantía, f. guarantee; (com. and law) warranty, guaranty, security.—**garantizar,** vti. [a] to guarantee, vouch for.

garañón, m. stallion.

garapiña, f. (cook.) icing.—**garapiñado,** a. candied, sugarcoated.—**garapiñar,** vt. (cook.) to ice.

garbanzo, m. chickpea.

garbo, m. grace, gracefulness, elegant carriage.—**garboso,** a. graceful, sprightly.

gardenia, f. gardenia.

garete, m.—*al g.,* (naut.) adrift.

garfio, m. hook; gaff.

garganta, f. throat; gullet; gorge.—**gargantilla,** f. necklace.

gárgara, f., **gargarismo,** m. gargle, gargling.—*hacer gárgaras,* to gargle.—**gargarizar,** vii. [a] to gargle.

garita, f. sentry box; lodge, hut.—*g. de señales,* (RR.) signal tower.

garito, m. gambling house or den.

garlopa, f. (carp.) jack plane, long plane.

garra, f. claw, paw, talon; hook.—*echarle g.,* (coll.) to arrest, grasp.—*sacar de las garras de,* to free from.

garrafa, f. carafe, decanter.—**garrafal,** a. great, huge.—**garrafón,** m. large carafe.

garrapata, f. (entom.) tick.—**garrapatear,** vi. to scribble, scrawl.

garrocha, f. (sports) pole; goad stick.

garrotazo, m. blow with club or cudgel.—**garrote,** m. club, cudgel; garrote (for capital punishment).—*dar g.,* to garrote.—**garrotero,** n. beater; (coll.) usurer.

garrucha, f. pulley.

garza, f. heron.

garzo, a. blue-eyed.

gas, m. gas; vapor; (coll.) gaslight.—*g. hilarante,* laughing gas.—*g. lacrimógeno,* tear gas.—*g. mostaza,* mustard gas.—*g. neurotóxico* or *nervioso,* nerve gas.—*g. propano,* propane gas.

gasa, f. gauze.

gaseosa, f. soda water.—**gaseoso,** a. gaseous.—**gasificar,** vti. [d] to gasify.—**gasolina,** f. gasoline, gas.—*g. normal,* regular gasoline.—*g. sin plomo,* unleaded gasoline.—*g. super,* high-octane gasoline.—**gasolinera,** f. filling station, service station.

gastable, a. expendable.—**gastado,** a. worn-out; shabby; blasé.—*g. por el tiempo,* timeworn.—**gastador,** a. lavish, prodigal.—n. spender, spendthrift.—**gastar,** vt. to spend, expend; to waste, wear out; to use.—vr. to become old or useless; to waste away, wear out; to fray.—**gasto,** m. expenditure, outlay, expense; consumption; spending, consuming.—*g. deducible,* tax deduction.—*gastos de explotación,* operating or working expenses.—

gastos de representación, incidental expenses.

gastrónomo, *m.* gourmet.

gatas, *f. pl.—andar a g.,* on all fours.— **gatazo,** *m.* large cat; (coll.) artful trick, cheat.—**gatear,** *vi.* (of children) to creep; to climb up; to go upon all fours.

gatillo, *m.* trigger.

gato, *n.* cat.—*m.* (mech.) jack; (coll.) shrewd fellow.—*cuatro gatos,* (contempt.) just a few people.—*dar* or *meter g. por liebre,* (coll.) to cheat, to give chalk for cheese.—*aquí hay g. encerrado,* (coll.) there is something fishy here.—*g. macho,* tomcat.

gauchada, *f.* artifice; act of a Gaucho.—*hacer una g.,* (Arg.) to do a favor.—**gauchaje,** *m.* (Am.) Gaucho folk, group of Gauchos.—**gaucho,** *n.* Gaucho, pampas cowboy (-girl).

gaulteria, *f.* wintergreen.

gaveta, *f.* drawer.

gavilán, *m.* sparrow hawk.

gavilla, *f.* bundle or sheaf of grain; gang of thugs.

gaviota, *f.* sea gull, gull.

gay [gei], *a. & m.* gay.—*f.* lesbian.— **gayo,** *a.* (literary) gay, festive, cheerful, bright.

gaza, *f.* loop of a bow.

gazapo, *m.* young rabbit; (coll.) blunder, mistake.

gazmoñería, *f.* prudery.—**gazmoño,** *a.* prudish, priggish.

gaznápiro, *n.* churl; simpleton.

gaznate, *m.* throttle; windpipe.—**gaznatón,** *m.* (Am.) slap in the face.

gazofia, *f.* = BAZOFIA.

gel, *m.* gel.—*g. de baño,* bath gel.—*g. para el pelo,* hair gel.—**gelificarse,** *vr.* to gel.

gelatina, *f.* gelatine; jelly.—**gelatinoso,** *a.* gelatinous.

gema, *f.* jewel, gem, precious stone; bud.

gemelo, *n.* twin.—*m.* cufflink.—*pl.* binoculars; opera, field or marine glasses.

gemido, *m.* moan; whine; whimper.— **Géminis,** *m.* or **Gemelos,** *m. pl.* (astr.) Gemini.—**gemir,** *vii.* [29] to moan; to whine; to whimper.

gen, *m.* = **gene,** *m.* gene.

gendarme, *mf.* (Am.) gendarme, policeman (-woman).

genealogía, *f.* genealogy.

generación, *f.* generation.—**generador,** *n. & a.* generator; generating.— *m.* (mech., elec.) generator.

general, *a.* general; usual.—*por lo g.,* in general, generally.—*m.* (mil.) general.—**generalidad,** *f.* generality.— **generalizar,** *vti.* [a] to generalize.— *vri.* to become general, usual, or popular.

genérico, *a.* generic.—**género,** *m.* genus; class; kind; sort; material, cloth; (literary) genre; (gram.) gender.—*pl.* dry goods; (com.) merchandise—*g. humano,* mankind.

generosidad, *f.* generosity.—**generoso,** *a.* generous.

génesis, *f.* genesis.—**genetic,** *a.* genético.—**genética,** *f.* genetics.

genial, *a.* genial; pleasant.—**genio,** *m.* genius; temperament, disposition; temper; character; spirit.—*mal g.,* ill temper.

geniecillo, *m.* elf.

genital, *a.* genital.—*m.* testicle.

gente, *f.* people, folk, crowd; race, nation; (coll.) folks, family.—*g. baja,* lower classes; mob.—*g. bien,* upper class.—*g. de bien* honest people.— *g. de edad,* senior citizens.—*g. de paz,* friends.—*g. menuda,* children, small fry.

gentil, *a.* graceful, genteel; polite.— *mf.* gentile; pagan.—**gentileza,** *f.* gentility, gracefulness; courtesy.

gentío, *m.* crowd, multitude.—**gentuza,** *f.* rabble, riffraff; mob.

genuflexión, *f.* genuflection.—*hacer una g.,* to genuflect.

genuino, *a.* genuine; unadulterated.

geografía, *f.* geography.—**geográfico,** *a.* geographical.—**geógrafo,** *n.* geographer.—**geología,** *f.* geology.— **geólogo,** *n.* geologist.—**geometría,** *f.* geometry.—**geométrico,** *a.* geometrical.—*g. del espacio,* solid geometry.

geranio, *m.* geranium.

gerencia, *f.* (com.) management, administration.—**gerente,** *mf.* (com.) manager.

germen, *m.* germ; source.—**germinación,** *f.* (bot.) germination.—**germinar,** *vi.* to germinate.

gerundio, *m.* gerund.

gestación, *f.* gestation, pregnancy.

gestión, *f.* management, negotiation; effort.—**gestionar,** *vt.* to manage; to negotiate; to undertake.

gesto, *m.* facial expression; grimace; gesture.—*hacer gestos,* to make faces.

giba, *f.* hump, hunch.—**giboso,** *a.* humpbacked.

gigante, *mf.* giant; giantess.—*a.* gigantic.—**gigantesco,** *a.* gigantic.

gimnasia, *f.* calisthenics, gymnastics.—*g. respiratoria,* breathing exercises.—**gimnasio,** *m.* gymnasium.—**gimnasta,** *mf.* gymnast.—**gimnástica,** *f.* gymnastics.

gimotear, *vi.* (coll.) to whine.—**gimoteo,** *m.* whining.

ginebra, *f.* gin (liquor).

ginecología, *f.* gynecology.—**ginecólogo,** *n.* gynecologist.

girador, *n.* (com.) drawer of draft.—**girar,** *vi.* to whirl, revolve, rotate; to turn; (com.) to draw (checks, drafts).—*g. contra* or *a cargo de,* to draw on.—*g. sobre un eje,* to swivel.—**girasol,** *m.* sunflower.—**giratorio,** *a.* revolving, rotary.—*m.* revolving bookcase.—**giro,** *m.* turn; rotation; bend; trend, bias; turn of phrase; (com.) draft; line of business.—*g. en descubierto,* overdraft.—*g. postal.* money order.—*tomar otro g.* to take another course.

gitano, *a.* gypsy; gypsylike; honey-mouthed.—*n.* gypsy.

glacial, *a.* glacial.—**glaciar,** *m.* glacier.

gladiolo, *m.* gladiolus.

glándula, *f.* gland.—*g. tiroides,* thyroid gland.—**glandular,** *a.* glandular.

global, *a.* global, overall.—**globo,** *m.* globe, sphere; balloon.—*en g.,* as a whole; in bulk.—*g. aerostático,* hot-air balloon.—*g. ocular,* eyeball.—*g. sonda,* trial balloon; observation balloon.—*g. terráqueo* or *terrestre,* (the) globe, (the) earth.—**globular,** *a.* globular.—**glóbulo,** *m.* globule; corpuscle.—*g. blanco/rojo,* white/red corpuscle.

gloria, *f.* glory, fame; heavenly state, bliss; splendor.—*saber a g.,* to taste delicious.—**gloriarse,** *vr.* (**de** or **en**) to boast (of), to take delight (in).—**glorieta,** *f.* traffic circle; bower, arbor.—**glorificación,** *f.* glorification; praise.—**glorificar,** *vti.* [d] to glorify; to exalt; to praise.—*vri.* = GLORIARSE.—**glorioso,** *a.* glorious.

glosa, *f.* gloss; (mus.) variation of a theme.—**glosar,** *vt.* to gloss, comment; (mus.) to vary (a theme).—**glosario,** *m.* glossary.

glotón, *n.* & *a.* glutton; gluttonous.—**glotonería,** *f.* gluttony.

gluglú, *m.* gurgle, gurgling sound.

gnomo, *m.* gnome.

gobernación, *f.* government.—**gobernador,** *n.* governor; ruler.—**gobernante,** *mf.* ruler.—*a.* ruling.—**gobernar,** *vti.* [1] & *vii.* to govern, rule.—*vri.* to manage (one's affairs), carry on.—**gobierno,** *m.* government; management, direction; control (of a business, an automobile, an airplane); helm, rudder.—*g. exiliado,* government in exile.—*para su g.,* for your guidance.

goce, *m.* enjoyment; joy; fruition.

godo, *n.* & *a.* Goth(ic); (Colombia, pol.) conservative, Spaniard.

gol, *m.* (sports) goal scored.—*g. de campo,* (football) field goal.

gola, *f.* ruff; gullet, throat.

goleta, *f.* (naut.) schooner.

golf, *m.* golf.—**golfista,** *mf.* golfer.

golfo, *m.* gulf; sea; bum; ragamuffin.

gollería, *f.* dainty; delicious morsel; superfluity, excess.

gollete, *m.* throttle, gullet; neck of a bottle.

golondrina, *f.* (ornith.) swallow.

golosear, golosinear, *vi.* to nibble on sweets.—**golosina,** *f.* dainty, delicacy, sweet morsel, tidbit; daintiness; trifle.—**goloso,** *a.* fond of tidbits or sweets.

golpe, *m.* blow; stroke, hit, knock, beat; shock, clash; attack, spell; action.—*de g.,* suddenly.—*g. bajo,* low blow, cheap shot.—*g. de estado,* coup d'état.—*g. de fortuna,* stroke of luck.—*g. de mar,* large wave.—*g. de timón,* change of direction.—*g. de vista,* glance, look.—**golpear,** *vt.* to strike, hit, hammer.—*vi.* to beat; to knock, pound (as a piston).—**golpetazo,** *m.* (fam.) clunk.—**golpetear,** *vt.* & *vi.* to rattle; to pound, pummel.—*vi.* to clunk.—**golpeteo,** *m.* knocking, pounding, rattling.

goma, *f.* gum; rubber; glue; tire; rubber band; rubber eraser; overshoes, rubbers; (Am.) hangover.—*g. de borrar,* rubber eraser.—*g. de mascar,* chewing gum.—*g. de pegar,* glue.—*g. dos,* plastic explosive.—*g. espuma,* foam rubber.—*g. laca,* lacquer.—**gomoso,** *a.* gummy; gum-producing.

gonce, *m.* hinge.

góndola, *f.* gondola.—**gondolero,** *n.* gondolier.

gong, *m.* gong.

gonorrea, *f.* gonorrhea.

gordinflón, *a.* (coll.) chubby, flabby, fat.—**gordo,** *a.* fat, plump; fatty, greasy; coarse; thick, chunky; enormous, large; hard (water).—*m.* fat man; fat, suet; (fam.) jackpot, first prize (in lottery).—*f.* fat woman.—*adv.*—*hablar g.*, (fam.) to talk big.—**gordura,** *f.* fatness, plumpness, stoutness, corpulence; fat, grease.

gorgojo, *m.* grub, weevil; (coll.) dwarfish person.

gorgotear, *vi.* to gurgle.—**gorgoteo,** *m.* gurgle, gurgling sound.

gorguera, *f.* ruff.

gorila, *m.* gorilla; (fam.) thug; (fam.) bodyguard; (fam.) bouncer.

gorjear, *vi.* to warble, trill.—*vr.* to gabble (as a child).—**gorjeo,** *m.* warble, trilling; gabble of a child.

gorra, *f.* cap; sponging, bumming.—*de g.*, at other people's expense.—*g. de baño,* bathing cap; shower cap.—*g. de marinero,* sailor's hat.—*g. de vasco,* beret.—*g. de visera,* peaked hat.—*ir, comer, andar, etc., de g.*, (coll.) to sponge.

gorrión, *m.* sparrow.

gorrista, *mf.* (coll.) sponger.—**gorro,** *m.* cap, coif.—*g. de baño,* bathing cap; shower cap.—*g. de cocinero,* chef's hat.—*g. de dormir,* night cap.—*g. de ducha,* shower cap.—**gorrón,** *n.* sponger, parasite.

gota, *f.* drop of liquid; gout.—*sudar la g. gorda,* (coll.) to sweat blood.—*una g. en el mar,* a drop in the bucket.—*pl.* drops.—*g. nasales,* nose drops.—*g. para los oídos,* eardrops.—**gotear,** *vi.* to drop, drip, dribble, leak; to sprinkle, begin to rain.—**gotera,** *f.* leak, leakage; drip, dripping.

gótico, *a.* Gothic.

gotoso, *a.* gouty.

gozar, *vti.* [a] to enjoy; to have possession or result of.—*vii.* (**de**) to enjoy, have possession (of).—*vri.* to rejoice.

gozne, *m.* hinge.

gozo, *m.* joy, pleasure, gladness.—*saltar de g.,* to be in high spirits, to be very happy.—**gozoso,** *a.* joyful, cheerful, merry.

grabado, *a.* engraved, carved, cut.—*m.* engraving; art of engraving; cut, picture, illustration; recorded.—*g. al agua fuerte,* etching.—*g. en madera,* wood engraving, wood carving.—**grabación,** *f.* recording, taping, cutting; recording, tape.—*g. en cinta,* tape recording.—*g. en video,* video recording.—**grabador,** *n.* engraver, carver; cutter, sinker.—**grabadora,** *f.* tape recorder.—*g. de alambre,* wire recorder.—*g. de cassettes,* cassette recorder.—*g. de cinta,* tape recorder.—**grabar,** *vt.* to engrave; to cut, carve; to impress upon the mind; to record (on a CD, tape, etc.).—*g. en cassette,* to audiotape.—*g. en cinta,* to tape-record.—*g. en video,* to videotape.

gracejo, *m.* graceful, winsome way.—**gracia,** *f.* grace; gracefulness; benefaction; graciousness; pardon, mercy; remission of a debt; witticism, wit; joke, jest; name of a person.—*pl.* thanks; accomplishments.—*caer en g.,* to please, to be liked.—*hacer g.,* to please; to amuse, strike as funny.—*tener g.,* to be witty; to be funny.—**grácil,** *a.* slender.—**gracioso,** *a.* graceful, pleasing; witty, funny; gracious.

grada, *f.* step of a wide staircase; harrow.—*pl.* stands, seats of bullring or amphitheater.—**gradación,** *f.* (mus.) gradation; graded series of things or events.—**gradería,** *f.* series of steps or seats at bullring or stadium stands.

grado, *m.* degree; step of a staircase; (mil.) rank; grade, class.—*de g.,* or *de buen g.,* willingly, with pleasure.—**graduación,** *f.* graduation; (mil.) rank.—**gradual,** *a.* gradual.—**graduar,** *vt.* to graduate, give a degree or a military rank; to grade; to gauge; to adjust.—*vr.* (**en**) to graduate (from), to take a degree.

gráfico, *a.* graphic(al); clear, vivid.—*diseño g.,* graphics.—*n.* graph, diagram.—*pl.* graphics.—*g. de alta resolución,* high-resolution graphics.—**grafismo,** *m.* graphics.—*g. por computadora,* computer graphics.

grafito, *m.* graphite.

grafospasmo, *m.* writer's cramp.

grajo, *m.* jackdaw; rook.

grama, *f.* grama grass; lawn.

gramática, *f.* grammar.—**gramatical,** *a.* grammatical.—**gramático,** *a.* grammatical.—*n.* grammarian.

gramo, *m.* gram (weight). See Table.

gran, *a. contr.* of GRANDE.—*g. danés,* Great Dane.—*grandes almacenes,* department store.—*g. ópera,* grand opera.—*g. supermercado,* large supermarket.—**Gran Bretaña,** *f.* Great Britain.

grana, *f.* scarlet color; scarlet cloth.

granada, *f.* pomegranate; (mil.) gre-

nade.—*g. de mano*, hand grenade.—
g. de mortero, mortar shell.—**granado**, *a.* remarkable, illustrious;
mature; select, choice.—*m.* pomegranate tree.—**granangular**, *a.* wide-angle.—*objetivo g.*, wide-angle lens.
—**granar**, *vi.* to bloom, mature,
come to fruition.—**granate**, *m.* garnet; maroon (color); claret.

grande, *a.* large, big; great; grand.—*en
g.*, on a large scale.—*mf.* grandee.
—**grandeza**, *f.* greatness; grandeur;
grandeeship; bigness; size, magnitude.—**grandiosidad**, *f.* greatness;
grandeur; abundance.—**grandioso**,
a. grandiose, grand, magnificent.
—**grandullón**, *a.* overgrown.

granear, *vt.* to sow (grain); to stipple;
to grain (lithographic stone).—**granel**, *m.* heap of grain.—*a g.*, in a
heap; (com.) in bulk.—**granero**, *m.*
granary, barn; grange; cornloft.

granito, *m.* granite; small grain; pimple; granule.

granizada, *f.* hailstorm; shower of objects, facts, etc.; water ice.—**granizar**, *vii.* [a-50] to hail.—**granizo**, *m.*
hail.

granja, *f.* grange, farm, farmhouse.
—**granjear**, *vt.* to gain, earn,
profit.—*vt. & vr.* to get, win (as the
good will of another).—**granjería**, *f.*
gain, profit, advantage.—**granjero**,
n. farmer.

grano, *m.* grain; cereal; each single
seed; pimple.—*pl.* (com.) cereals,
corn, breadstuffs.—*ir al g.*, to come
to the point.

granuja, *mf.* rogue; waif, urchin.

granulación, *f.* granulation.—**granular**,
vt. to granulate.—*vr.* to become covered with granules or pimples.—*a.*
granular, grainy.—**granuloso**, *a.* granulous, granular.

grapa, *f.* staple; paper clip; clamp,
clasp.—**grapador**, *m.* stapler.—**grapón**, *m.* brace, hook.

grasa, *f.* grease; fat; suet; oil.—**grasiento**, *a.* greasy; filthy.—**graso**, *a.*
fat, unctuous.—**grasoso**, *a.* greasy.

gratificación, *f.* reward; gratuity; tip;
fee; gratification.—**gratificar**, *vti.*
[d] to reward, recompense; to tip,
fee; to gratify, please.—**gratis**, *adv.*
gratis, free.—**gratitud**, *f.* gratitude,
gratefulness.—**grato**, *a.* pleasing,
pleasant; grateful.—**gratuito**, *a.* gratis; gratuitous, uncalled-for; unfounded.

grava, *f.* gravel.

gravamen, *m.* tax, scot; charge, obligation; nuisance; (law) mortgage,
lien.—**gravar**, *vt.* to burden; to tax;
(law) to encumber.

grave, *a.* weighty, heavy; grave, serious; (mus.) grave; deep (voice).
—**gravedad**, *f.* gravity, graveness; seriousness.

gravitación, *f.* gravitation.—**gravitar**,
vi. to gravitate; to rest, press (on).

gravoso, *a.* costly; onerous; vexatious.

graznar, *vi.* to croak, caw, cackle.
—**graznido**, *m.* croak, caw, cackle;
croaking.

greda, *f.* clay, chalk, marl, potter's clay.

green [grin], *m.* (sports) putting green.

gremio, *m.* guild; society, brotherhood; trade union.

greña, *f.* entangled or matted mop of
hair.—*andar a la g.*, (of women) to
pull each other's hair; to argue excitedly.—**greñudo**, *a.* with long, disheveled hair; shy (horse).—*m.* shy
horse.

gresca, *f.* wrangle, brawl, row.

grial, *m.* grail.—*el santo G.*, the holy
Grail.

griego, *n. & a.* Greek, Grecian.—*m.*
the Greek language; unintelligible
language.

grieta, *f.* crevice, crack; chink, fissure;
scratch in the skin.

grifo, *a.* (print.) script; bristling (hair,
fur); kinky, tangled (of hair).—*m.*
griffin or griffon; faucet, spigot,
cock.—*pl.* frizzled hair.

grillete, *m.* fetter, shackle.—**grillo**, *m.*
(entom.) cricket.—*pl.* fetters.

grima, *f.* fright, horror.—*dar g.*, to set
the teeth on edge.—**grimoso**, *a.* horrible; repulsive.

gringo, *n.* (Am.) foreigner (esp. English
or American).

gripe, *f.* grippe.

gris, *a.* gray.—*m.* gray color.—**grisáceo**, *a.* grayish.

grita, *f.* clamor, outcry; screaming;
hooting.—**gritar**, *vi.* to shout, cry
out, scream; to hoot.—**gritería**, *f.*
outcry, uproar, shouting.—**grito**, *m.*
cry, scream; hoot, whoop.—*a gritos*,
a g. pelado, a todo g., at the top of
one's voice.—*estar en un g.*, to be in
continual pain.—*poner el g. en el
cielo*, to complain loudly.

grosella, *f.* currant; gooseberry.

grosería, *f.* rudeness, ill-breeding; discourtesy; clumsiness; vulgarity.—

grosero, *a.* coarse, rough, gross; rude, discourteous, crass; vulgar, uncouth.

grosor, *m.* thickness.

grúa, *f.* crane, derrick.—*g. de auxilio,* wrecking crane.

gruesa, *f.* gross (12 dozen).

grueso, *a.* thick; bulky, corpulent; fleshy.—*m.* thickness; bulk, corpulence; main part; main body of an army.

grulla, *f.* (ornith.) crane.

grumete, *m.* apprentice sailor; cabin boy.

grumo, *m.* clot.—**grumoso,** *a.* full of clots, clotted.

gruñido, *m.* grunt.—**gruñir,** *vii.* [27] to grunt.—**gruñón,** *n.* & *a.* crank, irritable.

grupa, *f.* croup, rump of a horse.

grupo, *m.* group; set; clump, cluster.

gruta, *f.* cavern, grotto.

guacamayo, *m.* (ornith.) macaw.

guacho, *a.* & *n.* (Am.) orphan, foundling; solitary, forlorn; odd (only one of a pair).

guaco, *m.* (Am.) grouse.

guadaña, *f.* scythe.—**guadañar,** *vt.* to mow.

guagua, *f.* (Am.) insect that destroys fruit; trivial thing; omnibus; baby.—*de g.,* free, gratis.—**guagüero,** *n.* (Am.) bus driver; sponger.

guajalote, *m.* (Am.) turkey.

guajiro, *n.* & *a.* Cuban peasant.

guanaco, *m.* (Am.) a kind of llama; boor, rustic; (coll.) simpleton, idiot.

guanajo, *n.* (Am.) turkey.—*a.* & *n.* (coll.) fool.

guano, *m.* guano; palm leaves; (coll., Cuba) money.

guante, *m.* glove.—*echarle (a uno) el g.,* (coll.) to seize, grasp; to imprison.—**guantelete,** *m.* gauntlet.—**guantera,** *f.* (aut.) glove compartment.

guapear, *vi.* (coll.) to boast of courage.—**guapetón,** *a.* daring, bold.—**guapo,** *a.* (coll.) brave, daring; good-looking or handsome; spruce, neat; ostentatious; gay, sprightly.—*m.* gallant, beau; brawler, quarrelsome person.—*ponerse g.,* (Am.) to get angry.

guaraní, *a.* & *mf.* Guarani.—*m.* Guarani language.

guarapo, *m.* juice of the sugar cane.

guarda, *mf.* guard; keeper.—*g. forestal,* forest ranger.—*g. jurado,* security guard.—*f.* custody; trust, wardship, safe-keeping; observance of a law; outside rib or guard (of a fan, etc.); ward of a lock or of a key.—**guardabarrera,** *m.* (RR.) gatekeeper.—**guardabarro,** *m.* fender, splashboard.—**guardabosque,** *m.* forester; game warden.—**guardacantón,** *m.* protective stone at corner of buildings.—**guardacostas,** *m.* Coast Guard; (naut.) revenue cutter.—**guardafango,** *m.* = GUARDABARRO.—**guardafrenos,** *m.* (RR.) brakeman.—**guardamonte,** *m.* guard of a gunlock; forester, keeper of a forest. —**guardamuebles,** *m.* warehouse. —**guardapuerta,** *f.* storm door.—**guardar,** *vt.* to keep; to guard, protect, watch over; to store, save, reserve.—*vr.* (**de**) to guard (against), avoid, beware (of), take care not (to).—**guardarropa,** *m.* wardroom; wardrobe; cloakroom.—**guardarropía,** *f.* (theat.) wardrobe, properties.—**guardavientos,** *m.* windbreak; chimney pot.—**guardia,** *f.* guard; defense, protection.—*m.* uniformed policeman.—**guardiamarina,** *m.* midshipman.—**guardián,** *n.* keeper, watchman.

guarecer, *vti.* [3] to shelter, protect.—*vri.* to take refuge or shelter.—**guarida,** *f.* den, cave; lair of a wild beast; shelter; lurking place, cover, haunt.

guarnecer, *vti.* [3] to garnish, adorn, decorate; (sew.) to trim, bind, line; (jewelry) to set in gold, silver, etc.; (mason.) to plaster; (mil.) to garrison.—**guarnición,** *f.* trimming, etc.; setting; (mech.) packing; guard of a sword; garrison; adornment.—*pl.* harness; fittings; accessories.—**guarnicionero,** *m.* harness maker.

guasa, *f.* joking, jesting; joke, jest.

guaso, *m.* lasso; Chilean cowboy.

guasón, *a.* (coll.) jocose, witty.—*n.* joker, wag.

Guatemala, *f.* Guatemala.—*salir de G. para entrar en Guatepeor,* to jump out of the frying pan into the fire.

guatemalteco, *n.* & *a.* Guatemalan.

guayaba, *f.* guava.—**guayabo,** *m.* guava tree.

gubernamental, *a.* governmental.—**gubernativo,** *a.* administrative, governmental, gubernatorial.

gubia, *f.* (carp.) gouge, centering chisel.

guedeja, *f.* long lock of hair; forelock; lion's mane.

guerra, *f.* war, warfare.—*dar g.,* to cause annoyance or trouble.—*g. bacteriológica,* germ warfare.—*g. civil,* civil war.—*g. fría,* cold war. —*g. de las dos Rosas,* War of the Roses.—*g. de precios,* price war.— **guerrear,** *vi.* to war, wage war, fight.—**guerrera,** *f.* (mil.) tunic.— **guerrero,** *a.* martial, warlike.— *m.* warrior, fighter.—**guerrilla,** *f.* guerrilla.—**guerrillero,** *m.* guerrilla fighter.

guía, *mf.* guide; leader.—*f.* guidebook; (mech.) guide, rule, guide pin, guide screw, etc.—*g. de datos,* (comput.) data dictionary, data directory.—*g. social,* social register.—**guiar,** *vt.* to guide, lead; to drive (auto, etc.).—*vr.* (**por**) to go or be governed (by); to follow.

guija, *f.* pebble; gravel.—*pl.* (coll.) force, vigor.—**guijarro,** *m.* pebble, cobble.—**guijo,** *m.* gravel.

guiñada, *f.* wink; (naut.) yaw; lurch.

guiñapo, *m.* tatter, rag; ragamuffin.

guiñar, *vt.* to wink; (naut.) to yaw; to lurch.—**guiño,** *m.* wink.

guión, *m.* hyphen; dash; (theat., radio, T.V.) script; explanatory text or reference table; cross (carried before a prelate in a procession); leader (among birds and animals); leader in a dance.—**guionista,** *mf.* script-writer.

guirnalda, *f.* garland, wreath.

güiro, *m.* (Am.) fruit of the calabash tree; bottle gourd; gourd used as a musical instrument.

guisa, *f.* manner, fashion.—*a g. de,* like, in the manner of.

guisante, *m.* pea.—*g. de olor,* sweet pea.

guisar, *vt.* to cook or dress (food); to arrange, prepare.—**guiso,** *m.* cooked dish; seasoning, condiment.

guitarra, *f.* guitar.—*g. eléctrica,* electric guitar.—**guitarrista,** *mf.* guitarist.

gula, *f.* gluttony, inordinate appetite.

gusano, *m.* worm, grub, caterpillar; meek, dejected person.

gustar, *vt.* to taste, try.—*vi.* to be pleasing; to cause pleasure.—*gustarle a uno una cosa,* to like something.— **gusto,** *m.* taste; tasting; pleasure; liking; choice; discernment.—*a g.,* to one's taste or judgment.—*con mucho g.,* with pleasure.—*dar g.,* to please.—**gustoso,** *a.* savory; tasty; cheerful; pleasing; willing.

H

haba, *f.* broad bean; lima bean.

habano, *m.* Havana cigar.

haber, *vti.* [21] to have (used as *aux.*).— *hágase seguir,* please forward.—*hay (habia, hubo, etc.),* there is, there are (there was, there were).—*hay que,* one must, it is necessary.—*no hay de que,* don't mention it.—*m.* (bookkeeping) credit.—*pl.* property, assets; estate.

habichuela, *f.* kidney bean.—*h. verde,* string bean.

hábil, *a.* capable, skillful.—*día h.,* work day.—**habilidad,** *f.* ability, skill.—*pl.* accomplishments.

habilitación, *f.* habilitation; outfit, equipment.—**habilitar,** *vt.* to qualify, enable; to fit out, equip.

habitable, *a.* habitable.—**habitación,** *f.* room, chamber, suite of rooms, apartment; lodging; (law) caretaking.—**habitante,** *a.* inhabiting.— *mf.* inhabitant.—**habitar,** *vt.* to inhabit, live, reside.

hábito, *m.* habit, custom; dress of ecclesiastics.—*tomar el h.,* to become a nun or a monk.—**habitual,** *a.* habitual, usual, customary.—**habituar,** *vt.* to accustom, habituate.—*vr.* to become accustomed, accustom oneself, get used to.

habla, *f.* speech; language; talk.—*de h. española,* Spanish-speaking.—*de h. inglesa,* English-speaking.—*ponerse al h.,* to communicate, get in touch, speak.—**hablador,** *a.* talkative.—*n.* talker, gabber.—**habladuría,** *f.* gossip, empty talk.—**hablar,** *vi.* to speak; to talk.—*h. a tontas y a locas,* to speak recklessly.—*h. claro,* or *en plata,* to speak in plain language, to call a spade a spade.—*h. por h.,* to talk for the sake of talking.—*h. por los codos,* to talk incessantly; to chatter.—*vt.* to speak.—*vr.* to speak to each other; to be on speaking terms.—**hablilla,** *f.* rumor, gossip.

hacedero, *a.* feasible, practicable.—**hacedor,** *m.* maker.—*el Supremo H.,* the Maker, the Creator.

hacendado, *n.* landholder, farmer, rancher.—**hacendoso,** *a.* industrious.

hacer, *vti.* [22] to make; to produce; to do; to gain, earn; to suppose, think; to cause.—*h. alarde,* to boast.—*h. caso,* to mind, pay attention.—*h. daño,* to hurt, harm.—*h. de,* to act as.—*h. juego,* to match.—*h. la vista gorda,* to wink at, to connive at.—*h. una pregunta,* to ask a question.—*no le hace,* never mind, let it go.—*v. impers.*—*¿cuánto (tiempo) hace?* how long ago?—*¿cuánto (tiempo) hace que?* since when?—*hace años,* many years ago.—*hace calor,* it is warm.—*hace tiempo,* a long time ago.—*hace un año,* a year ago, or, it is now one year.—*hace viento,* it is windy.—*vri.* to become, grow; to pretend to be.—*h. a,* to become accustomed.

hacha, *f.* ax; hatchet; torch.—**hachazo,** *m.* blow or stroke with an ax.—**hachero,** *m.* lumberjack; torchbearer.—**hachuela,** *f.* hatchet.

hacia, *prep.* toward; near, about.—*h. abajo,* downward.—*h. arriba,* upward.—*h. atrás,* backward.

hacienda, *f.* landed property; plantation; ranch; estate, fortune; finance.—*h. pública,* public treasury; public finances.

hacina, *f.* stack; pile.—**hacinamiento,** *m.* accumulation; heaping or stacking.—**hacinar,** *vt.* to stack; to pile; to accumulate.

hada, *f.* fairy.—**hado,** *m.* fate, destiny, doom.

haitiano, *n. & a.* Haitian.

halagador, *a.* flattering; coaxing.—*n.* flatterer, cajoler, coaxer.—**halagar,** *vti.* [b] to cajole; to flatter; to coax, allure; to fondle.—**halago,** *m.* cajolery, allurement, flattery; caress. —**halagüeño,** *a.* flattering; alluring.

halar, *vt.* to haul, pull, tow.—*vi.* to pull ahead.

halcón, *m.* falcon.

hálito, *m.* breath; vapor.

hallar, *vt.* to find; to find out; to discover.—*vr.* to be (in a place or condition); to feel (as to health); to fare.—

hallazgo, *m.* find, thing found; discovery; reward.

halo, *m.* halo.

halógeno, *a. & m.* halogen.

haltera, *f.* dumbbell.—**halterofilia,** *f.* weightlifting.—**halterófilo,** *n.* weightlifter.

hamaca, *f.* hammock.

hambre, *f.* hunger; appetite; famine.—*h. canina,* inordinate hunger.—*tener h.,* to be hungry.—**hambrear,** *vt.* to starve, famish.—*vi.* to be hungry.—**hambriento,** *a.* hungry; starving; starved; greedy, covetous; longing.

hamburgués, *a.* from or pertaining to Hamburg.—**hamburguesa,** *f.* hamburger.—*h. con queso,* cheeseburger.

hampa, *m.* underworld.—**hampón,** *m.* gangster, bully, rowdy.

hangar, *m.* (neol.) hangar.

haragán, *n.* idler, loiterer, loafer; lazy person.—*a.* lazy, indolent, idle. —**haraganear,** *vi.* to be lazy; to lounge, idle, loiter.—**haraganería,** *f.* idleness, laziness, sloth.

harapiento, *a.* ragged, tattered.—**harapo,** *m.* tatter, rag.

hardware, *m.* (comput.) hardware.

harén, *m.* harem.

harina, *f.* flour, meal.—*h. de otro costal,* another matter, a horse of a different color.—**harinoso,** *a.* mealy.

hartar, *vti.* [49] & *vri.* to glut, gorge; to sate, satiate; to satisfy; to fill to excess.—**hartazgo,** *m.* satiety, fill.—**harto,** *ppi.* of HARTAR.—*a.* sufficient, full, complete.—*adv.* enough or sufficiently; very much, abundantly.—**hartura,** *f.* satiety, fill; superabundance.

hasta, *prep.* till, until; up to, down to; as far as; even (emphatic).—*h. después,* or *h. luego,* good-by, so long.—*h. la vista,* (in parting) so long, see you later.—*h. mañana,* (in parting) see you tomorrow.—*conj.* even.—*h. que,* until.

hastiar, *vt.* to disgust; to cloy, sate.—**hastío,** *m.* disgust; boredom.

hatillo, *m.* small bundle; a few clothes.—*coger el h.,* (coll.) to quit, to pack and go.

hato, *m.* herd of cattle; flock of sheep; (Am.) farm or cattle ranch; shepherd's lodge; lot; gang, crowd.

hawaiano, *a. & n.* Hawaiian.

hay, *impers. irreg.* of HABER; there is, there are.

haya, f. beech tree.

haz, m. fagot, bundle, bunch; (agr.) sheaf; beam.—*h. de electrones,* electron beam.—*h. de láser,* laser beam.

hazaña, f. feat, heroic deed.

hazmerreír, m. laughing stock.

hebilla, f. buckle, clasp.

hebra, f. thread fiber; string; strand.

hebreo, n. & a. Hebrew.—m. Hebrew (language).

hechicería, f. witchcraft, enchantment; charm; sorcery, wizardry.—**hechicero,** n. witch; wizard; sorcerer; charmer, enchanter; medicine man, witch doctor.—a. charming, bewitching.—**hechizar,** vti. [a] to bewitch, enchant; to charm.—**hechizo,** m. charm (used to bewitch), enchantment.

hecho, ppi. of HACER.—a. made; done; ready-made; finished; ripe or developed.—*h. a la medida,* custom-made.—*h. de encargo,* custom-made, made-to-order (furniture).—*h. y derecho,* real; complete.—*ya h.,* ready-made.—m. fact; act, action, deed.—*de h.,* in fact, as a matter of fact.—**hechura,** f. making, make; workmanship; form; build (of a person); creature, creation.

heder, vii. [18] to stink.—**hediondez,** f. stench, stink.—**hediondo,** a. stinking, fetid.—**hedor,** m. stench, stink.

helada, f. frost; nip.—**heladera, heladora,** f. refrigerator; ice-cream dish.—**helado,** a. icy; freezing, frosty; cold.—m. ice cream.—**helar,** vti. [1] & vii. to freeze; to amaze.—vri. to freeze, be frozen.

helecho, m. fern.

hélice, f. propeller; helix.

helicóptero, m. helicopter.

helio, m. helium.

hembra, f. female; (mech.) nut of a screw.

hemisférico, a. hemispherical.—**hemisferio,** m. hemisphere.

hemorragia, f. hemorrhage.—*h. nasal,* nosebleed.—**hemorrágico,** a. hemorrhagic.

hemorroides, f. pl. piles, hemorrhoids.

henchir, vti. [29] to fill, stuff.—vri. to fill or stuff oneself.

hender, vti. [19] to crack, split; to cut (as the water).—**hendidura,** f. fissure, crack, cut.

heno, m. hay.—*campo de h.,* hayfield.

hepatitis, f. hepatitis.

heráldica, f. heraldry.—**heraldo,** m. herald; harbinger.

herbazal, m. grassy place; pasture ground.

heredad, f. improved piece of ground; country estate, farm.—**heredar,** vt. to inherit; to deed to another.—**heredero,** n. heir; heiress; inheritor; successor.—*h. forzoso,* general or legal heir.—**hereditario,** a. hereditary.

hereje, mf. heretic.—**herejía,** f. heresy; injurious expression.

herencia, f. inheritance, heritage; heredity.

herético, a. heretical.

herida, f. injury, wound.—**herido,** a. & n. wounded (person).—*mal h.,* dangerously wounded.—**herir,** vti. [39] to wound; to hurt, harm; to strike; to offend (the senses).

hermanar, vt. to mate, match, pair; to suit.—vi. to fraternize; to match.—**hermanastro,** n. stepbrother; f. stepsister.—**hermandad,** f. fraternity, brotherhood.—**hermano,** n. brother; (f. sister); twin (app. to objects).—*h. de sangre,* blood brother.—*media h.,* half sister.—*medio h.,* half brother.—*h. de leche,* foster brother.—*hermanos siameses,* Siamese twins.—*h. político,* brother-in-law.

hermético, a. hermetic, air-proof, airtight; close-mouthed.—**hermetismo,** m. secrecy, complete silence.

hermosear, vt. to beautify, embellish.—**hermoso,** a. beautiful, handsome.—**hermosura,** f. beauty; belle.

hernia, f. hernia.

héroe, m. hero.—**heroicidad,** f. heroism; heroic deed.—**heroico,** a. heroic.—**heroína,** f. heroine.—**heroísmo,** m. heroism.

herpes, m. pl. or f. pl. herpes; cold sore; shingles.

herradura, f. horseshoe.—**herraje,** m. ironwork; iron or metal fittings or accessories, hardware (gen. pl.).—**herramienta,** f. tool; implement; set of tools.—*h. motriz,* power tool.—**herrar,** vti. [1] to shoe (horses); to brand (cattle); to garnish or trim with iron.—**herrería,** f. smithy; forge; ironworks.—**herrero,** n. blacksmith.

herrumbre, f. rust; iron taste.—**herrumbroso,** a. rusty, rusted.

hervidero, m. boiling; bubbling, seething; hot spring; swarm, multitude, crowd.—**hervir,** vti. [39] & vii. to boil; to seethe.—vii. to become choppy (the sea); to bubble.—

hervor, *m.* boiling; fervor, heat.—*h. de sangre,* rash.

heterodoxo, *a.* unorthodox.

heterogéneo, *a.* heterogenous.

hexágono, *m.* hexagon.

hez, *f.* sediment, dregs of liquor; scum.—*pl.* dregs; excrement.

hibrido, *n.* & *a.* hybrid.

hidráulica, *f.* hydraulics.—**hidráulico,** *a.* hydraulic.—**hidroavión,** *m.* seaplane.—**hidrógeno,** *m.* hydrogen.—**hidroplano,** *m.* seaplane.

hiedra, *f.* ivy.

hiel, *f.* gall, bile; bitterness.

hielo, *m.* ice; frost; coolness, indifference.—*h. seco,* dry ice.

hiena, *f.* hyena.

hierba, *f.* grass; weed; herb; herbage; (Am.) maté.—*mala h.,* weed; bad character; marijuana.—**hierbabuena,** *f.* mint.

hierro, *m.* iron; brand stamped with a hot iron.—*pl.* fetters, shackles, irons, handcuffs.—*a h. caliente batir de repente,* strike while the iron is hot.—*h. colado* or *fundido,* cast iron.—*h. forjado,* wrought iron.

hígado, *m.* liver.—*pl.* courage, bravery.—*echar el h.* or *los hígados,* to work very hard.

higiene, *f.* hygiene; sanitation.—**higiénico,** *a.* hygienic, sanitary.—**higienizar,** *vti.* [a] to make sanitary.

higo, *m.* fig.—**higuera,** *f.* fig tree.

hija, *f.* daughter, child.—*h. de leche,* foster daughter.—*h. política,* daughter-in-law.—**hijastro,** *m.* stepchild.—**hijo,** *m.* son, child; (bot.) shoot; fruit; result; Junior, Jr., p.ej., **Daryl Wayne Brown,** hijo, Daryl Wayne Brown, Jr.—*pl.* children, offspring.—*h. de leche,* foster son.—*h. de sus propias obras,* self-made man.—*h. natural,* illegitimate child.—*h. político,* son-in-law.

hijito, *m.* sonny, junior.

hila, *f.* line.—*a la h.,* in a row, single file.—*pl.* (surg.) lint.—**hilacha,** *f.,* **hilacho,** *m.* fraying, shred, filament or thread raveled out of cloth.—*pl.* lint.—**hilada,** *f.* row or line; (mason.) course.—**hilado,** *m.* spinning; yarn.—**hilandera,** *f.* woman spinner.—**hilandería,** *f.* spinning mill.—**hilandero,** *n.* & *a.* spinner; spinning.—*m.* spinning room, spinnery.—**hilar,** *vt.* & *vi.* to spin.

hilaza, *f.* yarn; fiber; uneven thread.—*pl.* lint.

hilera, *f.* row, line, file.

hilo, *m.* thread; yarn; filament, fiber; linen; wire.—*al h.,* along the thread, with the grain.

hilván, *m.* (sew.) tacking, basting.—**hilvanar,** *vt.* to tack, baste; to plan.

himen, *m.* hymen.—**himeneo,** *m.* hymen, nuptials.

himno, *m.* hymn.—*h. nacional,* national anthem.

hincapié, *m.* stamping the foot.—*hacer h.,* to emphasize, stress.—**hincar,** *vti.* [d] to thrust, drive; to plant.—*h. el diente,* to bite; to slander.—*h. la rodilla,* or *hincarse de rodillas,* to kneel down.

hinchabocas, *f.* (fam.) jawbreaker (candy).

hinchar, *vt.* to swell; to inflate.—*vr.* to swell; to become arrogant, conceited or puffed up.—**hinchazón,** *m.* swelling; ostentation, vanity, airs; inflation.

hinojo, *m.* fennel; knee.—*de hinojos,* kneeling.

hipar, *vi.* to hiccough; to pant.

hipertensión, *f.* high blood pressure.

hípico, *a.* equine, pertaining to horses.

hipo, *m.* hiccough.

hipocresía, *f.* hypocrisy.—**hipócrita,** *mf.* & *a.* hypocrite; hypocritical.

hipódromo, *m.* race track.

hipoteca, *f.* mortgage.—**hipotecar,** *vti.* [d] to mortgage.

hipótesis, *f.* hypothesis.

hiriente, *a.* hurting, cutting, offensive.

hirsuto, *a.* hairy, bristly.

hirviente, *a.* boiling.

hispánico, *a.* Hispanic.—**hispano,** *a.* Hispanic, Spanish.—*n.* Spaniard.—**hispanoamericano,** *n.* & *a.* Spanish-American.—**hispanohablante,** *a.* Spanish-speaking.—*mf.* Spanish speaker.

histérico, *a.* & *n.* histeric(al); hysterics.—**histerismo,** *m.,* **histeria,** *f.* hysteria.

historia, *f.* history; tale, story.—*dejarse de historias,* to come to the point.—**historiador,** *n.* historian.—**histórico,** *a.* historic(al).—**historieta,** *f.* short story; comics, comic strip.

histrión, *n.* actor, player; buffoon, juggler.

hito, *m.* landmark; guidepost; milestone; signpost.—*mirar de h. en h.,* to stare at.

hocicar, *vti.* [d] to root (as hogs).—*vii.* to fall on one's face; to muzzle; to nuzzle.—**hocico,** *m.* snout, muzzle, nose (of animal).—*de hocicos,* face downwards.—*meter el h.,* to meddle.

hockey, *m.* hockey.—*h. sobre hielo, h. sobre patines,* ice hockey.—*h. sobre hierba* or *césped,* ground or field hockey.

hogar, *m.* home; hearth, fireplace.—*h. de adopción,* foster home.

hogaza, *f.* large loaf of bread.

hoguera, *f.* bonfire; blaze; pyre.

hoja, *f.* leaf; petal; sheet of paper or metal; blade.—*doblemos la h.,* no more of that.—*h. de cálculo,* (comput.) spreadsheet.—*h. de lata,* tin plate.—*h. de nenúfar,* lily pad.—*h. de presencia,* timecard.—*h. de pedidos,* order blank.—*h. de servicios,* service record.—**hojalata,** *f.* tin plate.—**hojalatería,** *f.* tinware; tin shop.—**hojalatero,** *n.* tinsmith.

hojarasca, *f.* dead leaves; excessive foliage; trash, rubbish.

hojear, *vt.* to turn the leaves of; to glance at (a book), look over hastily.

hojuela, *f.* small leaf; flake; thin pancake.—*h. de estaño,* tin foil.

¡hola! *interj.* hello! hi!

holandés, *n.* & *a.* Dutch.—*m.* Dutch language.

holgado, *a.* loose, wide; large, spacious; at leisure; well-off.—**holganza,** *f.* leisure; idleness.—**holgar,** *vii.* [12-b] to rest; to quit work; to be idle; to be needless or useless.—*vri.* to be glad; to idle; to relax, amuse oneself.—**holgazán,** *a.* idle, lazy.—*n.* idler, loiterer, lounger.—**holgazanear,** *vi.* to idle; to loiter; to lounge.—**holgazanería,** *f.* idleness, laziness.—**holgorio,** *m.* frolic, spree.—**holgura,** *f.* ease, comfort; roominess; (mech.) play.

hollar, *vti.* [12] to tread or trample on.

hollejo, *m.* skin, peel, pod, husk.

hollín, *m.* soot, lampblack.

hombrada, *f.* manly action; impulse.—**hombre,** *m.* man.—*¡hombre al agua!,* man overboard!—*h. de la calle,* man in the street.—*h. de las cavernas,* caveman.—*h. del tiempo,* weatherman.—*h. de negocios,* businessman.—*h. de paja,* straw man, front man, puppet.—*h. lobo,* werewolf.—*h. mono,* missing link.—*h. rana,* frogman.

hombrera, *f.* shoulder pad; shoulder armor.

hombría, *f.* manliness.—*h. de bien,* probity, integrity, honesty.

hombro, *m.* shoulder.—*arrimar el h.,* to lend a hand.—*encogerse de hombros,* to shrug one's shoulders.—*en hombros,* piggyback.

hombruno, *a.* mannish.

homenaje, *m.* homage, honor.—*h. del autor,* compliments of the author.

homicida, *a.* homicidal.—*mf.* murderer, homicide (person).—**homicidio,** *m.* homicide (act).

homogeneidad, *f.* homogeneity.—**homogéneo,** *a.* homogeneous.

homosexual, *a.* & *mf.* homosexual.

honda, *f.* slingshot.

hondo, *a.* deep, profound.—*m.* depth.—**hondón,** *m.* bottom; depths.—**hondonada,** *f.* dale, glen; gully, ravine.—**hondura,** *f.* depth; profundity.—*meterse en honduras,* (fig.) to go beyond one's depth. —**hondureño,** *a.* & *n.* Honduran.

honestidad, *f.* decency, decorum; honesty; chastity; modesty.—**honesto,** *a.* honest; decent, decorous; chaste.

hongo, *m.* mushroom; fungus; derby hat.—*h. no comestible,* toadstool.

honor, *m.* honor; dignity; reputation. *pl.* rank, position, honors.—**honorable,** *a.* honorable; illustrious; reputable.—**honorario,** *a.* honorary.— *m. pl.* professional fees.—**honorífico,** *a.* honorary; honorable.

honra, *f.* honor; reputation; chastity.—*pl.* obsequies.—**honradez,** *f.* honesty, probity, integrity.—**honrado,** *a.* honest, honorable, reputable.—**honrar,** *vt.* to honor, do honor to; to respect; to be an honor for.—*vi.* to honor; to be honored.—**honrilla,** *f.* keen sense of honor or duty; punctiliousness.—**honroso,** *a.* honorable; decorous; honoring, honorgiving.

hora, *f.* hour; time.—*altas horas,* small hours.—*dar la h.,* to strike the hour; to tell the time.—*de última h.,* up-to-date.—*h. de,* time to, time for.— *h. de aglomeración,* rush hour.—*h. de cenar, h. de comer,* dinner time.—*h. de salida,* checkout time.—*h. de verano,* daylight saving time.—*h. legal* or *oficial,* standard time.—*h. libre,* free period.—*horas de menor consumo,* off-peak hours.—*horas de oficina* or *consultorio,* office hours. —*horas de trabajo,* working hours. —*horas de valle,* off-peak hours. *horas de visita,* visiting hours.— *horas extraordinarias,* overtime.—

horas libres, spare time.—*h. pica* or *punta*, rush hour, peak hour.

oradar, *vt.* to perforate, bore; to burrow.

orario, *m.* timetable, schedule; hour hand of a clock or watch.

orca, *f.* gallows; pitchfork; forked prop; rope or string of onions or garlic.

orcajadas, *f. pl.*—*a h.*, astride or astraddle.

orcón, *m.* forked pole, forked prop; post; (Am.) roof.

orda, *f.* horde.

orizontal, *a.* & *f.* horizontal.—**horizontalidad**, *f.* horizontality.—**horizonte**, *m.* horizon.

orma, *f.* mold; shoemaker's last; hatter's block; (mason.) dry wall; shoe tree.

ormiga, *f.* ant.—**hormigón**, *m.* (eng.) concrete.—*h. armado*, reinforced concrete.—**hormigonera**, *f.* concrete mixer.—**hormiguear**, *vi.* to itch; to swarm, teem.—**hormigueo**, *m.* itching.—**hormiguero**, *m.* ant hill or hillock; ant hole or nest; swarm of people or little animals.—*oso hormiguero*, anteater.

ormona, *f.* hormone.

ornacina, *f.* niche.

ornada, *f.* batch of bread, baking; melt (of a blast furnace).—**hornilla**, *f.* burner; grate (of a stove). —**hornillo**, *m.* portable furnace or stove.—**horno**, *m.* oven; kiln; furnace.—*h. crematorio*, crematorium.—*h. de microondas*, microwave oven.

orquilla, *f.* forked pole, bar, pipe, etc.; pitchfork; hairpin; double-pointed tack.

orrendo, *a.* hideous, awful.—**horrible**, *a.* horrid, horrible; hideous, heinous.—**hórrido**, *a.* horrible, hideous.—**horripilante**, *a.* horrifying, harrowing.—**horripilar**, *vt.* & *vi.* to cause or feel horror.—*vr.* to be horrified.—**horrísono**, *a.* of a terrifying noise.—**horror**, *m.* horror; enormity, frightfulness.—**horrorizar**, *vti.* [a] to horrify, terrify.—*vri.* to be terrified.—**horroroso**, *a.* horrible; hideous, frightful.

ortaliza, *f.* vegetable.—*pl.* garden produce, vegetables.

osco, *a.* sullen, gloomy.

ospedaje, *m.* lodging, board.—**hospedar**, *vt.* to lodge, harbor.—*vi.* & *vr.*

(*en*) to lodge or take lodging (at); to live (in).

hospicio, *m.* hospice; orphan asylum.

hospital, *m.* hospital.—*h. de sangre*, (mil.) field hospital.—**hospitalario**, *a.* hospitable.—**hospitalidad**, *f.* hospitality.

hosquedad, *f.* sullenness.

hostia, *f.* (eccl.) Host.

hostigamiento, *m.* chastisement; vexation.—**hostigar**, *vti.* [b] to lash, scourge, chastise; to vex, trouble; to gall.

hostil, *a.* hostile.—**hostilidad**, *f.* hostility.—**hostilizar**, *vti.* [a] to commit hostilities against, be hostile to, antagonize.

hotel, *m.* hotel.—**hotelero**, *n.* hotel manager.

hoy, *adv.* today; at the present time.— *de h. a mañana*, before tomorrow; when you least expect it.—*de h. en adelante*, hence forward, in the future.—*h. día*, or *h. en día*, nowadays.—*h. mismo*, this very day.—*h. por h.*, at the present time; this very day.

hoya, *f.* hole, pit; grave; valley, dale, glen; basin (of a river).—**hoyo**, *m.* hole, excavation; dent, hollow; pockmark; grave.

hoz, *f.* sickle; narrow pass.

hozar, *vti.* [a] to root (as hogs).

huacal, *m.* (Am.) crate.

huarache, *m.* (Am.) Mexican leather sandal.

huaso, *m.* (Am.) Chilean cowboy; peasant; halfbreed; lasso.—*a.* rustic, uncouth.

hucha, *f.* money box, bank; savings.

huchear, *vi.* to hoot, shout, cry out, call.

hueco, *a.* hollow; empty; vain, emptyheaded; resonant.—*m.* hole; hollow, gap; interval of time or space, recess.

huelga, *f.* labor strike, walkout; rest, repose.—*declararse en h.*, to strike.— *h. de sentados, h. de brazos caídos*, sitdown strike.—*h. de celo*, work-to-rule.—*h. de hambre*, hunger strike.—*h. patronal*, lockout.—*h. salvaje*, wildcat strike.—**huelguista**, *mf.* striker.

huella, *f.* track, footprint; trace, sign; trail

húerfano, *n.* & *a.* orphan(ed).

huero, *a.* vain, empty; (Am.) blonde.

huerta, *f.* orchard; vegetable garden;

irrigated land.—**h. de hortalizas,** truck garden.—**huerto,** *m.* small orchard; garden patch.

hueso, *m.* bone; stone; pit; core, center.—*estar en los huesos,* to be very thin.—*h. de la cadera,* hipbone.—*h. duro de roer,* (sl.) a hard nut to crack.—*la sin h.,* the tongue.—**huesoso,** *a.* = HUESUDO.

huésped, *n.* guest, roomer, lodger; host.—*casa de huéspedes,* boarding house.

hueste, *f.* host, army.

huesudo, *a.* bony, having large bones; rawboned.

hueva, *f.* spawn of fishes, roe.—**huevo,** *m.* egg.—*h. de Pascua,* Easter egg.—*h. duro,* hard-boiled egg.—*huevos escalfados,* poached eggs.—*huevos fritos,* fried eggs.—*huevos pasados por agua,* soft-boiled eggs.—*huevos revueltos,* scrambled eggs.

huída, *f.* flight, escape.—**huidizo,** *a.* elusive; fugitive, fleeing.—**huir,** *vii.* [23-e] & *vri.* to flee; to escape; to run away; to slip away; (**de**) to keep away (from), shun, avoid.—*h. la cara de,* to avoid, keep away from.

hule, *m.* oilcloth, oilskin; (Am.) India rubber.

hulla, *f.* mineral coal.—*h. blanca,* white coal (water power).—*h. grasa,* soft coal.

humanidad, *f.* humanity; mankind; humaneness; (coll.) corpulence, fleshiness.—*pl.* humanities.—**humanitario,** *a.* humanitarian.—**humano,** *a.* human; humane.—*m.* man, human being.

humarada, *f.* great deal of smoke.—**humazo,** *m.* dense and abundant smoke.—**humeante,** *a.* smoking, steaming, fuming.—**humear,** *vi.* to smoke; emit smoke, fumes, o[r] vapors.

humedad, *f.* humidity, moistur[e] dampness.—**humedecer,** *vti.* [3] t[o] moisten, dampen.—**húmedo,** *a[.]* wet, humid, moist, damp.

humildad, *f.* humility, humblenes[s] meekness.—**humilde,** *a.* humbl[e] meek; lowly.

humillación, *f.* humiliation; hum[i-] bling.—**humillar,** *vt.* to humiliate; t[o] humble; to subdue.—*vr.* to humbl[e] oneself; to lower oneself.

humo, *m.* smoke; fume.—*pl.* air[s] conceit.

humor, *m.* humor, wit; dispositio[n] temper, mood.—**humorada,** *f.* pleas[-] ant joke, humorous saying.—**h[u-] morismo,** *m.* humor; humorism.—**humorístico,** *a.* humorous; amus[-] ing; facetious.

hundimiento, *m.* sinking; cave-i[n] downfall, collapse.—**hundir,** *vt.* t[o] submerge, sink; to stave in, crus[h] to destroy, ruin.—*vr.* to sink; to cav[e] in, fall down.

húngaro, *n.* & *a.* Hungarian.

huracán, *m.* hurricane.

huraño, *a.* unsociable, shy.

hurgar, *vti.* [b] to stir; to poke; to st[ir] up, excite.

¡hurra!, *interj.* hurrah!

hurtadillas. —*a h.,* by stealth, on th[e] sly.—**hurtar,** *vt.* to steal, rob of; t[o] cheat in weight or measure.—*h. [el] cuerpo,* to flee; to dodge, shy awa[y] to hide.—**hurto,** *m.* theft, robber[y] stealing.

husmear, *vt.* to scent, smell; (coll.) [to] pry, peep.

huso, *m.* spindle; bobbin.—*h. horari[o]* time zone.

I

ibérico, *a.,* **ibero,** *n.* & *a.* Iberian.—**iberoamericano,** *n.* & *a.* Ibero-American.

ictericia, *f.* jaundice.—**icterlclado,** *a.* jaundiced.

ida, *f.* departure; going.—*i. y vuelta,* round trip.

idea, *f.* idea.—*i. genial* or *luminosa,* brainstorm, bright idea.—**ideal,** *a.* & *m.* ideal.—**idealismo,** *m.* ideal-ism.—**idealista,** *mf.* & *a.* idealis[t] idealistic.—**idealizar,** *vti.* [a] to idea[l-] ize.—**idear,** *vt.* to conceive the id[ea] of; to devise.

ídem, *a.* & *pron.* ditto, the same.

idéntico, *a.* (**a**) identical (with).—**ide[n-] tidad,** *f.* identity.—*de i.,* identific[a-] tion (as *a.*).—**identificación,** *f.* iden[-] tification.—*i. de llamadas,* (tel[.)] Caller ID.—**identificar,** *vti.* [[c]

to identify.—*vri.* to identify one-self.

ideología, *f.* ideology.—**ideológico,** *a.* ideological.

idioma, *m.* language, tongue.—**idiomático,** *a.* idiomatic.

idiota, *mf.* & *a.* idiot; idiotic.—**idiotez,** *f.* idiocy.—**idiotismo,** *m.* expression, idiom; idiotic action.

ido, *ppi.* of IR.

idólatra, *a.* idolatrous; heathen.—*mf.* idolater; (coll.) ardent lover.—**idolatrar,** *vt.* to idolize, worship.—**idolatría,** *f.* idolatry; idolization.—**ídolo,** *m.* idol.

idóneo, *a.* fit, able, suitable.

iglesia, *f.* church.

ignición, *f.* ignition.

ignífugo, *a.* fireproof, fire resistant, fire retardant.

ignorancia, *f.* ignorance.—**ignorante,** *a.* ignorant.—**ignorar,** *vt.* to be ignorant of, not to know.

igual, *a.* equal; even, flat; unvarying; equal sign.—*(me) es i.,* it is all the same (to me).—*m.* equal.—*al i.,* equally.—*sin i.,* unrivaled, matchless; without parallel.—**iguala,** *f.* stipend on agreement.—**igualar,** *vt.* to equalize; to match; to level, smooth; to adjust; to equate.—*vi.* to be equal; (sports) to be tied (in score).—*vr.* (**a, con**) to put oneself on the same plane (as).—**igualdad,** *f.* equality.

ijada, *f.,* **ijar,** *m.* flank (of an animal).—*dolor de i.,* pain in the side.

ilación, *f.* inference; connection.

ilegal, *a.* illegal, unlawful.—**ilegalidad,** *f.* illegality, unlawfulness.

ilegible, *a.* illegible.

ilegitimidad, *f.* illegitimacy.—**ilegítimo,** *a.* illegal, unlawful; illegitimate.

ileso, *a.* unhurt; uninjured.

ilícito, *a.* illicit; unlawful.

ilimitado, *a.* unlimited.

ilógico, *a.* illogical; irrational.

iluminación, *f.* illumination; (art) painting in distemper.—**iluminar,** *vt.* to illuminate; to enlighten.

ilusión, *f.* illusion; delusion; eagerness.—*hacerse ilusiones,* to delude oneself.—**ilusionar,** *vt.* to cause illusion; to delude.—*vr.* (**con**) to have illusions; to get up hopes (of); to bank on.—**ilusionista,** *mf.* magician.—**iluso,** *a.* deluded, deceived.—*m.* dreamer.

ilustración, *f.* illustration; elucidation,

explanation.—**ilustrar,** *vt.* to illustrate.—*vr.* to acquire knowledge, learn.—**ilustrativo,** *a.* illustrative.—**ilustre,** *a.* illustrious, distinguished.

imagen, *f.* image.—**imaginable,** *a.* imaginable.—**imaginación,** *f.* imagination; imagining.—**imaginar,** *vt.* & *vr.* to imagine; to suspect.—**imaginaria,** *f.* (mil.) reserve guard; (math.) imaginary.—**imaginario,** *a.* imaginary, imagined; mythical.—**imaginativa,** *f.* imagination.—**imaginativo,** *a.* imaginative.

imán, *m.* magnet; magnetism, charm.—**imanar, imantar,** *vt.* to magnetize.—**imantación,** *f.* magnetization.

imbécil, *mf.* & *a.* imbecile.—**imbecilidad,** *f.* imbecility.

imborrable, *a.* indelible; unforgettable.

imitable, *a.* imitable.—**imitación,** *f.* imitation.—**imitador,** *n.* & *a.* imitator; imitating.—**imitar,** *vt.* to imitate.

impaciencia, *f.* impatience.—**impacientar,** *vt.* to vex, irritate, make (one) lose patience.—*vr.* to become impatient.—**impaciente,** *a.* impatient.

impacto, *m.* impact.

impar, *a.* odd.—*m.* odd number.

imparcial, *a.* impartial.—**imparcialidad,** *f.* impartiality.

impartir, *vt.* to impart.

impás, impase or **impasse,** *m.* impasse; (bridge) finesse.

impasibilidad, *f.* impassiveness.—**impasible,** *a.* impassive, unmoved.

impávido, *a.* impassive, stolid; fearless; impudent.

impecable, *a.* impeccable.

impedido, *a.* disabled, crippled.—**impedimento,** *m.* impediment; obstacle, hindrance.—**impedir,** *vti.* [29] to impede, hinder, prevent.—*i. el paso,* to block (the way).

impeler, *vt.* to impel; to spur, stimulate.

impenetrable, *a.* impenetrable, impervious.

impenitente, *a.* impenitent, unrepentant.

impensado, *a.* unforeseen, unexpected.

imperante, *a.* commanding, reigning.—**imperar,** *vi.* to command; to prevail.—**imperativo,** *a.* imperative, urgent; domineering, bossy.—*m.* (gram.) imperative.

imperceptible, *a.* imperceptible.

imperdible, *a.* that cannot be lost.—*m.* safety pin.

imperdonable, *a.* unpardonable, unforgivable.

imperfecto, *a.* imperfect, defective.

imperial, *a.* imperial.—**imperialismo,** *m.* imperialism.—**imperialista,** *mf.* & *a.* imperialist; imperialistic.

impericia, *f.* unskillfulness, inexpertness.

imperio, *m.* empire; rule; influence; pride.—*I. romano,* Roman Empire.—**imperioso,** *a.* imperious, overbearing; pressing, urgent.

impermeabilizado, *a.* water-repellent, water-resistant.—**impermeabilizar,** *vt.* to waterproof.

impermeable, *a.* waterproof; watertight; impervious.—*m.* raincoat.

impersonal, *a.* impersonal.

impertérrito, *a.* serene; stolid.

impertinencia, *f.* impertinence, folly, nonsense.—**impertinente,** *a.* not pertinent; impertinent, meddlesome.—*m. pl.* lorgnette.

imperturbable, *a.* imperturbable, undisturbed, unruffled.

ímpetu, *m.* impetus, impulse.—**impetuoso,** *a.* impetuous, violent.

impiedad, *f.* impiety; irreligion, infidelity.—**impío,** *a.* impious; godless.—*n.* impious person; enemy of religion.

implacable, *a.* implacable.

implicar, *vti.* [d] to implicate, involve; to imply.

implícito, *a.* implicit.

implorar, *vt.* to implore, beg, entreat.

imponente, *a.* imposing.—**imponer,** *vti.* [32–49] to impose; to command (respect, fear).—*vri.* to assert oneself, impose one's authority; to command respect.

imponible, *a.* taxable.

impopular, *a.* unpopular.—**impopularidad,** *f.* unpopularity.

importación, *f.* (com.) importation, imports.—**importador,** *n.* & *a.* importer; importing.

importancia, *f.* importance.—**importante,** *a.* important.—**importar,** *vi.* to be important; to concern.—*eso no importa,* that doesn't matter.—*eso no le importa a Ud.,* that is none of your business.—*no importa,* never mind.—*no me importa,* I don't care; that makes no difference to me.—*¿qué importa?* what does it matter? what difference does it make?.—*vt.*

to import; to amount to; to be worth; to imply.—**importe,** *m.* amount, price, value.

importunar, *vt.* to importune, pester.—**importuno,** *a.* inopportune; persistent, annoying.

imposibilidad, *f.* impossibility.—**imposibilitado,** *a.* helpless, without means; disabled, unfit for service.—**imposibilitar,** *vt.* to disable, make unfit for service.—**imposible,** *a.* impossible.

imposición, *f.* imposition (of a duty, etc.); tax, burden.

impostor, *n.* impostor.—**impostura,** *f.* imposture.

impotencia, *f.* impotence.—**impotente,** *a.* impotent, powerless.

impracticable, *a.* impracticable.

impregnación, *f.* impregnation.—**impregnar,** *vt.* to impregnate; to saturate.—*vr.* to become impregnated.

imprenta, *f.* printing; printing office or house; press.

imprescindible, *a.* indispensable, essential.

impresión, *f.* impression; print, printing; stamping; footprint.—*i. digital,* fingerprint.—**impresionable,** *a.* impressionable, emotional.—**impresionar,** *vt.* to impress; to affect.—*vr.* to be moved.—**impreso,** *ppi.* of IMPRIMIR.—*a.* printed; stamped.—*m.* publication; printed matter, print; blank.—**impresor,** *n.* printer.—**impresora,** *f.* (comput.) printer.—*i. láser,* printer.

imprevisión, *f.* lack of foresight; improvidence.—**imprevisto,** *a.* unforeseen, unexpected.—*m. pl.* incidental or unforeseen expenses.

imprimir, *vti.* [49] to print, stamp, imprint.

improbable, *a.* improbable, unlikely.

ímprobo, *a.* laborious, painful, arduous.

improcedente, *a.* contrary to law.

impromptu, *m.* (mus.) impromptu performance.

improperio, *m.* insult, indignity.

impropio, *a.* inappropriate, unfitting; improper, unbecoming.

improvisación, *f.* improvisation, ad lib, impromptu.—**improvisado,** *a.* makeshift, improvised; ad-lib, impromptu.—**improvisar,** *vt.* to improvise; to ad-lib.—**improviso,** *a.* unexpected, unforeseen.—*de i.,* suddenly.

Imprudencia, *f.* imprudence, indiscretion.—**Imprudente,** *a.* imprudent, indiscreet.

Impudicia, *f.* immodesty.—**Impúdico,** *a.* immodest; impudent; revealing (of a dress).

Impuesto, *ppi.* of IMPONER.—*a.* imposed; informed.—*estar,* or *quedar i. de,* to be informed about.—*m.* tax, duty.—*i. al* or *sobre el valor agregado* or *añadido,* value-added tax.—*i. de consumo, i. interno,* excise tax.—*i. de lujo,* luxury tax.—*i. de retención* or *retenido,* withholding tax.—*i. sobre la plusvalía,* capital gains tax.—*i. sobre los ingresos, i. sobre rentas,* income tax.—*i. sobre las utilidades excedentes* or *ganancias excesivas,* excess profits tax.—*i. sobre las ventas,* sales tax.—*i. sucesorio, i. sobre sucesiones, i. a la herencia,* inheritance tax.—*i. único,* flat tax.

Impulsar, *vt.* to impel, move; (mech.) to drive, force.—**Impulsión,** *f.* impulsion, impulse, impetus.—**Impulsivo,** *a.* impulsive.—**Impulso,** *m.* impulsion; impulse.

Impureza, *f.* impurity; unchastity.—**Impuro,** *a.* impure; defiled.

Inacabable, *a.* everlasting, endless.—**Inacabado,** *a.* unfinished.

Inaccesible, *a.* inaccessible, unapproachable.

Inacción, *f.* inaction, inactivity.

Inactividad, *f.* inactivity.—**Inactivo,** *a.* inactive.

Inadecuado, *a.* inadequate.

Inadaptable, *a.* unadaptable.—**Inadaptación,** *f.* maladjustment.

Inadmisible, *a.* inadmissible.

Inadvertencia, *f.* inadvertence, oversight.—**Inadvertido,** *a.* careless; unseen, unnoticed.

Inaguantable, *a.* unbearable.

Inalámbrico, *a.* wireless; cordless.

Inalienable, *a.* inalienable.

Inamovible, *a.* immovable; tenured.—**Inamovilidad,** *f.* tenure.

Inanición, *f.* starvation.

Inanimado, *a.* inanimate, lifeless.

Inapelable, *a.* irrevocable.

Inapetencia, *f.* lack of appetite.

Inaplazable, *a.* that cannot be deferred.

Inaplicable, *a.* irrelevant.

Inapreciable, *a.* invaluable; imperceptible.

Inasequible, *a.* unattainable, unobtainable, unavailable.

Inastillable, *a.* shatterproof.

Inaudito, *a.* unheard of, most extraordinary.

Inauguración, *f.* inauguration.—**Inaugurar,** *vt.* to inaugurate; to open (exhibition, etc.); to unveil (statue, monument, etc.).

Inca, *mf.* & *a.* Inca.—**Incaico,** *a.* Inca.

Incalculable, *a.* incalculable; innumerable.

Incalificable, *a.* extremely bad, most reprehensible.

Incandescencia, *f.* incandescence.—**Incandescente,** *a.* incandescent.

Incansable, *a.* indefatigable, tireless.

Incapacidad, *f.* incapacity; incompetence.—**Incapacitar,** *vt.* to incapacitate, disable.—**Incapaz,** *a.* incapable; unable; incompetent.

Incauto, *a.* unwary; gullible.

Incendiar, *vt.* to set on fire.—*vr.* to catch fire.—**Incendiario,** *n.* & *a.* arsonist; incendiary.—**Incendio,** *m.* fire, conflagration.—*i. forestal,* forest fire.—*i. provocado,* arson attack.

Incensar, *vti.* [1] (eccl.) to incense; to bestow excessive praise or adulation.

Incentivo, *m.* incentive, inducement; encouragement.

Incertidumbre, *f.* uncertainty; quandary.

Incesante, *a.* unceasing, incessant.

Incesto, *m.* incest.

Incidencia, *f.* incident; incidence.—**Incidental,** *a.* incidental.—**Incidente,** *a.* incidental.—*m.* incident.—**Incidir,** *vi.* (**en**) to fall (into) (as an error).

Incienso, *m.* incense.

Incierto, *a.* uncertain; untrue; unknown.

Incinerar, *vt.* to incinerate, cremate.

Incisión, *f.* incision, cut.—**Incisivo,** *a.* incisive; keen, sharp.

Incitante, *a.* inciting, exciting.—**Incitar,** *vt.* to incite, spur, instigate.—**Incitativo,** *a.* inciting.—*m.* incitement.

Incivil, *a.* uncivil; rude.

Inclasificable, *a.* unclassifiable, nondescript.

Inclinación, *f.* inclination; tendency, proclivity, bent; pitch; slope; (RR.) grade.—**Inclinado,** *a.* inclined; sloping; disposed.—**Inclinar,** *vt.* to incline; to bow; to influence.—*vr.* to incline, slope; to lean; to stoop, bow.

Incluir, *vti.* [23–49-e] to include; to enclose.—**Inclusión,** *f.* inclusion.—**In-**

clusive, *adv.* inclusively.—**inclusivo,** *a.* inclusive.—**incluso,** *ppi.* of IN-CLUIR.—*a.* enclosed; including, included.

incobrable, *a.* (com.) uncollectable.

incógnito, *a.* unknown.—*de i.,* incognito.—*f.* (math.) unknown (quantity).

incoherencia, *f.* incoherence.—**incoherente,** *a.* incoherent.

incoloro, *a.* colorless.

incólume, *a.* sound, safe, unharmed.

incombustible, *a.* fireproof.

incomible, *a.* inedible, uneatable.

incomodar, *vt.* to disturb, inconvenience, trouble.—*vr.* to become vexed or angry.—**incomodidad,** *f.* inconvenience; discomfort; nuisance, annoyance.—**incómodo,** *a.* inconvenient; uncomfortable; ill at ease.

incomparable, *a.* incomparable.

incompetencia, *f.* incompetence.—**incompetente,** *a.* incompetent, unqualified.

incompleto, *a.* incomplete.

incomprensible, *a.* incomprehensible.—**incompresión,** *f.* misunderstanding; lack of understanding.

incomunicado, *a.* isolated; in solitary confinement.—**incomunicar,** *vti.* [d] to isolate, put in solitary confinement.

incondicional, *a.* unconditional; unqualified.

inconexo, *a.* unconnected, not pertinent; incoherent.

inconfundible, *a.* unmistakable.

incongruente, *a.* incongruous, out of place.

inconmensurable, *a.* immeasurable; vast.

inconmovible, *a.* unrelenting, unshakable.

inconsciencia, *f.* unconsciousness; (the) unconscious; unawareness; (coll.) irresponsibility.—**inconsciente,** *a.* unconscious; unaware; (coll.) irresponsible.

inconsecuencia, *f.* inconsistency.—**inconsecuente,** *a.* inconsistent.

inconsistente, *a.* unsubstantial, unstable.

inconstancia, *f.* inconstancy, fickleness, mutability.—**inconstante,** *a.* inconstant, fickle, mutable.

incontable, *a.* countless, innumerable.

incontestable, *a.* unanswerable.

incontrovertible, *a.* unanswerable.

inconveniencia, *f.* inconvenience; discomfort.—**inconveniente,** *a.* inconvenient, uncomfortable.—*m.* difficulty, obstacle.

incopiable, *a.* inimitable; priceless.

incorporar, *vt.* to incorporate, embody; to make (someone) sit up.—*vr.* to incorporate; to join (as a mil. unit); to form a corporation; to sit up.

incorpóreo, *a.* bodiless, ethereal, immaterial.

incorrección, *f.* incorrectness; impropriety.—**incorrecto,** *a.* incorrect; improper.

incredulidad, *f.* incredulity.—**incrédulo,** *a.* incredulous.—*n.* unbeliever.—**increíble,** *a.* incredible, unbelievable.

incrementar, *vt.* (neol.) to increase, make bigger.—*vi.* to be increased.—**incremento,** *m.* increment, increase.

increpar, *vt.* to rebuke.

incriminar, *vt.* to incriminate.

incrustar, *vt.* to incrust; to encase; to inlay.

incubación, *f.* incubation; hatching.—**incubadora,** *f.* incubator (apparatus); hatchery.—**incubar,** *vt.* to incubate; to hatch.

inculpar, *vt.* to accuse, blame.

inculto, *a.* uncultured, untutored; uncultivated.—**incultura,** *f.* lack of culture.

incumbencia, *f.* incumbency; concern.—**incumbir,** *vt.* to concern, pertain.

incumplimiento, *m.* nonfulfillment.

incurable, *a.* incurable.

incurrir, *vi.* (en) to incur, become liable (to); to commit (error or crime).

incursión, *f.* (mil.) incursion, raid.

indagación, *f.* investigation, search, inquiry.—**indagar,** *vti.* [b] to investigate, inquire into or about.

indebidamente, *adv.* unduly; improperly; illegally.—**indebido,** *a.* improper; illegal.

indecencia, *f.* indecency; obscenity.—**indecente,** *a.* indecent, obscene.

indecible, *a.* inexpressible, untold.

indecisión, *f.* indecision, irresolution.—**indeciso,** *a.* hesitant, irresolute; undecided.

indecoroso, *a.* indecorous, unbecoming; undignified.

indefectible, *a.* unfailing.

indefendible, *a.* indefensible.—**indefenso,** *a.* defenseless.

indefinible, *a.* undefinable.—**indefinido,** *a.* indefinite; undefined.

indeleble, a. indelible.

indemne, a. undamaged, unhurt.—**indemnización,** f. compensation; indemnity.—**indemnizar,** vti. [a] to indemnify, compensate; to recoup.

independencia, f. independence.—**independiente,** a. independent.—**independizar,** vti. [a] to free, emancipate.—vri. to become independent, win freedom.

indescifrable, a. undecipherable.

indescriptible, a. indescribable.

indeseable, a. undesirable, unwelcome.

indesmallable, a. runproof.

indeterminado, a. indeterminate, undetermined.

india, f. gang, mob.—**la India,** f. India.—**las Indias Occidentales,** f. pl. the West Indies.—**las Indias Orientales,** f. pl. the East Indies.

indicación, f. indication; hint.—**indicar,** vti. [d] to indicate, suggest, show.—**indicador,** m. (aut.) sign; gauge.—i. de velocidad, speedometer.—**indicativo,** a. indicative, pointing.—m. (gram.) indicative.—i. de la emisora, (rad./TV) station identification.

índice, m. index; catalog; pointer; forefinger.—i. con pestañas, thumb index.—i. de audiencia, (TV) ratings.—i. del costo de (la) vida, cost-of-living index.—i. de materias, i. temático, table of contents.—i. de mortalidad, death rate.—i. de natalidad, birth rate.—i. de precios al consumo, consumer prices index.—**indicio,** m. indication, clue, sign.

indiferencia, f. indifference.—**indiferente,** a. indifferent.

indígena, a. native, indigenous; (Am.) Indian.—mf. native; (Am.) Indian.

indigestarse, vr. to cause indigestion; to suffer from indigestion; to be unbearable.—**indigestión,** f. indigestion.—**indigesto,** a. indigestible.

indignación, f. indignation.—**indignar,** vt. to irritate, anger.—vr. to become indignant.—**indignidad,** f. indignity; unworthy act.—**indigno,** a. unworthy, undeserving; unbecoming, contemptible; low.

indigo, m. indigo.

indio, n. & a. Indian; Hindu.—fila india, Indian file.

indirecta, f. innuendo, hint.—echar indirectas, to make insinuations.—**indirecto,** a. indirect.

indisciplina, f. lack of discipline.—**indisciplinado,** a. undisciplined; untrained.

indiscreción, f. indiscretion.—**indiscreto,** a. indiscreet.

indiscutible, a. unquestionable, indisputable.

indispensable, a. indispensable, vital.

indisponer, vti. [32–49] to indispose; to make ill; (con) to prejudice (against).—vri. to become ill; to fall out (with a person).—**indisposición,** f. indisposition, slight ailment; dislike.—**indispuesto,** ppi. of INDISPONER.—a. indisposed; ill.

indistinto, a. indistinct, vague.

individual, a. individual.—**individualidad,** f. individuality.—**individuo,** n. individual, person; fellow.

indivisible, a. indivisible.

indochino, a. & n. Indo-Chinese.

indócil, a. headstrong, unruly.

indocto, a. ignorant, untaught, untutored.

índole, f. class, kind; disposition, nature.

indolencia, f. indolence.—**indolente,** a. indolent.

indomable, a. untamable, indomitable; unmanageable.—**indómito,** a. untamed; unruly.

indostánico, a. Hindu.

inducción, f. inducement, persuasion; (elec., log.) induction.—**inducir,** vti. [11] to induce; to persuade.—**inductor,** a. (elec.) inducive.—m. magnetic field.

indulgencia, f. indulgence; forbearance; forgiveness.—**indulgente,** a. indulgent, forbearing.

indultar, vt. to pardon.—**indulto,** m. pardon, amnesty.

indumentaria, f. garb, apparel, garments.

industria, f. industry.—caballero de i., swindler; confidence man.—**industrial,** a. industrial.—mf. industrialist.—**industrializar,** vti. [a] to industrialize.—**industrioso,** a. industrious.

inédito, a. unpublished.

ineficacia, f. inefficacy.—**ineficaz,** a. ineffectual, ineffective.

inelegible, a. ineligible.

ineludible, a. inevitable, unavoidable.

inenarrable, a. inexplicable; inexpressible, ineffable.

ineptitud, f. ineptitude, incompetency.—**inepto,** a. inept, incompetent, unqualified.

inequívoco, *a.* unmistakable.

inercia, *f.* inertia; inertness, inactivity.—**inerte,** *a.* inert; slow, sluggish.

inescrutable, *a.* inscrutable; unconfirmable.

inesperado, *a.* unexpected.

inestabilidad, *f.* instability.—**inestable,** *a.* unstable, unsteady.

inestimable, *a.* inestimable, invaluable.

inevitable, *a.* inevitable, unavoidable.

inexactitud, *f.* inexactness; inaccuracy; unfaithfulness.—**inexacto,** *a.* inexact, inaccurate.

inexistente, *a.* nonexistent.

inexorable, *a.* inexorable, relentless.

inexperiencia, *f.* inexperience.—**inexperto,** *a.* inexperienced, unskillful; unpractical.

inexplicable, *a.* inexplicable, unexplainable, unaccountable.

inexplotado, *a.* undeveloped.

inexpresivo, *a.* inexpressive, wooden.

infalible, *a.* infallible, unerring, failsafe.

infame, *a.* & *mf.* infamous (person).—**infamia,** *f.* infamy; baseness; dishonor; opprobrium.

infancia, *f.* infancy; childhood.—**infante,** *n.* infante, prince; (*f.* infanta, princess).—**infantería,** *f.* infantry.—**infantil,** *a.* infantile, childlike; children's; innocent; (pej.) childish.

infarto, *m.* heart attack.

infatigable, *a.* untiring, tireless.

infausto, *a.* unlucky; unhappy.

infección, *f.* infection.—**infeccioso,** *a.* infectious.—**infectar,** *vt.* to infect; to corrupt.—*vr.* to become infected.

infecundo, *a.* barren, sterile.

infelicidad, *f.* unhappiness, infelicity.—**infeliz,** *a.* unhappy, unfortunate.—*mf.* poor devil.

inferencia, *f.* inference.

inferior, *a.* inferior; lower; · under (part).—*mf.* subordinate.—**inferioridad,** *f.* inferiority.

inferir, *vti.* [39] to infer; to imply; to inflict (as a wound).

infernal, *a.* infernal, hellish.

infestar, *vt.* to infest, plague; to infect.

inficionar, *vt.* to infect; to corrupt.

infidelidad, *f.* infidelity; unfaithfulness.—**infiel,** *a.* unfaithful, faithless; infidel, pagan; inaccurate.—*mf.* infidel.

infiernillo, *m.* spirit lamp.—**infierno,** *m.* hell, inferno.

infiltración, *f.* infiltration.—**infiltrar,** *vt.* & *vr.* to infiltrate, filter through.

ínfimo, *a.* lowest; least.

infinidad, *f.* infinity; infinite number, lot.—**infinitivo,** *m.* & *a.* infinitive.—**infinito,** *a.* infinite.—*adv.* infinitely, immensely.—*m.* infinity.

inflación, *f.* inflation; conceit, airs.

inflamable, *a.* inflammable.—**inflamación,** *f.* inflammation.—**inflamar,** *vt.* to inflame; to set on fire.—*vr.* to catch fire; to become fiery; (med.) to become inflamed.

inflar, *vt.* to inflate; to exaggerate.—*vr.* to swell; to puff up (with pride, etc.).

inflexibilidad, *f.* inflexibility; stiffness, rigidity.—**inflexible,** *a.* inflexible, rigid, steely; unbending, unyielding.—**inflexión,** *f.* inflection; accent, modulation.

infligir, *vti.* [c] to impose (a penalty); condemn to.

influencia, *f.* influence.—**influenza,** *f.* influenza, grippe.—**influir,** *vti.* [23-e] to influence; to act on.—*vii.* (**en**) to have influence (on); to contribute (to).—**influjo,** *m.* influence.—**influyente,** *a.* influential.

infolio, *m.* folio.

información, *f.* information; report; inquiry; (law) brief.—**informal,** *a.* informal; unreliable; unconventional.—**informalidad,** *f.* informality; breach of etiquette; unreliability.—**informar,** *vt.* to inform, report to.—*vi.* (law) to plead.—*vr.* (**de**) to acquaint oneself (with), to inquire (into); to find out (about).—**informático,** *a.* computer.—*n.* computer specialist; computer programmer.—*f.* computer science, computing.—**informativo,** *a.* instructive, informative; newsy.—*m.* news.—**informe,** *a.* shapeless.—*m.* information; report; news; account; (law) pleading.

infortunado, *a.* unfortunate, unlucky.—**infortunio,** *m.* misfortune, ill luck; mishap; misery.

infracción, *f.* infraction, infringement, transgression.

infranqueable, *a.* insurmountable.

infrascrito, *a.* undersigned; hereinafter mentioned.

infrecuente, *a.* unusual, infrequent.

infringir, *vti.* [c] to infringe, violate, break.

infructuoso, *a.* fruitless; unsuccessful, unavailing.

ínfulas, *f. pl.* conceit, airs.—*darse í.,* to put on airs.

infundado, *a.* groundless, baseless.

infundio, *m.* (coll.) fib, story.

Ingeniería, *f.* engineering.—*i. civil,* civil engineering.—*i. de sistemas,* systems engineer.—*i. eléctrica, i. electricista,* electrical engineering.—*i. genética,* genetic engineering.—*i. química,* chemical engineering.—**Ingeniero,** *n.* engineer.—*i. civil,* civil engineer.—*i. electrotécnico, i. electricista,* electrical engineer.—*i. de sistemas,* systems engineer.—*i. químico,* chemical engineer.—**Ingenio,** *m.* talent; wit; cleverness, ingenuity; (Am.) sugar mill; device.—**Ingeniosidad,** *f.* ingeniousness, ingenuity.—**Ingenioso,** *a.* ingenious; witty, sparkling; resourceful.

Ingénito, *a.* inborn, innate.

Ingenuidad, *f.* ingenuousness, candor.—**Ingenuo,** *a.* ingenuous, candid, unsophisticated.

Ingerencia, *f.* interference, meddling.—**Ingerir,** *vti.* [39] to insert, introduce.—*vri.* to interfere.

Ingle, *f.* groin.

Inglés, *a.* English.—*n.* Englishman (-woman).—*m.* English language.

Ingratitud, *f.* ingratitude, ungratefulness.—**Ingrato,** *a.* ungrateful; thankless; disagreeable.

Ingravidez, *f.* weightlessness.—**Ingrávido,** *a.* weightless.

Ingrediente, *m.* ingredient.

Ingresar, *vt.* (en) to enter; to deposit (money); to join (a party, group). —**Ingreso,** *m.* entrance; entering; joining; (com.) entry, money received.—*pl.* receipts; earnings.

Inhábil, *a.* unable; incompetent; unfit, unskillful.—**Inhabilitación,** *f.* disabling or disqualifying; disqualification; disability.—**Inhabilitar,** *vt.* to disqualify; to disable, render unfit.—*vr.* to lose a right; to become disabled.

Inhabitable, *a.* uninhabitable.

Inhalación, *f.* inhalation.—**Inhalar,** *vt.* to inhale.

Inherente, *a.* inherent.

Inhibición, *f.* inhibition; prohibition.—**Inhibir,** *vt.* to inhibit.—**Inhibitorio,** *a.* inhibitory.

Inhospitalario, *a.* inhospitable; unsheltering.—**Inhóspito,** *a.* inhospitable.

Inhumano, *a.* inhuman, cruel.

Iniciación, *f.* initiation, introduction.—**Inicial,** *mf.* & *a.* initial.—**Iniciar,** *vt.* to initiate; to begin, start.—*vr.* to be initiated.—**Iniciativa,** *f.* initiative; resourcefulness.

Inicuo, *a.* iniquitous, wicked.

Inimaginable, *a.* unimaginable, inconceivable, unthinkable.

Inimitable, *a.* inimitable.

Ininteligible, *a.* unintelligible.

Injerencia, *f.* interference.

Injerir, *vti.* & [39] *vri.* = INGERIR.

Injertar, *vt.* to graft.

Injuria, *f.* offense, insult, affront.—**Injuriar,** *vt.* to insult, offend.—**Injurioso,** *a.* injurious; insulting, offensive.

Injusticia, *f.* injustice.—**Injustificable,** *a.* unjustifiable.—**Injustificado,** *a.* unjustified, unjustifiable.—**Injusto,** *a.* unjust, unfair.

Inmaculado, *a.* immaculate.

Inmanente, *a.* inherent.

Inmaterial, *a.* immaterial.

Inmaturo, *a.* immature.

Inmediación, *f.* contiguity.—*pl.* suburbs; neighborhood.—**Inmediato,** *a.* close, adjoining, immediate.

Inmejorable, *a.* most excellent.

Inmensidad, *f.* immensity, vastness; infinity; great multitude or number.—**Inmenso,** *a.* immense; infinite; countless.

Inmerecido, *a.* unmerited, undeserved.

Inmersión, *f.* immersion.

Inmigración, *f.* immigration.—**Inmigrante,** *mf.* immigrant.—**Inmigrar,** *vi.* to immigrate.—**Inmigratorio,** *a.* immigration.

Inminencia, *f.* imminence, nearness.—**Inminente,** *a.* imminent, near.

Inmiscuir, *vti.* [23-e] (fig.) to discuss elements alien to the question.—*vri.* to interfere; to meddle.

Inmodestia, *f.* immodesty.—**Inmodesto,** *a.* immodest.

Inmoral, *a.* immoral.—**Inmoralidad,** *f.* immorality.

Inmortal, *a.* immortal.—**Inmortalidad,** *f.* immortality.—**Inmortalizar,** *vti.* [a] to immortalize.—*vri.* to become immortal.

Inmovible, *a.* immovable.—**Inmóvil,** *a.* motionless; fixed; unshaken.—**Inmovilidad,** *f.* immovability, fixedness.—**Inmovilizar,** *vti.* [a] to immobilize, fix.

Inmueble, *a.* (law) immovable, real (property).—*m.* (law) immovables.

Inmundicia, *f.* filth, dirt; garbage; filthiness; uncleanliness; impurity.—**Inmundo,** *a.* unclean, filthy.

inmune, *a.* immune; exempt.—**inmunidad,** *f.* immunity; exemption.—**inmunizar,** *vti.* [a] to immunize.

innato, *a.* innate; inborn.

innecesario, *a.* unnecessary.

innegable, *a.* undeniable.

innoble, *a.* ignoble.

innovación, *f.* innovation.—**innovador,** *n.* & *a.* innovator; innovating. —**innovar,** *vt.* to innovate.

innumerable, *a.* innumerable, numberless.

inocencia, *f.* innocence.—**inocente,** *a.* innocent.—**inocentón,** *n.* simpleton.

inoculación, *f.* inoculation.—**inocular,** *vt.* to inoculate; to contaminate.

inodoro, *a.* odorless.—*m.* toilet, lavatory.

inofensivo, *a.* inoffensive, harmless.

inolvidable, *a.* unforgettable.

inopinado, *a.* unexpected, unforeseen.

inoportuno, *a.* inopportune, untimely.

inorgánico, *a.* inorganic.

inoxidable, *a.* nonrusting.

inquebrantable, *a.* unbreakable; unshakable; inflexible.

inquietante, *a.* disquieting, disturbing.—**inquietar,** *vt.* to disquiet, trouble, worry; to vex, harass; to stir up or excite.—*vr.* to become uneasy or restless; to fret, worry. —**inquieto,** *a.* restless; uneasy, worried.—**inquietud,** *f.* restlessness, uneasiness, anxiety.

inquilinato, *m.* occupancy; lease, leasing.—**inquilino,** *n.* tenant, lodger, renter, lessee.

inquina, *f.* (coll.) aversion, hatred, grudge.

inquirir, *vti.* [2] to inquire, search, investigate.

inquisición, *f.* inquest, examination, inquiry; Inquisition, Holy Office.

insalubre, *a.* unhealthful, unsanitary.—**insalubridad,** *f.* unhealthfulness.

insania, *f.* insanity.—**insano,** *a.* insane, crazy.

insatisfecho, *a.* dissatisfied; unsatisfied.

inscribir, *vti.* [49] to inscribe, register, record, book.—*vri.* to register; to enroll.—**inscripción,** *f.* inscription; record, register, entry; registration; matriculation; government bond.—**inscrito,** *ppi.* of INSCRIBIR.

insecticida, *m.* & *a.* insecticide; insecticidal.—*i. en aerosol,* insect spray.—**insecto,** *m.* insect.

inseguridad, *f.* insecurity; uncertainty.—**inseguro,** *a.* insecure, unsafe; uncertain.

inseminación, *f.* insemination.—*i. artificial,* artificial insemination.

insensatez, *f.* stupidity, folly.—**insensato,** *a.* stupid; mad.

insensibilidad, *f.* insensitivity; (med.) numbness.—**insensibilizar,** *vti.* [a] to desensitize; (med.) to numb.—**insensible,** *a.* insensitive, thickskinned; imperceptible; unfeeling.

inseparable, *a.* inseparable; undetachable.

inserción, *f.* insertion; grafting.—**insertar,** *vti.* [49] to insert.—**inserto,** *ppi.* of INSERTAR.

inservible, *a.* unserviceable, useless.

insidia, *f.* ambush, snare.—**insidioso,** *a.* insidious, sly, guileful.

insigne, *a.* noted, famous, renowned.

insignia, *f.* decoration, medal, badge, standard; (naut.) pennant.—*pl.* insignia.

insignificancia, *f.* insignificance; trifle.—**insignificante,** *a.* insignificant.

insinuación, *f.* insinuation; hint, suggestion.—**insinuar,** *vt.* to insinuate, hint, suggest.—*vr.* to ingratiate oneself; to creep in.

insípido, *a.* insipid, tasteless; unsavory; spiritless, flat; unseasoned.

insistencia, *f.* persistence, insistence, obstinacy.—**insistir,** *vi.* (en) to insist (on), persist (in); to dwell (upon), emphasize.

insolación, *f.* sunstroke.

insolencia, *f.* insolence.—**insolentar,** *vt.* to make bold.—*vr.* to become insolent.—**insolente,** *a.* insolent.

insólito, *a.* unusual, unaccustomed.

insomnio, *m.* insomnia, sleeplessness.

insondable, *a.* unfathomable, fathomless; inscrutable.

insoportable, *a.* unbearable, intolerable.

insostenible, *a.* indefensible.

inspección, *f.* inspection; inspector's office.—**inspeccionar,** *vt.* to inspect.—**inspector,** *n.* inspector; supervisor, overseer.

inspiración, *f.* inspiration; inhalation.—**inspirar,** *vt.* to inspire; to inhale.

instalación, *f.* installation.—**instalar,** *vt.* to install.—*vr.* to establish oneself, settle.

instancia, *f.* instance; petition; request.

instantáneo, *a.* instantaneous.—

snapshot.—**instante**, *m*. instant, moment, trice.—*al i.*, immediately.

instar, *vt*. to press, urge.—*vi.* to be urgent.

instaurar, *vt*. to establish; to renovate.

instigador, *n*. instigator, abettor.—**instigar**, *vti*. [b] to instigate, incite.

instintivo, *a*. instinctive.—**instinto**, *m*. instinct.

institución, *f*. institution, establishment.—**instituir**, *vti*. [23-e] to institute, establish, found.—**instituto**, *m*. institute.—**institutriz**, *f*. governess.

instrucción, *f*. instruction; education, learning; tutoring; (law) court proceedings.—*pl*. instructions, orders.—**instructivo**, *a*. instructive.—**instruir**, *vti*. [23-e] to instruct, teach, train; to inform; to put in legal form.

instrumentación, *f*. (mus.) instrumentation, orchestration.—**instrumental**, *a*. (mus.) instrumental; (law) pertaining to legal instruments.—*m*. set of instruments.—**instrumentista**, *mf*. instrumentalist.—**instrumento**, *m*. instrument, implement, apparatus; instrument, musical instrument.—*i. de cuerda*, stringed instrument.—*i. de viento*, wind instrument.—*i. de viento de madera*, woodwind.

insubordinación, *f*. insubordination.—**insubordinar**, *vt*. to incite to insubordination.—*vr*. to rebel, mutiny.

insubstituible, *a*. irreplaceable.

insuficiencia, *f*. insufficiency.—**insuficiente**, *a*. insufficient.

insula, *f*. isle, island.—**insular**, *a*. insular.

insulso, *a*. insipid; dull, heavy.

insultar, *vt*. to insult.—**insulto**, *m*. insult, affront.

insuperable, *a*. insuperable, impassable.

insurgente, *mf*. & *a*. insurgent.

insurrección, *f*. insurrection, rebellion.—**insurreccionar**, *vt*. to cause to rebel.—*vr*. to rebel.—**insurrecto**, *n*. & *a*. insurgent, rebel.

insustancial, *a*. unsubstantial.

intacto, *a*. untouched, intact, whole, undisturbed.

intachable, *a*. unexceptionable, irreproachable.

intangible, *a*. intangible, untouchable.

integración, *f*. integration.—**integral**, *a*. integral; whole.—**integrar**, *vt*. to integrate; to compose, make up; (com.) to reimburse.—**integridad**, *f*. wholeness; integrity, honesty; virginity.—**íntegro**, *a*. entire, complete, whole; upright, honest; unabridged; unexpurgated.

intelecto, *m*. intellect.—**intelectual**, *a*. & *mf*. intellectual.—**intelectualidad**, *f*. intelligentsia.—**inteligencia**, *f*. intelligence; understanding (between persons).—**inteligente**, *a*. intelligent; smart, clever.

intemperancia, *f*. intemperance, excess.—**intemperante**, *a*. intemperate.—**intemperie**, *f*. rough or bad weather.—*a la i.*, in the open air, outdoors, unsheltered.

intempestivo, *a*. unseasonable, inopportune.

intención, *f*. intention, purpose.—*de primera i.*, provisionally, tentatively.

intendencia, *f*. intendancy; administration; office or district of an intendant.—**intendente**, *n*. intendant; administrator; (mil.) quartermaster.

intensidad, *f*. intensity; vehemence.—**intensivo**, **intenso**, *a*. intense, intensive, vehement.

intentar, *vt*. to try, attempt, endeavor; to intend; (law) to enter (an action), commence (a lawsuit).—**intento**, *m*. intent, purpose.—*de i.*, purposely, knowingly.—*i. fallido*, false start.—**intentona**, *f*. (coll.) rash attempt.

intercalar, *vt*. to interpolate, place between.

intercambiar, *vt*. & *vi*. to interchange.—**intercambio**, *m*. interchange, intercourse.

interceder, *vi*. to intercede.

interceptar, *vt*. to intercept, cut off.

intercesión, *f*. intercession, mediation.

interdicción, *f*. interdiction, prohibition.

interés, *m*. interest.—*pl*. interests.—*intereses creados*, vested interests.—**interesado**, *a*. interested; mercenary, selfish.—*n*. associate; person interested; (law) party in interest.—**interesante**, *a*. interesting.—**interesar**, *vi*. & *vr*. (**en**, **por**, **con**) to be concerned (with) or interested (in); to take an interest.—*vt*. to invest; to give an interest; to interest.

interfaz or **interface**, *f*. interface.

interfecto, *n*. (law) murdered person, victim.

Interferencia, f. interference.—**Interferir,** vi. to interfere; to meddle.

ínterin, adv. meanwhile, interim.—**Interino,** a. provisional, temporary, acting, interim.

Interior, a. interior, inner, inside; domestic (as commerce, etc.).—m. interior; inside; inner part; mind, soul.—pl. entrails, intestines, (coll.) insides.—**Interioridades,** f. pl. family secrets; inwardness.

Interjección, f. interjection.

Interludio, m. (mus.) interlude.

Intermediario, a. intermediary.—n. intermediary; mediator; middleman.—**Intermedio,** a. intermediate, interposed.—m. interval, interim; (theat.) interlude, intermission; (rad./TV) station break.

Interminable, a. interminable, endless.

Intermisión, f. intermission, interruption.

Intermitente, a. intermittent.—m. (aut.) turn signal.

Internacional, a. international.

Internado, m. boarding school; boarding.—**Internar,** vt. to intern, confine; to place in an institution.—vi. to enter.—vr. (en) to go into the interior (of); to go deeply (into).—**Interno,** a. interior, internal, inward; boarding.—n. boarding student; interne.

Interpelar, vt. to interrogate, question.

Interponer, vti. [32–49] to interpose, place between; to appoint as a mediator; (law) to present (a petition) to a court.—vri. to go between, to interpose.—**Interposición,** f. mediation; interjection; interposal; intervention.

Interpretación, f. interpretation; rendering.—**Interpretar,** vt. to interpret.—**Intérprete,** mf. interpreter.

Interpuesto, ppi. of INTERPONER.—a. interposed.

Interrogación, f. interrogation, questioning; question mark.—**Interrogante,** a. interrogative; interrogating.—mf. interrogator, questioner.—m. question mark.—**Interrogar,** vti. [b] to question, interrogate.—**Interrogatorio,** m. questioning, examination, grilling; (law) cross-examination.

Interrumpir, vt. to interrupt.—**Interrupción,** f. interruption.—**Interruptor,** n. interrupter.—m. (elec.) switch; circuit-breaker.—i. de encendido, ignition switch.

Intersección, f. intersection.

Intervalo, m. interval; interlude.

Intervención, f. intervention; mediation, auditing of accounts; (surg.) operation.—i. de precios, price control.—**Intervenir,** vii. [45] to intervene, mediate, intermediate; to interfere; (tel.) to wiretap.—vt. to supervise; to audit; to control.—**Interventor,** n. comptroller; supervisor; auditor.

Intestino, a. intestine, internal; civil, domestic.—m. intestine.—i. delgado, small intestine.—i. grueso, large intestine.

Intimación, f. intimation, hint.—**Intimar,** vt. to intimate, indicate.—vr. to pierce, penetrate.—**Intimidad,** f. intimacy.

íntimo, a. internal, innermost; intimate.

Intocable, a. untouchable.

Intolerable, a. intolerable, unbearable.—**Intolerancia,** f. intolerance.—**Intolerante,** a. intolerant.

Intoxicación, f. poisoning.—i. por alimentos, food poisoning.—**Intoxicar,** vti. [d] to poison.—vri. to get poisoned.

Intraducible, a. untranslatable.

Intranquilidad, f. restlessness, uneasiness.—**Intranquilizar,** vti. [a] to worry, make uneasy.—vri. to become disquieted, to worry.—**Intranquilo,** a. uneasy, restless.

Intransferible, a. not transferable.

Intransitable, a. impassable; impracticable.

Intransitivo, a. (gram.) intransitive.

Intrepidez, f. intrepidity, bravery.—**Intrépido,** a. intrepid, daring.

Intriga, f. intrigue.—**Intrigante,** mf. & a. intriguer; intriguing, scheming.—**Intrigar,** vti. [b] to arouse (one's) interest or curiosity; to mystify.—vii. to intrigue.—vri. to be interested (in) or curious (about).

Intrincado, a. intricate, involved.

Introducción, f. introduction.—**Introducir,** vti. [11] to introduce; to usher in, put in, insert; to present (a person).—vri. (en) to gain access (to); to get in; to ingratiate oneself (with); to interfere (in).

Intromisión, f. influx; interference, meddling.

Intrusión, f. intrusion, obtrusion.—**Intruso,** a. intrusive, intruding.—n. intruder, outsider.

Intuición, f. intuition.—**Intuir,** vti. [23-

e] to know or perceive by intuition.—**intuitivo**, *a.* intuitive.

inundación, *f.* inundation, flood.—**inundar**, *vt.* to inundate, flood.

inusitado, *a.* unusual, rare.

inútil, *a.* useless; fruitless, unavailing; needless.—**inutilidad**, *f.* uselessness; needlessness.—**inutilización**, *f.* spoilage.—**inutilizar**, *vti.* [a] to render useless; to disable; to spoil, ruin.—*vri.* to become useless.

invadir, *vt.* to invade; to encroach upon.

invalidar, *vt.* to invalidate, nullify; to quash.—**inválido**, *a.* invalid; crippled; feeble; null, void.—*n.* invalid.

invariable, *a.* invariable, constant.

invasión, *f.* invasion.—**invasor**, *n. & a.* invader; invading.

invectiva, *f.* invective.

invencible, *a.* invincible, unconquerable.

invención, *f.* invention.

invendible, *a.* unsalable.—**invendido**, *a.* unsold.

inventar, *vt.* to invent; to fib.

inventariar, *vt.* to inventory, take inventory of.—**inventario**, *m.* inventory.

inventiva, *f.* inventiveness, ingenuity, resourcefulness.—**invento**, *m.* invention.—**inventor**, *n.* inventor.

invernadero, *m.* winter quarters; hothouse.—**invernal**, *a.* winter, wintry.—**invernar**, *vii.* [1] to winter, pass the winter.

inverosímil, *a.* unlikely, improbable.

inversión, *f.* inversion; (com.) investment.—**inversionista**, *mf.* (neol.) investor.—**inverso**, *ppi.* of INVERTIR.—*a.* inverse, inverted.—**invertido**, *a. & n.* invert.—*a.* inverted.—**invertir**, *vti.* [39–49] to invert; to reverse; to spend (time); (com.) to invest.

investidura, *f.* ceremonial investment, installation.

investigación, *f.* investigation, research; inquest.—**investigador**, *n. & a.* investigator; investigating.—*i. de campo*, fieldworker.—**investigar**, *vti.* [b] to investigate, ascertain, inquire into; to do research work.

investir, *vti.* [29] to invest; to confer upon.

inveterado, *a.* inveterate, ingrained.

invicto, *a.* invincible, unconquered.

invierno, *m.* winter.

invisible, *a.* invisible.

invitación, *f.* invitation.—**invitado**, *n.* guest.—*i. de piedra*, unwanted guest.—*i. especial*, special guest.—**invitar**, *vt.* to invite; to entice; to treat.

invocación, *f.* invocation.—**invocar**, *vti.* [d] to invoke, implore.

involucrar, *vt.* to involve.

involuntario, *a.* involuntary, unintentional.

inyección, *f.* injection.—*poner una i.*, to give an injection.—**inyectado**, *a.* bloodshot, inflamed.—**inyectar**, *vt.* to inject.

iodo, *m.* = YODO.

ir, *vii.* [24] to go; to walk; to be becoming; to fit, suit.—*¿cómo le va?* how are you?—*i. a*, to go to; to be going to, to purpose or intend to.—*i. a buscar*, to get, fetch.—*i. a caballo*, to ride, to be riding on horseback.—*i. a medias*, to go halves.—*i. a pie*, to walk.—*i. pasando*, to be so-so, to be as usual, to be getting along.—*no me va ni me viene*, it does not affect me in the least.—*¡qué va!* nonsense!—*¡vámonos!* let's go!—*¡vamos a ver!* let's see!—*vri.* to go, go away.—*i. abajo*, to topple down.—*i. a pique*, to founder, go to the bottom.

ira, *f.* ire, anger.—**iracundo**, *a.* wrathful; angry, enraged.—**irascible**, *a.* irascible, irritable, short-tempered.

iridiscente, *a.* iridescent.

iris, *m.* (anat.) iris.—*arco i.*, rainbow.—**irisado**, *a.* rainbow-hued.

irlandés, *a.* Irish.—*m.* Irishman; Irish language.—*f.* Irishwoman.

ironía, *f.* irony.—**irónico**, *a.* ironical, sarcastic.

irracional, *a.* irrational, unreasoning.

irradiación, *f.* radiation.—**irradiar**, *vt.* to radiate.

irrazonable, *a.* unreasonable, impracticable.

irreal, *a.* unreal.—**irrealidad**, *f.* unreality.—**irrealizable**, *a.* unrealizable.

irrebatible, *a.* indisputable.

irreemplazable, *a.* irreplaceable.

irreflexión, *f.* rashness, thoughtlessness.—**irreflexivo**, *a.* thoughtless, impulsive, unthinking.

irregular, *a.* irregular.—**irregularidad**, *f.* irregularity.

irreligioso, *a.* irreligious.

irrellenable, *a.* nonrefillable.

irrespetuoso, *a.* disrespectful.

irrespirable, *a.* not fit to be breathed.

irresponsable, *a.* irresponsible.

irreverencia, *f.* irreverence.—**irreverente**, *a.* irreverent.

Irrevocable, *a.* irrevocable.

Irrigación, *m.* irrigation.—**Irrigar,** *vti.* [b] to irrigate, water.

Irrisión, *f.* derision, ridicule.—**irrisorio,** *a.* derisive.

Irritable, *a.* irritable.—**irritación,** *f.* irritation.—**irritante,** *a.* irritating; irritant.—**irritar,** *vt.* to irritate.

Irrogar, *vti.* [b] to cause (harm or damage).

Irrupción, *m.* raid, incursion.

isla, *f.* island.—*i. desierta,* desert island.—*i. peatonal,* safety or traffic island.—**Islam,** *m.*—*el I.,* Islam.—**Islámico,** *a.* Islamic, Muslim.—**islandés, islándico,** *a.* & *n.* Icelandic.—**isleño,** *n.* & *a.* islander; (Cuba) native of the Canary Islands.

—**islote,** *m.* small barren island, key.

Israelí, *a.* & *mf.* Israeli.—**israelita,** *a.* & *mf.* Israelite.

istmo, *m.* isthmus.

italiano, *n.* & *a.* Italian.—*m.* Italian language.—**itálico,** *a.* Italic; italic.

ítem, *m.* section, clause, article; addition.—*í.,* or *í. más,* also, likewise, furthermore.

itinerario, *a.* itinerary.—*m.* itinerary; railroad guide, timetable, schedule.

izar, *vti.* [a] to hoist, heave, haul up.

izquierda, *f.* left hand; (pol.) left wing.—*a la i.,* to the left.—**izquierdista,** *mf.* & *a.* (pol.) leftist, radical.—**izquierdo,** *a.* left-handed; left, left-hand side.

J

jaba, *f.* (Am.) basket; crate.

jabalí, *m.* wild boar.—**jabalina,** *f.* sow of a wild boar; javelin.

jabón, *m.* soap; a piece of soap.—*j. de olor, j. de tocador,* toilet soap.—**jabonadura,** *f.* washing.—*pl.* suds or soap suds; lather.—**jabonera,** *f.* soap dish.—**jabonería,** *f.* soap factory or shop.

jaca, *f.* pony, cob; gelding.

jacal, *m.* (Mex.) Indian hut.

jacarandoso, *a.* blithe, merry, gay.

jacinto, *m.* hyacinth.

jaco, *m.* sorry nag, jade.

jactancia, *f.* boasting.—**jactancioso,** *a.* boastful, vainglorious.—**jactarse,** *vr.* to boast, vaunt.

jaculatoria, *f.* short prayer.

jade, *m.* (jewel.) jade.

jadeante, *a.* panting, out of breath.—**jadear,** *vi.* to pant.—**jadeo,** *m.* pant, palpitation.

jaez, *m.* harness; trappings; (fig.) manner, kind, quality.—*pl.* trappings.

jaiba, *f.* (Am.) (ichth.) a kind of crab; a cunning, crafty or sneaky person.

jalar, *vt.* = HALAR.—*vr.* (Am.) to get drunk.

jalea, *f.* jelly.

jalear, *vt.* to animate dancers by clapping hands.—**jaleo,** *m.* (coll.) carousal; clapping of hands to encourage dancers.

jaletina, *f.* (Am.) calf's foot jelly; gelatine.

jalón, *m.* landmark, stake; (Am.) pull, jerk.—**jalonar,** *vt.* to stake out, mark.—**jalonear,** *vt.* (Am.) to pull, jerk.

jamaiquino, *n.* & *a.* Jamaican.

jamás, *adv.* never.—*nunca j.,* never, nevermore.—*por siempre j.,* forever and ever.

jamba, *f.* jamb.

jamelgo, *m.* swaybacked nag.

jamón, *m.* ham.—**jamona,** *f.* (coll.) middle-aged woman; (Am.) spinster.

japonés, *n.* & *a.* Japanese; Japanese language.

jaque, *m.* (chess) check; bully.—*j. mate,* checkmate.

jaqueca, *f.* migraine; headache.

jáquima, *f.* part of a halter which encloses the head.—**jaquimazo,** *m.* (coll.) blow; displeasure; disappointment.

jarabe, *m.* syrup; any sweet mixed drink; (Am.) a Mexican folk dance.—*j. de pico,* empty talk, prattling.

jarana, *f.* (coll.) carousal, revelry.—**jaranear,** *vi.* (coll.) to carouse.—**jaranero,** *a.* jolly.

jarcia, *f.* (naut.) rigging and cordage; shrouds.

jardín, *m.* flower garden.—*j. derecho, izquierdo,* (baseball) right, left field.—*j. entre rocas,* rock garden.—**jardinería,** *f.* gardening.—**jardi-**

nero, n. gardener; (baseball) outfielder.—f. flowerstand.

jaretón, m. (sewing) hem.

jarra, f. jar; pitcher.—en j., or de jarras, akimbo.

jarrete, m. hock (of an animal).

jarro, m. pitcher, jug, pot.—**jarrón,** m. flower vase; large jar.

jaspe, m. (min.) jasper.—**jaspeado,** a. mottled, variegated.

jaula, f. cage; (Am.) cattle or freight car; cell (in a prison).—j. para pájaros, birdcage.

jauría, f. pack of hounds.

javanés, a. & n. Javanese.

jazmín, m. jasmine.

jazz, m. jazz.—banda de j., conjunto de j., jazz band.—**jazzístico,** a. jazz.

jeans, m. pl. jeans.—unos j., a pair of jeans.

jefatura, f. position or headquarters of a chief.—j. de policía, police headquarters.—**jefe,** n. chief, head, leader; (fam.) boss; (mil.) commanding officer.—j. de bomberos, fire chief.—j. de cocina, chef.—j. de estación, stationmaster.—j. de Estado Mayor, Chief of Staff.—j. de gobierno, prime minister; president.— j. de redacción, editor-in-chief.—j. de taller, supervisor, foreman.—j. de ventas, sales manager.

jején, m. (Cuba) gnat.

jengibre, m. ginger.

jerarquía, f. hierarchy.

jerez, m. sherry wine.

jerga, f. jargon; gibberish; slang.

jergón, m. straw bed; mattress, pallet; zircon.

jerigonza, f. (coll.) jargon; gibberish; slang.

jeringa, f. syringe.—**jeringar,** vti. [b] to inject with a syringe; to bother, vex.—**jeringazo,** m. injection; squirt.—**jeringuilla,** f. mock orange, syringa.—j. hipodérmica, syringe.

jeroglífico, m. hieroglyph.—a. hieroglyphic.

jersey, m. sweater, pullover.

jesuita, m. Jesuit.

jet [dʒet], m. (aer.) jet.

jeta, f. hog's snout; (rostro de una persona) (fam.) face, mug; (boca) (sl.) trap.—¡cállese la j.!, shut your trap!

jet lag [dʒétlæg], m. jet lag.

jíbaro, a. (Am.) wild, rustic.—n. countryman(-woman).

jibia, f. cuttlefish.

jícara, f. (Am.) small chocolate or coffee cup; bowl made out of a gourd.

jiga, f. jig (dance and tune).

jigote, m. hash, minced meat.

jilguero, m. linnet.

jinete, m. trooper; cavalryman; horseman, rider, equestrian.—**jinetear,** vt. (Am.) to break in (a horse).—vi. to ride around on horseback, mainly for show.

jip, m. jeep.

jipijapa, f. Panama hat.

jira, f. picnic, outing; tour.

jirafa, f. giraffe.

jirón, m. shred, tear; rag; small part (of anything).

jitomate, m. (Am.) tomato.

jockey, m. jockey.

jocoso, a. jocose, humorous, facetious.

jofaina, f. washbasin, washbowl.

jolgorio, m. = HOLGORIO; boisterous frolic.

jornada, f. one-day march; working day; stage, journey, travel, trip; (mil.) expedition; act of a play.—**jornal,** m. salary; day's wages.—a j., by the day.—j. mínimo, minimum wage.—**jornalero,** n. day laborer.

joroba, f. hump; (coll.) importunity, annoyance, nuisance.—**jorobado,** a. crooked, humpbacked.—n. hunchback.—**jorobar,** vt. (coll.) to importune, bother, annoy.

jota, f. name of the letter j; jot, tittle, bit; iota; an Aragonese dance and tune.

joven, a. young.—mf. youth; young man; young woman; young person.

jovial, a. jovial, gay, cheerful.—**jovialidad,** f. joviality, gaiety.

joya, f. jewel, gem; piece of jewelry. —**joyería,** f. jeweler's shop.—**joyero,** n. jeweler.—m. jewel case.

juanete, m. bunion.

jubilación, f. retirement; pension. —**jubilar,** vt. to retire; to pension off.—vr. to become a pensioner; to be retired.—**jubileo,** m. jubilee.— **júbilo,** m. glee, merriment, rejoicing.—**jubiloso,** a. joyful, merry, gay.

judaico, a. Judaical, Jewish.—**Judaísmo,** m. Judaism.—**judía,** f. bean, string bean.—j. de la peladilla, Lima bean.

judicatura, f. judicature; judgeship. —**judicial,** a. judicial, juridical.

judío, n. Jew.—a. Jewish.

juego, m. play, sport, game; gambling; set of cards; movement, work, working (of a mechanism); set; (mech.) play, free space.—hacer j., to match, to fit; to bet (in games of chance).—*j. de azar*, game of chance.— *j. de ingenio*, guessing game.—*j. de llaves*, set of keys.—*j. de manos*, legerdemain.—*j. de mesas*, nest of tables.—*j. de palabras*, pun, play on words.—*j. de tejo*, shuffleboard.— *juegos malabares*, juggling.—*Juegos Olímpicos*, Olympic games, Olympics.

juerga, *f.* spree, carousal.

jueves, *m.* Thursday.

juez, *m.* judge, justice; umpire.—*j. de paz*, justice of the peace.

jugada, *f.* play, act of playing; a throw, move, stroke; ill turn.—**jugador,** *n.* player; gambler.—**jugar,** *vti.* [25-b] & *vii.* to play; to sport; to gamble; to stake; to move in a game; to take active part in an affair; to intervene; to make game of.—*j. a cara o cruz*, to bet on the toss of a coin.— *j. a la bolsa*, to dabble in stocks.—*j. al tócame tú*, to play tag.—*vri.* to gamble, to risk (one's salary, one's life).—*jugarse el todo por el todo*, to stake all, to shoot the works.—**jugarreta,** *f.* (coll.) bad play; bad turn, nasty trick.

juglar, *m.* juggler; minstrel.

jugo, *m.* juice, sap; marrow, pith, substance.—*j. de frutas*, fruit juice.—*j. de naranja*, orange juice.—*j. de uva*, grape juice.—**jugosidad,** *f.* succulence, juiciness.—**jugoso,** *a.* juicy, succulent, full of sap.

juguete, *m.* toy.—**juguetear,** *vi.* to play, frolic; trifle, toy.—**juguetería,** *f.* toyshop, toy trade.—**juguetón,** *a.* playful, frolicsome, rollicking, waggish.

juicio, *m.* judgment; decision; prudence, wisdom; thinking; good behavior; (law) trial.—*estar fuera de su j.*, to be crazy.—*perder el j.*, to become insane.—*tener j.*, to be wise; to be cautious; to be well-behaved.— **juicioso,** *a.* judicious, wise; wellbehaved.

julio, *m.* July.

juma, *f.* (coll.) spree.

jumento, *m.* donkey; stupid person.

junco, *m.* (bot.) reed, rush; Chinese junk.

jungla, *f.* (Am.) jungle.

junio, *m.* June.

junquillo, *m.* (bot.) jonquil; reed, rattan.

junta, *f.* board, council; meeting, conference; session; joint; coupling.— *j. de instrucción pública*, school board.—*j. de perdones*, pardon board.—*j. directiva*, board of directors.—**juntar,** *vt.* to join, connect, unite; to assemble, congregate; to amass, collect; to pool (resources).—*vr.* to join, meet, assemble; to be closely united; to copulate; (**con**) to associate (with). —**junto,** *adv.* near, close at hand, near at hand; at the same time. —*j. a*, next to, by, beside.—*j. con*, together with.—*a.* united, joined; together.—**juntura,** *f.* juncture, joining.

jurado, *m.* jury; juryman.—*j. de acusación*, grand jury.—**juramentar,** *vt.* to swear in.—*vr.* to be sworn in, take an oath.—**juramento,** *m.* oath; act of swearing; curse, imprecation. —**jurar,** *vt.* & *vi.* to swear; to take an oath.—*j. en falso*, to commit perjury.—*jurársela(s) a uno*, to threaten one with revenge.—**jurídico,** *a.* legal, juridical.—**jurisconsulto,** *n.* jurist; lawyer.—**jurisdicción,** *f.* jurisdiction; territory.—**jurisprudencia,** *f.* jurisprudence; laws, legislation.—**jurista,** *mf.* jurist; lawyer.

justa, *f.* joust, tournament; contest.

justicia, *f.* justice, rightness.—*j. de la soga*, lynch law.—**justiciero,** *a.* just and strict.—**justificable,** *a.* justifiable.—**justificación,** *f.* justification, defense; production of evidence. —**justificar,** *vti.* [d] to justify; to vindicate.—**justipreciar,** *vt.* to appraise.—**justo,** *a.* just; pious; correct, exact, strict; fit; tight, close. —*m.* just and pious man.—*adv.* tightly.

juvenil, *a.* juvenile, youthful.—**juventud,** *f.* youthfulness, youth; young people.

juzgado, *m.* court of justice; courthouse.—*j. de tráfico*, traffic court. —**juzgar,** *vti.* [b] & *vii.* to judge; to pass or render judgment (on).

K

kaki, *m.* khaki.
kaleidoscopio, *m.* kaleidoscope.
kermesse or **kermés,** *f.* bazaar; village or country fair.
kerosén, *m.,* **keroseno,** *m.,* **kerosina,** *f.* kerosene.
kilo, *m.* kilo, kilogram.—**kilogramo,** *m.* kilogram.—**kilolitro,** *m.* kiloliter.

—kilométrico, *a.* kilometric; mileage (ticket); (coll.) very long, interminably long.—**kilómetro,** *m.* kilometer.—**kilovatio,** *m.* kilowatt.
kiosco, *m.* kiosk, small pavilion; newsstand.
knock-out [nákau̯t], *m.* knockout.
K.O., *abbr.* (**knock-out**) K.O.

L

la, *art. f. sing.* the.—*pron. pers. f. sing.* her, it.—*m.* (mus.) la, A.
laberinto, *m.* labyrinth, maze.
labia, *f.* (coll.) gift of gab, palaver, fluency.—**labial,** *a.* labial; lip.—**labio,** *m.* lip.—**labiolectura,** *f.* lip reading.
labor, *f.* labor, task; work; (sew.) needlework; trimming.—**laborable,** *a.* workable; tillable.—*día l.,* working day.—**laborar,** *vt. & vi.* to work; to till.
laboratorio, *m.* laboratory.—*l. de idiomas,* language laboratory.—*l. espacial,* Skylab, space laboratory.
laboriosidad, *f.* laboriousness; industry.—**laborioso,** *a.* laborious; industrious.
labrado, *a.* cultivated, tilled; wrought; figured, hewn.—*m.* cultivated land.—**labrador,** *n.* farmer, peasant, tiller.—**labranza,** *f.* cultivation, tillage; farming.—**labrar,** *vt.* to till, cultivate; to carve (stone); to work (metals).—**labriego,** *n.* farmer, peasant; rustic.
laca, *f.* lacquer; shellac; hair spray.
lacayo, *m.* lackey, footman.
lacio, *a.* straight (as hair); flaccid, languid.
lacónico, *a.* laconic.
lacra, *f.* mark left by illness; fault, defect.
lacrar, *vt.* to seal with sealing wax.—**lacre,** *m.* sealing wax.
lacrimoso, *a.* tearful.
lactancia, *f.* weaning period; nursing (of a baby).—**lactar,** *vt.* to nurse; to feed with milk.—*vi.* to suckle; to

feed on milk.—**lácteo,** *a.* milky.—*Vía Láctea,* Milky Way.
ladeado, *a.* tilted; twisted; lopsided.—**ladear,** *vt. & vr.* to tilt, tip, incline to one side.—*vi.* to skirt; to deviate.—*vr.* to lean; to tilt, incline to one side.—**ladeo,** *m.* inclination or motion to one side; tilt.
ladera, *f.* slope, hillside.
ladino, *a.* cunning, crafty.
lado, *m.* side, edge.—*al l.,* just by; near at hand; next door.—*a un l.,* aside.—*hacerse a un l.,* to get out of the way, to move aside.—*l. a l.,* side by side.—*l. contrario,* wrong side.—*por otro l.,* on the other hand.
ladrador, *n. & a.* barker (dog); barking.—**ladrar,** *vi.* to bark.—**ladrido,** *m.* barking, bark.
ladrillazo, *m.* blow with a brick.—**ladrillo,** *m.* brick, tile.
ladrón, *n.* thief; robber.—**ladronzuelo,** *n.* petty thief.
lagaña, *f.* bleariness.—**lagañoso,** *a.* blear-eyed.
lagartija, *f.,* **lagartijo,** *m.* small lizard.—**lagarto,** *m.* lizard; (Am.) alligator; (coll.) sly, artful person.
lago, *m.* lake.
lágrima, *f.* tear.—**lagrimal,** *m.* tearduct.—**lagrimar, lagrimear,** *vi.* to shed tears.—**lagrimeo,** *m.* shedding tears.—**lagrimoso,** *a.* tearful; (of eyes) watery.
laguna, *f.* lagoon; gap.
laico, *a.* lay, laic.—*laicos,* laiety.
laja, *f.* flagstone; slab.
lamedura, *f.* lick, act of licking.

lamentable, *a.* lamentable, deplorable.—**lamentación,** *f.* lamentation, wail.—**lamentar,** *vt.* to lament, mourn.—*vi. & vr.* to lament, grieve, wail; to complain; to moan.—**lamento,** *m.* lament, moan.

lamer, *vt.* to lick; to lap.

lámina, *f.* plate, sheet; print, illustration.—**laminado,** *a.* laminated; (of metals) rolled.—**laminar,** *vt.* to roll or beat (metal) into sheets.

lámpara, *f.* lamp.—*l. de pie,* floor lamp.—*l. de rayos ultravioletas,* sun lamp.—**lamparón,** *m.* large grease spot; (med.) scrofula.

lampazo, *m.* mop, swab.

lampiño, *a.* beardless.

lana, *f.* wool.—*l. mineral,* rock wool.—**lanar,** *a.* wool, woolen.

lance, *m.* cast, throw; incident, episode; event; quarrel; move or turn in a game.—*l. de honor,* duel.

lancear, *vt.* to wound with a lance.—**lancero,** *m.* lancer.—**lanceta,** *f.* (surg.) lancet.

lancha, *f.* boat; launch; flagstone, slab.—*l. cañonera,* gunboat.—**lanchón,** *m.* (naut.) barge, scow.

langaruto, *a.* (coll.) tall and skinny; thin.

langosta, *f.* lobster; locust.—**langostino,** *m.* crayfish.

languidecer, *vii.* [3] to languish.—**languidez,** *f.* languor, pining.—**lánguido,** *a.* languid, faint.

lanilla, *f.* nap (of cloth), down; fine flannel.—**lanudo,** *a.* woolly, fleecy; (Am.) crude; ill-bred; dull.

lanza, *f.* lance, spear.—**lanzacohetes,** *m.* rocket launcher.—**lanzada,** *f.* thrust or blow with a lance.

lanzadera, *f.* shuttle.—*l. espacial,* space shuttle.

lanzador, *n.* thrower, ejecter; (baseball) pitcher.—**lanzamiento,** *m.* launching, casting, or throwing; (law) dispossessing, eviction.—*l. a la Luna,* moon shot.—**lanzaminas,** *m.* mine layer; mine-laying boat.—**lanzar,** *vti.* [a] to throw, fling; to launch; to throw (a ball) up; (law) to evict, dispossess; (baseball) to pitch; to bowl.—*vr.* to rush or dart; to launch forth; to engage or embark (in).—**lanzatorpedos,** *m.* torpedo boat; torpedo tube.

lanzazo, *m.* thrust or blow with a lance.

lapa, *f.* barnacle.

lapicero, *m.* mechanical pencil.

lápida, *f.* tombstone, gravestone; memorial tablet.

lápiz, *m.* pencil; crayon.—*l. de cejas,* eyebrow pencil.—*l. de labios, l. labial,* lipstick.—*l. de ojos,* eye pencil.—*l. estíptico,* styptic pencil.

lapón, *n.* Laplander.—*a.* pertaining to Lapland or Laplanders.

lapso, *m.* lapse, slip.

lardo, *m.* lard.

larga, *f.* (gen. in the *pl.*) delay, procrastination.—*a la corta o a la l.,* sooner or later.—*a. la la l.,* in the end, in the long run.—*dar largas,* to delay, put off.

largar, *vti.* [b] to loosen; to let go, set free; to expel; to give (as a slap); to heave (as a sigh).—*vri.* (coll.) to get out, quit, leave.—**largo,** *a.* long; generous; shrewd, cunning.—*a lo l.,* lengthwise; at full length.—*l. de lengua,* loose-tongued.—*traje l.,* evening dress.—*m.* length.—*de l.,* in length, long.—*pasar de l.,* to pass by without stopping.—*adv.* largely, profusely.—*interj.* ¡l.! or ¡l. de ahí! get out!—**largor,** *m.* length.—**larguero,** *m.* jamb post; stringer.—**largueza,** *f.* liberality, generosity.—**larguirucho,** *a.* (coll.) long and thin.—**largura,** *f.* length.

laringe, *f.* larynx.

larva, *f.* larva.

las, *art. pl.* of LA, the.—*pron. f.* them.

lasca, *f.* slice; chip from a stone.

lascivia, *f.* lasciviousness.—**lascivo,** *a.* lascivious.

lasitud, *f.* lassitude, weariness, faintness.

lástima, *f.* pity; compassion; pitiful object.—*dar l.,* to arouse pity or regret.—*es l.,* it's a pity.—**lastimadura,** *f.* sore, hurt.—**lastimar,** *vt.* to hurt; to injure, damage.—*vr.* to hurt oneself; to get hurt.—**lastimero, lastimoso,** *a.* pitiful, sad, doleful.

lastrar, *vt.* to ballast.—**lastre,** *m.* ballast.

lata, *f.* tin plate or tinned iron plate; tin can; annoyance, nuisance; lath.—*dar (la) l.,* (coll.) to pester.

latente, *a.* latent.

lateral, *a.* lateral, side.

latido, *m.* beat, beating, throb.

latifundio, *m.* large entailed estate.

latigazo, *m.* lash, whipping; crack of a whip.—**látigo,** *m.* whip.

latín, *m.* Latin (language).—**latino,** *a.* Latin.

Latinoamérica, *f.* Latin America. —**latinoamericano,** *a.* Latin American.

latir, *vi.* to palpitate, throb, beat.

latitud, *f.* latitude; breadth.

latón, *m.* brass.—**latoso,** *a.* boring, annoying.

latrocinio, *m.* robbery, larceny, thievery.

laúd, *m.* (mus.) lute.

laudable, *a.* laudable, praiseworthy.—**laudatorio,** *a.* laudatory, full of praise.—**laudo,** *m.* (law) award; finding (of an arbitrator).

laureado, *a.* laureate.—**laurear,** *vt.* to honor, reward; to crown with laurel.—**laurel,** *m.* laurel; honor.—**lauro,** *m.* glory, honor; laurel.

lava, *f.* lava.—*de lava y pon,* drip-dry, wash and wear.

lavabo, *m.* lavatory; washstand; washroom.—**lavadero,** *m.* washing place; laundry.—**lavado,** *m.* wash, washing; laundry work; (de dinero) laundering (of money).—*l. automático,* carwash.—*l. de cerebro,* brainwashing.—**lavadora,** *f.* washing machine.—**lavafrutas,** *m.* finger bowl.—**lavamanos,** *m.* lavatory; washstand.

lavanda, *f.* lavender.

lavandera, *f.* laundress, washerwoman.—**lavandería,** *f.* laundry.—**lavandero,** *m.* launderer, laundryman.—**lavaplatos,** *mf.* dishwasher.—*m.* (mech.) dishwasher.—**lavar,** *vt.* to wash; to launder; (mason.) to whitewash.—**lavarropas,** *m.* washing machine.—**lavativa,** *f.* enema; syringe; nuisance.—**lavatorio,** *m.* washing; lavatory; washstand.

laxante, *m.* & *a.* laxative.

lazada, *f.* bowknot; (sew.) bow.—**lazar,** *vti.* [a] to lasso, capture with a lasso.

lazareto, *m.* leper hospital.

lazarillo, *m.* blind person's guide.

lazarino, *a.* leprous.—*n.* leper.

lazo, *m.* bow, loop; trap or snare (for persons); lasso, lariat; slipknot; tie, bond.—*l. de amor,* truelove knot, love knot.

le, *pron.* him; you; to him; to her; to you.

leal, *a.* loyal; (pol.) stalwart.—**lealtad,** *f.* loyalty.

lebrel, *n.* greyhound.

lección, *f.* lesson; lecture; reading.—

dar una l., to say or recite a lesson; to give a lesson.

lechada, *f.* mixture of water and plaster; whitewash.

leche, *f.* milk.—*l. condensada,* condensed milk.—*l. de magnesia,* milk of magnesia.—*l. desnatada* or *descremada,* skim milk.—*l. en polvo,* powdered milk.—*l. entera,* whole milk.—*l. esterilizada,* sterilized milk.—*l. homogeneizada,* homogenized milk.—*l. pasteurizada,* pasteurized milk.—**lechera,** *a.* milch (app. to animals).—*f.* milkmaid; dairymaid; milk jug; milk can.—**lechería,** *f.* dairy.—**lechero,** *a.* milky.—*m.* milkman.

lecho, *m.* bed; bed of a river.—*l. de enfermo,* sickbed.—*l. de muerte,* deathbed.

lechón, *n.* pig; suckling pig.

lechoso, *a.* milky.—*f.* (Am.) papaya.

lechuga, *f.* (bot.) lettuce.—**lechuguino,** *m.* (coll.) dandy, dude.

lechuza, *f.* barn owl.

lector, *a.* reading.—*n.* reader; lecturer.—*l. del contador,* meter reader.—*l. mental,* mind reader.—*m.* (comput.) optical character reader.—*l. digital,* digital scanner.—*l. óptico,* optical scanner.

lectura, *f.* reading; reading matter or material; (comput.) readout.—*l. rápida* or *veloz,* speed reading.—**leer,** *vti.* [e] to read.—*l. a libro abierto, l. a primera vista,* to sight-read.—*l. (en) los labios,* to lip-read.—*l. entre líneas,* to read between the lines.

leer, *vti.* [e] to read.

legación, *f.* legation.—**legado,** *m.* (law) legacy; legate.

legajo, *m.* docket, file, bundle of papers.

legal, *a.* legal, lawful; faithful.—**legalidad,** *f.* legality, lawfulness.—**legalización,** *f.* legalization.—**legalizar,** *vti.* [a] to legalize.

legaña, *f.* = LAGAÑA.—**legañoso,** *a.* = LAGAÑOSO.

legar, *vti.* [b] to send as a legate; (law) to bequeath.—**legatario,** *n.* (law) legatee.

legendario, *a.* legendary.

legible, *a.* legible, readable.

legión, *f.* legion.—**legionario,** *n.* & *a.* legionary.

legislación, *f.* legislation.—**legislador,**

n. & *a.* legislator; legislating, legislative.—**legislar**, *vt.* to legislate.—**legislativo**, *a.* legislative.—**legislatura**, *f.* legislature; term of a legislature.

legitimidad, *f.* legitimacy, legality.—**legítimo**, *a.* legitimate, lawful, rightful; genuine.

lego, *a.* lay, laic; ignorant.—*m.* layman.—*pl.* laiety.

legua, *f.* league (measure of length).—*a la l., de cien leguas,* or *desde media l.,* very far, at a great distance.

leguleyo, *m.* petty lawyer; shyster.

legumbre, *f.* vegetable, garden stuff.

leído, *a.* well-read, well-informed.—*l. y escribido,* (coll. & contempt.) affecting learning.

lejanía, *f.* distance, remoteness; remote place.—**lejano**, *a.* distant, far.—*L. Oeste,* Far West.—*L. Oriente,* Far East.

lejía, *f.* lye; (coll.) severe reprimand.

lejos, *adv.* far away, far off, afar.—*a lo l.,* in the distance.—*m.* perspective, background.

lelo, *a.* stupid, dull.

lema, *m.* theme; motto; slogan.

lencería, *f.* linen goods; linen-draper's shop; linen room.

lengua, *f.* (anat.) tongue; language.—*írsele, a uno la l.,* to give oneself away.—*l. de gestos,* signing.—*l. gestual* or *de gestos, l. por señas,* sign language.—*l. de ordenador, de programación,* or *de máquina,* computer language.—*l. madre* or *materna,* mother tongue.—*morderse la l.,* to hold one's tongue.

lenguado, *m.* (ichth.) sole, flounder.

lenguaje, *m.* language; speech; style.—**lenguaraz**, *a.* loquacious.—**lengüeta**, *f.* tongue (of a shoe); (mus.) languette; (mec.) feather, wedge; (coll.) bill, tab.—**lengüetada**, *f.* act of licking.—**lengüilargo**, *a.* (coll.) garrulous; scurrilous.

lenidad, *f.* leniency, mildness.

lente, *m.* lens.—*pl.* glasses, spectacles.—*l. bifocales,* bifocals.—*l. negros, oscuros,* or *de sol,* sunglasses.—*l. de aumento, de fórmula,* or *ópticos,* prescription glasses.

lenteja, *f.* lentil.—**lentejuela**, *f.* spangle, sequin.

lentilla, *f.* contact lens.

lentitud, *f.* slowness, tardiness.—**lento**, *a.* slow.

leña, *f.* firewood, kindling wood; (coll.) beating.—*echar l. al fuego,* to add fuel to the fire.—*l. seca,* dead wood.—**leñador**, *n.* woodman(-woman), woodcutter; logger.—**leñazo**, *m.* cudgeling.—**leñero**, *m.* woodshed.—**leño**, *m.* log; timber.

Leo, *m.* (astr.) Leo.

león, *m.* lion; brave man.—**leona**, *f.* lioness; undaunted woman.—**leonera**, *f.* cage or den of lions; (coll.) disorderly room.—**leonino**, *a.* leonine; (law) one-sided, unfair.

leontina, *f.* watch chain.

leopardo, *m.* leopard.

leotardo, *m.* leotard.

lépero, *n.* (Am.) one of the rabble.

lepra, *f.* leprosy.—**leproso**, *a.* leprous.—*n.* leper.

lerdo, *a.* slow, heavy; dull, obtuse.

les, *pers. pron.* them; to them; you; to you.

lesión, *f.* lesion, wound, injury; damage.—**lesionar**, *vt.* to injure, wound; to damage, impair.—**lesivo**, *a.* prejudicial, injurious.

lesna, *f.* = LEZNA.

letal, *a.* mortal, deadly, lethal.

letanía, *f.* (eccl.) litany.

letargo, *m.* lethargy, drowsiness.

letra, *f.* letter; handwriting; (print.) type; motto, inscription; literal meaning; lyrics.—*l. bastardilla, cursiva,* or *itálica,* italics.—*l. mayúscula,* capital letter.—*l. negrita* or *negrilla,* boldface.—*l. pequeña* or *menuda,* fine print, small print.—*pl.* letters, learning.—*l. de cambio,* (com.) draft, bill of exchange.—*l. de molde,* print, printed letter.—**letrado**, *a.* learned, erudite.—*n.* lawyer.—**letrero**, *m.* sign, notice; label; legend.

letrina, *f.* privy, latrine.

letrista, *mf.* lyricist.

leucemia, *f.* leukemia.

leva, *f.* (naut.) act of weighing anchor; (mil.) levy, press; (mech.) cam.—**levadura**, *f.* leaven, yeast.—*l. en polvo,* baking powder.—**levantador**, *n.*—*l. de pesas,* weightlifter.—**levantamiento**, *m.* elevation, raising; insurrection, uprising.—*l. de pesas,* weightlifter.—**levantar**, *vt.* to raise; to lift, pick up; to erect, build; to rouse; to impute; to stand up.—*vr.* to rise, get up (from bed, chair, etc.); to rise up.—**levante**, *m.* Levant, east coast of Spain.—**levantino**, *a.* & *n.*

Levantine.—**levantisco**, *a.* turbulent, restless.—**levar**, *vt.* (naut.) to weigh (anchor).—*vr.* to set sail.

leve, *a.* light, of little weight; trifling; slight.

levita, *f.* frock coat; Levite.

léxico, *m. a.* lexical.—*m.* lexicon.—**lexicográfico**, *a.* lexicographic(al).—**lexicógrafo**, *n.* lexicographer.—**lexicografía**, *f.* lexicography.—**lexicología**, *f.* lexicology.

ley, *f.* law; rule of action; loyalty.—*de buena l.*, sterling.—*de mala l.*, vicious; crooked; low, base.—*l. del embudo*, oppressive law.—*l. marcial*, martial law.—**leyenda**, *f.* reading; legend, inscription; motto.

lezna, *f.* awl.

liar, *vt.* to tie, bind, do up; (coll.) to embroil, draw into an entanglement.—*vr.* to bind oneself; to get tangled up.

libar, *vt.* to suck; to taste.

libelo, *m.* libel.

libélula, *f.* dragon fly.

liberación, *f.* liberation; (law) quittance.—**liberal**, *a.* & *mf.* liberal.—**liberalidad**, *f.* liberality, generosity.—**liberalismo**, *m.* Liberalism.—**libertad**, *f.* liberty, freedom; familiarity; unconventionality; ransom.—*l. bajo fianza* or *palabra*, *l. provisional*, bail.—*l. condicional*, parole.—*l. de cátedra*, academic freedom.—*l. de cultos*, freedom of worship.—*l. de expresión* or *palabra*, freedom of speech.—*l. de prensa*, freedom of the press.—*l. de reunión*, freedom of assembly.—*l. vigilada*, probation.—**libertador**, *n.* & *a.* liberator, rescuer; liberating.—**libertar**, *vt.* to free, liberate; to exempt; to acquit; to rid, clear.—**libertinaje**, *m.* licentiousness.—**libertino**, *n.* & *a.* libertine, (fam.) wolf; dissolute.

líbico, *a.* & *n.* Libyan.

libidinoso, *a.* lustful.

libio, *a.* & *n.* Libyan.

libra, *f.* pound (weight, coin).—*L.*, (astr.) Libra.

librador, *n.* deliverer; (com.) drawer of a check or draft.—**libramiento**, *m.* delivery, delivering; warrant, order of payment.—**libranza**, *f.* (com.) draft, bill of exchange.—**librar**, *vt.* to free, deliver; to exempt; to pass (sentence); to issue (a decree); (com.) to draw.—*l. batalla* or *combate*, to engage in battle.—*vr.* (**de**) to

escape, avoid, be free (from); get rid (of).—**libre**, *a.* free; unencumbered; independent; vacant; disengaged; clear, open; exempt; single, unmarried.—*l. de impuestos*, tax-free.

librea, *f.* livery, uniform.

librería, *f.* bookstore.—**librero**, *n.* bookseller.—*m.* bookcase.—**libreta**, *f.* notebook, copybook.—*l. de ahorro*, (com.) passbook.—*l. de espiral*, spiral-bound notebook.—*l. de manejar*, driver's license.—*l. militar*, military service record.—**librettista**, *mf.* librettist.—**libreto**, *m.* libretto.—**librito**, *m.*—*l. de fósforos* or *cerillas*, matchbook.—**libro**, *m.* book.—*l. blanco*, (pol.) white paper.—*l. de bocetos*, *l. de esbozos literarios*, sketchbook.—*l. de bolsillo*, paperback.—*l. de chistes*, joke book.—*l. de texto*, textbook.—*l. de vuelo*, (aer.) logbook.—*hacer l. nuevo*, to turn over a new leaf.

licencia, *f.* permission, license; licentiousness, wantonness; (mil.) furlough; degree of licentiate; leave of absence.—*l. de conducción*, driver's license.—**licenciado**, *n.* licentiate; (Am.) lawyer.—**licenciamiento**, *m.* graduation as a licentiate; (mil.) discharge.—**licenciar**, *vt.* to license; to confer a degree on; (mil.) to discharge.—*vr.* to get a master's degree.—**licenciatura**, *f.* degree of licentiate; graduation as a licentiate.—**licencioso**, *a.* licentious, dissolute.

licitar, *vt.* & *vi.* to bid (on, for) at auction or on public works.—**lícito**, *a.* licit, lawful; just.

licor, *m.* liquor; liqueur.

lid, *f.* contest, fight.

líder, *mf.* leader.

lidia, *f.* battle, fight; bullfight.—**lidiar**, *vi.* to fight; to struggle.—*vt.* to run or fight (bulls).

liebre, *f.* hare; coward.

liendre, *f.* nit, egg of a louse.

lienzo, *m.* linen cloth; (art) canvas.

liga, *f.* garter; birdlime; league, alliance; alloy; rubber band.—**ligadura**, *f.* ligature; subjection.—**ligamento**, *m.* bond, tie; ligament.—**ligar**, *vti.* [b] to tie, bind, fasten; to alloy; to join.—*vii.* to combine cards of the same suit.—*vri.* to league, join together; to bind oneself.

ligereza, *f.* lightness; swiftness; inconstancy, fickleness.—**ligero**, *a.* light;

fast, nimble; (of cloth) thin; gay; unsteady, giddy; unimportant, trifling; easily disturbed (as sleep).—*a la ligera,* superficially.—*l. de lengua,* loose-tongued.—*adv.* fast, rapidly.

lija, *f.* sandpaper.—**lijar,** *vt.* to sandpaper.

lila, *f.* lilac tree; lilac flower; lilac color.

liliputiense, *mf.* & *a.* midget; Lilliputian.

lima, *f.* sweet lime; (mech.) file; finish, polishing.—*l. para las uñas,* nail file.—**limar,** *vt.* to file; to polish; to touch up.

limaza, *f.* slug.

limero, *m.* lime tree.

limitación, *f.* limitation, limit.—**limitar,** *vt.* to limit; to bound; to restrict; to reduce (expense).—*vr.* to confine oneself to.—**límite,** *m.* limit; boundary; cutoff point.—*l. del bosque maderable,* timber line.—**limítrofe,** *a.* bounding.

limo, *m.* slime, mud.

limosna, *f.* alms.—**limosnero,** *a.* charitable.—*n.* (Am.) beggar.

limón, *m.* lemon.—**limonada,** *f.* lemonade.—**limonero,** *m.* lemon tree.

limpia, *f.* cleaning; dredging.—**limpiabotas,** *mf.* bootblack; shoeshine boy.—**limpiador,** *n.* & *a.* cleaner, scourer; cleaning.—**limpiametales,** *m.* metal polish.—**limpiapipas,** *m.* pipe cleaner.—**limpiar,** *vt.* to clean, cleanse; (coll.) to steal; (coll.) to clean out.—*l. con algodón,* (surg.) to swab.—*l. con chorro de arena,* to sandblast.—**límpido,** *a.* limpid, crystal-clear.—**limpieza,** *f.* cleanness, cleanliness; neatness, tidiness; purity; honesty.—*l. de cutis,* facial.—*l. en* or *a seco,* drycleaning.—**limpio,** *a.* clean; clear; neat; (coll.) broke.—*poner en l.,* to make a clear copy.—*sacar en l.,* to conclude, infer; to make out, understand.

linaje, *m.* lineage, descent, ancestry.

linaza, *f.* linseed.

lince, *m.* lynx; very keen person.—*a.* keen-sighted, observing.

linchamiento, *m.* lynching.—**linchar,** *vt.* to lynch.

lindar, *vi.* to be contiguous, to border.—**linde,** *m.* landmark; boundary.—**lindero,** *m.* limit, boundary.

lindeza, *f.* neatness, elegance, prettiness.—*pl.* pretty things; (ironic) improprieties, insults.—**lindo,** *a.* pretty.—*de lo l.,* very much;

wonderfully; greatly.—**lindura,** *f.* beauty; beautiful thing.

línea, *f.* line; (of persons) lines, figure; boundary, limit; progeny; (mil.) file.—*l. aérea,* airline.—*l. de flotación,* water line.—*l. de montaje,* assembly line.—*l. de pleamar,* high-water mark.—**lineal,** *a.* lineal, linear.—**lineamiento,** *m.* lineament, feature.

lingote, *m.* (foundry) ingot; slug.

lingüista, *mf.* linguist.—**lingüística,** *f.* linguistics.—**lingüístico,** *a.* linguistic.

lino, *m.* flax; linen.

linóleo, *m.* linoleum.

linotipia, *f.* linotype.—**linotipista,** *mf.* linotypist.—**linotipo,** *m.* linotype.

linterna, *f.* lantern; flashlight.

lío, *m.* bundle; (coll.) mess, confusion, scrape.—*armar un l.,* to tangle, mess up, make difficulties.—**liofilizado,** *a.* freezedried.—**liofilizar,** *vt.* to freezedry.

liquidación, *f.* liquidation, settlement; bargain sale.—**liquidar,** *vt.* to liquefy; (com.) to liquidate, sell out; to settle, pay up; to squander; (coll.) to wipe out; to murder.—*vr.* to liquefy.—**líquido,** *a.* liquid; (econ.) liquid; (com.) net.—*m.* liquid; (com.) balance, net profit.

lira, *f.* (mus.) lyre; lira.—**lírico,** *a.* lyric(al).—*f.* lyric poetry.

lirio, *m.* lily.

lirón, *m.* dormouse; (coll.) sleepy head.

lirondo, *a.* pure, clean, neat.

lis, *f.* (heraldry) lily; iris.

lisiar, *vt.* to cripple.—*vr.* to become crippled.

liso, *a.* smooth, even, flat; plain, unadorned; straight (hair); plaindealing.—*l. y llano,* clear, evident.

lisonja, *f.* flattery.—**lisonjear,** *vt.* to flatter.—**lisonjero,** *n.* flatterer.—*a.* flattering; complimentary.

lista, *f.* list; strip; stripe.—*l. de correos,* Post Office general delivery.—*l. de control,* checklist.—*l. de envío,* mailing list.—*l. de espera,* waiting list.—*pasar l.,* to call the roll.—**listado,** *a.* striped, streaky.—*m.* list, roll; (comput.) printout.

listo, *a.* ready; quick, prompt; clever, resourceful.—*estar l.,* to be ready.

listón, *m.* ribbon; tape; (carp.) strip; lath.

lisura, *f.* smoothness, evenness; sincerity, candor.

litera, *f.* litter, stretcher; berth; bunk bed.

literal, *a.* literal.—**literario,** *a.* literary.—**literato,** *n.* writer.—**literatura,** *f.* literature.

litigar, *vti.* [b] & *vii.* to litigate.—**litigio,** *m.* litigation, lawsuit.

litografía, *f.* lithography.

litoral, *a.* coastal.—*m.* coast, shore.

litro, *m.* liter. (See Table.)

liturgia, *f.* liturgy.—**litúrgico,** *a.* liturgical.

liviandad, *f.* lightness; levity, frivolity; lewdness.—**liviano,** *a.* light (not heavy); inconstant, fickle; frivolous; slight; lewd.

lividez, *f.* lividness.—**lívido,** *a.* livid.

llaga, *f.* ulcer, sore.—**llagar,** *vti.* [b] & *vri.* to ulcerate.

llama, *f.* flame, blaze; (zool.) llama.

llamada, *f.* call; beckoning; (print.) reference mark to a note.—*l. a las armas,* call to arms.—*l. al orden,* call to order.—*l. interurbana* or *a larga distancia,* long-distance call.—*l. telefónica,* telephone call.—*l. urbana,* local call.—**llamamiento,** *m.* calling; call; appeal; convocation.—**llamar,** *vt.* to call, summon; to beckon; to invoke; to name.—*ll. la atención,* to attract attention; to call to task.—*ll. por teléfono,* to telephone.—*vi.* to ring; to knock (at the door).—*ll. a capítulo,* to call to account.—*vr.* to be called or named.—*¿cómo se llama Ud.?* what is your name?

llamarada, *f.* sudden blaze; flash; sudden flush.

llamativo, *a.* showy, gaudy, flashy; causing thirst.

llameante, *a.* blazing, flaming.—**llamear,** *vi.* to blaze; to flame.

llanero, *n.* plainsman (-woman).—**llaneza,** *f.* plainness, simplicity; familiarity.—**llano,** *a.* even, level, smooth; plain, unadorned; open, frank.—*de ll.,* openly; clearly.—*m.* plain.

llanta, *f.* rim (of vehicle wheel); (auto) tire.

llanto, *m.* crying, weeping; tears.

llanura, *f.* plain, prairie; flatness.

llave, *f.* key; faucet, spout; (print.) brace; clock winder; key, explanation of anything difficult; switch; (mus.) clef, key.—*bajo ll.,* under lock and key.—*echar ll.,* to lock.—*ll. de caja* or *de cubo,* socket wrench.—*ll. de cierre, ll. de paso,* stopcock.—*ll. inglesa,* monkey wrench.—*ll. maestra,* master key, passkey.—*ll. para tubos,* pipe wrench.—**llavero,** *m.* key ring.—**llavín,** *m.* latch key; key.

llegada, *f.* arrival, coming.—*ll. a la meta,* (sports) photofinish.—**llegar,** *vii.* [b] to arrive; to come; to reach, go as far as; to amount.—*ll. a las manos,* to come to blows.—*ll. a saber,* to find out, get to know.—*ll. a ser,* to become, get to be.—*no ll. a,* not to amount to; not to come up, or be equal, to.—*vri.* (**a**) to approach; to go up to.

llenar, *vt.* to fill, stuff, pack; to pervade; to satisfy, content.—*vr.* to fill, fill up; (**de**) to become full (of), or covered (with); (coll.) to lose patience; to get crowded, packed; (of the moon) to be full.—**lleno,** *a.* full, filled, replete; complete; teeming.—*de ll.,* fully, totally.—*m.* fill, fullness; (theat.) full house.

llevadero, *a.* tolerable, bearable.—**llevar,** *vt.* to carry; to bear; to take; to bring; to take off, carry away; to lead (a life); to wear (clothing, etc.); to spend (time); to keep (books).—*ll. a cabo,* to accomplish, carry out.—*ll. a cuestas,* to carry on one's back; to support.—*ll. el compás,* to beat or keep time.—*ll. en viaje corto,* to shuttle.—*ll. la contra,* to oppose, antagonize.—*ll. la delantera,* to be ahead.—*lleva un año aquí,* he has been here one year.—*me lleva cinco años,* he is five years older than I.—*vr.* to take or carry away; to get along.—*ll. bien* (or *mal*), to be on good (or bad) terms.—*ll. chasco,* to be disappointed.

llorar, *vi.* to cry, weep.—*vt.* to weep over, bewail, mourn.—**lloriquear,** *vi.* to whimper, whine, snivel, sniffle.—**lloriqueo,** *m.* whining; whimper.—**lloro,** *m.* weeping, crying.—**llorón,** *a.* given to weeping.—*n.* weeper, crybaby.—**lloroso,** *a.* mournful, sorrowful, tearful.

llover, *vii.* [26] to rain; to shower.—**llovizna,** *f.* drizzle, sprinkling.—**lloviznar,** *vi.* to drizzle, sprinkle.—**lluvia,** *f.* rain.—*l. acida,* acid rain.—*l. de estrellas,* meteor shower.—*l. nuclear, l. radiactiva,* nuclear fallout.—*lluvias aisladas,* scattered showers.—**lluvioso,** *a.* rainy.

lo, *art. neut.* the.—*pron.* him; you; it;

so; that.—*lo de*, that of; that matter of, what.—*lo de siempre*, the same old story.—*lo que*, what, that which.—*sé lo hermosa que es*, I know how beautiful she is.

loable, *a.* laudable, praiseworthy.—**loar**, *vt.* to praise.

lobanillo, *m.* wen, tumor.

lobato, lobezno, *m.* wolf cub.—**lobo**, *n.* wolf.—*l. solitario*, lone wolf.

lóbrego, *a.* murky, obscure; sad, somber.—**lobreguez**, *f.* obscurity, darkness.

local, *a.* local.—*m.* place, site, premises.—*en el l. mismo*, on the premises.—**localidad**, *f.* locality, location; (theat., etc.) seat.—**localización**, *f.* localization.—**localizar**, *vti.* [a] to localize; to find out where.

loción, *f.* lotion.

loco, *a.* insane, crazy; excessive.—*n.* insane person, lunatic.

locomoción, *f.* locomotion.—**locomotora**, *f.*, **locomotriz**, *a.* locomotive.

locuacidad, *f.* loquacity, talkativeness, volubility.—**locuaz**, *a.* loquacious, talkative.—**locución**, *f.* diction; phrase, locution.

locura, *f.* madness, insanity; folly.

locutor, *n.* radio announcer or speaker.—*l. deportivo*, sportscaster.

lodazal, *m.* bog, mire.—**lodo**, *m.* mud, mire.—**lodoso**, *a.* muddy, miry.

lógica, *f.* logic.—**lógico**, *a.* logical.

logicial, *m.* (comput.) software.

lograr, *vt.* to get, obtain; to attain.—*vr.* to succeed, be successful.—**logro**, *m.* gain, profit, benefit; success, accomplishment; usury.

loma, *f.* little hill.

lombarda, *f.* red cabbage.

lombriz, *f.* earthworm.—*l. solitaria*, tapeworm.

lomo, *m.* loin; back of an animal; chine of pork; back of a book or cutting tool.

lona, *f.* canvas.

longaniza, *f.* pork sausage.

longevidad, *f.* longevity.

longitud, *f.* length; longitude.—**longitudinal**, *a.* longitudinal.

loncha, *f.* thin slice.

lonja, *f.* (com.) exchange; grocer's shop; warehouse; slice (of meat); strip; leather strap.

lontananza, *f.*—*en l.*, far away, in the distance.

loquero, *n.* attendant in an insane asylum; (Am.) insane asylum.

loro, *m.* parrot.

los, *art. m. pl.* the.—*pron. m. pl.* them.—*l. que*, those who, those which; which.

losa, *f.* slab, flagstone; gravestone; grave.—**loseta**, *f.* tile.

lote, *m.* lot; share, part.

lotería, *f.* lottery; raffle; lotto.

loza, *f.* chinaware; porcelain; crockery.

lozanía, *f.* luxuriance; freshness; vigor, lustiness.—**lozano**, *a.* luxuriant; fresh; brisk, spirited.

lubricación, *f.* lubrication.—**lubricante**, *m. & a.* lubricator; lubricating.—**lubricar**, *vti.* [d] to lubricate.

lucero, *m.* bright star; light hole; star on the forehead of horses; brightness, splendor.

lucha, *f.* struggle, strife; wrestling, wrestle; dispute, argument.—*l. a puñetazos*, fistfight.—*l. de la cuerda*, tug of war.—**luchador**, *n.* wrestler; fighter.—**luchar**, *vi.* to fight, struggle; to wrestle.

lucidez, *f.* brilliancy; brightness; success.—**lucido**, *a.* magnificent, splendid, brilliant; most successful.—**lúcido**, *a.* clear, lucid; brilliant, shining.—**luciente**, *a.* shining, luminous, bright.—**luciérnaga**, *f.* glowworm, firefly.—**lucimiento**, *m.* brilliance; success.—**lucir**, *vii.* [3] to shine, glitter, glow; to outshine, exceed; to look, appear.—*vti.* to light, illuminate; to show off, display, exhibit.—*vri.* to shine, be brilliant; to dress to advantage; to be very successful; to do splendidly.

lucrar, *vt. & vr.* to profit.—**lucrativo**, *a.* lucrative, profitable.—**lucro**, *m.* gain, profit.

luctuoso, *a.* sad, mournful.

luego, *adv.* presently, immediately; afterwards; next; later.—*desde l.*, of course, naturally.—*hasta l.*, so long, see you later.—*l. que*, after, as soon as.—*conj.* therefore.

lugar, *m.* place, spot, site; town, village; room, space; seat; employment; time, opportunity; cause, reason.—*dar l. a*, to cause, give occasion for.—*en l. de*, instead of.—*hacer l.*, to make room.—*l. común*, cliché.—*l. de veraneo*, summer resort.—*tener l.*, to take place, happen.—**lugareño**, small town.—**lugarteniente**, *mf.* second in command, deputy, substitute.

lúgubre, *a.* sad, gloomy, dismal.

lujo, *m.* luxury.—**lujoso**, *a.* showy, luxurious; lavish.

lujuria, *f.* lewdness, lechery, lust; excess.—**lujuriante**, *a.* lusting; luxuriant, exuberant.—**lujurioso**, *a.* lustful, lecherous, lewd.

lumbre, *f.* fire (in stove, fireplace, etc.);light (from a match, etc.); splendor.—**lumbrera**, *f.* luminary; louver.

luna, *f.* moon; mirror plate; plate glass.—**lunar**, *a.* lunar.—*m.* mole; beauty spot.—**lunático**, *a.* & *n.* lunatic.

lunes, *m.* Monday.

luneta, *f.* lens; orchestra chair in a theater.—*l. posterior*, (aut.) rear window.

lupa, *f.* magnifying glass.

lupanar, *m.* brothel.

lúpulo, *m.* hops.

lustrar, *vt.* to polish.—**lustre**, *m.* polish, glaze, sheen; splendor, glory; shoeshine.—**lustroso**, *a.* lustrous, glossy, shining.

luterano, *n.* & *a.* Lutheran, Protestant.

luto, *m.* mourning; grief.—*pl.* mourning draperies.—*de l.*, in mourning.

luz, *f.* light.—*pl.* culture, enlightenment.—*a todas luces*, evidently.—*dar a l.*, to give birth to; to publish.—*entre dos luces*, by twilight.—*l. de antorcha*, torchlight.—*l. de parada*, stop light.—*l. de tráfico*, traffic light.—*l. verde*, (fig.) green light; all clear.

M

macabro, *a.* macabre; ugly, hideous.

macaco, *m.* monkey.—*m. de la India*, rhesus (monkey).

macadán, *m*, **macadam**, *m.* macadam.

macana, *f.* (Am.) club, cudgel; (Am.) blunder; fib, joke.

macarela, *f.* (Am.) mackerel.

macarrones, *m. pl.* macaroni.

maceración, *f.*, **maceramiento**, *m.* maceration, steeping.—**macerar**, *vt.* to macerate, steep.

macero, *m.* mace bearer; sergeant-at-arms.

maceta, *f.* flowerpot; mallet; stonecutter's hammer; (Am.) slow person.—**macetero**, *m.* flowerpot stand.

machacar, *vti.* [d] to pound; to crush.—*vii.* to importune; to harp on a subject.—**machacón**, *a.* monotonous; tenacious.

machetazo, *m.* blow with a machete.—**machete**, *m.* machete.—**machetero**, *n.* (Am.) sugar cane cutter.

machihembrar, *vt.* (carp.) to dovetail.

macho, *a.* male; masculine, robust.—*m.* male; he-man; he-mule; hook (of hook and eye); bolt (of a lock); sledge hammer; ignorant fellow; (arch.) buttress; spigot.—*m. cabrío*, he-goat, buck.

machucar, *vti.* [d] to pound; to bruise; to crush.

machuno, *a.* mannish, masculine.

macilento, *a.* pale; emaciated; haggard.

macis, *f.* (bot.) mace.

macizo, *a.* solid; massive; firm.—*m.* massiveness; massif; flower bed.

madeja, *f.* hank, skein; lock of hair.

madera, *f.* wood; timber, lumber.—*m. laminada*, plywood.—*m. prensada*, wallboard.—**maderaje, maderamen**, *m.* timber; timber work; woodwork.—**madero**, *m.* beam; timber; piece of lumber; log; blockhead.

madrastra, *f.* stepmother.—**madre**, *f.* mother; origin, source; womb; bed (of a river); dregs.—*m. alquilada, madre suplente, m. de alquiler*, surrogate mother.—*m. política*, mother-in-law.—*m. soltera*, single or unmarried mother.—*salirse de m.*, to overflow.—**madreperla**, *f.* mother-of-pearl.—**madreselva**, *f.* (bot.) honeysuckle.

madriguera, *f.* burrow; den, lair, nest.

madrileño, *a.* & *n.* Madrilenian, native of Madrid.

madrina, *f.* godmother; bridesmaid; protectress, patroness.—*m. de guerra*, war mother.—*primera m. de boda*, maid of honor.

madrugada, *f.* dawn; early morning; early rising.—*de m.*, at daybreak.—**madrugador**, *a.* early rising.—*n.*

early riser.—**madrugar**, *vii.* [b] to rise early; to anticipate, to be beforehand.—**madrugón**, *m.* (coll.) very early rising.

madurar, *vt.* & *vi.* to ripen; to mature.—**madurez**, *f.* maturity; ripeness; wisdom.—**maduro**, *a.* ripe; mature; wise, judicious; middle-aged.

maestra, *f.* teacher, schoolmistress, professor; (mason.) guide line.—**maestría**, *f.* mastery; great skill.—**maestro**, *a.* masterly; master.—*m. de ceremonias*, master of ceremonies; ringmaster.—*m. de coro*, choir director.—*m. de escuela*, schoolteacher.—*obra m.*, masterpiece.—*m.* master; teacher, professor; expert; skilled artisan.—*m. de obras*, builder.

magia, *f.* magic, wizardry.—**mágico**, *a.* magic(al).

magín, *m.* (coll.) imagination.

magisterio, *m.* mastery; mastership; teaching profession.—**magistrado**, *m.* judge, magistrate.—**magistral**, *a.* magisterial, masterly, masterful.—**magistratura**, *f.* judges (as a body).

magnánimo, *a.* magnanimous, generous.

magnate, *m.* magnate; (coll.) tycoon.

magnético, *a.* magnetic.—**magnetismo**, *m.* magnetism.—**magnetizar**, *vti.* [a] to magnetize; to hypnotize.

magnificencia, *f.* magnificence, grandeur, splendor.—**magnífico**, *a.* magnificent; excellent.

magnitud, *f.* magnitude; quantity.—**magno**, *a.* great.

mago, *n.* magician, wizard.—*pl.* magi.—*los Reyes Magos*, The Three Wise Men.

magra, *f.* slice of ham.—**magro**, *a.* meager, lean.

magulladura, *f.* bruise.—**magullar**, *vt.* to bruise; to mangle.

Mahoma, *m.* Muhammad.

maíz, *m.* corn, maize.—**maizal**, *m.* cornfield.

majada, *f.* sheepfold; dung.

majadería, *f.* foolish act, foolishness.—**majadero**, *a.* silly, foolish.—*n.* bore, fool; pestle.—**majar**, *vt.* to pound, bruise, mash; (coll.) to importune, vex, annoy.

majestad, *f.* majesty; stateliness.—**majestuosidad**, *f.* majesty, dignity.—**majestuoso**, *a.* majestic, grand.

majo, *a.* gay, gaudy, handsome, pretty.—*n.* low class dandy or belle.

mal, *a. contr.* of MALO.—*m.* evil; harm, disease, illness.—*m. de Alzheimer*, Alzheimer's disease.—*mal de (las) altura(s)*, altitude sickness.—*m. de ojo*, evil eye.—*m. de Parkinson*, Parkinson's disease.—*m. de rayos*, radiation sickness.—*adv.* badly, wrongly; deficiently.

malabarista, *mf.* juggler.

malla, *f.* mesh (of a net); (naut.) net work.—*pl.* tights.

malagradecido, *a.* ungrateful.

malandanza, *f.* misfortune, misery.

malanga, *f.* (Am.) (bot.) arum.

malaria, *f.* malaria.

malayo, *n.* & *a.* Malayan.

malbaratador, *n.* spendthrift, squanderer.—**malbaratar**, *vt.* to squander; to undersell.

malcriado, *a.* ill-bred, rude; spoiled.—**malcriar**, *vt.* to spoil (a child).

maldad, *f.* wickedness, iniquity, badness.

maldecir, *vti.* [14–49] to damn, curse, accurse.—**maldición**, *f.* curse, malediction; damnation.—**maldito**, *ppi* of MALDECIR.—*a.* damned, accursed; perverse, wicked.—*¡m. lo que me importa!* little do I care!

maleable, *a.* malleable.

maleante, *mf.* & *a.* rogue; roguish.—**malear**, *vt.* to pervert, corrupt.

malecón, *m.* dike, mole; quay, jetty.

maledicencia, *f.* slander, calumny.

maleficio, *m.* spell; witchcraft, charm, hex.—**maléfico**, *a.* evil-doing, harmful.

malentendido, *m.* misunderstanding.

malestar, *m.* indisposition, slight illness; discomfort.

maleta, *f.* valise, suitcase; (fam.) bungler; (Am.) hump.—*hacer la m.*, to pack.—**maletero**, *m.* porter, (coll.) red cap.—**maletín**, *m.* small valise or case, overnight bag, satchel.

malévolo, *a.* malevolent, malignant, wicked.

maleza, *f.* weeds; underbrush, shrubbery; thicket, undergrowth.

malgastar, *vt.* to waste, squander.

malhablado, *a.* foul-mouthed.

malhadado, *a.* wretched, unfortunate, ill-starred.

malhechor, *n.* evildoer, criminal.

malherir, *vti.* [39] to wound badly.

malhumorado, *a.* ill-humored, peevish.

malicia, *f.* malice, malignity; suspicion; shrewdness.—**maliciar,** *vt.* to suspect.—**malicioso,** *a.* malicious; wicked, knavish; suspicious.

malignidad, *f.* malignity; viciousness.—**maligno,** *a.* malignant; vicious; harmful; baleful.

malintencionado, *a.* ill-intentioned.

malla, *f.* mesh (of a net); (naut.) network.—*pl.* tights.

mallete, *m.* (sports) mallet.

malo, *a.* bad, evil, wicked; ill, sick; difficult, hard.—*estar de malas,* to be unlucky; to be ill-disposed.—*mala hierba,* weed.—*mala pasada,* dirty trick.—*por buenas o por malas,* willy-nilly.

malograr, *vt.* to waste, lose.—*vr.* to fail, miscarry.

malparir, *vi.* to miscarry.

malquerencia, *f.* ill-will, hatred.

malquistar, *vt.* to estrange; to create prejudice against.—*m. a uno con,* to set one against.—*vi.* to incur dislike, make oneself unpopular.

malsano, *a.* unhealthy, sickly; noxious.

malta, *f.* malt.

maltratar, *vt.* to ill-treat, abuse; to use roughly, maul.—**maltrato,** *m.* ill-treatment; rough usage.—**maltrecho,** *a.* ill-treated; in bad condition, damaged; badly off, battered.

malvado, *a.* wicked, fiendish.—*n.* wicked man (woman).

malvavisco, *m.* (bot.) marshmallow.—*bombón de malvavisco,* marshmallow.

malversación, *f.* misuse of funds, embezzlement.—**malversador,** *n.* one who misapplies funds, embezzler.—**malversar,** *vt.* to misapply (funds); to embezzle.

mamá, *f.* mamma (mother).—**mama,** *f.* breast.

mamada, *f.* (coll.) act of sucking, suckling.—**mamadera,** *f.* (Am.) nursing bottle.—**mamar,** *vt.* & *vi.* to suck, suckle.—*vr.* (Am.) to get drunk.

mamarracho, *m.* daub; grotesque figure or ornament.

mameluco, *m.* (Am.) child's nightdress; (Am.) overalls; (coll.) dolt.

mamífero, *n.* mammal.—*a.* mammalian.

mamón, *a.* & *n.* suckling.

mamotreto, *m.* bulky book or bundle of papers.

mampara, *f.* screen.

mampostería, *f.* masonry, rubble work.

mamut, *m.* mammoth.

manada, *f.* herd; flock; drove.

manantial, *m.* spring, source; origin.—**manar,** *vi.* to issue, flow out; to ooze; to abound.

manatí, *m.* manatee.

manceba, *f.* mistress.

mancilla, *f.* stain, blemish, smirch.—**mancillar,** *vt.* to stain, smirch, sully.

manco, *n.* armless, handless; one-handed or one-armed person.—*a.* handless; armless; one-handed; one-armed; maimed; faulty.

mancha, *f.* stain, spot, blot; patch of ground or vegetation.—*m. de sangre,* bloodstain.—**manchado,** *a.* spotted, speckled.—**manchar,** *vt.* to stain, soil; to tarnish.

mandadero, *n.* messenger, porter; errand boy or girl.—**mandado,** *m.* mandate, order; errand.—**mandamiento,** *m.* order, command; commandment; (law) writ, court order.—*los diez M.,* the Ten Commandments.—**mandar,** *vt.* & *vi.* to command, order; to send.

mandarina, *f.* tangerine.

mandarria, *f.* iron maul, sledge hammer.

mandatario, *n.* proxy; representative; (law) attorney.—**mandato,** *m.* mandate; command, injunction, order, behest.

mandíbula, *f.* jaw; jawbone.

mando, *m.* command, power; control.—*alto m.,* high command.—*con m. a distancia,* remote-controlled.—*m. a distancia,* remote control.—**mandón,** *a.* imperious, domineering.—*n.* imperious, haughty person; (Am.) (min.) boss or foreman.

mandril, *m.* baboon; (mech.) collet.

manducar, *vti.* [d] (coll.) to chew; to eat.

manear, *vt.* to hobble (a horse).

manecilla, *f.* small hand; (print.) fist (☞); hand of a clock or watch.

manejable, *a.* manageable, tractable.—**manejar,** *vt.* to manage, handle; (Am.) to drive (a vehicle, a horse, etc.); to run (an engine, a business).—vr. to behave; to get along, manage.—m. pegado al vehículo de delante, to tailgate.—**manejo,** m. handling; management, conduct; driving.—m. doméstico, housekeeping.

manera, f. manner, way, mode; fly of trousers; side placket of skirt.—pl. ways, customs; manners.—de mala m., blunderingly; roughly; reluctantly.—de m. que, so that, so as to.—de ninguna m., in no way; by no means, not at all.—de otra m., otherwise.—de tal m., in such a way; so much.—de todas maneras, at any rate.—sobre m., exceedingly.

manga, f. sleeve; (water) hose; straining bag; fish trap.—en mangas de camisa, in shirt-sleeves.—m. de incendio, fire hose.—m. de viento, whirlwind; (aer.) windsock.—tener m. ancha, to be broadminded.

mangana, f. lasso, lariat.

manganeso, m. manganese.

manglar, m. grove of mangrove trees.—**mangle,** m. mangrove.

mango, m. handle, haft; tiller; (bot.) mango.

mangonear, vi. (coll.) to meddle for power, to interfere in order to dominate.—**mangoneo,** m. (coll.) domination.

manguera, f. (watering) hose; waterspout.

mangulto, m. muff; wristlet, half-sleeve; oversleeve; (mech.) muff.

maní, m. (Am.) peanut.

manía, f. mania; whim, fancy.

maniatar, vt. to handcuff; to manacle.

maniático, a. & n. crank; queer, mad (person).—**manicomio,** m. insane asylum, madhouse.

manicura, f. manicurist; manicure.

manido, a. commonplace, trite.

manifestación, f. manifestation, statement; (public) demonstration.—**manifestante,** mf. (public) demonstrator.—**manifestar,** vti. [1–49] to state, declare; to manifest, reveal; to tell, let know.—vri. to make a demonstration.—**manifesto,** ppi. of MANIFESTAR.—a. manifest, plain, self-evident.—m. manifesto, public declaration; (com.) custom-house manifest.—poner de m., to make evident; to show plainly; to make public.

manigua, f. (Am.) thicket, jungle.

manija, f. handle, haft; crank; (mech.) brace, clamp.

manilla, f. small hand; bracelet; manacle, handcuff.

maniobra, f. maneuver; operation, procedure.—**maniobrar,** vt. & vi. to maneuver.

manipulación, f. manipulation.—**manipular,** vt. to manipulate, handle.

maniquí, m. manikin; tailor's dummy; mannequin; puppet.—f. model.

manirroto, n. squanderer.—a. lavish, prodigal, wasteful.

manivela, f. (mech.) crank; crankshaft.

manjar, m. food, dish; delicacy, morsel.

mano, f. hand; forefoot; hand of a clock or watch; first hand at cards; round of any game; power or means of making or attaining something; coat (of paint, varnish, etc.).—a la m., near, at hand.—a m., by hand; at hand, near by.—a manos llenas, liberally, abundantly.—de la m., by the hand; hand in hand.—de manos a boca, suddenly, unexpectedly.—entre manos, in hand.—m. a m., in friendly cooperation, together; on equal terms.—m. de cerdo, pig's foot.—m. de obra, work force, labor.—¡manos a la obra! lend a hand! to work!—m. sobre m., idle, doing nothing.—**manojo,** m. bunch; handful; bundle.—**manopla,** f. gauntlet.—**manosear,** vt. to fumble; to touch, feel of.—**manoseo,** m. handling, fingering.—**manotazo,** m. slap, blow with the hand.—**manotear,** vi. to gesticulate.—**manoteo,** m. gesturing with the hands.

mansalva, adv.—a m., without risk or danger; in a cowardly manner.

mansedumbre, f. meekness; tameness.

mansión, f. stay, sojourn; mansion, abode; residence.

manso, a. tame; gentle, mild; calm; soft, quiet; meek.—m. bellwether.

manta, f. blanket; (Am.) poncho.—m. de algodón, wadding.

manteca, f. lard; fat.—**mantecado,** m. butter cake; (Am.) ice cream.—**mantecoso,** a. greasy, buttery.

mantel, m. tablecloth; altar cloth.—**mantelería,** f. table linen.—**manteleta,** f. lady's shawl.

mantener, vti. [42] to support; to maintain; to defend or sustain (an opinion); to keep up (conversation, correspondence).—*vri.* to support oneself; to remain, continue (in one place).—**mantenimiento**, *m.* maintenance, support; living.

mantequilla, *f.* butter.—*m. de maní, m. de cacahuete*, peanut butter.—**mantequillera**, *f.* butter dish.

mantilla, *f.* mantilla; saddlecloth.—**manto**, *m.* cloak, mantle; robe; (min.) layer, stratum.—**mantón**, *m.* large shawl; (Am.) mantilla.—*m. de Manila*, embroidered silk shawl, Spanish shawl.

manuable, *a.* easy to handle, handy.—**manual**, *a.* manual; handy.—*m.* manual, handbook.

manubrio, *m.* handle; crank.

manufactura, *f.* manufacture.—**manufacturar**,*vt.* & *vi.* to manufacture.—**manufacturero**, *a.* manufacturing.—*n.* manufacturer.

manuscrito, *m.* & *a.* manuscript.

manutención, *f.* maintaining; maintenance, support.

manzana, *f.* apple; block (of houses), square.—**manzanilla**, *f.* (bot.) common camomile; dry white sherry wine.—**manzano**, *m.* apple tree.

maña, *f.* skill, cleverness, knack; cunning; evil habit or custom.—*darse m.*, to contrive, manage.

mañana, *f.* morning.—*m.* [the] future.—*de la m.*, A.M.—*de m.*, in the morning; very early.—*por la m.*, in the morning.—*adv.* tomorrow; in the future.—*hasta m.*, until tomorrow, see you tomorrow.—*m. mismo*, tomorrow without fail.—*m. por la m.*, tomorrow morning.—*pasado m.*, day after tomorrow.—**mañanero**, *a.* early rising.

mañoso, *a.* skillful, handy, clever; cunning, shifty, careful; (Am.) lazy.

mapa, *m.* map, chart.—*m. itinerario, m. de carreteras* or *rutas*, road map.

mapache, *m.* raccoon.

mapamundi, *m.* map of the world.

maqueta, *f.* mock-up, dummy, rough cut.

maquillaje, *m.* make-up.—*m. teatral*, greasepaint.—**maquillar**, *vt.* & *vr.* (neol.) to make-up, paint.

máquina, *f.* machine, engine.—*a toda m.*, at full speed.—*m. de afeitar eléctrica*, electric razor or shaver.—*m. de calcular*, calculator.—*m. de coser*, sewing machine.—*m. de discos*, jukebox.—*m. de escribir*, typewriter.—*m. de frutas*, slot machine.—*m. expendedora de sellos*, stamp-vending machine.—*m. fotográfica, m. de fotos*, camera.—*m. trilladora*, threshing machine.—**maquinación**, *f.* machination, plotting; plot.—**maquinal**, *a.* mechanical; unconscious, automatic.—**maquinar**, *vt.* & *vi.* to machinate, scheme, plot.—**maquinaria**, *f.* machinery.—**maquinilla**, *f.* small device.—*m. de afeitar* or *seguridad*, safety razor.—*m. para cortar el pelo*, (hair) clippers.—**maquinista**, *mf.* engineer; machinist.

mar, *m.* & *f.* sea.—*alta m.*, high seas.—*hacerse a la m.*, to put out to sea.—*la m.*, (coll.) a great deal, a lot, lots.—*m. de fondo*, (sea) swell.

maraña, *f.* tangle, snare; puzzle; intrigue, plot; undergrowth.

maravilla, *f.* wonder, marvel; (bot.) marigold.—*a las mil maravillas*, wonderfully well.—**maravillar**, *vt.* to surprise, astonish.—*vr.* (**de**) to wonder (at), marvel.—**maravilloso**, *a.* wonderful, marvelous.

marbete, *m.* label, tag; index card; baggage check.—*m. engomado*, sticker.

marca, *f.* mark, stamp; sign; make, brand.—*de m.*, excellent, reputed.—*m. de agua, m. de nivel de agua*, watermark.—*m. de contraste, m. de ley*, hallmark.—*m. de fábrica*, trademark, trade name.—*m. de nacimiento*, birthmark.—*m. registrada*, registered trademark.—**marcador**, *m.* marker; (sports) score board; scorer; felt-tip pen, felt pen.—**marcapaso**, *m.* (med.) pacemaker.—**marcar**, *vti.* [d] to mark, stamp, impress, brand; (sports) to score; to dial (telephone); to note.—*m. el compás*, to beat time, keep time.

marcha, *f.* march; progress; turn, course, run; departure; (naut.) speed; movement of a watch.—*apresurar la m.*, to hurry, speed up.—*¡en marcha!* forward march! go on! let's go!—*m. en fila apretada*, lock step.—*m. nupcial*, wedding march.—*poner en m.*, to start, put in motion.—*sobre la m.*, at once, right away.

marchamo, *m.* custom-house mark on goods.

marchante, *mf.* dealer; (Am.) customer, buyer.

marchar, *vi.* to march, parade; to progress, go ahead; to work, run, go (as a machine, engine, clock, etc.).—*m. en ralentí, m. en vacío,* (aut.) to idle.—*vr.* to go; to go away, leave.

marchitar, *vt.* to wither, fade.—*vr.* to wither, fade, decay.—**marchito,** *a.* faded, withered.

marcial, *a.* martial, warlike, soldierly.

marco, *m.* frame; (com.) mark.—*m. de ventana,* window frame.

marea, *f.* tide.—*contra viento y m.,* against all odds; come what may.—*m. negra,* oil slick.—**mareado,** *a.* seasick; dizzy.—**marear,** *vt.* to navigate; (coll.) to vex, annoy, bother.—*vr.* to get dizzy, seasick, carsick.—**marejada,** *f.* swell, surf; tidal wave; commotion, disturbance.—**maremágnum,** *m.* (coll.) confusion, bedlam.—**mareo,** *m.* dizziness, seasickness, carsickness; nausea; (coll.) vexation.

marfil, *m.* ivory.—**marfileño,** *a.* ivory.

margarina, *f.* margarine.

margarita, *f.* common daisy; (print.) daisy wheel.

margen, *mf.* margin; border; edge; bank (of a river).—*dar m.,* to give an opportunity or an occasion.—*m. de beneficio,* profit margin.—*m. de error,* margin of error.—**marginal,** *a.* marginal.—**marginar,** *vt.* to leave a margin on; to make marginal notes.

marica, maricón, *m.* (pej. & of.) fag, queer, faggot.

marido, *m.* husband.

mariguana or **marihuana** or **marijuana,** *f.* marijuana.

marimacho, *m.* (coll.) shrew, mannish woman.

marina, *f.* shore, sea coast; seascape; seamanship; navy, fleet, marine.—**marinería,** *f.* seamanship; body of seamen; ship's crew.—**marinero,** *a.* seaworthy.—*m.* sailor, seaman.—*m. de cubierta,* deck hand.—**marino,** *a.* marine, sea.—*m.* seaman, mariner.

mariposa, *f.* butterfly; moth.—**mariposear,** *vi.* to flutter about.

mariscal, *m.* (mil.) marshal.

marisco, *m.* shellfish.

marisma, *f.* marsh, swamp.

marital, *a.* marital.

marítimo, *a.* maritime, marine, sea.

marmita, *f.* kettle, pot, boiler.

mármol, *m.* marble (stone).—**marmóreo,** *a.* marbled, marble.

marmota, *f.* (zool.) marmot; (coll.) sleepy head.—*m. de América,* woodchuck.

maroma, *f.* rope, cable; (Am.) acrobat's performance.—**maromero,** *n.* (Am.) tight-rope dancer, acrobat.

marqués, *m.* marquis.—**marquesa,** *f.* marchioness, marquise.—**marquesina,** *f.* marquee, awning.

marquetería, *f.* marquetry.

marrana, *f.* sow, female pig; (coll.) dirty woman.—**marranada,** *f.* (coll.) hoggish action; nastiness.—**marrano,** *m.* hog; (coll.) dirty man.

marrón, *a.* maroon; brown.

marroquí, *mf. & a.* Moroccan.

marrullería, *f.* wheedling, cajolery.—**marrullero,** *n.* wheedler, coaxer, cajoler.

marsopa, *f.* porpoise.

marta, *f.* sable.

martes, *m.* Tuesday.

martillar, *vt.* to hammer.—**martillazo,** *m.* blow with a hammer.—**martilleo,** *m.* hammering; clatter.—**martillo,** *m.* hammer.—*m. neumático,* pneumatic drill.

martinete, *m.* drop hammer; pile driver; hammer of a piano.

mártir, *mf.* martyr.—**martirio,** *m.* martyrdom; torture; grief.—**martirizar,** *vti.* [a] to martyr; to torture; to torment.

marzo, *m.* March.

mas, *conj.* but, yet.—**más,** *a. & adv.* more; most; (math.) plus.—*a lo m.,* at the most.—*a m.,* besides.—*a m. tardar,* at the latest.—*m. bien,* rather.—*no m. que,* only.—*por m. que,* however much.—*sin m. ni m.,* without more ado.

masa, *f.* dough, mash; (mason.) mortar; (phys.) mass; volume; crowd of people.

masacre, *m.* (neol.) massacre.

masaje, *m.* massage.—**masajear,** *vt.* to massage.—**masajista,** *mf.* massagist; masseur, masseuse.—**masar,** *vt.* to massage.

mascada, *f.* chewing; (Am.) chew of tobacco; (Mex.) silk handkerchief.—**mascar,** *vti.* [d] to chew; (coll.) to mumble.

máscara, *f.* mask.—*pl.* masquerade.—*mf.* mask, masquerader.—*m. antigás,* gas mask.—**mascarada,** *f.* masquerade.—**mascarilla,** *f.* death mask; half mask.

mascota, f. mascot; (baseball) catcher's mitt.

masculino, a. masculine; male.

mascullar, vt. to mumble; to munch.

masilla, f. putty.

masón, m. freemason.—**masonería,** f. freemasonry, masonry.

masticación, f. chewing.—**masticar,** vti. [d] to chew.

mástil, m. mast, post; tent-pole; neck (of violin or guitar).

mastín, n. mastiff.

mastuerzo, m. dolt, simpleton; (bot.) common cress.

mata, f. (bot.) plant; sprig, blade; grove, orchard.—m. de pelo, head of hair.

matadero, m. slaughterhouse; drudgery.—**matador,** n. & a. killer; killing.—m. matador.—**matadura,** f. sore, gall.—**matanza,** f. slaughter, butchery.—**matar,** vt. to kill.—a mata caballo, in a great hurry.—m. de hambre, to starve.—vr. to kill oneself; to get killed; to commit suicide.—**matarife,** m. slaughterer.—**matarratas,** m. rat poison; (fam.) rotgut.—**matasanos,** m. (coll.) quack, charlatan, quack doctor.—**matasellos,** m. postmark.

mate, a. dull, lusterless, mat.—m. (chess) checkmate; (bot.) Brazilian holly; maté, Paraguay tea.—dar m., to checkmate.—dar m. ahogado a, to stalemate.—m. ahogado, stalemate.

matemática(s), f. (pl.) mathematics.—**matemático,** a. mathematical.—n. mathematician.

materia, f. matter; material, stuff; subject, topic; (med.) matter, pus.—entrar en m., to come to the point.—m. prima, raw material.—**material,** a. material.—m. material, stuff; ingredient; (elec. and RR.) equipment.—**materialismo,** m. materialism.—**materialista,** mf. & a. materialist(ic).—**materializar,** vti. [a] to materialize.—vri. to become (morally) materialistic.

maternal, a. maternal.—**maternidad,** f. maternity.—**materno,** a. maternal, motherly; mother.

matinal, a. of the morning; morning.—**matiné,** m. matinée.

matiz, m. tint, hue, shade; nuance.—**matizado,** a. many-hued.—**matizar,** vti. [a] to blend (colors); to tint, shade.

matojo, m. bush; (bot.) glasswort.

matón, m. (coll.) bully.

matorral, m. thicket; bush.

matraca, f. wooden rattle.—dar m., to banter.

matrero, a. cunning, shrewd; (Am.) suspicious.—n. trickster, swindler; (Am.) cattle thief.

matriarca, f. matriarch.

matrícula, f. register, list; matriculation; license; car license plate.—**matricular,** vt. & vr. to matriculate, register, enroll.

matrimonial, a. matrimonial.—**matrimonio,** m. marriage, wedlock, matrimony; married couple.—proponer m., to propose.

matriz, a. first, principal, main.—f. womb; mold, form, matrix; screw nut.

matrona, f. matron.

matutino, a. morning.—m. (Am.) morning newspaper.

maula, f. rubbish, trash, junk; cunning, craft; deceitful trick.—mf. (coll.) malingerer, sluggard; cheat, tricky person.

maullar, vi. to mew, to meow.—**maullido,** m. mew(ing), meow(ing).

mausoleo, m. mausoleum.

máxima, f. maxim, proverb; rule.—**máxime,** adv. especially, principally.—**máximo,** m. & a. maximum.

maya, mf. Maya (people and language).—a. Mayan.—f. daisy.

mayar, vi. to mew.

mayo, m. May.

mayonesa, f. mayonnaise.

mayor, a. greater; greatest; larger; largest; older, elder; oldest, eldest; senior; main, principal; major.—altar m., high altar.—m. superior; (mil.) major.—pl. ancestors, forefathers; superiors; elders.—al por m., (by) wholesale.—m. de edad, of age.

mayoral, m. foreman, overseer; head shepherd; coach driver.

mayordomo, m. butler, steward; major-domo.

mayoría, f. majority (in age or number); superiority.

mayorista, mf. wholesale merchant or dealer.

mayúscula, a. & f. capital (letter).—**mayúsculo,** a. large, good-sized; important, prominent.

maza, f. mace; drop hammer; war club; roller of a sugar-cane mill.

mazacote, *m.* concrete; dry, tough mass.

mazmorra, *f.* dungeon.

mazo, *m.* mallet, maul, wooden hammer; bundle, bunch.

mazorca, *f.* ear of corn.

me, *pron.* me; to me; for me; myself.

Meca, *f.—la M.,* Mecca.

mecánico, *a.* mechanical.—*n.* mechanic; engineer; technician; serviceman, repairman, repairwoman.—**mecanografía,** *f.* typewriting.—**mecanógrafo,** *n.* typist, stenographer.

mecate, *m.* (Mex.) maguey rope or cord.

mecedora, *f.* rocking chair.—**mecer,** *vti.* [a] to rock; to swing; to move (a child) gently; to shake.—*vri.* to rock, swing, sway.

mecha, *f.* wick; fuse (of explosive); slice of bacon (for larding); (Am.) lock of hair.—*m. de lámpara,* lampwick.—**mechar,** *vt.* to lard (meat, etc.).—**mechero,** *m.* lamp burner; gas burner; cigarette lighter; (sl.) shoplifter.—**mechón,** *m.* large lock of hair.

medalla, *f.* medal.—**medallón,** *m.* locket; medallion.

médano, *m.* sand bank; dune.

media, *f.* stocking; hose; (Am.) sock; (math.) mean.—*medias de nilón,* nylon stockings, nylons.—**mediación,** *f.* mediation; intercession.—**mediado,** *a.* half-filled, half-full.—*a mediados de,* (of period of time) about the middle of.—**mediador,** *n.* mediator; intercessor.—**medianamente,** *adv.* middling, so-so, fairly.—**medianería,** *f.* partition wall.—**medianero,** *a.* mediating, interceding; intermediate.—*n.* mediator; adjacent owner.—**medianía,** *f.* halfway; average; mediocrity; moderate means.—**mediano,** *a.* moderate, middling, medium; middle sized; mediocre, tolerable; half full.—**medianoche,** *f.* midnight.—**mediante,** *a.* interceding, intervening.—*adv.* by means of, through.—**mediar,** *vi.* to be at the middle; to intercede, mediate; to intervene.

medicación, *f.* medication.—**medicamento,** *m.* medicine, medicament.—**medicastro,** *m.* quack doctor.—**medicina,** *f.* medicine; remedy.—**medicinal,** *a.* medici-

nal.—**medicinar,** *vt.* to prescribe c give medicines (to a patient).

medición, *f.* measurement, measuring

médico, *a.* medical.—*n.* physician.-*m. de medicina general,* general prac titioner.—*m. forense,* coroner.

medida, measure; (shoe, etc.) siz number; gauge; measuring, mea surement; rule; moderation, pru dence.—*a la m.,* to order, custom made.—*a m. del deseo,* accordin to one's wishes.—*a m. que,* a according as, while.—*sin m.,* t excess.—*tomar medidas,* to tak measures or steps.—**medidor,** measurer.

medieval, *a.* medieval.

medio, *a.* half; medium; middl mean, intermediate.—*a m. asa* (cook.) medium.—*a m. camin* half-way.—*media naranja,* (fam better half, wife.—*media vuelt* right about face.—*m.* middle, cer ter; (often *pl.*) means, resources; ex pedient, measure; environment.-*justo m.,* golden mean.—*m. transmisión de datos,* (comput.) da link.—*por m. de,* by means of.—*a half; partially.—*de m. a m.,* con pletely, entirely.—*de por m.,* b tween.—*m. hecho,* (cook.) mediu rare.

mediocre, *a.* mediocre.—**mediocrida** *f.* mediocrity.

mediodía, *m.* midday; noon, noo time; south.—*en pleno m.,* at hig noon.

medioeval, *a.* = MEDIEVAL.

medir, *vti.* [29] to measure; to sca (verses).—*vri.* to be moderate; to a with prudence.

meditabundo, *a.* pensive, musing.-**meditación,** *f.* meditation.—**me tar,** *vt.* & *vi.* to meditate, muse.-**meditativo,** *a.* meditative.

mediterráneo, *a.* Mediterranean.

médium, *mf.* medium.

medrar, *vi.* to thrive, prosper.

medroso, *a.* timorous, faint-hearte cowardly; dreadful, scary.

médula, *f.* marrow; pith; substance, e sence.—*m. espinal,* spinal cord.

medusa, *f.* jellyfish.

megáfono, *m.* megaphone.

mejicano, *n.* & *a.* Mexican.

mejilla, *f.* cheek.

mejillón, *m.* mussel.

mejor, *a.* better, best.—*el m. día,* som

fine day.—*lo mejor,* the best thing.—*m. después del primero,* second-best.—*m. postor,* highest bidder.—*adv.* better; rather.—*a lo m.,* perhaps, maybe.—*m. que,* rather than, instead of.—**mejora,** *f.* improvement, betterment; higher bid.—**mejoramiento,** *m.* improvement.

mejorana, *f.* marjoram.

mejorar, *vt.* to improve, better, enhance; to outbid.—*vi. & vr.* to recover from a disease; to improve; to reform.—**mejoría,** *f.* improvement; betterment; advantage; improvement in health.

mejunje, *m.* concoction.

melado, *m.* cane-juice syrup.

melancolía, *f.* melancholia, gloom, blues.—**melancólico,** *a.* melancholy, gloomy.

melaza, *f.* molasses.—**melcocha,** *f.* (Am.) molasses candy, taffy.

melena, *f.* long hair; mane.—**melenudo,** *a.* bushy-haired.

melifluo, *a.* honeyed (of speech and voice).

melindre, *m.* a sort of fritter; fastidiousness; prudery.—**melindroso,** *a.* prudish, finicky.

mella, *f.* notch, nick, dent; jag in edged tools; gap.—*hacer m.,* to make an impression on the mind; to strike home.—**mellado,** *a.* gaptoothed.—**mellar,** *vt.* to jag, notch; to injure (as honor, credit).

mellizo, *n. & a.* twin (brother, sister).

melocotón, *m.* peach.—**melocotonero,** *m.* peach tree.

melodía, *f.* melody, tune.—**melodioso,** *a.* melodious.

melón, *m.* melon; muskmelon; cantaloupe.—*m. de agua,* (Am.) watermelon.—**melosidad,** *f.* sweetness; mildness.—**meloso,** *a.* honeyed, sweet, syrupy; soft-voiced; gentle.

membrana, *f.* membrane.

membrete, *m.* letterhead; heading.

membrillo, *m.* quince; quince tree.

membrudo, *a.* strong, robust, muscular.

memo, *a.* silly, foolish.

memorable, *a.* memorable.—**memorándum,** *m.* memorandum.—**memoria,** *f.* memory; remembrance, recollection; memoir; report, statement.—*pl.* memoirs; regards, compliments.—*de m.,* by heart.—*hacer*

m., to remember.—*m. de acceso aleatorio, m. de acceso ROM,* read-only memory (ROM).—*m. de acceso aleatorio o directo,* (comput.) random-access memory (RAM).—**memorial,** *m.* memorial; petition, application; (law) brief.

mención, *f.* mention.—**mencionar,** *vt.* to mention.

mendicidad, *f.* beggary.—**mendigar,** *vti.* [b] & *vii.* to beg; to entreat.—**mendigo,** *n.* beggar.

mendrugo, *m.* crumb of bread.

menear, *vt.* to stir; to shake; to wag, waggle.—*vr.* (coll.) to hustle, be active, get a move on; to waggle.—**meneo,** *m.* shake, shaking; wagging, wriggling; (coll.) drubbing, beating.

menester, *m.* need, want; employment, occupation, office.—*pl.* natural or bodily necessities.—*ser. m.,* to be necessary.—**menesteroso,** *a. & n.* needy, indigent (person).

mengano, *n.* (Mr. or Mrs.) so-and-so.

mengua, *f.* diminution, waning, decrease.—**menguar,** *vii.* [b] to diminish, decrease, wane.

menor, *a.* smaller, lesser, younger; smallest, least, youngest; minor.—*mf.* minor.—*m. de edad,* minor, underage.—*por m.,* by retail.—*m.* (mus.) minor.—**menoría,** *f.* inferiority, subordination; underage (person).

menos, *a.* less; least.—*adv.* less; least; except, save.—*al m.* or *a lo m.,* at least.—*a m. que,* unless.—*de m.,* less; wanting, missing.—*echar de m.,* to miss.—*m. mal,* it could be worse, not so bad.—*poco más o m.,* more or less, about.—*por lo m.,* at least.—*venir a m.,* to decline; to become poor.—*prep.* minus, less.—*las ocho m. veinte,* twenty minutes to eight.—**menoscabar,** *vt.* to lessen, diminish; to impair, damage; to discredit.—**menoscabo,** *m.* impairment, damage, detriment.—**menospreciar,** *vt.* to underrate, undervalue; to despise, scorn.—**menosprecio,** *m.* undervaluation; contempt; scorn.

mensaje, *m.* message; errand.—**mensajero,** *n.* messenger; errand boy or girl.

menstruación, *f.* menstruation, period.—**menstruar,** *vi.* to menstruate.—**menstruo,** *m.* menstruation.

mensual, *a.* monthly.—**mensualidad,** *f.* monthly salary or allowance; monthly installment.

ménsula, *f.* bracket; rest for the elbows.

mensurable, *a.* mensurable, measurable.

menta, *f.* mint; peppermint.

mental, *a.* mental.—**mentalidad,** *f.* mentality.—**mentalizar,** *vt.* to make aware of.—*vr.* to get into the right frame of mind, to psych oneself.

mentar, *vti.* [1] to mention, name.

mente, *f.* mind; intelligence.—*m. directora,* mastermind.

mentecatería, mentecatez, *f.* foolishness, silliness.—**mentecato,** *a.* silly, foolish, stupid.—*n.* fool.

mentir, *vti.* [39] & *vii.* to lie.—**mentira,** *f.* lie, falsehood; fib.—*de mentiras,* in jest.—**mentiroso,** *a.* lying, untruthful.

mentón, *m.* chin.

menú, *m.* menu, bill of fare.

menudear, *vt.* to repeat; to do over and over again.—*vi.* to occur frequently; to go into details; to sell by retail.—**menudencia,** *f.* trifle; minuteness.—*pl.* small matters.—**menudeo,** *m.* (com.) retail.—*al m.,* by retail.—**menudo,** *a.* small, little; minute; insignificant.—*m.* small coins, change.—*pl.* entrails of an animal.—*a m.,* often, frequently.

meñique, *a.* little (finger).—*m.* little finger.

meollo, *m.* brain; marrow; judgment; substance.

meple, *m.* (Am.) maple.

mequetrefe, *m.* coxcomb, busybody.

mercachifle, *m.* peddler, hawker, huckster; cheap fellow.—**mercadeo,** *m.* marketing.—**mercader,** *m.* merchant, dealer.—**mercadería,** *f.* commodity, merchandise; trade.—*pl.* goods, wares, merchandise.—**mercado,** *m.* market; marketplace.—*m. alcista,* bull market.—*m. bajista, m. en baja,* bear market.—*m. de valores,* stock market.—*m. monetario* or *m. de dinero,* money market.—*m. negro,* black market.—**mercancía,** *f.* merchandise, goods, wares.—**mercante, mercantil,** *a.* merchant, mercantile, commercial.—**mercar,** *vti.* [d] to buy, purchase.

merced, *f.* favor, grace; mercy.—*estar a*

m. de, to be or to live at the mercy of.—*m. a,* thanks to.

mercenario, *a.* mercenary.—*n.* mercenary soldier.

mercería, *f.* small wares, haberdashery, notions.

mercología, *f.* marketing.

mercurial, *a.* mercurial.—**mercurio,** *m.* mercury, quicksilver.

merecedor, *a.* deserving, worthy.—**merecer,** *vti.* [3] to deserve, merit.—**merecido,** *m.* fitting punishment—*a.* deserved.—**merecimiento,** *m.* merit.

merendar, *vti.* [1] to snack on.—*vii.* to have a snack.—**merendero,** *m.* lunchroom; picnic grounds.

merengue, *m.* meringue, sugarplum.

meretriz, *f.* prostitute.

meridiano, *a.* meridian; meridional (section, cut).—*m.* meridian.—**meridional,** *a.* southern, southerly.—*mf.* southerner.

merienda, *f.* (afternoon) snack; packed meal; picnic; lunch.—*m. al lado de coche,* (aut.) tailgating, tailgate party.—*m. campestre,* picnic.

mérito, *m.* merit; excellence, value.—*hacer méritos,* to make oneself deserving.—**meritorio,** *a.* meritorious, deserving.—*n.* apprentice, unpaid probationer.

merluza, *f.* hake; (coll.) drunkenness.

merma, *f.* decrease; shrinkage.—**mermar,** *vi.* to decrease, wear away.—*vt.* to lessen, reduce, decrease.

mermelada, *f.* marmalade; jam.

mero, *a.* mere, pure, simple; (Am.) real, true; (Am.) very, very same.—*m.* (ichth.) halibut.

merodeador, *n.* marauder.—**merodear,** *vi.* to maraud.—**merodeo,** *m.* marauding.

mes, *m.* month; monthly salary; menstruation.

mesa, *f.* table; desk; executive board; plateau.—*m. de baraja,* card table.—*m. centro, m. de té,* coffee table.—*m. de comedor,* dinner table.—*m. de noche,* bedside table.—*m. de trucos,* pool table.—*m. operatoria,* operating table.—*poner la m.,* to set the table.

mesada, *f.* monthly wages or allowance.

meseta, *f.* plateau; landing of a staircase, tableland.

mesilla or **mesita,** *f.* small table.—*m. baja,* coffee table.—*m. de noche,* bedside table.—*m. de té,* teacart.

mesón, *m.* inn, hostel.—**mesonero,** *n.* innkeeper.

mestizaje, *m.* diverse group.—**mestizo,** *a.* hybrid.—*n.* & *a.* mestizo.

mesura, *f.* civility, politeness; moderation.—**mesurar,** *vr.* to control oneself.

meta, *f.* goal, aim; boundary; finish line.

metáfora, *f.* metaphor.

metal, *m.* metal; (mus.) brass.—*m. de voz,* tone or timbre of the voice.—*m. laminado,* sheet metal.—**metálico,** *a.* metallic.—*m.* cash.—**metalizar,** *vti.* [a] to metallize.—*vri.* to become mercenary.—**metalurgia,** *f.* metallurgy.

metamorfosear, *vt.* & *vr.* to metamorphose, transform.—**metamorfosis,** *f.* metamorphosis, transformation.

metano, *m.* methane.

metemuertos, *m.* stagehand; busybody, meddler.—**metesillas,** *m.* stagehand.

meteórico, *a.* meteoric.—**meteoro,** *m.* meteor.—**meteorología,** *f.* meteorology.—**meteorológico,** *a.* meteorological.—*parte m.,* weather report.—**meteorologista,** *mf.* weather reporter.—*m.* weatherman.

meter, *vt.* to put in(to), insert, introduce; to make (as a noise); to cause (as fear); to induce, get (one into business, etc.).—*vr.* to meddle, intrude; to plunge into.—*m. a,* to undertake to; to turn to; to set oneself up as, pretend to be.—*m. con,* to pick a quarrel with.—*m. en,* (coll.) to meddle with, poke one's nose into.

meticuloso, *a.* meticulous, scrupulous.

metódico, *a.* methodical.—**método,** *m.* method; technique.

metralla, *f.* grapeshot; shrapnel.

métrico, *a.* metric(al).—**metro,** *m.* meter; subway.

metro, *m.* meter; tape measure; ruler.—*m. cuadrado,* square meter.—*m. cúbico,* cubic meter.—*m. de carpintero,* carpenter's rule.

metrónomo, *m.* metronome.

metrópoli, *f.* metropolis.—**metropolitano,** *a.* metropolitan.—*m.* subway.

mexicano, *n.* & *a.* V. MEJICANO.

mezcal, *m.* Mexican alcoholic beverage.

mezcla, *f.* mixture; medley; mortar; mixed cloth.—**mezclar,** *vt.* to mix, mingle; blend.—*vr.* to mix; to intermarry; to intermeddle.

mezclilla, *f.* pepper and salt cloth.

mezcolanza, *f.* (coll.) mix-up, hodgepodge.

mezquindad, *f.* niggardliness, stinginess.—**mezquino,** *a.* niggardly, stingy; petty, puny.

mezquita, *f.* mosque.

mi, *pron.* me.—*a.* my.

miaja, *f.* = MIGAJA.

mico, *n.* monkey.

microbio, *m.* microbe.—**microchip,** *m.* microchip.—**microcirugía,** *f.* microsurgery.—**microcomputadora,** *f.* microcomputer.—**microcosmo,** *m.* microcosm.—**microficha,** *f.* microfiche, microcard.—**microfilm,** *m.* microfilm.—**microfilmar,** *vt.* to microfilm.—**micrófono,** *m.* microphone.—*m. oculto,* hidden microphone, bug.—**microinformática,** *f.* microcomputing.—**microonda,** *f.* microwave.—*pl.* microwave oven.—**microordenador,** *m.* microcomputer.—**micropelícula,** *f.* microfilm.—**microscopio,** *m.* microscope.—*m. electrónico,* electron microscope.—**microsurco,** *m.* microgroove.—**microteléfono,** *m.* handset.

miedo, *m.* fear.—*m. al público,* stage fright.—*tener m.,* to be afraid.—**miedoso,** *a.* fearful, afraid.

miel, *f.* honey; molasses.—*m. de abejas,* bee's honey.

miembro, *m.* member; limb; penis.

mientes, *f.* thoughts, ideas.—*parar m. en,* or *poner m. en,* to consider, reflect on.—*traer a las m.,* to remind.

mientras, *adv.* & *conj.* while; whereas.—*m. más,* the more.—*m. que,* while, as long as, so long as.—*m. tanto,* meanwhile, in the meantime.

miércoles, *m.* Wednesday.

mies, *f.* ripe grain; harvest time.—*pl.* grain fields.

miga, *f.* crumb, soft part of bread; fragment, bit; (coll.) marrow, substance, pith.—*hacer buenas (malas) migas,* (coll.) to get on well (badly) with.—**migaja,** *f.* crumb or bit of bread; fragment, chip or bit; (coll.)

little or nothing.—*pl.* leavings; bits of foods.

migración, *f.* migration.

migraña, *f.* migraine, headache.

migratorio, *a.* migrating, migratory.

milagro, *m.* miracle.—**milagroso,** *a.* miraculous.

mildeu, *m.* mildew.

milésima, *f.* thousandth; mill (part of a dollar).

milicia, *f.* militia; science of war; military profession.—**miliciano,** *n.* militiaman.

militar, *vi.* to serve in the army; to militate.—*m. contra,* to be against.—*a.* military, soldierly.—*m.* soldier, military man; serviceman.

milla, *f.* mile.—*m. náutica,* sea mile.

millar, *m.* thousand.—*pl.* (fig.) a great number.—**millón,** *m.* million; (fig.) a great deal.—*pl.* (fig.) a multitude, a great number.—**millonario,** *n.* & *a.* millionaire.

millonésimo, *a.* & *s.* millionth.

mimar, *vt.* to pet, fondle; to pamper, spoil (a child); to coax.

mimbre, *m.* osier; willow; wicker.—**mimbrera,** *f.* willow.

mímica, *f.* pantomime, sign language.—**mímico,** *a.* mimic; imitative.

mimo, *m.* caress, petting; pampering; coaxing.—**mimoso,** *a.* soft, spoiled; delicate; fastidious, finicky.

mina, *f.* mine; lead of pencil.—*m. de oro,* gold mine.—**minar,** *vt.* to mine, excavate; to undermine; to consume; to ruin.—**mineraje,** *m.* mining.—*m. a tajo abierto,* strip mining.—**mineral,** *a.* mineral; rich mine.—**mineralogía,** *f.* mineralogy.—**minería,** *f.* mining; force of miners.—**minero,** *a.* pertaining to mines.—*m.* miner; mine operator; source, origin.

mingo, *s.* (billiards) object ball.

miniatura, *f.* miniature.—**miniaturización,** *f.* miniaturization.

mínimo, *a.* least, smallest, minimal.—*m.* minimum.

ministerio, *m.* ministry; office and term of a cabinet minister; government department and building.—**ministril,** *m.* minstrel.—**ministro,** *m.* cabinet minister; minister; judge or justice.—*primer m.,* prime minister.

minoría, *f.* minority (in age or in number).—**minoridad,** *f.* minority (in age).

minucia, *f.* minuteness, smallness; mite.—*pl.* minutiae.—**minuciosidad,** *f.* minuteness, thoroughness; trifle; small detail.—**minucioso,** *a.* minutely precise, thorough.

minúsculo, *a.* very small, tiny; of little importance.—*f.* small letter, lower-case letter.

minuta, *f.* first draft; lawyer's bill; memorandum; list.—*pl.* minutes (of a meeting).

minutero, *m.* minute hand.—**minuto,** *m.* minute (in time and geom.).—*al m.,* at once, right away.

mío, mía. —*pl.* **míos, mías,** *pron.* mine.—*a.* my, of mine.

miope, *a.* near-sighted, myopic; short-sighted.—*mf.* near-sighted person.—**miopía,** *f.* myopia, near-sightedness.

mira, *f.* sight (firearms and instruments); vigilance; design, purpose, intention, view.—*estar a la m.,* to be on the lookout, to be on the watch.—**mirada,** *f.* glance, gaze, look.—*echar una m.,* to glance, cast a glance.—**mirado,** *a.* considerate; circumspect, prudent; considered, reputed.—*bien m.,* carefully considered; looking well into the matter; in fact.—**mirador,** *m.* veranda; bay window, vantage-point; gazebo.—**miramiento,** *m.* consideration, reflection; circumspection, prudence; attention, courtesy.—*pl.* fuss, bother, worry.—**mirar,** *vt.* to look, look at; to gaze, gaze upon; to view, survey; to see, regard; to consider, think; to have regard for, esteem; to watch, be careful; to watch, spy; to notice; to concern.—*m. de hito en hito,* to stare at.—*m. de reojo,* to look askance.—*m. por encima,* to examine slightly, glance at.—*vi.* to look.—*m. a,* to face, front on.—*m. por,* to take care of; look after.—*vr.* to look at oneself; to look at each other, one another.

miríada, *f.* myriad, large quantity or number.

mirilla, *f.* peephole; sight (firearms, etc.).

mirlo, *m.* blackbird.—*m. blanco,* (fig.) rare bird.

mirón, *n.* spectator, onlooker; kibitzer; busybody, gazer.—*a.* inquisitive, curious.

mirra, *f.* myrrh.

mirto, *m.* myrtle.

misa, *f.* (eccl.) Mass.—*m. mayor,* high Mass.—*no saber de la m. la media,* to know nothing.—**misal,** *m.* missal.

miscelánea, *f.* miscellany.—**misceláneo,** *a.* miscellaneous.

miserable, *a.* miserable, wretched, unhappy.—*mf.* wretch, cur, cad.—**miseria,** *f.* misery, wretchedness; need, squalor, poverty; stinginess; trifle, pittance.—**misericordia,** *f.* mercy, mercifulness, pity.—**misericordioso,** *a.* merciful.—**mísero,** *a.* = MISERABLE.

misil, *m.* missile.—*m. antibalístico,* antiballistic missile.—*m. balístico,* ballistic missile.—*m. de aire a aire,* air-to-air missile.—*m. de crucero,* cruise missile.—*m. superficie-superficie,* surface-to-surface missile.—*m. tierra-aire,* ground-to-air missile.—*m. teledirigido,* guided missile.

misión, *f.* mission; errand.—**misionero,** *n.* missionary.—**misiva,** *f.* missive, letter.

mismo, *a.* same; similar, like; equal, selfsame.—*ahora m.,* right now.—*el hombre m.,* the man himself.—*el m. hombre,* the same man.—*este m. mes,* this very month.—*lo m.,* the same thing.—*lo m. da,* it is all the same.—*yo m.,* I myself.

misógino, *m.* woman hater.

misterio, *m.* mystery.—**misterioso,** *a.* mysterious.

místico, *n.* & *a.* mystic(al).

mistificador, *n.* = MIXTIFICADOR.—**mistificar,** *vti.* [d] = MIXTIFICAR.

mitad, *f.* half; middle, center.—*cara m.,* better half, spouse.—*m. de precio,* half price.—*a. y m.,* fifty-fifty.—*por la m.,* in two.

mítico, *a.* mythical.

mitigar, *vti.* [b] to mitigate, alleviate, soothe.

mitin, *m.* political meeting; rally.

mito, *m.* myth.—**mitología,** *f.* mythology.—**mitológico,** *a.* mythological.

mitón, *m.* mitt, mitten.

mitra, *f.* miter; bishopric.

mixtificador, *n.* cheat, deceiver.—**mixtificar,** *vti.* [d] to cheat, deceive.

mixto, *a.* mixed, mingled; composite; halfbreed; assorted.—**mixtura,** *f.* mixture, compound.

mobiliario, moblaje, *m.* household furniture.

mocasín, *m.* moccasin (shoe and snake).—**mocasina,** *f.* moccasin (shoe).

mocedad, *f.* youth; youthfulness.—**mocetón,** *n.* strapping youth; lad.

mochar, *vt.* to cut, lop off.

mochila, *f.* knapsack; haversack.

mocho, *a.* cropped, shorn, cut-off; maimed, mutilated.—*m.* butt end.

mochuelo, *m.* red owl.

moción, *f.* motion.

moco, *m.* mucus, snivel, snot.—*llorar a m. tendido,* (coll.) to cry like a child.—**mocoso,** *a.* snotty.—*n.* child; inexperienced youth.

moda, *f.* fashion, mode, style.—*de m.,* in style, in vogue.—*pasado de m.,* out of style.

modales, *m. pl.* manners.—*de malos m.,* ill-mannered.

modelado, *m.* modeling.—**modelar,** *vt.* to model.—**modelo,** *f.* model, pattern, copy.—*mf.* life model.

módem, *m.* (comput.) modem.

moderación, *f.* moderation.—**moderador,** *n.* & *a.* moderator, moderating.—**moderar,** *vt.* to moderate, regulate, curb.—*vr.* to calm down, moderate, refrain from excesses.

modernizar, *vti.* [a] & *vri.* to modernize.—**moderno,** *a.* modern.

modestia, *f.* modesty.—**modesto,** *a.* modest, unpretentious; unobtrusive; unassuming.

módico, *a.* reasonable, economical.

modificación, *f.* modification.—**modificar,** *vti.* [d] to modify.

modismo, *m.* idiom, idiomatic expression.

modista, *f.* dressmaker, modiste.—*m. de sombreros,* milliner.—**modisto,** *m.* couturier, fashion designer.

modo, *m.* mode, way, manner; (gram.) mood.—*a m. de,* like, by way of.—*de buen* (*mal*) *m.,* politely (impolitely).—*de m. que,* so that; and so.—*de ningún m.,* by no means, under no circumstances.—*de otro m.,* otherwise.—*de todos modos,* at any rate, anyway.

modorra, *f.* drowsiness.

modoso, *a.* temperate, well-behaved.

modulación, *f.* modulation.—**modular,** *vt.* & *vi.* to modulate.—**módulo,** *m.* module; unit.—*m. de maniobra y mando,* command module.—*m. lunar,* lunar module.

mofa, *f.* mockery, jeering, ridicule.—**mofar,** *vi.* & *vr.* to jeer, scoff, mock.—*mofarse de,* to mock, sneer at, make fun of, razz.

mofeta, *f.* skunk.

mofiete, *m.* fat cheek.—**mofletudo,** *a.* fat-cheeked.

mogol, *a.* & *n.* Mogul, Mongol.

mohín, *m.* grimace, gesture.—**mohino,** *a.* gloomy, sulky; sad, mournful; (of horses, etc.) black.

moho, *m.* mold, mildew; rust.—**mohoso,** *a.* rusty; moldy, musty, mildewed.

mojado, *a.* wet.—*n.* (pej. & off.) wetback.—**mojadura,** *f.* drenching, moistening, wetting.—**mojar,** *vt.* to wet, drench; to moisten, dampen; (coll.) to stab.—*vr.* to get wet.

mojicón, *m.* bun; punch, blow.

mojigatería, mojigatez, *f.* hypocrisy, sanctimoniousness; bigotry; prudery.—**mojigato,** *n.* prude, hypocrite; bigot, fanatic.—*a.* hypocritical, sanctimonious; prudish; bigoted.

mojón, *m.* landmark; milestone; heap, pile; (Am.) solid excrement.

molar, *a.* molar.

molde, *m.* mold, cast; pattern; (eng.) form; (print.) form ready for printing.—**moldear,** *vt.* to mold.—**moldura,** *f.* molding.

mole, *f.* huge mass or bulk.—*m.* (Mex.) chilli gravy.

molécula, *f.* molecule.—**molecular,** *a.* molecular.

moler, *vti.* [26] to grind, mill; to overtire; to vex, bore; to waste, consume.—*m. a palos,* to give a sound beating.

molestar, *vt.* to disturb; to trouble; to annoy, vex; to tease.—*vr.* (**en**) to bother, put oneself out.—**molestia,** *f.* annoyance, bother; inconvenience, trouble; discomfort; hardship; grievance.—**molesto,** *a.* annoying, vexatious, bothersome; troublesome; uncomfortable.

molicie, *f.* softness; effeminacy.

molienda, *f.* milling, grinding; season for grinding (sugar cane, etc.).—**molimiento,** *m.* grinding, pounding; fatigue, weariness.—**molinero,** *n.* miller, grinder.—**molinete,** *m.* little mill; pinwheel; ventilating wheel; friction roller.—**molinillo,** *m.* hand mill; coffee grinder.—**molino,** *m.* mill.

molleja, *f.* gizzard.

mollera, *f.* crown of head; (fig.) intelligence.—*ser duro de m.,* to be dull or obstinate.

molusco, *m.* mollusk.

momentáneo, *a.* momentary; prompt.—**momento,** *m.* moment, trice; opportunity.—*a cada m.,* continually, every minute.—*al m.,* in a moment, immediately.

momia, *f.* mummy.

mona, *f.* female monkey; (coll.) ludicrous imitator; (coll.) drunkenness.—*dormir la m.,* to sleep off a drunk.—**monada,** *f.* grimace; fawning, flattery; a pretty person or thing.

monaguillo, *m.* (eccl.) acolyte, altar boy.

monarca, *m.* monarch.—**monarquía,** *f.* monarchy; kingdom.—**monárquico,** *a.* monarchical.

monasterio, *m.* monastery.—**monástico,** *a.* monastic.

mondadientes, *m.* toothpick.—**mondadura,** *f.* cleaning, cleansing.—*pl.* paring, peelings.—**mondar,** *vt.* to clean, cleanse; to trim, prune; to hull, peel.—**mondo,** *a.* neat, pure, unmixed.—*m. y lirondo,* (coll.) pure, without adornment.

mondongo, *m.* tripe; intestines.

moneda, *f.* coin; money; specie; coinage.—*m. corriente,* currency.—*m. legal,* legal tender.—*m. suelta,* small change.—**monedero,** *n.* coiner.—*m.* purse.

monería, *f.* grimace, mimicry, monkeyshine; cunning action.

monetario, *a.* monetary.

mongol, *n.* Mongol.—**mongólico,** *a.* Mongolian, Mongolic.

monigote, *m.* puppet.

monitor, *n.* monitor; (comput.) monitor; (sports) coach, instructor.

monja, *f.* nun.—**monje,** *m.* monk.

mono, *n.* monkey.—*m.* overalls; dungarees.—*a.* (coll.) dainty; (coll.) cute.

monóculo, *m.* monocle.

monogamia, *f.* monogamy.

monograma, *m.* monogram.

monologar, *vii.* [b] to soliloquize.—**monólogo,** *m.* monologue, soliloquy.

monopolio, *m.* monopoly.—**monopolizar,** *vti.* [a] to monopolize.

monorriel, *m.* monorail.

monosilábico, *a.* monosyllabic.—**monosílabo,** *m.* & *a.* monosyllable; monosyllabic.

monotonía, *f.* monotony.—**monótono,** *a.* monotonous.

monóxido, *m.*—*m. de carbon,* carbon monoxide.

nonserga, f. (coll.) gabble, gibberish; annoyance.

nonstruo, m. monster, freak.—**monstruosidad,** f. monstrosity; monstrousness.—**monstruoso,** a. monstrous; huge; hideous; hateful; shocking.

nonta, f. act of mounting; amount; sum total.—*poca m.,* little value; little importance.—**montacargas,** m. hoist, winch; freight elevator.—**montador,** n. mounter; installer (electrician, etc.).—**montaje,** m. setting up, installing; assembling; mounting.—**montante,** m. (carp. & mech.) upright, standard, post, strut, jamb; (arch.) transom; (com.) amount.—**montaplatos,** m. dumbwaiter.

nontaña, f. mountain.—**montañés,** a. mountain, of or from the mountains or highlands.—n. mountaineer, highlander; native of Santander, Spain.—**montañoso,** a. mountainous.

nontar, vi. to mount, get on top; to ride horseback; to amount; to be of importance.—*m. en cólera,* to fly into a rage.—vt. to ride, straddle; to amount (to); to cover (as a horse, etc.); (mech.) to mount, set up; to establish; to assemble; (jewelry) to set; to cock (as a gun); (mil.) to mount (guard).—*m. a horcajadas,* to straddle.—vr. (**en**) to get into, board (vehicles); to mount (saddle animals).

nontaraz, a. wild, untamed; uncouth, boorish.—**monte,** m. mountain, mount; woods, forest, woodland.—*m. de piedad,* pawnshop.—**montés,** a. wild, undomesticated, uncultivated.—**montículo,** m. mound.

nonto, m. sum (of money); amount; sum total.—**montón,** m. heap, pile; great number; mass; mound.—*m. de basuras,* dump, landfill, dumpyard.—*m. de leña,* woodpile.—*a montones,* abundantly, in heaps.—*del m.,* mediocre, run of the mill.

nontuno, a. pertaining to the highlands; rustic, boorish.—**montuoso,** a. mountainous, hilly.

nontura, f. riding horse, mount; saddle trappings; (jewelry) frame, setting; mounting.

nonumental, a. monumental.—**monumento,** m. monument.

noña, f. (Am.) dressmaker's manne-

quin; doll; (coll.) drunkenness; rosette, ribbon head ornament; elaborate badge on bull's neck when in the arena.

moño, m. (of hair) topknot; chignon, bun; crest, tuft.

moquear, vi. to sniffle, snivel; to run from the nose.—**moquita,** f. sniffle, snivel; running from the nose.

mora, f. blackberry; mulberry; Moorish woman.

morada, f. habitation, residence; stay.—**morado,** a. purple.—**morador,** n. resident, inhabitant.

moral, a. moral.—f. morals, morality; morale; mulberry tree.—**moraleja,** f. moral, maxim, lesson.—**moralidad,** f. morality, morals.—**moralizar,** vti. [a] & vii. to moralize.

morar, vi. to inhabit, dwell, reside.

morbidez, f. softness, mellowness.—**mórbido,** a. morbid; soft, mellow, delicate.—**morbo,** m. disease, infirmity.—**morboso,** a. diseased, morbid.

morcilla, f. blood sausage; (theat., coll.) gag, ad-libbing.

mordacidad, f. pungency, sharpness, sarcasm.—**mordaz,** a. corrosive, biting; sarcastic, trenchant.

mordaza, f. gag; muzzle.

mordedor, n. & a. biter; biting.—**mordedura,** f. bite; sting.—**morder,** vti. [26] to bite; to eat away; to backbite; to nip.—**mordiscar,** vti. [d] to nibble.—**mordisco, mordiscón,** m. bite; biting; bit, piece bitten off.

moreno, a. brown; dark, swarthy; brunette.—n. dark-haired person; (Am.) colored person.

morfina, f. morphine.—**morfinómano,** n. drug addict.

morigeración, f. temperance, moderation.

morillos, m. pl. andirons.

morir, vii. [17-49] & vri. to die; to die out (as fire).—*m. por,* to crave for.

mormón, a. & s. Mormon.

moro, a. Moorish.—n. Moor.

morón, m. moron; hillock, mound.

morosidad, f. slowness, tardiness.—**moroso,** a. slow, tardy; sluggish.

morral, m. nose bag; game bag; knapsack.

morralla, f. small fry (fish); rubbish; rabble.

morriña, f. (coll.) homesickness; sadness, blues.

morro, *m.* muzzle; snout; promontory; thick lip.

morsa, *f.* walrus.

mortaja, *f.* shroud, winding sheet.—**mortal,** *a.* mortal, fatal, deadly.—*mf.* mortal.—**mortalidad,** *f.* mortality; death rate.—**mortandad,** *f.* mortality; slaughter; butchery.—**mortecino,** *a.* dying away or extinguishing; pale, subdued (color).

mortero, *m.* mortar.

mortífero, *a.* death-dealing, fatal.—**mortificación,** *f.* mortification; humiliation.—**mortificar,** *vti.* [d] & *vri.* to mortify; to subdue (passions); to vex; to bother; to humiliate.—**mortuorio,** *a.* mortuary.—*m.* burial, funeral.

moruno, *a.* Moorish.

mosaico, *a.* Mosaic.—*m.* mosaic (work); concrete tile.

mosca, *f.* fly; (coll.) dough, money; nuisance, pest.—*aflojar la m.*, to give or spend money.—*m. muerta,* one who feigns meekness.—*papar moscas,* to gape with astonishment.—**moscardón, moscón,** *m.* bumblebee; (coll.) bore, pest.—**mosquearse,** *vr.* to show resentment.

mosquitero, *m.* mosquito bar or net.—**mosquito,** *m.* gnat; mosquito.

mostacho, *m.* bushy mustache.

mostaza, *f.* mustard.

mosto, *m.* must, grape juice.

mostrador, *m.* counter (in a shop); stand.—*m. de facturación,* check-in desk or counter.—*m. de revisión,* checkout counter.—**mostrar,** *vti.* [12] to show; to point out.—*vri.* to appear; to show oneself, prove to be.

mostrenco, *a.* (coll.) homeless; unclaimed, unowned; masterless; stray; dull, stupid.

mota, *f.* small knot (in cloth); mote, speck.

mote, *m.* nickname; motto.

motear, *vt.* to speckle, mottle.

motejar, *vt.* to chaff, call offensive names; to censure.—*m. de,* to brand as.

motín, *m.* mutiny, riot.

motivar, *vt.* to give a reason or motive for; to cause; to motivate.—**motivo,** *m.* motive, cause, reason, occasion; (mus.) motif, theme.—*con m. de,* owing to, by reason of; on the occasion of.

moto, motocicleta, *f.* motorcycle.—*m.*

acuática, jet ski.—**motociclista,** *m* motorcyclist.—**motoneta,** *f.* moto scooter.—**motor,** *n.* & *a.* move moving.—*m.* motor; engine.—*m.* chorro, *m. de reacción,* jet engine.-*m. a inyección,* fuel-injected en gine.—*m. de combustión interna* c *de explosión,* internal combustio engine.—*m. de propulsión a chorre* jet engine.—*m. fuera de borde* outboard motor.—**motorista,** *m* motorman (-woman); motoris driver.—**motorización,** *f.* mechan zation.—**motosegadora,** *f.* powe lawnmower, power mower.—**mot** **sierra,** *f.* chainsaw.—**motorizar,** *vt* [a] to mechanize.—**motriz,** *a* moving.

movedizo, *a.* movable; shaky, ur steady; inconstant, shifting.-**mover,** *vti.* [26] to move; to mak move; to drive, propel; to persuade induce; to prompt; to incite, pro mote; to stir.—*m. el intestino, m. a vientre,* to move one's bowels.—*vr* to move, stir.—**movible,** *a.* movable mobile; changeable, fickle.—**móvi** *a.* movable; mobile; unsteady, po table.—*m.* motive, incentive, in ducement; mover, motor; mov ing body.—**movilidad,** *f.* mobility movableness; fickleness; unstead iness.—**movilización,** *f.* mobiliza tion.—**movilizar,** *vti.* [a] & *vri.* to mo bilize.—**movimiento,** *m.* movemen move, activity; stir, agitation; life liveliness; animation; motion; (art distribution of lines, etc., tech nique; (mus.) tempo, time.

mozalbete, *m.* teenager, youth.—**mozo,** *a.* young, youthful; singl unmarried.—*m.* lad; manservan waiter; porter.—*m. de estaciór* redcap.—*f.* lass, maid.—*buen m* good-looking.

mu, *m.* lowing of cattle, moo.

mucamo, *n.* (Am.) servant.

muchacha, *f.* girl; maid (servant).-**muchachada,** *f.* boyish act; prank.-**muchachería,** *f.* boyish trick; crow of boys.—**muchacho,** *m.* boy, lad.

mucosidad, *f.* mucosity, mucous ness.—**mucoso,** *a.* mucous; slim viscous.—*f.* mucous membrane.

muchedumbre, *f.* multitude; crowc populace, rabble.

mucho, *a.* much, a great deal o (of time) long.—*pl.* many.—*ad* much, very much; a great deal; in great measure; often; (of time) long very.—*ni con m.*, not by far; far from it.—*ni m. menos*, nor anything like it.—*no es m.*, it is no wonder.—*no ha m., no hace m.*, not long since.—*por m. que*, no matter how much.

muda, *f.* change, alteration; change of underwear; molt, molting; change of voice in boys; roost of birds of prey.—**mudable,** *a.* changeable; fickle; shifty.—**mudanza,** *f.* change; mutation; removal, moving (residence); inconstancy; fickleness.—**mudar,** *vt.* to change; to remove; to vary, alter; to molt.—*vi.* (**de**) to change (opinion, mind, etc.).—*vr.* to reform, mend, change; to change one's clothes; to move, change one's place of residence.

mudez, *f.* dumbness.—**mudo,** *a.* & *n.* dumb; silent; mute.

mueblaje, *m.* = MOBILIARIO.—**mueble,** *a.* movable.—*m.* piece of furniture.—*pl.* chattels, furniture, household goods.

mueca, *f.* grimace, wry face, grin.

muela, *f.* molar tooth; millstone, grindstone.—*m. del juicio*, wisdom tooth.

muelle, *m.* (naut.) pier, wharf; (RR.) freight platform; metal spring.—*m. helicoidal*, coil spring.—*a.* delicate, soft, voluptuous.

muérdago, *m.* mistletoe.

muerte, *f.* death; murder.—*a la m.*, at the point of death.—*de mala m.*, miserable, of no account.—*de m.*, implacably.—*m. cerebral*, brain death.—*m. de cuna*, crib death.—**muerto,** *ppi.* of MORIR.—*a.* dead, deceased, killed; languid; slaked.—*clínicamente m.*, brain-dead.—*estar m. por*, (coll.) to be crazy about.—*m. de*, (fig.) dying with.—*n.* dead person, corpse; (in cards) dummy.—*echarle a uno el m.*, (coll.) to put the blame on one.—*tocar a m.*, to toll.

muesca, *f.* notch, groove, indentation.

muestra, *f.* sample, specimen; shop sign; placard, bill; model, pattern, copy; sign, indication.—**muestrario,** *m.* collection of samples; specimen or sample book.

mugido, *m.* lowing of cattle, moo.—**mugir,** *vii.* [c] to low, bellow.

mugre, *f.* grease, grime, filth; squalor.—**mugriento,** *a.* greasy, grimy, filthy.

mujer, *f.* woman; wife, mate.—**mujeriego,** *a.* fond of women.—*m.* (coll.) wolf.—**mujeril,** *a.* womanish, womanly, feminine.—**mujerío,** *m.* gathering of women.—**mujerzuela,** *f.* woman of no account.

muladar, *m.* dungheap; rubbish heap.

mulato, *n.* & *a.* mulatto.

muleta, *f.* crutch.—**muletilla,** *f.* pet word or phrase often repeated in talking.

mullir, *vti.* [27] to fluff, make soft, mollify.

mulo, *n.* mule.

multa, *f.* (money) fine.—**multar,** *vt.* to fine.

multicolor, *a.* many-colored, variegated, motley.—**multiempleo,** *m.* moonlighting.—**multilingüe,** *a.* multilingual.—**multiple,** *a.* multiple, complex; (int. combust. eng.) manifold.—**multiplicación,** *f.* multiplication.—**multiplicar,** *vti.* [d] & *vri.* to multiply.—**múltiplo,** *m.* & *a.* multiple.

multitud, *f.* multitude; crowd; the masses.

mundanal, *a.* mundane, worldly.—**mundanidad,** *f.* worldliness, sophistication.—**mundano,** *a.* = MUNDANAL.—**mundial,** *a.* world, worldwide.—**mundo,** *m.* world; (coll.) great multitude, great quantity; social life, circle; experience.—*gran m.*, high society.—*medio m.*, many people.—*ser hombre de m.*, to be a man of experience.—*todo el m.*, everybody.

munición, *f.* ammunition; small shot; birdshot; charge of firearms.

municipal, *a.* municipal.—**municipalidad,** *f.* municipality; town hall; municipal government.—**municipio,** *m.* municipality.

munificencia, *f.* munificence, liberality.

muñeca, *f.* wrist; doll; (mech.) puppet; polishing bag.—*m. de papel*, paper doll.—**muñeco,** *m.* puppet, manikin; boy doll; soft fellow; ventriloquist's dummy.

munición, *f.—pl.* municions.

munón, *m.* stump (of mutilated limb).

mural, *a.* mural.—*m.* mural painting.—**muralla,** *f.* rampart; wall (of a city).—**murar,** *vt.* to wall.

murciélago, *m.* (zool.) bat.

murmullo, *m.* whisper, whispering; murmuring, murmur; muttering.

murmuración, *f.* backbiting, gossip.—**murmurar,** *vi.* to purl, ripple; to whisper, murmur; to gossip, backbite.

muro, *m.* wall; (fort.) rampart.

murria, *f.* (coll.) blues; surliness, sullenness.

musa, *f.* Muse, poetic inspiration.—*pl.* (The) Muses.

musaraña, *f.* shrew-mouse; any small animal, insect or vermin.—*mirar a,* or *pensar en las musarañas,* to be absent-minded.

muscular, *a.* muscular.—**músculo,** *m.* muscle.—**musculoso,** *a.* muscular, brawny.

muselina, *f.* muslin.

museo, *m.* museum.—*m. de cera,* waxworks, wax museum.

musgo, *m.* moss.—**musgoso,** *a.* mossy, moss-covered.

música, *f.* music; band; musical composition; sheet music.—*m. de fondo,* background music.—*m. en hojas sueltas,* sheet music.—**musical,** *a.* musical.—**músico,** *a.* musical.—*n.* musician.

musitar, *vi.* to mumble, mutter, whisper.

muslo, *m.* thigh.

mustio, *a.* withered; sad, languid.

musulmán, *a.* & *n.* Muslim.

mutabilidad, *f.* mutability; fickleness.—**mutación,** *f.* mutation, change; (theat.) change of scene.

mutilación, *f.* mutilation.—**mutilar,** *vt.* to mutilate.

mutis, *m.* (theat.) exit.

mutismo, *m.* muteness, silence.

mutualidad, *f.* mutual benefit association.—**mutuo,** *a.* mutual, reciprocal.

muy, *adv.* very; greatly, most.

N

nabo, *m.* turnip (plant and root).

nácar, *m.* mother-of-pearl; pearl color.

nacer, *vii.* [3–49] to be born; to sprout, grow (as branches, plants); to rise (as the sun); to originate, start; to spring (as a stream, a river).—*n. de pies,* to be born lucky.—**nacido,** *a.* & *n.* born.—*los nacidos,* those born.—*n. muerto,* stillborn.—**naciente,** *a.* rising (sun).—*m.* Orient, East.—**nacimiento,** *m.* birth; beginning; origin; source of a river or spring; crèche.—*n. de pelo,* hairline.

nación, *f.* nation.—*naciones en vía de desarrollo,* developing nations.—*Naciones Unidas,* United Nations.—**nacional,** *a.* national.—**nacionalidad,** *f.* nationality; citizenship.—**nacionalización,** *f.* nationalization; naturalization.—**nacionalizar,** *vti.* [a] to nationalize; to naturalize.—**nacista,** *a.* & *mf.* Nazi.

nada, *f.* nothing, naught; nothingness; nil.—*indef. pron.* nothing, not anything.—*de n.,* insignificant, good-for-nothing; (after thanks) you are welcome! don't mention it!—*n. de eso,* none of that; not so.—*por n.,* for nothing; under no circumstances; (Am.) you are welcome!—*adv.* not at all, by no means.

nadador, *n.* & *a.* swimmer; swimming.—**nadar,** *vi.* to swim; to float.

nadería, *f.* (coll.) insignificant thing, trifle.

nadie, *indef. pron.* nobody, no one, none; (after negative) anybody, anyone.

nafta, *f.* naphtha.—**naftalina,** *f.* naphthalene.

naipe, *m.* (playing) card.—*pl.* cards; pack or deck of cards.

nalga, *f.* buttock, rump.—*pl.* (fam.) hams.—**nalgada,** *f.* spanking.—*dar una n.,* to spank.

nana, *f.* (coll.) child's nurse; lullaby.

naranja, *f.* orange.—*media n.,* (coll.) better half (spouse).—*n. de ombligo,* naval orange.—**naranjada,** *f.* orangeade.—**naranjal,** *m.* orange grove.—**naranjo,** *m.* orange tree.

narciso, *m.* narcissus; daffodil; coxcomb.

narcótico, *a.* & *m.* narcotic, dope.—**narcotizar,** *vti.* [a] to drug, dope.

nardo, *m.* spikenard.

nariz, *f.* nose; nostril; sense of smell.—*meter la n. en todas partes,* to nose about.

narración, *f.* narration, account.—**narrador,** *n.* narrator; storyteller.—**narrar,** *vt.* to narrate, relate, tell.

—narrativa, *f.* narrative.**—narrativo,** *a.* narrative.

nasal, *a.* & *f.* nasal.**—nasalizar,** *vt.* to nasalize.

nata, *f.* cream; prime or choice part; elite.**—***pl.* whipped cream with sugar.

natación, *f.* swimming.

natal, *a.* natal, native.**—***m.* birthday, birth.**—natalicio,** *m.* birthday.**—natalidad,** *f.* birth rate.

natatorio, *a.* swimming.

natilla, *f.* custard.

natividad, *f.* nativity; Christmas, Yuletide.**—nativo,** *a.* native.

natural, *a.* natural; native; inherent; common, usual; unaffected; plain.**—***mf.* native.**—***m.* temper, disposition, nature.**—***al n.,* without art or affectation.**—***del n.,* (art) from life, from nature.**—naturaleza,** *f.* nature; constitution; sort, character, kind; nationality; temperament or disposition.**—***n. muerta,* still life.**—naturalidad,** *f.* naturalness; birthright, nationality.**—naturalista,** *mf.* & *a.* naturalist(ic).**—naturalización,** *f.* naturalization.**—naturalizar,** *vti.* [a] to naturalize; to acclimatize.**—***vri.* to become naturalized; to get accustomed to.

naufragar, *vii.* [b] to be shipwrecked; to fail.**—naufragio,** *m.* shipwreck; failure.**—náufrago,** *a.* & *n.* shipwrecked (person).

náusea, *f.* nausea, disgust, squeamishness.**—nauseabundo,** *a.* nauseous, sickening, loathsome.

náutica, *f.* navigation.**—náutico,** *a.* nautical.

navaja, *f.* claspknife; jack knife, penknife.**—***n. de afeitar,* razor.**—***n. barbera,* straight razor.**—navajazo,** *m.* thrust or gash with a claspknife or razor; stab wound.

naval, *a.* naval.**—nave,** *f.* ship, vessel; (arch.) nave; aisle.**—***n. capitana* or *insignia,* flagship.**—***n. espacial,* spacecraft, spaceship.**—***n. lateral,* aisle.**—navegable,** *a.* navigable.**—navegación,** *f.* navigation; sea voyage.**—***n. aérea,* aviation.**—***n. espacial,* space travel.**—navegante,** *m.* & *a.* navigator; navigating.**—navegar,** *vii.* to navigate, sail, steer.

navidad, *f.* Nativity; Christmas.**—***pl.* Christmas season.

naviero, *a.* shipping, ship.**—***n.* ship owner.**—navío,** *m.* ship, vessel.

nazi, *a.* & *mf.* Nazi.

neblina, *f.* fog, mist.**—nebulosa,** *f.* nebula.**—nebulosidad,** *f.* cloudiness; mistiness; nebulousness.**—nebuloso,** *a.* nebulous, hazy, misty.

necedad, *f.* stupidity, foolishness; nonsense; (coll.) tripe.

necesario, *a.* necessary.**—neceser,** *m.* dressing case, toilet case.**—***n. de costura,* sewing case.**—necesidad,** *f.* necessity; need, want.**—***por n.,* from necessity; necessarily.**—necesitado,** *a.* & *n.* indigent, needy (person).**—necesitar,** *vt.* to need; to necessitate.**—***vi.* (de) to be in need (of).

necio, *a.* stupid, idiotic, foolish.**—***n.* fool.

necrópolis, *f.* cemetery.

nefando, *a.* nefarious, heinous.**—nefasto,** *a.* sad, ominous, unlucky.

negación, *f.* negation; denial; want or total privation; (gram.) negative particle.**—negar,** *vti.* [1-b] to deny; to refuse, withhold; to prohibit; to disown.**—***n. a reconocer,* (law) to repudiate.**—***n. el saludo,* to give the cold shoulder to.**—***vri.* to decline, refuse.**—negativa,** *f.* negative, refusal.**—negativo,** *a.* negative.**—***n.* (photog.) negative.

negligencia, *f.* negligence, neglect, carelessness.**—negligente,** *a.* negligent, careless, neglectful.

negociable, *a.* negotiable.**—negociación,** *f.* negotiation; business transaction, deal.**—negociado,** *m.* bureau, division or section in official departments.**—negociante,** *a.* negotiating, trading.**—***mf.* dealer, merchant, trader.**—negociar,** *vi.* to trade; to negotiate.**—negocio,** *m.* business; transaction.**—***pl.* business, commercial affairs.**—***n. redondo,* good bargain.

negrear, *vi.* to turn black; to look black.**—negrero,** *m.* slave driver; slave trader.**—negrita, negrilla,** *f.* (print.) boldface.**—negro,** *a.* black; tanned.**—***m.* black (color).**—***n. azabache,* jet-black; jet black.**—***n. de humo,* lampblack.**—***n.* (person) black, Black, Afro-American, African-American, African American; (obs.) Negro.**—negrura,** *f.* blackness.**—negruzco,** *a.* blackish, dark brown.

nena, *f.* baby girl; babe.**—nene,** *m.* (coll.) infant, baby boy; dear, darling.

nenúfar, m. or **ninfea,** f. water lily.

neo, m. neon.—**neón,** m. neon.

neolatino, a. & m. Neo-Latin.—a. Romance.

neologismo, m. neologism.

neozelandés, n. New Zealander.—a. of or from New Zealand.

nervio, m. nerve; energy, stamina, vigor.—**nerviosidad,** f., **nerviosismo,** m. nervousness; strength, vigor.—**nervioso,** a. nervous.—**nervudo,** a. strong, sinewy, vigorous.

neto, a. neat, pure; (com.) net (profit, etc.).

neumático, m. tire.—a. pneumatic.—n. recauchutado, recap.

neumonía, f. (med.) pneumonia.—**neumónico,** a. pneumonic; pulmonary.

neurastenia, f. neurasthenia.—**neurasténico,** n. & a. neurasthenic.—**neurosis,** f. neurosis.—**neurótico,** n. & a. neurotic.

neutral, a. neutral, neuter.—**neutralidad,** f. neutrality.—**neutralizar,** vti. [a] to counteract; to neutralize.—**neutro,** a. (gram.) neuter; neutral.—**neutrón,** m. neutron.

nevada, f. snowfall.—**nevado,** a. white as snow.—m. snow-covered peak.—**nevar,** vii. [1] to snow.—vti. to make white as snow.—**nevera,** f. icebox, refrigerator.—**nevisca,** f. gentle fall of snow.

nexo, m. bond, tie, union.

ni, conj. neither, nor; not even.—ni con mucho, not by a good deal.—ni siquiera, not even.

nicaragüense, mf. & a. Nicaraguan.

nicho, m. niche; alcove; recess.

nicotina, f. nicotine.

nidada, f. nestful of eggs, nest; brood, covey; sitting.—**nidal,** m. nest; nest egg; basis, motive; haunt.—**nido,** m. nest; haunt; den.

niebla, f. fog, mist, haze.

nieto, n. grandson (f. granddaughter).

nieve, f. snow.

nilón, m. nylon.

nimbo, m. halo.

nimiedad, f. superfluity, prolixity; excess.—**nimio,** a. prolix.

ninfa, f. nymph.

ningún, (contr. of) **ninguno,** a. no, not one, not any.—de ningún modo, de ninguna manera, by no means.—ninguna cosa, nothing.—**ninguno,** pron. nobody, none, no one, not one.—n. de los dos, neither of the two.

niñada, f. puerility, childishness.—**niñera,** f. nurse, nursery-maid.—**niñería,** f. puerility, childish action; child's play; plaything; trifle.—**niñez,** f. childhood, infancy.—**niño,** a. childish, childlike; young; inexperienced.—n. child.—desde n., from childhood.—n. de los azotes, whipping boy, scapegoat.—n. explorador, boy scout.—n. probeta, test-tube baby.—n. prodigio, child prodigy.—niña del ojo, pupil of the eye.—niñas de los ojos, (coll.) apple of one's eye; treasure.—niña exploradora, girl scout.

nipón, n. & a. Nipponese, Japanese.

níquel, m. nickel.—**niquelar,** vt. to plate with nickel.

nitidez, f. neatness; brightness, clarity.—**nítido,** a. neat; bright, clear.

nitrato, m. nitrate.—**nítrico,** a. nitric.—**nitro,** m. niter, saltpeter.—**nitrógeno,** m. nitrogen.

nivel, m. level; levelness; watermark.—a n., level, true; on the same level.—n. de aire or de burbuja, spirit level.—n. de la vida, standard of living.—n. del mar, sea level.—**nivelación,** f. leveling; grading.—**nivelar,** vt. to level; to grade; to make even.—vr. to level off.

nmo, abbr. (**enésimo**) nth.—elevado a la potencia n, to the nth degree.

no, adv. no, not, nay.—interrog. isn't it? isn't that so? do you see?—n. bien, no sooner.—n. más, only; no more.—n. obstante, notwithstanding.—n. sea que, lest; or else.—n. tal, no such thing.—por sí o por n., just in case, anyway.

noble, a. noble.—mf. nobleman (-woman).—**nobleza,** f. nobleness; nobility; noblesse.

nocaut, m. (sports) knockout.

noche, f. night; evening (after sunset); (fig.) obscurity, ignorance.—ayer n., last night.—buenas noches, good evening; goodnight.—la n. vieja, New Year's Eve.—n. de bodas, wedding night.—n. de estreno, opening night.—**Nochebuena,** f. Christmas eve.

noción, f. notion, idea; element, rudiment.

nocivo, a. noxious, harmful, injurious.

nocturno, *a.* nocturnal, night.—*m.* (mus., lit.) nocturne.

nodo, *m.* (med., astr.) node.

nodriza, *f.* wet nurse.

nódulo, *m.* small node.

nogal, *m.* walnut.

nómada, *mf.* & *a.* nomad; nomadic.

nombradía, *f.* renown, fame, reputation.—**nombramiento,** *m.* nomination, naming; appointment.—**nombrar,** *vt.* to name; to nominate; to appoint.—**nombre,** *m.* name; fame, reputation; (gram.) noun; watch-word.—*n. artístico,* stage name.—*n. comercial,* trade name.—*n. de cariño,* pet name.—*n. de lugar,* place name.—*n. de pila* or *de bautismo,* first name.—*n. de soltera,* maiden name.—*n. impropia,* misnomer.—*n. masivo* or *no numerable* or *no contable,* mass noun.—*n. y apellidos,* full name.

nómina, *f.* payroll; roster, roll, register.—**nominal,** *a.* nominal.—**nominar,** *vt.* to name.—**nominativo,** *a.* & *m.* (gram.) nominative.

non, *a.* odd, uneven.—*m.* odd number.—*pl.* refusal.—*estar de n.,* to be unpaired.—*dar* or *echar nones,* to say no.

nonada, *f.* trifle, nothing.

nonagésimo, *a.* & *m.* ninetieth.

nordeste, *m.* northeast.—**nórdico,** *n.* & *a.* Nordic.

noria, *f.* waterwheel; Ferris wheel, big wheel.

norma, *f.* standard, norm, rule.—**normal,** *a.* normal; standard.—*f.* normal school; (geom.) normal.—**normalidad,** *f.* normality.—**normalizar,** *vti.* [a] to normalize; to standardize.—*vri.* to become normal, return to normal.

noroeste, *m.* northwest.—**norte,** *m.* north; northwind; rule, guide, clue, direction.—**norteamericano,** *n.* & *a.* North American, American, from the U. S.—**norteño,** *n.* & *a.* Northerner; northern.

noruego, *n.* & *a.* Norwegian.

norueste, *m.* = NOROESTE.

nos, *pron.* us, to us; ourselves.—**nosotros,** *pron.* we; ourselves; us (after preposition).

nostalgia, *f.* nostalgia, longing, homesickness.—**nostálgico,** *a.* nostalgic, homesick.

nota, *f.* note; mark (in exam); anno-

tation; memorandum; (com.) account, bill, check; fame.—**notabilidad,** *f.* notability; a notable (person).—**notable,** *a.* notable, remarkable, telling; distinguished, prominent.—**notación,** *f.* note; notation.—**notar,** *vt.* to note, observe; to notice, take notice of.—**notaría,** *f.* notary's office.—**notario,** *m.* notary public.

noticia, *f.* news item; news; notice, information.—**noticiario,** *m.* newsman, reporter; news; newsreel.—*n. deportivo,* sports news.—*n. radiofónico,* newscast.—**noticioso,** *a.* newsgiving.—**notificación,** *f.* notification; notice.—**notificar,** *vti.* [d] to notify.

notoriedad, *f.* quality of being well-known; notoriety.—**notorio,** *a.* well-known; evident.

novatada, *f.* hazing (in colleges).—**novato,** *n.* novice, beginner.

novecientos, *a.* & *m.* nine hundred.—*n. uno,* nine hundred one.

novedad, *f.* novelty; newness; surprise, recent occurrence; fad; change.—**novel,** *a.* new, inexperienced.

novela, *f.* novel; story, fiction.—*n. policíaca* or *policial,* detective story.—**novelero,** *a.* fond of novels, fads, and novelties; newfangled; fickle.—*n.* newsmonger, gossip.—**novelesco,** *a.* novelistic, fictional; fantastic.—**novelista,** *mf.* novelist.

noveno, *a.* & *m.* ninth.—**noventa,** *a.* & *m.* ninety.—*n. y uno,* ninety-one.—**noventavo,** *a.* & *m.* ninetieth.

novia, *f.* bride; fiancée; sweetheart, girl friend.—**noviazgo,** *m.* engagement, betrothal; courtship.

noviciado, *m.* (eccl.) novitiate; apprenticeship; probation.—**novicio,** *a.* new, inexperienced.—*n.* novice, probationer; freshman.

noviembre, *m.* November.

novilla, *f.* young cow, heifer.—**novillada,** *f.* fight with young bulls; drove of young cattle.—**novillero,** novice fighter; (coll.) truant, idler.—**novillo,** *m.* young bull.—*hacer novillos,* (coll.) to play truant or hooky.

novio, *m.* bridegroom; fiancé; sweetheart, boyfriend.—*los novios,* the bride and groom.

nubarrón, *m.* storm cloud.—**nube,** *f.* cloud; film on the eye; shade in pre-

cious stones; crowd, multitude.—
n.-hongo, mushroom cloud.—
nublado, a. cloudy.—m. thunder-
cloud; (fig.) threat of danger.—
nublar, vt. to cloud, obscure.—vr. to
become cloudy.

nuca, f. nape or scruff of the neck.

nuclear, a. nuclear.—**núcleo,** m. nucleus; center.

nudilleras de metal, fpl. brass knuckles.

nudillo, m. knuckle; small knot.

nudismo, m. nudism.—**nudista,** mf.
nudist.

nudo, m. knot; tangle; (bot.) node;
joint; knotty point, intricacy; crisis
of a drama.—n. corredizo, granny
knot.—**nudoso,** a. knotty, knotted,
gnarled.

nuera, f. daughter-in-law.

nuestro, a. our, ours.—pron. ours.

nueva, f. news, tidings.—**nuevo,** a.
new.—de n., again, once more.—
Nueva York, New York.—¿qué hay de
n.? what's the news? what's new?

nueve, a. & m. nine.

nuez, f. walnut; nut; Adam's apple.—
n. moscada, nutmeg.

nulidad, f. nullity; inability, incompetency; incompetent person, a no-
body.—**nulo,** a. null, void; of no account.—n. y sin valor, nul and void.

numeración, f. numeration; number-
ing.—**numeral,** a. & m. numeral.—
numerar, vt. to number; to enumerate.—**numerario,** a. numerary.—m.
cash, coin, specie.—**numérico,** a.
numerical.—**número,** m. number;
numeral; size (shirt, etc.); number
issue (magazine, etc.).—n. arábigo,
Arabic numeral.—n. de identificación personal, Personal Identification Number, PIN number.—n. de
matrícula, license number.—n. de
serie, serial number.—n. de teléfono,
telephone number.—n. equivocado,
wrong number.—n. impar, odd
number.—n. medio, median.—n.
par, even number.—n. Romano, Roman numeral.—**numeroso,** a. numerous.

nunca, adv. never.—n. jamás, never,
never more.

nupcial, a. nuptial.—**nupcias,** f. pl.
nuptials, wedding.

nutria, f. otter.

nutrición, f. nutrition, nourishing.—
nutrido, a. full, abundant, numerous, dense.—**nutrir,** vt. to nourish,
feed.—**nutrimento,** m. nourishment; nurture.—**nutritivo,** a. nutritive, nourishing.

Ñ

ñame, m. yam.

ñandú, m. (Am.) ostrich.

ñaño, a. intimate; spoiled, pam-
pered.—n. bosom friend.

ñapa, f. (Am.) something over or extra.—de ñ., to boot, into the
bargain.

ñato, a. (Am.) pug-nosed.

ñeque, a. strong, vigorous; bullying,
swaggering.

ño, abbr. (**Señor**) (sl.) sir, e.g., **Ño Antonio,** Sir Anthony (used only before
the first name).

ñongo, n. (coll.), (Cuba), peasant.—a.

(Chile) lazy, good-for-nothing; (Co-
lomb.) (of dice) loaded.—f. (Chile)
laziness.

ñoñería, ñoñez, f. dotage, senility,
drivel; shyness; silliness.—**ñoño,**
a. (coll.) timid, shy; stupid; soft,
feeble; flimsy; babyish; insipid,
tasteless; senile, whiny.

ñoque, ñoqui, m. (cook.) gnoccho.—
pl. gnocchi.

ñu, m. (zool.) gnu, wildebeest.

ñudo, m. knot.

ñudoso, a. knotty, knotted.

O

o, *conj.* or, either.—*o sea,* that is.

oasis, *m.* oasis.

obedecer, *vti.* [3] to obey.—**obediencia,** *f.* obedience.—**obediente,** *a.* obedient.

obelisco, *m.* obelisk.

obertura, *f.* (mus.) overture.

obesidad, *f.* obesity, fatness.—**obeso,** *a.* obese, fat.

óbice, *m.* obstacle, hindrance.

obispado, *m.* bishopric; episcopate.—**obispo,** *m.* bishop.

obituario, *m.* obituary.

objeción, *f.* objection.—**objetar,** *vt.* to object to, oppose.

objetivo, *a.* objective.—*m.* (opt.) objective, eyepiece.—**objeto,** *m.* object; subject matter; thing; purpose; aim; target.—*o. volador no identificado* or *o. volante no identificado (OVNI),* unidentified flying object (UFO).

oblea, *f.* wafer.

oblicuo, *a.* oblique, slanting.

obligación, *f.* obligation, duty; bond, security.—*pl.* engagements; (com.) liabilities.—**obligar,** *vti.* [b] to obligate, compel, bind; to oblige.—*vri.* to obligate or bind oneself.—**obligatorio,** *a.* obligatory, compulsory.

óbolo, *m.* donation, alms, contribution; mite.

obra, *f.* work, creation; literary work; manufacture; structure; building; repairs in a house; toil, labor.—*o. de arte,* work of art.—*o. maestra,* masterpiece.—*o. muerta,* (naut.) gunwale.—**obrar,** *vt.* to work; to act; to operate; to perform, execute.—*vi.* to act; to ease nature.—**obrero,** *n.* worker, workman (-woman), laborer.—*o. autónomo,* self-employed worker.—*o. especializado,* skilled worker.—*o. inexperto,* roustabout.

obscenidad, *f.* obscenity.—**obsceno,** *a.* obscene.

obscurecer, = OSCURECER.—**obscuridad,** *f.* = OSCURIDAD.—**obscuro,** *a.* = OSCURO.

obsequiar, *vt.* to treat, entertain; to make presents to; to present, make a gift of.—**obsequio,** *m.* courtesy, attention shown; gift, present.—*en o. de,* for the sake of, out of respect to.—*o. del autor,* compliments of the author.—**obsequioso,** *a.* obsequious; compliant; attentive, obliging.

observación, *f.* observation; remark, note.—*en o.,* under observation.—**observador,** *n.* & *a.* observer; observing.—**observancia,** *f.* observance, fulfillment.—**observar,** *vt.* to observe; to notice, remark, spot; to watch; to conform to (a rule, etc.).—**observatorio,** *m.* observatory.

obsesión, *f.* obsession.—**obsesionar,** *vt.* to obsess.

obstaculizar, *vti.* [a] to impede, obstruct.—**obstáculo,** *m.* obstacle; stumbling block.

obstar, *vi.* to oppose, obstruct, hinder.—*no obstante,* notwithstanding; nevertheless, however.

obstetra, *mf.* obstetrician.—**obstetricia,** *f.* obstetrics.

obstinación, *f.* obstinacy, stubbornness.—**obstinado,** *a.* obstinate, stubborn, headstrong.—**obstinarse,** *vr.* (en) to be obstinate (about), to persist (in); to insist (on).

obstrucción, *f.* obstruction, stoppage.—**obstruccionismo,** *m.* obstructionism.—**obstruccionista,** *mf.* & *a.* obstructionist(ic).—**obstruir,** [23-e] to obstruct, block, stop up.—*vri.* to become obstructed, clogged up.

obtención, *f.* obtainment, attainment.—**obtener,** *vti.* [42] to obtain, get, procure; to attain.

obturador, *m.* (photog.) shutter; throttle; plug, stopper.

obtuso, *a.* obtuse; blunt, dull.

obús, *m.* howitzer, mortar.

obviar, *vt.* to obviate, remove, prevent.—*vi.* to hinder.—**obvio,** *a.* obvious, evident.

ocasión, *f.* occasion; opportunity; cause, motive.—*de o.,* secondhand; at a bargain.—*en ocasiones,* at times.—**ocasional,** *a.* occasional, accidental, casual.—**ocasionar,** *vt.* to cause, occasion.

ocaso, *m.* sunset; setting of any heavenly body; decadence, decline; west.

occidental, *a.* occidental, western.
—occidente, *m.* occident, west.

oceánico, *a.* oceanic.**—océano,** *m.*
ocean.

ochenta, *a.* & *m.* eighty.**—o. y uno,**
eighty-one.**—ochentavo,** *a.* & *m.*
eightieth.

ocho, *a.* & *m.* eight.**—ochocientos,**
a. & *m.* eight hundred.**—o. uno,**
eight hundred one.

ocio, *m.* leisure, idleness; pastime, diversion.**—ratos de o.,** spare time.**—
ociosidad,** *f.* idleness, leisure.**—ocioso,** *a.* idle; fruitless; useless.

oclusión, *f.* occlusion.

octava, *f.* (mus.) octave.

octavo, *a.* & *m.* eighth.**—octogésimo,**
a. & *m.* eightieth.

octubre, *m.* October.

ocular, *a.* ocular.**—testigo o.,** eye witness.**—m.** eyepiece.**—oculista,** *mf.*
oculist.

ocultar, *vt.* to hide, conceal.**—oculto,**
a. hidden, concealed; occult.

ocupación, *f.* occupation; employment, trade, business.**—ocupado,** *a.*
occupied, busy, engaged.**—
ocupante,** *mf.* occupant.**—ocupar,**
vt. to occupy; to take possession of;
to hold (a job); to employ; to engage
the attention.**—vr. (en or de)** to busy
oneself (with); to be engaged (in),
devote oneself (to); to pay attention (to).

ocurrencia, *f.* occurrence, incident;
notion; witticism.**—ocurrente,** *a.*
occurring; humorous, witty.**—ocurrir,** *vi.* to occur, happen.**—vr.** to occur (to one); to strike one (as an
idea).

oda, *f.* ode.

odiar, *vt.* to hate.**—odio,** *m.* hatred.**—
odioso,** *a.* odious, hateful, revolting.

odisea, *f.* odyssey.

odre, *m.* wine skin; (coll.) drunkard.

oeste, *m.* west; west wind.

ofender, *vt.* to offend; to make
angry.**—vr.** to become angry; to take
offense.**—ofensa,** *f.* offense.**—ofensivo,** *a.* offensive; attacking.**—f.** offensive.**—ofensor,** *n.* & *a.* offender;
offending.

oferta, *f.* offer; offering.**—o. de matrimonio,** proposal.**—o. y demanda,**
supply and demand.

oficial, *a.* official.**—mf.** officer, official;
skilled worker; clerk.**—o. de adua-
nas,** customs officer.**—oficialidad,** *f.*
(mil.) body of officers.**—oficiar,** *vi.*

(eccl.) to officiate, minister; to notify officially.**—o. de,** to act as.
—oficina, *f.* office; bureau; workshop.**—o. de empleo,** unemployment office.**—o. de objetos perdidos,**
lost-and-found department.**—o. de
turismo,** travel bureau.**—oficinesco,**
a. departmental, office; white collar.**—oficinista,** *mf.* clerk, employee;
office worker.**—o. de a bordo,** (naut.)
yeoman.**—oficio,** *m.* employ, work
or occupation, vocation; function;
official letter; trade or business.**—
pl.** (eccl.) office, service.**—de o.,** officially; by trade, by occupation or
profession.**—oficioso,** *a.* diligent;
officious, meddlesome; useful,
fruitful; semi-official, unofficial.

ofrecer, *vti.* [3] to offer; to promise; to
show.**—vri.** to offer, occur, present
itself; to offer oneself.**—¿se le ofrece
algo?** what do you want? may I help
you?**—ofrecimiento,** *m.* offer, offering.**—ofrenda,** *f.* offering, gift.
—ofrendar, *vt.* to present offerings.

oftamólogo, *n.* oculist.

ogro, *m.* ogre, fabulous monster.

ohmio, *m.* ohm.

oído, *m.* sense of hearing; ear.**—al o.,**
whispering, confidentially.**—dar
oídos,** to lend an ear.**—de o.,** by
ear.**—de oídas,** by hearsay.**—oír,** *vti.*
[28] to hear, to listen; to attend (as
lectures).**—o. decir,** to hear (it
said).**—o. hablar de,** to hear of.

ojal, *m.* buttonhole; loop.

¡ojalá! *interj.* God grant! would to God!
I wish.

ojeada, *f.* glance, glimpse.**—ojear,** *vt.*
to eye, look at, stare at; to startle,
frighten.**—ojera,** *f.* circle under the
eye.**—ojeriza,** *f.* spite, grudge, ill-
will.**—ojeroso,** *a.* haggard, with
circles under the eyes.**—ojete,** *m.*
(sew.) eyelet.**—ojo,** *m.* eye; eye of a
needle; hole; arch of a bridge.**—a los
ojos de,** in the presence of.**—a ojos
cerrados,** blindly, without reflection.**—costar un o.,** to cost a fortune.**—en un abrir y cerrar de ojos,** in
the twinkling of an eye.**—o. avizor,**
sharp lookout.**—o. de agua,** spring
(of water).**—o. de la cerradura,** key-
hole.**—o. morado,** black eye.**—o. por
o.,** an eye for an eye.**—interj.** take
notice! look out!

O.K., *a.* & *adv.* O.K., okay.

ola, *f.* wave, billow.**—o. de frío,** cold
wave.**—o. de marea,** tidal wave.

—oleada, *f.* big wave; surge, swell of the sea; surging of a crowd.

oleaginoso, *a.* oily; unctuous.

oleaje, *m.* continuous movement of waves.

óleo, *m.* oil; extreme unction; holy oil.—*al ó.,* in oil colors.—**oleoso,** *a.* oily.

oler, *vti.* [28] to smell, scent.—*vii.* to smell; to smack of.—**olfatear,** *vt.* & *vi.* to smell, scent, sniff.—**olfato,** *m.* sense of smell.—**oliente,** *a.* smelling.—*mal o.,* (coll.) smelly.

Olimpiadas, *fpl.* Olympics; Olympic games.—**Olímpico,** *a.* Olympic.—*juegos Olímpicos,* Olympic games.

oliva, *f.* olive; olive tree.—**olivar,** *m.* olive grove, yard.—**olivo,** *m.* olive tree.

olmo, *m.* elm tree.

olor, *m.* smell, fragrance; odor; suspicion, smack.—**oloroso,** *a.* fragrant; (coll.) smelly.

olvidadizo, *a.* forgetful, short of memory.—**olvidar,** *vt.* to forget.—*vr.* to be forgotten, to forget.—**olvido,** *m.* forgetfulness; oversight; oblivion.—*echar al o.* or *en o.,* to forget; to cast into oblivion.

olla, *f.* pot, kettle.—*o. de grillos,* great confusion, pandemonium.—*o. exprés,* pressure cooker.

ombligo, *m.* navel.

ominoso, *a.* ominous, foreboding.

omisión, *f.* omission; carelessness, neglect.—**omiso,** *ppi.* of OMITIR.—*a.* neglectful, remiss.—**omitir,** *vti.* [49] to omit.

ómnibus, *m.* omnibus, stagecoach; bus.—*o. escolar,* school bus.

omnipotencia, *f.* omnipotence.—**omnipotente,** *a.* omnipotent.

once, *a.* & *m.* eleven.—**onceavo** or **onceno,** *a.* & *m.* eleventh.

onda, *f.* wave; ripple.—*o. corta,* short wave.—*o. de choque,* shock wave.—**ondear,** *vi.* to wave, ripple, undulate; to flicker.—**ondulación,** *f.* wave, or wavy motion.—**ondulado,** *a.* undulated, rippled; scalloped, wavy; corrugated.—**ondulante,** *a.* waving, undulating; rolling.—**ondular,** *vt.* to undulate; to ripple.

oneroso, *a.* burdensome, onerous.

onomástico, *a.* onomastic, nominal.—*m.* saint's day, name day.

ONU [oúnu], *abbr.* (**Organización de las Naciones Unidas**) UN.—*la ONU,* the UN.

onza, *f.* ounce. See Table.

opaco, *a.* opaque; dark; dull.

ópalo, *m.* opal.

opción, *f.* option, choice; right.—**opcional,** *a.* optional.

ópera, *f.* opera.—*ó. bufa,* ó *cómica,* comic opera.—*gran ó.,* grand opera.

operación, *f.* operation; process.—**operar,** *vt.* to operate; (surg.) to operate on.—*vi.* to operate, act, work.—**operario,** *n.* workman (-woman); operator.

opereta, *f.* operetta, light opera.—**operístico,** *a.* operatic.

opinar, *vi.* to be of the opinion.—**opinión,** *f.* opinion.

opiato, *m.* opiate.

opio, *m.* opium.

opíparo, *a.* sumptuous (of a meal).

oponente, *mf.* & *a.* opponent.—**oponer,** *vti.* [32–49] to oppose, place against.—*vri.* to oppose, resist; to act against; to be opposed to; to compete.

oporto, *m.* port wine.

oportunidad, *f.* opportunity; timeliness.—**oportunismo,** *m.* (pol.) opportunism.—**oportunista,** *mf.* & *a.* (pol.) opportunist; opportunistic.—**oportuno,** *a.* opportune, timely.

oposición, *f.* opposition, clash; competition for official position.—**oposicionista,** *mf.* & *a.* (pol.) oppositionist.—**opositor,** *n.* opponent; competitor (for a position).

opresión, *f.* oppression.—**opresivo,** *a.* oppressive.—**opresor,** *n.* oppressor.—**oprimir,** *vt.* to oppress.

optar, *vi.* (por) to choose, select.—*o. por,* to opt for or to.—**optativo,** *a.* optional.

óptica, *f.* optics.—**óptico,** *a.* optic(al).—*n.* optician.

optimismo, *m.* optimism.—*o. a ultranza,* wishful thinking.—**optimista,** *mf.* & *a.* optimist; optimistic.

óptimo, *a.* very best.

opuesto, *ppi.* of OPONER.—*a.* opposite.

opulencia, *f.* opulence.—**opulento,** *a.* opulent, wealthy.

oquedad, *f.* hollow, cavity.

ora, *conj.* whether; either; or.

oración, *f.* (gram.) sentence; speech; prayer; dusk.

oráculo, *m.* oracle.

orador, *n.* orator, speaker.—**oral,** *a.* oral, vocal.—**orar,** *vi.* to pray.

orangután, *m.* orang-utan.

orate, *mf.* lunatic, crazy person.

oratoria, *f.* oratory, eloquent speaking.—**oratorio**, *a.* oratorical.—*m.* oratory, chapel; (mus.) oratorio.

orbe, *m.* orb, sphere; the earth.

órbita, *f.* orbit; eye socket.

orden, *m.* order, orderliness, tidiness; class, group; proportion, relation.—*de segundo o.*, second-rate.—*o. de batalla*, battle formation.—*o. de colocación*, word order.—*o. del día*, agenda.—*o. sacerdotal* or *sagrado*, ordination.—*f.* order, command; (com.) order; religious or honorary order.—*pl.* orders, instructions.—*o. de allanamiento*, search warrant.—*o. de arresto* or *detención*, arrest warrant.—*o. del día*, (mil.) order of the day.—**ordenación**, *f.* arrangement; disposition; array; ordination.—**ordenador**, *m.* computer.—*o. central*, mainframe.—*o. de a bordo*, onboard computer.—*o. de sobremesa* or *de mesa*, desktop computer.—*o. digital*, digital computer.—*o. doméstico*, home computer.—*o. personal*, personal computer.—*o. portátil*, laptop computer.—**ordenamiento**, *m.* ordaining, regulating.—**ordenanza**, *f.* method, order; statute, ordinance; military regulation; ordination.—*m.* (mil.) orderly.—**ordenar**, *vt.* to arrange, put in order; to order, command; to ordain.—*vr.* (eccl.) to be ordained.

ordeñadero, *m.* milk pail.—**ordeñar**, *vt.* to milk.

ordinal, *m.* & *a.* ordinal.

ordinariez, *f.* rough manners, ordinariness.—**ordinario**, *a.* ordinary, usual; coarse, unrefined.—*n.* unrefined person.—*de o.*, usually, ordinarily, regularly.

orear, *vt.* to air, expose to the air.—*vr.* to take an airing.

oreja, *f.* ear (external); flap of a shoe; small flap; flange.—*aguzar las orejas*, to prick up one's ears.—*bajar las orejas*, to come down from one's high horse.—**orejera**, *f.* ear muff, earcap.—**orejudo**, *a.* flap-eared, long-eared.

oreo, *m.* airing; ventilation.

orfanato, *m.* orphan asylum, orphanage.—**orfandad**, *f.* orphanage (the state of being an orphan).

orfebre, *mf.* goldsmith, silversmith.—**orfebrería**, *f.* gold or silver work.

orfeón, *m.* glee club; choral society.

orgánico, *a.* organic.—**organillero**, *m.* organ-grinder.—**organillo**, *m.* hand organ, barrel organ.—**organismo**, *m.* organism; organization, association.—**organista**, *mf.* (mus.) organist.—**organización**, *f.* organization; arrangement.—**organizar**, *vti.* [a] to organize, set up; to arrange.—**órgano**, *m.* (physiol., & mus.) organ; instrument, agency; pipe organ.

orgasmo, *m.* orgasm.

orgía, *f.* orgy.

orgullo, *m.* pride; haughtiness.—**orgulloso**, *a.* proud; haughty; conceited.

orientación, *f.* orientation; bearings.—**oriental**, *a.* oriental, eastern.—*mf.* Oriental.—**orientar**, *vt.* to orientate, orient.—*vr.* to find one's way about, get one's bearings.—**oriente**, *m.* east, orient; luster (in pearls); east wind.—*extremo O.*, *lejano O.*, Far East.—*gran o.*, grand lodge.—*O. Medio*, Middle East.—*O. Próximo*, *Cercano O.*, *Próximo O*, Near East.

orificación, *f.* (dent.) gold filling.

orificio, *m.* orifice, small hole, opening.

origen, *m.* origin; source; beginning.—**original**, *a.* original, new; quaint, odd.—*m.* original, first copy; (print.) manuscript.—**originalidad**, *f.* originality.—**originar**, *vt.* to originate, create; to start.—*vr.* to originate, arise, spring.—**originario**, *a.* originating; native; derived.

orilla, *f.* border, margin; edge; bank (of a river); shore; sidewalk.

orín, *m.* rust.—*pl.* urine.—**orina**, *f.* urine.—**orinal**, *m.* urinal; chamber pot.—**orinar**, *vt.* & *vi.* to urinate.

oriundo, *a.* native, coming (from).

orla, *f.* fringe, trimming; matting; ornamental border.—**orlar**, *vt.* to border with an edging.

ornamentación, *f.* ornamentation.—**ornamentar**, *vt.* to adorn, decorate.—**ornamento**, *m.* ornament; decoration; accomplishment.—**ornar**, *vt.* to adorn, embellish, garnish.—**ornato**, *m.* ornament, decoration, embellishment.

ornitología, *f.* ornithology.

oro, *m.* gold; gold color.—*o. en polvo*, gold dust.—*pl.* a suit of cards named **oros**.

orondo, *a.* pompous, showy; hollow.

oropel, *m.* tinsel; brass foil; glitter.

oropéndola, *f.* golden oriole.

orquesta, *f.* orchestra.—**orquestación**,

f. orchestration.—**orquestar,** *vt.* to orchestrate.

orquídea, *f.* orchid.

ortiga, *f.* nettle.

ortodoxia, *f.* orthodoxy.—**ortodoxo,** *a.* orthodox.

ortografía, *f.* orthography, spelling.—**ortográfico,** *a.* orthographical.

oruga, *f.* (entom.) caterpillar; (bot.) rocket.

orzuelo, *m.* (med.) sty.

os, *pron.* you; to you; yourselves.

osadía, *f.* audacity, daring.—**osado,** *a.* daring, bold, audacious.—**osar,** *vi.* to dare, venture; to outdare.

oscilación, *f.* oscillation.—**oscilar,** *vi.* to oscillate.—**oscilatorio,** *a.* oscillatory.

oscuras, —*a o.,* in the dark.—**oscurecer,** *vti.* [3] to obscure, darken; to dim; to tarnish; (art) to shade.—*vii.* to grow dark.—*vri.* to become dark; to cloud over.—**oscurecimiento,** *m.* darkening; blackout.—**oscuridad,** *f.* obscurity; darkness; gloominess.—**oscuro,** *a.* obscure; dark; gloomy; dim.

óseo, *a.* bone, bony.

osezno, *m.* whelp or cub of a bear.—**oso,** *m.* (zool.) bear.—*o. blanco,* polar bear.—*o. gris,* grizzly bear.—*o. hormiguero,* anteater.—*o. marino,* fur seal, seal.

oso, *n.* bear.—*Osa Mayor,* Great Bear, Big Dipper.—*Osa Menor,* Little Bear, Little Dipper.—*o. blanco* or *polar,* polar bear.—*o. de felpa* or *peluche,* teddy bear.—*o. hormiguero,* anteater.—*o. panda,* panda.—*o. pardo,* brown bear; grizzly bear.—*o. perezoso,* sloth.

ostensible, *a.* ostensible, apparent.—**ostentación,** *f.* ostentation.—**ostentar,** *vt.* to make a show of, exhibit.—*vi.* to boast, brag; to show off.—**ostentoso,** *a.* sumptuous, magnificent.

ostión, *m.* large oyster.—**ostra,** *f.* oyster.—**ostracismo,** *m.* ostracism.—**ostrero,** *m.* oyster bed.

otear, *vt.* to observe, examine, pry into.—**otero,** *m.* hill, knoll.

otoñal, *a.* autumnal.—**otoño,** *m.* autumn, fall.

otorgamiento, *m.* grant, granting; (law) executing an instrument.—**otorgar,** *vti.* [b] to consent, agree to; (law) to grant.

otro, *a.* another, other.—*pron.* other one, another one.

ovación, *f.* ovation.—**ovacionar,** *vt.* to give an ovation to; to acclaim.

oval, ovalado, *a.* oval.—**óvalo,** *m.* oval.

ovario, *m.* ovary.

ovas, *f. pl.* roe.

oveja, *f.* sheep.—**ovejuno,** *a.* pertaining to sheep.

overol, *m.,* **overoles,** *m. pl.* (Am.) overalls; dungarees.

ovillar, *vt.* to wind (thread) in a ball or skein.—*vr.* to curl up.—**ovillo,** *m.* skein, ball of yarn.

OVNI, *abbr.* (**objeto volador** or **volante no identificado**) UFO.

oxiacanta, *f.* hawthorn.

oxidar, *vt. & vr.* to oxidize; to rust.—**óxido,** *m.* oxide; rust.

oxígeno, *m.* oxygen.

oyente, *mf.* hearer.—*pl.* audience.

ozono, *m.* ozone.

P

pabellón, *m.* building; pavilion; summerhouse; bell (of a musical instrument); flag, banner.—*p. auricular,* outer ear.—*p. de aduanas,* customs house.—*p. de caza,* hunting lodge.—*p. de la oreja,* outer ear.—*p. de los condenados a muerte,* death row.—*p. deportivo* or *p. de deportes,* sports building.—*p. separado,* annex.

pablo, *m.* wick (of candle); burnt end of wick.

pábulo, *m.* encouragement; nourishment, food.—*dar p.,* to give basis for (gossip); to stimulate (gossip).

paca, *f.* bale of goods.

pacana, *f.* pecan nut; pecan tree.

pacer, *vii.* [3] to pasture; to graze.

pachorra, *f.* sluggishness, slowness.

paciencia, *f.* patience.—**paciente,** *a.* patient.—*mf.* patient, sick person.—*p. de consulta externa,* outpatient.—**pacienzudo,** *a.* long-suffering.

pacificador, *n.* pacifier, peacemaker.—**pacificar,** *vti.* [d] to pacify, appease.—*vri.* to become calm.—**pacífico,** *a.* peaceful, pacific.—**pacifismo,** *m.* pacifism.—**pacifista,** *mf.* & *a.* pacifist; pacifistic.

paco, *m.* alpaca; sniper.

pacotilla, *f.* (com.) venture.—*de p.,* of poor or inferior quality.

pactar, *vt.* to make an agreement, contract; to stipulate.—**pacto,** *m.* agreement, pact; treaty.

padecer, *vti.* [3] to suffer.—*vii.* (de) to suffer (from).—**padecimiento,** *m.* suffering; ailment.

padrastro, *m.* stepfather.—**padre,** *m.* father; priest; principal author; Senior, p.ej., **Juan Cruz, padre,** John Cruz, Senior, John Cruz, Sr.—*pl.* parents, father and mother; ancestors.—*P. Eterno,* our Father, God Almighty.—**padrenuestro,** *m.* Lord's Prayer.—**padrino,** *m.* godfather; second (in a duel); best man; patron, sponsor.

paella, *f.* dish of rice with meat, chicken and shellfish.

paga, *f.* payment; wages, salary; pay.—**pagadero,** *a.* payable.—**pagador,** *n.* payer; paymaster; paying teller.—**pagaduría,** *f.* paymaster's office.

paganismo, *m.* paganism, heathenism.—**pagano,** *m.* & *a.* pagan, heathen.—*n.* sucker, dupe.

pagar, *vti.* [b] to pay; to pay for; to requite.—*p. contra entrega,* C.O.D.—*p. el pato,* to get the blame; to be the scapegoat.—*p. por anticipado or adelantado,* to pay in advance.—*p. una visita,* to visit, return a call.—*vri.* (de) to be pleased (with); to boast (of); to be conceited (about).—**pagaré,** *m.* (com.) promissory note; I.O.U.

página, *f.* page (of a book); folio.—**paginar,** *vt.* to page (a book, etc.), paginate.

pago, *m.* payment; requital.—*a.* (coll.) paid.

país, *m.* country, nation; land, region.—*del p.,* domestic, national.—*p. en vías de desarrollo,* developing country.—*p. satélite,* satellite country.—**paisaje,** *m.* landscape.—*p. lunar,* moonscape.—**paisano,** *a.* from the same country.—*n.* fellow countryman(-woman); civilian; peasant.

paja, *f.* straw; chaff, trash.—*un quítame allá esas pajas,* an insignificant reason; a jiffy.—**pajar,** *m.* barn, straw loft.

pajarera, *f.* aviary; large bird cage.—**pajarería,** *f.* pet shop (specializing in birds).—**pájaro,** *m.* bird; shrewd, sly fellow.—*p. carpintero,* woodpecker.—*p. de cuenta,* person of importance, big shot; shrewd, sly fellow.—*p. mosca,* hummingbird.—**pajarraco,** *m.* large bird; (coll.) shady character.

paje, *m.* page, valet.

pajizo, *a.* made of straw; straw-colored.

pajonal, *m.* (Am.) place abounding in tall grass.

pala, *f.* shovel; spade; scoop; trowel; blade of an oar; blade of the rudder; artifice; (coll.) fix, thrown game.—*p. mecánica,* power shovel.—*p. mecánica de vapor,* steam shovel.

palabra, *f.* word.—*interj.* honestly! my word of honor!—*bajo p.,* on (one's) word.—*de p.,* by word of mouth.—*mala p.,* dirty word.—*p. de matrimonio,* promise of marriage.—*p. de moda,* buzzword.—*pedir la p.,* to ask for the floor (at a meeting).—*p. familiar,* colloquial word.—**palabrería,** *f.* wordiness, palaver, empty talk, verbosity, wind.—*p. de vendador,* sales talk.—**palabrero,** *a.* long-winded.—**palabrota,** *f.* coarse expression, dirty word.

palacio, *m.* palace.—*p. de justicia,* courthouse.

paladar, *m.* palate; taste; relish.—**paladear,** *vt.* to taste with pleasure, to relish.—**paladeo,** *m.* act of tasting or relishing.

paladín, *m.* champion.

palafrenero, *m.* stableboy, groom, ostler.

palanca, *f.* lever; bar, crowbar; pole for carrying a weight.—*p. de cambio, p. de velocidades,* gearshift.

palangana, *f.* washbowl, basin.

palanqueta, *f.* small lever; (Am.) dumbbell.

palco, *m.* (theat.) box, loge; stand with seats.

palear, *vt.* (Am.) to shovel.

palenque, *m.* palisade; arena.

paleta, *f.* (cooking) ladle; lollipop; (anat.) shoulder blade; (mason.) trowel; blade; (art) palette; little shovel.—**paletada,** *f.* trowelful.—**paletilla,** *f.* shoulder blade.

palidecer, *vii.* [3] to pale, turn pale.—**palidez,** *f.* paleness, pallor.—**pálido,** *a.* pale, pallid, pasty.

palillo, *m.* toothpick; drumstick; small stick.—*pl.* castanets; chopsticks.

pallo, *m.* cloak, mantle; pallium, pall.

palique, *m.* (coll.) chitchat, small talk.

paliza, *f.* beating, thrashing.

palizada, *f.* palisade; (fort.) stockade.

palma, *f.* palm tree; leaf of a palm tree; palm of the hand; emblem of victory or martyrdom.—*pl.* applause.—*ganar,* or *llevarse la p.,* to carry the day; to win the prize.—**palmada,** *f.* pat; clapping; slap.—**palmar,** *m.* palm grove.

palmario, *a.* clear, obvious, evident.

palmatoria, *f.* small candlestick.

palmear, *vt.* to clap (the hands); to pat.

palmera, *f.* palm tree.—**palmiche,** *m.* fruit of a palm tree.

palmípedo, *a.* web-footed.

palmo, *m.* span, measure of length.—*p. a p.,* foot by foot.—**palmotear,** *vi.* to clap hands.—**palmoteo,** *m.* hand clapping.

palo, *m.* stick; pole; timber, log; wood (material); (Am.) tree; blow with a stick; suit at cards; (Am.) a drink; (naut.) mast.—*pl.* blows, cudgeling.—*dar (de) palos,* to thrash, club, beat.—*p. de golf,* golf club.

paloma, *f.* pigeon; dove; meek, mild person.—*p. mensajera,* carrier pigeon.—*p. torcaz,* wild pigeon.—*pl.* white caps.—**palomo,** *m.* cock pigeon.

palpable, *a.* palpable, obvious, evident.—**palpar,** *vt.* to feel (of); to touch; to see as self-evident; (med.) to palpate.—*vi.* to feel by touching; to grope in the dark.

palpitación, *f.* palpitation; throbbing.—**palpitante,** *a.* vibrating, palpitating.—**palpitar,** *vi.* to palpitate, throb, quiver.

palúdico, *a.* malarial.—**paludismo,** *m.* malaria.

pampa, *f.* pampa, prairie.—*estar a la p.,* (Am.) to be outdoors.—**pampeano, pampero,** *a.* of or from the pampas.—*n.* pampa man (woman).

pamplina, *f.* (coll.) trifle, frivolity.

pan, *m.* bread; loaf; wheat; leaf (of gold, silver).—*pl.* breadstuffs.—*p. ácimo* or *ázimo,* unleavened bread.—*p. blanco* or *candeal,* white bread.—*p. de carne,* meatloaf.—*p. de centeno,* rye bread.—*p. de oro finí-*

simo, gold leaf.—*p. integral,* whole wheat bread.—*p. negro* or *moreno,* brown bread.—*p. rallado,* breadcrumbs.—*llamar al p. p. y al vino vino,* to call a spade a spade.—*ser p. comido,* to be easy as pie; to be a pushover.

pana, *f.* corduroy, plush.

panadería, *f.* bakery.—**panadero,** *n.* baker.

panal, *m.* honeycomb; hornet's nest; a sweetmeat.

Panamá, *m.* Panama.—*el Canal de P.,* the Panama Canal.—*p.,* Panama hat.

panameño, *n. & a.* Panamanian.

panamericano, *a.* Pan-American.

pandear, *vt., vi. & vr.* to bend, warp, bulge out.—**pandeo,** *m.* bulge, bulging.

pandereta, *f.,* **pandero,** *m.* tambourine.

pandilla, *f.* gang, band.—**pandillero,** *n.* (Am.) gangster.

panecillo, *m.* roll (bread); biscuit.

panel, *m.* (art, elec.) panel.

panetela, *f.* (Am.) sponge cake.

panfleto, *m.* tract, pamphlet; lampoon; libel.

paniaguado, *n.* protégé, henchman.

pánico, *m. & a.* panic(ky).

panocha, *f.* ear of grain.

panqué, panqueque, *m.* (Am.) pancake; cupcake.

pantaletas, *f. pl.* (Am.) panties.—**pantalón,** *m.* (gen. *pl.*) trousers; panties; slacks.—*p. corto,* shorts; Bermuda shorts.—*pl.* pants, trousers.—*p. bombachos,* baggy pants.—*p. de dril,* jeans.—*p. de peto,* overalls, dungarees.—*p. tejanos* or *vaqueros,* jeans.—**pantaloncitos,** *m. pl.* (Am.) panties.

pantalla, *f.* lamp shade; screen.—*p. de chimenea,* fire screen.—*p. televisora,* television screen.

pantano, *m.* swamp, marsh, bog.—**pantanoso,** *a.* swampy, marshy, miry; full of difficulties.

pantera, *f.* panther.

pantomima, *f.* pantomime.

pantorrilla, *f.* calf (of leg).

pantufla, *f.* slipper.

panza, *f.* belly, paunch.—**panzada,** *f.* (coll.) bellyful.—**panzón, panzudo,** *a. & n.* big-bellied, paunchy (person).

pañal, *m.* diaper.—*estar en pañales,* to have little knowledge or experience.—**paño,** *m.* cloth, woolen ma-

terial; washcloth, washrag; wiper.—
pl. clothes, garments.—*paños
calientes,* half measures.—*paños menores,* underclothes.—*p. de cocina,*
washrag.—**pañoleta,** *f.* triangular
shawl.—**pañolón,** *m.* large square
shawl.—**pañuelo,** *m.* handkerchief,
kerchief.

papa, *m.* pope.—*f.* potato; (Am.) easy
job; (coll.) food, grub; lie, fib.—*papas fritas, papas a la francesa,* French
fries.

papá, *m.* (coll.) dad, daddy, papa, pop.

papada, *f.* double chin; dewlap.

papagayo, *m.* macaw; parrot.

papal, *a.* papal.

papalina, *f.* sunbonnet.

papalote, *m.* (Am.) kite.

papamoscas, *m.* flycatcher, flyeater;
(coll.) ninny.—**papanatas,** *m.* (coll.)
simpleton, dolt, ninny.

paparrucha, *f.* (coll.) fake, humbug;
nonsense, silliness.

papaya, *f.* papaya.

papel, *m.* paper; piece of paper; document; (theat.) part, role; character,
figure.—*desempeñar un p.,* to play a
role.—*hacer buen* (o *mal*) *p.,* to cut a
good (or bad) figure.—*p. alquitranado,* tar paper.—*papeles usados,*
waste paper.—*p. carbon, carbónico,*
or *calco,* carbon paper.—*p. cebolla,*
onionskin paper.—*p. celofán,* cellophane.—*p. crepé* or *crêpe,* crepe paper.—*p. de carta,* writing paper, note
paper.—*p. de cartas,* stationery.—*p.
de cera,* wax paper.—*p. de copia,*
bond paper.—*p. de desecho,* waste
paper.—*p. de diario* or *periódico* or *p.
prensa,* newsprint.—*p. de embalar* or
reglo or *envolver,* wrapping paper.—
p. de empeño, pawn ticket.—*p. de escribir,* writing paper.—*p. de estaño* or
plata or *aluminio,* tinfoil, aluminum
foil.—*p. de estraza,* brown or gray
wrapping paper.—*p. de inodoro* or
water or *p. higiénico,* toilet paper.—
p. de lija, sandpaper.—*p. de seda,* tissue paper.—*p. de soporte,* mounting.—*p. encerado* or *parafinado,* wax
paper.—*p. mojado* or *para apuntes,*
scrap paper, waste paper.—*p. principal,* title role.—*p. secante,* blotting
paper.—**papeleo,** *m.* red tape.—**papelera,** *f.* paper case; paper mill.—
papelería, *f.* stationery; stationery
shop.—**papelero,** *n.* paper maker;
stationer.—**papeleta,** *f.* card, ticket,
slip.—**papelucho,** *m.* worthless
paper.

papera, *f.* goiter.—*pl.* mumps.

papilla, *f.* pap; guile, deceit.—*hacerse
p.,* to break into small pieces.

paquete, *m.* packet, package; bundle
of papers; (coll.) dandy, dude.—*de
p.,* (cook.) ready-mix.—*p. regalo,*
gift wrapping.

par, *a.* even (number).—*m.* pair,
couple; peer; (elec.) cell.—*a la p.,*
jointly, equally; (com.) par; at par;
(horse racing) in a dead heat.—*de p.
en p.,* (of a door, etc.) wide open.—
sin p., peerless, incomparable.

para, *prep.* for, to, in order to, toward,
to the end that.—*estar p.,* to be on
the point of, about to.—*p. mi capote,*
to myself.—*¿p. qué?* what for?—*p.
que,* so that, in order that.—*sin qué
ni p. qué,* without rhyme or reason.

parabién, *m.* congratulation, felicitation, greeting.

parábola, *f.* parable; (geom.) parab-
ola.—**parabólico,** *a.* parabolic.

parabrisa, *m.* windshield.

paracaídas, *m.* parachute.—**paracaí-
dista,** *mf.* parachutist; (mil.) paratrooper.

parachoques, *m.* (auto) bumper.

parada, *f.* stop (as a train, etc.); (mil.)
halt, halting; parade; review; stakes,
bet; (fencing) parry.—*p. de descanso,*
rest stop.—*p. de taxis,* taxi stand.—
p. en firme or *en seco,* dead stop.—**paradero,** *m.* halting place; (Am.)
(R.R.) depot, station; whereabouts.

parado, *a.* unoccupied; (of a clock)
stopped; shut down (as a factory);
(Am.) standing.—*a.* & *n.* unemployed.

paradoja, *f.* paradox.

parafina, *f.* paraffin.

paraguas, *m.* umbrella.

paraguayo, *n.* & *a.* Paraguayan.

paragüero, *n.* umbrella maker, repairer
or seller; (coll.) Sunday driver.—*m.*
umbrella stand.

paraíso, *m.* paradise; heaven; (theat.,
coll.) upper gallery.—*p. fiscal,* tax
haven.—*p. terrenal,* Paradise, garden of Eden.

paraje, *m.* place, spot.

paralela, *f.* parallel line.—**paralelo,** *a.*
parallel; similar.—*m.* parallel, resemblance; (geog.) parallel.

parálisis, *f.* paralysis.—**paralítico,** *n.* &
a. paralytic; paralyzed.—**paraliza-
ción,** *f.* paralyzation; (com.) stagnation.—**paralizado,** *a.* (com.) dull,
stagnant.—**paralizar,** *vti.* [a] to paralyze; to impede, stop.

páramo, *m.* bleak plateau, moor; desert.

parangón, *m.* comparison.—**parangonar,** *vt.* to compare.

paraninfo, *m.* assembly hall in a university.

paranoico, *m.* paranoiac.

parapeto, *m.* (mil.) parapet.

parar, *vt.* to stop, detain; (fencing) to parry; (Am.) to stand, place in upright position.—*p. mientes en,* to consider carefully.—*vi.* to stop, halt; to come to an end; (en) to become, end (in); to stop or stay (at).—*ir a p. a o en,* to become, end in, finally to get to.—*vr.* to stop, halt; (Am.) to stand up.—*sin pararse,* without delay, instantly.—**pararrayos,** *m.* lightning rod.

parásito, *m.* & *a.* parasite; parasitic.

parasol, *m.* parasol.

parcela, *f.* parcel of land, lot.—**parcelar,** *vt.* to divide into lots.

parche, *m.* patch, mending; (pharm.) plaster, sticking plaster; (mil.) drum-head; drum.

parcial, *a.* partial.—*mf.* follower, partisan.—**parcialidad,** *f.* partiality, bias; party, faction.

parco, *a.* sparing, scanty; sober, moderate.

pardal, *m.* (ornith.) sparrow, linnet; crafty fellow.

pardo, *a.* brown; dark gray, dun.—*n.* (Am.) mulatto.—**pardusco,** *a.* grayish, grizzly.

parear, *vt.* to match, mate, pair.

parecer, *vii.* [3] to appear, show up; to seem, look like.—*al p.,* apparently. —*vri.* to look alike, resemble. —*m.* opinion, thinking; look, mien; appearance.—*a mi parecer,* in my opinion.—**parecido,** *a.* (a) resembling, like, similar (to).—*bien (mal) p.,* good-(bad-) looking.—*m.* resemblance, likeness.

pared, *f.* wall.—*entre cuatro paredes,* confined; imprisoned.—*p. maestra,* main wall.—*p. medianera,* partition wall.

pareja, *f.* pair, couple; match; dancing partner.—*parejas mixtas,* (games) mixed doubles.—**parejo,** *a.* equal, even; smooth; (horse racing) neck and neck.

parentela, *f.* kinsfolk, relatives.—**parentesco,** *m.* kindred, relationship.

paréntesis, *m.* parenthesis.—*entre p.,* by the bye, by the way.

pargo, *m.* red snapper.

parhilera, *f.* ridgepole.

parla, *m.* outcast.

paridad, *f.* parity, equality.

pariente, *n.* relative, relation.

parihuela, *f.* handbarrow; litter; stretcher.

parir, *vt.* & *vi.* to give birth.—*poner a p.,* to constrain, force (a person).

parisiense, *mf.* Parisian.

parking, *m.* parking lot, parking garage.

parlamentar, *vi.* to parley; to converse.—**parlamentario,** *a.* parliamentary, parliamentarian.—*n.* member of parliament; envoy to a parley.—**parlamento,** *m.* parliament; legislative body; parley.

parlanchín, *n.* & *a.* chatterbox, jabberer, talker; chattering, jabbering, talkative.—**parlero,** *a.* loquacious, talkative; chirping (birds); babbling (brooks).—**parlotear,** *vi.* to prattle, prate, chatter.—**parloteo,** *m.* chat, prattle, talk.

paro, *m.* lockout.—*p. forzoso,* unemployment.

parodia, *f.* parody.

parótida, *f.* parotid gland.—*pl.* mumps.

parpadear, *vi.* to wink; to blink, twinkle.—**parpadeo,** *m.* winking; blinking, twinkling.—**párpado,** *m.* eyelid.

parque, *m.* park; (Am.) ammunition; playpen.—*p. de atracciones, diversiones,* or *entretenciones,* amusement park.—*p. empresarial,* industrial park.—**parquear,** *vt.* & *vi.* (Am.) to park (auto).—**parquímetro,** *m.* parking meter.

parra, *f.* grapevine.

párrafo, *m.* paragraph.

parranda, *f.* revel, carousal, spree.—**parrandear,** *vi.* to go on a spree.—**parrandero,** *a.* fond of carousing.—*n.* carouser, reveler.

parricida, *mf.* parricide (person).—**parricidio,** *m.* parricide (act).

parrilla, *f.* grill, broiler; toaster; (furnace) grate.

párroco, *m.* parish priest.—**parroquia,** *f.* parish; parish church; (com.) customers.—**parroquial,** *a.* parochial. —*f.* parochial church.—**parroquiano,** *n.* parishioner; (com.) customer, client.

parsimonia, *f.* moderation, calmness.

parte, *f.* part; portion; share; place; (law) party; (theat.) role.—*pl.* (coll.) the genitals.—*dar p.,* to inform, notify.—*de algún tiempo a esta p.*, for some time past.—*de mi p.*, for my part; on my side; in my name.—*de p. a p.*, from side to side, through.—*de p. de*, from, in the name of; in behalf of.—*en alguna p.*, somewhere.—*en ninguna p.*, nowhere.—*en todas partes*, everywhere.—*la mayor p.*, most.—*la tercera (cuarta, etc.) p.*, one-third (-fourth, etc.).—*p. de la oración*, part of speech.—*por mi p.*, as for me.—*por otra p.*, on the other hand.—*m.* communication, dispatch, report, telegram, telephone message.—*p. de defunción*, death certificate.—*p. facultativo* or *médico*, medical report.—*p. meteorológico*, weather report.—*adv.* in part, partly.

partenogénesis, *f.* parthenogenesis.

partera, *f.* midwife.

partición, *f.* division, partition, distribution.—**participación,** *f.* participation, share; communication; (com.) copartnership.—**participante,** *mf. & a.* participant, sharer; notifier; participating, sharing; notifying.—**participar,** *vt.* to notify, communicate.—*vi.* (de) to share (in); (en) to participate, take part (in).—**partícipe,** *mf.* participator, participant.—**participio,** *m.* participle.

partícula, *f.* particle.

particular, *a.* particular, peculiar, special; personal; private; individual; odd, extraordinary.—*m.* private person, individual; topic, point.—*en p.*, particularly.—*p. a p.*, (tel.) person-to-person.—**particularidad,** *f.* particularity, peculiarity; detail.

partida, *f.* departure; item in an account; entry; game; band, gang; (com.) shipment, consignment.—*p. de bautismo,* (matrimonio, defunción), certificate of birth (marriage, death).—*p. de campo*, picnic.—**partidario,** *n.* supporter; follower; retainer.—**partido,** *a.* divided; broken.—*m.* (pol.) party; advantage, profit; game, contest, match; odds, handicap; territorial division or district.—*p. de boxeo profesional*, prize fight.—*p. de desempate*, (sports) play-off.—*p. de exhibición*, exhibition game.—*p. de lucha*, wrestling match.—*sacar p. de*, to turn to advantage.—*tomar p.*, to take sides.—

partir, *vt.* to split; to divide; to break, crush, crack.—*vi.* to depart, leave.—*a p. de*, starting from.—*vr.* to break; to become divided.

partitura, *f.* (mus.) score.

parto, *m.* childbirth.—*p. muerto*, stillbirth.—*p. virginal*, virgin birth.

parvedad, *f.* smallness, minuteness; light breakfast.

párvulo, *a.* very small; innocent; humble, low.—*n.* child.

pasa, *f.* raisin; (naut.) narrow channel.

pasable, *a.* passable, able to be traversed, crossed, etc.—**pasada,** *f.* passage, passing; pace, step.—*de p.*, on the way; hastily.—*mala p.*, (coll.) bad turn, mean trick.—**pasadero,** *a.* supportable, sufferable; passable, so-so, tolerably good.—*m.* stepping stone.—**pasadizo,** *m.* passageway, aisle; alley.—**pasado,** *a.* past; last (day, week, etc.); stale; (of fruit) spoiled; antiquated, out of date or fashion.—*p. mañana*, day after tomorrow.—*m.* past.—**pasador,** *m.* door bolt; window fastener; pin; woman's brooch.

pasaje, *m.* passage, passageway; fare; number of passengers in a ship; (naut.) strait, narrows.—**pasajero,** *a.* passing, transient, transitory; provisional.—*n.* traveler, passenger, rider.—*p. de entrepuente*, (naut.) steerage passenger.—*p. de pie*, standee.

pasamano, *m.* handrail, banister.

pasamontañas, *m.* ski mask.

pasaporte, *m.* passport.

pasar, *vt.* to pass; to take across, carry over; to pass, hand; to go to, in, by, across, over, around, beyond, through; to filter; to surpass; to tolerate; to endure; to pass, spend (as time).—*p. a cuchillo*, to put to the sword.—*p. el rato*, to kill time.—*p. (la) lista*, to call the roll.—*p. la pelota*, (fam.) to kick the bucket.—*pasarlo bien (mal)*, to have a good (bad) time.—*p. por alto*, to overlook.—*p. por las armas*, to shoot, execute.—*¿qué (le) pasa?* what's the matter with (him)?—*vi.* to pass; to live; to get along; to pass, happen, turn out.—*p. de*, to exceed.—*p. de largo*, to pass by without stopping; to skim through.—*p. por*, to be considered as, to be taken for.—*p. sin*, to do without.—*vr.* to become spoiled, tainted or stale; to slip from one's memory; to go too far; to exceed; to be overcooked.

pasarela, f. gangplank; (theat.) runway; catwalk; footbridge.

pasatiempo, m. amusement, pastime.

pascua, f. Passover; Easter; Christmas; Twelfth-night; Pentecost.—*estar como una p.* or *unas pascuas,* to be as merry as a lark.—*felices Pascuas,* Merry Christmas.—*P. de Navidad,* Christmas.—*P. florida,* or *P. de Resurrección,* Easter.

pase, m. pass, permit; (fencing) thrust.

paseante, mf. walker, stroller.—**pasear,** vi. & vr. to take a walk; to ride, drive or sail for pleasure; to walk up and down, pace.—vt. to take out to walk (as a child).—**paseo,** m. walk; promenade; stroll; drive; ride; boulevard; parade.—*dar un p.,* to take a walk, ride, etc.—*echar* or *enviar a p.,* to dismiss or reject rudely or without ceremony.—*p. en trineo,* sleigh ride.—*p. espacial,* space walk.

pasillo, m. passage, corridor; aisle; short step.

pasión, f. passion.

pasivo, a. passive; inactive.—m. (com.) liabilities.

pasmar, vt. to stupefy, stun; to amaze, astound.—vr. to wonder, marvel; (of plants) to freeze.—**pasmo,** m. astonishment; wonder, awe.—**pasmoso,** a. marvelous, wonderful.

paso, m. pace, step; pass, passage; passing, gait, walk; footstep.—*apretar el p.,* to hasten.—*ceder el p.,* to yield the right of way.—*de p.,* in passing; on the way.—*p. a nivel,* (R.R.) grade crossing.—*p. de ganso,* goose step.—*p. de peatones,* crosswalk.—*p. de tortuga,* snail's pace.—*p. elevado,* overpass.—*p. inferior,* underpass.—*prohibido el p.,* no trespassing, keep out.—*salir del p.,* to get out of the difficulty; to get by.—adv. softly, gently.

pasquín, m. lampoon; anonymous satiric public poster.—**pasquinar,** vt. to ridicule, lampoon, satirize.

pasta, f. paste; dough; pie crust; noodles; board binding (for books).—*buena p.,* good disposition.

pastadero, m. pasture, grazing field.—**pastar,** vi. to pasture, graze.—vt. to lead (cattle) to graze.

pastel, m. pie; combine, plot; (art) pastel.—*p. de boda,* wedding cake.—

pastelear, vi. (coll.) (pol.) make a deal.—**pastelería,** f. pastry shop; pastry.—**pastelero,** n. pastry cook; (pol.) deal-maker.

pasteurizar, vti. [a] to pasteurize.

pastilla, f. tablet, lozenge, pastille, drop; cake (of soap).—*p. de silicio,* microchip, silicon chip.

pastizal, m. pasture ground.—**pasto,** m. pasture, grazing; grass for feed; pasture ground; food.—*a p.,* abundantly; excessively.—*a todo p.,* freely, abundantly and unrestrictedly.—**pastor,** n. shepherd(ess); pastor, clergyman.—**pastoral,** f. pastoral; idyl.—a. pastoral.—**pastorear,** vt. to pasture; to keep, tend (sheep).—**pastoreo,** m. pasturing.—**pastoril,** a. pastoral.

pastoso, a. pasty, soft, mellow, doughy, mushy.

pata, f. foot or leg of an animal; drumstick; leg of a piece of furniture, an instrument, etc.; female duck.—*a.or en cuatro patas,* on all fours.—*a la p. la llana,* plainly, unaffectedly.—*a p.,* (coll.) on foot.—*estirar la p.,* (coll.) to kick the bucket.—*meter la p.,* to put one's foot in.—*patas arriba,* topsy-turvy, head over heels; upside down.—*patas de gallina* or *de gallo,* crow's-foot wrinkles.—*patas de rana,* flippers.—*p. de cabra,* crowbar.—*p. de palo,* wooden leg.—**patada,** f. kick.—**patalear,** vi. to kick about violently.—**pataleo,** m. kicking; pattering.—**pataleta,** f. (coll.) fainting fit; convulsion; tantrum.

patata, f. potato.—*patatas fritas, patatas a la francesa,* French fries.

patatús, m. (coll.) swoon, fainting fit.

pateadura, f., **pateamiento,** m. kicking, stamping of the feet.—**patear,** vt. & vi. to kick; to stamp the foot; to tramp.

patentar, vt. to patent.—**patente,** a. patent, manifest, evident, self-evident.—f. patent; privilege, grant.—**patentizar,** vti. [a] to make evident.

paternal, a. paternal, fatherly.—**paternidad,** f. paternity, fatherhood.—**paterno,** a. paternal, fatherly.

patético, a. pathetic.—**patetismo,** m. dramatic quality; pathos.

patibulario, a. harrowing; criminal looking.—**patíbulo,** m. gallows.

patidifuso, a. (coll.) astounded.

patillas, f. pl. sideburns; side whiskers.

patín, *m.* skate; (aer.) skid; small patio; (theat.) orchestra.—*p. de cuchillo,* ice skate.—*p. de mar,* surfboard.—*p. de ruedas,* roller skate.—**patinador,** *n.* skater; ice skater.—**patinaje,** *m.* skating.—*p. sobre hielo,* ice skating.—*p. sobre las olas,* surf-riding.—**patinar,** *vi.* to skate; (of vehicles) to skid.—*p. sobre hielo,* to ice skate.—**patinazo,** *m.* skid.

patio, *m.* yard, patio, courtyard.

patituerto, *a.* crook-legged, knock-kneed.—**patizambo,** *a.* knock-kneed, bowlegged.

pato, *m.* duck.—*pagar el p.,* to get the blame, be the scapegoat.

patochada, *f.* blunder; nonsense.

patología, *f.* pathology.—**patológico,** *a.* pathological.

patoso, *a.* (coll.) boring; awkward.

patraña, *f.* fabulous story; fake, humbug.

patria, *f.* native country, fatherland.

patrio, *a.* native; home.—**patriota,** *mf.* patriot.—**patriótico,** *a.* patriotic.—**patriotismo,** *m.* patriotism.

patrocinar, *vt.* to sponsor; to protect, favor.—**patrocinio,** *m.* sponsorship, auspices; protection, patronage.—**patrón,** *n.* patron(ess); host(ess); landlord (-lady); patron saint.—*m.* master, boss; pattern; standard; (naut.) skipper.—**patronato,** *m.* board of trustees; employers' association; foundation.—**patrono,** *n.* patron, protector; trustee; employer; patron saint.

patrulla, *f.* patrol; gang, squad.—**patrullar,** *vt.* to patrol.

paulatino, *a.* slow, gradual.

pausa, *f.* pause; rest, repose.—**pausado,** *a.* slow, calm, quiet.—*adv.* slowly.

pauta, *f.* guide lines; standard, rule, pattern.

pava, *f.* turkey hen; (Am.) joke, fun.—*pelar la p.,* to carry on a flirtation.

pavesa, *f.* embers, hot cinders.—*pl.* ashes.

pavimentación, *f.* paving; pavement.—**pavimentar,** *vt.* to pave.—**pavimento,** *m.* pavement.

pavo, *m.* turkey; gobbler.—*p. real,* peacock.—*p. silvestre,* wood grouse.—**pavonearse,** *vr.* to strut, show off.

pavor, *m.* fear, fright.—**pavoroso,** *a.* awful, frightful, terrible.

payasada, *f.* clownish joke or action.—**payaso,** *m.* clown.

paz, *f.* peace.—*en p.,* quits, even.

pazguato, *n.* dolt, simpleton.

peaje, *m.* (bridge, road, etc.) toll.

peana, *f.* pedestal stand; (mech.) ground plate; step before an altar.

peatón, *m.* pedestrian, walker.

pebete, *m.* punk (joss stick).

peca, *f.* freckle.

pecado, *m.* sin.—*p. capital, grave,* or *mortal,* deadly or mortal sin.—**pecador,** *n.* & *a.* sinner; sinning.—**pecaminoso,** *a.* sinful.—**pecar,** *vii.* [d] to sin.—*p. de listo,* to be too wise.

pececillo, *m.* minnow, little fish.

pecera, *f.* fishbowl, fish tank; aquarium.

pechera, *f.* shirt bosom; shirt frill; chest protector; breast strap (of a harness).—**pecho,** *m.* chest, thorax; breast; bosom; teat; courage.—*abrir el p.,* to unbosom oneself.—*dar el p.,* to nurse, suckle; (coll.) to face it out.—*tomar a p.,* to take to heart.—**pechuga,** *f.* breast of a fowl; white meat; slope; (coll.) bosom.

pecoso, *a.* freckled.

peculado, *m.* (law) embezzlement.

peculiar, *a.* peculiar.—**peculiaridad,** *f.* peculiarity.

peculio, *m.* private property.

pedagogía, *f.* pedagogy.—**pedagógico,** *a.* pedagogical.—**pedagogo,** *n.* pedagogue; teacher; educator.

pedal, *m.* pedal; (mech.) treadle.

pedazo, *m.* piece, fragment, bit.—*a pedazos,* or *en pedazos,* in bits, in fragments.

pedernal, *m.* flint.

pedestal, *m.* pedestal; stand; base.

pedestre, *a.* pedestrian; low, vulgar, common.

pedicuro, *n.* chiropodist.

pedido, *m.* demand, call; (com.) order.—*p. postal,* mail order.—*p. urgente,* rush order.—**pedigrí,** *m.* pedigree.—**pedigüeno,** *a.* persistent in begging.—**pedir,** *vti.* [29] to ask for, request, beg, solicit; to demand; to wish, desire; to require; (com.) to order; to ask for in marriage.—*a p. de boca,* just right.—*p. prestado,* to borrow.

pedrada, *f.* throw of a stone; blow or hit with a stone.—**pedrea,** *f.* stone-throwing, stoning; hailstorm.—**pedregal,** *m.* stony ground.—**pedregoso,** *a.* stony, rocky.—**pedrería,** *f.* precious stones; jewelry.—**pedrusco,** *m.* rough piece of stone.

ega, f. joining, cementing together; (coll.) jest, practical joke; (ichth.) remora.—**pegajoso,** a. sticky; catching, contagious.—**pegar,** vti. [b] to stick, glue, cement; to fasten; to post (bills); to sew on; to pin; to patch; to attach; to infect with; to hit, beat, slap.—*no p. los ojos,* not to sleep a wink.—*p. fuego a,* to set fire to.—*p. un tiro,* to shoot.—vii. to make an impression on the mind; to join; to be contiguous; to fit, match; to be becoming, fitting, appropriate.—*esa no pega,* (coll.) that won't go.—vri. to stick; adhere.—**pegote,** m. sticking plaster; coarse patch; sponger.

eina, f. = PEINETA.—**peinado,** m. hairdo.—**peinador,** n. hairdresser.—m. dressing gown, wrapper.—**peinar,** vt. to comb or dress (the hair); to touch or rub slightly.—**peine,** m. comb.—**peineta,** f. ornamental shell comb (to wear in the hair).

eladilla, f. sugar almond; small pebble.

elado, a. plucked; bared; peeled, stripped; hairless; treeless; bare; penniless, broke.—n. penniless person.—m. Mexican peasant; haircut.—**peladura,** f. paring, peeling.—**pelafustán,** m. (coll.) nobody, idler, vagrant.—**pelagatos,** m. nincompoop, poor wretch.—**pelaje,** m. character or nature of the hair or wool; disposition.—**pelar,** vt. to cut the hair of; to pluck; to skin, peel, husk, shell; to cheat, rob; to break the bank.—*duro de p.,* exceedingly difficult, hard to crack.—vri. to get one's hair cut; to peel off, flake; to lose the hair (as from illness).

eldaño, m. step of a staircase.

elea, f. fight; scuffle, quarrel.—*p. a tiros,* gunfight.—**pelear,** vi. to fight; to quarrel; to struggle.—vr. to scuffle, come to blows.

elele, m. stuffed figure, dummy; puppet; nincompoop.

eletería, f. furrier's trade or shop; (Am.) leather goods or shop; furrier.—**peletero,** n. furrier; (Am.) dealer in leather goods; skinner.

llagudo, a. (coll.) arduous, difficult.

lícano, m. pelican.

lícula, f. film; moving picture reel; moving picture.—*p. casera,* home movie.—*p. de dibujos animados,*

(cine) cartoon.—*p. del Oeste* or *de vaqueros,* Western.—*p. de miedo* or *terror,* horror movie.—*p. muda,* silent movie.—*p. sonora,* sound movie.

peligrar, vi. to be in danger.—**peligro,** m. danger, peril.—*correr p.,* to be in danger.—**peligroso,** a. dangerous, perilous, risky.

pelillo, m. fine hair; trifle, slight trouble.—*echar pelillos a la mar,* to become reconciled.—**pelirrojo,** a. red-haired, red-headed.—**pelirrubio,** a. blond, light-haired.

pelleja, f. skin, hide.—**pellejo,** m. skin; rawhide; peel, rind.—*jugarse el p.,* to risk one's life.

pelirrojo, n. redhead.—a. red-haired.

pellizcar, vti. [d] to pinch; to nip; to clip.—**pellizco,** m. pinch; pinching; nip; small bit.

pelmazo, m. crushed or flattened mass; undigested food in the stomach; nuisance, sluggard.

pelo, m. hair; fiber, filament; nap, pile (of cloth); hairspring (in watches and firearms); grain (in wood).—*de medio p.,* of little account; would-be important.—*de p. áspero,* wirehaired.—*de p. en pecho,* brave, daring.—*en p.,* bareback; unsaddled.—*no tener p. de tonto,* to be bright, quick, clever.—*no tener pelos en la lengua,* to be outspoken.—*tomar el p. a,* to make fun of, pull one's leg.—*venir al p.,* to be to the point, fit the case to a tee.—**pelón,** a. hairless, bald.

pelota, f. ball; ball game; (Am.) baseball (game).—*p. de golf,* golf ball.—*en p.,* stark-naked; penniless.—**pelotazo,** m. blow or stroke with a ball.—**pelotear,** vi. to play ball; to throw (as a ball); to argue, dispute.—**pelotera,** f. quarrel, tumult, riot.—**pelotero,** m. (Am.) baseball player.—**pelotilla,** f. small ball; pellet.—**pelotón,** m. large ball; (mil.) platoon.—*p. de ejecución* or *fusilamiento,* firing squad.—*p. de salvamento,* rescue party.

peluca, f. wig, toupee.—**peludo,** a. hairy, shaggy.—m. shaggy mat.—**peluquería,** f. hairdressing shop; barber shop.—**peluquero,** n. hairdresser; barber.—**pelusa,** f. down; floss, fuzz, nap; (coll.) envy.

pena, f. penalty; punishment; affliction, sorrow, grief; (Am.) embarrassment.—*a duras penas,* with great difficulty, just barely.—*estar con (mucha) p.,* to be (very) sorry.—*merecer la p.,* to be worthwhile.—*p. capital* or *de muerte,* death penalty.—*p. corporal,* corporal punishment.—*p. pecuniaria,* fine.

penacho, *m.* tuft of feathers, plumes, crest.

penado, *n.* convict.—**penal,** *m.* penitentiary, prison.—*a.* penal.—**penalidad,** *f.* trouble, hardship; (law) penalty.—**penalizar,** *vti.* [a] to penalize.—**penar,** *vi.* to suffer; to crave, long for.—*vt.* to impose penalty on.

penco, *m.* swaybacked nag.

pendencia, *f.* quarrel, fight.—**pendenciero,** *a.* quarrelsome, rowdy.

pender, *vi.* to hang, dangle; to be pending or suspended.—**pendiente,** *a.* pendent, hanging; dangling; pending.—*m.* earring, pendant; watch chain.—*f.* slope.

pendón, *m.* standard, banner.

péndulo, *m.* pendulum.

pene, *m.* penis.

penetración, *f.* penetration, penetrating; acuteness, sagacity.—**penetrante,** *a.* penetrating; keen, acute; deep.—**penetrar,** *vt.* to penetrate, pierce; to break or force in; to fathom, comprehend.

penicilina, *f.* penicillin.

península, *f.* peninsula.—**peninsular,** *a.* inhabiting or pert. to a peninsula.

penitencia, *f.* penitence; penance.—**penitenciaría,** *f.* penitentiary.—**penitente,** *a.* penitent, repentant.—*mf.* penitent.

penoso, *a.* painful; laborious, arduous; distressing; embarrassing.

pensado, *a.* deliberate, premeditated.—*bien p.,* wise, proper.—*mal p.,* unwise, foolish.—*tener p.,* to have in view, to intend.—**pensador,** *n.* thinker.—**pensamiento,** *m.* mind; thought, idea; thinking; epigram, maxim; (bot.) pansy.—**pensar,** *vii.* [1] to think; to reflect.—*vti.* to think over, or about, consider; to intend, contemplate.—**pensativo,** *a.* pensive, thoughtful.

pensión, *f.* pension; boarding-house; board; fellowship for study abroad.—*p. completa,* room and board.—**pensionado,** *n.* pensioner, pensionary; fellow (study).—**pensionar,** *vt.* to impose on or to grant pensions on or to.—**pensionista,** *mf.* boarder, pensioner.

pentagrama, *m.* (mus.) ruled staff.

Pentecostés, *m.* Pentecost.

penúltimo, *a.* next to the last.

penumbra, *f.* dimness.

penuria, *f.* destitution, indigence.

peña, *f.* rock; boulder.—**peñasco,** *m* large rock.—**peñascoso,** *a.* rocky.—**peñón,** *m.* large rock; rocky cliff.—*p de Gibraltar,* Rock of Gibraltar.

peón, *m.* day laborer; foot soldier; spinning top; pawn (in chess); pedestrian.

peonía, *f.* (bot.) peony.

peonza, *f.* top (toy).

peor, *adv.* & *a.* worse; worst.

pepa, *f.* (Am.) seed, stone, pit.

pepino, *m.* cucumber.—*no importarl un p.,* not to give a fig.

pepita, *f.* pip or seed of fruit; nugget (veterinary med.) pip.

pequeñez, *f.* smallness; childhood; trifle; pettiness; mean act or conduct.—**pequeño,** *a.* little, small; of tender age; lowly, humble.—*n* child.

pera, *f.* (bot.) pear; goatee.—*pedi peras al olmo,* to expect the impossible.—**peral,** *m.* pear tree.

percal, *m.* percale, calico.

percance, *m.* misfortune; mishap.

percatar, *vi.* & *vr.* to think; consider; to beware.—*p. de,* to notice.

percepción, *f.* perception.—*p. a posteriori, p. tardía,* hindsight.—**perceptible,** *a.* perceptible, perceivable.—**percibir,** *vt.* to perceive; to receive; collect.

percha, perch, pole; hat or clothes rack; roost; snare for birds.—**perchero,** *m.* clothes rack or hanger.

percolador, *m.* percolator.

percudir, *vt.* to tarnish, stain, soil.

percusión, *f.* percussion; collision.

perdedor, *n.* loser.—**perder,** *vti.* [18] to lose; to forfeit; to squander away; to ruin; to miss (train, opportunity etc.).—*echar a p.,* to spoil, ruin.—*p los estribos,* to lose one's poise; to become reckless.—*¡pierda Ud. cuidad* don't worry! forget it!—*vii.* to lose.—*vri.* to get lost, lose one's way to miscarry; to be lost, confounde to be ruined; to go astray; to b spoiled or damaged (as fruits, crop etc.); to disappear.—*perderse vista,* to get out of sight; to be ver shrewd.—**pérdida,** *f.* loss; detri ment, damage; waste; (com.) leak age.—**perdidamente,** *adv.* despe ately; uselessly.—**perdido,** *a.* los mislaid; misguided; profligate, dissolute.—*m.* (fig.) black sheep.

perdigón, *m.* young partridge; buckshot; pellet.—**perdigonada,** *f.* peppering of buckshot.—**perdiguero,** *n.* setter, retriever (dog).—**perdiz,** *f.* partridge.

perdón, *m.* pardon, forgiveness; remission.—*interj.* pardon! excuse me!—*con p.,* by your leave.—**perdonable,** *a.* pardonable.—**perdonar,** *vt.* to pardon, forgive; to remit (a debt); to excuse.

perdulario, *a.* reckless, heedless.—*n.* good-for-nothing, ne'er-do-well.

perdurable, *a.* lasting, everlasting.—**perdurar,** *vi.* to last long.

perecedero, *a.* perishable, not lasting.—**perecer,** *vii.* [3] to perish.

peregrinación, *f.,* **peregrinaje,** *m.* traveling; pilgrimage.—**peregrinar,** *vi.* to travel, roam.—**peregrino,** *a.* foreign; traveling, migratory; strange, odd, rare.—*n.* pilgrim.

perejil, *m.* parsley.

perenne, *a.* perennial, perpetual.

perentorio, *a.* urgent, decisive; peremptory.

pereza, *f.* laziness; slowness, idleness.—**perezoso,** *a.* lazy, indolent, idle.—*m.* (zool.) sloth.

perfección, *f.* perfection; perfect thing.—*a la p.,* perfectly.—**perfeccionamiento,** *m.* perfecting, improvement, finish.—**perfeccionar,** *vt.* to improve, perfect.—**perfecto,** *a.* perfect.

perfil, *m.* profile, side view; outline.—**perfilado,** *a.* streamlined.—**perfilar,** *vt.* to outline, profile.—*vr.* to place oneself sideways; to dress carefully.

perforación, *f.* perforation, hole, puncture; drilling, boring.—**perforador,** *a.* & *n.* perforator, driller; perforating, drilling.—**perforadora,** *f.* drill, rock drill.—*p. mecánica,* power drill.—**perforar,** *vt.* to perforate; to bore, drill.

perfumar, *vt.* to perfume.—**perfume,** *m.* perfume.—**perfumería,** *f.* perfumery; perfumer's shop.—**perfumista,** *mf.* perfumer.

pergamino, *m.* parchment, vellum; diploma.

pericia, *f.* skill, expertness.

perico, *n.* parakeet; small parrot.

perifollos, *m. pl.* ribbons, tawdry ornaments of dress.

perilla, *f.* small pear; pear-shaped ornament; knob; pommel of a saddle;

goatee; lobe of the ear.—*de p.,* to the purpose.

perillán, *n.* rascal; sly, crafty person.

perímetro, *m.* perimeter.

periódico, *a.* periodic(al).—*m.* newspaper; periodical, journal.—*p. sensacional,* tabloid.—**periodismo,** *m.* journalism.—**periodista,** *mf.* journalist.—**periodístico,** *a.* journalistic.—**período,** *m.* period, age; sentence; menstruation, period; (elec.) cycle; (pol.) term, tenure.—*p. de prueba,* probation.

peripecia, *f.* situation, incident, episode.

peripuesto, *a.* dolled up; dressy.

periquete, *m.* (coll.) jiffy, instant.

periquito, *m.* parakeet, lovebird.

periscopio, *m.* periscope.

peritaje, *m.* expertness; appraisal.—**perito,** *a.* skillful, able, experienced.—*n.* expert; appraiser.

perjudicar, *vti.* [d] to damage, impair, harm.—**perjudicial,** *a.* harmful.—**perjuicio,** *m.* damage.

perjurar, *vi.* to commit perjury; to swear.—*vr.* to perjure oneself.—**perjurio,** *m.* perjury.—**perjuro,** *a.* perjured, forsworn.—*n.* forswearer, perjurer.

perla, *f.* pearl; (fig.) jewel.—*de perlas,* perfectly; to a tee.

permanecer, *vii.* [3] to stay, remain.—**permanencia,** *f.* stay, sojourn; duration, permanence.—**permanente,** *a.* permanent.—*f.* permanent (in hair).

permeable, *a.* porous, permeable; not waterproof.

permisible, *a.* permissible.—**permiso,** *m.* permission; permit.—*¡con p.!* excuse me!—*p. de conducir,* driver's license.—**permitir,** *vt.* to permit, allow, let; to grant, admit.

permuta, *f.* barter; exchange.—**permutar,** *vt.* & *vi.* to exchange, barter.

pernera, *f.* trouser leg.—**perneta,** *f.*—*en pernetas,* barelegged.

pernicioso, *a.* pernicious; harmful.

pernil, *m.* hock (of animals).

perno, *m.* nut and bolt; spike; joint pin.

pernoctar, *vi.* to pass the night.

pero, *conj.* but; except; yet.—*m.* (coll.) fault, defect.—*poner pero(s),* to find fault.

perogrullada, *f.* (coll.) obvious truth, truism; platitude.

perol, *m.* kettle.

peroración, *f.* peroration.—**perorar,** *vi.*

to deliver a speech or oration; to declaim.—**perorata**, *f.* (coll.) harangue, speech.

perpendicular, *f.* & *a.* perpendicular.

perpetrar, *vt.* to perpetrate, commit (a crime).

perpetuar, *vt.* & *vr.* to perpetuate.—**perpetuidad**, *f.* perpetuity.—**perpetuo**, *a.* perpetual, everlasting.

perplejidad, *f.* perplexity; quandary.—**perplejo**, *a.* uncertain, perplexed.

perra, *f.* bitch, female dog; slut; drunken state; tantrum.—**perrada**, *f.* mean, base action.—**perrera**, *f.* kennel.—**perrería**, *f.* pack of dogs; angry word; vile action.—**perrero**, *m.* dogcatcher.—**perro**, *m.* dog.—*no se admiten perros*, no dogs allowed.—*p. caliente*, (cook.) hot dog.—*p. de caza*, bird dog.—*p. de hortelano*, dog in the manger.—*p. guardián* or *de guard a*, guard dog, watchdog.—*p. guía* or *lazarillo*, guide dog, Seeing-Eye Dog.—*p. que ladre no muerde*, barking dogs don't bite.—*p. viejo*, (fam.) shrewd old bird.—**perruno**, *a.* doggish, canine; currish; doglike, doggy.

persa, *a.* & *n.* Persian.

persecución, *f.* persecution; pursuit.—**perseguidor**, *n.* persecutor; pursuer.—**perseguir**, *vti.* [29-b] to pursue; to persecute.

perseverancia, *f.* perseverance.—**perseverante**, *a.* persevering.—**perseverar**, *vi.* to persevere, persist.

persiana, *f.* blind, shutter; Venetian blind.

persignarse, *vr.* to cross oneself.

persistencia, *f.* persistence; obstinacy.—**persistente**, *a.* persistent; firm.—**persistir**, *vi.* to persist.

persona, *f.* person.—*en p.*, in person, personally.—*p. desplazada*, displaced person.—**personaje**, *m.* personage; (theat., lit.) character.—**personal**, *a.* personal, private.—*m.* personnel, staff.—**personalidad**, *f.* personality; individuality; (law) person; legal capacity.—*p. desdoblada*, split personality.—**personalizar**, *vti.* [a] to personalize; to become personal.—**personarse**, *vr.* to appear personally; (law) to appear as an interested party.—**personificar**, *vti.* [d] to personify.

perspectiva, *f.* perspective; view; prospect, outlook; appearance.

perspicacia, *f.* perspicacity, sagacity.—**perspicaz**, *a.* acute, sagacious, clear-sighted.

persuadir, *vt.* to persuade.—*vr.* to be persuaded.—**persuasión**, *f.* persuasion.—**persuasivo**, *a.* persuasive.

pertenecer, *vii.* [3] to belong, pertain; to concern.—**perteneciente**, *a.* belonging, pertaining.—**pertenencia**, *f.* possession, holding property.

pértiga, *m.* bar, pole, rod.

pertinente, *a.* pertinent, apt; (law) concerning, pertaining.

pertrechar, *vt.* & *vr.* (mil.) to supply, store, equip; to arrange, prepare.—**pertrechos**, *m. pl.* (mil.) stores; tools.

perturbación, *f.* perturbation, disturbance; agitation.—**perturbar**, *vt.* to perturb, disturb, unsettle; to confuse.

peruano, *n.* & *a.* Peruvian.

perversidad, *f.* perversity, wickedness.—**perversión**, *f.* perversion, perverting; depravity, wickedness.—**perverso**, *a.* perverse, wicked, depraved.—*n.* pervert.—**pervertido**, *a.* perverted.—*n.* pervert.—**pervertir**, *vti.* [39] to pervert; to corrupt.—*vri.* to become depraved.

pesa, *f.* weight (in scales, clocks).—*pl.* bar bells.—**pesadez**, *f.* heaviness; slowness; drowsiness; trouble, pain, fatigue.—**pesadilla**, *f.* nightmare.—**pesado**, *a.* heavy; deep, sound (sleep); stuffy (air, atmosphere); cumbersome; tedious, tiresome; dull; slow; clumsy; fat, corpulent; importunate, annoying.—*n.* bore, tease.—**pesadumbre**, *f.* grief, affliction, sorrow; heaviness.—**pésame**, *m.* condolence, sympathy.—**pesantez**, *f.* gravity; heaviness.—**pesar**, *vi.* to weigh, have weight; to be weighty or important; to cause regret, sorrow or repentance; to preponderate.—*vt.* to weigh; to examine, consider.—*m.* sorrow, grief, regret; repentance.—*a p. de*, in spite of, notwithstanding.—*a p. mío*, or *a mi p.*, in spite of me, against my wishes.—**pesaroso**, *a.* sorrowful, regretful; sorry, sad.

pesca, *f.* fishing; fishery; catch, fish caught.—**pescadería**, *f.* fish market.—**pescadero**, *n.* fishmonger.—**pescado**, *m.* fish (caught).—**pescador**, *n.* fisherman, fisher.—**pescar**, *vti.* [d] & *vii.* to fish; to catch fish.—*p. a la cacea*, to troll.—*vti.* to find or pick up; to catch in the act, surprise.

escozón, *m.* slap on the neck.—**pescuezo,** *m.* neck; throat.

esebre, *m.* manger; crib, rack.

esimismo, *m.* pessimism.—**pesimista,** *mf.* & *a.* pessimist(ic).—**pésimo,** *a.* very bad, very worst.

eso, *m.* weight, heaviness; weighing; importance; burden, load; judgment, good sense; peso, monetary unit.—*caerse de su p.,* to be self-evident; to go without saying.—*en p.,* suspended in the air; bodily; totally.—*p. gallo,* bantamweight.—*p. ligero* or *liviano,* lightweight.—*p. mediano ligero* or *welter,* welterweight.—*p. medio* or *mediano,* middleweight.—*p. mosca,* flyweight.—*p. pesada,* heavyweight; (fig.) heavyweight.—*p. pluma,* featherweight.

espunte, *m.* backstitching.

esquería, *f.* fishing, fishing trip.—**pesquero,** *a.* fishing.

esquisa, *f.* inquiry, investigation, search.

estaña, *f.* eyelash; (sewing) fringe, edging; (mech.) flange; index tab.—*quemarse las pestañas,* to burn the midnight oil.—**pestañear,** *vi.* to wink; to blink.—**pestañeo,** *m.* winking; blinking.

este, *f.* pest, plague, pestilence; epidemic; foul smell, stink; (coll.) excess, superabundance.—*p. bubónica,* bubonic plague.—*pl.* offensive words.—**pestilencia,** *f.* pest, plague, pestilence; foulness, stench.—**pestilente,** *a.* pestilent, foul.

estillo, *m.* door latch; bolt of a lock.

etaca, *f.* cigar case; (Am.) leather trunk or chest; (Am.) suitcase; tobacco pouch.

etalo, *m.* petal.

etardo, *m.* (artil.) petard; bomb.

etate, *m.* (Am.) sleeping mat; (coll.) luggage, baggage.—*liar el p.,* (coll.) to pack up and go.

etición, *f.* petition, request.

etimetre, *m.* fop, coxcomb, beau.

etirrojo, *m.* robin.

etreo, *a.* rocky; stony, of stone.

etróleo, *m.* crude oil, (fuel, gas or diesel) oil.—**petrolero,** *a.* oil.—*n.* person in the oil industry, oil man; incendiary.—*m.* (naut.) oil tanker.

etulancia, *f.* petulance; insolence; flippancy.—**petulante,** *a.* petulant, insolent, pert.

petunia, *f.* petunia.

pez, *m.* fish (not caught).—*f.* pitch, tar.—*p. espada,* swordfish.—*p. gordo,* (fam.) bigwig, big shot, big wheel, big cheese.—*p. volador,* flying fish.

pezón, *m.* stem of fruits; leaf stalk; nipple of a teat.

pezuña, *f.* hoof.

piada, *f.* chirping, peeping, peep.

piadoso, *a.* pious, godly; merciful.

piafar, *vi.* (of horses) to paw, to stamp.

pianista, *mf.* pianist.—**piano,** *m.* piano.—*p. de cola,* grand piano.—*p. de media cola,* baby grand.

piar, *vi.* to peep, chirp.

piara, *f.* herd (of swine).

pica, *f.* pike, lance; stonecutter's hammer.—*poner una p. en Flandes,* to achieve a triumph.

picacho, *m.* top, peak, summit.

picada, *f.* pricking, bite; (aer.) dive; diving.—**picadero,** *m.* riding school.—**picadillo,** *m.* hash, minced meat.—**picado,** *a.* decayed, rotten; (fam.) miffed.—*m.* grinding, mincing, chopping.—*p. con motor,* power dive.—*caer en p.,* to nosedive.—**picador,** *m.* horse-breaker; horseman armed with a goad in bullfights; chopping block; paper pricker.—**picadura,** *f.* pricking; pinking; puncture; bite; sting; pipe tobacco.—**picante,** *a.* pricking, piercing; biting; spicy, racy, highly seasoned.—*m.* piquancy, pungency, acrimony.—**picapleitos,** *m.* shyster, pettifogger; (coll.) litigious person.

picaporte, *m.* spring latch; latchkey; (Am.) door knocker.

picar, *vti.* [d] to prick, pierce, puncture; to sting, bite (as insects); to mince, chop, hash; (of birds) to peck; (of fish) to bite; to nibble, pick at; to spur, goad, incite; to pique, vex.—*vii.* to sting, bite (as insects) (of fish) to bite; to itch, burn; to scorch, burn (as the sun); (aer.) to dive.—*p. alto,* to aim high.—*p. con motor a toda marcha,* to power-dive.—*vri.* to be offended or piqued; to be motheaten; to stale, sour (as wine); to begin to rot (as fruit); to begin to decay (of teeth, etc.); (naut.) (of the sea) to get choppy.

picardía, *f.* knavery, roguery; malice; foulness; wanton trick, wantonness; lewdness.—**picaresco,** *a.*

roguish, knavish, picaresque.—**pícaro**, *a.* knavish, roguish; vile, low; mischievous; crafty, sly.—*n.* rogue, knave, rascal.—**picarón**, *n.* great rogue, rascal.

picazón, *f.* itching, itch.

pichón, *m.* young pigeon, squab.—*n.* (coll.) darling, dearest.

pico, *m.* beak or bill of a bird; sharp point; pick, pickaxe; spout; peak, top, summit; small balance of an account; (coll.) mouth; loquaciousness; (coll.) a lot of cash.—*costar un p.,* to be very expensive.—*p. de oro,* man of great eloquence.—*treinta y p.,* thirty odd.

picota, *f.* pillory, stocks; top, peak, point.

picotada, *f.,* —**picotazo**, *m.* blow with the beak, peck.—**picotear**, *vt.* & *vi.* to strike with a beak, to peck; (Am.) to cut into small pieces.

pictórico, *a.* pictorial.

pie, *m.* foot; leg, stand, support; base; foot, bottom (of a page); motive, occasion.—*al p.,* near, close to; at the foot.—*al p. de la letra,* literally, exactly.—*a p.,* on foot.—*a p. juntillas,* firmly; most emphatically.—*de p.,* standing.—*en p.* = DE PIE; pending, undecided.—*p. calcáneo, pie talo, p. equino,* clubfoot.—*p. de amigo,* prop, shore.—*p. de atletea,* (med.) athlete's foot.—*p. de fotografía,* caption.—*p. de imprenta,* imprint, printer's mark.

piedad, *f.* piety; mercy.

piedra, *f.* stone; cobblestone; (med.) gravel; hail.—*no dejar p. sobre p.,* to raze to the ground, to destroy entirely.—*p. angular,* cornerstone.—*p. de amolar* or *de afilar,* whetstone, grinding stone.—*p. falsa,* imitation (precious) stone.—*p. miliaria,* milestone.—*p. pómez,* pumice.

piel, *f.* skin; hide; leather; fur.—*p. de serpiente,* snakeskin.

pienso, *m.* fodder.

pierna, *f.* leg.—*dormir a p. suelta,* to sleep soundly.

pieza, *f.* piece; part (of a machine, etc.); bolt or roll of cloth; room (in a house); (theat.) play.—*de una p.,* solid, in one piece.—*p. de convicción,* piece of evidence.

pifia, *f.* miscue at billiards; error, blunder.

pigmento, *m.* pigment.

pigmeo, *a.* dwarfish.—*n.* pygmy, dwarf.

pignorar, *vt.* to pledge, give as security

pijama, *m.* or *f.* pajama.

pila, *f.* sink; (eccl.) font, holy water ba sin; pile, heap; stone trough or ba sin; (elec.) battery, cell.—*nombre d p.,* Christian or given name.—**pila** *m.* pillar, column, post; basin of fountain.

píldora, *f.* pill, pellet.—*p. para dormi* sleeping pill.

pileta, *f.* kitchen sink, washbowl, dish pan; swimming pool.

pillaje, *m.* pillage, plunder, maraud ing.—**pillar**, *vt.* to pillage, rifle, plun der; (coll.) to catch, grasp.—**pilleria** *f.* gang of rogues; piece of rasca ity.—**pillo**, *a.* roguish, knavish shrewd, sly.—*n.* knave, rogue, ra cal; petty thief.—**pilluelo**, *n.* littl rogue, urchin.

pilón, *m.* mortar (for pounding); lo (of sugar); watering trough; basin a fountain; rider, sliding weight (a balance).—*de p.,* to boot, in ac dition.

pilote, *m.* (eng.) pile.

pilot(e)ar, *vt.* to pilot.—**piloto**, *n* (naut., aer.) pilot, navigator.—*p.* pruebas,* (aer.) test pilot.

piltrafa, *f.* skinny flesh; hide pa ings.—*pl.* scraps of food.

pimentón, *m.* Cayenne or red peppe paprika.—**pimienta**, *f.* pepp (spice); black pepper.—*p. de J maica,* (bot.) allspice (tree).—*p. i glesa,* (cook.) allspice.—**pimient** *m.* pepper (vegetable).

pimpollo, *m.* rosebud; spruce, live youth; sprout, shoot.

pináculo, *m.* pinnacle, summit.

pinar, *m.* pine grove.

pincel, *m.* fine paintbrush.—**pinc lada**, *f.* stroke with a brush, touch.

pinchadiscos, *mf.* disk jockey.

pinchar, *vt.* to prick, punctur pierce.—**pinchazo**, *m.* prick, pun ture, stab.

pinche, *m.* kitchen boy.

pincho, *m.* thorn, prickle; goa skewer.

pingajo, *m.* (coll.) rag, tatter.—**ping** *m.* rag; (Am.) saddle horse.—*f* worthless clothes, duds.

pingüe, *a.* plentiful; fat, greasy, oily.

pingüino, *m.* penguin.

pino, *m.* pine.—**pinocha**, *f.* pin needle.

pin-pón, *m.* ping-pong.

pinta, *f.* spot, mark; appearance, a pect; drop; pint. (See Table.)

intada, f. (Am.) mackerel; guinea hen.

intar, vt. to paint; to picture; to describe, portray; to fancy, imagine.—vi. to begin to ripen; to show, give signs of.—vr. to make up (one's face).—**pintarrajear,** vt. (coll.) to daub.

intiparado, a. perfectly like, closely resembling; pat, fit.

into, a. (Am.) pinto, spotted.—**pintor,** n. painter.—p. de brocha gorda, house or sign painter; dauber.—**pintoresco,** a. picturesque.—**pintura,** f. painting; (art) picture, painting; color, paint, pigment; portrayal, description.—p. mural, mural.—p. rupestre, cave painting.—**pinturero,** a. (fam.) fashion-conscious.—n. (fam.) show-off.

inzas, f. tweezers, pincers; claws (of lobsters, etc.).

iña, f. pineapple; pine cone; cluster, gathering; game of pool.—**piñón,** m. the edible nut of the nut pine; (mech.) pinion.

io, a. pious; mild, merciful.—m. peeping of chickens.

ojo, m. louse.—**piojoso,** a. lousy.

onero, n. (neol.) pioneer.

pa, f. cask, butt, hogshead; fruit seed; tobacco pipe.—p. ceremonial, peace pipe.—**pipote,** m. keg.

que, m. pique, resentment.—a p. de, in danger of, on the point of.—echar a p., to sink (a ship).—irse a p., (naut.) to founder, sink; fall.

queta, f. pickaxe; mason's hammer.

quete, m. pricking; sting; small hole; stake, picket; (mil.) picket.

ra, f. pyre, funeral pile.

ragua, f. dugout, canoe.

rámide, f. pyramid.

rata, m. pirate.—p. aéreo, (aer.) hijacker.—p. informático, (comput.) hacker.—**piratear,** vi. to pirate.—**piratería,** f. piracy.—p. aéreo, (aer.) hijacking.—p. informático, (comput.) hacking.

ropear, vt. & vi. (coll.) to flatter; to compliment.—**piropo,** m. (coll.) flattery; compliment.

rulí, m. lollipop.

sada, f. footstep; footprint; treading.—**pisapapeles,** m. paperweight.—**pisar,** vt. to tread on, trample, step on; to press; to press on; to stamp on the ground.

saverde, m. (coll.) fop, coxcomb, dude.

piscina, f. swimming pool; fishpond.

Piscis, m. (astr.) Pisces.

piscolabis, m. (coll.) snack.

piso, m. floor; pavement, flooring; loft, flat, apartment; ground level; story; (Am.) fee for pasturage rights.—p. bajo, ground floor, street floor, first floor.—p. principal, primer piso, second floor; (G.B.) first floor.—**pisotear,** vt. to trample, tread under foot.—**pisotón,** m. heavy step or stamp of the foot.

pista, f. trail, track, trace, clue; race track; race course; circus ring; dancing floor; tennis court; (aer.) runway; landing strip.—p. cubierta, indoor track.—p. de aterrizaje, (aer.) runway.—p. de atletismo, athletics track.—p. de baile, dance floor.—p. de esquí, ski slope.—p. de patinaje, skating rink.

pistilo, m. (bot.) pistil.

pistola, f. pistol.—p. pulverizadora, spray gun.—**pistolera,** f. holster.—**pistoletazo,** m. pistol shot.

pistón, m. (mech.) piston; (mus.) piston of a brass instrument.

pita, f. agave plant, maguey; string, cord.

pitada, f. blow of a whistle.

pitanza, f. pittance; (coll.) daily food; salary.

pitar, vi. to blow a whistle; to hiss.—**pitazo,** m. sound or blast of a whistle.

pitillera, f. cigarette case.—**pitillo,** m. cigarette.

pito, m. whistle; (coll.) cigarette.—no me importa or no se me da or me importa un p., (coll.) I don't care a bit.—no tocar pitos en, to have no part in.

pitón, m. (of deer, etc.) horn just starting to grow; spout, nozzle; python.

pivote, m. (mech.) king pin; pivot.

piyama, m. or f. = PIJAMA.

pizarra, f. slate; blackboard.—**pizarrín,** m. slate pencil.—**pizarrón,** m. blackboard.

pizca, f. (coll.) mite, speck, sprinkling, crumb, particle.

placa, f. plate; badge insignia; plaque, tablet.—p. de matrícula, license plate.

placebo, m. placebo.

pláceme, m. congratulation.

placentero, a. joyful, pleasant.—**placer,** vti. [30] to please.—m. pleasure.

placero, a. pertaining to the marketplace.—n. seller at a market; gadder.

plácido, a. placid, quiet, calm.

plaga, *f.* plague; calamity; scourge; pest.—**plagar**, *vti.* [b] to plague, infest.—*vri.* (de) to be full of, infested with.

plagiar, *vt.* to plagiarize; (Am.) to kidnap.—**plagiario**, *n.* & *a.* plagiarist; plagiarizing.—**plagio**, *m.* plagiarism; (Am.) kidnapping.

plan, *m.* plan; design, scheme.—*p. de estudios*, curriculum, syllabus.

plana, *f.* page; copy; level ground, plain; (mason.) trowel.—*enmendar la p. a*, to find fault with, criticize.—*p. mayor*, (mil.) staff.—*primera p.*, front page.

plancha, *f.* plate, sheet; slab; flatiron, iron; (coll.) blunder, boner; (naut.) gangplank; photographic plate.—*p. caliente*, (cook.) steam table.—*p. de vapor*, steam iron.—**planchador**, *n.* ironer.—**planchar**, *vt.* to iron, to press.—*p. el asiento*, (fam.) to be a wallflower.

planeador, *m.* (aer.) glider.—**planear**, *vt.* & *vi.* to plan, design.—*vi.* (aer.) to glide.

planeta, *m.* planet.—**planetario**, *a.* planetary.—*m.* planetarium.

planicie, *f.* plain.

planilla, *f.* (Am.) list; payroll; (Mex.) list of candidates; ticket; (Cuba) application form, blank.

plano, *a.* plane; level; smooth, even.—*m.* plan, blueprint; map; flat (of a sword, etc.); (geom.) plane; (aer.) plane, wing.—*de p.*, openly, clearly; flatly.—*primer p.*, foreground.

planta, *f.* sole of the foot; (bot.) plant; (eng.) plan, horizontal projection; top view; floor plan; plant, works; site of a building.—*p. baja*, first floor, ground floor, street floor.—**plantación**, *f.* plantation; planting.—**plantar**, *vt.* (agr.) to plant; to erect, set up, fix upright; to strike (a blow); to set, put, place; to leave in the lurch, disappoint; to jilt.—*vr.* (coll.) to stand upright; to stop, halt, balk.

plantear, *vt.* to plan, try; to put into action; to state or tackle (a problem); to raise (an issue).

plantel, *m.* nursery, nursery garden; establishment, plant; educational institution.

plantilla, *f.* first sole, insole (shoes); model, pattern; roster, staff; plan, design.

plantío, *m.* planting; plot, bed.

plañidero, *a.* mournful, weeping, moaning.—**plañido**, *m.* moan, lamentation, crying.—**plañir**, *vii.* [41] to lament, grieve; to whimper.

plasma, *m.* plasma.—**plasmar**, *vt.* to mold, shape.

plasta, *f.* soft mass; anything flattened; (coll.) anything poorly wrought.

plasticidad, *f.* plasticity.—**plástico**, *a.* & *m.* plastic.

plata, *f.* silver; silver coin; (Am.) money.—*en p.*, in plain language.

plataforma, *f.* platform.—*p. de lanzamiento*, launching pad.—*p. espacial*, space platform.

platal, *m.* great quantity of money, great wealth.

platanal, **platanar**, *m.* banana grove or plantation.—**plátano**, *m.* banana (plant and fruit).

platea, *f.* (theat.) orchestra; pit.

platear, *vt.* to silver, plate with silver.—**platería**, *f.* silversmith's shop or trade.—**platero**, *m.* silversmith, jeweler.

plática, *f.* talk, chat, conversation; address, lecture; sermon.—**platicar**, *vii.* [d] to converse, talk, chat.

platillo, *m.* saucer; pan (of a balance); cymbal.

platina, *f.* platen; tape deck; slide (of microscope).

platino, *m.* platinum.

plato, *m.* dish, plate; dinner course; (tiro) clay pigeon; (béisbol) home plate.—*p. de entrada*, side dish.—*p. fuerte*, main course.—*p. hondo* or *sopero*, soup dish.—*p. llano*, *liso* or *playo*, dinner plate.

platónico, *a.* Platonic.—**platonismo**, *m.* Platonism.

plausible, *a.* plausible.

playa, *f.* beach, shore.

plaza, *f.* plaza, square; marketplace; (com.) emporium, market; room, space; office, position, employment.—*p. de toros*, bull ring, arena.—*p. fuerte*, stronghold.—*p. mayor*, main square.—*sentar p.*, to enlist.

plazo, *m.* term, time, date, day of payment; credit.—*a corto p.*, short term.—*a plazos*, in installments, on credit.

plazoleta, **plazuela**, *f.* small square.

pleamar, *f.* high water, high tide.

plebe, *f.* common people, populace.—**plebeyo**, *n.* & *a.* plebeian.—**plebi-**

cito, *m.* (pol.) plebiscite; referendum.

legable, plegadizo, *a.* pliable, folding.—**plegadura,** *f.* plait, fold; plaiting, folding, doubling; crease.—**plegar,** *vti.* [1-b] to fold; to plait; to crease.—*vri.* to fold; to bend; to submit, yield.

legaria, *f.* prayer, supplication.

leitear, *vi.* to plead, litigate; to wrangle.—**pleitista,** *mf.* litigious person.—*a.* litigious.—**pleito,** *m.* lawsuit; litigation; proceedings in a case; dispute, contest, debate, strife.—*poner p. (a),* to sue, bring suit (against).

lenario, *a.* complete, full; (law) plenary.—**plenilunio,** *m.* full moon.—**plenipotenciario,** *n.* & *a.* plenipotentiary.—**plenitud,** *f.* plenitude, fullness, abundance.—**pleno,** *a.* full, complete; joint (session).

letina, *f.* platen; tape deck.

leuresia, *f.* pleurisy.

llego, *m.* sheet (of paper).—*p. de condiciones,* specifications; tender, bid.—**pliegue,** *m.* fold, plait; crease.

lisar, *vt.* to pleat, plait.

lomada, *f.* plumb, lead weight, plummet.—**plomería,** *f.* lead roofing; leadware shop; plumbing.—**plomero,** *n.* plumber.—**plomizo,** *a.* leaden; lead-colored.—**plomo,** *m.* lead (metal); piece of lead; plummet; bullet; (coll.) dull person, bore.—*andar con pies de p.,* to proceed with the utmost caution.—*a p.,* true, plumb.—*caer a p.,* to fall down flat.

luma, *f.* feather; plume; quill; writing pen; penmanship; (fig.) style.—*al correr de la,* or *a vuela p.,* written in haste.—*p. atómica,* ball-point pen.—*p. estilográfica, p. fuente,* fountain pen.—**plumaje,** *m.* plumage; plume, crest.—**plumazo,** *m.* pen stroke.—**plumero,** *m.* feather duster.—**plumífero,** *m.* ski jacket.—**plumón,** *m.* down, feather bed.—**plumoso,** *a.* feathered.

lural, *m.* & *a.* plural.—**pluralidad,** *f.* plurality.—**pluralizar,** *vti.* [a] to pluralize.—**pluriempleo,** *m.* moonlighting.—**plurilingüe,** *a.* multilingual.

lus, *m.* (mil.) extra pay; bonus; extra.

•NB, *m.* (**Producto Nacional Bruto**) GNP.

oblación, *f.* population; populating; city, town, village.—**poblado,** *a.* populated, inhabited.—*m.* inhabited place, town, settlement.—**poblador,** *n.* settler.—**poblar,** *vti.* [12] & *vii.* to populate, settle; to inhabit; to stock; to breed fast.—*vri.* to bud, leaf.

pobre, *a.* poor; needy; barren; pitiable, unfortunate.—*mf.* poor person; beggar.—**pobrete,** *m.* poor man.—**pobreza,** *f.* poverty; need; scarcity, dearth.

pochismo, *m.* (Mex.) (derog.) expression in Spanish (used by Latinos in the U.S.).

pocilga, *f.* pigsty, pigpen; dirty place.

pocillo, *m.* chocolate cup.

pócima, *f.,* **poción,** *m.* drink, draft; potion.

poco, *a.* little; scanty, limited; small.—*pl.* few, some.—*m.* a little, a bit, a small quantity.—*adv.* little, in a small degree; a short time.—*a p.,* immediately; shortly afterward.—*dentro de p.,* in a short time, soon.—*de p. más o menos,* of little account.—*p. a p.,* little by little, gradually, slowly.—*p. después,* shortly afterward.—*p. más o menos,* more or less.—*por p.,* almost, nearly.

poda, *f.* pruning, lopping; pruning season.—**podadera,** *fpl.* pruning shears.—**podar,** *vt.* to prune, lop, trim.

podenco, *m.* hound (dog).

poder, *vti.* & *vii.* [31] to be able; can; may.—*a. más no p.,* or *hasta más no p.,* to the utmost, to the limit.—*no p. con,* not to be able to bear, manage, etc., to be no match for.—*no p. menos de,* to be necessary; cannot but, cannot fail to.—*puede que venga,* (or *que no venga*), he may come (or, he may not come).—*m.* power; faculty, authority; might; proxy; (law) power or letter of attorney.—**poderío,** *m.* power, might; dominion, jurisdiction; wealth.—**poderoso,** *a.* powerful, mighty; wealthy.

podre, *m.* pus; rotten substance.—**podredumbre,** *f.* decay; pus; putrid matter; corruption.—**podridero, podrimento,** *m.* = PUDRIDERO, PUDRIMENTO.—**podrido,** *pp.* of PODRIR, PUDRIR.—**podrir,** *vti.,* [33] *vii.* & *vri.* = PUDRIR.

poema, *m.* poem.—**poesía,** *f.* poetry; poetical composition, poem.—

poeta, *m.* poet, bard.—**poética**, *f.* poetics.—**poético**, *a.* poetic(al).—**poetisa**, *f.* poetess.

pogromo, *m.* pogrom.

polaco, *a.* Polish.—*m.* Polish language.—*n.* Pole.

polaina, *f.* legging.

polar, *a.* polar.—**polaridad**, *f.* polarity.

polea, *f.* pulley; tackle block, block pulley.

polen, *m.* pollen.

policía, *f.* police.—*mf.* policeman (-woman).—*p. de tráfico* or *de tránsito*, traffic police, highway patrol.—*p. secreta*, secret police.—**policíaco, policial**, *a.* pertaining to police, police.

políglota, *a.* & *mf.* multilingual (person).

polígono, *m.* polygon; (artil.) practice ground.

polilla, *f.* moth; clothes moth.

polinesi(an)o, *n.* & *a.* Polynesian.

polio, *f.* polio.—**poliomielitis**, *f.* poliomyelitis.

polista, *mf.* polo player.

política, *f.* policy; politics.—**politicastro**, *n.* petty politican.—**político**, *a.* political; polite; suave.—*n.* politician.—*pariente p.*, in-law.—**politiquería**, *f.* (Am.) low politics; political talk and doings, political trash.—**politiquero**, *n.* (Am.) one that indulges in, or is fond of, common politics; political busybody.

póliza, *f.* (com.) policy; scrip; check, draft; voucher, certificate.

polizón, *m.* stowaway; vagrant.

polizonte, *m.* (coll.) cop, policeman.

polla, *f.* pullet; (cards) pool, (coll.) girl.—**pollada**, *f.* flock of young fowls; hatch, covey.—**pollera**, *f.* chicken roost, chicken coop; gocart; (Am.) skirt; hooped petticoat.—**pollería**, *f.* poultry shop or market.—**pollero**, *m.* poulterer; poultry yard.

pollino, *n.* donkey, ass.

pollo, *m.* chicken; (coll.) young person.—**polluelo**, *n.* little chicken, chick.

polo, *m.* (geog. & astr.) pole; (sports) polo.—*p. de agua,* water polo.

polonés, *a.* Polish.—*f.* polonaise.

polución, *f.* (med.) ejaculation, pollution.—*p. nocturna,* nocturnal emission.

polvareda, *f.* cloud of dust; (fig.) scandal.—**polvera**, *f.* (cosmetic) powde[r] box.—**polvo**, *m.* dust; powder.—*p[olvos de]* toilet powder.—*en p.,* powdered.—*p. de hornear,* baking powder.—**pól[vora]**, *f.* gunpowder.—**polvorear**, *vt[.]* to powder, sprinkle powder on.—**polvoriento**, *a.* dusty.—**polvorín**, *m[.]* (mil.) powder magazine; (fig.) powder keg, tinderbox.

pomada, *f.* pomade.

pómez.—*piedra p.,* pumice.

pomo, *m.* small bottle, flask, flagon; pommel; doorknob.

pompa, *f.* pomp, ostentation; bubble.—**pomposidad**, *f.* pomposity, pompousness.—**pomposo**, *a.* pompous, turgid; magnificent, splendid; inflated.

pómulo, *m.* cheek bone.

ponche, *m.* punch.—**ponchera**, *f.* punch bowl.

poncho, *m.* (Am.) poncho; military coat.—*a.* lazy, soft; heedless.

ponderación, *f.* consideration, deliberation; exaggeration.—**ponderar**, *vt.* to weigh, ponder, consider; to exaggerate; to praise highly.

poner, *vti.* [32–49] to put, place, lay; to dispose, arrange, set (as the table); to impose, keep (as order); to oblige, compel; to wager, stake; to appoint, put in charge; to write, set down; to lay eggs; to cause; to become or turn (red, angry, etc.).—*p. al corriente,* to inform.—*p. al día,* to bring up to date.—*p. como nuevo,* to humiliate, reprimand or treat harshly, dress down.—*p. coto a,* to stop, put a limit to.—*p. de manifiesto,* to make public.—*p. en claro,* to make clear; to clear up.—*p. en duda,* to question, doubt.—*p. en práctica,* to start doing, get (a project, etc.) underway.—*p. en ridículo,* to make ridiculous.—*p. en vigor,* to enforce.—*vri.* to apply oneself to; to set about; to put on (as a garment); to become, get (as wet, angry, dirty); to set (as the sun); to reach, get to, arrive.—*p. a,* to begin to, start to.—*p. a cubierto,* to shelter oneself from danger.—*p. colorado,* to blush.—*p. de acuerdo,* to reach an agreement.—*p. en camino,* to set out, start, take off.—*p. en pie,* to stand up.—*p. en razón,* to become reasonable.

poniente, *m.* west.

pontaje, pontazgo, *m.* bridge toll.

pontifical, *a.* pontifical, papal.—**pontifice,** *m.* pontiff.—*Sumo Pontifice,* Pope.

pontón, *m.* pontoon.

ponzoña, *f.* poison, venom.—**ponzoñoso,** *a.* poisonous.

popa, *f.* (naut.) poop, stern.

popelina, *f.* (neol.) poplin.

populachero, *a.* vulgar, common.—*n.* rabble rouser.—**populacho,** *m.* populace, mob, rabble.—**popular,** *a.* popular.—**popularidad,** *f.* popularity.—**popularizar,** *vti.* [a] to popularize, make popular.—*vri.* to become popular.—**populoso,** *a.* populous.

popurrí, *m.* (mus.) medley; potpourri; mess, confusion.

poquito, *a.* very little; weak of body and mind.—*m.* a wee bit.—*a poquitos,* little by little; a little at a time.

por, *prep.* by; for; through; as; across; about, nearly; per; after, for; for the sake of; in behalf of, on account of; in order to; by way of; in the name of; without, not yet, to be.—*p. cuanto,* inasmuch as, whereas.—*p. docena,* by the dozen.—*p. escrito,* in writing.—*p. la mañana (tarde, noche),* in the morning (afternoon, evening).—*p. más que,* or *p. mucho que,* however much, no matter how much; notwithstanding.—*p. poco,* almost.—*p. qué,* why.—*¿p. qué?* why?—*p. si,* or *p. si acaso,* in case; if by chance.—*p. sí o p. no,* to be sure; to be on the safe side.—*p. supuesto,* of course.

porcelana, *f.* porcelain; chinaware.

porcentaje, *m.* percentage.

porción, *f.* portion, part; lot.

porche, *m.* porch, portico; covered walk.

pordiosero, *n.* beggar.

porfía, *f.* tussle, dispute, competition, obstinate quarrel.—*a p.,* in competition; insistently.—**porfiado,** *a.* obstinate, stubborn, persistent; importunate.—**porfiar,** *vi.* to contend, persist, insist; to importune.

pormenor, *m.* detail, particular.—**pormenorizar,** *vti.* [a] to detail, itemize.

pornografía, *f.* pornography.

poro, *m.* pore.—**porosidad,** *f.* porosity.—**poroso,** *a.* porous.

porque, *conj.* because, for, as; in order that.—**porqué,** *m.* reason, motive.

porquería, *f.* filth, squalor; vile, dirty act; nasty trick; trifle, worthless thing.—**porquerizo, porquero,** *n.* swineherd.

porra, *f.* bludgeon, club, truncheon; maul.—**porrazo,** *m.* blow, knock; fall; thump.

porta, *f.* porthole.

portaaviones, *m.* aircraft carrier.

portada, *f.* portal, porch; frontispiece; cover (of a magazine, etc.); title page.

portador, *n.* bearer, carrier; (com.) holder, bearer.

portaestandarte, *mf.* color guard, standard bearer.

portaféretro, *m.* pallbearer.

portal, *m.* porch, vestibule; portico.

portalámpara, *m.* (elec.) socket; lamp holder.

portalápiz, *m.* pencil case; pencil holder.

portalibros, *m.* book strap.

portalón, *m.* gangway.

portamonedas, *m.* purse.

portapliegos, *m.* large portfolio.

portaplumas, *m.* penholder.

portañuela, *f.* (Am.) fly of trousers.

portar, *vt.* to carry (as arms).—*vr.* to behave, act.—**portátil,** *a.* portable.—*s.* (comput.) laptop.—**portavoz,** *mf.* spokesman, representative; loudspeaker, megaphone.

portazgo, *m.* toll.

portazo, *m.* slam of a door.

porte, *m.* cost of carriage; freight; postage; bearing (of persons).—**portear,** *vt.* to carry or convey for a price.

portento, *m.* prodigy, wonder; portent.—**portentoso,** *a.* prodigious, marvelous.

porteño, *a.* & *n.* of or from Buenos Aires.

portería, *f.* porter's lodge or box; janitor's quarters.—**portero,** *n.* gatekeeper, porter; superintendent, janitor.—**portezuela,** *f.* (vehicles) door.

pórtico, *m.* portico; porch.

portilla, *f.* opening, passage; (naut.) porthole.—**portillo,** *m.* opening, gap, breach; wicket; gate; pass between hills.—**portón,** *m.* front door or gate.

portorriqueño, *n.* & *a.* Porto Rican.

portugués, *n.* & *a.* Portuguese.—*m.* Portuguese language.

porvenir, *m.* future, time to come.

posada, *f.* inn; lodging house; lodging.—**posadero,** *n.* innkeeper.—*f. pl.* buttocks.

posar, *vi.* (art) to pose.—*vt.* to lay down.—*vr.* to land, alight, sit (on).—**posavasos,** *m.* coaster (for drinks).

posdata, *f.* postscript.

poseedor, *n.* possessor, holder, owner.—**poseer,** *vti.* [e] to possess, own; to hold; to master (an art, language, etc.).—**posesión,** *f.* possession; ownership; property.—**posesionar,** *vt.* to give possession; to install, induct.—*vr.* to take possession.—**posesivo,** *n.* & *a.* (gram.) possessive.—**poseso,** *ppi.* of POSEER.—*a.* possessed (by evil spirits).

posfecha, *f.* postdate.—**posfechar,** *vt.* to postdate.

posguerra, *f.* postwar period.

posibilidad, *f.* possibility.—**posibilitar,** *vt.* to render possible, facilitate.—**posible,** *a.* possible.—*m. pl.* personal means.

posición, *f.* position; placing, placement; standing, status.

positivo, *a.* positive, certain; absolute, real; matter-of-fact; (math., elec., photog.) positive.

posma, *f.* (coll.) sluggishness, sloth, dullness.—*n.* (coll.) dull, sluggish person.

poso, *m.* sediment, dregs.

posponer, *vti.* [32–49] (a) to postpone, put off, defer; to subordinate; to put after.—**posposición,** *f.* postponement; subordination.—**pospuesto,** *ppi.* of POSPONER.

postal, *a.* postal.—*giro p.,* money order.—*f.* post card.

postdata, *f.* = POSDATA.

poste, *m.* post, pillar.—*p. de flagelación,* whipping post.—*p. de guía,* signpost.—*p. ilustrada,* picture postcard.—*p. indicador,* road sign.

postergación, *f.* delaying; leaving behind.—**postergar,** *vti.* [b] to delay, postpone; to disregard someone's rights; to hold back, to pass over.

posteridad, *f.* posterity.—**posterior,** *a.* posterior, rear; later, subsequent.

postguerra, *f.* = POSGUERRA.

postigo, *m.* wicket; peep window; shutter.

postilla, *f.* scab on wounds.

postizo, *a.* artificial, not natural; false (teeth).—*m.* false hair.

postmeridiano, *a.* postmeridian (p.m.).

postración, *f.* prostration, proneness; kneeling; dejection.—**postrar,** *vt.* to prostrate; to weaken, exhaust.—*vr.* to prostrate oneself, kneel down; to be exhausted.

postre, *m.* dessert.—*a la p.,* at last.

postrer(o), *a.* last; hindmost.

postulado, *m.* postulate.—**postular,** *vt.* to postulate; to nominate a candidate.—*vr.* to become a candidate.

postura, *f.* posture, position, stance; bid (auction); wager, bet; egglaying.—*p. relajada,* slouch.

potable, *a.* potable, drinkable.

potaje, *m.* pottage; porridge; medley.

potasa, *f.* potash.

pote, *m.* pot, jar.

potencia, *f.* power; potency; dominion; faculty of the mind; power, strong nation; force, strength.—*en p.,* potentially.—**potencial,** *a.* & *m.* potential.—**potentado,** *m.* potentate.—**potente,** *a.* powerful.—**potestad,** *f.* power, dominion, jurisdiction; potentate.—**potestativo,** *a.* optional.

potingue, *m.* (coll.) medicinal concoction.

potra, *f.* filly; hernia.—**potranca,** *f.* filly.—**potrero,** *m.* pasture ground; cattle ranch.—**potril,** *m.* pasture for young horses.—**potro,** *m.* colt, foal.

póstumo, *m.* posthumous.

poyo, *m.* stone seat against a wall.

poza, *f.* puddle.—**pozo,** *m.* (water) well.—*p. de inspección,* manhole.—*p. séptico, negro,* or *ciego,* septic tank.

práctica, *f.* practice; habit; practicing; exercise; manner, method, routine.—**practicable,** *a.* practicable, feasible.—**practicante,** *a.* practicing.—*mf.* nurse; student teacher; churchgoer.—**practicar,** *vti.* [d] to practice; to make; to perform, do, put in execution; to practice, go in for.—**práctico,** *a.* practical; skillful, experienced.—*m.* (naut.) harbor pilot.

pradera, *f.* prairie, meadow, meadowland.—**prado,** *m.* lawn; field, meadow; pasture.

preámbulo, *m.* preamble; (coll.) evasion.

precario, *a.* precarious.

precaución, *f.* precaution.—**precaver,** *vt.* to prevent, obviate.—*vr.* (de) to guard, be on one's guard (against).

precedencia, *f.* precedence, priority;

seniority.—**precedente**, *a.* prior, precedent.—*m.* precedent.—**preceder**, *vt.* to precede; to be superior to.

precepto, *m.* precept.—**preceptor**, *n.* teacher, tutor.

preciar, *vt.* to value, price, appraise.—*vr.* (de) to boast, brag (about); to take pride, glory (in).

precintar, *vt.* to strap, hoop, bind; to seal.

precio, *m.* price; importance, worth.—*p. de catálogo* or *tarifa*, list price.—**preciosidad**, *f.* worth, preciousness; rich or beautiful object, [a] beauty.—**precioso**, *a.* precious; beautiful.

precipicio, *m.* precipice, chasm; violent fall.

precipitación, *f.* rash haste, unthinking hurry; (chem.) precipitation.—*p. radiactiva*, nuclear fallout.—**precipitado**, *a.* headlong; hurried, hasty.—*m.* (chem.) precipitate.—**precipitar**, *vt.* to precipitate; to rush, hasten.—*vr.* to throw oneself headlong; to rush, hurry.

precisar, *vt.* to fix, set, determine; to compel, oblige; to be urgent or necessary.—**precisión**, *f.* necessity; compulsion; preciseness, exactness; precision, accuracy.—**preciso**, *a.* necessary; indispensable; precise, exact, accurate; distinct, clear; concise.

preconizar, *vti.* [a] to praise, eulogize.

predecesor, *n.* predecessor.

predecir, *vti.* [14–49] to foretell, predict, forecast.

predestinación, *f.* predestination.—**predestinar**, *vt.* to predestine, foreordain.

predeterminar, *vt.* to predetermine.

prédica, predicación, *f.* preaching; sermon.—**predicado**, *m.* predicate.—**predicador**, *n.* preacher.—**predicar**, *vti.* & *vii.* [d] to preach; to praise.

predicción, *f.* prediction.—**predicho**, *ppi.* of PREDECIR.

predilección, *f.* predilection.—**predilecto**, *a.* preferred, favorite.

predisponer, *vti.* [32–49] to prejudice, predispose; to prearrange.—**predisposición**, *f.* predisposition; prejudice.—**predispuesto**, *ppi.* of PREDISPONER.—*a.* predisposed, biased, inclined.

predominante, *a.* predominant, prevailing.—**predominar**, *vt.* & *vi.* to predominate, prevail; to rise above,

overlook, command.—**predominio**, *m.* predominance, superiority.

prefabricado, *a.* prefabricated.

prefacio, *m.* preface, prologue.

preferencia, *f.* preference.—**preferente**, *a.* preferential; preferring; preferable.—**preferible**, *a.* preferable.—**preferir**, *vti.* [39] to prefer.

prefijar, *vt.* to predesignate, set beforehand.—**prefijo**, *a.* prefixed.—*m.* prefix.

pregón, *m.* hawker's cry.—**pregonar**, *vt.* to hawk, proclaim, cry out; to make known.—**pregonero**, *n.* hawker, town crier.

pregunta, *f.* question, query.—**preguntar**, *vt.* & *vi.* to ask, question, inquire.—*vr.* to wonder.—**preguntón**, *a.* inquisitive.

prejuicio, *m.* prejudice, bias.—**prejuzgar**, *vti.* [b] to prejudge.

prelación, *f.* preference.

prelado, *m.* prelate.

preliminar, *a.* preliminary.—*m.* preliminary; protocol.

preludio, *m.* introduction; (mus.) prelude.

prematuro, *a.* premature; untimely; unripe.

premeditación, *f.* premeditation, willfulness.—**premeditar**, *vt.* to premeditate.

premiar, *vt.* to reward, remunerate; to award a prize.—**premio**, *m.* prize; reward; recompense; (com.) premium, interest.—*primer p.*, blue ribbon.

premisa, *f.* premise.

premura, *f.* urgency, pressure, haste.

prenda, *f.* pledge, token; piece of jewelry; garment; person dearly loved.—*pl.* endowments, natural gifts, talents.—*soltar p.*, to commit oneself.—**prendarse** *vr.* (de), to fall in love with, take a great liking (to).

prendedor, *m.* breastpin; brooch; safety pin; tiepin.—**prender**, *vti.* [49] to seize, grasp, catch, apprehend; to fasten, clasp.—*p. fuego a*, to set on fire.—*p. la luz*, to turn on the light.—*vii.* to take root; to catch or take fire.—**prendería**, *f.* pawnshop.—**prendero**, *m.* pawnbroker.

prensa, *f.* press; printing press.—**prensar**, *vt.* to press.

preñada, *a.* pregnant (esp. of animals).—*preñado de*, full of.—**preñez**, *f.* pregnancy.

preocupación, *f.* worry, preoccupation, concern.—**preocupar,** *vt.* to worry, to preoccupy.—*vr.* to worry.

preparación, *f.* preparation; preparing; compound; medicine.—*p. de datos,* (comput.) data preparation.—**preparar,** *vt.* to prepare, make ready.—*vr.* to be prepared, get ready, make preparations.—**preparativo,** *a.* preparatory.—*m. pl.* preparations, arrangements.—**preparatorio,** *a.* preparatory.

preponderancia, *f.* preponderance, sway.—**preponderar,** *vi.* to have control; to prevail.

preposición, *f.* preposition.

prepotencia, *f.* predominance.—**prepotente,** *a.* predominant.

prerrogativa, *f.* prerogative.

presa, *f.* capture, seizure; (mil.) booty; quarry, prey; (water) dam; morsel; tusk, fang; claw.

presagiar, *vt.* to presage, foretell.—**presagio,** *m.* presage, omen, prognostication.

presbiteriano, *n.* & *a.* Presbyterian.—**presbítero,** *m.* priest; presbyter.

prescindir, *vi.* (de) to dispense (with), do (without); to set aside, ignore, omit.

prescribir, *vti.* [49] to prescribe, specify.—**prescrito,** *ppi.* of PRESCRIBIR.

presencia, *f.* presence; appearance.—*p. de ánimo,* coolness, presence of mind.—**presenciar,** *vt.* to witness, see; to attend.—**presentación,** *f.* presentation, exhibition; personal introduction.—**presentador, presentadora,** *n.* presenter; (TV) master or mistress of ceremonies, host or hostess; (TV) anchorman or anchorwoman.—**presentar,** *vt.* to present; to put on (a program, etc.); to display, show.—*vr.* to appear, present oneself, report; to turn up; to offer one's services.—**presente,** *a.* present, current.—*hacer p.,* to state; to remind of, call attention.—*tener p.,* to bear in mind.—*m.* present, gift; present (time).

presentimiento, *m.* presentiment; misgiving.—**presentir,** *vti.* [39] to have a presentiment of; to forebode, predict.

preservación, *f.* preservation, conservation.—**preservar,** *vt.* to preserve, guard, keep, save.—**preservativo,** *m.* contraceptive, condom.

presidencia, *f.* presidency; presidential chair; chairmanship; presidential term.—**presidencial,** *a.* presidential.—**presidente,** *n.* president, chairman; any presiding officer.—*p. del tribunal,* chief justice.

presidiario, *m.* convict.—*p. fidedigno* trusty.—**presidio,** *m.* penitentiary.

presidir, *vt.* to preside over, or at; to govern, determine.

presilla, *f.* loop, fastener; clip.

presión, *f.* pressure.—*p. de inflado,* tire pressure.—*p. sanguínea,* blood pressure.—**presionar,** *vt.* to press, urge.

preso, *ppi.* of PRENDER.—*a.* arrested, imprisoned.—*n.* prisoner; convict.

prestación, *f.* provision.—*pl.* benefits, assistance.—*p. por desempleo,* unemployment compensation.

prestamista, *mf.* money lender.—**préstamo,** *m.* loan.

prestar, *vt.* to lend, loan.—*p. atención,* to pay attention.—*p. ayuda,* to help.—*p. un servicio,* to do a favor.—*vr.* to offer oneself or itself; to adapt oneself or itself.

presteza, *f.* quickness, promptness.—**prestidigitación,** *f.* legerdemain, sleight of hand; jugglery.—**prestidigitador,** *n.* juggler; magician.

prestigio, *m.* prestige; influence; good name.—**prestigioso,** *a.* renowned, well-reputed.

presto, *a.* quick, swift, prompt; ready, prepared.—*adv.* soon; quickly.

presumible, *a.* presumable.—**presumido,** *a.* presumptuous, conceited.—**presumir,** *vti.* [49] to presume, surmise, conjecture.—*vii.* (de) to boast (of being), claim (to be); to be conceited.—**presunción,** *f.* presumption, conjecture; presumptuousness, conceit.—**presunto,** *ppi.* of PRESUMIR.—*a.* presumed.—**presuntuosidad,** *f.* presumptuousness.—**presuntuoso,** *a.* presumptuous, conceited.

presuponer, *vti.* [32–49] to presuppose; to estimate; to budget.—**presuposición,** *f.* presupposition.—**presupuestario,** *a.* budgetary.—**presupuesto,** *ppi.* of PRESUPONER.—*m.* budget, estimate.—*a.* presupposed; estimated.

presuroso, *a.* prompt, quick.

pretender, *vti.* [49] to pretend; to aspire to; to seek, solicit; to try; to intend; to court.—*p. decir,* to mean, be driv ing at.—**pretensión,** f. pretension, claim; presumption.—**pretenso,** ppi. of PRETENDER.

preterir, vti. [50] to ignore, overlook.—**pretérito,** m. & a. preterit, past.

pretextar, vt. to give as a pretext.—**pretexto,** m. pretext, pretense, excuse.

pretil, m. railing, battlement.

pretina, f. girdle, waistband; belt; fly (of trousers).

prevalecer, vii. [3] to prevail.

prevención, f. prevention; foresight; warning; prejudice; police station.—**prevenir,** vti. [45] to prevent, avoid; to arrange, make ready; to foresee.—vri. to be ready, prepared, or on guard; to take precautions.—**preventivo,** a. preventive.

prever, vti. [46–49] to foresee, anticipate.—**previo,** a. previous, foregoing.—**previsión,** f. foresight.—**previsor,** a. far-seeing.—**previsto,** ppi. of PREVENIR.

prieto, a. blackish, very dark; tight.

prima, f. female cousin; (mus.) treble; (com.) premium; bounty.—**primacía,** f. primacy; superiority; priority.—**primario,** a. principal, primary.

primavera, f. spring, springtime; primrose; robin.—**primaveral,** a. spring.

primer(o), a. first; former; leading; principal.—de buenas a primeras, suddenly.—de primera, of superior quality.—p. piso, second floor; (G.B.) first floor.—adv. first; rather, sooner.

primicia, f. first fruit.—pl. first production, maiden effort.

primitivo, a. primitive, original.

primo, n. cousin; (coll.) simpleton.—coger a uno de p., to deceive someone easily.—número p., prime number.—p. carnal, or p. hermano, first cousin.—p. segundo, second cousin.—a. first; superior, prime.—**primogénito,** n. & a. first-born.—**primogenitura,** f. state of being the first-born child; seniority.

primor, m. beauty; nicety.

primordial, a. primal.

primoroso, a. neat, fine, exquisite; beautiful; skillful.

princesa, f. princess.—**principado,** m. princedom.—**principal,** a. principal, main; first; famous.—m. (com.) principal, capital, stock; chief or head.—**príncipe,** m. prince.—p. de

Gales, Prince of Wales.—p. heredero, crown prince.

principiante, a. beginning.—mf. beginner.—**principiar,** vt. to commence, begin, start.—**principio,** m. principle, tenet; beginning; start; original cause; rule of action.—a principios de, at the beginning of.—al p., at first.—en p., in principle.

pringoso, a. greasy, fatty.—**pringue,** m. or f. grease, fat; grease stain.

prior, m. (eccl.) prior, superior; rector, curate.—**prioridad,** f. priority, precedence.

prisa, f. haste, promptness; urgency.—a p., quickly.—darse p., to make haste, hurry.—de p., quickly.—estar de p., or tener p., to be in a hurry.

prisión, f. seizure, capture; prison; imprisonment.—**prisionero,** n. prisoner.

prisma, m. prism.

prístino, a. pristine.

privación, f. privation; lack.—**privado,** a. private, secret; personal.—**privar,** vt. to deprive.—vi. to prevail, be in favor or in vogue.—vr. to deprive oneself.—**privativo,** a. privative; special, distinctive, particular; exclusive.

privilegiar, vt. to favor; to grant a privilege to.—**privilegio,** m. privilege; grant, concession.

pro, m. or f. profit, benefit, advantage.—en p. de, in behalf of, for the benefit of.—los pros y los contras, the pros and cons.

proa, f. bow, prow.

probabilidad, f. probability.—**probable,** a. probable.

probador, m. fitting room.—**probar,** vti. [12] to try, test; to prove; to taste; to sample (as wine); to attempt, try; to try on (as a coat).—p. fortuna, to take one's chances.—vii. to suit, agree with.—vri. to try on (as a coat).

probeta, f. pressure gauge; test tube; beaker.

probidad, f. probity, honesty, integrity.

problema, m. problem.

probo, a. upright, honest.

procaz, a. impudent, bold, insolent.

procedencia, f. origin; source; place of sailing.—**procedente,** a. coming or proceeding (from); according to law.—**proceder,** vi. to proceed; to go on; to arise; to be the result; to behave; to act; to take action.—*m.* behavior, action.—**procedimiento**, *m.* procedure; process; method; (law) proceeding.

prócer, *a.* tall, lofty, elevated.—*mf.* hero, leader, dignitary.

procesado, *a.* (law) related to court proceeding; included in the suit; prosecuted, indicted.—*n.* defendant; (comput.) enhanced.—**procesamiento**, *m.* (law) prosecution, trial; (comput.) processing.—*p. de datos*, data processing.—*p. de textos* or *palabras*, word processing.—*p. por lotes*, batch processing.—**procesador**, *m.* processor.—*p. de textos* or *de palabras*, word processor.—*p. de datos*, data processor.—**procesar**, *vt.* to sue; to indict; (comput.) to enchance.

procesión, *f.* procession.

proceso, *m.* process; course, development; (law) criminal case; proceedings of a lawsuit, trial.—*p. de datos*, data processing.

proclama, *f.* proclamation; publication; banns of marriage.—**proclamación**, *f.* proclamation.—**proclamar**, *vt.* to proclaim; to acclaim.

procrear, *vt.* to father, procreate; to sire.

procuración, *f.* care, diligence; proxy, power or letter of attorney; procurement, procuring; office of an attorney.—**procurador**, *n.* (law) solicitor, attorney.—**procurar**, *vt.* to endeavor, try; to procure; (Am.) to look for.—*vi.* to act as a solicitor.

prodigalidad, *f.* prodigality, wastefulness; abundance.—**prodigar**, *vti.* [b] to lavish; to squander.

prodigio, *m.* prodigy; marvel.—**prodigioso**, *a.* prodigious, marvelous.

pródigo, *a.* prodigal, extravagant, wasteful; liberal, generous.—*n.* spendthrift.

producción, *f.* production; produce.—**producir**, *vti.* [11] to produce; to bring about; to yield.—*vri.* to explain oneself; to be produced; to come about; to break out.—**productivo**, *a.* productive; profitable, fruitful.—**producto**, *m.* product; article (of trade, etc.); production; produce.—*P. Nacional Bruto (PNB)*, Gross National Product (GNP).—**productor**, *a.* productive.—*n.* producer.

proeza, *f.* prowess, feat.

profanación, *f.* profanation, desecration.—**profanar**, *vt.* to profane, desecrate.—**profano**, *a.* profane; secular; irreverent; uninformed, ignorant.—*n.* layman; uninitiated person.

profecía, *f.* prophecy.

proferir, *vti.* [39] to utter, express, speak.

profesar, *vt.* to practice (a profession); to profess, declare; to show, manifest.—*vi.* to take vows.—**profesión**, *f.* profession, vocation.—**profesional**, *a.* professional.—**profesor**, *n.* professor, teacher, schoolteacher; (de universidad) professor.—*p. de piano*, piano teacher.—**profesorado**, *m.* professorship; faculty; teaching profession; teacher training.

profeta, *m.* prophet.—**profético**, *a.* prophetic(al).—**profetizar**, *vti.* [a] & *vii.* to prophesy.

proficiente, *a.* proficient, advanced.

profiláctico, *a.* prophylactic, preventive.—*m.* prophylactic.

prófugo, *n.* & *a.* fugitive from justice.

profundidad, *f.* depth; profoundness.—**profundizar**, *vti.* [a] to deepen; to go deep into.—**profundo**, *a.* deep; profound.

profusión, *f.* profusion; lavishness, prodigality.—**profuso**, *a.* profuse, plentiful; lavish.

progenie, *f.* progeny, offspring; issue.

progenitor, *m.* progenitor, ancestor.

programa, *m.* program.—*p. concurso*, game show.—*p. de exploración espacial*, space program.—*p. de ordenador*, computer program.—*p. de preguntas y respuesta*, (TV) quiz show.—*p. para computadora*, software.—**programación**, *f.* organization, planning; (comput. & rad./TV) programing, programming.—**programador**, *n.* (comput. & electron.) programer, programmer.—**programar**, *vt.* to draw up a program for, to schedule, to plan; (comput.) to program.

progresar, *vi.* to progress; to advance.—**progresión**, *f.* progression.—**progresista**, *a.* & *mf.* progressive.—**progresivo**, *a.* advancing, progressive.—**progreso**, *m.* progress, civilization; advancement, development.—*pl.* progress, strides (in an undertaking, school, etc.).

prohibición, *f.* prohibition, forbidding.—**prohibir**, *vt*. to prohibit, forbid.—*prohibida la entrada*, no entry, no admittance, no entrance, no trespassing.—*se prohibe fumar*, no smoking.—**prohibitivo**, *a*. prohibitive, forbidding.

prohijar, *vt*. to adopt.

prójimo, *m*. fellow creature, neighbor.

prole, *f*. progeny, offspring.—**proletariado**, *m*. proletariat.—**proletario**, *a*. proletarian; belonging to the working classes.—*n*. proletarian.

prolífico, *a*. prolific, fruitful.

prólogo, *m*. prologue.

prolongación, *f*. prolongation, lengthening; extension.—**prolongar**, *vti*. & *vri*. [b] to prolong; to extend, continue.

promediar, *vt*. (com.) to average.—*vi*. to mediate.—**promedio**, *m*. average.

promesa, *f*. promise, offer; pious offering.—**prometedor**, *a*. promising.—**prometer**, *vt*. to promise; to bid fair.—*vi*. to show promise.—*vr*. to expect with confidence; to become engaged.—**prometido**, *n*. fiancé, fiancée, betrothed.—*m*. promise.

prominencia, *f*. elevation; prominence; protuberance.—**prominente**, *a*. prominent, outstanding; salient.

promiscuidad, *f*. promiscuity.—**promiscuo**, *a*. promiscuous.

promisorio, *a*. promissory.

promoción, *f*. promotion.

promontorio, *m*. promontory; anything bulky and unwieldy.

promotor, *n*. promoter, advancer.—**promover**, *vti*. [26] to promote; to advance.

pronombre, *m*. pronoun.

pronosticar, *vti*. [d] to prognosticate, foretell.—**pronóstico**, *m*. forecast, prediction; omen.

prontitud, *f*. promptness; quickness.—**pronto**, *a*. prompt, quick, fast; ready.—*m*. sudden impulse. *adv*. soon; promptly, speedily, quickly.—*de p.*, suddenly, without thinking.—*por lo p.*, for the time being.

pronunciación, *f*. pronunciation.—**pronunciar**, *vt*. to pronounce; to deliver, make (a speech).—*vr*. to declare oneself.

propagación, *f*. propagation; spreading, dissemination.—**propagador**, *n*. & *a*. propagator; propagating.—**propaganda**, *f*. propaganda.—**propagandista**, *mf*. propagandist.—**pro-**

pagar, *vti*. [b] to propagate; to spread, disseminate.—*vri*. to spread; to propagate; to multiply.

propalar, *vt*. to publish, divulge.

propasarse, *vr*. to go too far; to go to extremes.

propender, *vii*. [49] to tend, be inclined.

propensión, *f*. tendency, proclivity, proneness.—**propenso**, *ppi*. of PROPENDER.—*a*. inclined, disposed.

propiciar, *vt*. to propitiate.—**propicio**, *a*. propitious, favorable.

propiedad, *f*. ownership, proprietorship; property, holding; propriety, fitness; dominion, possession.—*p. horizontal*, condominium.—*p. industrial*, patent rights.—*p. inmobiliaria*, real estate.—*p. intelectual*, copyright.—*p. privada*, private property.—**propietario**, *n*. proprietor, landlord; home owner.—*a*. proprietary.

propina, *f*. tip, gratuity.—**propinar**, *vt*. to deal (a beating, a kick, etc.).

propio, *a*. one's own; proper, appropriate; characteristic, typical.—*m*. messenger.

proponer, *vti*. [32–49] to propose, propound; to present or name (as candidate).—*vri*. to purpose, plan, intend.

proporción, *f*. proportion; opportunity, chance.—**proporcionado**, *a*. proportioned, fit, relevant.—**proporcional**, *a*. proportional.—**proporcionar**, *vt*. to proportion; to supply, provide, furnish; to adjust, adapt.

proposición, *f*. proposition; proposal; motion (in congress, etc.).

propósito, *m*. purpose, intention; aim, object.—*a p.*, for the purpose; fit; incidentally, by the way.—*a p. de*, in connection with, apropos of.—*buenos propósitos*, good resolutions.—*de p.*, on purpose, purposely.—*fuera de p.*, irrelevant.

propuesta, *f*. proposal, offer; nomination.—**propuesto**, *ppi*. of PROPONER.

propugnar, *vt*. to advocate, defend strongly, promote.

propulsar, *vt*. to propel.—**propulsión**, *f*. propulsion.—*p. a chorro*, jet propulsion.—**propulsor**, *n*. & *a*. propeller; propelling.

prorrata, *f*. apportionment.—*a p.*, pro rata, in proportion.—**prorratear**, *vt*. to allot in proportion.—**prorrateo**, *m*. pro rata division.

prórroga, f. prolongation, extension (of time).—**prorrogable,** a. that may be prolonged or extended (in time).—**prorrogar,** vti. [b] to prolong, extend (in time).

prorrumpir, vi. to break forth, burst out.

prosa, f. prose.—**prosaico,** a. prosaic.—**prosista,** mf. prose writer.

proscribir, vti. [49] to proscribe, banish; to outlaw.—**proscripción,** f. proscription, banishment.—**p. de las pruebas nucleares,** nuclear test ban.—**poscrito,** ppi. of PROSCRIBIR.—n. exile; outlaw.

proseguir, vti. [29-b] to continue; to carry on with; to resume.—vii. to keep going, proceed.

prosodia, f. prosody.

prosperar, vi. to prosper, thrive.—**prosperidad,** f. prosperity, success.—**próspero,** a. prosperous; favorable.

próstata, f. prostate, prostate gland.

prosternarse, vr. to prostrate oneself.

prostitución, f. prostitution.—**prostituir,** vti. [23–49-e] to prostitute, corrupt, debase.—vri. to sell one's honor; to turn prostitute.—**prostituto,** ppi. of PROSTITUIR.—n. prostitute; streetwalker.

protagonista, mf. protagonist, hero(ine).

protección, f. protection; favor.—**p. de datos,** (comput.) data protection.—**protector,** n. protector.—**proteger,** vti. [c] to protect.—**protegido,** n. protégé.

proteína, f. protein.

protesta, f. protestation; protest.—**protestante,** a. protesting.—mf. & a. Protestant.—**protestantismo,** m. Protestantism.—**protestar,** vt. (com.) to protest; to assure, protest, asseverate; to profess (one's faith).—**p. contra,** to protest, deny the validity of.—**p. de,** to protest against.—**protesto,** m. (com.) protest (of a bill).

protocolo, m. protocol; registry, judicial record.

protoplasma, m. protoplasm.

prototipo, m. prototype, original; model.

protuberancia, f. protuberance; nub.

provecho, m. benefit; advantage; profit, gain; proficiency, progress.—**provechoso,** a. profitable; beneficial, good; useful, advantageous.

proveedor, n. purveyor, provider; supplier.—**proveer,** vti. [49-e] to provide, furnish; to supply with provisions; (law) to decide.—vri. (de) to provide oneself (with), get one's supply (of).

provenir, vii. [45] to come, originate, arise; to be due.

proverbial, a. proverbial.—**proverbio,** m. proverb.

providencia, f. providence, foresight; Providence; act of providing; (law) decision, sentence.—**providencial,** a. providential.

provincia, f. province.—**provincial,** a. provincial.—**provinciano,** n. & a. provincial.

provisión, f. provision; supply, stock; measure, means.—**provisional,** a. provisional, interim.—**provisorio,** a. provisional, temporary.—**provisto,** ppi. of PROVEER.—a. provided, stocked, supplied.

provocación, f. provocation, irritation.—**provocador,** n. provoker; inciter.—**provocar,** vti. [d] to provoke, excite, incite, anger; to promote; to tempt, arouse desire in.—**provocativo,** a. inciting; tempting; provoking, irritating.

proximidad, f. proximity.—**próximo,** a. next; nearest, neighboring; close.

proyección, f. projecting; projection.—**proyectar,** vt. to design; to project, plan, devise; to shoot or throw forth; (geom.) to project; to cast (as a shadow); to show (a movie).—vr. to be cast, fall (as a shadow).—**proyectil,** m. projectile, missile.—**proyectista,** mf. planner; designer; (pej.) schemer.—**proyecto,** m. project, plan; design.—**proyector,** m. projector; searchlight.

prudencia, f. prudence; moderation.—**prudente,** a. prudent, cautious.

prueba, f. proof; evidence; trial, test; probation; sample; testing; temptation; trial, fitting.—a p., on trial; according to the best standards.—a p. de, proof against.—a p. de impericia, foolproof.—hacer la p., to try.—poner a p., to try, put to the test.—p. negativa, (phot.) negative.

prurito, m. itching; excessive desire.

prusiano, n. & a. Prussian.

psicoanálisis, m. psychoanalysis.—**psicoanalista,** mf. psychoanalyst.—**psicoanalizar,** vti. [a] to psychoana-

lyze.—**psicología,** f. psychology.—
psicológico, a. psychological.—**psi-cólogo,** n. psychologist.—
psicópata, mf. psychopath.—
psicosis, f. psychosis.—**psicótico,**
n. & a. psychotic.—**psique,** f. psyche.—**psiquiatra,** mf. psychiatrist.—**psiquiatría,** f. psychiatry.—
psíquico, a. psychic(al).

psitacosis, f. parrot fever.

púa, f. prick, barb; prong; thorn; spine
or quill (of porcupine); (coll.) tricky
person.

pubertad, f. puberty.

publicación, f. publication.—**publicar,**
vti. [d] to publish; to publicize.—
publicidad, f. publicity.—**público,**
a. & m. public.—en p., publicly.

puchero, m. cooking pot; stew; dinner,
food; pouting.—hacer pucheros,
(coll.) to pout.

pudiente, a. powerful; wealthy.

pudín, m. pudding.—p. inglés con pasas, plum pudding.

pudor, m. decorousness, modesty.—
pudoroso, a. modest; bashful, shy.

pudrir, vti., vii. & vri. [33] to rot, decay.

pueblecito, m. hamlet, whistle stop.

pueblo, m. town, village; people; population; common people; nation.—
p. natal, home town.

puente, m. bridge.—p. aéreo, shuttle
flight.—p. colgante, suspension
bridge.—p. de peaje, toll bridge.—p.
giratorio, swing bridge.—p. levadizo,
drawbridge.

puerco, a. filthy, dirty, foul; low, base,
mean.—n. pig, hog; (fig.) dirty, base
or low person.

pueril, a. childish, puerile.

puerta, f. door; doorway, gateway;
gate; entrance.—a p. cerrada, privately, secretly.—p. de embarque,
(aer.) gate.—p. falsa, back door, side
door.—p. franca, open door, free entrance; free entry.—p. giratoria, revolving door.—p. lateral, side door.

puerto, m. port; mountain pass; harbor; (fig.) shelter, refuge.

puertorriqueño, n. & a. Puerto Rican.

pues, conj. because, for, as; since;
then.—p. bien, now then, well
then.—p. no, not at all, not so.—p.
que, since.—¿p. qué? what? what
about it? so what?—p. sí, yes, indeed, most certainly.—¿y p.? so? is
that so? how is that?—adv. so; certainly; anyhow, just the same.

puesta, f. (astr.) set, setting; stake (at
cards).—p. de sol, sunset.—p. en
marcha, starting, start.

puesto, ppi. of PONER.—bien (mal) p.,
well (badly) dressed.—p. que, since,
inasmuch as, as long as.—m. place;
vendor's booth or stand; position,
job; post, dignity, office; military
post; blind for hunters; breeding
stall.

pugilato, m. boxing; boxing bout.—
pugilista, mf. boxer, pugilist, prize
fighter.

pugna, f. combat, struggle; conflict.—
estar en p., to be in conflict, disagree.—**pugnar,** vi. to fight, struggle;
(con) to conflict (with), be opposed
(to); to persist.

puja, f. outbidding or overbidding at
an auction; higher bid.—**pujante,** a.
powerful, strong.—**pujanza,** f. push,
might, strength.—**pujar,** vi. to outbid or overbid; to strive, struggle.—
pujido, pujo, m. grunt; strenuous
effort.

pulcritud, f. neatness, tidiness.—**pulcro,** a. neat, trim.

pulga, f. flea.—ser de or tener malas pulgas, to be ill-tempered.—**pulgada,** f.
inch.—**pulgar,** m. thumb.—**pulgón,**
m. green fly, plant louse.

pulimentar, vt. to burnish, gloss, polish.—**pulimento,** m. polish; glossiness.—**pulir,** vt. to polish, burnish;
to beautify; to render polite.—vr. to
beautify or deck oneself; to become
polished.

pulla, f. cutting remark, taunt, quip;
hint.

pulmón, m. lung.—**pulmonar,** a. pulmonary.—**pulmonía,** f. pneumonia.

pulpa, f. pulp, flesh; fruit or wood
pulp.—**pulpería,** f. (Am.) retail grocery or general store; tavern.—**pulpero,** n. (Am.) grocer.

púlpito, m. pulpit.

pulpo, m. cuttlefish, octopus.

pulsación, f. pulsation, throb; pulse,
beating.—**pulsar,** vt. to feel the
pulse of; to finger (a string instrument); to explore, sound, or examine.—vi. to pulsate, beat.—**pulsear,**
vt. to arm-wrestle, to hand-wrestle.—**pulsera,** f. bracelet; wrist
bandage.—reloj de p., wrist
watch.—**pulso,** m. pulse; beat;
firmness or steadiness of hand;
(Am.) bracelet.—a p., freehand;

with the strength of the hand.—*tomar el pulso a*, to take the pulse of, to feel the pulse of.

pulular, *vi.* to swarm; to multiply with great rapidity; to bud, sprout.

pulverización, *f.* pulverization.—**pulverizador**, *m.* atomizer, spray; pulverizer.—**pulverizar**, *vti.* [a] to pulverize; to spray.

puma, *m.* puma, American panther; cougar.

puna, *f.* (Am.) cold, desertlike tableland of the Andes; (Am.) desert; (Am.) mountain sickness.

punching, *m.* punching bag.

pundonor, *m.* point of honor.

punición, *f.* punishment.

punta, *f.* point, sharp end; end, tip; apex, top; cape, promontory; touch, trace, suggestion; stub of a cigar or cigarette.—*de p.*, point first.—*de p. en blanco*, all dressed up; in full regalia.—*estar de p.*, to be on bad terms.—*p. de alfiler*, pinpoint.—*p. de lanza*, spearhead.—**puntada**, *f.* stitch; hint.—**puntal**, *m.* prop, support.—**puntapié**, *m.* kick.—**puntear**, *vt.* to play (the guitar); (art) to stipple; (sew.) to stitch.—**puntería**, *f.* aiming or pointing of a weapon; marksmanship.—**puntero**, *m.* pointer; chisel; (sports) front-runner.—**puntiagudo**, *a.* sharp, spiky; pungent.—**puntilla**, *f.* lace edging; tack; joiner's nail.—*de*, or *en puntillas*, softly, gently; on tiptoe.—*p. francesa*, finishing nail.—**puntilloso**, *a.* sensitive, easily offended.—**punto**, *m.* point, dot; period in writing; point of a pen; sight in firearms; stitch; mesh; place; instant, moment; stop, rest, recess; end, object, aim; pip (on card or dice).—*al p.*, immediately, at once.—*a p. de*, on the point of, about to.—*a p. fijo*, exactly.—*dos puntos*, colon.—*en p.*, on the dot, (of the hour) sharp.—*p. ciego*, blind spot.—*p. decimal*, decimal point.—*p. de interrupción*, (comput.) break point.—*p. de partido*, starting point.—*p. de ruptura*, (tennis) break point.—*p. de venta a precios reducidos*, outlet.—*p. en boca*, silence.—*p. final*, stop; full stop.—*p. medio*, median; golden mean.—*p. muerto*, standstill.—*p. y coma*, semicolon.—*puntos suspensivos*, leaders.—**puntuación**, *f.* punctuation.—**puntual**, *a.*

prompt, punctual.—**puntualidad**, *f.* punctuality.—**puntualizar**, *vti.* [a] to give a detailed account of.—**puntuar**, *vt.* to punctuate; to point.

punzada, *f.* prick, puncture; sharp pain.—**punzante**, *a.* pricking, sharp; poignant.—**punzar**, *vti.* [a] to punch, bore, perforate; to prick, puncture; to cause sharp pain; to grieve.

punzó, *a.* (Am.) deep scarlet red.

punzón, *m.* punch; puncher; driver, point, awl.

puñada, *f.* blow with the fist.—**puñado**, *m.* handful; a few.—**puñal**, *m.* dagger, poniard.—**puñalada**, *f.* stab (with a dagger); sharp pain.—*p. trapera*, stab in the back.—**puñetazo**, *m.* = PUÑADA.—**puño**, *m.* fist; grasp; handful; cuff, wristband (of garment); hilt of a sword; haft (of a tool); handle (of an umbrella, etc.); head of a staff or cane.

pupila, *f.* (anat.) pupil.

pupilaje, *m.* room and board; boarding house.—**pupilo**, *n.* ward; boarding-school pupil; boarder.

pupitre, *m.* writing desk; school desk.

puré, *m.* thick soup, purée.—*p. de papas*, or *p. de patatas*, mashed potatoes.

pureza, *f.* purity, chastity; genuineness.

purga, *f.* physic, cathartic.—**purgación**, *f.* purge, purgation; gonorrhea, clap.—**purgante**, *a.* purging, purgative.—*m.* purgative, cathartic, physic.—**purgar**, *vti.* [b] to purge, purify; to expiate; to refine, clarify; to drain; to purge.—*vri.* to take a purgative; to clear oneself of guilt.—**purgatorio**, *m.* purgatory.

purificación, *f.* purification.—**purificador**, *n.* & *a.* purifier; purifying.—**purificar**, *vti.* [d] to purify.—*vri.* to be purified.

puritano, *a.* & *n.* Puritan.

puro, *a.* pure; unadulterated; mere, only, sheer.—*m.* cigar.

púrpura, *f.* purple shell; purple; dignity of a cardinal.—**purpúreo, purpurino**, *a.* purple.

purulento, *a.* purulent.—**pus**, *m.* pus.

pusilánime, *a.* faint-hearted, spineless.

pústula, *f.* pimple.

puta, *f.* whore, harlot; tart.

putter, *m.* (sports) putter.

puya, *f.* goad, goad stick.

Q

quántum, *m.* quantum.

quásar, *m.* quasar.

que, *rel. pron.* that; which; who, whom.—*el q.,* he who, the one who, the one that.—*lo q.,* what, which.—*por más q.,* no matter how.—*conj.* that, than; because, for.—*más q.,* more than.—*por mucho q.,* no matter how much.—*¿que? interrog. pron.* what? which? how?—*¿para q.?* what for?—*¿por qué?* why?—*¿q. hay, amigo?,* (fam.) what's up, mac?—*¿q. tal?* how goes it?—*interj.* what a! how!

quebrada, *f.* ravine; gorge; (Am.) gulch; stream.—**quebradizo,** *a.* brittle, fragile; frail, sickly.—**quebrado,** *a.* broken; (com.) bankrupt; rough, uneven (ground); (med.) ruptured.—*m.* (arith.) common fraction.—**quebrantar,** *vt.* to break, crush; to burst open; to pound; to transgress; to violate, break (as a contract); to vex; to weaken.—**quebranto,** *m.* (com.) loss, damage; breaking, crushing; grief, affliction.—**quebrar,** *vti.* [1] to break; to crush.—*vii.* (com.) to fail, become bankrupt.—*vri.* to be ruptured; to break (as a plate, a bone, etc.); to be broken.

quechua, *mf. & a.* Quechua; Quechuan (Indian and language).

quedar, *vi.* to remain; to stay, stop in a place; to be or be left in a state or condition.—*q. bien,* (mal), to acquit oneself well (badly); to come out well (badly).—*q. en,* to agree to; to have an understanding.—*vr.* to remain.—*quedarse atrás,* to get, or be left, behind.—*quedarse con,* to retain, keep.

quedo, *a.* quiet, still, noiseless; easy, gentle.—*adv.* softly, gently; in a low voice.

quehacer, *m.* occupation, business, work.—*pl.* chores; duties.

queja, *f.* complaint; grumbling, moan; grudge.—**quejarse,** *vr.* to complain; to grumble; (de) to regret, lament.—**quejido,** *m.* moan.—**quejoso,** *a.* complaining.—**quejumbroso,** *a.* grumbling; plaintive.

quema, *f.* burning, fire, conflagration.—*huir de la q.,* to get away from trouble, get out.—**quemado,** *a.* burnt, crisp; sunburned.—*m.* burnt down forest or thicket.—**quemadura,** *f.* burn, scald.—**quemar,** *vt.* to burn; to scald; to scorch; to set on fire; to dispose of at a low price; to annoy.—*vi.* to burn, be too hot.—*vr.* to get burned, burn oneself; to burn, be consumed by fire; to feel very hot.—**quemarropa,**—*a q.,* at close range, point-blank.—**quemazón,** *f.* fire, conflagration; (coll.) smarting, burning; (Am.) bargain sale.

querella, *f.* complaint; quarrel; (law) plaint, complaint.—**querellante,** *mf. & a.* complainant; complaining.—**querellarse,** *vr.* to complain; (law) to file a complaint, bring suit.

querer, *vti.* [34] to will; to want, desire, wish; to like, love.—*q. decir,* to mean.—*vii.* to be willing.—*como quiera,* in any way.—*como quiera que,* since; however, no matter how.—*como quiera que sea,* in any case.—*como Ud. quiera,* as you like; let it be so.—*cuando quiera,* at any time, whenever.—*donde quiera,* anywhere, wherever.—*sin q.,* unwillingly; unintentionally.—*v. impers.* to look like (rain, etc.), threaten.—*m.* love, affection; will; desire.—**querido,** *a.* dear; beloved. —*n.* lover; mistress.

querosén, *m.* (Am.) kerosene.

querubín, *m.* cherub.

quesería, *f.* dairy.—**quesera,** *f.* cheese dish.—**quesero,** *n.* cheesemaker.—**queso,** *m.* cheese.—*q. crema,* cream cheese.—*q. suizo,* Swiss cheese.

quicio, *m.* hinge of a door.—*sacar de q.,* to unhinge; to exasperate.

quichua, *mf. & a.* = QUECHUA.

quid, *m.* main point, gist.

quídam, *m.* (coll.) person; a nobody.

quiebra, *f.* crack, fracture; gaping fissure; loss, damage; (com.) failure, bankruptcy.

quiebro, *m.* dodge, swerve; (mus.) trill.

quien, *pron.* (*pl.* QUIENES) who, whom, he who (*pl.* those who); whose.—**quienquiera,** *pron.* (*pl.* QUIENESQUIERA) whoever, whosoever, whomsoever.—**quién,** *interrog. pron.* (*pl.* QUIENES) who?

quieto, *a.* quiet, still; steady, undisturbed.—**quietud,** *f.* stillness, quietness; tranquility.

quijada, *f.* jaw, jawbone.

quijotesco, *a.* quixotic.

quilate, *m.* (jewelry) carat or karat; degree of excellence.

quilo, *m.* (med.) chyle.—*sudar el q.,* to work hard.

quilla, *f.* (naut.) keel.

quimbombó, *m.* (Am.) okra, gumbo.

quimera, *f.* fancy, absurd idea; quarrel.—**quimérico,** *a.* imaginary; wildly fanciful.

química, *f.* chemistry.—**químico,** *a.* chemical.—*n.* chemist.

quimono, *m.* kimono.

quina, *f.* = QUININA.

quincalla, *f.* (com.) hardware; small wares.—**quincallería,** *f.* hardware trade or store; small wares store.

quince, *a.* & *m.* fifteen.—**quinceavo,** *a.* & *m.* fifteenth.

quincena, *f.* fortnight.—**quincenal,** *a.* fortnightly, semi-monthly.

quincuagésimo, *a.* & *m.* fiftieth.—**quindécimo,** *a.* & *s.* fifteenth.—**quingentésimo,** *a.* five-hundredth.—**quinientos,** *a.* & *m.* five hundred.—*q. uno,* five hundred one.

quinina, *f.* quinine.

quinta, *f.* country seat, villa; manorhouse; (mil.) draft; (mus.) fifth.

quintaesencia, *f.* quintessence.

quintal, *m.* quintal. (See Table.)

quinteto, *m.* (mus.) quintet.

quintillizos, *npl.* quintuplets.

quinto, *a.* & *m.* fifth.—*quinta columna,* (pol.) fifth column.

quintuples, *mfpl.* quintuplets.

quíntuplo, *a.* quintuple, fivefold.

quiosco, *m.* kiosk.—*q. de necesidad,* public toilet.

quirófano, *m.* (surg.) operating room.

quiromancia, *f.* palmistry.—**quiromántico,** *n.* palmist.

quirúrgico, *a.* surgical.

quisquilla, *f.* bickering, trifling dispute; shrimp; (coll.) small man.—**quisquilloso,** *a.* fastidious; touchy, peevish.

quitamanchas, *m.* cleaner, spot remover.—*m.* dry cleaner.

quitanieves, *m.* snow plow.

quitapintura, *f.* paint remover.

quitar, *vt.* to take away; to subtract; to take off, remove; to separate, take out; to free from; to rob of, deprive of; to forbid, prohibit; (fencing) to parry.—*vr.* to abstain, refrain; to quit, move away, withdraw; to get rid of; to take off (a garment); to come out (as a stain).—**quite,** *m.* parry, dodge.

quitasol, *m.* sunshade, parasol.

quizá, quizás, *adv.* perhaps, maybe.

R

rabadilla, *f.* coccyx; rump.

rábano, *m.* radish.—*r. picante,* horseradish.—*tomar el r. por las hojas,* (coll.) to be off the track.

rabí, *m.* rabbi.

rabia, *f.* rabies.—*tenerle r. a,* to have a grudge against.—**rabiar,** *vi.* to have rabies; to rage; to rave; to suffer racking pain.—*r. por,* to long eagerly for.—**rabieta,** *f.* tantrum.

rabínico, *a.* rabbinical.—**rabino,** *m.* rabbi.

rabión, *m.* rapids of a river.

rabioso, *a.* rabid; suffering from rabies; enraged.

rabo, *m.* tail; tail end, back, or hind part.—*con el r. entre las piernas,* (coll.) (fig.) with the tail between the legs, crestfallen.—*mirar con el r. del ojo,* to look askance, or out of the corner of the eye.

racha, *f.* flaw; gust of wind; streak of luck.

racial, *a.* racial, race.

racimo, *m.* bunch; cluster.

ración, *f.* ration; supply, allowance.

racional, *a.* rational; reasonable.

racionamiento, *m.* rationing.—**racionar,** *vt.* to ration.

radar, *m.* radar.

radiación, *f.* radiation.—**radiador,** *m.* radiator.—**radial,** *a.* radial; radio.—

radiante, *a.* radiant, brilliant, beaming.—**radiar,** *vi.* to radiate.—*vt.* & *vi.* to radio; to broadcast.

radical, *a.* radical.—*mf.* (pol.) radical; (gram. & math.) root.

radicar, *vii.* [d] to take root; to be (in a place).—*vr.* to settle, establish oneself.

radio, *m.* radius; radio set; radiogram; radium; circuit, district; rung.—*mf.* radio.—*r. de acción,* range.—**radio-actividad,** *f.* radioactivity.—**radioactivo,** *a.* radioactive.—**radiodespertador,** *m.* clock radio.—**radiodifundir,** *vt.* & *vi.* to broadcast.—**radiodifusión,** *f.* broadcast; broadcasting. —**radiodifusora, radioemisora,** *f.* broadcasting station.—**radioescucha,** *mf.* radio listener.—**radiofaro,** *m.* radio beacon.—*r. de aterrizaje,* landing beacon.—**radiografía,** *f.* X-ray, radiography.—**radiografiar,** *vt.* to X-ray.—**radiográfico,** *a.* X-ray.— **radiograma,** *m.* radiogram.— **radiólogo,** *n.* radiologist.—**radiorreceptor,** *m.* radio receiver.—**radiotransmisor,** *m.* radio transmitter.— **radioyente,** *mf.* radio listener.

raer, *vti.* [8] to scrape; to rub off, fray; to erase.

ráfaga, *f.* gust of wind; flash or gleam of light; burst (of an automatic weapon).—*r. de aire,* waft.

raíces, *pl.* of RAÍZ.—*bienes r.,* real estate.

raído, *a.* frayed, worn out, threadbare; shameless.

raigón, *m.* large strong root; root of a tooth.

rail, *m.* (RR.) rail.

raíz, *f.* root; base, foundation; origin.—*a r. de,* immediately, right after.—*de r.,* by the roots, from the root; entirely.—*echar raíces,* to take root, become settled or fixed.

raja, *f.* split, rent, crack; slice (as a fruit).—**rajadura,** *f.* cleft, crack; crevice.—**rajar,** *vt.* to split; to slice (food).—*vr.* to split, crack.—*vi.* (coll.) to chatter.—*a rajatabla(s),* in a great haste.

ralea, *f.* race, breed, stock; kind, quality.—**ralo,** *a.* thin, sparse, not dense.

rallador, *m.* grater.—**rallar,** *vt.* to grate; (coll.) to vex.

rama, *f.* branch, twig, limb, bough.— *andarse por las ramas,* to beat around the bush.—*en r.,* raw.—**ramaje,** *m.* mass of branches; foliage.—**ramal,**

m. branch, ramification; (RR.) branch road; strand of a rope; halter.—**ramalazo,** *m.* lash, stroke with a rope; mark left by a lash; blow; spot on the face caused by blows or disease.

ramera, *f.* prostitute, whore.

ramillete, *m.* bouquet; cluster.—**ramo,** *m.* bough; branch (of trade, science, art, etc.); branchlet; cluster, bouquet; line of goods.—**ramonear,** *vi.* to lop off twigs; to browse.

rampa, *f.* ramp.

ramplón, *a.* coarse, rude, vulgar, common.

rana, *f.* frog.

ranchera, *f.* station wagon.

ranchería, *f.* settlement; cluster of huts; camp.—**ranchero,** *m.* mess cook; small farmer; (Am.) rancher.—**rancho,** *m.* (mil.) mess, chow; messhall; hut; camp; (Am.) cattle ranch.

rancio, *a.* rank, rancid, stale.—*vino r.,* mellow wine.

rango, *m.* rank, class, position, status.

ranura, *f.* groove, notch; slot.

rapacidad, *f.* rapacity.

rapadura, *f.* shaving; hair cut.—**rapapolvo,** *m.* (coll.) sharp reprimand, dressing down.—**rapar,** *vt.* to shave; to crop (the hair); to plunder, snatch, rob.

rapaz, *a.* rapacious, predatory.—*f. pl.* (RAPACES) birds of prey.—*n.* young boy (girl).

rape, *m.* (coll.) hurried shaving or hair cutting.—*al r.,* cropped, clipped, cut close or short.

rapidez, *f.* rapidity, swiftness.—**rápido,** *a.* rapid, swift.—*m.* rapids; express train.

rapiña, *f.* rapine, plundering.—*de r.,* (of birds) of prey.—**rapiñar,** *vt.* (coll.) to plunder; to steal.

raposa, *f.* vixen, fox; (fig.) cunning person.

rapsodia, *f.* rhapsody.

raptar, *vt.* to abduct; to kidnap (a woman).—**rapto,** *m.* kidnapping; abduction, ravishment; rapture, ecstasy.

raqueta, *f.* (sports) racket.—*r. de nieve,* snowshoe.

raquítico, *a.* rachitic, rickety; feeble, skinny.

raquitis, *f.* or **raquitismo,** *m.* (med.) rickets.

rareza, *f.* rarity, uncommonness;

queerness; freak; curiosity; oddness.—*por* or *de r.*, rarely, seldom.—**raro**, *a.* rare; scarce; thin, not dense; queer, odd.—*rara vez*, seldom.

ras, *m.* level, flush.—*al r. con* or *de*, even or flush with.—**rasante**, *a.* leveling, grazing.—*f.* (RR.) grade, grade line.—**rasar**, *vt.* to strike or level with a straight edge; to graze, touch lightly.

rascacielos, *m.* (coll.) skyscraper.—**rascar**, *vti.* [d] to scratch; to rasp; to scrape.—*vri.* to scratch oneself.

rasete, *m.* sateen.

rasgado, *a.* torn, open; generous.—*ojos rasgados*, large eyes.—*m.* tear, rip.—**rasgadura**, *f.* rent, rip.—**rasgar**, *vti.* [b] to tear, rend, rip.—**rasgo**, *m.* stroke, flourish; stroke (of wit, kindness, etc.); feature (of face); characteristic.—*a grandes rasgos*, broadly, in outline.—**rasgón**, *m.* rent, tear.

rasguñar, *vt.* to scratch.—**rasguño**, *m.* scratch.

raso, *a.* clear; plain; flat.—*a campo r.*, in the open air.—*m.* satin.—*soldado r.*, private.

raspadura, *f.* erasure; rasping; scraping; shavings.—**raspar**, *vt.* to scrape, rasp; to erase; to steal.

rastra, *f.* sled; dray; (Am.) trailer; (agr.) harrow, rake; anything dragging.—*a rastras*, dragging; by force, unwillingly.—**rastreador**, *n.* tracer; scout.—**rastrear**, *vt.* to trace, scent; to track down, trail; (agr.) to harrow, rake; to follow a clue to.—*vi.* to fly very low.—**rastrero**, *a.* creeping, dragging; trailing; flying low; abject; low.—**rastrillar**, *vt.* to hackle, dress (flax), comb; to rake.—**rastrillo**, *m.* hackle, flax comb; (agr.) rake.—**rastro**, *m.* track, scent, trail; trace; (agr.) rake, harrow; slaughterhouse; sign, token; vestige.—**rastrojo**, *m.* stubble.

rata, *f.* rat.—*r. de alcantarilla*, sewer rat.—*m.* (coll.) pickpocket.—**ratería**, *f.* larceny, petty theft; (coll.) meanness, stinginess.—**ratero**, *n.* pickpocket.—*r. de tiendas*, shoplifter.

ratificación, *f.* ratification, confirmation.—**ratificar**, *vti.* [d] to ratify, confirm.

rato, *m.* short time, while.—*al poco r.*, presently, very soon.—*a ratos*, from time to time, occasionally.—*buen r.*, a great while; a pleasant, good time.—*mal r.*, a hard time.—*pasar el r.*, to pass the time, while away the time.

ratón, *m.* mouse; (Am.) hangover; (comput.) mouse.—*r. de biblioteca*, (fam.) bookworm.—**ratonera**, *f.* mousetrap, rat trap.

raudal, *m.* torrent; plenty, abundance.

raudo, *a.* rapid, swift.

ravioles or **raviolis**, *mpl.* ravioli.

raya, *f.* stroke, dash, streak, stripe, line; crease (in trousers); parting in the hair; (print.) dash, rule.—*tener a uno a r.*, to hold one at bay; (ichth.) ray, skate.—**rayado**, *a.* streaky.—**rayano**, *a.* neighboring, contiguous, bordering.—**rayar**, *vt.* to draw lines on; to rule; to scratch, mar; to stripe, streak; to cross out.—*vi.* to excel, surpass; to border (on).—*r. el alba*, to dawn.—**rayo**, *m.* ray, beam; spoke of a wheel; thunderbolt; flash of lightning; lively, ready genius; great power or efficacy of action.—*de rayos X*, X-ray.—*r. de sol*, sunbeam.—*r. lunar*, moonbeam.—*r. X*, X-ray.

rayón, *m.* (neol.) rayon.

raza, *f.* race, lineage; breed.—*de r.*, pure-breed.

razón, *f.* reason; reasonableness; right; account, explanation; information; (Am.) message; (math.) ratio.—*a r. de*, at the rate of.—*con r. o sin ella*, rightly or wrongly.—*dar la r. a*, to agree with.—*entrar en r.*, to be, or become, reasonable, listen to reason.—*no tener r.*, to be wrong or mistaken.—*perder la r.*, to become insane.—*r. social*, (com.) firm, firm name.—*tener r.*, to be right.—**razonable**, *a.* reasonable; moderate; fair, just.—**razonamiento**, *m.* reasoning.—**razonar**, *vi.* to reason.

Rdo., *abbr.* (**Reverendo**) Rev.

reabastecer, *vti.* & *vri.* [3] to supply again.

reabrir, *vti.* & *vri.* [49] to reopen.

reacción, *f.* reaction.—*r. exagerada*, overreaction.—*r. de forma exagerada*, overreact.—*r. en cadena*, chain reaction.—**reaccionar**, *vi.* to react.—**reaccionario**, *n.* & *a.* reactionary.

reacio, *a.* obstinate, stubborn; reluctant.

reacondicionar, *vt.* to recondition.

reactivo, *a.* reactive.—*m.* (chem.) reagent; reactor.

reactor, *m.* (phys.) reactor; jet engine;

jet plane.—*r. nuclear,* nuclear reactor.

readaptación, *f.* readjustment.—**readaptar,** *vt.* to readjust, adapt again.

reajuste, *m.* readjustment.

real, *a.* real, actual; royal, kingly.—*m.* real, a silver coin; camp, encampment.

realce, *m.* excellence; luster, splendor; raised work, embossment; enhancement.—*dar r.,* to enhance.

realeza, *f.* royalty, regal dignity.—**realidad,** *f.* reality, fact; truth.—*en r.,* truly; really; in fact.—**realismo,** *m.* realism; royalism.—**realista,** *mf.* realist; royalist.—**realización,** *f.* realization, fulfillment; (com.) sale.—**realizar,** *vti.* [a] to realize, fulfill, carry out, perform; (com.) to sell out.

realzar, *vti.* [a] to raise, elevate; to emboss; to brighten the colors of; to make prominent; to heighten, enhance.

reanimar, *vt.* to cheer, encourage; to revive; reanimate.

reanudación, *f.* renewal; resumption.—**reanudar,** *vt.* to renew, resume.

reaparecer, *vii.* [3] to reappear.—**reaparición,** *f.* reappearance.

rearme, *m.* rearmament.

reasegurar, *vt.* (com.) to reinsure.—**reaseguro,** *m.* (com.) reinsurance.

reasumir, *vt.* to retake; to resume.

reata, *f.* rope, lariat; string of horses.

reavivar, *vt.* & *vr.* to revive, reanimate.

rebaja, *f.* (com.) discount; deduction, diminution.—**rebajar,** *vt.* to abate, lessen, diminish; to reduce, lower, cut down.—*vr.* to be dismissed; to lower oneself.

rebanada, *f.* slice.—**rebanar,** *vt.* to slice; to cut.

rebaño, *m.* herd; flock.

rebasar, *vt.* to exceed; to overflow.

rebatir, *vt.* to beat or drive back, repel; to refute.—**rebato,** *m.* alarm, alarm bell; call to arms; commotion; (mil.) sudden attack.

rebelarse, *vr.* to revolt, rebel.—**rebelde,** *a.* rebellious; stubborn.—*mf.* rebel; (law) defaulter.—**rebeldía,** *f.* rebelliousness, contumacy; stubbornness; (law) default.—**rebelión,** *f.* rebellion, revolt.

rebencazo, *m.* (Am.) blow with a whip.—**rebenque,** *m.* (Am.) whip.

reblandecer, *vti.* & *vri.* [3] to soften.—**reblandecimiento,** *m.* softening.

rebobinar, *vt.* to rewind.

reborde, *m.* flange, border; rim.—**rebordear,** *vt.* to flange.

rebosar, *vi.* to overflow; (de) to abound (in); to teem (with).

rebotar, *vi.* to rebound.—*vt.* to cause to rebound; to repel; to vex.—**rebote,** *m.* rebound, rebounding, bounce, bound.—*de r.,* on the rebound; indirectly.

rebozar, *vti.* [a] to muffle up; to dip (food in flour, etc.).—*vri.* to muffle oneself up.—**rebozo,** *m.* muffler; woman's shawl.—*sin r.,* frankly, openly.

rebullir, *vii.* & *vri.* [27] to stir, begin to move; to boil up.

rebusca, *f.* search; research; searching; gleaning.—**rebuscar,** *vti.* [d] to search carefully; to glean; to dig up.

rebuznar, *vi.* to bray.—**rebuzno,** *m.* braying (of a donkey).

recabar, *vt.* to obtain by entreaty.

recado, *m.* message, errand; present; gift; regards; daily provision or marketing; voucher; equipment; precaution.

recaer, *vii.* [8-e] to fall back, relapse; to fall or devolve; to behoove.—**recaída,** *f.* relapse.

recalar, *vi.* to make, sight, or reach port.—*vt.* to soak, drench, saturate.

recalcar, *vti.* [d] to cram, pack, press; to emphasize, stress.—*vri.* to harp on a subject.

recalentar, *vti.* [1] to reheat; to overheat; to warm over; to superheat.—*vri.* to become overheated or superheated.

recamar, *vt.* to embroider with raised work.

recámara, *f.* dressing room; boudoir; (Mex.) bedroom; (artil.) breech of a gun.

recambiar, *vt.* to exchange or change again; (com.) to refill.

recapacitar, *vi.* to refresh one's memory; to think carefully.

recargar, *vti.* [b] to reload; to overload; to overcharge; to recharge.—*vri.* (de) to have in abundance, have an abundance (of).—**recargo,** *m.* overload; overcharge; surtax, additional tax, charge, etc.; extra charge.

recatado, *a.* prudent, circumspect, unobtrusive; shy; modest.—**recatar,** *vt.* to secrete, conceal.—*vr.* to act modestly; to be cautious.—**recato,** *m.* prudence, caution; modesty; bashfulness.

recaudación, f. collecting, collection.—**recaudador,** n. tax collector.—**recaudar,** vt. to gather; to collect (rents or taxes).—**recaudo,** m. collection of rents or taxes; precaution, care; (law) bail, bond, security.—a buen r., well guarded, under custody, safe.

recelar, vt. to fear, suspect.—vr. (de) to fear, be afraid or suspicious (of), to beware (of).—**recelo,** m. misgiving, fear, suspicion.—**receloso,** a. suspicious, fearful, distrustful.

recental, a. suckling (lamb or calf).

recepción, f. reception, receiving, admission; registration desk, reception desk.—**recepcionista,** mf. receptionist; desk clerk, room clerk.

receptáculo, m. receptacle.—**receptivo,** a. receptive.—**receptor,** n. receiver; abettor; (baseball) catcher.—r. telefónico, telephone receiver.—**receptoría,** f. receiver or treasurer's office; (law) receivership.

recesar, vi. (Am.) to recess, suspend temporarily.—**recesión,** f. (com.) recession.—**receso,** m. recess; separation, withdrawal.

receta, f. prescription; recipe.—**recetar,** vt. to prescribe (medicines).

rechazado, a. rejected; defeated; unclaimed (mail).—**rechazar,** vti. [a] to repel, repulse, drive back; to reject; to rebuff; recoil.—**rechazo,** m. rebound; rebuff; recoil; rejection.

rechifla, f. hissing (in derision); hooting; mockery, ridicule.—**rechiflar,** vt. to hiss; to mock, ridicule.

rechinar, vi. to creak, squeak; to gnash the teeth.

rechoncho, a. (coll.) chubby, stocky.

recibidor, n. receiver; (com.) receiving teller.—m. reception room; vestibule.—**recibimiento,** m. reception; greeting, welcome.—**recibir,** vt. to receive; to take, accept; to admit; to experience (an injury).—vr. (de) to graduate (as); to be admitted to practice (as).—**recibo,** m. reception; (com.) receipt; sales slip.—acusar r., (com.) to acknowledge receipt.—estar de r., to be at home to callers.

recién, adv. (before pp.) recently, lately, newly.—r. casados, newlyweds.—r. llegado, newcomer.—r. nacido, newborn.—**reciente,** a. recent; new; modern; fresh.

recinto, m. enclosure; place (building, hall, etc.); precinct.—r. ferial, fairgrounds.

recio, a. strong, robust, vigorous; loud; rude; hard to bear; severe, rigorous (weather).—adv. strongly; rapidly; vigorously; loud.

recipiente, a. receiving.—m. receptacle; container; recipient.

reciprocar, vti. & vri. [d] to correspond.—**reciprocidad,** f. reciprocity.—**recíproco,** a. reciprocal, mutual.

recitación, f. recitation, recital.—**recital,** m. (mus.) recital.—**recitar,** vt. to recite; to rehearse.

reclamación, f. reclamation; (com.) complaint; claim.—**reclamante,** mf. & a. complainer; claimer; complaining; claiming.—**reclamar,** vt. to claim, demand; to decoy (birds); (law) to reclaim.—vi. to complain.—**reclamo,** m. decoy bird; lure (of birds); call; claim; complaint; advertisement.

reclinar, vt. to incline, recline, lean.—vr. to recline, lean back.—**reclinatorio,** m. pew; couch, lounge; prayer desk.

recluir, vti. [23-e] to shut up; to seclude.—**reclusión,** f. seclusion; place of retirement; arrest; jail, prison.—**recluso,** ppi. of RECLUIR.

recluta, f. (mil.) recruiting.—m. recruit.—**reclutamiento,** m. (mil.) recruiting.—**reclutar,** vt. (mil.) to recruit.

recobrar, vt. & vr. to recover, recuperate, regain; to recoup.—**recobro,** m. recovery, recuperation; resumption.

recocer, vti. [26-a] to boil too much; to boil again; to reheat.—vri. to burn with rage.

recodo, m. turn, winding, bend, angle.

recoger, vti. [c] to draw, pick; to pick up, take up; to take in, collect; to take in, shelter.—vri. to take shelter; to retire.—**recogida,** f. withdrawal; harvesting; (com.) retiral.—**recogimiento,** m. concentration, abstraction.

recolección, f. gathering, harvest; compilation; summary.—**recolectar,** vt. to gather, collect, harvest.

recomendable, a. commendable, laudable.—**recomendación,** f. recommendation; request; praise; merit; testimonial.—**recomendar,** vti. [1]

to recommend; to commend; to entrust; to ask, request.

recompensa, f. compensation; recompense, reward.—*en r.,* in return.—**recompensar,** vt. to compensate; to recompense, reward.

reconcentrar, vt. to concentrate; to dissemble.—*vr.* to concentrate (one's mind).

reconciliación, f. reconciliation.—**reconciliar,** vt. to reconcile.—*vr.* to become reconciled; to make up; to renew friendship.

reconocer, vti. [3] to recognize; to admit; (por) to acknowledge (as); to acknowledge; (mil.) to scout, reconnoiter.—**reconocimiento,** m. recognition; acknowledgment; gratitude; recognizance; examination, inquiry; (mil.) reconnoitering; (surv.) reconnaissance.

recontar, vti. [12] to recount; to relate.

reconvención, f. charge, accusation; reproach.—**reconvenir,** vti. [45] to accuse, reproach; (law) to countercharge.

recopilación, f. summary, compilation; (law) digest.—**recopilar,** vt. to compile, digest.

recordación, f. remembrance; recollection.—**recordar,** vti. [12] to remember, to remind.—*vri.* to remember.—**recordatorio,** m. reminder.

recorrer, vt. to go over; (mech.) to pass over, travel; to read over; to travel in or over; to overhaul.—*vi.* to resort; to travel.—**recorrido,** m. run; space or distance traveled or passed over, course; (auto) mileage.

recortar, vt. to cut away, trim, clip; to cut out; to cut to size; to outline (a figure).—**recorte,** m. cutting, paring; clipping (from newspaper, etc.); outline.—*pl.* trimmings, parings.

recostar, vti. [12] to lean, recline.—*vri.* to go to rest; to repose; to lean back (against), to recline.

recoveco, m. turning, winding; nook, cranny; sly approach.

recreación, f. recreation.—**recrear,** vt. to amuse, delight.—*vr.* to amuse oneself; to be pleased; to divert oneself.—**recreo,** m. recreation; place of amusement; (school) recess.

recrudecer, vii. & vri. [3] to increase; to recur.

rectángulo, a. rectangular; right-angled (triangle, etc.).—*m.* rectangle.

rectificar, vti. [d] to rectify; to correct, amend.

rectitud, f. straightness; righteousness, rightness, rectitude; accuracy, exactitude.—**recto,** a. straight; erect; righteous, just, fair; literal; right.—*m.* rectum.

rector, n. rector, curate; president (of a university, college, etc.); principal.—**rectorado,** m. rectorship; directorship; rector's office.—**rectoría,** f. rectory, curacy; rectorship; rector's or director's office.

recua, f. herd of beasts of burden; multitude, pack of things.

recuento, m. recount; inventory.—*r. de vocabulario,* word count.

recuerdo, m. remembrance; memory; recollection; souvenir; keepsake, memento.—*pl.* compliments, regards.

reculada, f. recoil, recoiling.—**recular,** vi. to recoil, back up; (coll.) to yield, give up, turn back.

recuperación, f. recovery, recuperation.—**recuperar,** vt. & vr. to recover, regain, recuperate.

recurrir, vi. to resort, apply; to revert.—**recurso,** m. recourse; resource, resort; return, reversion; memorial, petition; (law) appeal.—*pl.* resources, means.

recusar, vt. to reject, decline; to challenge (a juror).

red, f. net; network, netting; bag net; snare, trap; system (of RR., tel., etc.).

redacción, f. wording; editing; editorial rooms; editorial staff.—**redactar,** vt. to edit, be the editor of; to write, word.—**redactor,** n. editor.

redada, f. casting a net; catch, haul.

redargüir, vti. [23-e] to retort; (law) to impugn.

redecilla, f. hair net.

rededor, m. surroundings, environs.—*al* or *en r.,* around.

redención, f. redemption.—**redentor,** n. & a. redeemer; redeeming.

redil, m. sheepfold.

redimible, a. redeemable.—**redimir,** vt. to redeem, rescue, ransom; to liberate; (com.) to redeem, pay off.

rédito, m. (com.) revenue, interest, yield.

redoblar, vt. to double; to clinch; to repeat; (mil.) to roll (a drum).—**re-**

doble, *m.* (mil. & mus.) roll of a drum.

redoma, *f.* vial, flask.

redomado, *a.* artful, sly, crafty.

redonda, *f.* neighborhood, district.—*a la r.,* roundabout.—**redondamente,** *adv.* clearly, plainly, decidedly.—**redondear,** *vt.* to round, make round; to round off; to perfect.—*vr.* to clear oneself of debts; to obtain good profits (of a business).—**redondel,** *m.* (coll.) circle; round cloak; bull ring, arena.—**redondez,** *f.* roundness, rotundity.—*r. de la Tierra,* face of the Earth.—**redondilla,** *f.* quatrain.—**redondo,** *a.* round, rotund; clear, straight; (fig.) nice, honest.—*en r.,* all around.—*negocio r.,* (fig.) profitable business.

reducción, *f.* reduction, decrease; discount.—*r. de impuestos,* tax cut.—**reducido,** *a.* limited; small; narrow; compact.—**reducir,** *vti.* [11] to reduce; to diminish, decrease; (a) to convert (into); to subdue; to condense, abridge.—*vri.* to adjust oneself, adapt oneself; to be compelled, to decide from necessity.

reducto, *m.* (fort.) redoubt.

redundancia, *f.* redundance.—**redundante,** *a.* redundant, superfluous.—**redundar,** *vi.* to overflow; to be redundant; (en) to redound (to), lead (to).

reduplicar, *vti.* [d] to duplicate again, redouble.

reedificar, *vti.* [d] to rebuild.

reelección, *f.* reëlection.—**reelecto,** *ppi.* of REELEGIR.—**reelegir,** *vti.* [29–49] to reëlect.

reembolsar, *vt.* to reimburse, refund, pay back.—**reembolso,** *m.* reimbursement, refund.

reemplazar, *vti.* [a] to replace; to substitute.—**reemplazo,** *m.* replacement; substitution; (mil.) substitute.

reentrada, *f.* reentry (of a space vehicle).

reenvasar, *vt.* (com.) to refill.

reestreno, *m.* (theat.) revival.

reexpedir, *vti.* [29] to forward (mail, etc.).

refacción, *f.* refreshment, luncheon; reparation; (Am.) spare part; financing.

refajo, *m.* underskirt; petticoat.

referencia, *f.* reference; narration.—**referéndum,** *m.* referendum.—**referente,** *a.* referring, relating.—**referir,** *vti.* [39] to refer, relate; to tell, narrate.—*vri.* (a) to refer (to), have relation (to).

reflón, —*de r.,* obliquely, askance.

refinamiento, *m.* refinement; refining.—**refinar,** *vt.* to refine, purify; to make polite or refined.—**refinería,** *f.* refinery.

reflector, *a.* reflecting, reflective.—*m.* searchlight; reflector.—**reflejar,** *vt.* to reflect.—*vr.* to be reflected.—**reflejo,** *a.* reflected; (gram.) reflexive; (physiol.) reflex.—*m.* reflex; glare; reflection; light reflected.—*r. rotuliano,* knee jerk.—**reflexión,** *f.* reflection; thinking.—**reflexionar,** *vi.* to think, reflect.—**reflexivo,** *a.* reflexive; reflective; thoughtful.

reflujo, *m.* ebb or ebb tide.

reforma, *f.* reform; reformation; alteration, correction, improvement.—**reformador,** *n.* & *a.* reformer; reforming.—**reformar,** *vt.* to reform; to amend, improve.—*vr.* to reform; to mend.—**reformatorio,** *a.* corrective, reforming.—*m.* reformatory.—**reformista,** *mf.* & *a.* reformer; reforming, reformist.

reforzar, *vti.* [12-a] to strengthen, reinforce.

refrán, *m.* proverb, saying.

refrenar, *vt.* to restrain, check; to rein, curb.

refrendar, *vt.* to legalize, authenticate, countersign.

refrescante, *a.* cooling, refreshing.—**refrescar,** *vti.* [d] to refresh; to cool.—*vii.* & *vri.* (of the weather) to get cool; to take the fresh air; to take refreshment; to cool off.—**refresco,** *m.* refreshment.

refriega, *f.* affray, scuffle, fray.

refrigeración, *f.* refrigeration.—**refrigerador,** *a.* refrigerating, freezing, cooling.—*m.* refrigerator, freezer, ice box.—**refrigerar,** *vt.* to cool, refrigerate.—**refrigerio,** *m.* coolness; refreshment, refection.

refuerzo, *m.* reinforcement; strengthening; welt (of shoe); aid, help.

refugiado, *n.* refugee.—**refugiar,** *vt.* to shelter.—*vr.* to take shelter or refuge.—**refugio,** *m.* refuge, shelter.—*r. antiaéreo,* air-raid shelter.—*r. antinuclear,* fallout shelter.—*r. fiscal,* tax shelter.

refundir, *vt.* to remelt or recast; to rearrange, recast, reconstruct.—*vi.* to redound.

refunfuñar, vt. to growl, grumble, mutter.—**refunfuño**, m. grumbling, growl, snort.

refutar, vt. to refute.

regadera, f. watering can, sprinkling can.—**regadío**, a. & m. irrigated (land).

regalar, vt. to present, give as a present, make a present of; to regale, entertain; to gladden, cheer, delight.—vr. to feast sumptuously.

regalía, f. regalia, royal rights; (Am.) advance payment or royalty to owner of patent, etc.; privilege, exemption.

regalo, m. present, gift; pleasure; dainty; comfort, luxury.

regañadientes. —a r., reluctantly, grumbling.—**regañar**, vi. to growl, grumble; mutter; to quarrel.—vt. (coll.) to scold, reprimand.—**regaño**, m. scolding, reprimand.—**regañón**, n. growler, grumbler; scolder, scold.—a. growling, grumbling; scolding.

regar, vti. [1-b] to water; to irrigate; to sprinkle; to scatter.

regata, f. regatta, boat race.—**regatear**, vt. to haggle about, beat down (the price), to resell at retail; to bargain; to dodge, dribble (soccer)—vi. to haggle; to wriggle; (naut.) to race.—**regateo**, m. chaffer, bargaining, haggling.

regazo, m. lap (of body).

regente, a. ruling, governing.—mf. regent; manager, director.—**regentear**, vi. to rule, boss, manage.—**regidor**, a. ruling, governing.—m. alderman or councilman.

régimen, m. regime; management, rule; (gram.) government; (med.) regimen, treatment.—r. alimenticio, diet.—r. de hambre, starvation diet.

regimental, a. regimental.—**regimentar**, vt. to regiment.—**regimiento**, m. (mil.) regiment; administration, government; town council.

regio, a. royal, regal; sumptuous, magnificent.

región, f. region.—**regional**, a. regional, local.

regir, vti. [29-c] to rule, govern, direct; to manage.—vii. to be in force.

registrador, n. register; registrar, recorder, master or clerk of records; searcher, inspector.—a. registering.—**registrar**, vt. to inspect, examine; to search; to register, record.—vr. to register, be registered or matriculated.—**registro**, m. search, inspection, examination; census, registry, registration; enrollment; record, entry; enrolling office; certificate of entry; register book; bookmark; (mus.) register, organ stop; regulator (of a timepiece).

regla, f. rule, regulation, precept; order, measure, moderation; (drawing) ruler, straight edge; menstruation.—en r., thoroughly, in due form, in order.—r. de oro, golden rule.—**reglamentar**, vt. to establish rules; to regulate by rule, law or decree.—**reglamento**, m. by-laws; rules and regulations.

regocijado, a. merry, joyful, festive.—**regocijar**, vt. to gladden, cheer, rejoice.—vr. to rejoice, be merry.—**regocijo**, m. joy, gladness; merriment; rejoicing.

regodearse, vr. to take delight, rejoice.—**regodeo**, m. joy, delight.

regordete, a. (coll.) chubby, plump.

regresar, vi. to return.—**regreso**, m. return, coming or going back.

reguero, m. trickle, drip; irrigating furrow.

regulación, f. regulation; adjustment.—**regulador**, a. regulating, governing.—m. (mech.) regulator; governor; register; controller (of electric car).—**regular**, vt. to regulate; to adjust.—a. regular; moderate, sober; ordinary; fairly good, soso.—por lo regular, usually, as a rule.—**regularidad**, f. regularity; common usage, custom.—**regularizar**, vti. [a] to regularize.

rehabilitación, f. rehabilitation; renovation.—r. del habla, speech correction.

rehacer, vti. [22–49] to remodel, make over, remake; do over, redo; to renovate, mend, repair.—vri. to regain strength and vigor; (mil.) to rally, reorganize.—**rehecho**, ppi. of REHACER.

rehén, m. (gen. pl.) hostage.

rehuir, vti., vii. & vri. [23-e] to shun, avoid; to reject, decline, refuse.

rehusar, vt. to refuse, decline, reject, withhold.

reimpresión, f. reprint; reissue.—**reimprimir**, vti. [49] to reprint.

reina, f. queen.—**reinado**, m. reign.—**reinante**, a. reigning; prevailing.—

reinar, *vi.* to reign; to prevail, predominate.

reincidir, *vi.* to relapse; to backslide.

reingreso, *m.* reentry.

reino, *m.* kingdom.—*R. Unido*, United Kingdom.

reintegrar, *vt.* to reintegrate, restore; (com.) to reimburse, refund.—*vr.* (de) to recover, recuperate.—**reintegro**, *m.* reimbursement, restitution.

reír, *vii.* & *vri.* [35] to laugh.—*r. a carcajadas*, to laugh loudly, guffaw.—*reírse de*, to laugh at; to mock.

reiterar, *vt.* to reiterate.

reja, *f.* grate, grating, railing; plowshare; plowing.—**rejilla**, *f.* small lattice or grating; latticed wicket; cane for backs and seats of chairs.

relación, *f.* relation, relationship, dealing; ratio; narration, account; (law) report, brief; (theat.) speech.—*pl.* relations, connections; acquaintance; courting, engagement.—*en* or *con r.* regarding (to or with).—**relacionar**, *vt.* to relate, connect; to make acquainted.—*vr.* to get acquainted, make connections; to be related.

relajación, *f.*, **relajamiento**, *m.* relaxation, laxity; slackening; hernia.—**relajar**, *vt.* to relax, slacken; to release from an obligation; to amuse, divert.—*vr.* to become relaxed, loosened, weakened; to grow vicious; to be ruptured.—**relajo**, *m.* (Am.) disorder, mix-up; (Am.) depravity; diversion.

relamer, *vt.* to lick again.—*vr.* to lick one's lips; to relish; to boast.

relámpago, *m.* lightning; flash; (fig.) quick person or action.—**relampaguear**, *vi.* to lighten; to flash, sparkle.—**relampagueo**, *m.* lightning; flashing.

relatar, *vt.* to relate, narrate.

relatividad, *f.* relativity.—**relativo**, *a.* relative.

relato, *m.* statement; narration; report, account.—**relator**, *n.* narrator.

releer, *vti.* [e] to read over again; to revise.

relegar, *vti.* [b] to relegate, banish; to set aside.

relente, *m.* night dew, night dampness.

relevador, *m.* (elec.) relay.

relevante, *a.* excellent, great, eminent.—**relevar**, *vt.* (mil.) to relieve, substitute; to emboss; to bring into relief; to relieve, release; to forgive, acquit; to exalt, aggrandize.—*vi.* (art) to stand out in relief.—**relevo**, *m.* (mil.) relief.—*carrera de relevos*, relay race.

relicario, *m.* locket; reliquary.

relieve, *m.* relief, raised work, embossment.—*poner de r.*, to bring out, throw into relief, emphasize.—*pl.* (of food) leavings; (fig.) highlights or high points.

religión, *f.* religion.—**religiosidad**, *f.* religiosity; religiousness.—**religioso**, *a.* religious; scrupulous.—*n.* religious, member of a religious order.

relinchar, *vi.* to neigh.—**relincho**, *m.* neigh, neighing.

reliquia, *f.* relic; remains; trace, vestige.

rellano, *m.* landing (of a stair).

rellenar, *vt.* to refill; to fill up; (cook.) to stuff; (sewing) to pad; (mason.) to point.—*vr.* to stuff oneself.—**relleno**, *a.* stuffed.—*m.* stuffing, dressing, filling; (mech.) packing, gasket; (sewing) padding, wadding.

reloj, *m.* clock; watch.—*estar como un r.*, (fam.) to be in perfect trim.—*r. de arena*, hourglass, sandglass.—*r. de bolsillo*, pocket watch.—*r. de cuco* or *cucú*, cuckoo clock.—*r. de pie*, tallcase clock, grandfather's clock.—*r. de pulsera*, wrist watch.—*r. de segundos muertos*, stop watch.—*r. de sol*, sundial.—*r. despertador*, alarm clock.—*r. eléctrico*, electric clock.—*r. registrador*, time clock.—**relojero**, *n.* watchmaker.

reluciente, *a.* shining, glittering, bright.—**relucir**, *vii.* [3] to shine, glow, glitter; to be brilliant.

relumbrante, *a.* resplendent.—**relumbrar**, *vi.* to sparkle, shine, glitter.—**relumbrón**, *m.* luster, dazzling brightness; tinsel.—*de r.*, showy, pompous.

remachar, *vt.* to clinch; to rivet; to secure, affirm.—**remache**, *m.* rivet; riveting; flattening, clinching.

remanente, *m.* remains, remnant, residue.—*a.* residual.

remangar, *vti.* [b] to tuck up (sleeves, etc.).

remanso, *m.* backwater; dead water; eddy.

remar, *vt.* & *vi.* to row, paddle.

rematado, *a.* sold (at auction); finished.—*estar r.*, (coll.) to be completely crazy.—**rematar**, *vt.* to end, finish; (com.) to auction; to give the finishing stroke; (sewing) to fasten off (a stitch).—vr. to be utterly ruined or destroyed; to become completely crazy.—**remate**, m. end, finish, conclusion; punch line (of a joke); (com.) auction, public sale; (arch.) finial, pinnacle.—de r., utterly, completely, hopelessly.—r. de cuentas, closing of accounts.

emedar, vt. to imitate, copy, mimic.

emediar, vt. to remedy; to help; to repair (mischief); to avoid.—no poder r., not to be able to help (prevent).—**remedio**, m. remedy; medicine; help; amendment.—no hay más r. (que), there's nothing else to do (but).—no tener r., to be unavoidable; to be irremediable; to be no help for.—sin r., inevitable; hopeless.

ememorativo, a. reminiscent, reminding, recalling.

emendar, vti. [1] to patch, mend, repair; to darn.—**remendón**, n. cobbler; botcher, patcher.

emero, m. rower, oarsman.

emesa, f. (com.) shipment; remittance.—**remesar**, vt. (com.) to ship; to send, remit.

emlendo, m. patch; mending piece; darning; repair.—a remiendos, by patchwork, piecemeal.

emiligado, a. affected, prudish, squeamish.—**remilgo**, m. affected nicety, prudery, squeamishness.

eminiscencia, f. reminiscence.

emirar, vt. to review, look at or go over again.—vr. (en) to take great pains with; to inspect or consider with pleasure.

emisión, f. remission, sending back, remitting, remitment; pardon, forgiveness; remissness, indolence; relaxation, abatement.—entrar en r., (med.) to go into remission.—**remiso**, a. remiss, careless, slack.—**remitente**, mf. & a. remitter, sender; remitting, sending.—**remitir**, vt. to remit; to forward; to pardon; to refer; (law) to transfer, remit to another court.—vt., vi. & vr. to remit, abate.—vr. (a) to refer (to); to quote from.

emo, m. oar; leg (of quadruped); (coll.) arm or leg (of person).

emoción, f. removal, removing; dismissal.

emojar, vt. to steep, soak, drench.—

remojo, m. steeping, soaking, soakage.

remolacha, f. (bot.) beet.

remolcador, m. tug, tugboat, towboat.—**remolcar**, vti. [d] to tow, tug, take in tow; to haul.

remolino, m. whirl, whirlwind; whirlpool; twisted tuft of hair; crowd, throng; commotion.

remolón, a. indolent, lazy, soft.—n. malingerer.

remolque, m. towing, towage; trackage; towline.—a r., in tow.—dar r., to tow.

remontar, vt. (Am.) to go up (river); to repair, resole, revamp (shoes).—vt. & vr. to elevate, raise, rise.—vr. to soar (as birds); to take to the woods; to go back to, date from.

rémora, f. hindrance, obstacle; cause of delay; (ichth.) remora.

remordimiento, m. remorse.

remoto, a. remote, far off; unlikely.

remover, vti. [26] to move, remove, stir, disturb; to dismiss.

rempujar, vt. to jostle, shove, push.—**rempujón**, m. jostle, push, shove.

remuneración, f. remuneration; gratuity, consideration.—**remunerar**, vt. to remunerate.

renacer, vii. [3] to be born again; to spring up again, grow again.—**renacimiento**, m. renaissance, renascence, new birth.

renacuajo, m. tadpole; (coll.) little squirt.

rencilla, f. grudge; heartburning.

renco, a. = RENGO.

rencor, m. rancor, animosity, grudge.—**rencoroso**, a. rancorous, spiteful.

rendición, f. rendition, surrendering, yielding; profit, yield, product.—**rendido**, a. obsequious; devoted; fatigued, tired out.

rendija, f. crevice, crack, cleft.

rendimiento, m. submission; yield; income; output; (mech.) efficiency.—**rendir**, vti. [29] to subdue, overcome; to surrender, yield, give up; to render, give back; to do (homage); (com.) to produce, yield; to fatigue, tire out.—r. las armas, to throw down the arms, to surrender.—vri. to become exhausted, tired, worn out; to yield, submit, give up, surrender.

renegado, n. renegade, apostate; wicked person.—**renegar**, vti. [1-b]

to deny, disown; to detest.—*vii.* to turn renegade, apostatize; to blaspheme, curse; (de) to deny, renounce; to blaspheme, curse.

renegrido, *a.* blackish.

renglón, *m.* written or printed line; (com.) line of business, staple, item.—*a r. seguido,* immediately after; the next moment.—*pl.* lines, writings.

rengo, *a.* lame.—**renguear,** *vi.* to limp, hobble.

reno, *m.* reindeer.

renombrado, *a.* renowned, famous.—**renombre,** *m.* surname, family name; renown.

renovación, *f.* renovation, renewing; change, reform; replacement.—**renovador,** *n.* & *a.* renovator; renewing.—**renovar,** *vti.* [12] to renew; to renovate; to replace; to repeat.

renquear, *vi.* = RENGUEAR.

renta, *f.* profit; annuity; tax, contribution; revenue, income.—*r. de aduanas,* customs duties.—*r. gravable* or *imponible,* taxable income.—*r. vitalicia,* life annuity.—**rentar,** *vt.* to produce, bring, yield; to rent for.—**rentista,** *mf.* financier; bondholder; one who lives on a fixed income.

renuente, *a.* unwilling, reluctant.

renuevo, *m.* sprout, shoot.

renuncia, *f.* resignation; renunciation; renouncement; waiving.—**renunciamiento,** *m.* renouncement.—**renunciar,** *vt.* to renounce; to resign; to disown; to waive; to reject; to abandon, relinquish.—*vi.* to resign.

reñir, *vti.* & *vii.* [9] to wrangle, quarrel, fight; to fall out; to scold.

reo, *a.* guilty, criminal.—*mf.* criminal, culprit; (law) defendant.

reojo, *m.*—*mirar de r.,* to look askance.

reorganización, *f.* reorganization.—**reorganizar,** *vti.* [a] to reorganize; to reconstitute.

reóstato, *m.* rheostat.

repantigarse, *vri.* [b] to stretch (oneself) in a chair.

reparación, *f.* reparation, repair, indemnity; atonement.—**reparador,** *n.* repairer; restorer; faultfinder.—**reparar,** *vt.* to repair, recondition; to restore; to observe, notice; to consider, heed; to make up for, indemnify for; to atone for.—**reparo,** *m.* repair, restoration; observation, warning, notice; difficulty; objec-

tion.—*poner reparos,* to make obje tions.

repartición, *f.* distribution; dealing. *r. errónea,* misdeal.—**repartide** *a.* distributing.—*n.* distributor; a sessor of taxes.—**repartimiento,** *m* division, distribution, apportio ment; assessment.—**repartir,** *vt.* divide, distribute, apportion; to a sess.—*r. mal,* to misdeal.—**repart** *m.* = REPARTIMIENTO; (theat.) cast characters; delivery (of goods, ma etc.).—*r. de acciones gratis,* sto split.

repasar, *vt.* to pass again; to reëxan ine, revise; to glance over; to men darn; to review (as a lesson).—**r paso,** *m.* review (of a lesson); rev sion, reëxamination; final inspe tion; mending.

repecho, *m.* short, steep incline.

repelar, *vt.* to pull out the hair of.

repelente, *a.* repellent.—*m.* (de i sectos) insect repellent.

repeler, *vt.* to repel, repulse; to refut dispute.

repente, *m.* sudden movement or im pulse.—*de r.,* suddenly.—**repentin** *a.* sudden.

repertorio, *m.* repertory, repertoire.

repetición, *f.* repetition; (theat.) er core.—**repetir,** *vti.* & *vii.* [29] to re peat.—*vri.* to repeat oneself.

replicar, *vti.* [d] to peal, ring (bells); mince, chop.—**repique,** *m.* ringing pealing (bells).—**repiquetear,** *vt.* t ring, peal (bells); to tap (with finger or shoes).—**repiqueteo,** *m.* ringin of bells; tapping, clicking.

repisa, *f.* mantelpiece; shelf, consol bracket.—*r. de ventana,* window sil

replegar, *vti.* [1-b] to fold severa times.—*vri.* (mil.) to fall back, re treat in order.

repleto, *a.* replete, very full.

réplica, *f.* reply, answer; retort, rejoir der; objection; exact copy, rep lica.—**replicar,** *vii.* [d] to reply, an swer; to contradict, argue.

repliegue, *m.* doubling, folding; (mil orderly retreat.

repollo, *m.* cabbage; round head (of plant).

reponer, *vti.* [32–49] to replace, pu back; to reinstall; to restore.—*vri.* t recover lost health or property.

reportaje, *m.* (journalism) report, re porting.—**reportar,** *vt.* to contro restrain, check; to obtain, get, at tain; to carry; to bring.—*vr.* to refrain, forbear, control oneself.—**repórter**, *mf.*, **reportero**, *n.* reporter.

posado, *a.* quiet, restful.—**reposar**, *vi.* to rest, repose; to stand (on), be supported (by); to take a nap; to lie down; to lie (in the grave).—*vr.* to settle (as liquids).

posición, *f.* replacement, reinstatement; recovery (in health); (theat.) revival.—**repositorio**, *m.* repository.

poso, *m.* rest, repose; sleep; tranquillity.

posteria, *f.* confectionery, pastry shop.—**repostero**, *n.* pastry cook.

prender, *vt.* to scold, reproach, reprehend.—**reprensión**, *f.* reprimand, reproach.

presa, *f.* dam, dike, sluice; damming; stopping, holding back.

presalia, *f.* reprisal.

presentación, *f.* representation; description; (theat.) performance, play; figure, image, idea.—**en r. de**, as a representative of.—**representante**, *a.* representing, representative.—*mf.* representative; agent.—**representar**, *vt.* to represent, typify; (theat.) to perform, act.—*vr.* to image, picture to oneself, conceive.—**representativo**, *a.* representative.

presión, *f.* repression, check, control.—**represivo**, *a.* repressive, restrictive.

primenda, *f.* reprimand.—**reprimir**, *vt.* to repress, check, curb, quash.

probable, *a.* blameworthy.—**reprobación**, *f.* reproof.—**reprobado**, *a.* flunked.—**reprobar**, *vti.* [12] to reprove, disapprove, condemn; to damn; to flunk, fail.—**réprobo**, *n.* & *a.* reprobate.

prochar, *vt.* to reproach, censure; to challenge (witnesses).—**reproche**, *m.* reproach, reproof; repulse, rebuff.

producción, *f.* reproduction; (art) copy.—**reproducir**, *vti.* & *vri.* [11] to reproduce.—**reproductor**, *n.* & *a.* reproducer; reproducing.

ptil, *m.* reptile; crawler, creeper.

pública, *f.* republic.—**republicano**, *a.* & *n.* republican.

pudiar, *vt.* to repudiate; to reject; to divorce.—**repudio**, *m.* repudiation; rejection; divorce.

puesto, *ppi.* of REPONER.—*a.* recovered.—*m.* store, stock, supply.—**de r.**, extra; spare.

repugnancia, *f.* reluctance; aversion; loathing; disgust.—**repugnante**, *a.* loathsome; repulsive, disgusting.—**repugnar**, *vt.* to cause disgust; to do with reluctance.

repulgar, *vti.* [b] (sewing) to hem.

repulsa, *f.* refusal, rebuke, repulse.—**repulsión**, *f.* repulsion. **repulsivo**, *a.* repelling.

reputación, *f.* reputation.—**reputar**, *vt.* to repute; to estimate, appreciate.

requebrar, *vti.* [1] to woo, court, make love to; to flatter, wheedle; to break again.

requemar, *vt.* to reburn; to overcook; to inflame (the blood).

requerimiento, *m.* summons; requisition, demand.—**requerir**, *vti.* [39] to summon; to notify; to require, need; to court, woo, make love to.

requesón, *m.* pot cheese, cottage cheese; curd.

requiebro, *m.* flattery, compliment; endearment.

requilorios, *m.* (coll.) useless ceremony; circumlocution.

requisa, *f.* tour of inspection; requisition.—**requisar**, *vt.* to make the rounds of; to requisition.—**requisito**, *m.* requisite, requirement.

res, *f.* head of cattle; beast.

resabio, *m.* unpleasant aftertaste; viciousness; bad habit.

resaca, *f.* surge; surf, undertow; (com.) redraft; (Am.) hangover.

resaltar, *vi.* to stand out; to jut out, project; to rebound; to come off, get loose; to be evident.

resarcimiento, *m.* compensation, reparation, indemnity.—**resarcir**, *vti.* [a] to compensate, indemnify, make amends to; to mend, repair; to recoup.

resbaladizo, *a.* slippery; glib; elusive; tempting, alluring.—**resbalar**, *vt.* & *vr.*, to slip, slide, glide; to skid; to err, go astray.—**resbalón**, *m.* slip, slipping; fault, error, break.—**resbaloso**, *a.* (Am.) slippery.

rescatar, *vt.* to ransom; to redeem, recover; to rescue; to exchange, barter, commute.—**rescate**, *m.* ransom; redemption; ransom money; exchange, barter; reward.

rescindir, *vt.* to rescind, annul.—**rescisión**, *f.* cancellation, annulment.

rescoldo, *m.* embers, hot ashes; scruple, doubt, apprehension.

resecar, *vti.* & *vri.* [d] to dry up; to

parch.—**reseco**, *a*. too dry; very lean.

resentimiento, *m*. resentment, grudge; impairment.—**resentirse**, *vri*. [39] to be impaired or weakened; to resent, be offended or hurt.

reseña, *f*. brief description; book review; sketch, summary, outline; (mil.) review.—**reseñar**, *vt*. to review, summarize, outline; (mil.) to review.

reserva, *f*. reserve, reticence; reservation; discretion; (mil.) reserve; salvo; second-string.—*a r. de*, intending to.—*de r.*, extra, spare.—*en r.*, confidentially.—*guardar r.*, to act with discretion.—*r. de materias primas*, stockpile.—*sin r.*, openly, frankly.—**reservación**, *f*. reservation.—**reservado**, *a*. reticent, reserved, circumspect.—**reservar**, *vt*. to reserve, keep; to retain, hold; to postpone; to exempt; to conceal.—*vr*. to bide one's time; to keep for oneself; to beware, be cautious.

resfriado, *m*. cold (illness).—**resfriarse**, *vr*. to catch cold.—**resfrío**, *m*. = RESFRIADO.

resguardar, *vt*. to preserve, defend, protect.—*vr*. to take shelter; (de) to guard (against); protect oneself (from).—**resguardo**, *m*. security, safety, safeguard, defense, protection; (com.) guarantee, collateral.

residencia, *f*. residence, domicile.—*r. estudiantil (en el campus)*, dormitory, dorm, residence hall.—**residencial**, *a*. residential.—**residente**, *a*. residing, resident, residential.—*mf*. dweller, inhabitant.—**residir**, *vi*. to reside, live; dwell; (fig.) to consist.

residuo, *m*. remainder, remnant; residue; (arith.) difference.—*r. líquido*, runoff.—*pl*. refuse, leavings.

resignación, *f*. resignation; submission.—**resignar**, *vt*. to resign, give up.—*vr*. to resign oneself, be resigned.

resina, *f*. resin, rosin.—**resinoso**, *a*. resinous.

resistencia, *f*. resistance, endurance.—**resistente**, *a*. resisting; resistant, tough.—**resistir**, *vi*. to resist, offer resistance.—*vt*. to resist; to bear, stand; to endure.—*vr*. to put up a struggle, resist.

resma, *f*. ream (of paper).

resol, *m*. glare of the sun.

resollar, *vii*. [12] to breathe noisily, pant; (coll.) to breathe; (coll.) give signs of life.

resolución, *f*. resolution; resoluteness; determination, courage; solution (of a problem).—*en r.*, in short.—**resolver**, *vti*. [47–49] to resolve, determine; to sum up; to solve (a problem).—*vri*. to resolve, determine; (med.) to resolve, be reduced.

resonancia, *f*. resonance.—*tener r.*, cause a stir, attract attention.—**resonante**, *a*. resonant, resounding, sounding.—**resonar**, *vii*. [12] to resound, clatter.

resoplar, *vi*. to puff, breathe audibly; snort.—**resoplido**, *m*. puff; snort.

resorte, *m*. (mech.) spring; resilience, spring, elasticity; means; motivation.—*tocar resortes*, (fam.) to pull strings or wires.

respaldar, *vt*. to indorse; to back; to answer for, guarantee.—*m*. back of seat.—**respaldo**, *m*. back of a seat; backing; back of a sheet of paper; indorsement.

respectivo, *a*. respective.—**respecto**, *m*. relation, proportion; relativeness; respect.—*a este r.*, with respect to this.—*al r.*, relatively, respectively.—*con r. a*, *r. a*, or *r. de*, with respect to, with regard to.—**respectuosamente**, *adv*. respectfully.

respectabilidad, *f*. respectability.—**respetable**, *a*. respectable, considerable; worthy; honorable, reliable.—**respetar**, *vt*. to respect, revere, honor.—**respeto**, *m*. respect; deference, attention; observance.—*faltar al r. a*, to be disrespectful to.—**respetuoso**, *a*. respectful; respectable.

respingar, *vii*. [b] to kick, wince; to grunt; (coll.) to mutter; to talk back.—**respingo**, *m*. muttering, grumbling; gesture of unwillingness.

respirable, *a*. breathable.—**respiración**, *f*. respiration, breathing.—*artificial*, artificial respiration.—**respiradero**, *m*. vent, air hole; ventilator.—**respirar**, *vi*. & *vt*. to rest, take rest or respite; to catch one's breath; to breathe freely; to exhale scents or odors.—**respiratorio**, *a*. respiratory.—**respiro**, *m*. breathing; moment of rest; respite; (com.) extension, time.

resplandecer, *vii*. [3] to glitter, glisten, shine.—**resplandeciente**, *a*. aglow,

—resplandor, *m.* light, splendor, brilliance, radiance; glare.

esponder, *vt.* & *vi.* to answer, reply; to respond; to acknowledge; to requite; to yield, produce; to have the desired effect; (com.) to correspond.—*vi.* (**de**) to answer (for), be responsible (for), vouch (for), guarantee.—**respondón,** *a.* saucy, pert, insolent.

esponsabilidad, *f.* responsibility; reliability.—**responsable,** *a.* responsible; reliable.

esponso, *m.* (eccl.) responsory for the dead.

espuesta, *f.* answer, reply; response, rejoinder; refutation.—*r. pronta y aguda,* retort.—*r. viva,* repartee.

esquebra(ja)dura, *f.* crack, cleft, fissure.—**resquebrajar,** *vt.* & *vr.* to crack, split.

esquicio, *m.* slit, crevice, crack; chance, opportunity.

esta, *f.* (arith.) subtraction; remainder, difference.

establecer, *vti.* [3] to restore, reestablish, reinstate.—*vri.* to recover (from illness).—**restablecimiento,** *m.* reëstablishment; restoration; recovery.

estallar, *vi.* to crack (a whip); to crackle.

estante, *a.* remaining.—*m.* remainder.

estañar, *vt.* to stanch (wounds); to stop the flow of (blood).

estar, *vt.* to deduct; (arith.) to subtract.—*vi.* to be left, remain; (arith.) to subtract.

estauración, *f.* restoration.—**restaurante,** *m.* restaurant.—*r. autoservicio,* cafeteria.—**restaurar,** *vt.* to restore; to recondition.

estitución, *f.* restitution.—**restituir,** *vti.* [23-e] to restore; to return, give back.—*vri.* to return, come back.

esto, *m.* remainder, balance, rest; limit for stakes at cards.—*pl.* remains.—*echar el r.,* to stake one's all; to do one's best.

estorán, *m.* (Am.) restaurant.

estregar, *vti.* [1-b] to rub, scrub.—**restregón,** *m.* scrubbing, hard rubbing.

estricción, *f.* restriction, limitation.—**restrictivo,** *a.* restrictive, restricting.—**restringir,** *vti.* [c] to restrain, restrict, confine.

resucitar, *vt.* to resuscitate, revive; to renew.—*vi.* to rise from the dead, return to life.

resuelto, *ppi.* of RESOLVER.—*a.* resolute, determined, quick.

resuello, *m.* breath, breathing; puffing, snorting.

resulta, *f.* result, effect, consequence.—*de resultas,* in consequence.—**resultado,** *m.* result.—**resultar,** *vi.* to result, follow; to turn out; to turn out to be; (coll.) to work (well or badly).

resumen, *m.* summary, résumé.—*en r.,* in brief.—**resumir,** *vt.* to abridge; to summarize, sum up.—*vr.* to be reduced or condensed.

resurrección, *f.* resurrection.

retablo, *m.* series of historical pictures; (eccl.) altarpiece.

retador, *n.* challenger.—*a.* challenging.

retaguardia, *f.* rear, rear guard.

retahíla, *f.* string, series; line.

retar, *vt.* to challenge, dare.

retardado, *a.* retarded.—**retardar,** *vt.* to retard, slow up; to delay, detain.—*vr.* to fall behind, be slow.—**retardo,** *m.* retardation; delay.

retazo, *m.* piece, remnant; cutting; fragment, portion.

retemblar, *vii.* [1] to tremble, shake, quiver.

retención, *f.* retention, keeping or holding back.—**retener,** *vti.* [42] to retain, withhold; to detain.—**retentivo,** *a.* retentive, retaining.—**retentiva,** *f.* retentiveness, memory.

reticencia, *f.* reticence.—**reticente,** *a.* reticent.

retina, *f.* retina of the eye.

retinto, *a.* very black.

retintín, *m.* tinkling, jingle; ringing (in the ears). (coll.) sarcastic undertone.

retirada, *f.* withdrawal; (mil.) retreat; retirement.—**retirado,** *a.* retired; isolated; distant; pensioned.—**retirar,** *vt.* to withdraw; to put aside, reserve; to repel.—*vr.* to withdraw; to retire; to recede; (mil.) to retreat.—**retiro,** *m.* retirement; retreat; secluded place.—*r. obrero,* social security.

reto, *m.* challenge; threat, menace.

retocar, *vti.* [d] to retouch; to touch up, finish.

retoñar, *vi.* to sprout; to reappear.—**retoño,** *m.* sprout, shoot.

retoque, *m.* retouching, finishing touch.

retorcer, *vti.* [26-a] to twist; to contort; to distort, misconstrue.—*vri.* to writhe, squirm.—**retorcimiento,** *m.* twisting; writhing.

retórica, *f.* rhetoric.—*pl.* (coll.) sophistries, quibbles, subtleties.—**retórico,** *a.* rhetorical.

retornar, *vi.* & *vr.* to return, come back.—*vt.* to return; to give back.—**retorno,** *m.* return, coming back; repayment, requital.

retorta, *f.* (chem.) retort.—**retortero,** *m.*—*andar al r.,* to hover about.

retortijón, *m.* curling up, twisting up.—*r. de tripas,* cramps, bellyache.

retozar, *vii.* [a] to frisk, romp, frolic.—**retozo,** *m.* romping, frolic; wantonness.—**retozón,** *a.* frolicsome, rollicking.

retractación, *f.* retraction.—**retractar,** *vt.* & *vr.* to retract, to recant.

retraer, *vti.* [43] to bring again; to dissuade; (law) to redeem.—*vri.* to take refuge or shelter; to withdraw from, shun; to keep aloof, retire.—**retraimiento,** *m.* retirement; refuge; aloofness.

retranca, *f.* (Am.) brake.—**retranquero,** *m.* (Am., RR.) brakeman.

retransmitir, *vt.* to relay (a message, etc.); to broadcast again.

retrasado, *a.* & *n.* retarded; retarded person.

retrasar, *vt.* to defer, postpone; to delay; to set back (timepiece).—*vi.* to go back, decline.—*vr.* to be backward; to be behindhand, late, behind time; (of timepiece) to run slow.—**retraso,** *m.* delay, deferment, lateness.

retratar, *vt.* to portray; to imitate, copy; to photograph.—*vr.* to be reflected; to be depicted; to sit for a portrait or photograph.—**retratista,** *mf.* portrait painter; photographer.—**retrato,** *m.* portrait, picture; photograph; copy, resemblance; description.

retrechero, *a.* (coll.) wily; attractive, winsome.

retreparse, *vr.* to lean back; to recline in a chair.

retrete, *m.* toilet, rest room.

retribución, *f.* retribution; recompense, fee.—**retribuir,** *vti.* [23-e] to remunerate, reward.

retroactividad, *f.* retroactivity.—**retroactivo,** *a.* retroactive.

retroceder, *vi.* to fall back, move backward; (auto) to back up; to recede, to retrogress.—**retroceso,** *m.* backward motion; (med.) relapse; recession; (mech. & cine) rewind.—**retrocohete,** *m.* retrorocket.—**retrodisparo,** *m.* retrofiring.

retrospectivo, *a.* retrospective.

retruécano, *m.* pun.

retumbante, *a.* resonant, resounding, pompous, bombastic.—**retumbar,** *vi.* to resound, rumble.

reuma, *m., reumatismo,* *m.* rheumatism.—**reumático,** *a.* rheumatic.

reunión, *f.* reunion; meeting; gathering; rendezvous (in space).—**reunir,** *vt.* to unite; to reunite; to gather; to collect, accumulate; to join.—*vr.* to join, to unite; to meet, get together, assemble.

revalidar, *vt.* to ratify, confirm; to renew.

revancha, *f.* revenge.

revelación, *f.* revelation.—**revelador,** *n.* & *a.* revealer; revealing, telltale.—*m.* (photog.) developer.—**revelar,** *vt.* to reveal; (photog.) to develop.

revendedor, *n.* retailer; ticket scalper.—**revender,** *vt.* to resell; to retail.—**reventa,** *f.* resale.

reventar, *vii.* [1] to blow up, blow out; to burst forth; to explode; to sprout, shoot, blossom.—*vti.* to burst; to break; to crush, smash; to tire, wear out; to vex, annoy.—*vri.* to burst; to blow up, blow out; to break.—**reventón,** *a.* bursting.—*m.* bursting, blowout, explosion.

rever, *vti.* [46] to review, revise, look over again; (law) to try again.—**reverberar,** *vi.* reverberate.

reverdecer, *vii.* [3] to grow green again; to sprout again; to acquire new freshness and vigor.

reverencia, *f.* reverence; curtsy, bow; (eccl.) reverence (title).—**reverenciar,** *vt.* to venerate, revere; to hallow.—**reverendo,** *a.* reverend, worthy of reverence.—**reverente,** *a.* reverent.

reversible, *a.* (law) returnable, revertible; (phys.) reversible.—**reverso,** *m.* reverse (in coins); back, rear side.—*el r. de la medalla,* the opposite in every respect.

evertir, *vii.* [39] to revert.

vés, *m.* reverse, back, wrong side; backhand slap, shot or stroke; counterstroke; misfortune.—*al r.,* on the contrary, contrariwise; in the opposite or wrong way or direction; wrong side out.

vestimiento, *m.* (mason.) covering, facing, coat(ing); finish.—**revestir,** *vti.* [29] to dress, clothe; to cover, face; to line; (fig.) to cloak; (mason.) to coat, cover with a coating.—*vri.* to be invested with.

evisar, *vt.* to revise, review; to reëxamine, check.—**revisión,** *f.* revision, reviewing; reëxamination.—**revisor,** *m.* reviser, corrector; auditor; ticket collector; (RR.) conductor.—**revista,** *f.* (mil.) review, parade; review, magazine; (theat.) revue.—*pasar r.,* to review; to examine, go over.—*r. de historietas,* comic book.—**revistero,** *n.* reviewer.

evivir, *vi.* to revive.

evocable, *a.* revocable.—**revocación,** *f.* revocation; abrogation.—*r. de una sentencia,* (law) reversal.—**revocar,** *vti.* [d] to revoke, repeal, reverse; to whitewash, plaster.—**revoco,** *m.* whitewashing, plastering.

evolcar, *vti.* [12-d] to knock down, tread or trample upon; (coll.) to floor (an opponent).—*vri.* to wallow; to be stubborn.

evolotear, *vi.* to flutter, fly about.—**revoloteo,** *m.* fluttering.

evoltijo, revoltillo, *m.* mess, mass, medley, jumble.—*r. de huevos,* scrambled eggs.—**revoltoso,** *a.* turbulent; rebellious; mischievous.—**revolución,** *f.* revolution.—**revolucionario,** *a.* & *n.* revolutionary; revolutionist.—**revolver,** *vti.* [47–49] to turn over, turn upside down; to stir; to agitate; to wrap up; to mix up.—*vri.* to move to and fro; to rebel; to change (as the weather).—**revólver,** *m.* revolver.

evuelco, *m.* rolling.—**revuelo,** *m.* fluttering; commotion, stir, disturbance.

evuelta, *f.* revolution, revolt; change.—**revuelto,** *ppi.* of REVOLVER. —*a.* mischievous; confused, mixed up; intricate, difficult; topsy-turvy.—*huevos revueltos,* scrambled eggs.

ey, *m.* king.

reyerta, *f.* dispute, wrangle, quarrel.

rezagado, *n.* straggler.—**rezagar,** *vti.* [b] to leave behind; to outstrip; to put off, defer.—*vri.* to fall behind, lag.—**rezago,** *m.* remainder, leftover.

rezar, *vti.* [a] to say, recite (prayers); to say, read, state (of books, etc.).—*vii.* to pray.—*r. con,* to concern, be the business or duty of.—**rezo,** *m.* prayer; praying, devotions.

rezongar, *vii.* [b] to grumble, mutter, growl.—**rezongón,** *n.* grumbler, mutterer, growler.

rezumadero, *m.* dripping place; cesspool.—**rezumar,** *vi.* & *vr.* to ooze, exude, percolate, filter through; (coll.) to transpire; to leak out.

ría, *f.* estuary.—**riachuelo,** *m.* rivulet, rill; small river.

ribazo, *m.* sloping bank; mound, hillock.

ribera, *f.* shore, beach, bank.—**ribero,** *m.* levee.

ribete, *m.* (sewing) binding; trimming; pretense.—**ribetear,** *vt.* to bind.

ricacho, ricachón, *n.* (coll.) vulgar, rich person.

ricino, *m.* castor-oil plant.

rico, *a.* rich, wealthy, abundant, plentiful; delicious, exquisite; cute (child).

ridiculez, *f.* ridiculous thing or action; ridiculousness.—**ridiculizar,** *vti.* [a] to ridicule.—**ridículo,** *a.* ridiculous.—*ponerse en r.,* or *quedar en r.,* to make oneself ridiculous.—*m.* ridicule.

riego, *m.* irrigation; watering.

riel, *m.* (RR.) rail.—*pl.* tracks.

rienda, *f.* rein of a bridle; (fig.) moderation, restraint.—*pl.* reins, ribbons; government, direction.—*a r. suelta,* with a free rein.—*soltar las riendas,* to act without restraint.

riesgo, *m.* risk.—*de alto r.,* high-risk.

rifa, *f.* raffle, scuffle, wrangle.—**rifar,** *vt.* to raffle.—*vi.* to quarrel.

rifle, *m.* rifle.

rigidez, *f.* rigidity; sternness.—*r. cadavérica,* rigor mortis.—**rígido,** *a.* rigid, stiff; rigorous, inflexible; puritanical.

rigor, *m.* rigor; sternness.—**rigoroso, riguroso,** *a.* rigorous; exact; absolute; strict, severe, puritanical.—**rigurosidad,** *f.* rigorousness; severity.

rima, f. rhyme; heap, pile.—pl. poems.—**rimar,** vi. to rhyme.

rimbombante, a. resounding; bombastic.

rincón, m. (inside) corner, nook; cozy corner.—**rinconera,** f. corner cupboard, stand, bracket.

ringla, ringlera, f. (coll.) row, file, line, tier; swath.

rinoceronte, m. rhinoceros.

riña, f. quarrel, scuffle, dispute.—r. de gallos, cockfighting.

riñón, m. kidney.—tener cubierto el r., to be rich, to be well off.—**riñonada,** f. layer of fat about the kidneys; dish of kidneys.

río, m. river.—r. abajo, down the river.—r. arriba, up the river.

ripio, m. residue, rubbish; padding, useless words.—no perder r., not to miss the least occasion.

riqueza, f. riches, wealth; richness; abundance; fertility.

risa, f. laugh, laughter.

risco, m. crag, cliff.

risible, a. laughable, ludicrous.—**risotada,** f. outburst of laughter, loud laugh.

ríspido, a. harsh, gruff.

ristra, f. string (of onions, garlic, etc.).

risueño, a. smiling; pleasing, agreeable.

rítmico, a. rhythmic.—**ritmo,** m. rhythm; rate (of increase, etc.).

rito, m. rite, ceremony.—**ritual,** m. (eccl.) ritual, ceremonial.—a. ritual.

rival, mf. rival.—**rivalidad,** f. rivalry.—**rivalizar,** vii. [a] to rival, compete.

rivera, f. brook, creek, stream.

rizar, vti. [a] to curl.—vri. to curl naturally.—**rizo,** a. naturally curled or frizzled.—m. curl, ringlet.—rizar el r., (aer.) to loop the loop.

robar, vt., vi. & vr. to rob, steal; to abduct; to kidnap.

roble, m. oak; (fig.) very strong person or thing.

robo, m. robbery, theft; plunder, loot.

robot, m. robot.

robustecer, vti. [3] to make strong.—**robustez,** f. robustness, ruggedness, hardiness.—**robusto,** a. robust, vigorous, hale.

roca, f. (geol.) rock; cliff.—**rocalloso,** a. rocky.

roce, m. friction, rubbing; contact, familiarity.

roclada, f. sprinkling; reprimand.—**rocladera,** f or **rociador,** m. sprin-

kling can, sprinkler.—**rociar,** vi. to fall (of dew).—vt. to sprinkle, to spray; to strew about.

rocín, m. decrepit nag.

rocío, m. dew; spray, sprinkle; light shower.

rocoso, a. rocky.

rodada, rodadura, f. wheel track, rut, tread.

rodaja, f. small wheel or disk; round slice.—**rodante,** a. rolling.—**roda pié,** m. (arch.) skirting; foot rail dado.—**rodar,** vii. [12] to roll; to rotate, revolve, wheel; to run on wheels; to wander about; to go up and down.—vt. to shoot (a film movie, etc.).

rodear, vt. & vi. to surround, encircle.—vi. to go around; to make a detour.—vr. to turn, twist, toss about.—**rodeo,** m. turn, winding roundabout course, method or way round-up, rodeo; circumlocution beating around the bush; evasion subterfuge; corral.

rodilla, f. knee.—de rodillas, on one' knees.—doblar or hincar las rodillas to kneel down.—**rodillazo,** m. push or blow with the knee.—**rodillera,** f knee guard; knee patch; bagging o trousers at the knee.

rodillo, m. roll, roller; (cook.) rolling pin.

roedor, n. & a. rodent.—**roer,** vti. [36] to gnaw, eat away; to gnaw at; to corrode; to harass, annoy.

rogar, vti. [12-b] to request, beg, entreat.

rojez, f. redness, ruddiness.—**rojizo,** a reddish, sandy; ruddy.—**rojo,** a. red ruddy, reddish.—m. red color.

rol, m. list, roll, catalogue; muster roll.

roldana, f. sheave, pulley wheel; caster

rollizo, a. plump, stocky.—m. log.

rollo, m. roll; roller, rolling pin.

romadlzo, m. cold in the head snuffles; hay fever.

romance, m. Romance (language) Spanish vernacular (language) Spanish ballad.—en buen r., in plain language.

romanesco, a. Roman; characteristi of novels.—**románico,** a. (arch.) Ro manesque; Romance (language).—**romano,** n. & a. Roman.

romanticismo, m. romanticism.—**romántico,** a. romantic.—n. romanti cist.—**romanza,** f. (mus.) romance.

ombo, *m.* (geom.) rhombus; lozenge, diamond.

omería, *f.* pilgrimage; picnic.

omero, *m.* (bot.) rosemary; pilgrim.

omo, *a.* obtuse; blunt.

ompecabezas, *m.* puzzle, riddle; jigsaw puzzle.—**rompehielos,** *m.* ice breaker; ice plow (of a boat).—**rompeolas,** *m.* breakwater, jetty.—**romper,** *vti.* [49] to break, smash, shatter; to fracture (bone); to tear; to pierce.—*vii.* to burst; to break; to burst forth; to fall out, quarrel; (of the day) to dawn; to begin, start; to sprout, bloom; to break out, spring up; (of light, sun, etc.) to break through.—*vri.* to break.—**romplente,** *a.* breaking.—*m.* reef, shoal.—**rompimiento,** *m.* break, breakage, rupture; breach; quarrel.

on, *m.* rum.

oncar, *vii.* [d] to snore; to roar; (coll.) to brag.—**ronco,** *a.* hoarse, raucous; rasping.

oncha, *f.* welt; blotch.

onda, *f.* night patrol; rounds (by a night watch), beat; round (card game, drinks, cigars); serenade.—**rondar,** *vt.* & *vi.* to patrol, go the rounds; to walk the streets by night; to haunt, hover about; to impend.

onquedad, ronquera, *f.* hoarseness; rasp.—**ronquido,** *m.* snore; raucous sound.

onronear, *vi.* to purr.

onzal, *m.* halter.

oña, *f.* filth, grime; scab (in sheep); stinginess; (Am.) ill-will; infection.—**roñoso,** *a.* scabby, leprous; dirty, filthy, rusty; (coll.) niggardly, stingy; (Am.) spiteful.

opa, *f.* clothes, clothing; garments.—*a. quema r.,* at close range, point-blank.—*r. blanca,* household linen; underwear.—*r. de baño,* swim suits, bathing trunks.—*r. de cama,* bedclothes.—*r. de mesa,* table linen.—*r. hecha,* ready-made clothing.—*r. interior,* underclothes.—*r. interior de mujer,* lingerie.—*r. íntima,* underwear and swimwear.—*ropas civiles,* civvies.—**ropaje,** *m.* vestments; garb; (art) drapery.—**ropero,** *m.* wardrobe, closet.—**ropón,** *m.* wide, loose gown.

oque, *m.* rook (in chess).

orro, *m.* (coll.) babe in arms.

osa, *f.* (bot.) rose; red spot on any part of the body; rose color.—*r. náu-*

tica, or *de los vientos,* (naut.) mariner's compass.—**rosáceo,** *a.* rose-colored.—**rosado,** *a.* rose-colored; rose.—**rosal,** *m.* rose plant, rose-bush.—**rosaleda,** *f.* rosary, rose garden.—**rosario,** *m.* rosary.

rosbif, *m.* roast beef.

rosca, *f.* screw and nut; screw thread; ring-shaped biscuit or bread.

róseo, *a.* rosy.—**roseta,** *f.* small rose; rosette.—**rosetón,** *m.* large rosette; (arch.) rose window; rosette.

rosquilla, *f.* ring-shaped fancy cake.

rosillo, *a.* light red, roan (of horses).

rostro, *m.* face, countenance; rostrum.

rotación, *f.* rotation.—**rotar,** *vi.* to roll, rotate.—**rotativo,** *a.* rotary, revolving.—*f.* rotary printing press.—**rotatorio,** *a.* rotary, rotating.

roto, *ppi.* of ROMPER.—*a.* broken, chipped, shattered; torn; ragged; destroyed.—*m.* tear (in clothes); (Am.) man of the poorer classes; (Am.) hole.

rotonda, *f.* rotunda.

rótula, *f.* knee-joint.

rotulación, *f.* labeling.—**rotulador,** *a.* labeling.—*m.* felt-tip pen., felt pen.—**rotular,** *vt.* to label, put a title to.—**rótulo,** *m.* label, mark; show bill, placard.

rotundidad, *f.* roundness, rotundity.—**rotundo,** *a.* round, rotund; (of voice) full, sonorous; plain.

rotura, *f.* rupture, fracture; breakage, breach, opening.—**roturación,** *f.* breaking up new ground.—**roturar,** *vt.* to break up.

rozadura, *f.* friction; chafing.

rozagante, *a.* pompous, showy; trailing on the ground (as a gown).

rozamiento, *m.* friction; rubbing; disagreement, clashing.—**rozar,** *vti.* [a] to stub; to nibble; to gall, chafe; to graze, pass lightly over.—*vii.* to graze, rub.—*vri.* (con) to have to do with, be on familiar terms with.

rubí, *m.* ruby; red color.—**rubia,** *f.* (aut.) station wagon.—**rubicundez,** *f.* ruddiness; rosiness.—**rubicundo,** *a.* reddish, ruddy.

rubio, *a.* blond(e), golden, fair.—*r. ceniza,* ash-blond.—*r. platino,* platinum blond.

rubor, *m.* blush, flush; bashfulness.—**ruborizarse,** *vri.* [a] to blush, flush.—**ruboroso,** *a.* bashful.

rúbrica, *f.* mark, flourish; (after signature) rubric; title, heading.—*de r.,* according to rules or custom.—**ru-bricar,** *vti.* [d] to sign with a flourish; to sign and seal.

rucio, *a.* (of animals) light silver gray.

rudeza, *f.* roughness, ruggedness, rudeness, coarseness.—**rudimen-tario,** *a.* rudimentary, undeveloped.—**rudimento,** *m.* rudiment, embryo; vestige.—*pl.* rudiments, elements.—**rudo,** *a.* rude, rough, unpolished; hard, rigorous; stupid.

rueca, *f.* distaff (for spinning).

rueda, *f.* wheel; circle of persons; round slice; turn, time, succession; rack (torture).—*hacer la r.,* to cajole, wheedle; to court.—*r. de agua, r. de paletas,* (naut.) water wheel.—*r. de feria, r. gigante,* Ferris wheel, big wheel.—*r. de fuegos artificiales,* pinwheel.—*r. del timón,* (naut.) (steering) wheel.—*r. de prensa,* press conference.

ruedo, *m.* bull ring, arena; rotation; circuit; circumference, edge of a wheel or disk; round mat or rug; (Am.) (sewing) hem of a skirt; hemline.

ruego, *m.* request, plea, petition, supplication.

rufián, *m.* ruffian, rowdy, tough; pimp, pander.—**rufianismo,** *m.* rowdyism.

rufo, *a.* sandy (haired); curled.

rugido, *m.* roar; rumbling.—**rugir,** *vii.* [c] to roar, bellow, howl.

ruido, *m.* noise; din; rumor; report.—*hacer* or *meter r.,* to attract attention; to create a sensation; to make a noise.—**ruidoso,** *a.* noisy, loud; clamorous.

ruin, *a.* mean, vile, despicable; puny; stingy; insidious; (of an animal) vicious.—*m.* wicked, mean or vile man.—**ruina,** *f.* ruin, downfall; overthrow, fall.—*pl.* ruins, debris.—**ruindad,** *f.* baseness; avarice; base action.—**ruinoso,** *a.* decayed, ramshackle; ruinous; worthless.

ruiseñor, *m.* nightingale.

ruleta, *f.* roulette.

rumano, *n. & a.* Rumanian.

rumbo, *m.* bearing, course, direction; (coll.) pomp, show; generosity.—*con r. a,* in the direction of; heading or sailing for.—**rumboso,** *a.* pompous, magnificent; liberal, lavish.

rumiante, *m. & a.* ruminant.—**rumiar,** *vt.* to ruminate.

rumor, *m.* rumor; sound of voices; murmur.—**rumorarse,** *vr.* (Am.) to be said or rumored, be circulating as a rumor.

runrún, *m.* (coll.) rumor, report.

ruptura, *f.* rupture; fracture, breaking.

rural, *a.* rural.

ruso, *n. & a.* Russian.—*m.* Russian language.

rusticidad, *f.* rustic nature; rudeness, clumsiness.—**rústico,** *a.* rustic, rural; coarse, clumsy; unmannerly.—*en rústica,* (bookbinding) in paper covers, unbound.—*n.* peasant.

ruta, *f.* route, way.—*r. marítima,* seaway.

rutilante, *a.* sparkling, starry.

rutina, *f.* routine, custom, habit.—**rutinario,** *a.* routine.

Rvdo., *abbr.* (**Reverendo**) Rev.

S

S.A., *abbr.* (**Sociedad Anónima**) Inc. (Incorporated).

sábado, *m.* Saturday; Sabbath.

sábalo, *m.* shad.

sábana, *f.* sheet (for a bed).—*pegársele a uno las sábanas,* to rise late.—*s. ajustale* or *de cuatro picos,* fitted sheet.—*s de arriba* or *encimera,* top sheet.

sabana, *f.* (Am.) savanna, grassy plain.

sabandija, *f.* small nasty reptile.—*pl.* vermin.

sabañón, *m.* chilblain.

saber, *vti.* [37] to know; to be able, know how to, can; to be aware of, know about.—*vii.* to know; to be very sagacious.—*a s.,* namely, to wit.—*que yo sepa,* as far as I know, to my best knowledge.—*¿quién sabe?* perhaps, who knows?—*s. a,* to taste of, taste like.—*s. de,* to know, be familiar with; to hear of or from, have news about.—*s. todas las tretas,* (fam.) to know the ropes.—*m.* learning, knowledge, lore.—**sabi-duría,** *f.* wisdom; learning, knowledge.—**sabiendas.**—*a s.,* knowingly, consciously.—**sabihondo,** *a.* know-it-all.—**sabio,** *n.* sage, wise person.—*a.* wise, learned.

sablazo, *m.* blow with or wound from a saber; (coll.) borrowing or sponging.—**sable,** *m.* saber, cutlass.—**sablear,** *vt.* (coll.) to sponge, borrow.—**sablista,** *mf.* (coll.) sponger, one who asks for petty loans.

sabor, *m.* taste, flavor, savor.—**saborear,** *vt.* to flavor, savor; to give a relish or zest to.—*vt.* & *vr.* to relish, enjoy; to smack one's lips.

sabotaje, *m.* sabotage.—**saboteador,** *n.* saboteur.—**sabotear,** *vt.* & *vi.* to sabotage.

sabroso, *a.* savory, tasty, palatable, delicious; pleasant.

sabueso, *m.* hound; bloodhound; (fig.) bloodhound (detective).

sacabocado(s), *m.* (hollow) punch.—**sacabullas,** *m.* (fam.) (Mex.) bouncer.—**sacacorchos,** *m.* corkscrew.—**sacamuelas,** *mf.* (coll.) tooth extractor, quack dentist.—**sacapintura,** *f.* paint remover.—**sacapuntas,** *m.* pencil sharpener.—**sacar,** *vti.* [d] to extract, draw out, pull out; to take out; to put out; to take (a photo); to bring out; to get, obtain; to deduce, infer; to draw, win (a prize); (games) to serve (the ball); to kick off); to unsheathe (a sword); to make, take (a copy).—*s. a bailar,* to lead out for a dance.—*s. a luz,* to print, publish.—*s. de quicio,* to make one lose patience.—*s. (a uno) de sus casillas,* (fig.) to drive crazy, to exhaust one's patience.—*s. en claro,* or *en limpio,* to conclude, arrive at the conclusion.—*s. la cara,* to stand for, defend.—*s. la cuenta,* to figure out.

sacarina, *f.* saccharin.

sacerdocio, *m.* priesthood.—**sacerdote,** *m.* priest.—**sacerdotisa,** *f.* priestess.

saco, *m.* sack, bag; sackful, bagful; coat, jacket; (mil.) sack, plunder.—*entrar a s.,* to plunder, loot.—*no echar en s. roto,* not to forget, not to ignore.—*s. de noche,* hand bag, satchel.

sacramento, *m.* sacrament.

sacrificar, *vti.* [d] to sacrifice.—*vri.* to sacrifice oneself, give up one's life.—**sacrificio,** *m.* sacrifice, offering.

sacrilegio, *m.* sacrilege.—**sacrílego,** *a.* sacrilegious.

sacristán, *m.* sexton, sacristan.—**sacristía,** *f.* sacristy, vestry.

sacro, *a.* holy, sacred.—*m.* (anat.) sacrum.—**sacrosanto,** *a.* very holy, sacrosanct.

sacudida, *f.* shake, shaking, jerk.—**sacudimiento,** *m.* shake, shaking; shock, jerk, jolt.—**sacudir,** *vt.* to shake; jolt, jerk; to beat (to remove dust); to spank, drub; to shake off.—*vr.* to reject, drive away, shake off.

sádico, *a.* sadistic.—**sadismo,** *m.* sadism.

saeta, *f.* arrow, dart.

Sagitario, *m.* (astr.) Sagittarius.

sagrado, *a.* sacred.

sahumar, *vt.* to perfume; to smoke; to fumigate.—**sahumerio,** *m.* smoke; vapor, steam; fumigation; fuming.

sainete, *m.* (theat.) short farce; flavor sauce; tidbit.

sajón, *n.* & *a.* Saxon.

sal, *f.* salt; wit; grace, winning manners; (Am.) bad luck.—*s. de compas,* rock salt.—*s. de mesa, s. fina,* table salt.—*sales aromáticas,* smelling salts.—*sales de baño,* bath salts.—*s. gema,* rock salt.—*s. yodada,* iodized salt.

sala, *f.* living room, parlor; hall; courtroom, court of justice (room and judges); tribunal.—*s. de conciertos,* concert hall.—*s. de conferencias,* assembly room, lecture hall.—*s. de descanso,* lounge.—*s. de embarque, s. de preembarque,* departure lounge.—*s. de espera,* waiting room.—*s. de estar,* sitting room.—*s. de exhibición* or *muestras,* showroom.—*s. de exposiciones,* gallery.—*s. de fiestas,* night club.—*s. de juntas,* boardroom.—*s. de lectura,* reading room.—*s. del trono,* throneroom.—*s. de máquinas,* engine room.—*s. de partos,* delivery room.—*s. de reuniones,* clubroom.—*s. de subastas,* auction room.—*s. de tribunal, s. de justicia,* courtroom.—*s. de trucos,* poolroom.—*s. de urgencias,* emergency room.

saladillos, *mpl.* salted peanuts.

salado, *a.* salty, salted; briny; witty; graceful, winsome; (Am.) unlucky; (Am.) expensive.

salamandra, *f.* salamander.

salar, *vt.* to salt; to season or preserve with salt; to cure or corn (meat); to brine; (Am.) to bring bad luck; to spoil, ruin.

salario, *m.* wages, salary.

salchicha, *f.* sausage.—**salchichón,** *m.* salami.—*s. de Frankfurt,* frankfurter, frank, hot dog.

salcochar, *vt.* (cook.) to boil with water and salt.

saldar, *vt.* (com.) to settle, liquidate, balance.—**saldo,** *m.* (com.) balance; settlement; remnants sold at low price; sale.

saledizo, *a.* salient, projecting.—*m.* projection, ledge.

salero, *m.* saltcellar; salt pan; (coll.) gracefulness, winning ways, charm.—**saleroso,** *a.* (coll.) witty; lively, jolly, winsome.

salida, *f.* start, setting or going out, departure; exit; outlet; issue, result; subterfuge, pretext; witty remark; sally; projection; expenditure, outlay; (comput.) output.—*s. a escena,* (theat.) curtain call.—*s. de baño,* beach robe.—*s. del sol,* sunrise.—*s. en falso,* (sports) false start.—*s. impresa,* (comput.) printout.—*sin s.,* dead end.—*s. lanzada,* (sports) running start.—**saliente,** *a.* salient, projecting.—*f.* projection, lug.

salino, *a.* saline.—*f.* salt works, salt mine.

salir, *vii.* [38] to go or come out; to depart, leave; to get out, get off (of a vehicle); to rise (as the sun); to spring; to be issued or published; to come out, do (well, badly); to lead to; to open to; to say or do a thing unexpectedly or unseasonably; (theat.) to enter, appear.—*s. a,* to resemble, look like.—*s. adelante,* to be successful.—*s. al encuentro,* to come out to meet.—*s. de,* to dispose of; to part with; to get rid of.—*s. ganando,* to come out a winner, gain.—*vri.* to leak; to overflow.—*s. con la suya,* to accomplish one's end, to have one's way.

salitre, *m.* saltpeter, niter.

saliva, *f.* saliva, spittle.

salmo, *m.* psalm.

salmón, *m.* salmon.

salmuera, *f.* brine; pickle.

salobre, *a.* brackish, briny, saltish.

salón, *m.* salon, large parlor; living or assembly room.—*s. de actos,* auditorium.—*s. de baile,* ballroom.—*s. de belleza,* beauty salon.—*s. de exhibición* or *de ventas,* showroom,

salesroom.—*s. de exposiciones,* exhibition hall, showroom.—*s. de fiestas,* reception room.—*s. de juegos, s. recreativo,* amusement arcade.—*s. del automóvil,* automobile show.—*s. de té,* tearoom.—**saloncillo,** *m.* rest room (of a theater).

salpicadura, *f.* splash, spatter, spattering.—**salpicar,** *vti.* [d] to spatter, sprinkle, splash.

salpimentar, *vti.* [1] to season with pepper and salt.

salpullido, *m.* (med.) rash.

salsa, *f.* sauce, dressing, gravy.—**salsera,** *f.* gravy dish, tureen.

saltamontes, *m.* grasshopper.—**saltar,** *vi.* to jump, leap, spring, hop; to skip; to bound; to snap, break in pieces; to come off (as a button).—*s. a la vista,* to be self-evident.—*s. a tierra,* to land, debark.—*vt.* to leap or jump over; to skip.

salteado, *a.* assorted.

salteador, *n.* highwayman(-woman); hold-up man, robber.

Salterio, *m.* Psalter.

saltimbanqui, *mf.* acrobat.—**salto,** *m.* jump, leap; skip; omission; gap.—*a saltos,* leaping, by hops.—*dar un s.,* to jump, leap.—*de un s.,* at one jump; in a flash.—*s. de agua,* waterfall, falls, cataract.—*s. con garrocha, s. con pértiga,* pole vault.—*s. de altura, s. (en) alto,* high jump.—*s. de(l) ángel,* swan dive.—*s. de cama,* negligée.—*s. de carpa,* (swimming) jackknife.—*s. de esquí,* ski jump.—*s. de longitud, s. (en) largo,* long jump.—*s. desde grandes alturas,* high diving.—*s. en paracaídas,* parachute jump.—*s. mortal,* somersault.

saltón, *a.* jumping, hopping; protruding.—*ojos saltones,* bulging eyes.—*m.* grasshopper.

salubre, *a.* salubrious, healthful.—**salubridad,** *f.* salubrity, healthfulness.—**salud,** *f.* health; public weal; welfare.—*pl.* compliments, greetings.—*a. su s.,* to your health (in drinking).—*mala s.,* ill health.—**saludable,** *a.* healthy; salutary, wholesome.

saludar, *vt.* to greet, how to, salute, hail.—**saludo,** *m.* bow, salute, salutation, greeting.—**salutación,** *f.* salutation, greeting, salute, bow.

salva, *f.* (artil.) salvo; salver, tray.

salvación, *f.* salvation.

salvado, *m.* bran.

salvador, *n.* savior, rescuer, redeemer.
salvadoreño, *n.* & *a.* Salvadoran.
salvaguardar, *vt.* to safeguard, protect.—**salvaguardia,** *m.* safeguard, security, protection; guard; watchman.—*f.* safe-conduct, passport.
salvajada, *f.* savage word or action.—**salvaje,** *a.* savage, uncivilized; (of plants, animals) wild; rough, wild (country).—*mf.* savage.—**salvajismo,** *m.* savagery.
salvamento, *m.* salvage; safety; rescue.—*bote de s.,* lifeboat.—**salvar,** *vt.* to save, rescue; to avoid (a danger); to jump over, get over (ditch, creek, etc.), clear (an obstacle); to overcome (a difficulty); to excuse, make an exception of.—*s. las apariencias,* to keep up appearances.—*vr.* to be saved; to escape from danger.—**salvavidas,** *m.* life preserver; lifesaver.
¡salve! *interj.* hail!
salvedad, *f.* reservation, exception, qualification; salvo.
salvia, *f.* (bot.) sage.
salvo, *a.* saved, safe; excepted, omitted.—*adv.* save, saving, excepting, barring.—*s. que,* unless.—**salvoconducto,** *m.* safe-conduct; permit, pass.
samaritano, *a.* & *n.* Samaritan.
san, *a. contr.* of SANTO.
sanar, *vt.* to heal, cure.—*vi.* to heal; to recover from sickness.—**sanatorio,** *m.* sanatorium, sanitarium; asylum (for mental illness); nursing home.
sanción, *f.* sanction; ratification.—**sancionar,** *vt.* to sanction; to ratify.
sandalia, *f.* sandal.
sandez, *f.* foolishness, stupidity.
sandía, *f.* watermelon.
sandio, *a.* foolish, stupid.
sandunga, *f.* gracefulness; charm.—**sandunguero,** *a.* (coll.) graceful, charming.
sandwich [sǽngwch], *m.* sandwich.—*s. caliente,* toasted sandwich.—*s. club, sandwich de dos pisos,* club sandwich.
saneamiento, *m.* drainage (of land); sanitation; (law) waiver of lien.—**sanear,** *vt.* to drain, dry up (lands); (law) to indemnify.
sangrar, *vt.* to bleed; to drain.—*vi.* to bleed.—**sangre,** *f.* blood; lineage.—*a s. fría,* in cold blood.—*a s. y fuego,* by fire and sword.—*de sangre caliente,* (zool.) warm-blooded.—*s.*

fría, calmness, presence of mind.—**sangría,** *f.* bleeding; drain, outflow; sangria (red-wine punch).—**sangriento,** *a.* bloody, gory.—**sanguijuela,** *f.* leech.—**sanguinario,** *a.* sanguinary, bloody.—**sanguinolento,** *a.* bloody; bloodstained.
sanidad, *f.* health; healthfulness; health department.—**sanitario,** *a.* sanitary, hygienic.—*m.* health officer; rest home.—**sano,** *a.* healthy, sound; honest.—*s. y salvo,* safe and sound.
sanseacabó, *m.* (coll.) that's all.
santabárbara, *f.* (naut.) magazine; powder room.
santiamén, *m.* (coll.) instant, moment, jiffy.
santidad, *f.* sanctity, sainthood, saintliness, holiness.—**santificar,** *vti.* [d] to sanctify, to consecrate, hallow; to keep.—**santiguar,** *vt.* to bless; to heal by blessing.—*vr.* to cross oneself.—**santo,** *a.* saintly, holy; saint; sacred.—*todo el s. día,* the whole day long.—*n.* saint; saint's day.—*s. y seña,* (mil.) password.—**santuario,** *m.* sanctuary.—**santurrón,** *a.* sanctimonious, self-righteous.
saña, *f.* anger, rage, fury.—**sañudo,** *a.* furious, enraged.
sapo, *m.* toad.
saque, *m.* (sports) service; server (in tennis); kick-off (in football).
saqueador, *n.* looter, pillager.—**saquear,** *vt.* to plunder, loot, pillage.—**saqueo,** *m.* pillage, loot, plunder.
sarampión, *m.* measles.
sarao, *m.* dance; evening party.
sarape, *m.* (Am.) serape; blanket.
sarcasmo, *m.* sarcasm.—**sarcástico,** *a.* sarcastic.
sardina, *f.* sardine.
sargento, *m.* (mil.) sergeant.
sarmiento, *m.* vine shoot or branch.—**sarmentoso,** *a.* vinelike, gnarled, knotty.
sarna, *f.* itch, scabies; mange.—**sarnoso,** *a.* itchy; scabbed; mangy.
sarpullido, *m.* = SALPULLIDO.
sarraceno, *n.* Saracen; Moor.—*a.* Saracen; Moorish.
sarro, *m.* tartar on teeth.
sarta, *f.* string, series, row.
sartén, *m.* & *f.* frying pan; skillet.—*tener la s. por el mango,* to have the control or command.
sastre, *m.* tailor.—**sastrería,** *f.* tailor's shop.

satánico, *a.* satanic.

satélite, *m.* satellite; follower, henchman.—*s. espía,* spy satellite.—*s. meteorológico,* weather satellite.

satén, *m.* sateen.

sátira, *f.* satire.—**satírico,** *a.* satirical; sarcastic.—**satirizar,** *vti.* [a] to satirize, lampoon.—**sátiro,** *m.* lewd man; satyr.

satisfacción, *f.* satisfaction; apology, excuse.—**satisfacer,** *vti.* [22–49] to satisfy; to pay in full, settle.—*s. una letra,* (com.) to honor a draft.—*vri.* to satisfy oneself; to be satisfied; to take satisfaction; to be convinced.—**satisfecho,** *ppi.* of SATISFACER.—*a.* satisfied, content; arrogant, conceited.

saturación, *f.* saturation.—**saturar,** *vt.* to saturate.—*vr.* to become saturated; to fill, satiate.

sauce, *m.* willow, osier.

saurio, *m.* lizard.

savia, *f.* sap.

saxofón, saxófono, *m.* saxophone.

saya, *f.* skirt.—**sayuela,** *f.* (Am.) petticoat.

sazón, *f.* maturity, ripeness; season; taste, relish, flavor; occasion, opportunity.—*a la s.,* then, at that time.—*en s.,* ripe, in season.—**sazonar,** *vt.* (cook.) to season; to mature.—*vr.* to ripen, mature.

se, *3d. pers. refl. pron.* oneself, herself, itself, himself, themselves, each other, one another.—Replaces **le** to him, to her, to you (*formal*), to them.

sebo, *m.* tallow, fat.

seca, *f.* drought; dry season.—*a. secas,* simply; plain, alone.—**secador,** *a.* drying.—*m.* dish towel, tea towel; dryer.—*s. de pelo,* hairdryer.—**secadora,** *f.* clothes dryer.—**secante,** *f.* (geom.) secant.—*a.* drying.—*a.* & *m.* blotting (paper).—**secar,** *vti.* [d] to dry (out); to parch; to wipe dry; to tease, vex.—*vri.* to dry, dry up; to become lank, lean, or meager; to decay; to wither.

sección, *f.* act of cutting; section; division.—**seccionar,** *vt.* to section.

secesión, *f.* secession.

seco, *a.* dry; dried up; arid; dead (leaves); lean, meager; abrupt, curt; cold; sharp (noise).—*en s.,* high and dry; without cause or reason.—*parar en s.,* to stop suddenly.

secoya, *f.* sequoia.

secreción, *f.* (med.) secretion.—**secretar,** *vt.* (physiol.) to secrete.

secretaría, *f.* secretary's office; secretaryship.—**secretario,** *n.* secretary; actuary.—**secretear,** *vi.* (coll.) to whisper.—**secreteo,** *m.* (coll.) whispering.—**secreto,** *a.* secret; hidden.—*m.* secret; secrecy.—*s. a voces,* open secret.

secta, *f.* sect.—**sectario,** sectarian.

sector, *m.* sector, group, area.—*s. de distribución,* (elec.) power line.

secuaz, *mf.* follower, supporter, partisan.

secuela, *f.* sequel, result; fallout (side effect).

secuencia, *f.* sequence.

secuestrador, *n.* kidnapper.—**secuestrar,** *vt.* to kidnap, abduct; (law) to sequestrate.—**secuestro,** *m.* kidnapping, abduction; (law) sequestration.

secular, *a.* centenary; agelong; secular, lay.

secundar, *vt.* to second, aid, favor.—**secundario,** *a.* secondary; subsidiary.—*m.* second hand (of timepiece).

sed, *f.* thirst; longing, desire.—*tener s. de,* to be thirsty for; to thirst or hunger after.

seda, *f.* silk.—*como una s.,* sweet-tempered; smoothly.—**sedán,** *m.* sedan.

sedal, *m.* fishline.

sedante, sedativo, *m.* & *a.* sedative.

sede, *f.* see, seat.

sedeño, *a.* silken, silky.—**sedería,** *f.* silks; silk shop.—**sedero,** *a.* silk.—*n.* silk weaver or dealer.

sedición, *f.* sedition.—**sedicioso,** *a.* seditious; mutinous.

sediento, *a.* thirsty; (**de**) eagerly desirous, anxious (for).

sedimento, *m.* sediment, dregs, settling; grouts, grounds.

sedoso, *a.* = SEDEÑO.

seducción, *f.* seduction, deceiving.—**seducir,** *vti.* [11] to seduce; to charm, captivate.—**seductivo,** *a.* seductive, enticing.—**seductor,** *a.* fascinating, attractive, tempting.—*n.* seducer, deceiver; delightful person.

segador, *n.* reaper; harvester.—*f.* harvester, mowing machine.—**segar,** *vti.* [1-b] to mow; to harvest; to cut off, mow down.

seglar, *a.* secular, lay.—*mf.* layman (-woman).

segmento, *m.* segment.

segregación, *f.* segregation, separation.—*s. racial,* racial segregation.—**segregar,** *vti.* [b] to segregate, separate; (med.) to secrete.

segueta, *f.* jig saw, marquetry saw.

seguida, *f.*—*en s.,* at once, immediately.—**seguidamente,** *adv.* right after that, immediately after.—**seguido,** *a.* continued, successive; straight, direct.—**seguidor,** *n.* follower.—**seguimiento,** *m.* pursuit, following; continuation; tracking.—**seguir,** *vti.* [29-b] to follow; to pursue; to prosecute; to continue; to keep on.—*vri.* to ensue, follow as a consequence.

según, *prep.* according to.—*s. y como,* or *s. y conforme,* just as; it depends.—*conj.* as; according as.

segundero, *m.* second hand (of watch or clock).—**segundo,** *a.* & *n.* second.—*segunda intención,* double meaning.—*m.* (time) second.

seguridad, *f.* safety; security; certainty.—*s. social,* social security.—**seguro,** *a.* safe; secure; sure, certain, positive; dependable, trustworthy.—*m.* assurance; (mech.) click; safety catch (of a pistol); tumbler of a lock; (com.) insurance, assurance.—*a buen s.,* or *de s.,* certainly, undoubtedly.—*s. contra incendios,* fire insurance.—*s. contra terceros,* liability insurance.—*s. de accidentes,* accident insurance.—*s. de desempleo,* unemployment insurance.—*s. de enfermedad,* health insurance.—*s. de responsabilidad civil,* liability insurance.—*s. de vida, s. sobre la vida,* life insurance.—*sobre s.,* without risk.

seis, *a.* & *m.* six.—**seiscientos,** *a.* & *m.* six hundred.—*seiscientos uno,* six hundred one.

selección, *f.* selection, choice.—**seleccionar,** *vt.* to select, choose.—**selecto,** *a.* select, choice, distinguished.

self-service, *m.* self-service restaurant, cafeteria.

sellar, *vt.* to seal; to stamp; to conclude, finish; to cover, close.—**sello,** *m.* seal; stamp (sticker, mark or implement); signet.—*s. de correo,* postage stamp.

selva, *f.* jungle, forest.—*s. tropical,* rain forest.

semáforo, *m.* traffic lights.—*un s. en rojo,* a red light.

semana, *f.* week.—*entre s.,* any weekday except Saturday.—**semanal,** *a.* weekly.—**semanario,** *m.* weekly publication.

semántica, *f.* semantics.—**semántico,** *a.* semantic.

semblante, *m.* mien, countenance, look, expression; aspect.—**semblanza,** *f.* portrait, biographical sketch.

sembrado, *m.* cultivated field, sown ground.—**sembradura,** *f.* sowing, seeding.—**sembrar,** *vti.* [1] to sow, seed; to scatter, spread.

semejante, *a.* similar, like; such, of that kind.—*m.* fellow creature, fellow man.—**semejanza,** *f.* resemblance, similarity, similitude.—*a s. de,* like.—**semejar,** *vi.* & *vr.* to be like; to resemble.

semen, *m.* semen, sperm; (bot.) seed.—**semental,** *a.* & *m.* breeding (horse).

semestre, *m.* semester.

semicircular, *a.* semicircular.—**semicírculo,** *m.* semicircle.

semidiós, *m.* demigod.—*f.* demigoddess.

semilla, *f.* seed.—**semillero,** *m.* seed bed, seed plot; nursery; hotbed.

seminario, *m.* seminary.—**seminarista,** *m.* seminarist.

semita, *a.* Semitic.—*mf.* Semite.—**semítico,** *a.* Semitic.

semi-remolque, *m.* semitrailer.

sempiterno, *a.* eternal, everlasting.

senado, *m.* senate.—**senador,** *n.* senator.

sencillez, *f.* simplicity; plainness, naturalness; candor.—**sencillo,** *a.* simple; slight, thin; plain; harmless; natural, unaffected, unsophisticated; unadorned; single.

senda, *f.* path, footpath, way.—**sendero,** *m.* path, footpath, byway.

sendos, *a. pl.* one each, one for each.

senectud, *f.* old age, senility.—**senil,** *a.* senile.

seno, *m.* breast, bosom; womb; lap of a woman; cavity; sinus; bay; innermost recess; (math.) sine.

sensación, *f.* sensation.—**sensacional,** *a.* sensational.

sensatez, *f.* good sense, wisdom.—**sensato,** *a.* sensible, judicious, wise.

sensibilidad, *f.* sensibility; sensitiveness.—**sensible,** *a.* perceptible; sensitive, keen; regrettable; (photog.) sensitive, sensitized.—**sensiblería,** *f.* false sentimentality.—**sensitivo,** *a.* sensitive; sensual; appreciable.

sensual, *a.* sensuous; sensual; sexy.—**sensualidad,** *f.* sensuality, voluptuousness.

sentar, *vti.* [1] to seat; to establish, set up (a precedent, etc.).—*dar por sentado,* to take for granted.—*vii.* to fit, become, suit; to agree with (of food).—*vri.* to sit, sit down.

sentencia, *f.* (law) sentence, verdict, judgment; maxim.—*pronunciar s.,* to pass judgment.—**sentenciar,** *vt.* (law) to sentence; to pass judgment on.

sentido, *a.* sensitive, touchy; heartfelt; offended.—*m.* sense; meaning; direction, course.—*en el s. de que,* to the effect that; stating that.—*perder el s.,* to lose consciousness; to faint.—*sin s.,* meaningless; unconscious.

sentimental, *a.* sentimental; emotional, soulful.—**sentimentalismo,** *m.* sentimentality.—**sentimiento,** *m.* sentiment, feeling; sensation; grief, sorrow, regret.

sentina, *f.* (naut.) bilge; sewer.—*s. de vicios,* place of iniquity.

sentir, *vti.* [39] to feel, experience; to perceive by the senses; to grieve, regret, mourn; to be sorry for.—*vii.* to feel; to foresee.—*sin s.,* without noticing, inadvertently.—*vri.* to complain; to feel (well, bad, sad); to resent.—*m.* feeling; opinion, judgment.

seña, *f.* sign, mark, token; nod, gesture; signal.—*pl.* address; personal description.—*hablar por señas,* to talk in a sign language.—*señas personales,* physical description.—**señal,** *f.* signal; sign, mark; indication; trace, vestige; scar; token.—*s. de carretera,* road sign.—*s. de comunicando, s. de ocupado,* (tel.) busy signal.—*s. de la cruz,* sign of the cross.—*s. de tráfico,* traffic sign, traffic signal.—*s. horaria,* time signal.—*s. luminosa,* (radar) blip.—**señalado,** *a.* distinguished, noted.—**señala-miento,** *m.* date, appointment.—**señalar,** *vt.* to stamp, mark; to point out; to name; to determine; to sign; to assign.—*vr.* to distinguish oneself, to excel; to call attention to oneself.

señor, *m.* mister, Mr.; sir; man, gentleman; lord, master.—*muy s. mío,* Dear Sir (in letters).—**señora,** *f.* Mrs.; lady; madam; dame.—**señorear,** *vt.* to master; to domineer, lord it over; to excel; to control (one's passions).—**señoría,** *f.* lordship.—**señorial,** *a.* lordly; manorial.—**señorío,** *m.* dominion, command; arrogance; lordship; domain, manor.—**señorita,** *f.* Miss; young lady; miss; Miss; (coll.) mistress of the house.—**señorito,** *m.* Master (title); (coll.) master of the house; (coll.) playboy.

señuelo, *m.* decoy, lure; bait; enticement.

separable, *a.* separable, detachable, removable.—**separación,** *f.* separation.—**separado,** *a.* separate, apart.—*por s.,* separate, separately.—**separar,** *vt.* to separate; to divide; to detach; to remove, take away or off; to lay aside; to dismiss, discharge.—*vr.* to separate; to part company; to withdraw.—**separata,** *f.* offprint.

sepello, *m.* burial.

septentrional, *a.* northern, northerly.

séptico, *a.* septic.—**séptimo,** *a.* & *m.* seventh.—**septuagésimo,** *a.* & *m.* seventieth.

septiembre, *m.* September.

septillizos, *npl.* septuplets.

sepulcro, *m.* sepulcher, grave, tomb.—**sepultar,** *vt.* to bury, inter; to hide, conceal.—**sepultura,** *f.* burial; tomb, grave, sepulcher.—*dar s.,* to bury.—**sepulturero,** *n.* gravedigger, sexton.

sequedad, *f.* aridity, dryness; gruffness.—**sequía,** *f.* drought.

ser, *vii.* [40] to be; to exist; to happen.—*es la una,* it is one o'clock.—*es tarde,* it is late.—*esto es,* that is to say.—*no sea que,* lest.—*¿qué ha sido de Juan?* what has become of John?—*sea lo que juere, sea como fuere,* be that as it may; anyhow, anyway.—*s. humano,* human being.—*son las dos,* it is two o'clock.—*soy yo,* it is I.—*m.* existence; being; essence.

serenar, vt. to calm down, pacify.—vr. (of weather) to clear up, become calm.

serenata, f. serenade.

serenidad, f. serenity, calmness; tranquility.—**sereno**, a. serene, calm; clear, cloudless.—m. night watchman; night dew.

serie, f. series; sequence.—fabricación en s., mass production.

seriedad, f. seriousness, gravity; earnestness.—**serio**, a. serious, grave, dignified; grand, solemn; earnest; sincere.—en s., seriously.

sermón, m. sermon; reprimand.—**sermonear**, vt. to sermonize; (coll.) to lecture, reprimand.—**sermoneo**, m. (coll.) repeated admonition, sermonizing.

serpentear, vi. to meander; to wind; to wriggle, squirm.—**serpentín**, f. coil (of a heater, etc.).—**serpentina**, f. (min.) serpentine; paper streamer. —**serpiente**, f. serpent, snake.—s. boa, boa constrictor.—s. de cascabel, rattlesnake.

serranía, f. sierra; mountainous region.—**serrano**, a. mountain, highland.—n. mountaineer, highlander.

serrar, vti. [1] to saw.—**serrín**, m. sawdust.—**serrucho**, m. handsaw.

servible, a. serviceable, adaptable.—**servicial**, a. serviceable; obsequious; obliging, kind.—**servicio**, m. service; servants; (Am.) toilet, water closet; tea or coffee set.—s. a domicilio, (home) delivery service.—s. de enlace, shuttle service.—s. de grúa, towing service.—s. de mesa, set of dishes.—s. secreto, servicios de inteligencia, secret service.—**servidor**, n. servant.—de Vd. atento y seguro s., respectfully yours.—s. de Ud., at your service.—**servidumbre**, f. (staff of) servants or attendants; servitude; (law) right of way.—s. de acceso, right of access.—s. de paso, right of way.—**servil**, a. servile, slavish, abject; lowly, humble.—**servilismo**, m. servility, abjectness.

servilleta, f. napkin.

servio, n. & a. Serb, Serbian.

servir, vii. [29] to serve; to be of use.—no s. para nada, to be good for nothing.—para s. a Ud., at your service.—s. de, to act as, to be used as.—s. para, to be for, be used or useful for; to be good for; to do for.—

vti. to serve; to do a service or a favor to.—vri. to please; to help oneself (as at table).—s. de, to make use of; to employ.

servodirección, f. (aut.) power steering.—**servofreno**, m. power brake.

sésamo, m. sesame.—¡S. ábrete!, open sesame!

sesgado, a. oblique, slanting, bias.—**sesgar**, vti. [b] to slope, slant; to cut on the bias.—vii. to take an oblique direction.—**sesgo**, m. bias, slope, obliqueness; turn (of an affair).

sesenta, a. & m. sixty.—s. y uno, sixty-one.—**sesentavo**, a. & m. sixtieth.

sesión, f. session, meeting; conference, consultation.—levantar la s., to adjourn the meeting.—s. de espiritistas, séance.—**sesionar**, vi. to be in session.

seso, m. brain; brains, intelligence.—levantarse la tapa de los sessos, to blow out one's brains.—perder el s., to go crazy; (fig.) to lose one's head.—sin seso(s), scatterbrained.

sestear, vi. to take a nap.

sesudo, a. judicious, discreet, wise.

seta, f. mushroom.

setecientos, a. & m. seven hundred.—s. uno, seven hundred one.—**setenta**, a. & m. seventy.—s. y uno, seventy-one.—**setentavo**, a. & m. seventieth.

seto, m. fence, inclosure.—s. vivo, hedge.

seudónimo, m. pseudonym, pen name.

severidad, f. severity, austerity, strictness; seriousness.—**severo**, a. severe, rigorous; rigid, strict; serious; puritanical.

sexagenario, n. & a. sexagenarian.

sexagésimo, a. & m. sixtieth.

sex, m. sex.—**sexual**, a. sexual.

sí, adv. yes; indeed.—un s. es no es, somewhat, a trifle.—m. yes, consent.—3rd. pers. refl. pron. (after prep.) himself, herself, yourself, itself, oneself, themselves, yourselves.—dar de s., to stretch, give. —metido en s., pensive, introspective.—**si**, conj. if; whether.—por s. acaso, just in case.—s. bien, although.

siamés, n. & a. Siamese, Thai.—n. pl. Siamese twins, Siamese.

sibila, f. prophetess.

siciliano, n. & a. Sicilian.

sicoanálisis, sicología, siquiatría, etc.,

V. PSICOANALIS, PSICOLOGIA, PSIQUIA-
TRIA, etc.

SIDA, *abbr.* **(síndrome de inmunodeficiencia adquirida)** AIDS (acquired immune-deficiency syndrome).

siderurgia, *f.* iron and steel industry.

sidra, *f.* cider.

slega, *f.* reaping, harvest, mowing.

siembra, *f.* sowing, seeding; seedtime; sown field.

siempre, *adv.* always.—*para* or *por s. (jamás),* forever (and ever).—*s. que,* provided; whenever.

sien, *f.* (anat.) temple.

sierpe, *f.* serpent, snake.

sierra, *f.* saw; mountain range.—*s. de armero,* hacksaw.—*s. de arco,* hacksaw.—*s. de cadena,* chainsaw.—*s. de vaivén,* jig saw.

siervo, *n.* serf.—*s. de la gleba,* serf.

siesta, *f.* siesta, afternoon nap; hottest part of the day.—**siestecita,** *f.* short nap, snooze.

siete, *a.* & *m.* seven.

sietemesino, *a.* & *n.* prematurely born (baby).—*m.* puny.

sifón, *m.* siphon; siphon bottle.

sigilo, *m.* secrecy, concealment, reserve.—**sigiloso,** *a.* silent, reserved.

siglo, *m.* century; age; period; the world, worldly matters.—*s. de Acuario,* Age of Aquarius.

significación, *f.* significance; sense, meaning; implication; importance.—**significado,** *m.* meaning, definition (of a word, etc.).—**significar,** *vti.* [d] to signify, mean; to indicate; to make known; to import, be worth.—**significativo,** *a.* significant.

signatario, *n.* & *a.* signatory.

signo, *m.* sign, mark, symbol; signal.—*s. de igual,* equal sign.—*s. de interrogación, s. de pregunta,* question mark.

siguiente, *a.* following, next.

sílaba, *f.* syllable.—**silabario,** *m.* primer; reader, speller.

silba, *f.* (theat.) hiss, hissing (of disapproval).—**silbar,** *vi.* to whistle.—*vt.* & *vi.* (theat.) to hiss, boo.—**silbato,** *m.* whistle (instrument).—**silbido,** *m.* whistle, whistling sound; hiss.

silenciador, *m.* (auto) muffler; silencer (on gun, etc.).—**silencio,** *m.* silence; noiselessness; taciturnity; secrecy; stillness; quiet; (mus.) rest.—*guardar s.,* to keep quiet.—**silencioso,** *a.* silent, noiseless; still, quiet.

silicio, *m.* silicon.

silla, *f.* chair; saddle; (eccl.) see.—*s. alta (para niños),* high chair.—*s. de cubierta,* deck chair.—*s. de la reina,* chair (made by two people linking arms).—*s. de manos,* sedan chair.—*s. de montar,* riding saddle.—*s. de orejas,* wing chair.—*s. de ruedas,* wheelchair.—*s. de tijera,* folding chair, camp chair.—*s. eléctrica,* electric chair.—*s. giratoria,* swivel chair.—*s. plegable,* folding chair.—**silleta,** *f.* small chair; low stool; bedpan.—**silletazo,** *m.* blow with a chair.—**sillín,** *m.* light riding saddle; saddle (on bicycle, etc.).—**silo,** *m.* silo.—**sillón,** *m.* armchair; easy chair; sidesaddle.—**silo,** *m.* silo.

silueta, *f.* silhouette; (of person) figure.

silvestre, *a.* wild; uncultivated; rustic, savage.—**silvicultura,** *f.* forestry.

sima, *f.* deep cavern; abyss.

simbólico, *a.* symbolical.—**simbolismo,** *m.* symbolism.—**simbolizar,** *vti.* [a] to symbolize, represent, typify.—**símbolo,** *m.* symbol; mark, device.

simetría, *f.* symmetry.—**simétrico,** *a.* symmetrical.

simiente, *f.* seed; germ; semen, sperm.

símil, *m.* resemblance, similarity; simile.—**similar,** *a.* similar, like, alike, resembling.—**similitud,** *f.* similitude, similarity.

simio, *n.* simian, ape.

simpatía, *f.* charm, attractiveness; congeniality; liking, friendly feeling; (med.) sympathy.—**simpático,** *a.* congenial; appealing; charming.—**simpatizar,** *vii.* [a] to be congenial with; to have a liking for; to be attracted by.

simple, *a.* simple; mere; foolish; artless, ingenuous; plain, unmixed, unadorned.—*mf.* simpleton.—**simpleza,** *f.* silliness, foolishness; silly thing; rusticity, rudeness.—**simplicidad,** *f.* simplicity.—**simplificación,** *f.* simplification.—**simplificar,** *vti.* [d] to simplify.—**simplón,** *m.* simpleton.

simulación, *f.* simulation, feigning.—**simulacro,** *m.* image, idol; show, semblance; pretense; sham battle.—**simulador,** *n.* simulator; malingerer.—*a.* simulative.—**simular,** *vt.* to simulate, pretend, sham.

simultaneidad, *f.* simultaneity.—**simultáneo,** *a.* simultaneous.

sin, *prep.* without; but for; besides, not including.—*s. embargo,* notwithstanding, nevertheless, however.—*s. que,* without.

sinagoga, *f.* synagogue.

sinapismo, *m.* mustard plaster; (coll.) nuisance, bore.

sincerar, *vt.* to justify.—*vr.* to excuse, justify, or vindicate oneself.—**sinceridad,** *f.* sincerity, good faith.—**sincero,** *a.* sincere.

síncope, *f.* (med.) swoon, fainting fit.

sincronizar, *vti.* [a] to synchronize.

sindéresis, *f.* common sense, discretion, good judgment.

sindicalismo, *m.* trade unionism.—**sindicato,** *m.* labor union.

síndico, *m.* trustee; (law) assignee, receiver.

síndrome, *m.* syndrome.—*s. de abstinencia,* withdrawal symptoms.—*s. de inmunodeficiencia adquirida (SIDA),* acquired immune-deficiency syndrome (AIDS).—*s. tóxico,* poisoning.

sinfín, *m.* countless number.

sinfonía, *f.* symphony.—**sinfónico,** *a.* symphonic.

singular, *a.* singular; unique; unusual; odd; excellent.—**singularizar,** *vti.* [a] to single out; to distinguish.—*vri.* to be conspicuous; to be singled out; to distinguish oneself.

siniestro, *a.* sinister; left (side); vicious.—*m.* disaster; catastrophe.—*f.* left hand; left-hand side.

sino, *conj.* but; except, besides; solely, only.—*m.* fate, destiny.

sinónimo, *a.* synonymous.—*m.* synonym.

sinopsis, *f.* synopsis.

sinrazón, *f.* wrong, injury, injustice.

sinsabor, *m.* displeasure; trouble, grief, sorrow.

sinsonte, *m.* (Am.) mockingbird.

sintaxis, *f.* syntax.

síntesis, *f.* synthesis.—**sintético,** *a.* synthetical.—**sintetizar,** *vti.* [a] to synthesize; to sum up.

síntoma, *m.* symptom; sign.—*s. de abstinencia,* withdrawal symptom.

sinnúmero, *m.* countless number.

sinvergüenza, *mf.* (coll.) scoundrel, rascal; brazen, shameless person.—*a.* shameless.

siquiera, *adv.* even, at least.—*conj.* even if; even.—*ni s.,* not even.

sirena, *f.* siren, mermaid; whistle, foghorn; temptress, vamp.

sirvienta, *f.* servant girl, maid.—**sir-**

viente, *m.* (domestic) servant; waiter.

sisa, *f.* petty theft; (sewing) dart.—**sisar,** *vt.* to pilfer, filch; (sewing) to take in.

sisear, *vi.* to hiss.—**siseo,** *m.* hiss, hissing.

sísmico, *a.* seismic.—**sismógrafo,** *m.* seismograph.

sistema, *m.* system.—*s. de alarma anticipada, s. de alerta avanzada,* early-warning system.—**sistemático,** *a.* systematic.—**sistematización,** *f.* systematization.—**sistematizar,** *vti.* [a] & *vii.* to systematize.

sitial, *m.* seat of honor, presiding chair.

sitiar, *vt.* (mil.) to lay siege to; to surround, hem in, compass.—**sitio,** *m.* place, space, spot, room; stand; seat; location, site; country house, country seat, villa; (Cuba) small farm; (mil.) siege.—*quedar en el s.,* to die on the spot.

sito, *a.* situated, lying, located.—**situación,** *f.* situation; position; site, location; condition, circumstances.—**situar,** *vt.* to place, locate, situate; (com.) to remit or place (funds).—*vr.* to settle in a place; to station oneself.

smoking, *m.* tuxedo, dinner jacket.

so, *prep.* under.—*s. capa de,* or *s. color de,* under color of; on pretense of.—*s. pena de,* under penalty of.—*s. pretexto,* under the pretext of.—*interj.* whoa!

sobaco, *m.* armpit; (bot.) axil.

sobado, *a.* shopworn.

sobaquera, *f.* (tailoring) armhole.—**sobaquina,** *f.* bad odor of the armpit.

sobar, *vt.* to knead; to massage, squeeze, soften; to pummel, box; to handle (a person) with too much familiarity.

soberanía, *f.* sovereignty; rule, sway.—**soberano,** *a.* sovereign; supreme; royal; superior.—*n.* sovereign.

soberbia, *f.* excessive pride, haughtiness; presumption; magnificence, pomp; anger.—**soberbio,** *a.* overproud, arrogant, haughty; superb, grand; lofty, eminent.

sobornar, *vt.* to suborn, bribe.—**soborno,** *m.* subornation, bribe; incitement, inducement; bribery.—*s. de testigo,* (law) subornation of perjury.

sobra, *f.* surplus, excess; leftover, leaving.—*de s.,* over and above; more than enough.—*estar de s.,* (coll.) to be one too many; to be superfluous.—**sobrante**, a. extra; excess; leftover.—m. surplus, remainder.

sobrar, vt. to surpass; to have in excess.—vi. to be in excess; to be intrusive; to remain, be left over.

sobre, prep. on, upon; over; above; about, concerning; about, more or less; to, toward, near.—m. envelope (for letters); package, packet.—de s., (cook.) ready-mix.—s. con el nombre y dirección del remitente, self-addressed envelope.

sobrealimentar, vt. to overfeed.

sobrecama, f. coverlet, bedspread.

sobrecargar, vti. [b] to overload, overburden; (com.) to overcharge.—**sobrecargo**, m. (naut.) purser, supercargo.

sobrecoger, vti. [c] to surprise, catch unaware; to startle.—vri. to become afraid or apprehensive.—**sobrecogimiento**, m. fear, apprehension.

sobrecoser, vt. (sewing) to fell, sew the edge of a seam flat.

sobreexcitación, f. overexcitement.—**sobreexcitar**, vt. to overexcite.—**sobreexposición**, f. (phot.) overexposure.—**sobregiro**, m. overdraft.

sobrehumano, a. superhuman.

sobrellevar, vt. to ease (another's burden); to carry, bear, endure; to overlook, be lenient about.

sobremanera, adv. beyond measure; exceedingly, most.

sobremesa, f. tablecloth; after-dinner chat.—de s., afternoon; after-dinner.

sobrenadar, vi. to float.

sobrenatural, a. supernatural.

sobrenombre, m. sobriquet; nickname.

sobrentender, vti. [18] to understand, deduce, infer.—vri. to be understood, go without saying.

sobrepasar, vt. to exceed, surpass.

sobrepeso, m. overweight.

sobreponer, vti. [32-49] to superimpose, overlap.—vri. to control oneself.—s. a, to master, overcome (difficulties, hardships).

sobreprecio, m. extra charge, raise.

sobreprenda, f. overdress.

sobreproducción, f. overproduction.

sobrepujar, vt. to excel, beat, surpass.

sobresaliente, a. outstanding; projecting.—mf. substitute, understudy.—**sobresalir**, vii. to excel, be prominent, stand out; to project, just out, flange.

sobresaltar, vt. to rush upon, assail; to frighten, startle.—vi. to stand out.—vr. to be startled.—**sobresalto**, m. assault; startling surprise; sudden dread or fear.

sobrescrito, m. envelope address.

sobreseer, vti. [e] to desist from a design; to relinquish a claim; (law) to stay a judgment, etc.

sobresolar, vt. to resole.

sobretensión, f. (elec.) surge.

sobretiro, m. offprint.

sobretodo, m. overcoat.

sobrevenir, vii. [45] to happen, take place; to follow.

sobrevidriera, f. window screen.

sobreviviente, mf. & a. survivor; surviving.—**sobrevivir**, vt. & vi. to survive, outlive.

sobrevolar, vti. [12] to fly over; (mil.) to overfly.

sobriedad, f. sobriety, frugality.

sobrina, f. niece.—**sobrino**, m. nephew.

sobrio, a. sober, temperate, frugal.—**socarrón**, a. cunning, sly, crafty.—**socarronería**, f. cunning, artfulness, craftiness.

socavar, vt. to excavate, undermine.

sociabilidad, f. sociableness, sociability.—**sociable**, a. sociable, companionable.—**social**, a. social.—**socialismo**, m. socialism.—**socialista**, mf. & a. socialist(ic).—**socialización**, f. socialization.—**socializar**, vti. [a] to socialize.—**sociedad**, f. society; social intercourse; (com.) society, corporation, company.—constituido en s. anónima, incorporated.—s. anónima, corporation.—s. de ahorros y préstamos, savings and loan company.—s. de control, holding company.—**socio**, n. partner, copartner; companion; member, fellow; (sl.) buddy, mister, mac.—**sociología**, f. sociology.

socorrer, vt. to assist, help, succor; to favor.—**socorrido**, a. furnished, well-supplied; (coll.) handy; hackneyed, trivial.—**socorro**, m. succor, aid, help.—puesto de s., first-aid station.

soda, f. (chem.) = SOSA.

sodio, m. sodium.

sodomía, f. sodomy.

soez, a. mean, vile, base, coarse.

sofá, *m.* sofa; couch.—*s.-cama,* studio couch.

sofisma, *m.* fallacy; sophism.—**sofisticar,** *vti.* [d] to falsify, pervert or distort by fallacy.

sofocación, *f.* suffocation; smothering, choking.—**sofocante,** *a.* suffocating, stifling.—**sofocar,** *vti.* [d] to choke, suffocate, smother; to quench, extinguish; to stifle; to oppress, harass; to importune, vex; to provoke; to make blush.—**sofoco,** *m.* suffocation; vexation; embarrassment.—**sofocón,** *m.* (coll.) vexation, chagrin.

sofreír *vti.* [35–49] to fry lightly.

sofrenar, *vt.* to check (a horse) suddenly; to reprimand severely; to check (a passion).

sofrito, *ppi.* of SOFREÍR.

soga, *f.* rope, halter, cord.

soja, *f.* soy; soy bean.

sojuzgar, *vti.* [b] to conquer, subjugate, subdue.

sol, *m.* sun; sunlight; (mus.) sol.—*de s. a s.,* from sunrise to sunset.—*hacer s.,* to be sunny.—*tomar el s.,* to bask in the sun, sunbathe; (naut.) to take the altitude on the sun.—**solana,** *f.* intense sunlight; sunny place.—**solanera,** *f.* sunburn; sunny place; sun porch.

solapa, *f.* lapel; flap; pretense.—**solapado,** *a.* sly, artful, sneaky.—**solapar,** *vt.* to put lapels on; to overlap, lap; to cloak, conceal.—*vi.* to overlap (as a lapel).

solar, *m.* lot, ground plot; manor house, ancestral mansion.—*a.* solar.—**solariego,** *a.* manorial; of old lineage.

solaz, *m.* solace, consolation; relaxation, comfort; enjoyment.—**solazar,** *vti.* [a] to solace, comfort.—*vri.* to be comforted; to rejoice, have pleasure.

soldada, *f.* wages, salary.—**soldadesca,** *f.* soldiery; undisciplined troops.—**soldadesco,** *a.* soldierly.—**soldadito,** *m.*—*s. de plomo,* tin soldier.—**soldado,** *m.* soldier.—*s. raso,* private.—*s. de cavallería,* trooper.—*s. de juguete,* toy soldier.—*s. desconocido,* unknown soldier.

soldador, *m.* solderer; welder; soldering iron.—**soldadura,** *f.* soldering; welding; solder; correction.—**soldar,** *vti.* [12] to solder; to weld; to correct.

soleado, *a.* sunny.—**solear,** *vt.* to sun.

soledad, *f.* solitude, loneliness; lonely place.

solemne, *a.* solemn; imposing; ceremonious; (coll.) great, downright.—**solemnidad,** *f.* solemnity; religious pomp; grand ceremony.—*pl.* formalities.—**solemnizar,** *vti.* [a] to solemnize, celebrate with pomp.

soler, *vii.* [26–50] to be in the habit of, accustomed to, used to.

solera, *f.* vintage wine; lees or mother of wine; crossbeam.

solevantamiento, *m.* upheaval.

solfa, *f.* musical annotation, notes; music, harmony; (coll.) sound beating or flogging.—*estar,* or *poner en s.,* to appear (or present) in a ridiculous light.—**solfeo,** *m.* solfeggio; (coll.) beating, drubbing.

solicitar, *vt.* to solicit; to apply for; to woo, court.—**solícito,** *a.* solicitous, diligent, careful.—**solicitud,** *f.* solicitude; importunity; diligence; petition, application, request; (com.) demand.—*a s.,* on request, at the request (of).—*s. de ingreso,* application for admission.

solidaridad, *f.* solidarity; union.—**solidario,** *a.* solidary; mutually binding.—**solidarizarse,** *vri.* [a] to act together in a common cause.

solideo, *m.* skullcap.

solidez, *f.* solidity; firmess; strength; stability; compactness.—**solidificación,** *f.* solidification.—**solidificar,** *vti.* & *vri.* [d] to solidify.—**sólido,** *a.* solid; firm; compact; strong.—*m.* (geom. & phys.) solid.

soliloquio, *m.* soliloquy, monologue.

solista, *mf.* (mus.) soloist.—**solitaria,** *f.* tapeworm.—**solitario,** *a.* solitary, lonely, isolated, secluded.—*m.* recluse, hermit; solitaire.

solivantar, *vt.* to induce, incite, rouse.

sollozar, *vii.* [a] to sob.—**sollozo,** *m.* sob.

solo, *a.* alone, unaccompanied; only, sole; unaided, unattended; solitary, lonely.—*a solas,* alone; unaided.—*m.* (mus.) solo.—**sólo,** *adv.* = SOLAMENTE.

solomillo, solomo, *m.* sirloin; loin of pork.

soltar, *vti.* [12] to untie, unfasten, loosen; to turn on (the water); to turn loose; to cast off, set free, discharge; to let go, drop; to throw down, throw out; (coll.) to utter, let out (laughter, etc.).—*vri.* to get loose; to come off; to become expert; to lose restraint; to break out (laughing, crying, etc.).—*s. a,* to begin, start.

soltería, *f.* celibacy, bachelorhood.—**soltero,** *a.* single, unmarried.—*m.* bachelor, unmarried man.—*f.* spinster, unmarried woman.—**solterón,** *m.* old bachelor.—**solterona,** *f.* old maid, maiden lady.

soltura, *f.* freedom, abandon, ease; fluency; agility, nimbleness; laxity, licentiousness.

solubilidad, *f.* solubility.—**soluble,** *a.* soluble; solvable.—**solución,** *f.* loosening or untying; climax or denouement in a drama or epic poem; pay, satisfaction; (math., chem.) solution.—**solucionar,** *vt.* to solve; to meet (a difficulty).

solvencia, *f.* (com.) solvency.—**solventar,** *vt.* to settle (accounts); to solve.—**solvente,** *a.* solvent, dissolving; (com.) solvent.

sombra, *f.* shade; shadow; darkness; spirit, ghost; protection; sign, vestige.—*buena s.,* wit; good luck.—**sombrear,** *vt.* to shade.—**sombrerería,***f.* hat factory or shop.—**sombrero,** *m.* hat.—*s. de copa,* or *de copa alta,* silk hat, high (silk) hat.—*s. de jipijapa,* Panama hat.—*s. de paja,* straw hat.—*s. hongo,* derby.—*s. nuclear,* nuclear umbrella.—**sombrilla,** *f.* parasol, sunshade.—**sombrío,** *a.* gloomy, somber; overcast.

somero, *a.* superficial, shallow; concise, summary.

someter, *vt.* to subject; to submit, subdue; to put (to the test, etc.).—*vr.* to humble oneself; to submit; to surrender.—**sometimiento,** *m.* submission, subjection, subduing.

somnolencia, *f.* drowsiness, somnolence.

son, *m.* sound; tune; (Am.) popular song and dance.—*¿a son de qué?* why? for what reason?—*en s. de,* as, like, in the manner of.—*sin ton ni s.,* without rhyme or reason.

sonaja, *f.* jingles; tambourine; rattle.—**sonajero,** *m.* baby's rattle.

sonambulismo, *m.* sleepwalking.—**sonámbulo,** *n.* sleepwalker.

sonante, *a.* sounding, ringing.

sonar, *vti.* [12] to sound, to ring; (mus.) to play.—*vii.* to sound; to ring; (of clock) to strike; to be mentioned, talked about; (a) to sound or look

(like); to seem; to sound familiar.—*vri.* to blow one's nose.

sonda, *f.* (naut.) sounding (line); lead, sounder, plummet; surgeon's probe.—*s. espacial,* space probe.—**sondaje,** *m.* sounding.—**sondar, sondear,** *vt.* (naut.) to sound; to try, sound out (another's intentions); to explore, fathom; to probe; to poll, question, canvass.—**sondeo,** *m.* sounding; exploring, exploration; test drilling; poll, survey, canvass.—*s. de opinion,* opinion poll.—*s. informal de opinión,* straw vote.

soneto, *m.* sonnet.

sónico, *a.* sonic.

sonido, *m.* sound; noise; report.—**sonoridad,** *f.* sonority, sonorousness.—**sonorizado,** *a.* (phon.) voiced.—**sonoro,** *a.* sonorous; sounding, clear, loud.

sonreír, *vii.* & *vri.* [35] to smile; to smirk.—**sonriente,** *a.* smiling.—**sonrisa,** *f.* smile; smirk.

sonrojar, *vt.* to make (one) blush.—*vr.* to blush.—**sonrojo,** *m.* blush; blushing.

sonrosado, *a.* pink, rosy.

sonsacar, *vti.* [d] to pilfer; to draw (one) out; to entice, allure; to elicit information.

sonsonete, *m.* singsong (voice).

soñador, *a.* dreamy.—*n.* dreamer.—**soñar,** *vti.* & *vii.* [12] to dream.—*s. con* or *en,* to dream of.—**soñoliento,** *a.* sleepy; somnolent; soporific.

sopa, *f.* soup; sop.—*hecho una s.,* (coll.) drenched, wet through to the skin.—*s. de ostras,* oyster stew.—*s. de pastas* or *fideos,* noodle soup.

sopapear, *vt.* (coll.) to chuck under the chin; to vilify, to abuse.—**sopapo,** *m.* chuck under the chin; (coll.) box, blow, slap; (mech.) stop valve.

sopera, *f.* soup tureen.

sopesar, *vt.* to test the weight of by lifting.

sopetón, *m.*—*de s.,* suddenly.

soplar, *vi.* to blow; (coll.) to tattle.—*vt.* to blow; to blow out; to fan; to fill with air, inflate; to rob or steal in an artful manner; to prompt, tell what to say.—**soplete,** *m.* blowpipe; blow torch.—**soplido,** *m.* blowing; blast.—**soplo,** *m.* blowing; blast, gust, puff of wind; breath, instant; hint, tip, secret advice or warning; secret accusation.—**soplón,** *n.*

(fam.) tattletale; canary, stool pigeon.

soponcio, *m.* fainting fit, swoon.

sopor, *m.* drowsiness, lethargic sleep.—**soporífero,** *a.* soporific.

soportable, *a.* bearable, endurable.

soportal, *m.* portico; front porch.—*pl.* arcades.

soportar, *vt.* to bear, put up with; to support.—**soporte,** *m.* support; rest; bearing.

soprano, *m.* soprano voice.—*f.* soprano singer.

sor, *f.* (eccl.) sister.

sorber, *vt.* to sip, suck; to imbibe, soak, absorb; to swallow.—**sorbete,** *m.* sherbet, water ice.—**sorbo,** *m.* imbibing; absorption; sip, draft, swallow, gulp.

sordera, *f.* deafness.

sordidez, *f.* sordidness.—**sórdido,** *a.* sordid.

sordina, *f.* (mus.) mute; damper (piano).

sordo, *a.* deaf; silent, noiseless, quiet; muffled, stifled; dull; unmoved, insensible; (phon.) voiceless.—*n.* deaf person.—**sordomudo,** *a.* & *n.,* deaf and dumb; deaf mute.

sorna, *f.* slyness; ironic undertone; sneer.

sorprendente, *a.* surprising.—**sorprender,** *vt.* to surprise, astonish; to take by surprise.—**sorpresa,** *f.* surprise.—*de s.,* by surprise.

sortear, *vt.* to draw or cast lots for; to raffle; to elude or shun cleverly.—**sorteo,** *m.* casting lots; drawing, raffle.

sortija, *f.* finger ring; curl of hair.

sortilegio, *m.* spell, charm; sorcery, sortilege.

sosa, *f.* (chem.) soda; (bot.) glasswort.

sosegar, *vti.* [1-b] to appease, calm, quiet; to lull.—*vii.* to rest, repose.—*vri.* to become quiet, calm or composed; to rest quiet.

sosera, sosería, sosez, *f.* tastelessness; dullness.

soslego, *m.* tranquillity, calm, quiet.

soslayar, *vt.* to do or place obliquely.—**soslayo,** *m.*—*al s.,* or *de s.,* askance; slanting.

soso, *a.* insipid; dull.

sospecha, *f.* suspicion.—**sospechar,** *vt.* & *vi.* to suspect.—**sospechoso,** *a.* suspicious; suspecting.

sostén, *m.* support (person or thing); prop; brassiére; upkeep.—**sostener,** *vti.* [42] to support, hold up; to maintain, keep; to assist, help; to encourage; to hold (a conference).—*vri.* to support or maintain oneself.—**sostenido,** *a.* supported; sustained.—*m.* (mus.) sharp.—**sostenimiento,** *m.* sustenance, maintenance; support.

sota, *f.* (cards) jack; hussy, jade.

sotabanco, *m.* garret, attic.

sotana, *f.* cassock.

sótano, *m.* cellar, basement.

sotavento, *m.* leeward, lee.

soterrar, *vti.* [1] to bury, put under ground; to hide.

soto, *m.* grove, thicket.

sóviet, *m.* soviet.—**soviético,** *a.* soviet.

soya, *f.* (Am.) = SOJA.

Sr., *abbr.* (**Señor**) Mr.

Sra., *abbr.* (**Señora**) Mrs.; Ms.

Srta., *abbr.* (**Señorita**) Miss; Ms.

Sta., *abbr.* (**Santa; Señorita**) Saint; Miss; Ms.

su, *a. poss.* (*pl.* **sus**), his, her, its, their, your, one's.

suave, *a.* smooth, soft; easy, tranquil; gentle, tractable, docile, suave;—**suavidad,** *f.* softness, smoothness; ease; suavity; gentleness; lenity, forbearance.—**suavizar,** *vti.* [a] to soften, smooth, mitigate; to ease; to temper.

subarrendar, *vti.* [1] to sublet, sublease.

subasta, *f.* auction, auction sale.—*poner en* or *sacar a pública s.,* to sell at auction.—**subastar,** *vt.* to sell at auction.

subconsciencia, *f.* subconscious.—**subconsciente,** *a.* subconscious.

subdesarrollado, *a.* underdeveloped.—**subdesarrollo,** *m.* underdevelopment.

subdirector, *n.* assistant director.

súbdito, *mf.* subject (of a state, etc.).

subdividir, *vt.* to subdivide.

subida, *f.* ascent, going up; climb; taking or carrying up; rise; increase; slope.—**subir,** *vi.* to rise; to come up, go up, climb, mount; to grow; to increase in intensity; (com.) to amount to.—*vt.* to raise, place higher; to take up, bring up; to set up.—*vr.* to go up; to climb; to rise.

súbito, *a.* sudden.—*de s.,* suddenly.

subjetividad, *f.* subjectivity.—**subjetivo,** *a.* subjective.

subjuntivo, *m.* & *a.* (gram.) subjunctive.

sublevación, *f.* insurrection, revolt.—

sublevar, *vt.* to incite to rebellion, raise in rebellion.—*vr.* to rise in rebellion.

sublimar, *vt.* to heighten, elevate, exalt; (chem.) to sublimate.—**sublime,** *a.* sublime.—**sublimidad;** *f.* sublimity.

submarinista, *m.* frogman; skin diver.

submarino, *a.* & *m.* submarine.

subordinación, *f.* subordination; subjection.—**subordinado,** *a.* subordinate, subservient.—*n.* subordinate.—**subordinar,** *vt.* to subordinate; to subject.

subproducto, *m.* by-product.

subrayar, *vt.* to underscore, underline; to emphasize.

subrepticio, *m.* surreptitious.

subsanar, *vt.* to excuse; to mend, correct, repair; to obviate, get over.

subscribir, *vti.* & *vri.* [49] = SUBSCRIBIR.—**subscripción,** *f.* = SUSCRIPCION.—**subscripto,** *ppi.* = SUSCRITO.—**subscriptor,** *n.* = SUSCRITOR.

subsecretaría, *f.* office and employment of an assistant secretary.—**subsecretario,** *n.* assistant secretary.

subsecuente, *a.* subsequent.

subsidiario, *a.* subsidiary; branch; auxiliary.—**subsidio,** *m.* subsidy, monetary aid.

subsiguiente, *a.* subsequent, succeeding.

subsistencia, *f.* livelihood, living; permanence, stability; subsistence.—**subsistir,** *vi.* to subsist, last; to live, exist.

substancia, *f.* = SUSTANCIA.—**substancial,** *a.* = SUSTANCIAL.—**substancioso,** *a.* = SUSTANCIOSO.—**substantivo,** *a.* & *m.* = SUSTANTIVO.

substitución, *f.* = SUSTITUCION.—**substituir,** *vti.* [23-e] = SUSTITUIR.—**substituto,** *pp.i.* of SUSTITUIR = SUSTITUTO.

substracción, *f.* = SUSTRACCION.—**substraer,** *vti.* [43] = SUSTRAER.

subteniente, *m.* second lieutenant.

subterráneo, *a.* subterranean, underground.—*m.* any place underground; (Arg.) subway.

suburbano, *a.* & *n.* suburban(ite).

suburbio, *m.* outskirt; suburb.

subvención, *f.* subsidy, money aid.—**subvencionar,** *vt.* to subsidize.—**subvenir,** *vti.* [45] to aid, assist; to provide, supply.

subversión, *f.* subversion, overthrow.—**subversivo,** *a.* subversive, destructive.—**subvertir,** *vti.* [18] to subvert, destroy, ruin.

subyacente, *a.* underlying.

subyugación, *f.* subjugation, subjection.—**subyugador,** *n.* & *a.* subjugator; subjugating.—**subyugar,** *vti.* [b] to subdue, subjugate.

succión, *f.* suction, suck.

sucedáneo, *a.* & *m.* substitute; surrogate.—**suceder,** *vi.* to succeed, follow; to happen.—**sucesión,** *f.* succession.—**sucesivo,** *a.* successive.—*en lo s.,* hereafter, in the future.—**suceso,** *m.* event, happening; issue, outcome.—**sucesor,** *n.* successor.

suciedad, *f.* nastiness, filthiness; dirt, filth.

sucinto, *a.* brief, succinct, concise.

sucio, *a.* dirty, nasty, filthy, squalid; soiled; untidy; low.

sucumbir, *vi.* to succumb; to submit, yield.

sucursal, *a.* subsidiary; branch.—*f.* branch of a commercial house.

sud, *m.* south; south wind.—**sudamericano,** *n.* & *a.* South American.

sudar, *vi.* to sweat, perspire; to ooze; to toil, labor.—**sudario,** *m.* shroud (for corpse).—**sudor,** *m.* sweat, perspiration.—**sudoroso,** *a.* sweating, perspiring freely.

sueco, *a.* Swedish.—*n.* Swede.—*m.* Swedish language.—*hacerse el s.,* to pretend not to hear.

suegra, *f.* mother-in-law.—**suegro,** *m.* father-in-law.

suela, *f.* sole (of shoe); shoe leather.—*de siete suelas,* downright.

sueldo, *m.* salary, stipend.

suelo, *m.* ground; soil; land, earth; pavement; floor, flooring; bottom.—*s. franco,* loam.

suelto, *ppi.* of SOLTAR.—*a.* loose; light; expeditious; swift, able; free, bold, daring; fluent; odd, disconnected, unclassified; single (copy); blank (verse).—*s. de lengua,* outspoken.—*m.* editorial paragraph; newspaper item or paragraph; loose change.

sueñecillo, sueñecito, *m.* nap, snooze.—*echar* or *descabezar un s.,* to take a nap, to snooze.

sueño, *m.* sleep; sleeping; drowsiness, sleepiness; dream.—*conciliar el s.,* to get to sleep.—*descabezar* or *echar un s.,* to take a nap.—*en sueños,* dreaming; in dreamland.—*tener s.,* to be sleepy.

suero, *m.* whey; serum (of blood).

suerte, *f.* fortune, luck, chance; piece of luck; lot, fate; sort, kind; trick, feat (bullfighting).—*buen s.,* good luck.—*mala s.,* bad luck.—*de s. que,* so that; and so.—*echar suertes,* to draw lots.—*tener s.,* to be lucky.—*tocarle a uno la s.,* to fall to one's lot.

suficiencia, *f.* sufficiency; capacity, ability; self-importance.—**suficiente,** *a.* sufficient; fit, competent.

sufijo, *a.* suffixed.—*m.* suffix.

sufragar, *vti.* [b] to defray, pay; to favor; to aid; (Am.) to vote for.—**sufragio,** *m.* suffrage; vote; favor, support, aid.—**sufragista,** *mf.* suffragette.

sufrible, *a.* tolerable, sufferable.—**sufrido,** *a.* patient, long-suffering.—*color s.,* color that does not show dirt.—*mal s.,* rude.—**sufrimiento,** *m.* suffering; sufferance.—**sufrir,** *vt.* to suffer, bear up; to undergo (a change, an operation, etc.); to sustain, resist (an attack); to permit, tolerate.—*vi.* to suffer.

sugerencia, *f.* insinuation, hint.—**sugerir,** *vti.* [39] to suggest, hint, insinuate.—**sugestión,** *f.* suggestion, insinuation, hint.—**sugestionable,** *a.* easily influenced.—**sugestionar,** *vt.* to hypnotize; to influence.—**sugestivo,** *a.* suggestive; revealing (of a dress).

suicida, *a.* suicidal.—*mf.* suicide (person).—**suicidarse,** *vr.* to commit suicide.—**suicidio,** *m.* suicide (crime).

suizo, *n.* & *a.* Swiss.

sujeción, *f.* subjection; control; subordination; submission; connection.—**sujetapapeles,** *m.* paper clip.—**sujetar,** *vti.* [49] to subject, subdue; to hold fast, fasten, grasp.—*vri.* to control oneself; to submit; (a) to abide (by), to observe.—**sujeto,** *ppi.* of SUJETAR.—*a.* subject, liable; amenable.—*m.* subject; person; individual, fellow; (logic & gram.) subject.

sulfa, *f.* (pharm.) sulfa.

sulfato, *m.* sulfate.

sulfurar, *vt.* to irritate, anger.—*vr.* to become furious.

suma, *f.* sum; addition; aggregate; amount; total; summary.—*en s.,* in short.—**sumadora,** *f.* adding machine.—**sumando,** *m.* (math.) addend.—**sumar,** *vt.* to add; to amount to; to sum up, recapitulate.—*máquina de s.,* adding machine.—**su-**

mario, *a.* concise; plain; brief; (law) summary.—*m.* summary, abstract; (law) indictment.

sumarísimo, *a.* (law) swift, with dispatch.

sumergible, *a.* submersible.—*m.* submarine.—**sumergir,** *vti.* [c] to immerse; to submerge; to sink.—*vri.* to dive, to plunge; to submerge; to sink.—**sumersión,** *f.* submersion, immersion.—**sumidero,** *m.* sewer, drain, sink, gutter.

suministrar, *vt.* to supply, furnish, provide.—**suministro,** *m.* supply, providing.—*suministros para oficinas,* office supplies.

sumir, *vt.* & *vr.* to sink; to plunge; to submerge.—**sumisión,** *f.* submission.—**sumiso,** *a.* submissive, humble, meek.

sumo, *a.* high, great, supreme.—*a lo s.,* at most.

suntuosidad, *f.* magnificence, sumptuousness.—**suntuoso,** *a.* sumptuous, magnificent.

supeditación, *f.* subjection; oppression.—**supeditar,** *vt.* to subdue, oppress; to reduce to subjection.

superar, *vt.* to overcome, conquer; to surpass; to exceed.

superávit, *m.* (com.) surplus.

superficial, *a.* superficial, shallow.—**superficialidad,** *f.* superficiality; shallowness.—**superficie,** *f.* surface; area.

superfluo, *a.* superfluous.

superhombre, *m.* superman.

superintendencia, *f.* superintendence, supervision.—**superintendente,** *n.* superintendent, manager; inspector; overseer, supervisor.

superior, *a.* superior; upper; better, finer; higher (algebra, math, studies).—*m.* superior.—*f.* mother superior.—**superioridad,** *f.* superiority.

superlativo, *m.* & *a.* superlative.

superponer, *vti.* [32–49] to superimpose.—**superposición,** *f.* superposition.—**superpuesto,** *ppi.* of SUPERPONER.

superstición, *f.* superstition.—**supersticioso,** *a.* superstitious.

supervisar, *vt.* (neol.) to supervise.—**supervisión,** *s.* (neol.) supervision.—**supervisor,** *m.* (neol.) supervisor.

supervivencia, *f.* survival.—**superviviente,** *mf.* & *a.* survivor; surviving.

suplantación, *f.* supplanting.—**su-**

plantar, vt. to supplant; to forge (as a check).

suplementario, a. supplementary.—**suplemento,** m. supply, supplying; supplement.

suplente, a. & mf. supply, substitute; substituting; second-string.

súplica, f. entreaty; supplication; request.—**suplicar,** vti. [d] to entreat; to supplicate; to petition.

suplicio, m. torture; execution; gallows; grief, suffering, anguish.

suplir, vt. to supply, furnish; to act as a substitute for; to make good, make up for.

suponer, vti. [32–49] to suppose, assume; to entail (expense, etc.).—vii. to have weight or authority.—**suposición,** f. supposition, assumption; imposition, falsehood.

supositorio, m. (med.) suppository.

supremacía, f. supremacy.—**supremo,** a. supreme; last, final.

supresión, f. suppression; omission; elimination.—**suprimir,** vt. to suppress; to cut out; to omit; to clear of.

supuesto, ppi. of SUPONER.—s. que, allowing that; granting that; since.—por s., of course.—m. supposition; assumption.

supuración, f. suppuration.—**supurar,** vi. (med.) to suppurate.

sur, m. south; south wind.—**suramericano,** a. & n. = SUDAMERICANO.

surcar, vti. [d] to plow, furrow; to move through.—**surco,** m. furrow; rut; wrinkle.

surgir, vii. [49-c] to spout; to issue, come forth; to appear, arise; to sprout.

surí, m. (Am.) ostrich.

surtido, a. (com.) assorted.—m. assortment; stock, supply.—**surtidor,** n. purveyor, caterer.—m. jet, fountain.—**surtir,** vt. to supply, furnish, stock.—s. efecto, to have the desired effect, to work.—vi. to spout, spurt.

suscitar, vt. to stir up; to raise; to originate.—vr. to rise, start, originate.

suscribir, vti. [49] to subscribe; to sign; to endorse; to agree to.—vi. to subscribe (periodicals, etc.).—**suscrición,** f. subscription.—**suscrito,** ppi. of SUSCRIBIR.—**suscritor,** n. subscriber.

susodicho, a. aforementioned, aforesaid.

suspender, vti. [49] to suspend; to hang up; to stop, delay, interrupt; to discontinue; to fail (in exam); to adjourn (a meeting).—**suspensión,** f. suspension, interruption; reprieve; discontinuance.—**suspenso,** ppi. of SUSPENDER.—m. failing mark (in exam); failure; suspense.—en s., suspended (sentence).—**suspensorio,** m. athletic supporter, jockstrap.

suspicacia, f. suspiciousness.—**suspicaz,** a. suspicious, distrustful.

suspirar, vi. to sigh.—s. por, to crave, long for.—**suspiro,** m. sigh; brief pause.

sustancia, f. substance; essence; (coll.) judgment, sense.—**sustancial,** a. substantial; essential.—**sustancioso,** a. juicy; nourishing; substantial.—**sustantivo,** a. substantive.—m. substantive, noun.

sustentación, f. support, sustenance.—**sustentar,** vt. to sustain, support, bear; to feed.—**sustento,** m. sustenance, maintenance; support.

sustitución, f. substitution.—**sustituir,** vti. [23-e] to substitute, replace.—**sustituto,** n. substitute; supply.—ppi. of SUSTITUIR.—s. provisional, stopgap.

susto, m. scare, fright, shock.—dar un s., to frighten; to startle.

sustracción, f. subtraction.—**sustraer,** vti. [43] to subtract, remove, take off, deduct.—vri. to withdraw oneself; to elude.

susurrar, vi. to whisper; to murmur; to rustle; to hum gently (as the air).—vr. to be whispered about.—**susurro,** m. whisper, humming, murmur, rustle.—s. en voz alta, stage whisper.—**susurrón,** a. & m. whispering.—n. whisperer.

sutil, a. thin, slender; subtle, cunning; keen; light, volatile.—**sutileza,** f. thinness, slenderness, fineness; sublety, cunning; sagacity; nicety.

sutura, f. seam; suture.

suyo, a. & pron. poss. (f. **suya.**—pl. **suyos, suyas**) his, hers, theirs, one's; his own, its own, one's own, their own.—de s. intrinsically; spontaneously.—salirse con la suya, to get one's own way.—una de las suyas, one of his pranks or tricks.

T

tabacalero, *a.* tobacco.—*n.* tobacco grower or dealer.—**tabaco,** *m.* tobacco; cigar.

tábano, *m.* (entom.) gadfly, horsefly.

tabaquera, *f.* cigar case; tobacco pouch.—**tabaquería,** *f.* cigar store.—**tabaquero,** *n.* cigar maker; tobacconist.

taberna, *f.* tavern, saloon, barroom.

tabernáculo, *m.* tabernacle.

tabernero, *m.* tavern keeper, barkeeper.

tabique, *m.* partition wall, partition.

tabla, *f.* (carp.) board; plank; slab; tablet, plate (of metal); pleat; table, list.—*pl.* (theat.) stage; draw, stalemate (in a game).—*a raja t.,* at any price, ruthlessly.—*hacer t. rasa de,* to ignore entirely; to set at nought.—*salvarse en una t.,* to have a narrow escape.—*t. del piso,* floorboard,—*t. de materias,* table of contents.—*t. de planchar,* ironing board.—*t. de salvación,* last resource.—*T. Redonda,* Round Table.—**tablado,** *m.* stage, scaffold, platform; (theat.) stage boards.—**tablero,** *m.* board, panel; sawable timber; drawing board; chessboard, checkerboard; (Am.) blackboard; shop counter; door panel.—*t. de distribución,* (elec.) switchboard.—**tableta,** *f.* tablet; writing pad; (pharm.) tablet, pastille, lozenge.—**tabletear,** *vt.* to rattle clappers.—**tableteo,** *m.* rattling sound of clappers.—**tablilla,** *f.* tablet, slab; bulletin board; (surg.) splint.—*t. de persiana,* louver.—**tablón,** *m.* plank, thick board.—**tabloncillo,** *m.* flooring board.

tabú, *m.* taboo.

tabulador, *m.* (neol.) tabulator, computer.—**tabular,** *vt.* (neol.) to tabulate.

taburete, *m.* taboret; stool.

tacañería, *f.* stinginess.—**tacaño,** *a.* stingy, niggardly.

tacha, *f.* fault, defect, blemish, flaw.—**tachar,** *vt.* to censure, blame, charge; to find fault with; to cut out, cross out.

tachón, *m.* ornamental nail; trimming; crossing out (in writing).—

tachonar, *vt.* (sew.) to adorn with trimming.

tachuela, *f.* tack, small nail.

tácito, *a.* tacit, implied; silent.—**taciturno,** *a.* taciturn, reserved; sad, melancholy; silent.

taco, *m.* plug, stopper; (artil.) wad, wadding; billiard cue; (coll.) snack; (Am.) dandy; (Am.) heel (of shoe).—*echar tacos,* (coll.) to swear; to curse.

tacón, *m.* heel (of shoe).—**taconazo,** *m.* blow with a shoe heel.—**taconear,** *vi.* (coll.) to walk or strut loftily on the heels.—**taconeo,** *m.* noise made with the heels.

táctica, *f.* tactics.—**táctico,** *a.* tactical.

tacto, *m.* touch, sense of touch; tact, carefulness.

tafetán, *m.* taffeta.—*t. inglés,* court plaster, sticking plaster.

tagarnina, *f.* (coll.) bad cigar.

tahalí, *m.* shoulder belt, sword belt.

tahur, *m.* gambler, gamester; sharper, card sharp.

taimado, *a.* sly, cunning, crafty.

taita, *m.* (Am.) (coll.) daddy, dad.

tajada, *f.* slice; (coll.) cut.—**tajar,** *vt.* to cut, cleave, chop.—**tajo,** *m.* cut; incision; cutting edge; steep cliff; chopping block.

tal, *a.* such, such as.—*t. cual,* such as; such as it is.—*pron.* such, such a one, such a thing.—*no hay t.,* there is no such thing.—*t. para cual,* two of a kind.—*t. por cual,* (a) nobody.—*adv.* thus, so, in such manner.—*con t. que, con t. de que,* provided, on condition, that.—*¿qué t.?* hello! how do you do?

tala, *f.* felling, cutting.—*t. de árboles,* logging.

talabarte, *m.* sword belt.—**talabartero,** *m.* saddler; harness maker.

taladrar, *vt.* to bore, drill; to pierce (the ears).—**taladro,** *m.* drill, bit, borer, auger; bore, drill hole.—*t. eléctrico,* power drill.

tálamo, *m.* bridal chamber or bed.

talanquera, *f.* picket fence.

talante, *m.* mode or manner; mien; desire, will, disposition.—*de mal t.,* unwillingly, grudgingly.

talar, *vt.* to fell (trees).

talco, *m.* talc; talcum powder.

talega, *f.* bag, sack; money bag; diaper.—**talego**, *m.* bag or sack; clumsy, awkward fellow; duffel bag.

talento, *m.* talent; cleverness.—**talentoso**, *a.* smart, clever, talented.

tallón, *m.* retaliation, requital.

talismán, *m.* talisman, charm, amulet.

talla, *f.* carving, wood carving; (jewelry) cut, cutting; height, stature (of person).—*de t.*, (of person) prominent.—**tallar**, *vt.* to carve; to engrave; (jewelry) to cut; to appraise.—*vi.* (card games) to deal.

tallarín, *m.* noodle (for soup).

talle, *m.* form, figure; waist; (tailoring) fit; bodice.

taller, *m.* workshop, factory; atelier; studio.—*t. de laminación*, rolling mill.—*t. de reparaciones*, repair shop; (auto) service station.—*t. franco*, open shop.

tallo, *m.* (bot.) stem, stalk; shoot, sprout.

talón, *m.* (anat., shoe) heel; (com.) check, draft; stub; coupon.—**talonario**, *m.* stub book.—*libro t.*, check book.

talud, *m.* slope, bank.

tamal, *m.* (Am.) tamale.

tamaño, *m.* size.—*t. natural*, full size.—*a.* so great; so big, so small; huge.

tambalear, *vi.* & *vr.* to stagger, totter, reel.—**tambaleo**, *m.* reeling, staggering, tottering.

también, *adv.* also, too; as well; likewise.

tambor, *m.* drum; drummer; band pulley, rope barrel.—**tambora**, *f.* bass drum.—**tamboril**, *m.* tabor, small drum.—**tamborilear**, *vi.* to drum.—*vt.* to praise, extol.—**tamborilero**, *m.* taborer, drummer.

tamiz, *m.* sieve, sifter; bolting cloth.—**tamizar**, *vti.* [a] to sift.

tampoco, *adv.* neither, not either; either (after negative).

tampón, *m.* stamp pad; (pharm.) tampon.

tan, *adv. contr.* of TANTO: as so, so much, as well, as much.—*¡qué mujer t. bella!* what a beautiful woman.—*t. solo*, only, merely.

tanda, *f.* turn, rotation; task; gang of workmen, shift; relay; set, batch; each game of billiards.

tangente, *f.* & *a.* (geom.) tangent.—

salir or *salirse por la t.*, to confuse the issue.

tangerina, *f.* tangerine.

tangible, *a.* tangible.

tanque, *m.* tank; (Am.) swimming pool.

tantear, *vt.* to try, test, measure; to feel out; to make an estimate of; to consider carefully; to scrutinize.—*vi.* to keep the score.—**tanteo**, *m.* estimate, calculation; test, trial; points, score (in a game).—*al t.*, by eye; as an estimate; by trial.

tanto, *a.* & *pron.* so much, as much.—*pl.* as many, so many.—*adv.* so, thus; so much, as much; so long, as long; so hard, so often.—*m.* undetermined sum or quantity; counter, chip; point (in games).—*a las tantas*, in the small hours.—*al t.*, posted about, up to date.—*en t.*, or *entre t.*, in the meantime.—*no ser para t.*, not to be so bad as that.—*otro t.*, as much; the same again.—*por lo t.*, therefore.—*t. así*, so much.—*t. más cuanto*, all the more because.—*t. mejor*, so much the better.—*t. peor*, so much the worse.—*t. por ciento*, percentage, rate.—*t. que*, so much that.—*treinta y tantos*, thirty odd.

tañer, *vti.* [41] to play (a musical instrument).—**tañido**, *m.* playing; tune; ringing.

tapa, *f.* lid, cover, cap; cover (of book); heel lift (of shoe).—*t. de los sesos*, top of the skull.—**tapaboca**, *m.* (coll.) slap on the mouth; muffler, scarf.—**tapadera**, *f.* loose lid, cover of a pot.—**tapar**, *vt.* to hide, cover up, veil; to stop up, plug; to close up, obstruct.—**taparrabo**, *m.* loin cloth.

tapete, *m.* cover for a table or chest; small carpet, rug.—*t. verde*, gaming table.

tapia, *f.* wall fence.—*más sordo que una t.*, deaf as a post.—**tapiar**, *vt.* to wall up; to wall in; to close or block up.

tapicería, *f.* tapestry; tapestry making; upholstery; tapestry shop.—**tapicero**, *m.* tapestry maker; upholsterer; carpet layer.

tapioca, *f.* tapioca.

tapiz, *m.* tapestry.—**tapizar**, *vti.* [a] to hang with tapestry; to upholster.

tapón, *m.* cork, stopper; plug; (elec.) fuse; (surg.) tampon.—*t. de algodón*, (surg.) swab.—*t. de desagüe*, drain plug.—*t. de radiador*, radiator cap.—

t. de tráfico, traffic jam.—**taponar,** *vt.* to cork, plug; (surg.) to tampon.

tapujo, *m.* muffle; (coll.) pretext, subterfuge.

taquigrafía, *f.* stenography.—**taquígrafo,** *n.* stenographer.

taquilla, *f.* letter file; booking office; ticket window; (theat., RR.) ticket office.—**taquillero,** *n.* booking clerk; ticket agent.

tara, *f.* (com.) tare, weight of container; defect.

tarambana, *mf.* giddy person; madcap.

tararear, *vt.* & *vi.* to hum (a tune).—**tarareo,** *m.* humming.

tarascada, *f.* bite, wound with the teeth; (coll.) pert, rude answer.

tardanza, *f.* delay; slowness, tardiness.—**tardar,** *vi.* & *vr.* to delay, tarry; to take a long time; to be late.—*a más t.,* at the latest.—**tarde,** *f.* afternoon.—*de t. en t.,* now and then, once in a while.—*adv.* late; too late.—**tardío,** *a.* late, too late; slow, tardy.—**tardo,** *a.* slow, sluggish; tardy; dull, thick.

tarea, *f.* task.

tarifa, *f.* tariff; price list, fare, rate.

tarima, *f.* stand; movable platform; low bench, footstool.

tarjeta, *f.* card.—*t. de buen deseo,* greeting car.—*t. de cobro automático,* debit card.—*t. de crédito,* credit card.—*t. de pago,* credit card.—*t. de embarque,* boarding pass.—*t. de Navidad,* Christmas card.—*t. de visita,* business card, calling card.—*t. índice,* index card.—*t. postal,* postcard.—*t. registradora,* timecard.—*t. telefónica,* phonecard.—*t. verde,* green card (for resident noncitizens).—**tarjetero,** *m.* cardcase; index file; wallet.

tarro, *m.* jar; (Am.) horn (of an animal); (Am.) can, pot; (beer) mug.

tarta, *f.* tart; cake.

tartamudear, *vi.* to stutter, stammer.—**tartamudeo,** *m.,* **tartamudez,** *f.* stuttering, stammering.—**tartamudo,** *n.* & *a.* stutterer, stammer; stuttering, stammering.

tartera, *f.* baking pan for pastry; dinner pail.

tarugo, *m.* wooden peg or pin; stopper, plug; (fig.) blockhead.

tasa, *f.* measure, rule; standard; rate; scot, valuation, appraisement.—**tasación,** *f.* appraisement, appraisal, valuation.—**tasador,** *n.* appraiser.

tasajo, *m.* jerked beef.

tasar, *vt.* to appraise; to rate; to stint.

tata, *m.* (Am., coll.) dad, daddy; nursemaid; younger sister.

tatarabuelo, *n.* great-great-grandfather(-mother).—**tataranieto,** *n.* great-great-grandson(-daughter).

tatuaje, *m.* tattooing; tattoo.—**tatuar,** *vt.* & *vr.* to tattoo.

Tauro, *m.* (astr.) Taurus.

taxi, taxímetro, *m.* taxi, taxicab.—**taxista,** *mf.* taxi driver, cab driver.

taza, *f.* cup; cupful; bowl; basin of a fountain; cup guard of a sword.—**tazón,** *m.* large bowl; basin.

te, *m.* tea.

te, *pers.* & *refl. pron.* (*obj. case* of TU) you, to you; yourself; thee.

tea, *f.* torch.

teatral, *a.* theatrical.—**teatrero,** *n.* theatergoer.—**teatro,** *m.* theater; stage; dramatic art; scene.—*t. de guiñol, marionetas,* or *titeres,* puppet theater.—*t. de la ópera,* opera house.—*t. de variedades,* vaudeville.

techado, *m.* roof, roofing; ceiling; shed.—**techar,** *vt.* to roof; to cover with a roof.—**techo,** *m.* = TECHUMBRE; (aer.) absolute ceiling.—*t. corredizo,* sunroof.—*t. de cristal,* glass ceiling.—**techumbre,** *f.* ceiling; roof, roofing; cover; shed.

tecla, *f.* key (of a piano, typewriter, etc.).—*dar en la t.,* to find the way.—*t. de escape,* margin release.—*t. de espacios,* space key.—*t. de mayúsculas,* shift key.—**teclado,** *m.* keyboard.

técnica, *f.* technique; technical ability.—**tecnicismo,** *m.* technical term; technology.—**técnico,** *a.* technical.—*n.* technician.—**tecnología,** *f.* technology.

tecolote, *m.* (Mex.) owl.

tedio, *m.* boredom, tediousness.—**tedioso,** *a.* tedious, boresome, boring, tiresome.

teja, *f.* roof tile; (bot.) linden tree.—**tejado,** *m.* roof; shed.—**tejamanil,** *m.* shingle.—**tejanos,** *mpl.* blue jeans.—**tejar,** *m.* tile kiln.—*vt.* to tile.

tejedor, *n.* weaver.—**tejemaneje,** *m.* (coll.) skill, cleverness; (Am.) scheming, trick.—**tejer,** *vt.* to weave; (Am.) to knit; to devise.—**tejido,** *m.* texture; weaving; fabric, textile, web; (anat.) tissue.

tejón, *m.* (zool.) badger.

tela, *f.* cloth, fabric; pellicle, film.—*en t. de juicio,* in doubt; under careful consideration.—*t. aisladora,* friction tape.—*t. de cebolla,* onion skin; thin cloth.—*t. metálica,* wire cloth.—**telar,** *m.* loom.—**telaraña,** *f.* cobweb.—*t. mundial,* World-Wide Web.

tele, *f.* (fam.) TV, television.—**telebanco,** *m.* automated-teller machine, ATM.—**telecabina,** *m.* or *f.* cable car.—**telecine,** *m.* **telefilm,** *m.* television movie.—**telecomando,** *m.* **telecontrol,teledirección,** *f.* **telemando,** *m.* remote control.—**telecomunicación,** *f.* telecommunication.—**teleconferencia,** *f.* (tel.) conference call.—**teleculebra,** *f.* (fam.) soap opera.—**telediario,** TV news.—**teledirigido,** *a.* remote-controlled, guided.—**telefax,** fax.—**teleférico,** *m.* cable railway.

telefonear, *vt. & vi.* to telephone.—**telefonema,** *m.* telephone message.—**telefónico,** *a.* telephonic.—**telefonista,** *mf.* (telephone) operator.—**teléfono,** *m.* telephone.—*t. celular,* cellular telephone, cellphone.—*t. inalámbrico, t. sin hilos,* cordless telephone.

telegrafía, *f.* telegraphy.—**telegrafiar,** *vt.* to telegraph; to wire.—**telegráfico,** *a.* telegraphic.—**telegrafista,** *mf.* telegrapher.—**telégrafo,** *m.* telegraph.—**telegrama,** *m.* telegram.

telegulado, *a.* remote-controlled, guided.—**teleimpresor,** teleprinter, teletype.—**telemárketing,** *m.* telemarketing.—**telemática,** data transmission.—**telenovela,** *f.* soap opera.—**telepatía,** *f.* telepathy.—**telerreceptor,** *m.* television set.

telescópico, *a.* telescopic.—**telescopio,** *m.* telescope.—*t. espacial,* space telescope.—**telesilla,** *m.* chair lift.—**telespectador,** *n.* television viewer.—**telesquí,** *m.* ski lift.—**teletipo,** *m.* Teletype (TM).—*transmitir por t.,* to teletype.—**televisar,** *vt.* to televise.

televisión, *f.* television.—*t. en blanco y negro,* black-and-white television. —*t. en circuito cerrado,* closed-circuit television.—*t. en color* or *en colores,* color television.—*t. por abonados,* pay-per-view television.—*t. por cable,* cable television.—**televisor,** *m.* television set.

telón, *m.* (theat.) curtain.—*bajar el t.,* to drop the curtain.—*t. de acero,* Iron Curtain.—*t. de fondo,* (theat.) backdrop.—*t. de boca,* drop curtain.

tema, *m.* theme, subject; text, thesis; (mus.) theme, motive.—*t. central,* theme song.—*f.* mania, obsession.—**temario,** *m.* agenda.

temblar, *vii.* [1] to tremble, shake, quake, quiver; to shiver.—**temblequear,** *vi.* (coll.) to tremble, shake, shiver.—**temblor,** *m.* trembling, tremor, thrill; quake.—*t. de tierra,* earthquake.—**tembloroso,** *a.* trembling, tremulous, shivering, shaking.

temer, *vt. & vi.* to fear, dread.—**temerario,** *a.* rash, imprudent; reckless.—**temeridad,** *f.* temerity, rashness, recklessness; foolhardiness.—**temeroso,** *a.* dread; timid; timorous; fearful.—**temible,** *a.* dread, terrible.—**temor,** *m.* dread, fear.

témpano, *m.* kettledrum; drumhead; piece, block.—*t. de hielo,* iceberg.

temperamento, *m.* temperament, constitution; climate.—**temperatura,** *f.* temperature.

tempestad, *f.* tempest, storm.—**tempestuoso,** *a.* tempestuous, stormy.

templado, *a.* moderate (esp. of climate); tempered; lukewarm; fair; brave, firm; (mus.) tuned.—**templanza,** *f.* temperance, moderation; mildness (of temperature or climate).—**templar,** *vt.* to temper, moderate; to temper, quench (metals); (mus.) to tune.—*vr.* to be moderate.—**temple,** *m.* temper (of metals, of persons); courage; disposition; (mus.) temperament.

templo, *m.* temple; church.

temporada, *f.* season; period (of time); spell (of weather).—*t. baja,* off-season.

temporal, *a.* temporal; temporary; secular, worldly.—*m.* tempest; storm; long rainy spell.—**temporero,** *a.* temporary (laborer).

tempranero, *a.* early.—**temprano,** *a.* early.—*adv.* early; in good time.

ten, *m.*—*t. con t.,* tact, wisdom.

tenacidad, *f.* tenacity; tenaciousness, perseverance.—**tenacillas,** *f.* small tongs; pincers; sugar tongs; curling irons.—**tenaz,** *a.* tenacious; strong, firm; stubborn; purposeful, persevering.—**tenaza(s),** *f.* claw (as a lobster's).—*pl.* tongs, nippers, pliers; (dent.) forceps.

tendal, *m.* tent, awning, tilt; piece of canvas.

tendedero, *m.* drying place.—*f.* (Am.) clothesline.—**tendencia,** *f.* tendency, proclivity; trend, drift.—**tendencioso,** *a.* tendentious.—**tender,** *vti.* [18] to stretch, stretch out; to spread out; to hang out (washing); to lay (tablecloth, rails, etc.).—*vii.* to have a tendency, tend.—*vri.* to stretch out, lie full length.

tendero, *n* .retail shopkeeper.—*t. de ultramarinos o comestibles,* grocer.

tendido, *a.* lying, spread out.—*m.* washing hung or spread out to dry.—*pl.* uncovered seats in the bullring; bleachers.

tendón, *m* .tendon, sinew.

tenebroso, *a.* dark, gloomy.

tenedor, *m.* (table) fork; keeper; (com.) holder.—*t. de libros,* bookkeeper.—**teneduría,** *f.* position of bookkeeper.—*t. de libros,* bookkeeping.

tenencia, *f.* tenure, occupancy, possession, holding; (mil.) position of a lieutenant.

tener, *vti.* [42] to have, possess; to hold; to contain.—*no tenerlas todas consigo,* to be worried, to be anxious.—*t. a bien,* to please; to find it convenient.—*t. cuatro años,* to be four years old.—*t. cuidado de,* to take care of.—*t. dos metros de ancho,* to be two meters wide.—*t. en cuenta,* to take into account.—*t. gana* or *ganas,* to wish, desire (to); to have in mind (to); to feel like.—*t. gracia,* to be funny.—*t. gusto en,* to be glad to.—*t. hambre (sed, etc.),* to be hungry (thirsty, etc.).—*t. presente,* to bear in mind.—*t. prisa,* to be in a hurry.—*t. razón,* to be right.—*t. suerte,* to be lucky.—*vai.* to have.—*tengo dicho,* I have said.—*tengo entendido,* I understand.—*tengo escritas dos cartas,* I have two letters written.—*tengo pensado,* I intend.—*vri.* to hold fast or steady; to stop, halt.—*t. en pie,* to keep on one's feet, remain standing.

tenería, *f.* tannery.

tenia, *f.* tapeworm.

teniente, *m.* lieutenant.

tenis, *m.* tennis.—*t. de mesa,* table tennis.—**tenista,** *mf.* tennis player.

tenor, *m.* (mus.) tenor; condition, nature; kind; literal meaning.

tensión, *f.* tension; (mech.) stress; strain; (elec.) voltage, tension.—*t. arterial,* blood pressure.—**tenso,** *a.* tense, tight, taut, stretched.

tentación, *f.* temptation.

tentáculo, *m.* tentacle.

tentador, *n.* & *a.* tempter; tempting, tantalizing.—*el t.,* the devil.—**tentar,** *vti.* [1] to touch, feel with the fingers; to grope; to tempt; to attempt, try; to test; (surg.) to probe.—**tentativa,** *f.* attempt.—**tentativo,** *a.* tentative.

tentemplé, *m.* (coll.) light luncheon, snack, refreshment.

tenue, *a.* thin, tenuous; worthless; (art) subdued.

teñir, *vti.* [9–49] to dye, tinge; to stain; (art) to darken (a color).

teologal, *a.* theologic(al).—**teología,** *f.* theology.—**teológico,** *a.* = TEOLOGAL.

teorema, *m.* theorem.

teoría, *f.* theory.—**teórico,** *a.* theoretical.—*mf.* theorist.—**teorizar,** *vii.* [a] to theorize.

terapia, *f.* therapy.—*t. de electrochoque,* (med.) shock treatment.

tercer, *a.* third.—*en t. lugar,* thirdly.—*T. Mundo,* Third World.—**tercería,** *f.* pandering, procuring.—**tercero,** *a.* third.—*n.* third; mediator; third person; go-between.

terciar, *vt.* to place sidewise; to sling diagonally; to divide into three parts; (mil.) to carry (arms.)—*vi.* to mediate, arbitrate; to go between; to join (in conversation).—**tercio,** *a.* third.—*m.* one-third; (Sp.) Foreign Legion; (Am.) (coll.) fellow, guy.—*hacer mal t.,* to do a bad turn.

terciopelo, *m.* velvet.

terco, *a.* stubborn.

tergiversar, *vt.* to misrepresent, distort.

terliz, *m.* ticking.

terminación, *f.* termination; end, ending.—**terminal,** *a.* terminal, final, last.—*m.* (elec.) terminal.—**terminante,** *a.* ending, closing; final, decisive.—**terminar,** *vt.* & *vi.* to end, terminate, conclude.—**término,** *m.* end, ending, completion; term, word; boundary; terminus; manner, behavior; outlying district; period, limit; aim, goal; (math., log.) term.—*en buenos términos,* in kind language.—*en último t.,* finally; in the background.—*primer t.,* (art) foreground.—*t. medio,* average.

termita, *f.,* **termite,** *m.* termite.

termodinámico, *a.* thermodynamic.—**termonuclear,** *a.* thermonuclear.

termómetro, *m.* thermometer.—**termo(s),** *m.* thermos bottle.—**termóstato,** *m.* thermostat.

ternero, *n.* calf.—*f.* veal.

terneza, *f.* softness; tenderness; affection, caress.—*pl.* sweet nothings.

terno, *m.* set of three, trio; tern (in lottery); bad word; suit of clothes; (jewelry) set.

ternura, *f.* tenderness, softness, fondness.

terquedad, *f.* stubborness, obstinacy.

terrado, *m.* terrace; flat roof of a house.

terral, *m.* land breeze.

terramicina, *f.* terramycin.

terraplén, *m.* (RR.) embankment; mound; terrace.

terrateniente, *mf.* landowner, landholder.

terraza, *f.* terrace; border in a garden; veranda; sidewalk safé.

terremoto, *m.* earthquake.—**terrenal,** *a.* wordly, earthly.—**terreno,** *a.* earthly, terrestrial; wordly, mundane.—*m.* land, ground, soil; terrain; piece of land, lot; field, sphere of action.—**terrestre,** *a.* terrestrial.

terrible, *a.* terrible.—**terrífico,** *a.* terrific, frightful.

territorio, *m.* territory; region.

terrón, *m.* clod; lump.

terror, *m.* terror.—**terrorismo,** *m.* terrorism.—**terrorista,** *mf.* & *a.* terrorist; terroristic.

terruño, *m.* native land; piece of ground.

tesauro or **tesoro,** *m.* thesaurus.

terso, *a.* smooth, polished, glossy.—**tersura,** *f.* smoothness, polish; cleanliness, terseness.

tertulia, *f.* social gathering for entertainment; party; conversation; (Am.) (theat.) gallery.

tesis, *f.* thesis, dissertation; opinion.

tesón, *m.* tenacity, firmness, endurance.—**tesonero,** *a.* (Am.) persistent, tenacious.

tesorería, *f.* treasury; treasurership.—**tesorero,** *n.* treasurer; bursar (of a college, univ.).—**tesoro,** *m.* treasure; treasury.

testa, *f.* (coll.) head; top or crown of the head; front, face; (coll.) brains, cleverness.

testaferro, *m.* man of straw, dummy, figurehead.

testamento, *m.* will, testament.—**testar,** *vi.* to make a will.—*vt.* to scratch out.

testarudez, *f.* hardheadedness, stubbornness, willfulness.—**testarudo,** *a.* stubborn, hardheaded.

testículo, *m.* testicle.

testificar, *vti.* [d] to attest, witness, testify.—**testigo,** *mf.* witness.—*t. de cargo,* witness for the prosecution.—*t. ocular,* eyewitness.—**testimoniar,** *vt.* to attest, to bear witness to.—**testimonio,** *m.* testimony; affidavit; attestation.

testuz, *m.* nape or forehead (of some animals).

teta, *f.* teat, breast; nipple; udder.

tétano, tétanos, *m.* tetanus, lockjaw.

tetera, *f.* teapot, teakettle. (Am.) nursing bottle.—**tetilla,** *f.* teat.

tétrico, *a.* sad, sullen; dark, gloomy.

textil, *a.* textile.

texto, *m.* text; quotation; textbook.—**textual,** *a.* textual; verbatim.

tez, *f.* complexion (of the face).

ti, *pron.* 2d. pers. sing. (after *prep.*) (*obj. case* of TU) you.

tía, *f.* aunt.—*no hay tu t.,* there's no use.

tibia, *f.* tibia, shin bone.

tibieza, *f.* tepidity, lukewarmness; coolness.—**tibio,** *a.* tepid, lukewarm; remiss.

tiburón, *m.* shark.

tibor, *m.* Chinese vase; (Am.) chamberpot.

tictac, *m.* tick, ticking; tick-tock.

tiempo, *m.* time; (mus.) tempo, meter; (gram.) tense; weather.—*andando el t.,* in time, in the long run.—*a su t.,* in due time.—*a t.,* timely, in or on time.—*cuanto t.,* how long.—*fuera de t.,* out of season; inopportunely.—*hace t.,* long ago.—*los buenos tiempos,* the good, old days.—*tiempos de paz,* peacetime.—*t. muerto,* time out.

tienda, *f.* shop, store; tent.—*ir de tiendas,* to go shopping.—*t. de comestibles, t. de ultramarinos,* grocery.—*t. de objetos de regalo,* gift shop.—*t. de variedades,* general store.—*t. máquina,* (comput.) computing time.—*t. real,* (comput.) real time.

tienta, *f.* (surg.) probe.—*andar a tientas,* to grope; to feel one's way.—*a tientas,* gropingly.

tiento, *m.* touch, act of feeling; blind man's stick; tact; steady hand; (coll.) blow, cuff; (coll.) swig.—*perder el t.,* to get out of practice, to get rusty.

tierno, *a.* tender, soft; delicate; affectionate; sensitive; young; green, unripe.

tierra, *f.* earth, world; land; soil; ground; native country.—*a t.,* ashore.—*besar la t.,* (coll.) to bite the dust.—*dar en t. con,* or *echar por t.,* to overthrow; to ruin, destroy.—*echar t. a,* to hush up, forget, drop (a matter).—*irse a t.,* to fall down, to topple over.—*t. de las maravillas,* wonderland.—*t. de nadie,* no man's land.—*t. firme,* mainland; firm, solid ground.—*t. natal,* native land.—*tomar t.,* to land; to anchor.—*venirse a t.,* = IRSE A TIERRA.

tieso, *a.* stiff; tight, taut; stuck up; too grave or circumspect.

tiesto, *m.* potsherd; flowerpot.

tiesura, *f.* stiffness; rigidity.

tifo, *m.* typhus.—**tifoidea,** *a.* & *f.* typhoid (fever).

tifón, *m.* whirlwind; typhoon.

tifus, *m.* typhus.

tigre, *m.* tiger.—**tigresa,** *f.* tigress.

tijera, *f.* (usually in *pl.*) scissors; sawbuck.—*cama de t.,* folding bed, cot.—*silla de t.,* folding chair.—*tijeras de trasquilar,* shearing clippers.—**tijeretada,** *f.,* **tijeretazo,** *m.* a cut with scissors, clip, snip.—**tijeretear,** *vt.* to cut with scissors; to snip, clip; to gossip.—**tijereteo,** *m.* clipping.

tildar, *vt.* to cross or scratch out; to put a tilde over; to criticize.—*t. de,* to accuse of, or charge with being.—**tilde,** *f.* tilde, diacritic (~) of the letter *ñ*; blemish; jot.

timador, *n.* swindler.—**timar,** *vt.* to cheat, swindle.

timba, *f.* gambling party; gambling den; (Am.) guava paste or jelly.—**timbal,** *m.* kettledrum; (cook.) casserole.

timbrar, *vt.* to stamp.—**timbre,** *m.* seal; postage stamp; call or door bell; ringing (of phone); timbre, tone; crest (heraldry).—*t. de gloria,* glorious deed.

timidez, *f.* timidity; bashfulness.—**tímido,** *a.* timid, shy, bashful.

timo, *m.* (coll.) cheat, swindle, con, con game.

timón, *m.* helm, rudder.—*t. de profundidad,* (aer.) elevator.—**timonear,** *vt.* & *vi.* (naut.) to helm; to steer.—**timonel,** *m.* helmsman, steersman; coxswain.

timorato, *a.* timorous, chickenhearted.

tímpano, *m.* (anat.) eardrum; kettledrum.

tina, *f.* large earthen jar; vat; tub, wash tub; bathtub.—**tinaco,** *m.* wooden trough, tub, or vat.—**tinaja,** *f.* large earthen jar.—**tinajón,** *m.* very large earthen water jar, or tank.

tinglado, *m.* shed, shed roof; temporary board floor; machination, intrigue.

tiniebla, *f.* (usually in *pl.*) darkness.

tino, *m.* skill; steady and accurate aim; judgment; tact; knack.

tinta, *f.* ink; tint, hue, color.—*de buena t.,* from or on good authority.—*t. china,* India ink.—*t. de imprenta,* printer's ink.—*t. simpática,* invisible ink.—**tinte,** *m.* dyeing, staining; tint, hue; paint, color, stain; dye; (fig.) guise, color.—**tinterillo,** *m.* (Am.) shyster lawyer.—**tintero,** *m.* inkpot, inkwell.—*dejarse en el t.,* (coll.) to forget to mention.

tintinear, *vi.* to clink, tinkle, jingle.—**tintineo,** *m.* clink, tinkling.

tinto, *ppi.* of TEÑIR.—*a.* tinged; (dark) red; (Am.) black, strong (coffee).—**tintorería,** *f.* cleaner or dyer's shop.—**tintorero,** *n.* cleaner, dyer.—**tintura,** *f.* tincture; tint, color; stain; dye; smattering.

tiña, *f.* (med.) scab; ringworm.—**tiñoso,** *a.* scabby, scurvy; stingy, mean.

tío, *m.* uncle; (coll.) good old man; fellow.

tiovivo, *m.* merry-go-round.

típico, *a.* typical, characteristic.

tiple, *m.* (mus.) treble, soprano voice; treble guitar.—*f.* soprano singer.

tipo, *m.* type, pattern; standard, model; (coll.) (of person) figure, physique; (Am.) (com.) rate; (print.) type; (zool.) class; (coll. contempt.) fellow, guy.—*t. de letra,* typeface.—*t. impositivo,* tax rate.—*t. menudo,* small print.—**tipografía,** *f.* printing; typography.—**tipográfico,** *a.* typographical.—**tipógrafo,** *n.* typographer.

tira, *f.* long, narrow strip.—*t. de película, t. proyectable,* filmstrip.

tirabuzón, *m.* corkscrew; corkscrew curl.

tirada, *f.* cast, throw; distance; (print.) edition, issue.—**tirador,** *n.* thrower; drawer; sharpshooter; marksman, good shot.—*m.* handle, knob.—**tirafondo,** *m.* wood screw.—**tiraje,** *m.* (phot.) print.

tiranía, *f.* tyranny.—**tiranizar,** *vti.* [a] to tyrannize.—**tirano,** *a.* tyrannical.—*n.* tyrant.

tirante, *a.* drawing, pulling; taut, tense, stretched; strained (as relations).—*m.* trace, gear (of harness); brace, strap.—*pl.* suspenders, braces.—**tirantez,** *f.* tenseness, tightness; stretch; strain; tension.—**tirar,** *vt.* to throw, cast, pitch (as a ball); to cast off, throw away (as a garment); to print; to fire, shoot (as a gun); to draw (a line); to waste, squander.—*t. de,* to pull (on).—*vi.* to draw, border, pull; (a) to have a shade (of), border (on); to tend, incline (to).—*vr.* to throw oneself; to abandon oneself; to jump (at), spring (upon).

tirita, *f.* Band-Aid (TM).—*t. tobillera,* ankle strap.

tiritar, *vi.* to shiver.

tiro, *m.* throw, shot; shot, discharge, report (of a firearm); target practice; range; team of draught animals; landing of a stairway; draught of a chimney.—*al t.,* (Am.) right away, immediately.—*a tiros,* with shots, by shooting.—*de t.,* draft (horse).—*de tiros largos,* in full dress, in full regalia.—*errar el t.,* to miss the mark; to be mistaken.—*ni a tiros,* (coll.) not for love or money, absolutely not.—*t. al blanco,* target practice; shooting gallery.—*t. al blanco* or *al vuelo,* trapshooting.—*t. de la pesa,* (sports) shot-put.

tirón, *m.* pull, haul, tug; effort, yank.—*de un t.,* at once, at one stroke.

tirotear, *vi.* & *vr.* to exchange shots, to skirmish.—**tiroteo,** *m.* skirmish; shooting, shoot-out.

tirria, *f.* (coll.) aversion, dislike, grudge.

tísico, *n.* & *a.* (med.) consumptive.—**tisis,** *f.* consumption, tuberculosis.

tisú, *m.* tissue, gold or silver tissue.

títere, *m.* puppet; whipper-snapper.—*no dejar t. con cabeza,* to upset everything; to leave no one to tell the tale.

titilar, *vi.* to twinkle, flicker.

titiritar, *vi.* to shiver with cold or fear.

titiritero, *n.* juggler, acrobat; pup peteer.

titubear, *vi.* to hesitate; to totter; t(toddle (as a child); to stagger.—**titu beo,** *m.* hesitation; tottering.

titular, *vt.* to title, entitle, name, call.—*vr.* to call oneself; to be entitled.—*a(* titular; nominal.—*f.* headline (of (newspaper).—**título,** *m.* title; head ing, headline; claim, privilege c right; (law) legal title to property diploma; professional degree (com.) certificate, bond.—*a t. (de* under pretext (of); on the authorit' (of).—*t. de propiedad,* title deed.

tiza, *f.* chalk; clay.

tiznar, *vt.* to smut, smudge; to stain tarnish.—**tizne,** *m.* soot, coal smut stain.

tizón, *m.* firebrand; (agr.) blight, rust stain; mildew (of plants).

toalla, *f.* towel.—*t. rusa, t. de felp(gruesa,* Turkish towel.—*t. sin fir* roller towel.—**toallero,** *m.* towe rack.

tobogán, *m.* slide, chute; toboggan.

tobillo, *m.* ankle.

toca, *f.* hood, coif, bonnet, wimple.—**tocadiscos,** *m.* record player.—*t. au tomático de moneda,* jukebox.

tocado, *a.* (fig.) touched (in the head' perturbed; tainted.—*m.* hairdc hairdress, coiffure.—**tocador,** *n* dressing table; dressing room, bou doir; dressing case; player (of a mu sical instrument).—**tocante,** *a.*—*a,* respecting, concerning, with re gard to.—**tocar,** *vti.* [d] to touch feel; (mus.) to play; to toll, ring (bell); to blow (a horn); to knock rap; to tag (a player).—*t. de cerca,* t(concern, affect closely.—*t. fondo,* t(strike ground.—*vii.* to touch; be hoove, concern; to be one's turn; t call at a port; to border on; to be re lated.

tocayo, *n.* namesake.

tocino, *m.* bacon; salt pork.

tocólogo, *n.* obstetrician.

tocón, *m.* stump of a tree.

todavía, *adv.* still; yet; even.

todo, *a.* all, every, each; whole, en tire.—*t. aquello que,* whatever.—*aquél que,* whoever.—*t. el mund(* everybody.—*m.* all; whole; every thing.—*pl.* everybody.—*ante t* first of all.—*con t.,* nevertheless however.—*del t.,* entirely, wholly. —*en un t.,* together, in all its parts.— *jugar el t. por el t.,* to stake or risk all.—*sobre t.,* above all.—*adv.* entirely, totally.—*así y t.,* in spite of everything.—**todopoderoso,** *a.* almighty.

oga, *f.* robe or gown (worn by judges, professors, etc.); toga.

oldo, *m.* awning; tarpaulin; (Am.) Indian hut; tent.

olerable, *a.* tolerable, bearable; permissible.—**tolerancia,** *f.* toleration; tolerance.—**tolerante,** *a.* tolerant. —**tolerar,** *vi.* to tolerate, endure, permit; to be indulgent; to overlook.

olete, *m.* (Am.) club, cudgel.

oma, *f.* taking, receiving; take; (mil.) capture, seizure; dose (of a medicine); (hydraul.) intake; (elec.) outlet; tap (of a water main or electric wire).—*t. de datos,* (comput.) data capture.—**tomacorriente,** *m.* (Am.) (elec.) socket, plug.

omaína, *f.* ptomaine.

omar, *vt.* to take; to drink; to eat.—*t. a mal,* to take ill.—*t. asiento,* to take a seat, sit down.—*t. el pelo a,* (fam.) to make fun of, to tease.—*t. en cuenta,* to consider.—*t. la delantera,* to excel; to get ahead.—*vi.* to drink (liquor).—*vr.* to drink; to eat; to rust.

omate, *m.* tomato.

omillo, *m.* thyme.

omo, *m.* volume, tome.—*de t. y lomo,* of weight and bulk; of importance.

on, *m.*—*sin t. ni son,* without rhyme or reason.

onada, *f.* tune, song.—**tonalidad,** *f.* tonality.

onel, *m.* cask, barrel.—**tonelada,** *f.* ton.—**tonelaje,** *m.* tonnage, displacement; (com.) tonnage dues.

ónico, *a.* tonic; (gram.) accented or inflected.—*m.* tonic.—*f.* (mus.) keynote, tonic.—**tonificador, tonificante,** *a.* tonic, strengthening.— **tonificar,** *vti.* [d] (med.) to tone up.— **tono,** *m.* tone; tune; pitch; conceit; manner, social address.—*darse t.,* to put on airs.—*de buen t.,* stylish, fashionable, polite.—*t. de marcar, t. de discado,* dial tone.—*t. de ocupado,* (tel.) busy signal.

onsila, *f.* (anat.) tonsil.

ontada, tontera, tontería, *f.* foolishness, silliness, nonsense.—**tonto,** *a.* silly, foolish, stupid.—*n.* fool, dunce, dolt.—*a tontas y a locas,*

without order, haphazard.—*hacerse el t.,* to play dumb.

topacio, *m.* topaz.

topar, *vt.* to collide with; to meet with by chance; to find.—*vi.* to butt, strike; to stumble upon.—**tope,** *m.* butt, end; top; summit; (mech.) stop; (RR.) buffer, collision, knock.—*hasta el t.* or *los topes,* up to the top, or the brim.—**topera,** *f.* **topinera,** *f.* molehill.—**topetazo, topetón,** *m.* butt, knock, blow, collision.

tópico, *a.* topical.—*m.* commonplace, trite idea; topic.

topo, *m.* (zool.) mole; (coll.) awkward person.

toque, *m.* touch, touching; ringing (of bells); (mil.) bugle call; beat (of a drum).—*t. de diana,* reveille.—*t. de difuntos,* death knell, taps.—*t. ligero,* dab.

tórax, *m.* thorax.

torbellino, *m.* whirlwind; whirlpool; vortex; (fig.) hustling, restless person.

torcaz, torcaza, *f.* wild pigeon.

torcedura, *f.* twisting; sprain.—**torcer,** *vti.* [26-a] to twist, twine, wind (as strands); to sprain; to bend; to distort.—*no dar el brazo a t.,* to be obstinate.—*vii.* to turn (to right or left).—*vri.* to become twisted, bent or sprained; to go crooked or astray.—**torcimiento,** *m.* twist(ing); sprain; winding; bend.

tordillo, *a.* grayish, grizzled.—**tordo,** *a.* dappled (of horses).—*m.* (ornith.) thrush, throstle.

torear, *vi.* to fight bulls in the ring.— *vt.* to fight (bulls); to banter; to provoke.—**toreo,** *m.* bullfighting.—**torero,** *m.* bullfighter.—*a.* pertaining to bullfighters.

tormenta, *f.* storm, tempest; hurricane; misfortune.—*t. de arena,* sandstorm.—*t. de nieve,* snowstorm.—*t. eléctrica,* electric storm. —**tormento,** *m.* torment, torture.— **tormentoso,** *a.* stormy; boisterous; turbulent.

tornado, *m.* tornado, twister.

tornar, *vt.* to return, restore; to turn; to change, alter.—*vi.* to return, come back; to do again.—*vr.* (en) to change (into), to become.—**tornasol,** *m.* (bot.) sunflower; iridescence, sheen; litmus.—**tornasolado,** *a.* changeable, iridescent.

tornear, *vt.* & *vi.* to turn (in a lathe); to do lathe work.—**torneo,**; (sports) tournament.—*t. de preguntas y respuestas,* quiz game.—**tornero,** *n.* lathe operator.

tornillo, *m.* screw, bolt; vise, clamp.

torniquete, *m.* turnstile; turnbuckle; (surg.) tourniquet.

torno, *m.* lathe; winch, windlass; revolving dumbwaiter; turn; spindle.—*en t.,* round about.

toro, *m* .bull.—*agarrar el t. por los cuernos,* to take the bull by the horns.—*los toros,* bullfighting.

toronja, *f.* grapefruit.

torpe, *a.* slow, heavy, torpid, wooden; dull, stupid; bawdy, lewd.

torpedear, *vt.* to torpedo.—**torpedeo,** *m.* torpedoing.—**torpedero,** *m.* torpedo boat.—**torpedo,** *m.* torpedo.

torpeza, *f.* heaviness, dullness; torpor; lewdness.

torre, *f.* tower; turret; steeple; (chess) castle or rook.—*t. de apartamentos,* high rise.—*t. de perforación,* drilling rig.

torrencial, *a.* torrential; overpowering.—**torrente,** *m.* torrent; rush; plenty.

torreón, *m.* fortified tower.—**torrero,** *m.* lighthouse keeper.

tórrido, *a.* torrid; parched, hot.

torsión, *f.* twist; twisting.

torso, *m.* trunk of the body or of a statue.

torta, *f.* cake, pie; loaf; (coll.) blow, slap.—**tortazo,** *m.* (fam.) blow, slap, clout.—*dar un t. a,* to clout.

tortícolis, *m.* stiff neck.

tortilla, *f.* omelet; (Am.) cornmeal cake, pancake.—*hacer t.,* to smash to pieces.

tórtola, *f.* (ornith.) turtledove.

tortuga, *f.* turtle; tortoise.

tortuoso, *a.* tortuous, winding, sly, sneaky.

tortura, *f.* torture; grief.—**torturar,** *vt.* to torture.

torvo, *a.* fierce, stern, severe, grim.

tos, *f.* cough.—*t. ferina* or *convulsiva,* whooping cough.

tosco, *a.* coarse, rough; unpolished; slipshod.

toser, *vi.* to cough.

tosiguero, *m.* poison ivy.

tosquedad, *f.* roughness, coarseness; rudeness; clumsiness.

tostada, *f.* [slice of] toast.—**tostador,**

n. toaster; coffee roaster.—**tostadura,** *f.* toasting.—**tostar,** *vti.* [12] to toast; to roast; to tan (as the sun).

total, *a.* total; general.—*m.* total; totality; result, upshot.—*en t.,* in short, to sum up.—**totalidad,** *f.* totality; whole.—**totalitario,** *a.* & *n* totalitarian.—**totalitarismo,** *m.* totalitarianism.—**totalizar,** *vti.* [a] to sum up; to find the total of.

tóxico, *a.* toxic.—*m.* poison.—**toxicómano,** *m.* drug addict.—**toxina,** *f* (med.) toxin.

toza, *f.* log; block of wood; piece o bark.

tozudo, *a.* stubborn, obstinate.

traba, *f.* tie, bond, brace, clasp, locking device; anything that binds together; ligament, ligature; hobble clog; obstacle, hindrance.

trabajador, *a.* industrious; hardworking.—*n.* worker; laborer.—**trabajar** *vt.* & *vi.* to work, labor; to shape form; to endeavor.—**trabajo,** *m* work, labor; piece of work; employment; obstacle, hindrance; trouble hardship.—*pasar trabajos,* to have troubles, to experience hardships o. privation.—*t. por turnos,* shif work.—*trabajos forzados,* hard la bor.—**trabajoso,** *a.* difficult, hard laborious.

trabalenguas, *m.* tongue twister, jaw breaker.—**trabar,** *vt.* to seize, fetter fasten; to impede; to link; to engage in, join in.—*vr.* to become locked interlocked; to become confused rattled.—**trabazón,** *f.* juncture union, bond, connection.

trac, *m.* stage fright.

tracción, *f.* traction; cartage; (mech. tension.—*t. delantera,* (aut.) front wheel drive.—**tractor,** *m.* tractor.

tradición, *f.* tradition.—**tradicional,** *a* traditional.

traducción, *f.* translation; rendering.—**traducir,** *vti.* [11] to trans late.—**traductor,** *n.* translator.

traer, *vti.* [43] to bring, fetch; to cause to wear (as a garment); to carry.—*t a colación,* to bring up for discussion.—*t. a mal t.,* to go hard with one; to disturb, trouble, vex.—*t. en tre manos,* to be engaged in, busy with.

tráfago, *m.* commerce, trade; drudgery; bustle, hustle.

traficar, *vii.* [d] to traffic, deal, trade; to

travel, journey, roam.—**tráfico**, *m.* trade, business; traffic.—*t. de influencias,* influence peddling.

tragaderas, *f.* gullet.—*tener buenas t.,* to be very gullible.—**tragadero,** *m.* gullet; pit.—**tragaldabas,** *mf.* glutton.—**tragaluz,** *m.* skylight, bull's-eye.—**tragar,** *vti.* [b] to swallow; to devour; to swallow up, engulf.—*vri.* to swallow; to dissemble.—**tragasables,** *mf.* sword swallower.

tragedia, *f.* tragedy.—**trágico,** *a.* tragic.—*n.* tragedian.

trago, *m.* gulp, swallow; drink.—*a tragos,* by degrees, slowly.—*echar un t.,* to take a drink.—*mal t.,* calamity, misfortune.—*t. antes de acostarse,* nightcap.—**tragón,** *n.* & *a.* glutton(-ous).—**tragonería,** *f.* gluttony.

traición, *f.* treason; treachery; betrayal.—*a t.,* treacherously.—**traicionar,** *vt.* to betray.—**traicionero,** *a.* treacherous.—**traidor,** *a.* traitorous; treasonable; treacherous.—*n.* traitor; betrayer.

traílla, *f.* leash, lash; packthread; (agr.) leveling harrow; road leveler; road scraper.

traje, *m.* dress; suit; gown; apparel.—*t. de baño,* swimming trunks; bathing suit.—*t. de calle,* business suit; street clothes.—*t. de campaña,* battledress.—*t. de chaqueta, t. sastre,* suit.—*t. de etiqueta, t. de gala, t. de noche, t. largo,* evening dress.—*t. de montar,* riding habit.—*t. de novia,* wedding dress, bridal gown.—*t. de paisano,* civvies.—*t. de pantalon,* pantsuit.—*t. espacial,* space suit.—*t. fiesta,* evening gown.—*t. hecho,* ready-made suit.—*t. hecho a medida,* tailor-made suit.—*trajes deportivos* or *de sport,* sports clothes, sportswear.

trajín, *m.* transport, haulage; traffic; coming and going, bustle, commotion.—**trajinar,** *vt.* to carry from place to place.—*vi.* to bustle about; (coll.) to fidget.

tralla, *f.* whip; whiplash.

trama, *f.* weft or woof of cloth; intrigue, scheme; (lit.) plot.—**tramar,** *vt.* to weave; to plot, scheme.

tramitación, *f.* procedure; transaction, action, carrying out.—**tramitar,** *vt.* to transact, carry through, conduct.—**trámite,** *m.* the carrying on (of administration, etc.), the trans-acting (of business, etc.); step; (law) proceeding.

tramo, *m.* parcel of ground; flight of stairs; stretch, span, section; panel (of a bridge).

tramoya, *f.* (theat.) stage machinery.—**tramoyista,** *mf.* (theat.) stage machinist; stage carpenter, stagehand.

trampa, *f.* trap, snare, pitfall; trapdoor; falling board of a counter; flap or spring door; cheat, fraud, deceit, trick; bad debt.—*hacer trampa(s),* to cheat.—**trampear,** *vi.* (coll.) to cheat; to swindle; to get along, pull through.—*vt.* to defraud.

trampolín, *m.* springboard; diving board; ski jump.

tramposo, *a.* tricky, deceitful.—*n.* cheater, swindler.

tranca, *f.* crossbar, bolt (for door); club, stick, truncheon; (Am., coll.) drunken spell.—**trancar,** *vti.* [d] to bar (a door).—**trancazo,** *m.* blow with a club; (coll.) influenza.

trance, *m.* plight, predicament; trance, rapture.—*a todo t.,* at all costs, at any price.—*en t. de muerte,* at the point of death.

tranco, *m.* long stride; threshold.—*a trancos,* hurriedly, carelessly.

tranquilidad, *f.* tranquility, peace quiet.—**tranquilizador,** *a.* quieting soothing, reassuring.—**tranquilizante,** *a.* reassuring, soothing; (med.) tranquilizing.—*m.* (med.) transquilizer.—**tranquilizar,** *vti.* [a] & *vri.* to calm, quiet down.—**tranquilo,** *a.* tranquil, calm, quiet.

transacción, *f.* transaction, negotiation; compromise, settlement.—**transar,** *vt.* & *vr.* (Am.) to compromise, adjust, settle.

transatlántico, *a.* transatlantic.—*m.* ocean liner; cruise ship.

transbordador, *a.* transferring.—*m.* transfer boat, car, etc.; ferry.—*t. espacial,* space shuttle.—**transbordar,** *vt.* to transfer.—**transbordo,** *m.* transfer.

transcribir, *vti.* [49] to transcribe.—**transcripción,** *f.* transcription.—**transcripto,** *ppi.* of TRANSCRIBIR.

transcurrir, *vi.* (of time) to pass, elapse.—**transcurso,** *m.* lapse, course.

transeúnte, *a.* transient; transitory.—*mf.* pedestrian, passer-by; nonresident, transient.

transferencia, f. transference, transfer.—**transferible,** a. transferable.—**transferir,** vti. [39] to transfer.

transformación, f. transformation.—**transformador,** n. & a. transformer; transforming.—m. (elec.) transformer.—t. portátil, power pack.—**transformar,** vt. & vr. to transform.—vr. to be or become transformed.

tránsfuga, mf. deserter; fugitive; turncoat.

transfusión, f. transfusion.—t. de sangre, blood transfusion.

transición, f. transition.

transido, a. worn out; famished.

transigencia, f. tolerance.—**transigente,** a. accommodating, pliable, compromising; tolerant.—**transigir,** vti. [c] to compromise, settle.—vii. to give in, agree.

transistor, m. transistor; transistor radio.

transitable, a. passable, practicable.—**transitar,** vi. to go from place to place (as traffic); to flow.—**transitivo,** a. transitive.—**tránsito,** m. transit; traffic; passing; passage; transition; death.—**transitorio,** a. transitory.

translación, etc. = TRANSLACION, etc.

transmisible, a. transmissible.—**transmisión,** f. transmission; (radio) broadcast.—**transmisor,** a. transmitting.—m. (elec.) transmitter.—t. de datos, (comput.) data transmission.—t.-receptor portátil, walkie-talkie.—f. (radio) broadcasting station.—**transmitir,** vt. to transmit; to broadcast.

transparencia, f. transparency.—**transparentarse,** vr. to be transparent; to show through.—**transparente,** a. transparent.—m. window shade; stained glass window.

transpiración, f. perspiration.—**transpirar,** vi. to perspire; to transpire; (fig.) to seep through.

transponer, vti. [32–49] to transpose; to transfer; to transplant.—vri. (of sun, etc.) to set below the horizon; to go behind; to be rather drowsy.

transportación, f. transportation, transport.—**transportar,** vt. to transport, carry; (mus.) to transpose.—t. en viaje corto, to shuttle.—vr. to be in a transport; to be carried away.—**transporte,** m. transport(ation), conveyance; cartage; fit; rapture, ecstasy.

transposición, f. transposition.—**transpuesto,** ppi. of TRANSPONER.

transversal, a. transversal.—sección t., cross section.—**transverso,** a. transverse.

tranvía, m. streetcar, trolley car.

trapacear, vi. to cheat, defraud.—**trapacería,** f. fraud, cheating.—**trapacero,** n. & a., **trapacista,** mf. & a. cheat; cheating.

trapecio, m. trapezium; trapeze.

trapero, n. ragpicker; rag dealer.

trapezoide, m. trapezoid.

trapiche, m. grinding machine (in sugar mills, etc.).—**trapichear,** vi. (coll.) to contrive, shift.—**trapicheo,** m. (coll.) contriving, shifting.

trapisonda, f. (coll.) bustle, clatter; (coll.) deception, trickery; brawl, scuffle; escapade.

trapo, m. rag; tatter; sails of a ship; (coll.) bullfighter's cloak.—a todo t., with all one's might; (naut.) all sails set.—poner como un t., to reprimand severely, to dress down.—soltar el t., (coll.) to burst out (crying or laughing).

tráquea, f. trachea, windpipe.

traquetear, vt. & vi. to rattle; to shake, jolt; to crack, crackle.—**traqueteo,** m. shaking, jolting; cracking, creaking; (Am.) confused, noisy movement.—**traquido,** m. snapping, rattle; creaking, cracking.

tras, prep. after, behind; beyond; besides; in search of.—t. de, after, back of; besides, in addition to.

trasanteayer, trasantier, adv. three days ago.

trasatlántico, a. = TRANSATLANTICO.

trasbordador, etc. = TRANSBORDADOR etc.

trascendencia, f. importance, consequence.—**trascendental,** a. transcendental; far-reaching; momentous, highly important.—**trascender,** vii. [18] to transcend; to spread beyond; to be pervasive; to become known, seep out.

trascribir, trascripción, etc. = TRANSCRIBIR, etc.

trascurrir, trascurso, etc. = TRANSCURRIR, etc.

trasegar, vti. [1-b] to upset, overturn; to change the place of; to pour into another vessel.

trasera, f. back part, rear.—**trasero,** a. hind, back, rear.—m. buttock, rump.

trasferencia, etc. = TRANSFERENCIA, etc.

trasfiguración, etc. = TRANSFIGURACIÓN, etc.

trasformación, etc. = TRANSFORMACIÓN, etc.

trásfuga = TRANSFUGA.

trasgo, m. goblin, sprite.

trasgredir, etc. = TRANSGREDIR, etc.

trashumante, a. (of flocks) nomadic.

traslego, m. upsetting; transfer (of wine, etc.).

traslación, f. (astr.) movement, passage; (math.) translation.—**trasladar,** vt. to move, remove, transfer; to translate; to transcribe copy.—**traslado,** m. transfer; transcription, copy.—t. de jurisdicción, (law) change of venue.

trasmisible, etc. = TRANSMISIBLE, etc.

traslúcido, = TRANSLUCIDO.—**traslucirse,** vri. [3] to be translucent.—**trasluz,** m. light seen through a transparent body; (art) transverse light.—al t., against the light.

trasnochado, a. tired from lack of sleep; haggard; stale, worn-out; trite, hackneyed.—**trasnochador,** n. nighthawk; night owl.—**trasnochar,** vi. to stay out all night; to spend a sleepless night.

traspapelar, vt. to mislay.—vr. to become mislaid.

traspasar, vt. to pierce; to pass over; to cross over; to go beyond, exceed limits; to transfer (a business); to trespass.

traspié, m. slip, stumble.—dar traspiés, to stumble; to slip; to err.

trasplantar, vt. to transplant.—vr. to migrate.—**trasplante,** m. transplantation; migration.

trasponer = TRANSPONER.

trasportación, etc. = TRANSPORTACION, etc.

trasposición, etc. = TRANSPOSICION, etc.

traspunte, mf. (theat.) prompter.

trasquilar, vt. to shear (sheep); to lop; to cut down.

trastada, f. (coll.) inconsiderate act; bad turn.

trastazo, m. whack, thump, blow.

traste, m. fret of a guitar; utensils, implements.—dar al t. con, to spoil, ruin, destroy.

trasto, m. (pej.) piece of furniture; junk; (coll.) useless person, washout.—pl. tools, paraphernalia.

trastornar, vt. to upset; to turn upside down; to disorder, disarrange; to excite; to confuse, perplex, unsettle (the mind).—**trastorno,** m. upsetting; upheaval; disturbance, disorder, confusion; trouble; disarrangement.

trastrocar, vti. [12-d] to change the order of; to disarrange.—**trastrueco, trastrueque,** m. disarrangement; transposition; rearrangement.

trasudar, vt. to sweat, perspire slightly.

trasunto, m. faithful image, likeness; copy.

trasversal, etc. = TRANSVERSAL, etc.

trata, f. trade.—t. de blancas, white slavery.—**tratable,** a. sociable; compliant.—**tratado,** m. treaty; treatise.—**tratamiento,** m. treatment; manners; title or form of address.—t. por electrochoque, electric shock treatment.—**tratante,** mf. dealer, trader.—t. de esclavos, slave trader.—**tratar,** vt. to handle; to treat (a subject, a person, a patient, a substance); to deal with; (con) to have dealings with; to discuss; (de) to try, attempt; to address as, give the title of; to call, charge with being.—vi. to treat; to deal, trade.—t. sobre or acerca de, to treat of, deal with (a subject).—t. de, to treat (of a subject).—t. en, to deal in.—vr. to look after oneself; to be on good terms.—tratarse de, to concern, be a question of.—**trato,** m. treatment; social behavior; manner; pact, agreement, deal; trade, commerce; friendly intercourse; title or form of address.—t. de esclavos, slave trade.—tener buen t., (coll.) to be pleasant, nice.—tener mucho t., to be close friends.

trauma, m. trauma.—**traumático,** a. traumatic.

través, m. bias, inclination; misfortune.—a(l) t. de, across, through.—de t., crosswise.—**travesaño,** m. crosspiece, crossbar; bolster; rung; (RR.) tie.—**travesía,** f. crossing; crossroad, cross passage; sea voyage.

travesura, f. prank, frolic; mischief; lively fancy.—**travieso,** a. frolicsome, mischievous.

trayecto, m. distance between two points; run, stretch, way.—**trayectoria,** f. trajectory, path.

traza, f. looks, appearance; trick, ruse; sign, indication.—**trazado,** a.

traced, outlined.—*m.* sketch, outline, plan; (act of) drawing.—**trazar,** *vti.* [a] to design, plan out; sketch, draw up; to trace, mark out; to draw (as a line).—**trazo,** *m.* outline; line, stroke (of a pen or pencil).

trebejo, *m.* implement, tool, utensil.

trébol, *m.* clover, shamrock.

trece, *a.* & *m.* thirteen.—*mantenerse en sus t.,* to stand pat, to stand one's ground.

treinta, *a.* & *m.* thirty.—*t. y uno,* thirty-one.—**treintavo,** *a.* & *m.* thirtieth.

trecho, *m.* space, distance; lapse.—*de t. en t.,* at intervals.

tregua, *f.* truce; reprieve, respite.

tremebundo, *a.* dreadful, frightful, fearful.

tremedal, *m.* quagmire, bog.

tremendo, *a.* tremendous; huge; excessive.

trementina, *f.* turpentine.

tremolar, *vt.* & *vi.* to wave (as a flag).—**tremolina,** *f.* rustling of the wind; (coll.) uproar.—**trémolo,** *m.* (mus.) tremolo.—**trémulo,** *a.* tremulous, quivering, shaking.

tren, *m.* train; outfit; equipment; following, retinue; show, pomp.—*t. búho* or *nocturno,* night train.—*t. de aterrizaje,* (aer.) landing gear.—*t. de mercancías,* freight train.

trencilla, *f.* braid.—**trenza,** *f.* braid; plait; tress.—**trenzar,** *vti.* [a] to braid; to plait.

trepador, *a.* climbing.—*m.* climber.—*f.* (bot.) climber, creeper.—**trepar,** *vi.* to climb, mount.—*vr.* (Am.) to climb; to perch.

trepidación, *f.* trepidation; vibration, trembling.—**trepidar,** *vi.* to shake, vibrate, jar; to quake.

tres, *a.* & *m.* three.—**trescientos,** *a.* & *m.* three hundred.—*t. uno,* three hundred one.

treta, *f.* trick, wile, craft; (fencing) feint.

triángulo, *m.* triangle.—*t. rectángulo,* right-angled triangle.

tribal, *a.* tribal.—**tribu,** *f.* tribe.

tribulación, *f.* tribulation, affliction.

tribuna, *f.* rostrum, platform; tribune; grandstand.—**tribunal,** *m.* tribunal, court of justice.—*t. de apelación,* court of appeals.—*t. militar,* court martial, military court.—**tribuno,** *m.* orator; tribune.

tributación, *f.* tribute, contribution; system of taxation.—**tributar,** *vt.* to pay (taxes, etc.); to pay, render

(homage, respect).—**tributario,** *a.* tributary.—*n.* taxpayer; tributary river.—**tributo,** *m.* tribute; tax, contribution; gift, offering.

triciclo, *m.* tricycle.

tricornio, *m.* three-cornered hat.

trifulca, *f.* (coll.) squabble, row.

trigal, *m.* wheat field.—**trigo,** *m.* wheat.

trigésimo, *a.* & *m.* thirtieth.

trigonometría, *f.* trigonometry.

trigueño, *a.* brunette, swarthy, dark.

trilla, *f.* (agr.) threshing.—**trillado,** *a.* hackneyed, trite, commonplace.—**trillador,** *n.* thresher.—**trilladora,** *f.* thresher, threshing machine.—**trilladura,** *f.* (agr.) threshing.—**trillar** *vt.* (agr.) to thresh, beat; to frequent to repeat.—**trillo,** *m.* (Am.) footpath.

trilogía, *f.* trilogy.

trimestral, *a.* quarterly.—**trimestre,** *m.* quarter; quarterly payment.

trinar, *vi.* (mus.) to trill; to quaver; to warble; (coll.) to fume (with fury).

trincar, *vti.* [d] to tie, bind, make fast.

trinchar, *vt.* to carve (food).

trinchera, *f.* (mil.) trench; deep cut ditch; trench coat.

trineo, *m.* sleigh, sledge; sled, bobsled.

trinidad, *f.* Trinity, trinity.—*la (Santísima) Trinidad,* the (Holy) Trinity.

trino, *a.* threefold, triple.—*m.* (mus.) trill; warbling.

trío, *m.* trio.

tripa, *f.* gut, intestine; (coll.) belly.—*pl.* insides, entrails.

triple, *a.* triple, treble.—**triplicar,** *vti.* [d] to treble, triple.—**trípode,** *m.* tripod.

tripulación, *f.* crew (or ship, etc.).—**tripulante,** *mf.* one of the crew.—*pl.* crew.—**tripular,** *vt.* to man (ships).

triquina, *f.* trichina.

triquiñuela, *f.* (coll.) trickery, subterfuge.

triquitraque, *m.* crack, clashing; firecracker.

tris. —*en un t.,* almost, coming pretty near.

triscar, *vii.* [d] to romp, frisk, frolic; to walk lively, to hustle.

triste, *a.* sad, sorrowful; dismal.—**tristeza,** *f.* sadness, sorrow, grief.—**tristón,** *a.* rather sad, melancholy.

tritón, *m.* merman.

triturar, *vt.* to crush, grind, pound.

triunfador, *n.* conqueror, victor.—**triunfal,** *a.* triumphal.—**triunfante,** *a.* triumphant.—**triunfar,** *vi.* to con quer; to triumph; to trump (at cards); to win.—**triunfo,** *m.* triumph, victory; trump card.—*sin t.,* no-trump.

ivial, *a.* trivial, trifling; trite, banal.—**trivialidad,** *f.* triviality; triteness.

iza, *f.* fragment.—*hacer trizas,* to knock to pieces; to tear to bits.

ocar, *vti.* [12-d] to exchange; to change, alter; to interchange; to distort, pervert.—*vri.* to change; to be changed, transformed or reformed.

ocha, *f.* (Am.) cross path, short cut; rough road, trail; military road.

ofeo, *m.* trophy; spoils of war; memorial.

oj(e), *f.* granary, barn.

ole, *m.* trolley.

omba, *f.* waterspout.

ombón, *m.* trombone.

ombosis, *f.* (med.) thrombosis.

ompa, *f.* trumpet; (mus.) horn; trunk of an elephant; (Am.) thick lips; (RR.) cowcatcher, pilot (of a locomotive).—**trompada,** *f.,* **trompazo,** *m.* (coll.) heavy blow.—**trompeta,** *f.* trumpet; bugle.—*m.* trumpeter; bugler.—**trompetazo,** *m.* trumpet blast; bugle blast or call.—**trompetear,** *vi.* (coll.) to sound the trumpet.—**trompeteo,** *m.* sounding the bugle or trumpet.—**trompetilla,** *f.* small trumpet; ear trumpet; (Am. coll.) raspberry, Bronx cheer.

ompicón, *m.* stumbling.

ompo, *m.* spinning top.

onada, *f.* thunderstorm.—**tronar,** *vii.* [12] to thunder, rumble; (coll.) to be ruined, come down in the world.—*por lo que pueda t.,* as a precaution, just in case.

onco, *m.* trunk; stem, stalk; stock, origin; team of horses; unfeeling person.

onchar, *vt.* & *vr.* to break off.—**troncho,** *m.* stalk.

onera, *f.* (fort.) embrasure; loophole; porthole; pocket hole (billiards).—*m.* madcap, man about town.

onido, *m.* thunder, loud report.

ono, *m.* throne.

onquista, *m.* (U.S.) teamster; coachman.

opa, *f.* troops, soldiers; multitude; (Am.) herd of cattle.—*pl.* forces, army.

opel, *m.* rush, hurry, confusion; huddle; crowd.—*en t.,* tumultuously, in a throng.—**tropelía,** *f.* rush, hurry; injustice, outrage.

tropezar, *vii.* [1-a] to stumble; (**con**) to strike (against); to stumble, trip (over); to meet (with); to stumble, light (on), happen to find.—**tropezón,** *m.* stumbling; stumble; slip.—*a tropezones,* by fits and starts.—*dar un t.,* to stub one's toe.

tropical, *a.* tropical.—**trópico,** *m.* tropic.

tropiezo, *m.* stumble; obstacle, hitch, stumbling block; slip, fault; quarrel, dispute.

troquel, *m.* die (as for coining).

trotar, *vt.* & *vi.* to trot.—**trote,** *m.* trot.—*al t.,* trotting, at a trot; (coll.) in haste.—**trotón,** *a.* trotting.—*n.* trotter.—*m.* horse.

trovador, *n.* troubadour, minstrel.

trozo, *m.* piece, fragment, part; selection (of music); passage (from a book, etc.).

trucha, *f.* trout.

truchimán, *n.* (coll.) expert buyer; shrewd trader.

truco, *m.* trick.—*pl.* pool (game).

truculento, *a.* truculent.

trueno, *m.* thunder.

trueque, *m.* exchange, barter.

trufa, *f.* truffle.

truhán, *n.* rascal, scoundrel, knave.—**truhanería,** *f.* rascality.

truncar, *vti.* [49-d] to truncate; to maim; to mutilate (a speech, quotation, etc.).

tú, *pron.* you (*sing.* fam. form); thou.—*tratar de tú,* to be on intimate terms with.—**tu,** *a.* (*pl.* **tus**) your (when on intimate terms); thy.

tubérculo, *m.* (bot.) tuber; (med.) tubercle.—**tuberculosis,** *f.* (med.) tuberculosis.—**tuberculoso,** *a.* & *n.* tubercular; sufferer from tuberculosis.

tubería, *f.* tubing; piping.—**tubo,** *m.* tube; pipe; lamp chimney.—*t. de desagüe,* drainpipe.—*t. de ensayo,* test tube.—*t. de estifa, t. de hornillo,* stovepipe.—*t. de imagen* or *televisión,* (TV) picture tube.—*t. digestivo,* alimentary canal.—**tubular,** *a.* tubular.

tuerca, *f.* (mech.) nut.—*t. de aletas, t. (de) mariposa,* wing nut.

tuerto, *a.* one-eyed.—*n.* one-eyed person.—*m.* tort, wrong, injustice.

tueste, *m.* toaste, toasting (by heat).

tuétano, *m.* marrow; pith.—*hasta los tuétanos,* to the marrow.

tufo, *m.* vapor, emanation; (coll.) offensive odor; conceit, airs, snobbishness.

tugurio, *m.* hovel; dive, saloon.

tul, *m.* tulle, net.—**tula,** *f.* duffel bag.

tulipán, *m.* (bot.) tulip.

tullir, *vti.* [27] to cripple, maim.—*vri.* to be crippled.

tumba, *f.* tomb, grave.—**tumbar,** *vt.* to fell, throw down; (coll.) to knock down.—*vi.* to tumble, fall down.—*vr.* (coll.) to lie down, tumble into bed.—**tumbo,** *m.* tumble, fall; somersault.

tumefacción, *f.* swelling.

tumor, *m.* tumor.—*t. maligno,* cancer.

túmulo, *m.* tomb.

tumulto, *m.* tumult; mob.—**tumultuario, tumultuoso,** *a.* tumultuous.

tuna, *f.* (bot.) prickly pear, tuna.

tunante, *n.* truant, rake; rascal, rogue.

tunda, *f.* (coll.) trouncing, whipping.—**tundidora,** *f.*—*t. de césped,* lawnmower.—**tundir,** *vt.* to whip, thrash; to shear.

túnel, *m.* tunnel.

tungsteno, *m.* tungsten.

túnica, *f.* tunic; robe, gown.

tuno, *a.* roguish, cunning.—*m.* truant, rake, rascal.

tuntún, *m.*—*al buen t.,* (coll.) heedlessly, haphazard.

tupé, *m.* toupee; (coll.) nerve, cheek.

tupir, *vt.* to pack tight; to make thick or compact; to choke, obstruct; to block or stop up.—*vr.* to stuff or glut oneself.

turba, *f.* crowd, rabble, mob; peat.

turbación, *f.* confusion, embarrassment.—**turbador,** *n.* disturber.—*a.* disturbing.—**turbamulta,** *f.* mob.—**turbante,** *a.* disturbing.—*m.* turban.—**turbar,** *vt.* to disturb; to embarrass.—*vr.* to be disturbed, embarrassed.

turbina, *f.* turbine.

turbio, *a.* muddy, turbid; obscure (language).

turbión, *m.* windy shower; sweeping rush.—**turbonada,** *f.* squall, pelting shower.

turco, *a.* Turkish.—*n.* Turk.—*m.* Turkish language.

turgencia, *f.* (med.) swelling.—**turgente,** *a.* turgid, swollen.

turismo, *m.* tourism, touring.—**turista,** *mf.* & *a.* tourist; touring.

turnar, *vi.* & *vr.* to alternate; to take turns.—**turno,** *m.* turn, alternation.—*de t.,* open for service (of a store, etc.); on duty (of a person).

turquesa, *f.* turquoise.

turquí, *a.* deep blue.

turrón, *m.* nougat, almond paste.

turulato, *a.* (coll.) dumbfounded, stupefied.

tutear, *vt.* to use the familiar TU in addressing a person.

tutela, *f.* guardianship, tutelage, protection.

tutiplén, —*a t.,* (coll.) abundantly.

tutor, *n.* tutor.—**tutoría,** *f.* tutelage, guardianship.

tuyo, *a.* & *pron. poss.* (*f.* **tuya.**—*pl.* **tuyos, tuyas**) your(s) (*fam.* form corresp. to TU).

U

u, *conj.* (replaces **o** when preceding a word beginning with **o** or **ho**) or.

ubérrimo, *a.* very fruitful; exceedingly plentiful.

ubicación, *f.* situation, location, position.—**ubicar,** *vti.* & *vii.* [d] to locate; to lie; to be located or situated.—**ubicuidad,** *f.* ubiquity.—**ubicuo,** *a.* ubiquitous.

ubre, *f.* udder; teat.

ufanarse, *vr.* to boast, pride oneself.—**ufanía,** *f.* pride; conceit; joy, pleasure.—**ufano,** *a.* conceited, proud; cheerful.

ujier, *m.* doorman; usher.

úlcera, *f.* ulcer; open sore.—*ú. de de cúbito,* bedsore.—**ulceración,** *f.* ulceration.—**ulcerar,** *vt.* to ulcerate.—*vr.* to become ulcerated.

ulterior, *a.* ulterior, farther; subsequent.

ultimar, *vt.* to end, finish, close.—**último,** *a.* last, latest; farthest; ultimate; final; latter; most valuable.—*ú. disposición,* last will and testament.—*ú. palabra,* last word.

ultracongelación, *f.* deep freezing.—**ultracongelar,** *vt.* to deep-freeze.

ultrajar, *vt.* to outrage, offend, abuse

to despise; to revile.—**ultraje,** m. outrage, insult; contempt; abuse.

ultramar, m. overseas.—**ultramarino,** a. oversea.—**ultrarrojo,** a. infra-red.—**ultrasónico,** a. ultrasonic.—**ultratumba,** f.—*de le u.* or *en u.,* beyond the grave.—**ultraviolado, ultravioleta,** a. ultraviolet.

ulular, vi. to screech, hoot.

umbilical, a. umbilical.

umbral, m. threshold; (arch.) lintel; beginning, rudiment.

umbrío, a. shady.—**umbroso,** a. shady.

un (f. **una**) art. a, an.—a. (abbr. de UNO) one.

unánime, a. unanimous.—**unanimidad,** f. unanimity.—*por u.,* unanimously.

unción, f. unction; religious fervor.

uncir, vti. [a] to yoke.

undécimo, a. & m. eleventh.

ungimiento, m. unction.—**ungir,** vti. [c] to anoint.

ungüento, m. unguent, ointment.

único, a. only, sole; unique, rare, unmatched, unparalleled.

unidad, f. unity; unit.—*u. de disco,* (comput.) disk drive.—**unificación,** f. unification.—**unificar,** vti. [d] to unify.

uniformar, vt. to standardize, make uniform; to put into uniform.—**uniforme,** a. & m. uniform.—*de gran u.,* in full uniform.—**uniformidad,** f. uniformity.

unilateral, a. unilateral.

unión, f. union; harmony; concord; marriage; joining, joint; (com.) consolidation, merger.

unir, vt. to join, unite; to connect; to mix; bring together.—vr. to join, get together; to wed; (com.) to consolidate, merge.

unisonancia, f. state of being unisonal; monotony.—**unísono,** a. (mus.) unisonal; unisonous; unanimous.

unitario, a. & n. (eccl.) Unitarian; (pol.) supporter of centralization.

universal, a. universal.—**universidad,** f. university.—**universitario,** a. university.—n. undergraduate; university graduate.—**universo,** m. universe.

uno, a. (f. **una**) one; only, sole.—pl. some; nearly, about.—*u. que otro,* (only) a few.—pron. one, someone.—pl. some, a few (people).—*cada u.,* each one.—*u. a otro,* each other, mutually.—*u. y otro,* both.—

unos a otros, one another.—*unos cuantos,* a few.—*unos y otros,* all, the lot (of them).—n. one (number).—*a una,* unanimously, of one accord.—*de u. en u.,* one by one; in single file.—*la una,* (time) one o'clock.—*u. por u.,* one after another; one by one, one at a time.

untar, vt. to anoint; to smear; to grease, oil; to bribe.—*u. las manos,* to grease the palm; to bribe.—vr. to be greased or smeared; to embezzle.—**unto,** m. grease, fat of animals; unguent, ointment.—**untuoso,** a. unctuous, greasy.—**untura,** f. unction; ointment, liniment.

uña, f. fingernail; toenail; hoof, claw; pointed hook of instruments.—*a u. de caballo,* at full gallop, in great haste.—*enseñar* or *mostrar las uñas,* to show one's true nature.—*hincar* or *meter la u.,* to overcharge; to sell at an exorbitant price.—*largo de uñas,* filcher.—*ser u. y carne,* to be hand and glove, to be fast friends.—**uñero,** m. ingrowing nail.

uranio, m. uranium.

urbanidad, f. urbanity, civility, manners.—**urbanización,** f. urbanization.—**urbanizar,** vti. [a] to lay out (land) for a town; to polish, render polite.—**urbano,** a. urban; urbane, courteous.—**urbe,** f. large modern city, metropolis.

urdimbre, f. warp (of cloth).—**urdir,** vt. to warp (cloth); to plot, scheme.

urgencia, f. urgency.—**urgir,** vii. [c] to be urgent.

urinario, a. urinary.—m. urinal.

urna, f. urn, casket; glass case; ballot box.

urraca, f. magpie.—*u. de América,* blue jay.

urticaria, f. (med.) hives.

uruguayo, a. & n. Uruguayan.

usado, a. secondhand, used; worn out.

usanza, f. usage, custom.—**usar,** vt. to use; to make use of; to wear; to wear out.—vr. to be in use or fashion; to be customary.—**uso,** m. use; usage, custom; wearing, wear; wear and tear; (com., law) usance.—*a(l) u.,* according to usage.—*en buen u.,* in good condition.—*u. de razón,* discernment, understanding, thinking for oneself (esp. of a child).

usted, pron. (usually abbreviated **V., Vd., U., Ud.**) you.—pl. **ustedes** (abbrev. **VV., Vds., UU., Uds.**) you.—*de*

Ud., your, yours.—*de Vd. atto. y S.S.,* yours truly, sincerely yours.

usual, *a.* usual, customary.—**usuario,** *n.* user.

usufructo, *m.* (law) usufruct; use, enjoyment; profit.—**usufructuar,** *vt.* to hold in usufruct; to enjoy the use.

usura, *f.* usury.—**usurario,** *a.* usurious.—**usurero,** *n.* usurer; money lender, loan shark.

usurpación, *f.* usurpation.—**usurpador,** *n.* & *a.* usurper; usurping.—**usurpar,** *vt.* to usurp.

utensilio, *m.* utensil; tool, implement.

uterino, *a.* uterine.—**útero,** *m.* (anat.) uterus, womb.

útil, *a.* useful; profitable.—*m. pl.* utensils, tools; outfit, equipment.—**utilidad,** *f.* utility; profit; usefulness.—**utilitario,** *a.* utilitarian.—**utilizable,** *a.* utilizable, available.—**utilizar,** *vti.* [a] to utilize.—*vri.* to be made profitable.

utopía, *f.* utopia.—**utópico,** *a.* utopian.

uva, *f.* grape.—*hecho una u.,* dead drunk.—*u. pasa,* raisin.

úvula, *f.* uvula.

uxoricida, *m.* uxoricide. (person).—*a.* uxoricidal.—**uxoricidio,** *m.* uxoricide (act).

V

vaca, *f.* cow.—*carne de v.,* beef.—*hacer una v.,* or *ir en una v.,* to pool money (two or more gamblers).—*v. lechera* or *de leche,* dairy cow.

vacación, *f.* vacation.—*pl.* holidays, summer recess.—*de vacaciones,* on holidays.

vacada, *f.* herd of cows.

vacante, *a.* vacant; unoccupied.—*f.* vacancy.—**vacar,** *vii.* [d] to give up work or employment temporarily; to be vacant.

vaciado, *m.* plaster cast.—**vaciar,** *vt.* to empty; to pour out; to cast, mold; to hone, grind.—*vi.* to flow (into) (as rivers).—*vr.* to spill; to be drained; to become empty or vacant.—**vaciedad,** *f.* nonsense, silly remark.

vacilación, *f.* hesitation; vacillation; wavering.—**vacilante,** *a.* hesitating, irresolute; unstable.—**vacilar,** *vi.* to vacillate, fluctuate; to hesitate; to reel.

vacío, *a.* empty; hollow; vain, presumptuous; vacant, unoccupied.—*m.* void, empty space; vacuum; opening; hollowness; blank; gap.—*en el v.,* in vacuo.

vacuna, *f.* vaccine; vaccination; cowpox.—**vacunación,** *f.* vaccination.—*v. de recuerdo,* (med.) booster shot.—**vacunar,** *vt.* to vaccinate.—**vacuno,** *a.* bovine.—*ganado v.,* (bovine) cattle.

vadear, *vt.* to wade through, ford.—**vado,** *m.* ford of a river; expedient.

vagabundear, *vi.* (coll.) to wander, rove

or loiter about.—**vagabundo,** *n.* vagabond, vagrant, rover; roamer, tramp.—*a.* roving, roaming, tramping, vagrant.—**vagancia,** *f.* vagrancy.—**vagar,** *vii.* [b] to rove, roam, loiter about, wander; to be idle.—*m.* leisure, idleness, loitering.—**vago,** *a.* roving, roaming; vagrant; vague; wavering; loose; (art) hazy; indistinct.—*n.* vagabond, loafer, vagrant, tramp.

vagón, *m.* (RR.) car; wagon.—*v. cisterna,* tank car.—*v. de cola,* caboose.—**vagoneta,** *f.* (RR.) small open car; (Am.) open delivery cart; (aut.) station wagon.

vaguear, *vi.* = VAGAR.

vaguedad, *f.* vagueness; vague statement.

vahído, *m.* vertigo, dizziness.

vaho, *m.* vapor, fume, steam; odor.

vaina, *f.* scabbard, sheath, case; (bot.) pod, capsule; (Am.) nuisance, annoyance.

vainilla, *f.* vanilla.

valvén, *m.* fluctuation, oscillation, sway; unsteadiness, inconstancy; giddiness; rocking; (mech.) swing, seesaw.—*pl.* ups and downs.—*sierra de v.,* jig saw.

vajilla, *f.* table setting, tableware, dinner set; crockery.—*v. de plata,* silverware.

vale, *m.* (com.) bond, promissory note, IOU; voucher; sales slip.—*v. respuesta,* reply coupon.—**valedero,** *a.* valid, efficacious, binding.—

valedor, *n.* protector, defender; (Am.) chum, pal.

valenciano, *n.* & *a.* Valencian.

valentía, *f.* valor, courage, bravery; heroic exploit; brag, boast.—**valentón,** *a.* blustering, arrogant.—*m.* hector, bully.

valer, *vti.* [44] to protect, favor; to cost; to cause, bring upon or to (one) (discredit, fame); to amount to; to be worth, be valued at; to be equal to.—*hacer v.,* to assert (one's rights); to avail oneself of.—*ni cosa que lo valga,* nor anything of the kind, or like it.—*v. la pena,* to be worth while.—*vii.* to be valuable; to be worthy; to possess merit or value; to prevail, avail; (of coins) to be legal and current; to be valid or binding; to be important or useful; to be or serve as a protection; to be equivalent to; to mean.—*hacer v.,* to turn to account.—*(impers.) más vale, más valiera,* it is better, it would be better.—*más vale tarde que nunca,* better late than never.—*v. por,* to be equal to, to be worth.—*¡válgame Dios!* good Heavens! bless me!—*vri.* to help oneself, take care of oneself.—*no poderse v.,* to be helpless.—*v. de,* to make use of, have recourse to.—*m.* value; merit, worth.—**valeroso,** *a.* brave, courageous.—**valía,** *f.* value, worth; favor, influence.—**validar,** *vt.* to validate.—**validez,** *f.* validity; soundness; vigor, strength.—**válido,** *a.* valid.

valiente, *a.* valiant, brave, courageous.—*mf.* brave person.

valija, *f.* valise, suitcase; mail bag; mail.

valimiento, *m.* benefit, advantage; favor, support; favoritism.—**valioso,** *a.* valuable; highly esteemed, of great influence; wealthy.—**valor,** *m.* value; price; worth; activity, power; valor, bravery; (fig.) cheek, nerve.—*v. adquisitivo,* purchasing power.—*v. alimenticio,* nutritional value.—*v. añadido,* value added.—*v. de uso,* practical value.—**valoración,** *f.* appraisement, valuation.—**valorar,** *vt.* **valorizar,** *vti.* [a] to appraise, value, price.

valla, *f.* fence, stockade; barrier, barricade; obstacle, impediment.—**valladar,** *m.* = VALLADO; obstacle.—**vallado,** *m.* stockade; inclosure; stone wall.

valle, *m.* valley; vale, dell.

vals, *m.* waltz.

valuación, *f.* appraisement, valuation.—**valuar,** *vt.* to rate, price, value, appraise.

valva, *f.* valve (of a mollusk).—**válvula,** *f.* valve.

¡vamos!, *interj.* well! come, now! go on! let's go!

vampiro, *m.* ghoul; vampire; (fig.) bloodsucker.

vanagloria, *f.* vainglory, boast, conceit.—**vanagloriarse,** *vr.* to be vainglorious; to glory; to boast.

vanguardia, *f.* vanguard.

vanidad, *f.* vanity; nonsense; shallowness.—**vanidoso,** *a.* vain, conceited.—**vano,** *a.* vain; hollow; inane, empty, shallow, insubstantial; unavailing.—*m.* opening in a wall (as for a door).

vapor, *m.* vapor, steam; mist; steamer, steamship.—**vaporización,** *f.* vaporization.—**vaporizador,** *m.* vaporizer.—**vaporizar,** *vt.* & *vi.* to vaporize.—**vaporoso,** *a,* vaporous, misty, cloudy.

vapulear, *vt.* (coll.) to whip, flog, beat.—**vapuleo,** *m.* (coll.) whipping, flogging, beating.

vaquería, *f.* dairy; stable for cows.—**vaquero,** *n.* cowherd.—*m.* cowboy.—*pl.* blue jeans.—*a.* pertaining to a cowherd.—**vaqueta,** *f.* sole leather.

vara, *f.* twig; pole, staff; stick, rod, wand; yard, yardstick.—*v. alta,* sway, high hand.

varadero, *m.* shipyard.—**varar,** *vt.* to beach (a boat).—*vi.* & *vr.* (naut.) to run aground, be stranded; to be at a standstill.

variable, *a.* variable, changeable.—*f.* variable.—**variación,** *f.* variation.—**variado,** *a.* varying, varied; variegated.—**variante,** *a.* varying; deviating.—*f.* difference, discrepancy (in texts).—**variar,** *vt.* to vary, change; to shift; to variegate.—*vi.* to vary, change; to differ.

várice, varice, *f.* varicose vein.

varicela, *f.* (med.) chicken pox.

variedad, *f.* variety; change, variation.—*pl.* miscellany of things or items; variety show.

varilla, *f.* rod; spindle, pivot; wand; rib (of an umbrella, a fan, etc,); whalebone, stay.—*v. de nivel,* (aut.) dipstick.

vario, *a.* various, different; inconstant, changeable.—*pl.* various; some, several.

varón, *m.* male, man.—*santo v.*, (coll.) good but simple fellow.—**varonil**, *a.* manly; virile; vigorous.

vasco, vascongado, *n.* & *a.* Basque.

vaselina, *f.* vaseline.

vasija, *f.* vessel, container, receptacle (for liquids).—**vaso**, *m.* (drinking) glass; vessel, receeptacle; glassful; vase.—*v. sanguíneo*, blood vessel.

vástago, *m.* stem, sapling, shoot; scion, offspring.

vasto, *a.* vast, huge, immense.

vate, *m.* bard, poet.—**vaticinar**, *vt.* to divine, predict, foretell.—**vaticinio**, *m.* prediction.

vatio, *m.* (elec.) watt.

¡vaya!, *interj.* go! come! indeed! certainly! well!

Vd., *abbr.* (**usted**) you.—**Vdes., Vd., (ustedes)** you.

vecinal, *a.* neighboring, adjacent.—**vecindad**, *f.* neighborhood, vicinity.—*casa de v.*, tenement.—**vecindario**, *m.* population of a district, ward, etc.; neighborhood, vicinity.—**vecino**, *a.* neighboring, next, near by.—*n.* neighbor; resident; citizen.

veda, *f.* prohibition, interdiction by law; closed season (hunting, etc.).—**vedar**, *vt.* to prohibit, forbid; to impede.

vega, *f.* flat lowland; (Am.) tobacco plantation.

vegésimo, *a.* & *m.* twentieth.

vegetación, *f.* vegetation.—**vegetal**, *a.* & *m.* vegetable, vegetal, plant.—**vegetar**, *vi.* to vegetate.

vehemencia, *f.* vehemence.—**vehemente**, *a.* vehement; persuasive; vivid; keen.

vehículo, *m.* vehicle.—*v. interplanetario*, space vehicle.

veinte, *a.* & *m.* twenty.—**veinteno**, *a.* & *m.* twentieth.—*f.* score, twenty; about twenty.—**veintésimo**, *a.* & *m.* twentieth.—**veintidós**, *a.* & *m.* twenty-two.—**veitiún**, *a.* twenty-one.—**veintiuno**, *a.* & *m.* twenty-one.—*f.* blackjack, twenty-one.

vejación, *f.*, **vejamen**, *m.* vexation, annoyance; oppression.—**vejar**, *vt.* to vex, tease, annoy; to oppress.

vejestorio, *m.* (coll.) valueless finery; shriveled old person.—**vejete**, *m.* (coll.) ridiculous old man.—**vejez**, *f.* old age.

vejiga, *f.* bladder; blister.

vela, *f.* candle; (naut.) sail; vigil, wakefulness; wake; watch; watchfulness.—*a toda v.*, with all sails up and full of wind; in full swing.—*en v.*, vigilantly, without sleep.—*hacerse a la v.*, to set sail.—*v. mayor*, mainsail.—*v. romana*, roman candle.

velada, *f.* evening party or celebration.—**velador**, *n.* watchman(-woman), nightguard.—*m.* small round table.—**velamen**, *m.* (naut.) canvas; set of sails.—**velar**, *vi.* to watch; to be awake; to observe; to be vigilant; (por) to watch (over), protect.—*vt.* to veil; to cover, hide.

veleidad, *f.* fickleness; versatility.—**veleidoso**, *a.* fickle, inconstant.

velero, *a.* (naut.) swift-sailing.—*m.* sailboat, bark.

veleta, *f.* weathercock, vane.—*mf.* fickle person.

vello, *m.* down; nap; fuzz.

vellón, *m.* fleece, wool of one sheep; lock of wool; ancient copper coin.

velloso, *a.* downy, hairy, fuzzy.—**velludo**, *a.* = VELLOSO.—*m.* shag, velvet.

velo, *m.* veil; curtain.—*v. del paladar*, (anat.) soft palate, velum.

velocidad, *f.* velocity.—*a toda v.*, at full speed.—**velocímetro**, *m.* speedometer.

velorio, *m.* wake, watch (over a dead person); (Am.) boring party.

veloz, *a.* fast, quick, swift, rapid.

vena, *f.* vein; (min.) vein, seam, lode.—*estar en v.*, to be in the mood; to be inspired.—*v. de loco*, fickle disposition.

venablo, *m.* javelin, dart.

venado, *m.* deer, stag; venison.

venático, *a.* (coll.) cranky, erratic, daft.

vencedor, *a.* winning, victorious; conquering.—*n.* winner, victor; conqueror.—**vencer**, *vti.* [a] to conquer, subdue, defeat, vanquish; to surpass; to surmount, overcome; to win.—*vii.* to conquer; to win; (com.) to fall due, mature; to expire.—*vri.* to control oneself.—**vencido**, *a.* (com.) due; payable; conquered; defeated.—**vencimiento**, *m.* defeat; (com.) maturity, expiration.

venda, *f.* bandage.—**vendaje**, *m.* bandage; bandaging.—*v. enyesado*, plaster cast.—**vendar**, *vt.* to bandage, to tape.

vendaval, *m.* gale wind.

vendedor, *n.* seller; salesclerk; salesman; saleswoman; vendor.—**vender**, *vt.* & *vi.* to sell.—*v. al mayor*, to sell at wholesale.—*v. al por* *menor,* or *v. al detalle,* to sell at retail.—*v. a plazos,* to sell on credit.—*vr.* to sell out, accept a bribe; to expose oneself to danger.—*v. caro,* to sell (be sold) dear.—**vendido,** *a.* sold; betrayed.—*estar v.,* to be duped; to be exposed to great risks.—*v. directamente al comprador,* over-the-counter.

endimia, *f.* vintage.

enduta, *f.* (Am.) small vegetable store; (Am.) auction.

eneno, *m.* poison, venom.—**venenoso,** *a.* poisonous, venomous.

enerable, *a.* venerable.—**veneración,** *f.* veneration; worship.—**venerar,** *vt.* to venerate, revere; to worship.

enéreo, *a.* venereal.

enero, *m.* water spring; (min.) bed, lode; origin, source.

enezolano, *n.* & *a.* Venezuelan.

engador, *n.* avenger; revenger.—*a.* avenging; revenging.—**venganza,** *f.* vengeance; revenge.—**vengar,** *vti.* [b] to avenge.—*vri.* (de) to take revenge (on).—**vengativo,** *a.* revengeful, vindictive, vengeful.

enia, *f.* pardon, forgiveness; leave, permission; bow with the head.

enial, *a.* venial; pardonable.

enida, *f.* arrival, return; flood, freshet; rashness, rush.—**venidero,** *a.* future, coming.—**venir,** *vii.* [45] to come; to arrive; to fit, suit; to occur (to one's mind).—*¿a qué viene eso?* what has that to do with the case?—*la semana que viene,* next week.—*si a mano viene,* perhaps.—*v. a buscar,* to come for, or to get.—*v. a las manos,* to come to blows.—*v. a menos,* to decay, to decline.—*v. a ser,* to get to be, become; to turn out to be.—*v. bien,* to suit, to be becoming.—*v. como anillo al dedo,* or *v. de perilla,* to come in the nick of time; to fit the case, be to the point.

venoso, *a.* venous; veined.

venta, *f.* sale; selling; roadside inn.—*de v.* or *en v.,* for sale.—*v. al descubierto,* (com.) short sale.—*v. (al) por mayor,* wholesale.—*v. (al) por menor,* retail sale; retailing.—*v. de garage,* garage sale.—*v. pública,* public auction sale.

ventaja, *f.* advantage; gain, profit; handicap (in races, sports, etc.).—**ventajoso,** *a.* advantageous; profitable; advisable.

ventalla, *f.* valve; (bot.) pod.

ventana, *f.* window; (carp.) window

frame.—*echar la casa por la v.,* to go to a lot of expense.—*v. de la nariz,* nostril.—*v. panorámica,* picture window.—**ventanilla,** *f.* window (vehicles, banks, theaters, etc.); ticket window.—**ventanillo,** *m.* small window shutter; peephole.

ventarrón, *m.* stiff wind, gust; windstorm.—**ventear,** *vt.* to smell; to scent, sniff (as dogs); to investigate, inquire; to air.

ventilación, *f.* ventilation.—**ventilador,** *m.* ventilator; (ventilating) fan.—**ventilar,** *vt.* to ventilate, air; to discuss.

ventisca, *f.* snowstorm, blizzard.—**ventisquero,** *m.* snowstorm, snowdrift; glacier; snow-capped mountain.

ventolera, *f.* gust of wind; whim, notion; scurry.

ventorrillo, *m.* poor inn or tavern.

ventosear, *vi.* to break wind.—**ventosidad,** *f.* flatulence, windiness.—**ventoso,** *a.* windy; flatulent.

ventrílocuo, *m.* ventriloquist.

ventura, *f.* happiness; luck; fortune; chance, hazard; risk.—*buena v.,* fortune told by cards, etc.—*por v.,* by chance; fortunately.—**venturoso,** *a.* lucky; successful, prosperous.

ver, *vti.* & *vii.* [46] to see; to look into, examine; to look; to look at.—*¡a v.!* let's see!—*no poder v. a,* to abhor or detest (can't bear).—*no tener que v. con,* to have nothing to do with.—*v. de,* to try to.—*v. el cielo abierto,* to see a great opportunity.—*vri.* to be seen; to be conspicuous; to find oneself (in a situation), be; to meet, have an interview; to see oneself or look at oneself (in a mirror); to see each other, one another; to meet one another.—*ya se vé,* it is obvious.—*m.* sense of sight, seeing.—*a mi modo de v.,* in my opinion, to my way of thinking.

vera, *f.* edge, border.—*a la v. de,* close, by the side of.

veracidad, *f.* veracity, truthfulness.

veraneante, *mf.* summer resident or vacationer.—**veranear,** *vi.* to summer.—**veraneo,** *m.* summering, summer vacation.—**veraniego,** *a.* summer.—**verano,** *m.* summer.

veras, *f. pl.* reality, truth.—*de v.,* really, in truth, in earnest.—**veraz,** *a.* veracious, truthful.

verbal, *a.* verbal; oral.

verbena, *f.* (bot.) verbena, vervain;

night carnival (on a saint's day eve).

verbigracia, *adv.* for example, for instance.

verbo, *m.* verb.—*el Verbo,* the Word, second person of the Trinity.—**verboso,** *a.* wordy, verbose.

verdad, *f.* truth, verity.—*a decir v.,* to tell the truth; in reality, in fact.—*a la v.,* truly, really, in truth.—*bien es v. que,* it is true that.—*decir cuatro verdades,* to speak one's mind freely.—*de v.* or *a la v.,* in earnest; real.—*en v.,* truly, really.—*¿no es v.?* isn't it? isn't that so?—*ser v.,* to be true.—*¿v.?* isn't it? isn't that so? is that so?—**verdadero,** *a.* true; real, actual; truthful.

verde, *a.* green; verdant; unripe; young, blooming; unseasoned (wood); off-color, obscene.—*están verdes,* sour grapes.—*m.* green (color); verdure; vert.—**verdear,** *vi.* to grow green; to look green.—**verdín,** *m.* mildew; verdigris.—**verdinegro,** *a.* dark green.—**verdor,** *m.* greenness; verdure, verdancy.—**verdoso,** *a.* greenish.

verdugo, *m.* executioner; shoot of a tree; lash, scourge; wale, welt; torturer, very cruel person.—**verdugón,** *m.* large wale or welt.

verdulera, *f.* market woman; (coll.) coarse, low woman.—**verdura,** *f.* verdure, verdancy; greenness.—*pl.* greens, vegetables.—**verdusco,** *a.* dark greenish.

vereda, *f.* path, trail; (Am.) sidewalk.

veredicto, *m.* verdict.

vergel, *f.* flower garden.

vergonzoso, *a.* bashful, shy; shameful, disgraceful.—**vergüenza,** *f.* shame; bashfulness, shyness; modesty; disgrace.—*pl.* private parts.—*tener v.,* to be ashamed; to be shy; to have shame.

vericueto, *m.* rough and pathless place.

verídico, *a.* truthful.—**verificación,** *f.* verification, confirmation.—**verificar,** *vti.* [d] to verify, confirm; to test, adjust (an instrument); to fulfil, accomplish, carry out.—*vri.* to be verified; to take place, occur.

verja, *f.* grate, grating; iron railing.

vernáculo, *a.* vernacular, native.

verosímil, *a.* credible, probable; true to life.—**verosimilitud,** *f.* verisimilitude, probability.

verraco, *m.* male hog or boar.

verruga, *f.* wart.

versado, *a.* versed, conversant.—**versar,** *vi.*—*v. acerca de* or *sobre,* to treat of, deal with.—*vr.* to become versed or conversant.

versátil, *a.* changeable, fickle shifty.—**versatilidad,** *f.* versatility.

versículo, *m.* (eccl.) versicle.

versificación, *f.* versification.—**versificador,** *n.* versifier, verse maker.—**versificar,** *vti.* & *vii.* [d] to versify.

versión, *f.* version; translation.

verso, *m.* line (of poetry).—*pl.* poems.

vértebra, *f.* (anat.) vertebra.—**vertebrado,** *n.* & *a.* vertebrate.

vertedero, *m.* landfill, dumping ground; garbage dump. small dam spillway.—**verter,** *vti.* [18] to pour spill, shed, cast; to empty; to dump, to translate; to construe, interpret.—*vii.* to run, flow.

vertical, *a.* vertical.—*f.* vertical line.—**verticalidad,** *f.* verticality.

vértice, *m.* vertex; apex, top.

vertiente, *f.* watershed; slope.

vertiginoso, *a.* giddy.—**vértigo,** *m.* giddiness, dizziness, vertigo.

vesania, *f.* insanity.—**vesánico,** *a.* mentally deranged.

vesícula, *f.* blister, vesicle.—*v. biliar,* gall bladder.

vespertino, *a.* evening.—*m.* evening paper.

vestíbulo, *m.* vestibule, hall, lobby.

vestido, *m.* dress; apparel, clothing.—*v. espacial,* space suit.—**vestidura,** *f.* vesture.—*pl.* (eccl.) vestments.

vestigio, *m.* vestige, trace; relic.—*pl.* remains.

vestimenta, *f.* clothes, garments.—**vestir,** *vti.* [29] to clothe, dress; to deck, adorn; to don, put on; to wear; to cover.—*vii.* to dress; to be dressy.—*vri.* to dress oneself; to be covered; to be clothed.—**vestuario,** *m.* apparel, wardrobe, clothes, clothing, dress; (eccl.) vestry; (theat.) wardrobe, dressing room.

veta, *f.* (min.) vein; grain (in wood).

vetar, *vt.* to veto.

veteado, *a.* striped, veined, grained, mottled.—**vetear,** *vt.* to grain, mottle.

veterano, *a.* (mil.) veteran; having had long experience.—*n.* veteran, old hand.

veterinario, *m.* veterinarian.

veto, *m.* veto; prohibition, interdict.

vetusto, *a.* very ancient.

vez, *f.* turn, time, occasion.—*a la v.,* at a time; at the same time; at one time.—*a la v. que,* while.—*alguna v.* (in a question) ever.—*alguna que otra v.,* once in a while, occasionally.—*algunas veces,* sometimes; some times.—*a su v.,* in his (one's) turn; on his (one's) part.—*a veces,* sometimes, occasionally.—*cada v.,* each time, every time.—*cada v. más,* more and more.—*cada v. que,* every time that, whenever.—*de una v.,* all at once; at one time.—*de v. en cuando,* occasionally, from time to time, at intervals.—*en v. de,* instead of.—*otra v.,* again, once more; some other time.—*pocas* or *raras veces,* seldom, rarely; only a few times.—*tal v.,* perhaps, maybe, perchance.—*todas las veces que,* whenever, as often as.—*una que otra v.,* once in a while, a few times.—*una v. que,* since, inasmuch as; after.

vía, *f.* way, road; route; carriage track; (RR.) track, line; gauge; manner, method; duct, conduit; passage.—*en v. de,* in the process of.—*por v. de,* by way of, as.—*v. muerta,* siding.—**viable,** *a.* viable; feasible, practicable.—**viaducto,** *m.* viaduct, overpass.

viajante, *a.* traveling.—*mf.* traveler.—*m.* traveling salesman.—**viajar,** *vi.* to travel, journey.—**viaje,** *m.* journey, voyage, travel, trip.—*v. de ida y vuelta,* round trip.—*v. de negocios,* business trip.—*v. de novios,* honeymoon.—*v. de vuelta,* return trip.—*viajes por el espacio,* space travel.—*v. organizado,* package tour.—*v. relámpago,* quick trip.—**viajero,** *n.* traveler, voyager; passenger.

vianda, *f.* food, viands.—*pl.* (Am.) vegetables for a stew.

viandante, *mf.* walker, pedestrian; tramp, vagabond.

víbora, *f.* viper; (fig.) perfidious person.

vibración, *f.* vibration.—**vibrar,** *vt.* to vibrate; to brandish; to throw, dart.—*vi.* to vibrate.—**vibratorio,** *a.* vibratory.—**viceversa,** *adv.* vice versa.

vicepresidente, *n.* vice president.—**vicesecretario,** *n.* assistant secretary.—**vicetesorero,** *n.* assistant treasurer.

viciar, *vt.* to vitiate, spoil; to adulterate; to pervert, corrupt; to falsify; to misconstrue.—*vr.* to become corrupt.—**vicio,** *m.* vice; (bad) habit; defect; craving.—*de v.,* by habit or custom.—**vicioso,** *a.* vicious; defective; licentious.

vicisitud, *f.* vicissitude.—*pl.* ups and downs.

víctima, *f.* victim.

victoria, *f.* victory, win, triumph.—**victorioso,** *a.* victorious, triumphant.

vid, *f.* (bot.) vine, grapevine.

vida, *f.* life; living, livelihood; activity, animation.—*darse buena v.,* to live comfortably.—*de por v.,* for life, during life.—*en v.,* while living, during life.—*ganarse la v.,* to earn one's living.—*v. airada,* licentious life.—*v. mía,* dearest, darling.

vidente, *a.* seeing.—*mf.* seer, prophet.

video or **vídeo,** *m.* video; videotape, videocassette; videocassette recorder, VCR; video recording.—*grabación en v.,* video recording.—*grabar en v.,* to record on video.—**videocámara,** *f.* video camara, camcorder.—**videocasete** or **videocassette,** *m.* **videocinta,** *f.* videocassette, videotape, video.—**videograbación,** *f.* video recording or taping.—**videograbadora,** *f.* video recorder, videocassette recorder.—**videograbar,** *vt.* to videotape, to video, to record on video.—**videojuego,** *m.* videogame.—**videopiratería,** *f.* video piracy.—**videoproyector,** *m.* videoprojector.—**videoteca,** *f.* video library.—**videoteléfono,** *m.* videophone.—**videoterminal,** *f.* (comput.) terminal, VDU.

vidriar, *vt.* to glaze (earthenware).—**vidriera,** *f.* glass window or partition; (Am.) glass case, show case, show window.—**vidriero,** *n.* glazier; glassblower; glass dealer.—**vidrio,** *m.* glass;—*v. cilindrado,* plate glass.—**vidrioso,** *a.* glassy; brittle; slippery (from sleet); peevish, touchy.

viejo, *a.* old, aged; ancient, antiquated; stale; worn-out; old-fashioned.—*V. Mundo,* Old World.—*n.* old man (woman).—*v. verde,* lecherous old man; girlish old woman.

viento, *m.* wind; bracing rope; scent of dogs; vanity.—*a los cuatro vientos,* in all directions.—*beber los vientos por,* to be crazy about.

vientre, *m.* abdomen; belly; bowels; womb; pregnancy.

viernes, *m.* Friday.—*V. Santo,* Good Friday.

viga, *f.* beam, girder; rafter.—*v. maestra,* chief supporting beam.

vigencia, *f.* currency; operation (of a law); life (of a ruling body, etc.).—**vigente,** *a.* (law) in force; standing.

vigía, *f.* watchtower; watch; watching; (naut.) shoal, rock; surveillance.—*m.* watchman, lookout.—**vigilancia,** *f.* vigilance, watchfulness.—**vigilante,** *a.* vigilant, watchful.—*m.* watchman.—*v. de incendios,* firewarden.—*v. nocturno,* night watchman.—**vigilar,** *vt.* & *vi.* to watch (over); to keep guard; to look out (for); (coll.) to tail.—**vigilia,** *f.* vigil, wakefulness; (eccl.) vigil, fast.

vigor, *m.* vigor, stamina; validity.—*en v.,* in force, in effect.—**vigorizar,** *vti.* [a] to strengthen, invigorate; to encourage.—**vigoroso,** *a.* vigorous; substantial; trenchant.

viguería, *f.* set of girders or beams; timberwork.—**vigueta,** *f.* small beam; joist; beam.

VIH, *abbr.* (**Virus de Inmunodeficiencia Humana**) HIV (Human Immunodeficiency Virus).

vihuela, *f.* guitar.

vil, *a.* vile, low, despicable, soulless.—**vileza,** *f.* baseness, meanness, vileness; base act or conduct.—**vilipendiar,** *vt.* to scorn, revile, vilify.—**vilipendio,** *m.* contempt; reviling.

villa, *f.* village; villa, country house.

villancico, *m.* Christmas carol.

villanía, *f.* meanness; villainy, villainousness; vile, base deed.—**villano,** *a.* villainous; rustic, boorish.—*n.* villain.

villorrio, *m.* small village or hamlet.

vilo, *m.*—*en v.,* in the air; insecurely; in suspense.

vinagre, *m.* vinegar; acidity, sourness.—**vinagrera,** *f.* vinegar cruet.—**vinajera,** *f.* (eccl.) wine vessel for the Mass.—**vinatero,** *a.* pertaining to wine.—*n.* vintner, wine merchant.

vinculación, *f.* entail; binding; grounding.—**vincular,** *vt.* to entail; to tie, bond, unite; to ground or found upon.—**vínculo,** *m.* tie, bond; entail.

vindicar, *vti.* [d] to vindicate; to avenge; to assert (as rights), defend; (law) to reclaim.

vinícola, *a.* wine-growing.—**vinicult-**ura, *f.* winegrowing.—**vinilo,** *m.* vinyl.—**vino,** *m.* wine.—*v. de Jerez,* sherry wine.—*v. tinto,* red table wine.

viña, *f.,* **viñedo,** *m.* vineyard.

viñeta, *f.* (print. & photog.) vignette.

violáceo, *a.* violet-colored.

violación, *f.* violation; ravishment.—**violado,** *pp.* of VIOLAR.—*a.* violet (color).—**violador,** *m.* violator; rapist.—**violar,** *vt.* to violate; to rape; to desecrate; to tarnish.—**violencia,** *f.* violence; compulsion; force; rape, outrage.—**violentar,** *vt.* to do violence to; to break into; to distort.—*vr.* to force oneself (to do something distasteful); to control one's unwillingness.—**violento,** *a.* violent; impulsive; irascible; forced, unnatural; exceedingly intense or severe.

violeta, *f.* (bot.) violet.

violín, *m.* violin; violinist.—**violinista,** *mf.* violinist.—**violón,** *m.* bass viol, double bass; bass-viol player.—*tocar el v.,* to do or say something absurd or nonsensical; to talk through one's hat.—**violoncelista,** *mf.* (violon)cellist.—**violoncelo,** *m.* (violon)cello.

viperino, *a.* viperish.

virago, *f.* mannish woman; shrew, harpy.

virar, *vt.* to turn, turn around, change direction; (naut.) to tack.—**virazón,** *f.* sea breeze.

virgen, *f.* & *a.* virgin.—**virginal, virgíneo,** *a.* virginal, virgin.—**virginidad,** *f.* virginity.—**virgo,** *m.* (anat.) hymen; (**V.**) (astr.) Virgo, Virgin; virginity.

viril, *a.* virile, manly.—**virilidad,** *f.* virility, manhood; vigor; strength.

virreinato, virreino, *m.* viceroyalty.—**virrey,** *m.* viceroy.

virtual, *a.* apparent; virtual; potential.

virtud, *f.* virtue; power.—**virtuoso,** *a.* virtuous, righteous; chaste.—*a.* & *n.* (mus.) virtuoso.

viruela, *f.* (med.) pock; smallpox.

virulencia, *f.* virulence.—**virulento,** *a.* virulent.—**virus,** *m.* (med.) virus.

virus, *m.* virus.—*v. de inmunodeficiencia humana,* (VIH) human immunodeficiency virus (HIV).—*v. de ordenadores, v. de computadora,* computer virus.

viruta, *f.* wood shaving.—**virutilla,** *f.* thin shaving.—**virutillas de acero,** steel wool.

visa, *f.,* **visado,** *m.* visa.

visaje, *m.* grimace, grin, smirk.—*hacer visajes,* to make wry faces.

visar, *vt.* to issue a visa; to countersign; to O.K.

víscera, *f.* vital organ.—*pl.* viscera.—**visceral,** *a.* visceral.

viscosidad, *f.* viscosity, stickiness.—**viscoso,** *a.* viscous, sticky.

visera, *f.* visor of a cap or helmet; eye-shade.

visibilidad, *f.* visibility.—**visible,** *a.* visible; evident; conspicuous.

visillo, *m.* window curtain or shade.—**visión,** *f.* sight; vision; fantasy; phantom, apparition; revelation; (coll.) grotesque person, sight.—**visionario,** *a.* & *n.* visionary.

visita, *f.* visit; call; visitor(s); visitation, inspection.—*pagar una v.,* to return or make a call.—*v. a domicilio,* house call.—*v. de cumplido* or *de cumplimiento,* formal call.—*v. guiada,* guided tour.—**visitante,** *mf.* visitor; inspector.—**visitar,** *vt.* to visit; to call on; to inspect, search, examine.—*vr.* to visit one another, call on one another.—**visiteo,** *m.* frequent visiting or calling.

vislumbrar, *vt.* to glimpse, have a glimmer of; to see imperfectly at a distance; to know imperfectly; to suspect, surmise.—*vr.* to loom, to be glimpsed.—**vislumbre,** *f.* glimpse, glimmer; glimmering; conjecture, surmise; appearance, semblance.

viso, *m.* gloss, sheen (of fabric); glass curtain; lady's slip.—*pl.* aspect, appearance.

visón, *m.* mink.

víspera, *f.* eve, day before; forerunner; time just before.—*pl.* vespers.—*en v. de,* on the eve of.—*la v. de año nuevo,* New Year's Eve.

vista, *f.* sight, seeing, vision; view, vista; eye, eyesight; glance, look; aspect, looks; (law) trial.—*a la v.,* at sight; in sight; before one's eyes.—*a la v. de,* in the presence of.—*a simple v.,* at first sight; with the naked eye.—*estar a la v.,* to be obvious.—*hacer la v. gorda,* to wink at, overlook.—*hasta la v.,* good-by.—*perder de v.,* to lose sight of.—*tener v. a,* to face, look out on.—*v. cansada,* far-sightedness.—*m.* customs officer.—**vistazo,** *m.* glance.—*dar un v. a,* to glance at, to look over.—**visto,** *pp.* of VER.—*a.* obvious, evident, clear; (law) whereas.—*bien v.,* proper or approved, good form.—*mal v.,* improper or disapproved, bad form.—*v. bueno* (*V*⁰·*B*⁰·), correct, approved, O.K.—*v. que,* considering that, since.—**vistoso,** *a.* showy; beautiful; flaring, loud.—**visual,** *a.* visual; of sight.—*f.* line of sight.—**visualizar,** *vt.* to visualize; to display.

vital, *a.* vital; essential, necessary.—**vitalicio,** *a.* lasting for life; during life.—**vitalidad,** *f.* vitality.

vitamina, *f.* vitamin.

vitela, *f.* vellum, parchment.

vítor, *m.* cheer, applause.—*interj.* hurrah!—**vitorear,** *vt.* to cheer, acclaim.

vítreo, *a.* vitreous, glassy.—**vitrina,** *f.* show case; (Am.) show window.—**vitrinear,** *vi.* to window-shop.

vitriolo, *m.* vitriol.

vituallas, *f. pl.* victuals, provisions, food.

viuda, *f.* widow.—**viudez,** *f.* widowhood.—**viudo,** *m.* widower.

viva, *interj.* viva.

vivac, vivaque, *m.* (mil.) bivouac; (Am.) police headquarters.

vivacidad, *f.* vivacity, liveliness; brilliance.—**vivaracho,** *a.* lively, frisky.—**vivaz,** *a.* lively, active; ingenious; bright, witty.

víveres, *m. pl.* provisions, foodstuffs.

vivero, *m.* hatchery; (bot.) nursery.

viveza, *f.* liveliness; vivacity; quickness; witticism; perspicacity.—**vívido,** *a.* vivid, bright.—**vivienda,** *f.* dwelling; housing; domicile.—**viviente,** *a.* living.—**vivificar,** *vti.* [d] to animate, enliven.—**vivir,** *vi.* to live, be alive; to last, endure.—*vt.* to live, experience; to dwell.—*¡viva!,* hurrah! long live!.—*¿quién vive?* (mil.) who goes there?—*m.* life, living, existence.—*mal v.,* riotous living.—**vivo,** *a.* alive, live; lively; intense; (of color) vivid; acute, ingenious; quick, bright, smart; lasting, enduring.—*a lo v., al v.,* vividly.—*de viva voz,* by word of mouth.—*en v.,* living, alive; (rad./TV) live.—*tocar en lo v.,* to cut or hurt to the quick.—*m.* (sewing) edging, piping.

vizcaíno, *a.* & *n.* Biscayan, Basque.

vizconde, *m.* viscount.—**vizcondesa,** *f.* viscountess.

vocablo, *m.* word, term.—**vocabulario,** *m.* vocabulary, lexicon.

vocación, *f.* vocation, calling; occupation.

vocal, *a.* vocal, oral; (gram.) vowel.—*f.* vowel.—*mf.* voting member of a governing body.—**vocalista,** *mf.* vocalist.—**vocalizar,** *vii.* [a] to vocalize.

vocear, *vi.* to cry out, shout.—*vt.* to cry, publish, proclaim; to call, hail.—**vocería,** *f.,* **vocerío,** *m.* clamor, outcry, shouting.—**vocero,** *n.* spokesman (for another).—**vociferar,** *vi.* to vociferate, shout.—**vocinglero,** *a.* vociferous; prattling, chattering; loudmouthed.—*n.* loud babbler.

volador, *a.* flying.—*m.* skyrocket.—**voladora,** *f.* flywheel of a steam engine.—**voladura,** *f.* blast, explosion; blasting.—**volante,** *a.* flying, fluttering, unsettled.—*m.* steering wheel; balance wheel; handbill, circular; ruffle, frill; escapement (of a watch); (sports) shuttlecock.—**volar,** *vii.* [12] to fly; to flutter, hover (as insects); to run or move swiftly; to vanish, disappear; to make rapid progress; to explode, burst.—*vti.* to blow up; to blast.—**volátil,** *a.* volatile; fickle; mercurial.—**volatinero,** *n.* tightrope walker; acrobat.

volcán, *m.* volcano.—**volcánico,** *a.* volcanic.

volcar, *vti.* [12-d] to upset, overturn; to tilt.—*vri.* to overturn.

volibol, *m.* volleyball.

volición, *f.* volition.—**volitivo,** *a.* volitional.

volquete, *m.* **volqueta,** *f.* dump truck.

volt, *m.* volt.—**voltaje,** *m.* voltage.

voltear, *vt.* to turn; to revolve; to overturn; (arch.) to arch; to vault.—*vi.* to turn; to revolve; to roll over; to tumble (as an acrobat).—*vr.* to turn over; to upset; (coll.) to change one's party or creed.—**volteo,** *m.* whirl; whirling; turn; turning; overturning; felling; tumbling.—**voltereta,** *f.* tumble, somersault.

voltio, *m.* volt.

volubilidad, *f.* volubility.—**voluble,** *a.* easily moved about; voluble; fickle; versatile.

volumen, *m.* tome; volume, size, bulk; corpulence.—*v. sonoro,* (phon. & mus.) volume.—**voluminoso,** *a.* voluminous; bulky.

voluntad, *f.* will; goodwill, benevolence; desire; disposition; consent.—*a v.,* optional, at will.—*de (buena) v.,* with pleasure, willingly.—*de mala v.,* unwillingly.—*mala v.,* ill will.—**voluntariedad,** *f.* voluntariness; willfulness.—**volun-**

tario, *a.* & *n.* voluntary; volunteer.—**voluntarioso,** *a.* willful, self-willed.

voluta, *f.* (arch.) volute; spiral.

volver, *vti.* [47] to turn; to turn up, over, upside down, inside out; to return; to repay; to give back, restore; to send back.—*v. loco,* to drive crazy.—*vii.* to return, come, or go back; to come again; to turn (to the right, etc.).—*v. a cantar,* to sing again.—*v. atrás,* to come, or go, back.—*v. en sí,* to recover consciousness, come to.—*v. por,* to stand up for, to defend.—*vri.* to turn, become; to turn about, turn around; to change one's views.—*v. atrás,* to flinch; to back out.—*v. loco,* to lose one's mind.

vomitar, *vt.* to vomit, puke.—**vomitivo,** *m.* & *a.* emetic.—**vómito,** *m.* vomiting; vomit.

vorágine, *f.* vortex, whirlpool.

voraz, *a.* voracious, greedy; fierce (as fire).

vórtice, *m.* vortex, whirlpool, whirlwind; center of a cyclone.

vosotros, *pron. pl.* (*f.* **vosotras**) (fam.) you.

votación, *f.* voting, vote, balloting.—*segunda v.,* runoff election.—**votar,** *vi.* & *vt.* to vote; to vow.—*¡voto a tal!* goodness!—**voto,** *m.* vote; vow; votive offering; oath, curse.—*hacer votos de,* to vow to.—*hacer votos por,* to pray for; to wish.

voz, *f.* voice; sound; clamor, outcry; word, term; rumor, report.—*a media v.,* in a whisper.—*a una v.,* unanimously.—*a v. en cuello,* at the top of one's voice.—*a voces,* clamorously.—*correr la v.,* to be said, to be rumored; to spread the rumor.—*dar voces,* to scream, shout.—*secreto a voces,* open secret.—*ser v. común,* to be a common rumor.

vuelco, *m.* tumble, overturning, upset.

vuelo, *m.* flight; flying; sweep, space flown through; fullness of clothes; ruffle or frill; (arch.) projection, jut.—*al v.,* on the fly; quickly, in a moment; in passing.—*alzar* or *levantar v.,* to fly; to take off, depart.—*tomar v.,* to progress; to grow.

vuelta, *f.* turn; revolution (of a wheel, etc.); turning; return; reverse side; returning, giving back; (money) change; stroll, walk.—*a la v.,* on returning; round the corner; (turn) over (the page); (bookkeeping) carried over, carried forward.—*a la v. de*, within (time).—*a. v. de correo*, by return mail.—*dar la v. a*, to turn; to go around.—*dar una v.*, to take a stroll.—*dar vueltas*, to turn; to walk to and fro; to fuss about; to hang around.—*de la v.*, brought forward.—*de v.*, on returning.—*estar de v.*, to be back; to be knowing.—*no tener v. de hoja*, to be self-evident.—*poner de v. y media*, (coll.) to give a dressing down, or a going over, to.—**vuelto**, *ppi.* of VOLVER.—*m.* (Am.) (money) change.

vuestro, *pron.* & *a.* (coll.) your, yours.

vulcanización, *f.* vulcanization; mending (a tire, etc.).—**vulcanizar**, *vti.* [a] to vulcanize; to mend (a tire, etc.).

vulgar, *a.* vulgar, coarse; common, in general use.—**vulgaridad**, *f.* vulgarity; triteness.—**vulgarización**, *f.* vulgarization.—**vulgarizar**, *vti.* [a] to vulgarize, popularize.—*vri.* to become vulgar.—**vulgo**, *m.* common people; populace.

vulnerable, *a.* vulnerable.—**vulnerar**, *vt.* to harm, injure, damage.

X

X, x, *f.* X, x; (cine, E.U.) prohibida para menores de 18 años.—*el señor X*, Mr. X.—*XXX*, besos.

xantoma, *m.* (med.) xanthoma.

xenia, *f.* (bot.) xenia.

xenofilia, *f.* friendliness toward strangers.

xenófilo, *n.* xenophile.

xenofobia, *f.* xenophobia.

xenófobo, *n.* xenophobe.

xerocopia, *f.* Xerox (TM), Xerox copy, photocopy.

xerocopiar, *vt.* to photocopy, to make a Xerox (TM) of, to make a Xerox copy of.

xerografía, *f.* xerography.

xerografiar, *vt.* to make a Xerox (TM) copy of, to make a Xerox of.

xerográfico, *a.* xerographic.

Xerox, *m.* Xerox (TM).

xilema, *f.* (bot.) xylem.

xilófono, *m.* xylophone.

xilografía, *f.* xylography.

Y

y, *conj.* and.—*¿y bien? ¿y qué?* and then? so what?

ya, *adv.* already; now; at once; presently; in time; once, formerly.—*interj.* oh yes! I see.—*ya lo creo*, naturally, of course.—*ya no*, no longer.—*ya que*, since, seeing that.—*ya se ve*, yes, indeed! it is clear, it is so.

yac, *m.* (zool.) yak.

yacaré, *m.* (Am.) alligator.

yacer, *vii.* [48] to lie in the grave; to lie, be located; to be lying down.—*aquí yace*, here lies (inscription on tombstone).—**yacimiento**, *m.* (geol.) bed; deposit, field.

yaguar, *m.* (zool.) jaguar.

yanqui, *n.* & *a.* Yankee.

yak, *m.* yak.

yarda, *f.* yard (measure).

yatagán, *m.* saber dagger.

yate, *m.* yacht.

yaya, *f.* wound, injury; damage; jam, fix.

yedra, *f.* (bot.) ivy.

yegua, *f.* mare.—**yeguada**, *f.* herd of mares.

yeísmo, *m.* pronunciation of Spanish *ll* as *y*.

yelmo, *m.* helm, helmet.

yema, *f.* yolk (of an egg); bud; candied egg yolk; heart, center.—*dar en la y.*, to hit the nail on the head.—*y. del dedo*, fleshy tip of the finger.

yerba, *f.* = HIERBA.—**yerbabuena**, *f.* = HIERBABUENA.—**yerbajo**, *m.* weed.

yermo, *a.* barren, sterile.—*m.* wasteland, desert.

yerno, *m.* son-in-law.

yerro, *m.* error, mistake; fault.

yerto, *a.* stiff, motionless; rigid, tight.

yesca, *f.* tinder, punk. (fig.) fuel, incentive.—*pl.* tinderbox.

yeso, *m.* gypsum; plaster; plaster cast; chalk.—*y. mate,* plaster of Paris.

yídish, *a.* & *m.* Yiddish.

yo, *pron.* I.—*y. mismo,* I myself.—*m.* ego.

yodado, *a.* iodized.—**yodo,** *m.* iodine.

yoga, *m.* yoga.

yogur, yoghurt, yogurt, *m.* yogurt.

yugo, *m.* yoke; marriage tie.—*sacudi* *el y.,* to throw off the yoke.

yuguero, *m.* plowman.

yugular, *a.* jugular.

yunque, *m.* anvil; (anat.) incus.

yunta, *f.* couple, pair, yoke of draft an imals.

yute, *m.* jute (fiber).

yuxtaponer, *vti.* [32–49] to juxtapose to place next to each other.—**yuxta posición,** *f.* juxtaposition.—

yuxtapuesto, *ppi.* of YUXTAPONER.

Z

zafado, *a.* (Am.) brazen, shameless; (Am.) alert, wide-awake; (Am.) crazy, crackbrained.—**zafar,** *vt.* to loosen, untie.—*vr.* to loosen oneself or itself; to run away; to keep out of the way; to dodge; to slip away.—*z. de,* to get rid of; to avoid.

zafarrancho, *m.* turmoil, confusion.—*z. de combate,* (naut.) clearing for battle.

zafio, *a.* coarse, uncivil, ignorant, uncouth.

zafir(o), *m.* sapphire.

zafra, *f.* sugar cane crop; sugar cane harvest time; sugar-making season.

zaga, *f.* rear, back.—*a la z.* or *en z.,* behind.—*no ir en z. a,* to be equal to.

zagal, *m.* shepherd boy; country lad.—**zagala,** *f.* shepherdess; **lass,** maiden.—**zagalón,** *n.* overgrown boy or girl.

zaguán, *m.* entrance hall, vestibule.

zaguero, *a.* rear, hind; lagging behind.—*m.* (sports) backstop, defense player.

zaherir, *vti.* [39] to censure, blame, reproach, upbraid.

zahorí, *mf.* seer, clairvoyant.

zahurda, *f.* pigsty, pigpen; unclean establishment.

zaino, *a.* chestnut-colored (horse); vicious (animal); treacherous, false.

zalamería, *f.* flattery, wheedling.—**zalamero,** *n.* flatterer.—*a.* flattering.—**zalema,** *f.* bow, curtsy.—*pl.* flattery.

zamarra, *f.* sheepskin jacket.

zambo, *a.* bowlegged.

zambullida, *f.* dive, plunge.—**zambullir,** *vti.* [27] to plunge, immerse; to give

a ducking to.—*vri.* to plunge, dip dive.

zambullo, *m.* chamber pot; toilet.

zampar, *vt.* to stuff away; to conceal hurriedly; to devour eagerly.—*vr.* t(rush in; to gatecrash; to scoff; t(devour.

zanahoria, *f.* (bot.) carrot.

zanca, *f.* long shank or leg; large pin.—**zancada,** *f.* long stride.—**zancadilla,** *f.* sudden catch to trip one; trick, deceit.—**zancajear,** *vi.* & *vt.* to run, rush about.—**zanco,** *m.* stilt.—**zancudo,** *a.* long-legged.—*m.* (Am.) mosquito.

zanfona, *f.* hurdy-gurdy.

zanganada, *f.* impertinence.—**zanganear,** *vi.* to idle.—**zángano,** *m.* drone; (coll.) idler, sponger; (Am.) rascal; wag.

zangolotear, *vi.* (coll.) to shake violently; to fuss, fidget.—*vr.* to rattle, swing or slam.—**zangoloteo,** *m.* fuss, bustle; swinging, rattling.

zanguanga, *f.* (fam.) malingering; (fam.) flattery.—*hacer la z.,* (fam.) to pretend to be ill in order to avoid work.

zanguango, *a.* (coll.) lazy, sluggish; silly.—*m.* dunce, fool.—*f.* (coll.) feigned illness, malingering; wheedling, fawning.

zanja, *f.* ditch, trench.—**zanjar,** *vt.* to cut ditches in; to excavate; to settle amicably; to obviate, surmount.—**zanjón,** *m.* deep ditch; large drain.

zapa, *f.* trenching spade; (fort.) sap.—**zapador,** *m.* mining engineer; miner.—**zapapico,** *m.* pickaxe.—**zapar,**

vt. (fort.) to sap, mine; (fig.) to undermine.

zapateado, *m.* tap dance.—**zapatear,** *vt.* to strike with the shoe.—*vi.* to tap-dance.—**zapateo (americano),** *m.* (Mex.) tap dancing.—**zapatería,** *f.* trade of shoemaker; shoemaker's shop.—**zapatero,** *m.* shoemaker; shoe dealer.—**zapateta,** *f.* caper, leap.—

zapatilla, *f.* slipper, pump; (mec.) washer.—*zapatillas (de deporte),* sneakers.—**zapato,** *m.* shoe.—*zapatos de tacón,* high heels.

zaquizamí, *m.* garret; small wretched room.

zarabanda, *f.* saraband; bustle, noise.

zaragata, *f.* turmoil; scuffle, quarrel.

zaranda, *f.* sieve, sifter.

zarandajas, *f. pl.* trifles, odds and ends.

zarandear, *vt.* to winnow; to sift; to shake (coll.) to stir and move nimbly.—*vr.* to be in motion; to move to and fro; to stalk, strut.—**zarandeo,** *m.* sifting or winnowing; shaking; stalking; strut.

zarcillo, *m.* eardrop.

zarco, *a.* light blue (of eyes).

zarpa, *f.* claw, paw of an animal.—*echar la z.,* to grasp, grip.—**zarpar,** *vi.* (naut.) to weigh anchor; to sail.—**zarpazo,** *m.* blow with a paw; bang, thud, whack.

zarrapastroso, *a.* ragged, slovenly, shabby.—*n.* ragamuffin.

zarza, *f.* bramble; blackberry bush.—**zarzal,** *m.* bramble thicket.—**zarzamora,** *f.* blackberry.—**zarzaparrilla,** *f.* sarsaparilla.

zarzuela, *f.* Spanish musical comedy.

zascandil, *m.* (coll.) busybody.

zepelín, *m.* zeppelin.

zigzag, *m.* zigzag.—**zigzaguear,** *vi.* to zigzag.—**zigzagueo,** *m.* zigzagging.

zinc, *m.* zinc.

zipizape, *m.* (coll.) row, rumpus, scuffle.

zócalo, *m.* base of a pedestal; baseboard; (Mex.) main square.

zocato, *a.* (of fruits) overripe.

zoco, *m.* market; market place.

zodíaco, *m.* zodiac.

zollo, *m.* malicious critic.

zona, *f.* zone, belt; district, area, region.—*z. parachoque,* buffer zone.

zonzo, *a.* dull.—*n.* (Am.) simpleton, dunce.

zoología, *f.* zoology.—**zoológico,** *a.* zoologic(al).

zopenco, *a.* (coll.) doltish, dull.—*n.* dolt, blockhead, fool.

zopilote, *m.* (Am.) buzzard.

zoquetada, *f.* foolishness, foolish words or acts.—**zoquete,** *m.* (carp.) chump, chunk; bit of stale bread; (coll.) dolt, dunce; (Am.) slap.

zorra, *f.* (zool.) fox; foxy person; truck.—**zorro,** *a.* cunning, foxy.—*n.* fox; foxy person.

zorzal, *m.* (ornith.) thrush.

zote, *a.* dull and ignorant.—*m.* dolt.

zozobra, *f.* worry, anxiety; (naut.) foundering, sinking.—**zozobrar,** *vi.* (naut.) to sink. founder; to capsize; to be in great danger.

zueco, *m.* sabot, wooden soled shoe.

zumba, *f.* mule bell; banter, raillery; sarcasm.—**zumbar,** *vi.* to buzz, hum; to whiz; (of the ears) to ring.—**zumbido,** *m.* humming, buzzing, whiz; ringing in the ears.—**zumbón,** *a.* waggish; sarcastic.—*n.* wag, joker.

zumo, *m.* sap, juice.

zuncho, *m.* metal band or hoop.

zurcido, *m.* (sewing) darning.—**zurcir,** *vti.* to darn, mend; (coll.) to concoct (lies).

zurdo, *a.* left-handed.—*n.* left-handed person.

zurra, *f.* beating, thrashing.—**zurrar,** *vt.* to thrash, flog.

zurrapa, *f.* sediment, dregs; rubbish, trash.

zurrón, *m.* shepherd's pouch; game bag; leather bag.

Zutano, *n.* (coll.) Mr. So-and-So.—*Fulano, Z. y Mengano,* Tom, Dick and Harry.

GEOGRAPHICAL NAMES THAT DIFFER IN ENGLISH AND SPANISH

A

Abisinia, Abyssinia.
Adriático, Adriatic.
Afganistán, Afghanistan.
Alejandría, Alexandria.
Alemania, Germany.
Alpes, Alps.
Alsacia y Lorena, Alsace-Lorraine.
Alto Volta, Upper Volta.
Amazonas, Amazon.
Amberes, Antwerp.
América del Norte, North America.
América del Sur, South America.
América Española, Spanish America.
América Meridional, South America.
Andalucía, Andalusia.
Antillas, Antilles, West Indies.
Apeninos, Apennines.
Arabia Saudita, Saudi Arabia.
Aragón, Arragon.
Argel, Algiers.
Argelia, Algeria.
Argentina, Argentine.
Asia Menor, Asia Minor.
Asiria, Assyria.
Atenas, Athens.
Atlántico, Atlantic.

B

Babilonia, Babylon.
Baja California, Lower California.
Báltico, Baltic.
Basilea, Basel.
Baviera, Bavaria.
Belén, Bethlehem.
Bélgica, Belgium.
Belgrado, Belgrade.
Belice, Beliza, Belize; British Honduras.
Berbería, Barbary.
Berlín, Berlin.
Berna, Bern.
Birmania, Burma.
Bizancio, Byzantium.
Bolonia, Bologna.
Bona, Bonn.
Borgoña, Burgundy.
Bósforo, Bosporus.
Brasil, Brazil.

Bretaña, Bretagne, Brittany.
Bruselas, Brussels.
Bucarest, Bucharest.
Burdeos, Bordeaux.

C

Cabo de Buena Esperanza, Cape of Good Hope.
Cabo de Hornos, Cape Horn.
Cachemira, Kashmir.
Calcuta, Calcutta.
Caldea, Chaldea.
Cambrige, Cambridge.
Camerón, Cameroons.
Canadá, Canada.
Canal de la Mancha, English Channel.
Canarias, Canary (Islands).
Caribe, Caribbean.
Carolina del Norte, North Carolina.
Carolina del Sur, South Carolina.
Cartagena, Carthagena.
Cartago, Carthage.
Caspio, Caspian (Sea).
Castilla (la Nueva, la Vieja), Castile (New C., Old C.).
Cataluña, Catalonia.
Cáucaso, Caucasus.
Cayena, Cayenne.
Cayo Hueso, Key West.
Ceilán, Ceylon.
Cerdeña, Sardinia.
Colonia, Cologne.
Columbia Británica, British Columbia.
Constantinopla, Constantinople.
Copen(h)ague, Copenhagen.
Córcega, Corsica.
Córdoba, Cordova.
Corea, Korea.
Corinto, Corinth.
Costa del Marfil, Ivory Coast.
Costa de Oro, Gold Coast.
Creta, Crete.
Croacia, Croatia.
Curasao, Curazao, Curaçao.

CH

Champaña, Champagne.
Checoslovaquia, Czechoslovakia.

Chile, Chili, Chile.
Chipre, Cyprus.

D

Dakota del Norte, North Dakota.
Dakota del Sur, South Dakota.
Dalmacia, Dalmatia.
Damasco, Damascus.
Danubio, Danube.
Dardanelos, Dardanelles.
Delfos, Delphi.
Dinamarca, Denmark.
Dresde, Dresden.
Duero (Río), Douro (River).
Dunquerque, Dunkirk.
Duvres, Dover.

E

Edimburgo, Edinburgh.
Egeo, Ægean.
Egipto, Egypt.
Elba, Elbe.
Escandinavia, Scandinavia.
Escocia, Scotland.
Escorial, Escurial.
Eslavonia, Slavonia.
Eslovaquia, Slovakia.
Eslovenia, Slovenia.
Esmirna, Izmir, Smyrna.
España, Spain.
Española, Hispaniola; Santo Domingo, Haiti.
Esparta, Sparta.
Espoleto, Spoleto.
Estados Federados de Malaya, Malay Federated States.
Estados Unidos de América, United States of America.
Estambul, Istanbul.
Estocolmo, Stockholm.
Estonia, Esthonia.
Estrasburgo, Strasbourg.
Estrecho de Magallanes, Strait of Magellan.
Etiopía, Ethiopia.
Eufrates, Euphrates.
Europa, Europe.

F

Fenicia, Phoenicia.
Filadelfia, Philadelphia.
Filipinas, Philippines.

658

Finlandia, Finland.
Flandes, Flanders.
Florencia, Florence.
Francfort del Mein,
Frankfort-on-the-Main.
Francia, France.

G

Gales, Wales.
Galia, Gaul.
Galilea, Galilee.
Gante, Ghent.
Gascuña, Gascony.
Génova, Genoa.
Ginebra, Geneva.
Golfo Pérsico, Persian Gulf.
Gran Bretaña, Great Britain.
Grecia, Greece.
Groenlandia, Greenland.
Guadalupe, Guadeloupe.
Guaján, Guam, Guam.
Guayana, Guiana.

H

Habana, Havana.
Haití, Haiti.
Hamburgo, Hamburg.
Hauai, Hawai, Hawaii.
Haya (La), Hague.
Hébrides, Hebrides.
Hispano-América,
Hispanoamérica, Spanish
America.
Holanda, Holland.
Honduras Británicas,
British Honduras.
Hungría, Hungary.

I

Indias (Occidentales,
Orientales), Indies (West
I., East I.).
Indostán, Hindustan, India.
Inglaterra, England.
Irlanda, Ireland.
Isla de San Salvador,
Watling Island.
Islandia, Iceland.
Islas Baleares, Balearic
Islands.
Islas Británicas, British Isles.
Islas Filipinas, Philippine
Islands.
Islas Vírgenes, Virgin
Islands.
Italia, Italy.

J

Japón, Japan.
Jericó, Jericho.
Jerusalén, Jerusalem.
Jonia, Ionia.
Jutlandia, Jutland.

K

Kartum, Khartoum.
Kenia, Kenya.
Kurdistán, Kurdistan.

L

Laponia, Lapland.
Lasa, Lhasa.
Lausana, Lausanne.
Leningrado, Leningrad.
Letonia, Latvia.
Líbano, Lebanon.
Libia, Libya.
Lieja, Liége.
Liorna, Leghorn.
Lisboa, Lisbon.
Lituania, Lithuania.
Lombardía, Lombardy.
Londres, London.
Lorena, Lorraine.
Lucerna, Lucerne.
Luisiana, Louisiana.
Luxemburgo, Luxemburg.

M

Madera, Madeira.
Malaca, Malay.
Mallorca, Majorca.
Mar de las Indias, Indian
Ocean.
Mar del Norte, North Sea.
Mar Muerto, Dead Sea.
Mar Negro, Black Sea.
Mar Rojo, Red Sea.
Marañón, (upper reaches of
the) Amazon.
Marruecos, Morocco.
Marsella, Marseilles.
Martinica, Martinique.
Meca, Mecca.
Mediterráneo,
Mediterranian.
Méjico, Mexico.
Menfis, Memphis.
Menorca, Minorca.
Misisipí, Mississippi.
Misuri, Missouri.
Mobila, Mobile.
Mompeller, Montpellier.
Montañas Rocosas (o
Rocallosas), Rocky
Mountains.
Montes Apalaches,
Appalachian Mountains.
Moscú, Moscow.
Mosela, Moselle.

N

Nápoles, Naples.
Navarra, Navarre.
Nazaret, Nazareth.
Niasalandia, Nyasaland.
Nilo, Nile.
Niza, Nice.
Normandía, Normandy.
Noruega, Norway.
Nueva Escocia, Nova Scotia.
Nueva Gales del Sur, New
South Wales.
Nueva Inglaterra, New
England.
Nueva Orleáns, New
Orleans.
Nueva York, New York.

Nueva Zelandia, New
Zealand.
Nuevo Brúnswick
(Brúnsvick), New
Brunswick.
Nuevo Méxcio (or Méjico),
New Mexico.
Nuremberga, Nuremberg.

O

Oceanía, Oceania, Oceanica.
Océano Índico, Indian
Ocean.
Olimpo, Olympus.
Omán, Masqat.
Ostende, Ostend.

P

Pacífico, Pacific.
Países Bajos, Low Countries,
Netherlands.
Palestina, Palestine.
Panamá, Panama.
París, Paris.
Parnaso, Parnassus.
Paso de Calais, English
Channel.
Pekín, Peking.
Peloponeso, Peloponnesus.
Pensilvania, Pennsylvania.
Perú, Peru.
Pirineos, Pyrenees.
Polinesia, Polynesia.
Polonia, Poland.
Pompeya, Pompeii.
Praga, Prague.
Provenza, Provence.
Providencia, Providence.
Provincias Vascas (or
Vascongadas), Basque
Provinces.
Prusia, Prussia.
Puerto (de) España, Port of
Spain.
Puerto Príncipe, Port-au-
Prince.
Puerto Rico, Porto Rico,
Puerto Rico.

R

Reino Unido, United
Kingdom.
Renania, Rhineland.
Rhin, Rin, Rhine.
Rocallosas, Rocosas, Rocky
(Mountains).
Ródano, Rhone.
Rodas, Rhodes.
Rodesia, Rhodesia.
Roma, Rome.
Ruán, Rouen.
Rusia, Russia.

S

Saboya, Savoy.
Sajonia, Saxony.
Sena, Seine.
Servia, Serbia.
Seúl, Seoul.
Sevilla, Seville.

Sicilia, Sicily.
Sierra Leona, Sierra Leone.
Sión, Zion.
Siracusa, Syracuse.
Siria, Syria.
Somalia, Somaliland.
Sud-África, Sudáfrica, South Africa.
Sud-América, Sudamérica, South America.
Sudán, Sudan.
Suecia, Sweden.
Suiza, Switzerland.
Sur-América, Suramérica, South America.

T

Tabago, Tobago.
Tahití, Tahiti.
Tajo, Tagus.
Támesis, Thames.
Tanganica, Tanganyika.
Tánger, Tangier.
Tebas, Thebes.

Tejas, Texas.
Terranova, Newfoundland.
Thailandia, Thailand.
Tierra del Labrador, Labrador.
Tierra Santa, Holy Land.
Tirol, Tyrol.
Tokío, Tokyo.
Tolosa, Toulouse.
Toscana, Tuscany.
Tracia, Thrace.
Trento, Trent.
Troya, Troy.
Túnez, Tunis (City), Tunisia (Country).
Turquestán, Turkestan.
Turquía, Turkey.

U

Ucrania, Ukraine.
Unión Soviética, Soviet Union.
Unión Sudafricana, Union of South Africa.

URSS (Unión de Repúblicas Socialistas Soviéticas), USSR (Union of Soviet Socialist Republics).

V

Varsovia, Warsaw.
Venecia, Venice.
Versalles, Versailles.
Vesuvio, Vesuvius.
Viena, Vienna.
Virginia Occidental, West Virginia.
Vizcaya, Biscay.

Y

Yugoeslavia, Yugoslavia, Jugoslavia.

Z

Zanzíbar, Zanzibar.
Zaragoza, Saragossa.
Zelandia, Zealand.
Zululandia, Zululand.

PROPER NAMES OF PERSONS, INCLUDING THOSE OF HISTORICAL, LITERARY, AND MYTHOLOGICAL PERSONAGES

(Only those which differ in English and Spanish are included)

A

Abelardo, Abelard.
Abrahán, Abraham.
Adán, Adam.
Adela, Adele.
Adelaida, Adelaide.
Adolfo, Adolf, Adolph.
Adriano, Hadrian.
Ágata, Águeda, Agatha.
Agustín, Augustine.
Alano, Allan, Allen.
Alberto, Albert.
Alejandro, Alexander.
Alfonso, Alphonso.
Alfredo, Alfred.
Alicia, Alice.
Alonso, Alphonso.
Ana, Ann(e), Anna, Hannah.
Andrés, Andrew.
Ángel, Angel.
Aníbal, Hannibal.
Antonio, Anthony.
Aquiles, Achilles.
Aristófanes, Aristophanes.
Aristóteles, Aristotle.
Arminio, Herman.
Arnaldo, Arnold.
Arquímedes, Archimedes.
Arturo, Arthur.

Atila, Attila.
Augusto, Augustus.

B

Baco, Bacchus.
Bartolomé, Bartholomew.
Basilio, Basil.
Beatricz, Beatrice.
Benita, Benedicta.
Benito, Benedicto.
Benjamín, Benjamin.
Bernardo, Bernard.
Berta, Bertha.
Bibiana, Vivian.
Bruto, Brutus.
Buda, Buddha.
Buenaventura, Bonaventura.

C

Calvino, Calvin.
Camila, Camille.
Camilo, Camillus.
Carlomagno, Charlemagne.
Carlos, Charles.
Carlota, Charlotte.
Carolina, Caroline, Carolyn.
Casandra, Cassandra.
Catalina, Catharine,

Catherine, Katharine, Katherine.
Catón, Cato.
Catulo, Catullus.
Cecilia, Cecile.
Cenón, Zeno.
César, Caesar.
Cicerón, Cicero.
Ciro, Cyrus.
Claudio, Claude.
Clemente, Clement.
Clodoveo, Clovis.
Colón, Columbus.
Confucio, Confucius.
Constancia, Constance.
Constantino, Constantine.
Constanza, Constance.
Cristina, Christine.
Cristo, Christ.
Cristóbal, Christopher.

D

Dalila, Delilah.
Demóstenes, Demosthenes.
Diego, James.
Diógenes, Diogenes.
Dionisio, Dennis, Dionysius.
Domingo, Dominic.
Dorotea, Dorothy.

660

E

Edita, Edith.
Edmundo, Edmund.
Eduardo, Edward.
Elena, Ellen, Helen.
Elisa, Eliza.
Eloísa, Eloise.
Ema, Emma.
Emilia, Emily.
Emilio, Emil.
Eneas, Æneas.
Engracia, Grace.
Enrique, Henry.
Enriqueta, Henrietta.
Epicuro, Epicurus.
Erasmo, Erasmus.
Ernestina, Ernestine.
Ernesto, Ernest.
Escipión, Scipio.
Esopo, Æsop.
Esquilo, Æschylus.
Esteban, Stephen, Steven.
Ester, Esther, Hester.
Estrabón, Strabo.
Estradivario, Stradivarius.
Euclides, Euclid.
Eugenia, Eugénie.
Eugenio, Eugene.
Eva, Eve.
Ezequías, Hezekiah.
Ezequiel, Ezekiel.

F

Federica, Frederica.
Federico, Frederick.
Fedra, Phaedra.
Felicia, Felicia.
Felipa, Philippa.
Felipe, Filipo (de
    Macedonia), Philip.
Felisa, Felicia.
Fernando, Ferdinand.
Florencia, Florence.
Francisca, Frances.
Francisco, Francis.

G

Galeno, Galen.
Gaspar, Jasper.
Geofredo, Jeffrey, Geoffrey.
Gerarda, Geraldine.
Gerardo, Gerard, Gerald.
Gerónimo, Jerome.
Gertrudis, Gertrude.
Gilberto, Gilbert.
Godofredo, Godfrey.
Graco, Gracchus.
Gregorio, Gregory.
Gualterio, Walter.
Guillermina, Wilhelmina.
Guillermo, William.
Gustavo, Gustave, Gustavus.

H

Haroldo, Harold.
Heriberto, Herbert.
Herodes, Herod.
Herodoto, Herodotus.
Hipócrates, Hippocrates.
Hipólito, Hippolytus.
Homero, Homer.
Horacio, Horace, Horatio.
Hortensia, Hortense.
Huberto, Hubert.
Humberto, Humbert.
Hunfredo, Humphrey.

I

Ignacio, Ignatius.
Ildefonso, Alphonso.
Inés, Inez, Agnes.
Inocencio, Innocent.
Isabel, Isabella, Elizabeth.
Isidoro, Isidro, Isidor(e).

J

Jacobo, Jaime, James.
Javier, Xavier.
Jehová, Jehovah.
Jenofonte, Xenophon.
Jerjes, Xerxes.
Jerónimo, Jerome.
Jesucristo, Jesus Christ.
Joaquín, Joachim.
Jonás, Jonah.
Jonatán, Jonatás, Jonathan.
Jorge, George.
José, Joseph.
Josefa, Josefina, Josephine.
Juan, John.
Juana, Jane, Joan.
Juana de Arco, Joan of Arc.
Judit, Judith.
Julia, Juliet.
Julián, Juliano (el
    Emperador), Julian.
Julieta, Juliet.
Julio, Julius.
Justiniano, Justinian.

L

Lázaro, Lazarus.
Leandro, Leander.
Lenora, Lenore, Leonora.
León, Leo, Leon.
Leonardo, Leonard.
Leonor, Eleanor, Elinor.
Leopoldo, Leopold.
Licurgo, Lycurgus.
Livio, Livy.
Lorenzo, Laurence,
    Lawrence.
Lucano, Lucan.
Lucas, Luke.
Lucía, Lucy.
Luciano, Lucian.
Lucrecia, Lucretia.
Lucrecio, Lucretius.
Luis, Lewis, Louis, Aloysius.
Luisa, Louise.
Lutero, Luther.

M

Magallanes, Magellan.
Magdalena, Magdalen.
Mahoma, Mohammed,
    Mahomet.
Manuel, Em(m)anuel.

Manuela, Emma.
Marcial, Martial.
Marco, Marcos, Mark.
Margarita, Margaret,
    Marjorie, Daisy.
María, Mary, Miriam.
Mariana, Marian, Marion.
Marta, Martha.
Marte, Mars.
Mateo, Matthew.
Mauricio, Maurice, Morris.
Mercurio, Mercury.
Mesías, Messiah.
Miguel, Michael.
Miguel Angel,
    Michelangelo.
Moisés, Moses.

N

Nabucodonosor,
    Nebuchadnezzar.
Natán, Nathan.
Nataniel, Nathaniel.
Neptuno, Neptune.
Nerón, Nero.
Nicolás, Nicholas.
Noé, Noah.

O

Octavio, Octavius.
Oliverio, Oliver.
Orlando, Roland.
Otón, Otto.
Ovidio, Ovid.

P

Pablo, Paul.
Patricio, Patrick.
Paulina, Pauline.
Pedro, Peter.
Perseo, Perseus.
Pilatos, Pilate.
Píndaro, Pindar.
Pío, Pius.
Pitágoras, Pythagoras.
Platón, Plato.
Plauto, Plautus.
Plinio, Pliny.
Plutarco, Plutarch.
Pompeyo, Pompey.
Poncio, Pontius.
Prometeo, Prometheus.

Q

Quintiliano, Quintilian.
Quintín, Quentin.

R

Rafael, Raphael.
Raimundo, Raymond.
Ramón, Raymond.
Randolfo, Randolph.
Raquel, Rachel.
Rebeca, Rebecca.
Reinaldo, Reginald.
Renaldo, Ronald.
Renato, René.
Ricardo, Richard.
Roberto, Robert.

Rodolfo, Ralph, Rudolph.
Rodrigo, Roderick.
Rogelio, **Rogerio**, Roger.
Rolando, Roland.
Rómulo, Romulus.
Rosa, Rose.
Rosalía, Rosalie.
Rosario, Rosary.
Rubén, Reuben, Rubin.
Ruperto, Rupert.

S

Saladino, Saladin.
Salomé, Salome.
Salomón, Solomon.
Salustio, Sallust.
Sansón, Samson.
Santiago, James.
Sara, Sarah.
Satanás, Satan.
Saturno, Saturn.
Sila, Sulla.
Silvestre, Sylvester.
Sofía, Sophia.

Sófocles, Sophocles.
Solimán, Suleiman.
Suetonio, Suetonius.
Susana, Susan.

T

Tácito, Tacitus.
Tadeo, Thaddeus.
Tamerlán, Tamerlane.
Teócrito, Theocritus.
Teodoro, Theodore.
Teófilo, Theophilus.
Terencio, Terence.
Teresa, Theresa.
Tertuliano, Tertullian.
Tiberio, Tiberius.
Ticiano (el Ticiano), Titian.
Timoteo, Timothy.
Tito, Titus.
Tolomeo, Ptolemy.
Tomás, Thomas.
Trajano, Trajan.
Tristán, Tristram, Tristan.
Tucídides, Thucydides.

U

Ulises, Ulysses.
Urano, Uranus.
Urbano, Urban.
Urías, Uriah.

V

Valentina, Valentine.
Valeriano, Valerian.
Ventura, Bonaventura.
Veronés, Veronese.
Vespasiano, Vespasian.
Vespucio, Vespucci.
Vicente, Vincent.
Virgilio, Vergil, Virgil.

Y

Yugurta, Jugurtha.

Z

Zacarías, Zachary.
Zenón, Zeno.
Zoroastro, Zoroaster.
Zuinglio, Zwingli.

ABBREVIATIONS MOST COMMONLY USED IN SPANISH

A

a., área.
(a), alias.
@, arroba.
ab., abril.
A.C., antes de Cristo.
admón., administración.
admor., administrador.
afmo., afectísimo.
afto., afecto.
ag., agosto.
ap., aparte.
atto., atento.
Av., Avenida.

B

B.L.M., besa la mano.
bto., bulto; bruto.

C

c/, cargo; contra.
C.A., corriente alterna.
cap., capítulo.
C.C., corriente continua.
c. de., en casa de.
cg., centigramo(s).
Cía., Compañía.
cl., centilitro(s).
cm., centímetro(s).
Co., Compañía.
Const., Constitución.
corrte., corriente.
cta., cuenta.

cta. cte., cuenta corriente.
cts., céntimos.
c/u, cada uno.

D

D., don.
Da., doña.
D.C., después de Cristo.
dcha., derecha.
descto., descuento.
d/f, días fecha.
dg., decigramo(s).
Dg., decagramo(s).
dic., diciembre.
dl., decilitro(s).
Dl., decalitro(s).
dls., dólares ($).
dm., decímetro(s).
Dm., decámetro(s).
dna(s)., docena(s).
dom., domingo.
d/p, días plazo.
Dr., Doctor.
dup., duplicado.
d/v, días vista.

E

E., Este, oriente.
EE. UU., Estados Unidos.
E.M., Estado Mayor.
en., enero.
E.P.D., en paz descanse.
E.P.M., en propia mano.

etc., etcétera.
E.U., Estados Unidos.
E.U.A., Estados Unidos de
   América.
Exc., Excelencia.
Excmo., Excelentísimo.

F

f/, fardo(s).
fact., factura.
F.C., f.c., ferrocarril.
feb., febrero.
fol., folio.
Fr., Fray.
fra., fractura.

G

g., gramo(s).
gnte., gerente.
gob., gobierno.
gobr., gobernador.
gral., general.
gte., gerente.

H

hect., hectáreas.
Hg., hectogramo(s).
Hl., hectolitro(s).
Hm., hectómetro(s).
H.P., caballo(s) de fuerza.
id., ídem.
Ilmo., Ilustrísimo.

662

Ing., Ingeniero.
izda., izdo., izquierda, -do.

J

J.C., Jesucristo.
juev., jueves.
jul., julio.
jun., junio.

K

Kg., kg., kilogramo(s).
Kl., kl., kilolitro(s).
Km., km., kilómetro(s).
k.w., kilovatio.

L

L/, letra.
Ldo., Licenciado.
l., litro(s).
lb(s)., libra(s).
lun., lunes.

M

m., minuto(s); metro(s); mañana (A.M.).
M., Madre.
m/., mes; mi(s); mío(s).
Ma., María.
mar., marzo.
mart., martes.
m/f, mi favor.
mg., miligramo(s).
mierc., miércoles.
M/L, mi letra.
ml., mililitro(s).
mm., m/m, milímetro(s).
m/o, mi orden.
m/ o m/, más o menos.
Mons., Monseñor.

N

n., noche (P.M.)
N., Norte.
n/, nuestro.
Nª Sª, Nuestra Señora.
N.B., Nota bene.
n/cta., nuestra cuenta.
no., nro., número.
nov., noviembre.
N.S.J.C., Nuestro Señor Jesucristo.
nto., neto.

O

O., Oeste.
o/, orden.
ob., obpo., obispo.
oct., octubre.
O.E.A., Organización de Estados Americanos.
O.N.U., Organización de las Naciones Unidas.
onz., onza.
orn., orden.

P

P., Padre; pregunta.
pág., págs., página(s).
Part., Partida.
P.D., Posdata.
p.ej., por ejemplo.
P.O., por orden.
P.P., Porte pagado; por poder.
ppdo., próximo pasado.
pral., principal.
prof., profesor.
prov., provincia.
próx., próximo.
ps., pesos.
ptas., pesetas.
pte., parte.
pza., pieza.

Q

q., que.
Q.B.S.M., que besa su mano.
Q.D.G., que Dios guarde.
q.e.g.e., que en gloria esté.
q.e.p.d., que en paz descanse.
q.e.s.m., que estrecha su mano.
qq., quintales.

R

R., Reverendo.
Rbí., Recibí.
Rda. M., Reverenda Madre.
Rdo. P., Reverendo Padre.
R.I.P., Requiescat in pace.
r.p.m., revoluciones por minuto.
rúst., rústica.

S

S., San(to); Sur.
s/, su(s); sobre.
sáb., sábado.
S.A.R., Su Alteza Real.
S.C., s.c., su casa.
s/c, su cuenta.
s/cta., su cuenta.
sept., septiembre.
set., septiembre.
S.E. u O., salvo error u omisión.
S.M., Su Majestad.
S.N., Servicio Nacional.
Sr., Señor.
Sra(s), Señora(s).
Sres., Señores.
Sría., Secretaría.
Srta., Señorita.
S.S., Su Santidad.
S.S.S., s.s.s., Su seguro servidor.
Sta., Santa; Señorita.
Sto., Santo.

T

t., tarde.
tít., título.
tpo., tiempo.
trib., tribunal.
tom., tomo.

U

U., Ud., usted.
Uds., UU., ustedes.

V

V., usted; venerable; véase.
Vers., Versículo.
Vd., usted.
Vds., ustedes.
V.E., Vuestra Excelencia.
vg., verbigracia.
v.gr., verbigracia.
vier., viernes.
Vto. Bno., Visto Bueno.
Vol., volumen; voluntad.
vols., volúmenes.
vta., vto., vuelta, vuelto.

TABLES OF WEIGHTS AND MEASURES

Metric Weights
(Unidades Métricas de Peso)

1 gramo (g.) = .03527 ounces (oz.)
1 kilogramo (kg.) = 1.000 gramos = 2.2046 pounds (lb.)
1 quintal métrico = 100 kg. = 220.55 pounds.
1 tonelada métrica = 10 quintales = 2,205 pounds

Old Weights Still Encountered
(Unidades antiguas todavía en uso)

1 libra = 16 onzas = 0,460 kg. = 1.014 lb.
1 arroba = 25 libras = 11,51 kg. = 25.36 lb.
1 quintal = 4 arrobas = 46,09 kg. = 101.43 lb.
1 tonelada = 20 quintales = 922 kg. = 2,028 lb.

Metric Liquid and Dry Measures
(Unidades métricas de capacidad)

1 litro (l.) = 1 decímetro cúbico (dm.) = .908 qt. U.S. dry measure = 1.0567 qt. U.S. liquid measure
1 decálitro (dl.) = 10 litros = 9.08 U.S. qt. dry measure = 2.64 gal. U.S. liquid measure = 2.837 bushels
1 hectólitro (hl.) = 100 l. = 26.417 gal.
1 kilólitro (kl.) = 1.000 l. = 28.337 bushels = 264.17 gal.

Old Measures Still Encountered
(Unidades antiguas todavía en uso)

1 cuartillo = 0,005 l. = 1.05 qt.
1 celemín = 4 cuartillos

Metric Linear Measures
(Unidades métricas de longitud)

1 milímetro (mm.) = .039 inches (in.)
1 centímetro (cm.) = 10 mm. = .393 inches
1 decímetro (dm.) = 10 cm. = 3.94 inches
1 metro (m.) = 10 dm. = 3.28 feet (ft.)
1 kilómetro (km.) = 1,000 m. = 3,280 feet, approx. 5/8 of a mile

Old Measures Still Encountered
(Unidades antiguas todavía en uso)

1 pulgada = 2,3 cm. = .92 inches
1 pie = 12 pulgadas
1 vara = 3 pies
1 legua = 6,666 varas = 5,572 km.

Metric Square Measures
(Unidades métricas de superficie)

1 centiárea = 1 metro cuadadro (m.^{2}) = 1.196 square yards (sq. yd.)
1 área = 100 metros cuadrados = 119.6 square yards
1 hectárea = 1.000 metros cuadrados = 2.471 acres

THERMOMETER

0 centigrade (freezing point) = 32 Fahrenheit
100 centigrade (boiling point) = 212 Fahrenheit

To reduce degrees centigrade to degrees Fahrenheit multiply by 9/5 and add 32.